DOLLARWISE

USA

EDOUARD de BLAYE

Introduction by
Susan Poole

Edited by
Maxwell R.D. Vos

□

1989–1990

Translation by Maxwell R.D. Vos

Published by Prentice Hall Trade Division
A Division of Simon & Schuster Inc.
15 Columbus Circle
New York, NY 10023

ISBN 0-13-217787-0

ISSN 0899-2797

Text design by Levavi & Levavi, Inc.

Manufactured in the United States of America

CONTENTS

Part Three   THE MIDWEST

Part Four   THE MOUNTAIN STATES

Part Eight HAWAII AND ALASKA

Maps

SYMBOLS & ABBREVIATIONS

Abbreviations in Hotels, Restaurants, Sights, Museums, & Shopping

A/C	air-conditioned		M	moderate (price range)
adj.	adjoining		Mon.-Fri.	Monday through
AE	American Express			Friday
	(credit card)		Mon.-Sat.	Monday through
B	budget (price range)			Saturday
CB	Carte Blanche (credit card)		nr.	near
d.	double (room)		rest.	restaurant
DC	Diners Club credit card		resv.	reservations
dwntwn	downtown		rm(s)	room(s)
E	expensive (price range)		s.	single (room)
gar.	garage		s/d	single or double rooms
grdn	garden		svce	service
hr(s)	hour(s)		w.	with
hrdrsr	hairdresser		V	VISA (credit card)
I	inexpensive (price range)		VE	very expensive
J&T	jacket and tie required			(price range)
jkt	jacket required		vic.	vicinity
MC	MasterCard (credit card)		wknd	weekend
min.	minutes		ZIP	ZIP code

Abbreviations on the Road

Ave.	Avenue		mi.	miles
Blvd.	Boulevard		Pkwy.	Parkway
Dr.	Drive		Pl.	Place
Expwy.	Expressway		Rd.	Road
Fwy.	Freeway		Sq.	Square
Hwy.	Highway		Tpke.	Turnpike
km	kilometers			

What the Symbols Mean

HOTELS

Modest but acceptable, with a good price-to-quality ratio.

A quality establishment, but with shortcomings in service or comfort.

Worth a detour.

Exceptional comfort or service, among the best in the U.S. Try to fit it into your trip.

One of the dozen best hotels in the country. Don't miss it.

RESTAURANTS

Modest but acceptable, with a good price-to-quality ratio.

A quality establishment, but with shortcomings in service or cuisine.

Worth a detour.

Exceptional standard in service or cuisine, among the best in the U.S. Try to fit it into your trip.

One of the dozen best restaurants in the country. Don't miss it.

BUILDINGS, MUSEUMS, OR NATURAL FEATURES

Interesting and worth a visit or at least a look.

Remarkable and should be seen.

A building, museum, or natural feature that should not be missed.

Unique of its kind, and worth a journey in itself.

CITIES OR AREAS

Interesting and worth a visit.

Remarkable and should be seen.

A city or area that should not be missed.

Exceptionally interesting, and worth a journey in itself.

OF SPECIAL INTEREST

Highly recommended as an unusual and worthwhile experience, of very special interest.

INTRODUCTION

□ □ □

Any traveler in the United States will find the very vastness of the country—some 3,628,062 square miles (9,396,681 sq km)—impressive, perhaps even a trifle intimidating. Within this huge area, the 50 states of the Union, including Alaska, separated from the contiguous 48 by about 500 miles, and Hawaii, 2,500 miles offshore in the Pacific, offer the traveler a bewildering range of options: from the semitropical Everglades to San Francisco Bay, from the Indian reservations of Arizona to the little fishing villages of New England, from the arid landscape of Nevada to the deep woods of Vermont, from the Great Plains of the Dakotas to the beaches of California, from the fiery volcanoes of Hawaii to the glaciers of Alaska, from the tawny deserts of New Mexico to the sprawling megalopolis of Boswash (the conurbation that stretches from Boston through Providence, Hartford, New York, Philadelphia, Wilmington, and Baltimore to Washington along the northeastern corridor).

The choice of diversions is equally limitless. You can hunt big game or fish for salmon; run the Colorado River rapids on a rubber raft; follow the trail of the pioneers in a covered wagon; see the Indianapolis 500, the world's most dangerous automobile race; or watch a rocket launching from Cape Canaveral. You can explore America in an RV, a real home on wheels, or if you prefer and can afford it, spend a dream vacation at a super-luxury California spa/resort. You can discover the intoxication of virgin powder in the ski resorts of the Rockies or the Sierra Nevada, encounter the future at EPCOT and good ole Mickey at Walt Disney World, and wonder at some of the world's great natural marvels—from the Grand Canyon to Death Valley, from Niagara Falls to the geysers of Yellowstone National Park. And then of course there are America's wondrous cities—New York, Los Angeles, Chicago, San Francisco, Washington—all repositories of great art, culture, and architecture, providing some of the premier urban experiences of the world.

For Americans setting out to get to know their own country, the options may indeed seem endless—for the foreign visitor they can be overwhelming—so let's try to make some sense out of this welter of options.

WHERE AND WHEN

For practical purposes the United States can be divided into eight great tourist regions.

THE NORTHEAST AND MID-ATLANTIC: From the Canadian frontier to the Potomac and from the shores of Maine to Niagara Falls, this is the cradle of Anglo-Saxon Protestant America. Its principal regions are New England, with its slightly old-fashioned charm, and Boswash, the extensive conurbation sheltering 50 million people along the Boston–Washington corridor. American History with a capital *H* is evident everywhere, from Philadelphia's Independence Park to Boston's Freedom Trail, from New York's Federal Hall to Washington's Capitol Hill. So, too, are the great names associated with science and learning: Yale, Harvard, Columbia, and Princeton. See the chapters on Boston, Cape Cod, New

York, Niagara Falls, the Atlantic Coast, Philadelphia, Pittsburgh, Baltimore, and Washington.

Best Time to Visit: Cities in the spring and fall, beaches in summer. Fall foliage colors are at their peak in Vermont in late September, and move south to New York state by mid-October. Winter skiing begins in late November.

THE SOUTH: From Washington, D.C., along the Atlantic coast to Florida and west to Louisiana and Arkansas, this is the homeland of bourbon, of the great plantations of the legendary *Gone with the Wind*. Traces of this Old South exist in the historic cities of Alexandria, Williamsburg, Charleston, and Savannah, and in the plantation country along the Mississippi River in Louisiana and Mississippi. This region has given birth to much that is original in American culture—jazz (from New Orleans), the blues (from Memphis), and country music (from Nashville). Today the romance of Rhett Butler's and Scarlet O'Hara's South has been replaced by the bright progressive New South represented by such cosmopolitan cities as Atlanta, New Orleans, and Miami. See the chapters on Charleston, Savannah, Atlanta, Nashville, Memphis, New Orleans, Florida's East Coast, Tampa/St. Petersburg, Orlando, and Miami/Miami Beach.

Best Time to Visit: Spring, fall, and winter; summers tend to be hot and humid with temperatures averaging 80°–90°F (26.6°–32.2°C) in Florida and along the Gulf Coast.

THE MIDWEST: From North Dakota to the Great Lakes and from Missouri to Kansas, this region is often called the Heartland of America, where the plains stretch to a vast horizon and where grain and cattle have been, and still are, king. Although few tourists go there, many of its cities—St. Louis, Kansas City, Minneapolis, and above all, Chicago—are well worth seeing. See the chapters on Detroit, Cleveland, Cincinnati, Chicago, Milwaukee, Minneapolis/St. Paul, Indianapolis, St. Louis, and Kansas City.

Best Time to Visit: Spring and fall; winters are harsh (20°F,–6.6°C, and lower in the northernmost states); scorching summer temperatures can rise above 100°F (38°C) on the plains.

THE MOUNTAIN STATES: Montana, Wyoming, Idaho, Colorado, and Utah—a spectacular scenic playground, this is one of the country's most beautiful and dramatic regions. Colorado and Utah with their dozens of national parks and awesome landscapes are worth a trip in themselves. City highlights also include Salt Lake City, the terminus of the great Mormon trek overland, and Denver, a thoroughly modern city that has not entirely shaken off its earlier heritage as a wild and wooly frontier town. Great summer hiking and winter skiing. See the chapters on Denver, the Rocky Mountains, Salt Lake City, Utah National Parks, Yellowstone National Park, and the Black Hills and Mount Rushmore.

Best Time to Visit: Year round. Summers are sunny and moderately hot, except in desert areas where the thermometer can register 110°F (44°C) plus. Spring and fall are temperate, although temperatures can drop mightily at night.

THE SOUTHWEST: From Texas to Arizona, including the adjoining states of New Mexico and Oklahoma, a land of tawny, rust-colored deserts and lunar landscapes, of splendid canyons and Indian reservations, it also boasts archeological remains from the dawn of civilization. Fascinating culturally and historically, especially for those in search of the Old West. See the chapters on Dallas/Fort Worth, Houston, Albuquerque, San Antonio, Santa Fe, Navajoland, the Grand Canyon, Phoenix, and Tucson.

Best Time to Visit: Fall, winter, and spring, before the temperatures rise.

THE NORTHWEST: The beautiful countrysides of Oregon and Washington—rugged coastline, mountain peaks, lakes, rivers, rich farmland, and burgeoning wine country—are attracting more visitors. The two major cities, Portland and Seattle, are also attracting more and more people to their livable cosmopolitan environments. See the chapters on Portland, Seattle, and the Pacific Coast.
Best Time to Visit: Summer and fall—least rainfall in July.

THE WEST: The Pacific Coast of California along with Nevada. California, America's experimental social laboratory sets the pace for the rest of the country exporting its technology, lifestyle, and social trends, fads, and fashions to the other 49 states. An eclectic mix of European, Asian, and Latin American cultures; movie stars and millionaires; computer age technology; alternative lifestyle devotees, natural wonders, and fine wineries. And then, of course, there's glitter gulch Las Vegas in nearby Nevada. See the chapters on Las Vegas, Death Valley, Reno, San Francisco, Sequoia National Park, Yosemite National Park, Los Angeles, San Diego, and the California Coast.
Best Time to Visit: Anytime except in the rainy early spring.

ALASKA AND HAWAII: While not a region per se, the states of Alaska and Hawaii are major destinations for both Americans and foreign visitors. See the chapters on Anchorage and Alaska, and Honolulu and the Hawaiian Islands.
Best Time to Visit: Spring and summer for Alaska, year round for Hawaii.

Average Temperatures, in ° Fahrenheit, for Representative Cities

	Jan.	Feb.	Mar.	Apr.	May	Jun.	Jul.	Aug.	Sept.	Oct.	Nov.	Dec.
Anchorage	23	25	28	35	46	57	62	58	48	39	33	28
Atlanta	44	47	52	62	70	76	80	82	71	62	52	44
Chicago	25	27	35	48	57	68	73	71	64	55	41	30
Dallas	44	48	55	64	73	80	86	86	77	66	55	48
Denver	30	32	37	48	58	66	73	71	62	51	39	32
Kansas City	30	33	44	55	66	73	80	78	69	59	44	33
Las Vegas	44	50	57	66	73	86	93	91	82	68	57	48
Los Angeles	55	55	57	59	62	66	68	69	68	62	51	55
Miami	68	68	71	73	77	80	82	82	80	78	71	69
Minneapolis	13	15	30	44	57	66	73	69	62	50	33	19
New York	30	30	39	48	60	69	77	75	66	55	44	33
San Francisco	50	51	53	55	55	59	59	60	62	60	57	51
Washington, D.C.	37	39	44	55	66	73	78	77	69	59	48	39

The daily newspaper *USA Today,* on sale in all large cities, carries a daily weather map, detailed and in color, as well as forecasts for the whole U.S.

SPECIAL VACATION IDEAS

NATIONAL PARKS AND FORESTS: Scattered throughout the United States are 48 national parks—about 27 million acres of land that has been set

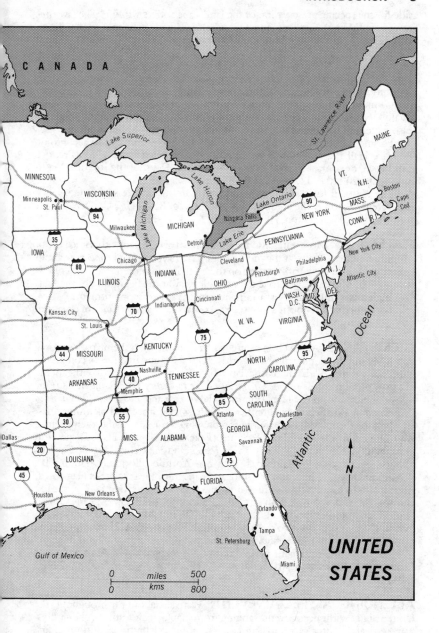

CANADA

Lake Superior

MINNESOTA

WISCONSIN

Minneapolis
St. Paul

94

Milwaukee

35

Lake Michigan

Lake Huron

MICHIGAN

IOWA

80

Chicago

Detroit

Lake Erie

INDIANA

ILLINOIS

70

Indianapolis

OHIO

Cincinnati

Cleveland

Lake Ontario

Niagara Falls

90

NEW YORK

PENNSYLVANIA

Pittsburgh

Philadelphia

St. Lawrence River

MAINE

VT.
N.H.

MASS.
Boston
Cape
Cod

CONN. R.I.

New York City

N.J.

Atlantic City

Kansas City

St. Louis

44

MISSOURI

Baltimore

WASH. MD.
D.C.

DEL.

Ocean

W. VA.

VIRGINIA

KENTUCKY

75

ARKANSAS

40

Nashville

TENNESSEE

Memphis

NORTH

CAROLINA

95

30

55

65

85

SOUTH

CAROLINA

Charleston

Dallas

20

MISS.

ALABAMA

Atlanta

GEORGIA

45

LOUISIANA

Savannah

Atlantic

N

75

Houston

New Orleans

FLORIDA

Orlando

Tampa

St. Petersburg

Miami

Gulf of Mexico

**UNITED
STATES**

| 0 | miles | 500 |
| 0 | kms | 800 |

aside for the specific preservation of the landscape and its wildlife. The favorites are: Acadia (Maine), Glacier (Montana), Grand Canyon (Arizona), Grand Teton (Wyoming), Great Smoky Mountain (Tennessee and North Carolina), Hawaii Volcanoes (Hawaii), Mammoth Cave (Kentucky), Mount Rainier (Washington), Olympic (Washington), Rocky Mountain (Colorado), Sequoia/Kings Canyon (California), Shenandoah (Virginia), Yellowstone (Wyoming, Montana, and Idaho), Yosemite (California), and Zion (Utah).

Camping facilities, ranging from primitive campsites to rustic cabins, are usually open from late spring to early fall (year round at some parks). Rates are reasonable, and because of the parks' popularity, it's wise to reserve ahead.

For more information, refer to *The National Park Guide* by Michael Frome (Prentice Hall Press), or his *America's Favorite National Parks 1989* (Prentice Hall Press), or contact the **National Park Service,** Dept. of the Interior, Washington, DC 20240 (202/343-1100).

The national forests are less well known and usually less crowded. For a complete list, contact the **National Forest Service,** Box 2417, US Department of Agriculture, Washington, DC 20013 (202/447-3957).

STATE PARKS: Most states also maintain state parks, often with some type of camping facilities. Again, at the more popular parks you'll need to reserve ahead —for example, in New York to camp on the Long Island shoreline at Hither Hills State Park in Montauk, you have to enter a lottery at the beginning of the year. Although this is unusual, reservations are wise to avoid disappointment.

For **information about state parks,** contact each state's tourism organization. See the Appendix.

THEME PARKS: Almost every state worth its name has a theme park of some sort. They run the gamut from Sea World to Opryland and include, of course, the stars, Walt Disney World and Disneyland. If you're planning a trip to either of the last two, pick up copies of *The Unofficial Guide to Disney World and EPCOT* by Bob Sehlinger and John Finley (Prentice Hall Press) and *The Unofficial Guide to Disneyland* by Bob Sehlinger (Prentice Hall Press). Both are vital planning aides.

Just for the record, here are the top-drawing amusement and theme parks: Walt Disney World and EPCOT center (Lake Buena Vista, Fla.), Disneyland (Anaheim, Calif.), Knott's Berry Farm (Buena Vista, Calif.), Busch Gardens (Tampa, Fla.; also in Williamsburg, Va.), Sea World of Florida (Orlando, Fla.; also in San Diego, Calif.; Aurora, Ohio; and San Antonio, Texas); Six Flags Great Adventure (Jackson, N.J.; also in Arlington, Texas; Atlanta, Ga.; St. Louis, Mo.; Gurnee, Ill.; and Valencia, Calif.); Cedar Point (Sandusky, Ohio); Kings Island (Cincinnati, Ohio); Opryland USA (Nashville, Tenn.); Marriott's Great America (Santa Clara, Calif.); AstroWorld (Houston, Texas); and Hersheypark, the granddaddy of them all (Hershey, Penna.).

For a list of amusement parks, contact the **International Association of Amusement Parks and Attractions,** 4230 King St., Alexandria, VA 22302 (703/671-5800).

ATTENDING A SPECIAL EVENT: Festivals abound throughout the United States with special events ranging from maple sugar festivals, cherry blossom festivals, winter carnivals, crafts fairs, ethnic celebrations, antiques fairs, fleamarkets—everything from Mardi Gras to Oktoberfest—as well as blockbuster cultural events like the Spoleto Festival in Charleston or Tanglewood in Massachusetts. In each chapter you'll find major special events highlighted, but for a full list, contact any state's tourist organization (see the list in the Appendix). Inquire well in advance. Some events draw large audiences.

VISITING NATIONAL MONUMENTS: These are monuments that recall the great moments of American history—places like Gettysburg, Penna.; Custer Battlefield, Mont.; the Alamo, Texas; and Minute Man National Historical Park, Mass. For information contact the **National Park Foundation,** Suite 210, 1850 K Street NW, Washington, DC (202/785-4500). A good resource is *The Complete Guide to America's National Parks* (Prentice Hall Press).

ACTIVE VACATIONS: For up-to-date information about specialty travel in general, obtain a copy of *Specialty Travel Index,* a bi-yearly magazine, either from your travel agent, your library, or by subscription from Specialty Travel Index, 305 San Anselmo Ave., Suite 217, San Anselmo, CA 94960. Cost is $8 for one year.

Here's a very brief resource list to stimulate ideas:

Ballooning: Contact the **Balloon Federation of America,** P.O. Box 246, Indianola, IA 50125 (515/961-8809).

Bicycling: *Bicycle USA,* published nine times a year, puts out an issue called *Tourfinder,* which lists tour operators around the U.S. It's available to the public for $4. Contact Bicycle USA, Suite 209, 6707 Whitestone Rd., Baltimore, MD 21207 (301/944-3399).

Birdwatching: Contact the **National Audubon Society** Headquarters, 950 Third Ave., New York, NY 10022 (212/832-3200).

Camping and Hiking: Contact the **Sierra Club,** Outing Department, 730 Polk St., San Francisco, CA 94109 (415/776-2211).

Skiing: Two good sources of information here: the **U.S. Ski Association,** U.S. Olympic Complex, 1750 E. Boulder St., Colorado Springs, CO 80909 (303/578-4600); and the **U.S. Recreational Ski Association,** 221 W. Dyer Rd., Santa Ana, CA 92707 (714/641-0724).

Spelunking: The **National Speleological Society,** Cave Ave., Huntsville, AL 35810 (205/852-1300), can put you in touch with fellow enthusiasts.

Tennis: Contact the **U.S. Tennis Association,** 1220 Ave. of the Americas, New York, NY 10036 (212/302-3322).

Wilderness Trips: The major source is the **Sierra Club** (see address above), which organizes wilderness treks to various forests and parks. Other organizations include:

Appalachian Mountain Club, 5 Joy St., Boston, MA 02108 (617/528-0636). Single annual membership is $40; family membership is $65.

American Wilderness Alliance, 7600 E. Arapahoe Rd., Suite 114, Englewood, CO 80112 (303/771-0380).

American Forestry Association, P.O. Box 2000, Washington, DC 20013 (202/667-3300; toll free 800/368-5748).

Nature Expeditions International, P.O. Box 11496, Eugene, OR 97440 (503/484-6529).

Yosemite Institute, P.O. Box 487, Yosemite, CA 95389 (209/372-4441).

TRAVEL FOR PARTICULAR GROUPS

FOR STUDENTS: It's worth using your high school or college ID to obtain an International Student Identity Card, because although it's not as widely recognized in the U.S. as it is abroad, it still delivers some savings. Available from the **Council on International Educational Exchange (CIEE),** 205 E. 42nd St., New York, NY 10017 (212/661-1414), and 312 Sutter St., Room 407, San Francisco, CA 94108 (415/421-3473).

Student travel tour operators include: **Contiki Holidays,** 1432 E. Katella Ave., Anaheim, CA 92805 (toll free 800/626-0611), for ages 18 through 35; for ages 15 through 20, **Arista Student Travel Association, Inc.,** 11 E. 44th St.,

New York, NY 10017 (212/687-5121; toll free 800/356-8861); and **Bailey Travel Service, Inc.,** 123 E. Market St., York, PA 17401 (717/854-5511).

FOR SINGLES: The only way to avoid the extra cost of the single supplement is to find someone to share those "doubles" rates. The following organizations specialize in matching up individuals for this purpose (most charge modest monthly or annual membership fees):

Travel Companion Exchange, P.O. Box 833, Amityville, NY 11701 (516/454-0673 or 516/454-0880); **Travel Mates International,** 49 W. 44th St., New York, NY 10036 (212/221-6565); and **Saga International Holidays,** 120 Boylston St., Boston, MA 02116 (toll free 800/343-0273), for ages 60 and over.

Singleworld, 401 Theodore Fremd Ave., Rye, NY 10580, specializes in arranging cruises and group tours for singles. Membership is $18 a year.

FOR FAMILIES: Careful planning makes all the difference between a successful enjoyable vacation and one that ends with exhausted, irritable parents and cranky kids. Here are just a few hints to help:

1. Get the kids involved. Let them, if they're old enough, write to the tourist offices for information and color brochures. Give them a map on which they can outline the route; let them help decide the itinerary.

2. Packing. Although your home may be toddler-proof, accommodations are not. Bring portable gates for stairways and other off-limit areas, and also some blank plugs to cover outlets.

3. En route. Carry a few simple games to relieve boredom in the car. A few snacks will also help and will save money. In some states it's mandatory for children under age 2 to have an infant's car seat; you may want to bring your own on a fly-drive trip. Check AMTRAK for special family discounts; the airlines, too, have reduced air fares for those under 17; both let under-2s travel free.

4. Accommodations. Children under a certain age usually stay free in their parents' room. Look for establishments that have pools and other recreational facilities. Reserve equipment such as cribs and playpens in advance.

5. Resources. What to do with the kids this year: *Traveling with Children in the U.S.A.* by Leila Hadley (Morrow), *Travel with Children* by Maureen Wheeler (Lonely Planet), and *How to Take Trips with Your Kids* by Joan and Sanford Portnoy (Harvard Common Press).

Traveling by Train or Bus

On AMTRAK, children under 2 travel free. Children 2 to 12 travel for half fare. Also don't forget to ask about special family fares and promotions.

On Greyhound, when accompanied by an adult, children under 5 travel free; children 5 to 11 pay half fare.

FOR THE DISABLED: Standards of accessibility vary so widely that planning is crucial. Here are a few helpful hints:

1. Accessibility Information. Unfortunately there are few centralized sources. Three of the best are: the **Travel Information Service,** Moss Rehabilitation Hospital, 12th and Tabor Rd., Philadelphia, PA 19141 (215/456-9602), which charges nominally for mailing materials; **The Itinerary,** P.O. Box 1984, Bayonne, NJ 07002, a bi-monthly newsletter for disabled travelers costing $9 per year; the **Access Foundation for Accessibility by the Disabled,** P.O. Box 356, Malvern, NY 11565, a clearinghouse of specialist tour operators and travel agents which will respond to individual queries on specific destinations and recommend organizations offering tours for the disabled; their monthly newsletter; *Access: International,* is $25 a year.

2. Golden Access Passport. This admits a disabled person and companion into a national park, forest, or wildlife refuge for free. At some sites a 50% discount on camping and other facilities is also given. For information, call the National Park Service (202/485-9666).

3. Tour Packagers. There are many, but two that are recommended and have been in the business a long time are: **Evergreen Travel Service / Wings on Wheels Tours,** 19505 44th Ave., W. Lynnwood, WA 98036 (206/776-1184), which has tours everywhere, even to China and Thailand; and **Whole Person Tours,** P.O. Box 1084, Bayonne, NJ 07002 (201/858-3400).

4. Book Resources. *Access to the World: A Travel Guide for the Handicapped* by Louise Weiss (H. Holt & Co.) and *Travel for the Disabled: A Handbook of Travel Resources & 400 Worldwide Access Guides* by Helen Hecker (Twin Peaks Press).

Traveling by Bus and Train

A companion can accompany a disabled person for free aboard Greyhound. This is only available to disabled people who have a letter from their doctor certifying that they are handicapped and will also only be extended to those who cannot negotiate the bus steps alone.

AMTRAK has a standard handicapped person's fare, which discounts at least 25% off the regular fare ticket. AMTRAK also provides wheelchair-accessible sleeping accommodations in both eastern and western trains. Although pets are not allowed, guide dogs are permissible and travel free of charge. In all cases, notify your reservation agent for the lowest possible fare and authorization for any special needs.

FOR SENIORS: For the fastest-growing travel group, there's a lot available:

1. Discounts. To find them, there's one major resource: *The Discount Guide for Travelers Over Fifty-Five* by Caroline and Walter Weinz (E.P. Dutton). The only other way to find them is to ask for them everywhere—at cinemas, theaters, museums, hotels, restaurants, attractions, and on local transit.

2. Information Sources. The **American Association of Retired Persons (AARP),** 1909 K. St. NW, Washington, DC 20049 (202/872-4700); **Mature Outlook,** 3701 W. Lake Ave., Glenview, IL 60025 (toll free 800/336-6330); and the **National Council of Senior Citizens,** 925 15th St. NW, Washington, DC 20005 (202/347-8800).

3. Tour and Other Specialists. Fascinating, reasonably priced learning vacations are offered by **Elderhostel, Inc.,** 80 Boylston St., Suite 400, Boston, MA 02116 (617/426-8056); the **AARP Travel Service,** 5855 Green Valley Circle, Culver City, CA 90230 (toll free 800/227-7737); **Saga International Holidays,** 120 Boylston St., Boston, MA 02116 (617/451-6808; toll free 800/343-0273); and **Grand Circle Travel, Inc.,** 347 Congress St., Boston, MA 02210 (617/350-7500). The last two concentrate on foreign destinations.

4. Book Resources. *Travel Easy: The Practical Guide for People over 50* by Rosalind Massow (AARP).

RECOMMENDED TOURING ITINERARIES: It is relatively easy to take in all the major sights of widely separated regions by flying to a major transportation hub and then renting a car with unlimited mileage. Below you will find suggestions for touring itineraries lasting from one week to one month, covering the main tourist areas of the United States. Note that the cheapest available rates for rental cars and motor homes are currently offered in California (for the West Coast) and Florida (for the East Coast). For the Northeast, choose Boston over Washington as your home base, and avoid New York, which has the highest car rental rates in the whole country.

For a detailed description of the sights, museums, scenery, and nearby excursions for the cities and touring areas listed in the itineraries below, consult the chapters corresponding to the names marked with an asterisk (see the index at the end of the book).

Region	Cities or Tourist Areas	Length of Stay (in days)	Mileage	Via Highway No.
	If you only have a week . . .			
Arizona	1. Phoenix*	2	—	
	2. Navajoland* & Monument Valley	2	395	I-17, U.S. 89, U.S. 160, U.S. 163.
	3. Grand Canyon*	2	173	U.S. 160, U.S. 89, Ariz. 64.
	4. return to Phoenix	1	218 / 736	U.S. 180, I-17.
S. Dakota	1. Rapid City	1	—	
	2. Badlands Nat'l Park	2	70	I-90, S.Dak. 240.
	3. Mt. Rushmore*	1	86	S. Dak. 44, U.S. 16.
	4. Devil's Tower Nat'l Monument	1	153	U.S. 85, I-90, U.S. 14.
	5. Spearfish	1	84	U.S. 14, I-90.
	6. return to Rapid City	1	53 / 446	I-90.
East Coast	1. Boston*	2	—	
	2. Cape Cod* & Martha's Vineyard or Nantucket	3	89	Mass. 3, U.S. 6.
	3. Newport, R.I.	1	86	U.S. 6, R.I. 24, R.I. 138.
	4. return to Boston	1	68 / 243	R.I. 138, R.I. 24, Mass. 24.
East Coast	1. Boston*	2	—	
	2. Salem & Gloucester	2	37	Mass. 1A, Mass. 128.
	3. Portland, Maine	1	91	Mass. 128, Mass. 133, Mass. 1A, I-95.
	4. Portsmouth, N.H.	1	50	I-95.
	5. return to Boston	1	55 / 233	I-95.
East Coast	1. Washington*	3	—	
	2. Annapolis	1	28	U.S. 50.
	3. Chincoteague	1	113	U.S. 50, U.S. 13, Va. 175.
	4. Williamsburg	1	176	U.S. 13, I-64, Va. 31.
	5. return to Washington	1	205 / 522	U.S. 60, I-64, I-95.

Florida	1. Orlando*, Kennedy Space Center, and Disney World	3	—	
	2. West Palm Beach	1	161	Fla. Tpke.
	3. Fort Lauderdale	1	42	U.S. 1.
	4. Miami*	2	25	U.S. 1.
			228	
Great Lakes	1. Chicago*	2	—	
	2. Milwaukee*	1	87	I-94.
	3. Sault Ste. Marie	1	398	U.S. 43, U.S. 41, U.S. 2 I-75.
	4. Mackinaw City	1	56	I-75.
	5. Holland	1	284	U.S. 31.
	6. return to Chicago	1	140	U.S. 31, I-94.
			965	
Rockies	1. Denver*	1	—	
	2. Colorado Springs	1	76	I-25.
	3. Canon City	1	44	Colo. 115, U.S. 50.
	4. Gunnison	1	121	U.S. 50.
	5. Glenwood Springs	1	173	U.S. 50, Colo.92, Colo. 133, Colo. 82.
	6. Dillon	1	91	I-70.
	7. return to Denver	1	76	I-70.
			581	
Rockies	1. Denver*	1	—	
	2. Great Sand Dunes & Alamosa	1	239	I-25, U.S. 160.
	3. Santa Fe*	2	140	U.S. 285.
	4. Durango and Mesa Verde	2	215	U.S. 84, U.S. 160.
	5. return to Denver	1	390	U.S. 160, I-25.
			984	
West	1. Los Angeles*	2	—	
	2. Las Vegas*	2	272	I-15.
	3. Palm Springs	1	309	I-15, I-10, Calif. 111.
	4. San Diego*	2	133	Calif. 111, Calif. 74, Calif. 79, I-15.
			714	
West	1. San Francisco*	2	—	
	2. Sacramento	1	86	I-80.
	3. Reno	1	136	I-80.
	4. Lake Tahoe*	2	56	U.S. 395, U.S. 50.
	5. return to San Francisco	1	204	U.S. 50, I-80.
			482	

If you have two weeks or more . . .

Florida & Georgia	1. Atlanta*	2	—	
	2. Savannah*	2	256	I-75, I-16.
	3. St. Augustine	1	175	I-95, U.S. 1.
	4. Orlando* & Disney World	3	200	I-95, I-4.
	5. Palm Beach	1	146	I-95, U.S. 1.
	6. Miami*	2	75	I-95,U.S. 1.
	7. Sarasota	1	212	U.S.41.
	8. St. Petersburg*	1	51	U.S. 41, I-275.
	9. Tallahassee	1	256	U.S. 19, U.S. 27.
	10. return to Atlanta	1	268	U.S. 319, I-75.
			1628	

Florida & Louisiana	1. Atlanta*	2	—	
	2. Great Smoky Mountains	2	231	U.S. 19, U.S. 441.
	3. Nashville*	2	225	U.S. 441, I-40.
	4. Memphis*	2	200	I-40.
	5. Vicksburg	1	231	I-55, I-20.
	6. New Orleans*	4	250	U.S. 61, I-10.
	7. Montgomery	1	312	I-10, I-65.
	8. return to Atlanta	1	168	I-85.
			1617	
Arizona & The Grand Canyon	1. Phoenix*	3	—	
	2. Grand Canyon*	2	218	I-17, U.S. 180.
	3. Las Vegas*	2	290	Ariz. 64, I-40, U.S. 93.
	4. Zion National Park	2	162	I-15, Utah 9.
	5. Monument Valley	2	256	Utah 9, U.S. 89, Ariz. 98, U.S. 160, U.S. 163.
	6. Canyon de Chelly	2	112	U.S. 163, U.S. 160, U.S. 191.
	7. Indian Pueblos	1	81	U.S. 191, Ariz. 264.
	8. return to Phoenix	1	281	Ariz. 264, U.S. 89, I-17.
			1375	
California	1. Los Angeles*	3	—	
	2. Death Valley*	2	306	I-15,
	3. Sequoia Nat'l Park*	1	362	Calif. 127, Calif. 190.
	4. Yosemite Nat'l Park*	2	177	Calif. 190, Calif. 178, Calif. 65, Calif. 198.
	5. San Francisco*	3	210	Calif. 198, Calif. 180, Calif, 41.
	6. California Coast*	3	487	Calif. 120, I-205, I-580.
	7. return to Los Angeles	1	1543	U.S. 101, Calif. 1.
California & Navajoland	1. Denver*	2	—	
	2. Mesa Verde Nat'l Park	2	416	I-25, U.S. 160.
	3. Monument Valley	2	158	U.S. 160, U.S. 163.
	4. Canyon de Chelly	2	112	U.S. 163, U.S. 160, U.S. 191.
	5. Santa Fe*	3	287	U.S. 191, Ariz. 264, I-40, I-25.
	6. Durango	1	215	U.S. 84., N. Mex. 96, N. Mex. 44, U.S. 550.
	7. Colorado Springs	2	316	U.S. 160, I-25.
	8. return to Denver	1	66	I-25.
			1573	
Colorado & Yellowstone	1. Denver*	2	—	
	2. Dinosaur Nat'l Park	1	303	I-70, Colo. 13, Colo. 64, U.S.40.
	3. Salt Lake City*	3	200	U.S. 40, I-80.
	4. Jackson, Wyo.	1	301	I-15, U.S. 26.
	5. Yellowstone Nat'l Park*	4	79	U.S. 89.
	6. Casper	1	293	U.S. 20, Wyo. 120, U.S. 20.

	7. Rocky Mountain Nat'l Park	2	275	I-25, U.S. 34.
	8. return to Denver	1	70	U.S. 34, U.S. 36.
			1521	
Texas & Louisiana	1. Dallas*	3	—	
	2. Austin	1	192	I-35
	3. San Antonio*	2	80	I-35.
	4. Houston*	3	196	I-10.
	5. Baton Rouge	1	281	I-10.
	6. New Orleans*	3	81	I-10.
	7. Vicksburg	1	253	I-10, U.S. 61.
	8. return to Dallas	1	362	I-20.
			1445	

If you have three weeks or more . . .

East Coast & the South	1. Boston*	2	—	
	2. New York*	2	212	I-95.
	3. Philadelphia*	2	100	I-278, I-95.
	4. Washington*	2	134	I-95.
	5. Williamsburg	1	160	I-395, I-95, I-64.
	6. Roanoke	1	221	I-64, I-81.
	7. Great Smoky Mountains	1	303	I-81, U.S. 441.
	8. Atlanta*	2	231	U.S. 441, U.S. 19.
	9. Charleston*	2	306	I-20, U.S. 78, I-26.
	10. Raleigh	1	261	U.S. 52, I-95, U.S. 70.
	11. Virginia Beach	1	184	U.S. 64, I-95, U.S. 58.
	12. Assateague Island	1	106	U.S. 60, U.S. 13, Va. 175.
	13. Atlantic City	1	145 +Ferry	Va. 175, U.S. 13, U.S. 113, U.S. 9, Garden St. Pkway.
	14. New York*	1	128	I-95, I-278,
	15. return to Boston	1	212	I-95.
			2706	
California & Nevada	1. San Francisco*	4	—	
	2. Sacramento	1	93	I-80.
	3. Reno*	2	137	U.S. 50, U.S. 395,
	4. Death Valley*	2	380	I-80, Nev. 50, U.S. 95, Nev. 267.
	5. Zion Park & Bryce Canyon	3	381	Calif.190, Calif. 127, Nev. 373, U.S. 95, I-15, Utah 9.
	6. Grand CAnyon	2	312	U.S. 09, Ariz. 64.
	7. Las Vegas*	2	290	Ariz. 64, I-40, U.S. 93.
	8. Los Angeles*	3	282	I-15, I-10.
	9. return to San Francisco	2	487	Calif. 1, U.S. 101.
			2365	
California & Grand Canyon	1. Los Angeles*	3	—	
	2. San Diego*	2	125	Calif. 1, I-5.
	3. Phoenix*	2	356	I-8, Ariz. 85.
	4. Grand Canyon*	2	218	I-17, U.S. 180.
	5. Las Vegas*	2	290	Ariz. 64, I-40, U.S. 93.

	6. Death Valley*	2	143	U.S. 95, Nev. 373, Calif. 190.
	7. Sequoia Nat'l Park*	1	362	Calif. 190, Calif. 178, Calif. 65, Calif. 198.
	8. Yosemite Nat'l Park*	2	177	Calif. 180, Calif. 41.
	9. San Francisco*	3	210	Calif. 120, I-205, I-580, I-80.
	10. return to Los Angeles	2	487 2371	U.S. 101, Calif. 1.
Utah, Arizona, & Nevada	1. Las Vegas*	2	—	
	2. Zion Park & Bryce Canyon	3	243	I-15, Utah 9, U.S. 89, Utah 12.
	3. Salt Lake City*	2	262	Utah 12, U.S. 89, I-15.
	4. Canyonlands & Arches Park	3	243	I-15, U.S. 6, U.S. 191.
	5. Mesa Verde Park	2	150	U.S. 191, U.S. 666, U.S. 160.
	6. Monument Valley	2	158	U.S. 160, U.S. 163.
	7. Canyon de Chelley	1	112	U.S. 163, U.S. 160, U.S. 191,
	8. Indian Pueblos	1	81	U.S. 191, Ariz. 264.
	9. Glen Canyon	2	141	Ariz. 264, U.S. 89.
	10. Grand Canyon*	2	137	U.S. 89, Ariz. 64.
	11. return to Las Vegas	1	290 1840	Ariz. 64, I-40, U.S. 93.

If you have a month or more . . .

Colorado, Yellowstone, the Pacific Northwest, & California	1. Denver*	3	—	
	2. Rocky Mountain Nat'l Park	1	70	U.S. 36, U.S. 34.
	3. Casper	1	275	U.S. 34, I-25.
	4. Yellowstone Nat'l Park*	3	293	U.S. 20, Wyo. 120, U.S. 20.
	5. Butte	1	212	U.S. 89, I-90.
	6. Spokane	1	315	I-90.
	7. Seattle*	2	293	U.S. 2, Wash. 174, Wash. 155, U.S. 2, Wash. 522.
	8. Pacific Coast*	2	468	Ferry + U.S. 101, U.S. 30.
	9. Portland*	2	—	—
	10. Medford & Jacksonville	1	250	I-5.
	11. Sacramento	2	341	I-5.
	12. San Francisco*	3	93	I-80.
	13. Yosemite Nat'l Park*	2	210	I-580, I-205, Calif. 120, Calif. 41.
	14. Death Valley*	2	321	Calif. 41, Calif. 120, U.S. 395, Calif. 190.
	15. Las Vegas*	1	143	Calif. 190, Nev. 373, U.S. 95.
	16. Zion Park & Bryce Canyon	2	243	I-15, Utah 9, U.S. 89, Utah 12.
	17. Grand Junction	1	337	Utah 12, U.S. 89, I-70.
	18. return to Denver	1	259 4124	I-70.

BEFORE YOU LEAVE HOME

SOURCES OF INFORMATION: Begin planning as far in advance as possible, especially if you will travel during peak seasons. Every state has a central tourist information office and a series of regional offices; most cities also have convention and tourist bureaus; both will provide a lot of information. For a complete listing of state tourist organizations, see the Appendix; for city bureaus, see each city chapter under "Tourist Information."

You can also contact the **International Association of Convention and Visitors Bureaus,** P.O. Box 758, Champaign, IL 61820 (217/359-8881).

USING A TRAVEL AGENT: To use a travel agent successfully you need to find a good one, and you need to know where you want to go and what you want to do, so that you're free to go over the details with the agent, modifying your plans to incorporate his or her professional advice. The first can be achieved by asking for personal recommendations among your friends, or by contacting the **American Society of Travel Agents (ASTA),** 4400 MacArthur Blvd. NW, Washington, DC 20007, whose members have been in business a minimum of three years; or the **Institute of Certified Travel Agents,** 148 Linden St. (P.O. Box 56), Wellesley, MA 02181 (617/237-0280), whose certification means that the agent has taken an 18-month training course sponsored by the institute.

If your main interest is saving money on air fares, to really make good use of your travel agent, keep asking for the lowest fare and request the agent to check out the many ways that can be used to find the lowest price—flying to a destination in two or more segments to take advantage of discounts on particular highly competitive or infrequently flown routes, etc. If the agent is not willing to do this, you need to find one who will, although you may be charged a modest additional fee for these services.

WHAT AND HOW TO PACK: Just some brief hints:

1. Leave at home clothes that need to be ironed before each wearing, unless you're staying at a deluxe resort/hotel. Pack drip-dry coordinated separates so that you can vary your outfits easily.

2. Pack a pair of comfortable shoes.

3. Carry extra pairs of contact lenses and glasses, and copies of any prescriptions.

4. Travel light, even if you're driving—lugging heavy bags in and out of the trunk is tedious. Two small, light bags are better than one heavy, large one.

5. If you're flying, pack one carry-on bag with toiletries and other necessities, in case checked luggage gets lost. Airlines are strictly enforcing the limit of two carry-on bags; both must fit under the seat (about $9 \times 14 \times 22$ inches; $25 \times 35 \times 92$ cm) or in an overhead bin ($10 \times 14 \times 36$ inches; $23 \times 35 \times 56$ cm).

6. Pack an extra folding bag for shopping finds.

7. Make a list of all items to be packed a few weeks before you leave.

8. Take copies of any important documents and also record traveler's check numbers. Stow separately.

INSURANCE: If you're taking a prepaid package tour, cruise, or charter flight, you may want to take out a special traveler's insurance for a specific trip that covers baggage loss, cancellation/trip interruption, and medical emergencies. Always check the fine print for exclusions from coverage, limits, and restricted definitions of whatever sort. Be sure that the policy is adequate to cover nondiscounted air fares and unexpected hotel expenses, if you do have to interrupt your trip for any emergency reason. Such policies are obtainable from an insurance broker or travel agent. Whatever you do, before you leave home, check:

1. Your homeowner's insurance, for off-premises theft and loss; if it doesn't cover this you may want to purchase a floater to protect you during your vacation.

2. Your health insurance, for any pre-treatment emergency requirements—hot line numbers, etc. Most standard health insurance policies will cover you while on vacation.

3. Your auto insurance, for full coverage—accident insurance for medical expenses, injury to other passengers in your car, and loss of pay if you're injured; liability for injury you cause to another person or property; comprehensive and collision; and uninsured motorist protection if you're involved in an accident with an uninsured driver of another car.

4. Your personal insurance, because if it does not cover you for injury or death when flying, you may want to amend your policy. Although your plane ticket price automatically includes airline liability insurance, the limits are set by individual state laws and each claim is hard fought and consequently costly. Some credit-card companies automatically provide flight insurance if your ticket is charged to that account—American Express, for example.

A TRAVEL-PLANNING CHECKLIST: Here is a quick list of things to take care of in advance and at the very last minute:

In Advance

1. Leave with a friend a house key, your auto registration number, and a trip itinerary (including, if possible, names of specific accommodations, where you will be staying). As a further precaution, you can notify the police of your departure and tell them who has your key and travel plans.

2. Write or call state and local tourists boards along your route and at your destination for information on attractions, special events, and special weather conditions (remember the vagaries of weather when packing).

3. Have your car checked and serviced. Fluid levels and tire pressures should be up to capacity, oil and oil filter clean, and ignition system tuned.

4. Prepare an emergency road kit, including basic tools, flares, flashlight, a duplicate set of car keys (to be kept with you), and a first-aid kit; check the jack and spare tire.

5. Think about health needs (do you need a medical or dental checkup before you go?). Carry an adequate supply of any prescription drugs and medications you require, and take along a copy of important prescriptions, in case of loss. Have extras for other important personal items, such as a pair of glasses and contact lenses.

6. Store valuables at home in a safe place. You may want to rent a safe-deposit box for silverware and jewelry, or register major appliances (stereo, television) with the police (check your homeowner's insurance for theft coverage).

7. Check important documents and their expiration dates: driver's license, credit cards, auto insurance policy, auto registration, auto club membership card.

8. Purchase traveler's checks and record the check numbers in two places, keeping both lists separate from the checks.

9. Install automatic timers on a few lights in your home, or arrange for a friend to turn various lights on and off during your absence.

10. Discontinue deliveries, such as mail and newspapers, or arrange for a friend to pick up such items. Have someone check periodically for unexpected deliveries, pamphlets, or circulars, which tend to pile up at the door, sending a clear message to thieves that no one is home.

11. Arrange for yardwork at regular times.

12. The week before you leave, buy smaller quantities of perishable foods than usual.

At Departure

1. Remove perishable goods from the refrigerator.

2. Disconnect electrical appliances, lower the thermostat, and turn off gas jets, including the hot-water heater.

3. Set automatic timers on lights.

4. Make sure all the important documents get packed. Those traveler's checks can't help you if you leave them in the desk drawer.

5. Make a final check of all doors and windows as you are leaving the house.

6. And finally, check your travel documents, making sure that the destinations printed on your airline tickets are correct. Also, if you're flying, reconfirm your flight (even though that's not required for domestic flights).

GETTING AROUND

BY CAR: Although it may not be the least expensive way to go unless you're traveling with family or friends (with gasoline at $1 plus, the real cost of driving a medium-size car is about 30¢ a mile), it's certainly the most flexible.

Driving Your Own Car

PRE-TRIP PREPARATIONS. Inspect your car thoroughly before setting out on a long trip. The best time to do this is when the engine and tires are cool. Run through the following:

1. Check all lights—headlights, tail lights, parking lights, license-plate lights, and hazard lights. Test the brake lights, backup lights, and turn signals.

2. Make sure the horn, seatbelts, and windshield wipers are functioning properly.

3. Inspect the tires carefully and replace any tire that is cut, shows bulges on its sidewalls, or has bald patches on its tread. Also replace any tire whose tread depth is worn to one-16th inch or less. Check also for uneven wear. If there's any sign of this, take the car for wheel alignment. While the tires are cool, check the tire pressure and inflate to correct pressure. Don't forget to fill the spare.

4. With the engine off and the vehicle on a level surface, check all fluid levels: the oil level should be between "add" and "full" on the dipstick; top up the engine coolant (a 50/50 mixture of antifreeze and water) to the appropriate level, as marked on the plastic reservoir; check the power steering and automatic transmission fluid levels according to the instructions in the owner's manual. Fill the windshield washer bottle and test the system.

5. Check the battery. Make sure it's clean and dry. Top up the electrolyte (water) level, if necessary. It should be half an inch above the vertical plates in the battery. Replace the battery if the case is cracked or leaking. Also replace any battery cables that have damaged strands. Clean corroded battery and cable connections, and tighten any loose cable clamps on the battery posts.

6. Inspect the drive belts and replace any that are cracked frayed, glazed, or contaminated by grease or oil. Press the belt with your thumb midway between the pulleys. The belt needs tightening if it depresses more than half an inch.

7. Squeeze the radiator and heater hoses. If they feel brittle or spongy, replace them. With the engine running, check also for any leaks in the cooling system.

8. After inspection, road-test the car, checking to see if it pulls to the left or right on a straight road. If it does, it may need a front-end alignment. Also test the brakes. If the brake pedal feels spongy, have the brakes checked by a professional.

9. Before you leave, check that the following documents are still valid: vehicle registration, safety inspection sticker, auto insurance, auto club membership, and driver's license.

MAPS. There are several good road atlases: *The Mobil Road Atlas & Trip Planning Guide* (Prentice Hall Press); *The Rand McNally Road Atlas & Vacation Guide* is also very popular. Many auto clubs also supply maps to members (see below).

PACING. Don't drive more than 300 to 400 miles a day. Stop every two hours or so, and try to phone and make reservations for the night by mid-afternoon to avoid a wearying search at the end of an exhausting day's drive.

LEGAL ISSUES. Watch your speed limit. The recently voted higher speed limit of 65 mph is limited to Arizona, Arkansas, California, Colorado, Missouri, Nevada, New Mexico, North Dakota, Oklahoma, South Dakota, Texas, Utah, and Wyoming. Elsewhere, it's 55 mph.

Buckle up! Seatbelts for driver and front-seat passengers are mandatory in about half the states, most notably Connecticut, Illinois, Indiana, Iowa, Louisiana, Michigan, Mississippi, New Jersey, New Mexico, New York, Ohio, Oklahoma, and Utah. Seatbelts must be worn by all passengers in the District of Columbia, California, Massachusetts, and Washington. Note also that in all 50 states and in Washington, D.C., children under 4 must be in a child's seat or be buckled up.

AUTO CLUBS. Join one of the auto clubs. They will supply maps, recommended routes, guidebooks, accident and bail-bond insurance, and most important of all, emergency road service. The leader, with 850 offices and 26 million members, is the **American Automobile Association (AAA)**, 8111 Gatehouse Rd., Falls Church, VA 22047 (703/222-6000). Check telephone book for local offices. Membership for both U.S. citizens and foreign visitors range from $17 to $56, depending on which particular local office you join. AAA also has a 24 hr. emergency toll free number: 800/336-4357.

Other recommended auto clubs include the **Allstate Motor Club,** Allstate Pl., Northbrook, IL 60062 (312/402-5461); the **Amoco Motor Club,** P.O. Box 9046, Des Moines, IA 50369 (toll free 800/334-3300).

A NOTE FOR FOREIGN VISITORS. The AAA can provide you with a "Touring Permit" validating your driving license. Members of some foreign auto clubs that have reciprocal arrangements with AAA enjoy AAA's services for free.

Auto Rentals

To rent a car you need a major credit card or you'll have to leave a sizable cash deposit ($100 or more for each day). Minimum driver age is usually 21, and you'll need a valid driver's license.

SHOP AROUND. Rates vary from company to company, from location to location (airport vs. downtown, Florida vs. New York City). In addition, companies offer unlimited-mileage options vs. per-mile charges and also special discounts on weekends, for example. So it pays to shop around. Use the major companies' toll-free 800 numbers to do this. Other variable costs to check include drop-off charges if you're picking up the car in one city and leaving it in another; the cost of daily collision damage and personal accident insurance. And always return your car with a full tank—the rental companies charge excessive prices for gasoline.

THE COMPANIES. The majors are: **Hertz** (toll free 800/654-3131), **Avis** (toll free 800/331-1212), **National** (toll free 800/227-7368), **Budget** (toll free 800/527-0700), and **Dollar** (toll free 800/421-6868). Also check the smaller local companies and **Rent a Wreck** (toll free 800/535-1391), if there is one in a particular city.

BY RECREATIONAL VEHICLE (RV): Accommodating four to six people, these vehicles are ideal for long family trips. Air-conditioned, and equipped with showers, refrigerators, and a full kitchen, they're also comfortable. Throughout the U.S. campsites have hookups for electricity, water, and sewage disposal.

Book Resources

The *RV Park and Campground Directories*—one national book and two smaller editions covering the eastern U.S. and Canada and the western U.S. and Canada (Prentice Hall Press)—contain thousands of listings in easy-to-read chart format that are cross-referenced to maps, as well as establishments that sell and service RVs. The AAA also publishes regional campground directories.

Renting an RV

Check the *Yellow Pages* under "Recreational Vehicles—Renting & Leasing." Major companies include **Cruise America** (toll free 800/327-7778), **Rent Rite** (toll free 800/243-7483).

For information, contact the **Recreation Vehicle Dealer's Association,** 3251 Old Lee Hwy., Suite 500, Fairfax, VA 22030 (703/591-7130). The RVDA publishes *Rental Ventures,* a directory of rental agencies, for $5.

BY AIR: Since deregulation in 1987, shopping the airlines has become increasingly complex and travel by air increasingly irksome as airlines delay and often cancel flights without warning.

Shop Around

Use the toll-free lines to call all the airlines that go to your destination. Always ask the agent for the lowest-priced fare as opposed to a particular fare, such as an APEX (an advance purchase fare). This way you're asking them to search for the cheapest fare to your destination. Once you've located it and made a reservation, still check a day or so before your departure to see if there's been a fare change since you booked—you'll be due a refund if it has decreased, but no extra charge if it's increased—because airlines, as the departure date draws nearer, will make more seats available for discounting if the flight is not being booked. That's why, for example, you can call on Wednesday, June 23, and be told that no discount seats are available, and then call on Thursday, June 24, and obtain a discount seat. So it really is worth calling almost daily up to the departure time to see if any discounts have opened up.

The Regular Fare Structure

At the top there's **first class.** You're paying for larger seats, more leg room, superior service and meals. In **business class,** the next step down, you get a little extra leg room and some extra little services, including free drinks. A **coach** or **economy** fare puts you in cramped seating, and ensures typical airline food and service.

For all three classes above you can book at the last moment, incur no cancellation penalties, and your round-trip ticket will be good for a year, longer if you renew it.

Personal Rating of the Nine Major U.S. Airlines

Airline	Service	Punctuality
American		
United	Good	Good
Delta*	Good	Moderate
Pan Am**		
Northwest	Moderate	Moderate
Continental		
TWA**		
Eastern**	Mediocre	Mediocre
US Air		

*Acceptable food in flight.

**Very poor food in flight.

Discount Fares

Referred to variously as Excursion, Super Saver, or Advance Purchase (APEX), these offer savings as much as 35% to 45% of the regular fare—but they do have strings attached.

Usually they must be booked anywhere from one week to a month in advance; they carry penalties for changing either the date of departure or return, and also for cancellation.

To find these discount fares, check your local newspaper advertisements. Among them, sometimes you'll find incredible promotions like the recent offer by Northwest Airlines to senior citizens to discount any air fare on their domestic routes by the purchaser's age—if you were 100, you flew free; if you were 75, you flew for 75% off. All thanks to America's penchant for creative marketing.

Other money-savers are: flying off-season (mid-January through March and October through mid-December, except Thanksgiving weekend); off-hour flights (10 a.m. to 3 p.m. and after 8 p.m. departures); day-of-the-week reductions (usually Tuesday, Wednesday, Thursday, or Saturday when traffic is lightest); and routing with stops or connections (direct means stops but no change of plane; nonstop means exactly that).

Be aware, too, that you may be able to save a lot of money by splitting your trip into segments and taking advantage of particularly low fares on a given segment. For example, a travel agent looking for the lowest fare from Pittsburgh to Portland, Oregon, might see only an American Airlines fare of $505 each way, but if the agent "digs" he or she may find that you can fly on United from Pittsburgh to Denver and then from Denver to Portland for a total of only $320—a great savings. It's worth checking alternative routings either through an agent or by calling the airlines directly and asking them constantly, "Isn't there anything cheaper?"

Anyone requiring only a one-way fare should always look into the comparable price of a round-trip super-saver or other discount ticket. Sometimes it's simply cheaper to take the round-trip ticket and throw the return half away (better yet, you can sell it to someone). Anomalies like this can always be found.

Airline Passes, Charters, and Tour Packages

Often airlines will offer special passes for particular groups—like senior citizens or youths. For example, last year Eastern offered a pass to 62-year-olds-plus, good for one year's unlimited flying anywhere within their system.

Frequent-flyer plans can cut costs dramatically. Bonus points accumulate every time you fly, and recently the airlines have been offering triple-mileage bonuses. Estimates are that the public currently has billions of dollars' worth of free flying miles!

Often you can take advantage of an all-inclusive tour package which will deliver a very cheap air fare, and possibly some extra discounts on car rentals, accommodations, and sightseeing. These are most often offered in Florida and the Southwest. Remember that you don't have to use the whole package, but you may still save money by purchasing it and not using what you don't want.

Flying as an Air Courier

Although this fun low-cost way of flying is more available for foreign travel, there are one or two companies that recruit people to fly as couriers carrying packages to domestic destinations. Anyone can become a courier. All you do is give up your baggage allowance, except for a carry-on. The courier company handles the check-in and pickup of packages at each airport. Special arrangements do have to be made to enable two people to fly, often on staggered flights. The savings, though, are remarkable.

Here are just a couple of suggested companies: **Now Voyager Freelance Courier,** 74 Varick St., Mezzanine B, New York, NY 10013 (212/431-1616), with flights to Los Angeles and Miami only; and **Graf Airfreight,** 5811 Willoughby Ave., Hollywood, CA 90038 (213/461-1547), with flights to New York, Los Angeles, and Chicago only.

Notes and Special Air Fares for Foreign Visitors

There are about nine "major" airlines (although several are owned by the same corporate parent), a dozen somewhat smaller "nationals," and hundreds of local commuter carriers, offering day and night service at more than 1,000 airports. Taking the plane in the U.S.A. has become almost as simple as taking the subway or a cab. Some lines, like Eastern's or Pan Am's New York/Washington and New York/Boston shuttles, require no reservations and fares are paid in flight to an attendant.

SPECIAL AIR FARES. Foreign visitors can take advantage of the special promotional air fares that have been discussed above, but they can also obtain special passes *before they leave home* that allow unlimited flying anywhere on the airline's network for a stated time period, usually 21 days, one month, three months, etc. These passes do usually carry restrictions—blackout days of the week; holidays, etc.; no backtracking; and so on. Unfortunately, none are currently available, but they have been offered in the past and it's worth inquiring.

Some Easy Flying Hints

Use the secondary airports if you can, like Midway instead of O'Hare in Chicago; Dulles instead of National in Washington, D.C.; Newark instead of LaGuardia or Kennedy in New York.

Allow plenty of time between connecting flights; unless you have to, don't book the last flight of the day since you'll be stuck overnight if you miss it or are bumped.

To protect themselves against people who reserve seats and don't show up, the airlines do overbook their planes. If everyone shows up, obviously something has to give and passengers do get "bumped." The airlines, however, must abide by certain rules in resolving the situation. If the airlines can arrange alternative flights that arrive within one hour of the originally scheduled flight, then it does not have to pay compensation of any sort. If the delay is longer, compensation is mandatory. Airlines usually offer ticket vouchers. If you are bumped, find out immediately what the airline will do to make your enforced delay more comfortable—meal vouchers, overnight accommodations, etc. Speak to a supervisor if a reservations clerk cannot give you a good answer. Also, if you have connecting flights, make sure that those airlines are informed.

For a booklet entitled *Fly Rights* that discusses passengers' rights, send $1 to the Consumer Information Center, Department 156T, Pueblo, CO 81009 (303/948-3334).

If you have any complaints about the airlines—regarding lost baggage, bumping, or anything else—inform the Office of Community and Consumer Affairs, U.S. Department of Transportation, 400 7th St. SW, Room 10405, Washington DC 20590 (202/366-2220).

BY TRAIN: Although the savings over air travel may be negligible, going by train is a comfortable option if you have the time. It takes 49 hours by train from Chicago to San Francisco, 28 hours from New York to New Orleans, and 33 hours from Seattle to Los Angeles. On some routes—Washington to New York, for example—you're better off taking the Metroliner than the airplane. Total travel time by train will be about the same or less.

AMTRAK services some 600 cities, in all states except Maine, New Hampshire, Oklahoma, South Dakota, Hawaii, and Alaska. Facilities along the Boswash corridor and on long-distance lines west of the Mississippi are good, but a bit uneven elsewhere. Some of these trains boast panoramic cars from which you can admire the landscape—they include the *California Zephyr* (Chicago–San Francisco), the *Coast Starlight* (Seattle–Los Angeles), the *Southwest Chief* (Chicago–Los Angeles), the *Desert Wind* (Chicago–Salt Lake City–Los Angeles), the *Empire Builder* (Chicago–Seattle) and the *Sunset Limited* (New Orleans–Los Angeles). Long-distance trains have full dining and lounge cars; on others there's usually a snackbar and lounge.

Seat Types and Fares

Reclining day-coach seats are allocated on both a first-come, first-served basis and a reservation basis, depending on the train. The most economical for overnight is a reclining coach seat with a pull-up leg rest—pillows and blankets are provided as well.

Sleeping compartments vary between eastern and western trains. East of the Mississippi River, a single traveler can reserve a roomette, which consists of one lounge seat, which is stowed away when the bed is pulled down from the wall, a private toilet, and a closet. Or two travelers can reserve a bedroom with two lounge or bench seats, two berths, and toilet facilities. On trains running west of the Mississippi River, two different options are available. There's an economy room, with two lounge seats by day and two berths by night; or a deluxe bedroom, with showers and private toilet facilities. The price of sleeping accommodations is added on to the coach fare and includes three meals daily in the dining car.

Railpasses and Special Fares

All Aboard America passes can be purchased in the U.S. and allow unlimited travel within one of AMTRAK's regional divisions for 45 days, with two stopovers allowed in addition to your final destination. One-region travel is currently priced at $159 for coach accommodations (they can be upgraded). A two-region ticket is $239, and a three-region (total country) is $299. When one-way coach fares are $59 from New York to Chicago and $99 from New York to California, obviously the savings on such a pass are proportionate to the distance traveled.

AMTRAK also occasionally offers promotional fares like its **One-Way Plus $7,** which adds only $7 to a one-way fare over $60 to make it round trip.

The Auto Train

Running between Lorton, Va. (just south of Washington, D.C.), and Sanford, Fla. (just north of Orlando), this nonstop train will transport you *and* your car. Coach accommodations, dinner with wine, and a continental breakfast are provided. The Auto Train leaves daily at 4 p.m. (at both ends) and takes approximately 18 hours. Sleeping accommodations are available for an extra charge. Off-peak fares in 1988 were $135 one way for an adult, but they vary substantially from season to season.

AMTRAK Tours, Information, and Bookings

Get a copy of AMTRAK's National Timetable from any AMTRAK station, from travel agents, or by contacting AMTRAK, 400 N. Capitol St. NW, Washington, DC 20001 (toll free 800/USA-RAIL).

The reservation system is computerized; tickets can be purchased at stations and sales offices, from travel agents, or aboard the train for a small added fee. Some major stations now also have self-service machines that dispense reserved tickets (you must have booked by telephone and have an assigned reservation number).

AMTRAK offers some 75 tour packages throughout the U.S. For information, contact AMTRAK, Western Folder Distribution Co., Box 7700, 1549 W. Glen Lake Ave., Itasca, IL 60143 (312/773-3377).

For Foreign Visitors

AMTRAK offers the **USA Railpass,** available only overseas to non–U.S. citizens. This pass is unique in that it offers 45-day travel with an *unlimited* number of stopovers. Fares for regional plans vary from $45 for travel within Florida to $299 for travel within the whole of the continental U.S.

BY BUS: The least expensive way to travel, but often the most time-consuming (New York to Chicago takes 17 hours). Greyhound, which acquired its only major rival, Trailways in 1987, now reaches more than 8,000 cities and towns. Coaches are air-conditioned in summer (bring a sweater), heated in winter, and long-distance buses have toilets. Rest and meal stops are made about every four hours—best to bring your own snacks, though.

For longer trips, book an express or nonstop bus. Also, plan to arrive at your destination in daylight; some bus terminals are located in unsavory neighborhoods.

Always ask about promotional fares. For extensive travel, Greyhound's **Ameripass** is a real bargain, priced in 1988 at $189 for 7 days, $249 for 15 days, and $349 for 30 days.

No reservations are necessary, but you should arrive at least a half hour before departure time. Greyhound also offers reasonably priced package tours—for information, call toll free 800/528-6055.

For Information

Contact **Greyhound Bus Company,** Inter First Plaza, 901 Main St., 25th Floor, Dallas, TX 75202 (214/655-7000), or check the phone directory for the local number.

For Foreign Visitors

For foreign students, the best bet is the **International Ameripass,** which grants unlimited travel within the U.S. (it's also honored in Canada). Seven days of travel is $125, 15 days is $165, and 30 days is $250. The International Ameripass can be purchased in New York, Orlando, Miami, San Francisco, and Los Angeles with a student ID and a passport.

HITCHHIKING: Although hitching a ride is against the law in many states, people still do it. As a general rule it's forbidden on major highways and on limited-access roads (Interstates, freeways, expressways, and turnpikes).

The best way to find a ride is by contacting a ride-line group: Their telephone numbers can easily be obtained on any college campus, and the only cost is a few dollars' membership fee and a share of the gas costs.

Hitchhiking is either illegal or severely restricted in the following states: Alaska, Arizona, Arkansas, Colorado, Delaware, Georgia, Maryland, Michigan, Minnesota, Montana, New Jersey, North Dakota, South Carolina, Tennessee, Texas, and Utah.

GROUP TOURS/PACKAGES: These fly/drive, rail/drive, fully escorted, and various other types of tours save time and effort—and often money. Before booking though, you should:

1. Check to see if the tour operator is reliable. You can be pretty sure of this if the operator is a member of USTOA (United States Tour Operators Association), which requires for membership a minimum three years in business and hefty professional liability insurance. Write USTOA, 211 E. 51st St., Suite 12B, New York, NY 10022. Also, check with the local Better Business Bureau (212/944-5727).

2. Read the fine print. Make sure you know exactly what the overall price includes and what it doesn't; what the cancellation penalties are; and whether or not the company is free to cancel if not enough people sign up or to change the prices before departure.

DISCOUNT TRAVEL

The travel industry is so large and diverse that, like any other retail industry, there are an increasing number of professional discounters as well as newsletters and other information sources that clue you in on the latest travel discounts and bargains, from air fares to hotels and tour packages.

NEWSLETTERS: The following are reputable and useful:

Arthur Frommer's Travel Letter, 951 Broken Sound Pkwy., NW Suite 300, Boca Raton, FL 33431 (407/240-1800).

Consumer Reports Travel Letter, Subscription Department, P.O. Box 2886, Boulder, CO 80322 (303/447-9330; toll free 800/525-0643): Particularly useful for air fare discounts. A monthly, the subscription is $37.

Travel Smart, 40 Beechdale Rd., Dobbs Ferry, NY 10522 (914/693-8300): One of the oldest in the business. Published 12 times a year, an introductory subscription is $37, with a $44 renewal rate.

LAST-MINUTE TRAVEL CLUBS AND OTHER DISCOUNTERS: The first category purchases the excess inventory of travel suppliers and then sells it off at a discount to its membership. Members are given a toll-free hotline to call to obtain the latest offerings; occasionally, too, they receive newsheets detailing future offerings. Among such organizations are:

Discount Travel International, 114 Forrest Ave., Narberth, PA 19072 (215/668-2182; toll free 800/824-4000): Annual membership is $45.

Last Minute Travel Club, 132 Brookline Ave., Boston, MA 02215 (617/267-9800): Annual membership for one is $30; for two, $35.

Moment's Notice, 40 E. 49th St., New York, NY 10017: Annual fee is $45.

On Call to Travel, 14335 S.W. Allen Blvd., Suite 209, Beaverton, OR 97007 (503/643-7212): Annual fee is $39.

Stand Buys Ltd., 311 W. Superior St., Suite 404, Chicago, IL 60610 (312/943-5737; toll free 800/255-1488): Annual fee is $45.

Worldwide Discount Travel Club, 1674 Meridian Ave., Miami Beach, FL 33139 (305/534-2082): Family membership is $50; individual membership, $35.

Encore Marketing International, 4501 Forbes Blvd., Lanham, MD 20706 (301/459-8020), operates three specialty discounting organizations: Short Notice (annual membership is $36) gives you access to last-minute discounts on tour packages and organized trips; Encore (annual membership is $48) provides additional free nights at hotels and discounts on car rentals and air fares; Villas of the World ($60 for one year) delivers 20%- to 25%-per-night discounts on villa, resort, and hotel accommodations.

Recently, several specialist air fare discounters have appeared. They only deal in air tickets and for a fixed fee they will sell you a discount ticket. They are able to do this because they rebate part of the standard agent's commission to you, the customer.

McTravel, 130 S. Jefferson, Chicago, IL 60606 (312/876-1116; toll free 800/333-3335), is one of the better-known organizations in this area.

WHERE TO STAY

HOTELS AND MOTELS: For the last word in décor and facilities like health clubs or spas, there are the major players like Hilton, Hyatt, Ritz Carlton, Sheraton, Westin. In big cities, especially New York, Washington, Los Angeles, and Chicago, expect to pay $200 and up a night. Elsewhere, expect to pay $60 to $90 double in a two-star establishment, $90 to $140 in three- and most four-stars, and $140 to $200 in a few deluxe, four-star hotels. (*Money-Saving Hint:* Always ask about weekend packages, corporate rates, and any other special promotions being offered.)

Below the leaders are a host of motel chains offering comfortable rooms with full facilities at moderate prices. Sure they're standardized, but at least you know what to expect. Among them are Best Western, Holiday Inn, Howard Johnson, La Quinta Motor Inns, Ramada Inns, Rodeway Inns, Travelodge, and Vagabond. Doubles range from $40 to $80. (*Money-Saving Hint:* Again, ask about weekend packages and other discount rates. Use their toll-free numbers listed in the Appendix.)

Even more standardized, often located on the outskirts of cities and with limited facilities (sometimes without a restaurant) are the budget motel chains. Color TV and telephone, though, are standard. Look for Days Inns, Econo Lodges, Friendship Inns, Motel 6, Red Roof Inns, Holiday Inns' Hampton Inns, and Marriott's Fairfield Inns. Doubles can go as low as $20 and as high as $45.

INNS: Staying at a country inn is extremely popular across the whole country, although perhaps the greatest number of inns are in the Northeast, the South, and California. Many of these accommodations are historic homes that may have once served as stagecoach stops or even mansions for the wealthy. Usually they have a distinctive ambience, traditional antique or other noteworthy furnishings, and a personality that reflects the style and interests of the innkeepers. By definition, an inn should have a restaurant; otherwise, technically it's only a bed-and-breakfast establishment, but sometimes the definitions blur. Many inns often lack TV and room phone—the whole atmosphere is usually one of quiet relaxation. Inns and children do not usually mix—the kids find them boring—but the peace and quiet and personal charm of inns do appeal to most of us harried urban dwellers. The price tag can be high—from $80 and up, depending on the character and style of the particular inn.

How to Locate Them

Consult one of the many books available. In my opinion, the best among the many series is *Marilyn Wood's Wonderful Weekends* (Prentice Hall Press), which contains full descriptions of several hundred inns in the states surrounding New York City—Connecticut, Rhode Island, Massachusetts, Vermont, Pennsylvania, New York, New Jersey, and Delaware.

BED-AND-BREAKFAST: These establishments are increasingly popular and
also increasingly sophisticated. Some are beautifully renovated historic homes and breakfasts are lavish; others are simply homes and breakfast is taken with the family. Both types are very personal and a great way to meet the locals.

How to Locate Them

For a nationwide listing, contact the **Bed and Breakfast Registry,** P.O. Box 8174, St. Paul, MN 55108 (612/646-4238). Book resources include *Frommer's Bed & Breakfast North America* (Prentice Hall Press), which among other things lists all the bed-and-breakfast registries that you can contact to locate pre-inspected B&Bs. The *West Coast Bed & Breakfast Guide* and the *East Coast Bed & Breakfast Guide* (both Prentice Hall Press) describe and picture in four-color the prime B&B places.

YOUTH HOSTELS, Ys, AND UNIVERSITY ACCOMMODATIONS:
There are 270 youth hostels across the country that are open to members of any age. Annual membership is $20 for people ages 18 to 54, $10 for all others. Nightly charges run $5 to $10. Sleeping accommodations are usually in small single-sex dorms, although some hostels have private accommodations. Cooking and laundry facilities available.

For more information, contact **American Youth Hostels, Inc.,** National Administrative Offices, P.O. Box 37613, Washington, DC 20013 (202/783-6161).

The 40 or so YMCA (Young Men's Christian Association) and YMCA (Young Women's Christian Association) hostels are clustered in the bigger cities, charging $15 to $20 a night without bath or $30 to $40 with bath (you'll pay a little more in the major cities). Generally they are pleasant and well-equipped (pools, health clubs), with private rooms. Because of their popularity you should arrive early to secure a room.

The largest YMCA in New York City, **Sloane House,** 356 W. 34th St., New York, NY 10001 (212/760-5860 or 212/760-5856), will make advance reservations for you at other Ys, and also offers discount vouchers good at 42 YM/YWCAs.

During the summer many campus accommodations are open to travelers. Accommodations are usually very comfortable and low priced. For more information, contact the **Council on International Educational Exchange (CIEE),** Sloane House, 356 W. 34th St., New York, NY 10001 (212/563-3441), and ask for their publication *Where to Stay USA,* which is co-published with Prentice Hall Press and also available in bookstores.

CAMPING: There's an excellent network of 8,000 public and 8,000 private
campgrounds across the U.S., many with sites fully equipped with water, electricity, sewer connections, barbecues, showers, general store, and often with a swim-

ming pool and other recreational facilities. For a family tent site the fee is $12 to $15; $15 to $30 for a motor home. Send $2 to **Kampgrounds of America (KOA)**, P.O. Box 30558, Billings, MT 59114 (406/248-7444), for a list of campgrounds.

Book Resources: *RV Park & Campground Directories* (Prentice Hall Press); *Camp USA* (Prentice Hall Press). The AAA also publishes regional campground directories.

TIPS ON HAPPY STAYS: Make reservations particularly in peak tourist seasons and in large cities where conventions and other special events may block out accommodations. Small inns and bed-and-breakfasts also require advance bookings, particularly on weekends.

If you expect to arrive late, ask for "guaranteed late arrival"—that way your room will be held. When you book, make sure you understand the rate categories: European Plan (EP) is room only; Continental Plan (CP), room and continental breakfast; Modified American Plan (MAP), room, full breakfast, and dinner; American Plan (AP), room, breakfast, lunch, and dinner. Don't forget to include local and state taxes in the total price.

FOOD AND DRINK

The United States, this great melting pot of cultures, offers many cuisines to choose from: at one end of the spectrum are four-star restaurants serving "nouvelle cuisine"; at the other end, little Greek tavernas, Mexican eateries, and Thai restaurants with unbeatable prices. From the authentic New York "deli" (sorely missed in other parts of the country) to profoundly Italian *trattorie,* from authentic German beer cellars to Chinese restaurants better than any in Asia, the U.S. has them all.

CUISINE OF THE NORTHEAST: The whole Northeast, and especially New England, prominently features seafood, beginning with the typical Boston dish, *clam chowder,* a thick shellfish soup. Other respected specialties are *Boston baked beans* (salt pork, beans, onions, and molasses baked slowly in a clay crockpot), and *Yankee pot roast* (beef braised with onions, tomatoes, carrots, and celery). Cape Cod (*Chatham, Wellfleet, Cotuit*) and Long Island (*Blue Point*) are famous for their oysters. Chesapeake Bay, south of Baltimore, is well known for its blue crabs, scallops, and *Pocomoke* oysters. Chesapeake Bay crabs are the raw material for Maryland's great specialty, *crab cakes,* little crabmeat patties, breaded and sautéed.

The best *lobsters* come from Maine, the northernmost state of New England. They are the heart of a dish of American Indian origin, the *clambake,* which involves digging a hole in the sand at the bottom of which raw fish, clams, and lobsters are laid on a bed of red-hot stones and allowed to cook under a tarpaulin or a layer of branches.

Besides its shellfish, Long Island, to the east of New York City, is famous for its *Long Island ducklings.* Vermont, near the Canadian border, is the birthplace of *cheddar cheese soup* and the principal producer of *maple syrup,* traditionally served with pancakes and waffles. New England offers two desserts drawn from the cookbooks of the earliest settlers: sweet *pumpkin pie,* and *Indian pudding,* made from cornmeal and molasses and generally topped with whipped cream, which is an old Boston tradition.

Other northeastern specialties include: *clam fritters* (Maine and Rhode Island); *codfish balls* (New England); *crab Imperial,* crabmeat baked in a white-wine sauce (from Maryland); *fish stew,* a New England soup made from different kinds of fish or from oysters, clams, or other shellfish cooked in milk or cream, which unlike chowder contains no potatoes or other vegetables; *fried clams* (popular in

Maine and Rhode Island); *hoagie* or submarine, an enormous hero sandwich made with ham, salami, provolone, onions, tomatoes, lettuce, and fresh pepper, all doused in olive oil (a Philadelphia classic); *lobster pie,* a flaky pastry crust filled with lobster in white sauce (Maine); *Manhattan clam chowder,* a New York City variation on Boston clam chowder, with tomatoes, green pepper, carrots, and celery instead of milk and potatoes; *New England boiled dinner,* a local version of the classic French pot au feu; *New York cheesecake,* the best in the United States according to purists, served plain or with pineapple or strawberry topping; *oyster pie,* a country pie from Pennsylvania filled with oysters and mushrooms in a light white sauce; *pepper pot,* a thick, highly seasoned tripe soup (from Pennsylvania); *Philadelphia cheese steak,* a sandwich made from a thin slice of steak covered in fried onions and melted cheese; *red flannel hash,* made of corned beef, potatoes, and red beets cooked in a frying pan over a low flame, the New England treatment for leftovers; *shad roe,* rolled in bacon, broiled, and served on toast (a springtime specialty in Maryland); *shoofly pie,* a Pennsylvania-Dutch open tart with a filling of brown sugar and molasses; *snail salad,* cut into thin slices and served in a tart marinade (Rhode Island); *succotash,* a dish of American Indian origin consisting of sweet-corn kernels and lima beans cooked in milk over a low flame (Massachusetts and Rhode Island); and *Yankee chicken pie,* made of stewed chicken and vegetables covered with a thick crust of bread dough and then baked in the oven (from New England).

CUISINE OF THE SOUTH: Although more venturesome than that of New England, the cuisine of the South also draws heavily on the excellent seafood of the Atlantic and the Gulf of Mexico: oysters, scallops, *soft-shell crabs* (good with scallops), *stone crabs* (very hard-shelled crabs), shrimp, sea bass, swordfish, etc. Rice figures in many meat and fish dishes, notably *Hopping John* (rice, bacon, and red beans), *Limping Susan* (rice, bacon, and gumbo), or *dirty rice* (rice, vegetables, and chopped chicken liver).

But the two great dishes of the region are still *southern fried chicken,* crisp on the outside and moist on the inside, and the famous *Virginia ham* (the best comes from Smithfield, near Norfolk), which Queen Victoria consumed in such quantity that she ordered 20 a month. Smoked for six weeks over a hickory-wood fire, from which it derives its delicate amber color, it is served baked with honey, wine, apricots or pineapple—a real treat.

Another great regional dish is *spareribs,* related to *soul food,* which was the cuisine of the slave quarters in the plantations of the Old South. It was a simple but delicious style of cooking based on ingredients spurned by whites, such as pigs' trotters, tripe, or catfish stewed with bacon, and accompanied by such poor man's vegetables as turnips, dandelion greens, and kale.

Spoon bread, the typical corn bread of the South, is served so soaked in sorghum syrup and butter that it can only be eaten with a spoon—hence the name. Florida citrus fruits (oranges, lemons, limes, grapefruit) are not the least important of the South's dependable delicacies, witness such classics as *orange bread pudding, orange baked custard,* or the most famous of all, *key lime pie.* Another famous southern dessert, *pecan pie,* is very sweet and on the heavy side. Students of liquid refreshment should take care to try a *mint julep* on a hot summer's day: bourbon (or cognac), fresh mint, and sugar poured over crushed ice.

Other southern specialties include: *banana pudding,* a rather stodgy dessert (Georgia, Florida, Louisiana); *Brunswick stew,* of pork and vegetables, usually served with a barbecue (Georgia and Alabama); *burgoo,* originally a ragoût of game, now a lamb-and-vegetable stew (Kentucky); *Carpetbagger steak,* stuffed with oysters (a favorite in Georgia, and also found in Louisiana); *chess pie,* made of sugared cream in a chessboard pattern (Kentucky, Tennessee, Virginia); *cobbler,* a fruit pie with a thick crust (Kentucky, Tennessee); *conch chowder,* thick soup made with conch, salt pork, and tomatoes (Florida); *fried pie,* batter turnovers filled with fruit, usually apples or peaches (Arkansas, Louisiana); *greens,* turnip-tops, kale, or mustard greens cooked slowly with a ham bone, a traditional black dish; *hominy grits,* thick corn gruel (Virginia); *hushpuppies,* fried balls of cornmeal; *peanut soup,* celery-and-carrot soup with peanut butter, sour cream, and chopped peanuts (Virginia and Georgia); *picadillo,* chopped pork, onion, and olives, highly spiced and served with rice and beans (of Cuban origin, now a Florida classic); *pork skin,* large pieces of fried pork crackling served before a meal (South Carolina); *potlikker,* a broth made by slowly simmering green vegetables (Georgia); and *red rice,* cooked with tomatoes and ham (very popular in Savannah).

CRÉOLE CUISINE: Créole or Louisiana cooking is a very successful synthesis of several strains—French, Spanish, African, and Caribbean. The interaction produces deftly seasoned delicacies exemplified by the two best-known dishes: *gumbo,* a thick meat-and-vegetable soup to which may be added a choice of sausage, chicken, shrimp, crab, fish, and okra, the whole seasoned with gumbo filé (powdered sassafras leaves); and *jambalaya,* a kind of New World paella made with rice, tomatoes, shrimp or crayfish, oysters, sausage, and chicken.

Also worth looking for are *shrimp remoulade* New Orleans style, *oysters Benedict* (fried oysters wrapped in bacon and covered with hollandaise sauce), *oysters Bienville* (baked, with mushrooms, shrimp, and white-wine sauce), *oysters Casino* (baked and served under a layer of bacon with cocktail sauce), *oysters Rockefeller* (baked with spinach, au gratin, and flavored with Pernod), the *crayfish* (or *crawfish*) which abound in Louisiana's "bayous," and two delicious fish from the Gulf of Mexico, *pompano,* usually served "en papillote" (cooked in paper), and *red snapper.* Rice, fish, and shellfish figure in almost every Créole main dish.

Contrary to expectation, *pig's ears,* a New Orleans favorite, have nothing to do with pigs or ears; they are horns of batter filled with cream. Other desserts are the famous *bananas Foster* (caramelized bananas with a dash of rum served with vanilla ice cream), *sweet-potato pudding, beignets* (square sugar doughnuts) eaten with the traditional *café au lait* (made with chicory), as served in the morning at the Café du Monde in New Orleans, and *pain perdu,* an old French country recipe (stale bread soaked in milk, eggs, brandy, and lemon juice, and fried in butter). And don't miss paying your respects to *café brûlot* (black coffee with cognac flambé, lemon peel, cloves, cinnamon) and spices: "black as night, soft as love and hot as hell," in the words of the poet.

Other Créole specialties include: *andouille,* Cajun (Louisiana French) seasoned pork sausage (a Louisiana specialty); *blackened redfish,* filets of red snapper broiled over a high flame till the outside is blackened, a very typical Cajun dish; *boudin,* pork-and-rice sausage, highly spiced (*boudin rouge* is seasoned blood-and-lard sausage); *Calas cakes,* little fried ricecakes flavored with cinnamon or orange-flower water (a standard New Orleans dessert); *crab Imperial, New Orleans style,* crabmeat, red pepper, and green onions, covered in a spicy mayonnaise and glazed in the oven (not to be confused with crab Imperial, Maryland style); *filet mignon debris,* a medium filet mignon covered in a rich brown sauce made with burgundy, cognac, and crisp little pieces of leftover roast beef, the debris of the name (a New Orleans specialty); *muffuletta,* the great Créole sandwich, served on a round roll and made with salami, mortadella, provolone, and ham, garnished with olives; *poor boy* (or *po' boy*), a New Orleans–style hero of roast beef, ham, or sausage; *red beans and rice,* staple Monday fare in New Orleans; and *sauce remoulade New Orleans style,* a must when eating shrimp Créole—mayonnaise with mustard, anchovies, and horseradish, not to be confused with the classic French remoulade which is simply a vinaigrette with gherkins, capers, and shallots.

MIDWESTERN CUISINE: This country of wide-open spaces and great herds of cattle is not distinguished for the originality of its cuisine, in spite of a flow of immigrants from Germany, Italy, and Scandinavia. The always-dependable dishes are *meat and potatoes* or *freshwater fish* from the region's lakes and rivers. The reputation of such restaurants as Morton's in Chicago, the Hereford House in Kansas City, and the Iowa Beef Steak House in Des Moines—to name only a few—rests on their red meats: *T-bone steak, sirloin* or *New York steak, rib-eye* or *Delmonico steak, porterhouse steak* or *chateaubriand, tournedos, filet mignon, top loin* or *shell steak,* etc., usually served with *french fries,* of which the best are made from Idaho potatoes. Idaho is "the Potato State."

Other midwestern specialties are: *barbecued ribs,* spareribs brushed with barbecue sauce and cooked over an open fire of wood or charcoal till glazed (they have made the name of such restaurants as Carsons, in Skokie, Illinois); *deep-dish pizza,* which originated in Chicago, a pizza with a very thick, soft crust baked in a casserole; *five-way chili,* made with beans, spaghetti, chopped beef, onions, and cheese (comes from Cincinnati and should not be confused with Tex-Mex chili); *pan-fried chicken* (a specialty in Indiana, Missouri, and Ohio); *pasties* are turnovers filled with meat (Michigan); *sour-cream raisin pie,* a thick, creamy, raisin-filled cake covered in meringue (encountered in Indiana), Minnesota, and Wisconsin); and *toasted ravioli,* a specialty of St. Louis, is fried meat-filled ravioli.

SOUTHWESTERN CUISINE: Better known as Tex-Mex, this is essentially an adaptation of Mexican dishes (and particularly their explosive chili sauces) for the North American palate. Among the best-known dishes from this region north of the Rio Grande are *chili con carne* (chopped beef with red beans, minced onions, cumin or paprika, tomatoes, and chili); *tortillas* (flat cornmeal cakes used instead of bread); *frijoles refritos* (boiled beans mashed, seasoned with chili, and refried in a pan; traditional cowboy fare); *enchiladas* (tortillas stuffed with meat, beans, or cheese and baked in the oven); *tamales* (patties of chopped meat, cornmeal, and chili powder, steamed in a cornhusk); and *barbecue* (beef or pork brushed with a special spicy sauce and cooked over a wood or charcoal fire; usually eaten with corn on the cob). To wash it all down there's nothing better than a few generously proportioned *margaritas* (tequila and lime juice, served over crushed ice in a frosted glass whose rim has been dipped in salt).

Other southwestern specialties include: *carne adovada,* pork marinated in a chili sauce; *chicken-fried steak,* thin slices of steak floured and sautéed, a cowboy tradition; *chiles rellenos,* green peppers stuffed with meat or cheese, brushed with egg and fried; *hot links,* spicy Texan sausages broiled over a barbecue; *jerky,* air-dried beef (Oklahoma, Texas); *menudo,* tripe and cornmeal stew (New Mexico, Texas); *Rocky Mountain oysters,* fried bull's (although usually lamb's) testicles, a Colorado specialty; *sopaipilla,* fried honey-dipped bread served hot (Arizona, New Mexico).

WESTERN AND NORTHWESTERN CUISINE: Geography and climate have endowed the Pacific coast, and particularly California, with an abundance of fine foodstuffs. *Dungeness crabs,* superb salmon (*chinook, king, coho, sockeye*), *Dolly Varden trout, Rex* and *Petrale* sole, halibut, tuna, anchovy, *geoduck clams* (great shellfish whose meat weighs up to 15 pounds, served sliced and grilled as steak or chopped in tasty soup; a Washington state specialty), *razor clams,* turtles, oysters (*Olympia, Petit Points, Pigeon Points, Quilcene, Tamales Bay, Drakes Bay, Yakima Bay,* and others), and above all the delectable—but now strictly protected—*abalone* are its glories of seafood.

There are so many fruits and vegetables that it's hard to choose: figs in the San Joaquin Valley, tomatoes in the Sacramento Valley, vineyards in the Sonoma and Napa Valleys, avocados in the San Diego Valley, dates in the Coachella Valley, lettuce and melons in Imperial Valley, are among the best in the country.

Two unexpected discoveries in the region: crusty, tasty, yeasty *sourdough bread* (the best is from San Francisco), and *chop suey,* a stew or stir-fry of meat, beansprouts, mushrooms, and celery, served with rice, country fare of the Chinese workers who helped to build the first California railroads. Failing chop suey, lovers of Chinese food can choose among thousands of Cantonese, Mandarin, Hunan, or Szechuan restaurants, most of them better than their counterparts in the Far East.

Other western specialties include: *artichoke soup* (from California); *barbecued salmon,* fresh marinated salmon cooked over hot coals or a wood fire (the great northwestern specialty); *Caesar salad,* romaine lettuce, chopped hard-boiled egg, toast croutons, anchovies, and Parmesan cheese; *cioppino,* seafood stew seasoned with spices, herbs, and fresh tomatoes; *crab (or shrimp) Louie,* salad made with lettuce, hard-boiled egg, crabmeat, and mayonnaise blended with chili sauce (found all along the Pacific coast); and *Hangtown Fry,* scrambled eggs with oysters (California, Washington).

FOR FURTHER READING

To attempt to present an overview of U.S. history, economics, politics, and culture in the space permitted in this introduction seems folly indeed. Instead, I've chosen to compile this selective booklist. Readers can pick and choose from the following titles in the areas that interest them, whether it be a history of the blacks in America (*From Slavery to Freedom* by John Hope Franklin and Alfred Moss) or a recent novel about New York City in the '80s (*Bonfire of Vanities* by Tom Wolfe).

Economic, Political, and Social History

Acuno, Rodolfo. *Occupied America: A History of Chicanos* (2nd ed.).

Algren, Nelson. *Chicago: City on the Make.*

Bailyn, Bernard. *The Ideological Origins of the American Revolution.*

Beard, Charles M. *An Economic Interpretation of the Constitution of the United States.*

Becker, Carl L. *The Declaration of Independence: A Study of the History of Political Ideas.*

Birmingham, Stephen. *America's Secret Aristocracy.*

Boorstin, Daniel J. *The Exploring Spirit: America and the World, Then and Now.*
—————.*The Americans* (3 vols.).

Brandon, William. *The Last American: The Indian in American Culture.*

Bridenbaugh, Carl, and Jessica Bridenbaugh. *Rebels and Gentlemen: Philadelphia in the Age of Franklin.*

Brown, Dee. *Bury My Heart at Wounded Knee: An Indian History of the American West.*

Burns, James MacGregor. *The Vineyard of Liberty.*

Cather, Willa. *My Antonia.*

Catton, Bruce, and the American Heritage Editors. *American Heritage Picture History of the Civil War.*

Chen, Jack. *The Chinese of America.*

Commager, Henry Steele, ed. *The American Destiny.*

Connell, Evan. *Son of Morning Star: Custer and the Little Big Horn.*

Cooke, Alistair. *The Americans: Fifty Talks on Our Life and Times.*

Dangerfield, George. *Awakening of American Nationalism, 1815–1828.*

De Voto, Bernard. *Course of Empire.*

Du Plessix Gray, Francine. *Hawaii, the Sugar-Coated Fortress.*

Edmonds, Walter D. *Drums Along the Mohawk.*

Fitzgerald, Frances. *Fire in the Lake: The Vietnamese and the Americans in Vietnam.*

Franklin, John Hope, and Alfred Moss. *From Slavery to Freedom: A History of Negro America.*

Galbraith, John Kenneth. *The Great Crash of 1929.*

Garreau, Joel. *The Nine Nations of North America.*

Genovese, Eugene D. *The Political Economy of Slavery: Studies in Economy and Society of the Slave South.*

Goldman, Eric. *Rendezvous with Destiny: A History of Modern American Reform.*

Goldman, Eric F. *The Crucial Decade and After: America, 1945–1960.*

Handlin, Oscar. *The Uprooted.* (rev.).

Hofstadter, Richard. *The Age of Reform: From Bryan to F.D.R.*

————. *The American Political Tradition and the Men Who Made It.*

Howe, Irving. *World of Our Fathers.*

Inge, M. Thomas, ed. *Handbook of American Popular Culture.*

Jordan, Winthrop D. *White over Black: American Attitudes Toward the Negro, 1550–1812.*

Lewis, David L. *When Harlem Was in Vogue.*

Lewis, Oscar. *La Vida: A Puerto Rican Family in the Culture of Poverty.*

Liebling, A. J. *Back Where I Come From.*

Marquis, Arnold. *Guide to America's Indians: Ceremonials, Reservations, and Museums.*

McPherson, James. *Battle Cry of Freedom.*

McPhee, John. *Coming into the Country.*

Mencken, H. L. *The American Language.*

Morison, Samuel Eliot. *The Growth of the American Republic.*

Parish, Peter J. *The American Civil War.*

Parrington, Vernon L. *Main Currents in American Thought.*

Rose, Al. *Storyville, New Orleans.*

Schlesinger, Arthur M., Jr. *The Age of Jackson.*

————. *The Rise of the City.*

Shannon, William V. *The American Irish.*

Terkel, Studs. *American Dreams: Lost and Found.*

————. *Division Street: America.*

————. *Hard Times: An Oral History of the Great Depression in America.*

Trudgill, Peter. *Coping with America* (2nd ed.).

Turner, Frederick J. *The Frontier in American History.*

Whitman, Walt. *Democratic Vistas and Other Papers.*

Williams, Juan. *Eyes on the Prize: America's Civil Rights Years, 1954–1965.*

Wilson, Edmund, and Joseph Mitchell. *Apologies to the Iroquois: With a Study of the Mohawks on High Street.*

Wilson, Robert A., and Bill Hosokawa. *East to America: A History of Japanese in the United States.*

Woodward, Bob, and Carl Bernstein. *All the President's Men.*

Woodward, C. Vann. *The Origins of the New South, 1877–1913.*

Zinn, Howard. *The Twentieth Century: A People's History.*

Art, Architecture, Photography, and Film

Adams, Ansel. *Classic Images.*

Agee, James. *Agee on Film.*

Baigell, Matthew. *Dictionary of American Art.*

Barnouw, Erik. *Tube of Plenty: The Evolution of American Television* (rev. ed.).

Everson, William. *American Silent Film.*

Goldberger, Paul. *The City Observed: New York. A Guide to the Architecture of Manhattan.*
Highwater, Jamake. *Song from the Earth: American Indian Painting.*
Jacobs, Jane. *The Death and Life of Great American Cities.*
Jacobs, Lewis. *The Rise of the American Film.*
Kael, Pauline. *Deeper into the Movies.*
Kidder-Smith, G. E. *The Architecture of the United States.*
Larkin, Oliver W. *Art and Life in America.*
Mumford, Lewis. *The Culture of Cities.*
Novotny, Ann. *Alice's World: The Life and Photography of an American Original: Alice Austin, 1866–1952.*
Rifkind, Carole. *A Field Guide to American Architecture.*
Rose, Barbara. *American Art Since 1900* (rev. and expanded ed.).
Sklar, Robert. *Movie-Made America: A Cultural History of American Movies.*
Steichen, Edward. *Steichen: A Life in Photography.*
Trachtenberg, Allan. *America and Lewis Hine.*

Fiction, Poetry, and Travel

Adams, Henry. *The Education of Henry Adams.*
Baldwin, James. *Go Tell It on the Mountain.*
Bellow, Saul. *The Adventures of Augie March.*
Brooks, Van Wyck. *The Flowering of New England, 1815–65.*
Chandler, Raymond. *The Raymond Chandler Omnibus.*
Cooper, James Fenimore. *The Last of the Mohicans.*
———————. *The Deerslayer.*
Crane, Stephen. *The Red Badge of Courage.*
Dickens, Charles. *American Notes.*
Dickinson, Emily. *Collected Poems of Emily Dickinson.*
Didion, Joan. *Play It as It Lays.*
Doctorow, E. L. *Ragtime.*
Dos Passos, John. *USA.*
Dreiser, Theodore. *Sister Carrie.*
Ehrlich, Eugene, and Gorton Carruth. *The Oxford Illustrated Literary Guide to the United States.*
Ellison, Ralph. *The Invisible Man.*
Erdrich, Louise. *Love Medicine.*
Faulkner, William. *The Sound and the Fury.*
———————. *Absalom! Absalom!.*
Fitzgerald, F. Scott. *The Great Gatsby.*
Garland, Hamlin. *Main Travelled Roads.*
Hammett, Dashiell. *The Maltese Falcon.*
Harte, Bret. *The Outcasts of Poker Flat.*
Hawthorne, Nathaniel. *The Scarlet Letter.*
Hemingway, Ernest. *In Our Time.*
Howells, William Dean. *The Rise of Silas Lapham.*
Irving, Washington. *Diedrich Knickerbocker's A History of New York.*
James, Henry. *The American Scene.*
———————. *The Wings of the Dove.*
Kerouac, Jack. *On the Road.*
Kingston, Maxine Hong. *The Woman Warrior: Memories of a Girlhood Among Ghosts.*
La Farge, Oliver. *Laughing Boy.*
Lee, Harper. *To Kill a Mockingbird.*
London, Jack. *Call of the Wild.*
MacDonald, Ross. *The Underground Man.*

Mailer, Norman. *The Deer Park*.
——————. *The Armies of the Night*.
McInerney, Jay. *Bright Lights, Big City*.
Melville, Herman. *Bartleby the Scrivener*.
Michener. James A. *Hawaii*.
Mitchell, Margaret. *Gone with the Wind*.
Moon, William Least Heat. *Blue Highways: A Journey into America*.
Morris, Jan. *Manhattan '45*.
Mukherjee, Bharati. *Darkness*.
Nabokov, Vladimir. *Lolita*.
Norris, Frank. *McTeaque: A Story of San Francisco*.
Raban, Jonathan. *Old Glory: An American Voyage*.
Reeves, Richard. *American Journey: Traveling with Tocqueville in Search of Democracy in America*.
Roth, Philip. *Portnoy's Complaint*.
Sinclair, Upton. *The Jungle*.
Steffens, Lincoln. *The Shame of Cities*.
Stein, Gertrude. *The Making of Americans*.
Steinbeck, John. *The Grapes of Wrath*.
——————. *Travels with Charley in Search of America*.
Stevenson, Robert Louis. *Travels in Hawaii*.
Twain, Mark. *The Adventures of Huckleberry Finn*.
——————. *Roughing It*.
Updike, John. *Rabbit Run*.
Walker, Alice. *The Color Purple*.
Warren, Robert Penn. *All the King's Men*.
Waugh, Evelyn. *The Loved One* (rev. ed.).
West, Nathanael. *The Day of the Locust*.
Wharton, Edith. *The Age of Innocence*.
White, E. B. *Here Is New York*.
White, Edmund. *States of Desire: Travels in Gay America*.
Whitman, Walt. *Leaves of Grass*.
Wilson, Edmund. *Patriotic Gore: Studies in the Literature of the American Civil War*.
Wright, Richard. *Native Son*.

Biography

Amory, Cleveland. *The Proper Bostonians*.
Burns, James MacGregor. *Roosevelt: The Lion and the Fox*.
Flexner, James Thomas. *Washington: The Indispensable Man*.
Goodwin, Doris Kearns. *Lyndon Johnson and the American Dream*.
Link, Arthur S. *Woodrow Wilson and the Progressive Era, 1910–1917*.
Miller, Merle. *Plain Speaking: An Oral Biography of Harry S Truman*.
McCullough, David. *Mornings on Horseback*.
Morris, Edmund. *The Rise of Theodore Roosevelt*.
Padover, Saul. *Jefferson*.
Sandburg, Carl. *Abraham Lincoln: The Prairie Years and the War Years*.
Schlesinger, Arthur M., Jr. *A Thousand Days*.
Van Doren, Carl C. *Benjamin Franklin*.
Vidal, Gore. *Lincoln*.

FOR THE FOREIGN VISITOR

□ □ □

Although American fads and fashions have spread across Europe and other parts of the world so that America may seem like familiar territory before your arrival, there are still many peculiarities and uniquely American situations that any foreign visitor will encounter. This chapter is meant to clue you in on what they are.

International visitors should also read the Introduction carefully.

PREPARING FOR YOUR TRIP

NECESSARY DOCUMENTS: Except for Canadian nationals (who must have proof of residence), and British and Japanese nationals (who no longer need a visa, only a passport), foreigners entering the U.S. must have two documents:

□ a valid **passport,** with an expiration date at least six months later than the scheduled end of the visit to the U.S.; and

□ a **tourist visa,** available without charge from the nearest U.S. Consulate; you must fill out a special form and provide a passport photograph.

Usually you will be given your visa at once, or within 24 hours at most; try to avoid the summer rush in June-July-August. If applying by mail, enclose a large stamped, self-addressed envelope, and expect an average wait of two weeks. Visa application forms are also available at airline offices or from leading travel agents as well as from U.S. Consulates. The U.S. tourist visa (visa B) is theoretically valid for a year, and for any number of entries, but the U.S. Consulate that gives you the tourist visa will determine the length of stay for a multiple- or single-entry visa. However, there is some latitude here, and if you are of good appearance and can give the address of a relative, friend, or business connection living in the U.S. (useful, too, for car rental, passage through Customs, etc.), you have an excellent chance of getting a longer permit if you want one.

MEDICAL REQUIREMENTS: No inoculations are needed to enter the U.S. unless you are coming from, or have stopped over in, areas known to be suffering from epidemics, especially of cholera or yellow fever. Applicants for immigrants' visas (and only they) must undergo a screening test for AIDS under a law passed in 1987.

If you have a disease requiring treatment with medications containing narcotics or drugs, carry a valid, signed prescription from your physician to allay any suspicions that you are smuggling drugs. Ditto for syringes.

TRAVEL INSURANCE (BAGGAGE, HEALTH, AND LOSS): All such insurance is voluntary in the U.S.; however, given the very high cost of medical care, I cannot too strongly advise every traveler to arrange for appropriate coverage before setting out. There are specialized insurance companies that will, for a relatively low premium, cover:

□ loss or theft of your baggage;
□ trip-cancellation costs;
□ guarantee of bail in case you are sued;
□ sickness or injury costs (medical, surgical, and hospital);
□ costs of an accident, repatriation, or death.

Such packages (for example, "Europe Assistance" in Europe) are sold by automobile clubs at attractive rates, as well as by banks and travel agencies.

GETTING TO THE U.S.

Travelers from overseas can take advantage of the **APEX (Advance Purchase Excursion) fares** offered by all the major U.S. and European carriers. Aside from these, attractive values are offered by **Icelandair** on flights from Luxembourg to New York or Orlando; and by **Virgin Atlantic** from London to New York/Newark or Miami.

Some large airlines (for example, TWA, Eastern, Northwest, United, and Delta) offer travelers on their transatlantic or transpacific flights special discount tickets under the name **Visit USA,** allowing travel between any U.S. destinations at minimum rates. They are not on sale in the U.S., and must therefore be purchased before you leave your foreign point of departure. This system is the best way of seeing the U.S. at low cost. You should obtain information well in advance from your travel agent or the office of the airline concerned, since the conditions attached to these discount tickets can be changed without advance notice.

GETTING AROUND

For information on transportation around the U.S., see the "For Foreign Visitors" sections in the Introduction under each mode of transportation.

ABC'S FOR THE FOREIGN TRAVELER

ACCOMMODATIONS: See the Introduction.

AUTOMOBILE ORGANIZATIONS: See "By Car," in the Introduction.

BUSINESS HOURS: Public and private **offices** are usually open from 9 a.m. to 5 p.m. Monday through Friday, except in Hawaii and parts of California (7:30 or 8 a.m. to 4 p.m.).

Banking hours are generally 9 a.m. to 3 p.m. Monday through Friday, but in some cases till 6 p.m. on Friday, and sometimes also on Saturday morning.

Post offices are open from 8 a.m. to 5:30 or 6 p.m. Monday through Friday and 8 a.m. to noon on Saturday.

Store hours are 9:30 or 10 a.m. to 5:30 or 6 p.m. Monday through Saturday, though often till 9 p.m. one or two evenings a week. Shopping centers, drugstores, and supermarkets are open from 9 a.m. to 9 p.m. six days a week (seven days, and even in some cases 24 hours, in certain large cities).

Museum hours vary widely. The norm for big cities is 10 a.m. to 5 p.m. six days a week (closing day is usually Monday). Some art museums stay open till 9 p.m. one or, rarely, two evenings a week.

CLIMATE: Any season is a good time for travel in the U.S.—provided you understand how to juggle climates and distances! Summer is hot and humid in the East and the Southeast from New York to Louisiana. From Texas to California it can be scorching—95°F (35°C) in the shade is not unusual. On the other hand, it's a delightful time to visit the Northwest and the Rockies. Winter is severe across the North and a good deal of the Central Tier—the mercury often goes down to $10°–15°F$ $(-12°$ to $-9.5°C)$ in Chicago and Denver—but very agreeable in Florida and California. From coast to coast, the best seasons for travel are spring and (even more) fall, which can be very mild during the "Indian Summer." See the table of average temperatures for representative cities in the Introduction.

CURRENCY AND EXCHANGE: The U.S. monetary system has a decimal base: one **dollar** ($1) = 100 **cents** (100¢).

The commonest **bills** (all green) are the $1 ("a buck"), $5, $10, and $20 denominations. There are also $2 (seldom encountered), $50, and $100 bills (the two latter are not welcome when paying for small purchases).

There are six denominations of **coins:** 1¢ (one cent, or "penny"); 5¢ (five cents, or "nickel"); 10¢ (ten cents, or "dime"); 25¢ (twenty-five cents, or "quarter"); 50¢ (fifty cents, or "half dollar"); and rare—and prized by collectors—the $1 piece (both the older, large silver dollars and the newer, small Susan B. Anthony coin).

Traveler's Checks and Credit Cards

Traveler's checks denominated in *dollars* are accepted without demur at most hotels, motels, restaurants, and large stores. But as any experienced traveler knows, the best place to change traveler's checks is at a bank.

However, the method of payment most widely used is the **credit card:** VISA (BarclayCard in Britain, Chargex in Canada), MasterCard (EuroCard in Europe, Access in Britain, Diamond in Japan, etc.), American Express, Diners Club, and Carte Blanche, in descending order of acceptance. You can save yourself trouble by using "plastic money," rather than cash or traveler's checks, in 95% of all hotels, motels, restaurants, and retail stores (except for those selling food or liquor). A credit card can serve as a deposit when renting a car, as proof of identity (often carrying more weight than a passport), or as a "cash card," enabling you to draw money from banks that accept them.

Note: The "foreign-exchange bureaus" so common in Europe are rare even at airports in the U.S., and nonexistent outside major cities. Try to avoid having to change foreign money, or traveler's checks denominated other than in U.S. dollars, at a small-town bank, or even a branch bank in a big city; in fact, leave any currency other than U.S. dollars at home—it may prove more nuisance to you than it's worth.

CUSTOMS AND IMMIGRATION: Every adult visitor may bring in, free of duty: one liter of wine or hard liquor; 1,000 cigarettes or 100 cigars (but *no* cigars from Cuba) or three pounds of smoking tobacco; $400 worth of gifts. These exemptions are offered to travelers who spend at least 72 hours in the U.S. and who have not claimed them within the preceding six months. It is altogether forbidden to bring into the country foodstuffs (particularly cheese, fruit, cooked meats, and canned goods) and plants (vegetables, seeds, tropical plants, etc.). Foreign tourists may bring in or take out up to $5,000 in U.S. or foreign currency with no formalities; larger sums must be declared to Customs on entering or leaving.

The visitor arriving by air, no matter what the port of entry—New York, Boston, Miami, Honolulu, Los Angeles, or the rest—should cultivate patience and resignation before setting foot on U.S. soil. The U.S. Customs and Immigration Services are among the slowest and most suspicious on earth. On some days, especially summer weekends, you may wait to have your passport stamped at Miami or New York's John F. Kennedy Airport for nearly two hours, sometimes three. The situation is just as bad at other major international airports. Add the time it takes to clear Customs and you will see that you should make very generous allowance for delay in planning connections between international and domestic flights—an average of two to three hours at least.

In contrast, for the traveler arriving by car or by rail from Canada, the border-crossing formalities have been streamlined to the vanishing point. And for the traveler by air from Canada, Bermuda, and some points in the Caribbean, you can go through Customs and Immigration at the point of *departure,* which is much quicker and less painful.

DRINKING LAWS: As with marriage and divorce, every state, and sometimes every county and community, has its own laws governing the sale of liquor. The only federal regulation (based on a judgment of the U.S. Supreme Court on June 23, 1987) restricts the consumption of liquor in public places anywhere in the country to persons aged 21 or over (states not respecting this rule may be penalized by a withdrawal of federal highway funds).

Hours of operation for liquor stores, as well as for bars and nightclubs, are strictly limited in certain states; in most, establishments selling liquor are closed on Sunday and public holidays. In Alabama, Maine, New Hampshire, Ohio, Oregon, Pennsylvania, Utah, and Vermont, liquor may be sold by the bottle only in state-owned outlets.

Not all restaurants are licensed to serve beer, wine, or hard liquor, though you may generally bring your drink with you. As far as possible, restaurants not having beverage licenses are noted as such in this book.

ELECTRIC CURRENT: U.S. wall outlets give power at 110–115 volts, 60 cycles, compared to 220 volts, 50 cycles, in most of Europe. Besides a 110-volt converter, small appliances of non-American manufacture, such as hairdryers or shavers, will require a plug adapter with two flat, parallel pins.

EMBASSIES AND CONSULATES: All embassies are located in the national capital, Washington, D.C.; some consulates are located in major cities, and most nations have a mission to the United Nations in New York City.

Listed here are the embassies and consulates of the major English-speaking countries—Australia, Canada, Ireland, New Zealand, and the United Kingdom. If you are from another country, you can get the telephone number of your embassy by calling "information" in Washington, D.C. (202/555-1212).

Australia

EMBASSY. 1601 Massachusetts Ave. NW, Washington, DC 20036 (202/797-3000).

CONSULATES. **Chicago**—Quaker Tower, 321 N. Clark St., Suite 2930, IL 60610 (312/645-9440). **Honolulu**—1000 Bishop St., Penthouse, HI 96813 (808/524-5050). **Houston**—3 Post Oak Central A.H., 1990 Post Oak Blvd., Suite 800, TX 77056 (713/629-9131 or 520-3179). **Los Angeles**—611 N. Larchmont Blvd., CA 90004 (213/469-4300). **New York**—International Building, 636 Fifth Ave., NY 10111 (212/245-4000). **San Francisco**—360 Post St., CA 94108 (415/362-6160).

Canada

EMBASSY. 1746 Massachusetts Ave. NW, Washington, DC 20036 (202/785-1400).

CONSULATES. **Atlanta**—One CNN Center, Suite 400 South Tower, GA 30303

(404/577-6810). **Boston**—3 Copley Pl., Suite 400, MA 02116 (617/536-1731). **Buffalo**—One Marine Midland Center, Suite 3550, NY 14203 (716/825-1345). **Chicago**—310 S. Michigan Ave., Suite 1200, IL 60604 (312/427-1031). **Cleveland**—Illuminating Bldg., 55 Public Square, OH 44113 (216/771-0150). **Dallas**—St. Paul Place, 750 N. St. Paul, Suite 1700, TX 75201 (214/922-9806). **Detroit**—660 Renaissance Center, Suite 1100, MI 48243 (313/567-2340). **Los Angeles**—300 S. Grand Ave., 10th floor, CA 90071 (213/687-7432). **Minneapolis**—701 Fourth Ave. South, MN 55415 (612/333-4641). **New York**—1251 Ave. of the Americas, NY 10020 (212/586-2400). **San Francisco**—One Maritime Plaza, Golden Gateway Center, CA 94111 (415/981-8541). **Seattle**—412 Plaza 600, Sixth and Stewart, WA 98101 (206/443-1777).

Ireland

EMBASSY. 2234 Massachusetts Ave. NW, Washington, DC 20008 (202/462-3939).

CONSULATES. Boston—Chase Bldg., 535 Boylston St., MA 02116 (617/267-9330). **Chicago**—400 N. Michigan Ave., IL 60611 (312/337-1868). **New York**—515 Madison Ave., NY 10022 (212/319-2555). **San Francisco**—655 Montgomery St., Suite 930, CA 94111 (415/392-4214).

New Zealand

EMBASSY. 37 Observatory Circle NW, Washington, DC 20008 (202/328-4800).

CONSULATES. Los Angeles—Tishman Bldg., 10960 Wilshire Blvd., Suite 1530, CA 90024 (213/477-8241). **New York**—630 Fifth Ave., Suite 530, NY 10111 (212/698-4650). **San Francisco**—Citicorp Center, 1 Sansome St., Suite 810, CA 94104 (415/788-7404).

United Kingdom

EMBASSY. 3100 Massachusetts Ave. NW, Washington, DC 20008 (202/462-1340).

CONSULATES. Atlanta—225 Peachtree St. North, Suite 912, GA 30303 (404/524-5856). **Chicago**—33 N. Dearborn St., IL 60602 (312/346-1810). **Houston**—601 Jefferson, Suite 2250, TX 77002 (713/659-6270). **Los Angeles**—3701 Wilshire Blvd., Suite 312, CA 90010 (213/385-7381). **New York**—845 Third Ave., NY 10022 (212/752-8400). **San Francisco**—1 Sansome St., Suite 850, CA 94104 (415/981-3030).

EMERGENCIES: In all major cities you can call the police, an ambulance, or the fire brigade through the single emergency telephone number **911.** Another useful way of reporting an emergency is to call the telephone-company operator by dialing **0** (zero, *not* the letter "O"). Outside major cities, call the county sheriff or the fire brigade at the number you will find in the local telephone book.

If you encounter such travelers' problems as sickness, accident, or lost or stolen baggage, it will pay you to call **Travelers' Aid,** an organization which specializes in helping distressed travelers, whether American or foreign. Check the local telephone book for the nearest office, or dial 0 and ask the telephone operator.

GASOLINE: See Introduction.

HOLIDAYS: On the following legal national holidays, banks, government offices, post offices, and many stores, restaurants, and museums are closed:

> January 1 (New Year's Day)
> Third Monday in January (Martin Luther King Day)
> Third Monday in February (Presidents Day, Washington's Birthday)
> Last Monday in May (Memorial Day)
> July 4 (Independence Day)
> First Monday in September (Labor Day)
> Second Monday in October (Columbus Day)
> November 11 (Veteran's Day/Armistice Day)
> Last Thursday in November (Thanksgiving Day)
> December 25 (Christmas Day)

Also celebrated in some cities and states are the following:

> February 12 (in the North) (Lincoln's Birthday)
> March 17 (St. Patrick's Day)
> April 19 (Patriot's Day)

In addition, many states and cities have their own special holidays.

Finally, the Tuesday following the first Monday in November is Election Day, and is a legal holiday in presidential-election years.

INFORMATION: See the opening of each chapter and the Appendix for a list of state tourism information offices.

LEGAL AID: The foreign tourist, unless positively identified as a member of the Mafia or of a drug ring, will probably never become involved with the American legal system. If you are pulled up for a minor infraction (for example, of the highway code, such as speeding), never attempt to pay the fine directly to a police officer; you may wind up arrested on the much more serious charge of attempted bribery. Pay fines by mail, or directly into the hands of the clerk of the court. If accused of a more serious offense, it is wise to say and do nothing before consulting a lawyer. Under U.S. law, an arrested person is allowed one telephone call to a party of his choice. Call your embassy or consulate.

MAIL: If you want your mail to follow you on your vacation, you need only fill out a change-of-address card at any post office. The post office will also hold your mail for up to one month. If you aren't sure of your address, your mail can be sent to you, in your name, **c/o General Delivery** at the main post office of the city or region where you expect to be. The addressee must pick it up in person, and produce proof of identity (driver's license, credit card, passport, etc.).

Generally to be found at intersections, mailboxes are blue with a red-and-white stripe, and carry the inscription "U.S. MAIL." If your mail is addressed to a U.S. destination, don't forget to add the five-figure postal code or ZIP (Zone Improvement Plan) Code, after the two-letter abbreviation of the state to which the mail is addressed (CA for California, MA for Massachusetts, NY for New York, and so on).

MEASUREMENTS: While most of the rest of the world is on the metric system, for nonscientific purposes the United States still adheres to its own units of measurement. The following tables will help you with conversions, for both standard measurements and clothing and shoe sizes.

THE METRIC SYSTEM–IN A NUTSHELL

Length
    1 millimeter = 0.04 inches (*or* less than 1/16 in)
    1 centimeter = 0.39 inches (*or* just under ½ in)
    1 meter   = 1.09 yards (*or* about 39 inches)
    1 kilometer = 0.62 mile (*or* about ⅔ mile)

To convert kilometers to miles, take the number of kilometers and multiply by .62 (for example, 25 km × .62 = 15.5 mi).

To convert miles to kilometers, take the number of miles and multiply by 1.61 (for example, 50 mi × 1.61 = 80.5 km).

Capacity
    1 liter = 33.92 ounces
            = 1.06 quart
            = 0.26 gallons

To convert liters to gallons, take the number of liters and multiply by .26 (for example, 50 liters × .26 = 13 gallons).

To convert gallons to liters, take the number of gallons and multiply by 3.79 (for example, 10 gal × 3.79 = 37.9 liters).

Weight
    1 gram   = 0.04 ounces (*or* about a paperclip's weight)
    1 kilogram = 2.2 pounds

To convert kilograms to pounds, take the number of kilos and multiply by 2.2 (for example, 75 kg × 2.2 = 165 lbs.).

To convert pounds to kilograms, take the number of pounds and multiply by .45 (for example, 90 lbs. × .45 = 40.5 kg).

Area
    1 hectare (km²) = 2.47 acres

To convert hectares to acres, take the number of hectares and multiply by 2.47 (for example, 20 ha × 2.47 = 49.4 acres).

To convert acres to hectares, take the number of acres and multiply by .41 (for example, 40 acres × .41 = 16.4 ha.).

Temperature

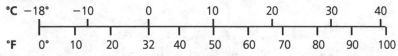

To convert degrees C to degrees F, multiply degrees C by 9, divide by 5, and add 32 (for example 9/5 × 20°C + 32 = 68°F).

To convert degrees F to degrees C, subtract 32 from degrees F, multiply by 5, then divide by 9 (for example, 85°F − 32 × 5/9 = 29°C).

Clothing Sizes

Women's Dresses, Coats, and Skirts

American	3	5	7	9	11	12	13	14	15	16	18
Continental	36	38	38	40	40	42	42	44	44	46	48
British	8	10	11	12	13	14	15	16	17	18	20

Women's Blouses and Sweaters

American	10	12	14	16	18	20
Continental	38	40	42	44	46	48
British	32	34	36	38	40	42

Women's Stockings

American	8	8½	9	9½	10	10½
Continental	1	2	3	4	5	6
British	8	8½	9	9½	10	10½

Women's Shoes

American	5	6	7	8	9	10
Continental	36	37	38	39	40	41
British	3½	4½	5½	6½	7½	8½

Note: Foot width should also be taken into account.

Children's Clothing

American	3	4	5	6	6X
Continental	98	104	110	116	122
British	18	20	22	24	26

Children's Shoes

American	8	9	10	11	12	13	1	2	3
Continental	24	25	27	28	29	30	32	33	34
British	7	8	9	10	11	12	13	1	2

Men's Suits

American	34	36	38	40	42	44	46	48
Continental	44	46	48	50	52	54	56	58
British	34	36	38	40	42	44	46	48

Men's Shirts

American	14½	15	15½	16	16½	17	17½	18
Continental	37	38	39	41	42	43	44	45
British	14½	15	15½	16	16½	17	17½	18

Note: Shirts are sized on a combination of collar and sleeve length.

Men's Shoes

American	7	8	9	10	11	12	13
Continental	39½	41	42	43	44½	46	47
British	6	7	8	9	10	11	12

Note: Foot width should also be taken into account.

Men's Hats

American	6⅞	7⅛	7¼	7⅜	7½	7⅝
Continental	55	56	58	59	60	61
British	6¼	6⅞	7⅛	7¼	7⅜	7½

MEDICAL EMERGENCIES: See "Emergencies," above.

NEWSPAPERS AND MAGAZINES: With a few exceptions, such as the *New York Times, USA Today,* the *Wall Street Journal,* and the *Christian Science Monitor,* daily newspapers in the U.S. are local, not national. Most large cities have at least two daily papers, of which the most important, after those mentioned above, are the *Washington Post,* the *Chicago Tribune,* and the *Los Angeles Times.* These papers are much larger than the great dailies of Europe or Australia; their Sunday editions can weigh six or seven pounds.

There are also innumerable newsweeklies like *Newsweek, Time, U.S. News & World Report,* and specialized periodicals, such as the monthly magazines each devoted to a single city—*New York* magazine (weekly), *Chicago* magazine, *Los Angeles* magazine, *The Washingtonian*—ideal starting points for your voyage of discovery into the city concerned.

The airmail editions of foreign newspapers and magazines are on sale only belatedly, and only at the airports and international bookstores in the largest cities.

POST: See "Mail."

RADIO AND TELEVISION: Audio-visual media, with three coast-to-coast networks—ABC, CBS, and NBC—joined in recent years by the Public Broadcasting System (PBS) and the cable network CNN, play a major part in American life. In the big cities, televiewers have a choice of about a dozen channels (including the UHF channels), most of them transmitting 24 hours a day, without counting the pay-TV channels showing recent movies or sports events. In smaller communities the choice may be limited to four TV channels (there are 1,200 in the entire country), and a half dozen local radio stations (there are 6,500 in all), each broadcasting a particular kind of music—classical, country, jazz, pop, gospel—punctuated by news broadcasts and frequent commercials.

SAFETY: In general, the U.S. is safer than most other countries, particularly in rural areas, but there are "danger zones" in the big cities, pinpointed in this guide, which should be approached only with extreme caution.

As a general rule, isolated areas such as gardens and parking lots should be avoided after dark. Elevators and public-transport systems in off-hours, particularly between 10 p.m. and 6 a.m., are also potential crime scenes. You should drive through decaying neighborhoods with your car doors locked and the windows closed. Never carry on your person valuables like jewelry or large sums of cash; traveler's checks are much safer.

TAXES: In the U.S. there is no VAT (Value-Added Tax), or other indirect tax at a national level. Every state, and each city in it, is allowed to levy its own local tax on all purchases, including hotel and restaurant checks, airline tickets, etc. It is automatically added to the price of certain services such as public transportation, cab fares, phone calls, and gasoline. It varies from 4% to 10% depending on the state and city, so when you are making major purchases such as photographic equipment, clothing, or high-fidelity components, it can be a significant part of the cost.

Here are the **sales tax rates** for certain major cities:

Atlanta	8.00%
Boston	5.50%
Chicago	8.00%
Dallas	5.00%
Denver	11.00%
Los Angeles	7.00%
Miami	5.00%
New Orleans	9.00%
New York	8.25%
Philadelphia	6.00%
San Francisco	6.50%
Washington, D.C.	6.00%

TELEPHONE, TELEGRAPH, TELEX: Public **telephones** and call boxes are an integral part of the American landscape. You will find them everywhere: at street corners, in bars, restaurants, public buildings, stores, service stations, along highways, etc. Outside the metropolitan areas public telephones are more difficult to find. Stores and gas stations are your best bet.

Unlike the mail and the railroads, the telephone is not a public-service system. It is run by private corporations, which perhaps explains its high standard of service. Throughout the country it is almost completely automated, and local calls cost only 20¢–30¢.

For **long-distance or international calls,** stock up with a supply of quarters; the pay phone will instruct you when, and in what quantity, you should put them into the slot. For direct overseas calls, first dial 011, followed by the country code (Australia, 61; Republic of Ireland, 353; New Zealand, 64; United Kingdom, 44; and so on), and then by the city code (for example, 1 for London, 21 for Birmingham) and the number of the person you wish to call. For Canada and long-distance calls in the U.S., dial 1 followed by the area code and number you want.

Before calling from a hotel room, always ask the hotel phone operator if there are any telephone surcharges. These are best avoided by using a public phone, calling collect, or using a telephone charge card.

For **reversed-charge or collect calls,** and for **person-to-person calls,** dial 0 (zero, *not* the letter "O") followed by the area code and number you want; an operator will then come on the line, and you should specify that you are calling collect, or person-to-person, or both. If your operator-assisted call is international, ask for the overseas operator.

For local **directory assistance** ("information"), dial 411; for long-distance information dial 1, then the appropriate area code and 555-1212.

Like the telephone system, **telegraph and telex** services are provided by private corporations like ITT, RCA, and above all, Western Union, the most important. You can bring your telegram in to the nearest Western Union office (there are hundreds across the country), or dictate it over the phone (a toll-free call, 800/552-5959). You can also telegraph money, or have it telegraphed to you, very quickly over the Western Union system.

TELEPHONE DIRECTORY: See "Yellow Pages," below.

TIME: The U.S. is divided into four **time zones** (six, if Alaska and Hawaii are included). From east to west, these are: Eastern Standard Time (EST), Central Standard Time (CST), Mountain Standard Time (MST), Pacific Standard Time (PST), Alaska Standard Time (AST), and Hawaii Standard Time (HST). Always keep changing time zones in mind if you are traveling (or even telephoning) long distances in the U.S. For example, noon in New York City (EST) is 11 a.m. in Chicago (CST), 10 a.m. in Denver (MST), 9 a.m. in Los Angeles (PST), 8 a.m. in Anchorage (AST), and 7 a.m. in Honolulu (HST).

Daylight Saving Time is in effect from the last Sunday in April through the last Saturday in October (actually, the change is made at 2 a.m. on Sunday) except in Arizona, Hawaii, part of Indiana, and Puerto Rico.

TIPPING: This is part of the American way of life, on the principle that you must expect to pay for any service you get. Here are some rules of thumb:

Bartenders: 10%–15%.
Bellhops: at least 50¢ per piece; $2–$3 for a lot of baggage.
Cab drivers: 15% of the fare (20% in large cities).
Cafeterias, fast-food restaurants: no tip.
Chambermaids: $1 a day; more in big-city hotels.
Cinemas, movies: tipping not obligatory, 50¢ optional in theaters.
Checkroom attendants (restaurants, theaters): 50¢ a garment; $1 in large cities.
Doormen (hotels or restaurants): not obligatory, but $1 at top hotels.
Gas-station attendants: not obligatory.
Hairdressers: 15%–20%.
Parking-lot attendant: 50¢ ($1 in hotels).
Redcaps (airport and railroad station): at least 50¢ per piece; $2–$3 for a lot of baggage.
Restaurants, nightclubs: 15%–20% of the check.
Sleeping-car porters: $1 per night to your attendant.

TOILETS: Foreign visitors often complain that public toilets are hard to find in most U.S. cities. True, there are none on the streets, but the visitor can usually find one in a bar, restaurant, hotel, museum, department store, or service station —and it will probably be clean (although the last-mentioned sometimes leaves much to be desired). Note, however, a growing practice in some restaurants and bars of displaying a notice that "toilets are for the use of patrons only." You can ignore this sign, or better yet, avoid arguments by paying for a cup of coffee or soft drink which will qualify you as a patron. The cleanliness of toilets at railroad stations and bus depots may be more open to question, and some public places are equipped with pay toilets, which require you to insert one or two 10¢ coins (dimes) into a slot on the door before it will open.

YELLOW PAGES: There are two kinds of telephone directory available to you. The general directory is the so-called **White Pages,** in which private and business subscribers are listed in alphabetical order. The inside front cover lists the emergency number for police, fire, and ambulance, and other vital numbers (like the Coast Guard, poison control center, crime-victims hotline, etc.). The first few pages are devoted to community service numbers, including a guide to long-distance and international calling, complete with country codes and area codes.

The second directory, printed on yellow paper (whence its name, *Yellow Pages*), lists all local services, businesses, and industries by type of activity, with an index at the back. The listings cover not only such obvious items as automobile repairs by make of car, or drugstores (pharmacies), often by geographical location, but also restaurants by type of cuisine and geographical location, bookstores by special subject and/or language, places of worship by religious denomination, and other information that the tourist might otherwise not readily find. The *Yellow Pages* also include city plans or detailed area maps, often showing postal ZIP Codes and public transportation routes.

PART ONE

THE NORTHEAST AND MID-ATLANTIC

CHAPTER 1

BOSTON ⚜

□ □ □

Cradle of American puritanism and the largest city in New England, Boston has played a starring role in U.S. history since the 17th century. In 1630 a group of 800 English colonists led by governor-to-be John Winthrop landed at **Charlestown,** on the north shore of the Charles River. During the following months the settlers acquired the south shore and moved there, on what is now **Beacon Hill.** They established a village of fishermen, craftsmen, and fur traders (commerce with the Native Americans flourished for a long time) known originally as **Tremont** because of its three hills. But the new arrivals, being loyal subjects of His Majesty, quickly renamed the town Boston, after their small Lincolnshire birthplace. Despite its deep Anglo-Saxon roots, Boston was the scene of the 1770 revolt against British rule (the Boston Massacre), which snowballed into the 1773 Boston Tea Party. And nearby **Lexington, Concord,** and **Bunker Hill** became the theater two years later for the first major battles against British colonialism. After its 1776 liberation by George Washington, Boston grew and prospered, quickly becoming the third-largest American city, with a population of 93,000 in 1840, 360,000 in 1890, and more than 500,000 in 1914. After World War I the city passed through almost four decades of eclipse, suffering economic setbacks, and political and racial conflicts, which culminated in 1927 with the Sacco and Vanzetti affair. The city lost a third of its inhabitants during this troubled time.

Under the guidance of newly elected officials in the early 1960s, the capital of Massachusetts initiated an exemplary urban-renewal plan. Witness the **Government Center,** with its futurist architecture; the sweeping gray-green silhouette of the **John Hancock Tower,** designed by I. M. Pei (62 stories: 768 ft, 235 m); as well as the new business district near the harbor. Boston's renaissance coincided, not accidentally, with the presidency of one of the city's most illustrious sons, John Fitzgerald Kennedy, the first Roman Catholic president in the country's history.

With the possible exception of New York, Boston has undoubtedly produced more noteworthy politicians, writers, and intellectuals than any other U.S. city: from Paul Revere to Ralph Waldo Emerson, from John Hancock to John Adams, from Benjamin Franklin to Samuel Morse (inventor of the telegraph), and from Edgar Allan Poe to architect Louis Sullivan and actor Jack Lemmon. Boston also prides itself on the first American newspaper, the *Boston Newsletter,* published by postmaster John Campbell from 1704 to 1776.

Taking pride, as it understandably does, in its glorious history, Boston is the most European of American cities. If you follow the red arrows of the **Freedom Trail** along the small, winding downtown streets, you will encounter all the landmarks of Boston life over 350 years: the venerable **Boston Common,** the country's first public park (1634); charming **Faneuil Hall,** known as "the cradle of American liberty"; the one-time British governor's mansion (**Old State House**); the elegant patrician homes of **Beacon Hill;** and the old red-brick houses of the **North End,** a once-seedy area now the heart of picturesque Little Italy, with Italian food stores, cafés, and restaurants. Some old Boston buildings, like the **Paul Revere House** (1677), are among the oldest still standing in the country.

Important waves of immigrants (mostly Roman Catholic)—especially Irish, but also Italian, Polish, and more recently, Puerto Rican—have transformed this sanctuary of American puritanism into a vast, expanding industrial center (navy yards, electronics, machine tools, clothing), a port city, and a very active university town: one Bostonian in six is a student. Home of two of the world's most prestigious universities—**Harvard,** which recently celebrated its 350th anniversary, and the **Massachusetts Institute of Technology (M.I.T.)**—a world-renowned symphony orchestra, countless museums, libraries, and more, Boston is, not surprisingly, still referred to as "the Athens of North America."

BASIC FACTS: Capital of the state of Massachusetts. Area Code: 617. Time Zone: Eastern Time. ZIP code (of central post office): 02109. Founded: 1630. Approximate population: city, 570,000; metropolitan area, 4,060,000. Seventh-largest metropolitan area in the U.S.

CLIMATE: Except for a brief and sunny spring, Boston's climate is less than ideal. Summer is heavy with humidity (mean July temperature, 72°F, 22°C), and winter is freezing and snow-covered (mean Jan. temperature, 29°F,–2°C). Outside of spring, the best time to visit Boston is during the chilly but clear days of autumn.

DISTANCES: Chicago, 965 mi. (1,545 km); Montreal, 318 mi. (508 km); New York, 209 mi. (335 km); Niagara Falls, 480 mi. (768 km); Washington, 431 mi. (690 km).

ARRIVAL & TRANSIT INFORMATION

AIRPORT: Logan International Airport (BOS): 3 mi. (5 km) east. Information: 800/235-6426.

DOMESTIC AIRLINES: American (542-6700), Bar Harbor (262-3700), Braniff (toll free 800/272-6433), Continental (569-8400), Delta (567-4100), Eastern (262-3700), Midway (toll free 800/621-5700), Northwest (267-4885), Pan Am (toll free 800/221-1111), PBA (567-6090), TWA (367-2800), United (482-7900), USAir (482-3160).

FOREIGN CARRIERS: Aer Lingus (toll free 800/223-6537), Air Canada (toll free 800/422-6232), British Airways (toll free 800/247-9297), Lufthansa (toll free 800/645-3880), QuébecAir (toll free 800/361-4940), Swissair (423-7778).

CITY LINK: Cab fare to city center, about $10–$12; time, 20–25 min. Bus: Airways Transportation Co. (267-2981); leaves every 30 min.; serves major dwntwn hotels; fare, $5.50; time, 25–30 min. There is a not-too-convenient dwntwn connection by subway (MBTA Blue Line). Boat: Airport Water Shuttle (toll free 800/235-6426), motorboat service to two dwntwn quays, Long Wharf and Rowes Wharf; time, 7 min.; leaves every 15 min.; fare, $5. Unless you are planning some East Coast excursions, the proximity of the airport and the compact layout of dwntwn Boston may make car rental superfluous. There is also a good public transportation system which combines bus and subway (MBTA) (722-3200).

CAR RENTAL (all at the airport): Avis (424-0800), Budget (569-4000), Dollar (569-5300), Hertz (569-7272), National (569-6700). For dwntwn locations, consult the local phone directory.

LIMOUSINE SERVICES: Carey Limousine (623-8700), Cooper's Limousine (482-1000), Fifth Avenue Limousine (286-1590).

TAXIS: Taxis are few and expensive. They may be hailed on the street, but priority response goes to waiting lines at the major hotels and phone orders. Major companies: Checker Cab (536-7000) and Town Taxi (536-5000).

TRAIN: AMTRAK, South Station, Atlantic Ave. & Summer St. (482-3660).

BUS: Greyhound, 10 St. James Ave. (292-4707).

INFORMATION & TOURS

TOURIST INFORMATION: Greater Boston Convention & Tourist Bureau, Prudential Plaza, MA 02199 (617/536-4100).
   Visitor Information Center, Tremont St. at Boston Common (338-1976).
   Foreign Visitor Center, 15 State St. (536-4100).
   Recorded phone message giving an up-to-date listing of cultural events and shows: 617/267-6446.

GUIDED TOURS: American Cruise Lines (boat). Information: 1 Marine Park, Haddam, CT 06438 (toll free 800/243-6755). Has 7- and 14-day cruises along the New England coast to Georgia on 100-berth luxury yachts.
   Bay State Cruises (harbor cruise), 20 Long Wharf (617/723-7800): mid-May to late October.
   Boston by Foot (guided walking tours), 77 N. Washington St. (617/367-2345): daily, May-Oct.
   Clipper Cruise Lines (boat). (See "Guided Tours" in the chapter on Baltimore.)
   Gray Line Tours (bus), Statler Office Bldg., 20 Park Plaza St. (617/426-8800): guided tours of the city and environs.
   Horse & Carriage Tours (Old Boston tours in horse-drawn carriage), 82 Commercial St. (617/523-5256): Resv. necessary. Tues.-Sun.
   Old Town Trolley (bus), 329 W. 2nd St. (617/269-7010); 90-min tours of historic Boston.

SIGHTS, ATTRACTIONS, & ACTIVITIES

ADVENTURE TOURS: The New England Aquarium (Central Wharf) organizes daily **whale-watching boat trips** May-Oct. Cost, $22; resv. needed (973-5277).

ARCHITECTURAL HIGHLIGHTS: ▵ **Government Center,** City Hall Plaza: Complex of ultramodern administrative buildings including **City Hall,** a commanding brick-and-concrete structure humorously nicknamed "the Aztec Tomb" by Bostonians, and the **J. F. Kennedy Federal Building,** designed by I. M. Pei. Worth a look.
      ☼ ▵▵ **John Hancock Tower,** Copley Square (247-1976): Very handsome curtain-wall skyscraper by I. M. Pei, 768 ft (240 m) tall. (See "Panoramas," below.) Open daily. Worth seeing.
      ▵▵ **Massachusetts Institute of Technology (M.I.T.),** Massachusetts Ave. at Memorial Dr., Cambridge: The country's (and perhaps the world's) most prestigious university of science and technology, M.I.T. is home to 9,000 students who make up a veritable breeding ground of future academics and Nobel Prize winners. The many interesting buildings on

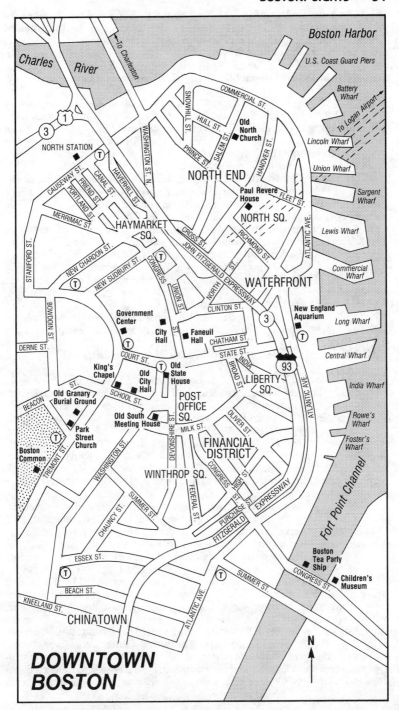

DOWNTOWN BOSTON

the 127-acre campus include I. M. Pei's **Green Building** (Pei was a student at M.I.T.) and the chapel designed by Eero Saarinen. Open Mon.-Fri. **Information Center:** 77 Massachusetts Ave. (253-4795). An absolute must-see.

⚓ **Prudential Tower,** 800 Boylston St. (236-3318): This modern, 752-ft- (229-m-) tall skyscraper offers a very lovely panorama from the **Skywalk** on the 50th floor (see "Panoramas," below). Open daily.

CHURCHES/SYNAGOGUES: ※ ⚓ King's Chapel, Tremont and School

Sts. (523-1749): Boston's first Episcopalian church. The present building, on the site of an Anglican chapel dating from 1686, was erected in 1754. A favorite of British sovereigns, the church has received many royal gifts: the communion plate is from George III, the pulpit from James II, and the red velvet cushions from Queen Anne. See it. Open Tues.-Sun.

👀 **Old North Church,** 193 Salem St. (523-6676): One of the prettiest and the most history-laden of Boston's churches. The two lanterns hanging in this church's bell tower on the night of April 18, 1775, warned Bostonians of the British offensive against Concord and Lexington (an episode immortalized in the words of Longfellow, "One if by land, two if by sea"). Very beautiful interior decoration. Not to be missed. Open daily.

⚓ **Park Street Church,** 1 Park St. (523-3383): One of Boston's most famous churches (1809) was a powder magazine during the War of 1812. William Lloyd Garrison here delivered the first public speech against slavery (1829), and the hymn "America" was first sung here (July 4, 1831). See it. Open daily.

⚓ **Trinity Church,** Copley Square (536-0944): Romanesque Episcopalian church completed in 1877. Henry Hobson Richardson's interesting architecture was inspired by Spain's Salamanca cathedral. Sumptuous interior. Absolutely worth a look. Open daily.

HISTORIC BUILDINGS: ⚓ U.S.S. Constitution, 55 Water St., Charlestown

(426-1812): The renowned frigate launched in 1797, undefeated in 42 engagements at sea, is nicknamed *"Old Ironsides"* and is the oldest commissioned ship in the U.S. Navy. Don't miss it. Open daily.

👀 **Faneuil Hall,** Merchants Row (227-1638): Former indoor market (1742), beautifully restored. Scene of the first public meetings protesting British rule, thus the nickname "Cradle of Liberty." The place offers many historic sights, including relics from the **Ancient & Honorable Artillery Company,** the country's oldest military school (1638). Attracts ten million visitors each year. Not to be missed. Open daily.

⚓ **Granary Burying Ground,** Tremont St.: Boston's oldest cemetery (1660), with the graves of Samuel Adams, John Hancock, Paul Revere, Benjamin Franklin's parents, and the five casualties of the Boston Massacre (see "Monuments," below). Worth a visit. Open daily.

👀 **Harvard University,** around Harvard Square, Cambridge: Temple of secular learning, Harvard (16,000 students) is the country's oldest (1636) and most famous university. Attended by the cultural and political elite (from poet Henry Longfellow to Pres. John F. Kennedy), its ivy-covered buildings have become the symbol of the East Coast's Ivy League, whose members include Columbia, Harvard, Princeton, and Yale. Among the university's many interesting modern buildings are the **Graduate Center,** designed by Walter Gropius, and the **Carpenter Center,** conceived by Le Corbusier. Many remarkable museums, as well: the **Peabody Museum** (archeology and pre-Columbian art) and the **Fogg Museum** (classic and modern paintings and sculptures, Chinese art). The campus **(Harvard Yard)** was used as the setting of the film *Love Story*. Open Mon.-Sat. **Information Center:** 1350 Massachusetts Ave. (495-1573). Don't miss it.

    Old Corner Bookstore, School & Washington Sts. (523-6658): Once a library frequented by Henry Wadsworth Longfellow, Harriet Beecher Stowe, Nathaniel Hawthorne, and other celebrated writers, one of Boston's oldest buildings (1712) is today an interesting bookstore specializing in works on New England history. Open daily. See it.

    Old State House, 206 Washington St. (242-5655): The former British governor's mansion dating from 1713, where the Declaration of Independence was read from the balcony, and where John Hancock was sworn in as Massachusetts' first governor (1789). Also Boston's City Hall from 1830 to 1841, it now houses many historic relics and temporary exhibitions. Its elegant architecture is overborne by surrounding skyscrapers. An absolute must-see. Open daily.

    Paul Revere's House, 19 North Square (523-2338): Boston's oldest (1677) house, carefully restored, contains period furniture and much personal memorabilia of the renowned Revolutionary War hero, Paul Revere. Picturesque little square and surrounding area. Not to be missed. Open daily.

MARKETS: ✳ 𝍤 **Quincy Market,** Merchants Row (227-1638): Picturesque indoor market in the heart of historic Boston comprising three spacious concourses dating from the 19th century. The city's hottest tourist attraction (12 million visitors each year) with boutiques, restaurants, terraced cafés, Sunday flea market. A tremendously colorful scene that shouldn't be missed. Open daily.

MONUMENTS: 𝍤 **Boston Massacre Site,** 30 State St.: A circle of stones marks the site of the "bloodbath of March 5, 1770," the historic episode during which British soldiers, stoned by the crowd, opened fire on the demonstrators and killed five people, including Crispus Attucks, the first black victim of the Revolutionary War.

    Bunker Hill Monument, Monument Square, Charlestown (252-5641): This 214-ft (67-m) granite obelisk on the far side of the Charles River commemorates the Battle of Bunker Hill (June 17, 1775), the baptism by fire of the Minutemen facing British troops. Fine panorama of the city and the harbor from the top of the obelisk (294 steps; no elevator). Worth a look. Open daily.

    Not far from the Bunker Hill Monument is the **State Prison of Charlestown,** where anarchists Nicola Sacco and Bartolomeo Vanzetti were executed on August 23, 1927, after a seven-year court battle that divided the nation.

MUSEUMS OF ART: 𝍤 **Institute of Contemporary Art,** 955 Boylston St. (266-5151): Has 20th-century art plus notable concerts, films, and temporary exhibitions. The building is a former police station. Worth a visit. Open Wed.-Sun.

    ☀𝍤𝍤𝍤 **Isabella Stewart Gardner Museum,** 280 The Fenway (566-1401): Startling baroque "palazzo" with a wonderful colonnaded courtyard in the Venetian style. Remarkable collection of European masters, Italian primitive art, and Flemish tapestries. Among the most famous works: Fra Angelico's *The Assumption of the Virgin,* Vermeer's *The Concert,* Rembrandt's *Storm on the Sea of Galilee,* Tintoretto's *Woman in Black,* Titian's *The Rape of Europa,* Matisse's *Terrace in St. Tropez,* and Degas' *Madame Gaujelin.* Boston's loveliest museum. Free concerts Tues., Thurs., and Sun. Open Tues.-Sun. in summer; Wed.-Sun. the rest of the year. Not to be missed.

Museum of Fine Arts, 465 Huntington Ave. (267-9300): Hundreds of masterworks from Rembrandt to Morris Louis and from Monet to Gauguin (see especially his famous painting *Who are we? Where do we come from? Where are we going?*). Among its other notable works: a Greek head of Aphrodite from the 4th century B.C., Van der Weyden's *St. Luke Painting the Virgin,* El Greco's *Portrait of Brother Paravicino,* Renoir's *Dance at Bougival,* Cézanne's *Winding Road,* Van Gogh's *House at Auvers,* and Jackson Pollock's *Number Ten.* Very fine collections of Asian and Egyptian art. The West Wing was designed by I. M. Pei. Don't miss it. Open Tues.-Sun.

Public Library, 666 Boylston St. (536-5400): Rich public library (more than three million volumes). Italian Renaissance architecture by Charles McKim. Remarkable interior decoration. Open Mon.-Sat.

MUSEUMS OF SCIENCE & HISTORY: **Bell's Laboratory,** 185 Franklin St.: Interesting little telephone museum in the lobby of the New England Telephone Building. Includes notably an exact replica of Alexander Graham Bell's studio.

Boston Tea Party Ship & Museum, Congress St. Bridge (338-1773): The spot where the revolt against the British began (1773). Life-size replica of the British sailing ship *The Beaver,* whose cargo of tea was dumped overboard by protesting Bostonians. Historic exhibition and, of course, tea is served. Not to be missed. Open daily.

Bunker Hill Pavilion, 55 Constitution Rd., Charlestown (241-7575): Neighbor of the frigate *Constitution* (see "Historic Buildings," above) and the Bunker Hill Monument (see "Monuments," above), this specially conceived hall offers a multimedia show which reproduces the Battle of Bunker Hill on 14 movie screens and seven soundtracks. Hear Israel Putnam's immortal words, "Don't fire until you see the whites of their eyes." Worth a look. Open daily.

Christian Science Publishing House, 1 Norway St. (450-2000): Inside is a concave glass terrestrial globe, 28 ft (9 m) in diameter, that is truly astonishing. Open daily. In the Administration Building next door is the headquarters of the Church of Christ, Scientist (300,000 members worldwide). See it.

Computer Museum, Museum Wharf, 300 Congress St. (423-6758): From the good old UNIVAC 1 of the 1950s to the massive AN/FSQ-7, the biggest computer in the world (175 tons), this museum offers a complete panorama of the history of data processing. Demonstrations of state-of-the-art technology. Marvelous. Open daily in summer; Tues.-Sun. the rest of the year.

John F. Kennedy Library, University of Massachusetts, Columbia Point Campus, 5 mi. (8 km) SE on I-93 (929-4523): The life of the 35th president in movies, documents, and photographs in a very effective futurist setting designed by I. M. Pei. Very lovely view of the skyline and the ocean. Open daily.

John F. Kennedy National Historic Site, 83 Beals St., Brookline (566-7937): The birthplace of the president on the outskirts of Boston. JFK lived in the house from 1917 to 1921. Period furniture and Kennedy family memorabilia. Simple and moving. See it. Open daily.

Museum of Science & Hayden Planetarium, Science Park (589-0100): Large, ultramodern science museum devoted to technology and natural history, including a life-size dinosaur replica. The interesting medical section has a giant model of the human heart. Boasts the largest Omnimax 360° film screen in the world (73 ft, 22 m, in diameter; 84 speakers).

For science and astronomy buffs. Open Tues.-Sun.

    New England Aquarium, Central Wharf (742-8870): Huge, four-story glass aquarium with more than 7,000 fish and marine creatures of all kinds, from sea lions to sharks. Worth a visit. Open daily. (See also "Adventure Tours," above.)

    Old South Meeting House, Washington & Milk Sts. (523-6676): Built in 1729 on the site of an earlier house of worship where Benjamin Franklin was baptized in 1706, this red-brick building, once a religious and public meeting center, is today home to the historical museum of the city. This was also the starting point of Bostonians (some disguised as Indians) who took part in the Boston Tea Party (see above). A definite must-see. Open Mon.-Sat.

    State House, Beacon St. (727-2121): The Massachusetts legislative building, designed by Charles Bulfinch (1795). Its unique historical archives contain notably the passenger list of the *Mayflower* and the original Massachusetts Constitution of 1780, the country's first written constitution. Very lovely Hall of Flags. Not to be missed. Open daily.

PANORAMAS: Bunker Hill Monument (see "Monuments," above).

    John Hancock Observatory, 200 Clarendon St. (247-1976): Splendid panorama of the city and harbor from the 60th floor of the John Hancock Tower. Absolutely worth a look. Open daily until 11 p.m.

    Prudential Tower, 800 Boylston St. (236-3318): The observation platform on the 50th floor affords a 360° panorama of the city that is almost as impressive as the view from the John Hancock Observatory. Worth a look. Open daily until 11 p.m.

PARKS & GARDENS: Arnold Arboretum, Arborway, Jamaica Plain (524-1717): This very lovely 265-acre park was designed by Frederick Law Olmsted, the renowned landscape architect. It contains more than 6,000 kinds of trees and shrubs, and offers floral exhibits year round. 25 min. from dwntwn.

    Boston Common, Tremont, Park, & Beacon Sts.: The first of the country's large public parks (1634), it encompasses 48 acres of trees, lawns, and shrubberies in the heart of Boston. Once a training ground for the redcoats, it is much enjoyed by amblers and soapbox orators, but should be avoided after nightfall. The Bostonian gathering point for all great occasions, the Common was the site of Pope John Paul II's outdoor mass before 200,000 people (1979). The adjacent **Public Garden** has a lake for boating in summer and skating in winter.

    Mount Auburn Cemetery, Mt. Auburn St., Cambridge: The country's oldest garden cemetery, this flower-filled park overlooking the Charles contains the graves of such notables as Henry Wadsworth Longfellow, Justice Oliver Wendell Holmes, and Mary Baker Eddy, founder of the Church of Christ, Scientist. Worth a detour. Open daily.

PERFORMING ARTS: For a daily listing of all shows and cultural events, consult the entertainment pages of the daily papers *Boston Globe* (morning), *Boston Herald-American* (morning), and *Christian Science Monitor* (morning); the weekly *Boston Phoenix;* and the monthly magazine *Boston.* **Bostix,** a kiosk in Faneuil Hall Marketplace, Faneuil Hall Square (723-5171), sells half-price tickets for all shows on the day of performance.

    Boston Center for the Arts, 539 Tremont St. (426-5000): Concerts, recitals, avant-garde theater, ballet. Year round.

    Charles Playhouse Theatre, 106 Boylston St. (426-6912): Drama, comedy, modern theater.

Hatch Shell, Esplanade, Memorial Dr.: Open-air Boston Pops Orchestra concerts and Boston Ballet Company performances. Summer only.

Loeb Drama Center, 64 Brattle St., Cambridge (547-8300): Home of the American Repertory Theater, offering classical and modern works.

Next Move Theatre, 1 Boylston Pl. (423-5572): Experimental theater.

Opera Company of Boston, 539 Washington St. (426-2786): Boston's new grand opera house, with artistic director Sarah Caldwell.

Shubert Theatre, 265 Tremont St. (426-4520): Broadway shows (often previews). Year round.

Symphony Hall, Huntington & Massachusetts Aves. (266-1492): Home of the celebrated Boston Symphony Orchestra, one of the country's "big six" orchestras (principal conductor: Seiji Ozawa); Sept.-Apr. Also the home of the Boston Pops Orchestra (principal conductor: John Williams); May-July.

Wang Center for the Performing Arts, 268 Tremont St. (542-3945): Home of the Boston Ballet Company.

Wilbur Theatre, 246 Tremont St. (423-4008): Modern theater, Broadway shows. Year round.

SHOPPING: The Coop, 1 Federal St. at Harvard Square, Cambridge: The world's biggest student-oriented store: from textbooks to blue jeans, from posters to backpacks, and from records to the latest in microcomputers. A classic since 1882.

Copley Place, 100 Huntington Ave.: Gigantic shopping center with a futurist look (interior gardens, huge waterfalls), plus dozens of luxury boutiques, from Neiman-Marcus to Gucci and Vuitton to Tiffany's. Spectacular.

☀ **Filene's,** 462 Washington St.: A real landmark. In the famous basement of this crowded store are Boston's best deals on cut-rate clothing—in a hurly-burly atmosphere. Many other interesting stores close by, along Washington and Summer Sts.

Newbury Street: Boston's chic shopping street, with fashionable boutiques, art galleries, famous food stores. Worth a look.

Tower Records, Massachusetts Ave. & Newbury St.: The biggest and most up-to-date record and video store in the world (more than 40,000 square ft, 3,730 m²). Impressive. Close to Symphony Hall.

SPECIAL EVENTS: For the exact schedule of events below, consult the **Greater Boston Convention & Tourist Bureau** (see "Tourist Information," above).

Patriots Day Celebration (mid-April): Parades, celebrations, and the Boston Marathon.

Esplanade Concerts (first two weeks of July): Free open-air concerts by the world-famous Boston Pops Orchestra at the Hatch Memorial Shell (on the banks of the Charles River). Don't miss it.

Harborfest (July): Fireworks, concerts.

Charles River Regatta (last Sun. in Oct.): Boat races on the Charles, a classic of the Boston season.

Harvard-Yale Football Game (Nov.): When the great rivals Harvard and Yale clash, the famous match-up guarantees excitement and a great atmosphere. The game is played in Cambridge and New Haven, alternating every two years.

SPORTS: Boston has four professional teams:

Baseball (Apr.-Oct.): Red Sox, Fenway Park (267-8661).

Basketball (October-late Apr.): Celtics, Boston Garden (523-3030).

Football (Sept.-Dec.): New England Patriots, Sullivan Stadium (543-1776).

Ice Hockey (Oct.-Apr.): Bruins, Boston Garden (227-3200).

Horse Racing
Suffolk Downs, on Mass. 1A, East Boston (567-3900), year round.

STROLLS: ☼ ▲▲ **Freedom Trail:** This red-arrow-marked circuit begins at Beacon and Park Sts. and winds for 2½ mi. (4 km) through the streets and sites of Old Boston. You'll see the principal historic monuments of the city. Don't miss it.

☀️▲ **Beacon Hill,** around Mt. Vernon St.: Boston's aristocratic neighborhood, with old gas lamps, cobblestoned streets, lovely private homes with elegant façades and carefully polished brass nameplates. A whiff of nostalgia. An absolute must-see (especially, gorgeous **Louisburg Square).**

▲ **North End,** bordered by Commercial St. and John F. Fitzgerald Expwy: Surrounded by warehouses and the docks of Boston's old harbor, this picturesque area composed of small, narrow streets with red-brick houses has become the local **Little Italy** over the years. Numerous agreeable restaurants, bars, and food stores contribute to a colorful atmosphere (especially during religious festivals). From Commercial St. or Atlantic Ave., you can enjoy an unobstructed view of the port and its maritime traffic.

THEME PARKS: See **Old Sturbridge Village,** in "Farther Afield," below.

WINTER SPORTS RESORTS: Boston Hills (26 mi., 42 km, north on Mass. 28 and 125; 508/683-2733): Four lifts, open mid-Dec. to mid-Mar.
Crotched Mountain (100 mi., 160 km, NW on Mass. 2, Mass. 12, U.S. 202, and N.H. 47; 603/588-6345): Three lifts, open mid-Nov. to Apr.
Temple Mountain (87 mi., 139 km, NW on Mass. 2, Mass. 12, U.S. 202, and N.H. 101; 603/924-6949): Three lifts, open Dec.-Apr.
Wachusett Mountain (58 mi., 93 km, NW on Mass. 2 and Mass. 140; 508/464-5101): Three lifts, open Dec.-Mar.

ACCOMMODATIONS
See the listing of toll-free numbers in the Appendix.

Room Rates in Boston	
B (Budget)	up to $30
I (Inexpensive)	$30–$60
M (Moderate)	$60–$90
E (Expensive)	$90–$140
VE (Very Expensive)	$140 and up

Personal Favorites (in order of preference)
♛♛♛♛♛ **Ritz Carlton Hotel** (dwntwn), 15 Arlington St., MA 02117 (617/536-5700; toll free 800/241-3333). 278 rms, A/C, color TV. AE, CB, DC, MC, V. Gar. $12, health club, sauna, two rests. (including the Ritz Carlton Dining Room), two bars, 24-hr rm svce, hrdrsr,

drugstore, concierge, free crib. *Note:* "The" grand palace of Boston since 1927 and one of the 12 best hotels in the country, across from the Public Garden. Elegant, refined décor, irreproachable comfort w. period furniture and ultracorrect svce. Renowned bar and rests. (the Ritz Café is the "in" place for working breakfasts). VIP floor. Recently received a $25-million facelift. Free limousine service to and from the business district. **VE**

☼ 🛏🛏🛏 **The Bostonian** (dwntwn), Faneuil Hall Marketplace, MA 02109 (617/523-3600; toll free 800/343-0922). 155 rms. A/C, cable color TV. AE, CB, DC, MC, V. Valet gar. $15, rest. (the Seasons), bar, 24-hr rm svce, free crib. *Note:* The hotel's modern red-brick architecture is perfectly integrated into the Old Boston setting. Inside is an elegant fourstory glass atrium and cramped but comfortable rms with exposed beams and fireplaces (some w. balconies). Intimate, sophisticated atmosphere and impeccable svce, plus an excellent rest. (the Seasons). The best location in Boston, across from Faneuil Hall and Quincy Market. **VE**

🛏🛏🛏 **Royal Sonesta** (vic.), 5 Cambridge Pkwy., Cambridge, MA 02142 (617/491-3600; toll free 800/343-7170). 397 rms. A/C, color TV, in-rm movies. AE, CB, DC, MC, V. Free parking, two pools, health club, three rests. (including the Rib Room), four bars, rm svce, disco, hrdrsr, free crib. *Note:* Large, post-modern convention hotel, recently enlarged. Irreproachable comfort and facilities. The interior is adorned w. numerous original works of contemporary art, from Roy Lichtenstein to Buckminster Fuller. Spacious rms with mini-bars. VIP floors. Excellent svce and a very lovely view of Boston from the opposite side of the Charles River. Business clientele. Convenient to M.I.T. An excellent location, 20 min. from dwntwn. **E-VE**

☼ 🛏🛏🛏 **Omni Parker House** (dwntwn), 60 School St., MA 02107 (617/227-8600; toll free, see Omni). 540 rms. A/C, cable color TV. AE, CB, DC, MC, V. Gar. $15, health club, sauna, three rests (including The Last Hurrah), coffeeshop, three bars, 24-hr rm svce, disco, hrdrsr, drugstore. *Note:* In this venerable (dates from 1855), history-laden palace in the heart of Boston, Charles Dickens stayed, Ho Chi Minh was a bellboy, and the Kennedys are a familiar sight. Marble, woodwork, and Oriental rugs abound in the sumptuously renovated building. The rms are elegantly comfortable and the atmosphere calm and distinguished. Reception and svce of the highest quality. Good rests. A favorite of connoisseurs. **E-VE**

🛏🛏 **The 57 Park Plaza Hotel** (dwntwn), 200 Stuart St., MA 02116 (617/482-1800; toll free, see Howard Johnson's). 345 rms, A/C, color TV, in-rm movies. AE, CB, DC, MC, V. Free parking, pool, sauna, rest. (57 Restaurant), bar, rm svce, disco, hrdrsr, free crib. *Note:* Rather ordinary modern architecture, but a very good location just off the Common. Functional rms w. balconies and a satisfactory rest. Fair svce. Business clientele. VIP suites on the 23rd floor. Movie theaters. **E**

🛏🛏 **Boston Park Plaza Hotel** (dwntwn), 50 Park Plaza, MA 02117 (617/426-2000; toll free 800/225-2008). 956 rms, A/C, color TV, in-rm movies. AE, CB, DC, MC, V. Gar. $2, health club, rest. (Fox & Hounds), coffeeshop, bars, 24-hr rm svce, disco, hrdrsr, drugstore, boutiques, free crib. *Note:* Massive, aging palace near the Common w. slightly faded interior decoration but comfortable rms. Svce. so-so, and the group and convention clientele is somewhat obtrusive. Very good location. **E-VE**

🛏 **Chandler Inn** (nr. dwntwn), 26 Chandler St., MA 02116 (617/482-3450; toll free, see Quality Inns). 56 rms, A/C, color TV. AE, CB, DC, MC, V. Parking $12, bar. *Note:* Small, modest, and inviting hotel, five min. from dwntwn. Free breakfast. Recently renovated. Very good value for those on a budget. **I**

℄ **Quality Inn Downtown** (dwntwn), 275 Tremont St., MA
02116 (617/426-1400). 350 rms, A/C, color TV. AE, CB,
DC, MC, V. Rest., bar. *Note:* Oldish but well-maintained hotel in the theater district. Regular clientele. Recently renovated. A good overall value. **M–E**

Other Accommodations (from top bracket to budget)

℄℄℄℄ **Four Seasons** (dwntwn), 200 Boylston St., MA 02116 (617/
338-4400; toll free, see Four Seasons). 288 rms, A/C, cable
color TV. AE, CB, DC, MC, V. Valet gar. $12, pool, health club, sauna, two
rests. (including Aujourd'hui), two bars, 24-hr rm svce, disco, free crib. *Note:*
Open in 1985, this elegant, modern 15-story hotel overlooking the Public Garden is a favorite of financial-industry executives. Spacious, comfortable rms w.
mini-bars (the most pleasant have a view of the park). The décor complements
the hotel's period furniture and unassuming modernism. Personalized svce of
great distinction. Excellent nouvelle cuisine rest. One of Boston's finest. **VE**

℄℄℄℄ **Westin Hotel** (nr. dwntwn), 10 Huntington Ave., MA 02117
(617/262-9600; toll free, see Westin). 800 rms, A/C, cable
color TV. AE, CB, DC, MC, V. Parking $10, pool, gym, sauna, three rests. (including Ten Huntington), coffeeshop, three bars, 24-hr rm svce, disco. *Note:*
Brand-new 36-story building which towers over Copley Place Shopping Center.
Spectacular lobby w. waterfalls and interior gardens. Ultramodern comfort w.
vast, well-equipped rms (those on the top floors have a very lovely view of the
city). Efficient, diligent svce. Houses Boston's most expensive suite ($1,500 a
night). Frequented by VIPs and business people. Very good location. **VE**

☀℄℄℄ **Marriott Long Wharf** (dwntwn), 296 State St., MA 02116
(617/227-0800; toll free, see Marriott). 400 rms, A/C, color
TV, in-rm movies. AE, CB, DC, MC, V. Valet parking $8, two pools, sauna,
health club, two rests. (including Harbor Terrace), coffeeshop, two bars, rm svce,
disco, free crib. *Note:* One of the most recent additions to the Boston hotel family, just off Quincy Market. Unusual design in the shape of an inverted ship's hull
(due to the proximity of the harbor, no doubt). Ultracomfortable rms w. balconies and efficient svce w. no frills. Mediocre rests. like all Marriotts, good recreational facilities, and a pretty view of the harbor. Interesting wknd packages. **VE**

℄℄℄ **Meridien** (dwntwn), 250 Franklin St., MA 02110 (617/451-
1900; toll free, see Meridien). 328 rms, A/C, color TV, in-rm
movies. AE, CB, DC, MC, V. Gar. $12, pool, health club, sauna, two rests. (including Julien), two bars, 24-hr rm svce, disco, boutiques, free crib. *Note:* Italian
Renaissance–style palace dating from 1922 which once housed the Federal Reserve Bank. Luxurious, well-conceived rms w. mini-bars. Attentive reception and
service with a touch of elegance à la française. Excellent nouvelle cuisine rest. that
is much enjoyed by business people (Julien). Very central location. Business clientele. Recommended. **VE**

℄℄℄ **Hyatt Regency Cambridge** (vic.), 575 Memorial Dr., Cambridge, MA 02139 (617/492-1234; toll free, see Hyatt). 478
rms, A/C, color TV, in-rm movies. AE, CB, DC, MC, V. Gar. $8, three rests.
(including the Spinnaker), bar, 24-hr rm svce, disco, boutiques, drugstore, free
crib. *Note:* Futurist pyramid overlooking the Charles River w. a spectacular 16-
story atrium. Spacious, comfortable rms w. private balconies (no-smoking rms
available). Rather cold modern architecture, but good svce. VIP floor. Five min.
from Harvard. **E–VE**

℄℄ **Holiday Inn Government Center** (dwntwn), 5 Blossom St.,
MA 02114 (617/742-7630; toll free, see Holiday Inns). 300
rms, A/C, color TV, in-rm movies. AE, CB, DC, MC, V. Parking $7, pool, tennis, rest. (Lobster Trap), coffeeshop, bar, rm svce, disco, boutiques, free crib.
Note: Functional, modern 15-story tower à la Holiday Inn but more inviting

than usual. Comfortable rms, group clientele. Quite close to the Charles and to City Hall. Interesting wknd packages. **E**

Sheraton Commander (vic.), 16 Garden St., Cambridge, MA 02138 (617/547-4800; toll free, see Sheraton). 175 rms, A/C, color TV, in-rm movies. AE, CB, DC, MC, V. Free parking, rest. (Brandywine), bar, rm svce, disco, drugstore, free crib. *Note:* Inviting hotel rebuilt as new. Close to Harvard and M.I.T., it offers comfortable colonial-style rms, good svce, and an agreeable ambience. 20 min. from dwntwn. **E**

Copley Square Hotel (nr. dwntwn), 47 Huntington Ave., MA 02116 (617/536-9000; toll free 800/225-2008). 130 rms, A/C, color TV, in-rm movies. AE, CB, DC, MC, V. Gar. $8, rest. (Café Budapest), coffeeshop, bar, free crib. *Note:* Small, rather well-worn hotel in the shadow of the Prudential Tower. The décor and svce leave something to be desired, but the rms are vast and comfortable, and the location very practical for those on business. Excellent rest. (Café Budapest). Recently acquired by the Golden Tulip hotel chain. Good overall value. Good reduced wknd rates in winter. **M–E**

Midtown Hotel (nr. dwntwn), 220 Huntington Ave., MA 02115 (617/262-1000; toll free 800/343-1177). 160 rms., A/C, color TV. AE, CB, DC, MC, V. Free parking, pool, health club, sauna, rest., bar, rm svce, hrdrsr. *Note:* Relatively modern motel across from the Prudential Tower. Spacious, comfortable rms. The svce fluctuates. Interesting wknd packages. **M–E**

Eliot Hotel (nr. dwntwn), 370 Commonwealth Ave., MA 02215 (617/267-1607). 100 rms, A/C, color TV. AE, CB, DC, MC, V. Parking, adjacent bar. *Note:* All the rms in this modern, tranquil hotel are mini-suites with or without kitchenettes. Interesting deals for longer stays. International clientele. A good value. Ten min. from dwntwn. **M**

Quality Inn Cambridge (vic.), 1651 Massachusetts Ave., Cambridge, MA 02138 (617/491-1000; toll free, see Quality Inns). 135 rms, A/C, color TV, in-rm movies. AE, CB, DC, MC, V. Free parking, pool, rest., bar, rm svce. *Note:* Classic, modern-style motel w. pleasant reception and svce and comfortable rms. Close to Harvard. 20 min. from dwntwn. **M**

Susse Chalet (vic.), 800 Morrissey Blvd., MA 02122 (617/287-9100; toll free 800/258-1980). 177 rms, A/C, color TV. AE, MC, V. Free parking, pool, adjacent coffeeshop, crib $3. *Note:* Relatively old but well-maintained motel 15 min. from dwntwn on the Southeast Expwy. Inviting rms. Close to the University of Massachusetts and to Kennedy Library. Ideal if you're driving through. Very good value. **I**

Airport Accommodations

Hilton Logan Airport (vic.), 75 Service Rd., Logan Airport, MA 02128 (617/569-9300; toll free, see Hilton). 550 rms, A/C, color TV, in-rm movies. AE, CB, DC, MC, V. Free parking, pool, three rests. (including Appleton's), bar, rm svce, disco, free crib. *Note:* This entirely renovated convention hotel offers comfortable, well-soundproofed rms w. private balconies and cheerful svce. Business clientele. 25 min. from dwntwn. **E–VE**

YMCAs / Youth Hostels

Boston International Hostel (nr. dwntwn), 12 Hemenway St., MA 02115 (617/536-9455). 175 beds. Youth hostel, Ten min. from dwntwn.

YMCA Boston (nr. dwntwn), 316 Huntington Ave., MA 02115 (617/536-7800). 300 rms, pool, health club, rest. Men and women.

RESTAURANTS

Boston Restaurant Prices	
(per person, excluding drinks and service charges)	
B (Budget)	up to $15
I (Inexpensive)	$15–$25
M (Moderate)	$25–$40
E (Expensive)	$40–$60
VE (Very Expensive)	$60 and up

Personal Favorites (in order of preference)

ౠౠౠౠ **Le Marquis de Lafayette** (dwntwn), in the Lafayette Swissôtel, 1 Ave. de Lafayette (451-2600). A/C. Lunch Mon.-Fri.; dinner Mon.-Sat.; closed Sun., hols. AE, CB, DC, MC, V. J&T. Specialties: clam ravioli, eggs au caviar, aiguillete of duck in maple syrup, filet of beef with marrow, veal medallions with mango and ginger, remarkable pastries. The menu changes regularly. Very fine wine list (with some finds at reasonable prices). *Note:* This newcomer to the Boston gastronomic scene has won a place of honor in just a few months under the guidance of Louis Outhier, owner of the famous three-star Oasis restaurant in La Napoule (France). He skillfully modifies classic *grande cuisine* with nouvelle cuisine tendencies, and the results are brilliant. The décor is of a sober elegance w. beveled mirrors, period furniture, and crystal chandeliers. Ultracorrect but unsmiling svce. Resv. a must long in advance given the limited seating in the dining room (60 seats). One of the best on the East Coast. *French.* **E–VE**

ౠౠౠ **L'Espalier** (nr. dwntwn), 30 Gloucester St. (262-3023). A/C. Dinner only, Mon.-Sat.; closed Sun., holidays. AE, CB, DC, MC, V. J&T. Specialties: squab with artichokes and truffles, lamb ravioli, veal sautéed in honey and lemon, pigeon mousse in pastry shell, grilled bass w. soy and lemon sauce, filet of beef bordelaise w. green peppercorns, excellent desserts, and a rich wine list. The menu changes regularly. *Note:* The temple of Boston nouvelle cuisine since Dodin Bouffant moved to New York, it offers light, inspired cuisine from chef Moncef Meddeb. Pretty, antique décor in an elegant, Edwardian three-story house in the Back Bay section. Very lovely floral arrangements. Exemplary svce. Trendy clientele. Resv. a must. Valet parking $5. *French-Continental.* **E–VE**

ౠౠౠ **Café Budapest** (nr. dwntwn), 90 Exeter St., at Huntington Ave. (734-3388). A/C. Lunch/dinner daily; closed holidays. AE, CB, DC, MC, V. Jkt. Specialties: cherry soup, paprika chicken, stuffed cabbage, goulash, beef Stroganoff. *Note:* As the name indicates, the cuisine is Hungarian-inspired, as is the wine list. The menu's originality, the svce, the musicians and the nicely kitsch decor are enough to explain the years of success this rest. has enjoyed. Resv. necessary (especially on wknds). In the basement of the Copley Square Hotel. *Continental.* **M**

☼ ౠౠ **Locke Ober Café** (dwntwn), 3 Winter Pl. (542-1340). A/C. Lunch/dinner daily; closed holidays. AE, CB, DC, MC, V. J&T. Specialties: lobster Savannah, duckling bigarade, sole bonne femme, sweetbreads Eugénie, filet Mirabeau, steak tartare, Nesselrode sundae, Indian pudding. *Note:* The most famous eating place in Boston. Since 1875 this venerable institution has retained its Victorian woodwork and its old-world club atmosphere. The only break with tradition: women are now admitted to the mezzanine, or most elegant, dining room. Cuisine and svce exemplary on all counts. Resv. advised. A favorite of Boston society (especially the late President Kennedy). *Continental-American.* **I–M**

Anthony's Pier 4 (dwntwn), 140 Northern Ave. (423-6363). A/C. Lunch/dinner daily; closed Dec. 25. AE, CB, DC, MC, V. Jkt. Specialties: lobster and remarkable seafood of all kinds that are fresh and reasonably priced. Good wine list. *Note:* Criticized by purists for its "eating factory" appearance, Anthony's Pier 4 is, according to a *Boston Globe* poll, the favorite restaurant of Bostonians. Not surprisingly, it is often jam-packed despite the imposing dimensions of the windowed dining rm. Generous portions, diligent svce, and an agreeable view of the harbor. Rather amusing marine bric-a-brac décor. No dinner resv., unfortunately. Valet parking. *Seafood.* **I–M**

Ye Olde Union Oyster House (dwntwn), 41 Union St. (227-2750). A/C. Lunch/dinner daily; closed Thanksgiving, Dec. 25. AE, CB, DC, MC, V. Specialties: clam chowder, oysters, coquilles St-Jacques, lobster, fish of the day. *Note:* Boston's oldest oyster bar (1826) in a more-than-three-centuries-old little one-story house is a tourist favorite. Superb raw bar on the mezzanine. Charming period décor. Cheerful svce. Resv. are useless. *Seafood.* **I**

Brandy Pete's (dwntwn), 267 Franklin St. (439-4165). A/C. Lunch/dinner Mon.-Fri.; closed Sat., Sun., holidays. MC, V. Specialties: beef with noodles, roast turkey, steak, lamb chops, fish of the day, bread pudding. *Note:* This friendly regulars' tavern for half a century has lost none of its appeal after a recent move to more spacious quarters. The décor is forgettable but the cuisine is solid and the portions generous. Relaxed, noisy atmosphere and efficient svce. Very popular at lunchtime. *American.* **I**

Other Restaurants (from top bracket to budget)

Aujourd'hui (dwntwn), in the Four Seasons (see "Accommodations," above) (338-4400). A/C. Breakfast/lunch/dinner daily. AE, CB, DC, MC, V. J&T. Specialties: cream of lentil soup with lobster, rack of lamb à la Szechuan, fish of the day nouvelle cuisine, fresh figs with ice cream and custard. The menu changes regularly. Remarkable wine list. *Note:* Superb, elegant rest. with airy, inventive French cuisine from the wonderful Mark Baker. Opulent décor of somber woodwork, floral upholstery, and large bay windows overlooking the Public Gardens. Ultra-polished svce. Big business clientele. One of Boston's most fashionable places. Resv. strongly advised. *French.* **M–E**

Restaurant Jasper (dwntwn), 240 Commercial St. (523-1126). A/C. Dinner only, Mon.-Sat.; closed Sun., holidays. AE, CB, DC, MC, V. Jkt. Specialties: boudin of lobster and cabbage, rack of lamb with grilled leeks, breast of pigeon with oysters. The menu changes regularly. *Note:* Inventive, elegant American nouvelle cuisine from chef Jasper White, but the prices are painful. Pretty pastel décor w. elegant floral arrangements. Efficient if starchy svce. Trendy clientele. Quite close to the harbor. Resv. a must. Valet parking. *Ameican.* **M–E**

Another Season (dwntwn), 97 Mt. Vernon St. (367-0880). A/C. Lunch Tues.-Fri; dinner Mon.-Sat.; closed Sun. AE, MC, V. Jkt. Specialties: lamb nivernaise, poached sole with orange mousseline, fried trout with pecans, filet of beef with roquefort, very good desserts. The menu changes regularly with the seasons (hence the name). Rather skimpy wine list. *Note:* Charming, fashionable little bistro that offers modern, innovative cuisine. Pleasant, Paris-1900 décor. Svce is exceedingly competent. An excellent spot. *French-Continental.* **I–M**

Suntory (dwntwn), 212 Stuart St. (338-2111). A/C. Lunch Mon.-Sat.; dinner daily. AE, CB, DC, MC, V. Jkt. Specialties: sushi, shabu-shabu, tempura, teppanyaki, yakitori. *Note:* Experts consider this the best Japanese rest. in Boston. It is one of a dozen luxury rests. around the world (including one in Chicago and one in Honolulu) owned by the renowned Japanese distillery, Suntory. Sober, elegant Oriental décor. The customer has a choice between the sushi bar and the upstairs dining rms, specializing in different types of Japanese cuisine. An excellent locale. Resv. advised given its success. *Japanese.* **I–M**

Casa Romero (nr. dwntwn), 30 Gloucester St. (enter through the adjacent alley (536-4341). A/C. Dinner only, daily; closed holidays. AE, CB, DC, MC, V. Jkt. Specialties: higaditos, marinated pork, chicken with coriander. *Note:* Very elaborate Mexican cuisine in a pretty hacienda setting. Elegantly romantic atmosphere and attentive svce. No resv. *Mexican.* **I**

Durgin Park (dwntwn), 30 N. Market St. (Faneuil Hall) (227-2038). A/C. Lunch/dinner daily. No credit cards. Specialties: Yankee pot roast, prime rib, roast duck, oyster stew, fish of the day, shellfish, Indian pudding. *Note:* A Boston classic since 1830. Excellent regional fare with generous portions in a noisy, relaxed atmosphere. Communal tables. Efficient, if rather brusque, svce. No resv. Other location: 100 Huntington Ave. at Copley Place (266-1964). *American.* **I**

Felicia's (dwntwn), 145A Richmond St. (second floor) (523-9885). A/C. Dinner only, daily; closed Easter, Thanksgiving, Dec. 25. AE, MC, V. Jkt. Specialties: fresh homemade pasta, shrimp Toscano, chicken with verdicchio, seafood cannelloni, veal Margarita. *Note:* Wholly authentic Italian trattoria with charming period décor and diligent, courteous svce. Locally popular for more than 30 years. No resv., unfortunately. *Italian.* **I**

Jimmy's Harborside (nr. dwntwn), 242 Northern Ave., on the waterfront (423-1000). A/C. Lunch/dinner Mon.-Sat.; closed Sun., Dec. 25. AE, CB, DC, MC, V. Jkt. Specialties: clam chowder, excellent seafood. *Note:* The best clam chowder in all Boston. Remarkable seafood at reasonable prices and a very lovely view of the harbor (especially from the second floor). Locally very popular for more than a half century. Very efficient svce. One disappointment: Jimmy's closes relatively early (9:30 p.m.). Resv. advised. Valet parking. *Seafood.* **I**

The Last Hurrah (dwntwn), in the Omni Parker House (see "Accommodations," above) (227-8600). A/C. Lunch/dinner daily (until midnight). AE, CB, DC, MC, V. Jkt. Specialties: Boston scrod (haddock), clam chowder, prime rib, daily specials. *Note:* A favorite hangout of Boston journalists and politicians in the basement of the venerable Parker House Hotel. Pleasant atmosphere, especially at lunch (the orchestra is a bit obtrusive in the evening). Pretty, retro décor w. a mahogany bar and Tiffany lamps. Resv. advised. *American.* **I**

Legal Seafoods (dwntwn), 35 Columbus Ave. (426-4444). A/C. Lunch/dinner daily; closed Thanksgiving, Dec. 25. AE, CB, DC, MC, V. Specialties: huge variety of seafood that is cooked, steamed, fried, or grilled to perfection. Chowder, smoked hake pâté, cioppino, mussels au gratin. *Note:* One of the country's best seafood restaurants in a vast, modern, and luminous setting of mirrors, polished brass, and a dining rm spread over several levels. Legal Seafoods is at once a rest. chain and a retail fish store, and the more than 30 tons of fresh seafood it sells each week are its best recommendation. No resv. Inevitable waits, sometimes lengthy ones. Other locations: 43 Boylston St., in Newton (277-7300); and Kendall Square, in Cambridge (864-3400). Excellent value. *Seafood.* **B–I**

    ♀ **Imperial Teahouse** (dwntwn), 70 Beach St. (426-8543). A/C. Lunch/dinner daily (until 2 a.m.). AE, CB, DC, MC, V. Specialties: dim sum (at lunch), soup of eight delights, char siu ding, braised duck. *Note:* A highly commendable rest. in the heart of Boston's Chinatown. Vast and inviting, w. elegant Oriental décor and good svce. Resv. are possible but waits are inevitable on the wknd. *Chinese.* **B–I**

    ♀ **No Name** (dwntwn), 15½ Fish Pier (338-7539). A/C. Lunch/dinner Mon.-Sat. (until 9:30 p.m.); closed Sun. No credit cards. Specialties: clam chowder, grilled fish, fried clams. *Note:* On the pier itself, this seafood rest. w. rather Spartan décor is one of the most popular in Boston. The seagulls and the ship horns add to the local color. The cuisine is as simple as the décor, but the seafood is the highest quality. Efficient svce and an excellent value. A Boston classic since 1917. *Seafood.* **B–I**

Top of the Hub (nr. dwntwn), Prudential Bldg. (536-1775). As in most skyscraper rests., the panorama is the prime reason for coming here. Pleasant bar and view. *American.* **E**

Cafeterias / Fast Food

    ☼ **Elsie's** (vic.), 71 Mt. Auburn St., Cambridge (354-8781). Lunch/dinner daily. No credit cards. *Note:* Entire generations of Harvard students have sung the praises (and continue to do so) of Elsie's huge sandwiches. A "must" for all (preferably famished) visitors.

Ken's at Copley (dwntwn), 549 Boylston St. (266-6149). Open daily, 7 a.m. to 3 a.m. *Note:* Large, very popular deli offering very good sandwiches.

Museum of Fine Arts Cafeteria (nr. dwntwn), 465 Huntington Ave. (267-9300). Lunch only, Tues.-Sun. *Note:* Excellent cafeteria cuisine.

BARS & NIGHTCLUBS

As in New York, there is a magic telephone number in Boston, **Jazzline** (262-1300), listing all the jazz club programs.

    ☼ **Bull & Finch Pub** (dwntwn), Hampshire House, 84 Beacon St. (227-9600). Very lively pub (especially on weekends) and by far the most popular bar in Boston. Was the model for the television show "Cheers." Trendy restaurant on the second floor. Rather pleasant retro décor.

Daisy Buchanan's (nr. dwntwn), 240A Newbury St. (247-8516). Relaxed, comfortable singles bar, frequented by local football and baseball stars.

Jason's (nr. dwntwn), 131 Clarendon St. (262-9000). Open daily. Very popular piano bar that offers backgammon, a fashionable disco, and a decent restaurant. Rather posh clientele.

Metro (nr. dwntwn), 15 Landsdowne St., at Kenmore Square (262-2424). New wave, video-equipped disco; the "in" club.

Nick's Comedy Stop (dwntwn), 100 Warrenton St. (482-0930). A very crowded comedy club in the heart of the theater district and a classic on the Boston scene for more than 30 years.

The Ritz Bar (dwntwn), in the Ritz Carlton Hotel (see "Accommodations," above). (536-5700). Open daily. Classy, very British bar. "High society" describes the décor, the svce, and the prices.

Ryles (vic.), Inman Square, Cambridge (876-9330). Live jazz, pop, and blues with the biggest stars. Locally popular.

T.G.I. Friday's (nr. dwntwn), 26 Exeter St. (266-9040). Open daily. Pleasant, usually packed bar offering generous portions and an adequate rest. in hip/comfortable surroundings.

Zanzibar (dwntwn), 1 Boylston Pl. (451-1955). Hot pop-music dance club with jungle motif décor.

NEARBY EXCURSIONS

CONCORD (20 mi., 32 km, NW on Mass. 2): Known as "the cradle of the Republic," this charming historic New England town owes its name to the treaty, or concord, signed with the Native Americans soon after it was settled in 1635. A bloody confrontation at the North Bridge between British troops and the Minutemen on April 19, 1775, set the Revolutionary War in full motion. There are many historical landmark houses and museums here, including the **Old Manse** (Monument St.; open Thurs.-Mon.), **Orchard House** (399 Lexington Rd.; open daily), **Concord Antiquarium Museum** (200 Lexington Rd.; open daily); and **Concord Art Association** (37 Lexington Rd.; open Tues.-Sun.). Many famous writers are buried in the **Sleepy Hollow Cemetery** (Bedford St.), including Ralph Waldo Emerson and Nathanial Hawthorne. Well worth the trip. Makes a good joint excursion with Lexington (see below).

GLOUCESTER (35 mi., 56 km, NE on U.S. 1 and Mass. 128): Old fishing village with narrow, picturesque streets and very lovely beaches and cliffs nearby. Don't miss the **Hammond Castle Museum** (80 Hesperus Ave.; open daily), a startling medieval-style building built by inventor John Hays Hammond.

LEXINGTON (12 mi., 19 km, NW on Mass. 2): With Concord, another hallmark town of the Revolutionary War. There are a number of historic structures and relics here, including the **Hancock-Clarke House** (36 Hancock St.; open daily), where Paul Revere sounded warning for the Minutemen; **Buckman Tavern** (1 Bedford St.; open daily), on the site of the battle against the British (April 19, 1775): and **Munroe Tavern** (1232 Massachusetts Ave.; open daily), which served as a hospital for British troops. Worth a side trip.

LINCOLN (18 mi., 29 km, NW on Mass. 2 and 126): See the **Gropius House**, 68 Baker Bridge Rd. (617/227-3956). The Gropius family residence and the first of his designs realized in this country. This house's unadorned lines were considered avant-garde at the time of its construction (1937). Original Bauhaus furniture. Open Fri.-Sun. A "must" for all architecture lovers. A recommended joint excursion with Concord (see above).

MARBLEHEAD (17 mi., 27 km, NE on Mass. 1A): On a large Massachusetts Bay promontory, this former fishing port was founded in 1629 by British sailors from Cornwall and has since become a well-known summer resort. Numerous interesting colonial houses. Don't miss **Town Hall** (Washington Square; open daily) and its famous painting, *Spirit of '76*. Very popular boat races on summer wknds.

PLYMOUTH (39 mi., 65 km, SE on Mass. 3): A name known to every American. The first permanent British colony of New England was founded on Dec. 21, 1620, by the pilgrims of the *Mayflower*. (For more details, see the chapter on the Atlantic Coast.)

☼ 🛆🛆 **PORTSMOUTH** (55 mi., 88 km, NE on I-95): With its old waterfront neighborhood known as **Strawbery Banke,** this former New Hampshire capital of British colonial times offers one of the most handsome groups of historic buildings in the country. (For more details, see the chapter on the Atlantic Coast.)

🛆 **ROCKPORT** (38 mi., 61 km, NE on U.S. 1, Mass. 128 and 127): Charming little port that has become a haven for artists. See especially the famous **Paper House,** 52 Pigeon Hill St. (508/546-2629)—a baroque monument to the glory of the newspaper. A recommended combined excursion w. Gloucester (see above).

🛆 **ROUTE 128** (at the I-95N and I-95S fork): Along 26 mi. (42 km), this Boston beltway encompasses the largest complex of science and space research laboratories in the country. Some 700 firms, including all the giants of the electronics industry (General Electric, Honeywell, Raytheon, Wang, Digital, Geodyne, etc.), are represented, as well as NASA and U.S. Army research centers. Overall, some 50,000 scholars, engineers, and technicians make the famous Rte. 128 one of the most highly concentrated centers of brain power in the world. Also known as the "Silicon Valley of the East Coast."

☼ 🛆🛆 **SALEM** (16 mi., 26 km, NE on Mass. 1A): First capital of Massachusetts (1626–1630) and scene of the infamous witch trials of 1692 (described quite realistically in Arthur Miller's famous play *The Crucible*), which ended only after the hanging of 19 victims of religious fanaticism. Lovely old houses carefully preserved in the harbor area **(Maritime National Historic Site)** and around Chestnut St., notably. Many remarkable museums including the **House of Seven Gables,** 54 Turner St. (open daily), dating from 1668, which inspired Nathaniel Hawthorne's famous novel; **Witch House,** 310½ Essex St. (open daily), where the "witches" were interrogated; the **Peabody Museum,** E. Indian Square (open daily), and its rich naval collections; and the **Witch Museum,** 19½ Washington Square (open daily), which offers a detailed re-creation of a witch trial. The **Information Center,** Derby St. (617/744-4323), offers relatively complete brochures and written material. An excursion not to be missed.

🛆 **SAUGUS** (8 mi., 13 km, NE on U.S. 1): Cradle of the American iron and steel industry, Saugus was the site of the continent's first foundry (1646). Don't miss the **Iron Works National Historic Site,** 224 Central St., a minutely detailed replica of the period's first smelting furnaces with forging demonstrations. Open daily, Apr.-Oct. Worth the detour.

FARTHER AFIELD

☼ 🛆 **CAPE COD** (202 mi., 323 km, r.t. on Mass. 3S and U.S. 6E): A virtual island, this sandy, 60-mile- (97-km-) long area is where the Pilgrims of the *Mayflower* landed in 1620. Charming old fishing villages and beautiful seascapes. The two neighboring islands—**Martha's Vineyard** and **Nantucket**—are favorite vacation spots of well-to-do New Yorkers and Bostonians, offering fishing, sailing, and a temperate summer climate. (For more details, see the chapter on Cape Cod.) An excursion not to be missed.

🛆🛆 **OLD STURBRIDGE VILLAGE** (65 mi., 104 km, SW on the Massachusetts Tpke. and U.S. 84) (508/347-3362): Faithful rendition of an 18th-century New England village, with more than 40 old houses, stalls, workshops, and people in period dress. Interesting slice of history. Also, a nearby car museum, the **Sturbridge Automuseum,** 2 mi. (4 km) west on U.S. 20. Worth a visit. Open daily, Apr.-Oct.; Tues.-Sun. the rest of the year.

Heading back to Boston, turn off at ⚓ **Webster** (via Mass. 131 and 197), a small industrial town on the edge of the largest natural body of water in Massachusetts. Renamed **Lake Webster** for convenience sake, the lake's official name is actually **Lake Chargoggagoggmanchauggagoggchaubunagungamaug,** a term which, in the Indian Nipmuc dialect, means "you fish on your side, I fish on my side, no one fishes in the middle." In addition to having the longest and most complicated name in U.S. geography, the lake is also a fishing paradise, with trout, perch, and pike. Worth going out of your way for.

Where to Stay En Route

IN STURBRIDGE. The ☕☕ **Publick House Inn,** Mass. 131, Sturbridge, MA 01566 (508/347-3313). 17 rms. A charming little colonial inn dating from 1771 with a very satisfactory restaurant. **M**

☼ **THE BERKSHIRES** (336 mi., 538 km, r.t. on I-90W and U.S. 20N to Pittsfield): With its undulating landscapes, dense forests, and dozens of lakes and charming old New England villages, the Bershires region is a favorite vacation haven in all seasons: in winter for cross-country skiing; in summer for its music and theater festivals (Tanglewood Music Festival, the Williamstown Theater Festival, and the Berkshire Theater Festival are among the most popular in the country); and from mid-Sept. to late Oct., for the sumptuous colors of its autumn leaves.

Crossing through the Berkshires from the Vermont border north to southern Connecticut, U.S. 7 allows a complete picture of the area and its most remarkable locales: **Lenox,** the picturesque town celebrated by Nathaniel Hawthorne *(Tanglewood Tales)*, has been the backdrop each spring for half a century for the **Tanglewood Music Festival** (late June to late Aug.) with the Boston Symphony Orchestra (for information, call 413/637-1940).

Pittsfield offers, among other attractions, the **Berkshire Museum,** 39 South St., with its collection of European paintings (Rubens, Van Dyck, etc.); **Arrowhead,** 780 Holmes Rd., the residence-museum where Herman Melville wrote *Moby-Dick;* and the very lovely Shaker village of **Hancock** (5 mi., 8 km west on U.S. 20), a religious community founded in 1790 and where some 20 period buildings still stand. A visit not to be missed.

Stockbridge, a magnificent little summer community which seems to come straight out of an old picture book, has attracted many artists (sculptor Daniel Chester French, painter Norman Rockwell, author Norman Mailer, etc.) and is home to the renowned **Berkshire Theater Festival** (late June to Sept.; for information, call 413/298-5576). Two stops not to be missed: the **Norman Rockwell Museum,** on Main St., and the **studio of Daniel Chester French,** on Mass. 183.

Williamstown, another charming little village typical of the Berkshires with its old houses in pastel tones, has a very beautiful art museum with rich impressionist collections, the **Sterling and Francine Clark Institute,** 225 South St. Home of venerable **Williams College** (est. 1793) and of the **Williamstown Theater Festival** (late June to late Aug.), which offers modern and classical theater with famous actors. An absolute must since 1954. (For information, call 413/458-8109.)

A visit to the Berkshires is not to be missed for all lovers of art and culture. For regional tourist information, contact the **Berkshire Hills Visitors Bureau,** Berkshire Commons South, Pittsfield, MA 01201 (413/443-9186).

Where to Stay En Route

IN LENOX. ❄ 🍴🍴 **Apple Tree,** 224 West St., Lenox, MA 01240 (413/637-1477). 33 rms. Century-old inn amid lovely gardens. **M–E**

IN PITTSFIELD. 🍴🍴 **Hilton Inn,** Berkshire Common & West St., Pittsfield, MA 01201 (413/499-2000). 175 rms. Modern comfort. **M**
　　　　🍴 **Heart of the Berkshires,** 970 W. Housatonic, MA 01201 (413/443-1225). 16 rms. Small, functional motel. **I**

IN STOCKBRIDGE. ❄ 🍴🍴🍴 **Red Lion Inn,** Main St. at U.S. 7, Stockbridge, MA 01262 (413/298-5545). 100 rms. Charming inn dating from 1773. **I–E**

IN WILLIAMSTOWN. 🍴🍴🍴 **Orchards,** 222 Adams Rd., Williamstown, MA 01267 (413/458-9611). 49 rms. Elegant little colonial-style inn. **E**
　　　　🍴 **Berkshire Hills,** Cold Spring Rd. (U.S. 7S), MA 01267 (413/458-3950). 21 rms. Small motel in the woods. **I–M**

🔭 VERMONT AND THE NEW HAMPSHIRE MOUNTAINS:

(568 mi., 908 km, round trip from Boston via I-93N, N.H. 106N, U.S. 3N, N.H. 25E, N.H. 16N, U.S. 302W, N.H. 10S, U.S. 4W, U.S. 7S, Vt. 9E, N.H. 9E, N.H. 101E, U.S. 3S, Mass. 128W, and Mass. 2E): This trip, requiring at least three or four days and taking you through some of the most beautiful wooded country in the U.S., is suitable for all seasons: the long winter snows, the lovely New England spring, the radiant summer, or the splendid autumn which sets the forests of New Hampshire's **White Mountains** and Vermont's **Green Mountains** ablaze with color.

Leaving Boston northward along I-93, you soon come to your first stop, **Concord**, the capital of New Hampshire. See the 1819 **Statehouse**, on Main St. (603/271-2154), open Mon.-Fri., with its hall of flags and its characteristic dome. If you enjoy handcrafts you'll certainly want to visit the ⛵ **Concord Arts and Crafts Center,** 36 N. Main St., open Mon.-Sat.

Farther north on N.H. 106 you'll come to ⛵ **Canterbury Shaker Village**, on Shaker Rd. off N.H. 106 (603/783-9511), open Tues.-Sat. from mid-May through October. Founded in 1792 and today one of the only two active Shaker villages remaining in the U.S., it can still show half a dozen of its original buildings and a little museum illustrating the unusual Shaker lifestyle. Well worth the side trip.

The next stop is ❄ **Laconia**, a popular summer resort in the heart of the "lakes region" (one of the lakes is New Hampshire's largest, Lake Winnipesaukee). Continue north to ❄ **White Mountain National Forest**, a wooded tract of 741,000 acres (300,000 ha.) whose highest peak, 🔭 **Mount Washington**, rises to 6,288 ft. (1,917 m). A road reached from **Glen House** on N.H. 16, and a **cog railway** whose terminus is a little north of Crawford House on U.S. 302 (603/846-5404), will take you to the top of Mt. Washington from the end of May till Oct., and give you a breathtaking view. Many winter-sports resorts and spectacular gorges are nearby: **Crawford Notch, Dixville Notch, Franconia Notch, Pinkham Notch**, etc.

A very lovely scenic drive, the ⛵ **Kancamagus Highway** (N.H. 112), crosses the White Mountains from side to side. On your way, don't fail to visit the lovely resort of ⛵ **Bretton Woods**, famous as the scene of a 1944 international monetary conference which fixed the price of gold at $35 per ounce and created the International Bank for Reconstruction and Development (World Bank).

Regaining the right bank of the Connecticut River at **Woodsville**, your route stays on it for about 50 mi. (80 km) on the beautiful, scenic N.H. 10, passing the historic little town of ❊ **Hanover**, the home of famous Dartmouth College, founded in 1796. ❊ ⛆ **Woodstock**, the next stop, with its charming old houses, is one of Vermont's best-known ski resorts. Continuing toward the Green Mountains and **Sherburne Pass**, you'll come to **Rutland** and its renowned marble quarries; at the ⛆ **Vermont Marble Exhibit**, 61 Main St. (802/459-3311), open daily from late May through Oct., see how marble is quarried and then turned into works of art.

Manchester, the next stop, has been a popular summer and winter resort for more than a century. The ❊ ⛆ **Equinox Skyline Drive**, a mountain road rising as high as 3,835 ft. (1,169 m), will give you a magnificent view of the endless woodlands of the **Green Mountain National Forest**; it can be reached from U.S. 7, 6 mi. (9 km) south of Manchester. Road open May-Oct.; difficult in rainy or foggy weather. Don't miss it. There's a very popular classical-music festival every summer at the **Southern Vermont Art Center**, West Rd.; call 802/362-1405 for programs and schedules.

The trip ends at ❊ **Bennington**, where in 1777, in one of the decisive engagements of the War of Independence, Ethan Allen's "Green Mountain Boys" held off the British under General Burgoyne. Lovely old Colonial houses at ⛆ **Old Bennington**, and a remarkable **city museum** on W. Main St. (802/447-1571), open dailyMar.-Nov., with paintings by the American primitive, Grandma Moses. Don't miss it.

Finally, back to Boston across the Appalachian foothills, following various scenic highways: Vt. 9, N.H. 9 and N.H. 101. A spectacular excursion for lovers of unspoiled nature.

Where to Stay En Route

IN BENNINGTON, VT. 🏨 **Vermonter**, Vt. 9W, Bennington, VT 05201 (802/442-2529). 32 rms and cottages. Comfortable, well-run little motel on a lake with sand beach. Closed March and April. **I**
.

IN BRETTON WOODS, N.H. ❊ 🏨🏨 **Mount Washington**, on U.S. 302, Bretton Woods, N.H. 03575 (603/278-1000). 21 rms. Charming old Edwardian-style hotel against a splendid mountain backdrop. **E–VE (Modified American Plan).**

IN CONWAY N.H. ❊ 🏨🏨 **Merrill Farm**, N.H. 16, Conway, NH 03818 (603/447-3866). 43 rms. Picturesque country inn whose oldest parts date from 1780, on a river. Open May-Oct. **M–E**

IN WOODSTOCK, VT. 🏨🏨🏨 **Woodstock Inn and Resort**, Village Green, Woodstock, VT 05091 (802/457-1100). 120 rms. Luxurious resort hotel with a clear view over the town. **E–VE**

☼🏨🏨 **Kedron Valley,** Vt. 106, South Woodstock, VT 05071 (802/457-1473). 29 rms. Charming old inn built in 1840 and prettily restored. Closed April. **M–E**

Where to Eat En Route

IN MENDON, VT. ❊ 🍴🍴 **Countryman's Pleasure**, Townline Rd. (802/773-7141). Dinner only, Tues.-Sat. poached salmon, rack of lamb. Century-old Colonial-style house; open-air dining in good weather. **I–M**

IN NORTH CONWAY, N.H. ☼ 𝕏𝕏 **Scottish Lion,** on U.S. 302 (603/356-6381). Lunch/dinner daily. 1872 country inn; Scottish-inspired food. **I**

OTHER FROMMER TRAVEL GUIDES: *Dollarwise USA* complements 13 other Dollarwise Guides and 3 $-A-Day Guides dealing with individual U.S. states and areas: *Dollarwise Alaska, Dollarwise Florida, Dollarwise New York State, Dollarwise California & Las Vegas, Dollarwise Texas, Dollarwise Cruises, Dollarwise Mid-Atlantic States, Dollarwise New England, Dollarwise South-Atlantic States, Dollarwise Northwest, Dollarwise Southwest, Hawaii on $50 a Day, New York on $50 a Day,* and *Washington, D.C., & Historic Virginia on $40 a Day.*

The Frommer series also boasts 10 City Guides focusing on U.S. destinations: *Frommer's Atlantic City & Cape May, Frommer's Boston, Frommer's Las Vegas, Frommer's Los Angeles, Frommer's Minneapolis/St. Paul, Frommer's New Orleans, Frommer's New York, Frommer's Philadelphia, Frommer's San Francisco,* and *Frommer's Washington, D.C.*

In contrast to the book you are now reading, which highlights 57 U.S. cities and scenic areas, each of the above guides treats one particular city, state, or area in the fullest detail, setting forth scores of hotel, restaurant, and sightseeing suggestions. Frommer travel guides can be obtained at and sightseeing suggestions. Frommer travel guides can be obtained at most bookstores, or by mailing the appropriate amount (turn to the last few pages in this guide) to Frommer Books, Prentice Hall Trade Division, One Gulf + Western Plaza, New York, NY 10023.

CHAPTER 2

CAPE COD

□ □ □

With Martha's Vineyard and Nantucket

It was in **Provincetown** Bay, at the northern end of Cape Cod, that on Nov. 19, 1620, the 101 Pilgrim Fathers disembarked from the *Mayflower* and set foot for the first time on American soil. The long, sandy promontory, for years a region of simple fishing villages, has undergone a profound change since the beginning of the 20th century: it is now one of the most sought-after, and one of the most select, resort areas in the country. The peninsula of Cape Cod, shaped strangely like a lobster's claw, is a 70-mile stretch of sanddunes, pine forests, immaculate beaches discreetly hidden from the highway, nature reserves such as the **Cape Cod National Seashore** and **Monomoy National Wildlife Refuge** (once a haunt of pirates), and spruce little towns of old houses and unobtrusive newer estates such as **Brewster, Chatham, Falmouth, Harwich, Orleans, Sandwich,** and **Yarmouth.**

The whole political and financial establishment of New York and Boston, headed by the Kennedy family, has taken to summering at the Cape or on one of the two delightful islands nearby, **Martha's Vineyard** and **Nantucket.** The price of this success is that the "sold out" notices go up all along the Cape seashore in July and August, particularly over weekends. The best times to go are spring and, even more, fall; the favorite amusements (besides idling or strolling on the 275 mi., 440 km, of fine sand beaches), are sailing, surfing, and above all deep-sea fishing. There are more than a dozen species of big-game fish in these waters, including a highly prized variety of giant tuna.

BASIC FACTS: State of Massachusetts. Area Code: 508. Time Zone: Eastern Time. First colonized: 1637 (Sandwich); 1639 (Hyannis-Yarmouth); 1642 (Martha's Vineyard). Approximate population: 175,000 year round; 500,000 in July-Aug.

CLIMATE: Although the city of Boston is quite close, Cape Cod enjoys a much less extreme climate due to the sea breezes in summer (mean temperature in July 71°F, 22°C) and the Gulf Stream in winter (mean temperature in January 38°F, 4°C). Spring and fall offer enjoyable temperatures and plenty of sunshine.

DISTANCES: Boston, 55 mi. (89 km); New York, 270 mi. (432 km).

ARRIVAL & TRANSIT INFORMATION

AIRPORTS: Hyannis Barnstable Municipal Airport (HYA), 1 mi. north. Cab, $4. Information: 775-2020.

Martha's Vineyard Airport (MVY), 6 mi. west of Edgartown. Cab, $15. Information: 693-0550.

Nantucket Memorial Airport (ACK), 3 mi. south. Cab, $10. Information: 228-2765.

AIRLINES: Delta Connection (toll free 800/345-3400), Hyannis and Nantucket to Boston; PBA (toll free 800/525-0280), Hyannis, Martha's Vineyard, and Nantucket to Boston and New York.

BUS OR CAR RENTAL? Given the distances involved, the bus or a rental car are the only ways of seeing Cape Cod. Greyhound buses provide direct connections between Hyannis or Woods Hole (from which the ferry leaves for the islands) and Boston or New York. Bonanza Bus Lines offers several buses a day from Hyannis or Provincetown to the station in Providence, R.I., where connections can be made with AMTRAK trains.

CAR RENTAL: Avis, Hyannis-Barnstable Airport (775-2888); Budget, on Mass. 132, Hyannis (775-3832); Hertz, Hyannis-Barnstable Airport (775-5825); National, on Mass. 132, Hyannis (771-4353); Thrifty, on Mass. 132, Hyannis (771-0450).

TRAIN: Nearest AMTRAK station: 100 Gaspee St., Providence, R.I. (401/751-5416). From May to Sept. there is regular svce (6 hrs) between New York and Hyannis; for information, call toll free 800/872-7245. Also between Boston (Braintree T Station) and Hyannis, Mar.-Dec.; for information, call 617/771-1145.

BUS: Greyhound: Elm & Centre Sts., Hyannis (775-5524).
Bonanza: Elm & Centre Sts., Hyannis (775-5524); Boston (617/423-5810); Provincetown (487-9007); Woods Hole (548-5011).

FERRY: Boston-Martha's Vineyard, Bay State-Spray Cruises (June–Sept.). 3 hrs by catamaran. 20 Long Wharf, Boston (617/723-7800). **Falmouth–Martha's Vineyard,** from the end of May to mid-Oct., on the *Island Queen* (548-4800).

Hyannis–Martha's Vineyard and Nantucket, Hyline (May-Dec.), Pier 1, Ocean St. Dock (775-7185); Steamship Authority (in summer), Ocean St. Dock (771-4000).

Woods Hole–Martha's Vineyard and Nantucket (year round), Steamship Authority (540-2022; toll free 800/352-7144).

INFORMATION & TOURS

TOURIST INFORMATION: Cape Cod Chamber of Commerce, U.S. 6 & Mass. 132, Hyannis, MA 02061 (508/362-3225); **Martha's Vineyard Chamber of Commerce,** Beach Rd., Vineyard Haven, MA 02568 (508/693-0085); **Nantucket Island Chamber of Commerce,** Main St., Nantucket, MA 02554 (508/228-1700).

GUIDED TOURS: Hyline, Pier 1, Ocean St. Dock, Hyannis (775-7185): Boat excursions, summer only.

Cape Cod & Hyannis Railroad, 252 Main St., Hyannis (771-1145): Entertaining round trip between Hyannis and Woods Hole in a little steam train. May–Oct, daily.

Whale Watcher cruises, P.O. Box 254, Barnstable Harbor (775-1622): Narrated 4-hour whale watching excursion. Twice daily, early Apr.-late Oct. Rsv. required.

REGIONAL HIGHLIGHTS

CAPE COD NATIONAL SEASHORE (26 mi., 41 km, NE of Hyannis along U.S. 6): A 44,000-acre nature reserve along the shore, offering beautiful seascapes, camera safaris, fishing, picnic grounds, and beaches. There are Visitor Centers at Provincetown and at Eastham (349-3785). Worth going out of your way for.

MARTHA'S VINEYARD AND NANTUCKET (respectively 5 mi., 8 km, and 30 mi., 48 km, off Woods Hole): These islands, once home to a very active whaling community in the 18th century, have now become fashionable summer resorts with a wealth of attractions for holidaymakers. They have many charming small villages with beautiful old houses, the climate is generally temperate, and there are ferries all year from Woods Hole. Martha's Vineyard is also a naturalist's paradise. Both are worth visiting. Off Martha's Vineyard lies the half-wild little island of **Chappaquiddick,** where in 1969 a mysterious auto accident resulted in the death of Ted Kennedy's secretary, and gravely compromised the political career of the Kennedy dynasty's standard-bearer.

MONOMOY NATIONAL WILDLIFE REFUGE (3 mi, 5 km, off Chatham): Designated a wilderness area by the Federal Government in 1970, Monomoy Island attracts tens of thousands of migrating birds to its dunes (late May to Nov.). Access by boat only from Chatham. For further information: Refuge manager, Morris Island, Chatham, MA 02633 (508/945-0594).

PROVINCETOWN (50 mi., 80 km, NE of Hyannis along U.S. 6): The first landfall for the Pilgrim Fathers (see the introduction to this chapter). A picturesque little port at the tip of Cape Cod, whose waters attracted at the turn of the century a large colony of Portuguese fishermen, still plying their trade today. Today the town is an artists' colony and hosts a large gay community. A 247-ft (77-mi) granite tower with a splendid view over the Cape, and a little historical museum, commemorate the landing of the Pilgrim Fathers. An absolute must-see.

YARMOUTH (4 mi., 6 km, north of Hyannis by Willow Rd.): One of the oldest (1639) villages on the Cape, with an authentic New England atmosphere. Not to be missed.

MUSEUMS: At Brewster, the **Drummer Boy Museum,** 2½ mi. (4 km) west on Mass. 6A (896-3823), is housed in a converted windmill built in 1750; devoted to Revolutionary history. Worth the detour. Open daily, end of May to end of Oct. only.

At Nantucket, the **Whaling Museum,** Broad St. (228-1736), depicts the life of the Nantucket whalers that inspired Herman Melville to write *Moby-Dick*. Fascinating. Open daily in summer, wkends the rest of the year.

At Provincetown, the ⚓ **Historical Museum** and **Pilgrim Monument,** Town Hill (487-1310), gives the history of the *Mayflower* and the Pilgrim Fathers. Open daily in summer, Wed.-Sun. the rest of the year.

At Sandwich, the **Glass Museum,** in Town Hall Square (888-0251). Interesting museum of glass-making with a collection of 3,000 exhibits; open daily in summer, wknds the rest of the year. The ⚓ **Heritage Plantation,** Grove & Pine Sts.(888-3300), is a small historical museum housed, as its name suggests, in a 19th-century plantation house. It has a fine collection of classic cars, including a fabulous 1931 Duesenberg which belonged to Gary Cooper. Don't miss it. Open daily from the end of May to the end of Oct., closed the rest of the year.

ACCOMMODATIONS

See the listing of toll-free numbers in the Appendix.

Room Rates on and around Cape Cod	
B (Budget)	up to $30
I (Inexpensive)	$30–$60
M (Moderate)	$60–$90
E (Expensive)	$90–$140
VE (Very Expensive)	$140 and up

Personal Favorites (in order of preference)

☀️🛏🛏🛏 **Jared Coffin House,** 29 Broad St. at Centre St., Nantucket, MA 02554 (508/228-2400). 58 rms, color TV (in most). AE, CB, DC, MC, V. Free parking, rest., bar, rm svce, free crib. *Note:* Old private house artistically restored, to which five adjoining buildings, dating from 1720 to 1870, have been added after an elegant job of renovation. Comfortable rms w. period furniture, each decorated in a different style. Romantic atmosphere, beautiful gardens, exemplary svce and reception. Very acceptable rest. Resv. required. Open year round. **M–E**

🛏🛏🛏 **New Seabury Inn,** Mass. 28 and 151 (P.O. Box B, New Seabury), Popponesset Beach, MA 02649 (508/477-9111; toll free 800/222-2044). 200 rms (some with kitchenettes), A/C, color TV. AE, CB, DC, MC, V. Free parking, private beach, two golf courses, 16 tennis courts, boating, rest., bar, rm svce, disco. *Note:* Resort complex offering both comfort and luxury, standing in its own 1,900+ acres, with 5 mi. (8 km) of private beach. Individual villas or spacious rms with patios. Efficient svce but so-so rest. Sailboats available to guests; very comprehensive sports facilities. Resv. advised, well in advance. Open year round. **VE**

☀️🛏🛏 **Old Yarmouth Inn,** Mass. 6A, Yarmouth Port, MA 02675 (508/362-3191). 14 rms, color TV. AE, MC, V. Free parking, rest., bar. *Note:* Charming little inn housed in Cape Cod's oldest (1692) building. Huge, comfortable rms; excellent rest. serving traditional American food;

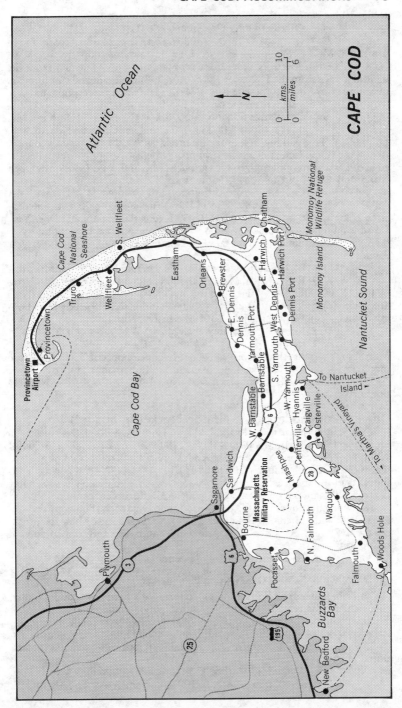

svce a little inattentive. Resv. a must. Open Mar.–Nov. **M–E**

☀☖☖ **Charlotte Inn,** 27 S. Summer St., Edgartown (Martha's Vineyard), MA 02539 (508/627-4751). 24 rms, color TV in some. AE, MC, V. Free parking, rest. (L'Étoile), antique shop, free breakfast. *Note:* The best in Martha's Vineyard, with both style and refinement; four delightful houses from the 1820s lovingly restored. Rms elegant and comfortable, w. antique furniture and private patios. Well-regarded rest.; reception and svce with a smile. A few steps from the harbor. **E–VE**

☖☖ **Coonamessett Inn,** Jones Rd. at Gifford St., Falmouth, MA 02541 (508/548-2300). 22 rms, A/C, color TV. AE, CB, DC, MC, V. Free parking, rest., bar, free breakfast. *Note:* Typical small country farmhouse, Cape Cod style, in its own fine gardens beautifully situated at the edge of a lake. Interior arrangements at once lavish and cozy. Good rest. Open year round. **E, but out-of-season reductions**

☖ **Captain Gosnold Village,** 230 Gosnold St., Hyannis, MA 02601 (508/775-9111). 54 rms and cottages with kitchenettes, color TV, in-rm movies. AE, MC, V. Free parking, pool, gardens. *Note:* Likeable motel near the beach, w. friendly reception and svce. Very pleasant gardens. Free airport limo. Ideal for families. Good value out of season. Open year round. **M**

☖ **Earl of Sandwich Motor Manor,** Old Kings Hwy., Mass. 6A, E. Sandwich, MA 02537 (508/888-1415). 24 rms, A/C, color TV. AE, CB, DC, MC, V. Free parking, nearby coffeeshop, free breakfast, crib $5. *Note:* Comfortable little motel in vaguely Tudor style; friendly reception; good value; open year round. **I, but out-of-season reductions**

☖ **Americana Holiday,** 99 Main St., West Yarmouth, MA 02673 (508/775-5511). 154 rms, A/C, color TV, in-rm movies. MC, V. Free parking, three pools, sauna, nearby coffeeshop, crib $5. *Note:* Classic motel style, modest but well maintained, w. utilitarian comforts. Family clientele. Good overall value. Open Mar.-Nov. **I–M, but out-of-season reductions**

Other Accommodations (from top bracket to budget)

☖☖☖ **Nantucket Inn,** 27 Macy's Lane, Nantucket (Nantucket Island), MA 02554 (508/228-6900; toll free 800/343-7000). 100 rms, A/C, color TV. AE, CB, DC, MC, V. Free parking, two pools, two tennis courts, health club, rest. (Windsong), bar, rm svce. *Note:* A newcomer to the ranks of the area's deluxe hotels. Modern architecture which gives the effect of an island rising out of an attractive garden. All the rms are commodious and comfortable mini-suites furnished in period style. Svce of the highest order. Caters to VIPs and conferences. Free bus service to the beach and dwntwn Nantucket; time, 5 min. A fine place; open year round. **VE, but out-of-season reductions**

☖☖☖ **Tara Dunfey Hotel,** 35 Scudder Ave., Hyannis, MA 02601 (508/775-7775; toll free, see Omni). 225 rms, A/C, cable color TV. AE, CB, DC, MC, V. Free parking, two pools, golf, tennis court, health club, saunas, rest. (Silver Shell), coffeeshop, bar, rm svce, disco, hrdrsr, cinema, free crib. *Note:* A comfortable, luxurious modern hotel, 5 min. from the beach, surrounded by more than 50 acres of gardens. Very comprehensive sports facilities. Spacious rms with patios or balconies. Good svce. Group clientele. Attractive vacation packages. Open year round. **E–VE, but out-of-season reductions**

☖☖ **Wychmere Harbor Club,** 23 Snow Inn Rd., Harwich Port, MA 02646 (508/432-1000). 115 rms, color TV. AE, MC, V.

Free valet parking, pool, sauna, tennis court, golf, boating, rest., bar, rm svce, disco, crib $5. *Note:* Elegant older hotel right on the harbor; peerless layout and amenities. Rms w. private balconies or patios, the nicest overlooking the water. Well-thought-of rest. with open-air terrace in good weather. Thoughtful svce. Private beach and lovely garden open to guests. Open early May to Oct. **E–VE (modified American Plan), but out-of-season reductions**

☀️🍳🍳 **Queen Anne Inn,** 70 Queen Anne Rd., Chatham, MA 02633 (508/945-0394). 30 rms, most A/C, color TV in public rms. MC, V. Free parking, pool, boating, rest., bar. *Note:* Gracious Victorian house very near the beach; enormous antique-furnished rms (some with balconies), the best overlooking garden and bay. A warm welcome here; also admirable cooking. Observation trips by boat offered during whale migrations. This small hotel can be warmly recommended. Open year round. **E**

🍳🍳 **Sheraton–Ocean Park Inn,** U.S. 6, Eastham, MA 02642 (508/255-5000; toll free, see Sheraton). 107 rms, A/C, cable color TV. AE, CB, DC, MC, V. Free parking, two pools, tennis court, health club, sauna, rest., bar, rm svce, disco, crib $5. *Note:* Congenial hotel at the entrance to Cape Cod National Seashore. Comfortable rms, good sports facilities, efficient svce. Free bus to beach in season. Good value out of season. Interesting full American Plan rates. Open year round. **E, but out-of-season discounts**

🍳🍳 **Bradford Gardens,** 178 Bradford St., Provincetown, MA 02657 (508/487-1616). 18 rms (doubles only, 10 with kitchenettes), color TV. AE, MC, V. Free parking. *Note:* Two elegant cottages dating from 1820, w. comfortable rms, patios, and balconies. No bar, no rest. Open from April to the end of Nov. Near beach. **M–E, but out-of-season reductions**

☀️🍳🍳 **Daggett House,** 59 N. Water St., Edgartown (Martha's Vineyard), MA 02539 (508/627-4600). 26 rms, cable color TV in suites. MC, V. Free parking. *Note:* Inviting rms in a charming 17th-century house and two adjoining cottages; atmosphere very characteristic of New England. Beautiful gardens; no bar, no rest. Private beach. Open year round. **M–E, but out-of-season reductions**

🍳 **Green Harbor,** Acapesket Rd., East Falmouth, MA 02536 (508/548-4747). 40 rms (doubles only, 17 with kitchen), A/C, color TV. AE, CB, DC, MC, V. Free parking, pool, beach. Boats available to guests. *Note:* Small, quiet, comfortable motel ideal for families. No bar, no rest. Open year round. **M, but out-of-season discounts**

🍳 **Lewis Bay Motel,** 53 South St., Hyannisport, MA 02601 (508/775-6633). 63 rms (doubles only), A/C, color TV. AE, CB, DC, MC, V. Free parking, pool, rest., bar. *Note:* Typical motel near the terminal of the Nantucket ferry, looking out over the harbor and marina. Run-of-the-mill comfort, affable svce, good overall value. Open year round. **M, but out-of-season reductions**

🍳 **Cranberry Cottages,** Box 146, U.S. 6, Eastham, MA 02642 (508/255-0602). 14 cottages for two to four persons, 7 with kitchen. Color TV. No credit cards. Free parking. *Note:* Pleasing little Cape Cod cottages in a shady grove. No bar, no rest. Ideal for families; open year round. **I–M**

🍳 **Iyanough Hills Motor Lodge,** Iyanough Rd., Hyannis, MA 02601 (508/771-4804). 104 rms, A/C, cable color TV. AE, MC, V. Free parking, free breakfast, pool, sauna, tennis court, golf. Adjoining coffeeshop, gardens. *Note:* Congenial, well-run motel 5 min. from Hyannis airport. Huge, comfortable rms, some with kitchenettes. Good-natured svce. A good place for golfers. Attractive family packages. Very good overall value. Open year round. **I–M, but out-of-season reductions**

RESTAURANTS

Cape Cod Restaurant Prices	
(per person, excluding drinks and service charges)	
B (Budget)	up to $15
I (Inexpensive)	$15–$25
M (Moderate)	$25–$40
E (Expensive)	$40–$60
VE (Very Expensive)	$60 and up

Personal Favorites (in order of preference)

☼ ♟♟♟♟ **Chillingsworth Restaurant,** 2449 Main St., Brewster (896-3460). A/C. Lunch Tues–Sun. all yr; dinner nightly late June to mid-Sept., wkends only in spring and fall; brunch Sun.; closed Nov. to the end of May. AE, CB, DC, MC, V. Jkt. Specialties: magret de canard with figs, broiled shrimp in sauce chinois, escalope of salmon with asparagus, filet of beef Kempinski, ragoût of sweetbreads and lobster. Menu changes regularly. Rather sparse wine list. *Note:* French-inspired cuisine in an enchanting colonial house almost three centuries old amid wonderful gardens. Handsome Louis XV décor. Polished reception and svce. A truly remarkable place. *French-Continental.* **M–E (prix fixe)**

♟♟♟ **Chanticleer,** 40 New St., Siasconset, on Nantucket (257-6231). Lunch/dinner Thurs.-Tues.; closed Wed. and Nov. to early May. MC, V. Jkt. Specialties: scallops with truffles, bass with sorrel, quail with brandy, roast rack of lamb with herbs, fruit sherbets. Fine wine list. *Note:* An oasis for those who love to eat, wholly French and under the masterly direction of the admirable chef, J. Charles Berruet. Engaging, urbane décor and atmosphere; the best rest. on the island. Resv. advised. *French.* **I–M**

☼ ♟♟ **Jared Coffin House,** in the hotel of the same name (see "Accommodations," above), 29 Broad St., Nantucket (228-2400). Lunch/dinner daily. AE, CB, DC, MC, V. Jkt. Specialties: shrimp Victoria, sautéed scallops, quail, tournedos, fish of the day. *Note:* Elegant dining room in a carefully restored 19th-century house. Romantic atmosphere w. classical background music. Patio open in summer. Resv. advised. *Continental-Seafood.* **I–M**

♟♟ **L'Étoile,** in the Charlotte Inn (see "Accommodations," above), 27 S. Summer St., Edgartown, Martha's Vineyard (627-5187). Dinner only, daily; brunch Sun. AE, MC, V. Jkt. Specialties: lobster w. cognac and cream, rack of lamb w. red wine and garlic, sautéed scallops w. wild mushrooms, pheasant w. plums. Fine wine list. *Note:* This hotel rest., very busy during the season, is one of the most elegant and highly regarded on the island. Refined French-inspired cuisine with a menu which changes regularly. Attractive Victorian setting; irreproachable svce, resv. a must. *French-Continental.* **M (prix fixe)**

♟♟ **The Paddock,** W. Main St. at W. End Rotary, Hyannis (775-7677). A/C. Lunch daily (summer only); dinner daily, mid-Apr. to mid-Nov.; closed the rest of the year. AE, CB, DC, MC, V. Jkt. Specialties: coq au vin, rack of lamb, roast duckling, lobster, scampi. *Note:* A fashionable place, done up in the purest Victorian idiom. Cuisine very worthy, but devoid of imagination. Open-air terrace for fine days. Excellent svce, resv. a must, valet parking. *Continental-Seafood.* **I–M**

☼♈♈ **Cap'n Linnell House,** Skaket Rd., Orleans (255-3400). Dinner only, daily; brunch Sun.; closed Dec. 25. AE, CB, DC, MC, V. Specialties: scallops, tournedos, chicken provençale, Mandarin duck. *Note:* Modest, inviting sea captain's home from the 1850s. Rather elaborate cooking. Open-air dining in summer; live jazz in season. Very popular locally, so resv. advised. *Continental-Seafood.* **I**

Other Restaurants (from top bracket to budget)

♈♈♈ **Anthony's Cummaquid Inn,** 2 Main St. (Mass. 6A), Yarmouth Port (362-4501). A/C. Dinner only, daily; brunch, Sun.; closed Dec. 25. MC. Jkt. Specialties: fish and shellfish, red meats. *Note:* Same management, excellent fare, and slightly touristy atmosphere as the well-known Anthony's Pier 4 in Boston—a top character reference! Elegant colonial décor and most engaging country ambience. Very good svce. One of the most sought-after places on the Cape, so resv. are advised. Valet parking. *Steak-Seafood.* **I–M**

☼♈♈ **Daniel Webster Inn,** 149 Main St., Sandwich (882-3622). A/C. Lunch/dinner daily. AE, CB, DC, MC, V. Jkt. Specialties: fish and shellfish of the day, veal Oscar, red meats, roast duckling. Fine wine list. *Note:* Decent but unimaginative cooking. Magnificently reconstructed interior of an 18th-century tavern. Excellent svce. Very popular locally, so resv. are advised. Beautiful English-style gardens. *Steak-Seafood.* **I–M**

♈♈ **The Straight Wharf,** Straight Wharf, Nantucket (228-4499). Dinner only, Tues.-Sun.; closed Mon. and from the end of Sept. to mid-June. AE, CB, DC, MC, V. Specialties: sauteed soft-shell crabs, sushi. The menu, built around fresh fish and garden produce, changes daily. *Note:* Noteworthy modern cuisine under the direction of Marian Morash, author of several bestselling cookbooks. Ultra-professional svce. Pretty seaside décor with unobstructed view of the harbor. Open-air terrace for fine days. Resv. must be made well in advance. *Continental-Seafood.* **I–M**

♈ **Riverway Lobster House,** Mass. 28, Bass River Bridge, South Yarmouth (398-2172). A/C. Dinner only, daily; brunch Sun.; closed Monday out of season, Christmas Day. AE, CB, DC, MC, V. Specialties: lobster, roast beef, souvlaki, fish of the day. *Note:* Appealing colonial atmosphere with big open fireplaces. Excellent fish and shellfish. Locally popular; excellent value. *American-Seafood.* **I–M**

☼♈♈ **Bishop Terrace,** 118 Main St., West Harwich (432-0253). A/C. Lunch/dinner daily. MC, V. Jkt. Specialties: stuffed lobster, roast duckling, ribs of beef, swordfish steak. *Note:* Pleasant glassed-in terrace in an inviting 250-year-old colonial house. Classic, appetizing fare; friendly svce. Resv. advised. Valet parking. *Continental-Seafood.* **I**

♈♈ **Coonamessett Inn,** in the hotel of the same name (see "Accommodations," above), Jones Rd. at Gifford St., Falmouth (548-2300). A/C. Lunch/dinner daily. AE, CB, DC, MC, V. Jkt. Specialties: absolutely fresh lobster and fish of the day. *Note:* Impressive dining rm with lake view and a cathedral ceiling. Built in 1796. Cooking and svce both urbane. Resv. advised; a fine place. Dancing in summer. *Seafood.* **I**

♈ **Captain's Chair,** 166 Bay View St., Hyannis (775-5000). A/C. Lunch/dinner daily; closed Mon. in winter, Thanksgiving, Dec. 25. AE, CB, DC, MC, V. Specialties: fish of the day, sautéed scallops, roast beef, duck a l'orange. *Note:* Country setting with a fine view of the bay. Piano bar. Unfussy, unaffected cooking and svce. *Steak-Seafood.* **B–I**

♈ **Landfall,** Water St. at the Wharf, Woods Hole (548-1758). Lunch/dinner daily; closed from the end of Sept. to mid-June. AE, CB, DC, MC, V. Specialties: sandwiches (at lunch), broiled swordfish, baked lobster, fish of the day. *Note:* This likeable fish-and-seafood restaurant stands right on the docks and offers a very fine view of the harbor. Appropriate 100% maritime décor. Friendly svce, good value. *American.* **B–I**

☼♈ **Moors,** Beach Rd. and Bradford St., Provincetown (487-0840). Lunch/dinner daily; closed Oct.-Mar. AE, CB, DC, MC, V. Specialties: Portuguese dishes, caldeirada, broiled fish. *Note:* The setting is a very picturesque reconstruction of an old whaler's house. Tasty, unpretentious food, relaxed atmosphere. *Continental-Seafood.* **B–I**

♈ **Zachariah's,** Kelley St., Edgartown, Martha's Vineyard (627-4394). A/C. Breakfast/lunch/dinner Mon.-Sat.; brunch Sun. AE, MC, V. Specialties: fish of the day, steak, some very acceptable French dishes. *Note:* Pleasant, friendly inn dating from 1742. Food worthy but no more than that; svce assiduous. A short distance from the Chappaquiddick ferry. *Continental-American-Seafood.* **B–I**

BARS & NIGHTCLUBS

Asa Bearse House, 415 Main St., Hyannis (771-4131). Sophisticated modern jazz. Open nightly, summer only.

Atlantic Connection, 126 Circuit Ave., Oak Bluffs, Martha's Vineyard (693-7129). The Vineyard club of choice. DJ dancing, jazz, big-name dance bands. Open Thurs.–Sun., summer only.

Fiddlebee's, 72 North St., Hyannis (771-6032). Live classic rock music. Open nightly, summer only.

Muse, 44 Atlantic Ave., Nantucket (228-9716). Rock, reggae, and ska bands. Also DJ dancing. Open nightly, March 1–late Dec.

Surf Club, 315 A Commercial St., Provincetown (487-1367). The Provincetown jug band, now in its twenty-second season. Pop and rock music live seven nights a week. Open summer only.

Wellfleet Beachcomber, Old Cahoon Hollow Rd., Wellfleet (349-6055). Rock-and-roll and reggae club packed with a college-age crowd. Converted old Coast Guard station which sits smack on the Atlantic in the Cape Cod National Seashore. Open nightly, Memorial Day–Labor Day.

Woodshed, Route MA 6A, Brewster (896-7771). Boisterous summer club with live music in a rustic, informal setting. Open nightly, summer only.

NEARBY EXCURSIONS

🔭 **NEWPORT** (60 mi., 96 km, SW of Sagamore Bridge via U.S. 6, Mass. 124, and R.I. 138): American yachting capital (see the chapter on the Atlantic Coast).

🔭 **PLYMOUTH** (12 mi., 19 km, NW of Sagamore Bridge on Mass. 3): Pretty little port which has come down in history because of its connection with the epic of the *Mayflower* (see the chapter on the Atlantic Coast). Not to be missed.

CHAPTER 3

NEW YORK

□ □ □

New York has 120 or more skyscrapers, around whose feet swirl crowds of all nations, colors, and tongues. But it is not—repeat, not—America. New York is everything, and the opposite of everything: a unique melting pot of races, cultures, and religions. Any adjective you can conceive of can be applied to this symbol of the New World, visited each year by 18 million tourists (including three million foreigners), all singing the same chorus: "I love New York!"

It was a little more than 4½ centuries ago in 1524 that Giovanni da Verrazano, a Florentine navigator in the service of King François I of France, dropped anchor—the first European to do so—in the bay of what was to become the most exciting, the most electric, and the most neurotic city of our times, the city which the architect Le Corbusier described as "a magnificent catastrophe on an enormous scale." In 1609 a British navigator employed by the Dutch East India Company, Henry Hudson, sailed up the river that bears his name as far as Albany, now the capital of New York State, 155 mi. (250 km) north of the river's mouth, thereby giving the Dutch their claim to the region. And 17 years later, in 1626, Peter Minnewit (or Minuit, as it is more commonly spelled), the first governor-general of New Netherland, purchased the island of Manhattan, 12½ mi. (20 km) long and 2½ mi. (4 km) wide at its widest point, from the Algonquin Indians for the moderate amount of 60 florins ($24), paid in cloth, glass beads, and other trinkets. He had his 200 Batavian and Walloon colonists build the fort of Nieuw Amsterdam on the site of what is now **Wall Street.**

Over the next half century the British, asserting a prior claim based on the explorations of John Cabot in 1497–1498, pushed steadily toward New Amsterdam from the north and northeast. By 1664 the town's position was so untenable that when a British fleet sailed into the bay, the Dutch governor, Peter Stuyvesant, surrendered without a fight. New Netherland was given by King Charles II of England to his brother, the Duke of York (later the ill-fated King James II), and divided into the twin colonies of New York, named in honor of its new patron, and New Jersey. It was briefly recaptured and held by the Dutch in 1673–1674, but otherwise remained British until the Revolution.

When it was designated the first official capital of the young United States in 1784, the city already boasted 33,000 inhabitants, and it has never stopped growing. In 1898 the original city on Manhattan Island was swelled by the accession of four more boroughs, **Brooklyn, Queens, The Bronx,** and **Staten Island,** each with its own style, ethnic mix, and individual character. Indeed, few of the world's great cities present a wider gamut of characteristics than New York.

Where can more striking contrasts be found than between the trend-setters haunting the fashionable stores on Madison Ave. or Fifth Ave. and the homeless who sleep curled in corners at nearby Grand Central Terminal? or between the twin 1,350-ft. (412-m), 110-story towers of the World Trade Center, or the luxury apartment houses of the Upper East Side or Battery Park City, and the wretched slums of Harlem, of "Loisaida" (a phonetic rendering by Hispanics of "Lower East Side"), or Fort Apache, the most disreputable neighborhood in the Bronx? If temples of haute cuisine like Lutèce, the Quilted Giraffe, and Le Bernardin are called "restaurants" in New York, how can the greasy spoons of the Bowery or the South Bronx bear the same name? What can the trendy lovers of opera and classical music who flock to Lincoln Center and the gaudy crowds of Greenwich Village, Chinatown, or La Marqueta, the popular marketplace for Puerto Rican foods, have in common? There's no obvious link except that "the Big Apple" (New York's nickname, "The Big Apple" came from New Orleans jazz musicians who during the 1920s saw New York as a succulent fruit to bite into) simply *is* all these things at once—a giant melting pot for more than nine million human beings, of whom a quarter were born in foreign lands.

According to the latest available census figures, there were almost 2.3 million blacks (a quarter of the total population) in the New York metropolitan area, including 300,000 Haitians (half the population of Port-au-Prince); 14,000 Native Americans, ranging from Sioux to Navajo; 1.8 million Hispanics, mostly Puerto Ricans, with three Spanish-language TV stations and eight radio stations (New York is the largest Puerto Rican city in the world, twice the size of San Juan); 400,000 Greeks (almost as many as in Salonika); 300,000 Asians, including 100,000 crowded into the minuscule area of Chinatown, and more than 60,000 Japanese; 800,000 Italians of recent or older vintage who make Little Italy, as well as some Queens and Brooklyn neighborhoods, look and sound like suburbs of Naples or Palermo; two million Jews from around the globe, making New York, rather than Jerusalem or Tel Aviv, the world's largest Jewish city; 400,000 Poles or people of Polish descent; 600,000 Irish (as many as Dublin)—to say nothing of the Slavs, Lebanese, Germans, Indians, and Scandinavians whose presence had made New York a sort of symbolic world capital, long before the U.N. erected its famous "glass palace" on the East River.

The mixture of races is reflected in a mixture of tongues, which has in turn engendered a flourishing foreign-language press. New York boasts no fewer than three daily papers in Chinese, along with others in Spanish, Italian, Polish, German, Korean, Greek, and even Russian.

The sheer size of New York is at the root of most of its problems—pollution, unemployment, the crime rate, the traffic snarls, the homeless, the lack of coherent city planning—and sometimes even calls into question its ability to survive. The Big Apple nearly went broke in 1975, and had to be bailed out by the federal government. But although the city lost 400,000 jobs during the dark days of the 1970s, it has experienced a kind of economic, architectural, and cultural renaissance since the beginning of the 1980s. Whereas in 1979 there were more than 5,000 uninhabited buildings, Manhattan is now being renewed. In a skyline which changes like a kaleidoscope, the old surfaces of stone or brick are giving way to arrogant façades of steel, glass, and concrete: New York, "the upright city," is reaching for the sky to express its superabundance of energy. The former massive exodus of "yuppies" and other middle-class whites toward distant suburbs has suddenly reversed itself, causing an unprecedented real-estate boom in Manhattan and restoring to the city its almost-forfeited title as the world's financial and cultural torchbearer.

Not content with being the country's literary and artistic capital, New York is also its greatest port, through which 30,000 ships pass every year; its biggest stock market (Wall Street handles more than 70% of all the country's financial transactions); the center for its communications and media businesses; its biggest industrial city; and—for good measure—the second-largest airport in the world. Of the 500 largest corporations in America, 118 have their headquarters here; more than 1,800 foreign corporations, including at least 300 banks, maintain branches or representatives' offices here. The revenues of New York businesses, at some $350 billion annually, exceed the gross national product of such countries as Brazil and Canada, and represent one-tenth of the GNP of the United States.

Obviously the tourist can't hope to see all this in two or three days. You should set aside at least a week for any kind of worthwhile overview of the modern Babylon, this enormous, jovial city which boasts no fewer than 350 theaters, 700 art galleries, and more than 150 museums devoted to every form of human self-expression, no matter how far-fetched. As the publicity leaflets of the New York Visitors Bureau proudly proclaim, "You name it, and New York has a museum for it."

The city's numberless shops, boutiques, and department stores, its thousands of restaurants, its bars, its jazz dives, and its nightclubs warrant a visit all by themselves. Not to mention the famous "sidewalks of New York," for this is a city where life is often to be seen out on the street—even when it takes the form of potholes and piles of garbage.

Here are some of the scenes that make Manhattan "the world's greatest show":

□ A walk up Avenue of the Americas (Sixth Ave.), through the high-rises of Rockefeller Center;

□ The sight of the Pan Am building astride Park Ave., the most chic residential street in the city;

□ A bird's-eye view, from a helicopter, of Manhattan's more than 120 skyscrapers, of which a full third are of recent construction;

□ A ride around Central Park in a horse-drawn cab (for those who enjoy tourist picture postcards);

□ A trip on the Staten Island Ferry, which gives you, for 25¢, the best view of the city; for backdrop you'll have the Statue of Liberty, which celebrated its 100th birthday with appropriate festivities in 1986;

□ The modern-day bohemian picture of Washington Square, with its rollerskaters, chess players, and buskers;

□ The very "in" art galleries and wild and crazy fashion boutiques of Soho;

□ The magic panorama of New York by night from the top of the Empire State Building;

□ The Visitors' Gallery at the New York Stock Exchange, with the crowd of shouting, gesticulating brokers below;

□ The faces of "intellectuals," straight out of a Woody Allen movie, to be seen thronging the counterculture shrines and avant-garde galleries of Soho and Tribeca;

□ The screaming neon signs and Oriental-bazaar atmosphere of Times Square.

As the writer John Dos Passos used to say, "If you can be bored in New York, you're in sorry shape."

Manhattan is laid out in a grid system (dating from 1811), with streets running from east to west and numbered from 1 to 220, and avenues running from north to south and numbered from 1 to 12, with three of the most famous—Lexington, Park, and Madison—sandwiched between Third and Fifth Aves. Broadway is the only major deviation from the grid pattern: it slants across the city from west (in the north) to east (in the south). In Lower Manhattan, below Houston (or "Zero") St., the oldest section of the city, most streets are named rather than numbered, and the grid system of midtown is practically nonexistent. Fifth Ave. is the boundary between the east and west sides, and all midtown and uptown addresses are numbered according to their distance from it. For New Yorkers, "uptown" means north of where you are, "downtown" means south, and "crosstown" refers to anywhere east or west of your location: this is crucial when asking for directions.

Some 12,000 "Yellow Cabs," 4,500 buses, and 250 mi. (400 km) of subway lines (carrying more than four million riders every working day) serve Manhattan and the adjoining boroughs. Aside from a few notoriously tough neighborhoods such as the Bowery around E. Houston St., Hell's Kitchen (along the Hudson between W. 42nd St. and W. 59th St.), and the north end of Harlem between 125th and 155th Sts., New York is no more unsafe for tourists than any other great city. In spite of the persistent legend to the contrary, FBI figures rank New York 27th among U.S. cities in terms of homicides (19 per 100,000 inhabitants), far behind Miami, Atlanta, Detroit, or St. Louis. Sensible caution should still be exercised: don't walk alone after dark in Central Park, on the Lower East Side between Second Ave. and the East River, or around Times Square after midnight. And stay out of the subway late at night.

There are about 15,000 restaurants, cafeterias, and fast-food outlets in New York, and 100,000 hotel rooms in all categories. But demand exceeds supply, so reserve your hotel room (unless you're in search of adventure, avoid New York hotels charging less than $60 a night). It's a good idea to make reservations, too, at any restaurant with two or more stars.

New York has dozens of tourist agencies that run conducted tours of the city; some of these are mentioned under "Guided Tours," below. But the fun way to see the Big Apple is to set out through its streets on foot, without any very precise destination in mind. It is by rubbing shoulders with the nine million people, of all sorts and sizes, who live here that you'll capture the real flavor of the city. Manhattan's big attraction is not the Statue of Liberty or even its incredible skyline, but the endless ebb and flow of the nameless multitudes in "the city that never sleeps."

You'd need a good-sized phone book to list all the famous people who were born in one or another of New York's five boroughs. President Theodore Roosevelt was born here; so were the physicist Robert J. Oppenheimer, the 19th-century railroad tycoon Cornelius Vanderbilt, and Jonas Salk, inventor of the polio vaccine. You can add the publisher DeWitt Wallace, founder of *Reader's Digest;* the playwrights Arthur Miller, Eugene O'Neill, and Neil Simon, and the violinist Yehudi Menuhin. Then there's the choreographer Jerome Robbins and the composers George Gershwin and Aaron Copland, the sculptor George Segal, the designer Louis Comfort Tiffany, and the singers Harry Belafonte and Barbra Streisand. How about the movie directors Stanley Kubrick, Martin Scorsese, and Woody Allen; actresses Mae West, Lauren Bacall, Rita Hayworth, and Jane Fonda; actors Groucho Marx, Humphrey Bogart, Danny Kaye, Mickey Rooney, Burt Lancaster, Walter Matthau, Tony Perkins, Robert De Niro, Alan Alda, and Al Pacino? To say nothing of the writers Washington Irving, Henry James, J. D. Salinger, Henry Miller, James Baldwin, Irwin Shaw, Robert Ludlum, Mario Puzo, Norman Mailer, James Michener, Harold Robbins, and Herman Wouk, and the tennis player John McEnroe. Want more? Let's close with a list of famous jazzmen: Benny Carter, Sonny Rollins, Buddy Rich, Bud Powell, Artie Shaw, Fats Waller, and Gerry Mulligan.

BASIC FACTS: State of New York. Area Codes: 212 (Manhattan, the Bronx); 718 (Queens, Brooklyn, Staten Island). Time Zone: Eastern Time. ZIP Code : 10001. Founded: 1615. Approximate population: city, 7,260,000; metropolitan area, 9,170,000. Largest city and largest metropolitan area in the U.S. The "New York / Northeastern New Jersey Standard Consolidated Area," lying in a 50-mi. (80-km) radius around Manhattan and taking in parts of New Jersey and Connecticut, has a population of 18 million.

CLIMATE: Its climate is one of the principal drawbacks of New York. Aside from a few weeks of agreeable weather in spring (mid-Apr. to mid-May) and fall (mid-Sept. to mid-Oct.) the rest of the year swings between sweating and shivering weather. Summer is usually hot and muggy, with an average temperature of 77°F (25°C) in July, but 100% humidity. Luckily, all public buildings, stores, hotels, and restaurants are heated and air-conditioned, but watch out for the rise —or fall—in temperature when you leave. Winter is often severe, with temperatures dropping to −5°F (−20°C), particularly when the icy winds out of the north whistle down the glass-and-steel canyons of Manhattan's avenues. There's no rainy season, but it rains intermittently year round (except in winter, when it snows) to make up for it. It's wise to bring raincoats and umbrellas in spring and fall.

DISTANCES: Boston, 209 mi. (335 km); Chicago, 806 mi. (1,290 km); Dallas, 1,550 mi. (2,480 km); Denver, 1,768 mi. (2,830 km); Detroit, 634 mi. (1,015 km); Los Angeles, 2,790 mi. (4,465 km); Miami, 1,309 mi. (2,095 km); Montréal, 378 mi. (605 km); New Orleans, 1,335 mi. (2,136 km); Niagara Falls, 410 mi. (656 km); Philadelphia, 100 mi. (160 km); Washington, D.C., 234 mi. (375 km).

ARRIVAL & TRANSIT INFORMATION

AIRPORTS: The three New York airports, served by 108 airlines, collectively handle the world's heaviest passenger traffic: 78 million travelers a year.
    John F. Kennedy International Airport (JFK), in Queens, 15 mi. (24 km) SE of Manhattan. (718/656-4444).
    La Guardia Airport (LGA), in Queens, 8 mi. (13 km) NE of Manhattan. (718/656-4444).
    Newark International Airport (EWR), in Newark, N.J., 16 mi. (25 km) SW of Manhattan. (201/961-2000).

U.S. AIRLINES (212 area code unless otherwise indicated): Allegheny Commuter (736-3200), American (619-6991), Braniff (toll free 800/272-6433), Continental (319-9494), Delta (239-0700), Eastern (986-5000), Midway (toll free 800/621-5700), New York Helicopter (toll free 800/645-3494), Northwest (732-1220), Pan Am (687-2600), P.B.A. (247-0088), TWA (290-2121), United (718/803-2200), and USAir (736-3200).

FOREIGN CARRIERS (212 area code unless otherwise indicated): Aer Lingus (557-1110), Air Canada (869-1900), Air France (247-0100), British Airways (toll free 800/247-9297), El Al (486-2600), Icelandair (967-8888), Japan Air Lines (838-4400), KLM (784-2000), Lufthansa (718/895-1277), Sabena (936-7800), S.A.S. (718/657-7700), Swissair (718/995-8400), Varig (682-3100), and Virgin Atlantic (800/862-8621).

CITY LINK: There is comparatively easy access between all three of the metropolitan airports and Manhattan.

John F. Kennedy International
    Cab fare to mid-Manhattan, about $28–$35; time, about 45 min., but 1 hr or more at peak traffic periods. Traffic can be nightmarish at rush hours.
    Bus: Carey Transportation (718/632-0500), departs every 15–30 min. for Grand Central Terminal (E. 42nd St. and Park Ave.) and the Port Authority Bus Terminal (W. 40th St. and Eighth Ave.) with intermediate stops at selected midtown hotels. Fare, $8; time, 50 min. to 1 hr and 15 min.

Subway: JFK Express (718/858-7272), makes eight stops in Brooklyn and Manhattan, terminating at W. 56th St. and Ave. of the Americas; runs every 20 min. from 5:30 a.m. till 12:30 a.m. Price, including bus link at the airport, $7; time, 1 hr. and 20 min.

Helicopter: New York Helicopter (toll free 800/645-3494), departs approx. every 40 min., linking the Manhattan heliports at the World Trade Center and E. 34th St. to the TWA Terminal at JFK. Fare, $60; time, 18–20 min.

La Guardia

Cab fare from La Guardia to midtown Manhattan, about $18–$22; time, about 30–40 min.

Bus: Carey Transportation (718/632-0500), departs every 15 min., serving Grand Central Terminal (E. 42nd St. and Park Ave.) and the Port Authority Bus Terminal (W. 40th St. and Eighth Ave.) with intermediate stops at selected hotels. Fare, $6; time, 35–45 min.

Helicopter: New York Helicopter (toll free 800/645-3494), leaves approx. every 40 min., linking the Manhattan heliports at the World Trade Center or E. 34th St. to the American Airlines terminal at La Guardia. Fare, $60; time, about 6–8 min.

Newark International

Cab fare from Newark to midtown Manhattan, about $30–$38; time, about 35–45 min.

Bus: NYC Minibus Service (201/961-2535), departs approx. every 35 min., serving the principal Manhattan hotels. Fare, $14; time, 50 min. to 1 hr.

New Jersey Transit (201/460-8444), departs every 30 min. for the Port Authority Bus Terminal; fare, $5; time, 30 min.

Olympia Trails (212/964-6233), departs every 15 min. for the World Trade Center and Grand Central Terminal. Fare, $7; time, about 30 min.

Helicopter: New York Helicopter (toll free 800/645-3494), departs approx. every 45 min., linking the Manhattan heliports at the World Trade Center or E. 34th St. to the United Airlines terminal at Newark. Fare, $60; time, about 10–12 min.

CAR RENTAL (all serving the three New York airports as well as operating out of the in-town locations listed): Avis, ten Manhattan offices (toll free 800/331-1212); Budget, nine Manhattan offices (807-8700); Dollar, two Manhattan offices (406-1751); Hertz, ten Manhattan offices (toll free 800/654-3131); National, nine Manhattan offices (toll free 800/328-4567); and Thrifty, three Manhattan offices (toll free 800/367-2277).

LIMOUSINE SERVICES: Allstar Limousine Service (718/784-7766), Carey Limousine (212/599-1122), Farrell's Limousine Service (212/988-4441), London Towncars (212/988-9700), and Scripps Edward Limousine (212/371-2460).

TAXIS: New York City has two kinds of taxis, both licensed and regulated by a city agency: metered cabs and unmetered ("gypsy") cabs. The tourist unfamiliar with New York is advised to stick to metered cabs where the fare is as shown on the meter. If going to (or even more, if returning from) one of the outer boroughs (except at the airports), a metered cab may be hard to find; in that case it may be advisable to telephone a local unmetered cab company or "car service," taking care to agree beforehand on the fare.

Easily recognized because they're painted yellow, metered cabs may be hailed on the street, or taken from the waiting lines outside the major hotels; some may also be called by phone: **Citywide Taxi** (212/295-1122) and **Two-Way Radio** (212/741-0070). Many of the drivers are recent immigrants, ill-acquainted with the topography of New York and even with the English language. A tip equivalent to 20% of the meter fare is expected.

PUBLIC TRANSPORTATION: Car-rental rates in New York are among the highest in the nation; parking lots and garages are crowded and very expensive; fines for illegal parking are hard to avoid. Taxis (abundant and relatively inexpensive), buses, and subways are the best means of getting around Manhattan. The subway is noisy, dirty, and aging, but it runs around the clock (late-evening and night trips should be avoided), and is much the quickest and cheapest way of traveling; the fare is $1 regardless of how far you ride. You'll need exact change or a token on New York City buses, where the fare is the same; tokens only (purchased when you enter the station) on the subway. Trains run either local or express, and provide very complete service in Manhattan and the outer boroughs. For information, call the New York Transit Authority (718/330-1234).

TRAIN: AMTRAK has two major stations in Manhattan:
    Grand Central Terminal, Park Ave. and E. 42nd St. (736-4545): Trains to Chicago, Niagara Falls, Montréal, and Toronto.
    Pennsylvania Station, Eighth Ave. and W. 31st St. (736-4545): All other destinations. For reservations on the Metroliner (fast train to Philadelphia, Baltimore, and Washington) *only,* call 736-3967.
    And there's also the **Rockefeller Center Ticket Office,** 12 W. 51st St. (736-4545).

BUS: Greyhound, Port Authority Bus Terminal, 8th Ave. and 41st St. (971-6363).

MANHATTAN: AREAS AND NEIGHBORHOODS

    Manhattan—an Indian word meaning "the island of hills"—is a mosaic of neighborhoods, each of which is pretty much a separate village with its own distinct character. The island does indeed constitute a huge multiracial, socially diverse patchwork, with the boundaries between the patches sharply drawn.
    Note: Given the size of Manhattan, the different hotels, restaurants, buildings, museums, etc., referred to below are classified by these areas or neighborhoods. From south to north, Manhattan's principal neighborhoods are:

LOWER MANHATTAN (WALL STREET AND THE FINANCIAL DISTRICT) (around Wall and Broad Sts., from City Hall to the Battery): Here you'll find the banks, the financial institutions, and the New York Stock Exchange. Wall Street takes its name from the wooden palisade built in 1653 by Gov. Peter Stuyvesant to protect Nieuw Amsterdam against incursions by the English and the Indians. This district, whose narrow streets are fenced in by high-rises, is the historic heart of Manhattan. Like most business districts it's at its liveliest during office hours, but such major tourist attractions as the South Street Seaport, apartment complexes like Battery Park City, and the stores and restaurants that grow up around them keep the streets fairly busy on evenings and weekends too.

TRIBECA (below Canal St. to City Hall, and west of W. Broadway): An acronym of "*TRI*angle *BE*low *CA*nal St.," this neighborhood, originally called "Lower Broadway," has succeeded Soho as the fashionable hangout for the city's intelligentsia. Real-estate speculation has reached fever pitch here; run-down

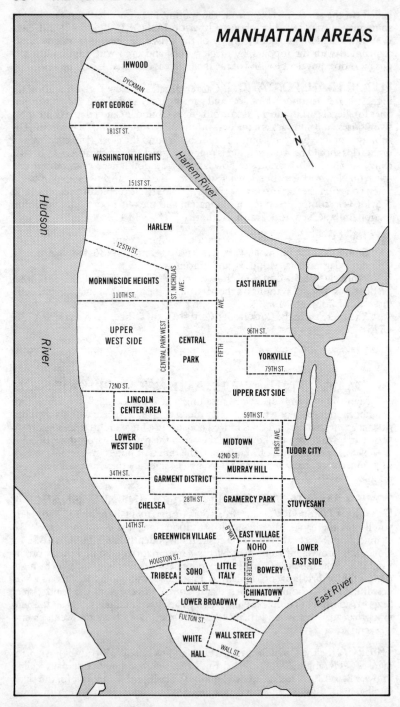

MANHATTAN AREAS

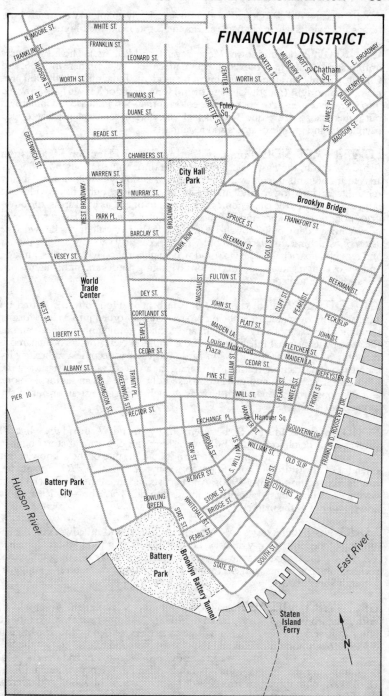

FINANCIAL DISTRICT

warehouses and old abandoned workshops are slowly giving way to trendy boutiques and to lofts where big-name artists and actors make their homes.

CHINATOWN (around lower Mott, Bayard, and Pell Sts.): The first Chinese immigrant is said to have moved into a small, closet-like room here in 1865, and Chinatown grew up around him almost by accident. Today almost 100,000 people of Asian origin (mostly Chinese from Hong Kong or Taiwan) are crowded into this tiny Far Eastern enclave, less colorful than San Francisco's Chinatown but nonetheless picturesque, with its lanterns, dragon carvings, pagoda-topped payphones, and jumble of stores and restaurants.

LOWER EAST SIDE (from Canal St. north to E. Houston St. and from Broadway east to the East River): An area that once housed thousands of newly arrived immigrants in cold-water tenements, it is slowly—very slowly—being rehabilitated into lower- and middle-income housing, but still provides the homes for many of the city's poorest residents. In one of its local areas, the **Bowery** (around the Bowery and Delancey St.), Peter Stuyvesant, last governor of Nieuw Amsterdam, built himself a farm outside the city wall; it was known as *de bouwerij,* which means "farm" in old Dutch. A century ago this was the theater and red-light district. Today it is a run-down neighborhood where bums, junkies, and winos congregate—a district of sordid lodging houses and punk nightspots. For slice-of-life addicts.

LITTLE ITALY (around Mulberry St. south of E. Houston St.): Butted up against Chinatown (and today being progressively absorbed into it), this former stronghold of Neapolitan, Calabrian, and Sicilian immigrants has been all but forsaken by its original inhabitants. Of the 800,000 New Yorkers of Italian origin, only 5,000–10,000 still live in Little Italy. It has become a rather tawdry ethnic tourist attraction, featuring pizzerias, the aroma of espresso, statues of the Madonna, restaurants, and groceries tricked out in the Italian national colors, and religious processions which look as though they come straight out of the movie *The Godfather.*

SOHO (south of Houston St. between Crosby St. and W. Broadway): Just 20 years ago this neighborhood of huge workshops and department stores built in the mid-19th century was practically abandoned, in spite of the acknowledged splendor of its cast-iron façades. Soho, an acronym of *SO*uth of *HO*uston St., began its recovery in the early 1960s, when artists and intellectuals, driven out of Greenwich Village by spiraling rents, invaded the lofts of Soho—which are now also priced out of the market.

NOHO (*NO*rth of *HO*uston St. between the Bowery and Broadway): At the beginning of the 19th century this was the "swell" neighborhood, where Cornelius Vanderbilt, the Croesus of the day, chose to live. Now it's full of young punk rockers, loft apartments, and electronics and microcomputer stores—a doggedly trendy part of town.

GREENWICH VILLAGE (around Washington Square at the lower end of Fifth Ave., from Canal St. north to W. 14th St. and from Broadway west to the Hudson River): It began as a real village of farmers, settled by the first English colonists out among the fields and the woods. New Yorkers still call it "the Village," but by the 19th century it had already become an artists' and writers' colony, numbering among its inhabitants Edgar Allan Poe, Henry James, and John Dos Passos. With its narrow streets, little brick houses, small shops, and taverns, the Village was long regarded as New York's literary and bohemian center. Now the upper middle class and the tourists have taken over, but the neighborhood is still picturesque. Stay away on summer weekends because of the crowds.

EAST VILLAGE (around Tompkins Square Park, from E. Houston St. north to E. 14th St. and from the Bowery east to the East River): This neighborhood, north of the Lower East Side, is where new cultural movements and schools of avant-garde art ("graffiti art," "real art," "street art") are born. It's also one of the few left in Manhattan where rents are still fairly affordable. Hence the influx of young, creative people who have made it one of the most lively, newsworthy parts of the city. Many art galleries. As you proceed farther east past First Ave. to Aves. A, B, C, and D, the area becomes progressively more blighted and progressively more dangerous, especially at night.

CHELSEA (around Chelsea Park at Eighth, Ninth, and Tenth Aves., from W. 14th to W. 30th Sts. and from Fifth Ave. to the Hudson River): Forty years ago this was largely a district of Hispanic immigrants, as witness the many Spanish-language store signs still to be seen on 14th Street. Now Chelsea has become typical of New York's "mixed bag" neighborhoods, where old New Yorkers live cheek by jowl with new arrivals, where run-down, grimy brick buildings and old, elegant brownstones stand shoulder to shoulder with modern high-rises. For some reason New York's best art and fashion photographers seem to live here.

GRAMERCY PARK (around Gramercy Park at Lexington Ave. and 20th St., from E. 14th St. north to E. 30th St. and from Fifth Ave. east to the East River): Includes both the high-rise apartments of Stuyvesant Town (east of First Ave. between E. 14th and E. 19th Sts.) and the elegant little brownstones and town houses around Gramercy Park itself, as well as the office towers along lower Third Ave. and Park Ave. South and the huge hospitals between First Ave. and the East River in the E. 20s.

MIDTOWN (from 30th to 59th Sts., river to river): Takes in the whole center of Manhattan, south of Central Park. From the frantic bustle of the **Garment District** (Sixth and Seventh Aves. between 30th and 39th Sts.), where fabrics and ready-to-wear clothing are manufactured, to the permanent Big Top of **Broadway and the Theater District** (from Sixth to Eighth Aves. between W. 43rd and W. 53rd Sts.), the heart of America's show business, with more than 50 theaters and music halls and dozens of cinemas, their lights blazing through the crush of nighttime idlers (not a safe district after midnight); from the magical reflections off the glass façades of the **Rockefeller Center** high-rises to the porno movie houses and the drug and sex industry of **Times Square** (soon, it is hoped, to fall before a giant urban-renewal project), by way of the big new office buildings of **Murray Hill** (between Third and Madison Aves. south of E. 42nd St.) and the little island of tranquility of 1920s-style fantasy of **Tudor City** (around First Ave. between E. 38th and E. 44th Sts.), where a cluster of apartment houses, in an unusual neo-Tudor idiom, stands on a huge elevated platform overlooking the East River and the "glass palace" of the U.N. (many diplomats and U.N. officials live here)—midtown is a microcosm of the city itself.

UPPER WEST SIDE (from Central Park to the Hudson River between W. 60th and W. 110th Sts.): At the end of the 19th century this was an upscale "WASP" neighborhood, the chicest in Manhattan. At the end of the 1930s it started a long process of deterioration, which was only halted in the 1970s. Now it has become fashionable again, attracting a young, well-to-do, trendy crowd of actors, musicians, movie directors, bankers, and intellectuals who have made the

SOHO, LITTLE ITALY, AND CHINATOWN AREA

MIDTOWN MANHATTAN

To Lincoln Center

Columbus Circle

CENTRAL PARK SOUTH

Port Authority Bus Terminal

Penn Station and Madison Square Garden

EIGHTH AVE.

THEATER DISTRICT

BROADWAY

SEVENTH AVE.

Times Square

Carnegie Hall

City Center

Radio City

AVE. OF THE AMERICAS

Rockefeller Center

Museum of Modern Art

ROCKEFELLER PL.

FIFTH AVE.

St. Patrick's

Bryant Park

Empire State Bldg.

Public Library Main Branch

MADISON AVE.

VANDERBILT AVE.

PARK AVE.

Grand Central Station

LEXINGTON AVE.

Chrysler Bldg.

THIRD AVE.

Citicorp Center

SECOND AVE.

Hammarskjold Plaza

FIRST AVE.

United Nations

Tudor City

BEEKMAN

SUTTON PL.

FDR DRIVE

EAST RIVER DR.

QUEENS MIDTOWN TUNNEL

East River

QUEENSBORO BRIDGE

W. 40TH ST., W. 41ST ST., W. 42ND ST., W. 43RD ST., W. 45TH ST., W. 46TH ST., W. 47TH ST., W. 48TH ST., W. 49TH ST., W. 50TH ST., W. 51ST ST., W. 52ND ST., W. 53RD ST., W. 54TH ST., W. 55TH ST., W. 56TH ST., W. 57TH ST., W. 58TH ST.

E. 40TH ST., E. 41ST ST., E. 42ND ST., E. 43RD ST., E. 45TH ST., E. 46TH ST., E. 47TH ST., E. 48TH ST., E. 49TH ST., E. 50TH ST., E. 51ST ST., E. 52ND ST., E. 53RD ST., E. 54TH ST., E. 55TH ST., E. 56TH ST., E. 57TH ST., E. 58TH ST., E. 59TH ST.

N

area along Columbus Ave. into a sort of smart new version of Greenwich Village. It includes the huge Lincoln Center for the Performing Arts complex.

UPPER EAST SIDE (from Fifth Ave. to the East River between E. 59th and E. 96th Sts.): The gilt-edged ghetto of New York's upper classes, symbolized by the uniformed chauffeurs and their long limousines gliding silently down Park Ave., and by the luxurious apartment houses that run the length of East End Ave. The only lighter note to be found in this money-oriented universe is provided by the little restaurants and singles bars of First and Second Aves.

"EL BARRIO" (East Harlem around Lexington and Fifth Aves. between E. 105th and E. 125th Sts.): *Barrio* is the Spanish for "neighborhood," and this is the Puerto Rican neighborhood, its heart the renowned Marqueta, the colorful covered market with its swirling crowds and hundreds of stalls. It's a Hispanic enclave in the heart of Harlem.

HARLEM (between Central Park North, or 110th St., and 155th St.): Originally named Nieuw Haarlem after the town in the Netherlands, and founded as a community for Dutch settlers in 1658 by Gov. Peter Stuyvesant, Harlem was, in the latter part of the 19th century, one of the most elegant residential districts in Manhattan, as witness the imposing upper-class houses of Convent Ave., Mount Morris Park West, and Strivers Row. The first blacks arrived around 1910, and with the coming of the first jazz bands at the famous Cotton Club, the Savoy Ballroom, and the Apollo Theater, Harlem became for a while the center of New York's nightlife. Today its community of 300,000 blacks makes it the symbol of Black America. However, the real-estate speculators are slowly moving in on behalf of their yuppie clients. Several museums and some distinguished turn-of-the-century architecture merit your attention, but stay away from the high-risk areas such as Lenox Ave. around W. 125th St. and Eighth Ave. around W. 116th.

UPPER MANHATTAN (WASHINGTON HEIGHTS) (north of 155th St.): Most of this area is taken up by middle-class apartment buildings, but the George Washington Bridge and its bus station are at 177th St., and at the northern tip of Manhattan is Fort Tryon Park and the Cloisters.

INFORMATION & TOURS

TOURIST INFORMATION: The **New York Convention and Visitors Bureau** (midtown), 2 Columbus Circle, NY 10019 (212/397-8222).
Information Desk (midtown), in the lobby at 30 Rockefeller Plaza (212/806-7000). Multilingual hostesses; guided tours of Rockefeller Center.
Times Square Information Center (midtown), 158 W. 42nd St. (212/397-8222).

GUIDED TOURS: Adventures on a Shoestring (walking tours) (midtown), 300 W. 53rd St. (212/265-2663): Conducted walking tours of Chinatown, Greenwich Village, and other picturesque neighborhoods. For lovers of the unexpected.
American Sightseeing / Short Line Tours (bus) (midtown), 166 W. 46th St. (212/354-4740): Conducted tour of the city in glass-roofed sightseeing bus; shuttle connection with principal hotels.
Circle Line (boat) (midtown), Pier 83, W. 43rd St. at the Hudson River (212/563-3200): Around Manhattan Island by boat; a spectacular three-hour ride. Daily, Apr. to mid-Nov.

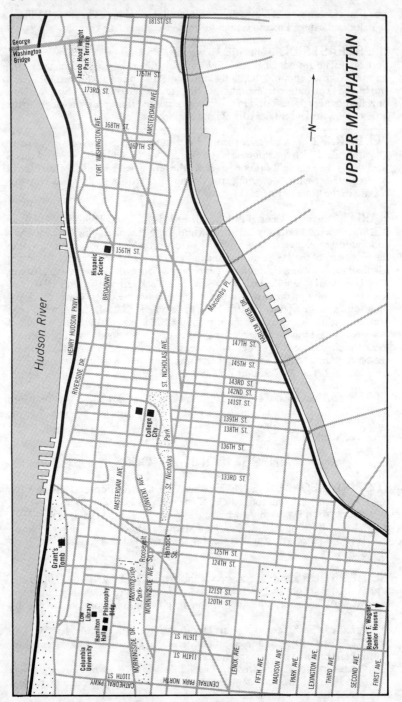

Gray Line Tours (bus) (midtown), 900 Eighth Ave., at W. 53rd St. (212/397-2600): Conducted tours of the city and surroundings.

Island Helicopters (helicopter) (midtown), E. 34th St. Heliport, at the Hudson River (212/895-1626): Flights over Manhattan and the Statue of Liberty. Unforgettable. Fare: $30–$50, according to duration of flight.

New York Big Apple Tours (bus) (midtown), 22 W. 23rd St. (212/691-7866): Conducted tours of Manhattan with multilingual guides—French, German, Italian, Spanish, etc. For foreign visitors.

Penny Sightseeing Harlem Tours (bus and walking tour) (midtown), leave from 303 W. 42nd St. at Eighth Ave. (212/410-0080): Conducted tours of Harlem on Tues., Thur., Sat., and Sun. mornings.

SIGHTS, ATTRACTIONS, & ACTIVITIES

ARCHITECTURAL HIGHLIGHTS: ⌂ **The Beresford** (Upper West Side), Central Park West and 81st St.: Luxury apartment building dating from 1929, designed by the architect Emery Roth. With its ocher sandstone façade, rococo carvings, and three unusual towers, this designated historic landmark has been, and still is, home to many celebrities such as violinist Isaac Stern, tennis star John McEnroe, and TV newscaster Peter Jennings. Definitely worth a look.

　　☼⌂ **Dakota Apartments** (Upper West Side), 1 W. 72nd St. at Central Park West: Perhaps the most prestigious address in New York. A strange blend of English Victorian and German neo-Gothic, this 1884 structure by Henry Hardenbergh was New York's first luxury apartment building. Among its present residents are Lauren Bacall and Leonard Bernstein; John Lennon, who also lived here, was assassinated outside the entrance to the building. A sight you shouldn't miss.

　　☼⌂ **Federal Reserve Bank** (Lower Manhattan), 33 Liberty St. (720-6130): The world's largest hoard of gold—900,000 ingots worth $114 billion—slumbers in the armored vaults here, 80 ft. (24 m) underground and protected by a steel door weighing 90 tons. Visits, by appointment only, Mon.-Fri.; no still or movie cameras permitted. For daydreaming.

　　☼⌂⌂ **Jacob K. Javits Convention Center** (midtown), Eleventh Ave. and W. 35th St. (216-2000): Designed by the great I. M. Pei, this futuristic convention center, largest of its kind in the Western world, has an immense façade of glass made up of more than 16,000 individual panes, supported by a web of metal girders; the design was inspired by London's famous Crystal Palace, and will delight all lovers of contemporary architecture. Opened in April 1986 at a cost of more than $500 million. Positively worth seeing.

　　☼⌂⌂ **Lincoln Center for the Performing Arts** (Upper West Side), Broadway and W. 64th St. (877-1800): This renowned cultural center comprises five elegant, modernist theaters and concert halls arranged in a harmonious pattern around a central plaza. **Avery Fisher Hall,** designed by Max Abramovitz, is the home of the New York Philharmonic; **Alice Tully Hall,** home of the Chamber Music Society, and the adjoining **Juilliard School of Music** are by Pietro Belluschi; Philip Johnson designed the **New York State Theater,** which houses the New York City Ballet and New York City Opera; the **Vivian Beaumont Theater** is the work of Eero Saarinen, while the **Metropolitan Opera House,** home of the world-famous Metropolitan Opera or "Met," with its Chagall murals, is from the hand of Wallace K. Harrison. The very lovely marble fountain in the central plaza, designed by Philip Johnson, is illuminated at night. This is a visit you should certainly make.

　　⌂ **Madison Square Garden** (midtown), 4 Pennsylvania Plaza, Seventh Ave. and W. 32nd St. (563-8300): A 20,000-seat covered stadium (the Arena), which with its adjoining little brother, the Felt Forum, draws more than five million spectators a year to various events. For a century it has been the scene of the most important sporting events, shows, and political occasions in New York City. The present building dates from 1968. Penn Station (trains to Boston, Miami, New Orleans, and Washington) is on the levels below Madison Square Garden.

☀️🏛️ **New York Stock Exchange** (Lower Manhattan), 20 Broad St. (656-3000): The center of the U.S. financial community; gesticulating brokers and frantic agitation. Don't miss the show from the visitors' gallery.

🏛️ **Radio City Music Hall** (midtown), Ave. of the Americas at W. 50th St. (757-3100): The largest movie theater in the world, with 6,000 seats and a stage 144 ft. (44 m) across and 65 ft. (20 m) deep. Splendid art deco lobby with giant chandeliers in crystal weighing two tons apiece. Home of the world-renowned precision-dancing Rockettes; draws more than eight million visitors a year. Conducted tours daily. Don't miss it.

☀️🏛️ **United Nations** (midtown), First Ave. between E. 42nd and 48th Sts. (754-4440): Designed by Le Corbusier and Oscar Niemeyer, this 1952 "glass palace" of the Secretariat towers over the East River with its 39 floors. Conducted tours daily; you should see it, preferably between early Sept. and mid-Dec. when the General Assembly is in session.

Skyscrapers

☀️🏛️ **AT&T Building** (midtown), 550 Madison Ave. at E. 56th St.: Its salmon-colored granite façade and pediment drawn from a Chippendale breakfront make this building by the well-known duo, Philip Johnson and John Burgee one of the most innovative of post-modern high-rises. In the lobby is a deliberately old-fashioned statue of Mercury and an exhibition of AT&T's technological achievements. A must-see.

🏛️ **Chase Manhattan Bank Building** (Lower Manhattan), 1 Chase Manhattan Plaza, 60 stories of steel and glass—one of the world's largest bank buildings (about 15,000 people work here), designed by the firm of Skidmore, Owings & Merrill. The underground vault is protected by six armored doors weighing 45 tons each. There is a strange sculpture by Jean Dubuffet on the plaza. Worth a look.

☀️🏛️🏛️ **Chrysler Building** (midtown), 405 Lexington Ave. at E. 42nd St.: The crowning glory of art deco, designed by William Van Alen in 1930; 77 stories rising 1,048 ft. (319 m), capped by a stainless-steel spire which looks like the jawbone of a swordfish. Superb lobby with remarkable wood inlays and modernist wall paintings. You'll be able to admire the architecture while visiting **Con Edison's Conservation Center,** an interesting little energy exhibit on the ground floor. Nearly 9,000 people come to work here every day. Open Tues.-Sat.

☀️🏛️ **Citicorp Center** (midtown), Lexington Ave. and E. 54th St.: An unusual modern (1978) 79-story building designed by Hugh Stubbins, with a roofline angled to receive and store solar energy. "The Market" is an enticing, very popular atrium-garden with cafés, restaurants, shops, bookstores, and even a church. Definitely worth visiting.

☀️🏛️ **Empire State Building** (midtown), 34th St. and Fifth Ave.: Built in 1929–1931 on the site of the original Waldorf Hotel, this world-famous skyscraper, designed by Shreve, Lamb and Harmon, was long the tallest building in the world, and the symbol of New York. Its construction required 60,000 tons of steel; it is solid enough that when, on a foggy day in 1945, a B-25 bomber flew straight into the 79th floor and 14 people were killed—but the building sustained no damage whatsoever. The 102 floors are served by 73 elevators. For further details, see "Panoramas," below. Don't miss it.

Equitable Building (Lower Manhattan), 120 Broadway at Cedar St.: One of the earliest (1915) high-rises in the city; its monumental mass led to the adoption of the city's first zoning law in the following year. Should be seen.

Flatiron Building (Gramercy Park), 175 Fifth Ave. at E. 23rd St.: The first true office skyscraper built in New York (1902). Its name derives from its 22-floor height and its dramatic triangular form. The architect was D. W. Burnham. Worth a look.

Ford Foundation Building (midtown), 320 E. 42nd St.: Beautiful 1967 glass-and-brick building by Kevin Roche and John Dinkeloo; headquarters of the Ford Foundation, which sponsors research in the physical and social sciences. A splendid tree-planted lobby serves as an indoor garden. Worth a look.

I.B.M. Building (midtown), 590 Madison Ave. at E. 56th St.: Edward Larrabee Barnes designed this 40-floor tower of polished green granite and green glass; the head office of the giant international computer company is one of New York's loveliest modern skyscrapers. There's an unexpected tropical greenhouse with giant reeds and a Japanese garden on the ground floor. Interesting temporary art exhibitions. Don't fail to visit it.

Lever House (midtown), 380 Park Ave. at E. 54th St.: This elegant 24-story Skidmore, Owings & Merrill building, dating from 1952, is one of the earliest all-glass curtain-wall buildings. A classic of its kind, and worth seeing.

Marriott Marquis Hotel (midtown), 1535 Broadway at W. 45th St.: Splendid 52-story high-rise designed by John Portman; its looming mass dominates Times Square. It's one of the most comprehensive hotel facilities in the world; note the 46-floor glass-walled lobby, which absolutely must be seen.

Morgan Guaranty Trust Building (Lower Manhattan), 60 Wall St.: This brand-new giant by architect Kevin Roche rears its 50-story bulk of pure post-modernism far above its downtown neighbors; worth a look.

Pan Am Building (midtown), 200 Park Ave. at E. 45th St.: The masterpiece of the great Walter Gropius, completed in 1963. This elegant 59-story octagon, 810 ft. (247 m) tall, atop Grand Central Terminal, is one of the world's biggest office buildings, housing 25,000 workers. The best view is the Park Ave. view. A sight not to be missed.

Park Avenue Tower (midtown), 65 E. 55th St.: One of Manhattan's most flamboyant buildings, with its astonishing marble and granite lobby, pyramidal cap, and ever-changing surface colors—pink to chestnut to metallic gray. It's half *Star Wars,* half art deco, and all the work of the prolific Chicago architect Helmut Jahn. Worth seeing.

Philip Morris Building (midtown), Park Ave. at E. 42nd St.: This ultramodern high-rise, headquarters of a cigarette conglomerate, is principally noteworthy for the annex of the **Whitney Museum** on its ground floor, with sculptures by Calder, Segal, Claes Oldenburg, Nevelson, etc., standing in an indoor garden open to the public. Should not be missed.

Rockefeller Center (midtown), between Fifth and Sixth Aves. from W. 48th to W. 52nd Sts.: A breathtaking forest of skyscrapers, 21 in all, built during the early '30s in the heart of Manhattan. Among the best-known and most often visited are the 70-story **RCA Building,**

where NBC has its TV studios, with a restaurant on the 65th floor and an observation platform on the 70th; **Radio City Music Hall** (see "Architectural Highlights," above); the 51-floor **McGraw Hill Building,** where the audio-visual show *The New York Experience* (see "Museums of Science and History") is located; the **Exxon Building** (54 floors); and the **Time-Life Building** (48 floors). You must see the whole complex, and visit the buildings.

Seagram Building (midtown), 375 Park Ave. at E. 52nd St.: Lovely skyscraper of steel and bronze-tinted glass, a 1958 work of Ludwig Mies van der Rohe and the crowning achievement of the International School. The splendid interior décor was designed by Philip Johnson around works by Picasso, Chagall, Rodin, and others. An absolute must-see.

Trump Tower (midtown), 725 Fifth Ave. between 56th and 57th Sts.: This 68-story tower with a profusion of gilding and pink marble had cost a mere $150 million by the time it was completed in 1983. The six-floor lobby, with an unbelievable indoor waterfall 82 ft. (25 m) high, is tenanted by some of the world's most upscale boutiques: Charles Jourdan, Fred Cartier, Loewe, and the like. The quintessence of nouveau riche ostentation. It has to be seen.

Waldorf-Astoria Hotel (midtown), 301 Park Ave., at E. 50th St.: When it was opened in 1931, this imposing structure with its 47 floors and 1,900 rooms was described as "the largest and most luxurious hotel in the world." It has retained, through several facelifts, some vestiges of its original glory such as its magnificent art deco lobby and its unique ballroom, the Starlight Roof, whose roof really does open to the stars. Worth seeing.

Woolworth Building (Lower Manhattan), 233 Broadway at Barclay St.: A curious Gothic Revival skyscraper originally described as a "cathedral of commerce." It was the world's tallest building from its construction in 1913 until the completion of the Chrysler Building in 1930. Rising 60 floors and 792 ft. (241 m), it is the work of the great Cass Gilbert. Wonderful entrance hall with delightful stone gargoyle carvings and gold-leaf mosaics; the building's tower is modeled after the campanile of St. Mark's Basilica in Venice. Very much worth seeing.

World Trade Center (Lower Manhattan), West, Church, Vesey, and Liberty Sts.: Twin shimmering silver towers, designed by architects Minoru Yamasaki and Emery Roth, 110 floors high and rising 1,377 ft. (420 m) above the ground. These are the tallest buildings in New York and the second-tallest (after Chicago's Sears Tower) in the world. Opened in 1977, they took 15 years to build. Now 70,000 people work in them, and 80,000 tourists visit them, every day. If you want to know what New York looks like from a bird's-eye view, you really have no other place to go—you must come here. See "Panoramas," below.

BEACHES: ₰ **Coney Island Beach,** Surf Ave. between Ocean Ave. and W. 37th St., Brooklyn: The Konijn Eiland (Rabbit Island) of the original Dutch settlers has become New York's most popular beach; on some summer days more than a million people can be found on its 3.2 mi. (5 km) of fine sand or in the nearby amusement park. The best hot dogs in the city are to be had at **Nathan's Famous,** Surf and Stillwell Aves. The overall effect is kitsch, but amusing. Directly accessible by subway.

Jacob Riis Park, Beach 149 to Beach 169 Sts., Queens: A mile- (1.6-km-) long sandy beach with a huge parking lot; a spot particularly favored by gay nudists. Access is via the Marine Pkwy. Bridge, or subway and bus.

Jones Beach State Park, Bay Pkwy. and Meadowbrook Pkwy., Long Island: Farthest from Manhattan, but also the nicest beach in the metropolitan area. It's a huge state park of 2,413 acres (977 ha.) along the ocean, with 6 mi. (10 km) of splendid sand beach. Metro Apple Express buses (718/788-8000) depart for the beach from E. 56th St. and Second Ave. in Manhattan.

🔔 **Manhattan Beach,** Ocean Ave. between Oriental Blvd. and Mackenzie St., Brooklyn: The favorite beach of the city's young, it's relatively uncrowded though near Manhattan. Accessible by subway and bus.

🔔 **Rockaway Beach,** Beach 1st St. to Beach 149th St., Queens: Fine 10-mi.- (16-km-) long beach on a narrow spit of land which closes off the southern end of Jamaica Bay. Direct subway access.

BROADCASTING AND MOVIE STUDIOS: The principal New York TV studios allow public audiences to watch their shows being taped. In general, reservations must be made days or even weeks in advance, because of the limited number of seats. Some shows admit only spectators over 18, and none admit children under six months old. Write or call:

ABC Guest Relations, 36A W. 66th St., New York, NY 10023 (212/887-3537).

CBS Ticket Bureau, 524 W. 57th St., New York, NY 10019 (212/975-2476).

NBC Ticket Bureau, 30 Rockefeller Plaza, New York, NY 10112 (212/664-3055). NBC also offers conducted tours of its studios Mon.-Sat. (644-7174).

The **New York Convention and Visitors Bureau,** 2 Columbus Circle (397-8222), usually has some free same-day tickets for TV shows; out-of-town or foreign visitors are given priority.

CHURCHES/SYNAGOGUES: 🔔 **Church of the Ascension** (Greenwich Village), 36 Fifth Ave. at 10th St. (254-8620): Designed by Richard Upjohn; the first church (1841) built in New York in the Gothic Revival style then popular in England. Extensively restored in 1885–1889 under the direction of Stanford White. Very fine mural of the Ascension, and stained-glass windows, by John La Farge. Carvings of angels by Louis Saint-Gaudens. Worth seeing. Open daily.

☀🔔 **Cathedral of St. John the Divine** (Upper West Side), Amsterdam Ave. at 112th St. (316-7540): Largest Gothic cathedral in the world, 601 ft. (183 m) long, 124 ft. (38 m) wide, and capable of seating 10,000 people; the great rose (west) window is 40 ft. (12 m) across. The work of Ralph Adams Cram, it was begun in 1892. The transept and twin towers were never completed, though work has been resumed on them in the last five years. Must be seen.

☀🔔 **St. Patrick's Cathedral** (midtown), Fifth Ave. and 50th St. (753-2261): The Roman Catholic cathedral of New York, built in 1888. A fine, flamboyant example of Gothic by James Renwick, somewhat overshadowed by the surrounding high-rises despite its 330-ft. (100-m) spires. Very rich interior. Worth a visit. Open daily.

☀🔔 **St. Paul's Chapel** (Lower Manhattan), Broadway and Fulton St. (732-5564): The oldest (1766) church in the city, designed by Thomas McBean; George Washington had his private pew in the north aisle, while Jefferson and Cornwallis were other famous parishioners. The elegant Georgian design is reminiscent of London's St. Martin-in-the-Fields. Should be seen. Open daily.

☀🔔 **Temple Emanu-El** (Upper East Side), Fifth Ave. and 65th St. (744-1400): The largest synagogue in the country, with 2,500 seats, built in 1929 in majestic Romano-Byzantine style. Open daily.

Trinity Church (Lower Manhattan), Broadway and Wall St. (285-0872): Dwarfed today by the surrounding skyscrapers of the financial district, the steeple of this church was, when it was built in 1846 on the site of two earlier churches, the tallest structure in New York. Its churchyard is the oldest in the city (1681); in it may be found the tombs of Robert Fulton, inventor of the steamboat, and Alexander Hamilton. A favorite place for lunchtime picnics among Wall Street workers. Must positively be seen.

HISTORIC BUILDINGS AND STRUCTURES: Brooklyn Bridge
(Lower Manhattan), between City Hall Park, Manhattan, and Cadman Plaza, Brooklyn: The first (1883) steel-cable suspension bridge in the world, designed by engineer Johann August Roebling. A triumph of technical skill with its two piers resting on hydraulic caissons, this magnificent structure also offers an impressive view of Manhattan, especially at night. A sight not to be missed.

Carnegie Hall (midtown), 154 W. 57th St. at Seventh Ave. (247-7800): One of New York's two famous concert halls, the other being Avery Fisher Hall at Lincoln Center. The 1891 inaugural concert in this lovely 2,700-seat auditorium was conducted by Tchaikovsky himself. In 1986 it reopened after a $50-million renovation had restored all its former splendor, but some feel its once-outstanding acoustics have been somewhat compromised. For concert schedules, consult the entertainment pages of the daily papers.

City Hall (Lower Manhattan), Broadway at Murray St. (566-5200): An elegant Renaissance-style 1811 building of marble and brown sandstone. All civic processions and parades begin here. Should be seen.

Columbia University (Upper West Side), Broadway and 116th St. (280-2845): Founded in 1754 as King's College, this is one of the oldest and most respected of American universities—a member, along with Harvard, Yale, Princeton, and others, of the famous "Ivy League." Its campus, attended by 19,000 students, has 60 buildings, of which the most interesting are Low Memorial Library, whose Palladian style is reminiscent of the Pantheon in Rome; University Hall; and Butler Library, which contains five million books. Conducted tours of the campus Mon.-Fri.

Dyckman House (Upper Manhattan), 4881 Broadway at W. 204th St. (397-3188): The only 18th-century Dutch Colonial house still standing in modern Manhattan. Built by William Dyckman in 1782, it is decorated and furnished in a style typical of the wealthy farmers of the period. Worth the side trip. Open Tues.-Sun.

Ellis Island, opposite Battery Park, in New York Harbor (269-5755): Between 1892 and 1954, 17 million faceless immigrants filed through these enormous brick buildings (now being restored), on their way to try their luck on U.S. soil. A moving sight. An immigration museum will open here during 1989; 1.5 million visitors are expected yearly.

Federal Hall National Memorial (Lower Manhattan), 26 Wall St. (264-8711): As steeped in history as any building in Manhattan: the first City Hall was built here in 1699; here the Stamp Act imposed by the British in 1765 was rejected by the colonists; here the British made their headquarters during the War of Independence; here George Washington delivered his inaugural address as first president of the U.S. in 1789; here the first Congress met in 1789–1790. The present building, in the Doric style, dates from 1842. J.Q.A. Ward's statue of Washington dominates the façade. Don't miss it. Open Mon.-Fri.

Gracie Mansion (Upper East Side), East End Ave. at E. 88th St. (570-4751): Pretty country house in the Federal style, built in 1799 by a wealthy merchant named Archibald Gracie; now the official residence of the mayor of New York. Visits by appointment on Wed. from Apr. to Nov.

Grand Central Terminal (midtown), E. 42nd St. and Lexington Ave. (935-3960): Busiest railroad station in the world. This magnificent example of the Beaux Arts style, dating from 1912, is a kind of underground cathedral, and is a designated historic landmark. The central hall has a lovely ceiling. The flood of humanity which descends on the station at rush hours (150,000 commuters daily) must be seen to be believed. Trains to Chicago, Montréal, Niagara Falls, etc. Conducted tours on Wed.

Theodore Roosevelt Birthplace National Historic Shrine (Gramercy Park), 28 E. 20th St. (260-1616): Birthplace of the 26th president, the much-loved "Teddy" Roosevelt, with his furniture and personal memorabilia. He lived here from 1858 to 1872. The original house burned to the ground; the present replica dates from 1923. Regular classical concerts and temporary exhibitions. Open Tues.-Sat.

Yeshiva University (Upper Manhattan), 500 W. 185th St. (960-5390): The oldest (1886) and largest (7,000 students) Jewish university in America. Interesting buildings both Oriental in feeling—with Byzantine domes, like Tanenbaum Hall—or modern like the Science Center; museum devoted to Jewish history, architecture, and art, with particularly interesting models of synagogues from the 3rd to the 19th century. Open Tues., Thur., and Sun. during the academic year.

MARKETS: **Essex Street Market** (Lower East Side), Essex St. between Broome and Stanton Sts.: Built in 1938 by then-Mayor Fiorello La Guardia, this enormous covered market, the city's largest, is worth visiting not only for its many stalls overflowing with all kinds of foodstuffs, but for the variety of languages you'll hear—Yiddish, Spanish, Greek, Italian, Polish, Vietnamese, and many more. Worth seeing. Open daily except Jewish holidays.

Fulton Fish Market (Lower Manhattan), at South and Fulton Sts.: Adjacent to the South Street Seaport Museum (see "Museums of Science and History," below), this fish market, in existence since 1869 though the present building dates only from 1907, is one of the most important on the East Coast. Atmosphere and local color guaranteed, from 4 a.m. on, six days a week.

La Marqueta (El Barrio), Park Ave. between 110th and 116th Sts.: Puerto Rican covered market displaying all the exotic fruit, vegetables, seeds, spices, smoked meats, and fish from that Caribbean island. One of the most colorful (and aromatic) places in New York.

Paddy's Market (midtown), Ninth Ave. between W. 37th and W. 42nd Sts.: Once the stronghold of Greek and Italian grocers and produce merchants, this has become a kind of U.N. of the food business, displaying products of all nations. Its annual International Food Festival takes place in May, and is much appreciated by New Yorkers.

MONUMENTS: **General Grant National Memorial** (Upper West Side), Riverside Dr. and W. 122nd St. (666-1640): Tomb of Gen. Ulysses S. Grant, commander of the Union armies during the Civil War and 18th president of the U.S., and his wife. The marble and granite memorial is derivative of the mausoleum of Halicarnassus, one of the seven wonders of the ancient world, and is beautifully situated on a height overlooking the Hudson. The surrounding park should be avoided after dark. Open Wed.-Sun.

Statue of Liberty National Monument, Liberty Island, in New York Harbor (269-5755): Probably the most famous statue in the world. Affectionately known as "Miss Liberty," or "The Green Lady," this colossal work of the French sculptor Frédéric-Auguste Bartholdi and the French engineer Gustave Eiffel is 152 ft. (46 m) tall (305 ft., 93 m, including its base), and consists of 300 plates of copper fitted around a steel armature; the whole weighs 225 tons. A gift from the people of France to the people of the United States, since she was unveiled in 1886 *Liberty Enlightening the World* has become a symbol of the U.S., and is once again open to the public after a two-year rehabilitation project for the centennial in 1986. An elevator takes you to the statue's feet, and you then climb a spiral staircase of 168 steps to the top, where 40 people can enter the head, without crowding, and enjoy the magnificent view it affords of New York. There is an interesting little museum of immigration in the statue's base. A must for every visitor, but bear in mind that in summer, when 12,000 tourists make the trip every day, you may have to wait a couple of hours. Access by ferry from Battery Park at the southern tip of Manhattan. Open daily.

Washington Arch (Greenwich Village), Washington Square at the foot of Fifth Ave.: An 86-ft. (26-m) triumphal arch by Stanford White, erected in 1892–1895 to mark the centennial of George Washington's election to the presidency. The surrounding park is the heart of Greenwich Village. You should certainly see it.

MUSEUMS OF ART AND DESIGN: American Craft Museum (midtown), 40 W. 53rd St. (956-3535): The youngest (1987) of the city's art museums is entirely devoted to handcrafts in wood, metal, fabric, ceramics, etc. There are hundreds of objects on display, from an art deco rocking chair to blown glass. This triumph of the unusual occupies the ground floor of a 30-story high-rise opposite the Museum of Modern Art (see below). Don't miss it. Open Tues.-Sun.

Brooklyn Museum, 200 Eastern Pkwy. at Washington Ave., Brooklyn (718/638-5000): One of the country's most richly stocked and innovative museums, best known for its fine Egyptian collection and its primitive art, particularly from North America, Africa, and Polynesia; also offers interesting special exhibitions. Among the major works on display are *Palazzo Dogale in Venice* by Monet, *Mlle Fiocre* by Degas, *The Lady in Red* by Thomas Anshutz, and 12 bas-reliefs from the palace of the Assyrian king Assurbanipal at Nimrud. A new display area houses one of the world's largest collections of sculpture by Auguste Rodin, recently presented to the museum. Not to be missed. Open Wed.-Mon. Directly accessible by subway.

The Cloisters (Upper Manhattan), Fort Tryon Park at Fort Washington Ave. and W. 193rd St. (923-3700): Medieval French and Spanish cloisters acquired at the turn of the century by the millionaire art patron John D. Rockefeller, and transported stone by stone to the U.S. from the monasteries of St. Michael de Cuxa, Saint-Guilhem-le-Désert, and Bonnefont-en-Comminges, as well as others. Admirable collection of medieval art including the famous series of 15th-century "Unicorn Tapestries," and the almost equally famous Mérode Altarpiece painted around 1425. Lovely gardens overlooking the Hudson make up a magnificent whole which you mustn't miss. One of the most beautiful and least-known museums in the city. Open Tues.-Sun.

Cooper-Hewitt Museum (Upper East Side), 2 E. 91st St. at Fifth Ave. (860-6868): In what was once the sumptuous private house of the Carnegie family, this museum, entirely devoted to the decorative arts, displays a rich collection of furniture, ceramics, old fabrics (including a silken bonnet and mittens from China that are more than 2,000 years old), wallpaper, bronzes, architectural drawings, etc., as well as interesting temporary exhibitions. Should be seen. Open Tues.-Sun.

🔔 **El Museo del Barrio** (Upper East Side), 1230 Fifth Ave. at 104th St. (831-7272): Exhibitions of painting, sculpture, and photography by Latin American artists, in the heart of the Puerto Rican quarter ("El Barrio") of New York. Also public concerts, movies, plays, etc. Fascinating. Open Wed.-Sun.

🔔 **Forbes Collection** (Greenwich Village), 60 Fifth Ave. at 12th St. (620-2389): A highly eclectic private museum belonging to the publisher and businessman Malcolm Forbes. It includes the world's largest collection of Fabergé Easter eggs, some old paintings, 500 ship models, and an army of 12,000 lead toy soldiers. Unexpected. Open Tues.-Sat.

☼🔔🔔 **Frick Collection** (Upper East Side), 1 E. 70th St. at Fifth Ave. (288-0700): European masters (Velázquez, Vermeer, Gainsborough, Boucher, Van Eyck, and many others of equal stature) and fine furniture displayed in a lovely little Renaissance-style palace designed by architect Thomas Hastings for the Pittsburgh steel magnate Henry Clay Frick. Delightful covered courtyard. Among the most famous paintings on exhibition: *Man in a Red Hat* by Titian, *Self-Portrait* by Rembrandt, *Portrait of Philip IV* by Velázquez. Perhaps New York's most exquisite museum; not to be missed. Open Tues.-Sun.

☼🔔🔔🔔 **Guggenheim Museum** (Upper East Side), 1071 Fifth Ave. at E. 89th St. (360-3500): One of the world's most beautiful and original museum buildings, truly a work of art in its own right, designed in 1959 by Frank Lloyd Wright, the greatest American architect, in the form of an inverted spiral supposedly inspired by the legendary Tower of Babel. Splendid collection of impressionist and modern painting and sculpture by Kandinsky, Paul Klee, Delaunay, Picasso, Rauschenberg—but also by Renoir, Cézanne, Van Gogh, Manet, and the like. In all, some 5,000 paintings, sculptures, and drawings including such acknowledged masterpieces as Kandinsky's *Blue Mountain,* Picasso's *Moulin de la Galette,* Jackson Pollock's *Ocean Greyness,* Chagall's *Green Violinist,* and *The Watchmaker* by Paul Cézanne. You should plan not to leave New York without coming to the Guggenheim. Open Tues.-Sun.

🔔 **International Center of Photography** (Upper East Side), Fifth Ave. at 94th St. (860-1777): The only museum in New York entirely devoted to photography. Temporary exhibitions and a permanent collection by the greatest masters of the lens: Robert Capa, Henri Cartier-Bresson, Ernst Haas, David Seymour, Marc Riboud, Ken Heyman, Edward Weston, and Ansel Adams. Fascinating. Open Tues.-Sun.

☼🔔🔔🔔🔔 **Metropolitan Museum of Art** (Upper East Side), Fifth Ave. and E. 82nd St. (535-7710): Familiarly known to New Yorkers as "the Met," this cultural colossus is the world's largest art museum: more than three million objects are displayed in 236 galleries plus a very fine Rooftop Sculpture Garden with a clear view of the Manhattan skyline. The presentation is admirable: from Egyptian temples to Gauguin and from medieval art to Jackson Pollock, the Met offers you a complete panorama of mankind's artistic evolution over the last 5,000 years. You should take care to see the new Lila Acheson Wallace Wing, devoted to 20th-century art. Among the world-famous works of art you will see are Giovanni Pisano's *Head of King David,* the *Mezzetin* of Antoine Watteau, Rembrandt's *Aristotle Contemplating the Bust of Homer,* Vermeer's *Woman at a Window,* an *Annunciation* by Hans Memling and another by Botticelli, a *Crucifixion* by Jan van Eyck, *The Harvest* by Peter Breughel the Elder, Ingres' *Princesse de Broglie,* Gauguin's *Ia Orana Maria,* Picasso's *Portrait of Gertrude Stein,* and *Autumn Rhythm* by Jackson Pollock. Five million people visit the museum every year; you should allow at least two full days for it. It is in itself worth the trip to New York. Good cafeteria. Open Tues.-Sun.

Museum of Holography (Soho), 11 Mercer St. (925-0526): The world's first museum devoted to holography, a process invented in 1949 in which the exposure of photographic film by laser light permits the development of three-dimensional images. Spectacular and surprising. Open Tues.-Sun.

Museum of Modern Art (MOMA) (midtown), 11 W. 53rd St. (708-9400): From impressionism to cubism, from expressionism to abstract art, MOMA's collection of 100,000 priceless works covers the spectrum from Dali to Monet, from Bacon to Chagall, and from Andy Warhol to de Kooning and Mark Rothko. Recently modernized, and enlarged by the construction of an adjoining 52-story tower designed by Cesar Pelli with an enormous glassed-in atrium, MOMA also boasts a superb garden court with modern sculpture by Lipchitz, Rodin (*The Burghers of Calais*), Picasso, Nevelson, Henry Moore, Reginald Butler, and others. With its 5,000 visitors a day, this is one of the most popular museums in the country. Its most cherished canvas, Picasso's *Guernica,* was returned to Spain in 1981, but you can still admire the same artist's famous *Demoiselles d'Avignon,* along with such other masterpieces as Van Gogh's *Starry Night,* Matisse's *The Dance,* Douanier Rousseau's *Sleeping Gypsy,* the waterlily triptych by Monet, *Dog* by Francis Bacon, and *Christina's World* by Andrew Wyeth. This museum alone could justify the trip to New York. Open Thur.-Tues.

Studio Museum (Harlem), 144 W. 125th St. (864-4500): This little-known museum in the heart of Harlem has interesting temporary exhibitions of the work of black artists, both American and Third World. Worth the trip. Open Wed.-Sun.

Whitney Museum of American Art (Upper East Side), 945 Madison Ave. at E. 75th St. (570-3676). Founded in 1930 by the sculptor Gertrude Vanderbilt Whitney, this remarkable museum displays the most representative works by contemporary American artists, from Georgia O'Keeffe and Louise Nevelson to Edward Hopper and George Segal. The odd granite-and-concrete building in the shape of a truncated Aztec pyramid dates from 1954, and is the work of Marcel Breuer. Major exhibits: *Circus* by Calder, *Early Sunday Morning* by Edward Hopper, *Dempsey and Firpo* by George Bellow, Charles Demuth's *My Egypt,* and Jackson Pollock's *Number 27.* Don't miss it. Open Tues.-Sun.

MUSEUMS OF SCIENCE AND HISTORY: American Museum of the Moving Image/AMMI (Queens), 35th Ave. at 36th St. (718/784-0077): The nation's first public museum wholly devoted to chronicling the history of cinema, television and video art. This $15 million shrine to the motion picture, inaugurated in Sept. 88, is part of the old Astoria Studios, once Paramount Pictures' production center for silent films. The 60,000-item-collection includes vintage movie cameras and television sets, old posters, photographs, souvenirs, costumes of movie and TV stars, and three theaters where visitors can see films or TV serials rarely seen. A must for movie buffs. Open Wed.-Sat.

American Numismatic Society (Upper Manhattan), Audubon Terrace, Broadway at 155th St. (234-3130): The largest numismatic library in the world, and one of the greatest collections ever assembled of coins, medals, and decorations. A collector's paradise. Open Tues.-Sun.

Fraunces Tavern Museum (Lower Manhattan), 54 Pearl St. (425-1778): This picturesque tavern in dull-brown brick is as faithful a replica as can be made of the original structure, dating from 1719, which was razed by two successive fires in 1837 and 1852; it belonged to Samuel Fraunces (the name is a corruption of "Français," French), a black man from the

Antilles who became steward to George Washington. It was here that Washington gave a farewell banquet for his generals before temporarily leaving New York for Philadelphia in 1783. Museum, with historical collection, open Mon.-Fri. On the ground floor there's a very acceptable restaurant with incomparable American Colonial atmosphere; breakfast/lunch/dinner Mon.-Fri. Don't miss it.

Hayden Planetarium (Upper West Side), Central Park West and W. 81st St. (769-5000): This famous planetarium, and its comprehensive museum of the history of astronomy, form an integral part of the Museum of Natural History (see below). You'll be interested in a 30-ton meteorite found in Greenland in 1897, a reproduction of the solar system, and an exact representation of the moon's surface. For ardent amateur astronomers. Exciting. Open daily.

Intrepid Sea-Air-Space Museum (midtown), Pier 86 at W. 46th St. (245-2533): The famous World War II and Vietnam War aircraft carrier, 890 ft. (270 m) long, now converted into a floating museum with aircraft, helicopters, and space capsules. Interesting audio-visual show. Impressive. Open Wed.-Sun.

Jewish Museum (Upper East Side), 1109 Fifth Ave. at E. 92nd St. (860-1888): The world's largest Jewish museum illustrates the history of Judaism by means of painting, sculpture, manuscripts, ceremonial objects, etc. Samuel Friedenberg numismatic collection. Take care to see the beautiful composition by the sculptor George Segal, entitled *Holocaust.* In 1991, the museum will begin a $15 million expansion. Open Sun.-Thur.

Morris-Jumel Mansion (Upper Manhattan), W. 160th St. and Edgecombe Ave. (923-8008): With its four-column portico, this elegant 1765 Georgian mansion was Washington's headquarters before the battle of Harlem Heights in 1776. It's considered the oldest Colonial private house left in Manhattan. Very fine old furniture. For lovers of glimpses from the past. Open Tues.-Sun.

Museum of the American Indian (Upper Manhattan), Audubon Terrace, Broadway at 155th St. (283-2420): The most comprehensive collection of Native American art in the country, with more than a million objects—of which, for reasons of space, only 10,000 can be exhibited at any one time. A remarkable panorama of Indian culture from North, Central, and South America. Among the curiosities are personal possessions of such famous Indian chiefs as Geronimo, Sitting Bull, and Crazy Horse. Important groups of pre-Columbian art, of kachina dolls, and of Iroquois masks. Even though badly run-down, this museum should not be missed. Open Tues.-Sun.

Museum of Broadcasting (midtown), 1 E. 53rd St. (752-7684): Enormous archive of tapes on which are stored the most important radio and TV broadcasts by the three networks—ABC, CBS, and NBC—from 1946 to the present day; more than 20,000 programs, from which the visitor may select favorites for replay. For those who believe that the Golden Age of radio and TV is past. Open Tues.-Sat.

Museum of the City of New York (Upper East Side), Fifth Ave. and E. 103rd St. (534-1672): New York history in models, dioramas, paintings, prints, toys, old furniture, etc., from the foundation of New Amsterdam in the 17th century. Multimedia show on "the Big Apple." Fascinating. Open Tues.-Sun.

Museum of Natural History (Upper West Side), Central Park West at W. 79th St. (769-5100): Some 34 million objects in inventory enrich the collection of this, the largest natural-history museum in the world. Particularly important zoology and anthropology sections, with every animal in creation, including dinosaurs and a 98-ft. (30-m) blue whale. Many dioramas showing the habitats of the people, and animals, of America, Asia, Africa, and the Pacific. Gallery of meteorites and minerals. Enormous collection of fossils. One of the world's largest assemblages of gemstones, including some unique and valuable specimens. Movies shown on the giant "Naturemax" screen. Don't miss this one. Open daily.

The New York Experience (midtown), 1221 Ave. of the Americas at W. 48th St. (869-0345): Amazing audio-visual show, with spectacular effects, on New York and its history. Worth seeing. Open daily.

New-York Historical Society (Upper West Side), 170 Central Park West at 77th St. (873-3400): An indispensable complement to the Museum of the City of New York (see above), with a very rich collection of American decorative art (Tiffany lamps, silverware, toys), and in particular 433 of the 435 famous original watercolors by John James Audubon of the *Birds of America*. History of transportation in New York. The library has more than four million manuscripts, prints, photos, engravings, and rare books relating to New York. Must certainly be seen. Open Tues.-Sun.

New York Public Library (midtown), Fifth Ave. and 42nd St. (930-0730): Imposing Italian Renaissance structure, guarded by two enormous marble lions and housing the second-largest public library in the country, after the Library of Congress in Washington: 30 million works, paintings, posters, etc. Among the rarities: a letter from Christopher Columbus dated 1493, and a rough draft of the Declaration of Independence in the handwriting of Thomas Jefferson. Very interesting temporary exhibitions. Open Mon.-Sat.

Pierpont Morgan Library (midtown), 29 E. 36th St. (685-0610): This magnificent library, assembled by the financier and art patron J. Pierpont Morgan, specializes in valuable manuscripts and rare books. Since 1906 it has been housed in a sumptuous Renaissance palazzo by McKim, Mead & White, opened to the public in 1924. It has, among its other treasures, three Gutenberg Bibles, the 15th-century illuminated *Book of Hours* of Catherine of Cleves, 9th-century Coptic manuscripts, the oldest-known edition of Boccaccio's *Decameron* (1473), and autograph letters by Shakespeare, Byron, Shelley, Dickens, etc. Its temporary exhibitions are wonderful. The book lover's paradise. Open Tues.-Sun.

Queens Museum, Flushing Meadows–Corona Park, Grand Central Pkwy. and Roosevelt Ave., Queens (718/592-5555): Since 1972 this museum has occupied the former New York City building of the 1964 World's Fair. Halfway between Kennedy and La Guardia airports, it's worth a sidetrip because of its extraordinary 9,000-sq.-ft. scale model of New York. A sight not to be missed. Open Tues.-Sun.

South Street Seaport Museum (Lower Manhattan), East River at the foot of Fulton St. (669-9400): The historic port district of old New York converted into an open-air museum, with carefully restored 19th-century houses, pubs, restaurants, shops, a covered market, and street musicians. Along its piers are moored old ships such as the very fine four-master *Peking* (1911), the *Ambrose* lightship (1907), the three-master *Wavertree* (1885), and the schooner *Lettie G. Howard* (1893). The setting is admittedly touristy, but lively and colorful; it could have come straight out of an old picture book. Stay away Thur. and Fri. evenings when the horde of Wall St. brokers comes out to play. Don't miss it. Open daily.

NIGHTTIME ENTERTAINMENT: No city in the world offers a gamut of nighttime diversions equal to New York's. Leaving aside its dozens of theaters, concert halls, and opera houses, including the prestigious Met and Carnegie Hall, the visitor may find it hard to choose among several hundred bars, discos, comedy clubs, jazz dives, dance halls, and nightclubs—ranging from smart to sleazy. When it comes, specifically, to nightclubs, bars, and discos, the problem is to pick the "in" places; on the New York scene, discos, in particular, can be born, flourish, and die in less than a year. Some safe bets will be found listed under "Bars and Nightclubs," below.

For lovers of theater and musicals, no visit to New York can be complete without at least one evening on Broadway, "the greatest show on earth." The 42 theaters around Times Square generally present high-grade entertainment, from Shakespeare to Arthur Miller and from Neil Simon to the latest musicals. Elsewhere in the city, more than 300 "off-" and "off-off-" Broadway houses are home to avant-garde plays or comedy clubs which may become tomorrow's big hits. Most of New York's theaters may be old and uncomfortable, but with ten million playgoers a year the "Sold Out" signs are often up, so tickets should be obtained well in advance. You can use a ticket broker, or charge tickets on your credit card through Telecharge (239-6200) or Teletron (947-5850). **TKTS**, at Broadway and 47th St. (midtown) or the mezzanine of 2 World Trade Center (Lower Manhattan), sells tickets at half price; the drawback is that they are available only on the day of the performance—matinee tickets from noon on and evening tickets from 3 p.m. There's another TKTS outlet in Bryant Park behind the Public Library at W. 42nd St. and Ave. of the Americas), which sells tickets on the same terms for operas, ballets, and concerts. You can't make advance reservations, and the waiting lines are often long. Finally, in the big hotels, the concierge may be induced by the suggestive rustle of $10 bills to unearth the ticket(s) that you have been told are not to be had. For other information, see "Performing Arts," below.

OUTDOOR ART AND PLAZAS: The streets and squares of New York boast many important works of art, including an amusing 40-ft. (12-m) Fiberglas composition by Jean Dubuffet entitled *Group of Four Trees,* in the Chase Manhattan Plaza, in Lower Manhattan. In front of Lincoln Center (Upper West Side), are *Reclining Figure,* a monumental bronze by British sculptor Henry Moore, and *The Ticket Window* by Alexander Calder. Other noteworthy pieces include *The Alamo,* an enormous cubic structure by Tony Rosenthal on Astor Pl. (Noho); *Shadows and Flags,* a group of seven abstracts in black-painted steel by Louise Nevelson at Liberty and William Sts. (Lower Manhattan); a strange mobile globe in bronze by the German Fritz Koenig in the World Trade Center Plaza (Lower Manhattan); and a giant Jacques Lipchitz outside the Law School at Columbia University, Broadway and 116th St. (Harlem). In a more classical vein are the monumental 45-ft. (14-m) *Atlas* and the famous *Prometheus* by P. Manship in gilt bronze dominating the lower plaza of Rockefeller Center (midtown).

PANORAMAS: ☼ 🔭 **Brooklyn Bridge** (Lower Manhattan), between City Hall Park in Manhattan and Cadman Plaza, Brooklyn: The city's oldest (1883) suspension bridge; a beautiful piece of functional architecture in steel, whose pedestrian walkway affords a superb view of downtown Manhattan. A sight not to be missed.

☼ 🔭 **Brooklyn Heights,** Columbia Heights between Remsen and Orange Sts., Brooklyn: Smart residential neighborhood on a hill overlooking the East River. The writer Truman Capote used to live here; Norman Mailer is a current resident. Splendid view of the skyline and the southern tip of Manhattan from the promenade that runs below the Brooklyn–Queens Expwy. You should definitely see it.

Empire State Building (midtown), 34th St. and Fifth Ave. (736-3100): Probably the world's most famous skyscraper, particularly to *King Kong* fans. Its 102 stories and 223 ft. (68 m) of TV transmitting antenna add up to a total height of 1,454 ft. (439 m). There are two observation platforms, one in the open air on the 86th floor, the other closed and glassed-in on the 102nd floor. On a clear day you can see more than 60 mi. (100 km) over four states. New York's most astonishing view, especially by night, attracting 2 million visitors a year. Open daily till 11:30 p.m. Don't miss it. For more details, see "Skyscrapers," above.

RCA Building (midtown), 30 Rockefeller Plaza (489-2947): Although "a mere" 70 stories tall, this Rockefeller Center building gives you a unique view out over the forest of high-rises. A must-see. Open daily.

Roosevelt Island Aerial Tramway (Upper East Side), Second Ave. at E. 60th St. (832-4555): Running 200 ft. (60 m) above the waters of the East River, parallel to the Queensboro Bridge, this cable car connecting Manhattan and Roosevelt Island gives you a fine view of the East Side skyline. Runs every 15 min., daily.

Staten Island Ferry (Lower Manhattan), Ferry Terminal, Peter Minuit Plaza (718/727-2508): New York's most spectacular view for 25¢. The ferry links the southern tip of Manhattan to Staten Island, and passes near the Statue of Liberty. It runs daily around the clock, leaving every 15 min. in rush hours, once an hour late at night. The trip takes about 20 min. each way. An experience not to be passed up.

Statue of Liberty, Liberty Island, in New York Harbor (390-5253): Reached by an elevator and a spiral staircase (trying), and 12 stories high, the statue's head offers a splendid view of New York and the bay through the windows in the crown. Advisable only for those in good physical condition. Open daily; accessible by ferry from Battery Park.

World Trade Center (Lower Manhattan), West, Church, Vesey, and Liberty Sts. (466-7397): These twin towers, 1,377 ft. (420 m) tall, took the championship away from the Empire State Building, but were themselves defeated by the 1,454-ft. (443-m) Sears Tower in Chicago. Unique panorama of New York from the Observation Deck on the 107th floor, or the open terrace on the 110th floor of the No. 2 tower. Open daily till 9:30 p.m. An absolute must for every visitor. For more information, see "Architectural Highlights—Skyscrapers," above.

PARKS AND GARDENS: **Battery Park** (Lower Manhattan), Battery Pl. and State St.: Standing at the tip of Manhattan Island, with a magnificent view of New York Bay and the Statue of Liberty, this park marks the spot where Giovanni da Verrazano is supposed to have made his first landfall in 1524. The lowering bulk of **Castle Clinton,** a fort built in 1811 to defend the city against British warships, was an immigrant processing center in 1855–1890. Nearby is the terminal for the Statue of Liberty, Ellis Island, and Staten Island ferries. For those who like to take souvenir photographs, a stroll around here is definitely indicated.

Bowling Green (Lower Manhattan), Battery Pl. and Broadway: According to legend, this is where Peter Minuit bought Manhattan from the Indians. There is still lawn bowling here as there was in Dutch Colonial days—the distant ancestor of present-day American ten-pin bowling. Should be seen.

Brooklyn Botanic Gardens, Eastern Pkwy. at Washington Ave., Brooklyn (718/622-4433): On a 50-acre (20.5-ha.) site tucked between Olmsted and Vaux's masterly **Prospect Park** and the Brooklyn Museum you'll find azaleas and rhododendrons, lilacs, wisteria, one of the country's most beautiful rose gardens, a Japanese water garden, an unspoiled tract of New York woodland, a lovely grove of cherry trees, and more. The greenhouses reopened in 1988 after a two-year expansion project; they house among other attractions an unequalled collection of bonsai (Japanese miniature trees). The gardens are scrupulously maintained—no graffiti or litter—and it's hard to believe you're in the city. Combine this with a visit to the adjoining Brooklyn Museum (see "Museums of Art and Design," above) for a day's escape.

Central Park, between Fifth Ave. and Central Park West from 59th to 110th Sts.: This magnificent park, covering 840 acres (340 ha.) in the center of the city (twice the size of the principality of Monaco) is Manhattan's lung; it was designed by Frederick Law Olmsted and Calvert Vaux, fathers of American landscape architecture. Much frequented by New York joggers and cyclists. Pleasantly undulating, and stitched together by more than 30 mi. (50 km) of surfaced roads, footpaths, and riding trails, it also has several lakes (on some of which boating is available), a herb garden, a small zoo with a special children's zoo, an ice-skating rink, a carousel, and other attractions. Many tourists take a daytime ride through the park in a horse-drawn carriage, but the park is less safe at night; avoid dark, deserted sections. Many festivals and free concerts in summer. Should certainly be seen.

Fort Tryon Park (Upper Manhattan), between Riverside Dr. and Broadway from W. 192nd St. to Dyckman St.: A gift of the Rockefeller family to the city, this park occupies the site of the old Fort Washington, which played an important role during the War of Independence. There's a splendid view of the Hudson flowing below. Lovely terraced flower gardens. Don't miss it. In the middle of the park stands the Cloisters (see "Museums of Art and Design," above).

Gramercy Park, Lexington Ave. between E. 20th and E. 21st Sts.: In the middle of a square lined with fine century-old buildings stands this quiet, green oasis in mid-Manhattan, the last private square in New York. Only residents, and guests at the Gramercy Park Hotel on the square, have access to it. You should see it.

Inwood Hill Park (Upper Manhattan), bounded by the Hudson and Harlem Rivers, Dyckman St., and Payson Ave.: 434 acres (176 ha.) of hilly woods along the river, centuries-old trees, and lawns much appreciated by picnickers, at the northern tip of Manhattan. Here once stood the village of Shorakkopoch, consisting in part of cave dwellings belonging to the Algonquins who, in 1626, sold Manhattan Island to Peter Minuit for a mess of pottage.

New York Botanical Gardens, 200th St. and Southern Blvd., The Bronx (220-8777): This splendid 250-acre (102.5-ha.) tract of greenery has everything: the only first-growth timber still standing within the city limits; acres of tree-studded lawns; beautiful flowerbeds; the tremendous, recently renovated Enid Haupt Conservatory with its stunning seasonal flower shows; a rushing country stream, beside which stands an 18th-century snuff mill where you can have a snack. Less elegant and intimate than the Brooklyn gardens, but more spacious. Free, unless you bring your car (parking $4).

Washington Square (Greenwich Village), Fifth Ave. at Waverly Pl.: A square whose triumphal arch (by Stanford White) is dedicated to George Washington, in the heart of bohemian Greenwich Village. Here was once the burial ground for black slaves and executed criminals. Today jam sessions, roller skaters, artists, and sidewalk orators of every kind may be found here; a lively, colorful place, though overwhelmed by tourists. Unfortunately it has for several years been one of the city's top open-air drug markets. Nevertheless, don't fail to see it.

Woodlawn Cemetery, Jerome Ave. at E. 233rd St., The Bronx (920-0500): Huge landscaped cemetery with 250,000 graves, some sumptuous crypts, and beautiful gardens, now a designated bird sanctuary. Among the illustrious dead here are the writer Herman Melville (*Moby-Dick*), Duke Ellington, newspaperman and publisher Joseph Pulitzer (founder of the prizes that bear his name), the 19th-century railroad magnate Jay Gould, the five-and-dime king Frank W. Woolworth, and the great New York City mayor Fiorello La Guardia. Worth a visit. Open daily.

PERFORMING ARTS: For daily listings of the innumerable shows and cultural events in New York, consult the entertainment pages of the **daily papers** *New York Times* or *New York Daily News* (morning) and *New York Post* (morning and evening), as well as the weeklies *The Village Voice, New York* magazine, and *The New Yorker,* or call **New York City On Stage** (587-1111) for current theater schedules.

Alice Tully Hall (Upper West Side), Lincoln Center, 140 W. 65th St. (877-1800): Recitals, chamber concerts, movies.

American Place Theater (midtown), 111 W. 46th St. (247-0393): Off-Broadway theater.

Astor Place (Noho), 434 Lafayette St. (254-4370): Musicals, off-Broadway theater.

Avery Fisher Hall (Upper West Side), Lincoln Center, 140 W. 65th St. (877-1800): Home of the New York Philharmonic, one of the world's great orchestras (principal conductor, Zubin Mehta).

Booth Theatre (midtown), 222 W. 45th St. (239-6200): Contemporary theater.

Broadhurst Theater (midtown), 235 W. 44th St. (239-6200): Contemporary theater.

Broadway Theater (midtown), 1681 Broadway at W. 52nd St. (239-6200): Musicals.

Brooklyn Academy of Music, 30 Lafayette St., Brooklyn (718/636-4100): Concerts, contemporary theater, opera, ballet.

Brooklyn Center for the Performing Arts, Nostrand Ave. and Ave. H, Brooklyn (718/434-1900): Ballet, recitals.

Brooks Atkinson Theater (midtown), 256 W. 47th St. (719-4099): Contemporary theater.

Carnegie Hall (midtown), 154 W. 57th St. (247-7800): Concerts, recitals.

Charles Ludlam Theater (Greenwich Village), 1 Sheridan Square (691-2271): Off-Broadway theater.

Cherry Lane Theater (Greenwich Village), 38 Commerce St. (989-2020): The oldest Off-Broadway theater.

Circle in the Square (Greenwich Village), 159 Bleecker St. (254-6330): Musicals, off-Broadway theater.

Circle Repertory Company (Greenwich Village), Seventh Ave. at W. 4th St. (924-7100): Off-Broadway theater.

City Center Theater (midtown), 131 W. 55th St. (581-7907): Ballet.

Delacorte Theater (Upper West Side), W. 81st St. in Central Park (861-7277): Open-air theater; the New York Shakespeare Festival is staged here every summer.

Douglas Fairbanks Theater (midtown), 432 W. 42nd St. (239-4321): Musicals, recitals.

Edison Theater (midtown), 240 W. 47th St. (757-7164): Musicals.

Ensemble Studio Theater (midtown), 549 W. 52nd St. (247-4982): Contemporary theater.

Ethel Barrymore Theater (midtown), 243 W. 47th St. (239-6200): Contemporary theater.

Eugene O'Neill Theater (midtown), 230 W. 49th St. (246-0220): Contemporary theater.

Forty-Sixth Street Theater (midtown), 226 W. 46th St. (221-1211): Contemporary theater.

Gershwin Theater (midtown), 1633 Broadway at W. 51st St. (586-6510): Musicals.

Golden Center for the Performing Arts, Queens College, Kissena Blvd., Queens (718/793-8080): Concerts, ballet, recitals.

Guggenheim Bandshell (Upper West Side), Lincoln Center, 140 W. 65th St. (887-1800): Open-air concerts.

Helen Hayes Theater (midtown), 240 W. 44th St. (944-9450): Contemporary theater.

Imperial Theater (midtown), 249 W. 45th St. (239-6200): Musicals.

Joyce Theater (Chelsea), 175 Eighth Ave. at W. 19th St. (242-0800): Ballet.

The Kitchen (Chelsea), 512 W. 19th St. (255-5793): Experimental theater.

La Mama Experimental Theater Club (East Village), 74 E. 4th St. (475-7710): Avant-garde theater.

Lamb's Theater (midtown), 130 W. 44th St. (997-1780): Contemporary theater.

Longacre Theater (midtown), 220 W. 48th St. (239-6200): Musicals.

Majestic Theater (midtown), 247 W. 44th St. (239-6200): Musicals.

Manhattan Theater Club (Upper East Side), 321 E. 73rd St. (472-0600): Off-Broadway theater.

Marquis Theater (midtown), Broadway at 46th St. (398-8383): Musicals.

Martin Beck Theater (midtown), 302 W. 45th St. (246-6363): Musicals.

Merkin Concert Hall (Upper West Side), 129 W. 67th St. (362-8719): Concerts, recitals.

Metropolitan Opera House (Upper West Side), Lincoln Center, 140 W. 65th St. (877-1800): Home of the New York Metropolitan Opera (musical director, James Levine).

Minskoff Theater (midtown), Broadway at W. 45th St. (869-0550): Musicals.

Mitzi E. Newhouse Theater (Upper West Side), Lincoln Center, 140 W. 65th St. (877-1800): Concerts, recitals, musicals.

Neil Simon Theater (midtown), 250 W. 52nd St. (247-2234): Contemporary theater.

Nederlander Theater (midtown), 208 W. 41st St. (921-8000): Contemporary theater.

New York State Theater (Upper West Side), Lincoln Center, 140 W. 65th St. (877-1800): Home of the New York City Opera (director, Christopher Keene). Performances by the New York City Ballet.

Norman Thomas Theater (midtown), 111 E. 33rd St. (685-3233): Musicals.

Playwrights Horizon (midtown), 416 W. 42nd St. (564-1235): Avant-garde theater.

Plymouth Theater (midtown), 236 W. 45th St. (239-6200): Contemporary theater.

Promenade Theater (Upper West Side), 2162 Broadway at W. 76th St. (580-1313): Musicals.

Provincetown Players (Greenwich Village), 133 MacDougal St. (477-5048): One of the best-known off-Broadway theaters.

Public Theater (Noho), 425 Lafayette St. (598-7150): Very popular; off-Broadway and classical theater.

Ritz Theater (midtown), 225 W. 48th St. (582-4022): Musicals, modern theater.

Roundabout Theater (Gramercy Park), 100 E. 17th St. (420-1883): Off-Broadway theater.

St. James Theater (midtown), 246 W. 44th St. (398-0280): Musicals.

Second Avenue Theater (East Village), Second Ave. at 12th St.

Second Stage Theater? Bwy & 75th or 74th? (246-0102): Musicals.

Shubert Theater (midtown), 225 W. 44th St. (239-6200): Musicals.

Sullivan St. Playhouse (Greenwich Village), 181 Sullivan St. (674-3838): Off-Broadway theater. The musical *The Fantasticks* had a 14-year run here.

Theater Four (midtown), 424 W. 55th St. (246-8545): Contemporary theater.

Vivian Beaumont Theater (Upper West Side), Lincoln Center, 140 W. 65th St. (877-1800): Musicals, light opera.

Westside Arts Theater (midtown), 470 W. 43rd St. (541-8394): Contemporary theater.

Winter Garden Theater (midtown), 1634 Broadway at W. 51st St. (239-6200): Operetta, musicals.

WPA Theater (Chelsea), 519 W. 23rd St. (206-0523): Off-Broadway theater.

SHOPPING:

In spite of high state and local sales taxes (8.25%), New York is a shoppers' paradise for at least three reasons: (1) the tremendous range of choice in a city with almost 200,000 shops, stores, and merchants of all kinds; (2) the generally attractive level of prices; (3) the clustering of certain kinds of stores in certain neighborhoods, making the shopper's task easier. Note also that if you have your purchases shipped to an address outside New York State, you should not be charged the 8.25% sales tax. If you can't find what you want through these listings, consult the *Yellow Pages*.

Shopping Areas

The concentrations of various kinds of retailers in New York is roughly as follows:

Antique Dealers and Art Galleries: Second and Third Aves. between E. 47th and E. 57th Sts., Madison Ave. between E. 57th and E. 80th Sts., Columbus Ave., Greenwich Village, Soho.

Books: *New*—Fifth and Madison Aves. from E. 46th to E. 57th Sts., Greenwich Village; *Secondhand*—around Fourth Ave. from E. 8th to E. 13th Sts., E. 59th St. between Madison and Third Aves.

Cameras, Photography, Electronics: W. 32nd to W. 34th Sts. between Sixth and Seventh Aves., Essex St. (Lower East Side), W. 45th to W. 47th Sts. between Fifth and Sixth Aves.

Clothing: From Washington Square to W. 42nd St. between Fifth and Seventh Aves.; W. 26th to W. 41st Sts. between Broadway and Seventh Ave. ("Fashion Ave."); Soho and Greenwich Village (trendy boutiques); Orchard, Grand, and Delancey Sts. (Lower East Side) for bargains.

Fabrics: W. 35th and 41st Sts. between Fifth and Eighth Aves., Broadway between Canal and 8th Sts.

Flowers: W. 28th St. and Sixth Ave., Canal St.

Furs: W. 26th to W. 30th Sts. between Broadway and Sixth Ave.

Jewels and Diamonds: W. 47th St. between Fifth and Sixth Aves. ("Diamond Row"), Fifth Ave. between 42nd and 59th Sts.

Luxury Items (Fashion, Perfumes): Fifth Ave. between 34th and 59th Sts., Park and Madison Aves. between E. 48th and E. 59th Sts.

Shoes: W. 8th St. between Broadway and Sixth Ave.

TV/Stereo Equipment: Canal St.; W. 45th St.; Leonard, Warren, and Chambers Sts. between Broadway and Greenwich St. (Tribeca).

Some Recommended Establishments

BOOKS. **Barnes and Noble** (Greenwich Village), 105 Fifth Ave. at 18th St.; **B. Dalton** (midtown), 666 Fifth Ave.; **Doubleday** (midtown), 673 Fifth Ave. at 53rd St.; **Strand** (East Village), Broadway at 12th St., with secondhand books in carload lots.

DEPARTMENT STORES. **Bergdorf Goodman** (midtown), Fifth Ave. and 58th St.; **Bloomingdales** (midtown), 1000 Third Ave., at 59th St., New York's chicest, to see and be seen; ※ **Macys** (midtown), W. 34th St. and Broadway, largest store in the world, with 400,000 items, 150,000 customers per day; **Saks Fifth Ave.** (midtown), 611 Fifth Ave. at 50th St., with very yuppie customers.

FOOD. **Balducci's** (Greenwich Village), 422 Ave. of the Americas at W. 9th St.; **Fay and Allen's Foodworks** (Upper East Side), 1241 Third Ave. at 72nd St.; **Zabar's** (Upper West Side), Broadway at W. 80th St., the biggest food store in the country, offering an unbelievable range of choice, which is best visited like a museum.

GADGETS AND GIFTS. **Hammacher Schlemmer** (midtown), 147 E. 57th St., with every kind of gift idea for the home, including the silliest (and the most expensive).

MICROCOMPUTERS AND VIDEO GAMES. **Computer Factory** (midtown), 485 Lexington Ave. at 72nd St.; **47th St. Photo** (see "Photographic Equipment," below).

MILITARY SURPLUS, T-SHIRTS, LOW-PRICED CLOTHING. **Canal Jean Co.** (Soho), 504 Broadway, at Spring St.; **Hudson's** (East Village), Third Ave. at 13th St.; **Unique Clothing Warehouse** (East Village), 726 Broadway at Waverly Pl.

OUTLET AND THRIFT STORES. **Job Lot** (Lower Manhattan), 140 Church St. at Warren St.; **Romano** (midtown), Twelfth Ave. and W. 45th St.

PHOTOGRAPHIC EQUIPMENT. **47th St. Photo** (midtown), 67 W. 47th St.; **Hirsch** (midtown), 699 Third Ave. at E. 44th St.; **Willoughby's** (midtown), 110 W. 32nd St.

POSTERS. **L'Affiche Galerie** (Soho), 145 Spring St., for modern art posters; **Jerry Ohlinger** (Greenwich Village), 242 W. 14th St., for movie posters; **The Old Print Shop** (Gramercy Park), 150 Lexington Ave. at 29th St., for old art posters; **Triton Gallery** (midtown), 323 W. 45th St., for theater posters.

RECORDS. **Disc-O-Mat** (midtown), Lexington Ave. and E. 58th St.; **King Karol** (midtown), 126 W. 42nd St.; **Sam Goody's** (midtown), 51 W. 51st St., at Sixth Ave.; **Tower Records** (Noho), 692 Broadway at 4th St., with one of the country's largest selections, 400,000 records in all; **J and R Music World** (Lower Manhattan), 23 Park Row.

SPORTING GOODS. Herman's (midtown), 135 W. 42nd St. or 845 Third Ave. at 51st St.; **Paragon** (Gramercy Park), 867 Broadway at 17th St.

STEREO AND ELECTRONIC EQUIPMENT. ABC Trading Co. (Soho), 31 Canal St.; **Rabson's** (midtown), 119 W. 57th St., with equipment for European and foreign voltages; **Harvey Electronics** (midtown), 2 W. 45th at Fifth Ave., also with equipment for any voltage you need; **Uncle Steve** (Chinatown), 343 Canal St., with unbeatable prices.

TOYS. ❄ **F.A.O. Schwarz** (midtown), 767 Fifth Ave., between 58th and 59th Sts., the world's largest toyshop, with 100 boutiques and a children's barbershop—Shooting Star Hair Parlour.

SPECIAL EVENTS: For the exact schedule of events below, consult the **New York Convention and Visitors Bureau** (see "Tourist Information," above).

Chinese New Year (Jan.-Feb.): Ten days of gargantuan banquets, processions, fireworks, and the dragon parade through the streets of Chinatown. Colorful.

St. Patrick's Day Parade (March 17): On this feast day of the Irish, the sons and daughters of Erin parade up Fifth Ave.

Easter Parade (Easter Sunday): Parade on Fifth Ave. near St. Patrick's Cathedral; more like a fashion show than a religious occasion.

Washington Square Art Show (last weekend in May/first in June; last weekend in Aug./first in Sept.): Transforms the sidewalks of Washington Square and the surrounding streets into a huge open-air art gallery, where hundreds of artists exhibit their work.

52nd Street Festival (mid-June): Concerts, exhibitions, open-air restaurants; very lively.

Festa di San Antonio / Feast of St. Anthony of Padua (mid-June): An Italian street "festa" with music, games of chance, and glorious aromatic food for sale. In Little Italy—a spring must.

Lesbian and Gay Pride Day Parade (last Sunday in June): Since 1970, a yearly procession along Fifth Ave. of all New York's homosexual groups, with more than 80,000 marchers. Colorful.

Jazz Festival–New York (late June to early July): Two weeks of concerts around the city, with the biggest names in jazz. For information, call 787-2020.

New York Shakespeare Festival (June-Sept.): Free open-air performances of Shakespeare's and other great plays at the Delacorte Theater in Central Park.

Harbor Festival (July 1–4): Naval review and parade of boats in the harbor.

San Paolino Festival (mid-July): Spectacular procession of the "Giglio," a three-story tower borne on men's backs through the streets of Williamsburg; the biggest Italian religious festival in Brooklyn.

Greenwich Village Jazz Festival (late Aug. to early Sept.): The leading jazz performers play for ten days in a dozen clubs in the Village.

Caribbean Festival (Labor Day weekend): Starting on Thursday with nightly music performances representing different parts of the Caribbean—including reggae, steel band, and calypso—this colorful celebration culminates in an exuberant parade on the Monday of Labor Day. Spicy food, dancing in the streets—the closest thing to Mardi Gras in New York. Takes place on Eastern Pkwy. in Brooklyn.

Feast of San Gennaro (ten days in Sept.): The feast of the patron saint of Naples, and of New York's Little Italy. Pizza and chianti at every street corner in Little Italy. Plenty of atmosphere.

Columbus Day Parade (Oct. 12): Spectacular parade on Fifth Ave., commemorating the discovery of America by Christopher Columbus—the great Italian-American occasion. On the previous day (Oct. 11) there is an equally spectacular procession of the Latin American communities—the **Hispanic-American Day Parade.**

New York City Marathon (late Oct. to early Nov.): 20,000 marathoners compete along a course from the Staten Island end of the Verrazano-Narrows Bridge through Brooklyn, Queens, and the southern Bronx, and into Manhattan to the finish line in Central Park. Spectacular.

Macy's Thanksgiving Day Parade (fourth Thurs. in Nov.): The prettiest parade of the year, with tens of thousands of participants, bands, floats, and giant balloons in procession the whole length of Broadway. You might call it New York's Carnival. Don't miss it.

Times Square New Year (Dec. 31): If you want to wish yourself a Happy New Year, you have to be in Times Square for the 12 strokes of midnight. A must for New Yorkers since 1904.

SPORTS: New York boasts eight major-league teams in four professional sports:

Baseball (Apr.-Oct.): Mets, Shea Stadium, Queens (718/507-8499); Yankees, Yankee Stadium, Bronx (293-6000).

Basketball (Oct.-Apr.): Knicks, Madison Square Garden, midtown (564-4400); New Jersey Nets, Byrne Meadowlands Arena, E. Rutherford, N.J. (201/935-3900).

Football (Sept.-Dec.): Giants, Giants Stadium, E. Rutherford, N.J. (201/935-8222); Jets, Giants Stadium, E. Rutherford, N.J. (201/421-6600).

Ice Hockey (Sept.-Apr.): Islanders, Nassau Coliseum, Hempstead, Long Island (516/794-9100); Rangers, Madison Square Garden, midtown (563-8000).

Horse Racing

Aqueduct Race Track, Rockaway Blvd., Ozone Park, Queens (718/641-4700), with racing Jan.-May and Oct.-Dec.

Belmont Park Race Track, Hempstead Tpke. at Plainfield Ave., Belmont, Long Island (718/641-4700), with racing May-July and Sept.-Oct.

Meadowlands Racetrack, at the Meadowlands, E. Rutherford, N.J. (201/935-8500), with trotters Jan.-Aug. and thoroughbred racing Sept.-Dec.

Yonkers Raceway, Central and Yonkers Aves., Yonkers (914/968-4200), with racing Mar. to mid-Apr., June to mid-July, Sept.-Oct., and Dec.

STROLLS: ⚓ **Battery Park City** (Lower Manhattan), along West St. between Battery Pl. and Chambers St.: New residential complex on land reclaimed from the Hudson at the southern tip of Manhattan. The fill was excavated from the site of the nearby World Trade Center. Pleasant walkway along the river, and a splendid tropical garden in an enormous glass-roofed atrium 128 ft. (40 m) high (the Winter Garden at World Financial Center). A sight to be seen.

　　　　☀☖ **Chinatown,** around lower Mott, Bayard, and Pell Sts.: Picturesque Chinese district next door to Little Italy. Countless stalls, groceries, restaurants, and stores with souvenirs (often made in Japan). Uncommonly gaudy and crowded, especially on Mott St., Chinatown's main drag. Interesting little museum of Chinese culture, religion, and art at 8 Mott St., open daily. A stroll you shouldn't miss.

　　　　☖ **Columbus Ave.** (Upper West Side), around Lincoln Center: Long overlooked by well-to-do New Yorkers, this neighborhood regained its lost youth a couple of decades ago, and now attracts yuppies, artists, and intellectuals. Many trendy boutiques, fashionable restaurants, outdoor cafés. The style is well-heeled intelligentsia crossed with screwy. Amusing.

Diamond Row (midtown), W. 47th St. between Fifth and Sixth Aves.: The New York diamond-merchants' street, where a polyglot crowd of dealers haggles in all languages—from Flemish to Yiddish—over 80% of all the precious stones bought and sold in the U.S. Take a look at all the diamonds, rubies, and emeralds glittering in the display windows.

Fifth Ave. (midtown), between E. 48th and E. 59th Sts.: The stores here are a *Who's Who* of international high fashion: Cartier, Tiffany, Van Cleef & Arpels, Saks Fifth Avenue, Valentino, Gucci, Ted Lapidus. For well-lined bank accounts.

Greenwich Village, around Washington Square: New York's bohemian quarter, with old houses and narrow streets. Many inviting bars and little restaurants. Bookstores, art galleries, dress shops, antique dealers, jazz clubs, and souvenir stores are all there to tempt the idler. The people are an amusing intellectual-hippy mix, but you'll find junkies here too. Although it appeals blatantly to the tourist trade, it's worth a visit.

Harlem, between Central Park North (110th St.) and W. 155th St.: "The black capital of America," with several interesting museums, the Apollo Theater, and some lovely 19th-century houses, particularly along Striver's Row (139th St. between Seventh and Eighth Aves.), which are worth visiting. Don't walk alone after dark; the rate of deaths by violence is, according to police statistics, twice as high in Harlem as in the rest of Manhattan.

Little Italy, around Mulberry St.: With its typically Italian grocery stores, bars, *trattorias,* and funeral parlors, this is a postcard Italy of chianti, pizza, and espresso—but it's being slowly swallowed by its neighbor, Chinatown. Guaranteed local color, especially on such saints' days as San Antonio (mid-June) or San Gennaro (mid-Sept.). Worth the detour.

Soho, around W. Broadway south of Houston St.: The artists' quarter, with art galleries, far-out boutiques, and trendy restaurants. Many lofts—former commercial or light-industrial space converted into artists' studios or luxury apartments for yuppies. Lovely old cast-iron façades around Broome and Greene Sts. Not safe late at night.

Times Square and the Theater District (midtown), Broadway between W. 42nd and W. 52nd Sts.: Dozens of theaters and movie houses with their neon signs flashing, but also porno houses and the headquarters of the retail drug traffic. Currently in the midst of a vast urban-renewal project. Fascinating—but imprudent alone after midnight.

THEME PARKS: ⚜ ⚱ **Coney Island Astroland Park,** W. 10th St. between Surf Ave. and the Boardwalk, Brooklyn (718/372-0275): The granddaddy of American amusement parks, born 1884. Numerous attractions, including the famous 60-year-old giant roller-coaster *Cyclone,* and a spectacular ferris wheel. Kitsch but picturesque. Overrun by New Yorkers on summer weekends. Open weekends only, Apr. and May; daily, June to mid-Sept.; weekends only to mid-Oct.; closed the rest of the year.

Six Flags Great Adventure, in Jackson, N.J., 82 mi. (131 km) SW on the N.J. Tpke., I-195E, and N.J. 537S (201/928-3500): Enormous 450-acre (182-ha.) theme park with more than 100 attractions —carousels and giant roller-coasters, as well as a safari zoo with 2,000 wild animals which you see from your car. Variety and other shows. Open daily, Apr.-Sept.; closed the rest of the year.

WINTER SPORTS RESORTS: Although most New York skiers prefer the slopes of the Adirondacks (see "Farther Afield," below), there are some very acceptable resorts nearer the city, notably the following in the Catskills:

🔔 **Bellayre Mountain,** 154 mi. (246 km) NW on I-87N and N.Y. 28W (914/254-5600): 7 lifts. Open Dec.-Mar. For snow conditions, call toll free 800/942-6904.

🔔 **Holiday Mountain,** 101 mi. (162 km) NW along I-87N and N.Y. 17W (914/796-3161): 9 lifts. Open Dec.-Mar.

🔭 **Hunter Mountain Ski Bowl,** 155 mi. (248 km) NW on I-87N and N.Y. 23A West (518/263-4223): 16 lifts. Open Nov.-Apr.

ZOOS: ☀ 🔭 **Bronx Zoo,** Fordham Rd. and Bronx River Pkwy., Bronx (367-1010): One of the world's largest, with 3,600 creatures of 700 different species on 252 acres (102 ha.). Although the overall layout of a zoo dating from 1899 has to be somewhat antiquated, this one has some interesting reconstructions of natural habitats: "Wild Asia," "Jungle World," "World of Darkness" for nocturnal animals, etc. The "World of Birds" is a splendid collection of tropical birds. You can visit the zoo by monorail or by a miniature safari train. Reached by subway directly from Manhattan: East Side IRT (Green) Line no. 5 to E. Tremont Ave. Very well worth visiting. Open daily.

🔔 **New York Aquarium,** Boardwalk and W. 8th St., Coney Island, Brooklyn (718/266-8500): Very well-stocked aquarium where you can see 200 species of marine creatures, from the giant octopus to the shark and from the beluga whale to the electric eel. Shows by trained sea creatures. Reached by subway directly from Manhattan: IND (Orange) Lines F or D to W. 8th St. Worth the trip. Open daily.

☀🔔 **Staten Island Zoo,** Barrett Park, 614 Broadway, W. New Brighton, Staten Island (718/442-3100). Best known for its reptiles, this interesting little zoo exhibits animals as strange as they are rarely seen, including 32 varieties of rattlesnake (the world's largest collection), scorpions, alligators, crocodiles, and other reptiles and amphibians. Fascinating. Open daily.

ACCOMMODATIONS

See the listing of toll-free numbers in the Appendix.

Room Rates in New York	
B (Budget)	up to $30
I (Inexpensive)	$30–$60
M (Moderate)	$60–$90
E (Expensive)	$90–$140
VE (Very Expensive)	$140 and up

PERSONAL FAVORITES (in order of preference)

🏰🏰🏰🏰🏰 **Carlyle** (Upper East Side), Madison Ave. at E. 76th St., NY 10021 (212/744-1600). 500 rms, A/C, color TV, in-rm movies. AE, CB, DC, MC, V. Garage $30, two rests. (including Café Carlyle), bar, 24-hr rm svce, nightclub, concierge. *Note:* Splendid and refined, w. rooms for servants and luxury kennels, the Carlyle is the most elegant and chic hotel in New York, favored by the Kennedy family among others. Spacious and luxuriously inviting rms w. mini-bars and VCRs. Exemplary, personalized svce. Discreet, plush ambience. Perfection—at a price. Good rest., ideal for lunch. Very popular piano bar. 80% of the rms are rented by the year. Voluptuous luxury in its purest form. Probably the best hotel in the U.S. **VE**

🐚🐚🐚🐚 **Sherry Netherland** (Upper East Side), 781 Fifth Ave. (at 59th St.), NY 10022 (212/355-2800). 370 rms, A/C, color TV, in-rm movies. AE. Garage $26, rest., bar, rm svce, nightclub, hrdrsr, crib $10. *Note:* Quiet and distinguished, with one of New York's best locations, facing Central Park and a stone's throw from the smart Fifth Ave. stores. The building is slightly kitsch Gothic Revival, but the rms and suites are very elegant, some w. balconies or terraces. Many clients rent by the year. Exceptionally polished svce; Italian rest. which doesn't deserve its high reputation. The only grand hotel in New York which accepts only one credit card. One of the dozen best hotels in the country; the movie stars' favorite. **VE**

🐚🐚🐚 **Plaza Athénée** (Upper East Side), 34 E. 64th St., NY 10021 (212/734-9100; toll free 800/255-3050). 160 rms. A/C, color TV, in-rm movies. AE, CB, DC, MC, V. Valet garage $30, rest. (La Régence), bar, 24-hr rm svce, free crib, concierge. *Note:* This newcomer on the New York hotel scene is an outpost of the luxurious and very exclusive Paris hotel of the same name. Same refined elegance, same intimate, protected atmosphere. Remarkably comfortable rms and suites w. French furniture and refrigerators, some w. private terraces, solariums, and dining rms. Flawless personalized svce. Remarkable rest. w. sumptuous turn-of-the-century décor. Lots of class, but pricey; one duplex suite goes for $1,800 a night. Belongs to Britain's Trusthouse Forte hotel chain. Draws VIPs and leaders of the European financial community. Very near Central Park. **VE**

🐚🐚🐚 **Grand Hyatt New York** (midtown), Park Ave. at E. 42nd St., NY 10017 (212/883-1234; toll free, see Hyatt). 1,400 rms, A/C, color TV, in-rm movies. AE, CB, DC, MC, V. Valet garage $24, two rests. (including Trumpet's), bars, 24-hr rm svce, nightclub, boutiques, drugstore, free crib. *Note:* Ultramodern, w. a tinge of poetry, built by Donald Trump, New York's leading real-estate developer. The huge 30-story glass façade reflects the surrounding high-rises. Splendid four-story lobby adorned by a giant sculpture. Luxurious and comfortable rms, but often short on space. Efficient multilingual help; exemplary rm svce. Unhappily no physical-fitness facilities in the hotel. Mediocre rest. Interesting wknd discounts. Adjacent to Grand Central Terminal on the site of the old Commodore Hotel. VIP suites on the top two floors. **VE**

☀🐚🐚🐚 **Waldorf-Astoria** (midtown), 301 Park Ave. (at E. 49th St.), NY 10022 (212/355-3000; toll free, see Hilton). 1,752 rms, A/C, color TV, in-rm movies. AE, CB, DC, MC, V. Valet garage $22, five rests. (including Bull & Bear), three bars, 24-hr rm svce, nightclub, hrdrsr, boutiques, free crib, concierge. *Note:* A landmark since 1931; everybody of any importance on the planet has stayed in this immense rococo caravanserai. The art deco lobby is superb, and the *Starlight Roof* is the only ballroom in New York whose roof opens to the stars. The rms have been entirely redecorated and refurnished at a cost of $150 million. Very good rm svce; inadequate reception. Excellent location. A favorite w. foreigners, since the help speaks 37 languages. Luxurious VIP suites in the adjoining Waldorf Towers. Interesting wknd packages. **VE**

🐚🐚 **Doral Tuscany Hotel** (midtown), 120 E. 39th St., NY 10016 (212/686-1600; toll free 800/847-4078). 127 rms, A/C, color TV, in-rm movies. AE, CB, DC, MC, V. Garage $18, rest., bar, 24-hr rm svce, nightclub, free crib. *Note:* Remarkable reception and atmosphere in one of New York's best small hotels. Spacious, elegant rms w. refrigerators and VCRs.

Faultless comfort; polished svce. Regular clientele. A favorite w. those in-the-know, half a block from Park Ave. Good rest. (Da Vinci). Interesting wknd discounts. **VE**

☼🎎 **Algonquin** (midtown), 59 W. 44th St., NY 10036 (212/840-6800). 160 rms, A/C, color TV. AE, CB, DC, MC, V. Garage $18, rest., bar, rm svce, drugstore, crib $12. *Note:* Turn-of-the-century hotel popular w. distinguished writers and theater-goers, since it's a stone's throw from Broadway. The 1900 décor is a little wilted but the reception and svce are still attentive. The rms are cosily old-fashioned. The Blue Bar is famous; the after-theater buffet is fashionable but so-so. There's a slight aura of the past, for those who hanker for the bohemian 1930s. Sir John Gielgud and Lord Olivier have long been among the hotel's titled patrons. Designated historic landmark. **E**

🛏🛏 **Gramercy Park Hotel** (Gramercy Park), 2 Lexington Ave. (at E. 21st St.), NY 10010 (212/475-4320; toll free 800/221-4083). 509 rms, A/C, color TV. AE, CB, DC, MC, V. Parking adjoining, rest., bar, rm svce. *Note:* Quiet, agreeable 1920s hotel far from Manhattan's high-rises. Courteous reception and svce. Comfortably renovated. Regular clientele w. many Europeans. Relaxed, inviting atmosphere. The best rms overlook Gramercy Park. Very acceptable rest. A good place to stay. **E**

🛏 **Tudor Hotel** (midtown), 304 E. 42nd St., NY 10017 (212/986-8800). 525 rms, A/C, color TV. AE, CB, DC, MC, V. Garage $16, rest., bar, rm svce. *Note:* Good value a couple of blocks from the U.N., w. a very cosmopolitan clientele. Vaguely Tudor décor; rms skimpy but comfortable enough. Facilities entirely renovated. The svce leaves something to be desired. **M–E**

🛏 **Best Western Milford Plaza** (midtown), 270 W. 45th St., NY 10036 (212/869-3600; toll free, see Best Western). 1,310 rms, A/C, color TV, in-rm movies. AE, CB, DC, MC, V. Garage $12, two rests., bar, rm svce, nightclub. *Note:* The old Royal Manhattan renovated and improved. Rms small and functional at best; most have refrigerators. Many package tours and airline crews come here from abroad. The only plus: accommodation and show-ticket packages at very attractive prices ("Show Time New York"). In the heart of the Broadway theater district—not a safe neighborhood after midnight. **M–E**

Other Hotels (From top bracket to budget)

🛏🛏🛏 **Marriott Marquis** (midtown), 1535 Broadway (at W. 44th St.), NY 10036 (212/398-1900; toll free, see Marriott). 1,876 rms, color TV, in-rm movies. AE, CB, DC, MC, V. Valet garage $20, health club, sauna, three rests. (including The View revolving rest. on the top floor), coffeeshop, four bars, 24-hr rm svce, theater, boutiques, concierge. *Note:* The most eye-catching luxury hotel in New York: an ultramodern 52-story high-rise by the architect John Portman. The glass-walled lobby is 46 floors high, w. fountains, indoor gardens, and glass-walled elevators. Exceptionally spacious, comfortable rms, w. unobstructed views of Manhattan from the top two floors. Impersonal but efficient svce. As in all Marriotts, the rests. are mediocre. Overlooks Times Square and the theater district. Two VIP floors. **VE**

🛏🛏🛏 **Regency Hotel** (Upper East Side), 540 Park Ave. (at 61st St.), NY 10021 (212/759-4100; toll free, see Loews). 350 rms, A/C, color TV, in-rm movies. AE, CB, DC, MC, V. Valet garage $25, health club, sauna, rest. (540 Park), bar, 24-hr rm svce, nightclub, hrdrsr, concierge, crib $10. *Note:* Favored by the financial upper crust. All the charm of a European luxury hotel; elegant rms w. mini-bars and period furniture, some w.

kitchenettes. Quiet, distinguished atmosphere. Excellent rm svce. The very good rest. is the ideal place for a working breakfast or lunch. Many rms rented by the year. Elegant and urbane. Recently underwent a $15-million facelift. **VE**

♔♔♔ **Drake Swissôtel** (midtown), 440 Park Ave. (at E. 56th St.), NY 10022 (212/421-0900; toll free 800/372-5369). 640 rms, A/C, color TV, in-rm movies. AE, CB, DC, MC, V. Valet garage $20, two rests. (including Lafayette), bar, 24-hr rm svce, nightclub, free crib, concierge. *Note:* Since it was bought by Swiss interests this venerable, and indeed somewhat decrepit, pile has been restored to its former luster by a multi-million-dollar facelift. Its spacious peach-and-ivory rooms w. marble bathrooms and refrigerators, exemplary svce, and excellent rest. (Lafayette) supervised by the great French chef Louis Outhier, combine to make it one of the best places to stay on Park Ave. Free a.m. limo to Wall St. Draws many business travelers from Europe. **VE**

♔♔♔ **Essex House Nikko** (formerly the Marriott; midtown), 160 Central Park South, NY 10019 (212/247-0300; toll free 800/645-5687). 715 rms, A/C, color TV, in-rm movies. AE, CB, DC, MC, V. Valet garage $25, rest. (Devereux's), bar, 24-hr rm svce, piano bar, hrdrsr, free crib, concierge. *Note:* Elegant, comfortable older hotel whose 40 stories overlook Central Park. Slightly antiquated décor but a pleasant atmosphere and attentive reception. Spacious, entirely renovated rms, some w. refrigerators, the best w. park views. Very international clientele, and the help speaks 18 languages. Belongs to the Nikko hotel chain of Japan, a subsidiary of Japan Air Lines. Acceptable rest.; well-equipped business center. **VE**

♔♔♔ **Grand Bay Hotel at Equitable Center** (midtown), 152 W. 51st St., NY 10019 (212/765-1900; toll free, see Preferred). 179 rms, A/C, color TV, in-rm movies. AE, CB, DC, MC, V. Valet garage $25, two rests. (including Mezzanine), bar, rm svce, concierge on every floor. *Note:* Brand-new (1987) grand hotel in the great European luxury hotel tradition. The decoration and furnishings are sumptuous, w. Italian marble, Oriental rugs, crystal chandeliers, and an abundance of works of art. Remarkably spacious, comfortable rms w. mini-bars, two TV sets, and marble bathrooms. Ultrapolished svce. Mediocre rests. Free a.m. limo to Wall St. Big business clientele. Admirably located halfway between Rockefeller Center and the theater district, on the site of the old Taft Hotel. **VE**

♔♔♔ **Helmsley Palace Hotel** (midtown), 455 Madison Ave. (at E. 49th St.), NY 10022 (212/888-7000; toll free 800/321-2323). 964 rms, A/C, color TV, in-rm movies. AE, CB, DC, MC, V. Garage $30, two rests. (including the Trianon), two bars, 24-hr rm svce, nightclub, hrdrsr, boutiques, free crib, concierge. *Note:* Extravagant grand hotel deluxe built at a cost of $100 million. The attempt to integrate the modern 51-story glass tower w. an 1882 Renaissance revival house, the Villard Mansion, doesn't come off. The opulence is often strident but the comfort and rm svce are incomparable. Opposite St. Patrick's Cathedral. One triplex suite rents for $1,800 a night plus taxes and svce. Very successful since its 1980 opening. **VE**

♔♔♔ **Helmsley Park Lane** (midtown), 36 Central Park South, NY 10019 (212/371-4000; toll free 800/321-2323). 640 rms, A/C, color TV, in-rm movies. AE, CB, DC, MC, V. Garage $28, rest., bar, rm svce, nightclub, hrdrsr, free crib. *Note:* 46 floors of glass and steel overlooking Central Park. Huge, very comfortable rms w. refrigerators, the best w. park views. Big business clientele. Rm svce on the surly side. The Park Room is a so-so rest. Multilingual help. **VE**

♔♔♔ **New York Hilton and Tower** (midtown), 1335 Ave. of the Americas (at W. 54th St.), NY 10019 (212/586-7000; toll free, see Hilton). 2,117 rms, A/C, color TV, in-rm movies. AE, CB, DC, MC, V. Valet garage $24, rest., coffeeshop, three bars, 24-hr rm svce, disco, hrdrsr, drugstore, free crib. *Note:* Huge 46-floor tourist mill. Modern, functional rms, some very small. Public areas and rests. crowded and noisy. Svce often overburdened. A new 1,200-rm tower will make this one of the largest hotels in the world. Excellent location. Draws American and Japanese business travelers. Interesting wknd discounts. VIP suites in the Executive Tower from the 39th to the 44th floors. Business Center. **VE**

Parker Meridien (midtown), 118 W. 57th St., NY 10019 (212/245-5000; toll free, see Meridien). 697 rms, A/C, color TV, in-rm movies. AE, CB, DC, MC, V. Valet garage $20, pool, health club, sauna, tennis court, two rests. (including Maurice), bar, 24-hr rm svce, nightclub, crib $20. *Note:* The first French-owned hotel in New York, belonging to the hotel chain of Air France. Unimaginative modern building, but elegant, refined interior w. many works of art. Rms on the diminutive side, w. mini-bars. Very complete fitness facilities. Hard-working rm svce. Very good nouvelle cuisine rest. Business clientele. A favorite w. those in-the-know. Interesting wknd discounts. A stone's throw from Central Park. **VE**

Morgan's (midtown), 237 Madison Ave. (at E. 38th St.), NY 10016 (212/686-0300; toll free 800/334-3408). 114 rms, A/C, color TV, in-rm movies. AE, CB, DC, MC, V. Valet garage $20, rest. (Pierpoint Restaurant), bar, 24-hr rm svce. *Note:* Conceived by the promoters of the famous old Studio 54 and the Palladium, Steve Rubell and Ian Schrager, Morgan's is the most original, the most amusing, and the most "with-it" luxury hotel in Manhattan. White, black, and gray décor w. hi-tech stainless-steel bathrooms by Andrée Putnam. Smallish rms w. *Star Wars* TV/stereo/hi-fi equipment. The help—young, smiling, and relaxed—wear uniforms designed by Calvin Klein and Giorgio Armani. Movie stars, leading dress designers, and trendy artists stay here (Cher, Margaux Hemingway, and Giorgio Armani are regulars). The "in" place. **VE**

The Pierre (Upper East Side), 2 E. 61st St. (at Fifth Ave.), NY 10021 (212/838-8000; toll free, see Four Seasons). 197 rms, A/C, color TV, in-rm movies. AE, CB, DC, MC, V. Garage $22, rest. (Café Pierre), bar, rm svce, nightclub, hrdrsr, boutiques, free crib, concierge. *Note:* The Pierre long enjoyed a reputation as New York's best hotel, but doesn't deserve it today. Plush but depressing interior decoration; svce sometimes defective. Wonderfully situated opposite Central Park. So-so rest. Thronged w. aristocratic and/or wealthy Europeans. Along w. the Stanhope, one of New York's most expensive hotels. **VE**

The Royalton (midtown), 44 W. 44th St. at Ave. of the Americas, NY 10036 (212/730-1344). 175 rms, A/C, color TV, in-rm movies. AE, CB, DC, MC, V. Garage $26, rest. (Royalton Grill), bar, 24-hr rm svce, concierge. *Note:* A 90-year-old neo-Georgian limestone building turned into a haven for well-traveled sophisticates by superstar of french design Philippe Starck. Reopened in Oct. 88 after 18 months and more than $40 million renovation program. Spacious suitelike rms w. minimalist décor, startling contemporary furniture and stainless steel bathrooms (some rms w. working fireplaces). Spectacular columned lobby that stretches from 43rd to 44th Sts. Faultless svce. The Royalton Grill restaurant is notable. Same management as the famed Morgan's (see above). **VE**

Stanhope Hotel (Upper East Side), 995 Fifth Ave. (at 81st St.), NY 10028 (212/288-5800; toll free 800/828-1123). 117 rms (of which 91 are suites), A/C, color TV, in-rm movies. AE, CB, DC, MC, V. No private parking; rest. (Stanhope Dining Room), bar, rm svce, nightclub, free crib. *Note:* On elegant Fifth Ave. opposite the Metropolitan Museum of Art, this small, intimate, ultra-luxurious hotel was completely renovated in 1986 at a cost of $26 million. Its discreet, refined decorative scheme weds Louis XVI furniture, Baccarat crystal chandeliers, impressionist paintings, cream-colored leather and silk. Free Chanel toiletries in every bathroom. Extremely polished svce. The rest. is of the highest order, but the prices are even higher than that. Among the most expensive hotels in town, where single rooms start at $275 a night. **VE**

United Nations Plaza (midtown), 1 United Nations Plaza (at E. 44th St.), NY 10017 (212/355-3400; toll free, see Preferred). 444 rms, A/C, color TV, in-rm movies. AE, CB, DC, MC, V. Valet garage $26, pool, health club, sauna, tennis court, rest. (Ambassador Grill), bar, rm svce, free crib. *Note:* The hotel begins on the 28th floor of an ultramodern 40-story glass tower by architect Kevin Roche. Pool and tennis court in the sky. Comfortable, inviting rms w. refrigerators, all w. superb view of New York. Efficient svce. Overlooks the East River and the U.N. building. Good French rest. Clientele of diplomats and big-business travelers; free a.m. Wall St. limo. A favorite w. those in-the-know. **VE**

Vista International Hilton (Lower Manhattan), 3 World Trade Center, NY 10048 (212/938-9100; toll free, see Hilton). 829 rms, A/C, color TV, in-rm movies. AE, CB, DC, MC, V. Garage $20, pool, health club, sauna, tennis court, two rests. (including the American Harvest), two bars, 24-hr rm svce, concierge. *Note:* The only hotel of quality in the Wall St. district. Ultramodern and comfortable; very inviting rms w. mini-bars, some w. Statue of Liberty views. Comprehensive physical-fitness facilities. Business clientele. Good rest. specializing in modern American cuisine (The American Harvest). Not really suitable for tourists; the neighborhood is almost deserted at night. **VE**

Barbizon (Upper East Side), 140 E. 63rd St., NY 10021 (212/838-5700; toll free 800/344-1212). 350 rms, A/C, color TV, in-rm movies. AE, CB, DC, MC, V. Garage $15, health club, rest. (Barbizon Restaurant), coffeeshop, bar, rm svce, crib $10. *Note:* A true landmark, which for years accepted women only, this '30s hotel in a tall, austere neo-Gothic tower now caters to travelers of both sexes. Rms a little cramped, but pleasant and comfortable. Some terraced suites have a wonderful view of the Manhattan skyline. Excellent svce; fine location a block or two from the smart stores of Lexington Ave. Interesting wknd discounts. **E–VE**

Dorset (midtown), 30 W. 54th St., NY 10019 (212/247-7300; toll free 800/227-2348). 210 rms, A/C, color TV, in-rm movies. AE, MC, V. Garage $20, rest., coffeeshop, bar, rm svce, free crib. *Note:* Discreet, charming, polished small hotel a stone's throw from the Museum of Modern Art and the smart Fifth Ave. stores. Inviting, comfortable rms, the best overlooking the interior court. Coffeeshop very popular w. TV and show-business people at lunchtime. A fine place. **E–VE**

Mayflower (Upper West Side), 15 Central Park West, NY 10023 (212/265-0060; toll free 800/223-4164). 577 rms, A/C, color TV. AE, CB, DC, MC, V. No private parking; rest. (Conservatory), bar, rm svce, free crib. *Note:* The favorite place to stay for theater-goers, music lovers, and opera buffs; Lincoln Center is a few minutes' walk. Décor and furnishings completely renovated; spacious, comfortable rms (ask for one overlooking Central Park). Cordial, efficient svce; pleasant but expensive rest. Interesting wknd discounts. **E–VE**

New York Penta (formerly the Statler Hilton; midtown), 401 Seventh Ave. (at W. 33rd St.), NY 10001 (212/736-5000; toll free 800/225-3456). 1,700 rms, A/C, color TV, in-rm movies. AE, CB,

DC, MC, V. Garage $22, three rests. (including the Globetrotter), two bars, rm svce, nightclub, hrdrsr, boutiques, concierge, crib $15. *Note:* Huge group-and-convention hotel across the street from Madison Square Garden and five blocks from the Javits Convention Center. Recently renovated at a cost of $35 million. Comfortable rms, some too small; svce sometimes overworked. **E–VE**

Novotel (midtown), 226 W. 52nd St. (at Broadway), NY 10019 (212/315-0100, toll free 800/221-3185). 478 rms, A/C, color TV, in-rm movies. AE, CB, DC, MC, V. Valet parking $16, rest. (Cafe Skylight), two bars, rm svce, nightclub, free crib. *Note:* The second French hotel in New York, on the top 17 floors of an ungraceful new building a few blocks from Times Square. Ultramodern furnishings; spacious, well-equipped rms; good rests.; inviting wine bar. Reception and svce in the French manner. Business clientele. **E–VE**

Roosevelt (midtown), Madison Ave. at E. 45th St., NY 10017 (212/661-9600; toll free 800/344-1212). 1,070 rms, A/C, color TV. AE, CB, DC, MC, V. Valet garage $24, two rests. (including Crawdaddy's), two bars, rm svce, concierge. *Note:* One of the best locations in the city, in the heart of the midtown business district, two blocks from Grand Central Terminal and the airport limo for Kennedy and La Guardia. Massive, unattractive building, but renovated, comfortable interior. Good Créole rest. popular at lunchtime. Svce a little undependable. Business clientele. **E–VE**

Sheraton Centre (formerly the Americana; midtown), Seventh Ave. at W. 52nd St., NY 10019 (212/581-1000; toll free, see Sheraton). 1,818 rms, A/C, color TV, in-rm movies. AE, CB, DC, MC, V. Garage $22, two rests., coffeeshop, two bars, rm svce, disco, hrdrsr, drugstore, free crib. *Note:* Enormous 50-story concrete tower crowded w. groups and conventions. The top five floors have luxurious VIP suites. Functionally comfortable; svce sometimes defective. The favorite hotel of former President Carter. Recently renovated. Interesting wknd and vacation packages. Near the theater district. **E–VE**

Days Inns New York (formerly the Holiday Inn Coliseum; midtown), 440 W. 57th St., NY 10019 (212/581-8100; toll free, see Days Inn). 603 rms, A/C, color TV, in-rm movies. AE, CB, DC, MC, V. Garage $16, open-air pool (in summer), rest., bar, rm svce. *Note:* The most attractive things about this reasonably modern 18-floor motel are its location near Lincoln Center and its rooftop pool in summer. Functionally comfortable; svce undependable. Caters to groups and conventions (special rates). **E–VE**

Ramada Inn (midtown), 790 Eighth Ave. (at W. 49th St.), NY 10019 (212/581-7000; toll free, see Ramada Inns). 366 rms, A/C, color TV, in-rm movies. AE, CB, DC, MC, V. Garage $16, pool, rest., bar, valet svce, free crib. *Note:* Typical convention and package-tour hotel. Rms quite large and functionally comfortable. Reception and svce undependable. Well-located near the theater district. Rooftop swimming pool (open in summer). **E**

Roger Smith Winthrop (midtown), 501 Lexington Ave. (at E. 47th St.), NY 10017 (212/755-1400; toll free 800/445-0277). 183 rms, A/C, color TV. AE, CB, DC, MC, V. Public parking adjacent; rest., bar, free crib. *Note:* Older, elegant small hotel in the heart of midtown. Spacious, comfortable rms done in pastel shades, all w. refrigerators and some w. terraces and fireplaces. Free breakfast on wknds. Good svce; central location. **E**

Century Paramount (midtown), 235 W. 46th St., NY 10036 (212/764-5500; toll free 800/223-9868). 600 rms, A/C, color TV. AE, CB, DC, MC, V. Garage $12, coffeeshop, bar, hrdrsr, crib $15.

Note: Small but quite comfortable rms; the svce falls short. Package tours and flight attendants—much of the clientele is foreign. Always crowded. In the heart of the theater district. **M–E**

Comfort Inn Murray Hill (midtown), 42 W. 35th St., NY 10001 (212/947-0200; toll free 800/228-5150). 118 rms, A/C, cable color TV. AE, CB, DC, MC, V. No private parking; rest., bar, free crib. *Note:* Completely renovated at a cost of $4.5 million, this once run-down small hotel now offers you modern, comfortable, inviting rms. Friendly, efficient svce. Business clientele. Free morning coffee. A couple of blocks from the Garment District and the Empire State Building. **E**

Edison (midtown), 228 W. 47th St., NY 10036 (212/840-5000; toll free 800/223-1900). 1,000 rms, A/C, color TV. AE, CB, DC, MC, V. Garage $12, rest., coffeeshop, two bars, free crib. *Note:* Massive, antiquated 50-year-old hotel; deplorable svce but functionally comfortable. Recently renovated. Clientele largely of groups and Europeans. Smack in the middle of the theater district. Cafeteria (Polish Tea Room) much frequented by theater people. **M–E**

Empire (Upper West Side), 63rd St. and Broadway, NY 10023 (212/265-7400; toll free 800/223-9868). 500 rms, A/C, cable color TV. AE, CB, DC, MC, V. Parking $12, adjoining rest., bar, valet svce, free crib. *Note:* Pleasant, comfortable hotel a stone's throw from Lincoln Center. The rms (some without bath) have been completely renovated. A fine place; try to reserve well ahead. Special rates for foreign visitors. Very good value. **M–E**

Esplanade (Upper West Side), 305 West End Ave. (at 74th St.), NY 10023 (212/874-5000; toll free 800/367-1763). 200 rms, A/C, cable color TV. AE, CB, DC, MC, V. No private parking. *Note:* Charming, older hotel in the heart of the Upper West Side. Huge, agreeably decorated rms, some w. kitchenettes, the best w. views of Riverside Park and the Hudson River. Svce w. a smile. Interesting wknd discounts. Clientele of regulars. **M–E**

Gorham (midtown), 136 W. 55th St., NY 10019 (212/245-1800). 116 rms, A/C, color TV. AE, CB, DC, MC, V. Parking adjoining, $16; rest., bar, rm svce, crib $10. *Note:* One of the best of New York's charming small hotels. Spacious, comfortable rms w. kitchenettes and refrigerators. Pleasing reception and svce. Favored by Europeans. Excellent value. **M–E**

Palace International (Gramercy Park), 429 Park Ave. South (at 29th St.), NY 10016 (212/532-4860; toll free 800/922-7002). 45 rms, A/C, cable color TV. AE, CB, DC, MC, V. Parking $20, 24-hr rm svce. *Note:* Built in the early 1980s, this modern hotel off the beaten tourist path is one of New York's best buys. Its reasonable rates and proximity to the Garment District attract textile and clothing executives. Inviting, comfortable rms; good svce; good overall value. Interesting wknd discounts. **M–E**

Salisbury (midtown), 123 W. 57th St., NY 10019 (212/246-1300; toll free 800/223-0680). 320 rms, A/C, color TV. AE, CB, DC, MC, V. No parking; coffeeshop, rm svce, free crib. *Note:* Opposite Carnegie Hall, this charming, scrupulously clean old hotel is run by the Calvary Baptist Church; hence no alcoholic beverages are served in Salisbury's Café. Vast, comfortable rms, most w. refrigerators; friendly reception and svce. Caters mostly to musicians and theater-goers. Good value. **M–E**

Wellington (midtown), 55th St. and Seventh Ave., NY 10019 (212/247-3900; toll free 800/652-1212). 700 rms, A/C, color TV. AE, CB, DC, MC, V. Garage $14, rest., coffeeshop, bar. *Note:* Slightly cramped rms, some w. kitchenettes, recently renovated. Very acceptable standard of comfort. Attracts musicians (Carnegie Hall is two blocks away) and groups. Good value overall. **M–E**

🔑 **Wentworth** (midtown), 59 W. 46th St., NY 10036 (212/ 719-2300; toll free 800/223-1900). 195 rms, A/C, color TV. AE, CB, DC, MC, V. No private parking; rm svce. *Note:* Near as it is to the Garment District, this is a favorite hotel for out-of-town buyers. Aging and functionally comfortable, it offers good value. Clean, prettily decorated rms; courteous, efficient svce. **M–E**

🔑 **Wales** (Upper East Side), 1295 Madison Ave. (at E. 92nd St.), NY 10128 (212/876-6000). 97 rms, A/C, cable color TV. AE, CB, DC, MC, V. No private parking; coffeeshop (Sarabeth's Kitchen), rm svce. *Note:* Modest, well-run turn-of-the-century hotel. Rms a little confining, but inviting and scrupulously clean; most have kitchenettes, and some overlook Central Park. Pleasant coffeeshop. A nice district, a 10-min. walk from the Metropolitan Museum of Art. Good value; regular clientele. **M–E**

🔑 **Excelsior** (Upper West Side), 45 W. 81st St., NY 10024 (212/ 362-9200; toll free 800/368-4575). 150 rms, A/C, color TV. AE, MC, V. Nearby parking, coffeeshop, valet svce. *Note:* Older family-style hotel a block from Central Park and the Hayden Planetarium. Rms w. kitchenettes. Very acceptable comfort level. The rms on the uppermost floors have a fine view of the city. Pleasant neighborhood; good value. **I–M**

🔑 **Times Square Hotel** (midtown), 255 W. 43rd St., NY 10036 (212/354-7900; toll free 800/242-4343). 700 rms, A/C, cable color TV. AE, DC, MC, V. Free parking, 24-hr coffeeshop, 24-hr rm svce, free breakfast. *Note:* One of the best buys in Manhattan. The rms are commendably comfortable, and you get some bonuses thrown in, such as free breakfast and free parking, despite the unbeatably low prices. A stone's throw from Broadway and the theater district, but don't go for a solitary walk here after midnight. Ideal for tight budgets. **M**

Airport Accommodations

🔑🔑🔑 **Holiday Inn JFK,** 144-02 135th Ave., Jamaica (Queens), NY 11436 (718/659-0200; toll free, see Holiday Inns). Free parking, pool, health club, sauna, rest., (Claudine's) bar, rm svce, nightclub, crib $10. *Note:* Brand-new; the first hotel built near JFK in 20 years. Comfort and facilities above the Holiday Inn average. Rms perfectly soundproofed, spacious, and well designed. Efficient svce. Free airport limo. Caters to groups and business travelers; ideal for a stopover between flights. **E–VE**

🔑🔑 **Holiday Inn La Guardia,** 100-15 Ditmars Blvd., East Elmhurst (Queens), NY 11369 (718/898-1225; toll free, see Holiday Inns). 224 rms, A/C, color TV, in-rm movies. AE, CB, DC, MC, V. Free parking, rest., bar, rm svce, nightclub, free crib. *Note:* A typical Holiday Inn 3 min. from La Guardia. Completely renovated rms w. refrigerators. Free 24-hr airport limo. Efficient svce. **E**

YMCA / Youth Hostels

International House (Upper West Side), 500 Riverside Dr. (at 122nd St.), NY 10027 (212/316-8400). 500 rms. Students' residence open from the end of May to the end of Aug. Good facilities.

McBurney YMCA (midtown), 215 W. 23rd St., NY 10011 (212/741-9226). 270 rms. Men only. Limited standard of comfort. Health club.

Sloane House YMCA (midtown), 356 W. 34th St., NY 10001 (212/760-1707). 1,500 rms. The most comfortable and inviting YMCA in New York.

Men, women, couples, and families w. children. Coffeeshop, health club.

Vanderbilt YMCA (midtown), 224 E. 47th St., NY 10017 (212/755-2410). 435 rms. Men, women, and families. Good facilities (pool, health club), coffeeshop. Down the road from the U.N.

West Side YMCA (Upper West Side), 5 W. 63rd St., NY 10023 (212/787-4400). 558 rms. Men, a limited number of women. Pool, health club, coffeeshop. A stone's throw from Lincoln Center.

RESTAURANTS

New York Restaurant Prices	
(per person, excluding drinks and service charges)	
B (Budget)	up to $15
I (Inexpensive)	$15–$25
M (Moderate)	$25–$40
E (Expensive)	$40–$60
VE (Very Expensive)	$60 and up

Personal Favorites (in order of preference)

Lutèce (midtown), 249 E. 50th St. (752-2225). A/C. Lunch Tues.-Fri., dinner Mon.-Sat.; closed Sun. and Aug. until Labor Day. AE, CB, DC. J&T. *Specialties:* sweetbreads in white wine w. capers, scallops sautéed w. truffles, baby lamb w. fresh noodles and spring vegetables, medallion of veal w. morels, filets de St. Pierre (John Dory) w. fresh mint, navarin of lobster w. Pernod, filet mignon in pastry shell, chicken w. tarragon, bitter-chocolate mousse, tarte tatin. Menu changes regularly. Very fine wine list, balanced and clear (there are 20,000 bottles in the cellar). *Note:* Classic French *grande cuisine* at its best; for a quarter of a century Lutèce has earned the title of New York's best rest. Under the direction of André Soltner, from Alsace, the menu is progressively enriched and refined. Pretty winter garden on the ground floor; elegant little rms, recently renovated, upstairs. Flawless reception and svce. Resv. a must, many days or even weeks ahead. President Reagan's special favorite is the filet of salmon w. mustard. One of the country's 12 finest rests. *French.* **M (lunch), VE (dinner)**

Le Bernardin (midtown), 155 W. 51st St. (489-1515). A/C. Lunch/dinner Mon.-Sat.; closed Sun. and holidays. AE, CB, DC, MC, V. J&T. *Specialties:* oysters and shellfish, sea urchins in butter, marinated sea bass w. coriander and basil, scallop salad w. cream and juice of truffles, slice of salmon w. julienne of fennel, poached halibut w. warm herbed vinaigrette, filet of pompano w. parsley, carpaccio of tuna. Menu changed regularly. Good wine list at reasonable prices. *Note:* This remarkable, relatively young (1986) seafood rest. quickly established itself in a place of honor on the New York gastronomic scene. The credit goes to its chef and owner, the talented Gilbert Le Coze, whose former rest. in Paris rated a coveted two stars from Michelin. The exceptional quality of the seafood, the short cooking times, and a particular talent for refined simplicity explain its unprecedented popularity (it almost requires a miracle to get a dinner resv.). Elegant London club interior w. Danish teak woodwork, bluish-gray tones, and rather hackneyed maritime paintings. Exemplary service supervised by the omnipresent Maguy Le Coze, Gilbert's sister.

Resv. absolutely essential. One of the 12 best rests. in the country. *Seafood.* **M (lunch), VE (dinner)**

🍷🍷🍷🍷 **Quilted Giraffe** (midtown), 15 E. 55th St., at Madison Ave. (593-1221). A/C. Lunch/dinner Mon.-Sat.; closed Sun., holidays, and the month of July. AE, MC, V. J&T. *Specialties:* "Beggar's Purses" (pancakes stuffed w. beluga caviar and crème fraîche, sweetbread sautéed w. pecan nuts, duck cutlet w. lime and ginger, rack of lamb w. Chinese mustard, ragoût of lobster and monkfish, poached salmon w. red pepper and dill. Remarkable desserts. Wine list a little disappointing and overpriced. *Note:* The unchallenged shrine of nouvelle cuisine in New York. Long cramped into three very small, slightly kitschy rooms, its huge new premises and their futurist décor of steel and marble are more in keeping w. the inventive contemporary cuisine. The proprietor, Barry Wine, used to be a lawyer; driven by a lust for perfection he has (almost unbelievably) taught himself to be a great chef. Ultra-professional svce. Fashionable and/or very-big-business clientele. Resv. a must, some days (or weeks) ahead. A very good place indeed. *French.* **E (lunch), VE (dinner)**

🍷🍷🍷 **Palio** (midtown), 151 W. 51st St. (245-4850). A/C. Lunch Mon.-Fri., dinner Mon.-Sat.; closed Sun. and holidays. AE, CB, DC, MC, V. J&T. *Specialties:* carpaccio, risotto w. quails, ricotta croquettes w. truffled butter, steamed sea bass w. zucchini, gnocchi w. frogs' legs and garlic, squab w. sage, prosciutto-stuffed chicken breast w. green sauce, black polenta pudding. Fine list of Italian and California wines at sensible prices. *Note:* Chef Andrea Hellrigl, the presiding genius here, is one of the finest exponents of the Italian *nuova cucina,* and brought here from the well-reputed Villa Mozart in Merano (Italy) a light, delicate cuisine which will be a revelation to lovers of traditional Italian food. Wall paintings by Sandro Chia, superbly depicting the "Palio" race in Siena, lend warmth and color to the bar. The dining rm, upstairs, is elegant in a more discreet fashion. One of the best contemporary Italian rests. in the country. Resv. a must. Business clientele. Valet parking. *Italian.* **M–E**

🍷🍷🍷 **Shun Lee Palace** (midtown), 155 E. 55th St. (371-8844). A/C. Lunch/dinner daily; closed Thanksgiving. AE, CB, DC. Jkt. *Specialties:* hot-and-sour soup, Szechuan lobster, mu shu pork, Peking duck, frogs' legs w. broccoli, jellyfish w. hot mustard and thousand-year-old eggs, carp w. ginger and shallots. So-so desserts. *Note:* Purists might find cause for regret in the slight over-Americanization of chef T. T. Wang's cuisine in this excellent Chinese rest., but the result is still delectable. There are Szechuan, Hunan, and Mandarin dishes, more elaborate at dinner than at lunch. Elegant, intimate Far Eastern setting; discreet but efficient svce. *Chinese.* **M**

☀️🍷🍷 **Arizona 206** (Upper East Side), 206 E. 60th St. (838-0440). A/C. Lunch/dinner Mon.-Sat.; closed Sun. and Dec. 25. AE, CB, DC, MC, V. Jkt. *Specialties:* chili of game and black beans, broiled scallops w. coriander and tomatillos, tuna tartar w. salsa, lamb in salad w. artichokes and chayote, broiled rib-eye steak w. jalapeño sauce, barbecued quail w. polenta, chocolate-and-walnut cake. Short but pleasant list of California wines. *Note:* One of New York's most original American rests., no less for its southwestern décor, w. adobe walls, open hearth, and natural-wood tables than for the inventive genius of its young chef Brendan Walsh, whose southwestern food is natural, simple, and remarkable. Warm, relaxed but sometimes noisy setting; svce w. a smile. Since the yuppies have taken enthusiastically to the place, resv. are a must. Don't miss it. *American.* **M**

☀️🍷🍷 **Oyster Bar and Restaurant** (midtown), in Grand Central Terminal at E. 42nd St. and Vanderbilt Ave. (490-6650). A/C. Lunch/dinner Mon.-Fri.; closed Sat., Sun., and holidays. AE, CB, DC,

MC, V. Jkt. *Specialties:* every kind of oyster, broiled fish and shellfish, clam chowder, bouillabaisse, Florida stone crab (in season), pan-roasted shellfish, cheesecake. Splendid list of California wines. *Note:* A vast, tile cavern on the lower level of Grand Central Terminal. Usually crowded and noisy, particularly at lunch, but still one of the best selections of fish and shellfish in the entire country, at prices that are reasonable given the quality of the food. Svce sometimes distracted. Resv. advised. A New York landmark since 1913. *Seafood.* **I—M**

Palm (midtown), 837 Second Ave. at E. 45th St. (687-2953). A/C. Lunch Mon.-Fri., dinner Mon.-Sat. (until midnight); closed Sun. and holidays. AE, CB, DC, MC, V. Jkt. *Specialties:* shrimp sautéed w. herbs, steak, prime cuts, lamb chops, Maine lobster, cheesecake. *Note:* A living legend for six decades among those who like solid food. Superb steaks, enormous lobsters, and some passable Italian dishes. The portions are gargantuan. The caricatures on the walls are amusing, but the place is very noisy and resolutely macho, down to the sawdust on the floor. Svce efficient but disagreeable. The annex across the avenue (Palm Too) is less picturesque, but the meat is of the same high quality. Resv. accepted for lunch only. *Steak-seafood.* **M—E**

Hatsuhana (midtown), 17 E. 48th St. (355-3345). A/C. Lunch Mon.-Fri., dinner Mon.-Sat.; closed Sun. and holidays. AE, CB, DC, MC, V. Jkt. *Specialties:* sushi, chawan mushi, sashimi, sukiyaki, tempura. *Note:* Purists maintain that you will find here the widest choice of the best sushi in all New York. Modern, comfortably furnished setting w. dining rms on two levels, and sushi bars behind which the artist-chefs, past masters in the preparation and presentation of their 35 varieties of raw fish, go about their business. Generally crowded, especially at lunch. Svce overburdened. Many Japanese businessmen come here; resv. advised. Also at 237 Park Ave. (661-3400). *Japanese.* **M**

Rosa Mexicano (midtown), 1063 First Ave. at 58th St. (753-7407). A/C. Lunch/dinner daily (till midnight). AE, CB, DC, MC, V. *Specialties:* taquitos, guacamole, carnitas, chiles en mogada, snapper w. coriander, shell steak w. sautéed chilis poblanos, budin azteca. Excellent margaritas. *Note:* A worthy representative of Mexico, this likeable, fashionable rest. will give you, as it were, a foretaste of exotic vacations. The food is completely authentic, the atmosphere congenial, the bar inviting though crowded, and the rustic décor executed in a beautiful shade of pink. Efficient, smiling svce. Resv. a must. A fine place. *Mexican.* **I—M**

Man Ray (Chelsea), 169 Eighth Ave. (627-4220). A/C. Dinner only, nightly (until midnight). AE. *Specialties:* merguez (Moroccan sausage) and chickpeas, scallops w. beurre blanc, cassoulet, choucroute, salad of confit of duck, broiled filet of lamb w. potatoes au gratin, Coho salmon w. red butter, crème caramel, Paris-Brest (pastry filled w. praline-flavored cream). Short, intelligently selected wine list. *Note:* Named after the famous American surrealist painter-photographer Man Ray, whose works adorn the walls and the bar, this art deco bistro is a successful re-creation of the 1930s Paris that the artist painted. Even the waiters, w. their big white aprons, suspenders, and weird ties enhance the Jazz Age effect. Pleasant, tasty *cuisine bourgeoise;* svce undependable; atmosphere lively. The fashionable place in the heart of Chelsea. Resv. advised. *French.* **I—M**

Frank's (Greenwich Village), 431 W. 14th St. (243-1349). A/C. Breakfast/lunch/dinner Mon.-Fri. (from 2 a.m. to 10 p.m.); dinner only, Sat. (from 5 to 11 p.m.); closed Sun. No credit cards. *Specialties:* tagliarini puttanesca (pasta w. capers, olives, and anchovies), tripe Florentine, rack of lamb, steak, roast beef, veal cutlets, broiled kidney. *Note:* A stone's throw from Gansevoort Market, headquarters of the city's wholesale meat business, this stronghold of meat eating makes a point of opening its doors at 2 a.m. to feed breakfast to the neighborhood butchers. Manly food, sturdy portions, and prime meat as you would expect, all at very attractive prices. The long mahogany bar, lazy ceiling fans, and sawdusted floor contribute to a friendly, unpretentious setting. Efficient svce. A very good place indeed; a Manhattan landmark since 1912. *Steak.* **I—M**

Other Restaurants (from top bracket to budget)

Cellar in the Sky (Lower Manhattan), at Windows on the World, 1 World Trade Center (938-1111). A/C. Dinner only (single sitting at 7:30 p.m.), Mon.-Sat.; closed Sun. AE, CB, DC, MC, V. J&T. *Specialties:* The prix-fixe menu changes twice a month and comprises seven main dishes, hors d'oeuvres, and desserts accompanied by five different wines. Some regular features: lobster w. beurre blanc and truffles, lamb ravioli w. tomatoes and ginger, smoked salmon w. tarragon sabayon, squab w. cabbage and Pinot Noir sauce. Excellent selection of wines. *Note:* One of New York's most unusual rests., both for its location on the 107th floor of the World Trade Center, and for its pricing policy—a prix-fixe menu for $75, wines included, not unreasonable in view of the excellent cuisine and wines. Intimate, cozy atmosphere, but the view out over the city is impeded by the wine racks lined up along the glass walls. Exemplary svce; since only 40 people can be seated, you should reserve a long way ahead. Free parking. *Continental-American.* **VE (prix fixe)**

Gloucester House (midtown), 37 E. 50th St. (755-7394). Lunch and dinner Mon.-Sat., closed Sun. AE, DC, MC, V. J&T. *Note:* Remarkably fresh seafood at enormously high prices against a backdrop of seafaring décor. **VE**

Le Cirque (Upper East Side), 58 E. 65th St. (794-9292). Lunch and dinner Mon.-Sat.; closed Sunday. AE, CB, DC. Trend-setting rest. whose patrons range from Richard Nixon and Fiat chairman Giovanni Agnelli to Liza Minelli and the Greek shipowner Livanos. Super-high prices. President Reagan has occasionally honored the place w. his presence. **VE**

Rainbow Room (midtown), 30 Rockefeller Plaza (632-5100). Dinner only Tues.-Sat.; brunch Sat. and Sun. AE. On the 65th floor of the RCA Bldg., this dazzling recently remodeled art deco rest. is so New York City, it offers a splendid view of the lighted skyline and nostalgic dining and dancing. Prices are predictably steep. **VE**

La Côte Basque (midtown), 5 E. 55th St. (688-6525). A/C. Lunch/dinner Mon.-Sat.; closed Sun., holidays, and the month of July. AE, CB, DC, MC, V. J&T. *Specialties:* couronne (crown) of seafood, mousse of two fish, sweetbreads au Madère, duck in peppered vinaigrette, roast lamb w. thyme, pomponettes of truffles, lobster ragoût w. morels, dacquoise, frozen raspberry soufflé. Fine wine list at outrageous prices. *Note:* Founded 30 years ago as an affiliate of the legendary Pavillon, once New York's greatest French rest., La Côte Basque is now its worthy successor. Pretty, flowery décor w. wall painting of the port of St. Jean de Luz. Grand cuisine which contrives to be both traditional and light, from the hand of the excellent chef Jean-Jacques Bachou. Svce and presentation are flawless, but the place is a little noisy. Resv. must be made some days ahead. Very "in" clientele. *French.* **E—VE**

An American Place (midtown), 2 Park Ave. at 32nd St. (517-7660). A/C. Dinner only, Mon.-Sat.; closed Sun. and holidays. AE, CB, DC, MC, V. J&T. *Specialties:* broiled duck sausage w. shallots, terrine of smoked fish w. three caviars, sautéed lobster w. chives, filet of venison w. wild bilberries and pepper sauce, roast salmon in cider vinegar, broiled chicken w. fettuccine and wild mushrooms, chocolate pudding, mile-high strawberry shortcake. Very fine list of American wines at reasonable prices. The menu changes regularly. *Note:* Modern American cuisine admirable in its elegance and simplicity. Chef Larry Forgione, a virtuoso of short cooking times and light sauces, uses American products exclusively (even the caviar). Fashionable Art Deco interior; svce usually faultless. Resv. a must. *American.* **E–VE**

♈♈♈ **Aurora** (midtown), 60 E. 49th St. (692-9292). A/C. Lunch Mon.-Fri., dinner Mon.-Sat.; closed Sun. and holidays. AE, CB, DC, MC, V. Jkt/J&T. *Specialties:* mousse of zucchini w. marinated lobster and shrimp, salad of duck confit w. walnuts, roast squab w. sweet garlic, poached lobster (w. ginger, lime, and Sauternes), salmon w. tomato butter and apples, broiled guinea fowl in lime juice, lemon-and-walnut cake, hot chocolate mousse. Fine wine list at acceptable prices. Menu changes daily. *Note:* When he worked in Paris, Gerard Pangaud, the chef of this very distinguished New York rest., rated two stars in Michelin. He felicitously applies the techniques of French nouvelle cuisine to American raw materials; the result is light, simple dishes that are always innovative and surprising, as w. his many variations on the potato. Rather grotesque post-modern décor in pastel tones. The svce is ultra-professional but unfriendly. Resv. absolutely essential, several days ahead. Trendy clientele. *French.* **E–VE**

♈♈♈ **Parioli Romanissimo** (Upper East Side), 24 E. 81st St. (288-2391). A/C. Dinner only, Tues.-Sat.; closed Sun., Mon., holidays, and the month of Aug. AE, CB, DC. J&T. *Specialties:* tortellini alla panna, trenette w. fresh cêpes (*funghi porcini*), carpaccio of lamb w. purée of red peppers, scaloppine Capriccio, seafood veneziana. Decent wine list at indecent prices. *Note:* This Upper East Side rest. pays tribute to the culinary achievements of Italy, w. northern Italian dishes that are subtle and refined, particularly in the combination of flavors accompanying the homemade fresh pasta. Elegant décor w. subdued lighting, mirrors, and paneling. Svce highly polished but a little pretentious. Resv. a must. A fine place despite its exorbitant prices. *Italian.* **E–VE**

Four Seasons (midtown), 99 E. 52nd St. (754-9494). Lunch and dinner Mon.-Sat.; closed Sunday. AE, CB, DC, MC, V. The "Pool Room" w. its enormous skylight and marble pool is a triumph of elegant modern design. The wine list is exhaustive. A favorite of New York's publishing community in particular. Super expensive. **E–VE**

♈ **Café des Artistes** (Upper West Side), 1 W. 67th St. (877-3500). Lunch Mon.-Fri., brunch Sat. and Sun., dinner daily. AE, DC, MC, V. *Specialties:* seafood gazpacho, confit of duck w. white beans, bourride w. aioli, snapper w. crushed pine nuts, steak au poivre vert, veal chop w. scallion-port sauce. Great dessert place. *Note:* Ultimately, the plush Central European atmosphere and the exquisite painted murals are what draw regulars to this festive rest. However, the food is not as consistently pleasing as the setting. *Continental.* **E**

☼ **Tavern on the Green** (Upper West Side), Central Park West at W. 67th St. (873-3200). A/C. Lunch Mon.-Fri., brunch Sat. and Sun., dinner daily. AE, CB, DC, MC, V. *Specialties:* lobster bisque, scallops w. Chinese cabbage, veal chop w. braised endive, chateaubriand, sautéed shrimp w. ginger, chocolate truffle cake. *Note:* The food is at best uneven, but it's worth visiting for the spectacular setting on the edge of Central Park—a veritable fairyland in winter when the snow is on the ground and a gala flower-filled bosky scene in summer. The dining rms are exuberantly decorated w. chandeliers, stained glass, etched and carved mirrors, and pastel plaster ceiling featuring fantastic animal and flower motifs. Go for cocktails or a snack. Sheer New York. *Continental.* **E**

Elaine's (Upper East Side), 1703 Second Ave. at E. 88th St. (534-8103). Dinner daily. AE, MC, V. The watering place for celebrities and show-business personalities. Elaine stands guard by the door; only regulars like Woody Allen, Leonard Bernstein, Willie Nelson, or Luciano Pavarotti are allowed in without argument. Go if you insist on seeing the famous feeding. *Italian/Continental.* **E**

  "21" (midtown), 21 W. 52nd St. (582-7200). Lunch and dinner Mon.-Sat.; closed Sun. AE, CB, DC, MC, V. Movers and shakers make this their "club" for socializing and deal making. A famous old speakeasy, recently renovated for the '90s, it's a famed New York "power" spot. The food is only one of the issues —the "21" burger is $24. **E**

  ☖☖☖ **Sofi** (Chelsea), 102 Fifth Ave. at 15th St. (463-8888). A/C. Lunch Mon.-Fri., dinner Mon.-Sat.; closed Sun. AE, CB, DC, MC, V. Jkt. *Specialties:* garden salad, cucumber soup w. dill, terrine of cassoulet, Castlebay lobster, filet of lamb cutlet w. timbale of vegetables, broiled Dover sole w. red wine, hazelnut-praline ice cream. Interesting, reasonably priced wine list. *Note:* The name of this newish, smart rest. defines both it and its location: SOFI is a contraction either of "Southern Fifth Ave." or "South of Flatiron," the famous triangular high-rise at 23rd St. where Broadway and Fifth Ave. meet. This rest. undoubtedly serves some of the most original, interesting food in New York; the cuisine of talented young chef Dennis MacNeil is contemporary American modified by French, Italian, or Asian influences. It's a huge but congenial and comfortable place w. a dining rm on two levels in the manner of a 1930s luxury-hotel rest. Flawless svce. Resv. a must. The trendy place to eat. *American-continental.* **M–E**

  ☖☖ **Auntie Yuan** (Upper East Side), 1191A First Ave. at E. 65th St. (744-4040). A/C. Lunch/dinner daily (until midnight). AE, DC. Jkt. *Specialties:* barbecued quail w. garlic, Chinese noodles w. sesame sauce and shallots, steamed salmon w. black beans, orange beef, Peking duck, mediocre desserts. *Note:* Unlike the general run of neon-and-Formica eating places in Chinatown, this is one of the most beautiful rests. in New York: black Chinese lacquer, elegant flower arrangements, indirect lighting, luxury tableware, and waiters in tuxedos. The Taiwanese nouvelle cuisine of chef David Keh and his team is above criticism; so is the svce, which is uncommon in a Far Eastern rest. A fine place. Resv. required. Valet parking. *Chinese.* **M–E**

  ☖☖ **Christ Cella** (midtown), 160 E. 46th St. (697-2479). A/C. Lunch Mon.-Fri., dinner Mon.-Sat.; closed Sun. and holidays. AE, CB, DC, MC, V. J&T. *Specialties:* steak, lamb chops, veal cutlets, lobster, roast beef, catch of the day, Caesar salad, Napoleon. Rather skimpy wine list. *Note:* Since 1926, New York's only steakhouse that can challenge the famous Palm. The steaks and lobster here are almost as big, and the svce a touch friendlier. The waiters will tell you the daily specials. Atmosphere and clientele resolutely masculine. Resv. a must. *Steak-seafood.* **M–E**

  ☼☖☖ **Coach House** (Greenwich Village), 110 Waverly Pl. (777-0303). A/C. Dinner only, Tues.-Sun.; closed Mon., holidays, and the month of Aug. AE, CB, DC, MC, V. J&T. *Specialties:* black-bean soup, oyster soup, crab cakes, Virginia ham, rack of lamb, chicken pie, steak au poivre, blueberry pie, chocolate cake. Good list of California wines. *Note:* The Coach House has for 40 years been a leading exponent of the American culinary tradition, and by now has achieved landmark status. Charming colonial-inn setting a stone's throw from Washington Square in the heart of Greenwich Village. Exceptionally attentive, courteous svce. If you want to rediscover the authentic flavor of traditional American food, you must pay your respects here. Resv. a must. *American.* **M–E**

  ☖☖ **Hubert's** (Upper East Side), 575 Park Ave. at E. 63rd St. (826-5911). A/C. Lunch Mon.-Fri., dinner Mon.-Sat.; closed Sun. and holidays. AE, MC, V. Jkt. *Specialties:* rabbit-meat sausage w. mole sauce, poached salmon w. horseradish sauce, shrimp and cucumber in sesame and honey sauce, rack of lamb and lasagne w. goat cheese, roast duck w. vegetable and quince strudel, sauté of pork w. mustard sauce. Superb desserts. Fine list of American wines. Menu changed regularly. *Note:* Its recent move to larger and smarter premises has in no way impaired the exceptional qualities of this rest., a longtime leader in American nouvelle cuisine. Len Allison chooses to depart from traditional recipes in search of new, sometimes disconcerting, tastes, almost always surprising but agreeable. Friendly, relaxed svce. Recommended to all who enjoy leaving the culinary beaten track. Resv. a must. *American.* **M–E**

    Il Nido (midtown), 251 E. 53rd St. (753-8450). A/C. Lunch/dinner Mon.-Sat.; closed Sun. and holidays. AE, CB, DC, MC, V. Jkt. *Specialties:* ravioli malfatti, carpaccio, chicken salad, porcini mushrooms w. truffles (in season), crostini di polenta, veal pizzaiola, scampi w. capers, zuppa di pesce, zabaglione w. Cointreau and champagne. Fine wine list. *Note:* In the early '80s Il Nido was regarded as one of Manhattan's two or three best Italian rests.; what remains today is still very fine, though the Tuscan cuisine is unimaginative and a little too orthodox. Elegantly rustic farmhouse décor. Ultra-professional svce. Business clientele; resv. a must. *Italian.* **M–E**

    River Café, 1 Water St., Brooklyn (718/522-5200). A/C. Lunch/dinner daily. AE, CB, DC, MC, V. Jkt./J&T. *Specialties:* sautéed oysters w. endives and artichokes, snails in puff pastry, Black Angus steak w. bourbon sauce, broiled pheasant w. risotto of wild mushrooms, lamb cutlets w. charlotte of eggplant, braised sea bass w. morel mushrooms and tomatoes, mignon of veal w. pears, chocolate terrine, raspberry cheesecake. Exceptional wine list, particularly the California section. Menu changes regularly. *Note:* By day, and even more by night, one of the most fabulous sights New York has to offer. From a charming barge moored below the Brooklyn Bridge, you can see at a glance the distant Statue of Liberty and the skyscrapers of dwntwn Manhattan. The rest. was once so-so; now it serves a sophisticated, contemporary American cuisine using only U.S. raw materials, including the caviar and the olive oil. Ultra-professional svce; resv. essential many days ahead. Ask for a table near the bay window or, in summer, on the terrace. A must for tourists, but also draws many bankers from nearby Wall St. at lunchtime. *American.* **M (lunch), E (dinner)**

    Smith & Wollensky (midtown), 201 E. 49th St. at 3rd Ave. (753-1530). A/C. Lunch Mon.-Fri., dinner nightly; closed Jan. 1 and Dec. 25. AE, CB, DC, MC, V. Jkt. *Specialties:* crabmeat cocktail, steak, T-bone, filet mignon au poivre, veal cutlet, lobster, broiled fish of the day, chocolate-mousse cake. Exceptional wine list, one of the best in New York. *Note:* In a huge two-story turn-of-the-century building, this typical New York steakhouse serves man-sized portions of choice red meat to a following of devotees. Its wine list, especially the California cabernet sauvignons, is also praiseworthy. Warm, efficient svce; a fine place in spite of prices on the high side. Resv. recommended. *Steak-seafood.* **M–E**

    Canton (Lower Manhattan), 45 Division St. (226-0921). A/C. Lunch/dinner Wed.-Sun.; closed Mon., Tues., and from mid-July to mid-Aug. No credit cards. *Specialties:* lettuce roll stuffed w. pigeon, roast duck, lobster w. black-bean sauce, boned chicken w. herbs and shallots, steamed pike w. quenelles. No wine, beer, or liquor; you may bring your own. *Note:* Laudably original Cantonese food, stimulated by delicate touches of French or Italian provenance. The slightly chilly modern setting is in no way Oriental, but the Canton is one of the best places in Chinatown for those w. a taste for gastronomic subtleties. Friendly reception and svce; resv. advised. *Chinese.* **M**

🍷 **Darbar** (midtown), 44 W. 56th St. (432-7227). A/C. Lunch/dinner daily, buffet lunch Sat. and Sun. AE, CB, DC, MC, V. Jkt. *Specialties:* samosas, chicken pakora, reshmi kebab (baked chicken en brochette), marinated lamb w. cardamom and cumin, ghosht vindaloo (ragoût of lamb), baygan ghurta (broiled eggplant w. tomatoes, onions, and spices), kheer (rice pudding w. cardamom). *Note:* The most sought-after and elegant of New York's Indian rests., on several levels, w. a friendly bar on the ground floor, fabric-covered walls, and magnificent decorative objects in hammered copper. Darbar serves a refined version of Mogul (northern Indian) food; the seasonings are added w. a careful hand but some dishes, like the murgh Madras, are volcanic. Svce efficient but a little brusque. Resv. advised. *Indian.* **M**

🍷 **John Clancy's Restaurant** (Greenwich Village), 181 W. 10th St. at Seventh Ave. (242-7350). A/C. Dinner only, nightly; closed holidays. AE, CB, DC, MC, V. Jkt. *Specialties:* oysters on the half shell, gravlax, lobster bisque, swordfish en brochette, barbecued jumbo shrimp, halibut w. sesame sauce, broiled sea bass w. coriander, English trifle. Good wine list. *Note:* Serving exclusively seafood—broiled over mesquite, raw, baked, or steamed—this Greenwich Village rest. has a host of groupies. The food is as fresh as can be, and cooked to perfection. Elegant, intimate setting in tones of pearl and gray, occupying two floors of a charming century-old town house. Svce relatively efficient and relaxed. Resv. advised. *Seafood.* **M**

☀️🍷 **Gage & Tollner,** 372 Fulton St., Brooklyn (718/875-5181). A/C. Lunch Mon.-Fri., dinner Mon.-Sat.; closed Sun. and holidays. AE, CB, DC, MC, V. Jkt. *Specialties:* Virginia crabmeat, soft clam-belly broil, pan-fried oysters, catch of the day, English mixed grill (mutton chops w. veal kidney and sausages), steak, lamb chops, hazelnut cheesecake. Huge selection of beer. *Note:* A landmark of authentic American cooking since 1879; the wall-mounted gas jets (recently wired for electricity) and the paneling are of the period. So, it might seem, are the waiters, proudly wearing their long-service stripes on their sleeves. Absolutely fresh seafood and wonderful meat as well. A designated landmark. Worth the 30-min. drive across the East River. *American.* **M**

Sardi's (midtown), 234 W. 44th St. (221-8440). The name is Italian but the cuisine is more continental/American. Still a quintessential haunt of theater and movie folk. Caricatures of leading entertainers on the walls. **I–M**

🍷 **Kitcho** (midtown), 22 W. 46th St. (575-8880). A/C. Lunch Mon.-Fri., dinner Sun.-Fri.; closed Sat. and holidays. AE, CB, DC. Jkt. *Specialties:* sushi, sashimi, kushi-katsu (fried pork), tempura, stone-cooked beef, teriyaki. *Note:* This modern but uncomely rest. on three levels (tatami rm upstairs) draws a regular and enthusiastic Japanese clientele. Experts consider it New York's best *kaiseki* (Japanese haute cuisine) rest.; it's a subsidiary of a very well-regarded chain w. establishments in Tokyo, Osaka, and Kyoto. Friendly, hard-working svce. Generally crowded for lunch. Resv. advised. *Japanese.* **M**

🍷 **Odeon** (Tribeca), 145 W. Broadway (233-0507). A/C. Lunch Mon.-Fri., dinner nightly (until 2:30 a.m.). AE, V. Jkt. *Specialties:* consommé of duck w. julienne of vegetables, fresh pasta w. broiled shrimp and Chardonnay sauce, poached oysters, baked red snapper w. saffron, pan-fried steak, cassoulet, poached salmon w. green peppercorn sauce, fricassee of sole, roast lamb w. garlic, chocolate terrine à l'orange, poached peaches w. Sauternes sabayon. Good wine list. *Note:* Successful American nouvelle cuisine in a rather chilly 1930s setting of subdued chromium and marble. Trendy clientele from punk to banker; congenial but noisy atmosphere, especially at night. Efficient, smiling long-aproned servers. A godsend if you're up late in Tribeca. Resv. advised. *French.* **M**

☼ ♈♈ **Windows on the World (the Restaurant)** (Lower Manhattan), 1 World Trade Center (938-1111). A/C. Lunch Mon.-Fri. (private club; $8 entrance fee for nonmembers), dinner Mon.-Sat., brunch and dinner Sun. (till 7:30 p.m.). AE, CB, DC, MC, V. J&T. *Specialties:* sautéed shrimp w. leeks and broccoli, pâté of wild boar w. morels, broiled salmon w. orange-and-chive sauce, scaloppine w. wild mushrooms, marinated pheasant w. wild thyme, rack of lamb, stuffed trout in pastry shell, good desserts including amaretto soufflé. *Note:* The highest skyscraper rest. in the world, 107 floors and 1,318 ft. (402 m) above the sidewalk could easily have turned into a tourist trap, w. a wonderful view of Manhattan on a clear day. As it turns out, the food is on a par w. the view (and what a view it is!), and the superb wine list boasts 800 labels. The svce, though not genial, is efficient. Resv. must be made days, or weeks, in advance. Free parking under the tower. *Continental.* **M**

☼ ♈ **Peter Luger,** 178 Broadway, Brooklyn (718/387-7400). A/C. Lunch/dinner daily. No credit cards. Jkt. *Specialties:* shrimp cocktail, steak, roast beef, creamed spinach, cheesecake, chocolate mousse. Rickety wine list. *Note:* Since 1887 this venerable, vaguely Germanic tavern has been serving the best T-bone and porterhouse steaks in the city on its scrubbed wooden tables. The svce is rough. You should eat here, though the surrounding streets are not inviting after dark. 30 min. from midtown. Resv. advised. *Steak.* **M**

♈ **Russian Tea Room** (midtown), 150 W. 57th St. (265-0947). A/C. Lunch/dinner daily (till 12:30 a.m.). AE, CB, DC, MC, V. Jkt. *Specialties:* borscht, caviar w. blinis, zakuski, Kiev cutlet, lamb steak, Caucasian shashlik, pirozhki, broiled salmon w. lemon butter. The desserts and wine list are unworthy of a good rest. *Note:* The rest. is sandwiched between skyscrapers, the clientele is well-heeled, the décor is Christmas-tree primitive—and the place is crowded seven days a week. The Russian food is adequate, the prices high. You may see such stars of stage, screen, and concert hall as Woody Allen, Dustin Hoffman, and Isaac Stern. Svce so-so. A place to see and be seen. Resv. advised. *East European.* **M**

♈♈ **Mitsukoshi** (midtown), 461 Park Ave. at E. 57th St. (935-6444). A/C. Lunch/dinner Mon.-Sat.; closed Sun. and holidays. AE, CB, DC, MC, V. Jkt. *Specialties:* sushi, sashimi, sukiyaki, tempura, shabu-shabu. *Note:* The favorite rest. of Manhattan's Japanese business community. Those who enjoy raw fish and salty garnishes will find a very wide range of sushi at very stiff prices. You can eat either Western style or at tatami. Svce (in kimono) w. a smile, but not always prompt. Resv. recommended. *Japanese.* **M**

☼ ♈ **Bridge Café** (Lower Manhattan), 279 Water St. (227-3344). A/C. Lunch Mon.-Fri., dinner nightly, brunch Sat. and Sun. AE, DC. *Specialties:* soft-shell crab (in season), curried oysters vinaigrette, duck w. green peppercorns, sautéed salmon, chicken breast w. black beans and garlic. Apple-and-walnut cake w. rum sauce. *Note:* This early-19th-century seamen's tavern, now a lunchtime meeting place for yuppies, is often graced by His Honor Edward I. Koch, the mayor of New York, as well as a clutch of Wall St. bankers. The cuisine is uneven, w. good and bad appearing side by side. Pleasant atmosphere; good-mannered but muddle-headed svce. A fashionable place in the shadow of the Brooklyn Bridge. No resv., and sometimes a long wait. *American.* **I-M**

♈♈ **Provence** (Greenwich Village), 38 MacDougal St. (475-7500). A/C. Lunch/dinner Tues.-Sun. AE. *Specialties:* fish soup, Provençal onion-and-anchovy tart, rabbit pâté in aspic, skate w. caper sauce, roast lamb w. ratatouille, poached seafood in broth w. aioli, grilled rabbit (w. mustard, sage, and braised cabbage), crème brûlée. *Note:* A popular French bistro serving good, honest cuisine using fresh ingredients. Svce is gracious and the atmosphere comfortable. The garden w. fountain is especially appealing in summer. Extensive wine list. Reserve well ahead, especially for wknds. *French.* **M**

♀ **El Rincon de España** (Greenwich Village), 226 Thompson St. (475-9891). A/C. Lunch/dinner daily; closed holidays. AE, CB, DC, MC, V. *Specialties:* shrimp à la Carlos, mariscada (ragoût of seafood), paella valenciana, cod Galician style, octopus w. tomato. Mediocre desserts. *Note:* Small, dark, and usually crowded, this typical tavern a few blocks from Washington Square serves as tasty Spanish food as you'll find. The servings are generous, the Rioja wine flows like water, and the svce is as relaxed as the atmosphere. Inevitable background music provided by guitars. Resv. desirable. *Spanish.* **I–M**

♀ **Gallagher's Steak House** (midtown), 228 W. 52nd St. (245-5336). A/C. Lunch/dinner daily (until midnight). AE, CB, DC, MC, V. Jkt. *Specialties:* steak, roast beef, lamb chops, steak-and-kidney pie, brains w. hazelnut butter, lobster, broiled catch of the day. *Note:* Long considered one of New York's best steakhouses, the fabled Gallagher's has lost some of its luster in the course of half a century. Its meats, still displayed for your inspection in a large glass-walled freezing locker as you come in, are as good as ever, but there are weaknesses in the kitchen, and the svce is less professional than it used to be. Unchanged are the gallery of yellowing photos of entertainers and early sports greats on the walls, and the elderly barmen working behind the oval bar in the middle of the room. Resv. advised. *Steak.* **I–M**

♀ **La Gauloise** (Greenwich Village), 502 Ave. of the Americas at W. 13th St. (691-1363). A/C. Lunch/dinner Tues.-Sun., brunch Sat. and Sun.; closed Mon. and holidays. AE, DC, MC, V. *Specialties:* lamb chops w. sweet garlic, magret of duck, skate w. brown-butter sauce, rabbit w. tarragon and mustard, steak au poivre, saddle of veal, paillard of salmon, roast chicken, crème brûlée, pears in red wine. Good wine list but overpriced. *Note:* Authentic re-creation of a Parisian brasseries 1920s style complete w. art deco lamps, dark paneling, and lovely mirrors. Excellent bistro food, and at attractive prices. Svce a little out of control. Congenial, very Greenwich Village clientele and atmosphere. Very good value overall. Resv. advised. *French.* **I–M**

♀ **Nanni** (midtown), 146 E. 46th St. (697-4161). A/C. Lunch Mon.-Fri., dinner Mon.-Sat.; closed Sun. and holidays. AE, CB, DC, MC, V. Jkt. *Specialties:* capellini alla Nanni, fresh homemade pasta, chicken ortolana, sea bass alla marecchiara, veal cutlet milanese, game (in season). *Note:* The best little *trattoria* in New York. Modest, unpretentious setting, praiseworthy food at very reasonable prices. Quick, efficient svce. Often noisy and crowded. A very good place. *Italian.* **I–M**

♀ **Sabor** (Greenwich Village), 20 Cornelia St. (243-9579). A/C. Dinner nightly. AE, MC, V. *Specialties:* white-bean soup, shrimp in lime sauce, red snapper w. salsa verde, ropa vieja (shredded beef w. tomatoes and cinnamon), pork filet w. pineapple, escabeche (pickled fish), fried plantains, key lime pie, coco quemado (baked coconut dessert). *Note:* A Greenwich Village landmark serving flavorful, highly spiced Cuban food. The décor is minimal—cream-washed exposed brick and wicker baskets. Diligent, efficient svce. Generally crowded; resv. advised. Good value on balance. *Latin American.* **I–M**

♀ **Café 43** (midtown), 147 W. 43rd St. (869-4200). A/C. Lunch Mon.-Fri., dinner Mon.-Sat.; closed Sun. AE, DC, MC, V. *Specialties:* seafood stew, grilled prawns w. lemon grass and ginger, swordfish w. lemon and basil, pan-grilled rib steak, penne w. pancetta, asparagus, and mushrooms. Special desserts every day. *Note:* Good value. Popular w. the theater crowd. Svce is prompt and smooth. The broad menu allows for economical dining w. pasta and sandwich selections as well as modestly priced main dishes. *Continental.* **I–M**

☀☻♆ **Sweet's** (Lower Manhattan), 2 Fulton St. (825-9786). Lunch/dinner Mon.-Fri.; closed Sat., Sun., and holidays. No credit cards. *Specialties:* oysters and shellfish, crab, catch of the day, broiled scallops. Good imported beers, mediocre wine list. *Note:* The most authentic (and oldest) seafood rest. in the city; opened in 1842 in the middle of the Fulton Fish Market, it has scarcely changed since. Absolutely fresh (but often overcooked) fish. The Manhattan clam chowder is recommended. Crowded at both lunch and dinner, but unfortunately no resv. accepted. For lovers of good seafood and local color. *Seafood.* **I–M**

♆ **The Nice Restaurant** (Chinatown), 35 E. Broadway (406-9510). A/C. Lunch/dinner daily. AE. *Specialties:* spring rolls w. shrimp, chopped squab in lettuce leaf, fried prawns, roast sucking pig, lacquered duck, salted chicken, melon-and-coconut soup. *Note:* Huge (ask to be seated upstairs) and frantic though it is, this is one of Chinatown's best. Truly outstanding Cantonese food; unusually (for a Chinese rest.) efficient svce. The elaborate décor might be described as Hong Kong through the eyes of Hollywood. Popular enough that resv. are advised. *Chinese.* **I–M**

♆♆ **Japonica** (Greenwich Village), University Pl. at E. 12th St. (243-7752). A/C. Lunch/dinner daily. AE, CB, DC. *Specialties:* avocado Japonica, gyoza, kyoage, nabeyaki udon, negimaki, sushi, sashimi. *Note:* This small, pretty, unpretentious rest. is well known for the ultra-fresh quality of its sushi and sashimi. Svce is swift and courteous; the décor above the sushi bar changes to reflect the seasons. Expect to wait if you arrive after 7:30 p.m., particularly on wknds. *Japanese.* **I**

☀☻♆ **Spring Street Natural** (Soho), 62 Spring St. at Lafayette St. (966-0290). A/C. Lunch/dinner daily. AE, CB, DC, MC, V. *Specialties:* hummus, black-bean soup, shrimp tempura, baked bluefish (w. red onion, mushrooms, leeks, and sake), breast of chicken w. broccoli, melted Brie w. lemon butter, stir-fried vegetables w. brown sauce. Daily specials ensure freshness. Modest wine list. Good fish and salad dishes. *Note:* Large loft-style rest. w. polished wood décor, plenty of greenery, and classical music in the background. Svce can be a little "relaxed." *Seafood-vegetarian.* **I**

☀☻♆♆ **Sylvia's** (Harlem), 328 Lenox Ave. at 126th St. (996-0660). A/C. Breakfast Mon.-Sat., lunch/dinner daily. No credit cards. *Specialties:* typical southern food: smothered steak, stewed chicken w. dumplings, fried chicken, turnips and collard greens, barbecued spareribs, butter beans w. ham bone, sweet-potato pie. *Note:* Sylvia Woods' rest. in the heart of Harlem has been an institution for more than 20 years. The flavors and spices of her cuisine are as savory and colorful as the Deep South where she was born. The décor is unobtrusive and the neighborhood unattractive; you should come and go by cab. But the atmosphere is warm and the svce congenial. The clientele is made up mostly of regulars and local politicians, w. a sprinkling of celebrities and tourists who come, in increasing numbers, to discover Harlem and Sylvia's food. v. A fine place. *American.* **I**

♆ **Cabana Carioca** (midtown), 123 W. 45th St. (581-8088). A/C. Lunch/dinner Mon.-Sat.; closed Sun. AE, CB, DC, MC, V. *Specialties:* caldo verde (vegetable soup), feijoada (the Brazilian national dish—stewed beef, sausage, and black beans), shrimps Paulista (cooked in white wine), mixed grill, broiled pork chops w. rice and black beans, steak. Excellent caipirinhas (a punch made w. lime juice and cachaça, a high-octane Brazilian spirit). *Note:* The unchallenged shrine of Brazilian cooking, Cabana Carioca is one of the most pleasing and authentic ethnic rests. in Manhattan. Its enormous helpings and diminutive prices keep the regulars coming back in crowds, and draw every Brazilian passing through town. Colorful tropical atmosphere and décor. Another location, half a block away, is Cabana Carioca II (midtown), 133 W. 45th St. (730-8375). *Brazilian.* **I**

🍸 **Cinco de Mayo** (Soho), 349 W. Broadway (226-5255). A/C. Lunch/dinner daily. AE, DC, MC, V. *Specialties:* ceviche, camarones (sautéed shrimp in a mustard-and-jalapeña vinaigrette), enchiladas de mole poblano, pollo en salsa de cacahuate, flan de chocolate, batido de Kahlúa. *Note:* Practically the only Mexican rest. rated in the *New York Times* as coming close to authentic by a visiting Mexican food expert. Lively bar scene up front; less noisy in back. Attractive, not hokey décor. Menu w. rarely featured regional dishes. Punchy margaritas and a selection of tequilas to go along w. them. *Mexican.* **I**

🍷 **Lou G. Siegel's** (midtown), 209 W. 38th St. (921-4433). A/C. Lunch Sun.-Fri., dinner Sun.-Thur.; closed Sat. and Jewish holidays. AE, CB, DC, MC, V. *Specialties:* brisket, roast beef, broiled veal cutlets, gefilte fish, stuffed cabbage, goulash, chopped liver. *Note:* Authentic Jewish food since 1917: from pastrami to roast beef and from matzoh balls to pastry, everything is scrupulously kosher. At both lunch and dinner it's packed w. workers from the nearby Garment District. Friendly, efficient svce. Depressing décor. Styles itself "the world's most famous kosher rest." *Continental.* **I**

🍷 **Avgerino's** (midtown), 153 E. 53rd St. (688-8828). A/C. Lunch/dinner daily; closed holidays. AE, CB, DC, MC, V. *Specialties:* gyro, dolmades (stuffed vine leaves), pita (spinach pie), moussaka, souvlaki, baklava. *Note:* Tucked away in the luminous, futurist courtyard of Citicorp Center, this warm, intimate little rest. serves authentic Greek food, prepared, as it should be, under your very eyes. Svce (in Greek national dress) is deft and smiling. Very good value; ideal for quick before- or after-theater dinners. *Greek.* **B−I**

🌟🍸 **Hard Rock Café** (midtown), 221 W. 57th St. (489-6565). A/C. Lunch/dinner daily (till 4 a.m.). AE, MC, V. *Specialties:* pig sandwich (roast pork), hamburgers, salads, ice-cream sundaes. *Note:* A pretty faithful copy of London's famous establishment of the same name, this funky landmark of rock 'n' roll serves excellent hamburgers and sandwiches, and praiseworthy desserts. Far-out décor w. a 45-ft. (14-m) bar in the shape of a guitar, and the rear half of an elderly 1959 Cadillac Biarritz cemented into the façade. Very high-level sound system. Very popular w. the New York young; serves between 1,800 and 2,500 customers a day. No resv. Also a crowded rock joint. *American.* **B−I**

🍷 **Bayamo** (Noho), 704 Broadway near E. 4th St. (475-5151). A/C. Lunch/dinner daily; closed Thanksgiving and Dec. 25. AE, CB, DC, MC, V. *Specialties:* ropa vieja (traditional Cuban beef stew), picadillo de camarones (spicy shrimp minced w. cheese, tortilla, and guacamole), chicken w. ginger, pan-fried lo mein noodles. *Note:* Named for a Cuban village where Chinese settlers had immigrated in the early 1900s, this busy duplex rest. is in the heart of the action along lower Broadway. The rm is dominated by a huge papier-mâché red pepper simulating the boats of the Chinese immigrants to Cuba, and the brilliant wall frescoes are interesting to contemplate while you sip one of the house special margaritas or Foster's beer. Curious combination of Chinese-Latino cuisine. Stick to the simpler dishes. Good for a snack or a full dinner. *Cuban-Chinese.* **I**

🍷 **Acme Bar & Grill** (Noho), 9 Great Jones St. (420-1934). A/C. Lunch/dinner daily; closed Thanksgiving and Dec. 25.

No CC. *Specialties:* golden fried oysters, jambalaya, chicken fried steak, fish grilled over pecan wood, grilled chicken. *Note:* A no-frills, American-diner ambience at this big, bright, cheerful meeting place for neighborhood loft dwellers and newly arrived gentry in trendy Noho. Renowned for its jukebox and the shelf of hot sauces that runs the length of the rest. From "Cajun Power Garlic Sauce" (Louisiana) to "Acme Almost Flammable Hot Sauce of Chile Habanero" (Mexico) or the fearsome "Pepper Creek Farms Jalapeño TNT" (Texas). No resv. accepted. *American-Cajun.* **I**

▽ **Gaylord** (East Village), 87 First Ave. at E. 7th St. (529-7990). A/C. Lunch/dinner daily. AE, MC, V. *Specialties:* samosa, crab bhuna, tandoori chicken, beef Madras, vegetarian thali, nan stuffed w. minced lamb, cold chicken and cucumber in tamarind sauce. *Note:* Really good, nongreasy Indian food served in an elegant atmosphere. If you can't secure a table here, then turn the corner and check into any one of the many Indian rests. that line E. 6th St. between First and Second Aves. Although Gaylord is somewhat pricier than most of these, it's worth it. Resv. recommended. *Indian.* **I**

▽ **Abyssinia** (Soho), 35 Grand St. (226-5959). A/C. Dinner daily, brunch Sat. and Sun. AE. *Specialties:* kitfo (raw chopped beef seasoned w. spiced butter and topped w. hot chili powder), ye'beg tibs (lamb w. tomato, onion fried w. rosemary, and black pepper), doro wot (chicken marinated in hot Berber sauce, served w. boiled egg), shuro (purée of chickpeas, tomatoes, onions, garlic, and other herbs), chocolate-chip cake, pear-and-almond tart. *Note:* A mecca for a young crowd who come here for the great-value cuisine eaten sans tableware, using the large, round bread as plate and scoop. You sit on traditional wooden stools at low, round, woven basket tables in two small rms decorated w. authentic Ethiopian artifacts too. Fun and different. Brief wine and beer selection. *Ethiopian.* **B**

▽▽ **Grand Palace** (Chinatown), 94–98 Mott St. (219-3088). A/C. Lunch/dinner daily. AE. *Specialties:* shark's-fin soup, sliced pigeon and vegetable, fried crab w. ginger and onion, chicken in salt, Peking duck. *Note:* On wknds if you can push your way through the crowds outside, you'll discover a vast hall filled w. large, round tables all occupied by Chinese families and friends, dining on everything from cuttlefish and abalone to ducks' feet and frog—a veritable slice of Hong Kong / Canton life. *Chinese.* **B**

▽ **Siam Inn** (midtown), 916 Eighth Ave. between W. 54th and W. 55th Sts. (489-5237). A/C. Lunch Mon.-Fri., dinner daily. AE, DC. *Specialties:* Tom Yum Koong soup, beef w. basil leaves and chili, broiled salmon w. green curry, masaman curry (w. jumbo shrimp, avocado, coconut milk, peanuts, spices, and chili), pad Thai. *Note:* Among the many Thai rests. that have opened recently in New York, this small, simply decorated place offers some of the most authentic cuisine. Svce is gracious. *Thai.* **B**

☼▽ **Carnegie Delicatessen** (midtown), 854 Seventh Ave. at 55th St. (757-2245). A/C. Breakfast/lunch/dinner daily (till 4 a.m.). No credit cards. *Specialties:* corned beef, brisket, pastrami, roast beef, smoked herring and salmon, cheese blintzes, Jewish specialties. Excellent cheesecake. *Note:* Generally acknowledged to be New York's best deli, the place is overrun at lunchtime. Gigantic sandwiches, remarkable desserts. The ideal place to eat on the run, before or after a show. A lively local institution since 1935; part of Woody Allen's movie *Broadway Danny Rose* was shot here. No resv. Beer but no liquor. *American.* **B**

Cafeterias / Specialty Spots/Fast Food

☼ **Broadway Diner** (midtown), 1726 Broadway at W. 55th St. (765-0909). Breakfast/lunch/dinner daily (from 7 a.m. to 11 p.m.). Corned-beef hash w. poached eggs, hamburgers, very good sandwiches, and broiled chicken in an *American Graffiti*–style luncheonette, all Formica, chromium, and stainless steel. For 1940s enthusiasts.

☀ **Exterminator Chili** (Lower Manhattan), 305 Church St. (219-3070). Breakfast/lunch/dinner daily. As the name implies, the house specialty is the excellent chili—75 varieties, from vegetarian to hot-as-Hades. Also laudable omelets, hamburgers, and hot dogs. Super-kitsch décor, Elvis Presley style; amusing clientele, half-bohemian, half-punk.

Hamburger Harry's (Lower Manhattan), 157 Chambers St. (267-4446). Lunch/dinner daily (till 11:30 p.m.). Some 16 kinds of hamburgers (connoisseurs call them the best in New York) and champagne by the glass, a stone's throw from the World Trade Center. Other locations. 145 W. 45th St., midtown (840-0566).

Katz's Delicatessen (Lower East Side), 205 E. Houston St. at Ludlow St. (254-2246). Breakfast/lunch/dinner daily. No credit cards. Cafeteria-style deli w. the authentic New York flavor. Gigantic sandwiches of brisket, corned beef, tongue, roast beef, etc.

☀ **Museum of Modern Art Garden Café** (midtown), 11 W. 53rd St. (708-9400). Lunch Thurs.-Tues. The tourists' favorite: big bay windows w. unobstructed view of the Sculpture Garden. Crowded out at lunch. Praiseworthy food.

Nathan's Famous (midtown), 1482 Broadway at W. 43rd St. (382-0620). Open daily from 7 a.m. to 3 a.m. New York's best hot dogs, excellent french fries and sandwiches, but so-so burgers. Three other locations in Manhattan and Brooklyn, besides the famous original at Coney Island (see "Nearby Excursions," below).

☀ **Tap Room Manhattan Brewing Co.** (Soho), 40-42 Thompson St. (219-9250). A/C. Open Tues.-Sun. (until 1 a.m.). Large tavern dominated by the huge copper vats of the Manhattan Brewing Co. in the heart of Soho. Several house brews are on tap, accompanied by acceptable British-pub style food; buffet brunch on wknds.

WHERE TO EAT WHAT

American: An American Place (♟♟♟), Sofi (♟♟♟), Arizona 206 (♟♟), Coach House (♟♟), Gage & Tollner (♟♟), Hubert's (♟♟), River Café(♟♟), Sylvia's (♟♟), Acme Bar & Grill (♟), Bridge Café(♟), Carnegie Delicatessen (♟), Hard Rock Café(♟), Manhattan Brewing Co. (♟)

Chinese: Shun Lee Palace (♟♟♟), Auntie Yuan (♟♟), Grand Palace (♟♟), Canton (♟♟), Nice, Restaurant (♟)

Continental: Cellar in the Sky (♟♟♟), Sofi (♟♟♟), Windows on the World (♟♟), Lou Siegel's (♟), Café des Artistes (♟), Café 43 (♟)

Cuban-Chinese: Bayamo (♟)

East European: Russian Tea Room (♟)

Ethiopian: Abyssinia (♟)

Fast Food/Cafeterias: Broadway Diner, Exterminator Chili, Hamburger Harrys, Katz's Delicatessen, Museum of Modern Art cafeteria, Nathan's Famous, Tap Room Manhattan Brewing Co.

French: Lutèce (♟♟♟♟), La Côte Basque (♟♟♟♟), The Quilted Giraffe (♟♟♟), Aurora (♟♟♟), Provence (♟♟♟), Odeon (♟♟), La Gauloise (♟), Man Ray (♟)

Greek: Avgerino's (♟)

Hamburgers: Hamburger Harry's (see "Fast Food"), Hard Rock Café(♟)

Indian: Darbar (♟♟), Gaylord's (♟)

Italian: Palio (♟♟♟), Parioli Romanissimo (♟♟♟), Il Nido (♟♟), Nanni (♟)

Japanese: Hatsuhana (♟♟), Kitcho (♟♟), Mitsukoshi (♟♟), Japonica (♟♟)

Latin American: Cabana Carioca (♟), Sabor (♟)

Mexican: Rosa Mexicano (♟♟), Cinco de Mayo (♟♟)
Seafood: Le Bernardin (♟♟♟♟), John Clancy's (♟♟), Oyster Bar (♟♟), Spring Street Natural (♟), Sweet's (♟)
Spanish: El Rincon de España (♟)
Steak: Christ Cella (♟♟), Palm (♟♟), Smith & Wollensky (♟♟), Frank's (♟), Gallagher's (♟), Peter Luger (♟)
Thai: Siam Inn (♟)

BARS & NIGHTCLUBS

In a city with some 15,000 bars, discos, nightclubs, dance halls, strip joints, etc., it isn't easy to make a current list of the "in" places. Here are some dependable values, classified by type.

BARS/PUBS: The Ballroom (Chelsea), 253 W. 28th St. (244-3005). An unusual nightspot which contrives to be simultaneously a cabaret, comedy club, off-off-Broadway theater, commendable restaurant, and excellent "tapas" bar, serving the highly esteemed Spanish hors d'oeuvres. One of the most popular places in Chelsea. Karen Akers is one of the stars who appear here regularly. Open Tues.-Sat.

Café Carlyle (Upper East Side), in the Hotel Carlyle (see "Accommodations," above) (744-1600). Preppy piano bar, enlivened for the last two decades by the talented Bobby Short. Also a restaurant. Open nightly.

Café Skylight (midtown), in the Novotel (see "Accommodations," above) (315-0100). On a terrace on the seventh floor of the Novotel, this wine bar has a panoramic view of Broadway and Times Square. Large selection by the glass or the bottle. Excellent sandwiches, cheeses, and pâtés to accompany the wine. Spectacular view after dark. Open nightly till 1 a.m.

Chumley's (Greenwich Village), 86 Bedford St. (675-4449). The entrance is unmarked—a reminder that this was originally a speakeasy. Sawdust on the floor, fire burning in winter. Bar area is small and decorated with book jackets, reminders of the original denizens. A Greenwich village literary landmark. Good burgers. Open nightly until 2 a.m.

Clarke's (midtown), 915 Third Ave. at E. 56th St. (759-1650). Only the uninitiated refer to this very lively bar by its full name, P.J. Clarke's. Rather hearty masculine atmosphere. So-so restaurant. Crowded at night. Open nightly.

Landmark Tavern (midtown), 626 Eleventh Ave. at W. 46th St. (757-8595). A/C. AE. Authentic Victorian style bar built in 1868 w. tin ceiling, tile floor, and pot-belly stove. Good Irish style food too, available at lunch and dinner. Open daily noon until midnight.

Lion's Head Ltd. (Greenwich Village), 59 Christopher St. nr. Seventh Ave. (929-0670). Likeable, relaxed bar full of intellectual scribblers; very Greenwich Village. Also a restaurant. Open nightly until 4 a.m.

McSorley's Old Ale House (East Village), 15 E. 7th St. (473-9148). Classic alehouse serving beer. Young, student crowd along w. locals from the Ukrainian neighborhood. Historic atmosphere—one of Brendan Behan's haunts. The corned-beef sandwiches are also famous. Open daily 11 a.m. to 1 a.m.

☀ **White Horse Tavern** (Greenwich Village), 567 Hudson St. (243-9260). One of Manhattan's oldest literary cafés (1880), once the favorite of Dylan Thomas. Gently bohemian clientele; excellent hamburgers. Open daily from noon to 3 a.m.

COUNTRY AND WESTERN MUSIC: The **Lone Star Café** (Greenwich Village), 61 Fifth Ave. at 13th St. (242-1664). The temple of country music; western décor crowned by the famous rooftop iguana 32 ft. (10 m) long. Big country-music stars. Mechanical steer. Noisy. Also a mediocre restaurant. Open nightly.

O'Lunney's (midtown), 915 Second Ave. at E. 49th St. (751-5470). Another place for country music lovers, *Urban Cowboy* style, with bluegrass as well on Sun. Also a passable restaurant. Open nightly.

DISCO/ROCK: ※ **Au Bar** (midtown), 41 E. 58th St. (308-9455). Intimate, very upscale bar-restaurant modeled on a smart London club. Dance floor, elegant dining room, library(!), and smoking room. A world away from the ear-splitting modern disco. Thronged by well-brought-up yuppies. Open nightly.

B2/Be Square (formerly Area)(Tribeca), 157 Hudson St. (966-5881). Classical Art Deco disco for the Wall Street crowd (there is even an automatic teller machine, the first in a New York club). Wed.-Sat.

China Club (Upper West Side), 2130 Broadway at W. 75th St. (877-1166). One of the most amusing "in" discos in the city. The décor, Far Eastern crossed with art deco, is bizarre. Frequented by New York celebrities and entertainers. Open nightly.

El Morocco (midtown), 307 E. 54th St. (750-1500). The famous '30s nightspot restored to its original splendor, with big swing band, artificial palm trees, and zebra-skin upholstery. A triumph of kitsch, modestly self-styled "the world's most famous nightclub." Open nightly.

Emerald City (formerly Red Parrot) (midtown), 617 W. 57th St. (247-1530). Fashionable disco popular with leading figures from the world of high fashion. There are parrots flying around above the dance floor. Jazz and New Wave music. Open Wed.-Sat.

Limelight (Chelsea), 660 Ave. of the Americas at W. 20th St. (807-7850). This enormous disco, in an old church, seats 1,000 people on three floors. The bar is in the adjoining chapel. Very "in" atmosphere. Open nightly.

Nell's (Greenwich Village), 246 W. 14th St. (675-1567). Very trendy semi-private nightclub which draws New York's artistic and literary crowd. Sumptuously venerable Victorian décor; background music ranges from modern jazz to Dvorak. For with-it intellectuals. Open nightly.

※ **Palladium** (East Village), 126 E. 14th St. (473-7171). World's biggest disco, 320,000 sq. ft. (30,000 m²) on seven floors. The famous architect Arato Isozaki did the interior, where 3,500 people can be comfortable. Far out. Open Tues.-Sun.

Ritz (East Village), 119 E. 11th St. (254-2800). Old movie house now a rendezvous for rockers. Ear-splitting audio. Adventure movies on big screen. Very with-it atmosphere. Open nightly.

※ **Roseland** (midtown), 239 W. 52nd St. (247-0200). Enormous 1930s dance hall, straight out of *They Shoot Horses, Don't They?* Super-kitsch in a very populist way; some evenings you can count 3,000 dancers. Guaranteed atmosphere; patriotic décor with huge star-spangled banner. A sight to be seen. Open Wed.-Sun.

S.O.B. (Sounds of Brazil) (Greenwich Village), 204 Varick St. at W. Houston St. (924-5521). Fashionable super-disco; Latin rhythms to an American beat. One of the "hottest" places in town. Open Wed.-Sun.

Stringfellow's (Gramercy Park), 35 E. 21st St. (254-2444). Aggressively hi-tech disco, a triumph of multicolored neon. Waitresses in pink tutus. A fashionable place. Open nightly.

☼ **The Tunnel** (Chelsea), 220 Twelfth Ave. at W. 27th St. (714-9886). Giant disco (can hold up to 2,500) in an old dockside railroad terminal; the rails are still on the ground, and form an integral part of the décor. Off-the-wall rock ambience. Neighborhood unsafe at night; arrange for a cab. Open nightly.

COMEDY CLUBS: Caroline's (Lower Manhattan), Pier 17 at 89 South St. (233-4900). One of the most famous comedy clubs in the country, with Jay Leno, Billy Crystal, or Howie Mandel at the head of the bill. Preppy atmosphere and patrons. Open Tues.-Sun.

Catch a Rising Star (Upper East Side), 1487 First Ave. at E. 77th St. (794-1906). As the name suggests, specializes in discovering new talent.

Chicago City Limits (Upper East Side), 351 E. 74th St. (772-8707). An old reliable of satire, political and other. Open Wed.-Sat.

Improvisation (The Original) (midtown), 358 W. 44th St. (765-8268). The oldest (1963) of New York's comedy clubs, which has showcased such future superstars as Richard Pryor, Joe Piscopo, and Robin Williams. Casual ambience and décor with no affectations. Open nightly.

JAZZ: The magic **Jazzline** telephone number (718/465-7500) gives current programs for all the jazz clubs.

Blue Note (Greenwich Village), 131 W. 3rd St. (475-8592). The biggest stars of the day. Restaurant as well. Open nightly.

Bottom Line (Greenwich Village), 15 W. 4th St. (228-7880). Free jazz, rock, blues. Switched-on clientele. Reservations a must.

Carlos I (Greenwich Village), 432 Ave. of the Americas at W. 10th St. (982-3260). Restaurant-jazz club featuring some solid performers. Agreeable décor; praiseworthy Caribbean cooking. Open nightly.

Fat Tuesday's (Gramercy Park), Third Ave. and E. 17th St. (533-7902). Modern and traditional jazz; restaurant as well. Open nightly.

Michael's Pub (midtown), 211 E. 55th St. (758-2272). New Orleans jazz; restaurant. Every now and then Woody Allen still turns up on a Monday evening to play clarinet. Open nightly.

Sweet Basil (Greenwich Village), 88 Seventh Ave. South (242-1785). Modern jazz; several stars appear regularly, including Art Blakey and the Jazz Messengers. Pretty rustic décor; likeable atmosphere. Open nightly.

Village Gate (Greenwich Village), Bleecker and Thompson Sts. (475-5120). Very famous jazz club; Dizzy Gillespie comes here. Open nightly.

Village Vanguard (Greenwich Village), 178 Seventh Ave. (255-4037). The jazz shrine of New York City since 1935; probably the world's most famous jazz club. All the biggest names in jazz put in an appearance here. Generally crowded. Open nightly.

LATE NIGHT SERVICE (closing time in parentheses): Auntie Yuan (midnight), Carnegie Delicatessen (4 a.m.), Frank's (open from 2 a.m. until 10 p.m.) Gallagher's (midnight), Hard Rock Café (4 a.m.), Man Ray (midnight), Odeon (2:30 a.m.), Palm (midnight), Rosa Mexicano (midnight), Russian Tea Room (12:30 a.m.).

NEARBY EXCURSIONS

🔔 **CONEY ISLAND** (Surf Ave., Brooklyn): Beach very crowded in summer (see "Beaches," above). Kitsch but entertaining amusement park (see "Theme Parks," above). Famous aquarium (see the New York Aquarium under "Zoos," above), and New York's best hot dogs at

Nathan's Famous, Surf and Stillwell Aves. (718/266-3161). In a word, don't miss it, but avoid the summer weekend crush.

☼⚲ **STATEN ISLAND** (10 mi., 16 km, SW via the Brooklyn-Battery Tunnel, I-278, and the Verrazano-Narrows Bridge, or via ferry from Battery Park, in Lower Manhattan): Facing Manhattan across New York Bay, this small island, only 14 by 8 mi. (22 by 12 km), still retains a rural touch with its many parks, old villages, and rolling hills that invite you to a stroll.

You should certainly see **Richmondtown Restoration,** 441 Clarke Ave. at Arthur Kill Rd. (718/351-1617), a museum village with 30 or so carefully restored buildings from the 17th to 19th centuries, including the Voorlezer's House, the country's oldest surviving school, built around 1690.

Not far away is the curious **Jacques Marchais Center of Tibetan Art,** 338 Lighthouse Ave. (718/987-3478), open Fri.-Sat. afternoons in Apr., Oct., and Nov.; Wed. and Sun. afternoons May-Sept. This interesting museum of Buddhist art stands in its own fine Oriental garden.

The **Snug Harbor Cultural Center,** 1000 Richmond Terrace (718/448-2500), open daily, is a cultural and creative-arts center in what used to be a sailors' retirement home dating from the early 19th century. Interesting Greek Revival and Victorian buildings, art museum, fine sculpture garden, and 80-acre (39-ha.) park.

An oasis of peace and calm within New York's city limits, 30 min. from Manhattan by the Staten Island Ferry.

☼⚲⚲ **VERRAZANO-NARROWS BRIDGE** (9 mi., 15 km, SW via the Brooklyn-Battery Tunnel and I-278): The bridge connecting Brooklyn to Staten Island was designed by Othmar Ammann, an architect of Swiss origin. It's the world's longest suspension bridge, with a total length of 13,700 ft. (4,176 m); the central span is 4,260 ft. (1,299 m) long. The piers are 689 ft. (210 m) high; there are two decks, each with six lanes. Opened in 1964, it cost $305 million. More than 50 million vehicles cross it every year. A truly riveting sight. **Fort Wadsworth,** at the Staten Island approach to the bridge, has a fine view of New York Bay. Don't miss it.

FARTHER AFIELD

☼⚲⚲ **THE HUDSON VALLEY** (229 mi., 366 km, round trip via U.S. 9N, N.Y. 9A, U.S. 9N, N.Y. 199W, N.Y. 28N/S and N.Y. 375N/S, I-87S, U.S. 9W, Palisades Interstate Pkwy., and the George Washington Bridge): A car trip along a very lovely valley, which reminds seasoned travelers of the Rhine. Next to Manhattan this may be richer in historical associations than any other part of New York State. Leave Manhattan on U.S. 9, the northward extension of Broadway, and begin the tour with a visit to ⚱ **Philipse Manor Hall State Historic Park,** Warburton Ave. and Dock St., Yonkers (914/965-4027) (visit by appointment, Wed.-Sun. from end of May to Nov.). Built in 1682, this was the home of a family of noble loyalists from England. Superb Georgian-style interior decoration. Not far is the **Hudson River Museum,** 511 Warburton Ave. (914/963-4550), open Wed.-Sun., where exhibits bearing on the art and history of the Hudson Valley are housed in an imposing 19th-century home.

Tarrytown, 11 mi. (17 km) north, was founded in the 17th century by the Dutch, and made famous by Washington Irving, whose house, ⚱ **Sunnyside,** W. Sunnyside Lane (914/631-8200), is open daily. Many other fine old homes have been restored at the expense of the Rockefeller family. They include **Lyndhurst,**

635 S. Broadway (914/631-0046), open Tues.-Sun., Apr.-Oct. (weekends only, the rest of the year), a splendid 1833 Gothic Revival estate overlooking the river; and ☖☖ **Philipsburg Manor,** Kingsland Point Park (914/631-7766), open daily, a beautiful 1683 manor house, still with its old mill, where a very popular classical-music festival is held every summer. Near here, see the old Dutch church built in 1685 and the charming little **Sleepy Hollow cemetery,** with the graves of Washington Irving, Andrew Carnegie, and William Rockefeller.

U.S. 9 continues northward through **Ossining,** with the famous **Sing Sing Federal Penitentiary** (no visitors), on its way to **Croton-on-Hudson** and the lovely ☖ **Van Cortlandt Manor,** Croton Point Ave. (914/631-8200), open daily, dating from the War of Independence and built on the old post road to Albany; fine 18th-century garden. Between Garrison and Cold Spring, on a height of land overlooking the river, see ☖ **Boscobel,** built in 1805 in the Federal style by States Morris Dyckman, with its beautiful orangery.

North another 23 mi. (36 km) is **Poughkeepsie,** home of **Vassar College,** long the most famous women's college in the country, co-ed since 1969; its campus on Raymond Ave. is worth a look.

On to **Hyde Park,** birthplace of Franklin D. Roosevelt; visit the ☀ ☖☖ **Roosevelt-Vanderbilt National Historic Sites,** on U.S. 9 (914/229-9115), open daily. You'll see the house where the 32rd president was born; his tomb, and that of his wife, Eleanor, are in the rose garden. There's a museum, a library with Roosevelt's private papers, and the sumptuous mansion of the railroad magnate Frederick Vanderbilt, built in 1898 to the Beaux Arts design of McKim, Mead and White. Don't miss it.

A little off U.S. 9 at **Staatsburg,** the ☖ **Mills Mansion Historic Site** (914/889-4100), a magnificent 65-room 1895 classical revival building by Stanford White, certainly deserves a visit. Elegant Louis XV and Louis XVI furniture. Open Wed.-Sun., Apr.-Oct.

☀☖ **Rhinebeck,** a little distance north, has two claims to fame: the oldest inn in the country (see the Beekman Arms, under "Where to Stay," below), and a wonderful collection of early aircraft at the **Old Rhinebeck Aerodrome,** Stone Church Rd. (914/758-8610). Weekend air shows mid-May to Oct.; museum open daily, mid-May to Oct. Then take the opposite bank of the Hudson River on to ☀ ☖ **Woodstock,** at the foot of the Catskills. This agreeable little summer resort and artists' colony is famous for its chamber-music festival (started in 1916), and also as the scene (Aug. 15–18, 1969) of the legendary rock festival, which was attended by almost half a million people, and which in a sense marked the end of the '60s. Should be seen.

Head back to Manhattan via ☀ **Kingston,** founded by the Dutch in 1652 and the first capital of New York State before it was burned by the British. Many interesting buildings including the ☖ **Senate House Historic Site** of 1676 at 312 Fair St. (914/338-2786), open Wed.-Sun. (weekends only, Jan.-Mar.).

George Washington made his headquarters in ☀ **Newburgh,** 34 mi. (55 km) south, from April 1782 to Aug. 1783 during the War of Independence, and it was from here that he made the official announcement of the end of hostilities. You may visit the site at 84 Liberty St. (914/562-1195), Wed.-Sun., Apr.-Dec. (weekends only, Jan.-Mar.). Also see the **New Windsor Cantonment Site,** Temple Hill Rd. (914/561-1765), open Wed.-Sun. from late Apr. through Oct., the last encampment of the Continental Army. Interesting museum. Don't miss this page of history.

On your way to West Point, make a detour along N.Y. 32 to the ☀ **Storm King Art Center,** Old Pleasant Hill Rd. in Mountainville (914/534-3115), open daily Apr.-Nov., a fine museum of modern art in a superb 350-acre (142-ha.) park adorned with monumental sculpture. Don't miss it.

☀ 🔭🔭 **West Point,** home of the U.S. Military Academy, founded in 1802, turns out 4,000 cadets a year. **Fort Putnam** (1779), dominating the campus, the **Cadet Chapel,** and the **West Point Museum** are all worth visiting. At the **Information Center,** at Thayer Gate (914/938-2638), you can obtain dates and times of parades in Apr.-May and Sept.-Oct. Don't miss it.

☀ **Bear Mountain State Park,** just south of West Point, is a lovely wooded park of some 5,000 acres (2,000 ha.) overlooking the Hudson. **Perkins Memorial Drive,** a scenic highway, will take you to the top of Bear Mountain and give you a splendid view across the valley. If you like flea markets you should stop at ☀ 🜍 **Nyack** (where the painter Edward Hopper was born) to see its **Arts & Crafts & Antiques,** with almost 100 art galleries, handcraft shops, and antiques dealers (914/358-8443), open Tues.-Sun.

Finally, back to Manhattan by the Palisades Interstate Pkwy. and the George Washington Bridge; allow two to three days for this exciting tour.

Where to Stay En Route

The following hotels, motels, and inns are recommended as suitable places for a stopover.

IN BEAR MOUNTAIN STATE PARK. The 🍴 **Bear Mountain Inn,** U.S. 9W, Bear Mountain, NY 10911 (914/786-2731). 60 rms. Small rustic motel inside the park. **I–M**

HYDE PARK. The 🍴 **Roosevelt Inn,** 38 Albany Post Rd., Hyde Park, NY 12538 (914/229-2443). 26 rms. Modest but very well-run motel w. modern comforts. Open May-Dec. **I**

LAKE MOHONK / NEW PALTZ. The ☀ 🍴🍴🍴 **Mohonk Mountain House,** N.Y. 299, New Paltz, NY 12561 (914/255-1000; 212/233-2244 in New York City). 300 rms, some without bath. Flamboyant castle-hotel dating from 1879; the Victorian structure is a designated historic landmark. Resv. strongly advised at all times, and as far in advance as possible during the summer. **VE (AP)**

NEWBURGH. The 🍴🍴 **Diplomat Motor Inn,** 845 Union Ave., Newburgh, NY 12550 (914/564-7550). 80 rms. Small, comfortable hotel overlooking Washington Lake. **I**

RHINEBECK. The ☀ 🍴🍴 **Beekman Arms,** Beekman Square, Rhinebeck, NY 12572 (914/876-7077). 48 rms. The oldest inn (1766) in the country; period décor and atmosphere but modern standards of comfort. **I–M**

WEST POINT. The ☀ 🍴 **Hotel Thayer,** S. Entry (off N.Y. 218), U.S. Military Academy, West Point, NY 10996 (914/446-4731). 200 rms. Venerable old hotel on the academy campus looking out on the Hudson. **I–M**

Where to Eat En Route

The following restaurants and inns are suitable places for a meal, if you're following the above itinerary.

GARRISON. The ☀ 🍴🍴 **Bird and Bottle Inn,** Old Albany Post Rd. (914/424-3000). Lunch/dinner daily (closed Mon. and Tues. from mid-Nov. to Apr.). Authentic Revolutionary-period tavern attractively restored. French-inspired cuisine of refinement. **M**

HYDE PARK. The 🍴🍴🍴 **Escoffier Room,** on U.S. 9, 3 mi. (5 km) north of town

(914/471-6608). Lunch/dinner Tues.-Sat. This is the dining rm of the Culinary Institute of America, where the country's future culinary greats are trained. Very carefully prepared French-inspired cuisine. Resv. a must. **M**

KINGSTON. 🍸🍸 **Hillside Manor,** 240 Boulevard (914/331-4386). Lunch Mon.-Fri., dinner nightly. Tasty Italian food; romantic country-inn décor w. wonderful views. **M**

POUGHKEEPSIE. The ※ 🍸🍸 **Treasure Chest,** 568 South Rd. (914/462-4545). Lunch Mon.-Fri., dinner Mon.-Sat. Charming inn in a 250-year-old building. Excellent continental cooking. **I**

RHINEBECK. The ※ 🍸🍸 **Beekman Arms,** Beekman Square (914/876-7077). Lunch/dinner daily. This is the oldest inn (1766) in the country; period décor and atmosphere. Classic cuisine. **M–E**

STORMVILLE. 🍸🍸🍸 **Harrald's,** N.Y. 52 (914/878-6595). Dinner only, Wed.-Sat. One of the finest rests. on the East Coast; with refined continental cuisine and exemplary svce. **E (prix fixe)**

WOODSTOCK. ※ 🍸 **Deanie's Towne Tavern,** junction of N.Y. 212 and N.Y. 375 (914/679-6508). Dinner only, Wed.-Mon. Turn-of-the-century tavern serving very commendable classic cuisine. **I**

🔭🔭 **LONG ISLAND** (244 mi., 390 km, round trip by the Queens-Midtown Tunnel, Long Island Expwy., N.Y. 25A, N.Y. 106N, N.Y. 25A West, N.Y. 25W, ferry from Greenport to Shelter Island, N.Y. 114S, N.Y. 27W, N.Y. 27E, Robert Moses Pkwy. South, Ocean Pkwy. West, Loop Pkwy., the beaches at Long Beach, Atlantic Beach, Rockaway Beach, Flatbush Ave., the Belt Pkwy., the Brooklyn-Queens Expwy., and the Brooklyn-Battery Tunnel): White-sand beaches, dozens of little museums, old homes that recall the island's past, and picturesque fishing harbors, all just two or three hours' drive from the center of New York. Long Island has always been the favorite country retreat of celebrities, including Pres. Theodore Roosevelt, Albert Einstein (who worked out his General Theory of Relativity between two sailing trips), painters Willem de Kooning and Jackson Pollock, sculptor Isamu Noguchi, writers James Fenimore Cooper, John Steinbeck, Saul Bellow, Truman Capote, Edward Albee, and Kurt Vonnegut, and many others.

Leaving Manhattan to the east via the Queens-Midtown Tunnel and the Long Island Expwy. (I-495), stop first at **Kings Point,** home of the ⚓ **U.S. Merchant Marine Academy** with its thousand students, at King's Point Rd. (516/773-5000), open daily; there are parades of the midshipmen Sat. in spring and fall.

Another 15 mi. (24 km) east is ※ **Oyster Bay,** a busy pleasure-boat harbor at the head of a long, narrow bay. See the ⚓ **Raynham Hall Museum,** 20 W. Main St. (516/922-6808), open Tues.-Sun. This old farmhouse, which was bought by Samuel Townsend in 1738, has been scrupulously restored; it played an important part in the War of Independence, particularly as the headquarters of the "Queens Rangers." ※⚓ **Sagamore Hill Historic Site,** 304 Cove Neck Rd. (516/922-4447), open daily, May-Sept. (Tues.-Sun., Oct.-Apr.), was the Summer White House from 1901 to 1909, and the final home of Theodore Roosevelt, who died in 1919. Authentic furnishings and many personal memorabilia of "Teddy"; not to be missed. It's only a short distance to the ⚓ **Theodore Roosevelt Memorial Sanctuary,** E. Main St. at Cove Rd., open daily, tomb of the 26th president in an 11-acre (4-ha.) park which is also a sea-bird sanctuary. Should be seen (516/922-3200).

On to the interesting ⚓ **Whaling Museum,** commemorating a trade that once flourished on these shores, at **Cold Spring Harbor,** on Main St. (516/367-3418), open Tues.-Sun. At nearby **Huntington,** lovers of poetry will be sure to pay their respects at the ⚓ **birthplace of Walt Whitman** at 246 Old Walt Whitman Rd. (516/427-5240), with a museum and library devoted to the famous poet, open Wed.-Sun.

Continuing eastward, don't fail to visit ☀ 🏛🏛 **"Eagles Nest, "** Little Neck Rd. in **Centerport** (516/261-5656), open Tues.-Sun., May-Oct., a lovely house belonging to the Vanderbilt family, which stands in a 43-acre (17-ha.) park looking out over **Northport Bay.** It is now the home of the **Vanderbilt Museum,** with its natural-history collection. N.Y. 25A now passes part of **Sunken Meadow State Park,** a well-laid-out recreation area with huge sand beach and golf course, on its way to ☀ **Stony Brook,** a delightful seaside village founded in 1655 by settlers from Boston, which seems to have changed very little since colonial times. Several old houses and a remarkable group of small museums of art and history, 🏛🏛 **The Museums at Stony Brook,** Main St. at N.Y. 25A (516/751-0066), open Wed.-Mon. Don't miss them—particularly the unique collection of 250 horse-drawn vehicles, coaches, and carriages. The road now passes through **Port Jefferson,** terminal of the ferry for Bridgeport, Conn., and rejoins N.Y. 25, passing through **Riverhead** (interesting **Suffolk County Historical Museum,** 300 W. Main St., open Mon.-Sat.) on its way to **Greenport** and the ferry.

☀ 🔔 **Sag Harbor,** at the head of Gardiners Bay, was once one of the most important whaling ports in the world; it inspired James Fenimore Cooper to write several stories about sailors and the sea. Besides the little streets lined with charming small houses, you should see the **Custom House,** on Main St., a late-18th-century building which also served as the post office, and the **Whaling and Historical Museum,** Garden and Main Sts. (516/725-0770), open daily mid-May to Sept.

At **East Hampton,** founded in 1648 and also once a prosperous whaling port, the fishermen have by now given way to artists and wealthy summer sojourners. In and around the town are many 19th-century windmills, including one at 14 James Lane (516/324-0713), open daily June-Oct. and by appointment the rest of the year; this is the ⚓ **birthplace of John Howard Payne** (1791–1852), who wrote the words of "Home, Sweet Home." On to the east, and after a look at the **Town Marine Museum** in **Amagansett** on Bluff Rd. (516/267-6544), open Tues.-Sun. in summer (by appointment the rest of the year), with its delightful ship models, you reach ☀ **Montauk,** at the eastern tip of the island, a busy and picturesque fishing port (swordfish, tuna). Its miles of deserted beach, and the facilities for leasing sailboats, make it a very appealing resort. From ⚓ **Montauk State Park,** with its 1795 lighthouse built on the orders of George Washington, you'll have a splendid view of the ocean. Don't miss it.

On your way back to the city along N.Y. 27W, stop at ⚓ **Southampton,** one of the island's two oldest towns (1640). With its many Colonial houses, it is today an elegant beach resort noted for its luxurious homes and fashionable shops. See the **Old Halsey Homestead** (1648), the oldest wooden house in all New York State, on S. Main St. (516/283-3527), open Tues.-Sun. from mid-June to mid-Sept. Return to Manhattan via N.Y. 27W as far as **Bay Shore,** where the Robert Moses Pkwy. leads off on the left to the long beach at **Jones Beach State Park,** very popular with New Yorkers during the summer. In the last stage of the trip you follow a succession of coastal highways between **Long Beach** and **Brooklyn.** On the way, lovers of lonelier beaches can explore **Fire Island National Seashore,** a thin belt of pine-planted sand dunes 31 mi. (50 km) long abounding in fish and wildlife; it can be reached at either end of the park by bridge, or by ferry from Sayville or Bay Shore.

A very full two- to three-day trip.

Where to Stay En Route

The following hotels, motels, and inns are recommended as suitable places for a stopover.

EAST HAMPTON. The ☼ ⚑⚑ **1770 House–Philip Taylor,** 143 Main St., East Hampton, NY 11937 (516/324-1770). 10 rms. Charming old inn dating from 1770, elegantly and comfortably furnished. **E–VE**

EAST NORWICH. ⚑⚑ **Burt Bacharach's Inn,** jct. N.Y. 25A and N.Y. 106, East Norwich, NY 11732 (516/922-1500). 72 rms. Modern, very comfortable motel; acceptable rest. **E**

GREENPORT. The ⚑⚑ **Sound View Inn,** North Rd., Greenport, NY 11944 (516/477-1910). 70 rms. Comfortable motel w. private beach. **M–E**

MONTAUK. The ⚑⚑⚑ **Montauk Yacht Club and Inn,** Star Island, Montauk, NY 11954 (516/668-3100). 107 rms. One of the most comfortable hotel-marinas on the eastern seaboard. **VE**

SHELTER ISLAND. The ⚑⚑ **Pridwin,** Shore Rd., Shelter Island, NY 11964 (516/749-0476). 40 rms. Comfortable motel on its own beach. Open May-Oct. **M–E**

SOUTHAMPTON. The ⚑⚑ **Sandpiper,** on N.Y. 27, Southampton, NY 11968 (516/283-7600). 64 rms. Inviting motel on Peconic Bay. **M**

⚑ **Shinnecock,** 240 Montauk Hwy., Southampton, NY 11968 (516/283-2406). 30 rms. Functional motel a stone's throw from the beach. **M**

Where to Eat En Route

The following inns and restaurants are suitable places for a meal, if you're following the above itinerary.

BAYVILLE. ⚏⚏ **Steve's Pier 1,** 33 Bayville Ave. (516/628-2153). Lunch/dinner daily. Continental rest. on Long Island Sound. Excellent value. **I**

COLD SPRING HARBOR. The ⚏⚏ **Old Whaler,** 105 Harbor Rd. (516/367-3166). Lunch/dinner daily. Good, reasonably priced seafood rest. in a charming inn dating from 1680 with view of the harbor. **I**

EAST HAMPTON. The ⚏⚏ **Maidstone Arms,** 207 Main St. (516/324-5006). Dinner Wed.-Mon. Pleasant French country inn setting, praiseworthy continental cuisine. **M**

EAST HILLS. ⚏⚏⚏ **L'Endroit,** 290 Glen Cove Rd. (516/621-6630). Lunch/dinner Mon.-Sat. Excellent contemporary French cuisine in a delightful rustic setting. **I–M**

MONTAUK. The ⚏⚏ **Blue Marlin,** Edgemere and Flamingo Sts. (516/668-9880). Lunch/dinner daily; closed Jan.-Feb. Good seafood rest. in a pretty Early American setting. Good value. **I**

SOUTHAMPTON. ☎☎ Herb McCarthy's Bowden Square, N. Sea Rd. (516/283-2800). Lunch/dinner daily. Tasty food with a slight Irish accent. Dinner on the terrace in summer. **M**

STONY BROOK. The **☎☎☎ Three Village Inn,** 150 Main St. (516/751-0555). 1785 Colonial inn with very good country food. A great place. **M**

ᗊᗊ FINGER LAKES (785 mi., 1,256 km, round trip via the George Washington Bridge, Palisades Interstate Pkwy., U.S. 6W, N.Y. 17N, I-81N, N.Y. 175W, U.S. 20W, N.Y. 89S, N.Y. 79W, N.Y. 14N, U.S. 20W, N.Y. 21S, N.Y. 53S, N.Y. 54S, N.Y. 17E, I-81S, Penna. 106S, U.S. 6E, N.J. 23S, I-80N, I-95N, and the George Washington Bridge): With its 11 lakes extended like fingers (the Iroquois legend says that God wanted to leave his handprint on the most beautiful place in his creation), its famous vineyards with about 40 growers, its green hills, caves, gorges, and waterfalls, the Finger Lakes region draws more than half a million holidaymakers a year. As well as its beautiful landscapes, this quietly charming countryside offers a foothold in history, as the birthplace of some of the ideas and institutions that have helped to shape America: the abolition of slavery (Auburn), women's rights (Seneca Falls), and the Mormon church (Palmyra).

Head NE out of Manhattan by the George Washington Bridge, the Palisades Interstate Pkwy., and N.Y. 17 (also known as the Southern Tier Expwy.) on to I-81. Your first stop will be at ※ **Syracuse,** capital of the lakes district, 270 mi. (430 km) NE of New York, famed for its parks and its museums. Make a point of seeing the **Everson Museum of Art,** 401 Harrison St. (315/474-6064), open Tues.-Sun., the first museum designed by I. M. Pei, with a fine collection of American painting and ceramics; the **Erie Canal Museum,** Erie Blvd. and Montgomery St. (315/471-0593), open Tues.-Sun., with exhibits on the construction of the historic canal; and ᗊ **Onondaga Lake Park,** Onondaga Lake Pkwy. (315/457-2990), open daily May-Oct., where you'll find an interesting **Salt Museum** as well as a faithful reconstruction of **Fort Ste. Marie de Gannentaha,** the first camp set up here by the French in the 17th century.

After a stop at the delightful tourist town of **Skaneateles,** on the northern shore of the lake of the same name, go on to **Auburn** at the tip of **Owasco Lake,** a site settled by Native Americans since the 11th century. In the 19th century it had two famous residents: William H. Seward, the secretary of state who bought Alaska from the Russians for a trifling consideration (see "Farther Afield" in Chapter 57 on Anchorage), and Harriet Tubman, a former slave whose influence and determination were instrumental in bringing about abolition; she saved more than 300 black slaves in flight from their Southern masters through her network of secret helpers, the Underground Railroad. The ᗊ **Tubman House** at 180 South St. (315/253-2621), now a museum, may be visited by appointment only; don't miss it.

Some 16 miles (25 km) farther west, ※ **Seneca Falls** is a place of pilgrimage for American feminists; here, in 1848, was held the first Convention for Women's Rights. The ᗊ **National Women's Hall of Fame,** 76 Fall St. (315/568-2936), open daily, commemorates two centuries of the struggle for equal rights, and pays tribute to such past leaders as Amelia Jenks Bloomer, Elizabeth Cady Stanton, Mary Cassatt, Abigail Adams, Helen Hayes, and Marian Anderson.

The route now runs along the left shore of **Cayuga Lake,** 40 mi. (64 km) long, and after a stop to admire **Taughannock Falls,** higher than Niagara (215 ft., 65 m), you'll arrive in **Ithaca,** home of renowned ※ **Cornell University** with 17,500 students. Visit the campus in its magnificent natural setting w. two gorges formed by glacial runoff that cut off the campus and plummet about 100 ft at their steepest point. The ⚓ **Herbert F. Johnson Museum,** Central Ave. (607/255-6464), open Tues.-Sun., is an interesting art museum which you shouldn't miss. In summer this former capital of the silent movies presents many concerts, plays, and ballets.

Going on to the west, you come next to 🏔 **Watkins Glen,** at the southern tip of beautiful **Seneca Lake,** the deepest in the region (630 ft., 192 m). Best known for its race track and **racing-car museum,** at 110 N. Franklin St. (607/535-4202), open Thur.-Sun. afternoon, June-Aug. (by appointment the rest of the year), the town is scored across by the impressive glens that give it its name. Don't fail to see it.

Now drive northward along the whole length of Seneca Lake as far as **Geneva;** if you enjoy fishing you'll want to know that summer visitors call it "the fisherman's paradise." ❄ **Canandaigua** is a little summer resort 17 mi. (27 km) farther west at the tip of the lake of the same name; don't fail to stop at the **Sonnenberg Gardens,** a lovely 50-acre (20-ha.) landscaped park on N.Y. 21N, open daily May-Oct.; also see the ⚓ **Granger Homestead,** 295 N. Main St. (716/394-1472), the splendidly restored 1816 house of Gideon Granger, Postmaster General under Presidents Jefferson and Madison. Complete with period furniture and a collection of horse-drawn carriages.

History buffs are advised to turn aside to **Palmyra,** 16 mi. (25 km) north, where in 1820 the prophet Joseph Smith had the vision of the angel Moroni that led him to found the Mormon religion. See his childhood home, now a museum, on Stafford Rd., open daily; also **Hill Cumorah,** the hill where the prophet is said to have found the golden pages of the Book of Mormon. Visitor center on N.Y. 21 (315/597-5851), open daily.

Head on past Lake Canandaigua to 🏔 **Hammondsport,** New York State's largest wine-growing center; the first vines were brought here from Germany and Switzerland in 1829. Many vineyards give conducted tours of their storehouses, among them **Bully Hill Vineyards,** Bully Hill Rd. via N.Y. 54A (607/868-3610), open Mon.-Sat.; and **Taylor Wineries,** on Pleasant Valley Rd. via N.Y. 54 (607/569-2111), open daily May-Oct. (Mon.-Sat. the rest of the year), with the largest and finest cellars in the region. Two other places you won't want to miss here: the **Wine Museum of Greyton H. Taylor,** with everything about vines and wine, on G. H. Taylor Memorial Dr. via N.Y. 54A (607/868-4814), open daily May-Oct.; and the **Glenn H. Curtiss Museum,** birthplace of one of the great early figures of aviation, now a historical museum, at Lake and Main Sts. (607/569-2160), open daily July-Sept., Mon.-Sat. in spring and fall, closed the rest of the year. Hammondsport shouldn't be bypassed.

Next stop is 🏔 **Corning,** the world's glass capital, where the giant 200″ (5-m) mirror of the Mount Palomar telescope was cast. Don't miss the **Corning Glass Center,** Centerway (607/974-8271), open daily, with its fascinating museum containing a unique collection of 23,000 glass objects, some of them 3,500 years old. Also interesting is the ⚓ **Rockwell Museum,** Denison Pkwy. & Cedar St. (607/937-5386), specializing in western art with pictures by Remington, Russell, Bierstadt, etc., and also displaying the very fine glass collection of Baron Steuben. Open daily.

At the end of the tour lies ❄ **Elmira,** famous as Mark Twain's favorite vacation spot; the author of *Huckleberry Finn,* who came here regularly for 20 years, is buried in **Woodlawn Cemetery** on Walnut St. You should also see his ⚓ writing study on the campus of **Elmira College,** Park Pl. (607/734-3911), open by appointment only; a must.

Back to Manhattan by way of **Binghamton,** an industrial city at the confluence of the Chenango and Susquehanna Rivers; the **Roberson Center for the Arts and Sciences,** 30 Front St. (607/772-0660), open Tues.-Sun., has interesting collections of art and historical material. Then through the foothills of the **Pocono Mountains.**

A trip of at least four to five days, ideal for nature lovers.

Where to Stay En Route

The following hotels, motels, and inns are recommended as suitable places for a stopover.

GENEVA. ☼ ⌘⌘⌘ **Geneva on the Lake,** 1001 Lochland Rd., Geneva, NY 14456 (315/789-7190). 29 suites. Lovely old villa overlooking Lake Seneca; period furniture and romantic atmosphere. **E–VE**

☀⌘♟♟ **Belhurst Castle,** on N.Y. 14, Geneva, NY 14456 (315/781-0201). 12 rms. A small castle in the Romanesque style built on the shores of Lake Seneca in 1885 w. décor and furniture of the period. **M–E**

HIMROD. The ⌘ **Rainbow Cove,** on N.Y. 14, Himrod, NY 14842 (607/243-7535). Inviting, likeable small motel on Lake Seneca. Very good value. Closed Oct. to mid-May. **I**

SKANEATELES. The ☼ ⌘⌘ **Sherwood Inn,** 26 W. Genesee St., Skaneateles, NY 13152 (315/685-3405). Charming 1807 inn w. rest on Lake Skaneateles. Good value. **I–M**

Where to Eat En Route

The restaurants and inns that follow are suitable places for a meal, if you're following the above itinerary.

ELMIRA HEIGHTS. ☼ ♟♟♟ **Pierce's 1894,** 228 Oakwood Ave. (607/734-2022). Dinner only, Tues.-Sun.; brunch Sun. Cuisine of a very high order in a lovely Victorian rest., run by the Pierce family since 1894. **I–M**

GENEVA. The ☼ ♟♟ **Belhurst Castle,** on N.Y. 14 (315/781-0201). Impeccably prepared and served continental cuisine in this small castle in the Romanesque style built on the shores of Lake Seneca in 1885 with décor and furniture of the period; terrace on fine days. **I–M**

ITHACA. ☼ ♟♟♟ **L'Auberge du Cochon Rouge,** 1152 Danby Rd. (607/273-3464). Dinner only, nightly; Sun. brunch. Some of the best food in the region— magnificent, refined French cuisine. Elegant old farmhouse with duck pond. **I–M**

♟♟ **Turback's,** 919 Elmira Rd. (607/272-6484). Dinner only, nightly; Sun. brunch. Luxurious Victorian manor; very skilled continental cuisine. **I**

SKANEATELES. The ☼ ♟♟ **Sherwood Inn,** 26 W. Genesee St. (315/685-3405). Charming 1807 inn on Lake Skaneateles w. lake-view rest. and flawless traditional hotel cuisine. **I**

SYRACUSE. ♟♟♟ **Pascale Wine Bar and Restaurant,** 304 Hawley Ave. (315/471-3040). Dinner only, Mon.-Sat. Wonderful French food at painless prices, and an elegant Victorian setting, account for the success of this very good rest. **I**

TRUMANSBURG. The ♟♟ **Taughannock Farms Inn,** on N.Y. 89 (607/387-7711). Dinner only, nightly; Sun. brunch. In this old farmhouse overlooking Cayuga

Lake and Taughannock Park, you'll be served excellent family cooking at reasonable prices. Very good value. I

ADIRONDACK PARK (806 mi., 1,290 km, round trip via the Saw Mill River Pkwy., Taconic State Pkwy., I-90W, U.S. 4N, N.Y. 29W, I-87N, N.Y. 9N, N.Y. 22N, N.Y. 86W, N.Y. 30S, N.Y. 8W, I-90E, N.Y. 28S, N.Y. 80E, I-90E, I-87S, Palisades Interstate Pkwy. South, and the George Washington Bridge): There are places steeped in history like Lake George, Saratoga, and Ticonderoga, but also, and just as important, there are 2,800 lakes, 1,200 mi. (1,920 km) of rivers, thousands of miles of brooks and streams, 42 mountains more than 4,000 ft. (1,200 m) high, deep forests, peaks crowned with snow in winter, dozens of campgrounds, 750 mi. (1,200 km) of marked trails. The Adirondacks (from the Iroquois name for the Algonquin, "Ha-de-ron-dah," or "skin-eaters"), are a paradise for lovers of unspoiled nature.

Leaving Manhattan northward along the Henry Hudson, Saw Mill River, and Taconic State Pkwys., make your first stop 155 mi. (248 km) from Manhattan at ☀ **Albany,** the capital of New York State. Visit the **State Capitol,** a fine 1898 French Renaissance-style building on State St. (518/474-2418), open daily, and the **State University** on its beautiful campus at Washington and Western Aves. (518/442-5571), open Mon.-Fri. Also, take time to admire the **Empire State Plaza,** one of the most successful complexes of modern architecture in the country, comprising a dozen striking structures devoted to administrative or cultural uses, including the **Performing Arts Center** (familiarly known as "the egg" on account of its shape), the 44-story **Corning Tower Building,** with an observation platform at the top, and the fascinating ▲▲ **New York State Museum** (518/474-5877), open daily. There are a number of ▲ architecturally interesting old buildings you should see, including the 1761 **Schuyler Mansion** at 32 Catherine St.; the 1798 **Ten Broeck Mansion,** 9 Ten Broeck St., open Tues.-Sun.; and **Historic Cherry Hill,** dating from 1787, at 523½ Pearl St., open Tues.-Sun.

Then on to ☀ ▲▲ **Saratoga National Historic Park,** where in engagements on Sept. 19 and Oct. 7, 1777, American forces under the command of Gen. Horatio Gates inflicted a decisive defeat on Gen. John Burgoyne's British army, as a result of which France decided to make common cause with the Americans. Visitor center-museum open daily (518/664-9821), and marked road around the battlefield. Don't miss it. Not far away is **Saratoga Springs,** whose renowned hot springs, two racecourses, and a polo ground attract every year a crown of racegoers—not to mention lovers of classical music and ballet: the ☀ **Saratoga Performing Arts Center,** S. Broadway (518/587-3330), is open July and Aug. Also see the very unusual ▲ **Petrified Sea Gardens,** 3 mi. west on N.Y. 29 (518/584-7102), open daily late June through Aug., with its fossils of prehistoric plants.

Glens Falls, which owes its name to the falls on the Hudson south of the town, has a beautiful art museum, the **Hyde Collection** at 161 Warren St. (518/792-1761), open afternoons Tues.-Sun., with many paintings by such masters as Rembrandt, Rubens, and Picasso. Between mid-July and August it is also the scene of the very popular ▲ **Lake George Opera Festival** (for information, call 518/793-6641).

Continue on I-87N to ☀ ▲ **Lake George,** a pretty little resort town at the southern end of the lake of the same name. **Fort William Henry Museum,** Canada St., open daily May-Oct., is an exact replica of a British fort built in 1755. The **Lake George Steamboat Co.,** Beach Rd. (518/668-5777), offers one- to four-hour lake cruises, May-Oct.

Follow the lovely N.Y. 9N, which traces the shore of Lake George for almost 35 mi. (56 km), to ☀ ▲▲ **Ticonderoga,** another summer resort with historic interest. For almost two centuries it was the storm-center of countless battles and bloody engagements among Indians, French, British, Canadians, and Americans, witness the history of **Fort Ticonderoga,** built by the French in 1755 under the name of Fort Carillon and destroyed by the British in 1777, after it had been occupied by Ethan Allen and his Green Mountain Boys in the early morning of May 10, 1775. Now restored to its original condition and converted to a military museum, it should be visited by all history buffs; you'll find it on N.Y. 74 (518/585-2821), open daily mid-May to mid-Oct.

Next comes a 50-mi. (80-km) scenic drive on N.Y. 9 N and N.Y. 22 N along the great and magnificent ※ **Lake Champlain** as far as ※ ⚓ **Ausable Chasm,** 200-ft. (60-m) gorges carved by the Ausable River and spilling into Lake Champlain in a series of torrential falls, a sight to be seen. Continuing westward, you come upon some more spectacular gorges (like the **High Falls Gorge,** near **Wilmington,** on N.Y. 86), before you reach ※ ⚓⚓ **Lake Placid,** the famous resort town where the Winter Olympics have been held twice: in 1932 and 1980. With the 5,344-ft. (1,629-m) crest of New York State's highest mountain, Mount Marcy, looming in the background, Lake Placid draws a full house of tourists in winter and summer alike.

Leaving Lake Placid, the route touches, like gems on a long necklace, the countless lakes and resort areas of the Adirondacks: **Saranac Lake, Tupper Lake, Long Lake, Blue Mountain Lake**—where you should be sure to visit the splendid ⚓ **Adirondack Museum,** devoted to the history of the region, on N.Y. 30 (518/352-7311), open daily mid-June to mid-Oct.—before reaching ※ ⚓⚓ **Utica,** a small industrial city on the Mohawk River distinguished by possessing one of the finest art museums in the entire state, the **Munson-Williams-Proctor Institute,** 310 Genesee St. (315/797-0000), open Mon.-Fri. Works of Picasso, Jackson Pollock, Kandinsky, Paul Klee, and Thomas Cole, and sculptures by Calder and Henry Moore among others. Don't miss it.

Last stop is ※ ⚓⚓ **Cooperstown,** on Otsego Lake, a town dear to all American sports fans because it was here, in 1839, that Gen. Abner Doubleday devised the game of baseball; that's why it is now the site of the ※ **National Baseball Hall of Fame and Museum,** Main St. (607/547-9988), open daily, devoted to the history of the national sport and its greatest players. Also see the **Farmers' Museum,** N.Y. 80N (607/547-2533), open daily May-Oct., illustrative of rural life in the 19th century, and **Fenimore House,** on N.Y. 80N (607/547-2533), open daily May-Oct., a lovely museum of American folklore dedicated to the writer James Fenimore Cooper, whose father founded the town in 1786. Don't miss it.

Then back to Manhattan on I-90 and I-87. This trip, to which you should devote five days at least, can easily be combined with the tour of the Hudson Valley, since both follow the same highways for part of their routes (see "Hudson Valley," above).

Where to Stay En Route

The following hotels, motels, and inns are recommended as suitable places for a stopover.

BLUE MOUNTAIN LAKE. 🍴**Hemlock Hall,** N.Y. 30, Blue Mountain Lake, NY 12812 (518/352-7706). 23 rms. Inviting little country motel on a lake. Closed Oct. 15 to May 15. **M–E**

BOLTON LANDING. The ※ 🍴🍴🍴 **Sagamore Omni Hotel,** N.Y. 9N, Bolton Landing, NY 12814 (518/644-9400; toll free, see Omni). 350 rms. Wonderful Victorian palace, built in 1883 and now a designated historic landmark. Wonderfully situated on Lake George. Elegant and distinguished. Open year round. **VE (MAP)**

COOPERSTOWN. The ※ 🍴🍴🍴 **Otesaga Hotel,** Lake St., Cooperstown, NY 13326

(607/547-9331). 135 rms. Elegant, luxuriously furnished grand hotel in the Georgian style on Otsego Lake. Closed late Oct. through Apr. **E–VE**

🍸 **Lake View Motel,** 6 mi. (10 km) north on N.Y. 80, Cooperstown, NY 13326 (607/547-9740). 13 rms. Small, engaging hotel w. direct access to the lake. Closed Oct. 15 to May 15. **I–M**

LAKE GEORGE. 🍸🍸 **Dunham's Bay Lodge,** N.Y. 9N, Lake George, NY 12845 (518/656-9242). 54 rms. Modern, comfortable motel on Lake George. Closed Oct. 15 to May 15. **I–M**

🍸🍸 **Tahoe Beach Club,** N.Y. 9N, Lake George, NY 12845 (518/668-5711). 73 rms. Large, modern motel-marina on the lake. Closed from the end of Oct. to mid-Apr. **I–M**

LAKE PLACID. The ☀ 🍸🍸 **Mirror Lake Inn,** 5 Mirror Lake Dr., Lake Placid, NY 12946 (518/523-2544). 100 rms. Luxury motel w. elegant Colonial interior on the lake. Rebuilt after a fire. Open year round. **M–E**

🍸 **Alpine Air Motel,** 99 Saranac Ave., Lake Placid, NY 12946 (518/523-9261). 24 rms. Small motel w. inviting cottages on a riverbank. **I**

LONG LAKE. The 🍸 **Shamrock Motel,** N.Y. 30, Long Lake, NY 12847 (518/624-3861). 15 rms. Rustic but comfortable motel on a lake. Open year round. **I**

SARANAC LAKE. The ☀🍸🍸 **Hotel Saranac,** 101 Main St., Saranac Lake, NY 12983 (518/891-2200). 92 rms. Venerable hotel built in the '20s, now run w. masterly touch by the pupils of the hotel school at Paul Smith's College. Open year round. **I–M**

SARATOGA SPRINGS. The ☀🍸🍸 **Inn at Saratoga,** 231 Broadway, Saratoga Springs, NY 12866 (518/583-1890). 40 rms. Delightful late-19th-century inn, elegantly comfortable. Open year round. **M–E** (except Aug. during race meet)

🍸 **Turf and Spa,** 140 Broadway, Saratoga Springs, NY 12866 (518/584-2550). 42 rms. Conventional but well-run motel. **I** (except Aug.)

Where to Eat En Route

The following restaurants and inns are suitable places for a meal, if you're following the above itinerary.

ALBANY. ☀ 🍴🍴 **Jack's Oyster House,** 42 State St. (518/465-8854). Lunch/dinner daily. One of the city's oldest rests., passed from father to son since 1913. Excellent continental food. **M**

GLENMONT. The 🍴🍴 **Stone Ends Restaurant,** U.S. 9W (518/465-3178). Dinner only, Mon.-Sat. Excellent contemporary American cuisine in a rustic mountain-chalet setting. **I–M**

LAKE GEORGE. The 🍴 **Trolley Steak and Seafood,** Canada St. (518/668-3165). Lunch/dinner daily; closed Nov. to mid-May. Appealing steakhouse w. very attractive prices. Terrace in summer. **B–I**

LAKE PLACID. The 🍴 **Alpine Cellar,** Wilmington Rd. (518/523-2180). Dinner only, nightly; closed April to mid-May and Nov. to mid-Dec. Bavarian setting and atmosphere. Very laudable German food. **I**

SARATOGA SPRINGS. The ☀ 🍴🍴 **Union Coach House,** 139 Union Ave.

(518/5846440). A coaching inn dating from 1872, as does the décor. Praiseworthy continental cuisine. **M**

UTICA. ☎☎ **The Metro,** 606 Huntington St. (315/733-4130). Lunch/dinner Mon.-Sat. Elegant rest. serving continental cuisine, in a 1920s building which once housed a bank. **I**

CHAPTER 4

NIAGARA FALLS

□ □ □

Although of modest size (35 mi., 55 km, long), the Niagara River ("thundering waters" in the Iroquois language) has the most famous, the most visited, and the most photographed falls in the world. Formed during the last glacial period 30,000 to 50,000 years ago, the falls, located midway between Lake Erie and Lake Ontario (which differ 324 ft., 99 m, in water level), offer visitors a fabulous spectacle. Viewing the roaring waters of the **Horseshoe Falls** and the **American Falls** hurtling down from as high as 184 feet (56 m) is an awesome experience, especially from the Canadian side of the river—or better yet, on board the *Maid of the Mist* amid the swirling waters near the base of the falls.

Legend has it that the French explorer Jacques Cartier, in 1535, was the first "paleface" to be dazzled by the falls. Their "official discovery" 78 years later is credited to another Frenchman, Samuel de Champlain. Defining the border between New York State and the Canadian province of Ontario, the falls have become over the years one of the top tourist attractions in the United States (15 million visitors each year). Despite Oscar Wilde's celebrated witticism—"the wedding trip brings two disappointments, the second being Niagara Falls"—tens of thousands of newlyweds have made Niagara Falls the country's honeymoon capital since 1804. This pleasant tradition will no doubt endure for some time to come; while the falls recede about 11.8 inches (30 cm) every year, it will take at least 125,000 years before they reach Lake Erie and totally disappear!

Although the falls were formally given parkland status by the state of New York in 1885, the chemical and metallurgical industries, heavy consumers of electricity (the power station built below the falls is one of the most powerful in the United States), pollute and disfigure the American side. Also distressing to the eye is the scene on the Canadian side of the falls, which has been gradually transformed into a giant amusement park of dismaying vulgarity. But in spite of these ecological affronts, the falls remain an incredible living spectacle, even in winter when the water is frozen. Maximum rate of flow is approximately 740,000 gallons (2.8 million liters) per second.

BASIC FACTS: State of New York. Area Codes: U.S. side, 716; Canadian side, 416. ZIP Code: 14302. Time Zone: Eastern Time. First discovery by a European, 1535?/1613. Approximate population of Niagara Falls: American side, 72,000; Canadian side, 70,000.

CLIMATE: Summer temperatures are relatively high, averaging 77° F (25° C) in July and Aug., but much more tolerable and a lot less humid than in New York City. Spring and autumn, both quite brief, are sunny but chilly. Winters—from the end of Oct. to the end of April—are glacial, to the point where the falls themselves are frozen.

DISTANCES: Boston, 480 mi. (768 km); Cleveland, 200 mi. (320 km); Montreal, 421 mi. (674 km); New York, 410 mi. (656 km); Toronto, 145 mi. (232 km); Washington, 405 mi. (648 km).

ARRIVAL & TRANSIT INFORMATION

AIRPORT: Buffalo International Airport (BUF): 22 mi. (35 km) SE. Information: 632-3115.

AIRLINES: American (856-7050), Continental (852-1223), Eastern (852-3170), Northwest (854-0903), United (856-2900), USAir (632-3000).

CITY LINK: The **cab** fare from Buffalo Airport to Niagara Falls is about $25–$30; time, 35–40 min. **Bus:** Niagara Scenic Lines (648-1500), departing every hour between 8:30 a.m. and 8:30 p.m., serves the major hotels of Niagara Falls; fare, $8 (American side) or $9 (Canadian side); time, 50–60 min.

There is ample bus service in the Niagara Falls/border area; renting a car with unlimited mileage is thus not necessary unless you are planning an excursion to outlying places.

CAR RENTAL (all at the Buffalo International Airport): Avis (632-4662); Budget (632-4662); Dollar (631-9880); Hertz (632-4772); National (632-1510).

LIMOUSINE SERVICES: Buffalo Limousine (835-4997), Carey Limousine (881-5466).

TAXIS: Although in theory you can hail a taxi on the street, the best way is to telephone **LaSalle Cab** (284-8833) or **United Cab** (285-9331).

TRAIN: AMTRAK Station, Hyde Park Blvd. and Lockport Rd., Niagara Falls, N.Y. (285-4224).

BUS: Greyhound has bus stations on both sides of the border: **in the U.S.** at 343 4th St., Niagara Falls (716/282-1331), and **in Canada** at 6761 Oakes Dr., Niagara Falls (416/732-3501).

INFORMATION & TOURS

TOURIST INFORMATION: The **Niagara Falls Convention & Visitors Bureau** (U.S.), 345 3rd St., Niagara Falls, NY 14303 (716/285-2400).

Niagara Falls Visitor & Convention Bureau (Canada), 4610 Ontario Ave., Niagara Falls, Ont. L2E 3P9 (416/356-6061).

GUIDED TOURS (AMERICAN SIDE): Gray Line Tours (bus) (716/694-3600): Guided tour of both sides of the falls and surrounding areas, serving major hotels.

Maid of the Mist (boat), Prospect Tower (716/284-4233): Boat tour to the foot of the falls through clouds of foam and spray; passengers are furnished with rain slickers. This is an unforgettable experience, not to be missed. Daily from May to Oct.

Niagara Viewmobile (bus), Prospect Point (716/282-0028): Tour by miniature train along the falls. Daily from mid-May to mid-Oct.

Rainbow Helicopter Tours (helicopter), 454 Main St. (716/284-2800): Tour of the falls by air, lasting 6–7 min.; $35. Impressive.

GUIDED TOURS (CANADIAN SIDE): Double Deck Tours (bus), 3957

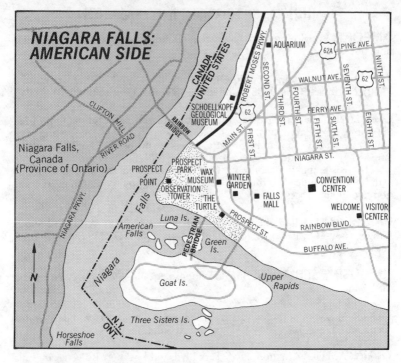

Bossert Rd. (416/295-3051): Tour along the falls in an English double-decker bus. Pleasantly quaint.

Gray Line Tours (bus), 6761 Oakes Dr. (416/354-4524).

Maid of the Mist (boat), Niagara River Pkwy. (416/358-5781): Boat tour to the foot of the falls through clouds of foam and spray; rain slickers furnished. An unforgettable experience, not to be missed. Daily from May to Oct.

Niagara Helicopters (helicopter), 3731 Victoria Ave. (416/357-5672): Helicopter flights above the falls. Impressive. Year round.

SIGHTS, ATTRACTIONS, & ACTIVITIES— AMERICAN SIDE

THE FALLS: ☼ ⚌⚌ **American Falls,** between the east bank and Goat Island, 1,082 ft. (330 m) wide, 184 ft. (56 m) high. More headlong than the Canadian falls. Best viewing is in the morning from Prospect Point.

☼ ⚌⚌ **Cave of the Winds,** at the foot of Goat Island (716/282-8979): Underground grotto at the foot of the American falls. Spectacular observation point. Access is by elevator and then by tunnel. Wooden footbridges allow you to venture within a few feet of **Bridal Veil Fall** (slickers and rubber boots provided). Open daily, mid-May to mid-Oct. Don't miss this!

MUSEUMS: ⚐ Aquarium of Niagara Falls, 701 Whirlpool St. (716/285-3575): From piranhas and sharks to dolphins and electric eels, more than 2,000 marine animals from the world over can be seen here. The aquarium is of modern design and surrounded by beautiful gardens graced with outdoor sculpture. Worth seeing. Open daily.

    🔔 **Native American Center for the Living Arts,** 25 Rainbow Mall (716/284-2427): Curiously designed in the shape of a tortoise's shell. Inside you'll find temporary art exhibitions, crafts boutiques, a restaurant, etc. Worth a look. Open daily in summer; Wed.-Sun. the rest of the year.

    🔆🔔 **Schoellkopf Geological Museum,** Prospect Park (716/278-1780): Features the geological history of the falls. Interesting as much for its spiral design as for its collection of minerals tracing the evolution of the falls area over 500 million years. Lovely view of the Niagara River gorge. Altogether captivating. Open daily in summer; Wed.-Sun. the rest of the year.

PANORAMAS: 🔆 👓 **Goat Island,** in the Niagara River between the American and Canadian sides: Offers a striking view of the Horseshoe Falls from **Terrapin Point,** located at the extreme SW tip of the island. You'll enjoy an equally fantastic vista of the American falls, and especially the Bridal Veil Falls, from tiny **Luna Island,** reached by footbridge from the extreme NW point of Goat Island. Truly a must for every visitor.

    🔆👓 **Prospect Point Observation Tower,** Prospect Park (716/278-1770): A 282-ft. (86-m) tower with a long footbridge over the void offering a magnificent scenic view of the American falls. The *Maid of the Mist* tour boat leaves from the foot of the tower; see "Guided Tours (American Side)," above. Absolutely must be seen. Open daily.

PARKS AND GARDENS: 🔆 👓 **Goat Island,** in the Niagara River between the American and Canadian sides: Auto and footbridges permit access to this little island planted squarely in the middle of the roaring Niagara River. Visitors will enjoy both splendid viewing and the chance for a pleasant stroll among the island's trees and flowers. It was here, in times past, that local Indian tribes practiced human sacrifice and buried their chiefs. Not to be missed.

    🔔 **Wintergarden,** Rainbow Blvd. (716/278-8196): Immense seven-story greenhouse of ultramodern design. More than 7,000 plants and tropical trees flourish within the futuristic décor created by overhead walkways, glass elevators, waterfalls, and lagoons. Very pleasant atmosphere. Open daily.

SPECIAL EVENTS: Artpark, 7 mi. (11 km) north on Robert Moses Pkwy. (June-Sept.): Modern-art festival displaying current, original works of art in a vast 200-acre (80-ha.) park setting. Jazz, dance, opera, theater. For information, call 716/754-9001.

    Tuscarora Indian Nation Picnic, 5 mi. (8 km) NE on N.Y. 104. (mid-July): Annual fair of the Tuscarora Indian reservation. Shows, dances, craft exhibitions.

SIGHTS, ATTRACTIONS, & ACTIVITIES— CANADIAN SIDE

THE FALLS: 🔆 👓 **Horseshoe Falls,** between the west bank and Goat Island, 2,099 ft. (640 m) across, 176 ft. (54 m) high. The most spectacular falls; in sunny weather magnificent rainbows form above it, especially during the afternoon. Strikingly illuminated evenings by four-billion-candlepower floodlights. Can be viewed clearly from **Table Rock.**

MUSEUMS: 🔆 🔔 **Niagara Falls Museum,** 5651 River Rd. (416/356-2151): One of the oldest museums in North America (1827). Note especially the display tracing the history of daredevil attempts to survive a trip over the falls in an amazing variety of contraptions (small boats, barrels, inner tubes). It's also worth taking a look at the picturesque bric-a-brac of the other exhibits. Open daily in summer; weekends the rest of the year.

PANORAMAS: ⚱ **Niagara Spanish Aerocar,** Niagara River Pkwy., 3½ mi. (5 km) north (416/354-5711): A sort of open cable car. Its 1,800-ft. (549-m) route goes over the Niagara River rapids. Worth seeing. Open daily from mid-April to mid-Oct.

⚱ **Minolta Tower,** 6732 Oakes Dr. (416/356-1501): A 325-ft. (99-m) tower with a 360° panoramic view of the falls. Superb observation point. Open daily.

Skylon Tower, 5200 Robinson St. (416/356-2651): Soaring to 518 ft. (158 m), the tower offers unobstructed viewing and the most beautiful bird's-eye view of both the American and the Canadian falls. The revolving restaurant at the top of the tower is mediocre, but don't miss the views! Open daily.

Table Rock, Queen Victoria Park, Niagara River Pkwy. (416/358-3268): Awesome viewing from this observation platform located 25 ft. (8 m) above the river's surface at the base of the Canadian falls. This is a sight not to be missed (slickers and rubber boots are furnished). Open daily.

PARKS AND GARDENS: **Queen Victoria Park,** Niagara River Pkwy.: A lovely English garden with flower-planted slopes stretching along the Niagara River. Splendid panoramic view of the American and Horseshoe Falls. A must-see.

SHOPPING: **Maple Leaf Village,** 5685 Falls Ave. (416/374-4444): Both an amusement park and a giant shopping center. An additional feature is the 350-ft. (107-m) observation tower. Shops, food stalls, restaurant. Open daily.

Skylon Centre, 5200 Robinson St. (416/356-2651): Shops, restaurants, a museum of automatons, and the **Imax Theatre,** an astonishing pyramidal movie house with a giant screen six stories tall. Worth a look. A stone's throw from the falls. Open daily.

THEME PARKS: **Marineland,** 7657 Portage Rd., 1 mi. (1.6 km) south of the falls (416/356-9565): Modern zoo with performing animal shows, from bears to killer whales. Amusement park with gigantic roller coaster. Open daily year round.

OTHER FROMMER TRAVEL GUIDES: *Dollarwise USA* complements 13 other Dollarwise Guides and 3 $-A-Day Guides dealing with individual U.S. states and areas: *Dollarwise Alaska, Dollarwise Florida, Dollarwise New York State, Dollarwise California & Las Vegas, Dollarwise Texas, Dollarwise Cruises, Dollarwise Mid-Atlantic States, Dollarwise New England, Dollarwise South-Atlantic States, Dollarwise Northwest, Dollarwise Southwest, Hawaii on $50 a Day, New York on $50 a Day,* and *Washington, D.C., & Historic Virginia on $40 a Day.*

In contrast to the book you are now reading, which highlights 57 U.S. cities and scenic areas, each of the above guides treats one particular state or area in the fullest detail, setting forth scores of hotel, restaurant, and sightseeing suggestions. Frommer travel guides can be obtained at most bookstores, or by mailing the appropriate amount (turn to the last few pages in this guide) to Frommer Books, Prentice Hall Trade Division, One Gulf + Western Plaza, New York, NY 10023.

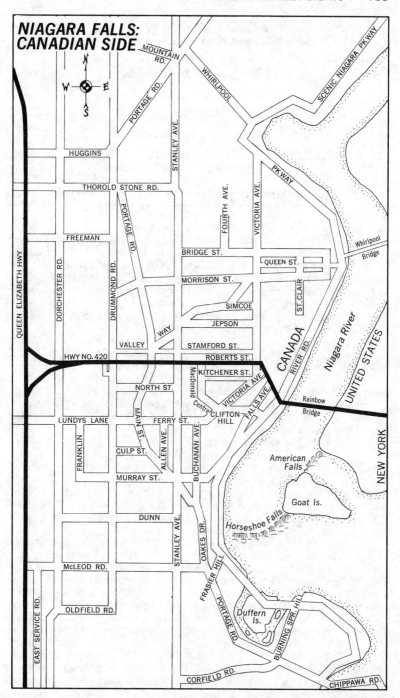

ACCOMMODATIONS

See the listing of toll-free numbers in the Appendix.

Room Rates in Niagara Falls	
B (Budget)	up to $30
I (Inexpensive)	$30–$60
M (Moderate)	$60–$90
E (Expensive)	$90–$140
VE (Very Expensive)	$140 and up

Personal Favorites (in order of preference)

Hilton Niagara (dwntwn), Mall and 3rd St., Niagara Falls, NY 14303 (716/285-3361; toll free, see Hilton). 396 rms, A/C, color TV, in-rm movies. AE, CB, DC, MC, V. Garage $2, pool, health club, sauna, rest., coffeeshop, bars, rm svce, nightclub, free crib. *Note:* Modern, functional hotel in the heart of the dwntwn area. Very complete facilities; spacious rms, some w. refrigerators; very efficient svce, pleasant pool. Favored by groups and convention-goers (direct access to the Convention Center). A 5-min. walk from the falls. **M–E, but lower rates out of season**

Oakes Inn (dwntwn), 6546 Buchanan Ave., Niagara Falls, Ont. L2G 3W2, Canada (416/358-5926). 153 rms, A/C, color TV, in-rm movies. AE, CB, DC, MC, V. Free parking, three pools, sauna, health club, miniature golf, rest., bar, rm svce, disco, crib $10. *Note:* Large 12-story modern motor hotel overlooking Horseshoe Falls on one of the best sites in the entire city. Large, comfortable rms (the best—especially on the top three floors —look out on the falls). Cheerful reception and svce. A fine place. **M–E, but lower rates out of season**

Michael's Inn (dwntwn), 5599 River Rd., Niagara Falls, Ont. L2E 3H3, Canada (416/354-2727). 130 rms, A/C, cable color TV. AE, CB, DC, MC, V. Free parking, sauna, rest. (Embers Open Hearth), bar, rm svce, crib $10. *Note:* One of the best locations in Niagara Falls. Many rms have a view of the falls or of the Niagara River; some have refrigerators. Modern and comfortable. Courteous, pleasant reception. Good steakhouse. Across from the Rainbow Bridge. **M–E, but lower rates out of season**

Ramada Inn (nr. dwntwn), 401 Buffalo Ave., Niagara Falls, NY 14303 (716/285-2541; toll free, see Ramada Inns). 190 rms, A/C, color TV, in-rm movies. AE, CB, DC, MC, V. Free parking, pool, bowling, rest. (Circle), bar, rm svce, disco, free crib. *Note:* A classic motel, modern and comfortable, a few steps away from the Convention Center. The terrace overlooks the Niagara River. Spacious rms w. balconies. Very acceptable rest. Frequented by groups and conventioneers. Good value. A 5-min. walk from the falls. **M–E, but lower rates out of season**

Park Inn International (formerly Hotel Niagara; dwntwn), 201 Rainbow Blvd., Niagara Falls, NY 14303 (716/285-9321). 220 rms, A/C, color TV. AE, CB, DC, MC, V. Free parking, rest., bar, rm svce, disco, crib $3. *Note:* Antiquated but well-maintained hotel w. a view of the Niagara River rapids. Spacious rms, some w. refrigerators. Friendly reception and service. Favored by groups and organized tours. Two minutes' walk from the base of the falls. Good value overall. **M, but lower rates out of season**

    Cascade Inn (dwntwn), 5305 Murray St., Niagara Falls, Ont. L2G 2J3, Canada (416/354-2796). 67 rms, A/C, color TV, in-rm movies. AE, CB, DC, MC, V. Free parking, rest. (breakfast only), rm svce, free crib. *Note:* Pleasant little motel open year round, close to the Skylon Tower. Comfortable and well maintained. Some rms have balconies and a view of the falls. Three minutes by foot from the falls. **M, but lower rates out of season**

    Inn by the Falls (dwntwn), 5525 Victoria Ave., Niagara Falls, Ont. L2G 3L3, Canada (416/357-2011). 60 rms, A/C, color TV. AE, DC, MC, V. Free parking, adjacent coffeeshop, rm svce, crib $5. *Note:* Comfortable little English-style hotel nr. the falls. Spacious rms, pleasant reception. Closed from Nov. to mid-March. **I–M, but lower rates out of season**

Other Accommodations (from top bracket to budget)

    Sheraton Hotel (dwntwn), 5685 Falls Ave., Niagara Falls, Ont. L2E 6W7, Canada (416/357-3090; toll free, see Sheraton). 405 rms, A/C, color TV, in-rm movies. AE, CB, DC, MC, V. Garage $5, pool, rest., bar, rm svce, disco. *Note:* Relatively modern grand hotel of massive, ungraceful design. Many rms have balconies and views of the falls. Somewhat deficient in svce. Pool and rest. offer panoramic viewing. Frequented by groups and conventioneers. A 10-min. walk from the falls. **E–VE**

    Best Western Your Host (nr. dwntwn), 5551 Murray Hill St., Niagara Falls, Ont. L2G 2J4, Canada (416/356-0551; toll free, see Best Western). 280 rms, A/C, color TV, in-rm movies. AE, CB, DC, MC, V. Free parking, two pools, saunas, rest. (Coach Room), coffeeshop, bar, rm svce, free crib. *Note:* Huge functional motel close to the falls. Comfortable and spacious rms w. private balconies or patios and refrigerators. Good svce. Ideal for families. The Skylon Tower is close by. **M–E, but lower rates out of season**

    Holiday Inn Downtown (dwntwn), 114 Buffalo Ave., Niagara Falls, NY 14303 (716/285-2521; toll free, see Holiday Inns). 194 rms, A/C, color TV, in-rm movies. AE, CB, DC, MC, V. Free parking, pool, health club, sauna, holidome (indoor recreation center), rest., bar, rm svce, disco. *Note:* Typical Holiday Inn, two minutes' walk from the falls. Functional comfort. Good facilities. Clientele of groups and organized tours. Rates seem high for a plain motel. Excellent location for visiting the falls. **M–E, but lower rates out of season**

    Radisson (formerly the Niagara Royale; dwntwn), 240 Rainbow Blvd., Niagara Falls, NY 14301 (716/282-1212; toll free, see Radisson). 217 rms, A/C, color TV, in-rm movies. AE, CB, DC, MC, V. Free parking, pool, rest., coffeeshop, bar, rm svce. *Note:* Big new motel adjacent to the Wintergarden. Welcoming, comfortable rooms. Very acceptable rest. Good svce. Frequented by business travelers and groups (very close to the Convention Center). Three min. on foot to the falls. **M–E**

    Quality Inn Intown (dwntwn), 443 Main St., Niagara Falls, NY 14301 (716/284-8801; toll free, see Quality Inns). 166 rms, A/C, color TV. AE, CB, DC, MC, V. Free parking, pool, rest., bar, rm svce, disco, crib $3. *Note:* A comfortable motel, recently renovated. Middling rest. Clientele mainly groups and organized tours. Five minutes' walk from the falls. Good value overall. Right in the middle of dwntwn. **M, but lower rates out of season**

    Ameri-Cana Motor Inn (nr. dwntwn), 8444 Lundy's Lane, Niagara Falls, Ont. I2H 1H4, Canada (416/356-8444; toll free 800/263-3508). 120 rms, A/C, color TV, in-rm movies. AE, MC, V.

Free parking, pool, two tennis courts, rest., coffeeshop, bar, rm svce, free crib. *Note:* Classic type of motel, but very well maintained and surrounded by 25 acres of lawns and gardens. It's 15 min. by car to the falls; there's also free shuttle service during the summer. Spacious, comfortable rms. The rest. is adequate. Ideal for families. Generally a group clientele. Good value. **I–M, but rates are lower out of season**

Lincoln Motor Inn (nr. dwntwn), 6417 Main St. (Portage Rd.), Niagara Falls, Ont. L2G 5Y3, Canada (416/356-1748). 60 rms, A/C, color TV, in-rm movies. AE, MC, V. Free parking, pool, rest. (Traveller's Delight), bar, crib $5. *Note:* Comfortable, well-kept little motel 5 min. by car from the falls. The rms are spacious; the rest. is adequate. Friendly reception. Good value. **I–M, but lower rates out of season**

Hotels in the Vicinity

Holiday Inn Conference Center (vic.), 100 Whitehaven Rd. (at E. River), Grand Island, NY 14072 (716/773-1111; toll free, see Holiday Inns). 265 rms, A/C, color TV, in-rm movies. AE, CB, DC, MC, V. Free parking, three pools, health club, sauna, golf, two tennis courts, marina, fishing, cross-country skiing in winter, rest., coffeeshop, bar, rm svce, disco, free crib. *Note:* Large, modern, comfortable six-story motel on the banks of the Niagara River. Ideal for physical-fitness buffs. Pleasant rms w. balconies; good svce. Holiday Inn style, only better. Groups and conventioneers make up much of the clientele. It's a 15-min. driving distance from the falls or from Buffalo Airport. **M–E, but lower rates out of season**

YMCAs/Youth Hostels

Niagara Falls Frontier Hostel (nr. dwntwn), 1101 Ferry Ave. (at Memorial Pkwy.), Niagara Falls, NY 14301 (716/282-3700): Youth hostel with 44 beds.

YMCA (nr. dwntwn), 1317 Portage Rd., Niagara Falls, NY 14301 (716/285-8491): Men only. 58 rms, gym, pool.

RESTAURANTS

Niagara Falls Restaurant Prices	
(per person, excluding drinks and service charge)	
B (Budget)	up to $15
I (Inexpensive)	$15–$25
M (Moderate)	$25–$40
E (Expensive)	$40–$60
VE (Very Expensive)	$60 and up

Personal Favorites (in order of preference)

Ports of Call (nr. dwntwn), Niagara Ave. and 30th St., Niagara Falls, NY (716/282-3262). A/C. Dinner only, nightly. AE, CB, DC, MC, V. Jkt. *Specialties:* steak, prime rib, fresh seafood. *Note:* One of the most popular rests. on the American side. Very pleasing antique décor, carefully prepared food, romantic, intimate atmosphere. Very good svce. Next door is the Bakery nightclub. Resv. advised. An 8-min. drive from dwntwn. *Steak-American.* **I–M**

🍷🍷 **Victoria Park** (dwntwn), Niagara Pkwy., Queen Victoria Park, Niagara Falls, Ont. (416/356-2217). Lunch/dinner daily; closed mid-Oct. to mid-May. AE, MC, V. *Specialties:* fresh salmon, roast beef, homemade pastry. *Note:* Venerable Victorian-style rest. w. open terrace facing the park and the falls. Pleasant gardens. Rather pretentious cuisine. Excellent svce. *Continental.* I

☼🍷🍷 **Donna Felicia** (vic.), 490 Center St., Lewiston, NY (716/754-7901). A/C. Dinner Tues.-Sun.; closed Mon., Tues., Thanksgiving, Christmas Day, and the first three weeks in Jan. AE, MC, V. Jkt. *Specialties:* fettuccine Alfredo, filet of sole Florentine, veal cutlet al Nero, manicotti del mare. Good desserts. *Note:* One of the best tables in the region, featuring solid Italian cooking and good homemade pasta. The sauces are a bit too rich. Pleasant rustic décor; good svce. A 10-min. drive from the falls. Resv. advised. *Italian.* I–M

🍷🍷 **The Happy Wanderer** (dwntwn), 6405 Stanley St., Niagara Falls, Ont. (416/354-9825). A/C. Lunch/dinner daily; closed holidays. AE, DC, MC, V. *Specialties:* wienerschnitzel, sauerbraten, rouladen, schweinebraten. *Note:* Typical Bavarian-style chalet 2 min. from the falls. Rather kitschy interior décor. A classic of its kind for over 20 years. The German cuisine is hearty and the servings generous. *German.* I

🍷 **Embers Open Hearth** (dwntwn), in Michael's Inn (see "Accommodations," above) (416/354-2727). A/C. Breakfast/lunch/dinner daily; closed Dec. 25. AE, CB, DC, MC, V. *Specialties:* steak, prime rib, roast chicken, roast piglet. *Note:* Excellent broiled meats and spitted fowl, prepared while you watch, are the main attractions of this rest. Highly regarded by Niagara Falls residents. Honest, unimaginative cuisine. Diligent svce, good value. *Steak-American.* I

☼🍷 **Riverside Inn** (vic.), 115 Water St., Lewiston, NY (716/754-8206). A/C. Lunch Mon.-Sat., dinner nightly. AE, MC, V. *Specialties:* Alaska king crab, roast beef, steak, catch of the day. *Note:* Charming rustic inn on the American side of the Niagara River. Conventional, no-frills cuisine. Good wine list. Popular locally. Resv. advised. *Steak-Seafood.* I

Other Restaurants (from top bracket to budget)

🍷🍷 **Clarkson House** (vic.), 810 Center St., Lewiston, NY (716/754-4544). A/C. Dinner only, Tues.-Sun.; closed Mon. and Dec. 25. AE, MC, V. Jkt. *Specialties:* charbroiled steak, lamb chops, Maine lobster, roast beef. Good homemade desserts. *Note:* Old inn dating from the 19th century and retaining the elegant décor of that era. The cooking, however, is uneven. Popular w. local residents. 10 min. from Niagara Falls. Resv. desirable. *Steak.* I

🍷🍷 **Red Coach Inn** (dwntwn), 2 Buffalo Ave., Niagara Falls, NY (716/282-1459). A/C. Lunch/dinner daily; closed Dec. 25. AE, MC, V. Jkt. *Specialties:* trout meunière, roast duck, roast beef, veal boursin, chicken alouette. *Note:* Very pleasant décor in the style of an old English inn. During the summer, diners on the outdoor terrace enjoy a view of the Niagara River rapids. The cooking is respectable, the svce efficient. Good wine list. Resv. recommended. Heavily patronized by tourists. *Continental-American.* I

🍷 **Queenston Heights** (vic.), 6 mi. (9.5 km) north on Niagara Pkwy., Niagara Falls, Ont. (416/262-4274). A/C. AE, MC, V. Lunch/dinner daily, Sunday brunch; closed Dec. 25. *Specialties:* ribs, roast beef, roast pork, leg of lamb, quail, rabbit stew. *Note:* Lovely view of the Niagara River from the glassed-in terrace. Tudor décor, w. a pleasant patio for summer dining. The cooking is estimable and the svce friendly. A 10-min. drive from the falls. Resv. advised. *Continental.* I

♀♀ **Suisha Gardens** (dwntwn), 5705 Falls Ave., Niagara Falls, Ont. (416/357-2660). A/C. Lunch daily during the summer; dinner nightly, year round; closed Dec. 25. AE, CB, DC, MC, V. Jkt. *Specialties:* tempura, sukiyaki, teriyaki. *Note:* Located on the second floor of the Maple Leaf Village Shopping Center, Suisha is the only Japanese restaurant in Niagara Falls worthy of the name. The cuisine is 100% authentic, although the décor is all-purpose Oriental. The cooks show off their dexterity w. the chopping knife right in front of your eyes. Resv. advised during the summer and on wknds. *Japanese.* **I**

♀ **Alps** (nr. dwntwn), 1555 Military Rd., Niagara Falls, NY (716/297-8990). A/C. Lunch/dinner Tues.-Sun.; closed Mon. AE, CB, DC, MC, V. *Specialties:* roast beef, Greek dishes, lobster, baklava. *Note:* Some good Greek-inspired dishes in a restaurant whose décor suggests a mountain chalet. The quality of the cooking doesn't seem to suffer much from this curious mix of styles. *American-Greek.* **B–I**

♀ **Carlos O'Brians** (dwntwn), 5645 Victoria Ave., Niagara Falls, Ont. (416/357-1283). A/C. Lunch/dinner daily (until midnight); closed Mon. from Nov. to March, and on Dec. 25. AE, DC, MC, V. *Specialties:* steak, prime rib, catch of the day, shellfish. *Note:* Pleasant tavern w. inviting rustic décor. Good broiled prime cuts and fish dishes. Relaxed atmosphere, friendly svce. Popular w. the locals. Resv. suggested wknds. *Steak-seafood.* **B–I**

Como Restaurant (nr. dwntwn), 2220 Pine Ave., Niagara Falls, NY (716/285-9341). A/C. Lunch/dinner daily (until midnight); closed Dec. 25. AE, MC, V. *Specialties:* homemade pasta, Italian dishes, steaks, sandwiches. *Note:* Both a deli and an Italian rest., this establishment run by the same family since 1927 has become a local institution. You'll enjoy good, honest Italian-American cooking in a pleasant, relaxed atmosphere. Excellent value. 8 min. from dwntwn. *Italian-American.* **B–I**

♀ **John's Flaming Hearth** (nr. dwntwn), 1965 Military Rd., Niagara Falls, NY (716/297-1414). A/C. Lunch/dinner daily. AE, DC, MC, V. *Specialties:* steak, surf and turf (steak and lobster), catch of the day, pumpkin ice-cream pie. *Note:* Enormous rest. 10 min. from the falls. A true local institution. The USSR's Premier Kosygin ate here during his visit to the States in 1967. Good value. Usually crowded and noisy. Pleasant atmosphere. *Steak-seafood.* **B–I**

♀ **Ye Olde Barn** (nr. dwntwn), 7280 Lundy's Lane, Niagara Falls, Ont. (416/356-7075). A/C. Breakfast/lunch/dinner daily; closed Dec. 25 and Jan. 1. AE, DC, MC, V. *Specialties:* barbecued ribs, catch of the day, roast chicken. *Note:* Excellent barbecued ribs in a setting resembling a rustic old barn, as the name suggests. Exposed beams enhance the comfortable, pleasing ambience. Each year the Barn serves over 60,000 lbs. of barbecued spareribs. Very good svce. An excellent place. 10 min. from dwntwn. *American-Seafood.* **B–I**

In the Vicinity

☀♀♀ **Schimschacks** (vic.), 2943 Upper Mountain Rd., Sanborn, NY (716/731-4111). A/C. Dinner nightly, Sunday brunch; closed Mon. and Tues. Dec.-Apr., also Dec. 24–25. AE, CB, DC, MC, V. Jkt. *Specialties:* Florida stone crab (in season), charcoal-broiled baby back ribs, steak, catch of the day, peanut-butter pie. *Note:* Located on the heights overlooking Lake Ontario—on a clear day you can see Toronto—this rest. offers excellent country cooking. Colonial-style décor w. a terraced dining room. Legend holds that Marilyn Monroe first met Joe Di Maggio here during the filming of the movie *Niagara*. Good svce. Definitely worth the 20-min. drive from Niagara Falls (via N.Y. 104, N.Y. 31, and N.Y. 429). *Steak-Seafood.* **I**

NEARBY EXCURSIONS IN NEW YORK STATE

AMERICAN SIDE: ☀ ⚄ **OLD FORT NIAGARA** (14 mi., 22 km, north on Robert Moses Pkwy.) (716/745-7611): French military fortress dating from 1726; its well-preserved fortifications tower above Lake Ontario. Occupies the site of an earlier fortress built in 1679. Numerous artillery pieces from bygone eras are on display in the fort **museum,** and in the summer there are military parades featuring soldiers in period uniforms. Fort Niagara played an important role in the War of 1812. Worth a side trip. Open daily year round.

⚓ **GRAND ISLAND** (6 mi., 9 km, south on I-190): Very popular summer vacation spot. Numerous parks, campsites, and picnic areas dot this 7½-by-5½-mi. (12-by-9-km) island located in the middle of the Niagara River upstream from the falls. Amusement park **(Fantasy Island)** open in summer. (716/773-7591).

☀⚓ **NIAGARA POWER PROJECT** (5 mi., 8 km, north via Lewiston Rd./N.Y. 104) (716/285-3211): Inaugurated in 1963, this is one of the most powerful hydroelectric power stations in the U.S.; with a continuous output of 2.5 million kilowatts per hour, it can more than meet all the electricity needs of a city the size of Chicago. There's an arresting panoramic view of the river gorge from the **observation platform,** and an interesting model of the power station in the **Visitor Center.** Don't miss seeing this. Open daily.

NEARBY EXCURSIONS IN CANADA

CANADIAN SIDE: ☀ ⚓ **FORT GEORGE** (14 mi., 23 km, north on the Niagara River Pkwy.) (416/468-4257): Constructed in 1796, this imposing fortress, sheltered behind massive ramparts, was formerly the principal British stronghold along the Canadian frontier. Particularly active during the War of 1812. Open daily, mid-May through Oct.; visit by appointment during the rest of the year. An absolute must-see.

☀⚄ **NIAGARA-ON-THE-LAKE** (14 mi., 22 km, north on the Niagara River Pkwy.): Formerly the capital of Upper Canada, this picturesque town founded in 1776 is one of the region's main tourist attractions. Built on a lovely site along Lake Ontario, the town contains dozens of carefully restored old houses (the town was put to the torch in 1813 during the second British-American war). Charming Edwardian-vintage ambience.

The **Shaw Festival Theatre** is very popular in the summer. For information, call 416/468-2172.

Visit not to be missed.

Where to Stay and Eat
Two 19th-century inns are highly recommended:

☀♋♋ **Pillar & Post Inn,** King and John Sts., Niagara-on-the-Lake, Ont. L0S 1J0 (416/468-2123). 91 rms. Also a good restaurant. **M–E**

♋♋ **Prince of Wales,** 6 Picton St., Niagara-on-the-Lake, Ont. L0S 1J0 (416/468-3246): 104 rms. Also a very decent restaurant. **M–E**

WHIRLPOOL RAPIDS (2 mi., 3.5 km., north on the Niagara River Pkwy.): Very lovely view of the Niagara River's rapids
and whirlpools. Should be seen.

OTHER FROMMER TRAVEL GUIDES: *Dollarwise USA* comple-
ments 13 other Dollarwise Guides and 3 $-A-Day Guides dealing with indi-
vidual U.S. states and areas: *Dollarwise Alaska, Dollarwise Florida,
Dollarwise New York State, Dollarwise California & Las Vegas, Dollarwise
Texas, Dollarwise Cruises, Dollarwise Mid-Atlantic States, Dollarwise New
England, Dollarwise South-Atlantic States, Dollarwise Northwest,
Dollarwise Southwest, Hawaii on $50 a Day, New York on $50 a Day,* and
Washington, D.C., & Historic Virginia on $40 a Day.

The Frommer series also boasts 10 City Guides focusing on U.S. destina-
tions: *Frommer's Atlantic City & Cape May, Frommer's Boston, Frommer's
Las Vegas, Frommer's Los Angeles, Frommer's Minneapolis/St. Paul,
Frommer's New Orleans, Frommer's New York, Frommer's Philadelphia,
Frommer's San Francisco,* and *Frommer's Washington, D.C.*

In contrast to the book you are now reading, which highlights 57 U.S.
cities and scenic areas, each of the above guides treats one particular city,
state, or area in the fullest detail, setting forth scores of hotel, restaurant,
and sightseeing suggestions. Frommer travel guides can be obtained at
most bookstores, or by mailing the appropriate amount (turn to the last few
pages in this guide) to Frommer Books, Prentice Hall Trade Division, One Gulf
+ Western Plaza, New York, NY 10023.

CHAPTER 5

THE ATLANTIC COAST

□ □ □

From the Canadian Border to New York City

The Atlantic seaboard, for a stretch of some 900 mi. (1,400 km) between the border with the Canadian province of New Brunswick and New York City, is at once the historic cradle of the United States, the theater of its seafaring destiny, and an eye-opening testimony to its diverse countrysides and landscapes.

The rocky, jagged shores of **Maine;** the gentle, eye-pleasing sands of **Long Island Sound** or the dunes of **Cape Cod;** the little fishing ports and pleasure harbors of New England with their innumerable churches and old brick or pastel-washed frame houses, like **Bar Harbor, Mystic, Gloucester,** or **New Bedford,** are a wonderful background to the giant megalopolis of Boston and New York. The stark Canadian winters and blizzards of **Acadia National Park** will help take your mind off New York's hot, sticky summers. And the futurist high-rises of Boston and New York must share your attention with some of the oldest buildings in this country, some of them going back more than 300 years. For it was along this coast, which you can drive from end to end in a matter of hours, that America first saw the light. From **Plymouth,** where the Pilgrim Fathers landed, the earliest permanent settlements in the northern U.S. are strung out like beads on a necklace: **Hartford** (1623), **New York** (1626), **Salem** (1626), **Boston** (1630), **Cambridge** (1630), **Portland** (1631), **Newburyport** (1635), **Providence** (1636), **New Haven** (1638), **Hyannis** (1639), and so on. The Atlantic seaboard between New York and Boston is, to this day, that part of the country most thickly populated by immigrants from the Old World and their descendants.

Besides these cities and history-laden harbor towns, there is much to attract lovers of the seashore, from the endless beaches of Massachusetts to the dozens of islands, big and little, scattered along the coast—including **Monhegan Island,** offshore from Maine, where according to some historians the Viking Leif Ericson made landfall around the year 1000, almost 500 years before Christopher Columbus "discovered" America. Big-game fishermen can indulge their passion at **Martha's Vineyard, Marblehead,** or **Nantucket Island,** all three also fashionable resorts. Art enthusiasts will not fail to visit such museum towns as **Portsmouth** and above all **Newport,** with its dream mansions; Newport, long the scene of the America's Cup races, is also well known for its regattas (see Chapter 1 on Boston, Chapter 2 on Cape Cod, and Chapter 3 on New York).

BASIC FACTS: States of Maine, New Hampshire, Massachusetts, Rhode Island, Connecticut, and New York. Area Codes: 207 (Maine), 603 (New Hampshire), 617 and 518 (Massachusetts), 401 (Rhode Island), 203 (Connecticut), and 212, 718, 914, and 516 (New York). Time Zone: Eastern Time. Distance as the crow flies from New York City to the Canadian border at Calais, Maine: 810 mi. (1,300 km).

CLIMATE: With the cold Labrador Current washing its entire coastline, the climate of the New England littoral tends to extremes. Harsh and snowy—indeed, in the case of Maine or New Hampshire, downright icy—winters (Jan. mean temperature, 21°F, –6°C) are followed by a short, temperate spring and a summer that is rarely too hot but often very humid, particularly in the coastal strip from New York City to Cape Cod (avg. temperature for July, 69°F, 21°C). By far the best time to visit the Atlantic coast is the fall, with its crisp, dry days (about 59°F, 15°C), to say nothing of the glorious coloring of the leaves during the "Indian summer." Except in late summer and fall you'll do well to bring your umbrella.

ARRIVAL & TRANSIT INFORMATION

AIRPORTS: The **Bangor** International Airport (BGR), 2 mi. (3.5 km) NW.
    Boston: Logan International Airport (BOS) (see Chapter 1 on Boston).
    Hartford: Bradley International Airport (BDL), 11 mi. (17 km) north.
    New York: John F. Kennedy International Airport (JFK), La Guardia Airport (LGA), and Newark International Airport (EWR) (see Chapter 3 on New York).
    Portland: International Jet Port (PWM), 2 mi. (3 km) west.
    Providence: T. F. Green State Airport (PVD), 7 mi. (11 km) south.

U. S. AND FOREIGN AIRLINES: In **Hartford** (area code 203): Air Canada (toll free 800/422-6232), American (527-5141), Continental (549-3673), Delta (527-1811), Eastern (525-0141), TWA (563-9943), United (522-4131), and USAir (522-2161).
    Providence (area code 401): American (272-1200), Continental (351-7020), Eastern (831-4460), United (831-6950), and USAir (274-5600).
    Boston, Cape Cod, New York: See Chapters 1, 2, and 3.

BUS OR CAR RENTAL: The Greyhound Bus Company has excellent service along the entire coast from New York to the Canadian border. However, the innumerable opportunities for side trips in the area strongly suggest renting a car or mobile home with unlimited mileage. (But don't do it in New York, where the rates are among the highest in the country.)

CAR RENTAL: See Chapters 1, 2, and 3 on Boston, Cape Cod, and New York. For rentals elsewhere, consult the local telephone directory.

TRAIN: AMTRAK has stations on Union Pl. in **Hartford,** Conn. (203/525-4580); Union Ave. in **New Haven,** Conn. (203/777-4002); and at 100 Gaspee St. in **Providence,** R.I. (401/751-5416).
    For the terminal in **Boston,** see Chapter 1; for the terminals in **New York,** see Chapter 3.

BUS: The **Greyhound Bus Co.** has terminals or stops at 158 Main St., **Bangor,** Me. (207/945-3000); 409 Church St., **Hartford,** Conn. (203/522-9267); 45

George St., **New Haven,** Conn. (203/772-2470); 104 Broadway, **Newport,** R.I. (401/846-1820); 946 Congress St., **Portland,** Me. (207/772-6587); 9 Congress St., **Portsmouth,** N.H. (603/436-0163); and at Sabin and W. Exchange Sts., **Providence,** R.I. (401/751-8800).

For the terminal in **Boston,** see Chapter 1; for the terminal in Cape Cod, see chapter 2; for the terminal in **New York,** see Chapter 3.

INFORMATION, TOURS, & ADVENTURES

TOURIST INFORMATION: You'll find a flood of tourist information available from both state-government and local sources. On the road, feel free to stop at the local chambers of commerce or convention and visitors bureaus for on-the-spot assistance and information.

State-Government Sources
Connecticut Department of Economic Development, 210 Washington St., Hartford, CT 06106 (203/566-3948).

Maine Publicity Bureau, 97 Winthrop St., Hallowell, ME 04347 (207/289-2423).

Massachusetts Division of Tourism, 100 Cambridge St., Boston, MA 02202 (617/727-3201).

New Hampshire Hospitality Association, 15 Pleasant St. (P.O. Box 1175), Concord, NH 03301 (603/228-9585).

Rhode Island Tourist Promotion Division, 7 Jackson Walkway, Providence, RI 02903 (401/277-2601).

Local Sources
Augusta Office of Tourism, 189 State St., Augusta, ME 04333 (207/289-5710).

Bangor Chamber of Commerce, 519 Main St. (P.O. Box 1443), Bangor, ME 04401 (207/947-0307).

Bar Harbor Chamber of Commerce, 93 Cottage St. (P.O. Box 158), Bar Harbor, ME 04609 (207/288-5103).

New Bedford–Bristol County Development Council, 70 N. 2nd St. (P.O. Box BR-976), New Bedford, MA 02741 (508/997-1250).

New Haven Convention and Visitors Bureau, 900 Chapel St., New Haven, CT 06510 (203/787-8367).

Newport County Chamber of Commerce, 10 America's Cup Ave. South, Long Wharf Mall, Newport, RI 02840 (401/847-1600).

Portland Chamber of Commerce, 142 Free St., Portland, ME 04101 (207/772-2811).

Portsmouth Chamber of Commerce, P.O. Box 239, Portsmouth, NH 03801 (603/436-1118).

Providence Convention and Visitors Bureau, 30 Exchange Terrace, Providence, RI 02903 (401/274-1636).

GUIDED TOURS: In addition to the information below, see also Chapters 1 and 2 on Boston and Cape Cod. For all other locations, see the local *Yellow Pages* under "Sightseeing."

Newport, R.I.
Viking Tours (bus), 10 America's Cup Ave. (401/847-6921): Conducted bus tour of the city and surroundings, year round. Serves the principal hotels.

Viking Queen (boat), Goat Island Marina, Washington St.

(401/847-6921): One-hour trip on Newport Bay and Rhode Island Sound, allowing you a view from offshore of the mansions of bygone millionaires. May to mid-Oct., daily.

Portland, Me.

Casco Bay Lines (boat), Custom House Wharf, Commercial St. (207/774-7871): Scenic-cruises around Portland Harbor and lovely Casco Bay with its 136 islands. Daily, year round.

Portsmouth, N.H.

Portsmouth Harbor Cruises (boat), 64 Ceres St., Old Harbor (603/436-8084): Boat trips in the harbor and to the Isles of Shoals. Daily, June-Oct.

ADVENTURES: Here are special cruises/trips available along the Atlantic coast.

Brunswick, Me.

Unicorn Expeditions (boat), P.O. Box T, Brunswick, ME 04011 (207/725-2255): One to six days rafting down the upper Hudson in New York State or the Kennebec and Penobscot Rivers in Maine. Spectacular. Apr.-Oct., daily.

Camden, Me.

Maine Windjammer Cruises (boat), P.O. Box 617, Camden, ME 04843 (207/236-2938): Three- to six-day cruises along the Maine coast aboard an authentic schooner from the olden days; a whiff of adventure. About $450 for six days. May-Oct.

Schooners *Roseway* and *Adventure* (boat), P.O. Box 696, Camden, ME 04843 (207/236-4449): See "Maine Windjammer Cruises," above.

Schooner *Stephen Taber* (boat), 70 Elm St., Camden, ME 04843 (207/236-3520): See "Maine Windjammer Cruises," above.

Conway, N.H.

Saco Bound Northern Waters (boat), U.S. 302E, Center Conway, NH 03813 (603/447-2177): One to several days' descent by raft or kayak of the Kennebec and Penobscot Rivers. Spectacular. Apr.-Oct., daily.

Portland, Me.

Balloon Sports (balloon), 146 Glenwood Ave., Portland, ME 04103 (207/772-4401): Dirigible trips over Casco Bay and the Portland area; $85 per person. An unforgettable sight. Daily, year round.

New England Whitewater Center (boat), 10 Exchange St., Portland, ME 04101 (207/772-4480): Rafting down the Kennebec, Dead, and Penobscot Rivers, with comfortable lodging at the Sugarloaf Inn at Sugarloaf Mountain. Also, in spring, descent of the Swift River in New Hampshire. Spectacular. Daily, Apr.-Oct.

Providence, R.I.

Stumpf Balloons (balloon), P.O. Box 1143, Providence, RI 02901 (401/253-0111): Balloon trips over Narragansett Bay and the Providence area; an unforgettable sight. Daily, year round.

SPECIAL EVENTS: For exact dates of the events listed below, check with the state-government and local sources listed earlier in this chapter under "Tourist Information," as well as with those listed below:

Boothbay Harbor Chamber of Commerce, Box 356, Boothbay Harbor, ME 04538 (207/633-2353).

Bridgeport Chamber of Commerce, 180 Fairfield Ave. (P.O. Box 999), Bridgeport, CT 06601 (203/335-3800).

Newburyport Chamber of Commerce, 29 State St., Newburyport, MA 01950 (508/462-6680).

Ogunquit Chamber of Commerce, P.O. Box 2289, Ogunquit, ME 03907 (207/646-5533).

Plymouth Chamber of Commerce, 91 Samoset St., Plymouth, MA 02360 (508/746-3377).

Rockland Chamber of Commerce, P.O. Box 508, Rockland, ME 04841 (207/596-0376).

Augusta, Me.

Whatever Week (late June to early July): All kinds of boat races ("anything that floats") on the Kennebec River. Giant barbecue, parade, fireworks.

Bar Harbor, Me.

Art Exhibit (third weekends of July and Aug.): Work by local artists.

Boothbay Harbor, Me.

Windjammer Cruises (mid-July): Review of old schooners in the bay; very picturesque.

Bridgeport, Conn.

Barnum Festival (late June to early July): Parades, concerts, and art exhibitions bearing on the history of the circus.

Newburyport, Mass.

Yankee Homecoming (late July to early Aug.): Boat races, parades, food festival.

New Haven, Conn.

Powder House Day (late Apr. to early May): Pageant showing the capture of the arsenal during the Revolutionary War.

Newport, R.I.

Music Festival (two weeks in mid-July): Chamber-music concerts in the mansions of 19th-century millionaires; for information, call 401/846-1133.

Jazz Festival (mid-Aug.): With all the big stars.

Wooden Boat Show and Classic Yacht Regatta (mid-Aug.): Annual yachting competition, very popular with sailboat buffs.

Ogunquit, Me.

Ogunquit Playhouse (late July to Labor Day): Plays of high quality and musicals; for information, call 207/646-5511.

Plymouth, Mass.

Thanksgiving Week (Nov.): Commemorating the first celebration of Thanksgiving by the Pilgrim Fathers.

Portland, Me.

New Year's Eve Portland (Dec. 31): Shows, parades, fireworks, concerts.

Portsmouth, N.H.

Jazz Festival (late June to early July): Jazz concerts on the historic Portsmouth waterfront; for information, call 603/436-7678.

Rockland, Me.

Maine Lobster Festival (first weekend of Aug.): Three days of joyous gluttony devoted to that most illustrious denizen of Maine's waters—the lobster.

A NORTH TO SOUTH ITINERARY

The section of this guide devoted to the Atlantic coast has been organized as an itinerary, starting at Calais, Me., and ending in New York City, a distance of almost 900 miles (1,440 km). You may choose not to drive the whole distance; key towns such as Bangor, Portland, Boston, Portsmouth, Providence, Hartford, and New York are linked by air, bus, and train, while car rentals are available everywhere. In that case, you may select from the following travel plan the parts that appeal to you most.

Distances Down the Atlantic Coast

From	*To*	*Distance*
Calais, Me.	Roosevelt/Campobello	53 mi. (84 km)
Roosevelt/Campobello	Bar Harbor	110 mi. (176 km)
Bar Harbor	Camden	78 mi. (125 km)
Camden	Augusta	42 mi. (67 km)
Augusta	Wiscasset	18 mi. (29 km)
Wiscasset	Boothbay Harbor	12 mi. (19 km)
Boothbay Harbor	Bath	22 mi. (36 km)
Bath	Brunswick	10 mi. (16 km)
Brunswick	Portland	26 mi. (44 km)
Portland	Kennebunkport	30 mi. (45 km)
Kennebunkport	Ogunquit	11 mi. (18 km)
Ogunquit	York	7 mi. (11 km)
York	Portsmouth, N.H.	6 mi. (10 km)
Portsmouth, N.H.	Newburyport, Mass.	21 mi. (33 km)
Newburyport, Mass.	Boston area (Gloucester, Marblehead, Rockport, Salem)	28–72 mi. (45–115 km)
Boston area	Quincy	9 mi. (15 km)
Quincy	Hull	15 mi. (24 km)
Hull	Plymouth	32 mi. (51 km)
Plymouth	Sagamore	18 mi. (29 km)
Sagamore	New Bedford	30 mi. (48 km)
New Bedford	Providence, R.I.	29 mi. (46 km)
Providence, R.I.	Bristol	14 mi. (23 km)
Bristol	Portsmouth	6 mi. (9 km)
Portsmouth	Newport	10 mi. (16 km)
Newport	Narragansett Pier	17 mi. (27 km)
Narragansett Pier	Mystic, Conn.	30 mi. (48 km)
Mystic, Conn.	Groton	6 mi. (10 km)
Groton	New London	2 mi. (3 km)
New London	Hartford	44 mi. (71 km)
Hartford	New Haven	40 mi. (64 km)
New Haven	Stratford	12 mi. (19 km)
Stratford	Bridgeport	3 mi. (5 km)
Bridgeport	Stamford	20 mi. (32 km)
Stamford	Greenwich	7 mi. (11 km)
Greenwich	Rye Brook, N.Y.	6 mi. (9 km)
Rye Brook, N.Y.	New York City	22 mi. (36 km)

Room Rates along the Atlantic Coast

See the listing of toll-free numbers in the Appendix.

B (Budget)	up to $30
I (Inexpensive)	$30–$60
M (Moderate)	$60–$90
E (Expensive)	$90–$140
VE (Very Expensive)	$140 and up

Atlantic Coast Restaurant Prices

(per person, excluding drinks and service charges)

B (Budget)	up to $15
I (Inexpensive)	$15–$25
M (Moderate)	$25–$40
E (Expensive)	$40–$60
VE (Very Expensive)	$60 and up

CALAIS: Small market town on the Canadian border. Some 15 mi. south, a marker at the side of U.S. 1 marks the 45th parallel and tells you that you are precisely halfway between the Equator and the North Pole. Still on this stretch of U.S. 1, opposite Red Beach, the **St. Croix Island International Historic Site** marks the place of the first attempted European settlement on the Atlantic coast north of Florida, in 1604 by the French explorer Samuel de Champlain and 78 of his companions. The park is not open to the public.

ROOSEVELT CAMPOBELLO INTERNATIONAL PARK (at Lubec): Campobello Island, at the mouth of the St. Croix River, is jointly owned by the U.S. and Canada, and marks the border between the two countries. It was here that Franklin D. Roosevelt had his summer home, where he contracted polio. The Visitor Center, with movies of the life and career of the 32nd president of the U.S., is on Maine 189 (506/752-2922), open daily from Memorial Day to the end of Oct. Should be seen.

BAR HARBOR: Charming old fishing village on **Mount Desert Island,** a site explored by the French at the beginning of the 17th century. Much favored by vacationers for the last 100 years because of the neighboring **Acadia National Park** (see below). The town, almost entirely rebuilt after a blaze in 1947, boasts dozens of hotels and restaurants in all price ranges. Boats may be hired for big-game fishing. A car-ferry, the ***Bluenose,*** connects Bar Harbor to Yarmouth, Nova Scotia, in Canada, in six hours from mid-

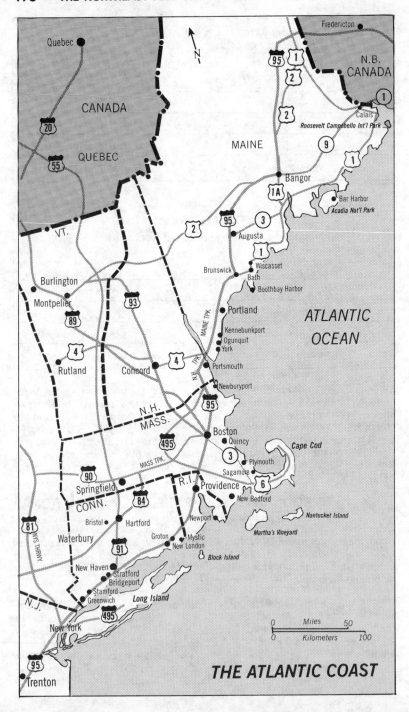

THE ATLANTIC COAST

June through Sept.: Ferry Terminal (207/288-3395), daily. Don't fail to visit Bar Harbor.

Acadia National Park

☀☖ Discovered in 1604 by the French explorer Samuel de Champlain, and part of French Acadia until 1713, the site of Acadia National Park is a perfect representation on a small scale of all the natural beauties of the Maine seaboard. On its 64 sq. mi. (168 km²) of splendid landscapes, the only large national park in the Northeast finds room for jagged coastlines, pine forests, little fishing villages, deep blue lakes, steep cliffs, clear streams, storm-beaten granite islands, and mountains: **Cadillac Mountain,** at 1,530 ft (466 m), is the highest on the Atlantic coast of the U.S.

The **Loop Road,** a 33-mi. (55-km) scenic drive, takes you along the shore of the park's largest island, with fine views of its fjords (particularly **Somes Sound**) and its lakes; you should follow it in a clockwise direction, beginning from the **Visitors Center** at Hulls Cove on Maine 3, about 3 mi. (5 km) NW of Bar Harbor. The **Abbe Museum of Indian Artifacts,** on Maine 3 at Sieur de Monts Springs (207/288-3519), open daily mid-May to mid-Oct., displays some interesting Indian material evidencing that Mount Desert Island has been inhabited since the Stone Age.

There is year-round ferry service between the mainland harbors and the little islands scattered offshore like **Isle-au-Haut, Little Cranberry Island,** and **Great Cranberry Island.** Many campsites, beaches with facilities, and 120 mi. (193 km) of trails.

Opened in 1919, Acadia National Park is ranked second among national parks in the number of its visitors (4.5 million a year). For information, contact the Superintendent, Acadia National Park, P.O. Box 177, Bar Harbor, ME 04069 (207/288-3338). A nature lover's dream; don't miss it.

Where to Stay

♛♛♛ **Bayview Waterfront Resort,** 111 Eden St., Bar Harbor, ME 04609 (207/288-5861). 38 rms, A/C, cable color TV. AE, CB, DC, MC, V. Free parking, pool, rest., bar, valet service, disco in season. *Note:* Elegant Georgian-style mansion standing in a fine garden. Spacious, tastefully decorated rms, period furniture, private patios, and open fireplaces. Excellent svce. Great charm and great quality. Open year round. **E–VE**

♛♛ **Atlantic Oakes,** Eden St. at Maine 3, Bar Harbor, ME 04609 (207/288-5801). 109 rms, no A/C; cable color TV. MC, V. Free parking, pool, marina, five tennis courts, nearby coffeeshop, free breakfast, free crib. *Note:* Friendly, comfortable motel adjoining the *Bluenose* ferry terminal. Huge, inviting rms, all w. ocean view. Private marina; garden. Affable reception. Open year round. **M–E, but lower rates out of season**

♛ **Testa's Hotel,** 53 Main St., Bar Harbor, ME 04609 (207/288-3327). 16 rms, A/C; cable color TV. AE, CB, DC, MC, V. On-street parking, rest., crib $8. *Note:* Modest but well-kept small hotel opposite the beach. Reception with a smile. Likeable Italian rest. Very good value. Closed mid-Oct. to mid-June. **I**

Where to Eat

♟ **Testa's,** in Testa's Hotel (see "Where to Stay," above) (207/288-3327). A/C. Breakfast/lunch/dinner daily (till midnight); closed mid-Oct. through June. AE, CB, DC, MC, V. *Specialties:* broiled or steamed lobster, clams, steak, Italian dishes. *Note:* Modest, unpretentious little *trattoria* serving excellent seafood and some decent Italian dishes. Run by the same family for the last half century. Locally popular. Friendly svce; very good value. *American-Italian.* **B–I**

♆ **Tripp's,** 45 Main St. (207/288-5001). A/C. Lunch/dinner daily; closed Nov. to mid-Apr. AE, DC, MC, V. *Specialties:* clams and oysters on the half shell, broiled lobster, baked stuffed shrimp, ice-cream pie. *Note:* Very attractively priced fish and shellfish served in generous portions. A landmark since 1939; the homemade desserts alone make it worth eating here. Very good value. *Seafood.* **B–I**

IN NEARBY HANCOCK. ☀ ♙♙♙ **Le Domaine,** U.S. 1, 18 mi. north of Bar Harbor (207/422-3916). Dinner only, Tues.-Sat.; closed Sun., Mon., and Nov.-May. AE, MC, V. *Specialties:* magret of duck w. cherries, rabbit w. prunes, catch of the day broiled w. fennel, sautéed sweetbreads, calves' liver dijonnaise, émincé of beef w. aioli. *Note:* The cooking of Nicole Purslow, and the décor of this enchanting little country inn, w. its huge fireplace and open-hearth grill, smell sweetly of France. All the vegetables and herbs come from her own garden. The breakfasts here are memorable too. Applauded by tourists for more than four decades. *French.* **I–M**

IN NEARBY SEAL HARBOR. ♆ **Jordan Pond House,** Park Loop Rd., 2 mi. (3.2 km) north of Seal Harbor (207/276-3316). Lunch/dinner daily; closed Nov.-May. AE, DC, MC, V. Jkt. *Specialties:* steak, broiled lobster, broiled chicken, homemade ice cream. *Note:* Charming rest. in a little farmhouse, more than a century old, on the grounds of Acadia National Park, which was generously donated to the National Parks Service in 1945 by John D. Rockefeller, Jr. Painstaking but unimaginative cuisine; open-air dining on fine days. Good value. *American.* **B–I**

☀ ♊♊ **CAMDEN:** In its splendid natural setting where the mountains plunge steeply into Penobscot Bay, with its mosaic of little islands, this town is particularly lively in summer, with many productions at the **Camden Amphitheatre,** on Atlantic Ave. (207/236-4404). From here many sailboats offer three- to six-day cruises along the Maine coast (see "Adventures," above). You should stop here.

Where to Stay

♙♙ **High Tide,** Belfast Rd. at U.S. 1, Camden, ME 04843 (207/236-3724). 26 rms and 3 cottages. No A/C; color TV. MC, V. Free parking, beach, tennis court, adjoining golf course, nearby coffeeshop, free crib. *Note:* Charming old (1901) house on a private beach. Pleasant rms w. private balconies; 7 acres (3 ha.) of lovely garden overlooking Penobscot Bay. Serene, relaxing atmosphere; good value. Closed mid-Oct. to early June. **I–M**

IN NEARBY LINCOLNVILLE. ♙ **Mt. Battie,** U.S. 1, Lincolnville, ME 04849 (207/236-3870). 21 rms, A/C, color TV. AE, MC, V. Free parking, nearby coffeeshop, free morning coffee. *Note:* Acceptable, small budget motel, functionally comfortable. Great ocean view. Good value. Closed late Oct. to early May. **B–I**

IN NEARBY ROCKPORT. ♙♙♙ **Samoset,** Warrenton St., Rockport, ME 04856 (207/594-2511). 150 rms, A/C, cable color TV. AE, CB, DC, MC, V. Free parking, two pools, health club, saunas, tennis court, golf course, marina, boats, rest. (Marcel's), bar, valet svce, disco, free crib, concierge. *Note:* Luxurious resort complex, modern and comfortable, overlooking Penobscot Bay. Spacious, comfortable rms w. private patios (most w. ocean view), in small buildings scattered around 230 acres (93 ha.) of green gardens and woods. Elegant rest.; attentive svce. A fine place. Interesting vacation packages. Open year round. **M–E, but lower rates out of season**

IN NEARBY ROCKLAND. ⚑ **Navigator Motor Inn,** 520 Main St., Rockland, ME 04841 (207/594-2131). 62 rms, A/C, cable color TV. AE, MC, V. Free parking, rest., bar, rm svce. *Note:* Typical but inviting motel on the ocean, opposite the ferry terminal. Comfortable rms w. balconies and refrigerators, some w. kitchenettes. Efficient svce. Good overall value. **I–M, but lower rates out of season**

Where to Eat

※ 🍷🍽 **Aubergine,** 6 Belmont Ave. (207/236-8053). Dinner only, Tues.-Sun.; closed Mon. and from Nov. to mid–May. AE, CB, DC, MC, V. Jkt. *Specialties:* terrine of duck, médaillons of lobster, classic French dishes. *Note:* Light, inspired French cuisine in a pretty Victorian setting w. furniture in period. Romantic atmosphere; classical background music. Somewhat starchy svce. Resv. advised. *French.* **I–M**

IN NEARBY BELFAST. 🍽🍽 **Penobscot Meadows Country Inn,** on U.S. 1 (207/338-5320). A/C. Dinner only, nightly; closed Tues. and Wed. from mid-Sept. to Memorial Day. *Specialties:* tomato soup w. cognac, shrimp w. ginger, chicken w. raspberries, lobster in pastry shell, catch of the day. *Note:* Pretty Victorian setting w. a clear view of Penobscot Bay and Blue Hill. Elegant ambience; very good svce; agreeable background music. Resv. advised. *American.* **I**

IN NEARBY LINCOLNVILLE. ※ 🍽🍽 **Lobster Pound,** on U.S. 1 (207/789-5550). A/C. Lunch/dinner daily; closed Nov.-Apr. AE, CB, DC, MC, V. *Specialties:* lobster, catch of the day, roast turkey, steak, fried clams, good desserts. *Note:* As the name implies, the specialty is lobster, in a ragoût, broiled, or steamed; shellfish lovers can go to town here. Dining rm overlooking Penobscot Bay, or eat in the open on the wharf. Efficient, smiling svce; a local landmark for 30 years. *American.* **I–M**

IN NEARBY ROCKPORT. 🍽🍽 **The Helm,** U.S. 1 (207/236-4337). A/C. Lunch/dinner Tues.-Sun.; closed Mon. and from mid-Oct. to early Apr. MC, V. *Specialties:* onion soup, steak au poivre, catch of the day, shellfish. *Note:* Locally popular little rest. serving good *cuisine bourgeoise* of French inspiration, and tasty homemade desserts. Friendly svce.; good value. *French-American.* **I***

IN NEARBY ROCKLAND. 🍽🍽 **Marcel's,** in the Samoset (see "Where to Stay," above) (207/594-2511). A/C. Breakfast/lunch/dinner daily. AE, CB, DC, MC, V. Jkt. *Specialties:* Maine lobster, highest-quality prime cuts and fish. *Note:* Elegant rest. w. view of Penobscot Bay and the ocean; classic grand-hotel food, impeccably prepared and served (by tuxedoed waiters). Pianist at dinner. Valet parking. Resv. advised. *Continental.* **I–M**

※ **AUGUSTA:** Maine's picturesque capital on the Kennebec River was founded in 1628 by settlers from Plymouth, Mass. Imposing **State House** (1832), on State and Capitol Sts. (207/289-2301), open Mon.-Fri., by the celebrated Charles Bulfinch, who also designed the Massachusetts State House in Boston. Across the river, **Fort Western** was built in 1754 for protection against the Indians, and has been carefully restored. Should be seen.

※ 🔭 **WISCASSET:** Tucked into the side of a hill at the mouth of the Sheepscot River, this enchanting little harbor, long the home of shipping tycoons and sea captains, is now an artists' and writers' colony. Louis-Philippe, king of France, landed here when he went into exile in the U.S.

Charming early-19th-century houses along Main St. The **Musical Wonder House,** 16–18 High St. (207/882-7163), open daily, June to mid-Oct., is an interesting museum of old music boxes and other automata. See also the picturesque **Lincoln County Museum and Old Jail,** built in 1811, the first penitentiary in the state, on Federal St. (207/882-6817), open daily July to Labor Day, by appointment the rest of the year. Should positively be seen.

BOOTHBAY HARBOR: With its old jetties and neat little houses, it gives you an engaging, representative picture of the seaports of Maine. A well-known regatta, Windjammer Days, is held in July. Should be seen.

Where to Stay

Linekin Bay, on Maine 27, Boothbay Harbor, ME 04538 (207/633-2494). 35 rms and 33 bungalows. No A/C; color TV in lounge. No credit cards. Free parking, pool, tennis court, marina, boats, fishing, waterskiing. *Note:* Rustic motel w. youthful, relaxed atmosphere reminiscent of a summer camp. Functionally comfortable (a little less in the bungalows). Wonderful for water-sports enthusiasts. Family clientele. Good value on balance. Closed mid-Sept. to mid-June. **I–M (American Plan)**

IN NEARBY SOUTHPORT. **Ocean Gate Motor Inn,** Maine 27, Southport, ME 04576 (207/633-3321). 55 rms, no A/C; color TV. AE, CB, DC, MC, V. Free parking, pool, tennis court, marina, boats, rest. (May-Oct.), bar, valet svce, crib $5. *Note:* Inviting, comfortable motel on the ocean. Agreeable rms w. offshore or harbor view, some w. private porches; also cottages for two to six people. Reception and svce w. a smile. 85 acres (34 ha.) of pretty woods and gardens. A fine place. Closed Dec.-May. **M–E, but lower rates out of season**

Where to Eat

Brown Bros., Atlantic Ave. (207/633-5440). A/C. Breakfast and dinner daily; closed late Sept. to mid-June. AE, CB, DC, MC, V. *Specialties:* lobster, catch of the day. *Note:* Picturesque rest. in an 18th-century salt shed overlooking the water; the menu emphasizes local seafood. In the hands of the same family for almost half a century. Relaxed atmosphere; good value. No lunch served. *Seafood.* **B–I**

BATH: Harbor town on the Kennebec River, with fine old houses and famous shipyards from which more than 4,000 vessels have been launched since the beginning of the 18th century. See the splendid **Maine Maritime Museum,** Washington St. (207/443-1316), open daily, May-Oct.; call ahead the rest of the year. Its exhibits cover three centuries of shipbuilding. Worth the side trip.

BRUNSWICK: This historic little port, dating from 1628, has wonderful old houses the whole length of Park Row and Federal St. Among them is the 1806 **Stowe House,** 63 Federal St. (207/725-5543), where Harriet Beecher Stowe wrote *Uncle Tom's Cabin;* the building is now a hotel and restaurant. See also **Bowdoin College,** founded in 1794, whose alumni include the writers Nathaniel Hawthorne and Henry Wadsworth Longfellow; the 14th president of the U.S., Franklin Pierce; and the first man to reach the North Pole, Adm. Robert Peary. The campus and its museums may be visited Tues.-Sun., year round (Maine and College Sts. 207/725-3000). Must be seen.

PORTLAND: The most important fishing port north of Boston, on beautiful **Casco Bay,** whose 136 islands attract many summer vacationers. The **Portland Historic Trail** through the streets of the old port town takes you to several historic 18th-century homes, including **Tate House,** 1270 Westbrook St. (207/774-9781), open Tues.-Sun. from mid-June to mid-Sept.; and the **Wadsworth-Longfellow House,** birthplace of the poet, 487 Congress St. (207/772-1807). Open Tues.-Sat. from June to mid Oct.

And don't overlook the **Portland Museum of Art,** 7 Congress Square (207/775-6148), open Tues.-Sun., where you'll find choice works by such American artists as Andrew Wyeth, Winslow Homer, and John Marin.

Four mi. (6.5 km) south on Maine 77, the **Portland Headlight,** dating from 1791 and built by order of George Washington, is the oldest lighthouse in the U.S. still in service. Worth seeing.

Don't miss trips on Casco Bay (see above under "Guided Tours"). A car-ferry, the *Scotia Prince,* links Portland to Yarmouth, Nova Scotia (Canada), in 11 hours, daily, mid-May to Oct., from the International Terminal (207/775-5616).

Don't fail to visit Portland.

Where to Stay

🍸🍸 **Ramada Inn,** 1230 Congress St., Portland, ME 04102 (207/774-5611). 149 rms, A/C, cable color TV. AE, CB, DC, MC, V. Free parking, pool, sauna, rest., bar, rm svce, disco, free crib. *Note:* Large, comfortable motel midway between the airport and dwntwn. Huge, functional rms; comprehensive facilities. Impersonal but efficient svce. Free limos to airport and dwntwn. Business clientele. Open year round. **M–E**

IN NEARBY PROUT'S NECK. 🍸🍸🍸 **Black Point Inn,** Maine 207, Prout's Neck, ME 04074 (207/883-4126). 81 rms, A/C, cable color TV. MC, V. Free parking, two pools, tennis court, putting green, sauna, private beach, boats, rest., bar, rm svce, nightclub, hrdrsr, free crib. *Note:* Handsome resort hotel in a lovely setting on the ocean. Spacious, comfortable rms; efficient svce. If you love calm and tranquility, this is the place for you. Closed Nov.-May. **E–VE (American Plan), but lower rates out of season**

Where to Eat

🍷🍷🍷 **Brattle Street,** 19 Brattle St. (207/772-4658). A/C. Dinner only, Mon.-Sat.; closed Sun., and holidays. AE, CB, DC, MC, V. Jkt. *Specialties:* roast lobster w. leeks, filet of salmon w. cucumbers and dill sauce, lamb ravioli w. rosemary and basil, duck w. lemon sauce and raspberries. *Note:* The excellent young chef, Dale Gussett, serves an ambitious, distinguished French nouvelle cuisine. The rest., one of Portland's most fashionable, occupies an elegantly restored old brick house in the historic district. Polished svce; successful enough that resv. are advisable. A fine place to eat. *French.* **M**

☀🍷🍷 **Boone's,** 6 Custom House Wharf (207/774-5725). A/C. Lunch/dinner daily; closed Thanksgiving and Dec. 25. AE, CB, DC, MC, V. *Specialties:* clam chowder, fisherman's stew, clambake, enormous choice of seafood broiled, steamed, sautéed, or fried, but also some praiseworthy beef dishes and game in season. *Note:* The ads truthfully term it "A Waterfront Tradition Since 1898," while the building has been there since 1840. Superb, absolutely fresh lobster and catch of the day. Picturesque seafaring décor. Relaxed atmosphere; very good value. *Seafood.* **B–I**

🔔 **KENNEBUNKPORT:** Well-known beach resort with an interesting streetcar museum displaying 150 vehicles from all periods and places, from horse-drawn trams to cable cars: **Seashore Trolley**

Museum, Log Cabin Rd. (207/967-2712), open daily, mid-June to early Sept.; call ahead the rest of the year. Worth going out of your way for.

Where to Stay

☀ ⓛⓛⓛ **The Colony,** Ocean Ave. and Kings Rd., Kennebunkport, ME 04046 (207/967-3331). 139 rms, no A/C; color TV. AE, MC, V. Free parking, pool, tennis court, putting green, private beach, rest., bar, rm svce, disco, cinema, crib $5. *Note:* Charming old 1920s-style hotel w. direct access to beach. Lovely gardens. Elegant, comfortable rms; faultless svce. One of the best places to stay on the coast. Closed mid-Sept. to mid-June. **E–VE (American Plan)**

ⓛ **Nonantum,** Ocean Ave., Kennebunkport, ME 06046 (207/967-4050). 67 rms, some w. A/C, cable color TV. AE, MC, V. Free parking, pool, boats, rest., bar, valet svce. *Note:* Aging hotel of conventional type on the Kennebunk River. Functional comfort; the best rms overlook the river. 5 min. on foot from beach. Good value overall. Closed Nov. to mid-May. **E–VE (Modified American Plan), but lower rates out of season**

☀☀ⓑ **OGUNQUIT:** The jagged, rocky shores of Maine here yield to sandy beaches; this is another delightful fishing port, as much for its setting as for the high quality of its lobsters. In summer, an important artists' colony exhibits in the Shore Rd. galleries. Beautiful fine-sand beach, 3 mi. (5 km) long, ideal for surfing. Worth seeing.

Where to Stay

ⓛ **Terrace by the Sea,** 11 Wharf Lane, Ogunquit, ME 03907 (207/646-3232). 60 rms, A/C, cable color TV. No credit cards. Free parking, pool, tennis court, beach, free breakfast. No bar, no rest. *Note:* Typical motel w. direct beach access. Comfortable rms w. balconies, patios, and refrigerators. Picnic tables. Efficient svce. Closed Dec.-May. **M–E, but lower rates out of season**

IN NEARBY MOODY. ⓛⓛ **River Plantation,** U.S. 1, Moody, ME 03907 (207/646-9611). 80 rms, A/C, cable color TV. AE, MC, V. Free parking, pool, adjoining coffeeshop, free breakfast, free crib. *Note:* Modern, elegant motel on the Ogunquit River. Spacious, comfortable rms w. balconies and refrigerators, all w. ocean or river view. Beach 5 min. by car (free jitney). Good svce. Very good value. Closed Nov.-Apr. **I–M**

☀☀ⓑ **YORK:** A picturesque anachronism, York could be taken for a small fragment of the Colonial period that has escaped the burden of the years. Many historic buildings, dating from 1720 to 1760, along York St. and Lindsay Rd.: the **Old Gaol,** whose cells were in use until the 1860s; the **Old School House** (1755); **Jefferd's Tavern** (1759); **First Parish Congregational Church** (1747); the **Elizabeth Perkins House** (1730); etc. All may be visited daily, June-Sept.

Busy **York Harbor** provides the economic underpinnings for this little piece of a bygone era, with many charter companies offering trips on the ocean and deep-sea fishing parties. Must definitely be seen.

Where to Eat

🍷🍷 **Dockside Dining Room,** Harris Island Rd. (207/363-4800). A/C. Lunch/dinner Tues.-Sun.; closed Mon. and from mid-Oct. through May. MC, V. *Specialties:* oven-baked sole stuffed w. lobster, roast duckling, steak teriyaki, broiled fish. *Note:* This light-filled rest. w. its huge picture windows stands right on York Harbor, overlooking the yacht basin. The food, though unimaginative, is pleasant and tasty. Good svce. *American.* **I**

PORTSMOUTH: Founded in 1630, the same year as Boston, the former capital of New Hampshire allows you to immerse yourself in 17th- and 18th-century America. In the Old Harbor neighborhood, **Strawbery Banke,** at Hancock and Marcy Sts. (603/433-1100), you can see three dozen craftsman's shops and old houses, built between 1695 and the end of the 19th century and carefully restored; open to visitors daily, May-Oct.; signposted pedestrian trail.

See also some fine upscale homes such as the **John Paul Jones House,** once the home of the famous naval commander, at 43 Middle St. (603/436-8420), open Mon.-Sat., mid-May to mid-Oct.; the **John Langdon House,** which George Washington termed "the handsomest house in Portsmouth," 143 Pleasant St. (603/436-3205), open Wed.-Sun., June to mid-Oct.; or the **Wentworth-Coolidge Mansion,** one of the oldest in the city (1695), on Little Harbor Rd. (603/436-6607), open daily, mid-June to Labor Day.

Fort Constitution, on the site of a post built in 1632 which had its moment of glory during the War of Independence, is also worth a side trip; the present structure, imposing in granite, dates from 1808. Go 4 mi. east on N.H. 1B to New Castle (603/431-0113); open daily mid-June to mid-Sept.; weekends only from mid-May to mid-June and mid-Sept. to mid-Oct.

For history lovers, a visit to Portsmouth is a must.

Where to Stay

Holiday Inn, 300 Woodbury Ave., Portsmouth, NH 03801 (603/431-8000; toll free, see Holiday Inns). 130 rms, A/C, color TV. AE, CB, DC, MC, V. Free parking, pool, health club, rest., bar, rm svce, disco, free crib. *Note:* A typical Holiday Inn, modern and comfortable, 5 min. from the Strawbery Banke historic district. Spacious rms; efficient svce; business clientele. Open year round. **M–E**

Where to Eat

Blue Strawbery, 29 Ceres St. (603/431-6420). A/C. Dinner only, nightly; closed Mon. and Tues. from Oct. through May, and Dec. 25. No credit cards. Jkt. *Specialties:* mussel soup, pork filet stuffed w. walnuts and cheese, broiled salmon w. squash and blueberries, striped bass w. scallops, cognac, and sour cream; menu changes regularly. Large wine list. *Note:* One of the best places to eat in New England, as chef Philip McGuire turns out sophisticated, contemporary American cuisine. Lovely old décor in a magnificently restored 1797 ship's chandlery. Ultra-polished svce. Much charm and distinction. Resv. a must. *American.* **M (prix fixe)**

NEWBURYPORT: The main thoroughfare of this harbor town with its three-centuries-old shipyards, **High Street** is a journey 200 years back through time. A living museum of American Federalist architecture, High St. displays rows of big, square, three-story houses, built around 1800 by rich shipowners or long-haul sea captains in an architectural idiom reminiscent of nearby Salem. Newburyport, at the mouth of the Merrimack River, is also renowned as the birthplace of the U.S. Coast Guard in 1790. Worth going out of your way for.

Where to Eat

IN NEARBY SALEM. **Courtyard Café,** Salem Inn, 7 Summer St.

(508/741-0680). A/C. Lunch/dinner daily. AE, CB, DC, MC, V. *Specialties:* stuffed lobster, sole meunière, mussel stew, broiled scrod, catch of the day. *Note:* This 1840s sea captain's house has been prettily converted into an inn, w. a charming patio where you can dine out on fine days. Excellent seafood. Svce with a smile. *Seafood.* **I**

BOSTON, GLOUCESTER, MARBLEHEAD, ROCKPORT, SALEM:
See Chapter 1 on Boston.

☼ 🔔 **QUINCY:** An important industrial town founded in 1625, this Boston suburb is the home of the famous Adams family of statesmen and patriots, whose origin can be traced back to 1636 in the colony's earliest days. Among their number is John Adams, second president of the U.S., and his son, John Quincy Adams, sixth president. See the **John and John Quincy Adams Birthplaces,** two 17th-century saltbox houses at 133 and 141 Franklin St. (617/773-1177), open daily, mid-Apr. to mid-Nov.; also the **Adams National Historic Site,** 135 Adams St. (same phone number and visiting days as the preceding), built in 1731, acquired by John Adams in 1787 and retained in the family until 1946, still with its original fixtures and furniture. The tombs of the two presidents are not far away, in the **United First Parish Church** (the only church in the country with crypts of *two* presidents), 1306 Hancock St. (617/773-1290), open Mon.-Sat., mid-May to Labor Day; by appointment the rest of the year. John Hancock, the first signer of the Declaration of Independence, was also a native of Quincy. Should be seen.

☼ 🔔 **HULL:** At the tip of **Nantasket Peninsula,** Hull boasts the oldest lighthouse in the country, the **Boston Light (Little Brewster Island).** The original, built in 1716, was destroyed 60 years later by the British when they were forced to evacuate Little Brewster Island; the present lighthouse, dating from 1783, is worth seeing.

☼ 🔔🔔 **PLYMOUTH:** It was on these desolate, windswept shores that on Dec. 21, 1620, after an Atlantic crossing which lasted 66 days, the *Mayflower* cast anchor in the lee of **Plymouth Rock,** with her passenger list of 102 men, women, and children collectively known as the "Pilgrim Fathers." That first winter was terrible. Half the colonists perished, and were buried in secret, at night, on **Cole's Hill** so that the terrifying Wampanoag Indians should not be able to determine how few were the survivors. All the same, but for these Indians and their gifts of food, there might well have been no survivors.

Plymouth, affectionately referred to as "America's Hometown," was the first permanent British settlement north of Virginia, and to this day it looks like something from an old book of prints. The precious relics of the first settlers are carefully arranged in the **Pilgrim Hall Museum,** 75 Court St. (508/746-1620), open daily. There are many old houses around Water and Summer Sts., including the oldest in the city, the **Richard Sparrow House,** built in 1640 at 42 Summer St.

The *Mayflower II* is a full-size replica of her illustrious namesake, and like her, built in England. Having crossed the Atlantic in 1957, the *Mayflower II* is now at State Pier. The ship may be visited daily from Apr. to Nov.

See also on Water St. **Plymouth Rock** itself, now sheltered behind a Greek Revival columned portico in granite; this is the exact spot where the Pilgrims made their landfall.

Three mi. (5 km.) south along Mass. 3 A., the museum-village of **Plimoth Plantation** is a faithful reconstruction of the life of the original colonists in the

1620s, with costumed extras and a facsimile of a Wampanoag Indian encampment. Find it on Mass. 3 A (508/746-1622), open daily Apr.-Nov.

Plymouth is an absolute must.

Where to Stay

Sheraton Plymouth at Village Landing, 180 Water St., Plymouth, MA 02360 (508/747-4900; toll free, see Sheraton). 175 rms, A/C, cable color TV. AE, CB, DC, MC, V. Free parking, pool, health club, sauna, rest., bar, rm svce, nightclub, concierge, crib $10. *Note:* Big vacation motel on the Plymouth waterfront. Spacious, very comfortable rms, some w. balconies, the best overlooking the ocean. Acceptable rest. Good svce. A stone's throw from Plymouth's principal tourist attractions. Open year round. **M–E**

Cold Spring, 188 Court St., Plymouth, MA 02360 (508/ 746-2222). 31 rms, A/C, color TV. AE, MC, V. Free parking, nearby coffeeshop, free breakfast, crib $5. *Note:* Smart little motel in a typical New England building; functionally comfortable. Friendly reception. Good value. Closed Dec. to mid-Mar. **I**

SAGAMORE: The access port for **Cape Cod,** at the junction of U.S. 6 and Mass. 3. There are charming old fishing towns and splendid seascapes the whole 60-mi. (100-km) length of Cape Cod, while the nearby islands of **Martha's Vineyard** and **Nantucket** are the favorite country retreat for well-off Bostonians and New Yorkers. Fishing, sailing, and a temperate climate in summer. For more details on the peninsula, see Chapter 2 on Cape Cod, above.

NEW BEDFORD: Although by now partly given over to textile production, New Bedford has retained intact its seafaring traditions and its very large fishing fleet. The port, which is home to some 10,000 sailors, including a Portuguese colony which goes back almost to the town's foundation in 1640, was in the 19th century the world's largest whaling port, and inspired Herman Melville to write *Moby-Dick.* Readers of that great work will find fascinating new viewpoints opened to them, probably more than at any of the region's other museums devoted to man and the sea, at the superb **New Bedford Whaling Museum,** 18 Johnny Cake Hill (508/997-0046), open daily.

Be sure also to see the lovely old houses of the **County Street Historic District,** which once belonged to wealthy merchants and whaler captains. Well worth the side trip.

Car-ferry service in summer between New Bedford and the island of Martha's Vineyard: **Cape Island Express Lines,** 1494 E. Rodney French Blvd. (508/997-1688), daily, mid-May to Sept.

PROVIDENCE: Sheltered at the head of the enormous **Narragansett Bay,** the capital of Rhode Island was christened "[Divine] Providence" by its founder, Roger Williams, a religious leader of British origin who in 1636 took refuge here from the dogmatic intolerance of the Salem puritans. The rich historical inheritance of this liberal, hard-working, business-oriented city is reflected in its ❄ **old neighborhoods,** of which Kennedy Plaza and Benefit St. are the finest examples.

Built at the beginning of the 20th century, the **Rhode Island State House,** on Smith St. (401/277-2311), open daily, with its imposing dome of white Georgia marble, fittingly sets off the downtown office high-rises. In it you may see the charter originally granted by King Charles II in 1663 to the new Rhode Island colony. Dating from 1762, the **Old State House,** 150 Benefit St. (401/ 277-2678), open Mon.-Fri., is still dear to Rhode Islanders because it was here that the Declaration of Independence was originally signed on May 4, 1776 —two full months before it was ratified by the original 13 colonies in Philadelphia.

The splendid Georgian **John Brown House** (1786), 52 Power St. (401/331-8575), open Tues.-Sun., was described by John Quincy Adams as "the most magnificent mansion in the continent," and very definitely deserves a visit. Nearby, you should also see the ☀ **First Baptist Church in America,** 75 N. Main St., open daily, the oldest Baptist church in the country, founded by Roger Williams in 1638; the present building, a very fine work by architect Joseph Brown, dates from 1775.

While you're here, in the adjoining suburb of **Pawtucket** you should see the extremely interesting ☀ **Slater Mill Historic Site** (1793), often termed "the cradle of American industry." Its mill and its antique machines give you a vivid picture of America at the beginning of her Industrial Revolution in the very early 19th century. See it at Roosevelt Ave. and Main St. (401/725-8638), open daily from Memorial Day to Labor Day; weekends only the rest of the year.

Where to Eat

🍸 **Al Forno,** 7 Steeple St. (401/273-9760). A/C. Dinner only, Tues.-Sat.; closed Sun., Mon., and holidays. AE, MC, V. *Specialties:* baked clams w. tomato sauce, fresh homemade pasta and pizza, hot sausage roasted w. vegetables, sautéed squid, filet of pork à l'orange, grilled tuna vinaigrette. *Note:* The gloomy exterior of this tiny rest. is discouraging, but the light, inventive cuisine of George Germond and his wife, Johanne, are worth going out of your way for. One negative: Al Forno accepts no reservations, so— small as it is (seating only 32), and successful as it is—you may have a long wait. *American-Italian.* **I**

🏛 **BRISTOL:** A busy port in the 19th century (in 1800–1810 it was fourth in importance in the nation), Bristol can show you a rich gamut of Colonial houses, particularly along **Hope Street,** as well as some charming small museums. Among the latter, on Tower Rd., 1 mi. (1.6 km) east along Metacom Ave. (401/253-8388), you'll find the **Haffenreffer Museum of Anthropology,** open Tues.-Sun., June-Aug.; weekends only the rest of the year. It has a remarkable collection in the areas of Eskimo, Indian, and Polynesian culture.

☀🏛 **PORTSMOUTH:** The **Green Animals Topiary Gardens** on R.I. 114 (401/847-1000), open daily, May-Sept. (weekends only in Oct.; closed the rest of the year), is one of the most original examples of the landscape gardener's art on the eastern seaboard. You'll see dozens of shrubs and bushes trimmed into the shape of giant animals: elephant, lion, giraffe, antelope, etc. Very beautiful rose garden. Well worth the side trip.

Where to Eat

☀🍸 **Sea Fare Inn** (formerly Le Rochambeau), 3352 E. Main Rd. at R.I. 138 (401/683-0577). A/C. Lunch Tues.-Fri., dinner Tues.-Sun.; closed Mon. and mid-Feb. to mid-Mar. AE, MC, V. J&T. *Specialties:* remarkable seafood prepared in an infinite variety of ways. Also choice beef and fowl. Menu changes daily. *Note:* Everything you could ask from a luxury inn. This rest., in an enormous 19th-century English-style manor house with crystal chandeliers, six open fireplaces, and nine dining rooms, is one of the most elegant in New England. Chef George Karousos turns out refined cuisine and light-as-air sauces. Svce exemplary in all respects. A fine place. *Continental-seafood.* **I–M**

☼☊ 👓👓 **NEWPORT:** America's yachting capital; in the bay off this famous Rhode Island resort the America's Cup races were held every four years for more than a century (1870–1983). It was this engaging little city, steeped in history, that in 1657 welcomed the first Quaker settlers from Europe and only a year later the first 15 Jewish families (from Holland) to come to the New World.

In the latter part of the 19th century Newport became the favorite summer home of New York millionaires such as the Astors, Belmonts, Vanderbilts, Stuyvesants, and McAllisters. It still preserves from its glory days some splendid residences, worthy of Scott Fitzgerald's *The Great Gatsby:* **Marble House,** on Bellevue Avenue, modeled after Versailles, and **The Breakers,** a 70-room palace on Ochre Point Ave., both belonging to the Vanderbilt family; **Rosecliff,** with its huge ballroom, on Bellevue Ave.; and again on Bellevue Ave. such fantasy estates as the Victorian **Château-Sur-Mer, The Elms** (a copy of the old chateau at Asnières near Paris), the Louis XIII–style **Belcourt Castle,** and so on. All these houses are open daily, Apr.-Oct.; for information, call 401/847-1000.

Among the town's other notable buildings are **Hammersmith Farm** on Ocean Dr., where John and Jackie Kennedy were married; the **Redwood Library,** at 50 Bellevue Ave. (401/847-0292), open daily, believed to be the oldest library in the U.S. still in operation (1748); and the **Touro Synagogue,** 85 Touro St. (401/847-4794), open Sun.-Fri. from late June to Labor Day (Sun. only the rest of the year), an architectural treasure which, dating from 1763, is the oldest synagogue in the continental U.S.

Tennis fans won't want to miss the remarkable museum at the **International Tennis Hall of Fame,** Newport Casino, 194 Bellevue Ave. (401/849-3990), open daily June-Apr. (closed in May), entirely devoted to the glories of that great game.

The world-famous **Jazz Festival** has returned to Newport after many years in eclipse, and again draws crowds in Aug. of each year, as does the chamber-music festival in mid-July.

Newport alone is enough to justify your journey to the Atlantic seaboard.

Where to Stay

🛏🛏🛏 **Sheraton Islander Inn,** Goat Island (causeway from Washington St.), Newport, RI 02840 (401/849-2600; toll free, see Sheraton). 253 rms, A/C, color TV. AE, CB, DC, MC, V. Free parking, two pools, health club, tennis court, marina, rest., coffeeshop, bars, rm svce, disco, hrdrsr, free crib. *Note:* Luxurious convention hotel on a little island in dwntwn Newport, w. its own marina and heliport. Spacious, well-laid-out rms w. private balconies or patios. Very good svce. VIP floor. Caters to big businessmen and well-heeled vacationers. Open year round. **E–VE**

🛏🛏 **Treadway Resort and Marina,** 49 America's Cup Ave., Newport, RI 02840 (401/847-9000; toll free, see Treadway Inns). 133 rms, A/C, color TV. AE, CB, DC, MC, V. Free parking, pool, sauna, rest., bar, rm svce, free crib. *Note:* Very comfortable hotel-marina overlooking the harbor and the bay w. spectacular views. Huge, inviting rms w. balconies. Flawless svce. Excellent dwntwn location a stone's throw from Newport's main tourist attractions. Open year round. **M–E**

Where to Eat

☼ 🍷🍷🍷 **White Horse Tavern,** Marlborough and Farewell Sts. (402/849-3600). A/C. Lunch/dinner daily, Sun. brunch; closed Jan. 1 and Dec. 25. AE, CB, DC, MC, V. Jkt. *Specialties:* rack of lamb, beef Wellington, ratatouille w. five kinds of mushrooms, roast duck, steak Diane.

Good wine list. *Note:* Gracious Colonial inn in one of the oldest (1673) buildings in New England. Slightly affected continental cuisine; svce of a very high order. Resv. advised. *Continental.* **I–M**

NARRAGANSETT PIER: Among New England's most magnificent beaches. You should try to see the **Point Judith Lighthouse** at the south entrance to Narragansett Bay in heavy weather, when the enormous waves breaking over the rocky promontory offer mute testimony of past shipwrecks.

BLOCK ISLAND: Sighted in 1524 by Verrazano, the discoverer of New York, this picturesque little island, 12 miles (19 km) out to sea from **Point Judith,** temperate in summer and winter alike, was a pirate stronghold as late as 1815. A treeless moor with many little ponds, a sanctuary for seabirds, and a paradise for fishermen (tuna, swordfish, sea bass, etc.), the island has some fine cliffs at **Mohegan Bluffs,** and strange black-sand beaches.

A favorite vacation resort in summer, it is reached by the **ferries** of the Interstate Navigation Co. from New London, Conn. (daily, mid-June to Labor Day), from Providence and Newport, R.I. (daily, late June to Labor Day), and from Point Judith, R.I. (daily, year round). For information, call 203/442-9553 in Connecticut, 401/789-3502 in Rhode Island.

MYSTIC: This old whaling port, founded in 1654 and built athwart the Mystic River, has the country's finest maritime museum, **Mystic Seaport**. This is a fascinating reconstruction of a 19th-century seaport, with old houses, craftsmen's workshops, sailing boats anchored at the docks, and staff in period costume. Allow at least three to four hours for your visit. On Conn. 27 (203/572-0711), open daily, year round. Don't miss it.

Where to Stay

Inn at Mystic, U.S. 1 and Conn. 27, Mystic, CT 06355 (203/536-9604). 67 rms, A/C, cable color TV. AE, MC, V. Free parking, pool, tennis court, boats, rest. (Flood Tide), bar, rm svce, crib $10. *Note:* Comfortable motel near Mystic Seaport and its living museum. Inviting rms w. fireplaces and whirlpool baths, some w. private balconies or patios. Very good svce; agreeable setting at ¼ mi from the ocean. Open year round. **E, but lower rates out of season**

Days Inn, 26 Michelle Lane, Mystic, CT 06355 (203/572-0574; toll free, see Days Inn). 122 rms, A/C, cable color TV. AE, CB, DC, MC, V. Free parking, pool, coffeeshop, valet svce, free crib. *Note:* Typical modern motel near Mystic Seaport. Functionally comfortable rms; reception and svce w. a smile. Good value overall. Open year round. **I–M**

Where to Eat

Flood Tide, in the Inn at Mystic (see "Where to Stay," above) (203/536-8140). A/C. Breakfast/lunch/dinner daily; closed Dec. 24–25. AE, MC, V. *Specialties:* duck w. peaches, Maine lobster, roast rack of lamb, jumbo shrimp stuffed w. crab and garnished w. bacon, beef Wellington, Caesar salad. *Note:* On a hill overlooking Mystic Harbor, this quiet, comfortable hotel rest. serves carefully prepared classic food. Attentive, polished svce. Resv. highly advisable. *Continental-American.* **I–M**

GROTON: Important naval base where the first diesel-powered submarine was built in 1912, and the first nuclear-powered submarine, U.S.S. *Nautilus,* in 1975. The *Nautilus* is now a floating museum, at Crystal Lake Rd. at Conn. 12 (203/449-3174), open Tues.-Sun.; closed June, Sept., and Dec.

NEW LONDON: Old seaport at the mouth of the Thames River (whence its name), since 1876 home of the **U.S. Coast Guard Academy,** on I-95, exit 83 (203/444-8270). The Visitor Center and museum are open daily May-Oct., Mon.-Fri. the rest of the year; cadet parades on Fri. in spring and fall.

Opposite the base, the **Lyman Allyn Museum,** 625 Williams St. (203/443-2545), open Tues.-Sun., is rich in classical art and antiquities, 18th- and 19th-century American furniture, and enchanting old dolls and dollhouses. Downtown, on Huntington St., see **Whale Oil Row** with its early-19th-century classical revival shipowners' homes.

Ferry connection with Orient Point, at the NE tip of Long Island, N.Y.: 2 Ferry St. (203/443-5281), daily year round.

Where to Eat

IN NEARBY ESSEX. ☼ 🍽 **Griswold Inn,** Main St. (203/767-0991). A/C. Lunch/dinner daily; closed Dec. 24–25. AE, DC, MC, V. *Specialties:* filet of beef w. fried oysters and sauce béarnaise, roast beef, broiled haddock, seafood of the day, meat pie, homemade sausages. *Note:* Founded in 1776, this delightful inn w. its historic décor is well worth a visit, as much for the inimitable atmosphere as for the quality of its praiseworthy, flavorful food. Superb old bar. Youthful, smiling svce. Resv. advised. A fine place. *American.* **I**

HARTFORD: The world's insurance capital, where no fewer than 35 corporate headquarters buildings reach proudly for the sky, Hartford, founded by Dutch settlers in 1623, presents a happy mix of old and modern architecture. With their futuristic towers and their dozens of stores, boutiques, and restaurants, **Constitution Plaza** and the **Civic Center,** both in the heart of downtown, are among the most remarkable achievements of urban renewal in the country.

Lovers of the grand antique would sooner visit the 1796 **Old State House,** by Charles Bulfinch, where there is a fine portrait of George Washington by Gilbert Stuart. It's at 800 Main St. (203/522-6766), open daily. Or there's the 1782 **Butler-McCook Homestead,** with its ornate interior, at 396 Main St. (203/522-1806), open Tues., Wed., Thur., and Sun., mid-May to mid-Oct.

Book-lovers will want to see the charming 1870s home where Mark Twain wrote part of *Huckleberry Finn* and *Tom Sawyer* (and the adjoining cottage, once the home of Harriet Beecher Stowe, who wrote *Uncle Tom's Cabin*): **Nook Farm,** Farmington Ave. and Forest St. (203/525-9317), open daily, June-Aug.; Tues.-Sun. the rest of the year.

Another absolute must is the ☼ 🏛 **Wadsworth Atheneum,** 600 Main St. (203/278-2670), open Tues.-Sun., one of the oldest and richest art museums in America, with several hundred major works by artists both European (Caravaggio, Zurbaran, Rembrandt, Goya, Picasso, Monet, Gauguin) and American (Church, Sargent, Whistler, Wyeth, Calder).

Hartford prides itself on possessing the oldest continuously published daily paper in the country, the *Hartford Courant,* which was founded in 1764 and became a daily in 1837. Hartford is the birthplace of Noah Webster, author of the first American dictionary (1828).

Where to Stay

🔑🔑🔑 **Hilton Parkview,** 1 Hilton Plaza, Hartford, CT 06103 (203/249-5611; toll free, see Hilton). 383 rms, A/C, color TV, in-rm movies. AE, CB, DC, MC, V. Garage $5, health club, rest. (Terrace on the Park), bar, rm svce, disco, hrdrsr, free crib. *Note:* Great tower of glass, 18 floors high, looming over the Capitol and Bushnell Park. Décor and furnishings completely renovated. Huge, comfortable rms w. refrigerators, the best over-looking the park. Efficient svce; acceptable rest. Business clientele. A block or two from the Civic Center. Open year round. **E–VE**

Ramada Inn–Capitol Hill, 440 Asylum St., Hartford, CT 06103 (203/246-6591; toll free, see Ramada Inns). 96 rms, A/C, color TV. AE, CB, DC, MC, V. Free parking, rest., bar, valet svce. *Note:* Elderly hotel recently renovated; functionally comfortable. Undependable svce. Very centrally located. Good value. Open year round. **M**

Where to Eat

L'Americain, 2 Hartford Square West (203/522-6500). A/C. Lunch Mon.-Fri., dinner Mon.-Sat.; closed Sun. and hol-idays. AE, MC, V. Jkt. *Specialties:* oyster-and-mushroom ravioli, lobster-stuffed vine leaves, roast saddle of rabbit w. honey, broiled blackfish w. corn kernels, fruit Charlotte. *Note:* Local business people enjoy lunching at this elegant rest., dis-creetly decorated in shades of peach w. original paintings and antique chande-liers. The cuisine of chef Chris Pardue is remarkable for its imagination and refinement, and the svce. is ultraprofessional. A splendid place right in the busi-ness district. Resv. a must. *American.* **I–M**

NEW HAVEN: Although only 75 mi. (120 km) from New York, New Haven is a typical New England port, on whose stones 350 years of history (it was founded in 1638) have left their mark.

As Harvard has done for Cambridge, so rival **Yale University** has raised New Haven to a place of eminence in science and learning. Founded in 1701 at **Brandford** and moved to New Haven in 1716, the university owes its name to a bygone patron of letters, Elihu Yale. On the old campus with its charming ivied buildings, mostly English Gothic Revival or Romanesque, see the **Peabody Mu-seum of Natural History,** with its spectacular collection of prehistoric animals, at 170 Whitney Ave. (203/432-5050), open daily. The **Sterling Memorial and Beinecke Libraries,** Wall and High Sts. (203/432-2977), open daily, house be-tween them more than three million works, including such rarities as a Guten-berg Bible, the Yale archives, and an unparalleled collection of playing cards. Louis I. Kahn's 1976 **Center for British Art and Studies,** 1080 Chapel St. (203/432-2800), open Tues.-Sun., houses the most important public collection outside Great Britain of that country's art, including works by Hogarth, Consta-ble, Turner, and many others. You should take a **guided tour of the campus,** given daily; apply to the University Information Office, Phelps Gateway, 344 College St. (203/432-2300).

On **The Green,** a 16-acre (6-ha.) park contemporary with the city, see **three lovely churches** of Georgian design from 1813–1814. Al Capp, the cre-ator of "Li'l Abner," was born in New Haven.

Where to Stay

Park Plaza and Conference Center, 155 Temple St., New Haven, CT 06510 (203/772-1700). 300 rms, A/C, color TV. AE, CB, DC, MC, V. Garage $2, pool, rest. (Top of the Park), bar, rm svce, disco, crib $10. *Note:* Modern 19-story building overlooking dwntwn and the Yale campus; rest. w. panorama on top floor. Spacious, comfortable rms. Good svce on balance. Business clientele; open year round. **M–E**

Where to Eat

Robert Henry's, 1032 Chapel St. (203/789-1010). A/C. Lunch Mon.-Fri., dinner Mon.-Sat.; closed Sun. and holidays. AE, CB, DC, MC, V. Jkt. *Specialties:* artichoke hearts braised w. basil, lobster w. hazelnut butter, lamb on a skewer w. goat's-cheese ravioli, confit of duck w. apples, tuna tartare, broiled duck w. wild rice, good homemade desserts. *Note:* One of the handsomest rests. in New England, in the former Union League Club of New Haven, w. its high ceilings, marble columns, and elaborate Oriental décor. Light, imaginative American cuisine; very good svce. Locally popular; resv. advised. A stone's throw from the Yale campus. *American.* **I–M**

      ♀ **Delmonaco's,** 232 Wooster St. (203/865-1109). A/C. Lunch daily exc. Tues. & Sat., dinner Wed.-Mon.; closed Tues. and holidays. AE, CB, DC, MC, V. *Specialties:* spaghetti alla carbonara, fresh homemade pasta, sautéed scallops, veal cutlet Milanese. *Note:* Large, noisy *trattoria* serving straightforward, tasty Italian food. Likeable atmosphere; very efficient svce. Good value. *Italian.* **I**

STRATFORD: In 1955 Stratford acknowledged the destiny inseparable from its name and paid tribute to William Shakespeare with the **American Shakespeare Theatre,** a replica of London's original Globe Theatre, and an annual summer festival inspired by the original held at its namesake city, Stratford-upon-Avon in England, the poet's birthplace. This is one of the most important classical-theater festivals in the country. For programs and schedules, contact 1850 Elm St., Stratford, CT 06497 (203/375-5000). Worth the detour.

BRIDGEPORT: An important industrial town on Long Island Sound, which is best known as the longtime winter home of the famous Barnum Circus, "The Greatest Show On Earth." Its principal attraction, a 28-inch (70-cm) dwarf known as "General Tom Thumb," was himself a Bridgeport native; his tomb, with life-size effigy, is in Mountain Grove Cemetery, North Ave. and Dewey St. See the **Barnum Museum,** 820 Main St. (203/576-7320), open Tues.-Sun., with many personal memorabilia of the circus's founder, P. T. Barnum, who served for a time as mayor of Bridgeport, and of Gen. Tom Thumb. There is a **Barnum Festival,** with parades, concerts, and exhibitions of circus art, every year in late June or early July.

    Daily year-round **car-ferry service** between Bridgeport and Port Jefferson, Long Island, N.Y., from Union Square Dock (203/367-8571).

STAMFORD: Both a residential suburb of New York and — by latest count—home to 24 of the Fortune 500 largest corporations, Stamford also has many scientific laboratories and research centers.

    See the astonishing 1958 **First Presbyterian Church** by Wallace Harrison in the shape of a giant fish; 1101 Bedford Ave., open daily.

Where to Eat

IN NEARBY WESTPORT. ♀ **Panda Pavilion,** 1300 Post Rd. East (203/255-3988). A/C. Lunch/dinner daily. AE, MC, V. *Specialties:* spareribs w. sesame seeds, Hunan chicken w. honeyed walnuts, duck w. ginger and bamboo shoots, sesame beef, eggplant w. shrimp. *Note:* The food is absolutely authentic Chinese, though the setting—a maze of little rooms with wall paintings of romping pandas—is not. Pleasant, quick svce. Very good value. *Chinese.* **B–I**

GREENWICH: A smart suburb for well-to-do New Yorkers, with a very New England vintage charm. Among its most remarkable and historic buildings are the 1685 **Bush-Holley House,** 39 Strickland Rd. (203/869-6899), open Tues.-Sun., housing many works of art and pieces of antique furniture; and the 1690 **Putnam Cottage,** where Gen. Israel Putnam, a Revolutionary hero, was detained by, and escaped from, the British in 1779; it's at 243 E. Putnam Ave. (203/869-9697), open Mon., Wed., and Fri., or by appointment. Worth seeing.

Where to Eat

☀️ 🍸🍸🍸 **Bertrand,** 253 Greenwich Ave. (203/661-4459). A/C. Lunch Mon.-Fri., dinner Mon.-Sat.; closed Sun. and holidays. AE, MC, V. Jkt. *Specialties:* seafood in puff pastry w. leeks and basil, salmon marinated w. aniseed, confit of duck w. chanterelle mushrooms, red snapper braised in white wine, sautéed breast of chicken w. cream of basil, very good desserts. Large wine list. *Note:* The chef of this newish rest., Christian Bertrand, was once the associate of André Soltner at New York's Lutèce (see Chapter 3 on New York). That tells you all you need to know about the quality and delicacy of the food. The décor, running to Roman arches, vaulted ceilings, and a glassed lobby, is on the elaborate side. Polished svce; resv. a must. Has quickly established itself as one of the best rests. in the New York area. *French.* **M–E**

☀️ 🔔 **RYE BROOK:** This out-of-the-way little town north of White Plains, on the New York/Connecticut state border, reached by the Merritt Pkwy. and Conn. 15 from Greenwich, is the home of one of the most unexpected of America's museums: the 🔔 **Museum of Cartoon Art,** entirely devoted to the characters of comic strips and cartoon movies. Has more than 60,000 pieces of original "cartoon art" from 1870 to the present day, and hundreds of cartoon movies, the oldest dating from 1899. The museum is housed in an 1876 medieval fortress which is itself a kind of museum piece, being the first American house built using poured concrete reinforced with iron beams. Everyone who enjoys the comics will want to visit it, on Comly Ave. (914/939-0234), open daily except Mon. and Sat.

NEW YORK: See Chapter 3 on New York City.

CHAPTER 6

PHILADELPHIA🍦🍦

□ □ □

With Atlantic City and the
Pennsylvania Dutch Country

There is no properly brought-up U.S. citizen who doesn't know that Philadelphia is "the cradle of our nation." Here the Declaration of Independence was drawn up and adopted; here the Constitution, the cornerstone of the American government, was approved; here George Washington presided, for the eight years 1790–1797, over the destiny of the new nation. Philadelphia can also claim the country's first bank, its first daily newspaper, its first hospital, its first stock exchange, its first zoo, its first mint, and its first school for black children.

In the 18th century London was the only English-speaking city in the world larger than Philadelphia, and from so illustrious a past the American city has retained a sense of history, and a love of old buildings. Not far from the spot on the Delaware River where the Englishman William Penn (who gave his name to the state of Pennsylvania) led the first Quaker settlers ashore in 1682 may still be found some of the country's best-known public buildings: **Independence Hall** with its famous **Liberty Bell**; **Congress Hall**, the **Old City Hall**; the **Jacob Graff House,** where Thomas Jefferson drafted the Declaration of Independence; **Carpenters' Hall,** where the first Continental Congress was held; **Franklin Court,** where stood the home of Benjamin Franklin, one of Philadelphia's most illustrious citizens; the house of **Betsy Ross,** who sewed together the first American flag. For the bicentennials of the Declaration of Independence (1976) and the Constitution (1987), much restoration and rehabilitation was done in **Independence National Park,** known as "America's most historic square mile."

Some of the nearby side streets with their pretty little red-brick houses, such as **Elfreth's Alley,** the oldest street in the U.S., are strangely reminiscent of 18th-century London. Art galleries, antiques shops, and above all, restaurants elbow each other in these little streets near Independence Mall. Philadelphia, which once had little enough to offer the gourmet, has become a place of pilgrimage; in the last dozen years more than 300 new restaurants, some of the highest order, have opened their doors here.

Lovers of the picturesque will make a point of visiting **Little Italy,** the domain of *Rocky,* of little family-owned *trattorie,* and open-air markets. To the north of the city, **Germantown,** founded by Mennonite settlers in the 17th century, is another interesting ethnic enclave; around Germantown Avenue, an Indian trail in pre-Colonial days, there are many very lovely old homes.

Philadelphia (in classical Greek, "the city of brotherly love") is a thriving center of industry and commerce, with strong representation in health care, publishing, pharmaceuticals, petrochemicals, and electronics. Handling more than 40 million tons of cargo annually, it's also one of the world's largest river ports.

In spite of uncertainties in municipal politics, dozens of corporations have moved their head offices here, attracted by Philadelphia's strategic position halfway between New York and Washington, its abundant labor supply, its rich cultural life—and a booming real-estate market. U.S. 202, on the city's northern periphery, fills the role of the local Silicon Valley, as does the more famous "Route 128" in Boston.

"Philly," as its citizens affectionately call it, takes pride in a long-standing tradition of intellectual and artistic activity: it boasts no fewer than 1,400 churches, synagogues, and other places of worship; 90 museums; eight universities, including the renowned **University of Pennsylvania** and **Temple University;** and a world-famous symphony orchestra. In spite of its size, it is still a city on a human scale, watched over by the statue of William Penn, perched 548 ft (167 m) in the air atop the astonishing City Hall.

According to FBI figures, Philadelphia's crime rate (16 homicides per 100,000 inhabitants) is one of the lowest for any major U.S. city.

Famous children of "Philly" include the movie directors Sidney Lumet and Arthur Penn, the painter-photographer Man Ray, the sculptor Alexander Calder, the late Princess Grace of Monaco (Grace Kelly), comedians W. C. Fields and Bill Cosby, actor Richard Gere, singer Patti LaBelle, jazzmen Rex Stewart and Sam Wooding, and the late anthropologist Margaret Mead.

BASIC FACTS: State of Pennsylvania. Area Code: 215. Time Zone: Eastern Time. ZIP Code: 19014. Founded: 1682. Approximate population: city, 1,640,000; metropolitan area, 4,680,000. Fifth-largest metropolitan area in the country.

CLIMATE: Spring and fall, usually sunny and cool, are the best times for a visit, but the climate of the Atlantic seaboard is unpredictable at best, so bring an umbrella and a raincoat. Winter is cold, though the temperature rarely drops below 23°F (−5°C), and the Jan. average is 35°F (2°C). The weather is hot and sticky from June to Sept., with July averaging 78°F (25°C).

DISTANCES: Baltimore, 94 mi. (150 km); Niagara Falls, 385 mi. (623 km); New York, 100 mi. (160 km); Pittsburgh, 308 mi. (498 km); Washington, 134 mi. (215 km).

ARRIVAL & TRANSIT INFORMATION

AIRPORT: Philadelphia International Airport (PHL), 7 mi. (11 km) SW, is a very up-to-date terminal. For information, call 215/492-3181.

U. S. AIRLINES: American (365-4000), Continental (592-8005), Delta (928-1700), Eastern (923-3500), Midway (toll free 800/621-5700), Northwest (563-7501), TWA (923-2000), United (568-2800), and USAir (563-8055).

FOREIGN AIRLINES: British Airways (toll free 800/247-9297) and Lufthansa (toll free 800/645-3880).

CITY LINK: The **cab** fare from the airport to dwntwn is about $16–$18; time, about 20–30 min. Express train from the airport to dwntwn, the **SEPTA Airport Line,** leaves every 30 min.; serves the 30th St., 16th St., and Market St. East stations dwntwn; fare, $4; time, 25 min.

Taxis are expensive, but the **public transportation** system (bus, subway, and streetcar) is efficient and cheap (though to be avoided at night). For information, call SEPTA (574-7800).

The dwntwn area is small enough that you shouldn't need to rent a car, unless you're planning trips to Atlantic City or Pennsylvania Dutch Country.

CAR RENTAL (at the airport unless otherwise indicated): Avis (492-0900); Budget (492-5500); Dollar (492-2692); Hertz (492-7205); National (492-2750); and Thrifty, 6401 Passyunk Ave. (365-3900). For dwntwn locations, consult the local telephone directory.

LIMOUSINE SERVICES: Carey Limousine (492-8402), Dav-El Limousines (334-7900), and Royal Limo & Coach (800/248-7557).

TAXIS: Abundant during daylight hours; may be hailed in the street, or taken from the waiting lines at the major hotels or the downtown cab stands. After 5 p.m. it's better to phone: **Quaker City Cab** (215/728-8000), **United Cab Assoc.** (215/625-2881), or **Yellow Cab** (215/922-8400).

TRAIN: AMTRAK Station, 30th and Market Sts. (824-1600). There's a ticket office at 1708 John F. Kennedy Blvd. (824-1600); for information and reservations for the Metroliner, call 824-4224.

BUS: Greyhound, 1001 Filbert St. (931-4000).

INFORMATION & TOURS

TOURIST INFORMATION: The **Philadelphia Convention and Visitors Bureau,** 1515 Market St., PA 19102 (636-3300).
International Visitors Center, 34th St. and Civic Center Blvd. (823-7261), has multilingual personnel.
Visitors Center, 16th St. and John F. Kennedy Blvd. (636-1666), open daily year round.
For a **recorded message** with current listing of shows and cultural events, call 568-7255.

GUIDED TOURS: Audio Walk and Tour, Norman Rockwell Museum, 601 Walnut St. (925-1234): Rent a "Walkman" with prerecorded cassettes and visit the Historic District on foot. Open daily year round.
Centipede Tours, 1315 Walnut St. (735-3123): A 90-minute walk through the Historic District with Colonial-costumed guides. Original and instructive. Mid-May to mid-Oct. on Wed., Fri., and Sat. in good weather. Resv. advised.
Fairmount Park Trolley (bus): Trip around Fairmount Park and its museums in a replica of a turn-of-the-century trolley; get on and off as often as you like. Also a two-hr conducted tour across the city. Daily, Apr.-Nov.
Gray Line Tours (bus), 1525 John F. Kennedy Blvd. (922-5224): Conducted tours of the city year round; serves the major hotels.
Philadelphia Carriage Co. (carriage), 500 N. 13th St. (922-6840): Carriage trip around the city center, leaving from the Liberty Bell Pavilion. Daily, Feb.-Dec.
Philadelphia Tours (bus): A two-hr conducted tour in a London double-decker bus; leaves 16th St. and John F. Kennedy Blvd. at 10 a.m. Tues.-Sat. (271-2999).
R. & S. Harbor Tours (boat), Penn's Landing, Delaware Ave. and Lombard St. (928-0972): Guided tour of the harbor and trip on the Delaware River. Daily, mid-Apr. to Oct.

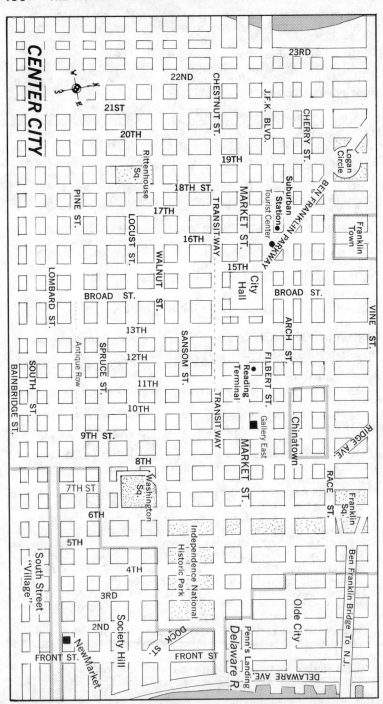

SIGHTS, ATTRACTIONS, & ACTIVITIES

ARCHITECTURAL HIGHLIGHTS: ⚓ **Boat House Row,** Kelly Dr., in Fairmount Park: Picturesque Victorian boathouses along the Schuylkill River, used by the many local rowing clubs. Afternoon regattas throughout the summer (for information on times, call 686-2176). Should be seen.

City Hall, Broad and Market Sts. (567-4476): John McArthur designed this flamboyant 1894 building in French-Renaissance style. The 548-ft (167-m) tower is crowned by a bronze statue of William Penn. With 750 rooms, it's the biggest City Hall in the country, and took 20 years to build. Open daily; don't miss it.

One Liberty Place, 1 Liberty Pl.: Very fine 61-story skyscraper, whose conical crest recalls New York's famous Chrysler Building, was designed by Helmut Jahn and opened in 1987. At 816 ft (248 m), or 921 ft (280 m) with its needle, it was the first building to violate the hallowed limit of 548 ft (167 m)—the height of William Penn's hat on the City Hall statue—above which no building in Philadelphia had previously been allowed to rise. Should be seen.

U.S. Mint, 5th and Arch Sts. (597-7350): The world's largest, producing 25,000 coins a minute. Visitors' gallery and display of old coins and medals in the Rittenhouse Room. Interesting. Open daily in summer; Mon.-Fri. the rest of the year.

CHURCHES/SYNAGOGUES: ⛪ **Christ Church,** 2nd St. between Market and Arch Sts. (922-1695): A handsome 1754 Colonial church, once attended by George Washington, Benjamin Franklin, and other historic figures. In the churchyard and the neighboring cemetery at 5th and Arch Sts. are buried seven signers of the Declaration of Independence, including Franklin. Should be seen. Open daily.

Gloria Dei Church, 916 S. Swanson St. (389-1513): The oldest place of worship in Pennsylvania (1700). Called "Old Swedes' Church" because many of the first Scandinavian settlers worshipped here. Worth a visit. Open daily.

Old St. Mary's Church, 252 S. 4th St., between Locust and Spruce Sts. (923-7930): Built in 1763 as the city's original Roman Catholic cathedral. The tomb of Commodore John Barry, "Father of the U.S. Navy," is behind the church. Open daily.

St. George's United Methodist Church, 235 N. 4th St. (925-7788): The oldest (1769) Methodist church in the country; the first black Methodist minister was ordained here in 1799. An interesting Colonial building; see the chalice which belonged to John Wesley, the English theologian who founded the Methodist church. Worth a visit. Open daily.

HISTORIC BUILDINGS: The largest group of historic buildings are in Independence National Historic Park, but others are scattered around town.

Independence National Historical Park

Called "America's most historic square mile." For information on all the buildings listed below, phone 597-8974.

Carpenters' Hall, 320 Chestnut St. (925-0167): The 1770 Hall of the Carpenters' Guild; the First Continental Congress met here in 1774. Museum. Open Tues.-Sat. Should be seen.

City Tavern, 2nd and Walnut Sts. (923-6059): A careful reconstruction of a famous Revolutionary tavern, once described by President John Adams as "the most elegant tavern in America." Here, two centuries ago, came the most famous people in the young Republic. Today it has become an appealing (and successful) restaurant with lunch/dinner daily.

Congress Hall, 6th and Chestnut Sts.: Adjoining Independence Hall, this 1789 building housed the meetings of the first Congress of the United States from 1790 to 1800, while the Capitol in Washington was under construction. The reelection of George Washington to the presidency in 1793, and the election of John Adams in 1797, took place here. You can see the chambers of the House of Representatives (first floor) and the Senate (second floor). Don't miss it. Open daily.

First Bank of the U.S., 3rd St. between Walnut and Chestnut: The oldest American bank, founded in 1791 by Alexander Hamilton. Closed to visitors.

Franklin Court, Market St. between 3rd and 4th Sts.: Group of old buildings conceived and designed by Benjamin Franklin. His house, where he died in 1790, was destroyed by fire in 1812. An underground museum is devoted to this genial inventor and statesman. A visit you should make. Open daily.

Independence Hall, Chestnut St. between 5th and 6th Sts. (627-1776): With its rounded bell tower, four-faced clock, and elegant Georgian façade in ocher brick, Independence Hall is one of the most historically meaningful public buildings in the U.S. The Declaration of Independence was signed here on July 4, 1776, and the Constitution was adopted here in 1787. In the former assembly hall, now renovated, you can see several pieces of historic furniture, including Washington's armchair. Independence Hall, open daily, is worth the trip all by itself.

Jacob Graff House, 701 Market St. at 7th St.: A 1975 reconstruction of the house where Thomas Jefferson was living in 1776 while he worked on the text of the Declaration of Independence. The two rooms he occupied have been carefully re-created. A short film is shown on this historic episode. A must. Open daily.

Liberty Bell Pavilion, Independence Mall between Market and Chestnut Sts.: The bell here, which once was perched on the tower of Independence Hall, was the first to be rung after the first public reading of the Declaration of Independence on July 8, 1776. Bearing on its side the engraved inscription (Leviticus 10:25) "Proclaim liberty throughout all the land unto all the inhabitants thereof," the bell was cracked in 1835 and has not sounded since 1846. This symbol of Liberty is now housed in a glass structure built in 1976 in the center of the mall. A must—on no account to be missed—for every visitor to Philadelphia.

Old City Hall, 5th and Chestnut Sts.: In spite of its name this building was never City Hall; it was the first seat of the U.S. Supreme Court from 1791 to 1800. Museum devoted to life in 18th-century Philadelphia. Interesting. Open daily.

Todd House, 4th and Walnut Sts.: Handsome middle-class home dating from 1785, where Dolley Todd lived before she married President James Madison and became first lady. Interesting reconstruction of life in a middle-class Quaker family of the period. Open daily.

Historic Buildings Outside the Park

"A Man Full of Trouble" Tavern, 127-129 Spruce St. (922-1759): Picturesque tavern built in 1759 and splendidly restored to its original condition. Furniture and handcrafts of the 17th and 18th centuries. By appointment only; should be seen.

☼🔔 **Betsy Ross House,** 239 Arch St. (627-5343): Pretty little Colonial house which once belonged to the seamstress Betsy Ross, and where (so the story goes), at the request of George Washington, she sewed the first American flag ("Old Glory," with, at that time, only 13 stars). Don't miss it. Open daily.

☼🔔 **Edgar Allan Poe National Historic Site,** 532 N. 7th St., at Spring Garden St. (597-8780): Home of Edgar Allan Poe in 1843–1844, where he wrote some of his most famous poems and stories, particularly *The Raven* and *The Gold Bug*. This is the illustrious author's only national memorial. A must for all book lovers. Open daily.

☼🔔 **Penn's Landing,** Delaware Ave. and Chestnut St. (923-8181): Maritime museum, marina, and cultural center, this huge recreation complex on the banks of the Delaware River stands where the first Quaker settlers, led by William Penn, are believed to have landed. The floating museum comprises half a dozen big sailing ships and old vessels including the U.S.S. *Olympia,* Admiral Dewey's flagship during the Spanish-American War of 1898, and the *Mosholu,* one of the biggest four-masters in the world. Should be visited. Open daily.

MARKETS: ☼🔔 **Italian Market,** along 9th St. between Christian and Federal Sts.: Open-air market in the heart of Little Italy; used as background in the movie *Rocky*. Colorful. Tues.-Sat.

☼🔔 **Reading Terminal Market,** 12th and Filbert Sts. (922-2317): A real institution since 1893, with every kind of food known to land or sea piled in picturesque disorder on dozens of stalls. A wonderful place for a quick snack, where you can sample some of the local specialties such as cheese-steak sandwiches, snapper soup, and the famous Bassett's ice cream. A sight that should be seen. Open Mon.-Sat.

MONUMENTS: ☼🔔 **Tomb of the Revolutionary War's Unknown Soldier,** Washington Square at Walnut and 6th Sts.: In the west sector of huge Washington Square, this tomb of an unknown soldier from the War of Independence is watched over by a life-size statue of George Washington. Also buried here are hundreds of other Revolutionary combatants, as well as civilian victims of yellow-fever epidemics.

MUSEUMS OF ART: 🔔 **Athenaeum of Philadelphia,** 219 S. 6th St. (925-2688): Paintings, sculpture, and Empire furniture which once belonged to Joseph Bonaparte, brother of Napoléon. Library devoted to the architecture and decorative arts of the 19th century—the building itself is a fine 1847 example of Victorian architecture. Should be seen. Open Mon.-Fri.

☼🔔🔔 **Barnes Foundation,** 300 N. Latch's Lane in Merion, 7 mi. (12 km) NW on I-76 and City Ave. (667-0290): One of the world's most extraordinary private collections, comprising a full 1,000 paintings, mostly impressionist and modern, including 150 Renoirs and 60 Cézannes. They include Renoir's *Women Bathing in the Forest* and *Woman Reading,* Cézanne's *Card Players,* Seurat's *Three Sitters,* and Picasso's *Comedians*. Unfortunately it admits no more than 200 visitors on Fri. and Sat., and only 100 on Sun. Closed in July and Aug. Reservations an absolute must—but in spite of the inconveniences, don't fail to see it.

☼🔔 **Norman Rockwell Museum,** 601 Walnut St. (922-4345): Works on display from the 60-year career of this famous painter and illustrator include drawings, paintings, posters, lithographs, etc., with a faithful reconstruction of his studio. Should be seen. Open daily.

☀︎ 🛍🛍 **Pennsylvania Academy of the Fine Arts,** Broad and Cherry Sts. (972-7600): Founded in 1805 and now installed in an elegant Victorian building, this is the oldest academy of fine arts in the country. The museum has a fine collection of American painting from the 18th century to the present day, with works by Charles Willson Peale, Benjamin West, Thomas Eakins, Thomas Sully, etc. Should be seen. Open daily.

☀︎ 🛍🛍🛍 **Philadelphia Museum of Arts,** 26th St. and Benjamin Franklin Pkwy. (763-8100): One of the greatest, as well as one of the largest, art museums in America, with more than 500,000 paintings, sculptures, drawings, watercolors, prints, and other works of art. Imposing Greco-Roman building whose monumental staircase figured in the movie *Rocky*. Superb collections of medieval art, Oriental art, and European painting (particularly works by Marcel Duchamp). Among the most famous works on display: *The Crucifixion* by Rogier van der Weyden, Giovanni di Paolo's *Miracle of St. Nicolas of Tolentino*, Charles Willson Peale's *The Staircase Group*, Marcel Duchamp's *Nude Descending a Staircase*, Van Gogh's *Sunflowers*, Cézanne's *The Large Bathers*, and a *Self-Portrait* by Picasso. An absolute must for art lovers. Open Tues.-Sun.

☀︎ 🛍 **Rodin Museum,** 22nd St. and Benjamin Franklin Pkwy. (763-8100): The largest collection of Rodin sculptures, drawings, and watercolors outside France, including versions of *The Thinker, The Gates of Hell,* and *The Burghers of Calais*. Should be seen. Open Tues.-Sun.

🛍 **Rosenbach Museum,** 2010 Delancey Pl. at 20th St. (732-1600): Interesting period furniture, silverware, porcelains, art objects, rare books, and valuable manuscripts. Also temporary exhibitions. Should be seen. Open Tues.-Sun.; closed in Aug.

MUSEUMS OF SCIENCE AND HISTORY: ☀︎ 🛍 Academy of Natural Sciences Museum, 19th St. and Benjamin Franklin Pkwy. (299-1000): Many prehistoric animals, including a dozen dinosaurs; a panorama of the animal kingdom throughout the world, in facsimiles of its natural habitats; Egyptian mummies; an enormous selection of precious stones and minerals. A must-see. Open daily.

🛍 **Afro-American Historical and Cultural Museum,** 7th and Arch Sts. (574-0380): The first American museum entirely devoted to black art and culture in Africa and the U.S.; also a history of racial discrimination. A must-see. Open Tues.-Sun.

🛍 **Army-Navy Museum,** Chestnut St. between 3rd and 4th Sts. (597-8974): In a building **(Pemberton House)** which is a facsimile of the home of a wealthy Quaker merchant of the Colonial period, this museum recapitulates the history of the U.S. Army and Navy during the War of Independence. Interesting. Open daily.

🛍 **Civil War Library and Museum,** 1805 Pine St. (735-8196): With 12,000 different books and documents, this is one of the richest Civil War libraries in the country. Unique collection of period weapons, uniforms, flags, and other memorabilia. A must for all history buffs. Open Mon.-Fri.; weekends by appointment only.

🛍 **Fireman's Hall Museum,** 149 N. 2nd St. (923-1438): Unique collection of material relating to firefighting in the 18th and 19th centuries, the largest of its kind in the country. Housed in an 1876 fire station. Should be seen. Tues.-Sat.

☀︎ 🛍🛍 **Franklin Institute Science Museum,** 20th St. and Benjamin Franklin Pkwy. (448-1200): One of the country's most complete and up-to-date science museums. Everything on nuclear fission and fusion, computers, astronomy, space flight, and aviation. A giant human heart 20 ft

(6 m) high demonstrates the circulation of the blood. Also home of the highly regarded **Fels Planetarium.** Fine view of the city. Not to be missed. Open daily.

Historical Society of Pennsylvania, 1300 Locust St. (732-6201): Interesting small history museum with some important Colonial objects, from William Penn's furniture to Martha Washington's cookbook. Worth seeing. Open Tues.-Sat.

Marine Corps Memorial Museum, Chestnut St. between 3rd and 4th Sts. (597-8974): On the site of **New Hall,** built in 1791 by the Carpenters' Guild, this relatively new museum commemorates the birth and early days of the U.S. Marine Corps. For military-history enthusiasts. Open daily.

Mummers Museum, 2nd St. and Washington Ave. (336-3050): The "Mummers" parade — eight hours of spectacle and music along Broad St. on Jan. 1 (see "Special Events," below). The museum has memorabilia, costumes, video tapes, and sound recordings of past parades. Free concerts Tues. evenings May-Oct. Must be seen. Open Tues.-Sun.

National Museum of American Jewish History, 55 N. 5th St. (923-3811): Bears witness to the contributions that America's Jewish communities have made to the arts, the sciences, and society since 1654. Memorabilia of famous Philadelphians, including Haym Salomon, the financier of the War of Independence. There is a synagogue attached to the museum. Open Sun.-Thur.

Perelman Antique Toy Museum, 270 S. 2nd St. (922-1070): Charming museum of old toys — dolls, animals, piggy banks, mechanical toys, etc. — in the 1758 Abercrombie House. More than 4,000 exhibits in all, some of great value. Worth seeing. Open daily.

Philadelphia Maritime Museum, 321 Chestnut St. (925-5439): Smallish but well-laid-out maritime museum with many ship models, treasures recovered from shipwrecks, and an exhibition on underwater exploration. Should be seen. Open daily.

Please Touch Museum, 210 N. 21st St. (963-0666): Unusual museum for children under 7. In an inviting, colorful setting, the young visitors are encouraged to participate directly in educational experiences relating to art, technology, and natural science. Fascinating for young and old alike. Open Tues.-Sun.

Port of History Museum, Penn's Landing, Delaware Ave. and Walnut St. (925-3804): Temporary exhibitions of visual art, photography, design, etc.; also concerts, shows, dance, and a multimedia spectacle entitled *Philadelphia: Visions & Realities.* Should be seen. Wed.-Sun.

University Museum, 33rd and Spruce Sts. (898-4000): One of the finest museums of archeology and anthropology in the world. From Egyptian mummies to Eskimo or Polynesian art, and from African masks to Roman, Chinese, or Mayan antiquities, you will find here a complete panorama of the ancient cultures of five continents. Not to be missed. Open Tues.-Sun. (but closed Sun. in summer).

OUTDOOR ART AND PLAZAS: More than 200 modern sculptures embellish the greensward and avenues of **Fairmount Park.** Notable among them are the *Swann Memorial Fountain* by Alexander Calder (a native Philadelphian), *Washington Monument* by Rudolf Siemering, *Cowboy* by Frederic Remington, *Spirit of Enterprise* by Jacques Lipchitz, *Playing Angels* by Carl Milles, and *Stone Age in America* by John Boyle.

Another remarkable modern sculpture, this time downtown, is Claes Oldenburg's giant *Clothespin* in chromed steel, 45 ft (13 m) high, standing like a challenge in front of **City Hall** at 15th and Market Sts.

PANORAMAS: ♨ **City Hall,** Broad and Market Sts. (686-1776): Fine view of downtown Philadelphia and the Delaware Valley from the top of the Observation Tower at 548 ft (167 m). Undergoing renovation.

PARKS AND GARDENS: ☼ ♨♨ **Fairmount Park,** NW of the city on both sides of the Schuylkill River: 8,900 acres (3,600 ha.) of woods, lawns, and lovely gardens, designed by the famous landscape architect Frederick Law Olmsted, one of the two creators of Central Park in New York. The "lung" of Philadelphia, with more than 100 mi. (160 km) of paths for cycling and jogging. Many carefully restored Colonial houses, including the Georgian **Mount Pleasant Mansion** (1761) and the 1798 **Strawberry Mansion,** a blend of the Federal and Greek Revival styles. Open-air symphony concerts in summer at **Robin Hood Dell.** Highly regarded zoo (see below). Well worth a visit. For information, call 686-2176.

☼ ♨♨ **Independence Mall,** bounded by 5th and 6th Sts. between Race and Walnut Sts.: Shady, flower-planted promenade with lawns and fountains, in the heart of historic Philadelphia. The glass pavilion housing the Liberty Bell stands in the middle of the mall. Shouldn't be missed.

♨ **Laurel Hill Cemetery,** Randolph Dr.: Adjoining Fairmount Park and overlooking the Schuylkill River, this landscaped cemetery offers an unbelievably rich selection of funerary art, from Victorian crypts with marble angels or lions, to a replica of the Egyptian temple of Philae or giant obelisks in the style of the Washington Monument. The bronze statue of a goddess by Alexander Calder should also be seen. Worth a look. Open daily.

♨ **Pennsylvania Horticultural Society,** 325 Walnut St. (625-8250): The oldest horticultural society in the country, founded in 1765. Its garden contains flowers, plants, and shrubs typical of that period. Worth seeing. Open Mon.-Fri., Mar.-Sept.

PERFORMING ARTS: For a daily listing of all shows and cultural events, consult the entertainment pages of the daily papers *Philadelphia Inquirer* (morning) and *Philadelphia Daily News* (evening), and of the monthly *Philadelphia* magazine.

☼ **Academy of Music,** Broad and Locust Sts. (893-1930): A fine classical revival building dating from 1847; home of the Philadelphia Orchestra (principal conductor, Ricardo Muti), of the Opera Company of Philadelphia (director, Margaret Ann Everitt), and of the Pennsylvania Ballet (artistic director, Robert Weiss). Also big-name recitals.

Annenberg Center, University of Pennsylvania, 3680 Walnut St. (898-6791): Modern and classical theater, children's theater, musicals. Home of the Philadelphia Drama Guild.

Forrest Theater, 1114 Walnut St. (923-1515): Broadway and off-Broadway hits, musicals.

Mann Music Center, George's Hill, W. Fairmount Park (567-0707): Concerts by the Philadelphia Orchestra, June-Aug. Big-name recitals.

Plays and Players Theatre, 1714 Delancey St. (592-8333): Modern and classical theater; home of the Philadelphia Company.

Robin Hood Dell East, 33rd and Dauphin Sts., Fairmount Park (477-8810): Pop, jazz, gospel music concerts (summer only).

Schubert Theater, Broad and Locust Sts. (735-4768): Ballet performances by the Pennsylvania Ballet and other companies.

Society Hill Playhouse, 507 S. 8th St. (923-0210): Modern theater, off-Broadway shows.

The Spectrum, Broad St. and Pattison Ave. (574-1200): Concerts by leading pop and rock stars.

☼ **Walnut Street Theater,** 9th and Walnut Sts. (574-3550): One of the oldest theaters (1809) in the country. Comedy, drama, experimental theater, modern dance. Home of the Pennsylvania Opera Theater (artistic director, Barbara Silverstein).

SHOPPING: The Bourse, 5th St. between Market and Chestnut Sts. (625-0300): More than 50 boutiques, shops, and restaurants in a handsomely restored Victorian-style building, once the home of the Philadelphia Stock Exchange. Opposite the Liberty Bell Pavilion. Open daily.

The Gallery, 9th and Market Sts. (925-7162): The biggest shopping center in the city, with more than 230 stores, boutiques, and restaurants under one roof, with indoor gardens, fountains, and glass-walled elevators. Spectacular. Open daily.

☼ **Jewelers' Row,** 7th and Sansom Sts.: The diamond and jewelry district, with more than 300 stores—Philadelphia's answer to New York's W. 47th St. A sight not to be missed.

John Wanamaker, 13th and Market Sts. (422-2000): The most famous department store in Philadelphia, truly a city within the city, with a splendid nine-story rococo-columned main hall, post office, and free organ recitals at 11:15 a.m. and 5:15 p.m. Open daily.

New Market, 2nd St. between Pine and Lombard Sts. (627-7500): Modern all-glass shopping center, contrasting sharply with the surrounding red-brick structures; 50 boutiques and restaurants. Open daily.

SPECIAL EVENTS: For the exact schedule of events listed below, consult the **Philadelphia Convention and Visitors Bureau** (see "Tourist Information," above).

☼ **Mummers Parade** (Jan. 1): Big costumed parade, with bands and floats, down Broad St.; eight hours of colorful carnival. A solidly entrenched tradition since 1901; don't miss it.

☼ **Devon Horse Show** (nine days in late May to early June), 22 mi. (35 km) NW on U.S. 30 in Devon: One of the biggest horse shows in the country, with more than 1,200 horses competing. Harness races. Spectacular. For information on schedules, call 964-0550.

Elfreth's Alley Fête Day (last Sun. in June): Tour of the charming old houses on Elfreth's Alley (see "Strolls," below), with Colonially costumed guides. Don't miss it.

Freedom Week (late June to July 4): A week of festivities celebrating Independence, with processions, fireworks, fountain festival, nighttime Mummers Parade. Shouldn't be missed.

Thanksgiving Day Parade (Thanksgiving Day): Parade of giant floats through the downtown streets.

SPORTS: Philadelphia has four professional teams:

Baseball (Apr.-Oct.): Phillies, Veterans Stadium (463-1000).
Basketball (Oct.-Apr.): 76ers, Spectrum Sports Arena (339-7676).
Football (Aug.-Dec.): Eagles, Veterans Stadium (463-5500).
Ice Hockey (Oct.-Apr.): Flyers, Spectrum Sports Arena (465-4500).

Horse Racing

Garden State Park, N.J. 70 in Cherry Hill (609/488-8400): thoroughbred racing from mid-Feb. to mid-June; harness, Aug.-Dec.

STROLLS: ⚱ **Chinatown,** bounded by Franklin Square and 11th St. from Arch to Vine Sts.: With more than 15,000 people, this is one of the most important Chinese districts in America's great cities. There are no fewer than 80 restaurants and an interesting cultural center at 125 N. 10th St. (923-6767), with visits by appointment. Worth the side trip.

☀ ⚱⚱ **Elfreth's Alley,** 2nd St. between Arch and Quarry Sts.: Narrow cobbled lane dating from the late 1690s; probably the oldest street in the country. Still has around 30 original craftsmen's and sailors' houses, the oldest from 1728. There's a museum, with period furnishing and equipment, in **Elfreth's House,** no. 126 (574-0560), open daily. Not to be missed.

⚱ **Head House Square,** 2nd and Pine Sts.: Head House is an old hall built in 1775, surrounded by old buildings, boutiques, art galleries, restaurants, and the New Market Shopping Center (see "Shopping," above). Concerts in summer. Very lively atmosphere.

⚱ **Rittenhouse Square,** 18th and Walnut Sts.: One of the city's most elegant residential neighborhoods, a mixture of upscale 19th-century houses and luxurious modern apartment buildings, with a shady square in the middle where in spring and summer there are flower shows, concerts, and art exhibitions. Worth a look.

☀ ⚱⚱ **Society Hill Area,** bounded by Front, Walnut, 7th, and Lombard Sts.: So-called after the Free Society of Traders founded by William Penn. Many celebrated figures of the Revolutionary period once lived here. Their houses, now scrupulously restored, add to the charm of the neighborhood, which with its tree-lined streets and little red-brick houses is straight out of the 18th century. Don't miss it.

☀ ⚱ **South Philly,** bounded by Front and 20th Sts., Washington Ave. and South St.: Colorful working-class neighborhood which became widely known through the movie *Rocky*. There are many cafés and family *trattorie* around the **Italian Market,** making this local **Little Italy** a must for visitors; don't miss it.

THEME PARKS: ⚱ **Sesame Place,** 100 Sesame Rd. in Langhorne, 22 mi. (35 km) NE on I-95 (757-1100): Amusement park for small children, based on the TV program "Sesame Street" and its characters. More than 100 games and other attractions. The kingdom of the moppets. Open daily, May to early Sept.; weekends only, Labor Day to mid-Oct.; closed the rest of the year.

⚱ **Six Flags Great Adventure,** at Jackson, N.J., 56 mi. (90 km) NE via I-95, Pennsylvania Tpke. Connection, New Jersey Tpke. north, I-195E, and N.J. 537S (201/928-3500): Huge 450-acre (182-ha.) theme park, with a hundred attractions including carousels, giant roller coasters, and a safari-zoo with 2,000 wild animals (you stay in your car). Shows and vaudeville. Open daily, Apr.-Sept.; closed the rest of the year.

WINTER SPORTS RESORTS: ⚱ **Doe Mountain,** near Hereford, 58 mi. (92 km) along U.S. 76W, U.S. 422W, and Penna. 100N (682-7109): Seven lifts; open Dec. to mid-Mar.

⚱ **Spring Mountain Ski Area,** 36 mi. (57 km) via U.S. 76W, U.S. 422W, and Penna. 29N (287-7900): Six lifts; open mid-Dec. to mid-Mar.

ZOOS: ☀ ⚱ **Zoological Garden,** Fairmount Park, 34th St. and Girard Ave. (387-6400): Opened in 1874, this is the oldest zoo in the U.S. More than 1,600 animals; important collections of reptiles and primates. Children's zoo. Monorail tour. Worth a visit. Open daily.

ACCOMMODATIONS
See the listing of toll-free numbers in the Appendix.

Room Rates in Philadelphia	
B (Budget)	up to $30
I (Inexpensive)	$30–$60
M (Moderate)	$60–$90
E (Expensive)	$90–$140
VE (Very Expensive)	$140 and up

Personal Favorites (in order of preference)

Four Seasons (dwntwn), 1 Logan Square, PA 19103 (215/ 963-1500; toll free, see Four Seasons). 363 rms, A/C, color TV, in-rm movies. AE, CB, DC, MC, V. Valet garage $14, pool, health club, sauna, two rests. (including the Fountain), bar, 24-hr rm svce, concierge. *Note:* The most distinguished place to stay in Philadelphia; eight-floor modern building adjoining an office high-rise from which it is separated by a lovely landscaped courtyard and garden w. fountains. Spacious, ultra-comfortable rms decorated in Federal style, with balconies and mini-bars. Excellent svce. Sophisticated rest. Very well located a stone's throw from the museum district. Big business clientele. **VE**

The Barclay Hotel (dwntwn), Rittenhouse Square and 18th St., PA 19103 (215/545-0300; toll free 800/421-6662). 240 rms, A/C, color TV. AE, CB, DC, MC, V. Valet garage $12, rest. (Le Beau Lieu), bar, 24-hr rm svce, nightclub, free crib, concierge. *Note:* The charm of the '30s: a quiet, distinguished luxury hotel in the city's smartest neighborhood. Comfortable, tastefully furnished rms, most w. refrigerators, some w. kitchenettes. Exemplary svce. Since the Barclay is a stone's throw from the theater district it's the favorite hotel of entertainers, from Luciano Pavarotti to Bob Hope or Zubin Mehta. **E–VE**

Latham Hotel (dwntwn), 135 S. 17th St., PA 19103 (215/ 563-7474; toll free 800/228-0808). 141 rms, A/C, color TV, in-rm movies. AE, CB, DC, MC, V. Valet garage $10, rest. (Bogart's), bar, rm svce, nightclub, free crib, concierge. *Note:* Charming small hotel with a touch of European class. Intimate distinction is the keynote here. Elegant, spacious rms w. period furniture and ultra-luxurious bathrooms; some have refrigerators. Excellent svce. The rest. and bar are among Philadelphia's "in" places. A very good place to stay. **E–VE**

The Palace (dwntwn), Benjamin Franklin Pkwy. at 18th St., PA 19103 (215/963-2222; toll free 800/225-5843). 285 suites, A/C, color TV, in-rm movies. AE, CB, DC, MC, V. Garage $10, pool, sauna, rest. (Café Royal), coffeeshop, bar, 24-hr rm svce, free crib, concierge. *Note:* Large 28-floor cylindrical tower, a block or two from Logan Circle and the museum district. Has only suites, spacious, w. terraces and refrigerators. Ideal for long stays and/or business travelers (fully equipped Business Center). Caters mostly to groups and conventions. **E–VE**

Comfort Inn Penn's Landing (dwntwn), 100 N. Delaware Ave., PA 19107 (215/627-7900; toll free 800/228-5150).

185 rms, A/C, color TV. AE, CB, DC, MC, V. Adjacent parking, health club, bar, rm svce, free breakfast. *Note:* Brand-new ten-story motel on the banks of the Delaware River. Functional, comfortable rms overlooking river or city. Friendly reception and svce. Ideal for visiting Independence Mall and its historic monuments. Very good overall value. **I–M**

    🍴 **Days Inn–Cherry Hill** (formerly the Tudor Inn; vic.), N.J. 70W, Cherry Hill, NJ 08002 (609/665-1100; toll free, see Days Inn). 120 rms, A/C, color TV, in-rm movies. AE, CB, DC, MC, V. Free parking, pool, health club, sauna, rest., bar, rm svce. *Note:* Comfortable, well-equipped motel across the road from the Garden State Racetrack, 15 min. by car from dwntwn Philadelphia by the Benjamin Franklin Bridge. Spacious rms, most w. refrigerators. Ideal if you're driving. Good value. **I–M**

Other Accommodations (from top bracket to budget)

    🏨🏨🏨 **Sheraton Society Hill** (dwntwn), 1 Dock St., PA 19106 (215/238-6000; toll free, see Sheraton). 365 rms, A/C, color TV, in-rm movies. AE, CB, DC, MC, V. Valet garage $12, pool, health club, sauna, rest., bar, 24-hr rm svce, nightclub, free crib, concierge. *Note:* Very new hotel in an original version of the red-brick idiom, in the heart of the Society Hill historic district. Ultramodern furnishings and facilities. Spectacular four-story glass-walled lobby. Huge, very comfortable rms, some w. refrigerators. Efficient svce. Perfect for visiting Independence Mall. Interesting wknd discounts. **VE**

    ☀️🏨🏨🏨🏨 **The Warwick** (dwntwn), 17th and Locust Sts., PA 19103 (215/735-6000; toll free 800/523-4210). 180 rms, A/C, color TV, in-rm movies. AE, CB, DC, MC, V. Valet garage $10, rest. (Élan), coffeeshop, bar, 24-hr rm svce, disco, hrdrsr, drugstore, free crib, concierge. *Note:* Elegant, intimate little hotel dating from the '20s. Lobby sumptuously decorated w. rare rugs and period pieces. Spacious, inviting rms, some w. kitchenettes. Extremely polished svce. Conveniently located very near Rittenhouse Square and the business district. Clientele of wealthy businessmen. Has both charm and distinction; offers interesting wknd discounts. **E–VE**

    🏨🏨🏨 **Wyndham Franklin Plaza** (dwntwn), 2 Franklin Plaza, PA 19103 (215/448-2000; toll free 800/822-4200). 761 rms, A/C, color TV, in-rm movies. AE, CB, DC, MC, V. Valet garage $14, pool, health club, tennis court, sauna, three rests. (including the Terrace), coffeeshop, two bars, rm svce, disco, hrdrsr, drugstore, free crib. *Note:* Large, ultramodern convention hotel w. 26 floors, Philadelphia's biggest. Functional, comfortable rms w. refrigerators; impersonal but efficient svce; very good physical-fitness facilities. Caters mostly to groups and business travelers. Halfway between City Hall and the museum district. **E–VE**

    🏨🏨 **Holiday Inn City Line** (formerly the Best Western; nr. dwntwn), 4100 Presidential Blvd., PA 19131 (215/477-0200; toll free, see Holiday Inns). 350 rms, A/C, color TV, in-rm movies. AE, CB, DC, MC, V. Free parking, pool, health club, rest., bar, rm svce, crib $10. *Note:* Functional, comfortable eight-floor motel 15 min. from dwntwn and 20 min. from the airport on I-76, in the new business district on the western outskirts of the city. Entirely renovated. Group and convention clientele. **M–E**

    🏨🏨 **Holiday Inn Independence Mall** (dwntwn), 4th and Arch Sts., PA 19106 (215/923-8660; toll free, see Holiday Inns). 364 rms, A/C, color TV, in-rm movies. AE, CB, DC, MC, V. Free parking, rooftop pool, two rests. (including Benjamin's), bar, rm svce, disco, free crib. *Note:* Large, comfortable, very well-run motel; rooms and facilities recently modernized. Pool open in summer only. One of the best locations for visiting the Historic District. Group and tourist clientele. A better class of Holiday Inn. **M–E**

☼🔑🔑 **Lotus Suites Quality Inn** (dwntwn), 1010 Race St., PA 19016 (215/922-1730; toll free, see Quality Inns). 96 suites, A/C, color TV. AE, CB, DC, MC, V. Free garage, health club, sauna, rest. (The Lotus Inn), bar, rm svce. *Note:* Unusual all-suites hotel in the heart of Chinatown, in a building which used to be a rocking-chair factory—Victorian rococo, now pleasingly restored. Spacious, comfortable suites w. kitchenettes; good svce. Well situated, near City Hall and the picturesque Reading Terminal Market. Group clientele. **M–E**

🔑🔑🔑 **Penn Tower Hotel** (formerly the Hilton; nr. dwntwn), Civic Center Blvd. at 34th St., PA 19104 (215/387-8333; toll free 800/351-5656). 230 rms, A/C, color TV, in-rm movies. AE, CB, DC, MC, V. Garage $10, pool, health club, rest., coffeeshop, bar, rm svce, nightclub. *Note:* Large, very modern hotel on the University of Pennsylvania campus, w. completely renovated interior. Inviting, comfortable atmosphere; efficient svce. VIP floor. With the Civic Center and the Convention Hall nearby, attracts mostly groups and conventions. **M–E**

🔑🔑 **Quality Inn Center City** (formerly the Franklin Motor Inn; nr. dwntwn), 501 N. 22nd St., PA 19130 (215/568-3636; toll free, see Quality Inns). 280 rms, A/C, color TV, in-rm movies. AE, CB, DC, MC, V. Free parking, pool, rest., bar, rm svce, disco. *Note:* Recently renovated motel in the museum district. Comfortable rms, though some are on the small side; good svce. Good value on balance. Group clientele. 10 min. from dwntwn. **I–M**

🔑 **Days Inn–Roosevelt** (nr. dwntwn), 4200 Roosevelt Blvd. at U.S. 1, PA 19124 (215/289-9200; toll free, see Days Inns). 116 rms, A/C, color TV. AE, MC, V. Free parking, pool, rest., bar. *Note:* Motel north of the city. Functionally comfortable; acceptable rest. Great if you're driving; 15 min. from dwntwn. **I**

🔑 **Roosevelt Motor Inn** (vic.), 7600 Roosevelt Blvd., PA 19152 (215/338-7600). 101 rms, A/C, color TV. AE, MC, V. Free parking, pool, rest., bar. *Note:* Typical, well-run motel w. acceptable comforts and facilities. Ideal if you're driving; 25 min. from dwntwn. **I**

🔑 **St. Charles Hotel** (dwntwn), 1935 Arch St., PA 19103 (215/567-5651). 70 rms, A/C, color TV. AE, MC, V. No parking, bar, or rest. *Note:* Small hotel, aging but clean, near Logan Circle and the museum district. Decent levels of comfort; friendly reception. Caters mostly to students; great for the budget traveler. **I**

Airport Accommodations

🔑🔑 **Holiday Inn–Airport** (vic.), 45 Industrial Hwy., in Essington, PA 19029 (215/521-2400; toll free, see Holiday Inns). 307 rms, A/C, color TV, in-rm movies. AE, CB, DC, MC, V. Free parking, pool, rest., bar, rm svce (until midnight), disco, free crib. *Note:* Large modern six-story motel in true Holiday Inn style, 5 min. from the airport. Comfortable, well-soundproofed rms; free 24-hr airport limo. Business clientele. **M–E**

YMCAs/Youth Hostels

☼ **Chamounix Mansion** (nr. dwntwn), Chamounix Dr., Fairmount Park (215/878-3676). Inviting youth hostel in a renovated 19th-century farmhouse. Dormitories. Closed at Christmas.

International House (nr. dwntwn), 3701 Chestnut St. (215/387-5125). If you're on a tight budget, this is the best place in town (though reserved for students only). Nr. U. of Pennsylvania; acceptable rest.

RESTAURANTS

Philadelphia Restaurant Prices	
(per person, excluding drinks and service charges)	
B (Budget)	up to $15
I (Inexpensive)	$15–$25
M (Moderate)	$25–$40
E (Expensive)	$40–$60
VE (Very Expensive)	$60 and up

Personal Favorites (in order of preference)

Le Bec Fin (dwntwn), 1523 Walnut St. (567-1000). A/C. Lunch Mon.-Fri., dinner Mon.-Sat. (two sittings, at 6 and 9 p.m.); closed Sun. and holidays. AE, DC. J&T. *Specialties:* scallops sautéed w. sugar peas; squab w. cream sauce, thyme, and garlic; medaillons of veal w. morel mushrooms; oysters in millefeuille pastry shell; veal kidneys moutardier; civet of lobster. Remarkable desserts; large wine list. Menu changed regularly. *Note:* Along with New York's Lutèce and Chicago's Le Français, Le Bec Fin is one of the most honorable exponents of French haute cuisine in the country. Chef George Perrier, from Lyons, works wonders at his stoves; his dishes and sauces are marvels of delicacy and balance. Elegant, flower-decked setting w. only 14 tables, so that resv. must be made at least eight days ahead for weeknights, and weeks ahead for Fri. and Sat. evenings. Full of big-business people and celebrities passing through. Flawless svce. One of the 12 best rests. in the country. *French.* **M (lunch) – VE (dinner)**

The Fountain (dwntwn), in the Four Seasons (see "Accommodations," above) (963-1500). A/C. Breakfast/lunch/dinner daily. AE, CB, DC, MC, V. Jkt. *Specialties:* linguine w. shrimp and cream of saffron, cold tomato soup w. coriander, pâté of wild boar, roast pheasant w. cabbage and walnuts, sautéed veal cutlet w. turnips, chocolate ramekin. Very fine wine list, particularly strong on half bottles; low-calorie menu available. *Note:* This relatively new (1983) luxury-hotel rest. has quickly become recognized as offering some of the best food in Philadelphia. Luxurious, expensive décor featuring wood paneling, Italian marble floors covered in Oriental rugs, and magnificent flower arrangements. Unimpeded view of Logan Square and the fountain for which the rest. is named. Modern cuisine in every way remarkable. Ultrapolished svce. The fashionable place for entertaining. Resv. a must. *Continental.* **M–E**

The Garden (dwntwn), 1617 Spruce St. (546-4455). A/C. Lunch Mon.-Fri., dinner Mon.-Sat.; closed Sun. and holidays. AE, CB, DC, MC, V. Jkt. *Specialties:* carpaccio, pasta primavera, oyster stew, mussels and clams w. chives, roast chicken w. cognac, broiled Cornish hen w. wild rice and pecans, broiled breaded Dover sole, raspberry and chocolate cake. Rather skimpy wine list. *Note:* With its open-air garden, yellow umbrellas, and centuries-old trees surrounded by old Georgian houses, this dwntwn rest. offers you the loveliest setting you could ask for on a fine day. The five indoor dining rms are no less delightful. Excellent, unaffected bistro food; the meat is especially noteworthy. Friendly, smiling svce. Locally popular; resv. advised. *Continental-American.* **M**

ΥΥ **Bookbinder's Seafood House** (dwntwn), 215 S. 15th St. (545-1137). A/C. Lunch Mon.-Fri., dinner nightly; closed Thanksgiving, Dec. 25. AE, CB, DC, MC, V. Jkt. *Specialties:* oysters, snapper (snapping turtle) soup, mussels in red sauce, Florida stone crabs in season, crab Imperial, lobster Coleman, filet of flounder stuffed w. crabmeat. Weak on wines and desserts. *Note:* "Booky's," as Philadelphians call it, has been a landmark for half a century (by the way, don't confuse it with its near namesake, Old Original Bookbinders, a typical tourist rest. in the heart of the Historic District), and has belonged to four generations of the Bookbinder family. Dependable but unimaginative food; traditional seafaring décor w. the inevitable fishing trophies stuffed and mounted on the walls. Popular for business lunches; often crowded and noisy. Svce on the curt side. Resv. advised. *Seafood.* **I–M**

ΥΥ **Il Gallo Nero** (dwntwn), 254 S. 15th St. (546-8065). A/C. Lunch Tues.-Fri., dinner Tues.-Sat.; closed Sun., Mon., and holidays. AE, CB, DC, MC, V. Jkt. *Specialties:* fresh homemade pasta (w. truffles in season), paglia e fieno, sautéed porcini mushrooms, risotto, ossobuco, northern Italian dishes. Menu changes seasonally. Fine list of Italian wines. Low-calorie menu available. *Note:* Housed in a century-old building which was once a music conservatory, this rest., somewhat overdecorated in the rococo idiom, offers light food in the Tuscan tradition. Diligent svce. The favorite rest. of Luciano Pavarotti as well as other musical celebrities. Resv. advised. *Italian.* **M**

Υ **The Commissary** (dwntwn), 1710 Sansom St. (569-2240). A/C. Breakfast Mon.-Fri., lunch/dinner daily. AE, CB, DC, MC, V. *Specialties:* homemade soups and salads, fresh pasta, daily specials, excellent desserts. Menu changes daily. *Note:* Steve Poses, who owns this attractive place (ground-floor cafeteria and second-floor rest.), used to be a student of urban planning; here he has studied to ennoble the fast-food business. The setting is at once modern and comfortable, the food often original and well-prepared, the atmosphere gently Bohemian, the svce. efficient but relaxed. A fine place. *American.* **B–I**

⚡Υ **The City Tavern** (dwntwn), 2nd and Walnut Sts. (923-6059). A/C. Lunch/dinner daily; closed Jan. 1, Dec. 25. AE, MC, V. Jkt. *Specialties:* salmagundi salad, chicken w. cider, roast beef, catch of the day, Indian pudding. *Note:* This famous Revolutionary War tavern, rebuilt in 1974, perfectly recaptures the feeling of the 1770s, when John Adams described it as "the most elegant tavern in America." Period-costumed waitresses and a harpist at dinner. Unpretentious, praiseworthy food based on old recipes. Resv. advised. A must for history buffs. *American.* **I–M**

Υ **Ragozzino's** (dwntwn), 737 S. 10th St. (923-2927). A/C. Lunch/dinner Mon.-Sat. (until 2 a.m.); closed Sun. No credit cards. *Specialties:* hoagies (Philadelphia-style giant sandwiches). *Note:* The hoagie is a real Philadelphia institution: an enormous hero on a loaf sliced down the middle, w. ham, salami, provolone, onions, lettuce, tomato, and green pepper, the whole doused with olive oil. Dainty eaters stay away. Philadelphia's biggest, tastiest hoagies are to be had at Ragozzino's, a stone's throw from the Italian Market. *American.* **B**

Other Restaurants (from top bracket to budget)

ΥΥΥΥ **Déjà Vu** (dwntwn), 1609 Pine St. (546-1190). A/C. Lunch Tues.-Fri., dinner Tues.-Sat.; closed Sun., Mon., Jan. 1. AE, CB, DC, MC, V. J&T. *Specialties:* duck cutlet w. blueberries, lamb w. mustard and ginger, filet of young wild boar w. cider vinegar and shallots, blanquette of lobster, chocolate soufflé, herb and fruit sherbets. Menu changes regularly. Splendid wine list. *Note:* Derivatively French cuisine w. a Far Eastern touch of the exotic, remarkable desserts, and an unrestrained *nouveau riche* 18th-century décor. The overall effect is surprisingly congenial. The cellar is one of the best stocked on the eastern seaboard and the svce is flawless. A very fine place indeed. *French.* **E–VE**

A Propos (dwntwn), 211 S. Broad St. (546-4424). A/C. Breakfast/lunch/dinner daily; closed July 4. AE, CB, DC, MC, V. *Specialties:* fresh homemade pasta, a variety of pizzas, mesquite-broiled meat, fish, and chicken. The desserts, particularly the chocolate cake, are excellent. *Note:* Chef Aliza Green's California cuisine is as up-to-date as the décor, with its pretty winter-garden terrace. Youthful, hip clientele. A fashionable place; often noisy. *American.* **I–M**

Fish Market (dwntwn), 18th and Sansom Sts. (567-3559). A/C. Lunch Mon.-Fri., dinner nightly; closed holidays. AE, CB, DC, MC, V. Jkt. *Specialties:* crabmeat quiche, sole Oscar, bouillabaisse, catch of the day, shellfish. *Note:* The Fish Market, which started life as no more than a retail fishmonger's, over the years has become one of the best fish rests. in Philadelphia. The fish and shellfish are absolutely fresh, but sometimes overcooked. Preppy atmosphere. Always crowded at lunchtime; resv. advised. *Seafood.* **I–M**

Friday, Saturday, Sunday (nr. dwntwn), 261 S. 21st St. (546-4232). A/C. Lunch Mon.-Fri., dinner nightly. AE, DC, MC, V. *Specialties:* smoked bluefish w. horseradish cream, stuffed sea trout, curried duck, rack of lamb, Cornish hen Normandie stuffed w. apples and walnuts. *Note:* Elegant, romantic little bistro w. a truly Parisian flavor. The daily menu, scrawled on a chalkboard, is resolutely nouvelle cuisine. Trendy clientele; friendly, hard-working svce; a very good place. *Continental.* **I–M**

La Terrasse (nr. dwntwn), 3432 Sansom St. (387-3778). A/C. Lunch Mon.-Fri., dinner nightly, Sun. brunch; closed holidays. AE, CB, DC, MC, V. *Specialties:* snails with spinach, sea bass en papillote, salmi of duck, veal cutlet w. pink peppercorns, almond cheesecake. Menu changes regularly. Huge wine list at reasonable prices. *Note:* This charming rest., a stone's throw from the university, w. its riot of virgin-jungle-style greenery, is the favorite of local artists and intellectuals. Glassed-in terrace in winter (whence the name), but meals outdoors in good weather. Rather elaborate modern French cuisine; service w. a smile; background music of distinction. Resv. advised; a very good place. 15 min. from dwntwn. *French.* **I–M**

Siva's (dwntwn), 34 S. Front St. (925-2700). A/C. Lunch Mon.-Fri., dinner nightly. AE, CB, DC, MC, V. Jkt. *Specialties:* pakora (buns stuffed w. spiced meat or fish), chicken tandoori, bivyarri (ragoût of mutton, chicken, and rice), Indian-style fish. *Note:* One of the best and most authentic Indian rests. on the East Coast. Pretty Oriental décor with bronze-inlaid teak doors, Indian fabrics, ocher-and-gold color scheme, and cane chairs. Excellent northern Indian food; diligent svce. Resv. advised. A Philadelphia classic. *Indian.* **I–M**

Asakura at Tokyo Center (dwntwn), 1207 Race St. (988-0274). A/C. Lunch Mon.-Fri., dinner nightly. AE, MC, V. *Specialties:* sushi, tempura, sashimi, teriyaki, sukiyaki. *Note:* Chinatown's only Japanese restaurant. Chefs from Tokyo offer a wide variety of Japanese dishes from simple vegetable tempura to esoteric sushi. Dining is Western style at tables or Japanese style in the tatami room. Live jazz Fri.-Sat. Resv. advised. *Japanese.* **I**

Sansom Street Oyster House (dwntwn), 1516 Sansom St. (567-7683). A/C. Lunch/dinner Mon.-Sat.; closed Sun. and holidays. AE, CB, DC, MC, V. *Specialties:* oysters and clams, broiled fish of the day, crab Imperial. *Note:* Likeable seafood bistro where the décor is Formica-style unpretentious but the seafood is remarkably fresh. Locally popular; often noisy. No resv., so sometimes a long wait. Excellent value. *Seafood.* **B–I**

☀☖ **Famous 4th St. Delicatessen** (dwntwn), 4th and Bainbridge Sts. (922-3274). A/C. Breakfast/lunch/dinner daily (from 7 a.m. to 6 p.m., to 4 p.m. on Sun.); closed Jewish holidays. No credit cards. *Specialties:* corned beef sandwiches, pastrami, kugel, whitefish, lox, chocolate-chip cookies, milkshakes. *Note:* This New York–style deli is a favorite of those in-the-know. The décor and svce are without pretension or affectation, boasting collections of old telephones and old milk cartons. Generous servings; very popular locally. Has been in the same family for 60 years. *American.* **B**

☀☖ **Jim's Steaks** (dwntwn), 400 South St. at 4th St. (928-1911). A/C. Lunch/dinner daily (till 1 a.m.). No credit cards. *Specialties:* cheese steak, hoagies. *Note:* Undisputed master of these two local specialties. Hoagies are giant hero sandwiches of ham, provolone, and salami; cheese steaks are thin slices of steak broiled w. onion, green pepper, tomato sauce, and cheese, all served on a crusty loaf of Italian bread. Both are a real Philadelphia institution. You eat them here in a superb art deco setting—black-and-white tiles and sparkling chrome. Generally crowded at lunch. *American.* **I**

☀☖ **Melrose Diner** (nr. dwntwn), 1501 Snyder Ave. (467-6644). A/C. Breakfast/lunch/dinner around the clock daily. No credit cards. *Specialties:* chicken soup, scrapple (leftover pork, sliced and fried up w. buckwheat meal or cornmeal), hamburgers, pork chops, apple pie. *Note:* A South Philly favorite for more than half a century. Praiseworthy plain food served w. a smile in generous portions. Crowded at all hours of day and night. A real landmark. *American.* **I**

☖ **H. A. Winston & Co.** (dwntwn), 1500 Locust St. (546-7232). A/C. Lunch/dinner daily (until midnight). AE, CB, DC, MC, V. *Specialties:* onion soup, sandwiches, salads, hamburgers, broiled chicken, catch of the day. *Note:* In the opinion of experts, the best burgers in Philadelphia, in more than 25 varieties: from hamburger à la Russe w. caviar and sour cream to hamburger Hawaiian w. pineapple and coconut. Agreeable décor. Locally popular. *American.* **I**

In the Vicinity

☀☖☖☖ **Joe's,** 450 S. 7th St. at Laurel St., in Reading, 60 mi. (96 km) NW on I-76 and U.S. 422 (373-6794). A/C. Dinner only, Tues.-Sat.; closed Sun., Mon., and holidays. AE, CB, DC, MC, V. Jkt. *Specialties:* wild-mushroom soup, mushrooms in pastry shell, morels Marie stuffed w. mousse of pheasant, vol-au-vent w. wild mushrooms in cream, duck in sauce bourguignonne w. fresh mushrooms, squab stuffed w. mushrooms. Good homemade desserts. *Note:* One of Pennsylvania's best, and certainly one of its most original, rests. Owner Jack Czarnecki, an expert who picks his own wild mushrooms in the surrounding woodlands, knows them all and blends their different flavors to perfection; his food is delicate and inspired. The rest., which has been in the Czarnecki family since 1916, is well worth the hour-and-a-quarter trip from Philadelphia by car. Resv. a must. *Continental.* **M**

Cafeterias / Fast Food

Eden (nr. dwntwn), 3701 Chestnut St., in International House (387-2471). Lunch/dinner daily. No credit cards. *Specialties:* broiled chicken, fresh pasta, catch of the day, vegetarian and nouvelle cuisine daily specials. *Note:* Remarkable cafeteria food at modest prices. Same management as the Commissary (see above). Patronized by students. On fine days you can eat in the open air. **I**

BARS & NIGHTCLUBS

Borgia Café (dwntwn), 406 S. 2nd St. (574-0414). Excellent modern jazz —the purist's choice—in a smoke-filled room.

Comedy Works (dwntwn), 126 Chestnut St. (922-5997). Famous comedy club above the Middle East Restaurant. A landmark on the Philadelphia scene.

Downey's (dwntwn), 526 Front St. (629-0526). Irish pub favored by local sports figures; dance floor. Also praiseworthy rest. Usually crowded. Open nightly.

Flanigan's (dwntwn), 532 2nd St. (928-9898). The fashionable rock joint; elegant.

Going Bananas (dwntwn), 613 S. 2nd St. (925-3470). A local shrine of improvisation; all the big names perform here.

Magnolia (dwntwn), 1603 Latimer St. (546-4180). This popular bar draws a business-suited crowd of singles. Live music Mon.-Sat. Good creole-cajun eatery adjacent.

Polo Bay (dwntwn), in the Warwick (see "Accommodations," above) (545-4655). The favorite nightclub of Philadelphia's yuppies. Caribbean ambience.

P.T.'s (dwntwn), 6 S. Front St. (922-5676). Singles bar, jazz, disco, backgammon. Relaxed, comfortable atmosphere. Open nightly.

Revival (dwntwn), 22 S. 3rd St. (627-4825). The 20s-30s age bracket piles into the two large rooms for contemporary dance music, videos, and performance art. Wed.-Sun.

Spectacles (dwntwn), in the Sheraton Society Hill (see "Accommodations," above) (238-6000). Philadelphia's "in" disco. Very preppy. Spectacular contemporary décor.

NEARBY EXCURSIONS

CAMDEN (1 mi., 2 km, east by the Benjamin Franklin Bridge): This little New Jersey city, founded in 1681 and now an industrial suburb of Philadelphia, boasts the ▲ **house of Walt Whitman,** singer of the "American Dream," where he spent the last 20 years of his life, at 330 Mickle St. (609/964-5383), open Wed.-Sun. You'll find the original furniture, books, and personal memorabilia of the "Good Gray Poet." His tomb is in Harleigh Cemetery, Heddon Ave. and Vesper Blvd.

Camden is also the home of Campbell Soup, and has an unusual museum devoted to old soup tureens in silver, faïence, and porcelain: the ▲ **Campbell Museum,** Campbell Pl. (609/342-6440), open Mon.-Fri.

☼ **DOYLESTOWN** (28 mi., 44 km, north on Penna. 611): Capital of picturesque Bucks County, country retreat of many artists, writers, and theatrical people. Be sure to see the ▲ **home of Pearl Buck,** the novelist and Nobel laureate, at 520 Dublin Rd., Hilltown Township (249-0100), open Mon.-Fri., plus Sun. in May-Sept. It was here that she wrote her most famous novel, *The Good Earth,* which won the Pulitzer Prize in 1932.

While you're here, don't miss the ▲ **Mercer Museum** and its famous collection of old Americana at Pine and E. Ashland Sts. (345-0210), open daily, March-Dec.

You can conveniently combine this trip with visits to **New Hope** and **Washington Crossing Historical Park** (see below).

☼ ⚔ **GERMANTOWN** (7 mi., 11 km, north on Broad St. and Germantown Ave.): Settled toward the end of the 17th century by Mennonite immigrants from the Rhineland in Germany, this old village, now a residential neighborhood, has dozens of old houses that are designated historic monuments. Its main thoroughfare, **Germantown Avenue,** is an old Indian trail which is itself a "National Historic Landmark."

Among the most interesting buildings (all open to the public from Dec. to Apr.) are: **Cliveden,** a 1767 Georgian house at 6401 Germantown Ave.; George Washington's summer residence at 5442 Germantown Ave., the 1773 **Deshler-Morris House;** the **Germantown Historical Society Complex,** comprising several museums in houses built between 1745 and 1798, at 5214 Germantown Ave. (844-0514); the 1744 **Grumblethorpe House** at 5267 Germantown Ave.; **Stenton,** at 18th St. and Windrim Ave., constructed in 1730, which was Washington's headquarters during the Battle of Germantown; **Upsala,** 6430 Germantown Ave., a 1798 gem of Federal architecture; and the town's oldest house, the 1690 **Wyck** at 6026 Germantown Ave. Don't miss this visit.

LONGWOOD GARDENS (at Kennet Square, 31 mi., 49 km, SW on I-95S, U.S. 322N, and U.S. 1S): Magnificent 350-acre (140-ha.) park, once the property of Pierre S. DuPont, where something is in bloom almost any time of year; there are tropical greenhouses, lush Italian gardens, an arboretum, an orchid house, and pools covered with giant water lilies. Concerts and shows in summer. Open daily; for information, call 388-6741. Well worth the trip.

On the way see ☀ **Brandywine Battlefield,** on U.S. 1 at Chadds Ford (459-3342), where the colonists sustained a defeat at the hands of the British in 1777. Visitor Center; Washington's and Lafayette's headquarters. Open Tues.-Sun.

Another place you shouldn't miss is the ☀ 🔭 **Brandywine River Museum,** on U.S. 1 at Chadds Ford (388-7601), open daily, housed in a century-old mill. Contains Andrew Wyeth's private collection of his own works; those of his father, the famous illustrator N. C. Wyeth; and paintings by his father's teacher, Howard Pyle, and many other American artists.

NEW HOPE (46 mi., 73 km, NE on I-95N and Penna. 32): Charming 300-year-old village on the banks of the Delaware River, which has long proved irresistible to artists and writers. Many old houses, boutiques, art galleries, and inns. From Apr. to Nov. you can take a picturesque trip in a **mule-drawn barge** along the Old Delaware Canal; apply on New St. (609/862-2842).

On the way, be sure to visit ☀ **Washington Crossing State Park,** on either side of the Delaware River at the exact spot where Washington and 2,400 of his men crossed it in a snowstorm on the night of Dec. 25, 1776, on his way to capture the town of Trenton by surprise. This brilliant feat of arms, reenacted every year on Dec. 25 by costumed extras, was one of the turning points of the War of Independence. Memorials; museum on Penna. 32 (493-4076). Open daily; don't miss it.

OLD FORT MIFFLIN (Fort Mifflin Rd., 8 mi., 12 km, SW along Broad St. and Penna. 291) (365-9781): Sometimes called "the Alamo of the War of Independence"; scene of a fierce engagement against the British in the fall of 1777. Rebuilt in 1798. Open weekends only, Mar.-Dec. Military parades in period uniform on Sun. in summer. Should be seen.

POTTSTOWN (36 mi., 57 km, NW on I-76 and U.S. 422): Here, in 1714, the ironmaster John Potts opened Pennsylvania's first industrial foundry. His family home, **Pottsgrove Mansion,** a very fine 1752 example of Colonial architecture on W. King St. (326-4014), is open to visitors Tues.-Sun.

Some 13 mi. (20 km) SW along Penna. 724 and 345, look in on the ☀ ⚱ **Hopewell Furnace National Historic Site** (582-8773), a museum-village clustered around an old foundry which was active between 1770 and 1883, and has been restored in the style of the period 1820–1840. Interesting museum; demonstrations of blacksmithing in summer. Don't miss this page from American history. Open daily.

☀ **PRINCETON** (41 mi., 65 km, NE on I-95 and U.S. 206): Gracious little university town, steeped in history, which was briefly (June-Nov. 1783) the capital of the United States. While in session at Princeton, the Congress learned of the signing of the peace treaty ending the Revolutionary War in Sept. 1783; from here, too, Washington delivered his famous "Farewell Orders to the Armies."

With its 6,000 students and Anglo-English charm, the Ivy League ☀ ⚑⚑ **Princeton University,** founded in 1746, is one of the most socially exclusive as well as one of the most distinguished universities on the eastern seaboard. Its faculty has included eight Nobel Prize winners (one of them Albert Einstein, who died here in 1955). Interesting tour of the campus, open daily (609/452-3603), with its collection of modern sculptures by Calder, Picasso, Moore, Noguchi, Lipchitz, and others. See, too, the **Woodrow Wilson School of Public and International Affairs,** designed by Minoru Yamasaki, architect of New York's World Trade Center, and **Nassau Hall,** built in 1756, where the Second Continental Congress met in 1783. The **University Art Museum** has works by such painters as Raphael, Cranach, Van Dyke, Rubens, and Monet. Don't miss it.

You can visit Princeton along with **New Hope** and **Washington Crossing State Park** (see above).

☀⚱ **VALLEY FORGE NATIONAL HISTORICAL PARK** (N. Gulph Rd. and Penna. 23, 20 mi., 33 km, NW on I-76) (783-7700): George Washington's camp from Dec. 1777 to June 1778, one of the darkest periods of the Revolutionary War. Some 3,000 soldiers died here of cold, hunger, or disease during that terrible winter. Washington's headquarters, a commemorative chapel, and a museum are open daily; guided tours from the Visitor Center, mid-Apr. to Oct. Lovely countryside all around; don't miss it.

☀⚱ **WINTERTHUR MUSEUM AND GARDENS** (36 mi., 57 km, SW on I-95 and Del. 52) (302/654-1548): Once the 200-bedroom home of chemical tycoon Henry F. DuPont. Sumptuous collection of decorative art and American furniture from the 17th to the 19th century. Reservations a must for conducted tours of the principal collections. Magnificent 200-acre (80-ha.) English-style park. Open Tues.-Sun. Well worth going out of your way for. Combine it with a visit to **Longwood Gardens** and the **Brandywine Museum and Battlefield** (see above).

ATLANTIC CITY & CAPE MAY

☀⚱ **ATLANTIC CITY** (215 mi., 344 km, round trip via N.J. 42S the Atlantic City Expwy. east, N.J. 585S, the Garden State Pkwy. north, Atlantic City Expwy. west, and N.J. 42N): The trip begins at Atlantic City, Philadelphia's seaside entertainment extension. This seaside resort, flashy and kitsch, was founded as recently as 1852; after the introduction of legalized gaming it was considered Las Vegas' poor relation, but has become the new mecca for American gamblers. In 1976, when the New Jersey legislature legalized roulette wheels and slot machines, Atlantic City awoke from a 25-year sleep;

it now accommodates 30 million visitors every year, who leave behind them $2.5 billion. Its location—only 3 hours from New York and 1½ hours from Philadelphia, by car—has contributed greatly to its prosperity. Two other points of civic pride: the game of *Monopoly* was based on Atlantic City street names, and every year since 1921 Miss America has been crowned here.

The city's enormous **Convention Hall** is another curiosity in itself; it seats 41,000 people and has the largest organ in the world, with 32,000 pipes and 1,477 registers. A still-bigger convention center is under construction nearby, to be opened in 1991.

Along the 5-mi. (8-km) **Boardwalk** beside the ocean—the East Coast's answer to the Las Vegas Strip—and at the bay side are the flashy, luxurious casinos, which draw their flocks of conventioneers and package tourists. Well worth a visit.

Tourist Information

Convention & Visitors Bureau: 2314 Pacific Ave., Atlantic City, NJ 08401 (609/348-7100).

Transportation

Greyhound (bus), 2101 Arctic Ave. (609/345-5403): Service between Atlantic City and New York/Philadelphia/Washington.

New Jersey Transit (bus), Arctic and Arkansas Aves. (609/344-8181): Service between Atlantic City and Cape May/New York/Philadelphia.

Allegheny Commuter (airplane), Municipal Airport (609/344-7104): Flights to/from Cape May, New York, Philadelphia, Washington.

Trump Air (helicopter), Steel Pier Heliport (609/344-0833): To/from Manhattan.

AMTRAK (train) will resume on Apr. 1, 1989, its regular service with Philadelphia (five round trips daily; time, 1¼ hours) and New York (one round trip daily; time, 2 hours 20 min.). The AMTRAK station is on Ohio Ave. (toll free 800/872-7245).

Guided Tours and Excursions

Gray Line Tours (bus), 9 N. Arkansas Ave. (609/344-0965).

Where to Stay

Bally's Grand Hotel Casino (formerly the Golden Nugget), Pacific and Boston Aves., Atlantic City, NJ 08401 (609/347-7111; toll free 800/225-5977). 528 rms, A/C, cable color TV. AE, CB, DC, MC, V. Valet garage $10, pool, health club, sauna, beach, seven rests. and coffeeshops (some open around the clock), 24-hr bars, rm svce, nightclub, casino, shows, hrdrsr, free crib. *Note:* One of the largest, most up-to-date casinohotels in Atlantic City; outrageously flamboyant décor, but incomparable comfort and facilities. Ultra-professional svce; deluxe rest. (Victoria's). Direct beach access. 5-min. walk from the Convention Hall; group and convention clientele. **E–VE, but lower rates out of season**

Caesars Atlantic City, 2100 Pacific Ave., Atlantic City, NJ 08401 (609/348-4411; toll free 800/257-8555). 646 rms, A/C, cable color TV. AE, CB, DC, MC, V. Valet garage $10, two pools, health club, sauna, three tennis courts, beach, seven rests. (including Le Posh), two 24-hr coffeeshops, 24-hr bars, rm svce, casinos, shows, boutiques. *Note:* This cream of the local hotel crop has undergone a much-needed facelift; the exterior is strident and unconvincing, but the rms are inviting and comfortable. Same management as the famous Caesars Palace establishments at Las Vegas and Lake

Tahoe. Rest. (Le Posh) in the highest deluxe category; efficient svce. Direct beach access. The casino does the biggest business in Atlantic City. **E–VE, but lower rates out of season**

Harrah's Marina Hotel Casino, 1725 Brigantine Blvd., Atlantic City, NJ 08401 (609/441-5000; toll free 800/524-1351). 758 rms, A/C, color TV, in-rm movies. AE, CB, DC, MC, V. Free valet parking, pool, health club, sauna, tennis court, marina, four rests. (including the Meadows), 24-hr coffeeshop, 24-hr bars, rm svce, nightclub, casino, shows, hrdrsr, boutiques, free crib. *Note:* The best place to stay in Atlantic City, away from the hubbub of the Boardwalk. Large, ultramodern marina-hotel whose 18 floors overlook the yacht basin and Absecon Bay: a facsimile of the giant Las Vegas casino-hotels with the waterway thrown in. Spacious, very comfortable rms; efficient reception and svce; very complete facilities. Group and convention clientele. **E–VE, but lower rates out of season**

Showboat Hotel Casino, 801 Boardwalk, Atlantic City, NJ 08401 (609/343-4000; toll free 800/524-1351). 516 rms, A/C, cable color TV. AE, CB, DC, MC, V. Valet garage $10, pool, beach, bowling, 11 rests., coffeeshops, and bars, rm svce, nightclub, casino, shows. *Note:* Brand-new casino hotel, rather curiously designed with a cut-off corner facade, and direct access to beach. Other than the inevitable casino w. dozens of tables and hundreds of slot machines, the main attraction of the hotel is its 60-lane bowling alley. Flawless comfort and facilities; good svce. Group and convention clientele. **E–VE, but lower rates out of season**

The Admiral's Quarters, 655 Absecon Blvd., Atlantic City, NJ 08401 (609/344-2201; toll free 800/833-3242). 74 mini-suites, A/C, cable color TV. AE, CB, DC, MC, V. Parking, pool, no bar, no rest., 24-hr concierge, free breakfast. *Note:* Small, quiet, comfortable hotel 5 min. from the Boardwalk and 10 min. from the airport. Offers only mini-suites w. refrigerators, kitchenettes, and private balconies. Direct shuttle to beach and casinos. Business clientele. **M–E, but lower rates out of season**

Atlantis Casino Hotel (formerly the Playboy), 2500 Boardwalk, Atlantic City, NJ 08401 (609/344-4000; toll free 800/257-8672). 500 rms, A/C, color TV. AE, CB, DC, MC, V. Free valet parking, pool, health club, tennis court, beach, four rests. (including Jeanne's), 24-hr coffeeshop, 24-hr bars, rm svce, casino, shows, boutiques. *Note:* Big, elegantly designed 24-story glass tower adjoining the Convention Hall. Guaranteed comfort and comprehensive facilities, but deficient svce. Direct beach access. Group and convention clientele. **M–E, but lower rates out of season**

Best Western Inn, Pacific and Indiana Aves., Atlantic City, NJ 08401 (609/348-9175; toll free, see Best Western). 108 rms, A/C, cable color TV. AE, CB, DC, MC, V. Valet parking $8, pool, sauna, adjoining 24-hr coffeeshop, crib $10. *Note:* Modern motel a stone's throw from the big casinos, less expensive but no less comfortable than most of the local palaces. Right next to the beach. Friendly reception and svce. **M–E, but lower rates out of season**

Comfort Inn West, Black Horse Pike at Dover Pl., West Atlantic City, NJ 08232 (609/645-1818; toll free 800/228-5150). 198 rms, A/C, color TV, in-rm movies. AE, CB, DC, MC, V. Free parking, pool, coffeeshop, free crib. *Note:* Inviting, modern motel near the municipal airport. Very comfortable rms; reception and svce w. a smile. Free shuttle bus to casino district. Group clientele. **M, but lower rates out of season**

Fiesta Motel, Tennessee and Pacific Aves., Atlantic City, NJ 08401 (609/344-4193). 72 rms, A/C, cable color TV. AE, DC, MC, V. Free parking, pool, coffeeshop, rm svce. *Note:* Modest but well-run motel very nr. the Boardwalk, w. completely renovated décor and facilities. Friendly reception. Good overall value. **I–M, but lower rates out of season**

🍷 **Continental Motel,** 137 S. Illinois Ave., Atlantic City, NJ 08404 (609/345-5141). 60 rms, A/C, color TV. AE, MC, V. Free parking, pool, bar. *Note:* Aging small motel a block or two from the Boardwalk and the casinos. Decently comfortable; ideal for budget travelers. **I–M, but lower rates out of season**

Where to Eat

🍷🍷 **Knife & Fork Inn,** Albany and Atlantic Aves. (344-1133). A/C. Dinner only, nightly; closed Dec. 25, Yom Kippur. AE. Jkt. *Specialties:* mussels marinière, shellfish, lobster Thermidor, bouillabaisse, crab Newburg, catch of the day; also some meat dishes. *Note:* The best seafood rest., and quite simply the best rest., in the culinary wasteland called Atlantic City. The crabs and scallops are particularly worthwhile. Plush-type décor; uncommonly efficient svce. Resv. strongly advised. A local landmark since 1912. *Seafood.* **M**

🍷🍷 **Dock's Oyster House,** 2405 Atlantic Ave. (345-0092). A/C. Dinner only, Tues.-Sun.; closed Mon., Thanksgiving, and Dec.-Feb. AE, MC, V. *Specialties:* linguine w. clams, oyster stew, lobster broiled or stuffed w. crabmeat, catch of the day, steak, cheese pie. *Note:* Dock's Oyster House, in the hands of the Dougherty family for four generations, is the oldest (1897) seafood rest. in Atlantic City, notwithstanding its vaguely Scandinavian-contemporary décor. Its success is due to absolutely fresh fish and shellfish. Friendly, relaxed svce; resv. advised. *Steak-seafood.* **I–M**

🍷🍷 **Peking Duck House,** 2801 Atlantic Ave. (344-9090). A/C. Lunch/dinner daily. AE, CB, DC, MC, V. *Specialties:* shrimp lo-mein, shark's-fin soup, Peking duck, chicken w. lotus flour, beef w. tiger-lily flowers. *Note:* Chinese food at a high level, inventive and refined, from the skillets of the very talented Kenny Poo from Hong Kong. The décor, on the contrary, featuring beige-toned walls and subdued lighting, is not in the least Oriental. The Peking duck (order in advance) is remarkable. A very good place. Resv. advised, particularly on wknds. *Chinese.* **I–M**

🍷 **Angelo's Fairmount Tavern,** 2300 Fairmount Ave. (344-2439). A/C. Lunch/dinner daily. No credit cards. *Specialties:* fresh homemade soup and pasta, classical Italian dishes, Sicilian specialties. Everyone takes a caffè espresso. *Note:* This former speakeasy, frequented by local politicians and newspaper people, serves the kind of good, tasty food you'd expect from a typical Italian *trattoria.* The menu changes regularly at the whim of the owner Angelo "The Meatball" Mancuso. Excellent value. No resv. *Italian-American.* **I**

☼🍷 **Smithville Inn,** on U.S. 9 at Smithville, 10 mi. (16 km) north via U.S. 30 and U.S. 9 (652-7777). A/C. Lunch/dinner daily; closed Dec. 25. AE, CB, DC, MC, V. *Specialties:* chicken pot pie, stuffed pork chops, roast duck. *Note:* Picturesque Colonial-style inn in "The Historic Towne of Smithville," a careful replica of an 18th-century village. The food is acceptable but unimaginative. Much favored by tourists; resv. advised in summer. *American.* **I**

☼🍷 **White House Sub Shop,** 2301 Arctic Ave. (345-1564). A/C. Lunch/dinner daily (till midnight). No credit cards. *Specialties:* submarines, cheese steaks. *Note:* The unchallenged champion of the "submarine" sandwich, the local equivalent of the Philadelphian "hoagie" or the New York "hero": an Italian roll stuffed with salami, ham, turkey, prosciutto, provolone, lettuce, tomatoes, onions, green peppers, etc. The rest. proudly claims (and has signed photos on the wall to prove it) such famous patrons as Jerry Lewis, Frank Sinatra, Ray Charles, and Joan Rivers. The décor is pure art deco kitsch. A local landmark since 1946. *American.* **B**

SOUTH FROM ATLANTIC CITY: The trip continues along N.J. 585, a scenic route which follows the shoreline for almost 40 mi. (65 km), and offers some fine ocean views. At **Margate,** immediately south of Atlantic City, see the amazing ♙**Lucy,** a six-story building shaped like an elephant, constructed in 1881; you reach the beast's "stomach" by climbing spiral staircases in its legs. Worth seeing; open daily in Jul.-Aug., weekends only in spring and fall; closed the rest of the year. The next stop, 10 mi. (16 km) further south, is **Ocean City,** a beach resort whose resolutely sober family atmosphere is a striking contrast to Atlantic City; the town is "dry," and attracts a number of religious conventions every year.

☀☍ **CAPE MAY:** Farther along N.J. 585 you come to Cape May, the oldest seaside resort (1631) in the country; its famous visitors have included Presidents Lincoln and Grant, Horace Greeley, and the department-store magnate John Wanamaker. Its Victorian elegance, and its hundreds of pretty old pastel-washed houses with their white porches and lacy carpenter's-Gothic fretwork, seem to have come straight out of a 19th-century picture postcard. The whole town is a designated historic monument. On its magnificent beach, 4 mi. (7 km) long, you can pick up the so-called Cape May diamonds—pebbles of quartz polished by the action of the waves. You can tour the center of the town in a horse-drawn carriage, or in an imitation 19th-century streetcar, leaving from Beach Dr. at Gurney St. (609/884-5404). Paul Volcker, long head of the Federal Reserve Board, comes from Cape May. You shouldn't miss it.

Return back to Philadelphia by the Garden State Parkway and Atlantic City Expwy. An interesting, varied itinerary taking two to three days.

Where to Stay

☀☍☍ **The Chalfonte,** 301 Howard St., Cape May, NJ 08204 (609/ 884-8409). 103 rms. Picturesque old hotel in the purest gingerbread tradition. Closed Nov.-Apr. **M–E**

☀☍☍ **The Mainstay,** 635 Columbia Ave., Cape May, NJ 08204 (609/884-8690). 13 rms (9 w. private bath), all no-smoking. Charming Victorian structure dating from 1872. Minimum stay in summer is three days. Distinction and style. Closed Dec.-Mar. **M–E**

☀☍☍ **The Queen Victoria,** 102 Ocean St., Cape May, NJ 08204 (609/884-8702). 11 rms (7 w. private bath). Elegantly furnished Victorian villa. Minimum stay on wknds is two to four days. Open year round. **M–E**

Where to Eat

☍ **Lobster House,** Fisherman's Wharf (609/884-8296). Lunch/dinner daily; closed Tues. in winter. Excellent seafood rest. on the harbor; very popular locally. **B–I**

☀☍ **Watson's Merion Inn,** 106 Decatur St. (609/884-8363). Dinner only, nightly; closed Nov.-Mar. Good regional American food in an authentic 1885 Victorian setting. **I–M**

FARTHER AFIELD

☀☍ **GETTYSBURG BATTLEFIELD AND PENNSYLVANIA DUTCH COUNTRY** (274 mi., 441 km, round trip via

I-76W, U.S. 222S, U.S. 322W, U.S. 15S, U.S. 30E, U.S. 202N, and I-76E): After visiting **Valley Forge National Historical Park,** site of one of the darker pages of American military history (see "Nearby Excursions," above), you can drive on through Pennsylvania Dutch Country.

Pennsylvania Dutch Country

Begin your tour at ☀ ⚓ **Ephrata Cloister,** a rural religious community at 632 W. Main St., Ephrata, 6 mi. (9 km) south of the Pennsylvania Tpke. and I-76 on U.S. 222S and U.S. 322W (717/733-6600). Founded in 1732 by Conrad Beissel, a Baptist pastor from Germany, this contemplative community of country folk observed an ascetic rule of life: unmarried people of opposite sexes were segregated, wooden benches and headrests were used instead of beds, and so on. It continued its archaic lifestyle until 1934. You can still visit a dozen buildings from the period 1735–1750; open Tues.-Sun. Should not be missed.

This stop is a good introduction to a more detailed inspection of Pennsylvania Dutch Country, a region whose people are among the most unusual, and least known, in America. They are often, and wrongly, taken for people of Dutch descent; in fact their ancestors were German ("Deutsch") settlers who came here in the 17th century from the Rhineland and the Palatinate, whose original customs have been preserved almost intact. These austere, devout, hard-working country folk are divided into three main religious denominations: Amish, Moravian, and Mennonite. They agree, however, in rejecting almost everything that smacks of modernity, whether vaccination, chemical fertilizers, automobiles, radios, or quite simply electricity, which the more pious among them regard as an invention of the devil. The "Plain People," as they are called, use only buggies for conveyance and only kerosene lamps for light; they speak the same Low German as their ancestors and wear the same dark-hued, archaic dress vividly portrayed in the movie *Witness.* Some 15,000–20,000 Amish in Pennsylvania Dutch Country live in closed communities observing to the letter the teachings of the Bible. But these Americans from an earlier epoch are progressively disappearing. (There are also Amish communities of some hundreds of souls in Ohio, Indiana, Texas, and Canada. As for the Mennonites, who unlike the Amish have come to terms with some manifestations of progress, such as electricity, there are believed to be some 200,000 of them in the U.S. and Canada.)

For an unforgettable experience, you should visit the ☀ ⚓ **Amish farms and markets around Lancaster, York, Intercourse, Strasburg, or Bird-in-Hand.** Note, however, that for religious reasons the Amish reject any depiction of the human form, and thus forbid the use of still or movie cameras.

Paradoxically, a mere 40 mi. (64 km) from this region so firmly rooted in the past you will find the famous nuclear power plant at **Three Mile Island,** where in 1979 the beginning of a meltdown threw the whole of Pennsylvania into a panic. Three Mile Island has played a leading part in alerting mankind to the dangers of nuclear energy.

Some useful addresses for visitors to Pennsylvania Dutch Country:

INFORMATION. The **Mennonite Tourist Information Center,** 2209 Millstream Rd., Lancaster, PA 17601 (717/299-0954): Organizes guided tours and house visits with Mennonite families; open Mon.-Sat.

Other very active information centers are the **Pennsylvania Dutch Visitors Bureau,** 501 Greenfield Rd., Lancaster, PA 17601 (717/299-8901); and **People's Place,** Main St., Intercourse, PA 17534 (717/768-7171), with an Amish museum, movies, and a library; open Mon.-Sat.

⚓ **FARM VISITS.** The **Amish Homestead,** 3 mi. (5 km) east of Lancaster on Penna. 462 (717/392-0832), open daily; also **Amish**

Farm and House, 5 mi. (8 km) east of Lancaster on U.S. 30 (717/394-6185), open daily.

🔔 **MARKET VISITS.** The **Central Market,** Pennsylvania Square, Lancaster, held on Tues., Fri., and Sat.; **Meadowbrook Market,** 5 mi. (8 km) east of Lancaster at Leola, on Penna. 23, held on Fri. and Sat.; **Farmer's Market,** 6 mi. (10 km) east of Lancaster at Bird-in-Hand on Penna. 340, held on Wed., Fri., and Sat.; and the **Farmer's Market,** Market and Penn Sts. in York, held on Tues., Fri., and Sat.

SIGHTS. The 🔔 **Pennsylvania Farm Museum,** 2451 Kissel Hill Rd., Lancaster, 2 mi. (4 km) north on Penna. 272 (717/569-0401): 250,000 authentically old exhibits, from Conestoga wagons to spinning wheels. Interesting. Open Tues.-Sun.

🔔 **Strasburg Railroad,** 8 mi. (12 km) SE of Lancaster via U.S. 30 and Penna. 896 (717/687-7522): Trip on a steam train through Amish country. Also a railroad museum. Open daily, May-Oct.; weekends only, in Apr. and Nov.

🔔 Hershey

After a long look at Lancaster and the surrounding countryside, you go on to Hershey. Known as "the chocolate capital of the world," this smiling little town of 13,000 people, perpetually pervaded by the aroma of chocolate, is the home of the world's largest chocolate factory. Milton Hershey, founder of the Hershey Corporation in 1903, also gave his name to the town. At **Hershey's Chocolate World,** Park Blvd. (open daily), you can see the entire production cycle from the planting of a cocoa tree down to the finished chocolate bar. See also the very interesting **Hershey Museum of American Life,** with scenes from the life and history of the Pennsylvania Dutch and their Indian predecessors.

Hersheypark, on Park Blvd. (717/534-3900), is a big amusement park with dozens of carousels, roller coasters and other attractions; open daily mid-May to Sept.; closed the rest of the year. There's a large rose garden, where tulips and chrysanthemums are also grown in season, at **Hershey Gardens,** Park Blvd., open daily mid-Apr. to Oct. Must definitely be seen.

After another 50 mi. (80 km) of driving south, you arrive at—

☀ 🔔 Gettysburg National Military Park

The **Visitor Center** is on Penna. 134 (717/334-1124), open daily. Here, on July 1–3, 1863, was fought the bloodiest battle of the Civil War. The Confederate troops of Gen. Robert E. Lee sustained 28,000 casualties, and the Union forces under Gen. George Meade, 23,000. It was this welter of kindred blood which moved Lincoln to compose the famous *Gettysburg Address,* appealing for peace and reconciliation between North and South.

To visit the battlefield thoroughly you must make a circuit of more than 35 mi. (56 km). There are hundreds of commemorative objects, including 400 cannon and more than 1,300 monuments, engraved tablets, and markers. The **Battlefield Tower** observation tower is 295 ft (90 m) high, and nearby is a cyclorama with movies depicting the course of the battle. Don't miss this visit.

Not far from the battlefield is the ☀ 🔔 **Eisenhower National Historic Site,** reached only by bus from the Visitor Center (717/334-1124). No more than 1,100 persons may be admitted on any day; open daily Apr.-Oct., Wed.-Sun. the rest of the year. Many personal items associated with "Ike" and his wife, Mamie. Must certainly be seen.

Then back to Philadelphia via York and Lancaster, so that if need be you can catch anything you missed earlier in Pennsylvania Dutch Country. Fascinating three- to four-day trip; a must for all lovers of history—or of the unusual.

Where to Stay En Route

IN GETTYSBURG. The 🛏🛏 **Quality Inn Gettysburg Motor Lodge,** 380 Steinwehr Ave., Gettysburg, PA 17325 (717/334-1103). 89 rms. Comfortable, inviting motel next to the Battlefield Visitor Center. **I–M**

IN HERSHEY. The 🛏🛏 **Hershey Lodge,** Chocolate Ave. at University Dr., Hershey, PA 17033 (717/533-3311). 460 rms. Large, modern motel w. adjoining tennis courts and golf course. **M–E**

IN LANCASTER. The 🛏🛏🛏 **Willow Valley Resort,** 2416 Willow St. Pike (at U.S. 222), Lancaster, PA 17602 (717/464-2711). Luxurious motel in the heart of the country; does a heavy convention business. **M–E**

IN MOUNT JOY. The ☀ 🛏🛏 **Cameron Estates Inn,** Donegal Springs Rd., Mount Joy, PA 17552 (717/653-1773). 18 rms. Elegant 19th-century manor house surrounded by a beautiful garden. **I–M**

IN STRASBURG. The 🛏🛏 **Historic Strasburg Inn,** Penna. 896, Strasburg, PA 17579 (717/687-7691). 103 rms. Charming Colonial-style inn. **M–E**

Where to Eat En Route

IN BIRD-IN-HAND. The 🍷 **Plain and Fancy Farm Restaurant,** on Penna. 340 (717/768-8281). Breakfast/lunch/dinner (till 8 p.m.) Mon.-Sat. Tasty family cooking in an authentic Amish farm. **B**

IN MOUNT JOY. ☀ 🍷🍷 **Groff's Farm,** 650 Pinkerton Rd. (717/653-2048). Lunch/dinner (till 7:30 p.m.) Tues.-Sun. Typical, rather elaborate Pennsylvania Dutch cooking, in a pleasantly restored 1756 building. Resv. advised, particularly at dinner. **I–M**

CHAPTER 7

PITTSBURGH

□ □ □

Long known as "Smoky City," this once gloomy and polluted industrial center has been transformed in less than two decades into a modern, sparkling metropolis. The glass-and-steel high-rises of "Steel City"—another of Pittsburgh's nicknames—its luxury hotels, and its ultramodern office buildings now reach skyward around the "Golden Triangle," once a slum, now the heart of the business district.

Steel (almost 25% of U.S. output), glass, nuclear engineering (the first American nuclear power plant was built near Pittsburgh), aluminum, data processing, chemicals, robotics, and pharmaceuticals all contribute to the wealth of this dedicated, hard-working city—to say nothing of its busy river port, which handles more than 60 million tons of freight a year. For more than a century Pittsburgh was synonymous with steel and coal, and so renowned for its ugliness that after World War II, when the great architect Frank Lloyd Wright was asked how to go about modernizing the city, he replied that it would make more sense to tear it down and start over. Fortunately this pessimism was ignored when a gigantic urban-renewal plan was put into effect toward the end of the 1960s; it has already borne much fruit, and is still being carried forward through such reconstruction projects as **Renaissance II** (total cost, $6 billion) and the **Pittsburgh Technology Center,** now under construction on the site of an old steel mill on the banks of the Monongahela River.

The first settlement was French: Fort Duquesne, built in 1754 at the confluence of the Monongahela, Allegheny, and Ohio rivers. The British captured it in 1758 and renamed it in honor of their prime minister, William Pitt the Elder; later the fort passed its name on to the city. Pittsburgh was the arsenal of the Union during the War Between the States; three-quarters of a century later it played the same role during World War II. Today the capital of "America's Ruhr" (as Europeans refer to it) is still a stronghold of finance and industry, headquarters of Alcoa, Heinz Foods, Rockwell International, USX Corporation (formerly U.S. Steel), Westinghouse, and many other giant corporations. From the summit of **Mount Washington,** reached by cable car, the visitor can again enjoy the view of the city and the three rivers that run through it, now that stringently enforced antipollution laws have almost abolished the obscuring smog once spewed forth by its factories.

Thanks to the lavish donations of such local captains of industry and finance as Carnegie, Frick, and Mellon, Pittsburgh boasts some of the country's wealthiest and most beautiful museums, including the famous **Carnegie Institute,** a justly renowned symphony orchestra, and no fewer than seven universities and colleges of great quality such as Carnegie-Mellon University (6,000 students) and the University of Pittsburgh (35,000 students).

Famous people born in Pittsburgh include painter Andy Warhol; choreographer Martha Graham; dancer Gene Kelly; jazz musicians Art Blakey, Billy Eckstine, Roy Eldridge, Errol Garner, Earl Hines, Ahmad Jamal, and Kenny Clarke; conductor Billy May; and Stephen Foster, composer of "Swannee River," "My Old Kentucky Home," and other treasures of American folk song.

BASIC FACTS: State of Pennsylvania. Area Code: 412. Time Zone: Eastern Time. ZIP Code: 15230. Founded: 1758. Approximate population: city, 410,000; metropolitan area, 2,350,000. 15th-largest U.S. metropolitan area.

CLIMATE: With 200 days of rain a year, bring your umbrella in any season. Winter is moderately cold (January mean, 31°F, −1°C). In summer the thermometer rarely goes above 77°F (25°C); the July mean is 75°F (24°C). Spring and autumn are brisk.

DISTANCES: Buffalo, 219 mi. (350 km); Cincinnati, 290 mi. (465 km); Cleveland, 129 mi. (206 km); New York, 368 mi. (590 km); Philadelphia, 308 mi. (498 km); Washington, 247 mi. (396 km).

ARRIVAL & TRANSIT INFORMATION

AIRPORT: Greater Pittsburgh International Airport, 17 mi. (27 km) west. For information call 778-2525.

DOMESTIC AIRLINES: American (771-4437), Continental (391-6910), Delta (566-2100), Eastern (471-7100), Northwest (281-2088), Pan Am (toll free 800/221-1111), TWA (391-3600), United (288-9900), and USAir (922-7500).

FOREIGN CARRIERS: British Airways (toll free 800/247-9297) and Canadian (toll free 800/426-7000).

CITY LINK: The **cab** fare from the airport to downtown is about $28; time, 35 min. Bus: **Airlines Transportation Co.** (471-8900), leaves about every 30 min., serving principal downtown hotels; fare, $8; time, about 40–50 min.
   The **bus and subway public transportation** provided by Port Authority Transit/PAT (231-5707) is relatively efficient.
   The downtown area isn't big enough to require renting a car.

CAR RENTAL (at the airport unless otherwise indicated): Avis (262-5160); Budget (262-1500); Dollar (262-1300); Hertz (262-1705); National (262-2312); Thrifty, 1432 Beers School Rd. (264-1775). For downtown locations, consult the local telephone book.

LIMOUSINE SERVICES: Carey Limousine (731-8671), Limo Center (923-1650), and Riemer's Limousine (661-6054).

TAXIS: Cabs are few and dear. Theoretically they can be hailed on the street, but it's better to phone, at least 15–30 min. ahead of time: **Colonial Cab** (833-3300), **People's Cab** (681-3131), or **Yellow Cab** (665-8100).

TRAIN: AMTRAK Station, Liberty Ave. and Grant St. (621-4850).

BUS: Greyhound, 11th St. and Liberty Ave. (391-2300).

RIVER CRUISES: Three- to ten-day cruises on the Mississippi and Ohio Rivers aboard the *Delta Queen* or the *Mississippi Queen,* sternwheelers dating from the 1920s. Luxurious kitsch. See Chapter 15 on New Orleans.

INFORMATION AND TOURS

TOURIST INFORMATION: The **Greater Pittsburgh Convention and Visitors Bureau,** 4 Gateway Center, PA 15222 (412/281-7711).

Visitor Information Center, 18 Gateway Towers at Liberty Ave. (412/281-9222).

For a **telephone recording** with an up-to-date listing of cultural events and shows, call 412/391-6840.

GUIDED TOURS: The **Gateway Clipper Fleet** (boat), Monongahela Wharf, Station Square Dock (355-7980): Paddlewheeler trips on the three rivers; Apr.-Nov.

Gray Line Tours (bus) (761-7000): Conducted tours of the city and surroundings; serves principal downtown hotels. June-Sept.

SIGHTS, ATTRACTIONS, & ACTIVITIES

ARCHITECTURAL HIGHLIGHTS: ☀ ⚖ **Alcoa Building,** 425 Sixth Ave.: The 30-story aluminum-clad building is 410 ft (125 m) high and of revolutionary design; it was one of the first skyscrapers in the world with an aluminum frame. Worth a look, but not open to visitors.

☀⚖ **Cathedral of Learning,** University of Pittsburgh campus, Fifth Ave. and Bigelow Blvd. (624-6000): The only university skyscraper in the country, 520 ft (160 m) high, with 42 floors. The Gothic Revival design, now redolent of kitsch, dates from 1935. The 18 lecture rooms grouped around the entrance hall are each decorated in a different idiom: Byzantine, Roman, Renaissance, Tudor, Empire, and so on. Observation platform on the 36th floor. Conducted tours. Open daily; should be seen.

☀⚖ **Civic Arena,** Washington Pl. at Centre and Bedford Aves. (642-1800): Huge 20,000-seat arena with a roof that opens. The stainless-steel dome, three times larger than that of St. Peter's in Rome, can be folded back in 2½ minutes. Concerts, sports events, and conventions. Worth a look.

⚖ **CNG Tower,** Liberty Ave. and 7th St.: A 30-story post-modern tower in brown and buff granite, capped with a steel arch of unusual design. A 1987 work of architects Bob Evans and William Pedersen. Worth seeing.

⚖ **Heinz Hall,** 600 Penn Ave. (392-4800): A beautiful rococo 1920s movie house converted into a concert hall and now home to the famous Pittsburgh Symphony. Conducted tours by appointment; should be seen.

☀⚖⚖ **P.P.G. Place,** 1 PPG Pl. (434-3832): Symbol of the new Pittsburgh designed by the well-known architectural team of Philip Johnson and John Burgee: a group of six ultramodern neo-Gothic buildings, with façades all in glass, grouped around a huge plaza with a winter garden, shops, restaurants, and stores. The 40-story central tower, PPG Tower, stands 635 ft (193 m) high; its pinnacled silhouette recalls the Houses of Parliament in London. Open-air concerts on the plaza in summer. Very much worth seeing.

⚖ **Stephen Collins Foster Memorial Hall,** University of Pittsburgh campus, Forbes Ave. at Bigelow Blvd. (624-4100): Imposing monument commemorating Pittsburgh's native son Stephen Collins Foster, who wrote many well-loved songs. Library with personal memorabilia of the composer, and an auditorium where the Three Rivers Shakespeare Festival is held every year, as well as many concerts. For lovers of music history. Open Mon.-Fri.

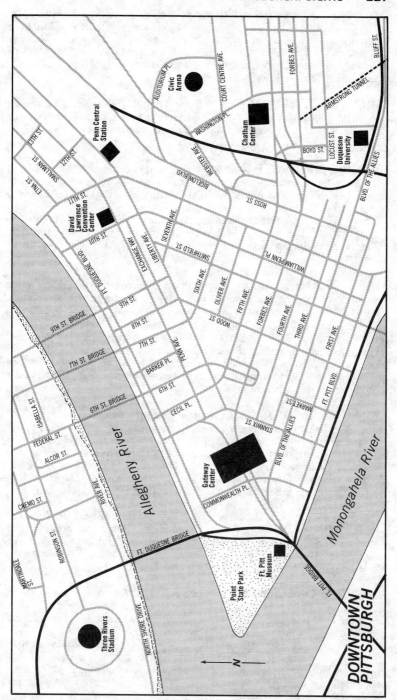

DOWNTOWN
PITTSBURGH

University of Pittsburgh, Fifth Ave. and Bigelow Blvd. (624-4141): One of the oldest (1787) and most famous of American universities, with 35,000 students. Of the 60 or so buildings scattered across its 132-acre (53-ha.) campus, several are worth going to see: the **Cathedral of Learning,** the **Heinz Chapel,** and the **Stephen Collins Foster Memorial,** in particular. Campus open daily.

CHURCHES/SYNAGOGUES: ⚓ **Heinz Chapel,** University of Pittsburgh campus, S. Bellefield Ave. (624-4157): Modern building in the French Gothic Revival style, with a series of splendid stained-glass windows, each 73 ft (22 m) high. Definitely worth seeing; open Sun.-Fri.

HISTORIC BUILDINGS: ☀ ⚓ **Allegheny County Courthouse,** Grant St. and Fifth Ave.: Remarkable Romanesque Revival building by Henry Hobson Richardson dating from 1888; one of the finest courthouses in the U.S. A sight not to be missed; open Mon.-Fri.

Fort Pitt Blockhouse, Point State Park (471-1764): Last vestige of the original fort built by the British in 1764; it saw some vigorous action during the French and Indian War. Worth a visit; open Tues.-Sun.

MARKETS: ⚓ **Market Square,** Market Place: Picturesque shopping area in the heart of downtown Pittsburgh; many bars, restaurants, and pubs in the vicinity. Very lively.

MONUMENTS: ☀ ⚓ **Point State Park Fountain,** Point State Park: Monumental fountain at the tip of Point State Park at the confluence of the Allegheny and Monongahela Rivers. The computer-controlled fountain, fed by an underground spring, issues in colorful plumes of water rising to 150 ft (45 m); Easter to mid-Nov. A spectacular sight.

MUSEUMS OF ART: ☀ ⚓⚓ **Carnegie Institute Museum of Art,** 4400 Forbes Ave. (622-3270): Lovely museum with an important collection of impressionists and post-impressionists (Sarah Scaife Gallery) alongside classical paintings and sculptures and antique furniture. Among its best-known works: *Virgin and Child with Angel* by Francesco Francia, *Toilette of Venus* by Simon Vouet, *Reefs near Dieppe* by Monet, *The Something-or-Other Circus* by Jean Dewasne, and George Segal's amazing *Tightrope Walker.* Should be visited; open Tues.-Sun.

Frick Art Museum, 7227 Reynolds St. (371-0600): European old masters (Tintoretto, Rubens, Fragonard, Boucher, and others) in an elegant Renaissance-style mansion once the home of the coal-and-steel magnate Henry Clay Frick; also many pieces of furniture that belonged to Marie Antoinette. Must certainly be seen; Wed.-Sun.

MUSEUMS OF SCIENCE AND HISTORY: ⚓ **Allegheny Observatory,** Perrysville Ave., Riverview Park (321-2400): One of the best-known observatories in the U.S., boasting a 30-in. (75-cm) telescope. Open to budding astronomers Wed.-Fri. evenings Apr.-Oct. Reservations a must.

Bessemer Court, Station Square (471-5808): Open-air museum displaying a giant ten-ton Bessemer converter (for converting pig iron into steel), the symbol of Pittsburgh's industrial might. Also antique cars, old railway carriages, and other relics of the golden age of transportation. Worth seeing; open Tues.-Sun.

Buhl Science Center, Allegheny Square (321-4300): Modern, well-designed science museum; temporary exhibitions on different aspects of science, particularly astronomy and computers. Also well-equipped planetarium, laser show, and model railroad much appreciated by the younger set (Nov.-Feb.). Worth a visit; open daily.

Carnegie Institute Museum of Natural History, 4400 Forbes Ave. (622-3313): Best known for its hall of dinosaurs, this very handsome natural history museum also has fine displays of minerals, precious stones, and zoology, as well as a fascinating exhibition devoted to the Arctic world. Not to be missed. Open Tues.-Sun.

Fort Pitt Museum, 101 Commonwealth Pl., Point State Park (281-9284): Interesting military museum on the French and Indian War. This facsimile of a fort occupies the site of the original (1764) Fort Pitt. Military parades in period uniform Sun. in summer. Worth a visit; open Wed.-Fri.

Historical Society of Western Pennsylvania, 4338 Bigelow Blvd. (681-5533): A journey back into 19th-century Pennsylvania, through collections of old furniture, unusual glass bottles, paintings, documents, and other historical items. For lovers of bygone days. Tues.-Sat.

Soldiers and Sailors Memorial Hall and Museum, Fifth Ave. and Bigelow Blvd. (621-4253): Weapons, uniforms, military mementoes, and flags from the country's wars. Should be seen; open daily.

PANORAMAS: Mount Washington: There are two cable cars to the top
of Mount Washington: the **Monongahela Incline** from W. Carson St. near Station Square and the **Duquesne Incline** from W. Carson St. near Fort Pitt Bridge. Fine view of the city and the Golden Triangle with its three rivers; shouldn't be missed.

U.S. Steel Building, 600 Grant St. (471-4100): Fine view of the city from the Top of the Triangle restaurant on the 62nd floor (admission fee). So-so food but congenial bar. Open Mon.-Sat.

PARKS AND GARDENS: Conservatory-Aviary, Ridge Ave. and Arch
St. (322-7855): Wonderful collection of the world's birds, more than 220 species inall,inreconstructionsoftheirnaturalhabitats.Asighttobeseen.Open daily.

Phipps Conservatory, Schenley Park, Schenley Dr.: Lovely tropical greenhouses and flower shows; splendid cactus and orchid gardens. Don't miss it; open daily.

Point State Park, at the west end of Fort Duquesne and Fort Pitt Blvds.: A 36-acre (15-ha.) park on the site of the first settlement, at the confluence of the Monongahela and Allegheny Rivers; panoramic view of the city and Mount Washington. Monumental fountain and traces of old Fort Pitt. Must be seen.

Schenley Park, Schenley Dr.: A stone's throw from the University of Pittsburgh, this 456-acre (185-ha.) park is popular at all times of year; there are several picnic areas, a public golf course, a small lake, several miles of trails, and a skating rink. Cross-country skiing in winter.

PERFORMING ARTS: For daily listings of all shows and cultural events, consult the entertainment pages of the daily papers *Pittsburgh Post-Gazette* (morning) and *Pittsburgh Press* (evening), as well as the monthly *Pittsburgh* magazine.

Benedum Theater for the Performing Arts, 719 Liberty Ave. (456-6666): The old Stanley Theater, entirely renovated in 1987. Home of the Pittsburgh Opera (director, Tito Capobianco), the Civic Light Opera, and the Pittsburgh Ballet Theater. Also Broadway hits.

Fulton Theater, 101 6th St. (471-9700): Classical concerts and recitals.

Heinz Hall, 600 Penn Ave. (281-5000): Home of the Pittsburgh Symphony, under principal conductor Lorin Maazel (Sept.-May). Concerts and recitals by distinguished soloists. Broadway hits.

Kresge Theater, Carnegie-Mellon University campus, Schenley Park (578-2407): Contemporary theater, musicals.

New City Theatre, Bouquet and Sennott Sts. (624-4101): Modern American theater; home of the City Theatre Company (Oct.-Apr.).

Pittsburgh Playhouse Theater Center, 222 Craft Ave. (621-4445): Contemporary and classic theater; children's shows.

Pittsburgh Public Theater, Allegheny Square (321-9800): Comedy, drama; the best of Pittsburgh's many theaters.

Stephen C. Foster Memorial Theater, U. of Pittsburgh campus, Forbes Ave. and Bigelow Blvd. (621-3342): Contemporary and classic theater, concerts; the Three Rivers Shakespeare Festival takes place here every year.

Syria Mosque, Bigelow Blvd. (621-8700): Former home of the Pittsburgh Symphony; contemporary theater, concerts.

SPECIAL EVENTS: For the exact schedule of events below, consult the **Greater Pittsburgh Convention and Visitors Bureau** (see "Tourist Information," above).

Folk Festival (end of May): The food, dance, music, and crafts of the many countries that have contributed to the great ethnic melting pot of Pittsburgh: Ireland, Scotland, Germany, Czechoslovakia, Hungary, Russia, and many more. Held at the David L. Lawrence Convention Center.

Three Rivers Shakespeare Festival (late May to mid-Aug.): Presents three new plays every year at the Stephen C. Foster Memorial Theater.

Three Rivers Art Festival (three weeks in June): Open-air art exhibitions, public concerts, movie festival, plays, etc.

Shadyside Art Festival (early Aug.): Draws artists, craftspeople, and spectators from the whole region.

Three Rivers Regatta (first weekend in Aug.): Very popular boat races (Formula I and rowing).

Jazz Festival (early Sept.): With the biggest names.

SPORTS: Pittsburgh has professional teams in three major sports:

Baseball (Apr.-Oct.): Pirates, Three Rivers Stadium (323-1150).

Football (Aug.-Dec.): Steelers, Three Rivers Stadium (323-1200).

Ice Hockey (Oct.-Apr.): Penguins, Civic Arena (642-1800).

Horse Racing

The Meadows, **Meadowlands,** at exit 8 from I-79 (563-1224), year round.

STROLLS: ⚱ **Bank Center Mall,** Fourth Ave. and Wood St.: Turn-of-the-century houses, charmingly restored, in what was once the heart of Pittsburgh's downtown business district. Fashion shops, stores, movie houses, restaurants. A pleasant place.

☀⚱⚱ **Station Square,** on the south bank of the Monongahela River at the foot of the Smithfield St. Bridge (261-9911): Terminal of the Pittsburgh & Lake Erie Railroad, no longer in use, now the favorite place for strolling, window-shopping, and distractions. Dozens of stalls, bars, and restaurants; lively and colorful day and night.

WINTER SPORTS RESORTS: ⚱ **Boyce Park Ski Area,** 18 mi. (28 km) east via I-376 and Penna. 286 (733-4665): Four lifts; open Dec.-Feb.

ZOOS: ♨ **Pittsburgh Zoo,** Highland Ave., Highland Park (665-3640): More than 2,000 animals in reconstructions of their natural habitat, and a very modern aquarium, in a 65-acre (26-ha.) park. Worth a visit; open daily.

ACCOMMODATIONS

See the listing of toll-free numbers in the Appendix.

Room Rates in Pittsburgh	
B (Budget)	up to $30
I (Inexpensive)	$30–$60
M (Moderate)	$60–$90
E (Expensive)	$90–$140
VE (Very Expensive)	$140 and up

Personal Favorites (in order of preference)

👤👤👤 **Vista International Hotel** (dwntwn), 1000 Penn Ave., PA 15222 (412/281-3700; toll free, see Hilton). 618 rms, A/C, color TV, in-rm movies. AE, CB, DC, MC, V. Valet parking $8, pool, health club, sauna, two rests. (including American Harvest), coffeeshop, bar, 24-hr rm svce, disco, boutiques, free dwntwn limo, free crib. *Note:* Newest of the big dwntwn hotels; large, massive 25-story tower across from the David L. Lawrence Convention Center w. direct access to it. Ultra-comfortable facilities and furnishings; spacious, inviting rms w. mini-bars; efficient svce. Good rest. serving American food; three VIP floors; business and convention clientele. Very well located. **E–VE**

👤👤👤 **Hyatt Pittsburgh** (dwntwn), 112 Washington Pl. at Chatham Center, PA 15219 (412/471-1234; toll free, see Hyatt). 404 rms, A/C, color TV, in-rm movies. AE, CB, DC, MC, V. Garage $6, pool, health club, sauna, rest. (Hugo's Rotisserie), coffeeshop, bars, rm svce, disco, free crib. *Note:* Occupies the top 11 floors of a modern, architecturally unattractive, 20-story office building. The hotel is very comfortable and well equipped, but rms are on the small side. Diligent svce; praiseworthy rest.; VIP suites on the top floor. Business clientele; in the heart of the business district. **E–VE**

👤👤 **Sheraton Hotel at Station Square** (nr. dwntwn), 7 Station Square Dr., PA 15219 (412/261-2000; toll free, see Sheraton). 293 rms, A/C, in-rm movies. AE, CB, DC, MC, V. Free parking, pool, health club, sauna, rest. (River's Edge), coffeeshop, bar, rm svce, disco, hrdrsr, boutiques, free crib. *Note:* Very modern 15-story hotel across the Monongahela River. Impeccable comfort and facilities; futurist seven-story lobby; spacious rms, the best overlooking the river and city. Reasonably efficient svce. In the center of Station Square, w. its dozens of trendy shops and rests. Group and convention clientele. **E**

👤👤 **Bigelow Apartment Hotel** (dwntwn), Bigelow Square, PA 15219 (412/281-5800). 270 suites, A/C, cable color TV. AE, CB, DC, MC, V. Parking $4, health club, rest. (Ruddy Duck), bar, rm svce. *Note:* Modern hotel w. suites only, spacious and comfortable. Excellently located right in the business district. Good svce; acceptable rest. Business clientele; good value. **M–E**

Envoy Inn Pittsburgh West (vic.), 100 Kisow Dr., PA 15205 (412/922-0120; toll free 800/227-7378). 118 rms, A/C, color TV, in-rm movies. AE, CB, DC, MC, V. Free parking, adjoining rest. *Note:* Economical, very acceptable motel; clean, inviting rms. 20 min. from dwntwn via I-279W, I-79N, and Penna. 60; 10 min. from airport; ideal if you're driving. Free a.m. coffee; good value. **B–I**

Motel 6 Pittsburgh (nr. dwntwn), 211 Beecham Dr., PA 15205 (412/922-9400). 125 rms, A/C, color TV, in-rm movies. DC, MC, V. Free parking, pool. *Note:* Brand-new motel offering unbeatable value 15 min. from dwntwn. Serviceable comfort; ideal for the budget traveler. **B**

Other Accommodations (from top bracket to budget)

Hilton Pittsburgh and Towers (dwntwn), Commonwealth Pl. in Gateway Center, PA 15222 (412/391-4600; toll free, see Hilton). 752 rms, A/C, color TV, in-rm movies. AE, CB, DC, MC, V. Valet garage $6, health club, sauna, two rests. (including Sterling's), two bars, rm svce, nightclub, hrdrsr, drugstore, free crib, concierge. *Note:* Recently renovated massive modern building w. the best view in Pittsburgh, from the point where the three rivers come together; ask for a room overlooking Point State Park. Comfortable but constricted rms; VIP suites on three top floors; efficient svce. Business and convention clientele. **E–VE**

Westin William Penn (dwntwn), 530 William Penn Pl., PA 15219 (412/281-7100; toll free, see Westin). 595 rms, A/C, color TV, in-rm movies. AE, CB, DC, MC, V. Garage $8, two rests. (including the Terrace Room), bar, 24-hr rm svce, nightclub, free crib, concierge. *Note:* Since 1906 many distinguished American personalities, including presidents, have seen the crystal chandeliers, the gilt, and the wood paneling in this revered local institution. The plush Edwardian décor is currently undergoing renovation. Huge, luxuriously comfortable rms; very good svce; big business and VIP clientele. The building is a designated historic landmark. **E–VE**

Marriott Pittsburgh Greentree (nr. dwntwn), 101 Marriott Dr., PA 15205 (412/922-8400; toll free, see Marriott). 480 rms, A/C, color TV, in-rm movies. AE, CB, DC, MC, V. Free parking, two pools, health club, sauna, two tennis courts, rest. (Ashley's), coffeeshop, two bars, rm svce, disco, hrdrsr, free airport limo, free crib. *Note:* Large, modern, functional convention hotel 10 min. from dwntwn on I-279. Spacious, well-soundproofed rms, agreeable décor and setting. Rest. satisfactory but no more; efficient svce. Group and business clientele. 15 min. from airport. **E**

Best Western–Parkway Center Inn (nr. dwntwn), 875 Greentree Rd., PA 15220 (412/922-7070; toll free, see Best Western). 151 rms, A/C, color TV, in-rm movies. AE, CB, DC, MC, V. Free parking, pool, health club, sauna, rest., bar, valet svce, hrdrsr, free airport limo, free breakfast. *Note:* Excellently run motel; agreeable rms, some w. kitchenettes and refrigerators. For a motel, very comprehensive facilities. 10 min. from dwntwn on I-279; ideal if you're driving. **M–E**

Holiday Inn–Allegheny Valley (vic.), 180 Gamma Dr., PA 15238 (412/963-0600; toll free, see Holiday Inns). 184 rms, A/C, color TV, in-rm movies. AE, CB, DC, MC, V. Free parking, pool, coffeeshop, bar, rm svce. *Note:* Typical functional motel, 20 min. from dwntwn on Penna. 28. Spacious rms. The Holiday Inn style. Group clientele. Ideal if you're driving. **M**

Howard Johnson Lodge–South (vic.), 5300 Clairton Blvd., PA 15236 (412/884-6000; toll free, see Howard Johnson's). 94 rms, A/C, color TV. AE, CB, DC, MC, V. Free parking, pool, adjoining coffeeshop, bar, rm svce, free breakfast. *Note:* Older but comfortable motel nr. Allegheny County Airport. Spacious, inviting rms; cheerful svce; good value. 15 min. from dwntwn on Penna. 51; ideal if you're driving. **I–M**

    Redwood Inn (vic.), 2898 Banksville Rd., PA 15216 (412/ 343-3000). 95 rms, A/C, color TV, in-rm. movies. AE, CB, DC, MC, V. Free parking, pool, coffeeshop, bar, rm svce, disco, free crib. *Note:* Conventional motel but w. huge, comfortable rms and friendly reception and svce. Very good overall value. 10 min. from dwntwn on I-279 and U.S. 19; ideal if you have a car. **I**

    Knights Inn–Pittsburgh (vic.), 4800 Steubenville Pike, PA 15205 (412/922-6900). 110 rms, A/C, color TV, in-rm movies. AE, CB, DC, MC, V. Free parking, pool, adjoining 24-hr coffeeshop, crib $2. *Note:* Good value 15 min. from dwntwn on Penna. 60. Very acceptable standards of comfort; some rms w. kitchenettes and refrigerators. Worthwhile reductions for long-term stays. Ideal if you're driving. **I**

Airport Accommodations

    Ramada Inn Airport (vic.), 1412 Beers School Rd., Coraopolis, PA 15108 (412/264-8950; toll free, see Ramada Inns). 135 rms, A/C, color TV, in-rm movies. AE, CB, DC, MC, V. Free parking, pool, rest. (Myron's), bar, rm svce, disco, free crib. *Note:* Inviting, comfortable six-floor motel a quarter mile (400 m) from the airport (free shuttle). Spacious, well-soundproofed rms; efficient svce. Business clientele. Perfect for a stopover between flights. **M**

YMCA/Youth Hostels

    Point Park College Youth Hostel (dwntwn), 201 Wood St., PA 15222 (412/392-3824 or 391-4100). 100 beds. Coffeeshop. Youth hostel open year round.

RESTAURANTS

Pittsburgh Restaurant Prices	
(per person, excluding drinks and service charges)	
B (Budget)	up to $15
I (Inexpensive)	$15–$25
M (Moderate)	$25–$40
E (Expensive)	$40–$60
VE (Very Expensive)	$60 and up

Personal Favorites (in order of preference)

    La Normande (nr. dwntwn), 4415 Fifth Ave. (621-0744). A/C. Lunch Fri. only, dinner Mon.-Sat.; closed Sun., holidays, and last two weeks in Aug. AE, CB, DC, MC, V. J&T. *Specialties:* truffle soup, fresh foie gras vinaigrette, duck cutlet, lobster w. caviar butter, Dover sole, mignons of veal w. tarragon, noisette of lamb w. spinach in pastry shell, game in season, delicious sherbets and pastries. Large wine list w. more than 400 labels. *Note:* Since 1983, all the local press surveys have placed La Normande highest among Pittsburgh's rests. for the quality of its food, its svce, and the elegance of its appointments. The cuisine is a happy blend of traditional and innovative, and the svce is exemplary, though the atmosphere is a little too stiff. Resv. a must, particularly on wknds. Valet parking. 20 min. from dwntwn. *French.* **E**

🍷🍷🍷 **The Colony** (vic.), Greentree and Cochran Rds. (561-2060). A/C. Dinner only, Mon.-Sat.; closed Sun. and holidays. AE, DC, MC, V. Jkt. *Specialties:* lump crabmeat, scampi, steak, filet mignon, veal chop, broiled swordfish. Good desserts; rather weak wine list. *Note:* A fine example of a rest. seriously, carefully devoted to American food. The menu is voluntarily limited to a dozen (remarkable) meat and (impeccably fresh) fish dishes. The décor and atmosphere are those of a luxurious country club, w. an open grill in the center of the rm; the svce is in all respects flawless. Clientele of business people and local VIPs. A Pittsburgh landmark since 1960; resv. advisable during the week, indispensable on wknds. Valet parking. 20 min. from dwntwn. *Steak-American.* **M–E**

🌣🍷🍷 **Grand Concourse** (nr. dwntwn), 1 Station Square (261-1717). A/C. Lunch Mon.-Fri., dinner nightly, brunch Sun.; closed Thanksgiving, Dec. 25. AE, CB, DC, MC, V. *Specialties:* oysters, fresh homemade pasta, broiled fish, shellfish, paella, rack of lamb. *Note:* One of the most unusual rest. settings in the country, in a turn-of-the-century railroad station. The enormous rest., in its wonderful rococo space with soaring vaults and stained-glass windows, specializes in the freshest possible seafood. Lively, congenial atmosphere; ask to be seated in the River Room, at a table w. a river view. Efficient, diligent svce. Locally popular, and a must for the visitor. In spite of its size, you'd be well advised to reserve ahead. *Seafood-American.* **I–M**

🍷🍷 **Papillon** (nr. dwntwn), 1910 Cochran Rd. (343-1000). A/C. Lunch/dinner Tues.-Sun.; closed Mon., Thanksgiving, Dec. 25. AE, CB, DC, MC, V. Jkt. *Specialties:* Sauteed rainbow trout w. pecan butter sauce, filet mignon w. wine sauce, tempting homemade desserts. *Note:* One of the city's best new restaurants. Memorable nouvelle cuisine, including first-rate seafood dishes, in casual elegance. Fine service and a selection of good wines to complement the excellence of the cuisine. Live jazz is featured Wed.-Sat. Locally popular. Resv. required. *French-American.* **I–M**

🌣🍷 **Klein's** (dwntwn), 330 Fourth Ave. (232-3311). A/C. Lunch Mon.-Fri., dinner Mon.-Sat.; closed Sun. and holidays. AE, CB, DC, MC, V. *Specialties:* crab Imperial, blackened redfish, clambake, bouillabaisse, broiled fish, Maine lobster. *Note:* Since it opened in 1900, this has been the favored resort of local seafood lovers. Everything's absolutely fresh and reasonably priced, though sometimes a little overcooked. Charmingly old-fashioned seafaring décor contemporary w. the establishment; diligent svce in a relaxed atmosphere. A real local landmark in the heart of dwntwn. Resv. advised. A very good place. *Seafood.* **I**

🍷 **Samreny's** (nr. dwntwn), 4808 Baum Blvd. (682-1212). A/C. Lunch/dinner Tues.-Sun. (until 1 a.m.); closed Mon. and holidays. No credit cards. *Specialties:* stuffed vine leaves, tabouleh, shish kebab, stuffed cabbage, kibbee nayaa (rice with pine nuts), baklava, Oriental pastries. *Note:* The best and most popular of Pittsburgh's many Middle Eastern rests.; while the décor verges on the tawdry, the food is authentic Lebanese and the prices are low. Prompt, friendly svce. Locally popular for more than 30 years. 20 min. from dwntwn. *Middle Eastern.* **B–I**

Other Restaurants (from top bracket to budget)

🍷🍷 **Carlton Restaurant** (dwntwn), 1 Mellon Bank Center at Grant St. (391-4099). A/C. Lunch Mon.-Fri., dinner Mon.-

Sat.; closed Sun and holidays. AE, CB, DC, MC, V. Jkt. *Specialties:* Charcoal-grilled prime meats and fresh seafood, Cajun dishes, own pastries. *Note:* A favorite with business people. Voted best steaks in Pittsburgh by readers of *Pittsburgh Magazine.* Tables are somewhat close together and the place can get noisy. Service attentive and discreet. Always crowded. Resv. strongly suggested. *American-Continental.* **M**

The Common Plea (dwntwn), 308 Ross St. (281-5140). A/C. Lunch Mon.-Fri., dinner nightly; closed holidays. AE, CB, DC, MC, V. Jkt. *Specialties:* scallops and shrimp Norfolk, bouillabaisse, roulade of veal w. crabmeat, broiled seafood platter, good homemade desserts. Menu changes regularly. *Note:* For more than 15 years this little rest., a stone's throw from the City Council Building and the Court House, has been the lunchtime favorite of local politicians and lawyers. The food is generally excellent, and emphasizes seafood. Very good svce; resv advised, a must at lunch. Ask to be seated upstairs. *Continental.* **I–M**

Le Pommier (nr. dwntwn), 2104 E. Carson St. (431-1901). A/C. Dinner only, Tues.-Sat.; closed Sun. and Mon. AE, MC, V. Jkt. *Specialties:* salmon cooked in foil, escalope of veal w. morel mushrooms, breast of chicken stuffed w. goat cheese, chocolate mousse and Grand Marnier cake. Menu changes regularly. *Note:* Remarkable food, inspired by modern French originals, in a prettily converted shop more than a century old. Elegant countrified décor; attentive, efficient svce; an excellent place to eat. Resv. a must; 15 min. from dwntwn. *French-American.* **I–M**

Louis Tambellini's (nr. dwntwn), 860 Saw Mill Run Blvd. (481-1118). A/C. Lunch/dinner Mon.-Sat. (until midnight); closed Sun. and holidays. AE, MC, V. Jkt. *Specialties:* homemade pasta and gnocchi, baked scampi, poached salmon w. vegetables, sautéed sole w. herbs, rack of lamb, steak, Italian dishes, caffè espresso. *Note:* In spite of its strong Italian overtones, the cuisine of the Tambellini family gives precedence to seafood—broiled, poached, or baked. Remarkable fish and shellfish. Very elegant modern décor; diligent, unfussy svce. Big enough that resv. are not needed. Valet parking; 15 min. from dwntwn. *Italian-seafood.* **I–M**

Jimmy Tsang's (nr. dwntwn), 5700 Centre Ave. (661-4226). A/C. Lunch Mon.-Sat., dinner nightly. AE, CB, DC, MC, V. Jkt. *Specialties:* honeyed shrimp, E. Show chicken, Peking duck, sweet-and-sour pork. Cantonese, Mandarin, and Szechuan dishes. *Note:* While the cuisine of chef-owner Jimmy Tsang (he's Korean, not Chinese) may appear somewhat "Americanized" to purists, this is still far and away the best Far Eastern rest. in Pittsburgh—one of the few major American cities without a Chinatown. Pretty Oriental décor; efficient if abrupt svce; noisy ambience. Resv. a must. *Chinese.* **I**

Froggy's (dwntwn), 100 Market St. (471-3764). A/C. Lunch Mon.-Fri., dinner Mon.-Sat.; closed Sun. and holidays. AE, MC, V. *Specialties:* sandwiches, salads, hamburgers, steaks. *Note:* In the Firstside, the old warehouse district along the Monongahela, this granddaddy of local singles bars is alleged to serve the best drinks in all of dwntwn, as well as excellent steaks and hamburgers. Draws yuppies and sports fans, particularly when there's a game at the nearby Three Rivers Stadium. A likeable, relaxed place. *American.* **B–I**

Max's Allegheny Tavern (nr. dwntwn), 537 Suismon St. (231-1899). A/C. Lunch/dinner daily, brunch Sun. AE, CB, DC, MC, V. *Specialties:* sauerbraten, würst platte (sausage plate), wienerschnitzel, weisswurst, apfelstrudel. Draft beer. *Note:* This picturesque turn-of-the-century tavern is one of the oldest on the Northside, a neighborhood across the Allegheny. Authentically German food and atmosphere at very attractive prices.

Pretty turn-of-the-century-type décor with Tiffany-style lamps, ceiling fans, tile floors, and superb bar in massive walnut. Noisy but congenial; locally popular. Resv. for parties of five or more only, so you'll have to wait. *German.* **B–I**

♀ **Tequila Junction** (nr. dwntwn), The Shops at Station Square (261-3265). A/C. Lunch/dinner daily. AE, CB, DC, MC, V. *Specialties:* crabmeat enchiladas, chili Colorado, tamales, burritos. *Note:* Charming Mexican-inn décor in brick and adobe; good, unpretentious food; svce more friendly than efficient. Locally popular; no resv. *Mexican.* **B–I**

Restaurants in the Vicinity

♕♕ **Hyeholde** (vic.), 190 Hyeholde Dr., Coraopolis (264-3116). A/C. Lunch Mon.-Fri., dinner Mon.-Sat.; closed Sun. and holidays. AE, CB, DC, MC, V. Jkt. *Specialties:* rack of lamb persillade, apple-stuffed breast of chicken w. sauce velouté, baked Virginia spots (a local fish; in season), squab w. champagne, filet mignon, Hyeholde trifle. Very fine wine list. *Note:* Very nr. the airport, this unexpected English Tudor manor house, w. exposed beams, open fireplaces, and wall hangings, serves very commendable classic *grande cuisine*—and charges prices to match. Dinner by candlelight and romantic atmosphere. Pretty gardens; attentive svce; resv. advised. Valet parking. *Continental.* **M–E**

Cafeteria / Fast Food

Applebee's (dwntwn), 411 Smithfield St. (261-2277). Lunch/dinner Mon.-Sat.; closed Sun. No credit cards. Excellent sandwiches, salads, roast beef, cookies, and home-baked pies; perfect for a meal on the run. An old standby of its kind.

Original Hot Dogs Shop (nr. dwntwn), 3901 Forbes Ave. (621-7388). Lunch/dinner daily; no credit cards. The "Big O," as the students at the nearby University of Pittsburgh fondly call it, is generally held to serve the best hot dogs in town.

BARS & NIGHTCLUBS

Froggy's (dwntwn), 100 Market St. (471-3764). The granddaddy of local singles bars; excellent drinks in a warm atmosphere; also a restaurant serving laudable meat dishes (see "Restaurants," above). Open Mon.-Sat.

Gandy Dancer Saloon (nr. dwntwn), 1 Station Square (261-1717). Congenial piano bar adjoining the Grand Concourse (see "Restaurants," above). Live music; oyster bar. Open nightly.

Graffiti (nr. dwntwn), 4615 Baum Blvd. (682-4210). This nightclub presents a wide-ranging variety of music: jazz, folk, rock, classical. Youthful clientele and atmosphere. Wed.-Sat.

Hemingway's (nr. dwntwn), 3911 Forbes Ave. in Oakland (621-4100). One of the best-known jazz spots in town. Open nightly.

Tramp's (dwntwn), 212 Blvd. of the Allies (261-1990). Another very popular singles bar in what used to be a flourishing brothel. Amusing ambience.

NEARBY EXCURSIONS

☼☖♨ **AMBRIDGE** (18 mi., 28 km, NW on Penna. 65): **Old Economy Village** is the former community of the Utopian Christian "Harmony Society," founded around 1825 by a pastor of German origin, George Rapp. Many buildings of the period: communal kitchens, festival hall, workshops, church, granary, cellar, etc., with their original furniture. The community, which practiced celibacy and community property, survived until its dissolution in 1905. A fascinating visit. Open Tues.-Sun.

FALLINGWATER (at Mill Run, 70 mi., 112 km, SE via Penna. 51S, U.S. 40E, and Penna. 381N) (329-8501): With its terraces cantilevered out over Bear Run, this "house over the waterfall," dating from 1936, is one of the most celebrated achievements of Frank Lloyd Wright, the man who can almost be said to have invented the contemporary private house. Open Tues.-Sun., mid-Apr. to mid-Nov.; reservations advised. Well worth the detour; best combined with a visit to Fort Necessity (see below).

FORT NECESSITY NATIONAL BATTLEFIELD (58 mi., 93 km, SE via Penna. 51S and U.S. 40E) (329-5512): Site of the first major battle fought by George Washington, at the time a colonel in the British army, against the French and their Indian allies on July 3, 1754. The engagement, which resulted in a British defeat, marked the official beginning of the French and Indian War. Replica of the fort originally built by Washington, museum, early-19th-century tavern. Open daily; best visited in combination with Fallingwater (see above).

HARTWOOD ACRES (215 Saxonburg Blvd., 12 mi., 19 km, North via Penna. 8 and Saxonburg Blvd.) (767-9200): Faithful reproduction of a great English country house, with Gothic Tudor buildings, antique furniture, formal gardens, stud farm, etc. Worth going out of your way for. Open Tues.-Sun.

PRABHUPADA'S PALACE OF GOLD (near Wheeling, W. Va., 72 mi., 115 km, SW via I-79S, I-70W, W. Va. 88, U.S. 250S, and Limestone Hill Rd.) (304/843-1600): Sumptuous palace in the Indian style built by Hare Krishna devotees as a sanctuary dedicated to their spiritual director Srila Prabhupada. More than 8,000 sq. ft (740 m²) of 22-karat gold leaf was used in its construction, as well as 52 different kinds of marble, carved teakwood furniture, and crystal chandeliers imported from Austria. Fine gardens with rose gardens, fountains, and original sculptures. Restaurant. Definitely worth visiting; open daily.

PITHOLE CITY (102 mi., 163 km, north via I-79, U.S. 62E, and Penna. 227N) (814/589-7912): The drilling, on August 27, 1859, of the first U.S. oil well on the banks of Oil Creek, 4 mi. (6 km) west, made the fortune of Pithole—for a short while. In five months of the year 1865 its population rose from 15 to 10,000, but in 1867 its prosperity vanished as abruptly as it had come. The first boom town created by "black gold" is now totally abandoned, and only a few vestiges remain of its extraordinary past. Visitor Center open Tues.-Sun, Memorial Day to Labor Day. Should be seen.

TOUR-ED MINE (Red Belt West at Tarentum, 20 mi., 32 km, NW on Penna. 28) (224-4720): Former underground coal mine, first worked in the 1780s. Visit to the original plant and buildings. Interesting mining museum. Open daily, May to Labor Day.

CHAPTER 8

BALTIMORE

□ □ □

Hub of the 17th-century tobacco trade, Baltimore, like Boston and New York, is one of the continent's oldest regional centers. It is also one of the birthplaces of religious tolerance in America: the Royal Charter of 1649 expressly granted freedom of worship to the colony of Maryland, created 17 years earlier by a decree of King Charles I. Tucked away at the head of the huge Chesapeake Bay (187 mi., 300 km, long), Baltimore, named in honor of the first British "proprietor" of the colony, Cecilius Calvert, 2nd Baron Baltimore, has always been a bustling commercial crossroads between the East Coast and the South. Point of origin of the country's first railroad line (1827)—the legendary Baltimore & Ohio—Maryland's biggest city is still the principal Atlantic outlet for midwestern grain and Appalachian coal.

Port city and home to industry and business, Baltimore is also a bastion of culture: some of the people associated with the city are Edgar Allan Poe, who died here in 1849 in still-mysterious circumstances; Francis Scott Key, who wrote "The Star-Spangled Banner" here (1814); critic Henry L. Mencken (1880–1956); author Leon Uris, born here in 1924; and John Dos Passos, who died here in 1970. Baltimore is famous for its five universities—**Johns Hopkins** is one, with its prestigious medical center—an internationally known symphony orchestra, and an architectural heritage too often ignored by tourists. The city is an attractive blend of tradition and vitality: the glass-and-steel skyscrapers of **Charles Center** and the patrician homes of **Mount Vernon Place** rubbing shoulders with the picturesque row houses and cobblestone alleyways of **Fell's Point** and **Otterbein Homesteading;** the imposing Victorian architecture of **City Hall;** the delicate grace of the **Walters Art Gallery;** and the United States' oldest Catholic cathedral, the **Basilica of the Assumption** (1821), miraculously spared by the 1904 fire that destroyed much of the historic section. **Fort McHenry,** built in 1794–1805 with star-shaped fortifications characteristic of the period, and tenaciously held against the British during the War of 1812, attracts close to a million visitors each year. The new port area, the **Inner Harbor,** is one of the finest examples of urban renewal in the United States, with many lively and colorful boutiques, stores, and crowded seafood restaurants (Chesapeake Bay blue crabs and oysters are justly famous). This area alone is worth the trip to Baltimore. Other areas worth a look are the old ethnic neighborhoods: **Little Italy** (around High and Pratt Sts., Central and Eastern Aves.); **Greektown** (Eastern Ave. from nos. 3500 to 4800); **Little Lithuania** (Hollins and Carrollton Sts.); the Polish and Ukrainian neighborhoods of **Highlandtown** (around Patterson Park); and the old Jewish quarter, nicknamed **Corned Beef Row** because of a multitude of deli restaurants (Lombard St. around Lloyd St. and Central Ave.).

Some of Baltimore's famous native children are: Billie Holiday, the great jazz singer; drummer Chick Webb; jazz musician Eubie Blake; Wallis Warfield Simpson, who married Edward VIII of England (1937) and became the Duchess of Windsor; and the legendary Babe Ruth, known to baseball fans as the "Sultan of Swat."

BASIC FACTS: State of Maryland. Area Code: 301. Time Zone: Eastern

Time. ZIP Code (of central post office): 21233. Settled: 1661. Founded: 1729. Approximate population: city, 790,000; metropolitan area, 2,270,000. 17th largest U.S. metropolitan area.

CLIMATE: As in all the Northeast Corridor cities, the winter is cold (mean Jan. temperature, 37°F, 3°C), but with less snow than in Boston or New York. Summer is hot and humid with sudden downpours due to the proximity of Chesapeake Bay (mean July temperature, 79°F, 26°C). Autumn is rainy, and an umbrella is a must in Sept./Oct. The best season to visit Baltimore is spring which, although windy, is almost always pleasant.

DISTANCES: New York, 200 mi. (320 km); Philadelphia, 93 mi. (150 km); Pittsburgh, 218 mi. (350 km); Washington, 40 mi. (65 km).

ARRIVAL & TRANSIT INFORMATION

AIRPORT: Baltimore-Washington International Airport (BWI): 10 mi. (16 km) south of Baltimore, 32 mi. (51 km) north of Washington. Information: 859-7111.

AIRLINES: American (850-5800); Delta (768-9000); Eastern (768-3100); Northwest (821-0994); TWA (338-1156); United (850-4557); USAir (727-0825).

CITY LINK: Cab fare to city center about $15; time, 20 min. Cab fare to dwntwn Washington from BWI, $36–$40; time, 45 min. Bus: Airport Connection (859-3000); leaves every 30 min.; stops at the major dwntwn hotels; fare, $7; time, 25 min. Also stops at 16th St. NW and K St. in dwntwn Washington: fare, $10; time, 50 min.; leaves every 45 min. The proximity of the airport and the compact layout of downtown Baltimore may make car rental superfluous. Good public transportation system (MTA)—subway, bus, and tramway.

CAR RENTAL (all at the airport): Avis (859-1680); Budget (859-0850); Dollar (859-8950); Hertz (859-3600); National (859-8860). For dwntwn locations, consult the local telephone book.

LIMOUSINE SERVICES: Carey Limousine (233-7400); Chesapeake Limousine (366-3000).

TAXIS: Taxis can be hailed on the street or summoned by telephone. The major companies are Diamond Cab (947-3333) and Yellow Cab (685-1212). Baltimore cab fares are among the lowest in the nation.

TRAIN: AMTRAK, Pennsylvania Station, 1515 N. Charles St. (539-2112).

BUS: Greyhound, 210 W. Fayette St. (752-1393).

INFORMATION & TOURS

TOURIST INFORMATION: Baltimore Office of Promotion & Tourism, 34 Market Place, Suite 310, MD 21202 (301/752-8632).
  Visitor Center, Pratt St. & Pier 4 (301/837-4636).
  Recorded telephone message giving an up-to-date listing of cultural events and shows: 301/837-4636).

GUIDED TOURS: *Baltimore Patriot* (boat), Inner Harbor (685-4288). Harbor cruise, mid-Apr. to mid-Oct.

Clipper Cruise Line (boat). Information: 7711 Bonhomme Ave., St. Louis, MO 63105 (toll free 800/325-0010). Has 7-, 10-, and 14-day luxury yacht cruises (100 berths) along the Atlantic coast from Boston or Baltimore to Fort Lauderdale and the Virgin Islands.

Gray Line Tours (bus) (301/962-1611). Guided tour of the city. Leaves from major hotels.

Insomniac Tours (bus), 3414 Philips Dr. (301/653-2998). An original and highly successful idea, this guided tour of Baltimore for night owls leaves at 1:30 a.m. and returns at dawn, with dinner included. Reservations a must.

Port Welcome (boat), W. Bulkhead at Light St. (301/727-3113). Cruises along Chesapeake Bay to Annapolis (end of May to Sept.).

SIGHTS, ATTRACTIONS, & ACTIVITIES

ARCHITECTURAL HIGHLIGHTS: ☼ ⚐ **Charles Center,** Market Place and Liberty St.: New business district begun in the early 1960s. Among the 15 commercial and residential skyscrapers are the very handsome **One Charles Center,** 24 floors of bronze-colored glass, by Mies van der Rohe; and the 13,000-seat **Civic Center.** Fountains and modern sculptures (see "Outdoor Art and Plazas," below). Worth a glance.

⚐ **Social Security Headquarters,** 6401 Security Blvd.: Here 240 million social security files are available for reference in these immense archives, housed in the country's largest administrative building after the Pentagon. Computer enthusiasts will want to visit the impressive complex. Worth a look. Open Mon.-Fri.

⚐ **World Trade Center,** Pratt St. at Inner Harbor (837-4515): I. M. Pei's innovative pentagonal 30-story building. The observation platform on the 27th floor offers an unobstructed view of the city and the port (see "Panoramas," below).

CHURCHES/SYNAGOGUES: ☼ ⚐ **Basilica of the Assumption,** Cathedral and Mulberry Sts. (727-2564): Be sure to see the United States' oldest Catholic cathedral (1821), of interesting classical revival architecture. Visits by appointment.

HISTORIC BUILDINGS: ⚐ **Asbury House,** 10 E. Mt. Vernon Pl. (685-5290): Luxurious private residence dating from the 1850s, with decorative balconies and wrought-iron fences. Very lovely interior décor with a startling three-story spiral staircase. See it. Open Mon.-Fri.

⚐ **City Hall,** 100 N. Holiday St. (837-5424): Baltimore's City Hall is one of the finest examples of Victorian architecture in the United States (1875) and was entirely restored in 1975. Imposing dome, 252 ft (77m) high. Visits by appointment, Mon.-Sat.

☼⚐ **Edgar Allan Poe House,** 203 N. Amity St. (396-7932): The last residence of the famous writer who died in 1849 in still-mysterious circumstances. Open Wed.-Sat. His grave is close by, at **Westminster Presbyterian Church Yard,** Fayette and Greene Sts. (525-1274). A group of admirers leads a graveside ceremony each Oct. 7 at midnight to commemorate the anniversary of his death. Worth making the trip.

⚐⚐ **Fort McHenry,** Fort Ave. (962-4290): Splendidly restored early-19th-century fortress at the entrance to the harbor. When, from the English warship on which he was held prisoner, Francis Scott

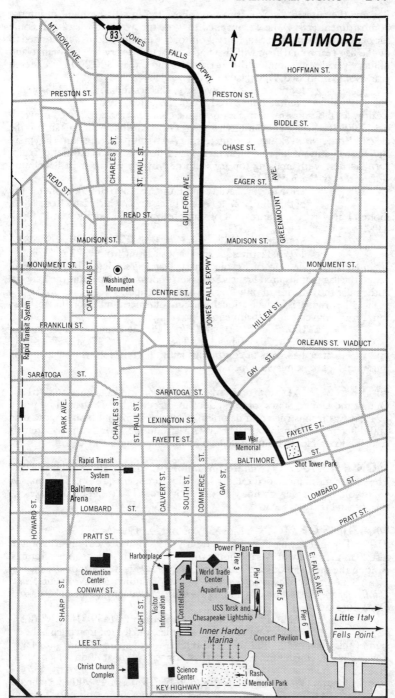

Key saw the tattered flag still streaming above the fort after a night of intense bombardment (1814), he was inspired to write the words to what has become the national anthem. Fort McHenry is one of five public buildings authorized to fly the flag year round. You will also find a museum, a very fine panorama, and military parades in summer; the fort attracts more than 800,000 visitors each year. Not to be missed. Open daily.

      ⚱ **Johns Hopkins University,** Charles and 34th Sts. (338-8000): Founded in 1876 through the generosity of Johns Hopkins, a wealthy local businessman, this is one of the country's most respected universities (3,000 students). The campus has many Georgian-style buildings such as the elegant **Homewood House,** the interesting **Archeological Museum** (Egyptian and Roman antiquities; open Mon.-Fri.), and the very original **Bufano Sculpture Garden,** with amusing topiary sculptures by the Italian artist Beniamino Bufano. See it. Open daily.

      ⚱ **Shot Tower,** Fayette and Front Sts. (396-5894): From the top of this slim, 227-ft (70-m) brick tower which dates from 1828, molten lead was poured into a vat of water below to make cannon balls. Open daily.

      ⚱ **Star-Spangled Banner Flag House,** 844 E. Pratt St. (837-1793): Picturesque small house dating from 1773 and home to an interesting collection of Revolutionary War relics. Here Mary Pickersgill sewed the flag that inspired Francis Scott Key's poem which became the national anthem; at the time it had only 15 stars and 15 stripes. The flag on display is a replica; the original is in the National Museum of American History in Washington. Period souvenirs and documents. Open daily.

      ⚱ **U.S. Frigate *Constellation*,** Pier 1, Pratt St., Inner Harbor (539-1797): The oldest U.S. warship (1797) still afloat. Laid up in 1945 after 148 years of continuous faithful service, she is now a floating museum. Not to be missed. Open daily.

MARKETS: ☀ ⛩ **Lexington Market,** Lexington and Eutaw Sts. (685-6170): One of the United States' oldest indoor markets (1782). Destroyed by fire in 1949, it was reconstructed in its original form in 1952 and houses more than 160 different food businesses. The city's gastronomic pride, with its extremely colorful décor. Not to be missed. Open Mon.-Sat.

MONUMENTS: ⚱ **Washington Monument,** Charles and Monument Sts.: The oldest monument dedicated to our first president (1842). This massive white column offers a very fine view of the city from 172 ft (54 m) up (no elevator). Open Fri.-Tues. See it.

MUSEUMS OF ART: ⛩⛩ **Museum of Art,** N. Charles and 31st Sts. (396-7100): This interesting museum, currently (1988) undergoing restoration, is just 20 min. from dwntwn. and houses many beautiful paintings and sculptures. Among the most famous are Titian's *Man with a Fur;* Rembrandt's *Portrait of Titus;* Renoir's *The Washerwomen;* 43 Matisses, including *Blue Nude* and *Seated Odalisque;* and 16 Picassos, including *Portrait of Allan Stein.* Not to be missed. Open Tues.-Sun.

      ☀⚱ **Peabody Institute,** E. Mt. Vernon Pl. (659-8100): With six-story atrium, interior balconies, and forged-iron pillars, the design of this library (300,000 volumes) is itself worth a visit. Also home of a renowned music conservatory, offering free concerts Wed. at noon. Open Mon.-Fri.

      ☀⛩ **Walters Art Gallery,** 600 N. Charles (547-9000): Archeology, old masters, jewelry, weapons from antiquity to modern times, and a very rich collection of Armenian manuscripts in the elegant Italian Renaissance–style home of philanthropist William T. Walters, and in the new wing opened in 1974. One of the country's best art museums, some of its most famous exhibits including Giovanni di Paolo's *Carrying of the Cross,* Raphael's *Madonna of the Candelabra,* Orcagna's *Crucifixion,* Corot's *Very Early Spring,* and Manet's *At the Café-Concert.* A definite must-see. Open daily.

MUSEUMS OF SCIENCE AND HISTORY: ☼ ▲▲ Babe Ruth Museum,
216 Emory St. (727-1539): The house in which the most famous baseball player of all time was born (1895) is now a museum devoted to the man known as the "Sultan of Swat." Open Wed.-Sun.

▲▲ **B & O Railroad Museum,** Mount Clare Station, Pratt and Poppleton Sts. (237-2387): The world's biggest collection of old locomotives in a Baltimore & Ohio Railroad station that is the oldest in the United States (1830). A visit not to be missed. Wed.-Sun. (In this same station, in 1844 Samuel Morse inaugurated the telegraph system that bears his name, transmitting from Washington the famous message: "What hath God wrought.")

▲ **Maryland Science Center,** 601 Light St. (685-2370): Unusual assembly of octagonal structures housing an ultra-sophisticated planetarium **(Davis Planetarium)** which reproduces a space voyage as well as various exhibits on the evolution of science and a giant model of a human cell. Fascinating. Tue.-Sun.

☼ ▲▲ **National Aquarium,** Pier 3, Pratt St., Inner Harbor (576-3810): One of the East Coast's most modern and spectacular aquariums. Futurist architecture in the form of a glass pyramid. 8,000 specimens of 600 different species, including a pair of very rare white (beluga) whales. Also, a shark tank and facsimilies of natural habitats. Attracts more than a million and a half visitors each year. An absolute must-see. Open daily.

▲ **Peale Museum,** 225 Holiday St. (396-1149): One of the United States' oldest museums (1814). Once the City Hall, it covers the history of Baltimore from the earliest settlement to the present. Interesting. Tue.-Sun.

OUTDOOR ART & PLAZAS: Charles Center, Market Place and Liberty
St.: This ultramodern architectural ensemble boasts numerous fountains, esplanades (among them, **Center Plaza,** which recalls Siena's famous Piazza del Campo), and sculpture (notably a 32-ft, 10-m, bronze flame by Francesco Somaini). Open-air concerts in summer.

PANORAMAS: Federal Hill Park: See "Parks & Gardens," below.
▲▲ **Top of the World,** Pratt St. (837-4515): Observation platform on the 27th floor of the **World Trade Center** (see "Architectural Highlights," above). The best panoramic view of the city and the harbor. Open daily.

Washington Monument: See "Monuments," above.

PARKS & GARDENS: ▲ Cylburn Arboretum, 4915 Greenspring Ave.: 168-
acre (70-ha.) landscaped park, 20 min. from dwntwn via the Jones Falls Expwy. A favorite of nature lovers, with its numerous trails and its countless varieties of plants. Open daily. The botanical museum **(Cylburn Mansion)** is open Mon.-Fri.

▲ **Druid Hill Park,** Druid Park Lake Dr.: Dating from the 1850s, this lovely urban park is home to a very substantial zoo (more than 1,000 animals), flower displays **(Conservatory),** lakes, groves, playing fields, and picnic grounds, all ten min. from dwntwn. via Jones Falls Expwy.

Federal Hill Park, Warren and Battery Aves.: Gardens at the southern end of the Inner Harbor affording a very fine view of the city and the harbor.

PERFORMING ARTS: For daily listings of all shows and cultural events, consult the entertainment pages of the daily papers: *Baltimore Sun* (morning) and *Baltimore Evening Sun* (evening); and of the monthly magazine *Baltimore*.

Arena Players, 801 McCulloh St. (728-6500): Modern theater, drama, comedy.

Center Stage, 700 N. Calvert St. (332-0033): Classical and modern theater.

Lyric Opera House, 1404 Maryland Ave. (685-5086): Baltimore Opera Company in residence, Feb.-June.

Meyerhoff Symphony Hall, 1212 Cathedral St. (837-5691): Home of the Baltimore Symphony Orchestra; principal conductor David Zinman. Oct.-May.

Morris A. Mechanic Theatre, 1 W. Baltimore St. (625-1400): Broadway hits.

Peabody Institute and Conservatory of Music, 1 E. Mt. Vernon Pl. (659-8100): Very popular chamber-music recitals.

Pier 6 Concert Pavilion, Pier 6, Inner Harbor (727-5580): Big-name concerts and shows, June-Sept.

Theatre Project, 45 W. Preston St. (752-8558): Experimental theater.

Vagabond Players, 806 S. Broadway (563-9135): One of the oldest "little theaters" in the United States. Drama, comedy, modern theater, Broadway shows.

SHOPPING: Harborplace, Light and Pratt Sts.: Some 150 food stores, stalls, fashionable boutiques, and restaurants (including Jean Claude's Caf and Phillips) in two huge glass pavilions on the basin of the Inner Harbor. Lively, picturesque ambience. Open daily.

SPECIAL EVENTS: For the exact schedule of the events below, consult the **Baltimore Office of Promotion & Tourism** (see "Tourist Information," above).

Preakness Festival Week (mid-May): Public concerts, exhibits, ballooning exhibitions, and shows the entire week preceding the Preakness Stakes, a famous horse race since 1873 and one of the three events that make up thoroughbred racing's Triple Crown.

Pier 6 Concerts (June-Sept.): Open-air concerts on the water's edge. Jazz, classical, variety. Locally very popular.

Showcase of Nations Festival (every wknd, June-Sept.): Festival dedicated to the folk music, crafts, and foods of the different ethnic groups living in Baltimore.

I Am an American Day (early Sept.): The United States' biggest patriotic parade, with more than 10,000 flags and 25 marching bands. A truly spectacular tradition for more than 50 years. Patterson Park.

City Fair (mid-Sept.): Open-air shows, parades, food festival. Inner Harbor.

New Year's Eve Extravaganza (Dec. 31): Concerts, fireworks, parades. Inner Harbor.

SPORTS: Baltimore has two professional teams:

Baseball (Apr.-Oct.): Orioles, Memorial Stadium (338-1300).

Ice Hockey (Oct.-Apr.): Skipjacks, Baltimore Arena (347-2010).

Horse Racing

Laurel Race Track, U.S. 1, in Laurel (725-0400), thoroughbred racing Sept.-Feb.; **Pimlico Race Course,** 5201 Park Heights Ave. (542-9400), racing Mar.-June, Sept.-Oct.

STROLLS: ※ ⚓ **Fells Point,** Broadway south of Eastern Ave.: These once seedy, run-down docks are today undergoing complete renovation, a unique group of more than 300 rowhouses, 2½ centuries old, lining narrow, picturesque cobblestone alleyways. With many restaurants and pubs, the area is lively and bustling after dark.

⚓⚓ **Inner Harbor,** Pratt and Calvert Sts.: The old harbor, now undergoing renovation, is lively and colorful with boutiques, restaurants, yacht marinas, ultramodern aquarium, and museums. It's worth coming to Baltimore just to see it.

※⚓⚓ **Mount Vernon Place,** Charles and Monument Sts.: A very handsome ensemble of opulent 19th-century patrician homes, including **Asbury House** (see "Historic Buildings," above), bordered by public gardens. Museums, elegant boutiques. The ideal place for a stroll, it should positively not be missed.

⚓ **Otterbein Homesteading,** around Sharp, Conway, and Hanover Sts.: A group of houses dating from 1780–1800, originally inhabited by German immigrants, still with original gas lamps and cobblestones. Present-day residents were able to buy the houses for a symbolic $1 each, on condition that they would renovate them at their own expense and preserve their original character. See especially the **Old Otterbein United Methodist Church,** Baltimore's oldest church (1786). Worth a look.

ACCOMMODATIONS

See the listing of toll-free numbers in the Appendix.

Room Rates in Baltimore	
B (Budget)	up to $30
I (Inexpensive)	$30–$60
M (Moderate)	$60–$90
E (Expensive)	$90–$140
VE (Very Expensive)	$140 and up

Personal Favorites (in order of preference)

※♟♟♟ **Peabody Court** (dwntwn), 612 Cathedral St., MD 21201 (301/727-7101; toll free 800/345-3457). 104 rms, A/C, color and satellite TV. AE, CB, DC, MC, V. Valet gar. $6, two rests. (including The Conservatory), bar, 24-hr rm svce, disco, concierge, crib $20. *Note:* "The" grand hotel of Baltimore, facing the very aristocratic Mount Vernon Square. Rather massive 1930s building, but w. an interior décor that is both intimate and elegant. Very comfortable rms with Empire-style furniture, marble bathrooms, and mini-bars. Service and reception are of rare quality, and the rest. (The Conservatory) is truly remarkable. VIP and big-business clientele; the favorite hotel of connoisseurs. Just off the business district. **E–VE**

♟♟♟ **Hyatt Regency** (dwntwn), 300 Light St., MD 21202 (301/528-1234; toll free, see Hyatt). 490 rms, A/C, color TV, in-rm movies. AE, CB, DC, MC, V. Valet gar. $6, pool, tennis, health club, two rests. (the Trellis Garden is one), coffeeshop, two bars, rm svce, disco, hrdrsr, free crib. *Note:* One of Baltimore's newest luxury hotels, in an ultramodern all-glass building. Its unique location—next to dwntwn on the edge of the Inner Harbor—offers direct access to the Convention Center. Large, very comfortable rms—the best have a view of the port. Very complete facilities. Efficient svce. Big-business clientele. Interesting wknd packages. VIP floor. **E–VE**

Admiral Fell Inn (dwntwn), 888 S. Broadway, MD 21231 (301/522-7377). 36 rms, A/C, color TV. AE, MC, V. Free parking, rest., bar, rm svce, concierge. *Note:* Charming little hotel in the heart of the picturesque Fells Point section (see "Strolls," above). It offers luxury without ostentation in spacious, comfortable rms w. private patios and ultra-professional svce. Very creditable rest. Free breakfast. An excellent location, eight min. from dwntwn. **E–VE**

Belvedere (nr. dwntwn), 1 E. Chase St., MD 21202 (301/332-1000; toll free 800/692-2700). 167 rms, A/C, color TV. AE, CB, DC, MC, V. Gar. $4, pool, health club, two rests., two bars, rm svce, disco, hrdrsr, boutiques, free crib. *Note:* A classic hotel, elderly but comfortable, ten min. from the business district. Spacious, pleasing rms (some are a bit dated) and a good rest. (John Eager Howard Room). Svce varies. Group clientele. Interesting wknd packages. **M–E**

Comfort Inn (dwntwn), 24 W. Franklin St., MD 21201 (301/576-8400; toll free 800/228-5150). 200 rms, A/C, color TV, in-rm movies. AE, CB, DC, MC, V. Parking $3, pool, sauna, coffeeshop, bar, rm svce, free crib. *Note:* Modern, comfortable motel just off the business district (free shuttle to and from the Inner Harbor). Spacious rms. Business clientele. Good value. No-smoking rms. **M**

Friendship Inn (dwntwn), 306 W. Franklin St., MD 21201 (301/539-0227; toll free, see Friendship Inns). 118 .rms, A/C, color TV, in-rm movies. AE, CB, DC, MC, V. Parking $3, rest., bar, disco, crib $2. *Note:* Excellent value in the heart of dwntwn Baltimore. Modern comfort w. friendly reception and svce. No-smoking rms. Business clientele. **I**

Other Accommodations (from top bracket to budget)

Cross Keys Inn (vic.), 5100 Falls Rd., MD 21210 (301/532-6900; toll free 800/532-5397). 150 rms, A/C, color and cable TV. AE, CB, DC, MC, V. Free parking, pool, tennis, health club, rest. (Crossroads), coffeeshop, bar, rm svce, disco, hrdrsr, boutiques, free crib. *Note:* Very comfortable, luxurious motel w. first-rate reception and svce. Some rms have private patios or balconies. Group and business clientele. Good rest. Excellent location 15 min. from the hurly-burly of dwntwn via the Jones Falls Expwy. Free shuttle to and from dwntwn. **E–VE**

Harbor Court (dwntwn), 550 Light St., MD 21202 (301/234-0550; toll free 800/824-0076). 204 rms, A/C, color and cable TV. AE, CB, DC, MC, V. Gar. $5, pool, rest., bar, rm svce. *Note:* Brand-new hotel of pleasant modern architecture, on the waterfront of the Inner Harbor. Rms are ultracomfortable and well-equipped mini-suites (the best have a view of the port). Attentive, personalized svce and a very adequate rest. An excellent location, five min. from dwntwn. **E–VE**

Sheraton Inner Harbor (dwntwn), 300 S. Charles St., MD 21201 (301/962-8300; toll free, see Sheraton). 334 rms, A/C, color and cable TV. AE, CB, DC, MC, V. Gar. $6, pool, health club, sauna, two rests., two bars, 24-hr rm svce, disco, free crib. *Note:* Brand-new 15-story hotel of rather characterless modern architecture. Spacious, comfortable rms and good sports facilities. Svce sometimes overburdened. Group and convention clientele. Very convenient to the Inner Harbor and the business district, with direct access to the Convention Center. No-smoking rms. **E–VE**

Holiday Inn Inner Harbor (dwntwn), 301 W. Lombard St., MD 21201 (301/685-3500; toll free, see Holiday Inns). 360 rms, A/C, color TV. AE, CB, DC, MC, V. Parking $2, pool, rest., bar, rm svce, free crib. *Note:* Classic Holiday Inn style, with functional comfort and less-than-perfect svce. Group and convention clientele. Across from the Civic Center. Interesting wknd packages. **M–E**

Lord Baltimore Clarion (dwntwn), 20 W. Baltimore St., MD 21201 (301/539-8400; toll free, see Clarion). 440 rms, A/C, color TV, in-rm movies. AE, CB, DC, MC, V. Free parking; valet parking $6, health club, two rests., two bars, rm svce, drugstore, free crib. *Note:* Massive 1930s palace in the heart of Baltimore, entirely renovated. Spacious, pleasing rms, an adequate rest., and fair svce. Overall, a good value. Two VIP floors. No-smoking rms. Linked to the Convention Center by an overpass. **M–E**

Days Inn Inner Harbor (dwntwn), 100 Hopkins Pl., MD 21201 (301/576-1000; toll free, see Days Inns). 250 rms, A/C, color TV, in-rm movies. AE, CB, DC, MC, V. Parking $2, pool, coffeeshop, bar, free crib. *Note:* Modern, nine-story motel in the middle of dwntwn. Functional comfort and facilities. Well-conceived, spacious rms and relatively friendly reception. Business clientele. **M**

Best Western Hallmark (formerly the Howard House; dwntwn), 8 N. Howard St., MD 21201 (301/539-1188; toll free, see Best Western). 93 rms, A/C, color TV. AE, MC, V. Parking $3, rest. (Gallery), bar, free crib. *Note:* Small and aging, but well placed in the heart of the business district; welcoming and intimate. Entirely modernized rms. A very good value. Regular clientele. Free airport shuttle. **I–M**

Howard Johnson's (vic.), 5701 Baltimore National Pike, Catonsville, MD 21228 (301/747-8900; toll free, see Howard Johnson's). 147 rms, A/C, color TV, in-rm movies. AE, CB, DC, MC, V. Free parking, pool, tennis, 24-hr coffeeshop, rm svce, free crib. *Note:* Classic motel w. direct access to the Baltimore Beltway, exit 15. Modern comfort. Some rms have balconies. Ideal if you're driving—25 min. from dwntwn. Good value. **I–M**

Abbey Hotel (nr. dwntwn), 723 St. Paul St., Madison, MD 21202 (301/332-0405). 35 rms, A/C, color TV. AE, MC, V. Parking $4, adjacent coffeeshop, free breakfast. *Note:* Small, antiquated hotel but nicely located quite close to Mount Vernon Pl. Rather cramped but pleasant rms (some have no bathroom). Cheerful service. Good value. **I**

Airport Accommodations

International Hotel (vic.), Baltimore-Washington Airport, MD 21240 (301/859-3300; toll free 800/638-5855). 196 rms, A/C, color TV, in-rm movies. AE, CB, DC, MC, V. Free parking, pool, rest. (Michener's), bar, rm svce, disco, free crib. *Note:* Comfortable, functional motel with modern facilities. Very adequate rest. Free airport shuttle; 20 min. to dwntwn. Steep rates for a motel. **E–VE**

YMCA/Youth Hostels

Baltimore Hostel (youth hostel, dwntwn), 17 W. Mulberry St., MD 21201 (301/576-8880). 40 beds.

RESTAURANTS

Baltimore Restaurant Prices (per person, excluding drinks and service charges)	
B (Budget)	up to $15
I (Inexpensive)	$15–$25
M (Moderate)	$25–$40
E (Expensive)	$40–$60
VE (Very Expensive)	$60 and up

Personal Favorites (in order of preference)

☼ 🍷🍷🍷 **The Conservatory** (dwntwn), in the Peabody Court (see "Accommodations") (727-7101). A/C. Dinner only, Tues.-Sun.; closed Mon. AE, CB, DC, MC, V. J&T. Specialties: goat cheese in pastry shell with Devonshire sauce, duckling à la rouennaise, lobster with vanilla sauce, chocolate mousse cake with raspberries. The menu changes regularly. Fine wine list but astronomical prices. *Note:* The view of Baltimore from the top floor of the Peabody Court Hotel is splendid, as are the cuisine and the setting. Enchanting if rather extravagant art deco conservatory décor, and an atmosphere as romantic as your heart could desire. Ultrarefined svce. By far, Baltimore's most chic and expensive rest. *French.* **E**

🍷🍷 **Maison Marconi's** (nr. dwntwn), 106 W. Saratoga St. (727-9522). A/C. Lunch/dinner Tues.-Sat.; closed Sun., Mon. MC, V. Jkt. Specialties: filet of sole Marguéry, sautéed soft-shell crabs, oysters Pauline, sweetbreads bordelaise, rack of lamb, fish of the day, Italian dishes, ice cream sundaes. *Note:* For more than half a century Marconi's has won the hearts of lovers of fine cuisine. The décor and the waiters seem to be of the same period. No resv., unfortunately, and the place is often packed. Another disappointment: it closes very early—8 p.m. *Italian-Continental.* **I–M**

🍷🍷 **Brass Elephant** (nr. dwntwn), 924 N. Charles St. (547-8480). A/C. Lunch Mon.-Fri.; dinner daily. AE, MC, V. J&T. Specialties: fresh homemade pasta, northern Italian cuisine (the menu changes regularly). Very good desserts. *Note:* In an elegant Victorian residence that once belonged to a rich 19th-century businessman, this rest. of great quality is a favorite of local society people. Light, inspired Italian cuisine. Very effective décor of woodwork, marble, and crystal. Excellent svce. The only good Italian rest. outside of Baltimore's Little Italy. *Italian.* **I–M**

🍷🍷 **Café des Artistes** (nr. dwntwn), 1501 Sulgrave Ave. (664-2200). A/C. Lunch Mon.-Fri.; dinner daily. AE, CB, DC, MC, V. Jkt. Specialties: duck pâté, stuffed trout with salmon mousse, steak, roast rack of lamb, Dover sole au gratin. The menu changes regularly. Well-stocked wine list. *Note:* Formerly located near the Morris Mechanic Theater, this fashionable bistro offers very pleasing French-inspired cuisine in an ornate, intimate setting. The paintings and prints on display are themselves worth a visit. Irreproachable svce. Locally very popular. Resv. highly advised. 25 min. from dwntwn on the Jones Falls Expwy. Free valet parking. *French.* **I–M**

🍷 **Tandoor** (dwntwn), Harborplace, Light and Pratt Sts. (547-0575). Lunch/dinner daily; brunch Sat., Sun. AE, CB, DC, MC, V. Specialties: samosas, tandoori chicken, curry, marinated lamb. *Note:*

An exotic yet delicate cuisine, elegantly prepared and served—an interesting gastronomic experience. Modern, vaguely Eastern décor. Attentive svce. Dinner resv. advised. Fairly touristy ambience (the rest. is one of Harborplace's two large glass pavilions along the Inner Harbor). *Indian.* **I**

☼� **John W. Faidley Seafood** (dwntwn), Lexington Market, 400 W. Lexington St. (727-4898). Lunch only, Mon.-Sat.; closed Sun. No credit cards. Specialties: Specialties: fresh Maryland oysters and crabs, clams, crabcakes. *Note:* Superb seafood bar in the picturesque enclosed Lexington Market. Baltimore's most authentic bistro, serving seafood that couldn't be fresher. Pleasant ambience. No resv. Open for lunch only. A local favorite for close to a century. *Seafood.* **B–I**

Other Restaurants (from top bracket to budget)

♔♔ **Danny's** (nr. dwntwn), 1201 N. Charles St. (539-1393). A/C. Lunch Mon.-Fri.; dinner Mon.-Sat.; closed Sun. and the last two weeks of July. AE, CB, DC, MC, V. Jkt. Specialties: crab imperial, beef Wellington, steak Diane, fresh salmon, very good desserts. *Note:* A good trendy rest. with faux Louis XV décor. The prices are somewhat excessive, the svce less than ideal—nevertheless, a Baltimore classic for almost a quarter century. *Continental.* **M**

☼♔♔♔ **Tio Pepe** (dwntwn), 10 E. Franklin St. (539-4675). A/C. Lunch Mon.-Fri.; dinner daily; closed holidays. AE, MC, V. Jkt. Specialties: gazpacho, gambas al ajillo, paella valenciana, roast suckling pig, filet of sole Alcazar, langosta a la cataluña, brazo gitano. Excellent house sangría and a good Spanish wine list. *Note:* Remarkable variations on Iberian cuisine in a sober but elegant Castilian cave setting. Impeccable svce. Resv. a must. Without a doubt Baltimore's most famous rest. *Spanish.* **I–M**

♔♔ **Haussner's** (nr. dwntwn), 3244 Eastern Ave. at Clinton St. (327-8365). A/C. Lunch/dinner Tue.-Sat.; closed Sun., Mon., Dec. 25. AE, MC, V. J&T. Specialties: sauerbraten, wienerschnitzel, hasenpfeffer, fish of the day. Very good desserts (try the strawberry pie). More than 100 dishes to choose from. German beer on tap. *Note:* Rather amusing kitsch décor w. an abundance of paintings and busts of Roman emperors in the best firehouse style. Rest. established in 1926. Locally very popular. Good svce. No resv. *German-American.* **I**

♔♔ **Sabatino's** (nr. dwntwn), 901 Fawn St., Little Italy (727-9414). A/C. Lunch/dinner daily (until 3 a.m.). Jkt. MC, V. Specialties: fresh homemade pasta, shrimps napoletana, veal marsala. *Note:* A favorite of Baltimore's Italian community, serving serious, unpretentious cuisine in generous portions. Diligent svce and a pleasant ambience. Open very late. *Italian.* **I**

☼♔ **Olde Obrycki's Crab House** (nr. dwntwn), 1729 E. Pratt St. (732-6399). A/C. Lunch Tue.-Fri.; dinner Tue.-Sun.; closed Mon. and Nov.-Mar. AE, MC, V. Specialties: blue crabs, crabcakes, seafood, fish of the day. *Note:* One of the best spots in Baltimore for sampling the famous Maryland crabs and washing them down with draft beer (the rest. is only open during crab season, Apr.-Oct.). Charming, colonial décor and a pleasant, if noisy, ambience. An excellent spot. *Seafood.* **I**

♔ **Uncle Lee's** (nr. dwntwn), 3317 Greenmount Ave. (366-3333). A/C. Lunch/dinner daily. AE, CB, DC, MC, V. Specialties: bird's-nest soup, moo shoo pork, spicy orange beef, lobster Cantonese. *Note:* One of the few acceptable Chinese rests. in Baltimore. Typical modern Oriental décor. Efficient if less-than-cheerful svce. 25 min. from dwntwn. Other location (the cuisine is rather less satisfying): 44 South St. (727-6666). *Chinese.* **I**

Bertha's (nr. dwntwn), 734 S. Broadway (327-5795). A/C. Lunch/dinner daily (bar open until 2 a.m.). AE, CB, DC, MC, V. Specialties: mussels marinière, fish of the day, omelets, steaks. *Note:* A truer-than-life old English pub in the picturesque Fells Point section. Daily specials are written on a blackboard. Honest, unpretentious cuisine. Diligent svce. English-style tea in the afternoon (resv. necessary). Locally very popular. *Continental-American.* **B–I**

Ikaros (nr. dwntwn), 4805 Eastern Ave. (633-9825). A/C. Lunch/dinner daily exc Tue. AE, MC, V. Specialties: stuffed grape leaves, lemon soup, calamari, moussaka, kapama (lamb and tomatoes), baklava. *Note:* The oldest and the best Greek rest. in the city. The décor is nothing special, but the cuisine is 100% authentic. Locally very popular. Inevitable waits on wknds. Resv. advised. *Greek.* **B–I**

Cafeteria / Fast Food

Woman's Industrial Exchange (dwntwn), 333 N. Charles St. (685-4388). Breakfast/lunch only, Mon.-Fri.; closed wknds. No credit cards. Specialties: crabcakes, chicken croquettes, sandwiches, salads, dishes of the day, homemade pies, floating island. *Note:* A real local institution, nearly a century old. *Cuisine bourgeoise,* not of the lightest, served in 1920s cafeteria-style décor that is nicely old-fashioned. Motherly svce. Locally very popular.

BARS & NIGHTCLUBS

Blues Alley (formerly Ethel's Place) (dwntwn), 1225 Cathedral St. (837-2288). Contemporary music and jazz with top-name performers. Open nightly.

P.T. Flagg's (formerly the Power Plant), Pier 4, Inner Harbor (244-7377). After its failure as an indoor amusement park, this old electric-utility generating station now hosts a large-scale nightclub with four different music spots. Among them a "members only" disco, big on lasers. Worth a glance. Nightly.

Thirteenth Floor Lounge, in the Belvedere (see "Accommodations") (547-8220). Open daily. A fashionable piano-bar on the 13th floor of the hotel with a relaxed atmosphere and a lovely view.

NEARBY EXCURSIONS

ELLICOTT CITY (11 mi., 18km, west on Md. 144): Former iron-working center, founded in 1774 on the banks of the Patapsco River. It was also the temporary terminus of the United States' first railroad, the Baltimore & Ohio (interesting museum in the old station, which dates from 1830). The city has conserved a good number of its early-19th-century stone and log houses on the hills overlooking the river and an interesting Historic District downtown. Well worth going out of your way. Visitor Information: 3430 Court House Dr. (301/992-2022).

ANNAPOLIS (28 mi., 45 km south on Md. 2): Charming colonial town more than 300 years old. Capital of Maryland and home of the U.S. Naval Academy (interesting naval museum). Very picturesque port quarter with beautiful old houses. See the chapter on Washington.

CARROLL COUNTY FARM MUSEUM (in Westminster, 28 mi., 45 km, northwest on Md. 140; 301/848-7775): Large agricultural estate dating from 1852, transformed into a living museum of the 19th century, with a Victorian-style dwelling house, forge, stables, craft shops, etc. Interesting slice of history. Open Tue.-Sun. in summer; weekends only, spring and autumn; closed the rest of the year. Worth the trip.

FARTHER AFIELD

    GETTYSBURG (110 mi., 180 km, round trip on Md. 140N, Md. 97N, and return): The Civil War's bloodiest battlefield. See the chapter on Philadelphia.

    PENNSYLVANIA DUTCH COUNTRY (130 mi., 210 km, round trip on I-83N/S): Here, the 17th century has left a clear imprint in modern America. See the chapter on Philadelphia.

    CHESAPEAKE BAY & WYE MILLS (165 mi., 264 km, r.t. on Md. 2S, U.S. 50E, Md. 33W): See **Wye Mills,** a picturesque little village which has kept its authentic 18th-century look; **Easton,** famous for its antique shops; **St. Michaels,** with its marvelous maritime museum **(Chesapeake Bay Museum);** and the gorgeous **St. Mary's Square,** with its old houses. Return via **Oxford,** capital of pleasure boating and point of origin for the 300-year-old Oxford–Bellevue ferry, oldest in the country. A very pleasant trip.

Where to Stay En Route

IN OXFORD. 🛎🛎**Robert Morris Inn,** on Md. 333 (301/226-5111). Charming little colonial-style inn with a view of the water. Good rest. 28 rms. **I–M**

IN EASTON. 🛎🛎**Tidewater Inn,** Dover and Harrison Sts. (301/822-1300). Elegant 200-year-old, historic landmarked building. Rest. renowned for its seafood. 120 rms. **I–M**

    ATLANTIC BEACHES (274 mi., 438 km, round trip on Md. 2S, U.S. 50E, Md. 528N, Del. 1N, U.S. 9S, Del. 18W, Del. 404W, U.S. 50W, and Md. 2N): Lots of beaches and fashionable seaside resorts between **Ocean City** (to the south) and **Rehoboth Beach** (to the north). See the chapter on Washington. On the way, you can see **Annapolis** (see above.)

CHAPTER 9

WASHINGTON, D.C. 🔥🔥🔥

□ □ □

The federal capital, that "city of heroes and monuments," the first city ever planned for a specific purpose, was brought into being by George Washington through an act of political will—and through the visionary genius of Maj. Pierre-Charles l'Enfant. This French architect, who served as a volunteer during the War of Independence, drew up an urban plan of majestic simplicity for a concentric city pierced by wide avenues—a plan which imparts to the city its ordered charm, at once graceful and austere. Even so, the capital of the young Republic almost failed to survive its rough handling in 1814 by the British, who sacked it and burned its principal buildings.

Here and there along the great green carpet of the **Mall** stand some of the most historic (and most visited) structures in the country. America's most famous address is 1600 Pennsylvania Avenue, better known as **The White House**, official residence of America's presidents since John Adams in 1800. Not far away, on a little hill, the imposing **Capitol** and its majestic dome, modeled on that of St. Peter's in Rome, dominate the city's skyline, as the architectural embodiment of American democracy properly should. A mile and a half to the west, interrupting the otherwise unbroken prospect down the Mall and across the **Potomac River** to **Arlington Cemetery**, the giant obelisk of the **Washington Monument** leaps skyward to honor the Father of his Country.

City of government offices and museums. City of embassies (154 of them at the time of writing), gardens, and statues. City of officials, reporters, and diplomats (some 20,000 in all, from heads of mission to clerical staff). City of monuments ranging from the extraordinary (the **Lincoln Memorial**, the **Jefferson Memorial**, the **National Gallery of Art East Wing**) to the downright disgraceful (the **Pentagon**, the **J. Edgar Hoover Building**). City of learning, with its five universities and 20 colleges—and strategic heart of the formidable power of the U.S.A. Washington is all these things and more, an elegant, cosmopolitan city like none other in the world.

Nevertheless, unlike their fellow Americans, the inhabitants of Washington are not fully enfranchised. The Founding Fathers, apparently concerned that the local population might loom too large in the eyes of the legislature, constitutionally denied it the right to vote. In 1961 the Congress finally acknowledged the anachronism and gave Washingtonians a vote in presidential elections. Since 1975 they have also been allowed to elect their own mayor—but they still have no vote in Congress.

Sadly, this great city has one of the highest unemployment rates in the country. Side by side with the 350,000 federal employees and the army of white-collar workers who cluster around the centers of power (among them, 12,000 lawyers and 90,000 duly registered lobbyists at last count), there is an economically distressed population of young people in black neighborhoods; among those under 21, the unemployment rate is 36%.

As a direct consequence of the unemployment rate and the high incidence of drug addiction, FBI statistics credit the nation's capital with a crime rate twice the national average—something of a paradox for a city that is the seat of the Supreme Court, and thus of the Law. But even so, Washington—with its classical revival buildings, its cluster of museums (including the renowned **Smithsonian Institution** and the **National Gallery of Art**) unmatched anywhere in the world, its wide tree-lined avenues, its reflecting pools fringed with Japanese cherries (try to be there when they're in flower, in late March or early April), and its appealing and historic **Georgetown** district—lacks nothing that the visitor could ask for. Some 17 million pilgrim-tourists, including a million foreigners, visit the capital every year.

Long considered a cultural desert, with the construction in 1971 of the **John F. Kennedy Center,** Washington acquired a world-class artistic and theatrical complex. Nevertheless, it remains after dark one of the starchiest, least lively places in the country. The only interest offered by Washington's nightlife is the extraordinary profusion of restaurants—French, Caribbean, Ethiopian, Créole, Italian, Chinese, East European, Vietnamese, Latin American, and any other kind you can think of—which have made the city a sort of gastronomic Tower of Babel. There are in all more than 6,500 restaurants, pizzerias, sushi bars, fast-food outlets, and cafeterias, and the prices they charge are steep even by New York standards.

Washington's famous children include Duke Ellington and his son, Mercer Ellington, the late FBI director J. Edgar Hoover, the late Secretary of State John Foster Dulles, playwright Edward Albee, author Frank Slaughter, comedian and actress Goldie Hawn, actor William Hurt, and singer-dancer Chita Rivera.

A Note on Orientation: The spider-web layout of Washington is divided into four geographic quadrants with the Capitol as their center: Northwest (NW), Northeast (NE), Southwest (SW), and Southeast (SE). Streets running north and south are designated by numbers; those running east and west, by letters of the alphabet. The grid system of numbered and lettered streets is slashed diagonally by wide avenues bearing the names of states of the Union: Massachusetts, Wisconsin, Pennsylvania, Connecticut, etc.

BASIC FACTS: District of Columbia. Area Codes: 202 (District of Columbia), 301 (Maryland), 703 (Virginia). Time Zone: Eastern Time. ZIP Code (of the central post office): 20013. Founded: 1790. Approximate population: city, 630,000; metropolitan area, 3,560,000. Ninth-largest metropolitan area in the country.

CLIMATE: The last word you would think of to describe the Washington climate is "agreeable." It's a hot, sticky steambath in summer (July average temperature, 79° F, 26° C), cold and very humid in winter with snowfalls and icy roads (Jan. average, 37° F, 3° C). That leaves spring and fall, which are usually sunny and pleasant (especially May and Oct.), as the best times of year to visit Washington.

DISTANCES: Atlanta, 608 mi. (975 km); Baltimore, 40 mi. (65 km); Chicago, 668 mi. (1,070 km); New York, 234 mi. (375 km); Niagara Falls, 425 mi. (680 km); Philadelphia, 134 mi. (215 km); Pittsburgh, 247 mi. (395 km); Savannah, 633 mi. (1,012 km).

ARRIVAL & TRANSIT INFORMATION

AIRPORTS: The **Baltimore-Washington International Airport** (BWI), 32 mi. (51 km) NE, for medium- and long-haul flights. Hard to reach from dwntwn Washington; for information, call 301/859-7111.

Dulles International Airport (IAD), 26 mi. (42 km) west, for medium- and long-haul flights; for information, call 703/471-4242.

Washington National Airport (DCA), 4 mi. (7 km) south, for medium-haul flights; for information, call 703/685-8000.

U.S. AIRLINES (area code 202 unless otherwise indicated): American (393-2345), Braniff (toll free 800/272-6433), Continental (478-9700), Delta (468-2282), Eastern (393-4000), Midway (toll free 800/621-5700), Northwest (737-7333), Pan Am (845-8000), Presidential (893-3400), TWA (737-7400), United (893-3400), and USAir (783-4500).

FOREIGN CARRIERS: All Nippon Airways (toll free 800/235-9262), British Airways (toll free 800/247-9297), Lufthansa (toll free 800/645-3880).

CITY LINK: The **cab** fare from Baltimore-Washington Airport to dwntwn is about $36–$40; time, 45 min. Cab fare from Dulles International to dwntwn, about $32–$38; time, 40 min. Cab fare from National Airport to dwntwn, about $8–$12; time, 15–20 min.

Bus: The **Washington Flyer** (202/685-1400); serves the Air Terminal at 16th and K Sts. NW and the major dwntwn hotels; leaves National Airport every 20 min. (fare, $5; time, 25 min.); leaves Dulles International every 30 min. (fare, $12; time, 45–60 min.). The Washington Flyer also connects National Airport and Dulles International, leaving every 30 or 60 minutes; fare, $10; time, 45 min. The **Airport Connection** (202/685-1400) connects Baltimore-Washington Airport and the Air Terminal at 16th and K Sts. NW, leaving every 45 min.; fare, $10; time, about 60–70 min.

A **subway** line (Metrorail Blue Line) connects National Airport to dwntwn Washington, leaving every 10 min.; fare, 80¢–$1; time, 18 min.

Public transportation by bus and subway (ultramodern and comfortable) covers the city effectively, but is complicated for visitors; for information on **Metrobus and Metrorail,** call 202/637-7000. With 11,000 cabs on the street there is no shortage, but not all of them are trustworthy.

The city is not so large that you'll need to rent a car, unless you plan to drive out into the country or along the eastern seaboard; rental rates with unlimited mileage are noticeably lower than in New York.

CAR RENTAL (area code for both airports is 703): Avis, Dulles Airport (661-8404), National Airport (379-4757); Budget, Dulles Airport (437-9373), National Airport (920-3360); Dollar, Dulles Airport (661-8577), National Airport (739-2255); Hertz, Dulles Airport (471-6020), National Airport (979-6300); National, Dulles Airport (471-5278), National Airport (783-1590); Thrifty, Dulles Airport (471-4544), National Airport (548-1600).

For dwntwn locations, consult the local telephone book.

LIMOUSINE SERVICES: Admiral Limousine service (554-1000), Carey Limousine (892-2000), Dav El Limousine (543-2300), Excelsior Limousine (789-0022), Scripps Edward Limousine (toll free 800/223-6710).

TAXIS: Washington cabs are not metered; they charge according to the number of "zones" they must pass through between starting point and destination (there should be a legible city map, with the zones marked, in the passenger compartment). The cabs may carry more than one passenger or party to the same destination, or different destinations in the same general direction; each passenger or party may be charged a separate fare. Many of the drivers are recent immigrants, only superficially acquainted with the English language (and the city).

Cabs may be hailed on the street, taken from the waiting lines outside major hotels, or called by phone. The principal companies are Barwood (984-1900), Capitol Cab (546-2400), Diamond Cab (387-6200), Liberty Cab (636-1600), Red Top Cab (522-3333), and Yellow Cab (544-1212).

TRAIN: The AMTRAK terminal is at Union Station, 50 Massachusetts Ave. NE (484-7540); the city ticket office, 1721 K St. NW (484-7540). For reservations and information for the Metroliner, call 484-5580.

BUS: Greyhound, 1005 1st St. at L St., NE (565-2662).

INFORMATION & TOURS

TOURIST INFORMATION: The **Washington Convention and Visitors Association,** 1212 New York Ave. NW (Suite 250), DC 20005 (202/789-7000).
International Visitors Information Service, 1575 I St. NW, DC 20005 (202/789-7000): Orientation for visitors from abroad.
Visitor Information Center, 1455 Pennsylvania Ave. NW (202/789-7000).
A **recorded message** giving a list of current shows and cultural events may be reached at 202/737-8866.

GUIDED TOURS: **Gray Line Tours** (bus), 333 E St. SW (479-5900): Conducted tours of the city and surroundings, serving major hotels.
Helicopter Sightseeing Tour (helicopter), National Airport, Hangar 4, Commuter General Aviation Terminal (920-9486): Helicopter flight over the capital; spectacular.
Old Town Trolley Tours (bus): Two-hour shuttle tour across the city in a replica of a turn-of-the-century streetcar. A ticket gives unlimited boarding rights. The best sightseeing tours in town. Daily, year round. For information, call 269-3020.
Tourmobile Sightseeing (bus): A very practical shuttle system which allows you to visit Washington's principal monuments, with a couple of dozen stops along the route. Get off and on again as often as you like. Runs daily year round. Fare is $7, payable on the bus. Also serves Arlington National Cemetery and Mount Vernon. For information, call 554-7950.
Washington Boat Lines (boat), 6th and Water Sts. SW (554-8000): Mini-cruises along the Potomac as far as Mount Vernon; Apr.-Oct. only.
The Washington Post, 1150 15th St. NW (334-7969): Guided tour around one of the largest daily papers in the country—the paper that blew the whistle on Watergate. Fascinating. By appointment only, Mon.-Fri.

SIGHTS, ATTRACTIONS, & ACTIVITIES

ADVENTURE TOURS: **Adventures Aloft** (balloon), Rockville, Md. (301/881-6262): Balloon rides over the Washington countryside from any of several different launch sites in Maryland or Virginia. Spectacular. Year round.
Balloons Unlimited (balloon): 115 Pleasant St., Vienna, Va. (703/281-2300): Balloon rides over the Washington countryside from any of several different launch sites in Virginia. Fare, $90 per person. Spectacular. Year round.
Blue Ridge Outfitters (boat), W.Va. 340, Harpers Ferry, W.Va.

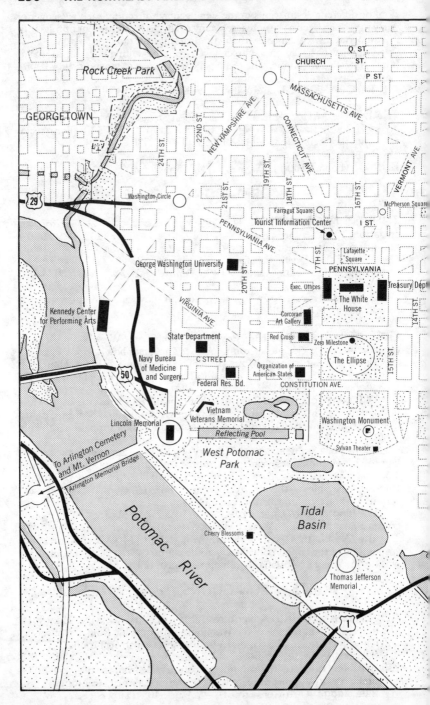

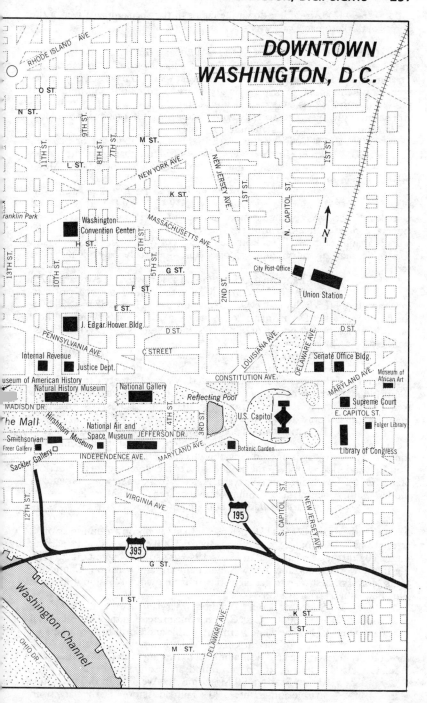

DOWNTOWN WASHINGTON, D.C.

(304/725-3444): Air-rafting down the rapids of the Shenandoah River or the gorges of the Potomac. Daily, Apr.-Oct.

ARCHITECTURAL HIGHLIGHTS: ※ ⚲ **Bureau of Engraving and Printing,** 14th and C St. SW (447-9709): Tens of billions of dollars in banknotes, Treasury notes, and stamps are printed here every year. From glassed-in galleries you can watch banknotes being printed and packaged (about $50 million are produced daily). Coins are struck at Philadelphia, Denver, and San Francisco. Not surprisingly, very strict security is imposed here; photography is forbidden. Open Mon.-Fri. An encouragement to daydreams.

⚲ **FBI Headquarters–J. Edgar Hoover Building,** E St. between 9th & 10th Sts. NW (324-3447): Headquarters of the war on crime—and one of the ugliest buildings in Washington. Conducted tours Mon.-Fri. Marksmanship demonstrations by G-men. For lovers of detective fiction.

※⚲ **John F. Kennedy Center for the Performing Arts,** New Hampshire Ave. and F St. NW (254-3600): Huge cultural complex on the banks of the Potomac, opened in 1971; opera house, theater, cinema, concert hall, and art gallery. The very successful modern design is the work of architect Edward Durrell Stone. The heart of Washington's cultural (and social) life, drawing four million visitors a year. Open daily. Must definitely be seen.

⚲ **Old Executive Office Building,** Pennsylvania Ave. and 17th St. NW (395-5895): Adjoining the White House, this interesting example of French classical revival architecture dating from 1871–1888 originally housed the Departments of State, the Navy, and War. It now accommodates the vice-president of the U.S. and members of the White House staff. Open Sat. by appointment.

※⚲ **Old Post Office,** Pennsylvania Ave. and 12th St. NW (289-4224): Imposing Romanesque building designed by Daniel Burnham and dating from 1899, surmounted by a Big Ben–style tower 315 ft. (96 m) high. Once the central post office, it now houses government offices as well as many boutiques and restaurants under an enormous glass roof. An appealing place which should definitely be seen. Open daily.

⚲ **Panamerican Union Building,** 17th St. and Constitution Ave. NW (789-3951): A strange compromise between Spanish Colonial and French Renaissance idioms, this graceful 1910 building, designed by Paul Cret and Albert Kelsey, is the headquarters of the Organization of American States (OAS). Lovely interior courtyard; Aztec garden; interesting museum of modern Latin American art adjoining. Should be seen. Open Mon.-Fri.

※⚲ **Pentagon Building,** bounded by Jefferson Davis Hwy., Washington Blvd., and Shirley Hwy., Arlington, Va. (703/695-1776): The heart and head of U.S. defense, with five floors on a groundplan of 32 acres (13 ha.), 17.5 mi. (28 km) of corridors, 32,000 employees, and a parking lot for 10,000 cars. Constructed in 1941–1943, it's still the biggest office building in the world. Imposing, but without architectural distinction. Conducted tours Mon.-Fri. Best ways to get there: bus 16 from dwntwn Washington or the Blue Line subway. Worth a look.

※ **Supreme Court Building,** Maryland Ave. and 1st St. NE (479-3030): Cass Gilbert's fine exercise in the classical revival style dates from 1935. The white Vermont marble and Corinthian columns are reminiscent of the days of ancient Greece. Majestic interior decoration. When the Court is in session the public is admitted to hearing cases (Mon., Tues., and Wed., Oct.-April). Open Mon.-Fri. year round; an absolute must.

※⚲ **Union Station,** 50 Massachusetts Ave. NE: In sheer size, this marble-and-granite 1907 railroad station is the largest in the country; its majestic design was inspired by the Baths of Diocletian in Rome. Reopened in the fall of 1988 after decades of neglect and decay. Daniel H. Burnham's building, now splendidly restored at a cost of $140 million, now houses around 100 boutiques, stores, restaurants, and movie houses on three levels, as well as the station itself.

      🔔 **Voice of America,** 330 Independence Ave. SW (485-6231): Transmits around the clock to five continents in 42 languages. Conducted tours Mon.-Fri. (resv. advised). For radio hams.

      ☀🔔 **Watergate,** New Hampshire and Virginia Aves. NW: Luxury complex beside the Potomac; scene of the political scandal that cost Richard M. Nixon the presidency in 1974. Smart shops, restaurants, luxury hotel. The elegant architecture is worth a look.

CHURCHES/SYNAGOGUES: 🔔 Franciscan Monastery, 1400 Quincy St.

NE (526-6800): This Romanesque monastery with its graceful cloister, standing in its own beautiful garden, houses the curious "Holy Land of America"—a faithful facsimile of some of the most sacred places in the Holy Land such as the crib at Bethlehem, the Garden of Gethsemane, and so on, as well as of the Roman catacombs and the grotto at Lourdes. Tours conducted daily by the friars.

      🔔 **Islamic Center,** 2251 Massachusetts Ave. NW (332-8343): America's largest mosque, and largest Islamic cultural center, built with funds contributed by all the Muslim countries that have diplomatic relations with the U.S. The center, an elegant building with fine surface carving and a 160-ft. (48-m) minaret, oriented toward Mecca, is open to visitors every day except during the Fri. prayers. Should be seen.

      ☀🔔 **National Shrine of the Immaculate Conception,** 620 Michigan Ave. NE (526-8300): The largest Roman Catholic church in the U.S., on the campus of Catholic University; its Romanesque-Byzantine nave is 459 ft (140 m) long and surmounted by a 331-ft (101-m) bell tower. The huge dome is blue, with touches of gold. Organ and carillon concerts on Sun. Worth seeing.

      ☀🔔 **St. John's Episcopal Church,** 16th and H Sts. NW (347-8766): On Lafayette Square across from the White House, St. John's Episcopal Church was built in 1816 to the design of Benjamin H. Latrobe, the city's first public architect. It has become known as "the Church of the Presidents," because more than a dozen have worshiped there, beginning with James Madison in the year after the church was built. Since then, Pew 54 has traditionally been reserved for the president of the U.S. Unquestionably worth a visit. Open daily.

      ☀ **Scottish Rite Supreme Council,** 1733 16th St. NW (232-3579): Dating from 1915, this building designed by J. Russell Pope is modeled on the famous tomb of King Mausolus of Halicarnassus, one of the seven wonders of antiquity. Its interior, embellished with purple ceilings, polished black marble columns and doors, and light fixtures in bronze, is sumptuous. Open daily by appointment; shouldn't be missed.

      ☀ **Washington National Cathedral,** Wisconsin and Massachusetts Aves. NW (537-6200): Very fine cathedral in the Gothic Revival style, Episcopalian but open to all denominations; one of the largest in the country. The interior, particularly the stained glass, is sumptuous. Begun in 1907 to the design of British architect George Bodley, it remains unfinished to this day. It stands atop Mount St. Alban, the capital's highest hill (419 ft, 128 m). Within is the tomb of President Woodrow Wilson. Library of rare books. Should definitely be visited.

      🔔 **Washington Temple,** 9900 Stoneybrook Dr., Kensington, at Beltway Exit 33 (587-0144): One of 40 Mormon temples around the world built on the model of the temple at Salt Lake City, to an unusual design executed in 1976. Non-Mormons may not enter the temple, but the Visitor Center is open daily. Particularly impressive when floodlit after dark.

HISTORIC BUILDINGS: ※ 🔔 **Blair House,** 1651-1653 Pennsylvania Ave. NW: Blair House and the adjoining **Blair-Lee House,** opposite the White House, have since 1942 served as the official residence of foreign heads of state when visiting the U.S. The two buildings, which have recently been extensively restored, are not open to the public. The 1824 Blair House has played an important part in American history. It was here, on April 18, 1861, that President Lincoln offered the command of the Union army to Gen. Robert E. Lee; Lee refused, and later became commander-in-chief of the Confederacy. President Truman lived at Blair House from 1948 to 1952 while the White House was being restored.

※🔔🔔 **The Capitol,** 1st St. between Constitution and Independence Aves. (224-3121): This imposing structure, home of the 435-member House of Representatives and the 100-member Senate, is capped by a dome 258 ft (79 m) high designed by Charles Bulfinch after the dome of St. Peter's in Rome. A 19-ft (6-m) statue of *Liberty,* by Thomas Crawford, crowns the whole. Originally erected in 1793–1812, burned by the British in 1814, and built anew in 1816–1829, the building has been enlarged several times, most recently in 1962. Very rich interior decoration with colossal statues and wall-paintings, especially in the main **Rotunda,** from which 40-min. conducted tours leave every 15 min., allowing access to the Visitors' Galleries of the House and the Senate. The **Senate Dining Room,** renowned for its bean soup, is also open to the public. See also, beneath the Rotunda, the crypt originally intended for the tomb of George Washington; here is the catafalque used for the funerary vigil of Abraham Lincoln, and of the unknown soldiers of World War II and the Korean War. From the west front you have a fine view along the Mall to the Washington Monument and the Lincoln Memorial in the distance. Don't miss the Capitol; it's worth the trip to Washington all by itself.

🔔 **Christian Heurich Mansion,** 1307 New Hampshire Ave. NW (785-2068): Home of the Columbia Historical Society, this luxurious 1892 private house, built of brown sandstone in the Renaissance Revival style, boasts no fewer than 43 rooms. Very fine Victorian furniture; library devoted to the history of the Capital. Should be seen. Open Wed.-Sat.

※🔔 **Decatur House,** 748 Jackson Pl. NW (673-4030): This red-brick town house a stone's throw from the White House, and itself rich in historical associations, was built in 1818 by Benjamin H. Latrobe for Commodore Stephen Decatur, hero of the war against the Barbary pirates. It has been home to a succession of distinguished men, including one future president (Martin Van Buren), three secretaries of state, and several other prominent politicians. For almost a century and a half it was one of the centers of Washington's social life. Splendid period furniture and decoration. Worth a visit. Open Tues.-Sun.

※🔔 **Dumbarton Oaks,** 1703 32nd St. NW (338-8278): Elegant small early-19th-century manor house in the heart of historic Georgetown. Since 1940 the house and its lovely landscaped gardens have belonged to Harvard University. It has important collections of Byzantine and pre-Columbian art, and a library of 80,000 books on art. In 1944 a conference of the four Great Powers (the U.S., Great Britain, China, and the Soviet Union) on international security was held here; this conference worked out the framework for the U.N. Don't fail to visit. Open Tues.-Sun.

※🔔 **Ford's Theater,** 511 10th St. NW (426-6927): Here Abraham Lincoln was assassinated, on April 14, 1865, by John

Wilkes Booth during the performance of a play. The oldest theater in Washington still in use. There is a small Lincoln museum in the basement. An absolute must. Open daily.

Georgetown University, 37th and O Sts. NW (625-4866): Founded in 1789 and still run by the Society of Jesus (the Jesuit order), this is the oldest Roman Catholic University in the U.S.; it has 12,000 students. On a bluff overlooking the Potomac, the campus has a number of interesting buildings in the Gothic style, including the Healy Building, which houses the administrative offices and the Information Center. Worth a look. Open daily.

Library of Congress, 10 1st St. SE (287-5000): The world's largest library, in an impressive Italian Renaissance granite building modeled on the Opéra in Paris. The interior is sumptuously decorated. The catalog lists 85 million books and other items in 470 languages, from a Gutenberg Bible to the original draft of the Declaration of Independence, not to mention Pierre-Charles l'Enfant's preliminary plan of Washington. Built around the 6,847 volumes from Thomas Jefferson's personal collection, which he sold to Congress for $23,950 after the original Library had been burned by the British in 1814, the Library of Congress today possesses more than 20 million books; it is a depositary library, and since 1870 has received two free copies of every book published in the United States. Don't fail to see the Library, and particularly the marble staircase of the Grand Hall and the dome of the main Reading Room. Open daily.

Octagon House, New York Ave. and 18th St. NW (638-3105): Unusual octagonal structure dating from 1798, which served as a temporary home for President Madison after the British burned the White House in 1814; now the headquarters of the American Institute of Architects. Temporary exhibitions; interesting period furniture. Open Tues.-Sun.

Old Stone House, 3051 M St. NW (426-6851): Believed to be the oldest surviving building in Washington from the pre-Revolutionary period (about 1765). The charming little two-story house with massive stone walls located in the heart of Georgetown was both a private home and a place of business. Magnificently restored in the original manner and décor of the 18th century. Worth a visit. Open Wed.-Sun.

Petersen House, 516 10th St. NW (426-6924): The house where President Lincoln was taken after Booth's fatal shot at Ford's Theater across the street (see above); he died here the next morning, April 15, 1865, at 7:22 a.m. Memorabilia of the affair that horrified America. Open daily.

The White House, 1600 Pennsylvania Ave. NE (456-7041): The most famous building in the U.S., home to every American president since John Adams in 1800. Designed by the architect James Hoban following the style of the Irish mansion of the Duke of Leinster, the White House owes its name to the whitewash with which its blackened frontage was hastily covered after the British burned it in 1814. Rebuilt in 1817, the original structure has been often enlarged and altered, particularly by the 1824 addition of a graceful elliptical portico along the side of the house facing the Mall. More than a million and a half visitors pass through the White House each year; tickets are free, and may be obtained from the kiosk in the Ellipse in front of the south front, but only five reception rooms, of the total of 32 rooms in the Executive Mansion, are open to the public; there is no admission either to the president's private quarters on the second floor, or to his office and the offices of his staff in the West Wing. On a busy day, particularly in summer, you may have to wait as long as two hours for your guided tour, but they are given from 10 a.m. until noon Tues.-Sat., except on Jan. 1 and Dec. 25. Visitors' entrance is the east gate on E. Executive Ave. If you write sufficiently far ahead to your (or a friendly) senator or congressman, you may be able to obtain a ticket for a "personalized" VIP visit to the White House, which will allow you to avoid the long waiting lines in summer. You should specify a choice of dates. Requests, in writing, should be addressed to a senator at the United States Senate, Washington, DC 20510, or a congressman at the United States House of Representatives, Washington, DC 20515. In any case, be sure to see the White House.

Woodrow Wilson House, 2340 S St. NW (673-4034): Home of former President Wilson from the end of his second term until his death in 1924, then of his widow until she died in 1961, this elegant red-brick Georgian-style town house is now a museum. Many personal memorabilia of the 28th president; reconstructs the atmosphere and the way of life of the upper middle class in the '20s. Should be seen. Open Tues.-Sat., Mar.-Dec.; weekends only in Feb.; closed Jan.

MONUMENTS:

Arlington National Cemetery, opposite Memorial Bridge, Arlington, Va. (703/692-0931): Overlooking the Potomac, this largest and most famous of America's national cemeteries shelters 201,000 of the dead, both illustrious like Presidents William H. Taft and John F. Kennedy (before whose tomb burns an eternal flame), Adm. Richard Byrd., Robert F. Kennedy, Gen. George Marshall, and Pierre-Charles l'Enfant, or nameless, like the Unknown Soldier, whose tomb commemorates the dead of the two World Wars and the Korean and Vietnam Wars. Lovely countryside, and a unique view of Washington from **Arlington House** (see "Panoramas," below). The changing of the guard, every hour exactly on the hour, is a spectacular sight. Every year more than four million people visit Arlington; bus trips daily, though the vehicles are not allowed to enter the cemetery itself. Don't miss it.

Jefferson Memorial, Tidal Basin, Potomac Park SW (426-6822): A graceful circular building by John Russell Pope (1943) in white marble, surrounded by an Ionic colonnade reminiscent of the Pantheon in Rome. Commemorates the author of the Declaration of Independence and third president of the U.S. A masterpiece of classical architecture which you have to see (try to be there in early Apr. when the Japanese cherries are in bloom). Open daily.

Lincoln Memorial, 23rd St. south of Constitution Ave. NW (426-6841): Washington's finest monument, the work of Henry Bacon (1922). Majestic white marble building inspired by the Parthenon in Athens, and setting off the Capitol at the other end of the Mall. A colossal statue of Lincoln by Daniel Chester French looks down on the visiting throngs. The memorial's 36 Doric columns correspond to the states of the Union at the time of Lincoln's death. Engraved on the walls of the two side rooms are the salient sentences from his second Inaugural Address and his famous Gettysburg Address of 1863. Open daily; don't miss it. Particularly impressive at sunset and when floodlit after dark.

Theodore Roosevelt Memorial, north end of Theodore Roosevelt Island, reached by footbridge from George Washington Memorial Pkwy. (285-2598): Erected in 1965 in memory of the 26th president of the U.S., this austere monument in its wooded setting is an allusion to Theodore Roosevelt's interest in nature conservation; the island is itself a wildlife reserve. Worth a look. Open daily.

U.S. Marine Corps War Memorial, Arlington Blvd., Arlington, Va. (703/433-4173): Impressive group in bronze, 64 ft (23 m) high, by Felix de Weldon. Inspired by Joe Rosenthal's photograph of marines raising Old Glory on the island of Iwo Jima in 1945. Fine view over Washington. Military parades on Tues. at 7 p.m. June-Aug. Must be seen.

☼🔔 **Vietnam Veterans Memorial,** Constitution Ave. at 21st St. NW (426-6700): A 492-foot-long (150 m) monument of polished black granite in the shape of a large letter "V," bearing the names of some 58,000 GIs reported dead or missing during the Vietnam War. The design, by Maya Ying Lin, a 21-year old architecture student at Yale, is both tragic and moving in its simplicity. It was unveiled in 1982. The memorial is the most popular in Washington, attracting 12,000 to 15,000 visitors daily.

☼🔔🔔 **Washington Monument,** the Mall near 15th St. NW (426-6839): A 555-ft (169-m) obelisk in white Maryland marbie designed by architect Robert Mills in 1885, in memory of the first president (see "Panoramas," below).

MUSEUMS OF ART: ☼🔔 Corcoran Gallery of Art, 17th St. and New York
Ave. NW (638-3211): The most important collection of American art after New York's Metropolitan Museum, with works by many artists including Mary Cassatt, Childe Hassam, John Singleton Copley, and Rembrandt Peale; also paintings by such European masters as Rembrandt, Corot, Daumier, and Degas from the Clark Collection. Highly regarded school of fine arts. Very popular temporary exhibitions. Must positively be seen. Open Tues.-Sun.

🔔 **Fondo del Sol Art Center,** 2112 R St. NW (483-2777): Unusual museum conceived as a way of presenting and promoting the work of contemporary Caribbean and Latin American artists and craftsmen. Also has a fine collection of pre-Columbian art and of *santos* (religious statues carved in wood). Interesting temporary exhibitions. Worth a look. Open daily.

☼🔔 **Museum of Modern Art of Latin America,** 201 18th St. at Constitution Ave. NW (458-6016): Part of the Panamerican Union Building (see "Architectural Highlights," above), this enchanting little museum displays a remarkable range of works by contemporary Caribbean and Latin American painters and sculptors; the exhibits are changed every six months. Lovely Aztec garden with giant statue of the god Xochipilli, the "Flower Prince." Should be seen. Open Tues.-Sat.

☼🔔🔔🔔 **National Gallery of Art,** Constitution Ave. between 3rd and 7th Sts. NW (737-4215): The cultural jewel of Washington, in a handsome 1941 classical revival setting by John Russell Pope. Along with New York's Metropolitan, this is one of the outstanding museums in the country, or the world. Fabulous collection of paintings from Leonardo da Vinci (his only canvas in the U.S.) to Kandinsky, from Botticelli to Salvador Dali. The new (east) wing of the museum, designed by I. M. Pei and linked to the main building by an underground passage, is a masterpiece of modern architecture (1978) and houses contemporary works of art by Robert Motherwell, Picasso, Henry Moore, Alexander Calder, and others. Among the gallery's most famous works are Fra Angelico's *Adoration of the Magi,* Titian's *Portrait of Doge Andrea Gritti,* El Greco's *St. Martin and the Beggar,* Rogier van der Weyden's *Portrait of a Woman,* Vermeer's *Woman Weighing Pearls,* a *Self-Portrait* by Rembrandt, and *Family of Acrobats* by Picasso. The eight million visitors who come here every year are the largest number for any art gallery in the world; allow at least one full day. Top-class temporary exhibitions (O'Keeffe, Gauguin . . .). Excellent cafeteria. The National Gallery justifies a trip to Washington all by itself.

🔔 **National Museum of Women in the Arts,** New York Ave. and 13th St. NW (783-5000): Founded as recently as 1987, this museum is entirely devoted to women artists. There are some 500 paintings, sculptures, and ceramics, from the Renaissance (Lavinia Fontana) through the impressionists (Mary Cassatt) to the moderns (Georgia O'Keeffe, Helen Frankenthaler, and so on). The impressive Renaissance Revival building dates from 1908 and was originally intended as a Masonic temple with a superb Grand Hall. Should be seen; open Tues.-Sun.

Phillips Collection, 1600 21st St. NW (387-2151): The country's oldest (1921) museum of modern art, with very fine European impressionists (Monet, Renoir, Cézanne, Van Gogh) and American abstractionists (Mark Rothko, Hans Hofmann, Jackson Pollock) in the Phillips family's elegant mansion. An absolute must. Tues.-Sun.

The Smithsonian Institution

The world's largest complex of museums and research centers for the arts, science, and history. Created in 1846, the foundation has 5,000 members and its establishments are visited by 25 million people annually. They include:

Freer Gallery, 12th St. and Jefferson Dr. SW (357-1300): Wonderful collection of Far Eastern art (Chinese bronzes, Hindu sculptures, Japanese screens), and some important American paintings by James McNeill Whistler, John Singer Sargent, Winslow Homer, and others, in an elegant "palazzo" in the Florentine tradition. Whistler's *Peacock Room* is worth a visit all to itself. Ongoing renovations until 1990.

Hirshhorn Museum, Independence Ave. and 8th St. SW (357-1300): Wonderful modern sculptures and paintings, from Rodin and Miró to Dali and Henry Moore, in a futurist circular museum designed by Gordon Bunshaft in 1974 and irreverently nicknamed "the doughnut." More than 4,000 paintings and 2,000 sculptures collected over a half century by Joseph H. Hirshhorn, a financier of Latvian origin, and donated by him to the Smithsonian in 1966. Among the most famous works on exhibition: Rodin's *Burghers of Calais,* Snelson's *Needle Tower,* Oldenburg's *Geometric Mouse,* Henry Moore's *Seated Woman,* Brancusi's *Sleeping Muse,* Jackson Pollock's *Aquatic Silhouette,* and *Heads of Jeanette* by Matisse. Not to be missed. Open daily.

National Museum of African Art, 950 Independence Ave. SW (357-4600): This wonderful underground museum designed by Junzo Yoshimura, along with the adjoining Sackler Gallery (see below), cost $73 million and opened in 1987. It houses the nation's largest collection of African art comprising some 6,000 objects in all, from Angolan ceremonial masks by way of Benin metal sculptures and wood figures from Zaire to copper vessels from the Lower Niger. Unusual and fascinating; don't miss it. Open daily.

National Museum of American Art, 8th and G Sts. NW (357-2700): Paintings, sculptures, and graphics by American artists from Colonial times to the present day, including works by Sargent, Homer, Wyeth, Prendergast, Whistler, and George Catlin, the greatest painter of Indians. Must be seen. In the south wing of the building is the **National Portrait Gallery,** 8th and F Sts. NW (357-2627), with busts and portraits of famous figures in American history, including Gilbert Stuart's well-known *George Washington* and a portrait of Mary Cassatt by Degas. Should be seen. Open daily.

Renwick Gallery, 1611 Pennsylvania Ave. NW (357-1300): Interesting museum of decorative art, with posters, drawings, etc. The fine flower of popular artistic expression. Unusual temporary exhibitions. Worth a visit. Open daily.

Arthur M. Sackler Gallery, 1050 Independence Ave. SW (357-4880): Another very fine underground museum opened in 1987, adjoining the National Museum of African Art, a flawless achievement aesthetically and architecturally. More than a thousand objects are displayed here from China, Southeast Asia, India, and the Middle East; the Chinese jades and Persian manuscripts are particularly beautiful. A must-see. Open daily.

MUSEUMS OF SCIENCE AND HISTORY: ☼⚜ Anderson House Museum, 2118 Massachusetts Ave. NW (785-0540): Home of the respected Society of the Cincinnati, a patriotic organization founded in 1783, this luxurious Beaux Arts mansion from 1906 displays a rich collection of historical items bearing on the War of Independence. Portraits, books, period weapons. Many antique art objects. For history buffs. Open Tues.-Sat.

⚜ **B'nai B'rith Klutznick Museum,** 1640 Rhode Island Ave. NW (857-6583): Jewish religious and folk art; history of Judaism in the U.S. (note a letter from George Washington to the Jewish community of Newport, R.I.) and of the Jewish contribution to the American trade union movement. Interesting. Open Sun.-Fri. except for Jewish holidays.

☼⚜ **Daughters of the American Revolution / DAR Museum,** 1776 D St. NW (879-3242): A complex of turn-of-the-century buildings occupied by the DAR, a patriotic organization now numbering some 200,000 members, which was founded in 1890 for descendants of those who fought in the War of Independence. Includes a museum of decorative art with 33 "State Rooms" decorated in the style of the Revolutionary period; one of the country's most important genealogical libraries, tracing the family trees of the earliest immigrants and their descendants; and **Constitution Hall,** a 3,800-seat auditorium. A must for history buffs. Open daily.

☼⚜ **Folger Shakespeare Library,** 201 E. Capitol St. SE (544-7077): The world's largest collection of Shakespeariana, with 180,000 works; also possesses an Elizabethan-style theater and a scaled-down replica of London's famous Globe Theatre (performances Oct.-July). Open daily, Apr.-Aug.; Mon.-Sat. the rest of the year.

☼⚜ **Frederick Douglass Memorial Home,** 1411 W St. SE (426-5961): The founder of the Black Liberation movement in America, the black activist Frederick Douglass, who was himself born a slave, lived here from 1877 until his death in 1895. Famous orator, journalist, lawyer, and for a time, U.S. Ambassador to Haiti, he is looked on as the father of the civil rights movement—a forerunner of Martin Luther King, Jr. Interesting personal museum and well-stocked library. Open daily; should be seen.

☼⚜ **Marine Corps Museum,** Bldg. 58, Washington Navy Yard, M and 9th Sts. SE (433-3534): 200 years of the United States Marine Corps' history, illustrated by its weapons, its uniforms, and other soldierly souvenirs, arranged in chronological order from the foundation of this elite unit in 1775. The museum is hard to reach without a car. Open daily.

⚜ **Martin Luther King Library,** 901 G St. NW (727-1111): In this austerely beautiful black building by Mies van der Rohe is a library devoted to the winner of the Nobel Peace Prize, with many works relating to the struggle for civil rights. Also books, movies, and photographs on the history of the city of Washington, and the archives of the now-defunct daily *Washington Star.*

☼⚜⚜ **National Archives,** Constitution Ave. between 7th and 9th Sts. NW (523-3183): Imposing Greek Revival building designed by John Russell Pope, containing the country's most prized historical documents, from the originals of the Constitution, the Bill of Rights, and the Declaration of Independence, to the 1783 Treaty of Paris bearing the signature of Benjamin Franklin and the seal of King George III of England, the 1945 instruments of surrender of Germany and Japan, and the notorious Watergate tapes. Among the innumerable other documents and curiosities of history is the photo album of Hitler's mistress, Eva Braun. Fascinating; must certainly be seen. Open daily.

☼⚜⚜ **National Building Museum,** 4th and F Sts. NW (272-2448): This building, perhaps the most unusual in Washington, originally built to house the proliferating offices of the Civil War veterans' pension administration, now displays temporary exhibitions. Splendid interior hall with 75-ft (22-m) Corinthian columns. A positive must-see. Open daily.

National Geographic Society, 17th and M Sts. NW (857-7000): Home of the world-famous *National Geographic* magazine. In Explorers Hall you'll find brilliantly conceived exhibitions devoted to the exploration of land, sea, and outer space, and a terrestrial globe 11 ft (3 m) in diameter. Should be seen. Open daily.

National Library of Medicine, 8600 Rockville Pike, Bethesda, Md. (301/496-6308): The world's largest medical library in an ultramodern building belonging to the National Institutes of Health, with four million books, professional periodicals, manuscripts, and other works in 70 languages, accumulated in the course of 150 years. Visitor Center and conducted tours. If you're a disciple of Hippocrates, this is for you. Open Mon.-Fri.

National Rifle Association Firearms Museum, 1600 Rhode Island Ave. NW (828-6194): More than 1,500 firearms, from 15th-century arquebuses to the latest in sub-machineguns; one of the largest in the world, as you would expect from an association numbering three million enthusiasts. Open daily.

Naval Observatory, 34th St. and Massachusetts Ave. NW (653-1543): Standing amid spacious gardens adjoining the official home of the vice-president of the U.S., this observatory administered by the U.S. Navy is responsible for determining standard American time. Interesting astronomical museum (admission at 2 p.m. Mon.-Fri.). Every Mon. when the moon is full, budding astronomers may scan the heavens through a 26-inch (65-cm) telescope.

Navy Museum, Bldg. 76, Washington Navy Yard, 9th and M Sts. SE (433-2651): From the mizzenmast of the famed frigate *Constitution* to a replica of the command station of a submarine, complete with periscope, and including a destroyer moored in front of the museum and open to visitors, you will find here a complete history of the U.S. Navy, from the engagements of the War of Independence to the age of nuclear missiles. Fascinating. Museum hard to reach except by car. Open daily.

The Smithsonian Institution

As well as the various art museums listed above, the Smithsonian Institution also comprises:

Anacostia Museum, 1901 Fort Pl. SE (357-2700): In a largely black neighborhood in the south of Washington, this museum reopened in 1987 at a new location. It presents temporary exhibitions dealing with the role of minorities, ethnic and other, in American society. Should be seen. Open daily.

National Air and Space Museum, Independence Ave. and 7th St. SW (357-1300): Possibly the most remarkable aeronautical museum in the world, designed by Gyo Obata and opened in 1976. Here, under an enormous vaulted roof, are displayed the most memorable machines in the history of flying and space exploration: the *Kitty Hawk Flyer,* the Wright Brothers' first plane; the *Spirit of St. Louis,* first aircraft to be flown solo across the Atlantic in 1927; the *Bell X-1,* the first aircraft to exceed the speed of sound; the fastest aircraft in the world, the *X-15,* which has reached Mach 6; a copy of *Sputnik 1,* the Soviet satellite which was the first to be placed in orbit around the earth; the *Apollo 11* module, which made the first lunar landing in 1969. There are extraordinary audiovisual shows, including *To Fly* and *Living Planet.* Ultramodern planetarium **(Albert Einstein Spacearium).** The most visited museum in the world—ten million people come here every year. Very good new restaurant and cafeteria. An absolute must. Open daily.

National Museum of American History, Constitution Ave. and 14th St. NW (357-1300): Immense museum of science and technology. On the ground floor is a 280-ton locomotive which had to be moved into place before the museum was built! Comprehensive collection of historic objects, from George Washington's false teeth and the ceremonial dresses of First Ladies to "Old Glory," the original star-spangled banner which inspired Francis Scott Key to write the words of the National Anthem, and from Alexander Graham Bell's first telephone to a wooden gunboat which lay for 200 years beneath the waters of Lake Champlain. Not to be missed. Open daily.

National Museum of Natural History, Constitution Ave. and 10th St. NW (357-1300): A comprehensive Museum of Man. A spectacular 92-ft (28-m) blue whale; the largest stuffed elephant in the world, weighing eight tons; a life-size diplodocus. Anthropological material from the Western Hemisphere, Africa, and Asia. Extensive collection of minerals including the world-famous Hope Diamond of 44 carats. Archeology, biology, etc. An absolute must. Open daily.

PANORAMAS: Arlington House / Custis-Lee Mansion, Arlington National Cemetery, Arlington, Va. (703/557-0613): On a hill above Arlington National Cemetery (see "Monuments," above), this very fine Greek Revival house, once the home of Gen. Robert E. Lee, the Confederate commander-in-chief during the Civil War, has a splendid view of the Potomac River and downtown Washington. Lee abandoned Arlington House in 1861, at the beginning of the war, and never set foot there again. Overlooks the tomb of President John F. Kennedy. Don't miss the view. Open daily.

Bell Tower of the Old Post Office, Pennsylvania Ave. and 12th St. NW (523-5691): This 315-ft (96-m) Gothic Revival clock tower crowns the former central post office and has a spectacular view of downtown Washington. Elevator. Open daily, 10 a.m. to 5:45 p.m. Worth a look.

Washington Monument, The Mall, nr. 15th St. NW (426-6841): A 555-ft (169-m) white marble obelisk dedicated to the first president of the U.S. A masterpiece of simple grandeur, this monument, which has become the city's symbol, was unveiled in 1885 and opened to the public three years later. From an observation platform 502 ft (153 m) up, there is a truly spectacular panoramic view; on a clear day you can see the Blue Ridge Mountains 50 mi. (80 km) away. Elevator. Since more than two million tourists come here every year, you may have a long wait in line, particularly in summer. Open daily from 8 a.m. to midnight in summer; from 9 a.m. to 5 p.m. the rest of the year. Don't miss it.

Washington National Cathedral, Wisconsin and Massachusetts Aves. NW (537-6207): The Pilgrim Observation Gallery at the top of the cathedral's tower, 300 ft (91 m) above the ground, has a fine view of the northern part of the city as far as the banks of the Potomac. Worth seeing. Open daily, 10 a.m. to 3 p.m.

PARKS AND GARDENS: Botanic Garden Conservatory, Maryland Ave. between 1st and 2nd Sts. SW (225-8333): A tropical jungle under glass, and some beautiful gardens, at the foot of the Capitol: a botanic cross-section of all five continents. Worth seeing. Open daily.

Kenilworth Aquatic Gardens, Kenilworth Ave. and Douglas St. NE (426-6905): On the bank of the Anacostia River, a wonderful aquatic garden with lotus, water hyacinth, bamboo, and water lilies by the thousand (flowering spectacularly from June to Aug.). Worth seeing. Open daily.

Lafayette Square, Pennsylvania Ave., between Jackson and Madison Place NW: This charming tree-shaded little square in front of the main façade of the White House is a godsend to footsore tourists (and for demonstrators who want to express dissatisfaction outside the White House railings). Besides an equestrian statue (1853) of Andrew Jackson, seventh president, the square is embellished with statues of four foreign-born heroes of the War of Independence: the German Friedrich Wilhelm von Steuben, the Pole Tadeusz Kosciuszko, and two Frenchmen, the Comte de Rochambeau and the Marquis de Lafayette. On the north side of the square is St. John's Episcopal Church, attended by many presidents of the U.S. In the corner of the square, Blair House, at 1651 Pennsylvania Ave. NW, is the official residence of foreign heads of state visiting Washington (not open to the public). If you want to take souvenir snapshots in front of the White House, this is the place to do it.

The Mall, between the Capitol and the Potomac River: This broad green carpet runs through the center of Washington on either side of the 655-yard (600-m) **Reflecting Pool.** On the **Ellipse,** a great oval of lawn behind the White House, stands the Zero Milestone, placed there in 1923 to mark the zero mile of the great U.S. highways. One of the loveliest views in Washington, and a squirrels' paradise.

Meridian Hill Park, 16th St. between Euclid St. and Florida Ave. NW (426-6851): Hidden from public view behind high walls, this 12-acre (5-ha.) terraced park, though little-known to Washingtonians, is perhaps the most beautiful landscaped complex in the capital. Completed in 1936, the park, sometimes known as **Malcolm X Park,** comprises a garden in the French style with clumps of trees, stone benches, and a statue of Joan of Arc on horseback, as well as a baroque Italian garden with a magnificent 13-step waterfall reminiscent of the famous fountains of the Villa d'Este near Rome. A sight you shouldn't miss, but the neighborhood is unsafe after nightfall. Open daily.

National Arboretum, 3501 New York Ave. NE (475-4815): Floral displays throughout the year, particularly impressive in spring when the azaleas are in flower. Pretty Japanese garden and collection of bonsai (dwarf trees). On the banks of the Anacostia River. Worth a detour. Open daily.

Potomac Park, along Ohio Dr. SW (485-9666): Extensive tree-lined walk along the Potomac and Washington Channel on either side of the Jefferson Memorial. The beautiful cherry trees given by the Japanese government in 1912 are in flower in late March and early April around the Tidal Basin and East Potomac Park. Two golf courses; fishing; skating in winter; boat rental. A lovely sight in season. Much favored by joggers. Open daily.

Rock Creek Park, along Rock Creek Pkwy. and Beach Dr. NW (426-6829): 1,754 acres (710 ha.) of winding, rolling parkland on either side of Rock Creek, a tributary of the Potomac. Golf, tennis, horseback riding, open-air concerts in summer in the **Carter Barron Amphitheater.** A joggers' favorite, but don't go there after dark.

Roosevelt Island, Potomac River, reached by a footbridge from the George Washington Pkwy. at Arlington, Va. (285-2598): Unspoiled nature 10 min. from downtown, with a memorial dedicated to President Theodore Roosevelt. Open from sunrise to sunset, daily. Worth the trip.

PERFORMING ARTS: For a daily listing of all shows and cultural events, consult the entertainment pages of the daily papers *Washington Post* (morning) and *Washington Times* (morning), and of the monthly magazine *The Washingtonian.*

American Film Institute, Kennedy Center, New Hampshire Ave. NW at Rock Creek Pkwy. (785-4600): The depository library of the American cinema, with all the great classics.

Arena Stage, 6th St. and Maine Ave. SW (488-3300): Three contiguous theaters; musicals, contemporary and classical theater.

Carter Barron Amphitheater, Rock Creek Park, 4850 Colorado Ave. NW (829-3200): Open-air concerts in a 4,000-seat auditorium in the woods; folk, pop, and jazz. Mid-June to Aug.

D.C. Space, 7th and E Sts. NW (347-1445): Popular comedy club in the spirit of "Saturday Night Live."

Folger Theater, 201 E. Capitol St. SE (546-4000): Classical (Shakespeare) and modern theater.

Ford's Theater, 511 10th St. NW (347-4833): The theater where Abraham Lincoln was assassinated, now a designated historic monument with the original décor restored. Musicals, modern theater.

John F. Kennedy Center for the Performing Arts, New Hampshire Ave. NW at Rock Creek Pkwy. (254-3600): Major, ultramodern entertainment complex with five different halls and auditoriums: the **Concert Hall,** home of the National Symphony (principal conductor, Mstislav Rostropovich), concerts and recitals of classical music; the **Eisenhower Theater,** modern and classic plays and Broadway hits; the **Opera House,** home of the Washington Opera (director, Martin Feinstein), opera, ballet; the **Terrace Theater,** chamber music; **Theater Lab,** off-Broadway and experimental theater.

Lisner Auditorium, George Washington University, 21st and H Sts. NW (994-6800): Opera, classical concerts, jazz; recitals.

National Theater, 1321 E St. NW (628-6161): Musicals, Broadway hits.

New Playwrights Theater, 1742 Church St. NW (232-1122): Modern theater, comedy, drama.

Source Theater, 1835 14th St. NW (462-1073): Modern and experimental theater.

Trinity Theater, 36th and O Sts. NW (965-4680): Musicals, off-Broadway plays.

Warner Theater, 513 13th St. NW (626-1050): Modern theater, Broadway hits.

Washington National Cathedral, Wisconsin and Massachusetts Aves. NW (537-6200): Concerts of sacred music, recitals, organ recitals.

Wolf Trap Farm Park for the Performing Arts, 1624 Trap Rd. at Va. 676, Vienna, Va. (703/255-1868): Big open-air auditorium used in summer for shows and concerts—jazz, classical, pop, opera, folk, ballet. Enormously popular. June-Sept. For details, see "Special Events," below.

Ticket Place, 12th and F St. Plaza NW (842-5387): Sells tickets at half price for all same-day performances: shows, ballet, concerts, plays, etc. Open Mon.-Sat. from 11 a.m. to 7 p.m.

SHOPPING: **Georgetown** (see "Strolls," below) has innumerable boutiques and fashion shops. In the **Watergate** building, **Les Champs** is a shopping arcade with some 30 luxury boutiques and shops (Valentino, Gucci, Yves St. Laurent, Saks Fifth Avenue, etc.).

The Shops (1331 Pennsylvania Ave. NW), **International Square** (1850 K St. NW), **The Pavilion at the Old Post Office** (1100 Pennsylvania Ave. NW), and **Esplanade Mall** (1990 K St. NW) are four ultramodern downtown shopping malls, each with dozens of trendy boutiques and shops as well as plenty of bars and restaurants.

Another successfully designed, modern-style shopping center is **Georgetown Park Mall,** 3222 M St. NW, with a round 100 establishments doing business in a pretty Victorian-rococo setting.

The traditional department stores have for the most part fled to the huge shopping plazas on the outskirts of the city, the smartest and most accessible of which is **Mazza Gallerie** at Wisconsin and Western Aves. NW, in Chevy Chase, Md.; there's a subway stop right outside.

Highly recommended for the transient visitor are the gift shops of the various museums on the Mall; their gifts are original and usually affordable as well.

If food is important to you, visit **Sutton Place Gourmet,** 3201 New Mexico Ave. NW, or better still, at 10323 Old Georgetown Rd. in Bethesda, Md., Washington's answer to Zabar's in New York or Fauchon's in Paris.

SPECIAL EVENTS: For the exact schedule of events below, consult the **Washington Convention and Visitors Association** (see "Tourist Information," above).

Cherry Blossom Festival (late Mar. to early Apr.): Parades, concerts, balls when the Japanese cherries are in flower.

Flying Circus (May-Oct.): Displays of aerobatics in old propeller-driven craft of the barnstorming era, every Sunday at 2 p.m. Picturesque and entertaining. You'll find it at the end of a 40-min. drive from downtown Washington along I-66W, U.S. 211W, and U.S. 17S, on U.S. 17 at Bealeton, Va. (703/439-8661). If you're nostalgic about goggles and leather helmets, this is for you.

Friday Evening Parade (mid-May to mid-Sept.): Unusually spectacular; the marines on parade Fridays at 8:15 p.m., U.S. Marines Barracks, 8th and I Sts. SE. You have to reserve several days ahead (433-6060).

Memorial Day Ceremony (Memorial Day): The president lays a wreath on the tomb of the Unknown Soldier in Arlington National Cemetery. In the evening, the National Symphony gives an open-air concert on the lawn in front of the Capitol.

Festival of American Folklife (late June to July): Colorful display of America's folklore heritage on the Mall.

Outdoor Concerts on the Mall (June-Aug.): Places and times vary from day to day; consult the newspapers or call 426-4011.

Kool Jazz Festival (early June): The world's biggest names in jazz come to the Kennedy Center for 48 hours.

July 4th Celebration (July 4): Concerts and fireworks on the Mall.

Wolf Trap Festival (June-Sept.): Open-air concerts of classical music, jazz, ballet, opera, etc.; draws 600,000 spectators yearly. At Wolf Trap Farm, Vienna, Va. (703/255-1868), 14 mi. (22 km) NW on George Washington Memorial Pkwy., I-495S, and Dulles Airport Rd.

SPORTS: Washington has three professional teams:

Basketball (Oct.-Apr.): Bullets, Capital Center, Landover, Md. (301/350-3400).

Football (Aug.-Dec.): Redskins, RFK Stadium (546-2222).

Ice Hockey (Oct.-Apr.): Capitals, Capital Center, Landover, Md. (301/350-3400).

Horse Racing

Laurel Race Track, Baltimore-Washington Pkwy. exit to Md. 198, 18 mi. (28 km) NW in Laurel, Md. (301/725-0400), for thoroughbred racing, Sept.-Feb.

Rosecroft Raceway, 6336 Rosecroft Dr., 8 mi. (13 km) SE, in Oxon Hill, Md. (301/567-4000), has harness racing Jan.-May and Oct.-Dec.

STROLLS: ⚲ Adams Morgan, bounded by Columbia Rd., Florida Ave., and

18th St. NW: A sort of local melting pot where blacks rub shoulders with yuppies, Latin American exiles, Europeans, and riff-raff from around the world. Unlike the rest of Washington, it remains lively and bustling until 2 a.m. The neighborhood restaurants reflect the cosmopolitan crowd: Ethiopian, Créole, Chinese, Japanese, French, Mexican, Caribbean, Brazilian, and more. Worth a visit.

Potomac Banks (see the Potomac Park and Roosevelt Island entries under "Parks and Gardens," above): Very pleasant in fine weather.

Embassy Row, Massachusetts Ave. between Scott Circle and Belmont Rd. NW: The world's largest diplomatic quarter, with some 80 embassies, consulates, and legations in a span of less than one mile. You should see this national display of national flags and coats-of-arms.

Georgetown, around Wisconsin Ave. and M St. NW: In Colonial days, Georgetown was a leading port for the export of tobacco; today it's a charming residential district. While some of its former elitist glitter has worn off, it's still—with its old houses, little narrow streets, boutiques, nightclubs, and variety of restaurants—both the Greenwich Village and the Soho of the nation's capital. Particularly lively on weekends. You should make a point of seeing the **Old Stone House** at 3051 M St. NW, the city's oldest house (1765), and **Dumbarton Oaks,** 1703 32nd St. NW, with its fine collections of Byzantine and pre-Columbian art. You might like to do as many tourists do every summer—take a barge ride on the **C. & O. Canal.** The house where John F. Kennedy lived before his election to the presidency is at 3307 N St. NW; no visitors. **Washington Harbor,** 3030 K St. NW, is a vast terraced esplanade on the Potomac—an imaginative piece of post-modern design by Arthur Cotton Moore. And there are many more things to see; don't miss this stroll.

THEME PARKS: ☼ ⚲⚲ Kings Dominion, I-95 and Va. 30 at Doswell, Va., 78

mi. (124 km) SW on I-95 (804/876-5000): Comprehensive theme park on 800 acres (324 ha.), with a picturesque reconstruction of Old Europe, including a miniature Eiffel Tower, as well as dozens of attractions such as carousels and giant roller coasters. Big-name shows; safari zoo. Open daily, June to Labor Day; weekends only from late Mar. to June and from Labor Day to early Oct.

Wild World, 13710 Central Ave. at Md. 214, in Mitchellville, Md., 15 mi. (24 km) east on E. Capitol St. and Central Ave. (301/249-1500): Giant roller coaster ("Wild One"); pool holding one million gallons (3.8 million liters), with artificial waves for surfers, the biggest of its kind in the world; and dozens of other family attractions. 20 min. from downtown Washington. Open daily, early May through Sept.

WINTER SPORTS RESORTS: ⚲ Blue Knob, 150 mi. (240 km) NW on I-

270N and I-70N, Pennsylvania Tpke. west, U.S. 200N, and Penna. 869W (814/239-5111): 5 lifts.

Canaan Valley, 180 mi. (288 km) west on I-66W, Va. 55W, and W. Va. 32N (304/866-4121): 4 lifts; one of the best resorts in the region.

Massanutten, 125 mi. (200 km) SW on I-66W, I-81S, U.S. 33E, and Va. 644N (703/289-9441): 5 lifts.

Ski Liberty, 65 mi. (104 km) NW on I-270N, U.S. 15N, Md. 140W, Penna. 16W, and Penna. 116E (717/642-8297): 5 lifts.

♟♟ **Ski Roundtop,** 121 mi. (194 km) N on I-95N, I-695W, I-83N, Penna. 382W, and Penna. 177N (717/432-9631): 8 lifts.

☼♟♟ **Wintergreen,** 168 mi. (268 km) SW on I-66W, U.S. 29S, I-64W, Va. 6E, and Va. 151S (804/325-2200): 5 lifts.

ZOOS: ☼ ♟♟ **National Zoological Park,** 3001 Connecticut Ave. NW (673-4717): One of the finest and best-known zoos in the country; almost 3,000 animals representing 600 species, some of them very rare, such as the Indian white tiger, the only pair of Komodo dragons in the Western hemisphere, and pandas donated by the People's Republic of China, in facsimiles of their natural environment. Belongs to the Smithsonian Institution. A must-see. Open daily.

ACCOMMODATIONS

See the listing of toll-free numbers in the Appendix.

Room Rates in Washington, D.C.	
B (Budget)	up to $30
I (Inexpensive)	$30–$60
M (Moderate)	$60–$90
E (Expensive)	$90–$140
VE (Very Expensive)	$140 and up

Personal Favorites (in order of preference)

♟♟♟♟ **Four Seasons** (nr. dwntwn), 2800 Pennsylvania Ave. NW, DC 20007 (202/342-0444; toll free, see Four Seasons). 198 rms, A/C, color TV, in-rm movies. AE, CB, DC, MC, V. Valet parking $12, rest. (Aux Beaux Champs), coffeeshop, bar, 24-hr rm svce, nightclub, free crib, concierge. *Note:* The cream of Washington luxury hotels, its ocher brick intended to harmonize w. Georgetown's old houses. Elegantly comfortable; refined interior; polished, personalized svce. Spacious rms w. period furniture, some w. balconies, the best overlooking Rock Creek Park. Excellent rest. Free limo to dwntwn. The VIP's favorite. **VE**

♟♟♟♟ **Grand Hotel** (nr. dwntwn), 2350 M St. NW, DC 20037 (202/429-0100; toll free 800/848-0016). 265 rms, A/C, color TV, in-rm movies. AE, CB, DC, MC, V. Valet garage $10, pool, rest. (the Mayfair), piano bar, 24-hr rm svce, free crib, concierge. *Note:* Opened in 1985 as the Regent, this is one of the most elegant of Washington's new grand hotels. Subdued, distinguished post-modern design capped w. a copper dome. A profusion of marble and paneling, especially in the lobby. Comfortable, inviting rms w. immense Italian marble bathrooms. Extremely distinguished svce; rest. of a high order. Clientele of wealthy businessmen—the hotel is located right in the West End business district. **VE**

♟♟♟ **Madison** (dwntwn), 15th and M Sts. NW, DC 20005 (202/862-1600; toll free 800/424-8577). 365 rms, A/C, color TV, in-rm movies. AE, CB, DC, MC, V. Garage $6, two rests. (including the Montpelier Room), two bars, rm svce, crib $25, concierge. *Note:* Ungraceful modern building elegantly and tastefully decorated within, w. period furniture, master paintings, and rich Oriental rugs. Big businessmen, foreign dignitaries, prominent politicians, and entertainers (including Henry Kissinger, Frank Sinatra, Bob Hope, and David Rockefeller) have been coming here for a quarter of a century. Spacious, comfortable rms w. mini-bars. Thoughtful, discreet svce; overpriced, pretentious rest. Opposite the *Washington Post* building. Boasts one of Washington's most expensive suites, at $1,800 a night, plus tax. **VE**

🏩🏩🏩 **Watergate Hotel** (nr. dwntwn), 2650 Virginia Ave. NW, DC 20037 (202/965-2300; toll free 800/222-0939). 238 rms, A/C, color TV, in-rm movies. AE, CB, DC, MC, V. Valet garage $12, pool, health club, sauna, rest., coffeeshop, bars, rm svce, hrdrsr, boutiques. *Note:* Relatively modern luxury hotel of original design, part of the celebrated Watergate development on the Potomac, a stone's throw from the Kennedy Center. Inviting, comfortable rms, the best w. river view; elegant décor w. Far Eastern works of art. Remarkable rest. (Jean Louis); flawless svce. Attracts many well-heeled foreigners. Run by the British company Cunard, which owns London's famous Ritz Hotel. 10 min. from dwntwn. (free morning limo). **VE**

🏩🏩🏩 **Hilton-Capitol** (nr. dwntwn), 1001 16th St. NW, DC 20036 (202/393-1000; toll free, see Hilton). 549 rms, A/C, color TV, in-rm movies. AE, CB, DC, MC, V. Valet parking $8, health club, two rests. (including Trader Vic's), coffeeshop, bar, rm svce, nightclub, hrdrsr, boutiques, free crib, concierge. *Note:* After many years of neglect and decay, this wonderfully located convention hotel, in the heart of the business district and only three blocks from the White House, has recently undergone a $55-million facelift. Rms are now larger, redecorated, and w. mini-bars; facilities have been completely renovated. Four VIP floors w. their own elevator and concierge. New, fully equipped business center. Svce (at last) efficient and hustling. The airport buses have their terminal here. Business and convention clientele. **E-VE**

🏩🏩 **Embassy Row** (nr. dwntwn), 2015 Massachusetts Ave. NW, DC 20036 (202/265-1600; toll free 800/424-2400). 196 rms, A/C, color TV, in-rm movies. AE, CB, DC, MC, V. Valet garage $10, pool, rest. (Ambassador Grill), bar, 24-hr rm svce, concierge, free breakfast. *Note:* Elegant little hotel in the heart of the embassy district. Comfortable rms and suites, some with mini-bars. Foreign and diplomatic clientele. The help speaks a number of languages but the svce is undependable. Acceptable rest. Interesting wknd discounts. **E-VE**

🏩🏩 **Channel Inn** (nr. dwntwn), 650 Water St. SW, DC 20024 (202/554-2400; toll free 800/368-5668). 100 rms, A/C, color TV, in-rm movies. AE, CB, DC, MC, V. Free parking, pool, rest., bar, rm svce, disco, free crib. *Note:* Agreeable motel right on the water; comfortable, more-than-usually spacious rms w. balconies, the best overlooking Washington Channel and the marina. Efficient svce. 5 min. from the Mall and its museums. Tourist clientele. Good value on balance. **M-E**

🏩🏩 **Howard Johnson at Kennedy Center** (nr. dwntwn), 2601 Virginia Ave. NW, DC 20037 (202/965-2700; toll free, see Howard Johnson's). 194 rms, A/C, color TV. AE, CB, DC, MC, V. Free garage, rooftop pool, 24-hr rest., bar, free crib. *Note:* Traditional eight-floor motel a block or two from the Kennedy Center, opposite the Watergate complex and 10 min. from dwntwn. Functionally comfortable rms w. refrigerators, some w. balconies. Efficient reception and svce. Favored by show-business people. Good overall value. **M**

🏩 **Normandy Inn** (nr. dwntwn), 2118 Wyoming Ave. NW, DC 20008 (202/483-1350; toll free 800/424-3729). 74 rms, A/C, color TV, in-rm movies. AE, CB, DC, MC, V. Valet garage $6, rm svce. *Note:* Charming hotel, aging but very well maintained, in the heart of the embassy district, 10 min. from dwntwn. Functionally comfortable. Friendly reception and svce. Regular clientele; good value. **M**

    Allen Lee Hotel (dwntwn), 2224 F St. NW, DC 20037 (202/331-1224). 90 rms, A/C, color TV. No credit cards. *Note:* Small economy hotel very nr. the State Department and George Washington University. Limited comforts—some rms have no private bath—but agreeable atmosphere. Ideal for budget travelers. Youthful clientele. **I**

Other Accommodations (from top bracket to budget)

    Willard Inter-Continental (dwntwn), 1401 Pennsylvania Ave. NW, DC 20004 (202/628-9100; toll free, see Inter-Continental). 394 rms, A/C, color TV, in-rm movies. AE, CB, DC, MC, V. Valet parking $15, rest. (Willard Room), coffeeshop, bar, 24-hr rm svce, boutiques, free crib, concierge. *Note:* This venerable Beaux Arts building dates from 1901, is a designated historic monument, and has long been known as "the hotel of presidents." Long allowed to deteriorate, and indeed threatened with demolition, a $75-million restoration program completed in 1986 has restored all its old splendor as well as its sumptuous interior. All the world's great have stayed here, from Mark Twain to Richard Nixon. The standard rms are somewhat cramped and gloomy; the suites and studios, on the contrary, are unusually elegant and comfortable. The lobby promenade known as Peacock Alley was, at the turn of the century, a favorite meeting place for politicians and the representatives of special-interest groups—whence the term "lobbyist." Highly regarded but overpriced rest. The Round Robin Bar is famous. Svce of the highest order. Boasts Washington's most expensive suite—$2,000 a night, plus tax. One of the great names among American hotels. **VE**

    Grand Hyatt (dwntwn), 1000 H St. NW, DC 20001 (202/582-1234; toll free, see Hyatt). 907 rms, A/C, color TV, in-rm movies. AE, CB, DC, MC, V. Parking $8 (valet parking $12), three rests., two bars, 24-hr rm svce, disco, drugstore, free crib, concierge. *Note:* Big brand-new brick, stone and concrete cube, well-located across from the Convention Center, but completely lacking in architectural originality. Its 12-story lobby w. skylight, giant waterfall, pool, and indoor gardens is, on the other hand, an altogether praiseworthy piece of design. Huge, well-designed rms; unexpectedly efficient svce given the sheer size of the place. VIP floor; group and convention clientele. **VE**

    Hay-Adams Motel (dwntwn), 1 Lafayette Square NW, DC 20006 (202/638-6600; toll free 800/424-5054). 144 rms, A/C, color TV, in-rm movies. AE, CB, DC, MC, V. Valet garage $10; two rests. (including the John Hay Room), coffeeshop, bar, 24-hr rm svce, concierge. *Note:* The best location in town, right across from the White House. Charming old hotel in the European fashion, a favorite of visiting foreign statesmen and dignitaries for more than half a century. Spacious, elegant rms w. balconies and mini-bars, some w. fireplaces, the best looking out on Lafayette Square. Period furniture. Excellent svce, discreet and attentive. Good rests. Quality and style. **VE**

    Jefferson Hotel (dwntwn), 1200 16th St. at M St. NW, DC 20036 (202/347-2200; toll free 800/368-5966). 104 rms, A/C, color TV. AE, CB, DC, MC, V. Valet parking $10, two rests. (including the Hunt Club), bar, 24-hr rm svce, free crib, concierge. *Note:* Charming little '20s hotel, tastefully renovated. Each spacious, comfortable rm is decorated in a different style; most have four-poster beds. Exemplary svce. The Hunt Club is one of Washington's fashionable rests. Distinction and elegance near the embassy district and four blocks from the White House. Leonard Bernstein is a regular. **VE**

ggg **J. W. Marriott** (dwntwn), 1331 Pennsylvania Ave. NW, DC
20004 (202/393-2000; toll free, see Marriott). 774 rms,
A/C, color TV, in-rm movies. AE, CB, DC, MC, V. Valet parking $12, pool,
health club, three rests. (including Celadon), coffeeshop, bars, 24-hr rm svce,
nightclub, hrdrsr, boutiques, free crib, concierge. *Note:* The flagship hotel of the
Marriott chain, an ultramodern palace whose design earns no plaudits, strategi-
cally placed a stone's throw from the Mall and the White House. Luckily, the
interior decoration and equipment are more successful. Enormous, boastful lobby w. marble floors and huge crystal chandeliers; spacious, well-designed rms;
efficient though impersonal svce. As in all Marriotts, so-so rests. Business and
convention clientele. Two VIP floors ("Marquis Floors"); direct access to "The
Shops" at National Place, a shopping mall with 110 shops and 20 rests. The
movie *Broadcast News* was in part shot here. **VE**

ggg **Ritz-Carlton** (formerly the Fairfax; nr. dwntwn), 2100 Massachusetts Ave. NW, DC 20008 (202/293-2100; toll free 800/
424-8008). 240 rms, A/C, color TV. AE, CB, DC, MC, V. Valet parking $10,
rest. (Jockey Club), bar, 24-hr rm svce, nightclub, crib $20, concierge. *Note:* This
elegant, classy old hotel in the heart of the embassy district has undergone a
much-needed facelift, and is now smart and distinguished, achieving a harmonious combination of elegance and comfort. There are, however, still shortcomings in maintenance and svce. Spacious rms w. mini-bars; good hotel rest. (a
favorite of President Kennedy and Nancy Reagan). Big business and diplomatic
clientele. **VE**

ggg **Sheraton Grand** (dwntwn), 525 New Jersey Ave. NW, DC
20001 (202/628-2100; toll free, see Sheraton). 243 rms,
A/C, color TV, in-rm movies. AE, CB, DC, MC, V. Valet parking $10, rest.
(Signature Room), coffeeshop, bar, 24-hr rm svce, free crib, concierge. *Note:* The
newest of Capitol Hill's luxury hotels: an elegant, modern 15-story building w. a
vast pink-marble lobby, waterfall, and indoor garden in what is quickly becoming
the conventional manner. Comfortable, very well-equipped rms (personal computers, exercise equipment, refrigerators, etc.). Very acceptable rest. serving
American cuisine. Efficient svce. Free dwntwn limo. Business clientele. A block
or two from the Capitol and Union Station. **VE**

ggg **Hilton Washington and Towers** (nr. dwntwn), 1919 Connecticut Ave. NW, DC 20009 (202/483-3000; toll free, see
Hilton). 1,165 rms, A/C, color TV, in-rm movies. AE, CB, DC, MC, V. Valet
garage $7, pool, tennis court, health club, two rests., coffeeshop, two bars, rm
svce, disco, hrdrsr, drugstore, free crib. *Note:* Massive white tourist barracks in
the shape of two arcs of a circle, standing in 6 acres (2 ha.) of garden. Up-to-date
comfort. Spacious rms w. refrigerators, some w. balconies. Very complete facilities; rather distracted svce and average rests. Crowded out year round by groups
and conventions. Two top floors reserved for VIPs (Hilton Towers). It was in
front of this hotel that an attempt was made to assassinate President Reagan on
March 30, 1981. 10 min. from dwntwn. **E–VE**

ggg **Loews L'Enfant Plaza** (nr. dwntwn), 480 L'Enfant Plaza SW,
DC 20024 (202/484-1000; toll free, see Loews). 372 rms,
A/C, color TV, in-rm movies. AE, CB, DC, MC, V. Valet parking $7, pool, two
rests., bar, rm svce, disco, boutiques, free crib, concierge. *Note:* Successful essay in
futurist architecture, occupying the top four floors of an ultramodern office complex w. underground shopping mall and direct subway access. Luxurious, comfortable rms w. mini-bars, most w. balconies. Inviting open-air pool on 12th
floor. Very good svce. A few blocks from the Mall and its museums. Business and
group clientele. A good place to stay. **E–VE**

ggg **One Washington Circle** (dwntwn), 1 Washington Circle
NW, DC 20037 (202/872-1680; toll free 800/468-3532).

152 suites, A/C, color TV. AE, CB, DC, MC, V. Parking $9, pool, rest., bar, rm svce, nightclub, concierge, free breakfast. *Note:* Modern, very comfortable hotel halfway between the White House and Georgetown. Suites only, spacious and w. kitchenettes and refrigerators (most w. balconies). Elegantly decorated and furnished. Irreproachable svce. Business clientele. Inviting little garden. An excellent place to stay. **E–VE**

Ramada Renaissance (nr. dwntwn), 1143 New Hampshire Ave. NW, DC 20037 (202/775-0800; toll free, see Ramada Inns). 356 rms, A/C, color TV, in-rm movies. AE, CB, DC, MC, V. Parking $9, rest., coffeeshop, bar, rm svce, disco, hrdrsr, free crib, concierge. *Note:* Luxurious, inviting hotel in the West End business district. Unappealing modern building and no physical-fitness facilities, but spacious, very comfortable rms and relatively efficient svce. Business clientele, VIP floor. Interesting wknd and vacation packages. **E–VE**

Holiday Inn Capitol (dwntwn), 550 C St. SW, DC 20024 (202/479-4000; toll free, see Holiday Inns). 529 rms, A/C, color TV, in-rm movies. AE, CB, DC, MC, V. Parking $6, pool, rest. (Smithson's), bar, rm svce, nightclub, hrdrsr, boutiques, free crib. *Note:* Huge modern nine-floor motel a stone's throw from the Mall and the Capitol. A typical Holiday Inn, w. comfortable rms, efficient reception and svce. Group and convention clientele; interesting wknd discounts. Ideal base for visits to the Mall museums. **E–VE**

Quality Inn Capitol Hill (dwntwn), 415 New Jersey Ave. NW, DC 20001 (202/638-1616; toll free, see Quality Inns). 340 rms, A/C, color TV, in-rm movies. AE, CB, DC, MC, V. Free parking, pool, rest. (Coach and Parlor), bar, rm svce. *Note:* Comfortable ten-floor motel 5 min. from the Capitol and Union Station. Functional rms; efficient reception and svce; so-so rest. Caters to groups and conventions. Rooftop pool open in summer w. view of the city. **M–E**

Washington Hotel (dwntwn), 515 15th St. NW, DC 20004 (202/638-5900; toll free 800/424-9540). 350 rms, A/C, color TV, in-rm movies. AE, CB, DC, MC, V. Garage $8, rest. (Two Continents), coffeeshop, bar, rm svce, free crib. *Note:* Massive, aging luxury hotel now entirely renovated. Very well located 3 min. from the White House and 5 min. from the Mall and its museums. Spacious, comfortable rms; efficient svce. The top-floor rest.-bar has one of the finest views of the city. Interesting wknd discounts. A Washington landmark since 1918. **M–E**

Comfort Inn (dwntwn), 500 H St. NW, DC 20001 (202/289-5959; toll free 800/228-5150). 197 rms, A/C, color TV, in-rm movies. AE, CB, DC, MC, V. Parking $8, health club, sauna, rest., bar, valet svce. *Note:* Brand-new hotel very nr. the Convention Center. Comfortable, well-designed rms; efficient reception and svce. Business and group clientele. **M–E**

Hotel Bellevue (dwntwn), 15 E St. NW, DC 20001 (202/638-0900). 140 rms, A/C, color TV. AE, DC, MC, V. Free parking, rest. (Tiber Creek), bar, rm svce. *Note:* One of Washington's oldest hotels, but comfort and facilities are maintained at a very acceptable level. Entirely renovated rms, some w. refrigerators; inviting rest. and pub. Friendly svce. A stone's throw from the Capitol and Union Station. Good overall value; interesting wknd discounts. **M–E**

Tabard Inn (dwntwn), 1739 N St. NW, DC 20036 (202/785-1277). 42 rms, A/C, color TV, in-rm movies. MC, V. Street parking, rest., bar. *Note:* Charming little hotel, elderly and a touch bohemian (built in 1860, it's the oldest in Washington). Comfortable Victorian-style rms, some without private bathrooms. Four floors, no elevator. Clientele of artists and intellectuals, creating a very European atmosphere. Pleasant rest. and bar. 5 min. from the White House. Worthwhile wknd discounts. **M–E**

🔑 **Days Inn Connecticut Ave.** (formerly the Best Western; nr. dwntwn), 4400 Connecticut Ave. NW, DC 20008 (202/244-5600; toll free, see Days Inns). 155 rms, A/C, color TV, in-rm movies. AE, CB, DC, MC, V. Free parking, pool, rest., free breakfast. *Note:* Relatively elderly but comfortable motel, recently renovated. Spacious rms; smiling reception. Interesting family rates. Very good value. 7 min. from dwntwn by subway. **M**

🔑 **Harrington Hotel** (dwntwn), 11th and E Sts. NW, DC 20004 (202/628-8140; toll free 800/424-8532). 308 rms, A/C, color TV. AE, CB, DC, MC, V. Free parking, coffeeshop (Kitcheteria), bar, sandwich shop. *Note:* Elderly but acceptable grand hotel in a fast-improving neighborhood nr. the Mall and the White House, a few blocks from Pennsylvania Ave. Very commendable standard of comfort. Group clientele. Reductions to YMCA members. Very good value. **I–M**

Airport Accommodations

🔑🔑🔑 **Ramada Renaissance Dulles Airport** (vic.), 13869 Park Center Rd., Herndon, VA 22071 (703/478-9286; toll free, see Ramada Inns). 301 rms, A/C, cable color TV. AE, CB, DC, MC, V. Free valet parking, two pools, tennis court, health club, sauna, rest., coffeeshop, bars, 24-hr rm svce, disco, hrdrsr, free crib. *Note:* Luxurious, modern airport hotel 2 min. from the terminal (free shuttle). Spacious, well-equipped rms w. refrigerators. Comprehensive facilities. Efficient reception and svce. Ideal for a stopover between flights. Business clientele; two VIP floors. 40 min. from dwntwn. **E–VE**

YMCAs/Youth Hostels

International Guest House (nr. dwntwn), 1441 Kennedy St. NW, DC 20011 (202/726-5808). Priority given to visitors from abroad. Operated by the Mennonite church, and w. the lowest rates in Washington. Very acceptable comfort.

International Hostel (dwntwn), 1009 11th St. NW, DC 20001 (202/737-2333). 250 rms. Youth hostel open to members and nonmembers. Very central.

RESTAURANTS

Washington, D.C., Restaurant Prices	
(per person, excluding drinks and service charges)	
B (Budget)	up to $15
I (Inexpensive)	$15–$25
M (Moderate)	$25–$40
E (Expensive)	$40–$60
VE (Very Expensive)	$60 and up

Personal Favorites (in order of preference)

🍷🍷🍷🍷🍷 **Jean Louis** (nr. dwntwn), in the Watergate Hotel (see "Accommodations," above) (298-4488). A/C. Dinner only,

Mon.-Sat.; closed Sun. AE, CB, DC, MC, V. J&T. *Specialties:* ragoût of cèpes, Belon oysters w. leek purée, blanquette of fish w. fresh mint, magret of duck w. honey and dates, sweetbreads w. truffles, lobster w. caviar butter, fresh foie gras w. peaches, saddle of rabbit w. wild mushrooms. Remarkable desserts. Well-stocked but overpriced wine list. The menu is changed periodically. *Note:* French-style nouvelle cuisine triumphant, under the command of one of the great chefs of his generation, the young Jean Louis Palladin, whose prestigious La Table des Cordeliers in Le Gers, France, rated two stars in Michelin. Sauces light as air, refined but simple preparation, the choicest (American) raw materials, perfect cooking, and elegant preparation combine to make his cuisine a genuine masterpiece. Elegant, flowery décor in pastel tones. Service exemplary in all respects. Since there are only 42 seats, you should reserve a number of days ahead. President Reagan had his 70th birthday dinner here. One of the dozen best rests. in the country, but prices to match. *French.* **VE**

🍷🍷🍷 **Windows** (nr. dwntwn), 1000 Wilson Blvd., in Arlington, Va. (703/527-4430). A/C. Lunch Mon.-Sat., dinner nightly. AE, CB, DC, MC, V. Jkt. *Specialties:* California-style pizza (w. smoked salmon, w. caviar, w. shrimp and mussels, w. duck sausage, etc.), sautéed fresh foie gras, chilled parsley soup, broiled salmon w. vinaigrette of champagne and papaya, swordfish steak w. almond-and-orange butter, sautéed veal w. wild mushrooms, broiled tuna w. hazelnut-and-mint sauce, lemon-curd tart w. blackberries. The menu changes seasonally. *Note:* Across the Potomac on the eighth floor of the futurist *USA Today* building, Windows gives you a clear view of the Washington skyline and an imaginative, distinguished modern American cuisine. Chef Henry Dinardo is a virtuoso of delicate sauces. Dining room on two levels, w. lacquered walls and elegant flower arrangements. Only the svce doesn't quite measure up. Big business clientele; resv. a must. Free parking in the evening. 15 min. from dwntwn. *American.* **E**

🍷🍷🍷 **Morton's** (nr. dwntwn), 3251 Prospect St. NW, Georgetown (342-6258). A/C. Dinner only, Mon.-Sat.; closed Sun. and holidays. AE, CB, DC, MC, V. Jkt. *Specialties:* wonderful aged beef, veal or lamb chops, catch of the day, Maine lobster, so-so desserts. *Note:* This pillar of the local dining scene has been acclaimed for a decade as Washington's best steakhouse. Steak, porterhouse, and ribs of beef that are quite exceptional, but also fine fish and gigantic lobsters, broiled to perfection. Comfortable, elegant London club-style interior, w. an interesting collection of paintings by LeRoy Neiman. Excellent svce, quick and efficient. No resv. after 7 p.m. Same management as the well-known Morton's in Chicago. Rather noisy; a favorite with local politicians and lobbyists. *Steak-Seafood.* **M–E**

🍷 **Primi Piatti** (dwntwn), 2013 I St. NW (223-3600). A/C. Lunch Mon.-Fri., dinner Mon.-Sat.; closed Sun. and holidays. AE, DC, MC, V. *Specialties:* mixed antipasti, inventive pizzas cooked over a wood fire, fresh homemade pasta, fritto misto, fish, chicken and meat broiled with polenta, chocolate terrine with strawberry coulis. Good list of Italian wines. *Note:* Here you will find no sophisticated fare or trendy sauces; the emphasis is rather on basic Italian dishes such as mixed hors d'oeuvres, various kinds of homemade pasta, broiled foods, and pizza, all of them nonetheless pleasing and tasty. Hence the name of this huge, modern, likeable *trattoria* in the heart of dwntwn. Noisy, relaxed atmosphere; yuppie patrons; fashionable place. Resv. not honored so you'll have to wait, especially at lunchtime. *Italian.* **I–M**

🍷 **Szechuan Restaurant** (dwntwn), 615 I St. NW, Chinatown (393-0130). A/C. Lunch/dinner daily. AE, MC, V. *Specialties:* Hot-and-sour soup, duck smoked over tea leaves, fish rolls, shrimp Szechuan, sesame chicken, pork tripe w. chili and black mushroom, sweet-hot crispy beef,

Mongolian pork, lamb in garlic sauce. Dim sum at Sat. and Sun. lunch. *Note:* By general consent Washington's best Chinese rest., serving excellent Hunan and Szechuan food. Very popular with residents who frequent Chinatown, especially on wknds. Modernized, light-filled décor; service surly but efficient. Very good value; resv. advised. *Chinese.* **I**

⚙🍸🍸 **Old Ebbitt Grill** (dwntwn), 675 15th St. NW (347-4801). A/C. Breakfast/lunch/dinner daily (until 1 a.m.). AE, DC, MC, V. *Specialties:* spaghetti w. four cheeses, cannelloni w. spinach, crab cake, hamburgers, sautéed veal scaloppine, baked scrod, broiled fish of the day, calves' liver w. onions, roast pork w. applesauce, chicken pot pie. Good homemade desserts. *Note:* Founded in 1856, the Old Ebbitt Grill is Washington's oldest saloon, though the present building, once a vaudeville theater, dates only from the turn of the century. The menu includes all the great American classics and some specialties as well. Pretty Victorian setting w. marble floors, Persian rugs, oak beams, and gas lamps; fine bar. Locally popular. Same management as Clyde's (see below). *American.* **I–M**

🍸🍸 **Crisfield** (vic.), 8012 Georgia Ave., Silver Spring, Md. (301/589-1306). A/C. Lunch/dinner Tues.-Sun.; closed Mon., Dec. 25, and the last week in Aug. No credit cards. *Specialties:* clam chowder, oysters on the half shell, crab cake, crab Imperial, catch of the day sautéed or stuffed with crabmeat. *Note:* Seafood rest. with no mannerisms or affectations; the décor is period Formica, but the seafood is absolutely fresh and cooked to perfection. You can eat standing at the counter. Quick, efficient svce. Very popular locally; unfortunately no resv., so you'll have to wait. 25 min. from dwntwn. *Seafood.* **I**

⚙🍸 **Le Gaulois** (dwntwn), 2133 Pennsylvania Ave. NW (466-3232). A/C. Lunch Mon.-Fri., dinner Mon.-Sat.; closed Sun. and holidays. AE, MC, V. *Specialties:* scallops with Pernod, quenelles de brochet, confit of duck, braised tongue w. mustard, pot-au-feu, brains w. sauce Gribiche. Good homemade fruit tarts. Menu changes daily. *Note:* Attractive French-bistro food and setting; always crowded. Resv. advised at all times, but the waiting line can still be long, especially at lunch. Svce often overburdened. Regular clientele; excellent value. *French.* **I–M**

🍸 **El Caribe** (nr. dwntwn), 3288 M St. NW, Georgetown (338-3121). A/C. Lunch/dinner daily; closed holidays. AE, CB, DC, MC, V. *Specialties:* Empanadas, shrimp w. garlic, paella, zarzuela of seafood, roast pork w. bananas, arroz con pollo, beef tongue w. tomato, squid stuffed w. ham, South American dishes. *Note:* A real Georgetown "find": traditional Spanish dishes and some very successful Latin American specialties. The setting is that of a nice little Spanish home. Efficient svce; very good value; resv. advised. Also located at 1828 Columbia Rd. NW (234-6969). *Latin-American/Spanish.* **I**

🍸 **Sushi Ko** (nr. dwntwn), 2309 Wisconsin Ave. NW, Georgetown (333-4187). A/C. Lunch Tues.-Fri., dinner Tues.-Sun.; closed Mon. AE, MC, V. *Specialties:* sushi, miso soup, shrimp tempura, teriyaki, yakitori. *Note:* Many of the patrons of this small, unimaginatively decorated Japanese bistro come from the nearby Japanese Embassy; in spite of the downbeat setting it's the best sushi bar in Washington. Poker-faced svce. *Japanese.* **I**

Other Restaurants (from top bracket to budget)

🍸🍸🍸 **Le Lion d'Or** (dwntwn), 1150 Connecticut Ave. NW, w. entrance on 18th St. (296-7972). A/C. Lunch Mon.-Fri., dinner Mon.-Sat.; closed Sun. and holidays. AE, CB, DC, MC, V. J&T. *Specialties:* mousse of seafood, sautéed morels w. fresh pasta (in season), ravioli of foie gras, navarin of lobster, civet of duck w. red wine, filet of lamb w. herbs, rockfish in pastry shell, game in season. Very good desserts and soufflés; large wine list at reasonable prices. Menu changes regularly. *Note:* The owner, Jean Pierre Goyenvalle, is one of the most talented French chefs now working in the U.S.; his splendid, very elaborate cuisine is a happy marriage of the traditional with nouvelle tendencies (such as shorter cooking times). The décor is an elegant, old-fashioned, commonplace, the svce is courteous and polished. Can be noisy. Resv. a must, since this is the favorite rest. of local VIPs. One of the best places to eat on the East Coast. Free parking at dinner. *French.* **E–VE**

ℙℙℙ **Cantina d'Italia** (dwntwn), 1214A 18th St. NW (659-1830). A/C. Lunch/dinner Mon.-Fri.; closed Sat., Sun., and holidays. AE, CB, DC, MC, V. J&T. *Specialties:* stuffed wild mushrooms, polentina, splendid fresh homemade pasta, duck w. grapes, snapper baked in parchment, sautéed kidneys, bagna cauda, escalope Sorrentina, fricassee of rabbit w. peppercorns and rosemary. Great cholcolate-espresso cheesecake. Good wine list at outrageous prices. Menu changes regularly. *Note:* A Washington landmark for more than two decades. Delicate, tasty Italian food served in serious portions. Attentive svce. The décor, however—gloomy, cramped, and underground—is somewhat claustrophobic; if the setting were more inviting, this rest. would rate a fourth glass. Business and diplomatic clientele; resv. necessary. *Italian.* **M–E**

☀ℙℙℙ **Occidental** (dwntwn), 1475 Pennsylvania Ave. NW (783-1475). A/C. Lunch/dinner daily (until 11:30 p.m.); closed holidays. AE, CB, DC, MC, V. Jkt. *Specialties:* crab cakes w. sauce tartare, hamburgers, steak, pepper salmon, pheasant w. wild mushrooms, rack of lamb w. garlic and cream, médaillon of beef w. shallots, bread pudding in bourbon sauce, squash ice cream. Fine list of American wines. *Note:* Once known as "the restaurant where statesmen dine," as witness the 2,500-odd photographs of leading politicians on the walls, this turn-of-the-century rest., now splendidly restored, is a true Washington classic. In the Grill, on the ground floor, the food is agreeably bistro style; upstairs in the Restaurant it's a more sophisticated American nouvelle cuisine. Efficient, smiling svce. Resv. advised. An excellent place a stone's throw from the White House. *American.* **M (Grill), E (Restaurant)**

ℙℙℙ **Twenty-one Federal** (dwntwn), 1736 L St. NW (331-9771). A/C. Lunch Mon.–Fri., dinner Mon.–Sat.; closed Sun. and holidays. AE, MC, V. Jkt. *Specialties:* wild-mushroom ravioli, herb-crusted sole w. tomatoes and chive butter, roast loin of pork w. chiles, black beans and corn pudding, veal loin w. purée of shallots, mixed grill of quail, calves' liver, duck sausage and sweet breads, "palette" of chocolate desserts. Fairly priced. *Note:* Named after its Nantucket forebear, this newcomer deserves its early success. The cuisine of chef and part-owner Bob Kinkead is modern-American cooking at its best. Luxurious décor w. exotic blond woods and a marble mosaic floor. Frequented by journalists, lobbyists, lawyers, and politicians (Edward Kennedy, John Chancellor, and Art Buchwald are regulars). Service is attentive yet unobtrusive. Good wine list. Getting a table is a problem; book *at least* a day or two ahead. *American.* **M–E**

ℙℙ **Dar Es Salam** (nr. dwntwn), 3056 M St. NW, Georgetown (342-1925). A/C. Dinner only, nightly (until 2 a.m.). AE, MC, V. Jkt. *Specialties:* b'stila (flaky pastry pie w. pigeon or chicken filling), tagine (mutton or chicken stew), couscous, shish kebab, chicken w. olives and lemon, calves' tongue stew w. cumin, Oriental pastries. *Note:* The only worthy representative of the justly renowned gastronomic traditions of Morocco. Luxuriously extravagant *Thousand and One Nights* décor, w. mosaics, carved wood, and overstuffed couches. Attentive, gracious svce. The height of the exotic in the heart of Georgetown. Locally popular; resv. advised. *Middle Eastern.* **M**

ℙℙℙ **Germaine's** (nr. dwntwn), 2400 Wisconsin Ave. NW (965-1185). A/C. Lunch Mon.-Fri., dinner nightly; closed Jan. 1,

Dec. 25. AE, CB, DC, MC, V. Jkt. *Specialties:* Vietnamese spring rolls, Korean kimchi, Thai beef w. basil, Indonesian sate, Japanese chicken teriyaki, Peking duck. Good wine list. *Note:* Germaine Swanson, the very talented Vietnamese who created this enormously popular rest., offers you a tasty cross-section of Far Eastern cuisines: Vietnamese, Korean, Chinese, Japanese, Thai, and more. Some of her dishes, like her "pine cone fish," have already become classics. Light-filled, elegant setting w. a huge skylight. Flawless svce. An excellent place to eat. Resv. advised. *Far eastern.* **M**

🍸🍸 **Joe and Mo's** (dwntwn), 1211 Connecticut Ave. NW (659-1211). A/C. Breakfast/lunch Mon.-Fri., dinner Mon.-Sat.; closed Sun. and holidays. AE, CB, DC, MC, V. Jkt. *Specialties:* crab cakes, steak, veal chops, roast beef, filet mignon, rack of lamb, broiled catch of the day. *Note:* A Washington landmark beloved of businessmen, reporters, and politicians, especially for the excellent breakfast and at lunchtime. Top-quality meat and fish; the roast beef is the best in town. Classic steakhouse décor and atmosphere; courteous, efficient svce. Resv. advised at lunch. *Steak.* **M**

🍸🍸 **La Colline** (dwntwn), 400 N. Capitol St. NW (737-0400). A/C. Breakfast/lunch Mon.-Fri., dinner Mon.-Sat.; closed Sun. and holidays. AE, CB, DC, MC, V. Jkt. *Specialties:* smoked salmon house style, fresh foie gras, shrimp Créole, salmon w. beurre blanc and baby turnips, braised sweetbreads w. zucchini, parsleyed ham, bouillabaisse, breast of duck w. blackcurrant; skip desserts. Good wine list at reasonable prices. *Note:* The likeable, bearded, 40-ish chef Robert Greault has worked a miracle: he serves excellent, elegant, varied bistro food at half the prices charged by other French rests. of the same caliber. Huge, modern, comfortable dining rm; ultra-professional svce. Very popular w. the locals, so resv. advised. At the foot of Capitol Hill near Union Station. *French.* **I–M**

🍸🍸 **New Orleans Emporium** (dwntwn), 2477 18th St. NW (328-3421). A/C. Lunch/dinner daily, brunch Sat. and Sun.; closed holidays. AE, CB, DC, MC, V. *Specialties:* oysters Rockefeller, barbecued shrimp, beignets of catfish, crayfish à l'étouffée, jambalaya, gumbo, blackened redfish, bread pudding w. brandy sauce, pecan pie. Skimpy wine list. *Note:* Tasty Créole/Cajun food in a very New Orleans setting, noisy and relaxed. Inviting bar; efficient svce; locally popular so resv. advised. A fine place. *Créole.* **I–M**

🍸 **Old Europe** (nr. dwntwn), 2434 Wisconsin Ave. NW, Georgetown (333-7600). A/C. Lunch/dinner daily; closed Dec. 25. AE, CB, DC, MC, V. *Specialties:* smoked loin of pork, sauerbraten, bratwurst, wienerschnitzel, schnitzel à la Holstein, game in season, apfelstrudel. Fine list of German wines. *Note:* Typically German food and setting, w. a fine collection of beer steins. The best thing here is the venison dishes, in season. Smiling, efficient waitresses. Resv. advised. This is where you come to celebrate Oktoberfest. *German.* **I–M**

🍸 **China Inn** (dwntwn), 631 H St. NW, Chinatown (842-0909). A/C. Lunch/dinner daily (until 3 a.m.). AE, MC, V. *Specialties:* spiced shrimps, clams w. black-bean sauce, Cantonese roast duck, smoked crabmeat, roast pork Chow Mai Fun, lemon chicken, steamed sea bass w. ginger. So-so desserts. *Note:* A Chinatown classic for more than half a century, serving good Cantonese food at prices very easy on the wallet. Recently modernized and enlarged. Friendly svce (unusual for a Chinese rest.). Locally popular; very good value. *Chinese.* **I**

🍸🍸 **Enriqueta's** (nr. dwntwn), 2811 M St. NW, Georgetown (338-7772). A/C. Lunch Mon.-Fri., dinner nightly; closed holidays. AE, CB, DC, MC, V. *Specialties:* tacos, enchiladas verdes, tamales, mussels w. chili, stuffed green pepper, mole poblano (turkey in chocolate sauce), shrimp w. coriander, ceviche, cremitas. *Note:* Enriqueta's dishes have the true Mexican flavor; the setting, too, is as lively, noisy, and colorfully decorated as you could hope for south of the Rio Grande. Diligent svce. Since the place is as small as it is (and as successful), resv. are advised. Also at 1832 Columbia Rd. NW (328-0937); dinner only. *Mexican.* **I**

Filomena (nr. dwntwn), 1063 Wisconsin Ave. NW, Georgetown (338-8800). A/C. Lunch Mon.-Fri., dinner nightly (until midnight); closed holidays. AE, CB, DC, MC, V. *Specialties:* fresh homemade pasta, zuppa di pesce, chicken Tetrazzini, veal alla zingara. Good list of Italian wines. *Note:* Chrome, copper, and houseplants give this huge brasserie more of a Californian than an Italian air, but the food is 100% authentic, and in generous portions. Diligent, friendly svce. Locally popular, so resv. advised. *Italian.* **I**

Tandoor (nr. dwntwn), 3316 M St. NW, Georgetown (333-3376). A/C. Lunch/dinner daily, brunch Sat. and Sun. AE, CB, DC, MC, V. *Specialties:* samosas, shrimp biriani, chicken tandoori, chicken tikka, curries, lamb vindaloo. *Note:* Lovers of exotic food will be captivated by these delicate, disconcerting dishes, which are ill-matched by the chilly, impersonal décor. Excellent svce.; very good value; resv. advised. *Indian.* **I**

The American Café (dwntwn), 227 Massachusetts Ave. NE (547-8500). A/C. Lunch/dinner daily (till 1 a.m.). AE, MC, V. *Specialties:* Excellent sandwiches and homemade soups, pizza, salads, sesame pasta, tarragon chicken, food broiled over mesquite wood, chili, daily specials. *Note:* In this modern, agreeable setting you'll enjoy a late supper or a lunch on the run. Interesting specialty salads. Young, trendy clientele. A stone's throw from the Capitol and Union Station. Relaxed svce. Very good value. Also at 1211 Wisconsin Ave. NW (944-9464) and 1331 Pennsylvania Ave. NW (626-0770). *American.* **I**

Calvert Café (nr. dwntwn), 1967 Calvert St. NW (232-5431). A/C. Lunch/dinner daily (until midnight). AE, MC, V. *Specialties:* kibbee, hummus, couscous, stuffed eggplant and vine leaves, baked lamb shank, shish kebab, baklava. *Note:* The colorful Mama Ayesha, owner of this quiet neighborhood rest., is everywhere at once in the dining room no less than the kitchen—and has been for the last 30 years. Tasty, moderately seasoned dishes. The décor is as unpretentious as the prices. Friendly svce; excellent value. *Middle Eastern.* **B–I**

Clyde's (nr. dwntwn), 3236 M St. NW (333-9180). A/C. Lunch/dinner daily (until 2 a.m.), brunch Sat. and Sun. AE, CB, DC, MC, V. *Specialties:* sandwiches, hamburgers, omelets, steak tartare, specialty salads, broiled foods. *Note:* Once favored by Washington's gilded youth, this likeable New York–style bistro still has a devoted following, especially among visitors. Good hamburgers (except when they're overcooked). Lovely greenhouse setting in the back dining room. Often crowded and noisy; relaxed atmosphere; svce disorganized but good-humored. Good value on balance. A landmark in Washington for more than 20 years. *American.* **B–I**

Restaurants in the Vicinity

L'Auberge Chez François (vic.), 332 Springvale Rd. (Va. 674), Great Falls, Va. (703/759-3800). A/C. Dinner only, Tues.-Sun; closed Mon. and holidays. AE, MC, V. Jkt. *Specialties:* quiche, salmon soufflé, Alsatian choucroute, sautéed kidneys, filet of lamb w. tarragon, truffled sweetbreads, duckling bigarade, navarin of seafood, coq au riesling. Very good homemade ice cream and tarts. Fine list of Alsatian wines. Menu changes regularly. *Note:* The food and the atmosphere are those of a deluxe inn in France. Some country dishes (tripe, homemade pâté de campagne), and some more sophisticated (salmon soufflé). Charming rustic décor; irreproachable svce; resv. a must some days (or weeks) ahead, considering its success. 35 min. from dwntwn. A fine place. *French.* **M**

☀♀ **Evans Farm Inn** (vic.), 1696 Chain Bridge Rd. (Va. 123), McLean, Va. (703/356-8000). A/C. Lunch/dinner daily; closed Dec. 25. AE, CB, DC, MC, V. *Specialties:* roast beef, barbecued chicken, Smithfield ham, barbecued spareribs, roast duckling. *Note:* Charming Colonial-style inn 30 min. by car from Washington. The dining rms overlook the garden and herb garden where the farm's vegetables and herbs are grown (ask to be seated in the dining rm nr. the entrance, w. its big stone hearth). Open-air meals in summer. Country food harking back to traditional Virginia recipes; family clientele. Usually crowded on wknds. Waiters in 18th-century costume. *American.* **I**

Cafeterias / Specialty Spots

☀ **Au Pied de Cochon** (nr. dwntwn), 1335 Wisconsin Ave. NW, Georgetown (333-5440). A/C. Breakfast/lunch/dinner daily (open around the clock). No credit cards. *Specialties:* omelets, rillettes, cold cuts, onion soup, quiches, pig's trotters, shallot steak, beef bourguignon, coq au vin, etc. *Note:* Picturesque French bistro w. a terrace, in the heart of Georgetown. Svce on the brusque side, but an entertaining place. Usually crowded; good value.

National Gallery Garden Café (dwntwn), Constitution Ave. and 4th St. NW (347-9401). A/C. Lunch/dinner daily (till 7:30 p.m. in summer, 4:30 p.m. in winter). No credit cards. *Specialties:* sandwiches, soup, quiches. *Note:* Ultramodern, inviting museum cafeteria overlooking the Mall; very acceptable food.

Sholl's Colonial Cafeteria (dwntwn), 1990 K St. NW in Esplanade Mall (296-3065). A/C. Lunch/dinner Mon.-Sat. (until 8 p.m.); closed Sun., Jan. 1, and Dec. 25. No credit cards. *Specialties:* calves' liver w. onions, spaghetti, roast chicken, daily specials, homemade pastry. *Note:* A popular cafeteria, much appreciated by Washingtonians. Offers excellent value; usually crowded at lunch. No alcoholic beverages. A Washington landmark since 1928.

Where to Eat in Washington?

American: Windows (♀♀♀); Twenty-one Federal(♀♀♀); New Orleans Emporium (♀♀); Occidental (♀♀); Old Ebbitt Grill (♀♀); The American Café (♀); Clyde's (♀); Evans Farm Inn (♀).

Cafeterias/Specialty Spots: Au Pied de Cochon; National Gallery Terrace Café; Sholl's Colonial Cafeteria.

Chinese: Szechuan Restaurant (♀♀); China Inn (♀).

French: Jean Louis (♀♀♀♀♀); Le Lion d'Or (♀♀♀♀); L'Auberge (♀♀♀); Chez François (♀♀♀); La Colline (♀♀); Le Gaulois (♀).

German: Old Europe (♀).

Hamburgers: Old Ebbitt Grill (♀♀); The American Cafe (♀); Clyde's (♀).

Indian: Tandoor (♀).

Italian: Cantina d'Italia (♀♀♀); Filomena (♀♀); Primi Piatti (♀♀).

Japanese: Sushi Ko (♀).

Latin-American: El Caribe (♀).

Middle Eastern: Dar Es Salam (♀♀); Calvert Café (♀).

Mexican: Enriqueta's (♀♀).

Oriental: Germaine's (♀♀♀).

Seafood: Crisfield (♀♀).

Spanish: El Caribe (♀).

Steak: Morton's (♀♀♀); Joe and Mo's (♀♀).

Late Night Service (closing time in parentheses): The American Café (midnight, 1 a.m., or 3 a.m. according to location); China Inn (3 a.m.); Clyde's (2 a.m.); Dar Es Salam (2 a.m.); Filomena (midnight); Old Ebbitt Grill (1 a.m.); Au Pied de Cochon (open round the clock).

BARS & NIGHTCLUBS

Bayou (nr. dwntwn), 3135 K St. NW, Georgetown (333-2897): Live rock and New Wave; youthful, relaxed ambience. Open nightly.

The Birchmere (vic.), 3901 Mt. Vernon Ave., Alexandria, Va. (703/549-5919): One of the best clubs in the country for folk and bluegrass; the biggest names appear here. Tues.-Sat.

Blues Alley (nr. dwntwn), on the alley behind 1073 Wisconsin Ave. NW, Georgetown (337-4141). The oldest jazz club in Washington, and still the best. All the big names from Dizzy Gillespie to Chick Corea and McCoy Tyner. Also acceptable Créole rest. Open nightly; two or three shows an evening.

Brickskeller (nr. dwntwn), 1523 22nd St. NW (293-1885). Very popular bar serving 500 varieties of domestic and imported beer; also rest. (so-so). Usually crowded. Open nightly until 2 a.m.

Chelsea's (nr. dwntwn), 1055 Thomas Jefferson St. NW, Georgetown (298-8222). Fashionable disco with live music, Latin rhythms. Open Tues.-Sun.

Comedy Café (dwntwn), 1520 K St. NW (638-5653). Oldest and best-known comedy club in Washington, presenting all the big names and young local talent as well. Open Thur., Fri., and Sat.; resv. advised.

Dakota (dwntwn), 1777 Columbia Rd. NW (265-6600). The fashionable disco in the trendy Adams Morgan neighborhood. Also acceptable rest. Patronized by students and yuppies. Open Tues.-Sun.

The Dubliner (dwntwn), 520 N. Capitol St. NW (737-3773). An authentically noisy, friendly Irish pub. Irish jigs and whisky are a must. Also average rest. Open nightly.

Fifth Column (dwntwn), 915 F St. NW (393-3632): Luxurious disco in a former branch bank. Marble dance floor, video music, and spectacular laser shows. Also acceptable rest. and art gallery. Clientele on the smart side. Open Tues.-Sat.

Rumors (nr. dwntwn), 1900 M St. NW (466-7378). Very popular singles bar in a handsome Colonial setting, ceiling fan included. Disco. Elegant clientele. Open nightly.

F. Scott's (nr. dwntwn), 1232 36th St. NW, Georgetown (342-0009). Well-known, congenial bar frequented by students from nearby Georgetown U. and intellectuals. Pretty art nouveau décor. Also undistinguished rest. Open nightly.

1063 (nr. dwntwn), 1063 Wisconsin Ave. NW, Georgetown (342-7373). Preppy disco; elegant clientele in an elegant setting. Don't go in blue jeans. Open nightly.

Tracks (nr. dwntwn), 1111 1st St. SE (488-3320). The fashionable gay club, drawing a very mixed crowd. Disco w. live music. Lots of action. Open nightly (until 6 a.m. on Fri. and Sat.).

NEARBY EXCURSIONS

ALEXANDRIA, VA. (7 mi., 11 km, south on George Washington Memorial Pkwy. and Washington St.; area code 703): Founded in the mid-18th century by Scottish merchants, this appealing little Colonial town on the Potomac has not kept pace with its mighty neighbor, Washington. With its cobbled streets, traditional streetlamps, and enchanting old houses, ☼ ♙♙ **Old Town Alexandria,** around King and Fairfax Sts., looks like a print from an old British book. No visit to Washington is complete without a pilgrimage to Mount Vernon (see below) and the other historic spots in Alexandria which are intimately associated with the life of George Washington: **Gadsby's Tavern,** 134 N. Royal St. (838-4242), open Tues.-Sun.; **Carlyle House,** 121 N. Fairfax St. (549-2997), open Tues.-Sun.; the **Stabler-Leadbeater Apothecary Shop,** 105 S. Fairfax St. (836-3713), open Mon.-Sat.; the **Lee-Fendall House,** 614 Oronoco St. (548-1789), open Tues.-Sun.; **Old Presbyterian Meeting House,** with the tomb of the Unknown Soldier of the War of Independence, 321 S. Fairfax St. (549-6670), open Mon.-Sat.; and **Christ Church,** 118 N. Washington St. (549-1450), open daily. All these places were frequented by the "Father of Our Country."

For other historic buildings in Alexandria, inquire at the **Alexandria Tourist Council,** itself quartered in the oldest house in town, **Ramsay House** (ca. 1724), 221 King St. (549-0205), open daily.

See also the ☼ ♙ **George Washington Masonic National Memorial,** an unusual Masonic temple with a 333-ft (102-m) tower copied from the famous Pharos (lighthouse) of Alexandria, one of the seven wonders of antiquity, with an observation platform at the top. It's at Shooter's Hill, W. King St. and Russell Rd. (683-2007), open daily, and well worth the side trip. Alexandria should not be missed.

Where to Eat

    ♉♉ **La Bergerie,** 218 N. Lee St. (683-1007). Lunch/dinner Mon.-Sat. AE, DC, MC, V. Excellent Basque food in a charming antique setting. **I-M**

    ♉♉ **Taverna Cretekou,** 818 King St. (548-8688). Lunch/dinner Tues.-Sun. AE, DC, MC, V. The best Greek rest. in the Washington, D.C., area. **I**

☼♙♙ **ANNAPOLIS, MD.** (31 mi., 50 km, east on U.S. 50; area code 301): Briefly the capital of the U.S. (Congress met here from Nov. 26, 1783, to Aug. 13, 1784), and capital of Maryland since 1695, this lovely 300-year-old harbor town is best known today as the home of the U.S. Naval Academy. It offers a wide range of diversions to the visitor.

You can **cruise the harbor** and the Severn River aboard the *Harbor Queen,* boarding at City Dock at the foot of Main St. (268-7600), daily from Memorial Day to Labor Day.

You can visit the **State House** (1772–1779), the oldest legislative building still in use in the country, at State Circle (974-3400), open daily. It was here, in 1783, that George Washington laid down his office as commander-in-chief of the Continental Army. Here, too, in 1784, the Treaty of Paris, which had been signed at Versailles the previous year, was ratified, ending the War of Independence.

Stroll among the beautifully restored old houses of Cornhill St., Maryland Ave., or Prince George St.: the **Hammond-Harwood House, Chase Lloyd House, William Paca House,** and so on.

Watch a noon parade of uniformed midshipmen, admire the model sailing ships at the maritime museum, or meditate before the ☼ **tomb of John Paul Jones** in the chapel of the ♙ **U.S. Naval Academy** at the foot of King George St. (263-6933). There are conducted tours daily from March to Thanksgiving; more than a million visitors come here annually. Rediscover the 18th century in an old tavern near the docks.

For further information, contact the **State House Visitor Center,** State Circle (974-3400), open daily. Don't fail to visit Annapolis.

Where to Eat

☼♈ **Middleton Tavern,** 2 Market Pl. (263-3323). Lunch/dinner daily. AE, MC, V. Seafood in a 1750 building with a fine view of the harbor. **I**

☼♈♈ **Treaty of Paris (Maryland Inn),** Church Circle at Main St. (263-2641). Lunch/dinner daily. AE, CB, DC, MC, V. Historic (1776) inn serving excellent traditional food. **I**

☼⚱⚱ **DULLES INTERNATIONAL AIRPORT** (in Chantilly, Va., 26 mi., 42 km, west via the George Washington Memorial Pkwy., I-495, and Dulles Airport Rd.) (703/471-4242): Lovers of architecture will appreciate the pure lines of the terminal designed in 1962 by the great Finnish-American architect Eero Saarinen. This was the first U.S. airport specifically intended for the jet age, and its roof, in-curved like a hammock and secured by cables, has served as a model for many other buildings around the world. The airport is named after John Foster Dulles, President Eisenhower's much-traveled secretary of state. Worth seeing.

☼⚱⚱ **FREDERICKSBURG, VA.** (50 mi., 80 km, south on I-95; area code 703): Halfway between Washington and Richmond, the capital of Virginia, this charming vestige of the past occupies a proud place in American history. Capt. John Smith, founder of Jamestown, the first permanent British settlement on the continent, visited the site in 1608. George Washington spent his childhood here, James Madison practiced law here before going on to become the fifth president of the U.S., and some of the bloodiest battles of the Civil War were fought here, as the town changed hands seven times between 1862 and 1864.

Houses that have seen the passage of one or two centuries line Charles St. and Caroline St. in the heart of the historic district. Among them are: the **Rising Sun Tavern,** 1306 Caroline St. (371-1494), open daily, which was built in 1760 by George Washington's youngest brother, Charles; the **Mary Washington House,** 1200 Charles St. (373-1569), open daily, which George Washington presented to his mother in 1772 and where she lived until her death; the **James Monroe Museum,** 908 Charles St. (373-8426), open daily, where the future president lived; the **Hugh Mercer Apothecary Shop,** 1020 Caroline St., open daily, with its authentic 18th-century interior; and **Kenmore,** 1201 Washington Ave. (373-3381), open daily, one of Virginia's loveliest historic homes, built in 1752 by Col. Fielding Lewis, George Washington's brother-in-law.

Don't fail to visit Fredericksburg.

☼⚱⚱ **MOUNT VERNON** (15 mi., 25 km, south on the George Washington Memorial Pkwy. and Mount Vernon Memorial Hwy.) (703/780-2000): This splendid Colonial mansion following a design by Washington overlooks the Potomac, and is where George Washington died on Dec. 14, 1799. The main building, with its white, colonnaded Georgian façade turned to the river, was begun in 1754 on land that had been in the family since 1674. Washington lived here as a planter with his wife, the former Martha Custis, for 15 years, from 1759 until 1775 when he became commander-in-chief of the Continental Army. Returning in 1783, he continued to enlarge the house and its gardens. After eight years as president he retired here finally in 1797 and remained until his death two years later. After the death of Martha in 1802, Mount Vernon remained in the Washington family until 1858, when it was purchased, along with 198 acres (80 ha.), by the Mount Vernon Ladies Association, carefully restored, and operated as a national memorial.

In part built by Washington himself, the main block has 19 rooms, of which the most interesting are the president's library and the room where he died. Very beautiful original furniture. A feature of the main reception room is the key to the Bastille, a gift from La Fayette. A little apart are the kitchen, the workers' and slaves' quarters, and the Washington family vault with the caskets of George and Martha Washington.

Drawing a million people a year, this is one of the most-visited places in the U.S.; long waiting lines on weekends and in summer. The access road is a scenic highway along the river. Open daily; don't miss it.

NASA–GODDARD SPACE FLIGHT CENTER AND MUSEUM (Baltimore Pkwy., Exit 22, Greenbelt, Md.) (301/ 286-8101): The whole gamut of NASA rockets, satellites, and space capsules. Temporary exhibitions illustrating the history of NASA, and movies on the conquest of space. Fascinating. 25 min. from dwntwn along New York Ave., U.S. 50E, and Baltimore Pkwy. North. Open Wed.-Sun.

NATIONAL AIR AND SPACE MUSEUM–PAUL E. GARBER FACILITY (Old Silver Hill Rd., Suitland, Md.): The restoration workshop and annex of the famous museum in downtown Washington. A hundred craft, old (the 1914 Blériot Type XI) and new (the cruise missile) are displayed side by side with machines in process of restoration like the *Enola Gay,* from which the atom bomb was dropped on Hiroshima.

An absolute must for aviation buffs, 30 min. from dwntwn along Independence Ave., Pennsylvania Ave. SE, and Old Silver Hill Rd. Conducted tours by appointment only; reservations should be made at least two weeks ahead with the Tour Scheduler at the dwntwn museum (202/357-1300).

WOODLAWN PLANTATION (18 mi., 29 km, south via George Washington Memorial Pkwy. and Mount Vernon Memorial Hwy.) (703/673-4000): Splendid home adjoining Mount Vernon, built between 1800 and 1805 by William Thornton, one of the architects of the Capitol, on land given by George Washington to his adopted daughter as a wedding present. The mansion is a typical Virginia plantation house.

Also on the grounds is the **Pope-Leighey House,** designed by the great Frank Lloyd Wright; this cypress wood, brick, and glass structure was originally erected at Falls Church, Va., in 1940 and was moved to its present location in 1964. It's well worth going out of your way to visit these two very dissimilar houses.

Woodlawn Plantation is open daily; Pope-Leighey House, weekends only, Mar.-Dec.

FARTHER AFIELD

SHENANDOAH NATIONAL PARK (76 mi., 122 km, west on I-66 to Front Royal at the north entrance to the park): This magnificent wooded park covering 300 sq. mi. (777 km²) is 80 mi. (129 km) long but only 2–13 mi. (3–21 km) wide; encompassing the crests of the **Blue Ridge Mountains,** it is traversed from end to end by one of the most spectacular scenic highways in the country, ✵ **Skyline Drive.** The Blue Ridge Mountains, the easternmost ridge of the Appalachians, owe their name to the veil

of bluish mist that usually clings to most of the peaks. Shenandoah Park (it means "daughter of the stars" in the local Indian tongue), which averages about 2,000 ft (610 m) above sea level, is almost entirely covered in a thick forest of conifers, oaks, and birches, which shelter a numerous and varied wildlife including brown bears, deer, foxes, lynx, and more than 200 species of birds. Along the Skyline Drive more than 75 overlooks have been constructed, allowing you views all the way west to the Shenandoah Valley or east to the Piedmont plateau.

Skyline Drive is continued to the S by an equally spectacular mountain road, the **Blue Ridge Parkway,** which is the best route to **Great Smoky Mountains National Park,** 750 mi. (1,200 km) to the south (see Chapter 13 on Nashville).

Shenandoah Park and the neighboring **George Washington Forest** are at their best in spring, and even more at the peak of the fall foliage display. They also boast some of the finest caves on the East Coast: **Skyline Caverns,** near Front Royal; ❄ **Luray Caverns** and **Endless Caverns,** near Luray; and **Grand Caverns,** near Grottoes.

☀ **Natural bridge,** south of Lexington, is also worth a detour. A limestone arch 215 ft (66 m) high and 65 million years old, it has been termed "one of the Seven Wonders of the New World."

The park is open year round. For information, contact the Superintendent, Rte. 4, Box 292, Luray, VA 22835 (703/999-2266). A must for nature lovers.

Some 25 mi. (40 km) east of Shenandoah Park, don't fail to visit ❄ 🔭 **Monticello,** on Va. 53 near Charlottesville (804/295-8181). The luxurious estate of Thomas Jefferson, third president of the U.S., is one of the finest surviving examples of 18th-century American architecture, spectacularly situated on a height of land. Designed and built by Jefferson over a period of 40 years. Period furniture and decoration. The tomb of Thomas Jefferson is in the nearby family graveyard. Open daily; don't miss it.

Where to Stay and Eat En Route

IN CHARLOTTESVILLE. ❄ 🍷🍷🍷 **Boar's Head Inn,** Ivy Rd. (U.S. 250), Charlottesville, VA 22905 (804/296-2181). 175 rms. Delightful country inn built around an 1834 grain-mill. Remarkable comfort and facilities. **M–E**

IN NEW MARKET. 🍷 **Shenvalee,** U.S. 11, New Market, VA 22844 (703/740-3181), half a mile south of town. 42 rms. Inviting, comfortable motel on 200 acres (80 ha.) of park and garden. Tennis and golf. Excellent value. **I**

IN WASHINGTON, VA. ❄ 🍷🍷🍷🍷 **Inn at Little Washington,** Middle and Main Sts., Washington, VA 22747 (703/675-3800). Dinner only, Tues.-Sun. Modern, delicate, inventive cuisine and svce of the highest order in a plush English-inn setting. Some of the best food in the entire region, as well as ten luxuriously comfortable rms. Resv. a must, well in advance. **E–VE**

🔭 **EASTERN SHORE** (395 mi., 632 km, round trip via U.S. 50E, U.S. 113S, U.S. 13S, Va. 175E and 175W, U.S. 13N, and U.S. 50W—about 500 mi., 800 km, if you go and return via the Chesapeake Bay Bridge-Tunnel): Leaving Washington on New York Ave. and U.S. 50 (John Hansen Hwy.), you'll soon come to your first stop, **Annapolis** (see "Nearby Excursions," above). The road then follows the shoreline of **Chesapeake Bay,** a great arm of the sea 185 mi. (300 km) long and parallel to the Atlantic Ocean, famous for its seafood. After passing through 🔱 **Wye Mills,** a picturesque little village whose authentic 18th-century character has been preserved, you come to **Easton,** capital of the Eastern Shore and an antique lover's paradise. There are many old houses to see, as well as the superb Courthouse Square. The Third Haven Friends

Meeting House, 405 S. Washington St., open daily, was built by Quaker settlers in 1682 and is one of the oldest religious buildings in the country.

Before continuing toward Cambridge and Ocean City, go out of your way to the charming little fishing port of ※ ⌂ **St. Michaels,** where you'll find a fascinating maritime museum on Waterside (301/745-2916), open daily Apr.-Dec., as well as the enchanting St. Mary's Square with its old houses.

Another worthwhile side trip is to **Oxford,** a pleasure-sailing center and terminus of the oldest ferry in the U.S., the **Oxford–Bellevue Ferry,** which has been in operation for three centuries.

Southwest of **Cambridge,** another little Colonial port, take Md. 16 as far as ⌂ **Church Creek,** where you will come upon Old Trinity Church (1675), one of the oldest in the country. Back on U.S. 50, when you're 5 mi. (8 km) west of Mardela Springs, look out for the **Mason-Dixon Line Marker,** the first stone placed in 1763 on the historic line marking the traditional boundary between the northern and southern U.S. (The Mason-Dixon Line owes its name to Charles Mason and Jeremiah Dixon, two British surveyors who in 1763 were instructed to determine the boundaries of the land given 130 years earlier by the Crown to Cecilius Calvert, Second Baron Baltimore, and to William Penn. Following the line of latitude 39 degrees 42 minutes 26.3 seconds from the sea to the Alleghenies, the Mason-Dixon Line forever divides the Yankee North from the Dixie South.)

Then on to ⌂ **Ocean City,** Maryland's only Atlantic coast resort, with a beautiful fine-sand beach 3 mi. (5 km) long, and dozens of hotels and motels in all price ranges—but also huge crowds in summer.

Your last stop will be at ⌂⌂ **Assateague Island National Seashore,** a long chain of sand dunes alternating with marshes and pinewoods which are home to myriads of birds and to many wild ponies, said to be descended from those brought here by the first Spanish explorers in their galleons. On the last Wednesday and Thursday and Friday of July the ponies are swum across the arm of the sea which separates **Assateague Island** from **Chincoteague Island** to be sold at auction; in the week before this yearly ritual of "pony penning," the whole region devotes itself to carnival—and pony races. A visit to this nature reserve, famous also for its oysters and shellfish, is worth the trip all by itself. For information, contact the Superintendent, Assateague Island National Seashore, Rte. 2, Box 294, Berlin, MD 21811 (301/641-1441), or the Refuge Manager, Chincoteague National Wildlife Refuge, P.O. Box 62, Chincoteague, VA 23336 (804/336-6122).

You can return to Washington either the same way you came, along U.S. 13 and U.S. 50, or by going farther south to the very spectacular 17-mi. (28-km) **Chesapeake Bay Bridge-Tunnel** and then jogging back north along I-64 and I-95. This will enable you to visit Williamsburg, Yorktown, and Richmond (see below). Allow at least three to four days for this very comprehensive trip, which you shouldn't miss.

Where to Stay En Route

IN EASTON, MD. ※ 🍴🍴 **Tidewater Inn,** Dover and Harrison Sts., Easton, MD 21601 (301/822-1300) 120 rms. Elegant two-century-old building, now a designated historic monument. Rest. highly regarded for its seafood. **I–M**

IN OXFORD, MD. 🍴🍴 **Robert Morris Inn,** Md. 333, Oxford, MD 21654 (301/226-5111). 33 rms. Closed Feb. Charming little Colonial-style inn overlooking the water. Praiseworthy rest. **I–M**

IN OCEAN CITY, MD. 🍴🍴🍴 **Sheraton Fontainebleau Inn,** 10100 Ocean Hwy.,

Ocean City, MD 21842 (301/524-3535; toll free, see Sheraton). 250 rms. Big, ultramodern 16-story tower on the beach. **M–E**

🔔🔔 **Plim Plaza Hotel,** Boardwalk and 2nd St., Ocean City, MD 21842 (301/289-6181). 181 rms. Standard motel. **M–E**

IN CHINCOTEAGUE, VA. ☼ 🔔🔔 **Driftwood,** Beach Rd. at Assateague Bridge, Chincoteague, VA 23336 (804/336-6557). 52 rms. Congenial little motel at the entrance to the park. For lovers of the sea. **I–M**

🔔🔔 **The Refuge,** one block west of Assateague Bridge, Chincoteague, VA 23336 (804/336-5511). 68 rms. Inviting motel with view of the wildlife refuge. **I–M**

Where to Eat En Route

IN ST. MICHAELS, MD. 🍷 **The Harbor,** St. Michaels, Md. (301/745-2900). Lunch/dinner Tues.-Sat. This restaurant's reputation is founded on its blue crabs and other Chesapeake Bay seafood. **I**

IN OXFORD, MD. 🍷 **The Masthead Club,** Mill St. at the Strand (301/226-5303). Dinner only, nightly; brunch Sat. and Sun. Excellent local seafood. **I**

☼🏛 **GETTYSBURG AND PENNSYLVANIA DUTCH COUNTRY** (265 mi., 424 km, round trip via I-270N, U.S. 15N, U.S. 30E and 30W, I-83S, and I-95S): The greatest and most glorious battlefield of the Civil War, and in Amish country, a 17th-century survival (for details, see Chapter 6 on Philadelphia). On the way, stop in **Catoctin Mountain Park** on Md. 77 west of Thurmont. In this lovely rolling, wooded landscape is hidden **Camp David,** country retreat of the presidents and scene of many famous diplomatic meetings, among others that of Sept. 1978, at which Anwar Sadat and Menachem Begin negotiated a peace treaty between Egypt and Israel. No visitors. A two-day trip interesting on account of its variety. (For recommended accommodations and restaurants, see Chapter 6 on Philadelphia.)

Washingtonians will find a foretaste of Amish country at the **Dutch Country Farmers Market** in Burtonsville, Md., at the intersection of U.S. 29 and Md. 198 (301/421-4046). A score of stands kept by Amish countryfolk wearing traditional garments and head coverings sell farm products from vegetables to meat and from cheese to home-baked pastry—all guaranteed to contain no chemical additives or pesticides. Locally popular; open Fri. and Sat. 30 min from dwntwn Washington.

🏛 **POTOMAC VALLEY** (165 mi., 264 km, round trip via the George Washington Memorial Pkwy., River Rd. West, Whites Ferry, U.S. 15S, Va. 7W, Va. 9W, Va. 671N, Md. 65N, Md. 34E, Alt. U.S. 40E, and I-270S): Picturesque drive running for much of its length along the Potomac River. It begins with a visit to the ☼🏛 **Chesapeake & Ohio Canal National Historical Park and Great Falls.** Begun in 1828, the canal was intended to link Georgetown, now a suburb of Washington, with the Ohio Valley, but work was abandoned in the 1870s because of competition from the railroads. There survives to this day, on the stretch near the Great Falls of the Potomac, an entire system of bridges and locks, now surrounded by a pretty wooded park which is maintained jointly by the states of Maryland and Virginia. Interesting little museum; open daily (301/739-4200).

Cross the Potomac at **Whites Ferry** (toll ferryboat) and continue to 🏛 **Leesburg,** a charming little Colonial town founded in 1758 and in great part restored to its original appearance. Be sure to see the **Loudoun County Historical Museum** at 16 W. Loudoun St. (703/777-7427), open daily. Today Leesburg is an important thoroughbred center.

Now on to ☀ ♨ **Harpers Ferry,** proudly standing at the confluence of the Shenandoah and Potomac rivers. In this Civil War landmark town, the old U.S. Army arsenal has been completely restored; there are also many historic houses in the Old Town. It is best known as the scene of John Brown's rebellion against slavery in 1859, which later became a symbol to the northern states. It ended in his execution by hanging at **Charles Town,** 8 mi. (13 km) south, where the ambience of the 18th century has also been scrupulously preserved. Don't fail to visit John Brown's Fort, rebuilt on the exact site of the drama, on Arsenal Square, open daily.

Continuing northward, you'll come to ☀ ♨ **Antietam National Battlefield Site and Cemetery,** where the defeat of the Confederate troops of General Lee ended the South's first invasion of the North. This, Sept. 17, 1862, was the single bloodiest day of the entire Civil War, with 23,000 killed and wounded in a matter of a few hours. The battlefield may be visited. Visitor Center and museum on Md. 65 (301/432-5124), open daily.

The last stop is at ☀ **Frederick,** a place of strategic importance during the Civil War with a magnificently preserved historic district. Be sure to see the **Francis Scott Key Museum,** 123 S. Bentz St. (301/663-8703), open by appointment only, birthplace of the author of the words of the National Anthem. His tomb, marked by the U.S. flag, may be seen at Mount Olivet Cemetery at the south end of Market St., open daily. Then back to Washington on I-270. A one-day trip particularly worthwhile in warm weather.

Where to Eat En Route

IN LEESBURG. ☀ ♨♨ **Green Tree,** 15 S. King St. (703/777-7246). Lunch/dinner daily; authentic 18th-century recipes in a very lovely antique setting. An unusual experience. I

♨♨ **WILLIAMSBURG AND COLONIAL VIRGINIA** (320 mi., 512 km, round trip via I-95S and I-64E, and the reverse route returning): Your first stop will be at ☀ ♨ **Richmond,** capital of Virginia since 1780 and capital of the Confederacy from 1861 to 1865. Founded in 1607 as a trading post for the first settlers and the Indians, Richmond soon flourished thanks to its tobacco business; on the eve of the Civil War it had some 40 curing plants.

While skyscrapers and modern buildings now cluster along the banks of the James River, bearing witness to the economic and industrial vigor of present-day Richmond, the older neighborhoods of the center city are still a living museum of Virginia's great Colonial epoch. The warehouses of **Shockoe Slip,** at E. Cary and 13th Sts., the oldest part of the city, are now home to artists, boutiques, and fashionable restaurants. The respectable middle classes live in the **Fan District,** in the shade of the trees in **Monroe Park. Church Hill** is the district around the wooden church of the Revolutionary patriots, **St. John's Church,** at 25th and Broad Sts. (804/648-5015), open daily; here Patrick Henry made his immortal pronouncement: "As for me, give me Liberty, or give me Death." Somehow the neighborhood has preserved a subtle aura of the 19th century. A more solemn note is struck by ☀ **Monument Avenue,** Richmond's processional boulevard, lined with trees, mansions, and monuments in honor of its most illustrious citizens, particularly Jefferson Davis and Gen. Robert E. Lee.

Try not to miss the **State Capitol** (1788), on Capitol Square (804/786-4344), open daily, whose design closely follows that of the Maison Carrée in

Nîmes; also the ✳ **White House of the Confederacy** and the adjoining museum, rich in historical material, at 1201 E. Clay St. (804/649-1861), open daily; here Jefferson Davis made his home during the Civil War.

You should see the lovely ▲▲ **Virginia Museum of Fine Arts,** at Boulevard and Grove Ave. (804/257-0844), open Tues.-Sun., with fine art nouveau and art deco material, jewelry by Fabergé, and paintings by great European masters.

Driving east from Richmond you will come next to ✳ ▲▲ **Williamsburg,** capital of Virginia from 1698 to 1780, and the most famous museum-town in the U.S., looking just as it did in the 18th century. Thanks to funding from John D. Rockefeller, Jr., Williamsburg was able to launch, in 1926, a gigantic salvage operation involving almost 150 old buildings. The many craftsmen's workshops, booths, taverns, and displays with people in 18th-century attire attract more than a million visitors to Williamsburg every year. The evidences of the past lie all around you here, from the 1705 **State Capitol** on Duke of Gloucester St., rebuilt on the original foundations, to the 1693 ✳ **College of William and Mary,** the second oldest in the U.S. after Harvard, also on Duke of Gloucester St., by way of the (British) **Governor's Palace and Gardens** on Palace Green and the ✳ **Raleigh Tavern** on Duke of Gloucester St., frequented by Jefferson, Henry, and other Revolutionary leaders. Most of these historic buildings are open to visitors daily throughout the year. The **Visitor Center,** on Colonial Pkwy. at Va. 132 (804/229-1000), provides useful information, leaflets, and museum tickets, and will make hotel reservations for you.

Williamsburg is worth the trip all by itself, but there are three places nearby that are worth the detour. ✳ **Jamestown,** 9 mi. (14 km) SW on Colonial Pkwy., was the first permanent British settlement in North America (1607), and has many historic buildings including the 1639 ▲ **Old Church Tower.**

☀▲ **Yorktown,** 13 mi. (20 km) SE on Colonial Pkwy., was the scene of the last engagement of the War of Independence, where the American and French troops of Washington and Rochambeau, on Oct. 19, 1781, accepted the surrender of General Cornwallis, putting an end to British rule over the Thirteen Colonies. The battlefield may be visited; Visitor Center open daily (804/898-3400).

Finally, ✳ ▲ **Busch Gardens–The Old Country,** 3 mi. (5 km) east on U.S. 60 (804/253-3350), is a 360-acre (121-ha.) theme park with recreated of picturesque European villages; open daily mid-May to Labor Day, weekends only in spring and fall; closed the rest of the year.

On your way back to Washington along I-64W and I-95N, be sure to see **Fredericksburg** and **Alexandria** (see "Nearby Excursions," above). This is a trip which will appeal to lovers of History with a capital H; allow at least three days. Don't miss it.

Where to Stay En Route

IN RICHMOND. ✳ ♜♜♜♜ **Sheraton Jefferson Hotel,** Franklin and Adams Sts., Richmond, VA 23220 (804/788-8000). 276 rms. One of the finest old hotels (1895) in the country. Sumptuous interior superbly restored; the Rotunda and its grand staircase are worth a visit in themselves. **E–VE**

♜♜ **John Marshall Hotel,** 5th and Franklin Sts., Richmond, VA 23219 (804/644-4661). 418 rms. Comfortable old hotel a stone's throw from the Capitol and the financial district. **I–M**

IN WILLIAMSBURG. ✳ ♜♜♜♜ **Williamsburg Inn,** Francis St., Williamsburg, VA 23185 (804/229-1000). 102 rms. Elegant Colonial building in the heart of the Historic District, with remarkably good facilities and standards of comfort. Regency décor and furnishings. **VE**

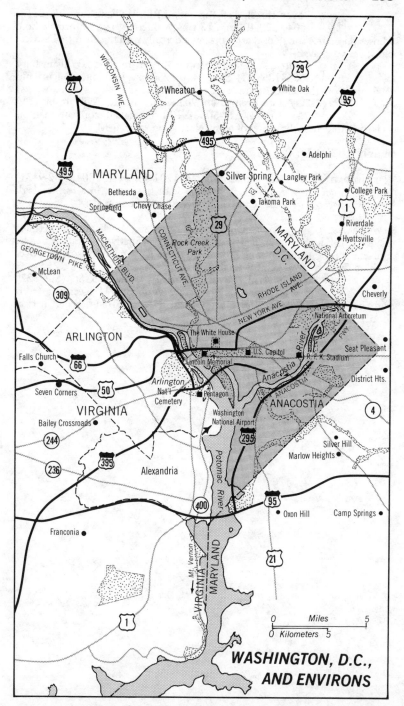

WASHINGTON, D.C., AND ENVIRONS

    💶💶💶 **Royce Hotel,** 415 Richmond Rd., Williamsburg, VA 23185
(804/229-4020). 313 rms. Modern, very comfortable hotel
whose appearance and décor harmonize wonderfully with the Historic District a
block or two away. **E–VE**

    💶💶 **George Washington Inn,** 500 Merrimac Trail, Williamsburg,
VA 23185 (804/220-1410). 253 rms. Inviting, congenial motel 5 min. from the center of town; very good value. **I–M**

    💶 **Days Inn Downtown,** 902 Richmond Rd., Williamsburg, VA
23185 (804/229-5060). 100 rms. Small, conventional, but
well-run motel near the center of town. Very good value. **I–M**

Where to Eat En Route

IN RICHMOND. ✳ 🍷🍷 **Tobacco Company,** 1201 Cary St. (804/782-9431).
Lunch/dinner daily. A rest. very popular with the locals, in a former 19th-
century tobacco warehouse. Excellent conventional cooking. **I–M**

IN WILLIAMSBURG. ✳ 🍷🍷 **Trellis,** Duke of Gloucester St., Merchants Square (804/
229-8610). Lunch/dinner daily, brunch Sun. Imaginative, delicate American
nouvelle cuisine; some of the best food in Virginia at extremely reasonable prices.
Inviting shady terrace. A fine place. **I**

    ✳🍷 **King's Arms Tavern,** Duke of Gloucester St. (804/229-
2141). Lunch/dinner daily. Authentic 18th-century tavern
with its original Colonial décor attractively restored. Traditional American
food. **I–M**

PART TWO
SOUTH

CHAPTER 10

CHARLESTON 🍦🍦

□ □ □

Called "The Holy City" because of its many churches and dozens of bell towers, Charleston—formerly spelled "Charles Towne," for King Charles II—is one of the most gracious cities in the United States, and one of the most popular among tourists. Under British rule Charleston was the largest Atlantic port south of Philadelphia, enjoying a strategic position at the junction of the Ashley and Cooper Rivers. Elegant and cosmopolitan, Charleston attracted a large Huguenot (French Protestant) colony in the 18th century (until 1928 there were still religious services conducted in French), as well as strong currents of Irish, German, Scottish, and even West Indian immigration.

Charleston surrendered to General Sherman in February 1865 after a two-year siege. Despite the wounds of war, a terrible earthquake in 1886, and many devastating fires and hurricanes, this charming, aristocratic city of the Old South, bypassed by time, has conserved a number of interesting traces of the past: **Fort Sumter,** whence came the spark that ignited the Civil War; the **Dock Street Theatre,** the country's oldest (1736); **Cabbage Row,** immortalized as "Catfish Row" in the opera *Porgy and Bess*; the **Charleston Museum,** founded in 1773 (the country's first); the venerable houses of **Old Charleston,** with their Doric columns and wrought-iron balconies; and dozens of plantations with lush tropical gardens. Each spring since 1977 Charleston has played host for the American version of Italy's famous **Spoleto Festival,** offering ballet, theater, and classical and contemporary music to enthusiasts from all over the country.

Center of the rice and indigo trades in colonial times, then a prosperous slave market before the Civil War, Charleston is presently an active port at the heart of a highly mechanized agricultural region, with a booming tourist trade (more than two million visitors each year), but a hotel capacity that is still relatively limited. Charleston is 14th on the list of the 20 American cities experiencing the most rapid economic growth.

BASIC FACTS: State of South Carolina. Area Code: 803. Time Zone: Eastern Time. ZIP Code: 29401. Founded: 1670. Approximate population: city, 69,000; metropolitan area, 380,000.

CLIMATE: Almost any season is a good one to discover Charleston. Winter is generally mild (avg. Jan. temperature, 50°F, 10°C) and summer hot (avg. July temperature, 80°F, 27°C), although raincoats and umbrellas are in order due to tropical storms. Spring (gardens bloom in Mar. and Apr.) and autumn, Oct. and Nov. especially, are the ideal seasons to visit this popular tourist destination.

DISTANCES: Atlanta, 289 mi. (462 km); Miami, 455 mi. (728 km); Savannah, 106 mi. (170 km); Washington, 527 mi. (844 km).

ARRIVAL & TRANSIT INFORMATION

AIRPORT: International Airport (CHS): 12 mi. (20 km) NW. Information: 767-7009.

AIRLINES: American (722-7108); Continental (723-4407); Delta (577-3230); Eastern (723-7851); United (747-0591).

CITY LINK: Cab fare to city center, about $16; time, about 20 min. Bus: Airport Limousine (767-7111); fare, $8; time, about 30 min. Although cab fares are reasonable, renting a car with unlimited mileage is advisable for visiting the numerous parks and plantations surrounding the city. Rather inadequate public transportation (bus) system (SCE&G). Information: 722-2226.

CAR RENTAL (all at the airport): Avis (767-7030); Budget (554-8070); Dollar (552-7275); Hertz (767-7047); National (723-8266). For dwntwn locations, consult the local telephone book.

LIMOUSINE SERVICES: Dav El Limousines (800/922-0343); Parker Limousine Service (723-7601).

TAXIS: Taxis cannot be hailed on the street but can be summoned by phone: Yellow Cab (577-6565).

TRAIN: AMTRAK, 4565 Gaynor Ave. (toll free 800/872-7245).

BUS: Greyhound, 89 Society St. (722-1115).

INFORMATION & TOURS

TOURIST INFORMATION: Historic Charleston Foundation, 51 Meeting St., SC 29401 (803/723-1623).
    Visitor Information Center, Arch Building, 85 Calhoun St., SC 29402 (803/722-8338). Offers the best printed material.

GUIDED TOURS: American Sightseeing (bus), 28½ Alexander St. (722-2988). Guided tour of the city and environs.
    Charleston Carriage Co. (city tour in horse-drawn carriage), 96 N. Market St. (577-0042).
    Gray Line Tours (bus), Radisson Hotel, King and Calhoun Sts. (722-4444). Guided tour of the city and environs. Leaves from major dwntwn hotels.
    Gray Line Water Tours (harbor cruise), Municipal Marina, Lockwood Blvd. (722-1112). Offers a view of the U.S. Navy's famous Polaris submarines. Open daily, year round.
    Fort Sumter Tour, Municipal Marina, Lockwood Blvd. (722-2628). Worth going out of your way for. Open daily except Dec. 25.

SIGHTS, ATTRACTIONS, & ACTIVITIES

ARCHITECTURAL HIGHLIGHTS: ▲ **The Citadel,** Moultrie St. and Elmwood Ave. (792-5006): Also known as "the West Point of the South," this celebrated military academy, founded in 1842 (1,900 students), occupies the site of an early-19th-century fort built to quell slave revolts. Commanding fortress-style architecture with battlements and turrets, a military museum, and archives of

Gen. Mark Clark, World War II hero. Cadet parades on Fri. at 3:30 p.m. Worth a look. Open daily.

☀☖ **U.S.S. *Yorktown,*** Patriots Point, left bank of the Cooper River (884-2727): This World War II aircraft carrier, which has been transformed into a floating museum with planes, helicopters, and weapons, also affords a very lovely view of the city, the harbor, and Fort Sumter. Anchored not far from here is the **Savannah,** the first nuclear-powered freighter, and other U.S. Navy ships. Worth the trip. Open daily.

CHURCHES/SYNAGOGUES: ☖ **Huguenot Church,** 138 Church St.: Consecrated in 1687, rebuilt in 1796 and again in 1845 after two fires, this is the only church in the country that has retained the Calvinist liturgy of the Huguenots. Until 1928 services were conducted in French. Worth a look. Open daily.

☀☖ **Kahal Kadosh Beth Elohim,** 90 Hasell St.: The country's second-oldest synagogue, founded in 1749 (the oldest is in Newport, R.I.). The present building, which dates from 1840, is considered one of the most beautiful examples of the Greek Revival style in the country. Open Mon.-Fri. Worth a glance.

☖ **St. Michael's Church,** Meeting and Broad Sts.: With its 186-ft- (57-m-) tall bell tower, this unusual church is Charleston's oldest (1761) and was attended by George Washington. The organ dates from 1768. Worth a look. Open daily.

☀☖ **St. Philip's Church,** 142 Church St.: On this site the first Anglican church south of Virginia was built in 1670, the year Charleston was founded. The present building dates from 1838; its soaring steeple was an aiming point for northern gunners during the Civil War. The adjacent cemetery is the resting place of many notables, including Edward Rutledge, one of the signers of the Declaration of Independence. See it. Open daily.

HISTORIC BUILDINGS: ☀☖ **Dock Street Theatre,** Church and Queen Sts. (723-5648): This hall opened in 1936 on the site of the country's oldest theater (1736). The architecture, inspired by the Georgian theaters of the 19th century, includes a carefully restored section of the former Planter's Hotel (1809). Open Mon.-Fri. in summer, Mon.-Sat. the rest of the year. See it.

☖ **Fort Moultrie,** W. Middle St., Sullivan's Island (883-3123): Col. William Moultrie dealt the English one of their first and gravest defeats of the Revolutionary War here in 1776. The present fort, rebuilt in 1809, served as a prison, in the last year of his life, for the captured Osceola, who led the revolt of the Seminoles in Florida, the bloodiest of the Indian wars. See it. Open daily.

☖☖ **Fort Sumter,** (722-1691): One of the hallowed places of American history. Built on a man-made island in the middle of Charleston's harbor, Fort Sumter was the target both of the South's surprise attack which touched off the Civil War (4:30 a.m., April 12, 1861), and of a bloody northern siege from 1863-1865. Can be reached only by boat from the Municipal Marina. Interesting military museum and a very lovely view of the old city's skyline. A visit not to be missed. Open daily.

☀☖☖ **Old Charleston,** around Meeting, George, and Church Sts.: Very lovely vignette of the past—pastel houses with wrought-iron railings and small, narrow cobbled streets. There are many historic homes to see, such as the **Nathaniel Russell House,** 51 Meeting St., a fine example of the Adam style with its splendid staircase (1808); the imposing Greek Revival **Edmonston-Alston House,** 21 E. Battery St. (1828); the **Heyward-**

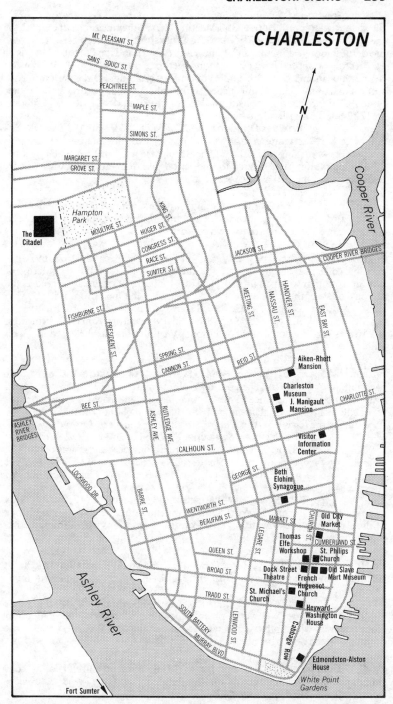

CHARLESTON

N

Cooper River

MT. PLEASANT ST.

SANS SOUCI ST.

PEACHTREE ST.

MAPLE ST.

SIMONS ST.

MARGARET ST.
GROVE ST.

KING ST.

Hampton
Park

The
Citadel

MOULTRIE ST.

HUGER ST.

CONGRESS ST.

RACE ST.

SUMTER ST.

JACKSON ST.

COOPER RIVER BRIDGES

FISHBURNE ST.

PRESIDENT ST.

MEETING ST.

NASSAU ST.

HANOVER ST.

EAST BAY ST.

SPRING ST.

REID ST.

Aiken-Rhett
Mansion

CANNON ST.

Charleston
Museum
J. Manigault
Mansion

CHARLOTTE ST.

BEE ST.

RUTLEDGE AVE.

ASHLEY
RIVER
BRIDGES

ASHLEY AVE.

CALHOUN ST.

Visitor
Information
Center

LOCKWOOD DR.

GEORGE ST.

Beth
Elohim
Synagogue

BARRE ST.

WENTWORTH ST.

Old City
Market

BEAUFAIN ST.

MARKET ST.

CHURCH ST.

LEGARE ST.

Thomas
Elfe
Workshop

CUMBERLAND ST.

St. Philips
Church

QUEEN ST.

BROAD ST.

Dock Street
Theatre

French
Huguenot
Church

Old Slave
Mart Museum

TRADD ST.

St. Michael's
Church

Heyward-
Washington
House

Ashley River

SOUTH BATTERY

LENWOOD ST.

MURRAY BLVD.

Cabbage Row

Edmondston-Alston
House

White Point
Gardens

Fort Sumter

Washington House, 87 Church St., once home to George Washington (1772); the **Joseph Manigault House,** 350 Meeting St., another magnificent example of the Adam style (1803); the **Thomas Elfe Workshop,** 54 Queen St., former studio of the famous cabinetmaker Thomas Elfe (1760); and the **Calhoun Mansion,** 16 Meeting St., noted for its sumptuous Victorian interiors (1870). With more than 2,000 landmarked 18th- and 19th-century buildings, Old Charleston constitutes one of the nation's most spectacular collections of historic architecture. For detailed information, consult the **Visitor Information Center,** 85 Calhoun St. (722-8338). A visit not to be missed.

      Provost Dungeon, 122 E. Bay St. (792-5020): The **Old Exchange Building** (1771) was a small British fort where American patriots were imprisoned during the Revolutionary War (Provost Dungeon). Interesting exhibition dedicated to this period, plus films about Charleston's artistic heritage. Open Tues.-Sun. See it.

MARKETS: ✳️⚜️ **The Market,** Meeting and Market Sts.: A mixture of flea market and yard sale with merchandise of all kinds. Lively and colorful, it has been the center of local commerce for two centuries.

MUSEUMS OF ART: ✳️⚜️ **City Hall Art Gallery,** 80 Broad St. (577-6970): A very fine collection of famous portraits, including John Trumbull's rendering of George Washington, in an interesting 1801 building. It originally served as the regional office of the Bank of the United States. See it. Open Mon.-Fri.

      Gibbes Art Gallery, 135 Meeting St. (722-2706): An interesting collection of 18th- and 19th-century American paintings, miniatures, and Japanese prints. Temporary exhibitions, as well. See it. Open daily.

MUSEUMS OF SCIENCE & HISTORY: ⚜️ **Charleston Museum,** 360 Meeting St. (722-2996): The country's oldest museum (1773), in a modern, well-designed building since 1980. Natural history, anthropology, fine arts, relics of colonial times. Contains notably the life-size replica of the first submarine used during the Civil War, the *Hunley*. An absolute must-see. Open daily.

      Old Powder Magazine, 79 Cumberland St. (722-3767): This former Revolutionary War gun-powder factory was part of the original city fortifications and is Charleston's oldest structure (1713). Today it houses a history museum run by the National Society of Colonial Dames of America. Worth a look. Open Mon.-Fri.

      Old Slave Mart Museum, 6 Chalmers St. (722-0079): This former slave market is now a museum dedicated to the history of the slave trade and slave handcrafts from the plantations. Afro-American art. Not to be missed. Open daily.

PARKS & GARDENS: ⚜️ **Hampton Park,** Rutledge Ave. and Cleveland St.: A splendid array of blooming camellias and azaleas in spring and roses in summer. Open daily.

      White Point Gardens, Murray Blvd. and E. Battery St.: A lovely flowered promenade at the junction of the Ashley and Cooper Rivers which offers a spectacular view of the city, the harbor, and Fort Sumter. A scene not to be missed. Open daily.

PERFORMING ARTS: For daily listings of all shows and cultural events, consult the entertainment pages of the daily papers *Charleston News & Courier* (morning) and *Charleston Evening Post* (evening).

Dock Street Theatre, Church and Queen Sts. (723-5648): Classical and modern theater, from Shakespeare to Broadway, Oct.-May.

Spoleto Festival/USA, Middleton House Plantation (722-2764): From classical music to theater and from jazz to opera and dance, the nation's most famous and most comprehensive festival. Late May to early June.

SHOPPING: Charleston Place, 130 Market St.: Dozens of luxury boutiques —from Gucci to Ralph Lauren and from Laura Ashley to Godiva chocolates— brought together in a very effective faux antique décor. Right in the center of Charleston. A must for all visitors. Open daily.

SPECIAL EVENTS: For the exact schedule of events below, consult the **Visitor Information Center** (see "Tourist Information," above).

Festival of Houses (mid-Mar. to mid-Apr.): The most beautiful old homes, specially opened to the public. Try to time your visit for it. For information, call 723-1623.

Spoleto Festival/USA (late May to early June): American annex of the famous Italian "Festival of Two Worlds" founded by Gian Carlo Menotti. Classical music, ballet, jazz, opera, theater, art exhibitions, and more. Not to be missed. For information, contact P.O. Box 157, Charleston, SC 29402 (803/722-2764).

House & Garden Tours (mid-Oct.): Nocturnal, candlelit walks through the city's gardens and loveliest historic homes. Spectacular. For information, call 722-4630.

International Film Festival (late Oct. to early Nov.): Annually presents more than 500 works of filmmakers worldwide, plus film symposia.

STROLLS: ⚐ **Cabbage Row,** 89-91 Church St.: The picturesque cluster of old rowhouses that inspired George Gershwin's setting for *Porgy and Bess* (called "Catfish Row" in the opera). An absolute must-see.

👓👓 **Old Charleston:** See "Historic Buildings," above.

ACCOMMODATIONS

See the listing of toll-free numbers in the Appendix.

Room Rates in Charleston	
B (Budget)	up to $30
I (Inexpensive)	$30–$60
M (Moderate)	$60–$90
E (Expensive)	$90–$140
VE (Very Expensive)	$140 and up

Personal Favorites (in order of preference)

☀ 🐚🐚🐚🐚 **Planters Inn** (dwntwn), 112 N. Market St., SC 29401 (803/722-2345; toll free 800/845-7082). 45 rms, A/C, color TV. AE, CB, DC, MC, V. Parking, rest. (Silks), bar, 24-hr rm svce, concierge, free crib. *Note:* Charming little luxury hotel that has become a favorite of connoisseurs. Elegant, carefully restored 19th-century building. Spacious rms w. antique furniture (some have fireplaces). Personalized service in an elegant, cushy atmosphere. Creditable American-cuisine rest. Class and style. **M–E**

Omni at Charleston Place (dwntwn), 130 Market St., SC 29401 (803/722-4900; toll free, see Omni). 450 rms, A/C, color TV. AE, CB, DC, MC, V. Gar. $5, pool, health club, sauna, two rests. (including Shaftesbury's), two bars, 24-hr rm svce, disco, boutiques. *Note:* Ultramodern palace with architecture that blends with the Old Charleston setting. Elegant, refined décor and vast, well-conceived rms with stylish furniture. Impeccable svce and reception. VIP and big-business clientele. At the very heart of historic Charleston, with direct access to Charleston Place Mall and its luxury boutiques. An excellent location. **E–VE**

Battery Carriage House (dwntwn), 20 S. Battery, SC 29401 (803/723-9881; toll free 800/845-7638). 10 rms, A/C, color TV. AE, MC, V. Parking, pool, rm svce, mini-bars in rms, private garden, bicycles. *Note:* Elegant 1860s residence in the heart of Old Charleston with fourposter beds and free breakfast in bed. Charm and class, plus a very lovely view of the harbor. Resv. must be made many weeks in advance. Extremely attentive svce. **E**

Heart of Charleston (nr. dwntwn), 200 Meeting St., SC 29401 (803/723-3451; toll free 800/845-2504). 118 rms, A/C, color TV. AE, CB, DC, MC, V. Parking, pool, rest., bar, rm svce. *Note:* This comfortable, well-maintained motel with excellent svce is a very good value. A few minutes' walk from Charleston's principal tourist attractions. **I–M**

Two Meeting Street Inn (formerly Carr's Guest House; nr. dwntwn), 2 Meeting St., SC 29401 (803/723-7322). 9 rms, A/C, no TV, no single rms, no credit cards. Parking, bar. *Note:* The charm of an old family-run European pension in a small, late-19th-century villa. Spacious, inviting rms (some without private bathroom). View of the bay. Good value. Resv. a must. **I–M**

Days Inn Historic District (dwntwn), 155 Meeting St., SC 29401 (803/722-8411; toll free; see Days Inns). 124 rms, A/C, color and cable TV. AE, DC, MC, V. Free parking, pool, coffeeshop (no alcohol), free crib. *Note:* Classic motel particularly well situated for a visit to Old Charleston. Comfortable rms. Good value. **I**

Other Accommodations (from top bracket to budget)

Holiday Inn Mills House (formerly the Hyatt House; dwntwn), 115 Meeting St., SC 29401 (803/577-2400; toll free, see Holiday Inns). 210 rms, A/C, color TV. AE, CB, DC, MC, V. Gar. $4, pool, rest. (Barbadoes Room), bar, rm svce, free crib. *Note:* Comfort and svce above the norm for a Holiday Inn. Elegant décor, stylish furniture, and a deftly reconstructed colonial atmosphere. In the heart of Old Charleston. **E, but low out-of-season rates**

Sheraton Charleston Hotel (nr. dwntwn), 170 Lockwood Dr., SC 29403 (803/723-3000; toll free, see Sheraton). 338 rms, A/C, color TV, in-rm movies. AE, CB, DC, MC, V. Free parking, pool, four tennis courts, rest., coffeeshop, bar, rm svce, disco, free crib. *Note:* One of the most recent additions to the local hotel scene, with spacious, very comfortable rms with balconies (the best have a view of the Ashley River) and good svce. Very complete facilities. Adequate rest. (Charleston Terrace). Three min. from the center of historic Charleston (free shuttle bus). **M–E**

Indigo Inn (dwntwn), 1 Maiden Lane, SC 29401 (803/577-5900; toll free 800/922-1340). 40 rms, A/C, color TV.

AE, MC, V. Parking, adjacent coffeeshop, rm svce. *Note:* An artistically renovated, early-19th-century warehouse, this small, luxurious hotel offers elegant, tastefully decorated, stylishly furnished rms. Delightful private patio. Excellent svce. Just off the City Market in the very heart of Charleston. **M–E**

Vendue Inn (dwntwn), 19 Vendue Range, SC 29401 (803/577-7970; toll free 800/845-7900). 33 rms, A/C, color TV. AE, MC, V. Free parking, bicycles, rest. (Morton's), rm svce. *Note:* Charming little luxury hotel in a lovely three-story residence dating from 1824. Period decor as romantic as can be. Exceptionally polished reception and svce. Well-regarded rest. Free breakfast. A very classy place. **M–E**

Holiday Inn Riverview (nr. dwntwn), 301 Savannah Hwy., SC 29407 (803/556-7100; toll free, see Holiday Inns). 178 rms, A/C, color and cable TV. AE, CB, DC, MC, V. Free parking, pool, rest., bar, rm svce, disco, free crib. *Note:* This 14-story tower with a view of the Ashley River offers functional, balconied rms and a scenic rest.-bar at the top. Holiday Inn style. Good value. 10 min. from dwntwn. **M, but out-of-season reductions**

Best Western Dorchester Motor Lodge (vic.), 3668 Dorchester Ave., SC 29405 (803/747-0961; toll free, see Best Western). 200 rms, A/C, color TV, in-rm movies. AE, CB, DC, MC, V. Free parking, rest., bar, rm svce. *Note:* Typical but comfortable motel in the northern end of Charleston. Cheerful reception. Its location, just 10 min. from dwntwn on I-26, makes it ideal if you're driving. **I**

Lord Ashley (nr. dwntwn), 1501 Savannah Hwy., SC 29407 (803/766-1611). 48 rms, A/C, color and cable TV. AE, DC, MC, V. Free parking, 24-hr adjacent coffeeshop, crib $2. *Note:* Small, modest but well-maintained motel, 10 min. from dwntwn on U.S. 17. Functional comfort and a good value. **I**

Motel 6 (vic.), 2058 Savannah Hwy., SC 29407 (803/571-0560). 111 rms, A/C, color TV, free in-rm movies. DC, MC, V. Free parking, pool, free crib. *Note:* Ultra-economical, modern, and functional motel that is an excellent value and ideal if you're driving—15 min. from dwntwn (at the intersection of S.C. 7 and U.S. 17). **B**

Accommodations in the Vicinity

Kiawah Island Inn (vic.), Kiawah Island (P.O. Box 12910), SC 29455 (803/768-2121; toll free 800/845-2471). 150 rms, A/C, color and cable TV. AE, DC, MC, V. Free parking, four pools, tennis, two golf courses, health club, two rests. (including Jasmine Porch), bar, rm svce, disco, crib $5. *Note:* Luxurious vacation complex that is ideal for water sports offering a 9½-mi. (15-km) private beach, boat rentals, and waterskiing. Comfortable rms w. balconies and patios. Also available are 350 cottages and villas w. kitchenettes. Svce leaves a bit to be desired. Interesting wknd packages. 20 mi. (32 km) south of Charleston on U.S. 17, S.C. 171, and S.C. 700. **E–VE, but with out-of-season reductions**

Airport Accommodations

La Quinta (vic.), 2499 La Quinta Lane, SC 29418 (797-8181; toll free, see La Quinta). 122 rms, A/C, color TV, in-rm movies. AE, CB, DC, MD, V. Free parking, pool, rest., bar, rm svce, free morning coffee, free crib. *Note:* Brand-new motel five min. from the airport. Comfortable, spacious rms plus cheerful reception and svce make this a very good value. 20 min. from dwntwn. **I**

RESTAURANTS

Charleston Restaurant Prices	
(per person, excluding drinks and service charges)	
B (Budget)	up to $15
I (Inexpensive)	$15–$25
M (Moderate)	$25–$40
E (Expensive)	$40–$60
VE (Very Expensive)	$60 and up

Personal Favorites (in order of preference)

Robert's (dwntwn), 42 N. Market St. (577-7565). A/C. Dinner only, Tues.-Sat. (svce until 8 p.m.); closed Sun., Mon. AE, MC, V. Jkt. Specialties: seafood mousse w. lobster bisque, chateaubriand béarnaise or périgourdine, excellent desserts. *Note:* Tiny dining room, seating no more than 30 at most, with Regency décor. Resv. must therefore be made days (or weeks) in advance. A remarkable experience despite chef Robert Dickson's passion for *bel canto*. The menu always includes six different dishes or entrees. Good service. Free parking. *Continental-French.* **E (prix fixe)**

The Colony House (dwntwn), 35 Prioleau St. (723-3424). A/C. Lunch Mon.-Sat.; dinner nightly; closed holidays. AE, MC, V. Specialties: she-crab soup, crab gratinée, stuffed plaice, fish of the day. *Note:* The best broiled and baked fish in Charleston in a pleasantly laid-out dock warehouse. The same establishment as the Wine Cellar (see below), but less chic. Resv. advised. Locally popular. Free parking. *Seafood-American.* **I**

Marianne's (dwntwn), 235 Meeting St. (722-7196). A/C. Dinner only, Mon.-Sat.; closed Sun., Thanksgiving, Dec. 25, Jan. 1. AE, MC, V. Jkt. Specialties: house pâtés, rack of lamb, baron of beef, paupiettes of red snapper, excellent homemade pastries. The menu changes regularly. *Note:* French bistro-style cuisine and décor. Good wine list. Friendly svce. Resv. advised. *French.* **I–M**

A. W. Shuck's (dwntwn.), 70 State St. (723-1151). A/C. Lunch/dinner Mon.-Sat; closed Sun. AE, CB, DC, MC, V. Specialties: oysters, clams, scampi, fish of the day. *Note:* Seafood bistro which serves first-rate fish year round. Generous portions at the bar. Pleasant ambience. *Seafood.* **I**

Atlantic House (vic.), 301 W. Atlantic Ave., at Folly Beach (588-9563). Lunch/dinner daily. AE, MC, V. Specialties: broiled fish of the day, shellfish, lobster, steak. *Note:* This seafood restaurant sits where it was originally built, on piles over the water, 20 min. from dwntwn. The fish is prepared without great imagination but is impeccably fresh. Pleasant, if somewhat noisy, ambience. Good svce. A favorite tourist rest. *Seafood-American.* **B–I**

Other Restaurants (from top bracket to budget)

The Wine Cellar (dwntwn), 35 Prioleau St. (723-9463). A/C. Dinner only, Mon.-Sat.; closed Sun.(in winter), Dec. 25, Jan. 1. AE, MC, V. Jkt. Specialties: parsleyed rack of lamb, pompano sautéed with almonds, red snapper in chablis, tournedos, duckling à l'orange. The menu changes regularly. Fine wine list. *Note:* Modern, carefully prepared French-American cuisine served in an elegantly rehabilitated old storeroom. A favorite of the local smart set. Resv. a must. Very good svce. Parking. *French-American.* **M (prix fixe)**

🍷🍷🍷 **Jilich's on East Bay** (dwntwn), 188 E. Bay St. (577-4338).
🍷🍷🍷 A/C. Lunch Mon.-Fri.; dinner Mon.-Sat.; closed Sun. AE, CB, DC, MC, V. Jkt. Specialties: blue crab soup with sherry, barbecued shrimp with grits, good seafood, praline cheesecake with pecan sauce. *Note:* This newcomer to the local gastronomic scene offers typical Carolina Low Country cuisine. Pretty, rustic décor of exposed brick walls and beams under an elegant skylight. An "in" spot with an ambience that is both romantic and relaxed. Good svce. Resv. advised. *American.* **I–M**

🔆🍷🍷 **East Bay Trading Co.** (dwntwn), East Bay and Queen Sts.
🔆🍷🍷 (722-0722). A/C. Lunch Mon.-Fri.; dinner Mon.-Sat.; closed Sun., holidays. AE, DC, MC, V. Specialties: beef Wellington, roast lamb, roast beef au jus, fish of the day, good homemade desserts. *Note:* In an old harbor warehouse with picturesque, if overelaborate, décor, this pleasant restaurant offers excellent European-inspired cuisine. Cheerful svce. Locally popular. Resv. advised. *Continental-American.* **I**

🍷🍷 **82 Queen** (dwntwn), 82 Queen St. (723-7591). A/C.
🍷🍷 Lunch/dinner daily; closed Thanksgiving, Dec. 25. AE, MC, V. Jkt. Specialties: fish of the day, regional dishes. The menu changes regularly. *Note:* An "in" place in a charming early-19th-century residence. Carefully prepared cuisine centering on seafood. First-rate svce. Locally very popular. Resv. highly recommended. The adjacent Wine Bar is the ideal spot for a before- or after-dinner drink. *Seafood.* **I**

🔆🍷🍷 **Ferrante's** (dwntwn), 32 N. Market St. (723-3614). A/C.
🔆🍷🍷 Dinner only nightly; closed holidays. AE, CB, DC, MC, V. Jkt. Specialties: fresh pasta, scaloppine al marsala, fish of the day, roast duck, lamb cacciatore. *Note:* Pleasant rest. with Italian-inspired cuisine in an old fishermen's chapel complete w. stained glass and frescoes. Irreproachably fresh seafood and very creditable meat dishes. Svce varies. Resv. advised. *Italian-Seafood.* **I**

🍷 **Charleston Ice House** (dwntwn), 188 Meeting St. (723-
🍷 6123). A/C. Breakfast/lunch/dinner daily (until midnight); closed Thanksgiving, Dec. 25. AE, MC, V. Specialties: fish of the day, Greek dishes, sandwiches, excellent desserts. *Note:* Picturesque, lively atmosphere in the heart of the Old City Market. Honest, unpretentious cuisine. Excellent value. Locally popular. *Greek-American.* **B–I**

🍷 **Marina Variety Store** (nr. dwntwn), Municipal Marina,
🍷 Lockwood Blvd. (723-6325). A/C. Lunch/dinner daily. No credit cards. Specialties: clam chowder, fish of the day, Kentucky-style fried chicken, hamburgers. *Note:* Generally jam-packed at lunchtime, this very popular bistro on the banks of the Ashley River offers decent cuisine at very reasonable prices. Efficient svce. Pleasant view of the yacht basin. *Seafood-American.* **B**

Cafeterias / Specialty Spots

Gaulart & Maliclet (dwntwn), 98 Broad St. (577-9797). Breakfast/lunch/dinner daily. AE, MC, V. Specialties: gazpacho, homemade soups, pâtés, sandwiches, and daily specials that can be eaten at the counter. Fine wine list. *Note:* Small, pleasant bistro especially popular among lawyers and bankers at lunch hour. An excellent spot.

Reuben's Downtown Delicatessen (dwntwn), 251 Meeting St. (722-6883). Lunch daily; dinner Mon.-Sat. (until 10 p.m.) No credit cards. Specialties: New York–style deli offering hearty sandwiches, homemade soups, and salads. *Note:* Usually packed with locals. Located in old building (1880s). No resv.

BARS & NIGHTCLUBS

A. W. Shuck's (dwntwn), 70 State St. (723-1151). Inviting oyster bar (see "Restaurants," above). Mon.-Sat.

Myskyn's Tavern (dwntwn), 83 Market St. (577-5595). Congenial pub and rest. with live jazz. Mon.-Sat.

Watercolors (dwntwn), in the Omni Hotel, 130 Market St. (722-4900). The area's classiest disco attracts a young professional crowd.

NEARBY EXCURSIONS

BOONE HALL (8 mi., 13 km, NE on U.S. 17; 803/884-4371): Former cotton plantation dating from 1681. Only the slave quarters and the outbuildings are original. The classic Georgian-style house is 50 years old and served as the setting for *Gone With the Wind*. Very lovely avenue of century-old oaks. Worth a visit. Open daily.

CHARLES TOWNE LANDING (1500 Old Towne Rd.; 803/556-4450): This colonial village, rebuilt at the spot where the English landed in 1670, faithfully reconstructs the life and atmosphere of the first British colonists. The grounds include 660 acres (267 ha.) of parks, plantations, and gardens, plus a replica of the 17th-century merchant ship *Adventure*. Not to be missed. Open daily.

CYPRESS GARDENS (23 mi., 37 km, north on U.S. 52) (803/553-0515): Superb camellia and azalea gardens and giant cypresses amid pools, once a part of the Dean Hall Plantation (1725). Boat rides. Not to be missed. Open daily.

FRANCIS MARION NATIONAL FOREST (18 mi., 29 km, northeast on U.S. 17 or S.C. 41): Dotted with lakes and swamps, this 250,000+-acre (100,000+-ha.) forest contains subtropical vegetation and many remains of Indian and colonial plantings. Camping, boating, fishing, hunting, and a hiker's paradise. For information, contact District Ranger, Rte. 3, Box 630, Moncks Corner, SC 29461 (803/887-3311).

MAGNOLIA PLANTATION (10 mi., 16 km, northwest on S.C. 61): One of the country's most beautiful gardens, it dates from the late 1670s and boasts 900 varieties of camellias (some more than two centuries old), 250 varieties of azaleas and magnolias, and a majestic avenue of moss-covered, century-old oaks.

On the way, visit **Drayton Hall,** 2 mi. north on S.C. 61 (803/766-0188), one of the oldest plantations of the Southeast (1738), inhabited until 1974 by seven successive generations of the Drayton family. Beautiful Palladian architecture. An absolute must-see. Open daily.

MIDDLETON PLACE (14 mi., 22 km, northwest on S.C. 61; 803/556-6020): The oldest and one of the most beautiful landscaped gardens in the country, with cypress groves and thousands of azaleas (1741). The gardens and the Tudor-style wing, miraculously spared by Civil War battles, house the Spoleto Festival/USA each year (see "Special Events," above). Not to be missed. Open daily.

OLD DORCHESTER STATE PARK (20 mi., 32 km, northwest on S.C. 642) (803/873-1740): Archeological reserve close to the source of the Ashley River on the site of a village founded by Massachusetts colonists (1696). The British occupied it during the Revolutionary War and then razed it in 1781. Traces of Fort Dorchester and the church remain. Archeological digs in process. Interesting museum. Worth going out of your way for. Open daily.

FARTHER AFIELD

ATLANTIC ISLANDS (318 mi., 509 km, round trip on U.S. 17S, S.C. 700, S.C. 174, U.S. 21, S.C. 281, S.C. 170, U.S. 278, and U.S. 17N): Vacation excursion for three or more days for lovers of beaches, water sports, and semitropical wildlife more or less untamed. The suggested circuit includes visits (in the following order) to:

Kiawah Island: 9,600 acres (4,000 ha.) of lush, subtropical vegetation plus 10 mi. (16 km) of superb beaches, woods, and ponds haunted by alligators, deer, sea turtles, and 140 different species of birds. Accessible by road. The **Kiawah Island Inn,** a very comfortable three-star hotel, organizes island tours by Jeep and by boat (768-2121; see "Accommodations in the Vicinity," above). Visit not to be missed.

Edisto Island: The best public beach in South Carolina (**Edisto Beach State Park**)—1.8 mi. (3 km) of immaculate sand and a real treasure trove for seashell collectors.

Hunting Island: 4,800 acres (2,000 ha.) of semi-wild nature, deserted beaches, subtropical forests, and swamps. Campgrounds and hiking trails. Island accessible by U.S. 21. Park open year round.

Parris Island: Settled in 1562 by the French Huguenot Jean Ribaut (there is a monument to him here), Parris Island is today home to a well-known U.S. Marines training camp. Military museum. Open daily.

Hilton Head Island: The largest island on the Atlantic coast between New Jersey and Florida, a fashionable summer getaway since the early 1960s, offers 12 mi. (19 km) of beach, 18 golf courses, more than 200 tennis courts, and six marinas, plus a marvelous climate year round and an unpolluted sea. A vacation paradise. There are a dozen luxury hotels and motels, including the ♔♔♔♔ **Inter-Continental,** 135 S. Port Royal Dr., Hilton Head, SC 29928 (803/681-4000), 415 rms, **E–VE;** and the ♔♔ **Sea Crest Motel,** Avocet St., Hilton Head, SC 29928 (803/785-2121), 90 rms, **M–E.** Hilton Head is accessible by U.S. 278. Well worth going out of your way.

On the trip back to Charleston, see ☼ ♙♙ **Beaufort:** Built on the island of Port Royal, this pretty little town of 8,600 with charming old houses was home to the first Protestant colony in America (1562), the French Huguenots. Numerous antebellum structures, including St. Helena Episcopal Church (1724), the Arsenal (1795), and the John Mark Verdier House Museum (1790). Visitor Center, 910 Bay St. (803/524-3163). Not to be missed.

CHAPTER 11

SAVANNAH ♖♖

□ □ □

Once a major cotton and tobacco trading center, today the headquarters of the paper industry, Savannah is also, like its neighbor and rival, Charleston, a living page from the book of history. It is also one of the most beautiful cities in the U.S. The 13th—and last—of the colonies founded by the British on American shores, Savannah was conceived in 1733 as the continent's first "modern" city. Its founder, Gen. James Oglethorpe, an ecologist ahead of his time, created a checkerboarded urban plan which would be a harmonious alternation of gardens, houses, and squares—green oases planted with mossy oaks, pines, and azaleas. Its cover of trees gives Savannah some shelter from the heat of a climate, which can be truly oppressive in summer.

Since no house here is like its neighbor, the city displays the whole gamut of southern architectural styles; more than Atlanta, Charleston, or New Orleans, Savannah is *the* city of the Deep South. The colonnaded verandas, ornate façades, and flowered gardens along **Bull Street,** the wrought-iron balconies and pastel-washed houses with their stoops on **Abercorn Street,** come together in a living picture of peaceful, romantic charm straight out of *Gone With the Wind*.

The urban-restoration project in the **Savannah Historic District,** begun more than two decades ago, has been energetically implemented. But though Savannah boasts a complex of old buildings unequalled in America, it is no drowsy, languishing museum city. Miraculously spared during the Civil War by General Sherman because its inhabitants gave him a kindly reception at the end of his famous "March to the Sea," Savannah is today a city on the move; you have only to walk along the docks on the **Savannah River,** or around **Riverfront Plaza,** the old cotton-mill district, to satisfy yourself of that.

The actor Stacy Keach was born in Savannah.

BASIC FACTS: State of Georgia. Area Code: 912. Time Zone: Eastern Time. ZIP Code (of the central post office): 31402. Founded: 1733. Approximate population: 142,000.

CLIMATE: A winter almost as mild as Florida's (Jan. average, 52° F, 11°C) is succeeded by an early, riotous spring (don't miss the azaleas in bloom in mid-Apr.). After the hot, sticky summer (81° F, 27°C, average in July) comes the sunny fall, both typically subtropical with sudden late-afternoon downpours from mid-June to Sept. Every season has something to offer to the visitor.

DISTANCES: Atlanta, 251 mi. (401 km); Charleston, 106 mi. (170 km); Miami, 496 mi. (794 km); Orlando, 292 mi. (467 km); Washington, 633 mi. (1,012 km).

ARRIVAL & TRANSIT INFORMATION

AIRPORT: Savannah International Airport (Travis Field) (SAV), 8 mi. (13 km) NW; for information call 966-5637.

AIRLINES: American (233-9988), Delta (234-1221), Eastern (236-4411), United (234-9800).

CITY LINK: The **cab** fare from the airport to dwntwn is about $14–$16; time, about 20 min. Bus: **Regal Limos** (toll free 800/334-8264) serves major dwntwn hotels; leaves according to published schedule; fare, $8; time, 25 min.

Since the airport is close in and the city compact, you won't need to rent a car unless you plan excursions into the country around.

Cabs are relatively inexpensive, and public (bus) transportation by the **Savannah Transit Authority** (233-5767) is reasonably efficient.

CAR RENTAL (at the airport unless otherwise indicated): Avis (964-1781); Budget (964-9186); Hertz (964-1220); National (964-1771); Thrifty, Dean Forest Rd. (964-2341). For dwntwn locations, consult the local telephone directory.

LIMOUSINE SERVICES: Dav El Limousine (toll free 800/922-0343), Regal Limo Service (toll free 800/334-8264).

TAXIS: Cabs may be hailed on the street, taken from the waiting lines outside the major hotels, or—most conveniently—called by phone: **Yellow Cab** (236-1133).

TRAIN: AMTRAK Station, 2611 Seaboard Coast Line Dr. (toll free 800/872-7245).

BUS: Greyhound, 610 W. Oglethorpe Ave. (233-7723).

INFORMATION & TOURS

TOURIST INFORMATION: The **Savannah Convention and Visitors Bureau,** 222 W. Oglethorpe Ave., GA 31499 (912/944-0456).

Savannah Visitors Center, 301 W. Broad St. (912/233-3067 or 233-6651), open daily.

For a **recorded message** giving a current list of shows and cultural events, call 233-2787.

GUIDED TOURS: **AAA Savannah Scenic Tours** (bus), 1113 Winston Ave. (355-4296): Conducted tours of the city and surroundings; serves leading dwntwn hotels.

Cap'n Sam's Cruises (boat), River and Bull Sts. (234-7248): Cruises in the harbor and on the Savannah River, daily year round.

Carriage Tours (horse-drawn carriage), Madison Square (236-6756): Around Savannah in a horse-drawn carriage; unusual and pleasing.

Clipper Cruise Line (boat): 7-, 10-, or 14-day cruises along the Atlantic coast aboard 100-berth luxury yachts (see "Guided Tours" in Chapter 8 on Baltimore).

Gray Line Tours (bus), 215 W. Boundary St. (236-9604): Two-hour guided tour of the Historic District, serving major hotels and the Visitors Center.

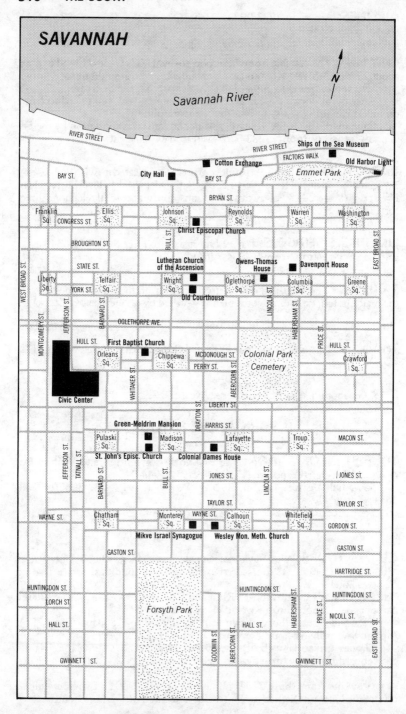

Historic Savannah Foundation Tours (bus), Hilton–De Soto Hotel (233-3597): Conducted tours of Savannah's rich architectural heritage.

SIGHTS, ATTRACTIONS, & ACTIVITIES

ARCHITECTURAL HIGHLIGHTS: ⌂ **City Hall,** Bull and W. Bay Sts. (233-9321): Fine turn-of-the-century classical revival building capped by a gilded copper dome. Note the two British cannon in bronze, captured at the Battle of Yorktown and given to the city of Savannah by George Washington in 1791.

⌂ **U.S. Customs House,** Bull and E. Bay Sts. (944-4253): Erected in 1850 on the site where the city's founder, Englishman James Oglethorpe, built his first home in 1733. The capitals of its imposing granite columns are carved into the shape of tobacco leaves, as a tribute to this important local source of wealth.

BEACHES: ⌂ **Savannah Beach,** 18 mi. (28 km) east on U.S. 80: Lovely fine-sand beach, some 6 mi. (9.5 km) long, on **Tybee Island.** Many hotels, motels, and restaurants. Very popular in the warm weather.

CHURCHES/SYNAGOGUES: ⌂ **Christ Episcopal Church,** Johnson Square between E. St. Julian and E. Congress Sts. (232-4131): The first church in the colony (1733); among its famous rectors were John Wesley and George Whitefield, founders of the Methodist church. The present church with its immaculate white columns, dating from 1838, is the third to occupy the site. Should be seen. Open Tues.-Fri.

⌂ **Congregation Mikve Israel,** 20 E. Gordon St. (233-1547): The only Gothic Revival synagogue in the country, built in 1878 for a congregation of German and Portuguese Jews which was founded in 1733. Museum with many ancient manuscripts, historical documents, letters from Presidents Washington, Jefferson, and Madison, etc. Conducted tours Mon.-Fri. Should be seen.

☼⌂ **First African Baptist Church,** 23 Montgomery St. (233-6597): Home of the oldest black congregation in the country, founded in 1777 at Brampton Plantation. The present church dates from 1861. Should be seen; open daily.

☼⌂ **Independent Presbyterian Church,** Bull St. and W. Oglethorpe Ave. (236-3346): Founded in 1755 by members of the Church of Scotland; the design recalls the famous London church St. Martin-in-the-Fields on Trafalgar Square. Georgian interior. Should be seen; open Mon.-Fri.

HISTORIC BUILDINGS: ☼ ⌂⌂ **Savannah's Historic District,** a 2.2 square mile area bounded by the Savannah River, Gaston St., and E. and W. Broad Sts.: More than a thousand 19th-century buildings scrupulously restored—the country's largest group of historic houses. Among the most interesting and elegant are:

The **Andrew Low House,** 329 Abercorn St. (233-6854), open daily except Thur., a charming home dating from 1848. Among its illustrious guests are numbered Gen. Robert E. Lee and the British writer William Makepeace Thackeray. Belonged at one time to Juliette Gordon Low, who founded the Girl Scouts in 1912.

Davenport House, Columbia Square (236-8097), open daily, is a fine example of the Georgian "Federal" style dating from 1820, with superb old furniture and original ellyptical staircase.

The **Green-Meldrim House,** Madison Square (233-3845), open Mon.-Sat., an interesting Gothic Revival building with a characteristic wrought-iron portico, was General Sherman's headquarters at the end of the Civil War.

The **Juliette Gordon Low Birthplace,** Oglethorpe Ave. and Bull St. (233-4501), open daily except Wed., is an elegant 1821 house in Regency style, birthplace of the woman who founded the Girl Scouts.

The **Owens-Thomas House,** 124 Abercorn St. (233-9743), open daily (closed in Sept.), is one of the loveliest examples of the Regency idiom in the U.S., built in 1816 to the design of the British architect William Jay. Lafayette stayed here.

The **William Scarbrough House,** 41 W. Broad St. (233-7703), open Mon.-Fri., another remarkable example of the Regency style, dates from 1819. It's the home of the Historic Savannah Foundation, with a museum devoted to the process of rehabilitating old houses.

Don't fail to visit the Historic District.

MUSEUMS OF ART: ❋ ▵ Telfair Mansion and Art Museum, 121 Barnard St. (232-1177): Fine old porcelain, silverware, and traditional 18th- and 19th-century painting and sculpture from Europe and America, displayed in an elegant upper-class mansion in the Regency style, the work of William Jay. Be sure to see the splendid Octagon Room. This was the residence of the British governor from 1760 until the end of the War of Independence. Open Tues.-Sun.; not to be missed.

MUSEUMS OF SCIENCE AND HISTORY: ❋ ▵ Great Savannah Exposition, 303 W. Broad St. (238-1779): Temporary exhibitions and remarkable audiovisual shows illustrating the history of Savannah and the state of Georgia, in a 19th-century locomotive barn cunningly restored. Open daily; not to be missed.

▵ **Savannah Science Museum,** 4405 Paulsen St. (355-6705): Botany, zoology (interesting collection of reptiles and amphibians), aquarium. Exhibitions on medicine and physics. Well-designed planetarium. Should be seen; open Tues.-Sun.

▵ **Ships of the Sea Museum,** 503 E. River St. (232-1511): Interesting maritime museum on the banks of the Savannah River, with many ship models, old figureheads, and a fine scrimshaw collection. Reconstructions of a ship's carpenter's shop and a chandlery. Worth a visit. Open daily.

PANORAMAS: ▵ Talmadge Memorial Bridge, north of W. Boundary St.: From this bridge across the Savannah River you'll get a very good view of the city and of Riverfront Plaza along a line from north to south. Worth a look.

PARKS AND GARDENS: ❋ ▵▵ City's Squares, along Abercorn, Barnard, Bull, Habersham, and Houston Sts.: Wonderful public gardens, planted with azaleas, palm trees, pines, and moss oaks, in the heart of the Historic District. The finest are those along Bull St.: **Chippewa Square, Johnson Square, Madison Square, Monterey Square,** and **Wright Square.** A sight to be seen.

▵ **Forsyth Park,** Gaston and Bull Sts.: With its great fountain, reminiscent of the one in Paris's Place de la Concorde, and its Confederate Monument, this is the largest public park in Savannah. Try to see it, particularly in spring when the azaleas are in bloom.

☀ 🔔 **Trustee's Garden Site,** E. Broad St. at E. Bryan St.: Originally the site of a botanic garden planted in 1733 by the first English settlers on the model of the Chelsea Gardens in London, with a view to raising medicinal plants, vines, and mulberry trees for silkworms. The first peaches planted here are the origin of Georgia's renowned peach crop. In 1762 a fort was built here; it was captured in 1782 by Gen. "Mad Anthony" Wayne during the war against the British. Today you'll find here several elegantly restored 19th-century houses, as well as the **Pirate's House,** a sailors' tavern reminiscent of that described by Robert Louis Stevenson in *Treasure Island*. (See "Restaurants," below). Should be seen.

PERFORMING ARTS:
For a daily listing of all shows and cultural events, consult the entertainment pages of the daily papers *Savannah Morning News* (morning) and *Savannah Evening Press* (evening).

Savannah Civic Center, Orleans Square (234-6666): This auditorium is the home of the Savannah Symphony Orchestra; also ballet, Broadway hits, musicals.

Savannah Theater, Chippewa Square (233-7764): One of the oldest theaters in the country. Drama, comedy, contemporary theater.

SPECIAL EVENTS:
For the exact schedule of events below, consult the **Savannah Visitors Center** (see "Tourist Information," above).

Georgia Week (Feb.): Parades, concerts, exhibitions; a colorful commemoration of the founding of Georgia.

St. Patrick's Day (mid-Mar.): One of the biggest popular parades on the East Coast, drawing more than 250,000 participants every year.

Christ Episcopal Church Tour of Homes and Gardens (late Mar. to early Apr.): Conducted tours, by daylight or by candlelight, of some 30 historic private houses and their gardens. Sponsored by Christ Episcopal Church and the Historic Savannah Foundation. For information, call 234-8054.

Night in Old Savannah (third wknd in Apr.): Folklore and food festival; jazz concerts.

Christmas in Savannah (Dec.): A month of festivities in the Historic District, with parades, concerts, house tours, cultural events, etc.

STROLLS:
☀ 🔔 **Bull Street,** between Bay St. and Forsyth Park: Savannah's elegant main street, with many old houses, historic churches, and superb flower-planted squares. A walk you should take.

🔔 **Factors Walk,** between Bull and E. Broad Sts.: Running between old buildings formerly used in the cotton business, these narrow cobbled ramps, reached by a network of wrought-iron footbridges, have retained all the flavor of the 19th century. Their cobblestones were once ballast in ships coming here from Europe. A sight not to be missed.

☀ 🔔 **Waterfront Area,** around John P. Rousakis Riverfront Plaza: Old brick warehouses along the Savannah River, now converted into boutiques, restaurants, pubs, art galleries, nightclubs. Lively and colorful by day and night alike. At sunrise and sunset the view from the quays is magnificent. One of the finest examples of urban renovation in the U.S.; don't miss it.

ACCOMMODATIONS
See the listing of toll-free numbers in the Appendix.

Room Rates in Savannah	
B (Budget)	up to $30
I (Inexpensive)	$30–$60
M (Moderate)	$60–$90
E (Expensive)	$90–$140
VE (Very Expensive)	$140 and up

Personal Favorites (in order of preference)

☼ ♟♟♟♟ **Mulberry Inn** (dwntwn), 601 E. Bay St., GA 31401 (912/ 238-1200; toll free 800/554-5544). 125 rms, A/C, color TV, in-rm movies. AE, DC, MC, V. Free parking, pool, rest. (Christopher's), bar, rm svce, free crib. *Note:* Small, gracious, unusually designed luxury hotel. The main building began life as a livery stable in the 1860s, was converted into a Coca-Cola bottling plant, and has now been tastefully restored, w. an elegant classical revival décor. Period furniture, many art objects; pretty interior garden. Spacious rms, some w. mini-bars; impeccable svce; very good hotel rest. Distinction and charm in the heart of Old Savannah. **E, but lower rates out of season**

☼ ♟♟♟ **Foley House Inn** (dwntwn), 14 W. Hull St., GA 31401 (912/ 232-6622). 20 rms, A/C, color TV, in-rm movies. AE, MC, V. Street parking, hot tub, valet svce, free breakfast, free crib. *Note:* Charming, luxuriously restored 19th-century mansion looking out on Chippewa Square in the heart of the Historic District. Original Victorian setting and period furniture. Each room is decorated in its own style, most having private patios, Jacuzzis, and fireplaces. Ultra-polished reception and svce. Since there is no elevator, avoid the rms on the third and fourth floors. For those who love glimpses of the past. Resv. advisable, a good while ahead. **E–VE, but lower rates out of season**

♟♟♟ **Hilton–De Soto** (dwntwn), Liberty and Bull Sts., GA 31402 (912/232-9000; toll free, see Hilton). 250 rms, A/C, color TV, in-rm movies. AE, CB, DC, MC, V. Free parking, pool, bicycles for rent, rest. (Pavilion), coffeeshop, bar, 24-hr rm svce, nightclub, free airport limo, free crib. *Note:* The most famous hotel in Savannah, on the site of the old, and now legendary, De Soto Hotel. The modern building agrees well enough w. its surroundings. Comfortable rms, some w. private balconies or patios. Attentive svce. A favorite w. those in-the-know. Very centrally located. **M–E**

♟♟ **Ramada Inn Civic Center** (dwntwn), 201 W. Oglethorpe Ave., GA 31401 (912/233-3531; toll free, see Ramada Inns). 202 rms, A/C, cable color TV. AE, CB, DC, MC, V. Free parking, pool, sundeck, rest., bar, rm svce, hrdrsr, free crib. *Note:* Modern, comfortable motel in brick w. wrought-iron balconies. Friendly reception and svce; very acceptable rest. Good value in the heart of the Historic District. **I–M**

♟ **Quality Inn Heart of Savannah** (dwntwn), 300 W. Bay St., GA 31401 (912/236-6321; toll free, see Quality Inns). 53 rms, A/C, color TV. AE, CB, DC, MC, V. Free parking, valet svce, adjoining coffeeshop, free breakfast. *Note:* Modest but very well-run small motel in the heart of dwntwn. Functionally comfortable; good reception. Excellent value. I

Other Accommodations (from top bracket to budget)

♀♀♀ **Hyatt Regency** (dwntwn), 2 W. Bay St., GA 31401 (912/
🛏🛏🛏 238-1234; toll free, see Hyatt). 346 rms, A/C, color TV, in-rm movies. AE, CB, DC, MC, V. Valet garage $6, pool, marina, rest. (Windows), coffeeshop, bar, rm svce, disco, boutiques, free crib, concierge. *Note:* The giant among local hotels. Modern, graceless building but spacious, very comfortable rms w. balconies, the best overlooking the Savannah River. Moorings, for a fee. Efficient svce; business and group clientele. Very well located on the river, a couple of blocks from City Hall. **E**

※🛏🛏🛏 **Planters Inn Savannah** (formerly the Royal Colony; dwntwn), 29 Abercorn St., GA 31401 (912/232-5678; toll free 800/554-1187). 60 rms, A/C, color TV. AE, CB, DC, MC, V. Free valet garage, bar, rm svce, free breakfast, free crib, concierge. *Note:* Urbane, intimate small hotel looking onto Reynolds Square in the center of the Historic District. Elegant, comfortable layouts w. four-poster beds, period furniture, and private balconies. Exceptionally attentive svce. An excellent place to stay. **M–E**

※♀♀ **17 Hundred 90 Inn** (dwntwn), 307 E. President St., GA
🛏🛏 31401 (912/236-7122). 14 rms, A/C, color TV, in-rm movies. AE, CB, DC, MC, V. Free garage, rest., bar, rm svce, free breakfast, crib $6. *Note:* Delightful old Colonial home dating, as the names indicates, from 1790. Each rm is decorated in different fashion, but all in the Georgian style of the last century. Oversize beds and antique furniture. Personalized reception and svce. Praiseworthy rest. One of the most charming places to stay in Savannah. **M–E**

♀ **Days Inn Historic District** (dwntwn), 201 W. Bay St., GA
🛏 31401 (912/236-4440; toll free, see Days Inns). 252 rms, A/C, color TV, in-rm movies. AE, DC, MC, V. Free parking, pool, 24-hr rest., valet svce, free crib. *Note:* Modern motel in the heart of the Historic District; spacious, comfortable rms, some w. kitchenettes, the best overlooking the Savannah River. Efficient svce. Group clientele. Good value. **I–M**

♀ **Holiday Inn Downtown** (dwntwn), 121 W. Boundary St.,
🛏 GA 31401 (912/236-1355; toll free, see Holiday Inns). 206 rms, A/C, color TV, in-rm movies. AE, CB, DC, MC, V. Free parking, two pools, rest., bar, rm svce, free crib. *Note:* Typical Holiday Inn a stone's throw from the Historic District. Spacious, functional rms; friendly reception. Good value. I

♀ **Howard Johnson's Downtown** (dwntwn), 224 W. Bounda-
🛏 ry St., GA 31401 (912/232-4371; toll free, see Howard Johnson's). 89 rms, A/C, color TV, in-rm movies. AE, CB, DC, MC, V. Free parking, pool, rest., bar, valet svce, crib $10. *Note:* Small motel, typical but comfortable, a block or two from the Historic District. Huge, inviting rms, some w. private patios. Reception w. a smile. Good value. I

In the Vicinity

※🛏🛏🛏 **Sheraton Savannah Resort and Country Club** (vic.), 612 Wilmington Island Rd., GA 31401 (912/897-1612; toll free, see Sheraton). 200 rms (in the hotel) or cottages, A/C, color TV, in-rm movies. AE, CB, DC, MC, V. Free parking, pool, sauna, health club, golf course, putting green, five tennis courts, horseback riding, private beach, boats, fishing, water sports, two rests., two bars, rm svce, disco, free crib. *Note:* Very lovely resort hotel on the Wilmington River less than 15 min. by car from Savannah, completely renovated and tastefully decorated. Comfortable cottages and villas clustering around a charming old 1920s hotel. Acceptable rests.; attentive svce. Ideal for open-air sports, w. one of the finest golf courses in the country. The American Plan is very good value. Interesting wknd discounts. **E (hotel) and VE (cottages), but lower rates Nov.-Mar.**

RESTAURANTS

Savannah Restaurant Prices (per person, excluding drinks and service charges)	
B (Budget)	up to $15
I (Inexpensive)	$15–$25
M (Moderate)	$25–$40
E (Expensive)	$40–$60
VE (Very Expensive)	$60 and up

Personal Favorites (in order of preference)

Elizabeth on 37th (nr. dwntwn), 105 E. 37th St. (236-5547). A/C. Lunch/dinner Tues.-Sat.; closed Sun., Mon., holidays, and mid-July to mid-Aug. AE, MC, V. Jkt. *Specialties:* wild-mushroom pies, broiled quail w. oyster sauce, rack of lamb w. pistachios, flounder stuffed w. mousse of fish and served in hollandaise sauce flavored w. basil, oysters and country ham w. leeks in cream sauce, poached salmon w. mushrooms and saffron rice, green onion pancake; superb desserts. Good wine list at reasonable prices. *Note:* Since it opened in 1981 this wonderful rest., classified as "southern nouvelle," has won plaudits from all the food critics. Imagination, lightness, and top-quality materials (especially seafood) are the three golden rules of Elizabeth Terry, the extraordinary self-taught chef. Her husband, Michael, a former Atlanta lawyer and a wine lover, makes a wonderful sommelier. The rest. occupies a very lovely old house, elegantly restored. Praiseworthy svce. A wonderful place to eat, 10 min. from dwntwn. Resv. a must. *American.* **I–M**

Pirate's House (dwntwn), 20 E. Broad St. (233-5757). A/C. Lunch/dinner daily, brunch Sun. AE, CB, DC, MC, V. Jkt. *Specialties:* seafood bisque, "shrab" (combination of shrimp and crabmeat), gumbo, oysters Savannah, jambalaya, seafood w. red rice, honeyed chicken w. pecans, catch of the day, steak. Very good desserts. *Note:* This huge, picturesque museum-tavern, 2½ centuries old, houses one of Georgia's best rests., serving many regional specialties such as "red rice" Savannah style (w. tomatoes and spices). Legend has it that Captain Flint, of Stevenson's classic adventure story *Treasure Island,* drew his last breath here. Amusing maritime décor; splendid bar. An experience not to be missed—but take care not to lose yourself; the place boasts no fewer than 23 rooms! Resv. advised. *Seafood-American.* **I–M**

Johnny Harris (nr. dwntwn), 1651 E. Victory Dr. (354-7810). A/C. Lunch/dinner Mon.-Sat.; closed Sun., Jan. 1, and Dec. 25. AE, CB, DC, MC, V. Jkt. (J&T required on Fri. and Sat. evenings.) *Specialties:* roast beef, crabmeat au gratin, steak, barbecued pork, southern fried chicken. *Note:* a three-generation-old institution for lovers of good, solid food. The beef and the barbecued spareribs, served w. fresh vegetables (something uncommon enough to deserve mention), are highly recommended. Diligent svce. Uninspiring rustic décor. A 10-min. drive from dwntwn. Locally very popular; resv. recommended. *American.* **I**

🍸🍸 **Shrimp Factory** (dwntwn), 313 E. River St. (236-4229). A/C. Lunch/dinner daily; closed Jan. 1, Thanksgiving, Dec. 25. AE, CB, DC, MC, V. *Specialties:* cassolette of seafood, broiled fish of the day, variety of salads. *Note:* This pleasant old place on the river specializes, as its name suggests, in seafood, perfectly fresh and perfectly cooked. Touristy but congenial atmosphere; nice view of the passing boats. *Seafood.* **B–I**

🍸 **Mrs. Wilke's Boarding House** (dwntwn), basement of 107 W. Jones St. (232-5997). A/C. Breakfast/lunch Mon.-Fri.; closed Sat. and Sun. No credit cards. *Specialties:* barbecued spareribs, southern fried chicken, collard greens, ham and gravy, swordfish steak, homemade cakes, banana pudding. *Note:* Colorful family boarding house, serving authentic regional food—all you can eat—in a somewhat minimal setting. The best value in Savannah. No resv. Locally popular. *American.* **B**

Other Restaurants (from top bracket to budget)

🍸🍸🍸 **45 South** (nr. dwntwn), in the Best Western Central at 20 E. Broad St. (354-0444). A/C. Lunch Mon.-Fri., dinner Mon.-Sat.; closed Sun. and holidays. AE, DC, MC, V. Jkt. *Specialties:* mussels and artichokes w. ginger, poached oysters w. leeks, snapper filet w. julienne of vegetables, strawberry puff pastry. *Note:* Inspired, delicate American nouvelle cuisine, particularly noteworthy for its light-as-air sauces. Uninteresting modern décor; very good svce. Over the past couple of years has established a strong local following; resv. advised. *American.* **I–M**

🔆🍸🍸🍸 **Olde Pinke House** (dwntwn), 23 Abercorn St. (232-4286). A/C. Lunch Mon.-Sat., dinner nightly; closed Dec. 25. AE, MC, V. Jkt. (tie suggested). *Specialties:* seafood crêpes, crabcakes, gumbo, chateaubriand, chicken Cordon Bleu. *Note:* A designated historic monument, this attractive pink mansion (whence the name) serves excellent traditional European food and some local dishes as well. Charming 18th-century décor, w. waitresses in period dress. Resv. recommended. Congenial tavern in the cellar. *Seafood-continental.* **I–M**

🍸🍸 **River's End** (vic.), 3122 River Rd., in Thunderbolt (354-2973). A/C. Dinner only, Mon.-Sat.; closed Sun. and holidays. AE, CB, DC, MC, V. Jkt. *Specialties:* scampi, catch of the day, shellfish, steak, Maine lobsters, homemade pies. *Note:* Elegant, polished cuisine whose billing—"direct from fishing boat to cooking stove"—is fully justified. Fine view of the Wilmington River and the yacht basin (customers can moor their own boats in front of the rest.). Preppy crowd; resv. advised. *Seafood.* **I–M**

🍸🍸 **William Seafood** (vic.), 8010 Tybee Rd., U.S. 80E (897-2219). A/C. Lunch/dinner daily; closed Thanksgiving, and Dec. 15 to Jan. 15. No credit cards. *Specialties:* oysters, scallops, broiled shrimp, catch of the day, fried chicken, hamburgers. *Note:* A good bet in Savannah since 1936. Irreproachably fresh seafood in a nondescript décor. Diligent svce; locally popular. Resv. advised; 15 min. from dwntwn. *Seafood.* **B–I**

🔆🍸 **Crystal Beer Parlor** (dwntwn), 301 W. Jones St., at Jefferson (232-1153). A/C. Lunch/dinner Mon.-Sat.; closed Sun. AE, MC, V. *Specialties:* hamburgers, fried chicken, crab stew, gumbo, supersandwiches. *Note:* Congenial, very popular pub with pleasantly faded décor—yellowed photos on the walls, ceiling fans, worn wood floor. Excellent draft beer. A Savannah landmark since 1933. Relaxed atmosphere; no resv. *American.* **B–I**

♈ **Garibaldi's Escape Café** (dwntwn), 315 W. Congress St. (232-7118). A/C. Dinner only, nightly; closed Thanksgiving and Dec. 25. AE, CB, DC, MC, V. *Specialties:* fresh homemade pasta, northern Italian dishes, broiled duck, catch of the day. *Note:* Charming *trattoria* in a converted 1870s firehouse in the heart of the Historic District. Praiseworthy Italian food; excellent espresso; youthful, trendy atmosphere; resv. advised. *Italian.* **B–I**

Cafeterias / Fast Food

Morrisson's (dwntwn), Bull and Bryan Sts. (232-5264). Lunch/dinner daily (till 8:30 p.m.). MC, V. Roast beef, daily specials, salads, sandwiches. Good cafeteria food in an old Savannah setting. Locally popular. Also located at Oglethorpe mall (352-3521).

BARS AND NIGHTCLUBS

Emma's (dwntwn), Riverfront Plaza (232-1223). Trendy disco, lots of action. Open nightly.

Planter's Tavern (dwntwn), 23 Abercorn St. (232-4286). Elegant piano bar with an open fireplace, on the ground floor of the Olde Pink House (see "Restaurants," above). Open nightly.

Spanky's (dwntwn), 317 E. River St. (236-3009). Congenial saloon on the banks of the Savannah River; an amusing contrast between the historic setting and the youthful atmosphere. Pizzas and sandwiches. Locally popular. Open nightly.

NEARBY EXCURSIONS

FORT JACKSON (3 mi., 5 km, east on Islands Expwy.) (232-3945): Situated on the banks of the Savannah River and surrounded by moats, this is one of the oldest (1809) forts in Georgia to survive intact. Its moments of glory were in the War of 1812 and the War Between the States. Now it houses many 19th-century military accessories and devices illustrating the history of its construction and its battles. Interesting. Open Tues.-Sun. from Mar. through Nov.; weekends only the rest of the year.

FORT McALLISTER HISTORIC PARK (25 mi., 40 km, south on U.S. 17 and Ga. 144) (727-2339): Carefully restored Civil War fort, originally built by the Confederates for the defense of Savannah. Its capture by Union forces on Dec. 13, 1864, spelled the downfall of the city and marked the end of Sherman's "March to the Sea." Military museum. Open Tues.-Sun.; worth the side trip.

FORT PULASKI NATIONAL MONUMENT (15 mi., 24 km, east on U.S. 80) (786-5787): One of the largest and best-known defense works on the eastern seaboard, named after the Revolutionary War hero who was killed at the Battle of Savannah in 1779. Witnessed fierce artillery exchanges between North and South during the Civil War. Completely restored before World War II. Museum. Open daily; well worth the detour.

HILTON HEAD ISLAND (38 mi., 60 km, NW on U.S. Alt. 17, S.C. 170, S.C. 46, and U.S. 278): Discovered by the Spaniards in 1526, this inviting island has become one of the most sought-after summer resorts in the country, by virtue of its superb beaches, piney woods, and old plantation houses. Dozens of hotels, motels, vacation cottages, art galleries, and elegant boutiques; 200 tennis courts, 18 golf courses, six marinas, etc. Worth the detour. For details, see Chapter 10 on Charleston.

FARTHER AFIELD

☼ CUMBERLAND ISLAND NATIONAL SEASHORE
(145 mi., 232 km, SW on I-95, Ga. 40, and a ferry): Along the entire Atlantic coast, this is the island most nearly in an unspoiled, natural state. Long uninhabited, this island 16 mi. (26 km) long by 1½–3 mi. (2–5 km) wide, covered in moss oaks and dwarf palmettos, with its marshes and empty beaches, teems with ibis, duck, alligators, and wild ponies. Reached by boat from **St. Mary's,** daily in summer, Thur.-Mon. from Sept. to June; resv. necessary (for information, call 912/882-4335). Limited number of camping sites available. The tiny (ten-rm) ☼ ⌘ **Greyfield Inn** (904/261-6408) occupies an old Colonial-style villa built by the millionaire Thomas Carnegie, who once owned the island. A memorable experience for lovers of nature-in-the-raw. Should be combined with the trip to **Golden Isles** (see below).

☼ ⌘ OKEFENOKEE NATIONAL WILDLIFE REFUGE (122
mi., 195 km, SW on U.S. 17, Ga. 196, U.S. 82, and U.S. 1): The largest wetlands park in the country after Florida's Everglades, with an area of 700 sq. mi. (2,080 km²). Enormous variety of flora and fauna: black bear, deer, lynx, alligators, water birds, etc. Canoe trips through the swamp, daily year round. For information, call the refuge manager (912/496-3331). Well worth the detour; combine it with the excursion to Golden Isles (see below).

☼ ⌘⌘ GOLDEN ISLES (about 180 mi., 288 km, round trip via I-
95S and U.S. 17N): According to legend, the isles owe their name to the many hoards of treasure buried in their sands by the famous pirate Edward Teach, better known as Blackbeard. Another version attributes it to the wonderfully warm and sunny climate of the Georgia coast. Either way, you'll find some of the lushest, most gracious islands on the Atlantic coast.

First you come to **Jekyll Island,** the smallest but also the most chic of the Golden Isles, originally named Île de la Somme by the French Huguenots who landed here in 1562; the last shipload of African slaves to enter the U.S. was unloaded here in 1858. Jekyll became an exclusive winter resort for titans in American industry and finance from 1885 to the end of World War II: Rockefeller, Gould, J. P. Morgan, Vanderbilt, Joseph Pulitzer, and Goodyear were among those who built sumptuous villas here, which are now open to visitors.

On **St. Simons Island,** where until the Civil War there were rich plantations, the English General Oglethorpe, the founder of Savannah, built Fort Frederica, now **Fort Frederica National Monument** (638-3639), in 1736. Burned down in 1758, the fort and the little town it protected were abandoned. Open daily. Wonderful beaches lined with forests of oak, pine, and palm trees.

Sea Island boasts many beautiful seaside homes as well as **The Cloister** (638-3611), one of the grandest grand hotels on the Georgia coast. Luxurious accommodations (764 rms or cottages. Rates: **VE**).

As well as their dozens of oceanfront hotels and motels, the Golden Isles offer a whole gamut of vacation activities: fishing, golf, sailing, horseback riding, etc. Don't miss them.

CHAPTER 12

ATLANTA

□ □ □

Atlanta, known and loved by generations of movie-goers through *Gone With the Wind,* was the paragon of southern cities at the time of the Civil War: brilliant, lavish, and cultured. After one of the most ferocious battles of that war—117 days of siege by General Sherman (1864)—90% of the city lay in ruins. The only traces that remain from this tragic period are the partly restored **Underground Atlanta** and its famous **Zero Mile Post** marking the terminus of the first Western & Atlantic Railroad line (1837). Not far from here is **Peachtree Street,** dear to the heart of Scarlett O'Hara and today Atlanta's most elegant and lively downtown thoroughfare. Founded as Terminus in 1837 and incorporated as Marthasville in 1843, the city received its present name in 1845, perhaps reflecting a feminine form of Atlantic in the railroad's name.

Like a phoenix, Atlanta rose from the ashes of the Civil War to become the economic and cultural capital of the Deep South. Today it is a modern, ever-expanding metropolis, and ranks ninth among the American cities in terms of economic growth rate. Testifying to Atlanta's extraordinary financial and industrial vitality are more than 1,800 factories (automobile, aviation, chemical, paper, steel, food); the CNN television empire; 130 banks; and dozens of multinational corporations (including Georgia Pacific, Nabisco, and especially, Coca-Cola, maker of the universally famous beverage, which Doc Pemberton invented here in 1886).

A veritable turntable for road, rail, and air transportation, Atlanta possesses the busiest airport in the world, Hartsfield International Airport. Georgia's capital also boasts some of the most spectacular modern structures in the U.S., including the country's tallest hotel (the **Westin Peachtree Plaza,** an immense glass-and-steel, 73-story tower) and the brand-new **Carter Presidential Center,** both library and international conference center.

In 1973 Atlanta became the third major American city to elect a black mayor (after Cleveland and Los Angeles). Atlanta was the birthplace of Nobel Peace Prize winner Martin Luther King, Jr.—don't miss the **Martin Luther King, Jr., Historic District** in the heart of downtown; her children also include historian Daniel Boorstin and the architect who revolutionized contemporary hotel construction, John Portman.

BASIC FACTS: Capital of the state of Georgia. Area Code: 404. Time Zone: Eastern Time. ZIP Code (of central post office): 30301. Founded: 1837. Approximate population: city, 430,000; metropolitan area, 2,400,000. 13th-largest metropolitan area in the country.

CLIMATE: Spring is rather brief but pleasant, especially May. Summer is hot and sticky (mean July temperature, 80°F, 27°C, but with 70% humidity). Winter is relatively mild but rainy (mean Jan. temperature, 45°F, 5°C). The best season to visit Atlanta is autumn; Sept., Oct., and Nov. are the sunniest months.

DISTANCES: Miami, 659 mi. (1,055 km); Nashville, 242 mi. (387 km); New

Orleans, 481 mi. (770 km); Savannah, 251 mi. (401 km); Washington, 608 mi. (975 km).

ARRIVAL & TRANSIT INFORMATION

AIRPORT: Hartsfield Atlanta International Airport (ATL): 9 mi. (14 km) SW. Its new terminal is the largest in the world. It is, with 43 million passengers each year, the world's busiest airport. Information: 530-6000.

DOMESTIC AIRLINES: American (521-2655), Continental (436-3300), Delta (765-5000), Eastern (435-1111), Northwest (577-3271), TWA (522-5738), United (394-2234), USAir (toll free 800/428-4322).

FOREIGN CARRIERS: British Airways (toll free 800/247-9297); Lufthansa (toll free 800/645-3880); Sabena (toll free 800/645-3790).

CITY LINK: Cab fare to city center, about $18; time, 30 min. Bus: Atlanta Airport Shuttle (766-5312); leaves every 20 min.; serves major dwntwn hotels; fare, $9; time, 40 min. Direct subway (MARTA) connection to dwntwn; leaves every 20 min.; fare, 75¢. The proximity of the airport and the compactness of dwntwn Atlanta may mean that you don't need to rent a car. Atlanta also has an efficient public transportation system (bus, subway), currently being expanded (MARTA) (848-4711).

CAR RENTAL (all at the airport): Avis (530-2700), Budget (530-3000), Dollar (530-3120), Hertz (530-2900), National (530-2800). For dwntwn locations, consult the phone directory.

LIMOUSINE SERVICES: Carey Limousine (681-3366), Dav El Limousine (toll free 800/922-0343).

TAXIS: Expensive and undependable, taxis may not be hailed on the street but must be summoned by phone. The best are Checker Cab (525-5466) and Yellow Cab (521-0200).

TRAIN: AMTRAK, Peachtree Station, 1688 Peachtree St. NW (688-4417).

BUS: Greyhound, 81 International Blvd. (584-1729).

INFORMATION & TOURS

TOURIST INFORMATION: Convention & Visitors Bureau, 233 Peachtree St. NE, Suite 200, GA 30342 (404/521-6600).
   Visitor Information Center, Peachtree Center Mall (404/521-6633).

GUIDED TOURS: American Sightseeing (bus) (768-7676). Guided tour of the city and environs, serving principal downtown hotels.
   Gray Line Tours (bus) (767-0594). Same as above.
   Wheels Across Atlanta (horse-drawn carriage), 1385 Niskey Lake Rd. (768-0414). Carriage rides in good weather.

SIGHTS, ATTRACTIONS, & ACTIVITIES

ARCHITECTURAL HIGHLIGHTS: ※ ⚜ **Federal Reserve Bank,** 104 Marietta St. NW (521-8747): Imposing Greek Revival building on the site of the

Jacobs Pharmacy where, in May 1886, John Pemberton created the famous Coca-Cola formula. Today it houses immense, rigorously guarded workshops where many millions of banknotes are printed each day. Interesting currency museum. Open Mon.-Fri. by appointment only.

IBM Building, 1207 W. Peachtree St. NW (877-6800): Atlanta's most dramatic building (1987). Beautiful post modern skyscraper, crowned by a 100-ft- (30-m-) high copper pyramid topped by a lantern. Philip Johnson/ John Burgee designed, 50 story and 825-ft-, (251-m-) high, the building detailing is "American Gothic" and inspired by the famous Tribune Tower in Chicago. Worth a look.

Peachtree Center, 230 Peachtree St. NE: Futurist complex of office skyscrapers, an ultramodern 73-story hotel, and a giant shopping mall with luxury boutiques, restaurants, bars, and interior gardens. One of the country's most spectacular architectural assemblies. An absolute must-see.

BROADCASTING & MOVIE STUDIOS: CNN (formerly Omni) **Center,**
Marietta St. and Techwood Dr. NW: One of dwntwn Atlanta's most recent additions. Its ultramodern, sometimes assertive buildings include the **Cable News Network** studios, office buildings, restaurants, movie theaters, hotels, and sports and convention centers. Worth a look.

HISTORIC BUILDINGS: Fox Theatre, 660 Peachtree St. NE (892-5685):
Once a Masonic temple dating from 1929 with an onion dome and minarets, and then a movie theater with rather dizzying Hollywood-Moorish architecture, the Fox, a historical landmark, is now a 4,500-seat concert hall. An absolute must-see. Guided tours by appointment.

Georgia State Capitol, Capitol Square: Georgia's legislative building, dating from 1889, is a replica of the Washington Capitol. The 237-ft- (72-m-) high dome is covered with gold leaf from the Dahlonega mines north of Atlanta. The complex includes a very lovely Hall of Flags and an interesting museum of science and industry. Open Mon.-Fri.

Oakland Cemetery, 248 Oakland Ave. SE: Landscaped, 84-acre cemetery with tens of thousands of graves, the oldest dating back to the Civil War. The site also has many grand mausoleums in the Victorian style, including that of Margaret Mitchell Marsh, author of *Gone With the Wind.* Visitor Center open daily.

Underground Atlanta, Pryor and Alabama Sts.: Beneath the modern city, a labyrinth of cobblestoned streets and houses spared by the fire of 1864. This area was used as a hospital during the battle of Atlanta. Under the Central Ave. bridge stands the **Zero Mile Post,** marking the point where the Western & Atlantic Railroad line, and the city, began.

MARKETS: Atlanta State Farmers' Market, in Forest Park, 10 mi. (16
km) south on I-75 (366-6910): The largest open-air market in the Southeast (144 acres, 60 ha.). Hundreds of farmers display their produce every day, 24 hours a day. Worth a look.

MUSEUMS OF ART: High Museum of Art, 1280 Peachtree St. NE
(892-4444): Rich collection of European paintings and sculptures, especially from the Renaissance. Richard Meier designed the ultramodern setting of pure geometric forms, and won the Pritzker Prize (in comparable terms, the Nobel Prize of architecture) for the beauty and originality of his work. The museum is part of the vast **Robert W. Woodruff Arts Center,** built in 1968 in memory of the 122 members of the Atlanta Arts Association who died in an air disaster in

Paris (1962). (The French government gave Rodin's *L'Ombre* to the association.) Among the museum's most famous works: Bellini's *Virgin and Child,* Veronese's *Rest on the Flight from Egypt,* Annibale Carracci's *Crucifixion,* and many Picasso etchings. The Robert Woodruff Arts Center also includes a concert hall **(Symphony Hall),** home of the Atlanta Symphony Orchestra; two theaters (including the **Alliance Theater**); and the **Atlanta College of Art.** A visit not to be missed. Open Tue.-Sun.

MUSEUMS OF SCIENCE & HISTORY: 🔔 Atlanta Historical Society,

3101 Andrews Dr. NW (261-1837): Interesting architectural models of Georgian houses, à la *Gone With the Wind.* You can see everything from an 1840s plantation farm **(Tullie Smith House)** to aristocratic Palladian homes **(Swan House)** and slave quarters **(Coach House).** Very lovely old furniture. Not to be missed. Open daily.

🔔 **Carter Presidential Center,** 1 Copenhill Ave. NE (331-3942): Built on the wooded hill from where, according to legend, General Sherman watched Atlanta burn, this group of ultramodern circular buildings includes an international conference center, a museum, and a library with 27 million written and on-film documents concerning the 39th president of the United States. It contains, notably, a faithful replica of the White House's Oval Office. More than 600,000 visitors each year. The complex includes a very beautiful Japanese garden and a lovely view of the Atlanta skyline. Worth the trip. Open daily.

🔔 **Cyclorama,** in Grant Park, Cherokee and Georgia Aves. SE (624-1071): This huge fresco of the Battle of Atlanta is the largest circular wall mural in the world (390 by 48 ft, 22 by 15 m). Painted in 1885–1886 by a group of 12 Polish and German artists, it has recently been restored. Sound-and-light show. An absolute must-see. Open daily.

🔔 **Fernbank Science Center,** 156 Heaton Park Dr. NE, in Decatur (378-4311): In the middle of a 62-acre (26-ha.) park, the center includes an observatory and one of the country's largest planetariums. For astronomy buffs. Open daily.

🔔🔔 **Martin Luther King, Jr., Historic District,** 407 Auburn Ave. NE (331-3919): The life of the Nobel Peace Prize winner, assassinated in a Memphis hotel in 1968, is retraced in the **King Library and Archives.** His grave is in the middle of an ornamental lake behind the **Ebenezer Baptist Church,** where Martin Luther King, Jr., pursued his pastoral mission from 1960 until his death. In front of the grave burns an eternal flame illuminating the simple words "Free at last." The **King Birthplace** is close by at 501 Auburn Ave. There's an **Information Center** at 413 Auburn Ave. A moving visit. Open daily.

🔔 **Toy Museum of Atlanta,** 2800 Peachtree Rd. NE (266-8697): Very handsome toy museum displaying priceless 19th-century specimens. More than 100,000 items, some of which are incredibly rare. An absolute must-see. Open daily.

PANORAMAS: The ☀ 🔔🔔 Sun Dial bar and revolving restaurant on the 73rd

floor of the Westin Peachtree Hotel offers the most spectacular view of Atlanta (admission fee).

PARKS & GARDENS: 🔔 Central City Park, Peachtree and Auburn Sts.: Gift

of the Coca-Cola magnate Robert W. Woodruff, this spot in the heart of Atlanta is very popular with lunch-hour picnickers.

🔔 **Grant Park,** Cherokee Ave. SE: Vast landscaped park housing a very modern zoo and Civil War fortifications **(Fort Walker),**

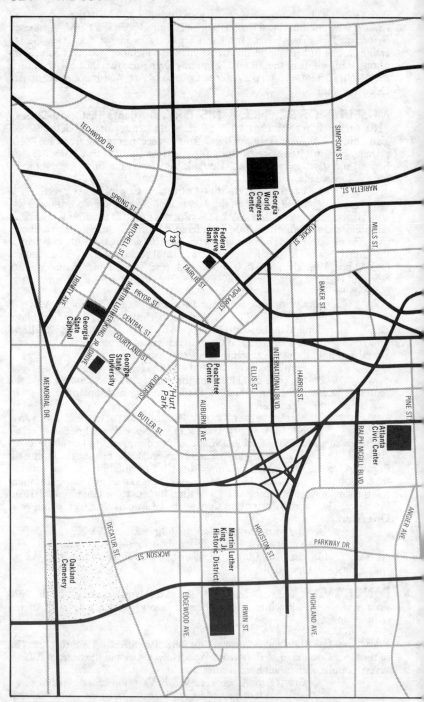

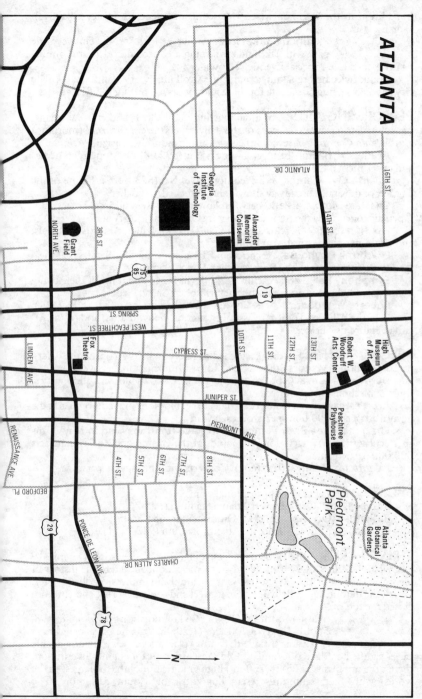

in addition to the Cyclorama (see "Museums of Science & History," above). Worth a visit.

Piedmont Park, Piedmont Ave. at 14th St. NE: This very fine park with lake and swimming area accommodates the annual **Arts Festival** (see "Special Events," below).

Think twice before taking a nighttime stroll in any of Atlanta's parks. The city has seen a rising crime rate for the last few years, according to FBI statistics.

PERFORMING ARTS: For a daily listing of all shows and cultural events, consult the entertainment pages of the daily papers *Atlanta Journal* (morning) and *Atlanta Constitution* (evening), as well as the monthly magazine *Atlanta*.

Academy Theater, 581 Peachtree St. NE (892-0880): Modern comedies and experimental theater.

Atlanta Civic Center, 395 Piedmont Ave. NE (523-6275): Home of the Theater of the Stars (Broadway shows) and of the Atlanta Ballet.

Chastain Memorial Park, between Powers Ferry Rd. and Lake Forrest Dr.: Open-air concerts by the Atlanta Symphony Orchestra, June-Aug.

Fox Theatre, 660 Peachtree St. NE (881-1977): Ballet, concerts, musicals, and a summer film festival. Year round.

Peachtree Playhouse, Peachtree and 13th Sts. (237-8829): Classical theater and performances by the Ruth Mitchell Dance Company.

Symphony Hall, 1280 Peachtree St. NE (892-2414): Home of the Atlanta Symphony Orchestra (principal conductor: Robert Shaw). Sept.-May.

Robert W. Woodruff Arts Center, 1280 Peachtree St. NE (892-2414): Home of the Alliance Theater (classical theater, comedy, drama) and of the Atlanta Children's Theater.

SPECIAL EVENTS: For the exact schedule of events below, consult the **Atlanta Convention & Visitors Bureau** (see "Tourist Information," above).

Dogwood Festival (Apr.): Concerts, parades, shows, hot-air balloon rides, tours of old houses.

Arts Festival (May): Concerts, ballets, art exhibitions in Piedmont Park; the festival attracts 2,000,000 spectators each year.

Chattahoochee River Ramblin' Raft Race (third weekend in May): This spectacular, crazy raft race along the rapids of the Chattahoochee River attracts 300,000 participants.

Atlanta Jazz Festival (late June): Concerts with the biggest stars.

SPORTS: Atlanta has three professional teams:

Baseball (Apr.-Oct.): Braves, Atlanta Stadium (522-763).
Basketball (Oct.-Apr.): Hawks, Omni Center (681-3605).
Football (Sept.-Dec.): Falcons, Atlanta Stadium (945-1111).

THEME PARKS: **Six Flags over Georgia,** 7561 Six Flags Rd. (12 mi., 19 km, west on I-20; 948-9290): This giant theme park dedicated to the history of Georgia boasts more than 100 attractions, including an impressive roller coaster. Worth the detour. Open daily June-Sept.; weekends only in spring and autumn; closed the rest of the year.

Stone Mountain (16 mi., 26 km, northeast on U.S. 78; 498-5600): Large, 3,200-acre (1,295-ha) theme park including a Civil War memorial, an authentic 19th-century plantation, a car museum, a cable car, a paddle-boat lake ride, and an Old West–style steam engine. In addition, there's the impressive, 825-ft- (250-m-) high granite monolith (the largest in the world) with giant sculptures resembling those of Mount Rushmore. The

165- by 72-ft- (55- by 24-m) bas-relief represents three southern heroes: Confederate Pres. Jefferson Davis, Gen. Robert E. Lee, and Gen. "Stonewall" Jackson. Not to be missed. Open daily year round.

ACCOMMODATIONS

See the listing of toll-free numbers in the Appendix.

Room Rates in Atlanta	
B (Budget)	up to $30
I (Inexpensive)	$30–$60
M (Moderate)	$60–$90
E (Expensive)	$90–$140
VE (Very Expensive)	$140 and up

Personal Favorites (in order of preference)

Ritz-Carlton Buckhead (nr. dwntwn), 3434 Peachtree Rd. NE, GA 30326 (404/237-2700; toll free 800/241-3333). 550 rms, A/C, color TV, in-rm movies. AE, CB, DC, MC, V. Valet parking $8, pool, health club, tennis, two rests. (including The Dining Room), coffeeshop, two bars, 24-hr rm svce, disco, boutiques, concierge, free crib. *Note:* In the heart of the new business and entertainment district of Buckhead, this modern, 22-story structure is one of the most recent additions to the local luxury-hotel scene. Its décor and amenities are in the grand tradition, and its svce impeccable. The period-furnished rooms are spacious and elegant, and colored in pastel tones. The hotel also boasts an excellent rest. (Atlanta's best), and adjacent luxury shopping areas. Two VIP floors. Big-business clientele. Interesting wknd packages. Highly recommended. **E–VE**

Westin Peachtree Plaza (dwntwn), 210 Peachtree St. at International Blvd., GA 30343 (404/659-1400; toll free, see Westin). 1,080 rms, A/C, color TV, in-rm movies. AE, CB, DC, MC. Valet gar. $9, pool, health club, four rests. (including the Sun Dial), five bars, 24-hr rm svce, disco, boutiques, hrdrsr, free crib. *Note:* This futurist, glass-and-steel tower by John Portman is the world's tallest hotel—73 stories high—with waterfalls and interior gardens on eight floors. It offers total comfort, despite rather cramped rms, and efficient svce, despite the hotel's immense size. One of the country's most spectacular buildings, and the most eye-catching spot in Atlanta. Good rest. (the Southern Café). Business and group clientele. No-smoking floors. Recently underwent a $30-million renovation. **E–VE**

Omni Hotel at CNN Center (formerly Omni International) (dwntwn), 100 CNN Center, GA 30335 (404/659-0000; toll free, see Omni). 471 rms, A/C, color TV, in-rm movies. AE, CB, DC, MC, V. Valet gar. $8, pool, health club, skating rink, two rests. (including Bugatti's), coffeeshop, three bars, 24-hr rm svce, disco, hrdrsr, drugstore, free crib. *Note:* Rather chilling sci-fi décor w. 15-story lobby and glass elevators. Rooms are comfortable, w. balconies and mini-bars, and the svce is efficient. In the heart of the business district, the hotel is directly connected to the Georgia World Congress Center. Fairly obtrusive group and business clientele. VIP floor. **E–VE**

American (dwntwn), 160 Spring St., GA 30303 (404/688-8600; toll free 800/621-7885). 325 rms, A/C, cable color TV. AE, CB, DC, MC, V. Gar. $4, pool, rest. (Gatsby's), bar, rm svce, disco, hrdrsr, free crib. *Note:* Modern, comfortable, eight-story motel. Rms have patios or balconies. The svce is good, as is the value. Business clientele. Next to the Georgia World Congress Center. VIP floor. **M–E**

      Ibis Hotel (nr. dwntwn), 101 International Blvd., GA 30303 (404/524-5555; toll free 800/535-0707). 260 rms, A/C, cable color TV. AE, CB, DC, MC, V. Gar. $3, pool, rest., bar, free crib. *Note:* Ultramodern motel next to the Georgia World Congress Center. Inviting interior décor and comfortable, well-conceived rms. Cheerful reception with a European flavor, and a very adequate rest. with buffet. Excellent value. A favorite among business people. **M**

      Quality Inn Habersham (dwntwn), 330 Peachtree St. NE, GA 30308 (404/577-1980; toll free, see Quality Inns). 92 rms, A/C, cable color TV. AE, CB, DC, MC, V. Free parking, sauna, coffeeshop, bar, rm svce, free crib. *Note:* Aging but well-maintained hotel in the heart of dwntwn. Comfortable rms with kitchenettes. Good svce and value. Excellent location. **M**

      Days Inn Downtown (dwntwn), 300 Spring St. NE, GA 30303 (404/523-1144; toll free, see Days Inns). 260 rms, A/C, color TV, in-rm movies. AE, CB, DC, MC, V. Free parking, pool, coffeeshop, rm svce, free crib. *Note:* Modern, comfortable motel, quite centrally located. Very agreeable rms plus efficient reception and svce. Convention and group clientele. Good value. **M**

      Holiday Inn I-85 (nr. dwntwn), 1944 Piedmont Circle, GA 30324 (404/875-3571; toll free, see Holiday Inns). 251 rms, A/C, color TV, in-rm movies. AE, CB, DC, MC, V. Free parking, pool, rest., bar, rm svce, free crib. *Note:* Functional Holiday Inn–style comfort 20 min. from dwntwn on I-85. Spacious rms, some with balconies. Fair svce and reception. Ideal if you're driving. **M**

Other Accommodations (from top bracket to budget)

      Marriott Marquis (dwntwn), 265 Peachtree Center Ave., GA 30303 (404/521-0000; toll free, see Marriott). 1,675 rms, A/C, color TV, in-rm movies. AE, CB, DC, MC, V. Gar. $8, pool, tennis, health club, sauna, five rests. (including J.W.'s), four bars, rm svce, disco, boutiques, hrdrsr, crib $5. *Note:* This brand-new hotel is one of the most spectacular and tallest in the South—50 stories of glass and concrete in the heart of Atlanta, designed by John Portman. The 520-ft- (160-m-) high atrium houses interior gardens and glass elevators. Spacious, ultracomfortable rms and very complete amenities. Six VIP floors. Efficient svce, but a very average rest. (like all Marriotts). Interesting wknd packages. **E–VE**

      Colony Square Hotel (nr. dwntwn), Peachtree & 14th Sts., GA 30361 (404/892-6000; toll free, see Preferred). 502 rms, A/C, color TV, in-rm movies. AE, CB, DC, MC, V. Valet gar. $7, pool, health club, three rests., coffeeshop, bars, 24-hr rm svce, disco, boutiques, concierge, free crib. *Note:* Quiet, luxurious, 27-story hotel close to dwntwn. The rms are very comfortable and the interior decoration elegant and urbane. Excellent svce. Business clientele. A favorite among connoisseurs despite its rather mediocre rests. VIP floor. **E–VE**

      Hilton & Towers (dwntwn), 255 Courtland St. NE at Harris St., GA 30084 (404/659-2000; toll free, see Hilton). 1,220 rms, A/C, color TV, in-rm movies. AE, CB, DC, MC, V. Valet parking $8, pool, health club, tennis, sauna, four rests. (including Nikolai's Roof), 24-hr coffeeshop, three bars, rm svce, disco, boutiques, hrdrsr, free crib. *Note:* Immense, 30-story tourist barracks completely taken over by group and convention clientele. All the usual Hilton comfort, but the svce is a little overburdened. Spacious, well-furnished rms. Five-story atrium with glass elevators. Very good luxury rest. (Nikolai's Roof) and good recreational facilities. Three VIP floors. In the heart of dwntwn Atlanta. Interesting wknd packages. **E–VE**

☀ 🛏🛏🛏 **Hyatt Regency** (dwntwn), 265 Peachtree St. NE, GA 30303 (404/577-1234; toll free, see Hyatt). 1,285 rms, A/C, color TV, in-rm movies. AE, CB, DC, MC, V. Valet gar. $7, pool, health club, three rests., bars, rm svce, disco, boutiques, hrdrsr, free crib. *Note:* A hotel classic dating from 1967, with a 23-story atrium, interior gardens, and glass elevators. Vast rms with balconies offer lavish comfort. The svce is rather uncertain but the panoramic view of Atlanta from the revolving restaurant at the top, Polaris, is spectacular. No-smoking rms. The first of the grand hotels designed by John Portman. Two VIP floors. Group clientele. Recently renovated. **E–VE**

🛏🛏 **Pierremont Plaza** (dwntwn), 590 W. Peachtree St. NW, GA 30308 (404/881-6000; toll free 800/531-6660). 505 rms, A/C, color TV, in-rm movies. AE, CB, DC, MC, V. Gar. $6, pool, rest., bar, rm svce, disco, hrdrsr, free crib. *Note:* Modern, serviceable hotel close to the business district. The rms are spacious and comfortable; the svce leaves a bit to be desired. Business clientele. A good value overall. **M–E**

🛏🛏 **Terrace Garden Inn** (vic.), 3405 Lenox Rd., GA 30326 (404/261-9250; toll free 800/241-8260). 372 rms, A/C, cable color TV. AE, CB, DC, MC, V. Free indoor parking, two pools, four tennis courts, health club, sauna, two rests. (including the Garden Tree), bar, rm svce, disco, hrdrsr, free crib. *Note:* Very comfortable luxury motel with lovely gardens and spacious, balconied rms. Good svce. An excellent location, 20 min. from dwntwn on I-85. Ideal for the car traveler. Good recreational facilities. Business clientele. **M–E**

🛏🛏 **Ramada Capitol Plaza** (dwntwn), 450 Capitol Ave. SE, GA 30312 (404/688-1900; toll free, see Ramada Inns). 390 rms, A/C, cable color TV. AE, CB, DC, MC, V. Free parking, pool, rest., bar, rm svce, disco, free crib. *Note:* This typical, 15-story motel across from Atlanta Stadium offers spacious rms with mini-bars and utilitarian comfort. The reception and svce could use some work. Business clientele. A 2-min. walk to the State Capitol. **M**

🛏🛏 **Lenox Inn** (nr. dwntwn), 3387 Lenox Rd. NE, GA 30326 (404/261-5500; toll free 800/241-0200). 180 rms, A/C, cable color TV. AE, CB, DC, MC, V. Free parking, two pools, tennis, health club, rest. (open Mon.-Sat.), bar, rm svce, disco, free crib. *Note:* Comfortable, pleasant hotel away from the hustle and bustle of dwntwn. Spacious, inviting rms and ultraprofessional service in a tranquil, relaxing atmosphere. A very good value. Ideal if you're driving (10 min. from dwntwn on I-85N). **I–M**

🛏 **Days Inn Peachtree** (formerly the York Hotel; dwntwn), 683 Peachtree St. NE, GA 30308 (404/874-9200; toll free, see Days Inns). 138 rms, A/C, cable color TV. AE, CB, DC, MC, V. Free parking, adjacent coffeeshop, free crib. *Note:* Oldish, recently renovated hotel. Inviting rms and agreeable svce. Excellent location across from the Fox Theatre. Overall good value. Tourist and group clientele. **I–M**

🛏 **Travelodge Central** (dwntwn), 311 Courtland St. NE, GA 30303 (404/659-4545; toll free, see Travelodge). 70 rms, A/C, cable color TV. AE, CB, DC, MC, V. Free parking, pool, adjacent 24-hr coffeeshop, rm svce, free crib. *Note:* Small, three-story motel in the heart of dwntwn. Slightly threadbare décor and comfort, but very adequate rms (some with balconies). Overall good value. **I–M**

🛏 **Motel 6 West** (vic.), 4100 Wendell Dr. SW, GA 30336 (404/696-0757). 175 rms, A/C, color TV, free in-rm movies.

DC, MC, V. Free parking, pool, free crib. *Note:* Modern comfort at ultra-economical prices. Located 25 min. from dwntwn and 20 min. from Stone Mountain Park. One of the best values in the area. Ideal for the motorist. **B**

Airport Accommodations

㋡㋡㋡ **Holiday Inn Crowne Plaza** (vic.), 1900 Sullivan Rd., in College Park, GA 30337 (404/997-2770; toll free, see Holiday Inns). 399 rms, A/C, color TV, in-rm movies. AE, CB, DC, MC, V. Free parking, two pools, tennis, health club, rest. (Canard's), bar, rm svce, crib $10. *Note:* Modern, comfortable, 12-story hotel affording direct access to the Convention Center (near the airport). Spacious, well-soundproofed rms and efficient svce. VIP floor. Group and business clientele. Free airport shuttle. **M–E**

RESTAURANTS

Atlanta Restaurant Prices	
(per person, excluding drinks and service charges)	
B (Budget)	up to $15
I (Inexpensive)	$15–$25
M (Moderate)	$25–$40
E (Expensive)	$40–$60
VE (Very Expensive)	$60 and up

Personal Favorites (in order of preference)

㋡㋡㋡㋡ **The Dining Room** (nr. dwntwn), in the Ritz-Carlton Buckhead (see "Accommodations," above) (237-2700). A/C. Lunch/dinner Mon.-Sat.; closed Sun., holidays. AE, CB, DC, MC, V. J&T. Specialties: cream of coriander with lobster, beet ravioli with caviar, salmon with asparagus and truffles, rack of lamb with sweet-pepper sauce, strudel of crayfish, poppyseed-and-raspberry parfait. The menu changes daily. Splendid wine list with great vintages sold by the glass (cruvinet). *Note:* Once the owner of the renowned Boheneck restaurant in the Black Forest of Germany (two stars in Michelin), the very talented chef Guenter Seeger has made this classic, elegant palace restaurant into one of the finest in the South. Inspired nouvelle cuisine happily unites innovation with a meticulous attention to detail. Vast marble-and-mahogany dining room with stylish furniture and hunting pictures. Exemplary white-gloved svce. Wealthy clientele. By far the best rest. in Atlanta. Resv. a must. Valet parking. 15 min. from dwntwn. *French-Continental.* **E–VE**

㋡㋡㋡ **Pano's & Paul's** (nr. dwntwn), 1232 W. Paces Ferry Rd. (261-3662). A/C. Dinner only, Mon.-Sat.; closed Sun., holidays. AE, CB, DC, MC, V. J&T. Specialties: lobster tails with mustard sauce, red snapper with hazelnut butter, quail with wild mushrooms, coquilles St-Jacques in champagne, chocolate crêpes, Mississippi mud pie. Very fine wine list. *Note:* One of the best rests. in Atlanta. Classic, French-inspired cuisine impeccably presented. Ideally romantic Victorian décor. Distinguished music in the background. Discreet but ultraprofessional svce. Trendy clientele. Resv. recommended. 25 min. from dwntwn on I-75 and Northside Pkwy. *Continental.* **M–E**

☼ ♈♈ **Coach and Six** (nr. dwntwn), 1776 Peachtree Rd. NW (872-6666). A/C. Lunch Mon.-Sat.; dinner daily; closed holidays. AE, CB, DC, MC, V. Jkt. Specialties: black-bean soup, Florida stone crabs, lobster, fish of the day. Meat in all forms—steak, roast beef, lamb chops—has brought fame to this restaurant. Excellent desserts. *Note:* A veritable local institution with opulent, elegant old English club décor. The ambience is pleasant, if often overcrowded and noisy. Resv. advisable (but rarely honored, unfortunately). Diligent svce. A favorite spot among Atlanta carnivores for more than 20 years. Valet parking. *American.* **I–M**

♈♈ **Bone's** (nr. dwntwn), 3130 Piedmont Rd. NE (237-2663). A/C. Lunch Mon.-Sat.; dinner daily; closed holidays. AE, CB, DC, MC, V. Jkt. Specialties: excellent meats, Maine lobster, fish of the day. Average desserts and wine list. *Note:* A local red-meat shrine, this New York–style steakhouse is famous for the high quality of its meat (corn-fed Iowa cattle) and for its generous servings. Rather brusque but efficient svce. Amusing caricatures on the walls as well as old photographs of Atlanta. Business clientele. The tab can climb quickly if you choose lobster over T-bone steak. Resv. advised. Valet parking. *Steakhouse.* **I–M**

♈♈ **La Grotta** (nr. dwntwn), 2637 Peachtree Rd. NE (231-1368). AE, CB, DC, MC, V. J&T. A/C. Dinner only, Tues.-Sat.; closed Sun., Mon., holidays. Specialties: tortellini verdi, carpaccio, scaloppine al pesto, vitello tonnato. Very good list of Italian wines at reasonable prices. *Note:* Authentic Italian cuisine—especially the remarkable fresh pasta—in a pretty, rustic setting with terraced garden offering open-air dining in nice weather. Very good svce. Resv. advised. Valet parking. 20 min. from dwntwn. *Italian.* **I–M**

♈♈ **Lennox's** (nr. dwntwn), 2225 Peachtree Rd. NE (351-0921). A/C. Lunch Mon.-Fri.; dinner daily. AE, DC, MC, V. Specialties: redfish Créole, Bayou Teche eggplant, steamed crayfish jambalaya, gumbo. *Note:* Authentic Cajun cuisine in an agreeable New Orleans–style setting. Friendly, diligent svce. Requisite Dixieland music and a very lively ambience. Locally popular. No resv. A very commendable spot. *American.* **I**

☼ ♈ **Aunt Fanny's Cabin** (vic.), 2155 Campbell Rd., in Smyrna (404/436-5218). A/C. Lunch Mon.-Fri.; dinner daily; brunch Sun.; closed five days at Christmas. AE, CB, DC, MC, V. Specialties: Virginia ham, rainbow trout, fried chicken, steak, traditional southern dishes. *Note:* Occupies former slave quarters more than a century old. Picturesque décor, friendly reception, and pleasant music. No resv. Valet parking. 30 min. from dwntwn on I-75N. A "must" for all Atlanta visitors. *American.* **B–I**

☼ ♈ **Mary Mac's Tea Room** (nr. dwntwn), 224 Ponce de Leon Ave. NE (876-6604). A/C. Lunch/dinner Mon.-Sat. (until 8 p.m.); brunch Sun.; closed holidays. No credit cards. Specialties: fried chicken, southern-style shrimp, peanut-butter pie. *Note:* Only the name suggests a tea room. Rustic, flavorful southern cooking in a relaxed, if generally noisy and overcrowded, atmosphere. An excellent spot with unbeatable prices. Near Georgia Tech. Inevitable waits (sometimes fairly long). *American* **B**

Other Restaurants (from top bracket to budget)

♈♈ **Nikolai's Roof** (dwntwn), in the Hilton & Towers (see "Accommodations," above) (659-3282). A/C. Dinner only, daily; closed Jan. 1, Dec. 25. AE, CB, DC, MC, V. J&T. Specialties: borscht, coulibiac of salmon, pheasant à la normande, duck in muscadet, tournedos

Esterhazy, soufflés. The menu changes every 15 days. *Note:* Intimate, luxurious décor with an unimpeded view of downtown Atlanta from the 30th floor of the Hilton. "Tasting" prix-fixe menu with five dishes and desserts; Franco-Russian nouvelle cuisine. Impeccable svce despite the Cossack apparel of the servers. Resv. a must, several days in advance. Two sittings nightly, at 6:30 and 9:30 p.m. One of Atlanta's smartest rests. *Continental-East European.* **M (prix fixe)**

The Abbey (nr. dwntwn), 163 Ponce de Leon Ave. NE (876-8831). A/C. Dinner only, daily; closed holidays. AE, CB, DC, MC, V. Jkt. Specialties: escargots de Bourgogne, salmon and truffles, lamb in pastry shell, sole "Abbaye," filet mignon Aïda, chicken suprême with shrimp. Fine wine list. *Note:* Predominantly European cuisine, elegantly prepared and served. The unique décor—a turn-of-the-century church with stained glass and a 50-ft- (15-m-) high vaulted ceiling—produces a very medieval ambience. Servers are appropriately attired in monk's habits. Resv. advised. *Continental.* **I–M**

Bugatti's (dwntwn), in the Omni Hotel (see "Accommodations," above) (659-0000). A/C. Lunch Mon.-Fri.; dinner daily; brunch Sun. AE, CB, DC, MC, V. J&T. Specialties: fresh homemade pasta, osso buco milanese, shrimps in bagna cauda, veal Florentine. *Note:* This excellent hotel rest. is one of the best Italian rests. in Atlanta. Elegantly urbane modern décor and savory, appetizing cuisine. Impeccable svce. *Italian.* **I**

Fish Market (nr. dwntwn), 3393 Peachtree Rd. NE (262-3165). A/C. Lunch/dinner Mon.-Sat.; closed Sun., holidays. AE, CB, DC, MC, V. Jkt. Specialties: lobster tails in mustard sauce, seafood pastas, sautéed Dover sole, Florida stone crabs, fish of the day, chocolate pecan cake. Fine wine list. *Note:* Elegant rest. with Mediterranean décor offering Atlanta's largest choice of seafood. Everything is truly fresh, and grilled, fried, or poached to perfection. Excellent svce. Dinner resv. necessary. Locally very popular. Valet parking. *Seafood.* **I–M**

Midnight Sun (dwntwn), 225 Peachtree St. NE (Peachtree Center) (577-5050). A/C. Lunch Mon.-Fri.; dinner daily; closed holidays. AE, CB, DC, MC, V. Jkt. Specialties: very elaborate, French-inspired cuisine. The menu changes regularly. *Note:* Elegant Scandinavian décor embellished with statues and a huge marble fountain. Distinguished atmosphere and efficient svce. Locally very popular. Resv. advised. **I–M**

Trotter's (nr. dwntwn), 3215 Peachtree Rd. NE (237-5988). A/C. Lunch Mon.-Fri.; dinner daily; brunch Sun.; closed holidays. AE, CB, DC, MC, V. Specialties: fish broiled over a wood fire, fresh homemade pasta. The menu changes regularly. *Note:* Susan De Rose and Richard Lewis are masters of modern American cuisine and of natural foods (they grow their own herbs). The result is always original and innovative. Pure art deco, 1920s ambience, with equestrian motifs on the wall. Rather uncertain svce. A fashionable place. Valet parking. *American.* **I–M**

Nakato (nr. dwntwn), 1893 Piedmont Rd. NE (873-6582). A/C. Dinner only, daily; closed Dec. 25, Jan. 1. AE, CB, DC, MC, V. Specialties: sushi, sukiyaki, sashimi, teppanyaki, tempura. *Note:* Truly authentic Japanese cuisine. Very handsome Oriental décor with separate dining rms. Efficient, if slightly abrupt, svce. Locally popular. Resv. advised on wknds. *Japanese.* **I**

Pittypat's Porch (dwntwn), 25 International Blvd. (Peachtree Center) (525-8228). A/C. Dinner only, daily; closed holidays. AE, CB, DC, MC, V. Specialties: roast pheasant, stuffed quail, barbecued meat, a bison steak, fish of the day, southern dishes. *Note:* Has a *Gone With the Wind* atmosphere and décor with friendly svce and an agreeable bar; appeals greatly to tourists. Amusing collection of rocking chairs. *American.* **I**

☼ ⚲ **Sun Dial** (dwntwn), 73rd floor of the Westin Peachtree Plaza (see "Accommodations," above) (659-0099). A/C. Lunch/ dinner daily; brunch Sun. AE, CB, DC, MC, V. Jkt. Specialties: shrimp provençale, peanut soup, meat broiled over a wood fire. *Note:* One of the highest revolving rests. in the world. Creditable cuisine at best, but an exceptional view of Atlanta and her skyscrapers. Resv. necessary. A "must" for tourists. Very good value at lunch. *Steakhouse.* **I–M**

⚲ **Casa Gallardo** (vic.), 2728 New Spring Rd., Smyrna (404/ 435-2405). Lunch/dinner daily; closed Thanksgiving, Dec. 25. AE, CB, DC, MC, V. Specialties: chimichangas, chiles rellenos, burritos de sarita, fajitas. *Note:* The best and most authentic Mexican rest. in Atlanta. Agreeable hacienda décor, attentive svce, and a colorful, pleasant atmosphere. Well worth the 30-min. drive from dwntwn on I-75N and U.S. 41. *Mexican.* **B–I**

⚲ **Great Wall** (dwntwn), 240 CNN Center (522-8213). A/C. Lunch/dinner daily; closed holidays. AE, CB, DC, MC, V. Specialties: Great Wall shrimp, moo shoo pork, Mongolian beef, garlic chicken, Peking duck (on order). *Note:* One of the few authentic Chinese rests. in dwntwn Atlanta. Rather elegant Oriental décor and efficient svce. Locally popular. *Chinese.* **B–I**

⚲ **The Varsity** (nr. dwntwn), 61 North Ave. (881-1706). Lunch/dinner daily (until 2 a.m.). No credit cards. Specialties: hamburgers, chili dogs, sandwiches, orange freezes, apple pie. *Note:* By general consensus, the best hamburgers in Atlanta for close to 50 years. Also prides itself on being the largest drive-in rest. in the world, with two floors for parking. An absolute must-see. Right next to Georgia Tech. An authentic local institution. *American.* **B**

Cafeteria / Fast Food

David Bros. Cafeteria (vic.), State Farmers' Market, Forest Park (404/366-7414). Breakfast/lunch/dinner daily (until 8:30 p.m.). Specialties: roast beef, fried chicken, hamburgers, fried fish, excellent vegetables, pastries. *Note:* This excellent, lively, locally popular spot is in the heart of the Farmers' Market. 20 min. from dwntwn on I-75.

BARS & NIGHTCLUBS

Atlanta Nights (dwntwn), 505 Peachtree St. NE (892-4998). Since its opening in 1986, this disco has become a favorite "meet place" for upscale Atlantans. Studio 54. . . . Southern style. Tue.-Sun.

☼ **Dante's Down the Hatch** (nr. dwntwn), 3380 Peachtree Rd. NE (266-1600). Jazz and folk music in an old galleon setting that is both picturesque and pleasant. Supper served until midnight. Open nightly.

Élan (vic.), Park Place, 4505 Ashford-Dunwoody Rd. (393-1333). Deluxe singles bar/disco. Trendy clientele. A rest. as well (mediocre). Locally very popular. 20 min. from dwntwn. Open Mon.-Sat.

Hemingway's (vic.), 3910 N. Druid Hills Rd. (325-3094). Live country-rock music in a spirited ambience. Guaranteed cowboy atmosphere. Open nightly.

Limelight (nr. dwntwn), 3330 Piedmont Rd. NE (231-3520). The biggest disco in the South. Spectacular. Open nightly.

Manuel's Tavern (nr. dwntwn), 602 N. Highland Ave. (525-3447). Pleasant and very popular singles bar with English pub décor and a clientele of journalists and politicians. A classic of its kind for 20 years.

Walter Mitty's Jazz Café (nr. dwntwn), 816 N. Highland Ave. NE (876-7115). Excellent modern jazz.

Waverly Hotel (nr. dwntwn), 2450 Galleria Pkwy. (953-4500). Very crowded tea dances every Friday evening with orchestras à la Glenn Miller and Woody Herman. Attracts hundreds of devotees each wknd.

NEARBY EXCURSIONS

☼♙♙ **CALLAWAY GARDENS** (86 mi., 138 km, southwest on I-85S and U.S. 27S in Pine Mountain): One of the most beautiful botanic gardens in the country, with 2,400 acres (1,000 ha.) of splendid gardens and woods, 13 lakes (fishing, boating, waterskiing), four golf courses, and more than 12½ mi. (20 km) of hiking trails. Attracting many thousands of visitors annually, it is well worth the 90-min. car ride from Atlanta. Open Mar. to late Sept.

In **Warm Springs,** 15 mi. (24 km) farther west, visit the ⚓ **Little White House,** summer home of Pres. Franklin D. Roosevelt, where he died on April 12, 1945. Worth the trip.

Where to Stay En Route

IN PINE MOUNTAIN. **Callaway Gardens Hotel** (404/663-2281). Four-star hotel.

CHAPTER 13

NASHVILLE

□ □ □

And the Great Smoky Mountains

The mecca of country music, deftly portrayed by director Robert Altman in his movie *Nashville,* is today a mixture of southern conservatism and razzle-dazzle prosperity show business, publishing, banking, insurance, etc. It was founded in 1779 as Fort Nashborough by a group of North Carolina pioneers under the leadership of James Robertson. The little fort of rough-hewn logs named after the Revolutionary hero Gen. Francis Nash may still be seen, scrupulously restored, on the west bank of the Cumberland River.

From its past as a city of the Old South, the capital of Tennessee has retained its gracious, spacious upper-class homes and magnificent gardens, its taste for religion (707 churches), a fondness for education (the city boasts no fewer than 16 colleges and universities) and some venerable traditions. From the more recent past, since the popularity of country music began to explode in the 1950s generating an influx of tourists, Nashville derives a multitude of record shops and souvenir stores; a network of urban highways; the new-money palaces of the country-music stars, with their year-round congregation of busloads of worshipful fans; and endless suburbs punctuated with screaming neon signs, hamburger joints, and used-car lots. The recording industry contributes to the wealth of "Music City USA" at the rate of $800 million a year; here, where the famous "Nashville Sound" was born, a hundred recording studios turn out, in good years and bad alike, more than half the country's pop music.

It should, then, come as no surprise that the city's most famous monument is not the life-size replica of the **Parthenon** (whence the name "Athens of the South," bestowed on the city by its inhabitants), not the beautiful **Cheekwood Botanical Garden,** not even the elegant **Hermitage,** where Pres. Andrew Jackson ended his days—but rather that shrine for all lovers of country music, the **Grand Ole Opry.** Into this huge modern auditorium, designed to serve also as a recording studio, thousands of enthusiastic spectators squeeze every weekend to witness the videotaping of TV shows whose popularity, now a full 50 years old shows no signs of abating. Dreamed up by radio pioneer George D. Hay, the "Grand Ole Opry" (the local pronunciation of "Grand Old Opera") came into the world in November 1925 over the airwaves of a little local radio station, 650 WSM; before long it was to be relayed across the country over the NBC network. It was, and remains, the principal instrument of the triumph of country music, and thus of Nashville's prosperity.

From Nashville you can easily reach several interesting tourist destinations: Chattanooga and the Tennessee Valley, the Great Smoky Mountains, and Mammoth Cave National Park, among others. "Music City USA" ranks 15th among U.S. cities in terms of its economic growth rate.

The singer Rita Coolidge was born in Nashville.

BASIC FACTS: Capital of the State of Tennessee. Area Code: 615. Time Zone:

Central Time. ZIP Code: 37202. Founded in: 1779. Approximate population: city, 490,000; metropolitan area, 800,000. Rank among U.S. cities: 22nd.

CLIMATE: The summer in Nashville is a little less humid than in Memphis, but just as hot, averaging 80°F (27°C) in July. From March through July the humidity is accentuated by storms, which are sometimes violent. The winters are moderately cold, with January temperatures averaging 38°F (3°C). The fall, when the weather is cool but fair, is the best time to visit Tennessee.

DISTANCES: Atlanta, 242 mi. (387 km); Cincinnati, 269 mi. (430 km); Memphis, 210 mi. (336 km); St. Louis, 328 mi. (525 km).

ARRIVAL & TRANSIT INFORMATION

AIRPORT: The brand-new Nashville Metropolitan Airport (BNA) is 6 mi. (10 km) SE. Information: 275-1675.

AIRLINES: American (244-5500), Delta (244-9860), Eastern (244-3780), Northwest (242-8381), Pan Am (toll free 800/221-1111), Southwest (255-1221), TWA (244-9010), United (toll free 800/241-6522), USAir (256-1944).

CITY LINK: The **cab** fare to city center is about $12–$14; time, 15–20 min. Bus: **Airport Shuttle Service** (275-2555), serving principal hotels; fare, $8; time, 25 min. Also **city bus (MTA)** leaving from Fourth Ave. North and The Arcade: fare, 80¢; time 30 min.

Public transportation is by bus, provided by the Metropolitan Transit Authority/MTA (242-4433); it's inefficient, but unless you plan on excursions out of town (recommended), or a visit to the Grand Old Opry, the city is small enough that you may not need to rent a car.

CAR RENTAL: (at the airport unless otherwise noted): Avis (361-1838); Budget (366-0800); Dollar (366-0449); Hertz (361-3131); National (361-7467); Thrifty, 1315 Vultee Blvd. (361-6050).

LIMOUSINE SERVICE: Carey Limousine (889-5304), Dav El Limousines (toll free 800/922-0343), Imperial Limousines (361-3055).

TAXIS: In theory cabs may be hailed on the street, but it's difficult to find one cruising. It's best to telephone: **Checker** (254-5031), **Nashville Cab** (242-7070), **Yellow Cab** (256-0101).

BUS: Greyhound, 200 Eighth Ave. (256-6141).

MISSISSIPPI CRUISES: Three- to ten-day cruises aboard the 1920s paddlewheelers *Delta Queen* or *Mississippi Queen*. Luxurious kitsch. See Chapter 15 on New Orleans.

INFORMATION & TOURS

TOURIST INFORMATION: The **Nashville Chamber of Commerce–Visitors Division,** 161 Fourth Ave. North, TN 37219 (615/259-3900).

Tourist Information Center, Exit 85 from I-65 at J. Robertson Pkwy. (615/242-5606).

GUIDED TOURS: **Belle Carol Riverboat Co.** (boat), First Ave. N. and Broadway (244-3430): Trips on the Cumberland River aboard the heroic-age paddlewheeler *Music City Queen.* Mar.-Dec.

General Jackson (boat), 2812 Opryland Dr. (889-6611): Three-hour musical mini-cruises and dinner cruises aboard the giant (1,200-passenger) paddlewheeler *General Jackson.* Year round.

Gray Line Tours (bus), 314 Hermitage Ave. (244-7330): Conducted tour of city and surroundings; serves principal hotels.

Grand Ole Opry Tours (bus), 2810 Opryland Dr. (889-9490): Conducted tour of the Grand Ole Opry, the city's principal attractions, and the homes of country-music stars.

SIGHTS, ATTRACTIONS, & ACTIVITIES

ARCHITECTURAL HIGHLIGHTS: ⚑ **The Parthenon,** Centennial Park East End and 25th Ave. N. (259-6358): A surprising life-size replica, in marble and reinforced concrete, of the famous Athenian temple of Pericles' time. This version, dating from 1931, houses temporary cultural exhibitions. It shouldn't be missed. Open Tues.-Sun.

⚘⚑ **Ryman Auditorium,** 116 Fifth Ave. North (254-1445): This former church in red brick is considered the *real* "Mecca of Country Music" by purists; it was here that the Grand Ole Opry made its home from 1943 until the present auditorium was opened in 1974. Once celebrated for its acoustics, the Ryman Auditorium used to host a very different kind of performer: Sarah Bernhardt, Enrico Caruso, and the like. Today it is a gallery of country-star souvenirs. An absolute must for fans. Open daily.

BROADCASTING AND MOVIE STUDIOS: ⚑⚑⚑⚑ **Grand Ole Opry House,** 2802 Opryland Dr., 10 mi. (16 km) NE via I-40 and Briley Pkwy. (889-3060): The largest (4,400 seats) recording studio in the world, where the biggest stars of country music perform every Fri. and Sat. evening (two shows), with additional Tues., Thurs., Sat., and Sun. matinee performances in summer. Tickets may be purchased only at the box office, or by mail from 2802 Opryland Dr., TN 37214; in summer reservations must be made many weeks ahead. This is a visit you shouldn't miss.

⚑ **Recording Studios of America,** 1510 Division St. (254-1282): For a mere $10 you can have yourself recorded here with a "canned" accompaniment; a godsend for aspiring singers. Open Mon.-Sat.

⚘⚑ **Studio B,** Country Music Hall of Fame, 4 Music Square East (256-1639): The historic RCA studio where the likes of Elvis Presley, Chet Atkins, Charley Pride, and Eddy Arnold recorded some of their biggest hits. You can visit it along with the Country Music Hall of Fame (see "Museums of Science and History," below). Don't miss it. Open daily.

CHURCHES/SYNAGOGUES: ⚑ **Presbyterian Church,** Church St. and Fifth Ave. North (254-7584): Remarkable example of the Egyptian Revival architecture so much in vogue at the end of the 19th century; it was used as a hospital for Union casualties during the Civil War. Worth seeing. Open Mon.-Fri.

⚑ **Upper Room Chapel,** 1908 Grand Ave. (327-2700): This Georgian-style chapel holds, among its other treasures, a giant reproduction in polychromed wood of Leonardo's *Last Supper.* Religious-art kitsch of the highest order. Open Mon.-Sat.

HISTORIC BUILDINGS: ⚘ ⚑⚑ **Belle Meade Mansion,** Harding Rd. and Leake Ave., 7 mi. (12 km) SW on West End Ave. (356-0501): With its elegant portico and enormous state room, this very lovely 1854 plantation house was once the home of one of the country's most renowned stud farms (it produced Iroquois, the first American horse to win the English Derby, in 1881). Fine collection of old carriages. A definite must-see. Open daily.

Belmont Mansion, 1900 Belmont Blvd. at Acklen Ave. (269-9537): This luxurious 1850s Palladian home was a center of Nashville social life for more than half a century, and has now been magnificently restored to all its former grandeur. On the campus of Belmont College. Positively must be seen. Open Tues.-Sat.

Fisk University, 17th Ave. North and Jackson (329-8555): In the heart of Nashville's historic district, this university, founded in 1866, possesses some interesting old buildings, including the **Carl Van Vechten Art Gallery.** Worth a look.

Fort Nashborough, 170 First Ave. North at Church St. (255-8192): Built on the site of the first white settlement in 1779, this exact replica of an 18th-century fort, surrounded by its palisade, admirably reconstructs the daily life of the pioneers, with walk-ons in period clothing. Don't fail to visit it. Open Tues.-Sat.

The Hermitage, 4580 Rachel's Lane, in Hermitage, 12 mi. (19 km) NE via I-40 and Old Hickory Blvd. (889-2941): Andrew Jackson's country house, built in 1819 and enlarged in 1834 after a fire, is one of the finest classical revival buildings in the Deep South. Superb original furniture. The tombs of the seventh president and his wife, Rachel, stand amid lovely gardens. Don't miss it. Open daily.

State Capitol, Sixth and Charlotte Aves. (741-3211): Built on a hill overlooking the city, this classic of the Greek Revival style is the work of architect William Strickland, who in 1859 was buried within its walls. On the main lawn is the tomb of James Polk, 11th president of the U.S., and statues of local heroes including Pres. Andrew Jackson and Sgt. Alvin York, the most decorated U.S. soldier of World War I. Open daily. Should be seen.

Travellers' Rest, 636 Farrell Pkwy., 6 mi. (9 km) south on U.S. 31 (832-2962): Plantation house dating from the early 1800s, standing among groves of giant magnolias and maples. Often visited by Andrew Jackson, Lafayette, and other notables. Worth a visit. Open daily.

MUSEUMS OF ART: ☀ ▲▲ **Cheekwood Fine Arts Center,** Forrest Park Dr., 7 mi. (11 km) SW via U.S. 70S and Tenn. 100 (352-5310): 18th-century English furniture; 19th-century European and American paintings. Temporary exhibitions. Imposing 1932 building in the Georgian style surrounded by an outstandingly lovely botanic garden, with orchids, camellias, rose gardens, Japanese garden, etc. You should certainly go. Open Tues.-Sun.

MUSEUMS OF SCIENCE AND HISTORY: ☀ ▲ **Country Music Hall of Fame and Museum,** 4 Music Square East (256-1639): Innumerable memorabilia of all the idols of country music; Chet Atkins' first guitar, the car used by Burt Reynolds in the movie *Smokey and the Bandit,* Dolly Parton's show dresses, Elvis Presley's massive gold Cadillac. Enthralling; an absolute must for all fans. You will also visit the legendary **Studio B** (see "Broadcasting and Movie Studios," above). Don't miss this one.

Country Music Wax Museum, 118 16th Ave. South (256-2490): A pantheon in wax: 60 or so of country music's greatest stars in their authentic stage costumes and their original musical instruments. Very touristy, but a must for all country-music fans. Also live concerts. Souvenir shop and restaurant adjoining. Open daily.

Cumberland Museum, 800 Ridley Ave. (259-6099): Interesting material on zoology and Native American history; also a very up-to-date planetarium. Open Tues.-Sun.

Museum of Tobacco Art and History, 800 Harrison St. at Eighth Ave. North (242-9218): Traces the history of tobacco from its origins among the earliest Native Americans. Fine collection of old pipes, snuffboxes, and tobacco jars. Curious and interesting. Open daily.

State Museum, James K. Polk Bldg., 505 Deaderick St. (741-2692): Colorful presentation of Tennessee history from the Stone Age to the War Between the States, illustrated by a display of more than 5,000 old objects. Worth visiting. Open daily.

NIGHTTIME ENTERTAINMENT: The capital of country music has, as you might expect, one of the country's heaviest concentrations of nightclubs, bars, and dance halls to the square mile. Certain tourist traps should be given a wide berth: they're to be found on Printer's Alley or Broadway, the two "hot" streets in the entertainment district. Besides the Grand Ole Opry and the clubs listed further on in this chapter, don't miss a trip to the **Ernest Tubb Midnight Jamboree,** 2414 Music Valley Dr. (889-2474). It's a sort of country-music jam session which meets every Saturday in a well-known record store at midnight, after the show at the nearby Grand Ole Opry. Public admitted free. Very popular locally.

PARKS AND GARDENS: **Opryland Hotel Conservatory,** 2800 Opryland Dr. (889-1000): The 10,000 trees and tropical plants arrayed here in a six-story-high greenhouse make this wonderful winter garden, with its streams, waterfalls, and statues, a must for all who visit Opryland, whether or not they stay at the hotel. Should be seen. Open daily; 10 min. from dwntwn.

Tennessee Botanical Gardens–Cheekwood, Forrest Park Dr. (352-5310): Beautiful 30-acre botanic garden surrounding the Cheekwood Fine Arts Center (see "Museums of Art," above). Besides greenhouses with a simulated tropical forest and numberless varieties of camellias and orchids, the garden boasts several lovely specialty gardens: rose garden, Japanese garden, wildflower garden, herb garden. Don't fail to visit. Open Tues.-Sun.

PERFORMING ARTS: For current listings of shows and cultural events, consult the entertainment pages of the two daily papers, *The Tennessean* (morning) and *The Nashville Banner* (evening), as well as the monthly *Nashville*.

Centennial Park, W. End and 25th Aves. (259-6399): Open-air concerts by the Nashville Symphony, every weekend from June to Aug. Also folk and country-music concerts.

Grand Ole Opry, 2802 Opryland Dr., 10 mi. (16 km) NE via I-40 and Briley Pkwy. (889-3060): The shrine of country music. Shows and live concerts every Fri. and Sat. evening year round; matinees Tues., Thur., Sat., and Sun. in summer. You must reserve—as far ahead as possible.

Municipal Auditorium, 417 Fourth Ave. North (259-6461): Hosts political meetings, conventions, and live concerts.

Music Village USA, Music Village Blvd. in Hendersonville, 20 mi. (32 km) NE via I-65, Two Mile Pkwy., and U.S. 31E (822-1800): Shows and live concerts by the biggest stars in country music. Concerts Mon.-Sat. May-Aug., weekends only in Sept. and Oct.; closed the rest of the year.

Nashville Academy Theater, 724 2nd Ave. S. (254-7045): Specializes in classical theater and children's shows.

Opryland, 2802 Opryland Dr., 10 mi. (16 km) NE via I-40 and Briley

Pkwy. (889-6700): Live TV shows, live pop, jazz, blues, country, gospel, or rock 'n roll concerts, Broadway-style revues. Adjoining are the Grand Ole Opry and a giant amusement park. Open daily Memorial Day to Labor Day; weekends only in spring and fall; closed the rest of the year.

Tennessee Performing Arts Center, 505 Deaderick St. (741-2787): Ultra-modern complex of three adjoining auditoriums: **Andrew Jackson Hall,** offering concerts (home of the Nashville Symphony, under principal conductor Kenneth Schermerhorn) from Sept. to May; the **James K. Polk Theater,** for drama, comedy, operetta, chamber-music recitals (home of the Tennessee Repertory Theater); and the **Andrew Johnson Theater,** a theater-in-the-round for modern and avant-garde material (Sept.-May; also big-name shows).

War Memorial Auditorium, Memorial Square, Seventh Ave. and Union St. (741-5383): Pop and classical concerts.

SHOPPING: The Arcade, between Fourth and Fifth Ave. North: Picturesque turn-of-the-century shopping arcade under an elegant glass roof. Dozens of unusual shops and stalls in the heart of dwntwn.

Fountain Square, Metrocenter Blvd. and I-265: The newest and most colorful of the local shopping centers. Boutiques, stores, cafés, restaurants, cinemas, and open-air concerts on the shores of a charming little lake 5 min. from dwntwn.

Record Stores

Many specialized stores around Music Row, including **Conway's Twitty,** 1530 Demonbreun; **Country Music Factory Outlet,** 319 11th Ave. S.; **Ernest Tubb,** 417 Broadway; **The Great Escape,** 1925 Broadway—offering a huge selection of country-music records at bargain prices.

Western Wear

Lovers of cowboy boots and western clothing will find an unequalled selection in the innumerable outlets for this kind of merchandise which abound in Nashville. Some of these are: **Alamo of Nashville,** 324 Broadway; **Boot Country,** 2412 Music Valley Dr.; **Loretta Lynn's Western Stores,** 120 16th Ave.; and **Genesco Manufacturing Outlets,** 511 Main St. (discount clothing and boots).

SPECIAL EVENTS: For exact dates, consult the **Nashville Chamber of Commerce** (see "Tourist Information," above).

Iroquois Steeplechase (May): The country's oldest and most important steeplechase, an American racing classic since 1941.

Tennessee Crafts Fair (May): A handcrafts fair which draws more than 150 of the state's best-known craftspeople; very popular locally.

International Country Music Fan Fair (mid-June): Country music's great annual festival, which attracts tens of thousands of fans every year. Don't miss it.

Longhorn Rodeo Series (every weekend, July-Sept.): One of the most famous professional rodeos east of the Mississippi; local color guaranteed.

National Quartet Convention (Sept.-Oct.): Very popular gospel-music festival.

SPORTS: Nashville has no major-league teams, but has a minor-league team in—**Baseball** (Apr.-Oct.): Sounds, Greer Stadium (242-4371).

THEME PARKS: ☼ 🏛 **Opryland USA,** 2802 Opryland Dr., 10 mi. (16 km) NE via I-40 and Briley Pkwy. (889-6700): Adjoining the legendary Grand Ole Opry, this huge, inventive amusement park features popular music of all kinds

—country, jazz, blues, folk, rock, musical comedy, etc.—but also offers dozens of carousels, roller coasters, bars, restaurants, boutiques, and even a mini-zoo for children. Don't miss it. Open daily Memorial Day to Labor Day; weekends only in spring and fall; closed the rest of the year.

ACCOMMODATIONS
See the listing of toll-free numbers in the Appendix.

Room Rates in Nashville	
B (Budget)	up to $30
I (Inexpensive)	$30–$60
M (Moderate)	$60–$90
E (Expensive)	$90–$140
VE (Very Expensive)	$140 and up

Personal Favorites (in order of preference)

The Hermitage (dwntwn), 231 Sixth Ave. North, TN 37219 (615/244-3121; toll free 800/251-1908). 112 suites, A/C, color TV, in-rm movies. AE, CB, DC, MC, V. Valet parking $5, rest. (Hermitage Dining Room), two bars, rm svce, nightclub, boutiques, concierge. *Note:* Elegant small turn-of-the-century hotel, splendidly restored; one- and two-bedroom suites, luxuriously decorated, w. mini-bars and antique furniture. Faultless svce. Good rest. Free breakfast, served on a pretty porch. Elegant and charming; the favorite hotel of those in-the-know, in the heart of dwntwn. **E**

Radisson Plaza–Union Station (dwntwn), 1001 Broadway, TN 37203 (615/726-1001; toll free, see Radisson). 128 rms, A/C, color TV, in-rm movies. AE, CB, DC, MC, V. Valet parking $5, three rests. (including the Roosevelt), bar, rm svce, concierge, free crib. *Note:* The most innovative of the local luxury hotels. Opened in 1987, this elegant, comfortable establishment occupies seven floors of the old Union Station, an imposing turn-of-the-century structure in Railroad Gothic crowned by a tall Big Ben–style tower. Very spacious, well-equipped rms; excellent svce. Halfway between dwntwn and Music Row; a fashionable place to stay. **E**

Maxwell House Clarion (nr. dwntwn), 2025 Metro Center Blvd., TN 37228 (615/259-4343; toll free, see Clarion). 290 rms, A/C, color TV, in-rm movies. AE, CB, DC, MC, V. Free parking, pool, two tennis courts, health club, two rests. (including Crown Court), bar, rm svce, disco, free crib. *Note:* Modern, elegant hotel 5 min. from dwntwn; spacious, comfortable rms, recently renovated (some w. refrigerators). Attentive svce; very acceptable rest. VIP floor. Business clientele; a good place to stay. **M–E**

La Quinta (nr. dwntwn), 2001 Metro Center Blvd., TN 37228 (615/259-2130; toll free, see La Quinta). 121 rms, A/C, color TV, in-rm movies. AE, CB, DC, MC, V. Free parking, pool, 24-hr coffeeshop adjoining, free crib. *Note:* Rustic, but functional and comfortable, motel; friendly reception and svce. Very good value. 8 min. from dwntwn. **I**

Travelodge Nashville (dwntwn), 800 James Robertson Pkwy., TN 37203 (615/244-2630; toll free, see Travelodge). 83 rms, A/C, cable color TV. AE, CB, DC, MC, V. *Note:* Small four-story hotel

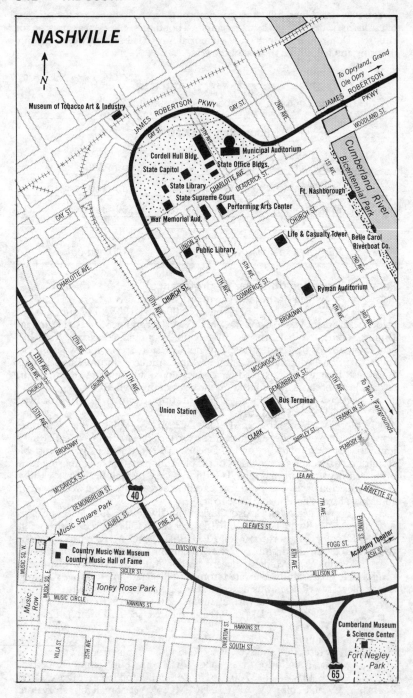

NASHVILLE

N

To Opryland, Grand
Ole Opry

JAMES ROBERTSON PKWY

Museum of Tobacco Art & Industry

Cumberland River

Bicentennial Park

Cordell Hull Bldg.
State Office Bldgs.
State Capitol
Municipal Auditorium
State Library
Ft. Nashborough
State Supreme Court
Performing Arts Center
War Memorial Aud.

Life & Casualty Tower
Belle Carol
Riverboat Co.

Public Library

Ryman Auditorium

Union Station

Bus Terminal

Music Square Park

Country Music Wax Museum
Country Music Hall of Fame

Toney Rose Park

Academy Theater

Cumberland Museum
& Science Center

Fort Negley
Park

at the foot of the State Capitol; modest but well run. Friendly reception. Some rms w. balconies. Good value. **I**

Other Hotels (from top bracket to budget)

Opryland Hotel (vic.), 2800 Opryland Dr., TN 37214 (615/889-1000). 1,067 rms, A/C, color TV, AE, CB, DC, MC, V. Valet parking $6, pool, six tennis courts, three rests. (including the Old Hickory Room), coffeeshop, four bars, 24-hr rm svce, disco, shows, hrdrsr, boutiques, free crib. *Note:* Enormous vacation complex oriented to mass tourism; ideal for visiting Opryland and the Grand Ole Opry, which it adjoins. Flashy Deep South interior. Spacious, comfortable rms, the best overlooking a lovely indoor botanic garden; mediocre rests. Obtrusive package-tour and convention clientele. Rates tend toward the exorbitant. 20 min. from dwntwn. **E–VE**

Stouffer Hotel (dwntwn), 611 Commerce St., TN 37203 (615/255-8400; toll free, see Stouffer). 673 rms, A/C, color TV, in-rm movies. AE, CB, DC, MC, V. Parking $6, pool, health club, sauna, rest., coffeeshop, bar, rm svce, disco, free crib. *Note:* Elegant, ultramodern tower whose 25 stories dominate the Convention Center—an excellent location in the heart of dwntwn. Huge, very comfortable rms; efficient svce; business and convention clientele. Two top floors reserved for VIPs. **E**

Doubletree Hotel (formerly the Radisson; dwntwn), 2 Commerce Pl., TN 37219 (615/244-8200; toll free 800/528-0444). 337 rms, A/C, color TV, in-rm movies. AE, CB, DC, MC, V. Garage $5, pool, health club, sauna, two rests. (including the Hunt Room), two bars, rm svce, disco, boutiques, free crib. *Note:* This modern building makes no appeal to the eye, but the rooms and interior decoration are elegant and comfortable. Right in the heart of dwntwn Nashville. Efficient svce. The 12th (top) floor is reserved for VIPs. Business clientele. **M–E**

Best Western–Opryland (vic.), 2600 Music Valley Dr., TN 37214 (615/889-8235; toll free, see Best Western). 212 rms, A/C, color TV. AE, CB, DC, MC, V. Free parking, pool, rest., bar, disco, free crib. *Note:* Large, modern, comfortable motel, very near the Grand Ole Opry and the Opryland theme park. Spacious, inviting rms; friendly reception and svce. Good value. **I–M**

Holiday Inn Vanderbilt (nr. dwntwn), 2613 W. End Ave., TN 37203 (615/327-4707; toll free, see Holiday Inns). 301 rms, A/C, color TV, in-rm movies. AE, CB, DC, MC, V. Free parking, pool, rest., bar, rm svce, disco, free crib. *Note:* Modern 14-floor building very near Vanderbilt University. Functionally comfortable in the Holiday Inn manner. Good value. 5 min. from dwntwn. **I–M**

Quality Inn Hall of Fame (nr. dwntwn), 1407 Division St., TN 37203 (615/242-1631; toll free, see Quality Inns). 103 rms, A/C, color TV, in-rm movies. AE, CB, DC, MC, V. Free parking, pool, rest., bar, rm svce, disco, crib $6. *Note:* Recently renovated motel, well placed for a visit to the Country Music Hall of Fame and the attractions of Music Row. Comfortable rms; smiling reception. Family and group clientele. **I–M**

Days Inn Downtown (dwntwn.), 711 Union St., TN 37219 (615/242-4311; toll free Days Inns). 100 rms, A/C, color TV, in-rm movies. AE, DC, MC, V. Free parking, coffeeshop, free breakfast, free crib. *Note:* Typical well-run motel very near the Capitol. Functionally comfortable. Some rms w. refrigerators. Very centrally located; good value. **I**

Motel 6 South (vic.), 95 Wallace Rd., TN 37211 (615/834-1231). 126 rms, A/C, color TV, free in-rm movies. DC, MC, V. Free parking, pool, nearby coffeeshop. *Note:* Inviting economy motel 20 min. from dwntwn, 10 min. from the airport and Grand Ole Opry. Unbeatable value; ideal for the budget traveler. **B**

Airport Accommodations

Days Inn Executive Center (formerly the Admiral Benbow Inn; vic.), 823 Murfreesboro Rd., TN 37217 (615/367-1234; toll free Days Inns). 294 rms, A/C, color TV, in-rm movies. AE, CB, DC, MC, V. Free parking, three pools, health club, rest., coffeeshop, rm svce, free airport limo. *Note:* Very good value 5 min. from the airport. Modern comfort surrounded by gardens; huge rms recently renovated. Good svce. Perfect for a stopover between flights. **I–M**

RESTAURANTS

Nashville Restaurant Prices	
(per person, excluding drinks and service charges)	
B (Budget)	up to $15
I (Inexpensive)	$15–$25
M (Moderate)	$25–$40
E (Expensive)	$40–$60
VE (Very Expensive)	$60 and up

Personal Favorites (in order of preference)

Julian's (nr. dwntwn), 2412 W. End Ave. (327-2412). A/C. Dinner only, Mon.-Sat.; closed Sun. and holidays. AE, CB, DC, MC, V. Jkt. *Specialties:* duck à l'orange, salmon Florentine in pastry shell, roast quail w. peaches, rack of lamb, fruit soufflés, good desserts. Fine wine list. *Note:* Gracious and elegant, Nashville's best rest. has chosen as its home a charming old house w. columns in the best Deep South style. The cuisine is flawlessly classic, the svce exemplary. Only 55 people can be seated here, so resv. are strongly advised. *French.* **M–E**

Mario's (nr. dwntwn), 2005 Broadway (327-3232). A/C. Dinner only, Mon.-Sat.; closed Sun. and holidays. AE, CB, DC, MC, V. Jkt. *Specialties:* fresh homemade pasta, zuppa di pesce, osso buco, veal marsala, roast duck, broiled fish. Excellent wine list. *Note:* The jovial Mario Ferrari serves excellent northern Italian food at relatively reasonable prices in his locally popular rest. The svce has too much to do and the place is often noisy. Favored by local celebrities. Resv. strongly advised. *Italian.* **I–M**

Tavern on the Row (nr. dwntwn), 26 Music Square (255-3900). A/C. Lunch/dinner Mon.-Sat. (till 3 a.m.); closed Sun. AE, MC, V. *Specialties:* sandwiches; broiled meat and fish, sautéed lamb chops, tournedos Bombay, daily specials. *Note:* Nashville's new "in" place, offering modern, often imaginative cuisine. Agreeable tavern setting w. open patio for good weather. Youthful, relaxed atmosphere. *American.* **B–I**

Dynasty (nr. dwntwn), 3415 W. End Ave. (269-0188). A/C. Lunch/dinner daily; closed Thanksgiving. AE, MC, V. *Specialties:* Peking duck, Mongolian beef, sweet-and-sour fish. *Note:* The best Chinese rest. in Nashville, serving elegant, authentic food. All-purpose Far Eastern décor; diligent svce; very good value. Resv. advised. *Chinese.* **B–I**

☼♈️ **Elliston Place Soda Shop** (nr. dwntwn), 211 Elliston Pl. (327-1090). A/C. Breakfast/lunch/dinner Mon.-Sat. (until 9 p.m.); closed Sun. No credit cards. *Specialties:* fried chicken, country ham, spaghetti Créole, roast beef au jus, roast turkey, excellent fresh vegetables, banana split. *Note:* An early (1939) precursor of today's fast-food establishments, and a monument of local gastronomy. Nothing in the décor or the atmosphere has changed since it opened, nor has the dependable, tasty family-style cooking. The place is as clean as ever; the waitresses are as motherly as ever; even the original soda fountain is still in action. Most of the patrons are students from nearby Vanderbilt U. A very good place to eat. *American.* **B**

Other Restaurants (from top bracket to budget)

♈️♈️♈️ **Arthur's** (nr. dwntwn), 2174 Abbott Martin Rd. (383-8841). A/C. Lunch Mon.-Fri., dinner nightly, brunch Sun.; closed holidays. AE, CB, DC, MC, V. J&T. *Specialties:* veal normande, beef Wellington, Dover sole meunière, flaming desserts; the menu changes regularly. Good wine list. *Note:* The classical French-inspired haute cuisine and the elegantly luxurious setting have made this rest. a favorite with notables, whether local or visiting. The svce is a touch pretentious. Resv. necessary. *Continental.* **M (prix fixe)**

♈️♈️ **Sperry's** (vic.), 5109 Harding Rd. (353-0809). A/C. Dinner only, nightly; closed holidays. AE, CB, DC, MC, V. Jkt. *Specialties:* snails, stuffed mushrooms, Alaska crabmeat, fine broiled meat and fish, banana Foster. *Note:* A small, quite intimate rest. near the Belle Meade Mansion, got up as an English pub in the Tudor style. The cuisine, though unimaginative, is polished. Good svce. 20 min. from dwntwn. *Steak-seafood.* **I**

☼♈️♈️ **Stock-Yard** (dwntwn), 901 Second Ave. (255-6464). A/C. Lunch/dinner Mon.-Sat.; closed Sun. and holidays. AE, CB, DC, MC, V. *Specialties:* all kinds of prime beef, pork and lamb chops, broiled chicken. Good desserts. *Note:* Located as its name suggests in the old slaughterhouses dwntwn, this picturesque place serves the best broiled steak in Nashville. Country music and dancing every evening in the adjoining Bullpen Lounge. Locally popular; free parking. *Steak.* **I**

♈️ **Jimmy Kelly's** (nr. dwntwn), 217 Louise Ave. (329-4349). Dinner only, Mon.-Sat. (till midnight); closed Sun. AE, DC, MC, V. *Specialties:* steak, Virginia ham, fried chicken, fish of the day. *Note:* A Nashville landmark for more than half a century, across from the Vanderbilt U. campus. Pleasing Victorian décor, relaxed atmosphere. Very good steaks and authentic southern food. A fine place. *American.* **I**

♈️♈️ **Crawdaddy's** (nr. dwntwn), 14 Oldham St., at the river (255-5434). A/C. Lunch Mon.-Fri., dinner nightly, Sunday brunch. AE, CB, DC, MC, V. *Specialties:* gumbo, fish Créole style, Cajun dishes, steaks. *Note:* No unworthy representative, this, of New Orleans cooking, in a charming (but hard-to-find) Victorian setting beside the Cumberland River. Very good svce, inviting bars. Also dancing. Resv. suggested. *American.* **B–I**

♈️ **Captain Ray's Sailmaker** (vic.), 4243 Harding Rd. (298-2645). A/C. Lunch/dinner daily; closed Dec. 25. AE, MC, V. *Specialties:* broiled meats, crab, fish of the day. *Note:* Inviting seafood rest., also serving good steak and roast beef. Everything is absolutely fresh. The seafaring décor is imaginative. Good svce. Very good value. 15 min. from dwntwn. *Steak-seafood.* **B–I**

Cafeterias/Fast Food

☼ **Loveless Motel & Restaurant** (vic.), on Tenn. 100 at Rte. 5, 15 mi. (24 km) SW (646-9700). Breakfast/lunch/dinner

Tues.-Sun. (till 9 p.m.). Well worth the 20-min. drive from dwntwn. Despite its dingy appearance, this motel serves some of the best country cooking in all Tennessee. Remarkable ham and fried chicken; excellent homemade biscuits and jam. No alcoholic beverages; no credit cards. In view of its popularity, you should make resv.

Morrison's (nr. dwntwn), 1000 Two Mile Pkwy. at Rivergate Mall (859-1359). A/C. Lunch/dinner daily (till 8 p.m.). MC, V. Cafeteria-buffet offering very good value. Roast beef, and desserts worth your attention.

BARS & NIGHTCLUBS

The capital of country music offers its visitors numberless nightclubs, bars, strip joints, dance halls, and dives where jazz, folk, or country music may be heard. There are, however, tourist traps to be avoided on Printers Alley and Broadway. The list given below includes the best places for lovers of authentic folk and country music.

Bluebird Café (vic.), 4104 Hillsboro Rd. (383-1461). Live country, folk, and jazz; highly recommended. Good rest. Open nightly. 20 min. from dwntwn.

Bluegrass Inn (nr. dwntwn), 1914 Broadway (329-1112). For lovers of real bluegrass; opposite the Vanderbilt campus. Wed.-Sat.

Boots Randolph's (dwntwn), 209 Printers Alley (256-5500). The well-known sax player (and owner) Boots Randolph puts on an excellent performance, but the atmosphere is touristy. Also a so-so rest. Open Mon.-Sat.

Bullpen Lounge (dwntwn), 901 Second Ave. (255-6464). Pleasing bar-disco adjoining the Stock-Yard rest. (see above). Open nightly.

Captain's Table (dwntwn), 313 Church St. (256-3353). Las Vegas–style shows; also a mediocre rest. Open nightly.

Western Room (dwntwn), 208 Printers Alley (256-9339). This club showcases new country-music talent. Open Mon.-Sat.

Exit Inn (nr. dwntwn), 2208 Elliston Pl. (321-4400). One of the best country-music joints; Robert Altman filmed *Nashville* here. Also a fair-to-middling rest. Open nightly.

Station Inn (dwntwn), 402 12th Ave. (255-3307). Shrine of local bluegrass and "newgrass." Open Tues.-Sun.

Wrangler (vic.), 1204 Murfreesboro Rd. (361-4440). Locally popular disco offering country and western. Nice atmosphere. Near the airport and 20 min. from dwntwn. Open nightly.

Zanies Comedy Showplace (nr. dwntwn), 2025 Eighth Ave. South (269-0221). Very popular comedy club with a star-studded schedule. Also mediocre rest. Open Tues.-Sun.

NEARBY EXCURSIONS

CHEATHAM LAKE (30 mi., 48 km, NW on Tenn. 12): Large body of water formed by a dam and locks on the Cumberland River. Water sports, fishing, camping; wildlife reserve. Fine scenic drive along the Cumberland River. Worth the side trip.

CUMBERLAND CAVERNS PARK (80 mi., 128 km, SE on I-24 and U.S. 70) (668-4396): Impressive patchwork of underground caves, once a saltpeter mine. It includes some of the largest and most impressive caverns in the country, particularly the "Hall of the Mountain King," 600 ft. (183 m) wide and 140 ft. (43 m) high. The temperature in the caves stays around 56° F (13°C) winter and summer alike. Conducted 90-min. tour daily, June to the end of Aug.; weekends only in spring and fall; by appointment Nov.-Apr. Worth going out of your way for.

FARTHER AFIELD

☼ 🔭 CHATTANOOGA AND THE TENNESSEE VALLEY

(515 mi., 824 km, round trip via I-24S, U.S. 231S, Tenn. 82S, Tenn. 50E, U.S. 64E, I-24S, U.S. 72W, U.S. Alt. 72W, U.S. 45N, Tenn. 22N, U.S. 64E, U.S. 43N, and U.S. 31N): The trip begins with a visit to the famous 🏛 **Jack Daniel's Distillery** at Lynchburg, the country's oldest (1866) registered whisky distillery. The rule here is "look but don't taste"—Lynchburg is in a "dry" county! Open daily; reservations advised (759-4221).

Next stop is **Chattanooga,** a thriving commercial town on the banks of the Tennessee River. Near here, in 1863, was fought one of the decisive engagements of the War Between the States, "the battle above the clouds" on 2,225-ft. (678-m) 🔭 **Lookout Mountain,** which dominates the town and offers a fine view over four states. The amazing cable car, which rises at an angle of 72° has its lower terminus at 3917 St. Elmo Ave. (841-4224); operates daily year round. Fine railroad museum, the 🏛 **Tennessee Valley Railroad Museum,** at 4119 Cromwell Rd. (894-8028); open daily from May to the end of Aug.; weekends Sept.-Nov.

Nine mi. (14 km) south of Chattanooga, see 🏛 **Chickamauga and Chattanooga National Military Park,** the country's most visited battlefield. Here, on Sept. 19–20 and Nov. 23–25, 1863, Confederates under Gen. Braxton Bragg and Union troops under Gen. George H. Thomas fought two bloody battles, ending in a Northern victory which left 34,000 dead and wounded on both sides. You can drive around the battlefield on a 3-mi. (5-km) signposted road. Visitor Center open daily; worth the detour.

Then on to the ☼ 🔭 **NASA Space and Rocket Center,** on Governors Drive in Huntsville (205/837-3400), with the world's largest space museum. Life-size replica of a lunar crater, simulated test flights into space, simulated launching ramp, museum of rockets and lunar modules, astronaut training center, etc. Fascinating; mustn't be missed.

Before ending this trip with a tour of the battlefield of **Shiloh** (see Chapter 14 on Memphis), be sure to turn aside to Florence for a glimpse of the huge ☼ 🏛 **Wilson Dam,** one of the largest in the world, and its giant lock on the Tennessee River. Visitor Center open daily.

This is a very full three- to four-day trip.

Where to Stay En Route

IN CHATTANOOGA. 🍷🍷🍷 **Chattanooga Choo-Choo,** 1400 N. Market St., Chattanooga, TN 37402 (615/266-5000). 327 rms. Built, as you might expect, in the old railroad terminal; original décor. **M**

IN HUNTSVILLE. 🍷🍷 **Holiday Inn Space Center,** 3810 University Dr., Huntsville, AL 35816 (205/837-7171). 181 rms. Typical modern Holiday Inn 3 min. from the Space Center. **I–M**

🍷 **Comfort Inn,** 3788 University Dr., Huntsville, AL 35816 (205/533-3291). 66 rms. Conventional small, well-run hotel 3 min. from the Space Center. **I**

IN FLORENCE. 🍷 **Regency Inn,** 1241 Florence Blvd., Florence, AL 35630 (205/764-5421). 84 rms. Comfortable, inviting motel. **B–I**

☼ 🏛 GREAT SMOKY MOUNTAINS NATIONAL PARK AND SURROUNDINGS (605 mi., 968 km, round trip

along I-40E, Tenn. 441S, U.S. 23N, and I-40W): This vacation trip for nature lovers begins, ironically enough, with a visit to "Atom City"—**Oak Ridge,** where the bomb dropped on Hiroshima was manufactured. Visit the 🔍 **American Museum of Science and Energy,** largest of its kind in the world, at 300 S. Tulane Ave. (576-3200), open daily. Several atomic facilities are open to the public; for a complete list, check with the Oak Ridge Convention and Visitors Bureau, 300 S. Tulane Ave. (482-7821).

Your second stop will be at 🔍 **Great Smoky Mountain National Park,** which draws more visitors (nine million a year) than any other in the country. Within its limited compass—50 mi. (80 km) long and 15–19 mi. (25–30 km) wide—it contains all the glories of the Appalachians, the oldest mountain range in North America, with more than 20 peaks rising above 6,560 ft. (2,000 m), as well as 812 mi. (1,300 km) of hiking trails. Its deep forests, home to black bear, deer, and other wildlife, are often wreathed in the mist and tattered clouds that give it its name.

Once the unapproachable realm of the Cherokee Indians, Great Smoky Mountains park now offers the tourist some magnificent landscapes (particularly from June to mid-July when the rhododendrons are in bloom), and some spectacular scenic drives. You should come to Nashville if only to see it. For information, contact the Superintendent, Great Smoky Mountain National Park, Gatlinburg, TN 37738 (615/436-1200).

Gatlinburg, a popular tourist resort at the edge of the park, and its next-door neighbor **Pigeon Forge,** where the singer Dolly Parton operates her theme park **Dollywood,** Dollywood Lane (428-9401), open daily May-Oct., both have many hotels and restaurants.

A fitting close to this trip is a visit to the picturesque little hot-springs town of **Asheville,** nestling in the woods east of the park. Birthplace of the writer Thomas Wolfe, Asheville boasts some noteworthy buildings including ☀ 🔍 **Biltmore House,** once the summer home of the millionaire George W. Vanderbilt. This imposing château in French Renaissance style is said to be the world's largest private house, with 255 rooms of which barely a quarter are open to the public. The garden was designed by Frederick Law Olmsted, who designed New York's Central Park. You'll find it on U.S. 25 (704/274-1776). Open daily; don't miss it. A popular festival of music and Appalachian folk dancing is held here every August.

You should certainly make this four- to five-day trip; it can be combined with the foregoing itineraries into a feature-packed tour lasting ten days to two weeks.

Where to Stay En Route

IN GATLINBURG. 🍸🍸🍸 **Park Vista Hotel,** Airport Rd., Gatlinburg, TN 37738 (615/436-9211). 315 rms in an 18-story tower w. a scenic view of the mountains. Ultramodern comfort. **M**

🍸🍸 **River Terrace,** River Rd., Gatlinburg, TN 37738 (615/436-5161). 209 rms. Comfortable, well-equipped motel. **M**

🍸 **Johnson's Inn,** Baskins Creek Rd., Gatlinburg, TN 37738 (615/436-4881). 31 rms. Inviting small motel located on the bank of a stream. **I**

IN ASHEVILLE. ☀ 🍸🍸🍸 **Grove Park Inn,** 290 Macon Ave., Asheville, NC 28804 (704/252-2711). 389 rms. Turn-of-the-century palace patronized by all the world's notables. Urbane and elegant. **E**

☀🔍 **Pisgah View Ranch,** N.C. 151S, Candler, NC 28715 (704/667-9100). 50 rms. A country inn lost in the forest 13 mi. (20 km) from Asheville. Highly recommended. Open May-Oct. **I–M**

☀ ☀ ☀ ⚓ **MAMMOTH CAVE NATIONAL PARK AND KEN-TUCKY COUNTRY** (520 mi., 832 km, round trip via I-65N, Ky. 70, Ky. 84E, Ky. 61N, U.S. 31W, 31N, and 31S, Blue Grass Pkwy. N, U.S. 68S, U.S. 150N, Blue Grass Pkwy. S, and I-65S): Discovered in 1799 by a bear hunter, the ⚓⚓ **Mammoth Caves** deserve their name: they are the longest system of underground caves in the world, but only 300 mi. (483 km) have been explored so far. They are interspersed with caverns, deep sink-holes, and spectacular underground lakes and rivers. Some chambers are 196 ft. (60 m) high. Guided tours (tiring), daily year round. Wear sturdy shoes and warm clothes. Call 502/758-2328 for information on schedules. The recommended approach is via Ky. 70. Don't miss it.

Continue to ⚓ **Abraham Lincoln's Birthplace,** a stately marble-and-granite memorial, erected in 1911 by public subscription of more than 100,000 anonymous contributors. Inside is the log cabin where the 16th president was born on Feb. 12, 1809. The museum should not be missed. Open daily year round; for information, call 502/358-3874.

Go a little out of your way to see the legendary ☀ **Fort Knox,** on U.S. 31W (502/624-3351), site of the **United States Bullion Depository,** the country's second-largest gold reserve. The treasure is kept in a two-level steel-and-concrete cave, proof against bombs and sealed by an armored door weighing 28 tons. Unhappily it's closed to visitors, but on its grounds you may visit the ⚓ **Patton Museum,** with its rich collection of tanks and other weapons of war; open daily year round.

On the way to **Lexington** and the famous **Kentucky Horse Park** (see Chapter 22 on Cincinnati), don't miss **Bardstown,** where you can make a sentimental pilgrimage to ☀ **"My Old Kentucky Home"** on U.S. 150 (502/348-3502), open daily year round; this lovely 18th-century Colonial house inspired Stephen Foster to write his immortal song. See also the **Oscar Getz Museum of Whisky,** 5th St. at Xavier Dr. (502/348-2999), open daily in summer, which traces the history of that popular beverage, and ⚓ **St. Joseph's Cathedral,** 310 W. Stephen Foster Ave. (502/348-3126), open daily; built in 1816, this was the first Roman Catholic cathedral west of the Alleghenies. It has a number of paintings presented by King Louis-Philippe of France during his exile.

The last stage of the journey takes you to ☀ **Harrodsburg,** the first white settlement in Kentucky (1774). ⚓ **Old Fort Harrod,** on U.S. 68 (606/734-3314), open daily year round, is an exact replica of the original fort; don't miss it. Two other nearby attractions are: the ☀ **Shaker Town at Pleasant Hill,** 3500 Lexington Rd. (606/734-5411), open daily year round, a museum village once inhabited by the Shakers and boasting no fewer than 27 of the original 19th-century buildings; and the ⚓ **Perryville Battlefield,** on U.S. 68 (606/332-8631), open daily Apr.-Oct., where there is a museum with a diorama of the battle, one of the bloodiest of the War Between the States.

This itinerary is interesting for its variety, and for the beautiful landscapes through which it takes you.

Where to Stay En Route

IN MAMMOTH CAVE NATIONAL PARK. 🛏 **Mammoth Cave,** 3 mi. inside the park on Ky. 70 Park Rd., Mammoth Cave Nat'l Park, KY 42259 (502/758-2225). 58 rms. Typical functional motel near the entrance to the caves. **I**

IN BARDSTOWN. 🛏 **Parkview,** 418 E. Stephen Foster Ave., Bardstown, KY 40004 (502/348-5983). 32 rms. Small, inviting motel opposite "My Old Kentucky Home." **I**

IN LEXINGTON. 🍸🍸 **Campbell House Inn,** 1375 Harrodsburg Rd., Lexington, KY 40504 (606/255-4281). 300 rms. Luxurious, comfortable motel with golf course. **I–M**

IN HARRODSBURG. 🍸🍸 **Inn at Pleasant Hill,** 3500 Lexington Rd., Harrodsburg, KY 40330 (606/734-5411). 72 rms. Comfortable rms built into the original structure of a 19th-century Shaker village. Picturesque old-fashioned charm. Good rest. **I–M**

CHAPTER 14

MEMPHIS

□ □ □

It was in 1541, near the site of modern Memphis, that Hernando de Soto, the first Spanish explorer of the interior, crossed the wide and muddy Mississippi River. His feat was replicated 132 years later by the French explorers Marquette and Jolliet; they in turn were followed by Robert Cavelier de La Salle, who during his 1682 voyage down the Mississippi to the Gulf of Mexico proclaimed French sovereignty over the region.

Memphis occupies a strategic position at a point where the Mississippi bends to welcome the Wolf River. Dominating the Mississippi from a commanding height, much as the ancient Memphis of the Pharaohs towered above the Nile, the city served briefly during the Civil War years as the capital of the Confederacy. This status ended abruptly in 1862, when Memphis was taken by Northern troops in a bloody naval battle in which some 30 ships were engaged.

Memphis owes its prosperity primarily to cotton—often referred to as "white gold"—for which it has long been the major market in the world. Soybeans and hardwood also play important roles in its economy. Its port activity (12 million tons shipped annually) and its dense railroad network have made Memphis one of the busiest shipping centers in the South. The city has mushroomed, growing 28% in population between 1960 and 1980. Fond of calling itself the "Home of the Blues," Memphis has come to be a comfortable blend of highways and skyscrapers with traces of a more gracious past such as **Overton Square** and **Beale Street,** picturesque examples of successful renovation in the old city. It was on Beale Street, close by the banks of the Mississippi, that the legendary composer W. C. Handy wrote "Memphis Blues" and "St. Louis Blues," two great classics of traditional jazz. In later years Memphis became the adopted home of Elvis Presley; although the singer died in 1977, idolatrous fans by the tens of thousands still flock to visit his grave and the gardens of **Graceland,** the Presley mansion.

Memphis is the proud birthplace (in 1952) of the first Holiday Inn, now part of one of the largest hotel empires in the world, whose headquarters are still in the city. So are those of Federal Express, a leading air-courier service, and for more than 800 other enterprises concentrated for the most part in the port area of **Presidents Island.** In a recent national poll, Memphis was voted the cleanest, most orderly, and most peaceful city in the United States. It was, however, in a Memphis motel that civil rights leader and Nobel Peace Prize winner Martin Luther King, Jr., was assassinated (Apr. 4, 1968). Among celebrated Memphis sons and daughters are the actor/comedian George Hamilton and singer Aretha Franklin.

BASIC FACTS: State of Tennessee. Area Code: 901. Time Zone: Central Time. ZIP Code: 31801. Founded in 1819. Approximate population: city, 66,000, metropolitan area, 910,000. Ranked 16th in size among the nation's cities and 41st among its metropolitan areas.

CLIMATE: The dominant presence of the Mississippi River guarantees humid-

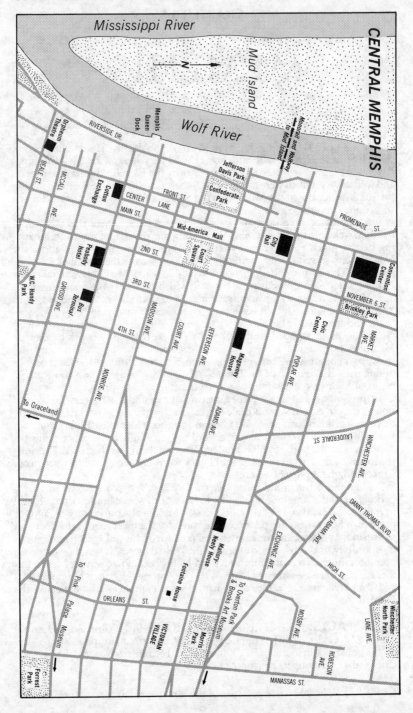

ity year round, even in winter when the temperature hovers around freezing. In July and August the city resembles a giant sauna, with temperatures around 82° – 86° F (28° – 30° C). Spring, and especially autumn, are the only two seasons recommended for your visit.

DISTANCES: Atlanta, 365 mi. (585 km); Chicago, 531 mi. (850 km); Dallas, 450 mi. (720 km); Nashville, 210 mi. (336 km); New Orleans, 390 mi. (625 km); St. Louis, 284 mi. (455 km).

ARRIVAL & TRANSIT INFORMATION

AIRPORT: Memphis International Airport (MEM), 10 mi. (6 km) SE. Information: 345-7777.

AIRLINES: American (526-8861), Delta (761-5441), Northwest (525-7681), TWA (toll free 800/221-2000), United (522-9222), US Air (526-7691).

CITY LINK: The **cab** fare from the airport to downtown is about $14; time, 25 min. Bus: **Yellow Cab** (526-2121) leaves every half hour and serves the principal downtown hotels; fare, $6; time, 30 min.

The city itself is not so large that renting a car is essential, but be warned that **public transportation** (bus) is inadequate; for information, call MATA (274-6282).

CAR RENTAL (at the airport unless otherwise noted): Avis (345-2847); Budget (767-1000); Dollar, 2031 E. Brooks Rd. (345-3890); Hertz (345-5680); National (345-0070); Thrifty (345-0170). Consult the local telephone directory for downtown rental locations.

LIMOUSINE SERVICES: DavEl Limousines (toll free 800/922-0343); Executive Limousine Service (396-7733).

TAXIS: Taxis may not be hailed in the street but can be summoned by telephone; try **United Cab** (525-0521) or **Yellow Cab** (526-2121).

TRAIN: AMTRAK Station, 545 S. Main St. (526-0052; toll free 800/872-7245).

BUS: Greyhound, 203 Union Ave. (523-7676).

MISSISSIPPI CRUISES: Three- to ten-day cruises are available on the **Delta Queen** or the **Mississippi Queen,** paddlewheelers dating from the 1920s. Luxurious kitsch. See Chapter 15 on New Orleans.

INFORMATION & TOURS

TOURIST INFORMATION: The **Memphis Convention and Visitors Bureau,** 50 N. Front St., Suite 450, TN 38103 (901/576-8181).

Visitor Information Center, 207 Beale St., TN 38103 (901/526-4880).

GUIDED TOURS: **Carriage Tours of Memphis,** 422 S. Main St. (527-7542);
Offers horse-drawn carriage tours of Old Memphis; daily.
  Gray Line Tours (bus), 2050 Elvis Presley Blvd. (942-4662): Guided bus
tours of the city; serves the principal hotels.
  Memphis Queen Line (boat), Monroe Ave. at Riverside Dr. (527-5694):
Offers boat tours on board the *Memphis Queen,* daily Mar.-Dec.

SIGHTS, ATTRACTIONS, & ACTIVITIES

ARCHITECTURAL HIGHLIGHTS: 🔔 **Civic Center,** Front and 3rd Sts. between Exchange and Adams Aves.: A costly (over $60-million) modern architec-
tural complex containing most of the city and Shelby County office buildings
(Federal Building, City Hall). There's also the Vincent de Frank Music Hall,
home of the Memphis Symphony Orchestra, and the immense Cook Convention Center used year round as a convention and exposition site. Worth a look.
  🔔 **Cotton Exchange Building,** Front St. and Union Ave. (525-
  3361): Skyscraper home of the nation's—and the world's—
most important cotton exchange. Nearly half of the U.S. cotton crop is traded
here. Visits arranged by appointment only; Mon.-Fri.

HISTORIC BUILDINGS: 🔔 **Court Square,** Court St. between 2nd St. and
Mid America Mall: Heart of Memphis's urban life for more than a century, this
pretty little square with its refreshing oases of green is surrounded by some of the
oldest and most interesting buildings in the city; the **Porter Building,** the **Tennessee Club Building,** and the **Lincoln American Tower** are especially noteworthy. Definitely not to be overlooked.
  ☼🔔 **Graceland,** 3797 Elvis Presley Blvd. (332-3322): For 20 years
  the home of Elvis Presley until his death on Aug. 16, 1977, at
the age of 42. The "King's" mansion features a lovely columned portico. The
graves of Elvis and his parents are in the nearby garden of meditation. Every year
a good half million tourists visit the museum, where an almost infinite number of
Presley souvenirs are on display. The whole is a triumph of artistic kitsch (note
especially the cast-iron entrance gate). Open daily Mar.-Oct. and every day but
Tuesday during the rest of the year. This is a must-see, whether or not you are an
Elvis fan.
  🔔 **Lorraine Motel,** 406 Mulberry St.: Site of the assassination of
  Dr. Martin Luther King, Jr., on Apr. 4, 1968, the motel is now
a memorial to the former civil rights leader and winner of the Nobel Peace Prize.
Undergoing renovation.
  ☼🔔 **Orpheum Theater,** 89 Beale St. (525-3000): A former movie
  house and vaudeville theater built in 1928. Superb rococo
décor, wonderfully restored, complete with large crystal chandeliers and a
mighty Wurlitzer. These days, the theater hosts musical comedies and various
other theatrical events.
  🔔 **Sun Recording Studio,** 706 Union Ave. (521-0664): Back in
  the 1950s singer Elvis Presley cut his first record in this studio.
Johnny Cash, Jerry Lee Lewis, and other famous pop stars also recorded here.
The Studio is now owned by Elvis Presley Enterprises. Of interest to rock fans.
Visits are by appointment only.
  Victorian Village (see "Strolls," below).

INDUSTRIAL TOURS: **Stroh Brewing Co.,** 5151 E. Raines Rd. (797-2331): Tour of the brewery and free beer-tasting. Open Mon.-Fri. year round. Pleasant Visitors Center shaped like an old Mississippi paddlewheeler.

MONUMENTS: ▲ *Memphis Belle,* Mud Island, access by monorail from Front St. (576-7241): On display is a World War II B-17 bomber, the first to finish 25 missions in the European theater before returning to the States. Worth seeing, especially for history lovers.

MUSEUMS OF ART: ▲ **Dixon Gallery and Gardens,** 4339 Park Ave. (761-5250): Formerly an elegant upper-class home, now a museum housing the works of French and American impressionist painters, English portraits, and historic furniture and porcelain. Surrounded by seven acres of very lovely landscaped gardens featuring outdoor sculpture and generous plantings of azaleas and camellias. Open Tues.-Sun.; closed Mon.

☼▲ **Memphis Brooks Museum of Art,** Overton Park at Poplar Ave. (722-3500): Known especially for its prestigious Samuel H. Kress Collection of valuable Italian Renaissance paintings, this lovely museum also has interesting contemporary American art, and European painting and sculpture from the 17th through the 19th centuries. Free Sun. concerts; also films on the history of art. Don't miss it. Open Tues.-Sun.; closed Mon.

☼▲ **National Ornamental Metal Museum,** 347 W. California Ave. (774-6380): A museum of decorative arts devoted entirely to the use of metal in art and architecture. The only museum of its kind in the United States. Demonstrations of iron-working at the forge. Worth a look. Open Tues.-Sun.; closed Mon.

▲ **University Gallery,** Norriswood Ave. (454-2224): Interesting collections of African and Egyptian art. Located on the campus of Memphis State University. Open Tues.-Sun.; closed Mon.

MUSEUMS OF SCIENCE AND HISTORY: ▲ **Memphis Pink Palace Museum,** 3050 Central Ave. (454-5600): A venerable museum of local history and natural history in a beautiful building made of pink marble from Georgia (hence its name). Displays of zoological and geological interest; history of the Civil War; collection of African hunting trophies. Also a planetarium. Worth seeing. Open Tues.-Sun.; closed Mon.

☼▲ **Mississippi River Museum,** Mud Island (576-7241): Features an astonishing giant model of the Mississippi River which reproduces, exactly to scale, the final 1,000 miles (1,600 km) of the river's course to the Gulf of Mexico. This is a spectacular display, not to be missed. Open daily.

NIGHTTIME ENTERTAINMENT: ☼ ▲ **Beale Street,** between Riverside Dr. and Hernando St.: The city's principal thoroughfare (Main St.) in the early 1800s became known, a century later, as the "cradle of the Blues." Today, Beale Street is the heart of the old town's pleasure district and its ebullient nightlife. Teems with bars, restaurants, nightclubs, movie houses, and theaters. A visit to the street is imperative (see "Strolls," below).

☼▲ **Overton Square,** Madison Ave. and Cooper St.: The only place in Memphis that can challenge Beale Street in terms of swinging nightlife. Restaurants, bars, shows. (See "Strolls," below.)

PARKS AND GARDENS: ~~Dixon Gallery Gardens~~ (see "Museums of Art," above).

🔔 **Jefferson Davis Park,** Riverside Blvd. at Jefferson Ave.: A pleasant little city park offering a lovely view of the Mississippi and the **Mud Island** amusement park. Faces **Confederate Park,** one of the battlefields of the Civil War. There are fortifications dating from the war, and also a statue of Jefferson Davis, president of the Confederacy, who lived in Memphis after the war.

🔔 **Memphis Botanic Garden,** 750 Cherry Rd., Audubon Park (685-1566): This 87-acre landscape contains 12 different kinds of gardens, from a rose garden to tropical plants and a Japanese garden. Spectacular. Open daily.

PERFORMING ARTS: For current listings of shows and cultural events, consult the entertainment pages of the daily morning newspaper, *Memphis Commercial Appeal,* and the monthly *Memphis.*

Circuit Playhouse, 1705 Poplar Ave. (726-5521): Contemporary theater, comedies, and musicals. Sept.-June.

Dixon Meyers Hall, Cook Convention Center, 225 N. Main St. (523-7645): Big live concerts.

Gaslight Dinner Theater, 1110 Brooks Rd. E. (396-7474): Broadway shows. Dinner theater.

Mid-South Coliseum, Fairgrounds at E. Parkway South and Southern Ave. (274-7400): Live rock and country music concerts.

Memphis Opera, Memphis State University Campus (454-2043): Home of the city's opera company, directed by Robert Driver. Oct.-Mar.

Orpheum Theater, 89 Beale St. (525-3000): Comedies, plays, musicals, ballet. A very lovely art deco building, elegantly restored. Open all year.

Playhouse-on-the-Square, 51 S. Cooper St., at Overton Square (726-4656): Broadway hits, contemporary theater. Year round.

Memphis Theater, 630 Perkins Rd. Ext. (682-8323): Contemporary and classical theater. Sept.-June.

Vincent de Frank Music Hall, Cook Convention Center, 225 Main St. (454-2043): Home of the Memphis Symphony Orchestra, under principal conductor Alan Balter. Sept.-May.

SPECIAL EVENTS: For exact dates, consult the **Memphis Visitor Information Center** (see "Tourist Information," above).

Memphis in May International Festival (May to early June): An entire month of artistic and cultural events dedicated to a different country each year.

Great River Carnival (June): Parades, dances, concerts, regattas. Very colorful.

Elvis Presley International Tribute Week (Aug.): A week long celebration of the myth and music of Elvis Presley.

Memphis Music Festival (Sept.): Jazz, blues, rock, and country music is performed in legendary Beale Street's many bars and restaurants.

Mid-South Fair (late Sept. to early Oct.): Renowned agricultural and commercial fair. Features the largest rodeo east of the Mississippi.

Liberty Bowl Football Classic (Dec.): One of the big events of the college football season.

SPORTS: Memphis has minor-league teams in two sports:
Baseball (Apr.-Oct.): Chicks, Tim McCarver Stadium (272-1687).
Football (Feb.-June): Showboats, Liberty Bowl Stadium (685-7469).

STROLLS: ☼ ♨ **Beale Street,** between Riverside Dr. and Hernando St.: The "cradle of the Blues." Made world-famous by W. C. Handy, composer of "Memphis Blues" and "St. Louis Blues," who lived on Beale Street in the early 20th century. At Beale and 3rd Streets you'll find **W. C. Handy Park** and the monument memorializing the composer. A monument to the late "King" of Rock is located nearby in **Elvis Presley Plaza.** This colorful section of the city bustles with activity generated by its many bars, restaurants, boutiques, and theaters. Must not be missed. (See also "Nighttime Entertainment," above.)

♨ **Mid America Mall,** between the Civic Center and Beale St.: Flanked by stores and skyscrapers, this street in the heart of the business district is reserved for pedestrian traffic. There are gardens and examples of modern sculpture. Very lively by day, often deserted at night. Worth a look.

☼♨ **Overton Square,** Madison Ave. and Cooper St.: Charming section of the old town, cleverly restored. You'll find oldtime stores, outdoor cafés, restaurants. One of the bastions of Memphis nightlife. Absolutely deserves a visit. (See also "Nighttime Entertainment," above.)

☼♨♨ **Victorian Village,** in the vicinity of 600 Adams Ave.: Delicious 19th-century architectural relic from the days when cotton was still "white gold," and Memphis its capital. The Village contains 20 or so remarkable old buildings, most now classified as historic monuments. Among the more noteworthy are: **Fontaine House,** 680 Adams Ave. (526-1469), open daily, a perfect example of the Second Empire style dating from 1870; **Magevney House,** 198 Adams Ave. (526-4464), open Tues.-Sat., the oldest building in Memphis, built in 1831 for Irish immigrant Eugene Magevney as recompense for his services as the city's first schoolteacher; and the **Mallory-Neely House,** 652 Adams Ave. (523-1484), open daily, an elegant Victorian residence in the Italian style, dating from 1852. All these buildings have been painstakingly restored with period furniture and décor. A visit to the Victorian Village is a must for those who enjoy beautiful architecture.

THEME PARKS: ♨ **Adventure River Water Park,** I-40 NW and Whitten Rd. (382-9283): Huge 25-acre park featuring aquatic attractions such as an oversize pool with waves for surf-lovers, giant slides, and swimming pools for children. Open every day from June to the end of Aug., weekends only in May and Sept.; closed the rest of the year.

♨ **Libertyland,** Fairgrounds at Central Ave. and East Pkwy. (274-1776): This unusual amusement park salutes our nation's past from the colonial period to the 1900s. Open daily mid-June to mid-Aug.; weekends only, Apr. to mid-June and mid-Aug. to late Sept.; closed the rest of the year.

☼♨♨ **Mud Island,** 125 N. Front St. (576-7241): On this island in the middle of the Mississippi are 50 acres of gardens, exhibitions, and an immense museum devoted to "Ol' Man River." (See the **Mississippi River Museum** in "Museums of Science and History," above.) Accessible by monorail from Front Street. With its numerous restaurants, bars, shops, shows, and exhibitions, the island is a lively place, especially in the evening. Open daily year round; hours vary.

ACCOMMODATIONS
See the listing of toll-free numbers in the Appendix.

Room Rates in Memphis	
B (Budget)	up to $30
I (Inexpensive)	$30–$60
M (Moderate)	$60–$90
E (Expensive)	$90–$140
VE (Very Expensive)	$140 and up

Personal Favorites (in order of preference)

Peabody (dwntwn), 149 Union Ave., TN 38103 (901/529-4000; toll free, see Preferred). 452 rms, A/C, color TV, in-rm movies. AE, CB, DC, MC, V. Valet parking $8, pool, sauna, health club, three rests. (including Chez Philippe), three bars, 24-hr rm svce, disco, hrdrsr, shops, free crib, concierge. *Note:* Fabulous luxury hotel dating from 1869, rebuilt in 1925 and recently restored to its former splendor. Elegant and comfortable. Resplendent entrance hall in Renaissance style w. colonnades and a marble fountain where ducks (symbol of the Peabody) swim and preen themselves. Exemplary svce. One of the best in the Deep South. A designated historic monument. **E–VE**

Radisson (dwntwn), 185 Union Ave., TN 38103 (901/528-1800; toll free, see Radisson). 283 rms, A/C, cable color TV. AE, CB, DC, MC, V. Parking $4, pool, health club, bar, rest. (The Veranda), rm svce, disco, crib $10. *Note:* Architecturally, a very pleasing blend of an ultramodern 11-story building w. a lovely old façade of the original historic building. Spectacular six-story lobby w. waterfalls and a winter garden. Comfortable, spacious rms; attentive svce. Good rest. offering Créole cuisine. Big business clientele because of the proximity of the financial district. Free bkfst. Free airport transportation. An excellent place to stay. **M–E**

Ramada Inn Convention Center (nr. dwntwn), 160 Union Ave., TN 38103 (901/525-5491; toll free, see Ramada). 190 rms, A/C, color TV, in-rm movies. AE, CB, DC, MC, V. Free parking, pool, rest. (Seasons), bar, rm svce, free crib. *Note:* Located in the heart of Memphis, this large modern motel is quite comfortable but without any distinctive appeal. Most of the guests are business people, for whom a special VIP floor is reserved. Spacious rms. **M–E**

Holiday Inn Overton Square (nr. dwntwn), 1837 Union Ave., TN 38104 (901/278-4100; toll free, see Holiday Inns). 143 rms, A/C, color TV, in-rm movies. AE, CB, DC, MC, V. Free parking, pool, rest. (Piper's), bar, room svce, free crib. *Note:* Modern eight-story motel nr. Overton Square and its nightlife. Functional comfort in typical Holiday Inn style. Good value. **I–M**

Best Western Riverbluff Inn (nr. dwntwn), 340 W. Illinois Ave., TN 38106 (901/948-9005; toll free, see Best Western). 99 rms, A/C, color TV, in-rm movies. AE, CB, DC, MC, V. Free parking, pool, rest. (Riverview), bar, rm svce, free crib. *Note:* Pleasant little motel on the banks of the Mississippi. The rms are spacious and comfortable; some have refrigerators. Friendly reception and svce. Good value. Lovely view of the Memphis skyline. **I–M**

    Admiral Benbow Inn Midtown (nr. dwntwn), 1220 Union Ave., TN 38104 (901/725-0630; toll free 800/321-2949). 190 rms, A/C, color TV, in-rm movies. AE, CB, DC, MC, V. Free parking, pool, rest., bar, rm svce. *Note:* Excellent value within 5 min. of dwntwn. Functional comfort, congenial svce. A very good place to stay. **I**

Other Hotels (from top bracket to budget)

    French Quarter Inn (nr. dwntwn), 2144 Madison Ave., TN 38103 (901/728-4000). 69 suites, A/C, color TV, in-rm movies. AE, CB, DC, MC, V. Free parking, health club, rest. (Café Toulouse), bar, 24-hr rm svce. *Note:* Small luxury hotel w. suites only, spacious and comfortable, w. mini-bars; some have private balconies. The rest. offers very acceptable Créole cooking. Personalized svce. Close by is Overton Square w. its shops and nightlife. Favored by those in-the-know. **E**

    Holiday Inn Crowne Plaza (dwntwn), 250 N. Main St., TN 38104 (901/527-7300; toll free, see Holiday Inns). 406 rms, A/C, color TV, in-rm movies. AE, CB, DC, MC, V. Valet parking $5, pool, sauna, health club, rest. (Chervil's), coffeeshop, two bars, rm svce, disco, shops, free crib. *Note:* Brand-new, centrally located 18-story hotel w. a view of the Mississippi. Beautiful contemporary design. Nothing is wanting in comfort and facilities. Spacious rooms w. balconies; most have refrigerators as well. Efficient svce; good rest. Caters to business people and groups; VIP floor. Direct access to Convention Center. **M–E**

    Hyatt Regency Memphis (vic.), 939 Ridge Lake Blvd., TN 38119 (901/761-1234; toll free, see Hyatt). 380 rms, A/C, color TV, in-rm movies. AE, CB, DC, MC, V. Free parking, pool, health club, rest. (Ducks & Co.), bar, rm svce, disco, free crib. *Note:* A 28-story circular tower made of glass designed by architect John Portman; locals call it "the glass silo." The décor is futuristic and rather chilly. Comfort and facilities are impeccable. Inviting rms with mini-bars. Good svce, so-so rest. Caters to business people and groups. 20 min. from dwntwn, 10 from the airport. **M–E**

    Sheraton Memphis Hotel (dwntwn), 300 N. 2nd St., TN 38105 (901/525-2511; toll free, see Sheraton). 243 rms, A/C, color TV, in-rm movies. AE, CB, DC, MC, V. Free parking, pool, rest., bar, rm svce, free crib. *Note:* Another favorite of business travelers, a few steps from the Convention Center. Comfortable and functional; recently renovated. Reception and svce no more than adequate. VIP floor. **M–E**

    Days Inn Downtown (formerly the Benchmark; dwntwn), 164 Union Ave., TN 38103 (901/527-4100; toll free, see Days Inns). 110 rms, A/C, color TV, in-rm movies. AE, MC, V. Free parking, rest., bar, rm svce, disco, hrdrsr, free crib. *Note:* Friendly, relatively modern hotel in the heart of the dwntwn area. Spacious rms, cheerful svce. An excellent value. **I–M**

    La Quinta Medical Center (nr. dwntwn), 42 S. Camilla St., TN 38104 (901/526-1050; toll free, see La Quinta). 130 rms, A/C, color TV, in-rm movies. AE, CB, DC, MC, V. Free parking, pool, adjoining 24-hr coffeeshop, valet svce, free crib. *Note:* This is the classic modern motel, comfortable and functional. Spacious rms, efficient svce. Ideal for those traveling by car. 8 min. from dwntwn. Recently renovated. **I**

    Rodeway Inn West (nr. dwntwn), 271 Alston Ave., TN 38106 (901/946-3301; toll free, see Rodeway Inns). 147 rms, A/C, color TV, in-rm movies. AE, CB, DC, MC, V. Free parking, pool, sauna, rest. (Riverside), bar. *Note:* Standard motel 8 min. from dwntwn and two steps from the industrial district of Presidents Island. Good value. **I**

    Travelodge Downtown (dwntwn), 265 Union Ave., TN 38103 (901/527-4305; toll free, see Travelodge). 74 rms, A/C, color TV. AE, CB, DC, MC, V. *Note:* Modest, unpretentious motel. Functional comfort w. no frills. A stone's throw from the Greyhound bus terminal. **I**

Airport Accommodations

    Winchester Plaza (vic.), 2201 Winchester Rd., TN 38116 (901/345-6251). 209 rms, A/C, color TV, in-rm movies. AE, CB, DC, MC, V. Free parking, health club, rest. (Fitzgeralds's), bar, rm svce, disco, free airport limo, free crib. *Note:* Very comfortable large motel nr. the airport, and 5 min. by car from Graceland. Spacious rooms w. balconies. Reception and svce are cheerful. Good value. **I**

RESTAURANTS

Memphis Restaurant Prices	
(per person, excluding drinks and service charges)	
B (Budget)	up to $15
I (Inexpensive)	$15–$25
M (Moderate)	$25–$40
E (Expensive)	$40–$60
VE (Very Expensive)	$60 and up

Personal Favorites (in order of preference)

    Chez Philippe (dwntwn), in the Peabody Hotel (see "Accommodations," above) (529-4188). A/C. Dinner only, Mon.-Sat.; closed Sun. AE, CB, DC, MC, V. Jkt. *Specialties:* warm salad of lobster prepared w. truffle butter, pigeon breast w. pears, medaillons of venison w. Pommard, roast veal w. morel mushrooms. Excellent wine list. *Note:* The cooking of Chez Philippe's young chef José Gutierrez is a miracle of creativity and balance. The rest.'s luxurious décor w. its painted trompe-l'oeil murals, crystal chandeliers, and sumptuous tableware is a feast for the eye. Svce is highly polished, and the total effect is close to perfection. This is the most prestigious rest. in Memphis, as your check will demonstrate. *French.* **E**

    Rendezvous (dwntwn), 52 S. 2nd St. (General Washburn Alley) (523-2746). A/C. Dinner only, Tues.-Sat. (until midnight); closed Sun. and Mon.; also two weeks late July and two weeks late Dec. AE, CB, DC, MC, V. *Specialties:* fantastic barbecued beef and pork. Beer but no wine. *Note:* Picturesque basement rest. which puts you in mind of a country general store; "decorated" with a profusion of posters, furnishings, and souvenirs of the Old South. The atmosphere is relaxed and the svce diligent. An excellent bet, right in the heart of Memphis. *American.* **I**

    Folk's Folly (vic.), 51 S. Mendenhall Rd. (767-8200). A/C. Dinner only, nightly; closed holidays. AE, CB, DC, MC,

V. Jkt. *Specialties:* broiled prime beef, Créole-style vegetables. *Note:* The biggest and the best steaks in Memphis. Pleasant décor and atmosphere. Very popular with locals. Resv. advised. 25 min. by car from dwntwn. *Steak.* **I–M**

☼♈ **Leonard's** (nr. dwntwn), 1140 S. Bellevue Blvd. (948-1581). A/C. Lunch daily (until 5 p.m.), dinner Thurs.-Sat. (until 8 p.m.). MC, V. *Specialties:* barbecued pork ribs and shoulders, lemon ice-box pie. *Note:* A Memphis tradition since 1932. Every day hordes of hungry patrons gather to devour mountains of superb barbecued pork ribs piled on platters by Leonard's comely waitresses. The décor is rustic and unpretentious. No resv. An experience not to be missed. *American.* **B–I**

♈ **Pete and Sam's** (nr. dwntwn), 3886 Park Ave. (458-0694). A/C. Lunch/dinner daily. AE, DC, MC, V. *Specialties:* steak, homemade pasta, pizza, classic Italian dishes. *Note:* Overall, one of the best values in all of Memphis. The cooking is honest and solid, and the price very reasonable. Resv. advised. *Italian.* **B–I**

Other Restaurants (from top bracket to budget)

♈♈♈ **Justine's** (nr. dwntwn), 919 Coward Pl. (527-3815). A/C. Dinner only, Mon.-Sat.; closed Sun. and holidays. AE, CB, DC, MC, V. J&T. *Specialties:* vichyssoise, crabmeat Justine, pompano Claudet, tournedos béarnaise, trout Marguéry, rum-cream pie. *Note:* Superb classic French cuisine, elegant vintage décor (the building dates from 1843), surrounded by beautiful gardens. Patrons can dine outdoors in good weather. One of the best rests. in the Deep South. Irreproachable svce. Resv. are indispensable. Valet parking. *French.* **M–E**

♈♈ **Dux** (dwntwn), in the Peabody Hotel (see "Accommodations," above) (529-4199). A/C. Breakfast/lunch/dinner daily. AE, CB, DC, MC, V. Jkt. *Specialties:* smoked catfish w. coriander, mussel-and-clam stew, filet of pork in mustard, scallops of veal sautéed in cream, fish of the day, and prime beef broiled over a wood fire. Delicious desserts. The menu changes frequently. *Note:* A rest. of palatial elegance and cooking of the first order. Lovely rococo décor, exemplary svce. Very "in" for business lunches. Dux's success makes resv. advisable. *Continental-seafood.* **I–M**

♈♈ **Four Flames** (nr. dwntwn), 1085 Poplar Ave. (526-3181). A/C. Dinner only Mon.-Sat.; closed Sun. and holidays. AE, CB, DC, MC, V. Jkt. *Specialties:* barbecued oysters, chateaubriand bouquetière, flaming desserts. *Note:* Charming 150-year-old planter's residence converted into a rest. Good southern cooking. Attentive svce. Resv. advised. *Continental-American.* **I**

♈♈ **Grisanti's** (vic.), 1489 Airways Blvd. (458-2648). A/C. Lunch Mon.-Fri., dinner Mon.-Sat.; closed Sun. and holidays. AE, DC, MC, V. Jkt. *Specialties:* fresh homemade pasta, cannelloni alla Gusi, veal cutlets milanese, steaks. Good wine list. *Note:* A Memphis favorite since 1909. The best local Italian rest. Resv. advised. Big John Grisanti, the owner, is a legendary local institution. *Italian.* **I**

♈ **Captain Bilbo's** (dwntwn), 263 Wagner Pl. (526-1966). A/C. Dinner nightly. AE, MC, V. *Specialties:* Maine lobsters, fish and oysters from the Gulf of Mexico, gumbo, prime cuts. *Note:* Pleasant seafood rest. located in an old warehouse overlooking the Mississippi. Appropriate nautical décor. Relaxed atmosphere. Friendly bar, live music every evening. *Seafood.* **I**

♈ **Formosa** (nr. dwntwn), 3735 Summer Ave. (323-4819). A/C. Dinner only, Tues.-Sun.; closed Mon. MC, V. *Specialties:* fried wonton, hot-and-sour soup, Chinese sausage w. shallots, 100-flower chicken, Mongol beef, scallops Kung Pao. *Note:* One of the few praiseworthy Oriental rests. in Memphis. Generally noisy and crowded. Svce somewhat curt. Resv. advised. *Chinese*. **B–I**

🍷 **Molly's La Casita** (nr. dwntwn), 2006 Madison Ave. (726-1873). A/C. Lunch/dinner daily. AE, CB, DC, MC, V. *Specialties:* tacos al carbon, burritos, chiles rellenos, enchiladas, tamales verdes. *Note:* One of the best places in town for aficionados of authentic Mexican cuisine. Pleasant atmosphere, typical but pretty décor. Very popular locally. Other location: 4972 Park Ave. (685-1616). *Mexican*. **B–I**

☼🍷 **Buntyn** (nr. dwntwn), 3070 Southern Ave. (458-8776). A/C. Lunch/dinner Mon.-Fri. (until 8 p.m.); closed Sat. and Sun. No credit cards. *Specialties:* fried chicken, meatloaf, fried catfish, Waldorf salad, special house-style vegetables, banana pudding, cobblers. *Note:* In spite of its unappealing neon and Formica décor, this immensely popular rest. has continued to attract faithful followers for over 40 years. Its southern-style fried chicken and platters of house-style vegetables are themselves worth a visit. No resv. accepted. *American*. **B**

Cafeterias/Fast Food

Morrison's (nr. dwntwn), 1331 Union Ave. (726-0969). Lunch/dinner daily (until 7 p.m.). *Specialties:* roast beef, daily specials, sandwiches. *Note:* Popular locally. For other locations, consult the local telephone directory.

BARS & NIGHTCLUBS

Alfred's (dwntwn), 197 Beale St. (525-3711). Popular downtown rock-and-roll spot. Nightly.

☼ **Blues Alley** (dwntwn), 60 Front St. (523-7144). Blues and jazz every night. An authentic local institution reminiscent of the smoke-filled saloons of blues king W. C. Handy's time. Also a rest. of sorts.

Mallards (dwntwn), in the Peabody Hotel (see "Accommodations," above) (529-4140). Very popular bar. Live jazz. Also a laudable rest. Open nightly.

Handy Hall (dwntwn), 174 Beale St. (528-0150). A showcase for veteran blues musicians.

Rum Boogie Café (dwntwn), 182 Beale St. (528-0150). Very popular jazz-rest. club. Open nightly.

T.G.I. Friday's (nr. dwntwn), 2115 Madison Ave. (725-7737). Bar-disco. Nice atmosphere. Open nightly until 1:30 a.m. Attractive Victorian-kitsch décor. Also very acceptable rest.

NEARBY EXCURSIONS

☼🔺🔺 **CHUCALISSA INDIAN VILLAGE** (Mitchell Rd., 10 mi., 16 km, SW on U.S. 61) (785-3160): Indian village dating from approximately 900 A.D. and mysteriously abandoned six centuries later. Numerous dwellings have been re-created based on the findings of ongoing archeological excavations; interesting museum of Choctaw arts and crafts. Well worth the trip. Open Tues.-Sun.

FARTHER AFIELD

☼🔺 **SHILOH NATIONAL MILITARY PARK** (230 mi., 368 km, round trip via U.S. 64 E. and Tenn. 22 S and return): Site of the first major land battle of the Civil War, April 6–7, 1862. Northern troops under Gen. Ulysses S. Grant won out after confused and unusually bloody combat—24,000 men were reported dead, wounded, or missing. Films are shown at the military museum, and visitors can take a self-guided 10-mi. (16-km) automobile tour of the battlefield. The surrounding countryside is lovely; of particular interest are the numerous tumuli from the pre-Columbian era. For history buffs. The Visitor Center is open daily (901/689-5275).

HOT SPRINGS NATIONAL PARK (396 mi., 634 km, round trip on I-40W, I-30W, and U.S. 70W and return): One of the most famous and popular in the United States. Well before Spanish explorer Hernando de Soto "discovered" the springs in 1541, Native Americans recognized their healing powers and revered the place as holy. Proclaimed a federal reservation in 1832 by the U.S. Congress and promoted in 1921 to the status of a national park, the springs and the picturesque charm of their locale annually attract hundreds of thousands of visitors seeking treatment for rheumatic and nervous conditions. Every day about a million gallons (4 million liters) of water gush forth, at a temperature of 143°F (62°C), from the 47 separate hot springs within the park. The surrounding countryside with its lakes and wooded mountains is very lovely. The Visitor Center at Reserve and Central Avenues is open daily (toll free 800/272-2081). Definitely worth the trip.

Where to Stay Near the Park

Arlington Resort, P.O. Box 5652, Central Ave. at Fountain St., Hot Springs, AR 71901 (501/623-7771; toll free 800/ 643-1502). 490 rms. A luxury hotel dating from the '20s, pleasingly renovated. **I–M**

Buena Vista, Buena Vista Dr., Rte. 3, Box 175, Hot Springs, AR 71913 (501/525-1321; toll free 800/255-9030), 4 mi. (6.5 km) south on Ark. 7S. 40 rms w. kitchenettes. Very pleasant motel on the shores of Lake Hamilton. **I–M**

Where to Eat

Hamilton House, 130 Van Lyell Dr. (501/525-2727), 6 mi. (10 km) south on Ark. 7S. Dinner only, nightly. Elegant antique décor, on the shores of Lake Hamilton. *Continental.* **I–M**

NASHVILLE (420 mi., 672 km round trip on I-40E and return): The capital of Country Music. Worth a visit. For details, see Chapter 13 on Nashville. Might well be combined with a visit to Shiloh National Military Park (see above).

CHAPTER 15

NEW ORLEANS 🎷🎷

□ □ □

And the Mississippi Delta

Birthplace of Louis Armstrong and Sidney Bechet, this most French of U.S. cities was founded in 1718 by Jean Baptiste Le Moyne, sieur de Bienville, Governor of Louisiana. Named in honor of Philippe, Duke of Orléans, Regent of France at the time, the city nowadays presents a fascinating fusion of races and cultures.

By turns French, Spanish, then French again, and finally sold to the U.S. in 1803 by Napoléon I under the terms of the Louisiana Purchase, the city has harmoniously blended its "Créole" inheritance from the first French and Spanish settlers with the "Cajun" influence of Acadian refugees from Canada in 1755, and has subsequently added dashes of Italian, Caribbean, German, Irish, and black. As a result, what was 250 years ago a village of trappers and gold prospectors is now a cosmopolitan city that has retained its liking for the open sea (its port is second in the U.S. only to New York City's) and for good food (New Orleans, New York, and San Francisco are the country's gastronomic capitals), as well as an inimitably attractive lifestyle. Beloved by European tourists, the "Gateway of the Mississippi" can claim, among its other distinctions, to have invented jazz. (Originally spelled "jass," the word had an indelicate significance in Créole, having to do with sexual intercourse; later it came to denote a kind of African dance.) As for its famous **Mardi Gras,** a festival of 19th-century origin lasting several weeks, its only rival anywhere in the world is the Carnival in Rio.

With its cobbled streets, balustraded old houses, flower-filled courtyards, and wrought-iron balconies, the **French Quarter (Vieux Carré,** literally "Old Square") is an architectural unity of a kind rare in North America. The strolling visitor will chance, unexpectedly but delightfully, on Mississippi docks that haven't changed since the days of the showboats; on the friendly crowds of **Jackson Square,** historic heart of the French Quarter, with its painters and street musicians; on 150-year-old bars still haunted by the memory of the pirate Jean Lafitte; on the authentic tradition of Dixieland in venerable **Preservation Hall;** on the impressive 1795 **Cabildo,** once the Spanish governor's palace, now a museum; on the slightly motheaten strip joints of Bourbon St., New Orleans's hot strip. To say nothing of those landmarks of local gastronomy, like Antoine's or Galatoire's, where the finest traditions of Créole cooking are still very much alive: oysters Rockefeller (baked and seasoned with Pernod), gumbo (a thick soup of shrimp, shellfish, crabmeat, and rice), jambalaya (an exotic mélange of rice, tomatoes, shrimps, oysters, and sausages or chicken), shrimp with sauce remoulade, bananas Foster (in liqueur, with ice cream), or pompano (a bass-like fish) en papillote, to name but a few.

Not far from the French Quarter, the delightful **Garden District,** with its old houses and aura of aristocracy, rubs shoulders with the new city created by black gold, with its inescapable high-rises including the prestigious 53-story

Place St. Charles Building and the colossal **Superdome,** which with its 90,000 seats is the world's largest indoor stadium. This huge 27-story concrete cathedral of football is entirely air-conditioned. Lovers of the picturesque will not feel that it compensates them for the disappearance of the fabled **Storyville,** a district of saloons, gaming houses, and brothels around Basin Street, which was demolished in 1917 at the request of the military, who wished to protect soldiers on leave from its temptations; its destruction was a heavy loss for "Big Easy," as jazz musicians have nicknamed the city.

The lower Mississippi Valley, and its immense delta opening onto the Gulf of Mexico, represents one of New Orleans's principal tourist attractions. Its lush vegetation of live oaks draped in Spanish moss, of creepers and water lilies; its endless network of bayous (creeks); its elegant 19th-century plantations — these make up the "Cajun country," where live 400,000 descendants of the French-speaking Acadians. There are no terms too strong for recommending a visit to this fascinating, little-known region.

The writer Truman Capote and the actress Dorothy Lamour were born here; among the great musicians who first saw daylight in "the cradle of jazz" are Red Allen, Barney Bigard, Lee Collins, Fats Domino, Baby and Johnny Dodds, Bunk Johnson, Nick Larocca, Albert Nicholas, Jelly Roll Morton — and of course, Louis Armstrong and Sidney Bechet.

FBI statistics put New Orleans near the top of the list of U.S. cities in terms of crime. It pays to be careful if you're walking alone, after dark, outside the French Quarter. Badly lit streets should always be avoided at night, especially in the area of the Bienville Housing Project, north of the French Quarter.

BASIC FACTS: State of Louisiana. Area Code: 504. Time Zone: Central Time. ZIP Code: 70140. Founded in: 1718. Approximate population: city, 550,000; metropolitan area, 1,390,000. Rank among U.S. metropolitan areas: 27th.

CLIMATE: From its proximity to the Gulf of Mexico, New Orleans derives a subtropical climate. The best time for a visit is between Oct. and March, since the winters are unusually mild (Jan. average, 53° F, 12° C), as is the autumn, with temperatures usually above 68° F (20° C) in Oct. Summer is disagreeably hot and sticky (July average, 82° F, 28° C). Between March and Sept. don't forget your raincoat and umbrella; it rains copiously and almost daily. The average annual rainfall of 60.88 in. (1,522 mm) is one of the highest in the country.

DISTANCES: Atlanta, 481 mi. (770 km); Dallas, 493 mi. (790 km); Houston, 356 mi. (570 km); Memphis, 390 mi. (625 km); Tampa, 633 mi. (1,012 km).

ARRIVAL & TRANSIT INFORMATION

AIRPORT: New Orleans International Airport (MSY), 12 mi. (19 km) NW. Information: 464-0831.

AIRLINES: American (523-2188), Continental (581-2965), Delta (529-2431), Eastern (524-4211), Northwest (525-0423), Southwest (523-5683), TWA (529-2585), United (toll free 800/241-6522), USAir (toll free 800/428-4322).

CITY LINK: The cab fare to city center is about $20; time, about 25–30 min.

Bus: **Orleans Transportation Service** (464-0611), leaves every 30 min., serving principal downtown hotels; fare, $8; time, 45 min.

The public transportation system by bus and streetcar is efficient and cheap; particularly useful are the **Central Business District Shuttle** and the **Vieux Carré Shuttle,** which operate only on working days. For information, call the Regional Transit Authority (569-2600).

If your visit is to be confined to the French Quarter and the Central Business District, you won't need to rent a car; on the other hand, if you follow my emphatic advice and travel to the "bayou" and plantation country, to Lake Pontchartrain, or to the shores of the Gulf of Mexico, you will.

CAR RENTAL (at the airport unless otherwise noted): Avis (464-9511); Budget (464-0311); Dollar (468-3643); Hertz (468-3695); National (466-4335); Thrifty, 1415 Airline Hwy., in Kenner (467-8796). For downtown locations, consult the local telephone directory.

LIMOUSINE SERVICES: Carey Limousines (523-5466), Dav El Limousines (toll free 800/922-0343), Cappel Limo Service (288-4696).

TAXIS: Taxis may be hailed on the street, taken from the waiting lines in front of the major hotels, or summoned by telephone. Fares are relatively low within the city limits. Recommended companies: Checker-Yellow Cabs (525-3311), Liberty Bell Cabs (822-5974), United Cabs (522-9771).

TRAIN: AMTRAK, Union Station, 1001 Loyola Ave. (525-1179).

BUS: Greyhound, 2101 Earhart Blvd. (525-9371).

MISSISSIPPI CRUISES: Three- to ten-day cruises on the Mississippi, Ohio, and Cumberland Rivers, aboard the *Delta Queen* or the *Mississippi Queen,* paddle-steamers built in the 1920s. Luxurious kitsch. For information, contact the **Delta Queen Steamboat Co.,** 30 Robin St. Wharf, New Orleans, LA 70130 (toll free 800/543-1949).

INFORMATION & TOURS

TOURIST INFORMATION: The Greater New Orleans Tourist and Convention Commission, 1520 Sugar Bowl Dr., LA 70112 (504/566-5011).

Jean Lafitte National Historical Park Visitor Center, French Market, 916 N. Peters St. (504/589-2636): Organizes a series of different daily walking tours of the French Quarter. Art exhibitions, concerts, audio-visual shows, etc.

Welcome Visitor Center, 529 St. Ann St. (504/568-5661): Also information on Louisiana and the Cajun country.

GUIDED TOURS: The Canal Street Ferry (boat), at the foot of Canal St.: Free Mississippi crossing; fine view of river and city. Last ferry leaves from the Canal St. terminal at 9:30 p.m.

Créole Queen Cruises (boat), Poydras St. Wharf (524-0814): Trips along the Mississippi to the battlefield of Chalmette; nightly jazz dinners aboard the *Créole Queen,* newest of the Mississippi paddlewheelers. Daily.

Cypress Swamp Tours (boat), 622 Napoleon Ave. (899-2027): Three-hour boat trip along the bayous, all among the tropical vegetation and the alligators. Spectacular; don't miss it. Daily.

Gay '90s Carriages (carriage), 1824 N. Rampart St. (943-8820): Carriage tour of the French Quarter leaving from Jackson St. Picturesque.

Gray Line Tours (bus), 1793 Julia St. (581-7222): Conducted tours of city and surroundings; serves principal dwntown hotels.

New Orleans Steamboat Co. (boat), Jackson Brewery, Decatur and St. Peter Sts. (586-8777): Mississippi and bayou trips aboard the paddlewheeler *Natchez* or *Jean Lafitte;* dinners with dancing aboard the riverboat *President,* the largest floating dance hall on the river. Daily.

Southern Seaplane (seaplane), 1 Coquille Dr., Belle Chasse (394-5633): Discover the city, Lake Pontchartrain, and the bayous as seen from above. Spectacular.

Saint Charles Avenue Streetcar (streetcar): Follows the route of Tennessee Williams' famous *Streetcar Named Desire;* you can visit the charming Garden District with its lovely old houses. Opened in 1835, this 13-mi.- (21-km-) long streetcar line is one of the oldest in the world. It's wiser not to ride it at night. Fare: 60 cents.

SIGHTS, ATTRACTIONS, & ACTIVITIES

ADVENTURES: **Honey Island Swamp Tours** (boat), 106 Holly Ridge Dr., in Slidell, 24 mi. (38 km) NE on I-10 (641-1769): Two-hour conducted tour into the heart of one of the country's wildest, remotest wetlands. Fascinating.

ARCHITECTURAL HIGHLIGHTS: 🔔 **Civic Center,** bounded by La Salle and Poydras Sts. and Loyola and Tulane Aves.: Heart of the **Central Business District,** with interesting high-rise buildings and the imposing 11-story **City Hall.** Worth a look.

🔔 **Loyola University,** 6363 St. Charles Ave. (865-3240): This highly regarded Catholic university dates from 1912, and has some fine Tudor Gothic buildings. Campus visits by appointment.

🔔 **Superdome,** Sugar Bowl Dr. (587-3810): Largest enclosed stadium in the world, with 90,000 seats; air-conditioned throughout. Scene every year of the famous Sugar Bowl. The dome is 262 ft. (80 m) high and 678 ft. (207 m) across. Absolutely riveting. Tours daily.

🔔 **World Trade Center,** 2 Canal St. (525-2185): A 33-story high-rise overlooking the harbor, with the offices of many international corporations as well as foreign consulates. The observation platform on the 31st floor and the revolving bar on the 33rd floor have a wonderful view of the French Quarter and the river. A definite must-see.

CHURCHES/SYNAGOGUES: 🔔 **Old Ursuline Convent,** Chartres and Ursuline Sts. (592-2001): This Ursuline convent, dating from 1745, once housed an orphanage as well as the city's first school for black children. Today it is the presbytery and record house of the adjoining Italian church of St. Mary's. It has been recently restored. Worth seeing; open to visitors Wed. afternoon only.

🔔 **St. Louis Cathedral,** Jackson Square (525-9585): Built in 1794 on the site of two earlier churches, both destroyed, this is one of the oldest Catholic cathedrals in the country. A fine classical building in the French style. Open daily.

HISTORIC BUILDINGS: ☀ 🔭 **Beauregard-Keyes House,** 1113 Chartres

(523-7257): Beautiful Greek Revival house built around 1826, now a designated historic monument. After the War Between the States, it was the home of Confederate Gen. Pierre G. T. Beauregard, and later of the novelist Frances Parkinson Keyes. Elegant patio and garden; period furniture. Don't miss it. Open Mon.-Sat.

Cabildo, 709 Chartres, at Jackson Square (568-6968): Built in 1795 as the Spanish Governor's Palace. The sale of Louisiana to the U.S. by Napoléon I (the Louisiana Purchase) was ratified here in 1803. Now houses part of the collection of the interesting **Louisiana State Museum** (maps, pictures, decorative arts), and Napoleoniana, including the emperor's authentic death mask. Don't miss it. Open Wed.-Sun.

Gallier House, 1118-1132 Royal St. (523-6722): Luxurious private house built in 1832 by architect James Gallier, with one of New Orleans's finest Victorian interiors. Open Mon.-Sat.; don't miss it.

Hermann-Grima Historic House, 820 St. Louis St. (525-5661): Plush home typical of New Orleans's "golden age" (1830–1860), with flower-planted patios, kitchens (demonstrations of Créole cooking in summer), slave quarters, and stables. Very fine old furniture; a beautiful vignette from the past. Open Mon.-Sat.

Longue Vue House and Gardens, 7 Bamboo Rd. (488-5488): Faithful 1942 replica of a great 19th-century Louisiana plantation, with lovely furniture of the period. Eight acres of magnificent garden, inspired in part by the famous Generalife at Granada in Spain. Worth seeing. Open Tues.-Sun.

Madame John's Legacy, 632 Dumaine St. (568-6968): One of the oldest houses in New Orleans; erected in 1727 and rebuilt after a fire in 1788, it was completely restored in 1981. Interesting collection of Louisianan folk art. Open Tues.-Sun.

Napoleon House, 500 Chartres St. (524-9752): Intended for Napoléon I by the mayor of New Orleans, Nicholas Girod, who had dreams of rescuing the fallen emperor from his imprisonment on St. Helena. Picturesque café on the ground floor. Worth seeing.

Old Absinthe House, 240 Bourbon St. (523-3833): The oldest and most famous bar in the Vieux Carré; here Gen. (later President) Andrew Jackson and the pirate Jean Lafitte drew up their plan for the Battle of New Orleans against the invading British. Don't miss it. (See "Bars and Nightclubs," below).

Pontalba Apartments, Jackson Square: Built in 1846–1849 by Baroness Pontalba, daughter of the last Spanish governor, these were the first apartments constructed in the U.S., in a lovely southern idiom with characteristic grace notes in wrought iron. The writer William Faulkner was among the illustrious tenants. **"The 1850 House,"** 523 St. Ann St. (568-6968), with original furniture and decoration of the period, may be visited Tues.-Sun. Another unusual museum is the **Pontalba Historical Puppetorium,** 514 St. Peter St. (522-0344), where the deeds-at-arms of the pirate Jean Lafitte, and other pages from the city's history, are portrayed by means of animated puppets. Don't miss it. Open Tues.-Sun.

Pitot House, 1440 Moss St. (482-0312): On the bank of Bayou St. John, this old plantation house once belonged to James Pitot, first elected mayor of New Orleans; dating from 1799, it is one of the last remaining examples of the Antillean style. Worth seeing. Wed.-Sat.

The Presbytère, 751 Chartres St. at Jackson Square (568-6968): Abutting on St. Louis Cathedral, this 1791 building, in the same style as but older than the Cabildo, long housed the Supreme Court under Spanish colonial administration. Now it, too, holds part of the collection of the **Louisiana State Museum,** including many articles and costumes relating to Mardi Gras, as well as fine ceramics in the Newcomb style and engravings of birds by the naturalist John James Audubon. Should not be missed.

        Preservation Hall, 726 St. Peter St. (522-2238 or 523-8939): Grandfather of jazz halls, dating from 1846. The décor is on its last legs but the ambience is incomparable. Open nightly; don't miss it.

        U.S. Custom House, Decatur and Canal Sts. (589-2997): Imposing 1848 edifice strangely blending the Greek Revival and Egyptian Revival styles. The famous marble lobby and scrupulously restored interior decoration should definitely be seen. Open Mon.-Fri.

MARKETS: ☀ ▲▲ **French Market,** N. Peters St. between Dumaine and Barracks Sts. (522-2624): A covered market dating from 1836 (the oldest portions from 1791) built on the site of an old Indian market. One of the most interesting sights of the French Quarter, with its picturesque displays of fruit and vegetables, its flea market, trinket merchants, strolling musicians, and terrace cafés, of which the legendary **Café du Monde** is open day and night. Amusing and colorful.

MONUMENTS: ▲ **Andrew Jackson Statue,** Jackson Square: This equestrian statue of Gen. Andrew Jackson, who defeated the British here in 1815, is the work of sculptor Clark Mills. It sits in the middle of the old "Place d'Armes" (Parade Ground), renamed Jackson Square when the city's best-known statue was placed here in 1856. Should be seen.

        Streetcar Named Desire, Barracks St. and French Market Place: This streetcar, which once ran along Royal St. and St. Charles Ave., was made famous in Tennessee Williams's play *A Streetcar Named Desire*. The car displayed here dates from 1906. Worth a look.

MUSEUMS OF ART: ▲ **Contemporary Arts Center,** 900 Camp St. (566-0233): Large cultural complex comprising two auditoriums and three art galleries, in a renovated former warehouse. Interesting temporary exhibitions, music recitals, shows, etc. Should be seen. Tues.-Sun.

        New Orleans Museum of Art/NOMA, Lelong Dr., City Park (488-2631): Fine Greek Revival building, inside which you'll find a remarkable microcosm of the history of art, from the primitive cultures of Asia, Africa, and the pre-Columbian Americas right down to cubism, via the great masters of the Renaissance (Samuel Kress Endowment) and a fabulous collection of Fabergé eggs. Among the best known of the works on display are Veronese's *Holy Conversation, Country House* by Monet, *Portrait of Estelle Musson* by Degas, and Max Ernst's *Everyone Here Speaks Latin*. A wealth of American art: Georgia O'Keeffe, Andy Warhol, Jacques Lipchitz, etc. Ceramic miniatures. Not to be missed; open Tues.-Sun.

MUSEUMS OF SCIENCE AND HISTORY: ☀ ▲ **Chalmette National Historical Park,** on Bernard Hwy. in Arabi, 6 mi. (10 km) east along St. Claude Ave. (277-8186): The spot where Gen. Andrew Jackson won his victory in 1815 in the last great battle of the War of 1812 against the British. Military museum and 98-ft. (30-m) memorial obelisk on the bank of the Mississippi. In the great National Cemetery adjoining lie 12,000 Union soldiers who fell during the Civil War. For history buffs. Open daily.

Confederate Museum, 929 Camp St. (523-4522): The oldest Civil War museum in Louisiana, with a memorial to Jefferson Davis, president of the Confederacy. Interesting. Open Mon.-Sat.

Historic New Orleans Collection, 533 Royal St. (523-4662): The history of Louisiana and New Orleans narrated by means of an interesting collection of maps, pictures, photographs, and historic documents displayed in two lovely old houses, **Merieult House** (1792) and the **Williams Residence** (about 1880). Temporary exhibitions. A positive must-see. Open Tues.-Sat.

Louisiana Maritime Museum, 130 Carondelet St. (581-1874): Maritime museum with a particularly remarkable collection of scale models of ships and ships' guns. Should be seen. Open Mon.-Sat.

Louisiana Science Center, Julia St. Wharf at Riverwalk (529-3622): Museum of science and astronomy opened in 1987. Visitors are invited to perform numerous scientific experiments, may program a computer, share in the sensations of an astronaut in space, or watch movies projected onto the giant screen of the IMAX Theater. Fascinating. Open daily.

Louisiana State Museum, housed in several different buildings (568-6968): Priceless historical collections going back to French and Spanish colonial times, housed in the Cabildo, The Presbytère (see above), or the Old U.S. Mint (see below). For details, see the names of the individual museums.

Old Pharmacy Museum, 514 Chartres St. (524-9077): An apothecary's store dating from 1823, "La Pharmacie Française," founded by Louis Dufilho, America's first licenced pharmacist. Very picturesque. Open Tues.–Sun.

Old U.S. Mint, 400 Esplanade Ave. (568-8213): This fascinating museum, opened in 1982, is housed in an Ionic temple which was once a mint. Displays souvenirs of the early jazz age (instruments that belonged to Louis Armstrong, Bix Beiderbecke, and the Original Dixieland Jazz Band are of special interest), and traces the evolution of the art form from its Afro-American origins to the present day. A must for all jazz fans. Also a museum of Carnival which you shouldn't miss. Open Wed.-Sun. Part of the Louisiana State Museum.

Voodoo Museum, 724 Dumaine St. (523-7685): Interesting small museum devoted to the cult of Voodoo, which commanded a large following among 19th-century black slaves, and its high priestess, the famous Marie Laveau. Should be seen. Open daily.

NIGHTTIME ENTERTAINMENT: The city which, at the beginning of the 20th century, gave birth to jazz, still proudly upholds its musical heritage, particularly in the Vieux Carré. After nightfall the quiet, slightly countrified streets of the **French Quarter** come briskly back to life. A throng of idlers moves along the brilliantly lit streets, some of which are closed to wheeled traffic, and which teem with bars, jazz clubs, and other more or less wholesome pleasure resorts. Typical is the famous **Bourbon Street:** you mustn't leave New Orleans without seeing it. For details, see "Bars and Nightclubs," below.

PANORAMAS: ⚓ **Greater New Orleans Bridge,** Pontchartrain Expwy.: Spanning the river from New Orleans to Algiers, this great work of art, constructed in 1958, is the second-largest metallic nonsuspension bridge in the country; looking north from it you have a nice view of the harbor and the Vieux Carré.

☼☖ **World Trade Center,** 2 Canal St. (525-2185): Observation platform on the 31st floor and revolving bar on the 33rd floor reached by outside glass-walled elevator. Fine view over the city, the Mississippi, and the harbor.

PARKS AND GARDENS: ☖ Audubon Park and Zoological Garden, St.

Charles Ave. opposite Tulane University (861-2537): Beautiful 400-acre park ringed with century-old oak trees, on the site of an old sugar plantation on the banks of the Mississippi. Well-known zoo with over 1,200 animals in reproductions of their natural habitats; lagoons, golf courses; picnic areas.

☼☖ **City Park,** Beauregard Circle (north of the city, almost at the edge of the great Lake Pontchartrain): In a bygone age, this is where duelists liked to settle their disputes, and on some Sundays a dozen duels were fought on the favorite ground of **Dueling Oaks.** Fine rose gardens, four public golf courses, many lagoons and lakes for canoeing. The park is almost 2½ mi. (4 km) long, and in the southern part is located the **New Orleans Museum of Art** (see above). You shouldn't fail to visit it.

☖ **Greenwood Cemetery and Metairie Cemetery,** Metairie Rd. and Pontchartrain Blvd.: Famous for their sumptuous tombs, particularly those of Gen. Stonewall Jackson and of Josie Arlington, a well-known madam who died in 1914—all standing amid magnolias and tropical trees. Should be seen—but don't go there alone.

☖ **Longue Vue Gardens,** 7 Bamboo Rd. (488-5488): Faithful reproduction of the famous Generalife Gardens at Granada (see "Historic Buildings," above). Worth a look. Open Tues.-Sun.

☖ **Louis Armstrong Park,** N. Rampart between St. Peter and St. Philip Sts.: Originally known as Congo Square and later renamed after the city's most famous jazz musician, this was once a meeting place for black slaves who came here on Sunday to dance, sing spirituals, and generally let off steam. Tradition has it that jazz was born here—where today, appropriately, stand the **Municipal Auditorium** and the **Theater for the Performing Arts.** Should be seen.

☖ **St. Louis Cemetery No. 1,** 400 Basin St.: One of the oldest cemeteries (1788) in the country, its splendid mausoleums raised well above the ground because of the high water table. Among them are those of the chessmaster Paul Morphy, and the voodoo queen Marie Laveau. Part of the movie *Easy Rider* was shot here. Don't fail to visit it—but don't venture alone into this unsafe neighborhood. Open daily.

PERFORMING ARTS: For current listings of shows and cultural events, con-

sult the entertainment pages of the daily *Times-Picayune/States-Item* (morning and evening), and the monthly *New Orleans* magazine.

Contemporary Arts Center, 900 Camp St. (523-1216): Concerts, ballet, modern and avant-garde theater.

Municipal Auditorium, 1201 St. Peter St. (587-3070): Concerts, opera, touring companies, ballet, etc. Year round.

Orpheum Theater, 129 University Pl. (525-0500): Home of the New Orleans Symphony, under principal conductor Maxim Shostakovich (Sept.-May).

Petit Théâtre du Vieux Carré / The Little Theater, 616 St. Peter St. (522-2081): The city's oldest theater (1797), with a magnificent antique interior. Drama, comedy, classical theater.

Saenger Performing Arts Center, 143 N. Rampart St. (525-1052): A 1920s movie house, an extravagant essay in the Renaissance style, now beautifully restored. Broadway hits, concerts.

Theater of the Performing Arts, 801 N. Rampart (525-7615): Home of the New Orleans City Ballet and the New Orleans Opera House Association. Also theater in the round.

SHOPPING: Canal Place, 365 Canal St. (523-4158): The city's most upscale shopping center, with 30 fashion boutiques and exclusive stores such as Gucci, Saks Fifth Avenue, and Brooks Brothers. Open Mon.-Sat.

Jackson Brewery, Decatur and St. Peter Sts. (529-1211): A 19th-century brewery transformed into a picturesque food bazaar, with more than 60 cafés, restaurants, and stores selling food and amusing gifts. Lively, likeable atmosphere. Open daily.

Magazine Street, between Canal St. and Napoleon Ave.: Charming 19th-century commercial thoroughfare with many antique shops; should be seen.

Riverwalk, Riverside between Canal and Poydras Sts. (522-1555): The newest of the great downtown shopping centers, with dozens of fashion boutiques, elegant stores, cafés, and restaurants. Has drawn crowds ever since its 1987 opening.

SPECIAL EVENTS: For exact dates, consult the **Greater New Orleans Tourist and Convention Commission** (see "Tourist Information," above).

Sugar Bowl (Jan. 1): Three days of popular celebration before the Sugar Bowl football game.

Mardi Gras (Feb.-Mar.): The only carnival of its kind in the world, and for 150 years New Orleans's most popular annual event. It celebrates Mardi Gras (literally "Fat Tuesday," but more commonly known in English as "Shrove Tuesday"), the eve of Ash Wednesday, the first day of Lent. Carnival was raised to its present level of splendor in 1857 by a secret society known as "The Mystic Krewe of Comus," and although often threatened with prohibition because of the fistfights and public disorders it occasioned, has survived in the teeth of all opposition thanks to the goodwill of 60 or so colorful associations, the "Krewes." It is these Krewes who sweep through the streets on the day of the great final parade, with their gaudy banners and frenzied bands going on before them, each following a different route. The Rex Parade, led by the King ("Rex") and followed by the mostly white Krewes, goes down St. Charles Ave. to Canal St., where the mayor of New Orleans is waiting to drink a toast with the Rex to the glory of the city. The Zulu Parade, with its "Zulu King," and the Indian Parade, both made up of black Krewes, twist and turn through the downtown streets and the suburbs, never mixing with the parade of the Rex and his subjects, the Mystic Krewe of Comus, Knights of Momus, Krewe of Porteus, Knights of Hermes, Krewe of Cronus, and the rest. But in any of the parades the costumes, masks, and floats will be magnificent, the Krewes setting no limit to their imagination and sense of humor. The Carnival season really begins in early January with an unbroken series of masked balls, parades, and torchlit processions, culminating on Shrove Tuesday in the country's greatest popular celebration. It's worth going to New Orleans just to see it.

French Quarter Festival (Apr.): Free open-air concerts, dancing in the streets, boat races on the Mississippi; the Vieux Carré's own festival.

Spring Fiesta (four days long, one week after Easter): Costume parades, public balls, art exhibitions. The city's oldest houses and the plantations in the vicinity are open to the public especially for the festival.

New Orleans Jazz and Heritage Festival (Jazzfest) (late Apr. to early May): One of the most famous of all jazz festivals, drawing the greatest performers in the medium; also rock, gospel, rhythm and blues, country and western, blues, Cajun, folk, Latin American, and African concerts—the great annual music festival.

Food Festival (late June to early July): Well-known gastronomic festival, a must for all lovers of Créole and Cajun food.

SPORTS: New Orleans boasts a professional football team:
Football (Aug.-Dec.): Saints, Superdome (587-3663).

Horseracing

The Fairgrounds, 1751 Gentilly Blvd. (944-5515); racing Wed.-Sun., Apr.-Nov. One of the oldest tracks (1872) in the country.

Jefferson Downs Racetrack, 1300 Sunset Blvd., in Kenner (466-8521). On the shore of Lake Pontchartrain. Racing Apr.-Nov.

STROLLS: ☼ 🔔 **Bourbon Street,** between Canal St. and Ursulines Ave.: On these ten blocks, New Orleans has turned sin into a pedestrian mall, with innumerable bars, nightclubs, jazz dives, strip joints, and (sometimes slightly sordid) peep shows. Noisy and colorful by night, silent and depressing by day. This is the Place Pigalle or Barbary Coast of the Old South; you should take a look.

☼ **Garden District,** around St. Charles Ave. between Jackson and Louisiana Aves.: 19th-century upper-class homes standing in delightful gardens; don't miss this page from the past. Take the picturesque St. Charles Ave. streetcar (it used to be the streetcar named Desire) from Canal St.—but don't come here after dark.

☼ 🔔🔔 **Jackson Square,** bounded by Decatur, Chartres, St. Peter, and St. Ann Sts.: The oldest public garden in New Orleans, and its historic center; in French Colonial times it was called "The Parade Ground." On it stand some of the city's most notable buildings: the Cabildo, St. Louis Cathedral, the Pontalba Apartments, the old Jackson Brewery, and others, overlooking the equestrian statue of the seventh president of the U.S., which reigns unchallenged over the square. Lively, appealing atmosphere thanks to the crowds of strollers, painters, and street musicians; don't miss it.

🔔 **Levee and Docks,** along the Mississippi between Canal St. and the Greater New Orleans Bridge: A picturesque walk along the docks of a busy commercial harbor: Banana Docks, Coffee Terminal, General Cargo Wharf, etc. For reasons of safety, smoking on the docks is forbidden. Don't come here alone after nightfall.

🔔 **Moon Walk,** along the quays in front of Jackson Square: Elevated walkway along the bank of the Mississippi, with a superb view of the heart of the French Quarter and the shipping on Ol' Man River. Owes its name not to its suitability for moonlight walks, but to a former mayor of the city, Moon Landrieu. A sight to be seen.

🔔 **Pirate's Alley,** between Chartres and Royal Sts.: Once a place of assembly for pirates and smugglers, this narrow alleyway in the shadow of the cathedral now belongs to painters and artists. Worth a look.

☼ 🔔🔔 **Royal Street,** between Esplanade Ave. and Canal St.: The Vieux Carré's smart street; almost every building on it is worth your attention: the **Gallier House** (no. 118), **Miro House** (no. 529), **Merieult House** (no. 533), **Court of Two Sisters** (no. 613), **Maison Le Monnier** (no. 640). Many boutiques, art galleries, antique shops, restaurants, etc. The first Carnival ball was held at no. 127 in 1857, thus inaugurating the Mardi Gras festival. A walk not to be missed.

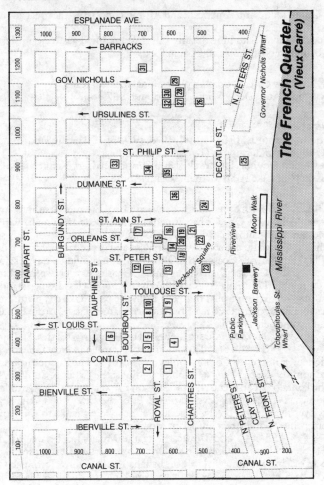

KEY TO THE NUMBERED REFERENCES ON THE FRENCH QUARTER MAP: 1. Old Bank of Louisiana; 2. Old Bank of the U.S.; 3. Old La. State Bank; 4. New Orleans Court Building; 5. Casa Faurie; 6. The Hermann House; 7. Maison Seignouret; 8. Merieult House; 9. Casa de Comercio; 10. Court of Two Lions; 11. LeMonnier House; 12. Maison de Fléchier; 13. Maison LeMonnier; 14. Spanish Arsenal; 15. LaBranche House; 16. St. Anthony's Garden; 17. Salle d'Orléans; 18. Père Antoine's Alley; 19. The Presbytère; 20. St. Louis Cathedral; 21. The Cabildo; 22. Pirates Alley; 23. Pontalba Buildings; 24. 1850 House; 25. Court of the Two Sisters; 26. Old Ursulines Convent; 27. Beauregard House; 28. Soniat House; 29. Clay House; 30. LaLaurie House; 31. Thierry House; 32. The Gallier House; 33. Lafitte's Blacksmith Shop; 34. cornstalk fence; 35. Miltenberger Houses; 36. "Madame John's Legacy."

ACCOMMODATIONS
See the listing of toll-free numbers in the Appendix.

Room Rates in New Orleans	
B (Budget)	up to $30
I (Inexpensive)	$30–$60
M (Moderate)	$60–$90
E (Expensive)	$90–$140
VE (Very Expensive)	$140 and up

Personal Favorites (in order of preference)

☼🛏🛏🛏🛏 **Omni Royal Orleans** (dwntwn), 621 St. Louis St., LA 70140 (504/529-5333; toll free, see Omni). 356 rms, A/C, color TV, in-rm movies. AE,CB, DC, MC, V. Valet parking $8, pool, health club, four rests. (including the Rib Room), three bars, 24-hr rm svce, nightclub, hrdrsr, concierge, free crib. *Note:* Splendidly situated on the site of the old St. Louis Exchange Hotel in the heart of the Vieux Carré, a stone's throw from Antoine's, Brennan's, and other landmarks of local gastronomy, as well as from the antique shops of Royal St. Luxuriously elegant 1920s-style décor and atmosphere, w. Italian marble lobby, lavish flower arrangements, and crystal chandeliers. Rms very comfortable, though a little on the small side. Excellent svce; good rests.; fabulous rooftop pool. The favorite hotel of those in-the-know. **E–VE**

🛏🛏🛏🛏 **Windsor Court** (dwntwn), 300 Gravier St., LA 70140 (504/523-6000; toll free 800/223-6800). 280 suites and 50 rms, A/C, color TV, in-rm movies. AE, CB, DC, MC, V. Valet garage $8, pool, health club, two rests. (including the Grill Room), two bars, 24-hr rm svce, nightclub, concierge, free crib. *Note:* Luxurious, ultramodern palace very nr. the French Quarter, its façade elegantly clad in pink granite, with balconies and bay windows. Well-bred interior decoration w. fine collection of old English pictures. Ultra-comfortable rms and suites with mini-bars (some w. kitchenettes) and marble bathrooms; the ultimate luxury is an underwater stereo system in the pool! Excellent luxury hotel rest.; thoughtful, polished svce; fashionable clientele. An establishment of the highest class. **E–VE**

☼🛏🛏🛏 **Pontchartrain Hotel** (nr. dwntwn), 2031 St. Charles Ave., LA 70140 (504/524-0581; toll free, see Preferred). 80 rms, A/C, cable color TV. AE, CB, DC, MC, V. Valet Garage $6, rest. (Caribbean Room), coffeeshop, bar, rm svce, free crib. *Note:* A little removed from the Vieux Carré and its nightlife, this *grande dame* of local hotels has been in the hands of its founding family, the Aschaffenburgs, for three generations. Its small size, and the high quality of its svce, make it a haven of peace, much frequented by VIPs and visiting celebrities. Elegant rms w. mini-bars and period furniture; rest. of high quality which appeals to business people for breakfast or lunch. 10 min. from dwntwn. **E–VE**

☼🛏🛏 **Soniat House** (dwntwn), 1133 Chartres St., LA 70116 (504/522-0570). 28 rms, A/C, color TV. AE, MC, V. Valet parking $10, bar, limited-menu rm svce, concierge, free breakfast. *Note:* Very lovely old 1830s dwelling house w. carriage entrance and majestic staircase. The rms or suites are huge and tastefully decorated, w. beds of hand-carved wood and period furniture. Inviting patio w. fountain and tropical plants. Personalized reception and svce. An excellent place to stay, partaking fully of the charm of the Vieux Carré. **E–VE**

Maison Dupuy (dwntwn), 1001 Toulouse St., LA 70112 (504/586-8000; toll free 800/535-9177). 196 rms, A/C, cable color TV. AE, CB, DC, MC, V. Valet garage $8, pool, health club, rest. (Le Bon Créole), bar, rm svce, nightclub, free crib. *Note:* A large hotel, modern and elegant, on the edge of the French Quarter, built around a delightful flower-planted patio w. a fountain and a heated pool. Very successful imitation-antique décor. Huge, comfortable rms w. balconies, the best overlooking the patio. Efficient svce; acceptable rest. Good value; recommended. **E**

Le Richelieu (dwntwn), 1234 Chartres St., LA 70116 (504/529-2492; toll free 800/535-9653). 88 rms, A/C, color TV. AE, CB, DC, MC, V. Free parking, pool, rest., bar, rm svce, concierge, free crib. *Note:* One of the best values in the French Quarter, the Richelieu occupies what used to be a luxurious private house belonging to an old macaroni factory. Like most hotels in the Vieux Carré it is built around an inviting interior courtyard, with big, welcoming rms tastefully decorated, and all the engaging charm of the slightly outdated. Friendly reception and svce. **M**

Château Motor Hotel (dwntwn), 1001 Chartres St., LA 70116 (504/524-9636). 40 rms, A/C, color TV. AE, CB, DC, MC, V. Free garage, pool, coffeeshop, bar, rm svce. *Note:* With its red-brick walls, its shutters and its creeper-covered façade, this winsome little hotel in the heart of the Vieux Carré offers excellent value. Largish, comfortable rms, the best overlooking the courtyard with its banana palms, azaleas, and fountain. Pleasing terrace for coffee. A good place to stay. **I–M**

La Salle Hotel (dwntwn), 1113 Canal St., LA 70112 (504/523-5831; toll free 800/521-9450). 60 rms, A/C, color TV. AE, CB, DC, MC, V. Parking (charge) next door, rm svce (breakfast only). *Note:* Small economy hotel, now half a century old, on the edge of the French Quarter. A commendable standard of comfort is maintained, though some rms lack private baths. Friendly reception; youthful clientele. Ideal for budget travelers. **I**

Other Hotels (from top bracket to budget)

Fairmont (formerly the Roosevelt; dwntwn), University Pl., LA 70140 (504/529-7111; toll free, see Fairmont). 735 rms, A/C, color TV. AE, CB, DC, MC, V. Valet parking $8, pool, two tennis courts, two rests. (including Sazerac), 24-hr coffeeshop, 24-hr bars, 24-hr rm svce, disco, hrdrsr, drugstore, concierge, free crib. *Note:* An elderly luxury hotel of Victorian elegance, a few steps from the Vieux Carré and on the edge of the Central Business District. Ultra-comfortable, lavishly decorated rms, though some are on the cramped side. Exemplary svce. Very commendable luxury rest. Big business clientele. A landmark among local hotels. Recently renovated. **E–VE**

Hilton Riverside and Towers (dwntwn), 2 Poydras St., LA 70140 (504/561-0500; toll free, see Hilton). 1,600 rms, A/C, color TV, in-rm movies. AE, CB, DC, MC, V. Valet parking $8, two pools, health club, sauna, 11 tennis courts, three rests. (including Winston's), two coffeeshops, four bars, 24-hr rm svce, disco, hrdrsr, concierge, free crib. *Note:* Enormous tourist barracks on the river, its massive silhouette by no means improving the view from Riverwalk. All rms overlook the city, the harbor, or both. Irreproachably comfortable; efficient svce; mediocre rests. Well-regarded jazz club. The top three floors are reserved for VIPs; on one is a Presidential Suite at $1,000 a night. Group and convention clientele of an obtrusive kind; the Convention Center and the French Quarter are nearby. **E–VE**

Inter-Continental (dwntwn), 444 St. Charles Ave., LA 70130 (504/525-5566; toll free, see Inter-Continental). 497 rms, A/C, color TV, in-rm movies. AE, CB, DC, MC, V. Valet parking $8, pool, health club, two rests. (including Les Continents), two bars, 24-hr rm svce, nightclub, hrdrsr, boutiques, concierges. *Note:* Ultramodern luxury hotel in the heart of the Central Business District and 5 min. from the French Quarter, of ungraceful exterior but elegant and urbane within, boasting many contemporary sculptures and other works of art. Spacious and remarkably comfortable rms w. mini-bars, some w. balconies. Very complete facilities; flawless svce; rest. of quality. Big business clientele. **E–VE**

Maison de Ville (dwntwn), 727 Toulouse St., LA 70130 (504/561-5858; toll free 800/634-1600). 21 rms, suites, or cottages, A/C, color TV. AE, DC, MC, V. Valet parking $12, pool, rest. (Bistro at Maison de Ville), bar, 24-hr rm svce, 24-hr concierge. *Note:* The most luxurious and exclusive small hotel in the French Quarter, its main building dating from the mid-19th century, while the adjoining cottages (200-year-old former slave quarters) bear the name of the naturalist John James Audubon, who once lived there. The whole has been lavishly and effectively restored, with period furniture. Shady patios and inviting pool. Reception and svce of the highest order. Excellent rest. The favorite of those in-the-know. **E–VE**

Westin Canal Palace (dwntwn), 100 Rue Iberville, LA 70130 (504/566-7006; toll free, see Westin). 438 rms, A/C, color TV, in-rm movies. AE, CB, DC, MC, V. Valet garage $8, pool, three rests. (including Le Jardin), two bars, 24-hr rm svce, nightclub, hrdrsr, boutiques, concierge, free crib. *Note:* One of the newest luxury hotels in the city, overlooking the Mississippi and the elegant Canal Place Shopping Center from the eminence of its 16 stories. Exceptionally huge, comfortable rms, w. marble bathrooms, mini-bars, and clear views over the river or the French Quarter. Ultra-professional svce. Very well situated a stone's throw from the Vieux Carré and the World Trade Center. Business clientele. **E–VE**

Monteleone Hotel (dwntwn), 214 Royal St., LA 70140 (504/523-3341; toll free 800/535-9595). 600 rms, A/C, color TV. AE, CB, DC, MC, V. Valet parking $6, pool, putting green, two rests. (including Le Café), four bars (one revolving), rm svce, disco, hrdrsr, boutiques, free crib. *Note:* Inviting older hotel at the entrance to the Vieux Carré. The package-tour and convention guests make a lot of noise, but the comfort and svce are flawless. Acceptable rest.; very agreeable nightclub and terrace w. pool on the top floor. A New Orleans landmark for the past century. **E–VE**

Radisson Suite Hotel (formerly the Sugar House Park; dwntwn), 315 Julia St., LA 70130 (504/525-1993; toll free, see Radisson). 243 suites, A/C, color TV, in-rm movies. AE, CB, DC, MC, V. Parking $6, pool, rest. (Sugar House), bar, rm svce, jazz club, concierge. *Note:* Typical hotel for the business traveler, very near the Convention Center. Spacious, inviting suites w. private balconies or patios and refrigerators. Spectacular six-story glass-walled lobby. Business and convention clientele. Good value. Recently redecorated and refurnished. **E–VE**

Holiday Inn French Quarter (dwntwn), 124 Royal St., LA 70130 (504/529-7211; toll free, see Holiday Inns). 252 rms, A/C, color TV. AE, CB, DC, MC, V. Free parking, pool, rest. (Jambo's), bar, crib $6. *Note:* The functional Holiday Inn style at the entrance to the Vieux

Carré. Comfortable rms. The rest. makes a praiseworthy effort. Package-tour and group clientele. Good value, considering the location. **M–E**

Provincial (dwntwn), 1024 Chartres St., LA 70116 (504/ 581-4995; toll free 800/535-7922). 97 rms, A/C, color TV. AE, CB, DC, MC, V. Free parking, pool, rest., rm svce, free crib. *Note:* Delightful older hotel, as quiet and discreet as its name implies, in the Vieux Carré very nr. the French Market. Inviting, comfortable rms w. period furnishings and private balconies. Pretty inner courtyards. The clients are mostly regulars, because they know this is a good place to stay. **M–E**

Avenue Plaza Hotel (nr. dwntwn), 2111 St. Charles Ave., LA 70130 (504/566-1212; toll free 800/535-9575). 200 rms. A/C, cable color TV. AE, CB, DC, MC, V. Parking $4, pool, sauna, health club, two rests., bar, hrdrsr, crib $15. *Note:* In the Garden District 10 min. from dwntwn by the St. Charles Ave. streetcar, this hotel offers good athletic facilities and inviting rms w. kitchenettes and refrigerators. Good value overall. The perfect place for viewing the Mardi Gras procession as it passes. **M–E**

The Columns (nr. dwntwn), 3811 St. Charles Ave., LA 70115 (504/899-9308). 17 rms, A/C. AE, DC, MC, V. Valet parking $6, rest., bar, rm svce. *Note:* A prosperous Victorian's elegant home built in 1833 and now a designated historic monument. Enormous rms furnished in period, but some lacking private baths. Movies such as *Tightrope* and *Pretty Baby* have been shot here. Romantic ambience; reception and svce of the friendliest. In the heart of the Garden District, 15 min. from dwntwn by the St. Charles Ave. streetcar. **I–M**

Days Inn Canal Street (nr. dwntwn), 1630 Canal St., LA 70112 (504/586-0110; toll free, see Days Inns). 216 rms, A/C, color TV, in-rm movies. AE, DC, MC, V. Free parking, pool, rest., bar, free crib. *Note:* Typical functional motel, recently renovated; 5 min. by car from the Superdome or the French Quarter. Comfortable rms, some w. balconies; efficient reception and svce. Good value overall. **I–M**

Quality Inn Midtown (nr. dwntwn), 3900 Tulane Ave., LA 70119 (504/486-5541; toll free, see Quality Inns). 104 rms, A/C, color TV, in-rm movies. AE, CB, DC, MC, V. Free parking, pool, rest., bar, rm svce, disco, crib $3. *Note:* Comfortable, attractive motel a little away from the center. Spacious rms w. balconies. Friendly reception and svce. Great if you're driving; easily accessible from the Pontchartrain Expwy. Good value 10 min. from dwntwn. **I–M**

French Quarter Maisonnettes (dwntwn), 1130 Chartres St., LA 70116 (504/524-9918). 7 rms, A/C, black-and-white TV. No credit cards. Parking $6, nearby coffeeshop. *Note:* Gracious little Vieux Carré home built in 1825. The rms, each w. kitchenette and tastefully decorated, open on a pretty shaded courtyard. Reception w. a smile. Excellent value. You'll need to book a number of weeks ahead. Closed in July. A very good place. **I–M**

La Quinta Gretna (nr. dwntwn), 50 Terry Pkwy., in Gretna, LA 70053 (504/368-5600; toll free, see La Quinta). 154 rms, A/C, color TV, in-rm movies. AE, CB, DC, MC, V. Free parking, pool, nearby 24-hr coffeeshop, free crib. *Note:* Excellent value 10 min. from dwntwn across the Mississippi. Modern comforts; reception and svce w. a smile. Ideal if you're driving. **I**

St. Charles Inn (nr. dwntwn), 3636 St. Charles Ave., LA 70115 (504/899-8888). 40 rms, A/C, color TV. AE, CB, DC, MC, V. Parking $5, rest., bar, free breakfast. *Note:* Well-run small budget motel 10 min. from dwntwn on the St. Charles Ave. streetcar. Pleasantly decorated rms; friendly reception. Excellent value. **I**

Airport Accommodations

Hilton Airport (vic.), 901 Airline Hwy., in Kenner, LA 70062 (504/469-5000; toll free, see Hilton). 324 rms, A/C, color TV, in-rm movies. AE, CB, DC, MC, V. Free parking, pool, two tennis courts, health club, rest., bar, rm svce, nightclub, free airport limo. *Note:* relatively modern and comfortable motel right across from the airport. Spacious, well sound-proofed rms overlooking pool or garden. Efficient svce. Business clientele. Great if you're stopping over between flights. 25 min. from dwntwn. **M–E**

YMCA/Youth Hostels

Marquette House International Hostel (nr. dwntwn), 2253 Carondelet St. (504/523-3014). 100 beds. Youth hostel in the Garden District.

YMCA International Center (nr. dwntwn), 936 St. Charles Ave. (504/568-9622). 139 rms. Pool, health club, rest. Men and women.

RESTAURANTS

New Orleans Restaurant Prices	
(per person, excluding drinks and service charges)	
B (Budget)	up to $15
I (Inexpensive)	$15–$25
M (Moderate)	$25–$40
E (Expensive)	$40–$60
VE (Very Expensive)	$60 and up

A Note on New Orleans Food: For more than 150 years New Orleans rightly prided itself on its gastronomic skills. During this period, half a dozen great restaurants have in turn enjoyed their days of glory: Antoine's, which created Créole cuisine in the 19th century; Galatoire's, at the beginning of the 20th century; Arnaud's, in the 1920s and '30s; Brennan's, in the years following World War II; Le Ruth's, Mosca's, and Commander's Palace, for the past 15 years. These seven "greats" have had their ups and downs over the years, but they are still counted among the best restaurants in the city.

The two great cuisines of New Orleans, ranked by many among the country's greatest gastronomic resources, are "Créole" (the more delicate) and "Cajun" (the earthier). They have one thing in common: both, in the words of Paul Prudhomme, the truculent figure who is the best-known chef in New Orleans today, are "Louisiana-born with French roots." But if Créole and Cajun food still acknowledge a predominantly French inheritance, they also pay tribute to other cuisines which immigration has brought to the city: Spanish, African, Italian, Caribbean, Native American. However—still quoting Prudhomme—the most compelling influence on Créole cuisine was undoubtedly that of the blacks, who had charge of the kitchen in many Louisiana plantation homes.

Personal Favorites (in order of preference)

Commander's Palace (nr. dwntwn), 1403 Washington Ave. (889-8221) A/C. Lunch/dinner daily, brunch Sat. and Sun.;

closed Shrove Tuesday, Dec. 24–25. AE, CB, DC, MC, V. Jkt. (J&T at dinner). *Specialties:* turtle soup, crabmeat Choron, oysters marinière, filet mignon Debris, veal Marcelle, pompano en papillote, pancakes with lemon. Fine wine list. *Note:* In the heart of the charming old Garden District, a stately Victorian house accommodates New Orleans's most elegant rest., belonging to the senior branch of the well-known Brennan family. While the cuisine has its passing moments of weakness, there are some dishes, such as the veal Marcelle or the filet mignon Debris, which belong in anyone's anthology of great food. Exquisite flower-planted courtyard in summer; Dixieland at brunch (very crowded) Sat. and Sun. Courteous and efficient svce; resv. a must. 10 min. from dwntwn; valet parking. One of the dozen best rests. in the country. *Créole.* **M–E**

Le Ruth's (vic.), 636 Franklin St., in Gretna (362-4914). A/C. Dinner only, Tues.-Sat.; closed Sun., Mon., holidays, Shrove Tuesday, and the month of July. MC, V. J&T. *Specialties:* oyster-and-artichoke soup, crab St. Francis, roast duck w. oysters, lake trout Oliva, roast rack of lamb w. fried parsley, veal Marie. Superb sherbet and homemade ice cream, almond tart. Louisiana's finest wine list, backed by a 25,000-bottle cellar. *Note:* This obscure neighborhood on the other side of the river has little to recommend it; nor does the appearance of the rest. itself, apart from a few fine paintings. But the food is among the best to be found. Their light sauces—unusual in New Orleans—and their talent for innovation make of Larry and Lee Le Ruth, the sons of founder Warren Le Ruth, the Bocuse brothers of the region. Flawless svce. You'll need to make resv., and do it some days ahead. Well worth the 15-min. drive from the Vieux Carré. *Créole.* **M–E**

Antoine's (dwntwn), 713 St. Louis St. (581-4422). A/C. Lunch/dinner Mon.-Sat.; closed Sun., Shrove Tuesday, and holidays. AE, CB, DC, MC, V. Jkt. *Specialties:* oysters Rockefeller, oysters Foch, pompano en papillote, étouffée of crayfish, filet of beef Robespierre, tournedos marchand de vin, chicken Rochambeau, soufflèed potatoes. Vast wine list backed by 35,000 bottles in the cellar. *Note:* The oldest rest. in the Vieux Carré is by now a sort of living legend. It was here that, in the 19th century, Antoine Alciatore created some of the most renowned Créole dishes, such as oysters Rockefeller and pompano en papillote. The décor has not changed since it was new (in 1840), and the present proprietor, Bernard Guste, is a fifth-generation descendant of the legendary Antoine. The waiters, some of whom have worked here for more than three decades, can be abrupt, but in spite of its slightly touristy atmosphere this is still one of the three or four best places to eat in the city. Ask to be seated in the big dining rm at the back, with its dark paneling. Resv. strongly advised. *Créole.* **M**

Galatoire's (dwntwn), 209 Bourbon St. (525-2021). A/C. Lunch/dinner Tues.-Sun.; closed Mon., Shrove Tuesday, and holidays. No credit cards. J&T at dinner. *Specialties:* shrimp remoulade, eggs Sardou, crabmeat ravigote, trout Marguéry, sweetbreads financière, chicken Clemenceau, oysters en brochette. *Note:* Another landmark since the beginning of the 20th century; the attractive 1900 décor, w. its mirrors and ceiling fans, is guaranteed authentic. Only Ruth's and the Commander's Palace can rival the food, and the svce is exemplary. This is a noisy place, and—another black mark—Galatoire's accepts no resv., inexcusable in a rest. of this quality. The wine list is poor. *Créole.* **I–M**

K. Paul's Louisiana Kitchen (dwntwn), 416 Chartres St. (942-7500). A/C. Dinner only, Mon.-Fri.; closed Sat., Sun., and holidays. AE. *Specialties:* Cajun popcorn (fried crayfish), jambalaya, shrimp Bayou Tèche, duckling à l'étouffée, blackened redfish, sweet-potato/pecan pie. Menu changes regularly. *Note:* This bistro began the revolution in local gastronomy. The chef, Paul Prudhomme, is a man of weight, both literally and figuratively, who came here from the Commander's Palace; he is the moving cause of the fashion for Louisiana food throughout the U.S. The food here is authentically Cajun, and the ambience relaxed, w. Formica décor and paper napkins. The svce does not aim to please. Always crowded, w. unavoidable waiting lines (no resv. accepted)—in spite of which, you should definitely eat here. *Cajun*. **I–M**

🍷🍷 **Mr. B's** (dwntwn), 201 Royal St. (523-2078). A/C. Lunch/ dinner daily, jazz brunch Sun.; closed Shrove Tuesday, Dec. 25. AE, CB, DC, MC, V. Jkt. *Specialties:* oysters Madras, gumbo, jambalaya, pasta, fish and meat broiled over wood fire, veal sauté w. fettuccine Alfredo, bread pudding. Good list of California wines. *Note:* The fresh homemade pasta and the Créole-style broiled dishes are the house specialties of this congenial place, developed by the Brennan family who also own the prestigious Commander's Palace. Décor and atmosphere are reminiscent of a London club, and this is a favorite luncheon spot for businesspeople. Its popularity makes resv. advisable. *Créole*. **I–M**

🍷🍷 **Ruth's Chris Steak House** (nr. dwntwn), 711 N. Broad Ave. (486-0810). A/C. Lunch/dinner daily; closed holidays. AE, CB, DC, MC, V. Jkt. *Specialties:* the finest of red meats, mediocre desserts. *Note:* For decades the favorite spot of New Orleans meat-eaters. Remarkable meats (especially the Porterhouse steak for two), and an inimitable butter sauce. Attentive svce. Clientele of businesspeople and leading figures in local sports or politics. The neighborhood is unattractive after dark; take a cab. Open till 11:30 p.m. *Steak*. **I–M**

🍷🍷 **Bon Ton Café:** (dwntwn), 401 Magazine St. (524-3386). A/C. Lunch/dinner Mon.-Fri.; closed Sat. and Sun. AE, MC, V. Jkt. *Specialties:* turtle soup, crayfish étouffée, jambalaya, crabmeat au gratin, fried catfish, bread pudding with whisky. *Note:* This old rest., a New Orleans classic for three decades, w. its countrified atmosphere and charming checked red gingham tablecloths, serves some of the most authentic Cajun food going. Generally crowded and noisy at lunch, quieter in the evening. Very near the Vieux Carré. Resv. a must. *Cajun*. **I**

☀️🍷 **Chez Hélène** (nr. dwntwn), 1540 N. Robertson St. (947-1206). A/C. Lunch daily, dinner Tues.-Sun. No credit cards. *Specialties:* oysters Rockefeller, gumbo, "dirty rice" (rice w. chopped chicken livers), trout Marguéry, fried chicken Créole, red beans and sausages, bread pudding with whisky. *Note:* By general consent the city's best value for lovers of real Créole cooking. The excellent chef Austin Leslie, nephew of the foundress, draws on old family recipes. Chez Hélène, with its nonexistent décor, democratic atmosphere, and soul-music jukebox, was the model for the TV series "Frank's Place." Svce very slow; neighborhood unsafe after dark—take a cab. *Créole*. **B–I**

☀️🍷 **Felix's** (dwntwn), 739 Iberville St. (522-4440). A/C. Lunch/dinner daily (till midnight); closed holidays. AE, MC, V. *Specialties:* oysters, gumbo, fish of the day. *Note:* Oyster bar and rest. which is crowded out midday and evening by hungry customers. Regulars usually sit at the counter to avoid the long wait for a table. Absolutely fresh oysters and seafood, very attractively priced. Noisy, genial atmosphere. No resv. *Seafood*. **B–I**

Other Restaurants (from top bracket to budget)

🍷🍷🍷 **Arnaud's** (dwntwn), 813 Bienville St. (523-5433). A/C. Lunch Mon.-Fri., dinner nightly, jazz brunch Sun.; closed holidays. AE, CB, DC, MC, V. Jkt. (J&T at dinner). *Specialties:* shrimp Arnaud, oysters Bienville, crab Imperial, pompano in pastry shell, tournedos Charlemond, rack of lamb diablo, bananas Foster. *Note:* Founded by Count Arnaud Cazenave in 1918, and restored to its original splendor in 1978, this elegant, polished establishment was New Orleans's most distinguished rest. in the years between the two World Wards. Like the décor, the food has completely recaptured its former glory. Excellent svce; resv. a must. A very fine place. *Créole.* **M–E**

Crozier's (vic.), 7033 Read Lane (241-8220). A/C. Lunch Tues.-Fri., dinner Tues.-Sat.; closed Sun., Mon., and holidays. AE, MC, V. Jkt. *Specialties:* pâté of duck, coq au vin, tournedos Gerard, trout w. fennel, steak au poivre, sweetbreads meunière. Weakish wine list. *Note:* Chef Gerard Crozier's food is—most unusually for New Orleans—100% French, without any Créole tinge. Charming reception and svce in a plush villa in the suburb of Lake Forest, almost on the shores of Lake Pontchartrain. Efficient svce; resv. a must. Very well worth the 20-min. drive from the French Quarter. *French.* **M–E**

Restaurant Jonathan (dwntwn), 714 N. Rampart (586-1930). A/C. Dinner only, nightly. AE, CB, DC, MC, V. Jkt. *Specialties:* mousse of trout w. dill mayonnaise, crab Entremont, calves' liver à l'orange, tournedos Thomas. Very good desserts. *Note:* The Restaurant Jonathan, a triumph of art deco, almost qualifies as a museum, w. signed originals by Erté, Idart, and Lalique, and an astonishing two-story glass rm divider. The food prepared by chef Tom Cowman is as brilliant as it is inventive. Svce of a high order. Resv. indispensable at this very successful rest. *Créole-continental.* **M–E**

Versailles (nr. dwntwn), 2100 St. Charles Ave. (524-2535). A/C. Dinner only, Mon.-Sat.; closed Sun., Shrove Tuesday, and one week in July. AE, CB, DC, MC, V. Jkt. *Specialties:* snails in pastry shell, crabmeat Florentine, Madras shrimp curry, bouillabaisse, duck w. port wine, trout sautéed w. capers, orange mousse. Good wine list (especially the German section). *Note:* Like a great wine, this rest. belonging to Günter Preuss continues to improve w. the years. Classic French-Créole food flawlessly prepared and served. Elegant paneling-and-mirror décor. Very popular locally, so resv. highly advisable. Valet parking. 10 min. from dwntwn. *Créole-French.* **M–E**

Bistro at Maison de Ville (dwntwn), in the Maison de Ville (see "Accommodations," above) (528-9206). A/C. Lunch/ dinner daily. AE, DC, MC, V. Jkt. *Specialties:* tapenade of eggplant, broiled shrimp w. coriander, cod cakes w. tomato purée, confit of duck salad, softshell crabs w. mustard Créole style, lemon tart, gratin of fruit. *Note:* Charming, romantic little hotel rest. w. dark paneling, intimate bar, and red upholstery. The cuisine is a happy marriage of classical Créole tradition w. contemporary French ideas. Since the rest. seats only 40, resv. are a must. *Créole-French.* **M**

Brennan's (dwntwn), 417 Royal St. (525-9711). A/C. Lunch/dinner daily; closed Dec. 25. AE, MC, V. Jkt. (at dinner). *Specialties:* eggs Sardou, crabmeat béarnaise, oysters 2-2-2, chicken Pontalba, tournedos Chanteclair, shrimp Clemenceau, bananas Foster. Superb wine list, especially the bordeaux. *Note:* Brennan's is the most widely known rest. in New Orleans—and also one of the most delightful. Standing in the heart of the Vieux Carré, it achieved its greatest triumphs in the 1940s. Since 1973, when the family split into two rival branches (the senior branch now presides over Commander's Palace and Mr. B's), the food has gone noticeably downhill. Now little more than a conventional tourist rest., Brennan's nonetheless retains the unique appeal of its courtyard, shaded by banana palms. Its famous breakfasts are much better than the lunches or dinners. The svce is confused and uninterested. Resv. recommended, but not always honored. *Créole.* **M**

Restaurant de la Tour Eiffel (nr. dwntwn), 2040 St. Charles Ave. (524-2555). A/C. Lunch/dinner daily. AE, CB, DC, MC, V, J kt. *Specialties:* rillettes of salmon, stuffed mussels w. sauce Pernod, softshell crabs meunière, sweetbreads grenobloise, Dover sole Bocuse, filet mignon Zingara, raspberry soufflé. Good wine list. *Note:* The farthest-out interior in New Orleans, this huge glass cage in the purest art nouveau style is—believe it or not—the old rest. from the Eiffel Tower in Paris, disassembled into 11,000 separate metal parts and reassembled on its present site in 1987. The talented chef, Daniel Bonnot, prepares remarkable contemporary French cuisine. Flawless svce; the fashionable place to eat. Resv. absolutely indispensable. *French.* **M**

♙♙♙ **Willy Coln's Chalet** (vic.), 2505 Whitney Ave., in Gretna (361-3860). A/C. Lunch Thurs. and Fri., dinner Tues.–Sat.; closed Sun.–Mon. AE, DC, MC, V. Jkt. *Specialties:* Bahamian chowder, ceviche, roast knuckle of veal, duckling Madagascar, choucroute maison (homemade sauerkraut), steak au poivre, Black Forest cake. Good wine list, particularly of Rhine wines. *Note:* German food in New Orleans? Indeed yes, and remarkable German food at that. The hunting-lodge interior, w. its open fireplace, looks incongruous in such a climate. The svce may not be polished, but it's efficient. Locally popular; resv. advised. 15 min. from dwntwn, across the Mississippi.*Créole-German.* **M**

♙♙ **Mike Anderson's** (dwntwn), 215 Bourbon St. (524-3884). A/C. Lunch/dinner daily; closed holidays. AE, MC, V. *Specialties:* gumbo, crayfish bisque, ragoût of shrimp, catch of the day Créole style. *Note:* Next door to the famous Galatoire's, Mike Anderson's is a godsend for those who are tired of the latter's long waiting lines. While it doesn't pretend to rival Galatoire's perfection, Mike Anderson's Créole dishes and Louisiana-style fish are definitely praiseworthy. Pleasant nautical décor w. huge aquariums. Diligent svce. *Seafood-Créole.* **I–M**

☼♙♙ **Pascal's Manale** (nr. dwntwn), 1838 Napoleon Ave. (895-4887). A/C. Lunch Mon.-Fri., dinner nightly; closed Dec. 25. AE, CB, DC, MC, V. *Specialties:* barbecued shrimp, crabmeat Rockefeller, gumbo, spaghetti Collins, veal au marsala, snapper Catherine. Skimpy wine list. *Note:* Another old (1913) landmark of local good food, which harmoniously blends the Créole influence into a basically Italian repertory. What matters here is the food, not the setting or the svce. Generally crowded and noisy; resv. rarely honored, so long waits are inevitable, especially at wknds. Not a good neighborhood at night; take a cab. *Créole-Italian.* **I–M**

☼♙ **Acme Oyster Bar** (dwntwn), 724 Iberville St. (522-5973). A/C. Lunch/dinner Mon.-Sat. (until 7 p.m.); closed Sun. and holidays. No credit cards. *Specialties:* oysters, "poor boys" (Créole sandwiches), oyster loaf. Draft beer. *Note:* The most representative of the Vieux Carré's oyster bars; the belons, Blue Points, Whitstables, Plaquemines, and so forth are fresh from the sea, and opened under your very eyes. Connoisseurs eat them standing, leaning an elbow on the old counter, and wash them down w. a draft beer. Relaxed atmosphere, full of local color. *Seafood-Créole.* **B**

♙ **Eddie's** (nr. dwntwn), 2119 Law St. (945-2207). A/C. Lunch/dinner Mon.-Sat. (until midnight); closed Sun. and holidays. AE, MC, V. *Specialties:* gumbo, pork chop stuffed w. oysters, Créole fried chicken, red beans and rice w. sausage, bread pudding w. whisky. *Note:* This little rest., tucked away in a nondescript building in the black district, is not easy to find, but it offers Créole food as authentic and tasty as you could ever hope for. Unpretentious décor but friendly reception and svce. One of the best underground-gourmet places in New Orleans. 10 min. from dwntwn. (take a cab). *Créole.* **B**

♙ **Mandina's** (nr. dwntwn), 3800 Canal St. (482-9179). A/C. Lunch/dinner daily. No credit cards. *Specialties:* poor boy sandwiches, shrimp remoulade, spaghetti w. meatballs, gumbo, jambalaya, Dobergé cake. *Note:* The king of the "poor boy" (a roast beef or sausage sandwich), also serving other commendable Créole dishes. Crowded at lunchtime, this likeable neighborhood rest. nonetheless represents one of the best values in the entire city. The atmosphere and the svce are unaffected and unconstrained. *Créole.* **B**

Restaurants in the Vicinity

♟♟♟ **La Provence** (vic.), on U.S. 190 in Lacombe (626-7662). A/C. Dinner only, Wed.-Sun.; closed Mon., Tues., Dec. 25, and the month of Sept. AE, MC, V. Jkt. *Specialties:* salmon mousse, médaillon of veal w. tarragon, duck w. Madagascar green peppercorns, steak au poivre Robert Aymes, rack of lamb w. herbs from Provence. Handsome wine list at decent prices. *Note:* In spite of his name, Chris Kerageorgiou is from France, and what's more, from Provence. His remarkable and wholly French cuisine can accommodate itself to influences of Greek and Créole origin. Agreeable country setting; romantic atmosphere and dedicated svce. Successful enough that you'll need resv. 40 min. from dwntwn. along the spectacular Pontchartrain Causeway. A fine place. *French.* **M**

☀♟♟♟ **Mosca's** (vic.), 4137 U.S. 90 in Waggaman, 5 mi. (8 km) west of the Huey Long Bridge (436-9942). A/C. Dinner only, Tues.-Sat.; closed Sun., Mon., and holidays. No credit cards. *Specialties:* baked oysters Mosca, marinated crabmeat salad, spaghetti bordelaise, shrimp à l'Italienne, chicken cacciatore, game in season. Unimpressive wine list. *Note:* The most original Italian rest. in Louisiana. The unpretentious white building, w. its rather shabby décor, is a full 20 min. by car from dwntwn and hard to find after nightfall. But the marriage of Italian and Créole cuisines achieved by the Mosca family reaches a perfection unequalled anywhere else, particularly in the fresh homemade pastas. The servings are generous, the svce efficient and casual. Often crowded and noisy, so resv. are definitely advised (but none are accepted on Sat.). *Créole-Italian.* **I–M**

CAFETERIAS / FAST FOOD: ☀ **Café du Monde** (dwntwn), 800 Decatur St., at Ann St. (525-4544). Old café inside the French Market, open round the clock seven days a week, and immensely popular. The doughnuts are renowned. There's an inviting terrace. A New Orleans classic. No credit cards.

☀ **Central Grocery** (dwntwn), 923 Decatur St. (523-1620). Authentic turn-of-the-century grocery carrying foods of all nations. It prides itself on having originated the famous "muffuletta sandwich" — ham, mozzarella, salami, provolone, and mortadella on a hard roll. Local color (and aroma) guaranteed. Open from 8 a.m. to 5 p.m. Mon.-Sat. No credit cards.

D. H. Holmes (dwntwn), 819 Canal St. (561-6140). Department-store cafeteria serving soup, "poor boys," and very acceptable daily specials at modest prices. Lunch/dinner Mon.-Sat. AE, MC, V.

WHERE TO EAT WHAT

Cajun: Bon Ton Café(♟♟); K. Paul's Louisiana Kitchen(♟♟)
Créole: Chez Hélène(♟); Eddie's(♟); Mandina's(♟)
Créole-Continental: Willie Coln's Chalet(♟♟♟); Mr. B's(♟♟); Restaurant Jonathan(♟♟).
Créole-French: Commander's Palace(♟♟♟♟); Le Ruth's(♟♟♟♟); Antoine's (♟♟♟); Arnaud's(♟♟♟); Galatoire's(♟♟♟); Versailles(♟♟♟); Bistro at Maison de Ville(♟♟); Brennan's(♟♟).
Créole-Italian: Mosca's(♟♟♟♟); Pascal's Manale(♟♟).
Fast Food / Cafeterias: Café du Monde; Central Grocery; D. H. Holmes.
French: La Provence(♟♟♟); Crozier's(♟♟); Le Restaurant de la Tour Eiffel(♟♟).
Seafood: Mike Anderson's(♟♟); Acme Oyster Bar(♟); Felíx's(♟).
Steak, Meat: Ruth's Chris Steak House(♟♟).

Late-Night-Service (closing time in parentheses): Café du Monde (never closes); Eddie's (midnight); Felix's (midnight); Ruth's Chris Steak House (11:30 p.m.).

BARS & NIGHTCLUBS

Crescent City Jazz Hall (dwntwn), 739 Conti St. (566-1056): Similar to Preservation Hall (see below), but offers drinks and theater seating; Thurs.-Sun.

Flagons (nr. dwntwn), 3222 Magazine St. (895-6471): Popular wine bar and early 1900's style bistro. A favorite of the young professional crowd, on Garden District edge. Nightly.

Lulu White's Mahogany Hall (dwntwn), 309 Bourbon St. (525-5595). New Orleans jazz by the well-known Dukes of Dixieland. Open nightly.

Maple Leaf Bar (vic.), 8316 Oak St. (866-9359). The local shrine of Cajun music, rhythm and blues. Generally crowded, especially when Beausoleil, the top group in the Cajun music hit parade, plays for its multitude of fans. Exciting ambience.

Napoleon House (dwntwn), 500 Chartres St. (524-9752). Comfortable, intimate bar serving very good cocktails and fast meals (muffuletta sandwiches). The period décor is of guaranteed authenticity (see "Historic Buildings," above).

Old Absinthe Bar (dwntwn), 400 Bourbon St. (525-8108). In the 1920s it was a speakeasy; now it's an excellent club offering modern jazz, rhythm and blues; the biggest stars appear here regularly. Very popular locally. Open nightly.

Old Absinthe House (dwntwn), 240 Bourbon St. (523-3181). The oldest (1806) and best-known bar in the Vieux Carré, its walls papered with thousands of visiting cards from patrons around the world. Always crowded, but don't fail to pay your respects (see "Historic Buildings," above). Open nightly.

Pat O'Brien's (dwntwn), 718 St. Peter St. (525-4823). The piano bar is noisy, but there's a pretty shaded courtyard. The cocktails are good (try a "Hurricane.") Open nightly till 4 a.m.

Pete Fountain's (nr. dwntwn), in the Hilton Hotel (see "Accommodations," above) (523-4374). New Orleans jazz by the renowned clarinettist Pete Fountain. Tues.-Sat.

Preservation Hall (dwntwn), 726 St. Peter St. (523-8939). The principal shrine of New Orleans jazz. No refreshments. Concerts nightly. See "Historic Buildings," above.

Rain Forest (nr. dwntwn), in the Hilton Hotel (see "Accommodations," above) (587-7246). Trendy disco on the 29th floor, open until 4 a.m. Often crowded. Open nightly.

Snug Harbor (dwntwn), 626 Frenchmen St. (949-0696). Very good modern-jazz club just outside the French Quarter. Also rest.

Storyville Jazz Hall (dwntwn), 1104 Decatur St. (525-8199). A sort of friendlier, more comfortable Preservation Hall, with authentic New Orleans jazz. Open Mon.-Sat.

Tipitina's (nr. dwntwn), 501 Napoleon Ave. (895-8477). Disco, jazz, Cajun music; very far from smart, but definitely amusing. Very popular locally. 15 min. from dwntwn. Open nightly. Also rest.

Tyler's Beer Garden (nr. dwntwn), 5234 Magazine St. (891-4989). Locally popular oyster bar open late; also contemporary jazz on Thurs., Fri., and Sat. 15 min. from dwntwn. Open Mon.-Sat.

NEARBY EXCURSIONS

☀🔔 **LAKE PONTCHARTRAIN** (north of the city, reached via Pontchartrain Expwy. and West End Ave. or by Elysian Fields

Ave.): A saltwater lake 40 by 25 mi. (64 by 40 km) in extent, and nowhere more than 20 ft. (6 m) deep. Ideal for fishing, water sports, and swimming, with many inviting beaches. Scenic drive along Lake Shore Dr. and Hayne Blvd. And don't miss the ※ ▲▲ **Lake Pontchartrain Causeway,** a spectacular over-water toll road opened in 1969, whose two separate but parallel highways run 24 mi. (39 km) from one shore of the lake to the other. This is the longest highway bridge in the world, and a riveting sight.

FARTHER AFIELD

SUGGESTED TOURING ITINERARIES

▲▲ **CAJUN COUNTRY** (420 mi., 672 km round trip via U.S. 90W, U.S. 167N, U.S. 190E, La. 1S, and U.S. 90E): After two centuries, the Cajun country still has some 400,000 French-speaking inhabitants, descendants of the Acadian colonists expelled from Canada by the British in 1755. (The word "Cajun" was originally written "Acadian," and referred to the people of the former French territories in Canada; local pronunciation modified it first to "Cadian," then to "Cagian," and finally to the present "Cajun.")

You begin your tour at **Houma,** capital of Terrebonne Parish (a parish is the Louisiana equivalent of a county), an old fishing port specializing in shellfish and dubbed "the Venice of America." Visit the ▲ **Southdown Plantation,** a hybrid of Greek Revival and Victorian traditions built in the latter part of the 19th century and now a museum of Cajun history; it's on La. 311W (504/851-0154), and open daily. Then on to **Morgan City,** an important shrimping harbor, and headquarters for offshore oil exploration. Here you should see the **Swamp Gardens,** a strange marshy botanic garden with foot trails. On your way to **New Iberia,** founded as its name indicates during the Spanish supremacy in Louisiana, don't fail to stop off at ※ ▲▲ **Oaklawn Manor Plantation** in Franklin, a sumptuous 1830s dwelling in lovely gardens on Bayou Tèche; you'll find it on U.S. 90 (318/828-0434); open daily. There are several other attractions worth stopping for at New Iberia: the pretty Bouligny Plaza at the town's center; **Shadows-on-the-Tèche,** 117 E. Main St. (504/369-6446), open daily, a fine 1834 classical revival plantation house; **Avery Island,** birthplace of Tabasco, a big salty island where you should look for ※ ▲▲ **Jungle Gardens,** a riot of azaleas, camellias, and tropical plants as well as a wildlife refuge for migratory birds, on La. 329; open daily. Another extraordinary garden nearby is **Live Oaks Gardens** on La. 14 in Jefferson Island, open daily; the moss-grown trees for which it is named are more than a century old.

Your next stop will be at ※ **St. Martinville,** the most French of Cajun towns, renowned for its "butcher's festival" the Sunday before Mardi Gras. Founded in 1760 by those Acadian immigrants whose tribulations inspired Longfellow to write his *Evangeline,* this charming little town straight out of old France was once known as "little Paris" because of its splendidly worldly way of life. There is a fine ▲ **Church of St. Martin of Tours** at 103 Main St., with memorabilia of Louis XVI and Marie Antoinette.

Nine miles (14 km) north is ※ **Lafayette,** capital of the new Acadia, a busy commercial center almost half of whose inhabitants are French-speaking. Visit the **Lafayette Museum** at 1122 Lafayette St. (318/234-2208), open Tues.-Sun., in what used to be the home of Alexandre Mouton, the first governor of Louisiana (1836); also the interesting **Acadian Village** on U.S. 167, open daily, with its scrupulously restored 19th-century buildings. A local festival you should try to catch is the ▲▲ **Acadian Festival** in mid-September: two days of music and culinary delights.

Now you proceed to ▲ **Opelousas,** another center of the Acadian influence in Louisiana, with its charming antebellum houses and its museum dedicated to Jim Bowie, a hero of the Battle of the Alamo, who lived for a time in this area: **Jim Bowie Museum,** U.S. 190W and Academy St., open Mon.-Fri.

On your way back to New Orleans, don't fail to visit **Baton Rouge,** the state capital (see "Plantation Country," below), making a detour to take in ✵ 🏛 **Madewood Plantation House** on La. 308 near Napoleonville, an 1846 plantation which is one of the best preserved in the entire South (504/524-1988), open daily.

Allow four to five days for this trip, which will give you a good idea of this little "France in the Southland," little known but extremely picturesque. If you'd like to learn more about the defense of the French language in Cajun country, and its cultural activities, contact **Codofil,** 810 Jefferson St., Lafayette, LA 70501 (318/233-1020).

Where to Stay En Route

IN LAFAYETTE. 🔑🔑 **Acadiana,** 1801 W. Pinhook Rd., Lafayette, LA 70508 (318/233-8120). 300 rms. Modern, friendly hotel. **I–M**

🔑🔑 **Lafayette Hilton and Towers,** 1521 Pinhook Rd., Lafayette, LA 70508 (318/235-6111). 328 rms. Big modern 15-story tower. **M–E**

🔑 **La Quinta Motor Inn,** 1810 U.S. 167N, Lafayette, LA 70501 (318/233-5610). 139 rms. Conventional but comfortable motel. **I**

IN NEW IBERIA. ✵ 🔑🔑 **Mintemere Plantation,** 1400 E. Main St., New Iberia, LA 70560 (318/364-6210). 5 rms with a charm all their own, in an authentic 19th-century plantation house. No credit cards. **E**

🔑🔑 **Holiday Inn,** 2801 Center St., New Iberia, LA 70560 (318/367-1201). 180 rms. A Holiday Inn modern style. **I**

🔑 **Best Western,** 2700 Center St., New Iberia, LA 70501 (318/364-3030). 103 rms. Motel. **I**

Where to Eat En Route

IN BREAUX BRIDGE. 🍸 **Mulate's,** La. 94 (318/332-4648). Breakfast/lunch/dinner daily. AE, MC, V. Excellent Cajun food. Dancing. Truly a local institution. **B–I**

IN HENDERSON. 🍸 **Robin's,** La. 352 (318/228-7594). Lunch/dinner daily. AE, DC, MC, V. One of the best places to eat in Cajun country. **B–I**

IN LAFAYETTE. 🍸 **Café Vermilionville,** 1304 Pinhook Rd. (318/237-0100). Lunch Mon.-Fri., dinner nightly, jazz brunch Sun. AE, MC, V. The oldest (1800) rest. in Lafayette, w. excellent Cajun food. **B–I**

🍸 **Don's Seafood,** 301 E. Vermilion St. (318/235-3551). Lunch/dinner daily. AE, CB, DC, MC, V. Very good Cajun-style fish and broiled steak. **B–I**

🍸 **Randol's,** 2320 Kaliste Saloom Rd. (318/981-7080). Lunch/dinner daily. MC, V. The place is famous for crab. **B–I**

IN NEW IBERIA. ✵ 🍸🍸 **Patout's,** 1846 Center St. (318/365-5206). Lunch Sun.-Fri., dinner nightly. AE, CB, DC, MC, V. The best rest. in Cajun country, with one of its best chefs, Alex Patout. Don't miss the experience. **I**

🔭 GULF COAST, FROM NEW ORLEANS TO MOBILE, ALABAMA

(330 mi., 528 km, round trip via I-10E, Miss. 607S, U.S. 90E, Miss. 163S, Miss. 188N, and I-10W): Fine shorescapes and historic seafaring towns make this trip a natural extension of your visit to New Orleans.

You begin with a dive into the future at the ☀ ⚓ **National Space Technology Laboratories** (601/688-2370), NASA's second-largest research center, where all space-vehicle engines are tested; it's at Exit 2 from I-10. Open daily. Then take a scenic ocean drive along I-90 through the beach resorts of **Bay St. Louis, Pass Christian,** and **Long Beach,** with their luxurious seaside homes once thronged by rich southern families, and on to **Gulfport** and its celebrated **Marine Life Aquarium,** in the Small Craft Harbor (601/863-0651), open daily.

Don't miss the excursion to ☀ **Gulf Islands National Seashore** and a visit to ☀ ⚓ **Old Fort Massachusetts,** an imposing defense work constructed 1859–1866. It was on these islands, the cradle of French-speaking civilization in the southern U.S. from 1699 to 1753, that in 1721 there disembarked 80 "casket girls," who came from France with their dowries and their trousseaux to ensure that Louisiana should not remain unpopulated. Fort Massachusetts was used for a while as a prisoner-of-war camp for Confederate soldiers during the War Between the States. You reach it from Gulfport on the *Pan American Clipper,* Small Craft Harbor (601/684-1014); it's open daily from mid-May through Aug.

Drive on to the lovely ⚓ **home of Jefferson Davis,** president of the Confederacy, on W. Beach Blvd. in Beauvoir (601/388-1313), (now a museum) open daily. Nearby, at ⚓ **Biloxi,** a very busy shrimp and oyster port founded by the French in 1699, there are many lovely old houses standing in stunning tropical gardens. The town also has beaches so magnificent that in summer it becomes a much-sought-after resort.

Farther east, at ⚓ **Pascagoula** with its "singing river" (the Pascagoula River gives off a strange sound, something like a swarm of bees, particularly on summer and fall evenings), visit the Old Spanish Fort (1718), which in spite of its name was built by the French, and is splendidly preserved; it's at 4602 Fort St. (601/769-1505), and is open Fri.-Wed.

At the end of your journey you'll have time for a detailed inspection of ☀ 🔭 **Mobile,** with its old neighborhoods full of fine colonial houses in the French style, and gardens where the azaleas bloom from Feb. to Apr.; look for these around Church Street, de Tonti Square, and Old Dauphinway. See Fort Condé, built by the French in 1724, at 150 S. Royal St., open daily; the Cathedral of the Immaculate Conception at Dauphin at Clairborne Sts., an imposing Greek Revival basilica dating from 1835, open daily; Oakleigh, a magnificent antebellum mansion which derives its name from the centuries-old oaks in its very lovely gardens, 350 Oakleigh Pl. at Savannah St. (205/432-1281), open daily; and the majestic battleship ☀ **U.S.S. Alabama,** covered with glory from World War II and the Korean War, which lies at anchor opposite the harbor, on Battleship Pkwy. via the George C. Wallace Tunnels (205/433-2703), open daily.

On the way back to New Orleans, make a detour via ☀ **Bellingrath Gardens and Home,** 20 mi. (32 km) south of Mobile, to see its sumptuous gardens planted with hundreds of different varieties of flowers, including 250,000 azaleas, some of which were brought from France in 1754; it's on Bellingrath Hwy. at Mon Louis (205/973-2217), open daily. Near ⚓ **Dauphin Island,** a well-known resort town, on Aug. 5, 1864, was fought the sea battle which led to the blockade of Mobile Bay by a Union fleet under the command of Adm. David G. Farragut. Visit Fort Gaines, captured by Union troops on Aug. 23, 1864. Wonderful fine-sand beaches and a bird sanctuary.

This is a very full four- to five- day trip.

Where to Stay En Route

IN BILOXI. 🛎🛎 **Royal d'Iberville,** 3420 W. Beach Blvd., Biloxi, MS 39531 (601/ 388-6610). 264 rms. Comfortable luxury hotel on the ocean. **M**

IN MOBILE. 🛎🛎🛎 **Stouffer Riverview Plaza,** 64 Water St., Mobile, AL 36602 (205/438-4000). 375 rms. Ultramodern 28-floor tower. **M–E**

※🛎🛎 **Malaga Inn,** 359 Church St., Mobile, AL 36602 (205/438-4701). 40 rms. Charming 1862 home designated as a historic monument. **I–M**

Where to Eat En Route

IN BILOXI. ※ 🍴🍴 **Mary Mahoney's Old French House,** Rue Magnolia and Rue Water (601/374-0163). Lunch/dinner Mon.-Sat. Créole and Cajun specialties in a charming upper-class home dating from 1737. **B–I**

🔭 **PLANTATION COUNTRY** (285 mi., 456 km, round trip via U.S. 90W, La. 18W, La. 1N, U.S. 61N, La. 66N, La. 10E, La. 68S, U.S. 61S, La. 30S, La. 75E, La. 44S, U.S. 61S, and La. 48S): Settled from the beginning of the 18th century by planters, wealthy Créole gentry of French or Spanish origin who exported to Europe the cotton, tobacco, rice, and indigo raised by armies of black slaves, the lower Mississippi Valley still displays its garland of luxurious plantations as silent witness of an urbane, elegant past. Your three-day journey through some of the finest plantations in Louisiana begins with a visit to ※ 🔭 **Oak Alley Plantation,** on La. 18 at Vacherie (504/ 523-4351), open daily. Built in 1839 by a rich French sugar planter, Jacques Telesphore Roman, it has been called "the queen of Louisiana plantations" because of its elegant Doric design and the extraordinary span of 300-year-old oak trees which overshadows its main driveway.

Then on to ※ 🔭 **Nottoway Plantation,** on La. 1 at White Castle (504/ 525-2730), open daily. With 64 rooms, this is the largest plantation home in the Southland, built in a gracious blend of Italianate and Greek Revival styles, with a double staircase in the hallway, an impressive ballroom, and a columned front.

As you pass, admire the **Plaquemine Locks** on La. 1 at Plaquemine, huge locks built at the beginning of the 20th century with a lookout tower rising above the Mississippi (504/925-3830), open Wed.-Sun. La. 1 takes you on to ※ **Baton Rouge,** the capital of Louisiana. Take a look at "Catfish Town," a huge, picturesque covered market in what were once warehouses along the Mississippi, now with dozens of shops and restaurants; it's on Government Street on the River Front (504/346-8888), open daily. You should also see the ⚓ **State Capitol,** dominated by its massive 450-ft. (135-m) tower built in 1932 with stone and marble from many countries; from its summit there is an all-around view of the city. It's at Riverside Mall and Spanish Rd. (504/342-7317), open daily. Two museums you must certainly see are the ⚓ **Louisiana Arts and Science Center,** occupying a splendid old railroad station no longer in use, at 100 S. River Rd. (504/344-9463), open Tues.-Sun.; and the ⚓ **Louisiana State University Rural Life Museum,** where you'll find a score of buildings and craftsmen's workshops from the 19th century, at 6200 Burden Lane at the junction of I-10 (504/766-8241), open Mon.-Fri.

Drive on to ※ ⚓ **Port Hudson Battlefield,** on U.S. 61, 14 mi. (22 km) north of Baton Rouge, scene of the longest (and one of the bloodiest) sieges of the Civil War, where 6,800 Confederate troops held off 30,000–40,000 Union soldiers from May 23 to July 9, 1863. Observation towers, museum. Open Thur.-Sun.

A little farther north, stop at ※ **St. Francisville,** with its charming old houses dating from the day when this little town, built on a ridge overlooking the river, was an important staging point for traffic traveling the Mississippi between New Orleans and Natchez. In the countryside around are many very beautiful plantations, including the 1830 ※ 🚲 **Greenwood Plantation,** regarded as the most perfect example of the southern colonial style of architecture; many movies have been made here. It's on Highland Rd. (504/655-4475), open Wed.-Sun. Also 🚲 **Myrtles Plantation,** with its fine wrought-iron balustrade running the whole length of the veranda, on U.S. 61 (504/635-6277), open daily; ※ 🚲 **Rosedown Plantation,** built in 1835, one of Louisiana's most sumptuous antebellum homes, standing in superb formal gardens in the French style, on La. 10 (504/635-3332), open daily; and 🚲 **Asphodel Plantation,** built 1820–1833, another favorite of Hollywood movie directors, on La. 68 (504/654-6868), open Mon.-Fri.

After returning to Baton Rouge, your route follows the curves of the Mississippi and brings your journey to a close with visits to five of Louisiana's most famous plantations. These are, in order:

※ 🚲🚲 **Ashland-Belle Hélène,** which, standing behind its majestic two-story colonnade, perpetuates the lordly, romantic classicism of the Old South; on La. 75 between Geismar and Darrow (504/473-1328), open daily.

※ 🚲🚲 **Houmas House Plantation,** on La. 942 at Burnside (504/473-7841), open daily, a sugar plantation built in 1840 in splendid Greek Revival style, with beautiful antique furniture.

🚲 **Tezcuco Plantation,** on La. 44 in Burnside (504/562-3929), open daily, a lovely building now designated as a historic monument.

※ 🚲🚲 **San Francisco Plantation,** La. 44 at Garyville (504/535-2341), open daily, an elegant 1854 Gothic Revival plantation house with a magnificent grand staircase and ornate interior decoration.

Finally we come to ※ 🚲 **Destrehan Plantation,** on La. 48 at Destrehan (504/764-9315), open daily, the oldest plantation in the Mississippi Delta.

This itinerary is expressly designed for those who love vivid glimpses of the past; don't miss it.

Where to Stay En Route

IN BATON ROUGE. 🛎🛎🛎 **Embassy Suites,** 4914 Constitution Ave., Baton Rouge, LA 70808 (504/924-6566). 224 suites. Very modern suites-only hotel. **M–E**

※ 🛎🛎 **Mt. Hope Plantation,** 8151 Highland Rd., Baton Rouge, LA 70802 (504/766-8600). 10 rms. Authentic Old South–style plantation house built in 1817. **M**

IN JACKSON. ※ 🛎🛎 **Asphodel Plantation,** La. 68, Jackson, LA 70748 (504/654-6868). 18 rms. A luxurious 1830s antebellum home. **M–E**

🛎 **Glencoe,** La. 68, Jackson, LA 70748 (504/629-5387). 8 rms. Fine example of late Victorian Gothic. **M**

IN ST. FRANCISVILLE. ※ 🛎🛎 **Cottage Plantation,** U.S. 61, St. Francisville, LA 70775 (504/635-3674). 12 rms. Typical Louisiana plantation house dating from 1795. **M**

🛎 **St. Francisville Inn,** 118 N. Commerce St., St. Francisville, LA 70775 (504/635-6502). 8 rms. Big Victorian home in a very handsome park. **M**

IN WHITE CASTLE. ※ 🛎🛎 **Nottoway Plantation,** La. 1, White Castle, LA 70788

(504/545-2730). 12 rms. Lousiana's largest plantation house, and one of its most beautiful. **E**

Where to Eat En Route

IN BATON ROUGE. ♝♝♝ Chalet Brandt, 7655 Old Hammond Hwy. (504/927-6040). Dinner only, Tues.-Sat. The fish soup and the veal w. chanterelle and morel mushrooms are among the successful achievements of this excellent continental-Créole rest. Pretty interior. **I–M**

IN BURNSIDE. ♝ The Cabin, La. 44 and La. 22 (504/473-3007). Lunch daily, dinner Thur., Fri., Sat. Excellent fish and Créole dishes in former slave quarters a century and a half old. **I**

IN DONALDSONVILLE. ❊ Lafitte's Landing, Sunshine Bridge Service Rd. (504/473-1232). Lunch daily, dinner Tues.-Sun. Créole and Cajun food. The building on the bank of the Mississippi, dating from 1797, may once have belonged to the pirate Jean Lafitte. **I**

IN PLAQUEMINE. ❊ Godfrey's, 602 Main St. (504/687-7578). Lunch only, Sun.-Fri. Créole food. Huge Victorian-style house. **B–I**

Chapter 16

FLORIDA'S EAST COAST

□ □ □

Florida's Atlantic coast, where swimsuits and suntan oil hold undisputed sway, unrolls its hundreds of miles of white sand beaches and coconut trees from **Amelia Island** on the Georgia border in the north to **Miami** in the south. It has remarkably comprehensive facilities to offer vacationers, often at very attractive prices—as witness the arrival every year of some 25 million U.S. tourists (mostly from the big cities of the Northeast), more than a million Canadians, and some hundreds of thousands of visitors from Europe and Latin America. In reality, the great beach resorts of **Daytona Beach** (famous for its auto races), the elegant and upscale **Palm Beach,** the more easy-going **Fort Lauderdale** and **Pompano Beach, Boca Raton,** and **Miami** (see the Miami chapter) form a single agglomeration of hotels—one of the largest in the world.

But Florida (discovered by Juan Ponce de León on Easter Day 1513, it owes its name to this accident of the calendar—the Spanish for "Easter Sunday" is *Pascua Florida)* is more than a string of immaculate beaches, wild mangrove swamps, or a network of fish-filled lakes and rivers. It boasts some of America's most popular tourist attractions, such as **St. Augustine,** the oldest city in the United States. It was founded by the Spanish conquistador Don Pedro Menéndez de Avilés in 1565—just 19 years after Sir Walter Raleigh's short-lived attempt to settle Roanoke Island, "the lost colony," and 55 years before the British colonists disembarked from the *Mayflower* at Plymouth. **Marineland** is the oldest marine zoo in the world and one of the most popular. The **Kennedy Space Center,** headquarters of the astronauts, has been internationally famous since the moon landing and the first shuttle launches. Visitors to Florida should make a point of putting the Space Center on their itinerary. **Lake Okeechobee,** one of the largest freshwater lakes in the country (30 by 40 mi., 60 by 48 km), is a paradise for bass and catfish fishermen. **Daytona Beach** is a popular resort, invaded every year by tens of thousands of car-racing enthusiasts come to watch the Daytona 24 Hours, the Daytona 500, and other famous races.

Finally, less than two hours by car from the Atlantic coast, two of the world's greatest theme parks await the tourist: the enchanted kingdom of **Walt Disney World** and its twin attraction, **Epcot,** the amazing 21st-century amusement park whose 18-story steel-and-concrete sphere has become the new symbol of the state of Florida. And let's not forget **Sea World,** an enormous marine zoo where sharks, killer whales, and dolphins frolic in the public gaze (see the Orlando chapter).

BASIC FACTS: State of Florida. Area Codes: 904 (St. Augustine and Daytona Beach); 305 or 407 (all others). Time Zone: Eastern Time. Founded in: 1565 (St. Augustine); 1567 (first Spanish garrison at Miami). Distance from Amelia Island to Miami Beach: approx. 400 mi. (640 km).

CLIMATE: Florida is well known for its sunshine. Winter is the ideal time for a visit—also the most crowded and expensive. The sun shines continually and the mercury swings between 60° and 68°F (16° and 20°C)—perfect for walking, even if too cool for swimming. Summer is hot and humid, with short but frequent tropical downpours, not to speak of prowling hurricanes. Spring and autumn are consistently sunny and pleasant, justifying the legend on Florida auto registration plates which reads "The Sunshine State."

ARRIVAL & TRANSIT INFORMATION

AIRPORTS: There are seven major airports that act as gateways to the Florida east coast.
　　Daytona Beach Regional Airport (DAB), 5 mi. (8 km) west.
　　Fort Lauderdale–Hollywood International Airport (FLL), 4 mi. (6.5 km) south.
　　Jacksonville International Airport (JAX), 15 mi. (24 km) north.
　　Melbourne Regional Airport (MLB), 1 mi. (2 km) NW.
　　Miami International Airport (MIA) (see the Miami chapter).
　　Orlando International Airport (MCO) (see the Orlando chapter).
　　West Palm Beach International Airport (PBI), 3 mi. (5 km) west.

AIRLINES: **Fort Lauderdale**—American (467-3040), Continental (525-4126), Delta (763-2211), Eastern (463-1515), Northwest (525-7204), PanAm (462-6600), TWA (522-1100), United (525-7321), USAir (toll free 800/428-4322).
　　Jacksonville—American (354-2593), Continental (354-3452), Delta (398-3011), Eastern (355-7392), TWA (toll free 800/221-2000), United (toll free 800/241-6522), USAir (toll free 800/428-4322).
　　Miami—See the Miami chapter.
　　Orlando—See the Orlando chapter.

CAR RENTAL: To cover this large area adequately you will need a car, and besides, rental rates are comparatively reasonable. In addition to the many car-rental agencies in **Miami** and **Orlando** (see those chapters for details), rentals are available at the following gateway cities (at airport locations unless noted):
　　Fort Lauderdale—Avis (761-7115); Budget, 1501 N. Federal Hwy. (921-8585); Dollar (921-6244); Econo Car, 2125 S. Federal Hwy. (763-7369); Hertz (525-5281); National (525-3633).
　　Jacksonville—Avis (757-2327); Budget (757-3555); Hertz (757-2151); National (757-7580); Thrifty (757-3366).

TRAIN: In addition to the AMTRAK stations in Miami and Orlando (see those chapters for details), there are stations/stops along the Florida east coast at 200 W. 21st Terrace, Fort Lauderdale (toll free 800/872-7245); 3570 Clifford Lane, Jacksonville (904/731-1600); and Tamarind Ave. & Datura St., West Palm Beach (toll free 800/872-7245).

BUS: In addition to the Greyhound offices in Miami and Orlando (see those chapters for details), there are Florida east coast offices at 282 N. Federal Hwy.,

Boca Raton (407/395-6696); 138 S. Ridgewood Ave., Daytona Beach (904/255-7076); 513 N.E. 3rd St., Fort Lauderdale (305/764-6551); 10 N. Pearl St., Jacksonville (904/356-1841); and 100 1st St., West Palm Beach (407/833-8534).

INFORMATION, TOURS, & SPECIAL EVENTS

TOURIST INFORMATION: For general information on the region, write or call the **Florida Division of Tourism,** 126 Van Buren St., Tallahassee, FL 32301 (904/487-1462). For more specific information, when in the area, contact:

Boca Raton Chamber of Commerce, 1800 N. Dixie Hwy., FL 33432 (407/395-4433).

Cocoa Beach Chamber of Commerce, 400 Fortenberry Rd., FL 32952 (407/459-2200).

Daytona Beach Chamber of Commerce, P.O. Box 2775, FL 32015 (904/255-0415).

Fort Lauderdale Chamber of Commerce, 208 S.E. Third Ave., FL 33301 (305/462-6000).

Grant (see the Melbourne Chamber of Commerce).

Hallandale Chamber of Commerce, P.O. Box 249, FL 33009 (305/454-0541).

Jacksonville Convention & Visitors Bureau, 33 S. Hogan St., FL 32202 (904/353-9736).

Jensen Beach Chamber of Commerce, 1910 Jensen Beach Blvd., FL 33457 (407/334-3444).

Kissimmee Convention & Visitors Bureau, P.O. Box 2007, FL 32742 (407/847-5000).

Melbourne Chamber of Commerce, 1005 E. Strawbridge Ave., FL 32901 (407/724-5400).

Miami Department of Tourism & Conventions (see the chapter on Miami).

Orlando Area Chamber of Commerce (see the chapter on Orlando).

Palm Beach Chamber of Commerce, 45 Coconut Row, FL 33480 (407/655-3282).

Pompano Beach Chamber of Commerce, 2200 E. Atlantic Blvd., FL 33062 (305/941-2940).

St. Augustine Chamber of Commerce, 75 King St., FL 32084 (904/824-5681).

Titusville Chamber of Commerce, 2000 S. Washington St., FL 32780 (407/267-3036).

West Palm Beach Chamber of Commerce, 501 N. Flagler Dr., FL 33401 (407/833-3711).

GUIDED TOURS: For the Miami and Orlando areas, see the chapters on those cities. In other localities on the Florida east coast, consult the local *Yellow Pages* under "Sightseeing."

SPECIAL EVENTS: For exact dates of the events listed below, check with the chambers of commerce and visitors bureaus listed above under "Tourist Information."

Boca Raton
High Goal Polo (Jan.-Apr.): A popular polo championship event.

Cocoa Beach
National Surfing Tourneys (Easter and Labor Day).

Daytona Beach
Auto Races: Daytona 24 Hours (early Feb.); Daytona 500 (mid-Feb.).
AMA Motorcycle Races (early March).
Stock-car Races: Like the Firecracker 400 (July 4).

Fort Lauderdale
Winterfest and Boat Parade (Dec.): Three weeks of cultural, artistic, and sporting events culminating in a spectacular parade on the water.

Grant
Seafood Festival (Feb.): A gigantic fish, shellfish, and seafood blowout, attracting 50,000 participants to a glutton's festival which lasts 48 hrs.

Hallandale
Seminole Indian Tribal Fair (early Feb.): A Native American cultural event in which every tribe in North America participates. Dance displays, handcraft exhibition, ethnic cooking. For information, call 305/583-7112.

Jacksonville
Mayport Jazz Festival (Oct.): One of the country's best-known modern-jazz events.

Jensen Beach
Turtle Watch (June-July; every evening): Visitors may see enormous (220–440 lbs., 100–200 kg, and up) sea turtles crossing the sand to lay their eggs at the water's edge.

Kissimmee
Silver Spurs Rodeo (3rd weekend in Feb., wknd of July 4): For lovers of the real Old West.
Florida State Air Fair (end of Oct. to beginning of Nov.): Complete with parachute jumps, aerobatics, etc.

Melbourne Beach
Turtle Crawl (June-Aug.): Thousands of newly hatched baby turtles struggling to reach the sea. Spectacular.

Pompano Beach
Boat Parade (July 4 and mid-Dec.): The boats are decorated and illuminated.

St. Augustine
Cross & Sword (Mon.-Sat. from mid-June to Sept.): A musical celebration of the founding of the city.
Days in Spain (mid-Aug.): Processions, shows, and fiesta in honor of the first Spanish conquistadors.

Titusville
Valiant Air Command Show (early Mar.): The world's greatest air show, featuring exclusively World War II combat planes. Aerobatics, ground displays, etc.

West Palm Beach
   Silver Sailfish Derby (mid-Jan. to early Feb.): Big-game fishing championship events.

DEEP-SEA FISHING: Almost three million visitors go deep-sea fishing in Florida every year, from Fernandina Beach to Key West on the Atlantic coast (sea bream, mackerel, barracuda, swordfish), and from Naples to Pensacola along the Gulf of Mexico (blue marlin, tarpon). Rates for fully equipped big-game fishing boats are around $350 for a half day (6 hrs) or $450 for a full day (10 hrs). Some recommendations:
   Jacksonville: Ray Barnes (904/744-4771).
   Fort Pierce: Ken Moore (407/465-2101).
   Fort Lauderdale: Ray McCleary (305/463-1357).

A NORTH TO SOUTH ITINERARY

   The section of this guide devoted to the east coast of Florida has been organized as an itinerary, starting at Amelia Island and ending in Miami Beach, a distance of almost 400 miles (640 km). You may choose not to drive the whole distance; key towns such as Jacksonville, Daytona, Orlando, Palm Beach, Fort Lauderdale, and Miami are linked by air, bus, and train, and car rentals are available everywhere (at some of the lowest rates in the country, particularly off-season). In that case, you can select from the following travel plan the parts that appeal to you most!

DISTANCES DOWN THE FLORIDA EAST COAST

From	To	Distance
Amelia Island	Fort Caroline	30 mi. (48 km)
Fort Caroline	Jacksonville	14 mi. (22 km)
Jacksonville	St. Augustine	40 mi. (64 km)
St. Augustine	Fort Matanzas	15 mi. (24 km)
Fort Matanzas	Marineland of Florida	5 mi. (7 km)
Marineland of Florida	Daytona Beach	32 mi. (51 km)
Daytona Beach	Kennedy Space Center	52 mi. (83 km)
Kennedy Space Center	Orlando	46 mi. (75 km)
Orlando	Sea World	13 mi. (21 km)
Sea World	Walt Disney World	7 mi. (11 km)
Epcot	Cypress Gardens	34 mi. (54 km)
Cypress Gardens	Cocoa Beach	97 mi. (155 km)
Cocoa Beach	Patrick AFB	5 mi. (8 km)
Patrick AFB	Vero Beach	48 mi. (74 km)
Vero Beach	Fort Pierce	14 mi. (22 km)
Fort Pierce	Jensen Beach	19 mi. (31 km)
Jensen Beach	Lake Okeechobee	39 mi. (62 km)
Lake Okeechobee	Jupiter Beach	33 mi. (52 km)
Jupiter Beach	Palm Beach	18 mi. (28 km)
Palm Beach	Boca Raton	28 mi. (45 km)
Boca Raton	Pompano Beach	8 mi. (12 km)
Pompano Beach	Fort Lauderdale	7 mi. (11 km)
Fort Lauderdale	Hollywood	8 mi. (12 km)
Hollywood	Miami Beach	17 mi. (26 km)

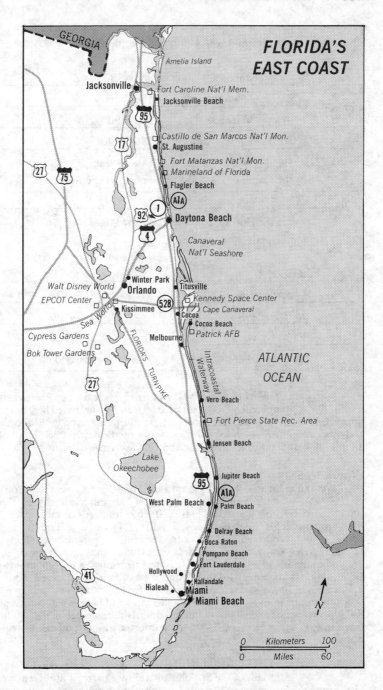

FLORIDA'S
EAST COAST

GEORGIA

Amelia Island

Jacksonville
□ *Fort Caroline Nat'l Mem.*
95
Jacksonville Beach

17

27 **75**

□ *Castillo de San Marcos Nat'l Mon.*
□ St. Augustine
□ *Fort Matanzas Nat'l Mon.*
□ *Marineland of Florida*
Flagler Beach

92 (1) (A1A)
4 Daytona Beach

Canaveral Nat'l Seashore

Winter Park
Walt Disney World Orlando Titusville
EPCOT Center □ *Kennedy Space Center*
□ Kissimmee (528) *Cape Canaveral*
Sea World Cocoa
Cocoa Beach
Cypress Gardens Melbourne □ *Patrick AFB*
Bok Tower Gardens □

27 *Intracoastal Waterway*

ATLANTIC OCEAN

FLORIDA'S TURNPIKE

Vero Beach

□ *Fort Pierce State Rec. Area*

Jensen Beach

Lake Okeechobee

Jupiter Beach
95
(A1A)
West Palm Beach ● Palm Beach

Delray Beach
Boca Raton
Pompano Beach
Fort Lauderdale

Hollywood
41 Hallandale
Hialeah Miami
Miami Beach

N

| 0 | Kilometers | 100 |
| 0 | Miles | 60 |

Room Rates Along the Florida Coast	
B (Budget)	up to $30
I (Inexpensive)	$30–$60
M (Moderate)	$60–$90
E (Expensive)	$90–$140
VE (Very Expensive) $140 and up	

See the listing of the toll-free numbers in the Appendix.

Florida Coast Restaurant Prices	
(per person, excluding drinks and service)	
B (Budget)	up to $15
I (Inexpensive)	$15–$25
M (Moderate)	$25–$40
E (Expensive)	$40–$60
VE (Very Expensive)	$60 and up

AMELIA ISLAND: By turns French (a group of Huguenots, or French Protestants, led by Jean Ribaut landed here in 1562), Spanish, British, Mexican, and American—and often a stronghold for pirates and other adventurers—this small island is not on the beaten track, but it offers 14 mi. (20 km) of magnificent beaches, and is a fisherman's dream.

Where to Stay
Amelia Island Plantation, 3000 First Coast Hwy. (on Fla. A1A, 6 mi., 10 km, south of Fernandina Beach), FL 32034 (904/261-6161; toll free 800/874-5510). 625 rms, A/C, cable color TV. Mini-apartments for two to eight people. AE, CB, DC, MC, V. Free parking, 20 pools, 24 tennis courts, three golf courses, health club, private beach, horseback riding, bicycles, sauna, rest. (Dune Side Club), coffeeshop, bars, rm svce, disco, hrdrsr, beauty parlor, grocery, crib $10. *Note:* Luxurious resort complex in a rustic setting on the ocean, with 4 mi. (6 km) of magnificent beaches and more than 1,300 acres of dunes and woods. A paradise for lovers of sports and fresh air. Spacious rms or mini-apartments w. kitchenettes and private patios. Reception and svce on the impersonal side—but still one of the best hotels in the Southeast. Interesting vacation packages. **E –VE (apartments, VE), but off-season reductions**

FORT CAROLINE: Fort Caroline was erected in 1564 at the mouth of the St. John's River by a party of 300 French colonists under the leadership of René de Laudonnière. A few months later the fort was taken by the Spaniards and its entire garrison (except for 70 women and children) put to the sword. In 1568 the French launched a reprisal raid against the Spaniards and burned the fort to the ground. It was partially rebuilt by the British, and achieved its moment of glory during the Civil War. Open daily. For information, call 904/641-7155.

JACKSONVILLE: With its half million population and cluster of ultramodern skyscrapers along the banks of the St. John's River, Jacksonville is one of the Southeast's busiest ports, handling large shipments of automobiles from Japan and Korea. Very busy airport. In terms of economic growth it ranks 16th among major American cities. The **Mayport Naval Base**, at the mouth of the river, is one of the navy's most important. With an area of 840 sq. mi. (2,180 sq km), Jacksonville covers more ground than any other U.S. city. The **Cummer Gallery of Art**, 829 Riverside Ave. (904/356-6857), is an interesting art museum with a collection of 700 pieces of Meissen (Dresden) china; open Tues.-Sun.

Where to Stay

Omni Hotel, 245 Water St., FL 32202 (904/355-6664; toll free, see Omni). 354 rms, A/C, color TV, in-rm movies. AE, CB, DC, MC, V. Parking $6, pool, health club, two rests., bars, 24-hr rm svce, disco, boutiques. *Note:* Latest of the area's luxury palaces—six stories of austerely post-modern glass and steel at the edge of the St. John's River. Forms part of the brand-new Enterprise Center, a huge complex of office buildings, stores, and rests. Spacious, well-equipped rms; elegant interior, ultra-professional svce. Strategically located in the heart of dwntwn Jacksonville. Business clientele. **E–VE**

Jacksonville Hotel, 565 S. Main St., FL 32207 (904/398-8800). 292 rms, A/C, color TV, AE, DC, MC, V. Free garage, pool, rest. (Wharf), coffeeshop, bar, rm svce, disco, hrdrsr, boutiques, free crib. *Note:* Modern ten-story grand hotel on the bank of the St. John's River. Large, comfortable rms w. private balconies, the best overlooking the river. Efficient reception and svce. Well located. Group and business clientele. Interesting vacation packages. **M–E**

Best Western Inn South, 5221 University Blvd. West, FL 32216 (904/737-1690; toll free, see Best Western). 187 rms, A/C, color TV, in-rm movies. AE, CB, DC, MC, V. Free parking, pool, tennis court, rest., bar, rm svce, disco, free crib. *Note:* Typical up-to-date motel 10 min. from dwntwn along I-95. Comfortable, home-like rms, friendly svce, inviting garden. Ideal if you're driving. **I**

Motel 6, 6107 Youngerman Circle, FL 32244 (904/772-8228). 126 rms, A/C, color TV, free in-rm movies. DC, MC, V. Free parking, pool, free crib. *Note:* Ideal for motorists; a good value. **B**

IN NEARBY JACKSONVILLE BEACH. **Holiday Inn**, 1617 N. 1st St., FL 32250 (904/249-9071; toll free, see Holiday Inns). 150 rms, A/C, color TV. AE, CB, DC, MC, V. Free parking, pool, sauna, health club, tennis court, rest. (Kelly's), bar, rm svce, disco, crib $5. *Note:* Standard vacation hotel w. direct access to beach. Functional rms w. balconies and refrigerators; impersonal reception and svce. Typical Holiday Inn style. **M–E**

Where to Eat

Crawdaddy's, 1643 Prudential Dr. (904/396-3546). A/C. Lunch Mon.-Sat.; dinner daily. AE, CB, DC, MC, V. Specialties: chicken Cajun, jambalaya, seafood gumbo. *Note:* This fisherman's-hut setting will fulfill your wildest dreams of the exotic; the New Orleans cooking is excellent, and the svce attentive. There's dancing too, and the place has a big local following, so resv. are advisable. *Créole.* **I**

Wharf, in the Jacksonville Hotel (see "Where to Stay," above) (904/398-5235). A/C. Lunch/dinner daily. AE, DC, MC, V. Jkt. Specialties: shrimp Wellington, roast beef, fish of the day. *Note:* Very creditable hotel rest. w. excellent seafood. Basic maritime décor; efficient svce; dancing Mon.-Sat. Resv. advised. *Continental-Seafood.* **I**

Patti's, 7300 Beach Blvd. (904/725-1662). A/C. Dinner only, daily; closed Thanksgiving, Dec. 24–25. AE, DC, MC, V. Specialties: fresh homemade pasta, lasagne, chicken parmigiana. *Note:* Completely authentic little trattoria; food ditto, if a little unimaginative. Locally popular. *Italian.* **I**

ST. AUGUSTINE: The oldest city in the U.S., founded in 1565 by Don Pedro Menéndez de Avilés, this bastion of Spanish colonialism retains a few interesting monuments (scrupulously restored) from its troubled past.

The Sights

Castillo de San Marcos, Castillo Dr. & Menendez Ave. (904/829-6506): Impressive fortress built in 1672 which commands Matanzas Bay. Its 13-ft- (4-m-) thick walls make it a weighty symbol of the Spanish military presence in Florida. Open daily. Don't miss it.

Casa del Hidalgo, St. George & Hypolita Sts. (904/829-6460): Preserves for us the atmosphere of 17th-century St. Augustine. Open Mon.-Fri.

Fountain of Youth, 155 Magnolia Ave. & William St. (904/829-3168): Supposed site of the "Fountain of Youth" discovered by the sailors of Ponce de León in 1513, when they first landed in Florida—making it the first place in North America on which Western Europeans set foot. Indian cemetery and planetarium nearby.

Lightner Museum, Cordova & King Sts. (904/824-2874): Occupying the 300 rms of the former Alcazar Hotel built in 1888, this museum, bequest of a wealthy Chicago publisher, displays a collection of 19th-century art objects. Open daily.

Oldest House, 14 St. Francis St.: The oldest house (1703) still standing in the city. Open daily.

Oldest Store Museum, 4 Artillery Lane: Amusing 19th-century bazaar, with more than 100,000 period objects on display. Open daily.

Nombre de Dios Mission, San Marcos Ave.: Site of the country's oldest mission, where the first Mass was celebrated in 1565; its huge stainless-steel cross, the highest in the U.S., rises 192 ft (60 m).

Zorayda Castle, 83 King St. (904/824-3097): A replica, constructed in 1833, of the Alhambra of Granada in Spain. Open daily.

And, especially, don't forget **San Augustin Antiguo** (Old St. Augustine), around St. George St., with its picturesque cobbled alleyways and balconied houses made of the local building material, "coquina," a conglomerate of seashells and sand.

A visit to this city is a must. The **Visitor Information Center** is at 10 Castillo Dr. (904/824-3334).

Where to Stay

☀☟🛎🛎 **Ponce de Leon Resort,** 4000 Ponce de Leon Blvd. (U.S. 1), FL 32085 (904/824-2821; toll free 800/824-2821). 200 rms, A/C, cable color TV. AE, DC, MC, V. Free parking, pool, tennis court, golf course, rest., bar, rm svce, disco, free airport limo, free crib. *Note:* Excellent value five min. by car from the beach or the Old City. Enormous, attractive rms w. balconies. Svce usually w. a smile. Interesting American Plan and vacation packages. The golfer's or tennis-player's dream. **M**

🛎 **Comfort Inn,** 1111 Ponce de Leon Blvd., FL 32084 (904/ 824-5554; toll free 800/228-5150). 86 rms, A/C, color TV, in-rm movies. AE, CB, DC, MC, V. Free parking, pool, coffeeshop, bar, disco, crib free. *Note:* A brand-new motel near St. Augustine's Old City. Comfort and facilities up to snuff; cordial reception and svce. Very good value. **I–M, but lower rates out of season**

🛎 **Monterey,** 16 Avenida Menendez, FL 32084 (904/824-4882). 54 rms, A/C, cable color TV. AE, CB, DC, MC, V. Free parking, pool, adjoining coffeeshop, free airport limo, crib $5. *Note:* Modest but well-run little motel opposite the Castillo San Marcos. The best rms overlook the bay. Interesting vacation packages. **I, but lower rates out of season**

Where to Eat

🍸🍸 **Chimes,** 12 Menendez Ave. (904/829-8141). A/C. Breakfast/lunch/dinner daily; closed Dec. 25. AE, DC, MC, V. Specialties: fish of the day, steamed shrimp, steak, leg of lamb. Good desserts. *Note:* St. Augustine's best rest.; very commendable cooking but slowish svce. Fine view of the bay and Castillo de San Marcos; an agreeable place. *Steak-Seafood.* **I–M**

🍸 **Columbia,** 98 St. George St. (904/824-3341). A/C. Lunch/ dinner daily; brunch Sun. AE, CB, DC, MC, V. Specialties: black-bean soup, paella, red snapper Alicante. *Note:* Charming early-20th-century "meson" in the Castilian style; Spanish- and Cuban-inspired food at very refreshing prices. Agreeable background music, friendly svce. In the heart of St. Augustine's historic quarter. *Spanish-Latin American.* **B–I**

🔔 **FORT MATANZAS:** The Spanish name means "Fort of the Massacres," and on the site of this fortified bastion built in 1740 (restored in 1924), more than 250 French Huguenots were indeed massacred by the Spaniards in 1565. Reached by boat from the Visitor Center; open daily. For information, call 904/471-0016. Worth a look.

🔔 **MARINELAND OF FLORIDA** (on Fla. A1A) (904/471-1111): The world's oldest marine zoo, opened in 1938, where hundreds of sharks, barracuda, porpoises, dolphins, moray eels, and the like may be watched through portholes in two enormous pools. Florida's other great sea zoo, Sea World at Orlando (see below), is more up-to-date and definitely more spectacular. Nevertheless, this one is worth going out of your way for. Open daily.

🔔 **DAYTONA BEACH:** A very popular beach resort (particularly among surfers), with 18 mi. (40 km) of sand along which cars may drive freely (though slowly) at low tide; there are also dune buggies for hire.

The town is also famous for its auto and stock-car races: the Daytona 24 Hours and Daytona 500 in February, the Firecracker 400 on July 4, etc. The ⚑ **Daytona International Speedway,** 1801 Speedway Blvd. (904/254-6767), where these events are held, can accommodate 125,000 spectators, and has parking for 35,000 cars! Open to visitors year round.

You should also see the ⚑ **Museum of Arts & Sciences,** 1040 Museum Blvd. (904/255-0285), where a fine collection of Latin American and Caribbean art is displayed in a building of ultramodern design. Open Tues.-Sun.

And take in the ⚑ **Ponce de Leon Inlet Lighthouse,** south of the town. Dating from 1884, the 175-ft (53-m) tower has been converted into an original kind of maritime museum. Well worth the side trip.

Where to Stay

Hilton Daytona, 2637 S. Atlantic Ave., FL 32018 (904/767-7350; toll free, see Hilton). 215 rms, A/C, color TV, in-rm movies. AE, CB, DC, MC, V. Free parking, two pools, tennis court, health club, sauna, putting green, boats, rest., coffeeshop, bars, rm svce, disco, crib free. *Note:* Rather ponderous modernist structure, but very spacious, comfortable rms w. their own balconies. Every facility of a great resort hotel. Efficient svce. Caters to groups and conventions. There is a laudable rest. on the top floor. **M–E, but lower rates out of season**

Holiday Inn Surfside, 2700 N. Atlantic Ave., FL 32018 (904/672-3770; toll free, see Holiday Inns). 383 rms, A/C, color TV, in-rm movies. Free parking, two pools, tennis court, rest., bar, rm svce, disco, crib free. *Note:* Modern 12-story tower on the beach; the Holiday Inn style at its friendliest and most comfortable. Group clientele. Interesting vacation packages. **I–M, but lower rates out of season**

Days Inn Beachside, 1909 S. Atlantic Ave., FL 32018 (904/255-4492; toll free, see Days Inns). 196 rms, A/C, color TV, free in-rm movies. AE, DC, MC, V. Free parking, pool, rest., bar, crib free. *Note:* Comfortable, unpretentious family motel directly on the beach. Rms w. private patios, the best overlooking the ocean. No alcoholic beverages in the rest. **I–M, but lower rates out of season**

Where to Eat

Asian Inn Restaurant, 2516 S. Atlantic Ave. (904/788-6269). A/C. Dinner only nightly exc. Tues.; closed Tues., Jan. 1st. AE, CB, DC, MC, V. *Specialties:* Chinese and Japanese cuisine. *Note:* You have to travel if you want good Chinese food along Florida's east coast, but this place is usually worth the detour. Does especially well with Cantonese and Szechuan dishes. Decor is standard Chinese rest. Excellent svce. Resv. suggested.

Cafeteria / Fast Food

Morrison's, 200 N. Ridgewood (904/258-6396). Lunch/dinner daily, till 8:30 p.m. No credit cards. Specialties: fried shrimps, fish of the day, roast beef. *Note:* Honest cafeteria food.

KENNEDY SPACE CENTER: Originally known as Cape Canaveral, the **John F. Kennedy Space Center** is America's largest interplanetary target range. Since the first rocket (a converted German V2) was launched in 1950, and including the most recent space shuttles, more than 2,200 devices have been launched into space from this NASA facility, which employs more than 25,000 technicians on its narrow seaside peninsula. It was from here that, on July 16, 1969, Apollo XI carried Neil Armstrong, Michael Collins, and Edward Aldrin on their historic mission—Armstrong and Aldrin were the first men to set foot on the moon.

Open buses take guided tours to the giant hangar where Saturn rockets and space vehicles are assembled; this **Vehicle Assembly Building,** 512 ft (160 m) high, is the largest of its kind in the world. Other highlights of the tour are the astronaut training center and several launching zones. There is a well-stocked space museum, and a cinema with a five-story screen (IMAX theater) where films of space shuttle launches are shown.

Open daily except Dec. 25. For information on timetables, call 407/452-2121. Don't miss this one. Inside Florida there is a toll-free number (800/432-2153) which will give you advance information on launchings.

Where to Stay in the Area

Hilton, 1550 N. Atlantic Ave., in Cocoa Beach, FL 32931 (407/799-0003; toll free, see Hilton). 300 rms, cable color TV. AE, CB, DC, MC, V. Free valet parking, pool, putting green, boats, rest., bar, rm svce, disco, free crib. *Note:* Ultramodern six-story hotel on the ocean, w. huge, comfortable rms. VIP floor. Efficient svce. 15 min. by road from Kennedy Space Center. Caters mostly to tourists. **M–E**

Holiday Inn, 260 E. Merritt Island Causeway, in Merritt Island, FL 32952 (407/452-7711; toll free, see Holiday Inns). 128 rms, A/C, cable color TV. AE, CB, DC, MC, V. Free parking, pool, tennis court, rest. (C. W. Dandy's), bar, rm svce, disco, free crib. *Note:* Modern, functional Holiday Inn–style motel on the banks of the Indian River; ideal for visitors to Cape Kennedy, which is 15 min. by car. **I–M, but lower rates out of season**

Travelodge Apollo, 3810 S. Washington Ave. (U.S. A1A), in Titusville, FL 32780 (407/267-9111; toll free, see Travelodge). 112 rms, A/C, cable color TV. AE, CB, DC, MC, V. Free parking, pool, rest., bar, rm svce, crib $5. *Note:* On the Indian River only 15 min. by car from Cape Kennedy; offers very acceptable standards of comfort, a cordial reception, and a good view over the center's firing ranges. Very good value overall. **I**

Motel 6, 3701 N. Atlantic Ave., in Cocoa Beach, FL 32931 (407/783-0890). 104 rms, A/C, color TV, free in-rm movies. DC, MC, V. Free parking, pool, free crib. *Note:* Unsurpassed value a quarter of an hour from Cape Kennedy; ideal for motorists. Facing beach; no rest. or bar. **B**

IN NEARBY MELBOURNE (25 mi, 40 km, south). **Radisson Suite Hotel Oceanside,** 3101 N. Fla. A1A, Indialantic, FL 32903 (407/773-9260; toll free, see Radisson). 168 suites, A/C, color TV. AE, CB, DC, MC, V. Free parking, pool, health club, sauna, rest., bar, rm svce. *Note:* Luxury hotel of original post-modern design at the water's edge. Spacious and remarkably comfortable suites w. their own balconies, the best overlooking the ocean. Brand-new facilities; excellent svce; 30 min. by car from Kennedy Space Center. Very acceptable rest. Clientele of well-to-do vacationers. **E–VE**

Days Inn, 4455 New Haven Ave., FL 32904 (407/724-5840; toll free, see Days Inns). 237 rms, A/C, color TV. AE, DC, MC, V. Free parking, pool, tennis court, rest., free crib. *Note:* A great place at very reasonable prices. Inviting rms w. balconies; garden w. small artificial lake. 45 min. by car from the Kennedy Space Center. Very good value. No alcoholic beverages permitted in rest. **I, but lower rates out of season**

Where to Eat in the Area

      Bernard's Surf, 2 S. Atlantic Ave., Cocoa Beach (407/783-2401). A/C. Lunch Mon.-Sat.; dinner daily; closed Dec. 25. AE, DC, MC, V. Specialties: red snapper, stuffed avocado, steak, shrimp Louie. *Note:* A very large menu and a softly romantic atmosphere of an evening are the two main attractions of this rest.; the food is commendable but unimaginative. Resv. advised. *Steak-Seafood.* **B–I**

    Lobster Shanty, 2000 S. Orlando, Cocoa Beach (407/783-1350). A/C. Lunch/dinner daily; closed Thanksgiving, Dec. 25. Specialties: rock shrimp, scallops, sea trout, red snapper. *Note:* Very good fish rest. right on the dock, often packed at peak hrs, so resv. a must. Attractive paneled décor highlighted by aquariums. Painstaking svce. A fine place, 25 min. by road from Kennedy Space Center. *Seafood.* **B–I**

    ORLANDO (46 mi., 70 km, west of the Kennedy Space Center): The tourist capital of Florida, with a thronged airport and a multitude of hotels, motels, and restaurants. Very near Walt Disney World and other major attractions. For detailed tourist information, see the chapter on Orlando.

    SEA WORLD (61 mi., 95 km, SW of the Kennedy Space Center): Enormous, ultramodern sea zoo. Shark aquarium with glass tunnel for sightseers; trained orcas (killer whales) and dolphins, sea lions, giant turtles, etc. Waterskiing displays. A spectacle that beggers description —and attracts almost three million tourists yearly. Well worth going out of your way for. Open daily. For detailed tourist information, see the chapter on Orlando.

    WALT DISNEY WORLD (71 mi., 115 km, SW of the Kennedy Space Center): The largest, and most famous, theme park in the world, visited by more than 200 million people since it opened in 1971. With an area of 28,000 acres—twice that of Manhattan Island—this is an amusement park on a planetary scale. It's open every day, 12 months a year. If there were nothing else to see in Florida, you should go just for this. For detailed tourist information, see the chapter on Orlando.

    EPCOT (71 mi., 115 km, SW of the Kennedy Space Center): This youngest child of the Walt Disney family, opened in 1982, is a 21st-century theme park with many of the attractions of a World's Fair. Designed to accommodate 18 million visitors a year, it cost $1 billion to build—2½ times more than Walt Disney World and four times more than Disneyland. Connected by monorail to Walt Disney World, this futuristic amusement park, overshadowed by its 18-story steel-and-concrete sphere, is also worth the trip to Florida all by itself. For detailed tourist information, see the chapter on Orlando.

    CYPRESS GARDENS (101 mi., 164 km, SW of the Kennedy Space Center): For more than a quarter of a century these magnificent tropical gardens on the shores of Lake Eloise have been one of Florida's principal tourist attractions. Underwater displays; waterskiing ballets in wonderful Esther Williams–style kitsch. Definitely worth the side trip. Open daily. For detailed tourist information, see the chapter on Orlando.

    COCOA BEACH: Several miles of fine beaches, celebrated for the beauty of their sunsets. A great place for surfing, big-game fishing—or picnicking while you watch the launches from the nearby Kennedy Space Center.

PATRICK AIR FORCE BASE: Examples of most of the types of spacecraft launched from the Kennedy Space Center are on exhibition in front of the base's Technical Laboratory, reached on Fla. A1A. Impressive. Open daily.

VERO BEACH: Enormous, uncrowded beach, much appreciated by those in the know. The charming little town is liberally adorned with flowerbeds.

Where to Stay

Holiday Inn Oceanside, 3384 Ocean Dr., FL 32963 (407/231-2300; toll free, see Holiday Inns). 104 rms, A/C, cable color TV. AE, CB, DC, MC, V. Free parking, pool, tennis court, rest., bar, rm svce, disco, free airport limo, free crib. *Note:* Holiday Inn style right on the beach. Serviceably comfortable; some balconies overlooking the ocean. Good value in summer. **M–E, but lower rates out of season**

Where to Eat

The Patio, 1103 Miracle Mile (Fla. 60) (407/567-7215). A/C. Lunch/dinner daily (open till 1 a.m.). AE, MC, V. Specialties: crab au gratin, scampi, chicken Kiev, filet mignon. *Note:* Some of the Italian-inspired dishes are successful. The décor, as the name suggests, is Spanish inspired, and the two together make for an agreeable stop. *Italian-Continental.* **B–I**

FORT PIERCE: Between the ocean and the Indian River lies a 332-acre nature reserve, open to the public. There are 21 mi. (30 km) of beaches, surfing, swimming, saltwater fishing, and freshwater fishing in the St. Lucie River. The **St. Lucie County Museum,** at 414 Seaway Dr. (407/464-6635), is interesting; it has a reproduction of a Seminole village. Open Wed.-Sat. Oct.-June.

JENSEN BEACH: Once the pineapple capital of Florida, this popular beach resort now specializes in big-game and freshwater fishing.

Where to Stay

Frances Langford's Outrigger Resort, 1405 N. Indian River Dr. (Fla. 707), FL 33457 (407/287-2411). 28 apartments, A/C, cable color TV. AE, CB, DC, MC, V. Indoor parking, pool, marina, boating, rest. (Outrigger), bar, disco, free crib. *Note:* Charming little Polynesian-style hotel w. gardens, verandas, and a clear view of the Indian River. Docking for pleasure boats. Comfortable mini-apartments w. kitchenettes. Affable reception. Very good rest. A fine place to stay. **I–E, but lower rates out of season**

IN NEARBY PORT ST. LUCIE (18 mi., 29 km, north) ☀ 🗝🗝🗝 **Club Med Sandpiper,** 3500 SE Morningside Blvd., FL 33452 (407/335-4400; toll free 800/258-2633). 273 rms, A/C, color TV, in-rm movies. American Plan only. AE, CB, DC, MC, V. Free parking, five pools, 19 tennis courts, three golf courses, health club, marina, boating, rest., bar, disco, free airport limo. *Note:* The country's first Club Med, open year round. Relaxed, comfortable atmosphere and attractive natural décor, set in 960 acres of gardens and woodlands on the St. Lucie River. All rms are mini-suites w. balconies. Excellent sports facilities. This is a youthful, informal place. **VE**

Where to Eat

🍸 **Outrigger,** in Frances Langford's Outrigger Resort (see "Where to Stay," above) (407/287-2411). A/C. Lunch/ dinner daily. AE, CB, DC, MC, V. Specialties: Tahitian delight, lobster Cantonese, Polynesian barbecued pork. *Note:* Tasty and often innovative cuisine (like the "Mystery Steak"!) in a Polynesian setting; open-air dining in good weather. Very good svce; dancing; valet parking. Resv. advised. *Polynesian.* **B–I**

☀🪣 **LAKE OKEECHOBEE** (38 mi., 62 km, SW of Jensen Beach on Fla. 76): The largest freshwater lake in Florida, with an area of 720 sq. mi. (1,865 sq km). A fisherman's heaven, with perch, bream, and large mouth bass, of which 500 tons are caught annually. You'll find a choice of boat rentals, motels, and campsites at **Belle Glade** and **Okeechobee.**

🪣 **JUPITER BEACH:** Several very beautiful nature reserves dedicated to birds and marine animals (**Joseph Verner Reed Sanctuary, Hobe Sound Refuge,** etc.), some of which can be reached only by boat, are well worth visiting. Also the usual beach diversions. Very nearby, **Jonathan Dickinson State Park** marks the spot where the *Reformation,* carrying a group of Quaker settlers, was shipwrecked in 1696; the survivors, captured by Seminole Indians, succeeded in making their way back to St. Augustine, 225 mi. (360 km) to the north, on foot.

Where to Eat

🍷 **Harpoon Louie's,** 1065 Fla. A1A (407/744-1300). A/C. Breakfast/lunch/dinner daily; closed Thanksgiving, Dec. 25. AE, MC, V. Specialties: fish of the day, broiled meats. *Note:* Agreeable little rest. at the water's edge, overlooking the Jupiter lighthouse. Simple but good food; svce w. a smile; locally popular. *American-Seafood.* **B–I**

☀🪣 **PALM BEACH (AND WEST PALM BEACH):** This beach resort is celebrated for its royal palms, its high fashion, and its social exclusiveness; in the eyes of rich Florida vacationers it easily outshines Miami Beach. Worth Ave. and Royal Poinciana Plaza are lined with luxury boutiques. With no fewer than nine polo grounds, the town is considered the world capital for this sport—but with 110 championship courses, it is no less a paradise for golfers.

It still boasts many magnificent mansions built by 19th-century giants of finance, including that of Henry Flagler, co-founder of Standard Oil and builder of Florida's first trunk railroad between Daytona Beach and Key West: his 🏛 **Whitehall,** a marble palace dating from 1901 with 55 opulently decorated rooms, must certainly be seen. It's at Coconut Row at Whitehall Way (407/655-2833), and is open Tues.-Sun.

Another remarkable museum, housed in an intelligently redesigned movie house, is the 🏛 **Lannan Museum,** at 601 Lake Ave., in Lake Worth (407/582-0006). It displays one of the country's richest private collections of modern art, including paintings and sculpture by Julian Schnabel, Morris Louis, Sandro Chia, and others. The overall effect is exceptionally striking. Open Tues.-Sat.

At West Palm Beach, don't miss the 🏛 **Union Congregational Church,** at 2727 Georgia Ave., with its enormous (75-by-27-ft, 23-by-8-m) stained-glass window, assembled like a mosaic from 10,000 pieces of colored glass.

Going west 18 mi. (28 km) along U.S. 98, you will come to ▲ **Lion Country Safari,** on Southern Blvd. West (407/793-1084). This modern wild-animal park covers 640 acres, and has more than 1,000 wild animals roaming free. It's open daily; visits by car only.

Where to Stay

The Breakers, S. County Rd., Palm Beach, FL 33480 (407/655-6611; toll free, see Preferred). 566 rms, A/C, color TV. Modified American Plan in winter. AE, CB, DC, MC, V. Free parking, two pools, 19 tennis courts, two golf courses, beach, sauna, masseur, two rests. (including the Florentine Room), bars, rm svce, disco, hrdrsr, cinema, drugstore, boutiques. *Note:* A jewel among U.S. hotels. Imposing Italianate palace w. white marble colonnades, Flemish tapestries, and crystal chandeliers. Roomy, comfortable (though slightly somber) rms w. mini-bars, superb English-style gardens, and direct access to beach. Reception and svce of the highest quality (in season, the hotel has about 1,100 on staff). The Florentine Room is an excellent rest. Comprehensive sports facilities. Interestihg wknd packages. Very upscale clientele. One of the 12 best hotels in the country. **E–VE, but lower rates out of season**

P.G.A. Sheraton Resort, 400 Ave. of the Champions, Palm Beach Gardens, FL 33418 (407/627-2000; toll free, see Sheraton). 333 mini-suites, A/C, cable color TV. AE, CB, DC, MC, V. Free valet parking, three pools, 19 tennis courts, four golf courses, private beach, boats, bicycling, health club, sauna, three rests. (including Explorers), three bars, rm svce, disco, hrdrsr, free crib. *Note:* Paradise for tennis players and golfers at the edge of a large lake, set in 2,160 acres of park and garden. Modern and very comfortable. Spacious mini-suites w. refrigerators and private balconies; also fully equipped villas. Attentive svce. 15 min. from the sea by car. Trendy group clientele. **E–VE, but lower rates out of season**

Palm Beach Lakes Inn, 1800 Palm Beach Lakes Blvd., West Palm Beach, FL 33401 (407/683-8810; toll free 800/331-9569). 200 rms, A/C, color TV. AE, CB, DC, MC, V. Free parking, pool, tennis court, golf course, nearby coffeeshop. *Note:* Relatively modern, functional motel w. large, balconied rms. Group clientele. Good overall value. **M, but lower rates out of season**

Days Inn, 2300 W. 45th St., West Palm Beach, FL 33407 (407/689-0450; toll free, see Days Inns). 238 rms, A/C, cable color TV. AE, CB, DC, MC, V. Free parking, pool, putting green, coffeeshop, rm svce, free airport limo, crib free. *Note:* Representative motel, 10 min. from downtown Palm Beach. Comfortable rms, quite friendly reception and svce. Rms for nonsmokers. Good value. **I–M, but lower rates out of season**

IN NEARBY BOYNTON BEACH (13 mi., 21 km, north). **Best Western Sage-n-Sand,** 1935 S. U.S. 1, FL 33435 (407/732-8196; toll free, see Best Western). 54 rms, A/C, cable color TV. AE, CB, DC, MC, V. Free parking, pool, two tennis courts, putting green, coffeeshop, crib free. *Note:* Likeable small motel a mile (1.6 km) from the beach. Comfortable rms w. private balconies or patios. Cordial reception; good value. **I–M, but lower rates out of season**

Where to Eat

Florentine Room, in The Breakers (see "Where to Stay," above) (407/659-8440). A/C. Dinner only, daily (w. two seatings, at 6 and 8:30 p.m.). AE, CB, DC, MC, V. Jkt. Specialties: ragoût fin en coquilles, navarin of lamb, filet of beef bordelaise, pear Belle Hélène. *Note:* The luxury-hotel rest. at its splendid best; wonderful Italianate frescoes, Venetian-glass chandeliers. The highest quality of cuisine and svce, but a weak wine list. Dinner-dances. Should appeal to your nostalgia for the '20s—but remember to make resv. *French.* **E**

♟♟♟ **Café l'Europe,** 150 Worth Ave., on the Esplanade (407/655-4020). A/C. Lunch/dinner Mon.-Sat.; closed Sun. and hols. AE, CB, DC, MC, V. J&T (at dinner). Specialties: scallops St-Jacques au Noilly, mignonette of beef w. peppercorns, veal cutlet w. watercress, poached salmon w. beurre blanc, roast lamb en croûte, very good desserts; remarkable wine list. *Note:* One of Florida's smartest rests. in an ideally romantic setting of paneling, mirrors, and brasswork. Refined and elegant cuisine; svce (in tuxedos) impeccable. Pleasant classical background music. On its way to becoming one of the greatest rests. on the East Coast. Resv. necessary. *Continental.* **M–E**

☼♟ **Testa's Restaurant,** 221 Royal Poinciana Way (407/832-0992). A/C. Breakfast/lunch/dinner daily (until 1 a.m.); closed 12/1–5/15. AE, MC, V. Specialties: stone crabs, steak, seafood, Italian dishes, strawberry pie. *Note:* Family owned since 1921, Testa's has become a landmark. Basically Italian, the cuisine does well also with native seafoods. Beautiful glass-roofed tropical garden patio or sidewalk cafe. Good svce. Resv. advised. *Italian-Seafood* **B–I**

IN NEARBY BOYNTON BEACH (12 mi., 19 km, south). ☼ ♟♟♟ **Bernard's,** 1730 N. Federal Hwy. (U.S. 1) (407/737-2236). A/C. Dinner only, daily; closed Dec. 25 and Mon. May-Oct. AE, CB, DC, MC, V. Jkt. (at dinner). Specialties: Bahamian chowder, chicken New Orleans, steak au poivre, poached salmon with dill, filet of grouper, gâteau nougatine. *Note:* The elegant setting—a Spanish-style home from the 1920s—and the delicacy of the cooking make this one of the most sought-after rests. in the area. Lovely tropical garden, illuminated in the evening. Ultraprofessional svce; valet parking. Resv. advised. *Continental-American.* **I–M**

IN NEARBY DELRAY BEACH (15 mi., 24 km, south). ♟♟ **Roberto,** 640 E. Atlantic Ave. (407/278-8351). A/C. Dinner only, Tues.-Sun.; closed Mon., hols, Aug.-Sept. AE, MC, V. Jkt. Specialties: duck w. cassis, veal cutlet w. madeira. Menu changes regularly. Fine Italian wines. *Note:* Chef Roberto Tempo, a master of the Chaîne des Rôtisseurs, dishes up excellent classic cuisine in this gracious Louis XV–style setting. Impeccable svce; resv. indispensable. Prix fixe. *Continental.* **E**

Cafeteria / Fast Food

S. & S., 7925 Dixie Hwy. (U.S. 1), West Palm Beach (407/686-4169). Lunch/dinner daily (until 8 p.m.); closed Dec. 25. No credit cards. Clean, carefully prepared cafeteria food.

☼♟ **BOCA RATON:** Charming, and rapidly growing, beachfront city. Seat of **Florida Atlantic University,** with 10,000 students, and the research laboratories of IBM. The **Boca Raton Hotel & Club** (see "Where to Stay," below), a magnificent 1930s luxury hotel, is worth the side trip by itself.

Where to Stay

☼ ♞♞♞♞ **Boca Raton Hotel & Club,** 501 E. Camino Real, FL 33432 (407/395-3000; toll free 800/368-1888). 1,000 rms, A/C, color TV, in-rm movies. Modified American Plan. AE, CB, DC, MC, V. Valet parking $5, four pools, 22 tennis courts, golf course, marina, boats, waterskiing, skeet shooting, health club, sauna, seven rests., eight bars, rm svce, disco, hrdrsr, boutiques, cinema, crib $7. Free jitney to the beach. *Note:* A Spanish baroque luxury hotel from the 1930s is here surprisingly wedded to a modern

27-floor tower overlooking Lake Boca Raton. The best rms (those in the older section) look out on 540 acres of lush tropical gardens; the tower rms, w. balconies, face the lake. Exemplary svce, but the group clientele is often quite obtrusive. Remarkable sports facilities and interesting golf/tennis packages. One of the great hotels of the East Coast. **VE, but lower rates out of season**

Best Western University Inn, 2700 N. U.S. 1, FL 33431 (407/395-5255; toll free, see Best Western). 90 rms, A/C, color TV. AE, CB, DC, MC, V. Free parking, pool, tennis court, coffeeshop, bar, rm svce, crib $6. *Note:* A classic small motel, a few steps from the campus of Florida Atlantic University and IBM's Research Laboratory. Huge, comfortable rms; agreeable svce; free breakfast. Good value out of season. **I–M, but lower rates out of season**

IN NEARBY DEERFIELD BEACH (2 mi., 3.2 km, south). **Days Inn,** 1250 Hillsboro Blvd., FL 33441 (305/427-2200; toll free, see Days Inns). 277 rms, A/C, color TV, in-rm movies. AE, CB, DC, MC, V. Free parking, pool, coffeeshop, crib free. *Note:* Relatively modern convenient hotel halfway between Boca Raton and Pompano Beach. Comfortable rms, some w. kitchenettes. Good overall value; five min. from the beach. **I–M, but lower rates out of season**

Where to Eat

La Vieille Maison, 770 E. Palmetto Park Rd. (407/391-6701). A/C. Dinner only, daily (two sittings, at 6:30 and 9:30 p.m.); closed hols. AE, CB, DC, MC, V. Jkt. Specialties: terrine of trout w. truffles, crayfish à la crème, shrimp in Pernod, pompano w. pecans, quails w. grapes, médaillon of lamb, lemon soufflé pancake. Superb wine list. *Note:* Almost perfect classic haute cuisine; w. a little more care in presentation and svce this rest. would definitely rate a fourth star. Sumptuous Mediterranean-style 1920s villa w. a patio; very beautiful cut flowers and antique furniture. Valet parking. Resv. required. Prix fixe. *French-Continental.* **E**

Fuji, Del Mar Shopping Village, Palmetto Park Rd. (407/392-8778). A/C. Lunch Mon.-Sat.: dinner daily. AE, CB, DC, MC, V. Specialties: sushi, sashimi, shabu-shabu, tempura. *Note:* One of the few authentic Japanese rests. on the Florida coast. You may choose between Western-style seating and tatami mats. Everything is as fresh as can be. Interesting modern décor w. flags and banners hanging from the ceiling. Efficient svce. *Japanese.* **B–I**

Tom's Place, 1198 N. Dixie Hwy. (407/368-3502). A/C. Lunch/dinner Wed.-Sat.; closed Sun., Mon., Tues. No credit cards. Specialties: hushpuppies, conch fritters, spareribs, catfish, barbecued chicken. *Note:* The local shrine of soul food, offering lavish portions of all the South's classic dishes wonderfully well prepared (especially the ribs). Neon-and-Formica setting. Very popular locally. *American.* **B**

POMPANO BEACH: Perhaps because of its 7 miles (11 km) of beach, this resort has for some time been experiencing the fastest growth in tourism on Florida's Gold Coast. At the **Goodyear Blimp Visitor Center,** 1500 N.E. Fifth Ave. (305/946-8300), you may pay your respects close up to the famous Goodyear blimp, which is based here every year from Nov. to May. Open daily.

Where to Stay

Palm Aire Hotel & Spa, 2501 Palm Aire Dr., FL 33069 (305/972-3300; toll free 800/327-4960). 195 rms, A/C, color TV, in-rm movies. AE, CB, DC, MC, V. Free parking, five pools, golf course, 37 tennis courts, sauna, private beach, water sports, three rests., bars, rm svce, disco, hrdrsr, crib free. *Note:* Luxurious, comfortable convention hotel standing in 1,800 acres of parkland right on the beach; commodious rms w. private patios (some w. kitchenettes). Hot springs. Family and Modified American Plan (MAP) packages worth looking into. Very good svce and some of the most comprehensive sports facilities in Florida. A wonderful place for lovers of sports and fresh air. **E–VE, but lower rates out of season**

> **Motel 6,** 1201 N.W. 31st Ave., FL 33069 (305/977-8011). 127 rms, A/C, color TV, free in-rm movies. DC, MC, V. Free parking, pool, crib free. *Note:* Up-to-date comfort at a modest price, 20 min. from dwntwn. One of the best values in the region. Ideal if you're driving. **B**

Where to Eat

> **Harris Imperial House,** 50 N. Ocean Blvd. (305/941-2200). A/C. Lunch Mon.-Fri.; dinner nightly. AE, CB, DC, MC, V. Specialties: Cantonese dishes, sesame chicken, steak, South Seas Supreme. *Note:* The run-of-the-mill Far Eastern décor may lead you to expect a ho-hum Chinese rest.—but the cooking is an unusual harmony of good old American steak w. Cantonese dishes, by way of Scandinavian smörgåsbord and the delicacies of Polynesia. The result may disconcert you—but the buffet is a good value. Valet parking. Locally popular, so resv. advisable. *Chinese-American.* **B–I**

FORT LAUDERDALE: Nicknamed "The Venice of America" because of its 165 miles (260 km) of canals and the 30,000 boats moored there year round, Fort Lauderdale is indeed a tourist attraction of Venetian caliber. Its 5 miles (11 km) of beaches, hundreds of hotels, motels, and rooming houses with a total of 20,000 rooms, 2,500 restaurants of all kinds and in all price ranges, the fashionable boutiques of Las Olas Blvd., one of the world's biggest pleasure-boat harbors (the Bahia Mar Yacht Basin, to which every pleasure sailor would like to make a pilgrimage)—all these attractions have made this busy, friendly city one of the leading tourist resorts in Florida. It doesn't hurt, either, that with 3,000 hours of sunshine annually, Fort Lauderdale holds the U.S. record.

For boat trips around the canals and the Intra-Coastal Waterway, try **Jungle Queen Cruises,** Bahia Mar Yacht Basin, Fla. A1A (305/462-5596), which offers them daily year round.

Don't miss the splendid, brand-new **Museum of Art,** a masterpiece from the hand of architect Edward Larrabee Barnes, at 1 E. Las Olas Blvd. (305/525-5500), open Tues.-Sun.; or **Ocean World,** 1701 S.E. 17th St. Causeway (305/525-6611), the classic marine zoo in Florida. Dozens of sea creatures, from sharks to dolphins, from sea lions to giant turtles—some of them trained to do the most wonderful tricks. Open daily.

Where to Stay

> **Bonaventure Hotel & Spa,** 250 Racquet Club Rd., FL 33326 (305/389-3300; toll free 800/382-3002). 500 rms, A/C, color TV, in-rm movies. AE, CB, DC, MC, V. Free parking, three pools, two golf courses, 23 tennis courts, health club, horseback riding, rest., coffeeshop, bars, rm svce, disco, hrdrsr, boutiques, free crib. *Note:* One of the best-known luxury hotels on the east coast of Florida. Its superb tropical setting, hot springs, and unrivaled sports facilities have made it a favorite of VIPs. Lavish décor and ultracomfortable layout. Excellent svce. If you're a physical-fitness buff, this is the place for you. **E–VE, but lower rates out of season**

> **Pier 66 Hotel & Marina,** 2301 S.E. 17th St. Causeway, FL 33316 (305/525-6666; toll free, see Preferred). 388 rms,

A/C, cable color TV. AE, CB, DC, MC, V. Valet parking $5, two pools, three tennis courts, health club, marina, boats, two rests., two bars (one a revolving bar on the top floor), 24-hr rm svce, disco, hrdrsr, free jitney to beach, free crib. *Note:* This is Fort Lauderdale's most famous building, a great white 17-story tower topped by a revolving bar in the shape of a flying saucer; it recently underwent a $21-million facelift. Capacious rms, most w. balconies or patios, and a view of the ocean or the marina. Outside glass elevator. Group clientele; efficient svce. Windows on the Green is a good rest. Very comprehensive sports facilities. All in all, a very good place to stay. **E–VE, but lower rates out of season**

Holiday Inn–Fort Lauderdale Beach, 999 N. Atlantic Blvd., FL 33304 (305/563-5961; toll free, see Holiday Inns). 240 rms, A/C, color TV. AE, CB, DC, MC, V. Valet parking $2, pool, two rests., bars, rm svce, free crib. *Note:* A great modern 12-story pile, Holiday Inn style, right on the ocean and very near the famous Galeria Mall w. its 150 stores and boutiques. Most rms (some w. balconies) overlook the beach. Svce on the impersonal side. **M–E, but lower rates out of season**

Merrimac, 551 N. Atlantic Blvd., FL 33304 (305/564-2345). 37 apartments, A/C, color TV. AE, CB, DC, MC, V. Free parking, pool, nearby coffeeshop. *Note:* Modest but well-maintained cluster of mini-apartments (most w. kitchenettes), w. balconies and ocean view; ideal for families. Direct access to the beach. **I–M, but lower rates out of season**

Villas by the Sea, 4500 Ocean Dr., in Lauderdale-by-the-Sea, FL 33308 (305/772-3550). 95 rms, A/C, color TV. MC, V. Free parking, pool, tennis court, nearby coffeeshop, free crib. *Note:* Friendly small motel right on the beach; serviceable rms w. balconies (most have kitchenettes). Good value. **I–M, but lower rates out of season**

Motel 6, 1801 Fla. 84, FL 33315 (305/760-7999). 108 rms, A/C, color TV. DC, MC, V. Free parking, pool, free crib. *Note:* Good value at an unbeatable price. **B**

IN NEARBY DANIA (5 mi., 8 km, south). **Motel 6,** Dania Beach Blvd. and N.E. Seventh Ave., FL 33004 (305/921-5505). 163 rms, A/C, color TV. DC, MC, V. Free parking, pool, free crib. *Note:* Ideal for motorists. **B**

YMCA/Youth Hostel

Sol Y Mar/AYH, 2839 Vistamar St., FL 33304 (305/566-1023). Youth hostel w. 94 beds, near the beach.

Where to Eat

Casa Vecchia, 209 N. Birch Rd. (305/463-7575). A/C. Dinner only, daily; closed Memorial Day, July 4. AE, CB, DC, MC, V. Jkt. Specialties: cima alla genovese, fresh homemade pasta, osso buco, red snapper Leghorn style, trout primavera. Also cannoli, fruit sherbets. The Italian wine list has more show than substance. *Note:* This 1930s mansion, set in beautiful gardens, once belonged to the Pond (cosmetics) family, and boasts period furniture, art objects, and much greenery. The northern Italian cuisine is as elegant as the interior; the service is on the same level. View of the gardens and the Intra-Coastal Waterway w. the passing vessels. One of the best places to eat on the Florida east coast, w. the same management as La Vieille Maison in Boca Raton (see above). Resv. a must. Valet parking. *Italian.* **E**

Down Under, 3000 E. Oakland Park Blvd. (305/563-4123). A/C. Lunch Mon.-Fri.; dinner daily; closed hols. AE, CB, DC, MC, V. Jkt. Specialties: duck w. green peppercorns, chicken Madagascar, red snapper Louisiana style, oysters Créole, trout imperial, Indian veal curry. *Note:* From the amusing Victorian-rococo interior you will have a fine view of the

Intra-Coastal Waterway and its traffic. Innovative, delicate French-inspired food w. a touch of the exotic. Fine list of California wines. Sometimes very noisy. Same management as La Vieille Maison in Boca Raton (see above). Valet parking. Resv. advised. One of Florida's great rests. *French-Continental*. **I–M**

☼ ♈♈ **Mai Kai,** 3599 N. Federal Hwy. (305/563-3272). A/C. Dinner only, daily (served till midnight); closed hols. AE, CB, DC, MC, V. Jkt. Specialties: shrimp Szechuan, lemon chicken, tea-smoked duck, steamed trout, roast pigeon, lobster Tahiti. *Note:* The Mai Kai offers you an original selection of food, w. Cantonese and Szechuan dishes predominating, but also including excellent steaks and fabulous Polynesian cocktails (try the "Mystery Drink"). No one could ask for a more exotic décor than this Hollywood-style corner of the South Seas w. its pool, waterfall, and Siamese temple. Impeccable svce. Very popular locally, so don't forget to reserve ahead. Polynesian floor show. Valet parking. A classic of its kind since the 1950s. *Chinese-Polynesian*. **I–M**

♈♈ **15th Street Fisheries,** 1900 S.E. 15th St. (305/763-2777). A/C. Lunch/dinner daily. AE, CB, DC, MC, V. Specialties: fish and shellfish; good wine list. *Note:* A remarkable seafood rest., one of the best on the Florida east coast. All the seafood is as fresh as can be, cooked or broiled to perfection, and very reasonably priced. Superbly sited right on the Intra-Coastal Waterway. Relaxed but efficient svce. Very popular locally, so resv. advised. *Seafood*. **I**

♈♈ **Paesano,** 1301 Las Olas Blvd. (305/467-3266). A/C. Lunch/dinner daily; closed Thanksgiving. AE, MC, V. Fresh homemade pasta, saltimbocca, crostata di vitello, snapper Adriatico. *Note:* You'll think you're in a Roman trattoria, and you'll find some of the best Italian food in the region at enticingly low prices. Very popular locally, and deservedly so. Resv. suggested. *Italian*. **I**

♈ **Nathan's Famous,** 1930 E. Sunrise Blvd. (305/763-4934). A/C. Lunch/dinner daily (11 a.m. to 11 p.m.). No credit cards. Specialties: stuffed clams, pastrami, corned beef, hot dogs, very good homemade french fries. *Note:* The delicatessen sandwiches and daily specials here are praiseworthy, but no match for those at Miami Beach's Rascal House. But the place (a branch of the well-known Nathan's of New York) is very popular, especially at lunchtime. *American*. **B**

IN NEARBY PORT EVERGLADES. ♈♈ **Burt & Jack's,** Berth 23 (305/522-5225). A/C. Dinner only, daily; closed Dec. 25. AE, DC, MC, V. Jkt. Specialties: red meats, broiled fish. *Note:* An old Spanish mission on the ocean, surrounded on three sides by water; one of the owners is actor Burt Reynolds. Wonderful broiled dishes; huge fireplaces; romantic décor w. many art objects. Resv. a must. *Steak-Seafood*. **I–M**

Cafeteria / Fast Food

Morrison's, 1700 N. U.S. 1 (305/565-3242). Lunch/dinner daily till 8 p.m. MC, V. Roast beef, fish of the day. Locally popular.

⚓ **HOLLYWOOD:** Founded in the 1920s by a California real-estate promoter (whence the name), this beach resort has always been a great commercial success. With more than 20 public courses, it is the golfer's favorite beach. Don't fail to visit **Six Flags Atlantis,** 2700 Stirling Rd. (305/926-1000), one of the world's largest water-sports parks, with 80 attractions on some of 62 acres. Open daily June-Sept., wknds only Oct.-Dec. See, too, the **Seminole Indian Reservation** at 3551 N. State Rd. 7 (305/583-7112), one of the last inhabited Indian villages in Florida. Handcrafts, mini-zoo, bingo. Open daily.

Where to Stay

Diplomat Resort, 3515 S. Ocean Dr., FL 33022 (305/457-8111; toll free 800/327-1212). 1,160 rms, A/C, color TV, in-rm movies. AE, CB, DC, MC, V. Valet gar. $6, pool, two golf courses, 19 tennis courts, health club, boats, nine rests., five bars, rm svce, disco, hrdrsr, boutiques, free crib. *Note:* Enormous 15-floor tourist complex w. direct access to the beach. Exemplary comfort and layout; spacious rms w. refrigerators and private patios or balconies (some have kitchenettes). Excellent sports facilities. Svce not always dependable; group and convention clientele somewhat obtrusive. **E–VE, but lower rates out of season**

MIAMI BEACH: "The Pearl of Florida"! See the chapter on Miami.

CHAPTER 17

TAMPA AND ST. PETERSBURG⸕

□ □ □

This urban agglomeration of 1.8 million people, Florida's largest after Miami, comprises two distinct cities located on the same body of water. One, **St. Petersburg,** is an outward-looking vacation community. The more businesslike **Tampa,** with its office high-rises and flourishing industries, prides itself on being the site (in 1539) of the first Spanish encampment on U.S. soil. It was from this base camp, at the mouth of the Little Manatee River, just south of Tampa, that Hernándo de Soto and his 600 companions set out on their expedition across the southeastern U.S. in an extraordinary odyssey that took them 4,800 mi. (7,700 km), from Florida to Texas and Mississippi. Tampa also boasts one of the highest growth rates in the country: 53% in the last decade.

But it is not the tourist industry, buoyant though it may be, that has brought all this prosperity to Tampa. A youthful population, including many workers who have moved here from the North and a large concentration of refugees from Cuba (Tampa's **Ybor City** district is a kind of Little Havana), has contributed much. St. Petersburg, on the other hand, along with such neighboring resort towns as **Clearwater, Dunedin,** and **Treasure Island,** is best known for its immense beaches and the beauty of its offshore islands, which draw more than a million visitors a year. Tampa, a modern, dynamic port city, puts its major industries on parade along the bay: phosphates, uranium processing, breweries, tobacco. With so large a Cuban population, Tampa could scarcely escape becoming the cigar capital of the U.S.: it turns out more than three million of them every day.

Besides their splendid deep-water bay, Tampa and St. Petersburg have two principal tourist attractions: the numberless excursions that can be made from here either into central Florida (**Walt Disney World, EPCOT, Cypress Gardens, Sea World,** etc.) or along the shores of the Gulf of Mexico (Sarasota, Sanibel and Captiva Islands, etc.).

BASIC FACTS: State of Florida. Area Codes: 813. ZIP Codes (of the central post offices): 33733 (St. Petersburg); 33602 (Tampa). Founded: 1876 (St. Petersburg); 1823 (Tampa). Approximate population: city, 240,000 (St. Petersburg), 280,000 (Tampa); metropolitan area, 1,880,000. 20th-largest metropolitan area in the country.

CLIMATE: St. Petersburg earns its nickname of "Sunshine City"; the sun shines almost all the time, and the Tampa Bay area has one of the most agreeable climates in the U.S. Almost never does the mercury dip below 59°F (15°C) even in the depth of winter; the Jan. mean temperature is 61°F (16°C). In summer, the July mean is 82°F (28°C), and the high rarely exceeds 86°F (30°C). To put it succinctly: it's always spring here, and you'll have a pleasant stay any time of year.

DISTANCES: Atlanta, 455 mi. (728 km); Miami, 268 mi. (428 km); New Orleans, 633 mi. (1,012 km); Orlando, 83 mi. (132 km); Savannah, 341 mi. (545 km).

ARRIVAL & TRANSIT INFORMATION

AIRPORTS: The **St. Petersburg–Clearwater International Airport** (PIE), 9 mi. (14 km) north of St. Petersburg, 17 mi. (27 km) SW of Tampa. For information, call 813/535-7600.

Tampa International Airport (TPA), 16 mi. (26 km) NE of St. Petersburg, 5 mi. (8 km) NW of Tampa. An airport of revolutionary design, one of the most modern in the country. For information, call 813/276-3400.

U.S. AIRLINES (the Tampa phone number is given first; the St. Petersburg number, if any, follows): American (221-5831; 447-0330), Braniff (toll free 800/272-6433), Continental (874-7151), Delta (286-1800; 894-1861), Eastern (877-8811; 896-7631), Midway (toll free 800/621-5700), Northwest (885-7811; 896-3131), Pan Am (229-0951; 822-4261), TWA (229-7961; 898-3131), United (223-1751), and USAir (toll free 800/428-4322).

FOREIGN CARRIERS: Air Canada (toll free 800/422-6232) and British Airways (toll free 800/247-9297).

CITY LINK: From the two airports to the two cities there is a variety of transportation available.

To Downtown St. Petersburg: The **cab** fare from St. Petersburg–Clearwater Airport is $12; time, 20 min. From Tampa Airport: fare, about $22; time, about 40 min. Bus between Tampa Airport and St. Petersburg: **The Limo** (822-3333), serving principal hotels. Fare to St. Petersburg, $10; to St. Petersburg Beach, $12; time, about 40 min. to 1 hr.

To Downtown Tampa: The **cab** fare from Tampa Airport is about $10; time, about 15 min. Bus between Tampa Airport and downtown Tampa: **Central Florida Limo Service** (276-3730), serving principal hotels; fare, $9; time, 20 min. **City bus:** Line 30 serves downtown Tampa; fare, 60¢.

Public transportation (bus) is inefficient: in Tampa, HART (254-4278); in St. Petersburg, PSTA (530-9911).

Given the many interesting destinations for excursions around the area, and the very low rates prevailing in Florida, it makes a lot of sense to rent a car with unlimited mileage.

CAR RENTAL (all at Tampa International Airport): Avis (883-3500); Budget (877-6051); Dollar (883-3640); Hertz (874-3232); National (883-3782). For downtown locations in Tampa and St. Petersburg, consult the appropriate local telephone directory.

LIMOUSINE SERVICES: Carey Limousine (577-4189 in St. Petersburg, 228-7927 in Tampa) and Esquire Limo Service (725-1777 in St. Petersburg, 855-5600 in Tampa).

TAXIS: In theory cabs may not be hailed on the street, but may be taken from the waiting lines outside the major hotels, or more conveniently, summoned by phone. Recommended companies **in St. Petersburg** are Blue Star Cab (327-4104) and Yellow Cab (821-7777); **in Tampa,** United Cab (253-2424) and Yellow Cab (253-0121). Cab fares are on the high side.

TRAIN: AMTRAK has stations at 3601 31st St. North in St. Petersburg (522-9475) and at Nebraska Ave. and Twiggs St. in Tampa (229-2473).

BUS: Greyhound has terminals at 110 Central Ave. in St. Petersburg (895-4455) and 610 E. Polk St. in Tampa (229-1501).

INFORMATION & TOURS

TOURIST INFORMATION: The **St. Petersburg Chamber of Commerce,** 100 Second Ave. North, St. Petersburg, FL 33731 (813/821-4069).
    Suncoast Welcome Center, junction of Fla. 688 and I-275, St. Petersburg (813/576-1449).
    Tampa Chamber of Commerce, 801 E. John F. Kennedy Blvd., Tampa, FL 33601 (813/228-7777).
    Tampa/Hillsborough Convention and Visitors Association, 100 S. Ashley Dr., Suite 850, Tampa, FL 33601 (813/223-1111).

GUIDED TOURS: Both St. Petersburg and Tampa have several options for guided tours.

St. Petersburg
    Gray Line Tours (bus), 921 Third St. South (822-3577): Conducted bus tours of the city and surroundings, year round.
    Gray Line Water Tours (boat), 401 Second Ave. NE (823-1665 or 823-8171): Two-hour cruises on Tampa Bay aboard the *Belle of St. Petersburg.* Also dinner-dances. Year round.

Tampa
    Around the Town Tours (bus), 3450 W. Busch Blvd. (932-7803): Conducted bus tours of the city and surroundings; year round.
    Gray Line Tours (bus) (273-0845): Conducted bus tours of the city and surroundings, serving principal hotels; year round.
    SeaEscape Cruises (boat), Port of Tampa (toll free 800/432-0900): One-day mini-cruise on the Gulf of Mexico; on board are restaurants, bars, pool, and casino. Fare is $79 per person including buffet. Daily, year round.

TAMPA

SIGHTS, ATTRACTIONS, & ACTIVITIES

ARCHITECTURAL HIGHLIGHTS: ☼ ⚜ **Performing Arts Center,** W. C. MacInnes Pl. (222-1010): Opened in 1987 at a cost of $55 million, this ultramodern performing-arts complex comprises three adjacent auditoriums: **Festi-**

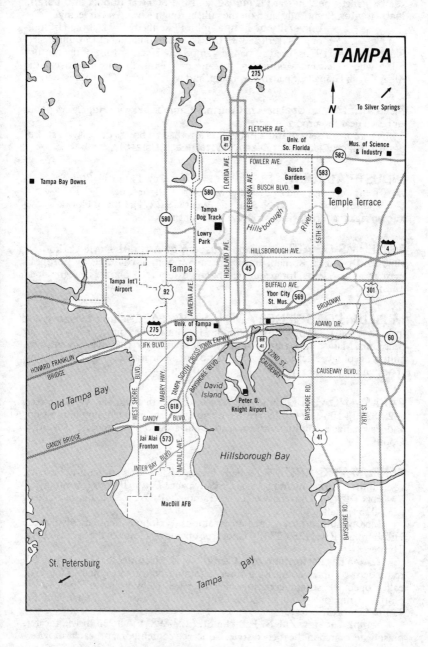

TAMPA

N

To Silver Springs

FLETCHER AVE.

BR 41

Univ. of So. Florida

Mus. of Science & Industry

582

FOWLER AVE.

583

Busch Gardens

BUSCH BLVD.

■ Tampa Bay Downs

580

Temple Terrace

FLORIDA AVE.

NEBRASKA AVE.

580

Tampa Dog Track

Lowry Park

Hillsborough River

56TH ST.

4

HILLSBOROUGH AVE.

HIGHLAND AVE.

45

Tampa

Tampa Int'l Airport

92

ARMENIA AVE.

BUFFALO AVE.

Ybor City St. Mus.

569

BROADWAY

301

275

Univ. of Tampa

60

ADAMO DR.

60

JFK BLVD.

BR 41

22ND ST.

CAUSEWAY

HOWARD FRANKLIN BRIDGE

WEST SHORE BLVD.

D. MABRY HWY.

TAMPA SOUTH CROSS-TOWN EXPWY.

BAYSHORE BLVD.

David Island

Peter O. Knight Airport

CAUSEWAY BLVD.

BAYSHORE RD.

78TH ST.

Old Tampa Bay

GANDY

618

BLVD.

41

GANDY BRIDGE

Jai Alai Fronton

573

Hillsborough Bay

INTER BAY BLVD.

MACDILL AVE.

MacDill AFB

St. Petersburg

BAYSHORE RD.

Tampa   Bay

val Hall, with 2,400 seats, home of the Florida Symphony Orchestra and the Tampa Ballet; the 900-seat **Playhouse;** and the 300-seat **Robert and Lorena Jaeb Theater.** Beautifully sited on the Hillsborough River. Worth seeing.

    ▲ **University of Tampa,** John F. Kennedy Blvd. at the Hillsborough River (253-3333): The main building of this university, founded in the 1930s, used to be the Tampa Bay Hotel, a turn-of-the-century palace whose Hispano-Moorish architecture and 13 minarets are imitative of the Alhambra in Granada (Spain). Surprising, and worth a look. Open Tues.-Sat.

BEACHES: ▲ **Municipal Beach,** Courtney Campbell Pkwy.: Huge, very popular beach near the airport; noisy.

    There are dozens of miles of beaches less than an hour's drive away, at **Bradenton Beach, Clearwater Beach, Crystal Beach, Sarasota,** etc.

INDUSTRIAL TOURS: The **Stroh's Brewing Co.,** 11111 N. 30th St. (971-7070): Brewery tour and free tasting, Mon.-Fri. Call for times.

    Villazon and Co., 304 N. Armenia Ave. (879-2291): One of Florida's best-known cigar factories; visits Mon.-Fri. Call for times.

MUSEUMS OF ART: ▲ **Tampa Museum of Art,** 601 Doyle Carlton Dr. (223-8130): Greek, Roman, and Egyptian antiquities; paintings by European masters and moderns. Interesting temporary exhibitions. Should be seen. Open Tues.-Sun.

MUSEUMS OF SCIENCE AND HISTORY: ▲ **Museum of Science and Industry,** 4801 E. Fowler Ave. (985-5531): One of the country's few open-air museums. Many displays and demonstrations relating to the environment, agriculture, geology, electricity, etc. Simulation of a hurricane; observation of sunspots with the aid of a heliostat. Don't fail to visit. Open daily.

PARKS AND GARDENS: ▲ **Lowry Park,** North Blvd. and W. Sligh Ave. (223-8230): 105-acre (42-ha.) park with zoo, currently undergoing renovation, and Fairyland, a children's theme park built around characters from Mother Goose.

PERFORMING ARTS: For a daily listing of all shows and cultural events, consult the entertainment pages of the daily paper *Tampa Tribune* (morning).

    Falk Theater, University of Tampa campus, 401 W. John F. Kennedy Blvd. (251-0254): Ballet, recitals.

    McKay Auditorium, U. of Tampa campus, W. John F. Kennedy Blvd. at the Hillsborough River (253-3333): Concerts, operettas. Home of the Spanish Lyric Theater.

    Tampa Bay Performing Arts Center, W. C. MacInnes Pl. (222-1010): Ultramodern complex comprising three adjoining performance halls. Concerts, ballet, opera, classic and contemporary theater, Broadway shows. Home of the Florida Symphony Orchestra, the Tampa Ballet (season Oct.-Mar.), and the Tampa Oratorio Society.

    Tampa Theater, 711 N. Franklin St. (223-8981): A 1926 movie theater, plushly decorated in the rococo style. Concerts, contemporary theater, movies.

SHOPPING: The **Market on Harbour Island,** 601 Harbour Island Blvd.

(229-5330): Ultramodern shopping mall which combines the atmosphere of a European open-air market, with cobbled streets, fountains, plazas, arcades, and an enormous carousel. More than 50 varied boutiques and stores as well as a score of restaurants, bars, and cafés. Lovely view of the waterfront. Connected to Tampa City by monorail. Very spectacular.

☼ **Ybor Square,** 13th St. and Eighth Ave.: Complex of boutiques and stores in a 19th-century cigar factory, now a designated historic monument. Imaginative décor; worth seeing.

SPECIAL EVENTS: For the exact schedule of events below, consult the Tampa/Hillsborough Convention and Visitors Association (see "Tourist Information," above).

Florida State Fair (Feb.): Very popular agricultural and business fair, with cattle show, handcraft market, flower shows (especially orchids), rodeos, pop concerts. At the Fairgrounds, I-4 and U.S. 301.

Gasparilla Pirate Invasion (Feb.): Boat parade, carnival, folklore parades; colorful. Commemorates the taking of Tampa by the pirate José Gaspar.

Latin America Fiesta (Mar.): Festival of South American art and folklore. Balls. Held in Ybor City.

SPORTS: Tampa boasts professional teams in two sports (one for spring training only):

Baseball (spring training, mid-Mar. to mid-Apr.): Cincinnati Reds, Al Lopez Field (873-8617).

Football (Aug.-Dec.): Buccaneers, Tampa Stadium (879-2827).

Horse Racing
Tampa Bay Downs, Race Track Rd., Oldsmar (855-4401), 11 mi. (17 km) NW of Tampa on Fla. 580. Thoroughbred racing Tues.-Sat., Dec.-Apr.

Jai Alai
Tampa Fronton, S. Dale Mabry Hwy. and Gandy Blvd. (831-1411), 5 mi. (8 km) SW of Tampa on I-275. Matches daily except Thurs. and Sun., Jan.-June.

STROLLS: ☼ ⚓ Waterfront, Davis Island, Water St. and 13th St.: The port district, always busy with the unloading of cargoes—fish, bananas, tropical fruit, or whatever. You'll have a good view of the impressive trawler fleet from the 22nd St. Causeway. A must.

☼ ⚓ **Ybor City,** bounded by Columbus Dr., 5th Ave., 22nd St., and Nebraska Ave.: A Cuban enclave in the heart of Tampa, complete with cigar factories and typical restaurants. The first Cuban immigrants to settle here were the cigar-manufacturing workers brought from Key West by Vicente Martinez Ybor in 1886. The scent of tobacco (no longer imported from Cuba, but from Puerto Rico, Honduras, and the Dominican Republic) perfumes a warm, colorful atmosphere embracing the descendents of Cuban and other Spanish-speaking immigrants, and many Italians as well. The **Ybor City State Museum,** 1818 9th Ave. (247-6323) traces the history of Cuban cigar manufacturing from its inception in the mid-19th century to the current industry in Florida. Open daily. Lively and picturesque, especially at night, Ybor City is not to be missed.

THEME PARKS NEARBY: ⚓ Adventure Island, 4545 Bougainvillea Ave. (971-7978): A 13-acre (5-ha) park entirely devoted to the pursuit of surfing, div-

ing, and swimming. You can splash in an enormous pool with artificial waves and waterfalls, or float down the artificial rapids. Entertaining. Open daily in summer, weekends only in spring and fall; closed in winter.

❀ ☟☟ **Busch Gardens—"The Dark Continent,"** 3000 Busch Blvd. (971-8282): One of the most famous theme parks in Florida, with a vast zoo, trained animal shows, and reconstructed African villages. Gigantic, thrilling roller coaster; rides by monorail, boat, or miniature train. Broadway-style shows. Tour of the Anheuser-Busch brewery. Not to be missed. Open daily year round.

❀ ☟☟ **Silver Springs,** 95 mi (152 km) NE of Tampa on I-75N and Fla. 40E (904/236-2121): The springs of the Silver River, the largest of which attains a record flow rate of half a billion gallons (two billion liters) a day, form a magnificent lake of remarkably clear water, where many TV movies and documentaries have been made. Glass-bottom-boat rides over the 100,000-year-old underwater grottoes—a truly spectacular sight. Impressive reptile zoo. The park attracts more than 1.5 million visitors a year; don't miss it. Open daily year round.

ACCOMMODATIONS

See the listing of toll-free numbers in the Appendix.

Room Rates in Tampa	
B (Budget)	up to $30
I (Inexpensive)	$30–$60
M (Moderate)	$60–$90
E (Expensive)	$90–$140
VE (Very Expensive)	$140 and up

Personal Favorites (in order of preference)

❀ ♙♙♙♙ **Saddlebrook** (vic.), 100 Saddlebrook Way, Wesley Chapel, FL 34249 (813/973-1111; toll free 800/237-7519). 500 suites, A/C, cable color TV. AE, CB, DC, MC, V. Free valet parking, pool, two golf courses, putting green, 37 tennis courts, sauna, health club, three rests. (including the Cypress Room), bar, rm svce, disco, hrdrsr. *Note:* If you enjoy golf or tennis you'll be in paradise here, 30 min. north of Tampa on I-75 (take exit 58). Luxurious vacation village standing amid 480 acres (194 ha.) of gardens, wooded hills, and lakes. Spacious, comfortable suites w. private balconies and refrigerators, some w. kitchenettes. Very acceptable rests. Extravagant outsize pool; as for the golf courses, they were laid out by Arnold Palmer himself. For exhausted businesspeople and lovers of outdoor sports. Worthwhile vacation discounts. One of the best places to stay in Florida. **E–VE, but lower rates out of season**

♙♙♙ **Wyndham Harbour Island Hotel** (nr. dwntwn), 725 S. Harbour Island Blvd., Harbour Island, FL 33602 (813/229-5000; toll free 800/822-4200). 300 rms, A/C, cable color TV. AE, CB, DC, MC, V. Valet garage $6, pool, health club, 15 tennis courts, marina, boats, two rests. (including Garrison's Harbour View), bar, rm svce, nightclub, boutiques, free breakfast, free crib, concierge. *Note:* Beautiful grand hotel on the water, w. splendid view of the bay and the Tampa skyline. Luxurious, comfortable rms w.

refrigerators and period furniture. Discreet, attentive svce; elegant rest. Adjoining the Market in Harbour Island with its dozens of shops and rests. Business clientele. 5 min. from dwntwn by Franklin St. Bridge, or 90 seconds by people mover. **E**

Bay Harbor Inn (nr. dwntwn), 7700 Courtney Campbell Causeway, FL 33607 (813/889-8900; toll free 800/237-7733). 260 rms, A/C, color TV, in-rm movies. AE, CB, DC, MC, V. Free parking, pool, two tennis courts, boats, windsurfing, rest. (Yankee Trader), bar, rm svce, disco, hrdrsr, free crib. *Note:* Big six-story hotel on the bay w. private beach. Faultless comfort; very complete facilities; attentive svce. Pretty tropical décor. Business and vacation clientele. Good value. 15 min. from dwntwn, 5 min. from the airport (free shuttle). **M–E**

Holiday Inn Downtown (dwntwn), 111 W. Fortune St., FL 33602 (813/223-1351; toll free, see Holiday Inns). 325 rms, A/C, color TV, in-rm movies. AE, CB, DC, MC, V. Free parking, pool, rest., bar, rm svce, nightclub, crib $10. *Note:* Modern 14-story building adjoining the Performing Arts Center; comfort and facilities above the Holiday Inn average. Spacious rms, some w. mini-bars. Well located in dwntwn Tampa, and a favorite w. business travelers. Very good value; free airport limo. **I–M**

Bahia Beach Resort (vic.), 611 Destiny Dr., Ruskin, FL 33570 (813/645-3291; toll free 800/372-2773). 84 rms, A/C, cable color TV. AE, CB, DC, MC, V. Free parking, two pools, tennis court, boating, bicycles, marina, rest. (Las Brisas), bar, disco, crib $3. *Note:* Engaging motel right on the beach, offering flawless comfort and svce. Spacious rms w. private balconies or patios, some w. kitchenettes. Good public facilities; fine view over the bay. Vacation clientele. Good value. 30 min. from dwntwn; private heliport. **M, but lower rates out of season**

Motel 6 (nr. dwntwn), 333 E. Fowler Ave., FL 33612 (813/932-4948). 150 rms, A/C, color TV, in-rm movies. DC, MC, V. Free parking, pool. *Note:* Unbeatable value right nr. the famous Busch Gardens. Modern and comfortable; 15 min. from dwntwn by I-275. Ideal for motorists and family parties. **B**

Other Accommodations (from top bracket to budget)

Sheraton Grand Hotel (nr. dwntwn), 4860 W. John F. Kennedy Blvd., FL 33609 (813/286-4400; toll free see Sheraton). 325 rms, A/C, color TV, in-rm movies. AE, CB, DC, MC, V. Valet garage $6, pool, two rests. (including J. Fitzgerald's), bar, 24-hr rm svce, disco, boutiques, free breakfast, free airport limo, free crib, concierge. *Note:* Eleven floors of spectacular glass-and-steel futurist design; beautiful glass-walled lobby w. indoor garden. Elegant, refined décor; spacious, ultra-comfortable rms w. refrigerators. Rest. of a high order; personalized svce. Two VIP floors. A favorite place with big-businesspeople; 10 min. from dwntwn and 5 min. from the airport. **E–VE**

Hyatt Regency (dwntwn), 2 Tampa City Center, FL 33602 (813/225-1234; toll free, see Hyatt). 540 rms, A/C, color TV, in-rm movies. Valet garage $6, pool, sauna, health club, two rests., coffeeshop, bars, rm svce, nightclub, free crib, concierge. *Note:* Rather massive tower a stone's throw from the Hillsborough River; spectacular lobby w. two-story waterfall and gardens. Ultramodern comfort and facilities; well-designed, spacious rms; efficient svce. Centrally located in the heart of the business district; attracts business travelers and groups. VIP floors. The largest of the dwntwn hotels. **M–E**

Hilton (dwntwn), 200 Ashley Dr., at John F. Kennedy Blvd., FL 33607 (813/223-2222; toll free, see Hilton). 265 rms, A/C, color TV, in-rm movies. AE, CB, DC, MC, V. Free parking, pool, health club, rest. (Riverside Café), bar, rm svce, disco, free crib, free airport limo. *Note:* Comfortable hotel on the banks of the Hillsborough River; very inviting rms w. patios, the best w. river view. Unfortunately, the svce leaves something to be desired. Good facilities. VIP floor. Good value on balance. Group and convention clientele. **M–E**

Days Inn Downtown (formerly the Sheraton; dwntwn), 515 E. Cass St., FL 33602 (813/229-6431; toll free, see Days Inns). 180 rms, A/C, color TV, in-rm movies. AE, CB, DC, MC, V. Free garage, pool, two rests., bar, rm svce, crib $5. *Note:* Typical motel in dwntwn Tampa; spacious, comfortable rms; entirely redecorated. Business clientele. Efficient svce; very good value. **I–M**

Tahitian Inn (nr. dwntwn), 601 S. Dale Mabry Hwy., FL 33609 (813/877-6721; toll free 800/541-2255). 80 rms, A/C, color TV, in-rm movies. AE, DC, MC, V. Free parking, pool, coffeeshop (breakfast and lunch only), rm svce, free crib. *Note:* Very acceptable small motel; relatively spacious, comfortable rms; friendly reception. Good value. 10 min. from dwntwn. **I–M**

Airport Accommodations

Marriott Airport (vic.), International Airport, Tampa, FL 33622 (813/879-5151; toll free, see Marriott). 300 rms, A/C, color TV, in-rm movies. AE, CB, DC, MC, V. Free valet parking, pool, health club, two rests. (including C.K.'s), bar, rm svce, nightclub, free crib. *Note:* Modern hotel in the airport terminal. Agreeable, well-soundproofed rms; very complete facilities; efficient svce. C.K.'s, a revolving rest. at the top, is praiseworthy. Business clientele; ideal for a stopover between flights. **E**

RESTAURANTS

Tampa Restaurant Prices	
(per person, excluding drinks and service charges)	
B (Budget)	up to $15
I (Inexpensive)	$15–$25
M (Moderate)	$25–$40
E (Expensive)	$40–$60
VE (Very Expensive)	$60 and up

Personal Favorites (in order of preference)

Bern's Steak House (nr. dwntwn), 1208 S. Howard Ave. (251-2421). A/C. Dinner only, nightly; closed Dec. 25. AE, CB, DC, MC, V. Jkt. *Specialties:* onion soup, red meats, lamb chops, sautéed chicken w. sesame, "wild fried steak," homemade pastry and sherbet. The enormous wine list weighs 7 lbs. (3 kg) and offers no fewer than 6,000 different labels. *Note:* Bern's likes to call itself "The World's Best and Most Famous Steak House," but joking apart, the charcoal-broiled steaks are truly remarkable, the vegetables are organically grown—and the prices are highly seasoned. To choose the degree of aging, weight, and cooking time for your steak, you almost need a slide rule. Kitschy opulent décor and a rather high noise level; excellent svce. Resv. strongly advised; valet parking. *Steak-American.* **M**

☀☆🍷 **Columbia** (dwntwn), 2117 E. Seventh Ave. (248-4961). A/C. Lunch/dinner daily. AE, CB, DC, MC, V. *Specialties:* red snapper Alicante, filet mignon criolla, chicken valenciana, paella. *Note:* Huge Spanish baroque-style house in the heart of Ybor City, Tampa's Cuban district. Lovely décor of *azulejos* (blue tiles) and houseplants. Tasty, Spanish-inspired food; flamenco music and show every evening except Sun. Diligent svce; a Tampa landmark since 1905. Resolutely tourist atmosphere; resv. advised. Valet parking. *Spanish–Latin American.* **I–M**

🍷🍷 **Café de Paris** (nr. dwntwn), 4430 W. John F. Kennedy Blvd. (287-8422). A/C. Lunch Mon.-Fri., dinner Mon.-Sat.; closed Sun., Jan. 1, and Dec. 25. AE, CB, DC, MC, V. Jkt. *Specialties:* chateaubriand bouquetière, shrimp Monte Carlo, bouillabaisse. *Note:* Somewhat pretentious cuisine in a deluxe bistro setting. The sauces could, w. advantage, be lighter, but the food is faultlessly prepared and presented. Courteous svce; good wine list at reasonable prices. Resv. necessary. *French.* **I–M**

🍷 **Mama Mia** (nr. dwntwn), 4732 N. Dale Mabry Hwy. (877-2489). A/C. Dinner only, nightly; closed Thanksgiving and Dec. 24–25. AE, CB, DC, MC, V. *Specialties:* fresh homemade pasta, lasagne, chicken cacciatore, veal parmigiana. *Note:* Modest, congenial little *trattoria.* Fun-style re-creation of an Italian village, w. fountain, grape arbors, and an array of antipasti served from flowered donkey carts. The homemade pastas are worth the trip. Efficient svce; good value. *Italian.* **I**

Other Restaurants (from top bracket to budget)

🍷🍷 **C.K.'s** (vic.), in the Marriott Airport (see "Accommodations," above) (879-5151). A/C. Lunch/dinner daily, brunch Sun. AE, CB, DC, MC, V. *Specialties:* chicken Florentine, prime rib, broiled red snapper, catch of the day, real caffè espresso. *Note:* This revolving rest. atop the Tampa airport, w. its private elevator, offers an unobstructed view of the runways and the coming and going of aircraft. Simply prepared but very acceptable food; efficient svce; locally popular, so resv. advised. Attracts many businesspeople at lunchtime. *Continental-American.* **I–M**

☀🍷🍷 **Tobacco Company Restaurant** (nr. dwntwn), 4115 E. Busch Blvd. (985-4062). A/C. Lunch Mon.-Fri., dinner nightly, brunch Sun.; closed Jan. 1 and Dec. 25. AE, DC, MC, V. *Specialties:* beef Bourbon with mushroom sauce, poached salmon hollandaise, broiled steak or fish, prime ribs. Remarkable wine list at bargain prices. *Note:* The enchanting Victorian décor w. genuine Tiffany windows, art objects, and the old cigar-rolling machines from which the rest. takes its name, are worth a visit all by themselves; so are the tropical gardens w. their peacocks and other exotic birds. Elegant, polished cuisine makes this incontestably Tampa's most original rest. Very good svce; resv. advised. Adjacent to Busch Gardens. *Steak–seafood.* **I–M**

🍷 **Café Pepe** (nr. dwntwn), 2006 W. John F. Kennedy Blvd. (253-6501). A/C. Lunch/dinner Mon.–Sat.; closed Sun. AE, DC, MC, V. *Specialties:* paella, shrimp suprema, Cuban rice and black beans, chicken w. rice, coconut sherbet. *Note:* With its whitewashed walls, flagons of sangría, and noisy, colorful atmosphere, Café Pepe is a little bit of Old Castile transplanted to Tampa. Locally very popular; resv. advised. *Spanish–Latin American.* **I**

Cafeterias / Fast Food

☀ **Silver Ring Café** (dwntwn), 1831 E. Seventh Ave. (248-2549). Breakfast/lunch only, Mon.–Sat.; closed Sun.

and July. The unchallenged king of the "Cuban sandwich" (ham, salami, pork, Swiss cheese on a toasted bun). A real local landmark.

BARS & NIGHTCLUBS

Ocean Club (nr. dwntwn), 4811 W. Cypress Ave., Tampa (875-6458). Singles bar-disco very popular with the youthful upper crust of the area. Good atmosphere.

Robiconti's (vic.), 14303 N. Dale Mabry Hwy., Tampa (961-4892). Youthful, trendy disco; laid-back atmosphere. Open Mon.-Sat.

Selena's (nr. dwntwn), 1623 Snow Ave., Tampa (251-2116). The fashionable Cajun rock joint, with live music; also very acceptable restaurant. Very popular with the locals. Open nightly.

ST. PETERSBURG

SIGHTS, ATTRACTIONS, & ACTIVITIES

ARCHITECTURAL HIGHLIGHTS: ⚓ **Municipal Marina,** 300 Second Ave. SE (893-7329): Lovely pleasure-boat basin on Tampa Bay, with 610 moorings. Worth a look.

☼⚓ **Pier Place,** 800 Second Ave. NE (893-7437): Curious five-story inverted pyramid of a building, overlooking the port's 2,400-ft (730-m) jetty. Many boutiques and restaurants. Fine view of the bay from the top-floor Observation Deck. A sight to be seen. Open daily.

☼⚓ **Sunshine Skyway Bridge** on I-275 linking St. Petersburg and Bradenton: Double road bridge, 12 mi. (19 km) long, consisting of one highway on piles dating from 1954, and a parallel, ultramodern structure opened in 1987 whose twin 426-ft (130-m) towers dominate the entrance to Tampa Bay. This is one of the most spectacular pieces of engineering in the U.S.; from it there's a wonderful view of the bay and the Gulf of Mexico, but don't try it if you suffer from dizzy spells.

BEACHES: ⚓ **Bay Beach,** N. Shore Dr. and 13th Ave. NE: Fine beach on Tampa Bay.

⚓ **Municipal Beach,** Gulf Blvd. at Treasure Island: The most popular of the public beaches, directly on the ocean; huge and well maintained.

⚓ **North Shore Beach,** North Shore Dr. and Eighth Ave.: Popular beach on the bay; many sports facilities.

⚓ **Spa Beach,** Second Ave. NE, The Pier: Most accessible of the St. Petersburg beaches, and often crowded. Many boutiques and restaurants nearby.

MUSEUMS OF ART: ⚓ **Museum of Fine Arts,** 255 Beach Dr. NE (896-2667): Small but comprehensive museum of painting, sculpture, and decorative arts, from Far Eastern and pre-Columbian art to contemporary American painters and photographers. Should be seen. Open Tues.-Sun.

☼⚓⚓ **Salvador Dalí Museum,** 1000 3rd St. South (823-3767): The Reynolds Morse Collection makes this the world's largest museum entirely devoted to Salvador Dalí. Comprises 93 oils, including *The Discovery of America by Christopher Columbus* and *The Hallucinogenic Toreador;* 200 original watercolors and drawings; and hundreds of sketches, lithographs, sculptures, and pop-art works by the Catalán artist. Initially opened in Cleveland,

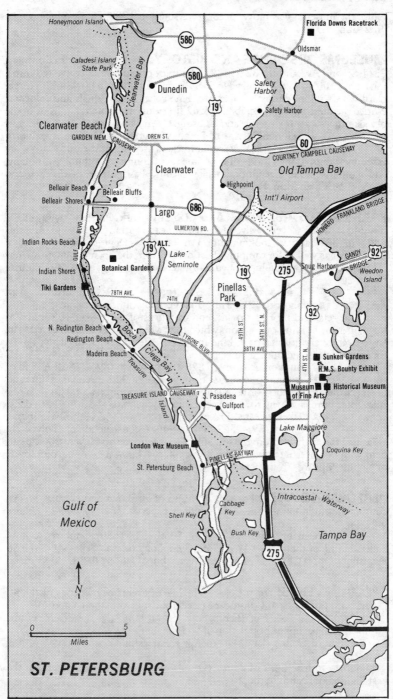

Honeymoon Island

586

Caladesi Island
State Park

580

US 19

Dunedin

Clearwater Bay

Florida Downs Racetrack

Oldsmar

Safety
Harbor

Safety Harbor

Clearwater Beach

GARDEN MEM. CAUSEWAY

DREW ST.

60

Courtney Campbell Causeway

Old Tampa Bay

Clearwater

Highpoint

Int'l Airport

Belleair Beach
Belleair Bluffs
Belleair Shores

Largo

686

ULMERTON RD.

HOWARD FRANKLAND BRIDGE

Indian Rocks Beach

19 ALT.

Lake
Seminole

Gulf Blvd

Indian Shores

Botanical Gardens

US 19

Gandy Bridge

92

Snug Harbor

Weedon
Island

Tiki Gardens

78TH AVE.

74TH AVE.

Pinellas
Park

275

92

Boca Ciega Bay

N. Redington Beach
Redington Beach
Madeira Beach

49TH ST.

34TH ST. N.

38TH AVE

4TH ST. N.

Sunken Gardens
H.M.S. Bounty Exhibit

Tyrone Blvd

Treasure Island

TREASURE ISLAND CAUSEWAY

S. Pasadena
Gulfport

Museum
of Fine Arts

Historical Museum

London Wax Museum

Lake Maggiore

St. Petersburg Beach

Pinellas Bayway

Coquina Key

Gulf of
Mexico

Cabbage
Key

Shell Key

Bush Key

Intracoastal Waterway

Tampa Bay

275

N

0   5
Miles

ST. PETERSBURG

Ohio, the museum was moved to St. Petersburg in 1982. Don't miss it. Open Tues.-Sun.

MUSEUMS OF SCIENCE AND HISTORY: ☼ ⚱ **Haas Museum Complex,** 3511 Second Ave. South (327-1437): Complex of old houses converted into a museum of life in 19th-century Florida. Reconstruction of a blacksmith's forge, hairdresser's salon, dentist's office, etc. Fine collection of shells and minerals. Notice the huge banyan tree, its trunk 62 ft (19 m) in diameter, in front of the blacksmith's forge. Instructive and amusing. Open Thur.-Sun.

⚘⚲⚲ **Science Center of Pinellas County,** 7701 22nd Ave. North (384-0027): Very educational science museum; visitors are asked to take part in all kinds of experiments in computer technology, botany, and natural science. Very modern planetarium. Fascinating for children and adults alike. Open Mon.-Fri.

PARKS AND GARDENS: ☼ ⚱ **Fort De Soto Park,** Pinellas Bayway at Fla. 679 (462-3347): Covering five little islands at the entrance to Tampa Bay, this 880-acre (356-ha.) park looking out on the ocean has facilities for every kind of water sport as well as for camping. Fort dating from the Spanish-American War (1898). Access by a long highway toll bridge. Worth seeing; open daily, sunrise to sunset.

⚘⚱ **Suncoast Seabird Sanctuary,** 18328 Gulf Blvd., Indian Shores (391-6211): Refuge for wounded seabirds: pelicans, herons, egrets, and ospreys. In all, representatives of more than 40 species, in huge open-air holding cages, from which they will be released when cured. The largest veterinary hospital of its kind in the U.S. Conducted tours daily; a must for animal lovers and camera buffs.

⚘⚲⚲ **Sunken Gardens,** 1825 4th St. North (896-3186): A kind of tropical paradise, with more than 7,000 species of plants and flowers from around the world, inhabited by parrots, monkeys, and exotic birds. A St. Petersburg landmark for half a century; must definitely be seen. Open daily.

⚱ **Tiki Gardens,** Fla. 699 at 196th Ave. and Gulf Blvd., Indian Shores (595-2567): Picturesque reconstruction of a Polynesian village, a stone's throw from the sea. Splendid mangroves and lovely tropical gardens with Polynesian temples and statues. Unusual boutiques. A must for lovers of picture postcards from faraway places. Open daily.

PERFORMING ARTS: For a daily listing of all shows and cultural events, consult the entertainment pages of the daily paper *St. Petersburg Times* (morning).

Bayfront Center Theater, 400 1st St. South (823-1870): Concerts, recitals, ballet. Home of the Florida West Coast Symphony (season Sept.-May), the St. Petersburg Opera Company, and the St. Petersburg Concert Ballet.

SPECIAL EVENTS: For the exact schedule of events below, consult the **St. Petersburg Chamber of Commerce** (see "Tourist Information," above).

International Folk Fair (Feb.): Folk festival honoring the diverse ethnic groups that make up the population of St. Petersburg.

Festival of States (late Mar. to Apr.): Art exhibitions, processions, fireworks, balls.

Florida Tournament of Bands (Dec.): Brings together in competition the best high-school bands in the state.

SPORTS: St. Petersburg hosts spring training for one major-league baseball team:

Baseball (mid-Mar. to mid-Apr.): St. Louis Cardinals, Al Lang Stadium (822-3384).

THEME PARKS NEARBY: ※ ⚏⚏ **Homosassa Springs Nature World,** 77 mi. (123 km) north of St. Petersburg on U.S. 19N (904/628-2311): A beautiful aquatic garden around the springs that are the source of the Homosassa River. They flow at a rate of 100,000 gal. (378,000 liters) a minute; the water is crystal clear, and at 72°F (22°C). For some reason which zoologists don't understand, saltwater as well as freshwater fish are attracted to the springs. Boat rides; underwater observation gallery. This is the only theme park in the country with a group of manatees in captivity, not to mention hippopotamuses as well as alligators and other saurians. Don't miss it. Should be combined with the visit to Weeki Wachee Springs (see below) and Tarpon Springs (see "Nearby Excursions," below).

⚏ **Sarasota Jungle Gardens,** 3701 Bayshore Rd., Sarasota, 38 mi. (60 km) south of St. Petersburg on I-275S and U.S. 41S (355-5305): More than 5,000 plant species, and hundreds of exotic birds flying free in a spectacular tropical jungle. Also very lovely landscaped gardens with flamingos, swans, and peacocks. A must-see; combine it with visits to Sarasota and De Soto National Memorial (see "Nearby Excursions," below).

※ ⚏ **Weeki Wachee Springs,** 57 mi. (91 km) north of St. Petersburg on U.S. 19N (904/596-2062): Aquatic displays and Esther Williams–style water nymphs make this one of Florida's most popular attractions. You'll find the world's only theater 16 ft (4 m) below the surface of the water, from which you can watch in comfort through huge walls of glass, 2⅞ in. (4 cm) thick, while the nymphs go through their evolutions—an amazing sight. Boat rides on the Weeki Wachee River. Very lovely orchid gardens. Don't miss it; open daily year round.

ACCOMMODATIONS

See the listing of toll-free numbers in the Appendix.

Room Rates in St. Petersburg	
B (Budget)	up to $30
I (Inexpensive)	$30–$60
M (Moderate)	$60–$90
E (Expensive)	$90–$140
VE (Very Expensive)	$140 and up

Personal Favorites (in order of preference)

※ ⚏⚏⚏⚏ **Don Cesar Beach Resort** (vic.), 3400 Gulf Blvd., St. Petersburg Beach, FL 33706 (813/360-1881; toll free 800/247-9810). 276 rms, A/C, color TV. AE, CB, DC, MC, V. Free parking, pool, health club, sauna, two tennis courts, boating, fishing, waterskiing, private beach, bicycles, four rests. (including King Charles), three bars, 24-hr rm svce, nightclub, hrdrsr, boutiques, free crib. *Note:* A 1930s luxury hotel—the light-hearted Spanish baroque building is painted a lovely pink, whence the hotel's nickname, "The Pink Lady." The best rooms, overlooking the Gulf of Mexico, are splendid, but those overlooking the parking lot are much less so. Excellent svce and very good rest. Clientele of upscale groups and trendy vacationers. Beautiful landscaped gardens; direct beach access. A landmark among Florida hotels. **E–VE, but lower rates out of season**

Dolphin Beach Resort (vic.), 4900 Gulf Blvd., St. Petersburg Beach, FL 33706. (813/360-7011; toll free 800/237-8916). 174 rms, A/C, color TV, in-rm movies. AE, CB, DC, MC, V. Free parking, pool, boating, waterskiing, rest., bar, rm svce, disco, free crib. *Note:* Attractive vacation motel on the beach; rms w. balconies and gulf view, half w. kitchenettes. Comprehensive facilities. Perfect for sailors. Good value; 20 min. from dwntwn St. Petersburg. **M–E, but lower rates out of season**

Days Inn Marina (formerly the Sheraton; nr. dwntwn), 6800 34th St., St. Petersburg, FL 33711 (813/867-1151; toll free, see Days Inns). 158 rms, A/C, color TV, in-rm movies. AE, CB, DC, MC, V. Free parking, two pools, five tennis courts, marina, boating, sailboat instruction, fishing, rest., bar, rm svce, disco, free crib. *Note:* Elderly but congenial motel on the bay. The redecorated rms are spacious and comfortable; one-third have kitchenettes and all have private balconies or patios. Also ten rustic bungalows. Efficient svce; pretty tropical gardens. The ideal vacation motel. Near the Sunshine Skyway, 10 min. from dwntwn. **M–E, but lower rates out of season**

Ponce de Leon (dwntwn), 95 Central Ave., St. Petersburg, FL 33731 (813/822-4139). 100 rms. A/C, color TV. AE, MC, V. Street parking, coffeeshop, bar. *Note:* Aging but well-run hotel w. commendable standards of comfort and svce, in dwntwn St. Petersburg a stone's throw from the yacht basin. Unbeatable value. The coffeeshop (Corner Café) is very acceptable. **B–I**

Other Accommodations (from top bracket to budget)

Hilton Inn (vic.), 5250 Gulf Blvd., St. Petersburg Beach, FL 33706 (813/360-1811; toll free, see Hilton). 152 rms, A/C, color TV, in-rm movies. AE, CB, DC, MC, V. Free parking, beach, boating, pool, rest., revolving bar (Bali Hi) on top floor, rm svce, nightclub. *Note:* Modern circular 11-story tower directly on the beach. Comfortable, functional rms w. private balconies or patios, the best w. gulf view. Friendly, diligent svce. 20 min. from dwntwn St. Petersburg. **E, but lower rates out of season**

Hilton and Towers (dwntwn), 333 1st St., St. Petersburg, FL 33701 (813/894-5000; toll free, see Hilton). 333 rms, A/C, color TV, in-rm movies. AE, CB, DC, MC, V. Free valet parking, pool, rest., bar, rm svce, disco, free crib, concierge. *Note:* Large modern hotel in dwntwn St. Petersburg, facing bay and yacht basin. Spacious, comfortable rms w. offshore view, some w. refrigerators. Efficient svce. Two VIP floors. Group clientele. **M–E, but lower rates out of season**

Alden (vic.), 5900 Gulf Blvd., St. Petersburg Beach, FL 33706 (813/360-7081; toll free 800/237-2530). 140 mini-suites and studios, A/C, color TV, in-rm movies. AE, CB, DC, MC, V. Free parking, two pools, windsurfing, adjoining 24-hr coffeeshop, rm svce. *Note:* Modern, comfortable motel on the beach. One- to three-rm suites w. private balconies or patios and kitchenettes. Agreeable environment; ideal for vacationers w. children. Good value on balance. Friendly reception. 20 min. from dwntwn St. Petersburg. **M–E, but lower rates out of season**

La Quinta (nr. dwntwn), 4999 U.S. 19N, St. Petersburg, FL 33714 (813/527-8421; toll free see La Quinta). 120 rms, no A/C; color TV, in-rm movies. AE, CB, DC, MC, V. Free parking, pool, 24-hr rest., bar, rm svce, free breakfast. *Note:* Charming Castilian-style hacienda in a splendid tropical garden w. fountain, palm trees, and gardenia bushes. Inviting, comfortable rms; excellent svce. Very good value; a fine place to stay. 10 min. from dwntwn. **I–M**

Quality Inn (nr. dwntwn), 2260 54th Ave., St. Petersburg, FL 33714 (813/521-3511; toll free, see Quality Inns). 116 rms, A/C, color TV, in-rm movies. AE, CB, DC, MC, V. Free parking, pool, sauna, health club, rest., bar, crib $5. *Note:* Relatively new, comfortable five-floor motel, recently renovated. Functional rms and facilities; reception w. a smile. Good overall value. 15 min. from dwntwn w. direct access to I-275, an ideal place to stay if you're driving. **I–M**

RESTAURANTS

St. Petersburg Restaurant Prices	
(per person, excluding drinks and service charges)	
B (Budget)	up to $15
I (Inexpensive)	$15–$25
M (Moderate)	$25–$40
E (Expensive)	$40–$60
VE (Very Expensive)	$60 and up

Personal Favorites (in order of preference)

King Charles (vic.), in the Don Cesar Beach Resort (see "Accommodations," above) (360-1881). A/C. Dinner only, Mon.-Sat., brunch Sun. AE, CB, DC, MC, V. Jkt. *Specialties:* chicken Florentine, veal Oscar, roast beef au jus, médaillons of lobster en bellevue (cold in jelly), game (in season), catch of the day, good desserts. *Note:* Luxurious grand-hotel rest. w. a view out over the Gulf of Mexico, serving distinguished classic food. Very preppy atmosphere. First-class svce; agreeable background music. Resv. a must. *Continental.* **M**

Pepin's (nr. dwntwn), 4125 4th St. (821-3773). A/C. Lunch Tues.-Fri., dinner Tues.-Sun.; closed Mon. and holidays. AE, MC, V. *Specialties:* salad Sevillana, shrimp w. almonds, chicken w. yellow rice, red snapper béchamel, baked pompano, steak. *Note:* Congenial Spanish-style tavern serving excellent fish and choice red meats. Friendly, efficient svce; locally very popular (especially for business lunches), so resv. strongly advised. A fine place to eat. *Spanish–Latin American.* **I–M**

Peter's Place (dwntwn), 208 Beach Dr. NE (822-8436). A/C. Lunch/dinner Tues.-Sat.; closed Sun., Mon., and for lunch May-Oct. CB, DC, MC, V. Jkt. *Specialties:* seafood crêpes, duck w. peaches, lobster thermidor, filet Cordon Bleu, mousse w. liqueur. Menu changes regularly. *Note:* A stone's throw from the city's pleasure-boat marina, this intimate, plush rest. is a favorite w. local society. The sauces are a little heavy but the food is a pleasure to eat. Polished svce. Resv. necessary. *Continental.* **I–M**

Siple's Garden Seat (vic.), 1234 Druid Rd., Clearwater (442-9681). A/C. Lunch/dinner daily, in season; dinner only, nightly, out of season. AE, CB, DC, MC, V. *Specialties:* clam chowder, roast duckling, baked shrimp, steak, roast beef, catch of the day, macadamia-nut pie. Skimpy wine list. *Note:* Since 1920 this inviting family home w. its country-club charm has been delighting lovers of wholesome, tasty food. Beautiful gardens and an unobstructed view of Clearwater Harbor, w. impressive sunsets. Friendly, efficient svce. A fine place. Resv. advised. *Continental-seafood.* **B–I**

Other Restaurants (from top bracket to budget)

🍷🍷 **Bradford's Coach House** (dwntwn), 1900 4th St. North (822-7982). A/C. Lunch/dinner Tues.-Sun.; closed Mon. and May-Sept. AE, MC, V. *Specialties:* shellfish, steak, roast beef, fish of the day. *Note:* Very popular steakhouse across from the Sunken Gardens serving very good red meat. Efficient svce; congenial English-pub atmosphere. *Steak-seafood.* **I**

☀🍷🍷 **Heilman's Beachcomber** (vic.), 447 Mandalay Ave., Clearwater Beach (442-4144). A/C. Lunch/dinner daily (until midnight). AE, DC, MC, V. *Specialties:* stone crab (in season), shrimp Rockefeller, calves' liver w. onions, roast lamb, steak, fried chicken, broiled fish of the day (snapper, grouper, swordfish, etc.), good homemade desserts. *Note:* The classic all-American rest., straight out of the 1940s w. décor, food, and waiters to match. Generous servings. Locally popular since 1948; a very fine place to eat, right on the beach. Resv. advised. *Steak-seafood.* **I**

🍷 **Aunt Hattie's** (vic.), 6340 Gulf Blvd., St. Petersburg Beach (367-3448). A/C. Lunch/dinner daily; closed Labor Day and Dec. 25. AE, CB, DC, MC, V. *Specialties:* langostinos, broiled chicken, roast beef hash. *Note:* Imaginative southern food in a charming old-fashioned setting. Often crowded and noisy. Excellent value. *American.* **B–I**

🍷 **The Kingfish** (vic.), 12789 Kingfish Dr., Treasure Island (360-0881). A/C. Lunch/dinner daily; closed Thanksgiving and Dec. 25. MC, V. *Specialties:* catch of the day, broiled or baked shellfish. *Note:* Traditional oyster bar and seafood rest. looking out over the Treasure Island yacht basin. Absolutely fresh seafood. Locally popular; very good value. *Seafood.* **B–I**

BARS & NIGHTCLUBS

Le Bistro (vic.), in the Don Cesar Beach Resort (see "Accommodations," above, St. Petersburg Beach) (360-1881). Snug, intimate bar with a view of the Gulf of Mexico; preppy clientele. Disco. Open nightly.

Le Pompano (vic.), 19325 Gulf Blvd., Indian Shores (596-0333). Congenial disco with live music. Also very praiseworthy French restaurant. Fine location on the water.

NEARBY EXCURSIONS

⚓ **DE SOTO NATIONAL MEMORIAL** (on Fla. 64 in Bradenton, 30 mi., 48 km, south of St. Petersburg along I-275 and U.S. 41) (792-0458): Museum of the Spanish Conquest built at the mouth of Tampa Bay, where Hernándo de Soto first dropped anchor on May 30, 1539. Recaptures the four-year expedition of the famous conquistador and his 600 companions to explore the Southeast, from Florida to Mississippi; their journey is retraced in detail by a movie shown at the Visitor Center. Small military museum. Well worth the side trip. Open daily.

☀🔭 **SARASOTA** (39 mi., 62 km, south of St. Petersburg via I-275 and U.S. 41): Sarasota is the birthplace of American golf (the first course in the country was laid out here in 1886 by Scotsman John Hamilton Gillespie), but it has been better known as the world capital of the circus since 1927, when "the King of the Circus," John Ringling himself, chose the town as the winter quarters of the Ringling Bros. & Barnum and Bailey Circus. Today it's the home of the great **Ringling Museum of Art** complex on U.S. 41 (355-5101), comprising four architecturally remarkable buildings. First is John Ringling's own home, **Ca' d' Zan,** a lavish replica of a 32-room Venetian Gothic palace complete with antique furniture and a 4,000-pipe organ. Then comes the superb art gallery with its collection of European masters: El Greco, Frans Hals, Rembrandt, Gainsborough, Poussin, and above all, Rubens. A new wing, recently built, displays contemporary works of art and revolving exhibitions. The **Asolo Museum Theater** is an authentic 18th-century Italian baroque theater, taken down and transported stone by stone to Florida in 1949 from the castle of Asolo, near Venice. Finally, there are a richly stocked **circus museum,** illustrating circus history from Roman times on, and some splendid gardens. Don't miss it; open daily year round.

TARPON SPRINGS (35 mi., 56 km, north of St. Petersburg on U.S. 19N): Picturesque little sponge-fishing port with an important Greek community. Pretty view of the docks from Dodecanese Blvd. Fine Greek Orthodox **Cathedral of St. Nicholas,** built in 1943 in the neo-Byzantine style, at 36 N. Pinellas Ave. (937-3540), open daily. Boat rides from the waterfront to the sponge-fishing grounds and demonstrations of sponge fishing. And don't fail to see the **Spongeorama** at Sponge Docks (937-4111), open daily, a museum entirely devoted to this unusual industry. You shouldn't miss Tarpon Springs.

Where to Eat

Louis Pappas, 10 W. Dodecanese Blvd. (937-5101). Lunch/dinner daily. AE, DC, MC, V. Local color guaranteed. *Greek.* **B–I**

FARTHER AFIELD

WALT DISNEY WORLD AND CENTRAL FLORIDA (160 mi., 256 km, round trip via I-4E, U.S. 17S, U.S. 27S, and Fla. 60W): A very crowded itinerary taking you to the fabulous **Disney World,** **EPCOT,** **Sea World,** **Wet 'n Wild,** and **Cypress Gardens** (for these five theme parks, among the most famous in the country, see Chapter 18 on Orlando). On the way you'll see **Bok Tower Gardens** at Lake Wales on U.S. 27A (676-1408), a bird sanctuary surrounded by splendid landscaped gardens. Unusual carillon concerts, with 53 bells weighing from 17 lb. (7 kg) to 11 tons, daily at 3 p.m. Also *Mystery of the Passion,* with 250 performers, on Tues., Thur., Sat., and Sun. from mid-Feb. to mid-Apr. Don't miss this trip; for hotels, motels, and restaurants, see Chapter 18 on Orlando.

EVERGLADES NATIONAL PARK (313 mi., 500 km, SE of Tampa on I-75S, U.S. 41E, U.S. 1S, and Fla. 997S): The only subtropical national park in the U.S. Its flora and fauna are of exceptional richness. For details, see Chapter 19 on Miami.

GULF OF MEXICO (256 mi., 409 km, round trip from St. Petersburg via I-275S and U.S. 41S, returning on I-75N &

U.S. 41N): Dozens of superb, uncrowded beaches: **Longboat Key, Lido Key, Siesta Key,** and **Venice** near Sarasota; **Fort Myers Beach, La Costa,** and **Sanibel** (the best beach in Florida for finding seashells) **and Captiva Islands** near Fort Myers.

On the way visit the **De Soto National Memorial** and the Ringling museums at Sarasota (see "Nearby Excursions," above). At **Fort Myers,** see the 🏛 **Thomas Edison Winter Home,** 2350 McGregor Blvd. (334-3614), where the famous inventor spent his winters for almost half a century. Open daily.

For boat rides on the rivers and swamps of Florida, **Everglades Jungle Cruise,** City Yacht Basin, Fort Myers (334-7474), daily year round.

This one- or two-day trip is perfect for nature lovers.

CHAPTER 18

ORLANDO 🍦🍦

□ □ □

With Walt Disney World, EPCOT, and Central Florida

"The city beautiful," as Orlando residents like to call their town, had modest beginnings as a simple military encampment during the war against the Seminole Indians (1835–1842). Today its purpose and chief claim to fame are to host the millions of American and foreign tourists who have made this central Florida area an enormous year-round vacation spot. **Walt Disney World, Cape Kennedy, Sea World, Daytona Beach, Cypress Gardens, St. Augustine, EPCOT, Silver Springs** . . . all are less than two hours by car from the Orlando airport, an ultramodern facility amply served by regular and charter flights coming from the northern states, Europe and Canada.

An important distribution center for citrus fruits and other Florida fruits and vegetables, this modern, dynamic commercial metropolis, whose population has more than doubled since the Cape Canaveral Space Center (now the **Kennedy Space Center**) was created in 1950, has one of the largest concentrations of hotel accommodations in America (56,000 rooms). Orlando's economy is the second fastest growing among major U.S. cities. This garden city, studded with parks and lagoons, is a winter resort favored by many northern residents, and a favorite honeymoon destination for young newlyweds. In addition, the surrounding countryside with its dozens of lakes makes the area a summer paradise for campers and caravaners.

Instead of impressive historical monuments, Orlando and its region offer some of the most famous tourist attractions in the world, beginning with Walt Disney World and its sister facility, the sprawling futuristic EPCOT (22 million visitors annually), or the fabulous **Cypress Gardens** featuring Esther Williams–style water ballet. In a more traditional vein but also worth visiting is the residential suburb of **Winter Park,** just north of Orlando, with its lovely European-style homes, music and art festivals, and canals reminiscent of Venice.

As a finishing touch, the inauguration in 1983 of the immense **Orange County Convention Center** has made the city one of the most important convention cities in the country.

BASIC FACTS: State of Florida. Area Codes: 407 (Orlando/Walt Disney World); 813 or 904 (other zones). ZIP Code: 32802 (city of Orlando). Founded: 1837. Approximate population: city, 130,000; metropolitan area, 880,000.

CLIMATE: As in all of Florida, winters in Orlando are mild and sunny (mean Jan. temperature, 62°F, 17°C). The summer is oppressive, with frequent showers, but somewhat less humid than at the Florida shore (average temperature in July is 82°F, 28°C). With the thermometer hovering around 71°–77°F (22°–25°C), spring and fall are uniformly pleasant.

DISTANCES: Atlanta, 436 mi. (698 km); Miami, 236 mi. (378 km); New Orleans, 644 mi. (1,030 km); New York, 1,160 mi. (1,856 km); Savannah, 292 mi. (467 km); Washington, 925 mi. (1,480 km).

ARRIVAL & TRANSIT INFORMATION

AIRPORT: Orlando International Airport (MCO): 8 mi. (13 km) SE. For information call 407/826-2001.

U.S. AIRLINES (Orlando telephone numbers unless otherwise indicated): American (896-2334), Continental (295-6000), Delta (849-6400), Eastern (843-7280), Midway (toll free 800/621-5700), Northwest (351-3190), Pan Am (422-0701), TWA (351-3855), United (859-0710), and USAir (toll free 800/428-4322).

FOREIGN CARRIERS: British Airways (toll free 800/247-9297) and Icelandair (toll free 800/223-5500).

CITY LINK: The cab fare from the airport to downtown Orlando is about $14; from the airport to Lake Buena Vista hotels, about $22; from the airport to Walt Disney World, about $35. Bus: Airport Limousine Service (407/423-5566); serves major hotels in Orlando and the area; fare, $8 to $15, according to destination.

    Although Orlando and all central Florida are amply served by regular long-distance and excursion bus lines, you should seriously consider renting a car with unlimited mileage for trips to Walt Disney World and other area attractions. Car-rental rates in Florida are among the most reasonable in the entire U.S., while municipal public bus service is woefully lacking. Information: OTA (407/841-8240).

CAR RENTAL (at the Orlando International Airport unless otherwise indicated): Avis (851-7600); Budget (855-6660); Dollar (851-3232); Hertz (859-8400); Thrifty, 2323 McCoy Rd. (859-6990). For downtown locations, consult the local telephone directory.

LIMOUSINE SERVICES: American Limousine (859-2250), Carey Limousine (352-6700), Dav El Limousines (toll free 800/922-0343).

TAXIS: Cabs can be hailed on the street or from waiting lines at designated taxi stations; you can also phone for taxi service, in which case try **City Cab** (422-5151) or **Yellow Cab** (422-4561).

TRAIN: AMTRAK Station, 1400 Sligh Blvd. (843-8460; toll free 800/424-1111).

BUS: Greyhound, 300 W. Amelia St. (407/843-7720).

INFORMATION & TOURS

TOURIST INFORMATION: The **Orlando Chamber of Commerce,** 75 E. Ivanhoe Blvd. (P.O. Box 1234), FL 32802 (407/425-1234).

Orlando Tourist Information Center, 8445 International Dr., Suite 152, FL 32819 (407/351-0412).

GUIDED TOURS: American Sightseeing Tours (bus), 9526 Boyce Ave. (407/859-2250): Guided tour of tourist attractions in the area, serving major hotels.

Gray Line Tours (bus) (407/422-0744): Guided tour of area attractions, serving major hotels.

Scenic Boat Tours (boat), Morse Blvd. at Lake Osceola (407/644-4056): Guided tour by boat on Winter Park's lagoons and canals. Daily.

SIGHTS, ATTRACTIONS, & ACTIVITIES

ADVENTURE TOURS: Phineas Phogg's Balloon Works (balloon tours/ ballooning), Church St. Station, Orlando (407/422-2434): Dawn departure on clear days. The tour lasts four hours and costs $140 per person, champagne brunch included. Spectacular.

MUSEUMS OF ART: 🏛 **Loch Haven Art Center,** 2416 N. Mills Ave., Orlando (407/896-4231): Pre-Columbian and primitive African art; also 20th-century American painting and sculpture. Interesting temporary exhibits. Worth a look. Open Tues.-Sun.

🏛 **Morse Gallery of Art,** 133 E. Welbourne Ave., Winter Park (407/644-3686): Very lovely art deco collection including lamps, blown glass, chandeliers, and stained-glass windows by Louis Comfort Tiffany. Also old ceramics, paintings, and furniture. Open Tues.-Sun.

MUSEUMS OF SCIENCE AND HISTORY: ☼ 🏛 **Beal-Maltbie Shell Museum,** Holt Ave., Winter Park (407/646-2000): One of the largest shell collections in the world, containing 2½ million specimens representing 100,000 different species. Also beautiful pearl and cameo collections. Worth a look. Open Mon.-Fri.

🏛 **Orange County Historical Museum,** 812 E. Rollins St., Orlando (407/898-8320): Traces the history of the settlement of Florida. From a re-created 19th-century saloon and grocery store to examples of Indian crafts. Worth a look. Open Tues.-Sun.

☼🏛 **Orlando Science Center,** 810 E. Rollins St., Orlando (407/ 896-7151): Comprehensive museum of science and technology. Be sure to see the exhibit devoted to space travel, including the model of a lunar space colony. Ultramodern planetarium. Open daily.

PARKS AND GARDENS: 🏛 **Bok Tower Singing Gardens,** at Lake Wales, 61 mi. (97 km) SW on I-4 and U.S. 27 (813/676-1408): 128-acre (52-ha.) botanical gardens with a bird sanctuary **(Mountain Lake Sanctuary)** and dominated by a 205-ft (62-m) bell tower, whose 53 bells weigh from 17 lbs. (7 kg) to ten tons. Marvelous carillon concerts daily at 3 p.m. In the nearby **Lake Wales Amphitheater,** on U.S. 27A (813/676-1495), visitors can enjoy performances of the Passion Play with 250 participants (Tues., Thur., Sat., and Sun., mid-Feb. to mid-Apr.). Spectacular. (The same troupe presents the Passion Play at Spearfish, June-Aug.; see Chapter 34 on Mount Rushmore.)

☼🏛🏛 **Cypress Gardens,** at Winter Haven, 55 mi. (89 km) SW by I-4, U.S. 27, and Fla. 540 (813/324-2111): For a good half century these fabulous tropical gardens on the shores of Lake Eloise have been among Florida's principal tourist attractions. There are tours via electric boat of flowers and foliage from five continents (more than 8,000 species from 70 coun-

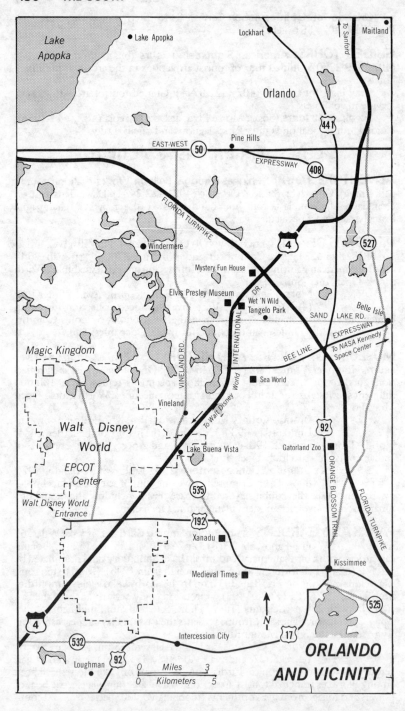

ORLANDO AND VICINITY

tries). Exotic birds swoop and chatter in the immense aviary. Exhibitions of synchronized waterskiing, Esther Williams style, are given four times a day, year round. Mustn't be missed.

🔔 **Eola Park,** Central Blvd., Orlando: Charming little public park located in the middle of the downtown area on the shore of Lake Eola. Flowerbeds; fountains illuminated after dark. Particularly dazzling when the azaleas are in flower, in Feb. and Mar.

🔔 **Leu Gardens,** 1730 N. Forest Ave., Orlando: Lovely tropical gardens in the center of Orlando. 56 acres (22 ha.) of camellias, orchids, roses, and azaleas. Not to be missed.

🔔 **Loch Haven Park,** Princeton Blvd. and Mills Ave., Orlando: City park which is the site of the principal museums in Orlando: the Loch Haven Art Center, the Orange County Historical Museum, and the Orlando Science Center (see "Museums of Art" and "Museums of Science and History," above).

PERFORMING ARTS: For a daily listing of all shows and cultural events, consult the entertainment pages of the daily paper *Orlando Sentinel* (morning and evening) and *Orlando* magazine.

Annie Russel Theater, Rollins College, Park and Holt Aves., Winter Park (407/646-2145): Modern theater, musical comedies. Year round.

Bob Carr Performing Arts Center, 401 W. Livingston Ave., Orlando (407/849-2577): Ballet, theater, concerts. Home of the Florida Symphony Orchestra (principal conductor, Kenneth Jean); season Sept.-May.

Central Florida Civic Theatre, 1010 E. Princeton, Orlando (407/896-7365): Classical and contemporary theater, musical comedies. Year round.

Once Upon a Stage, 3376 Edgewater Dr., Orlando (407/422-3191): Dinner-theater featuring musical comedies and Broadway-style reviews.

Tupperware Auditorium, U.S. 441S, Orlando (407/847-3111): Concerts, recitals, big-name entertainers.

SHOPPING: **Flea World,** U.S. 17/92 in Sanford (14 mi. NE): The largest flea market in the world. More than 1,000 vendors and mountains of varied merchandise. Open 8 a.m. to 5 p.m. Fri.-Sun. Worth the trip.

SPECIAL EVENTS: For the exact schedule of events below, consult the **Orlando Convention and Visitors Bureau** (see "Tourist Information," above).

Scottish Highland Games (end of Jan.): Festival of dance, music, and athletic events in the grand Scottish tradition (407/422-8226).

Central Florida Fair (Feb.-Mar.): Horse shows, entertainment, parades.

Bach Festival (end of Feb.): Concerts of classical music in Winter Park.

Autumn Art Festival (Sept.): Art exhibits, concerts. Winter Park.

Florida State Air Fair (end of Oct.): Festival of parachuting and aerobatics at Kissimmee. Many aircraft on display. Spectacular.

Citrus Sports Holiday (Dec.): Three weeks of sports and competitions culminating in the Citrus Bowl football game.

Christmas Parade (Christmastime): All the famous Walt Disney characters parade daily down Walt Disney World's "Main Street USA."

SPORTS: Orlando has two professional teams, and three major-league teams have spring training facilities here:

Baseball (Feb.-Mar): Houston Astros, Osceola Stadium, Kissimmee (407/933-5500); Kansas City Royals, Boardwalk Stadium, Haines City (407/648-5151); Minnesota Twins, Tinker Field, Orlando (407/849-6346).

Baseball (June-Sept.): Orlando Twins, Tinker Field, Orlando (407/849-6346).

Football (Aug.-Jan.): Renegades, Memorial Coliseum, Orlando (407/843-8735).

Horse Racing

Ben White Raceway, 1905 Lee Rd., Orlando (407/293-8721), Mon.-Sat., Oct.-May. Harness racing.

Jai Alai

Orlando Jai Alai Fronton, N. Fern Park, U.S. 17/92 (407/339-6221), Mon.-Sat., Sept.-Dec.

STROLLS: ※ ⚱ **Church Street Station,** 129 W. Church St., Orlando (407/422-2434): Quaint shops, saloons, restaurants, and nightclubs in a pleasing old-fashioned setting in the heart of Orlando's historical center. Picturesque and lively, especially in the evening. Open daily.

THEME PARKS: ⚱ **Boardwalk & Baseball,** junction of I-4 and U.S. 27 in Haines City (813/424-2424): This newly constructed park is an unexpected combination of two typically American institutions: amusement parks and baseball. A new 6,500-seat stadium hosts the Kansas City Royals for spring training and other sporting teams during the rest of the year. Visitors can practice their favorite sport. Nearby are concessions and rides—a Ferris wheel, giant roller coaster, etc. Open daily year round.

※ ⚱ **Silver Springs,** near Ocala, 86 mi. (138 km) NW by the Florida Tpke., U.S. 27, Fla. 35, and Fla. 40 (904/236-2121): Every year 1.5 million people visit the springs that feed the Silver River and the superb lake whose incredibly clear waters frequently attract moviemakers shooting underwater sequences. The springs produce 500 million gallons (2,000 million liters) of water per day. Tours in glass-bottom boats reveal underwater grottos more than 100,000 years old. Truly spectacular. Also a very beautiful park with deer, and a famous vivarium (Reptile Institute). Very much worth the detour. Open daily.

※ ⚱⚱⚱ **Walt Disney World,** 22 mi. (35 km) SW on I-4 at Lake Buena Vista (407/824-4500): The largest and most famous amusement park in the world, rising miraculously from Florida swampland. Opened to the public in 1971—five years after the death of its creator, Walt Disney—the park has already been visited by more than 210 million people. Park employees number over 19,000. Conceived along the lines of its older sister park, Disneyland (see Chapter 54 on Los Angeles), Walt Disney World—an amusement park taking the whole planet for its theme—stretches over 28,000 acres (twice the size of Manhattan); its parking facilities can accommodate 20,000 cars. In effect, Walt Disney World contains two distinct amusement parks linked by monorail: the Magic Kingdom and EPCOT.

The Magic Kingdom: Computer-controlled with chronometric precision, spectacular rides such as Cinderella's Castle, Mission to Mars, Twenty Thousand Leagues under the Sea, and Pirates of the Caribbean dazzle young and old alike. For convenience, the park is organized as six miniature villages, each with its own style: **Adventureland,** with its boat tour through the jungle; **Fantasyland,** inhabited by the loveable Disney characters; **Frontierland,** in traditional Far West style; **Liberty Square,** with its gallery of 40 U.S. presidents and a house haunted by 999 ghosts; **Main Street USA,** in the style of a turn-of-the-century small town; and **Tomorrowland,** with a space adventure theme.

EPCOT: Theme park of the 21st century, with overtones of a World's Fair, the most recent member of the Disney family opened its doors in October 1982. Expecting over 22 million visitors each year, EPCOT (acronym for "Experimental Prototype Community of Tomorrow") has only a tenuous thematic link with the fictional world of Mickey Mouse or Donald Duck. Several theme pavilions (Earth, Energy, Transportation, etc.), sponsored by such industrial giants as Exxon, IBM, General Motors, Kodak, and Bell Telephone, adjoin a "window on the world" where scrupulously re-created Japanese temples jostle the Eiffel Tower, Québec's Château Frontenac, St. Mark's Square in Venice, a Bavarian village, Mayan pyramids, a London street, Beijing's Temple of Heaven, etc. The whole ensemble is dominated by a giant 18-story sphere made of reinforced concrete and steel, reminiscent of a huge golf ball, which has become EPCOT's symbol. And there's the largest aquarium in the world, Living Seas, and its 7,500 sea creatures which visitors can observe from an underwater train moving through glass tunnels at the bottom of the gigantic six-million-gallon (22.6-million-liter) aquarium basin. The futuristic EPCOT, whose construction consumed five years and $1 billion (twice the cost of Walt Disney World and four times that of Disneyland), may well become the favorite among the three Disney parks.

In addition to the innumerable attractions of the Magic Kingdom and EPCOT, Walt Disney World offers visitors an immense 7,500-acre (3,000-ha.) forest reserve of cypress, pine, and laurel trees, two artificial lakes with 4.5 mi. (7 km) of sandy beaches, three golf courses, fully equipped camping facilities, and every imaginable sport, including tennis, swimming, waterskiing, sailing, fishing, horseback riding, etc.

There are four hotels ideally located for Walt Disney World visitors: the astounding **Contemporary Resort** (served by monorail), the brand new **Caribbean Beach Resort** or **Grand Floridian Beach Resort,** and the more intimate, highly successful **Polynesian Resort.** For reservations: Walt Disney World Central Reservations Office, P.O. Box 78, Lake Buena Vista, FL 32830 (407/934-7369).

Open daily all year, Walt Disney World is in itself worth the trip to Florida. Plan to spend at least two or three full days here, and avoid weekends and holidays. Admission fees: $30 per day for adults, $80 for three days. There's a 20% reduction for children aged 3 to 12 years. Albeit fatiguing, this is an experience that should not be missed by children, or by adults who don't want to grow up. Call 407/824-4321 for price and schedule information.

    Wet 'N Wild, in Orlando, 6 mi. (10 km) SW on I-4, exit 435S (407/351-3200): Aquatic fun park with some outstanding attractions: a giant six-story slide, a white-water course, and a lagoon with enormous artificial waves for would-be surfers. Spectacular. Open daily, mid-Feb. to mid-Oct.

ZOOS: **Gatorland Zoo,** at Kissimmee, 7 mi. (11 km) south on U.S. 17 (407/857-3845): 6,000 alligators, crocodiles, and giant turtles, as well as pink flamingos and zebras, in a 35-acre tropical park. Tour by miniature train. Open daily, year round.

    Sea World of Florida, 7007 Sea World Dr., Orlando (407/351-3600): One of the largest marine zoos in the world, surrounded by 150 acres of gardens. On display are sharks, a killer whale, sea lions, sea turtles, and trained dolphins performing on cue. Splendid view from the top of the 450-ft (140-m) revolving tower. There are also a Polynesian show and a buffet luau every evening. Sea World has almost three million visitors annually. Open daily, year round. A must-see.

ACCOMMODATIONS
See the listing of toll-free numbers in the Appendix.

Room Rates in Orlando and Central Florida	
B (Budget)	up to $30
I (Inexpensive)	$30–$60
M (Moderate)	$60–$90
E (Expensive)	$90–$140
VE (Very Expensive)	$140 and up

Personal Favorites (in order of preference)

Hyatt Regency Grand Cypress, 1 Grand Cypress Blvd., Orlando, FL 32819 (407/239-1234; toll free, see Hyatt). 750 rms, A/C, color TV, in-rm movies. AE, CB, DC, MC, V. Valet parking $5, pool, 12 tennis courts, two golf courses, private beach, marina, health club, three rests. (including Hemingway's), four bars, rm svce, disco, boutiques, free crib, concierge. *Note:* One of the most spectacular hotels in the U.S., built around a superb lagoon–swimming pool (the largest in the world) w. waterfalls and a giant slide. There's a magnificent 18-story atrium w. extensive plantings of flowers, waterfalls, and glass-walled elevators. Spacious rms w. balconies. Ultramodern comfort. The décor is elegant, w. master paintings and other works of art. Efficient svce. 1,000 acres (400 ha.) of gardens and groves; private lake with sandy beach. Home of the famous Jack Nicklaus Academy of Golf. 10 min. from dwntwn, 10 min. from Walt Disney World. The new paragon of Florida luxury hotelkeeping. Two VIP floors. **VE**

The Peabody, 9801 International Dr., Orlando, FL 32819 (407/352-4000; toll free 800/262-6688). 891 rms, A/C, color TV, in-rm movies. AE, CB, DC, MC, V. Valet parking $5, pool, tennis court, health club, sauna, three rests. (including Dux), coffeeshop, three bars, rm svce, nightclub, concierge. *Note:* Brand-new, palatial 27-story hotel in an impressive futuristic style. In the fountain of the exquisite marble lobby swim tame ducks, symbol of the Peabody Hotel chain. The rms are spacious and inviting, w. elegantly furnished interiors. There are raised gardens and a spectacular pool. Very good rests. Three VIP floors. Located directly across from Sea World and five min. away from Walt Disney World. Dwntwn is 15 min. away. A splendid place to stay. **E–VE**

Polynesian Resort, Walt Disney World, Lake Buena Vista, FL 32830 (407/824-2000; resv. 407/934-7639). 856 rms, A/C, cable color TV. AE, MC. Free parking, pool, golf, tennis court, health club, private beach, waterskiing, rest. (Papeete Bay Verandah), coffeeshop, bar, rm svce, nightclub, hrdrsr, boutiques, free crib. *Note:* Fragrance of the Southern Seas three min. by monorail from Walt Disney World. Lovely Polynesian-style pavilions on the shores of a lagoon. Rms are cramped but pleasant and the svce somewhat weak, but on balance the experience is positive. Pretty indoor gardens; good Polynesian rest. Three VIP floors. Clientele is mostly families. One of the best places to stay around Walt Disney World. **E–VE**

Gold Key Inn, 7100 S. Orange Blossom Trail, Orlando FL 32809 (407/855-0050; toll free 800/327-0304). 210 rms,

A/C, cable color TV. AE, CB, DC, MC, V. Free parking, pool, tennis court, sauna, putting green, rest. (Piccadilly), bar, rm svce, disco, free crib. *Note:* One of the best values in the Orlando area. Comfortable, well-equipped motel. The spacious rms have balconies; some have refrigerators. Reception is cheerful and pleasant. Good rest. Ideal for families. 10 min. by car from the airport and from Sea World, 20 min. from Walt Disney World (free shuttle bus). A fine place to stay. **M–E**

    Hilton Inn Florida Center, 7400 International Dr., Orlando, FL 32809 (407/351-4600; toll free, see Hilton). 400 rms, A/C, color TV, in-rm movies. AE, CB, DC, MC, V. Free parking, two pools, rest., bar, rm svce, disco, hrdrsr, free crib. *Note:* Large, relatively modern hotel 15 min. by car from Walt Disney World. Comfortable, inviting rms, some w. refrigerators, the best overlooking the outdoor pool. Good svce. Free airport shuttle. Good value. Ideal for families. **M**

    Chalet Suzanne, U.S. 27, Lake Wales, FL 33853 (813/676-6011). 30 rms, A/C, cable color TV. AE, CB, DC, MC, V. Free parking, pool, fishing, boating, rest., bar. *Note:* Charming lakeside inn, seemingly right out of a Hans Christian Andersen fairy tale. The décor leans rather heavily toward bric-a-brac, but the rms are comfortable and inviting. Very good rest.; excellent svce. 10 min. by car from Cypress Gardens and Bok Tower Gardens. Private airfield. A very good place to stay. **M–E**

    Days Inn Lakeside, 7335 Sandlake Rd., Orlando, FL 32811 (407/351-1900; toll free, see Days Inns). 702 rms, A/C, cable color TV. AE, MC, V. Free parking, three pools, rest., coffeeshop (no alcohol permitted), crib $6. *Note:* Large, standard-style motel on Spring Lake. Lovely views from most of the rms. Functional comfort 12 min. by car from Walt Disney World. Good value. **I**

    Motel 6, 5731 W. Irlo Bronson Hwy. (U.S. 192), Kissimmee, FL 32741 (407/396-6333). 347 rms, A/C, color TV, free in-rm movies. DC, MC, V. Free parking, pool, free crib. *Note:* Brand-new budget motel 5 min. by car from Walt Disney World. Ideal for families. One of the best values in the entire Orlando area. **B**

Other Accommodations (from top bracket to budget)

    Contemporary Resort, Walt Disney World, Lake Buena Vista, FL 32830 (407/824-1000; for resv., 407/934-7639). 1,046 rms, A/C, color TV. AE, MC, V. Free valet parking, two pools, health club, sauna, tennis court, beach, waterskiing, two rests. (including Top of the World), coffeeshop, bars, rm svce, disco, hrdrsr, boutiques, free crib. *Note:* Original, modern design. This enormous white truncated pyramid, 15 stories high, is accessed by a monorail which links it directly to Walt Disney World. Spacious, comfortable rms, all w. balconies or patios, overlooking the surrounding lagoons. The lobby is worth the visit all by itself. Svce is a bit vague but courteous. The rest. at the top is good and offers a panoramic view. VIP floor. The most spectacular accommodations in the Disney empire. Resv. far in advance are a must. **E–VE**

    Grenelefe Golf and Tennis Resort, 3200 Fla. 546, Winter Haven, FL 33844 (813/422-7511). 1,000 rms, A/C, cable color TV. AE, CB, DC, MC, V. Free parking, four pools, private beach, three golf courses, 13 tennis courts, waterskiing, marina, sauna, horseback riding, three rests., three bars, disco, rm svce, movie theater, crib $10. *Note:* Huge, luxurious vacation complex w. a lovely tropical lagoon. Comfortable rms w. balconies in two-story bungalows (most w. kitchenette) on the shores of Lake Marion. Svce beyond reproach. Exceptional sports facilities. 8 min. by car from Cypress

Gardens, 35 min. from Walt Disney World. **E–VE, but lower rates out of season**

Radisson Plaza Hotel, 60 Ivanhoe Blvd., Orlando, FL 32804 (407/425-4455; toll free, see Radisson). 324 rms, A/C, cable color TV. AE, CB, DC, MC, V. Free parking, pool, two tennis courts, sauna, health club, two rests. (including Thorndikes), two bars, rm svce, disco, free crib, concierge. *Note:* Large 15-story modern hotel located in the heart of dwntwn. Functional but elegant design. Rms are vast and well laid out. Faultless facilities and comfort; very good svce. Rests. are average. Business travelers and convention-goers are the staple clientele. Two VIP floors. Free airport shuttle. **E–VE**

Sheraton Orlando North Hotel and Towers, Maitland Blvd. and I-4, Orlando, FL 32853 (407/660-9000; toll free, see Sheraton). 400 rms, A/C, cable color TV. AE, CB, DC, MC, V. Free garage, pool, tennis court, sauna, health club, two rests., two bars, rm svce, nightclub, disco, hrdrsr, boutiques, free crib, concierge. *Note:* Ultramodern hotel w. an immense glass lobby housing a winter garden. Very comfortable, elegant rms w. balconies and refrigerators. Comprehensive facilities; attentive svce; rests. no more than adequate. Business and group clientele. VIP floor. 15 min. from Orlando's business section. **E**

Marriott Orlando, 8001 International Dr., Orlando, FL 32809 (407/351-2420; toll free, see Marriott). 1,079 rms, A/C, cable color TV. AE, CB, DC, MC, V. Free parking, three pools, four tennis courts, three rests. (including Grove Restaurant), bars, rm svce, disco, free crib. *Note:* Enormous tourist complex composed of two-story cottages surrounded by gardens and exotic lagoons. Spacious, comfortable rms, some w. kitchenettes and refrigerators. Ultra-professional svce and reception. Rests. are so-so. Frequented by convention and other groups. Good value. 10 min. from Walt Disney World, 15 min. from dwntwn. **M–E**

Sheraton Lakeside Inn, 7711 Irlo Bronson Memorial Hwy. (U.S. 192), Kissimmee, FL 32741 (407/828-8250; toll free, see Sheraton). 650 rms, A/C, cable color TV. AE, CB, DC, MC, V. Free parking, two pools, four tennis courts, pedalboats, miniature golf, two rests., coffeeshop, bars, rm svce, night club, free crib. *Note:* Large, comfortable, recently modernized motel. Large, inviting rms. Pleasant setting on a lagoon. Good svce overall. 10 min. from Walt Disney World. **M–E, but lower rates out of season**

Delta Courts of Flags (formerly the Ramada), 5715 Major Blvd., Orlando, FL 32819 (407/351-3340; toll free 800/268-3777). 824 rms, A/C, color TV, in-rm movies. AE, CB, DC, MC, V. Free parking, three pools, tennis court, sauna, two rests., two bars, rm svce, disco, hrdrsr, boutiques, free crib. *Note:* Large vacation and conference motel located halfway between dwntwn Orlando and Walt Disney World. The spacious rms w. balconies and refrigerators are in small three-story buildings surrounded by gardens. Reasonably complete facilities. Frequented by families and groups. Good value. 10 min. from dwntwn, 15 min. from Walt Disney World. **M**

Holiday Inn Main Gate East, 5678 E. Irlo Bronson Hwy., Kissimmee, FL 32741 (407/396-4488; toll free, see Holiday Inns). 512 rms, A/C, color TV, in-rm movies. AE, CB, DC, MC, V. Free parking, two pools, two tennis courts, rest., bar, rm svce, disco, free crib. *Note:* Modern, standard-type motel 5 min. from Walt Disney World. Comfortable rms, some w. kitchenettes. Children's rest. Shuttle bus to Walt Disney World. Good value. Ideal for families. **I–M, but lower rates out of season**

Imperial Inn, 830 Lee Rd., Orlando, FL 32810 (407/629-4000; toll free, see Imperial Inns). 145 rms, A/C, cable color TV. AE, CB, DC, MC, V. Free parking, sauna, health club, coffeeshop, bar, valet svce. *Note:* Comfortable, brand-new motel scarcely 5 min. from the dwntwn business district. Vast, inviting rms. Pleasant, cheerful svce. Business clientele. Good value. **I–M**

♀♀ **Quality Inn High Q,** 5905 International Dr., Orlando, FL 📞📞 32819 (407/351-2100; toll free, see Quality Inns). 300 rms, A/C, color TV. AE, CB, DC, MC, V. Free parking, pool, sauna, rest., bar, rm svce, disco, hrdrsr. *Note:* Large, round modern 21-story tower. Inviting rms. Functional facilities and comfort level; efficient svce. Very good value. 20 min. from Walt Disney World, 10 min. from dwntwn. **I–M, but lower rates out of season**

♀♀ **USA Inn,** 2639 Garfield Dr., Cypress Gardens, FL 33880 📞📞 (813/324-5950). 158 rms, A/C, cable color TV. AE, CB, DC, MC, V. Free parking, pool, rests., bar, rm svce, free crib. *Note:* Standard but comfortable motel. Functional rms w. balconies. Adequate rest. Good value. Efficient svce. 5 min. by car from Cypress Gardens, 40 min. from Walt Disney World. **I–M, but lower rates out of season**

♀ **Davis Park Motel,** 221 Colonial Dr. (Fla. 50), Orlando, FL 📞 32801 (407/425-9065). 75 rms, A/C, cable color TV. AE, CB, DC, MC, V. Free parking, pool, coffeeshop. *Note:* Small, modest, but very well-maintained motel right in the dwntwn area. Decent comfort. Some rms have refrigerators. Pleasant atmosphere. 40 min. by car from Walt Disney World. Good value. **I**

♀ **Orlando Motor Lodge,** 1825 N. Mills Ave., Orlando, FL 📞 32803 (407/896-4111). 85 rms, A/C, color TV. AE, DC, MC, V. Free parking, pool, coffeeshop. *Note:* Modest but very acceptable motel on Lake Rowena (boats available). Rms w. balconies, some w. kitchenettes. Good value. 30 min. drive to Walt Disney World. **I, but lower rates out of season**

♀ **Victorian Inn** (formerly the Comfort Inn), 200 Cypress Gardens Blvd., Winter Haven, FL 33880 (813/299-1151). 104 rms, A/C, cable color TV. AE, CB, DC, MC, V. Free parking, pool, tennis court, rest. nearby. *Note:* Typical but very well-run motel 3 min. from Cypress Gardens. Comfortable rms, pleasant reception and svce. Good value. 30 min. from Walt Disney World. **I, but lower rates out of season**

♀ **Motel 6 West,** 7455 W. Irlo Bronson Hwy., Kissimmee, FL 📞 32741 (407/396-6422). 148 rms, A/C, color TV, free in-rm movies. DC, MC, V. Free parking, pool. *Note:* Brand-new motel w. unbeatable rates. Functional comfort. 5 min. from Walt Disney World and EPCOT. Excellent value. Ideal for budget travelers. **B**

Airport Accommodations

♀♀♀ **Marriott Orlando Airport,** 7499 Augusta National Dr., Orlando, FL 32812 (407/851-9000; toll free, see Marriott). 484 rms, A/C, cable color TV. AE, CB, DC, MC, V. Free parking, pool, tennis court, health club, sauna, two rests. (including Courtney's), two bars, rm svce. *Note:* Large airport hotel, modern and comfortable. Rms are soundproof and very large. Reasonably complete facilities; efficient svce. Middling rests. VIP floor. Business clientele. 10 min. from dwntwn, 20 min. from Walt Disney World. Free airport shuttle. **M–E**

♀♀ **La Quinta Inn Florida Mall,** 8601 S. Orange Blossom Trail, Orlando, FL 32809 (407/859-4100; toll free, see La Quinta). 136 rms, A/C, color TV, in-rm movies. AE, CB, DC, MC, V. Free parking, pool, 24-hr coffeeshop, rm svce, free crib. *Note:* Inviting motel 10 min. from the airport and 20 min. from Walt Disney World. Very large, comfortable rms. Good value. Airport shuttle svce. **I–M**

RESTAURANTS

Orlando and Central Florida Restaurant Prices (per person, excluding drinks and service charges)	
B (Budget)	up to $15
I (Inexpensive)	$15–$25
M (Moderate)	$25–$40
E (Expensive)	$40–$60
VE (Very Expensive)	$60 and up

Personal Favorites (in order of preference)

La Belle Verrière, 142 Park Ave. South, Winter Park (407/645-3377). A/C. Lunch/dinner Mon.-Sat.; closed Sun. and holidays. AE, CB, DC, MC, V. Jkt. *Specialties:* veal Richard, Dover sole, rack of lamb, chateaubriand bouquetière, fish of the day. *Note:* Excellent classic French cooking impeccably prepared and served by Richard Cafarella, chef and owner of this very lovely rest. Superb authentic Tiffany stained glass and stylish furnishings enhance the elegant décor. Attentive and courteous svce. An excellent establishment. Resv. strongly advised. *French.* **I–M**

Maison et Jardin, 430 S. Wymore Rd., Altamonte Springs (407/862-4410). A/C. Dinner nightly; Sun. brunch; closed holidays. AE, CB, DC, MC, V. Jkt. *Specialties:* Rack of lamb diable, scampi Costa Brava, veal Oscar, chateaubriand bouquetière, sweetbreads bonne femme, bouillabaisse. Fine wine list (over 400 selections). *Note:* Framed by trees and shrubberies of jasmine and azalea, this lovely Mediterranean-style villa boasts one of the most flower-filled settings in Florida. Antique furniture and Oriental rugs contribute to the opulent décor. Excellent classic French cuisine, though a tad pretentious. Svce excellent. Resv. advised. 45 min. from Walt Disney World. *French-continental.* **I–M**

Chalet Suzanne, U.S. 27N, Lake Wales (813/676-6011). A/C. Breakfast/lunch/dinner daily; closed Mon. (from May-Nov.). AE, CB, DC, MC, V. Jkt. *Specialties:* romaine soup, lobster Newburg, curried shrimp, chicken Suzanne, lamb chops English style, rum cake, crêpes Suzettes. *Note:* One of the best rests. in Florida, in the middle of an orange grove. Picturesquely miscellaneous décor. The cuisine in general and the sauces in particular are meticulously worked out. Even the soups merit an award of excellence; some of them accompanied the *Apollo* astronauts to the moon. Cheerful, conscientious svce. Resv. advised. An excellent establishment which has already celebrated its 50th anniversary. *Continental.* **M–E**

Piccadilly, in the Gold Key Inn Motel (see "Accommodations," above) (407/855-0050). A/C. Breakfast/lunch/dinner daily. AE, CB, DC, MC, V. *Specialties:* scallops, scampi, steak Diane, veal Oscar, rack of lamb, Cajun-style red snapper. *Note:* This "veddy British" motel rest. offers one of the best values in all Florida. Dishes are carefully prepared, portions are generous, and the salad bar is enormous. Svce w. a smile, but nonetheless efficient for that. Fine wine list. Dancing too. 20 min. from Walt Disney World. *Continental.* **I**

♟ **Barney's Steak House,** 1615 E. Colonial Dr., Orlando (407/ 896-6864). A/C. Dinner only nightly; closed Thanksgiving, and Dec. 25. AE, CB, DC, MC, V. *Specialties:* broiled meats and fish, ribs of beef, giant salad bar. *Note:* The favorite steakhouse of Orlando residents, according to an *Orlando Sentinel* poll. Top cuts of meat, cooked to perfection. Modern décor, pleasant background music. Relaxed atmosphere, very good svce. No resv., unfortunately. *Steak.* **B–I**

♟ **Maison des Crêpes,** 348 N. Park Ave., Winter Park (407/ 647-4469). A/C. Lunch/dinner Mon.-Sat.; closed Sun., holidays, and early July. AE, CB, DC, MC, V. *Specialties:* pancakes (30 varieties), soups, fish of the day, filet Royal. *Note:* As the name indicates, pancakes of various types are the house specialty here, but the fish of the day and the chef's soups are equally worth recommending. Rustic, flowery setting. 40 min. from Walt Disney World. *French-seafood.* **B–I**

Other Restaurants (from top bracket to budget)

☼ ♟♟♟ **Empress Room,** aboard the *Empress Lilly riverboat,* Disney World Village, Lake Buena Vista (407/828-3900). A/C. Dinner only, nightly. AE, MC, V. J&T. *Specialties:* oyster soup w. spinach, snails en brioche, chicken in cider, turban of sole au champagne, wild boar w. blueberries, soufflé Grand Marnier, cloche au chocolat. Very fine wine list. *Note:* This life-size replica of a paddlewheeler is a fixture in the Disney empire. The dining room's Louis XV décor and the formal svce are impressive. The cuisine is rather pretentious, but dishes such as the sole stuffed w. salmon mousse are truly inspired. Be prepared for a hefty bill. Resv. indispensable (the rest. seats only 60). *Continental.* **M–E**

♟♟♟ **Le Cordon Bleu,** 537 W. Fairbanks Ave., Winter Park (407/ 647-7575).A/C. Lunch/dinner, Mon.-Sat.; closed Sun. and holidays. AE, CB, DC, MC, V. Jkt. *Specialties:* shellfish au gratin, red snapper Imperiale, bouillabaisse, tournedos Beaugency, duck in orange sauce, veal Oscar, lobster w. hazelnut butter. Excellent wine list. *Note:* Chef George Vogelbacher is Swiss, but his cooking is firmly in the French tradition. Prepared w. a daring and imaginative touch, his classic dishes are well-nigh irresistible. Décor suggests an elegant, vaguely Victorian bistro. Polished svce. 45 min. from Walt Disney World. *French-continental.* **M–E**

♟♟ **Freddie's Steak House,** U.S. 17, Fern Park, (407/339- 3265). A/C. Dinner only, Mon.-Sat. (until 1 a.m.); closed Sun., Dec. 25, and Jan. 1. AE, CB, DC, MC, V. Jkt. *Specialties:* beef ribs, roast duck, fish of the day (pompano, grouper). *Note:* For over 40 years the name "Freddie's" has been synonymous w. superb broiled meats and fish. Ambience is that of a rather intimate English club. Excellent svce. A fine place to eat; resv. advised. 30 min. from Walt Disney World. Popular with the locals. *Steak-seafood.* **I–M**

♟♟ **Top of the World,** in the Contemporary Resort (see "Accommodations," above) (407/824-3611). A/C. Breakfast/ lunch/dinner daily; Sun. brunch. AE, MC. Jkt. *Specialties:* roast duck Curaçao, veal cutlets Romanoff, broiled red snapper. Good desserts. *Note:* Located on the 15th and top floor of the astonishing Contemporary Resort, this rest. enjoys an incomparable view. Ultramodern setting and décor. The cooking is traditional European and somewhat lacking in imagination. Worthwhile for its unrestricted view of the Magic Kingdom. There's also dancing. Resv. a must, several days in advance. Valet parking. *Continental.* **I–M**

♟♟ **Christy's Sundown,** Ave. K and 3rd St. South (U.S. 17), Winter Haven (813/293-0069). A/C. Lunch/dinner, Mon.-Sat.; closed Sun. and holidays. AE, MC, V. *Specialties:* broiled red snapper, lobster, steak, shish kebab, chicken Florentine. *Note:* Rest. in rustic Mediterranean décor, very popular w. vacationers in the Cypress Gardens and surrounding areas. Solid, carefully prepared cuisine. Good desserts. Svce is rather dour but efficient. Resv. advised. 40 min. from Walt Disney World. Dancing. *Steakcontinental.* I

Lake Buena Vista Club, 2200 Club Lake Dr., Lake Buena Vista (407/828-3735). A/C. Breakfast/lunch/dinner daily; Sun. brunch. AE, MC, V. Jkt. (evenings). *Specialties:* onion soup au gratin, eggs Florentine, chateaubriand, steak Diane, gold brick sundae. *Note:* Elegant country club overlooking a golf course. The cooking is French-inspired and reasonably successful (at dinner). Intimate, inviting setting, cheerful svce. Resv. a must. 15 min. from Walt Disney World. Valet parking. Excellent value. *Frenchcontinental.* I

Lili Marlene's Aviators Pub, 129 Church St., Orlando (407/422-2434). A/C. Lunch/dinner daily (until midnight). *Specialties:* roast beef, steak aviateur, veal Cordon Bleu, fish of the day. *Note:* Located in the heart of Church Street Station with its yesteryear cottages and turn-of-the-century saloon, this pleasant, amusing pub offers a number of serviceable, adequately prepared dishes. Especially lively in the evening. 25 min. from Walt Disney World. *Steak-continental.* I

Papeete Bay Verandah, in the Polynesian Village Resort (see "Accommodations," above) (407/824-1391). A/C. Breakfast/lunch/dinner daily; Sun. brunch. AE, MC. *Specialties:* chicken Pago Pago, beef Bora Bora, pork ribs Fiji, ribs of beef. *Note:* The Tahitian setting is one of the most successful of the Walt Disney World creations. The décor and the savory Polynesian cooking together provide a truly exotic dining experience. Breakfast and lunch buffets are less convincing. Lovely view of the lagoon. Evenings, there's a Polynesian show. Dinner resv. advised. *Polynesian.* I

Samurai, 3911 E. Colonial Dr., Orlando (407/896-9696). A/C. Dinner only, nightly; closed Thanksgiving and Dec. 25. AE, CB, DC, MC, V. Jkt. *Specialties:* sushi, teppanyaki, tempura. *Note:* Japanese rest., very popular w. the business crowd. Cooking beyond reproach. Décor is uninspired Oriental. Svce excellent. Very central location. Resv. advised. *Japanese.* I

Gary's Duck Inn, 3974 S. Orange Blossom Trail, Orlando (407/843-0270). A/C. Lunch Mon-Fri., dinner nightly, brunch Sun.; closed Dec. 25. AE, MC, V. *Specialties:* steak, fish of the day, broiled chicken. *Note:* Enormous tavern w. seafaring décor. Honest, unpretentious cooking at a very reasonable price. Popular locally. 25 min. from Walt Disney World. *Steak-seafood.* **B–I**

La Cantina, 4721 E. Colonial Dr., Orlando (407/894-4491). A/C. Dinner only, Tues.-Sat.; closed Sun., Mon., Thanksgiving, and Dec. 25. AE, MC, V. *Specialties:* lasagne, veal parmigiana, Italian dishes, broiled steak. *Note:* Classic steakhouse w. nondescript décor offering decent Italian cooking and choice meats at very affordable prices. Popular w. the locals for over 40 years. No resv. accepted; be prepared to wait. 25 min. from Walt Disney World. *Italian-steak.* **B–I**

Steerman's Quarters, aboard the *Empress Lilly Riverboat,* Disney World Village, Lake Buena Vista (407/828-3900). A/C. Breakfast/lunch/dinner daily. AE, MC, V. *Specialties:* steak, meats, sandwiches, salads. *Note:* Located on the lower deck of this make-believe paddlewheeler, Steerman's serves very good broiled meats such as Texas-style T-bone steak. Children love breakfasting w. the familiar Disney characters (resv. a must). Pleasant, relaxed atmosphere. 15 min. from Walt Disney World. *American.* **B–I**

Ronnie's, 2702 E. Colonial Dr., Orlando (407/894-2943). A/C. Breakfast/lunch/dinner daily (7 a.m. to 11 p.m.). No credit cards. *Specialties:* Jewish deli delights, corned beef, pastrami, homemade desserts (excellent cheesecake). *Note:* New York–style delicatessen, w. gigantic sandwiches and waistline-destroying desserts. Often crowded at lunch. 25 min. from Walt Disney World. *American.* B

Cafeterias / Fast Food

Morrison's, 1840 E. Colonial Dr., Orlando (407/896-2091). Open daily until 8 p.m. MC, V. *Specialties:* roast beef, sandwiches, soups, salads, homemade pastry. *Note:* Cafeteria cooking, honest and well prepared. Other locations: 140 Winter Haven Mall, Winter Haven (813/293-1003), and 700 N. Orlando Ave., Winter Park (407/644-7853).

BARS & NIGHTCLUBS

Bonkerz, 4315 N. Orange Blossom Trail, Winter Park (407/298-2665). The best comedy club in the area, featuring the very top comedians.

Cheek to Cheek, 839 N. Orlando Ave., Winter Park (407/644-2060). Open Tues.-Sat. Preppy-style dancing to live music from the 1940s. Very decent Italian restaurant (Villa Nova).

J.J. Whispers, 904 Lee Rd., Winter Park, (407/629-4779). Disco music, live orchestras, several dance floors.

Park Avenue Club, 4315 N. Orange Blossom Trail, Orlando (407/295-3750). "In" disco with a youthful clientele. Generally crowded weekends.

Phineas Phogg's Balloon Works, Church St. Station, 129 W. Church St., Orlando (407/422-2434). Locally popular disco. Amusing ambience.

Rosie O'Grady's Goodtime Emporium, Church St. Station, 129 W. Church St., Orlando (407/422-2434). Dixieland jazz in turn-of-the-century setting. Very touristy atmosphere.

Sullivan's Trailway Lounge, 1108 S. Orange Blossom Trail, Orlando (407/843-2934). Trendy western club, featuring country music stars.

Village Lounge, Walt Disney World Village, Lake Buena Vista (407/828-3830). Live modern jazz. Also a decent rest.

NEARBY EXCURSIONS

KENNEDY SPACE CENTER (46 mi., 75 km, east on Fla. 50) (407/452-2121; toll free 800/432-2153): The primary American space-vehicle launch site. Since 1950 more than 2,200 spacecraft, including the famous Shuttle, have been launched from this narrow finger of land at the tip of Cape Canaveral. Participants on the guided bus tour visit the rocket and shuttle assembly areas, the astronaut training center, and the various launch sites. Interesting space museum. Open daily; closed Dec. 25. Should not be missed. Call the toll-free number for information on scheduled launchings. (For information on nearby hotels and restaurants, see Chapter 16 on Florida's East Coast.)

DAYTONA BEACH (55 mi., 89 km, NE on I-4): Immense beach, 25 mi. (40 km) long, accessible by car and dune buggy. Famous also for automobile racing (the Daytona 24-hour race in Feb., the Daytona 400 in July, etc.). Definitely worth a detour. (See Chapter 16 on Florida's East Coast.)

ST. AUGUSTINE (115 mi., 185 km, NE on I-4 and I-95): The oldest city in the U.S., founded in 1565 by Don Pedro Menendez de Áviles. Charming Spanish colonial city, cleverly restored (Castillo de San Marcos, Mission Nombre de Dios, Zorayda Castle, etc.). A visit here can readily be combined with a trip to Daytona Beach. (See chapter 16 on Florida's East Coast.)

FARTHER AFIELD

☼ ⚖⚖ **THE ATLANTIC COAST FROM CAPE CANAVE-RAL TO MIAMI** (390 mi., 625 km, round trip on Fla. AIA, U.S. 1, and I-95): Very satisfying vacation tour for devotees of sea and shore. Can also include visits to the Kennedy Space Center, Palm Beach, Fort Lauderdale, and Miami. See Chapter 16 on Florida's East Coast and Chapter 19 on Miami.

☼ ⚖⚖ **TAMPA / ST. PETERSBURG AND THE GULF OF MEXICO** (166 mi., 265 km, round trip on I-4): Many inviting beaches along the Gulf of Mexico: Treasure Island, St. Petersburg Beach, Longboat Key, Venice. Can also include the cities of Sarasota, Tarpon Springs, etc. See Chapter 17 on Tampa / St. Petersburg.

MIAMI AND
MIAMI BEACH 🔥🔥

□ □ □

With the Everglades and Key West

Originally known as Fort Dallas, a small military post established in 1835 at the mouth of the Miami River, the youngest of America's great cities officially saw the light in 1870 as a simple post office and trading post. It didn't begin to grow until 1896, when Henry M. Flagler, an enterprising railroad tycoon, decided to extend the East Coast Railroad south from Palm Beach and to build the Royal Palm Hotel at Miami. Today the city (whose name, from the Seminole *Mayami,* means a broad stretch of water) has become synonymous with vacations and lavish hotels, but it has higher aspirations.

First of all this enormous, complex metropolis, growing demographically at an explosive rate (35% in ten years), would like to outgrow its reputation, disseminated by the TV series "Miami Vice," as a drug dealers' paradise, and a racial melting-pot where Cubans, Haitians, Jamaicans, Salvadorans, and other Hispanics engage in confrontation rather than assimilation. It is indeed the case that in this tropical, cosmopolitan version of New York City, which in a comparatively few years has become the main financial clearinghouse for trade between the U.S. and Latin America, these different ethnic groups live beside one another or even on top of one another.

There are vacationers drawn to the beaches of **Miami Beach, Key Biscayne,** and **Surfside,** or to a dream cruise in the Caribbean (Miami is the world's cruise-ship capital). There are millionaires who, finding **Coconut Grove** or **Coral Gables** no longer exclusive enough for their tastes, are withdrawing from Miami in favor of the worldly social attractions of **Palm Beach** or **Naples.** There are retirees from New York and Chicago who have come to live out their lives in the Florida sun. There are business people and bankers of all nationalities—at last count there were more than 250 banks in Miami, 76 of them foreign. There are well-heeled South Americans doing their shopping in the smart stores of **Bal Harbor** or the **Miracle Mile.** There are big-game fishermen and boating buffs who can indulge their guilty passion here—43,000 pleasure boats claim Miami or Miami Beach as their port of registration, from little outboards to 120-ft (40-m) yachts; as to the fishing, biologists can point to no fewer than 600 species in the waters of southern Florida. There are Latin-American exiles, anti-Castro Cubans for the most part, who have come to try their luck in the U.S., making Miami the largest bilingual city in the country. Store signs on the picturesque **Calle Ocho** (8th St.), the Main Street of **Little Havana,** bear witness to this in a kind of American-flavored Spanish: "perros calientes," for example, for "hot dogs." In 1960 the "Port of the Americas," as Miami has been termed, was still 75% Anglophone; today, only 45%. The mayor of the city, Xavier Suarez, was born in Cuba.

The kindly climate brings down every year to Miami and other resort cities as far as **Fort Lauderdale** or even **Boca Raton** (see Chapter 16 on Florida's East Coast) hordes of shivering citizens nicknamed "snowbirds," in flight from the snows and blizzards of the North. Even the hot, humid summer weather has its devotees thanks to lower out-of-season prices. In all, almost 12 million visitors annually descend on the 850 hotels and motels and the 4,500 restaurants, cafeterias, and snackbars of Miami, making mass tourism the leading local industry (for the state of Florida as a whole it brings in $10 billion a year). The second industry is still the trade in early fruits and vegetables and in citrus crops, of which Florida is the country's largest producer. The third is believed to be the drug trade—over the past decade Miami has become the main market and principal drug clearinghouse in North America. In the light of this fact, it will not surprise you to learn that, according to FBI figures, Miami is one of the country's most dangerous cities. Once night has fallen in the downtown business district of Miami, only the rash go out alone on foot.

With its innumerable theme parks and its many theaters and museums, the superb, ultramodern **Metro-Dade Cultural Center,** its symphony orchestra, and its internationally famous Miami City ballet, the Floridian metropolis is in no sense a cultural desert. As well as its own attractions, Miami offers the visitor a whole range of interesting excursions: for example, to the famous **Everglades National Park** with its unending subtropical marshlands. Not to forget the **Florida Keys,** a chain of 43 small coral islands protruding like a huge comma into the Gulf of Mexico as far as **Key West,** barely 90 miles (144 km) from the coast of Cuba. Once the lair of pirates and smugglers, the Keys are today a paradise for deep-sea fishermen, and a sort of tourist annex of Miami.

The actor Sidney Poitier is perhaps the best-known of Miami's famous children.

BASIC FACTS: State of Florida. Area Code: 305. Time Zone: Eastern Time. ZIP Codes: 33101 (Miami); 33139 (Miami Beach). Founded: 1870. Approximate population: city, 350,000; metropolitan area, about 1,850,000 (of whom 900,000 are Hispanics). 11th in size of U.S. metropolitan areas.

CLIMATE: There is no need to dwell on Miami's benign winters, averaging 69°F (20°C) from Dec. to Feb.; it is this that draws the crowds of lucky vacationers. With its heavy heat (average in July, 82°F, 28°C), summer is much less pleasant. For the rest of the year the thermometer rarely goes above 77°F (25°C), ideal for ocean bathing or just doing nothing. But watch out for tropical hurricanes in the fall.

DISTANCES: Atlanta, 659 mi. (1,055 km); Key West, 161 mi. (258 km); New Orleans, 856 mi. (1,370 km); Orlando, 240 mi. (385 km); Savannah, 496 mi. (794 km); Washington, D.C., 1,075 mi. (1,720 km).

ARRIVAL AND TRANSIT INFORMATION

Note: In view of the sheer size of the Miami metropolitan area, which includes 27 different communities and stretches 40 mi. (64 km) from north to south, the different places, museums, and monuments referred to below are identified according to district: Miami, Miami Beach, Coral Gables, etc.

AIRPORT: Miami International Airport (MIA), 7 mi. (11 km) NW. There'll be a long wait at Arrivals on international flights. Information: 871-7021.

U.S. AIRLINES: American (358-6800), Braniff (toll free 800/272-6433), Continental (871-1400), Delta (448-7000), Eastern (873-3000), Midway (toll free 800/621-5700), Northwest (377-0311), Pan Am (874-5000), TWA (371-7471), United (377-3461).

FOREIGN CARRIERS: Air Canada (toll free 800/422-6232), British Airways (toll free 800/247-9297).

CITY LINK: The cab fare to city center is about $14; time, 20 min. Cab fare to Miami Beach, Coral Gables, or Key Biscayne is $16–$20, according to destination.

Airport bus: Red Top Sedan (526-5764) serves principal Miami and Miami Beach hotels (resv. a must when you're traveling *to* the airport); fare, $7–$9, according to destination; time, 30–45 min., according to destination.

Municipal bus: METROBUS (638-6700), Lines 3 and 20 to dwntwn; fare, $1; time, 45–50 min.

Cabs are costly because of the distances involved. Public bus transportation is inadequate and unsafe; the elevated rail system (METRORAIL) is modern but still in its infancy. The sensible solution is to rent a car with unlimited mileage; Florida rates are very low, and you may be able to leave the car in another city, such as Orlando, Fort Lauderdale, or Tampa, without surcharge.

Helicopter: Tropical Helicopter (374-6055) links the dwntwn Miami heliport to Miami International Airport and Fort Lauderdale–Hollywood International Airport. Flight time is 6–18 min., according to destination; fare, $40–$65, according to destination.

CAR RENTAL (all at Miami International Airport unless otherwise noted): Avis (526-3000); Budget (871-3053); Dollar (887-6000); Hertz (526-5646); National (526-5200); Reliable, 1130 5th St., Miami Beach (672-1250), a local firm with attractive rates. For downtown locations, consult the city telephone directory.

LIMOUSINE SERVICES: American Limo Service (871-2370), Carey Limousine (764-0615).

TAXIS: In theory cabs may be hailed on the street; in practice it's advisable to take them at the stands outside the major hotels, or simply to phone. The principal cab companies are Central Cab (532-5555), Metro Taxi (888-8888), and Yellow Cab (444-4444).

TRAIN: AMTRAK station, 8303 W. 37th Ave., Miami (691-0125).

BUS: Greyhound, 4111 N.W. 27th St., Miami (871-1810); and 7101 Harding Ave., Miami Beach (538-0381).

INFORMATION AND TOURS

TOURIST INFORMATION: The **Greater Miami Convention and Visitors Bureau,** 4770 Biscayne Blvd., Miami, FL 33137 (305/573-4300).

Florida Keys Promotion Board, 5900 S.W. 73rd St., South Miami, FL 33143 (305/666-5000): Information on the Keys and Key West.

Miami Beach Visitor and Convention Authority, 555 17th St., Miami Beach, FL 33139 (305/673-7080): Information on Miami Beach.

GUIDED TOURS: American Sightseeing (bus), 4300 N.W. 14th St., Miami (871-4992): Conducted tour of the city and surroundings; serves the principal hotels.

Gray Line Tours (bus), 1642 NE 21st Terrace, Miami (325-1000): Guided tour of the city and surroundings; serves the principal hotels.

Dade Helicopter, 1050 McArthur Causeway, Miami (374-3737): Impressive. Year-round service.

Island Queen (boat), Miamarina, 400 S.E. Second Ave., Miami (379-5119): Trips on the bay; year-round service.

Nikko Gold Coast Cruises (boat), 10800 Collins Ave., Miami Beach (945-5461): Trips to Biscayne Bay and the Florida Canal; year-round service.

Sea Escape (shipboard cruise), Port of Miami, Miami (379-0000): One-day mini-cruise to the Bahamas and back, with excursions on shore. Leaves at 8:30 a.m.; returns at midnight. On board are rests., bars, pool, casino. Fare is $99 per person, including three meals. Daily, year round.

SIGHTS, ATTRACTIONS, & ACTIVITIES

ADVENTURES: Wilderness Experiences, Inc. (Jeep and boat), Loop and Dill Rd., in Big Cypress National Preserve (813/695-3143): Airboat trip lasting one or more days across the swamps of Big Cypress National Preserve, north of Everglades National Park (see "National Parks Nearby," below). This 100-mi. (160-km) tour will reveal to you the fauna and flora unique to the Everglades. Year round, by resv. only. Don't miss it. For more information, write P.O. Box 440474, Miami, FL 33144.

ARCHITECTURAL HIGHLIGHTS: ❋ 🏛 **Art Deco District,** around Collins Ave. between 6th and 23rd Sts., Miami Beach: More than 800 fine 1930s buildings in pastel hues; the fine flower of art deco. The whole neighborhood is undergoing extensive rehabilitation. A sight not to be missed.

🏛 **Bacardi Buildings,** 2100 Biscayne Blvd., Miami: Modern structures with murals that recall the famous façade of the University of Mexico in Mexico City. Worth a look.

🏛 **Coral Castle,** 28655 U.S. 1 at S.W. 286th St., Homestead (248-6344): An extravaganza in the style of a fortified castle, carved from blocks of coral by a solitary craftsman from 1925 to 1940. Stone furniture; nine-ton swinging rock gate. Fantastic. Open daily.

☼🏛 **Metro Dade Cultural Center,** 101 W. Flagler St., Miami (372-7666): Ultramodern complex, very Mediterranean in flavor, designed by the architect Philip Johnson. Around a large plaza stand several remarkable buildings: the **Center for the Fine Arts** (see below), the **Historical Museum of Southern Florida** (see below), and the **Miami Public Library,** with 1.5 million volumes. The artistic and cultural heart of Miami; don't fail to see it.

☼🏛 **Miamarina,** Bayshore Dr., Bay Front Park, Miami (579-6955): Well-known, crowded boat basin for pleasure craft, with more than 200 berths. Boats may be rented for deep-sea fishing or boat trips on Biscayne Bay. A spectacular sight.

☼🏛 **Miami Beach Hotel Row,** Collins Ave. and Indian Creek between 21st and 71st Sts, Miami Beach: Grand hotels and other sumptuous buildings huddled on the narrow strip of land between the ocean and Indian Creek Canal. A remarkable sight.

🏛 **Miami Herald Building,** N. E. 1 Herald Plaza, Miami (376-2909): A superbly successful piece of modern architectural design; one of the loveliest buildings of its kind. Conducted tour of the newspaper on Mon., Wed., Fri.; resv. required.

☼🏛 **Port of Miami,** Port Blvd., Miami: This is the "Gate of the Americas," every year handling $9 billion in merchandise from all over the Western Hemisphere and Europe. Many liners, including the huge *Norway* (formerly the *France*), have their home port here; two million passengers pass through yearly. Note to photographers: The liners usually sail on Fri., Sat., Sun., and Mon. toward the end of the afternoon.

High-Rise Buildings

Centrust Savings, 101 E. Flagler St., Miami (376-5000): Spectacular 35-story building, 562 ft (175 m) high, by the distinguished architect I. M. Pei. Miami's finest skyscraper; must certainly be seen.

Southeast Financial Center, 1 S.E. Financial Center, Miami (375-7500): Florida's tallest high-rise at 764 ft (238 m), 55 floors. Worth a look.

BEACHES: Bill Baggs Cape Florida State Park, at the southern end of
Crandon Blvd., Key Biscayne: The local favorite. Pretty natural setting; picnic zones. Crowded on weekends.

Haulover Beach, 16 mi. (25 km) on Fla. 1A, North Miami Beach: Much favored by families; good for surfing and fishing.

Miami Beach, along Collins Ave.: The private beaches of the great hotels, side by side with several public beaches. The beach has recently been widened for a stretch of many miles. Access via 21st, 35th, 46th, 53rd, and 64th Sts.

South Beach, 5th St. and Collins Ave., Miami Beach: For surfers.

Venetian Pool, 2701 De Soto Blvd., Coral Gables: Wonderful Venetian-style lagoon in the heart of town.

Virginia Beach, 6 mi. (9 km) SE along Rickenbacker Causeway, Virginia Key: Ideal for scuba-diving.

CHURCHES/SYNAGOGUES: King Solomon Temple, 910 Lincoln Rd.,
Miami Beach (534-9776): Built in 1976 exactly according to the plan of King Solomon's temple in Jerusalem as described in the Old Testament. Worth seeing.

Spanish Monastery of St. Bernard, 16711 W. Dixie Hwy., North Miami Beach, 11 mi. (18 km) north (945-1461): Cloister of the monastery of St. Bernard, built in 1141 at Segovia in Spain. It was bought and transported, stone by stone, to the U.S. by the press baron William Randolph Hearst, and re-erected on its present site in 1952. It houses a number of medieval works of art. Now the property of the Episcopal church. Lovely gardens; well worth going out of your way for.

HISTORIC BUILDINGS: The Barnacle, 3485 Main Hwy., Coconut Grove
(448-9445): One of the most beautiful examples of the local Caribbean-style architecture of the last century. Owned originally by Commodore Ralph Munroe, this luxurious private home, dating from the 1880s, was built in the midst of tropical gardens that are alone worth the visit. A lovely breath of the past. Open Wednesday to Sunday.

Villa Vizcaya, 3251 S. Miami Ave., Miami (579-2813): Former residence of the International Harvester magnate James Deering, dates from 1912. This Venetian-style 72-room palace, which stands at the shore of the Atlantic, has fine collections of European art—paintings, furniture, sculpture, and antique rugs—in styles ranging from Renaissance to baroque, rococo, etc. The villa, which served as the meeting place in September 1987 for Pope John Paul II and President Reagan, is surrounded by 9.6 acres (4 ha.) of superb gardens. Don't miss it. Open daily.

MONUMENTS: ⚱ **Kennedy Memorial Torch of Friendship,** Bayfront Park, Biscayne Blvd. at 5th St., Miami: Fountain crowned by a "torch of friendship" with its eternal flame, and a plaque to the memory of the assassinated president. The torch symbolizes friendship among all the nations of the Western Hemisphere.

⚱ **Pepper Fountain,** Bayfront Park, Biscayne Blvd. and 5th St., Miami: A spectacular fountain honoring Claude Pepper, who has represented Florida in Congress for almost 60 years. Designed by the California sculptor Isamu Noguchi, its jets and lights are computer controlled. Definitely worth seeing.

MUSEUMS OF ART: ☀ ⚱⚱ **Bass Museum,** 2121 Park Ave., Miami Beach (673-7530): Recently reopened after major alterations, this very comprehensive art museum has a rich collection of European old masters (notably Rubens' *Holy Family*) and moderns, impressionists, and contemporary American painters, as well as a gallery of Far Eastern art. Definitely worth a visit. Open Tues.-Sun.

⚱ **Center for the Fine Arts,** 101 W. Flagler St., Metro-Dade Cultural Center, Miami (375-1700): Interesting modern works and temporary exhibitions in a very beautiful, austere building by Philip Johnson. Worth visiting. Open Tues.-Sun.

⚱ **Cuban Museum of Arts,** 1300 S.W. 12th Ave., Miami (858-8006): The whole museum is devoted to the cultural heritage of Miami's important Cuban community. Temporary exhibitions. Should be seen. Open Tues.-Sun.

⚱ **Lowe Art Museum,** 1301 Stanford Dr., Coral Gables (284-3535): Standing on the University of Miami campus, this ambitious art museum houses part of the famous Kress collection of Renaissance and baroque art, the Alfred I. Barton collection of primitive art, the Virgil Barker collection of American art, and interesting temporary exhibitions. Worth the side trip. Open Tues.-Sun.

☀⚱ **Metropolitan Museum and Art Center,** 1212 Anastasia Ave., Coral Gables (442-1448): Eclectic art museum in what was once the fine old Biltmore Hotel; houses important collections of modern painting and sculpture (including Jacques Lipchitz's lovely sculpture *Our Tree of Life*), and of pre-Columbian and African art, as well as a "costume museum" with more than 5,000 antique garments. Definitely worth a visit. Open Tues.-Sun.

Villa Vizcaya: See "Historic Buildings," above.

MUSEUMS OF SCIENCE AND HISTORY: ⚱ **Gold Coast Railroad Museum,** 12400 S.W. 152nd St. at Coral Reef Dr., South Dade (253-0063): Railroad museum with more than 200 steam locomotives and passenger cars from the olden days, including the legendary *Ferdinand Magellan,* which Presidents Franklin D. Roosevelt, Harry S Truman, and Dwight D. Eisenhower used as a "rolling White House." A must for railroad buffs. Open daily; it can conveniently be visited in conjunction with the nearby Metrozoo.

⚱ **Historical Museum of Southern Florida,** 101 W. Flagler St. in the Metro-Dade Cultural Center, Miami (375-1492): Fascinating historical museum that traces the evolution of southern Florida and the Caribbean from the Stone Age to modern times. Indian art; treasures salvaged by divers from shipwrecks. A must-see. Open daily.

 Δ **Miami Youth Museum,** 5701 Sunset Dr., Bakery Center,
 South Miami (661-2787): This is definitely a teaching museum; young (and not-so-young) visitors are encouraged to touch and handle all the objects on display. Also mounts very interesting temporary exhibitions. Open Tues.-Sun.

 ※ΔΔ **Museum of Science and Space Transit Planetarium,** 3280 S.
 Miami Ave., Miami (854-4247): Impressive museum of anthropology, devoted to the fauna and flora of Florida as well as biology and the development of modern science (chemistry, physics, energy sources). Also a giant planetarium with movies of journeys into space. Fascinating. Open Tues.-Sun.

 Δ **Weeks Air Museum,** Tamiami Airport, 12800 S.W. 137th
 Ave., South Dade (233-5197): Museum devoted to the preservation and restoration of aircraft from before World War II. More than 30 machines are on display, some of them very rare. For admirers of the intrepid birdmen. Open Tues.-Sun.

PANORAMAS: The most spectacular view of Miami and its skyscrapers may be obtained for a comparatively modest fare from a ※ **helicopter** (see "Guided Tours," above).

PARKS AND GARDENS: ※ ΔΔ **Bayfront Park of the Americas,** from N.E. 5th St. to S.E. 2nd St. between Biscayne Blvd. and Biscayne Bay, Miami: Lovely waterfront city park with a clear view of the city and the port. Contains several noteworthy monuments, including the **Kennedy Memorial Torch of Friendship** and the brand-new Pepper Fountain designed by the sculptor Isamu Noguchi (see "Monuments," above). Don't miss seeing it.

 Δ **Bill Baggs Cape Florida State Park,** south end of Crandon
 Blvd., Key Biscayne (361-5811): 400 acres of mangroves, woods, and inviting beaches 20 min. by car from Miami. You can see the oldest lighthouse in Florida, where there was a bitter battle with the Seminole Indians in 1836. Should be seen.

 ΔΔ **Fairchild Tropical Gardens,** 10901 Old Cutler Rd., Coral Gables (667-1651): One of the country's largest (83 acres) botanic gardens. Extraordinarily beautiful jungle and tropical gardens with more than 5,000 different varieties of exotic plants; you see all this from a mini-train. A must-see. Open daily.

 Δ **Hialeah Park,** 21st St. and E. Fourth Ave., Hialeah (887-
 4347): The famous racecourse, with superb tropical gardens and free-range pink flamingos. Worth a visit. Open daily.

 Δ **Japanese Garden,** Watson Park, McArthur Causeway, Miami
 (285-1027): Lovely little Japanese garden with pagoda, tea house, statues, lake, and waterfalls; romantically exotic. Open daily.

 Δ **Lummus Park,** 404 N.W. North River Dr. and N.W. 3rd St.
 Miami: On the banks of the Miami River, this park is now the site of the **Fort Dallas** camp, built in 1835 at the mouth of the river and once under the command of William Tecumseh Sherman. Abandoned in 1838, this unique example of pioneer architecture was later moved to its present location. Worth seeing. Open daily.

 ※ Δ ΔΔ **Venetian Pool,** 2701 De Soto Blvd., Coral Gables (442-6483):
 Lovely Italian garden with palm trees, waterfalls, and porticos. The wonderful swimming-pool lagoon, in the pit of an old coral-limestone quarry, is enough to justify the trip—an absolute must. Open daily.

PERFORMING ARTS: For current listings of shows and cultural events, consult the entertainment pages of the three daily papers, *Miami Herald* and *Diario de las Americas* (morning) and *Miami News* (evening), as well as the monthly *Miami*.

Coconut Grove Playhouse, 3500 Main Hwy., Coconut Grove (442-2662): Modern and classical theater; season Oct.-May.

Colony Theater, 1040 Lincoln Rd., Miami Beach (532-4880): Modern and avant-garde theater; performances by the Miami City Ballet.

Dade County Auditorium, 2901 W. Flagler St., Miami (547-5414): Ballet, opera, concerts. Home of the Greater Miami Opera (director, Robert Hever).

Gusman Center for the Performing Arts, 174 E. Flagler St., Miami (358-3338): Classical concerts, musical comedy, performances by the Miami City Ballet. Home of the Greater Miami Symphony Orchestra.

Miami Beach Theater of the Performing Arts (TOPA), 1700 Washington Ave., Miami Beach (673-8300): Symphony concerts, recitals by leading artists, Broadway hits. Undergoing renovation.

Miami Marine Stadium, 3601 Rickenbacker Causeway, Key Biscayne (361-6732): Nautical stadium with 6,500 seats; open-air concerts by the Summer Pops Orchestra. Aquatic shows. Open July-Aug.

Ring Theater, University of Miami, 1380 Miller Dr., Coral Gables (284-3355): Modern theater, drama, comedy; performs six plays a year.

Ruth Foreman Theater, N.E. 151st St. and Biscayne Blvd., North Miami Beach (891-1830): Contemporary theater.

SHOPPING: Bal Harbor Shops, 9700 Collins Ave., Bal Harbor (866-0311): Dozens of luxury boutiques and stores from Saint Laurent and Gucci to Cartier and Neiman-Marcus.

Bayside Marketplace, 401 Biscayne Blvd., Miami (577-3344): Brand-new shopping center running alongside Bayfront Park and its marina. The two great pavilions house dozens of unusual boutiques, cafés, and restaurants. Very lively atmosphere.

Lincoln Road Mall, Lincoln Rd. between Alton Rd. and Washington Ave., Miami Beach (531-8881): More than 175 very reasonably priced boutiques and stores along a pedestrian mall lined with plantings and fountains.

Mayfair Mall, Grand Ave. and Mary St., Coconut Grove (448-1700): One of the country's most elegant shopping centers; fashion boutiques (Balmain, Charles Jourdan), antique dealers, restaurants, nightclubs, etc.

Omni Shopping Mall, 1601 Biscayne Blvd., Miami (374-2033): 160 fashion boutiques and stores of all kinds, six movie houses, and 13 restaurants in a slightly chilly glass-and-steel setting.

Miracle Mile, S.W. 22nd St. between Douglas and Le Jeune Rds., Coral Gables: The Miami area's most popular shopping street, drawing a very cosmopolitan crowd.

SPECIAL EVENTS: For exact dates, consult the **Greater Miami Convention and Visitors Bureau** and the **Miami Beach Visitor and Convention Authority** (see "Tourist Information," above).

Orange Bowl Festival (Jan. 1): Eight days of festivities and parades culminating in the Orange Bowl football game.

Coconut Grove Arts Festival (Feb.): Hundreds of artists exhibit their work in the streets of Coconut Grove; there's also a food festival. Draws more than half a million visitors every year.

Miami Beach Festival of the Arts (Feb.): Concerts, art exhibitions, theater; a very popular festival.

International Boat Show (late Feb.): One of the biggest of its kind, at the Miami Beach Convention Center.

Grand Prix of Miami (late Feb. or early Mar.): Formula 1 Grand Prix held in the streets of downtown Miami. Spectacular.

Carnaval Miami (Mar.): Nine days of dancing, parades, and celebration along the famous Calle Ocho in Little Havana.

Miami Unlimited International Regatta (early June): Some of the world's fastest and most powerful boats compete in these outboard races on Biscayne Bay, starting from the Marine Stadium.

Festival of the Americas (late Oct.): All Miami's Hispanic communities, headed by the Cubans, meet in Tropical Park for this colorful, exuberant folklore festival.

SPORTS: Miami hosts a major-league baseball team for spring training (plus a farm team), and boasts a professional football franchise, three thoroughbred race-tracks, and a major sport uniquely its own—jai alai.

Baseball: Baltimore Orioles (Mar.-Apr.), Miami Stadium (635-4395); and Miami Marlins (Apr.-Aug.), Orange Bowl Stadium (579-6971).

Football (Sept.-Dec.): Dolphins, Joe Robbie Stadium (576-1000).

Horse Racing

Calder Race Course, 21001 N.W. 27th Ave., North Dade (625-1311), with racing from mid-May to mid-Jan.

Gulfstream Park, U.S. 1, Hallandale (944-1242), open Mon.-Sat., Jan.-Apr.

Hialeah Park Race Course, E. 4th Ave. at 25th St., Hialeah (885-8000), with races Mon.-Sat., Mar.-May.

Jai Alai

Jai Alai Fronton, 3500 N.W. 37th Ave., Miami (633-6400), has games nightly Mon.-Sat. from late Dec. to mid-Sept.

Deep-sea Fishing

Lovers of sports fishing may have trouble deciding among the dozens of boat-rental facilities in Miami and Miami Beach. Rates for fully equipped deep-sea fishing boats are around $350 for a half day of six hours, or $450 for a full day of ten hours. For a list of rentals, contact:

Crandon Park Marina, Crandon Blvd., Key Biscayne (361-1281).

Dinner Key Marina, 3400 Pan American Dr., Coconut Grove (579-6980).

Haulover Beach Park Marina, 10800 Collins Ave., Sunny Isles (947-3525).

Miamarina, Bayshore Dr., Bay Front Park, Miami (579-6955).

STROLLS: ☀ ⌂⌂ **Coconut Grove,** around S. Bayshore Dr. and S.W. 27th Ave.: The "Greenwich Village" of Miami, parts of which date back to 1870, owes its name to its many coconut palms. Many artists live here; there are also smart stores. A lively neighborhood by day or night; you should see it.

⌂ **Coral Gables,** around Coral Way and LeJeune Rd.: Elegant residential district with parks, Venetian-style canals, and broad, shady avenues. Beautiful homes in neo-Moorish and Mediterranean idioms. A well-known university. You should take a look.

⌂ **Key Biscayne,** around Crandon Blvd.: Luxury hotels, dream homes, and beautiful Crandon Park with its immense beaches combine to make this island, linked to Miami by a spectacular toll road, one of the favorite retreats of the great, including ex-President Richard Nixon.

☼ ⌂ **Little Havana,** around S.W. 8th St. (the famous "Calle Ocho") and S.W. 17th Ave.: Havana in the U.S., with Cuban

MIAMI AND VICINITY

restaurants, fruit stalls, craftsmen's shops (including some where cigars are still handmade after the Cuban manner), and Spanish signs. Lots of local color; don't miss a stroll here, especially in the evening. Information: 324-8127.

☼☖☖ **Miami Beach,** around Collins Ave.: Once a marshy, impenetrable, mosquito-ridden mangrove swamp, this narrow 8-mi. (13-km) peninsula has become synonymous with vacationing and with flashy luxury. Each year more than eight million tourists come here, summer and winter, to stay in the thousands of hotels, motels, rental apartments, and second homes. Principal attractions are the beaches, recently enlarged and renovated at a cost of $60 million, and the magnificent Art Deco District (see "Architectural Highlights," above). Linked to Miami by five causeways crossing Biscayne Bay. Don't miss it.

THEME PARKS: ☼☖ **The Bounty,** Bayside Marketplace, 401 Biscayne Blvd., Miami (375-0486): Life-size (169-ft-, 50-m-, long) replica of the famous "tall ship" whose crew mutinied in 1789. It was aboard this replica that the 1962 MGM movie, starring Marlon Brando and Trevor Howard, was filmed. She was once the pride of the pleasure-boat harbor at St. Petersburg on the west coast of Florida. Don't miss it. Open daily.

☖ **Everglades Holiday Park,** 21940 Griffin Rd. and U.S. 27, Fort Lauderdale (434-8111): Airboat trip through the swamps of the Everglades among the alligators and other wildlife. Organized camping, fishing, and hunting. Well worth the 40 min. by car from Miami. Open daily year round.

☖ **Monkey Jungle,** 14805 S.W. 216th St., South Dade (235-1611): Hundreds of primates, from baboons to gorillas, roaming free in a reproduction of an Amazon Basin forest. It's the visitors who are caged, on roads protected by chain-link fences. Worth a visit. Open daily. 30 min. from dwntwn on U.S. 1S.

☼☖☖ **Orchid Jungle,** 26715 S.W. 157th Ave., Homestead (247-4824): World's largest open-air orchid garden, with several thousand varieties on display. Trips through the jungle. Spectacular. Open daily. 40 min. from dwntwn on U.S. 1S.

☖ **Parrot Jungle,** 11000 S.W. 57th Ave., South Miami (666-7834): Many species of parrots, pelicans, marabou storks, and pink flamingos in a lush tropical garden. Shows by trained birds at set times. Open daily. 20 min. from dwntwn on U.S. 1S.

☼☖☖ **Planet Ocean,** 3979 Rickenbacker Causeway, Virginia Key (361-5786): More than 100 attractions devoted to the sea and man's dependence on it. From scuba-diving to a simulated hurricane by way of an "authentic" iceberg. Instructive, but also fascinating. Open daily. 5 min. from dwntwn.

☼☖ **Seaquarium,** 4400 Rickenbacker Causeway, Virginia Key (361-5705): One of the world's biggest marine zoos, with 12,000 fish and sea creatures. Home of the celebrated dolphin Flipper. Don't miss the fine tropical aquarium. Monorail tour. Opposite Planet Ocean (see above). Open daily. 5 min. from dwntwn.

☖ **Six Flags Atlantis,** 2700 Stirling Rd., Hollywood (926-1000): Huge watersports park with more than 80 different attractions. Giant pool with artificial waves for lovers of surfing; waterskiing shows; superslides, etc. Open daily, June-Sept.; weekends only, Mar.-May, and Oct.-Dec. 25 min. from dwntwn. on I-95.

ZOOS: ☼☖☖ **Metrozoo,** 12400 S.W. 152nd St. at Coral Reef Dr., South Dade

(251-0400): Big zoo of ultramodern design; the animals are semi-free with no bars or cages, on 265 acres of gardens and wilderness, reminiscent of the natural habitats of the 100 or so species on display, including the very rare white tigers from Bengal. You go around on a monorail. Wonderful and fascinating; not to be missed. Open daily.

ACCOMMODATIONS

See the listing of toll-free numbers in the Appendix.

Room Rates in Miami / Miami Beach	
B (Budget)	up to $30
I (Inexpensive)	$30–$60
M (Moderate)	$60–$90
E (Expensive)	$90–$140
VE (Very Expensive)	$140 and up

Note: Many hotels in Miami and Miami Beach require a checkout notice of 24 or 48 hours. Ask about the checkout policy when you register.

Personal Favorites (in order of preference)

ρρρρρ **The Alexander,** 5225 Collins Ave., Miami Beach, FL 33140 (305/865-6500; toll free 800/327-6121). 225 suites, A/C, color TV, in-rm movies. AE, CB, DC, MC, V. Valet garage $8, pool, marina, sauna, two rests. (including Dominique's), coffeeshop, three bars, 24-hr rm svce, nightclub, concierge, free crib. *Note:* Miami Beach's super-luxury hotel, standing in a lovely tropical garden adorned w. lagoon/swimming pools. High-toned and exclusive. Imposing lobby; spacious, elegant suites w. period furniture, each w. kitchenette, refrigerator, and private patio or balcony offering a splendid prospect of the ocean or Indian Creek. Personalized svce. Direct access to beach. VIP clientele; discreet, distinguished atmosphere. One of the 12 best hotels in the United States. **VE**

ρρρρ **Grand Bay,** 2669 S. Bayshore Dr., Coconut Grove, FL 33133 (305/858-9600; toll free 800/221-2340). 180 suites and mini-suites, A/C, color TV, in-rm movies. AE, CB, DC, MC, V. Valet garage $8, pool, health club, sauna, two rests. (including the Grand Café), bar, 24-hr rm svce, disco (Régine's), hrdrsr, concierge, crib $15. *Note:* With its modern truncated-pyramid design and unobstructed view over Biscayne Bay, this luxurious hotel, opened in 1984, has quickly become *the* place to stay in Miami. Elegant, very comfortable suites w. private balconies; the décor is a harmonious blend of modern art, crystal chandeliers, Oriental rugs, and period furniture. Remarkable svce. Good luxury hotel rest. In front of the hotel stands a fine modern sculpture by Alexander Liberman called *Windward*. The Grand Bay belongs to the Italian hotel chain Ciga. 10 min. from dwntwn. **VE, but lower rates out of season**

☼ρρρρ **Key Biscayne Hotel and Villas,** 701 Ocean Dr., Key Biscayne, FL 33149 (305/361-5431; toll free 800/327-7922). 175 rms or private cottages, A/C, color TV, in-rm movies. AE, CB, DC, MC, V. Valet garage $6, pool, golf course, sauna, 12 tennis courts, putting green, two rests.

(including the Spoonbill), bar, rm svce, disco, crib $5. *Note:* Entirely renovated, this wonderful small hotel offers every possible luxury in a lovely tropical setting with 16 acres of superb gardens. Large private ocean beach. Spacious, elegant rms or lavish private cottages. Quiet, sumptuous atmosphere; very good rest.; exemplary svce. One of the great places to stay in Florida. 10 min. from dwntwn. **VE, but lower rates out of season**

Inter-Continental, 100 Chopin Plaza, Miami, FL 33131 (305/577-1000; toll free, see Inter-Continental). 620 rms, A/C, color TV, in-rm movies. AE, CB, DC, MC, V. Valet garage $8, pool, health club, two tennis courts, four rests. (including the Pavillon Grill), 24-hr coffeeshop, bars, rm svce, nightclub, hrdrsr, concierge, free crib. *Note:* A big, massive, ultramodern 34-floor tower, groaning under its burden of marble, Flemish tapestries, and other ornaments in flamboyant style. Spacious, very comfortable rms w. refrigerators; very complete facilities; first-grade svce; first-class rest. Spectacular five-story lobby with a 70-ton monumental sculpture by Henry Moore. Surrounded by dwntwn's office high-rises; the business traveler's favorite. **E–VE**

Hotel Place St. Michel, 162 Alcazar Ave., Coral Gables, FL 33134 (305/444-1666). 28 rms, A/C, color TV. AE, CB, DC, MC, V. Parking $4, rest. (Restaurant St. Michel), piano bar, rm svce, concierge, free breakfast, free crib. *Note:* Delightful small hotel of great charm, built in the 1920s and elegantly restored. Every room is individually decorated w. period furniture and old paintings. Excellent French rest. Polished reception and svce; everything in the old European style. The favorite of those in-the-know, who keep coming back. 10 min. from dwntwn. **M**

Miami Lakes Inn, Main St., Miami Lakes, FL 33014 (305/821-1150; toll free 800/792-7367). 305 rms, A/C, color TV, in-rm movies. AE, CB, DC, MC, V. Free valet parking, two pools, nine tennis courts, two golf courses, health club, sauna, two rests. (including Legends), coffeeshop, two bars, rm svce, disco, boutiques, crib $10. *Note:* The resort hotel par excellence, far from the crowds of Miami and Miami Beach, in an elegant country club–like building surrounded by gardens. Spacious, inviting rms w. private balconies or patios; some w. refrigerators. Very good sports facilities. Service w. a smile and aiming to please. Wknd discounts. Good value. 15 min. from airport, 40 min. from dwntwn. **M–E, but lower rates out of season**

Mardi Gras, 3400 Biscayne Blvd., Miami, FL 33137 (305/573-7700). 50 rms, A/C, color TV, in-rm movies. AE, CB, DC, MC, V. Free parking, pool, rest., bar. *Note:* A modest but well-run small motel 5 min. from dwntwn. Some rms w. kitchenettes. Functionally comfortable; friendly reception. Good value. **I, but lower rates out of season**

Other Accommodations (from top bracket to budget)

The Biltmore Hotel, 1200 Anastasia Ave., Coral Gables, FL 33134 (305/445-1926; toll free 800/445-2586). 270 rms, A/C, color TV, in-rm movies. AE, CB, DC, MC, V. Parking $4, pool, health club, thermal baths, 12 tennis courts, golf course, two rests. (including Sardo's), bars, rm svce, nightclub, concierge. *Note:* Sumptuous 1926 art deco palace, surmounted by a high belltower which recalls the famous Giralda at Seville in Spain. Reopened December 1986 after several years (and $46 million) of renovation, which has recaptured its former splendor. Spacious, elegantly decorated rms; very polished svce; rests. somewhat lacking in character. Besides its well-known golf course and very lovely gardens w. tropical lagoons, the hotel has its own hot spring, particularly appreciated by those who enjoy this kind of therapy. The great lady among local hotels. 10 min. from dwntwn. **E–VE**

Doral-on-the-Ocean, 4833 Collins Ave., Miami Beach, FL 33140 (305/532-3600; toll free 800/327-6334). 420

rms, A/C, color TV, in-rm movies. AE, CB, DC, MC, V. Valet garage $8, pool, two tennis courts, health club, sauna, boats, panoramic rest. (Roof Garden, on top floor), coffeeshop, bar, rm svce, nightclub, drugstore, boutiques, crib $5. *Note:* Built of tinted glass, at the same time modern and baroque, the Doral-on-the-Beach is one of Miami's most luxurious hotels, its spacious, comfortable rms offering a very fine view of the ocean or of Indian Creek. Direct access to the beach. Excellent svce. Free limo connection with the five golf courses of the Doral Country Club. 15 min. from dwntwn. **E–VE, but lower rates out of season**

Doubletree Hotel (formerly the Coconut Grove), 2649 S. Bayshore Dr., Coconut Grove, FL 33133 (305/858-2500; toll free 800/528-0444). 152 rms, A/C, color TV, in-rm movies. AE, CB, DC, MC, V. Valet parking $7, pool, tennis court, sauna, fishing, boats, two rests. (including the Café Brasserie), bars, rm svce, disco, free crib. *Note:* Refined and distinguished—particularly the recently renovated interior. Spacious rms, most w. balcony and ocean view, some w. kitchenettes. Exemplary svce. Pleasant all-around view (but uneven food) in the top-floor rest. Opposite Coconut Grove Convention Center. 15 min. from dwntwn. **E–VE**

Fontainebleau Hilton, 4441 Collins Ave., Miami Beach, FL 33140 (305/538-2000; toll free, see Hilton). 1,204 rms, A/C, color TV, in-rm movies. AE, CB, DC, MC, V. Valet garage $7, two pools, health club, sauna, seven tennis courts, boats, beach, three rests. (including the Dining Galleries), two coffeeshops, four bars, rm svce, disco, hrdrsr, drugstore, concierge, boutiques, free crib. *Note:* The mammoth of local hotels. Since 1954 this giant vacation complex, now entirely renovated, has been Miami Beach's best-known address. Spacious, comfortable rms w. balconies and refrigerators. The overburdened svce at times leaves something to be desired. The lagoon/swimming pool with waterfalls and the tropical garden justify a visit in themselves. Direct beach access. Group and convention clientele. 20 min. from dwntwn. **E–VE, but lower rates out of season**

Hyatt Regency, 400 S.E. Second Ave., Miami, FL 33131 (305/358-1234; toll free, see Hyatt). 607 rms, A/C, color TV, in-rm movies. AE, CB, DC, MC, V. Valet parking $9, pool, two rests. (including the Esplanade), coffeeshop, bars, 24-hr rm svce, nightclub, boutiques, free crib. *Note:* Big 24-story tower on the bank of the Miami River; modern design with spectacular glass-walled lobby. Ultra-comfortable rms w. balconies. Very comprehensive facilities. Opposite the Convention Center in the heart of dwntwn, the hotel draws business and convention travelers. Two top floors reserved for VIPs. **E–VE, but lower rates out of season**

Omni International Hotel, 1601 Biscayne Blvd., Miami, FL 33132 (305/374-0000; toll free, see Omni). 535 rms, A/C, color TV, in-rm movies. AE, CB, DC, MC, V. Valet garage $9, pool, four tennis courts, two rests. (including the Fish Market), coffeeshop, two bars, rm svce, disco, boutiques, crib $10. *Note:* Truly a city within a city, this 30-story glass-and-concrete tower forms part of the immense Omni / Plaza Venetia Shopping Mall, w. its 160 stores and boutiques, six cinemas, and 13 rests. The interior is done in a rather chilly hi-tech, but the rms are very comfortable, the best overlooking Biscayne Bay. Efficient svce. Bar w. seafood rest. The favorite of visiting Latin American businessmen. **E–VE**

Sheraton–Bal Harbor (formerly the Americana), 9701 Collins Ave., Bal Harbour, FL 33154 (305/865-7511; toll free, see Sheraton). 675 rms, A/C, color TV, in-rm movies. AE, CB, DC, MC, V. Valet parking $8, two pools, health club, sauna, boats, two rests. (including

The Twenties), 24-hr coffeeshop, bars, rm svce, nightclub, drugstore, boutiques, free crib. *Note:* All the comfort you might expect from a modern, well-equipped luxury hotel; spacious rms w. mini-bars, most w. balconies too. Direct beach access; fine tropical garden on the ocean. Efficient svce. Attracts groups and conventions. Good value out of season. 25 min. from dwntwn. **E–VE, but lower rates out of season**

Sheraton—Brickell Point, 495 Brickell Ave., Miami, FL 33131 (305/373-6000). 600 rms, A/C, color TV, in-rm movies. AE, CB, DC, MC, V. Free parking, pool, two rests., bars, rm svce, disco, crib $10. *Note:* Ultramodern 18-story tower overhanging Biscayne Bay. Comfortable rms w. a view. For a Holiday Inn, the facilities are very comprehensive. Lovely tropical décor w. a flower-planted terrace. Acceptable rest. overlooking the bay. Well situated very nr. the financial district. **M–E**

Singapore, 9601 Collins Ave., Bal Harbour, FL 33154 (305/865-9931; toll free 800/327-4911). 238 rms, A/C, color TV. AE, CB, DC, MC, V. Free parking, pool, putting green, rest., coffeeshop, two bars, rm svce, disco, free crib. *Note:* Comfortable motel w. direct access to the beach; many rms have kitchenettes and private balconies. Friendly reception and svce. Good value. 25 min. from dwntwn. **M, but lower rates out of season**

Dupont Plaza, 300 Biscayne Blvd., Miami, FL 33131 (305/358-2541; toll free 800/327-3480). 295 rms, A/C, color TV. AE, CB, DC, MC, V. Valet garage $5, two pools, marina, rest., bar, rm svce, hrdrsr, boutiques. *Note:* Modern, functional hotel right on Biscayne Bay; the best rms have a fine view. Svce not always dependable. Group and convention clientele. In the heart of dwntwn Miami. Good value. **I–M, but lower rates out of season**

PLM Marina Park Hotel, 340 Biscayne Blvd., Miami, FL 33132 (305/371-4400; toll free 800/223-9862). 194 rms, A/C, color TV, in-rm movies. AE, CB, DC, MC, V. Free parking, coffeeshop, bar, rm svce. *Note:* Comfortable, completely renovated hotel at the edge of Bay Front Park and Biscayne Bay. Huge, inviting rms, some w. refrigerators, the best overlooking the harbor and the bay. Courteous svce. Clientele of groups and package tours. Good value. **I–M, but lower rates out of season**

Sans Souci, 3101 Collins Ave., Miami Beach, FL 33140 (305/531-8261; toll free 800/327-8470). 258 rms, A/C, color TV. AE, CB, DC, MC, V. Parking $3, pool, beach, rest., bar, disco. *Note:* Relatively modern nine-story hotel at the water's edge w. direct beach access; comfortable rms, some w. balconies. Reception and svce somewhat uneven. Good value out of season. Interesting American Plan packages. 15 min. from dwntwn. **I–M, but lower rates out of season**

Days Inn Medical Center, 1050 N.W. 14th St., Miami, FL 33136 (305/324-0200; toll free, see Days Inns). 214 rms, A/C, color TV, in-rm movies. AE, CB, DC, MC, V. Free parking, pool, 24-hr coffeeshop. *Note:* Typical functional motel 5 min. by car from dwntwn and near the Civic Center. Spacious, inviting rms. Good value. Ideal if you're driving. **I, but lower rates out of season**

Ocean Roc, 19505 Collins Ave, Sunny Isles, FL 33160 (305/931-7600). 95 rms, A/C, color TV, in-rm movies. AE, CB, DC, MC, V. Free parking, pool, coffeeshop, rm svce. *Note:* Elderly but very well-run small hotel on the beach; nice rms w. balconies and refrigerators (some w. kitchenettes), the best overlooking the ocean. Friendly reception. In summer, one of Miami Beach's best bargains. 35 min. from dwntwn. **I, but lower rates out of season**

♟ **Royalton Hotel,** 131 S.E. 1st St., Miami, FL 33132 (305/
374-7451). 130 rms, A/C. AE, CB, DC, MC, V. Parking (for
a fee) adjoining, coffeeshop, bar. *Note:* Older hotel w. small but functional rms in
the middle of the Cuban district. While reception and comfort are not of the
best, the prices can't be beat. **I, but lower rates out of season**

♟ **Bel Aire Hotel,** 6515 Collins Ave., Miami Beach, FL 33141
(305/866-6511). 111 rms, color TV. AE, CB, DC, MC, V.
Free parking, pool, coffeeshop, bar, rm svce. *Note:* Small vacation hotel, economical but well run, ideal for restricted budgets. Quiet family atmosphere. 20 min.
from dwntwn, and a few steps from a public beach. Very good value. **B–I**

Airport Accommodations

☀♟♟♟ **Hilton Miami Airport and Marina,** 5101 Blue Lagoon Dr.,
Miami, FL 33126 (305/262-1000; toll free, see Hilton). 500
rms, A/C, color TV, in-rm movies. AE, CB, DC, MC, V. Free valet parking,
pool, three tennis courts, health club, marina, boats, three rests. (including the
Cove), bars, rm svce, disco, free airport and dwntwn limos, free crib. *Note:* Immaculate 14-story building on a peninsula in the middle of a lagoon; first-grade
comfort and facilities. Elegant, comfortable rms, w. VIP suites on the three top
floors. Efficient svce. Business and convention clientele. **E–VE, but lower rates
out of season**

YMCA/Youth Hostel

Youth Hostel/AYH, 1438 Washington Ave., Miami Beach (305/534-
2988). Very central. 80 beds.

RESTAURANTS

Miami Restaurant Prices	
(per person, excluding drinks and service charges)	
B (Budget)	up to $15
I (Inexpensive)	$15–$25
M (Moderate)	$25–$40
E (Expensive)	$40–$60
VE (Very Expensive)	$60 and up

Personal Favorites (in order of preference)

♟♟♟♟ **Café Chauveron,** 9561 E. Bay Harbor Dr., Bay Harbor Island
(866-8779). A/C. Dinner only, nightly; closed June 1 to Oct.
15. AE, CB, DC, MC, V. Jkt. (tie advised). *Specialties:* quenelles de brochet sauce
Nantua, bouillabaisse, pheasant à la Perigourdine, rack of lamb w. spring vegetables, Dover sole bonne femme. The desserts, particularly the soufflés, are very
good; the wine list is large but the prices exorbitant. *Note:* One of the most distinguished and luxurious rests. on the eastern seaboard. After the death of the
founder, Roger Chauveron, in 1983, his son André took it firmly in hand, and it
remains the unchallenged temple of classic French cuisine in Miami. Flowery,
elegant interior w. a view of the bay, but on the noisy side. Exemplary recep-

tion and svce. Resv., far in advance, a must. Valet parking; private dock for boats. 25 min. from dwntwn. *French.* **E-VE**

♆♆♆ **Pavillon Grill,** in the Inter-Continental Hotel (see "Accommodations," above), Miami (372-4494). A/C. Lunch Mon.-Fri., dinner Mon.-Sat.; closed Sun. AE, CB, DC, MC, V. J&T. *Specialties:* marinated lamb w. fresh pasta, fresh tuna w. ginger and chilis, ragoût of lobster w. wild mushrooms, filet of beef w. papaya and lime, scallops w. asparagus. Large list of California wines. *Note:* Columns of green Italian marble, mahogany panels, and English leather make up the décor of this remarkable luxury hotel rest. Delicate, refined modern cuisine—but with prices to match. Service of the highest order. Resv. a must—this place is in fashion. Valet parking. *American.* **E**

♆♆♆ **Joe's Stone Crab,** 227 Biscayne St., Miami Beach (673-0365). A/C. Lunch Tues.-Sun., dinner nightly; closed May 15 to Oct. 15. AE, CB, DC, MC, V. Jkt. *Specialties:* everything that swims in the Atlantic or any other ocean; extraordinary stone crabs; Key lime pie. *Note:* A Miami landmark since 1913; its black-and-yellow stone crabs are famous coast to coast. Their high season runs from Oct. to Feb.; their claws are removed and they're thrown back into the sea, where the claws grow again. The rest. is often noisy and crowded. Excellent svce; unfortunately no resv., so waits are inevitable. Valet parking. *Seafood.* **M**

🔆♆♆ **Restaurant St. Michel,** in the Hotel Place St. Michel (see "Accommodations," above), Coral Gables (446-6572). A/C. Breakfast Mon.-Fri., lunch/dinner daily. AE, CB, DC, MC, V. Jkt. *Specialties:* rack of lamb bouquetière, poached salmon w. lobster sauce, veal scaloppine dijonnaise, duckling w. blackcurrants and pears. Very good desserts, but a rather lightweight wine list. *Note:* On the ground floor of the charming little Hotel Place St. Michel, this intimate rest. is a triumph of art deco elegance. Sophisticated modern cuisine of French derivation. Svce exemplary in all respects. Favorite lunchtime rest. for business people. Resv. advised; a fine place. *French-Continental.* **I–M**

♆♆ **Centro Vasco (Juanito's),** 2235 S.W. 8th St., Miami (643-9606). A/C. Lunch/dinner daily until midnight. AE, DC, MC, V. *Specialties:* zarzuela de mariscos, snapper in salsa verde, chicken Basque style, paella, filet Madrilène. So-so desserts. *Note:* Specializing in Basque food, this is one of Little Havana's most popular rests. The sangría is mixed, as it should be, at your table. The Spanish-tavern décor is agreeable, and the svce attentive. Resv. advised. Crowded bar serving excellent daiquiris. Valet parking. *Spanish.* **I**

♆♆ **Le Festival,** 2120 Salzedo St., Coral Gables (442-8545). A/C. Lunch Mon.-Fri., dinner Mon.-Sat.; closed Sun., holidays, and Sept.-Oct. AE, MC, V. Jkt. *Specialties:* salmon mousse, cheese soufflé, chicken normande, snapper Dugléré, tarte tatin, chocolate-mousse cake. *Note:* Small French bistro of the refined and elegant sort; chef Jacques Baudeau offers a flawless cuisine. Attentive svce. Well-chosen wine list. A fine place. *French.* **I–M**

♆ **Max's Place,** 2286 N.E. 123rd St., North Dade (893-6888). A/C. Dinner only, nightly. AE, CB, DC, MC, V. *Specialties:* pizza done over a wood fire, polenta w. cream of Gorgonzola cheese and basil, fresh homemade pasta, meat and fish broiled over mesquite, hot apple tart w. caramel. Skimpy wine list. *Note:* Florida version of the California-type rest. nowadays so much in vogue from New York to Los Angeles. Generally inventive cuisine; some simple dishes broiled over a wood fire. Has drawn crowds (mostly young, with-it crowds) ever since it opened. Resv. advised. Well worth the 25-min. drive (via Biscayne Blvd.) from dwntwn. *American.* **I**

♆ **La Esquina de Tejas,** 101 S.W. 12th Ave., Miami (545-5341). A/C. Breakfast/lunch/dinner daily till midnight. No credit cards. *Specialties:* fish soup, chicken w. rice, picadillo, pig's-trotter stew, roast pork w. rice and black beans, flan. Cuban coffee. *Note:* One of the small, traditional Cuban rests. of which there are so many in Little Havana, offering absolutely authentic food at very attractive prices. This one has some claim to celebrity in that President Reagan stopped here once on a visit to Miami and tried the chicken w. rice, w. side orders of black beans and fried plantain. Guaranteed atmosphere and local color. No resv. *Latin American.* **B**

Other Restaurants (from top bracket to budget)

�☐☐ **Vinton's,** in the La Palma Hotel, 116 Alhambra Circle, Coral Gables (445-2511). A/C. Lunch Mon.-Fri., dinner Mon.-Sat.; closed Sun., holidays. AE, CB, DC, MC, V. Jkt. *Specialties:* boudin of shrimp and scallops, ragoût of sweetbreads w. oysters, bouillabaisse, salmon w. sorrel, duck w. raspberries. Fine wine list, but no hard liquor. *Note:* One of the best prestige rests. in Miami. The food and the svce, both exemplary, run like a Swiss watch thanks to the brothers Hans and René Eichman. The décor is elegant and the atmosphere romantic (every lady is offered a flower, and a cushion for her feet). Resv. advised. *French-Continental.* **E**

☐☐☐ **Raimondo's,** 4612 S.W. Le Jeune Rd., Coral Gables (666-9919). A/C. Dinner only, nightly; closed holidays. AE, CB, DC, MC, V. Jkt. *Specialties:* zuppa di pesce, fettuccine Alfredo, canelloni alla romana, pompano en papillote. Remarkable homemade ice cream. *Note:* Miami's best Italian rest., warm and intimate. Modern, unpretentious setting; impeccable svce. Resv. advised. Valet parking. *Italian.* **M–E**

☐☐ **Christy's,** 3101 Ponce de León Blvd., Coral Gables (446-1400). A/C. Lunch Mon.-Fri., dinner nightly. AE, CB, DC, MC, V. Jkt. *Specialties:* steak, roast beef, filet mignon, fish of the day, lobster, lamb chops, Caesar salad. Slightly meager wine list. *Note:* First-rate meat and fish, in an urbane British-club setting, w. leather seats and velvet curtains. Very relaxed atmosphere; faultless svce. Business clientele. The fashionable place for meat eaters. Resv. a must. *Steak-Seafood.* **M**

☐☐ **The Depot,** 5830 S. Dixie Hwy., South Miami (665-6261). A/C. Dinner only, nightly until 2 a.m. AE, CB, DC, MC, V. Jkt. *Specialties:* ribs of beef, steak, Maine lobster, rack of lamb printanier, sautéed crabmeat. *Note:* The best red-meat rest. in Miami, with excellent seafood as well. Original railroad décor with displays of model trains. A nice place. Diligent svce. Popular locally; resv. advisable. Valet parking. 20 min. from dwntwn. *Steak-Seafood.* **I–M**

☐☐☐ **The Forge,** 432 Arthur Godfrey Rd., Miami Beach (538-8533). A/C. Dinner only, nightly until 2 a.m.; closed holidays. AE, CB, DC, MC, V. Jkt. *Specialties:* shrimp Merlin, steak Java, chicken w. walnuts, snapper Singapore, veal w. morel mushrooms. Wonderful desserts. Very fine wine list w. more than 3,000 labels. *Note:* Luxury rest. (w. disco) in an excessive art nouveau décor, w. molded ceilings, crystal chandeliers, much stained glass, and enough paintings and sculptures to turn many a museum green w. envy. Polished svce; fashionable diners; noisy atmosphere. Resv. advised. Valet parking. *Continental.* **I–M**

☐☐ **Gatti's,** 1427 West Ave., Miami Beach (673-1717). A/C. Dinner only, Tues.-Sun.; closed Mon., and from mid-May to Oct. AE, CB, DC, MC, V. Jkt. *Specialties:* excellent homemade fresh pasta, veal scaloppine alla Gatti, stone crabs, pompano amandine, osso buco, fish of the day. *Note:* A Miami classic since 1925, always in the hands of the Gatti family. Setting and food have much to recommend them, but the svce is inattentive unless you're a regular. Resv. advised. Valet parking. *Italian.* **I–M**

� **Malaga,** 740 S.W. 8th St., Miami (858-4224). A/C. Lunch/
dinner daily. AE, CB, DC, MC, V. *Specialties:* black-bean soup,
carne asada mechada (pot-au-feu), picadillo, hamhocks w. rice, pompano or red
snapper w. sauce Créole, paella, rice pudding. *Note:* Malaga is an exception to the
Miami rule that Cuban rests. have depressing interiors; with its charming shady
patio and domestic Castilian décor, it almost qualifies as a luxury rest. Tasty food
served in huge portions; svce with a smile. Very popular locally, so resv. advised.
Latin American. **I**

� **Prince Hamlet Restaurant,** 19115 Collins Ave., Sunny Isles
(932-8488). A/C. Lunch/dinner daily, brunch Sun.; closed
Dec. 25, Yom Kippur, Rosh Hashanah. DC, MC, V. *Specialties:* lavish cold buffet
(kolt bord), duck w. red cabbage. Copenhagen bouillabaisse, veal Oscar, Danish
pancakes. *Note:* A little corner of Scandinavia which has strayed under the palm
trees. The décor may be strange, but the food is serious and substantial, at very
reasonable prices. Interesting, varied menu w. Scandinavian overtones. Relaxed
and congenial atmosphere, despite amateurish svce. Resv. necessary. Has lost
none of its good qualities due to change of address. *Scandinavian-American.* **I**

� **Tiger Tiger Teahouse,** 5785 Sunset Dr., South Miami (665-
5660). A/C. Lunch/dinner daily. AE, CB, DC, MC, V. Jkt.
Specialties: hot-and-sour soup, sweet-and-sour fish, moo shu pork, Peking duck,
Mongolian hot-pot. *Note:* Miami's only Chinese rest. worthy of the name, serv-
ing excellent Mandarin and Szechuan food. Elegant Oriental décor, good svce.
Locally popular; resv. at dinner. *Chinese.* **I**

� **Joe's Seafood Restaurant,** 400 N.W. North River Dr., Miami (374-5637). A/C. Lunch/dinner daily. AE, CB, DC,
MC, V. Jkt. *Specialties:* ceviche, fried oysters, fish and shellfish of the day. *Note:*
Admirable seafood rest. on the bank of the Miami River; remarkably fresh seafood served in a marine-crossed-w.-rustic setting. Lunch or dinner outdoors in
fine weather. Inconsistent svce. Well located in the heart of Miami. *Seafood.* **I**

� **La Tasca,** 2741 W. Flagler St., Miami (642-3762). A/C.
Lunch/dinner daily. AE, CB, DC, MC, V. *Specialties:* white-
bean soup, shrimp enchilada, red snapper w. salsa verde, paella, diplomat pudding. *Note:* Likeable little outpost of Cuba a short distance from Little Havana;
old-style décor and svce. Clientele of regulars; a favorite with those in-the-know.
Latin American–Spanish. **B–I**

☼Y **Versailles,** 3555 S.W. 8th St., Miami (445-7614). A/C.
Lunch/dinner daily until 2 a.m. AE, CB, DC, MC, V. *Special-
ties:* Cuban sandwiches, homemade soups, chicken w. rice, picadillo, cheesecake.
Note: One of the most authentic Cuban rests. on the famous Calle Ocho, the
main drag of Little Havana. Straightforward, savory food. In spite of the mirrored ceilings, the name Versailles is not reflected in the décor. Usually crowded
and noisy, but a pleasant place. No resv. *Latin American.* **B–I**

☼Y **Rascal House,** 17190 Collins Ave., Miami Beach (947-4581).
A/C. Breakfast/lunch/dinner daily until 2 a.m. No credit
cards. *Kosher specialties:* soup, corned beef, pastrami, brisket; excellent (and enormously popular) deli items, homemade pastries. *Note:* Ideal for breakfast or a late
supper. At lunch customers come in droves. 35 min. from dwntwn. *American.* **B**

Cafeteria / Fast Food

☼ **Latin American Cafeteria,** 2940 Coral Way, Coral Gables
(448-6809). Typical cafeteria, open around the clock and serving enormous sandwiches and tasty, unpretentious Cuban food (fried pork w.
rice and beans, pan-fried steak, etc.). 1950s-style décor. Open daily. No credit
cards.

OTHER FROMMER TRAVEL GUIDES: *Dollarwise USA* complements 13 other Dollarwise Guides and 3 $-A-Day Guides dealing with individual U.S. states and areas: *Dollarwise Alaska, Dollarwise Florida, Dollarwise New York State, Dollarwise California & Las Vegas, Dollarwise Texas, Dollarwise Cruises, Dollarwise Mid-Atlantic States, Dollarwise New England, Dollarwise South-Atlantic States, Dollarwise Northwest, Dollarwise Southwest, Hawaii on $50 a Day, New York on $50 a Day,* and *Washington, D.C., & Historic Virginia on $40 a Day.*

BARS AND NIGHTCLUBS

The **Jazz Hotline** (382-3938) will give you details of current programming by local jazz clubs.

The great **hotels** of Miami and Miami Beach (Fontainebleau, Omni, Doral-on-the-Ocean, Hyatt, Sheraton–Bal Harbour, Doubletree Hotel, etc.) all have bars and discothèques. Other good places include:

Biscayne Babies, 3336 Virginia St., Coconut Grove (445-3751). Favorite of the trendy young; for lovers of rock 'n' roll.

Casanova's, 740 E. 9th St., Hialeah (883-8706). A shrine of salsa and disco. Trendy atmosphere and patrons.

Cye's Rivergate, 444 Brickell Ave., Miami (358-9100). Fashionable singles bar and disco under a handsome skylight; also a rest. Open Wed.-Sat.

Fire & Ice, 3841 N.E. Second Ave., Miami (573-3473). Three-level disco, futuristically decorated. Live music; big-screen TV. The "in" nightclub; also a rest. (average). Open nightly.

Les Violins, 1751 Biscayne Blvd., Miami (371-8668). Fashionable nightclub which puts on some far-out Latin American floor shows. Also a so-so rest.

Monty Trainer's, 2560 S. Bayshore Dr., Coconut Grove (858-1431). Amusing open-air bar-rest. serving very acceptable seafood. Live jazz and reggae; dancing. Youthful, congenial atmosphere. Open nightly.

Village Inn, 3131 Commodore Pl., Coconut Grove (445-8721). Fashionable jazz club, with a rest., in the artists' neighborhood of Coconut Grove.

NEARBY EXCURSIONS

MICCOSUKEE INDIAN VILLAGE (27 mi., 43 km, west on U.S. 41) (223-8380): Authentic Indian village of the Miccosukee tribe. Handicraft exhibitions, alligator wrestling, airboat trips into the swamps, rest. with authentic Indian food. Worth a visit. Open daily.

NATIONAL PARKS NEARBY

BISCAYNE NATIONAL PARK (30 mi., 48 km, SW on U.S. 1, on the Florida Tpke. at N. Canal Dr., in Homestead): Much the smallest of Florida's national parks, Biscayne, standing on the shore, comprises mostly a considerable stretch of water with a string of inhabited islands and some coral reefs teeming with fish. A paradise for scuba-diving, underwater fishing (snapper, mackerel, dorado), and birdwatching (blue herons, egrets, pelicans). Campsites, accessible only by boat. For information, contact P.O. Box 1369, Homestead, FL 33030 (305/247-7275). For lovers of nature in the raw.

☀ 🔔🔔 **EVERGLADES NATIONAL PARK** (45 mi., 72 km, SW on U.S. 1 and Fla. 27): Opened in 1947, this is the country's only tropical national park. Alligators, barracudas, sea turtles, pumas, lynxes, pelicans, egrets, pink flamingos, migratory birds, and at least a thousand varieties of fish abound in this enormous (2,100-sq.-mi., 5,440-km²) stretch of marshes, cypress stands, and mangrove swamps which the Seminole Indians knew by the beautiful name of Pay-Hay-Okee ("River of Grass"). A 50-mi. (80-km) asphalt road, the Flamingo Road, makes its way through the park; there are many observation platforms and elevated walkways from which you can admire the landscape. From May to Nov. visits are rendered unpleasant by clouds of mosquitos and other bloodthirsty insects, to say nothing of persistent rain during the summer; nevertheless, the rich wildlife and exotic vegetation are certainly worth seeing. Visitor Center at Flamingo.

It was in the Everglades that the Indians made their last stand in the terrible Seminole Wars of 1835–1842. After 2,000 warriors had successfully held off 20,000 soldiers for three years, they were wiped out or deported to Oklahoma. Although defeated, the Seminole never signed a peace treaty with the U.S. government, and are thus—theoretically—still in a state of war with it. For further information: Superintendent, Everglades National Park, Box 279, Homestead, FL 33030 (305/247-6211).

Where to Stay in the National Park
Flamingo Lodge, at the end of Fla. 27, Flamingo, FL 33030 (813/695-3101). 144 rms and bungalows; also houseboats for rent. AE, CB, DC, MC, V. Relatively modern and comfortable. **M**
Everglades Rod & Gun Club, at Everglades City, FL 33929 (813/695-2101). 20 rms. No credit cards. Comfortable in a rustic way. **I**

🔔🔔 **JOHN PENNEKAMP CORAL REEF PARK** (60 mi., 96 km, SW on U.S. 1, in Key Largo): The country's first underwater national park, dating from 1960, is 21.5 mi. (34 km) long by 6.5 mi. (10 km) wide; the water is nowhere deeper than 45 ft (15 m). There is a superb display of sea flora and fauna, with more than 60 varieties of tropical fish. Wonderful for scuba-divers; also trips in glass-bottomed boats. Spectacular. Open daily year round; for information, phone 305/451-1202.

Where to Stay in the Park
🤿🤿 **Jules' Undersea Lodge,** Key Largo, FL 33037 (305/451-2353). The only hotel of its kind in the world, with two fully equipped suites (bunks, kitchenette, closed-circuit TV) in a steel capsule 30 ft (10 m) below the surface. Patrons can reach it only by diving and passing through an airlock. Unobstructed view of the underwater life through huge portholes. Rates: $300 per person per day, including meals and unlimited diving. Resv. required, a long time ahead.

FARTHER AFIELD

☼🔭🔭 **FLORIDA EAST COAST** (640 mi., 1,024 km, round trip to St. Augustine on U.S. 1N, returning on I-95S): The great vacation artery of the Southeast. At least a week's trip with optional extensions to Orlando and Walt Disney World. For details, see Chapter 16 on Florida's East Coast and Chapter 18 on Orlando.

☼🔭🔭 **KEY WEST AND THE KEYS HIGHWAY** (330 mi., 528 km, on U.S. 1, round trip): Nicknamed Cayo Hueso (Bone Island) by the Spaniards and later anglicized as Key West, this old pirates' lair is the southernmost city in the continental U.S. Literary and bohemian, the picturesque town of Key West, now a little more than a century and a half old, is an important naval base, a fashionable vacation resort, and the favored retreat of such writers as the late playwright Tennessee Williams (*A Streetcar Named Desire*) and the novelist James Herlihy (*Midnight Cowboy*). From 1928 to 1939 Ernest Hemingway lived here and wrote some of his most successful works, including *Death in the Afternoon*. His house, at 907 Whitehead St. (294-1575), is open daily to visitors, and shouldn't be missed. Another well-known resident was the naturalist John James Audubon, whose former house at 205 Whitehead St. is today a small 🔲 **museum** (294-2116) devoted to the works of the distinguished artist-ornithologist; open daily. Pleasant strolls along the 🔲 **streets of old Key West.**

The ☀ **Overseas Highway,** by which Key West is reached, is built for the most part on a causeway over the water; the route involves a total of 40 bridges. There are spectacular seascapes, particularly from 🔭🔭 **Seven Mile Bridge** between Marathon and Key West.

A very worthwhile excursion is to the impressive **Fort Jefferson National Monument** on the Dry Tortugas, 70 mi. (112 km) offshore from Key West. The fort, nicknamed "the Gibraltar of the Gulf," was used as a prison at the end of the Civil War; Dr. Samuel Mudd, who gave medical assistance to John Wilkes Booth, the assassin of Abraham Lincoln, was among those detained there. It can be reached by seaplane from Stock Island; service provided by Key West Seaplanes (294-6978).

Key West is also one of the country's greatest centers for **big-game fishing.** Lovers of the sport will find dozens of places to rent boats. Prices are markedly lower than in Miami; a half-day charter averages $150–$200, and a full day runs $250–$300. Some recommended captains include Dick Stammers (296-7550), Patrick Hynes (296-4758), and Tom Pierce (294-6098).

Allow at least three to four days for this fascinating trip; it can conveniently be combined with a visit to Everglades National Park (see above).

Where to Stay in Key West

🛏🛏🛏 **Marriott's Casa Marina,** 1500 Reynolds St., Key West, FL 33040 (305/296-3535). 310 rms. AE, CB, DC, MC, V. *Note:* Facing the ocean; luxurious. **VE**

☼🛏🛏 **Pier House,** 1 Duval St., Key West, FL 33040 (305/294-9541). 120 rms. AE, MC, V. *Note:* In the center of town; comfortable in a baroque way. **E–VE, but lower rates out of season**

🛏 **Santa Maria,** 1401 Simonton St., Key West, FL 33040 (305/296-5678). 51 rms. AE, CB, DC, MC, V. *Note:* Modern, comfortable hotel with a commendable rest. **M–E, but lower rates out of season**

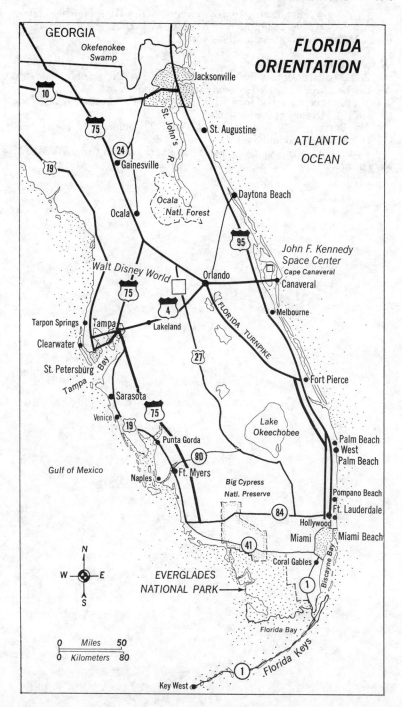

🔑 **Blue Marlin,** 1320 Simonton St., Key West, FL 33040 (305/ 294-2585). 53 rms. AE, MC, V. *Note:* A functional, well-run motel. **M, but lower rates out of season**

Where to Eat in Key West

A & B Lobster House, 700 Front St. (294-2536). Dinner only, Mon.-Sat. AE, CB, DC, MC, V. Broiled fish and shellfish; harbor view. **I—M**

Very near here, stop off for a drink at **Sloppy Joe's,** Greene and Duval Sts. (294-5717), Hemingway's favorite bar.

The Buttery, 1208 Simonton St. (294-0717). Dinner only, nightly. AE, CB, DC, MC, V. Steak and broiled fish; tropical décor. **I—M**

Kyushu, 921 Truman Ave. (294-2995). Lunch/dinner daily. AE, MC, V. Very commendable Japanese food; locally popular. **B—I**

PART THREE

THE MIDWEST

CHAPTER 20

DETROIT

□ □ □

"The automobile capital of the world," Detroit is America's most important industrial city after Chicago, accounting for 70% of domestic automobile production and more than half the country's output of weaponry (during World War II the city was known as "the arsenal of the democracies"). It would be more poetic to speak of it as the capital of soul music, the place where Diana Ross and the Supremes began their career.

The city's site, on a strait (in French, a *détroit,* hence the name) linking Lake Huron and Lake Erie, was first explored by the French in 1610. The city itself was founded 91 years later by an enterprising fur trader, Antoine de la Mothe Cadillac (whose name became world-famous a couple of centuries later when it was attached to a luxury automobile). This garrison town, originally called Fort Pontchartrain, was captured by the British in 1760 and renamed Detroit. The British successfully fended off attacks by a consolidated group of Indians led by the Ottawa chief Pontiac (another name destined for a famous automobile), but lost the city with the rest of the Northwest Territory to the Americans in the Revolutionary War. The British stirred up the Indians to attack the Americans in hopes of regaining the city, but Gen. ("Mad") Anthony Wayne defeated them decisively at the Battle of Fallen Timbers (1794). The opening of steam navigation on the Great Lakes in 1818 touched off Detroit's rocket-trip to prosperity, and when Henry Ford's first mass-produced automobile rolled off the production line in 1901 the rest became inevitable. The city's population rose from 20,000 in 1850 to 280,000 in 1900, 950,000 in 1920, and (suburbs included) over 4.5 million today.

Home to the three giants of the auto industry—General Motors, Ford, and Chrysler—Detroit is also the nation's largest used-car market, as witness the hundreds of billboards cheek by jowl along **Livernois Avenue,** an important petrochemical and space-industry complex. In addition it's the fifth-ranking freshwater port in the U.S., which can accommodate seagoing vessels of up to 25,000 tons coming through the St. Lawrence Seaway. In spite of all these advantages, "the city that put the world on wheels" bore the brunt of the world economic slump, with more than 250,000 layoffs in the five-year period 1978–1982. The unemployment rate is one of the highest in the country, with peaks of 30% (and up to 60% among young black workers). The crime rate has followed a similar curve; according to the FBI, Detroit leads the nation in violent crime, well ahead of Miami, New York, or Chicago.

After the race riots of July 1967, which left 43 dead and 2,000 wounded, the face of "Motown," as Detroit is often called, changed radically; an exodus of whites caused the population of the city proper to fall by more than 800,000. Stores, hotels, restaurants, offices, and movie-houses have forsaken "downtown" for outlying residential suburbs, leaving behind them a kind of no-man's-land, dark tumbledown ghettos, and urban throughways subject to asphyxiating pollution during rush hours. But since 1975 a successful program of urban renewal, pivoting on the **Civic Center,** has spread to the banks of the Detroit River facing the Canadian border. The heart of the program is the **Renaissance Center,** or

RenCen, an impressive $750-million architectural complex comprising six glass-clad futurist structures—four of them 39 floors high and two of them 21 stories—and the enormous 73-floor Westin Hotel tower, designed by the celebrated architect John Portman and opened in 1977. Another architectural landmark is the brand-new **Millender Center,** a huge modern cluster of offices, a hotel, stores, and restaurants linked to the RenCen by the **Skywalk,** a glassed-in overpass.

Famous children of Detroit include the father of the modern automobile industry, Henry Ford, born in the nearby town (now suburb) of Dearborn; director Francis Ford Coppola; actor George Peppard; the comedian and star of "Magnum P.I.," Tom Selleck; the legendary heavyweight champion Joe Louis; and singing star Diana Ross.

BASIC FACTS: State of Michigan. Area Code: 313. Time Zone: Eastern Time. ZIP Code: 48226. Founded in: 1701. Approximate population: city, 1,100,000; metropolitan area, 4,540,000. Sixth-largest metropolitan area in the U.S.

CLIMATE: Because of its unique geographical location, Detroit labors under a humid climate and extremes of temperature—chilling in winter (avg. Jan. temperature: 26°F, –3°C), warm and sticky in summer (avg. July temperature: 73°F, 23°C). Spring is rainy and uncomfortably cool. Only the fall, particularly October, offers attractive weather for the tourist.

DISTANCES: Chicago, 268 mi. (430 km); Cincinnati, 259 mi. (415 km); New York, 634 mi. (1,015 km); Niagara Falls, 392 mi. (628 km); Washington, 506 mi. (810 km).

ARRIVAL & TRANSIT INFORMATION

AIRPORT: Detroit Metropolitan Airport (DTW), 21 mi. (34 km) SW. Information: 942-3550.

DOMESTIC AIRLINES: American (965-1000), Braniff (toll free 800/272-6433), Continental (963-4600), Delta (355-3200), Eastern (965-8200), Midway (toll free 800/621-5700), Northwest (962-2002), Pan Am (toll free 800/221-1111), TWA (962-8650), United (336-9000), USAir (963-8340).

FOREIGN CARRIERS: Air Canada (883-3200), British Airways (toll free 800/247-9297), Sabena (toll free 800/645-3790).

CITY LINK: Cab fare to city center, about $28. Time, about 30-40 min. Bus: Commuter Transportation (941-3252) departs every 30 min., serving principal dwntwn hotels and the Renaissance Center; fare, $10; time, about 45 min. Inadequate public transportation system (bus), Department of Transportation (933-1300), but spectacular automated "People mover" operating through the entire downtown district. Since the metropolitan area is large and the airport a long way out, it's a good idea to rent a car with unlimited mileage, unless you plan to stay in the heart of dwntwn.

CAR RENTAL (all at the airport): Avis (942-3450), Budget (258-5877), Dollar (942-1710), Hertz (964-2678), National (941-5030). For dwntwn locations, consult the phone directory.

LIMOUSINE SERVICES: Carey Limousine (651-2300), Michigan Limo Service (546-6112).

TAXIS: An abundance of cabs at reasonable rates. You can hail them on the street, take them from the waiting lines outside the big hotels, or summon them by phone. The leading companies are Checker (963-7000) and Radio Cab (491-2600).

TRAIN: AMTRAK Station, 2405 W. Vernor (963-7396).

BUS: Greyhound, 130 E. Congress St. (961-8011).

INFORMATION & TOURS

TOURIST INFORMATION: The **Detroit Convention & Visitors Bureau,** 100 Renaissance Center (Suite 1950), MI 48243 (313/259-4333).

Department of Public Information, 608 City-County Bldg., 2 Woodward Ave., MI 48226 (313/224-3755).

For a **recorded announcement** with a list of current shows and cultural events, call 313/298-6262.

GUIDED TOURS: Boblo Steamers (boat excursions, May-Sept.), 661 Civic Center Dr. (313/843-8800).

Gray Line Tours (bus), Cobo Hall (Civic Center) and principal hotels (313/833-7692). Guided tours of the city.

SIGHTS, ATTRACTIONS, & ACTIVITIES

ARCHITECTURAL HIGHLIGHTS: ※ ▲ **Civic Center,** Woodward and Jefferson Aves. (224-1010): Ultramodern architectural complex on the banks of the Detroit River in the heart of downtown. Its constituent parts include the 20-story white marble tower of the **City-County Building,** protected by *The Spirit of Detroit,* Marshall Fredericks' massive bronze statue; **Cobo Hall,** one of the country's largest convention and exhibition halls, with 11,000 seats and roof parking for 1,700 vehicles; **Hart Plaza,** a wide esplanade near the spot where Cadillac and his French companions first came ashore in 1701, in the center of which is **Dodge Fountain,** a strange metallic construction with computer-controlled water jets and lights, designed by Isamo Noguchi; **Henry & Edsel Ford Auditorium,** a 3,000-seat, blue Swedish granite concert hall which is the home of the Detroit Symphony Orchestra; **Joe Louis Arena,** an indoor stadium with 15,000 seats; **Mariner's Church,** the city's oldest (1848), with a modern belfry and carillon, which was moved 780 ft (244 m) to its present site when the Civic Center was built; **Michigan Consolidated Gas Co. Building,** a 40-story glass skyscraper designed by Minoru Yamasaki. Don't miss this impressive sight.

▲ **Millender Center,** Randolph St. & Jefferson Ave. (222-1500): Latest of the new downtown architectural complexes, with office buildings, luxury hotel, stores, and restaurants, all linked by the Skywalk to the impressive Renaissance Center across Jefferson Ave. Worth a look.

※▲▲ **Renaissance Center,** Jefferson Ave. at Randolph St.: A spectacular grove of seven skyscrapers, ranging from 20 to 73 floors in height, at the edge of the Detroit River. The exceptional modern design bears the stamp of John Portman. Giant hotel, stores, restaurants, indoor gardens; symbol of the new Detroit. A sight not to be missed. (568-7800 for tours).

※▲ **Wayne State University,** 5050 Cass Ave. (577-2424): Founded in 1868, the university is highly regarded for its medical school—one of the finest in the country—and its architecturally distinguished campus, whose 100 buildings house 30,000 students. Among the most noteworthy: **McGregor Memorial Center,** the **College of Education Building,** and the **De Roy Auditorium,** all by Minoru Yamasaki, architect of New York's World Trade Center. Campus open to visitors Mon.-Sat.

HISTORIC BUILDINGS: 🔔 **Fisher Building,** 3011 W. Grand Blvd. (874-4444): A 28-story masterpiece of 1930s art deco by Albert Kahn, with restaurants, boutiques, and art galleries. Sumptuous interior. Well worth going out of your way for.

🔔 **Orchestra Hall,** 3700 Parsons at Woodward Ave. (883-3700): A 2,000-seat concert hall dating from 1920, "an acoustic miracle" according to the great cellist Pablo Casals. Recently renovated, and from 1989 on will again be the home of the Detroit Symphony Orchestra.

MARKETS: 🔔 **Eastern Market,** Russell St. at Fisher Fwy. (833-1560): Picturesque European-style open-air market dating from 1892. Worth a look. Open mornings only, Mon.-Sat.

MUSEUMS OF ART: ※ 🔔🔔 **Detroit Institute of Arts,** 5200 Woodward Ave. (833-7900): One of the country's finest, with great masters of European painting, Far Eastern art, superb murals by the Mexican Diego Rivera, and a fine collection of medieval armor. Among the most famous exhibits: Caravaggio's *Conversion of Mary Magdalene,* Titian's *Man with a Flute,* van Eyck's *St. Jerome,* Pieter Breughel the Elder's *A Village Wedding,* Frans Hals's *Portrait of Hendrick Swalmius,* Cézanne's *Mme Cézanne,* and a self-portrait by Gauguin. There are also works by contemporary American painters including Stuart Davis, Mark Rothko, Andy Warhol, and Charles Demuth. Not to be missed. Open daily.

MUSEUMS OF SCIENCE & HISTORY: 🔔 **Children's Museum,** 67 E. Kirby Ave. (494-1210): A fascinating place for children and adults alike, with collections relating to the history of Native Americans and exhibits on different cultures (African, Inuit, etc.). Fauna and flora of Michigan; planetarium next door. Amazing sculpture in the shape of a horse, made entirely of automobile bumpers (and what could be more appropriate to Detroit?). Open Mon.-Sat.

🔔 **Detroit Science Center,** 5020 John R St. (577-8400): This museum houses a wide-ranging cross section of pushbutton exhibits on diverse scientific subjects; the visitor is invited to participate in hands-on fashion. Spherical cinema with 360° projection of science films. Interesting to visit. Open Tues.-Sun.

※ 🔔 **Historical Museum,** 5401 Woodward Ave. (833-1805): Reconstructs the appearance and atmosphere of mid-19th-century Detroit: cobbled streets, stores, restored domestic interiors, models, and temporary exhibitions. For those who love glimpses of the past. Open Wed.-Sun.

🔔 **Money Museum,** 611 Woodward Ave. (225-1203): Traces the history of money from the Stone Age to the present day. Huge collection of Greek and Roman coins. An interesting display. Open Mon.-Fri.

🔔 **Public Library,** 5201 Woodward Ave. (833-1000): There are 2.5 million books housed in this 1921 Italian Renaissance building made of Vermont marble and decorated with enormous frescoes. They include very rare old volumes as well as many works on the history of the auto industry and of the trade union movement. Open Mon.-Sat.

OUTDOOR ART & PLAZAS: Other than the above-mentioned *Spirit of Detroit* by Marshall Fredericks and Dodge Fountain (see "Architectural Highlights," above), the visitor to the Civic Center may take pleasure in Giacomo Manzù's beautiful *Passo di Danza* and Isamo Noguchi's *Pylon.* On Cass St. in front of the Michigan Bell Telephone Bldg., you should take a look at a stabile by Alexander Calder known as *Young Lady and Her Suite.*

PANORAMAS: ※ 🏛 **The Summit** is a bar and restaurant on the 73rd floor of the Westin Hotel (see "Accommodations," below). You have to pay for the view —but it's the most spectacular in Detroit.

PARKS & GARDENS: 🏛 **Belle Isle,** MacArthur Bridge (267-7115): On a 3-mi.- (5-km-) long island in the Detroit River stands this 988-acre, 400-ha park: swimming, public golf course, jogging, aquarium, naval museum, mini-zoo. Free concerts in summer. Fine view of the city's skyline.

🏛 **Grosse Pointe Shore,** Lake Shore Dr.: An elegant residential neighborhood, with woods and lovely gardens, along Lake St. Clair; it boasts many affluent private houses. You should take a stroll there.

PERFORMING ARTS: For current listings of shows and cultural events, consult the entertainment pages of the two daily papers, *Detroit Free Press* (morning) and *Detroit News* (morning and evening); also the monthly magazines *Detroit Monthly* and *Metropolitan Detroit.*

Art Institute Auditorium, 5200 Woodward Ave. (833-7900): Concerts.

Attic Theater, 3031 W. Grand Blvd. (875-8284): Drama and comedy.

Fisher Theater, Second Ave. at Grand Blvd. (872-1000): Broadway hits. Year round.

Ford Auditorium, 20 Auditorium Dr. (224-1070): Home of the Detroit Symphony (music director: Gunther Herbig). Sept.-May.

Hilberry Theater, 4743 Cass Ave. (577-2972): Classical theater.

Music Hall Center for the Performing Arts, 350 Madison Ave. (963-7680): Dance, concerts.

Orchestra Hall, 3700 Parsons at Woodward Ave. (833-3700): Dance; classical and jazz concerts.

Theater Company–University of Detroit, 4001 W. McNichols Rd. (927-1130): Drama and comedy. Sept.-May.

SPECIAL EVENTS: For exact dates, consult the **Detroit Convention & Visitors Bureau** (see "Tourist Information," above).

Auto Show (Jan.): Very important auto exposition.

International Freedom Festival (late June to early July): Celebrates U.S.-Canadian friendship with parades, shows, open-air restaurants, and fireworks on either side of the international border.

Meadow Brook Music Festival (late June-Aug.): In Pontiac. Open-air concerts of classical music, pop, and jazz.

International Grand Prix (end of June): A spectacular Formula 1 Grand Prix race, run in downtown Detroit.

Detroit-Montreux Jazz Festival (late Aug. to early Sept.): The biggest stars in the jazz firmament; draws big crowds from the area.

SPORTS: Detroit boasts four professional teams:

Baseball (Apr.-Oct.): Tigers, Tiger Stadium (963-9944).

Basketball (Oct.-May): Pistons, Pontiac Silverdome (the world's largest inflatable dome), in Pontiac (313/338-4500).

Football (Sept.-Jan.): Lions, Pontiac Silverdome, in Pontiac (313/335-4151).

Ice Hockey (Oct.-May): Red Wings, Joe Louis Arena (567-6000).

Horse Racing

Hazel Park Race Track, 1650 E. 10 Mile Rd., in Hazel Park (313/398-1000), has racing Apr. to mid-Oct.

Ladbroke-DRC, 28001 Schoolcraft Rd., in Livonia (313/525-7300). Racing Apr.-Nov.

Northville Downs (harness racing), 301 S. Center St., in Northville (313/349-1000). Racing Jan.-Apr. and Oct.-Dec.

STROLLS: ⚓ **Greektown,** Monroe St. around Trappers Alley: The heart of Detroit's important Greek community; picturesque atmosphere with ethnic food stores, boutiques, and restaurants.

THEME PARK: ⚓ **Boblo Island:** On an island in Canadian territory, which can be reached only by two venerable cruise vessels dating from the early 1900s (the *Columbia* and the *Sainte Claire*), stands this big theme park with its giant roller coaster and 289-ft (96-m) observation tower; pretty walk along the riverbank. The dock for Boblo Steamers is at 661 Civic Center Dr. (843-8800). Open daily late May-Sept. 1.

TROLLEY: ⚓ **Washington Blvd. Trolley Car:** A picturesque old streetcar line whose ramshackle trams were once the pride of Lisbon, Portugal. It runs from the RenCen to Grand Circus Park, and boasts the world's last remaining open double-decker (933-1300).

WINTER SPORTS RESORTS: ⚓ **Alpine Valley,** 6775 E. Highland Rd., in White Lake Township (44 mi., 70 km, NW on I-75 and Mich. 59W) (313/887-2180): Nine lifts. Operates Nov.-March.

ZOOS: ⚓ **Royal Oak Zoo,** Woodward Ave. & 10 Mile Rd. (10 mi., 16 km, N) (398-0900): One of the best known in the U.S., with 400 species living in careful reconstructions of their natural habitat. The reptiles, penguins, and marine mammals are of particular interest. Miniature-railroad tour. Should be seen. Open daily.

ACCOMMODATIONS

See the listing of toll-free numbers in the Appendix.

Room Rates in Detroit	
B (Budget)	up to $30
I (Inexpensive)	$30–$60
M (Moderate)	$60–$90
E (Expensive)	$90–$140
VE (Very Expensive)	$140 and up

Personal Favorites (in order of preference)

☼♟♟♟♟ **Westin Hotel** (dwntwn), Renaissance Center, MI 48243 (313/568-8000; toll free, see Westin). 1,404 rms, A/C, color

TV, in-rm movies. AE, CB, DC, MC, V. Gar. $9, pool, health club, sauna, two rests. (one of which, The Summit, is a revolving rest. on the top floor), coffeeshop, four bars, 24-hr rm. svce, hrdrsr, cinema, boutiques, free crib. *Note:* Futuristic 73-story tower which bears the clear imprint of the famous architect John Portman. Eight-story-high lobby, w. indoor gardens and fountains. All rms are cramped but comfortable, and enjoy a panorama of the city or the Detroit River. La Fontaine is an acceptable rest. Efficient svce. Convention or business clientele. Detroit's most dazzling address. **E–VE**

♨♨♨ **Pontchartrain Hotel** (dwntwn), 2 Washington Blvd., MI 48226 (313/965-0200; toll free, see Preferred). 420 rms, A/C, cable color TV. AE, CB, DC, MC, V. Valet parking $6, pool, health club, sauna, two rests. (including Elaine's), two bars, 24-hr rm svce, disco, jazz (Fri. in summer), concierge, crib free . *Note:* A 23-story hotel no less up-to-date, but more intimate, than the Westin, built on the site of old Fort Pontchartrain. Elegant, comfortable rms, the best looking out over the Detroit River. Very good svce, very acceptable rest. The business traveler's favorite. Central location opposite Cobo Hall. No-smoking rms. Interesting wknd packages. Recently underwent a $15-million facelift. **E–VE**

☀♨♨♨ **Dearborn Inn** (vic.), 20301 Oakwood Blvd., in Dearborn, MI 48124 (313/271-2700); toll free 800/221-7236). 179 rms and cottages, A/C, color TV. AE, CB, DC, MC, V. Free parking, pool, tennis court, health club, three rests. (including the Early American Room), bar, rm svce, disco, crib free. *Note:* Built in 1931 by Henry Ford I, this big Georgian manor house sits in an enormous garden halfway between the airport and dwntwn, and very near the Ford Museum. Friendly colonial-style rms, as well as very comfortable individual cottages. Attentive reception and svce. Recently renovated and full of charm; ideal if you're driving. **M–E**

♨♨ **St. Regis Hotel** (nr. dwntwn), 3071 W. Grand Blvd., MI 48202 (313/873-3000; toll free 800/223-5560). 224 rms, A/C, color TV, in-rm movies. AE, CB, DC, MC, V. Free valet parking, rest. (Restaurant St. Regis), bar, rm svce, entertainment. *Note:* Charming older hotel, opposite the General Motors headquarters building, w. huge, inviting rms, polished svce, and an acceptable rest. Guests are mostly business people and regulars. Recently renovated. 10 min. from dwntwn. **VE**

♨ **Days Inn Downtown** (dwntwn), 231 Michigan Ave., MI 48226 (313/965-4646; toll free, see Days Inns). 287 rms, A/C, color TV, in-rm movies. AE, CB, DC, MC, V. Indoor parking $3, pool, health club, rest., bar, crib $5. *Note:* Large modern motel very near the Civic Center and Cobo Hall; large functional rms (some no-smoking). Business clientele. Rates on the high side for a motel. **M–E**

♨ **Balmar Motel** (nr. dwntwn), 3250 E. Jefferson Ave., MI 48207 (313/568-2000). 60 rms, A/C, color TV, in-rm movies. AE, DC, MC, V. Free parking, pool, rest. adjacent, private garden, crib free. *Note:* Modest but well-run small motel 15 min. from dwntwn; friendly reception and svce. Good value. **I**

Other Accommodations (from top bracket to budget)

♨♨♨ **Hyatt Regency Dearborn** (vic.), Michigan Ave. at Fairlane Town Center, in Dearborn, MI 48126 (313/593-1234; toll free, see Hyatt). 768 rms, A/C, color TV, in-rm movies. AE, CB, DC, MC, V. Free parking (valet parking $8), pool, sauna, three rests. (including La Rotisserie), coffeeshop, three bars, rm svce, disco, crib free. *Note:* Ultramodern steel-and-glass edifice w. a spectacular 16-story lobby and glass elevator shafts. Revolving bar on top floor. All the usual Hyatt comfort, very good svce, spacious rms. Business clientele. Very near Ford's manufacturing headquarters, 20 min.

from dwntwn, 5 min. from the airport—and has its own helicopter pad! Monorail link to a nearby shopping center. VIP floor. **E–VE**

🐚🐚🐚 **Omni International** (dwntwn), 333 E. Jefferson, MI 48226 (313/222-7700; toll free, see Omni). 258 rms, A/C, cable color TV. AE, CB, DC, MC, V. Valet indoor parking $9, pool, tennis court, sauna, two rests. (including 333 East), bar, rm svce, hrdrsr, boutiques, crib free. *Note:* Brand-new 20-story hotel in the recently constructed Millender Center; an elegant modern building w. commodious, comfortable rms (most w. balconies). Very comprehensive sports facilities. Efficient svce; group and business clientele. A good place to stay in the heart of dwntwn. Connected to RenCen by the Skywalk. **E–VE**

🐚🐚 **Hilton Southfield** (vic.), 17017 W. Nine Mile Rd., in Southfield, MI 48075 (313/557-4800; toll free, see Hilton). 390 rms, A/C, cable color TV. AE, CB, DC, MC, V. Free parking, pool, tennis court, rest., coffeeshop, bars, rm svce, hrdrsr, boutiques, crib free. *Note:* Up-to-date large motel, without much personality, north of Detroit. Large, comfortable rms, comprehensive facilities, good svce. Group and business clientele. 15 min. from dwntwn. **M–E**

🐚🐚 **Holiday Inn Dearborn** (vic.), 22900 Michigan Ave., in Dearborn, MI 48124 (313/278-4800; toll free, see Holiday Inns). 333 rms, A/C, cable color TV. AE, CB, DC, MC, V. Free parking, three pools, sauna, two rests. (one is Chambertin), bar, rm svce, night club, crib free. *Note:* Archetypal Holiday Inn; spacious balconied rms, some w. kitchenettes. Very creditable rest. Good value. Near the Ford Museum; 20 min. from dwntwn. **M**

🐚 **Shorecrest Motel** (dwntwn), 1316 E. Jefferson Ave., MI 48207 (313/568-3000; toll free 800/992-9616). 54 rms, A/C, color TV, in-rm movies. AE, CB, DC, MC, V. Free parking, coffeeshop, rm svce, crib free. *Note:* Aging but decent, comfortable motel; utilitarian rms, some w. refrigerators. Next to RenCen. Good value. **I–M**

🐚 **Red Roof Inn** (vic.), 26300 Dequindre Dr., in Warren, MI 48091 (313/573-4300; toll free 800/848-7878). 137 rms, A/C, color TV, in-rm movies. AE, CB, DC, MC, V. Free parking, nearby coffeeshop, crib free. *Note:* Modest small motel w. little to recommend it but its low rates. Functional comfort but nothing more. Free morning coffee. 15 min. from dwntwn. Ideal if you're driving. **I**

🐚 **Suez** (vic.), 3333 E. Eight Mile Rd., in Warren, MI 48091 (313/757-3333). 66 rms, A/C, color TV, in-rm movies. AE, MC, V. Free parking, garden, nearby 24-hr coffeeshop, crib free. *Note:* Modest, unpretentious little motel offering good overall value 15 min. from dwntwn. **I**

🐚 **Travelodge Dearborn** (vic.), 23730 Michigan Ave., in Dearborn, MI 48124 (313/565-7250; toll free, see Travelodge). 78 rms, A/C, color TV, in-rm movies. AE, CB, DC, MC, V. Free parking, pool, nearby coffeeshop, free crib. *Note:* Typical well-run motel; comfortable rms, some w. balconies. Free morning coffee. 5 min. from the Ford Museum and Greenfield Village, 20 min. from dwntwn. Good value. **I**

Airport Accommodations

🐚🐚 **Hilton Inn Airport** (vic.), 31500 Wick Rd., in Romulus, MI 48174 (313/292-3400; toll free, see Hilton). 272 rms, A/C, color TV, in-rm movies. AE, CB, DC, MC, V. Free parking, pool, health club, sauna, rest., bar, rm svce, night club, free crib. *Note:* The usual airport motel, recently renovated. Comfortable, sizeable rms, efficient svce. Business clientele. Free airport limo. **M–E**

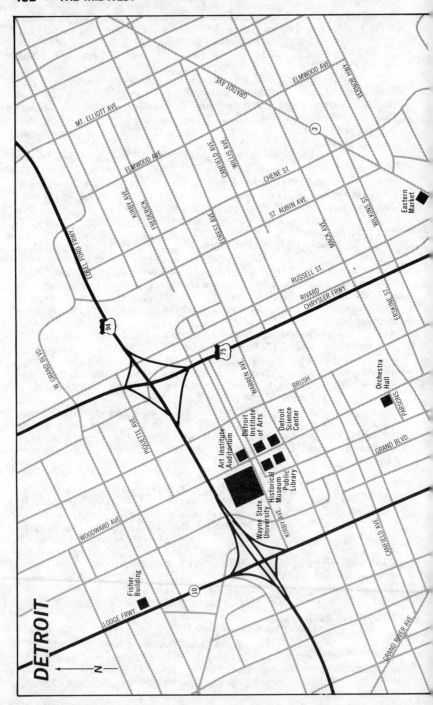

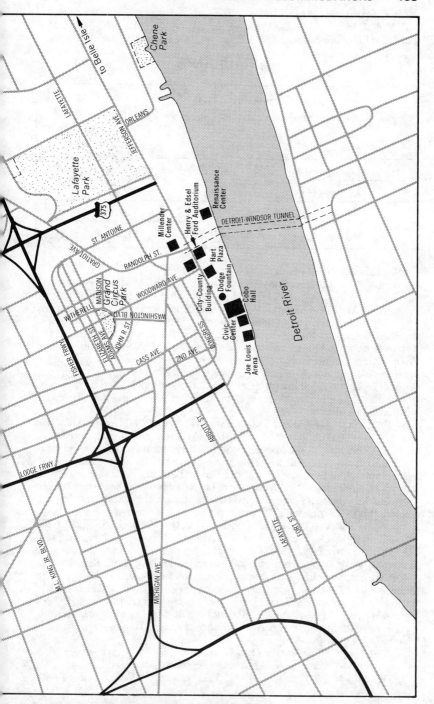

YMCA/Youth Hostel

YMCA (dwntwn), 2020 Witherell St., MI 48226 (313/962-6126). Men only; also functions as a youth hostel. 220 rms, pool, sauna, health club.

RESTAURANTS

Detroit Restaurant Prices	
(per person, excluding drinks and service charges)	
B (Budget)	up to $30
I (Inexpensive)	$30–$60
M (Moderate)	$60–$90
E (Expensive)	$90–$140
VE (Very Expensive)	$140 and up

Personal Favorites (in order of preference)

London Chop House (dwntwn), 155 W. Congress St. (962-0777). A/C. Lunch/dinner Mon.-Sat. (till 2 a.m.); closed Sun., hols. AE, CB, DC, MC, V. J&T. Specialties: fettucine w. seafood, lake perch, oysters au champagne, broiled venison cutlets w. cherries, rack of lamb w. mustard sauce, goujonettes de sole Murat, pheasant w. wild mushrooms, veal Oscar; frozen hazelnut soufflé. Excellent wine list w. more than 300 varieties. Menu changes regularly. *Note:* A local institution; everyone who's anyone in Detroit (including the Ford family), has eaten, eats, or will eat in this noisy, comfortable cellar decorated British style, w. caricatures of well-known customers on the walls. Exemplary svce; resv. a must. Don't miss this one. *American-Continental.* **E–VE**

Joe Muer's Seafood (nr. dwntwn), 2000 Gratiot Ave. (567-1088). A/C. Lunch Mon.-Fri.; dinner Mon.-Sat.; closed Sun., hols. AE, DC, MC, V. Jkt. Specialties: top-quality fish and shellfish; good list of California wines. *Note:* Also a local institution since 1929. This immense rest., w. its comfortable wood-paneled and exposed-brick rooms, is host every day to crowds of fish- and seafood-lovers, who are attracted by one of the broadest selections in the country. Two black marks: svce rather perfunctory; resv. not accepted. Private valet parking. 15 min. from dwntwn. *Seafood.* **M–E**

Van Dyke Place (nr. dwntwn), 649 Van Dyke St. (821-2620). A/C. Lunch Mon.-Fri.; dinner Mon.-Sat.; closed Sun., Dec. 23 to Jan. 1, early Aug. AE, MC, V. J&T. Specialties: boudin of duckling, assorted domestic caviars, paupiettes of braised veal, rack of lamb, abalone steak. Menu changes regularly. Very fine wine list. *Note:* Super-chic rest. housed in the mansion of a 19th-century captain of industry, elegantly decorated in Louis XVI style w. crystal chandeliers, gilt-framed pictures, and period furniture. The cuisine, while praiseworthy, doesn't quite measure up to the décor. Svce, while unpolished, is attentive. Resv., well in advance, a must. 10 min. from dwntwn. *American-Continental.* **M–E**

The Caucus Club (dwntwn), 150 W. Congress St. (965-4970). A/C. Lunch/dinner Mon.-Sat.; closed Sun., hols. AE, CB, DC, MC, V. Jkt. Specialties: Dover sole, corned beef hash, piccata of milk-fed veal, paillard of lamb w. noodles, spareribs, steak tartare, chili maison. *Note:* The less fashionable, less upscale younger sibling of the London Chop House (see above). Same high-quality food, same opulent London-club décor, same impeccable svce. Business clientele; generally packed at lunchtime. Resv. recommended. Valet parking. *American-Continental.* **I–M**

☼☆🍷☆ **Pontchartrain Wine Cellars** (dwntwn), 234 W. Larned St. (963-1785). A/C. Lunch Mon.-Fri.; dinner Mon.-Sat.; closed Sun., hols, and early Aug. AE, CB, DC, MC, V. Jkt. Specialties: escargots bourguignonne, gazpacho, escalope sauce Diable, leg of lamb w. ratatouille, veal Cordon Bleu, braised sweetbreads, fish of the day, pear Hélène. As you would expect from the rest.'s name, an excellent wine list; try a "cold duck" cocktail, made from champagne and burgundy. *Note:* Very successful French-inspired food, served in the romantic atmosphere of an old Paris bistro. Svce efficient but on the abrupt side. An outstanding rest. of its kinds since 1935. Resv. advised; valet parking. *Continental.* **I–M**

☼🍷 **Jacoby's** (dwntwn), 624 Brush St. (962-7067). A/C. Lunch/dinner Mon.-Sat.; closed Sun. AE, DC, MC, V. Specialties: schnitzel, sauerbraten, bratwurst, lake perch, sandwiches, German beer on draft. *Note:* The lawyers' and politicians' favorite since 1904. Looks and feels like a picturesque old brewhouse. Solid, honest food somewhat lacking in imagination. Svce w. a smile. *German-American.* **B–I**

Other Restaurants (from top bracket to budget)

🍷🍷🍷 **Golden Mushroom** (vic.), 18100 W. 10 Mile Rd., in South-field (16 mi, 25 km, N via Mich. 10N) (559-4230). A/C. Lunch/dinner Mon.-Sat.; closed Sun., hols. AE, CB, DC, MC, V. J&T. Specialties: sautéed wild mushrooms w. sherry, minced veal w. spaetzle, roast ribs of lamb w. onions and orange marmalade, mussels w. champagne, rainbow trout w. purée of leeks, calves' liver au poivre vert, foie gras sautéed w. port wine, gâteau Mozart. Menu changes regularly; fine wine list. *Note:* The food prepared by the Czech chef Miloš Čihelka, formerly of the London Chop House, which speaks well for him, is a little miracle of balanced inventiveness. Country-inn décor which achieves elegance in spite of the unpropitious neighborhood and the obtrusive proximity of a service station. Excellent svce. The only possible rival to the London Chop House for the best food in Detroit. Resv. advised. Valet parking. 20 min. from dwntwn. *Continental.* **M–E**

🍷🍷 **Carl's Chop House** (nr. dwntwn), 3020 Grand River Ave. (833-0700). A/C. Lunch/dinner daily (until 1 a.m.); closed Christmas Day. AE, CB, DC, MC, V. Specialties: the city's best prime ribs, steaks and lamb chops for more than half a century; also excellent pickled herring. *Note:* All the warmth of an AMTRAK waiting room and a strictly flea market décor, but efficient svce. Not far from Tiger Stadium, Carl's attracts many fans on game days. A good place. Valet parking. *Steakhouse-Seafood.* **I–M**

🍷🍷 **Money Tree** (dwntwn), 333 W. Fort St. (961-2445). A/C. Breakfast & lunch Mon.-Fri.; dinner Mon.-Sat.; closed Sun., hols. AE, CB, DC, MC, V. Jkt. Specialties: quiches, crêpes, and salads at lunch; catch of the day and more substantial dishes (rack of lamb w. mint, roast chicken w. ginger, roast veal w. basil, cassoulet, shrimp pêcheur) at dinner. Very good desserts. *Note:* A likeable, friendly café-restaurant in a modern setting; cuisine often inventive, svce relaxed and cheerful. Open-air terrace in summer. Agreeable background music. *Continental.* **I–M**

🍷🍷 **Roma Café** (nr. dwntwn), 3401 Riopelle, in the Eastern Market (831-5940). A/C. Lunch/dinner Mon.-Sat.; closed Sun., hols. AE, CB, DC, MC, V. Jkt. Specialties: fresh homemade pasta; well-prepared Italian cooking. *Note:* The city's oldest Italian rest.; tasty food and relatively easy on the wallet. Pleasant setting and background music. Resv. advised. Valet parking. *Italian.* **M**

    Chung's (nr. dwntwn), 3177 Cass Ave. (831-1100). A/C. Lunch/dinner daily. AE, DC. Specialties: shrimp in lobster purée, steak "Kew," wor hip harr, Cantonese specialties. *Note:* The best rest. in Detroit's Chinatown; wilted Far Eastern décor but many Chinese customers— always a good sign. *Chinese.* **I**

    New Hellas (dwntwn), 583 Monroe St. (961-5544). A/C. Lunch/dinner daily (until 2 a.m.). AE, MC, V. Specialties: moussaka, broiled lamb, squid, shish kebab, spanakopita (spinach-and-cheese pie), baklava. *Note:* An absolutely authentic Greek rest. in the heart of Greektown. Generally noisy and crowded. Open very late. No resv., so inevitable waits. *Greek.* **B–I**

    Sheik Restaurant (dwntwn), 316 E. Lafayette St. (964-8441). A/C. Lunch Tues.-Fri.; dinner Tues.-Sun.; closed Mon., hols. MC, V. Specialties: tabouleh, hummus, shish kebab, more than 20 different lamb dishes; rice pudding. *Note:* This rest. has been a family business since it opened in 1923; recently redecorated, it offers authentic Lebanese cooking at attractive prices. Friendly reception and svce, pleasant atmosphere. Very popular locally; excellent value. *Middle Eastern.* **B–I**

Restaurants In the Vicinity

    Chambertin (vic.), in the Holiday Inn in Dearborn (see "Accommodations," above) (278-6900). A/C. Lunch Mon.-Fri.; dinner nightly; brunch Sun. AE, CB, DC, MC, V. Jkt. Specialties: baked shrimp en chemise, filet of sole, beef Wellington. Nice wine list. *Note:* Generally successful French-inspired cooking—quite an achievement for a Holiday Inn. Pleasant atmosphere and svce. *French-Continental.* **I–M**

    La Cuisine (vic.), 417 Pelissier St., in Windsor, Canada (519/253-6432). A/C. Lunch/dinner Tues.-Sat.; closed Sun., Mon. AE, DC, MC, V. Jkt. Specialties: boeuf gros sel, kidneys w. mustard sauce, bouillabaisse. Good desserts. *Note:* A real French rest., well worth the jaunt into Canada (10 min. by car through the Windsor Tunnel; non–U.S. citizens should bring their passports). Congenial bistro atmosphere. Wine but no hard liquor. Resv. advised for dinner. *French.* **I–M**

Cafeterias / Specialty Spots

    American Coney Island (dwntwn), 114 W. LaFayette St. (961-7758). A/C. Breakfast/lunch/dinner daily (open around the clock). No credit cards. By general consent the best hot dogs in town. Locally popular since 1914.

BARS & NIGHTCLUBS

    Baker's Keyboard Lounge (vic.), 20510 Livernois (864-1200). One of the world's oldest and best-known jazz clubs, where you can hear all the stars. Open Tues.-Sun. 20 min. from dwntwn.

    Galligan's (dwntwn), 519 E. Jefferson Ave. (963-2098). Detroit's most popular Irish pub. Plenty of action. Disco music, bar food. Noisy and likeable. Open Mon.-Sat.

    Lindell AC (nr. dwntwn), 1310 Cass Ave. (964-1122). Popular, fun singles bar, much frequented by sports fans. Open daily.

    Soup Kitchen (dwntwn), 1585 Franklin St. (259-1374). Blues and jazz in a nice saloon setting; also a decent rest. Open Mon.-Sat.

    Watt's Mosambique (vic.), 8406 Fenkell (864-0240). Good black jazz in an outlying district, 25 min. from dwntwn.

NEARBY EXCURSIONS

ANN ARBOR (46 mi., 74 km, west on I-94): University town with a happy, youthful personality; seat of the **University of Michigan,** S. State St. & S. University Ave. (313/763-4636). One of the largest (35,000 students) and oldest (1817) universities in the Midwest, which moved here in 1837, 20 years after its founding in Detroit. Many buildings in the Gothic style; libraries; museums of art, archeology, and natural history. Also home to the **Gerald R. Ford Presidential Library,** 1000 Beal Ave. (313/764-0478), housing the personal archives of the 38th president. Campus open to visitors Mon.-Fri.; worth the trip.

CRANBROOK (500 Lone Pine Rd. in Bloomfield Hills, 25 mi., 40 km, NW by Woodward Ave. and Mich. 1) (313/645-3134): Internationally famous educational and cultural center on a 288-acre estate endowed early in this century by George G. Booth, publisher of the *Detroit News,* and his wife, Ellen. It includes among its facilities an academy of fine arts, a scientific institute with an observatory and planetarium, the very lovely neo-Gothic Christ Church, and an impressive manor house (Cranbrook House) in the Tudor style designed by Albert Kahn (visits by appointment; 313/645-3149), all standing amid beautiful landscaped gardens with groves and fountains. Open daily (gardens, May-Oct. only). Don't miss it.

FAIR LANE MANSION (Evergreen Rd., University of Michigan–Dearborn Campus, in Dearborn) (313/593-5590): Sumptuous private home built in 1915 for $2 million by Henry Ford; this pseudo-Scottish castle in rough stone boasts no fewer than 56 rooms and a garage for 12 cars! Open daily May-Sept.; Sun. only the rest of the year. Well worth the detour.

HENRY FORD MUSEUM AND GREENFIELD VIL-LAGE (23 Oakwood Blvd. in Dearborn, 10 mi., 16 km, west by Michigan Ave. and U.S. 12) (313/271-1620): Established in 1929 by Henry Ford, who was born here in 1863, the **Henry Ford Museum** is intended as a tribute to the dynamic qualities of the American people. It presents a complete panorama of the country's development from the days of the pioneers. To see it in detail requires at least two days. Very rich collection of art and handcrafts; impressive aircraft and automobile museum, including the first car built by Henry Ford, a great 600-ton Allegheny locomotive, and the Fokker aircraft in which Admiral Byrd first flew over the North Pole in 1926.

The adjacent **Greenfield Village** comprises 100 or so 17th-, 18th-, and 19th-century buildings drawn from all parts of the country and restored with scrupulous care. Among them are Henry Ford's birthplace, Edison's laboratory, and the courthouse in which Abraham Lincoln appeared as an attorney—a slice of living history that you shouldn't miss. It draws more than 1.5 million visitors a year. Open daily.

HISTORIC FORT WAYNE (6325 W. Jefferson Ave., 5 mi., 8 km, south of Detroit via Jefferson Ave.) (313/297-9360): Fort built in the period before the Civil War and in a fine state of preservation, with tunnels, a blockhouse, and its powder kegs. Interesting museum of military and Indian history. Open Wed.-Sun. May-Oct.

MEADOW BROOK (Adams Rd. in Rochester, 25 mi., 40 km, north on I-75) (313/370-3140): This enormous Tudor-style manor house on the campus of Oakland University was built in 1926 by the widow of automobile tycoon John Dodge, and contains around 100 richly furnished and decorated rooms. Open daily in summer; Sun. only, the rest of the year.

POINT PELEE NATIONAL PARK (32 mi., 51 km, SE by the Detroit-Windsor Tunnel and Ontario Rte. 3): This Canadian nature reserve of a little more than 2,400 acres is a paradise for wildlife enthusiasts; its expanse of marsh and woodland, standing on two of the great migratory routes between Canada and South America, is host to more than 340 different species of birds. Many trails and waterfront paths. Visitor Center. Camping not permitted. The perfect place for dedicated birdwatchers. Open daily, early Apr. to Sept. For information, phone 519/322-2365. (Non–U.S. citizens should bring their passports.)

WINDSOR (Canada): Cosmopolitan city of 200,000 across the Detroit River, reached by bridge or tunnel. Numerous parks, boutiques, restaurants. Spectacular view of the Detroit skyline, particularly after dark. (Non–U.S. citizens should bring their passports.)

CHAPTER 21

CLEVELAND⚡

□ □ □

This, now the second-largest city in Ohio (after Columbus) was founded on Lake Erie at the mouth of the **Cuyahoga River** by Gen. Moses Cleaveland. The spelling was later modified by the editor of a local newspaper who found the name too long for his taste. Sprawling over more than 50 mi. (80 km), Cleveland's metropolitan area is a riveting microcosm of America's industrial evolution over the last century. Interminable gray, polluted suburbs, home to steel mills, oil refineries, automobile factories, plus electronics and machine-tool plants, lie cheek by jowl with a few luxurious residential areas (**Shaker Heights, Beachwood**) around a downtown which now consists of no more than a couple of dozen blocks of houses surrounding the **Mall** and the completely renovated **Public Square**. The city's tallest building, the 52-story **Terminal Tower,** and the new **Standard Oil Co. tower** (45 stories) dominate the Square. Once the fifth most populous city in the country, Cleveland lost nearly a quarter of its population in the 1970s as a result of upheavals in the oil and steel industries; in 1980 the municipality barely avoided bankruptcy. Despite new-found economic activity, the unemployment rate is still well above 10%, and more than a third of Cleveland's inhabitants live below the poverty line.

Among its other claims to fame, Cleveland can boast the first modern striptease, in the person of an obscure tapdancer named Carrie Findel. Tired of the audience's boos, she declared one night, "I've a surprise for you. Each week, I'll take off one more part of my costume." The show lasted 52 weeks.

Two other truly American legends are associated with Cleveland: Superman, the famous comic-strip hero, who made his first appearance in 1938; and John Davison Rockefeller, the incarnation of capitalism triumphant, who, beginning in 1870, laid the foundations of the immense oil empire (originally known as the Standard Oil Company of Ohio) now known as Exxon. Cleveland is also headquarters for 35 of the most important U.S. industrial corporations. Medicine is another flourishing aspect of the local economy (the city has 45,000 doctors, researchers, and technicians). Besides schools and research institutes of renown like **Case Western Reserve University** and the **Cleveland State University Hospitals,** the city also has the **Cleveland Clinic,** known worldwide for the organ transplants and cardiac surgery performed here.

Ohio's industrial capital is a veritable mosaic of nationalities, with the second-largest concentration of Hungarians after Budapest, as well as Italian, Irish, Polish, German, Chinese, Greek, Serb, Czech, and Ukrainian communities —overall, a good 60 or so different nationalities are represented. With such a mix of ethnic groups, it's no wonder that Cleveland was the first major U.S. metropolis (1967) to elect a black mayor, Carl B. Stokes. Cleveland is also rich in first-rate cultural and theatrical institutions: its symphony orchestra is internationally renowned, and its **Museum of Art** is one of the best in the country.

Among Cleveland's famous natives are actor Paul Newman and composer and orchestra leader Henry Mancini.

BASIC FACTS: State of Ohio. Area Code: 216. Time Zone: Eastern Time. ZIP

Code: 44101. Founded: 1796. Approximate population: city, 550,000; metropolitan area, 1,850,000. 12th-largest metropolitan area in the United States.

CLIMATE: As in all the Great Lakes region, winter is very cold and snowy (avg. Jan. temperature: 27°F, 3°C) and summer hot and humid (avg. July temperature: 70°F, 22°C). Spring is normally very brief, and autumn mild and sunny; these are the two ideal seasons for visiting Cleveland.

DISTANCES: Chicago, 343 mi. (549 km); Cincinnati, 247 mi. (395 km); Detroit, 170 mi. (272 km); New York, 485 mi. (776 km); Washington, 350 mi. (560 km).

ARRIVAL & TRANSIT INFORMATION

AIRPORTS: Burke Lakefront Airport (BKL): 1 mi. (2 km) north. Delta Connection only. Information: 781-6411.
    Cleveland Hopkins International Airport (CLE): 10 mi. (16 km) SW. Information: 265-6000.

DOMESTIC AIRLINES: American (881-4341), Continental (771-8419), Delta (781-8800), Eastern (861-7300), Midway (800/621-5700), Northwest (267-0515), Pan Am (toll free 800/221-1111), TWA (781-2700), United (356-1311), USAir (696-8050).

FOREIGN CARRIERS: Air Canada (toll free 800/422-6232).

CITY LINK: Cab fare to city center from Hopkins International, about $16; time, 25–30 min. An airport–city center train leaves every 20 min. from the R.T.A. Terminal, Public Square; fare, $1; time, 25 min. Bus: Hopkins Airport Limousine (267-8282): leaves every 30 min.; serves major dwntwn hotels; fare, $6; time, 35–40 min. Unless your touring will be limited to the dwntwn area, you may wish to rent a car to cope with the sprawling metropolitan area and the difficulty of getting a taxi in the suburbs (the wait sometimes approaches an hour). A rather deficient public transportation system (bus and train); for R.T.A. information, call 621-9500.

CAR RENTAL (at Hopkins International Airport): Avis (265-3700), Budget (433-4433), Dollar (267-3133), Hertz (267-8900), National (267-0060). For dwntwn agencies, consult the phone directory.

LIMOUSINE SERVICES: American Limousines Service (221-9330), Park Avenue Limousines (871-9998).

TAXIS: Taxis may not be hailed on the street but may be summoned by phone. The fares are relatively reasonable. Major company: Yellow Zone Cab (623-1500).

TRAIN: AMTRAK, Lakefront Station, 200 E. Cleveland Memorial Shoreway Dr. (861-0105).

BUS: Greyhound, 1465 Chester Ave. (781-0520).

INFORMATION & TOURS

TOURIST INFORMATION: The **Cleveland Convention & Visitors Bureau,** 1301 E. 6th St., OH 44114 (216/621-4110; toll free 800/321-1001).

Recorded telephone message giving an up-to-date listing of cultural events and shows: 216/621-8860.

GUIDED TOURS: Gray Line Cleveland Tours (bus), 43 Harrison St., Bedford (216/232-4550): Guided tours of the city. Serves major dwntwn hotels.

Goodtime Cruises (boat): Lake Erie and Cuyahoga River cruises. Depart from the E. 9th St. Pier (216/861-5110), daily May-Oct.

Trolley Tours (bus), 1221 Washington Ave. (216/781-8819): City tour in a minibus that looks like a trolley car.

SIGHTS, ATTRACTIONS, & ACTIVITIES

ARCHITECTURAL HIGHLIGHTS: ☖ **City Hall,** Lakeside Ave. & E. 6th St. (664-2000): Cleveland's city hall, overlooking Lake Erie. Be sure to see the famous Archibald Willard painting, *Spirit of '76,* in the rotunda. Open Mon.-Sat.

☖ **Cleveland Clinic,** 9500 Euclid Ave. (444-2200): Second-largest private hospital in the country after the Mayo Clinic in Rochester, Minn. Employs 8,900 doctors, researchers, and staff. A pioneer in cardiac surgery since 1967, the clinic performs more than 3,000 open-heart operations each year. The world-renowned Cleveland Clinic has treated the likes of ex-King Khaled of Arabia, King Hussein of Jordan, and the former president of Brazil, General Figueiredo.

☖ **Playhouse Square,** 1900 E. 17th St.: Symbol of Cleveland's cultural renaissance, this urban-renewal project cost $20 million and endowed the city with one of the largest performance and concert hall complexes in the country. The three theaters and the cabaret, elegantly restored, present theatrical performances, ballet, opera, and classical and pop concerts. Open daily. For information on current performances, call 241-6000. Absolutely worth going out of your way for.

☖ **Public Square,** Ontario & Superior Aves.: The commercial heart of Cleveland, where all the major dwntwn thoroughfares converge: Euclid Ave., Ontario St., and Superior Ave. Towering above the square are the city's tallest building, the **Terminal Tower** (52 stories), and the brand-new **Standard Oil** skyscraper (45 stories). Quite lively by day, the area is deserted and unsafe at night. Imposing memorial: **Soldiers and Sailors Monument.** The appealing public park is adorned with statues.

HISTORIC BUILDINGS: ☖ **The Arcade,** 401 Euclid Ave. (621-8500): One of the oldest enclosed shopping areas in the world (1890), the Arcade offers very lovely art nouveau architecture crowned with an openwork metallic skylight, plus 112 bars, boutiques, and restaurants. Free concerts at noon. Don't miss a visit. Open Mon.-Sat.

MARKETS: ☖ **New Central Market,** E. 4th St. & Bolivar Rd. (781-5585): More than 100 food stalls in a vibrant, lively atmosphere. Open Tues.-Sun.

☼ ☖ **West Side Market,** Lorain Ave. at W. 25th St. (664-3386): Picturesque old European-style covered market with more than 100 food stalls offering products from all over the world. A colorful Cleveland classic. Open Mon., Wed., Fri., and Sat.

MUSEUMS OF ART: ☼ ☖☖☖ **Museum of Art,** 11150 East Blvd. at University

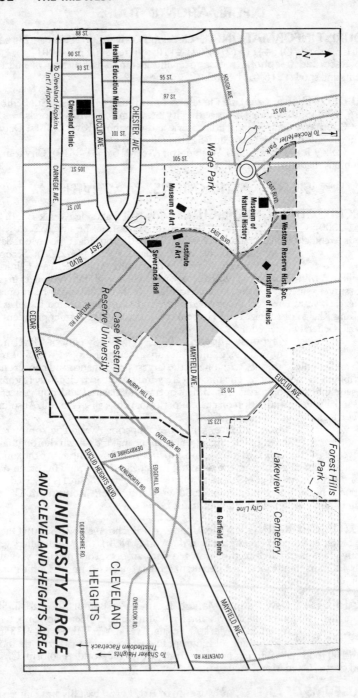

UNIVERSITY CIRCLE AND CLEVELAND HEIGHTS AREA

-N→

88 ST.
90 ST.
93 ST.
95 ST.
97 ST.
100 ST.
101 ST.
105 ST.
107 ST.
105 ST.
105 ST.
120 ST.
123 ST.

Health Education Museum

Cleveland Clinic

To Cleveland Hopkins Int'l Airport

CHESTER AVE.

EUCLID AVE.

CARNEGIE AVE.

HOUGH AVE.

To Rockefeller Park

Wade Park

Museum of Art

Museum of Natural History

Western Reserve Hist. Soc.

EAST BLVD.

EAST BLVD.

Institute of Art

Severance Hall

Institute of Music

Case Western Reserve University

ADELBERT RD.

CEDAR AVE.

MURRY HILL RD.

MAYFIELD AVE.

EUCLID AVE.

OVERLOOK RD.

DERBYSHIRE RD.

EDGEHILL RD.

KENILWORTH RD.

DERBYSHIRE RD.

EUCLID HEIGHTS BLVD.

OVERLOOK RD.

COVENTRY RD.

MAYFIELD AVE.

CLEVELAND HEIGHTS

To Shaker Heights
Thistledown Racetrack

Garfield Tomb

City Line

Lakeview Cemetery

Forest Hills Park

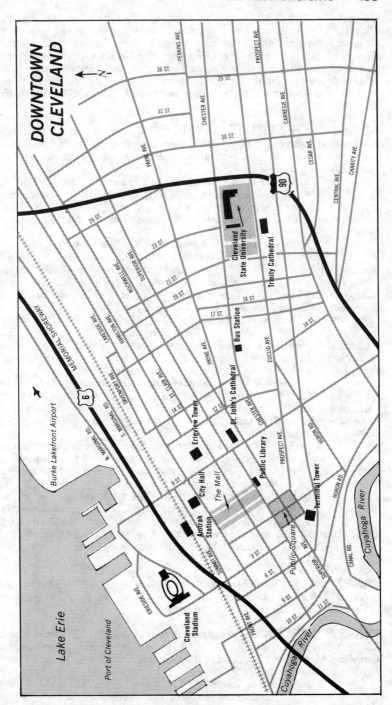

DOWNTOWN CLEVELAND

Lake Erie

Port of Cleveland

Burke Lakefront Airport

Cleveland Stadium

Amtrak Station

City Hall

Erieview Tower

St. John's Cathedral

Public Library

The Mall

Public Square

Terminal Tower

Bus Station

Cleveland State University

Trinity Cathedral

Cuyahoga River

MEMORIAL SHOREWAY

ERESIDE AVE.
N. MARGINAL RD.
S. MARGINAL RD.
DAVENPORT AVE.
HAMILTON AVE.
LAKESIDE AVE.
ROCKWELL AVE.
SUPERIOR AVE.
ST. CLAIR AVE.
PAYNE AVE.
PAYNE AVE.
EUCLID AVE.
CHESTER AVE.
PROSPECT AVE.
PROSPECT AVE.
HURON RD.
SUPERIOR
CANAL RD.
FRONT AVE.
SUMMIT AVE.
CEDAR AVE.
CARNEGIE AVE.
CENTRAL AVE.
CHARITY AVE.
PERKINS AVE.
CHESTER AVE.

9 ST.
14 S.
12 S.
3 ST.
6 ST.
9 ST.
10 ST.
11 ST.
14 ST.
17 ST.
18 ST.
19 ST.
21 ST.
23 ST.
26 ST.
30 ST.
32 ST.
35 ST.
36 ST.

6
90

Circle (421-7340): One of the top American art museums. From "The Treasure of the Guelphs" to Rauschenberg, the museum houses a sumptuous panorama of Oriental, European, and American art. Some of the best-known works: El Greco's *Christ on the Cross,* Velázquez's *The Clown Calabazas,* Rembrandt's *The Jewish Student,* Cézanne's *Mont Sainte Victoire,* and two famous Picassos, *Life* and *Harlequin with Violin.* The handsome, marble Greek Revival building faces the **Fine Arts Garden** and its sculptures. Itself worth a trip to Cleveland. Open Tues.-Sun.

MUSEUMS OF SCIENCE & HISTORY: ⚖ Dunham Tavern Museum,

6709 Euclid Ave. (431-1060): Former coaching inn along the Buffalo-Detroit route, now a historical museum with interesting temporary exhibitions. Open Wed.-Sun.

☼⚖⚖ **Health Education Museum,** 8911 Euclid Ave. (231-5010): The oldest (and one of the best) medical museums in the country, with an astonishing giant electronic brain and Juno, the transparent Plexiglass woman. In all, more than 150 giant anatomical models. Marvelous. Open daily.

⚖ **Howard Dittrick Museum of Medical History,** 11000 Euclid Ave. (368-3648): A natural complement to the Health Education Museum, this museum documents a complete panorama of the evolution of medicine, surgery, and pharmacology through a collection of more than 10,000 old and new medical objects. A must for all disciples of Hippocrates. On the fourth floor of the Allen Library. Open Mon.-Sat.

⚖ **Museum of Natural History,** Wade Oval Dr. at University Circle (231-4600): Very interesting museum displaying rich collections covering animals (dinosaurs, mammoths, giant insects), prehistoric times (including the three-million-year-old "Lucy" skeleton), Amerindian culture, geology, and more. An absolute must. Open daily.

⚖ **NASA Lewis Research Center,** 21000 Brookpark Rd. (433-2001): This NASA research center adjacent to Hopkins International Airport offers guided tours of research laboratories with, notably, a supersonic wind tunnel plus an exhibition and films on space exploration. Open daily.

⚖ **Ralph Mueller Planetarium,** Wade Oval Dr. at University Circle (231-4600): The renowned observatory and planetarium are an integral part of the Museum of Natural History (see above). Astronomy shows and other presentations. Open daily.

☼⚖⚖ **Western Reserve Historical Society Museum,** 18025 East Blvd. at University Circle (751-5722): Magnificently reconstructed U.S. history from independence to the present, including Shaker crafts and old costumes unique to the United States. Also houses a vast automotive and aeronautical museum with more than 200 old models. Absolutely worth a visit. Open Tues.-Sun.

PANORAMAS: ⚖ Terminal Tower, Public Square (621-7981): 52-story tower (761 ft, 238 m) with an observation platform on the 42nd floor. The best view of Cleveland and Lake Erie. Open wknds only.

PARKS & GARDENS: ⚖ Brookside Park, Denison Ave. & Fulton Pkwy.: Joggers will enjoy these 153 acres (64 ha) of gardens, which encompass the **Cleveland Metroparks Zoo,** one of the most highly rated zoos in the country (1,300 animals). Open daily.

☼⚖ **Lakeview Cemetery,** 12316 Euclid Ave. (421-2665): Splendid landscaped cemetery that overlooks Lake Erie, as the name indicates. Among noteworthy graves here are those of James Garfield, 20th president of the United States, whose enormous mausoleum affords a spectacular view of the city, and John D. Rockefeller, founder of the famous dynasty. See it. Open daily.

🔔 **Rockefeller Park,** along Liberty Blvd.: A calm, green oasis between Lake Erie and Case Western Reserve University. The park's 296 acres (120 ha) offer very fine Japanese gardens, greenhouses, and the **Shakespeare Cultural Gardens,** adorned with sculptures and architectural designs from 24 different countries. Worth a look.

PERFORMING ARTS: For daily listings of all shows and cultural events, consult the entertainment pages of the daily paper *Cleveland Plain Dealer* and the monthly *Cleveland* magazine.

Cleveland Play House, 2040 E. 86th St. (795-7000): One of the earliest permanent repertory troupes in the country. Classical and contemporary theater.

The Front Row Theatre, 6199 Wilson Mills Rd., Highland Heights (449-5000): Big-name stars.

Hanna Theater, 2067 E. 14th St. (621-5000): Musicals.

Karamu House & Theatre, 2355 E. 89th St. (795-7070): Experimental theater, concerts, and ballet.

Lakewood Little Theater, 17801 Detroit Ave., Lakewood (521-2540): Home of the Kenneth C. Beck Center for Cultural Arts. Sept.-June.

Playhouse Square Center, 1900 E. 17th St. (771-4444): These three contiguous halls—the **Ohio Theater,** the **State Theater,** and the **Palace Theater**—offer classical and modern theater, concerts, ballet, and opera, as well as the **Great Lakes Theatre Festival** (see "Special Events," below).

Severance Hall, 11001 Euclid Ave. at East Blvd. (231-1111): Home of the Cleveland Symphony Orchestra, one of the country's "big six" orchestras, under principal conductor Christoph von Dohnanyi. Sept.-May. The orchestra can be heard June-Sept. at the superb outdoor **Blossom Music Center,** 1145 W. Steels Corners Rd., Cuyahoga Falls (271-7300).

SPECIAL EVENTS: For the exact schedule of events below, consult the **Cleveland Convention & Visitors Bureau** (see "Tourist Information," above).

Jazz Festival (June): With the biggest stars.

Great Lakes Theatre Festival (late June to Oct.): One of the Midwest's best theater festivals.

All Nations Festival (Aug.): Ethnic folk groups from all over the United States.

National Air Show (Labor Day wknd): An exhibition of all types of planes and flight demonstrations over Lake Erie. A classic since 1929.

SPORTS: Cleveland boasts three professional teams:

Baseball (Apr.-Oct): Indians, Cleveland Stadium (241-5555).

Basketball (Oct. to late Apr.): Cavaliers, Coliseum, in Richfield (659-9100).

Football (Sept.-Dec.): Browns, Cleveland Stadium (696-5555).

Horse Racing

Northfield Park Raceway, Route 8 in Northfield (467-4101): Harness races year round.

STROLLS: 🔔 **Coventry Road,** enter from Chester Ave: The local Greenwich Village, with fashionable boutiques and numerous restaurants. Don't miss the annual festival here in July. Worth the trip.

    Hessler Road, enter from Bellflower Rd.: Cleveland's most bohemian street, with artists' studios, galleries, and pretty pastel houses. Worth a look.

    The Mall, between Lakeside & Rockwell Ave.: The monumental heart of the city, this vast rectangular esplanade adorned with gardens and fountains is bordered by Cleveland's major public buildings. Worth a look.

    Ohio City, around Lorain Ave. & W. 25th St.: Cleveland's old middle-class neighborhood, with fine Victorian houses, many antique shops, and restaurants.

    Shaker Heights, around N. Park Blvd. & Eaton Rd.: One of the country's plushest residential areas, with splendid, tree-shaded Tudor and Georgian turn-of-the-century homes. Take a look.

THEME PARKS: **Cedar Point,** near Sandusky (50 mi., 80 km, west on U.S. 6) (419/626-0830): On Lake Erie, this huge amusement park offers 55 attractions plus a zoo, aquarium, beach, restaurants, and marina. Open daily mid-May to Sept.

    On the way back, see the **Birthplace-Museum of Thomas Edison,** 9 Edison Dr., in Milan (17 mi., 27 km, farther south) (419/499-2968): Residence-turned-museum in memory of the great inventor. Open Tues.-Sun.

    Sea World, 11000 Sea World Dr., in Aurora (23 mi., 37 km, SE on Ohio 43) (216/562-8101): An enormous marine-life zoo in the middle of an 80-acre (32 ha) park, with sea lions, elephant seals, dolphins, and killer whales. Spectacular animal shows. Open daily May-Oct.

WINTER SPORTS RESORTS: **Alpine Valley,** 10620 Mayfield Rd., in Chesterland (30 mi., 48 km, east on U.S. 322): Five chair lifts. For information, call 216/285-2211.

ACCOMMODATIONS
See the listing of toll-free numbers in the Appendix.

Room Rates in Cleveland	
B (Budget)	up to $30
I (Inexpensive)	$30–$60
M (Moderate)	$60–$90
E (Expensive)	$90–$140
VE (Very Expensive)	$140 and up

Personal Favorites (in order of preference)
    Bond Court (dwntwn), E. 6th St. & St. Clair Ave., OH 44114 (216/771-7600; toll free 800/321-1090). 485 rms, A/C, color TV, in-rm movies. AE, CB, DC, MC, V. Gar. $4, rest. (Le Bistro), coffeeshop, two bars, 24-hr rm svce, disco, crib $12. *Note:* The best hotel in Cleveland, this modern, luxurious 22-story tower offers comfortable rms (the best have a view of Lake Erie), good svce, and a very adequate rest. Business clien-

tele. Adjacent to the Convention Center in the heart of the business district. VIP floor. No-smoking rms. **E**

Hollenden House (dwntwn), E. 6th St. & Superior Ave., OH 44114 (216/621-0700). 500 rms, A/C, color TV, in-rm movies. AE, CB, DC, MC, V. Gar. $4, pool, health club, sauna, rest. (Hollenden Tavern), coffeeshop, two bars, rm svce, crib free. *Note:* Relatively modern 14-story hotel in dwntwn Cleveland with comfortable, spacious rms and efficient svce. Business clientele. Pleasant rest. A good overall value. **E**

The Clinic Center (formerly The Clinic Inn; nr. dwntwn), 2065 E. 96th St., OH 44106 (216/791-1900; toll free 800/321-7100). 380 rms, A/C, color TV, in-rm movies. AE, CB, DC, MC, V. Free parking, pool, rest., coffeeshop, bar, rm svce, hrdrsr, crib free. *Note:* This modern hotel is a good value, ten min. from dwntwn and a few steps from the Cleveland Clinic. It offers spacious, inviting rms and a very satisfactory Olde English tavern –style rest. Efficient svce. **M**

Budget Inns of America (formerly Howard Johnson's; vic.), 14043 Brookpark Rd., OH 44142 (216/267-2350). 115 rms, A/C, cable color TV. AE, CB, DC, MC, V. Free parking, coffeeshop, bar, rm svce, crib free. *Note:* A very good value, this relatively modern motel is quite convenient to the international airport and offers vast rms with private patios or balconies and efficient, if hardly cheerful, svce. 8 min. from the airport (free shuttle) and 20 min. from dwntwn. Ideal for the motorist. **B–I**

Other Accommodations (from top bracket to budget)

Stouffer Tower City Plaza (dwntwn), 24 Public Sq., OH 44113 (216/696-5600; toll free, see Stouffers). 503 rms, A/C, color TV, in-rm movies. AE, CB, DC, MC, V. Parking $3, pool, health club, rest. (French Connection), coffeeshop, bar, rm svce, crib free. *Note:* Located in the heart of Cleveland, this old luxury hotel has undergone a $24-million renovation. It offers first-rate, comfortable, spacious rms (some are no-smoking) with private patios; impersonal reception and svce; well-regarded rest.; superb art deco pool and a spectacular ten-story atrium. Group and convention clientele. VIP floors. **E–VE**

Holiday Inn Lakeside (dwntwn), 1111 Lakeside Ave., at E. 12th St., OH 44114 (216/241-5100; toll free, see Holiday Inns). 400 rms, A/C, color TV. AE, CB, DC, MC, V. Free parking, pool, health club, sauna, rest., coffeeshop, bar, rm svce. *Note:* Modern 18-story building w. an unobstructed view of the city and of Lake Erie. Very satisfying comfort, Holiday Inn–style. Groups and business clientele. **M**

Howard Johnson Lodge–Lakefront (nr. dwntwn), 5700 S. Marginal Rd., OH 44103 (216/432-2220; toll free, see Howard Johnson's). 200 rms. A/C, color TV, in-rm movies. AE, CB, DC, MC, V. Free parking, pool, sauna, tennis, rest., bar, valet svce. *Note:* Modern and inviting motel five min. from dwntwn. Functional, comfortable rms (most with view of Lake Erie). Good svce. Rest. poor. Business clientele.

Days Inn (formerly the Airport Hilton; vic.), 4181 W. 150th St., OH 44135 (216/252-7700; toll free, see Days Inns). 144 rms, A/C, color TV. AE, CB, DC, MC, V. Free parking, pool, rest., bar, rm svce, disco, crib free. *Note:* Classic but comfortable five-story motel w. spacious rms and aggreeable reception and svce. 5 min. from the airport (free shuttle) and 20 min. from dwntwn. A good overall value. **I–M**

Skylight Inn (vic.), 3795 Orange Pl., Beachwood, OH 44122 (216/831-7200; toll free 800/321-6336). 128 rms, A/C, color TV, in-rm movies. AE, CB, DC, MC, V. Free parking, free breakfast, adjacent coffeeshop, crib free. *Note:* A convenient, well-kept motel not far from chic Shaker Heights. 15 min. from dwntwn on Ohio 422. Ideal for motorists. **I**

Airport Accommodations

👑👑 **Sheraton Hopkins Airport** (vic.), 5300 Riverside Dr., OH 44135 (216/267-1500; toll free, see Sheraton). 416 rms, A/C, color TV, in-rm movies. AE, CB, DC, MC, V. Free parking, pool, health club, sauna, rest. (Port Brittany), coffeeshop, bar, rm svce, night club, crib free. *Note:* A grand hotel w. immediate access to the airport terminal. Spacious, comfortable rms w. private patios or balconies. The facilities are very complete, the svce efficient. Free 24-hour airport shuttle. Very adequate rest. Business clientele. VIP floor. **M–E**

RESTAURANTS

Cleveland Restaurant Prices	
(per person, excluding drinks and service charges)	
B (Budget)	up to $15
I (Inexpensive)	$15–$25
M (Moderate)	$25–$40
E (Expensive)	$40–$60
VE (Very Expensive)	$60 and up

Personal Favorites (in order of preference)

🍷🍷🍷 **Contemporary Cuisine** (nr. dwntwn), 20600 Chagrin Blvd., Shaker Heights (991-1580). A/C. Dinner only Mon.-Sat.; closed Sun. AE, MC,V. Jkt. Specialties: veal medallions with caramelized soy sauce, grilled chicken breast with pommes frites, fresh tuna in madeira sauce. Rich desserts. The menu changes weekly. Remarkable wine list. *Note:* Critics may dislike the minimalist white decor, highlighted by abstract art, of this stark dining room on the ground floor of a highrise office building designed by Walter Gropius. But the menu of chef and owner, Zachary Bruell, adds a welcome sophistication to the locally standard upscale cuisine. The menu includes a variety of grilled entrees, all in California styling. The service is reliable and gracious. Resv. essential. *American.* **M–E**

☀️🍷🍷🍷 **That Place on Bellflower** (nr. dwntwn), 11401 Bellflower Rd. (231-4469). A/C. Lunch Mon.-Sat.; dinner nightly; closed hols. AE, DC, MC, V. Jkt. Specialties: turbot St-Germain, roast duck, veal Oscar, Renaissance salmon, scallops remoulade, good desserts. Fine wine list. *Note:* Eclectic, French-inspired cuisine (as its fleur-de-lys, or bellflower, requires) in a former coaching inn that has been elegantly restored. The menu changes periodically. Very good svce. Open-air dinner in summer. Resv. advised in light of its success. The pervasive noise at night sometimes detracts from the romantic atmosphere. *French-Continental.* **I–M**

🍷🍷 **Jim's Steak House** (nr. dwntwn), 1800 Scranton Rd. (216/241-6343). A/C. Lunch/dinner Mon.-Sat.; closed Sun. AE, CB, DC, MC, V. Specialties: steak, roast beef, lamb chops, fish of the day. *Note:* A local favorite, Jim's serves the best red meat in Cleveland, especially the remarkable T-bone steak, and very good broiled fish as well. You'll also get a lovely view of the city and the boats along the Cuyahoga. Efficient svce. Resv. advised. 5 min. from dwntwn. *Steakhouse.* **I–M**

☖☖ **Shujiro** (vic.), 2206 Lee Rd., Cleveland Heights (321-0210). A/C. Lunch Mon.-Fri.; dinner nightly; closed hols. MC, V. Specialties: sashimi, tempura, sushi, fried soft-shell crabs, grilled eel kabayaki. *Note:* The best local representative of Japanese cuisine, and one of Cleveland's most highly regarded spots. Modern décor of exposed woodwork and a dining room where one can eat Western-style or on tatami mats. Chef Hiroshi Tsuji blends Japanese simplicity and classicism w. French and Chinese influences. The kimono-clad servers are exceptionally attentive. Resv. advised. 20 min. from dwntwn. *Japanese.* **I**

☖ **Balaton** (vic.), 12523 Buckeye Rd. (921-9691). A/C. Lunch/dinner (until 9 p.m.) Tues.-Sat.; closed Sun., Mon. No credit cards. Specialties: goulash, paprika chicken, wienerschnitzel, stuffed cabbage, palacsinta, dobos torte. Hungarian wine and beer, but no hard liquor. *Note:* Exceptionally tasty Hungarian and German cuisine served in a Formica-and-paper-napkins setting. More than generous portions at very modest prices. A favorite rest. of Cleveland's large Hungarian community. *Continental-German.* **B–I**

☖ **The Mad Greek** (nr. dwntwn), Cedar Rd. at Fairmount Blvd. (421-3333). A/C. Lunch Mon.-Sat.; dinner nightly. AE, DC, MC, V. Specialties: moussaka, stuffed grape leaves, mezedakia, pita, and everything in between—the food and Greek wine here are truly authentic. Limited but interesting wine list. *Note:* An enjoyable ambience in a rustic patio setting enveloped by whitewashed walls and a profusion of greenery. It offers agreeable Greek cuisine at low prices as well as some very good Indian dishes: tikka chicken, curries (the owner is Indian and his wife Greek). Friendly, cheerful svce. Locally popular. *Greek.* **B–I**

Other Restaurants (from top bracket to budget)

☼☖☖ **French Connection** (dwntwn), in the Stouffer Tower City Plaza (see "Accommodations," above) (696-5600). A/C. Lunch/dinner daily; brunch Sun.; closed hols. AE, CB, DC, MC, V. J&T. Specialties: lobster bisque, sweetbread ravioli w. saffron, poached salmon w. vermouth, rack of lamb in pastry shell, roast veal w. grapefruit, lobster crêpes w. ginger, remarkable desserts. Fine list of French and California wines at sometimes excessive prices. *Note:* Far and away the most elegant and most luxurious rest. in Cleveland, the French Connection has been called one of the ten most romantic rests. in the country in a *USA Today* poll: paintings by the masters, period furniture, pastel tones, and windows that give a view of Public Square. Irreproachable luxury-hotel cuisine and first-rate svce. Resv. at must. *French.* **M–E**

☖☖ **Sammy's** (dwntwn), 1400 W. 10th St. (523-5560). A/C. Lunch/dinner Mon.-Sat.; closed Sun., hols. AE, CB, DC, MC, V. J&T. Specialties: sautéed sweetbreads w. pecans and madeira, pork medallion w. red cabbage, grilled tuna w. cucumbers. The menu changes regularly. Remarkable desserts (particularly the boule de neige). Fine wine list. *Note:* In an old warehouse on the Cuyahoga River, this fashionable rest. offers elegant, inventive cuisine and modern décor of exposed brick and large bay windows w. a view of the river. The svce is exemplary, the ambience rather noisy, and the clientele hip. Resv. a must, given its success. Valet parking. *American-Continental.* **M**

☖☖ **Guarino's** (nr. dwntwn), 12309 Mayfield Rd. (231-3100). A/C. Lunch/dinner Mon.-Sat.; closed Sun., hols. AE, CB, DC, MC, V. Jkt. Specialties: fettuccine Alfredo, cannelloni, snails marinara, veal marsala, very good grilled fish. Good list of Italian wines. *Note:* Since 1918 this trattoria in the heart of Little Italy has been a local institution. A favorite of musicians and fans of the Cleveland Symphony Orchestra (Severance Hall is nearby), the rest. offers al fresco dining in the garden in summer. 10 min. from dwntwn. *Italian.* **I**

Pier W (nr. dwntwn), 127000 Lake Ave., Lakewood (228-2250). A/C. Lunch Mon.-Fri.; dinner nightly; brunch Sun.; closed hols. AE, CB, DC, MC, V. Jkt. Specialties: fish of the day, shellfish, bouillabaisse. *Note:* Contrary to the regrettable reputation of most Stouffer chain rests., this one offers irreproachably fresh food that is impeccably prepared and served. Agreeable nautical décor and an unobstructed view of Lake Erie and the Cleveland skyline. Resv. necessary. 15 min. from dwntwn. *Seafood.* **I**

Pearl of the Orient (nr. dwntwn), 20121 Van Aken Blvd., Shaker Heights (751-8181). A/C. Lunch Mon.-Fri.; dinner nightly. AE, CB, DC, MC, V. Specialties: mu shu pork, hot-and-sour soup, Peking duck, steamed fish, spicy Szechuan dishes. *Note:* Entirely authentic Chinese cuisine in a rather cold modern décor. Attentive svce. Locally popular. Resv. advised. 15 min. from dwntwn. *Chinese.* **I**

Earth by April (vic.), 2151 Lee Rd., Cleveland Heights (371-1438). A/C. Lunch/dinner daily (until midnight); brunch Sun.; closed hols. AE, CB, DC, MC, V. Specialties: shrimp de Jonghe, salmon w. hollandaise sauce, eggplant parmesan, tempura, vegetarian dishes. *Note:* Pleasant rest. serving modern American cuisine in an agreeable décor of woodwork and greenery and a relaxed atmosphere. Resv. advised. Locally popular. 20 min. from dwntwn. *American-Continental.* **B–I**

James Tavern (vic.), 28699 Chagrin Blvd., Woodmere Village (464-4660). A/C. Lunch/dinner daily; brunch Sun. AE, CB, DC, MC, V. Specialties: roast beef, roast pork Savannah, chicken parmesan, veal madeira, fish of the day. *Note:* Warm, pleasant atmosphere of an old colonial tavern w. large fireplaces and old furniture. The very reasonably priced food is more substantial than refined. Friendly, efficient svce. Locally popular. Resv. advised. 25 min. from dwntwn. *American.* **B–I**

Hofbrau Haus (nr. dwntwn), 1400 E. 55th St. (881-7773). A/C. Lunch Mon.-Fri.; dinner nightly. AE, DC, MC, V. Specialties: bratwurst, wienerschnitzel, pork hocks. Good wine list. *Note:* Experts say it's the best German rest. in all of Cleveland. Authentic Germanic cuisine and ambience in a fairly noisy atmosphere, w. dancing on the wknds. Offers buffet or à la carte dishes. Locally popular. Resv. advised. *German.* **B–I.**

Miller's Dining Room (nr. dwntwn), 16707 Detroit Ave., Lakewood (221-5811). A/C. Lunch/dinner daily (until 8 p.m.); closed Memorial Day, July 4, Labor Day. No credit cards. Specialties: chicken à la king, veal chop Créole, roast pork, braised leg of lamb, excellent homemade tarts and desserts. *Note:* The most authentic home-cooking in Cleveland at prices you won't believe. The décor is 1930s-retro, and the servers seem to be of that era as well. Generous portions and a relaxed atmosphere. A remarkable value. Regular clientele. An address to remember. 10 min. from dwntwn. **B**

Cafeterias / Fast Food

Corky & Lenny's (vic.), 13937 Cedar Rd., South Euclid (321-3310). Breakfast/lunch/dinner daily. No credit cards. Specialties: superb sandwiches, homemade soup, smoked fish, and salads. *Note:* There is no décor to speak of in this very popular, rather noisy local hangout. 20 min. from dwntwn. Other location: 27091 Chagrin Blvd. (U.S. 422) in Woodmere (464-3838). Open Tues.-Sun.

BARS & NIGHTCLUBS

Bistro Nightclub (dwntwn), in Bond Court (see "Accommodations," above) (771-7600). Open Tues.-Sat. Quite popular disco and a satisfactory rest.

Club Isabella (nr. dwntwn), 2025 Abington Rd. (229-1177). Open daily. Very popular singles bar/rest. a few steps from the university. The décor is a pleasing blend of art deco and contemporary styles. Excellent live jazz. Very decent cuisine. An "in" place.

Peabody's (vic.), 2140 S. Taylor Rd. (321-4072). Folk music and blues, 20 min. from dwntwn.

The Theatrical Grille (dwntwn), 711 Vincent Ave. (241-6166). Open Mon.-Sat. Singles bar, shows, live jazz, as well as an average rest.

NEARBY EXCURSIONS

CUYAHOGA VALLEY RAILROAD (departure from 6311 Granger, at the intersection of Ohio 17 and 21 in Independence, south of Cleveland): An amusing, pleasing trip in a little steam-engine train along the picturesque Cuyahoga Valley to **Hale Farm** (see below) and **Akron.** Runs wknds only, mid-June to mid-Oct. For information, call 216/468-0797.

HALE FARM & VILLAGE (in Bath, 24 mi., 38 km, south on I-77, Bath Rd. exit) (216/861-4573): Small, carefully restored pioneer town from the early 19th century offers pottery making and other period craft demonstrations. Well worth the trip. Open Tues.-Sun. May-Oct. and in Dec.

KELLEYS ISLAND (50 mi., 80 km, west on U.S. 6, then by ferry): This charming little vacation island on Lake Erie gets very crowded in summer. Fishing, sailing, camping, beaches, etc. Accessible by ferry from Sandusky (runs daily, Apr.-Nov.). Worth a visit. This makes a good joint excursion with Cedar Point (see "Theme Parks," above).

KIRTLAND (22 mi., 35 km, NE on I-90): Site of the oldest Mormon temple in the country (1842), Kirtland was the place where the westward-bound Mormons made their first stop (see the Salt Lake City chapter). Non-Mormons may not enter the temple, on Chillicothe Rd. in Kirtland Village. Worth a look.

CHAPTER 22

CINCINNATI

□ □ □

Following the Roman example, Cincinnati is built around the terraced slopes of seven hills, on the northern bank of the Ohio River where it borders Kentucky and Indiana. Founded in 1788 as Losantiville, it was renamed Cincinnati in 1790 by Gov. Arthur St. Clair in honor of the Order of Cincinnati, a brotherhood founded in 1783 by Revolutionary War army officers who admired the famous Roman hero Lucius Quinctius Cincinnatus.

An Indian way-station before the region was settled, Cincinnati became an important hub of rail, river, and road communication in the 19th century. Despite seven cholera epidemics in less than a century and many catastrophic floods and disastrous harvests, tens of thousands of German and Irish immigrants, as well as a host of notable visitors—Charles Dickens, Harriet Beecher Stowe, John Audubon, Henry Clay, and John Quincy Adams—have helped to make Cincinnati the third-largest city in Ohio and the "queen city of the West," in the words of the poet Longfellow.

The home of many large multinational corporations, including Procter & Gamble, the worldwide leader in toiletries and detergents, Cincinnati is today one of the most dynamic commercial and industrial urban centers in the Midwest. The friendliness of its inhabitants and their taste for good food, music, and the arts make it one of the five or six most pleasant U.S. cities in which to live, according to polls. Once described by Winston Churchill as the most beautiful city of the American heartland, Cincinnati boasts a symphony orchestra of acknowledged reputation and two well-respected universities, but few praiseworthy monuments. In contrast to many other midwestern cities, Cincinnati has made it a point of honor to preserve the original character of the downtown district and of the **Riverfront** area along the Ohio, investing many millions of dollars in architectural renovation and in the construction of a vast, enclosed pedestrian walkway network, the **Skywalk System,** which connects old buildings with new downtown skyscrapers.

On a more prosaic note, Cincinnati was known as "Porkopolis" and the "pork capital of the U.S.A." because of its important meatpacking industry. It now prefers to proclaim itself "the world capital of baseball," having produced the country's first professional baseball team, the Red Stockings, now the Reds. Food-lovers won't want to miss another local specialty, the famous five-way chili, pride of Cincinnati since 1922: spaghetti smothered in ground beef, onions, beans, and cheese.

Some native children of Cincinnati are William Howard Taft, the 27th president; actors Tyrone Power and Doris Day; and director/producer Steven Spielberg.

BASIC FACTS: State of Ohio. Area Code: 513. Time Zone: Eastern Time. ZIP Code: 45202. Settled: 1788. Approximate population: city, 390,000; metropolitan area, 1,690,000. 23rd-largest metropolitan area in the country.

CLIMATE: A raincoat and umbrella are *de rigueur* in any season in Cincinnati.

Winter is cold (around 32°F, 0°C, in Jan.) and damp; summer is hot and sticky (avg. July temperature: 76°F, 24°C). Spring and autumn are the least soggy seasons and the most pleasant for visitors.

DISTANCES: Chicago, 290 mi. (465 km); Cleveland, 247 mi. (395 km); Detroit, 259 mi. (415 km); Nashville, 269 mi. (430 km); Philadelphia, 565 mi. (905 km).

ARRIVAL & TRANSIT INFORMATION

AIRPORT: Greater Cincinnati International Airport (CVG): 13 mi. (21 km) SW. Information: 606/283-3151.

AIRLINES: American (621-6200), Continental (381-8020), Delta (721-7000), Northwest (621-3264), TWA (381-1600), United (721-3303), USAir (621-9220).

CITY LINK: Cab fare to city center, about $16-$18; time, around 25 min. Bus: Shortway Lines (606/283-3702); leaves about every 30 min.; serves principal dwntwn hotels; fare, $7; time, about 35 min. Because corporate offices are dispersed throughout the Cincinnati suburbs, business people may want to rent a car, but tourists can easily do without, because of the compact layout of the city itself. Good public transportation system (bus), Queen City Metro (621-4455).

CAR RENTAL (all at the airport): Avis (606/283-3764), Budget (606/283-3131), Dollar (606/283-3571), Hertz (606/283-3535), National (606/283-3655). For dwntwn locations, consult the phone directory.

LIMOUSINE SERVICES: Carey Limousine (531-7321), Dav El Limousine (toll free 800/922-0343).

TAXIS: Taxis may not be hailed on the street but can be gotten by waiting on line in front of the major hotels or can be summoned by phone: Yellow Cab (241-2100).

TRAIN: AMTRAK station, 1901 River Rd. (579-8506).

BUS: Greyhound, 1005 Gilbert Ave. (352-6000).

INFORMATION & TOURS

TOURIST INFORMATION: The **Cincinnati Convention & Visitors Bureau,** 300 W. 6th St., OH 45202 (513/621-2142).

For a **recorded announcement** with an up-to-date listing of cultural events and shows, call 513/421-4636.

GUIDED TOURS: B.B. Riverboats (boat), at the end of Greenup St., Covington, Ky. (across the river by suspension bridge) (606/261-8500): Ohio River cruises, May-Oct.

    Gray Line (bus), 122A W. 5th St. (513/241-8000): Guided tours of the city.

STERNWHEELER RIVER CRUISES: Three- and ten-day cruises along the Mississippi and Ohio Rivers on the *Delta Queen* or the *Mississippi Queen* paddle-steamers dating from the 1920s. Luxurious kitsch. (See the New Orleans chapter.)

SIGHTS, ATTRACTIONS, & ACTIVITIES

ARCHITECTURAL HIGHLIGHTS: ⚓ **City Hall,** 801 Plum St. at 8th St. (352-3000): Imposing Romanesque city hall in pink granite. Its large marble staircase, stained-glass windows, and ceiling decoration are worth a look. Open Mon.-Fri.

    ⚓ **Hamilton County Courthouse,** 1000 Main St. (632-8331): One of the largest law libraries in the country housed in a fine example of Ionic-style architecture. Open Mon.-Fri.

    ⚓ **Riverfront Stadium,** 201 E. Pete Roseway (352-6333): The local shrine for baseball and football fans (60,000 seats). Superb location on the Ohio River. Open Apr.-Jan.

    ☼⚓ **Union Terminal,** 1301 Western Ave. (421-5650): No longer in use, this splendid art deco train station by Roland Wank (1931) has some very lovely wall mosaics and a huge rotunda. Currently undergoing reconstruction, the terminal will house the Museum of Natural History and the Historical Society Museum beginning in 1990.

CHURCHES/SYNAGOGUES: ☼⚓ **Basilica of the Assumption,** Madison Ave. & 12th St., Covington, Ky. (606/431-2060): A kind of small-scale pastiche of Notre-Dame in Paris (or the nearby Cathedral of St. Denis), with flying buttresses and gargoyles in the purest French Gothic style. Dating from 1901, this basilica has one of the largest stained-glass windows in the world. On the other side of the Ohio River. Open daily.

    ☼⚓ **Isaac M. Wise Temple,** 8th & Plum Sts. (793-2556): Built in 1865, this synagogue, in startling Byzantine-Moorish style topped with two minarets, is named for the founder of the Hebrew Union College (see "Historic Buildings," below). Visits by appointment. Don't miss it.

    ☼⚓ **St. Peter in Chains Cathedral,** 8th & Plum Sts. (421-5354): Seat of the archdiocese of Cincinnati, this 1845 cathedral, renovated in the late 1950s, has interesting Greek Revival architecture and a portico supported by 12 Corinthian columns. Striking interior décor. An absolute must-see. Open daily.

HISTORIC BUILDINGS: ⚓ **Hebrew Union College,** 3101 Clifton Ave. (221-1875): The oldest rabbinical school in the country (1875). Historical library and an interesting museum of archeology and religious art. Open Sun.-Fri.

    ☼⚓ **Music Hall,** 1241 Elm St. (621-1919): One of the most famous concert halls in the country, renowned for its exceptional acoustics, it is home to the Cincinnati Symphony Orchestra and the May Festival. Rich interior decoration and very lovely Victorian architecture from 1878.

△ **Showboat *Majestic*,** Public Landing on the Ohio River at the foot of Broadway: The last floating theater in the country, this authentic showboat is a historic landmark. For information on current shows, call 475-4163, Apr.-Oct.

△ **Suspension Bridge,** joining Cincinnati and Covington, Ky., across the Ohio River: Designed by John Roebling, this work of art was, at the time of its construction (opened 1876), the longest suspension bridge in the world. It also served as the model for the famous Brooklyn Bridge in New York, opened 16 years later. Presents a pretty view of the Cincinnati skyline.

△ **William H. Taft National Historic Site,** 2038 Auburn Ave. (684-3262): Birthplace of the 27th president, this elegantly restored building dates from 1840. Open daily in summer, Mon.-Fri. the rest of the year.

MARKETS: △ **Findlay Market,** Race & Elder Sts.: Picturesque open-air market dating from 1852. A bastion of local gastronomy. Open Wed., Fri., Sat.

MONUMENTS: △ **Tyler Davidson Fountain,** Fountain Square: This bronze fountain was cast in Munich in 1871 and is now the city's emblem. Especially worth a look at night when it's illuminated.

MUSEUMS OF ART: ☀ △△ **Art Museum,** Art Museum Dr. in Eden Park (721-5204): Greek Revival building dating from 1887 housing very rich collections of European paintings, especially impressionists and abstract painters. Among the best-known works: El Greco's *Christ on the Cross,* Gainsborough's *Portrait of Mrs. Thicknesse,* Cézanne's *Blue Still Life,* Gris's *Violin and Score,* Sargent's *Italian Girl,* Matisse's *The Gray Hat,* and Chagall's *The Red Chicken.* Large collection of Persian and medieval art as well. An absolute must-see. Open Tues.-Sun.

△ **Contemporary Arts Center,** 115 E. 5th St. (721-0390): On the second floor of the **Mercantile Center Building** with its very lovely arcade, this wonderful museum offers temporary exhibitions and events dedicated to modern art in every form. Open Tues.-Sun.

△ **Taft Museum,** 316 Pike St. (241-0343): European masters (Turner, Goya, Rembrandt) and Chinese and Limoges porcelain in a beautiful Federal-style upper-class residence, dating from 1820, once owned by President Taft's half-brother. See it. Open daily.

MUSEUMS OF SCIENCE & HISTORY: △ **Hebrew Union College** (see "Historic Buildings," above).

☀ △△ **Museum of Natural History,** 1720 Gilbert Ave. (621-3889): Remarkable reproductions of Indian dwellings and an astonishing artificial cavern with waterfalls. Exhibits of local fauna and flora as well as a planetarium. One of the best natural history museums in the country. Don't miss it. Open Tues.-Sun. The museum will move to Union Terminal (see "Architectural Highlights," above) in 1990.

△ **Stowe House,** 2950 Gilbert Ave. (632-5120): Harriet Beecher Stowe, author of *Uncle Tom's Cabin,* lived here while she was doing the documentary research for her famous novel. Interesting exhibition of black American history. Open Tues.-Sun.

☀ △ **Vent Haven Museum,** 33 W. Maple Ave., Fort Mitchell, Ky. (606/341-0461): Marvelous museum entirely dedicated

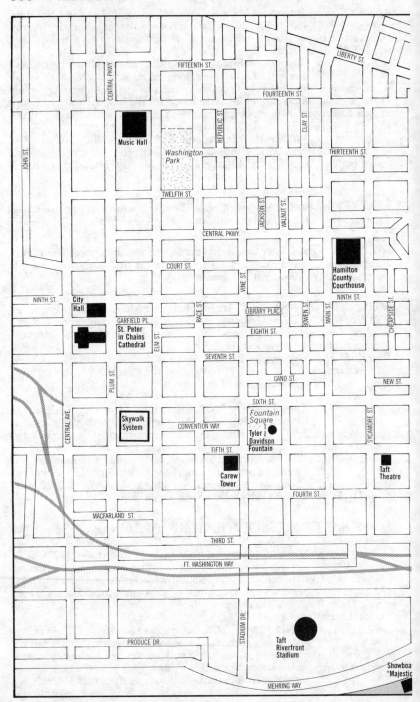

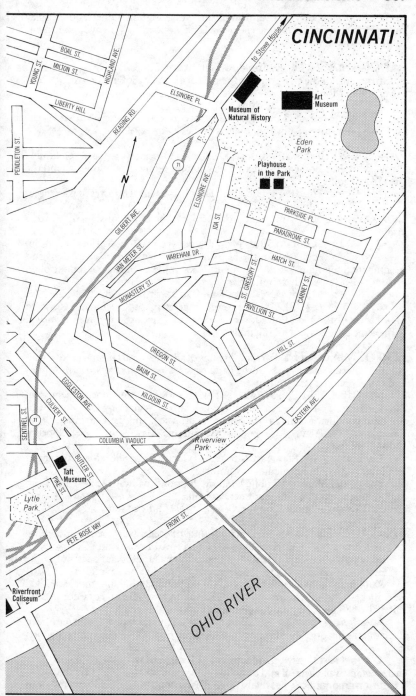

to the arts of puppetry and ventriloquism. Nearly 600 marionettes on display and a very rich specialized library. Unusual and wonderful. Visit by appointment Mon.-Fri. May-Sept.

PANORAMAS: ⚲ Carew Tower Observatory, 5th & Vine Sts. (381-3448):
Fine panorama of the city from the top of this 48-story (560-ft, 175-m) art deco tower. Open Mon.-Sat.

    ⚲ **Skywalk System,** around the Convention Center: Network of elevated enclosed walkways connecting major dwntwn hotels, buildings, and stores. Affords fine views of the skyline.

PARKS & GARDENS: ⚲ Ault Park, enter on Observatory Ave. or Columbia
Pkwy.: Very handsome park offering a panorama along the Ohio River and the city. Worth going out of your way for.

    ☼⚲ **Eden Park,** Eden Park Dr. (352-4086): 180 acres of park, floral exhibitions, and specialized botanic gardens (**Krohn Conservatory,** 352-4086) plus museums, overlooking the Ohio. Absolutely worth a visit.

    ⚲ **Fountain Square,** on 5th between Walnut & Vine Sts.: A bucolic oasis in the heart of the city with agreeable gardens and monumental fountain (see "Monuments," above). A popular spot for a stroll in good weather (especially at lunch hour).

    ⚲ **Mount Airy Forest and Arboretum,** 5080 Colerain Ave. (541-8176): The verdant getaway of Cincinnati. Close to 1,440 acres of forest and meadowland less than 9 mi. (15 km) from dwntwn, with picnic grounds and hiking trails.

PERFORMING ARTS: For daily listings of all shows and cultural events, con-
sult the entertainment pages of the daily papers *Cincinnati Enquirer* (morning) and *Cincinnati Post* (evening).

    Music Hall, 1241 Elm St. (621-1919): Home of the Cincinnati Opera, with director James de Blasis (Feb.-July); the Cincinnati Symphony Orchestra, with principal conductor Jesus Lopez Cobos (Sept.-May); and the Cincinnati Ballet Company (Sept.-May). Also houses the famous May Festival (see "Special Events," below).

    Playhouse in the Park, 962 Mt. Adams Circle (421-3888): Modern theater in winter and musical comedies in summer.

    Showboat *Majestic,* Public Landing, foot of Broadway (475-4163): Contemporary theater in spring, summer, and fall.

    Taft Theatre, 5th & Sycamore Sts. (721-0411): Road shows.

SPECIAL EVENTS: For the exact schedule of events below, consult the **Cin-
cinnati Convention & Visitors Bureau** (see "Tourist Information," above).

    May Festival (May): The oldest annual choral and operatic festival in the country (established 1873) features some of the world's finest soloists.

    Kool Jazz Festival (late July): One of the most famous and most attended jazz, rock, soul, and rhythm-and-blues festivals in the country. For information, call 321-6688. At Riverfront Stadium.

    Riverfest (Labor Day wknd): 48 hrs of festivities based on themes from Cincinnati's historical heritage. Spectacular fireworks, Ohio River cruises, sports events.

    Oktoberfest (last week of Sept.): The local version of the renowned Munich beer festival, cheerful and colorful.

    International Folk Festival (three days in mid-Nov.): Folk groups from more than 30 countries participate in this very lively festival dedicated to the food, arts, and crafts of different countries.

SPORTS: Cincinnati has two professional teams:
Baseball (Apr.-Oct.): Reds, Riverfront Stadium (421-4510).
Football (Sept.-Jan.): Bengals, Riverfront Stadium (621-3550).

STROLLS: ⚓ **Dayton Street,** between Baymiller & Linn Sts.: This was once known as "Millionaires' Street" because of its magnificent Italianate mansions built 1860–1890 by Cincinnati's richest families. One of these luxurious residences is now the **John Hauck House Museum,** 812 Dayton St. (721-3570), open to the public Tues., Thurs., Sun. Well worth the trip.

⚓ **Main Strasse,** 6th & Philadelphia Sts., Covington, Ky.: Dozens of different boutiques and stalls constitute this very lively shopping district, once inhabited exclusively by German immigrants. Overlooking it all is a pretty belfry 105 ft (33 m) high with a 43-bell carillon which plays at scheduled hours.

⚓ **Mount Adams,** Eden Park Dr.: The Greenwich Village or the Montmartre of Cincinnati, with narrow streets, museums, art galleries, boutiques, and numerous restaurants in a bohemian-chic setting. A visit not to be missed.

⚓ **Public Landing,** along the Ohio River at the end of Broadway: The exact point where Benjamin Stites, a Revolutionary War veteran, and 25 of his friends landed and founded Cincinnati on Dec. 28, 1788. Today it is the site for a nice stroll along the river's edge to view the large cruise ships moored on the Ohio. A lovely scene.

THEME PARKS: ⚓ **Kings Island,** 26 mi. (42 km) NE on I-71 at Kings Mills Rd., Kings Island (241-5600): Ultramodern amusement park on 1,600 acres. Some 40 attractions, giant roller coaster, mini-zoo, reconstructions of old villages, and a miniature Eiffel Tower. Open daily in summer, wknds only in spring and autumn. 25 min. from dwntwn.

Sports fans shouldn't miss the **Jack Nicklaus Sports Center** (241-5200), next door to Kings Island, with two superb golf courses and a 7,500-seat tennis stadium plus the ⚓ **College Football Hall of Fame** (398-5410), dedicated to great moments in college football. Films, exhibitions. Open daily in summer, wknds the rest of the year. A must for sports-lovers.

ZOOS: ⚓⚓ **Cincinnati Zoo,** 3400 Vine St. (281-4701): This famous zoo, the second-oldest zoo in the country, houses 800 animal species including a feline collection unmatched in the world: note particularly the white tigers and an impressive band of gorillas. Attracts a million visitors a year. An absolute must-see. Open daily.

ACCOMMODATIONS
See the listing of toll-free numbers in the Appendix.

Room Rates in Cincinnati	
B (Budget)	up to $30
I (Inexpensive)	$30–$60
M (Moderate)	$60–$90
E (Expensive)	$90–$140
VE (Very Expensive)	$140 and up

Personal Favorites (in order of preference)
Westin (dwntwn), Fountain Square, OH 45202 (513/621-7700; toll free, see Westin). 460 rms, A/C, cable color TV. AE, CB, DC, MC, V. Valet gar. $6, pool, health club, sauna, three rests. (including Delmonico's), two bars, 24-hr rm svce, night club, drugstore, boutiques, free crib. *Note:* The paragon of luxury hotels in Cincinnati. Ultramodern, comfortable 17-story building of rather cold concrete-and-glass design, but the rms are spacious and have mini-bars. Good svce and an excellent rest. In the heart of the business district, affording direct access to the Convention Center via the Skywalk. By far the best place to stay in town. No-smoking floors. **E–VE**

Cincinnatian Hotel (dwntwn), 601 Vine St., OH 45202 (513/381-3000; toll free, see Preferred). 149 rms, A/C, color TV, in-rm movies. AE, CB, DC, MC, V. Valet gar. $8, rest. (Palace), piano bar, 24-hr rm svce, concierge. *Note:* This Victorian palace w. a mansard roof is a historical landmark. Built in 1882, it reopened its doors in 1987 after a $23-million refurbishing that restored its old-world charm and former splendor. Spectacular eight-story atrium w. a large marble staircase. Exceptionally vast and comfortable rms w. period furniture and pastel walls, some w. private balconies overlooking the atrium. Impeccable, personalized svce and a first-rate rest. Another fine address in the heart of Cincinnati. **E–VE**

Hilton Terrace (dwntwn), 15 W. 6th St., OH 45202 (513/381-4000; toll free, see Hilton). 350 rms, A/C, color TV. AE, CB, DC, MC, V. Free valet parking, health club, two rests. (including Gourmet), bars, rm svce, entertainment, hrdrsr, drugstore, crib free. *Note:* Once the best hotel in Cincinnati, this elegant building was designed by Louis Skidmore. Business clientele. Impeccable comfort and very good svce. In the heart of dwntwn. **M–E**

Quality Inn Riverview (nr. dwntwn), 666 W. 5th St., Covington, KY. 41011 (606/491-1200; toll free, see Quality Inns). 236 rms, A/C, color TV, in-rm movies. AE, CB, DC, MC, V. Free parking, pool, tennis, revolving rest. on the top floor (Riverview Room), coffeeshop, bars, rm svce, night club, hrdrsr, drugstore, crib free. *Note:* Modern and comfortable round tower w. inviting, spacious rms. Offers a fine panorama of dwntwn Cincinnati from the other side of the Ohio (ask for a room with a river view). Business clientele. Very good value. A favorite of connoisseurs. Free Cincinnati and airport shuttles. **I–M**

Best Western Mariemont Inn (nr. dwntwn), 6880 Wooster Pike, OH 45277 (513/271-2100; toll free, see Best Western).

60 rms, A/C, cable color TV. AE, CB, DC, MC, V. Free parking, rest. National Exemplar), bar, rm svce, crib free. *Note:* Quaint little motel with English manor charm, a few steps from Ault Park. Inviting atmosphere, comfortable rms, and friendly, cheerful svce. Adequate rest. and a very good overall value. 15 min. from dwntwn on Columbia Pkwy. (U.S. 50E). An ideal spot for motorists. **I**

    Red Roof Inn (vic.), 11345 Chester Rd., Sharonville, OH 45246 (513/771-5141; toll free 800/848-7878). 109 rms, A/C, color TV. AE, MC, V. Free parking, adjacent coffeeshop, crib free. *Note:* Economical but well-kept motel which offers functional comfort and free coffee in the morning. 20 min. from dwntwn on I-75N (exit 15). **I**

Other Accommodations (from top bracket to budget)

    Hyatt Regency (dwntwn), 151 W. 5th St., OH 45202 (513/579-1234; toll free, see Hyatt). 485 rms, A/C, color TV, in-rm movies. AE, CB, DC, MC, V. Valet parking $10, pool, health club, two rests. (including Champs Restaurant), bar, rm svce, disco, boutiques, crib free. *Note:* Opened in 1984, this large, modern 22-story building has a spectacular, three-story lobby; its facilities and comfort are unparalleled. Vast, well-laid-out rms and ultraprofessional svce. VIP floor. Mediocre rests. Business and group clientele. Faces the Convention Center. Direct access to Skywalk. **E–VE**

    Omni Netherland Plaza (dwntwn), 35 W. 5th St., OH 45202 (513/421-9100; toll free, see Omni). 621 rms, A/C, color TV. AE, CB, DC, MC, V. Valet gar. $8, three rests. (including Orchids), bars, 24-hr rm svce, nightclub, hrdrsr, boutiques, concierge. *Note:* Lovely 1920s palace magnificently renovated to the tune of $25 million. The splendid art deco lobby is a historical landmark. Spacious, very comfortable rms and efficient, attentive svce. Very central location, steps away from the Convention Center. Excellent rest. Big business clientele. Direct access to the Skywalk. **E–VE**

    Clarion Cincinnati (formerly Stouffer's; dwntwn), 141 W. 6th St., OH 45202 (513/352-2100; toll free, see Clarion). 900 rms, A/C, color TV, in-rm movies. AE, CB, DC, MC, V. Parking $6, pool, health club, sauna, three rests., coffeeshop, bars, rm svce, disco, hrdrsr, boutiques, crib free. *Note:* Modern, functional hotel in two adjoining towers of 21 and 32 stories. Comfortable rms but rather mediocre svce and rests. Very centrally located. Group clientele (the hotel is directly across from the Convention Center). **M–E**

    Holiday Inn Downtown (nr. dwntwn), 800 W. 8th St., OH 45203 (513/241-8660; toll free, see Holiday Inns). 246 rms, A/C, color TV, in-rm movies. AE, CB, DC, MC, V. Free parking, pool, rest., bar, rm svce, disco, free airport shuttle, crib free. *Note:* Typical Holiday Inn, quite close to dwntwn. Functional, no-frills comfort w. impersonal reception and svce. **M**

    Vernon Manor (nr. dwntwn), 400 Oak St., OH 45219 (513/281-3300; toll free 800/543-3999). 160 rms, A/C, color TV. AE, CB, DC, MC, V. Valet gar., rest. (the Forum), coffeeshop, bar, rm svce, disco, hrdrsr, crib free. *Note:* An old Cincinnati classic tastefully renovated. Spacious rms with elegant décor and excellent svce. Regular clientele. 5 min. from dwntwn. **M**

Accommodations in the Vicinity

    Best Western Carrousel Inn (vic.), 8001 Reading Rd., OH 45237 (513/821-5110; toll free, see Best Western). 286 rms, A/C, cable color TV. AE, DC, MC, V. Free parking, three pools, health club, tennis, sauna, miniature golf, two rests. (including Brass Ring), bar, rm svce, nightclub, hrdrsr, boutiques, free crib. *Note:* Very comfortable country club–style motel on almost 15 acres of lovely gardens. Spacious rms w. private balconies or patios. Comprehensive recreational facilities, efficient svce, and a good rest. (Brass Ring). Group and convention clientele. Excellent value, 20 min. from dwntwn. **I–M**

Airport Accommodations

☼ 🍸🍸 **Cincinnati Drawbridge Motor Inn** (vic.), I-75 at Buttermilk Pike, Fort Mitchell, KY 41017 (606/341-2800; toll free 800/354-9794). 500 rms, A/C, cable color TV. AE, CB, DC, MC, V. Free parking, three pools, tennis, health club, sauna, two rests. (including Gatehouse Tavern), 24-hr coffeeshop, bar, rm svce, disco, hrdrsr, boutiques, crib free. *Note:* Vast motel with Tudor décor. Very appealing rms w. balconies, good recreational facilities, and agreeable reception and svce. Business clientele. Excellent value. Very adequate rest. (Gatehouse Tavern). Free airport shuttle. 8 min. from the airport; 10 min. from dwntwn. **I–M**

RESTAURANTS

Cincinnati Restaurant Prices	
(per person, excluding drinks and service charges)	
B (Budget)	up to $15
I (Inexpensive)	$15–$25
M (Moderate)	$25–$40
E (Expensive)	$40–$60
VE (Very Expensive)	$60 and up

Personal Favorites (in order of preference)

🍷🍷🍷🍷 **Maisonette** (dwntwn), 114 E. 6th St. (721-2260). A/C. Lunch Mon.-Fri.; dinner Mon.-Sat.; closed Sun., hols, and early July. AE, CB, DC, MC, V. J&T. Specialties: braised duck in beaujolais, sweetbreads w. paprika, sole stuffed w. scallops, salmon tartare w. caviar, rack of lamb w. morels, sautéed quails w. juniper berries, filet of brill in pastry shell. Very good soufflés and desserts. Long list of French and California wines. *Note:* One of the 12 best in the country. The svce is as polished as it is attentive; the rose-toned décor is luxurious without being ostentatious; and the classic cuisine is altogether remarkable. Resv. a must well in advance. Itself worth the trip to Cincinnati. Valet parking in the evening. A local institution for more than 30 years. *French.* **M–E**

🍷🍷🍷 **Pigall's** (dwntwn), 127 W. 4th St. (721-1345). A/C. Lunch Mon.-Fri.; dinner Mon.-Sat.; closed Sun., hols, and early Aug. AE, CB, DC, MC, V. J&T. Specialties: oysters Choron (in a tomato/béarnaise sauce), Dover sole w. basil, sweetbreads w. tarragon, duck w. green peppercorns, roast partridge périgourdine (sauce with truffles), soufflé Grand Marnier. A splendid wine list. *Note:* Another renowned Cincinnati table since 1956. Irreproachable French cuisine in the grand manner. Elegant décor w. crystal chandeliers and smoked mirrors. Svce somewhat unreliable. Resv. a must. *French.* **M**

🍷🍷 **Chester's Road House** (vic.), 9678 Montgomery Rd. (793-8700). A/C. Lunch Mon.-Sat.; dinner nightly; brunch Sun.;

closed Thanksgiving, Dec. 24 & 25, Jan. 1. AE, CB, DC, MC, V. Jkt. Specialties: rack of lamb, ribs of beef, trout meunière, liqueured cappuccino. Good wine list. *Note:* The bucolic, less refined version of the same owner's Maisonette. Simple but tasty cuisine in a pretty, rustic setting w. abundant greenery. A local favorite. An excellent locale. No resv. on Sat. 25 min. from dwntwn. *Continental-American.* **I**

☼🍷🦪🦪 **Lenhardt's** (nr. dwntwn), 151 W. McMillan (281-3600). A/C. Lunch/dinner Tues.-Sun.; closed Mon., first 15 days of Aug., Christmas hols. AE, CB, DC, MC, V. Specialties: wienerschnitzel, sauerbraten, jägerschnitzel, goulash, Viennese pastries. Fine list of German wines. *Note:* One of the best German rests. in all Ohio, in the former residence of a wealthy 19th-century brewer. Diligent svce. Resv. advised for evenings and wknds. A classic of its kind for more than 80 years. Very popular locally. *German.* **B–I**

Other Restaurants (from top bracket to budget)

🍷🍷🍷 **Delmonico's** (dwntwn), in the Westin (see "Accommodations," above) (621-7700). A/C. Dinner only, daily; closed Jan. 1. AE, CB, DC, MC, V. J&T. Specialties: wild boar paté, roast quail w. morels, Cajun-style scallops, wild game, meat and fish of the day. The menu changes regularly. Remarkable desserts (notably the soufflés). Fine wine list. *Note:* Elegant and refined grand-hotel rest. The French-inspired cuisine is a pleasing blend of "nouvelle" tendencies and traditional savoir-faire. Luxurious dining rm on two levels w. an enormous bay window and a lovely view of Fountain Square. The svce is exemplary in its diligence and attentiveness; the atmosphere is romantic. Resv. necessary one to several days in advance. *Continental.* **M–E**

🍷 **Charley's Crab** (vic.), 9769 Montgomery Rd. (891-7000). A/C. Dinner only, nightly; closed Jan. 1, Thanksgiving, Dec. 25. AE, CB, DC, MC, V. Jkt. Specialties: clam bake, paella, fish of the day, shellfish. *Note:* The best seafood rest. in Cincinnati, highly laudable despite often faltering svce. The marine décor is somewhat incongruous in this 1850s manor house. Resv. advised. Valet parking. 25 min. from dwntwn. *Seafood.* **I–M**

🍷🍷 **La Normandie** (dwntwn), 118 E. 6th St. (721-2761). A/C. Lunch Mon.-Fri.; dinner Mon.-Sat.; closed Sun., hols, and early July. AE, CB, DC, MC, V. Jkt. Specialties: steak, rack of lamb, fish of the day, seasonal game. *Note:* Pleasant bistro cuisine. Same owner as Maisonette and Chester's Road House—a guarantee of quality. Very British pub décor. Efficient svce. No resv., and waits at the bar are sometimes fairly long. *American-Continental.* **I**

🍷 **China Gourmet** (nr. dwntwn), 3340 Erie Ave., East Hyde Park Mall (871-6612). A/C. Lunch/dinner Mon.-Sat.; closed Sun., hols. AE, CB, DC, MC, V. Specialties: Chinatown shrimp, Cantonese lobster, Szechuan kung po, pike w. ginger. *Note:* Excellent Chinese cuisine—mostly Cantonese but Hunan and Szechuan dishes are served as well. Modern jungle-style Oriental décor. Friendly ambience. Locally popular. 15 min. from dwntwn. *Chinese.* **I**

🍷 **Cricket Tavern** (dwntwn), 6th & Vine Sts. (381-3000). A/C. Lunch Mon.-Sat.; dinner nightly. AE, CB, DC, MC, V. Specialties: fish bisque, poached salmon, steak. *Note:* Very good meat and fish at very reasonable prices. English pub ambience. A Cincinnati classic for half a century. Often packed at lunchtime despite its capacious premises. Business clientele. *American.* **I**

🍷 **Grammer's** (dwntwn), 1440 Walnut St. (721-6570). A/C. Lunch/dinner Mon.-Sat.; closed Sun., hols. AE, CB, DC,

MC, V. Specialties: sauerbraten, wienerschnitzel, fleisch teller (assorted meats), strudel, Black Forest cake. *Note:* Recently restored to its old splendor, this bastion of German cuisine is more than a century old and offers solid meals for big appetites. The svce, unfortunately, does not approach the stature of the setting or the cuisine. Open until 1 a.m. on Fri. and Sat. Resv. advised on wknds. An excellent value. *German-American.* **I**

☀☿ **Mike Fink's Riverboat Restaurant** (nr. dwntwn), at the end of Greenup St. on the Ohio River, Covington, Ky. (606/261-4212). A/C. Lunch/dinner daily (until midnight); closed Dec. 25. AE, CB, DC, MC, V. Specialties: fried catfish, Créole shrimp, Natchez-style halibut, fish of the day. *Note:* Very popular seafood rest. in an old riverboat from the good ol' days. Fine, authentic cuisine and a pleasant ambience. Lovely view of Cincinnati from the other side of the river. Resv. advised. *Seafood.* **I**

Restaurants in the Vicinity

☀☿☿ **Golden Lamb** (vic.), 27 S. Broadway, Lebanon (932-5065). A/C. Lunch/dinner daily; brunch Sun.; closed Dec. 25. AE, CB, DC, MC, V. Jkt. Specialties: braised leg of lamb, duck à l'orange, roast turkey, filet of pork w. sage, Shaker sugar pie. Average wine list. *Note:* This charming inn, once a stagecoach rest stop, dates from 1803 and has played host to ten presidents and countless celebrities. The cuisine is as simple and flavorful as the day it opened. Lovely antique décor. Pleasant ambience and svce. Well worth the 50-min. car ride from Cincinnati. Resv. advised. *American.* **B–I**

Cafeterias/Specialty Spots

Camp Washington Chili Inc. (nr. dwntwn), Colerain Ave. and Hopple St. (541-0061). Open 24 hrs a day Mon.-Sat. No credit cards. Purists consider this the best of the countless chili places in Cincinnati. Formica décor but friendly reception and svce.

Skyline Chili (dwntwn), 643 Vine St. (241-2020). Breakfast Mon.-Sat.; lunch/dinner daily (until midnight). No credit cards. A must for all visitors. Chili—as the name indicates—is the big house specialty, and it is served in many variations. More than 40 other branches in Cincinnati and the suburbs (consult the phone directory).

BARS & NIGHTCLUBS

The Blind Lemon (dwntwn), 936 Hatch St. (241-3885). Open nightly. Intimate and much-frequented singles bar w. live music nightly. One of the best spots in Mt. Adams, the heart of Cincinnati nightlife.

Conservatory (nr. dwntwn), 640 W. 3rd St., Covington, Ky. (on the other side of the river) (606/491-6400). Open Mon.-Sat. Jkt. A fashionable disco with a sophisticated ambience. A fair rest. as well.

Panorama Lounge (dwntwn), in the Hilton Terrace (see "Accommodations," above), 20th floor (381-4000). Elegant, comfortable piano bar.

The Precinct (nr. dwntwn), 311 Delta Ave. (321-5454). Open daily. A very popular rest./bar/disco in a former police station. Youthful, relaxed ambience. Very decent rest. ten min. from dwntwn.

Rookwood Pottery (nr. dwntwn), 1077 Celestial St. (721-5456). Open daily. This pleasant bar/disco in an old pottery factory at the top of Mt. Adams is very popular with the locals. Also an average rest.

NEARBY EXCURSIONS

🏛 **DAYTON** (60 mi., 80 km, NE on I-75): See the aviation museum at the **Wright-Patterson Air Force Base,** on Ohio 444

(513/255-3284), the largest museum of military aviation in the world: 160 machines on display, from the Wright Brothers' glider to the huge B-52 bomber and space rockets. An absolute must-see. Open daily. The graves of Orville and Wilbur Wright are in neighboring **Woodland Cemetery,** Woodland Ave.

FORT ANCIENT STATE MEMORIAL (36 mi., 58 km, NE on I-71 and Ohio 350E) (513/932-4421): Surprising fortified city constructed between 400 B.C. and A.D. 600 by Hopewell Indians (a tribe of the Mound Builder culture who lived at the beginning of our era in Ohio and Wisconsin and about whom historians know almost nothing). The still-visible earthen walls rise to 22 ft (7 m) in some places. Many burial mounds and other relics. Interesting archeological museum. Definitely worth the trip. Open Wed.-Sun. Apr.-Oct.

KENTUCKY HORSE PARK: (in Lexington, 72 mi., 115 km, south on I-75 & Iron Works Pike) (606/233-4303): In the heart of Bluegrass Land and its famous stud farms, this 960-acre equestrian museum attracts hundreds of thousands of visitors devoted to the cult of the thoroughbred. Visits to the stable (more than 600 stalls) and training field. Museum dedicated to horse-racing greats. Seasonal parade of stallions and a number of races, Apr.-Oct. A must for all admirers of "man's most noble conquest." Open daily Apr.-Sept., Wed.-Sun. the rest of the year.

MOUND CITY GROUP NATIONAL MONUMENT (in Chillicothe, 95 mi., 152 km, NE on U.S. 50E and Ohio 104N): 23 burial grounds of the Hopewell Indians (500 B.C. to A.D. 600). The densest concentration of prehistoric monuments of this kind in the country. Exhibition of religious relics. Worth the trip. Open daily.

Not far from here is the ▲ **Sugarloaf Mountain Amphitheater** (enter on U.S. 23N and Ohio 159), offering an interesting theatrical presentation of the heroic life and the death of Tecumseh, leader of the Shawnee tribe and last Indian warrior leader to resist the advance of the "palefaces" east of the Mississippi (1813). Open Mon.-Sat. until 8:30 p.m. mid-May to early Sept. For information, call 614/775-4100.

SERPENT MOUND STATE MEMORIAL (75 mi., 120 km, east on Ohio 32E, 41N, and 73W) (513/587-2796): Indian totem 1,302 ft (407 m) long in the form of a stylized serpent, made of stone and yellow clay between 800 B.C. and A.D. 1400. The largest mound of this type in the U.S. If the grass were clipped around the monument, this unusual work would look even more impressive. Well worth going out of your way for, nevertheless. Open Wed.-Sun. Apr.-Oct. A good joint excursion with Mound City Group National Monument (see above) and with ▲ **Fort Hill State Memorial** (15 mi., 24 km, NE of Serpent Mound State Memorial on Ohio 73S and 41N), former fortified camp of the Hopewell people built at the top of a hill. Museum of archeological finds. Open Wed.-Sun. Apr.-Oct.

SHARON WOODS VILLAGE (14 mi., 22 km, NE on U.S. 42) (563-9484): A very realistic portrayal of small-town life in Ohio in the mid–19th century. The authentic old houses were transported to Sharon Woods from their original locations. An absolute must-see. Open Wed.-Sun. May-Nov.

CHAPTER 23

CHICAGO ♛♛

□ □ □

An immense metropolis, with suburbs extending more than 62 miles (100 km) along the southwest bank of Lake Michigan, Chicago was the second-largest city in the U.S. until 1984, when it was ousted by Los Angeles. Two French explorers helped found Chicago, a name deriving from the Native American word "Checagou" (wild onion), a plant which once grew abundantly on the banks of the Chicago River. The Jesuit Fr. Jacques Marquette and the trapper Louis Jolliet were the first white men to visit the site, in 1673. Jean Baptiste Point du Sable, a black businessman from Santo Domingo, in 1796 created the first fur-trading post on the banks of Lake Michigan, a Native American name meaning "Great Lake." (This founding father is himself a symbol of the ethnic mix that has given the city its uniquely cosmopolitan character: his father was a Frenchman from Québec, his mother was a black slave from Santo Domingo, and Jean Baptiste Point du Sable married a Potawatomi Indian.) In 1803 a military encampment named Fort Dearborn was built at the mouth of the Checagou River. Its garrison was massacred by Indians nine years later and the fort was abandoned until 1816. With the mass settlement of homesteaders from the east around 1833, this cross-roads city between the Great Lakes and the plains of the Midwest entered a period of prodigious economic growth. Even the virtual destruction of the city by fire in 1871, when it had 300,000 inhabitants, could not check its burgeoning vigor. In 1900 its population had risen to 1.7 million and surpassed 3.5 million in 1960. Though its numbers have since fallen to just over 3,000,000 inhabitants, the third American city after New York and Los Angeles remains the capital of the American heartland.

A city of drive and superlatives—"the city that works," according to its late mayor, Richard J. Daley—Chicago claims the busiest airport in the world (**O'Hare International Airport**, with close to 55 million passengers per year), the largest railroad station, the largest inland port, the tallest skyscraper in the world (the **Sears Tower**, 110 stories and 1,454 feet (443 m), 90 feet (30 m) higher than New York's World Trade Center), the tallest church (the Chicago Temple, 568 feet, 173 m), the largest water-treatment plant in the world, the world's largest commercial building (**Merchandise Mart**), the world's most important grain exchange, and the largest convention center in the world (**McCormick Place**) among other outstanding civic achievements.

Chicago is the world capital of grain, chewing gum, agricultural machinery, mail order, frivolous magazines (the *Playboy* empire started here), electrical equipment, meat packing, the telephone, and the hamburger (the first McDonald's opened in 1955 in Des Plaines, near O'Hare Airport, and today enjoys the status of a relic). The second financial and industrial center of the U.S. after New York, Chicago also prides itself on possessing the world's first skyscraper (1884), the **Manhattan Building,** designed by William Le Baron Jenney. Of the ten tallest buildings in the world today, four are in Chicago.

The merest glance at Chicago's impressive skyline will disclose a greater wealth of architectural theory and practice than you are likely to find in any other

U.S. city. By the end of the last century, architects of the famous "Chicago School" (such as William Le Baron Jenney, Daniel Burnham, Dankmar Adler, and Louis Sullivan) had realized some of the masterpieces that anticipated by 20 –30 years the birth of art deco in Europe: The **Burnham's** with its 16 stories, at the time the tallest office building in the world; the **Auditorium Building;** the **Carson, Pirie, Scott & Co.** and **Marshall Field** department stores; and **The Rookery,** the world's oldest steel-frame skyscraper (1886), just to cite a few. Frank Lloyd Wright, Sullivan's favorite pupil and the greatest American architect of all time, created in the 1890s his revolutionary "Prairie Style" for individual houses, with low, uncluttered lines married harmoniously to the surrounding foliage and gardens. In the suburb of **Oak Park** you can admire a series of such houses, which, though constructed 90 years ago, still appear remarkably modern. With Wright's example to follow, a succession of architects both American (Root, Holabird and Roche, Raymond Hood, James Gamble Rogers) and foreign (the Germans Ludwig Mies van der Rohe and Walter Gropius, one-time members of the Bauhaus, and Finland's Eero Saarinen) has over the past century made Chicago into a shining light of urban architecture. Witness such classic structures as the **Chicago Tribune Tower,** the **Wrigley Building,** and especially Mies van der Rohe's **Lake Shore Drive Apartment Towers,** where in 1948 the "curtain wall" technique was first used in the United States. There is also Skidmore, Owings and Merrill's superb **John Hancock Center** (affectionately nicknamed "Big John" by Chicagoans) and Helmut Jahn's audacious **State of Illinois Center,** opened in 1986.

Many of us know Chicago as the brutal, opportunistic city seen in classic screen portrayals of the St. Valentine's Day Massacre, Al Capone, Dillinger, and Prohibition. The reality is far more complex: this city is home to one of the most extraordinary ethnic mixtures on the planet. Poles (Chicago is the largest Polish city in the world after Warsaw), Greeks, Italians, Slavs, blacks, Chinese, Mexicans, Irish, Swedes, Puerto Ricans, and Germans all have their neighborhoods, their lifestyles, their folklore, their museums, and their cuisine (the city has more than 6,000 restaurants of all kinds). Almost a third of current Chicagoans were born outside the United States, and a remarkable racial mix (48% white, 43% black, 7% Hispanic, 2% Asian) has enhanced the Homeric political contests that have become traditional at municipal elections.

A sprawling city full of contrasts—the chic galleries and stores of the **Magnificent Mile;** the black areas of the **South Side, Cabrini Green,** and **Bronzeville;** the frenetic activity of the **Loop,** the financial district constrained within the clangorous tracks of the Elevated; the luxury homes along **North Lake Shore Drive,** the chic restaurants and boutiques of **Printer's Row** and **River North**— Chicago has some of the most fascinating museums, public gardens (574 in all), and urban landscapes in America. Its seven universities include the **University of Illinois, Loyola** (Catholic), and the **University of Chicago,** where in 1942 Enrico Fermi achieved the world's first controlled atomic chain reaction. These plus the nuclear research center, **Argonne National Laboratory** in Darien, are among the most prestigious breeding-grounds for American Nobel Prize winners (53 to date). Chicago is the birthplace of Walt Disney, Jason Robards, Kim Novak, John Dos Passos, Edgar Rice Burroughs (the creator of Tarzan), and Ernest Hemingway (born, as was Burroughs, in the suburb of Oak Park), and is today one of the three great American art capitals (with New York and Los Angeles), offering a wealth of opportunity to lovers of theater, opera, jazz, and other cultural events. The **Chicago Symphony Orchestra,** long directed by the legendary Fritz Reiner, is considered by experts one of the two or three best instrumental ensembles in the world. A jazz capital since the 1920s and undisputed bastion of the blues, Chicago has also given birth to talents as varied as Benny Goodman, Gene

Krupa, Mezz Mezzrow, Bud Freeman, Jo Jones, Lennie Tristano, Muggsy Spanier, and Herbie Hancock. Finally, you may be surprised to learn that, according to the FBI, Chicago's crime rate is 12th among American cities.

BASIC FACTS: State of Illinois. Area code: 312. Time Zone: Central Time. ZIP Code: 60607. Settled: 1803. Approximate population: city, 3,000,000; metropolitan area: 8,100,000. Third-largest American city.

CLIMATE: The climate is very rigorous, with glacial winters (sometimes −22°F, −30°C) and lots of snow; spring and autumn are brief. Chicago owes its "Windy City" nickname to the terrible blizzards that blow in from northern Canada across the flat expanse of the Great Lakes. Summer, sometimes quite hot (avg. temperature 78°F, 26°C) but always breezy, is by far the best season to visit Chicago.

DISTANCES: Detroit, 268 mi. (430 km); Indianapolis, 181 mi. (290 km); Milwaukee, 87 mi. (139 km); Minneapolis, 406 mi. (650 km); New York, 806 mi. (1,290 km); St. Louis, 290 mi. (465 km); Washington, 668 mi. (1,070 km).

ARRIVAL & TRANSIT INFORMATION

AIRPORTS: Two major airports: **Midway Airport** (MDW), 11 mi. (17 km) SW, with aging facilities. Information:838-0001.

O'Hare International Airport (ORD), 18 mi. (29 km) NW, the busiest airport in the world (close to 55 million passengers per year), with a takeoff or landing every 20 seconds and served by 50 airlines. Information: 686-2200.

DOMESTIC AIRLINES: American (372-8000), Braniff (toll free 800/272-6433), Continental (686-6500), Delta (346-5300), Eastern (467-2900), Midway (767-3400), Pan Am (toll free 800/221-1111), TWA (558-7000), United (569-3000), USAir (726-1201).

FOREIGN CARRIERS: Air Canada (527-3900), Air France (782-6181), British Airways (786-1340), Iceland Air (toll free 800/223-5500), KLM (861-9300), Lufthansa (686-5800), Sabena (toll free 800/645-3790), Swiss Air (641-8830).

CITY LINK: Cab fare to city center **from O'Hare,** about $24–$28; time, about 45 min. Bus: Continental Air Transport (454-7800); leaves every 20 min.; stops at the major downtown hotels; time, about 50 min.; fare, $9.

Cab fare to city center **from Midway,** about $12–$14; time, about 20 min. Bus: Continental Air Transport (454-7800); leaves every 30 min.; time, about 35 min.; fare, $7.

Between high cab fares and O'Hare's distance from downtown, renting a car may be advisable if you're planning a prolonged stay. Chicago has a very efficient public transportation system (subway and bus), including notably an express subway connection between the Loop and O'Hare (CTA). Fare, $1; time, about 35 min. (call 836-7000 for information). CTA station is located under Terminal 4.

CAR RENTAL (all at O'Hare International Airport): Avis (694-5600), Budget

(686-4950), Dollar (671-5100), Hertz (686-7272), National (694-4640). For downtown agencies, consult the local telephone book.

LIMOUSINE SERVICES: Carey Limousines (663-1220), Dav El Limousines (toll free 800/922-0343), Lake Shore Limousine (334-2343).

TAXIS: Cabs may be hailed on the street, gotten in waiting lines at the entrances to the major hotels, or summoned by phone. The major cab companies are: American United (248-7600), Flash Cab (561-1444), and Yellow Cab (829-4222). Fares tend to be high.

TRAIN: AMTRAK, Union Station, 210 S. Canal St. (207-6550); ticket office, 500 N. Michigan Ave. (558-1075).

BUS: Greyhound, Clark & W. Randolph Sts. (781-2900).

INFORMATION & TOURS

TOURIST INFORMATION: Convention and Tourism Bureau, McCormick Place-on-the-Lake, IL 60616 (312/225-5000). Open Mon.-Fri.

Information Bureau (with multilingual hostesses), Water Tower, Chicago & Michigan Aves. (312/280-5740). Open daily.

Illinois Travel Information Center, 310 S. Michigan Ave. (312/793-2094). Open Mon.-Fri. Tourist information on the state of Illinois.

Recorded telephone announcement giving an up-to-date listing of cultural events and shows (312/225-2323).

GUIDED TOURS: Archi Center, 330 S. Dearborn St. (312/782-1776). Wonderful walking and bus tours around the major architectural achievements of Chicago and its suburbs. Also, photo exhibits, lectures, a well-stocked library, etc. Open daily.

American Sightseeing (bus), 530 S. Michigan Ave. (427-3100). Guided tour of the city. Serves major hotels.

CTA Culture Bus (bus), Art Institute, Michigan Ave. & Adams St. Stops at Chicago's major monuments and museums. You may get on and off as many times as you please. Sunday and holidays April-Sept. For information, call 836-7000.

Gray Line Tours (bus), 33 E. Monroe St. (346-9506). Guided tours of the city.

Mercury Sightseeing Boats, Wacker Dr. & Michigan Ave. (332-1353). Lake and Chicago River rides May-Sept.

Oak Park Tour Center (walking tours), 158 N. Forest Ave. & Lake St., Oak Park (312/848-1978). Guided tours of this residential area, cradle of the "Prairie House" style created by Frank Lloyd Wright. Visitors center open daily Mar.-Nov.

SIGHTS, ATTRACTIONS, & ACTIVITIES

ARCHITECTURAL HIGHLIGHTS: ♧ **Board of Trade,** 141 W. Jackson Blvd. (435-3626): The most important commodity exchange in the world, a huge building with 44 stories (588 ft, 184 m, high) crowned by a giant statue of

Ceres, goddess of the harvest. Visitors area is on the fifth floor. A sight not to be missed. Open Mon.-Fri.

City Hall, 121 N. La Salle St. (744-5000): Chicago's city hall and county administration building. Imposing neoclassical structure which dates from 1910. Admission by invitation only, Mon.-Fri. See it.

Federal Center, Adams & Dearborn Sts.: Courthouse with two Mies van der Rohe towers, 387 and 560 ft (121 and 175 m) high, it also houses various federal agencies. Imposing Calder sculpture in front of the south tower. Worth a glance.

Illinois Institute of Technology, 3300 S. Federal St. (567-3025): Technical university (6,000 students) whose campus, remarkable for the purity and simplicity of its lines, was designed by Mies van der Rohe (see especially Crown Hall). Campus tours on Saturday, Sept.-May: Perlstein Hall, 10 W. 33rd St. For architecture buffs.

Merchandise Mart, Wells & Kinzie Sts.: The largest commercial building in the world, it was erected in 1928 and has more than 900 furniture showrooms. An astonishing sight to see. Guided tours Tues. & Thurs. Reserv. 661-1443.

Richard J. Daley Center, Richard Daley Plaza: Elegant, modern skyscraper in bronze and steel tones (648 ft, 198 m, 31 stories) named for the former mayor of Chicago, it houses the city's administrative services. Be sure to see this building with its giant abstract sculptures by Picasso (48 ft, 15 m, tall) and Miró (34 ft, 11 m, tall) on the main esplanade.

State of Illinois Center, W. Randolph & La Salle Sts.: Be sure to see this, the most surprising and innovative building in all Chicago. A "hi-tech" masterpiece, this hemispherical tower of blue and pink tinted glass is built around a gigantic windowed atrium 17 stories tall. This building by Helmut Jahn houses administrative offices of the State of Illinois. Unusual fiberglass sculpture by Jean Dubuffet, *Monument with Standing Animal,* in front of the building.

United States Post Office, 433 W. Van Buren St. (765-3009): The largest post office in the world, it handles more than 40 million letters and 500,000 parcels each day. Interesting tours Mon.-Fri., Jan.-Nov.; you must make resv. several days in advance.

University of Chicago, 5801 S. Ellis Ave. (962-8374): Founded in 1890 by John D. Rockefeller, it is one of the most respected of American universities (8,000 students). There are a number of interesting buildings here by Frank Lloyd Wright, Mies van der Rohe, and Eero Saarinen among others. On **Stagg Field** (S. Ellis Ave. between E. 56th and E. 57th Sts.) a bronze composition by British sculptor Henry Moore marks the exact spot where on Dec. 2, 1942, history's first controlled nuclear chain reaction was set off by a team of researchers under the direction of Enrico Fermi, Italian Nobel Prize winner for physics. Not far from there is the **Oriental Institute** (1155 E. 58th St.) offering very rich collections of Assyrian and Egyptian art (open Tue.-Sun.), and the neo-Gothic **Rockefeller Memorial Chapel** (1156 E. 59th St.) with its 72-bell carillon (1910). Guided tour of the campus Mon.-Fri. at 10 a.m. Worth the trip.

University of Illinois, Circle Campus, Dan Ryan & Eisenhower Expwys. (996-5000): The most modern university in the United States (1965). Note the futurist architecture, especially the administration building with its 28 stories which get larger toward the top. On the campus is **Hull House** (800 Halsted), pioneering center for social work founded in 1889 by Jane Addams, Nobel Peace Prize winner. Interesting tours Mon.-Fri. (and Sun. in summer).

Water Tower Place, 835 N. Michigan Ave. (440-3165): The most luxurious and spectacular shopping center in the United States (see "Shopping," below). The **Water Tower** in the form of a medieval fortress is one of the few buildings spared by the great fire of 1871. It houses the local tourism office. A must-see.

Skyscrapers

Chicago Tribune Tower, 435 N. Michigan Ave. (222-3993): Raymond Hood's amazing octagonal neo-Gothic skyscraper, 36 stories high, dating from 1925. Home of the *Chicago Tribune*, the city's largest newspaper. Tours Mon.-Sat.; resv. necessary.

First National City Bank Building, 1 First National Plaza at Monroe & Dearborn Sts.: Built in 1969 by architects Murphy, Perkins and Will, it is the tallest bank in the world (60 stories) and should be seen.

John Hancock Center, 875 N. Michigan Ave. (751-3681): Superb derrick-shaped skyscraper with a façade of smoked glass and black and bronze aluminum, 1,097 ft/100 stories (343 m) high. The fifth-tallest skyscraper in the world, this work by Skidmore, Owings and Merrill is topped with two gigantic telecommunication antennas 336 ft tall. Since its construction in 1969, it has become the symbol of Chicago. The observation platform on the 96th floor should not be missed (see "Panoramas," below).

Marina City, 300 N. State St.: The twin 60-story cylindrical towers by architect Bertrand Goldberg date from 1964. The first floors constitute a parking garage with a spiral ramp. These, the most famous (and most photographed) apartment buildings in the United States dominate the Chicago River. Private marina. Should be seen.

Sears Tower, 233 S. Wacker Dr. (875-9696): The tallest skyscraper in the world, 1,454 ft (443 m) and 110 stories. 17,000 employees work in this huge, vertical ant's nest serviced by 102 elevators. Designed by the same team of architects that did the John Hancock Center, it is the property of Sears Roebuck & Co. Opened in 1974, its construction lasted four years. The installation of two TV antennas brought the tower to a total height of 1,753 ft (548 m). The lobby has a giant Calder mobile called *Universe*. (For more details, see "Panoramas," below.) Not to be missed.

Amoco Building, 200 E. Randolph Dr.: The second-tallest skyscraper in Chicago and the fourth tallest in the world, 1,107 ft/80 stories (346 m) high. Dating from 1973, its façade is completely covered in marble. No guided tours. Interesting Harry Bertoia "sonic" sculpture on the ornamental pool in front of the tower (see "Outdoor Art & Plazas," below).

Wrigley Building, 400 N. Michigan Ave.: One of the most famous monuments in Chicago and the headquarters of the Wrigley's chewing gum empire, this architecturally startling 35-story skyscraper (complete with Renaissance campanile) dates from 1924. The four huge clocks at the top of the tower are each two stories tall. Beautifully illuminated in the evening. A definite must-see.

BEACHES: ⚓ **North Ave. Beach** and ⚓ **Oak St. Beach** are the most popular Chicago beaches, just north of the city. The pollution level of Lake Michigan stays relatively low thanks to seven giant water-purification plants.

CHURCHES/SYNAGOGUES: ⚓ Chicago Temple, also known as the First

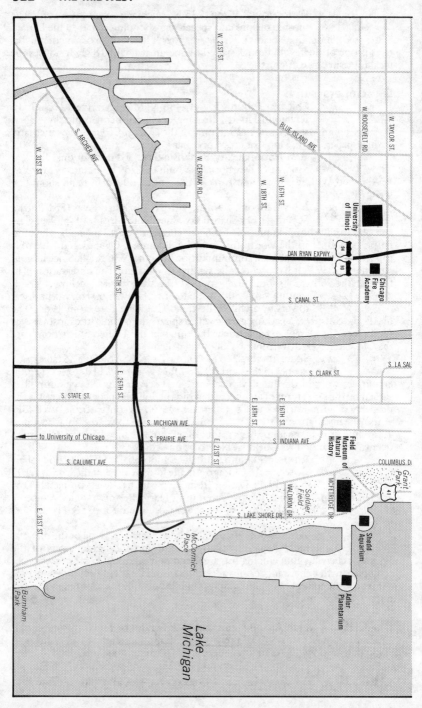

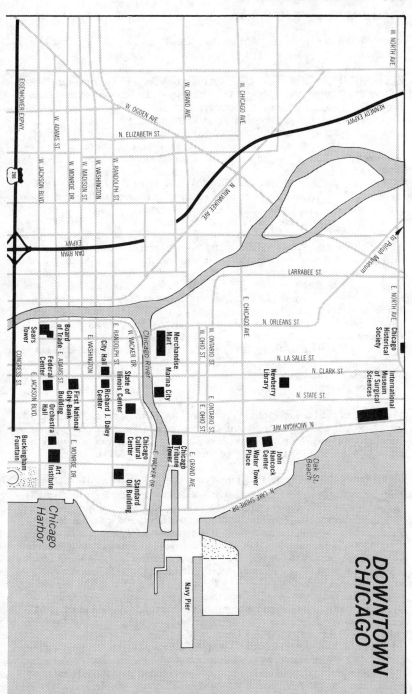

DOWNTOWN CHICAGO

Methodist Church, 77 W. Washington St. (236-4548): Built in 1924, the tallest church in the world—568 ft (173 m) including the cross on top of the Gothic tower—offers the interesting "Open-Air Chapel" on its roof. Worth a look. Open daily.

HISTORIC BUILDINGS: ☀☖ Auditorium Building, 430 S. Michigan Ave.:

Built in 1887-89 by Louis Sullivan and Dankmar Adler, it is one of the master-pieces of the Chicago School. Extraordinary interior décor. Both concert hall and headquarters of **Roosevelt University** (6,500 students). A must-see.

    ☀☖ **Manhattan Building,** 431 S. Dearborn St.: The first real sky-scraper in history (1884) though a mere eight stories, this William Le Baron Jenney building anticipated modern construction techniques. Worth a look.

    ☖ **Monadnock Building,** W. 53 Jackson Blvd. (922-1890): When completed in 1893, this was the tallest office skyscraper in the world; designed by Burnham and Root. For art history lovers.

    ☖ **Orchestra Hall,** 220 S. Michigan Ave. (435-8174): Dating from 1904, this acoustically perfect auditorium is home to the renowned Chicago Symphony Orchestra, whose current music director is Sir Georg Solti. The building figures on the national inventory of historic land-marks. Tours by appointment in advance. See it.

    ☀☖ **Robie House,** 5757 S. Woodlawn Ave. (962-8374): On the University of Chicago campus (see above), this brick building dating from 1909 is the forerunner of Frank Lloyd Wright's "Prairie House" style. Today it is home to the Institute of International Affairs. Open Mon.-Sat. A definite must-see.

    ☖ **The Rookery,** 209 S. La Salle St.: The oldest steel-frame sky-scraper in the world (1886); by Burnham and Root. The white-and-gold hall of this historic landmark was redesigned by Frank Lloyd Wright at the turn of the century. Worth a look.

MONUMENTS: ☖ Buckingham Fountain, Grant Park at the end of Congress

St.: A colossal public fountain in pink Georgia marble, with a jet rising to more than 131 ft (41 m) Dramatic illuminations and enchanting water shows in the evenings, May-Sept. Worth a look. (See also "Outdoor Art & Plazas," below.)

MUSEUMS OF ART: ☀☖☖☖ Art Institute, Michigan Ave. & Adams St. (443-

3500): Elegant Italian Renaissance-style palazzo, constructed for the World's Fair of 1893 and splendidly renovated. More than a thousand paintings by Euro-pean and American masters, from Rembrandt to Matisse and from Ben Shahn to Mark Rothko. Among the most famous: Caravaggio's *Resurrection,* El Greco's *Assumption of the Virgin,* Delacroix's *Lion Hunt,* Seurat's *Sunday Afternoon on the Isle of Grande-Jatte,* Van Gogh's *Vincent's Room in Arles,* Picasso's *The Old Gui-tarist,* Juan Gris's *Cubist Portrait of Picasso,* and Grant Wood's *American Gothic.* Also, wonderful stained glass by Chagall, and fine collections of Chinese sculp-ture and pre-Columbian art. Plays host to many prestigious traveling exhibitions. One of the most beautiful art museums in the United States and in the world, with a pleasant cafeteria and open-air restaurant in summer. The Art Institute alone is worth the trip to Chicago. Open daily.

    ☀☖☖ **Chicago Cultural Center,** 78 E. Washington St. (269-2922): In the former **Public Library,** this sumptuous, Renaissance-style building from the end of the 19th century houses distinguished temporary exhibitions. The interior is richly adorned with Carrara marble, mosaics, and Tiffany-style windows. Should be seen. Open Mon.-Sat.

Du Sable Museum of African-American History, 740 E. 56th Pl. (947-0600): Very rich, interesting collections of African and Afro-American art. Symbolically bears the name of a founder of Chicago, a black businessman from Santo Domingo (see the introduction to this chapter). Open Sun.-Fri.

Museum of Contemporary Art, 237 E. Ontario St. (280-2660): A truly marvelous little museum founded in 1967 housing modern and avant-garde art in all forms: painting, sculpture, poetry, film, music, dance, video, photography. Temporary exhibitions. Open Tues.-Sun. Not to be missed.

Newberry Library, W. 60 Walton St. (943-9090): Dating from 1887 and boasting more than 1.4 million volumes as well as several million manuscripts, this library is famous for its works on the Renaissance, Native Americans, and music history. Open Tues.-Sat.

Terra Museum of American Art, Erie St. at N. Michigan Ave. (664-3939): Rather small in size but big in content, the Terra Museum, which opened in 1987, is the newest museum of American art in the United States. A strange blend of modern architectural idioms (large bay windows, white marble from Vermont) adapted to older structures. 800 major works of classical and contemporary American artists: Bingham, Cassatt, Demuth, Homer, Hopper, Morse, Peale, Prendergast, Sargent, Sheeler, Whistler, Wyeth, etc. A must for all art-lovers. Right in the middle of the Magnificent Mile.

MUSEUMS OF SCIENCE & HISTORY: ☀ ⚖ Academy of Sciences, 2001 N. Clark St. (549-0606): Museum wholly devoted to the natural history and ecology of the Great Lakes region, notably a reconstruction of a 350-million-year-old forest with wildlife displays, as well as a "walk-through" cave and canyon. A definite must-see. Open daily.

Adler Planetarium, 1300 S. Lake Shore Dr. (322-0304): This world-renowned institution covers the history of astronomy from the ancients to our time. Space shows and telescope observation in summer. Exhibits on space explorations. (Voyager and Apollo II flights). Fine art deco architecture. Not to be missed. Open daily.

Chicago Fire Academy, 558 W. De Koven St. (744-6691): The famous fire-brigade school built on the site of Patrick O'Leary's stable, where legend puts the origin of the fire that totally ravaged Chicago on Oct. 8, 1871, and left more than 90,000 people homeless. Tours of the training center, Mon.-Fri. Resv. necessary. See it.

Chicago Historical Society, Clark St. at North Ave. (642-4600): A wonderful museum dedicated to American history —the Civil War and the life of Abraham Lincoln in particular—as well as to the evolution of Chicago from its founding to the present. Temporary exhibitions, demonstrations of old trades. Not to be missed. Open daily.

Field Museum of Natural History, Roosevelt Rd. at Lake Shore Dr. (922-9410): One of largest museums of natural history and ethnology in the world, with 200,000 exhibits ranging from reproductions of plants around the world to Egyptian tombs and meteorites. Section devoted to the history of Native Americans not to be missed. Open daily. A definite must-see.

International Museum of Surgical Sciences, 1524 N. Lake Shore Dr. (642-3555): This interesting museum of surgery from prehistoric times to the present includes displays of ancient instruments and of an apothecary's shop from the 19th century. Open Tue.-Sun.

☀ 🔱🔱🔱 **Museum of Science and Industry,** 57th St. & Lake Shore Dr. (684-1414): Science and industry from cave-dwelling days to the present, including a 15-ft- (5-m-) tall working model of a human heart. Authentic German U-boat from World War II. Old locomotives, cars, planes by the dozen, plus a re-creation of a working coal mine and an entirely mechanized midwestern farm. There are a number of robots which can be operated by visitors, plus a wing devoted to space research (**Crown Space Center**) with a 360° film-projection system, OMNIMAX. Three million visitors per year. The handsomest museum in Chicago. Open daily and not to be missed.

🔱 **Polish Museum,** 984 N. Milwaukee Ave. (384-3352): The second-largest Polish city in the world after Warsaw by right should and does have a museum devoted to Poland, its art, its culture, its folklore —and the Polish contribution to American history (among others, Gen. Tadeusz Kosciuszko, hero of the Revolutionary War, and the musician and statesman Ignace Jan Paderewski). Open daily.

🔱🔱 **Shedd Aquarium,** 1200 S. Lake Shore Dr. (939-2438): The largest aquarium in the world—more than 6,000 fish and marine animals from the dolphin to the piranha—with its own artificial coral reef. The 460,000 gallons of seawater required for the tanks is hauled by truck and rail from the Atlantic. Since 1929 this has been a must-see for every visitor. Open daily.

🔱 **Spertus Museum of Judaica,** 618 S. Michigan Ave. (922-9012): Rich collection of Jewish manuscripts, craft tools, and religious objects. Paintings, sculptures, temporary exhibitions. Open Tues.-Fri. and Sun.

NIGHTLIFE: 🔱 **Rush St.,** between Chicago Ave. and Division St.: The mecca of Chicago nightowls, full of bars, nightclubs, discos, jazz clubs. Guaranteed atmosphere. (Chicago has some of the most active nightlife of any city in the United States.)

OUTDOOR ART & PLAZAS: In addition to the previously mentioned giant sculptures by Picasso, Miró, and Dubuffet (see "Architectural Highlights," above), Chicago's streets and plazas offer numerous noteworthy works of art: a 3,000-sq.-ft (280-km²) Chagall mosaic, *The Four Seasons* (First National Plaza); *Batcolumn,* a kind of giant steel baseball bat 100 ft (31 m) tall by Claes Oldenburg (600 W. Madison); a 53-ft- (16-m-) high Calder sculpture, *Flamingo,* which weighs 50 tons (Federal Center Plaza); a giant bronze sundial by Henry Moore in front of the entrance to the Adler Planetarium (1300 S. Lake Shore Dr.); and a startling "sonic" sculpture by Harry Bertoia that sits above an ornamental pool in front of the Amoco Building (200 E. Randolph Dr.).

PANORAMAS: ☀ 🔱🔱 **John Hancock Center,** 875 N. Michigan Ave. (751-3681): At 1,097 ft (343 m), the fifth-tallest skyscraper in the world. The observation platform located on the 96th floor offers a unique, impressive view of the city and lake in clear weather. Platform open daily, 9 a.m.-midnight.

🔱 **Navy Pier,** at the end of E. Grand Ave.: This mile-long jetty extending into Lake Michigan dates from the beginning of the century and was once a berth for ocean-going vessels. It is a great place for strolling with its public benches, lawns, and turn-of-the-century gas lamps. Its unobstructed view of the Chicago skyline is not to be missed.

☀ 🔱🔱 **Sears Tower,** 233 S. Wacker Dr. (875-9696): The tallest skyscraper in the world at 1,454 ft (443 m) and equipped with the fastest elevator in the world (1,753 ft, 548 m per min.), it is the head office of

Sears Roebuck & Co. Its asymmetrical cubist structure was designed to offer maximum structural resistance to Chicago's windy weather. Observation platform on the 103rd floor open daily from 9 a.m. to midnight. In clear weather, you can see for 37 mi. (60 km). What a sight! Lovely giant Calder mobile, *Universe,* in the lobby. Not to be missed.

PARKS & GARDENS:

Garfield Park, 300 N. Central Park Blvd.: Splendid tropical greenhouses (the largest in the world) with palm trees, luxurious vegetation, 400 kinds of cactus, ornamental lakes, and water lilies. Beautiful floral exhibitions. Quite spectacular. Open daily.

Graceland Cemetery, 4001 N. Clark St.: A lovely landscaped cemetery among hills and ornamental ponds. Sumptuous mausoleums housing the mortal remains of rich Chicago families, bankers, industrial magnates, as well as famous architects Louis Sullivan and Daniel Burnham, the founders of the Chicago School. It also offers an unimpeded view of Lake Michigan and the city. Open daily.

Grant Park, along Lake Michigan between E. Randolph Dr. and McCormick Pl.: An enormous public park in the middle of the city with numerous museums and a fine view of the lake and the skyscrapers. See it.

Lincoln Park, along Lake Shore Dr. between La Salle Dr. and Hollywood Ave.: A sprawling park and lovely botanical garden extending close to five mi. along the shore of Lake Michigan, it is home to the famous zoo (one of the oldest in the United States) plus public beaches and marinas. A nice perspective on the city from a distance. During the tense days of the anti–Vietnam War demonstrations in 1968, it was the meeting spot of the "Yippies" (Youth International Party). Worth the walk.

(Just off Lincoln Park, in a garage that once stood at 2122 N. Clark St., the famous Saint Valentine's Day Massacre occurred on Feb. 14, 1929: seven gangsters were gunned down on the orders of Al Capone. He died in Miami in 1947, after spending eight years in Alcatraz. He is buried in lot 48 of Chicago's Mount Olivet Cemetery.)

PERFORMING ARTS:

For a listing of all shows and cultural events, consult the entertainment pages of the daily papers, the *Chicago Sun Times* (morning) and the *Chicago Tribune* (morning), of the weekly *The Reader,* and the monthly magazine *Chicago.* Or call 225-2323 for a recorded announcement of current cultural offerings. **Hot Tix,** a booth at State St. and Madison (977-1755), sells half price tickets for all shows on the day of the performance.

Apollo Theater Center, 2540 N. Lincoln Ave. (935-6100): Drama, comedy.

Arie Crown, McCormick Pl. (791-6000): Modern theater.

Auditorium Theatre, 70 E. Congress Pkwy. (922-2110): Concerts, recitals, ballet performances. Open year round.

Blackstone Theatre, 60 E. Balbo Ave. (977-1700): Broadway hits.

Body Politic Theatre, 2261 N. Lincoln Ave. (871-3000): Contemporary theater.

Chicago Theatre, 175 N. State St. (236-4300): Big-name concerts, Broadway hits.

Civic Opera House, 20 N. Wacker Dr. (372-7800): Home of the Chicago Opera Theatre and of the Lyric Opera of Chicago. Open Feb.-June.

Goodman Theatre, 200 S. Columbus Dr. (443-3800): The oldest theater in Chicago, offering everything from Shakespeare to contemporary theater.

Orchestra Hall, 220 S. Michigan Ave. (435-8111): Home of the Chicago

Civic Orchestra and of the Chicago Symphony Orchestra, one of the five best orchestras in the world (music director, Sir Georg Solti). Open Sept.-May.

Petrillo Music Shell, Columbus Dr. and Jackson Blvd., in Grant Park: Free outdoor concerts, late June to Aug.

Shubert Theatre, 22 W. Monroe St. (977-1700): Broadway hits and shows with big-name stars.

Steppenwolf Theatre, 2851 N. Halsted St. (472-4141): Drama, classical theater. One of the best theater buildings of the Chicago School.

Studebaker Theatre, 418 S. Michigan Ave. (435-0700): Modern theater.

Victory Gardens Theatre, 2257 N. Lincoln Ave. (549-5788): Specializing in plays by local playwrights.

SHOPPING: ※ **Marshall Field & Co.,** 111 N. State St.: The most beautiful and most famous department store in Chicago. This almost 100-year-old classic of the consumer society has a superb Tiffany-windowed dome comprising 1.6 million pieces of colored glass. Wonderful ice-cream sundaes for lovers of giant desserts can be found on the third floor (in the Crystal Palace). A must-see.

※ **Carson, Pirie, Scott & Co.,** 91 S. State St.: Another venerable representative of the local breed of department stores and a sample of Chicago School architecture from the end of the 19th century, designed by Louis Sullivan. Splendid rococo entrance hall of ornamental cast metal. See it.

State St., between Wacker Dr. and Congress Pkwy.: The main pedestrian and commercial street at the heart of the Loop. Boutiques and department stores by the dozen offer many a bargain.

※ **Water Tower Place,** 835 N. Michigan Ave.: The country's first "vertical" shopping center covering 2,140,000 square feet (200,000 sq. m.), with more than 125 stores, boutiques, 11 rests., and seven movie theaters. The shopping area is on the first eight floors of this 74-story tower which houses the Ritz Carlton Hotel. Luxurious, very stylish interior with fountains, gardens, and glass elevators.

SPECIAL EVENTS: For the exact schedule of events below, consult the **Chicago Convention & Tourism Bureau** (see "Tourist Information," above).

Chicago Auto Show (late Feb.): the most popular auto show in the United States.

St. Patrick's Day Parade (Mar. 17): pompoms, marching bands, and drum majorettes.

Ravinia Festival (June-Sept.): one of the most popular music festivals in the United States, with open-air symphonic concerts, ballet, jazz, and folk music. Highland Park.

Grant Park Concerts (late June to Aug.): free open-air classical concerts, plus a very famous blues festival.

Taste of Chicago (July/Aug., date varies): The world's largest culinary festival: 3,000,000 participants. All kinds of food are available for a whole week in Grant Park.

Chicago Sailboat Race (July): boat races on Lake Michigan.

Venetian Night Festival (mid-Aug.): shows and concerts on the lakeshore.

Jazz Festival (Sept.): with the greats.

SPORTS: Chicago has five professional teams:

Baseball (Apr.-Oct.): Cubs, Wrigley Field (281-5050); White Sox, Comiskey Park (924-1000).

Basketball (Oct. to late Apr.): Bulls, Chicago Stadium (943-5800).

Football (Sept.-Dec.): Bears, Soldier Field/Grant Park (663-5408).

Ice Hockey (Sept.-Apr.): Black Hawks, Chicago Stadium (733-5300).

Horse Racing

The racetracks are all in the suburbs: **Balmoral Park,** Dixie Hwy. & Elmscourt Lane, in Crete (312/568-5700); **Hawthorne Park,** 3501 S. Laramie Ave., Cicero (312/652-9400); **Maywood Park,** 8600 W. North Ave., Maywood (312/343-4800), racing daily; **Sportsman's Park,** 3301 S. Laramie Ave., Cicero (312/242-1121), racing Mar.-Dec.

STROLLS: ☖ **Chinatown,** around S. Wentworth Ave. and Cermak Rd.: Picturesque Chinese quarter with numerous characteristic stalls, rests., and guaranteed local color. See especially **City Hall,** the Buddhist temple, and the **Ling Long Museum.**

⛱☖☖ **Gold Coast,** Lake Shore Dr. between North Ave. and E. Ontario St.: The spectacular, luxurious face that Chicago presents to Lake Michigan, where skyscrapers abut opulent 19th-century palaces and estates.

☖ **Halsted St.,** around 2000 N. Halsted St.: Chicago's latest "in" neighborhood replete with trendy rests., galleries, and boutiques. Home of hip in Chicago.

⛱☖☖ **The Loop,** west of Michigan Ave. around State and Madison Sts.: Chicago's business district, complete with department stores, hotels, and rests., surrounded by the famous, clanking elevated train (the **"El"**). The heart of the Loop—the intersection of State and Madison Sts.—is nicknamed "the busiest corner in the world." City streets are oriented from this intersection: north-south in relation to Madison, east-west in relation to State. Animated and colorful by day, to be avoided at night if you're on foot. Absolutely worth a look.

⛱☖☖ **Magnificent Mile,** N. Michigan Ave. from the Chicago River to E. Oak St.: Lined with chic stores, hotels, boutiques, art galleries, and prestigious buildings, it is one of the most elegant—and snooty—thoroughfares in the United States. Go out of your way to see it.

☖ **Old Town,** around N. Wells and Division Sts.: The "Latin Quarter" or the "Greenwich Village" of Chicago, with its brick houses from the 19th century plus restaurants, nightclubs, antique stores, and fashionable boutiques. Very lively by night.

⛱☖☖ **Prairie Ave. Historic District,** Prairie Ave. around 18th and Cullerton Sts.: The 19th-century millionaire's neighborhood, currently undergoing renovation. Sumptuous private houses, cobblestone streets, gas lamps. Many old buildings should be seen: **Glessner House,** 1800 S. Prairie Ave., by Henry Hobson Richardson (1886), today houses the Chicago Architecture Foundation which organizes guided tours (Tue.-Sun.) of Chicago's architectural masterpieces; **Kimball House,** 1801 S. Prairie Ave., dates from 1890; **Coleman House,** 1811 S. Prairie Ave., from 1886; **Keith House,** 1900 S. Prairie Ave., from 1871. Neighboring **Clark House** is the oldest house in Chicago (1837). Not to be missed.

THEME PARKS: ☖ **Six Flags Great America,** in Gurnee, 40 miles (65 km.) north on I-94 (312/249-1776): Enormous (200 acres, 80 ha.) amusement park offering hundreds of attractions, with a giant roller-coaster. Facsimiles of pioneer villages plus shows and special events. Open daily in the summer; wknds only in spring and autumn; closed the rest of the year.

WINTER SPORTS RESORTS: ☖ **Holiday Park Ski Area** (42 mi., 68 km, NW on U.S. 12) (312/546-8222): Five ski lifts. Open Dec.-Mar.

    ⚑ **Pines Ski Area** (64 miles, 102 km. SE on I-90 and Ind. 49) (219/462-4179): Three lifts. Open Dec.-Mar.

    ⚑ **Ski Valley** (66 miles, 106 km. SE on I-90, U.S. 421, and Ind. 2) (219/326-0123): Six lifts. Open Dec.-Mar.

    ⚑ **Wilmont Ski Area** (54 miles, 87 km. NW on U.S. 12, Ill. 59 and 83, and WI Country C) (414/862-2301): Seven lifts. Open Nov.-Mar.

ZOOS: ☀ ♨ **Brookfield Zoo,** entrances at 31st St. and First Ave., 15 mi., (24 km) SW on W. Cermak Rd., and 22nd St. and First Ave. (485-0263): One of the largest and most modern zoos in the United States (192 acres, 80 ha.). Natural habitats from the Sahara Desert to tropical forests and from South America to the Pacific Islands. Mini-train tour (Mar.-Nov.). Definitely worth going out of your way to see. Open daily, year round.

ACCOMMODATIONS
See the listing of toll-free numbers in the Appendix.

Room Rates in Chicago	
B (Budget)	up to $30
I (Inexpensive)	$30–$60
M (Moderate)	$60–$90
E (Expensive)	$90–$140
VE (Very Expensive)	$140 and up

Note: Despite its 50,000 available rooms, and an ambitious hotel construction program going back to 1979, Chicago and the metropolitan area suffer from a chronic shortage of hotel space. It is advisable, therefore, to make reservations as far in advance as possible.

Personal Favorites (in order of preference)
    ♛♛♛♛♛ **The Drake** (nr. dwntwn), 140 E. Walton Pl., IL 60611 (312/787-2200; toll free 800/223-1146). 535 rms, A/C, color TV, in-rm movies. AE, CB, DC, MC, V. Valet gar. ($18), three rests. (including the Cape Cod Room), 24-hr coffeeshop, two bars, rm svce until midnight, hrdrsr, boutiques, drugstore, concierge, free crib. *Note:* A flawless palace in the shadow of the John Hancock Center. Here, all is tranquility, luxury, and pleasure. Spacious rooms (the best have a view of the lake) and an elegant, refined interior with an imposing marble lobby, grand staircase, and ultra-fashionable tea room. The pleasing svce and reception includes attention to such details as turning the mattress every evening. Its class and style make this the best hotel in Chicago and one of the 12 best in the United States; its Cape Cod Room is also one of the city's finest rests. A business clientele and traveling VIPs enjoy its exceptional location, facing Lake Michigan and a few steps from the Magnificent Mile (see "Strolls," above). One of the gems of the Hilton International group. Interesting wknd packages. The Drake recently celebrated its 66th anniversary and underwent renovation down to the last detail. **VE**

𝔏𝔏𝔏𝔏𝔏 **Ritz Carlton** (nr. dwntwn), 160 E. Pearson St., IL 60611 (312/266-1000; toll free, see Four Seasons). 431 rms, A/C, cable color TV, AE, CB, DC, MC, V. Valet parking, pool, health club, sauna, two rests. (including the Ritz Carlton Dining Room), coffeeshop, bar, 24-hr rm svce, live entertainment/dancing, hrdrsr, boutiques, giftshop, concierge, free crib. *Note:* An astonishingly successful venture which unites the modern conveniences of a 74-story skyscraper (the hotel occupies 20 floors) with a palace in the great European tradition. Elegant and luxurious, with huge and well-laid-out rooms that include mini-bars. A stylish, personalized reception is part of a very high-class whole. The ambitions of its high-priced rest. outstrip its performance. The very good location, quite close to the chic stores on the Magnificent Mile, make it a favorite of the Jet Set. The best rm svce and one of the 12 best hotels in the United States. No-smoking floors. Dominates the Water Tower Place Mall. **VE**

𝔏𝔏𝔏 **Mayfair Regent** (formerly the Lake Shore Drive Hotel; nr. dwntwn), 181 E. Lake Shore Dr., IL 60611 (312/787-8500; toll free 800/545-4000). 204 rms, A/C, color TV. AE, CB, DC, MC, V. Valet gar. ($7), two rests. (including Ciel Bleu), coffeeshop, bar, 24-hr rm svce, hrdrsr, concierge, free crib. *Note:* Venerable but now entirely renovated palace from the turn of the century, whose slightly dated décor houses smart comfort in the European tradition. Spacious rooms with mini-bars and marble bathrooms. Attentive svce which anticipates your wants. Fine rests., plus a much-frequented tea room. Beautiful view of the lake and the city. Part of the Hong Kong "Regent" chain of hotels. Interesting weekend packages. **VE**

𝔏𝔏𝔏 **Park Hyatt** (nr. dwntwn), on Water Tower Sq. at 800 Michigan Ave., IL 60611 (312/280-2222; toll free, see Hyatt). 255 rms, A/C, color TV, in-rm movies, AE, CB, DC, MC, V. Valet gar. ($15), pool, sauna, two rests. (La Tour is one), bar, 24-hr rm svce. *Note:* This extremely exclusive hotel—the most expensive in Chicago with one suite priced at $2,000 a night—accommodates neither groups nor conventions. It offers luxurious, elegant rooms with mini-bars, exemplary svce, a decent rest., and a pleasant tea room. A favorite hotel of big business. Interesting weekend packages. Faces the Water Tower in the midst of the Magnificent Mile. **VE**

☀︎𝔏𝔏 **Raphael** (nr. dwntwn), 201 E. Delaware Pl., IL 60611 (312/943-5000; toll free 800/821-5343). 175 rms, A/C, color TV, in-rm movies. AE, CB, DC, MC, V. Valet gar. ($18), rest., bar, 24-hr rm svce, free crib. *Note:* Small, calm, elegant hotel very close to the Magnificent Mile. Large, comfortable rms with mini-bars offer lovely views of the Gold Coast. Polished svce. A favorite of connoisseurs. **E**

𝔏𝔏 **Days Inn Lake Shore Drive** (nr. dwntwn), 644 N. Lake Shore Dr., IL 60611 (312/943-9200; toll free, see Days Inns). 580 rms, A/C, color TV, in-rm movies. AE, CB, DC, MC, V. Gar. ($6), pool, rest., coffeeshop, bar, rm svce, free crib. *Note:* The biggest attraction of this modern 33-story tower is its location directly on the shore of Lake Michigan, affording a splendid view of the lake and the city. A good idea if you're driving, because of the reduced-rate parking. Revolving rest. at the top. Less-than-ideal svce. Favored by rather obtrusive groups. A good overall value. **M–E**

𝔏𝔏 **Best Western Inn of Chicago** (formerly the St. Clair Hotel; nr. dwntwn), 162 E. Ohio St., IL 60611 (312/787-3100; toll free, see Best Western). 357 rms, A/C, color TV, in-rm movies. AE, CB, DC, MC, V. Gar. ($7), rest., 24-hr coffeeshop, bar, rm svce. *Note:* Old luxury hotel entirely modernized with marble lobby and very comfortable rms. Good svce and a very central location close to the Magnificent Mile. A favorite of business people. Interesting wknd packages. **M–E**

℞ **Comfort Inn** (nr. dwntwn), 601 W. Diversey Pkwy., IL 60614 (312/348-2810; toll free 800/228-5150). 73 rms, A/C, color TV. AE, CB, DC, MC, V. *Note:* Street parking. Neither bar nor rest., but free breakfast. Small, modern, and comfortable motel very nr. the Lincoln Park Zoo with spacious rms and friendly, pleasant reception. Good value. **I–M**

Other Accommodations (from top bracket to budget)

℞℞℞ **Tremont** (nr. dwntwn), 100 E. Chestnut, IL 60611 (312/751-1900; toll free 800/621-8133). 140 rms, A/C, cable color TV. AE, CB, DC, MC, V. Valet gar. ($18), health club, rest. (Cricket's), coffeeshop, bar, 24-hr rm svce, nightclub, concierge, free crib. *Note:* A hotel known for its excellence for more than half a century. Period furnishings and chandeliers; spacious, comfortable rms. Very British in style; notably good svce. The highly praised rest. is a facsimile of New York's 21 Club. Clientele of well-heeled regulars. **VE**

℞℞℞ **Westin Hotel** (formerly the Continental Plaza; nr. dwntwn), 909 N. Michigan Ave., IL 60611 (312/943-7200; toll free, see Westin). 747 rms, A/C, color TV, in-rm movies. AE, CB, DC, MC, V. Valet gar. ($18), pool, sauna, health club, two rests. (including The Consort), two bars, 24-hr rm svce, disco, hrdrsr, drugstore, free crib. *Note:* Modern, comfortable grand hotel, though architecturally undistinguished. Large, well-equipped rms and diligent svce. A favorite of politicians and movie stars, with a VIP floor. Very good location in the midst of the Magnificent Mile. No-smoking rms. Completely renovated décor. **VE**

℞℞℞ **Chicago Hilton & Towers** (dwntwn), 720 S. Michigan Ave., IL 60605 (312/922-4400; toll free, see Hilton). 1,610 rms, A/C, color TV, in-rm movies. AE, CB, DC, MC, V. Gar. ($8), pool, health club, sauna, three rests. (including Buckingham's), 24-hr coffeeshop, three bars, 24-hr rm svce, disco, hrdrsr, boutiques, business center, free crib. *Note:* Sturdy pioneer of the production-line hotel, restored to all its original splendor at a cost of $180 million. Heavy, forbidding architecture but a luxurious interior, especially the great lobby with its imposing staircase and the Versailles-style ballroom. Spacious, comfortable rms, the most pleasant of which have a view of Grant Park. Slightly overburdened svce. Convention and other groups. Three VIP floors and the most expensive suite in Chicago, at $4,000 a night. Good rest. with modern American cuisine (Buckingham's). Fine location next to the Loop. **E–VE**

℞℞℞ **Hyatt Regency** (nr. dwntwn), 151 E. Wacker Dr., IL 60601 (312/565-1234; toll free, see Hyatt). 2,031 rms, A/C, color TV, in-rm movies. AE, CB, DC, MC, V. V. Gar. ($12), health club, sauna, four rests. (Truffles is one), 24-hr coffeeshop, four bars, 24-hr rm svce, nightclub, hrdrsr, boutiques, drugstore, free crib. *Note:* Luxurious and comfortable rms in two adjoining towers of modern design. The spectacular atrium with pool and interior gardens on four floors is worth a look. Efficient, if impersonal, svce. One of the best locations in Chicago, on the Chicago River. Business clientele. The deluxe rest., Truffles, is highly overrated. Two floors, 35 and 36, reserved for VIPs. Interesting wknd packages. Recently renovated décor. **E–VE**

℞℞ **Omni Ambassador East** (nr. dwntwn), 1301 N. State Pkwy., IL 60610 (312/787-7200; toll free, see Omni). 274 rms, A/C, color TV. AE, CB, DC, MC, V. Gar. ($14), rest. (The Pump Room), coffeeshop, bar, 24-hr rm svce, disco, hrdrsr, drugstore, boutiques, free crib, free shuttle to and from the Loop. *Note:* Old-world charm, elegance, and comfort in a historic landmark building. Frequented by celebrities since 1926 (Humphrey Bogart and Lauren Bacall spent their honeymoon here). Very fine svce. Mediocre and overpriced rest. Total absence of exercise facilities. Recently renovated. Very close to Old Town and its nightlife. **E–VE**

🔑🔑 **Palmer House Hilton** (dwntwn), 17 E. Monroe St., IL 60690 (312/726-7500; toll free, see Hilton). 1,750 rms, A/C, color TV, in-rm movies. AE, CB, DC, MC, V. Gar. ($8), pool, five rests. (including the Empire Room), three bars, rm svce until midnight, nightlife, hrdrsr, drugstore, boutiques, free crib. *Note:* More than a century old, making it a survivor from an earlier age of Chicago hotels. Carefully restored décor and recently modernized facilities, but antiquated ambience and only moderate comfort. Less-than-agreeable svce. Conventions and other large groups. In the heart of the Loop. Two VIP floors. Interesting wknd packages. **E–VE**

🔑🔑 **Sheraton Plaza** (nr. dwntwn), 160 E. Huron St., IL 60611 (312/787-2900; toll free, see Sheraton). 340 rms, A/C, color TV, in-rm movies. AE, CB, DC, MC, V. Valet gar. ($14), pool, rest. (Bentley's), bar, rm svce, hrdrsr, free crib. *Note:* Modern and comfortable. All rms have a spectacular view of the city (the hotel occupies the top 27 stories of a 40-story tower). Good svce. Business clientele. Very central location. Beautiful rooftop pool. Recently renovated décor and layout. Interesting wknd deals. **E–VE**

🔑🔑 **Holiday Inn Mart Plaza** (nr. dwntwn), 350 N. Orleans St., IL 60654 (312/836-5000; toll free, see Holiday Inns). 525 rms, A/C, color TV, in-rm movies. AE, CB, DC, MC, V. Parking ($18), pool, rest., bar, rm svce, disco, hrdrsr, boutiques, crib ($10). *Note:* This modern and comfortable convention hotel occupies the top eight floors of the Apparel Center Building and faces the Merchandise Mart. Comfort and amenities above the norm for a Holiday Inn. Excellent location quite close to the Loop. Business clientele. Very nice view of the city from most rooms. Unsafe neighborhood at night; take a cab. **E**

🔑🔑 **Allerton Hotel** (nr. dwntwn), 701 N. Michigan Ave., IL 60611 (312/440-1500; toll free 800/621-8311). 450 rms, A/C, color TV. AE, CB, DC, MC, V. Adjacent valet parking, rest. (L'Escargot), bar, rm svce, hrdrsr. *Note:* A veteran of the 1920s in the heart of the Magnificent Mile, with renovated rms and amenities. Still has lots of charm, even if the svce doesn't always measure up. Highly recommendable rest. Interesting wknd packages. Overall, a good value. **M–E**

🔑🔑 **Hilton Hyde Park** (nr. dwntwn), 4900 S. Lake Shore Dr., IL 60615 (312/288-5800; toll free, see Hilton). 321 rms, A/C, color TV, in-rm movies. AE, CB, DC, MC, V. Free parking, pool, rest., coffeeshop, bar, rm svce, free crib, free shuttle to and from downtown. *Note:* Relatively modern and functional motel 10 min. from the Loop. Friendly reception and svce. Ideal for drivers. **M–E**

🔑 **Bismarck Hotel** (dwntwn), 171 W. Randolph St., IL 60601 (312/236-0123; toll free 800/643-1500). 525 rms, A/C, color TV. AE, CB, DC, MC, V. Valet parking ($10), two rests. (including the Walnut Room), bar, rm svce, disco, hrdrsr, free crib. *Note:* Located right in the heart of the Loop, this Chicago classic still retains much of its beauty. Entirely renovated décor and rm amenities. The svce leaves something to be desired but the rest. is still a favorite of local politicians. Rather obtrusive convention and other groups. Neighborhood unsafe at night; take a taxi. **M–E**

🔑 **Blackstone** (dwntwn), 636 S. Michigan Ave., IL 60605 (312/427-4300). 307 rms, A/C, color TV. AE, CB, DC, MC, V. Valet parking ($9), rest., bar, rm svce, nightclub, free crib. *Note:* An old hotel a bit past its prime facing Grant Park and Buckingham Fountain. Comfortable, but could use a facelift. Mediocre svce. Interesting family rates. **M–E**

🔑 **Essex Inn** (nr. dwntwn), 800 S. Michigan Ave., IL 60605 (312/939-2800; toll free 800/621-6909). 260 rms, A/C, color TV, in-rm movies. AE, CB, DC, MC, V. Valet parking $6, pool, rest., bar, rm svce, free crib, free shuttle to and from the Loop. *Note:* Pleasant, recently restored hotel nr. dwntwn. Efficient svce. Good value. Ideal location for museum visits. **M–E**

🔑 **Quality Inn Downtown** (formerly the Holiday Inn; nr. dwntwn), 1 Mid City Pl., IL 60606 (312/829-5000; toll free, see Quality Inns). 410 rms, A/C, color TV, in-rm movies. AE, CB, DC, MC, V. Free parking, pool, rest., bar, rm svce, nightclub, *Note:* Modern 17-story motel near Union Station. Comfortable rms w. balconies. Uneven svce. Direct access to the highway network makes it an ideal location if you're driving. Interesting wknd packages. **M–E**

🔑 **Avenue Motel** (nr. dwntwn), 1154 S. Michigan Ave., IL 60605 (312/427-8200; toll free 800/621-6909). 78 rms, A/C, color TV. AE, CB, DC, MC, V. Free parking, pool, coffeeshop, bar, rm svce., free shuttle to and from dwntwn. *Note:* Conventional but well-maintained motel located close to the Field Museum. Overall, a good value. **I–M**

🔑 **Ohio House** (nr. dwntwn), 600 N. La Salle St., IL 60610 (312/943-6000). 50 rms, A/C, color TV. AE, MC, V. Parking, adj. coffeeshop, free shuttle to and from the Loop. *Note:* Small, convenient motel close to the Merchandise Mart. No-frills comfort and a good value for those on a budget. Neighborhood unsafe at night; take a taxi. **I–M**

🔑 **Rodeway Inn** (formerly the Ramada Inn; nr. dwntwn), 506 W. Harrison St., IL 60607 (312/427-6969; toll free, see Rodeway Inns). 154 rms, A/C, color TV, in-rm movies. AE, CB, DC, MC, V. Free valet parking, pool, rest., bar, rm svce. *Note:* Typical motel offering modern comfort, quite close to the University of Illinois campus. Business clientele. Good value. Direct access to the highway network makes it an ideal location if you're driving. **I–M**

🔑 **Travelodge Downtown** (dwntwn), 1240 S. Michigan Ave., IL 60605 (312/427-4111; toll free, see Travelodge). 50 rms, A/C, color TV. AE, CB, DC, MC, V. Parking, rest. and bars nearby, free crib. *Note:* No-frills motel close to Soldier Field that offers clean, well-maintained rooms at reasonable prices. Efficient reception and svce. Overall, a good value. **I–M**

Airport Accommodations

🔑🔑 **Hilton O'Hare** (vic., 40 min. from dwntwn), O'Hare International Airport (P.O. Box 66414), IL 60666 (312/686-8000; toll free, see Hilton). 886 rms, A/C, color TV, in-rm movies. AE, CB, DC, MC, V. Valet gar. ($6), three rests., coffeeshop, bars, rm svce, nightclub, free crib. *Note:* Relatively modern hotel located within the airport itself. Moving walkway to and from the terminal. Enormous soundproof rms. Often overcrowded. So-so rests. and svce. Business and group clientele. **E–VE**

🔑 **Holiday Inn Midway** (vic., 15 min. from dwntwn), 7353 S. Cicero Ave., IL 60629 (312/581-5300; toll free, see Holiday Inns). 161 rms, A/C, cable color TV. AE, CB, DC, MC, V. Free parking, pool, rest., bar, rm svce, disco, free crib, free shuttle to and from Midway Airport. *Note:* Classic airport motel in the Holiday Inn style, offering no-frills comfort and facilities. **I–M**

YMCAs/Youth Hostels

International House—AYH (nr. dwntwn), 1414 E. 59th St., IL 60637 (312/753-2270). Youth hostel. Generally packed during the school year; easier to get into in the summer. **B**

YMCA (nr. dwntwn), 30 W. Chicago Ave., IL 60610 (312/944-6211). 500 rms, pool, health club. For men and women. **B**

RESTAURANTS

Chicago Restaurant Prices	
(per person, excluding drinks and service charges)	
B (Budget)	up to $15
I (Inexpensive)	$15–$25
M (Moderate)	$25–$40
E (Expensive)	$40–$60
VE (Very Expensive)	$60 and up

Personal Favorites (in order of preference)

Le Français (vic.), 269 S. Milwaukee Ave., in Wheeling (30 min. NW on I-94 and Ill. 68W) (312/541-7470). A/C. Dinner only, Tues.-Sun.; closed Mon., holidays, and all of Jan. AE, CB, DC, MC, V. J&T. Specialties: lobster ravioli with sauce Nantua, duck with cranberries, beef Brouilly with marrow, roast quail with cabbage, feuillantine of sole in champagne, fish in pastry shell à la Bocuse, turbot with leeks and oysters. Wonderful sherbets and desserts. The menu changes daily. A very fine wine list. *Note:* The likeable, bearded, 40-ish chef, Jean Banchet, friend and fellow-student of Bocuse, works wonders in this delightful country inn located in an obscure suburb of Chicago. Always in pursuit of new tastes, Jean Banchet's culinary art is a triumph of balance between the great classic cuisine of France and *cuisine moderne.* In addition to the usual menu, each night there are 15 or so different "dishes of the day" presented and explained to each table by the maître d'. Rich, elegant décor, but rather noisy. Reception and svce in the grand manner. Because of its limited 90-seat capacity, resv. should be made weeks in advance. Hollywood magnates and Texas oil millionaires don't hesitate to make a round trip to Chicago simply for a dinner at Le Français; O'Hare Airport is not very far. Two seatings each night, at 6 and 9 p.m. In my opinion, the best rest. in the U.S. Valet parking. 45 min. from dwntwn. *French.* **E–VE**

Le Perroquet (nr. dwntwn), 70 E. Walton Pl. (944-7990). A/C. Lunch Mon.-Fri., dinner Mon.-Sat.; closed Sun., holidays. AE, CB, DC. J&T. Specialties: salmon mousse, soft-shell crab in beurre blanc, quail "le Perroquet," escalope of swordfish with tomatoes, shrimp soufflé Madras, braised duck with green peppercorns, game in season. Very good desserts. Large wine list. *Note:* A touch on the formal side but remarkable classic cuisine and a menu that changes regularly. Luxurious décor with access by private elevator. Very polished svce. Resv. essential. One of the best tables in the Midwest. (Prix Fixe). *French.* **M–E**

Cape Cod Room (nr. dwntwn), in the Drake Hotel (see "Accommodations") (787-2200). A/C. Lunch/dinner daily (to midnight); closed Dec. 25. AE, CB, DC, MC, V. Jkt. Specialties: shrimp créole, pompano en papillote, red snapper soup, bouillabaisse, the finest fish and shellfish. Rather limited wine list. *Note:* The best seafood rest. in Chicago and one of the best in the United States. Amusing marine décor and impeccable svce. An authentic local institution since 1933. Resv. advised. Valet parking ($10). A highly recommendable spot. *Seafood.* **M**

☼♈♉♊ **Cricket's** (nr. dwntwn), in the Tremont Hotel (see "Accommodations") (280-2100). Lunch/dinner daily; New Orleans–style brunch Sun. AE, CB, DC, MC, V. J&T. Specialties: crab Diablo, sweetbread financière, mixed grill, grilled salmon, minced chicken Mornay, kidney dijonnaise, calves' liver with bacon, roast squab, chocolate sundaes. *Note:* Warm, club-like ambience and serious, irreproachable cuisine. Funny, eclectic décor including sports team pennants and airplane models recalling the 21 Club in New York. Exceptionally attentive, polished svce. The favorite restaurant of the tycoons. Resv. essential. Valet parking ($5). *Continental.* **M–E**

♈♉♊ **Gordon** (nr. dwntwn), 500 N. Clark St. (467-9780). A/C. Lunch Mon.-Fri., dinner nightly, brunch Sun. AE, CB, DC, MC, V. Jkt. Specialties: beignets of artichoke béarnaise, seafood stew, médaillon of pork with dates, roast turbot with thyme, duckling in pastry shell, tournedos with garlic and mustard, salmon in oyster sauce, "nouvelle cuisine" fish. *Note:* The menu changes daily. Insignificant desserts. Remarkable fish, light sauces prepared with style and imagination. Brilliant and original new décor. Fashionable clientele. Resv. necessary. Excellent location despite a less-than-attractive neighborhood. *Continental/Seafood.* **M**

♈♉♊ **Printer's Row** (dwntwn), 550 S. Dearborn St. (461-0780). A/C. Lunch Mon.-Fri., dinner Mon.-Sat.; closed Sun., holidays. AE, CB, DC, MC, V. Jkt. Specialties: fresh pasta with rosemary and wild mushrooms, spinach-and-goat-cheese tarte, rack of lamb with pepper and cream sauce, smoked chicken with curried mayonnaise, filet of beef in vermouth and ginger, ragoût of sweetbread with sorrel. Limited desserts and wine list. The menu changes regularly. *Note:* Modern, imaginative American cuisine with an occasional sublime touch from the very talented young chef, Michael Foley. Warm décor of pale paneling and claret tones in a former print shop. Efficient svce. One of Chicago's trendiest spots. Resv. advised. *American.* **I–M**

♈♉♊ **House of Hunan** (nr. dwntwn), 535 N. Michigan Ave. (329-9494). A/C. Lunch/dinner daily (closed Thanksgiving). AE, CB, DC, MC, V. Jkt. Specialties: hot-and-sour soup, mandarin lamb, imperial fried chicken, spicy Hunan beef, lobster Cantonese with ginger, sweet-and-sour pork. Characterless desserts. *Note:* Enormous menu with more than 100 dishes, from the spiciest to the mildest, harmoniously uniting recipes from China's four great culinary regions: Hunan, Szechuan, Canton, and Peking. The result is almost always remarkable. Very elaborate old-style décor. Svce is attentive and efficient—a distinction for a Chinese rest. By far the best Chinese rest. in Chicago. *Chinese.* **I**

☼♈♉♊ **Berghoff** (dwntwn), 17 W. Adams St. (427-3170). A/C. Lunch/dinner Mon.-Sat. (until 9:30 p.m.); closed Sun., holidays. AE, MC, V. Specialties: Bismarck herring, wienerschnitzel, ragoût à la Deutsch, Kassler rippchen (smoked pork), sauerbraten, roast goose, whitefish, lavish desserts. Draft beer from Munich plus a good wine list. *Note:* A Chicago classic since 1898, when it opened as a simple saloon. Authentic German brasserie ambience and cuisine offering efficient svce and generous portions. Often packed and noisy. Resv. for parties of six or more. Friendly bar. Excellent value. *German.* **I**

♈♉ **L'Escargot** (nr. dwntwn), in the Allerton Hotel (see "Accommodations") (337-1717). A/C. Lunch/dinner daily; closed holidays. AE, CB, DC, MC, V. Jkt. Specialties: rack of lamb in pastry shell, cassoulet toulousain, duckling à l'orange, rabbit à la crème, kidneys in mustard, mushroom-stuffed trout. Good house desserts. Fine wine list at reasonable prices. *Note:* Charming little French bistro located on the ground floor of the Hotel Allerton. Very fine cuisine bourgeoise and friendly svce. Locally popular.

Resv. advised. Good value. Other location: 2925 N. Halsted St. (535-5522). *French.* **I–M**

☼♀ **Blackhawk** (nr. dwntwn), 110 E. Pearson St. (943-3300). A/C. Lunch Mon.-Sat., dinner nightly; closed holidays. AE, CB, DC, MC, V. Jkt. Specialties: red meats, roast beef, fish of the day, Boston scrod (haddock), cheesecake. *Note:* One of Chicago's best places for meat-eaters. Intimate Mediterranean décor. Ideal for business meals. Quick, professional svce. The salad preparation alone is something to see. Locally popular. Resv. recommended. *Steak/Seafood.* **I–M**

Other Restaurants (from top bracket to budget)

♀♀♀ **Ambria** (nr. dwntwn), 2300 N. Lincoln Park West (472-5959). A/C. Dinner only, Mon.-Sat.; closed Sun., holidays. AE, DC, MC, V. Jkt. Specialties: foie gras sauté vinaigrette, gâteau d'escargots in beurre blanc, calves' liver with mustard seed, saddle of lamb piperade, sautéed duck with wild rice, salmon tartare. White chocolate mousse. *Note:* A must for all lovers of remarkable eating experiences. The "tasting/sampling" menu (must be ordered 24 hrs in advance) is a festival of modern culinary elegance. Rather depressing paneled décor, insufficiently relieved by touches of art nouveau. Diligent if sometimes disorganized svce. Resv. should be made several days in advance. Valet parking ($4). *French.* **E**

♀♀♀ **Nick's Fishmarket** (nr. dwntwn), 1 First National Plaza, Dearborn & Monroe Sts. (621-0200). A/C. Lunch Mon.-Fri., dinner Mon.-Sat.; closed Sun., holidays. AE, CB, DC, MC, V. Jkt. Specialties: fresh salmon, abalone, mahi mahi (dolphin à la Hawaiian), soft-shell crab meunière, sautéed scallops, all kinds of wonderful fish and shellfish. *Note:* Excellent seafood rest. in an elegant, intimate setting, complete with private booths. Sister rest. of the famous Nick's Fishmarkets in Honolulu and in Los Angeles. Impeccable svce. Resv. advised. Valet parking ($3). *Seafood.* **M–E**

♀♀♀ **Spiaggia** (nr. dwntwn), 980 N. Michigan Ave. (280-2750). A/C. Lunch Mon.-Sat., dinner nightly; closed holidays. AE, CB, DC, MC, V. Jkt. Specialties: farfalle rosse con verdure (butterfly pasta with tomatoes and green vegetables), carpaccio, vitello tonnato, lasagne, calves' liver veneziana, veal chop with sage, zabaglione. Fine Italian wine list. *Note:* Located in the mezzanine of the sparkling One Magnificent Mile Building and offering an unobstructed view of Lake Michigan through its immense bay windows, Spiaggia has rapidly become the best Italian rest. in Chicago. Northern Italian cuisine, modern and sophisticated in its preparation. The svce is very able and the post-modern décor a model of elegance. Resv. necessary. *Italian.* **M–E**

♀♀ **Morton's** (nr. dwntwn), 1050 N. State St. (266-4820). A/C. Dinner only, Mon.-Sat. (until midnight); closed Sun., holidays. AE, CB, DC, MC, V. Jkt. Specialties: shellfish, remarkable red meats, veal chops, Maine lobster, fish of the day. Soufflé Grand Marnier. Well-stocked wine list (especially California). *Note:* Fashionable steakhouse serving the highest-quality meats at commensurate prices. Charming English pub décor. Impeccable svce. No resv. unfortunately, which often means substantial waits, especially on wknds. "In" clientele. *Steak.* **M–E**

♀♀♀ **Yoshi's Café** (nr. dwntwn), 3257 N. Halsted St. (248-6160). A/C. Dinner Tues.-Sun., brunch Sun.; closed Mon. AE, MC, V. Jkt. Specialties: poached seafood sausage, warm wild-game pâté, braised rabbit in mustard, roulade of lamb with artichokes, snails with basil. The menu changes regularly. Remarkable desserts (notably the green-tea ice cream). *Note:* Japanese variations on the "nouvelle cuisine" theme by a culinary virtuoso and student of Jean Banchet (see Le Français), Yoshi Katsumura. Inventive, refined cuisine at relatively modest prices. Charming modern-art décor. Resv. necessary, given the limited seating (48 places) and the success of this fashionable bistro. *Continental*. **M**

☀︎ ❖🍸 **Eli's, The Place for Steak** (nr. dwntwn), 215 E. Chicago Ave. (642-1393). A/C. Lunch Mon.-Fri., dinner nightly; closed holidays and mid-Dec. to Jan. AE, CB, DC. Jkt. Specialties: very fine meats (as the name indicates), calves' liver with onions, and the best cheesecake in Chicago. *Note:* A favorite of local journalists and politicians as well as visiting celebrities. Rather busy décor, agreeable ambience, highest quality svce. Resv. advised. Very popular piano bar. Valet parking ($3). *Steak*. **I–M**

🍸 **Golden Ox** (nr. dwntwn), 1578 N. Clybourn Ave. (664-0780). A/C. Lunch Mon.-Sat., dinner daily; closed Sun. in July and Aug., Jan. 1. AE, CB, DC, MC, V. Jkt. Specialties: wienerschnitzel, Bavarian hotpot, sauerbraten, roast duck, zwiebelfleisch, Kassler rippchen, veal with paprika. Apple strudel. *Note:* This 110% German brasserie with "kolossal" portions, décor, and ambience plus a Bavarian orchestra on wknds has been a classic for more than 50 years. Valet parking. *German*. **I–M**

🍸🍸 **La Strada** (dwntwn), 155 N. Michigan Ave. (565-2200). A/C. Lunch Mon.-Fri., dinner Mon.-Sat.; closed Sun., holidays. AE, CB, DC, MC, V. J&T. Specialties: carpaccio, excellent homemade pasta, calves' liver veneziana, costoletta milanese, saltimbocca alla romana, involtini di melanzane. Extraordinary Italian wine list. *Note:* Very good northern Italian cuisine and one of the richest, most abundant selections of Italian wines in the United States. Opulent décor under an elegant skylight roof. Svce a bit overzealous. Resv. advised. *Italian*. **I–M**

🍸🍸 **Casbah** (nr. dwntwn), 514 W. Diversey Pkwy. (935-7570). A/C. Dinner only, daily; closed holidays. AE, CB, DC, MC, V. Jkt. Specialties: stuffed grape leaves, pastilla, couscous, shish kebab, trout Leila, kibbeh, Armenian dishes, baklava. *Note:* This warm, distinguished Middle Eastern restaurant has become a local favorite over the years. The décor is right out of a Chicago version of *1001 Nights,* music and ambience included. Attentive svce. Resv. advised. Excellent value. *Middle Eastern*. **I**

☀︎🍸🍸 **Frontera Grill** (nr. dwntwn), 445 N. Clark St. (661-1434). A/C. Lunch Tue.-Fri., dinner Tue.-Sat.; closed Sun., Mon. AE, CB, DC, MC, V. Jkt. Specialties: shrimp-stuffed avocados with garlic and lime, stuffed green peppers with chili-and-tomato sauce, turkey-stuffed tacos with coriander-spiced beans, grilled lamb chop, fried plantains with whipped cream. *Note:* The young and talented Rick Bayless is an American chef who is crazy about Mexican food, having lived and traveled south of the Rio Grande for many years. His rather elaborate cuisine is totally authentic and delicious. The décor is pleasantly rustic and the svce friendly. Has enjoyed much success since its 1987 opening. No resv. taken. Expect a long wait after 7 p.m. *Mexican*. **I**

🍸 **Hatsuhana** (nr. dwntwn), 160 E. Ontario St. (280-8287). A/C. Lunch Mon.-Fri., dinner daily; closed holidays. AE, CB, DC, MC, V. Jkt. Specialties: sushi, sashimi, tempura, teriyaki. *Note:* Excellent authentic Japanese rest. in a modern, immaculate setting. Svce of outstanding politeness and efficiency. American and Japanese business clientele. The dexterity with which the chefs handle their knives is a sight in itself. *Japanese*. **I**

🍸 **Yugo Inn** (nr. dwntwn), 2824 N. Ashland Ave. (348-6444). A/C. Dinner only, Wed.-Sun.; closed Mon., Tue. No credit cards. Specialties: ajvar, pjeskavica, moussaka, muckalica. *Note:* From moussaka to goulash, all the authentic flavors of the Balkans. Very good value. Resv. advised. *Balkan*. **I**

🍸 **Greek Islands** (nr. dwntwn), 200 S. Halsted St. (782-9855). A/C. Lunch/dinner daily (until midnight); closed Thanksgiving, Dec. 25. AE, CB, DC, MC, V. Specialties: pastitsio, gyros, moussaka, souvlaki, braised lamb, excellent grilled fish. *Note:* The best Greek restaurant in Chicago, a city full of Greeks. A modern setting and excellent, authentic cuisine at very good prices. Greek hospitality and a friendly, if noisy, ambience. Free valet parking. *Greek.* **B–I**

☕ **R. J. Grunt's** (nr. dwntwn), 2056 Lincoln Park West (929-5363). A/C. Lunch/dinner daily, brunch Sun.; closed Thanksgiving, Dec. 25. AE, CB, DC, MC, V. Specialties: hamburgers, roast beef, chili, barbecued fish, steak teriyaki, giant sandwiches. *Note:* Progenitor of a whole family of typically American rests., the "Lettuce Entertain You" chain, which boasts honest cuisine, reasonable prices, and an amusing atmosphere that is both "hip" and relaxed. Friendly, cheerful svce. Nice view of Lincoln Park. No resv. *American.* **B–I**

☕ **Su Casa** (nr. dwntwn), 49 E. Ontario St. (943-4041). A/C. Lunch Mon.-Fri., dinner Mon.-Sat. (to 12:30 a.m.); closed Sun., holidays. AE, CB, DC, MC, V. Jkt. Specialties: enchiladas, guacamole, tacos, chile relleno, ceviche, mole poblano, shrimp à la Veracruzana. *Note:* Typical Mexican dishes with several interesting variations like trout with garlic and coriander. Rather overwhelming hacienda décor. Svce is sometimes less than friendly. Resv. advised. Pleasant background music. Valet parking ($3). *Mexican.* **B–I**

☀☕ **Ed Debevic's** (nr. dwntwn), 640 N. Wells St. (664-1707). A/C. Lunch/dinner daily (until midnight); closed Thanksgiving, Dec. 25. No credit cards. Specialties: chili, hamburgers, fried chicken, meatloaf, chocolate milkshakes. *Note:* An amusing replica of a 1950s-style diner that seems to have come right out of *American Graffiti.* Even the background music is from that era. If there is nothing unforgettable about the food, the atmosphere is fun, the prices more than modest, and the crowd particularly diverse. Another success from the "Lettuce Entertain You" restaurant chain. No resv. *American.* **B**

☀☕ **Pizzeria Uno** (nr. dwntwn), 29 E. Ohio St. (321-1000). A/C. Lunch Tue.-Sun., dinner daily; closed Thanksgiving, Dec. 25. AE, CB, DC, MC, V. Specialties: Chicago-style pizza (thick yet light crust), salads, sandwiches, homemade soup. *Note:* The best pizza in Chicago and perhaps in America. Noisy atmosphere. Walls decorated with amusing graffiti. Generous portions (a "medium" pizza is plenty for two). Efficient svce. A local favorite since the 1940s. Other location: Pizzeria Due, 619 N. Wabash Ave. (943-2400). *Italian.* **B**

Restaurants in the Vicinity

☕☕☕☕☕ **Le Français** (see "Personal Favorites," above).

☀☕☕☕ **The Cottage** (vic.), 525 Torrence Ave., in Calumet City (312/891-3900). A/C. Lunch Tue.-Fri., dinner Tue.-Sat.; closed Sun., Mon., holidays. MC, V. Jkt. Specialties: duck ravioli, grilled lamb sausage with roast peppers, steak Madagascar, "Cottage" pork chop, salmon in pastry shell, roast duckling with raspberries, remarkable homemade desserts. The menu changes with the seasons. Weakish wine list. *Note:* Delightful little old-world inn that has become a shrine for fine-cuisine lovers. Chef Carolyn Buster deftly blends French, Austrian, and Californian influences in her quest for perfection. Rustic-opulent ambience. Very good svce. Worth the 30-min. car ride from downtown on I-94S and Sibley Blvd. Free parking. Resv. advised. *Continental-French.* **I–M**

Cafeterias/Specialty Spots

D. B. Kaplan's (nr. dwntwn), Water Tower Pl., 7th floor (280-2700). Lunch/dinner daily (closes at 11 p.m.). No credit cards. Specialties: salads, omelets, and giant sandwiches. *Note:* The best deli in Chicago. Ideal for a light meal before or after a show. **B**

Hemingway's Movable Feast (nr. dwntwn), 1825 N. Lincoln (943-1825). Lunch/dinner daily (to midnight). AE, MC, V. Specialties: 190 kinds of sandwiches, quiches, fresh pastas. *Note:* Pleasant ambience. **B**

Mr. Beef (nr. dwntwn), 666 N. Orleans St. (337-8500). Lunch only, Mon.-Fri. No credit cards. Specialties: remarkable Italian beef sandwiches (roast beef and roast peppers)—a Chicago specialty. *Note:* The rather depressing décor does not seem to discourage the clientele. **B**

Levy Delicatessen (dwntwn), in the Sears Tower (ground floor), 2335 Wacker Dr. (933-0220). Breakfast/lunch/dinner daily. No credit cards. Specialties: cabbage soup, Jewish dishes, corned beef, excellent sandwiches and home-made apple pie. *Note:* A very popular bistro at lunchtime. **B**

Where to Eat What

American: Printer's Row (♀♀); Ed Debevic's (♀); R. J. Grunt's (♀)

Balkan: Yugo Inn (♀)

Cafeterias: D. B. Kaplan's; Hemingway's Movable Feast; Mr. Beef; Levy Delicatessen

Chinese: House of Hunan (♀♀)

Continental: The Cottage (♀♀♀); Cricket's (♀♀♀); Yoshi's Café (♀♀♀); Gordon (♀♀)

French: Le Français (♀♀♀♀♀); Le Perroquet (♀♀♀♀); Ambria (♀♀♀); L'Escargot (♀♀)

German: Berghoff (♀♀); Golden Ox (♀)

Greek: Greek Islands (♀)

Italian: Spiaggia (♀♀♀); La Strada (♀♀); Pizzeria Uno (♀)

Japanese: Hatsuhana (♀)

Mexican: Frontera Grill (♀♀); Su Casa (♀)

Middle Eastern: Casbah (♀♀)

Seafood: Cape Cod Room (♀♀♀); Nick's Fishmarket (♀♀♀); Gordon (♀♀); Morton's (♀♀); Blackhawk (♀)

Steak: Eli's, The Place for Steak (♀♀); Morton's (♀♀); Blackhawk (♀)

Late-Night Choices: Cape Cod Room (open to midnight daily); Ed Debevic's (to midnight, 1 a.m. on Fri. & Sat.); Greek Islands (to midnight, 1 a.m. on Fri. & Sat.); Hemingway's Movable Feast (to midnight, 1 a.m. on Fri. & Sat.); Nick's Fishmarket (to 11:30 p.m. weekdays, 1 a.m. on Fri. & Sat.); Su Casa (to 12:30 a.m. Mon.-Sat.).

BARS & NIGHTCLUBS

As in New York and Boston, there is a magic telephone number in Chicago —**Jazz Institute Hot Line** (666-1881)—with a daily listing of all jazz club programs.

Andy's (nr. dwntwn), 11 E. Hubbard St. (642-6805): The best jazz club in Chicago, according to the experts. Lively, 1920s-style ambience. Rest. as well (jkt. required). Open daily.

B.L.U.E.S. (nr. dwntwn), 2519 N. Halsted St. (528-1012): A great blues place in a great blues city.

☀ **Butch McGuire's** (nr. dwntwn), 20 W. Division St. (337-9080). Chicago's most famous singles bar. A relaxed, pleasant atmosphere. Original décor. A quite good rest., too. A must for all visitors. Open Mon.-Sat.

Byfield's (nr. dwntwn), in the Omni Ambassador East, 1301 N. State Pkwy. (787-6433). Elegant, intimate comedy club which often features big-name stars.

☼ **Checkerboard Lounge** (nr. dwntwn), 423 E. 43rd St. (624-3240). Another famous locale for lovers of authentic blues. The guitarist Buddy Guy playing his own works. Rough neighborhood—take a cab.

Joe Segal's Jazz Showcase (dwntwn), in the Blackstone Hotel, 636 S. Michigan Ave. (427-4300). Renowned jazz club offering everything from be-bop to avant-garde jazz. Open Tue.-Sun.

☼ **John Barleycorn Memorial Pub** (nr. dwntwn), 658 W. Belden Ave. (348-8899). Very popular, intimate pub with classical background music and silent movies. Open daily.

Kingston Mines (nr. dwntwn), 2458 N. Halsted St. (447-4646). Jazz and blues in the heart of the North Side, a fashionable upper-class neighborhood. Locally popular. Open nightly.

Limelight (nr. dwntwn), Dearborn & Ontario Sts. (337-2985). Enormous discothèque with 1,700 seats, sister club to the famous Limelights of New York and Atlanta. Fashionable locale. Open daily.

McMahon's (nr. dwntwn), 1970 N. Lincoln Ave. (751-1700). Popular singles bar owned by the famous Bears quarterback, Jim McMahon. Sports clientele. Rest. as well. Open daily.

Old Town School of Folk Music (nr. dwntwn), 909 W. Armitage Ave. (525-7793). A temple of Chicago folk music, as the name indicates.

Park West (nr. dwntwn), 322 W. Armitage Ave. (929-5959). Big pop and jazz stars performing two shows a night. Rather snobby ambience.

☼ **Second City Theater** (nr. dwntwn), 1616 N. Wells St. (337-3992). A stronghold of improvisation, where comedians like Mike Nichols, Elaine May, and a good many of the "Saturday Night Live" troupe were discovered.

NEARBY EXCURSIONS

BATAVIA (36 mi., 56 km, west on Eisenhower Expwy. and East-West Tollway): Built on 6,800 acres (2,700 ha.) where peaceful herds of bison graze, the **Fermilab Particle Accelerator,** Kirk Rd. at Pine St., is the largest synchrotron particle accelerator in the world. Its annular tunnel, 4 mi. (6.4 km) in circumference, accelerates atomic particles to nearly the speed of light. The Visitors Center is located in **Wilson Hall,** a 15-story building in the center of the synchrotron. Guided tours are given Mon.-Fri. by appointment only (312/840-3351). A must for physics buffs.

ELMHURST (17 mi., 27 km, west on I-90): The **Lizzadro Museum of Lapidary Art,** 220 Cottage Hill Ave. in Wilder Park (312/833-1616), offers one of the world's largest collections of minerals and worked precious stones, notable jade figurines from the Far East. Open Tues.-Sun.

EVANSTON (12 mi., 19 km, north on Lake Shore Dr. and U.S. 41): Site of **Northwestern University** (10,000 students), this pretty residential area on the banks of Lake Michigan houses the headquarters of Rotary International. On the university campus, be sure to see the **Dearborn Observatory** (2131 Sheridan Rd.), the **Shakespeare Garden,** and the **Pick-Staiger Concert Hall.**

North of the campus is the **Grosse Point lighthouse,** Sheridan Rd. and Central St., erected after a shipwreck on Lake Michigan off Evanston took 300 lives (tours on Sat. and Sun. in summer).

The **Terra Museum of American Art,** 2600 Central Park (312/328-3400) (open Tue.-Sun.) makes for another interesting stop. An annex of the Terra Museum in downtown Chicago (see "Museums of Art," above), it is dedicated to American contemporary art.

OAK PARK (9 mi., 14 km, west on the Eisenhower Expwy.): The suburban cradle of the famous "Prairie School" which greatly influenced American architecture from the beginning of the century. There are at least a score of interesting buildings to see here, work of the famous Frank Lloyd Wright (see "Guided Tours," above). Among the most noteworthy are **Wright's house-studio,** at Forest and Chicago Aves. (open daily year round), in which he lived for more than 20 years; the **Harry Adams House,** 710 Augusta St. (dates from 1913); the **Unity Temple,** 875 Lake St. (dates from 1906); and the **River Forest Tennis Club,** 615 Lathrop Ave. There's a **Visitors Center** at 158 Forest Ave. (open daily, Mar.-Nov.). Definitely worth the trip.

Authors Ernest Hemingway and Edgar Rice Burroughs, the prolific creator of Tarzan (27 volumes from 1912 to 1964), also hail from Oak Park.

PULLMAN COMMUNITY (I-94 between 104th and 115th Sts.): This model company town, built in 1880 by the railroad magnate George Pullman for his employees, is an interesting sample of American social history. The **Visitors Center** is at 614 E. 113th St. (312/785-8181).

WILMETTE (16 mi., 26 km, north on Lake Shore Dr. and U.S. 41): Luxurious suburb on the shores of Lake Michigan complete with a fine sand beach. The startling **Baha'i House of Worship,** Sheridan Rd. and Linden Ave. (312/256-4400), religious center for the Baha'i faith, should definitely be seen. Founded in Iran in the last century, the faith has been flourishing in the United States for some 50 years. Innovative nine-sided design surrounded by nine gardens overlooking Lake Michigan. Open daily. Worth the trip.

FARTHER AFIELD

INDIANA DUNES NATIONAL LAKESHORE (92 mi., 148 km, r.t. on I-90E and U.S. 12E, returning the same way): A captivating landscape composed of giant sand dunes—some as high as 192 ft. (60 m)—of pine forests, of immense beaches with room for many thousands of bathers, and of marshes along the shores of Lake Michigan. Unique fauna and flora (notably carnivorous plants, cacti, oaks, and sumacs) flourish on the 14,227 acres (5,760 ha.) of the park, giving the whole an appearance of tropical vegetation in summer, the best season for a visit. There are also dozens of miles of rambling trails, picnic areas, and fully equipped campsites for nature-lovers. Visitor Center at the intersection of Kenil Rd. and U.S. 12. Definitely worth the trip. For further information, contact Superintendent, 1100 N. Mineral Springs Rd., Porter, IN 46304 (219/926-7561).

LAKE COUNTRY (124 mi., 199 km, r.t. on I-90N, U.S. 12N, Ill. 120E, and U.S. 14S): A string of rural lakes **(Long Lake, Fox Lake, Pistakee Lake, Grass Lake, Chain O'Lakes State Park),** this favorite fine-weather rural retreat for Chicagoans is a paradise for fishing, sailing, and strolling.

On the way back, go out of your way to pass through **Woodstock,** a peaceful little town of Victorian charm where Orson Welles spent his childhood and made his earliest appearances as a Shakespearean actor in the **Opera House,** 121 Van

Buren St. See also the **Old Courthouse Inn & Jail,** 101 N. Johnston St.; **Town Square;** etc.

☼☆ **GALENA & THE BANKS OF THE MISSISSIPPI** (406 mi., 650 km. west; r.t. on I-90N, U.S. 20W, Ill. 84S, and I-80 and I-55E): The charming little town of **Galena,** on the banks of the river of the same name, is a former mining town that made its fortune in the last century from lead. A visit here is a pleasant voyage back into history: 85% of its buildings are designated as landmarks, like the **Ulysses S. Grant Home,** 500 Bouthillier St. (815/777-0248), open daily, the former home of the commander-in-chief of Union forces during the Civil War. Photographers, and lovers of old buildings, will find here a wonderful glimpse of the past.

This two- or three-day trip leads next along the banks of the Mississippi (a beautiful scenic route) to **Rock Island,** former capital of the Saul and Fox Indians under Chief Black Hawk. The army defeated them in a decisive battle in 1832. **Black Hawk State Park,** with an observation tower overlooking the valley, as well as a Native American museum, commemorates the event. For information, call 309/788-9536. Also see the **Arsenal,** the **John M. Browning Museum** with a rich collection of arms (open Wed.-Sun.), and the reconstruction of old ☖ **Fort Armstrong.** Return to Chicago on I-80 and I-55, an ☆ ideal route for history lovers.

Where to Stay

IN GALENA. ☼ ♟♟ **DeSoto House,** 230 S. Main St., IL 61036 (815/777-0090). 55 rms. A more-than-100-year-old hotel, nicely restored. **M–E**

IN ROCK ISLAND. ♟♟ **Sheraton,** 17th St. at Third Ave., IL 61201 (309/794-1212). 177 rms. Modern and comfortable. **I–M**

CHAPTER 24

MILWAUKEE

□ □ □

From its Germanic antecedents the world's brewing capital has inherited a taste for order, work, classical music (its symphony orchestra is justly renowned), and solid food. In a strategic position on Lake Michigan at the confluence of three rivers—the Milwaukee, the Menominee, and the Kinnickinnic—the site of the city, whose original Indian name, Millioki, signifies "gathering-place by the waters," was visited in 1674 by the French missionary Jacques Marquette and the trapper Louis Jolliet. The present economic capital of Wisconsin was founded in 1818 as a trading post by the French fur trader Salomon Juneau; it attained stature as a major city in 1889, when the first modern brewery was opened.

Today Milwaukee produces more beer than any other city in the world, and two of the country's largest breweries, Pabst and Miller (both of German origin) have their headquarters here. Other well-known names in the roster of local industry include Harley-Davidson motorcycles, Allis-Chalmers heavy equipment, and Evinrude outboard motors; these and others have contributed to the economic growth of "the machine-shop of America," as Milwaukee has been called, taking advantage of the city's access to the ocean via the Great Lakes and the St. Lawrence Seaway.

"The German Athens"—another of Milwaukee's sobriquets—is an austere but by no means a charmless city, with its churches, its old buildings, its museum, and its lovely lakeside promenade. Every year it plays host, as it should, to a well-known beer festival, the Oktoberfest, reminiscent of the Munich event of the same name.

It is German immigration that has left the clearest stamp on Milwaukee, from the impressive **City Hall** to the **Pabst Theater,** not to mention the many cafés and "bier gartens," but the influence of other immigrant strains—Irish, Greek, and above all Polish—is also clearly evident. Witness America's first Polish cathedral, **St. Josaphat's Basilica,** built at the beginning of the 20th century, and the **Annunciation Greek Orthodox Church,** last major work of the great architect Frank Lloyd Wright.

Born here were the entertainer Liberace, the clarinetist Woody Herman, the actors Spencer Tracy and Gene Wilder, and the singer Al Jarreau.

BASIC FACTS: State of Wisconsin. Area Code: 414. Time Zone: Central Time. ZIP Code: 53201. Founded in: 1818. Approximate population: city, 635,000; metropolitan area, 1,550,000. Ranks 24th in size among U.S. metropolitan areas.

CLIMATE: Summer and fall are the best seasons for visiting Milwaukee. Temperatures are generally pleasant, though there can be sudden changes; mean temperature in July is 71°F (22°C). Winter is glacial and very windy; the mercury stays well under freezing, with a January average temperature of 22°F (−6°C). Spring is brief and brisk (41°–50°F, 5°–10°C).

DISTANCES: Chicago, 87 mi. (139 km); Duluth, 424 mi. (678 km); Minneapolis, 365 mi. (584 km); Omaha, 495 mi. (792 km); St. Louis, 376 mi. (602 km).

ARRIVAL & TRANSIT INFORMATION

AIRPORT: General Mitchell International Airport (MKE), 6 mi. (10 km) south. Information: 747-5300.

AIRLINES: American (344-6700), Continental (342-3099), Eastern (344-7910), Midwest (747-4646), Northwest (272-8920), TWA (933-8292), United (273-8400), USAir (toll free 800/428-4322).

CITY LINK: The **cab** fare to city center is about $16; time, 20–25 min. Bus: **American Airport Limousine** (423-1842) leaves every 30 min., serving principal dwntwn and outlying hotels; fare, $6.50–$12 according to destination; time, about 35 min.

Since the airport is near the city, which is not large, it may be unnecessary to rent a car unless you intend to take trips outside the city. Good public transportation system (bus): **Milwaukee County Transit System** (344-6711 for information).

CAR RENTAL (at the airport unless otherwise noted): Avis (744-2266); Budget (481-2409); Dollar (747-0066); Hertz (747-5335); National (483-9800); Thrifty, 4650 S. Howell Ave. (483-5870). For dwntwn locations, consult the local telephone directory.

LIMOUSINE SERVICES: Carey Limousine (271-5466), Dav El Limousine (toll free 800/922-0343).

TAXIS: Cabs may not be hailed on the street; they must be taken from the waiting lines outside the major hotels or summoned by phone. Principal companies are **Checker Cab** (542-4412), **City Veteran Taxicab** (643-1212), and **Yellow Cab** (271-1800).

TRAIN: AMTRAK Station, 433 W. St. Paul Ave. (933-3081).

BUS: Greyhound, 606 N. 7th St. (272-8900).

INFORMATION & TOURS

TOURIST INFORMATION: The **Milwaukee Convention & Visitors Bureau,** 756 N. Milwaukee St., WI 53202 (414/273-3950).

For a **recorded message** giving a list of current shows and cultural events, call 799-1177.

GUIDED TOURS: Gray Line Tours (bus), 1200 W. Wells (276-9588): Conducted tours of city and surroundings.

Iroquois Boat Line Tours (boat), Clybourn St. Bridge Dock (332-4194): Trips on Lake Michigan and the Milwaukee River (late June to Sept. 1).

Milwaukee County Transit System (bus), 1492 N. 17th St. (344-4550): Conducted tours of city and surroundings (June 1 to Sept. 1).

Star of Milwaukee (boat), Municipal Pier, Lincoln Memorial Dr. at E. Michigan Ave. (273-7827): Dinner-dances on Lake Michigan.

SIGHTS, ATTRACTIONS, & ACTIVITIES

ARCHITECTURAL HIGHLIGHTS: ⚓ **Civic Center Plaza,** between N. 7th and 9th Sts., north of W. Wells St.: Wide esplanade with fountain, statuary, and monumental bell tower, bordered by the **County Courthouse,** Police Headquarters, the huge **Convention Center (MECCA),** and the **Public Museum.** The heart of the city's government; worth a look.

⚓ **McKinley Marina,** 1750 N. Lincoln Memorial Dr. (273-5224): Lovely pleasure harbor with 650 moorings on Lake Michigan. Boats may be rented May-Oct. Must be seen.

☀⚓ **Performing Arts Center/PAC,** 929 N. Water St. (273-7206): This modern (1969), austerely geometric complex comprises four theaters and concert halls as well as an open-air auditorium. Home of the world-famous Milwaukee Symphony Orchestra, the Milwaukee Repertory Theater, the Milwaukee Ballet, and the Florentine Opera Company. Pretty gardens on the Milwaukee River. Visits by appointment only. Worth going out of your way for.

☀⚓ **War Memorial Complex,** 750 N. Lincoln Memorial Dr. (271-9508): This modern building by the great architect Eero Saarinen, splendidly situated on the shore of Lake Michigan, commemorates the dead of all wars. It houses the **Milwaukee Art Museum** (see "Museums of Art," below), and offers a fine view of lake and city. Don't miss it.

BEACHES: ⚓ **Bradford Beach,** N. Lincoln Memorial Dr. at Bradford Ave.: The best of the six public beaches along the lakefront. The water is very cold even at the height of summer; for dedicated swimmers only.

CHURCHES/SYNAGOGUES: ☀ ⚓ **Annunciation Greek Orthodox Church,** 9400 W. Congress St. (461-9400): Last major work of Frank Lloyd Wright; the imaginative Byzantine structure is crowned by a magnificent blue dome in the shape of a flying saucer. Visit by appointment. An absolute must-see.

⚓ **Central United Methodist Church,** 639 N. 25th St. (344-1600): A triumph of contemporary energy-saving design. Built partially underground, this unusual church, whose roof is also its garden, has a large bell tower which captures and stores solar energy. Worth seeing.

☀⚓ **St. Joan of Arc Chapel,** 601 N. 14th St. (224-7039): Authentic medieval French chapel from the 15th century, transported and reerected in 1965, stone by stone, on the campus of **Marquette University** (see "Historic Buildings," below). According to legend, Joan of Arc prayed here before going to the stake. Remarkable example of Gothic architecture, not to be missed. Open daily.

⚓ **St. Josaphat's Basilica,** 2336 S. 6th St. (645-5623): This is the oldest Polish basilica in North America, built at the turn of the century by Slavic immigrants with material salvaged from the demolition of the Federal Building in Chicago. Its majestic dome is reminiscent of St. Peter's in Rome; ornate interior with many pictures and relics of Polish saints. Worth a visit. Open daily.

HISTORIC BUILDINGS: ☀ ⚓ **Capt. Frederick Pabst Mansion,** 2000 W. Wisconsin Ave. (931-0808): Luxurious 1892 home of the 19th-century brewer Frederick Pabst; splendid upper-middle-class interior from the turn of the century with period furniture and decoration scrupulously restored. Worth a visit. Open daily.

☼☙ **City Hall,** 200 E. Wells St. (278-2221): Impressive in the purest Flemish Renaissance style, with monumental eight-story lobby surrounded by wrought-iron balconies, and a 393-ft. (122-m) belfry. Worth visiting. Open Mon.–Fri.

☙ **Kilbourntown House,** 4400 W. Estabrook St., Estabrook Park, 5 mi. (8 km) north on I-43 (273-8288): Beautiful Greek Revival house from 1844 with an interesting collection of furniture and art objects from the second half of the 19th century. Worth the side trip. Open Tues., Thur., Sat., and Sun., June-Sept.

☙ **Marquette University,** Wisconsin Ave. between N. 11th and 17th Sts. (224-7448): Well-known university founded in 1881; the campus has many interesting buildings, including the **Joan of Arc Chapel** (see above), the **Marquette Hall Carillon,** which with 48 bells of different sizes is one of the largest in the country (frequent recitals), and the **Haggerty Museum of Art,** with a permanent collection of 5,000 works of art, open daily. Worth a visit.

☼☙ **Pabst Theater,** 144 E. Wells St. (271-3773): Famous for its acoustics and its richly baroque interior, this fine theater, built in 1895, has been restored to all its original splendor. Classical concerts and chamber-music recitals. Worth seeing.

INDUSTRIAL TOURS: Your visit to Milwaukee wouldn't be complete without a visit to the breweries on which its fame and fortune are founded.

Miller, 4251 W. State St. (931-2337): Second-largest brewery in the world. Visits to the plant and museum, with free beer tasting, Mon.-Sat. Apr.-Oct.; Mon.-Fri. the rest of the year.

Pabst, 915 W. Juneau Ave. (223-3709): One of the city's oldest; plant tours and tasting Mon.-Sat. from June till the end of Aug.; Mon.-Fri. the rest of the year.

Sprecher, 730 W. Ogden St. (272-2337): This little batch brewery, specializing in premium beers, was the first to be licensed following the end of Prohibition. Visit by appointment.

MUSEUMS OF ART: ☙ **Charles Allis Art Museum,** 1801 N. Prospect Ave. at 1630 E. Royall Pl. (278-8295): Huge collection of Oriental art from China, Korea, Japan, and Persia, as well as French and contemporary American paintings — property of the late "king of farm machinery," Charles Allis — housed in a very beautiful Tudor-style home built in 1909. See it. Open Wed.-Sun.

♟♟ **Milwaukee Art Museum,** 750 N. Lincoln Memorial Dr. (271-9508): This very modern building by Eero Saarinen standing at the edge of Lake Michigan houses old masters, German expressionists, American painters (particularly of the "Ashcan School"), and interesting temporary exhibitions. Recently enlarged. Shouldn't be missed. Open daily.

☙ **Villa Terrace,** 2220 N. Terrace Ave. (271-3656): Charming villa in the Italian Renaissance style designed in 1923 by architect David Adler, with terraces and gardens overlooking Lake Michigan. Sculpture, 18th-century furniture, Shaker handcrafts, old porcelain. Definitely a must-see. Open Wed.-Sun., June to late Aug.; Wed., Sat., and Sun. the rest of the year.

MUSEUMS OF SCIENCE AND HISTORY: ☙ **Milwaukee County Historical Center,** 910 N. 3rd St. at Pere Marquette Park (273-8288): Housed in a former bank building from around 1910, this interesting little museum retraces the history of Milwaukee in lively fashion. Old workshops, exhibitions, etc. Should be seen. Open daily.

☼🔔🔔 **Milwaukee Public Museum,** 800 W. Wells St. (278-2700): One of the country's largest natural history museums. Besides important zoological (dinosaurs in a reconstruction of their natural habitat) and geological exhibits, there's a replica of Old Milwaukee, a European village, a Hopi pueblo, a New Delhi bazaar, a Mexican street scene, etc. Also a "wizard wing," which will appeal to budding scientists. Fascinating; don't miss it.

PANORAMAS: 🔔 **First Wisconsin Center,** 777 E. Wisconsin Ave. (765-4321): The tallest building in Milwaukee, with an observation deck on the 41st floor offering a unique view of the city and the lake. Open Mon.-Fri.

PARKS AND GARDENS: 🔔 **Boerner Botanical Gardens,** 5879 S. 92nd St. (425-1130): This very lovely botanical garden standing in the enormous **Whitnall Park** is best known for its rose gardens and its seasonal flower exhibitions. Open daily, mid-Apr. to mid-Oct.

🔔 **Juneau Park,** N. Lincoln Memorial Dr. from Wisconsin Ave. to McKinley Marina: Lovely verdant promenade with beautiful views along the shore of Lake Michigan. Worth seeing.

☼🔔🔔 **Mitchell Park,** 524 S. Layton Blvd. at W. Pierce St. (649-9800): This remarkable botanic garden, whose three glass cupolas are as tall as a seven-story building and cover an area half the size of a football field, exhibits a complete range of tropical and desert vegetation which, given the local climate, is somewhat unexpected. Spectacular flowers in Aug. An absolute must. Open daily.

🔔 **Père Marquette Park,** Old World 3rd St. between State and Kilbourn Aves.: This little triangular garden, in the heart of downtown on the bank of the Milwaukee River, marks the spot where the French Jesuit Fr. Jacques Marquette and the trapper Louis Jolliet are supposed to have first come ashore in 1674. Should be seen.

🔔 **Schlitz Audubon Center,** 1111 E. Brown Deer Rd. (352-2880): 185 acres of wild, wooded park on Lake Michigan, host to foxes, deer, and many other wild animals. Open Tues.-Sun.

PERFORMING ARTS: For current listings of shows and cultural events, consult the entertainment pages of the two daily papers, *Milwaukee Journal* (evening) and *Milwaukee Sentinel* (morning), as well as the monthly *Milwaukee*.

Emil Blatz Temple of Music, Washington Park, U.S. 41 and Washington Blvd. (278-4389): Open-air concerts of classical and pop music: "Music Under the Stars" (July-Aug.).

Helfaer Theater, on the campus of Marquette U., 13th and Clybourn Sts. (224-7504): Modern and classical theater; concerts.

Melody Top Theater, 7201 W. Good Hope Rd. (353-7700): Musical comedies, Broadway hits. Tues.-Sun. from early June to mid-Sept.

Pabst Theater, 144 E. Wells St. (271-3773): Musical comedy, concerts, and contemporary theater in a lovely turn-of-the-century baroque setting, superbly restored.

Performing Arts Center, 929 N. Water St. (273-7206): This ultramodern group of buildings houses the Milwaukee Symphony Orchestra, under principal conductor Zdenek Macal (Sept.-June); the Milwaukee Ballet, with artistic director Ted Kivitt (Sept.-May); the Milwaukee Repertory Theater, performing classic and contemporary plays (Sept.-July); and the Florentine Opera Company and Bel Canto Chorus, under music director John Gage (Nov.-May).

Riverside Theater, 116 W. Wisconsin Ave. (271-2000): Broadway hits, touring companies, big-star shows.

Skylight Comic Opera, 813 N. Jefferson St. (271-8815): Operettas, musical comedies.

SHOPPING: Grand Avenue Mall, Wisconsin Ave. between Boston Store and Plankinton Ave.: Enormous shopping mall on three levels, radiating out from a spectacular glassed-in rotunda. More than 160 stores, boutiques, restaurants, and cafés of all kinds. The heart of Milwaukee shopping.

Old World Third Street, 3rd St. between Wells St. and Highland Ave.: Well-known food shops such as Usinger's Famous Sausage and Wisconsin Cheese Mart, Inc., restaurants, antique dealers. A lively, colorful neighborhood, reminiscent of an old European city.

W. K. Walthers, Inc., N. 60th St. and Florist Ave. (527-0770): The world's largest store entirely devoted to model-railroad equipment; a 50-year-old tradition. A must for all buffs. Open year round.

SPECIAL EVENTS: For exact dates on the events listed below, consult the **Milwaukee Convention & Visitors Bureau** (see "Tourist Information," above).

Lakefront Festival of the Arts (June): Open-air concerts, art and craft exhibitions.

Summerfest (late June to early July): Public concerts, circus shows, music festival, boating displays on the lake. Colorful and crowded.

Great Circus Parade (July): The big annual circus festival, with a very spectacular street parade; it draws more than 800,000 spectators.

Wisconsin State Fair (ten days in Aug.): Very popular agricultural fair, also with big-name shows, auto races, fireworks, etc.

Oktoberfest (Sept.-Oct.): Oceans of beer and music, tons of food; lots of warmth. The country's biggest beer festival.

Holiday Folk Fair (Nov.): Folklore shows, food festival, and arts from around the world.

SPORTS: Milwaukee boasts professional teams in four major spectator sports:
Baseball (Apr.-Oct.): Brewers, County Stadium (933-1818).
Basketball (Oct.-Apr.): Bucks, Mecca Arena (272-8080).
Football (Sept.-Dec.): Green Bay Packers, County Stadium (342-2717).
Ice Hockey (Sept.-Apr.): Admirals, Mecca Arena (225-2400).

STROLLS: **Lakefront,** along Lincoln Memorial Dr.: One of the country's finest urban landscapes; beautiful gardens and opulent private homes along Lake Michigan. Definitely worth seeing.

Old World Third Street, 3rd St. between Wells St. and Highland Ave.: The shopping district of Old Milwaukee (see "Shopping," above). A stroll that shouldn't be missed.

THEME PARKS: **Old World Wisconsin,** Wisc. 59 in Eagle, 35 mi. (56 km) SW (594-2116): Picturesque museum-village, comprising 50 or so 19th-century buildings, scrupulously restored, with authentic furniture and equipment, and walk-ons in period dress. A pleasant glimpse of the past. Open daily, May-Oct. Well worth the side trip.

Six Flags Great America, on Grand Ave. in Gurnee, Illinois, 32 mi. (51 km) south on I-94 (312/249-1776): 200-acre theme park with giant roller coaster, waterfalls with giant slides, and more than 100 other attractions. Facsimile of a pioneer village. Shows. Open daily in summer, wknds only in spring and fall; closed the rest of the year.

WINTER SPORTS RESORTS: ⛷ **Alpine Valley,** 36 mi. (57 km) SW on Wisc. 15 and County D Rd. (642-7374): 17 lifts. Dec. to mid-Mar.

⛷ **Little Switzerland,** 30 mi. (48 km) NW on U.S. 41 and Wisc. AA Rd. (644-5020): 8 lifts. Nov.-Mar.

ZOOS: 🐾 **Milwaukee County Zoo,** 10001 W. Bluemound Rd., 7 mi. (11 km) west on U.S. 18 (771-3040): One of the best-designed and most comprehensive zoos in the country, with more than 3,000 animals from giant gorillas to white tigers. See it from the mini-train. Open daily year round. 10 min. from dwntwn.

ACCOMMODATIONS

See the listing of toll-free numbers in the Appendix.

Room Rates in Milwaukee	
B (Budget)	up to $30
I (Inexpensive)	$30–$60
M (Moderate)	$60–$90
E (Expensive)	$90–$140
VE (Very Expensive)	$140 and up

Personal Favorites (in order of preference)

☀🛏🛏🛏 **Pfister Hotel** (dwntwn), 424 E. Wisconsin Ave., WI 53202 (414/273-8222; toll free, see Preferred). 333 rms, A/C, color TV, in-rm movies. AE, CB, DC, MC, V. Valet parking $4, pool, health club, sauna, two rests. (including the English Room), coffeeshop, bars, 24-hr rm svce, disco, hrdrsr, concierge, free child's cot. *Note:* Much admired by Enrico Caruso, this luxury hotel from the 1890s was recently expanded with the addition of an ultramodern tower. Elegant décor w. many works of art. The rms in the old building, with lake views, are charming; in the tower, they are simply functional. Polished svce; very good rests.; the smartest address in Milwaukee. VIP floor. **M–E**

🛏🛏🛏 **Hyatt Regency** (dwntwn), 333 W. Kilbourn Ave., WI 53203 (414/276-1234; toll free, see Hyatt). 484 rms, A/C, color TV, in-rm movies. AE, CB, DC, MC, V. Garage $6, two rests. (one revolving on the top floor), coffeeshop, three bars, rm svce, nightclub. *Note:* Huge ultramodern glass-and-concrete cube w. spectacular 18-story lobby and glass-walled elevators. Typical Hyatt comfort, but svce leaves a little to be desired. Group and convention clientele; direct access to the Convention Center. VIP floor. "333" is a commendable rest. **M–E**

🛏🛏 **Marc Plaza** (dwntwn), 509 W. Wisconsin Ave., WI 53203 (414/271-7250; toll free, see Preferred). 500 rms, A/C, color TV, in-rm movies. AE, CB, DC, MC, V. Parking $3, pool, health club, two rests. (including Le Bistro), coffeeshop, bar, rm svce, nightclub, hrdrsr, boutiques, crib free. *Note:* The largest and one of the oldest hotels in Milwaukee, several times renovated and now w. heated indoor pool and sauna. A favorite of business travelers; a VIP section is reserved for them on the 20th through 24th floors. Very central. Excellent svce. Same management as the Pfister Hotel. No-smoking floors. **M–E**

Park East Hotel (dwntwn), 916 E. State St., WI 53202 (414/ 276-8800). 160 rms, A/C, color TV, in-rm movies. AE, CB, DC, MC, V. Free parking, health club, rest., coffeeshop, bar, rm svce. *Note:* A modern, functionally designed building within a stone's throw of the lake. Spacious, comfortable rms, some w. lake views. Friendly reception. Very good value. **I–M**

Knickerbocker (dwntwn), 1028 E. Juneau Ave., WI 53202 (414/276-8500). 300 rms, A/C, color TV. AE, MC, V. Parking adjoining; rest. (Sally's Steak House), coffeeshop, bar. *Note:* Elderly but well-maintained hotel; also apartments by the week or month. A very acceptable standard of comfort. Some rms have a view of nearby Lake Michigan. The Steak House is very popular. An old Milwaukee landmark. **I**

Ambassador Hotel (nr. dwntwn), 2308 Wisconsin Ave., WI 53233 (414/342-8400). 189 rms, A/C, color TV. AE, CB, DC, MC, V. Free parking, rest. (Chandelier Room), bar. *Note:* Massive, aging hotel from the 1930s. Functional comfort. Praiseworthy rest. Reception and svce uneven, but good value overall. Very near the Pabst Mansion; 5 min. from dwntwn. **I**

Other Hotels (from top bracket to budget)

Hilton Inn Milwaukee River (nr. dwntwn), 4700 N. Port Washington Rd., WI 53212 (414/962-6040; toll free, see Hilton). 164 rms, A/C, color TV, in-rm movies. AE, CB, DC, MC, V. Free parking, pool, health club, rest. (Anchorage), bar, rm svce. *Note:* Typical modern luxury motel on the bank of the Milwaukee River. Very good seafood rest. Efficient svce. Comfortable rms, the best w. views across the river. 10 min. from dwntwn. **M–E**

Astor Hotel (dwntwn), 924 E. Juneau Ave., WI 53202 (414/ 271-4220; toll free 800/558-0200). 90 rms, A/C, color TV, in-rm movies. AE, CB, DC, MC, V. Parking $4, rest., bar, crib free. *Note:* Venerable but charming hotel in a quiet residential neighborhood nr. the lake. Friendly reception and svce. Some rooms w. kitchenettes. Satisfactory rest. (Nantucket Shores). Free breakfast. Good value overall. 5 min. from dwntwn. **M**

Howard Johnson Plaza Hotel (formerly the Admiral Inn; dwntwn), 611 W. Wisconsin Ave., WI 53203 (414/273-2950; toll free, see Howard Johnson's). 248 rms, A/C, color TV, in-rm movies. AE, CB, DC, MC, V. Free parking, rest., bar, rm svce, free child's cot. *Note:* Functional ten-story motel adjoining the Convention Center (MECCA). Modern comforts; huge rms w. balconies; efficient svce. Group and convention clientele. **I–M**

Ramada Inn Downtown (dwntwn), 633 W. Michigan Ave., WI 53203 (414/272-8410; toll free, see Ramada). 152 rms, A/C, color TV, in-rm movies. AE, CB, DC, MC, V. Free parking, pool, rest., bar, rm svce, free child's cot. *Note:* Conventional motel near the business district; spacious, comfortable rms, some w. refrigerators. Good svce. Business clientele. Good value. **I–M**

Continental Motor Inn (nr. dwntwn), 3001 W. Wisconsin Ave., WI 53208 (414/344-7500). 54 rms, A/C, color TV, in-rm movies. AE, CB, DC, MC, V. Free parking, adjoining rest. *Note:* Well-run small motel nr. the County Stadium. Functionally comfortable; friendly reception; very good value. 10 min. from dwntwn. **I**

In the Vicinity

The American Club (vic.), Highland Dr., Kohler, WI 53044 (414/457-8000; toll free 800/458-2562), 50 mi. (80 km)

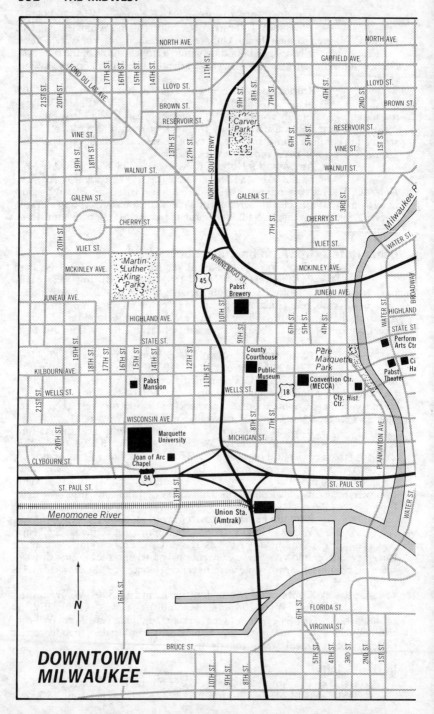

DOWNTOWN
MILWAUKEE

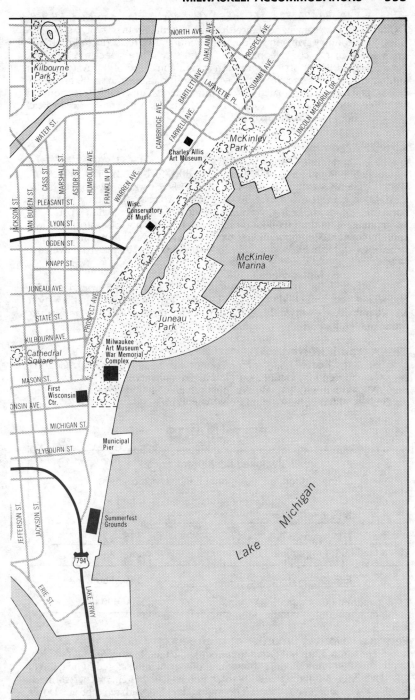

north on I-43 and Wisc. 23. 165 rms, A/C, color TV, in-rm movies. AE, CB, DC, MC, V. Free garage, pool, health club, 12 tennis courts, beach, sauna, canoes, cross-country skiing in season, trap shooting, two rests. (including Immigrant and Winery), coffeeshop, bar, 24-hr rm svce, disco, concierge, crib free. *Note:* Splendid British-style country inn standing in a beautiful private park, an authentic wildlife reserve. Spacious, lavishly comfortable rms in small three-story buildings which are designated historic monuments. Impeccable reception and svce. Very good sports facilities; rests. of real quality. A haven of peace and elegance one hour from Milwaukee. **E–VE**

Airport Accommodations

Red Carpet Hotel (vic.), 4747 S. Howell Ave., WI 53207 (414/481-8000; toll free 800/251-1962). 510 rms, A/C, color TV, in-rm movies. AE, CB, DC, MC, V. Free parking, two pools, health club, sauna, eight tennis courts, bowling alley, two rests. (including Harold's), bars, rm svce, disco, hrdrsr, cinema, free airport limo, free child's cot. *Note:* Huge, massive modern six-floor motel opposite the airport. Comfortable, well soundproofed rms, some w. private patios or balconies and mini-bars. Comprehensive sports facilities. Business clientele. Good value. 20 min. from dwntwn. **I–M**

Motel 6 (vic.), 5037 S. Howell Ave., WI 53207 (414/481-7800). 119 rms, A/C, color TV, free in-rm movies. DC, MC, V. Parking, pool, free child's cot. *Note:* Unbeatable value, across from the airport and 20 min. from dwntwn. Ideal if you're passing through by car, w. immediate access to I-94. **B**

YMCA/Youth Hostels

Red Barn Hostel (vic.), 6750 Loomis Rd. (414/529-3299). Country youth hostel open May-Oct.; 12 mi. (19 km) from dwntwn.

YMCA (dwntwn), 915 W. Wisconsin Ave. (414/291-5960). Men, women, families. 480 rms, health club, sauna. Very central.

RESTAURANTS

Milwaukee Restaurant Prices	
(per person, excluding drinks and service charges)	
B (Budget)	up to $15
I (Inexpensive)	$15–$25
M (Moderate)	$25–$40
E (Expensive)	$40–$60
VE (Very Expensive)	$60 and up

Personal Favorites (in order of preference)

Karl Ratzsch's (dwntwn), 320 E. Mason St. (276-2720). A/C. Lunch Tues.-Sun., dinner nightly; closed holidays. AE, CB, DC, MC, V. Jkt. *Specialties:* roast goose, sauerbraten, wienerschnitzel, hamhock with sauerkraut, lobster Thermidor, duckling with red cabbage, Dover sole. Superb 25-page list of German wines at reasonable prices. *Note:* A landmark of local gastronomy; the best German rest. in Milwaukee and—it inevitably follows—in the country. Atmosphere and décor haven't changed since 1903; even the classical-music trio at dinner is in period. Antique paneling and chandeliers. Exemplary svce. Resv. advisable at the end of the week. Still in the hands of the Ratzsch family, as it has been since it opened. *German-continental.* **I–M**

English Room (dwntwn), in the Pfister Hotel (see "Accommodations," above) (273-8222). A/C. Lunch Mon.-Fri., dinner nightly; closed holidays. AE, CB, DC, MC, V. J&T. *Specialties:* lobster, quenelles Nantua, crown of artichoke hearts, duck à la presse, sautéed sweetbreads w. garlic and red wine, truffled pheasant, bouillabaisse, flaming desserts. Marvelous wine list with 400 labels. *Note:* Luxury-hotel cuisine in all its splendor. Elegant, opulent décor; highly polished svce—w. prices to match. A classic of its kind since 1893. *Continental.* **I–M**

John Ernst Café (dwntwn), 600 E. Ogden Ave. (273-1878). A/C. Lunch/dinner Tues.-Sun.; closed Mon. AE, CB, DC, MC, V. Jkt. *Specialties:* sauerbraten with potato pancakes, Kassler rippchen, wienerschnitzel, jägerschnitzel, goulash, fish of the day. *Note:* A beautiful scene from 19th-century Germany, favored by local socialites since 1878. Authentic Bavarian décor w. huge open fireplace. Assiduous svce. Resv. advised at end of week. Milwaukee's oldest rest. *German.* **I–M**

Jack Pandl's Whitefish Bay Inn (vic.), 1319 E. Henry Clay St. (964-3800). A/C. Lunch/dinner Mon.-Sat.; closed Sun., holidays. AE, CB, DC, MC, V. *Specialties:* fish from Lake Michigan, German dishes, roast duck, schaum torte. *Note:* Another favorite of Milwaukee's German colony. Excellent broiled whitefish. Comfortable atmosphere; fine 75-year-old décor. Efficient svce; generous servings. German beer on draft. Resv. advised. 20 min. from dwntwn. *German-seafood.* **I**

Toy's Chinatown (dwntwn), 830 N. 3rd St. (271-5166). A/C. Lunch/dinner Tues.-Sun.; closed Mon. AE, MC, V. Jkt. *Specialties:* Cantonese food: chow mein, sweet-and-sour shrimps. *Note:* The food, and the elaborate Far Eastern décor, make this the best Chinese rest. in town. Svce on the abrupt side. Very good value. Opposite the Hyatt Regency Hotel. *Chinese.* **I**

Jake's Delicatessen (nr. dwntwn), 1634 W. North Ave. (562-1272). A/C. Lunch/dinner Mon.-Sat.; closed Sun. No credit cards. *Specialties:* corned beef, short ribs, giant sausage, pastrami, kosher specialties. *Note:* Likeable New York–style deli w. wonderful sandwiches to go. Often crowded at noontime. Resv. advised. *American.* **B–I**

Other Restaurants (from top bracket to budget)

Grenadiers (dwntwn), 747 N. Broadway (276-0747). A/C. Lunch Mon.-Fri., dinner Mon.-Sat.; closed Sun., holidays. AE, CB, DC, MC, V. J&T. *Specialties:* chicken w. morels, Calcutta lamb curry, breast of veal w. raspberries, fish of the day. The menu changes regularly; the wine list is good. *Note:* The young German chef, Knut Apitz, is indubitably producing some of the most inventive, delicate food around. Elegant Empire-style classical décor and a delightful glassed-in Garden Room. Very polished svce. One of the best places to eat in Milwaukee, in the heart of dwntwn. Valet parking; resv. necessary. *Continental.* **I–M**

Alioto's (vic.), 3041 N. Mayfair Rd., in Wauwatosa (476-6900). A/C. Lunch/dinner Mon.-Sat.; closed Sun. AE, CB, DC, MC, V. Jkt. *Specialties:* breaded steak Sicilian style, ribs of beef, traditional Italian dishes. *Note:* A very popular place w. lovers of prime beef and/or Italian cooking—even though the unmemorable décor reminds you of a railroad station waiting room. Good svce. 20 min. from dwntwn. A landmark since 1923. *Italian-steak.* **I**

 Boulevard Inn (nr. dwntwn), 4300 W. Lloyd St. (445-4221). A/C. Lunch/dinner daily. AE, CB, DC, MC, V. Jkt. *Specialties:* sauerbraten, sweetbreads w. shallots and champagne, New York steak, sautéed scallops, duckling w. red cabbage, fish of the day, cheesecake. *Note:* All the great standbys of German and continental cuisine, admirably prepared and served, in a pleasant country-inn setting 15 min. from dwntwn. Locally popular; resv. advised. *German-continental.* **I**

 Mader's (dwntwn), 1037 N. 3rd St. (271-3377). A/C. Lunch/dinner daily. AE, CB, DC, MC, V. Jkt. *Specialties:* oxtail, wienerschnitzel, hamhock Bavarian style, sauerbraten, Linzer torte. *Note:* Since 1902, yet another landmark for lovers of German food. Not as smart as Karl Ratzsch's or John Ernst, but just as popular, particularly for family parties. The Teutonic décor verges on kitsch; the svce is diligent and smiling. Resv. recommended in the latter part of the week. Free parking next door. Right in the heart of the celebrated Old World Third Street. *German.* **I**

 Café Siciliano (nr. dwntwn), 6904 N. Santa Monica Blvd. (352-5757). A/C. Dinner only, Mon.-Sat.; closed Sun., holidays. AE, CB, DC, MC, V. *Specialties:* fresh homemade pasta, chicken cacciatore, piccata of whitefish, shrimp Michelle, veal Grand Prix, cannoli. *Note:* A more authentic Italian *trattoria* you couldn't find in Italy; the food is from the southern part of the country, absolutely authentic and very reasonably priced. Reception and svce with a smile. Romantic Italian courtyard w. white stucco walls and tile floor. Well worth the 20-min. trip from dwntwn by car. Resv. advised. *Italian.* **I**

 Jake's (vic.), 6030 W. North Ave., in Wauwatosa (771-0550). A/C. Dinner only, nightly; closed Thanksgiving, December 24 and 25. AE, DC, MC, V. Jkt. *Specialties:* steak au poivre, filet of beef, scallops, fish of the day. Good wine list. *Note:* Superb meats broiled to perfection. Agreeable décor; friendly svce. 15 min. from dwntwn. Other location: 21445 W. Capital Dr., in Brookfield (781-7995), w. dinner nightly. *Steak.* **I**

 Sally's Steak House, in the Knickerbocker Hotel (see "Accommodations," above) (272-5363). A/C. Lunch Mon.-Fri., dinner Mon.-Sat.; closed Sun. AE, CB, DC, MC, V. *Specialties:* clam chowder, chicken Vesuvio, spiedini, steak Sicilian, duck stuffed w. chestnuts, very fine broiled meats. *Note:* Because of its substantial servings and generous drinks, this delightful hotel rest. has become a favorite of sports stars passing through town, and of actor Paul Newman, among other celebrities. Relaxed ambience and svce.; a fine place to eat. Resv. advised. *Steak-Italian.* **I**

 Old Town (nr. dwntwn), 522 W. Lincoln Ave. (672-0206). A/C. Lunch Tues.-Fri., dinner Tues.-Sun.; closed Mon. AE, MC, V. Jkt. *Specialties:* moussaka, baked lamb, paprika chicken, roast duckling, homemade pies and strudels. *Note:* Spicy but well-prepared Balkan food in a pretty setting. Efficient svce. Noisy background music. Resv. advised at the end of the week. 15 min. from dwntwn. *Continental.* **B–I**

 Turner's Bar & Restaurant (nr. dwntwn), 1034 N. 4th St. (273-5590). A/C. Lunch/dinner daily. AE, MC, V. *Specialties:* fish from Lake Michigan. *Note:* More than a century old, this is one of the city's most picturesque taverns. Particularly recommended on Fri. for the traditional fish fries. *Seafood.* **B**

Cafeterias/Fast Food

 Watts Tea Room (dwntwn), 761 N. Jefferson St. (276-6352). AE, MC, V. A century-old Milwaukee tradition; excellent daily specials, sandwiches, and house salads. Lunch only, Mon.-Sat. **B**

BARS & NIGHTCLUBS

Bogie's (dwntwn), 727 N. Van Buren (271-8771). Huge disco on several levels; also seafood bar and very acceptable rest. Locally popular. Open Mon.-Sat.

Bombay Bicycle Club (dwntwn), in the Marc Plaza (see "Accommodations," above) (271-7250). Excellent piano-bar; live jazz. Open Mon.-Sat.

Bryant's Cocktail Lounge (dwntwn), 1579 S. 9th St. (383-2620). The barmen have a repertory of 350 different cocktails. Comfortable, relaxing atmosphere. Open daily.

La Playa (dwntwn), in the Pfister Hotel (see "Accommodations," above) (273-8222). Tropical-style nightclub with large live orchestra. Superb view from the 23rd floor of the Pfister Hotel. Trendy crowd. Open Mon.-Sat.

Major Goolsby's (dwntwn), 340 W. Kilbourn Ave. (271-3414). This popular bar across from the MECCA Arena attracts mostly local sports stars and their fans. Good burgers. Open nightly.

Park Avenue (dwntwn), 500 N. Water St. (765-0891). Big-star shows; disco. Youthful atmosphere; locally popular. Open Tues.-Sat.

Safe House (dwntwn), 779 N. Front St. (271-2007). A rest. and nightclub in the James Bond tradition; you need a password and special codes for admission. The fashionable spot. Open nightly.

NEARBY EXCURSIONS

BROOKS STEVENS AUTOMOTIVE MUSEUM (10325 N. Port Washington, in Mequon, 10 mi., 16 km north on I-43N) (241-4185): Amazing collection of racing cars and production-line models from 1905 to the present day. One of the country's finest auto museums; a must for car buffs. Open daily.

LIZARD MOUND STATE PARK (County A Rd. at West Bend, 38 mi., 60 km, NW on U.S. 45N and Wisc. 144) (338-4445): Comprises 30 or so mounds of earth in the shape of beasts, birds, or geometric forms, the work of prehistoric Indians. Well worth the side trip. Open daily.

OSHKOSH (83 mi., 132 km, NW on U.S. 41N): On the banks of big Lake Winnebago, this friendly town of 50,000 people plays host for a week every year (late July to early Aug.) to the world's largest air show, the E.A.A. International Fly-in Convention, which attracts more than 300,000 spectators and participants. Thousands of early aircraft, from Mustangs to Spitfires and B-26s to World War I biplanes. Aerial acrobatics festival; flight demonstrations. For prop-plane enthusiasts. Interesting aeronautical museum, the **E.E.A. Air Museum,** 3000 Poberezny Rd. (426-4800), open daily. Don't miss this one. It should be combined with the excursion to Lizard Mound State Park (see above).

RACINE (29 mi., 46 km, SE on I-94S and Wisc. 20E): This pleasant little industrial town on Lake Michigan, most of whose inhabitants are of Danish descent, is the home of Johnson's Wax. The company's head office, built in 1939–1950 to the design of the great architect Frank Lloyd Wright, is an outright masterpiece of the modernist style. Conducted tour of the buildings at 14th and Franklin Sts., Tues.-Fri.; reservations (631-2154) a must. Don't miss it.

FARTHER AFIELD

☀️ 🔭 **SPRING GREEN AND WISCONSIN DELLS** (315 mi., 504 km, round trip via I-94 N. U.S.12S, Wisc. 60W, U.S. 14E, and I-94S): Three- to four-day trip beginning with a visit to 🔭 **Wisconsin Dells,** where the Wisconsin River has cut beautiful, wild gorges that can be reached only by boat. Guided sightseeing tours daily mid-Apr. to late Oct., 11 Broadway (608/254-8555). There is a Winnebago Indian village with a museum; tribal dances daily in summer. Many other tourist attractions. Well worth the trip.

Then on to ☀️ **Baraboo,** 12 mi. (19 km) south of Wisconsin Dells, with an interesting circus museum at 426 Water St. (608/356-8341), open daily mid-May to Sept., once the winter quarters of the famous Ringling Bros. circus. Parades, shows, menagerie, and more than 150 circus caravans of all ages; don't miss it. Also a very fine railroad museum at 🔭 **North Freedom,** 8 mi. (12 km) west on Wisc. 136 and County PF (608/522-4261), open daily mid-May to Sept., with a trip in a turn-of-the-century steam train. Amusing.

The next stop is at ☀️ 🔭 **Spring Green,** the town where the well-known architect Frank Lloyd Wright grew up, and where he built one of his houses, **Taliesin East,** 4 mi. (6 km) south on Wisc. 23 (608/588-2511). Open daily mid-May to mid-Oct; an absolute must-see. Another sight that shouldn't be missed is the extraordinary 🔭 **"House on the Rock,"** by architect Alexander Jordan, hanging 450 ft. (137 m) above the Wisconsin River, with its waterfalls, pools, and trees integrated spectacularly into the design of the building. It stands 9 mi. (14 km) south on Wisc. 23. Open daily from Apr. 1 to Nov. 15 (608/935-3639). Many other attractions nearby, including the world's largest carousel. A fascinating expedition, which shouldn't be missed.

Where to Stay in Wisconsin Dells

Shamrock Motel, 1321 Wisconsin Dells Pkwy., Wisconsin Dells, WI 53965 (608/254-8054). 48 rms. An inviting motel standing in its own gardens. Open mid-May to end-Oct. **I**

Tiki Motel, 1370 E. Hiawatha Dr., Wisconsin Dells, WI 53965 (608/253-4741). 32 rms. Small, congenial hotel on a lake. Open early May to mid-Oct. **I–M**

Where to Stay in Spring Green

The Prairie House, at the intersection of U.S. 14 and Wisc. 23, Spring Green, WI 53588 (608/588-2088). 31 rms. Modest but well-run motel open year round. **I**

CHAPTER 25

MINNEAPOLIS AND ST. PAUL

□ □ □

Lying on opposite sides of the Mississippi River, the Twin Cities complement each other harmoniously, while each retains its own distinct style and character. Minneapolis is dynamic, active, and mostly Scandinavian and Lutheran. St. Paul, the state capital, is more traditional; its people are mostly Irish or German, and Catholic. Minneapolis has its modern high-rises, its network of Skyways, its bustling nightlife, and the **Minnehaha Falls** of which Longfellow sang. St. Paul has fine classical buildings such as the **State Capitol,** designed by Cass Gilbert, the imposing **City Hall,** and **St. Paul's Cathedral,** one of the country's largest. Minneapolis is politically progressive and tolerant; Hubert Humphrey, the populist leader who was once vice-president of the U.S., was for many years first mayor of the city and then a senator from Minnesota. St. Paul may be more starchy and conservative, but the liberal Democrat Eugene McCarthy began his career here as a teacher at St. Thomas College. St. Paul is also the birthplace of F. Scott Fitzgerald, the chronicler of the "lost generation." Minneapolis, more prosaically, can lay claim to Charles Schulz, the creator of *Peanuts;* the late oil tycoon J. Paul Getty; the movie director George Roy Hill; and the rock singer Prince.

The site of the Twin Cities was explored in 1680 by the French missionary Fr. Louis Hennepin; their present prosperity began with the construction of the first flour mills in the 1850s. Successive waves of immigration—German, Irish, Polish, and above all, Scandinavian—did the rest. Minneapolis stands where the grain-growing prairies of the Dakotas and Minnesota (a name derived from two Sioux Indian words: "minne," meaning "water," and "sota," meaning "sky-colored") meet the waters of the Mississippi River where they are still—but only just—navigable; today it is still one of the country's principal agricultural markets. Along with St. Paul, it has also become the home of important electronic, chemical, forest-product, and food companies such as Honeywell, Control Data, General Mills, and 3M Corporation, as well as the hub for Northwest Airlines. While the winters are very harsh, Minneapolis and St. Paul rank among the greenest cities in the country, with 936 lakes and 513 parks or public gardens between them.

The Twin Cities pride themselves on being the intellectual capital of the Midwest, with the University of Minnesota, well-known symphony and chamber orchestras, an opera, many museums of high quality, and the famous **Guthrie Theater.** They are also the heart of a fabulous vacationland of deep forests, swift-running rivers teeming with fish, and numberless lakes, including **Lake Superior,** at 32,480 sq. mi. (84,130 km²) the world's largest body of fresh water. Such a wealth of tourist attractions has earned for Minneapolis/St. Paul the title of "Gateway of the Land of 10,000 Lakes," and for Minnesota the reputation of a hikers' and campers' paradise, at least during the summer months.

Last but not least, the Twin Cities represent in one sense a haven of peace and safety; by comparison with other great metropolitan areas their crime rate is among the lowest in the country (one-half Seattle's, one-sixth New York's).

BASIC FACTS: State of Minnesota (St. Paul is the state capital). Area Code: 612. Time Zone: Central Time. ZIP Codes: 55401 (Minneapolis); 55101 (St. Paul). Founded: 1840 (St. Paul); 1847 (Minneapolis). Approximate population: Minneapolis, 370,000; St. Paul, 270,000; metropolitan area, 2,260,000. Rank among U.S. metropolitan areas: 16th.

CLIMATE: With temperatures in July averaging 77°F (22°C), the summer is the only good time for a visit. The first snows of fall appear in mid-Oct. As to the winters, the only adjective that does them justice is "polar." January temperatures average 13°F (−10°C), with the mercury sometimes plunging to −22°F to −38°F (−30°C to −40°C), and demonstrating the value of the cities' "Skyways" —two networks of glassed-in, heated pedestrian walkways which link together the principal buildings of downtown Minneapolis and downtown St. Paul, respectively.

DISTANCES: Chicago, 406 mi. (650 km); Kansas City, 443 mi. (710 km); Milwaukee, 365 mi. (584 km); Rapid City, 633 mi. (1,012 km); St. Louis, 567 mi. (908 km); Winnipeg, 460 mi. (736 km).

ARRIVAL & TRANSIT INFORMATION

AIRPORT: Minneapolis/St. Paul International Airport (MSP), 10 mi. (16 km) SE of Minneapolis, 9 mi. (15 km) SW of St. Paul. Information: 726-5555.

U.S. AIRLINES: American (332-4168), Braniff (toll free 800/272-6433), Continental (332-1471), Delta (339-7477), Eastern (339-9520), Midway (toll free 800/621-5700), Northwest (726-1234), TWA (333-6543), United (339-3671), and USAir (338-5841).

FOREIGN CARRIERS: Air Canada (toll free 800/422-6232) and Canadian (toll free 800/426-7000).

CITY LINK: The **cab** fare to dwntwn Minneapolis is about $18; time, 30 min.; to dwntwn St. Paul, about $14; time, 40 min. Bus to both Minneapolis and St. Paul, **MSP & Suburban Limo** (726-6400), departs every 30 min. serving principal dwntwn hotels; fare, $7; time, 45 min.

Unless you intend to confine yourself to the two dwntwn districts with their covered walkways, the size of the metropolitan area and its profusion of green space make it advisable to rent a car with unlimited mileage.

The **public bus system, MTC** (827-7733), is trustworthy and practical for trips around dwntwn or between the Twin Cities.

CAR RENTAL (all at the airport): Avis (726-1723), Budget (726-5622), Dollar (726-9494), Hertz (726-1600), and National (726-5600). For dwntwn locations, consult the local telephone directory.

LIMOUSINE SERVICES: Carey Limousine (824-7665), Dav El Limousine (toll free 800/922-0343), Martin Limo Service (222-8544).

TAXIS: Cabs may be hailed on the street or taken from the waiting lines outside the big hotels, but are best summoned by phone. Recommended companies: **in**

Minneapolis, Blue & White (333-3331), and Yellow Cab (824-4444); **in St. Paul,** City Wide (292-1616) and Yellow Cab (222-4433).

TRAIN: AMTRAK, Midway Station, 730 Transfer Rd., St. Paul. (339-2382).

BUS: Greyhound, at 29 N. 9th St., Minneapolis (371-3311), and at 9th and St. Peter Sts., St. Paul (371-3311).

MISSISSIPPI CRUISES: Three- to ten-day cruises aboard the *Delta Queen* or the *Mississippi Queen,* paddlewheel steamers built in the 1920s. Luxurious kitsch. See Chapter 15 on New Orleans.

MINNEAPOLIS

INFORMATION & TOURS

TOURIST INFORMATION: The **Minneapolis Convention and Visitor Commission,** 15 S. 5th St., MN 55402 (612/348-4313).
For information on current shows and cultural events in the Twin Cities, call 922-9000.

GUIDED TOURS: Gray Line Tours (bus), 835 Decatur N. Minneapolis (591-0999): Conducted tours of the city and surroundings. Also serves St. Paul.

SIGHTS, ATTRACTIONS, & ACTIVITIES

ARCHITECTURAL HIGHLIGHTS: ☼ ⚖ **Guthrie Theater,** 725 Vineland Pl. (377-2224): This hall of ultramodern design is home to one of the country's best-known theatrical companies, founded in 1963 by the late Sir Tyrone Guthrie. The 1,400-seat hall occupies a 200° arc of a circle around an open stage. Year-round concerts and plays; don't miss these shows.

⚖ **Hennepin County Government Center,** Third Ave. and 5th St. (348-5596): Twin towers of pink granite, each 339 ft. (106 m) high, rise on either side of a huge lobby lit by picture windows, designed by architect John Carl Warnecke. This is the seat of the county government; worth a look.

⚖ **Hubert H. Humphrey Metrodome,** 900 S. 5th St. (332-0386): Impressive air-conditioned stadium with 60,000 seats, under a plastic dome; the Minnesota Twins and Minnesota Vikings make their headquarters here. Open Mon.-Fri.

☼ ⚖ **IDS Tower,** 80 S. 8th St. (372-3131): At 57 floors, 775 ft. (236 m), this is one of the tallest high-rises in the Midwest, designed by architects Philip Johnson and John Burgee. Splendid panorama from the 51st-floor Observation Deck. Visitor Information Center on the ground floor. You should take a look. Open daily.

⚖ **Minneapolis Grain Exchange,** 400 S. 4th St. (338-6212): The world's second-largest grain exchange, noisy and frenetic. Visitors' Gallery may be visited by appointment only. Open daily.

☼ ⚖ **Orchestra Hall,** 1111 Nicollet Ave. (371-5656): Home of the world-famous **Minnesota Orchestra** (formerly the Minneapolis Symphony Orchestra). The austere building has some of the finest acoustics ever achieved. See "Performing Arts," below.

☼📿 **Skyway,** around Marquette Ave. and Nicollet Mall: Ingenious system of heated walkways and footbridges connecting downtown's principal hotels, stores, and office buildings. Very useful in winter, when temperatures drop to −6°F to −22°F (−20°C to −30°C). You should certainly take a walk here.

☼📿 **Upper Lock,** at the foot of Portland Ave.: This giant lock, with a rise and fall of 49 ft. (15 m), marks the upper limit of the navigable waters of the Mississippi. An observation platform is open daily from Apr. 1 to Oct. 31. Spectacular.

CHURCHES/SYNAGOGUES: 📿 Basilica of St. Mary, Hennepin Ave. and

16th St. (333-1381): Renaissance-style building inspired by the basilica of St. John Lateran in Rome. Open daily; worth a look.

HISTORIC BUILDINGS: 📿 City Hall, 5th St. and Third Ave. South (348-

2491): The imposing 1891 City Hall, with its Big Ben clock tower, is a surprising contrast to its next-door neighbor, the ultramodern Hennepin County Government Center. Here you will find the *The Father of Waters,* the largest statue ever carved from a single block of Italian Carrara marble. Definitely should be seen. Open Mon.-Fri.

📿 **University of Minnesota,** Washington Ave. on either side of the Mississippi River (624-6504): One of the Midwest's oldest (1851) and most important universities, with 58,000 students. On its campus, one of the largest in the country, are two museums worth seeing: the **Bell Museum of Natural History,** open Tues.-Sun., and the **University Art Gallery,** open daily.

MUSEUMS OF ART: ☼📿📿 Minneapolis Institute of Arts, 2400 Third Ave.

South (870-3046): This very lovely museum of classical design is home to more than 70,000 art objects of all periods and places. Rich collection of great European masters from El Greco to Matisse; also Egyptian and Far Eastern art. Temporary exhibitions. Among the best-known works on display are *Temptation of Christ* by Titian, *Portrait of Cardinal Borghese* by Pietro da Cortona, Rembrandt's *Lucretia,* and Van Gogh's *Olive Grove,* as well as *Composition in Red* by Piet Mondrian, *White Feathers* by Matisse, and *Flayed Steer* by Chaim Soutine. Excellent cafeteria. An absolute must. Open Tues.-Sun.

☼📿📿 **Minneapolis Sculpture Garden,** 725 Vineland (375-7600): Open in September 1988 across from the Walker–Guthrie Theater complex, this sculpture garden, designed by the architect Edward Larrabee Barnes, has become one of the country's most important sites of its kind. Many of the 40 works displayed have been commissioned for this specific site, notably Spectacular Claes Oldenburg's 52 ft- (15m-) long fountain called "Spoonbridge and Cherry" and a Frank Gehry sculpture of a 22 ft- (6m-) high glass fish. Other works by Roy Lichtenstein, Henry Moore, Siah Armajani, Jacques Lipchitz, Richard Serra, Isamu Noguchi. . . . Open daily. Not to be missed.

☼📿📿 **Walker Art Center,** Hennepin Ave. at Vineland Pl. (375-7600): Contemporary art of all kinds—painting, sculpture, photography—as well as concerts, movies, and temporary exhibitions, in an interesting modern building whose new wing was designed by the distinguished Japanese architect Kenze Tangé. Twentieth-century American art is particularly well represented, with works by Edward Hopper, Andy Warhol, Robert

Rauschenberg, Clyfford Still, Barnet Newman, Louise Nevelson, George Segal, and others. Fascinating; shouldn't be missed. Open Tues.-Sun. Pleasant cafeteria.

MUSEUMS OF SCIENCE AND HISTORY: 🏛 American Swedish Institute, 2600 Park Ave. South (871-4907): This museum of Swedish art and folk tradition is housed in an amusing turn-of-the-century Roman Revival mansion. Also temporary exhibitions devoted to Swedish-American culture. Open Tues.-Sun.

🏛 **Hennepin County Historical Society Museum,** 2303 Third Ave. South (870-1329): Illustrates in lively fashion the history of the settlement of Minnesota from pioneer days to the turn of the century, with old workshops and reconstructions of domestic interiors. An absolute must. Open Tues.-Fri. and Sun.

🏛 **Minneapolis Planetarium,** Public Library, 300 Nicollet Mall (372-6644): Relatively small but well-designed planetarium, with a dome 40 ft. (12.5 m) high. For star-gazers. Open daily in summer; on Thur., Sat., and Sun. the rest of the year.

PANORAMAS: 🏛 IDS Tower, 80 S. 8th St. (372-1232): Observation deck on the 51st floor of this downtown skyscraper. On clear days you can see up to 30 mi. (48 km) away. Worth checking out. Open daily.

PARKS AND GARDENS: ☀ 🏛 Minnehaha Park, Minnehaha Parkway and Hiawatha Ave. South: This magnificent park on the banks of the Mississippi, famous for its 54-ft. (17-m) waterfall, was immortalized by Longfellow in *The Song of Hiawatha*, where he writes of its "laughing waters." Worth going out of your way for.

🏛 **Wirth Park,** Wayzata Blvd. and Wirth Pkwy.: Starting point of a panoramic drive through parks (**Eloise Butler Wild Flower Gardens**) and past lakes (**Lake Calhoun, Lake Harriet, Lake Hiawatha**) along the Minnehaha Parkway. Don't miss it.

PERFORMING ARTS: For current listings of shows and cultural events, consult the entertainment pages of the daily *Minneapolis Star & Tribune* (morning) and the monthly *Twin Cities*.

Dudley Riggs Theater, 2605 Hennepin Ave. (332-6620): Comedies, modern theater.

Guthrie Theater, 725 Vineland Pl. (377-2224): Classical and contemporary theater; one of the country's finest stock companies. Performances Tues.-Sat., May-Feb. Also concerts.

Hennepin Center for the Arts, 6th St. and Hennepin Ave. (332-4478): Home of the Minnesota Dance Theater, Feb.-May.

Met Center, 7901 Cedar Ave. S., in South Bloomington (853-9300): Big-name shows, musical comedies, circus shows.

Orchestra Hall, 1111 Nicollet Ave. (371-5656): Recitals, classical concerts. Home of the Minnesota Orchestra (principal conductor Edo de Waart). Oct.-Apr.

Showboat, University of Minnesota campus (625-4001): Melodrama, comedy, operetta on board an authentic "showboat" moored on the Mississippi in front of the university campus. June-Aug.

SHOPPING: Butler Square, 100 N. 6th St.: Agreeable stalls, boutiques, and restaurants in an old building in the warehouse district, cunningly restored. Very lively atmosphere.

Nicollet Mall, between Washington Ave. and Grant St.: One of the country's best-known pedestrian malls; many stores and boutiques. Pleasant promenade lined with trees and fountains. Worth a visit.

SPECIAL EVENTS: For exact dates, consult the **Minneapolis Convention and Visitors Commission** (see "Tourist Information," above).

Aquatennial Festival (late July): Colorful celebration of the many lakes and rivers of the Twin Cities. Parades on the Mississippi, boat races, sporting events, giant torchlight procession, open-air shows.

Sommerfest (July-Aug.): Much appreciated by music-lovers. Series of theme concerts by the Minnesota Orchestra, shows, opera.

SPORTS: Minneapolis is home to three professional teams:

Baseball (Apr.-Oct.): Twins, Hubert Humphrey Metrodome (375-7444).

Football (Sept.-Dec.): Vikings, Hubert Humphrey Metrodome (333-8828).

Ice Hockey (Sept.-Apr.): North Stars, Met Center (853-9300).

Horse Racing

Canterbury Downs, Minn. 101 and County Rd. 83 in Shakopee (445-7223), 20 mi. (32 km) by I-35W and Minn. 13 and Minn. 101. Racing Apr.-Nov.

STROLLS: **Nicollet Mall** (see "Shopping," above).

☀☖ **St. Anthony Falls,** Main St. SE and Central Ave.: These 45-ft. (15-m) falls mark the upper limit of navigation on the Mississippi. Spectacular walk along the dam and the locks. There are many cafés, stores, and restaurants on the riverbanks (River Place, St. Anthony Main, etc.).

THEME PARKS: ☀☖☖ **Murphy's Landing,** 2187 E. Minn. 101, in Shakopee, 22 mi. (35 km) southwest of Minneapolis on I-35W and Minn. 13 and Minn. 101 (445-6900): Replica of an 1850s pioneer village with church, school, blacksmith, grocer's, etc. Extras in period costume; craft demonstrations. The old buildings, all authentic, were moved here from their original sites elsewhere in Minnesota. Well worth the side trip. Open Tues.-Sun., May to late Oct., and in the month of Dec.

☖ **Valleyfair Amusement Park,** Minn. 101 in Shakopee, 20 mi. (32 km) SW of Minneapolis on I-35W and Minn. 13 and Minn. 101 (445-6500): Unusual amusement park laid out in turn-of-the-century style. Old carousels, old vehicles, streetcars. Also rafting down the river and giant roller coaster. Can conveniently be visited along with Murphy's Landing, above.

WINTER SPORTS RESORTS: ☖ **Afton Alps Ski Area,** 19 mi. (30 km) SE of St. Paul on U.S. 61 and Minn. 20 (436-5245): 18 ski lifts; open Nov.-Mar.

☖ **Birch Park Ski Area,** 20 mi. (32 km) NE of St. Paul on Minn. 5 and Wisc. 64 (439-2428): 11 ski lifts; open Nov.-Mar.

☖ **Buck Hill,** 18 mi. (29 km) south of Minneapolis on I-35W (435-7174): 7 ski lifts; open Nov.-Mar.

☖ **Hyland Hills,** 15 mi. (24 km) SW of Minneapolis on I-35W and 494 (835-4604): 7 ski lifts; open Nov.-Mar.

ZOOS: ☀☖☖ **Minnesota Zoo,** 20 mi. (32 km) via Cedar Ave. and Minn. 77 to Apple Valley (432-9000): Highly regarded ultramodern zoo covering 495 acres (200 ha.). From the monorail which takes you around, you can see more than 400 species in their natural habitats. Worth going out of your way for. Open daily, year round.

ACCOMMODATIONS
See the listing of toll-free numbers in the Appendix.

Room Rates in Minneapolis	
B (Budget)	up to $30
I (Inexpensive)	$30–$60
M (Moderate)	$60–$90
E (Expensive)	$90–$140
VE (Very Expensive)	$140 and up

Personal Favorites (in order of preference)

Radisson Plaza (dwntwn), 35 S. 7th St., MN 55402 (612/339-4900; toll free, see Radisson). 355 rms, A/C, color TV, in-rm movies. AE, CB, DC, MC, V. Parking $6, health club, sauna, two rests. (including Festival), coffeeshop, two bars, rm svce, nightclub, boutiques, free crib. *Note:* A brand-new tall tower of blue glass in the purest post-modern style, w. an impressive 18-story glass lobby. Huge, luxuriously comfortable rms; attentive, personal svce. Three VIP floors. Direct access to the Skyway. Business clientele; this is now *the* place to stay in dwntwn Minneapolis. **E–VE**

Vista Marquette (dwntwn), 710 Marquette Ave., MN 55402 (612/332-2351; toll free, see Hilton). 280 rms, A/C, color TV, in-rm movies. AE, CB, DC, MC, V. Garage $10, rest. (Marquis), coffeeshop, bar, 24-hr rm svce, drugstore, hrdrsr, concierge. *Note:* This elegant, modern hotel, much favored by business travelers, occupies 19 of the 57 floors of the immense IDS Tower. Remarkably spacious, inviting rms; exemplary comfort and facilities. Very good svce. Access via Skyway to principal dwntwn buildings. The Orion Room is a highly regarded rest. w. a panoramic view at the top of the IDS Tower. A good place to stay. **E–VE**

Hotel Luxeford (dwntwn), 1101 La Salle Ave., MN 55403 (612/332-6800; toll free 800/662-3232). 230 suites, A/C, color TV, in-rm movies. AE, CB, DC, MC, V. Parking $6, health club, sauna, rest., bar, rm svce, free breakfast, free crib. *Note:* Nothing but suites, comfortable and spacious, w. refrigerators; this new 12-story hotel is a favorite w. many business travelers. Very centrally located. Flawless reception and svce. A fine place to stay. **M–E**

Ritz Hotel (formerly the Sheraton Ritz; dwntwn), 315 Nicollet Mall, MN 55401 (612/332-4000; toll free 800/426-1987). 300 rms, A/C, color TV, in-rm movies. AE, CB, DC, MC, V. Parking $6, pool, health club, rest. (the Window Terrace), coffeeshop, bar, rm svce, free crib. *Note:* Modern, functional 19-story grand hotel; the four-story lobby is laid out as a tropical garden. Rms on the topmost floors are reserved for VIPs, and overlook the Mississippi River. Efficient svce; caters to groups and conventions. In the heart of dwntwn Minneapolis, w. direct access to the Skyway. Good value. **I–M**

Best Western Regency Plaza (dwntwn), 41 N. 10th St., MN 55403 (612/339-9311; toll free, see Best Western). 200 rms, A/C, color TV, in-rm movies. AE, CB, DC, MC, V. Free parking, pool, sauna, rest. (Harrigan's), coffeeshop, piano bar, rm svce, free crib. *Note:* Rela-

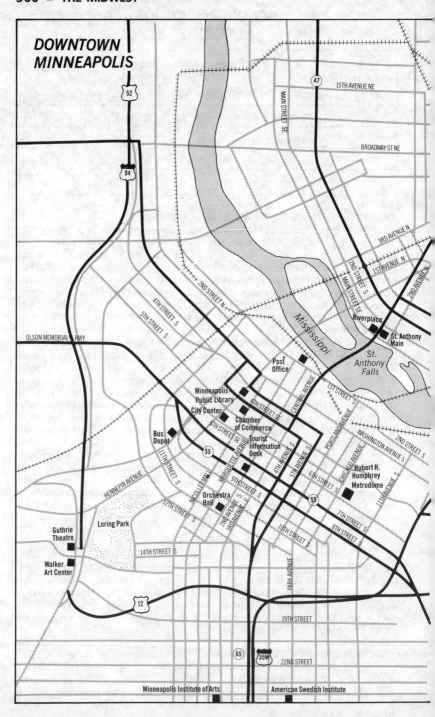

DOWNTOWN MINNEAPOLIS

tive ly modern but very comfortable hotel almost at the center of town, next to the Greyhound bus terminal. Large, well-designed rms; décor and facilities recently renovated. Friendly reception and svce. Business clientele. Very good value. **I–M**

Imperial Inn University (nr. dwntwn), 2500 University Ave. SE, MN 55414 (612/331-6000; toll free, see Imperial Inns). 80 rms, A/C, color TV. AE, CB, DC, MC, V. Free parking, pool, adjoining 24-hr coffeeshop, free breakfast, free crib. *Note:* Functional, well-kept motel nr. the university; inviting rms, some w. kitchenettes. Good value; 8 min. from dwntwn. **I**

Other Accommodations (from top bracket to budget)

Marriott City Center (formerly the Amfac; dwntwn), 30 S. 7th St., MN 55402 (612/349-4000; toll free, see Marriott). 582 rms, A/C, color TV, in-rm movies. AE, CB, DC, MC, V. Valet parking $13, health club, sauna, two rests. (including the Fifth Season), coffeeshop, two bars, rm svce, hrdrsr, drugstore, boutiques, free crib. *Note:* Here are 32 stories of glass and steel in the heart of dwntwn Minneapolis. Spacious, extremely comfortable rms (23 at the top of the tower are duplex rms), all w. spectacular view. Efficient svce. Two VIP floors. Very good luxury rest. Big business clientele. Direct access to Skyway. **E**

Radisson Hotel South (vic.), 7800 Normandale Blvd., MN 55435 (612/835-7800; toll free, see Radisson). 571 rms, A/C, color TV, in-rm movies. AE, CB, DC, MC, V. Free parking, pool, sauna, putting green, three rests. (including Aurora), two bars, rm svce, boutiques, free crib. *Note:* Huge convention hotel halfway between dwntwn and the airport. Décor and facilities recently renovated. Spacious rms, some w. private balconies or patios around the pool. VIP floors. Good svce; good luxury-hotel rest. Caters to business travelers and groups. 15 min. from dwntwn. **E**

Hyatt Regency Hotel (dwntwn), 1300 Nicollet Mall, MN 55403 (612/370-1234; toll free, see Hyatt). 540 rms, A/C, color TV, in-rm movies. AE, CB, DC, MC, V. Parking $6, pool, health club, four tennis courts, two rests. (including the Willows), two bars, 24-hr rm svce, nightclub, hrdrsr, boutiques, free crib. *Note:* An imposing white 20-story mammoth, a 5-min. walk from the Convention Center. All the comfort and facilities you'd expect of a Hyatt. Fine interior lobby with fountain. VIP floor, no-smoking floor. Ultraprofessional svce. Group and convention clientele. **M–E**

Holiday Inn Downtown (dwntwn), 1313 Nicollet Mall, MN 55403 (612/332-0371; toll free, see Holiday Inns). 324 rms, A/C, color TV, in-rm movies. AE, CB, DC, MC, V. Parking $5, pool, sauna, rest., coffeeshop, bar, nightclub, free crib. *Note:* Typical Holiday Inn right in dwntwn Minneapolis. Functional comfort; acceptable rest. Rather intrusive group and convention clientele. Interesting wknd packages. Very nr. the Convention Center. **M–E**

Days Inn–University (formerly the Cricket Inn; nr. dwntwn), 2407 University Ave. SE, MN 55119 (612/623-3999; toll free, see Days Inn). 130 rms, A/C, cable color TV. AE, CB, DC, MC, V. Free parking, nearby coffeeshop, free crib. *Note:* Functional six-floor motel nr. the U. of Minnesota campus. Huge, comfortable rms, some w. refrigerators. Good value. 8 min. from dwntwn. **I**

Fair Oaks (nr. dwntwn), 2335 Third Ave. South, MN 55404 (612/871-2000). 97 rms, A/C, color TV, in-rm movies. AE, CB, DC, MC, V. Free parking, rest. *Note:* Small, unpretentious, but acceptable hotel only 5 min. from dwntwn. Functional comfort; friendly reception. Ideal for budget travelers. **I**

YMCA/Youth Hostels

YMCA (dwntwn), 30 S. 9th St., MN 55402 (612/371-8750). 240 rms, pool, health club. Men and women.

RESTAURANTS

Minneapolis Restaurant Prices	
(per person, excluding drinks and service charges)	
B (Budget)	up to $15
I (Inexpensive)	$15–$25
M (Moderate)	$25–$40
E (Expensive)	$40–$60
VE (Very Expensive)	$60 and up

Personal Favorites (in order of preference)

510 Restaurant (nr. dwntwn), 510 Groveland Ave. (874-6440). A/C. Lunch Mon.-Fri., dinner Mon.-Sat.; closed Sun. and holidays. AE, CB, DC, MC, V. Jkt. *Specialties:* terrine of seafood, filet of pork Florentine, salmon or bass w. beurre blanc and Pernod, rack of lamb w. garlic sauce, breast of chicken broiled w. cucumbers and crème fraîche, fruit or Grand Marnier soufflé. Excellent list of French and California wines. *Note:* For those who enjoy classical French cooking in the grand manner, this is the best place to eat in the Twin Cities. The luxurious gray-and-ivory decorative scheme is complemented by thick carpets, crystal chandeliers, and Chippendale furniture. Efficient, competent svce. Much in favor with local society and visiting celebrities. Resv. indispensable. Valet parking. *French.* **M–E**

New French Café (dwntwn), 128 N. 4th St. (338-3790). A/C. Breakfast/lunch/dinner daily; closed holidays. AE, CB, DC, MC, V. *Specialties:* homemade terrines and pâtés, lamb chops w. green peppercorns, filet of salmon w. white wine and cream of shallots, rack of lamb w. zinfandel, poached halibut w. vermouth and lime, Queen of Sheba (blackberry-and-cream cake), mango sherbet. Very good list of French and California wines. *Note:* Dedicated to French-Californian nouvelle cuisine, and serving food that is usually inventive and elegant. The smooth white décor, under the high ceiling of this renovated warehouse, gives a rather chilly effect. The svce is pointlessly fussy; the patrons, mostly trendy, are artists and yuppies. Resv. strongly advised. *French-American.* **M**

Nigel's (dwntwn), 15 S. 12th St. (338-2235). A/C. Lunch/dinner Mon.-Sat.; closed Sun. AE, CB, DC, MC, V. *Specialties:* broiled meat and fish of the day, American nouvelle cuisine. Menu changes regularly. *Note:* Much enjoyed by local business people and visitors (mostly regulars), this likeable rest. offers creatively prepared food in a discreet, relaxed atmosphere. Very good svce. Resv. advisable, especially at lunchtime. *Continental-American.* **I–M**

Murray's (dwntwn), 26 S. 6th St. (339-0909). A/C. Lunch Mon.-Sat., dinner nightly. AE, CB, DC, MC, V. *Specialties:* barbecued shrimp, all kinds of meat including an excellent "Butter Knife Steak," catch of the day. *Note:* The steak lover's favorite for more than 40 years.

New-money décor and rather intrusive background music at dinner, but the meat is remarkable. Assiduous svce. A local institution. *Steak.* **I–M**

▼ **Black Forest Inn** (nr. dwntwn), 1 E. 26th St. (872-0812). A/C. Lunch/dinner daily (till 1 a.m.); closed holidays. AE, CB, DC, MC, V. *Specialties:* sauerbraten, wienerschnitzel, bratwurst, smoked pork chops w. sauerkraut, hot apfelstrudel, German beer. *Note:* A true-to-life German inn; inviting arbored patio w. pretty fountain for fine days. The clientele of artists and students (the College of Art and Design is a nr. neighbor) makes for a generally colorful, noisy atmosphere. Very efficient svce. Locally popular for two decades. *German.* **B–I**

▼ **Tejas** (dwntwn), 808 Nicollet Mall (375-0800). A/C lunch/ dinner daily. AE, MC, V. *Specialties:* duck empanada w. black bean sauce and green chile salsa, venison chile w. black beans and goat cheese. *Note:* This newcomer on the gastronomic scene offers innovative Southwestern cuisine supervised by famous chef and co-owner Stephan Pyles (Routh Street Cafe in Dallas, Texas). At $10 or so, the dinner entrees are a real bargain. In the basement of the new Conservatory Shopping Mall. Casual, elegant surroundings. Arrive early or late or expect to wait. *American.* **B–I**

Other Restaurants (from top bracket to budget)

▼▼ **Rosewood Room** (dwntwn), in the Omni Northstar Hotel, 618 Second Ave. S (338-2288). A/C. Breakfast/lunch daily, dinner Mon.-Sat. AE, CB, DC, MC, V. Jkt. *Specialties:* pheasant w. orange-and-herb sauce, Dover sole Colbert, noisettes of veal w. morel mushrooms and madeira, sweetbreads in brioche, chateaubriand. Very fine wine list. *Note:* Luxury-hotel cuisine near its best: impeccably traditional but a little old-fashioned. The same can be said of the 1930s décor. Frequented by local lawyers and bankers, especially at lunch. Faultless svce. Resv. recommended. Valet parking. *Continental-American.* **M**

☀ ▼▼ **Jax Café** (nr. dwntwn), 1928 University Ave. NE (789-7297). A/C. Lunch/dinner daily, Sunday brunch; closed holidays. AE, CB, DC, MC, V. Jkt. *Specialties:* steak, prime ribs, rainbow trout, baked salmon, chicken Kiev, duckling, tournedos béarnaise. *Note:* Trout lovers can catch their own here, in a specially designed pool complete with rustic brook and mill wheel. Excellent *cuisine bourgeoise* in a charming dining room built out over the garden. Very popular locally, especially for business luncheons, for the last half century. Resv. suggested. 10 min. from dwntwn. *Steak-seafood.* **I–M**

▼▼ **Coco Lezzone** (vic.), 5410 Wayzata Blvd., in Golden Valley (544-4014). A/C. Lunch/dinner Mon.-Sat.; closed Sun. AE, MC, V. *Specialties:* fresh homemade pasta, pizza, broiled chicken w. basil, fritto misto Tuscan style, catch of the day, homemade ice cream and sherbet, very good desserts. Excellent wine list. *Note:* Never trust appearances. In spite of its unappetizing name (literally "the filthy cook"), this elegant marble-floored *trattoria* w. its colonnades and lovely flower arrangements offers remarkably delicate northern Italian food at very reasonable prices. The odd name is a tribute to a famous rest. in Florence, L'Osteria del Coco Lezzone. Flawless svce. Resv. recommended. Valet parking. 20 min. from dwntwn along I-35W. *Italian.* **I**

▼ **Faegre's** (dwntwn), 430 First Ave. N (332-3515). A/C. Lunch Mon.-Sat., dinner nightly. AE, CB, DC, MC, V. *Specialties:* Caesar salad, Brazilian black-bean soup, fish stew w. saffron, fritto misto w. herbs and tomatoes, halibut w. olive oil and oregano, gâteau marjolaine. *Note:* One of the most popular dwntwn rests. among local yuppies. The modern décor emphasizes high glass walls and a sidewalk café which is very pleasant in fine weather. Innovative and often original American nouvelle cuisine. Also a crowded singles bar. *American.* **I**

Fuji Ya (dwntwn), 420 S. 1st St. (339-2226). A/C. Lunch/ dinner Mon.-Sat.; closed Sun. and holidays. AE, CB, DC, MC, V. Jkt. *Specialties:* sushi, teppanyaki, teriyaki, tempura, sukiyaki. *Note:* Charming Japanese rest. w. a modern, light-filled décor. The dexterity w. which the chefs handle their chopping knives is equalled only by their speed. Ask to be seated in the Teppanyaki Room on the ground floor. Fine view of the Mississippi and its locks. A very good place to eat; resv. advised. *Japanese.* **B–I**

Nankin Café (dwntwn), 2 S. 7th St. (333-3303). A/C. Lunch/dinner daily; closed holidays. AE, CB, DC, MC, V. *Specialties:* chow mein, chop suey, Cantonese and Szechuan dishes. *Note:* This venerable (1919) local institution boasts one of the country's largest menus, w. over 100 Chinese dishes, not to mention some traditional American offerings. Modern Far Eastern décor. Excellent value. *Chinese-American.* **B–I**

Nye's Polonaise Room (nr. dwntwn), 112 Hennepin Ave. (379-2021). A/C. Lunch/dinner daily (till midnight). AE, DC, MC, V. *Specialties:* pirogies, borscht, hamhock w. sauerkraut, T-bone steak, bigosz, spareribs. *Note:* Gigantic servings of hearty Polish-American food, w. waltzes and polkas in the background. Strong on atmosphere and local color. Moderate eaters don't belong here. Dinner-dances on wknds. Excellent value. *East European–American.* **B–I**

Pracna on Main (nr. dwntwn), 117 Main St. (379-3200). A/C. Lunch/dinner daily. AE, CB, DC, MC, V. *Specialties:* sandwiches, homemade soups, barbecued spareribs, steak, daily specials. *Note:* A likeable imitation of an oldtime saloon on the banks of the Mississippi. Simple but very acceptable food. Open-air terrace for fine weather. Youthful, relaxed atmosphere. Locally popular. *American.* **B–I**

Cafeteria / Fast Food

Ediner (nr. dwntwn), 3001 Hennepin Ave. (822-6011). Open daily. No credit cards. Cafeteria amusingly decorated in pastel shades, 1950s style. Hamburgers, daily specials. Good cafeteria food. **B**

BARS & NIGHTCLUBS

Jazzline (633-0329) gives detailed information on current programming at Twin Cities jazz clubs.

First Ave. and 7th St. Entry (dwntwn), 701 First Ave. N (338-8388). Rock and funky jazz; lots of warmth. Setting for Twin Cities rock singer Prince's movie *Purple Rain.*

Loon Café (dwntwn), 500 First Ave. North (332-8342). Best-known of the dwntwn singles bars; also so-so rest. Open nightly.

New French Bar (dwntwn), 128 N. 4th St. (338-3790). Very "in" singles bar frequented by artists and foundation people. Open nightly.

Rupert's (nr. dwntwn), 5410 Wayzata Blvd. (544-5035). Elegant disco with live jazz or swing and a big 1940s-style orchestra. Open Tues.-Sat.

Williams (nr. dwntwn), 2911 Hennepin Ave. S. (823-6271). Hot disco. Attracts a young uptown crowd. Open nightly.

ST. PAUL

INFORMATION & TOURS

TOURIST INFORMATION: The **St. Paul Convention and Visitors Bureau,** 600 NCL Tower, 445 Minnesota St., MN 55101 (612/297-6985).

For information of current shows and cultural events in the Twin Cities, call 922-9000.

GUIDED TOURS: Viking Explorer (boat): Three-day cruises on the Mississippi between St. Paul and La Crosse, Wisc.; summer only. For information, call toll free 800/328-1472.

Padelford Packet Boat Co. (boat), Harriet Island, St. Paul (227-1100): Two-hour mini-cruises on the Mississippi aboard two elderly paddlewheelers, the *Jonathan Padelford* and the *Josiah Snelling*. Early May to late Sept.

Gray Line Tours (bus): See above, Guided Tours Minneapolis.

SIGHTS, ATTRACTIONS, & ACTIVITIES

ADVENTURES: Inner Tube Rides, intersection of Wisc. 35 and Wisc. 64 at Somerset, Wisc., 27 mi. (43 km) NE of St. Paul on Minn. 5 and Wisc. 64 (715/247-3728): Shooting the rapids of the Apple River on inflated inner tubes. Time: 45 min. to 3 hrs., according to distance. The favorite local sport; entertaining and low risk. Open daily, mid-May to mid-Sept.

ARCHITECTURAL HIGHLIGHTS: ☀ ☖ ☖ **Ordway Music Theater,** 345 Washington St. (224-4222): Opened in 1985, this splendid auditorium with its glass façade and copper dome is now the home of the famous St. Paul Chamber Orchestra and the Minnesota Opera; many other concerts are also given here. A definite must-see.

☖ **Skyway,** around 6th and Cedar Sts.: Same network of heated walkways as in Minneapolis, connecting the main downtown buildings and department stores. Should be seen.

CHURCHES/SYNAGOGUES: ☖ **Old Muskego Church,** on the campus of Luther Theological Seminary, 2481 Como Ave. (641-3456): The first (1844) church in the country built by Norse immigrants; moved to its present site in 1904. Worth seeing.

☀ ☖ **Cathedral of St. Paul,** 239 Selby Ave. (228-1766): Built in 1915, this is a reasonably exact replica of St. Peter's in Rome, with its dome 175 ft. (53 m) high, its great west rose window, and its massive granite-and-travertine construction. Open daily; don't miss it.

HISTORIC BUILDINGS: ☖ **Alexander Ramsey House,** 265 S. Exchange St., at Walnut St. (296-0100): Fine Victorian house which was the home of the first governor of the Minnesota Territory (1872). Period furniture and decoration. Should be seen. Open Tues.-Sun. from Apr. to Dec.

☀ ☖ **City Hall and Court House,** 4th and Wabasha Sts. (298-4012): This 1932 building displays 19 floors of marble and rare woods from around the world. Impressive 60-ton statue, 44 ft. (13 m) high, in white onyx by the Swedish sculptor Carl Milles, of *The Indian God of Peace*. Shouldn't be missed. Open Mon.-Fri.

☀ ☖☖ **Fort Snelling,** Minn. 5 and Post Rd., 6 mi. (10 km) SW on Minn. 5 (726-1171): Former army fortress from the 1820s, scrupulously restored; attained its greatest importance in the wars against the Sioux and Chippewa. Picturesque site where the Mississippi and Minnesota rivers meet. Has retained all the flavor of the adventurous 19th-century frontier. Military parades in period uniform, daily May-Oct. Don't miss it.

☀ ☖ **Landmark Center,** 5th and Market Sts. (292-3225): This fine 1892 example of the Roman Revival style, once known as the Old Federal Courts Building, is capped by a tall belfry reminiscent of Trinity

1. Minnesota Office of Tourism
2. Ordway Music Hall
3. Civic Center
4. St. Paul Public Library
5. State Capitol
6. St. Paul Cathedral
7. Minnesota Museum of Art
8. Minnesota State Fairgrounds
9. Minnesota World Trade Center
10. Science Museum of Minnesota
11. 3M William L. McKnight Omnitheatre
12. Union Depot Place

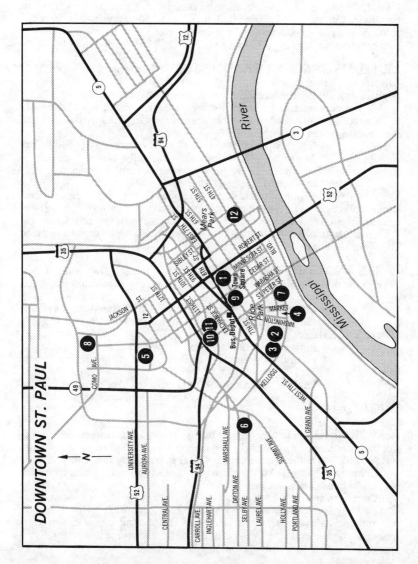

Church in Boston. Today it's an active cultural center with an auditorium, exhibition galleries, the **Schubert Piano Museum,** and part of the collection of the **Minnesota Museum of Art.** Open daily; don't miss it.

☼ 🔔🔔 **State Capitol,** Aurora Ave. between Cedar Park and Park Ave. (296-2881): The Minnesota legislature building, designed by the great Cass Gilbert, has one of the world's largest self-supporting domes, inspired by the work of Michelangelo in Rome. No fewer than 21 kinds of marble and 25 different types of stone are employed in this important building, whose foundation stone was laid in 1896. Open daily.

MUSEUMS OF ART: 🔔 Minnesota Museum of Art, St. Peter St. and Kellogg Blvd. (292-4355): This modest museum occupies two separate buildings: the **Landmark Center** (see "Historic Buildings," above) and the **Jemme Building.** It has an interesting collection of American art from the end of the 19th century to the present day, as well as African and Asian art. Open Tues.-Sun.

MUSEUMS OF SCIENCE AND HISTORY: 🔔 Children's Museum, 1217 Bandana Blvd. North (644-5305): Although this is a teaching museum, it's very popular with children. Among other attractions it has careful replicas of a TV studio, a grocery store, and a doctor's office, as well as computers and dozens of machines of all kinds which visitors can operate themselves. Open daily in summer, Tues.-Sun. the rest of the year.

🔔 **Gibbs Farm Museum,** 2097 W. Larpenteur Ave. (646-8629): Authentic 1850s farm, showing daily life of 19th-century country people. For lovers of living history; should be seen.

☼ 🔔🔔 **Science Museum of Minnesota,** 30 E. 10th St. (221-9488): Group of ultramodern buildings housing interesting natural-science collections in paleontology, biology, anthropology, geology, etc., as well as an auditorium and an innovative cinema with a giant hemispherical screen, the **William L. McKnight 3M Omnitheater.** Very dramatic. Open daily in summer, Tues.-Sun. the rest of the year.

PARKS AND GARDENS: 🔔 Cherokee Park, Cherokee Blvd. and Ohio St.: Lovely view from the heights of the park overlooking the Mississippi. Worth seeing.

🔔 **Como Park,** Lexington Pkwy. and W. Como Ave.: A 445-acre (180-ha.) park 15 mi. by car from dwntwn. Flower shows, zoo, 70-acre (28-ha.) lake.

🔔 **Indian Mounds Park,** Earl St. and Mounds Blvd.: Funerary mounds of Sioux chiefs on the banks of the Mississippi. Should be seen.

🔔 **Phalen Park,** Arcade St. and Larpenteur Ave.: Huge public garden around a lake, which draws many visitors winter and summer alike. Golf course.

PERFORMING ARTS: For current listings of shows and cultural events, consult the entertainment pages of the two daily papers, *St. Paul Dispatch* (evening) and *St. Paul Pioneer Press* (morning), as well as the monthly *Twin Cities.*

Chimera Theater, 30 E. 10th St. (293-1043): Dramas, comedies, children's shows, Broadway hits.

Civic Center, 143 W. 4th St. (224-7403): Live pop and rock concerts.

Ordway Music Theater, 345 Washington St. (224-4222): Opera, recitals, pop and classical concerts, dance. Home of the St. Paul Chamber Orchestra (principal conductor, Hugh Wolf) and of the Minnesota Opera (director, Kevin Smith). Lovely modern building.

O'Shaughnessy Auditorium, 2004 Randolph Ave. (690-6700): Classical concerts, opera.

World Theater, 10 E. Exchange St. (298-1300): Fine old theater beautifully restored. Shows and concerts. This was long the setting for the taping of the popular radio program "Prairie Home Companion."

SHOPPING: Town Square, 7th and Minnesota Sts.: More than 70 boutiques, stores, and cafés around a huge indoor public garden where waterfalls, pools, and tropical plants combine to create a beautiful setting. Spectacular.

SPECIAL EVENTS: For exact dates, consult the **St. Paul Convention and Visitors Bureau** (see "Tourist Information," above).

Winter Carnival (late Jan. to early Feb.): Processions, sporting events (marathon), parades through the city. Very popular since its inception in 1885; draws hundreds of thousands of spectators every year.

Minnesota State Fair (late Aug. to early Sept.): This very popular fair-exhibition draws more than a million visitors yearly. Horse shows. Plenty of atmosphere.

SPORTS: Same as Minneapolis.

STROLLS: ❋ ‍‍ **Summit Avenue,** around Lexington Ave.: Smart, elegant main drag with opulent churches and upper-class homes from the second half of the 19th century. They include the **James J. Hill House,** built by the railroad magnate in 1891 at 240 Summit Ave. (open Wed.-Sun.), and the house of author F. Scott Fitzgerald at 599 Summit Terrace (no visitors). Neither the very lovely 1862 **Burbank-Livingston-Griggs House** at 432 Summit Ave. nor the **Governor's Mansion** at 1106 Summit Ave. allows visitors. Well worth the side trip.

ACCOMMODATIONS
See the listing of toll-free numbers in the Appendix.

Room Rates in St. Paul	
B (Budget)	up to $30
I (Inexpensive)	$30–$60
M (Moderate)	$60–$90
E (Expensive)	$90–$140
VE (Very Expensive)	$140 and up

Hotels (from top bracket to budget)
Radisson Hotel St. Paul (dwntwn), 11 E. Kellogg Blvd., MN 55101 (612/292-1900; toll free, see Radisson). 475 rms, A/C, color TV, in-rm movies. AE, CB, DC, MC, V. Garage $6, pool, health club, two rests. (including Le Carrousel), coffeeshop, two bars, rm svce, disco, hrdrsr, free crib. *Note:* Modern luxury hotel of conventional type intended for

groups and conventions. Comfortable rooms, the best overlooking the attractive winter garden/pool. Revolving rest. on the 22nd floor w. a clear view of the city and the Mississippi River. Efficient svce. In the heart of dwntwn, with direct access to Skywalk. **M–E**

☀ 🛏🛏🛏 **St. Paul Hotel** (dwntwn), 350 Market St., MN 55102 (612/ 292-9292; toll free 800/457-9292). 254 rms, A/C, color TV, in-rm movies. AE, CB, DC, MC, V. Garage $8, rest. (L'Étoile), coffeeshop, bar, rm svce, nightclub, free crib, concierge. *Note:* Venerable turn-of-the-century luxury hotel in the European style, décor and facilities elegantly renovated. Quality and style; large, luxuriously comfortable rms; flawless svce. Excellent French rest. Centrally located with direct Skyway access; favored by those in-the-know. **M–E**

🛏🛏 **Holiday Inn Town Square** (dwntwn), 411 Minnesota St., MN 55101 (612/291-8800; toll free, see Holiday Inns). 250 rms, A/C, color TV, in-rm movies. AE, CB, DC, MC, V. Parking $5, rest., coffeeshop, bar, rm svce, piano bar, boutiques, free crib. *Note:* Rather futurist architecture in the heart of dwntwn St. Paul; 14-story glassed-in lobby w. indoor fountains and gardens. Comfort and facilities above the Holiday Inn standard; efficient svce. Direct access to Town Square Shopping Mall and the Skyways network. Business and group clientele. Interesting wknd discounts. **M**

🛏🛏 **Sheraton Midway** (nr. dwntwn), 400 Hamline Ave. North, MN 55104 (612/642-1234; toll free, see Sheraton). 197 rms, A/C, color TV, in-rm movies. AE, CB, DC, MC, V. Free parking, pool, health club, sauna, rest., bar, rm svce, disco, free crib. *Note:* Large conventional motel conveniently halfway between Minneapolis and St. Paul. Very comfortable; efficient svce. Ideal if you're driving, with direct access to I-94. **M**

🛏 **Center City Inn** (dwntwn), 77 E. 9th St., MN 55101 (612/ 227-7331). 96 rms, A/C, cable color TV. AE, CB, DC, MC, V. Parking $2, rest., bar, rm svce, free crib. *Note:* High-rise motel in the center of St. Paul, as its name suggests. Functional comfort; inviting rms w. balconies. Good value. **I**

🛏 **Travelodge St. Paul** (nr. dwntwn), 149 E. University Ave., MN 55101 (612/227-8801; toll free, see Travelodge). 50 rms, A/C, color TV, in-rm movies. AE, CB, DC, MC, V. Free parking, nearby rest., free crib. *Note:* Small, modest, unpretentious motel very nr. the State Capitol. Spacious rms w. balconies; functionally comfortable. Free morning coffee. Ideal for budget travelers. **I**

Airport Accommodations

🛏🛏🛏 **Hotel Sofitel** (vic.), 5601 W. 78th St., in Bloomington, MN 55435 (612/835-1900; toll free 800/328-6303). 288 rms, A/C, color TV, in-rm movies. AE, CB, DC, MC, V. Free valet parking, pool, health club, sauna, two rests. (including Chez Colette), coffeeshop, bar, rm svce, nightclub, free crib, concierge. *Note:* This modern hotel, part of the French-owned Sofitel chain, strongly upholds the gastronomic standards of its native country w. two good rests., one of which is open late, and a brasserie. Pleasant six-story lobby-garden. Very comfortable rms; smiling reception. Business clientele. 15 min. from dwntwn. Minneapolis, 10 min. from the airport. Interesting wknd discounts. **M–E**

YMCA/Youth Hostel

AYH Hamline (vic.), Snelling and Hewitt Aves., MN 55104 (612/641-2000). 14 beds. Youth hostel on the campus of Hamline University, halfway between Minneapolis and St. Paul. Open June to late Aug.

RESTAURANTS

St. Paul Restaurant Prices	
(per person, excluding drinks and service charges)	
B (Budget)	up to $15
I (Inexpensive)	$15–$25
M (Moderate)	$25–$40
E (Expensive)	$40–$60
VE (Very Expensive)	$60 and up

Restaurants (from top bracket to budget)

Blue Horse (nr. dwntwn), 1355 University Ave. (645-8101). A/C. Lunch Mon.-Fri., dinner Mon.-Sat.; closed Sun. and holidays. AE, CB, DC, MC, V. Jkt.; tie suggested. *Specialties:* fettuccine Alfredo, steak Diane, Dungeness crab w. sauce Poulette, sole amandine, roast duckling, broiled walleye pike. Imposing list of California and imported wines. *Note:* For more than 25 years the most fashionable and distinguished rest. in the Twin Cities. Elegant but intimate setting. Fish and seafood dishes can be highly recommended. Very polished svce. Resv. a must. 20 min. from Minneapolis. Valet parking. *Continental.* **M**

L'Étoile (dwntwn), in the St. Paul Hotel (see "Accommodations," above) (292-9292). A/C. Lunch Mon.-Fri., dinner Mon.-Sat.; closed Sun. and holidays. AE, CB, DC, MC, V. J&T. *Specialties:* lamb en croûte Paul Bocuse, catch of the day, roast veal w. wild mushrooms, rack of lamb, very good desserts. *Note:* Overlooking Rice Park, this rest., luxuriously decorated in shades of emerald, offers a delicate luxury-hotel-style cuisine in which Minnesota products are featured. Flawless svce. Draws big-business executives and local politicians. Resv. recommended. Valet parking. *French.* **M**

Forepaugh's (dwntwn), 276 S. Exchange St. (224-5606). A/C. Lunch Mon.-Fri., dinner nightly, Sunday brunch. AE, MC, V. Jkt. *Specialties:* seafood cassolette, scallops in beurre blanc, veal Cordon Bleu, filet mignon béarnaise, stuffed capon. Very good desserts; large wine list. *Note:* Successful union of classical and modern French cuisine under the skilled hand of chef Bernard Lagarde, in a big, elegant Victorian house (1870), tastefully restored. Svce of the highest order; romantic atmosphere; very popular locally. Resv. a must. valet parking. *French.* **I–M**

Lexington (nr. dwntwn), 1096 Grand Ave. (228-5878). A/C. Lunch/dinner Mon.-Sat. (until midnight); closed Sun., Dec. 24–25. No credit cards. Jkt. *Specialties:* steak, roast beef, fresh salmon, roast pheasant, catch of the day. *Note:* This well-established family rest. has enjoyed a solid reputation since 1934. The cooking is professional, but unimaginative despite the 35 dishes on the menu. The cocktails are generously poured. Very popular locally; resv. advised. 8 min. from dwntwn. *Steak-seafood.* **I–M**

Gallivan's (dwntwn), 354 Wabasha St. (227-6688). A/C. Lunch/dinner Mon.-Sat.; closed Sun. AE, MC, V. *Specialties:* broiled pike, steak, roast beef, fresh seafood. *Note:* Irish-style pub, usually noisy and crowded. A local institution, particularly favored by newspaper people and politicians. The food is simple but very acceptable. Also a piano bar w. dancing; an entertaining place. *American.* I

🍸 **Venetian Inn** (nr. dwntwn), 2814 Rice St. at Little Canada (484-7215). A/C. Lunch/dinner Mon.-Sat.; closed Sun. and holidays. AE, CB, DC, MC, V. *Specialties:* fresh homemade pasta, barbecued spareribs, steak, catch of the day. *Note:* The food is mostly Italian but the prime beef is also excellent and very reasonably priced. In the hands of the Vitale family for more than half a century. Friendly, smiling svce. Locally popular; this place can be confidently recommended. Resv. advised. 15 min. from dwntwn. *Italian.* B–I

Cafeteria/Fast Food

Café Latte (nr. dwntwn), 850 Grand Ave. (224-5687). Open daily. AE. Interesting soups and daily specials as well as excellent desserts, in a modern neon-and-chrome setting. Very popular locally. **B**

BARS AND NIGHTCLUBS

Jazzline (633-0329) gives detailed information on current programming in the Twin Cities jazz clubs.

Dixie (nr. dwntwn), 695 Grand Ave. (222-7345). Fashionable bar; trendy patrons.

Gallivan's (dwntwn), 354 Wabasha St. (227-6688). Friendly, jam-packed piano bar with dancing. Also a restaurant (see above). Open Mon.-Sat.

NEARBY EXCURSIONS

🛏 **ROCHESTER** (88 mi., 140 km, SE on U.S. 52): One of the capital cities of U.S. medicine. With its 800 doctors and hundreds of researchers and technicians, the **Mayo Clinic,** founded in 1898 by Dr. William Worrall Mayo and his sons, William James and Charles Horace, is world-renowned, particularly in the field of cardiac surgery. The research laboratories and diagnostic center, 200 1st St. SW (507/284-2511), are open to visitors Mon.–Fri. Also an interesting museum of medicine, the **Mayo Medical Museum,** 1st St. and Third Ave. SW (507/284-3280), open daily, and the lavish home of the Mayo family, **Mayowood** (507/282-9447), conducted tour by appointment daily except Mon. and Fri. (Tours leave from the corner of County Road 122 and Salem Road SW.) Well worth the side trip.

☀🛏🛏 **ST. CROIX VALLEY** (32 mi., 51 km, NE on I-35W and Minn. 36): Wonderful panoramic drive on Minn. 95 from **Stillwater** to **Taylor Falls,** 30 mi. (48 km) north, along "America's River Rhine," as the St. Croix River has been called.

From **Somerset,** on the right bank of the St. Croix, you can go down the Apple River on an inner tube (see St. Paul "Adventures," above). Don't miss it.

Where to Stay En Route

IN STILLWATER. ☀ 🛎🛎🛎 **Lowell Inn,** 102 N. 2nd St., Stillwater, MN 55082 (612/439-1100). 21 (very comfortable) rms. AE, DC, MC, V. The elegant colonial setting is more than a century old; the rest. is excellent. Boat trips are available on the St. Croix River. **M–E**

FARTHER AFIELD

GRAND PORTAGE NATIONAL MONUMENT (318 mi., 508 km, NE of Minneapolis via I-35 and U.S. 61): Owes its name to the "portage road" along Lake Superior, where the first French trappers, at the end of the 17th century, carried their canoes on their backs. The original 9-mi. (15-km) Indian trail is still there, but muddy and mosquito-infested. At Grand Portage, terminus of the ferry for Isle Royale National Park (see below), which operates from mid-June to the beginning of Sept. (call 218/728-1237 for information), the 1788 fur-trading post has been partially reconstructed to its original form and is worth a visit (open daily, mid-May to mid-Oct.). U.S. 61 offers you a panoramic drive along Lake Superior.

ISLE ROYALE NATIONAL PARK (343 mi., 548 km, NE of Minneapolis via I-35 and U.S. 61 and ferry from Grand Portage): This magnificent island, 45 by 8 mi. (72 by 13 km) in size, was so named by French trappers; it's a kind of open-air zoo, with dozens of animal species from the red fox to the elk and from the wolf to the fish-eagle. The only ways you can get around are by outboard boat (you can hire one there), by canoe, or on foot since no vehicles are allowed on the island. There are 155 mi. (250 km) of footpaths through the beautiful, unspoiled landscape, but beware of fog and mosquitos in summer.

Isle Royale is also the scene of many 19th-century shipwrecks, and has been designated a **national underwater museum,** with scuba-diving facilities and guided tours of underwater attractions provided by the National Parks Service. Note that scuba-diving should be attempted only by experts because of the low water temperature in Lake Superior (60°F, 16°C).

The park is open May-Oct. For lovers of nature and/or fishing, a visit (and a stay) here should on no account be missed. For further information, contact the Superintendent, Isle Royale National Park, 87 N. Ripley St., Houghton, MI 49931 (906/482-0984).

Where to Stay in the Park

There are 30 or so camping areas. In addition, ☼ ᵬ **Rock Harbor Lodge** has 60 comfortable rooms and 20 bungalows for rent from June to Sept., but reservations must be made very far ahead. In summer apply to National Park Concessions, P.O. Box 405, Houghton, MI 49931 (906/337-4993); out of season, National Park Concessions, Mammoth Cave, KY 42259 (502/773-2191).

VOYAGEURS NATIONAL PARK (294 mi., 470 km, north of Minneapolis via I-35 and U.S. 53): Another miraculously preserved wildlife sanctuary, covering 217,000 scenic acres (88,000 ha.) of lakes, islands, forests, and watercourses on the Canadian border, with a hundred camping areas but no hotels. Wear warm clothes, even in summer; not for nothing is the nearest city, **International Falls,** known as "America's Icebox" because of its year-round chill. A fisherman's paradise, with boats available for rent on the spot. For information, contact the Superintendent, Voyageurs National Park, P.O. Box 50, International Falls, MN 56649 (218/283-9821).

🔭 LAKE DISTRICT AND SUPERIOR NATIONAL FOREST (845 mi., 1,352 km, round trip via U.S. 10N, Minn. 27E, U.S. 169N, Minn. 18W, Minn. 371N, U.S. 2E, U.S. 169N, Minn. 1E, U.S. 61N, U.S. 615, and I-35S): An enthralling trip for devotees of nature in the raw, through the myriad lakes and endless forests of northern Minnesota.

The trip begins along a smooth-flowing stretch of the Mississippi, taking you to the 🏛 **birthplace of Charles A. Lindbergh,** the first man to make a non-stop solo flight across the Atlantic, with many personal mementos of the famous flyer (Lindberg Dr. at Little Falls. 612/632-3154). It is open daily from May to mid-Oct; winter and spring by reservation.

Then on along **Mille Lacs Lake** and **Leech Lake,** which between them boast 750 mi. (1,200 km) of shoreline (there are dozens of friendly inns and motels around 🔭 **Brainerd, Walker,** and **Grand Rapids**). Next, drive to 🔭 **Chippewa National Forest,** 3,400 sq. mi. (880,000 ha.) of dense standing timber with 2,000 lakes of all sizes—a paradise for hunters, fishermen, and canoeists. Superior National Forest is one of the last places in the country where wolves may be found in the wild.

On your way, stop at 🏛 **Hibbing,** "the iron-ore capital of the world," with the world's largest open-pit iron-ore mine, the Hull-Rust Mine, on Third Ave. (218/262-4900). You can inspect the enormous hole, 3 mi. (5 km) long and 535 ft. (163 m) deep, from an observation platform open daily, mid-May to mid-Sept. Well worth seeing. Hibbing has two famous children of whom it is equally proud: the Greyhound Bus Company and the singer Bob Dylan.

The excursion ends with a visit to **Grand Portage National Monument** and **Isle Royale National Park** (see above).

On the way back, **Duluth,** a busy commercial port with its astonishing Aerial Lift Bridge, is a stop you shouldn't fail to make.

You should allow at least a week for this spectacular drive—but you're not advised to make it in any season except summer!

Where to Stay En Route

As noted above, there are dozens of friendly inns and motels around Brainerd, Walker, and Grand Rapids.

IN DULUTH. 🛏🛏 **Best Western Edgewater East,** 2330 London Rd., Duluth, MN 55812 (218/728-3601). 120 rms. A functionally comfortable roadside motel. **I–M**

🛏🛏 **Best Western Edgewater West,** 2211 London Rd., Duluth, MN 55812 (218/728-5141). 59 rms. A small roadside motel with a view of Lake Superior. **M**

Where to Eat En Route

As noted above, there are dozens of friendly inns around Brainerd, Walker, and Grand Rapids.

IN DULUTH. 🍷 **Grandma's Saloon and Deli,** 522 Lake Ave. South, near the lift bridge (218/727-4192). Lunch/dinner daily. Honest, down-home food. **B–I**

CHAPTER 26

INDIANAPOLIS

□ □ □

Today a flourishing metropolitan area of more than 1,000,000 inhabitants, Indianapolis was not initially a pioneer encampment like so many other midwestern cities. Its site was determined by simple logic, rather than by some caprice of history or nature: Indianapolis is at the dead center of Indiana. The city's layout was inspired by that of Washington, D.C., and follows a rigorous geometry. Wide diagonal avenues converge on **Monument Circle** like the spokes of a wheel, and a right-angled grid of streets connects the city's principal monuments: the imposing **State Capitol**, the **World War Memorial Hall**, the **Soldiers and Sailors Monument**, the **Scottish Rite Cathedral**, and the national headquarters of the **American Legion**.

Indianapolis was long considered provincial, politically conservative (the John Birch Society originated here), and boring (it was once known as "Naptown"). But over the last dozen years the capital of Indiana has come to be perceived as a modern, lively, and safe city (the crime rate is one of the lowest in the country). Witness the renovation around picturesque **City Market, Union Station,** the **Hoosier Dome Complex** (an impressive enclosed stadium that seats 63,000), and the future **White River State Park.**

Neither Robert Cavelier, sieur de La Salle, the Frenchman who explored Indiana along the St. Joseph River (1679), nor Gen. William Henry Harrison, who defeated the great Shawnee chief Tecumseh in the battle of Tippecanoe (1811), could have dreamed that Indiana's capital would one day (since 1911) be world-famous for its Memorial Day weekend auto race, the thrilling and perilous "Indianapolis 500." At the heart of the famed corn belt, Indianapolis is one of the largest grain and cattle markets in the country. It is also the headquarters of the giant pharmaceutical company Eli Lilly (29,000 employees), as well as one of the most important hubs of rail and road communication in North America, where no fewer than four major Interstate highways converge. The state of Indiana is rightly called "the crossroads of America."

Some of the city's notable native children are guitarist Wes Montgomery, author Kurt Vonnegut, Jr., comedian and talk-show host David Letterman, the late actor Steve McQueen, and the famous bandit John Dillinger.

BASIC FACTS: Capital of Indiana. Area Code: 317. Time Zone: Eastern Time. ZIP Code: 46204. Founded: 1820. Approximate population: city, 775,000; metropolitan area, 1,190,000. 14th-largest city in the U.S.

CLIMATE: Indianapolis weather is typical of the midwestern Great Plains: radiant springs; oppressive, humid summers (mean July temperature 76°F, 24°C); mild, pleasant autumns; and rather harsh winters (mean Jan. temperature 28°F, −2°C). Spring is the ideal season to visit the area.

DISTANCES: Chicago, 181 mi. (290 km); Cincinnati, 106 mi. (170 km); Nashville, 297 mi. (446 km); St. Louis, 235 mi. (376 km).

ARRIVAL & TRANSIT INFORMATION

AIRPORT: Indianapolis International Airport (IND): 7 mi. (11 km) SW. Information: 248-9594.

AIRLINES: American (262-1054), Continental (635-0290), Delta (634-3200), Eastern (639-6611), Northwest (631-0377), TWA (635-4381), United (638-6363), USAir (248-1211).

CITY LINK: The **cab** fare from the airport to downtown is about $12–$14; time, about 15 min. **Bus:** AAA Airport Limo (247-7301), serving major downtown hotels, leaves every 20 min.; fare, $8; time, about 20 min. Unless you intend to make excursions outside the city, the relatively small downtown area makes renting a car unnecessary. The public transportation system (bus and trolley) is good: for information, call Metro Transit (635-3344).

CAR RENTAL (all at Indianapolis International Airport): Avis (244-3307), Budget (244-6858), Dollar (241-8206), Hertz (244-2413), National (243-7501). For downtown locations, consult the local telephone directory.

LIMOUSINE SERVICES: Carey Limousine (247-7307), VIP Limousine Service (635-2308).

TAXIS: Taxis are few and relatively expensive; they may be found outside the major hotels or simply summoned by phone: Checker Cab (637-5421), Metro Taxi (634-1112), Yellow Cab (637-5421).

TRAIN: AMTRAK station, 350 S. Illinois St. (632-1905).

BUS: Greyhound, 127 N. Capitol Ave. (267-3050).

INFORMATION & TOURS

TOURIST INFORMATION: The Indianapolis Convention and Visitors Bureau, One Hoosier Dome, Suite 100, IN 46225 (317/639-4282).
   Telephone recording with an up-to-date listing of cultural events and shows: 317/631-1500.

GUIDED TOURS: Gray Line Tours (bus), 155 W. Washington St. (317/634-4433). Guided tours of the city, serving the major hotels.

SIGHTS, ATTRACTIONS, & ACTIVITIES

ARCHITECTURAL HIGHLIGHTS: ※ ⚐ **Hoosier Dome,** 100 S. Capitol (262-3452): This 63,000-seat stadium with an inflatable dome opened in 1984 and is one of the largest in the country. Built at a cost of $65 million, it can accommodate conventions, auto shows, and trade fairs, as well as the Colts' home football games. The stadium is part of the enormous **Indiana Convention Cen-**

ter, with five exposition halls, two large ballrooms, and 55 meeting rooms. Impressive. Guided tours daily.

       🗿 **Indiana University–Purdue University at Indianapolis (IUPUI),** W. Michigan St. (264-2134): These two universities, with 23,000 students in all, were merged in 1969 into the present first-rate educational complex. With six hospitals and 90 clinics, faculties, and specialty schools, the **University Medical Center** enjoys a worldwide reputation in the areas of cancer, heart surgery, and organ transplants. IUPUI is also famous for its high-caliber sports teams. Interesting modern architecture. Campus visits Mon.-Fri.

       🗿🗿 **Indianapolis Motor Speedway,** 4790 W. 16th St.: Some 6 mi. (9 km) NW, this is the most celebrated auto raceway in the world. Nearly 400,000 spectators come here each May for the spectacular and sometimes deadly "Indy 500," staged on the 2.5-mi. (4-km) oval course. Bobby Rahal holds the track speed record set in 1986—an average of 170.722 mi./hr (273.12 km/hr). Interesting racing museum. Guided tour of the raceway (sorry —the bus goes no faster than 37 mph, 60 kph!). Open daily. For speed demons. (Seats for the Indianapolis 500 range from $15 to $60 and are scooped up weeks and months in advance. For reservations, call 317/241-2500, or write: 4790 W. 16th St., Speedway, IN 46224.)

CHURCHES/SYNAGOGUES: 🗿 Carmelite Monastery, 2500 Cold Spring Rd. (925-5654): The chapel, entranceway, and gardens of this medieval castle-like monastery are open to the public. Worth a look. Open daily.

       🌞🗿 **Scottish Rite Cathedral,** 650 N. Meridian St. (635-2301): This stunning Gothic-Tudor–style cathedral dates from 1929, and has a 212-ft (65-m) tower with a 54-bell carillon. The baroque interior, wood-carvings, and two organs with 5,500 pipes are an absolute must-see. Open Mon.-Fri.

HISTORIC BUILDINGS: 🗿 Benjamin Harrison Memorial Home, 1230 N. Delaware St. (631-1898): The former residence of the 23rd president houses interesting furniture, paintings, and period decoration (dates from 1874). See it. Open daily.

       🗿 **State Capitol,** between Washington and Ohio Sts. and Capitol and Senate Aves. (232-8687): The home of the state legislature is a Corinthian-style building from 1888, constructed of Indiana limestone and topped with a large brass dome. Worth a look. Visit by appointment Mon.-Fri.

       🌞🗿 **Union Station,** 39 Jackson Pl. (635-7955): A perfect example of urban renewal, this once-abandoned station dating from 1888 is now a vast shopping area with more than 70 stores and boutiques, 40 restaurants, three movie theaters, five nightclubs, and a hotel with unusual décor. Very lively ambience. Since reopening in 1986, it has attracted more than 20 million visitors. Don't miss it.

MARKETS: 🌞🗿 Old City Market, 222 E. Market St.: Picturesque enclosed market dating from 1886 in an original cast-iron structure. Dozens of food stalls, boutiques, little restaurants. Lively and colorful. Open Mon.-Sat. See it.

MONUMENTS: 🌞🗿 Soldiers and Sailors Monument, Monument Circle: This imposing monument rising 278 ft (87 m) in the heart of the city was erected in memory of those who died in the Revolutionary War. There is elevator access to the observation platform at the top. Not to be missed. Open daily.

       🗿 **World War Memorial,** 431 N. Meridian St.: Monument and commemorative exhibition room dedicated to the dead of the

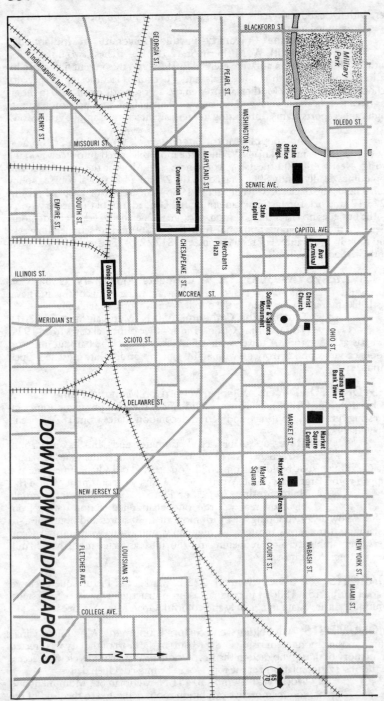

DOWNTOWN INDIANAPOLIS

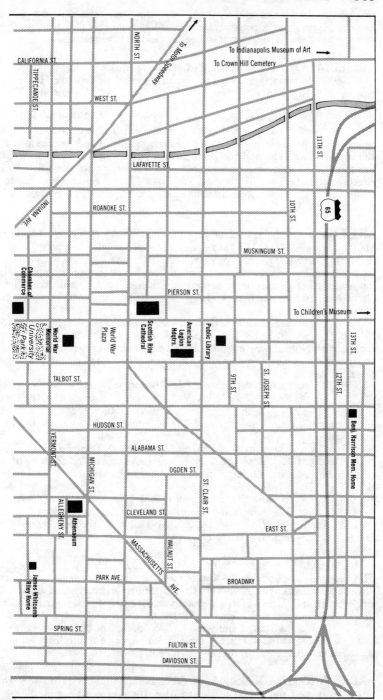

two World Wars, Korea, and Vietnam. Interesting military museum as well as gardens. Worth a visit. Open daily. In the northeast corner of the square is a four-story building that is the **American Legion** national headquarters.

MUSEUMS OF ART: ⚱ Morris-Butler House Museum, 1204 N. Park Ave.
(636-5409): Interesting museum of Victorian decorative arts (the Helena Rubinstein collection) in a building that dates from 1862. Worth a visit. Open Wed.-Sun.

☀⚱⚱ **Museum of Art,** 1200 W. 38th St. (923-1331): On a hill overlooking the White River, this remarkable art museum comprises three theme pavilions: Clowes Pavilion, medieval and Renaissance art; Krannart Pavilion, Oriental and primitive art; Lily Pavilion of Decorative Arts, European and American paintings (including Turner watercolors, works by El Greco, Claude Lorrain, Rembrandt, Van Dyck). Pretty gardens with modern sculptures, including Robert Indiana's pop masterpiece, *LOVE.* Not to be missed. Open Tues.-Sun.

MUSEUMS OF SCIENCE AND HISTORY: ⚱⚱ Children's Museum,
3000 N. Meridian St. (924-5431): This very instructional children's museum is the world's largest. It presents very lifelike collections and displays from the earliest times (an Indiana cave, a giant dinosaur, an Egyptian tomb complete with mummies) through the present (a huge miniature railroad network, computers, etc.). Wonderful for children of all ages. Open daily in summer, Tues.-Sun. the rest of the year.

⚱ **Indiana Basketball Hall of Fame,** 1241 N. Pennsylvania St. (872-4537): Consecrated to one of the country's favorite sports. With Notre Dame in South Bend and Indiana-Purdue in Indianapolis, Indiana is a major breeding ground for national basketball champions. Open Mon.-Sat.

⚱ **James Whitcomb Riley Home,** 528 Lockerbie St. (631-5885): Very lovely Victorian house dating from 1872, between 1892 and 1916 the home of James Whitcomb Riley, the "Hoosier poet" and creator of "Little Orphan Annie." Period décor and layout. See it. Open Tues.-Sun.

☀⚱ **Museum of Indian Heritage,** 6040 De Long Rd., Eagle Creek Park (293-4488): As you might expect in Indiana, one of the best American Indian museums in the country, with rich archeological collections. See it. Open Tues.-Sun.

⚱ **Indiana State Museum,** 202 N. Alabama St. (232-1637): This interesting museum, in the former City Hall, documents the natural and cultural history of Indiana, especially since the pioneer era. Giant Foucault pendulum in the entranceway. Open daily.

PANORAMAS: ⚱ Crown Hill Cemetery, 3402 Boulevard Pl. (925-8231):
This vast landscaped cemetery—one of the largest in the country—is the burial place of poet James Whitcomb Riley (his grave offers an unimpeded view of the city), President Benjamin Harrison, and the notorious John Dillinger. The monumental entranceway to the cemetery is itself worth a trip.

⚱ **La Tour,** 1 Indiana Sq. (635-3535): The best view of the city (admission fee) from the 35th floor of the Indiana National Bank Tower. Choose the bar over the restaurant. Open Mon.-Sat.

PARKS AND GARDENS: ⚱ Eagle Creek Park, 56th St. west of I-465: This
much-frequented and largely unspoiled (deer running wild) setting of 4,400

acres lies on the western edge of the city. It offers golf courses, canoeing, and walking areas for summer; cross-country skiing in winter.

🔔 **Riverside Park,** 2420 E. Riverside Dr.: Smaller than Eagle Creek Park, with "only" 902 acres, Riverside Park, steps away from downtown, is divided lengthwise by the White River. Golf courses, pool, and an inviting picnic area.

PERFORMING ARTS: For daily listings of all shows and cultural events, consult the entertainment pages of the daily papers *Indianapolis News* (evening) and *Indianapolis Star* (morning).

Beef 'n Boards, 9301 Michigan Rd. NW (872-9664): Dinner theater offering Broadway shows and recitals with big-name stars.

Circle Theater, 45 Monument Circle (635-6355): Home of the Indianapolis Symphony Orchestra (with principal conductor Raymond Leppard); performances Oct.-May. Offers many other musical shows as well.

Clowes Memorial Hall, 4600 Sunset Ave. (283-9696): Home of the Butler Ballet; season Oct.-Apr.

Hilton U. Brown Theatre, 304 W. 49th St. (926-1581): Open-air concerts and musical comedies in July and Aug.

Indiana Repertory Theatre, 140 W. Washington St. (635-5252): Classical and modern theater; performances Oct.-Apr.

Indianapolis Civic Theater, 1200 W. 38th St. (923-4597): One of the oldest theater troupes in the country, performing drama and comedy.

Murat Theater, 502 N. New Jersey (635-2433): Home of the Indianapolis Opera Company. The theater's Hollywood-Moorish architecture is as baroque as you could wish.

SPECIAL EVENTS: For the exact schedule of events below, consult the **Indianapolis Convention and Visitors Bureau** (see "Tourist Information," above).

500 Festival (May): A month chock-full of festivities leading up to the famous Indy 500: balls, parades, art festivals, and more. Gala ambience. Not to be missed.

Indiana State Fair (Aug.): One of the largest and most colorful agricultural fairs in the country, with horse racing, cattle shows, and more.

Indiana Speed Week (a week in early Sept.): The spectacular U.S. championship of drag racing at Indianapolis Raceway Park. For velocity lovers.

SPORTS: Indianapolis has four professional teams:

Baseball (Apr.-Sept.): Indians, Bush Stadium (632-5371).

Basketball (Oct.-Apr.): Pacers, Market Square Arena (639-2112).

Football (Sept.-Dec.): Colts, Hoosier Dome (632-4321).

Ice Hockey (Oct.-Apr.): Checkers, Market Square Arena (639-2112).

STROLLS: 🔔 **Lockerbie Square,** between N. York, College, Michigan, and East Sts.: Narrow, cobblestone streets and pretty, brightly colored 19th-century houses make this a fine area for a stroll.

WINTER SPORTS RESORTS: 🔔 **Nashville Alps Ski World Resort,** 59 mi. (94 km) south on Ind. 37 and 46 (812/988-6638): Two chair lifts. Slope of 310 ft (84 m). Open late Dec. to early Mar.

ZOO: 🔔 **Indianapolis Zoo,** 1200 W. Washington St. (638-8072): Brand new zoo, very complete and well-conceived with 2,000 animals roaming simulated environments. Rare birds and interesting section devoted to Australia. See it. Open daily.

ACCOMMODATIONS

See the listing of toll-free numbers in the Appendix.

Room Rates in Indianapolis	
B (Budget)	up to $30
I (Inexpensive)	$30–$60
M (Moderate)	$60–$90
E (Expensive)	$90–$140
VE (Very Expensive)	$140 and up

Note: Indianapolis hotels charge higher prices during the Indy 500 season (last Sunday in May), at which time a three-night minimum stay is also in effect.

Personal Favorites (in order of preference)

Canterbury (dwntwn), 123 S. Illinois St., IN 46225 (317/634-3000; toll free, see Preferred). 102 rms, A/C, cable color TV. AE, CB, DC, MC, V. Valet garage $5, rest. (The Restaurant), piano bar, rm svce, concierge, crib free. *Note:* This small, elegant European-style luxury hotel has been sumptuously renovated, 1920s style. Very comfortable rms, w. Chippendale furniture and refrigerators, though some are somewhat cramped. Intimate atmosphere; ultra-correct svce; first-rate rest. A favorite of connoisseurs, in the heart of the city. **VE**

Holiday Inn Union Station (dwntwn), 123 W. Louisiana St., IN 46206 (317/631-2221; toll free, see Holiday Inns). 276 rms, color TV, in-rm movies. AE, CB, DC, MC, V. Valet parking $5, pool, sauna, rest., bar, rm svce, disco, free airport shuttle. *Note:* The most innovative hotel in town stands in the enormous urban-renewal project around the former train station, amid dozens of bars, rests., and fashionable boutiques. Very lively ambience. The customer may choose between classic, comfortable hotel rms and the luxurious Pullman cars of yesteryear. Good overall svce. A delightful experiment by the Holiday Inn chain. Group and convention clientele. **M–E**

Sheraton Meridian (nr. dwntwn), 2820 N. Meridian St., IN 46208 (317/924-1241; toll free, see Sheraton). 290 rms, A/C, color TV, in-rm movies. AE, CB, DC, MC, V. Free parking, two pools, sauna, health club, two rests. (including Ramsgate Roof), two bars, rm svce, disco, hrdrsr, crib free. *Note:* Large modern motel w. 13 floors in a tranquil neighborhood close to the Children's Museum. Vast, comfortable rms. The many period furniture pieces blend nicely with the pseudo-Tudor décor. Efficient svce. Group clientele. Good value. 10 min. from dwntwn. **M–E**

Indianapolis Motor Speedway Motel (vic.), 4400 W. 16th St., IN 46222 (317/241-2500). 106 rms, A/C, cable color TV. AE, DC, MC, V. Free parking, pool, golf, coffeeshop, bar, rm svce, Indianapolis 500 museum. *Note:* Pleasant motel steps away from the famous auto raceway. Modern comfort. No resv. during Indy 500 time in May. Very good value. **I**

Days Inn East (nr. dwntwn), 7314 E. 21st St., IN 46219 (317/359-5500; toll free, see Days Inn). 120 rms, A/C, color TV, in-rm movies. AE, DC, MC, V. Free parking, pool, adjacent 24-hr coffeeshop, crib free. *Note:* Conventional motel near the new industrial area on the city's eastern periphery and convenient to the beltway (I-465). Functional comfort. Ideal for the motorist. 10 min. from dwntwn. Good value. **B–I**

Other Accommodations (from top bracket to budget)

Marriott (nr. dwntwn), 7202 E. 21st St., IN 46219 (317/ 352-1231; toll free, see Marriott). 250 rms, A/C, color TV, in-rm movies. AE, CB, DC, MC, V. Free parking, pool, health club, sauna, rest. (Durbin Junction), bar, rm svce, disco, crib free. *Note:* This large, modern motel on the eastern periphery of Indianapolis is close to the new industrial area. Unusual architecture. Comfortable, spacious rms and efficient svce. Group and business clientele. VIP floor. Interesting wknd packages. 10 min. from dwntwn on I-70. **E**

Hilton Indianapolis (dwntwn), Ohio and Meridian Sts., IN 46206 (317/635-2000; toll free, see Hilton). 371 rms, A/C, cable color TV. AE, CB, DC, MC, V. Parking $4, pool, two rests. (including Top of the Hilton), coffeeshop, bars, rm svce, disco, hrdrsr. *Note:* Relatively modern glass-and-concrete luxury hotel in the heart of dwntwn. The glass-walled elevator affords an unobstructed view of the city. Spacious, comfortable rms and good svce. Business clientele. Just off Monument Circle. **M–E**

Hyatt Regency (dwntwn), 1 S. Capitol Ave., IN 46204 (317/ 632-1234; toll free, see Hyatt). 496 rms, A/C, color TV, in-rm movies. AE, CB, DC, MC, V. Valet gar. $6, five rests and bars (including a revolving bar at the top), rm svce, disco, hrdrsr, drugstore, boutiques, free crib. *Note:* An ultra-luxurious hotel, modern and comfortable. The red-brick construction is rather massive but the 20-story glass-walled atrium is spectacular. Across from the Capitol and the Convention Center. Rather unreliable svce. Very acceptable rest. (Harrison's). VIP floor. A favorite of business people. **M–E**

Riverpointe Suites Hotel (nr. dwntwn), 150 N. White River Pkwy., IN 46222 (317/638-9866). 140 suites, A/C, cable color TV. AE, MC, V. Free parking, pool, tennis, health club, sauna, rooftop sundeck, valet svce, grocery store. *Note:* An ideal place for longer stays. While the hotel has neither bar nor rest., it offers spacious, well-equipped suites with kitchenettes, an inviting, comfortable layout, and a very good location on the White River, 5 min. from dwntwn. Agreeable reception and svce. Good value. **M**

Ramada Inn Downtown (dwntwn), 501 W. Washington St., IN 46204 (317/635-4443; toll free, see Ramada Inns). 232 rms, A/C, color TV, in-rm movies. AE, CB, DC, MC, V. Free parking, pool, 24-hr rest., bar, rm svce, free crib. *Note:* Chain motel w. no exceptional attraction or advantage apart from its very central location. Functional comfort. Some rms have patios and refrigerators. **I–M**

La Quinta East (nr. dwntwn), 7304 E. 21st St., IN 46219 (317/359-1021; toll free, see La Quinta). 122 rms, A/C, color TV, in-rm movies. AE, CB, DC, MC, V. Free parking, pool, adjacent 24-hr coffeeshop, bar, free crib. *Note:* This classic highway motel is modern and comfortable and 10 min. from dwntwn on I-70. Spacious, inviting rms (some no-smoking). Cheerful svce. Good value. **I**

Red Roof Inn South (nr. dwntwn), S. Emerson Ave. at I-465, IN 46203 (317/788-9551; toll free 800/848-7878). 106 rms, A/C, color TV, in-rm movies. AE, MC, V. Free parking, adjacent coffeeshop. *Note:* This modest, unassuming little motel on the southeastern edge of the city offers functional comfort and is ideal for the motorist passing through (direct access to the city beltway, I-465). Good overall value. **B–I**

🕯 **Motel 6** (nr. dwntwn), 2851 Shadeland Ave., IN 46219 (317/546-1501). 154 rms, A/C, color TV, free in-rm movies. DC, MC, V. Free parking, pool, free crib. *Note:* An unbeatable value, 10 min. from dwntwn. Functional comfort. Ideal for the motorist. **B**

Airport Accommodations

🛏🛏 **Holiday Inn Airport** (vic.), 2501 S. High School Rd., IN 46241 (317/244-6861; toll free, see Holiday Inn). 274 rms, A/C, color TV, in-rm movies. AE, CB, DC, MC, V. Free parking, pool, sauna, health club, rest. (Chanteclair), coffeeshop, bar, rm svce, disco, free airport shuttle, crib $10. *Note:* This typical Holiday Inn may not have a great deal of personality but it does have, strangely enough, one of the best rests. in town. Comfortable rms w. balconies. Efficient svce. **M-E**

YMCA/Youth Hostel

YMCA (nr. dwntwn), 860 W. 10th St. (317/634-2478). 87 rms. Pool, health club. Open to men and women, in a neighborhood that can be unsafe at night.

RESTAURANTS

Indianapolis Restaurant Prices	
(per person, excluding drinks and service charges)	
B (Budget)	up to $15
I (Inexpensive)	$15–$25
M (Moderate)	$25–$40
E (Expensive)	$40–$60
VE (Very Expensive)	$60 and up

Personal Favorites (in order of preference)

🍸🍸 **Chez Jean Restaurant Français** (vic.), 9027 S. Ind. 67, Mooresville (831-0870). A/C. Dinner only, Mon.-Sat.; closed Sun., holidays. AE, CB, DC, MC, V. Jkt. *Specialties:* duck à l'orange, lobster vol-au-vent, mussels marinière, sautéed tournedos chasseur. Good wine list. *Note:* The best French rest. (and the best rest., period) in Indianapolis. The country décor is a little too rustic, but the fine classic cuisine is very good indeed. Svce is a bit pretentious. A landmark since 1957. Resv. a must. 30 min. from dwntwn. *French.* **M-E**

☀🍸🍸 **St. Elmo Steak House** (dwntwn), 127 S. Illinois St. (635-0636). A/C. Dinner only, Mon.-Sat.; closed Sun., holidays, and the first 15 days of July. AE, DC, MC, V. Jkt. *Specialties:* Aged prime cuts, lamb chops, lobster, seafood. *Note:* A local institution since 1902 and "the" steakhouse par excellence. Pleasant old-fashioned décor. Excellent svce. Resv. advised. Generous cocktails. *Steak-seafood.* **I-M**

🍸 **Jonathan's Restaurant and Pub** (vic.), 96th St. and Keystone Crossing (844-1155). A/C. Lunch/dinner daily (until 2 a.m.); brunch Sun.; closed hols. AE, DC, MC, V. Jkt. *Specialties:* very fine red meat and fish broiled over a wood fire, spareribs, veal Oscar. *Note:* A delightful

British-style inn on the northern edge of Indianapolis. Well worth the 25 min. by car from dwntwn. Diligent svce. An excellent locale. Resv. advised. *Steak-seafood.* **I–M**

> **T.G.I. Friday's** (vic.), 3502 E. 86th St. (844-3355). A/C. Lunch/dinner daily. AE, CB, DC, MC, V. *Specialties:* steak, hamburgers, Mexican dishes, homemade soup. *Note:* An amusing bistro frequented by a young local crowd. Generous servings; pleasant ambience and décor; very crowded bar. 25 min. from dwntwn. *American-Mexican.* **B–I**

> **Dodd's Town House** (nr. dwntwn), 5694 N. Meridian St. (257-1872). A/C. Dinner only, Tues.-Sun.; closed Mon. AE, MC, V. *Specialties:* steak, fried chicken, grilled fish of the day, wonderful homemade cakes and pies. No alcoholic beverages. *Note:* The most popular rest. in town for more than a quarter century. The décor may be as modest as the prices, but Betty Dodd's cooking is very tasty and the portions copious. Efficient svce. Clientele of regulars. Resv. recommended. *American.* **B**

Other Restaurants (from top bracket to budget)

> **Chanteclair** (vic.), in the Holiday Inn Airport (see "Accommodations," above) (243-1040). A/C. Dinner only, Mon.-Sat.; closed Sun., holidays. AE, CB, DC, MC, V. Jkt. *Specialties:* mignonettes of venison, veal medallions with chanterelle mushrooms, pheasant Souvaroff, sweetbreads madeira, tournedos Rossini. Good wine list. *Note:* A first-rate rest. in a Holiday Inn may be surprising, but it's for real. Aside from some heavy sauces and uncertain svce, this is one of the best places to eat in Indianapolis. Elegant ambience. Resv. a must. *French-continental.* **I–M**

> **King Cole** (dwntwn), 7 N. Meridian St. (638-5588). A/C. Lunch Mon.-Fri., dinner Mon.-Sat.; closed Sun., holidays. AE, CB, DC, MC, V. Jkt. *Specialties:* roast duckling, baked clams, rack of lamb, pompano en papillote, fish of the day, lemon soufflé. Good wine list. *Note:* A favorite of local business people. Rich, cozy atmosphere w. old paintings, woodwork, and sumptuous table linens. Irreproachable cuisine and svce. Resv. highly recommended. *Continental.* **I–M**

> **Greenhouse** (vic.), 8702 Keystone Crossing (844-4556). A/C. Lunch/dinner daily; closed holidays. AE, CB, DC, MC, V. Jkt. *Specialties:* rack of lamb, chateaubriand, veal piccata. *Note:* A luxuriant tropical greenhouse justifies the name, and the European-inspired cuisine is impeccably prepared if not highly imaginative. Rather muddled svce. Adjoining piano bar with live jazz. Resv. recommended. 25 min. from dwntwn. *Continental.* **I**

> **Iron Skillet** (nr. dwntwn), 2489 W. 30th St. (923-6353). A/C. Dinner only, Wed.-Sun.; brunch Sun.; closed Mon., Tues. AE, CB, DC, MC, V. *Specialties:* fried chicken, steak, oven-baked pike. *Note:* In a 19th-century building, this pleasant rest. on the edge of a golf course presents the daily menu on a blackboard and offers honest, tasty regional fare. Attentive, friendly svce. Locally very popular. Resv. recommended. *American.* **B–I**

> **Hollyhock Hill** (vic.), 8110 N. College Ave. (251-2294). A/C. Dinner only, Tues.-Sun. (until 8 p.m.); brunch Sun.; closed Mon., Labor Day, Dec. 24 and 25. AE, MC, V. *Specialties:* southern fried chicken, steak, fish of the day. *Note:* Pleasant family rest. w. rather kitsch garden décor. Traditional, no-frills cuisine at very modest prices. Locally popular. 25 min. from dwntwn. *American.* **B–I**

> **Renee's French Delicatessen** (vic.), 839 E. Westfield Blvd. (251-4142). A/C. Lunch/dinner Mon.-Sat.; closed Sun. AE, DC, MC, V. *Specialties:* sandwiches, salads, homemade cakes, daily spe-

cials. *Note:* This excellent pastry-shop/rest. (emphasis on rest. at night) is an unbeatable value. 15 min. from dwntwn. *French-continental.* **B**

♀ **Shapiro's Delicatessen** (dwntwn), 808 S. Meridian St. (631-4041). A/C. Breakfast/lunch/dinner daily. No credit cards. *Specialties:* giant sandwiches, pastrami, corned beef, stuffed cabbage, brisket, chopped liver, cheesecake. *Note:* The experts agree that this is the best deli around; it's been a classic since 1905. Usually packed at lunchtime (inevitable waits). Other location: 2370 W. 86th St. (872-7255). *American.* **B**

Restaurants in the Vicinity

♅ **The Glass Chimney** (vic.), 12901 N. Meridian St., Carmel (844-0921). A/C. Dinner only, Mon.-Sat.; closed Sun., holidays. AE, MC, V. J&T. *Specialties:* lobster bisque w. cognac, pheasant chasseur, wild boar and game in season, duckling bigarade, rack of lamb, veal kidneys w. mustard sauce, Coho salmon. *Note:* A few remarkable dishes but also some weaknesses in the cooking and svce; the place could do better. Charming old décor and a pleasant patio-garden. Resv. advised. Locally popular. 35 min. from dwntwn. *Continental.* **I–M**

Cafeterias/Fast Food

Ayres Tea Room (dwntwn), 1 W. Washington St. (262-4411). Lunch only, Mon.-Sat. *Note:* Cafeteria in the department store of the same name. Dependable soups and daily specials. Good svce.

Laughner's Cafeteria (nr. dwntwn), 4030 S. East St. (787-3745). Lunch/dinner daily (until 8 p.m.). *Specialties:* fried chicken, roast beef, fish of the day, homemade desserts. *Note:* Very popular cafeteria with charming nostalgic décor.

BARS & NIGHTCLUBS

Crackers Comedy Club (vic.), 8702 Keystone Crossing (846-2500). Much-frequented comedy club with big-name stars. Open Wed.-Sat. Resv. advised.

☼ **Indiana Roof Ballroom** (dwntwn), 140 W. Washington (236-1870). Vast dance hall from the 1920s that has been superbly renovated. Amusing, very kitsch atmosphere. Open nightly.

Quincy's (vic.), in the Adam's Mark Hotel, 2544 Executive Dr. (248-2481). "In" disco w. an elegant atmosphere. Open Mon.-Sat.

Rick's Café (dwntwn), 33 Jackson Pl. (634-6666). One of the best local jazz clubs and a bastion of the "Naptown sound."

T.G.I. Friday's (vic.), 3502 E. 86th St. (844-3355). Hip bar and disco (see also "Restaurants," above). Open nightly.

Vogue (nr. dwntwn), 6259 N. College Ave. (259-7029). Excellent jazz-rock. One of the best nightspots in Indianapolis.

NEARBY EXCURSIONS

☼🔔 **COLUMBUS** (40 mi., 64 km, south on I-65): In the late 1930s this obscure prairie town launched an energetic construction program of buildings both public and private, commissioned from world-famous architects like Eliel and Eero Saarinen, Kevin Roche, I. M. Pei, and Harry Weese, and enriched with works by artists of the caliber of the sculptor

Henry Moore. To date some 50 outstanding examples have been completed. Guided tours from the Visitors Center, 506 5th St. (812/372-1954). Open daily in summer, Mon.-Sat. the rest of the year. An absolute must.

☼⚲ **CONNER PRAIRIE PIONEER SETTLEMENT** (13400 Allisonville Rd., Noblesville; 18 mi., 28 km, NE on Ind. 19) (776-6000): This authentic village-museum dating from the 19th century faithfully reproduces pioneer life between 1820 and 1840 with the help of 36 minutely restored old buildings, including the blacksmith's forge and the cobbler's workshop, as well as a plush, patrician residence in the Federal style. Handcraft demonstrations offered in period costume. For history lovers. Open Tues.-Sun., April to late Nov.

⚲ **MOUNDS STATE PARK** (in Anderson, 48 mi., 76 km, NE on I-69) (642-6627): A number of prehistoric tumuli including an earthwork 9 ft (2.7 m) tall and 1,280 ft (400 m) in circumference, built by Indian civilizations which remain an enigma to archeologists. Handsome, 247-acre park with campgrounds and picnic areas. Worth going out of your way for. Open daily.

☼⚲ **NASHVILLE** (43 mi., 68 km, south on Ind. 135): This charming pioneer town is now a haven for artists with numerous antique shops, art galleries, etc. A few miles south, see the **Brown County State Park:** 15,500 acres of wooded hills with splendid, glowing bronze tones in autumn; and enormous **Lake Monroe,** both of which offer ideal excursion destinations for nature lovers. (A good joint excursion with a visit to Columbus; see above).

⚲ **ZIONSVILLE** (12 mi., 19 km, north on U.S. 421): Charming little 19th-century town on the outskirts of Indianapolis with many elegant boutiques and an interesting pioneer museum, the **Patrick Henry Sullivan Museum,** 225 W. Hawthorne St. (873-4900). Open Tues.-Sat.

CHAPTER 27

ST. LOUIS⚡

□ □ □

Founded in 1764 by Pierre Laclède, a French fur trader and devotee of the sainted King Louis IX of France, then sold to the U.S. in 1803 by Napoleon as part of the Louisiana Purchase, the "Gateway to the West" stands at the confluence of the Illinois River with two greater rivers, the Mississippi and the Missouri. A crossroads for rail, road, and river traffic, its strategic position inevitably made it the starting point for the Westward Expansion in the 19th century. It was from St. Louis that Meriwether Lewis and William Clark started out on their famous expedition, 7,689 mi. (12,302 km) to the shores of Oregon and back again in 1804–1806. It was from St. Louis, too, that the covered wagons of the pioneers, the heavily laden Conestogas or "prairie schooners," lumbered off on their mission to open up the Middle West to the Pacific.

Once the city of jazz, of former black slaves, and of great paddlewheelers stemming the current of "Ol' Man River," St. Louis has also been, for a century or more, a thriving industrial center, the home of Monsanto, McDonnell Douglas, General Dynamics, Ralston Purina, and more. Second only to Detroit as a producer of automobiles in the U.S., the "Gateway to the West" prides itself most of all on its leading part in the history of flight. It was the *Spirit of St. Louis* in which Charles Lindbergh made the first solo flight across the Atlantic from west to east in 1927; its progeny descendants include the F-4 *Phantom*, F-15 *Eagle*, and F-16 *Fighting Falcon* jet pursuit planes, as well as the first *Mercury* and *Gemini* spacecraft.

As a legacy of the heavy inflow of German and Italian immigrants at the turn of the century, St. Louis still possesses the world's largest brewery (Anheuser-Busch) and the best Italian restaurants between New York and the West Coast. Two great culinary inventions, which have attained the status of national icons, first saw the light of day here at the Louisiana Purchase Exposition (St. Louis World's Fair) of 1904: the hot dog and the ice-cream cone. But the finest contemporary symbol of this midwestern city, with its touch of southern charm, is the **Gateway Arch.** The shining 630-ft (192-m) archway of stainless steel, designed by the Finnish-American architect Eero Saarinen, rises beside the Mississippi River. Dedicated to the memory of those durable pioneers who won the West, this gigantic double-downstroke has attracted two million visitors a year since it was unveiled in 1965.

Long considered the archetypical provincial town, graceless and boring, in the 1980s St. Louis has undergone an artistic, architectural, and cultural boom —witness the success of the St. Louis Symphony, which has become one of the best orchestras in the country. In the past decade the city has undertaken a tremendous program of urban renewal, but rather than mar the glorious view through the Gateway Arch with a jumble of high-rises, St. Louis made an inspired choice: it would make an old city over into a new one. Among the triumphs of renovation is **Laclede's Landing,** on the river, with its narrow cobblestone streets, cast-iron lamp standards, and dozens of boutiques, bars, and restaurants. Another resounding success is the former **Union Station,** now a shopping mall delightfully disguised as a medieval castle.

On the darker side, St. Louis has a crime rate which makes solitary walks at night inadvisable.

Famous St. Louis natives include the poet and critic T. S. Eliot, actresses Virginia Mayo and Marsha Mason, actors Vincent Price and Kevin Kline, and the singer Josephine Baker.

BASIC FACTS: State of Missouri. Area Code: 314. Time Zone: Central Time. ZIP Code: 63166. Founded: 1764. Approximate population: city, 450,000; metropolitan area, 2,420,000. 14th-largest metropolitan area in the U.S.

CLIMATE: Unavoidably, given the proximity of the Father of Waters, the climate is disagreeably hot and sticky from June to Sept., with a July mean temperature of 81°F (27°C). Winter is harsh (January mean, 33°F, 1°C), but snowfall is light. The spring is unusually rainy and windy, with tornados occurring in May and early June. There remains only the fall, by far the best season for a visit with its cool, sunny days.

DISTANCES: Chicago, 290 mi. (465 km); Indianapolis, 235 mi. (376 km); Kansas City, 259 mi. (415 km); Memphis, 284 mi. (455 km); Nashville, 328 mi. (525 km).

ARRIVAL & TRANSIT INFORMATION

AIRPORT: Lambert–St. Louis International Airport (STL), 10 mi. (16 km) NW; for information, call 314/426-8000.

AIRLINES: American (231-9505), Braniff (toll free 800/272-6433), Continental (241-7205), Delta (421-2600), Eastern (621-8900), Northwest (621-9177), Southwest (421-1221), TWA (291-7500), United (454-0088), and USAir (421-1018).

CITY LINK: The **cab** fare from the airport to downtown is about $18–$20; time, about 35 min. (1 hr. during rush hour). Bus: **Jetport Express** (427-8119), serving major downtown hotels, leaves every 20 min.; fare, $6; time, about 40–50 min. **City bus:** Bi-State has an express service between the airport and downtown, leaving every 40 min.; price, 75¢; time, 1 hr.

The size of the metropolitan area, and its distance from the airport, may make it advisable to rent a car unless you intend to confine yourself to seeing downtown St. Louis. The **public transportation system** (bus) is quite extensive but slow: for information, call Bi-State Transit System (231-2345).

CAR RENTAL (all at Lambert International Airport): Avis (426-7766), Budget (423-3000), Dollar (423-4004), Hertz (426-7555), National (426-6272), and Thrifty (423-3737). For downtown locations, consult the local telephone directory.

LIMOUSINE SERVICES: Carey Limousine (946-4114), Dav-El Limousines (toll free 800/922-0343), and Show Me Limo Service (382-6003).

TAXIS: Cabs may, at your pleasure, be hailed on the street, taken from the waiting lines in front of the major hotels, or summoned by phone. Recommended companies: Allen Cab (531-4545), Laclede Cab (652-3456), and Yellow Cab (361-2345).

TRAIN: AMTRAK, 550 S. 16th St. (241-8806).

BUS: Greyhound, Broadway and Delmar Blvd. (231-7800).

MISSISSIPPI RIVER CRUISES: Sternwheeler river cruises, three to ten days on the Mississippi aboard the *Delta Queen* or the *Mississippi Queen,* 1920s paddlewheelers. Luxurious kitsch. See Chapter 15 on New Orleans.

INFORMATION & TOURS

TOURIST INFORMATION: The **St. Louis Convention and Visitors Commission,** 10 S. Broadway, Suite 300, MO 63102 (314/421-1023; toll free 800/325-7962).

> **Visitors Center,** 330 Mansion House Center, Suite 211 (314/241-1764).
> For a **telephone recording** with an up-to-date listing of cultural events and shows, call 421-2100.

GUIDED TOURS: Gray Line Tours (bus), 7000 Collinsville Rd., East St. Louis, Ill. (618/241-1224): Conducted tours of the city and surroundings; serves principal downtown and midtown hotels. Daily, year round.

> **Fostaire Helicopter Ride** (helicopter), 400 N. Wharf St. (421-5440): Helicopter flights over the city; year round, weather permitting.

> **River Excursions** (boat), St. Louis Levee, beneath the Gateway Arch (621-4040): One-hour trips on the Mississippi aboard the paddlesteamer *Huck Finn, Tom Sawyer,* or *Becky Thatcher,* replicas of 19th-century steamboats. Daily, Apr.-Nov.

> **Riverboat *President*** (boat), St. Louis Levee, beneath the Gateway Arch (241-5500): Three-hour mini-cruises aboard the largest river excursion boat in the U.S. Dance cruises in the evening. Daily, June-Sept.

> **St. Louis Carriage Co.** (carriage) (621-3334): Rides in a horse-drawn carriage, serving downtown and the Riverfront. Year round, weather permitting. Reservations a must.

> **St. Louis Tram Tours** (bus), 516 Cerre St. (241-1400): Two-hour conducted tour across the city, in a replica of a turn-of-the-century open streetcar. Daily, Apr.-Oct.

SIGHTS, ATTRACTIONS, & ACTIVITIES

ARCHITECTURAL HIGHLIGHTS: ⚓ **Busch Stadium,** Walnut, Broadway, Spruce, and 7th Sts. (421-4040): Ultramodern circular stadium, seating 53,000, where Cardinals fans congregate for home games. Also home of the St. Louis Sports Hall of Fame (see "Museums of Science and History," below). Conducted tours of the stadium daily June-Aug., except on days of games. Should be seen.

> ⚓ **City Hall,** Memorial Plaza (622-4000): Huge building in the Renaissance style, an exact copy of the Hôtel de Ville in Paris. It is worth a look.

> ☼⚓🔍 **Fabulous Fox Theater,** 527 N. Grand Blvd. (534-1111): Originally considered to be one of the two or three finest movie theaters in the country, this 1929 architectural gem has been restored to all the fabulous rococo glory that its name implies. Now houses all kinds of performing arts: pop concerts, big-star shows, musicals, etc. Conducted tours by appointment Wed., Thur., and Sat. at 10:30 a.m. An absolute must.

> ⚓ **Powell Symphony Hall,** 718 N. Grand Blvd. (533-2500): This old (1925) movie theater also has a sumptuously kitsch

ivory-and-gold interior. Splendidly renovated in 1967, it has since then been home to the St. Louis Symphony Orchestra. Well worth a look.

☼☖☖ **Union Station,** 1820 Market St. (421-6655): St. Louis's old central station, dating from 1894 and once the largest in the world, architecturally a strange amalgam of railroad station and medieval fortress. Now houses a luxury hotel plus dozens of boutiques, stores, and restaurants. This gloriously successful urban-renewal project cost $135 million. Happy, relaxed atmosphere; definitely deserves a visit. Open daily.

☼☖ **S.S. Admiral,** Riverfront, at the foot of Washington Ave. (342-7200): From 1940 to 1979 this 378-ft (115-m) vessel with its wonderful art deco interior was the biggest river cruise ship in the world. Renovated in 1987 at a cost of $35 million, it is now a floating recreation center with a 200-seat restaurant (fine view of the river), rock disco, theater, nightclub, many boutiques, bars, dance floor with 1940s-style big band, etc. Very lively; don't miss it.

CHURCHES/SYNAGOGUES: ☖ Christ Church Cathedral, 1210 Locust
St. (231-3454): A perfect example of English Gothic, with its carved marble altar and Tiffany stained-glass windows, this beautiful place of worship was erected 1867–1911 on the site of the first Episcopalian parish (1819) built west of the Mississippi. Well worth a visit; open daily except Sat.

☖ **Old Cathedral,** 209 Walnut St. (231-3250): Erected in 1831 on the site of the first Roman Catholic church in St. Louis (1770), and given the status of a basilica by Pope John XXIII (its official title is Basilica of St. Louis King of France), it was also designated a national monument by Pres. John F. Kennedy shortly before his death. Religious museum in the crypt, open daily. The oldest Roman Catholic cathedral west of the Mississippi; definitely worth visiting.

☼☖☖ **St. Louis Cathedral,** 4431 Lindell Blvd. at Newstead Ave. (533-2824): This imposing Roman-Byzantine building, the city's "new" Roman Catholic cathedral, dates from 1907; it boasts a giant dome and a nave almost entirely clad in beautiful mosaics. The whole interior is richly decorated. Don't miss it. Open daily.

HISTORIC BUILDINGS: ☖ Campbell House, 1508 Locust St. (421-0325):
Museum-home of Robert Campbell, a rich fur trader in the latter part of the 19th century. Visitors can immerse themselves in the history of the local upper middle class. Original furniture, decorations, and clothing. Interesting. Open Tues.-Sun., Mar.-Dec.

☼☖ **Chatillon–de Menil Mansion,** 3352 De Menil Pl. (771-5828): This handsome 1848 Greek Revival house at the top of Arsenal Hill was long used as a landmark by Mississippi riverboats. Fine antique furniture. Open Tues.-Sun.; don't miss it. Also a laudable restaurant (lunch only).

☼☖ **Eads Bridge,** foot of Washington Ave.: The work of the architect James Eads, this was the first bridge (1874) on the central stretch of the Mississippi to span the entire river from side to side. It was also the first to be built with two decks and steel arches. Worth a look.

☖ **Goldenrod Showboat,** Riverfront, 700 N.L.K. Sullivan Blvd. (621-3311): Authentic 1909 showboat, one of the last still in existence. Presents melodramas, comedies, variety. Dinner-theater. Each year, too, the National Classic Jazz and Ragtime Festival (see "Special Events," below) takes place here. A must for those who crave local color.

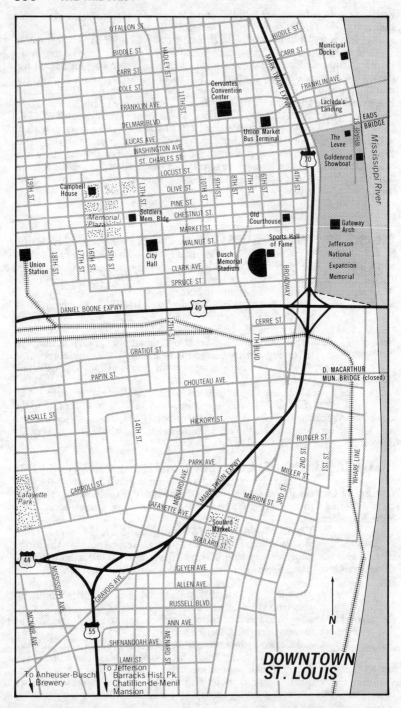

DOWNTOWN ST. LOUIS

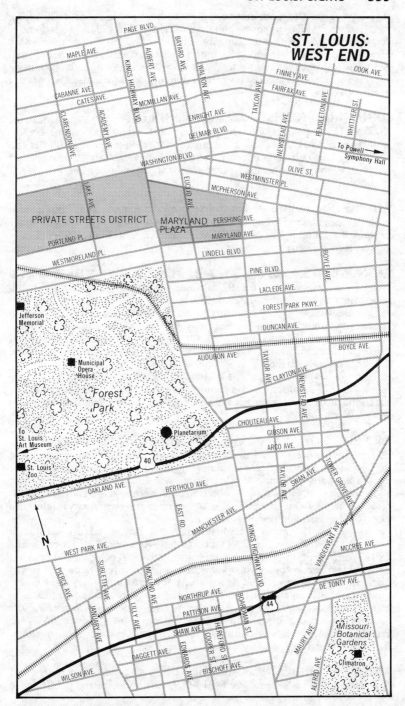

☀⚲🔔 **Old Courthouse,** 11 N. 14th St. at Market St. (425-4465): This imposing building, with its 173-ft- (53-m-) high dome of cast iron decorated with interesting historical frescoes, was completed in 1859. Here were heard, in 1846 and 1852, the first two trials in the famous case of Dred Scott, the first black man to contend that slavery could not be enforced outside the states where it was legal. Many memorabilia of this historic case. Well worth a visit; open daily.

INDUSTRIAL TOURS: ✸ **Anheuser-Busch Brewery,** 13th and Lynch Sts. (577-2626): The largest brewery in the world, whose two major brands, Budweiser and Michelob, sell at the rate of more than five million bottles and cans daily. Free tasting. Don't miss the stables of the famous Clydesdale draft horses, the symbol of Anheuser-Busch. Mon.-Sat., June-Aug.; Mon.-Fri. the rest of the year.

MARKETS: ⚱ **Soulard Market,** 7th St. and Lafayette Ave. (421-2008): From meat to vegetables and from homemade preserves to live animals, all the produce of the soil is found in this colorful covered market. A St. Louis landmark since 1847. Open Wed.-Sat.

MONUMENTS: ✸ ⚌ **Gateway Arch,** 11 N. 4th St. (425-4465): Colossal arch of stainless steel, 630 ft (192 m) high, designed by the famous Finnish-American architect Eero Saarinen. Completed in 1965, it symbolizes the Winning of the West by the 19th-century pioneers. An elevator composed of small capsules moving at an oblique angle takes you to the top, where the view is splendid. At the base is the interesting Museum of Westward Expansion (see "Museums of Science and History," below). The tallest and most imaginative memorial in the country; worth the trip to St. Louis all by itself. Open daily.

⚖ **Wedding of the Waters,** Aloe Plaza at Market St.: Monumental fountain comprising 14 figures in bronze, which symbolizes the confluence of the Mississippi and the Missouri, by the Swedish sculptor Carl Milles. Worth seeing.

MUSEUMS OF ART: ✸ ⚱ **Cupples Art Gallery,** 3673 W. Pine Blvd. (658-3025): This curious 1890s mansion in the Roman style stands on the campus of St. Louis University; its façade is abundantly ornamented with sculpture, while its 32 rooms are luxuriously decorated with wood paneling, Tiffany windows, and wrought iron. Houses a fine collection of modern engravings by Miró, Kandinsky, Chagall, Braque, and others, as well as interesting temporary exhibitions. Open Sun.-Fri.; should positively be seen.

☀⚌ **St. Louis Art Museum,** Forest Park, Art Hill (721-0067): Housed in Cass Gilbert's Fine Arts Palace, designed for the 1904 World's Fair, this great museum has recently been enlarged and houses a remarkable collection of art from prehistoric times to the present day. It's particularly strong in European and American painting and sculpture; also Chinese bronzes and African and pre-Columbian art. Among its best-known treasures: Hans Holbein's *Lady Guldeford,* Titian's *Ecce Homo,* Jordaens's *Suffer the Little Children to Come Unto Me,* Matisse's *Bathers with a Tortoise,* Maurice Prendergast's *Seashore,* Mark Rothko's *Red, Orange, Orange on Red,* and *Flesh Bathroom with Yellow Light Object* by Jim Dine. Don't miss it. Open Tues.-Sun.

MUSEUMS OF SCIENCE AND HISTORY: ⚱ **Eugene Field House and Toy Museum,** 634 S. Broadway (421-4689): Birthplace of the poet Eugene

Field, with many exhibits associated with the author of *Little Boy Blue*. Interesting collection of old toys and dolls. Worth a look; open Tues.-Sun.

    Magic House, 516 S. Kirkwood Rd., Kirkwood, 8 mi. (12 km) west on U.S. 44 (822-8900): A museum of the extraordinary intended specifically for children. Dozens of attractions including microcomputer games, an electrostatic generator that will literally make your hair stand on end, a three-story-high giant slide, a maze, and so on. An absolute must for kids. Open Tues.-Sun. 15 min. from downtown.

    McDonnell Douglas Prologue Room, McDonnell Blvd. and Airport Rd. (232-5421): Small aeronautical and space museum in the company's head-office building. Many preliminary designs, photographs, and scale models of planes and rockets illustrating the company's achievements since it was founded in 1920. Be sure to see the facsimiles of the *Mercury* and *Gemini* space capsules. For aviation buffs. Open Tues.-Sun., June-Aug.; 30 min. from downtown.

    Missouri Historical Society, Forest Park, Lindell Blvd. and De Baliviere Ave. (361-1424): Much material on the history of St. Louis, Missouri, and the West: weapons, clothing, models of boats, posters, etc. One section is devoted to the 1904 World's Fair. The Lindbergh Room displays material relating to the 1927 transatlantic flight of the *Spirit of St. Louis*. Fascinating. Open Tues.-Sun.

    Museum of Westward Expansion, at the base of Gateway Arch, 11 N. 4th St. (425-4465): Remarkable audio-visual display tracing the history of the settlement of the West, and of the construction of the arch. Dioramas, historical films, etc. Don't miss it. Open daily.

    National Museum of Transport, 3015 Barrett Station Rd., Barretts, 16 mi. (25 km.) SW on I-44W and I-270N (965-7988): From mule-drawn streetcars to electric locomotives, two centuries of transportation in the U.S. Hundreds of antique locomotives, railroad cars, buses, trucks, streetcars, horse-drawn vehicles, etc. Well worth the trip. Open daily. 25 min. from downtown.

    St. Louis Science Center, Forrest Park, 5100 Clayton Ave. (289-4400): Huge educational complex comprising the **McDonnell Planetarium** with its ultramodern equipment (laserium, Star Theater, etc.), the **Medical Museum,** and the **Museum of Science and Natural History.** Among them they offer a complete panorama of the natural sciences and the evolution of man, from a life-size dinosaur to a simulated earthquake. Fascinating; don't miss it. Open daily.

    St. Louis Sports Hall of Fame, Busch Stadium, 100 Stadium Plaza (421-3263): A must for all fans, particularly lovers of football and baseball. Many sports memorabilia, trophies, World Series movies, etc. A must-see; open daily year round.

    Across the street at 111 Stadium Plaza is the **National Bowling Hall of Fame,** which traces the history of bowling from Ancient Egypt to the present day. Exhibits associated with the great names in bowling. Should be seen; open daily.

PANORAMAS: **Gateway Arch,** 11 N. 4th St. (425-4465): From the top of Eero Saarinen's 630-ft (192-m) stainless-steel arch there's a spectacular view of the city and the Mississippi River. On a clear day you can see 30 mi. (48 km) in all directions. Access to the Observation Room is by an unusual elevator whose passenger capsules move on an inclined plane (see also "Monuments," above). A sight to be seen. Open daily.

PARKS AND GARDENS: ☼ ⚓ Forest Park, bounded by Lindell, Skinker, and Kingshighway Blvds. and Oakland Ave. (535-5050): 1,293 acres (482 ha.) of gardens, lakes, and groves less than 15 min. from downtown; the 1904 World's Fair was held here. Many museums and a well-known zoo; skating rink; two public golf courses. Worth a visit; open daily.

Grant's Farm, 10501 Gravois Rd., in Grantwood Village (843-1700): Deer and buffalo roam free on 281 acres (114 ha.) of park and woodland belonging to the Anheuser-Busch brewery. See the log cabin where, in 1856, lived Ulysses S. Grant, who went on to become Northern commander-in-chief during the Civil War and 18th president of the U.S.; plus the stables of the famous Clydesdales and a very fine collection of horse-drawn vehicles. A mini-train takes you around the exhibits. Open Tues.-Sun., June-Aug.; Thurs.-Sun. in spring and fall; closed the rest of the year. 25 min. from downtown on Mo. 30SW.

Laumeier Sculpture Garden, Geyer and Scott Rds. (821-1209): One of the country's finest modern-sculpture gardens, with works of such American and foreign artists as Donald Judd, Dennis Oppenheim, Michael Steiner, Giacomo Manzù, David von Schlegell, Lynn Chadwick, Jackie Ferrara, Ernest Trova, etc. Be sure to see *The Way,* a monumental sculpture by Jack Zehrt. An absolute must. Open daily; 20 min. from downtown on I-44.

Lone Elk Park, Mo. 141 and N. Outer Rd. (225-7395): Small wildland park with free-roaming animals—bison, Barbados sheep, elk, deer, etc., which you can see from your car along a scenic drive. Walking trails and picnic area. Well worth the trip. 25 min. from downtown on I-44W.

Missouri Botanical Garden, 4344 Shaw Blvd. (577-5100): Named Shaw Garden after the businessman and amateur botanist who laid it out in 1859, this magnificent 79-acre (32-ha.) botanic garden has a superb rose garden, waterfalls, a "scented garden" for the blind, and Seiwa En, the largest Japanese garden in North America. Tropical domed greenhouse, more than a century old, the Climatron. You tour the garden in a mini-train. Don't miss it; open daily.

PERFORMING ARTS: For daily listings of all shows and cultural events, consult the entertainment pages of the daily *St. Louis Post-Dispatch* (morning), the weekly *Riverfront Times,* and the monthly *St. Louis* magazine.

American Theater, 416 N. 9th St. (231-7000): The biggest Broadway hits. The building dates from 1917.

CASA/Conservatory and School for the Arts, 560 Trinity Ave. at Delmar (863-3033): Concerts, classical-music recitals, opera.

Edison Theater, Forsyth Blvd. and Hoyt Dr. (889-6543): Contemporary and avant-garde theater; ballet performances by the St. Louis Dancers. On the campus of Washington University.

Fabulous Fox Theater, 527 N. Grand Blvd. (534-1111): Pop concerts, big-name shows, musicals, etc. Wonderful rococo interior. Sept.-May.

Goldenrod Showboat, Riverfront, 700 N.L.K. Sullivan Blvd. (621-3311): Melodrama, comedy, variety; dinner-theater. Also the location of the annual National Classic Jazz and Ragtime Festival. It's an authentic 1909 showboat.

Loretto–Hilton Center, 130 Edgar Rd. (968-4925): Classical and contemporary theater; home of the Repertory Theater of St. Louis and the Opera Theater of St. Louis. Sept.-Apr.

Municipal Theater/MUNY, Forest Park (361-1900): 12,000-seat open-air amphitheater presenting musicals, ballet, operettas, Broadway hits. Mid-June to Aug.

Powell Symphony Hall, 718 N. Grand Blvd. (534-1700): Classical concerts and recitals in a richly decorated auditorium. Home of the renowned St. Louis Symphony, founded in 1880, the second oldest in the country (principal conductor, Leonard Slatkin). Mid-May to mid-Sept.

Theater Project Company, 4219 Laclede St. (531-1301): Off-Broadway shows.

Westport Playhouse, 600 West Port Pl. (878-3322): St. Louis's only theater-in-the-round. Contemporary theater, big-name shows, musicals.

SHOPPING: Maryland Plaza, between Kingshighway Blvd. and Euclid Ave.: Dozens of luxury stores and unusual boutiques: style and quality both.

Plaza Frontenac, Clayton Rd. at Lindbergh Blvd. (432-5800): Two floors of department stores (Saks Fifth Avenue, Neiman-Marcus), boutiques, and trendy restaurants in an ultramodern setting.

☀ **St. Louis Centre,** bounded by Washington Ave. and 6th, 7th, and Locust Sts. (231-5913): The largest urban shopping mall in the country. Opened in 1985, this enormous four-floor complex stretches across two full blocks in the heart of downtown, with more than 200 stores, shops, and restaurants.

Union Station, 1820 Market St. (421-6655): The old St. Louis Central Railroad Station, built at the turn of the century and now converted, at a cost of $135 million, into a vast shopping mall with more than 120 boutiques, stores, restaurants, and cafés, as well as fountains, a lagoon, and a luxury hotel.

SPECIAL EVENTS: For the exact schedule of events below, consult the **St. Louis Convention and Visitors Commission** (see "Tourist Information," above).

International Festival (last weekend in May): International food festival, dancing, folklore displays, and exhibitions of foreign handcrafts. Lively and colorful. Forest Park.

National Classic Jazz and Ragtime Festival (mid-June): Annual festival of New Orleans jazz and ragtime aboard the *Goldenrod Showboat;* a classic in the field since 1964. For information, call 621-3311.

Veiled Prophet Fair (four days around July 4): St. Louis's great popular festivity. Parades, fireworks, open-air concerts, marathon, art exhibitions, etc. Draws hundreds of thousands of participants. Riverfront.

Strassenfest (late July to early Aug.): The festival of the local German community; music, overeating, and beer flowing—in a manner of speaking—like water.

Jour de Fête à Ste. Geneviève (second weekend in Aug.): Parades, art exhibitions, old-house tours (see "Nearby Excursions," below). For information, call 883-5750.

Balloon Race (Sept.): Annual hot-air-balloon race, drawing contestants from all over the country. Forest Park.

SPORTS: St. Louis has two professional teams:
Baseball (Apr.-Oct.): Cardinals, Busch Memorial Stadium (421-3060).
Ice Hockey (Oct.-Apr.): Blues, Arena (644-0900).

Horse Racing
Fairmount Park, U.S. 40 at Collinsville, Ill. (618/345-4300): Thoroughbred-racing Mar.-Nov.; harness racing Nov.-Mar.

STROLLS: ▲ **The Hill,** around S. Kingshighway and Shaw Blvds.: The local "Little Italy," with food stores and *trattorie* more Italian than Rome; even the fire-hydrants are painted in the Italian national colors. Lively and colorful.

☼ ▲ **Laclede's Landing,** Riverfront north of Eads Bridge: The heart of historic St. Louis, come to life right out of the 1870s, bears witness to the city's prosperity right after the War Between the States. Cobbled alleys, cast-iron lamps, old shops, boutiques, nightclubs, and restaurants. A picturesque environment at the river's edge; you shouldn't miss this stroll.

☼ ▲▲ **The Levee,** Wharf St. between the Poplar St. Bridge and Eads Bridge: Beside this quay on the Mississippi are moored a number of craft: *Goldenrod Showboat,* a paddlewheeler from 1909 now converted into a floating theater (see "Historic Buildings," above); U.S.S. *Inaugural,* a World War II minesweeper, now a naval museum; and the river cruisers now used for short trips on the Mississippi, *Huck Finn, President, Tom Sawyer,* and S.S. *Admiral,* once the world's largest river cruiser, with a disco, cinema, theaters, restaurants, and bars (see "Architectural Highlights," above).

THEME PARKS: ▲ **Six Flags over Mid-America,** Allentown Rd., in Eureka, 30 mi. (48 km) SW on I-44 (938-4800): Enormous theme park with a round 100 carousels, roller coasters, and other attractions, including a huge Ferris wheel known as "Colossus." Open daily June-Aug., weekends only in spring and fall; closed the rest of the year.

ZOOS: ☼ ▲ **St. Louis Zoological Park,** Forest Park (781-0900): Well-stocked zoological garden with 2,800 animals in reconstructions of their natural habitat; be sure to see "Big Cat Country," where lions, tigers, and other big cats live in semi-freedom. Impressive "Jungle of the Apes," with gorillas, chimpanzees, and orangutans. Worth visiting in its mini-train. Open daily.

ACCOMMODATIONS
See the listing of toll-free numbers in the Appendix.

Room Rates in St. Louis	
B (Budget)	up to $30
I (Inexpensive)	$30–$60
M (Moderate)	$60–$90
E (Expensive)	$90–$140
VE (Very Expensive)	$140 and up

Personal Favorites (in order of preference)

♟♟♟ **Adam's Mark** (dwntwn), Fourth and Chestnut Sts., MO 63102 (314/241-7400; toll free 800/231-5858). 910 rms, A/C, color TV, in-rm movies. AE, CB, DC, MC, V. Valet garage $2, two pools, health club, sauna, racquetball, rest. (Faust's), coffeeshop, three bars, rm svce, disco, hrdrsr, boutiques, free crib, concierge. *Note:* The best location in St. Louis, at the foot of the Gateway Arch. Ultramodern twin 18-story towers w. unobstructed view of city, arch, or river. Richly decorated interior w. Flemish tapestries, Italian marble, French crystal chandeliers, two Ludovico De Luigi bronze horses in the lobby. Very spacious, comfortable rms, some w. refrigerators. Flawless reception and svce. Two VIP floors; big business clientele; in the heart of downtown. **E–VE**

☼ 🛏🛏🛏 **Omni International at Union Station** (dwntwn), 1820 Market St., MO 63103 (314/241-6664; toll free, see Omni). 546 rms, A/C, color TV, in-rm movies. AE, CB, DC, MC, V. Parking $8, rest. (American Rotisserie), coffeeshop, bar, 24-hr rm svce, nightclub, boutiques, free crib. *Note:* This new gem of the local hotel scene occupies a whole lavishly re-stored wing of the former Union Station, and boasts high vaulting, marble floors, stained glass, and magnificent turn-of-the-century décor (see "Architectural Highlights," above). Huge, elegant rms; ultramodern comfort; excellent svce. Direct access to Union Station Shopping Mall w. its 120 boutiques, cafés, and rests. An unusual, unusually successful, hotel w. a unique atmosphere. **E–VE**

☼ 🛏🛏🛏 **Chase Park Plaza Hotel** (nr. dwntwn), 212 N. Kingshighway Blvd., MO 63108 (314/361-2500; toll free 800/325-8989). 300 rms, A/C, color TV, in-rm movies. AE, CB, DC, MC, V. Free valet garage, pool, two rests. (including the Tenderloin Room), three bars, rm svce, disco, hrdrsr, boutiques, free crib, concierge. *Note:* Long-established grand hotel favored by celebrities passing through, a designated historic monument since 1977. Intelligently redecorated at a cost of $10 million. Spacious, comfortable rms w. balconies, some w. kitchenettes; very polished svce. Facing Forest Park, and a stone's throw from the smart stores on Euclid Ave. and Maryland Plaza. Very reasonably priced for a hotel of its class. Good rest. (Tenderloin Room); definitely a recommended place to stay. 15 min. from dwntwn. **M–E**

🛏🛏 **Radisson Hotel Clayton** (formerly the Clayton Inn; nr. dwntwn), 7750 Carondelet Ave., Clayton, MO 63105 (314/726-5400; toll free, see Radisson). 212 rms, A/C, color TV, in-rm movies. AE, CB, DC, MC, V. Free valet garage, two pools, health club, sauna, two rests., bar, rm svce, nightclub, hrdrsr, free crib. *Note:* Modern hotel in a new residential neighborhood on the west edge of the city. Spacious contemporary rms w. mini-bars. Good physical-fitness facilities; diligent svce; very acceptable rests. (the Café Clayton also offers a fine view of the city). Business and group clientele. Airport shuttle. 20 min. from dwntwn by car. **M–E**

🛏🛏 **Days Inn at the Arch** (formerly the Hilton Bel Air; dwntwn), 333 Washington Ave., MO 63102 (314/621-7900; toll free, see Days Inns). 182 rms, A/C, color TV, in-rm movies. AE, CB, DC, MC, V. Parking $5, pool, sauna, rest., bar, valet svce, free crib. *Note:* Large, modern 17-story tower halfway between the Gateway Arch and the Convention Center. Functional but inviting. Spacious rms w. balconies, some w. refrigerators, the best looking out on the arch. Business clientele. Good value on balance. **M**

🛏 **Forest Park Hotel** (nr. dwntwn), 4910 W. Pine Blvd., MO 63108 (314/361-3500; toll free 800/622-4910). 200 rms, A/C, color TV, in-rm movies. AE, CB, DC, MC, V. Free parking, pool, sauna, 24-hr coffeeshop, bar, nightclub, free crib. *Note:* Aging but spick-and-span hotel agreeably modernized. Rms a little cramped but comfortable. Friendly reception and svce. Very near Forest Park, 15 min. from dwntwn. Very good value; regular clientele. **I**

Other Accommodations (from top bracket to budget)

☼ 🛏🛏🛏 **Majestic Hotel** (dwntwn), 1019 Pine St., MO 63101 (314/436-2355; toll free 800/451-2355). 95 mini-suites, A/C, color TV. AE, CB, DC, MC, V. Valet garage $8, rest. (Richard Perry's), bar, 24-hr rm svce, free crib, 24-hr concierge. *Note:* Elegant small European-style hotel in an old dwntwn building luxuriously rehabilitated. Classy interior w. marble floors and Oriental rugs. All rms are spacious, comfortable mini-suites w. period furniture. Personalized reception and svce. VIP and big business clientele. Style and distinction. **VE**

ទ្ទ **Marriott's Pavilion** (dwntwn), 1 Broadway, MO 63102 (314/421-1776; toll free, see Marriott). 672 rms, A/C, color TV, in-rm movies. AE, CB, DC, MC, V. Garage $8, pool, sauna, health club, two rests. (including J. W. Carver's), bars, rm svce, hrdrsr, free crib, concierge. *Note:* A successful union of the former Spanish pavilion (whence the hotel's name) from the 1964 New York World's Fair, now the hotel lobby, with two modern, functional 25-story towers overlooking Busch Stadium. Comfortable, well-designed rms w. mini-bars, the best looking out on Gateway Arch. Efficient svce. Group and convention clientele. Very complete facilities. On the noisy side when there's a game at Busch Stadium, but excellent location in the heart of dwntwn. **E−VE**

ទ្ទ **Embassy Suites** (dwntwn), 901 N. 1st St., MO 63102 (314/241-4200; toll free 800/362-2779). 300 suites, A/C, color TV, in-rm movies. AE, CB, DC, MC, V. Parking $6, pool, health club, sauna, rest., bar, rm svce, disco, free breakfast, free crib. *Note:* Modern hotel for the business traveler; suites only, spacious and comfortable w. balconies, mini-bars, and refrigerators. Spectacular eight-floor-high lobby w. interior garden. Right in the Laclede's Landing neighborhood, w. its rests., boutiques, and lively nightlife. **E**

ទ្ទ **Clarion Hotel** (formerly Stouffer's; dwntwn), 200 S. 4th St., MO 63102 (314/241-9500; toll free, see Clarion). 853 rms, A/C, color TV, in-rm movies. AE, CB, DC, MC, V. Garage $8, two pools, health club, sauna, rest. (Top of the Riverfront), coffeeshop, bars, rm svce, hrdrsr, free crib. *Note:* Modern 28-floor circular towers on the Mississippi. Spacious, agreeable rms, some w. refrigerators. Svce functional, but no more. Acceptable revolving rest. on top floor; unobstructed view of Gateway Arch (ask for a rm overlooking the river). Rather obtrusive group and convention clientele. Three VIP floors. Recently redecorated and refurnished. **M−E**

ទ្ទ **Holiday Inn Riverfront** (dwntwn), 200 N. 4th St., MO 63102 (314/621-8200; toll free, see Holiday Inns). 444 rms, A/C, color TV, in-rm movies. AE, CB, DC, MC, V. Free garage, pool, sauna, rest., coffeeshop, bar, rm svce, nightclub. *Note:* Huge 30-story tower looking out on the Mississippi. Holiday Inn style, completely modernized. The better rms, w. balconies, overlook the river and the Gateway Arch. Efficient svce. Excellent location; business clientele. **M−E**

ទ **Best Western St. Louisian** (dwntwn), Tucker Blvd. at Washington Ave., MO 63101 (314/421-4727; toll free, see Best Western). 195 rms, A/C, color TV, in-rm movies. AE, CB, DC, MC, V. Free parking, pool, rest. (Greenfield's), bar, rm svce. *Note:* Relatively modern, functional motel 5 min. from Gateway Arch and the Convention Center. Comfortable rms; friendly svce; good overall value. **I−M**

ទ **Red Bird Inn** (formerly the Quality Inn Forest Park; nr. dwntwn), 5120 Oakland Ave., MO 63110 (314/531-7070). 168 rms, A/C, color TV, in-rm movies. AE, CB, DC, MC, V. Free parking, pool, rest., bar, rm svce. *Note:* Classic motel, recently renovated, on the edge of Forest Park. Comfortable rms; friendly reception. Good value; 15 min. from dwntwn. **I**

ទ **Motel 6 Northeast** (vic.), 1405 Dunn Rd., MO 63138 (314/869-9400). 81 rms, A/C, color TV, free in-rm movies. DC, MC, V. Free parking, pool. *Note:* Unbeatable value if you're traveling by car, 20 min. from dwntwn via I-70 and Mo. 367. Functionally comfortable. **B**

Airport Accommodations

☀♨♨♨♨ **Henry VIII Hotel and Conference Center** (vic.), 4690 N. Lindbergh Blvd., Bridgeton, MO 63044 (314/731-3040; toll free 800/325-1588). 400 rms, A/C, color TV, in-rm movies. AE, CB, DC, MC, V. Free parking, two pools, sauna, health club, two tennis courts, two rests. (including Henry VIII), two bars, rm svce (until 10 p.m.), disco, crib $2. *Note:* Huge English-style country inn, elegant and inviting. Spacious, comfortable rms w. refrigerators, some w. kitchenettes. Good facilities; good rest. Group clientele. Ideal for the business traveler between flights (free 24-hr airport shuttle) or for the motorist passing through. Very good value. 5 min. from airport, 40 min. from dwntwn. Interesting wknd discounts. **M**

YMCA/Youth Hostels

Huckleberry Finn (dwntwn), 1904 S. 12th St., MO 63104 (314/241-0076). 40 beds. Typical youth hostel.

RESTAURANTS

St. Louis Restaurant Prices	
(per person, excluding drinks and service charges)	
B (Budget)	up to $15
I (Inexpensive)	$15–$25
M (Moderate)	$25–$40
E (Expensive)	$40–$60
VE (Very Expensive)	$60 and up

Personal Favorites (in order of preference)

♟♟♟♟ **Tony's** (dwntwn), 826 N. Broadway (231-7007). A/C. Dinner only, Tues.-Sat.; closed Sun., Mon., holidays, and the first week in July. AE, CB, DC, MC, V. J&T. *Specialties:* fresh homemade pasta (tagliatelle marinara, cavatelli e broccoli), lobster albanello, veal piemontese, fish of the day, first-class red meats, zabaglione. Superb desserts. Menu changes regularly. Very fine list of European and American wines. *Note:* Since 1949 Vincent Bommarito has presided, diplomatically but firmly, over this shrine of Italian-American gastronomy. The antique décor and subdued lighting make for a romantic atmosphere. Reception and svce of the highest order, but no resv. accepted, and you may have to wait an hour or two. But for this important shortcoming, the rest. would deserve a place among the 12 best in the U.S. Prices to match. Valet parking. *Italian-continental.* **M–E**

♟♟♟ **Fio's La Fourchette** (nr. dwntwn), 1153 St. Louis Galleria, Brentwood Blvd. and Clayton Rd. (863-6866). A/C. Dinner only, Tues.-Sat.; closed Sun., Mon., and holidays. AE, MC, V. Jkt. *Specialties:* mousse of veal and Brie cheese in pastry shell, broiled sweetbreads w. leeks, roast duck w. fennel and rosemary, filet of beef w. Roquefort cheese, médaillons of veal w. mushroom-and-brandy cream, fish of the day, very good homemade desserts (particularly the soufflé praliné). Menu changes regularly. *Note:* With its modern, light-filled décor, luxuriant plants, and pastel-colored walls, this charming rest., hidden away in an outlying shopping center, has quickly established itself as the best local exponent of French nouvelle cuisine. Every dish bears witness to the imaginative elegance and refinement of the very talented young Swiss chef Fio Antognini, while the prices are surprisingly moderate. Very good svce. An excellent place to eat; resv. strongly advised. 25 min. from dwntwn. *French.* **M**

☖☖☖ **Richard Perry** (dwntwn), in the Majestic Hotel (771-4100). A/C. Lunch Mon.-Fri., dinner nightly, Sun. brunch. AE, CB, DC, MC, V. Jkt. *Specialties:* smoked scallops, seafood sausage, lamb cutlet w. red-currant sauce, lobster w. fresh pasta, roast duck w. dates, sole stuffed w. lobster mousse in green sauce, roast pork w. cassis. Very good list of American wines. *Note:* The rest.'s recent move and redecoration mellowed the atmosphere, but didn't change the excellence of Richard Perry's food, inspired by old American regional recipes. Diligent svce. Locally popular, so resv. advised. Valet parking evenings. *American.* **I–M**

☖☖ **Al Baker's** (nr. dwntwn), 8101 Clayton Rd. (863-8878). A/C. Dinner only, Mon.-Sat.; closed Sun., holidays, and two weeks in July. AE, CB, DC, MC, V. Jkt. *Specialties:* fresh homemade pasta, steamed mussels, hobo steak w. mustard sauce, lamb Monastiraki, beef w. marsala, sautéed yellowtail w. red-wine vinegar and shallots, veal Oscar New Orleans style, fish of the day. The best wine list in St. Louis. *Note:* Somewhat overornate décor w. a profusion of art objects, old paintings, tapestries, and period furniture, but the predominantly Italian food is elegant and relatively light. Remarkable svce. A St. Louis landmark; resv. advised. 25 min. from dwntwn. *Italian-continental.* **M**

☀☖☖ **Busch's Grove** (nr. dwntwn), 9160 Clayton Rd. (993-0011). A/C. Lunch/dinner Tues.-Sat.; closed Sun. and Mon. *Specialties:* toasted ravioli (a St. Louis specialty), "Russ's salad," calves' liver w. onions, roast beef, barbecued ribs, steak, fish of the day, peanut butter cream pie. *Note:* A local tradition for almost a century; if you can eat only one meal in St. Louis, eat it here—particularly in fine weather, when the regulars crowd into the garden w. its romantic arbors. The food is as serious, and flawless, as the svce. A very fine place. 20 min. from dwntwn. *American.* **I–M**

☖ **Café Zoe** (dwntwn), 1923 Park Ave. (241-9122). A/C. Lunch Mon.-Sat., dinner Fri. and Sat. only; closed Sun. AE, MC, V. *Specialties:* duck salad w. grapes, sandwiches, shrimp w. pesto sauce, broiled chicken w. rosemary, Thai marinated beef, very good desserts. Menu changes regularly. *Note:* Crowded daily at lunch by white-collar workers, Zoe's is the fashionable place for a quick meal. Imaginative dishes w. a touch of American nouvelle cuisine (particularly the specialty salads and the broiled foods) at very attractive prices. Relaxed atmosphere. Resv. advised for dinner. *American.* **B–I**

Other Restaurants (from top bracket to budget)

☖☖☖☖ **Anthony's** (dwntwn), Equitable Bldg., 10 S. Broadway (231-2434). A/C. Dinner only, Mon.-Sat.; closed Sun. and holidays. AE, DC, MC, V. J&T. *Specialties:* duck w. sauce bigarade, scallops poached in white wine, roast rack of lamb, scampi w. mustard, sweetbreads and chanterelle mushrooms in dill sauce, veal Francesca. Very good wine list. *Note:* Smoked mirrors and polished steel make for a rather chilly, impersonal setting, but the cuisine of Tony Bommarito (brother of Vince, the owner of Tony's) will quickly warm you up again. Some sophisticated dishes of French-Italian inspiration. Ultra-professional svce. Valet parking. Resv. strongly advised. *Continental.* **M–E**

☖☖☖ **Giovanni's** (nr. dwntwn), 5201 Shaw Ave. (772-5985). A/C. Dinner only, Mon.-Sat.; closed Sun., holidays, and the first week of July. AE, DC, MC, V. J&T. *Specialties:* "presidential bow tie" (smoked salmon pasta as served to President Reagan at his inaugural banquet), tagliatelle mare monte, calamari w. tomatoes and herbs, veal saltimbocca alla Giovanni, seafood ravioli, chicken fiorentina, broiled scampi. Very good desserts; large wine list. *Note:* All the gastronomic classics of northern Italy in an elegant peachcolored setting w. old paintings and crystal chandeliers. Warm, intimate atmosphere. Excellent svce. One of St. Louis's great rests.; resv. necessary. Valet parking. 10 min. from dwntwn. *Italian.* **M**

☙ **Cardwell's** (nr. dwntwn), 8100 Maryland Ave. (726-5055). A/C. Lunch Mon.-Sat., dinner nightly. AE, MC, V. Jkt. *Specialties:* salad of spinach, endive, and orange w. warm brie; smoked fish w. avocado, pigeon, and cabbage in Pinot Noir sauce; broiled pompano filet w. lime butter and papaya jelly; remarkable soufflés. Good wine list. Menu changes regularly. *Note:* St. Louis's most imaginative rest. serving American nouvelle cuisine. The young chef, Bill Cardwell, whose creative talents are becoming more and more evident, never ceases to surprise and to charm. The décor, on the other hand, is uninteresting and the atmosphere noisy. Svce a trifle helter-skelter. Resv. advised. *American.* **M**

☙ **Chez Louis** (nr. dwntwn), 26 N. Meramec Ave., Clayton (863-8400). A/C. Lunch/dinner Mon.-Sat.; closed Sun. and holidays. AE, DC, MC, V. *Specialties:* salad of smoked duck and endive, scallops w. lobster sauce, sea bass w. clams, fresh tuna béarnaise, lamb cutlets provençal. Very good desserts; splendid wine list with more than 100 labels. *Note:* Elegant little French bistro serving chef Bernard Douteau's light, imaginative cuisine. Smart décor and atmosphere w. a handsome collection of posters and artworks. Impeccable svce; successful enough for you to need resv. Valet parking. 20 min. from dwntwn on Daniel Boone Expwy. and Clayton Rd. *French.* **M**

☙ **Kemoll's** (nr. dwntwn), 4201 N. Grand Ave. (534-2705). A/C. Dinner only, Mon.-Sat.; closed Sun. and holidays. AE, DC, MC, V. *Specialties:* fried artichokes, fettuccine verdi, paglia e fieno, cannelloni, shrimp in mustard sauce, chicken Conti, saltimbocca alla romana. *Note:* Huge, popular Italian rest. serving excellent fresh homemade pasta and Italian regional specialties. Pleasant, noisy atmosphere; lots of regular patrons. Friendly svce; resv. advised. Run by the Kemoll family since 1927. *Italian.* **I–M**

☙ **Bevo Mill** (nr. dwntwn), 4749 Gravois Ave. at Morganford Rd. (481-2626). A/C. Lunch/dinner daily; closed Dec. 25. AE, CB, DC, MC, V. *Specialties:* sauerbraten, wienerschnitzel, German dishes, fish of the day, red meats, good desserts. *Note:* Don't let the décor (the place is done up as a Dutch windmill) fool you; the very kitschy setting (and cooking) are of purely German origin. Honest, unimaginative food at very reasonable prices; friendly svce. Locally popular, so resv. advised. 10 min. from dwntwn. *German-American.* **I**

☙ **Duff's** (nr. dwntwn), 392 N. Euclid Ave. (361-0522). A/C. Lunch/dinner Tues.-Sun., brunch Sun.; closed Mon. AE, CB, DC, MC, V. *Specialties:* barbecued shrimp New Orleans style, caponata, chicken marsala w. noodles, steak au poivre, chicken saltimbocca, bluefish w. salmon butter. Good homemade desserts; reasonably priced wine list. Menu changes regularly. *Note:* Inviting, relaxed, unaffected little rest. where blue jeans and business suits are both right at home. Excellent family cooking w. a strong French flavor; one of the best values in the area. Resv. advised. *French-American.* **B–I**

☙ **La Sala** (dwntwn), 513 Olive St. (231-5620). A/C. Lunch/dinner Mon.-Sat. (until midnight); closed Sun. and holidays. AE, DC, MC, V. *Specialties:* tacos, chiles, enchiladas. Good margaritas. *Note:* Very popular Mexican rest. a stone's throw from Busch Stadium. Agreeable folktype setting; good, unpretentious food. Crowded on days of games and evenings after shows. The buffet at lunch is good value. Pleasant background music. No resv. *Mexican.* **B–I**

🍷 **Yen Ching** (nr. dwntwn), 1012 S. Brentwood Blvd. (721-7507). A/C. Lunch Mon.-Fri., dinner nightly. AE, MC, V. *Specialties:* sizzling-rice soup, sweet-and-sour fish, Mongolian beef, Peking and Szechuan dishes. *Note:* One of the few acceptable Far Eastern rests. in St. Louis. The food is authentic and tasty, the décor totally uninteresting, and the svce. friendly. Locally very popular; resv. advised. *Chinese.* **B–I**

Cafeterias / Fast Food

Culpeppers (nr. dwntwn), 300 N. Euclid Ave. (361-2828). Lunch/dinner daily (until midnight). AE, MC, V. Remarkably good homemade soups (onion, vegetable, chicken, gazpacho, etc.) and substantial sandwiches have made the reputation of this nice, noisy bar.

Miss Hullings (dwntwn), 11th and Locust Sts. (436-0840). Open Mon.-Sat. (from morning till 8 p.m.). AE, DC, MC, V. Very respectable cafeteria food in a pleasant garden setting. Also located at 725 Olive St. (436-0404), Same hrs.

O'Connell's Pub (nr. dwntwn), 4652 Shaw Ave. at Kingshighway Blvd. (773-6600). Lunch/dinner Mon.-Sat. MC, V. By general consent the best hamburgers in town. Also excellent roast-beef sandwiches and several kinds of beer. Typical pub atmosphere.

BARS & NIGHTCLUBS

Brio's (vic.), 2136 Schuetz Rd. (993-8110). The trendy disco; youthful, highly charged atmosphere. 30 min. from dwntwn.

Goldenrod Showboat (dwntwn), Riverfront (621-3311). Bar, jazz, variety, melodrama on an old Mississippi sidewheeler. Amusing. Open Tues.-Sun.

Houlihan's (dwntwn), 147 St. Louis Union Station (436-0844). Popular, inviting singles bar with an acceptable rest. Open nightly.

Mississippi Nights (dwntwn), 914 N. 1st St. (421-3853). Fashionable nightclub in the heart of Laclede's Landing. Live music nightly.

Muddy Water Saloon (dwntwn), 724 N. 1st St. (421-5335). The best modern jazz club in town. Trendy clientele.

NEARBY EXCURSIONS

☼⌂ **BONNE TERRE** (62 mi., 99 km, SW via I-55 and U.S. 67): In this small town, where mining was actively pursued from 1870 to 1962, there still remain enormous excavations under its streets which are open to visitors; inquire at Park and Allen Sts. (358-2148), open daily year round. Don't fail to see the amazing **Billion Gallon Underground Lake,** with its 17 mi. (27 km) of navigable channels, visited every year by more than 7,000 scuba-divers. North of the town, **Washington State Park,** on Mo. 47 (586-2995), open daily year round, possesses hundreds of Indian petroglyphs. Worth seeing. Combine this with the trip to Sainte Geneviève (see below).

Where to Stay

☼🍴♨ **Mansion Hill Country Inn,** Mansion Hill Dr., Bonne Terre, MO 63628 (358-5311). 32 rms. Charming, elegantly restored Victorian home. **I–M**

☼⌂ **CAHOKIA MOUNDS STATE HISTORIC SITE** (9 mi., 15 km, east via I-70) (618/344-5268): One of the richest archeological sites in the country—a primitive community extending over 885 acres (380 ha.), inhabited between 700 and 1400 A.D. and with a population in the tens of thousands. There remain today only two score huge earthen mounds, of the 100 or so originally built, whose size and shape are reminiscent of Mayan pyramids. Particularly impressive is **Monks Mound,** a huge terraced earthwork rising 98 ft (30 m), which owes its name to the Trappist monastery built at its foot in 1809. Interesting archeological museum. Well worth the side trip. Open daily.

FORT KASKASKIA STATE HISTORIC SITE (52 mi., 83 km, SE over the Poplar Street bridge along Ill. 3) (618/589-3741): Built by the French in 1736, and destroyed by them in 1763 to prevent its passing into the hands of the British under the terms of the Treaty of Paris, this fort, of which only traces remain today, occupied a strategic position in a bend of the Mississippi. The nearby **Pierre Menard Mansion,** built in 1802 in the style of a Louisiana plantation house, at the foot of a bluff overlooking the river, is worth a visit. Nicknamed the "Mount Vernon of the West" on account of its elegant design, and today superbly restored, the house was visited by Lafayette in 1824. Well worth the side trip. Open daily year round. Combine this with the visit to Cahokia Mounds State Historic Site (above).

HANNIBAL (108 mi., 172 km, NW via I-70 and Mo. 79): Little Mississippi river port where Samuel Langhorne Clemens, better known as Mark Twain, passed much of his youth. Now entirely devoted to the cult of the famous author of *Tom Sawyer* and *Huckleberry Finn,* the city abounds in all kinds of museums. Make a point of seeing the ⌂ **Mark Twain Museum,** with numerous family souvenirs, in the house where he spent his childhood at 208 Hill St. (221-9010), open daily. Also the ⌂ **Mark Twain Cave,** 2 mi. (3 km) south on Mo. 79 (221-1656), open daily, Apr.-Oct., which gave him the idea for *The Adventures of Tom Sawyer.*

Mississippi trips aboard the paddlesteamer *Mark Twain,* Center St. Dock (221-3222), daily May-Oct.

Well worth the detour.

JEFFERSON BARRACKS HISTORICAL PARK (Broadway at Kingston Rd., 10 mi., 16 km, south on I-55) (544-5714): Military barracks built in 1826; many of the original buildings have been restored. Interesting military museum. The future Gens. Robert E. Lee and Ulysses S. Grant served here as young officers. Should be seen. Open Wed.-Sun.

MERAMEC CAVERNS (65 mi., 104 km, SW on I-44) (468-3166): Vast limestone caves on five levels, used to store gunpowder during the Civil War, and as a hiding place by Jesse James and his gang in the 1870s. The temperature remains constant at 60°F (16°C). Open daily, Mar.-Dec. A definite must-see.

POTOSI (62 mi., 100 km, SW on Mo. 21): The "Nation's Population Center" is located 10 mi. (16 km) NW of this little country town.

SAINTE GENEVIÈVE (64 mi., 102 km, south on I-55 and U.S. 61): One of the oldest (1720) French settlements in the Midwest. The town, which once rivaled St. Louis, still has 40 or so buildings dating from the late 18th and early 19th centuries, giving it something of the flavor of Old France. Among them are the 1785 **Bolduc House** at 123 S. Main St., the 1770 **Amoureaux House** on St. Mary's Rd., the 1790 **Green Tree Tav-**

ern at 224 St. Mary's Rd., and at 1 N. 4th St., the **Guibourd-Valle House,** dating from 1785. They are all open daily, Apr.-Nov. Interesting **historical museum** at Merchant and 3rd Sts. (883-3461), open daily year round.

Very popular festival in Aug. (see "Special Events," above). Don't miss Sainte Geneviève.

Where to Stay

☀ **St. Gemme Beauvais Inn,** 78 N. Main St., Sainte Geneviève, MO 63670 (883-5744). 12 rms, 7 with bath. Elegant 1847 mansion. **I–M**

☀ **Sainte Geneviève Inn,** Main and Merchant Sts., Sainte Geneviève, MO 63670 (883-2737). 14 rms. Charming little late 19th-century inn. **I**

CHAPTER 28

KANSAS CITY

□ □ □

Famous for its slaughterhouses (the country's largest) and the size of its steaks, Kansas City, which has been called "the heart of America," is yet much more than the simple "cow town" it was known as in the days of the Old West. First explored by French trappers, the region around Kansas City is unquestionably one of the richest agricultural areas of America, as well as the world's second-largest cattle market. Its strategic position midway between Chicago and the Rockies made it an obligatory stagecoach stop on both of the two great westward routes of the 19th century: the Santa Fe Trail to Albuquerque and the Mexican frontier, and the Oregon Trail to Portland and the Pacific Northwest. From its double historic role, as a center of communications and cattle raising, Kansas City has retained a tradition of hospitality, some first-class hotels, and some of the nation's finest steakhouses, beginning with the renowned Golden Ox in the very precincts of the famous **Stockyards.**

The city's political past is murky; under the Prendergast brothers, corruption and influence-peddling were elevated to a system of government. In the 1920s Kansas City boasted almost 300 speakeasies, brothels, gaming houses, and jazz clubs. Between the two World Wars these dozens of nightclubs, some respectable and some less so, along Vine and 18th Streets in a district known as "Little New York," produced musicians of the caliber of "Fats" Waller, Count Basie, Lester Young, and Charlie Parker, making Kansas City one of the great capitals of jazz. Missouri's second city still hosts, every September, a very popular jazz festival. Other remembrances of things past are the picturesque neighborhoods of **Westport Square** and the **City Market,** an open-air market more than a century and a half old, not far from the Missouri River. Kansas City is noted, too, as America's greeting-card and writing-paper capital, since it is headquarters of the vast Hallmark operation.

The broad avenues with their dozens of statues and fountains (many of European origin), the friendliness of the citizens and their taste for good, solid food, and the beauty of the surrounding countryside, particularly the **Lake of the Ozarks,** make Kansas City an attractive and often-overlooked destination, as well as a thriving metropolis. As early as 1946 André Maurois wrote in his *Journal de voyages,* "There are few in Europe, or even in America, who know that Kansas City is one of the most charming towns on earth."

Famous people born in Kansas City include the jazz musicians Charlie Parker and Ben Webster, the movie director Robert Altman, and the actor Ed Asner. Neighboring **Independence** is the birthplace of the movie star Ginger Rogers, but is perhaps best known as the beloved hometown of Pres. Harry S Truman.

BASIC FACTS: State of Missouri; its twin city is Kansas City, Kansas, across the state border. Area Code: 816. Time Zone: Central Time. ZIP Code: 64108. Founded: 1821. Approximate population: city, 450,000; metropolitan area, 1,450,000. Ranks 25th in size among U.S. metropolitan areas.

CLIMATE: The climate of the Midwest plains is pleasantest in the spring, apart from frequent showers, and in the fall, which is the ideal season for a visit. Summer is hot and humid, with average temperatures in July of 82°F (28°C). Winter is very harsh and often below freezing, especially in January with a mean temperature of 30°F (−1°C). *Warning:* There are often tornadoes in late spring.

DISTANCES: Chicago, 500 mi. (800 km); Dallas, 490 mi. (785 km); Denver, 600 mi. (960 km); Memphis, 450 mi. (720 km); Minneapolis, 443 mi. (710 km); St. Louis, 259 mi. (415 km).

ARRIVAL & TRANSIT INFORMATION

AIRPORT: Mid-Continent International Airport (MCI), 18 mi. (29 km) NW, one of the most up-to-date in the country. Information: 243-5237.

AIRLINES: Air Midwest (471-4353), American (221-7767), Braniff (472-4411), Continental (471-3700), Delta (471-1828), Eastern (471-4353), Midway (toll free 800/621-5700), Northwest (474-1104), Southwest (474-1221), TWA (842-4000), United (471-6060), USAir (toll free 800/428-4322).

CITY LINK: The cab fare to city center is about $25; time, about 30 min. BUS: KCI Airport Express (243-5950), serving the principal hotels, leaves every 30 min.; fare, about $10–$15; time, 45 min. Since the dwntwn district is compact, you may not need to rent a car, unless you intend to make the (very worthwhile) excursions available in the area. Public transportation (bus and trolley) is relatively efficient; call AREA TRANSIT AUTHORITY/ATA (221-0660) for information.

CAR RENTAL (all at Kansas City International Airport): Avis (243-5760), Budget (243-5755), Dollar (243-5600), Hertz (243-5765), National (243-5770), Thrifty (464-5670). For downtown locations, consult the local telephone directory.

LIMOUSINE SERVICES: Carey Limousine (587-4077), Mid-America Limousine (346-4848).

TAXIS: Cabs may not be hailed on the street, but they can be taken at the stands in front of the major hotels, or summoned by telephone: Quicksilver Taxi (262-0905) or Yellow Cab (471-5000).

TRAIN: AMTRAK Station, 2200 Main St. (421-4725).

BUS: Greyhound, 1111 Holmes St. (221-2885).

INFORMATION & TOURS

TOURIST INFORMATION: The **Kansas City Convention and Visitors Bureau,** City Center Square Bldg. (Suite 2550), 1100 Main St., MO 64105 (816/221-5242).

For a **tape-recorded list** of current cultural events and shows, call 816/474-9600.

GUIDED TOURS: **Gray Line Tours** (bus), 1212 E. 10th St. (471-5996): Guided tours of the city, serving principal dwntwn hotels.

Missouri River Excursions (boat, May-Nov.), Westport Landing, at the foot of Grand Ave. (842-0027): Trips along the Missouri on board the *Missouri River Queen.*

SIGHTS, ATTRACTIONS, & ACTIVITIES

ARCHITECTURAL HIGHLIGHTS: 🔔 **Board of Trade,** 4800 Main St. (753-7500): World's largest winter-wheat market. From the visitors' gallery on the third floor you can watch the frenzied brokers. Should be seen. Open Mon.-Fri.

🔔 **City Hall,** 414 E. 12th St. (274-2605): A building from the early '30s in the purest art deco style. From the 30th floor there's a fine view of the city (see "Panoramas," below).

🔔 **Crown Center,** Pershing St. and Grand Ave. (274-8444): Ultramodern commercial and office complex built on a rise overlooking the city at a cost of $300 million. Includes two luxury hotels; some 60 stores, boutiques, and restaurants; six movie houses; a theater, the **Hallmark Visitors Center,** focusing on the history of the greeting card industry; and a huge plaza with free concerts in summer and ice skating in winter. Lively, animated scene; you should see it. Open daily.

🔔 **Livestock Exchange and Stockyards,** Genesee and 17th Sts. (842-6800): Well-known slaughterhouses and the country's most important livestock exchange. Auctions Tues., Wed., Thurs. morning (visitors allowed). Guaranteed local color; don't miss it.

MARKETS: ☀🔔 **City Market,** Walnut and 3rd Sts. (274-1341): Picturesque open-air market in existence for more than a century and a half. Dozens of stalls and food stands. Justifies Kansas City's reputation for good food. Open Mon.-Sat.

MONUMENTS: 🔔 **Liberty Memorial,** 100 W. 26th St. (221-1918): This 217-ft (66-m) tower (elevator) offers a very fine view of the city. Museum dedicated to those who fought in World War I. A must-see. Open Tues.-Sun.

MUSEUMS OF ART: 🔔 **T. H. Benton Home,** 3216 Belleview Ave. (931-5722): Victorian house and studio which the famous painter Thomas Hart Benton occupied from 1937 until his death in 1975. Those who admire his work should not fail to visit it. Open daily.

☀🔔🔔 **Nelson-Atkins Museum,** 4525 Oak St. (561-4000): Art from ancient civilizations (Sumerian, Greek, and Egyptian). Many paintings by European masters from Titian to Van Gogh. Remarkable collection of Far Eastern (particularly Chinese) art. Among the best-known works on display are Caravaggio's *St. John the Baptist,* a *Virgin and Child* by Petrus Christus, Nicolas Poussin's *Triumph of Bacchus,* and Thomas Hart Benton's *Persephone.* Very fine modern-sculpture garden with works of Calder, Moore, Lipchitz, and Rodin. An absolute must. Open Tues.-Sun.

MUSEUMS OF SCIENCE AND HISTORY: 🔔 **Kansas City Museum,** 3218 Gladstone Blvd. (483-8300): Interesting museum of anthropology, housed in the sumptuous 72-room mansion of a 19th-century millionaire. Many Indian art objects. Plays up the importance of Kansas City in the Westward expansion. Also a planetarium. Open Tues.-Sun.

🔔 **Linda Hall Library,** Rockhill Rd. on the University of Missouri campus (363-4600): One of the country's richest libraries, entirely given over to science and technology, with works from as early as the 17th century. Interesting. Open Mon.-Sat.

☀🔔 **Toy & Miniature Museum,** 5235 Oak St. (333-2055): In a very beautiful, and carefully restored, 1911 building, this fascinating museum displays splendid collections of old toys, miniatures, and dollhouses. You have to see it. Open Wed.-Sun.

PANORAMAS: 🔔 **City Hall,** 414 E. 12th St. (274-2605): Observation platform on the 30th floor; worth seeing. Open Mon.-Fri.

PARKS AND GARDENS: 🔔 **Barney Allis Plaza,** 12th St. between Central and Wyandotte Aves.: Municipal park in the heart of dwntwn, opened in 1986, which has become very popular in fine weather for its shaded benches, hot-dog vendors, and enormous fountain (illuminated at night).

🔔 **Penn Valley Park,** 31st and Main Sts.: On the site of a former slum area once known as "Vinegar Hill," this beautiful 176-acre landscaped park designed by the architect George Kessler offers scenic footpaths among lawns and trees, as well as a small man-made lake.

🔔 **Swope Park,** Meyer Blvd. and Swope Pkwy.: A very large (1,730 acres) park at the southern edge of the city. Golf, tennis, boating, and a distinguished zoo. Open daily.

PERFORMING ARTS: For current listings of shows and cultural events, consult the entertainment pages of the daily *Kansas City Times* (morning) and *Kansas City Star* (evening).

Coterie Theater, Crown Center, 2400 Pershing St. (474-6552): Children's shows; very popular locally. Season is Feb. to mid-Dec.

Folly Theater, 12th St. and Central Ave. (474-4444): Modern drama and comedy; concerts. Designated historic monument.

Kansas City Ballet, 706 W. 42nd St. (931-2232): One of the best ballet companies in the Midwest. Performances Oct.-Mar.

Lyric Theater, 1029 Central Ave. (471-7344): Home of the Kansas City Symphony Orchestra (principal conductor William McGlaughlin), with performances Nov.-May; and of the Lyric Opera, April and mid-Sept. to mid-Oct.

Midland Center, 1228 Main St. (421-7500): Home of the Theater League. Broadway hits and theater tours.

Missouri Repertory Theater, 4949 Cherry St. (276-2704): Classical and modern theater on the U. of Missouri campus, with seasons July-Sept. and Jan.-Apr.

Municipal Auditorium, 1310 Wyandotte Ave. (421-8000): Musicals, concerts.

Starlight Theater, in Swope Park, 63rd St. and Swope Pkwy. (333-9481): Open-air concerts and big-star shows, May-Sept. A summer-season classic for the last 30 years.

SHOPPING: The **A.T.&T. Town Pavilion,** 1111 Main St. (472-9600): In the heart of the Petticoat Lane business district, this huge recently opened complex occupies three of the 38 floors of the new A.T.&T. tower. Comprises more than 70 boutiques, stores, and restaurants.

Country Club Plaza, 47th and Main Sts. (753-0100): The country's oldest (1922) shopping center, a monument to the consumer society. More than 160 boutiques, stores, restaurants, and nightclubs in a very successful Spanish-Moorish setting with fountains, statues, murals, and tree-lined walks. Well worth seeing.

Crown Center, 2400 Pershing Rd. (274-8444): Luxurious avant-garde shopping center with 60 or so boutiques and stores (see "Architectural Highlights," above).

SPECIAL EVENTS: For exact dates, consult the **Kansas City Convention and Visitors Bureau** (see "Tourist Information," above).

Kansas City Rodeo (late June to early July): For rodeo fans.

Jazz Festival (early Sept.): Very popular, featuring the biggest names in jazz.

American Royal Livestock Show and Rodeo (Nov.): A triumph of the cowboy idiom; one of the most renowned festivals in the Midwest, and a classic of its kind since 1899.

SPORTS: Kansas City has professional teams in two major sports:

Baseball (Apr.-Oct.): Royals, Harry S Truman Sports Complex (921-2200).

Football (Sept.-Dec.): Chiefs, Harry S Truman Sports Complex (924-9300).

STROLLS: ⚱ **Antiques and Art Center,** 45th and State Line: A score of antique shops and art galleries in the heart of one of Kansas City's oldest districts; well worth looking over.

☀⚱ **Westport Square,** Broadway at Westport Rd. (753-2611): This charming old district has managed to retain the full flavor of the past. Old shops, nicely restored 19th-century buildings, and inviting restaurants. One of the centers of the city's nightlife. Worth a look.

THEME PARKS: ⚱ **Benjamin's Stables Trail Town,** I-435S and E. 87th St. (761-5055): Facsimile of an Old West town, with riding, shows, rodeos in summer, and cowboy food. A pleasant place. Open daily.

⚱ **Oceans of Fun,** 12 mi. (19 km) NE along I-435 to Exit 54 (459-9283): Enormous lagoon-pool holding a million gallons (3.7 million liters) of water, with giant slides, artificial surf, and dozens of aquatic attractions. Adjoins the Worlds of Fun complex (see below). Open daily, Memorial Day to Labor Day.

⚱ **Worlds of Fun,** 10 mi. (16 km) NE along I-435 to Exit 54 (454-4545): A 163-acre amusement park with more than 100 different attractions, including a giant roller-coaster. Shows, public concerts. Open daily May-Sept., weekends only in spring and fall; closed the rest of the year.

ACCOMMODATIONS

See the listing of toll-free numbers in the Appendix.

Room Rates in Kansas City	
B (Budget)	up to $30
I (Inexpensive)	$30–$60
M (Moderate)	$60–$90
E (Expensive)	$90–$140
VE (Very Expensive)	$140 and up

Personal Favorites (in order of preference)

⚱⚱⚱ **Allis Plaza Hotel** (dwntwn), 200 W. 12th St., MO 64105 (816/421-6800), 572 rms, A/C, color TV, in-rm movies.

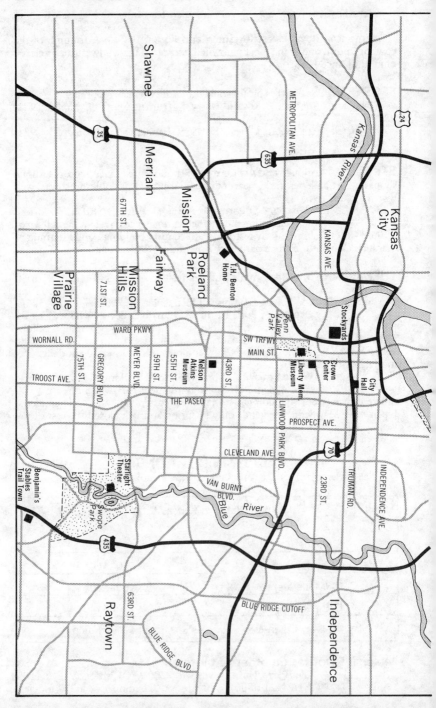

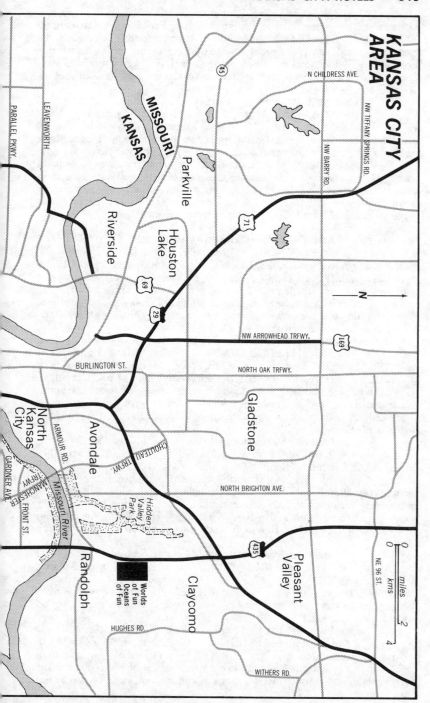

AE, CB, DC, MC, V. Valet garage $8, pool, two tennis courts, health club, sauna, two rests., bars, rm svce, disco, hrdrsr, boutiques, free crib. *Note:* An ungraceful ultramodern 22-story tower—but w. lavish interior and furnishings, and a spectacular indoor waterfall. Spacious, very comfortable rms, some with refrigerators. Two VIP floors and one no-smoking floor. Efficient reception and svce. Conveniently located very near the Convention Center. Business and convention clientele. **E–VE**

Hyatt Regency (nr. dwntwn), 2345 McGee St., MO 64108 (816/421-1234; toll free, see Hyatt). 732 rms, A/C, color TV, in-rm movies. AE, CB, DC, MC, V. Valet garage $8, two pools, health club, sauna, tennis court, two rests. (including Peppercorn Duck Club), coffeeshop, three bars (Skies is a revolving bar on the top floor), rm svce, concierge, free crib. *Note:* A 40-story building, more imposing than elegant, this new crown jewel among the city's deluxe hotels possesses, like most of the new Hyatts, a spectacular glass-walled foyer six floors high. Spacious, comfortable rms, most with refrigerators. Efficient svce. Entirely renovated after the 1981 collapse of two skywalks in the lobby left 111 dead. Group and convention clientele. Two VIP floors; no-smoking rms. **E–VE**

Adam's Mark (nr. dwntwn), 9103 E. 39th St., MO 64133 (816/737-0200; toll free 800/231-5858). 372 rms, A/C, color TV, in-rm movies. AE, CB, DC, MC, V. Free parking, two pools, health club, sauna, rest. (Remington's), coffeeshop, two bars, rm svce, nightclub, free crib. *Note:* Adjacent to the Harry S Truman Sports Complex, this modern luxury hotel is typical of its genre, and draws large numbers of groups and conventions. Huge well-laid-out rms; very good svce. Remington's is a well-regarded steakhouse. 15 min. from dwntwn on I-70. **M–E**

Raphael (nr. dwntwn), 325 Ward Pkwy., Country Club Plaza, MO 64112 (816/756-3800; toll free 800/821-5343). 124 rms, A/C, color TV, in-rm movies. AE, CB, DC, MC, V. Free garage, rest. (Raphael), bar, rm svce, free breakfast, free crib. *Note:* This is a small, elegant hotel in the European tradition, worlds away from the crowds of organized groups and conventions. Spacious rms with mini-bars; discreet svce which anticipates your needs. A good place to stay. Interesting wknd discounts. 15 min. from dwntwn. **M–E**

Embassy Suites (formerly the Granada Royale; nr. dwntwn), 220 W. 43rd St., MO 64111 (816/756-1720; toll free 800/362-2779). 266 suites, A/C, color TV, in-rm movies. AE, CB, DC, MC, V. Free parking, pool, sauna, coffeeshop, bar, rm svce, disco, free morning breakfast and evening cocktail, free crib. *Note:* Comfortable hotel comprising only suites, all equipped w. kitchenettes, refrigerators, and balconies. Inviting 12-story lobby w. an attractive fountain and glassed-in elevator—spectacular. An excellent choice for business travelers. 10 min. from dwntwn; 5 min. from Country Club Plaza. **E**

Rodeway Inn Downtown (dwntwn), 6th and Main Sts., MO 64106 (816/842-6090; toll free, see Rodeway Inns). 240 rms, A/C, cable color TV. AE, CB, DC, MC, V. Free parking, pool, 24-hr coffeeshop, bar, rm svce, hrdrsr. *Note:* Conventional (but well-run) motel a few steps from the business district. Functional layout; friendly reception and svce. Very good value. Repeat clientele. **I**

Budgetel Inn (nr. dwntwn), 2214 Taney St., North Kansas City, MO 64116 (816/221-1200; toll free 800/428-3438). 100 rms, A/C, cable color TV. AE, CB, DC, MC, V. Free parking, adjoining coffeeshop, rm svce. *Note:* Modest, unpretentious motel on the N bank of the river. Functionally comfortable; free morning coffee. Good value overall. 6 min. from dwntwn. **B–I**

Other Accommodations (from top bracket to budget)

Alameda Plaza (nr. dwntwn), Wornall Rd. at Ward Pkwy., MO 64112 (816/756-1500; toll free, see Preferred). 392 rms, A/C, color TV, in-rm movies. AE, CB, DC, MC, V. Free garage, pool, tennis court, health club, sauna, two rests. (including Alameda Roof), two bars, 24-hr rm svce, disco, drugstore, free crib. *Note:* Luxurious modern hotel w. an elegant and unusual Spanish interior. Comfortable rms w. mini-bars and private balconies. Excellent svce. Very good rest. w. panoramic view and glass-walled elevator. Inviting gardens w. waterfalls and statuary. Elegance with quality. Served as headquarters for Ronald Reagan during the 1976 Republican National Convention. 15 min. from dwntwn. **E–VE**

Westin Crown Center (nr. dwntwn), 1 Pershing Rd., MO 64108 (816/474-4400; toll free, see Westin). 724 rms, A/C, color TV, in-rm movies. AE, CB, DC, MC, V. Valet garage $6, pool, health club, sauna, putting green, tennis court, five rests. (including Trader Vic's), three bars, 24-hr rm svce, nightclub, hrdrsr, boutiques, cinemas, free crib. *Note:* Regarded simply as architecture the massive building doesn't quite come off, but the elegant interior boasts tropical gardens and a five-story waterfall. Comfortable rms w. balconies; friendly reception, good svce. No-smoking floor. Favored by business travelers. Interesting wknd discounts. 8 min. from dwntwn, adjoining the Crown Center w. its dozens of stores and boutiques. **E–VE**

Americana on Convention Square (formerly the Quality Inn; nr. dwntwn), 1301 Wyandotte St., MO 64105 (816/221-8800). 500 rms, A/C, color TV, in-rm movies. AE, CB, DC, MC, V. Garage $6, pool, rest., coffeeshop, bar, rm svce, nightclub. *Note:* Large (28-floor) modern motel opposite the Convention Center. Spacious, comfortable rms, but inefficient svce. Rather obtrusive group and convention clientele. Nevertheless, a good overall value. **M**

Holiday Inn Downtown (vic.), 424 Minnesota Ave., Kansas City, KS 66101 (913/342-6919; toll free, see Holiday Inns). 205 rms, A/C, color TV, in-rm movies. AE, CB, DC, MC, V. Free parking, pool, coffeeshop, rm svce, free crib. *Note:* A typical Holiday Inn, barely 5 min. from dwntwn across the Kansas border. Comfortably functional, w. good-humored reception. Very good value; ideal if you're driving. **I–M**

Howard Johnson's Central (dwntwn), 610 Washington St., MO 64105 (816/421-1800; toll free, see Howard Johnson's). 185 rms, A/C, color TV, in-rm movies. AE, CB, DC, MC, V. Free parking, pool, rest., bar, rm svce, entertainment, free crib. *Note:* Conventional seven-story motel, recently renovated and comfortably up-to-date. Well located very near the Convention Center. Favored by business travelers; good value. **I–M**

Best Western Inn Central (vic.), 501 Southwest Blvd., at 7th St., Kansas City, KS 66103 (913/677-3060; toll free, see Best Western). 115 rms, A/C, color TV, in-rm movies. AE, CB, DC, MC, V. Free parking, pool, coffeeshop, rm svce, free crib. *Note:* Inviting and comfortable small motel just across the Kansas border. Excellent reception; very good value. **I**

Motel 6 North (vic.), 8230 N.W. Prairie View Rd., MO 64152 (816/587-0287). 85 rms, A/C, color TV, free in-rm movies. DC, MC, V. Free parking, pool, free crib. *Note:* Unbeatable value 20 min. from dwntwn along U.S. 169. No bar or rest. Ideal for motorists. **I**

Travelodge Midtown (nr. dwntwn), 3240 Broadway, MO 64111 (816/531-9250; toll free, see Travelodge). 52 rms, A/C, color TV. AE, CB, DC, MC, V. Free parking, adjoining coffeeshop, free crib. *Note:* Low-priced but comfortable motel 5 min. from Crown Center and 10 min. from dwntwn. Free morning coffee. Good overall value. **I**

Airport Accommodations

Hilton Airport Plaza Inn (vic.), 112th St. NW and I-29, MO 64195 (816/891-8900; toll free, see Hilton). 350 rms, A/C, color TV, in-rm movies. AE, CB, DC, MC, V. Free parking, two pools, health club, sauna, tennis court, two rests., three bars, rm svce, nightclub, free airport limo, crib $5. *Note:* Modern, comfortable motel 3 min. from the airport. Good sports facilities; good svce. Spacious, well-soundproofed rms, some with refrigerators. Ideal for a stopover between flights. **M–E**

RESTAURANTS

Kansas City Restaurant Prices	
(per person, excluding drinks and service charges)	
B (Budget)	up to $15
I (Inexpensive)	$15–$25
M (Moderate)	$25–$40
E (Expensive)	$40–$60
VE (Very Expensive)	$60 and up

Personal Favorites (in order of preference)

The American Restaurant (nr. dwntwn), 25th St. and Grand Ave. (471-8050). A/C. Dinner only, Mon.-Sat.; closed Sun., holidays. AE, CB, DC, MC, V. Jkt. *Specialties:* sautéed shrimp in fennel butter, rack of lamb with green vegetables and hazelnuts, pheasant with juniperberries, Montana elk steak with blueberries, salmon poached in cream, carpetbagger (oyster-stuffed) steak. Delicious desserts, particularly the chocolate whisky cake. Fine list of California wines. *Note:* Delicate, inventive food; along with the rustic Golden Ox, this is the place to go in Kansas City. This multilevel rest. atop the Crown Center, elegantly decorated w. mirrors and paneling, affords a clear view over the city. Innovative cuisine, w. pride of place given to local produce. Exemplary svce. Resv. a must; valet parking. *American-continental.* **M–E**

Bristol Bar and Grill (nr. dwntwn), 4740 Jefferson St. (756-0606). A/C. Lunch Mon.-Fri., dinner nightly, brunch Sun.; closed December 25. AE, CB, DC, MC, V. Jkt. *Specialties:* clam chowder, gumbo, scampi sauté; extensive choice of absolutely fresh fish and shellfish, broiled, poached, or baked. Menu changes daily. Fine wine list. *Note:* One of the best fish rests. in all the Midwest; superb seafood flown in daily. Elegant Victorian décor; in the farthest room, a lovely Tiffany-style window. Exemplary svce. The bar is the favorite watering hole for the local yuppies; live jazz. Resv. a must. *Seafood.* **M**

Golden Ox (nr. dwntwn), 1600 Genesee St. (842-2866). A/C. Lunch Mon.-Fri., dinner nightly; closed December 24 and 25. AE, CB, DC, MC, V. *Specialties:* wonderful broiled red meats. *Note:* A landmark of local cuisine, in the precincts of the Kansas City stockyards, 15 min. from dwntwn. Even the somber, unoriginal western décor can't detract from the exceptional quality of the meats or the perfection with which they are prepared (the chefs do their work around enormous broilers in the middle of the dining room, under the eyes of the diners). Diligent svce. If you love to eat meat, this place belongs in your address book; it's the best steakhouse in Kansas City. Resv. advised. *Steakhouse*. **I**

Savoy Grill (dwntwn), 9th and Central (842-3890). A/C. Lunch Mon.-Sat., dinner nightly. AE, CB, DC, MC, V. Jkt. *Specialties:* world-famous Kansas City steaks, fresh fish, shrimp de Jonghe, Maine lobster, gumbo. *Note:* A Kansas City landmark since 1903; urbane old London club atmosphere, w. period service and décor guaranteed. Resv. advised. *Steak-seafood*. **I–M**

Arthur Bryant's Barbecue (nr. dwntwn), 1727 Brooklyn Ave. (231-1123). A/C. Lunch/dinner daily; closed December 25 and the month of Jan. No credit cards. *Specialties:* pork ribs, barbecued brisket, smoked ham, sandwiches. *Note:* Both the neighborhood and the décor could reasonably be described as shabby-looking, but lovers of the barbecue will find it here in generous portions, of remarkable quality, with subtly spiced sauces and lots of local color, neon-and-Formica style. The clientele is numerous, and comes back often. No resv. *American*. **B**

Stroud's Oak Ridge (vic.), 1015 E. 85th St. (333-2132). A/C. Lunch Fri.-Sun., dinner nightly; closed Thanksgiving, December 24 and 25. AE, MC, V. *Specialties:* fried chicken, fried catfish, chicken-fried steak. *Note:* This unassuming, discreetly decorated old roadhouse is a shrine to fried chicken Kansas style, and draws a crowd of regulars every day. Atmosphere relaxed and noisy; sometimes you'll have a long wait at the bar. *American*. **B**

Other Restaurants (from top bracket to budget)

Alameda Roof (nr. dwntwn), in the Alameda Plaza (see "Accommodations," above) (756-1500). A/C. Lunch/dinner daily, brunch Sun.; closed holidays. AE, CB, DC, MC, V. J&T (at dinner). *Specialties:* gazpacho, rack of lamb, scampi w. snail butter, Oriental beef. Good wine list. *Note:* Distinguished luxury-hotel rest. serving food on the pretentious side in an attractive Mediterranean setting w. a good view after dark (ask for a table near the glassed-in bay). Excellent svce. Overlooks the Country Club Plaza. *Continental*. **I–M**

La Méditerranée (nr. dwntwn), 4742 Pennsylvania Ave. (561-2916). A/C. Lunch Mon.-Fri., dinner Mon.-Sat.; closed Sun. and holidays. AE, CB, DC, MC, V. J&T. *Specialties:* bouillabaisse (must be ordered in advance), lobster w. truffle sauce, sole belle meunière, lamb w. purée of mushrooms, salmon w. pistachios, tournedos Gilbert. Magnificent wine list. *Note:* Even if the sauces are a little rich, chef Gérard Jahier's French food is excellent, as is the svce; the rest. has been agreeably redecorated. Free parking; resv. a must. *French-seafood*. **I–M**

Hereford House (dwntwn.), 2 E. 20th St. (842-1080). A/C. Lunch Mon.-Fri., dinner Mon.-Sat.; closed Sun. and holidays. AE, CB, DC, MC, V. Jkt. *Specialties:* the finest meats perfectly broiled over an open fire; also excellent hamburgers. *Note:* One of the steakhouses that endear Kansas City to meatlovers. Typical western décor; unfortunately no resv. are taken. A very fine place to eat. *Steak*. **I**

Jess & Jim's Steak House (vic.), 135th and Locust Sts., Martin City (942-9909). A/C. Lunch/dinner Mon.-Sat.; closed Sun. No credit cards. *Specialties:* excellent prime cuts at extremely reasonable prices. *Note:* Everything here, from the 8-oz. filet mignon to the 30-oz. porterhouse, including the baked potatoes that come with them, is enormous. Small appetites should stay away. The décor adds little to the value and no resv. are accepted, but the 45-min. trip from dwntwn is well worth while. Other location: **Jess & Jim's Annex,** 13035 Holmes Rd. (942-7454). *Steak.* **I**

☂ **Houlihan's Old Place** (nr. dwntwn), 4743 Pennsylvania Ave. (561-3141) A/C. Lunch/dinner daily; closed December 25. AE, CB, DC, MC, V. *Specialties:* onion soup, omelets, quiche, steak, hamburgers, salads. *Note:* Relaxed and friendly; the ideal place for a quick meal in an entertaining turn-of-the-century setting. Friendly svce. Open late (midnight or 1 a.m.). Trendy clientele; resv. advised. *American.* **B–I**

☂ **Italian Gardens** (dwntwn), 1110 Baltimore Ave. (221-9311). A/C. Lunch/dinner Mon.-Sat.; closed Sunday, holidays. AE, CB, DC, MC, V. *Specialties:* fresh homemade pasta, calves' liver alla Veneziana, classic Italian dishes, steak. *Note:* Nice, unassuming small family rest. Diligent svce. Popular in the community for half a century, especially for lunch. The only attempt at interior decoration is provided by photos of show-business stars. *Italian-American.* **B–I**

☂ **Prospect of Westport** (nr. dwntwn), 4109 Pennsylvania Ave. (753-2227). A/C. Breakfast/lunch/dinner daily; closed holidays. AE, CB, DC, MC, V. *Specialties:* fresh homemade pasta, fish, and daily specials; menu changes regularly. *Note:* Enchanting modern décor of exuberant greenery beneath a high skylight. Delicate, imaginative cooking; svce with a smile. Inviting open patio for fine days. One of Kansas City's fashionable spots; resv. advised. *American-Continental.* **B–I**

In the Vicinity

☀☂ **Stephenson's Apple Farm** (vic.), 16401 E. U.S. 40 at Lee's Summit Rd. (375-5400). A/C. Lunch/dinner daily; closed December 24 and 25. AE, CB, DC, MC, V. *Specialties:* meat, ham, and chicken smoked over a wood fire, steaks, homemade pies, apple fritters, cider. *Note:* Picturesque country inn occupying an old farmhouse 25 min. from dwntwn. Pleasant countrified setting; very crowded, so resv. advised at this successful rest. *American.* **B–I**

Cafeteria/Fast Food

Winstead's (nr. dwntwn), 101 Brush Creek Blvd. (753-2244). Drive-in and eat-in hamburger emporium. The hamburgers are made from fresh ground meat. Terrific ice cream and giant sundaes. Seven locations, including the original one at Brush Creek Blvd.

BARS & NIGHTCLUBS

As you would expect from the former jazz capital of the world, Kansas City, too, has a magic phone number—the **Jazz Hotline** (931-2888)—which will give you the programs at all the city's jazz concerts and jazz clubs.

Alameda Roof Lounge, (nr. dwntwn), in the Alameda Plaza (see "Accommodations," above) (756-1500). Elegant bar with live jazz adjoining the excellent rest. of the same name. Dancing. Open nightly.

The Funny Bone (vic.), 1148 W. 103rd St. (941-9857). Comedy club, very popular locally.

Harry T's (dwntwn), in the Phillips House Hotel, 12th and Baltimore Sts. (763-1018). Live jazz at a friendly bar; fashionable disco. Open nightly.

Houlihan's Old Place (nr. dwntwn), 4743 Pennsylvania Ave. (561-3141). Deservedly popular singles bar, adjoining the very acceptable rest. of the same name (see above). Open nightly.

NEARBY EXCURSIONS

FORT OSAGE (21 mi., 34 km, east on U.S. 24 and Sibley Rd. Sibley) (881-4431): The first fort built (1808) west of the Mississippi by the famous expedition of Lewis and Clark (see the Fort Clatsop National Memorial in chapter on the Pacific Coast), now carefully restored. Officers' cantonments, barracks for other ranks, museum, and trading post all look as though they had been lifted bodily from a period western. It's a good idea to combine this trip with a visit to Independence (see below). Open weekends only from the end of Dec. to mid-Mar., daily the rest of the year.

INDEPENDENCE (7 mi., 12 km, east via Independence Ave.): Starting point of the Santa Fe and Oregon Trails, and once the provisional capital of the Mormons.

The **Harry S Truman Library and Museum,** U.S. 24 at Delaware St. (833-1400), open daily, contains among other memorabilia an exact facsimile of the Oval Office at the White House. Also, don't miss the **Harry S Truman National Historic Site,** 219 N. Delaware St. (254-7199), a fine example of Victorian architecture where President Truman lived for more than half a century. Original furniture; open daily in summer, Tues.-Sun. the balance of the year.

On the way, stop at the **Mormon Visitors Center,** 937 W. Walnut St., which offers a complete history of the Church of Jesus Christ of the Latter-Day Saints as well as an organ with 6,300 pipes (daily recitals in summer).

Also take a look at the very picturesque **1859 Marshal's Home and Jail Museum** at 217 N. Main St. (252-1892), a genuine 19th-century prison and sheriff's office scrupulously restored. Open daily in summer, Tues.-Sat. the rest of the year. Well worth a visit.

KANSAS CITY, KANSAS (5 mi., 8 km, west on U.S. 24): The twin city across the Kansas River. There is a group of 400 interesting **Indian tombs** in Huron Park, at Center City Plaza between 6th and 7th.

The **Agricultural Hall of Fame,** 630 N. 126th St. (913/721-1075), offers a fascinating course in the development of midwestern farming by means of extensive collections of old agricultural equipment and period buildings. Open daily Apr.-Nov.; should be seen.

LIBERTY (15 mi., 24 km, NE on I-35 and Mo. 152): Visit the **Jesse James Bank Museum,** Old Town Sq. (781-4458), where in 1866 Jesse James, the legendary bandit of the Old West, committed the first bank holdup in the country's history. Open Mon.-Sat.

See also the **Historic Liberty Jail,** 216 N. Main St. (781-3188), open daily, where Joseph Smith, founder of the Mormons, was imprisoned with a number of his followers, and where he was vouchsafed many revelations about Mormon doctrine. Worth the side trip.

OLD SHAWNEE TOWN (18 mi., 29 km, SW along I-35 and Johnson Dr.) (913/268-8772 for information): Detailed reconstruction of a pioneer village in the period 1850–1900, with a dozen original buildings including the school and the jail, plus a score of facsimiles of structures from the time of the Westward expansion. Picturesque and amusing; worth going out of your way for. Open Tues.-Sun.

ST. JOSEPH (50 mi., 80 km, north on I-29): Founded in 1826 by a French fur trader, Joseph Robidoux, this little market town, birthplace of the great saxophonist Coleman Hawkins and the TV newscaster Walter Cronkite, still offers a whiff of adventure. It was the terminus of the Pony Express, which from April 1860 to October 1861 was the only link between Missouri and California thanks to its dauntless horsemen (the record time to Sacramento was 7 days, 17 hrs).

The horseman of the Pony Express, the most famous being the young Buffalo Bill, were, according to a contemporary newspaper advertisement, "young, slim, energetic and under 18. They must be consummate horsemen, ready to risk their lives every day. Orphans preferred. Pay: $25 a week." Every horseman covered about 90 mi., 145 km, with three changes of mount, before being relieved by another. Time allowed for change of mount: two minutes—and the fastest did it in 15 seconds. At the time it cost $5 (later reduced to $1) to send a half-ounce letter from Missouri to California. A mere four days after the opening of the first transcontinental telegraph line on Oct. 24, 1861, the Pony Express went out of business.

St. Joseph still displays some interesting links with the past: see the **Pony Express Stables Museum,** the company's birthplace, at 914 Penn St. (279-5059), open daily from April to Sept. only; the **Patee House Museum,** 12th and Penn Sts. (232-8206), open daily in summer, weekends only in spring and fall; and the **St. Joseph Museum,** 11th and Charles Sts. (237-8471), with many memorabilia of the Westward expansion, open year round.

Finally, visit the **Jesse James House,** 12th and Penn Sts. (232-8206), where the famous outlaw was killed in 1882 by a member of his own band for a $10,000 reward. Open daily May-Sept., weekends only in Apr. and Oct.

On the way, visit the little pioneer city of ☼ ⌂ **Weston,** on the banks of the Mississippi, with its dozens of interesting old houses. Particularly interesting is the **McCormick Distilling Co.,** 1 mi. (1.6 km) SE on County Rd. JJ, one of the oldest distilleries in the U.S.; call 386-2276 for visiting hours.

FARTHER AFIELD

☼ ♨ **LAKE OF THE OZARKS** (100 mi., 160 km, SE on U.S. 71 and Mo. 7): This superb artificial body of water, more than 93 mi. (150 km) long and surrounded by dense woods of oak and sassafras, was created in 1931 by the construction of the Bagnell Dam on the Osage River. Famous for its waterskiing, sailing, and fishing, this hilly region is attractive for the friendliness of its inhabitants, and for its wide range of all-season diversions: woodland walks in spring, water sports (more than 1,150 mi., 1,840 km, of waterfront) in summer, cross-country skiing and skating in winter, and in fall the dazzling sight of the turning leaves. Lake excursions on the paddlewheel steamer *Tom Sayer* from Bagnell dam, near Lake Ozark (314/365-3300), daily Apr.-Oct. Worth a protracted visit. There are hotels, motels, and rests. at Camdenton, Clinton, Lake Ozark, and Osage Beach; two recommended hotels are:

Where to Stay En Route
☼ ♟♟♟♟ **Marriott's Tan-Tar-A Resort,** State Rd. KK, Osage Beach, MO 65065 (314/348-3131). Luxurious resort complex right on the lake. 1,000 rms. Private marina. **E–VE**

♟♟ **Breckenridge on the Lake,** Lake Rd. 54-30 A., Osage Beach, MO 65065 (314/348-2293). Comfortable, friendly motel on the lake. 355 rms. **I–M**

PART FOUR

THE MOUNTAIN STATES

CHAPTER 29

DENVER

☐ ☐ ☐

Midway between the Pacific coast and Missouri, Denver lies at the foot of the Rockies against the magnificent natural backdrop of the mountains. The "mile-high city"—to use the attractive name conferred on it by its inhabitants—was dear to the heart of Buffalo Bill, whose grave overlooks the city from atop **Lookout Mountain.** More recently, Jack Kerouac eulogized it in his famous novel and bible of the beat generation, *On the Road.* A former gold and silver prospectors' camp, Denver served as a bridgehead for the Westward Expansion. Signs of the city's heroic past can be seen in structures like the **Capitol** dome, 243 ft (76 m) high, and covered in pure gold leaf from Colorado mines. The neoclassical architecture of the imposing Capitol forms a striking contrast with the ultra-futurist **Denver Art Museum,** on the other side of the **Civic Center** and its gardens. Not far from here, the picturesque **Larimer Square** marks the heart of historic Old Denver with art galleries, cafés, restaurants, and 19th-century gas lamps.

Like all the mushrooming cities of the West, the capital of Colorado experienced an economic boom after World War II. Specializing in growth industries such as oil and mineral exploration, aeronautics, defense, graphics, and electronics, it is one of the energy capitals of the country with its oil, gas, coal, uranium, solar energy, and synthetic fuels. Not surprisingly, Denver, like Dallas and Houston, was severely affected by the oil crisis of the 1980s.

The proximity of the Rockies has also made Denver "the queen city of the Plains," and one of the great capitals of American tourism. Less than two or three hours away by car are the famous resorts at **Aspen, Vail, Copper Mountain,** and **Winter Park,** all filled with visitors both summer and winter. A veritable turntable between the East and the West, **Stapleton International Airport** is the fifth-busiest airport in the country.

An effective mix of modern skyscrapers, wide tree-lined thoroughfares, and wealthy suburbs, Denver, "the green city," and its satellite, **Boulder,** have more than 200 public parks and gardens between them. The one drawback is that the walls of the Rockies form an impassable barrier for automobile emissions and industrial fumes, smothering Denver each winter in a thick cloud of atmospheric pollution whenever the winds blow westward or a temperature inversion occurs. This "brown cloud" even makes it necessary for local drivers to leave their cars in the garage according to a rotation system based on license plate numbers.

BASIC FACTS: Capital of Colorado. Area Code: 303. Time Zone: Mountain Time. ZIP Code: 80201. Settled: 1858. Approximate population: city, 500,000; metropolitan area, 1,820,000. 22nd-largest metropolitan area in the U.S.

CLIMATE: With close to 300 clear days per year, Denver is one of the sunniest cities in the country. The high altitude and the brisk, dry air make summer very agreeable (avg. temperature: 68°F, 20°C). In spring and autumn the air gets chilly even when the sun is shining. Winter brings blizzards from the Rockies and the temperature plunges to 5°F (−15°C), which can make outings dangerous (not to mention the frequent smog from mid-Nov. to mid-Jan.).

DISTANCES: Albuquerque, 421 mi. (675 km); Kansas City, 600 mi. (960 km); Los Angeles, 1,059 mi. (1,695 km); Salt Lake City, 506 mi. (810 km); Yellowstone, 638 mi. (1,022 km).

ARRIVAL & TRANSIT INFORMATION

AIRPORT: Stapleton International Airport (DEN): 7 mi. (11 km) NE. Information: 398-3977.

AIRLINES: American (595-9304), Aspen (320-4747), Continental (398-3000), Delta (696-1322), Eastern (623-4800), Northwest (825-6116), TWA (629-7878), United (398-4141), USAir (toll free 800/428-4322).

CITY LINK: Cab fare to city center, about $10–$12; time, 20 min. Bus: American Limousine Service (393-0703); leaves approximately every 30 min.; fare, $5. Many local bus lines (28, 32, and 52) which also serve the airport; fare, 70¢. Relatively efficient public transportation system (bus; R.T.D.) (778-6000). The proximity of the Rocky Mountains and the numerous excursion possibilities make it advisable to rent a car with unlimited mileage.

CAR RENTAL (at Stapleton International Airport): Avis (398-3725), Budget (399-3100), Dollar (398-2424), Hertz (355-2244), National (321-7990). For downtown locations, consult the telephone directory.

LIMOUSINE SERVICES: Carey Limousine (toll free 800/336-4646), Dav El Limousines (toll free 800/922-0343).

TAXIS: Taxis are few and may not be hailed on the street. There are taxi stations in front of all the major hotels, at the bus station, and at the AMTRAK station. They may also be summoned by phone. Major companies: Yellow Cab (292-1212) and Zone Cab (861-2323).

TRAIN: AMTRAK, Union Station, 17th & Wynkoop Sts. (893-3911).

BUS: Greyhound, 1055 19th St. (292-5699).

INFORMATION & TOURS

TOURIST INFORMATION: The **Denver Convention & Visitors Bureau,** 225 W. Colfax Ave., CO 80202 (303/892-1112 or 303/892-1505).

GUIDED TOURS: **Gray Line Tours** (bus), PO Box 38667 (303/289-2841). Guided tours of the city and around the Rockies. Serves principal hotels.

SIGHTS, ATTRACTIONS, & ACTIVITIES

ADVENTURES: **Colorado Adventure** (boat), 4300 E. 8th Ave. (333-7245):

Rafting on the Colorado and Green rivers (summer). For a list of other commercial operators, see chapter on The Rockies.

ARCHITECTURAL HIGHLIGHTS: ※ ⚲ **Boettcher Concert Hall,** 13th & Curtis Sts. (575-2637): Home of the Denver Symphony Orchestra, this building has remarkable architecture and acoustics: the orchestra is positioned in the center of the hall, totally surrounded by the audience. Worth a look.

⚲ **Denver Center for the Performing Arts,** 14th & Curtis Sts. (893-3272): Artistic and cultural heart of Denver, this ultramodern architectural complex includes notably three theaters **(Helen Bonfils Theater Complex),** a movie theater for art and experimental film, the Boettcher Concert Hall (see above), and a large shopping arcade under an 80-ft- (24-m-) high skylight. A sight not to be missed. Open daily.

⚲ **Public Library,** 1357 Broadway (571-2000): The largest library in the Mountain States, with 1.5 million volumes including an unrivaled collection of books, photographs, and documents on the history of the Old West.

HISTORIC BUILDINGS: ⚲ **Daniels & Fisher Tower,** Arapahoe & 16th St. Mall: This 328-ft (100-m) brick tower was inspired by the renowned campanile of the Piazza San Marco in Venice. At the time of its construction (1910) it was the tallest building in Denver. Not open to the public, unfortunately.

※ ⚲ **Molly Brown House,** 1340 Pennsylvania St. (832-4092): Nouveau riche Victorian house that belonged to Molly Brown, wife of a gold-mining magnate and famous as "Unsinkable Molly" because she survived the sinking of the *Titanic* in 1912. Lovely old furniture and interesting collections of clothing, tapestries, and turn-of-the-century memorabilia. An absolute must-see. Open daily in summer, Tues.-Sun. off-season.

⚲ **State Capitol,** E. Colfax Ave. at Sherman St. (866-2604): The seat of the state legislature, a formidable granite structure 243 ft (76 m) tall modeled on the Washington Capitol. The dome is covered in pure gold leaf from Colorado mines. Superb panorama from the gallery at the top (elevator and rather steep stairs). Open Mon.-Fri.

※ ⚲ **U.S. Mint,** 320 W. Colfax Ave. (844-3582): In business since 1862; turns out some 20 million coins each day. One of the three gold reserves in the country (Fort Knox and West Point, N.Y., are the other two), with heaps of ingots high enough to set you dreaming. Worth a visit. No picture-taking allowed. Open Mon.-Fri.

MUSEUMS OF ART: ※ ⚲⚲ **Denver Art Museum,** 100 W. 14th Ave. (575-2793): One of the best collections of American Indian and pre-Columbian art, including a unique group of reredos and sculpted religious figures (santos). Among its major works: Van der Weyden's *Portrait of Isabella of Portugal,* Arcimboldo's *Summer,* and Monet's *Waterloo Bridge,* as well as remarkable Oriental art. Surprising architecture in the form of a modern fortified castle covered in shining ceramic, by Gio Ponti and James Sudler. Not to be missed. Open Tues.-Sun.

⚲ **Museum of Western Art,** 1727 Tremont Pl. at 17th St. (296-1880): In the venerable **Old Navarre Building** (1880), which has successively housed a girls' school, restaurants, and a brothel, this wonderful art museum dedicated solely to the heroic age of the Far West offers works by Frederic Remington, Charles Russell, Georgia O'Keeffe, and Albert Bierstadt, notably. Not to be missed. Open Tues.-Sat.

MUSEUMS OF SCIENCE & HISTORY: ⚲ **Colorado State Museum,** 1300

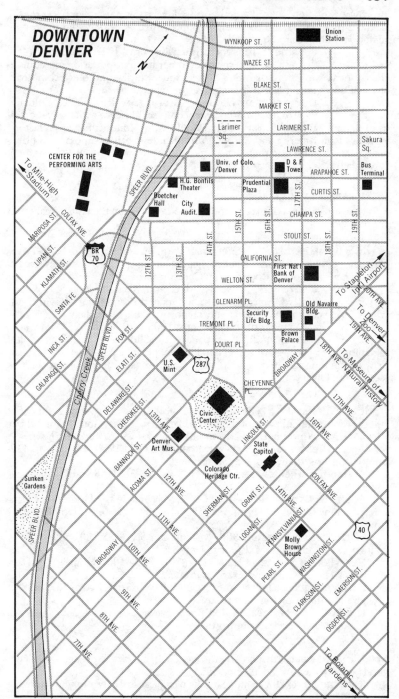

DOWNTOWN DENVER

N

WYNKOOP ST.
Union Station
WAZEE ST
BLAKE ST.
MARKET ST.
Larimer Sq.
LARIMER ST.
LAWRENCE ST.
Sakura Sq.
CENTER FOR THE PERFORMING ARTS
Univ. of Colo. /Denver
D & F Tower
ARAPAHOE ST.
Bus Terminal
To Mile-High Stadium
COLFAX AVE.
SPEER BLVD.
H.G. Bonfils Theater
Prudential Plaza
CURTIS ST.
Boetcher Hall
City Audit.
CHAMPA ST.
15TH ST.
16TH ST.
17TH ST.
18TH ST.
19TH ST.
STOUT ST.
MARIPOSA ST.
LIPAN ST.
KLAMATH ST.
SANTA FE
12TH ST.
13TH ST.
14TH ST.
CALIFORNIA ST.
BR 70
WELTON ST.
First Nat'l Bank of Denver
To Stapleton Int'l Airport
INCA ST.
CALAPAGO ST.
FOX ST.
ELATI ST.
GLENARM PL.
Old Navarre Bldg.
Security Life Bldg.
TREMONT PL.
Brown Palace
To Denver Zoo
19th AVE.
COURT PL.
CHEYENNE PL.
BROADWAY
To Museum of Natural History
18th AVE.
DELAWARE ST.
CHEROKEE ST.
U.S. Mint
287
Civic Center
LINCOLN ST.
17TH AVE.
Sunken Gardens
SPEER BLVD.
Cherry Creek
13TH AVE.
BANNOCK ST.
Denver Art Mus.
State Capitol
16TH AVE.
ACOMA ST.
12TH AVE.
Colorado Heritage Ctr.
SHERMAN ST.
GRANT ST.
14TH AVE.
COLFAX AVE.
11TH AVE.
LOGAN ST.
PENNSYLVANIA ST.
Molly Brown House
40
BROADWAY
10TH AVE.
PEARL ST.
WASHINGTON ST.
CLARKSON ST.
EMERSON ST.
9TH AVE.
8TH AVE.
OGDEN ST.
7TH AVE.
To Botanic Gardens

Broadway (866-3682): For Western history lovers, this museum retraces the life of the early pioneers and the Indians. Superb Anasazi pottery and interesting temporary exhibitions. Open daily.

☀☖ **Forney Transportation Museum,** 1416 Platte St. (469-2635): One of the most important transportation museums in the country, with more than 300 cars, various vehicles, and old locomotives, some of which are unique in the world. Open daily.

☀☖☖ **Museum of Natural History,** City Park, 2001 Colorado Blvd. (370-6363): Very complete museum with many dioramas of natural habitats, displaying the wildlife of five continents and prehistoric ways of life in America and Europe. Also includes a hall of dinosaurs, a planetarium, and a projection room with a four-story screen **(Phipps Imax Theater).** Open daily.

PANORAMAS: ☖ State Capitol, E. Colfax Ave. at Sherman St. (866-2604):
Spectacular panorama of the city and the mountains from the visitors' gallery at the top. Worth a look. Open Mon.-Fri.

PARKS & GARDENS: ☖☖ Cheesman Park, Franklin St. & E. Eighth Ave.:
Vast grass-covered park with a botanic garden and tropical greenhouses (see below). Superb view of the Rockies from Cheesman Memorial.

☖ **City Park,** between 17th & 26th Aves., York St. & Colorado Blvd.: Splendid 600-acre park in the center of town with a golf course, many lakes and fountains, and a renowned zoo. Open daily.

☖ **Denver Botanic Gardens,** 1005 York St. (575-2547): Incredibly beautiful floral park that includes a rose garden, tropical greenhouses displaying more than 850 kinds of plants, a gorgeous Japanese garden, and an unusual alpine garden with its own chalet. Part of Cheesman Park (see above). Open daily.

PERFORMING ARTS: For daily listings of all shows and cultural events, consult the entertainment pages of the daily papers *Denver Post* (morning) and *Rocky Mountain News* (morning), and the monthly magazines *Colorado* and *Denver*.

Arvada Center for the Arts & Humanities, 6901 Wadsworth Blvd. (422-8050): Concerts, drama, comedy. Year round.

Auditorium Theater, 14th & Curtis Sts. (573-7151): Broadway hits. Year round.

Boettcher Concert Hall, 14th & Curtis Sts. (572-2637): Home of the Denver Symphony Orchestra, with principal conductor Philippe Entremont. Sept.-June.

Elitch Gardens Theater, 38th & Tennyson Sts. (458-8801): One of the country's oldest theaters. Mid-June to late Aug.

Helen Bonfils Theater, 14th & Curtis Sts. (893-4100): Home of the Denver Center Theater Company. Classical theater.

Heritage Square Opera House, Colo. 40 & 93 in Golden (279-2789): Melodrama, dinner theater. Year round.

Red Rocks Amphitheater, Red Rocks Park, Colo. 26 (575-2637): Rock and pop open-air concerts. Summer only.

SHOPPING: Gart Brothers, Tenth Ave. & Broadway: The biggest sporting-goods store in the world. Unbelievable.

Kohleberg's, 1720 Champa St.: The best place in Denver for authentic Indian crafts.

Miller Stockman, 1555 Lawrence St.: From Stetson hats to cowboy boots and saddles, one of the best-stocked stores in the West. Seven other Miller Stockman stores throughout Denver.

SPECIAL EVENTS: For the exact schedule of events below, consult the **Denver Convention & Visitors Bureau** (see "Tourist Information," above).

Colorado Indian Market (mid-Jan.): Craft exhibits, Indian dances, and traditional cuisines of more than 90 tribes. A wonderfully colorful spectacle.

National Western Stock Show & Rodeo (ten days in mid-Jan.): The largest livestock fair and the biggest rodeo in the country. Cowboy gear is *de rigueur.* This classic has been around since 1906 and should not be missed.

Red Rocks Park Summer Concerts (throughout the summer): Classical concerts, ballets, musical comedies in an open-air amphitheater that seats 10,000. The amphitheater is in the middle of a very handsome rocky arena 15 mi. (24 km) SW of Denver.

Colorado Shakespeare Festival (July-Aug.): Mary Rippon Outdoor Theater (University of Colorado at Boulder) presents three Shakespeare works each summer.

SPORTS: There are three professional teams in the Denver area:

Basketball (Oct. to late Apr.): Nuggets, McNichols Sports Arena (893-3865).

Football (Sept.-Dec.): Broncos, Mile High Stadium (433-7466).

Ice Hockey (Oct.-Apr.): Colorado Flames, McNichols Sports Arena (572-7825).

STROLLS: ♙ The Financial District, 17th St. between Broadway & Arapahoe:

Known as "Wall Street West," this financial district brings together some of the most spectacular skyscrapers in the Mountain States, including the **Anaconda Tower,** 40 stories of smoked glass; the **First National Bank Building;** and the 30-story **Security Life Building.** For modern-architecture lovers.

Larimer Square, Larimer St. between 14th & 15th Sts.: The heart of Old Denver, with art galleries, cafés, boutiques, and restaurants, is especially lively by night. Charming turn-of-the-century town houses and gas lamps. Quite touristy but pleasant.

Sakura Square, 19th & Lawrence Sts.: A little piece of Japan in the middle of Colorado, "Cherry Blossom" Square has Oriental restaurants, boutiques, gardens, and a Buddhist temple. A welcome change of scenery.

16th Street Mall, 16th St. between Market St. & Cleveland Pl.: The business heart of Denver, with dozens of specialized boutiques and department stores, numerous bars, restaurants, theaters. A free shuttle bus runs along the mall. Fountains and public benches, as well as street musicians, mimes, and jugglers, make this tree-lined shopping street an agreeable place for a stroll.

THEME PARKS: ♙ Elitch Gardens, W. 38th Ave. & Tennyson St. (455-4771):

Very complete theme park with a giant roller coaster amid 28 acres of very lovely gardens. Also offers open-air concerts. Open wknds only in May, daily June-Sept., closed the rest of the year.

WINTER SPORTS RESORTS: With dozens of winter sports resorts, the Colorado Rockies are a skier's paradise. The most popular are:

Aspen and **Aspen Highlands,** 202 mi. (323 km) SW on I-70 and Colo. 82 (303/925-1220): 19 lifts. This is the luxury resort of the Rockies.

Breckenridge, 92 mi. (147 km) west on I-70 and Colo. 9 (303/453-2368): 14 lifts.

Copper Mountain, 86 mi. (137 km) west on I-70 (303/968-2882): 16 lifts.

Keystone, 78 mi. (124 km) west on I-70 (303/534-7712): 18 lifts.

Snowmass, 199 mi. (313 km) west on I-70 and Colo. 82 (303/925-1221): 14 lifts.

Steamboat Springs, 177 mi. (283 km) NW on I-70 and U.S. 40 (303/879-6111): 19 lifts.

Vail, 105 mi. (168 km) west on I-70 (303/476-5601): 16 lifts. The poshest of the Colorado resorts.

Winter Park, 71 mi. (113 km) NW on I-70 and U.S. 40 (303/726-5514): 17 lifts.

INDUSTRIAL TOURS: Coors, 13th & Ford Sts., in Golden (277-2337), 15 mi. (24 km) west on W. Colfax Ave. and U.S. 40: Tour of the brewery and beer tasting. Open Mon.-Sat. year round.

ACCOMMODATIONS

See the listing of toll-free numbers in the Appendix.

Room Rates in Denver	
B (Budget)	up to $30
I (Inexpensive)	$30–$60
M (Moderate)	$60–$90
E (Expensive)	$90–$140
VE (Very Expensive)	$140 and up

Personal Favorites (in order of preference)

Hyatt Regency (formerly the Fairmont; dwntwn), 1750 Welton St., CO 80202 (303/295-1200; toll free, see Hyatt). 540 rms, A/C, cable color TV. AE, CB, DC, MC, V. Gar. $8, pool, tennis, two rests. (including the Marquis Room), 24-hr coffeeshop, four bars, 24-hr rm svce, night club, concierge, free crib. *Note:* This elegant glass-and-steel tower (26 floors) is the last word in hotel comfort. Spacious, luxuriously arranged rms, each in its own style (most have refrigerators). Excellent svce and a fine rest. VIP and big business clientele. The best spot in Denver. **E–VE**

Burnsley Hotel (dwntwn), 1000 Grant St., CO 80203 (303/830-1000; toll free 800/345-3457). 82 suites, A/C, cable color TV. AE, CB, DC, MC, V. Free parking, pool, rest. (The Restaurant), bar, rm svce, night club, concierge. *Note:* Small, intimate hotel composed exclusively of suites. Luxurious, ultracomfortable facilities including vast bedrooms w. period furniture, refrigerators, private balconies, and a lovely view of the Rockies in the distance. Personalized svce, a very good rest., and renowned jazz club. A favorite of connoisseurs. **E–VE**

☼☐☐ **Oxford Alexis** (dwntwn), 1600 17th St., CO 80202 (303/ 628-5400; toll free 800/228-5838). 82 rms, A/C, color TV. AE, CB, DC, MC, V. Valet gar. $8, health club, rest. (Sage), bar, 24-hr rm svce, night club, free crib. *Note:* Denver's first luxury hotel (built more than a century ago) is a delightful little place that has been redone as good as new. The atmosphere is elegant and discreet, the rms comfortable and tastefully decorated, the rm svce excellent. Good rest. and a splendid art deco bar. Clientele of regulars. Free breakfast. **E–VE**

☐☐ **Best Western Regency Hotel** (nr. dwntwn), 3900 Elati St., CO 80216 (303/458-0808; toll free, see Best Western). 400 rms, A/C, color TV, in-rm movies. AE, CB, DC, MC, V. Free parking, two pools, tennis, health club, sauna, two rests. (including Jake's), coffeeshop, bar, rm svce, disco, hrdrsr, free crib. *Note:* Modern motel specializing in business and convention clientele w. big, comfortable rms, efficient reception and svce, a very adequate rest., and good recreational facilities. Free airport shuttle. 10 min. from dwntwn. **M**

☐☐ **Holiday Inn Sports Center** (nr. dwntwn), 1975 Bryant St., CO 80204 (303/433-8331; toll free, see Holiday Inns). 168 rms, A/C, color TV, in-rm movies. AE, CB, DC, MC, V. Free parking, pool, rest. (Fans), bar, rm svce, free crib. *Note:* Large, round 13-story tower a few steps from Mile High Stadium offering the functional style and comfort of a Holiday Inn. Group and convention clientele. 5 min. from dwntwn. Lovely view of the skyline and the mountains from the rest. at the top. A very good value. Free airport shuttle. **I–M**

☐ **La Quinta Central** (nr. dwntwn), 3500 Fox St., CO 80216 (303/458-1222; toll free, see La Quinta). 106 rms, A/C, color TV, in-rm movies. AE, CB, DC, MC, V. Free parking, pool, adjacent 24-hr coffeeshop, bar, rm svce, free crib. *Note:* Modern, comfortable motel 6 min. from dwntwn with spacious rms and efficient reception and svce. Good value. **I**

☐ **Motel 6 East** (nr. dwntwn), 12020 E. 39th Ave., CO 80239 (303/371-7410). 137 rms, A/C, color TV, free in-rm movies. DC, MC, V. Free parking, pool, free crib. *Note:* An unbeatable value in modern comfort quite close to the airport. Ideal for the motorist (direct access to the highways). **B**

☐ **Regal 8 West** (nr. dwntwn), 3050 W. 49th Ave., CO 80221 (303/455-8888; toll free 800/851-8888). 196 rms, A/C, color TV. AE, CB, DC, MC, V. Free parking, pool, adjacent 24-hr coffeeshop, free crib. *Note:* A classic motel 12 min. from dwntwn affording functional comfort. Ideal for the motorist. A good overall value. **B–I**

Other Accommodations (From top bracket to budget)

☼☐☐☐ **Brown Palace** (dwntwn), 321 17th St., CO 80202 (303/ 297-3111; toll free 800/321-2599). 230 rms, A/C, cable color TV. AE, CB, DC, MC, V. Valet gar. $8, four rests. (including the Palace Arms), two bars, rm svce, entertainment, hrdrsr, concierge, free crib. *Note:* The grande dame of Denver hotels has been frequented by every American president since Theodore Roosevelt. A slightly incongruous modern tower overhangs the original building (1890). Elegant, eight-story atrium and fairly spacious, entirely renovated rms enhance the hotel's urbane character. Personalized svce and a reputable rest. Interesting wknd packages. **E–VE**

☐☐☐ **Westin Tabor Center** (dwntwn), 1672 Lawrence St., CO 80202 (303/572-9100; toll free, see Westin). 420 rms, A/C, color TV, in-rm movies. AE, CB, DC, MC, V. Gar. $10, pool, health club, sauna, two rests. (including Augusta), coffeeshop, two bars, rm svce, disco, hrdrsr, boutiques, crib free. *Note:* This large 19-story building with rather ungraceful modern architecture offers direct access to the 16th Street Mall and its dozens of boutiques and stores. Luxurious, comfortable rms and very complete facilities. Very good svce and an exclusive, grand-hotel rest. Business clientele (the financial district is nearby). **E–VE**

      Marriott City Center (dwntwn), 1701 California St., CO 80202 (303/297-1300; toll free, see Marriott). 610 rms, A/C, color TV, in-rm movies. AE, CB, DC, MC, V. Valet gar. $6, pool, sauna, two rests. (including Marjolaine's), coffeeshop, three bars, rm svce, boutiques, night club, crib free. *Note:* On the first 20 floors of the Arco Tower (42 floors). Ultramodern architecture, irreproachable comfort and facilities, unreliable svce. Two VIP floors. Business clientele. A very good location at the heart of the business district. **M–E**

      Executive Tower Inn (dwntwn), 1405 Curtis St., CO 80202 (303/571-0300; toll free 800/525-6651). 335 rms, A/C, cable color TV. AE, CB, DC, MC, V. Gar. $6, pool, tennis, health club, rest., coffeeshop, bar, rm svce, crib free. *Note:* This large, modern and functional tower in the heart of dwntwn offers spacious, comfortable rms, good recreational facilities, and relatively efficient svce. Rather obtrusive group and convention clientele. The hotel from which Gary Hart announced his first withdrawal from the 1988 presidential race. **M–E**

      Radisson (formerly the Hilton; dwntwn), 1550 Court Pl., CO 80202 (303/893-3333; toll free, see Radisson). 750 rms, A/C, color TV, in-rm movies. AE, CB, DC, MC, V. Gar. $6, pool, health club, sauna, two rests., coffeeshop, bars, rm svce, night club, hrdrsr, boutiques, crib free. *Note:* This massive building is something of a tourist barracks. Entirely renovated facilities afford functional comfort and décor. Relatively efficient svce. VIP floor. Very central location. Skating rink open in winter. Group and convention clientele. **M–E**

      Writers' Manor Hotel (nr. dwntwn), 1730 S. Colorado Blvd., CO 80222 (303/756-8877; toll free 800/525-8072). 325 rms, A/C, color TV, in-rm movies. AE, CB, DC, MC, V. Free parking, two pools, tennis, health club, sauna, rest. (Churchill's), coffeeshop, bar, rm svce, night club, hrdrsr, crib free. *Note:* Attractive, comfortable motel 15 min. from dwntwn. Inviting rms w. private patios or balconies, and mini-bars. Good svce and a very adequate rest. Group and convention clientele. A very good value. **I–M**

      Friendship Inn South (nr. dwntwn), 4760 E. Evans Ave., CO 80222 (303/757-7601; toll free, see Friendship Inns). 78 rms, A/C, color TV, in-rm movies. AE, CB, DC, MC, V. Free parking, pool, health club, rest., bar, disco, crib $5. *Note:* Small, appealing motel 15 min. from dwntwn. Depressing surroundings, just off I-25, but a good overall value. Ideal for the motorist. No-smoking rms. **I**

      Motel 6 West (nr. dwntwn), 480 Wadsworth Blvd., CO 80226 (303/238-6471). 120 rms, A/C, color TV, free in-rm movies. DC, MC, V. Free parking, pool, crib free. *Note:* An unbeatable value in functional comfort that is ideal for the motorist, 15 min. from dwntwn. **B**

Airport Acccommodations

      Stouffer Concourse (nr. dwntwn), 3801 Quebec St., CO 80207 (303/399-7500; toll free, see Stouffer). 400 rms, A/C, color TV, in-rm movies. AE, CB, DC, MC, V. Indoor valet parking $3, two pools, health club, sauna, rest., bars, 24-hr rm svce, night club, concierge. *Note:* Remarkable futurist architecture in the shape of a trapezoid. All the comfort and luxury of a first-rate hotel in a splendid 12-story glass atrium. Vast, well-conceived rms w. refrigerators and private balconies (the best have a view of the mountains). Extremely well soundproofed. Very efficient svce and a mediocre rest., as in all Stouffers. Free airport shuttle. Three top floors are reserved for VIPs. One of the country's most spectacular hotels. 20 min. from dwntwn. **E**

 Stapleton Plaza Hotel & Athletic Center (nr. dwntwn), 3333 Quebec St., CO 80207 (303/321-3500; toll free 800/525-1315). 300 rms, A/C, color TV, in-rm movies. AE, CB, DC, MC, V. Free parking, two pools, health club, sauna, rest. (Antares), two bars, rm svce, hrdrsr, boutiques, crib free. *Note:* Modern motel w. futurist décor and a spectacular ten-story atrium w. glass elevators. Comfortable rms w. interior balconies and mini-bars. Very good recreational facilities. Business clientele. Efficient svce. Free airport shuttle. **M–E**

RESTAURANTS

Denver Restaurant Prices	
(per person, excluding drinks and service charges)	
B (Budget)	up to $15
I (Inexpensive)	$15–$25
M (Moderate)	$25–$40
E (Expensive)	$40–$60
VE (Very Expensive)	$60 and up

Personal Favorites (in order of preference)

 Rattlesnake Club (nr. dwntwn), 901 Larimer St. (Tivoli Center) (573-8900). A/C. Lunch/dinner daily; brunch Sun. AE, CB, DC, MC, V. Jkt. Specialties: smoked trout w. sour cream and blinis, Maine crab w. chives and mustard seed, roast duck w. shallots and grilled pear, roast veal w. vinegar and green peppercorns, ice cream w. white chocolate and passion fruit. The menu changes regularly. Superb wine list. *Note:* The most celebrated rest. in the Rockies is the creation of two renowned young American chefs (Michael McCarty of Michael's rest. in Santa Monica and the pleasant, mustachioed Jimmy Schmidt, formerly of Detroit's London Chop House). This splendid rest. w. contemporary décor—in tones of pink, with abstract paintings and a glass elevator shaft—occupies three levels of the former Tivoli brewery, now entirely remodeled. Jimmy Schmidt's superb modern cuisine is delicate and inventive, deriving its inspiration particularly from old Indian recipes. First-rate svce. VIP and gourmand clientele. Resv. are an absolute must, well in advance, except for the ground-floor Grill. One of the 12 best rests. in the United States. *American.* **M–E**

 Café Giovanni (dwntwn), 1515 Market St. (825-6555). A/C. Lunch Mon.-Fri.; dinner Mon.-Sat.; closed Sun., hols. AE, CB, DC, MC, V. Jkt. Specialties: fresh homemade pasta, chicken primavera, poached sweetbreads w. port, saltimbocca, roast duckling, fish of the day, very good soufflés. The menu changes regularly. Rather weak wine list. *Note:* The Leone brothers, young and talented owners of this excellent rest., have transformed an old, decrepit downtown warehouse into an inviting, comfortable refuge where

European-inspired cuisine (French and Italian, notably) reigns supreme. Flowery, elegant Victorian décor and first-rate svce. Resv. a must. One of Denver's best. *Continental-Italian.* **I–M**

🍷🍷 **Cliff Young's** (dwntwn), 700 E. 17th Ave. (831-8900). A/C.
🍷🍷 Lunch Mon.-Fri.; dinner Mon.-Sat.; closed Sun. AE, CB, DC, MC, V. Jkt. Specialties: rack of lamb encrusted in herbs, halibut in fruit sauce, salmon in lemon dill butter. Baked goods made fresh daily. Extensive wine list. *Note:* Most innovative address of Restaurant Row (17th Avenue), this elegant small restaurant serves creative American cuisine with southwestern flair. The menu is varied, its presentation unsurpassed. Attentive service. Resv. essential. *American.* **I–M**

☼🍷🍷 **The Broker** (dwntwn), 821 17th St. (292-5065). A/C. Lunch
Mon.-Fri.; dinner nightly; closed hols. AE, CB, DC, MC, V. Jkt. Specialties: Broker-style shrimp, roast beef au jus, beef Wellington, chicken Cordon Bleu, poor choice of desserts. *Note:* The rest. has retained the original décor of this former bank vault, and as is only fitting, the place is very popular among business people. An excellent locale. Resv. advised. *American-Continental.* **I–M**

🍷 **La Casa de Manuel** (nr. dwntwn), 2010 Larimer St. (295-
🍷 1752). A/C. Lunch/dinner Tues.-Sat.; closed Sun., Mon. No credit cards. Specialties: tacos, menudo, carnitas, burritos, enchilada verde, and some incredibly hot sauces. *Note:* Despite its modest location and décor, Casa de Manuel is the best of countless Denver rests. which call themselves Mexican. Cuisine is truly authentic, as are the colorful murals that decorate the walls. Rather brusque but efficient svce. Locally very popular. *Mexican.* **B**

🍷 **Berardi's** (nr. dwntwn), 1525 Blake St. (623-7648). A/C.
🍷 Lunch Mon.-Fri.; dinner nightly. AE, MC, V. Specialties: fresh homemade pasta, fettuccine Alfredo, cutlet milanese, veal marsala, chicken Abruzzi. Good list of Italian wines. *Note:* This locally popular rest. offers pleasant décor and ambience in a former butcher's shop that has been completely renovated. Generous portions and honest cuisine. *Italian.* **I**

Other Restaurants (from top bracket to budget)

🍷🍷 The **Marquis** (dwntwn), in the Hyatt Regency Hotel (see "Ac-
🍷🍷 commodations," above) (295-5825). A/C. Lunch Mon.-Fri., dinner nightly. AE, CB, DC, MC, V. Jkt. Specialties: rack of lamb, sole meunière, braised veal w. tender young vegetables. The menu changes regularly. One of Colorado's best wine lists, but at exorbitant prices. *Note:* Opulent décor w. crystal center lights, silver chandeliers, and period furniture. By far the most luxuriously elegant rest. in Denver, serving irreproachable, classic French-inspired cuisine. Ultracorrect svce. Resv. strongly advised. Valet parking. *French-Continental.* **M**

🍷🍷 **Strings** (nr. dwntwn), 1700 Humboldt (831-7310). A/C.
🍷🍷 Lunch Mon.-Sat.; dinner nightly. MC, V. Jkt. Specialties: grilled eggplant w. mozzarella, mixed salads, fresh homemade pasta, grilled swordfish w. cabbage and peppercorns, garlic chicken in tomatillo sauce, remarkable desserts. *Note:* Excellent variations on the California cuisine moderne theme. Hi-tech ocean-liner décor w. an open grill and a pleasant patio for al fresco meals. Friendly, cheerful svce. Hip clientele. Resv. a must in light of its success. *American.* **I–M**

🍷🍷 **Tante Louise** (nr. dwntwn), 4900 E. Colfax Ave. (355-4488).
🍷🍷 A/C. Lunch Mon.-Fri.; dinner Mon.-Sat.; closed Sun., hols. AE, CB, DC, MC, V. Jkt. Specialties: veal w. mustard, grilled filet of lamb, Peking duck, sweetbreads w. madeira. The menu changes regularly. Fine wine list. *Note:* This turn-of-the-century–style inn is elegant and intimate and offers

lovingly prepared, delicate, imaginative cuisine. Agreeable svce. Resv. advised. An excellent spot. 10 min. from dwntwn. *Continental.* **I–M**

Buckhorn Exchange (nr. dwntwn), 1000 Osage St. (534-9505). A/C. Lunch/dinner daily; closed hols. AE, CB, DC, MC, V. Specialties: huge cuts of red meat, T-bone steak, Rocky Mountain oysters, moose and bison steak, roast quail. *Note:* Patronized by Buffalo Bill in his day, the oldest rest. in Denver (1893) proudly displays the "No. 1" on its liquor license. Authentic western décor including a vast collection of guns and hunting trophies. Absolutely worth a visit. Locally very popular. Resv. advised. *Steakhouse.* **I**

Café Promenade (dwntwn), 1424 Larimer St. (893-2692). A/C. Breakfast/lunch/dinner Mon.-Sat.; closed Sun., hols. AE, CB, DC, MC, V. Jkt. Specialties: from fresh pasta to pastries, everything here is homemade. Veal is the great specialty of the house. Remarkable desserts. Good wine list. *Note:* Gracious old-world–style tavern in the heart of Larimer Square offering delicate French-Italian–inspired cuisine. The agreeable patio is open in good weather. Courteous, cheerful svce. Pleasant classical background music in the evening. A fine place for business lunches. Resv. advised. *Continental.* **I**

Baby Doe's Matchless Mine (nr. dwntwn), 2520 W. 23rd Ave. (433-3386). A/C. Lunch Sun.-Fri.; dinner nightly; closed Dec. 25. AE, CB, DC, MC, V. Specialties: bison steak, beef chops, chicken w. Calvados, duck à l'orange. *Note:* Reproduces the atmosphere of a famous Leadville (Colorado) gold mine from the 1880s. Amusing bric-a-brac décor. Very estimable, if not terribly original, cuisine. Rather touristy ambience. Dancing as well. *Steakhouse-American.* **I**

Gasho (dwntwn), 1627 Curtis St. (892-5625). A/C. Lunch/dinner daily. AE, CB, DC, MC, V. Specialties: hibachi steak, teriyaki, sashimi, sukiyaki. *Note:* Denver's best Japanese rest. offers classic knife-wielding performances by the cooks under the admiring gaze of the customers. Lovely décor taken from a 300-year-old Japanese farm. Business clientele. Locally popular. Other location: 5071 S. Syracuse St. (773-3277). *Japanese.* **B–I**

Casa Bonita (vic.), 6715 W. Colfax Ave., Lakewood (232-5115). A/C. Lunch/dinner daily; closed Sun., hols. AE, MC, V. Specialties: enchiladas, tacos, chili con queso, tamales. *Note:* Huge rest. (seating for 1,100) that is so wild, it's cool. Classic Mexican dishes served in a vibrant, carnival atmosphere: palm trees, a 30-ft (10-m) waterfall, mariachi music, staged shootouts, and puppet shows. Locally popular. *Mexican.* **B**

Daddy Bruce's Bar-B-Q (nr. dwntwn), 1629 E. Bruce Randolph Ave. (295-9115). A/C. Lunch Tues.-Sat.; dinner Tues.-Sun. (until midnight); closed Mon. No credit cards. Specialties: spareribs, chicken, barbecued pork, smoked turkey, sweet-potato pie. *Note:* A real institution; Denver's temple of soul food. The neighborhood is less than inviting and the décor is neo-Formica, but the barbecue is remarkable. A must for those in search of local color. No resv. *American.* **B**

Cafeteria / Fast Food

Furr's (nr. dwntwn), 4900 Kipling (423-4602). Open daily (until 8 p.m.). Honest, well-prepared cafeteria food, particularly the roast beef. No credit cards.

BARS & NIGHTCLUBS

Bay Wolf (nr. dwntwn), 231 Milwaukee St. (388-9221). Open nightly. Fashionable singles bar and rest. Excellent live jazz.

Corner Room (dwntwn), in the Oxford Alexis Hotel, 1600 17th St. (628-5400). Open Mon.-Sat. Inviting, pleasant art deco bar with an elegant atmosphere and live jazz.

☀ **Heritage Square Opera House** (vic.), intersection of U.S. 40 and Colo. 93, in Golden (279-7881). Open Tues.-Sun. Offers amusing parodies of classic melodramas and silent films. Well worth the 20-min. car ride from dwntwn. Buffet and bar.

Neo (nr. dwntwn), 350 S. Birch St. (320-0117). Open nightly. The "in" disco w. rather flashy décor and a funky ambience.

Turn of the Century (vic.), 8930 E. Hampden Ave. (694-4884). Open nightly. A disco offering big-name acts and an average rest.

NEARBY EXCURSIONS

☀ **BOULDER** (30 mi., 48 km, NW on U.S. 36): This residential extension of Denver is built in the foothills of the Rockies and has a young, upwardly mobile population keen on sports and the environment. Boulder is home to the **University of Colorado** (22,000 students), which includes a world-renowned medical school, and many leading scientific institutes, among them the laboratories of the National Bureau of Standards and the National Center for Atmospheric Research, housed in a futurist building by I. M. Pei at 1850 Table Mesa Dr. (497-8720), open Mon.-Fri.

An interesting pioneer museum is the **Boulder Historical Museum,** 1206 Euclid Ave. (449-3464), open Tues.-Sat. Don't miss a glance at the charming **Downtown Mall,** Pearl St. between 11th & 15th Sts., with its pedestrians-only street, boutiques, restaurants, and old town houses. Well worth going out of your way for. (For accommodations and restaurants, see the chapter on the Rockies.)

☀ **BUFFALO BILL GRAVE** (in Lookout Mountain Park, 18 mi., 28 km, west on I-70) (526-0747): A magnificent view over the city from the mountaintop where lies the tomb of the famous scout. Museum dedicated to his adventurous career. Well worth the trip. Open daily in summer, Tues.-Sun. the rest of the year. On the way, visit the **Colorado Railroad Museum** in Golden (see below).

☀ **CENTRAL CITY** (34 mi., 54 km, west on I-70 and Colo. 279): Spectacular little mining town from the days of the Gold Rush. The abundance of gold mined here earned it the nickname "the richest square mile on earth." Counting as many as 5,000 inhabitants in the 1870s, the town has barely 350 today. A walking tour of the town is fun but tiring (it was built on the side of a mountain; start at the top and work downward). See the very handsome **Opera House** from 1878, Eureka St. (571-4435), open June-Aug. The **Central Gold Mine,** 126 Spring St. (582-5574), is open daily May-Sept. The **Gold Coin Saloon** on Main St. has been in operation since 1878. The **Teller House,** Eureka St. (582-3200), is a charming little Victorian hotel built in 1872 with a famous bar. There is also a picturesque narrow-gauge railroad. Well worth going out of your way for.

☀ **COMANCHE CROSSING MUSEUM** (in Strasburg, 30 mi., 48 km, east on I-70 (622-4668): Open-air museum devoted to the builders of the 19th-century transcontinental railroad. Original buildings and historic memorabilia of all kinds. Open daily in June, July, and Aug. only.

☀ **GOLDEN** (15 mi., 24 km, west on W. Colfax Ave. and U.S. 40): The Colorado capital from 1862 to 1867. See the **Colorado Railroad Museum,** 17155 W. 44th Ave. (279-4591), with its interesting collection of old locomotives. Open daily. Don't miss **Heritage Square** (intersection of U.S. 40 and Colo. 93) with some 50 restaurants, bars, boutiques, and attractions in a pleasing Victorian setting from the 1880s; open daily. A recommended joint excursion with the nearby **Buffalo Bill Grave** (see above).

IDAHO SPRINGS (34 mi., 54 km, west on I-70): Old gold diggers' town in the midst of a still very active mining zone, now producing uranium, molybdenum, zinc, lead, tungsten. Today it is also a renowned tourist attraction with radioactive hot springs. The longest mine tunnel in the world (5 mi., 7 km) once joined Idaho Springs and Central City. Part of the tunnel still exists but is not open to the public. See the **Argo Gold Mill,** 23rd Ave. & Riverside Dr. (567-2421), a gold mine dating from 1913, open daily. Well worth going out of your way for. A recommended joint excursion with **Central City** (see above) and **Mount Evans Scenic Road** (see "Farther Afield," below).

RED ROCKS PARK (12 mi., 19 km, SW on W. Colfax Ave. and Colo. 26) (892-1505): A natural, 10,000-seat amphitheater carved out in the middle of reddish rocks more than 300 ft (100 m) high. Offers a spectacular view of the city plus public concerts, big-name performances, and open-air shows in summer. It is also the stage for an open-air Mass on Easter Sunday attended by thousands (Easter sunrise service).

NATIONAL PARKS NEARBY: Rocky Mountain National Park, 70 mi. (112 km) northwest on U.S. 36 and 34. The most mountainous national park in America boasts 65 peaks of more than 9,600 ft (3,000 m), including **Longs Peak** (13,904 ft, 4,345 m). Torrents, glaciers, eternal snows, fish-filled lakes, very dense forests, and more than 300 mi. (480 km) of hiking trails. Unspoiled nature and a paradise for mountain climbing, camping, and fishing. **Trail Ridge Road** crosses right through the park and offers splendid panoramas, as well as spectacular views of the mountain peaks. The road is closed mid-Oct. to mid-June. There are numerous hotels and motels open year round in **Estes Park, Grand Lake,** and **Granby.** The **Moraine Park Visitor Center and Museum** is 1 mi. (2 km) from the east entrance of the park on U.S. 36 (open daily June-Sept.). Information: 303/586-2371. An excursion not to be missed. (For accommodations, see the chapter on the Rockies.)

FARTHER AFIELD

MOUNT EVANS SCENIC ROAD (120 mi., 190 km, r.t. on I-70W, Colo. 103, & Colo. 5): The highest road in the country, peaking at 14,260 ft (4,346 m). Fabulous landscapes can be seen all along the road, which is open in summer only. A real trial for people and vehicles, but well worth the five hrs r.t. On the way, visit **Georgetown** and **Central City** (see "Nearby Excursions," above), two picturesque mining towns from the days of the Gold Rush. Not to be missed.

COLORADO SPRINGS (134 mi., 214 km, r.t. on I-25): Quaint garden city frequented year round by tourists and vacationers. Home of the **U.S. Air Force Academy** (10 mi. north on I-25. Visitor Center open daily; 719/472-2555), and headquarters of the U. S. North American Air Defense Command (NORAD). Numerous and very pretty excursions in the area, including:

Cheyenne Mountain Hwy.: A superb panoramic route and "shrine of the sun" dedicated to the famous Will Rogers.

Garden of the Gods: Splendid reddish rock formations, particularly spectacular at sunrise and sunset.

Manitou Springs: A charming mountain spa at 515 Ruxton Ave. in Manitou Springs (719/685-5401) is the terminus of the **Cog Railway,** picturesque route leading to Pike's Peak. The **Scenic Incline Railway,** 518 Ruxton Ave. (719/685-9086), is a cable car that goes to the summit of Mount Manitou, offering an impressive view. Operates May-Oct.

Pike's Peak (14,110 ft, 4,301 m): Accessible only in summer by a steep toll road or by the Cog Railway (see above). An excursion not to be missed.

Seven Falls: A very beautiful rocky canyon with waterfalls which are illuminated at dusk. Open daily year round. A wonderfully spectacular drive. (For more details, see the chapter on the Rockies.)

☼☖ **CHEYENNE** (200 mi., 320 km, r.t. on I-25): Founded in the 19th century by the army in an effort to protect Union Pacific Railroad builders against Sioux attacks, the capital of Wyoming has retained its frontier-town flavor. Witness the **State Museum,** Central Ave. & 24th St. (307/ 777-7024), open daily; the **Frontier Days Old West Museum,** Carey Ave. (307/778-7290), open daily; and the superb wall murals of the **State Capitol,** Capitol Ave., open Mon.-Fri. Cheyenne, named for the Indian tribe, has sponsored annually since 1897 the most fabulous **rodeo festival** in the country, late July to early Aug. For information, call 307/778-7200. Itself worth the trip.

Where to Stay in Cheyenne

🛏🛏 **Best Western Hitching Post Inn,** 1700 W. Lincolnway, WY 82001 (307/638-3301). 250 rms. First-rate comfort. **I–M**

🛏 **La Quinta Inn,** 2410 Lincolnway, WY 82001 (307/632-7117). 108 rms. Modern comfort. **I**

🛏 **Motel 6,** 1735 Westland Rd, WY 82001 (307/635-1676). 108 rms. A very good, economical value. **B**

CHAPTER 30

THE ROCKY MOUNTAINS♦♦♦

□ □ □

Comprising several parallel mountain chains, the Rocky Mountains form an impressive system more than 1,875 mi. (3,000 km) long, extending from New Mexico to Canada. This granite barrier of almost Himalayan proportions, with 53 peaks reaching more than 14,000 ft (4,260 m), marks the Continental Divide: east of the Rockies, the Missouri and its tributaries flow toward the Gulf of Mexico; to the west, the Colorado ("mother of all rivers" in the evocative phrase of writer James Michener) and its tributaries flow toward the Pacific. The central section of the Rocky Mountain chain, its peaks sculpted into fantastic shapes by erosion, makes Colorado one of the most beautiful states in America.

Some 70 million years old, the Rockies long remained uninhabited—the earliest traces of Native American settlement go back barely 2,000 years. It is as though the reverential awe that the sight of these wild, magnificent mountains must have inspired kept the local tribes away. Although the first white settlers arrived only in 1820, the westward expansion of the succeeding decades made the Rockies an obligatory way station for the famed riders of the Pony Express (eight days from Kansas to California) and for the heavy stagecoaches of the Wells Fargo and Overland companies. The gold rush of 1859–1860 caused a further influx of settlers into the mountains.

Today the Colorado Rockies have become one of the nation's great tourist attractions, favored equally by sun worshippers and skiers, with **Aspen Vail, Steamboat, Keystone Springs,** and **Copper Mountain** ranking among the most popular winter sports centers in the U.S. With Denver as their point of departure, motorists may enjoy numerous two- to ten-day touring itineraries, allowing them to discover such gorgeous landscapes as the peaks and alpine lakes of **Rocky Mountain National Park** to the north, the wild gorges of the **Colorado National Monument** to the east, the desert solitude of the **Great Sand Dunes** and the fabulous Native American archeological sites of **Mesa Verde National Park** to the south. Dozens of **ghost towns** from the gold-rush days, such as Georgetown, Central City, or Cripple Creek, as well as roads affording breathtaking panoramic views, such as those that wind up **Pikes Peak** and **Mount Evans** (at 14,260 ft, 4,346 m, the highest road in the U.S.), further enhance the unique appeal of the Colorado Rockies. All in all, this is a region not to be missed, as much for the incomparable beauty of its landscapes as for its aura of adventure (see also Chapter 29 on Denver).

BASIC FACTS: State of Colorado. Area Code: 303 or 719. Time Zone: Mountain Time. Population of Colorado: approx. 2.9 million.

CLIMATE: Very cold and snowy in winter (30°F, –1°C, on average), wonderfully sunny but cool in summer (70°F, 21°C, on average), the climate of the Colorado Rockies is a delight for tourists. Spring (47°F, 8°C, on average) and above all autumn (51°F, 11°C, on average) are the ideal seasons for avoiding the crowds of summer vacationers and winter sports enthusiasts. Sweaters and sunglasses are advisable in all seasons.

ARRIVAL & TRANSIT INFORMATION

NEAREST AIRPORT: Denver Stapleton International Airport (DEN), 65 mi. (105 km) SE of Rocky Mountain National Park; for information, call 303/398-3977.

Other airports giving access to the region are at Aspen, Durango, Grand Junction, Gunnison, Steamboat Springs, and Vail.

AIRLINES: See Chapter 29 on Denver. **Aspen Airways/United Express** (toll free 800/241-6522) and **Rocky Mountain Airways/Continental Express** (toll free 800/525-0280) serve the main regional airports, with departures from Denver.

BUS OR CAR RENTAL? Numerous bus companies, including Greyhound, link Denver with most of the cities in the Rockies. But considering the distances involved and the range of possible touring routes, a rental car with unlimited mileage is strongly recommended.

CAR RENTAL: See Chapter 29 on Denver. For all other cities, consult the local telephone directory.

LIMOUSINE SERVICES: See Chapter 29 on Denver. For all other cities, consult the local telephone directory.

TRAIN: AMTRAK (toll free 800/872-7245) has stations at 413 7th St., **Glenwood Springs;** Agate Ave., **Granby;** 2nd and Pitkin Sts., **Grand Junction;** and 420 Railroad Ave. at Fraser, **Winter Park.**

BUS: Several companies offer service from Denver: **Airport Transportation Service** (303/476-7576), to Aspen, Beaver, Creek, and Vail; **American Limo Service** (303/393-0703), to Boulder and Vail; **Aspen Limousine** (303/925-2400), to Aspen, Snowmass, and Vail; **Greyhound** (see Chapter 29 on Denver); **Resort Express** (303/468-7600), to Breckenridge, Copper Mountain, and Keystone; and **Rocky Mountain Coach Lines** (303/293-2871), to Granby, Winter Park, and Steamboat Springs.

INFORMATION & TOURS

TOURIST INFORMATION: The **Colorado Tourism Board,** 1625 Broadway, Denver, CO 80202 (303/592-5410; toll free 800/433-2656): Information on the entire Colorado Rockies region.

Other sources of local information include:

Aspen Resort Association, 303 Main St., Aspen, CO 81611 (303/925-1940).

Boulder Chamber of Commerce, 2440 Pearl St., Boulder, CO 80306 (303/442-1044).

Colorado Springs Convention and Visitors Bureau, 104 S. Cascade, Colorado Springs, CO 80902 (719/635-7506).

Denver (see Chapter 29 on Denver).

Durango Chamber Resort Association, 111 S. Camino del Rio, Durango, CO 81302 (303/247-0312).

Estes Park Chamber of Commerce, 500 Big Thompson Ave., Estes Park, CO 80517 (303/586-4431).

Grand Junction Convention and Visitors Bureau, 360 Grand Ave., Grand Junction, CO 81501 (303/242-3214).

Gunnison Chamber of Commerce, 500 E. Tomichi Ave., Gunnison, CO 81230 (303/641-1501).

Leadville Chamber of Commerce, 809 Harrison Ave., Leadville, CO 80461 (303/486-3900).

Rocky Mountain National Park: Contact the Superintendent, Rocky Mountain National Park, Estes Park, CO 80517 (303/586-2371).

Salida Chamber of Commerce, 406 W. Rainbow Blvd., Salida, CO 81201 (719/539-2068).

Steamboat Springs Chamber Resort Association, P.O. Box 774408, Steamboat Springs, CO 80477 (303/879-0740).

Telluride Chamber Resort Association, Telluride, CO 81435 (303/728-3041).

Vail Resort Association, 241 E. Meadow Dr., Vail, CO 81657 (303/476-1000).

GUIDED TOURS: Gray Line Tours (bus): Tours of one day or longer through the Colorado Rockies (see Chapter 29 on Denver). For all other cities, consult the local telephone directory.

SIGHTS, ATTRACTIONS, & ACTIVITIES

ADVENTURES: Adventure Bound (boat), 2392 H Rd., Grand Junction (303/241-5633): One- to five-day rafting trips down the Colorado, Green, and Yampa Rivers (May-Sept.).

Blazing Paddles (boat), Mill and Hyman Sts., Aspen (303/925-5651): Half-day to four-day rafting trips down the Roaring Fork, Arkansas, and Colorado Rivers (May-Sept.).

Brown's Rafting (boat), Brown's Fort, on U.S. 50, 7 mi. (11 km) west of Cañon City (719/275-5161): Half- or full-day rafting trips through the canyon of the Arkansas River (May to mid-Oct.).

Colorado Wagon Train (covered wagons), P.O. Box 73, Crawford, CO 81415 (303/921-3660): Six-night trips are offered weekly in summer. Vacationers sleep in tents, in a wagon, or under the stars. The cost is $530 a person; children under 14, $300. Meals included.

Ghost Town Scenic Jeep Tour (all-terrain vehicles), 11150 U.S. 50, Salida (303/539-2144): Jeep tours through the many ghost towns of the region.

River Rats, Inc. (boat), P.O. Box 3231, Aspen, CO 81612 (303/925-7648): Rafting trips down the Roaring Fork, Arkansas, Colorado, Dolores, and Green Rivers (mid-May to mid-Sept.).

River Runners Ltd. (boat), 11150 U.S. 50, Salida (303/539-2144): Half- to three-day rafting trips down the Arkansas River (mid-May to mid-Sept.).

Rocky Mountain River Expeditions (boat), P.O. Box 427, Westminster, CO 80030 (303/430-8333): Trips of varying lengths on the rivers of Colorado and Utah.

San Juan Scenic Jeep Tours (all-terrain vehicles), 480 Main St., Ouray (303/325-4444): Jeep tours in the mountains, with visits to abandoned mines, ghost towns, etc. Also jeep rentals. (June-Oct.).

Snowmass Whitewater (boat), 50 Village Square, Snowmass Village (303/923-4544): Half- to four-day rafting trips down the Arkansas, Colorado, and Roaring Fork Rivers (May-Sept.).

ATTRACTIONS: ⚙ **Estes Park Aerial Tramway,** 420 Riverside Dr., Estes

Park, 65 mi. (105 km) NW of Denver on U.S. 36 (303/586-3675): Cable car to the summit of Prospect Mountain (8,896 ft, 2,712 m). Spectacular view. Bar with picnic area at the summit. Open daily, mid-May to mid-Sept.

Mount Manitou Incline, 518 Ruxton Ave., Manitou Springs, 68 mi. (108 km) south of Denver on I-25 and U.S. 24 (719/685-9086): Funicular railway to the summit of Mount Manitou (8,856 ft, 2,700 m). Impressive. Open daily, May-Sept.

Pikes Peak Cog Railway, 515 Ruxton Ave., Manitou Springs, 68 mi. (108 km) south of Denver on I-25 and U.S. 24 (719/685-5401): One of the highest cog railways in the world (14,110 ft, 4,301 m). Tremendous view, not to be missed. Open May to Oct. 30; round trip takes three hours. Pikes Peak owes its name to Lt. Zebulon Pike, the first white man to explore the Rockies, in 1806, on orders from Pres. Thomas Jefferson.

Royal Gorge, 11 mi. (19 km) west of Cañon City on U.S. 50: Magnificent landscape of gorges along the Arkansas River. The suspension bridge over the canyon is the world's highest (1,053 ft, 321 m, above the river). The funicular railway that goes to the bottom is the steepest in the world (slope; 45°). A cable car offers a superb view of the gorges. You may combine all three. Not to be missed.

The Silverton, Durango, 38 mi. (60 km) east of Mesa Verde National Park on U.S. 160, and 379 mi. (606 km) SW of Denver on I-25 and U.S. 160 (303/247-2733): In operation since 1882, the Silverton is the last narrow-gauge railroad in regular service in the U.S. Four round trips daily between Durango and Silverton (50 mi., 80 km), mid-May to mid-Oct. Splendid scenery along the Animas Canyon. Recommended for Old West train buffs. Adults pay $38; children, $16. Reservations essential.

CITIES, SIGHTS, AND EXCURSIONS: ※ 🔔🔔 Aspen, 202 mi. (323 km)

SW of Denver on I-70 and Colo. 82: Once a very active mining town, today one of the most elegant resorts in the Rockies (it was Robert Kennedy's favorite). Superb powder skiing. Four mountains all over 13,120 ft (4,000 m) high. Exceptionally comfortable and pleasant. Very popular summer festival of classical music. Well worth the trip.

Beaver Creek, 10 mi. (16 km) west of Vail on I-70 and U.S. 24: Small winter resort opened in 1980. With its immaculate slopes, it could be mistaken for a '50s postcard of a Swiss or Tyrolean village. A real haven of peace and solitude compared to the crowds and commotion of its famous neighbor, Vail. The favorite resort of those in-the-know.

Black Canyon of the Gunnison National Monument, 70 mi. (112 km) west of Gunnison on U.S. 50: Gorges 2,600 ft (800 m) deep cut into the granite. Magnificent landscapes, wild and beautiful. Mule rides available. Access to the gorges is controlled. Open year round. Worth a side trip. For further information: Superintendent, P.O. Box 1648, Montrose, CO 81402 (303/249-7036)

Boulder, 30 mi. (48 km) NW of Denver on U.S. 36: A residential community in the mountains near Denver. Famous for its university and scientific research institutes (meteorology, etc.). Interesting museum of the pioneers (see Chapter 29 on Denver). Worth a visit.

Colorado Springs, 67 mi. (107 km) south of Denver on I-25: There is a very nice touring route about 62 mi. (100 km) long around Colorado Springs, passing by **Cheyenne Mountain Highway** (superb views from the road and a "Shrine of the Sun" dedicated to the famous cowboy humorist Will Rogers); the **Garden of the Gods** (amazing reddish rock formations, especially impressive at sunrise or sunset); **Manitou Springs,** a beautiful mountain hot spring, and nearby, the **Manitou Cliff Dwellings Museum**

on U.S. 24 Bypass (719/685-5242), open daily, May-Oct., devoted to ancient Native American cave dwellings; **Pikes Peak** (14,110 ft, 4,301 m), with its dizzyingly steep toll road; and finally, **Seven Falls,** a lovely rocky canyon whose waterfalls are illuminated by the setting sun. For more details, see Chapter 29 on Denver. A tour not to be missed.

Glenwood Springs, 202 mi. (270 km) SW of Denver on I-70: A vacation resort renowned for its hot thermal pools. Open-air bathing summer and winter. Rafting trips on the Colorado and Roaring Fork rivers. The famous gunman "Doc" Holliday died here in 1887; his tombstone bears the simple epitaph, "He Died in His Bed" (of tuberculosis, actually). A must.

Grand Lake, 115 mi. (184 km) NW of Denver on I-70 and U.S. 40: One of the highest yachting harbors in the world (8,380 ft., 2,554 m). Many other lakes nearby. Splendid alpine scenery.

Grand Mesa National Forest, 52 mi. (83 km) east of Grand Junction on I-70 and Colo. 65: An abundance of lakes and forests—a paradise for campers, and for fishing and hunting enthusiasts, at an average altitude of 9,840 ft (3,000 m).

Idaho Springs, 38 mi. (60 km) west of Denver on I-70: Renowned hot-springs resort in the middle of an area rich in minerals. The history of the gold rush is told at the **Argo Gold Mill,** 23rd Ave. and Riverside Dr. (303/567-2421), open daily. Many excursions in the vicinity, such as Mount Evans, Central City, Georgetown (see Chapter 29 on Denver).

Steamboat Springs, 177 mi. (283 km) NW of Denver on I-70 and U.S. 40: Very popular hot springs and winter-sports resort (nicknamed "Ski Town U.S.A."). **Tread of Pioneers Museum,** 5th and Oak Sts. (303/879-2214), open daily, late May to mid-Sept. Worth a side trip.

Telluride, 123 mi. (196 km) north of Durango on U.S. 550, Colo. 62, and Colo. 145: Surrounded on all sides by the sharp peaks and ridges of the San Juan Mountains, this picturesque little mining town, just over a century old, has scarcely aged since the gold-rush days. Its Main Street, which could come straight out of an old western, is a designated historic monument. Spared so far from the tourist invasion, Telluride offers superb ski slopes in winter and exciting music and film festivals every summer. Not to be missed.

Vail, 105 mi. (168 km) west of Denver on I-70: The classiest winter sports resort in Colorado. Fabulous slopes, and a well-deserved reputation for fine accommodations and dining. Former Pres. Gerald Ford's favorite vacation spot.

PANORAMAS: **Glenwood Canyon,** 15 mi. (24 km) east of Glenwood Springs on I-70: Very beautiful landscape of gorges along the Colorado River. Worth seeing.

Gold Camp Road, 5 mi. (8 km) west of Colorado Springs on Cheyenne Blvd.: A tortuous 35-mi. (56-km) unpaved road following the track of an abandoned gold-rush railroad. Visit the ghost towns of **Goldfield** and **Cripple Creek** en route. Splendid views. Road open late May to Sept. 30. Superb.

Independence Passroad, 24 mi. (38 km) SE of Aspen on Colo. 82: Fabulous landscapes high in the mountains, but a difficult road. Summit (12,095 ft, 3,686 m) closed in winter. Worth a side trip.

Million Dollar Highway, 23 mi. (36 km) along U.S. 550 from Ouray to Silverton: So named because of the large quantity of gold-bearing ore in the land over which it was built, this road offers some of the most beautiful scenery in the whole of Colorado. A must-see.

☼ 🔍🔍 **Mount Evans,** 64 mi. (102 km) west of Denver on I-70, Colo. 103, and Colo. 5: The highest road in the U.S. climbs up this mountain, reaching 14,260 ft (4,346 m). A tough ride for both car and driver, but fabulous views. Road open in summer only. Not to be missed.

☼ 🔍🔍 **Phantom Canyon,** 35 mi. (56 km) NE of Cañon City: One of the most spectacular panoramic routes in the U.S., with 25 mi. (40 km) of unpaved road between Cañon City and Cripple Creek. Wild and imposing. Road open only May to late Oct. Not recommended for mobile homes. Not to be missed.

☼ 🔍🔍🔍 **Pikes Peak,** 7 mi. (11 km) west of Manitou Springs on U.S. 24 and Pikes Peak Road: The most famous mountain road in the U.S., with 18 mi. (28 km) of sharp bends and steep climbs ending at 14,110 ft (4,301 m). In clear weather you can see Kansas, 165 mi. (264 km) east. It was the splendor of this scenery that inspired Katherine Lee Bates to write "America the Beautiful." Toll road open May to mid-Oct. Enough in itself to make your trip to the Rockies worthwhile.

🔍 **Skyline Drive,** 4 mi. (6 km) west of Cañon City on U.S. 50: This 3 mi.-long scenic drive offers a superb view of Cañon City 800 ft (244 m) below, and the surrounding mountains. Closed in bad weather. Worth seeing.

🔍🔍 **Trail Ridge Road,** 70 mi. (112 km) NW of Denver on U.S. 36: Following an old trail used by the Ute and Arapaho Indians, this section of U.S. 34 between Estes Park and Grand Lake peaks at over 12,168 ft (3,710 m)—a 4-mi. (6-km) stretch of the road is above 11,808 ft (3,600 m). Fantastic views of the mountains and the midwestern prairies in the distance. Open early June to mid-Oct. Not to be missed.

SPECIAL EVENTS: For detailed information on the festivals listed below, consult the chambers of commerce and visitors' bureaus listed under "Tourist Information," above.

Aspen
Music Festival and School (June-Aug.): A renowned festival of classical music and a much-sought-after music school, one of the best in the U.S.

Boulder
Colorado Shakespeare Festival (July-Aug.): Outdoor performances. Very popular locally.

Durango
Navajo Trail Fiesta (first weekend in Aug.): Rodeo, parades, horse races, square dances. Lively and colorful.

Leadville
Boom Days (last weekend in Aug.): Reconstructs the saga of the gold rush. Local color guaranteed.

Manitou Springs
Pikes Peak Marathon (Aug.): A 28-mi. (45-km) foot race up Pikes Peak. One of the most demanding sports events in the world.

Salida
Arkansas River Boat Race (third weekend in June): International kayak race, 26 mi. (42 km) long, on the tumultuous waters of the Arkansas River. Spectacular.

Telluride

Summer Festival: A series of festivals beginning with jazz (mid-July), followed by dance (late July), chamber music (late July to mid-Aug.), and ending with a very popular film festival (early Sept.).

WINTER SPORTS RESORTS: With dozens of winter sports resorts, the Colorado Rockies are a skier's paradise. The most popular resorts are:

Aspen and Aspen Highlands, 42 mi. (67 km) south of Glenwood Springs on Colo. 82 (303/925-1220): 19 lifts. Open Nov. to mid-Apr.

Beaver Creek, 10 mi. (16 km) west of Vail on I-70 and U.S. 24 (303/949-5750): 8 lifts. Open mid-Nov. to mid-Apr.

Breckenridge, 92 mi. (147 km) west of Denver on I-70 and Colo. 9 (303/453-2368): 14 lifts. Open mid-Nov. to mid-Apr.

Copper Mountain, 86 mi. (137 km) west of Denver on I-70 (303/968-2882): 16 lifts. Open Nov.-Apr.

Keystone, 78 mi. (124 km) west of Denver on I-70 (303/534-7712): 18 lifts. Open mid-Oct. to May.

Snowmass, 30 mi. (48 km) south of Glenwood Springs on Colo. 82 (303/925-1221): 14 lifts. Open Nov.-Apr.

Steamboat Springs, 177 mi. (283 km) NW of Denver on I-70, Colo. 90, and U.S. 40 (303/879-6111): 19 lifts. Open Nov. to mid-Apr.

Vail, 105 mi. (168 km) from Denver on I-70 (303/476-5601): 16 lifts. Open Nov. to mid-Apr.

Winter Park, 71 mi. (113 km) NW of Denver on I-70 and U.S. 40 (303/726-5514): 17 lifts. Open mid-Nov. to Apr.

GHOST TOWNS: The gold rush of 1859–1860 and the rich deposits of other minerals in the Rockies (silver, uranium, coal, tin, molybdenum) gave birth to dozens of mining camps, most of which have since become ghost towns. Some, such as St. Elmo, are completely abandoned today, while others, such as Leadville, still survive, though the luster of yesteryear has long since faded.

Ashcroft, 15 mi. (24 km) south of Aspen on Ashcroft Rd.: A well-preserved ghost town. Many buildings date from the 1880s. Worth a side trip.

Central City, 44 mi. (70 km) west of Denver on I-70, Colo. 119, and Colo. 279: Site of the first discovery of gold in 1859. Spectacular mountainside location. Many museums, hotels, and gold mines. A well-known opera house. Should definitely be seen. (For more details, see "Nearby Excursions" in Chapter 29 on Denver.)

Creede, 22 mi. (35 km) NW of South Fork on Colo. 149: Frequented in its heyday by such legendary figures as Butch Cassidy and Calamity Jane, this mining town hemmed in on all sides by the mountains is today half-deserted. Worth a side trip.

Cripple Creek, 40 mi. (64 km) west of Colorado Springs on Gold Camp Rd.: Nicknamed "the $300-million cow pasture." Its mines have yielded more than $500 million worth of gold and silver. In 1900 it boasted as many as 500 mines and a population of 25,000 (barely 600 today). Very beautiful 1890s bordello, the **Old Homestead,** 353 E. Myers Ave.; open daily, late May to Oct. Museum and visit to an underground gold mine at the **Mollie Kathleen Gold Mine** on Colo. 67, open daily late May to Sept. In passing, look over the forgotten ghost towns of **Goldfield** and **Victor.** The road can be treacherous in bad weather. Well worth a visit.

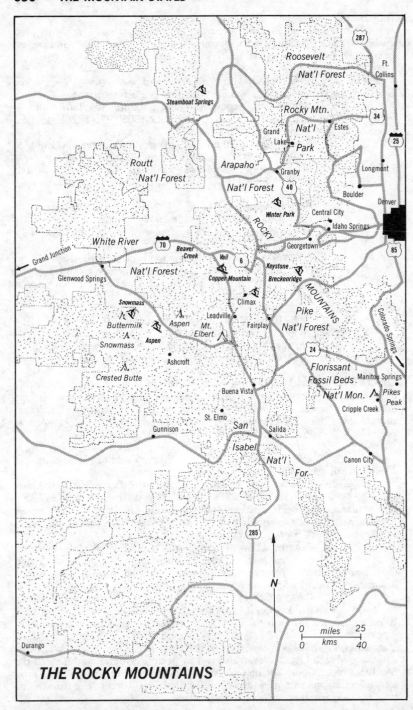

THE ROCKY MOUNTAINS

   Fairplay, 85 mi. (136 km) SW of Denver on U.S. 285: More than 30 carefully restored buildings from the gold-rush era. The **South Park City Museum,** 4th and Front Sts., open daily mid-May to mid-Oct., is worth looking over.

   Georgetown, 57 mi. (91 km) west of Denver on I-70: One of the most famous mining towns in Colorado. Many museums and buildings classified as historic monuments, including the legendary **Hotel de Paris,** 409 Sixth Ave., open daily, built in 1875. Equally interesting is the **Georgetown Loop Railroad** at exit 226 from I-70 (303/569-2403); a spectacular train ride operates daily, early June to early Oct. Not to be missed.

   Leadville, 103 mi. (164 km) SW of Denver on I-70 and Colo. 91: Boasting up to 40,000 inhabitants in its glory days, this picturesque town perched at 10,150 ft (3,100 m)—which makes it the highest town in the U.S.—today has a mere 3,800 (most of them employees of the Climax mine, from which 90% of the world's production of molybdenum is extracted). It was in one of Leadville's saloons in the 1880s that the famous sign "Don't shoot the pianist. He's doing his best." first appeared. Many museums and original buildings, among them the **Tabor Opera House,** at 308 Harrison Ave. (719/486-1147), open Sun.-Fri., end May-Oct., and the **Healey House,** built in 1878, 912 Harrison Ave., open daily, June-Aug. A must-see. **Mount Elbert,** Colorado's highest summit, 14,333 ft. (4,383 m) is 12 miles south via US 24.

   St. Elmo, 58 mi. (92 km) south of Leadville on U.S. 24 and Colo. 162: A spectacular, authentic ghost town from the gold-rush era, today completely abandoned. Worth a side trip. Caution: The last part of the road to the town is unpaved and passable only in dry weather.

NATIONAL PARKS NEARBY: **Colorado National Monument,** 4 mi. (6 km) west of Grand Junction on Colo. 340 (303/858-3617): Enormous red sandstone monoliths and deep gorges make for a sort of Monument Valley in miniature. Rim Rock Drive, a 22-mi. (35-km) scenic drive, crosses the park. Open daily year round. Not to be missed.

   Florissant Fossil Beds National Monument, 34 mi. (54 km) west of Colorado Springs on U.S. 24 (719/748-3253): About 35 million years ago volcanic lava flows fossilized all the life forms in this prehistoric lake. Exceptionally fine examples of fossilized animals and plants are displayed in the Visitor Center. Open daily year round. Worth a visit.

   Great Sand Dunes National Monument, 234 mi. (374 km) south of Denver on I-25, U.S. 160, and Colo. 150 (719/378-2312): Stunning sand dunes, some 700 ft (210 m) or more high, in a mountain setting. Spectacular at sunrise and sunset. Park open daily year round; worth a visit.

   Mesa Verde National Park, 430 mi. (688 km) SW of Denver on I-25 and U.S. 160: The most impressive Native American historic monument in the U.S. (see Chapter 39 on Santa Fe). Worth the trip all by itself. En route, visit Colorado Springs, the Great Sand Dunes National Monument, and The Silverton (see above).

   Rocky Mountain National Park, 70 mi. (112 km) NW of Denver on U.S. 36 and U.S. 34 (303/586-2371): The most mountainous of all American wilderness parks, with 65 peaks over 9,600 ft (3,000 m) high, including the Longs Peak (14,255 ft, 4,345 m). Rushing rivers, glaciers, snows that never melt, lakes teeming with fish, dense forests, and over 300 mi. (480 km) of hiking trails. Untouched wilderness. A paradise for climbers, campers, fishing enthusiasts, the park is visited by 2.5 million nature lovers annually. The **Trail Ridge Rd.,** which follows the route of an ancient Native

American trail, cuts right through the park and offers splendid views, as well as spectacular glimpses of the mountaintops (closed mid-Oct. to mid-June). Many hotels and motels are open year round in Estes Park, Grand Lake, and Granby (see "Accommodations," below). **Moraine Park Visitor Center** and museum are located 1 mi. (1.6 km) from the east entrance to the park on U.S. 36 (open daily, June-Sept.). Not to be missed.

ACCOMMODATIONS
See the listing of toll-free numbers in the Appendix.

Room Rates in the Colorado Rockies	
B (Budget)	up to $30
I (Inexpensive)	$30–$60
M (Moderate)	$60–$90
E (Expensive)	$90–$140
VE (Very Expensive)	$140 and up

Personal Favorites (by city)

ASPEN. ☼ � ♟ ♟ **Hotel Jerome**, 330 E. Main St., Aspen, CO 81611 (303/920-1000; toll-free 800/331-7213). 94 rms, A/C, cable color TV. AE, CB, DC, MC, V. Free indoor parking, pool, rest., bar, rm svce, concierge. *Note:* One of the oldest hotels in the Rockies (1889), and a designated historic monument. Exquisitely restored to its original elegance in 1985. Spacious rms, tastefully decorated. Considerate and polished svce. A great deal of distinction and charm, and you pay accordingly. Resv. well in advance essential. **VE, but lower rates out of season**

♟ ♟ **Aspen Meadows**, 845 Meadows Rd., Aspen, CO 81611 (303/925-3426). 92 rms, no A/C; cable color TV. AE, CB, DC, MC, V. Free parking, pool, health club, rest., bar, valet svce, free crib. *Note:* Charming rustic riverside motel. Comfortable rms w. private patios or balconies (some w. kitchenettes). Wide range of amenities. Surroundings and gardens very pleasant. Friendly svce. Interesting special wknd and ski packages. A fine place to stay. Hosts the Aspen Music Festival every summer. **E, but lower rates out of season**

♟ ♟ **Grand Aspen**, 515 S. Galena St., Aspen, CO 81611 (303/925-1150; toll free 800/242-7736). 175 rms, no A/C; color TV. AE, CB, DC, MC, V. Free parking, rest., bar, rm svce. *Note:* The biggest hotel in this resort town, right in the heart of Aspen. Pretty view of the mountains. Comfortable and well run. Caters to families and groups. Favored by those in-the-know. Recently renovated. **E–VE, but lower rates out of season**

♟ **Limelite Lodge**, 228 E. Cooper Ave., Aspen, CO 81611 (303/925-3025). 62 rms, no A/C; color TV, in-rm movies. AE, CB, DC, MC, V. Free parking, two pools, sauna, nearby coffeeshop, free breakfast. *Note:* Charming little mountainside hotel nr. Wagner Park. Spacious, comfortable rms w. refrigerators. Family atmosphere. Enticing ski packages. **M–E, but lower rates out of season**

BASALT. ♟ **Best Western Aspenalt,** Colo. 82, Basalt, CO 81621 (303/927-3191; toll free, see Best Western). 36 rms, no A/C; color TV, in-rm movies. AE, CB,

DC, MC, V. Free parking, adjoining coffeeshop-bar, free breakfast. *Note:* Stylish little motel in a pleasant setting on the banks of the Frying Pan River. Friendly reception. Good value. **I–M, but lower rates out of season**

BEAVER CREEK. ♟♟♟ **Charter at Beaver Creek,** 120 Offerson Rd., Avon, CO 81620 (303/949-6660). 59 rms in the hotel, 156 condos, A/C, color TV. AE, CB, DC, MC, V. Free parking, two pools, health club, tennis court and golf course nearby, skiing, snowmobiles, rest., bar, rm svce, concierge. *Note:* Luxurious vacation complex of very modern design, in a splendid setting. Spacious, comfortable rms w. refrigerators. Fully equipped condos w. kitchenettes and fireplaces. Excellent svce. Affluent tourist clientele. Free airport shuttle. **E–VE, but lower rates out of season**

BOULDER. ※ ♟♟♟ **Boulderado Hotel,** 2115 13th St., Boulder, CO 80302 (303/442-4344; toll free 800/433-4344). 103 rms, A/C, color TV, in-rm movies. AE, CB, DC, MC, V. Free valet parking, three rests. (incl. Winston's Seafood Grille), three bars, rm svce, nightclub, free crib. *Note:* Beautiful turn-of-the-century Victorian palace. Sumptuous rococo décor w. an abundance of marble and paneling. Comfortable rms w. balconies, some w. refrigerators. Polished svce. A wonderful place to stay, in a central dwntwn location. Adequate rest. Good value. **M–E**

♟ **Best Western Golden Buff,** 1725 28th St., Boulder, CO 80302 (303/442-7450; toll free, see Best Western). 112 rms, A/C, color TV, in-rms movies. AE, CB, DC, MC, V. Free parking, pool, sauna, health club, putting green, coffeeshop, crib $5. *Note:* Comfortable modern motel w. views of the mountains. Spacious rms w. refrigerators, some w. kitchenettes. Good svce. **I–M**

BRECKENRIDGE. ♟♟ **Hilton,** 550 Village Rd., Breckenridge, CO 80424 (303/453-4500; toll free, see Hilton). 208 rms, no A/C; color TV, in-rm movies. AE, CB, DC, MC, V. Free indoor parking, pool, health club, sauna, rest., coffeeshop, bar, nightclub (in winter only). *Note:* Charming mountain hotel, modern and comfortable. Ski slopes a stone's throw away. Huge inviting rms w. private balconies or patios and refrigerators. Good svce. Caters to groups. Interesting vacation packages. Very good value out of season. **M–E, but lower rates out of season**

CAÑON CITY. ♟ **Quality Inn,** 3075 U.S. 50E, Cañon City, CO 81212 (719/275-8676; toll free, see Quality Inns). 104 rms, A/C, cable color TV. AE, CB, DC, MC, V. Free parking, pool, sauna, putting green, rest., bar, rm svce, disco. *Note:* Functional modern motel surrounded by gardens. Spacious comfortable rms. Hot springs. Free airport shuttle. Good value. **I–M, but lower rates out of season**

COLORADO SPRINGS. ※ ♟♟♟ **Broadmoor,** Lake Circle and Lake Ave., Colorado Springs, CO 80906 (719/634-7711). 560 rms, A/C, color TV. AE, DC, MC, V. Garage $6, three pools, three golf courses, 16 tennis courts, health club, sauna, putting green, skiing, trapshooting, skating, boats, nine rests. and bars, rm svce, disco, movie theater, free crib. *Note:* Superb 1920s-style grand hotel built like a castle amid 3,000 acres (1,210 ha.) of park and private gardens. Luxurious, urbane interior; elegant, comfortable rms w. balconies (some w. kitchenettes or refrigerators). Exemplary svce. Ideal for devotees of every sport imaginable. One of the best hotels in the U.S. Caters to conventions and wealthy holiday-makers. **VE, but lower rates out of season**

♟♟ **Raintree Inn,** 314 W. Bijou St., Colorado Springs, CO 80905 (719/471-8680). 206 rms, A/C, color TV, in-rm movies.

AE, CB, DC, MC, V. Free parking, pool, rest, bar, rm svce, nightclub, free crib. *Note:* Pleasant motel surrounded by lovely gardens a stone's throw from dwntwn. Comfortable rms w. private balconies or patios. Efficient svce. Good value. **I–M, but lower rates out of season**

🅿️ 🛏️ **Motel 6,** 3228 N. Chestnut St., Colorado Springs, CO 80907 (719/520-5400). 84 rms, A/C, color TV, in-rm movies. DC, MC, V. Free parking, pool. *Note:* Modest but comfortable little motel 5 min. from dwntwn. Rms w. fine mountain views. One of the best values in the area. **B**

DILLON. 🛏️🛏️ **Best Western Lake Dillon Lodge,** intersection of U.S. 6 and I-70, Frisco, CO 80443 (303/668-5094; toll free, see Best Western). 126 rms, A/C, color TV, in-rm movies. AE, CB, DC, MC, V. Free parking, pool, tennis, boating, fishing, rest., bar, rm svce, boutiques, free crib. *Note:* A motel entirely sheathed in glass w. a view over the lake and the surrounding mountains. Ultramodern décor and amenities. Very good svce. Excellent value. **I–M, but lower rates out of season**

DURANGO. ☀️🛏️🛏️🛏️ **Tamarron Resort,** 18 mi. (28 km) north on U.S. 550, Durango, CO 81302 (303/247-8801; toll free 800/525-5420). 350 rms and condos, A/C, color TV. AE, CB, DC, MC, V. Free parking, pool, health club, sauna, three tennis courts, golf, putting green, skiing, skating rink, snowmobiles, horseback riding, two rests., bars, rm svce, disco, hrdrsr. *Note:* One of the most beautiful resort hotels in the U.S., in the heart of the San Juan National Forest. Spacious, extremely comfortable rms w. balconies and refrigerators. Condos w. fully equipped kitchenettes (some with two bedrooms). Very efficient, friendly svce. Superb location. Hotel organizes rafting trips on the river and Jeep tours. Hunting and fishing guides available. Paradise for lovers of sports and the outdoors. A great place to stay. **E–VE, but lower rates out of season**

☀️🛏️🛏️ **General Palmer House,** 567 Main Ave., Durango, CO 81301 (303/247-4747; toll free 800/523-3358). 39 rms, A/C, cable color TV. AE, CB, DC, MC, V. Nearby bar and rest., free crib. *Note:* Elegant Victorian building dating from the 1890s, marvelously restored. Comfortable rms furnished w. antiques. Friendly svce and reception. Minutes away from the Silverton train stations. **I–M, but lower rates out of season**

☀️🛏️ **Strater,** 699 Main Ave., Durango, CO 81301 (303/247-4431). 94 rms, A/C, cable color TV. AE, CB, DC, MC, V. Free parking, rest. (Henry's), bar, saloon, rm svce, boutiques. *Note:* Small rococo-style hotel built in the 1900s. Enormous rms, comfortable though not elegant. Woeful svce and reception, which denies the Strater its second star. The Old West–style saloon deserves a visit all by itself, however. Entertaining parody-melodramas performed in summer in the adjoining theater (Mon.-Sat., June-Sept.). A fine spot for lovers of the Old West. **I–M, but lower rates out of season**

ESTES PARK. ☀️🛏️🛏️🛏️ **Stanley Hotel,** 333 Wonderview Ave., Estes Park, CO 80517 (303/586-3371; toll free 800/762-5437). 100 rms, no A/C, cable color TV. AE, MC, V. Free parking, pool, tennis, rest., bar, rm svce, disco, crib $10. *Note:* Venerable, elegantly designed turn-of-the-century hotel situated at the east entrance to Rocky Mountain National Park. Very spacious rms, pleasantly decorated. Spectacular setting at the foot of the mountains. Friendly svce. Many cultural activities (concerts, theater, exhibitions, etc.). A fine place to stay. **M–E, but lower rates out of season**

☀️🛏️🛏️ **Longs Peak Inn and Guest Ranch,** Longs Peak Rte. 3A, Estes Park, CO 80517 (303/586-2110). 32 cottages and chalets, no A/C, TV in lounge. MC, V. Free parking, pool, horseback riding, fishing, rest., bar, movie theater. *Note:* Friendly vacation ranch w. lovely view of the mountains. Relaxed atmosphere. Ideal for lovers of the wide-open spaces. Adequate rest. Near Rocky Mountain National Park. Open June-Sept. **E–VE (MAP)**

Alpine Trail Ridge Inn (formerly the Friendship Inn), 927 Moraine Ave., Estes Park, CO 80517 (303/586-4585). 48 rms, no A/C,cable color TV. AE, CB, DC, MC, V. Free parking, pool, rest., bar, rm svce, crib $3. *Note:* Friendly small motel w. a superb view of the mountains. Comfortable rms, some w. balconies and refrigerators. Friendly, cheerful reception. Good value. Open early May to mid-Oct. **I–M, but lower rates out of season**

GLENWOOD SPRINGS. 🍴🍴 **Hot Springs Lodge,** 401 N. River Rd., Glenwood Springs, CO 81601 (303/945-6571). 107 rms, A/C, cable color TV. AE, CB, DC, MC, V. Free parking, pool, health club, miniature golf, rest., bar. *Note:* Congenial brand-new hotel for those who come to take the waters. Comfortable rms (some w. refrigerators). Excellent location on the banks of the Colorado River and just moments from the hot springs. Has one of the largest naturally heated pools in the world. Good value. **I–M**

GRANBY. ☼ 🍴🍴🍴 **C Lazy U Ranch,** Colo. 125, Granby, CO 80446 (303/887-3344). 6 rms in the inn, 35 one- to five-rm bungalows, no A/C. No credit cards. Free parking, pool, two tennis courts, health club, horseback riding, skiing, skating rink, fishing, hunting, rest., bar, open-air barbecue-buffets, disco. *Note:* Authentic western ranch some 8,200 ft (2,500 m) up on the shores of a mountain lake. Heaven for riding enthusiasts in summer and cross-country skiers in winter. The bungalow rms are prettily decorated, pleasant, and comfortable. Robust and abundant food. Friendly reception and atmosphere. The best vacation spot in the Colorado Rockies. Rodeos in summer. Closed late Sept. to early Dec. and in May. $750 and up per week in summer (AP); $140 and up per day in winter (AP).

GRAND JUNCTION. 🍴🍴 **Hilton Inn,** 743 Horizon Dr., Grand Junction, CO 81506 (303/241-8888; toll free, see Hilton). 269 rms, A/C, color TV. AE, CB, DC, MC, V. Free parking, pool, health club, three tennis courts, golf course nearby, rest. (Jockey Club), bar, rm svce, disco, free crib. *Note:* Vast modern motel of rather gloomy design; spacious, comfortable rms. Efficient svce and reception. Adequate rest. Free airport shuttle. VIP floor. A highly recommended stopover. **M–E, but lower rates out of season**

Motel 6, 776 Horizon Dr., Grand Junction, CO 81501 (303/243-2628). 100 rms, A/C, color TV, in-rm movies. DC, MC, V. Free parking, pool. *Note:* The best deal in town if you're passing through by car. Serviceable amenities at unbeatable prices. Airport nearby. **B**

GRAND LAKE. 🍴 **Western Riviera,** 419 Garmet St., Grand Lake, CO 80447 (303/627-3580). 17 rms, no A/C, cable color TV. MC, V. Free parking, snowmobiles, coffeeshop next door, free crib. *Note:* Charming little motel by the lake. Warm, comfortable rms. Beautiful natural surroundings. Closed Oct.-Nov. and in Apr. **I, but lower rates out of season**

GUNNISON. 🍴 **Friendship Inn Colorado West,** 400 E. Tomichi Ave., Gunnison, CO 81230 (303/641-1288; toll free, see Friendship Inns). 50 rms, A/C, color TV, in-rm movies. AE, CB, DC, MC, V. Free parking, coffeeshop next door, crib $2. *Note:* Pleasant, well-run little motel. Spacious rms. Friendly reception. Free airport shuttle. Good value. **I, but lower rates out of season**

KEYSTONE. 🛎🛎 **Keystone Resort,** U.S. 6, Keystone, CO 80435 (303/468-2316; toll free 800/222-0188). 888 rms and condo units, no A/C, color TV, in-rm movies. AE, CB, DC, MC, V. Free parking, ten pools, golf, 14 tennis courts, sauna, skiing, boats, four rests., coffeeshop, bars, rm svce, disco, boutiques, crib $3. *Note:* Huge ultramodern vacation complex on the banks of Lake Keystone in the heart of the Arapaho National Forest. Comfortable rms w. private balconies or patios. Studio and one- to four-bedroom condos. Very good sports facilities. Splendid panoramic view. Caters to conventions and groups. Rather average svce. Ordinary rests. (remember that the complex belongs to an animal-feed industry giant). Attractive family and vacation packages. **E–VE, but lower rates out of season**

LEADVILLE. 🛎 **Best Western Silver King Motor Inn,** 2020 N. Poplar St., Leadville, CO 80461 (303/486-2610; toll free, see Best Western). 56 rms, no A/C, cable color TV. AE, CB, DC, MC, V. Free parking, skiing, sauna, rest., bar, disco, crib $5. *Note:* Modern motel-chalet in the heart of this legendary gold-rush town. Spacious rms w. balconies. Decent rest. Friendly reception. Attractive vacation pkgs. (Take note of Leadville's high altitude—10,150 ft, 3,100 m—and its possible effects on your physical condition.) **I–M, but lower rates out of season**

SNOWMASS VILLAGE. 🛎🛎🛎 **Snowmass Club,** 239 Snowmass Club Circle, Snowmass Village, CO 81615 (303/932-5600; toll free 800/525-0710). 76 rms in the hotel, 62 separate villas. A/C, color TV, in-rm movies. AE, CB, DC, MC, V. Free parking, two pools, health club, sauna, 13 tennis courts, golf, squash, putting green, skiing, snowmobiles, rest., bar, rm svce, nightclub, concierge. *Note:* Paradise for sporting enthusiasts. Refined, elegant setting of modern design. Large rms, nicely decorated, w. private balconies or patios and refrigerators. Luxurious two- and three-bedroom villas. Worthwhile rest. Excellent svce. Free airport connection with Aspen. Caters to wealthy holiday makers. Closed mid-April to May and mid-Oct. to Nov. **E–VE, but lower rates out of season**

STEAMBOAT SPRINGS. 🛎🛎🛎 **Sheraton Steamboat Resort,** 2200 Village Inn Court, Steamboat Springs, CO 80477 (303/879-2220; toll free, see Sheraton). 287 rms, A/C, color TV, in-rm movies. AE, CB, DC, MC, V. Free parking, pool, four tennis courts, golf course, sauna, skiing, snowmobiles, rest., coffeeshop, bars, rm svce, disco, boutiques. *Note:* A vacation complex at the foot of Mount Werner, comprising a modern hotel and eight stories of comfortable studio condos w. kitchenettes. Ideal for families. Good vacation packages; good value overall. Closed mid-Apr. to May and mid-Oct. to mid-Nov. **M–E, but lower rates out of season**

🛎 **Inn at Steamboat** (formerly the Quality Inn Subalpine), 3070 Columbine Dr., Steamboat Springs, CO 80477 (303/879-2600; toll free 800/432-2628). 31 rms, no A/C, color TV, in-rm movies. AE, CB, DC, MC, V. Free parking, pool, sauna, rest., bar, free crib. *Note:* Quiet, friendly motel. Spacious rms w. balconies. Appealing winter sports packages. Good value. **M, but lower rates out of season**

TELLURIDE. ☀🛎🛎 **Skyline Guest Ranch,** 8 mi. (12 km) south on Colo. 145, Telluride, CO 81435 (303/728-3757). 16 rms and suites, no A/C, no TV. MC, V. Free parking, hot tub, sauna, skiing, horseback riding, fishing, rest. *Note:* Authentic Old West ranch hidden amid the mountains. Rustic but comfortable. Splendid view. The ranch organizes rafting trips, Jeep tours, climbing expeditions to the nearby peaks, fishing trips. Ideal for lovers of wilderness and the outdoor life. Resv. essential, well ahead. $600 and up per week in summer (AP); E in winter (EP)

VAIL. ☼ ♨ ♨ ♨ **Marriott's Mark Resort,** 715 W. Lionshead Circle, Vail, CO 81657 (303/476-4444; toll free, see Marriott). 350 rms, some w. A/C, color TV, in-rm movies. AE, CB, DC, MC, V. Free indoor parking, two pools, saunas, skiing, health club, four tennis courts, two rests. (including Windows), coffeeshop, two bars, rm svce, disco, hrdrsr, concierge, free crib. *Note:* Old luxury hotel, entirely renovated. Elegant, comfortable rms w. balconies, some w. kitchenettes. Thoughtful svce. Decent rest. The best hotel in the resort, two steps from the slopes. Caters to groups and conventions. Free airport shuttle. **VE, but lower rates out of season**

♨ ♨ ♨ **Westin Hotel,** 1300 Westhaven Dr., Vail, CO 81657 (303/476-7111; toll free, see Westin). 180 rms, no A/C, color TV, in-rm movies. AE, CB, DC, MC, V. Valet parking $5, pool, four tennis courts, health club, sauna, rest. (Alfredo's), coffeeshop, bars, rm svce, disco, drugstore, boutiques, concierge, free crib. *Note:* Very beautiful, brand-new alpine-style hotel. Elegant atmosphere. Spacious, comfortable rms w. mini-bars and private patios. Excellent svce. Decent rest. Nestled on the banks of Gore Creek. One of the best hotels in the Rockies. Free airport shuttle. **VE, but lower rates out of season**

☼ ♨ ♨ **The Lodge at Vail,** 174 E. Gore Creek Dr., Vail, CO 81657 (303/476-5011; toll free 800/237-1236). 350 rms, no A/C, color TV, in-rm movies. AE, CB, DC, MC, V. Free parking, pool, sauna, two rests. (including the Wildflower Inn), bar, rm svce. *Note:* Huge mountain hotel, quaint and charming. Many rms w. balconies and kitchenettes. Good communal facilities. Outstanding rest. Good svce. Caters to groups. **E–VE, but lower rates out of season**

♨ **Comfort Inn Vail,** 0161 W. Beaver Creek Blvd., Avon, CO 81620 (303/949-5511; toll free 800/228-5150). 147 rms, A/C, cable color TV. AE, CB, DC, MC, V. Free parking, pool, coffeeshop nearby, free breakfast. *Note:* Modern motel in the classic style. Pleasant, comfortable rms, some w. refrigerators. Friendly svce. 15 min. from dwntwn. Excellent value. **I, but lower rates out of season**

WINTER PARK. ♨ ♨ **Meadow Ridge Resort,** U.S. 40, Winter Park, CO 80482 (303/726-9401). 100 studios w. kitchenettes, no A/C, color TV. AE, MC, V. Free parking, pool, four tennis courts, health club, bar, free crib. *Note:* Comfortable mountaintop hotel. Spacious studios w. private balconies. Comprehensive facilities. Pleasant atmosphere. Ideal for families who enjoy winter sports. **M–E, but lower rates out of season**

YMCAs / Youth Hostels

COLORADO SPRINGS. Garden of the Gods, 3704 W. Colorado Ave., Colorado Springs, CO 80904 (719/475-9450). 48 beds. Youth hostel. Open Apr.-Oct.

ESTES PARK. H-Bar-G Ranch, 3500 H-Bar-G Rd., Estes Park, CO 80517 (303/586-3688). 130 beds. Youth hostel. Open late May to early Sept.

GRAND LAKE. Shadowcliff Youth Hostel, Tunnel Rd., Grand Lake, CO 80447 (303/627-9966). 32 beds. Youth hostel. Open June-Sept.

TELLURIDE. Oak Street Inn, 134 N. Oak St., Telluride, CO 81435 (303/728-3383). 83 beds. Youth hostel. Open year round.

WINTER PARK. Winter Park Hostel, U.S. 40 at Vasquez Rd., Winter Park, CO 80482 (303/726-5356). 20 beds. Youth hostel. Open year round.

RESTAURANTS

Colorado Rockies Restaurant Prices	
(per person, excluding drinks and service charges)	
B (Budget)	up to $15
I (Inexpensive)	$15–$25
M (Moderate)	$25–$40
E (Expensive)	$40–$60
VE (Very Expensive)	$60 and up

Personal Favorites (by city)

ASPEN. ♈♈♈ **Gordon's,** 205 Mill St. (303/925-7474). A/C. Dinner nightly; closed mid-Apr. to June and mid-Sept. to mid-Nov. AE, CB, DC, MC, V. *Specialties:* chiles rellenos w. goat cheese, potato pancakes w. golden caviar, free-range chicken w. sun-dried tomatoes and herbs, shrimp à la jamaïcaine w. black-bean sauce, grilled fresh tuna w. cheddar, tomatoes, and basil. Excellent desserts. *Note:* By far the best in town. Seductive, imaginative cuisine from the very talented Rebecca and Gordon Naccarato, formerly of Michael's in Santa Monica— quite a reference. Modern art adorns the walls. Friendly, obliging svce. Resv. highly recommended. An excellent place to dine. *American.* **I–M**

☀♈♈ **Sea Grill at the Copper Kettle,** 535 E. Dean Ave. (303/925-3151). Dinner only, Mon.-Sat.; closed Sun., Mon. (in summer), and April-May. AE, CB, DC, MC, V. *Specialties:* bouillabaisse, rack of lamb, fish of the day. *Note:* Serious, meticulous cuisine. Managed for over two decades by the same family, the rest. is housed in buildings that once belonged to a silver mine. Novel collection of antique copper. Friendly svce. *Continental.* **I–M**

☀♈♈ **Ute City Banque,** 501 E. Hyman St. (303/925-4373). A/C. Lunch/dinner daily; closed Apr. to mid-May. MC, V. *Specialties:* duck à l'orange, rack of lamb provençal, crab Diablo. *Note:* The bank décor is authentic and dates from 1885. Impeccable cooking, but lacks great imagination. Nice atmosphere. Good svce. Resv. recommended at dinner. *Continental.* **I–M**

♈ **La Cocina,** 308 E. Hopkins (303/925-9714). No A/C. Dinner nightly; closed Nov.-May. *Specialties:* Tacos, enchiladas, steak. *Note:* Small Mexican-style rest., modest and unpretentious. Popular locally. *Mexican-American.* **B**

BEAVER CREEK. ☀♈♈♈ **Mirabelle,** 55 Village Rd. (303/949-7728). A/C. Dinner Tues.-Sun.; closed Mon., May, and the first three weeks in Nov. AE, MC, V. Jkt. *Specialties:* Pâté de campagne, mousseline of fish in beurre blanc, poached salmon w. mussels and scallops, lamb cutlet w. hollandaise sauce, lobster w. tarragon. Exceptional desserts. Fine wine list. *Note:* Light, inventive cooking by the very talented chef Pierre Luc. Charming, old-fashioned, rustic décor (the building dates from 1898, which makes it one of the oldest ranches in the Vail area). Discreet, attentive svce. An outstanding rest. Many VIPs and wealthy people on vacation among the customers. Resv. highly recommended. *French.* **M**

BOULDER. ♙♙♙ **Flagstaff House,** Flagstaff Rd. (303/442-4640). A/C. Valet parking. Dinner only, nightly; closed Jan. 1 and Dec. 24–25. AE, DC, MC, V. Jkt. *Specialties:* escargots, oysters Rockefeller, crab Lausanne, elk steak, Colorado beef, roast quail. Very good wine list. *Note:* An elegant rest. w. a spectacular view of the mountains through huge bay windows. Romantic atmosphere. Terrace open in summer. Attentive svce. Some of the best fare in the region. Resv. recommended. *Continental.* **M**

♙♙ **John's,** 2338 Pearl St. (303/444-5232). A/C. Dinner only, nightly; closed holidays. AE, CB, DC, MC, V. Jkt. *Specialties:* scallops sautéed w. capers and lemon, pepper steak, salmon à la bretonne, veal chop w. green peppercorns. Rather scanty wine list. *Note:* Pleasant little Provençal-style inn w. a fireplace and old-fashioned décor. Very successful French-style cooking. Friendly, efficient svce. Resv. recommended. *French-continental.* **I–M**

BRECKENRIDGE. ♙ **Briar Rose,** 109 E. Lincoln St. (303/453-9948). No A/C. Dinner only, nightly. AE, DC, MC, V. *Specialties:* game, roast beef, quail, Alaska king crab. *Note:* Authentic 19th-century guesthouse. Charming old-fashioned décor. The game dishes (in season) are all to be recommended. Excellent svce. *Continental-American.* **I–M**

CENTRAL CITY. ❄ ♙♙ **Black Forest Inn,** Colo. 279 (303/279-2333). A/C. Lunch/dinner daily. No CC. *Specialties:* game (in season), roast pheasant, wild duck, elk steak. *Note:* One of the most famous rests. in the Rockies. The accent is definitely on wild game. Many German dishes too. Highly colorful German music and décor. *German-American.* **I**

COLORADO SPRINGS. ♙♙ **Edelweiss,** 34 E. Ramona Ave. (719/633-2220). A/C. Lunch Mon.-Fri., dinner nightly; closed Dec. 24. AE, CB, DC, MC, V. *Specialties:* wienerschnitzel, sauerbraten, veal Oscar. *Note:* Traditional Bavarian-chalet décor and praiseworthy German food. Dinner outdoors in summer. Efficient svce. Popular locally. Resv. recommended. *German-continental.* **I**

♙♙ **La Petite Maison,** 1015 W. Colorado Ave. (719/632-4887). A/C. Lunch Tues.-Fri., dinner Tues.-Sat.; closed Sun., Mon., July 4, and Dec. 25. AE, DC, MC, V. *Specialties:* classical French cuisine; menu changed regularly. *Note:* A charming little rest. housed in a nicely renovated former private residence. Honest, tasty food. Friendly reception and svce. Very good value. Resv. recommended. 5 min. from dwntwn. *French.* **B–I**

CRIPPLE CREEK. ❄ ♙ **Imperial Dining Room,** 123 N. 3rd St. (303/689-2922). No A/C. Breakfast/lunch/dinner daily; closed mid-Oct. to mid-May. AE, DC, MC, V. *Specialties:* steak, baron of beef, assorted buffet. *Note:* Magnificent Victorian dining rm in the Imperial Hotel, a registered historic monument dating from the gold-rush era of the last century. The décor alone makes a visit worthwhile. The food is worthy, but nothing more. Dinner theater Tues.-Sun. *American.* **B–I**

DURANGO. ❄ ♙♙ **Palace Restaurant,** 1 Depot Pl. (303/247-2018). A/C. Lunch/dinner daily; closed Thanksgiving and Dec. 25. AE, DC, MC, V. *Specialties:* honey chicken, sautéed trout Palace, mesquite-grilled steak, house salads and desserts. Good list of Californian wines. *Note:* One of the most agreeable and picturesque rests. in southern Colorado. Authentic Victorian décor w. Tiffany lamps and copper objets d'art (the building itself dates from 1881). Excellent

traditional American cooking. Relaxed atmosphere and svce. Very popular locally. Very good value. Resv. highly advisable in summer. Located near the famous
Silverton Railroad terminal. *American.* **B–I**

    Henry's, in the Strater Hotel (see "Accommodations," above)
(303/247-4431). A/C. Breakfast/lunch/dinner daily. AE,
CB, DC, MC, V. *Specialties:* scampi, fresh salmon, roast beef, red meats. *Note:*
Housed in the Strater Hotel, a picturesque Victorian building. Classic hotel cui-
sine. Rather inefficient svce. Pretty old-fashioned décor. *Continental-American.*
B–I

ESTES PARK. **Edelweiss Haus,** 100 E. Elkhorn Ave. (303/586-3400). A/C.
Lunch/dinner daily; closed Mon., Tues. in summer. DC, MC, V. *Specialties:*
duckling bigarade, wienerschnitzel, sauerbraten. *Note:* Bavarian style w. an unimpeded view over the lake and mountains. Accomplished German cuisine. Resv.
necessary. *German-American.* **B–I**

    Old Plantation, 128 E. Elkhorn Ave. (303/586-2800). A/C.
Lunch/dinner daily; closed Nov.-May. AE, CB, DC, MC, V.
Specialties: rainbow trout, roast duck, pot au feu. *Note:* Old southern colonial
décor—rather unlikely in this mountainous landscape. Generally pleasant rustic
cuisine. Efficient svce. A classic. Resv. recommended. *American.* **B–I**

    La Chaumière, 12 mi. (19 km) south on U.S. 36 in Pinewood
Springs (303/823-6521). A/C. Dinner only, Wed.-Sun.;
closed Mon., Tues., and Feb. AE. *Specialties:* veal sweetbreads, roast duck, fish of
the day, veal cutlet à la normande. *Note:* Lovely chalet dining rm w. a central
hearth. Very pleasant French-style cooking. Fixed-price menu. Unrestricted
view of the mountains. Friendly svce. Excellent value. Resv. recommended.
French-continental. **I (fixed-price)**

GEORGETOWN. **The Ram,** 606 6th St. (303/569-3263). A/C. Lunch/dinner
daily. AE, MC, V. *Specialties:* roast beef, steaks, good desserts. Good wine list.
Note: Located in the heart of Georgetown, an old gold-rush town, this 19th-
century saloon offers very good red-meat dishes at reasonable prices. Popular locally. *Steak.* **B–I**

GRAND JUNCTION. **Far East,** 1530 North Ave. (303/242-8131). A/C.
Lunch/dinner daily; closed holidays. AE, CB, DC, MC, V. *Specialties:* Cantonese and Mandarin dishes, beef teriyaki. *Note:* One of the few "exotic" rests. in the
Rockies. The Chinese-Polynesian décor is a success, as is the food. Popular locally. *Chinese-American.* **B–I.**

LEADVILLE. **Silver King,** in the Best Western Silver King Motor Inn (see "Accommodations," above) (303/486-2610). No A/C. Breakfast/lunch/dinner
Tues.-Sun.; closed Mon. and Nov.-Jan. AE, CB, DC, MC, V. *Specialties:* steak,
mountain lake trout. *Note:* A modest, unpretentious motel rest. Good red meats
and broiled dishes; friendly svce. *Steak-American.* **B–I**

LONGMONT. **Sebanton,** 424 Main St. (303/776-3686). A/C. Lunch
Tues.-Fri., dinner Tues.-Sat.; closed Sun., Mon., holidays, and mid-Aug. to mid-
Sept. AE, MC, V. Jkt. *Specialties:* oysters in mousseline sauce, Lyonnaise sausage,
duck à l'orange, fish of the day. Noteworthy desserts. *Note:* One of the best rests.
in the Rockies. The fixed-price dinner ($17) is a real bargain. Chef John Bomba's
cooking is worth a special trip, and the svce is beyond reproach. Typical bistro
décor w. checkered tablecloths. Rather noisy atmosphere. The menu changes
regularly. Resv. highly recommended, given the rest.'s popularity. Halfway between Denver and Rocky Mountain National Park. *French-continental.* **B–I**

LYONS. ♆♆ **Black Bear Inn,** 42 Main St. (303/823-6812). A/C. Lunch/dinner Tues.-Sun.; closed Mon., holidays, and mid-Jan. to mid-Feb. AE, CB, DC, MC, V. Jkt. *Specialties:* chateaubriand, veal casserole, fish of the day, apple strudel. *Note:* Elegant alpine-style inn w. a big fireplace and hunting trophies. Classical European cooking, w. delicacy. Diligent svce. Resv. recommended. A recommended stop midway between Denver and Rocky Mountain National Park. *Continental.* **B.**

MANITOU SPRINGS. ❀ ♈ **Stagecoach Inn,** 702 Manitou Ave. (719/685-9335). A/C. Lunch/dinner daily. AE, DC, MC, V. *Specialties:* broiled red meats, fish of the day, homemade pastries and preserves. *Note:* A pleasant rest. housed in a former coaching inn of the 1880s. Authentic period décor, in a rustic style w. big fireplaces. Honest, tasty cooking. A fine place. Resv. recommended. *American.* **B–I**

STEAMBOAT SPRINGS. ♈ **Pine Grove,** U.S. 40 (303/879-1190). A/C. Dinner only, nightly; closed Thanksgiving. AE, DC, MC, V. *Specialties:* roast beef, broiled trout, barbecued pork chops, fish of the day, game in season. *Note:* Pleasant ranch-style décor, and a welcoming atmosphere, w. open hearth and antique furniture. Honest, tasty cooking. Friendly svce. *American.* **I**

VAIL. ♆♆♆ **Wildflower Inn,** in The Lodge at Vail (see "Accommodations," above) (303/476-5011). No A/C. Dinner only, nightly. AE, CB, DC, MC, V. Jkt. *Specialties:* celeriac tart, fresh pâtés w. herbs, confit of poultry w. radicchio, filet of lamb w. green peppercorns, lamb cutlet w. vermouth sauce, braised breast of pheasant, hot plum tart. *Note:* The dining rm at The Lodge at Vail is a model of elegance and good taste (it won a Design of the Year Award). The cuisine, of French inspiration, is equally elegant. The svce is laudable and the whole amply deserves its three stars. By far the best in Vail. The menu changes regularly. *Continental.* **M**

♆♆ **Alpen Rose Tea Room,** 100 E. Meadow Dr. (303/476-3194). No A/C. Breakfast/lunch/dinner Tues.-Sun.; closed Mon., Memorial Day, late Apr. through June, and mid-Oct. to mid-Nov. AE, MC, V. *Specialties:* hausplatte, chicken Cordon Bleu, Mozart schnitte, roulade of beef w. red wine sauce. *Note:* This bakery-rest. is especially good at breakfast for its hot chocolate and cakes. More substantial fare at lunch, w. a strong emphasis on German dishes. Splendid view, and open-air terraces in fine weather. Popular locally. Resv. advised. Parking. *German-continental.* **I**

♆♆ **Left Bank,** Sitzmark Lodge, 183 Gore Creek Dr. (303/476-3696). No A/C. Dinner only, Thurs.-Tues.; closed Wed., mid-Apr. to mid-June, Oct.-Nov., and Dec. 25. *Specialties:* onion soup, scallops w. cucumbers, braised veal sweetbreads, Colorado trout. Good homemade desserts. Extensive wine list. *Note:* Pleasant mountain-chalet atmosphere, and cooking to match. Popular locally. Resv. recommended. *French-continental.* **I–M**

♈ **Cyrano's,** 298 Hanson Ranch Rd. (303/476-5551). No A/C. Lunch daily, dinner Mon.-Sat.; closed Sun. evening. MC, V. *Specialties:* sandwiches, omelets, pepper steak, tournedos, abalone, chicken Oscar. *Note:* Congenial small rest. Very acceptable food at reasonable prices. Very popular bar next door. Another location: **Cyrano's Too,** Lionshead Circle (303/476-1441). Renowned mainly for its desserts and its impressive wine list (225 labels). *American-steak.* **B–I**

CHAPTER 31

SALT LAKE CITY ⸙

□ □ □

The capital of Utah and the holy city of the Church of Jesus Christ of the Latter-Day Saints, more commonly known as the Mormon church, is situated about 15 miles south of the **Great Salt Lake,** for which it is named. The distant, usually snow-covered peaks of the **Wasatch Range,** more than 9,840 ft (3,000 m) high, enhance the beauty of the setting. In 1825 an adventurous fur trader named Jim Bridger was the first white man to set eyes on the Great Salt Lake, the largest body of water in the entire western United States. Some 22 years later, in July 1847, the Mormon preacher Brigham Young and 150 of his followers, fleeing religious persecution and open hostility in various East Coast and midwestern cities, founded Salt Lake City after a 1½-year forced march westward. Legend holds that Brigham Young, on seeing the Great Salt Lake and the site of the new Zion, exclaimed, "This is the place!" Today an imposing monument marks the spot where Young came upon this superb view. Baptized "Deseret" ("honeybee" in Mormon nomenclature), the early encampment soon became Great Salt Lake City, then simply Salt Lake City, once Utah was admitted to the Union in 1896.

An industrious and prosperous city (electronics, missiles, food processing, chemicals), the Mormon capital is today a modern metropolis, clean and inviting, carved out of the surrounding desert. Only the Mormons' extraordinary spirit of sacrifice and devotion to work can explain this astonishing transformation in less than a century and a half.

An ideal point of departure for magnificent trips to such national parks as **Zion, Bryce Canyon, Grand Teton, Yellowstone,** and **Canyonlands**—not to mention numerous nearby winter vacation spots—Salt Lake City boasts two monuments directly inspired by the Mormon religion: the **Temple,** a massive granite edifice in the Gothic Revival style (only Mormons are admitted), and the **Tabernacle,** shaped like an immense inverted ship's hull, which has become one of the world's most famous concert halls. The imposing **State Capitol,** built on a hill overlooking the town, is also a symbol of the city. In deference to the Mormon way of life, many Salt Lake City restaurants do not serve any alcoholic beverages, but diners can bring their own (purchased from state package stores). It's best to confirm this arrangement by an advance phone call to the restaurant of your choice.

THE MORMONS: Founded in 1830 in New York State by the visionary Joseph Smith, the Church of Jesus Christ of the Latter-Day Saints (LDS), the church's formal name, imposes a strict behavior code. Mormons, who comprise 70% of Utah's population, eschew drugs, tobacco, alcohol, tea, coffee, and even Coca-Cola. They practice tithing, returning to their rich and powerful church approximately 10% of their personal income.

Young Mormons of both sexes dedicate two years of their lives to missionary work; they may be sent at their own expense anywhere in the world to proselytize. There are nearly 6½ million Mormons today throughout the world, two-thirds of them in the United States. Their 20 or so temples are all modeled on the one in Salt Lake City. The Mormon practice of polygamy, which caused much of the anti-Mormon persecution during the last century (the church's founder, Joseph Smith, was lynched in 1844) and long delayed Utah's admission to the Union, was officially abolished in 1890. Highly moral, the Mormons are known for their religious zeal, their political conservatism, and their strong family ties.

BASIC FACTS: Capital of the State of Utah. Area Code: 801. Time Zone: Mountain Time. ZIP Code: 84101. Founded: 1847. Approximate population: city, 168,000; metropolitan area, 1,100,000. 37th largest metropolitan area in the country.

CLIMATE: With its magnificently sunny days and its colorful foliage, autumn is the ideal season for a visit to Salt Lake City and its nearby woodlands. Summers are quite hot but dry (average July temperature, 78°F, 26°C). Spring brings a disconcerting alternation of sun and sudden showers (sometimes with snow). Winter is pure pleasure for ski buffs, with the thermometer hovering consistently around 32°F (0°C) from Nov. to Feb.

DISTANCES: Denver, 506 mi. (810 km); Las Vegas, 439 mi. (702 km); Portland, 768 mi. (1,230 km); San Francisco, 750 mi. (1,200 km); Yellowstone, 325 mi. (520 km).

ARRIVAL & TRANSIT INFORMATION

AIRPORT: Salt Lake City International Airport (SLC), 3 mi. (5 km) west.

AIRLINES: America West (328-0121), American (521-6131), Continental (359-9800), Delta (532-7123), Northwest (toll free 800/225-2525), Pan Am (toll free 800/221-1111), TWA (539-1111), and United (328-8011).

CITY LINK: The cab fare from Salt Lake City Airport to downtown Salt Lake City is about $10; time, 15 min. Bus: The major hotels have their own free limousine service; time, about 20 min. City bus (UTA): Serves the downtown area; leaves every hour; fare, 50¢; time, 20 min.

Unless you plan on excursions, the size of the city makes car rental unnecessary. The public bus transportation system is not extensive (Utah Transit Authority, 801/263-3737).

CAR RENTAL (all at Salt Lake City Airport): Avis (539-1117), Budget (363-1500), Dollar (521-2590), Hertz (539-2683), and National (539-0200). For downtown locations, consult the local telephone directory.

LIMOUSINE SERVICES: Bonneville Limo (364-6520) and Dav-El Limousines (toll free 800/922-0343).

TAXIS: You'll find taxis in waiting lines at the major hotels; they cannot be hailed on the street. Your best bet is to phone Yellow Cab (521-2100).

TRAIN: AMTRAK station, 3rd St. South and Rio Grande St. (364-8562; toll free 800/872-7245).

BUS: Greyhound, 160 W. South Temple (355-4684).

INFORMATION & TOURS

TOURIST INFORMATION: The **Salt Lake City Convention and Visitors Bureau,** 180 S. West Temple St., UT 84101 (801/521-2822): Open Mon.-Fri.
Utah Travel Council, Council Hall, Capitol Hill, UT 84114 (801/538-1030): Information on Utah's national parks and tourist attractions.

The office is open daily in the summer, Mon.-Fri. the rest of the year.

Visitor Information Center, Temple Square, S. Temple and Main Sts. (801/531-2534): Information about the Mormon church. Open daily.

GUIDED TOURS: Gray Line Tours (bus), 553 W. 100 South (521-7060): Guided tours of the city and its outskirts, serving the major hotels.

Lewis Brothers Stages (bus), 549 W. 500 South (801/359-8677): Tour of the city in an open mini-train (summer only).

Western Leisure (bus), 142 E. 200 South (532-2113): Week-long tours to filming locations of well-known movies such as *Butch Cassidy and the Sundance Kid, Jeremiah Johnson,* etc. A must for movie buffs. Reservations essential.

SIGHTS, ATTRACTIONS, & ACTIVITIES

ADVENTURES: Adrift Adventures (boat), P.O. Box 81032, UT 84108 (485-5978; toll free 800/874-4483): Down the Colorado and Green Rivers in rubber rafts or rowboats. One- to seven-day trips (early Apr. through Oct.).

Colorado River and Trail Expeditions (boat), 5058 S. 300 West (261-1789): Raft trips on the Colorado, Green, San Juan, or Dolores Rivers (May-Sept.).

Holiday River Expeditions (boat), 544 E. 3900 South (266-2087; toll free 800/624-6323): Raft trips on the Colorado, Green, and San Juan Rivers (May-Sept.).

Moki Mac River Expeditions (boat), 1821 E. Ft. Union Blvd. (943-6707): Raft trips on the Colorado and Green Rivers, lasting 1-14 days (May–Sept.).

Western River Expeditions (boat), 7258 Racquet Club Dr. (toll free 800/453-7450): Raft trips on the Green and Colorado Rivers (May-Sept.).

ARCHITECTURAL HIGHLIGHTS: ⚲ **City and County Building,** Washington Square (535-7611): Built in 1894 along the lines of the Mansion House in London, this vast Romanesque edifice in dark sandstone served for 19 years as the State Capitol. Today it houses the city hall and the county's administrative offices. The building is set in a very lovely garden with 45 varieties of trees from around the world. Open Mon.-Fri. Worth seeing.

☀⚲ **LDS Church Office Building,** 50 E. North Temple St. (240-2673): The old Ionic-style building, inaugurated in 1917 (LDS Church Administration Bldg.), contains the offices of the president and the 12 "apostles" of the Mormon church. The new 30-story building, constructed in 1972, houses the largest genealogical library in the world. Tens of millions of computerized microfiches are said to make possible the reconstruction of genealogical trees for all U.S. citizens and many Europeans. Visitors can use the library Mon.-Sat. (Duplicate microfilm is stored in an underground vault dug out of a mountain in Little Cottonwood Canyon, 17 mi., 28 km, south of Salt Lake City.) An observation platform on the 26th floor offers a fine view of the city. Not to be missed. Open Mon.-Sat.

⚲ **Salt Palace Center,** bounded by W. Temple, 200 West, S. Temple, and 200 South Sts. (521-6060): Enormous arts complex and convention center covering two downtown blocks. Contains, among other facilities, the 200,000-sq.-ft. (18,000-m²) **Salt Palace,** which hosts many expositions, conventions, and sporting events (28,000 seats); the **Salt Palace Arena** (concerts, rodeos, shows of many kinds); the **Capitol Theatre** (see below); and the **Art Gallery** (art exhibitions). This is the cultural heart of Salt Lake City. Worth a look.

☀⚲ **State Capitol,** State St. and Capitol Hill (535-5900): One of the most imposing edifices of its type in the U.S. (1916). Inspired by the Capitol in Washington, D.C., its 285-ft (87-m) copper dome dominates the city. Constructed from marble and Utah State granite, the building

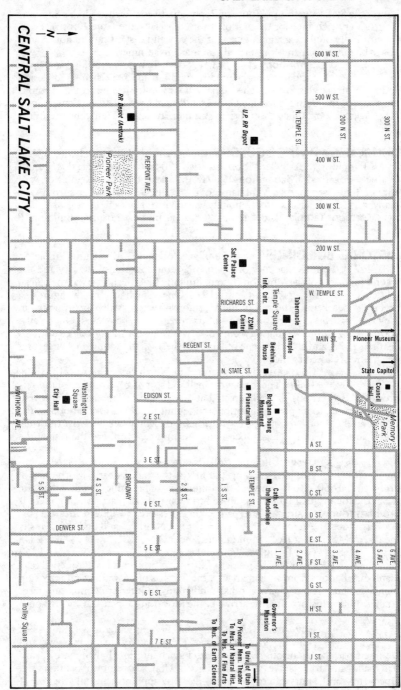

houses the State Senate and House of Representatives as well as Utah's Supreme Court. Very rich interior decoration (note especially the **Gold Room**). From Capitol Hill you'll have a grand view of the city and distant mountains. A visit not to be missed. Open Mon.-Fri. all year, daily in summer.

    Symphony Hall, 123 W. South Temple St. (533-5626): Spectacular modern building with an unusual chamfered design and an immense glass façade. The hall is well known for its fine acoustics, and is the home of the Utah Symphony Orchestra. Part of the Salt Palace Center Complex. Worth a look. Open Mon.-Fri. in summer, Tues. and Thurs. the rest of the year.

CHURCHES/SYNAGOGUES: ※ Cathedral of the Madeleine, 331 E.
South Temple St. (328-8941): Topped by two 220-ft (67-m) towers, this Spanish Gothic-style cathedral dating from 1909 features a richly decorated interior: varieties of Tennessee marble, Venetian mosaics, stained-glass windows from Germany, carved oak statues, etc. Definitely worth visiting. Open daily.

    Mormon Temple: See "Temple Square" under "Historic Buildings," below.

HISTORIC BUILDINGS: ※ ⚲ Beehive House, 67 E. South Temple St.
(531-2671): Former residence of Brigham Young, founder of the city and the second president of the Mormon church. Built in 1854, the house was the official residence of Mormon presidents until 1918. On its small tower is the figure of a beehive—betokening the zeal of the Mormons—which is also incorporated in the Utah State Seal. Interesting period furniture. Not to be missed. Open daily. (**Lion House,** next door, dating from 1856, was Brigham Young's office until his death in 1877, and also the scene of family gatherings for Young's 19 wives and 56 children. Closed to the public.)

    Council Hall, State and 300 North Sts., Capitol Hill (538-1030): The former city hall and seat of government for the Territory of Utah (1866). Initially erected at 1 E. South St., the hall was moved, stone by stone, to its present location and rebuilt in 1962. Today it houses the Utah Travel Council and its Visitor Information Center (see "Tourist Information," above). Worth seeing. Open daily in summer, Mon.-Fri. the rest of the year.

    Deseret Village, 2601 Sunnyside Ave. (533-5881): Museum village re-creating the life of the valley's early Mormon pioneers, circa 1850–1870. Some of the buildings are facsimiles, while others are the authentic original buildings, moved to their present place. Among them is **Brigham Young's** country home, painstakingly restored (**Brigham Young's Forest Farmhouse**). An interesting slice of history. Nearby you'll find the "This Is the Place" Monument (see "Monuments," below).

    Fort Douglas, Wasatch Dr. (524-4154): Constructed in 1862 by order of President Lincoln to protect transcontinental telegraph installations from Indian attacks, the fort has preserved several imposing buildings and fortifications of reddish sandstone. An interesting museum traces Utah's military history after the arrival of the Mormons. Open Tues.-Sat. Should be seen.

    Governor's Mansion, 603 E. South Temple (533-6459): Built in 1902 by Thomas Kearns, a wealthy mine owner and Utah senator, this luxurious residence with its rich interior (Italian marble, Russian mahogany) today serves as the residence of Utah's governor. Worth visiting. Open Tues. and Thurs. afternoons, May-Dec.; by appointment only the rest of the year.

Hotel Utah, S. Temple and Main Sts. (531-1000): After 76 years of welcoming famous visitors, this legendary palace of Italian Renaissance design, a designated historic monument, closed its doors in 1987. It has since reopened as an office building and meeting place for the Mormon church (to which it belongs), thus closing a chapter in Salt Lake City history. No visitors.

Temple Square, bounded by North Temple, South Temple, West Temple, and Main Sts. (531-2534): The historic heart and holy place of Joseph Smith's church. Enclosed within a 13-ft (4-m) wall of unbaked brick, the square contains those buildings that most symbolize the Mormon religion. First and foremost is the **Temple,** an imposing granite edifice in Mormon style, inaugurated in 1893 after 40 years in construction. At each of its two extremities are three pointed towers; the tallest, part of the main façade, measures 209 ft (64 m) in height and is crowned by Cyrus D. Dallin's gold statue of the angel Moroni. Reserved for baptism and marriage celebrations, sermons, and ordinations, the richly decorated Temple is off-limits to non-Mormons. The second noteworthy building, the **Tabernacle,** a vast 6,500-seat concert hall dating from 1867, has a wooden roof shaped like a turtle's carapace. Its exceptional acoustics are demonstrated daily via recitals on the 12,000-pipe organ. Recital times are noon Mon.-Fri., and 4 p.m. on Sat. and Sun. Concerts of the famous Mormon Tabernacle Choir are held Thurs. at 8 p.m. and on Sun. at 9:30 a.m. The last of the three major buildings, the **Assembly Hall** (1882), can accommodate as many as 3,000 people for religious observances, concerts, meetings, funerals, etc. Concerts Mon.-Sat. in summer, on Fri. and Sat. the rest of the year. There are also **visitor centers** with information on Mormon history and religion. Nearly three million visitors come to Temple Square each year. Don't miss it.

MONUMENTS: **Brigham Young Monument,** S. Temple and Main Sts.: Bronze statue of Salt Lake City's founder; note the figures of an Indian and a trapper at the base of the pedestal (1897). On the monument's north side is a plaque bearing the names of those Mormon pioneers who arrived with Brigham Young on July 24, 1847. Should be seen.

Eagle Gate, S. Temple and State Sts.: Originally constructed in 1859 to mark the entrance to Brigham Young's private property, this monumental sculpture, composed of the emblems of the United States (the eagle) and the State of Utah (the beehive) supported by four massive arches, overlooks one of the city's principal intersections. Really worth seeing.

Grave of Brigham Young, First Ave. between State and A Sts.: Tomb of the Mormon leader, three of his wives, and several of their children, in a modest garden surrounded by a wrought-iron railing. Lovely view of the city.

Seagull Monument, Temple Square: The figure of a seagull perches atop this bronze column (1913) in commemoration of the sea birds that in 1848 miraculously intervened to eat the grasshoppers threatening the harvest of the first settlers. Take a look.

"This Is the Place" Monument, Sunnyside Ave. at the entrance to Emigration Canyon: Erected in 1947 for the centennial celebration of the founding of Salt Lake City, the monument, designed by Brigham Young's grandson, Mahonry Young, marks the place from which the Mormon leader first discerned the site of the future capital of Utah (July 24, 1847). Lovely view of the valley. Visitor center open daily. A sight not to be missed.

MUSEUMS OF ART: ⚑ **Salt Lake Art Center,** 20 S. West Temple (328-4201): Temporary art exhibitions (paintings, photos, crafts). Sculpture garden. Numerous concerts, ballet, conferences, films on art, etc. Part of the huge Salt Palace Center cultural complex (see "Architectural Highlights," above). Open daily.

⚑ **Utah Museum of Fine Arts,** University of Utah campus, Wasatch Dr. (581-7049): Installed in the new building of the Art and Architecture Center, this relatively small but well-rounded museum offers a complete overview of the history of art, from Egyptian antiquities to contemporary American painting. Also a lovely collection of Louis XIV furniture and 17th-century tapestries. Worth seeing.

MUSEUMS OF SCIENCE AND HISTORY: ☀⚑ **Hansen Planetarium,** 15 S. State St. (538-2104): Well-known planetarium housed in a former turn-of-the-century public library building. A spectacular **Star Chamber** takes visitors on a vicarious tour of the planets. Space museum and specialty library. A must for astronomy buffs. Open daily.

☀⚑ **Pioneer Memorial Museum,** 300 N. Main St. (533-5759): Interesting museum focused on the Mormon era, just a few steps from the State Capitol. Created in 1950, the museum contains numerous and often-touching souvenirs from the time of the early Mormon pioneers (dolls, clothing, manuscripts, furniture, etc.). In the **Carriage House** next door, be sure to see the wagon used by Brigham Young in his 1847 trek to Salt Lake City. Should not be missed. Open daily, Jun.-Aug.; Mon.-Sat. the rest of the year.

⚑ **Utah Museum of Natural History,** University of Utah campus, Wasatch Dr. (581-6927): Rich geological, paleontological, and zoological collections. Outstanding display of five almost-complete dinosaur skeletons uncovered in earlier Utah excavations. Remarkable Hall of Minerals. Worth seeing. Open daily.

PANORAMAS: ☀⚑ **LDS Church Office Bldg.,** 50 E. North Temple St. (531-2190): The observation deck on the 26th floor offers (free) the best view of the city and surrounding mountains. Not to be missed. Open Mon.-Sat.

PARKS AND GARDENS: ⚑ **Jordan Park,** 1060 S. 9th West St.: Located on the shores of the Jordan River, this park and the adjacent **International Peace Gardens** features flowers and statues from 22 countries. Also a picnic area and a public swimming pool. Worth a look. Open daily, May-Sept.; closed the rest of the year.

☀⚑ **Liberty Park,** 1000 South and 600 East Sts. (972-7800): Very lovely 100-acre (41-ha.) park close to the center of the city. Notable features include a vast pond (boat rides), a children's amusement park, and the **Tracy Aviary.** Worth visiting. Open daily.

⚑ **State Arboretum,** University of Utah campus (581-5322): Spread over the university campus are more than 7,000 trees from 350 different species. Worth a look.

PERFORMING ARTS: For a daily listing of all shows and cultural events, consult the entertainment pages of the daily papers the *Salt Lake City Tribune* (morning) and the *Deseret News* (evening), and of the monthly magazine *Utah Holiday.*

Capitol Theatre, 50 W. 200 South St. (535-7905): Built in 1913, this very lovely rococo theater, sumptuously renovated, offers ballet, opera, top entertainers, and Broadway shows. Home of the Utah Opera Company (directed by Glade Peterson), the Ballet West, and the Repertory Dance Theatre.

Mormon Tabernacle, Temple Square (531-2534): Daily organ recitals (free), concerts of sacred music, and performances by the Mormon Tabernacle Choir on Thurs. and Sun. (see "Historic Buildings," above).

Pioneer Memorial Theatre, 300 South and University Sts. (581-6961): Classic and contemporary theater, musical comedies (Sept.-May). On the Utah State University campus.

Promised Valley Playhouse, 132 S. State St. (364-5677): Elegantly restored building dating from the end of the 19th century. Contemporary theater, drama, musical productions (Sept.-May). Musical comedy with the Mormon epic as theme, Tues.-Sat. all summer (free tickets at the Temple Square Visitor Center).

Salt Lake Acting Co., 168 W. 500 North (363-0525): Drama, comedy, contemporary theater.

Special Events Center, Hempstead Rd., Utah State University campus (581-6641): Circular dome-covered arena seating 15,000. Hosts the "Runnin' Utes" basketball team, also concerts and performances of top entertainers.

Symphony Hall, Salt Palace Center, W. Temple St. (533-6407): Very beautiful architecture and peerless acoustics. Concerts, classical-music recitals. Home of the Utah Symphony Orchestra, under principal conductor Joseph Silverstein.

SHOPPING: ☀ **Trolley Square,** bounded by 5th and 6th South Sts. and 6th and 7th East Sts. (521-9877): Former turn-of-the-century trolley depot, intelligently transformed into a business and entertainment center with 100 or so shops, booths, restaurants, and movie theaters. Strolling musicians and sidewalk artists. Lively, colorful atmosphere, lovely Victorian décor. Definitely deserves a visit. Open daily.

☀ **ZCMI,** Main and S. Temple Sts. (321-6179): Founded by Brigham Young himself in 1868, the Zion's Cooperative Mercantile Institution (ZCMI) is the oldest department store in the United States. Its ornamental cast-iron façade is a designated historic monument. Next door is the **ZCMI Center,** an enormous four-story modern shopping mall containing many shops, specialty stores, and restaurants.

SPECIAL EVENTS: For the exact schedule of events below, consult the **Salt Lake City Convention and Visitors Bureau** (see "Tourist Information," above).

Utah Arts Festival (end of June): Art exhibits, shows, concerts, international food festival, etc.

Pioneer Day (July 24): Commemorates the founding of Salt Lake City by the first Mormons. Parades, rodeo. Very colorful spectacle.

Promised Valley (July/Aug.): Musical show portraying the saga of Brigham Young and the early pioneers. Promised Valley Playhouse.

Utah State Fair (11 days in mid-Sept.): The biggest fair in the state of Utah.

SPORTS: Salt Lake City has three professional teams:

Baseball (mid-June to Sept.): Trappers, Derks Field (484-9900).
Basketball (Oct.-April): Utah Jazz, Salt Palace (355-5151).
Ice Hockey (Oct.-April): Golden Eagles, Salt Palace (521-6120).

STROLLS: ⚓ **Arrow Press Square,** West Temple St. across from Salt Palace Center: The old printers' and bookbinders' quarter, with beautifully restored early-19th-century buildings, boutiques, and trendy restaurants. Worth visiting.

☀⚓ **South Temple Street,** between Temple Square and 7th East St.: The most fashionable and historic street in Salt Lake City, featuring the elegant residences of 19th-century silver and copper magnates. Among these is the **Kearns Mansion** (see the Governor's Mansion under

"Historic Buildings," above). Note also the **Cathedral of the Madeleine** (see "Churches/Synagogues," above) and the **Masonic Temple,** 650 E. South Temple St. A stroll not to be missed.

☀ ⚓ **Trolley Square:** See "Shopping," above.

THEME PARKS: ☀ ⚓ **Lagoon Amusement Park and Pioneer Village,** 17 mi. (27 km) N. on I-15 (801/451-0101): Large amusement park with cleverly re-created 19th-century pioneer village. Stagecoach rides, vast lagoon/swimming pool. Rodeos in the summer, also musical shows. Truly worth the trip. Open daily from Memorial Day to Labor Day; weekends only from mid-April to Memorial Day and Labor Day to mid-Oct.

⚓ **Raging Waters,** 1700 W. 1200 West (973-9900): Aquatic amusement park with at least a dozen pools, with giant water slides, waterfalls, artificial surf, etc. Open daily, May-Sept.

WINTER SPORTS RESORTS: 🎿 **Alta,** 28 mi. (45 km) SE on Utah 152 and Utah 210 (801/742-3333): Ten lifts. Open mid-Nov. to mid-April.

🎿 **Brighton Bowl,** 31 mi. (49 km) SE on Utah 152 (801/359-3282): Five lifts. Open mid-Nov. to May.

⚓ **Deer Valley,** 30 mi. (48 km) SE on I-80 and Utah 224 (801/649-1000): Eight lifts. Open mid-Nov. to mid-April.

⚓ **Park West,** 26 mi. (41 km) East on I-80 and Utah 224 (801/649-5400): Seven lifts. Open Nov. to early April.

☀🎿 **Snowbird,** 29 mi. (46 km) SE on Utah 152 and Utah 210 (801/742-2222): Cable car and seven lifts. Open mid-Nov. to June.

⚓ **Solitude Ski Resort,** 23 mi. (36 km) SE on Utah 152 (801/534-1400): Five lifts. Open from the end of Nov. through April.

☀🎿 **Sundance Resort,** 63 mi. (100 km) SE on I-15, Utah 52, U.S. 189 and Utah 92 (801/225-4107): Four lifts. Managed by actor Robert Redford, who lives here. Far from the crowds and commotion of the typical ski resort.

ACCOMMODATIONS

See the listing of toll-free numbers in the Appendix.

Room Rates in Salt Lake City	
B (Budget)	up to $30
I (Inexpensive)	$30–$60
M (Moderate)	$60–$90
E (Expensive)	$90–$140
VE (Very Expensive)	$140 and up

Personal Favorites (in order of preference)

🛎🛎🛎 **Red Lion Salt Lake** (formerly Sheraton) (dwntwn), 255 S. West Temple St., UT 84101 (801/828-2000; toll free, see Red Lion Inns). 496 rms, A/C, color TV, in-rm movies. AE, CB, DC, MC, V. Free parking, pool, health club, sauna, rest., coffeeshop, bar, rm svce, nightclub. *Note:*

Large, very modern 18-story hotel next to the huge Triad Center architectural complex. Peerless comfort and facilities. Spacious, inviting rms, some w. refrigerators. Very good svce, acceptable rest. Frequented by businesspeople and convention-goers (the Salt Palace is close by). Two VIP floors. Free airport shuttle. **M–E**

Marriott Hotel (dwntwn), 75 S. West Temple St., UT 84101 (801/531-0800; toll free, see Marriott). 516 rms, A/C, color TV, in-rm movies. AE, CB, DC, MC, V. Free parking, pool, health club, tennis court, sauna, two rests. (including L'Abeille), two bars, rm svce, disco, boutiques, free crib. *Note:* Modern 15-story tower across from the Salt Palace Convention Center. Facilities and comfort are beyond reproach. Spacious rms w. balconies; attentive reception and svce. Rests. are so-so, as elsewhere in the Marriott chain. Business and group clientele. Interesting wknd packages. Free airport shuttle. Direct access to the adjacent shopping center. VIP floor. The best location in Salt Lake City. **M–E**

Brigham Street Inn (nr. dwntwn), 1135 E. South Temple, UT 84102 (801/364-4461). 9 rms, A/C, color TV. AE, MC, V. Free parking, valet svce, free breakfast. *Note:* Small luxury hotel, intimate and refined, in a charming Victorian residence dating from 1898. Rms are elegantly fitted out, each in its own style (some have fireplaces). Stylish reception and svce. Charm and distinction. 10 min. from dwntwn. **M–E**

Holiday Inn Downtown (nr. dwntwn), 230 6th South St., UT 84101 (801/532-7000; toll free, see Holiday Inns). 160 rms, A/C, color TV, in-rm movies. AE, CB, DC, MC, V. Free parking, pool, sauna, putting green, rest., bar, rm svce, free crib. *Note:* Typical Holiday Inn style, w. spacious rms and functional comfort. Free airport shuttle. Good value. **I–M**

Temple Square Hotel (dwntwn), 75 W. South Temple St., UT 84101 (801/355-2961; toll free 800/221-3151). 189 rms, A/C, color TV, in-rm movies. AE, CB, DC, MC, V. Free parking, rest., hrdrsr, free crib. *Note:* Old hotel in the heart of the city, completely renovated. Austere but functional décor. Very good value. **I**

Other Accommodations (from top bracket to budget)

Hilton Salt Lake (nr. dwntwn), 150 W. 500 South St., UT 84101 (801/532-3344; toll free, see Hilton). 351 rms, A/C, color TV, in-rm movies. AE, CB, DC, MC, V. Free parking, pool, sauna, three rests. (including Towne Hall), coffeeshop, bar, rm svce, disco, hrdrsr, free crib. *Note:* Large, modern, functional hotel. Rms are comfortable and spacious and have balconies and refrigerators. Svce somewhat lacking. A favorite of business travelers. Good rests. Two VIP floors. 5 min. from dwntwn. **M–E**

Little America (nr. dwntwn), 500 S. Main St., UT 84101 (801/363-6781; toll free 800/453-9450). 850 rms, A/C, color TV, in-rm movies. AE, CB, DC, MC, V. Free parking, two pools, health club, sauna, two rests. (including Little America), coffeeshop, bar, rm svce, nightclub, hrdrsr, shops, free crib. *Note:* A 17-story hotel, modern and comfortable, surrounded by lovely gardens. Spacious rms, some w. refrigerators. Comprehensive facilities. Efficient reception and svce. Good value. Frequented by convention-goers and other groups. Free airport shuttle. 5 min. from Temple Square and the Convention Center. **M–E**

Peery (dwntwn), 110 W. 300 South, UT 84101 (801/521-4300; toll free 800/331-0073). 77 rms, A/C, color TV, in-rm movies. AE, CB, DC, MC, V. Free parking, health club, two rests., bar, rm svce, free breakfast, free crib. *Note:* Constructed in 1910, this elegant small hotel, a designated historic monument, was completely renovated in 1985. Rms are huge and very comfortable. Svce is personalized. Free airport shuttle. Only a stone's throw from the Convention Center. A favorite of those in-the-know. **I–M**

Tri-Arc Hotel (formerly the Travelodge Tri-Arc; nr. dwntwn), 161 W. 600 South St., UT 84101 (801/521-7373). 375 rms, A/C, cable color TV. AE, CB, DC, MC, V. Free parking, pool, sauna, tennis, rest. (13th Floor Supper Club), coffeeshop, bar, rm svce, disco, free crib. *Note:* Modern 13-story building in the form of a triple arc. Completely renovated rms and facilities. Offers a lovely view of the mountains. Efficient svce. Group clientele. Good value. 5 min. from dwntwn. **I–M**

Shilo Inn (formerly the International Dunes; dwntwn), 206 S. West Temple St., UT 84101 (801/521-9500; toll free 800/222-2244). 200 rms, A/C, color TV, in-rm movies. AE, CB, DC, MC, V. Free parking, pool, sauna, 24-hr coffeeshop, bar, rm svce, shops, free breakfast, free crib. *Note:* Large hotel, comfortable and functional, in the center of town. Pleasant rms. w. balconies and mini-bars. Good value. Great location across from the Salt Palace. Free airport shuttle. **I–M**

Royal Executive Inn (dwntwn), 121 N. 300 West St., UT 84103 (801/521-3450). 94 rms, A/C, color TV, in-rm movies. AE, CB, DC, MC, V. Free parking, pool, coffeeshop next door, rm svce, free breakfast, crib $1. *Note:* Modest, unpretentious motel in the heart of dwntwn. Good reception, very decent comfort. Free airport shuttle. Good value. **I**

Motel 6 (nr. dwntwn), 176 W. 6th South St., UT 84101 (801/531-1252). 110 rms, A/C, color TV, free in-rm movies. DC, MC, V. Free parking, pool. *Note:* Small, super-economical but well-maintained motel, very nr. the center of town. An excellent value. Ideal for motorists. **B**

RESTAURANTS

Salt Lake City Restaurant Prices (per person, excluding drinks and service charges)	
B (Budget)	up to $15
I (Inexpensive)	$15–$25
M (Moderate)	$25–$40
E (Expensive)	$40–$60
VE (Very Expensive)	$60 and up

Personal Favorites (in order of preference)

La Caille at Quail Run (vic.), 9565 S. Wasatch Blvd., in Sandy (942-1751). A/C. Dinner nightly, Sun. brunch; closed holidays. AE, CB, DC, MC, V. Jkt. *Specialties:* oysters on the half shell, veal au citron, roast rack of lamb, duck à l'orange, lobster in red butter. Basque cooking on Sun. Wine and liquor available. *Note:* This elegant Louis XVI–style manor about 10 mi. (15 km) south of Salt Lake City is the site of one of the best rests. (if not the best) in Utah. The French-inspired cooking is of the first order, and the svce is courteous and distinguished. Lovely gardens. Resv. are a must. Valet parking. *Continental-French.* **I–M**

La Fleur de Lys (dwntwn), 165 S. West Temple St. (359-5753). A/C. Dinner only, Mon.-Sat.; closed Sun. and holidays. AE, CB, DC, MC, V. Jkt. *Specialties:* pheasant chasseur, roast duckling à l'orange, soufflés. Good desserts. Wine and liquor. *Note:* Classic French cuisine impeccably prepared and served. Elegant décor and pleasant background music create a romantic atmosphere on picturesque Arrow Press Square. Excellent svce; popular locally. Resv. advised. *French.* **I–M**

🍸 **Bird's Café** (vic.). 1355 E. 2100 South (466-1051). A/C. Lunch Mon.-Fri., dinner Mon.-Sat.; closed Sun. AE, CB, DC, MC, V. *Specialties:* homemade pasta, scallops au gratin, broiled lamb chops, catch of the day. The menu changes daily. Wine and liquor. *Note:* The modern, California-inspired cooking of chef Dennis Bird has made this rest. a Salt Lake City favorite. The daily specials, written on a blackboard, vary according to season and availability of ingredients. Dark paneling enhances the warm, intimate atmosphere. Svce is attentive. Dinner resv. indispensable. *American.* **I**

🍸 **Robintino's** (nr. dwntwn), 120 N. 900 West (596-2626). A/C. Lunch Mon.-Fri., dinner nightly; closed Easter, Thanksgiving, and Dec. 25. AE, DC, MC, V. *Specialties:* pizza, ravioli, steaks, Italian dishes. Beer and wine. *Note:* Small, modest, unpretentious *trattoria.* Very decent homemade pasta. Popular w. the locals. *Italian-steak.* **B–I**

🍸 **Mikado** (dwntwn), 67 W. 100 South St. (328-0929). A/C. Dinner only, Mon.-Sat.; closed Sun. and holidays. AE, DC, MC, V. *Specialties:* sushi, sukiyaki, tempura, chicken teriyaki, shabu shabu. Wine and liquor. *Note:* The only genuine Japanese rest. in Salt Lake City. Smiling, discreet svce (in kimono). Western- and tatami-style dining rms. Popular locally. Resv. advised. *Japanese.* **I**

Other Restaurants (from top bracket to budget)

🍸 **Liaison Restaurant** (nr. dwntwn), 1352 S. 2100 East (583-8144). A/C. Lunch Mon.-Fri., dinner Tues.-Sat.; closed Sun. and holidays. AE, CB, DC, MC, V. *Specialties:* Chinese-style sliced veal, roast lamb w. herbs, duck w. raspberries, trout au bleu, double-chestnut chocolate cake. Beer only (but you can bring wine or liquor w. you). *Note:* Located 20-or-so min. from the center of town, this small (34 seats), intimate rest. is the kingdom of the excellent chef "Bub" Horne, a virtuoso of light sauces. Elegant décor like a stylish New York bistro. Svce is very good. Resv. are a must. Frequented by trendy upscale crowd. A fine facility. *American.* **I–M**

🍸 **Log Haven** (vic.), 3800 S. Millcreek Canyon Rd. (272-8255). A/C. Dinner Wed.-Sun., Sun. brunch; closed Mon. and Tues. AE, CB, DC, MC, V. *Specialties:* steak, prime ribs, catch of the day, lobster, mud pie. Wine and liquor. *Note:* Pleasant steakhouse in a huge log cabin in open country, w. western-style décor. On nice days the open patio offers a panoramic view of the canyon. Diners enjoy top beef cuts, broiled to perfection. Relaxed atmosphere. Valet parking. 25 min. from dwntwn. *Steak-seafood.* **I–M**

🍸 **Ristorante Della Fontana** (dwntwn), 336 S. 4th St. East (328-4243). A/C. Lunch/dinner Mon.-Sat.; closed Sun., Memorial Day, July 4, and Dec. 25. AE, MC, V. Jkt. *Specialties:* lasagne, homemade pasta, Italian dishes. Wine and liquor. *Note:* Multicolored stained-glass windows and an indoor waterfall give this rest., converted from an old church, one of the most original settings ever. Very decent Italian cuisine, very good svce. Popular locally; resv. advised. *Italian.* **I**

🍸 **Market Street Grill** (dwntwn), 48 Post Office Pl. (322-4668). A/C. Breakfast/lunch Mon.-Sat., dinner nightly, Sun. brunch; closed holidays. AE, MC, V. *Specialties:* excellent meats and seafood cooked over a wood fire. Good desserts. Wine and liquor. *Note:* Oldtime steakhouse, very popular locally, in a building dating from the early 1900s. The ambience is pleasant, the svce rapid and efficient. Just a few steps from Temple Square. Very good value. No resv. *American-steak.* **B–I**

☼ ♆ **Lamb's Grill** (dwntwn), 169 S. Main St. (364-7166). A/C. Breakfast/lunch/dinner Mon.–Sat.; closed Sun. and holidays. AE, CB, DC, MC, V. *Specialties:* omelets, excellent homemade soups, fried trout, broiled snapper, corned beef and cabbage, braised lamb shank, rice pudding. Beer and wine. *Note:* The oldest rest. in Utah (1919). Local businesspeople prefer it for working breakfasts and lunches. Honest, serious family cooking. The pleasantly dated décor is charming and helps create a peaceful atmosphere. Excellent svce. This is a true Salt Lake City landmark. No resv. Very good value. *American.* **B–I**

♆ **The Old Salt City Jail** (nr. dwntwn), 460 S. 10th St. East (355-2422). A/C. Lunch/dinner daily; closed July 4, July 24, and Dec. 25. AE, DC, MC, V. *Specialties:* roast beef, steaks, barbecued meats. Beer and wine. *Note:* As its name indicates, this rest. is in a converted 19th-century jail. The quality of the meats is excellent, and the décor is amusing even if not authentic. The atmosphere and svce are congenial. Good value. *American-steak.* **B–I**

♆ **Rio Grande Café** (dwntwn), 270 S. Rio Grande Ave. (364-3302). A/C. Lunch/dinner daily; closed holidays. AE, CB, DC, MC, V. *Specialties:* tacos, enchiladas, chalupas, chimichangas. Wine and liquor. *Note:* The most authentic of the local Mexican rests. in both cooking and décor. Some of the sauces are dynamite. Very popular for lunch. Located in the former Denver & Rio Grande train station. No. resv. *Mexican.* **B**

Cafeterias/Fast Food

Marianne's Delicatessen (dwntwn), 149 W. 200 South (364-0513). Open from 11 a.m. to 3 p.m. Tues.-Sat.; closed Sun. and Mon. AE, MC, V. Excellent sandwiches, many German specialties (rouladen, sauerbraten, and bratwurst), good daily specials, and memorable desserts explain this deli's popularity among the locals. No resv.

BARS & NIGHTCLUBS

Bourbon Street (dwntwn), 78 W. 400 South St. (521-0589). Fashionable singles bar, popular locally. There's an entrance fee. Open Mon.-Sat.

D. B. Cooper's (dwntwn), 19 E. 200 South St. (532-2948). Very popular disco. Entrance fee. Open Mon.-Sat.; closed Sun.

Zephyr (dwntwn), 301 S. West Temple St. (355-9913). Live blues and jazz.

NEARBY EXCURSIONS

☼ ⚒ **BINGHAM CANYON COPPER MINE** (27 mi., 43 km, SW on I-15 and Utah 48): The largest open-pit copper mine in the world, owned by the Kennecott Co. The crater (2½ mi., 4 km, in diameter; 3,148 ft, 960 m, in depth) is the largest man-made excavation in the world. Five billion tons of rock and minerals have been mined since 1904. An impressive sight. Observation platform. Open daily. Not to be missed.

⚒ **BONNEVILLE SALT FLAT** (105 mi., 168 km, west on I-80): An immense desert of salt 200 mi. (322 km) long, as hard as cement. Used as an automobile test track since 1911. In 1970 the rocket vehicle *Blue Flame* set a then world speed record of 622.4 mph (1,001.4 km/h). Present record: 633.6 mph (1,019.7 km/h) attained by *Thrust 2,* driven by Richard Noble on Nevada's Black Rock Desert track on October 3, 1983. Races are held each year at the end of Sept., attracting a large crowd of fans. For speed freaks.

☼ ⚒⚒ **GREAT SALT LAKE** (31 mi., 49 km, NW on I-15): At 72 mi. (115 km) long and 30 mi. (48 km) wide, but with a maximum depth of barely 28 ft (8.5

m), Great Salt Lake, the remains of Lake Bonneville, a prehistoric sea 13 times greater in size, is the largest natural body of water in the western United States. With ongoing evaporation, the salt content of the lake now averages 25% (seven times that of the oceans); this makes it unlivable for any form of animal life except shrimp. The lake's surface area continues to shrink: from 2,393 sq. mi. (6,200 km²) in 1873 to 1,437 sq. mi. (3,724 km²) today. The salt content is so high that even nonswimmers float with ease. (It's wise to protect your eyes from the salty water.) Because of rising water and repeated flooding, **Antelope Island** and **Saltair Beach,** formerly very popular, are no longer accessible. This is truly a sight not to be missed.

⚓ TIMPANOGOS CAVE NATIONAL MONUMENT (36 mi., 58 km, SE via I-15 and Utah 92) (801/756-5238): Underground limestone caves at a constant temperature of 43°F (6°C). Splendid multicolored crystalline formations. Visiting the caves can be rather trying. Open daily, spring through fall; closed in winter.

❊ ⚓ WASATCH-CACHE NATIONAL FOREST: 1,235,000 acres (500,000 ha.) of forests, lakes, canyons, and mountains to the north, east, and southeast of Salt Lake City. Includes several **ski areas,** among them Alta, Park West, and Snowbird (see "Winter Sports Resorts," above). There are numerous camping and picnic areas. Hunting and fishing too. For **information,** contact the Supervisor, 8226 Federal Bldg., 125 S. State St., Salt Lake City, UT 84138 (801/524-5030). Nature unspoiled.

❊⚓ WHEELER HISTORIC FARM (6351 S. 900 East, 21 mi., 33 km, SE on I-15, exit I-215) (801/264-2241): Authentic farm from the end of the 19th century, magnificently restored. Re-creates to perfection the 1890s lifestyle of the Mormon farmers. Costumed guides conduct the tour; if they wish, visitors can help milk cows, gather eggs, or feed and water the farm animals. An original, historical slice-of-life. Open daily.

FARTHER AFIELD

❊ ⚓⚓ NORTH OF GREAT SALT LAKE (209 mi., 334 km, round trip via I-15N, Utah 83, and I-15S): Visit **Bear River Migratory Bird Refuge** near **Brigham City,** the largest migratory bird preserve in the U.S. Photo safaris encouraged. Open daily. Continue on to ⚓ **Golden Spike National Historic Site,** the place where, in 1869, the Central Pacific Railroad line coming from the west met the Union Pacific line from the east, creating the first transcontinental railroad. The anniversary of this event is celebrated each year on May 10 at 12:47 p.m., the exact day and hour of the original event. There's also a museum (801/471-2209) with exhibits and movies, open daily. Well worth the trip.

On your return, stop at the **Lagoon Amusement Park** (see "Theme Parks," above).

❊ ⚓⚓ SOUTH OF GREAT SALT LAKE (155 mi., 248 km, round trip via I-15S, Utah 48, Utah 68, Utah 73, Utah 36, and I-80E): Visit **Bingham Canyon Copper Mine** (see "Nearby Excursions," above), then the **Stagecoach Inn,** former relay station of the legendary Overland Stage Coach Company and the Pony Express. Go on to **Camp Floyd** (801/768-8932), formerly the largest military outpost in the United States during the wars against the Indians. Its visitor center is open daily, mid-March to mid-Nov. Next stop, **Ophir,** a famous ghost town of early pioneer days. Finally, of course, there is the **Great Salt Lake** itself (see "Nearby Excursions," above). A spectacular circuit.

For complete information on the three following parks, see Chapter 32 on Utah National Parks.

☀ ♨♨**CANYONLANDS** (248 mi., 396 km, SE via I-15, U.S. 6, U.S. 191, and Utah 313): Magnificent ocher-colored rocky cliffs tower over the Colorado River. Along the way, visit ♨♨ **Arches National Park,** where amid the reddish desert you'll find superb peaks and arches carved by erosion. An absolute must-see.

♨♨**DINOSAUR NATIONAL MONUMENT** (200 mi., 320 km, east via I-80 and U.S. 40): The quarries bear many footprints of prehistoric animals. The visitor center displays a remarkable fossil collection. Open daily.

On the way, visit ♨ **Flaming Gorge** and its exquisite scenery along the Green River, once the hideout of Butch Cassidy and the Sundance Kid. Worth a detour.

☀ ♨♨**GLEN CANYON** (319 mi., 510 km, south on I-15 and Utah 28, U.S. 89, Utah 24, and Utah 95): Multicolored cliffs bathed by the blue waters of **Lake Powell.**

En route, be sure to see the unspoiled natural beauty of ♨ **Capitol Reef National Park,** with its impressive but hard-to-reach canyons.

♨ **Natural Bridges National Monument,** 45 mi. (72 km) south of Glen Canyon, features gigantic rocky arches carved by erosion. Worth the trip.

♨ **PIONEER TRAIL** (90 mi., 144 km, round trip via I-15N, U.S. 89, I-84E, Utah 66, Utah 65, and Emigration Canyon Rd.): You'll go through **Farmington, Uintah, Weber Canyon, Morgan, East Canyon Lake,** and **Emigration Canyon.** A good third of this trip through gorgeous mountain scenery follows the old trail made by 19th-century Mormon pioneers.

☀ ♨ **UINTA NATIONAL FOREST** (138 mi., 220 km, round trip via I-15S, Utah 92, U.S. 189, Utah 52, and I-15N): You'll visit **Timpanogos Cave National Monument** (see "Nearby Excursions," above) aboard a quaint little steam-powered train, the *Heber Creeper,* which leaves daily, mid-May to mid-Oct., from 6th West and Center St. in **Heber City** (801/654-2900).

There are splendid views along **Deer Creek Lake** and the gorges of the **Provo River,** one of the most beautiful spots in the Uinta forest. Don't fail to admire the waterfalls at **Bridal Veil Falls**; there's a funicular railway (801/225-4461) on U.S. 189 between **Wildwood** and **Olmstead,** open daily, April-Nov.

To return to Salt Lake City, take I-15N. A trip packed with things to see.

☀ ♨♨♨♨**YELLOWSTONE AND GRAND TETON** (325 mi., 520 km, north via I-15, U.S. 26, and U.S. 89): The crown jewels among America's national parks (see Chapter 33 on Yellowstone), enough to justify the whole trip west.

On your way, I suggest stopping by the ♨ **Craters of the Moon National Monument** to see the astonishing lunar landscapes sculpted by volcanic eruptions. Closed in winter. For information, contact P.O. Box 29, Arco, ID 83213 (208/527-3257). Worth seeing.

☀ ♨♨**ZION NATIONAL PARK** (305 mi., 488 km, SW via I-15, Utah 17, and Utah 9): The only canyon in the United States whose floor is accessible by automobile. Lovely landscapes, not to be missed. See Chapter 32 on Utah National Parks.

En route, visit ♨ **Cedar Breaks** and its rocky plateaus pocked with strikingly colored amphitheater-shaped depressions. Be sure also to see ♨♨♨ **Bryce Canyon** with its breathtaking gorges and ravines, almost as awesome as those of the Grand Canyon. Not to be missed.

UTAH NATIONAL PARKS♛♛

□ □ □

With its ten great national parks for a population of less than 1.5 million inhabitants, the Mormon State is incontestably the most richly endowed from the point of view of the tourist or the ecologist. Mostly lying in the southern part of the state, these ten national parks or monuments boast some of the most breathtaking scenery in America. This is particularly true of **Zion National Park,** the only canyon in the country that can be entirely explored by car or on foot. Its many-colored gorges, several hundred feet high, bridling the headlong course of the Virgin River, are a sight not easily forgotten. Nearby **Bryce Canyon National Park** has, according to geologists, some of the most astonishing rock formations in the country, as well as a view almost as enthralling as the Grand Canyon of the Colorado. **Arches National Park** displays ranks of wonderful arches and windows carved by erosion out of the rusty rock of the desert. Its neighbor **Canyonlands National Park** is equally spectacular, with its great ocher-colored cliffs of rock looming above the serpentine curves of the Colorado River, an unforgettable sight at sunrise or sunset. More difficult of access, the wild canyons and rocky spurs of **Capitol Reef National Park** along the Fremont River are a perfect example of nature in the raw. Utah's other great national parks— **Natural Bridges National Monument, Glen Canyon National Recreation Area, Cedar Breaks, Dinosaur National Monument,** and **Rainbow Bridge** (one of the world's largest natural arches, 275 ft. (85 m) across)—rank, each in its degree, among the natural wonders of the United States. Allow at least one week to ten days just for the highlights.

BASIC FACTS: State of Utah. Area Code: 801. Time Zone: Mountain Time. Founded: Zion, 1909; Bryce Canyon, 1923; Arches National Park, 1929; Capitol Reef, 1937. Approximate combined area of the parks: 3,196 sq. mi. (8,280 km²).

CLIMATE: Utah's climate is like its scenery: beautiful but rugged. Summers are very hot, and winters icy. While in summer the mercury can climb to 95°F (35°C) by day, it can skid precipitously below 68°F (20°C) at night. There are frequent violent storms from July to Sept.; watch out, because the heavy rains can convert an unsurfaced road into a mudslide. The best times to escape both climatic extremes and crowds of tourists are May-June and Sept.-Oct. In any case, bring woolens for evening wear.

ARRIVAL AND TRANSIT INFORMATION

NEAREST AIRPORTS: See Chapter 47 on Las Vegas or Chapter 31 on Salt Lake City.

AIRLINES: See Chapter 47 on Las Vegas and Chapter 31 on Salt Lake City.

BUS OR CAR RENTAL?: Greyhound buses (for information call toll free 800/528-6055) serve many communities near Utah's national parks, but offer no direct access to them. Given the distances and the number of places you may wish to visit, it makes sense to rent a car with unlimited mileage. Rates in Nevada (Las Vegas) are more favorable than in Utah (Salt Lake City).

CAR RENTALS: See Chapter 47 on Las Vegas and Chapter 31 on Salt Lake City.

TRAIN: For AMTRAK, see Chapter 47 on Las Vegas and Chapter 31 on Salt Lake City. The nearest station to Arches and Canyonlands National Parks: Thompson D.R.G.&W. Station (toll free 800/872-7245). Nearest station to Bryce Canyon and Zion National Parks: Milford AMTRAK Station, East and South Sts. (toll free 800/872-7245).

BUS: The nearest long-distance Greyhound terminals are in Las Vegas (see Chapter 47) and Salt Lake City (see Chapter 31). The nearest local Greyhound stations are at 281 S. Main in Cedar City (586-9465) and 139 N. 2nd East in Green River (564-3421).

INFORMATION & ADVENTURE TOURS

TOURIST INFORMATION: The **Utah Travel Council,** Council Hall, Capitol Hill, Salt Lake City, UT 84114 (801/538-1030). Information on Utah's national parks and other great tourist attractions. For snow conditions, call 801/521-8102.

Visitor Centers
There are visitor centers in all the major parks:
Arches National Park, at the park entrance (801/259-8161).
Bryce Canyon National Park, 4 mi. (6 km) from Bryce Canyon Airport (801/834-5322).
Canyonlands National Park, at Island in the Sky Point (801/259-7164).
Capitol Reef National Park, 6 mi. (9 km) from the western entrance (801/425-3791).
Cedar Breaks National Monument, open from the end of May to mid-Sept. only (801/586-9451).
Dinosaur National Monument, at the park entrance on the Colorado side and 7 mi. (11 km) north of Jensen on the Utah side (303/374-2216).
Glen Canyon National Recreation Area, Glen Canyon Bridge at Page (602/645-2471).
Natural Bridges National Monument, at the park entrance (801/259-5174).
Zion National Park, at the south entrance (801/772-3256).

ADVENTURE TOURS: **Adventure River Expeditions** (boat), 245 N. Broadway, Green River (801/564-3648): Rafting down the Colorado, Green, San Juan, and Dolores Rivers. May-Sept.
Bryce Zion Trail Rides, Inc. (horseback): Rides on horseback or muleback in Bryce Canyon or Zion National Park; daily, Apr.-Sept. For information, call 801/834-5361 (Bryce) or 801/772-3967 (Zion).
Cedar City Air Service (airplane), Municipal Airport, Cedar City

(801/586-3881): Unforgettable flights over Cedar Breaks, Bryce Canyon, and Zion National Parks.

Del Webb Tours (boat), Wahweap Lodge, Page (602/645-3232): Boat cruises on Lake Powell and trips to Rainbow Bridge.

Don Hatch River Expeditions (boat), 411 E. 2nd North, Vernal (801/789-4316): One- to five-day air-rafting trips on the Green River and the Yampa River in Dinosaur National Park; May-Sept.

Lake Powell Air Service (airplane), Municipal Airport, Page (602/645-2494): Unforgettable flights, lasting 30 minutes to 2½ hours, over Lake Powell, Rainbow Bridge, Monument Valley, Bryce Canyon, etc.

Lin Ottinger's Scenic Tours (all-terrain vehicles), 137 N. Main St., Moab (801/259-7312): One-day trips in Arches and Canyonlands National Parks; Apr.-Nov.

North American's Adventures (boat), 534 N. Main St., Moab (801/259-5865): Down the Green and Colorado Rivers by air raft or jetboat; Apr.-Oct. Jeep trips in winter.

Red Tail Aviation (airplane), Canyonlands Field, on U.S. 191, 18 mi. (28 km) north of Moab (801/259-7421): Spectacular flights over Arches and Canyonlands National Parks, Lake Powell, or Monument Valley.

Tag-A-Long Tours (boat), 452 N. Main St., Moab (toll free 800/453-3292): Boat trips down the Green and Colorado Rivers and around Canyonlands National Park; Apr.-Oct.

NATIONAL PARKS & MONUMENTS

☼☖☖ **ARCHES NATIONAL PARK** (236 mi., 378 km, SE of Salt Lake City via I-15, U.S. 6, and U.S. 191): Dozens of stone arches and superb red sandstone spurs, carved over 150 million years by erosion, water, wind, sun, and frost in a dun-colored rocky wasteland. Among them are **Landscape Arch,** biggest natural arch in the world (288 ft., 88 m, across); **Park Avenue,** a spectacular rocky corridor between high vertical walls reminiscent of the famous street in New York; the sculptural group called the **Three Gossips;** the huge, precariously poised **Balanced Rock;** the unbelievably elegant **Delicate Arch,** spanning the sheer gorge of the Colorado, which can be reached by a footpath; and the fantastically shaped arches of the beautiful **Devil's Garden.**

There are 21 mi. (34 km) of surfaced roads and scores of miles of additional tracks for all-terrain vehicles, along which you can explore this open-air museum of natural architecture. The park is open year round, but beware extremes of temperature, winter and summer both. There are 53 authorized campsites.

For **information,** contact the Superintendent, Arches National Park, 125 W. 200 South, Moab, UT 84532 (801/259-8161 or 259-7164).

Don't leave it out of your itinerary.

☼☖☖☖ **BRYCE CANYON NATIONAL PARK** (241 mi., 385 km, NE of Las Vegas via I-15, Utah 9, U.S. 89, and Utah 12): One of the most beautiful national parks in America; its huge rock formations are almost as astonishing as those of the Grand Canyon of Colorado. Lying along the east side of the **Paunsaugunt Plateau** ("Country of the Beavers," in the Indian tongue), a limestone mesa 8,200 ft. (2,500 m) above sea level which, geologically speaking, is the bed of a 60-million-year-old sea, Bryce Canyon displays fairyland scenery of glittering rocks, cliff faces sculpted into gigantic organ pipes, and a dozen stepped amphitheaters in striking colors varying from yellow through orange to deep red (the famous **Pink Cliffs**). The scenic 17-mi. (27-km) **Rim Drive,** as well as a number of hiking trails leading to the bottom of the canyon, will take you to dozens of rock formations with strange shapes and poetic names—Cathedral, Queen's Castle, Wall of Windows, Mormon Temple, Tower Bridge, The Alligator—which have won for the park the nickname "Silent City." Particularly in summer you'll also see plentiful and varied wildlife: cougars, gray foxes, coyote, mule deer, prairie dogs, chipmunks, and more than 160 species of birds. There are unforgettable views from **Sunset Point, Inspiration Point,** and **Bryce Point.** Rim Drive is partly closed in winter. Camping permitted (218 sites).

For **information,** contact the Superintendent, Bryce Canyon National Park, Bryce Canyon, UT 84717 (801/834-5322).

All by itself it's worth the trip to Utah.

CANYONLANDS NATIONAL PARK (248 mi., 396 km, SE of Salt Lake City via I-15, U.S. 6, U.S. 191, and Utah 313: Huge, ocher-orange-colored rocky cliffs frowning down on the sinuous windings of the Green and Colorado Rivers, a fantasy world when seen at sunrise or sunset. Fabulous views from **Dead Horse Point, Grand View Point,** and **Needles Overlook.** Canyonlands National Park is a rocky maze cut out by 300 million years of erosion. The Colorado River, swollen with the waters of its Green River tributary, turns into a runaway bulldozer as it charges through **Cataract Canyon,** cutting gorges deep into the rock and carving out arches, columns, and needles which stand several hundred feet above the floor of the valley.

The park has only 25 mi. (40 km) of surfaced roads, in the **Island in the Sky** sector; the rest, in the **Needles** and **Maze** sectors, can be reached only by Jeep, on foot, or on horseback. Many hiking trails; 80 authorized tentsites. Park open year round.

For **information,** contact the Superintendent, Canyonlands National Park, 125 W. 2nd St., Moab, UT 84532 (801/259-7164).

Don't miss it.

CAPITOL REEF NATIONAL PARK (209 mi., 334 km, SE of Salt Lake City via I-15, Utah 28, U.S. 89, and Utah 24): Wild canyons, beetling cliffs, and rounded rocky domes reminiscent of the Capitol in Washington, whence the name. The interior of the park is difficult of access (the famous bandit Butch Cassidy once took refuge here). Along this enormous mountain wall runs a spectacular unsurfaced scenic highway, the **Scenic Drive,** following the rim of a 25-mi. (40-km) chain of gorges channeled by the Fremont River. Many rock paintings bear witness to Indian cultures from the 9th to the 13th centuries. The north of the park, reachable only by Jeep, displays the most beautiful rock formations, particularly **Cathedral Valley.** Authorized camping (40 sites). Park open year round.

For **information,** contact the Superintendent, Capitol Reef National Park, Torrey, UT 84775 (801/425-3791).

Well worth the side trip.

CEDAR BREAKS NATIONAL MONUMENT (215 mi., 344 km, NE of Las Vegas via I-15, Utah 14, and Utah 148): An enormous natural amphitheater created by erosion in the **Markagunt Plateau,** which rises to 9,840 ft. (3,000 m). Natural rock carvings in beautiful hues of red, orange, violet, and yellow make a vivid contrast with the deep greens of the conifers of Dixie National Forest and the alpine meadows on the mountain peaks, covered with wildflowers from mid-June to mid-Aug. Scenic drive (Rim Drive), 6 mi. (11 km) long. Camping permitted. Park open mid-May to mid-Oct.

For **information,** contact the Superintendent, Cedar Breaks National Monument, P.O. Box 749, Cedar City, UT 84720 (801/586-9451).

An absolute must-see.

DINOSAUR NATIONAL MONUMENT (200 mi., 320
km, east of Salt Lake City along I-80 and U.S. 40): Quarries with many vestiges of prehistoric animals. The **Dinosaur Quarry Visitor Center** has remarkable animal fossils, including an extremely rare 140-million-year-old stegosaurus. Excavations in progress.

The Colorado sector of the park, an area of rugged desert and canyons sometimes as much as 2,625 ft. (800 m) deep, offers unobstructed views of the Green and Yampa Rivers running below; access via U.S. 40, 2 mi. (3 km) east of Dinosaur, Colorado, and a 32-mi. (51-km) unsurfaced road (Harpers Corner Road). Camping permitted. Visitor center and excavation area open year round; rest of the park closed Mid-Nov. to mid-Apr. as dictated by snowfall.

For **information,** contact the Superintendent, Dinosaur National Monument, Harpers Corner Rd. and U.S. 40 (P.O. Box 210), **Dinosaur,** CO 81610 (303/374-2216). Must be seen.

On your way, take a side trip through the **Flaming Gorge National Recreation Area,** 55 mi. (88 km) NW of Dinosaur National Monument via U.S. 40 and U.S. 191, a huge recreation area brought into existence by the 502-ft.-(153-m-) high Flaming Gorge Dam on the Green River. The artificial lake, 91 mi. (146 km) long, offers fishing, sailing, water sports, and marinas. Lovely scenery. For information, contact the Ranger District Office, P.O. Box 157, Dutch John, UT 84023 (801/885-3315). Worth seeing.

It was in **Brown's Hole,** an inaccessible valley downstream from the dam and almost on the Colorado border, that Butch Cassidy, the Sundance Kid, and their "Wild Bunch" used to take refuge after their raids.

GLEN CANYON NATIONAL RECREATION AREA
(286 mi., 457 km, NE of Las Vegas via I-15, Utah 9, and U.S. 89): The park covers about a million acres (more than 4,000 km²), off the beaten tourist track. Its multicolored cliffs are washed by the blue waters of **Lake Powell,** 196 mi. (315 km) long and with 1,900 mi. (3,058 km) of desert shoreline, the second-largest artificial lake (after Lake Mead) in the country. All water sports and wonderful fishing for perch, rainbow trout, moonfish, etc. Superb sunsets. A paradise for hikers and campers. Boat trips from Page to **Rainbow Bridge,** one of the biggest natural rock arches in the world, 278 ft. (85 m) across by 290 ft. (88 m) high; no nature lover should fail to see it. Camping permitted. Park open year round.

For **information,** contact the Superintendent, Glen Canyon National Recreation Area, P.O. Box 1507, Page, AZ 86040 (602/645-2471).

Don't miss it. For further information, see Chapter 40 on Navajoland.

NATURAL BRIDGES NATIONAL MONUMENT (350
mi., 560 km, SE of Salt Lake City via I-15, Utah 28, U.S. 89, Utah 24, and Utah 95): In the comparatively small compass of 7,770 acres (3,148 ha.), this very beautiful, wild, colorful park, inaugurated in 1908, offers the visitor three great rock arches carved by two tributaries of the Colorado: **Kachina Bridge** (206 ft., 63 m, across), **Owachomo Bridge** (180 ft., 55 m, across), and **Sipapu Bridge** (258 ft., 82 m, across). The site, once settled by the legendary Anasazi Indians, has more than 200 interesting architectural ruins, easily reached by the visitor. **Bridge View Drive** is a splendid 8-mi. (13-km) scenic route winding across the canyons from the visitor center. Park open year round, but be careful in bad weather since the area is subject to violent storms.

For **information,** contact the Park Ranger, Star Route, Blanding, UT 84511

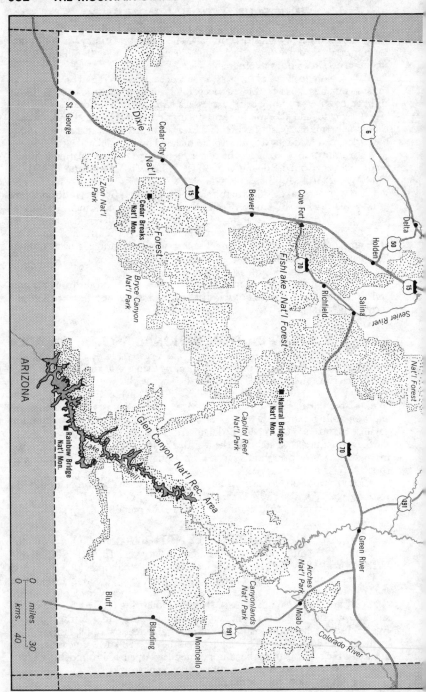

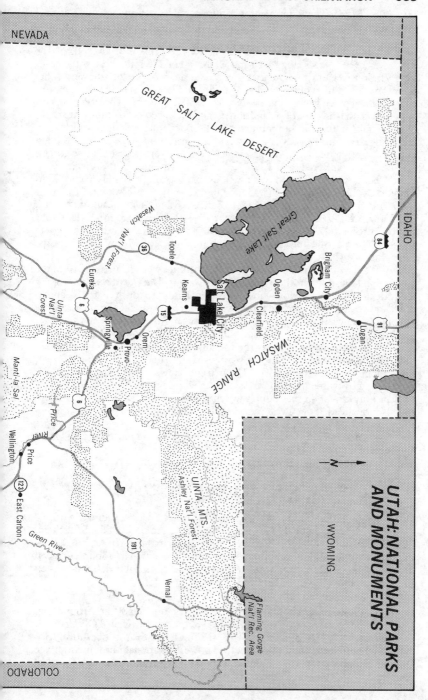

(801/259-5174). The monument is administered from Canyonlands National Park (see above).

※☖☖ **ZION NATIONAL PARK** (169 mi., 270 km, NE of Las Vegas along I-15 and Utah 9): For 225 million years the head-long Virgin River and its tributaries have carved their courses into the sandstone, limestone, and schists of the mighty **Markagunt Plateau,** creating an extraordinary tangle of precipitous gorges as deep as 2,950 ft. (900 m). The river's erosion has produced a landscape of pillars, domes, and rock needles assuming the shapes of cathedrals, statues, and monuments—all under a play of colors which vary, according to the time of day and season of the year, from grayish-white through orange and bright red to the deepest violet. **Zion Canyon,** largest of these gorges, splashed with pink, red, and white, follows the windings of the Virgin River North Fork, and is fringed with woods of poplar, oak, and maple. **Zion Canyon Scenic Drive,** 7 mi. (10 km) long, offers views of some of the most spectacular peaks—**The Sentinel** (7,157 ft., 2,181 m), **Mountain of the Sun** (6,723 ft., 2,049 m), **Lady Mountain** (6,940 ft., 2,115 m), **The Great White Throne** (6,744 ft., 2,056 m)—on its way to the end of the gorge and the **Temple of Sinawava,** a natural amphitheater which is at the same time a lush oasis.

Along the many hiking trails you will encounter some surprises. One of the most popular leads from the Temple of Sinawava to **The Narrows,** an amazing rocky defile through a canyon whose walls seem almost to touch overhead, and to **Weeping Rock Trail,** where the spring welling out from the cliff face appears to be weeping (whence the name). For the more adventurous, there's the **Hidden Canyon Trail** leading to the almost inaccessible canyon, **Zion Shangri La.**

The **Mukuntuweap Valley** (the Indian name for Zion Canyon), has been inhabited by several Indian cultures, particularly the Anasazi, Pueblo, and Paiute, since about the 6th century A.D. The present names, often biblical in origin, were bestowed by the Mormon missionaries who explored the area from 1861 on. The only canyon in the country which can be seen by car "from the inside," Zion National Park is open year round, and is visited by 1.8 million people annually. Camping permitted (376 sites).

For **information,** contact the Superintendent, Zion National Park, Springdale, UT 84767 (801/772-3256).

Worth the trip on its own account.

SUGGESTED TOURING ITINERARIES

※☖☖ **EAST UTAH PARKS** (707 mi., 1,131 km, round trip from/ to Salt Lake City via I-15S, U.S. 6, U.S. 191, Utah 95, Utah 24, U.S. 89, Utah 28, and I-15N): Comprehensive itinerary taking in Arches National Park, Canyonlands National Park, Natural Bridges National Monument, Glen Canyon National Recreation Area, and Capitol Reef National Park (for details on all these, see above).

※☖☖☖ **SOUTH UTAH PARKS** (712 mi., 1,139 km, round trip from/to Las Vegas via I-15N, Utah 14, Utah 148, Utah 14, U.S. 89, Utah 12, U.S. 89, Utah 9, and I-15S): One of the most beautiful trips the U.S. can offer, allowing you to see Cedar Breaks National Monument, Bryce Canyon National Park, Glen Canyon National Recreation Area, and Zion National Park (for details on all these, see above).

ACCOMMODATIONS & DINING
See the listing of toll-free numbers in the Appendix.

Room Rates in Utah National Parks Area	
B (Budget)	up to $30
I (Inexpensive)	$30–$60
M (Moderate)	$60–$90
E (Expensive)	$90–$140
VE (Very Expensive)	$140 and up

Utah National Parks Area Restaurant Prices (per person, excluding drinks and service charges)	
B (Budget)	up to $15
I (Inexpensive)	$15–$25
M (Moderate)	$25–$40
E (Expensive)	$40–$60
VE (Very Expensive)	$60 and up

PERSONAL FAVORITES: The following hotels and restaurants are grouped by location near or in individual parks.

Arches National Park and Canyonlands National Park

Apache Motel, 166 S. 4th St., Moab, UT 84532 (801/259-5727). 33 rms, A/C, color TV, in-rm movies. AE, CB, DC, MC, V. Free parking, pool, free morning coffee. *Note:* A small, inexpensive motel. Attentive svce. Some rms w. kitchenettes. Organizes river rafting trips. Good value. **B, but lower rates out of season.**

Best Western Green Well, 105 S. Main St., Moab, UT 84532 (801/259-6151; toll free, see Best Western). 71 rms, A/C, cable color TV. AE, CB, DC, MC, V. Free parking, pool, rest. (beer served), coffeeshop, bar, crib $4. *Note:* Typical functional motel; huge, comfortable rms; friendly reception. In the center of town. **I–M, but lower rates out of season**

Travelodge Moab, 550 S. Main St., Moab, UT 84532 (801/259-6171; toll free, see Travelodge). 56 rms, A/C, color TV, in-rm movies. AE, CB, DC, MC, V. Free parking, pool, rest., free crib. *Note:* Relatively old, but well-kept motel. Large rms. Friendly reception. Attractive family packages. **I, but lower rates out of season**

Grand Old Ranch House, 1266 N. U.S. 191, Moab, UT (259-5753). A/C. Dinner only, nightly. AE, CB, DC, MC, V. *Note:* The décor is a melange of Old West and Victorian styles (the building dates from 1896). Friendly, efficient svce. Good, German-inspired cuisine. Wine, beer, and liquor. A fine place. *Continental-American.* **I–M**

Bryce Canyon National Park

🍴🍴 **Best Western Ruby's Inn,** Utah 63 (1 mi. N. of the park entrance), UT 84764 (801/834-5341; toll free, see Best Western). 121 rms, A/C, color TV, in-rm movies. AE, CB, DC, MC, V. Free parking, pool, skiing and snowmobiles in winter, rodeos in summer, riding, rest., bar, boutiques, free crib. *Note:* A vast, efficient, modern hotel with a small private lake. Comfortable rms w. balconies and fireplaces. Very good location (5 min. from the park by car). Friendly reception and svce. Organizes helicopter tours of Bryce Canyon. An excellent place to stay. **I–M**

🍴 **Pink Cliffs Bryce Village,** at the intersection of Utah 12 and Utah 22 (2 mi., 3 km, north of the park entrance), Bryce Canyon National Park, UT 84717 (801/834-5303). 54 rms, most w. A/C, most w. color TV. MC, V. Free parking, pool, rest., bar, crib $4. *Note:* Country motel 5 min. by car from the park. Big, comfortable rms; friendly reception and svce. Free airport shuttle. Good value. Open Apr.-Oct. **I, but lower rates out of season**

🍴 **Bryce Canyon Pines,** Utah 12 (6 mi., 10 km, from the NW park entrance) Panguitch, UT 84759 (801/834-5336). 47 rms, most w. A/C, color TV. DC, MC, V. Free parking, pool, horseback riding, rest. (beer served), crib $3. *Note:* Small, inviting motel w. huge, prettily decorated rms, some w. fireplaces. Free airport shuttle. Horseback excursions into the canyon in summer. Good value. **I, but lower rates Nov.-June**

☼🍴 **Bryce Canyon Lodge,** Bryce Canyon National Park, UT 84717 (801/834-5361). 110 rms (cottages), a third w. A/C. AE, CB, DC, MC, V. Free parking, pool, horseback riding, rest., coffeeshop, cinema, grocery store. *Note:* Wonderful location in the heart of the park. Some rms modern and comfortable, others aging a little. Acceptable rest. Open mid-May to Sept.; closed the rest of the year. Horseback or muleback trips into the canyon. For reservations, contact T. W. Services, 451 N. Main St., Cedar City, UT 84720 (801/586-7686). **I–M**

Capitol Reef National Park

🍴 **Rim Rock,** on Utah 24, 3 mi. (5 km), east of Torrey, UT 84775 (801/425-3843). 21 rms, no A/C, cable color TV. AE, MC, V. Free parking, coffeeshop, private lake. *Note:* Rudimentary but acceptable levels of comfort; fine view of the park. Jeep excursions organized. Open Apr.-Oct. **I, but lower rates out of season**

Cedar Breaks National Monument

🍴🍴 **Best Western El Rey Inn,** 80 S. Main St., Cedar City, UT 84720 (801/586-6518; toll free, see Best Western), 26 mi. (41 km) from the park entrance. 73 rms, A/C, color TV, in-rm movies. AE, CB, DC, MC, V. Free parking, pool, sauna, rest. (beer served), rm svce, crib $4. *Note:* Comfortable, functional rms w. refrigerators. Reception w. a smile; acceptable rest. (Sullivan's). Free airport shuttle. **I, but lower rates out of season**

Dinosaur National Monument

🍴🍴 **Raintree Plaza** (formerly the Sheraton Inn), 1684 W. U.S. 40, Vernal, UT 84078 (801/789-9550), 19 mi. (30 km) west of the park entrance. 104 rms, A/C, color TV, in-rm movies. AE, CB, DC, MC, V. Free parking, pool, putting green, rest., bar, rm svce, disco, free breakfast, free crib. *Note:* Modern, comfortable motel; spacious rms; efficient reception and svce. The best place to stay in the region. **I–M**

⚲ **Weston Lamplighter Inn,** 120 E. Main St., Vernal, UT 84078 (801/789-0312), 19 mi. (30 km) west of the park entrance. 200 rms, A/C, color TV, in-rm movies. AE, CB, DC, MC, V. Free parking, pool, coffeeshop, valet svce, crib $5. *Note:* Inviting, well-run small motel; functionally comfortable. Good value. **I, but lower rates out of season**

Glen Canyon & Rainbow Bridge

⚲⚲ **Wahweap Lodge and Marina,** on U.S. 89, Page, AZ 86040 (602/645-2433; toll free 800/528-6154), 5 mi. (8 km) NW of Glen Canyon Bridge. 270 rms, A/C, color TV, in-rm movies. AE, CB, DC, MC, V. Free parking, pool, tennis court, beach, boating, fishing, rest., coffeeshop, bar, rm svce, disco, crib $5. *Note:* Modern building, splendidly located on Lake Powell. Spacious, comfortable rms w. balconies or patios, some w. refrigerators. Reception and svce on the chilly side. Free airport shuttle. One- or several-day excursions arranged on Lake Powell and to Rainbow Bridge. Resv. advised, well ahead. **I–M, but lower rates out of season**

⚲⚲ **Holiday Inn Page,** 287 N. Lake Powell Blvd., Page, AZ 86040 (602/645-8851; toll free, see Holiday Inns), 1 mi. (2 km) from Glen Canyon Bridge. 129 rms, A/C, color TV, in-rm movies. AE, CB, DC, MC, V. Free parking, pool, rest., bar, rm svce, hrdrsr, free crib. *Note:* Typical Holiday Inn; huge, comfortable rms w. balconies or patios, the best overlooking Lake Powell. Good svce. Free airport shuttle. **I–M, but lower rates out of season**

⚲ **Lake Powell Motel,** on U.S. 89, Page, AZ 86040 (602/645-2477), 5 mi. (8 km) northwest of Glen Canyon Bridge. 24 rms, A/C, color TV. AE, CB, DC, MC, V. Free parking, free a.m. coffee, crib $5. *Note:* Modest, unpretentious little motel w. a fine view of Glen Canyon and Lake Powell. Boats for rent; free airport shuttle. **I, but lower rates out of season**

⚱ **Glen Canyon Steak House,** 201 N. Lake Powell Blvd., Page, (602/645-3363). A/C. Lunch/dinner daily. MC, V. *Note:* Classic western steakhouse. Bar; dancing. **I**

Natural Bridges National Monument

⚲ **Best Western Gateway,** 88 E. Center St., Blanding, UT 84511 (801/678-2278; toll free, see Best Western), 46 mi. (74 km) east of the park entrance. 57 rms, A/C, color TV, in-rm movies. AE, CB, DC, MC, V. Free parking, pool, nearby coffeeshop. *Note:* Comfortable, inviting small motel 45-min. drive from Natural Bridges National Monument. Free airport shuttle. **I**

⚲ **San Juan Inn,** on U.S. 163 at the San Juan River, Mexican Hat, UT 84531 (801/683-2220). 22 rms, A/C, color TV. AE, MC, V. Free parking, coffeeshop (beer served), crib $4. *Note:* Modest but serviceable motel on the San Juan River, 15-min. drive from Monument Valley and 45 min. from Natural Bridges National Monument. Good value on balance. Arranges rafting trips down the river and conducted tours of Monument Valley. **I**

Zion National Park

☀⚲⚲ **Best Western Driftwood Lodge,** on Utah 9, Springdale, UT 84767 (801/772-3262; toll free, see Best Western), 2 mi. (3.5 km) south of the park entrance. 25 rms, A/C, color TV. AE, CB, DC, MC, V. Free parking, pool, rest. (beer and wine served), rm svce, crib $2. *Note:* Charming little motel surrounded by gardens and trees. Comfortable rms w. balconies, overlooking the park; friendly reception and svce. Very acceptable rest. An excellent place to stay. **I–M, but lower rates out of season**

☀️ 🛎 **Zion Lodge,** Scenic Dr., Zion National Park, UT 84767 (801/772-3213). 121 rms, A/C. AE, CB, DC, MC, V. Free parking, rest. (beer served), coffeeshop. *Note:* The only motel inside the park itself, in a superb natural setting. Friendly reception and svce; rustic comforts. Horseback excursions and conducted bus tours through the canyon arranged. For resv., contact T.W. Services, 451 N. Main St. (P.O. Box 400), Cedar City, UT 84720 (801/586-7686). Open May to mid-Oct. **I–M**

🛎 **Bumbleberry Inn,** 897 Zion Park Blvd. (Utah 9), Springdale, UT 84767 (801/772-3224), 1 mi. (1.6 km) south of the park entrance. 24 rms, A/C, color TV. CB, DC, MC, V. Free parking, pool, rest. *Note:* Well-run, functional small motel. Spacious rms, some w. balconies. Inviting garden. Good value. **I, but lower rates out of season**

🛎 **Pioneer Lodge,** 838 Zion Park Blvd. (Utah 9), Springdale, UT 84767 (801/772-3233), 1 mi. (1.6 km) south of the park entrance. 40 rms, A/C, color TV. MC, V. Free parking, pool, mini-golf, rest. *Note:* Unpretentious motel offering decent standards of comfort; caters mostly to families. **I, but lower rates out of season**

YELLOWSTONE NATIONAL PARK🔥🔥🔥

□ □ □

And Grand Teton National Park

A masterpiece of unspoiled nature, **Yellowstone National Park** is the most beautiful in the U.S., and probably in the world; nowhere else on the surface of the planet will you find such an astonishing variety of scenery gathered together in one place. With its boiling geysers, hot springs, steep canyons, mud volcanoes, frozen lakes, deep pine forests, dizzying waterfalls, and fossilized trees, Yellowstone is a glorious, untamed cross section of the North American continent— and one which, geologists tell us, has been three billion years in the making.

The wildlife is the entire animal kingdom in a nutshell: bison, elk, deer, pronghorn, black bear, grizzly, wild sheep, coyote, cougar, beaver, muskrat, and countless species of birds and fish. The whole great volcanic plateau, 60 mi. (100 km) long and 56 mi. (90 km) wide, lying some 7,870 ft. (2,400 m) above sea level, is stitched together by 250 mi. (400 km) of impeccably surfaced roads and more than 1,000 mi. (1,600 km) of marked trails. The park is open, weather permitting, from May 1 to Oct. 31, but its northern and northeastern entrances remain open year round (for snowmobiles only in winter). In all, almost 2½ million people every summer, and almost 100,000 every winter, visit the park, its six hotels and 12 campgrounds. Needless to say, reservations are a must for the peak months of July and Aug.

The uncanny alliance of the two normally hostile elements of fire and water constitute Yellowstone's principal tourist attractions. The park possesses no fewer than 10,000 hot springs and almost 200 geysers bubbling up from the bowels of the earth. To the amazement of many visitors, some geysers like the famous **Old Faithful** spew their columns of steam and boiling water dozens of feet into the air with clockwork regularity; others lie dormant for weeks, or years, before bursting forth again. All around lies an ominous landscape of evil-smelling fumaroles, multicolored pools, and boiling cauldrons of bubbling, sulfurous mud. Yet only a few miles away, the golden splendor of the **Grand Canyon of the Yellowstone** with its falls higher than Niagara's, or the azure depths of **Yellowstone Lake,** the largest mountain lake in the country at an elevation of 7,731 ft. (2,357 m), await to take your mind off the nightmare spectacle of **Mud Volcano** or **Dragon Mouth.**

Yellowstone is too large, and too varied, for a quick visit; many of its slopes are still untrodden, and can be reached only on foot or horseback. In spite of the catastrophic fires of the 1988 summer, that charred over 800,000 of the 2.2 million acres of the park, this wonder of nature, as large as the state of Rhode Island, is one of the last wilderness reserves in the civilized world.

Grand Teton National Park, only one-seventh the size of Yellowstone and more mountainous in its contours, is open year round. Its impressive mountain range numbers 31 peaks rising above 10,825 ft. (3,300 m); the highest, **Grand Teton** itself, soars to 13,770 ft. (4,197 m). This is a "young" granite range, little more than ten million years old. It owes its name to the romantic imagination of 19th-century French-Canadian trappers, who saw in these sparkling, pointed snow-capped peaks rising above the valley of **Jackson Hole,** some fancied likeness to a woman's breast. More than 187 mi. (300 km) of marked trails offer an unlimited choice of hiking or skiing excursions, according to the season. With the torrential **Snake River,** deep forests, lakes full of fish, and inaccessible mountain peaks, Grand Teton National Park encompasses some of the most beautiful natural landscapes in the U.S.

Wildlife Warning! While Yellowstone is a paradise for campers and mobile-home owners, camping is subject to very strict rules enforced by watchful rangers. As in all national parks, camping in the wild is strictly forbidden. There are also some simple precautions that must be taken regarding animals. Living free as they do, with no reason to fear human beings, animals will allow themselves to be photographed from quite close, especially around dawn and sunset. However, prudence is mandatory if you come suddenly face to face with a bear (there are about 500 black bear and 200 grizzly inside the park), an elk, or a buffalo, of which there are several thousand. Never feed, or hold food within reach of, an animal.

BASIC FACTS: State of Wyoming (with slight enroachments into the neighboring states of Idaho and Montana). Area Code: 307. Time Zone: Mountain Time. ZIP Codes: Yellowstone, 82190; Grand Teton, 83013. Inaugurated: 1872 (Yellowstone is the oldest nature reserve in the world); 1929 (Grand Teton). Area: Yellowstone, 3,472 sq. mi. (8,993 sq. km); Grand Teton, 486 sq. mi. (1,260 sq. km).

CLIMATE: At these altitudes, winter is long and icy at Yellowstone and Grand Teton; mean temperatures are 5°F (−15°C). Heavy snowfalls, sometimes 16 ft. (5 m) or more, make it very difficult to get around, even by snowmobile, from late Oct. through Apr. Summer is short, sunny, and cool; everyone wears a sweater in the evening. You should take a raincoat or poncho too, because of occasional heavy rain in the afternoon. Fall is the perfect time for the color photographer. Whatever the season, don't try a swim in the lakes; even in summer the water temperature never goes above 40°F (5°C), and if you were to fall in you wouldn't survive as long as half an hour.

DISTANCES: Denver, 638 mi. (1,022 km); Mount Rushmore, 549 mi. (875 km); Salt Lake City, 325 mi. (520 km); Seattle, 762 mi. (1,219 km).

ARRIVAL & TRANSIT INFORMATION

NEAREST AIRPORTS: Bozeman Gallatin Field (BZN), 131 mi. (210 km) NW of Yellowstone National Park; open year round.

Jackson Hole (JAC), 13 mi. (21 km) south of Grand Teton National Park and 79 mi. (128 km) south of Yellowstone National Park; open year round.

West Yellowstone (WYS), 30 mi. (48 km) west of Yellowstone National Park; open in summer only.

AIRLINES: Several airlines fly into the area's three airports: At **Bozeman Gallatin Field:** Continental (406/586-4749); Delta (toll free 800/221-1212), and Northwest (toll free 800/225-2525).

At Jackson Hole: Continental (307/733-9701) and Delta (toll free 800/221-1212).

At West Yellowstone: Delta Connection (toll free 800/453-9417), in summer only.

BUS OR CAR RENTAL?: Greyhound serves neither Yellowstone nor Grand Teton National Park.

The **Yellowstone National Park Co.** (307/344-7901) provides a shuttle bus from **Bozeman** (two departures daily), **Jackson** (two departures daily), and **West Yellowstone** (five departures daily) during the summer. The same company operates bus tours inside Yellowstone Park.

Given the distances, it makes sense to rent a car, but rates are relatively high and the choice of models is restricted.

CAR RENTAL: Rental cars are available at all three area airports. At Bozeman Gallatin Field: Avis (406/388-6414), Budget (406/388-4091), Hertz (406/388-6939), and National (406/388-6694).

At Jackson Hole: Avis (307/733-3422), Budget (307/733-1776), Hertz (307/733-2272), and National (307/733-4132).

At West Yellowstone Airport (summer only): Avis (406/646-7635), Budget (406/646-7882), Hertz (406/646-7753), and National (406/646-7670).

TRAIN: The nearest AMTRAK station is 135 mi. (215 km) SW of Grand Teton National Park at 300 S. Harrison Ave., Pocatello, Idaho (toll free 800/872-7245).

BUS: Greyhound has stations at 625 N. 7th St., Bozeman (406/587-3110), open year round; and at 127 Yellowstone Ave., West Yellowstone (406/646-7666), open in summer only.

INFORMATION & TOURS

TOURIST INFORMATION: The Cody County Chamber of Commerce, 836 Sheridan Ave. (P.O. Box 2777), Cody, WY 82414 (307/587-2297).

Grand Teton National Park: Superintendent, P.O. Drawer 170, Moose, WY 83012 (307/733-2880). There are visitors centers at Colter Bay, Jenny Lake, and Moose.

Jackson Hole Area Chamber of Commerce, 532 N. Cache St. (P.O. Box E-MTG), Jackson, WY 83001 (307/733-3316).

Yellowstone National Park: Superintendent, P.O. Box 168, Mammoth Hot Springs, WY 82190 (307/344-7381). There are visitors centers at Canyon Village, Fishing Bridge, Grant Village, Mammoth Hot Springs, Norris, and Old Faithful.

GUIDED TOURS: Gray Line Tours (bus): Conducted bus tours of Grand Teton and Yellowstone National Parks. Serves principal hotels in Jackson (307/733-4325) and West Yellowstone (406/646-9374).

TW Services, Inc. (bus/snowmobile) (307/344-7901): All-season tourist excursions in Yellowstone National Park; serves the park's principal hotels at Canyon Village, Fishing Bridge, Mammoth Hot Springs, and Old Faithful.

SIGHTS, ATTRACTIONS, & ACTIVITIES

ADVENTURES: Exum School of Mountaineering (climbing), P.O. Box 56,

Moose, WY 83012 (307/733-2297): Two-day climbs, with guides, in Grand Teton National Park (summer only). Also climbing school.

L.D. Frome Wagons West (covered wagons), Afton, WY 83110 (307/886-5240; toll free 800/433-1595): Back to the days of the pioneers with two- four-, or six-day covered-wagon trips. Serves the principal Jackson hotels; reservations a must. Mon.-Sat, late May to early Sept. Spectacular.

Jackson Hole Climbing School (climbing), P.O. Box 547, Teton Village, WY 83205 (307/733-4979): Climbing school and guided climbs in summer. For the dedicated.

Lewis & Clark Expeditions (boat), Crabtree Corner at Town Square, Jackson, WY 83001 (307/733-4022): Whitewater float trips down the Grand Canyon of Snake River, a three- to six-hour trip. June to mid-Sept. Amusing.

National Park Float Trips (boat), P.O. Box 120M, Moose, WY 83012 (307/733-5500): Boat or raft trips in Grand Teton National Park; bus connection from Jackson. Late May to mid-Sept.

Teton Country Prairie Schooner Holiday (covered wagons), Bar-T-Five Ranch, P.O. Box 2140, Jackson, WY 83001 (307/733-5386): Four-day covered-wagon trip between Yellowstone National Park and Grand Teton National Park; a guaranteed whiff of adventure. $400 per head, including meals. Mid June to Aug.

Wyoming River Trips (boat), 1701 Sheridan Ave., Cody, WY 82414 (307/527-7238): Float trips through Red Rock Shoshone Canyon; spectacular. June to mid-Sept.

GRAND TETON NATIONAL PARK: The entrance is 13 mi. (21 km) north of Jackson via U.S. 89.

Jackson Hole, 8 mi. (13 km) north from Jackson on U.S. 89: A huge basin ("hole" was the vernacular term for basin, or valley, among the *coureurs de bois*) of glacial origin, 50 mi. (80 km) long and 14 mi. (23 km) wide at its widest, traversed by the turbulent **Snake River** and dotted by clear lakes teeming with fish: **Jackson Lake, Jenny Lake, Phelps Lake, Emma Matilda Lake,** etc. This high alpine valley, moist and fertile, with an abundance of elk, deer, buffalo, white pelicans, duck, and wild geese, has some magnificent views across to the granite crests of the **Grand Teton Range,** a sight you shouldn't miss. Many **campsites,** particularly at Colter Bay, Jenny Lake, Lizard Creek, Gros Ventre, and Signal Mountain. **Boat rental** at Jackson and Jenny Lakes. The **John D. Rockefeller Pkwy.,** (U.S. 89), crossing the park from north to south, is usable year round. For information on road conditions, weather, and park activities, call (307)733-2220. Don't miss it.

Rendezvous Peak, 12 mi. (19 km) NW of Jackson via Wyo. 22 and Wyo. 390: Cable car from **Teton Village** to the top of Rendezvous Peak, 10,450 ft. (3,185 m) high. Wonderful view of Jackson Hole Valley and the Grand Tetons. Late May to late Sept. For information, call (307)733-2292. Don't miss it.

Scenic Drives

Bridger-Teton National Forest, 56 mi. (89 km) between Dubois and Moran Junction along U.S. 26: Splendid forest scenery; worth going out of your way for.

John D. Rockefeller Parkway, 58 mi. (92 km) between Jackson and Yellowstone National Park along U.S. 89: Follows the Snake River and the shore of Jackson Lake through very fine mountain scenery. Spectacular; not to be missed.

Signal Mountain Rd., 13 mi. (20 km) NE of Moose Junction via Teton Park Rd.: Scenic drive 5 mi. (8 km) long; from the top you'll have an unequalled view of Jackson Lake and the surrounding peaks. Well worth the detour.

☼ ♨♨♨ **YELLOWSTONE NATIONAL PARK:** The main entrance is 59 mi. (95 km) north of Jackson via U.S. 89; east entrance, 53 mi. (85 km) west of Cody via U.S. 20; north entrance, 85 mi. (136 km) SE of Bozeman via I-90 and U.S. 89.

♨ **Gibbon Falls,** 29 mi. (47 km) south of Mammoth Hot Springs on Grand Loop Rd.: Broad falls, with a drop of 84 ft. (26 m) along the river of the same name. Worth a look.

☼ ♨♨ **Grand Canyon of the Yellowstone,** 37 mi. (60 km) SE of Mammoth Hot Springs on Grand Loop Rd.: The most glorious scenery in the park. Two dizzying falls, the 308-ft. (94-m) **Lower Falls** (1½ times the height of Niagara) and the 109-ft. (33-m) **Upper Falls.** Wild gorges, up to 1,200 ft. (366 m) deep in places, with a perpetual play of yellow-to-orange color over their walls (whence the name of the Yellowstone River). A scenic drive links the main observation points, of which those at **Inspiration Point** and **Artist Point** are the most interesting. Worth the trip all by itself.

♨ **Obsidian Cliff,** 15 mi. (24 km) south of Mammoth Hot Springs on Grand Loop Rd.: A great cliff, 246 ft. (75 m) high and 885 ft. (270 m) wide composed of volcanic glass (obsidian), from which the Indians used to quarry material for their arrowheads. Should be seen.

♨ **Shoshone Lake,** 8 mi. (13 km) east of Old Faithful on Grand Loop Rd., then 2½ mi. (4 km) south by footpath: Beautiful wild isolated lake, reachable only on foot or on horseback. For lovers of unspoiled nature.

☼ ♨ **Tower Falls,** 21 mi. (33 km) east of Mammoth Hot Springs on Grand Loop Rd.: Spectacular 132-ft. (40-m) falls on the Yellowstone River; its name comes from its rock formations in the shape of towers or broken columns. Should definitely be seen.

♨ **Virginia Cascades,** 24 mi. (38 km) SE of Mammoth Hot Springs on Grand Loop Rd.: Beautiful waterfalls and rapids in the depths of the forest; one-way scenic drive. Well worth the side trip.

☼ ♨♨ **Yellowstone Lake,** 22 mi. (36 km) north of the southern entrance to the park on U.S. 89: The highest (7,731 ft., 2,357 m), and, with its azure-blue waters, perhaps the most beautiful mountain lake in the U.S. It covers 138 sq. mi. (360 sq. km) and is 308 ft. (94 m) deep at its deepest. The water is icy-cold even in summer. View clear over to the distant **Absaroka Range,** with a dozen peaks rising above 9,840 ft. (3,000 m). Boat trips from **Bridge Bay Marina** and **Grant Village Marina.** Don't miss it.

Geysers and Thermal Springs

Yellowstone National Park has almost 200 geysers, more than any other place in the world except Iceland and New Zealand, and some 10,000 hot springs. Among the most impressive are:

♨ **Artist Paint Pots,** between Norris Junction and Madison Junction along Grand Loop Rd.: A little footpath leads from Gibbon Meadows to these multicolored hot springs, which you should try to see.

♨ **Beryl Spring,** between Norris Junction and Madison Junction along Grand Loop Rd.: One of the most beautiful springs in the park; must be seen.

☼ ♨ **Lower Geyser Basin,** between Madison Junction and Old Faithful along Grand Loop Rd.: Comprises 25 geysers and 700

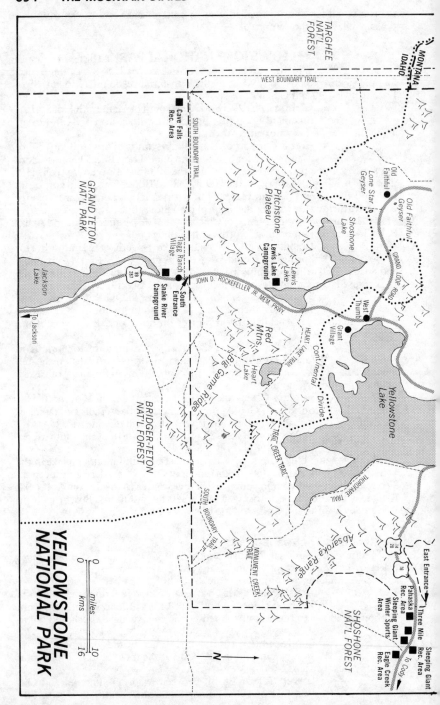

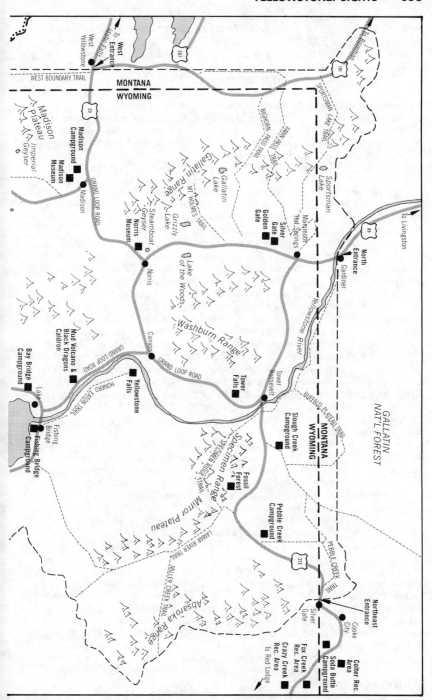

hot springs, among them **Fountain Paint Pot,** a flamboyant yellow-and-red cauldron, and two reliable geysers: **Great Fountain Geyser** erupts every six to ten hours to a height of 98–196 ft. (30–60 m), and **White Dome Geyser** erupts every 17–90 min. to a height of 19–29 ft. (6–9 m), with a fine concretion dome. An absolute must-see.

☀☗☗ **Mammoth Hot Springs,** 5 mi. (8 km) south of the northern entrance to the park on U.S. 89: Fantastic limestone terraces formed from suspended material deposited by some 60 hot springs issuing at temperatures from 64° to 165° F (18° to 74° C). The steps, in a variety of shades of white, bright yellow, ocher, and green, have been built up since prehistoric times to heights of as much as 196 ft. (60 m) in places. A wonder of natural beauty. Scenic drive to the top; don't miss it.

☀☗ **Midway Geyser Basin,** between Madison Junction and Old Faithful along Grand Loop Rd.: Famous for its colorful hot springs, particularly the **Excelsior Geyser,** a deep-blue lake 393 ft. (120 m) long on the site of a huge geyser which has been dormant since 1888, and the **Grand Prismatic Spring,** a great smoking pool whose waters refract all the colors of the rainbow (elevated observation road). Don't miss it.

☗ **Monument Geyser,** between Norris Junction and Madison Junction along Grand Loop Rd.: Along a little footpath from the bridge across the Gibbon River, you'll have a two-hour walk to this continually active geyser with a throw of 5–10 ft. (1.5–3 m). Worth seeing.

☀☗ **Mud Volcano and Black Dragon's Cauldron,** between Yellowstone Lake and Canyon Village along Grand Loop Dr.: Huge witches' cauldron, grumbling and boiling, whose superheated mud wells up and bursts in great evil-smelling bubbles. A fascinating sight, not to be missed.

☀☗☗ **Norris Geyser Basin,** 1 mi. (2 km) west of Norris Junction along Grand Loop Dr.: Has some of the park's most spectacular hot springs, including the lovely emerald-colored **Emerald Springs** and the astonishing rainbow-colored **Porcelain Basin** (elevated observation road), as well as such impressive geysers as **Constant Geyser** (erupts several times an hour to a height of 30–40 ft., 9–12 m), and **Steamboat Geyser,** the highest in the park, with a throw of 20–380 ft. (6–116 m) every 30–60 seconds. Visitor center at **Norris.** Don't miss it.

☀☗☗ **Old Faithful,** in front of the Old Faithful Inn at Old Faithful: The park's most famous, and most photographed, attraction. For more than a century Old Faithful has erupted with clockwork regularity for 2–5 min., to a mean height of 130 ft. (40 m), once an hour. Since 1986, however, it has shown signs of flagging, and now erupts only every 70 min., more or less. A boon to devotees of souvenir snapshots; don't miss it.

☗ **Sulphur Cauldron,** between Yellowstone Lake and Canyon Village along Grand Loop Rd.: Boiling springs emitting sulfurous steam along the steep banks of the Yellowstone River. Worth seeing.

☀☗☗ **Upper Geyser Basin,** between Madison Junction and Old Faithful along Grand Loop Rd.: Nearly 70 geysers clustered around Old Faithful; among the most spectacular are **Castle Geyser** (every 3–10 hr; 65–100 ft., 20–30 m), **Daisy Geyser** (irregular; 75 ft., 23 m), **Grand Geyser** (every 18–90 hr; 200 ft., 60 m), and **River Side Geyser** (every 6–9 hr; 75 ft., 23 m). Across Grand Loop Rd. in **Black Sand Basin** are countless petrified trees and a splendid emerald-green hot spring, **Emerald Pool,** issuing at 158° F (70° C). The most impressive group of geological phenomena in the park; don't miss it.

☗ **West Thumb Geyser Basin,** on the western shore of Yellowstone Lake by Grand Loop Rd.: Miniature geysers and an array of hot springs beside the lake; beautiful scenery. A must-see.

Scenic Drives

☀☖ **Buffalo Bill Highway,** 80 mi. (128 km) between Fishing Bridge, Yellowstone Lake, and Cody along U.S. 20: A two-hour drive of rare scenic splendor passing **Shoshone Canyon, Sylvan Pass,** and the **Absaroka Mountains.** Wonderful view of **Yellowstone Lake** from **Lake Butte** (8,344 ft., 2,544 m). Well worth the side trip.

☀☖☖ **Canyon Rim Scenic Road,** 1 mi. (1.6 km) east or 2½ mi. (4 km) south of Canyon Village on Grand Loop Rd.: A scenic drive of some 5 mi. (8 km), partly on a one-way highway, along both rims of the Grand Canyon of the Yellowstone. Wonderful views of gorges and falls from **Inspiration Point, Lookout Point, Artist Point,** and **Grandview Point;** don't miss it.

☀☖☖ **Grand Loop Road,** 22 mi. (35 km) north of the southern entrance to the park: Yellowstone Park's busiest road, a 142-mi. (227 km) "figure 8," linking all the park's scenic sights and tourist attractions. It's worth the trip all by itself.

☀☖☖ **Mount Washburn Trail,** 10 mi. (17 km) NE of Canyon Village along Grand Loop Rd.: If you make an 8-mi. (13-km) hike to the 10,243-ft. (3,122-m) top of **Mount Washburn** (6½-hr. round trip), you'll find the most beautiful view in the entire park, from the distant **Grand Tetons** to **Jackson Lake.** Only for seasoned walkers.

SPECIAL EVENTS: For the exact schedule of events below, consult the **Cody County Chamber of Commerce** and **Jackson Hole Area Chamber of Commerce** (see "Tourist Information," above).

Cody

Frontier Festival (late June): Music, dancing, craft shows, open-air meals, horse shows, games . . . the Old West come to life again.

Plains Indian Powwow (late June): Festival of traditional Indian music and dance; many tribes from the U.S. and Canada take part. Colorful.

Jackson

"The Shootout" (Memorial Day to Labor Day): Amusing parody of a western melodrama performed every evening in the Town Square.

Jackson Hole Rodeo (June-Aug.): Real cowboy atmosphere; nightly except Sun. and Tues. For information, call (307)733-6041.

Jackson Hole Fall Arts Festival (three weeks from mid-Sept. to early Oct.): Art shows, performances, dance, theater, film festival, etc.

Teton Village

Grand Teton Music Festival (July-Aug.): Symphony concerts, chamber music, classical recitals. More than 35 different programs. A very popular festival; for information, call (307)733-3155.

WINTER SPORTS RESORTS: ☖☖ **Alta-Grand Targhee Resort,** 42 mi. (67 km) NW of Jackson via Wyo. 22, Idaho 31, and Idaho 33 (307/353-2304): Three lifts; open mid-Nov. to mid-Apr.

☖ **Old Faithful,** 30 mi. (48 km) SE of West Yellowstone via U.S. 20 and Grand Loop Rd. (307/344-7381): No lifts; cross-country only. Open Mid-Dec. to mid-Mar.

☖ **Snow King Mountain,** 0.6 mi. (1 km) south of Jackson on U.S. 26 (307/733-5200): Three lifts; Open Dec.-Apr.

🔭 **Teton Village,** 13 mi. (20 km) NW of Jackson via Wyo. 22 and Wyo. 390 (703/733-2292): One cable car, eight lifts. Also cross-country skiing, climbing. Open Dec. to mid-Apr.

ACCOMMODATIONS

See the listing of toll-free numbers in the Appendix.

Room Rates in the Yellowstone National Park Area	
B (Budget)	up to $30
I (Inexpensive)	$30–$60
M (Moderate)	$60–$90
E (Expensive)	$90–$140
VE (Very Expensive)	$140 and up

Personal Favorites Inside the Parks (in order of preference)

GRAND TETON. For reservations for the three hotels listed, contact **Grand Teton Lodge Co.,** P.O. Box 250, Moran, WY 83013 (307/543-2855).

☀️🏨♿ **Jackson Lake Lodge,** on U.S. 89, Moran, WY 83013 (307/543-2855). 385 rms (42 in hotel, others in motel and bungalows), A/C. AE, MC, V. Free parking, pool, horseback riding, bicycles, rest. (Mural Room), bar, rm svce (until 10 p.m.), hrdrsr, airport shuttle, boutiques, free crib. *Note:* Large, modern, comfortable chalet-hotel overlooking Jackson Lake. The best rms (w. patios or balconies) are in the main building; the bungalows are more rustic. Magnificent view of the Grand Tetons; beautiful glass-walled dining rm overlooking the lake. Very acceptable food and svce. The best place to stay in Grand Teton National Park; open June to mid-Sept. only. **M–E**

☀️🏨♿ **Jenny Lake Lodge,** Jenny Lake Rd., Moran, WY 83013 (307/733-4647). 30 bungalows, no A/C. AE, MC, V. Free parking, fishing, horseback riding, bicycles, rest. *Note:* Log-cabin bungalows in the woods, w. private patios. Rustic comfort; for nature lovers. Has the best rest. in the park (resv. a must). Cheerful reception; airport shuttle. Open June-Sept. **VE (MAP)**

🏨 **Colter Bay Village,** on U.S. 89, Moran, WY 83013 (307/543-2855). 209 rms in bungalows, no A/C. AE, MC, V. Free parking, fishing, marina, horseback riding, rest., bar, coffeeshop, boutiques, free crib. Also campground and sites for motor homes. *Note:* Bungalows on Jackson Lake; pleasing rustic décor. Very good value. Open May-Sept. **I–M**

YELLOWSTONE. For reservations for the five hotels listed, contact **TW Recreational Services,** Yellowstone National Park, WY 82190 (307/344-7311). Unless otherwise indicated none of the hotels listed below is air-conditioned.

☀️🏨 **Old Faithful Inn,** Grand Loop Rd., Yellowstone National Park, WY 82190 (307/344-7311). 324 rms (only two-thirds w. baths). AE, MC, V. Free parking, coffeeshop, bar, nightclub, free crib. *Note:* A 1902 hotel in a diverting baroque-chalet style; wonderful entrance lobby, all in wood and four stories high. Rms are spacious but stark (ask for one overlooking the Old Faithful geyser). The plumbing could use some improvements, as could the food and the reception. The place is pleasant on balance, however—and its situation is like no other in the world. Open May to mid-Oct. only; the neighboring **Old Faithful Snow Lodge** (31 rms) is open Dec.-Mar. **I–M**

Lake Yellowstone Hotel, Grand Loop Rd., Yellowstone National Park, WY 82190 (307/344-7311). 290 rms (only 50% w. baths). AE, MC, V. Free parking, fishing, boating, rest., bar, hrdrsr., free crib. *Note:* Aging but still-elegant hotel beautifully situated on the shores of Yellowstone Lake. Huge, relatively comfortable rms (ask for a lake view); agreeable glass-walled dining rm; food and svce acceptable but no better. Open end of May through Sept. Also 110 bungalows offering rudimentary comforts. **I–M**

Canyon Village Lodge, Grand Loop Rd., Yellowstone National Park, WY 82190 (703/344-7311). 58 rms (chalets). AE, MC, V. Free parking, horseback riding, rest., bar, hrdrsr, boutiques, free crib. *Note:* Rustic motel of comfortable little cottages. Mediocre food, as everywhere in the park. Open May-Sept. **I–M**

Grant Village, 2 mi. south of Grand Loop Rd. on U.S. 89, Yellowstone National Park, WY 82190 (307/344-7311). 300 rms. AE, DC, MC, V. Free parking, coffeeshop, bar. *Note:* The newest (1984) and most up-to-date motel in the park, on Yellowstone Lake. Functionally comfortable. Open June-Sept. **I**

Mammoth Hot Springs Hotel, Grand Loop Rd., and U.S. 89, Yellowstone National Park, WY 82190 (307/344-7311). 94 rms (two-thirds w. baths) and 121 bungalows (half w. baths). AE, MC, V. Free parking, adjoining coffeeshop, bar, free crib. *Note:* Rundown old hotel 5 mi. (8 km) south of the northern park entrance. Ask for a bungalow overlooking the petrified hot springs. Dour reception; resolutely mediocre coffeeshop. Closed Oct.-Nov. and Apr.; open all the rest of the year. **B–I**

Personal Favorites Outside the Parks (in order of preference)

Jackson Hole Racquet Club, Star Route 362A, Teton Village, WY 83001 (307/733-3990); toll free 800/443-8616). 120 suites and apartments, cable color TV. AE, MC, V. Free parking, two pools, tennis court, health club, sauna, skiing, rest., bar, rm svce, grocery store, free crib. *Note:* The most luxurious resort hotel in the area. Elegantly countrified décor. Spacious, comfortable suites w. kitchenettes, fireplaces, and balconies or private patios; also two- or three-bedroom apartments. Flawless reception and svce; clientele of groups and racquets buffs. Open year round; reserve a long time ahead. Free shuttle to ski slopes. **E–VE, but lower rates out of season**

Best Western Alpenhof Lodge, on Wyo. 390, Teton Village, WY 83025 (307/733-3242; toll free, see Best Western). 40 rms, cable color TV. AE, CB, DC, MC, V. Free parking, pool, sauna, rest. (Alpenhof), rm svce, crib $6. *Note:* Charming little alpine chalet; inviting rms, most w. balconies. Attentive svce; excellent rest. (one of the best in the area). Ideal for winter sports or for visiting Grand Teton Park. A fine place to stay. Closed mid-Apr. to mid-May and Oct.-Nov. **M–E**

Snow King Resort, 400 E. Snow King Dr. (U.S. 89), Jackson, WY 83001 (307/733-5200; toll free 800/522-5464). 205 rms, A/C, cable color TV, AE, CB, DC, MC, V. Free parking, pool, sauna, skiing, rest., bar, rm svce, disco, hrdrsr. *Note:* Large, modern, comfortable seven-floor hotel. Huge, inviting rms, some w. balconies. Ideal for winter sports. Good svce; acceptable rest.; free airport shuttle. Open year round; group and convention clientele. Interesting wknd and vacation discounts. **E, but lower rates out of season**

Shoshone Lodge, on U.S. 20 (P.O. Box 790WT) Cody, WY 82414 (307/587-4044), 4 mi. (6 km) east of the eastern entrance to Yellowstone National Park. 16 cottages (3 w. kitchenettes). MC, V. Free parking, fishing, skiing, horseback riding, rest. *Note:* Small, inviting rustic motel on Grinnell Creek. Comfortable, individual log cabins. The kind of relaxed western atmosphere you associate w. campfires and square dances. The perfect place for nature lovers; run by the same family for three generations. Free airport shuttle; excellent value. Open May-Oct. **I**

☼ ♌ ♌ **Wort Hotel,** 50 N. Glenwood, Jackson, WY 83001 (307/733-2190; toll free 800/322-2727). 45 rms, A/C, color TV, in-rm movies. AE, CB, DC, MC, V. Free parking, nearby pool and tennis court (free shuttle), rest. (Goldpiece Dining Room), bar, rm svce, disco. *Note:* A hotel straight out of a western movie, decorated in rough wood, leather, and corduroy w. hunting trophies and frescoes of the Winning of the West. Huge, very comfortable rms; efficient, attentive svce; acceptable rest. The Silver Dollar Bar is very popular w. the locals. Free airport shuttle. **E, but lower rates out of season**

♌ **Signal Mountain Lodge,** Interpark Rd. (U.S. 89), Moran, WY 83013 (307/543-2831). 78 rms (a third w. kitchenettes). AE, MC, V. Free parking, rest., bar, grocery store. *Note:* Comfortable motel on Jackson Lake; friendly reception and svce. Many open-air activities available: fishing, swimming, boating, downstream rafting. Campsites adjoining. Open May-Oct. **I–M, but lower rates out of season**

♌ **Big Western Pine,** 234 Firehole Ave. (U.S. 191), West Yellowstone, MT 59758 (406/646-7622). 68 rms, color TV. AE, CB, DC, MC, V. Free parking, pool, sauna, snowmobile, rest. (Rustler's Roost). *Note:* Classic, well-run motel. Agreeable reception; acceptable rest. Located 600 yards (500 m) from the western entrance of Yellowstone National Park. Free airport shuttle. Open year round; good value. **I–M, but lower rates out of season.**

♌ **Motel 6,** 1370 W. Broadway, Jackson, WY 83001 (307/733-1620). 155 rms, A/C, color TV, free in-rm movies. DC, MC, V. Free parking, pool, nearby rest. *Note:* Unbeatable value for visitors to Grand Teton National Park. Functionally comfortable; friendly reception. Open year round. **B**

GUEST RANCHES: Guest ranches are legion around Grand Teton and Yellowstone National Parks. Some of them make their livelihood from the tourist business, organizing horseback riding, Jeep excursions, and rafting, hunting, or fishing parties. Others are authentic cattle ranches, where (paying) guests can follow the lifestyle of the last cowboys. Most of these ranches offer American Plan rates which include lodging, full board, and all the horseback riding you can handle. Since this kind of open-air vacation is becoming more and more popular, you should reserve a good way ahead. Some recommended establishments:

☼ ♌ **Bitterroot Ranch,** 76 mi. (122 km) SE of Moran Junction via U.S. 26 and East Fork Rd., Dubois, WY 82513 (307/455-2778). Ten bungalows w. baths. Free parking, pool, horseback riding, fishing, rest., bar. *Note:* A genuine stock ranch in its natural state. Rustic comforts; organized hikes; relaxed, inviting atmosphere. **E (AP)**

☼ ♌ **Diamond D Ranch,** P.O. Box 211, Moran, WY 83013 (307/543-2479), 12 mi. (19 km) east of Moran Junction via U.S. 26 and Buffalo Valley Rd. Accommodation for 40 people. Free parking, horseback riding, fishing, hunting, cross-country skiing, and snowmobiling in winter. Organizes downstream rafting trips. Rest. *Note:* A paradise for lovers of outdoor sports. Splendid view of the Grand Tetons. Rustic comforts. Big-game hunting parties in fall. Open year round. **E (AP)**

☼ ♌ **Moose Head Ranch,** 26 mi. (42 km) north of Jackson on U.S. 89 (P.O. Box 214), Moose, WY 83012 (307/733-3141).

14 bungalows. Free parking, horseback riding, fishing, rest., free crib. *Note:* Functionally comfortable bungalows w. verandas and fireplaces. Organizes mountain trips and rafting. For open-air lovers. Private lake on 123 acres (50 ha.) of woodland and pasture. Closed Oct. to mid-June. **E (AP)**

☼ ﬔ **Red Rock Ranch,** 30 mi. (48 km) NE of Jackson on U.S. 89 and Gros Ventre River Rd. (P.O. Box 38), Kelly, WY 83011, (307/733-6288). 15 cottages; minimum stay, one week. Free parking, heated pool, horseback riding, fishing, rest. *Note:* A real working stock-rearing ranch, whose very comfortable cottages stand in deep woods. Certified western atmosphere. Guests may join in the fall stock roundups. Open year round. **E (AP)**

YMCA / Youth Hostels

Teton Village Hostel, McCollister Dr., Teton Village, WY 83025 (307/733-3415). 240 beds. Typical youth hostel, open also to nonmembers both summer and winter. Nr. the snowfields.

RESTAURANTS

Yellowstone National Park Area Restaurant Prices	
(per person, excluding drinks and service charges)	
B (Budget)	up to $15
I (Inexpensive)	$15–$25
M (Moderate)	$25–$40
E (Expensive)	$40–$60
VE (Very Expensive)	$60 and up

Personal Favorites (in order of preference)

♟♟♟ **Stiegler's,** in the Jackson Hole Racquet Club (see "Accommodations," above) (733-1071). A/C. Lunch/dinner daily. AE, MC, V. Jkt. *Specialties:* rahmschnitzel (veal cutlet w. cream and paprika), bratwurst platte, western steak w. artichoke hearts, Rocky Mountain trout w. orange- and -lemon sauce, médaillons of elk w. venison sauce and poached pears, cherries Jubilee, apfelstrudel. Fine wine list. *Note:* The best food in the valley; elegant, refined cuisine from the hand of chef Peter Stiegler, brother of the Austrian grand champion Pepi Stiegler, who manages the Jackson Hole ski school. Lightly romantic décor; first-class svce. Resv. a must. *German-continental.* **I–M**

♟♟♟ **Strutting Grouse,** Jackson Hole Golf and Tennis Estates, 7 mi. (11 km) north of Jackson Hole on U.S. 89 (733-7788). A/C. Lunch/dinner Tues.-Sun.; closed Mon. and Oct. to mid-May. AE, MC, V. Jkt. *Specialties:* snails Florentine, poached salmon steak, veal w. lemon and mushrooms, remarkable chocolate mousse. *Note:* The view of the Grand Tetons is so spectacularly beautiful that there's a danger of overlooking the really excellent European-inspired food at this elegant country club. Modern décor w. beautiful hand-woven tapestries. Excellent svce. Resv. strongly advised, especially at dinner. A very good place. *Continental.* **I–M**

♟♟ **Jenny Lake Lodge,** in the Jenny Lake Lodge (see "Accommodations," above) (733-4647). No A/C. Breakfast/lunch/

dinner daily. Closed mid-Sept. to early June. AE, MC, V. *Specialties:* poached salmon w. capers in hollandaise sauce, roast leg of lamb boulangère, broiled rainbow trout, steak Delmonico w. bordelaise sauce. Menu changes regularly. Very fine wine list. *Note:* Excellent food in an unassuming log-cabin setting. Relaxed, cheerful atmosphere. Small enough that resv. are a must. A very good place to eat. *American-continental.* **I–M**

   ♀ **Vista Grande,** Teton Village Rd., 7½ mi. (12 km) NW of Jackson via Wyo. 22 and Teton Village Rd. (733-6964). A/C. Dinner only, nightly; closed Nov. MC, V. *Specialties:* chimichangas, fajitas, enchiladas, tacos al carbon. Excellent margaritas. *Note:* The Mexican food is as authentic and colorful as the décor, w. a fine view of the mountains thrown in. Cheerful svce. Locally popular, so resv. advised. Very good value. *Mexican.* **B–I**

NEARBY EXCURSIONS

   CODY (80 mi., 128 km) east of Fishing Bridge on Yellowstone Lake on U.S. 20): Founded in 1901 by the legendary "Buffalo Bill" (William Cody was his real name), and birthplace of the famous abstract painter Jackson Pollock, this picturesque pioneer settlement has retained its authentic far western flavor. Saloons, western boutiques, rodeos nightly June-Aug. (587-5155 for information).

The **Buffalo Bill Historical Center,** dedicated to the famous scout and buffalo-hunter, is at 720 Sheridan Ave. (307/587-4771), open daily May-Sept., Tues.-Sun. March-Apr. and Oct.-Dec. Closed Jan.-Feb. Under one roof it houses four different collections which make it one of the richest museums in the country on the Far West and its period. There are the **Buffalo Bill Museum** (personal memorabilia of William Cody); the **Winchester Arms Museum** (more than 1,500 firearms from the days of the Winning of the West); the **Whitney Gallery of Western Art** (fine paintings and sculptures by Bierstadt, Catlin, Miller, Moran, Remington, Russell, Wyeth, etc.); and the **Plains Indian Museum,** with an interesting collection of Indian ethnology: weapons, clothing, handcrafts, etc. Don't miss it.

   Nearby are the **Old Trail Town** and the **Museum of the Old West,** (1 mi., 1.6 km W. on Yellowstone Hwy. Open daily mid May-late Sept.), with authentic turn-of-the-century houses, which once stood beside the old stagecoach trail, now reerected on the original site of Cody; these, too, are worth the detour. Among the buildings in this open-air museum which recreate the authentic flavor of a frontier town are the inevitable saloon, the general store, school, forge, and so on.

   Lovers of the colossal won't overlook Gertrude Vanderbilt Whitney's **Buffalo Bill Monument,** believed to be the world's largest equestrian statue in bronze.

   Don't fail to visit Cody.

Where to Stay

   🛏🛏 **Holiday Inn,** 1701 Sheridan Ave., Cody, WY 82414 (587-5555). 184 rms. Very comfortable. **M**

Where to Eat

   ☼♀ **Irma Grill,** 1192 Sheridan Ave. (587-4221). Lunch/dinner daily. In Buffalo Bill's old hotel, a superb room of the period. *American.* **B–I**

🔔 **JACKSON** (57 mi., 92 km, south of the southern entrance to Yellowstone National Park): The ultimate cowboy town; relaxed, comfortable atmosphere. Many western boutiques. Don't miss the ☀ **"Million Dollar Cowboy Bar,"** 25 N. Cache St. (733-2207); the bar itself is 87 ft. (25 m) long, and the stools are shaped like western saddles. A must-see.

GHOST TOWNS: 🏚 **Virginia City,** 85 mi. (136 km) NW of West Yellowstone via U.S. 191, U.S. 287, and Mont. 287: One of the most picturesque and best-preserved ghost towns in the Northwest. Founded in 1863 by prospectors, this former capital of the Montana territory, along with its sister town of **Nevada City,** once boasted 10,000 inhabitants—today, barely 200 remain. There are many original buildings scrupulously restored: workshops, schools, brewery, Wells Fargo Express office, general store, offices of the *Montana Post* newspaper, opera house, Chinatown, and so on. So authentic is the setting that many westerns have been filmed here, notably *Little Big Man* and *The Missouri Breaks*. Interesting historical museum (Wallace St. in Virginia City) and railroad museum (Nevada City depot). Both recommended accommodations (below) date from the Gold Rush.

The ghost towns of Virginia City and Nevada City, connected by a narrow-gauge railroad, are open to visitors June-Aug. Don't miss them; they're worth the side trip.

Where to Stay

☀ **Fairweather Inn,** on Mont. 287, Virginia City, MT 59755 (406/843-5377). 15 rms (6 w. bath). MC, V. Adjoining coffeeshop. Closed May. **I**

☀🍴 **Nevada City Hotel,** on Mont. 287, Virginia City, MT 59755 (406/843-5487). 15 rms, 12 bungalows. MC, V. Gold-rush camp atmosphere.

CHAPTER 34

THE BLACK HILLS AND MOUNT RUSHMORE♵♵

□ □ □

Several of the country's most renowned tourist attractions lie within a two-hour drive of **Rapid City,** the second-largest town in South Dakota. The **Black Hills,** a huge, wooded outcrop of rock 93 mi. (150 km) long by 62 mi. (100 km) wide and rising in places to 6,400 ft. (2,000 m), frown across the great cereal-growing plains of the Dakotas (a Sioux word meaning "alliance of friends"). The Black Hills, rich in seams of ore, were the scene in 1875 of the country's penultimate gold rush, before that of Alaska's Klondike. Several ghost towns or almost-deserted mining camps remain to bear witness to those wild times, when fame alighted on adventurers like Wild Bill Hickok, Calamity Jane, and Preacher Smith, all three of whom lie buried in the Mount Moriah Cemetery at **Deadwood.** Southeast of the Black Hills, **Wind Cave National Park** has underground limestone caverns considered among the finest in the world.

Some 60 mi. (100 km) to the east, the glorious national park of the **Badlands** rears its contorted sandstone cliffs, whose savage beauty brings to mind the Grand Canyon of the Colorado; the colorful gorges are best seen at sunrise or sunset.

Finally, **Mount Rushmore National Memorial,** visited every year by 2½ million tourists, is one of the most extraordinary monuments in America. Here the features of Presidents George Washington, Thomas Jefferson, Abraham Lincoln, and Theodore Roosevelt, each some 60 ft. (20 m) high, have been carved from the living rock. These colossal portraits, the work of visionary artist Gutzon Borglum (and after his death, his son, Lincoln) required 14 years (1927–1941) of stubborn effort, and the removal of 450,000 tons of rock. After darkness falls, the sight of these enormous granite faces illuminated by floodlights is enthralling indeed. Not far from Mount Rushmore another solitary sculptor, Borglum's pupil, Korczak Ziolkowski, began work in 1948, with explosives, pneumatic drills, and bulldozers, on another huge mountainside statue: an equestrian figure, 564 ft. (172 m) high and 640 ft. (195 m) long of the renowned Sioux chief Crazy Horse, who defeated Colonel Custer at the battle of the Little Big Horn. Here, too, the sculptor's work was continued after his death (in 1982) by his sons. When finished, sometime around the year 2000, the **Crazy Horse Memorial** will be by far the largest statue in the world.

BASIC FACTS: State of South Dakota. Area Code: 605. Time Zone: Mountain Time. Zip Code: 57751.

CLIMATE: Summer, with mean July temperatures of 74°F (23°C) and occasional peaks of 95°F (35°C), or autumn, still sunny but cooler, are the best times to visit the Black Hills. Winter, too, has its own savage beauty, though the mercury rarely climbs above 14°F (−10°C) and the snow falls abundantly.

DISTANCES: Chicago, 896 mi. (1,434 km); Denver, 375 mi. (600 km); Minneapolis, 635 mi. (1,045 km); Salt Lake City, 680 mi., (1,088 km); Yellowstone, 549 mi. (878 km).

ARRIVAL & TRANSIT INFORMATION

NEAREST AIRPORT: Rapid City Regional Airport (RAP), 9 mi. (15 km) SE of the town.

AIRLINES: Continental (342-6707), Delta (toll free 800/221-1212), Northwest (343-5544), United (toll free 800/241-6522).

CITY LINK: An airport bus, **Airport Limo** (343-5358), serves the principal Rapid City hotels: fare, $6; time, 30 min.

CAR RENTAL (at the airport unless otherwise noted): Avis (393-0740); Budget (393-0488); Dollar, 410 N. Campbell, Rapid City (342-7071); Hertz (393-0160); National (343-9135); Thrifty, 510 N. Campbell, Rapid City (342-6945).
    Car-rental rates are high, and the choice of models is limited—but even so, you can't do better than rent a car with unlimited mileage, given the distances to be covered and the many interesting places to see.

BUS: Greyhound, 333 6th St., Rapid City (348-3300).

INFORMATION & TOURS

TOURIST INFORMATION: The **Rapid City Visitors and Convention Bureau,** 444 Mt. Rushmore Rd., Rapid City, SD 57709 (605/343-1744).
    Badlands National Park Visitor Center, Cedar Pass, SD 57750 (605/433-5361).
    Custer County Chamber of Commerce, 447 Crook St., Custer, SD 57730 (605/673-2244).
    Deadwood Chamber of Commerce, 735 Historic Main St., Deadwood, SD 57732 (605/578-1876).
    Mount Rushmore National Memorial Visitor Center, U.S. 16A, Keystone, SD 57751 (605/574-2523).

GUIDED TOURS: Gray Line Tours (bus), 1600 E. St. Patrick St., Rapid City (605/342-4461): Conducted tours around the whole region; serves principal Rapid City hotels.
    Jack Rabbit Bus Tours (bus), 333 6th St., Rapid City (605/348-3300): A nine-hour conducted tour of the whole region; serves principal Rapid City hotels.
    Jeep to the Buffalo (Jeep), State Game Lodge, U.S. 16A, Custer (605/255-4541): Jeep trips through the buffalo herds of Custer State Park—for wildlife photographers.
    Rushmore Helicopters (helicopter), Keystone Helipad, Keystone (605/666-4461): Trips lasting 4–20 min. over Mount Rushmore and the Black Hills. Spectacular. Mid-May to mid-Sept.

THE MAJOR SIGHTS & ATTRACTIONS

☀☖☖ **BADLANDS NATIONAL PARK** (83 mi., 132 km, east of Rapid City on I-90 and S.D. 240): Spectacular canyons carved by erosion in the multicolored hills of clay and sandstone—a spectacle whose singular beauty has fascinated travelers through the ages. Several herds of buffalo roam free here. Badlands National Park was set up in 1939. **Visitor Center** open daily, year round, at Cedar Pass, east of the park. For information, call 605/433-5361. Don't miss it.

☖ **BLACK HILLS** (10 mi., 16 km, west of Rapid City on U.S. 16): Glorious wooded mountains overlooking the vast Dakota plains, whose mineral wealth touched off a gold rush in 1875; several ghost towns still stand as witness. Once this land was held sacred by the Dakota Indians. Not to be missed.

☀☖☖ **CRAZY HORSE MEMORIAL** (41 mi., 65 km, SW of Rapid City on U.S. 16) (605/673-4681): The world's largest statue, 640 by 564 ft. (195 by 172 m), is being created here. The work, begun in 1948, has already required the removal of eight million tons of rock—18 times more than at Mount Rushmore. The Boston sculptor Korczak Ziolkowski, a pupil of Borglum's who at one time worked with him on the nearby Mount Rushmore Memorial, conceived and began this gigantic equestrian figure, carved with bulldozers and explosives from the granite of Thunderhead Mountain. The memorial pays tribute to the pride and greatness of Native Americans, in the person of the famous Crazy Horse, chief of the Oglala Sioux, and one of those who defeated Lt.-Col. George Armstrong Custer at the battle of the Little Big Horn. A model in the Visitor Center will give you an idea of the size and shape envisaged for the finished work: the horse's head will be as high as a 22-story building. After the sculptor died in October 1982, his wife, Ruth, and his ten sons took over the work and expect to complete it around the end of the century. An impressive sight; open daily, year round.

☀☖☖ **MOUNT RUSHMORE NATIONAL MEMORIAL** (24 mi., 38 km, SW of Rapid City on U.S. 16) (605/574-2523): Unique colossal sculptures, cut into a granite cliff 6,000 ft. (1,830 m) high. One of the most extraordinary memorials that history can record, the work of a single man (though completed by the hand of his son), John Gutzon de La Mothe Borglum, a sculptor of Danish descent from Idaho. Begun in 1927 when the sculptor was well over 50, these four gigantic portraits, each about 60 ft. (20 m) high and carved from the rock with explosives and pneumatic drills, were not completed until Oct. 1941, some months after his death. They symbolize the contribution made to U.S. history by four great presidents: George Washington, the struggle for independence; Thomas Jefferson, the foundation of a democratic state; Abraham Lincoln, the equality of all citizens and the preservation of the Union; Theodore Roosevelt, the influence of America on the world and the conservation of natural resources. Among others, Alfred Hitchcock's famous movie *North by Northwest* was shot here. Almost 2½ million people come here every year; the spectacular (in the most literal sense) sight is enough to make the trip worthwhile. Open daily, year round.

☀☖☖ **WIND CAVE NATIONAL PARK** (53 mi., 84 km, south of Rapid City on U.S. 16) (605/745-4600): One of the country's most beautiful natural caverns, lying at a depth of 196–328 ft. (60–100 m) beneath the slopes of the Black Hills. There is a pedestrian walkway running 1.2–8 mi. (2–12 km) through the colorful chambers of the cavern. Wear warm clothing and sturdy shoes—and don't try the walk unless you're in good shape physically. Discovered in 1881, the Wind Cave owes its name to the violent winds that blow between the cavern and the outer world according to changes in atmospheric pressure. Open for (exhausting) visits daily, year round.

OTHER SIGHTS, ATTRACTIONS, & ACTIVITIES

MUSEUMS OF SCIENCE AND HISTORY: ⚱ **Museum of Geology,** 500 E. St. Joseph St., Rapid City (394-2467): A rich collection of animal fossils (dinosaurs, *Tyrannosaurus*) and minerals; gold nuggets. A must-see. Open daily in summer; Mon.-Sat. the rest of the year.

Rushmore-Borglum Story and Gallery, Main St., Keystone (666-4449): An entire museum devoted to the sculptor of Mount Rushmore and his work. Photographs, paintings, models; history of the work. Interesting. Open daily May-Oct.

Sioux Indian Museum, 515 West Blvd., Rapid City (348-0577): One of the country's finest Indian museums. Interesting old utensils, Sioux handcrafts. The adjoining **Minnilusa Pioneer Museum** is devoted to the period of the Westward Expansion. Must be seen. Open daily in summer; Tues.-Sun. the rest of the year.

South Dakota Air & Space Museum, at Ellsworth Air Force Base, 6 mi. (10 km) east of Rapid City on I-90 (385-5188): Military museum whose special distinction is a score of different aircraft from the old reliable DC-3 to the giant B-52. Open daily in summer; weekends only the rest of the year. Also conducted tours of the base, Mon.-Fri., June-Aug. Should be seen.

SPECIAL EVENTS: **Black Hills Roundup** at Belle Fourche (July 4 weekend): One of the best-known rodeos in the Midwest; not to be missed.

Central States Fair at Rapid City (Aug.): Agricultural fair, rodeo, Indian dances, auto races, parades. Colorful.

Days of '76 at Deadwood (first weekend in Aug.): Big historical parade in honor of the gold-rush days; lively and colorful.

Black Hills Motorcycle Classic at Sturgis (first week in Aug.): Each August over 50,000 "bikers" and spectators celebrate this week long, internationally famous motorcycle racing extravaganza.

Fall Festival at Custer (second weekend in Sept.): Horse shows, giant barbecue, shows, concerts; very popular locally.

WINTER SPORTS RESORTS: ⚱ **Deer Mountain,** at Lead, 49 mi. (78 km) NW of Rapid City on I-90 and U.S. Alt 14 (584-3230): 5 lifts. Open Nov.-Mar.

Terry Peak, at Lead, 49 mi. (78 km) NW of Rapid City on I-90 and U.S. Alt 14 (584-2165): 5 lifts. Open Nov.-Mar.

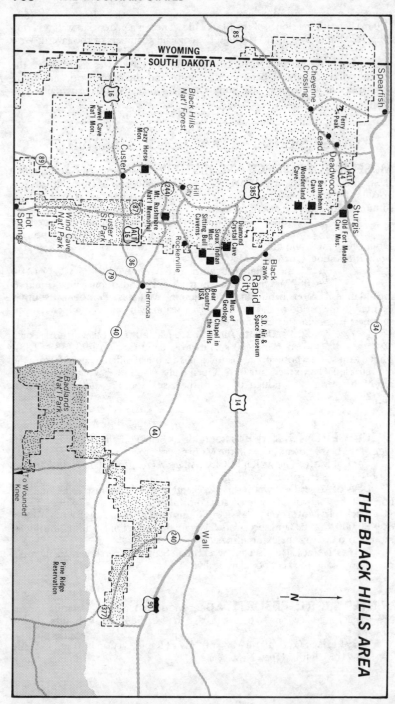

THE BLACK HILLS AREA

ACCOMMODATIONS IN THE AREA

See the listing of toll-free numbers in the Appendix.

Room Rates in the Black Hills Region	
B (Budget)	up to $30
I (Inexpensive)	$30–$60
M (Moderate)	$60–$90
E (Expensive)	$90–$140
VE (Very Expensive)	$140 and up

Personal Favorites (in order of preference)

Hilton Inn, 445 Mt. Rushmore, at Main St., Rapid City, SD 57701 (605/348-8300; toll free, see Hilton). 177 rms, A/C, color TV, in-rm movies. AE, CB, DC, MC, V. Free parking, rest. (Sylvan Room), coffeeshop, bar, rm svce, boutiques, crib free. *Note:* Modern grand hotel in the center of Rapid City. Comfortable, spacious rms, most w. views of the Black Hills. Efficient svce; acceptable rest. The best place to stay in town. Open year round. **I–M, but lower rates out of season**

Bavarian Inn, U.S. 16, Custer, SD 57730 (605/673-2802). 52 rms, A/C, color TV, in-rm movies. AE, CB, DC, MC, V. Free parking, pool, sauna, tennis court, rest., bar, crib free. *Note:* An agreeable small motel with distinction. Friendly reception; very commendable food. Near the Crazy Horse Memorial. One of the best places to stay in the region. Open year round. **I–M, but lower rates out of season**

Franklin Hotel, 700 Main St., Deadwood, SD 57732 (605/578-2241). 54 rms, cable color TV, AE, CB, DC, MC, V. Paid parking, rest. (1903 Dining Room), bar. *Note:* One of the oldest hotels (1903) in the Black Hills region. Elegant old décor, prettily restored. Nice rms, but avoid the annex on the other side of the street. An engaging breath of the past. Acceptable rest. Open year round. **I, but lower rates out of season**

Best Western Town and Country, 2505 Mt. Rushmore Rd., Rapid City, SD 57701 (605/343-5383; toll free, see Best Western). 100 rms, A/C, color TV, in-rm movies. AE, CB, DC, MC, V. Free parking, two pools, rest., bar, crib $4. *Note:* Comfortable, well-run motel on the road to Mount Rushmore. Friendly reception. Most rms have private balconies or patios. Open year round. **I–M, but lower rates out of season**

Alex Johnson, 523 6th St., Rapid City, SD 57701 (605/342-1210). 122 rms, A/C, color TV, in-rm movies. AE, DC, MC, V. Free valet parking, sauna, rest., bar, rm svce, disco, hrdrsr, crib free. *Note:* Charming old hotel, recently restored, in the center of Rapid City. Comfortable rms w. refrigerators. The Landmark Rest. is acceptable. Svce not always dependable. Open year round. **I–M, but lower rates out of season**

Cedar Pass Lodge, U.S. 16, Cedar Pass, SD 57750 (605/433-5460). 24 bungalows, A/C. AE, CB, DC, MC, V. Free parking, rest. *Note:* Spruce rustic cabins inside Badlands National Park, managed by the Oglllala Sioux tribe. For lovers of unspoiled nature. Beautiful view. Open May 1 to Oct. 15. **B–I**

♆ **Powder House Lodge,** U.S. 16, Keystone, SD 57751 (605/666-4646). 26 rms. AE, MC, V. Free parking, rest. *Note:* Comfortable cottages in the woods, 4 mi. (6 km) from Mount Rushmore. Friendly reception and svce. Very acceptable rest. Open May to the end of Sept. Good value. **I**

☼♆ **Sylvan Lake Resort,** S.D. 89, Custer State Park, SD 57730 (605/574-2561). 65 rms and bungalows. AE, MC, V. Free parking, fishing, beach, boats, rest., coffeeshop, bar. *Note:* There are 29 rms in the motel and 36 bungalows, some rms w. balconies on the lake. Rustic comfort; country atmosphere. Closed Oct.-May. **I–M**

♆ **Rushmore View Motor Lodge,** U.S. 16A, Keystone, SD 57751 (605/666-4466). 31 rms, A/C, color TV, in-rm movies. AE, CB, DC, MC, V. Free parking, rest., bar, child's cot $4. *Note:* Conventional small motel w. a view of Mount Rushmore. The Copper Room is an acceptable rest. Good value on balance. Closed Nov.-May. **I–M, but lower rates out of season**

♆ **Best Western Four Presidents,** U.S. 16A, Keystone, SD 57751 (605/666-4472; toll free, see Best Western). 30 rms, A/C, color TV. AE, CB, DC, MC, V. Free parking, adjoining coffeeshop, child's cot $3. *Note:* Conventional small motel 3 mi. (5 km) from Mount Rushmore. Functionally comfortable. Closed Dec. to the end of Mar. **I, but lower rates out of season**

♆ **Best Western Plains Motel,** 712 Glenn St., Wall, SD 57790 (605/279-2145; toll free, see Best Western). 74 rms, A/C, color TV, in-rm movies. AE, CB, DC, MC, V. Free parking, pool, coffeeshop, child's cot $3. *Note:* Typical but appealing small motel at the entrance to Badlands National Park. Comfortable rms. Closed Dec.-Mar. **I–M, but lower rates out of season**

♆ **Super 8 Motel,** 201 Main St., Hill City, SD 57745 (605/574-4141; toll free 800/843-1991). 34 rms, A/C, color TV, in-rm movies. MC, V. Free parking, nearby coffeeshop. *Note:* Modern, comfortable small motel. Spacious rms; friendly reception. Near the depot for the "1880 Train" (see the Hill City excursion, below). Open year round. **I**

YMCA/Youth Hostels

YMCA, 815 Kansas St., Rapid City (605/342-8538). Men and women; also youth hostel. Open in summer only. Pool.

RESTAURANTS IN THE AREA

Black Hills Region Restaurant Prices	
(per person, excluding drinks and service charges)	
B (Budget)	up to $15
I (Inexpensive)	$15–$25
M (Moderate)	$25–$40
E (Expensive)	$40–$60
VE (Very Expensive)	$60 and up

Personal Favorites (in order of preference)

Bavarian Inn (see the Bavarian Inn in "Accommodations in the Area," above), in Custer (673-4412). A/C. Breakfast/lunch/dinner daily. MC, V. *Specialties:* veal Cordon Bleu, wienerschnitzel, rouladen, spätzle, apfel strudel. *Note:* Classic German setting and food; likeable atmosphere. Dancing in season. Resv. advised. *German-American.* **I–M**

The Sluice, Heritage Dr., in Spearfish (642-5500). A/C. Lunch/dinner Tues.-Sun.; closed Mon. and holidays. AE, MC, V. *Specialties:* truite amandine, roast beef, "miner's stew," buffalo steak, homemade desserts. *Note:* Popular w. tourists and locals alike for its turn-of-the-century mining-camp décor. The menu, running to an unexpected 30 pages, adds to its appeal. Very estimable food, pleasant svce. A very good place. *American.* **B–I**

Powder House Lodge (see the Powder House Lodge in "Accommodations in the Area," above), in Keystone (666-4646). Breakfast/lunch/dinner daily; closed Oct.-May. AE, MC, V. *Specialties:* steak, roast beef, a variety of salads. *Note:* A rustic dining room in the heart of the woods. Very praiseworthy food. Good value. *American.* **B–I**

Dakota House (formerly Vern's Steakhouse), 815 E. North St., Rapid City (343-6541). A/C. Lunch/dinner daily; closed holidays. AE, MC, V. *Specialties:* roast chicken, barbecued meats, steak. *Note:* Likeable steakhouse decorated in traditional western style; solid, commendable food. *Steak-American.* **B–I**

Ruby House, U.S. 16A, in Keystone (666-4404). A/C. Lunch/dinner daily; closed end of Oct. to May. AE, CB, DC, MC, V. *Specialties:* meats broiled over wood fire, Italian dishes. *Note:* Picturesque Far West–style saloon rest., the dining room attractively decorated as a turn-of-the-century bawdy house. Attentive svce, laudable food. Worth a visit. *Steak.* **I**

Landmark Restaurant, in the Alex Johnson Hotel (see "Accommodations in the Area," above), Rapid City (342-1210). A/C. Breakfast/lunch/dinner daily. AE, CB, DC, MC, V. *Specialties:* steak, roast beef, fish of the day. *Note:* Hotel dining room somewhat in need of redecoration, but serving good meats. The svce could use some attention. *Steak.* **I**

1903 Dining Room, in the Franklin Hotel (see "Accommodations in the Area," above), Deadwood (578-2241). A/C. Breakfast/lunch/dinner daily; closed Dec. 25. AE, MC, V. *Specialties:* hamburger, steak, fish of the day. *Note:* The Victorian dining room of the venerable Franklin Hotel dates, as its name suggests, from the turn of the century; so do the decor and atmosphere. The food, though acceptable, is unimaginative, the svce efficient. Resv. suggested in tourist season. *American.* **B–I**

Legion Lake Resort Restaurant, in Custer State Park (255-4521). A/C. Breakfast/lunch/dinner daily; closed Oct.-May. No credit cards. *Specialties:* roast beef, lake trout. *Note:* The rustic dining room is pleasant enough, the food nourishing and unpretentious, the svce desperately slow. *American.* **B–I**

Copper Room, in the Rushmore View Motor Lodge (see "Accommodations in the Area," above), Keystone (666-4466). A/C. Breakfast/lunch/dinner daily; closed Nov.-May. AE, CB, DC, MC, V. *Specialties:* steak, broiled trout, salads. *Note:* Tiny motel dining room in neon and Formica; modest, unpretentious food. *American.* **B–I**

Chute Rooster, U.S. 385, in Hill City (574-2122). Lunch/dinner daily; closed Memorial Day, Dec. 24–25. MC, V. *Specialties:* steak, seafood, barbecued meats, beef stew. *Note:* A 19th-century barn turned into a western-style rest. Plentiful portions of solid food. Far West atmosphere, w. square dances in summer. Locally popular. *American.* **B–I**

☼☿ **Buffalo Room,** on S.D. 244 in Keystone (574-2515). A/C. Breakfast/lunch/dinner daily (till 8 p.m.); closed mid-Dec. to mid-Jan. AE, MC, V. *Specialties:* fried chicken, roast beef, good desserts. *Note:* A rustic cafeteria, w. its western décor and fine art by South Dakota artists; magnificent bay window overlooking Mount Rushmore and its sculptures. Very acceptable food; swift, efficient svce. *American.* **B**

☼☿ **Wall Drug Store,** 1 Main St., Wall (279-2175). A/C. Breakfast/lunch/dinner daily (till 10 p.m. in summer, 5 p.m. in winter); closed Sun. (in winter) and holidays. AE, MC, V. *Specialties:* steak, fried chicken, soups, sandwiches. *Note:* Self-service cafeteria in the middle of a huge, jumbled country store reminiscent of gold rush days. The sight is worth your time—the food, less so. Picturesque. *American.* **B**

NEARBY EXCURSIONS

☼☖ **BEAR COUNTRY USA** (8 mi., 12 km, south of Rapid City on U.S. 16) (343-2290): Wildlife reserve with bears, wolves, cougar, buffalo, elk, and other animals roaming free; you stay in your car. Guaranteed excitement. Open daily, May to mid-Oct.

☖ **CHAPEL IN THE HILLS** (5 mi., 8 km, west of Rapid City on S.D. 44 and Chapel Lane) (342-8281): Exact replica of the famous 12th-century Stavkirke church in Borgund, Norway; a magnificent building in carved wood. Well worth going out of your way for. Open daily, May-Sept.

☼☖☖ **DEADWOOD** (40 mi., 64 km, NW of Rapid City on I-90 and U.S. Alt. 14): Picturesque gold-prospectors' town, still haunted by the redoubtable shades of such as Wild Bill Hickok, Calamity Jane, Preacher Smith, and Potato Creek Johnny. Its gold-rush population of 25,000 has fallen to barely 2,000 today, but its **Main Street** is on the National Register of Historic Monuments. Visit the famous **Saloon # 10,** where Wild Bill Hickok was killed, at 657 Main St. (578-3346); open daily. At the **Old Town Hall,** on Lee St. (578-3583), you can see an amusing skit on his murderer's trial, Mon.-Sat., June-Aug. Other popular attractions: a gold mine, the **Broken Boot Mine,** on U.S. Alt. 14 (578-9997), open daily, May-Oct.; and the **Mount Moriah Cemetery,** with tombs of famous people, at **Boot Hill,** open daily. Don't miss it.

☼☖☖ **DEVILS TOWER NATIONAL MONUMENT** (86 mi., 140 km, NW of Rapid City via I-90 and Wyo. 24): Enormous (1,280-ft., 390-m) tower of streaked basalt, like the trunk of a giant tree, towering over the lovely Fourche River which washes its feet. The colors of this impressive volcanic bastion, which has inspired many legends and was used by Steven Spielberg as a setting for *Close Encounters of the Third Kind,* change with the time of day. Some thousand brave souls climb it every year. A truly riveting sight. Visitor Center open daily, May-Oct. For information, contact the Superintendent, P.O. Box 8, Devils Tower, WY 82714 (307/467-5370). Well worth the side trip.

☼☖ **HILL CITY** (28 mi., 44 km, SW of Rapid City on U.S. 16): This charming little mountain village at the foot of **Harney Peak,** South Dakota's highest at 7,242 ft. (2,207 m), boasts one of the Black Hills' best tourist draws: the **1880 Train.** Here you can travel to Keystone and back, a two-hr round trip, aboard an authentic steam train, Far Western style—a picturesque journey through lovely countryside. Open daily, mid-June to the end of Aug. For information, call 574-2222; resv. advised.

☼⚓ **HOT SPRINGS** (74 mi., 118 km, SW of Rapid City on U.S. 16 and U.S. 385): Highly regarded thermal springs, with the world's largest indoor pool of naturally heated water, the **Evans Plunge,** 1145 N. River St. (745-5165). Open daily year round.

Don't fail to visit the ☀ **Mammoth Site,** on U.S. 18 bypass (745-6017), a huge 26,000-year-old mammoth graveyard under active excavation by paleontologists; it's believed to have a larger store of bones of this type than any other deposit in the Western Hemisphere. A fascinating place to visit; don't miss it. Open daily.

☼⚓ **JEWEL CAVE NATIONAL MONUMENT** (59 mi., 94 km, SW of Rapid City on U.S. 16) (673-2288): One of the most beautiful caverns in the country; superb formations of crystalline calcite produce unique visual effects. You should be in good physical condition, wearing warm clothes and sturdy walking shoes—it's a tiring visit. Open daily, May-Oct. Worth the detour.

☼⚓ **LEAD** (49 mi., 78 km, NW of Rapid City via I-90 and U.S. Alt. 114): Clinging to its mountainside, this old pioneer village, now a very popular winter-sports resort, boasts the country's largest gold mine. Opened in 1876 and still in production, the **Homestake Gold Mine,** Main and Mill Sts. (584-3110), is also the country's deepest at 8,000 ft. (2,440 m); it takes 45 min. just to ride to the bottom in the elevator cage, and the temperature when you get there can be as high as 132° F (56° C). The surface installations of the mine are open to visitors Mon.-Fri. from May to Oct.

From the nearby 7,076-ft. (2,157-m) **Terry Peak,** accessible either by road or by cable car, there is a clear view of the Black Hills and the neighboring states of Wyoming, Montana, North Dakota, and Nebraska, a sight that shouldn't be missed.

☼⚓ **SPEARFISH** (47 mi., 75 km, NW of Rapid City on I-90): Famous for its trout hatcheries, Spearfish has also presented, June-Aug. of every year since 1939, the **Black Hills Passion Play,** with 250 characters; it may be seen every Tues., Thur., Sun. eves. at 400 St. Joe St. (642-2646).

The **Matthews Opera House,** 614 Main St. (642-3420), a fine baroque structure from 1906, stages amusing melodramas from the gold-rush era on Mon., Wed., and Fri. from June-Aug.; a must-see.

☼⚓ **STURGIS** (29 mi., 46 km, NW of Rapid City on I-90): The **Old Fort Meade Cavalry Museum,** 1 mi. (2 km) east on S.D. 34 (347-9822), may be visited daily, June-Sept. It was here that the 140 survivors of Lt.-Col. George Armstrong Custer's Seventh Cavalry regiment took refuge after their unit had been cut to pieces by 4,000 Sioux and Cheyenne under Sitting Bull and Crazy Horse at the battle of the Little Big Horn, on June 25, 1876. The museum has many memorabilia from those heroic times; all western-history buffs should see it. It was at Fort Meade, that "The Star-Spangled Banner" was first played in 1892 at official functions, a custom that led to its becoming the national anthem in 1931.

⚓ **WOUNDED KNEE** (89 mi., 142 km, SE of Rapid City via S.D. 44 and Indian Rd. 27): Here, on Dec. 29, 1890, the U.S. Army finally broke the resistance of the Sioux, killing 256 unarmed Indians including women and children. Some commentators have discerned in this sorry episode a sort of revenge exacted for Little Big Horn (see "Sturgis," above). Wounded Knee was also the scene of a symbolic Indian revolt in 1973. Monument marks the place of the massacre. For western-history fans. The visit can conveniently be combined with the trip to Badlands National Park (see "The Major Sights and Attractions," above).

GHOST TOWNS: ⚜Rockerville, 12 mi. (19 km) SW of Rapid City on U.S. 16 (342-0200): An authentic 1878 prospectors' village with old workshops, restaurant, saloon, and theater all carefully restored. Guaranteed local color. Open daily, mid-May to Oct. Worth seeing.

CUSTER STATE PARK (42 mi., 67 km, SW of Rapid City on U.S. 16): Some 73,000 acres of dense forests, lakes, and unspoiled natural beauty, with one of the country's largest buffalo herds as well as many deer, elk, mountain goats, and other creatures. The **Needles Highway Scenic Drive** (closed in winter) is a 14-mi. (22-km) panoramic road that you shouldn't miss. Well worth the detour.

PART FIVE

THE SOUTHWEST

CHAPTER 35

DALLAS AND
FORT WORTH ⚑

□ □ □

A city for the 21st century, "Big D" to its admirers, Dallas somehow captures the myth of modern America. Its futurist buildings and grand hotels worthy of Ancient Egypt rival in their brashness the New York and Chicago skylines: witness **City Hall**, with its unadorned, geometric lines; the **Dallas Theater Center;** the startling **Allied Bank Tower,** with its beveled architecture; the immense blue-tinted façade of the **Hyatt Regency Hotel;** and next door, the **Reunion Tower** and its geodesic dome, resembling an enormous crown when illuminated at night. With a more diversified economy than its great rival Houston (oil, textiles, aeronautics, banking, insurance, publishing, chemicals, electronics), Dallas continues to sustain an enviable economic growth rate, despite the depression that has gripped Texas for the past five or six years. It is a town of pioneers, founded less than 150 years ago by John Neely Bryan, a Tennessee lawyer who came seeking trade with the Caddo and Cherokee Indians. Named after then–Vice President George Mifflin Dallas, the city entered its great boom period after World War II. Known as "the New York of the South," Texas's second-largest city is also one of the country's three great fashion capitals; its designer houses and shops are particularly famous for their luxury and elegance. While it has been disparagingly identified with the unscrupulous "J.R." in its namesake TV series, Dallas rightly prides itself on its millionaire district—**Highland Park**—more like a city within a city, with private police, exclusive schools and clubs, dream houses, and its very own moral code. It is an indicator of its wealth that, outside Saudi Arabia, Dallas boasts more Cadillacs per capita than any other city in the world.

Dallas first built its fortune on cotton, then oil in the 1930s, and continues to be one of the country's most artistically and culturally active cities despite the current economic slump. This is in keeping with the spiritual tradition of the city's early settlers, a group of 200 Utopian scientists, painters, writers, and naturalists from France, Switzerland, and Belgium who came here in the 1850s. The Dallas of today boasts a nationally famous orchestra and opera—the **Dallas Symphony Orchestra** and the **Dallas Opera**—and one of the most prestigious schools in the South, **Southern Methodist University** (9,000 students). The recently opened **Museum of Art,** furthermore, is a remarkable achievement, and modern architecture rises proudly over the city, with works by I. M. Pei, Richard Keating, Frank Lloyd Wright, Philip Johnson, Martin Growald, and Edward Larrabee Barnes gracing the urban landscape.

Although the police force is regarded as quick on the draw, the Dallas–Fort Worth metropolitan area ranks ninth among the most dangerous cities in the country. John F. Kennedy was assassinated here on November 11, 1963, from the **Texas School Book Depository,** an undistinguished yellow-brick building which, with the nearby museum, continues to draw tens of thousands of the 35th president's admirers each year.

BASIC FACTS: State of Texas. Area Codes: 214 (Dallas), 817 (Fort Worth). ZIP Codes: 75221 (Dallas), 76101 (Fort Worth). Founded: 1841 (Dallas), 1849 (Fort Worth). Approximate population: city, 1,000,000 (Dallas), 430,000 (Fort Worth); metropolitan area (Dallas & Fort Worth), 3,500,000. Ninth-largest metropolitan area in the country.

CLIMATE: The Dallas climate fits the popular image of Texas: harsh and extreme. Brutal downpours punctuate the exceptionally hot, even torrid summer (mean July temperature, 86°F, 30°C, with peaks of 104°F, 40°C, and higher), but air conditioning reigns supreme. Winter is generally mild but punctuated by unpredictable temperature plunges (sometimes from 60°F, 15°C, to freezing in 24 hours). Spring and autumn are interspersed with often-violent thunderstorms and rather spectacular dust storms.

DISTANCES: Albuquerque, 637 mi. (1,020 km); Houston, 243 mi. (390 km); Memphis, 450 mi. (720 km); New Orleans, 493 mi. (790 km); San Antonio, 270 mi. (432 km).

ARRIVAL & TRANSIT INFORMATION

AIRPORTS: The **Dallas–Fort Worth International Airport** (DFW) is 13 mi. (21 km) west of Dallas, 17 mi. (28 km) east of Fort Worth. Ultramodern in conception, the Dallas–Fort Worth airport is the world's largest in surface area (16,800 acres)—as big as Manhattan. Third-busiest airport in the world. For information call 214/574-6720.
　　Dallas's **Love Field** (DAL) is 7 mi. (12 km) north, for commuter flights. For information call 214/352-2663.

U.S. AIRLINES (Dallas telephone numbers unless otherwise indicated): American (214/267-1151 in Dallas, 817/267-1151 in Fort Worth), Braniff (214/357-9511 in Dallas, 817/263-6110 in Fort Worth), Continental (214/263-0523), Delta (214/630-3200 in Dallas, 817/336-8341 in Fort Worth), Midway (toll free 800/621-5700), Northwest (214/988-0405), Pan Am (toll free 800/221-1111), Southwest (214/640-1221 in Dallas, 817/640-1221 in Fort Worth), TWA (214/741-6741), United (214/988-1004).

FOREIGN CARRIERS: Air Canada (toll free 800/422-6232), Air New Zealand (toll free 800/262-1234), British Airways (toll free 800/ 247-9297), Lufthansa (toll free 800/645-3880).

CITY LINK: Cab fare **from Dallas–Fort Worth Airport to downtown Dallas,** about $25; time, 35–40 min. Bus for the same route: Super-Shuttle (817/329-2000); provides door-to-door service to any Dallas destination; leaves every 30 min.; fare, $8; time, about 45 min.
　　Cab fare from Dallas-Fort Worth Airport **to downtown Fort Worth,** about $20; time, 30 min. Bus for the same route: Super-Shuttle (817/329-2000); provides door-to-door service to any Fort Worth destination leaves every hour; fare, $8; time, about 40 min.
　　Service is by Super-Shuttle **from Love Field:** fare to downtown Dallas, $5; cab fare, $12.
　　The bus system is thoroughly deficient (in Dallas, DART, 214/979-1111; in Fort Worth, CITRAN, 817/870-6200), the taxis few and expensive. This plus the enormous size of the metropolitan area makes renting a car with unlimited mileage a good idea.

CAR RENTAL (at Dallas–Fort Worth Airport unless otherwise indicated): Avis (214/574-4100); Budget (214/574-3300); Dollar, 4125 W. Airport Fwy. (214/256-4576); Hertz (214/574-2000); National (214/574-3400). For dwntwn locations, consult the phone directory.

LIMOUSINE SERVICES: Accent Limousine (214/358-1388), Limousines Inc. (214/827-7900), Scripps Edward Limousine (toll free 800/223-6710).

TAXIS: You'll find taxis in waiting lines at the major hotels; they may not be hailed on the street. The best arrangement, however, is to phone Yellow Cab (214/426-6262 in Dallas, 817/335-3333 in Fort Worth).

TRAIN: AMTRAK, Union Station, 400 S. Houston St., Dallas (214/653-1101).
AMTRAK Station, 1501 Jones St., Fort Worth (817/332-2931).

BUS: Greyhound, 205 S. Lamar St., Dallas (214/748-1142), or 901 Commerce St., Fort Worth (817/332-7611).

DALLAS

INFORMATION & TOURS

TOURIST INFORMATION: The **Dallas Convention & Visitors Bureau,** 1201 Elm St., TX 75270 (214/746-6677).
There is also an **information office** open daily at Union Station, 400 S. Houston St. (214/747-2355).

GUIDED TOURS: Gray Line Tours Dallas (bus) (214/824-2424): guided tour of the city, serving major hotels.

SIGHTS, ATTRACTIONS, & ACTIVITIES

ARCHITECTURAL HIGHLIGHTS: ⚐ **City Hall,** Municipal Plaza (670-5397): Impressive, futurist building in the shape of an inverted pyramid, a work of I. M. Pei. There is a lovely Henry Moore sculpture on the entrance plaza. Open Mon.-Fri.

⚐ **Dallas Market Center,** 2100 Stemmons Fwy. (655-6100): This group of ultramodern buildings (**Apparelmart, Dallas Trade Mart, Decorative Center District, Infomart, World Trade Center,** etc.) makes up the world's biggest wholesale market. Interesting modern sculptures dot the surrounding gardens (**Sculpture Garden**). Worth a look. Guided tours by appointment.

☼⚐ **Dallas Theater Center,** 3636 Turtle Creek Blvd. (526-8857): Two 460-seat halls and one of the country's most important theatrical companies. Daring cantilevered architecture by Frank Lloyd Wright. An absolute must-see.

☼⚐ **First Interstate Bank Tower,** Fountain Place: Designed by Henry Cobb, a pupil of I. M. Pei, this huge, beveled-glass prism stands 60 stories high and commands the 200 fountains and the cypresses of Fountain Place, a recently opened business center in downtown's north end. Well worth a look.

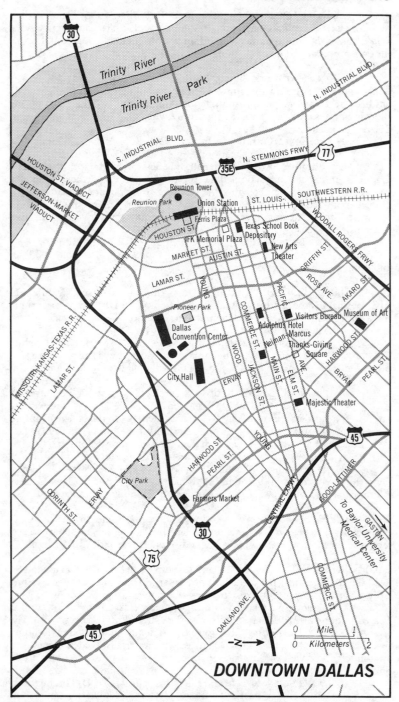

DOWNTOWN DALLAS

Infomart, 1950 Stemmons Fwy. (746-4636): This modern replica by Martin Growald of London's famous 1851 Crystal Palace houses the country's most important permanent marketing exhibition for the data-processing industry. Part of the Dallas Market Center complex. Worth a look.

Southfork Ranch, Murphy Rd., in Plano (214/442-6536): The Ewing family ranch in the renowned "Dallas" TV series has become a fashionable tourist attraction. Guided tours of the ranch during shooting breaks. For J.R. fans. 45 min. from dwntwn on I-75, Tex. 44. and FM 2551. Open daily.

Texas Commerce Tower, 2200 Ross Ave. (922-2300): The most spectacular building in Dallas. Designed by Richard Keating, of Skidmore, Owings & Merrill, this 55-story skyscraper of glass and granite is among the most compelling towers to rise in this decade in the U.S. Crowned by a great arch bringing the building to a dramatic conclusion, the Texas Commerce Tower presents a vast "hole"—75 ft. (22 m.) high, 22 ft. (6 m.) wide—that slices out the center of the 41st through the 49th floors. An absolute must-see.

Texas Stadium, Tex. 183 at Loop 12, in Irving (214/438-7676): One of the country's football shrines (holds 65,000) and home to the famous Cowboys. Worth a look.

HISTORIC BUILDINGS: **Hall of State,** in the center of State Fair Park (421-5136): A handsome art deco ensemble of huge wall murals, temporary exhibitions on the history of Texas, and memorabilia of famous Texas heroes. For those who enjoy the gigantic. Open daily.

John Neely Bryan Cabin, Main, Elm, & Market Sts.: Log cabin built in 1841 by the city's founder, it was later used as a post office and then a courthouse. It's not open to the public, but have a look at it anyway.

Southern Methodist University, Hillcrest Ave. at University Park (692-2000): Founded in 1915, this is one of the Southwest's most famous universities (9,000 students). On the 164-acre campus there are nearly 100 Georgian-style buildings, plus the **Owen Arts Center** (see "Museums of Art," below). Well worth going out of your way for.

Texas School Book Depository, 411 Elm St. (653-7011) According to the official version, Lee Harvey Oswald shot President Kennedy from this building, which is now the Dallas County Administration Building. The most photographed building in Dallas.

MONUMENTS: **John F. Kennedy Memorial,** J.F.K. (formerly Dealy) Plaza, at Main & Market Sts.: Granite cenotaph by Philip Johnson, sober and austere, near the place where President Kennedy was assassinated. Worth a look.

MUSEUMS OF ART: **Dallas Museum of Art,** 1717 N. Harwood St. (922-0220): The most recent (1984) of the large Texas museums houses pre-Columbian art, great European masters (Cézanne, Gauguin, Monet, Pissarro, Van Gogh), modern American painting (notably Jackson Pollock), as well as rich collections of African art. Don't miss the extraordinary giant sculpture by Claes Oldenburg, *Stake Hitch*. All this is housed in a splendid modern building by Edward Larrabee Barnes. Lovely gardens with waterfalls, shaded groves, and an uninterrupted view of the Dallas skyline. An absolute must-see. Open Tues.-Sun.

Owen Arts Center, Hillcrest Ave. (692-2614): This huge arts complex on the Southern Methodist University campus includes the **Bob Hope Theatre** (built with a donation from the famous comedian, but Shakespeare is the playwright of choice here); the **Meadows Museum,** dedicated to classical Spanish painting and also offering temporary exhibitions; and a very fine modern-sculpture garden. An absolute must-see. Open Tues.-Sun.

MUSEUMS OF SCIENCE & HISTORY: ⚒ Age of Steam Railroad Museum, 7226 Wentwood Dr., Fair Park (421-8711): Superb collection of old steam locomotives. Open Sun. only; daily during the State Fair.

⚒ **Biblical Arts Center,** 7500 Park Lane (691-4661): A surprising spectacle which includes a 124-by-20-ft (38-by-6-m) painting of the miracle of Pentecost with a sound-and-light show plus a replica of Christ's tomb. Open Tues.-Sun.

⚒ **Dallas Museum of Natural History,** Second & Grand Aves., Fair Park (421-2169): This neoclassical building is a museum of southwestern and Texas natural history. More than 50 facsimiles of natural habitats plus rich zoological and botanical collections, including a 90-million-year-old fossil fish. An absolute must-see. Open daily.

☀⚒ **Old City Park,** Gano & Harwood Sts. (421-5141): Authentic 19th-century Texas town restored in minutest detail, with a train station, booths, church, bank, school, etc. There are 40-some original buildings in all, from all over Texas. Well worth a visit. Open Tues.-Sun.

⚒ **The Science Place,** First Ave. & Martin Luther King, Jr., Blvd., Fair Park (428-8351): Remarkably conceived exhibits on science, energy, and ecology. History of anatomy depicted on transparent human bodies; a planetarium too. Worth a visit. Open daily.

OUTDOOR ART & PLAZAS: Apart from the **Sculpture Garden** in the middle of Dallas Market Center (see "Architectural Highlights," above), **City Hall** offers two interesting modern sculptures: Henry Moore's *The Dallas Piece*, three bronze blocks weighing 13 tons; and two "floating" sculptures by Marta Pan on an ornamental lake.

PANORAMAS: ⚒ First National Bank, Elm & Akard Sts. (744-8000): Impressive panorama from the 50th-floor platform. Open Mon.-Fri.

👓👓 **Reunion Tower,** 300 Reunion Blvd. (741-3663): This 50-story tower capped with a geodesic dome is the new symbol of Dallas. Observation deck at the top. Open daily until midnight.

PARKS & GARDENS: ⚒ Civic Garden Center, First Ave. & Martin Luther King, Jr., Blvd., Fair Park: Lovely botanic garden with rose gardens and a tropical hothouse. Open daily.

⚒ **Dallas Aquarium,** First Ave. & Martin Luther King, Jr., Blvd., Fair Park (670-8441): This modest-sized (and hence, perhaps, un-Texan) aquarium is one of the most modern and complete in the Southwest, with 350 species of fish, reptiles, and amphibians. Worth a visit. Open daily.

⚒ **L. B. Houston Park,** Tom Braniff Dr.: Kind of miniature nature reservation (20 min. from dwntwn on the Stemmons Fwy.) with gray fox, wild rabbit, beaver, racoon, and first-growth timber from a vast forest that was almost completely cleared at the turn of the century. One of the few green areas in Dallas.

☀⚒ **State Fair Park,** Parry & Second Aves. (565-9931): Immense, 240-acre fairground with fountains, ponds, floral exhibitions, an aquarium, and numerous museums (see above), as well as the famous

Cotton Bowl Stadium, where the Cotton Bowl is played each Jan. 1. In Oct. it is the site of the **Texas State Fair,** which attracts three million visitors annually.

⚓ **Thanks-Giving Square,** Bryan & Ervay Sts.: A green oasis in the heart of the city with an unusual spiral chapel and meditation garden designed by Philip Johnson, a striking contrast to neighboring skyscrapers.

PERFORMING ARTS: For a daily listing of all shows and cultural events, consult the entertainment pages of the daily papers *Dallas Morning News* (morning) and *Dallas Times Herald* (evening), and of the monthly magazine *D*.

Bob Hope Theatre, Owen Arts Center, Hillcrest Ave. (692-2573): Modern and classical theater on the Southern Methodist University campus.

Dallas Repertory Theatre, 1030 N. Park Center (369-8966): Classical theater, drama, comedy.

Dallas Theater Center, 3636 Turtle Creek Blvd. (526-8857): From Shakespeare to contemporary theater, Sept.-May. Daring Frank Lloyd Wright architecture.

Majestic Theatre, 1925 Elm St. (880-0137): Theater, recitals, and a variety of performances in a splendid, recently restored building.

Music Hall, First & Parry Aves., Fair Park (565-9100): Home of the Dallas Symphony Orchestra, with principal conductor Eduardo Mata (Sept.-May); the Dallas Opera (Nov.-Dec.); and the Dallas Ballet. Also offers Broadway hits (June-Aug.).

New Arts Theatre, 301 N. Market St. at Ross (761-9064): Contemporary theater.

Theatre Three, 2800 Routh St. (871-3300): Drama, comedy.

RODEOS: ⚓ **Kow Bell Indoor Rodeo,** U.S. 287 in Mansfield (15 mi. SW on I-20 and Tex. 157) (817/477-3092): The only rodeo in the country open year round, with events each Fri. at 8:30 p.m. (plus Sat. at 8 p.m., June to late Aug.). In an authentic breeding ranch that offers horseback riding daily. Don't miss it.

🔭 **Mesquite Rodeo,** I-635 at Military Pkwy. in Mesquite (13 mi. west on Tex. 352) (214/285-8777): Fri. and Sat. rodeos at 8:30 p.m., Apr.-Sept. Experts consider this the most demanding, most violent rodeo challenge in all Texas. Guaranteed local color.

SHOPPING: **The Galleria,** L.B.J. Fwy. & Dallas Pkwy.: A monument of modern shopping that has been often copied, never matched. More than 200 luxury boutiques, stores, theaters, restaurants, and even a skating rink, all in air-conditioned comfort (*de rigueur* in Texas) under an enormous glass dome. Not to be missed. 15 min. from dwntwn.

Luskey's, Forest Lane & Webb Chapel Rd.: Texas riding boots and all the necessary equipment for a real (or pretend) cowboy.

Neiman-Marcus, Main & Ervay Sts.: The most chic, most expensive department store in the country. You can find anything at Neiman-Marcus, even the most imagination-defying gift ideas. Those with thin billfolds are advised to stay away.

Resistol Hat Shop, 1505 Main St.: One of the largest assortments of cowboy hats in all Texas (no small claim, that).

SPECIAL EVENTS: For the exact schedule of events below, consult the **Dallas Convention & Visitors Bureau** (see "Tourist Information," above).

Cotton Bowl (Jan. 1): Eight days of festivities culminating in the famous football game. A classic since 1956.

Texas State Fair (Oct.): Shows, rodeos, sporting events—this animated fair attracts three million visitors each year. An absolute must-see.

SPORTS: Dallas has three professional teams:

Baseball (Apr.-Oct.): Texas Rangers, Arlington Stadium (817/273-5100).
Basketball (Oct.-Apr.): Dallas Mavericks, Reunion Arena (214/658-7068).
Football (Sept.-Dec.): Dallas Cowboys, Texas Stadium (214/556-2500).

THEME PARKS: ⛵ International Wildlife Park, I-30 at Wild Life Pkwy., Grand Prairie (214/263-2201): Drive your car through this vast zoo-safari and see wild animals (including African wildlife) in their natural habitat. Open daily year round.

☼⛵ **Six Flags Over Texas,** I-30 and Tex. 360, Arlington (817/640-8900): Huge, "Texas style" amusement park (192 acres) with more than 100 different attractions including a giant roller coaster. Events, performances, etc. Open daily in summer; wknds only in spring and autumn; closed the rest of the year.

ZOOS: The ⛵ Dallas Zoo, 621 E. Clarendon Dr. (946-5154): One of the most comprehensive zoos in the United States, with 2,000 animals on 48 acres. Worth a visit. Open daily.

ACCOMMODATIONS
See the listing of toll-free numbers in the Appendix.

Room Rates in Dallas	
B (Budget)	up to $30
I (Inexpensive)	$30–$60
M (Moderate)	$60–$90
E (Expensive)	$90–$140
VE (Very Expensive)	$140 and up

Personal Favorites (in order of preference)

♙♙♙♙ **Fairmont** (dwntwn), 1717 N. Akard St., TX 75201 (214/720-2020; toll free, see Fairmont). 600 rms, A/C, cable color TV. AE, CB, DC, MC, V. Gar. $9, pool, health club, two rests. (including the Pyramid Room), 24-hr coffeeshop, bars, 24-hr rm svce, disco, hrdrsr, drugstore, crib $25. *Note:* "The" chic palace of Dallas (the most expensive suite costs more than $1,500 a night). Two modern towers w. elegant, luxurious interior decoration and spacious, very comfortable rms. Svce is of the highest caliber in an opulent, tasteful atmosphere. Excellent rest. Wealthy Texan and big business clientele. No-smoking floor. In the heart of dwntwn. Recently renovated. **VE**

☼♙♙♙♙ **Hyatt Regency** (dwntwn), 300 Reunion Blvd., TX 75207 (214/651-1234; toll free, see Hyatt). 950 rms, A/C, color TV, in-rm movies. AE, CB, DC, MC, V. Valet gar. $6, pool, tennis, health club, two rests. (including Fausto's), coffeeshop, three bars, rm svce, disco, boutiques.

Note: This illustrious grand hotel displays a 27-story, blue-tinted glass façade that reflects neighboring skyscrapers. Waterfall and interior gardens in the 19-story lobby. Unparalleled facilities and comfort plus an extraordinary view from the revolving rest. at the top (Antares), although the cuisine is mediocre. Very efficient svce. Quite close to the business district. Interesting wknd packages. VIP floor. Has just undergone a $25-million facelift. **E–VE**

Plaza of the Americas (dwntwn), 650 N. Pearl Blvd., TX 75201 (214/979-9000; toll free 800/225-5843). 442 rms, A/C, color TV, in-rm movies. AE, CB, DC, MC, V. Valet gar. $9, health club, tennis, sauna, two rests. (including Café Royal), bar, rm svce, disco, hrdrsr, boutiques, concierge, free crib. *Note:* Some of the most luxury-hotel architecture in Texas, w. an immense 15-story plant-filled atrium overlooking a skating rink. Vast, luxurious rms w. balconies and modern, elegant décor. Very good svce and a renowned rest. Big business clientele. Part of the British group Trusthouse Forte, which owns the Travelodge chain. Very central location. **E–VE**

Hilton Dallas (dwntwn), 1914 Commerce St., TX 75201 (214/747-7000; toll free, see Hilton). 713 rms, A/C, color TV, in-rm movies. AE, CB, DC, MC, V. Gar. $6, solarium, rest., coffeeshop, bars, rm svce, boutiques, free crib. *Note:* The most central (but not the most modern) of Dallas's grand hotels. Practical comfort and good svce make it a good value and an excellent choice for the visitor. Interesting wknd packages. **M–E**

Marriott Market Center (nr. dwntwn), 2101 Stemmons Fwy., TX 75207 (214/748-8551; toll free, see Marriott). 415 rms, A/C, color TV, in-rm movies. AE, CB, DC, MC, V. Free parking, two pools, health club, rest., coffeeshop, bars, rm svce, disco, hrdrsr. *Note:* Large, modern, and comfortable motel offering spacious, balconied rms w. refrigerators. Near the World Trade Center and five min. from Love Field. Very popular w. business people. Interesting wknd packages. **M–E**

Best Western Market Center (nr. dwntwn), 2023 Market Center Blvd., TX 75207 (214/741-5041; toll free, see Best Western). 96 rms, A/C, color TV, in-rm movies. AE, CB, DC, MC, V. Free parking, pool, rest., bar, crib $4. *Note:* Conventional but comfortable motel quite close to the Market Center. Direct access to the highway network. Good-natured reception and svce. This very good value is ideal for the car traveler—eight min. from dwntwn and ten min. from Love Field. **I**

Days Inn Abrams (vic.), 9386 L.B.J. Fwy., TX 75231 (214/690-1220; toll free, see Days Inns). 279 rms, A/C, color TV, free in-rm movies. AE, DC, MC, V. Free parking, pool, rest. *Note:* A typical highway motel offering functional comfort. Ideal for the car traveler—five min. from the Galleria Shopping Center and 20 min. from dwntwn. **I**

Motel 6 South (nr. dwntwn), 4610 S. Thornton Fwy., TX 75224 (214/372-5924). 95 rms, A/C, color TV, free in-rm movies. DC, MC, V. Parking, pool, free crib. *Note:* Modern, ultra-economical motel located 15 min. from dwntwn. One of the best values in the area. Easy access to the highways makes it ideal for the car traveler. **B**

Other Accommodations (from top bracket to budget)

The Mansion on Turtle Creek (nr. dwntwn), 2821 Turtle Creek Blvd., TX 75219 (214/559-2100; toll free, see Preferred). 145 rms, A/C, cable color TV. AE, CB, DC, MC, V. Valet parking $9, pool, tennis, rest. (Mansion on Turtle Creek Restaurant), coffeeshop, bar, 24-hr rm svce, disco, concierge, free crib. *Note:* Elegant Moorish-style manor house dating from the 1920s standing in five acres of terraced park. Lovely period furniture w. pastel décor and flowers everywhere. Ultracomfortable rms w. balconies or private patios. Correct, attentive svce. First-rate rest. A big favorite of business people and celebrities. One of the great achievements of modern American hoteldom, owned by the wealthy Hunt family of Texas. **VE**

☼ ♟♟♟ **The Adolphus** (dwntwn), 1321 Commerce St., TX 75202 (214/742-8200; toll free 800/221-9083). 430 rms, A/C, cable color TV. AE, CB, DC, MC, V. Valet parking $9, health club, sauna, three rests., two bars, rm svce, hrdrsr, boutiques, concierge, free crib. *Note:* A venerable (1912) palace, engagingly sumptuous, and a historical landmark for its original rococo architecture. Inside are very lovely 17th-century Flemish tapestries and spacious, elegant rms w. stylish furniture and mini-bars (some have a private patio). Good svce and a very good rest. (The French Room). This celebrated locale in the heart of dwntwn Dallas hosts luminaries from all over the world. Has undergone $60 million worth of renovation. **VE**

♟♟♟♟ **Crescent Court Hotel** (nr. dwntwn), 400 Crescent Ct., TX 75201 (214/871-3200; toll free, see Preferred). 218 rms, A/C, cable color TV. AE, CB, DC, MC, V. Valet gar. $9, pool, rest. (Beau Nash), coffeeshop, bar, 24-hr rm svce, disco, boutiques, concierge, free crib. *Note:* This ultramodern palace designed by Philip Johnson is part Versailles, part Walt Disney World. But if the exterior provokes a bit of a giggle, the interior decoration is a masterpiece of classic elegance, w. numerous works of art and stylish furnishings. Vast, luxurious rms, and each suite decorated in a different style. Exemplary svce and a rest. that is full of business people at lunchtime. Free shuttle to and from dwntwn. An integral part of the vast Crescent Court commercial and office complex. **VE**

♟♟♟ **Loews Anatole** (nr. dwntwn), 2201 Stemmons Fwy., TX 75207 (214/748-1200; toll free, see Loews). 1,600 rms, A/C, color TV, in-rm movies. AE, CB, DC, MC, V. Free valet parking, pool, tennis, golf, health club, sauna, nine rests. (including The Plum Blossom), 24-hr coffeeshop, eight bars, rm svce, hrdrsr, boutiques. *Note:* A veritable city-within-a-city, the Anatole is the largest hotel in Dallas. The ultramodern interior (the exterior of this reddish monolith is somewhat reminiscent of a prison) includes a superb 14-story garden-lobby and very comfortable rms. Specializing in groups and convention clientele, this enormous futurist hotel is also a favorite of business people. Good svce and very complete recreational facilities w. a hot spring. Seven acres of gardens w. ponds, fountains, and groves, all quite close to the Dallas Market Center. Interesting wknd deals. **E–VE**

♟♟♟ **Westin Galleria** (vic.), 13340 Dallas Pkwy., TX 75240 (214/934-9494; toll free, see Westin). 440 rms, A/C, cable color TV. AE, CB, DC, MC, V. Free valet parking, pool, health club, sauna, two rests. (including Blom's), coffeeshop, bar, 24-hr rm svce, disco, hrdrsr, boutiques, free crib. *Note:* Modern, 21-story grand hotel in the famous Galleria Mall Shopping Center. The architecture lacks imagination but the comfort and facilities are remarkable. All rms have balconies and refrigerators. Very efficient svce. Business and group clientele. No-smoking floors. 20 min. from dwntwn. **E–VE**

♟♟ **Sheraton Dallas Hotel and Towers** (dwntwn), 400 N. Olive St., TX 75201 (214/922-8000; toll free, see Sheraton). 498 rms, A/C, color TV, in-rm movies. AE, CB, DC, MC, V. Valet gar. $12, three rests., three bars, rm svce, disco, boutiques. *Note:* Modern 30-story tower w. four VIP floors. Spacious, comfortable rms and relatively efficient svce. Entirely renovated décor and facilities. Obtrusive group clientele. No recreational facilities. In the heart of Dallas. **E–VE**

♟♟ **Aristocrat Hotel** (dwntwn), 1933 Main St., TX 75201 (214/741-7700; toll free 800/223-9815). 172 suites, A/C, cable color TV. AE, CB, DC, MC, V. Gar. $12, rest., bar, rm svce, free breakfast, free crib. *Note:* A venerable Conrad Hilton palace built in 1925, now a historical landmark. It was carefully restored in 1985 in all its antique splendor. Offers only spacious, comfortable mini-suites. Attentive, personalized svce. A good overall value in the heart of the business district. Very adequate rest. (Dallas Plaza Bar & Grill). **M–E**

☀️🦮🦽 **Omni Melrose** (nr. dwntwn), 3015 Oak Lawn, TX 75219 (214/521-5151; toll free, see Omni). 185 rms, A/C, color TV. AE, CB, DC, MC, V. Free parking, rest. (Garden Court), bar, rm svce, disco, library, concierge, free crib. *Note:* Charming 1920s hotel, entirely renovated to the tune of $12 million. Elegant art deco décor and spacious, comfortable rms. Attentive svce. Business clientele. Offering a free shuttle to and from Love Field, it is also close to the Dallas Theater Center. A favorite of connoisseurs. **M–E**

🦽 **Holiday Inn Downtown** (dwntwn), 1015 Elm St., TX 75202 (214/748-9951; toll free, see Holiday Inns). 312 rms, A/C, color TV, in-rm movies. AE, CB, DC, MC, V. Parking $7, pool, rest., bar, rm svce, disco, crib $7. *Note:* Functional Holiday Inn accommodations in a modern 19-story tower in the heart of Dallas. Spacious rms w. balconies and very mediocre svce. Business and group clientele. Close to the Medical Center. **M–E**

🦽 **Stoneleigh Hotel** (nr. dwntwn), 2927 Maple Ave., TX 75201 (214/871-7111; toll free 800/225-9299). 155 rms, A/C, color TV. AE, CB, DC, MC, V. Free gar. parking, pool, tennis, rest., bar, rm svce, hrdrsr. *Note:* Oldish but comfortable hotel surrounded by ten acres of gardens, close to dwntwn. A favorite of show-business people. Spacious rms, some w. kitchenettes. Svce fluctuates. Free shuttle to and from the Market Center. **M–E**

🦽🦽 **Quality Inn Market Center** (nr. dwntwn), 2015 N. Market Center Blvd., TX 75207 (214/741-7481; toll free, see Quality Inns). 280 rms, A/C, color TV, in-rm movies. AE, CB, DC, MC, V. Free parking, pool, health club, rest., bar, rm svce, free crib. *Note:* Modern 11-story motel offering easy access to Market Center, comfortable rms w. balconies or private patios, and friendly reception and svce. Business clientele. VIP floor. Good value. Eight min. from dwntwn and ten min. from Love Field. **I–M**

🦽 **Howard Johnson–Central** (nr. dwntwn), 10333 N. Central Expwy., TX 75231 (214/363-0221; toll free, see Howard Johnson's). 163 rms, A/C, color TV. AE, CB, DC, MC, V. Free parking, pool, tennis, sauna, rest., bar, rm svce, free crib. *Note:* Inviting motel not far from Southern Methodist University. Vast, well-laid-out rms w. private balconies and good svce. A good value and ideal if you're driving; ten min. from dwntwn. **I–M**

🦽 **Park Cities Inn** (nr. dwntwn), 6101 Hillcrest Ave., TX 75205 (214/521-0330). 53 rms, A/C, color TV, in-rm movies. AE, MC, V. Free parking, nearby coffeeshop, free breakfast, free crib. *Note:* Small, modest motel across from Southern Methodist University. Satisfactory comfort and facilities. Ten min. from dwntwn. **I–M**

🦽 **La Quinta Inn Central** (nr. dwntwn), 4440 N. Central Expwy., TX 75206 (214/821-4220; toll free, see La Quinta). 101 rms, A/C, cable color TV. AE, CB, DC, MC, V. Free parking, adjacent 24-hr coffeeshop, free crib. *Note:* A good value, 15 min. from dwntwn and close to Love Field. Spacious, comfortable (but rather dark) rms w. balconies; friendly reception and svce. Ideal for the car traveler. **I**

Accommodations in the Vicinity

🦽🦽🦽 **Marriott Mandalay** (formerly Four Seasons; vic.), 221 E. Las Colinas Blvd., Irving, TX 75039 (214/556-0800; toll free, see Marriott). 424 rms, A/C, cable color TV. AE, CB, DC, MC, V. Free parking, pool, tennis, health club, sauna, two rests. (including Enjolie), coffeeshop, three bars, 24-hr rm svce, boutiques, free crib. *Note:* An impressive 27-story white tower on the lake at Las Colinas, an enormous apartment complex known as Little Venice because of its canals and water taxis. Ultramodern facilities and comfort. Luxurious rms w. balconies and a spectacular view (the best overlook the lake). Efficient svce and a first-rate rest. Group and wealthy conventioneer clientele. Ten min. from dwntwn and ten min. from Dallas–Fort Worth Airport. **E–VE**

Airport Accommodations

Hyatt Regency Airport (formerly the Amfac; vic.), Dallas–Fort Worth Airport, TX 75261 (214/453-8400; toll free, see Hyatt). 1,460 rms, A/C, color TV, in-rm movies. AE, CB, DC, MC, V. Free parking, pool, eight tennis courts, two golf courses, health club, sauna, five rests., 24-hr coffeeshop, bars, rm svce, disco, hrdrsr, drugstore, free 24-hr airport shuttle. *Note:* This ultramodern hotel in the midst of the airport itself is the largest airport hotel in the world. Irreproachable comfort and efficient svce. Business, group, and convention clientele. Interesting wknd packages. Good recreational equipment. Two VIP floors. **E–VE**

La Quinta Inn Airport East (vic.), 4105 W. Airport Fwy., Irving, TX 75062 (214/252-6546; toll free, see La Quinta). 168 rms, A/C, cable color TV. AE, CB, DC, MC, V. Parking, pool, adjacent 24-hr coffeeshop, bar, disco, free crib. *Note:* Modern, functional motel w. huge, comfortable rms and efficient svce. A very good value, five min. from the airport (free shuttle). **I**

RESTAURANTS

Dallas Restaurant Prices	
(per person, excluding drinks and service charges)	
B (Budget)	up to $15
I (Inexpensive)	$15–$25
M (Moderate)	$25–$40
E (Expensive)	$40–$60
VE (Very Expensive)	$60 and up

Personal Favorites (in order of preference)

Routh Street Café (nr. dwntwn), 3005 Routh St. at Cedar Springs Rd. (871-7161). A/C. Dinner only, Tues.-Sat.; closed Sun., Mon., hols. AE, CB, DC, MC, V. Jkt. Specialties: the American nouvelle cuisine menu changes daily but may include catfish mousse w. smoked-tomato sauce, gazpacho w. coriander, fried chicken w. honey and thyme, quail w. goat cheese and black beans, chocolate nut cake w. tropical fruit. A fine list of American wines at reasonable prices. *Note:* The young and bearded chef, Stephen Pyles, is one of the most gifted cooks of his generation; his cuisine, based on regional food and wood-fire cooking, is a marvel of balance and invention. The décor is simultaneously austere and luxurious in shades of peach-pink and gray. Ultraprofessional svce. One of the 12 best rests. in the country, and a favorite of local yuppies. Resv. a must. *American*. **E (prix fixe)**

The French Room (dwntwn), in the Adolphus (see "Accommodations," above) (742-8200). A/C. Dinner only, Mon.-Sat.; closed Sun. AE, CB, DC, MC, V. J&T. Specialties: cold mussel soup w. basil, sweetbread terrine w. chanterelles, braised turbot w. noodles, saddle of lamb w. thyme and caviar sauce, oysters and asparagus in pastry shell w. lemon sauce, stuffed breast of capon, fruit in puff pastry, sherbet plate and praline mousse. The menu changes regularly. *Note:* Has stripped the "Favorite Restaurant of Wealthy Texans" title from the Fairmont Hotel's Pyramid Room. The cuisine—a remarkable updating of classic French recipes—is supervised by Jean Banchet, owner of the illustrious Le Français rest. in Wheeling, Ill. (see the Chicago chapter), and that says it all. Opulent baroque décor w. crystal chandeliers, cherubim on the ceiling, and Louis XVI furniture. The svce is of rare distinction. Resv. a definite must. Valet parking. *French.* **E**

Arthur's (vic.), 1000 Campbell Center (361-8833). A/C. Lunch Mon.-Fri.; dinner Mon.-Sat.; closed Sun., hols. AE, CB, DC, MC, V. Jkt. Specialties: superb meats, sweetbread medallions w. madeira sauce, lamb chops, calves' liver persillade, fresh poached salmon (in season). A very fine list of California wines. *Note:* A real Dallas classic, w. British club–style ambience and décor that is both relaxed and patrician. This much-praised spot offers an appealing bar and the finest svce. Resv. a must. Valet parking. 20 min. from dwntwn. *Steak-Continental.* **I–M**

Café Pacific (nr. dwntwn), 24 Highland Park Village, Preston Rd. & Mockingbird Lane (526-1170). A/C. Lunch/dinner daily; closed hols. AE, DC, MC, V. Jkt. Specialties: clam chowder, fried clams, fresh grilled salmon, sautéed seafood, steak Oscar. Complete wine list at appropriate prices. *Note:* Irreproachably fresh seafood makes this elegant rest. a favorite of connoisseurs. Modern, inviting décor of woodwork, polished brass, mirrors, and a wealth of plants. Attentive, considerate svce. Resv. advised, but the waits are sometimes long. An excellent place. *Seafood-American.* **I–M**

Mario's (nr. dwntwn), 135 Turtle Creek Village Shopping Center, Oaklawn Ave. at Blackburn (521-1135). A/C. Lunch Mon.–Fri.; dinner daily; closed hols. AE, CB, DC, MC, V. Jkt. Specialties: fresh homemade pasta (including spinach lasagne), scaloppine al marsala, fish of the day, meats. Rather short wine list. *Note:* A fashionable, Italian-inspired rest. that also offers very fine red meat (a Texas necessity). Elegant ambience, and décor that includes a magnificent collection of Chinese porcelain. Exemplary svce. Filled w. locals. Resv. necessary. Valet parking. *Italian-Continental.* **I–M**

Chiquita (nr. dwntwn), 3810 Congress St. (521-0721). A/C. Lunch/dinner Mon.-Sat.; closed Sun., Jan. 1, Thanksgiving, Dec. 25. AE, MC, V. Specialties: tacos al carbon, chile relleno, carne asada, mole poblano, bean soup. *Note:* The most authentic of the countless Mexican rests. in Dallas, w. a pleasant atmosphere and vibrant, colorful décor. Efficient svce. Locally very popular. No resv. *Mexican.* **B–I**

Sonny Bryan's (nr. dwntwn), 2202 Inwood Rd. (357-7120). A/C. Breakfast/lunch daily. No credit cards. Specialties: barbecue, ham, pork chops, and beef. Beer but no wine. *Note:* A contender, w. Dickey's Barbecue (see below), for the "Best Barbecue in Dallas" award. Cooked over hickory-wood fires and smothered in an inimitable sauce, Sonny's barbecue has inspired a cult following. Shabby décor and nonexistent svce. Close to the Medical Center. An authentic local legend for nearly 30 years. No resv. *American.* **B**

Dickey's Barbecue (nr. dwntwn), 14885 Inwood Rd. (239-8547). A/C. Lunch/dinner Mon.-Sat.; closed Sun. No credit cards. Specialties: pork chops, barbecued beef, and sausage. *Note:* This local institution offers one of the finest opportunities to sample truly authentic Texan cuisine at ludicrously low prices. No-frills décor and svce. Consult the phone directory for other locations around Dallas. *American.* **B**

Other Restaurants (from top bracket to budget)

☼♈♈♈♈ **Mansion on Turtle Creek** (nr. dwntwn), in the Mansion on Turtle Creek (see "Accommodations," above) (559-2100). A/C. Lunch/dinner daily; brunch Sat., Sun. AE, CB, DC, MC, V. J&T. Specialties: smoked-pheasant salad, tortilla soup, grilled red snapper w. chili vinaigrette, chicken w. wild rice. The menu changes regularly. Extensive wine list. *Note:* Ultrasophisticated cuisine combining French culinary finesse w. lively Tex-Mex flavors. Super-chic, Hispanic-Texan décor. Very correct svce. A favorite of the local moneyed elite. Resv. advised. Valet parking. *American-Continental.* **M–E**

♈♈♈ **The Plum Blossom** (nr. dwntwn), in the Loews Anatole (see "Accommodations," above) (748-1200). A/C. Dinner only, Mon.-Sat.; closed Sun. AE, CB, DC, MC, V. Jkt. Specialties: Mongolian pot au feu, Peking duck, coquilles St-Jacques w. oyster sauce, fried ice cream. *Note:* Chinese cuisine that is as remarkable as the décor—a six-foot-high bronze Buddha sits regally amid the diners. Very good svce. Resv. a must. An experience that should not be missed. Valet parking. *Chinese.* **M**

♈♈ **Baby Routh** (nr. dwntwn), 2708 Routh St. (871-2345). A/C. Lunch/dinner daily; brunch Sun. AE, CB, DC, MC, V. Specialties: black-bean and goat-cheese crêpes, cream of corn and green vegetable soup, barbecue, grilled shrimp and bacon on a brioche, banana-rum cake, crème brûlée w. pumpkin and ginger. *Note:* The more rustic, less snobby offshoot of the famous Routh Street Café (see above) offers inventive modern cuisine from the talented Amy Ferguson. Luminous, elegant décor w. a lovely patio. An "in" place. Resv. advised. *American.* **I–M**

☼♈♈ **Dakota's** (dwntwn), 600 N. Akard St. (740-4001). A/C. Lunch Mon.-Fri.; brunch Sun.; dinner nightly; closed hols. AE, CB, DC, MC, V. Specialties: homemade pasta, blackened red snapper, mesquite grilled steaks, game dishes. *Note:* With its marble walls, its cascading waterfall and its elegant patio, all below ground level, this restaurant draws Dallas's own VIP's as well as visiting celebrities. Good selection of grills, mainly steaks, chops and seafood. Service is first-rate. Resv. advised. *American.* **I–M**

♈♈ **Newport's** (dwntwn), 703 McKinney (954-0509). A/C. Lunch Mon.-Fri.; dinner Mon.-Sat.; closed Sun.; hols. AE/MC/V. Specialties: raw oysters, ceviche, mesquite-grilled seafood, fresh salmon and swordfish, toothsome cheesecake. *Note:* Another well-established favorite for business lunches and dinners. Located in a converted turn-of-the-century brewery, Newport's is one of the neatest rustic restaurants in town. The atmosphere is informal and relaxing, the fish superb. Pleasant svce. Resv. recommended. *Seafood.* **I–M**

♈♈ **Royal Tokyo** (vic.), 7525 Greenville Ave. (368-3304). A/C. Lunch Mon.-Fri; brunch Sun.; dinner daily. AE, CB, DC, MC, V. Jkt. Specialties: sashimi, tempura, sukiyaki, teppanyaki, sushi. *Note:* The experts agree that this is the best Japanese rest. in Dallas. Elegant Japanese décor w. a lovely water-garden. Very good svce. An excellent locale, 20 min. from dwntwn. Valet parking. *Japanese.* **I–M**

♈ **Raphael's** (nr. dwntwn), 3701 McKinney Ave. (521-9640). A/C. Lunch/dinner Mon.-Sat.; closed Sun., hols, and two weeks in June. AE, CB, DC, MC, V. Specialties: chile relleno, chicken mole, enchiladas, tamales, fajitas. *Note:* An old Dallas classic, w. vaguely Aztec décor and a warm, "ranchera" atmosphere. Very popular among local fans of authentic Mexican cuisine. Other location: 6718 Greenville Ave. (692-8431). *Mexican.* **B–I**

♈ **S. & D. Oyster House** (nr. dwntwn), 2701 McKinney Ave. (880-0111). A/C. Lunch/dinner Mon.-Sat.; closed Sun. AE, MC, V. Specialties: gumbo, oysters, Mexican Gulf shrimp, fish of the day.

Note: Irreproachably fresh seafood served in a usually packed house, w. very effective New Orleans décor and a noisy, friendly ambience. No resv. unfortunately. *Seafood.* **B–I**

☼☲ **Frank Tolbert Texas Chili Parlor** (nr. dwntwn), 4544 McKinney Ave. (953-1353). A/C. Lunch/dinner daily (until 2 a.m.). AE, CB, DC, MC, V. Specialties: "donkey tails" (hot dog tortillas), chili con carne. *Note:* The state's most celebrated chili parlor, a must for all visitors. Relaxed atmosphere. In case you're allergic to chili, try the Sonofabitch Stew, perfectly adequate sustenance despite the name. *American.* **B**

☼☲ **La Cave** (nr. dwntwn), 2019 N. Lamar St. (871-2072). A/C. Lunch/dinner Mon.-Sat.; closed Sun. AE, MC, V. Specialties: homemade pasta and soups, delicatessen meats, cheeses. *Note:* Congenial wine bistro w. very modest prices and an intimate atmosphere where Edith Piaf songs are *de rigueur.* An ideal spot for a quick bite. Stampeded by the white-collar crowd at noon. *French.* **B**

Cafeterias / Fast Food

Luby's (vic.), 10425 N. Central Expwy. at Meadow Central Mall (361-9024). A/C. Lunch/dinner daily (until 8 p.m.). No credit cards. Respectable fast-food cuisine, 20 min. from dwntwn. Other location: 5954 Alpha Rd. (233-3275).

Highland Park (nr. dwntwn), 4619 Cole St. (526-3801). A/C. Lunch/dinner Mon.-Sat. (until 8 p.m.). No credit cards. Excellent cafeteria w. low prices. Other location: 5100 Beltline Rd. (934-8025).

BARS & NIGHTCLUBS

Andrew's (nr. dwntwn), 3301 McKinney Ave. (220-0566). Open daily. The "in" bar w. a hip, youthful ambience; also a fair rest.

Belle Starr (nr. dwntwn), 7724 N. Central Expwy. (750-4787). Open daily. A saloon of typically Texan atmosphere w. dancing and the requisite country music.

Confetti (nr. dwntwn), 5201 Matilda (943-4013). Open daily. A disco filled w. locals.

☼☲ **Longhorn Ballroom** (nr. dwntwn), 216 Corinth (428-3128). Open Wed.-Sat. A country-music paradise for 20 years.

Starck (nr. dwntwn), 703 McKinney Ave. (720-0130). Refined décor by the French founder Philippe Starck and a trendy ambience. The most elegant disco in Dallas. Open Thurs.–Sun.

Strictly Tabu (nr. dwntwn), 4111 Lomo Alto (528-5200). One of the best jazz clubs in Dallas and an excellent spot.

FORT WORTH

Once a true cowboy town on the Trinity River, Fort Worth was known in the 19th century as the "gateway to the Far West" where the huge herds of Texas cattle were watered on the way to railhead in Kansas. Established in 1849 to defend the pioneers against the Comanches, this former garrison town attracted some of the most famous and formidable characters of the West, from Doc Holliday to Wyatt Earp, as well as Butch Cassidy and the Sundance Kid. Inseparable neighbors, Dallas and Fort Worth constitute a gigantic metroplex almost 50 mi. (80 km) long, criss-crossed with four-lane highways and nicknamed "Silicon Prairie" because of the area's high concentration of leading electronics companies. Despite its boots and Stetsons, the most Texan of Texas cities makes

good use of its aeronautical, oil, and computer resources. Fort ·Worth nevertheless remains one of the biggest livestock (see the famous **Stockyards)**
and grain markets in the country. Its famous rodeos continue to draw huge
crowds, as do the very popular **Amon Carter Museum,** dedicated to the era
of the Far West, and the splendid and futurist **Kimbell Art Museum.** The infamous "J.R." of "Dallas," Larry Hagman, is a famous celebrated son of Fort
Worth.

INFORMATION & TOURS

TOURIST INFORMATION: The **Fort Worth Convention & Visitors Bureau,** 100 E. 15th St., TX 76102 (817/336-8791).
    Visitor Information Center, 123 E. Exchange St. (817/624-4741).

GUIDED TOURS: Gray Line Tours Fort Worth (bus) (817/429-7563):
Guided tour of the city, serving major hotels.

SIGHTS, ATTRACTIONS, & ACTIVITIES

ARCHITECTURAL HIGHLIGHTS: ☼ ≜ **Water Gardens,** Houston & 14th
Sts.: Superb aquatic gardens in the middle of the city with concrete terraces,
plantings, and futurist waterfalls. The water flows at a rate of 19,000 gallons per
min. Designed by Philip Johnson; dates from 1974. An absolute must-see.
        ≜ **Will Rogers Memorial Center,** 3400 W. Lancaster St. (870-
        8150): Dedicated to the famous cinema cowboy and humorist,
this vast exhibition center includes **Memorial Coliseum** and the **Will Rogers Auditorium,** where the big concerts, rodeos, auto shows, and other Fort Worth
events take place, as well as several major museums of Fort Worth (see the Amon
Carter Museum, Kimbell Art Museum, and Museum of Science & History, below).

HISTORIC BUILDINGS: ≜ **Log Cabin Village,** 2100 Log Cabin Village Lane
(926-5881): A group of authentic pioneer homes dating from the mid–19th
century. For lovers of western history. Open daily.
        ☼≜ **The Stockyards,** Exchange Ave. & W. Main St. (626-3761):
        Fort Worth's original claim to fame, with numerous saloons,
western boutiques, and restaurants. The atmosphere is amusing although rather
touristy. Not to be missed.
        ☼≜ **Sundance Square,** Commerce, Houston, 2nd, & 3rd Sts.:
        The historic heart of Fort Worth, with old houses, brick side-
walks, and period gas lamps. Lots of restaurants, boutiques, and art galleries, as
well. Good for a bit of a stroll.
        ≜ **Thistle Hill,** 1509 Pennsylvania at Summit (336-1212): The
        last of the luxurious manors belonging to the surpassingly rich
"cattle barons" of the 19th century. Magnificently restored in all its Texan opulence. Worth a look. Open Sun.-Fri.

MUSEUMS OF ART: ☼ ≜≜ **Amon Carter Museum of Western Art,** 3501
Camp Bowie Blvd. (738-1933): American painting and sculpture, with special
attention to western lore (notably, paintings by Frederic Remington and Charles
Russell). The marvelous triangular Philip Johnson building also houses works by
contemporary artists such as Georgia O'Keeffe, Ben Shahn, Grant Wood, and
Stuart Davis. An absolute must-see. Open Tues.-Sun.
        ☼≜≜≜ **Kimbell Art Museum,** 3333 Camp Bowie Blvd. (332-8451):
        A Louis Kahn masterpiece from 1973, this building

houses all forms of art from prehistoric times to Picasso and includes one of the finest private collections of European masters in the country. Among its most famous holdings: Giovanni Bellini's *Christ in Benediction,* Goya's *Matador Pedro Romero,* Rembrandt's *Portrait of a Young Jew,* and Picasso's *Man with a Pipe.* A visit not to be missed. Open Tues.-Sun. The patio restaurant is agreeable in good weather.

MUSEUMS OF SCIENCE & HISTORY: ⚘ Museum of Science & History,
1501 Montgomery St. (732-1631): A very educational museum of man with a section on medical sciences and on anthropology as well as a 70-mm film projection room considered one of the most modern in the world **(Omni Theater).** See it. Open daily.

PARKS & GARDENS: ⚘ Botanic Gardens, 3200 Botanic Garden Dr. (870-7686): Very lovely botanic garden displaying more than 2,000 plant varieties as well as an enchanting Japanese garden with authentically Japanese tea houses. Open Tues.-Sun.

PERFORMING ARTS: For a daily listing of all shows and cultural events, consult the entertainment pages of the daily papers *Fort Worth News Tribune* (morning) and *Fort Worth Star Telegram* (morning and evening), and of the monthly magazines *Fort Worth* and *Texas Monthly.*
    Casa Mañana, 3101 W. Lancaster Ave. (332-9319): Broadway hits, concerts, modern theater.
    Circle Theater, 3460 Bluebonnet Circle (921-3040): Drama, comedy.
    Hip Pocket Theatre, 1672 Fairmount (246-1269): Open-air theater.
    Tarrant County Convention Center Theatre, 1111 Houston St. (332-9222): Home of the Fort Worth Opera, the Fort Worth Ballet, and the Fort Worth Symphony Orchestra, with principal conductor John Giordano (Sept.-May).
    Will Rogers Auditorium, 3301 W. Lancaster (332-0909): Concerts, recitals, shows with top stars.

RODEOS: ⚘ Cowton Coliseum, 123 E. Exchange at the Stockyards (871/625-1025): Saturday rodeos at 8 p.m., Mar. to late May and Sept. to mid-Nov., in a spirited atmosphere. Don't miss it.

SPECIAL EVENTS: For the exact schedule of events below, consult the **Fort Worth Convention & Visitors Bureau** (see "Tourist Information," above).
    Fat Stock Show & Rodeo (late Jan.-Feb.): One of the country's best-known rodeos, for fans of real flesh-and-blood cowboys. A nearly 100-year-old tradition.
    Chisholm Trail Roundup (second wknd in June): Lively and colorful cowboy parades, square dances, and barbecues.
    Shakespeare in the Park (June): Open-air, free performances.
    Pioneer Days Celebration (late Sept.): A lively celebration of the cult of the cowboy with carnivals, parades, and public dances.

THEME PARKS: See "Theme Parks" in Dallas, above.

ZOOS: ⚘ Zoological Park, 2727 Zoological Park Dr., Forest Park (817/870-7065): Modern, very well-conceived zoo in a wooded setting. More than 800 animal species; of particular interest, a spectacular seal pond and one of the world's richest collections of reptiles and amphibians (in the Herpetarium). Worth going out of your way for. Open daily.

ACCOMMODATIONS

See the listing of toll-free numbers in the Appendix.

Room Rates in Fort Worth	
B (Budget)	up to $30
I (Inexpensive)	$30–$60
M (Moderate)	$60–$90
E (Expensive)	$90–$140
VE (Very Expensive)	$140 and up

Personal Favorites (from top bracket to budget)

Worthington (formerly the Americana; dwntwn), 200 Main St., TX 76102 (817/870-1000; toll free 800/433-5677). 510 rms, A/C, color TV, in-rm movies. AE, CB, DC, MC, V. Valet parking $5, pool, health club, tennis, two rests., coffeeshop, bars, rm svce, disco, drugstore, boutiques, crib free. *Note:* The most recent, and most luxurious, of the local palaces, this architecturally startling hotel looks like a truncated pyramid. Spacious, ultracomfortable rms w. balconies and refrigerators, very complete facilities, a good rest. (Reflections), and excellent svce (the beds are turned daily). Big business clientele. In the heart of Fort Worth just off Sundance Square. **E**

Hyatt Regency (formerly the Texas Hotel; dwntwn), 815 Main St., TX 76102 (817/870-1234; toll free, see Hyatt). 515 rms, A/C, color TV, in-rm movies. AE, CB, DC, MC, V. Valet gar. $8, pool, health club, two rests. (including the Crystal Cactus Room), two bars, rm svce, disco, hrdrsr. *Note:* Massive 1940s-style palace in the heart of dwntwn. The hotel in which President Kennedy spent the night before he was assassinated in Dallas. Luxurious, comfortable layout w. spacious, well-conceived rms and a six-story atrium w. a waterfall and ornamental pools. Impeccable svce and fair rests. A favorite among business people. **E**

Stockyards Hotel (nr. dwntwn), 109 E. Exchange St., TX 76106 (817/625-6427; toll free 800/423-8471). 50 rms, A/C, color TV. AE, CB, DC, MC, V. Valet parking $5, rest., bar, rm svce, disco, crib free. *Note:* The city's oldest (1902) hotel, carefully renovated. Comfortable, congenial Old West ambience and décor. Good rest. and excellent svce. Local color seekers will enjoy the location, in the heart of the slaughterhouse district w. its rests. and nightlife. **M–E**

Green Oaks Inn (vic.), 6901 West Fwy., TX 76116 (817/738-7311; toll free 800/433-2174). 287 rms, A/C, color TV. AE, CB, DC, MC, V. Free parking, two pools, golf, health club, rest., bars, rm svce, disco, crib free. *Note:* Agreeable, Tudor-style motel amid ten acres of park and gardens. Spacious, comfortable rms and pleasant reception and svce. A good value and a favorite of connoisseurs, 15 min. from dwntwn. **M**

Holiday Inn Midtown (nr. dwntwn), 1401 S. University Dr., TX 76107 (817/336-9311; toll free, see Holiday Inns). 180 rms, A/C, color TV, in-rm movies. AE, CB, DC, MC, V. Free parking, pool, health club, rest. (Pipers), bar, rm svce, crib $3. *Note:* Holiday Inn–style functional, modern comfort not far from the museums. Interesting wknd packages. **I–M**

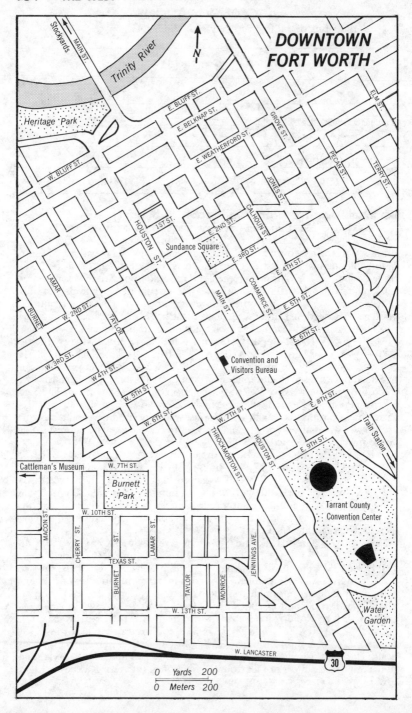

DOWNTOWN FORT WORTH

     Quality Inn South (nr. dwntwn), 4201 South Fwy., TX 76115 (817/923-8281; toll free, see Quality Inns). 98 rms, A/C, color TV, in-rm movies. AE, CB, DC, MC, V. Free parking, pool, coffeeshop, bar, rm svce, free crib. *Note:* Small, appealing, and functional motel w. comfortable rms and affable reception and svce. A very good value that is ideal for the car traveler, ten min. from dwntwn. **I**

     Motel 6 North (nr. dwntwn), 3271 I-35W, TX 76106 (817/625-4359). 106 rms, A/C, color TV, free in-rm movies. DC, MC, V. Parking, pool, free crib. *Note:* An unbeatable value ten min. from dwntwn, offering functional comfort and a warm welcome. **B**

RESTAURANTS

Personal Favorites (from top bracket to budget)

     Michel (nr. dwntwn), 3851 Camp Bowie Blvd. (377-8021). A/C. Lunch Tues.–Fri.; dinner Tues.-Sat.; closed Sun., Mon., hols. AE, CB, DC, MC, V. J&T. Specialties: rack of lamb, fish of the day, seasonal game. A good list of French and California wines. *Note:* Fort Worth's best French rest. offers classic cuisine but w. light sauces from chef Michel Baudouin. The menu changes daily according to what's fresh at the market. The prix-fixe menu (five courses) is particularly fine. Charming Victorian décor and excellent svce. Resv. a must. *French.* **I–M**

     Cattlemen's (nr. dwntwn), 2458 N. Main St. (Stockyards) (624-3945). A/C. Lunch Mon.-Fri.; dinner daily; closed hols. AE, CB, DC, MC, V. Jkt. Specialties: grilled steak, barbecued beef, calf fries. *Note:* The most famous steakhouse in Texas. A stronghold of red meat in an appropriately western setting. Very relaxed atmosphere. Locally popular for 40 years. No resv., hence, inevitable waits. *Steakhouse.* **I**

     Lombardi's (dwntwn), 2nd & Main Sts. (877-1729). A/C. Lunch Mon.-Fri.; dinner Mon.-Sat.; closed Sun., hols. AE, CB, DC, MC, V. Jkt. Specialties: fresh homemade pasta, zuppa di pesce, pork alla parmigiana, saltimbocca alla romana, rather undistinguished desserts. Adequate wine list. *Note:* Honest, tasty cuisine w. a tip of the hat to Italy. Pretty turn-of-the-century décor lighted by charming skylights, and very good svce. Resv. advised. Under the same management as the Ristorante Lombardi in Dallas. *Italian.* **I**

     Edelweiss (nr. dwntwn), 3801-A Southwest Blvd. (738-5934). A/C. Dinner only, Tues.-Sat.; closed Sun., Mon., hols. Specialties: sauerbraten, wienerschnitzel. *Note:* Totally authentic German brasserie w. very adequate, if unimaginative, cuisine. Rather noisy ambience w. the requisite Bavarian orchestra. Efficient svce. Locally popular. No resv. *German.* **B–I**

     Joe T. Garcia's (nr. dwntwn), 2201 N. Commerce St. (626-4356). A/C. Lunch Mon.-Fri.; dinner daily. No credit cards. Specialties: nachos, chile relleno, tacos, enchiladas, quesadillas, chimichangas, excellent margaritas. *Note:* A favorite of Tex-Mex connoisseurs for more than half a century, w. an agreeable patio and guaranteed local color. No resv. Locally very popular. Inevitable waits on the wknds. *American-Mexican.* **B–I**

     Szechuan (nr. dwntwn), 5712 Locke Ave. at Camp Bowie Blvd. (738-7300). A/C. Lunch Mon.-Sat.; dinner daily. AE, MC, V. Specialties: Szechuan chicken, Peking duck, sweet-and-sour shrimp. *Note:* The only Chinese rest. in Fort Worth that is worthy of the title, w. an extensive menu and generous portions. Classic Oriental décor and pleasant svce. *Chinese.* **B–I**

♀ **Tequillo's** (dwntwn), in the Hilton Hotel, 1701 Commerce
St. (335-7000). A/C. Lunch Mon.-Fri.; dinner Mon.-Sat.;
closed Sun. AE, CB, DC, MC, V. Jkt. Specialties: tacos, guacamole, tamales,
carne asada. *Note:* In a city w. dozens of Tex-Mex rests., Tequillo's is the only one
that offers authentic Mexican cuisine. Delightful patio-garden atmosphere w.
greenery, a large fountain, and mariachi band. The house margaritas come in 14
different flavors. Resv. advised. *Mexican.* **B–I**

Cafeterias / Fast Food
Colonial (nr. dwntwn), 1700 Rogers Rd. (335-9372). A/C. Lunch/
dinner daily (until 8 p.m.). No credit cards. Very adequate cafeteria food at modest prices. Close to the university.
☼ **Paris Coffee Shop** (nr. dwntwn), 704 W. Magnolia St. (335-
2041). Breakfast/lunch Mon.-Sat. No credit cards. A local institution. Whether you're a cowboy, a trucker, a Texas millionaire, or a society
lady, sooner or later you'll come to the Paris Coffee Shop. Very good chicken-
fried steak, enchiladas, and chili.

BARS & NIGHTCLUBS
Caravan of Dreams (dwntwn), 312 Houston St. (877-3000). Fashionable
nightclub w. excellent jazz and live blues.
Stagecoach Ballroom (nr. dwntwn), 2516 E. Belknap (831-2261). Huge,
locally popular western dance hall w. a guaranteed cowboy atmosphere.
☼ **The White Elephant Saloon** (nr. dwntwn), 106 E. Exchange
Ave. (624-1887). Open Mon.-Sat. Country-and-western mu-
sic just around the corner from the famous slaughterhouses; a classic for more
than a century, w. relaxed décor and ambience, plus decent barbecue.

NEARBY EXCURSIONS

☼ 🏛 **GRANBURY** (38 mi., 60 km, SW of Fort Worth on U.S.
377): Charming little Texas town that has conserved and re-
stored many of its buildings from the days of the great westward migration. Start
with the picturesque **Opera House,** dating from 1886 and reopened to the public in 1975 after 50 years of slumber. Performances Thurs.-Sun. Mar.-Dec. For
information, call 817/573-9191. Not to be missed.
On the way, see the 🏛 **Pate Museum of Transportation,** U.S. 377 between
Fort Worth and Cresson (14 mi., 22 km, south of Fort Worth) (871/332-1161):
Small transportation museum, from the double-decker bus to the DC-3 and
from the minesweeper to the venerable Model T. Rather jumbled but amusing.
Open Tues.-Sun.

Where to Eat
♀ **The Cuckoo's Nest,** 110 E. Pearl St. (817/573-9722): Origi-
nal décor in a remodeled 19th-century theater. Lunch/dinner
Tues.-Sun. **B–I**
♀ **Nutt House,** Town Square (817/573-9362): Delightful Vic-
torian décor from the 1890s. Lunch only, Tues.-Sun. The Nutt
House also has a dozen rms to rent, with old-fashioned but comfortable furni-
ture. **I**

☼ 🏛 **WAXAHACHIE** (30 mi., 48 km, south of Dallas on I-35E):
Called "Gingerbread City," Waxahachie boasts nearly 200
gingerbread-style and Victorian buildings, all historical landmarks and magnificently restored. Worth going out of your way for.

CHAPTER 36

HOUSTON 🔥

□ □ □

Where 150 years ago there was nothing but a muddy, mosquito-infested tent town, there stands today the Sunbelt's greatest city. Houston, once the capital of the Republic of Texas, owes its name to the first elected president of that short-lived nation—Sam Houston. One of the first Spanish explorers of the North American continent, Alvar Nuñez Cabeza de Vaca, remarked as early as 1528 on Houston's strategic position on the shore of Buffalo Bayou, and "The Bayou City," as Houston is sometimes called, is now the country's fourth-largest port (after New York, New Orleans, and Valdez). Its access to the sea is via the Ship Channel, a canal 50 mi. (80 km) long, 400 ft (122 m) wide, and 40 ft (12 m) deep, passable by the largest deep-water vessels and each year carrying more than 70 million tons of goods.

Like its neighbor and rival, Dallas, Houston is a boom town—a mushrooming city with congested freeways and a spectacular skyline. Surprisingly little affected by the first worldwide crude-oil crisis, Houston continued to flourish into the early 1980s, with annual economic and population growth averaging 15%. The second oil crisis and the slump in farm-product prices, however, have deeply depressed its principal industries—refining, petrochemicals, steel-making, electronic components, cotton, rice, etc.—since 1982, inflicting on the city a record rate of unemployment. Its citizens hope that this crisis, too, will soon be overcome, given the almost legendary drive and ambition of Texas's greatest city, where almost 200 giant corporations have chosen to build their headquarters.

The negatives of Houston include: no coherent city planning, almost non-existent public transportation, snarled auto traffic, a disturbing pollution level, a rising crime rate, and a police force generally regarded as quick on the draw.

The world capital of the oil industry, Houston is also a city of science, culture, and sport. The **Lyndon B. Johnson Space Center,** headquarters for America's conquest of space, guided man's first steps on the moon as well as every space flight launched from Kennedy Space Center or California. The first word spoken by the first man to set foot on the moon, on July 20, 1969, was "Houston." The **Texas Medical Center,** the world's largest hospital complex with its 6,000 beds, two million patients a year, and 52,000 doctors, nurses, and employees, is known around the world for its research on heart surgery and cancer treatment. Houston's six universities, its opera, and its symphony orchestra enjoy—and deserve—a high reputation. The **Astrodome,** an amazing covered stadium with 66,000 seats, 18 stories high, and air-conditioned throughout, is one of the most striking examples of contemporary American architecture.

Typically Texan, Houston is on the way to becoming a great cosmopolitan city as well; more than 45 consulates and 64 foreign banks have offices here.

Houston is the birthplace of the singer Kenny Rogers, the actress Shelly Duval, and the late billionaire businessman and movie producer, Howard Hughes.

BASIC FACTS: State of Texas. Area Code: 713. Time Zone: Central Time. ZIP Code: 77052. Founded: 1836. Approximate population: city, 1,720,000; metropolitan area, 3,650,000. Fourth-largest city and eighth-largest metropolitan area in the country.

CLIMATE: Due to the proximity of the Gulf of Mexico, Houston's winters are agreeably mild (average 51° F, 11° C, in Jan.), while spring and fall are relatively hot. In summer the temperature is high (average 86° F, 30° C, in July) and so is the humidity, but since everything is fiercely air-conditioned, you may need something warm to wear in hotels, restaurants, and office buildings. There are tornadoes, often violent, in the fall.

DISTANCES: Dallas, 243 mi. (390 km); New Orleans, 356 mi. (570 km); San Antonio, 197 mi. (315 km).

ARRIVAL & TRANSIT INFORMATION

AIRPORTS: Houston Intercontinental Airport (IAH), 20 mi. (32 km) north, handles 14.5 million passengers a year. Information: 230-3000.

 W. P. Hobby Airport (commuter flights) (HOU), 10 mi. (16 km) SE, has 7.5 million passengers a year. Information: 643-4597.

U.S. AIRLINES: American (222-9873), Continental (821-2100), Delta (448-3000), Eastern (738-8615), Northwest (868-9988), Pan Am (447-0088), Southwest (237-1221), TWA (222-7273), United (650-1055), USAir (toll free 800/428-4322).

FOREIGN CARRIERS: Air Canada (toll free 800/422-6232), Air France (toll free 800/237-2747), British Airways (toll free 800/247-9297), KLM (658-1781).

CITY LINK: Cab fare **from Houston Intercontinental Airport to city center,** is about $26; time, about 40 min. Bus: Airport Express (523-8888), every 20 min.; makes five stops downtown; fare, $8; time, about 60 min.

 Cab fare **from Hobby Airport to city center,** is about $15; time, 30 min. Hobby Airport Limo (644-8359) connects Hobby Airport to the city center; fare, $5.

 This is one of the country's most sprawling cities, and cab fares are high, so renting a car is probably the best solution, although for this, too, rates are among the highest in the country. Public (bus) transportation is almost nonexistent (Metropolitan Transit Authority/MTA; call 635-4000 for information).

CAR RENTAL (all at Houston Intercontinental Airport): Avis (443-2130), Budget (449-0145), Dollar (449-0161), Hertz (443-0800), National (443-8850), Thrifty (449-0126). For downtown offices, consult the local telephone directory.

LIMOUSINE SERVICES: Care Limousine Service (367-4759), River Oaks Limousine (880-5466), Scripps Edward Limo (toll free 800/223-6710).

TAXIS: Theoretically cabs can't be hailed on the street, but it's easy to find one outside any of the large hotels, or to call one by phone: Sky Jack Cab (523-6080), United Cab (654-4040), Yellow Cab (236-1111).

TRAIN: AMTRAK station, 902 Washington Ave. (toll free 800/872-7245).

BUS: Greyhound, 2121 Main St. (759-6581).

INFORMATION & TOURS

TOURIST INFORMATION: The **Houston Chamber of Commerce,** 1100 Milam St., TX 77002 (713/651-1313).

The **Houston Convention and Visitors Council,** 3300 Main St., TX 77002 (713/523-5050; toll free 800/231-7799).

GUIDED TOURS: Gray Line Tours (bus), 602 Sampson St. (223-8800): Guided tours of the city with departures from principal dwntwn hotels.

SIGHTS, ATTRACTIONS, & ACTIVITIES

ARCHITECTURAL HIGHLIGHTS: ☀ ⚖ **Astrodome,** Kirby Dr. and Loop 610 (799-9500): Second-largest (in height) covered stadium in the world, after that in New Orleans, with 66,000 seats. The plastic roof rises 18 stories. Used not only for sports events but also for concerts, exhibitions, and political meetings. Impressive; the most-visited building in Texas. Open daily.

☀⚖⚖ **Houston Civic Center,** I-45 at Milam St., between Texas and Dallas Aves.: A huge quadrilateral of ultramodern high-rises and municipal buildings in the heart of Houston, featuring the **Albert Thomas Convention Center,** a glass-and-steel building covering three city blocks; **Tranquility Park,** on 32 levels with its oversize fountain (see below); **City Hall;** the **Public Library** with an amusing sculpture (*Geometric Mouse*) by Claes Oldenburg; and an auditorium, **Jesse Jones Hall** (see below). Very eye-catching.

⚖ **Jesse Jones Hall for the Performing Arts,** 615 Louisiana St. (222-1103): A concert hall with remarkable acoustics, home of the Houston Symphony Orchestra. A daring design by the architect Caudill Rowlett Scott, with movable ceiling, which can be arranged to seat 1,800 to 3,000 people. Worth seeing.

☀⚖⚖ **Nina Vance Alley Theatre,** 615 Texas Ave., at Louisiana St. (228-8421): This futurist structure, comprising two auditoriums divided by a party wall, is one of Houston's most innovative buildings—a sort of 21st-century fortress designed by Ulrich Fransen. Should definitely be seen.

☀⚖⚖ **Pennzoil Towers, Pennzoil Place:** Twin towers shaped like oblique prisms, with interior gardens at ground level and a gigantic glass curtain wall rising 36 floors; a spectacular achievement of architects Philip Johnson and John Burgee. Definitely worth seeing.

⚖ **Republic Bank Bldg.,** Republic Bank Center: A strange 56-story postmodern skyscraper with a neo-Gothic gabled roof; another exciting building by the Johnson-Burgee team. The 105-ft.- (35-m.-) high entrance hall is reminiscent of Piranesi's drawings of the palaces of ancient Rome. Positively must be seen.

⚖ **Texas Commerce Tower,** Texas Ave. at Travis St.: Fine modern building, five-sided and 75 floors high—the highest in Texas. Worth seeing.

⚖⚖ **Texas Medical Center,** around Fannin St. and Holcombe Blvd.: Huge hospital complex covering 504 acres, considered the most up-to-date in the world. Its 12 hospitals and nine medical faculties attract researchers, students, and patients from all over the world. An acknowledged leader in cardiology, cancer care, rehabilitation, biomathematics, and space medicine. The Visitor Information Center (790-1136) arranges individual or guided-tour visits Mon.-Fri.

CHURCHES/SYNAGOGUES: ⚖ Christ Church Cathedral, 1117 Texas

Ave. (222-2593): The oldest church in Texas, dating from 1839 and rebuilt in 1893; interesting neo-Gothic building with Tiffany windows. You should see it. Open daily.

Rothko Chapel, 3900 Yupon St., at Sul Ross (524-9839): This octagonal chapel in an out-of-the-way district was designed by Philip Johnson in austere reinforced concrete. It houses a dozen enormous paintings by the famous American artist Mark Rothko, as well as Barnett Newman's very beautiful *Broken Obelisk,* a sculpture dedicated to Martin Luther King, Jr. Don't miss this wonderful setting for meditation and contemplation. Open daily.

HISTORIC BUILDINGS: Rice University, 6100 S. Main St. (527-4929): Small in size with only 3,500 students, but greatly renowned for its faculties of science and engineering, this university founded in 1912 boasts dozens of very beautiful neoclassical and Mediterranean-style buildings, including the **Sewall Art Gallery** and the **Media Center.** Don't miss a visit to the campus.

MUSEUMS OF ART: Bayou Bend Collection, 1 Westcott St. (529-8773): Beautiful collection of American furniture from the 17th through the 19th centuries, housed in 28 rooms of the vast Renaissance-style home of Ima Hogg, daughter of a former governor of Texas. Can be seen Tues.-Sat. by appointment.

Contemporary Arts Museum, 5216 Montrose Blvd. (526-3129): This strange silvered-aluminum parallelogram presents movies and temporary exhibitions of modern art and industrial design. Worth a look. Open Tues.-Sun.

Menil Collection, 1515 Sul Ross (525-9400): The personal collection of Dominique de Menil, which drew large crowds when it was exhibited a few years ago at the Petit Palais in Paris, is now housed in a building worthy of it. It comprises more than 10,000 works of art covering 5,000 years of history, from Etruscan and Anatolian sculpture to the works of such avant-garde painters as Pollock, Rothko, Rauschenberg, and Warhol and surrealists like de Chirico and Magritte. The remarkable, light-filled modern building was designed by Renzo Piano, the architect of many distinguished buildings, including Paris's famous Centre Pompidou. This is among the world's most highly regarded private museums and you shouldn't miss it. Open Tues.-Sun.

Museum of Fine Arts, 1001 Bissonnet (526-1361): A mixture of neoclassical and modern architecture (the interior of one of its modern wings, designed by Mies van der Rohe, presents an unusual theme of broken concrete shafts), this wonderful museum houses a splendid collection of European masters and well-known American painters (particularly Frederic Remington); it is rich in Indian pottery and pre-Columbian art, and has a very beautiful garden of modern sculpture **(Cullen Sculpture Garden)** designed by Isamu Noguchi. Some of the remarkable works on display are Fra Angelico's *Temptation of St. Anthony,* a *Virgin and Child* by Rogier van der Weyden, *Waterlilies* by Claude Monet, Van Gogh's *The Rocks,* and *Crab,* a futurist sculpture by Alexander Calder. Not to be missed. Open Tues.-Sun.

MUSEUMS OF SCIENCE AND HISTORY: Museum of Natural Science, 1 Hermann Circle, Dr. Hermann Park (526-4273): From the diplodocus to the space rocket and from oil wells to artificial earthquakes, this is one of the biggest and best natural-science museums in the country. Here, too, are the **Hall of Medical Science,** with its giant models of the human body, and the **Burke Baker Planetarium,** where visitors can follow the transit of comets and the motion of the planets against the star-studded dome. Open daily.

PANORAMAS: The finest ⚑ **overall view** of this city of skyscrapers is to be had at ground level from **Sam Houston Historical Park** (see below); it will give you a striking capsule history of American architecture from the 19th to the 21st century.

PARKS AND GARDENS: ⚑ **Allen's Landing,** Main and Commerce Sts.: A tiny park overshadowed by skyscrapers, on the spot where the city's founders (two New York promoters named Augustus and John Allen) first moored their boat in 1836. For a long time this was Houston's commercial harbor. Particularly fine view.

⚑ **Memorial Park,** Woodway and Loop 610: A 155-acre public park near downtown Houston. Paths for strollers; botanic garden. Houston's "lung."

⚑ **Sam Houston Historical Park,** 1100 Bagby St. (956-0480): Seven historic buildings (from a village church to a Texas-style plantation house) and stores dating from the 19th century, meticulously restored. Interesting journey into the past of the city and its inhabitants. Should be seen. Open daily.

☀⚑ **Tranquility Park,** bounded by Rusk, Bagby, Smith, and Walker Sts.: This very unusual park in the heart of downtown commemorates the historic *Apollo 11* mission of 1969—the first landing by a manned space vehicle on the moon, in the Sea of Tranquility. The park has a 32-level fountain covering two city blocks, and five rocket-shaped towers. At every entrance, bronze tablets commemorate the Apollo mission in 15 languages. A must-see.

PERFORMING ARTS: For current listings of shows and cultural events, consult the entertainment pages of the two daily papers, *Houston Post* (morning) and *Houston Chronicle* (evening), and the monthly *Texas Monthly*.

Alley Theatre, 615 Texas Ave. (228-8421): One of the country's most renowned stock companies; from classical to experimental theater. Performances Tues.-Sun. from Oct.-May.

Comedy Workshop, 2105 San Felipe (524-7333): Modern theater.

Jesse H. Jones Hall for the Performing Arts, 615 Louisiana St. (224-4240): Home of the Houston Symphony Orchestra. Season Sept.-May and July.

Miller Outdoor Theater, 100 Concert, Dr. Hermann Park (520-3290): Free open-air performances in summer. Shakespeare Festival, Houston Symphony Orchestra concerts, musical comedies, opera, pop concerts, etc.

Music Hall, 810 Bagby St. (853-8000): Home of the Theater Under the Stars (musical comedy, Broadway hits). Season Feb.-May and Oct.-Dec.

Tower Theater, 1201 Westheimer Rd. (529-5966): Drama, comedy, contemporary theater.

Wortham Theater Center, 550 Prairie (237-1439): Brand-new lyric theater opened in 1987. Home of the Houston Grand Opera (under director David Gockley), which performs Sept.-March; also of the Houston Ballet, the only permanent dance company in the South.

RODEOS: **Round Up Coliseum,** on Tex. 1093, in Simonton, 35 mi. (56 km) west along Westheimer Rd. (346-1534): Rodeo, western dancing, barbecue dinner every Sat. from 6 p.m. on. Open year round except Sept. Guaranteed local color. 45 min. from dwntwn, and worth the ride.

☀⚑⚑ **Texas Prison Rodeo,** at Huntsville, 71 mi. (113 km) north along I-45 (409/295-6371, ext. 418): Rodeo championship organized by the inmates of the famous state penitentiary at Huntsville, every Sun. in Oct. between 2 and 4 p.m. Election of Miss Texas Prison. Attracts more than 100,000 spectators every year. For lovers of the picturesque and unusual (see also "Nearby Excursions," below). A local institution since 1931; it shouldn't be missed.

SHOPPING: ❋ **Galeria Mall,** 5015 Westheimer Rd. (622-0663): A superb example of commercialized urban planning, with more than 250 luxury boutiques from Neiman Marcus to Tiffany's, restaurants, stores, bars, and even a public ice-skating rink, all air-conditioned under an enormous dome. Gigantism Texas style, elegant and spectacular.

SPECIAL EVENTS: For exact dates, consult the **Houston Convention and Visitors Council** (see "Tourist Information," above).
   Houston Rodeo and Livestock Show (late Feb. to early Mar.): Rodeos, concerts, parades; guaranteed western atmosphere. Shouldn't be missed.
   Houston Festival (late Mar.): Dance, theater, art exhibitions, concerts.
   Westheimer Art Show (Apr. and Oct.): Art exhibitions, public concerts on the "Strip." Worth seeing (see "Strolls," below).
   Offshore Technology Conference (late Apr. to early May): The world's biggest annual petroleum-industry exhibition.

SPORTS: Houston boasts professional teams in three major sports:
   Baseball (Apr.-Oct.): Astros, the Astrodome (799-9555).
   Basketball (Dec.-Apr.): Rockets, the Summit (627-0600).
   Football (Sept.-Dec.): Oilers, the Astrodome (797-1000).

STROLLS: ⚜ **Old Market Square,** bounded by Congress, Milam, Preston, and Travis: Boutiques, restaurants, and saloons in the style of the Old West's frontier days, all in attractively restored 19th-century row houses. Lively and colorful, particularly in the evening.
   River Oaks, River Oaks Blvd. between Westheimer Rd. and the River Oaks Country Club: Dream homes and sumptuous oil barons' mansions. Worth a look.
   The "Strip," Westheimer Rd. from about no. 100 to no. 1600: Terraced cafés, exotic restaurants, art galleries, antique shops, bookstores, nightclubs, flea market. Houston's liveliest district. Art festivals in Apr. and Oct.

THEME PARKS: ⚜ **AstroWorld,** South Loop 610 at Kirby Dr. (799-1234): Enormous (75-acre) amusement park with more than 100 attractions including the giant "Texas Cyclone" roller coaster. Shows; concerts. Open daily June-Sept., weekends only in spring and fall; closed the rest of the year.
   WaterWorld, Kirby Dr. and South Loop 610 (799-1234): Very popular aquatic amusement park adjoining AstroWorld. Enormous pool with artificial waves for surfers; giant slides; lagoon swimming pool with waterfalls. Spectacular. Open daily June-Aug., weekends only in May and Sept; closed the rest of the year.

ZOOS: ⚜ **Zoological Gardens,** Zoo Circle Dr. in Hermann Park (523-3211): Very fine zoo, known for its tropical jungle and its gorillas. The vampire bats eat lunch every day at 2:30 p.m. Huge aquarium.

ACCOMMODATIONS
See the listing of toll-free numbers in the Appendix.

Room Rates in Houston	
B (Budget)	up to $30
I (Inexpensive)	$30–$60
M (Moderate)	$60–$90
E (Expensive)	$90–$140
VE (Very Expensive)	$140 and up

Personal Favorites (in order of preference)
♕♕♕♕ **Remington on Post Oak Park** (nr. dwntwn), 1919 Briar Oaks Lane, TX 77027 (713/840-7600; toll free 800/223-6800). 248 rms, A/C, cable color TV. AE, CB, DC, MC, V. Valet parking $9, pool, three rests. (including the Conservatory and the Garden Room), bar, 24-hr rm svce, concierge, free crib. *Note:* The most elegant, and one of the newest, of Houston's luxury hotels, in the smart River Oaks section near Memorial Park. A beautiful melding of American efficiency and European charm. Furnishings include many works of art and old pictures. Spacious, very comfortable rms; personalized reception and svce. Rest. of great quality. Rich business clientele. Boasts the city's most expensive suite at $1,500 a night. 20 min. from dwntwn. **VE**

♕♕♕♕ **Hyatt Regency** (dwntwn), 1200 Louisiana St., TX 77002 (713/654-1234; toll free, see Hyatt). 958 rms, A/C, color TV, in-rm movies. AE, CB, DC, MC, V. Valet garage $9, pool, five rests. (including Hugo's Window Box), revolving bar (Spindletop) on the 33rd floor, entertainment, rm svce, free crib. *Note:* Typical Hyatt "smack in the eye" design; 30-floor foyer w. balconies, indoor gardens, and glass-caged elevators. Well-designed, friendly rms; irreproachable svce. Big business clientele. In the heart of Houston next to the Convention Center. VIP floor. Linked by "Skywalk" to other dwntwn buildings. **E–VE**

☼♕♕♕ **Lancaster Hotel** (dwntwn), 701 Texas Ave., TX 77002 (713/228-9500; toll free 800/345-3457). 93 rms, A/C, color TV. AE, CB, DC, MC, V. Valet parking $9, health club, rest. (Lancaster Grille), bar, 24-hr rm svce, concierge, free crib. *Note:* A luxurious little 1920s palace, elegantly renovated. Vast, welcoming rms furnished w. antiques. Very British atmosphere. Personalized svce. The rest. is a favorite w. audiences from the Jones Concert Hall and the Alley Theater, right across from the hotel. Charm and quality. Complimentary limousine dwntwn. **E–VE**

♕♕♕ **Hilton Nassau Bay** (vic.), 3000 NASA Rd. One, Clear Lake City, TX 77058 (713/339-9300; toll free, see Hilton). 244 rms, A/C, color TV, in-rm movies. AE, CB, DC, MC, V. Free parking, pool, fishing, water sports, marina, rest. (Compass Rose), bar, rm svce, disco, boutiques, drugstore, free limo to dwntwn Houston and the airports, free crib. *Note:* This 14-floor hotel-marina on Clear Lake is ideal for visiting NASA's Lyndon B. Johnson Space Center. Comfortable, ultramodern facilities; spacious rms. w. bal-

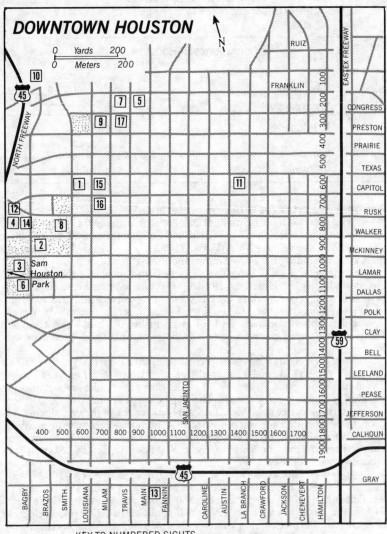

DOWNTOWN HOUSTON

N

Yards 200
Meters 200

KEY TO NUMBERED SIGHTS

1. Alley Theater
2. City Hall
3. Sam Houston Park
4. Sam Houston Coliseum
5. Pillot House
6. The Long Row
7. Old Cotton Exchange
8. Tranquility Park
9. Convention and Visitors Center
10. Amtrak Station
11. Greyhound Terminal
12. Music Hall
13. Trailways Terminal
14. Albert Thomas Space Hall of Fame
15. Jones Hall for Performing Arts
16. Pennzoil Towers
17. Old Market Square Park

conies and lake view; efficient svce. Very good value; a fine place to stay, 35 min. from dwntwn. **M–E**

Holiday Inn Downtown (dwntwn), 801 Calhoun St., TX 77002 (713/659-2222; toll free, see Holiday Inns). 600 rms, A/C, color TV. AE, CB, DC, MC, V. Free parking, sauna, rest., two bars, rm svce, disco, crib $10. *Note:* Huge, modern, well-laid-out 30-story hotel, very near the Exxon Building. Functionally comfortable in the Holiday Inn style. Efficient svce; business and group clientele. Interesting wknd discounts. **M**

Allen Park Inn (nr. dwntwn), 2121 Allen Pkwy., TX 77019 (713/521-9321; toll free 800/329-1499). 250 rms, A/C, color TV, in-rm movies. AE, CB, DC, MC, V. Free parking, pool, health club, 24-hr coffeeshop (Nashville Room), bar, 24-hr rm svce, hrdrsr, free crib. *Note:* Friendly, modern hotel of traditional type, nr. dwntwn. Spacious, comfortable rms w. balconies. Reception w. a smile. Very laudable rest. Caters largely to repeat customers; good value. **I–M**

La Quinta Inn Greenway (nr. dwntwn), 4015 Southwest Frwy., TX 77027 (713/623-4750; toll free, see La Quinta). 129 rms, A/C, cable color TV. AE, CB, DC, MC, V. Free parking, pool, coffeeshop, rm svce, free crib. *Note:* Modern, comfortable motel 20 min. from dwntwn. Friendly reception. Ideal if you're driving. Like all La Quinta motels, a good value. **I**

Comfort Inn Northwest (vic.), 16884 Northwest Frwy., TX 77040 (713/937-7056; toll free 800/228-5150). 114 rms, A/C, color TV, in-rm movies. AE, CB, DC, MC, V. Free parking, pool, 24-hr coffeeshop, free crib. *Note:* Modern, functional motel 20 min. from dwntwn. Cordial reception and svce. Perfect for motorists; good value. **I**

Other Accommodations (from top bracket to budget)

La Colombe d'Or (nr. dwntwn), 3410 Montrose Blvd., TX 77006 (713/524-7999). Six suites, A/C, color TV. AE, CB, DC, MC, V. Free parking, rest. (La Colombe d'Or), bar, rm svce, concierge. *Note:* Houston's most luxuriously extravagant place to stay, this 1923 mansion, once the home of Exxon chairman Walter Fondreu, has been transformed into a compact mini-palace with a mere six suites, each having its own huge bedroom, living room, and dining room, and all decorated with objets d'art and antique furniture. The service is polished to a high gloss. The name is that of a famous hotel at St-Paul-de-Vence on France's Côte d'Azur. Resv. must be made far in advance. **VE**

Inter-Continental (nr. dwntwn), 5150 Westheimer Rd., TX 77056 (713/961-1500; toll free, see Inter-Continental). 518 rms, A/C, color TV, in-rm movies. AE, CB, DC, MC, V. Free parking, pool, tennis court, health club, sauna, two rests. (including Les Continents), four bars, 24-hr rm svce, disco, boutiques, concierge, free crib. *Note:* Ultramodern 23-story luxury hotel opposite the celebrated Galeria Mall shopping center, offering remarkably high standards of layout and comfort. Spacious rms; luxurious foyer featuring works by contemporary Texan artists. Comprehensive sports facilities; impeccable svce; prosperous business clientele. 20 min. from dwntwn. **E–VE**

Four Seasons Inn on the Park (nr. dwntwn), 4 Riverway, TX 77056 (713/871-8181; toll free, see Four Seasons). 383 rms, A/C, color TV, in-rm movies. AE, CB, DC, MC, V. Valet parking $5, two pools, health club, four tennis courts, sauna, two rests., bar, 24-hr rm svce, disco, concierge, free crib. *Note:* A hotel of real quality in Houston's most elegant neighborhood; lavishly comfortable rms w. balconies and views of Memorial Park. Comprehensive facilities; La Reserve is an excellent rest. Personalized svce; caters to top business people and rich Texans. No-smoking floor. Inviting garden w. modern sculpture, a waterfall, and a little lake with black swans. **E–VE**

♀♀♀ **The Warwick** (nr. dwntwn), 5701 S. Main St., TX 77251
♀♀ (713/526-1991: toll free, see Preferred). 300 rms, A/C, cable
color TV. AE, CB, DC, MC, V. Parking $8, pool, sauna, two rests. (including
the Hunt Room), coffeeshop, bar, 24-hr rm svce, nightclub, hrdrsr, boutiques.
Note: Venerable 1920s luxury hotel in the European tradition, slightly disfigured
by a new wing. A wealth of marbles, Aubusson tapestry, and wood paneling.
Large, comfortable rms, some, two bathrooms. Exemplary svce; view of
Hermann Park. A place of elegance and charm; the favorite of politicians and visiting celebrities. **E–VE**

♀♀♀ **Westin Oaks** (nr. dwntwn), 5011 Westheimer Rd., TX 77056
♀♀ (713/623-4300; toll free, see Westin). 406 rms, A/C, color
TV, in-rm movies. AE, CB, DC, MC, V. Free parking (valet parking $8), pool,
health club, tennis court, two rests. (including the Savoy), two bars, 24-hr rm
svce, disco, hrdrsr, concierge, free crib. *Note:* Modern but graceless 21-story
building w. elegantly laid-out and decorated interior and period furnishings.
Spacious, comfortable rms w. refrigerators and private balconies. Very good facilities, diligent svce. Direct access to the Galleria Mall with its 250 stores and
boutiques, four movie houses, and indoor skating rink. No-smoking floor. 20
min. from dwntwn. **E–VE**

♀♀ **Wyndham at Travis Center** (nr. dwntwn), 6633 Travis St.,
♀♀ TX 77030 (713/524-6633; toll free 800/822-4200). 185
suites, cable color TV. AE, CB, DC, MC, V. Indoor valet parking $6, pool,
health club, rest., bar, piano bar, rm svce, free breakfast, free crib. *Note:* Very comfortable hotel offering only suites, very well laid out. Near Hermann Park and the
museum district. Courteous reception and svce. Business clientele. Good overall
value. **M–E**

♀♀ **Ramada Galleria West** (nr. dwntwn), 7787 Katy Frwy., TX
♀♀ 77024 (713/682-1611; toll free, see Ramada). 287 rms, A/C,
color TV, in-rm movies. AE, CB, DC, MC, V. Free parking, pool, rest., bar, rm
svce, disco, drugstore, free breakfast, crib $10. *Note:* Comfortable, up-to-date 11-
story motel at the western exit from the city on I-10. Comfortable and functional. Friendly rms w. balconies. Ideal if you're driving. Good value. Interesting
wknd packages. **I–M**

♀ **Best Western Greenspoint** (nr. dwntwn), 11211 North
♀ Frwy., TX 77037 (713/447-6311; toll free, see Best Western).
144 rms, A/C, cable color TV. AE, CB, DC, MC, V. Free parking, pool, rest.,
bar, crib $10. Typical motel at the northern exit from Houston on I-45. Func-
tional comfort; cheerful svce. Ideal if you're traveling by car. 25 min. from
dwntwn, 10 min. from Houston Intercontinental Airport (free 24-hr airport
limo.) Good value. **I**

♀ **Days Inn Wayside** (nr. dwntwn), 2200 S. Wayside Dr., TX
♀ 77023 (713/928-2800; toll free, see Days Inn). 100 rms,
A/C, cable color TV. AE, MC, V. Free parking, pool, rest. (no alcoholic beverages), free breakfast, free crib. *Note:* Comfortable, functional hotel; 20 min. from
dwntwn. **I**

♀ **Motel 6** (nr. dwntwn), 9638 Plainfield Rd., TX 77036 (713/
♀ 778-0008). 205 rms, A/C, color TV, free in-rm movies. DC,
MC, V. Free parking, pool. *Note:* Modern, appealing motel with very low rates,
20 min. from dwntwn by car. Ideal if you're driving. One of the best values in the
area. **B**

Airport Accommodations

♀♀♀ **Marriott Airport Hotel** (vic.), 18700 Kennedy Blvd., TX
♀♀ 77032 (713/443-2310; toll free, see Marriott). 570 rms,
A/C, color TV, in-rm movies. AE, CB, DC, MC, V. Free parking, pool, health

club, sauna, two rests. (one, C.K.'s, on the top floor, revolves), two bars, disco, rm svce, hrdrsr, boutiques. *Note:* The architecture of this hotel, in the airport complex, is original; the rms are comfortable and well soundproofed, w. refrigerators (some have private patios). Efficient svce, average rests. Business clientele. Free subway train to the terminal. Two VIP floors. **E**

YMCA/Youth Hostels

YMCA (dwntwn), 1600 Louisiana St. (713/659-8501). Men only. 147 rms, rest.

RESTAURANTS

Houston Restaurant Prices	
(per person, excluding drinks and service charges)	
B (Budget)	up to $15
I (Inexpensive)	$15–$25
M (Moderate)	$25–$40
E (Expensive)	$40–$60
VE (Very Expensive)	$60 and up

Personal Favorites (in order of preference)

Tony's (nr. dwntwn), 1801 Post Oak Blvd. (622-6778). A/C. Lunch Mon.-Fri., dinner Mon.-Sat.; closed Sun., holidays. AE, CB, DC, MC, V. J&T. *Specialties:* crab gazpacho, linguine pescatore, veal cutlet w. morels, red snapper Hemingway, rack of lamb, capon w. cherries, piccata of veal w. truffles, fruit soufflés. *Note:* Remarkable French-inspired cuisine, deftly and delicately prepared. Exemplary svce from waiters in tuxedos; plush, flowery setting worthy of the rest.'s reputation. One of the South's finest wine cellars, with 140,000 bottles. Resv. a must; the favorite of local VIPs. Valet parking; 20 min. from dwntwn. *Continental.* **E**

Uncle Tai's Hunan Yuan (nr. dwntwn), 1980 Post Oak Blvd. (960-8000). A/C. Lunch/dinner daily; closed Thanksgiving, Christmas Day. AE, DC, MC, V. Jkt. *Specialties:* three-color lobster, minced shrimp in garlic sauce, Hunan chicken, pork w. cashew nuts, Uncle Tai's beef, diced boneless pigeon, smoked duck, sesame banana fritters. *Note:* This used to be one of the best rests. in New York; since moving bag and baggage to Houston in 1979, it has become the best Chinese rest. in the southern U.S. Modern, elegant décor, but a little cold. Impeccable svce; 25 min. from dwntwn; resv. advised. An experience you shouldn't miss. *Chinese.* **I–M**

Maison de Ville (dwntwn), 1300 Lamar Ave. in the Four Seasons Hotel (650-1300, ext. 4184). A/C. Breakfast/lunch/dinner daily. AE, CB, DC, MC, V. Jkt. *Specialties:* oyster bisque, snapper soup w. mushrooms, filet of lamb w. raspberries, veal cutlet w. truffle sauce, sweetbreads au porto. *Note:* The archetype of a luxury rest. Innovative, refined cooking in the European fashion. Elegant, distinguished interior w. mahogany paneling, crystal, and Murano chandeliers reminiscent of the Edwardian era. Thoughtful, stylish svce; caters to senior executives and local VIPs. Resv. strongly advised. *French-Continental.* **I–M**

⚲ **Café Annie** (nr. dwntwn), 5860 Westheimer Rd. (780-1522). A/C. Lunch Tues.-Fri., dinner Tues.-Sat.; closed Sun., Mon., holidays. AE, CB, DC, MC, V. Jkt. *Specialties:* salmon prepared w. herbs and whisky, pasta salad w. mussels and shrimp, pheasant w. wild mushrooms, redfish w. coriander in sesame-seed crust, lamb cutlets w. stewed onions, broiled sweetbreads w. ginger and mint, broiled shrimp w. basil and chili. Very good wine list. *Note:* Few young Texan chefs of Robert Del Grande's generation offer so inventive and sophisticated a cuisine. The brown-and-mauve interior, no less avant-garde than the food, is enhanced by flower arrangements. Very good svce; successful enough to make resv. indispensable. *American.* **M–E**

⚲ **Ninfa's** (nr. dwntwn), 2704 Navigation (228-1175). A/C. Lunch/dinner daily; closed July 4, Thanksgiving, December 25. AE, CB, DC, MC, V. *Specialties:* tacos al carbon, flautas, carnitas, chalupas, queso a la parrilla, sopaipillas. *Note:* The best of the (numberless) Mexican rests. in Houston; a local institution, usually crowded, w. no interior decoration. No resv. are accepted over the wknd, and a wait is unavoidable. Other branches are at 6154 Westheimer Rd. (781-2740), 9333 Katy Frwy. (932-8760), and 8507 Gulf Frwy. (943-3183). *Mexican.* **B–I**

⚲ **Ballatori's** (nr. dwntwn), 4215 Leeland (224-9556). A/C. Lunch Mon.-Sat., dinner nightly; closed holidays. AE, CB, DC, MC, V. Jkt. *Specialties:* fresh homemade pasta, rolla di vitello, osso buco. *Note:* Far and away Houston's finest Italian rest. Agreeably old-fashioned décor, friendly svce. Resv. advisable. *Italian.* **I**

⚱ **Chili's** (vic.), 5930 Richmond (780-1654). A/C. Lunch/dinner daily. MC, V. *Specialties:* chili, hamburgers. *Note:* As the name implies, the house chili here (chopped beef, spiced according to a secret Texan recipe) deserves your whole attention, and you shouldn't miss the experience. Popular country-style atmosphere. For several other locations in Houston, consult the local telephone directory. *American.* **B**

⚱ **Tony Mandola's Blue Oyster Bar** (nr. dwntwn), 1608 N. Shepherd (864-0915). A/C. Lunch/dinner Mon.-Sat.; closed Sun. *Specialties:* gulf oysters, gumbo, red beans and rice, crayfish à l'étouffée, spaghetti w. shrimp and crab. *Note:* Wonderful Créole bistro whose flavorful, colorful food is worthy of the finest rests. in New Orleans. No pretensions to elegance, but friendly svce. Very popular locally; no resv.; 20 min. from dwntwn. Other location: 8105 Gulf Frwy. (640-1117). *Créole-Seafood.* **B–I**

Other Restaurants (from top bracket to budget)

⚲⚲⚲ **La Reserve** (nr. dwntwn), in the Four Seasons Inn on the Park (see "Accommodations," above) (871-8177). A/C. Lunch Mon.-Fri., dinner Mon.-Sat.; closed Sun. AE, CB, DC, MC, V. Jkt. (J&T at dinner.) *Specialties:* pheasant mousse w. myrtle vinegar, Dover sole w. caviar, lamb en croûte w. truffle butter, sautéed snails w. noodles and pesto, ragoût of lobster, remarkable desserts. Also, low-calorie diet menu. *Note:* As in all the luxury restaurants of the Four Seasons chain, you may choose between classic, elegantly prepared haute cuisine or a low-calorie menu limited in sodium and cholesterol. In either case, the food attains perfection. Beautiful flower arrangements in a luxurious setting; impeccable svce. Everything in the grand style—including prices. *French-continental.* **M–E**

⚲⚲⚲ **Brennan's** (nr. dwntwn), 3300 Smith St. (522-9711). A/C. Lunch/dinner daily, jazz brunch Sat. and Sun.; closed Dec. 25. AE, CB, DC, MC, V. Jkt. *Specialties:* turtle soup, shrimp remoulade, oysters Bienville, eggs Sardou, catfish w. pecans, veal cutlet Tchoupitoulas, bread pudding, bananas Foster. *Note:* Affiliated w. the famous Commander's Palace in New Orleans. Excellent Créole cuisine; pleasant setting in an old brick house w. a shady patio. Efficient svce; valet parking. Locally popular, especially for brunch, so resv. advised. *Créole.* **I–M**

Rotisserie for Beef and Bird (vic.), 2200 Wilcrest Dr. (977-9524). A/C. Lunch Mon.-Fri., dinner Mon.-Sat.; closed Sun., holidays, and two weeks in July. AE, MC, V. Jkt. *Specialties:* cream of pheasant soup, sautéed quail, mixed grill, roast goose, pheasant and game, aged prime steak and venison, very good homemade desserts. Fine wine list. *Note:* Lovers of unexpected delicacies will find here, year round, Asian venison, antelope, or Russian wild boar, but the more conventional dishes of game, venison, or ordinary red meat are equally recommended. The ovens and broilers are in full view of the patrons, enhancing the elegant country-club layout. Very good svce; yuppie clientele. *American-steak.* **I–M**

Confederate House (nr. dwntwn), 4007 Westheimer Rd. (622-1936). A/C. Lunch Mon.-Fri., dinner daily; closed holidays. AE, DC, MC, V. Jkt. (J&T at dinner.) *Specialties:* fish from the Gulf of Mexico, fried frogs' legs, lamb chops, roast beef, barbecued shrimp. *Note:* One of Houston's old reliables. Elegant Old South atmosphere; good wine list; exemplary svce; resv. advisable. A fine place. *American-continental.* **I–M**

Ruth's Chris Steak House (nr. dwntwn), 6213 Richmond Ave. (789-2333). A/C. Lunch Sun.-Fri., dinner nightly; closed holidays. *Specialties:* excellent broiled red meats, roast of beef, fried shrimp. Fine list of California wines. *Note:* As the name implies, the specialty here is steak, more steak, and steak again: from filet mignon to giant T-bone and from porterhouse to rib-eye. Affiliated w. New Orleans's famous restaurant of the same name. A few posters and other oil-company advertising constitute the entire scheme of decoration. Friendly, smiling svce; highly favored by local meat eaters; resv. advised. *Steak.* **I–M**

Cadillac Bar (nr. dwntwn), 1802 Shepherd Dr. (862-2020). A/C. Lunch/dinner daily; closed Thanksgiving, December 25. AE, CB, DC, MC, V. *Specialties:* fajitas, garrito, cabrito, barbecues, roast quail, chorizo and melted cheese. *Note:* Authentic northern Mexican cooking, tasty and highly spiced. Guaranteed local color from the shoeshine boy through the guitar player. Locally popular; resv. advised. *Mexican.* **B–I**

Las Cazuelas (nr. dwntwn), 2219 Fulton (223-0095). A/C. Breakfast/lunch/dinner 24 hrs daily. MC, V. *Specialties:* caldo de res, huevos rancheros, chiles rellenos, cabrito, enchiladas, burritos. Excellent house margaritas. *Note:* This noisy, lively "taqueria" in the heart of Houston's Mexican district is open 24 hrs a day, seven days a week. Honest, authentic 100% Mexican food; svce sometimes a little distracted. Locally popular. *Mexican.* **B–I**

André's (nr. dwntwn), 2515 River Oaks Blvd. (524-3863). A/C. Breakfast/lunch Mon.-Sat.; closed Sunday, holidays, and three weeks in June. No credit cards. *Specialties:* daily specials, quiches, omelets, coq au vin, and remarkable pastries at ridiculously low prices. One of Houston's biggest lunchtime attractions; unfortunately no dinner is served. The interior is a Texan version of a Swiss country inn. Regular clientele; no resv. *American-continental.* **B**

Captain Benny's Half Shell (nr. dwntwn), 7409 S. Main (795-9051). A/C. Lunch/dinner Mon.-Sat.; closed Sun. No credit cards. *Specialties:* oysters and shrimp from the gulf, stuffed crab, crayfish in season, fried catfish, gumbo. *Note:* Absolutely fresh seafood efficiently served—and the prices are a pleasant surprise. A favorite of connoisseurs and usually packed, so you'll have to wait. Unusual nautical décor. One of the best places to eat in Houston; for other locations, consult the city telephone directory. *Seafood.* **B**

Otto's Barbecue (nr. dwntwn), 5502 Memorial Dr. (864-2573). A/C. Lunch/dinner Mon.-Sat.; closed Sun. No credit cards. *Specialties:* barbecued brisket, hamburgers. *Note:* Generally agreed to offer Houston's best barbecued beef; Otto serves more than 1,400 lbs. (600 kg) daily—a reference in itself! Hamburger reigns supreme at the burger bar nr. the entrance. Unpretentious setting and svce. Locally very popular since 1950. *American.* **B**

Restaurant in the Vicinity

☼ ♈ **Frank's Café** (vic.), 603 E. U.S. 90, 37 mi. (60 km) east of Houston in Dayton (409/258-2598). A/C. Lunch/dinner daily. AE, MC, V. *Specialties:* oysters, crabs, shrimp, and red snapper from the gulf: fried catfish, filet mignon, club steak, ribs of beef Delmonico, home-made pies. *Note:* One of the most famous roadhouses in Texas, on the old U.S. 90 from Houston to New Orleans. Remarkably fresh seafood; superb meats stored in a glass-enclosed aging refrigerator with steaks on view, from which you can make your own choice—and all this at very reasonable prices. Cheerful, friendly svce. Frequented by people in the know since 1948 and well worth the 45-min. drive from the city. Resv. suggested. *American-steak.* **I**

Cafeterias / Fast Food

Luby's (nr. dwntwn), 5215 Buffalo Speedway (664-4852). Open till 8 p.m. daily. *Specialties:* Mexican dishes, fish of the day, steak, roast beef. *Note:* Decent food at very decent prices. There are 20 other locations in Houston; consult the city telephone directory.

BARS & NIGHTCLUBS

Al Mark's Melody Lane Ballroom (nr. dwntwn), 3027 Crossview (785-5301). Giant dance hall with live music; very popular locally, so local color guaranteed. 25 min. from dwntwn.

Cody's (nr. dwntwn), 3400 Montrose Blvd. (522-9747). A singles bar that is much frequented by yuppies after the day's toil; also very acceptable rest. and live jazz. Beautiful view of the city.

Comedy Workshop (nr. dwntwn), 2105 San Felipe St. (524-7333). Comedy club, very popular locally.

Confetti (nr. dwntwn), 14018 Memorial (497-8162). Fashionable disco; youthful, upscale ambience. Open nightly.

Cooter's (nr. dwntwn), 5164 Richmond Ave. (961-7494). Smart rock club with a very popular bar-rest. Open nightly.

☼ **Giley's** (vic.), 4500 Spencer Hwy., in Pasadena (941-7990). Enormous (5,000 seats) western dance hall, with a floor as large as a football field. Since John Travolta made *Urban Cowboy* here, it has become a shrine. Mechanical bucking bulls and top country performers; don't miss it. Open daily. 30 min. from dwntwn.

☼ **The Great Caruso** (vic.), 10001 Westheimer Rd. at Briar Park (780-4900). Original rest.-nightclub for lovers of opera and bel canto; even the waiters contribute to the illusion. Wonderful 1900s rococo opera-house décor. An entertaining place, well worth the 30-min. drive from dwntwn. Very acceptable food. Valet parking. Open nightly.

Jet Set Club (nr. dwntwn), 14918 North West Frwy. (680-3223). Trendy disco catering to the young and well-to-do.

Rockefeller's (nr. dwntwn), 3620 Washington Ave. (861-9365). Modern jazz, live, in a relaxed atmosphere. Open Mon.-Sat.

NEARBY EXCURSIONS

PORT OF HOUSTON (5 mi., 8 km, east along Clinton Dr.): You'll get a fine view of the port, which handles more than 6,000 vessels a year, from the observation platform at Wharf No. 9. Free boat tours of the harbor on Tues., Wed., Fri., Sat., and Sun. year round except for the month of Sept. (225-4044 for resv.). Worth seeing.

SAN JACINTO BATTLEGROUND (21 mi., 34 km, SE on I-45S, I-610N, and Tex. 225) (479-2421): Battlefield on which Gen. Sam Houston's Texas volunteers won a decisive engagement against the Mexican dictator Santa Anna, only two months after the latter's victory at the Alamo (see Chapter 37 on San Antonio). A gigantic memorial column (elevator), capped with the Lone Star of Texas, was erected in 1939; at 570 ft (174 m), it's the tallest monument in the world, 15 ft (5 m) higher than the Washington Monument. Made of concrete clad in polished limestone, it weighs a total of 32,000 tons. Nearby is the battleship *Texas,* veteran of two World Wars, which served as General Eisenhower's headquarters during the Normandy landings of 1944. At the foot of the monument is a Museum of the History of Texas. Open daily in summer, Tues.-Sun. the rest of the year. Well worth going out of your way for.

LYNDON B. JOHNSON SPACE CENTER (25 mi., 40 km, SE along I-45 and NASA Rd. 1 in Clear Lake City) (483-4321): The nerve center of NASA, from which guidance has been provided for all manned space flights since 1962 (including the *Gemini, Apollo,* and *Mercury* missions and the space-shuttle flights), with live TV coverage for viewers around the world. There are 40,000 technicians on the payroll. The wonderful **Space Museum** has several models of spacecraft, including the gigantic *Saturn V,* as well as *Apollo 17* and genuine moon rocks. Conducted tours of the **Control Center** and the astronaut training areas. Movies on various space missions. As exciting as the Kennedy Space Center; don't miss it. Open daily.

GALVESTON (51 mi., 82 km, south on I-45): This beach resort and busy port was almost totally destroyed in 1900 by a tidal wave which left 6,000 dead. There are many fine upper-class 19th-century homes along the Strand, between 20th and 25th Sts., and on Broadway, among them the **Bishop's Palace,** 1402 Broadway, open daily, and **Ashton Villa,** 2328 Broadway, open daily, which belongs to former Texas Gov. Ross Sterling. Very popular beaches. A must-see. **Railroad Museum** in the Santa Fe Union station, 123 Rosenberg (409/765-5700): the largest collection of restored railroad equipment in the southwest. On-the-way stop for a visit to the LBJ Space Center (see above).

Where to Stay in Galveston
Tremont House, 2300 Ship's Mechanic Row, Galveston, TX 77550 (409/763-0300). 110 rms. AE, CB, DC, MC, V. *Note:* An elegantly renovated 1880s hotel retaining its gracious Victorian atmosphere. **M–E**

HUNTSVILLE (71 mi., 113 km, north on I-45): Native city of Texas's founder and first elected president, Sam Houston. His birthplace, home, and tomb at 1836 Sam Houston Ave. (409/295-7824) may be seen Tues.-Sun.

Every fall a spectacular rodeo championship is held on the grounds of the state penitentiary here (see "Rodeos," above).

NATIONAL PARKS NEARBY

☼⚓ **PADRE ISLAND NATIONAL SEASHORE** (236 mi., 378 km, SW on U.S. 59, U.S. 77 and 37, and Tex. 358): A 113-mi.- (182-km) long peninsula with an average width of 3 mi. (5 km). Almost entirely uninhabited, this long sweep of sand, with dunes rising to 45 ft (15 m) in places, has once again become a paradise for campers (fully equipped camping grounds), fishermen, and sailors after sustaining severe damage from a disastrous oil slick in 1979. The spine of the peninsula, less contaminated by civilization, has been made into a nature reserve for some 350 species of birds. The park is connected to Corpus Christi by the John F. Kennedy Causeway. For lovers of unspoiled nature. For information, contact the Superintendent, Padre Island National Seashore, 9405 S. Padre Island Dr., Corpus Christi, TX 78418 (512/937-2621).

On the way, stop off at the ⚓ **King Ranch,** on Tex. 141 at Kingsville (37 mi., 59 km, SW of Corpus Christi via Tex. 44 and U.S. 77). Symbolic of Texan wealth and power, this ranch of about 820,000 acres, the size of the state of Rhode Island, is the largest privately held agricultural property in the world. Founded in 1853 by Richard King, an enterprising sea captain, the property is still owned by descendants of the King family. A 12-mi. (19-km) road tour (impassable in bad weather) will allow you to gain a good impression of life on the ranch. Open daily. Information: 512/592-8516. A must for lovers of wide-open spaces.

Where to Stay

There are hotels, motels, and restaurants at Corpus Christi (north of Padre Island) and at Port Isabel, to the south, almost at the Mexican border.

ₒₒₒ **Hilton South Padre Resort,** 500 Padre Blvd. at the Causeway, South Padre Island, TX 78597 (512/761-6511). 192 rms and 120 suites. Large modern hotel on the ocean. **E**

ₒₒ **Holiday Inn Padre Island,** 15202 Windward Dr., Corpus Christi, TX 78597 (512/949-8041; toll free, see Holiday Inns). 148 rms. Comfortable, functional motel right on the beach. **M–E**

ₒ **White Sands,** on Tex. 100, Port Isabel, TX 78578 (512/943-2414). Small and modest but well-run motel with private marina. 30 units. **I**

CHAPTER 37

SAN ANTONIO

□ □ □

The first of America's great cities to elect a mayor of Mexican origin (Henry Cisneros in 1981), San Antonio is a living symbol of the Hispanic influence north of the Rio Grande; every year it attracts ten million visitors.

Founded in 1718 as the Spanish military outpost of San Antonio de Bexar, with an accompanying Franciscan mission of San Antonio de Valero (both on the site of what is now the fort of the **Alamo**), the city was the capital of the Spanish province of Texas when, a century later, Mexico achieved independence. It shortened its name, changing its flag and its allegiance. But the restless settlers of Texas soon achieved confrontation with the Mexican authorities. On Feb. 23, 1836, the redoubtable Gen. Antonio López de Santa Anna, at the head of 5,000 Mexican soldiers, arrived to lay siege to the fort and mission of the Alamo, in the heart of San Antonio. After 13 days of furious fighting, the assault was mounted on March 6. The Mexicans lost 1,600 men in the battle, but they took the town and killed every last man of the heroic garrison: 187 American and foreign volunteers, including Col. William Travis and the two legendary scouts Davy Crockett and Jim Bowie. "Remember the Alamo" became the Texans' battle cry, until their final victory over the Mexicans a month later, at San Jacinto (see Chapter 36 on Houston). The famous Rough Riders, those volunteers who won so much renown in Cuba during the Spanish-American War, came into being in San Antonio in 1898. Among the recruiters of this army of firebrands was the future president Theodore Roosevelt, who signed up many of his Rough Riders at the bar of the famous **Menger Hotel,** still one of the city's greatest tourist attractions.

San Antonio has preserved many interesting architectural relics of its eventful past, perhaps the most important being the church of the Alamo, at once museum and historic shrine; a half dozen Franciscan missions, including the superb **San José Mission;** and the **Spanish Governor's Palace.** If you take into account the picturesque Mexican district with its colorful market, the **Mercado;** the German enclave of the **King William District** with its opulent 1870s homes; the **Paseo del Rio,** a pretty flower-planted promenade along the river with water buses, restaurants, cafés, and shops; or the charming **Villita,** a little bit of 18th-century Spain in the heart of the city, you'll see that San Antonio is unquestionably the most firmly rooted in history of all the great cities of Texas, though one of the most vigorous as well, with its food, garment, cement, and above all aircraft-maintenance industries (the huge **Kelly Air Force Base** is nicknamed "The Home of the Air Force"). San Antonio's growth rate ranks sixth among the country's major cities.

Famous San Antonians include Conrad Hilton, founder of the hotel chain that bears his name, and the actresses Carol Burnett and Joan Crawford.

BASIC FACTS: State of Texas. Area Code: 512. Time Zone: Central Time. ZIP Code: 78205. Founded: 1718. Approximate population: city, 915,000; metropolitan area, 1,235,000. 9th largest city, 31st-largest metropolitan area, in the U.S.

CLIMATE: Renowned for its year-round sunshine, San Antonio proudly proclaims itself "The City Where Sunshine Spends the Winter"; if you love fine weather, this is the place for you. While winter is pleasantly mild (rarely below 51°F, 10°C, in Jan.), summer is on the sultry side (July avg., 84°F, 29°C), only partly relieved by the occasional tropical storm coming up from the Gulf of Mexico.

DISTANCES: Albuquerque, 861 mi. (1,378 km); Dallas, 270 mi. (432 km); Houston, 197 mi. (315 km); New Orleans, 548 mi. (877 km); Tucson, 883 mi. (1,412 km).

ARRIVAL & TRANSIT INFORMATION

AIRPORT: San Antonio International Airport (SAT), 8 mi. (12 km) north. For further information call 821-3411.

AIRLINES: American (222-0121), Continental (828-8381), Delta (222-2354), Pan Am (toll free 800/221-1111), Southwest (696-1221), TWA (226-0626), United (223-2525), and USAir (toll free 800/428-4322).

CITY LINK: The cab fare from the airport to downtown is about $14; time, 15 min. Bus: Via Limousine Service (227-2020), leaves every 20 min.; serves major downtown hotels; fare, $6; time, about 20 min.

Good public transportation system by bus and streetcar: Metropolitan Transit System (227-2020). Cabs are quite numerous and affordable. Unless you intend to visit the Franciscan missions around the city, you won't need to rent a car.

CAR RENTAL (all at the airport): Avis (826-6332), Budget (349-4441), Hertz (826-0651), National (824-7544), and Thrifty (341-4677). For downtown locations, consult the local telephone directory.

LIMOUSINE SERVICES: Carey Limousine (385-5466) and Don's Limousine (923-7556).

TAXIS: Theoretically, cabs can be hailed on the street, but it's more usual to take one from the waiting lines outside the major hotels, or from one of the stands along the Paseo del Rio—or to phone. Major companies: Checker Cab (222-2151), United Cab (733-0852), and Yellow Cab (226-4242). There are also taxiboats operating along the Paseo del Rio (222-1701).

TRAIN: AMTRAK station, 1174 E. Commerce St. (223-3226; toll free 800/872-7245).

BUS: Greyhound, 500 N. St. Mary's St. (227-8351).

INFORMATION & TOURS

TOURIST INFORMATION: The **San Antonio Convention and Visitors Bureau,** 121 Alamo Pl. (P.O. Box 2277), TX 78298 (512/270-8700).
    San Antonio Conservation Society, 107 King William St. (512/224-6163): Information on the King William Historic District.
    Visitor Information Center, 317 Alamo Pl. (512/299-8155).

GUIDED TOURS: B. & T. Fuller Bus Tours (bus), 129 E. Summit St. (734-8706): Conducted tours in London-style double-decker bus; serves principal hotels.

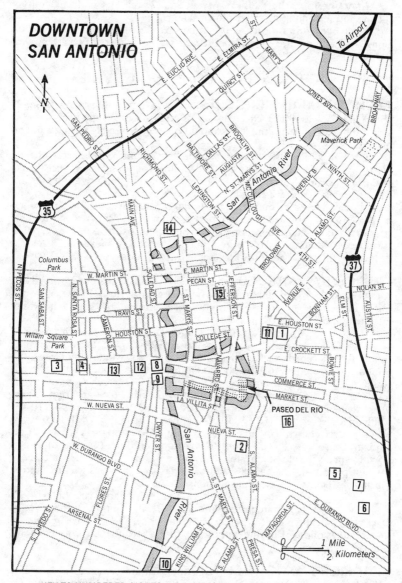

DOWNTOWN SAN ANTONIO

KEY TO NUMBERED SIGHTS
1. The Alamo
2. La Villita
3. Market Square
4. Fiesta Plaza
5. Tower of the Americas
6. The Institute of Texan Cultures
7. San Antonio Museum of Transportation
8. Main Plaza
9. Military Plaza
10. King William Historical Area
11. The Heart of Texas
12. San Fernando Cathedral
13. Spanish Governor's Palace
14. Southwest Craft Center
15. Travis Park
16. Convention and Visitors Bureau

Gray Line Tours (bus), 800 W. Myrtle St. (227-5251): Conducted tours of the city and surroundings; serves principal hotels.

River Boat Tours (boat), 430 E. Commerce St. (227-1701): Barge trips along the Paseo del Rio (seven landing stages); also dinner cruises. Daily, year round.

SIGHTS, ATTRACTIONS, & ACTIVITIES

ARCHITECTURAL HIGHLIGHTS: ☼ ♨ **Arneson River Theater,** 503 Villita St. (299-8610): Open-air theater of original design: the river flows between the spectators and the stage. Should be seen, preferably during a performance.

♨ **HemisFair Plaza,** bounded by Commerce, Market, Durango, and Alamo streets (299-8570): A huge esplanade, once the site of the HemisFair '68 World's Fair. There's an ultramodern **Convention Center** whose frontage displays a giant mosaic by the Mexican artist J. O'Gorman, and several other interesting buildings: the **Tower of the Americas,** the city's tallest high-rise (see "Panoramas," below), the **Museum of Transportation** (from the stagecoach to the automobile; open Tues.-Sun.), the **Institute of Mexican Cultures** (see "Museums of Art," below), and the **Institute of Texan Cultures** (see "Museums of Science and History," below). Worth a visit; open daily.

CHURCHES/SYNAGOGUES: ☼ 🔭 **San Antonio Missions National Historical Park:** Four Franciscan missions built between 1720 and 1731, and offering an interesting glimpse of Spanish Colonial culture in the 18th century. For information call 229-6000.

🔭 **Mission San José de Aguayo,** 6539 San José Dr., 5 mi. (9 km) south on Roosevelt Ave. (922-2731), is the most elegantly beautiful of all; superb chapel with richly carved sacristy window, and Indian encampment. Open daily. ♨ **Mission San Francisco de la Espada,** 10040 Espada Rd., 6 mi. (10 km) south on Roosevelt Ave. (627-2021), has been completely restored; note the dam and aqueduct built by the friars to supply the mission. Open daily. ♨ **Mission San Juan Capistrano,** 9101 Graf Rd., 6 mi. (10 km) south on Roosevelt Ave. (532-5840), is very near San Francisco de la Espada; the well-preserved church is still in use. Open daily. 🔭 **Mission de la Purisima Concepción de Acuña,** 807 Mission Rd. via Roosevelt Ave. (532-3158), is near downtown; it's the oldest unrestored Spanish mission in the country, and one of the best preserved. The chapel's wall paintings, and its acoustics, are famous. Open daily. Don't fail to visit the missions.

♨ **San Fernando Cathedral,** 114 Military Plaza (227-1297): Fine example of 19th-century (1873) Gothic, on the site of an earlier (1758) church built by settlers from the Canary Islands. The remains of the defenders of the Alamo are supposed to have been buried in its foundations. A must-see; open daily.

HISTORIC BUILDINGS: ☼ 🔭 **The Alamo,** Alamo Plaza (225-1391): Makes every Texan heart beat faster. Of the fort of the Alamo (the Spanish word for "poplar"), once so gallantly defended by Davy Crockett, Jim Bowie, Colonel Travis, and their 186 comrades-in-arms, there remain only the chapel, now a memorial of the battle, and the "Long Barrack," once the Franciscan convent, where the last defenders were killed on March 6, 1836. Today it houses a museum of Texas history. A visit not to be missed; open daily.

☼ ♨ **Cos House,** 416 La Villita (299-8610): The most famous building in the La Villita Historic District. It was here that Gen. Perfecto de Cos, on Dec. 10, 1835 (three months before the siege of the

Alamo), signed the instrument whereby the Mexicans surrendered the town to the patriots of Texas. Don't miss it; open daily.

☀️⚗️ **Menger Hotel,** 204 Alamo Plaza (223-4361): A local landmark since 1859. Historical figures of the caliber of Gens. Robert E. Lee and Ulysses S. Grant, not to mention Sam Houston, a founding father of the state of Texas, have frequented the place. At the bar here, in 1898, Theodore Roosevelt, the future president, recruited volunteers for his famous Rough Riders to serve in the Spanish-American War. A must for all history buffs.

☀️⚗️ **Navarro House State Historic Site,** 228 S. Laredo St. (226-4801): Interesting buildings of adobe (Indian-style unbaked bricks made in this instance of *caliche,* a mixture of gravel, clay, and limestone) and whitewashed stone, and blending a number of unrelated architectural styles: Spanish Colonial, German, French, Victorian. Built in the 1850s, these three houses, still with their original furniture and decoration, were the home of José Antonio Navarro, a rich Texan rancher and politician, born at San Antonio in 1795. Definitely worth a visit; open Tues.-Sat.

☀️⚗️ **Spanish Governor's Palace,** 105 Military Plaza (224-0601): Official residence of the Spanish governors, built in 1749—witness the date and the coats-of-arms of the Habsburgs and of King Philip V engraved on the keystone. A fine colonial building, still with its original furniture; the only one of its kind surviving in Texas. Shouldn't be missed; open daily.

⚗️ **Steves Homestead,** 509 King William St. (225-5924): This fine Gothic Revival home on the banks of the San Antonio River dates from 1876; it is a mute witness to the wealth and urbanity of the German merchants who in the 19th century lived in the King William Historic District (see "Strolls," below). Splendid old furniture; huge landscaped garden with an indoor pool (*River Haus*). Worth a visit; open daily.

INDUSTRIAL TOURS: ☀️⚗️ **Lone Star Brewing Co.–Buckhorn Hall of Horns,** 600 Lone Star Blvd. (226-8301 weekdays, 226-8303 weekends): This unusual museum, inside the brewery, displays an astonishing variety of hunting trophies from around the world—polar bears to African antelope—as well as the Hall of Fins (marine life) and the Hall of Feathers (mounted birds). Reconstruction of the 1887 Buckhorn Saloon; free beer tasting. The adjoining **Hall of Texas History** has exhibits dealing with the history of the state from the time of the first Spanish explorers. Worth a visit; open daily.

MARKETS: ☀️⚗️ **Market Square,** bounded by Dolorosa, San Saba, W. Commerce, and Santa Rosa Sts. (299-8600): The local retailing center for more than a century, it includes the **Farmers' Market,** dealing in fruit and vegetables; the Mexican market **El Mercado,** where you may haggle in a colorful, authentically Mexican environment; and the **Centro de Artes del Mercado,** an arts-and-crafts market in a restored 1922 building. All are open daily year round; some businesses are open around the clock. Very lively; don't miss it.

MUSEUMS OF ART: ⚗️ **Institute of Mexican Cultures,** HemisFair Plaza (227-0123): Mexican art, crafts, and archeology; revolving exhibits of work by contemporary Mexican artists. Interesting; open Tues.-Sun.

☀️⚗️ **Marion Koogler McNay Art Institute,** 6000 N. New Braunfels Ave. at U.S. 81 (824-5368): Some old master paintings, but mostly moderns (Picasso, Chagall, Cézanne, Gauguin, Van Gogh), pre-Columbian art, and 19th- and 20th-century bronzes, in a lovely Mediterranean-style villa overlooking San Antonio. Also temporary exhibitions. A must-see; open Tues.-Sun.

☀️🔔🔔 **San Antonio Museum of Art,** 200 W. Jones Ave. (226-5544): This new museum, housed in the former Lone Star Brewery (an 1880s building, magnificently restored and converted to its new use with interior overhead walkways and glass-walled elevators), is a complete success both artistically and architecturally. The important Robert W. Kinn and Nelson A. Rockefeller collections of pre-Columbian and Mexican art are on display here, as are Far Eastern and Spanish Colonial art, and 20th-century American painting and photography. Lovely modern-sculpture garden. All this in an inviting setting on the banks of the San Antonio River. Don't miss it; open Tues.-Sun.

MUSEUMS OF SCIENCE AND HISTORY: Buckhorn Hall of Horns and Hall of Texas History (see the Lone Star Brewery Co. under "Industrial Tours," above).

☀️🔔 **Fort Sam Houston Museum,** on I-35 at New Braunfels Ave., Bldg. 123 (221-1211): Headquarters of the Fifth U.S. Army, Fort Sam Houston is one of the oldest (1879) and most famous military posts in the southern U.S. It was here that the Indian chief Geronimo was imprisoned; here, too, U.S. military aviation was born in 1910. The museum contains thousands of objects from the 19th century (uniforms, weapons, documents, etc.). For military history buffs. Open Wed.-Sun.

☀️🔔 **Hertzberg Circus Collection,** 210 W. Market St. (299-7810): More than 20,000 items illustrating the history of the circus: posters, photographs, models of the Big Top, miniature circuses, souvenirs of Tom Thumb and the legendary Phineas T. Barnum. One of the most important collections of its kind in the world. Open daily May-Oct.; Mon.-Sat. the rest of the year. Should be seen.

🔔 **Institute of Texan Cultures,** HemisFair Plaza (226-7651): An entity of the University of Texas, this museum illustrates in lively visual fashion the historical and cultural contributions made by various nations and ethnic groups to the foundation and expansion of Texas. Spectacular. Open Tues.-Sun.

☀️ **Texas Ranger Museum Memorial Hall,** 3805 Broadway (824-2537): The history of the legendary Texas Rangers from their foundation in 1828 onward, illustrated by hundreds of drawings, photographs, old weapons, saddles, badges, souvenirs of pioneer days, etc. Interesting. Open Tues.-Sun., May-Aug.; Wed.-Sun. the rest of the year.

☀️🔔 **Witte Museum,** 3801 Broadway at Tuleta St. (226-5544): Fine museum of history, anthropology, and natural science entirely devoted to Texas. From dinosaurs and prehistoric Indian artifacts to houses of 19th-century pioneers, brought from different places across the state and rebuilt here. Don't miss this visit. Open Tues.-Sun.

PANORAMAS: ☀️🔔 Tower of the Americas, HemisFair Plaza (223-3101): Soaring concrete tower 741 ft (228 m) high including its crowning TV antenna, the tallest building in the city. The observation platform 622 ft (189 m) up offers a unique view, for a radius of 100 mi. (160 km) in fine weather. Revolving restaurant (mediocre) at the top. Open daily till 11 p.m.

PARKS AND GARDENS: Brackenridge Park, N. Broadway, 2 mi. (3.5 km) north of the city (732-8481): Lovely park on 340 acres (138 ha.) of rolling country a 5-min. drive from downtown. Celebrated zoo; miniature train and cable-car rides. Water gardens in the pit of an abandoned quarry (**Sunken Oriental Gardens**). **Texas Ranger Memorial Hall** and **Witte Museum** (see above). Many picnic areas. Worth a visit.

☀️🔔🔔 **San Antonio Botanical Gardens,** 555 Funston Pl. at N. New Braunfels Ave. (821-5115): On a height of land above the city (fine view from the Gazebo Observatory), this 33-acre (13-ha.) botanic garden includes a lovely rose garden, a little lake, a group of underground tropical greenhouses of revolutionary design (**Lucile Halsell Conservatory**), a garden for the blind labeled in Braille (**Touch-and-Smell Garden**), and an enormous sampling of the flora of Texas. Definitely worth a visit. Open Tues.-Sun.

PERFORMING ARTS: For daily listings of all shows and cultural events, consult the entertainment pages of the daily papers *San Antonio Express-News* (morning and evening) and *San Antonio Light* (morning and evening), and of the magazine *San Antonio Monthly*.

Alamo City Theater, 1150 S. Alamo St. (224-8666): Contemporary theater, comedy, drama.

Arneson River Theater, 503 Villita St. (299-8610): A theater of unprecedented design—the spectators are on one bank of the Paseo del Rio while the stage and the actors are on the other. Open-air music and theater (June-Aug.).

Convention Center Arena, 210 E. Market St. (299-8500): Pop, rock, and jazz concerts.

Joe and Harry Freeman Coliseum, 3201 E. Houston St. (224-6080): Country and western concerts.

Laurie Auditorium, 715 Stadium Dr. (736-8117): Chamber music, classical recitals.

Majestic Performing Arts Center, 212 E. Houston St. (226-9535): Broadway hits, touring companies. Beautiful 1920s interior splendidly restored.

San Pedro Playhouse, 800 W. Ashby (733-7258): Shows, contemporary theater. Sept.-May. Home of the San Antonio Little Theater.

Theater for the Performing Arts, Market St. and Bowie (299-8529): Concerts, ballet, opera. Home of the San Antonio Ballet (Oct.-Dec.) and the San Antonio Symphony, under principal conductor Sixten Ehrling (Dec.-Mar.).

SHOPPING: El Mercado / Mexican Market, W. Commerce and Santa Rosa Sts. (299-8600): Bargains for collectors of folk art: pottery, piñatas (ornamental pots filled with candies), handcrafts, silver jewelry, typical Mexican foodstuffs. Lively and colorful. Open daily; don't miss it.

Rivercenter Shopping Mall, 849 E. Commerce St. (225-1000): Ultramodern shopping center on the Paseo del Rio, opened in 1988 at a total cost of $200 million. Dozens of shops, stores, and restaurants. With its little bridges across the river, all-glass façades, and mariachi band, Rivercenter is an astonishing blend of Mexico, America, and Venice. Worth seeing.

SPECIAL EVENTS: For the exact schedule of events listed below, consult the **San Antonio Convention and Visitors Bureau** (see "Tourist Information," above).

Livestock Exposition and Rodeo (Feb.): Popular stock fair and rodeo.

Fiesta San Antonio (mid-Apr.): Parades, battle of flowers, processions on the river. One of Texas's most colorful festivals since 1891.

San Antonio Festival (late May through June): International arts festival offering classical concerts, opera, ballet, theater, jazz, pop, rock, chamber music, etc.

Fiesta Noche del Rio (June-Aug.): Open-air theater at Arneson River Theater.

Las Posadas (mid-Dec.): Nighttime processions along the Paseo del Rio; a tradition for more than 250 years.

SPORTS: San Antonio has two minor-league professional teams:

Baseball (Apr.-Aug.): Dodgers, Keefe Stadium (434-9311).
Basketball (Oct.-Mar.): Spurs, Convention Center Arena (224-9578).

STROLLS: ☀️⚓ El Mercado / Mexican Market, W. Commerce and Santa Rosa
Sts.: The heart of the Mexican quarter; food stalls, craft shops. Lively and color-ful; open daily (see "Shopping," above).

☀️⚓ **King William Historic District,** around King William and S.
St. Mary's Sts.: The 19th-century German district, now a resi-dential neighborhood. King William St. (so named in honor of William I of Ger-many) is the main drag, lined with fine homes dating from 1870–1890. Among them, no. 107, built in 1873, now houses the **San Antonio Conservatory Soci-ety** (free descriptive leaflets on the King William Historic District). Don't miss the **Steves Homestead** (see "Historic Buildings," above) at no. 509. This is a stroll you should take.

☀️👓👓 **Paseo del Rio,** along the San Antonio River: Pretty riverwalk,
shaded with palm trees and cypresses, along the San Antonio River. Lined with cafés, restaurants, hotels, shops, and art galleries. The river, its narrow bridges, and its water buses have won for San Antonio the nickname "Venice of the West." Don't miss it.

☀️⚓ **La Villita,** S. Presa, Alamo, and Nueva Sts.: A corner of 18th-century Spain in the middle of San Antonio. The old adobe
houses, deftly restored, now shelter galleries and craft shops surrounded by flower-planted patios, bougainvilleas, and banana palms. Don't overlook **Cos House,** where in 1835 was signed the first Mexican surrender to the Texans (see "Historic Buildings," above).

THEME PARKS: ☀️ 👓👓 Sea World of Texas, 10500 Sea World Dr. (523-
3611): The world's largest marine-life theme park, with dozens of attractions on its 250 acres (101 ha.): "Shamu" the killer whale, sea lions, walrus, trained-dolphin shows, waterski ballets. Ultramodern facilities opened in 1988. Worth the side trip.

⚓ **Water Park USA,** I-35 at Coliseum Rd. (227-1100): A surfers'
and divers' kingdom; pool with giant water slides and artificial
waves. Fine-sand beach; picnic area. Open daily, June-Sept.

ACCOMMODATIONS
See the listing of toll-free numbers in the Appendix.

Room Rates in San Antonio	
B (Budget)	up to $30
I (Inexpensive)	$30–$60
M (Moderate)	$60–$90
E (Expensive)	$90–$140
VE (Very Expensive)	$140 and up

Personal Favorites (in order of preference)
☀️ 🛏️🛏️🛏️🛏️ **St. Anthony Inter-Continental** (dwntwn), 300 E. Travis St.,
TX 78205 (512/227-4392; toll free, see Inter-Continental).

360 rms, A/C, color TV, in-rm movies. AE, CB, DC, MC, V. Valet garage $8, pool, health club, two rests. (including the Brasserie), bars, 24-hr rm svce, disco, free crib, concierge. *Note:* A major San Antonio landmark since 1909. Elegant and urbane, w. Oriental rugs and a profusion of marble and crystal. Spacious, completely renovated rms, some w. refrigerators. Period furnishings. Personalized svce. The best rms overlook Travis Park. Big business clientele; the best place to stay in the city. Good rest. serving American cuisine. **E–VE**

☼ 🐚🐚🐚 **La Mansion del Rio** (dwntwn), 112 College St., TX 78205 (512/225-2581; toll free, see Preferred). 337 rms, A/C, color TV, in-rm movies. AE, CB, DC, MC, V. Free parking, pool, rest. (Las Canarias), coffeeshop, bar, rm svce, free crib, concierge. *Note:* Opened in 1968, the Spanish Colonial hotel includes a part of the old building of St. Mary's University, skillfully restored. Pretty courtyard w. pool and bougainvilleas. Inviting but slightly constricting rms w. balconies and mini-bars. Efficient svce; elegant but expensive rest. Ask for a rm overlooking the Paseo del Rio. Business and group clientele. Excellent location. **E–VE**

🐚🐚🐚 **Hilton Palacio del Rio** (dwntwn), 200 S. Alamo St., TX 78205 (512/222-1400; toll free, see Hilton). 484 rms, A/C, color TV, in-rm movies. AE, CB, DC, MC, V. Valet garage $9, pool, sauna, rest. (El Comedor), coffeeshop, bar, rm svce, disco, drugstore, boutiques, concierge. *Note:* Huge, modern 22-story structure on the Paseo del Rio. High standard of comfort and facilities. Elegant Spanish interior. The rms on the higher floors look clear out over the river and city. Excellent svce; two VIP floors. Across from the Civic Center and a stone's throw from the Alamo. **E–VE**

☼ 🐚🐚 **Menger Hotel** (dwntwn), 204 Alamo Plaza, TX 78205 (512/223-4361; toll free 800/345-9258). 350 rms, A/C, color TV, in-rm movies. AE, CB, DC, MC, V. Garage $4, pool, rest., bar, rm svce, disco, drugstore, free crib. *Note:* An old hotel (1859) fraught w. history (see "Historic Buildings," above, for some of its illustrious guests). Has retained all its period flavor, but comfort and facilities leave something to be desired, as does the svce. Pleasant indoor garden; very famous bar (Roosevelt Bar). Unusually good location across from the Alamo. Good value. **I–M**

🐚🐚 **Travelodge on the River** (dwntwn), 100 Villita St., TX 78205 (512/226-2271; toll free, see Travelodge). 132 rms, A/C, color TV, in-rm movies. AE, CB, DC, MC, V. Free parking, pool, rest., bar, rm svce. *Note:* Newish motel overlooking the San Antonio River. Comfortable rms w. private balconies; charming Spanish-style interior. Efficient svce; good value. Free airport limo. **I–M, but lower rates out of season**

🐚 **La Quinta Convention Center** (dwntwn), 1001 E. Commerce St., TX 78205 (512/222-9181; toll free, see La Quinta Motor Inns). 140 rms, A/C, color TV, in-rm movies. AE, CB, DC, MC, V. Free parking, pool, rest., bar, valet svce, free crib. *Note:* Comfortable, serviceable motel a block or two from the Convention Center. Cheerful reception and svce; good value. Group and convention clientele. **I–M**

Other Accommodations (from top bracket to budget)

🐚🐚🐚 **Plaza San Antonio** (formerly Four Seasons) (dwntwn), 555 S. Alamo St., TX 78205 (512/229-1000; toll free 800/367-6046). 252 rms, A/C, color TV, in-rm movies. AE, CB, DC, MC, V. Valet parking $6, pool, two tennis courts, health club, sauna, two rests. (including the Anaqua Room), bars, 24-hr rm svce, free crib, concierge. *Note:* Very lovely modern hotel a stone's throw from La Villita and the Convention Center. Elegant and comfortable w. exotic touches. Luxurious rms w. private balconies overlooking a beautiful tropical garden. Very good svce; excellent rest. Upscale business clientele. A very fine place. **E–VE**

※❦❦❦ **Fairmount Hotel** (dwntwn), 401 S. Alamo St., TX 78205 (512/224-8800; toll free 800/642-3368). 37 rms and suites, A/C, color TV. AE, CB, DC, MC, V. Valet parking $8, rest. (Polo's), bar, 24-hr rm svce, concierge. *Note:* This luxurious three-story Victorian-style home, built in 1906, was transported some 550 yards (500 m) to its present location on a wheeled platform—a world's record in all respects. Refined interior w. old paneling and Italian marble; the suites, the most luxurious and best equipped of any San Antonio hotel, have three phones, four-poster beds, VCR, and built-in stereo. Polished svce; rest. of a high order. The favorite of those in-the-know. Opposite the Convention Center. **E–VE**

❦❦❦ **Hyatt Regency** (dwntwn), 123 Losoya St., TX 78205 (512/ 222-1234; toll free, see Hyatt). 633 rms, A/C, color TV, in-rm movies. AE, CB, DC, MC, V. Valet parking $7, pool, two rests. (including La Puerta), coffeeshop, bars, rm svce, disco, boutiques, concierge. *Note:* Futuristic 16-story building w. indoor gardens, waterfalls, and spectacular glass lobby. Ultra-comfortable rms w. private balconies, the best overlooking the San Antonio River. Very good svce. Group and business clientele; VIP floor; interesting wknd discounts. Very near the Alamo and the Convention Center. **E–VE**

※❦❦ **Crockett Hotel** (dwntwn), 320 Bonham St., TX 78205 (512/ 225-6500; toll free 800/292-1050). 203 rms, A/C, color TV, in-rm movies. AE, CB, DC, MC, V. Valet parking $6, pool, rest., coffeeshop, bar, rm svce, free crib, concierge. *Note:* Reopened in 1983 after a rejuvenation costing over $15 million, this elderly grand hotel from the 1910s has recaptured all the elegance and charm of its distinguished past. Many works of art, and period furniture. Rms a little cramped but comfortable and pleasantly decorated. Very good svce; charming patio-coffeeshop. VIP floor. Wonderfully located across from the Alamo. **M–E**

※❦❦ **Radisson Gunter** (dwntwn), 205 E. Houston St., TX 78205 (512/227-3241; toll free, see Radisson). 326 rms, A/C, color TV, in-rm movies. AE, CB, DC, MC, V. Valet garage $5, pool, health club, rest. (Café Suisse), coffeeshop, bar, rm svce, nightclub, hrdrsr, free crib. *Note:* This venerable institution dates from 1909, but furnishings and facilities have been completely renovated. Vast, inviting rms, some w. refrigerators; svce w. a smile. Wonderful location very nr. the Paseo del Rio and the Alamo. Group and convention clientele. A San Antonio landmark. **M–E**

❦❦ **Holiday Inn Downtown** (nr. dwntwn), 318 W. Durango St., TX 78207 (512/225-3211; toll free, see Holiday Inns). 317 rms, A/C, color TV, in-rm movies. AE, CB, DC, MC, V. Free parking, pool, rest., bar, rm svce. *Note:* A typical Holiday Inn a 5-min. drive from the Alamo and the Convention Center. Functional rms w. balconies; efficient svce; interesting wknd discounts. Good value on balance. **I–M**

❦ **El Tropicano** (dwntwn), 110 Lexington Ave., TX 78205 (512/223-9461). 320 rms, A/C, color TV, in-rm movies. AE, CB, DC, MC, V. Valet garage $4, pool, sauna, rest., bar, rm svce, nightclub, drugstore. *Note:* Good middle-category hotel on the San Antonio River. Comfortable rms w. balconies; reception and svce undependable. Group and convention clientele. Good value. **I–M**

❦ **Motel 6 East** (nr. dwntwn), 138 N.W. White Rd., TX 78219 (512/333-1850). 100 rms, A/C, color TV, free in-rm movies. DC, MC, V. Free parking, pool. *Note:* Unbeatable value 10 min. from dwntwn. Comfortable, serviceable rms. Direct access to the San Antonio bypass motorway. Ideal if you're driving through. **B**

Airport Accommodations

❦ **La Quinta Airport East** (vic.), 333 N.E. Loop I-410, TX 78216 (512/828-0781; toll free, see La Quinta Motor Inns).

198 rms, A/C, color TV, in-rm movies. AE, CB, DC, MC, V. Free parking, pool, rest., bar, rm svce. *Note:* Modern, comfortable motel; free airport limo. Also great if you're driving. **I**

YMCA / Youth Hostels

San Antonio International Hostel (nr. dwntwn), 621 Pierce St., TX 78208 (512/223-9426). 60 beds. Comfortable youth hostel in a fine old house. Open year round.

RESTAURANTS

San Antonio Restaurant Prices	
(per person, excluding drinks and service charges)	
B (Budget)	up to $15
I (Inexpensive)	$15–$25
M (Moderate)	$25–$40
E (Expensive)	$40–$60
VE (Very Expensive)	$60 and up

Personal Favorites (in order of preference)

Anaqua Room (dwntwn), in the Plaza San Antonio (see "Accommodations," above) (229-1000). A/C. Breakfast/lunch/dinner daily, brunch Sun. AE, CB, DC, MC, V. Jkt. *Specialties:* lobster ravioli, roast rack of lamb w. herbs, médaillons of venison w. tomatoes, very good desserts. Menu changed regularly. Fine wine list. *Note:* The luxury-hotel rest. at its best; classic grand cuisine, of French inspiration, superbly prepared and served. Elegant, intimate décor and a prospect of gardens, patios, and fountains. Open-air dining on fine days. Exemplary svce; resv. a must. Big business clientele. *Continental-French.* **M–E**

P.J.'s (dwntwn), 700 N. St. Mary's St. (225-8400). A/C. Lunch/dinner daily; closed Dec. 25. AE, CB, DC, MC, V. Jkt. *Specialties:* eye of lamb w. rosemary sauce, pinoch (seafood platter), steak California, fresh broiled salmon, mille-feuilles. Menu changes regularly. Very fine wine list. *Note:* Overlooking Riverwalk, P.J.'s is the favorite spot for a business lunch or dinner. Light, delicate food; ultra-polished svce (in tuxedo). Adjoining disco. The fashionable place; resv. advised. *French-American.* **I–M**

Fig Tree (dwntwn), 515 Villita St. (224-1976). A/C. Dinner only, nightly; closed Thanksgiving and Dec. 24–25. AE, CB, DC, MC, V. Jkt. *Specialties:* rack of lamb, duck à l'orange, coulibiac of salmon, catch of the day, game (in season). *Note:* In a charming 19th-century adobe house on the Paseo del Rio, this romantic luxury rest. serves food as perfect as the setting. Svce of the highest order; charming little covered patio. Resv. advised. Valet parking. *French-continental.* **M (prix fixe)**

Arthur's (nr. dwntwn), 4001 Broadway (826-3200). A/C. Lunch Mon.-Fri., dinner nightly. AE, DC, MC, V. *Specialties:* shrimp Martinique, seafood sausage w. saffron butter, lamb chop w. red-onion sauce, carpetbagger steak (stuffed w. fried oysters), médaillon of wild boar w. juniper-and-mustard sauce, exotic fruit pies. *Note:* The picture windows have an unobstructed view of Brackenridge Park. The quality of the materials (asparagus from France, fish delivered daily by air from both coasts) is matched only by the excellence of the cuisine. Elegant atmosphere; faultless svce. Yuppie clientele; live jazz at the bar. Resv. advised. 10 min. from dwntwn. *American-continental.* **I–M**

El Bosque (vic.), 12656 West Ave. (494-2577). A/C. Lunch/ dinner daily; closed holidays. DC, MC, V. *Specialties:* carne guisada, stuffed chile, enchiladas, guacamole salad, tamales. *Note:* One of San Antonio's first Mexican rests. Tasty food; country-garden setting inviting in good weather. Cheerful svce. 15 min. from dwntwn. *Mexican.* **B–I**

Earl Abel's (nr. dwntwn), 4200 Broadway (822-3358). A/C. Breakfast/lunch/dinner daily (around the clock); closed Dec. 25. AE, MC, V. *Specialties:* fried chicken, hamburgers, T-bone steak, fried catfish, broiled trout, pecan pie. *Note:* For more than half a century this worthy exponent of large-scale food service (more than a million meals a year) has been a family favorite. Decent, unpretentious food in generous portions; rather gloomy décor. Svce generally rushed. No resv.; 10 min. from dwntwn. *American-steak.* **B–I**

Other Restaurants (from top bracket to budget)

Chez Ardid (nr. dwntwn), 1919 San Pedro Ave. (732-3203). A/C. Lunch/dinner Mon.-Sat.; closed Sun., Jan. 1, and Dec. 25. AE, MC, V. Jkt. *Specialties:* seafood sausage, hot crabmeat Ardid, escalope of veal normande, tournedos périgourdine, rack of lamb w. herbs, red snapper w. truffles and pistachios. Good wine list. *Note:* San Antonio's worthy exponent of true French cuisine. Intimate atmosphere in a 19th-century mansion. Flawless svce; resv. recommended. 15 min. from dwntwn, 10 min. from airport. A very fine place. *French.* **M–E**

Polo's (dwntwn), in the Fairmount Hotel (see "Accommodations," above) (225-4242). A/C. Breakfast/lunch/dinner daily. AE, CB, DC, MC, V. Jkt. *Specialties:* tea-smoked duck w. plum sauce and sesame pancakes, deep-fried squab w. stir-fried cabbage, quesadillas of chorizo sausage w. mangos, crab enchiladas w. chipotle sauce, veal croquettes w. chili and aniseed sauce. Superb desserts. *Note:* The excellent chef, Bruce Alden, has devised an inventive, inspired American cuisine which combines Texas materials and recipes with a touch of the Far Eastern. Huge, elegant, light-filled hotel dining room; polished, attentive svce. Resv. a must. One of the best younger rests. in Texas. *American.* **M**

Boudreaux's (dwntwn), 421 E. Commerce St. (224-8484). A/C. Lunch/dinner daily. AE, MC, V. *Specialties:* gumbo (duck and sausage), redfish meunière w. pecans, blackened prime rib w. aromatic herb butter, bread pudding w. whisky sauce. *Note:* This charming rest. on the Paseo del Rio, w. its massive stone walls, serves the best Créole food (and quite simply, some of the best food) in San Antonio. Pleasant little shady patio. Good svce; very relaxed atmosphere. Resv. strongly advised. *Créole.* **I–M**

Grey Moss Inn (vic.), 19010 Scenic Loop Dr. (Texas 16) (695-8301). A/C. Dinner only, nightly; closed holidays. AE, CB, DC, MC, V. *Specialties:* squash au gratin, steak and chicken broiled over wood fire, pecan pie. *Note:* Some 15 mi. NW of San Antonio, this rustic cottage surrounded by trees serves excellent, wholesome, tasty Texas food. Open-air dining in summer. Good svce; resv. advised. *American-steak.* **I–M**

Paesano's (nr. dwntwn), 1715 McCullough Ave. (226-9541). A/C. Lunch Tues.-Fri., dinner Tues.-Sun.; closed Mon. AE, MC, V. *Specialties:* shrimp Paesano, steak pizzaiola, scaloppine Francesca, spumone. *Note:* Charming small *trattoria,* intimate and inviting. Genuine Italian cuisine; good svce. Popular among local politicians and sports fans; resv. advised. *Italian.* **I**

☼ ♈☕ **La Fonda** (nr. dwntwn), 2415 N. Main St. (733-0621). A/C. Lunch/dinner Mon.-Sat. (until 9 p.m.); closed Sun. and holidays. No credit cards. *Specialties:* chiles rellenos, enchiladas verdes, chalupas compuestas. *Note:* Best of the innumerable Mexican rests. in the city. The food is as authentic as the setting; svce friendly and attentive. Locally popular for more than 40 years. 10 min. from dwntwn. *Mexican.* **B–I**

♈ **The Barn Door** (vic.), 8400 N. New Braunfels Ave. (824-0116). A/C. Lunch Mon.-Fri., dinner Mon.-Sat.; closed Sun. and holidays. AE, MC, V. *Specialties:* fine prime cuts broiled over a wood fire. *Note:* Very popular steakhouse nr. the airport and 20 min. from dwntwn. Choice meats broiled to perfection, at very sensible prices. Engaging western décor. Very good value; given its popularity, resv. advised. *Steakhouse.* **B–I**

♈ **Hunan River Garden** (dwntwn), 506 Riverwalk (222-0808). A/C. Lunch/dinner daily. AE, MC, V. *Specialties:* classic Hunan and Szechuan dishes; highly seasoned sauces. *Note:* San Antonio's most picturesque Chinese rest., and its best, right on the Paseo del Rio. Generous portions; efficient svce; often crowded. Excellent value. *Chinese.* **B–I**

♈ **Mi Tierra** (dwntwn), 218 Produce Row (225-1262). A/C. Breakfast/lunch/dinner daily (around the clock). AE, MC, V. *Specialties:* baked cabrito (kid), fajitas, steak ranchero, enchiladas, menudo (tripe). *Note:* Popular and colorful, this Mexican rest. across from the famous Mercado is a favorite w. the local Mexican community as well as local gringos or tourists. Although open around the clock, it's usually full. Mariachi band evenings. No resv. An excellent place to eat. *Mexican.* **B**

Cafeterias / Fast Food

☼ **Mario's** (dwntwn), 325 S. Pecos St. (223-9602). A local shrine for Tex-Mex food. Excellent homemade soups and classic Mexican dishes. Open daily around the clock. Very popular locally, especially in the small hours. A stone's throw from the Mercado.

BARS & NIGHTCLUBS

Arthur's (nr. dwntwn), 4001 Broadway (826-3200). Excellent modern jazz Mon.-Sat. Relaxed atmosphere. Also a very good rest. (see above). 10 min. from dwntwn.

Farmer's Daughter (vic.), 542 N.W. White Rd. (333-7391). Big, colorful western-style dance hall, open daily. 15 min. from dwntwn.

Landing (dwntwn), 522 Riverwalk (223-7266). Live New Orleans jazz Tues.-Sat. Locally popular.

P.J.'s (dwntwn), 700 N. St. Mary's St. (225-8400). Fashionable disco; also a very popular rest. (see above). On the Paseo del Rio; open Mon.-Sat.

NEARBY EXCURSIONS

☼⚱ **AQUARENA SPRINGS** (32 mi., 51 km, NE on I-35) (396-8900): The springs of the San Marcos River, with splendid aquatic gardens; the crystal-clear water gives you a wonderful view of the rich vegetation and underwater life. Glass-bottom-boat rides; underwater shows in summer. Well worth the side trip. Open daily year round.

☼⚱ **AUSTIN** (78 mi., 124 km, NE on I-35): Founded as Waterloo in 1839 and later renamed in honor of Stephen F. Austin, one of the founders of Texas, the state capital is built on hills rising above the Colorado River (not to be confused with the river of the same name in the state of Colorado). **Old Pecan St.** is a charming historic district, with old houses, shops, and restaurants (6th St.). The imposing **State Capitol** in pink granite, north end of Congress Ave. (512/463-0063), is open daily. The **Lyndon B. Johnson Library and Museum,** on the University of Texas campus (512/482-5136), open daily, honors the 36th president of the U.S. The **French Legation,** at 802 San Marcos St. (512/472-8180), open Tues.-Sun., is the only foreign mission to the U.S. ever built outside Washington, D.C. (in 1840, when Texas was still an independent republic). The capital of Texas has also become the capital of "New Country Music" in the style of Willie Nelson and Waylon Jennings. Note the unusual downtown street-lighting system intended to produce "artificial moonlight." Definitely worth a visit.

CASCADE CAVERNS PARK (30 mi., 48 km, NW on I-10) (755-9285): Very fine limestone caves with illuminated 88-ft (27-m) waterfall. Many marine fossils in the walls. Conducted tours. Worth the side trip. Open daily.

NATURAL BRIDGE CAVERNS (17 mi., 27 km, NE via I-35 and FM 3009) (651-6101): Immense underground caves once inhabited by primitive man; among the finest in Texas. Many chambers with strange shapes and evocative names: "Sherwood Forest," with its columns shaped like totem poles; "The Castle of the White Giants," with its 40-ft- (12-m-) high "King's Throne," etc. The temperature inside the caves varies little, year round, from 70° (21°C). Conducted tours lasting about an hour. Open daily; definitely worth a visit.

FARTHER AFIELD

BIG BEND NATIONAL PARK (394 mi., 630 km, west via U.S. 90 and U.S. 385): One of the wildest and most beautiful of America's national parks. Impressive canyons along the Rio Grande, the river marking the Mexican border, whose right-angled "Big Bend" S of the **Chisos Mountains** gives the park its name. The rocky walls rise perpendicularly from the river to heights of 1,300 ft (400 m) at places such as **Santa Elena Canyon, Mariscal Canyon,** and **Boquillas Canyon.** The steep crests, once a refuge of the Comanche Indians, with their forests of oak, pine, and juniper and their great variety of wildlife (deer, coyote, peccary, mountain lion, and 400 species of birds), lie next to the Chihuahuan Desert, bristling with giant cactus and home to snakes, kangaroo rats, and roadrunners. There are also many dinosaur fossils in the park.

At its western edge are the ghost town of **Terlingua** and the little frontier town of **Lajitas,** whose Main Street comes straight out of a John Ford movie.

For air-rafting down the Rio Grande, contact **Big Bend River Tours,** P.O. Box 317, Terlingua, TX 79852 (915/424-3219).

Warning! There are no gas stations between Marathon on U.S. 90 and the park headquarters at **Chisos Basin,** 68 mi. (110 km) to the south.

Don't fail to visit Big Bend National Park; for **information,** contact the Superintendent, Big Bend National Park, TX 79834 (915/477-2251).

Sights En Route

On the way don't fail to see **Alamo Village** at **Brackettville,** 122 mi. (195 km) west on U.S. 90 (512/563-2580), a faithful reconstruction of San Antonio in the 1830s, built in 1959 for the shooting of John Wayne's famous movie *The Alamo.* From a classic saloon to an attack on a stagecoach, complete with enough musketry to make you laugh, every horse-opera cliché gets its turn. Indian museum. Open daily year round; amusing.

Also see the ⚓☀ **Judge Roy Bean Courtroom** at **Langtry,** 213 mi. (340 km) west on U.S. 90 (915/291-3340). The legendary Roy Bean was, at the time of the Wild West, in his own person "the law west of Pecos." He did justice, after his fashion, in his saloon-court, "The Jersey Lily" (named, like the town, after Lillie Langtry, "The Jersey Lily," a famous British beauty of the day), now a designated historic monument. A picturesque page of living history. Open daily.

Where to Stay En Route

IN THE PARK. The 🏨 **Chisos Mountain Lodge,** Chisos Basin, Big Bend National Park, TX 79834 (915/477-2291). 34 rms and bungalows. Rustic comforts; cafeteria. **I**

AT LAJITAS. The 🏨 **Badlands Hotel** and **Cavalry Post Hotel,** Star Rte. 70, Box 400, Lajitas, TX 79852 (915/424-3471). 81 rms. Picturesque replicas of original Far West hotels. **I—M**

🔭 HILL COUNTRY AND LYNDON B. JOHNSON RANCH (328 mi., 525 km, round trip via I-10W, Texas 46W, Texas 16N, Texas 27N, Texas 41W, I-10E, Texas 16N, U.S. 290E, and I-35S):

You come first to ⚓ **Boerne,** founded by German settlers in 1849; its old stone houses with narrow windows and gabled roofs still bear witness to their Germanic origins. Note the Kendall Inn, an old coaching inn built in 1859.

You now take Texas 46 to ☀ ⚓ **Bandera,** a picturesque little western town nicknamed "the cowboy capital of the world" (rodeos and open-air festivals). Interesting **Frontier Times Museum,** 506 13th St. (512/796-3864), open daily.

Near **Mountain Home,** 60 mi. (96 km) north, visit the ☀ ⚓ **Y.O. Ranch,** on Texas 41W (512/640-3222), one of the largest stock ranches in Texas (100 sq. mi., 259 km²). As well as a herd of more than 1,000 longhorns, the ranch has antelope, zebra, ostrich, and giraffe roaming free. Photo safaris arranged daily.

On to ☀ ⚓ **Fredericksburg,** the main destination of German immigrants to Texas in the 1850s, which has retained many of its original buildings and an unusual "Old European" flavor. Be sure to see the **Vereins Kirche,** a replica of the first church built in 1847, on Market Square, open Mon.-Fri., and the **Admiral Nimitz State Historical Park** at 340 E. Main St. (512/997-4379), open daily, a monument to the hero of World War II in the Pacific, who was a native of the town.

Continuing eastward, you come to **Lyndon B. Johnson State Historical Park,** 15 mi. west of Johnson City on U.S. 290, dedicated to the 36th president of the U.S.; free bus connection from the visitor center (512/644-2252), open daily, to the ☀ **LBJ Ranch House** and his birthplace; his tomb is in the family cemetery. Many memorabilia of the man who succeeded John F. Kennedy in the White House. At ⚓ **Johnson City** you can visit the Victorian **Boyhood Home,** one block south of Main St. (512/868-7128), open daily, where Lyndon B. Johnson lived from 1913 to 1934; don't miss it.

Now on to ☀ ⚓ **Austin,** capital of the state of Texas (see "Nearby Excursions," above).

Return to San Antonio via ☀ ⚓ **New Braunfels,** an engaging little German town founded in the 19th century by 5,000 German immigrants whose descendants have preserved unspoiled many of their inherited traditions: there's a very popular Wurstfest or sausage festival lasting for ten days at the beginning of Nov. On the way, stop to admire ☀ ⚓ **Aquarena Springs** near **San Marcos** (see "Nearby Excursions," above).

Your last stop on the return leg should be at ☀ ⚓ **Natural Bridge Caverns** (see "Nearby Excursions," above).

This picturesque trip, with lots to see, should take you three to four days.

Where to Stay En Route

IN AUSTIN. The 🛎🛎🛎 **Driskill Hotel,** 604 Brazos St., Austin, TX 78701 (512/474-5911). 185 rms. Luxury hotel of great quality dating from 1886. **M–E**

🛎 **Ramada Inn Capitol,** 300 E. 11th St., Austin, TX 78701 (512/476-7151). 145 rms. Typical motel, one block to state capitol. Recently renovated. **I–M**

IN FREDERICKSBURG. The 🛎 **Ad Dietzel Motel,** on U.S. 87 (1 mi., 1.6 km, west of town), Fredericksburg, TX 78624 (512/997-3330). 20 rms. A small and modest but very well-run motel. **I**

IN KERRVILLE. The 🛎🛎 **Best Western Inn of the Hills,** 1001 Junction Hwy., Kerrville, TX 78028 (512/895-5000). Large, modern, comfortable resort motel. **I–M**

☼🛎 **PADRE ISLAND NATIONAL SEASHORE** (165 mi., 264 km, SE via I-37 and Texas 358): Wildlife sanctuary for sea creatures and birds on a deserted sandspit 113 mi. (182 km) long; see Chapter 36 on Houston. Worth going out of your way for.

CHAPTER 38

ALBUQUERQUE ♛♛

□ □ □

And the Rio Grande Valley

Standing 5,300 ft (1,600 m) above sea level, in a ring of desolate mountains which define the valley of the **Rio Grande,** Albuquerque was founded in 1706 by Don Francisco Cuervo y Valdés, then governor of New Mexico. Named in honor of the Duke of Alburquerque (the first "r" has dropped out over the years), viceroy of New Spain, the city retains few traces of the colonial period. Only the **Old Town** with its fine **Plaza** bears witness to the past ascendancy of Spain, and here the atmosphere is distinctly touristy. Not far away are the ranks of impersonal office buildings and inevitable neon signs of the modern city.

Albuquerque was a staging-post on the Spanish colonial "Camino Real" between Mexico City and Santa Fe and, during the frontier days of the Far West, on the Santa Fe Trail. When the first transcontinental railroads were built in the last century, it was an important stop on the Santa Fe Railroad. Today it is the largest city in New Mexico, and its population, which quintupled between 1950 and 1980, is still growing. The city's industries—lasers, data processing, pharmaceuticals, solar energy, and nuclear weapons—face resolutely toward the future. In terms of industry and commerce Albuquerque ranks 12th among the 20 fastest-growing cities in the country. **Sandia Laboratories,** where in the years after 1942 the famous Manhattan Project resulted in history's first atomic bomb, employs 6,000 researchers and technicians and still dominates the city's industry. Noted for a very dry climate and an unusually cloudless sky (sunshine for 76% of the year), Albuquerque has become the world capital for ballooning, with a spectacular rally every October. The city is also an ideal point of departure for numerous excursions: toward **Santa Fe** (see that chapter); the cable car to the magnificent views at **Sandia Peak** (10,378 ft, 3,163 m); and the **Rio Grande Valley** (White Sands Desert, Valley of Fires, Mescalero Indian Reserve). Then there are the **Indian pueblos** of the fabled kingdom of Cibola, such as **Acoma** and **Zuñi,** and the **El Morro National Monument.**

BASIC FACTS: State of New Mexico. Area Code: 505. Time Zone: Mountain Time. ZIP Code: 87101. Founded: 1706. Approximate population: city, 380,000; metropolitan area, 480,000.

CLIMATE: Perpetual sunshine and low humidity make the climate of Albuquerque special. In summer the thermometer can run quickly up to 95° F (35° C) or higher. In winter, brisk but sunny weather and plentiful snowfall above 8,000 ft permit skiing on nearby Sandia Peak. Spring and, even better, fall are the ideal seasons for a trip.

DISTANCES: Dallas, 637 mi. (1,020 km); Denver, 421 mi. (675 km); Kansas

City, 790 mi. (1,265 km); Phoenix, 453 mi. (725 km); Salt Lake City, 609 mi. (975 km); Santa Fe, 61 mi. (98 km).

ARRIVAL & TRANSIT INFORMATION

AIRPORT: Albuquerque International Airport (ABQ), 5 mi. (8 km) SE. For information call 842-4366.

AIRLINES: America West (247-0737), American (242-9464), Delta (243-2794), Southwest (831-1221), TWA (842-4010), United (242-1411).

CITY LINK: Cab fare to city center, about $10; time, 15 min. City bus: SUNTRAN (route no. 50) until 7 p.m.; fare, 60¢; time, 25 min.

Bus to downtown Santa Fe (7 times a day): SHUTTLEJACK (982-4311); fare, $18; time, 1 hr. 10 min.

Since public transportation within the city is by an almost nonexistent bus service (SUNTRAN, 843-9200 for information), and excursions around the city are many and fascinating, it is highly advisable to rent a car with unlimited mileage.

CAR RENTAL (at airport unless noted): Avis (842-4080); Budget, 3000 Carlisle Rd. (884-2666); Dollar (842-4224); Hertz (842-4235); National (842-4222); Thrifty (842-8733). For downtown locations, consult the phone directory.

LIMOUSINE SERVICES: Capital City (998-2090), Dav El Limo (922-0343).

TAXIS: Cabs must be summoned by phone; they may not be hailed on the street. Yellow Cab: 247-8888.

TRAIN: AMTRAK Station, 314 1st St. SW (242-7816).

BUS: Greyhound, 300 2nd St. SW (243-4435).

INFORMATION & TOURS

TOURIST INFORMATION: Convention & Visitors Bureau, 625 Silver St. SW, NM 87125 (505/243-3696; toll free 800/284-2282).

GUIDED TOURS: Gray Line Tours (243-5501): Guided tours of city and surroundings. Depart from Sheraton Old Town Inn, 800 Rio Grande Blvd.

SIGHTS, ATTRACTIONS, & ACTIVITIES

ADVENTURES: World Balloon Co. (ballooning), 4800 Eubank Blvd. NE (293-6800): Leaves at dawn only when skies are clear. Best time of year: autumn or winter. About $100 per hour of flying time.

CHURCHES/SYNAGOGUES: ☼ ⌂ **Church of San Felipe de Neri,** on Old Town Plaza: The most representative building from the Spanish period. Built in

1793 on the site of a church of 1706 destroyed in 1790, this colonial-style church and the adjacent convent are still in use for religious purposes. See the spiral staircase in the choir, wrapped around the trunk of a spruce. Open daily.

HISTORIC BUILDINGS: ※ ⚖ University of New Mexico, E. Central Ave. & University Blvd. (277-4001): One of the oldest (1889) and most respected universities in the Southwest (24,000 students). Remarkable example of Pueblo Indian architecture, standing amid 672 acres (280 ha.) of gardens. Several museums (see below). Visitors Bureau in the Fine Arts Center. Well worth seeing.

MUSEUMS OF ART: ⚖ Albuquerque Museum, 2000 Mountain Rd. NW (243-7255): Interesting exhibits on the history of New Mexico; exhibitions of contemporary work by local artists. Open daily except Mon.

    ⚖ **Fine Arts Center,** Central & Cornell Aves. (277-4001): Large cultural complex including a fine-arts museum (**Art Museum**) mainly used for temporary exhibitions, the **Fine Arts Library,** and several theaters and concert halls (**Keller Hall, Rodey Theatre, Popejoy Hall,** etc.). On the university campus; worth a visit. Open daily except Mon.

    ※⚖⚖ **Indian Pueblo Cultural Center,** 2401 12th St. NW (843-7270): This cultural institute, operated by the Association of the 19 Pueblos of New Mexico, offers a complete overview of Indian art and customs. Original design derived from the architecture of Pueblo Bonito (see "Farther Afield," below). Traditional dances performed on weekends in summer. Craft shop. Authentic Indian restaurant. Guided tours of the pueblos. Don't miss. Open daily.

MUSEUMS OF SCIENCE & HISTORY: ※ ⚖⚖ Maxwell Museum of Anthropology, Grand Ave. NE & University Blvd. (277-4404): One of the finest museums in the country devoted to the culture of the American Indian. Everything about the "civilization of the Pueblos," particularly the mysterious Anasazi. Very fine Mimbres pottery. Equally rich in prehistoric material. Don't miss. On the university campus. Open daily.

    Museum of Geology and Meteoritics, 200 Yale Blvd. (277-4204): Unique collection of more than 200 meteorites from around the world. For students of astronomy. On the university campus. Open Mon.-Fri.

    ※⚖⚖ **New Mexico Museum of Natural History,** 1801 Mountain Rd. NW (841-8837): The first such museum to be opened in the U.S. in 50 years. The austere building, opened in 1986, offers a fascinating panorama of the land of the Rio Grande Valley, its plants and its animals, from prehistoric reptiles to a startling model of a volcano in eruption. An absolute must. Open daily.

    ⚖ **National Atomic Museum,** Kirtland Air Force Base, Bldg, 20358, on Wyoming Blvd. 7 mi. (11 km) from downtown (844-8443): Unusual museum devoted to nuclear weapons, with movies showing their effects, from the first A-bomb to the Minuteman missile. Pacificsts should stay away. Open daily.

    ⚖ **Rio Grande Nature Center,** 2901 Candelaria Rd. NW (344-7240): Standing on the east bank of the Rio Grande amid 7.2 acres (3 ha.) of park and woods, this all-glass structure houses rich collections of local geology, zoology, and history. Definitely worth seeing. Open daily.

PANORAMAS: ☀ **Sandia Peak,** Tramway Blvd. (5 mi. NE along I-25): With its summit 10,378 ft (3163 m) above sea level, the impressive Sandia Peak towers over Albuquerque and the Rio Grande Valley. On clear days (as they usually are) you can see the foothills of the Colorado Rockies 125 mi. (200 km) to the north, and as far as the Mexican border 187 mi. (300 km) south. Access by the longest cable car in the country (it rises 3,728 ft, 1,165 m, over a journey of 2.5 mi., 4 km). For information on timetables, call 298-8518. The High Finance rest. offers a panoramic view. A wonderful spectacle, not to be missed.

PARKS & GARDENS: ☀ ⚲ **Indian Petroglyph State Park,** Atrisco Rd. (9 mi., 14 km, west on I-40): Some 10,000 petroglyphs (figures carved from rock) —in this case, from lava by the ancestors of the Pueblo Indians between A.D. 1100 and 1600. Worth the trip. Open daily.

PERFORMING ARTS: For current listings of shows and cultural events, consult the entertainment pages of the two daily papers, *Albuquerque Journal* (morning) and *Albuquerque Tribune* (evening).
   Albuquerque Little Theatre, 244 San Pasquale SW (242-4750): Broadway hits, star-studded shows. Sept.-June.
   Keller Hall, U. of N.M. campus (277-3121): Concerts and recitals.
   Ki Mo Theatre, 423 Central Ave. NW (848-1370): Home of the Albuquerque Opera Theater (Sept.-May) and the New Mexico Repertory Theater (drama, comedy, classic theater).
   Popejoy Hall, U. of N.M. campus (277-3121): Home of the Albuquerque Civic Light Opera (musical comedy, operetta) and of the New Mexico Symphony Orchestra (music director: Neal Stulberg). Sept.-May. For information, call 842-8565. Also concerts; classic and modern dance theater.
   Rodey Theatre, U. of N.M. campus (277-4402): Modern theater.

SPECIAL EVENTS: For exact dates, consult the Albuquerque Convention & Visitors Bureau (see "Tourist Information," above).
   Old Town Fiesta (June): Concerts, art exhibitions, parades.
   New Mexico State Fair (September): Rodeo, horse races, country-music concerts. Local color guaranteed!
   International Balloon Fiesta (early October): World's greatest dirigible-balloon rally, attracting more than 500 participants from the U.S. and abroad. A splendid spectacle.
   Fiesta Encantada (December): Public concerts, folklore festivals, exhibitions; the Old Town is beautifully lit with candles.

STROLLS: **Old Town,** around Old Town Plaza: The heart of historic Albuquerque, with its beautiful tree-shaded Plaza, brick sidewalks, and bandstand. Several old buildings in Spanish Colonial idiom including above-mentioned Church of San Felipe de Neri. More than 100 boutiques, art galleries, souvenir shops, and restaurants. It flaunts its pitch for the tourist trade, but it's certainly picturesque.

WINTER SPORTS RESORTS: ⚲ **Sandia Peak Ski Area** (30 mi., 48 km, NE on I-40 and N.M. 14 and 44): 5 ski lifts. Operates Dec. to mid-Apr. Can also be reached by cable car from Tramway Rd. north of Albuquerque. For information on snow conditions, call 296-9585.

ZOOS: ⚲ **Rio Grande Zoo,** 903 10th St. SW (843-7413): More than 1,200 animals of all kinds in beautifully designed "natural" habitats, including a rain forest; picnic area and swimming pools nearby. Open daily.

ACCOMMODATIONS
See the listing of toll-free numbers in the Appendix.

Room Rates in Albuquerque	
B (Budget)	up to $30
I (Inexpensive)	$30–$60
M (Moderate)	$60–$90
E (Expensive)	$90–$140
VE (Very Expensive)	$140 and up

Personal Favorites (in order of preference)

Sheraton Old Town Inn (dwntwn), 800 Rio Grande Blvd., NM 87104 (505/843-6300; toll free, see Sheraton). 190 rms, A/C, color TV, in-rm movies. AE, CB, DC, MC, V. Free parking, pool, rest. (Customs House), coffeeshop, bar, rm svce, disco, hrdrsr, boutiques, free airport limo, free crib. *Note:* The best address in Albuquerque, right near Old Town Plaza. Spacious and comfortable rms, some with terraces and mini-bars. Svce and welcome impeccable. Decor warm and colorful. Rest. very acceptable. Caters mostly to tourists. **M–E**

Marriott (nr. dwntwn), 2101 Louisiana Blvd. NE, NM 87110 (505/881-6800; toll free, see Marriott). 410 rms, A/C, color TV, in-rm movies. AE, CB, DC, MC, V. Free parking, pool, tennis, health club, two rests. (incl. Nicole's), bar, rm svce, disco, boutiques, free crib. *Note:* Classic convention hotel, uninspired architecturally but with every modern convenience. Spacious, well-laid-out rms. Very efficient svce. Clientele mostly business people and conventions. Nicole's is an acceptable rest. One floor reserved for VIPs. Nr. new business district. **E**

La Posada de Albuquerque (formerly the Plaza; dwntwn), 125 2nd St. NW, NM 87102 (505/242-9090; toll free 800/621-7231). 114 rms, A/C, color TV. AE, CB, DC, MC, V. Free parking, rest. (Eulalia), coffeeshop, bar, rm svce, hrdrsr. *Note:* Charming old hotel from the late '30s. A recent facelift has retained its appealing period flavor—a pretty fountain in the lobby, heavy overhanging eaves, and murals. Rms are more comfortable than elegant. Rest. of very respectable quality. Welcome and service with a smile. Very well located, not 5 min. from the Plaza. Good quality-to-price ratio. An excellent place to stay. **M**

Barcelona Court (nr. dwntwn), 900 Louisiana Ave. NE, NM 87110 (505/255-5566). 164 suites w. kitchenettes, A/C, color TV, cable. AE, CB, DC, MC, V. Free parking, 2 pools, sauna. Coffeeshop next door, piano bar, rm svce, free airport limo. *Note:* This brand-new motel, 5 min. from the airport, has only spacious and welcoming suites, with kitchenettes and refrigerators. Private balconies or patios. Decor is elegant and full of light. Attentive svce. Free breakfast. Business clientele, since the new business district is a few steps away. **M–E**

Central Plaza (formerly the Quality Inn; dwntwn), 717 Central Ave. NW, NM 87102 (505/247-1501). 144 rms, A/C, color TV, in-rm movies. AE, CB, DC, MC, V. Free parking, pool, rest., bar, rm

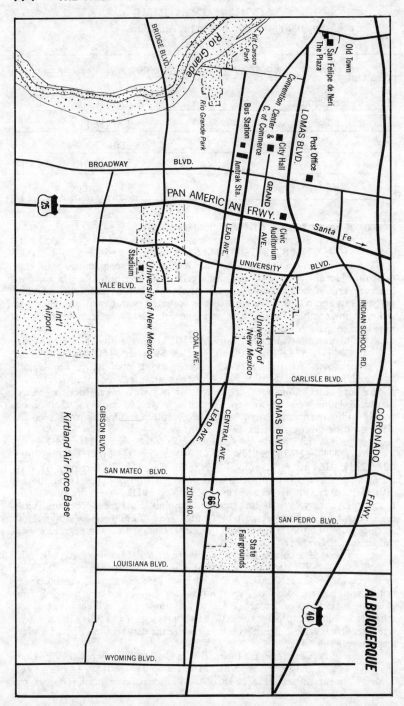

svce, free airport limo, free crib. *Note:* Functional six-floor motel, completely modernized. Rms are attractive; the best have a park view. Agreeable svce, very good price-to-quality ratio. 3 min. from Old Town by car. **I**

Motel 6 Midtown (nr. dwntwn), 1701 University Blvd., NM 87102 (505/843-9228). 118 rms, A/C, color TV, free in-rm movies. DC, MC, V. Free parking, nearby coffeeshop, free crib. *Note:* This motel, 5 min. from the city center, offers an unbeatable price-to-quality ratio. Down-to-earth comfort. Ideal for motorists. Nr. university campus. **B**

Other Accommodations (from top bracket to budget)

Hilton Inn (nr. dwntwn), 1901 University Blvd. NE, NM 87102 (505/884-2500; toll free, see Hilton). 450 rms, A/C, color TV, cable. AE, CB, DC, MC, V. Free parking, two pools, tennis, skating rink (Nov.-Mar.), sauna, rest. (The Rancher's Club), 24-hr coffeeshop, bar, rm svce, disco, hrdrsr, free airport limo, free crib. *Note:* Grand hotel, large and comfortable, with 12 floors, largest in Albuquerque. Efficient svce and welcome. Spacious rms w. refrigerators (some w. balconies). Restaurant renowned for its grill. Good recreational facilities. 5 min. from dwntwn by car. Guests mostly groups and conventions. Worthwhile weekend discounts. Two floors reserved for VIPs. **M–E**

Doubletree (formerly the Regent; dwntwn), 201 Marquette Ave. (at 2nd St.), NM 87103 (505/247-3344; toll free, 800/528-0444). 300 rms, A/C, color TV, in-rm movies. AE, CB, DC, MC, V. Free indoor parking, rest. (Mayfair), coffeeshop, bar, rm svce, disco, drugstore, free airport limo, free crib. *Note:* Massive 15-story tower with roof-garden overlooking the Convention Center. Utilitarian comfort and svce. Recently underwent major modernization. Very centrally located. Caters mostly to groups and conventions. **M–E**

Holiday Inn Midtown (nr. dwntwn), 2020 Menaul Blvd. NE, NM 87107 (505/884-2511; toll free, see Holiday Inns). 366 rms, A/C, color TV, in-rm movies. AE, CB, DC, MC, V. Free parking, pool, health club, rest., bar, rm svce, disco, free airport limo. *Note:* A typical Holiday Inn, 5 min. by car from dwntwn. Comfortable rms w. balconies. Svce and welcome impersonal. Good overall price-to-quality ratio. **I–M**

RESTAURANTS

Albuquerque Restaurant Prices	
(per person, excluding drinks and service)	
B (Budget)	up to $15
I (Inexpensive)	$15–$25
M (Moderate)	$25–$40
E (Expensive)	$40–$60
VE (Very Expensive)	$60 and up

Personal Favorites (in order of preference)

Al Monte's (nr. dwntwn), 1306 Rio Grande Blvd. NW (243-3709). A/C. Lunch/dinner Mon.-Sat.; closed Sun. and holidays. AE, DC, MC, V. Jkt. Specialties: veal Oscar, grilled squab, sole meunière, deviled crab. Good wine list. *Note:* Lavish but conventional decor. French-inspired classic cuisine, irreproachably prepared. Attentive service. Inviting bar with open fireplace; open-air dining in good weather. Res. advised. The local favorite. *Continental.* **I–M**

     Maria Teresa (dwntwn), 618 Rio Grande Blvd. NW (242-3900). A/C. Lunch/dinner daily; closed Thanksgiving, Dec. 25. No credit cards. Jkt. Specialties: steak, lobster, quail, truite amandine. Good wine list. *Note:* Beautiful hacienda (1840) standing in its own gardens, and designated as a historic monument. Very convincing decor. Meticulous presentation; svce on the slow side. Resv. advised. A few steps from Old Town Plaza. *Continental.* **I–M**

     El Pinto (nr. dwntwn), 10500 4th St. NW (898-1771). A/C. Lunch/dinner Tues.-Sun.; closed Mon., holidays. MC, V. Specialties: guacamole, chile con carne, enchiladas, sopaipillas. *Note:* Memorable Southwestern cooking in a hacienda setting. The inviting, tree-shaded courtyard with its fountain is one of Albuquerque's pleasantest spots. Friendly, ultra-professional svce. Very popular with locals, so resv. advised. Highly recommended. *Mexican-American.* **B–I**

     M. & J. Sanitary Tortilla Factory (dwntwn), 403 2nd St. SW (242-4890). A/C. Breakfast/lunch/dinner (till 8 p.m.) Mon.-Sat.; closed Sun., holidays. MC, V. Enchiladas, carne adovado, tacos. *Note:* Considered by purists one of the most authentic Mexican restaurants in the area. Decor Formica and neon, style, continuous Mexican music, relaxed atmosphere. Locally popular; excellent price-to-quality ratio. No resv. *Mexican.* **B**

Other Restaurants (from top bracket to budget)

     The Rancher's Club (nr. dwntwn), in the Hilton Inn (see "Accommodations," above) (884-2500). A/C. Lunch/dinner daily. AE, CB, DC, MC, V. Jkt. Specialties: finest-quality red meats grilled on a wood fire. *Note:* Albuquerque's best steakhouse. Stunning, rather overdone decor. The meat is excellent, and grilled to perfection over wood fires of different kinds at your choice (the mesquite is best). Impeccable service; ambience western-chic; locally very popular, so resv. a must. *Steakhouse.* **I–M**

     Casa Vieja (away from dwntwn), Corrales Rd. in Corrales (via Rio Grande Blvd. and N.M. 46 north) (505/898-4077). A/C. Dinner only Tues.-Sun.; closed Mon., Thanksgiving, Dec. 25, Jan 1. AE, MC, V. Jkt. Specialties: osso buco w. risotto alla milanese, homemade pâté maison, saltimbocca, veal marsala, lime pie. *Note:* Charming adobe hacienda, more than a century and a half old, 12 mi. north of Albuquerque. Nice colonial decor with open fires. Italian-leaning cuisine of excellent quality; rather restricted wine list. Efficient svce.; resv. advised. 25 min. from dwntwn. *Italian-Continental.* **I–M**

     The Cooperage (nr. dwntwn), 7220 Lomas Blvd. NE (255-1657). A/C. Lunch/dinner daily; closed Dec. 25. AE, MC, V. Jkt. Specialties: roast beef, barbecues, fish and shellfish, chicken Kiev. *Note:* Unusual building in the shape of a giant vat, but comfortable inside. Excellent meats and seafood. Intimate atmosphere, open late (till 11 p.m.); dancing Wed.-Sat. 10 min. from dwntwn. *Steak-American.* **I**

     Nob Hill Café (nr. dwntwn), 3500 Central Ave. NE (255-1792). Lunch Mon.–Fri., dinner Mon.–Sat.; closed Sun. AE, MC, V. Jkt. Specialties: excellent contemporary cuisine; daily change of menu. *Note:* The local temple for American (California-derived) nouvelle cuisine. Striking pink-and-black decor with art deco touches. Svce a little disorganized. Smart place; resv. strongly advised. *American.* **I**

New Chinatown (nr. dwntwn), 5001 Central Ave. NE (265-8859). A/C. Lunch/dinner daily; closed Thanksgiving, Dec. 25. AE, CB, DC, MC, V. Specialties: Cantonese-Szechuan. *Note:* The best Chinese rest. in Albuquerque. Modern Oriental decor; good food and exotic drinks. Svce leaves something to be desired. Open till 11 p.m. Very good price-to-quality ratio at the buffet lunch. 10 min. from dwntwn. *Chinese.* B–I

La Hacienda (dwntwn), 302 San Felipe NW (243-3131). A/C. Lunch/dinner daily; closed Thanksgiving, Dec. 25, Jan. 1. CB, DC, MC, V. Specialties: enchiladas, burritos, sopaipillas. *Note:* Pleasing, original Mexican-hacienda interior, with three great trees at the center of the dining room, but resolutely tourist atmosphere. Mexican-American cuisine no better than acceptable. Svce and welcome so-so. High noise level, agreeable music. Right on Old Town Plaza. Resv. advised. *Mexican.* B–I

Cafeterias/Fast Food

Furr's (nr. dwntwn), 2272 Wyoming Blvd. NE (298-6886). Lunch/dinner daily; open till 8 p.m. Specialties: roast beef, daily specials, sandwiches, baked fish. *Note:* Pleasant surroundings and atmosphere. Well-regarded locally. Other branches: 6100 Central Ave. SE (265-1022) and 109 Montgomery Plaza NE (881-3373).

BARS & NIGHTCLUBS

The Cooperage (nr. dwntwn), 7220 Lomas Blvd. NE (255-1657). Live jazz; dancing Wed.–Sat. Also an acceptable rest.

Nicole's Lounge (nr. dwntwn), at the Marriott (see "Accommodations," above) (881-6800). Fashionable disco; smart atmosphere. Also very acceptable rest. Open daily.

Palomino Club (nr. dwntwn), 2900 Coors Blvd. NW (831-2020). Country music; very cowboy atmosphere.

NEARBY EXCURSIONS

CIBOLA NATIONAL FOREST: 1,536,000 forested acres (640,000 ha.) surrounding Albuquerque, Mountainair, Grants, and Magdalena. Roads offering fine views, camping, hunting, fishing, skiing in mid-winter, etc. For information: 10308 Candelaria Rd. NE, Albuquerque, NM 87112 (505/766-2185).

CORONADO STATE PARK & MONUMENT (22 mi., 35 km, north via I-25 and N.M. 44N): Ruins of a Kuava pueblo dating from A.D. 1300. The Spanish conquistador Francisco Vásquez de Coronado pitched his camp here during his fruitless search for a mythical Eldorado known to historians under the name of "the seven golden cities of Cibola." Interesting Indian museum. Visit to a restored "kiva" (place of worship). Generally worth seeing. Open daily.

INDIAN PUEBLOS: There are 19 pueblos (villages) inhabited by 40,000 Indians, as well as another dozen abandoned or in ruins, in central New Mexico, all antedating the arrival of the Spanish colonists about 3½ centuries ago. The Anasazi Indians, close relatives of the Aztecs and great builders, built these too, between A.D. 700 and 1100. Bandelier National Monument (see "Nearby Excursions" in the chapter on Santa Fe), and especially Chaco Canyon (see "Farther Afield" in the chapter on Santa Fe), both now in ruins, are among the most important archeological monuments of Native American culture. The Pueblo or Zuñi Indians who live there today are the descendants of the legendary Anasazi. The most isolated of minorities, the Pueblo or Zuñi Indians of New Mexico, and their Hopi cousins in Arizona, have always been settlers, as distinct from such nomadic peoples as the Apaches and Navajos, who formed a large majority of the Native American population in the Southwest.

Half a dozen of their pueblos near Albuquerque are open to tourists between sunrise and sunset, generally for a fee of around $3–$4 per car. The best time for a visit is during the yearly festival or on days of religious ceremony; calendar from Albuquerque Convention & Visitors Bureau, 625 Silver St. SW (505/243-3696). *Note:* For religious reasons, some villages do not allow cameras (movie or still) or tape recorders. In others, photographers must pay a fee of $3–$6.

The most picturesque of these pueblos are: 🏛🏛 **Acoma Pueblo,** 65 mi. (104 km) west by I-40W and N.M. 23 (505/552-6606), the oldest continuously inhabited site in the U.S., believed to have been settled around A.D. 600. Perched 6,400 ft up on a rocky mesa, "Sky City," as historians have dubbed it, is by far the loveliest Indian pueblo in the country, and the least corrupted by Western civilization. Fine Spanish mission of San Esteban Rey (1629). Not to be missed. Photography permitted; fee $3.

🏛 **Isleta Pueblo,** 14 mi. (22 km) south on U.S. 85 (505/877-0370): Busy handcraft center. The original church of 1620 was destroyed during the Indian rebellion of 1680 and rebuilt 13 years later. Worth seeing. Photography permitted; fee $3.

🏛 **Jemez Pueblo,** 48 mi. (76 km) north by I-25 and N.M. 44 and 4: Renowned for its embroidery and basket-making; no photographs. Not far away, at Jemez Springs, is a beautiful Spanish mission dating from 1621.

🏛 **Zia Pueblo,** 34 mi. (54 km) north by I-25 and N.M. 44 (505/867-2196): Another pueblo well known for its pottery. Spanish mission dating from 1692. No photographs.

🔆🏛🏛 **Zuñi Pueblo,** 179 mi. (286 km) west via I-40 and N.M. 32 and 53 (505/782-5581): One of the "seven golden cities of Cibola." The Zuñi, a separate branch of the Pueblo people, are excellent potters and jewelers. Photography permitted; fee $3. Late November/early December is the season of the Zuñi "shalako" (council of the gods), the most beautiful, and spectacular, Indian ceremony in the U.S. By all means go—but movie/still cameras are not allowed during "shalako."

GHOST TOWNS: In New Mexico there are a round dozen old mining towns dating from last century's gold and silver rushes; some of them are now completely abandoned. Examples are **White Oaks** (15 mi, 24 km, NE of Valley of Fires State Park along U.S. 54 and N.M. 349) and 🏛 **Shakespeare** (46 mi., 73 km, SW of Silver City by N.M. 90 and U.S. 70), where most of the ornate exteriors are still standing.

Others are still more or less intact, but drained of their former vitality: **Chloride** (38 mi., 60 km, NW of **Truth or Consequences** along I-25 and N.M. 142 and 52), and **Hillsboro, Kingston,** and **Pinos Altos** (see "Farther Afield," below).

Among ghost towns closer to Albuquerque, the most picturesque are 🏛 **Cerrillos** (48 mi., 76 km, NE via I-40 and N.M. 14) and 🏛 **Madrid** (45 mi., 72 km, NE via I-40 and N.M. 14); for these two villages, see the chapter on Santa Fe.

FARTHER AFIELD

🔆🏛 **SANDIA LOOP DRIVE** (80 mi., 128 km, r.t. via N.M. 66E, 14N, 44N, and I-25S): A panoramic route, open approx. May

15 to Oct. 15, leading to the peak of **Sandia Mountain** (10,416 ft, 3,255 m). Wonderful view over the Rio Grande Valley and surrounding countryside. The **Sandia Peak Ski Area** can also be reached by cable car (see "Panoramas," above).

SANTA FE AND THE INDIAN PUEBLOS (240 mi., 384 km, r.t. via I-25N, N.M. 44N and 4E, U.S. 285S, and I-25S): Exhilarating two-day drive (longer if a visit is made to **Coronado State Park;** see "Nearby Excursions," above). The route continues through two typical Indian villages (see "Nearby Excursions," above), **Zia Pueblo** and **Jemez Pueblo,** best known for pottery and basketwork, respectively. Stop for a look at ☖ **Valle Grande,** ranked by geologists as the world's largest volcanic crater (area, 175 sq. mi., 453 sq. km.; mean depth, 486 ft., 152 m). Then on to the beautiful **Bandelier National Monument** (see "Nearby Excursions" in the chapter on Santa Fe); **Los Alamos,** the historic birthplace of the atom; and the pueblo of **San Ildefonso** with its beautiful plaza (see "Indian Pueblos," in the chapter on Santa Fe), before reaching the capital of New Mexico with its monuments and its museums (for places to stay, see the chapter on Santa Fe). Return to Albuquerque by I-25S. Set aside at least 48 hours for the trip, which mustn't be missed.

SKY CITY AND CHACO CANYON (473 mi., 758 km, r.t. via I-25N, N.M. 44N and 57S; I-40W; N.M. 32S, 53W, and 53E; I-40E; N.M. 38S and 23N; and I-40E): A full three- or four-day trip for devotees of archeology and Indian culture, it takes you first to **Coronado State Park** (see "Nearby Excursions," above), then on to the astonishing ☀ ☀ ☖ **Chaco Culture National Historical Park,** an archeological gem from our Amerindian past. Deserted by the Anasazi Indians around the end of the 13th century, this cluster of 75 ruined pueblos, one of which, Pueblo Bonito, boasted in its glory days no fewer than 800 rooms and 37 "kivas" (places of worship), well deserves a special trip. *Warning:* The road to Chaco Canyon is unsurfaced; dry weather only.

The third stage of the journey leads you to **Gallup,** "the Indian capital of the world." Every August some 50 Indian tribes from all over the U.S. and Canada meet for the ☖ "Intertribal Indian Ceremonial," a very lively four-day festival with dances, parades, rodeos, and handcraft displays. Don't miss it. Then on to **Zuñi Pueblo,** home of the famous Indian "shalako" ritual (see "Indian Pueblos," above), and ☖ **El Morro National Monument,** a shaft of rock 211 ft high with many Indian rock carvings as well as inscriptions by Spanish conquistadors and early settlers in the Old West—an interesting sight.

The trip ends with a leisurely visit to the beautiful **Acoma Pueblo,** or "Sky City" (see "Indian Pueblos," above), before returning to Albuquerque via I-40E. This exciting trip is strongly recommended; it can be prolonged to take in **Mesa Verde National Park,** an important center of Native American culture (see the chapter on Santa Fe), **Monument Valley,** or **Canyon de Chelly** (see the chapter on Navajoland).

Where to Stay En Route

IN GALLUP. Three motels are recommended: ☖ **Best Western–The Inn,** 3009 W. U.S. 66W, NM 87301 (505/722-2221). 124 rms. **I–M**

Motel 6, 3306 W. U.S. 66, NM 87301 (505/722-4084). 80 rms. **B**

Travelodge, 1709 W. U.S. 66, NM 87301 (505/863-9301). 50 rms. **I**

☼☼♨️ WHITE SANDS AND THE RIO GRANDE VALLEY

(582 mi., 932 km, r.t. via I-25S, U.S. 82E, N.M. 24N, U.S. 70E, U.S. 380W, and I-25N): After driving along the Rio Grande Valley for almost 225 mi. (360 km), you'll come to ♨️♨️ **White Sands National Monument,** an extraordinary desert of gypsum whose dazzling-white sand dunes, as much as 45 ft (15 m) high, create an ever-changing landscape of otherworldly beauty.

Then on to ♨️ **Cloudcroft,** an agreeable little winter-sports resort with a flourishing artists' colony and the highest golf course (8,700 ft, 2,650 m, above sea level) in the U.S. If you can, go on to visit **Mescalero,** capital of the lovely Apache reservation of the same name; museum, exhibition of ♨️ Indian handcrafts.

The fourth stage takes you to **Ruidoso,** a ski resort in the middle of a forest, and to **Lincoln,** famous in the days of the Old West and now a museum town. The legendary Pat Garrett, the man who killed Billy the Kid, was long its sheriff. Billy the Kid is buried at **Fort Sumner,** also famous during the winning of the West, about 125 mi. (200 km) north. Be sure to see the museum and the ♨️ **old courthouse** at Lincoln.

Finish the journey by crossing the ♨️♨️ **Valley of Fires,** a desert of gray-and-black lava from an old volcano. At ♨️ **Trinity Site** near Alamogordo, 30 mi. (50 km) west, on July 16, 1945, the first atomic bomb was tested as a trial run for Hiroshima and Nagasaki. Area open to the public the first Sat. of April and Oct. For information, call 505/437-6120. This beautiful three- or four-day trip can be combined with the visit to the ♨️♨️ **Gila Cliff Dwellings** (see below).

Where to Stay En Route

IN CLOUDCROFT. 🍽️🍽️ **The Lodge,** U.S. 82, NM 88317 (505/682-2566). 50 rms. Designated historic building. **I–M**

IN RUIDOSO. 🍽️ **Best Western Swiss Chalet Inn,** on N.M. 37, NM 88345 (505/258-3333), 82 rms. **M**

🛏️ **Super 8,** U.S. 70 at N.M. 37, NM 88345 (505/378-8180). 63 rms. **I**

☼♨️ GILA CLIFF DWELLINGS AND SILVER CITY (635

mi., 1,016 km, r.t. via I-25S; N.M. 90W, 35N, 15N, 15S; U.S. 180N; N.M. 12N; U.S. 60E; and I-25N): A journey of three to four days across the vast **Gila National Forest,** beginning with a visit to **Isleta Pueblo** and its lovely church built in 1693 (see "Indian Pueblos," above). At **Socorro,** 50 mi. farther south, you can admire the fine fortified mission of ♨️ **San Miguel,** 403 Camino Real (open Mon.-Fri.), built in 1615. Then on to ♨️ **Truth or Consequences** and its hot springs, and to **Hillsboro** and ♨️ **Kingston,** almost-deserted ghost towns from Gold Rush days. Kingston once had 22 saloons for its 1,800 inhabitants. Go on to see the ♨️ **Gila Cliff Dwellings,** very fine Indian cave dwellings from the 13th century, some 40 dwellings in caves cut into the living rock of the cliff; not to be missed. ♨️ Wonderful wooded surroundings.

Then drive to the old stagecoach stop of ♨️ **Silver City,** once thronged with gold and silver miners, scene of the early exploits of the famous outlaw Butch Cassidy. As you pass it, stop for a look at ♨️ **Pinos Altos,** a picturesque ghost town built by gold miners in the 19th century, and often under attack by the Apaches under Cochise and Geronimo. Its most famous inhabitant was Judge Roy Bean, known as the "hanging judge."

On the road back to Albuquerque, make a detour through **Mogollon** (74 mi., 118 km, north of Silver City via U.S. 80 and N.M. 78), another famous ghost town from the 19th century.

Where to Stay En Route

IN SILVER CITY. The **Best Western Holiday,** U.S. 180, NM 88061 (505/538-3711). 80 rms. **I–M**

Drifter Motel, 711 Silver Heights Blvd., NM 88061 (505/538-2916). 69 rms. **I**

CHAPTER 39

SANTA FE ❞❞

□ □ □

And the Indian Pueblos

A state capital of truly human dimension, "La Villa Real de la Santa Fe de San Francisco" (the Royal City of the Holy Faith of St. Francis), now called simply Santa Fe, is the offspring of an unusual amalgam of Native American, Hispanic, and Anglo-Saxon traditions. Instead of urban motorways or great avenues intersecting at right angles, you'll find shady streets, most of them narrow and winding. Neon signs are banned from downtown. No glass or concrete skyscrapers; just low-rise ocher or beige houses of adobe (sun-dried brick), typically in traditional Indian design. The lovely **Plaza,** standing at the historic heart of the city, where the legendary **Santa Fe Trail** ends; the 1610 **Mission de San Miguel,** one of the oldest churches in the country; the **Palace of the Governors,** also dating from 1610; even the modern **State Capitol,** whose massive rounded shape recalls the old kivas (Indian places of worship)—all evoke a sense of the past. And the city's museums house many treasures from the Indian civilizations. Indeed, Santa Fe is the only state capital in the country that won't permit commercial jets to land at its airport, lest its authenticity be impaired!

Vigilantly protecting its colonial heritage, more than 3½ centuries old (the city was founded in 1609—11 years before the Pilgrim fathers landed at Plymouth—by Don Pedro de Peralta, governor of the Spanish province of New Mexico), this oldest of the country's state capitals has never lacked for painters, sculptors, musicians, and writers. From D. H. Lawrence to Max Weber and Georgia O'Keeffe, from Ezra Pound to Aaron Copland, they came, attracted by the region's unique charm, the extraordinary luminosity of its skies, the majestic backdrop of the **Sierra Sangre de Cristo,** the southernmost spur of the Rocky Mountains.

Apart from the picturesque and colorful beauty of its own narrow streets and flower-filled patios, Santa Fe is the ideal starting point for many fascinating excursions to **Mesa Verde National Park** or to the surrounding **Hopi pueblos.** Some of these "pueblos" (villages) are already tainted by the "civilization" of electrical appliances and mass tourism. Others, such as **Taos Pueblo, San Ildefonso,** and **Santo Domingo,** have at least preserved their original appearance, if not their authentic character.

Note that, at an elevation of 7,000 ft (2,134 m), Santa Fe may give you a problem for your first few days, until you're accustomed to the altitude.

BASIC FACTS: Capital of the State of New Mexico. Area Code: 505. Time Zone: Mountain Time. ZIP Code: 87501. Founded: 1609. Approximate population, 56,000.

CLIMATE: With more than 300 days of sunshine annually, you could say that the sun is a year-round fixture in Santa Fe but, thanks to the altitude, it's never unpleasantly hot; the July avg. temperature is 71°F (22°C). The evenings are cool even in summer. There is heavy snow in winter, for the delectation of skiers, on the slopes of the Sierra Sangre de Cristo; Jan. avg. temperature, 35°F (2°C). In a word, it's always a good time of year to visit Santa Fe.

DISTANCES: Albuquerque, 61 mi. (98 km); Denver, 386 mi. (618 km); Grand Canyon National Park, 465 mi. (744 km); Phoenix, 521 mi. (834 km); Salt Lake City, 610 mi. (976 km).

ARRIVAL & TRANSIT INFORMATION

NEAREST MAJOR AIRPORT: Albuquerque International Airport (ABQ), 61 mi. (98 km) SW (505/842-4366).

AIRLINES (at the Albuquerque airport): America West (247-0737), American (242-9464), Delta (243-2794), Southwest (831-1221), TWA (842-4010), and United (242-1411).

CITY LINK: A minibus operated by Shuttlejack (505/982-4311) runs eight times a day between the Albuquerque airport and the principal Santa Fe hotels; fare, $15; time, about 75 min. Resv. advised.

However, given the distance from Albuquerque to Santa Fe and the countless tempting excursions in the surrounding countryside, it makes a lot of sense to rent a car with unlimited mileage. Moreover, there is no real public transportation system in Santa Fe, and cabs are hard to come by.

CAR RENTAL (at the Albuquerque airport, unless otherwise noted; if a second telephone number is given, it's for *free pickup at your place of residence in Santa Fe*): Avis (842-4080; 982-4361); Budget, 3000 Carlisle Blvd. (884-2666; 984-8028); Dollar (842-4224); Hertz (842-4235; 982-1844); National (842-4222; 983-2232); and Thrifty (842-8733).

TAXIS: Cabs may not be hailed on the street but may be summoned by phone. Recommended company: Capital City Cab (988-1211).

TRAIN: The nearest AMTRAK station is on N.M. 41 at Lamy, 19 mi. (30 km) south on U.S. 285 (toll free 800/872-7245).

A shuttle runs daily between downtown Santa Fe and the station; contact Lamy Shuttle Service, 1476 Miracerros Loop North (982-8829). Reservations advised.

BUS: **Greyhound,** 858 St. Michael's Dr. (471-0008).

INFORMATION & TOURS

TOURIST INFORMATION: The **Santa Fe Chamber of Commerce,** 333 Montezuma St., NM 87501 (505/983-7317).

Santa Fe Convention and Visitors Bureau, Sweeney Center, 201 W. Marcy St. (P.O. Box 909), NM 87504 (505/984-6760; toll free 800/777-2489).

New Mexico State Travel Division, J. M. Montoya Bldg., 1100 St. Francis Dr., NM 87503 (505/827-0291; or toll free 800/545-2040 outside New Mexico): Information on all New Mexico's treasures of tourism.

Visitor's Information Booth, The Plaza: Open Mon.-Sat.

GUIDED TOURS: Escort Guide Inc. (bus, limousine), 535 Cordova Rd. (988-7099): Guided tours of Santa Fe and environs for individuals or groups.

Gray Line Tours (bus), 220 N. Guadalupe St. (471-9200): Guided bus tours of the city and environs. Serves the main hotels.

SIGHTS, ATTRACTIONS, & ACTIVITIES

ADVENTURES: New Wave Rafting Co. (boat), 107 Washington Ave. (505/984-1444): White-water rafting down the Rio Grande, Rio Chama, and Arkansas rivers; half-day ($40), one-day ($60–$70), and two-day ($160–$200) trips. Summer only.

Rapid Transit (boat), P.O. Box A, Pilar, NM 87571 (505/758-9700): Rafting down the Rio Grande and Rio Chama; summer only.

Rio Bravo River Tours (boat), 1412 Cerrillos Rd. (505/988-1153; toll free 800/451-0708): Rafting down the Rio Grande and White Rock Canyon; summer only.

Southwest Safaris (airplane), P.O. Box 945, Santa Fe, NM 87504 (505/988-4246): One-day trips by plane to Grand Canyon National Park, Mesa Verde, Canyon de Chelly, Monument Valley, and Carlsbad Caverns. Spectacular. Departures year round from Santa Fe Municipal Airport.

ARCHITECTURAL HIGHLIGHTS: ☼ ⌂ **La Fonda,** 100 E. San Francisco St. (982-5511): One of the most history-laden hotels in the U.S., going back to the opening of the Santa Fe Trail in the 1870s. A favorite stopping place for trappers, pioneers, and early traders. Billy the Kid was a dishwasher here at the beginning of his career of adventure. Long known as "The Inn at the End of the Trail," and often rebuilt (the last time was in 1919), it is still one of the best hotels in the city. Worth seeing.

☼ ⌂ **Santa Fe Opera,** on U.S. 84, 7 mi. (11 km) north (982-3855): Splendid conch-shaped open-air auditorium built on a mesa at the foot of the Jemez Mountains; a very successful piece of modern design. Every summer it hosts a highly regarded opera festival (see "Special Events," below). Open afternoons, Mon.-Sat., during the opera season (June-Aug.); it's advisable to make reservations. Worth going out of your way for.

⌂ **State Capitol,** Old Santa Fe Trail and Paseo de Peralta (827-3773): One of the newest (1966) state capitols in the country; an unusual circular building reminiscent of a traditional Indian kiva (place of worship). The New Mexico legislature meets here. Open Mon.-Fri.

CHURCHES/SYNAGOGUES: ⌂ **Cathedral of St. Francis of Assisi,** Cathedral Plaza (892-5619): Built between 1869 and 1884 by Archbishop Jean Baptiste Lamy on the site of an older church destroyed by Indians in 1680, said to be the country's oldest Marian shrine. Its *La Conquistadora,* brought here by the Spaniards in 1692, is the oldest statue of the Virgin still in existence in the U.S. A classic piece of architecture in the French Romanesque Revival style. Worth a visit; open daily.

☼ ⌂ **Cristo Rey Church,** Canyon Rd. and Camino Cabra: The largest Indian-style church in the country; its adobe walls are 7 ft (2 m) thick. Valuable stone *reredos* (altar screen) dating from 1760; don't miss it. Open daily.

☼ ⌂ **Loreto Chapel,** 219 Old Santa Fe Trail (982-3376): Gothic Revival chapel modeled on the Sainte-Chapelle in Paris, with

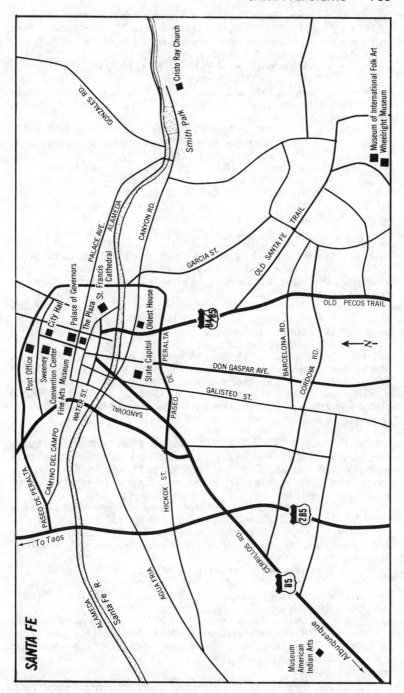

SANTA FE

Cristo Ray Church

Smith Park

GONZALES RD.

Museum of International Folk Art
Wheelright Museum

CANYON RD.

ALAMEDA

PALACE AVE.

GARCIA ST.

OLD SANTA FE TRAIL

St. Francis Cathedral

Palace of Governors

City Hall

The Plaza

Oldest House

OLD PECOS TRAIL

84 285

Post Office

Sweeney Convention Center

Fine Arts Museum

State Capitol

PASEO DE PERALTA

BARCELONA RD.

CORDOVA RD.

DON GASPAR AVE.

-N-

WATER ST.

SANDOVAL

GALISTEO ST.

PASEO DE PERALTA

CAMINO DEL CAMPO

HICKOX ST.

285

To Taos

ALAMEDA

Santa Fe R.

AGUA FRIA

CERRILLOS RD.

85

Albuquerque

Museum American Indian Arts

an amazing spiral staircase, "The Famous Staircase," the work of an unknown cabinetmaker in 1878. Its 33 treads rise to a height of 22 ft (7 m), and are held together without nails or any visible support. Loreto Chapel is sometimes called Our Lady of Light Chapel. Worth a look; open daily.

Mission of San Miguel, Old Santa Fe Trail and E. De Vargas St. (983-3974): The oldest church in the country still used for worship. Built between 1610 and 1636, its often-restored walls of thick adobe hide a wonderful interior, with a superb *reredos* (1798) and several old paintings. Shouldn't be missed; open daily.

Santuário de Guadalupe, 100 Guadalupe St. (988-2027): One of the oldest shrines of the Virgin in the country, dating from about 1796. Dedicated to Our Lady of Guadalupe, the patron saint of Mexico, it houses some interesting handcrafts and religious art from the Spanish Colonial period. Should definitely be seen; open Mon.-Sat.

Scottish Rite Temple, Washington Ave.: Enormous Masonic temple whose baroque design harks back to the Alhambra in Granada. No visitors, but worth a glance.

HISTORIC BUILDINGS: **Oldest House,** 215 E. De Vargas St.: Believed to be the oldest building in the country still in use, this Indian house built of clay and straw, whose walls and foundations are more than eight centuries old, is now a souvenir shop. A stone's throw from the Mission of San Miguel; worth seeing. Open daily.

Palace of the Governors, The Plaza (827-6460): Both palace and fortress, this massive, elegant building has been the home, successively, of Spanish, Mexican, and U.S. governors; it is the oldest (1610) public building in continuous use in the U.S. Partly destroyed in the Indian rebellion of 1680, the original building with its patios, storehouses, and outbuildings has been restored many times. The author Lew Wallace, at the time governor of New Mexico, used his idle moments here to write the major part of his famous novel *Ben Hur* in 1880. Interesting museum, Indian craft shop, and impromptu market under the portal (porch). Don't miss it; open daily Mar.-Dec., Tues.-Sun. the rest of the year.

MUSEUMS OF ART AND HISTORY: **Institute of American Indian Arts Museum,** 1369 Cerrillos Rd. (988-6281): A comprehensive panorama of modern Native American (including Inuit) arts and handcrafts: sculpture, pottery, textiles, jewelry, painting, etc. Fascinating. Temporary exhibitions. An absolute must. Open daily.

Laboratory of Anthropology / Museum of Indian Arts and Culture, 708-710 Camino Lejo (827-8941): Rich collection of Native American (particularly Navajo and Pueblo) art, from pottery to kachina dolls. Excellent specialized library. A must-see; open daily Mar.-Dec., Tues.-Sun. the rest of the year.

Museum of Fine Arts, 107 W. Palace Ave. (827-4455): More than 8,000 works of southwestern artists from 1898 to the present. Handsome traditional adobe building dating from the turn of the century. Open daily Mar.-Dec., Tues.-Sun. the rest of the year.

Museum of International Folk Art, 706 Camino Lejo (827-8350): One of the best American museums of popular art and tradition, displaying dolls, masks, toys, religious objects, clothing—more than 125,000 different objects. Must be seen; open daily Mar.-Dec., Tues.-Sun. the rest of the year.

Wheelwright Museum, 704 Camino Lejo (982-4636): All kinds of Indian art—jewelry, pottery, textiles, and wickerwork. The design of this 1937 museum is based on traditional Navajo hogans or earthen huts. Interesting Indian craft shop. Don't miss it; open daily May-Sept., Tues.-Sun. the rest of the year.

PARKS AND GARDENS: River Park, along the Santa Fe River between Old Santa Fe Trail and Don Gaspar Ave.: Pretty flower-planted, tree-shaded walk along the Santa Fe River, marking the boundary of the Analco district ("the other side of the river" in the Indian language), the old (11th- to 15th-century) Indian pueblo before the arrival of the Spanish settlers.

PERFORMING ARTS: For daily listings of all shows and cultural events, consult the entertainment pages of the daily papers, the *Albuquerque Journal* (morning) and *The New Mexican* (morning), particularly the latter's Friday supplement, *Pasatiempo*.

Armory for the Arts, 1050 Old Pecos Trail (988-1886): Musicals, ballet, children's theater.

Center for Contemporary Arts, 291 E. Barcelona Rd. (982-1338): Ballet, poetry recitals, big-name shows, theater.

Greer Garson Theater, College of Santa Fe campus, St. Michael's Dr. (473-6511): Contemporary and classic theater.

New Mexico Repertory Theater, 217 Johnson St. (983-2382): Drama, comedy, contemporary theater.

Paolo Soleri Outdoor Amphitheatre, Santa Fe's Indian School campus (988-6291): Big-name shows, rock concerts (summer only).

St. Francis Auditorium, 107 W. Palace Ave. (983-2075): Home of the renowned Santa Fe Chamber Music Festival (July-Aug.). Classical concerts, recitals.

Santa Fe Opera, on U.S. 84, 7 mi. (11 km) north (982-3855): Open-air opera; cycle of five operas every summer (June-Aug.). Nationally acclaimed.

SHOPPING: Deriving most of its income from tourism, Santa Fe abounds in Native American crafts shops, art galleries, and all kinds of stalls that put unseemly prices on their goods and generate an unpleasantly rapacious atmosphere. If you're a dedicated window-shopper, you may want to see:

Canyon Road (see "Strolls," below).

Santa Fe Village, 227 Don Gaspar St.: Two dozen shops and art galleries in a fake pueblo setting very near the Plaza.

Sena Plaza and Prince Plaza, 115 E. Palace Ave.: Some 40 luxury shops and restaurants around pretty patios in two elegant 19th-century mansions.

Among the shops offering authentic Native American art objects and handcrafts (and not Taiwanese, Mexican or Filipino knockoffs): **Packard's Indian Trading Co.** (61 Old Santa Fe Trail), **Bellas Artes Gallery** (301 García St.), and the museum shops at the Palace of the Governors and the Wheelwright Museum (see above).

SPECIAL EVENTS: For the exact schedule of events below, consult the **Santa Fe Chamber of Commerce** (see "Tourist Information," above).

Fiesta at Santo Domingo Pueblo (late July to early Aug.): The best-known and most colorful Indian fiesta in the Rio Grande valley.

Santa Fe Rodeo (mid-July): The great event for cowboys and rodeo lovers.

Spanish Market (last weekend of July): Exhibition of Hispanic crafts under the arcades of the Palace of the Governors.

Santa Fe Chamber Music Festival (six weeks in July and Aug.): One of the best classical-music festivals in the country; for information and reservations, call 983-2075.

Santa Fe Opera (July-Aug.): Opera in an open-air auditorium in the sierra. Few big names, but a nursery for young talent with a large, faithful audience of opera lovers. Reservations a must, well ahead.

Taos Summer Music Festival (mid-June to Aug.): Very popular chamber-music festival (776-2388).

Indian Market (mid-Aug.): One of the biggest Native American markets in the country; tribes from every quarter of the compass come to display their arts and crafts on the Plaza. Folk dances. 100,000 visitors each year. Don't miss it.

Santa Fe Fiesta (three days in mid-Sept.): Parades, processions, dancing; celebrated every year since 1712 to commemorate the reconquest of the town by the Spaniards after the Indian rebellion of 1680. One of the most famous popular festivals in the U.S.; don't miss it.

Sundown Dance at Taos Pueblo (late Sept.): Colorful festival.

Christmas Eve Celebrations in Santa Fe (Dec. 24): Lights, dancing, processions.

Dates of other **Indian festivals** may be obtained from the Santa Fe Convention and Visitors Bureau, 201 W. Marcy St. (984-6760).

SPORTS: Horse Racing (Wed. and weekends, early May to Labor Day): **The Downs,** 5 mi. (8 km) south on I-25 (471-3311). Thoroughbred racing.

STROLLS: ☼☖ **Canyon Road:** The old road to Pecos in the days of the Santa Fe Trail, now an arts-and-crafts street. More than 50 galleries, shops, and restaurants. Other studios and shops on nearby **Camino del Monte Sol.** Charming and picturesque.

☼☖☖ **The Plaza:** The historic heart of Santa Fe, a fine, lively, colorful sight with its gardens, its 1862 commemorative obelisk, its old houses, and its Indian market set up every morning in the arcades of the Palace of the Governors. In the SE corner, a plaque marks the end of the fabled Santa Fe Trail, linking Independence, Mo., with the Rio Grande Valley. It was opened in 1822 by William Becknell, a particularly enterprising Kansas City businessman. Don't miss it.

WINTER SPORTS RESORTS: ☖ **Santa Fe Basin,** 17 mi. (27 km) NE on N.M. 475 (982-4429): Six lifts; open Nov.-Apr.

☼☖☖ **Taos Ski Valley,** 89 mi. (142 km) NE via U.S. 84, N.M. 68, U.S. 64, and N.M. 150 (776-2291): Nine lifts; open Nov.-Apr.

For a recording giving **snow conditions** at different resorts, call 984-0606.

ACCOMMODATIONS
See the listing of toll-free numbers in the Appendix.

Room Rates in Santa Fe	
B (Budget)	up to $30
I (Inexpensive)	$30–$60
M (Moderate)	$60–$90
E (Expensive)	$90–$140
VE (Very Expensive)	$140 and up

Personal Favorites (in order of preference)

The Bishop's Lodge (vic.), Bishop's Lodge Rd. (3 mi., 5 km, north on N.M. 22), NM 87501 (505/983-6377). 65 rms, A/C, color TV. No credit cards. Free parking, pool, sauna, four tennis courts, trap shooting, boating, fishing, horseback riding, rest. (Bishop's Lodge Restaurant), bar, rm svce, nightclub, cinema (in summer), crib $10. *Note:* Luxurious vacation ranch on the outskirts of Santa Fe. Very comfortable rms w. private patios, some w. fireplaces; very complete facilities. Superb setting and surroundings on 1,000 acres (400 ha.) at the foot of the Sangre de Cristo Mountains. Attentive svce; rest. of quality. Once the home of Archbishop Jean Lamy, on whom Willa Cather based her famous novel *Death Comes for the Archbishop.* Closed Dec.-Feb. The best hotel in Santa Fe, 5 min. from dwntwn. **E–VE (MAP June-Aug.)**

Clarion Eldorado Hotel (dwntwn), 309 W. San Francisco St., NM 87501 (505/988-4455; toll free, see Clarion). 218 rms, A/C, color TV, in-rm movies. AE, CB, DC, MC, V. Valet garage $6, pool, saunas, two rests. (including the Old House), coffeeshop, bar, 24-hr rm svce, nightclub, boutiques, concierge. *Note:* The most elegant and one of the newest (1986) of the dwntwn hotels. A very successful design, deftly combining the imperatives of modern hostelry with the traditional esthetics of Santa Fe: adobe walls, exposed beams, and colorful décor w. Indian motifs. Luxurious, well-designed rms w. private balconies or patios and mini-bars (some w. fireplaces). Rooftop pool w. views clear across the city. Exemplary svce; very acceptable rests. Well-heeled tourist clientele. A stone's throw from the Plaza; an excellent place to stay. **E–VE, but lower rates out of season**

La Fonda (dwntwn), 100 E. San Francisco St., NM 87501 (505/982-5511; toll free 800/523-5002). 160 rms, A/C, color TV, in-rm movies. AE, CB, DC, MC, V. Free parking, rest. (La Plazuela), bars, rm svce, nightclub, art gallery, free crib. *Note:* Charming old Spanish Colonial–style hotel right on the Plaza. A genuine local institution (see "Architectural Highlights," above); the present building dates from 1919. Comfortable, tastefully decorated rms, some w. balconies and fireplaces. Pretty covered patio; acceptable rest.; romantic atmosphere. Very good value in spite of the utterly inefficient svce. The best location in Santa Fe. **M–E**

La Posada (dwntwn), 330 E. Palace Ave., NM 87501 (505/986-0000; toll free 800/531-6424). 112 rms, no A/C, color TV, in-rm movies. AE, CB, DC, MC, V. Free parking, pool, rest. (Staab House), bar, rm svce, hrdrsr, free crib. *Note:* Very pretty little older hotel in a lovely garden; elegant Spanish Colonial décor. Huge, comfortable rms in adobe casitas w. private patios. A stone's throw from the Plaza and the Palace of the Governors. Diligent svce; good rest. One of the best values in town. **M–E, but lower rates out of season**

☀� **Budget Inn** (nr. dwntwn), 725 Cerrillos Rd., NM 87501 (505/982-5952). 160 rms, no A/C, color TV, in-rm movies. MC, V. Free parking, pool, rest., crib $10. *Note:* Functional but definitely comfortable motel 5 min. from the Plaza. Spacious rms; efficient reception and svce. Good value on balance. Group and package-tour clientele. **I**

Other Accommodations (from top bracket to budget)

☀☀lll **Inn on the Alameda** (dwntwn), 303 E. Alameda, NM 87501 (505/984-2121; toll free, 800/552-0070, ext. 289). 36 rms and suites, A/C, cable color TV. AE, CB, DC, MC, V. Free parking, hot tub, nearby rest., bar, rm svce, free breakfast. *Note:* Small, intimately charming, comfortable hotel in Pueblo Indian style, 5 min. from the Plaza. Very inviting rms and suites, some w. private balconies or patios. Personalized svce. The favorite of those in-the-know. **E–VE, but lower rates out of season**

lll **Best Western Inn at Loreto** (dwntwn), 211 Old Santa Fe Trail, NM 87501 (505/988-5531; toll free, see Best Western). 139 rms, A/C, cable color TV. AE, CB, DC, MC, V. Free parking, pool, sauna, rest., coffeeshop, bar, rm svce, disco, hrdrsr, drugstore, free crib. *Note:* A good piece of modern architecture in the Native American style, well adapted to its surroundings. Comfortable, congenial hotel a block or two from the Plaza; spacious rms w. private balconies or patios. Very good reception; impeccable svce. Group and business clientele. **E, but lower rates out of season**

lll **Hilton Inn** (dwntwn), 100 Sandoval St., NM 87501 (505/988-2811; toll free, see Hilton). 150 rms, A/C, color TV, in-rm movies. AE, CB, DC, MC, V. Free parking, pool, rest. (Chamisa), coffeeshop, bar, rm svce, nightclub, free crib. *Note:* Relatively modern motel whose adobe design fits reasonably well into the colonial setting around it; 2-min. walk from the Plaza. Comfortable, well-equipped rms; efficient svce; so-so rest. Group and convention clientele. **M–E, but lower rates out of season**

ll **Garrett's Desert Inn** (dwntwn), 311 Old Santa Fe Trail, NM 87501 (505/982-1851). 82 rms, A/C, cable color TV. AE, MC, V. Free parking, pool, rest., bar, rm svce, nightclub, free crib. *Note:* Classic motel a few blocks from dwntwn. Very convincing colonial décor; vast, comfortable rms; attentive svce. A fine place to stay. **M, but lower rates out of season**

l **El Rey Inn** (nr. dwntwn), 1862 Cerrillos Rd., NM 87504 (505/982-1931). 56 rms, A/C, color TV. AE, DC, MC, V. Free parking, pool, adjoining coffeeshop, crib $4. *Note:* Engaging, well-run small motel in a verdant oasis 8 min. from dwntwn. Inviting rms, some w. kitchenettes and fireplaces. Attractive garden w. fountain. Good value. **I–M**

l **Motel 6** (nr. dwntwn), 3007 Cerrillos Rd., NM 87501 (505/473-1380). 104 rms, A/C, color TV, free in-rm movies. DC, MC, V. Free parking, pool. *Note:* Unbeatable value 8 min. from dwntwn in a rather depressing neighborhood. Inviting, functional rms; adjacent 24-hr coffeeshop. Perfect if you're driving. **B**

Accommodations in the Vicinity

☀lll **Rancho Encantado** (vic.), N.M. 4 (P.O. Box 57C), Tesuque, NM 87501 (505/982-3537), 8 mi. (13.5 km) north on U.S. 285. 58 rms (7 in the hotel, 51 in cottages or mini-apartments), A/C, color TV (in apartments). AE, CB, DC, MC, V. Free parking, two pools, tennis court, horseback riding, bar, rm svce, crib $15. *Note:* Luxurious resort complex nestled in the mountains north of Santa Fe, on the edge of the Tesuque Indian Reservation. Comfortable cottages and apartments in a beautiful garden. Private patios. Valuable Indian furnishings and artifacts. Upscale clientele. Renowned rest. (Rancho Encantado Dining Room). Library. Very good svce. Resv. should be made a number of weeks ahead, given the limited number of rms. One of the most famous hotels in the country; its guestbook has been signed by John Wayne, Maria Callas, Henry Fonda, and Gregory Peck. 15 min. from dwntwn. Closed Feb.-Mar. **E−VE**

YMCA / Youth Hostels

Santa Fe International Hostel (nr. dwntwn), 1412 Cerrillos Rd., NM 87501 (505/988-1153). Dormitories; rms for couples and families. Open year round.

RESTAURANTS

Santa Fe Restaurant Prices	
(per person, excluding drinks and service charges)	
B (Budget)	up to $15
I (Inexpensive)	$15–$25
M (Moderate)	$25–$40
E (Expensive)	$40–$60
VE (Very Expensive)	$60 and up

Personal Favorites (in order of preference)

ΨΨΨ **Coyote Café** (dwntwn), 132 W. Water St. (983-1615). A/C. Lunch/dinner Mon.-Sat.; closed Sun. AE, MC, V. *Specialties:* enchiladas w. green chile sauce, blue-corn tortillas w. goat cheese, chives, tomato, and coriander, lamb stew w. zucchini, squash, and juniper berries, broiled calamari w. sweet chili and yellow-tomato salsa, duck tamales w. mole sauce, chili of game and venison, carpaccio of tuna w. chili and lime. Menu changes regularly. *Note:* Mark Miller, former chef at Berkeley's famous Fourth Street Grill, is an anthropologist by training and draws inspiration from his travels through Mexico and the southwestern U.S. The result is a contemporary "ethnic" cuisine, rich in color and taste, which has been attracting an ever-growing number of devotees since the rest. opened in 1986. The rest., in what was once the Greyhound bus terminal, has high ceilings, bare walls enlivened by one or two modern paintings, and rustic benches which just accentuate the austerity of the décor. Friendly, smiling svce; successful enough that resv. are strongly advised. You'll have a memorable meal here. *American.* **I−M**

ΨΨΨ **Compound** (nr. dwntwn), 653 Canyon Rd. (982-4353). A/C. Lunch/dinner Tues.-Sun.; closed Mon., holidays, and Jan. AE. J&T. *Specialties:* fresh foie gras, squab w. champagne, sweetbreads and wild mushrooms, duck w. green peppercorns, roast filet of lamb w. spinach and pine-nut sauce, catch of the day. *Note:* A happy marriage of Spanish Colonial setting and modern atmosphere 5 min. from the Plaza. Elegantly intimate décor;

polished French-inspired cuisine. Pretty, open patio; a little stuffy svce in white gloves. Resv. advised. The chicest place in Santa Fe, and the only one to require a necktie. *Continental.* **M**

Pink Adobe (dwntwn), 406 Old Santa Fe Trail (983-7712). A/C. Lunch Mon.-Fri., dinner nightly; closed Jan. 1, Labor Day, Thanksgiving, and Dec. 25. AE, CB, DC, MC, V. *Specialties:* shrimp Créole, chicken Marengo, steak Dunigan (w. green chile), pork Napoleon w. madeira sauce, Mexican dishes. *Note:* One of the prettiest and most popular rests. in Santa Fe, in a three-centuries-old building. Charming setting w. a profusion of greenery and open patio in summer. The food is very good on the whole. Diligent svce. Often crowded and noisy; resv. a must. *Continental-Mexican.* **I**

La Tertulia (dwntwn), 416 Agua Fria St. (988-2769). A/C. Lunch/dinner Tues.-Sun.; closed Mon., Jan. 1, Labor Day, Thanksgiving, and Dec. 24–25. AE, MC, V. Jkt. *Specialties:* steak verde, paella, chile relleno, chalupas, Mexican dishes. *Note:* This elegant rest. in a converted 19th-century convent serves excellent Mexican-inspired food. Exemplary svce; locally popular; resv. advised. *American-Mexican.* **I**

Guadalupe Café (dwntwn), 313 Guadalupe St. (982-9762). A/C. Lunch/dinner Tues.-Sun.; closed Mon. and holidays. No credit cards. *Specialties:* sandwiches, enchiladas, chile relleno, steak w. green-chile salsa, sopaipillas. *Note:* Modest but inviting, this typical little down-at-the-heels bistro serves some of the most authentic food in the region. No wine or beer, but you may bring your own. Locally popular; local color guaranteed. *American-Mexican.* **B–I**

Other Restaurants (from top bracket to budget)

The Bull Ring (dwntwn), 414 Old Santa Fe Trail (983-3328). A/C. Lunch/dinner Mon.-Sat. (until 1 a.m.); closed Sun. MC. *Specialties:* shrimp à l'espagnole, steak, lamb chops, chateaubriand, catch of the day. *Note:* Charming 19th-century colonial-style building with patio, adobe walls, and big open fireplaces. Fine red meats and classic European cooking. As the capitol is just in back of the rest., it's a favorite w. local politicians, and the bar is very popular. Dancing. Resv. advised. *Steak-continental.* **I**

El Farol (nr. dwntwn), 808 Canyon Rd. (983-9912). Dinner only, Tues.-Sat.; closed Sun., Mon., and holidays. AE, CB, DC, MC, V. *Specialties:* tapas, chicken w. fruit, broiled lamb on a skewer, roast baby chicken. *Note:* Appealing little country rest. where you dine in the patio by candlelight. Some original dishes; congenial atmosphere. Locally popular. *American.* **I**

La Casa Sena (dwntwn), 20 Sena Plaza, 125 E. Palace Ave. (988-9232). A/C. Breakfast/lunch/dinner daily (until midnight); closed Dec. 25. AE, CB, DC, MC, V. *Specialties:* spicy meatball soup, enchilada Catalina, pasta w. red chili, trout baked in clay. *Note:* Excellent southwestern food in a charming adobe "mesón" dating from the 1860s in Old Santa Fe. It's near enough to the Plaza to attract a big tourist business, while the singing waiters at the bar provide unusual local color. A nice place. *Continental-Mexican.* **B–I**

Shohko Café (dwntwn), 321 Johnson St. at Guadalupe St. (983-7288). A/C. Lunch Mon.-Fri., dinner nightly; closed holidays. AE, MC, V. *Specialties:* Imperial rolls, tempura, sushi, teriyaki, sukiyaki. *Note:* This little Chinese-Japanese rest. behind the Hilton Hotel serves the best Far Eastern food in town. Simple and unpretentious. Resv. advised. *Chinese-Japanese.* **B–I**

Staab House (dwntwn), in La Posada (see "Accommodations," above) (983-6351). A/C. Breakfast/lunch/dinner daily. AE, CB, DC, MC, V. Jkt. *Specialties:* fajitas del norte, excellent broiled fish and meat. Good wine list. *Note:* Staab House, occupying a historic home dating from 1882, is one of the prettiest rests. in Santa Fe. Fine Victorian décor w. many Indian and Spanish handcrafts. Classic hotel food impeccably prepared and served; open-air eating on fine days. Excellent value. *Continental-American.* **B–I**

♈ **The Steaksmith** (nr. dwntwn), El Gancho, Old Las Vegas Hwy. (988-3333). A/C. Dinner only, Mon.-Sat.; closed Sun. and holidays. AE, MC, V. *Specialties:* steak, roast beef, catch of the day, good homemade desserts. *Note:* Generally crowded, this congenial, rustic steakhouse serves excellent beef cuts and remarkably fresh fish at very sensible prices. Relaxed atmosphere; locally popular. A fine place, 8 min. from dwntwn. *Steak-seafood.* **B–I**

☼� **The Shed** (dwntwn), 113½ E. Palace Ave. (982-9030). A/C. Lunch only, Mon.-Sat.; closed Sun. and holidays. No credit cards. *Specialties:* enchiladas, burritos, homemade desserts (mocha cake). *Note:* Delightful little rest. in the shadow of the cathedral, open for lunch only. Excellent Mexican-inspired food in a very picturesque colonial setting (the building dates from 1692). Locally popular. Wine and beer. Unfortunately, no resv. *American-Mexican.* **B**

Cafeterias / Fast Food

Furr's (nr. dwntwn), Coronado Center, 522 W. Cordova Rd. (982-3816). Lunch/dinner till 8 p.m. daily. No credit cards. Praiseworthy cafeteria food at very low prices: chicken-fried steak, baked fish, etc.

BARS AND NIGHTCLUBS

Bull Ring Lounge (dwntwn), 414 Old Santa Fe Trail (983-3328). Congenial bar, disco. Open nightly.

Club West (nr. dwntwn), 213 W. Alameda St. (982-0099). Live rock; *the* fashionable club.

NEARBY EXCURSIONS

☼🐌 **BANDELIER NATIONAL MONUMENT** (45 mi., 72 km, NW via U.S. 84 and N.M. 4) (672-3861): Ruins of Indian cave dwellings and cliff houses dating from the 13th century, in a lovely wild setting on Frijoles Canyon ("Canyon of Beans"). The monument is named after the Swiss ethnologist and writer Adolph Bandelier, who explored the area thoroughly in the 1880s. Along 70 mi. (113 km) of footpaths you, too, can explore the caves and ruins of the different pueblos in the park. Among them are **Tyuonyi,** a three-story circular ruin which once had 400 rooms and three kivas (places of worship); **Long House,** which once had more than 300 rooms; and the **Ceremonial Cave** kiva, in a cave 150 ft (46 m) above the valley floor which can be reached only by ladders. Visitor center with archeological museum. Open daily; quite a tiring visit. Combine it if possible with a trip to Los Alamos (see below).

☼🐌 **CORONADO STATE PARK AND MONUMENT** (45 mi., 72 km, south via I-25 and N.M. 44N) (867-5351): Ruins of a Kuava pueblo going back to A.D. 1300. The Spanish conquistador Francisco Vásquez de Coronado camped here in 1540 during his fruitless search for the mythical Eldorado known to historians as "the seven gold cities of Cibola." Interesting Indian museum. Visit to a restored kiva. Well worth the side trip. Open daily.

☼🐌 **LOS ALAMOS** (40 mi., 65 km, NW on U.S. 84 and N.M. 4): Once the secret city of atomic research ("Atomic City"), this is where Robert Oppenheimer and his team devised the first A-bomb in

1942–1943 as part of the so-called Manhattan Project. The **Bradbury Science Museum** on Diamond Dr. (667-4444), open daily, is an interesting museum of nuclear science and nuclear energy, with full-size models of "Little Boy" and "Fat Man," respectively the Hiroshima and Nagasaki bombs.

On the way, visit **San Ildefonso** (see "Indian Pueblos," below) and 🛆 **Puye Cliff Ruins** on N.M. 5 (753-7326), with a number of prehistoric dwellings and the ruins of a very large Indian pueblo five centuries old. Open daily Apr.-Oct.; definitely worth the visit.

🛆 **OLD CIENEGA VILLAGE MUSEUM** (10 mi., 16 km, SW on U.S. 85): Authentic museum-village tucked into the mountainside, depicting the life of the Spanish settlers between 1660 and the 19th century. Interesting; visits Mon.-Fri., Apr.-Oct., by appointment. Folklore festivals some weekends. For schedules, call 471-2261.

🌣🛆 **PECOS NATIONAL MONUMENT** (25 mi., 40 km, SE on I-25) (757-6032): Remains of a 14th-century pueblo which once had some 2,500 inhabitants; two magnificent kivas have been completely restored. The principal dwelling house was five stories high. Nearby are ruins of the first Spanish mission built in New Mexico (1542), destroyed during the Indian rebellion of 1680. Church rebuilt in 1701 and finally abandoned at the end of the 18th century. Open daily; worth the side trip.

🌣🛆🛆 **TAOS** (70 mi., 112 km, NE via U.S. 285 and N.M. 68): Picturesque little Spanish-Mexican-American community nestled in the foothills of the Sierra Sangre de Cristo ("Christ's Blood Mountains"), so called by the Spaniards because at twilight in winter the snow appears to take on a purplish cast. An artists' colony for more than a century, Taos now deploys dozens of art galleries and an unfortunate abundance of souvenir shops, but its museums and its pretty **Plaza** are enough to justify the trip. Among the more interesting museums: the **Ernest L. Blumenschein Home,** with its many works by local painters, at 13 Ledoux St., open daily; and the **Bent House Museum,** 18 Bent St., open daily, Mar.-Dec., residence of the first American governor of New Mexico, Charles Bent, who was killed and scalped there by Indians in 1847. You should also see the house, and tomb, of the famous scout Kit Carson, nicknamed "The Crack Shot of the West," who lived here for 24 years, at the **Kit Carson Home,** E. Kit Carson Rd. (758-4741), open daily; the beautiful Spanish mission of **San Francisco de Asis,** rebuilt in 1772, at Rancho de Taos, 4 mi. (6.5 km) south on N.M. 68 (758-2754), open daily; the **D. H. Lawrence Ranch,** 18 mi. (29 km) north on N.M. 3 (776-2245), open daily, where the British novelist who wrote *Lady Chatterley's Lover* is buried; and the great 🛆🛆 **Rio Grande Bridge** looking down on the river from its height of 650 ft (198 m), 10 mi. (16 km) NW on U.S. 64.

You'll find it a good idea to combine this with a trip to **Taos Pueblo** (see "Indian Pueblos," below).

On your way back to Santa Fe, take the "High Road to Taos" along N.M. 3 and N.M. 76, dotted with delightful little Spanish Colonial villages like **Chimayo** (beautiful old church with a legend of healing powers, weavers' workshops), **Truchas,** and **Cordova.** A trip full of worthwhile sights; don't miss it.

Where to Eat En Route

IN TAOS. 🍷 **Ogelvie's at Taos,** The Plaza (758-8866). Lunch/dinner daily. *Mexican-American.* **B–I**

IN CHIMAYO. The 🍴🍴 **Rancho de Chimayo,** on N.M. 520 (351-4444). Lunch/dinner daily in summer, Tues.-Sun. the rest of the year; closed Jan. One of the best regional rests. in the state. Don't miss it. *Mexican.* **B–I**

GHOST TOWNS: ⚱ **Cerrillos,** 28 mi. (44 km) SW via I-25 and N.M. 14: This old prospectors' town had 2,500 inhabitants, eight hotels, and 20 saloons in the 1880s; today its population is barely 200, but it still has many vestiges of its golden age. Sometimes used as a film set. Must be seen.

⚱ **Madrid,** 30 mi. (48 km) SW via I-25 and N.M. 14: Once an important coal-mining center, now down to 200 inhabitants. Interesting mining museum and dozens of abandoned houses. Open-air concerts in summer. An absolute must-see.

INDIAN PUEBLOS

There are more than a dozen still-inhabited Native American pueblos (the Spanish word for villages) within a 125-mi. (200-km) radius of Santa Fe, almost all going back beyond the arrival of the colonizing Spaniards 3½ centuries ago. Heirs of the famous Anasazi people of the Middle Ages, the Pueblo Indians fall into four major families: the Hopi (see Chapter 40 on Navajoland), the Zuñi and the Acoma in west-central New Mexico, and the Rio Grande Indians, who live around the valley of the same name. Their numbers, perhaps 20,000 when the Spaniards came, declined to 5,000–6,000 in the 19th century, but have now reached almost 40,000.

The pueblos of the Rio Grande Indians may be visited between sunrise and sunset on payment of a fee of $3–$4 per vehicle; try to make your visit coincide with the annual festival or a religious ceremony (Jan. 1, 22, 23; Feb. 2; Easter; May 3; June 13, 24; Aug. 10; Sept. 29, 30; Nov. 12; Dec. 12, 25, 31). *Warning:* You must not photograph the village or its people unless authorized to do so (usually for a fee) by the chief of the pueblo. Discreet and respectful behavior is appropriate at all times.

The **Santa Fe Convention and Visitors Bureau,** 201 W. Marcy St. (984-6760), will give you the dates of festivities; information may also be obtained from the Eight Northern Pueblos Council (852-4265). The most picturesque pueblos are:

☀⚱⚱ **Acoma Pueblo,** 127 mi. (204 km) SW via I-25S, I-40W, and N.M. 23 (552-6606): The oldest community in the U.S., believed to have been first settled around A.D. 600. Perched 6,560 ft (2,000 m) up on a rocky mesa, "Sky City," as the historians have dubbed it, is by far the country's most beautiful pueblo, and the least tainted by Western "civilization." Spanish Mission of San Estebán Rey (1629). A visit you shouldn't miss. Photography permitted for a $3 fee.

⚱ **Cochití Pueblo,** 30 mi. (48 km) SW via U.S. 85S and U.S. 22N (465-2244): Antedates the Spaniards; a center for the crafting of silver-and-precious-stone jewelry, ceramics, and drums, on the banks of the Rio Grande. No photographs.

☀⚱ **Jémez Pueblo,** 75 mi. (120 km) south via I-25S, N.M. 44N, and N.M. 4N (834-7359): Famous for its embroidery, weaving, and wickerwork. No photographs. Not far away, at **Jemez Springs,** is a pretty Spanish Franciscan mission dating from 1621, near a prehistoric village.

☀⚱ **San Ildefonso Pueblo,** 28 mi. (44 km) NW via U.S. 84 and N.M. 4 (455-2273): Lovely plaza with open-air market; best known for its Indian pottery and ceramics. One of the best-known Rio Grande pueblos. Photography permitted ($3).

⚱ **San Juan Pueblo,** 28 mi. (44 km) north on U.S. 285 (852-4400): Chosen by the Spaniards as the site of their first capital in 1598. The great rebellion of 1680 originated in San Juan; it culminated with the taking of Santa Fe and the massacre of all the Spanish garrisons. It took the forces of Don Diego de Vargas 12 years to put the rebellion down. Photography permitted ($3).

Santa Clara Pueblo, 27 mi. (43 km) NW on U.S. 84 (753-7326): A typical example of pueblo architecture; fine pottery. Photography permitted ($3).

Santo Domingo Pueblo, 32 mi. (51 km) SW via U.S. 85 and N.M. 22 (465-2214): The most authentic and traditional of the pueblos; turquoise jewelry and blankets. Photography permitted ($3).

Taos Pueblo, 72 mi. (115 km) NE via U.S. 285 and N.M. 68 (758-9593): The cultural capital of the Pueblo Nation, with the 13,000-foot peaks of the Sangre de Cristo as a distant backdrop. It retains the traditional 13th-century ground-plan of terraces in dark-yellow or brown adobe, with construction on four or five levels linked by rudimentary flights of steps. Ruins of Mission San Gerónimo (1598) are adjacent to the central plaza. A firmly tourist atmosphere but a splendid setting. Photography permitted ($5).

Tesuque Pueblo, 8 mi. (13 km) NW on U.S. 285 (983-2667): The site has been continuously inhabited since about A.D. 1250. A mission, now ruined, was built here at the beginning of the 18th century. Crafts (pottery, jewelry, embroidery) and remarkable dancing at different times of year.

Zía Pueblo, 65 mi. (104 km) SW via I-25S and N.M. 44N (867-3304): Also famous for its pottery. Fine natural site. Spanish Mission of Nuestra Señora de la Asunción (1692). No photographs.

For more details on this and other New Mexico pueblos, see Chapter 38 on Albuquerque.

FARTHER AFIELD

CUMBRES AND TOLTEC SCENIC RAILROAD (220 mi., 352 km, round trip on U.S. 84N and 84S): One of the highest and most spectacular railroads in the country, crossing the Cumbre Pass at an altitude of 9,860 ft (3,006 m). The little Far Western train makes a 64-mi. (102-km) trip to link **Chama,** N.M., and **Antonito,** Colo., through splendid mountain and forest scenery and along wild gorges. Time: seven hours round trip; operates daily, mid-June to mid-Oct. Round-trip fare: $42 for adults, $20 for children. Reservations a must, obtainable from P.O. Box 789, Chama, NM 87520 (756-2151). A must for steam-train buffs; can be combined with a visit to Taos (see "Nearby Excursions," above).

MESA VERDE NATIONAL PARK (580 mi., 930 km, round trip via U.S. 84N, N.M. 96E, N.M. 44W, U.S. 550N, U.S. 160W, and the reverse route to return): America's greatest monument from her Indian civilizations (8th through 13th centuries). Dozens of multilevel houses, towers, terraces, streets miraculously clinging to the cliff face, in a glorious setting of desert canyons. Every year 600,000 visitors confront the astonishing sight of these ghost villages, silent now for centuries. The sudden disappearance of their inhabitants, the Anasazi Indians, six centuries ago is still a riddle to historians: Was it an epidemic? a persistent drought? an invasion by wandering tribes? a slow leaching-out of the soil? A visit to these cliffs and their ruins, of which the most impressive are **Cliff Palace** (217 rooms and kivas) and **Spruce Tree House** (114 rooms, 8 kivas), is permitted only when accompanied by a ranger; it calls for stout shoes and good physical condition. Remarkable **Indi-**

an museum near the visitor center, open daily. Unique view of the states of Colorado, Utah, Arizona, and New Mexico from **Park Point Fire Lookout** at 8,572 ft (2,613 m), halfway between the park entrance and the visitor center. Park open to vehicles daily year round.

For **information,** contact the Superintendent, P.O. Box 8, Mesa Verde National Park, CO 81330 (303/529-4465).

Along the way, visit the ☀ ᎯᎯ **Chaco Culture National Historical Park,** with ruins of 16 Anasazi pueblos abandoned around the end of the 13th century, another Amerindian gem. Some of these pueblos, like Pueblo Bonito, have no fewer than 800 rooms and 37 kivas. Unsurfaced access road, passable only in dry weather. Don't miss this visit; visitor center 2 mi. (3.2 km) from the southern entrance on N.M. 57 (988-6727), open daily.

It's also well worth making the side trip to Ꭿ **Aztec Ruins National Monument** (334-6174), one of the best-preserved primitive pueblos in the Southwest. Large 13th-century kiva, splendidly restored. Open daily.

And don't miss taking a ride on the ᎯᎯ **Silverton,** a little Far Western train dating from 1882 which takes seven hours to cover the 50 mi. (80 km) from **Durango** to **Silverton,** and the return leg, through glorious mountain scenery; one of the most popular tourist attractions in the West. Operates daily, mid-May to mid-Oct. For reservations (a must), contact the railroad at 479 Main Ave., Durango, CO 81301 (303/247-2733). Round-trip fare: adults, $32; children, $16.

This 580-mi. (930-km) round trip from Santa Fe and back again is enough in itself to warrant visiting the city.

Where to Stay En Route

IN THE PARK. ᶓ ᶓ **Far View,** P.O. Box 277, Mancos, CO 81328 (303/529-4421). 150 rms w. mountain views. A comfortable motel inside the park. Open from the end of May through Sept. **I–M**

IN CORTEZ. The ᶓ **Ramada Inn,** 666 S. Broadway, Cortez, CO 81321 (303/565-3773). 87 rms. Open year round. **I–M**

　　　　　　　ᶓ **Best Western Sands,** 1000 E. Main St., Cortez, CO 81321 (303/565-3761). 81 rms. Open year round. **I**

IN DURANGO. The ☀ ᶓ **Strater Hotel,** 699 Main Ave., Durango, CO 81301 (303/247-4431). 94 rms. **I–M**

　☀ ᶓ ᶓ **General Palmer House,** 567 Main Ave., Durango, CO 81301 (303/247-4747). 39 rms. **I–M**

　☀ ᎯᎯ **NAVAJOLAND** (about 560 mi., 900 km, round trip via I-25S, I-40W, N.M. 264W, Ariz. 264W, and the reverse on the return trip): Spectacular scenery **(Monument Valley, Canyon de Chelly),** and the largest reservation in the U.S. See Chapter 40 on Navajoland.

On the way, visit the picturesque **Zuñi and Acoma Pueblos** (see Chapter 38 on Albuquerque). A spectacular itinerary; don't miss it.

CHAPTER 40

NAVAJOLAND ♀♀

□ □ □

With Monument Valley and Canyon de Chelly

Three times the size of the state of Massachusetts (and twice as large as the sovereign state of Belgium), the enormous territory of Navajoland offers its visitors some of the most spectacular natural wonders of the North American continent. It is a primitive landscape, with its desert canyons, its Indian pueblos perched on arid plateaus (the mesas), and the immense **Lake Powell.** Ironically nicknamed "the 51st State," Navajoland, or Navajo Country, is indeed the largest Indian reserve in the U.S. The Navajo, whose numbers at the end of the Indian Wars in 1864 had been reduced to a mere 8,000 by the depredations of Kit Carson and his soldiery, now administer the territory themselves from their capital at **Window Rock,** 112 mi. (180 km) west of Albuquerque.

The enormous mineral wealth underlying Navajo territory, estimated at 2.5 million tons of coal, 80 million tons of uranium ore, 100 million barrels of oil, and 26 billion cubic yards of natural gas, have all been leased to corporations by the auction method, and now bring in only $50 million a year in royalties to the Navajo. With an unemployment rate of 40% and per capita annual income of $2,400, they must rely on $80 million of subsidies from Washington every year if they are to survive.

The Navajo are generally tolerant of the tourists who visit them, but they impose some rules which must be respected. Indians and their homes may not be photographed without advance permission. Some sacred areas or monuments—for example, the Navajo Fortress in the Canyon de Chelly—are forbidden except to Indians. Additional information may be obtained on the spot.

The best known of the wonders of Navajoland is **Monument Valley,** not far from the Utah border; as the setting of countless Hollywood westerns, its twisted canyons and pillars of red rock 980 ft. (300 m) high (called the "cathedrals of the desert") are familiar to moviegoers the world over. A tour of Monument Valley by car takes two to three hours in dry weather and is an unforgettable experience. In winter you'll need a Jeep (see "Guided Tours," below).

The **Canyon de Chelly** (pronounced "de Shay"), 93 mi. (150 km) to the south, is another fascinating place that can be reached by car, but explored only in an all-terrain vehicle (see "Guided Tours," below); its Indian settlements, dating from the 4th century, are worth the visit by themselves.

The **Navajo National Monument,** not far from Monument Valley, can be reached only on horseback or on foot; it has well-preserved ruins of 13th-century Indian pueblos. Nearer the center of Navajoland are the mesas inhabited by the Hopi, traditional enemies of the Navajo, which frown down on the Arizona des-

ert from a height of many hundred feet. The Hopi are skilled craftspeople, producing silver jewelry, pottery, Kachina dolls, and beautiful basketwork.

As in all the country's Indian reservations, the sale of beer or liquor is forbidden in Navajoland.

A BRIEF HISTORY OF THE INDIANS OF NAVAJOLAND: When
Christopher Columbus first set foot on American soil, he thought he had arrived,
by a new westward route, at the Indies; under this misapprehension, he dubbed
the natives "Indians."

The peoples thus misnamed had always comprised two mutually hostile
groups: the settler tribes and the nomadic tribes. The **Navajo** (Navajo, or Navaho,
comes from an Indian word meaning "people of the soil") are settlers; a warrior
people, they came down from the northwest of Canada around the end of the
15th century and overran the lands hitherto occupied by the Hopi and Pueblo in
northern Arizona. Under the influence of the Spanish colonists, this nomadic
hunting tribe became, over the years, a people of shepherds and grazers, and
learned from the Pueblo Indians their techniques of cultivation, weaving, and
sand-painting. The Navajo, who in 1864 had been almost exterminated by the
famous scout Kit Carson and his white volunteers, are now the largest and most
powerful of America's Indian communities. The census figures show 1,450,000
Indians belonging to 570 different tribes across the country; 200,000 of these are
Navajo.

The Navajo speak an extraordinarily complex language belonging to the
Athapaskan linguistic family, which also includes the Apaches of New Mexico
and southern Arizona. They live in modest villages of traditional "hogans"—
windowless huts of earth and clay supported by logs. More open to outsiders
than the Pueblo or the Hopi, the Navajo generally allow strangers to be present at
the sacred rites and colorful religious ceremonies.

The **Hopi** (which means "peaceable people" in Indian) and their **Pueblo**
neighbors belong to the great Shoshone family of Indians, which includes the
Comanche, Ute, and Paiute tribes as well as others, all distant cousins of the Aztecs of Mexico. The Hopi are direct descendants of the Anasazi ("the Old
Ones"), a race of remarkable builders, as witness the ruins of Mesa Verde and
Chaco Canyon. Driven from their villages, probably during the 15th century, by
drought and famine, the Hopi, who today number around 6,000, were thrown
back onto the mesas by the conquering thrust of the Navajo. Like their blood-
brothers the Pueblo of New Mexico, the Hopi are a sedentary tribe, given over to
farming and stock breeding. For more than a thousand years they have cultivated
several strains of corn that can survive in arid country, and a number of plants
and vegetables indigenous to the Americas such as beans, pumpkin, tobacco,
squash, potatoes and tomatoes. In their isolated villages of stone-and-mortar
houses, which cling like eagles' aeries to the high plateaus of the mesas, the Hopi
practice the unusual talent they inherited from their Anasazi ancestors for the
working of silver and for basket weaving (the Anasazi are known to archeologists
as the "Basket Maker Pueblo"). They have also kept alive a religious tradition of
ritual dances to invoke rain and avert bad luck: fire dances, eagle dances, serpent
dances, and the like.

Their elaborate mythology is visibly manifested in the Kachina masks, which
embody the spirits of ancestors, animals, or plants. Kachina dolls, much prized
by visitors for their startling forms and colors, are a sort of miniature pantheon of
the Hopi deities. Unlike the Navajo, the Hopi are intensely suspicious of strangers, and try to keep outsiders away from their religious ceremonies. Even to visit a
Hopi village you must have advance authorization, which may be obtained from
the Hopi Cultural Center at Second Mesa. For the schedule of Navajo and Hopi
festivals, see "Special Events," below.

Those interested in the way of life, arts, and history of Native Americans should contact the Bureau of Indian Affairs, Office of Public Information, 18th and C Sts. NW, Washington, DC 20240 (202/343-1000).

BASIC FACTS: States of Arizona, New Mexico, and Utah. Area Code: 602. Time Zone: Mountain Time. Approximate area: 25,100 sq. mi. (65,000 km²). Reserve founded in: 1868. Nonmigrant Indian population: 180,000–200,000 Navajo and 6,000 Hopi.

CLIMATE: As in all semi-desert regions, summer (the season that draws most tourists) can be burning hot (95°–104°F, 35°–40°C) by day, but is much cooler at night. In spring and fall you'll need a sweater even in the daytime. August and September are the rainy season. In winter, the first snow falls on the mesas in November, and the mercury sometimes drops to 13°F (−10°C).

ARRIVAL & TRANSIT INFORMATION

NEAREST AIRPORTS: The **Albuquerque International Airport** (ABQ), 112 mi. (180 km) east of Window Rock.
   Flagstaff Pulliam Field (FLG), 180 mi. (290 km) SW of Monument Valley.
   Phoenix Sky Harbor International (PHX), 210 mi. (340 km) SW of the mesas.

AIRLINES AT ALBUQUERQUE (area code 505): American (242-9464), America West (247-0737), Delta (243-2794), Eastern (842-5240), Southwest (831-1221), TWA (842-4010), and United (242-1411).

BUS OR CAR RENTAL?: Given the distances to be covered, the sensible thing is to rent a car with unlimited mileage. There is no long-line bus service to Navajoland.

CAR RENTAL AT ALBUQUERQUE (area code 505; at the Albuquerque International Airport unless otherwise noted): Avis (842-4080); Budget, 3000 Carlisle Blvd. (884-2666); Dollar (842-4224); Hertz (842-4235); National (842-4222); Thrifty (842-8733). See also Chapter 41 on the Grand Canyon and Chapter 42 on Phoenix.

NEAREST TRAIN STATIONS: AMTRAK has stations at U.S. 66 and Santa Fe St., in **Gallup,** New Mexico (toll free 800/872-7245), and E. 2nd St., in **Winslow,** Arizona (toll free 800/872-7245).

NEAREST BUS STATIONS: Greyhound has terminals at 300 2nd St., **Albuquerque,** New Mexico (505/243-4435); 399 S. Malpais Lane, **Flagstaff,** Arizona (602/774-4573); and 105 S. Dean St., **Gallup,** New Mexico (505/863-3761).

INFORMATION & TOURS

TOURIST INFORMATION: Canyon de Chelly National Monument: Superintendent, P.O. Box 588, Chinle, AZ 86503 (602/674-5436). Visitor Center.
   Hopi Indian Reservation: Box 67, Second Mesa, AZ 86043 (602/734-2401). Cultural Center.
   Hubbell Trading Post: Ariz. 264 (P.O. Box 150), Ganado, AZ 86505 (602/755-3475). Visitor Center.

Navajo Indian Reservation: P.O. Box 308, Window Rock, AZ 86515 (602/871-6659). Visitor Center.

There are other Visitor Centers at **Monument Valley** and **Navajo National Monument.**

GUIDED TOURS:
You can visit the major sights of Navajoland on guided tours by car, bus, and airplane.

All-Terrain-Vehicle Excursions in Monument Valley
Crawley Tours, U.S. 163, Kayenta (602/697-3463). Full- and half-day trips.

Goulding's Lodge Valley Tour, U.S. 163, Gouldings (801/727-3231). Full- and half-day trips.

All-Terrain-Vehicle Excursions in Canyon de Chelly
Thunderbird Lodge Tours, Chinle (602/674-5841). Full- and half-day trips.

Bus Trips to the Hopi and Navajo Indian Reservations
Nava-Hopi Tours (Gray Line), 401 Malpais Lane, P.O. Box 339 Flagstaff (602/774-5003).

Flights Over Navajoland and Lake Powell
Lake Powell Air Service, Page Airport (602/645-2494).
Monument Valley Flying Service, Chinle (602/674-5657).

MONUMENTS & SIGHTS IN NAVAJOLAND

CANYON DE CHELLY NATIONAL MONUMENT
(225 mi., 360 km, NW of Albuquerque along I-40, U.S. 666, Ariz. 264, and U.S. 191): Spectacular landscapes which can be seen only from a Jeep (Apr.-Oct.). Indian cave dwellings from the 4th to the 14th centuries, including the **White House, Mummy Cave,** and **Antelope House.** In this savagely beautiful canyon there took place one of the last engagements between the troops of Kit Carson and the Indians who had taken refuge at the top of the **Navajo Fortress,** a huge rocky spur which is now sacred ground, forbidden to strangers. This is one of the few canyons in the country whose interior can be explored from an all-terrain vehicle. As well as the **Canyon de Chelly** itself, with its steep red sandstone walls, and **Spider Rock,** the 800-ft. (262-m) needle of rock which is its most remarkable feature, the monument also includes the lateral canyons, **Canyon del Muerto** ("Dead Man's Canyon"), **Black Rock Canyon,** and **Monument Canyon.** At the Visitor Center, open year round, there is an interesting small archeological museum. Don't miss this trip.

GLEN CANYON AND LAKE POWELL
(122 mi., 195 km west of Monument Valley along U.S. 163, U.S. 160, and Ariz. 98): **Lake Powell,** 196 mi. (315 km) long with 1,900 mi. (3,058 km) of shoreline, was created in 1963 by the construction of the **Page Dam** on the Colorado River; it has turned the **Glen Canyon National Recreation Area** into a tourist Mecca for lovers of watersports, with its beautiful landscapes where the red-brown-ocher cliffs are mirrored in the clear blue lake, and its wonderful fishing for oversize trout, carp, and pike. Glen Canyon is no less rich in its variety of land animals: Rocky Mountain sheep, deer, coyote, puma, and even the occasional, extremely rare, golden eagle.

At **Page** you can hire a comfortable houseboat, a sort of waterborne camper for six or eight, in which you can visit the lake and its dozens of magnificent desert canyons. Weekly rates are $980 in summer, $740 in spring and fall, $590 in winter; you can also rent for three or four days. Reservations must be made a long way ahead. For information, contact Del Webb Recreational Properties, Reservation Dept., P.O. Box 29040, Phoenix, AZ 85038 (602/278-8888; toll free 800/528-6154). An experience you will not quickly forget. See also Chapter 32 on Utah National Parks.

🔆🔔 **HOPI MESAS** (134 mi., 214 km, NE of Flagstaff along U.S. 89, U.S. 160, and Ariz. 264): Primitive Indian villages, some as much as eight centuries old, clinging like eagles' nests to the rocky plateaus (mesas). Spectacular views. Authorization for visits must be obtained from the Hopi Cultural Center at Second Mesa (see "Tourist Information," above). Don't miss it.

🔆🔔🔔🔔 **MONUMENT VALLEY** (170 mi., 272 km, NE of Flagstaff along U.S. 89, U.S. 160, and Ariz. 264): This is the country's best-known picture postcard, in glorious Technicolor: one of the most amazing landscapes in creation, more than 25 million years old. The "desert cathedrals," the red sandstone monoliths almost 2,000 ft. (over 600 m) high, with their evocative names—Camel Butte, Sentinel Mesa, Three Sisters, Big Chief, Elephant Butte—have provided the backdrop for countless westerns like *Stagecoach, Fort Apache,* and *Billy the Kid,* as well as for Walt Disney's famous *The Living Desert.*

The recent history of Monument Valley is closely linked with that of Harry Goulding, an enterprising businessman who in 1923 opened a trading post and coaching inn on the site of the motel that now bears his name (see "Motels and Restaurants," below). It was Goulding who, in 1938, persuaded John Ford to shoot his first major western, *Stagecoach,* in this magnificent natural setting, thus making Monument Valley a symbol of the Wild West in dozens of movies still to come.

Private cars are admitted during the summer for the 14-mi. (23-km) circuit, beginning at the Visitor Center; out of season, Jeeps only. For information, contact Park Headquarters, Monument Valley Navajo Tribal Park, P.O. Box 93, UT 84536 (801/727-3827). It's worth the journey here just to see the valley.

🔔 **NAVAJO NATIONAL MONUMENT** (135 mi., 216 km, NE of Flagstaff on U.S. 89 and U.S. 160): Very well-preserved 13th-century Indian cave dwellings, reachable on foot or horseback only. The most beautiful of the ruins, "Keet Seel," is 8 mi. (12 km) from the Visitor Center. For information, contact Navajo National Monument, HC 71, Box 3, Tonalea, AZ 86044 (602/672-2366).

MONUMENTS & SCENERY OUTSIDE THE NAVAJO RESERVE

GRAND CANYON OF THE COLORADO (181 mi., 288 km, SW of Monument Valley via U.S. 163, U.S. 160, U.S. 89, and Ariz. 64): See Chapter 41 on the Grand Canyon of the Colorado.

MESA VERDE NATIONAL PARK (159 mi., 254 km, NE of Monument Valley via U.S. 163 and U.S. 160): See Chapter 39 on Santa Fe.

🔆🔔 **METEOR CRATER** (40 mi., 56 km, east of Flagstaff on I-40): Some 22,000 years ago a two-million-ton meteorite crashed to earth here, forming the world's largest nonvolcanic crater, 4,160 ft. (1.2 km) across and 544 ft. (170 m) deep. It was used by NASA to train astronauts before their moon shots. Impressive. Open daily.

PETRIFIED FOREST NATIONAL PARK (102 mi., 163 km, SW of Canyon de Chelly on U.S. 191 and I-40): This petrified forest, the largest in the world, is 200 million years old. Countless animals and plants have been fossilized by the lakebed sediments or by volcanic ash. It's best to enter from the south at **Rainbow Forest,** with its interesting museum illustrating the petrifaction of wood. Visitor Center open daily. The **Painted Desert,** north of the Visitor Center, displays a blinding pattern of shimmering colors—blues, reds, and tawnies—particularly at sunrise and sunset. Scenic drive. For information, contact the Superintendent, AZ 86028 (602/524-6228).

RAINBOW BRIDGE (reached by boat from Page, on Lake Powell): One of the largest natural spans in the world, 278 ft. (85 m) across and 290 ft. (88 m) high. Well worth the side trip.

SUNSET CRATER (14 mi., 22 km, NE of Flagstaff on U.S. 89): Crater of a volcano that has been dormant for nine centuries; spectacular formations of reddish-orange lava. Worth seeing. Open daily.

WUPATKI NATIONAL MONUMENT (27 mi., 43 km, north of Flagstaff on U.S. 89): Ruins of an Indian village which was inhabited around A.D. 1100; the largest dwelling had some 100 bedrooms. Archeological museum. Worth the detour. Open daily.

OTHER SIGHTS, ATTRACTIONS, & ACTIVITIES

MUSEUMS: ⚱ **Hubbell Trading Post,** 42 mi. (67 km) south of Canyon de Chelly on Ariz. 264 at Ganado (602/755-3475): Picturesque trading post opened in 1876 by John Lorenzo Hubbell, an idealistic businessman who became a friend and protector to the Navajo. The present structure, with its unusual layout, dates from 1885; it houses an interesting ethnological collection, and is still a trading post for the Indians. Visit not to be missed. Open daily.

John Wesley Powell Memorial Museum, 6 N. Lake Powell Blvd. in Page, 130 mi. (208 km) north of Flagstaff (602/645-9496): This little-known small museum pays tribute to the intrepid 19th-century geologist John Wesley Powell, the first white man to shoot the Grand Canyon rapids in a canoe. Fascinating. Also an astonishing collection of fluorescent minerals. Days and times of opening depend on the time of year. Should definitely be seen.

Navajo Tribal Museum, 159 mi. (254 km) NW of Albuquerque on Ariz. 264 at Window Rock (602/871-6673): Remarkable Navajo jewelry, pottery, wickerwork, and weaving. Library, temporary exhibitions. Worth a visit. Open daily in summer; Mon.-Fri. the rest of the year.

SPECIAL EVENTS: Cameras, movie cameras, and tape recorders are not permitted at any Hopi or Navajo festivals.

Hopi Festivals

For information and exact dates call the **Hopi Cultural Center** (602/734-2401).

Niman or summer solstice festival (about June 21).

Hopi Home Dances (late July).
Snake or **Flute Dance** (Aug.): Tourists allowed, but subject to restrictions.
Soyal or winter solstice festival (about Dec. 31).

Navajo Festivals

For information and exact dates, call the **Navajo Indian Reservation** (602/871-6659).
All Indian Days (early July): Pow-wow and rodeo at Window Rock.
Squaw Dances (throughout the summer).
Navajo Nation Fair (early Sept.): One of the most important Indian occasions in the country; dancing, horse racing, rodeo, art exhibition. At Window Rock.
Yei-bi-chi, or Navajo Fire Dance (throughout the winter).

MOTELS AND RESTAURANTS

See the listing of toll-free numbers in the Appendix.

Room Rates in Navajoland	
B (Budget)	up to $30
I (Inexpensive)	$30–$60
M (Moderate)	$60–$90
E (Expensive)	$90–$140
VE (Very Expensive)	$140 and up

Personal Favorites (in order of preference)

IN MONUMENT VALLEY. ⬛ **Gouldings Monument Valley Lodge,** 2 mi. (3.2 km) west of U.S. 163, Monument Valley, UT 84536 (801/727-3231). 43 rms, A/C, color TV, in-rm movies (John Wayne classics). AE, MC, V. Resv. required. Free parking, coffeeshop. *Note:* Rustic motel at the foot of a towering cliff, decently comfortable and w. an unforgettable view. Rather cramped rms w. patios or balconies; Boy Scout summer camp atmosphere. If the reception and svce were friendlier, it would be a good place to stay. The coffee shop is only just acceptable —but it's the only one within 19 mi. (30 km). No alcoholic beverages. An ideal starting point for Jeep trips across Monument Valley ($36 for a full day). Don't miss stopping here. Hotel open year round; coffeeshop closed from Nov. 15 to March 1. **I–M**

⬛ **Holiday Inn,** Junction of U.S. 160 and U.S. 163, Kayenta, AZ 86033 (602/697-3221; toll free, see Holiday Inns). 100 rms, A/C, color TV. AE, CB, DC, MC, V. Free parking, pool, rest., rm svce; crib $6. *Note:* Typical motel, in the middle of the desert. Functionally comfortable. Open year round. 30 min. by road from Monument Valley (conducted tours by Jeep). **I–M, but lower rates out of season**

⬛ **Wetherill Inn,** U.S. 163, Kayenta, AZ 83033 (602/697-3231). 54 rms, cable color TV. AE, MC, V. Free parking, adjoining coffeeshop, free crib. *Note:* Rustic motel w. no air conditioning; limited comforts. Open year round. Organizes Jeep tours of Monument Valley. **I, but lower prices Nov.-Apr.**

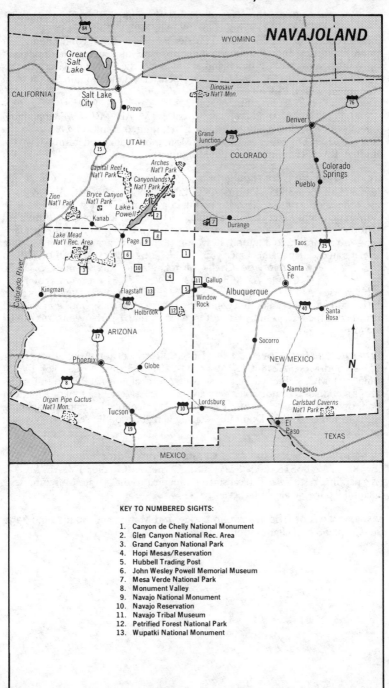

KEY TO NUMBERED SIGHTS:

1. Canyon de Chelly National Monument
2. Glen Canyon National Rec. Area
3. Grand Canyon National Park
4. Hopi Mesas/Reservation
5. Hubbell Trading Post
6. John Wesley Powell Memorial Museum
7. Mesa Verde National Park
8. Monument Valley
9. Navajo National Monument
10. Navajo Reservation
11. Navajo Tribal Museum
12. Petrified Forest National Park
13. Wupatki National Monument

♀ **Recapture Lodge,** U.S. 191, Bluff, UT 84512 (801/672-
2281). 18 rms, color TV. AE, MC, V. Free parking, pool, ad-
joining coffeeshop, free crib. *Note:* Tiny rustic motel w. no air conditioning, but
friendly reception and atmosphere; some rms have kitchenettes. Starting point
for conducted tours of the desert and rafting down the Colorado River. Also accommodations for groups and families. Open year round. 45 min. by car from
Monument Valley. **B–I**

♀ **San Juan Inn,** U.S. 163, Mexican Hat, UT 84531 (801/683-
2220). 22 rms, A/C, color TV. AE, MC, V. Free parking,
coffeeshop. *Note:* Small, unpretentious hotel; limited comforts. Overlooks the
San Juan River. Organizes excursions to Monument Valley and rafting down the
San Juan River. 15 min. by car from Monument Valley. **I**

IN CANYON DE CHELLY. ☼ ᵬ **Thunderbird Lodge,** 3 mi. SE of U.S. 191, Chinle, AZ
86503 (602/674-5841). 74 rms, A/C, cable color TV. AE, MC, V. Free parking, coffeeshop, crib $2. *Note:* Rustic but comfortable hotel at the entrance to
Canyon de Chelly. Reception w. a smile. Very acceptable coffeeshop open until
8:30 p.m. No alcoholic beverages. Organizes Jeep trips into the canyons; fare,
$15–$30 according to duration. Resv. advisable in summer. Don't miss staying
here; it's an excellent value. Open year round. **I, but lower rates out of season**

♀ **Canyon de Chelly Motel,** Navajo Rte. 7 (nr. U.S. 191),
Chinle, AZ 86503 (602/674-5875). 51 rms, A/C, color TV,
in-rm movies. AE, MC, V. Free parking, free child's cot. *Note:* Typical motel nr.
the canyon entrance; adjoining coffeeshop open 7 a.m. to 8 p.m. Designed and
furnished in the Navajo Indian style. Open year round. **I, but lower rates out of
season**

ON THE HOPI INDIAN RESERVATION. ☼ ᵬ **Hopi Cultural center,** Ariz. 264 at Pinon
Rd., Second Mesa, AZ 86043 (602/734-2401). 33 rms, A/C, color TV (in
some rms). MC, V. Free parking, rest. *Note:* Motel of unusual Pueblo Indian design, functionally comfortable. Very acceptable rest. serving Hopi or American
food, open till 9 p.m. (8 p.m. in summer). No alcoholic beverages. Adjoining
museum and craft shop. Don't miss staying here, but you'll need to reserve way
ahead. **I**

ON THE NAVAJO INDIAN RESERVATION. ᵬ **Window Rock Motor Inn,** Ariz. 264, Window Rock, AZ 86515 (602/871-4108). 52 rms, A/C, color TV. AE, MC, V.
Free parking, rest. *Note:* Typical small motel next to the Navajo Museum. Rest.
open till 9 p.m. No alcoholic beverages. **I**

IN RAINBOW BRIDGE. The Wahweap Lodge and Marina and **Holiday Inn Page**
(see Chapter 32 on Utah National Parks).

CHAPTER 41

GRAND CANYON OF THE COLORADO♣♣♣♣

□ □ □

Discovered in 1540 by the Spaniard Garcia Lopez de Cardenas, a member of Vásquez de Coronado's famous gold-seeking expedition, the Grand Canyon is one of the seven natural wonders of the world. It has taken more than 16 million years for the surging current of the Colorado River to carve its way down through the gray-white limestone, red sandstone, and green clay schist which today form the canyon's walls; wind, heat, and frost have done the rest. A true force of nature, the Colorado River in flood can run 224 ft (70 m) deep and 288 ft (90 m) wide. The river's intense yellow-brown color comes from the huge quantities of silt and alluvium that are continuously carried along. The gorges reach a height of 5,120 ft (1,600 m) in some places, and comprise an open book of terrestrial evolution: from the hard pre-Cambrian rocks (2 *billion* years old, the oldest on the planet), to the soft, fossil-rich tertiary rocks. Separated by 18 mi. (30 km) at their widest points, the canyon's two rims offer extraordinary vistas over the 277-mi. (445-km) stretch of canyon, and are accessible by car as well as on foot. The glorious views, notably at sunrise and sunset, make this masterpiece of creation one of the most astounding natural settings in the United States, and an ideal place for watching the wildlife, which includes 220 species of birds, 67 of mammals, 27 of reptiles, and 5 of amphibians.

The Grand Canyon of Colorado (situated in Arizona, despite its name) became a national park in 1919. The **South Rim**—the more accessible—is open year round; the **North Rim** is open in summer only. Near **Grand Canyon Village,** the two rims are connected by a steep footpath of 21 mi. (34 km); the road distance is closer to 218 mi. (350 km). In good weather, **Grand Canyon Airlines** also operates flights on request between the South and North Rims (if the latter is accessible).

Given the profusion of summer tourists and the relatively limited accommodations of the park, it is strongly advised that reservations be made weeks—if not months—in advance. This is true also for those who plan to go rafting down the Colorado and those wishing to descend into the canyon on mule-back (see "Adventure Tours," below). A total of three million people visit the Grand Canyon each year.

BASIC FACTS: State of Arizona. Area Code: 602. Time Zone: Mountain Time. ZIP Codes: 86023 (South Rim), 86052 (North Rim). First discovered by Europeans: 1540. Park dimensions: 1,770 sq. mi. (4,856 km²). A national park since 1919.

CLIMATE: In summer, the tourist season par excellence, the high country of

Arizona is very hot. Brief but violent downpours are a feature of virtually every July and Aug. noontime. Warning: If the ground-level temperature is 95° – 104° F (35° –40° C), it can easily reach 122° F (50° C) in the depths of the canyon. Winter is bitterly cold, with regular snowfalls which create a new and splendid landscape. The two ideal seasons for a visit to the Grand Canyon are autumn and especially spring, when the wildflowers are in bloom.

DISTANCES: Albuquerque, 404 mi. (647 km); Las Vegas, 291 mi. (465 km); Los Angeles, 533 mi. (852 km); Phoenix, 218 mi. (350 km); Salt Lake City, 518 mi. (828 km); San Francisco, 819 mi. (1,310 km).

ARRIVAL & TRANSIT INFORMATION

NEAREST AIRPORTS: There is one local airport, and two others nearby.

SOUTH RIM. **Grand Canyon Airport** (GCN): 6 mi. (10 km) south. Daily connections with Las Vegas and Phoenix.
   Flagstaff Pulliam Field (FLG): 80 mi. (129 km) SE. Daily connections with Phoenix.

NORTH RIM. **Page Municipal Airport** (PGA): 120 mi. (198 km) NE. Daily connections with Las Vegas and Salt Lake City.

AIRLINES: At **Grand Canyon Airport:** Air Nevada (638-2441), America West (toll free 800/247-5692), Scenic Airlines (toll free 800/634-6801).
   In **Flagstaff:** America West (525-1346), Sky West Airlines (toll free 800/453-9417).

CAR RENTAL (at Pulliam Airport in Flagstaff unless indicated): Avis (774-8421); Budget (779-0306); Dollar, Grand Canyon Airport, Grand Canyon (638-2625); Hertz (774-4452); National, 224 Mikes Pike, Flagstaff (779-1975).

BUS OR CAR RENTAL? Given the distances and the advantageous rental fees in Arizona as well as in neighboring California, renting a car with unlimited mileage is particularly recommended. Hitchhiking is prohibited inside Grand Canyon National Park.

TRAIN: The closest AMTRAK station is at 1 E. Santa Fe Ave., Flagstaff (toll free 800/872-7245).

BUS: Greyhound buses are not permitted in Grand Canyon National Park. The closest Greyhound station is at 399 S. Malpais Lane, Flagstaff (774-4573). Connections between Flagstaff and the Grand Canyon via Fred Harvey Bus Co. (638-2822).

SEEING THE GRAND CANYON

TOURIST INFORMATION: Write or phone the **Arizona Office of Tourism,** 1100 W. Washington St., Phoenix, AZ 85007 (602/255-3618); or Superintendent, P.O. Box 129, Grand Canyon National Park, AZ 86023 (602/638-7778).
   On site, go to the **Visitors Center,** Grand Canyon Village (eastern area). Open daily.
   For a **recorded telephone message** with weather conditions, tourist advice, and road conditions 24 hours a day, call 602/638-2245.

GUIDED TOURS: **Bus Tours:** Grand Canyon National Park Lodges, Grand Canyon Village (638-2631, ext. 6577).

Plane rides over the Grand Canyon: Grand Canyon Airlines, Grand Canyon Airport (10 mi., 16 km, south) (638-2407). Impressive.

Helicopter rides over the Grand Canyon: Grand Canyon Helicopters, Tusayan Heliport (8 mi., 13 km, south) (638-2419). Unforgettable.

ADVENTURE TOURS: **Rafting down the Colorado** (3–18 days): 22 authorized companies. For locations and rates, contact River Unit, Grand Canyon National Park, AZ 86023 (602/638-2401). Reservations must be made weeks (or months) in advance.

Walking excursions between the two rims (Kaibab Trail and Bright Angel Trail): 12 hrs minimum. This trek is physically trying, even for seasoned hikers, especially in summer, when the temperature can reach 122°F (50°C) at the bottom of the canyon. Be sure to bring reserves of water and food, and do not stray from the trails under any circumstances. For information, call 638-2474 Mon.-Fri.

Mule-back excursions between the two rims (reservations necessary): Grand Canyon National Park Lodges, Grand Canyon Village (638-2401). People weighing more than 200 lbs. (91 kg), pregnant women, children under age 12, and those susceptible to vertigo are prohibited. In winter the descent ends at Phantom Ranch (five-hr trip).

SIGHTS

SOUTH RIM: ☀ ⛰ **West Rim Drive,** 18 mi. (13 km) west of Grand Canyon Village: Splendid views over the Canyon at **Maricopa Point, Hopi Point, Mohave Point, Pima Point** (the most beautiful view of the South Rim), and **Hermit's Rest,** a large, rustic building which dates from 1914. Private cars are prohibited on this road between May and mid-Sept. (there is a free shuttle bus).

☀⛰ **East Rim Drive,** 23 mi. (37 km) east of Grand Canyon Village: Comprises, with West Rim Drive, one of the most beautiful spectacles in creation. Superb panoramas of the canyon at **Yavapai Point** (with an interesting museum), **Yaki Point, Grandview Point** (one of the loveliest views of the canyon), **Moran Point, Tusayan Ruins** (with an interesting museum), and **Desert View.** Enjoy an incomparable view of the **Painted Desert** and the neighboring forest from atop the restored **Indian Watchtower.** Private cars are permitted on this road year round.

NORTH RIM (open summer only): ⛰ **Bright Angel Point:** This spot offers a wonderful view of the canyon and is the point of departure for trips to the bottom of the gorge and toward the South Rim.

☀⛰ **Cape Royal:** The highest point of either rim, at an elevation of 8,576 ft (2,680 m), presents the most magnificent view of the canyon and the Painted Desert. On the way, don't miss the view from **Point Imperial.**

☀⛰ **Point Sublime:** Worthy of its name, this point is reachable only in dry weather via a 17-mi. (27-km) unpaved road.

☀⛰ **EXCURSIONS BETWEEN THE TWO RIMS** (218 mi., 350 km, via Ariz. 64E, U.S. 89N, Alt. U.S. 89W, and Ariz. 67S): Besides the rigorous Kaibab Trail and Bright Angel Trail, mentioned previously (see "Adventure Tours," above), there is a magnificent car route along the South Rim—the barren reaches of **Echo Cliffs** and **Vermilion Cliffs** and the

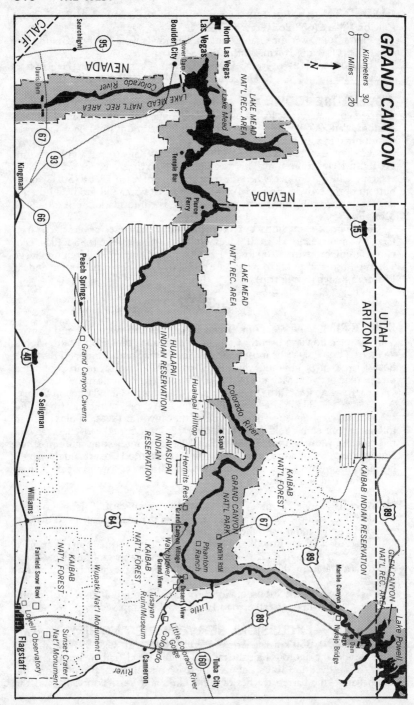

dense conifer forest of **Kaibab Plateau.** On the way you'll get a unique perspective on the Colorado River from **Navajo Bridge,** one of the most spectacular spots in Arizona, which overlooks the riverbed from a height of more than 467 ft (140 m). This is a two-day trip, with recommended lodging at the Grand Canyon Lodge or the Kaibab Lodge (see "Accommodations & Restaurants, North Rim," below). Don't miss it.

MUSEUMS: ⚱ **Tusayan Ruins,** 20 mi. (32 km) west of Grand Canyon Village: Traces of an Anasazi community from the 12th century and an archeological museum. Not to be missed. Open daily.

⚱ **Yavapai Museum,** Grand Canyon Village: An interesting geological history of the Grand Canyon. Open daily.

WINTER SPORTS RESORTS: ⚱ **Fairfield Snow Bowl,** 73 mi. (117 km) SE of the Grand Canyon on U.S. 180: Cross-country and downhill (2,300-ft, 690-m, slope) skiing. Eight chair lifts. Open mid-Nov. to mid-Apr. For information, call 779-6126 (or 779-4577 for snow conditions).

ACCOMMODATIONS & RESTAURANTS
See the listing of toll-free numbers in the Appendix.

Reservations Inside the National Park
The National Park Service has contracted out all of the food and lodging places inside Grand Canyon National Park to concessionaires, one for the North Rim and another for the South Rim. For reservations anywhere inside the park, contact the concessionaires directly:

South Rim: Contact Grand Canyon National Park Lodges, Grand Canyon, AZ 86203 (602/638-2401; toll free 800/528-6367).

North Rim: Contact T. W. Services, 451 N. Main St., Cedar City, UT 84720 (801/586-7686).

Room Rates in the Grand Canyon Area	
B (Budget)	up to $30
I (Inexpensive)	$30–$60
M (Moderate)	$60–$90
E (Expensive)	$90–$140
VE (Very Expensive)	$140 and up

Inside the Park (South Rim)
Note: In general, in all food and lodging places on the South Rim, the service is not up to par, the reception is barely civil, with unprofessional personnel who are perpetually snowed under, waits at the restaurants (where the cuisine is mediocre and expensive) can be two hours long and reservations are not always honored.

☼ 🍸 **El Tovar Hotel,** Village Loop Dr., AZ 86203 (602/638-2631; toll-free reservations through Grand Canyon National Park Lodges). 76 rms, A/C, cable color TV. AE, CB, DC, MC, V. Free parking, rest., bar, rm svce, disco, boutique, free airport shuttle, free crib. *Note:* Exceptional location on the edge of the canyon. The rustic 1905 architecture—a blend of tree trunks and boulders—may lack sophistication, but it has a certain charm. Functional rm comfort; there are a few suites w. balconies and a splendid view of the Grand Canyon. **E**

Maswik Deluxe, U.S. 180W, AZ 86023 (602/638-2631; toll-free reservations through Grand Canyon National Park Lodges). 160 rms, cable color TV. AE, CB, DC, MC, V. Free parking, coffeeshop, bar, free crib. *Note:* The latest addition to Grand Canyon motels offers functional rms w. private balconies. **M**

Kachina Lodge, Village Loop Dr., AZ 86023 (602/638-2631; toll-free reservations through Grand Canyon National Park Lodges). 48 rms, cable color TV. AE, CB, DC, MC, V. Free parking, check-in at the El Tovar Hotel, adjacent coffeeshop, free crib. *Note:* Relatively modern motel with functional rms, the best of which afford a view of the canyon. **M–E**

Thunderbird Lodge, Village Loop Dr., AZ 86023 (602/638-2631; toll-free reservations through Grand Canyon National Park Lodges). 55 rms, cable color TV. AE, CB, DC, MC, V. Free parking, check-in at the Bright Angel Lodge, adjacent coffeeshop, free crib. *Note:* Relatively modern motel that adjoins the Bright Angel Lodge. Functional rms, the best of which afford a view of the canyon. **M–E**

Bright Angel Lodge, W. Rim Dr., AZ 86023 (602/638-2631; toll-free reservations through Grand Canyon National Park Lodges). 37 rms (15 w. bath), 50 bungalows, cable color TV. AE, CB, DC, MC, V. Free parking, coffeeshop, bar, disco, hrdrsr, organized raft trips down the Colorado and mule-back excursions down into the canyon, free crib. *Note:* Old, rustic building surrounded by bungalows. Average comfort. A few rms w. views of the canyon. **I–M**

Yavapai Lodge, Mather Center, AZ 86023 (602/638-2631; toll-free reservations through Grand Canyon National Park Lodges). 351 rms, cable color TV. AE, CB, DC, MC, V. Free parking, coffeeshop, bar, disco, grocery store, free crib. *Note:* Functional motel in a pine grove across from the Visitors Center. **M**

Maswik Lodge, U.S. 180W, AZ 86023 (602/638-2631; toll-free reservations through Grand Canyon National Park Lodges). 90 rms, 38 bungalows. AE, CB, DC, MC, V. Free parking, coffeeshop, bar. *Note:* A tree-shaded rustic motel and individual bungalows. Rudimentary comfort. Closed Nov.-Apr. **M**

Phantom Ranch, Grand Canyon Village, AZ 86023 (602/638-2631; toll-free reservations through Grand Canyon National Park Lodges). 88 beds in the dormitory, bungalows. AE, CB, DC, MC, V. Pool, fishing, coffeeshop. *Note:* The Grand Canyon's most spectacular and most authentic motel. At the foot of a gorge, accessible only on foot or mule-back (at least a five-hr trip). Interesting mule-rental/lodging/meals package. Resv. necessary six months in advance for summer visits, as authorized descents into the canyon are limited to 90 people per day. Adventure accessible to everyone. **B–I**

Inside the Park (North Rim)

Grand Canyon Lodge, Bright Angel Point, AZ 86052 (602/638-2611; reservations through T. W. Services). 40 rms, 180 individual cottages. AE, DC, MC, V. Free parking, rest., coffeeshop, bar, grocery store, movie theater, crib $5. *Note:* The relatively modern, functional motel and the rustic cottages for two to five people (the "western cabins" are the best choice) afford a magnificent view of the canyon. Adequate rest. Organizes raft trips down the Colorado and mule-back trips down into the canyon. Closed Oct.-May. **I–M**

Outside the Park (South Rim)

☼ ♞ **Best Western Grand Canyon Squire Inn,** Ariz. 64 (2 mi., 3 km, south of the park entrance), AZ 86023 (602/638-2681; toll free, see Best Western). 150 rms, A/C, cable color TV. AE, CB, DC, MC, V. Free parking, pool, tennis, health club, bowling, sauna, rest., bar, disco, free crib. *Note:* This modern motel w. its excellent facilities is the most appealing and comfortable in the entire Grand Canyon area. Rustic, Indian-style décor. A 15-min. car ride from Grand Canyon Village. No-smoking rms. **M, w. lower rates mid-Oct. to mid-May**

♞ **Moqui Lodge,** Ariz. 64 (at the park entrance), AZ 86023 (602/638-2424; toll free 800/528-6367). 135 rms, color TV. AE, CB, DC, MC, V. Free parking, tennis, coffeeshop, bar, disco. *Note:* This convenient and basic motel offers reasonable comfort 10 min. from the canyon. Closed Jan. and Feb. **I–M w. lower rates in Nov., Dec., and Mar.**

♞ **Quality Inn Red Feather Lodge,** Ariz. 64 (1 mi., 1.6 km, south of the park entrance), AZ 86023 (602/638-2367; toll free, see Quality Inns). 180 rms, A/C, cable color TV. AE, DC, MC, V. Free parking, pool, coffeeshop, bar, rm svce, free shuttle between the airport and Grand Canyon Village. *Note:* Modern, comfortable motel w. spacious, balconied rms and cheerful reception. **M, w. lower rates Nov.-Mar.**

Outside the Park (North Rim)

♞ **Kaibab Lodge,** Ariz. 67, AZ 86022 (602/638-2389). 24 rms. MC, V. Free parking, pool, horseback riding, coffeeshop. *Note:* Small, pleasant motel away from the Grand Canyon crowds, 30 min. north of the North Rim. Ideal for the motorist. Fine location in the heart of Kaibab National Forest. Excellent value. Open mid-May to Oct. only. **I–M**

♞ **Jacob Lake Inn,** intersection of Alt. U.S. 89 and Ariz. 67, AZ 86051 (602/643-7232). 42 rms. AE, MC, V. Free parking, tennis, coffeeshop, grocery store. *Note:* Rustic motel in Kaibab Forest, 44 mi. (70 km) north of the North Rim. Modest but functional comfort. Motel units and cabins. Closed Dec. to mid-May. **I.**

YMCAs/Youth Hostels

American Youth Hostel, Tonto St., Grand Canyon (South Rim), AZ 86023 (602/638-9018).

Weatherford Hostel, 23 N. Leroux St., Flagstaff, AZ 86001 (602/774-2731). Individual rms or dormitory accommodations, close to the train station.

An alternative solution is **Motel 6** (nr. dwntwn), 2010 E. Butler Ave., Flagstaff, AZ 86001 (602/774-3533). 150 rms. Pool. DC, MC, V. **B**

NEARBY EXCURSIONS

☼ 👓 **HAVASUPAI INDIAN RESERVATION** (62 mi., 100 km, along unpaved road from Ariz. 66 after Grand Canyon Caverns, plus 8 mi., 13 km, on foot or horseback to the bottom of Grand Canyon): This primitive Indian reservation with its 300 inhabitants is completely cut off from the rest of the world. Camping is $10 per day per person, and there is an inexpensive 24-rm bungalow, but resv. are a must. Accommodations are available through Havasupai Tourist Enterprise, Supai, AZ 86435 (602/448-2121). The ultimate change of scene.

☼ 🔔 **LAKE POWELL** (138 mi., 220 km, NE on Ariz. 64W and U.S. 89N): Water sports and magnificent landscapes, including the celebrated **Rainbow Ridge,** the largest natural arch in the world (span of 272 ft, 85 m). An absolute must. For more details, see the chapter on Utah National Parks.

NATIONAL PARKS NEARBY: 🔭 **Bryce Canyon National Park,** 285 mi. (456 km) north via Ariz. 64W, U.S. 89N, Alt. U.S. 89, and Utah 9W: See the chapter on Utah National Parks.

🔭 **Glen Canyon National Recreation Area,** 138 mi. (220 km) NE via Ariz. 64W and U.S. 89N: See the chapter on Utah National Parks.

🔭 **Zion National Park,** 253 mi. (405 km) NW via Ariz. 64W, U.S. 89N, Alt. U.S. 89, and Utah 12: See the chapter on Utah National Parks.

FARTHER AFIELD

🔭 **HOPI AND NAVAJO INDIAN PUEBLOS** (280 mi., 450 km, r.t. from the Grand Canyon on Ariz. 64E, U.S. 89N, U.S. 160N, Ariz. 264E): See the Navajoland chapter.

FLAGSTAFF & VICINITY: (365 mi., 585 km, r.t. on Ariz. 64S, U.S. 180W, I-17S, U.S. 89N, and Ariz. 64W): You'll need at least two days to enjoy the wonderful variety this trip offers, including the interesting sights below. **Sedona** is a suggested stopover town (for more details, see "Suggested Touring Itineraries" in the Phoenix chapter). You won't want to pass up this outing.

🔔 **Lowell Observatory,** Mars Hill Rd., Flagstaff (602/774-2096): The country's oldest observatory (1894), where the planet Pluto was discovered in 1930. Guided tours Tues.-Sat. at 1:30 p.m. For astronomy lovers.

🔭 **Meteor Crater,** 40 mi. (56 km) east of Flagstaff: A meteor hit the earth 22,000 years ago on this site and left the world's best preserved crater—4,160 ft (1.2 km) in diameter and 557 ft (170 m) deep. NASA uses it for astronaut training. Impressive. For information, call 602/774-8350.

☼ 🔔 **Montezuma Castle,** 50 mi. (80 km) south of Flagstaff: Extraordinary, five-tier cave dwelling perched 64 ft (20 m) above the ground in a cliff shelter. Built by the Sinagua Indians in the 13th century, it is in remarkable condition. Not to be missed. For information, call 602/567-3322.

☼ 🔭 **Oak Creek Canyon,** 15 mi. (24 km) south of Flagstaff: Splendid rocky gorge landscapes that are almost as spectacular as the Grand Canyon; they've been used as the setting for many a western film. On the way, see **Sedona,** a picturesque little pioneer town that is today dedicated to modern painting and Native American crafts.

🔔 **Sunset Crater,** 14 mi. (22 km) north of Flagstaff: Volcanic crater that has been dormant for nine centuries. Spectacular red-orange lava formations. Worth a look. Open daily.

🔔 **Wupatki National Monument,** 30 mi. (48 km) north of Flagstaff: Ruins of a Sinagua Indian village from circa A.D. 1100. The main dwelling contains around 100 rooms. Archeological museum. Open daily. Worth going out of your way for. For information, call 602/527-7040.

LAS VEGAS (611 mi., 978 km, r.t. from the Grand Canyon on Ariz. 64S, U.S.

40W, U.S. 93, U.S. 95N): The world capital of gambling, in the heart of the desert (see the Las Vegas chapter). On the way, see:

  Grand Canyon Caverns, 124 mi. (198 km) SW of the Grand Canyon on Ariz. 64S, U.S. 40W, and Ariz. 66 (602/422-3223): Spectacular caverns 210 ft (64 m) underground (access by elevator) with a ¾-mi. (1-km) trail. Open year round. Interior temperature is 56°F (13°C). Worth the trip.

  Oatman, 193 mi. (308 km) SW of the Grand Canyon on Ariz. 64S, U.S. 40W, and old U.S. 66 SW of Kingman. Superb, remarkably preserved ghost town from the days of the Gold Rush. It had as many as 10,000 inhabitants around 1910; it has barely 100 today. Regularly used as the backdrop of western movies. Well worth the trip. For information, call 602/768-3424.

  Lake Mead and Hoover Dam, 259 mi. (415 km) west of the Grand Canyon on Ariz. 64S, U.S. 40W, and U.S. 93N: See the Las Vegas chapter.

CHAPTER 42

PHOENIX

□ □ □

Standing foursquare in the center of the **Valley of the Sun,** Arizona's capital, as you approach it from the air, looks like a verdant oasis in the midst of a sandy, mountainous desert. The Hohokam Indians, a people who mysteriously disappeared without trace around the year A.D. 1400, appear to have devised an irrigation system for the area, but around the turn of the century more up-to-date methods were initiated, and now Phoenix is the center of a green belt with market gardens, fields of cotton and alfalfa, citrus and olive groves, and even date palms. The city owes its name, too, to its Indian antecedents. As with the mythical bird which is reborn from its own ashes, the inhabitants of Phoenix have given new life to an arid plain which, after the disappearance of the Hohokam (an Indian word meaning simply "those who have vanished"), was long left empty to the scorching sun.

Less than a century old, Phoenix is a successful blend of the old, romantic West and the vigor of 20th-century America. A perfect base for excursions to such vacation wonderlands as the Grand Canyon of the Colorado, Navajoland, Tucson and southern Arizona, or the Apache Trail (in the 19th century the region witnessed savage battles with the Apache under Cochise and Geronimo), Phoenix itself has become, as time goes on, one of the principal tourist attractions of the West, especially in winter. Witness its 25,000 hotel rooms, its 80 golf courses, the **Heard Museum,** finest Indian museum in the country, and its dozen of luxury grand hotels, including the famous **Arizona Biltmore** designed by the great Frank Lloyd Wright. With 300 days of sunshine a year and low humidity, **Sun City,** as Phoenix calls itself, is also a dream come true for tens of thousands of well-to-do retirees.

Covering an enormous area 25 mi. (40 km) long by 40 mi. (65 km) wide with its low ranch or Spanish Colonial houses, and lacking any conspicuous buildings (or even a downtown, properly so called), Phoenix may be showing us the shape of cities to come—a sort of Los Angeles in the desert, with a dizzying rate of population growth. Between 1950 and 1987 the number of people living in the city and its inner suburbs (the super-smart **Scottsdale** and **Paradise Valley,** and the less exclusive **Glendale, Mesa,** and **Tempe**) rose from 200,000 to 1,850,000—more than 800% in less than a third of a century. It comes as no surprise, then, that Phoenix enjoys the third-fastest economic growth rate among America's major cities, right behind Austin and Orlando.

Besides its many high-tech industries, particularly electronics, telecommunications, and aerospace, Phoenix is the headquarters of the financial-services giant Greyhound, and of two of the largest hotel chains, Ramada Inns and Best Western.

BASIC FACTS: Capital of the state of Arizona. Area Code: 602. Time Zone: Mountain Time. ZIP Code: 85026. Founded: 1864. Approximate population: city, 930,000; metropolitan area, 1,850,000. 21st-largest metropolitan area in the U.S.

CLIMATE: With one of the largest amounts of sunshine (86% sunny days) in the U.S., the inhabitants of Phoenix are the spoiled children of nature. Winter is brilliantly sunny by day (Jan. avg., 54°F, 12°C) and cool at night. In summer the thermometer can easily rise above 95°F (35°C), but the dry desert air and the omnipresent air conditioning make the heat easy to take. Spring and fall are very pleasant, especially Apr. and Oct. The rainy season is July-Aug., with only an occasional downpour in winter.

DISTANCES: Albuquerque, 453 mi. (725 km); Denver, 805 mi. (1,288 km); Grand Canyon National Park, 218 mi. (350 km); Las Vegas, 285 mi. (456 km); Los Angeles, 390 mi. (625 km); Salt Lake City, 650 mi. (1,040 km); San Diego, 355 mi. (568 km).

ARRIVAL & TRANSIT INFORMATION

AIRPORT: Phoenix Sky Harbor International (PHX), 4 mi. SE (273-3300).

AIRLINES: Alaska (254-0303), America West (894-0737), American (258-6300), Braniff (244-8853), Continental (258-8911), Delta (258-5930), Midway (toll free 800/621-5700), Northwest (273-7325), Southwest (273-1221), TWA (252-7711), United (273-3131), and USAir (toll free 800/428-4322).

CITY LINK: The **cab** fare from the airport to downtown is $10–$14 (rates vary widely among different cab companies, so inquire in advance); time, 10–15 min. Bus: **Supershuttle** (244-9000); serves any address in Phoenix or the metropolitan area on request; fare, $5–$12; time, 15–20 min. Cab fares are very high, and the public bus transportation theoretically provided by **Phoenix Transit Systems/PTS** (253-5000) is almost useless in practice.

Given the size of the metropolitan area and the numerous excursion destinations around about, it makes a great deal of sense to rent a car with unlimited mileage, particularly at the low rates prevailing in Arizona.

CAR RENTAL (at the airport unless otherwise noted): Avis (273-3222); Budget (294-6124); Dollar (275-7588); General Rent-A-Car, 2800 E. Van Buren St. (273-0991); Hertz (267-8822); National (275-4771); and Thrifty, 4114 E. Washington St. (244-0311). For downtown locations, consult the local telephone directory.

LIMOUSINE SERVICES: Arizona Limousines/Dav El (267-7097), Carey Limousine (996-1955), and Desert Elegance Limousine (998-7711).

TAXIS: Taxis cannot be hailed on the street. Your best bet is to call **Arizona Taxi** (253-8294), **Checker Cab** (257-1818), or **Yellow Cab** (252-5071). Be sure to negotiate the fare in advance.

TRAIN: AMTRAK, Union Station, 401 W. Harrison St. (253-0121; or toll free 800/872-7245).

BUS: Greyhound, 525 E. Washington St. (248-4040).

INFORMATION & TOURS

TOURIST INFORMATION: The **Arizona Office of Tourism,** 1100 W.

Washington St., Phoenix, AZ 85007 (602/255-3618). Information covering the whole state of Arizona. Open Mon.-Fri.

Phoenix and Valley of the Sun Convention and Visitors Bureau, 505 N. 2nd St., Suite 300, Phoenix, AZ 85004 (602/254-6500; toll free 800/528-0483).

For a **telephone recording** with an up-to-date list of cultural events and shows, call 602/252-5588.

GUIDED TOURS: Arizona Air (airplane), 15000 N. Airport Dr., Scottsdale (991-8252): One-day air trips over the Grand Canyon, Monument Valley, Oak Creek Canyon, etc.; not to be missed.

Gray Line (bus), 1350 N. 22nd Ave., Phoenix (254-4550): Conducted tours of Phoenix and surroundings; serves principal hotels.

Sky Cab (airplane), 11115 N. Airport Dr., Scottsdale (998-1778): Half- and full-day flights over the Grand Canyon, Lake Powell, Monument Valley, Canyon de Chelly, etc. Spectacular.

SIGHTS, ATTRACTIONS, & ACTIVITIES

ADVENTURES: Arizona Awareness, 2422 N. 72nd Pl., Scottsdale (947-7852): Excursions on horseback, foot, or by Jeep through Arizona's mountains and deserts.

Arizona River Runners (boat), P.O. Box 47788, Phoenix, (867-4866): Rafting down the Colorado River through the Grand Canyon; three-, six- and eight-day round trips.

Balloon Voyage Inc. (balloon), 1701 E. Julie Dr., Tempe (838-4444): Balloon rides over Phoenix and the area. Spectacular.

Salt River Canyon Raft Trips (boat), 2319 E. Apache Blvd., Tempe (968-1552): Rafting near Phoenix; one-day or longer trips.

Unicorn Balloon Company (balloon), 7406 E. Butherus Dr., Scottsdale (991-3666): Dawn or afternoon balloon rides over Phoenix and the area; spectacular.

Wild West Jeep Tours, Inc. (Jeep), 7924 E. Chaparral Rd., Suite 104, Scottsdale (941-8355): One-day excursions into the mountain and desert country around Phoenix.

ARCHITECTURAL HIGHLIGHTS: ☼ ⚱ **Gammage Center for the Performing Arts,** the campus of Arizona State University, Apache Blvd., Tempe (965-3434): The last major work of Frank Lloyd Wright, opened in 1964 after his death. The huge auditorium, a great architect's celebration of the curved line, has astonishing acoustics. Open Tues., Thur., and Sat.; must certainly be seen.

⚱ **Mystery Castle,** 7 mi. (11 km) south on Central Ave. at 800 E. Mineral Rd., Phoenix (268-1581): A huge, bizarre sort of house at the foot of South Mountain Park, built by hand between 1927 and 1945 by the solitary eccentric Boyce Luther Gulley from a wide assortment of unusual salvage materials. It boasts no fewer than 18 rooms and 13 fireplaces, not to mention a chapel and a strange cantilevered staircase. Open Tues.-Sun. from Oct. 1 to July 4. Worth the side trip.

⚱ **State Capitol,** W. Washington St. and 17th Ave., Phoenix (255-4581): The home of the Arizona legislature is an imposing turn-of-the-century structure in limestone and Arizona granite, capped with a copper-plated dome. Interesting museum of western history, open Mon.-Fri. The beautiful gardens display a comprehensive selection of the local flora. Should be seen.

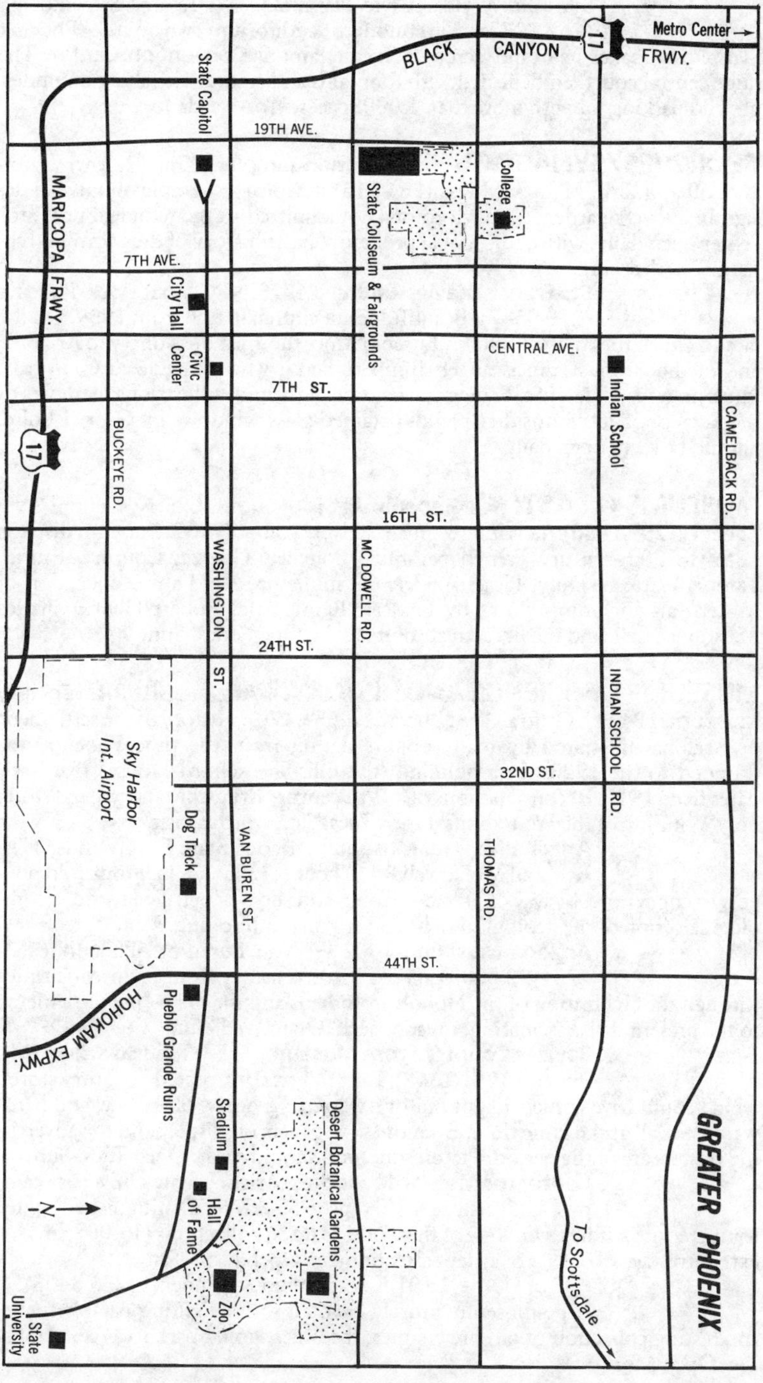

Metro Center →

BLACK CANYON FRWY.

17

MARICOPA FRWY.

State Capitol

19TH AVE.

7TH AVE.

City Hall

Civic Center

7TH ST.

State Coliseum & Fairgrounds

College

CENTRAL AVE.

Indian School

CAMELBACK RD.

17

BUCKEYE RD.

WASHINGTON ST.

16TH ST.

MC DOWELL RD.

24TH ST.

Sky Harbor Int. Airport

32ND ST.

INDIAN SCHOOL RD.

Dog Track

VAN BUREN ST.

THOMAS RD.

44TH ST.

HOHOKAM EXPWY.

Pueblo Grande Ruins

Stadium

Hall of Fame

Zoo

Desert Botanical Gardens

To Scottsdale

State University

-N→

GREATER PHOENIX

☼�� **Symphony Hall,** Civic Plaza, 225 W. Adams St., Phoenix (262-7272): Ultramodern auditorium where the Phoenix Symphony makes its home, across from the famous **Convention Center.** The huge central court, embellished with fountains and statues, lies above an underground parking lot with more than 1,000 spaces. Worth a glance.

CHURCHES/SYNAGOGUES: � Mormon Temple, 14 mi. (22 km) east on U.S. 60 at 525 E. Main St., Mesa (964-7164): Mormon Temple of unusual design in a lovely garden. Non-Mormons not admitted to the temple, but visitor center open daily, with audio-visual program on the history of the Mormon religion. Worth seeing.

� **St. Francis Xavier Church,** 4715 N. Central Ave., Phoenix (279-9547): Beautiful Jesuit church dating from 1959. On the façade, the statues of the Jesuit Fr. Eusebio Kino, the great missionary to Arizona, and of the famous Franciscan Fr. Junipero Serra, who evangelized California, stand on either side of St. Francis Xavier, one of the most illustrious members of the Society of Jesus. Inside, splendid stained-glass windows by Gabriel Loire. Should be seen; open daily.

MUSEUMS OF ART: ☼ � Phoenix Art Museum, 1625 N. Central Ave., Phoenix (257-1880): This interesting, relatively young (1969) museum displays 18th- to 20th-century French painting (Boucher, Greuze, Courbet, Fantin-Latour, Watteau, Dufy, Picasso), Oriental miniatures, and a fine collection of western art including works by Frederic Remington, Robert Henri, Charles Marion Russell, and the like. An absolute must. Open Tues.-Sun.

MUSEUMS OF SCIENCE AND HISTORY: � Arizona Historical Society Museum, 1242 N. Central Ave., Phoenix (255-4470): History of the settlement of Arizona illustrated by many objects dating from the time Phoenix was founded to the 1920s, in a building (the Ellis-Shackelford House) that itself dates from 1917. Reconstructions of a 19th-century drugstore and general store. For "Winning of the West" buffs. Open Tues.-Sat.; worth a visit.

� **Arizona Mineral Museum,** Arizona State Fairgrounds, 17th Ave. and McDowell Rd., Phoenix (255-3791): From gold nuggets to copper ore, by way of precious stones and slices of petrified wood, a complete selection of the geological riches of Arizona. Interesting. Mon.-Sat.

☼� **Arizona Museum,** 1002 W. Van Buren St., Phoenix (253-2734): 2,000 years of Arizona history from prehistoric times through the civilization of the Hohokam Indians and the first white settlements to the present day. Fascinating; must be seen. Open Wed.-Sun.

� **Bayless Country Store Museum,** 118 W. Indian School Rd., Phoenix (241-1368): Faithfully reconstructed "country store" which could have come straight out of a western: grocery, pharmacy, and hardware store all at the same time. Even the newspapers on display and the advertising posters are of the period. Picturesque; you should see it. Open Tues.-Sun.

� **Center for Meteorite Studies,** Arizona State University campus, University Dr., Tempe (965-3576): Distinguished center for meteorite studies, with one of the world's largest collections (1,400 items) of extraterrestrial objects. For ardent astronomers. Open Mon.-Sat.

� **Hall of Flame,** 6101 E. Van Buren St., Phoenix (275-3473): A large museum entirely devoted to fire-fighting paraphernalia. Interesting collection of old fire engines, the oldest going back to 1725. Amusing. Open Mon.-Sat.

※ ⚱⚱⚱ **Heard Museum,** 22 E. Monte Vista Rd., Phoenix (252-8840): The finest and one of the largest museums of anthropology and primitive art in the U.S., housed in an elegant Spanish Mission–style building. Although it has some African, Asian, and Oceanic pieces of quality, the museum has specialized since its foundation in 1929 in the Amerindian cultures, particularly those of the Southwest, and especially the Hohokam, Mogollon, Anasazi, and Pueblo. Fine hall of prehistoric arts and a splendid group of Kachina dolls given by former Sen. Barry Goldwater; also exhibitions of contemporary Indian art. Spanish Colonial room evidencing the Spanish cultural influence on the southwestern U.S. and Mexico. Don't fail to visit; open daily.

※ ⚱ **Pueblo Grande Museum,** 4619 E. Washington St., Phoenix (275-3542): Site of excavations that have unearthed an Indian village more than 2,000 years old. An observation platform allows you to follow the diggings under way, particularly on irrigation canals cut between the 6th and 8th centuries A.D. Remarkable archeological museum. Pueblo Grande was inhabited between 300 B.C. and A.D. 1450 by the mysterious Hohokam people. Worth the side trip; open daily.

PANORAMAS: ⚱ Golden Eagle, 201 N. Central Ave., Phoenix (257-7700):
Restaurant on the 37th floor of the Valley National Bank Building with the best view of the city and the mountains (admission fee). The food is unimpressive but the bar is congenial. Open Mon.-Sat. (till midnight).

※ ⚱ **South Mountain Park,** 10919 S. Central Ave., Phoenix (276-2221): Fine view of the city and the Valley of the Sun from **Dobbins Lookout** at 2,330 ft. (710 m). Well worth seeing.

PARKS AND GARDENS: ※ ⚱⚱ Desert Botanical Gardens, 1201 N. Galvin
Pkwy. at Papago Park, Phoenix (941-1225): All kinds of desert vegetation, including 1,400 different species of cactus, growing in a beautiful 150-acre (60-ha.) mountainside park. An energetic 45-min. walk, but well worth it. Spectacular cactus exhibition in Mar. Open daily.

⚱ **Encanto Park,** N. 15th Ave. and W. Encanto Blvd., Phoenix: Golf, tennis, and canoeing in the heart of town; the inviting lake is a wildlife reserve for waterfowl. Should be seen.

※ ⚱ **South Mountain Park,** 10919 S. Central Ave., Phoenix (276-2221): Large mountainous park covering 16,000 acres (6,475 ha.), with scenic drives, unspoiled canyons, weird rock formations, and dozens of miles of hiking trails—nature in the raw, 15 min. from downtown. Fine view of the city and valley; you should go there.

⚱ **Squaw Peak Recreation Area,** 2701 E. Squaw Peak Dr., Phoenix (262-6696): Northeast of town in the foothills of the Phoenix Mountains, this steeply contoured park has a 1.2-mi. (2-km) trail with a panoramic view of the city.

PERFORMING ARTS: For daily listings of all shows and cultural events, con-
sult the entertainment pages of the daily papers *Arizona Republic* (morning) and *Phoenix Gazette* (evening), as well as of the monthly *Phoenix* magazine.

Celebrity Theater, 440 N. 32nd St., Phoenix (267-1600): Comedy, drama.

Gammage Center for the Performing Arts, on the campus of Arizona State University, Apache Blvd., Tempe (965-3434): Contemporary theater, ballet, classical concerts in a Frank Lloyd Wright auditorium (see "Architectural Highlights," above).

Phoenix Little Theater, Civic Center, 25 E. Coronado Rd., Phoenix (254-2151): Contemporary theater (highly eclectic programs).

Sagebrush Theater, 7020 2nd St., Scottsdale (941-9875): Contemporary theater; home of the Scottsdale Community Players.

Scottsdale Center for the Arts, 7383 Scottsdale Mall, Scottsdale (994-2787): Contemporary and classic theater, dance, chamber music, concerts. Home of the Arizona Theatre Company. Annual Shakespeare Festival.

Sundome Theater for the Performing Arts, 19403 R. H. Johnson Blvd., Sun City West (584-3118): Big-name recitals.

Symphony Hall, Civic Center Plaza, 225 W. Adams St. (262-7272): Ultra-modern home of the Phoenix Symphony (principal conductor, Theo Alcantara) and the Arizona Opera Company.

Veterans Memorial Coliseum, 1826 W. McDowell Rd., Phoenix (252-6771): Rock concerts; leading pop stars.

SHOPPING: The **Biltmore Fashion Park,** 2470 E. Camelback Rd., Phoenix: 50 luxury stores and restaurants, including Saks Fifth Avenue, Gucci, and Ralph Lauren, in an ultramodern setting. High fashion.

The Borgata, 6166 N. Scottsdale Rd., Scottsdale: One of the most imaginative, luxurious shopping centers in the U.S., its architecture modeled on that of a medieval Italian village (whence the name). Some 50 stores and shops of surpassing elegance. Definitely worth seeing.

Fifth Avenue Shops, Fifth Ave., Scottsdale: 150 shops, art galleries, luxury ready-to-wear, and restaurants. Very elegant atmosphere.

Metrocenter, 9617 Metro Parkway, West Phoenix: Giant shopping center of strictly utilitarian appearance, with five department stores, more than 200 shops, 17 movie houses, and 47 restaurants, cafeterias, and snackbars. If you enjoy the colossal, this is for you.

Indian Art

For lovers of authentic Indian art, visit the **Heard Museum Shop,** 22 E. Monte Vista Rd., Phoenix; and **McGee's Indian Den,** 7239 First Ave., Scottsdale.

SPECIAL EVENTS: For the exact schedule of events below, consult the **Phoenix and Valley of the Sun Convention and Visitors Bureau** (see "Tourist Information," above).

Fiesta Bowl Classic (Jan. 1): Three days of festivities, parades, and concerts, culminating in the renowned Fiesta Bowl football game.

Arizona National Livestock Show (Jan.): Popular cattle show; guaranteed local color.

Phoenix Open Golf Tournament (Jan.): The world's greatest players compete at the Tournament Players Club, Scottsdale.

World's Championship JCs Rodeo of Rodeos (mid-Mar.): Rodeo championships, horseback parades; everyone's a cowboy on this day.

Indian Fair (Mar.): Exhibitions of Indian crafts; traditional dances; food festival. At the Heard Museum; don't miss it.

Arizona State Fair (late Oct. to early Nov.): One of the Southwest's biggest fair-exhibitions; cattle show, public concerts, games, etc. Plenty of atmosphere.

Thunderbird Balloon Race (Nov.): Air-balloon races drawing competitors from around the world.

SPORTS: Phoenix has one major and two minor-league professional teams:

Baseball (Apr.-Sept.): Firebirds, Municipal Stadium, Phoenix (275-0500).

Basketball (Oct.-May): Suns, Veterans Memorial Coliseum, Phoenix (263-7867).

Football (Sept.-Dec.): Cardinals, Sun Devil Stadium, Tempe (965-2381)

Dog Racing
Greyhound Park, 3801 E. Washington St., Phoenix (273-7181): Tues.-Sun., year round.

Horse Racing
Turf Paradise, 1501 W. Bell Rd., Phoenix (942-1101): Oct. to mid-May.

Tubing
Arizona's most popular summer sport: floating down the rapids of the Salt River or the Verde River on well-inflated inner tubes; helmets must be worn because of the rocks. Spectacular and not really risky. More than 20,000 enthusiasts meet every weekend (mid-Apr. to mid-Oct.) at **Saguaro Lake Guest Ranch,** 33 mi. (54 km) east via U.S. 60 (Apache Blvd.) and Bush Hwy.; for information, call 984-3305.

STROLLS: ☀☖ **Heritage Square,** E. Monroe & 7th Sts., Phoenix (262-5071): A group of perfectly restored 19th-century houses, including the very typical **Rosson House,** open Wed.-Sun., once the luxurious home of Dr. Roland Rosson who was mayor around 1895. The historic heart of Phoenix; shops and restaurants. Worth seeing.

☀☖ **Scottsdale,** around Scottsdale and Osborn Rds., Scottsdale: The smart suburb of Phoenix, with luxury hotels, fashionable restaurants, elegant shops, art galleries (around Fifth Ave. and Main St.), and the amazing **Borgata** at 6166 N. Scottsdale Rd. (see "Shopping," above), the last word in shopping centers. A sight to be seen.

THEME PARKS: ☀☖ **Big Surf,** 1500 N. Hayden Rd., Tempe (947-7873): Five-foot (2-m) artificial waves for surfers, in a huge lagoon-pool. Spectacular; open Tues.-Sun., Mar.-Sept.

☀☖ **Rawhide,** 23023 N. Scottsdale Rd., Scottsdale (563-5111): Reconstruction of a Far West village; shops, restaurants, rodeos, stagecoach rides, gunfire (for amusement only). Entertaining; if you love western movies, this is for you. Open daily.

ZOOS: ☖ **Phoenix Zoo,** 5810 Van Buren St., Papago Park, Phoenix (273-7771): Modern, comprehensive zoo with some 1,200 animals in reconstructions of their natural habitats, including a herd of very rare Arabian oryx. Pretty scenery; mini-train for visitors. A positive must-see; open daily.

ACCOMMODATIONS
See the listing of toll-free numbers in the Appendix.

Room Rates in Phoenix	
B (Budget)	up to $30
I (Inexpensive)	$30–$60
M (Moderate)	$60–$90
E (Expensive)	$90–$140
VE (Very Expensive)	$140 and up

Personal Favorites (in order of preference)

ℚℚℚℚℚ **Arizona Biltmore** (nr. dwntwn), 24th and Missouri Ave. Phoenix, AZ 85016 (602/955-6600; toll free, see Westin). 506 rms, A/C, color TV, in-rm movies. AE, CB, DC, MC, V. Free parking, three pools, health club, sauna, two golf courses, 18 tennis courts, putting green, bicycles, two rests. (including L'Orangerie), two bars, open-air buffet, rm svce, disco, boutiques, hrdrsr, free crib, concierge. *Note:* This luxurious grand hotel designed by Frank Lloyd Wright in a blend of art deco and traditional regional styles has been one of the glories of American hotelkeeping for more than half a century. Long favored by Hollywood stars and famous politicians, the Biltmore is among the dozen finest hotels in the country. Its superb gardens blazing w. flowers and planted with palm trees and cactus, pools, tennis courts, and two golf courses are all a fitting complement to the spacious, elegant rms (some w. private balconies or patios), faultless svce, and excellent food. VIP and big business clientele. Rates are more affordable in summer. 15 min. from dwntwn. A memorable place to stay. **VE, but lower rates out of season**

☀ℚℚℚℚ **The Pointe at Squaw Peak** (vic.), 7677 N. 16th St., Phoenix, AZ 85020 (602/997-2626; toll free 800/528-0428). 582 suites and villas, A/C, cable color TV. AE, CB, DC, MC, V. Free parking, seven pools, health club, sauna, eight tennis courts, putting green, four rests. (including Ianuzzi Pointe of View), two bars, rm svce, disco, cinema (on wknds), hrdrsr, crib $10, concierge. *Note:* Luxury hotel-village in a lovely natural setting. The Spanish Colonial design, w. shaded patios and fountains, comes off beautifully. Spacious suites or individual cottages w. mini-bars and private balconies. Unusually high level of comfort and physical-fitness facilities. Praiseworthy panoramic rest. Very good svce. Tourist and convention clientele. A hotel of great quality surrounded by 280 (113 ha) acres of unspoiled land and beautiful gardens. 20 min. from dwntwn. **VE, but lower rates out of season**

☀ℚℚℚ **Clarion Inn at McCormick Ranch** (vic.), 7401 N. Scottsdale Rd., Scottsdale, AZ 85253 (602/948-5050; toll free, see Clarion). 176 rms and villas, A/C, color TV, in-rm movies. AE, CB, DC, MC, V. Free parking, pool, sauna, two golf courses, four tennis courts, horseback riding, boats, windsurfing, rest., bar, rm svce, disco, crib $10, concierge. *Note:* Luxury motel on Camelback Lake. Very comfortable rms or individual villas w. private balconies and refrigerators. Decorated Castilian style. Splendid mountain view; attentive svce; comprehensive physical-fitness facilities and many outdoor activities, including hikes into the surrounding desert. Regular clientele. Very interesting summer discounts; a fine place to stay. **VE, but lower rates out of season**

ℚℚℚ **Hyatt Regency** (dwntwn), 122 N. 2nd St., Phoenix, AZ 85004 (602/252-1234; toll free, see Hyatt). 711 rms, A/C, color TV, in-rm movies. AE, CB, DC, MC, V. Valet garage $8, pool, solarium, two rests. (one revolving, on the top floor), bar, rm svce, nightclub, boutiques, free crib. *Note:* Modern, imposing 24-story glass-and-concrete building in the heart of Phoenix. Inviting, well-designed rms, some w. balconies; so-so rest. (Compass). Business and group clientele. Efficient svce; all the Hyatt comfort and glitter; excellent location a stone's throw from the Convention Center. Good value on balance. **E–VE, but lower rates out of season**

ℚℚ **Sunburst Resort Hotel** (vic.), 4925 N. Scottsdale Rd., Scottsdale, AZ 85251 (602/945-7666; toll free 800/854-2608). 212 rms, A/C, color TV, in-rm movies. AE, CB, DC, MC, V. Free parking, pool, eight tennis courts, putting green, rest., coffeeshop, bar, rm svce, disco, crib $5. *Note:* Inviting, comfortable vacation complex in a huge garden. Rustic Colonial décor. Spacious rms w. refrigerators and private balconies or patios. Attentive svce. 5 min. from the luxury Fifth Ave. stores. Group and convention clientele. Good overall value. Recently renovated. **M–E, but lower rates out of season**

🏦🏦 **Cornerstone Inn and Resort** (nr. dwntwn), 4301 N. 24th St., Phoenix, AZ 85016 (602/954-9220; toll free 800/227-8458). 125 mini-suites, A/C, cable color TV. AE, MC, V. Free parking, two pools, putting green, rest., valet svce, free breakfast, free crib, concierge. *Note:* Congenial hotel of Spanish design, surrounded by gardens. Mini-suites only, w. balconies and refrigerators, some w. kitchenettes. Friendly reception and svce. Group clientele. Free airport limo. Very good value. **M–E, but lower rates out of season**

🏦 **Quality Inn Desert Sky** (nr. dwntwn), 3541 E. Van Buren St., Phoenix, AZ 85008 (602/273-7121; toll free, see Quality Inns). 90 rms, A/C, color TV, in-rm movies. AE, CB, DC, MC, V. Free parking, pool, rest., bar, rm svce, free crib. *Note:* Comfortable, well-run small motel very nr. the airport; inviting garden and pool. Friendly svce; very good overall value. Package-tour and group clientele. 5 min. from dwntwn. **I, but lower rates out of season**

🏦 **Motel 6 Central** (nr. dwntwn), 2323 E. Van Buren St., Phoenix, AZ 85006 (602/267-7511). 245 rms, A/C, color TV, in-rm movies. DC, MC, V. Free parking, pool, rest. *Note:* Unbeatable value halfway from dwntwn to the airport. Functionally comfortable rms; excellent location 5 min. from dwntwn. Ideal if you're driving. **B**

Other Accommodations (from top bracket to budget)

☀️🏦🏦🏦🏦 **Hyatt Regency Scottsdale at Gainey Ranch** (vic.), 7500 E. Doubletree Ranch Rd., Scottsdale, AZ 85258 (602/991-3388; toll free, see Hyatt). 488 rms, suites, and individual villas; A/C, color TV, in-rm movies. AE, CB, DC, MC, V. Free valet parking, ten pools, health club, sauna, two golf courses, nine tennis courts, putting green, boats, two rests. (including the Gazebo), coffeeshop, three bars, 24-hr rm svce, nightclub, free crib. *Note:* Brand-new ultra-luxurious resort complex on a little lake w. private beach. Elegant Mediterranean-style buildings and spectacular lobby w. three-story-high modern sculpture. Spacious suites w. mini-bars and private balconies; individual villas w. two or four bedrooms. Very comprehensive sports facilities; excellent svce. 640 acres (256 ha.) of lawns and lush tropical gardens w. dozens of fountains, waterfalls, and palm trees. Tourist and big business clientele. **VE, but lower rates out of season**

☀️🏦🏦🏦🏦 **Marriott's Camelback Inn** (vic.), 5402 E. Lincoln Dr., Scottsdale, AZ 85252 (602/948-1700; toll free, see Marriott). 423 rms, A/C, color TV, in-rm movies. AE, CB, DC, MC, V. Free parking, two pools, health club, three golf courses, ten tennis courts, horseback riding, putting green, three rests. (including Chaparral), three bars, 24-hr rm svce, disco, hrdrsr, free crib, concierge. *Note:* A vacationers' paradise: little two-story cottages scattered through 125 acres (50 ha.) of splendid gardens w. the mountains as a backdrop. Almost as luxurious as the Arizona Biltmore, but less smart and—even more important—less stuffy. Spacious rms w. mini-bars and private patios or balconies; polished svce; food as indifferent as all Marriotts. Worthwhile vacation packages. Comprehensive physical-fitness facilities. Clientele of rich tourists. A real oasis in the desert, 20 min. from dwntwn. **VE, but lower rates out of season**

☀️🏦🏦🏦🏦 **The Wigwam** (vic.), Indian School and Litchfield Rds., Litchfield Park, AZ 85340 (602/935-3811; toll free see Preferred). 225 rms, A/C, color TV. AE, MC, V. Free parking, two pools, health club, saunas, three golf courses, eight tennis courts, horseback riding, trapshooting, rest., bar, rm svce, disco. *Note:* Superb country club in a class w. the Arizona Biltmore, occupying 70 acres (28 ha.) of very lovely gardens in the middle of the desert. Inviting, comfortable rms w. refrigerators and private patios, some w. fireplaces, in little adobe-style cottages. Efficient svce. Group and convention clientele. Interesting vacation packages. Closed from the end of May through Sept. Resv. essential, very far ahead. **VE (AP), but lower rates out of season**

Embassy Suites Biltmore (nr. dwntwn), 2630 E. Camelback Rd., Phoenix, AZ 85016 (602/955-3992; toll free 800/362-2779). 232 suites, A/C, color TV, in-rm movies. AE, CB, DC, MC, V. Free parking, pool, rest, bar, nightclub, boutiques, free breakfast, free crib, concierge. *Note:* Ultra-comfortable, elegant hotel, ideal for a long stay. Spacious suites w. kitchenettes and private patios; spectacular lobby w. tropical garden and goldfish pond. Excellent svce; free airport limo. Excellent location a stone's throw from Biltmore Fashion Park (see "Shopping," above). Business clientele. **E–VE, but lower rates out of season**

Doubletree Suites Gateway Center (nr. dwntwn), 320 N. 44th at Van Buren, Phoenix, AZ 85008 (602/225-0500; toll free 800/528-0444). 242 suites, A/C, color TV, in-rm movies. AE, CB, DC, MC, V. Free parking, pool, sauna, two tennis courts, rest., bar, 24-hr rm svce, nightclub, free breakfast, free crib. *Note:* Brand-new six-floor hotel very nr. the airport; suites only, huge and comfortable, w. kitchenettes and refrigerators. Lobby w. glass-walled elevators. Cheerful reception and svce. Business clientele. 10 min. from dwntwn. **E, but lower rates out of season**

Ramada Valley Ho Resort (vic.), 6850 Main St., Scottsdale, AZ 85251 (602/945-6321; toll free, see Ramada Inns). 282 rms, A/C, color TV, in-rm movies. AE, CB, DC, MC, V. Free parking, three pools, three tennis courts, putting green, rest. (Summerfield's), bar, rm svce, nightclub, hrdrsr, free crib. *Note:* Large, pleasant, comfortable motel nr. the smart Fifth Ave. stores in a huge tropical garden. Comfortable, spacious rms w. private patios or balconies and refrigerators. Efficient svce; good value out of season. Group and convention clientele. 15 min. from dwntwn. **E, but lower rates out of season**

Sheraton Phoenix Hotel (formerly Hilton Adams) (dwntwn), 111 N. Central Ave. at Adams St., Phoenix, AZ 85001 (602/257-1525; toll free, see Sheraton). 534 rms, A/C, color TV, in-rm movies. AE, CB, DC, MC, V. Parking $6, pool, health club, rest. (Sandpainter), coffeeshop, bar, rm svce, nightclub, hrdrsr, free crib. *Note:* Modern, clean-lined 19-story tower in the heart of dwntwn, a stone's throw from the Convention Center; light, spacious rms w. refrigerators, some w. private patios. Faultless standards of comfort; good svce. Group and business clientele. **M–E, but lower rates out of season**

Embassy Suites–Westside (nr. dwntwn), 3210 N.W. Grand Ave., Phoenix, AZ 85017 (602/279-3211; toll free 800/362-2779). 167 suites, A/C, color TV, in-rm movies. AE, CB, DC, MC, V. Free parking, pool, sauna, rest., bar, rm svce, free breakfast, free crib. *Note:* Very comfortable motel nr. the Arizona State Fairgrounds, 10 min. from dwntwn. Suites only, w. kitchenettes and private balconies or patios. Inviting indoor garden w. flowerbeds and palm trees. Efficient reception and svce. Business clientele. **M–E, but lower rates out of season**

Holiday Inn Financial Center (nr. dwntwn), 3600 N. Second Ave., Phoenix, AZ 85013 (602/248-0222; toll free, see Holiday Inns). 296 rms, A/C, color TV, in-rm movies. AE, CB, DC, MC, V. Free parking, two pools, rest. (C. W. Dandy's), bar, rm svce, nightclub, free crib. *Note:* Modern ten-floor motel adjoining Park Central Mall w. its 75 shops and rests. Typical Holiday Inn style; acceptable rest.; impersonal svce. Business clientele (the financial district is a block or two away). Free airport limo. **M—E, but lower rates out of season**

　　　　♀ **Warren House East** (nr. dwntwn), 2911 E. Indian School
　　　　♭ Rd., Phoenix, AZ 85016 (602/956-1345; toll free 800/331-7700). 47 rms, A/C, cable color TV. AE, MC, V. Free parking, pool, tennis court, adjoining coffeeshop, free crib. *Note:* Inviting, serviceable motel w. low rates. Comfortable rms, most w. kitchenettes and refrigerators. Friendly reception and svce. Very good value; 8 min. from dwntwn. **I**

　　　　♀ **Desert Rose** (nr. dwntwn), 3424 E. Van Buren St., Phoenix,
　　　　♭ AZ 85008 (602/275-4421). 56 rms, A/C, color TV. AE, CB, DC, MC, V. Free parking, pool, coffeeshop, rm svce, crib $2. *Note:* One of the best buys in Phoenix, 5 min. from dwntwn. Comfortable rms w. refrigerators and private balconies. Free airport limo. Ideal if you're driving. **B—I, but lower rates out of season**

Airport Accommodations

　　　　♀♀ **Fiesta Inn** (nr. dwntwn), 2100 S. Priest Dr., Tempe, AZ
　　　　♭♭ 85282 (602/967-1441; toll free 800/528-6481). 270 rms, A/C, color TV, in-rm movies. AE, CB, DC, MC, V. Free parking, pool, health club, sauna, three tennis courts, rest., bar, rm svce, disco, free crib. *Note:* The ideal motel for a stopover between flights. Spacious, comfortable rms w. refrigerators. Good physical-fitness facilities; good rest. (The Other Place); excellent svce. Pretty countrified décor w. original works of art. 8 min. from airport (free shuttle). Good value. **M—E, but lower rates out of season**

Accommodations in the Vicinity

　　　　☼♭♭♭♭ **The Boulders Resort and Club** (vic.), 34631 N. Tom Darling-
　　　　　　　　 ton Rd., Carefree, AZ 85377 (602/488-9009; toll free 800/233-7637). 120 casitas, A/C, color TV. AE, CB, DC, MC, V. Free parking, two pools, two golf courses, six tennis courts, putting green, horseback riding, two rests. (including Latilla Dining Room), bar, rm svce, disco, crib $3. *Note:* One of the most imaginative hotel buildings in the West. Built in the open desert at the foot of a huge rockfall, the adobe-style casitas (individual villas) blend into the dun-and-ocher landscape behind them. Spacious rms decorated w. Indian motifs, all w. refrigerators, fireplaces, and private patios. Exemplary svce; rest. of quality. Jeep trips organized into the desert. Clientele of well-heeled tourists; this is the perfect vacationers' grand hotel. Closed July to mid-Sept. 40 min. from dwntwn by Scottsdale Rd. **VE (MAP) but lower rates out of season**

Guest Ranch

　　　　☼♭♭♭♭ **Rancho de los Caballeros** (vic.), Vulture Mine Rd.,
　　　　　　　　 Wickenburg, AZ 85358 (602/684-5484). 73 rms, half w. A/C, color TV. No credit cards. Free parking, pool, golf course, four tennis courts, horseback riding, trapshooting, rest., bar. *Note:* At once a luxury hotel and a true stock ranch w. cattle and real cowboys. Rustic but comfortable ambience. More than 20,000 acres (8,000 ha.) of desert lie open to riders, in groups or alone. Friendly reception and svce. Interesting American Plan packages. Open Oct. 10 to early May. Resv must be made very far in advance at this successful place. One hour's drive from Phoenix by U.S. 89N. A highly recommended spot. **E-VE (AP) but lower rates out of season**

YMCA / Youth Hostels

Valley of the Sun International Hostel (nr. dwntwn), 1026 N. 9th St., Phoenix, AZ 85006 (602/262-9439). 40 beds. Conventional youth hostel, 5 min. from dwntwn.

YMCA–Phoenix (dwntwn), 350 N. First Ave., Phoenix, AZ 85003 (602/ 253-6181). Men and women. Pool, coffeeshop, health club. Very central location.

RESTAURANTS

Phoenix Restaurant Prices	
(per person, excluding drinks and service charges)	
B (Budget)	up to $15
I (Inexpensive)	$15–$25
M (Moderate)	$25–$40
E (Expensive)	$40–$60
VE (Very Expensive)	$60 and up

Personal Favorites (in order of preference)

Vincent Guerithault on Camelback (nr. dwntwn), 3930 E. Camelback Rd., Phoenix (224-0225). A/C. Lunch Mon.-Fri., dinner Mon.-Sat.; closed Sun. and holidays. AE, CB, DC, MC, V. Jkt. *Specialties:* broiled oysters w. pimento, lobster baked w. Pernod w. ratatouille of young vegetables, salmon w. tomatillo sauce, duck tamale, crème brûlée w. strawberries, lemon pie, sherbet. Splendid wine list. *Note:* Unquestionably the finest food in Phoenix and the surrounding area. The young, talented Vincent Guerithault, who learned his trade in France at the prestigious Oustau de Baumanière at Les Baux de Provence, serves a felicitous mix of recipes culled from his native France combined w. the ingredients and style of the American Southwest: his specialty, mesquite broiling. Warm, rustic décor, w. exposed beams, furniture of country charm, and flowers everywhere. Excellent svce; atmosphere at once elegant and relaxing. Resv. a must. A very fine place. Valet parking. *French-American.* **M–E**

L'Orangerie (vic.), in the Arizona Biltmore (see "Accommodations," above), Phoenix (954-2507). A/C. Lunch/dinner daily. AE, CB, DC, MC, V. J&T. *Specialties:* crayfish salad, shrimp w. orange and pistachio, veal Leonardo, lamb w. mint and spinach, pepper steak Mandalay, game (in season). Good desserts. Remarkable wine list (380 labels). *Note:* The luxury-hotel rest. at its splendid best, crystal chandeliers and all. Classic cuisine in the grand style, rather pompous (salmon Wellington, sautéed chicken w. madeira). Very polished svce in a setting from the hand of Frank Lloyd Wright. Agreeable background music. Resv. advised. *Continental.* **E**

The Other Place (vic.), 7101 E. Lincoln Dr., Paradise Valley (948-7910). A/C. Lunch Mon.-Fri., dinner nightly. AE, CB, DC, MC, V. *Specialties:* gazpacho, southern fried chicken, steak, roast beef, catch of the day. *Note:* One of the prettiest Mexican hacienda settings in the city; good, varied, tasty food. Rather noisy background music. Locally popular; no resv. Other locations: 1644 S. Dobson Rd. at Superstition Frwy. (831-8877); 2100 S. Priest Dr. at the Fiesta Inn (967-8721). *American-Mexican.* **B–I**

Le Petit Café (vic.), 7340 E. Shoeman Lane, Scottsdale (947-5194). A/C. Lunch/dinner Mon.-Sat.; closed Sun. and holidays. AE, CB, DC, MC, V. Jkt. *Specialties:* roast duckling w. peaches, broiled salmon w. tarragon sauce, chocolate soufflé. Menu changed regularly. Wine list limited but well balanced. *Note:* If you love modern, imaginative French cuisine, the excellent chef Jean Claude Poncet has made this the place for you. Charming Parisian-bistro décor; cheerful svce; congenial, relaxing atmosphere. Resv. strongly advised. *French.* **I–M**

☼☆🍸🍸 **The Stockyards** (nr. dwntwn), 5001 E. Washington St., Phoenix (273-7378). A/C. Lunch Mon.-Sat., dinner nightly; closed Dec. 25 and Sun. from June through Oct. AE, DC, MC, V. *Specialties:* "Rocky Mountain oysters," excellent meats of all kinds, steak, T-bone, prime ribs. Unimpressive desserts and wine list. *Note:* For almost 50 years this steakhouse has been serving prime beef cuts, broiled to perfection, at reasonable prices. Wonderful turn-of-the-century-style décor. The bar is worth a visit all to itself. Efficient svce. *Steak.* **I**

🍸🍸 **Shogun** (vic), 12615 N. Tatum Blvd., Scottsdale (953-3264). A/C. Lunch/dinner Mon.-Sat.; closed Sun. AE, MC, V. **Specialties:** Sushi, tempura, sukiyaki, karage chicken. *Note:* The best Japanese rest. in the Valley. Serenely attractive interior. Terrific sushi bar w. its two skilled craftsmen carving raw fish. Portions tend to be small, Japanese-style. Outstanding service. Resv. suggested. **I**

🍸 **Cafe' Casino** (nr. dwntwn), 1312 N. Scottsdale Rd., Scottsdale (947-1987). A/C. Breakfast/lunch/dinner daily; closed Dec. 25. MC, V. *Specialties:* quiche Lorraine, boeuf bourguignon, daily specials. *Note:* French-style cafeteria w. a sidewalk-café atmosphere, substantial, praiseworthy French-inspired food. Excellent homemade pastry; very good svce; remarkable value. Other location: 4842 N. 24th St. at Camelback Rd., Phoenix (955-3430). *French-continental.* **B**

🍸 **Garcia's Del Este Restaurant** (vic.), 7633 E. Indian School Rd., Scottsdale (945-1647). A/C. Lunch/dinner daily; closed Easter, Thanksgiving, and Dec. 25. AE, MC, V. *Specialties:* soup w. meatballs, chimichangas, quesadillas, fajitas. Excellent margaritas. *Note:* One of the lowest-priced and most authentic Mexican rests. in the region. Colorful setting and atmosphere; mariachi band evenings. Friendly, relaxed svce. No resv.; locally popular; generally crowded. Other locations: 3301 W. Peoria Ave., Phoenix (866-1850); 1604 E. Southern Ave., Tempe (820-0400). *Mexican-American.* **B–I**

Other Restaurants (from top bracket to budget)

🍸🍸🍸 **Etienne's Different Pointe of View** (nr. dwntwn), The Pointe at Tapatio Cliffs Hotel, 11111 N. 7th St., Phoenix (863-0912). A/C. Dinner only, nightly; Sun. brunch; closed Sun. June through Aug. AE, CB, DC, MC, V. Jkt. *Specialties:* poached salmon w. dill, filet mignon capella, duck à l'orange, crêpes Suzette. Wholly remarkable wine list. *Note:* Formal classic French-inspired cuisine, executed w. great success. Very handsome hi-tech setting and fabulous view of Phoenix and the Valley of the Sun at sunset (ask for a table near the picture window). Svce of a high order. Free shuttle (a Cadillac) from the hotel's parking lot at the foot of the hill. One of the best rests. in Phoenix. Resv. a must. Valet parking. *French-continental.* **M–E**

🍸🍸🍸 **The Palm Court** (vic.), Scottsdale Conference Center, 7700 E. McCormick Pkwy., Scottsdale (991-3400). Lunch/dinner daily; closed holidays. AE, CB, DC, MC, V. J&T *Specialties:* fettuccine Alfredo, lobster Lord Randolph, filet of venison w. blueberries, saddle of rabbit w. red pepper, stuffed quail, excellent seafood. Very good wine list. *Note:* Luxury rest. w. unobstructed view of Camelback Mountain and McCormick Lake. Elegant, refined cuisine in a typical Southwest-modern setting. Exceptionally polished svce (in tuxedo). One of the best rests. in the valley; resv. strongly advised. *Continental.* **M–E**

Le Relais (formerly Vincent's; vic.), 8711 E. Pinnacle Peak Rd., Scottsdale (998-0921). A/C. Dinner only, Mon.-Sat.; closed Sun. and holidays. AE, CB, DC, MC, V. Jkt. *Specialties:* Homemade fresh duck liver and smoked salmon, snail ravioli, warm sweetbread-and-squab salad, roast duck w. rosemary, poached lobster w. vanilla sauce. Remarkable desserts; large wine list. *Note:* Chris Ross is a great chef; his cuisine, a miracle of contemporary delicacy and imagination, has been lauded to the skies by many rest. critics. Uncommonly elegant décor, w. a collection of old paintings and art objects appraised at more than $3 million. Ultra-polished svce; very formal atmosphere. The patrons are rich snowbirds and local tycoons. The only rest. that can dispute Vincent Guerithault's claim to the title of the best in Phoenix. 30 min. from dwntwn. *French-American.* **M–E**

El Chorro Lodge (vic.), 5550 E. Lincoln Dr., Scottsdale (948-5170). A/C. Breakfast/lunch/dinner daily; closed June-Sept. AE, CB, DC, MC, V. Jkt. *Specialties:* chateaubriand, rack of lamb, good desserts. *Note:* One of the handsomest western settings in Arizona, w. enchanting patio for open-air dining. The cuisine is particularly polished, the svce impeccable, and the décor countrified elegant. A Phoenix landmark since 1937. Resv. a must; valet parking evenings. *Continental-American.* **M**

La Chaumière (vic.), 6910 Main St., Scottsdale (946-5115). A/C. Dinner only, Mon.-Sat.; closed Sun., holidays, and mid-July to mid-Aug. AE, DC, MC, V. Jkt. *Specialties:* poached salmon, chicken Cynthia, sole meunière, bouillabaisse, steak au poivre, rack of lamb, chocolate mousse. Good wine list. *Note:* Hidden in an orange-grove, this charming country inn with its big fireplace and vaulted ceiling serves serious French food, impeccably turned out. Very attentive svce; relaxed atmosphere. Resv. a must. Valet parking. *French.* **M**

Mancuso's (vic.), in the Borgata, 6166 N. Scottsdale Rd., Scottsdale (948-9988). A/C. Dinner only, nightly; closed Thanksgiving and Dec. 25. AE, CB, DC, MC, V. Jkt. *Specialties:* fresh homemade pasta, cannelloni Alfredo, chicken Agnesi, sautéed frogs' legs, duck à l'orange, sole Oscar, tournedos béarnaise. Good list of European and domestic wines. *Note:* Slightly theatrical décor in the style of a Renaissance château, but the mostly French and Italian food is of great quality. Exemplary svce. In the heart of the Borgata shopping center; heavily patronized by locals. Resv. advised; valet parking. *Italian-continental.* **M**

Avanti (nr. dwntwn), 2728 E. Thomas Rd., Phoenix (956-0900). A/C. Lunch Mon.-Fri., dinner nightly; closed Dec. 25. AE, MC, V. *Specialties:* ossobuco, fresh homemade pasta, veal Avanti, mussels marinière, catch of the day, French and Italian dishes. *Note:* The décor effectively highlights the green of plants against contrasting wall tones. As the name suggests, the food is predominantly Italian, but includes some interesting French and Spanish dishes. Good svce. Resv. advised. Valet parking. Other location: 3102 N. Scottsdale Rd., Scottsdale (949-8333). *Italian-continental.* **I–M**

Golden Belle (vic.), in Rawhide, 23023 N. Scottsdale Rd., Scottsdale (563-5600). A/C. Dinner only, nightly; brunch Sat. and Sun. AE, MC, V. *Specialties:* steak, broiled chicken, roast beef, barbecued meats. *Note:* Re-creation of a 19th-century saloon w. superb walnut bar. The meats are choice, and the cowboy atmosphere as real as can be. An entertaining place, and ideal for a quick dinner between two comic bandit attacks on a stagecoach at the picturesque western village of Rawhide (see "Theme Parks," above). Live country and western, just as it should be. *American-steak.* **I**

Monti's La Casa Vieja (vic.), 1st St. at Mill Ave., Tempe (967-7594). A/C. Lunch/dinner daily; closed Jan. 1 and Dec. 25. AE, CB, DC, MC, V. *Specialties:* steak, prime ribs, Maine lobster. *Note:* A real local landmark which prides itself on being the oldest rest. in town (1871). If you like good steak, it's also one of the best values in town. Pretty Spanish Colonial décor; good svce; resv. advised at lunch. Locally very popular. *Steak.* **I**

☀☿♈ **Pinnacle's Peak Patio** (vic.), 10426 E. Jomax Rd., Scottsdale (563-5134). A/C. Dinner only, nightly; brunch Sun.; closed Thanksgiving and Dec. 24–25. AE, MC, V. *Specialties:* charcoal-broiled T-bone steak (1 lb., 450 gm) and porterhouse steak (2 lbs., 900 gm), chateaubriand, hamburger. *Note:* Enormous (seats 2,000) western-style steakhouse; the view of the valley at sunset is worth the trip all by itself, but so are the enormous servings of prime beef. Relaxed svce; country music and dancing. Comic gunfights. Very touristic atmosphere; no resv.; no neckties. *Steak.* **B–I**

♈ **The Quilted Bear** (vic.), 6316 N. Scottsdale Rd., Scottsdale (948-7760). A/C. Breakfast/lunch/dinner daily; closed Dec. 25. AE, CB, DC, MC, V. *Specialties:* homemade soups, salads, sandwiches, steak, roast beef, catch of the day, fried chicken. *Note:* Huge cafeteria (at lunch) and conventional (at dinner) menu. Picturesque stained glass and a profusion of greenery. Locally popular. *American.* **B–I**

♈ **Aunt Chilada's** (nr. dwntwn), 7330 N. Dreamy Draw Dr., Phoenix (944-1286). A/C. Lunch/dinner daily. AE, CB, DC, MC, V. *Specialties:* tacos, tostadas, chimichangas, tamales, barbecued filet of pork, chicken w. raisins, calamari, steak. Very good margaritas. *Note:* In spite of its name, this old Phoenix landmark serves excellent Mexican food in a charming "mesón" setting with colorful flower-planted patios. Warm atmosphere; friendly, cheerful svce. Resv. unnecessary. Locally popular. Other location: 7777 S. Pointe Pkwy. (438-0992). *Mexican.* **B**

Cafeterias / Fast Food

Lunt Avenue Marble Club (vic.), 2207 W. Peoria Ave., Phoenix (863-9791). Quiches, sandwiches, pizza, crêpes at moderate prices, and the best hamburgers in town. Inviting décor. Open daily. Other locations: 2 E. Camelback Rd., Phoenix (265-8997); 6202 N. Scottsdale Rd., Scottsdale (998-3505).

Furr's (nr. dwntwn), Hayden Shopping Center, 3030 E. Thomas Rd., Phoenix (956-8650). Roast beef, sandwiches, chicken-fried steak, salads, catch of the day. Praiseworthy, well-prepared cafeteria food. Open daily till 8 p.m. Other location: 9115 Black Canyon Hwy., Phoenix (995-1588).

BARS & NIGHTCLUBS

Like other major cities, Phoenix has a magic phone number, the **Jazz Hotline** (254-4545), giving programs for all the jazz clubs.

Chuy's (vic.), 310 S. Mill Ave., Tempe (968-5568). The best modern-jazz club in town; college crowd.

Mr. Lucky's (nr. dwntwn), 3660 W. Grand Ave., Phoenix (246-0686). Live country music; typical cowboy atmosphere. Showcases the biggest names; also rock. Three dance floors.

Oscar Taylor (nr. dwntwn), 2420 E. Camelback Rd., Phoenix (956-5705). Singles bar got up like a Chicago speakeasy during Prohibition. Lots of action. Also an acceptable rest. Open nightly.

The Other Place (vic.), 7101 E. Lincoln Dr., Paradise Valley (948-7910). Live jazz; also a very good rest. (see above). Open nightly.

Rustler's Rooste (nr. dwntwn), The Pointe at South Mountain, 7777 S. Pointe Pkwy., Phoenix (231-9111). Very good live country music; dancing. Also an acceptable western rest. with a wonderful view of the city. Open nightly.

Seeker's Comedy Nite Club (vic.), 4519 N. Scottsdale Rd., Scottsdale (949-1100). Locally popular comedy club; the biggest names. Open nightly.

T.G.I. Friday's (nr. dwntwn), 1851 E. Camelback Rd., Phoenix (861-1737). Very popular singles bar; a nice place. Also an acceptable rest. Open nightly.

NEARBY EXCURSIONS

ARCOSANTI (65 mi., 104 km, north on I-17 to the Cordes Junction exit) (632-7135): A prototype of the city of the future, under construction since 1970; this first attempt at a synthesis of architecture and ecology has been dubbed "arcology." It's the work of the visionary Italian architect Paolo Soleri, with the help of many students and young volunteers; the desert megalopolis, still largely in embryo, displays strange, rounded shapes which are worth going out to see. Workshop open to visitors daily. See also Cosanti Foundation, below.

CASA GRANDE RUINS NATIONAL MONUMENT (52 mi., 84 km, SE via U.S. 60E and Ariz. 87S) (723-3172): One of the most amazing monuments of Native American civilization in the U.S. Built around 1350 by the Hohokam Indians (the word means "those who have disappeared"), the imposing structure, four stories high and with walls 4 ft. 11 in. (1.5 m) thick at the base, bears obvious resemblances to the ruins at Zacatecas in Mexico; it still constitutes a riddle for archeologists. Was it an official residence, a temple, an astronomical observatory, or a watch tower looking out over the valley? No one knows. The Hohokam, a race of remarkable builders and near relatives of the Anasazi and Pueblo Indians, left their mark on the valleys of the Gila and Salt rivers from 300 B.C. to A.D. 1400, when they mysteriously disappeared; in particular, they built dozens of miles of irrigation canals, 6 ft. 6 in. (2 m) wide and 3 ft. 3 in. (1 m) deep, to water their crops of beans, corn, squash, and cotton. The **Casa Grande** ("Big House," in Spanish) was so named by Fr. Eusebio Kino, the Jesuit missionary who explored southern Arizona in the 1690s. Built of caliche, a composition of clay gravel and calcium carbonate, Casa Grande has been protected since 1932 by a metal roof, not aesthetically appropriate but essential because caliche crumbles easily. Archeological museum. Don't miss it; open daily.

COSANTI FOUNDATION (6433 Doubletree Rd., Scottsdale (948-6145): Workshop of the famous Italian architect Paolo Soleri, a pupil of Frank Lloyd Wright's and the creator of Arcosanti (see above), the "city of the future" rising north of Phoenix. Exhibition of futurist urban projects, including a model of Arcosanti, and windbells by Paolo Soleri. Fascinating; don't miss it. Open daily.

FOUNTAIN HILLS (26 mi., 42 km, NE via Scottsdale Rd. and E. Shea Blvd.): The world's largest fountain, leaping 560 ft (170 m) from the middle of a little lake. The column of water weighs eight tons; should be seen.

SUN CITY (14 mi., 22 km, NW on Grand Ave., U.S. 60): Model community for well-to-do retirees, opened in the early '60s. **Sun City West,** another equally luxurious residential development, is under construction 2½ mi. (4 km) west. Both worth a look.

TALIESIN WEST (108th St. north of E. Shea Blvd., Scottsdale) (860-2700): Winter home and studio of the most famous American architect of the 20th century, Frank Lloyd Wright. The stone, glass, and steel buildings, modern and austere, contrast vividly with the surrounding desert; they house Wright's school of architecture, operated since his death in 1959 by the Taliesin Foundation. The buildings are a designated historic monument; you shouldn't miss them. Open daily except holidays and when it rains.

FARTHER AFIELD

APACHE TRAIL (168 mi., 268 km, round trip via Ariz. 88E and U.S. 60W): The old trail of Cochise and Geronimo, through wonderful desert-mountain scenery in violently contrasting colors. Your first stop is at **Tortilla Flat,** an old gold-prospectors' camp in the heart of the **Superstition Mountains,** complete with saloon, hotel, restaurant, and post office. Then drive along picturesque **Apache Lake,** a perch-fisherman's paradise, as far as the imposing ☀ ᐃ **Roosevelt Lake,** formed by the construction in 1910 of **Roosevelt Dam,** one of the largest dams in the world made entirely of hand-cut stone. Fishing, boat rentals. Very nearby is ☀ ᐃ **Tonto National Monument,** in the midst of a 1,100-acre (450-ha.) park covered in giant cactus. Clinging to the rock vault above the visitor center (467-2241; open daily) are two very fine Indian cave dwellings, each with a score of rooms, which can be reached with relative ease; dating from the 14th century, they are the work of the Salado Indians, cousins of the famous Anasazi. Don't miss them.

Then on to ☀ ᐃ **Globe,** once famous for its silver and copper mines. See the ☀ **Besh-Ba-Gowah Indian Ruins** on Jesse Hayes Rd., site of a huge cave dwelling inhabited by the Salado Indians between A.D. 1225 and 1400, with more than 200 rooms. Archeological excavations under way. Worth seeing.

At **Inspiration,** 3 mi. (5 km) west of Globe on U.S. 60, see also the immense open-pit copper mine of the **Consolidated Copper Co.,** open Mon.-Fri.

At **Superior,** 17 mi. (27 km) farther west, don't fail to visit the ☀ ᐃ **Boyce Thompson Southwestern Arboretum** on U.S. 60 (689-2811), open daily, a beautiful 39-acre (16-ha.) botanic garden with more than 10,000 species of desert plants from around the world, meticulously labeled; a must-see.

On the return trip, make a small detour between Florence Junction and Apache Junction, turning left off U.S. 60 to ᐃ **Kings Ranch,** an authentic 19th-century Far Western village where movies are often made. Worth seeing.

In **Mesa** is our last stop: ᐃ **Champlin Fighter Museum,** Falcon Field, 4636 Fighter Aces Dr., Mesa (830-4540), open daily. Here you'll find some 30 pursuit planes from World Wars I and II, splendidly restored, as well as souvenirs of U.S. fighter aces. A must for aviation buffs.

The trip is ideal for nature lovers, but take note that part of the road from Tortilla Flat to Roosevelt Lake is unsurfaced, and treacherous in wet weather. Allow one to two days.

Where to Stay En Route

NEAR GLOBE. The **Best Western Copper Hills Inn,** U.S. 60, Miami, AZ 85539 (602/425-7151). 68 rms. Conventional but very well-run motel. **I**

GRAND CANYON NATIONAL PARK (218 mi., 350 km, NW via I-17 and U.S. 180): One of the seven wonders of the world; see Chapter 41 on the Grand Canyon. Four hours' drive from Phoenix.

MOGOLLON RIM (239 mi., 382 km, round trip via Ariz. 87N, Ariz. 260E, Old Rim Rd. West, and Ariz. 87S): Leave

Phoenix by McDowell Rd. and Ariz. 87N. Wonderful scenery of wooded mountains, stretches of desert, lakes, and wild canyons as you cross ※ **Tonto National Forest.**

Your first stop will be at ※ ₰ **Payson,** an old gold-prospectors' town now known for its rustic cowtown heritage and its many festivals: the Festival of Country Music at the end of June; the Sawdust Festival, a national lumbermen's contest, at the end of July; a giant rodeo in mid-Aug.; and the Old Time Fiddlers Festival of folk music at the end of Sept. For schedules, call 602/474-4515. Local color guaranteed.

Near the little tourist resort of Kohl's Ranch, 17 mi. (27 km) east on Ariz. 260, visit ※ ₰ **Zane Grey's Cabin** (602/478-4243), open daily Mar.-Nov., a little mountain lodge where the famous author of westerns wrote some of his best-sellers, including *To the Last Man.*

After another ten miles on Ariz. 260, turn left on Old Rim Rd. toward the enchanting ※ **Woods Canyon Lake, Bear Canyon Lake,** and **Knoll Lake.** This picturesque little mountain road (to be avoided in winter or bad weather) snakes along the ridges of Tonto National Forest before rejoining Ariz. 87 a little north of **Strawberry,** a hill resort much appreciated by inhabitants of Phoenix seeking relief from the city's midsummer heat. Following Ariz. 87 about 5 mi. (8 km) south of the Mormon village of **Pine,** take a look at the ※ **Tonto Natural Bridge,** the world's largest natural arch of travertine limestone; 400 ft (121 m) across, it rises 183 ft (55 m) above the waters of Pine Creek, a tributary of the Verde River.

Return to Phoenix, 100 mi. (163 km) south, on Ariz. 87. This two- or three-day trip is particularly recommended for lovers of wide-open spaces and woodland hikes.

Where to Stay En Route

IN PAYSON. The **Paysonglo Lodge,** 1005 S. Beeline Hwy., Payson, AZ 85541 (602/474-2382). 33 rms. Small, very comfortable motel, the ideal base for a number of excursions into Tonto National Forest. **I–M**

※₰₰ **NAVAJOLAND** (Canyon de Chelly, Monument Valley, etc.; about 250 mi., 400 km, NE via I-17, U.S. 89, and U.S. 160): The land of the Hopi and Navajo; see Chapter 40 on Navajoland.

₰₰ **OAK CREEK CANYON** (322 mi., 515 km, round trip via I-17N, Ariz. 69N, U.S. Alt. 89N, Ariz. 179S, and I-17S): First stop is **Arcosanti,** the futurist city of architect Paolo Soleri (see "Nearby Excursions," above). Then follow Ariz. 69 to ※ ₰₰ **Prescott,** founded in 1864 and once capital of the Arizona Territory, which to this day retains something of a frontier-town flavor. Witness the interesting Indian material in the **Smoki Museum,** 143 N. Arizona Ave. (602/445-7615), open Tues.-Sun., June-Sept. (by appointment the rest of the year); also the group of buildings from 1860–1880 which constitutes the **Sharlot Hall Museum,** 415 W. Gurley St. (602/445-3122), open Tues.-Sun, including the **Governor's Mansion, Old Fort Misery,** and the **John C. Frémont House.** Don't miss it. Prescott is also the scene every July 4 of a rodeo famous throughout the West. Lovely pinewoods around the town.

Some 30 mi. (48 km) farther north, you'll come to the remarkable little mining town of ※ ₰₰ **Jerome,** now a kind of ghost town, with little wooden houses clinging to the mountainside; its population has fallen from 15,000 in 1929 to fewer than 500 today. Many craft shops, art galleries, and restaurants; mining museum on Main St., open daily. **Jerome State Historic Park** on U.S.

89A (602/634-5381), open daily, traces the history of Jimmy "Rawhide" Douglas, the picturesque founder of the United Verde Mine. You shouldn't miss Jerome.

Continue north on U.S. Alt. 89 to **Cottonwood,** a tourist resort in the Verde Valley, where you'll be very near **Tuzigoot National Monument,** the ruins of a 12th-century Indian pueblo with no fewer than 92 enormous rooms. Archeological museum, on Broadway (602/634-5564). Open daily. Worth the side trip.

Your next stop, the charming ☼ ⌂ **Sedona,** once a pioneer town, is now a renowned resort with a flourishing artists' colony; the painter Max Ernst lived here from 1945 to 1953. Stroll through the streets of **Tlaquepaque,** the business district with its original Mexican houses.

From Sedona you can conveniently visit ⌂⌂ **Oak Creek Canyon,** just north of the town: a splendid rocky gorge 16 mi. (26 km) long, whose walls display a range of ocher, yellow, and white hues; it's almost as spectacular as the Grand Canyon of the Colorado, and many westerns have been shot here. It's scenery you mustn't miss.

Leaving Sedona along Ariz. 179 and I-17S, you'll come to ☼ ⌂⌂ **Montezuma Castle National Monument,** an extraordinary cave dwelling five floors high, perched 70 ft (21 m) above the ground in a cleft of the cliff's rock. Built by the Sinagua Indians, it dates from the 13th century, and is so remarkably preserved that it is one of the finest monuments of primitive culture in the U.S. Although you're not allowed inside, you shouldn't miss it. Visitor center open daily; for information, call 602/567-3322.

On the way back to Phoenix, stop at the ☼ ⌂ **Fort Verde State Historic Park,** 2 mi. (3 km) east of Camp Verde. This 1870s cavalry fort on U.S. 279 (602/567-3275), open daily, was the U.S. Army's principal base for its many operations against the Apache Indians; it has now been splendidly restored, and is worth the side trip.

This very full three- to four-day journey would be worth the trip to Arizona all by itself, but you can combine it conveniently with a visit to the Grand Canyon (see Chapter 41) or to Navajoland (see Chapter 40).

Where to Stay En Route

IN PRESCOTT. The ⌂ **Sierra Inn,** 809 White Spar Rd., Prescott, AZ 86301 (602/445-1250). 49 rms. Inviting, comfortable motel, open year round. **I–M**

Motel 6, 1111 E. Sheldon St., Prescott, AZ 86301 (602/776-0160). Small, well-run low-priced motel; this place is ideal for budget travelers. **B**

IN SEDONA. ☼ ⌂⌂⌂ **Los Abrigados,** 160 Portal Lane, Sedona, AZ 86336 (602/282-1777). 187 suites. Luxurious Spanish Colonial–style tourist complex; lovely gardens. **E–VE**

Poco Diablo Resort, Ariz. 179, Sedona, AZ 86336 (602/282-7333). 144 rms. Charming little vacation hotel w. very comfortable individual villas standing in a garden. **M–E**

Sky Ranch Lodge, Airport Rd., Sedona, AZ 86336 (602/282-6400). 62 rms. Conventional but inviting motel overlooking Oak Creek Canyon. Good value. **I–M**

Where to Eat En Route

IN JEROME. The ⌂ **Jerome Palace,** 410 Clark St. (634-5262). Lunch/dinner Fri., Sat., and Sun. only. Picturesque little Victorian-style rest. **B–I**

IN SEDONA. ♟ **Shugrue's,** 2250 W. Ariz. 89A (602/282-2943). Breakfast/ lunch/dinner daily. Attractive, contemporary décor and cuisine. **B–I**

☀🔔 **PETRIFIED FOREST NATIONAL PARK** (225 mi., 360 km, NE via Ariz. 87 and I-40): The world's largest petrified forest, with innumerable animal and vegetable fossils. At the southern entry to the park, on U.S. 180, you can visit an interesting museum explaining the process of fossilization. The nearby **Painted Desert** displays canyons, mesas, and pillars of stratified rock in a striking palette of colors; well worth the detour. See Chapter 40 on Navajoland.

TUCSON AND SOUTHERN ARIZONA (370 mi., 592 km, round trip via Ariz. 87, I-10S, U.S. 80S, Ariz. 82W, Ariz. 83N, I-10N, and U.S. 89N): This spectacular tour, requiring four or five days, begins with a visit to ☀ 🔱🔱 **Casa Grande Ruins National Monument** (see "Nearby Excursions," above). Continuing south on I-10 you'll come to ☀ 🔱 **Saguaro National Monument** (602/ 883-6366), open daily year round, a fine wildland park full of giant cactus (saguaro) growing to 50 ft (15 m), such as you might find in the Sonora Desert. Spectacular flowering in May and June.

Next stop, ☀ **Tucson.** Rearing up like a mirage from its mountains and deserts, this former capital of Arizona has experienced, since its foundation in 1775, some of the most exciting times recorded in the Far West. Belonging in turn to the Apache, the Spaniards, the Mexicans, and finally the Americans, Tucson (which the locals pronounce "Too-Sahn") was described by 19th-century travelers as "the kingdom of crime, vice, and debauchery," or in short, "the worst hellhole in the West." Today a favorite stopping place for tourists as well as a vigorous commercial metropolis, Tucson has an interesting museum of Native American culture, the ☀ 🔱 **Arizona State Museum,** Park Ave. and University Blvd. (602/ 621-6281), open daily; the splendid ☀ 🔱🔱 **Mission San Xavier del Bac,** San Xavier Rd. (602/294-2624), open Mon.-Sat., a masterpiece of Spanish Colonial baroque; one of the most beautiful zoological/botanical gardens in the country, the 🔱🔱 **Arizona-Sonora Desert Museum,** Kinney Rd. (602/8831380), open daily; a remarkable museum of aviation displaying more than 130 aircraft of all periods, the 🔱🔱 **Pima Air Museum,** 6000 E. Valencia Rd. (602/574-9658); and 🔱 **Old Tucson,** an engaging mock–Far West village built in 1939 for making western movies, at 201 S. Kinney Rd. (602/883-6457), open daily.

Between Tucson and Tombstone, 70 mi. south, make a detour to 🔱 **Colossal Cave,** Colossal Cave Rd. (602/791-7677), open daily, a spectacular cavern with many marine fossils, proving that in a prehistoric era the Arizona desert was covered by the ocean.

Last stop, ☀ 🔱🔱 **Tombstone,** the Far West's most famous ghost town, scene of the bloody "Gunfight at the O.K. Corral." Immortalized in many westerns, Tombstone still has many buildings dating from its glory days; if you're nostalgic about the Winning of the West, here's the place to daydream. Don't miss it.

Back to Phoenix via U.S. 89, which runs from the Mexican to the Canadian border; also known as the 🔱🔱 **Pinal Pioneer Trail,** it's one of the most spectacular highways in the West.

For more details on the places, towns, and monuments mentioned in this itinerary, as well as for recommended accommodations and dining, see Chapter 43 on Tucson.

TUCSON ☖☖

□ □ □

And Southern Arizona

Rearing up like a mirage from the surrounding mountains and desert, this former capital (1867–1877) of the Arizona Territory has lived through more exciting times, in its two-century life span, than almost any other city in the Far West. First Indian, then Spanish (they built the first fort in 1776 to fend off the attacks of the Apaches), then Mexican, and finally American, Tucson (pronounced "Too-Sahn") was described in the 19th century as "the kingdom of crime, vice, and debauchery." With its dozens of dangerous saloons, dubious gaming houses, and ill-famed brothels, it was dubbed by contemporary newspapers "The Worst Hellhole in the West."

As in too many cities where the bulldozer has been allowed to run riot, Tucson has in the last three decades razed to the ground its old residential downtown, replacing it with graceless air-conditioned office buildings. But there are still interesting fragments of the city's heritage, such as the enchanting **Mission San Xavier del Bac,** called "the white dove of the desert," or **Frémont House.** And there are always wonderful things to see in southern Arizona: the giant cactus of **Saguaro National Park;** the wild landscapes of the **Chiricaua National Monument,** once the stronghold of the Indian chiefs Cochise and Geronimo; the Spanish mission at **Tumacacori;** the living museum of the **Arizona-Sonora Desert;** and the epic town of **Tombstone,** made notorious by the famous "Battle at the O.K. Corral."

A favorite stopping place for tourists, Tucson is also a lively business metropolis, ranking fifth among major American cities in its economic growth rate. Because of its exceptionally low humidity, it performed an odd service for the airline industry during the great world oil crisis of 1973–1974; many American and European airlines lacking fuel to fly their jets parked them at Tucson airport, where they could be left without fear of rust.

The singer Linda Rondstadt was born in Tucson.

BASIC FACTS: State of Arizona. Area Code: 602. Time Zone: Mountain Time. ZIP Code: 85702. Founded: 1775. Approximate population: city, 370,000; metropolitan area, 700,000.

CLIMATE: Tucson averages 318 days of clear skies every year, one of the highest figures in the U.S. The persistent sunshine results in oppressive temperatures in summer (July avg., 89°F, 32°C), and scarcely less so in spring and fall. However, the exceptionally dry air and the cool of the desert evening make the heat bearable. With a Dec.-Jan. average of 53°F (12°C), winter is a joy if you like your days brisk and sunny.

DISTANCES: Albuquerque, 441 mi. (705 km); Los Angeles, 512 mi. (819 km); Phoenix, 118 mi. (189 km); San Antonio, 883 mi. (1,412 km); San Diego, 415 mi. (664 km).

ARRIVAL & TRANSIT INFORMATION

AIRPORT: Tucson International Airport (TUS), 7 mi. (11 km) south (573-8000). First municipal airport opened in U.S. (1919).

AIRLINES: American (882-0331), America West (623-8917), Continental (623-3700), Northwest (622-2014), TWA (624-2771), United (622-1214), and USAir (toll free 800/428-4322).

CITY LINK: The cab fare from the airport to downtown is about $18–$20; time, 20 min. Bus: Arizona Stagecoach (889-9681), serves principal downtown hotels; fare, $8–$12; time, 25–35 min., depending on destination. Municipal bus: Sun Tran Line No. 8, until 10 p.m.; fare, 60¢.

The rudimentary public-transportation (bus) system provided by Sun Tran (792-9222), the very high cab fares given the size of the city, and the many fascinating excursions into the surrounding country combine to suggest the wisdom of renting a car with unlimited mileage.

CAR RENTALS (at Tucson International Airport unless otherwise noted): Allstate, 550 N. Alvernon Way (881-4322), a local renter with favorable rates; Avis (294-1494); Budget (889-8800); Dollar (573-1100); Hertz (294-7616); National (573-8050); and Thrifty, 7051 S. Tucson Blvd. (889-5761). For downtown locations, consult the local telephone directory.

LIMOUSINES: Carey Limousine (toll free 800/336-4646) and Dav El Limousines (toll free 800/922-0343).

TAXIS: Cabs may not be hailed on the street, but may be summoned by phone: Allstate Cab (798-1111), Checker Cab (623-1133), and Yellow Cab (624-6611).

TRAIN: AMTRAK station, 400 E. Toole St. (toll free 800/872-7245).

BUS: Greyhound, 2 S. Fourth Ave. (792-0972).

INFORMATION & TOURS

TOURIST INFORMATION: The **Tucson Convention and Visitors Bureau,** 130 S. Scott Ave., AZ 85701 (602/624-1889).

GUIDED TOURS: **Gray Line Tours** (bus) (622-8811): Conducted bus tours of the city and surroundings; serves principal hotels.

Classic Tours Co. (bus), 5741 N. Trisha Lane (327-3333): Conducted tours of the city and surroundings in double-decker London bus. Reservations needed.

SIGHTS, ATTRACTIONS, & ACTIVITIES

ADVENTURES: **Balloon America** (balloon), Westin La Paloma Resort, 3800 E. Sunrise (299-7744): Hot-air balloon trips over Tucson and the surrounding desert; spectacular. Free bus shuttle. Daily, year round.

Saguaro Whitewater (boat), 3223 E. Lee St. (326-6206). Rafting down Salt River Canyon; one-day trip. Spectacular. Daily, Feb.-Sept.

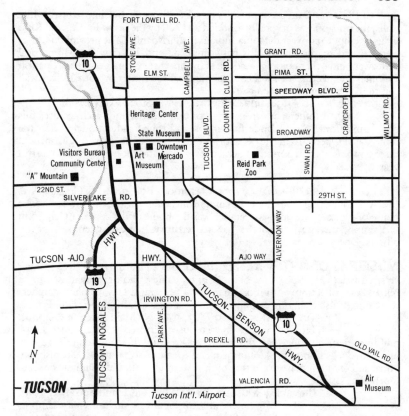

Southern Arizona Balloon Excursion (balloon), 926 W. Grant Rd. (624-3599): Hot-air-balloon trips over Tucson and the surrounding desert; spectacular. Daily, year round.

Sunshine Jeep Tours (Jeep), 2600 W. Ina Rd. (742-7000): Half-day or longer Jeep trips into the desert around Tucson.

ARCHITECTURAL HIGHLIGHTS: � **Pima County Courthouse,** 155 N. Church Ave. (792-8011): An old baroque building whose dome is covered with colored tiles in geometric patterns. A mixture of Spanish Colonial style, with columns, arches, and carved façade, and typical southwestern architecture. Pretty interior courtyard with fountain; you should certainly take a look. Open Mon.-Sat.

☀ **University of Arizona,** Park Ave. and University Blvd. (621-2211): Founded in 1885, this is now one of the most important universities in the Southwest, with 35,000 students. The huge campus, covering 325 acres (132 ha.), is embellished with lovely gardens and flowerbeds and several remarkable buildings: the **McKale Memorial Center,** the **College of Law,** the **Library,** and the **College of Medicine,** as well as several interesting museums described below. A sight you should see.

CHURCHES/SYNAGOGUES: ☀ ⛪ **Mission San Xavier del Bac,** San Xavier Rd., 9 mi. (14 km) SW of Tucson on I-19 (294-2624): Nicknamed "the white

dove of the desert" on account of its elegant silhouette and immaculate white walls, the mission was originally founded in 1700 by the Jesuit Fr. Eusebio Kino in his attempt to convert the Pima Indians to Christianity. The present buildings were erected by the Franciscans between 1783 and 1797; with asymmetrical belltowers and ocher-colored façade, it is the finest surviving example of Spanish Colonial architecture in the U.S. Splendid baroque interior with Indian wall paintings. Don't miss it; open daily.

    🔔 **St. Augustine Cathedral,** 192 S. Stone Ave. (623-6351): Another perfect example of Spanish religious architecture, this one dating from 1896. Wonderful carved sandstone façade, modeled after the cathedral at Querétaro in Mexico, surmounted by a statue of St. Augustine and three symbols of the desert: the yucca, the saguaro, and the horned toad. Worth a visit; open daily.

HISTORIC BUILDINGS: ☀️🔔 John C. Frémont House, 151 S. Granada Ave.

(622-0956): Dating from the 1880s and furnished in period, this modest adobe house of typically Mexican appearance was the home of the explorer Gen. John C. Frémont, then governor of the Arizona Territory. Interesting temporary exhibitions. Open Wed.-Sat.

MUSEUMS OF ART: ☀️🔔 Center for Creative Photography, 843 E. Uni-

versity Blvd. (621-7968): One of the country's finest photography museums. A remarkable collection, with more than 100 of the most famous photographers represented; also changing exhibits. A must for camera buffs. Open Sun.-Fri.

    🔔 **Tucson Museum of Art,** 140 N. Main Ave. (624-2333): Housed in six meticulously restored 19th-century adobe buildings that were once part of the Tucson Presidio, this museum offers a very impressive selection of pre-Columbian and Mexican art, as well as Spanish Colonial and contemporary art in the southwestern U.S. Should definitely be seen. Open Tues.-Sun.

    ☀️🔔 **University Museum of Art,** Olive Rd. and Speedway Blvd. (621-7567): Splendid art museum on the university campus, whose contents include a part of the famous Kress collection of Renaissance paintings, and an impressive group of modern paintings and sculptures from the Leonard Pfeiffer and E. J. Gallagher collections: Picasso, Rodin, Moore, Andrew Wyeth, etc. A must-see. Open daily.

MUSEUMS OF SCIENCE AND HISTORY: 🔔 Arizona Historical Society,

949 E. 2nd St. at Park Ave. (628-5774): History of Arizona from the Spanish settlers to the present day; geological specimens; costume museum; well-stocked library on the history of the West. Should be seen; open daily.

    🔔 **Arizona State Museum,** Park Ave. and University Blvd. (621-6281): Fascinating panorama of prehistoric (as far as 10,000 years back) and contemporary Native American culture; one of the best archeological collections in the Southwest. Don't miss it; open daily.

    ☀️🔔 **Grace H. Flandrau Planetarium,** Cherry Ave. and University Blvd. (621-7827): Very modern space museum and planetarium of innovative spherical design. Observations through the telescope every evening. For budding astronomers; open Tues.-Sun.

    ☀️🔔 **Fort Lowell Museum,** 2900 N. Craycroft Rd. (885-3832): Partly rebuilt military post, which was important in the Indian wars at the end of the 19th century. Interesting Apache Wars Museum. Must definitely be seen; open Wed.-Sat.

    🔔 **Mineralogical Museum,** North Dr. Geology Bldg. (621-4227): 10,000 different mineral specimens; large collection of precious stones from around the world and Arizona fossils. Should be seen; open Mon.-Fri.

☼☖☖ **Pima Air Museum,** 6000 E. Valencia Rd., 9 mi. (14 km) east to exit 269 on I-10 (574-9658): More than 130 civil and military aircraft, from the end of the '30s to the present day, collected in one place. One of the country's finest private aircraft collections; a spectacular history of American aviation from the venerable *Liberator* to the gigantic B-52 *Stratofortress.* Don't miss it; open daily.

PANORAMAS: ☼ ☖ Mount Lemmon, 35 mi. (56 km) NE on Mount

Lemmon Hwy.: Fine view over Tucson Valley and the surrounding mountains; reached over a lovely scenic highway.

☖ **Sentinel Peak Park,** Sentinel Peak Rd. at Congress St.: Spectacular view of the city, particularly at nightfall when the lights of Tucson are twinkling at your feet. The giant "A" on the mountainside is the brand of the University of Arizona. Park open from 7 a.m. to 10 p.m.

PARKS AND GARDENS: ☖ Randolph City Park, Broadway and Alvernon

Way (325-2811): Huge, shady park in the center of town; two public golf courses, pool, 24 tennis courts, rose garden, and mini-zoo. Open daily.

☖ **Reid Park,** 22nd St. and Country Club Rd. (791-4873): Pleasant oasis of greenery in the heart of Tucson. Pretty rose garden; small but well-designed zoo; picnic area; sizeable lake (fishing permitted). Open daily.

☼☖ **Tohono Chul Park,** 7366 N. Paseo del Norte (742-6455): Glorious 35-acre (14-ha.) garden displaying more than 400 species of arid-zone and desert plants, grouped by genus. Paths for strolling. Also a bird sanctuary: from roadrunners to hummingbirds and from cactus wrens to woodpeckers. A must for nature lovers. Open daily.

☼☖☖ **Tucson Mountain Park,** 12 mi. (19 km) west via Ariz. 86 and Kinney Rd. (883-4200): The "green lung" of Tucson; 16,000 acres (6,500 ha.) of sun-scorched ocher rocks, succulents, and giant cactus. This is the park most visited by tourists; the western part of the Saguaro National Monument (see "Nearby Excursions," below), including Old Tucson (see "Theme Parks," below) and the extraordinary zoological/botanic garden of the Arizona-Sonora Desert Museum (see "Nearby Excursions," below). Don't fail to see it. Open daily.

PERFORMING ARTS: For daily listings of all shows and cultural events, con-

sult the entertainment pages of the daily papers *Arizona Daily Star* (morning) and *Tucson Citizen* (evening).

Centennial Hall, University of Arizona Campus, University Blvd. (621-3341): Classical and jazz concerts, Broadway hits, ballet, top-performer recitals.

Community Center Music Hall, 260 S. Church Ave.: Concerts, recitals, opera. Home of the Arizona Opera (293-4336) and the Arizona Light Opera Company (Oct.-Mar.), and of the Tucson Symphony, under principal conductor Robert Bernhardt (882-8585) (Oct.-May).

Community Center Theater, 260 S. Church Ave. (622-2823): Contemporary and classic theater. Home of the Arizona Theater Company (Oct.-Apr.).

Gaslight Theatre, 7000 E. Tanque Verde Rd. (886-9428): Musical comedies, melodrama, family shows. Year round.

Invisible Theater, 1400 N. First Ave. (882-9721): Experimental and off-Broadway theater (Sept.-June).

Reid Park Bandshell, 22nd St. and Country Club Rd. (791-4873): Open-air classical concerts by the Tucson Pops Orchestra (May-July).

SHOPPING: Old Town Artisans, 186 N. Meyer Ave. (623-6024): Some 150 local artists and craftspeople exhibit their work in a picturesque 19th-century adobe building in the heart of old Tucson. Lovers of authentic Indian crafts will go to **Desert Son,** 2900 E. Broadway; **Kaibab Shop,** 2841 N. Campbell Ave.; and **Tom Bahti's,** 4300 N. Campbell Ave. Anywhere else, you may often find that your prized Indian artifact is stamped "Made in Hong Kong."

SPECIAL EVENTS: For the exact schedule of events below, consult the **Tucson Convention and Visitors Bureau** (see "Tourist Information," above).
   Fiesta de los Vaqueros (Feb.): Tucson's big annual event since 1928. History parade, concerts, dances, rodeos.
   Tucson Festival (Mar.-Apr.): Mexican fiesta, Indian dances, shows, opera, parades through town, craft exhibitions.
   Yaqui Indian Easter Celebration (Easter): Very colorful Indian festival.
   Pima County Fair (Apr.): Big agricultural fair; horse show, Indian art exhibition. Guaranteed local color.
   San Xavier Fiesta (Apr.): Religious procession, Indian dances, fireworks commemorating the founding of the San Xavier del Bac Mission.

SPORTS: Tucson is home to one professional major-league team for spring training, and a minor-league team:
   Baseball: Cleveland Indians, Hi Corbett Field (791-4096): spring training, Mar.; Tucson Toros, Hi Corbett Field (325-2621), Apr.-Aug.

THEME PARKS: ☼ ⚱ **Old Tucson,** 201 S. Kinney Rd. in Tucson Mountain Park (883-6457): Built in 1939 as a setting for the movie *Arizona,* this replica of Tucson in the 1860s has 100 houses and saloons, a prison, a gold mine, and a steam railroad. Has been and still is used from time to time for movies and TV series (*Rio Bravo, Gunfight at the OK Corral, High Chaparral,* and so on). Mock gunfights, stunt shows, stagecoach rides. Entertaining; open daily.

WINTER SPORTS RESORTS: ☼ ⚱ **Mount Lemmon Ski Valley,** 35 mi. (56 km) on Lemmon Hwy. (576-1321): Three lifts; open late Dec. to mid-Apr. The southernmost ski resort in the U.S.

ACCOMMODATIONS
See the listing of toll-free numbers in the Appendix.

Room Rates in Tucson	
B (Budget)	up to $30
I (Inexpensive)	$30–$60
M (Moderate)	$60–$90
E (Expensive)	$90–$140
VE (Very Expensive)	$140 and up

Personal Favorites (in order of preference)
   ☼ 🕯🕯🕯🕯 **Westin La Paloma** (vic.), 3800 E. Sunrise Dr., AZ 85718 (602/742-6000; toll free, see Westin). 486 rms, A/C, color

TV, in-rm movies. AE, CB, DC, MC, V. Free parking, pool, ten tennis courts, two golf courses, sauna, health club, three rests. (including La Villa), three bars, 24-hr rm svce, disco, free crib. *Note:* Brand-new luxury vacation and convention hotel a 15-min. drive from dwntwn, at the foot of the Santa Catalina Mountains on 650 acres (263 ha.) of beautiful untamed scenery. Very successful Spanish mission architecture, w. pastel-washed arcades and flower-filled gardens. Spacious, well-designed rms w. mini-bars; excellent svce; comprehensive sports facilities. Caters to upscale business clients and well-heeled tourists. The golf courses were designed by former U.S. champion Jack Nicklaus. Free airport shuttle. Lots of quality and style. **VE, but lower rates out of season**

Sheraton El Conquistador (vic.), 10000 N. Oracle Rd., AZ 85704 (602/742-7000; toll free, see Sheraton). 440 rms, A/C, color TV, in-rm movies. AE, CB, DC, MC, V. Free parking, two pools, 16 tennis courts, two golf courses, putting green, health club, sauna, horseback riding, two rests. (including the White Dove), coffeeshop, bars, 24-hr rm svce, nightclub, boutiques, free crib, concierge. *Note:* One of the most modern and luxurious resort hotels in the Southwest; a sort of oasis in the desert a 30-min. drive north of Tucson. Intimate, inviting little three-story buildings surrounded by gardens and palm trees in the shadow of the Santa Catalina Mountains. Elegant, comfortable rms w. mini-bars and private balconies or patios, the best overlooking the huge pool in the middle of the gardens. Exemplary reception and svce; very comprehensive sports facilities. If you want a complete change of scene, this is it. **E–VE, but lower rates out of season**

Doubletree Inn (nr. dwntwn), 445 S. Alvernon Way, AZ 85711 (602/881-4200; toll free 800/528-0444). 296 rms, A/C, color TV, in-rm movies. AE, CB, DC, MC, V. Free parking, pool, three tennis courts, rest. (Cactus Rose), coffeeshop, bar, 24-hr rm svce, disco, free crib. *Note:* Right opposite Randolph Park, this large, modern nine-story hotel is a favorite w. business travelers. Spacious rms w. refrigerators and private patios. Efficient, attentive svce; free airport limo. Group clientele; interesting wknd discounts. **E–VE, but lower rates out of season**

Holiday Inn Broadway (dwntwn), 181 W. Broadway, AZ 85701 (602/624-8711; toll free, see Holiday Inns). 310 rms, A/C, color TV, in-rm movies. AE, CB, DC, MC, V. Free garage, pool, rest., bar, rm svce, nightclub, hrdrsr, free crib. *Note:* Typical modern hotel a stone's throw from La Placita and its shopping. Serviceable comfort and facilities; so-so rest. Group and business clientele. A Holiday Inn at its best; very central location; good value on balance. **M–E, but lower rates out of season**

Motel 6 East (nr. dwntwn), 1031 E. Benson Hwy., AZ 85714 (602/628-1264). 146 rms, A/C, color TV, free in-rm movies. DC, MC, V. Free parking, pool, adjoining 24-hr coffeeshop. *Note:* The best buy in Tucson if you're driving through; functional comfort at unbeatable prices. 10 min. from dwntwn. **B**

Other Accommodations (from top bracket to budget)

Loews Ventana Canyon Resort (vic.), 7000 N. Resort Dr., AZ 85715 (602/299-2020; toll free, see Loews). 398 rms, A/C, color TV, in-rm movies. AE, CB, DC, MC, V. Free parking, two pools, ten tennis courts, two golf courses, putting green, health club, sauna, three rests. (including the Ventana Room), bars, 24-hr rm svce, disco, boutiques, free crib, concierge. *Note:* On a mesa w. a splendid view of Tucson Valley 3,000 ft (900 m) below and the surrounding mountains, this luxury hotel boasts a superb wild setting. The typically southwestern building overlooks an 80-ft (24-m) waterfall which feeds a little lake lying below the hotel. Spacious, inviting rms w. balconies and refrigerators; attentive svce; quality rest. Wonderful golf courses in the open desert. A very good place to stay, 20 min. from dwntwn. **VE, but lower rates out of season**

☀☃⚑⚑⚑ **Arizona Inn** (nr. dwntwn), 2200 E. Elm St., AZ 85719 (602/ 325-1541; toll free 800/421-1093). 85 cottages (three-quarters w. A/C), color TV. AE, MC, V. Free parking, pool, two tennis courts, outdoor sports, rest., bar, rm svce, free breakfast, free crib, concierge. *Note:* One of the most famous hotels in Arizona since 1932; a 14-acre (5-ha.) flowery, shady oasis dotted w. little adobe cottages. Elegant, luxurious rms w. private patios or balconies. Faultless reception and svce; very acceptable rest.; well-stocked library. Very interesting AP packages for a dream vacation. A stone's throw from dwntwn. **E–VE, but lower rates out of season**

☀☃⚑⚑⚑ **Westward Look** (vic.), 245 E. Ina Rd., AZ 85704 (602/297-1151; toll free 800/722-2500). 245 rms, A/C, color TV, in-rm movies. AE, CB, DC, MC, V. Free parking, three pools, eight tennis courts, health club, horseback riding, rest. (Gold Room), bar, rm svce, disco, free crib. *Note:* Luxury hotel in 84 acres (34 ha.) of garden and woodland in the foothills of the Santa Catalina Mountains, w. spectacular view over Tucson and the valley. Pretty one- or two-floor cottages around the pool, w. very comfortable rms (mini-bars and private patios). Worthwhile AP and MAP packages; the rest. is highly regarded. Cheerful, friendly svce. A Tucson landmark for 40 years. **E–VE, but lower rates out of season**

⚑⚑ **Best Western Aztec Inn** (nr. dwntwn), 102 N. Alvernon Way, AZ 85711 (602/795-0330; toll free, see Best Western). 156 rms, A/C, color TV. AE, CB, DC, MC, V. Free parking, pool, sauna, rest., bar, rm svce, hrdrsr, free crib. *Note:* Very engaging Spanish Colonial architecture and interior; comfortable rms w. refrigerators, the best overlooking the charming patio with pool. Rms w. kitchenettes and no-smoking rms available. Efficient reception and svce; good value 10 min. from dwntwn. **M, but lower rates out of season**

⚑ **La Quinta Inn** (nr. dwntwn), 665 N. Freeway, AZ 85705 (602/622-6491; toll free, see La Quinta Motor Inns). 132 rms, A/C, color TV, in-rm movies. AE, CB, DC, MC, V. Free parking, pool, adjacent 24-hr coffeeshop, valet svce. *Note:* Elegant Mexican-style building; huge, intelligently designed rms w. separate sleeping alcoves. Friendly reception; very good value. **I–M**

⚑ **Rodeway Inn** (nr. dwntwn), 810 E. Benson Hwy., AZ 85713 (602/884-5800; toll free, see Rodeway Inns). 100 rms, A/C, color TV, in-rm movies. AE, CB, DC, MC, V. Free parking, pool, adjoining rest. *Note:* Relatively modest but well-run motel; comfortable rms. Ideal if you're driving; halfway between the airport and dwntwn. **I**

GUEST RANCHES: Guest ranches, commonly known as "dude ranches," are the ideal solution if you like open-air vacations and horseback riding; they offer luxury comforts and svce while you play cowboy.

⚑⚑ **Hacienda del Sol** (vic.), 5601 N. Hacienda del Sol Rd., AZ 85718 (602/299-1501). 45 rms (a third w. A/C), color TV. AE, CB, DC, MC, V. Free parking, pool, tennis court, health club, horseback riding, outdoor sports, rest., bar, rm svce, library. *Note:* Traditional adobe buildings; very inviting rms w. views of nearby mountains. Friendly svce. Open Nov.-May only. 20 min. from dwntwn; free airport limo. **E–VE (AP)**

☀☃⚑⚑⚑ **Tanque Verde Guest Ranch** (vic.), 14301 E. Speedway Blvd., AZ 85710 (602/296-6275). 58 rms, A/C, color TV. AE, MC, V. Free parking, two pools, five tennis courts, health club, sauna, putting green, horseback riding, outdoor sports, rest., bar, disco, crib $15. *Note:* Old stock ranch and stagecoach station dating from 1868; picturesque rustic décor. Spacious rms w. refrigerators and private patios, some w. fireplaces. Open-air barbecues; excursions in the area. Informal but elegant atmosphere; a very good place. Free airport limo. Open year round. **VE (AP), but lower rates out of season**

☼ ♀♀ **White Stallion Ranch** (vic.), 9251 Twin Peaks Rd., AZ 85743 (602/297-0252). 30 rms, no A/C; color TV (in lounge only). No credit cards. Free parking, pool, two tennis courts, horseback riding, outdoor sports, rest., bar, free crib. *Note:* Authentic ranch, straight out of a western movie, with herds and real cowboys, on 4,000 acres (1,600 ha.) of untamed land. Comforts of rather a rustic nature, but engaging family atmosphere. Open-air barbecues, rodeos, horse-and-cart rides. Free airport limo. Open Oct.-May only. **E–VE (AP)**

Airport Accommodations

♀♀ **Best Western Inn at the Airport** (vic.), 7060 S. Tucson Blvd., AZ 85706 (602/746-0271; toll free, see Best Western). 148 rms, A/C, color TV, in-rm movies. AE, CB, DC, MC, V. Free valet parking, pool, rest. (The Other Place), bar, rm svce, free breakfast, free crib. *Note:* Typical airport motel, inviting and comfortable. Spacious, well-soundproofed rms w. balconies or patios, some w. refrigerators. Exceptionally friendly, cheerful svce. Free airport limo. Business clientele. Excellent value. **M–E**

YMCA/Youth Hostels

Lohse Memorial YMCA (dwntwn), 516 N. Fifth Ave. (602/624-7471). 26 rms; men only. Rather abridged comforts, but very central location. Pool.

RESTAURANTS

Tucson Restaurant Prices	
(per person, excluding drinks and service charges)	
B (Budget)	up to $15
I (Inexpensive)	$15–$25
M (Moderate)	$25–$40
E (Expensive)	$40–$60
VE (Very Expensive)	$60 and up

Personal Favorites (in order of preference)

☼ ♀♀♀ **Janos** (dwntwn), 150 N. Main Ave. (884-9426). A/C. Lunch Mon.-Fri., dinner Tues.-Sat.; closed Sun. and holidays. AE, MC, V. Jkt. *Specialties:* calzone w. goat cheese and spinach, roast duckling w. purée of red peppers and broiled shrimp, beef filet w. five kinds of pepper, sautéed veal w. pink peppercorns and salmon caviar, lobster w. papaya and champagne sauce, chicken w. chili and coriander stuffed w. broiled sausage. Menu changes regularly. Skimpy wine list. *Note:* The young chef Janos Wilder, 30-ish, bearded, and likeable, broke new ground when (in 1985) he opened the first rest. serving American nouvelle cuisine in Tucson, a city not theretofore overburdened w. good rests. Since then his success has never faltered. The rest. occupies a picturesque 19th-century adobe building w. exposed beams, a designated historic monument. Open-air dining on fine days. Excellent svce. Tucson's most inspired and imaginative food; resv. are a must. *American*. **M**

♟♟♟ **Café Terra Cotta** (nr. dwntwn), 4310 N. Campbell Ave. (577-8100). A/C. Lunch Mon.-Sat., dinner nightly; closed holidays. AE, DC, MC, V. *Specialties:* garlic custard w. warm salsa vinaigrette and herbed hazelnuts, roast chili pepper stuffed w. chicken and corn, prawns stuffed w. goat cheese, black bean and beef chili. Menu changes regularly. *Note:* Another talented newcomer on the local gastronomic scene. Inventive, praiseworthy contemporary southwestern cuisine; airy and comfortable décor; cheerful svce. Resv. requested. Excellent value. *American*. **I**

♟♟ **Scordato's** (nr. dwntwn), 4405 Speedway Blvd. (792-3055). A/C. Dinner only, Tues.-Sun.; closed Mon., early July, Thanksgiving, and Dec. 25. AE, CB, DC, MC, V. Jkt. *Specialties:* classic Italian food: veal Stresa, fresh homemade pasta, catch of the day, broiled prime cuts. Skimpy wine list. *Note:* On a height overlooking the city, this charming little house w. its tile roof is Tucson's oldest Italian rest., and one of the most popular. Elegant, romantic atmosphere. The veal, represented by no fewer than 13 different recipes on the menu, is the choicest reared in Wisconsin. Attentive svce; resv. requested. *Italian-continental*. **I–M**

♟♟ **La Fuente** (nr. dwntwn), 1749 N. Oracle Rd. (623-8659). A/C. Lunch/dinner Tues.-Sun.; closed Mon. and holidays. AE, MC, V. *Specialties:* flautas, tacos, enchiladas, carne a la tampiqueña, mole poblano (turkey in chocolate sauce). *Note:* The most authentic of Tucson's innumerable Mexican rests.; décor and atmosphere are tops in local color. The house margaritas are worth the trip. A landmark since 1963. Mariachi band evenings. *Mexican*. **B–I**

♟ **Pinnacle Peak** (vic.), 6541 Tanque Verde Rd. (886-5012). A/C. Dinner only, nightly; closed Thanksgiving and Dec. 25. MC, V. *Specialties:* choice steak and other meats, barbecued chicken, broiled fish. *Note:* Same successful formula as its sister spot in Phoenix: excellent beef cuts broiled over a mesquite fire. Pleasant western décor; locally popular. Well worth the 20-min. drive from dwntwn. No resv. *Steakhouse*. **I**

☼♟ **Samaniego House** (dwntwn), 222 S. Church Ave. (622-7790). A/C. Lunch/dinner Mon.-Sat.; closed Sun. and holidays. AE, CB, DC, MC, V. *Specialties:* sandwiches, ranch chow (steak w. spicy sauce), barbecued chicken, Mexican dishes, catch of the day. *Note:* Original 1881 colonial-style building with adobe walls and exposed beams. Typical local cuisine; nice atmosphere. In the heart of dwntwn Tucson. *American-Mexican*. **B–I**

Other Restaurants (from top bracket to budget)

☼♟♟♟ **Charles** (vic.), 6400 E. El Dorado Circle (296-7173). A/C. Lunch Mon.-Fri., dinner nightly; closed Memorial Day and July 4. AE, DC, MC, V. Jkt. *Specialties:* stuffed quail, lamb cutlets bouquetière, veal Charles béarnaise, game in season, steak Diane, cherries jubilee. Menu changes regularly. Fine wine list. *Note:* In an elegant freestone manor house which once belonged to the Pond cosmetics family, this luxury rest. serves some of the most refined traditional cuisine in Tucson. Very polished reception and svce; distinguished background music; prices to match. A lovely cypress avenue leads up to the rest. 20 min. from dwntwn; valet parking; resv. strongly advised. *Continental*. **I–M**

♟♟♟ **Daniel's** (nr. dwntwn), Plaza Palomino, 2900 N. Swan Rd. (742-3200). A/C. Lunch/dinner daily; closed holidays. AE,

CB, DC, MC, V. Jkt. *Specialties:* zuppa di pesce, spinach and smoked salmon pasta, seafood vermicelli, veal cutlet stuffed w. ham and cheese, lamb cutlet Provençal, filet of beef w. green peppercorns. Fine list of American wines. *Note:* The rest., opened in 1986 by Daniel Scordato, heir of a dynasty of local restaurateurs, is attempting to produce a contemporary version of classic French and Italian cuisine. Elegant modern décor in pastel tones of peach. Somewhat ceremonious svce. A fashionable place; resv. advised. *Italian-French.* **I–M**

Jerome's (vic.), 6958 E. Tanque Verde Rd. (721-0311). A/C. Lunch Tues.-Fri., dinner Tues.-Sun., Sun. brunch; closed Mon. and Dec. 25. AE, MC, V. Jkt. *Specialties:* Cajun calzone (w. spiced Louisiana sausage), blackened redfish, Créole and Cajun dishes, broiled fish. *Note:* With its paneled walls, exposed beams, and big brick fireplace, the décor is more Boston than Louisiana, but Jerome's food is authentic New Orleans. Swift, efficient svce; successful, so resv. advised. 25 min. from dwntwn. *Créole.* **I–M**

Palomino (nr. dwntwn), 2959 N. Swan Rd. (795-5561). A/C. Dinner only, Mon.-Sat.; closed Sun., holidays, and Aug. AE, CB, DC, MC, V. Jkt. *Specialties:* bouillabaisse, lamb chops bouquetière, sautéed sweetbreads, scampi, catch of the day. *Note:* The proprietor is of Greek origin, the setting typically Castilian, the food French or Italian inspired, and the result a complete success. Agreeable background music. Locally popular; resv. advised. *Continental-American.* **I–M**

Olive Tree (nr. dwntwn), 7000 E. Tanque Verde Rd. (298-1845). A/C. Lunch/dinner Mon.-Sat.; closed Sun. and holidays. AE, MC, V. *Specialties:* lamb chops, Greek dishes, broiled fish. *Note:* Enormously popular rest. 20 min. from dwntwn. Mainly Greek food, straightforward and tasty. Open patio w. fountain for open-air meals, or more romantic intimate dining room. Efficient svce; very good value; an excellent place. *Greek-continental.* **B–I**

El Charro (dwntwn), 311 N. Court Ave. (622-5465). A/C. Lunch/dinner daily, Sun. brunch; closed holidays. AE, CB, DC, MC, V. *Specialties:* tostada con carne seca, stuffed chile, chimichangas, topopo salad (chicken and avocado), burritos, pastelito de fruta, almendrado. *Note:* Typical Mexican rest., serving authentic food since 1922. In an 1887 building in the heart of old Tucson. Inviting patio for outdoor dining; diligent, friendly svce. Locally popular; excellent value. *Mexican.* **B**

Cafeterias / Fast Food

Piccadilly (nr. dwntwn), 6767 Broadway Blvd. (886-0529). Open daily (till 8:30 p.m.). No credit cards. Roast beef, fried chicken, homemade soups and desserts. Good cafeteria food at modest prices. Other location: 6767 Broadway Blvd. (886-0529).

BARS & NIGHTCLUBS

The Baron's (nr. dwntwn), 2401 S. Wilmot Rd. (747-3503). Trendy disco; locally popular. Open nightly. Also rest.

Doubletree Inn (nr. dwntwn), in the Doubletree Inn (see "Accommodations," above) (881-4200). Singles bar-disco much favored by the young professional crowd and the students of the nearby university. Noisy live rock. Open nightly.

Larry Colligan's Hidden Valley (vic.), 4825 N. Sabino Canyon Rd. (299-4941). Western disco with live music; warm atmosphere. Also a good steakhouse. Open nightly; 25 min. from dwntwn.

The Maverick (nr. dwntwn), 4700 22nd St. (748-0456). Country-and-western music; very cowboy atmosphere. Open nightly.

Paulo's Restaurant and Lounge (nr. dwntwn), 4915 E. Speedway Blvd. (325-2671). Piano bar, very popular locally; also a mediocre Greek rest. Open Mon.-Sat.

NEARBY EXCURSIONS

ARIZONA-SONORA DESERT MUSEUM (Tucson Mountain Park, 14 mi., 22 km, west via Ariz. 86 and Kinney Rd.) (883-1380): One of the country's most interesting zoological/botanical gardens, devoted to the plants and animals of the southwestern deserts. Hundreds of desert animals, from mountain lions and jaguars to prairie dogs, from tarantulas to rattlesnakes, living in their natural habitat. An underground gallery allows you to watch the behavior of creatures that live below the surface. Splendid wild scenery; don't miss it. Open daily.

CASA GRANDE RUINS NATIONAL MONUMENT (69 mi., 110 km, NW via I-10 and Ariz. 87) (723-3172): See Chapter 42 on Phoenix.

COLOSSAL CAVE (25 mi., 40 km, SE via I-10 and Colossal Cave Rd.) (791-7677): Unique natural caves with astonishing crystal formations. Many marine fossils bear witness that Arizona was once the bed of a prehistoric sea. The temperature in the caves stays at 72° F (22° C) year round. Only partially explored. Open daily; well worth the side trip.

CORONADO NATIONAL FOREST 1,790,000 acres (720,000 ha.) of forest and desert around Tucson, Nogales, Patagonia, Benson, and Wilcox. Scenic drives, camping, fishing, horseback riding, skiing in winter, etc. For information, contact the Supervisor, Federal Bldg., 300 W. Congress St., Tucson, AZ 85701 (629-6483). There's a **visitor center** at Sabino Canyon (see below).

KITT PEAK NATIONAL OBSERVATORY (56 mi., 90 km, SW via Ariz. 86 and Arix. 386) (325-9200): Considered by scholars one of the world's greatest astronomical observatories. At an elevation of 6,882 ft (2,098 m) up in the Sonora desert, it boasts the largest solar telescope in the world and the second-largest optical telescope in the U.S., 158 in. (4 m) in diameter and weighing 375 tons, housed in a 19-story building. Open daily; fascinating. Splendid surrounding scenery. Don't miss it.

SABINO CANYON (16 mi., 25 km, east via Tanque Verde Rd. and Sabino Canyon Rd.) (749-2327): A kind of green oasis in the desert of the Santa Catalina Mountains; forms part of the immense Coronado National Forest. No private cars are permitted in Sabino Canyon, but there are conducted bus tours every hour. A must for nature lovers.

SAGUARO NATIONAL MONUMENT (17 mi., 27 km, east via Broadway and Old Spanish Trail; or 16 mi., 25 km, west via W. Speedway Blvd. and Saguaro Rd.): America's most spectacular giant-cactus forest; some saguaros grow 52 ft (16 m) tall and live for two centuries. Wide variety of flora and fauna, including coyote, peccary, and various kinds of deer. The park is divided into two sections: the Rincon Mountain Unit (east of Tucson), the more spectacular, and the Tucson Mountain Unit (west of Tucson). Try to go in May and June, when the saguaros are in flower. Visitor centers open year round; hiking trails, camping permitted. For information, contact the Superintendent, 3693 Old Spanish Trail, Tucson, AZ 85730 (602/296-8576).

Where to Eat

🍷 **Saguaro Corners,** 3750 S. Old Spanish Trail (886-5424). Opposite Saguaro National Monument East. Open for lunch/dinner Tues.-Sun. **I**

☀☖ **TITAN MISSILE MUSEUM** (Duval Mine Rd. in Green Valley, 26 mi., 41 km, south on I-19 to exit 69) (791-2929): Former Titan II missile launch site converted to a museum. Guided tour (exhausting) of the silo containing the huge nuclear missile, 110 ft (33 m) high, deactivated in 1983 after standing on 24-hour alert for 19 years. Impressive. Open daily Oct.-May; Wed.-Sun. the rest of the year. Well worth the detour.

GHOST TOWNS: There are a good 20 ghost towns dating from the gold rush days in the area around Tombstone, Nogales, and Chiricaua National Monument. Some, such as Ruby (near Nogales), are closed to the public; others, such as Hilltop or Paradise (near Chiricaua National Monument) are very hard to reach. In addition to Tombstone—the liveliest, least ghostly ghost town in the west—(see Tombstone below), two others are well worth seeing: Charleston (6 mi., 11 km, SW of Tombstone) and above all Gleeson (16 mi., 26 km, east of Tombstone).

FARTHER AFIELD

☖ **CHIRICAUA NATIONAL MONUMENT** (121 mi., 194 km, SE via I-10E and Ariz. 186E): Picturesque rock formations of volcanic origin in a former Apache hunting ground (see "Tombstone," below).

☀☖ **NOGALES** (130 mi., 209 km, round trip via I-19S, Ariz. 82, Ariz. 83N, and I-10W): Picturesque excursion toward the Mexican border, beginning with a visit to the ☀ ⚌ **Mission San Xavier del Bac** (see "Churches/Synagogues," above). Drive on to ☖ **Tubac Presidio State Park,** on U.S. 89 (602/398-2252), open daily, the first Spanish settlement in Arizona. The remains of the fort, now a museum, date from 1752.

Then 5 mi. (8 km) south, at ☀ ☖ **Tumacacori National Monument,** see the Franciscan mission of San José, built around 1800, with a lovely courtyard garden. The Indian village of Tumacacori was first visited in 1691 by the Jesuit Fr. Eusebio Kino, the great Spanish missionary to Arizona (602/398-2341). Open daily.

At the end of I-19, **Nogales,** a very touristy border town bisected by high fences, is worth a look. No documents are required for U.S. citizens if you're just going to cross the border for a few hours of shopping (pottery, leather goods, baskets, glass, and tin items) or sightseeing. Some shops worth visiting are El Changarro (93 Calle Elias), El Continental (98 Obregón Ave.), and El Zarape (161 Obregón Ave.).

Continue east along the 200-acre (80-ha.) **Patagonia Lake,** complete with beach, marina, etc., and the picturesque little town of ☖ **Patagonia.** Don't miss the unusual **Stradling Museum of the Horse** at 350 McKeown Ave. (602/394-2264), open daily, containing everything that has to do with "man's noblest conquest," from classical Greece to the age of the cowboy. Not far from Patagonia, on Ariz. 82, is the wonderful ☖ **Patagonia-Sonoita Creek Sanctuary,** where willows, ash, and sycamores along the banks of the Sonoita brook shelter more than 250 different species of birds.

On the way back, visit the ☖ **Colossal Cave** (see "Nearby Excursions," above) and the ☀⚌ **Pima Air Museum** (see "Museums of Science and History," above). A wonderful expedition for nature lovers.

Where to Eat in Nogales

⚲ **La Rocca,** 91 Calle Elías, is a typical restaurant on the Mexican side. Open daily 11 a.m. to midnight (706/20-760).

☼🔔 ORGAN PIPE CACTUS NATIONAL MONUMENT

(139 mi., 222 km, west via Ariz. 86W and Ariz. 85S): One of the country's wildest and loveliest desert-land parks, on the Mexican border. The cactuses for which the park is named reach 20 ft (6 m) in height, with as many as 30 vertical arms stacked like organ pipes; they flower in May and June. Two scenic highways traverse this seldom-visited park, which is well worth the side trip. Visitor center open year round; camping permitted. For information, contact the Superintendent, Rte. 1, Ajo, AZ 85321 (602/387-6849).

☼🔔🔔 TOMBSTONE

(355 mi., 568 km, round trip via I-10E, U.S. 80E, an unsurfaced road between Rodeo–Portal and Chiricaua National Monument in summer only or U.S. 666N and Ariz. 181E in winter, Ariz. 186W, Apache Pass Rd., and I-10W): This spectacular trip, full of sights for the lover of frontier history, begins with a visit to ☼ 🔔🔔 **Tombstone,** "The Town Too Tough to Die," so called both because of its innumerable shoot-outs (such as the famous "Gunfight at the O.K. Corral" between the Earp brothers and the Clanton brothers, and for the series of catastrophes that overtook its gold and silver mines). Today it's a museum town, with many picturesque buildings from the 1880s: the **Boothill Graveyard,** on U.S. 80 (602/457-3348), with its unusual epitaphs; a **courthouse** dating from 1882 with many remembrances of the town's eventful past, at Toughnut and 3rd St. (602/457-3311), open daily; the **Bird Cage Theater,** Allen and 6th Sts. (602/457-3421), open daily, which was once dubbed "the wildest and wickedest spot between Basin St. and the Barbary Coast," and numbered the beautiful Lola Montez among its attractions; the **Crystal Palace Saloon,** 5th and Allen Sts., open daily, another house of ill-repute famous in the 1880s; the office of the *Tombstone Epitaph,* 5th St. and Allen St. (457-2211), the local daily paper founded in 1880 and published continuously since then; the **O.K. Corral** on Allen between 3rd and 4th Sts., scene of the famous gunfight; and more. No horse-opera buff can afford to miss Tombstone.

Next stop is ☼ **Bisbee,** a real pioneer town sprawled along the sides of Mule Pass Gulch with turn-of-the-century houses. Luckier than Tombstone, it remained prosperous for a full century, its last open-pit copper mines closing only in 1975. Visit the underground 🔔 **Queen Mine** copper mine, where the temperature in the bowels of the earth never rises above 49° F (9° C)—but take a sweater or a jacket even in summer—and its open-pit neighbor the **Lavender Pit,** on U.S. 80 (602/432-2071 for both mines), open daily. At the 🔔 **Bisbee Mining Historical Museum,** 5 Copper Queen Plaza (602/432-7071), open daily, are interesting souvenirs from Bisbee's mining days.

Continue south on U.S. 80 to **Douglas,** an engaging stagecoach-stop town on the Mexican border; don't fail to take a look at the extravagant 🔔🔔 **Gadsden Hotel,** originally built in 1907 and rebuilt after a fire in 1929; the sumptuously rococo interior has been used as a set for many westerns.

Your next stop is at 🔔 **Chiricaua National Monument,** whose spectacular landscape of volcanic rocks and deep gorges once gave sanctuary to the Indian chiefs Cochise and Geronimo. Wonderful scenic drive (Bonita Canyon Rd.) and dozens of miles of trails. Camping permitted. Visitor center (602/824-3560) at the park entrance on U.S. 186. Not far away, at 🔔 **Fort Bowie,** you'll see the ruins of two military posts built to protect the coaches of the legendary Butterfield Stage Coach line from Indian attacks. Small western museum (602/847-2500), open daily.

Drive back to Tucson along the Texas Canyon, by way of 🔔 **Willcox;** see the

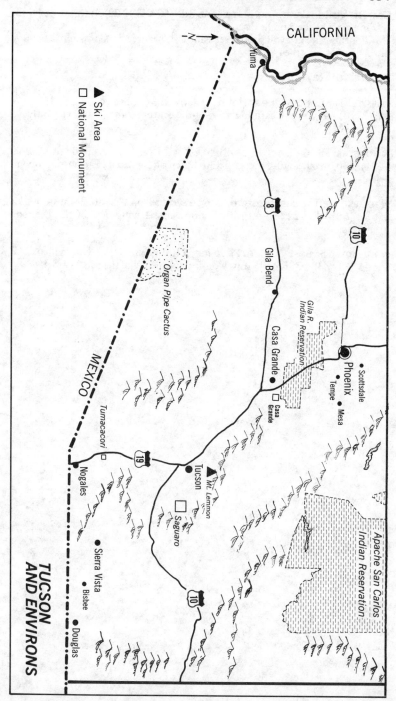

TUCSON
AND ENVIRONS

Cochise Visitor Center on Fort Grant Rd. (602/384-2272), open daily, the best museum of the Apache days.

For this itinerary you should set aside two or three days. If you're a western history buff, this is the trip for you.

Where to Stay En Route

IN BISBEE. The **Copper Queen Hotel,** 11 Howell Ave., Bisbee, AZ 85603 (602/432-2216). 43 rms. Charming turn-of-the-century hotel, now elegantly restored. I–M

IN DOUGLAS. The **Gadsden Hotel,** 1046 G Ave., Douglas, AZ 85608 (602/364-4481). 150 rms. Beautiful rococo 1920s hotel, a designated historic monument. I–M

IN TOMBSTONE. The **Best Western Lookout Lodge,** on U.S. 80, Tombstone, AZ 85638 (602/457-2223). 40 rms. Inviting motel with view of the Dragoon Mountains. I

IN WILLCOX. The **Best Western Plaza Inn,** 1100 W. Rex Allen Dr., Willcox, AZ 85643 (602/384-3556). 93 rms. Comfortable motel of the usual type. I

PART SIX

THE NORTHWEST

CHAPTER 44

PORTLAND

□ □ □

Dominated by the imposing, snow-crowned **Mount Hood** (11,235 ft., 3,424 m) in the distance, Portland figures consistently at the head of America's 243 major cities in various surveys having to do with the "quality of life." Downtown, where high-rises are few and all vehicular traffic is forbidden with the exception of (free) buses and cabs, the pedestrian zone of the **Mall,** with its stores, restaurants, fountains, and statues, is proof of the concern of Portland's inhabitants for their environment. By way of setting a good example, the mayor commutes to his office every day on a bicycle.

If you want to gather an overall impression of the "City of Roses," the best way is to drive around the 50-mi. (80 km) **Scenic Drive,** which encircles the city, from the heights above it through its innumerable parks and its botanic garden. Famous for its rose gardens (whence its nickname), its humidity, and its mountain scenery, Oregon's largest city is nonetheless a vigorous commercial and industrial metropolis, particularly important in lumber, electronics, food, clothing, and aluminum. But stern legislation has banished smog and pollution; salmon are once again being taken from the **Willamette River,** which divides the city in two, and the drinking water drawn from it is rated among the purest in the western U.S.

Although 112 mi. (180 km) from the ocean, Portland is one of the most active seaports on the Pacific coast, handling more than 20 million tons of cargo annually. It boasts the largest floating drydock in the western U.S.

Many excursions can be made, using Portland as a base, into the mountains of the **Cascade Range** and the **Coast Range,** or up the splendid **Columbia River Gorge.** The region is famous for its seafood: salmon and sturgeon from the **Columbia River,** trout and crawfish from the **Sun River,** oysters and crabs from the Pacific. So make a point of visiting some of the multitude of (excellent) seafood restaurants in town.

Among Portland's famous native sons are Linus Pauling, the Nobel Laureate in chemistry, and the food critic James Beard.

BASIC FACTS: State of Oregon. Area Code: 503. Time Zone: Pacific Time. ZIP Code: 97208. Founded: 1842. Approximate population: city, 380,000; metropolitan area, 1,330,000. 28th-largest metropolitan area in the U.S.

CLIMATE: With more than 150 days of rainfall a year, Portland is one of the wettest cities in the country, but it is precisely this fine, persistent, London-style drizzle that has made it a garden city. Winter (Jan. mean, 40°F, 4°C) is relatively mild, with little snow; spring is cool, but it rains, on average, every other day from Oct. to May. The best time to visit the city is between June and Sept., when the thermometer hovers around 68°F (20°C) and it sometimes doesn't rain for two weeks on end (whereupon the locals become anxious and talk about drought).

DISTANCES: Reno, 574 mi. (918 km); Salt Lake City, 768 mi. (1,230 km), San Francisco, 634 mi. (1,015 km); Seattle, 175 mi. (280 km).

ARRIVAL & TRANSIT INFORMATION

AIRPORT: Portland International Airport (PDX), 9 mi. (14 km) northeast. For information, call 234-8422.

AIRLINES: Alaska (224-2547), America West (228-0737), American (241-9145), Continental (224-4560), Delta (225-0830), Eastern (224-7550), Northwest (toll free 800/225-2525), TWA (toll free 800/221-2000), United (226-7211), and USAir (284-5193).

CITY LINK: The **cab** fare from the airport to downtown is about $20; time, about 25 min. Bus: **Raz Trans Airporter** (246-4676) leaves every 30 min., serving principal downtown hotels and the Greyhound terminal; fare, $5; time, 30 min. (60 min. during rush hour).

    Tri-Met, 701 S.W. 6th Ave. (233-3511) provides a remarkable public transportation by bus (free in the downtown area) and streetcar. However, since the metropolitan area is extensive and the number of (recommended) excursions into the surrounding country considerable, it's advisable to rent a car with unlimited mileage.

CAR RENTAL (at the airport unless otherwise indicated): Avis (249-4950); Budget (249-4550); Dollar (249-4792); Hertz (249-8216); National (249-4900); Thrifty, 5401 N.E. 82nd Ave. (254-6565). For downtown locations, consult the local telephone directory.

LIMOUSINE SERVICES: Dav-El Limousines (toll free 800/922-0343) and Oregon Limo Service (283-2275).

TAXIS: Taxis are comparatively few and dear; they may not be hailed on the street, but can be taken from the waiting lines outside the major hotels, or summoned by phone: **Broadway Cab** (227-1234) or **Radio Cab** (227-1212).

TRAIN: AMTRAK station, 800 N.W. Sixth Ave. (241-4290).

BUS: Greyhound, 550 N.W. Sixth Ave. (243-2323).

INFORMATION & TOURS

TOURIST INFORMATION: The **Portland Convention and Visitors Association,** 26 S.W. Salmon St., OR 97204 (503/222-2223).

    For a **recorded message** giving a list of all current cultural events and shows, call 233-3333.

GUIDED TOURS: Eagle Flight Center (airplane), Portland-Hillsboro Airport, Hillsboro (648-7151): Flights over Mount St. Helen's, the Columbia Gorge, or the Pacific coast (during the whale migrations). Spectacular. Year round, weather permitting.

    Gray Line Tours (bus), 400 S.W. Broadway (226-6755): Conducted bus tours of Portland and surroundings (Mount Hood, Columbia River, Mount St. Helens, etc.). Daily, mid-May through Oct.

    M/V Columbia Gorge (boat), N. Waterfront, 606 N.W. Front Ave. (223-3928): Sternwheeler trips on the Willamette and Columbia Rivers, on Fri., Sat., and Sun. from Oct. 1 to June 15. The rest of the year *Columbia Gorge* makes daily excursion trips through the Columbia Gorge, leaving from Cascade Locks.

    Yachts-O-Fun Riverboat Cruises (boat), P.O. Box 17252, Portland, OR

97217 (289-6665). One-day excursions on the Willamette River; brunch- and dinner-cruises. Reservations a must. Apr.-Dec.

SIGHTS, ATTRACTIONS, & ACTIVITIES

ADVENTURES: Go-for-it Adventures (boat), 15745 N.W. Norwich St., Beaverton (645-4337): Rafting down the Columbia, Clackamas, and Willamette Rivers; June-Sept.

River Drifters Whitewater Tours (boat), 13570 N.W. Lakeview Dr. (224-9625). Rafting down different rivers in the area; June-Sept.

ARCHITECTURAL HIGHLIGHTS ☼ ⚖ **Arlene Schnitzer Concert Hall,** 1037 S.W. Broadway (248-4496): Formerly the Paramount, this is a magnificent, flamboyantly rococo movie palace from the 1920s converted at a cost of $9 million into an auditorium, where you can hear concerts of classical music as well as jazz and pop. Home of the Oregon Symphony Orchestra. With three other contiguous performance facilities, it constitutes the **Portland Center for the Performing Arts.** An absolute must.

⚖ **Civic Auditorium,** 222 S.W. Clay St. (248-4496): Ultramodern concert hall, acoustically one of the finest in the U.S. Home of the Portland Opera Association and the Portland Ballet. In front of the building lies Ira's Fountain (see "Monuments," below) with its spectacular array of terraces, basins, and waterfalls. A sight you shouldn't miss.

⚑ **Portland Building,** 1120 S.W. Fifth Ave.: The most defiantly ultramodern building in the U.S.; a sort of gigantic concrete birthday cake (others think that "jukebox" is more appropriate), in pastel tones of blue, beige, and brown, housing federal government offices, shops, and a restaurant. It's a 1982 work of architect Michael Graves, and you should see it, if only out of curiosity.

⚖ **U.S. Bancorp Tower,** 111 S.W. Fifth Ave. (275-6111): An unexpected kind of skyscraper: beautiful pink granite and mirror glass, dubbed "Big Pink" by its admirers. One of the major features of the Portland skyline; a sight not to be missed.

CHURCHES/SYNAGOGUES: ⚖ **First Congregational Church,** 1126 S.W. Park Ave. (226-7219): A fine example of Venetian Gothic from around 1900. Its helical spire and downstairs gallery of contrasting beige and black stone are well worth seeing. Open daily.

☼⚖ **The Grotto (Sanctuary of Our Sorrowful Mother),** Sandy Blvd. and N.E. 85th Ave. (254-7371): Open-air cathedral carved out of the foot of a great rock face ten stories high. At the top of the cliff is a monastery surrounded by beautiful gardens, overlooking the Columbia River. Opened in 1924, this Marian sanctuary is visited each year by half a million of the faithful. Open daily; don't miss it.

HISTORIC BUILDINGS: The ⚖ **Bybee-Howell House,** Howell Park Rd., Sauvie Island, 14 mi. (22 km) N. via U.S. 30 (621-3344): A typical 19th-century farmhouse, originally built in 1856 and scrupulously restored. Illustrates the lifestyle of the first Oregon settlers; interesting little museum of agriculture. Worth the side trip; open Wed.-Sun., June to early Sept.

⚖ **City Hall,** 1220 S.W. Fifth Ave. (226-3161): Designed by architect William Whidden to look like an Italian palazzo, this unusual building is rich in rococo ornament and decoration in true 19th-century style; worth a look.

⚖ **Pioneer Courthouse,** 555 S.W. Yamhill St. (221-3800): This elegant Victorian courthouse, the first federal building in the

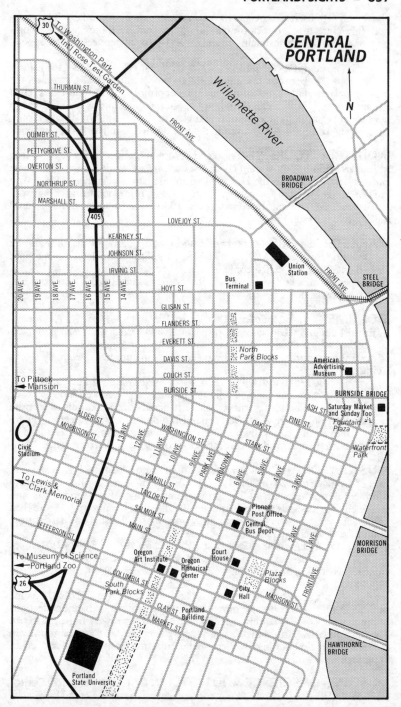

CENTRAL PORTLAND

N

Willamette River

30 To Washington Park,
Int'l Rose Test Garden

THURMAN ST.

QUIMBY ST.
PETTYGROVE ST.
OVERTON ST.
NORTHRUP ST.
MARSHALL ST.

405

FRONT AVE.

BROADWAY
BRIDGE

LOVEJOY ST.

KEARNEY ST.
JOHNSON ST.
IRVING ST.

20 AVE.
19 AVE.
18 AVE.
17 AVE.
16 AVE.
15 AVE.
14 AVE.

HOYT ST.

GLISAN ST.

FLANDERS ST.

EVERETT ST.

DAVIS ST.

COUCH ST.

BURSIDE ST.

Bus
Terminal

Union
Station

FRONT AVE.

STEEL
BRIDGE

North
Park Blocks

American
Advertising
Museum

BURNSIDE BRIDGE

To Pittock
Mansion

ALDER ST.

MORRISON ST.

Civic
Stadium

To Lewis &
Clark Memorial

JEFFERSON ST.

To Museum of Science,
Portland Zoo

26

13 AVE.
12 AVE.
11 AVE.
10 AVE.
9 AVE.
Park Ave.
BROADWAY
6 AVE.
5 AVE.
4 AVE.
3 AVE.
2 AVE.
1 AVE.
FRONT AVE.

WASHINGTON ST.

OAK ST.

STARK ST.

PINE ST.

ASH ST.

Saturday Market
and Sunday Too

Fountain
Plaza

Waterfront
Park

YAMHILL ST.

TAYLOR ST.

SALMON ST.

MAIN ST.

Pioneer
Post Office

Central
Bus Depot

Oregon
Art Institute

Oregon
Historical
Center

Court
House

City
Hall

Plaza
Blocks

MADISON ST.

MORRISON
BRIDGE

COLUMBIA ST.

South
Park Blocks

CLAY ST.

MARKET ST.

Portland
Building

HAWTHORNE
BRIDGE

Portland
State University

Northwest (1875), has recovered its original luster after long and careful restoration. Its architecture is one of the charms of Pioneer Courthouse Square, a complex of gardens with fountain, waterfall, and stepped terraces which appeals greatly to strollers. Should be seen.

Pittock Mansion, 3229 N.W. Pittock Dr. (248-4469): Built between 1909 and 1914 by the founder of *The Oregonian,* the most important daily paper in the city, this enormous manor house in French Renaissance style still has an abundance of antique furniture as well as 46 acres (19 ha.) of beautiful gardens. Wonderful view of the city and the distant mountains. Open daily; closed holidays and the first two weeks in Jan. A definite must.

INDUSTRIAL TOURS: The **Pendleton Woolen Mills,** 10505 S.E. 17th Ave., Milwaukie (654-0444), 6 mi. (10 km) south on Ore. 99E: Some of the finest sweaters and woolens in the U.S. come from the famous Pendleton plant. You can watch every stage in the manufacturing process, from the sorting of raw wool to washing and weaving. Interesting. Visits Mon.-Fri. by appointment; closed the first two weeks in July.

MARKETS: **Saturday Market and Sunday Too,** 108 W. Burnside St., under the Burnside Bridge (222-6072): Every Sat. and Sun. from 10 a.m. to 5 p.m. more than 300 artists, craftspeople, and farmers display their wares in this picturesque open-air market. Very popular with the locals since 1973. Open from Easter to Christmas; don't miss it.

MONUMENTS: **Ira's Fountain,** Third Ave. and S.W. Clay St.: A spectacular futurist design by Lawrence Halprin comprising basins, waterfalls, and fountains down which flows 13,000 gallons (49,500 liters) a minute. In the heart of downtown; much frequented by pickpockets in summer. Definitely worth seeing.

Portlandia, 1120 S.W. Fifth Ave.: This gigantic figure by Raymond Kasky, 35 ft. (10 m) high, represents a kind of marine Venus, on her knees with a trident in one hand. Its size never fails to surprise visitors. Standing in front of the Portland Building (see "Architectural Highlights," above), this comically pompous work in beaten copper turns out to be nothing but a giant reproduction of the city's official seal. Worth a glance.

MUSEUMS OF ART: **American Advertising Museum,** 9 N.W. Second Ave. at Couch St. (226-0000): The world's first museum entirely devoted to commercial publicity in all its forms, from 18th-century shop signs and sandwich-man's boards to modern radio and TV spot commercials. More than 7,000 ads, some of which are genuine works of art. Unusual and fascinating; don't miss it. Open Wed.-Sun.

Lawrence Gallery, 842 S.W. First Ave. (224-9442): Temporary exhibitions of painting, ceramics, sculpture, modern jewelry, etc., with more than 150 different artists represented. Should be seen. Open Mon.-Sat.

Oregon Art Institute, 1219 S.W. Park Ave. (226-2811): One of the best art museums in the Northwest, with fine collections of pre-Columbian, Far Eastern, African, and Pacific Northwest Indian material. The museum also features the very productive contemporary art community in the area. The main building, by Pietro Belluschi, dates from 1932. The open-air **Sculpture Mall** with its fountains is worth a visit all to itself. Open Tues.-Sun.

MUSEUMS OF SCIENCE AND HISTORY: **Oregon Historical Center,** 1230 S.W. Park Ave. (222-1741): A comprehensive panorama of the Indian civilizations of the Pacific Northwest, both before and after the coming of the white man. The history of the Oregon Trail and its pioneers is illustrated by collections of miniature covered wagons and boat models. Well-stocked library on the settlement of the Northwest. Interesting; open Mon.-Sat.

☀☖☖ **Oregon Museum of Science and Industry/OMSI,** 4015 S.W. Canyon Rd. (222-2828): A remarkable museum of science, instructive and up-to-date, covering the whole span from prehistory to outer space. Among its principal attractions are a robot with 3-D vision and a model of the space station of the future. Also the home of the **Kendall Planetarium.** Must certainly be seen. Open daily.

☖ **Western Forestry Center,** 4033 S.W. Canyon Rd. (228-1367): Across from **Washington Park Zoo,** this group of modern all-wood buildings has an information center on one of Oregon's principal natural resources: its forests. Exhibits relating to the forest-products industry; 70-ft. (21-m) "talking tree"; very realistic re-creation of a forest fire; model of a paper mill, etc. Interesting; open daily.

PANORAMAS: ☀ ☖☖ **Council Crest Park,** S.W. Greenway Ave. (796-5193): This little public park not far from downtown rises to a maximum elevation of 1,073 ft. (327 m), the highest point in the city. Belvedere with unobstructed view of the Willamette River, Mount Hood, Mount St. Helen's, and the Portland skyline below. A sight not to be missed.

☀☖ **Pittock Mansion:** See "Historic Buildings," above.

PARKS AND GARDENS: ☀☖ **Crystal Springs Rhododendron Garden,** S.E. 28th Ave. near S.E. Woodstock Blvd. (771-8386): A must for every visitor; more than 2,500 rhododendron bushes, as well as azaleas, flower here in April-May, and a superb sight they are. Open daily.

☖ **Mount Tabor Park,** S.E. 60th Ave. between Yamhill and Division Sts. (796-5193): The only municipal park in the country that occupies the crater of an extinct volcano. Fine view of the city and the mountains; public concerts in summer. Open daily.

Sauvie Island, 14 mi. (22 km) NW on U.S. 30: This island in the Columbia River is very popular in summer, the ideal place for picnics, fishing, walking, bicycling, or just doing nothing. Among its main attractions is the Bybee-Howell House (see "Historic Buildings," above). Worth the side trip.

Tom McCall Waterfront Park, SW Front Ave. between Burnside and Hawthorne Bridges: This pretty, tree-shaded 23-acre (9-ha.) park, the pride of Portland, occupies land originally intended for a riverfront highway. With its many shops and restaurants along the edge of the park, it's an agreeable place for a walk, a stone's throw from downtown.

☀☖☖ **Washington Park,** reached by West Burnside St. or Canyon Rd. (796-5193): This 145-acre (60-ha.) park overlooks Portland from its hilltop emplacement; it features the very beautiful **Japanese Garden** and the magnificent **International Rose Test Garden,** with more than 400 different varieties of roses. The best times for a visit are June and Sept. Splendid view of the city; don't miss it.

PERFORMING ARTS: For daily listings of all shows and cultural events, consult the entertainment pages of the daily paper *The Oregonian* (morning and evening) as well as the weekly *Willamette Week.*

Arlene Schnitzer Concert Hall, 1037 S.W. Broadway (248-4496): Very fine 1920s building, magnificently restored. Classical concerts and recitals. Home of the Oregon Symphony Orchestra (principal conductor, James De Preist).

Memorial Coliseum, 1401 N. Wheeler Ave. (239-4422): Pop and rock concerts; big-name shows.

New Rose Theatre, 904 S.W. Main St. (222-2487): Contemporary theater; off-Broadway shows.

Portland Civic Auditorium, 222 S.W. Clay St. (248-4496): Concerts, Broadway hits, musicals. Home of the Portland Opera Association (performances Sept.-May) and the well-known Portland Ballet.

Portland Civic Theater, 1530 S.W. Yamhill St. (226-3048): Contemporary theater, drama, comedy.

Storefront Actors' Theatre, 6 S.W. Third Ave. (224-4001): Contemporary theater, off-Broadway shows.

Washington Park Amphitheater, Washington Park (226-1561): Open-air public concerts and free recitals (late July to Aug.).

Willamette Repertory Theater, 25 S.W. Salmon St. (224-4491): Contemporary theater; wide-ranging program. The best local repertory company.

SHOPPING: **Lloyd Center,** N.E. Ninth Ave. and Multnomah St. (282-2511): One of the oldest and largest shopping centers in the country, with more than 100 shops and department stores. Flower-planted walkways. Skating rink in winter. Spectacular. Open daily.

Water Tower at John's Landing, 5331 S.W. Macadam Ave. (228-9431): Picturesque shopping center in a renovated turn-of-the-century furniture factory. Congenial shops, pubs, and restaurants around a delightful cobbled courtyard. Open daily.

Yamhill Marketplace, S.W. First Ave. and Yamhill St. (224-6705): Dozens of food shops, stores, and stalls of all kinds, around a glassed-in lobby five stories high. Lively and colorful, in the heart of downtown Portland.

SPECIAL EVENTS: For the exact schedule of events below, consult the **Portland Convention and Visitors Association** (see "Tourist Information," above).

Rhododendron Show (second weekend in May): Beautiful flower show at the Crystal Springs Rhododendron Garden.

Portland Rose Festival (15 days in June): Procession of flowered floats, carnival parades, flower show, auto races, dirigible-balloon rally, etc. Very popular since 1908.

Chamber Music Northwest (late June through July): A well-known chamber-music festival of 25 recitals; for information, call 223-3202.

Mount Hood Festival of Jazz (early Aug.): Two days of open-air jazz concerts, with leading performers, at Gresham, 15 mi. (24 km) east on I-84 (665-1131).

Artquake Festival (early Sept.): Concerts, ballets, art shows on the Mall and in Old Town; very popular.

Pacific International Livestock Show (Oct.): The biggest stock fair in the Northwest; rodeos, horse shows. Colorful.

SPORTS: Portland has teams in three professional sports:

Baseball (Apr.-Oct.): Beavers, Civic Stadium (248-4345).

Basketball (Oct.-Apr.): Trail Blazers, Memorial Coliseum (239-4422).

Ice Hockey (Oct.-Apr.): Winter Hawks, Memorial Coliseum (239-4422).

Horse Racing

Portland Meadows, 1001 N. Schmeer Rd. (285-9144), with thoroughbred and quarter horse racing Oct.-Apr.

STROLLS: ☀ ⚱ **The Mall,** S.W. Fifth and Sixth Aves. around S.W. Alder St.: A huge pedestrians-only zone with brick sidewalks and cobbled streets lined with shops and restaurants, and embellished with gardens, fountains, and statues. The only wheeled vehicles allowed are the (free) buses and cabs. Very lively.

☀☁🔔 **Old Town,** S.W. 1st St. to S.W. 5th Ave. on either side of W. Burnside St.: The historic heart of Portland along the Willamette River, with one of the country's finest remaining groups of 19th-century cast-iron building fronts. Antique dealers, amusing shops, restaurants, cafés. A likeable place.

WINERIES: Rex Hill Vineyards, 23 mi. (36 km) SW at 30835 N. Ore. 99W, in Newberg (538-0666): Tasting room open daily May-Dec.; Fri., Sat., Sun., and Mon. only, Jan.-Apr.

Sokol Blosser Winery, 5000 Sokol Blosser Lane, in Dundee, 26 mi. (42 km) SW on Ore. 99W (864-2672): The vineyards have a very fine view over the Willamette Valley and the mountains. Tasting room open daily, year round.

Tualatin Vineyards, Clapshaw Hill Rd., in Forest Grove, 30 mi. (48 km) west via U.S. 26 and Ore. 8 (357-5005): One of Oregon's largest wine cellars, which you may visit. Tasting room open daily, Feb.-Dec.

WINTER SPORTS RESORTS: ☀ 🔔🔔 **Mount Bachelor Ski Area,** 180 mi. (288 km) southeast via I-5, Ore. 22, U.S. 20, and Century Dr. (382-2442): The best resort in Oregon, with ten lifts; open Nov.-June.

🔔🔔 **Mount Hood Meadows,** 68 mi. (108 km) east via I-84, U.S. 26, and Ore. 35 (337-2222): Nine lifts; open Nov.-May.

🔔 **Summit Ski Area,** 57 mi. (91 km) east via I-84 and U.S. 26 (272-3351): Three lifts; open Nov.-Mar.

🔔🔔 **Timberline Lodge Ski Area,** 60 mi. (96 km) east via I-84 and U.S. 26 (272-3311): Seven lifts; open Nov.-May.

ACCOMMODATIONS

See the listing of toll-free numbers in the Appendix.

Room Rates in Portland	
B (Budget)	up to $30
I (Inexpensive)	$30–$60
M (Moderate)	$60–$90
E (Expensive)	$90–$140
VE (Very Expensive)	$140 and up

Personal Favorites (in order of preference)

☀🛎🛎🛎🛎 **The Heathman** (dwntwn), 1009 S.W. Broadway at Salmon, OR 97205 (503/241-4100); toll free, see Preferred). 152 rms, A/C, color TV, in-rm movies. AE, CB, DC, MC, V. Valet garage $8, rest. (Heathman Restaurant), bar, 24-hr rm svce, nightclub, boutiques, free crib, concierge. *Note:* After rejuvenation at a cost of $16 million, this time-honored 1920s palace, rife w. wood paneling, Italian marble, and white Spanish granite, has recovered all its old luster. Many works of art, including a collection of Andy Warhols, add something new to its plush elegance. Very spacious, comfortable rms; exemplary svce. Its rest. is the best in town. A stone's throw from the Center for the Performing Arts. By far the best place to stay in Portland. **E–VE**

    Marriott (dwntwn), 1401 S.W. Front Ave., OR 97201 (503/226-7600; toll free, see Marriott). 506 rms, A/C, color TV, in-rm movies. AE, CB, DC, MC, V. Valet garage $6, pool, health club, two rests. (including King's Wharf), two bars, rm svce, disco, hrdrsr, free crib. *Note:* Big, rather bulky convention hotel pleasantly located on the Willamette River. Ultra-modern comforts; spacious rms, some w. balconies and refrigerators, the best w. a view of the river and Mount Hood. Efficient svce; so-so rests. w. a beautiful view. Pretty Japanese garden. Group and business clientele; in the heart of dwntwn. **E**

    Hilton Portland (dwntwn), 921 S.W. Sixth Ave., OR 97204 (503/226-1611; toll free, see Hilton). 460 rms, A/C, color TV, in-rm movies. AE, CB, DC, MC, V. Valet garage $7, pool, sauna, rest. (Alexander's), coffeeshop, bar, rm svce, disco, hrdrsr, free crib. *Note:* Huge, relatively modern 23-story tower in the heart of the financial district. Completely redecorated. Inviting, comfortable rms; good svce. The rest. doesn't deserve its reputation but has a fine view of distant Mount Hood. Group and convention clientele. **M–E**

    Imperial Hotel (dwntwn), 400 S.W. Broadway at Stark, OR 97205 (503/228-7221; toll free 800/547-8282). 168 rms, A/C, in-rm movies. AE, CB, DC, MC, V. Free parking, rest., bar, rm svce, free crib. *Note:* Older, very well-run hotel in the center of Portland. The décor may be a little tired, but there's nothing at all wrong w. the comfort. Friendly reception and svce. Excellent value; regular and business clientele. **I–M**

    Red Lion Coliseum (formerly the Thunderbird Inn; nr. dwntwn), 1225 N. Thunderbird Way, OR 97227 (503/235-8311; toll free, see Red Lion Inns). 214 rms, A/C, color TV, in-rm movies. AE, CB, DC, MC, V. Free parking, pool, rest., coffeeshop, bar, rm svce, nightclub, crib $5. *Note:* Large, conventional motel on the Willamette River, very nr. the Memorial Coliseum. Spacious, well-designed rms; cheerful reception and svce; free airport limo. Excellent value; group clientele. **I–M**

    Mallory Hotel (nr. dwntwn), 729 S.W. 15th Ave. at Yamhill St., OR 97205 (503/223-6311). 144 rms, A/C, color TV, in-rm movies. AE, CB, DC, MC, V. Free parking, rest., bar, free crib. *Note:* Aging but inviting hotel, recently modernized, a stone's throw from dwntwn and across from the Portland Civic Theater. Agreeable, pleasantly furnished rms, some w. refrigerators. Perfect for budget travelers; good value. **I–M**

Other Accommodations (from top bracket to budget)

    Riverplace Alexis (dwntwn), 1510 S.W. Harbor Way, OR 97201 (503/228-3233; toll free 800/345-3457). 74 rms, A/C, color TV, in-rm movies. AE, CB, DC, MC, V. Valet garage $8, whirlpool, sauna, rest. (The Esplanade), bar, 24-hr rm svce, nightclub, boutiques, free breakfast, free crib, concierge. *Note:* A newcomer on the local scene, this small luxury hotel is part of an ultramodern real-estate development w. a marina, residential buildings, restaurants, etc., on the Willamette River. The interior decoration and furnishing are of unusual elegance. Spacious, comfortable rms in delicate pastel shades of pale yellow and lime green, w. balconies, the best overlooking the river. Reception and svce of a high order. Well-regarded rest. serving American cuisine. VIP and upscale business clientele; a very fine place to stay. **E–VE**

    Westin Benson (dwntwn), 309 S. Broadway, OR 97205 (503/228-2000; toll free, see Westin). 320 rms, A/C, color TV, in-rm movies. AE, CB, DC, MC, V. Parking $7, two rests. (including the London Grill), bar, 24-hr rm svce, free crib, concierge. *Note:* Massive grand hotel in the heart of dwntwn, built around 1910 and long regarded as the *grande dame* on the Portland scene. Comfortable, not to say plush, but the furniture of the rms is a touch outdated. Exemplary svce. The more famous of the two rests., the London Grill, isn't what it used to be. Business and convention clientele. Interesting weekend packages. **E–VE**

ᵠᵠᵠ **Red Lion Inn Columbia River** (vic.), 1401 N. Hayden Island
ᏝᏝᏝ Dr., OR 97217 (503/283-2111; toll free, see Red Lion Inns). 350 rms, A/C, color TV, in-rm movies. AE, CB, DC, MC, V. Free parking, pool, two tennis courts, putting green, sauna, rest. (Misty's), coffeeshop, bar, rm svce, disco, hrdrsr, boutiques, crib $5. *Note:* Luxury motel on the Columbia River. Inviting, well-designed rms w. private patios and balconies. Good physical-fitness facilities; agreeable garden and setting. Very good svce. Group and convention clientele; 15 min. from dwntwn, 10 min. from airport (free shuttle). Interesting wknd packages. A good place for the exhausted executive. **M–E**

ᵠᵠᵠ **Red Lion Inn Lloyd Center** (formerly the Sheraton; nr.
ᏝᏝᏝ dwntwn), 1000 N.E. Multnomah St., OR 97232 (503/281-6111; toll free, see Red Lion Inns). 520 rms, A/C, color TV, in-rm movies. AE, CB, DC, MC, V. Free parking, pool, health club, two rests. (including Maxi's), coffeeshop, bars, rm svce, disco, crib $5. *Note:* Large, comfortable, modern 15-story hotel, recently renovated, adjoining the enormous Lloyd Center shopping mall. Inviting, spacious rms w. views of the city, the river, or the mountains, many w. private balconies or patios. Efficient svce; acceptable rest. Group and business clientele. 5 min. from dwntwn; free airport limo. **M–E**

ᵠᵠ **Portland Inn** (dwntwn), 1414 S.W. Sixth Ave., OR 97201
ᏝᏝ (503/221-1611; toll free 800/231-2661). 175 rms, A/C, cable color TV. AE, CB, DC, MC, V. Free parking, pool, rest., bar, rm svce, free crib. *Note:* Older but completely renovated motel halfway between the Civic Auditorium and the university campus. Comfortable, inviting rms; efficient svce. Business and group clientele. Good value on balance. **I–M**

ᵠᵠ **Riverside Inn** (dwntwn), 50 S.W. Morrison St. at Front Ave.,
ᏝᏝ OR 97204 (503/221-0711; toll free 800/547-4262). 138 rms, A/C, color TV. AE, CB, DC, MC, V. Free parking, rest., coffeeshop, bar, rm svce, free crib. *Note:* Modern, functional motel at the foot of Morrison Bridge on the Willamette River. Comfortable and very well run; huge rms w. balconies; friendly, cheerful svce. Very good value in dwntwn Portland. **I–M**

ᵠ **Caravan** (nr. dwntwn), 2401 S.W. Fourth Ave., OR 97201
Ꮮ (503/226-1121). 40 rms, A/C, color TV, in-rm movies. AE, CB, DC, MC, V. Free parking, pool, coffeeshop, bar, valet svce, crib $4. *Note:* Modest but well-run small motel 8 min. from dwntwn. Spacious, serviceable rms; friendly reception and svce. Good value; ideal if you're driving since it offers direct access to the highway system. **I**

ᵠ **Motel 6** (nr. dwntwn), 3104 S. Powell Blvd., OR 97202
Ꮮ (503/238-0600). 70 rms, A/C, color TV, free in-rm movies. DC, MC, V. *Note:* Small, unpretentious economy motel 10 min. from dwntwn across the Ross Island Bridge. Very acceptable level of comfort; one of the best buys in Portland. Ideal for the budget traveler. **B**

Airport Accommodations

ᵠᵠ **Sheraton Inn Airport** (vic.), 8235 N.E. Airport Way, OR
ᏝᏝ 97220 (503/281-2500; toll free, see Sheraton). 216 rms, A/C, cable color TV. AE, CB, DC, MC, V. Free parking, health club, sauna, rest. (Première), coffeeshop, bar, 24-hr rm svce, disco, free crib. *Note:* Classic airport hotel 3 min. from the terminal (free shuttle). Comfortable and serviceable. Acceptable rest.; good svce; interesting wknd packages. Business clientele. **M–E**

YMCA / Youth Hostels

Portland International Hostel (nr. dwntwn), 3031 S.E. Hawthorne Blvd., OR 97214 (503/236-3380). 50 beds. Typical youth hostel; open year round.

RESTAURANTS

Portland Restaurant Prices	
(per person, excluding drinks and service charges)	
B (Budget)	up to $15
I (Inexpensive)	$15–$25
M (Moderate)	$25–$40
E (Expensive)	$40–$60
VE (Very Expensive)	$60 and up

Personal Favorites (in order of preference)

Heathman Restaurant (dwntwn), in the Heathman (see "Accommodations," above) (241-4100). A/C. Breakfast/lunch/dinner daily. AE, CB, DC, MC, V. Jkt. *Specialties:* Spanish-style tapas, Chinook salmon w. capers and horseradish sauce, Umpqua oysters w. mignonette of jalapeño pepper, Thai pork on a skewer w. apricots and mandarin sauce. Menu changes regularly. Fine, reasonably priced wine list. *Note:* The cuisine of this elegant, intimate luxury rest. emphasizes local produce, particularly seafood; it's prepared in ways that are often innovative and delicate. Very polished svce. The preferred dwntwn location for business meals; successful enough that resv. are strongly advised. *American-seafood.* **I–M**

Couch Street Fish House (dwntwn), 103 N.W. Third Ave. (223-6173). A/C, Dinner only, nightly; closed July 4, Thanksgiving, and Dec. 24–25. AE, CB, DC, MC, V. Jkt. *Specialties:* anything that swims, served broiled, poached, or in a sauce. Dungeness crab, Chinook salmon, Oregon sturgeon, excellent mahi-mahi (dolphin Hawaiian style). Good list of Northwest wines. *Note:* The best known of Portland's many seafood rests., in the heart of Old Town. Everything is absolutely fresh and impeccably cooked. Pretty Victorian décor on a background of exposed-brick and white walls. Svce a touch pompous. Valet parking. Resv. strongly advised. *Seafood.* **I–M**

Sweet Tibbie Dunbar (nr. dwntwn), 718 N.E. 12th Ave. (232-1801). A/C. Lunch Mon.-Fri., dinner nightly, brunch Sun.; closed Dec. 25. AE, MC, V. Jkt. *Specialties:* roast duck, roast beef, leg of lamb, catch of the day, seafood. *Note:* Fashionable rest. charmingly got up as an old English inn. Very polished cuisine at reasonable prices; the delightful adjoining pub allows you a pleasant wait until your table is free. Smooth svce; resv. advised. *American-seafood.* **I**

Ringside West (nr. dwntwn), 2165 W. Burnside St. (223-1513). A/C. Dinner only, nightly; closed holidays. AE, MC, V. Jkt. *Specialties:* Steak, prime rib, superb onion rings, fresh seafood. Mediocre wine list. *Note:* Long-established steakhouse, three blocks west of the Civic Stadium. Dimly-lit roadhouse atmosphere, w. sports decor and prize fight pictures (as the name implies). Excellent beef cuts moderately priced. New York strip is a favorite. Efficient tuxedo-clad waiters. Locally popular. Resv. essential. Other location: **The Ringside East,** 14021 NE Glisan (255-0750). Lunch Mon.–Fri.; dinner nightly. *Steak-seafood.* **I**

    Henry Thiele's (nr. dwntwn), 2305 W. Burnside St. (223-2060). A/C. Breakfast/lunch/dinner daily; closed Jan. 1, July 4, and Dec. 25. AE, CB, DC, MC, V. *Specialties:* German pancakes, wienerschnitzel, sesame chicken, frikadeller. Good desserts. *Note:* An honorable part of the local gastronomic scene since 1908; the food, predominantly German, is as solid and serious as the setting. Locally popular. Svce on the abrupt side, but very reasonable prices. *German-American.* **B–I**

Other Restaurants (from top bracket to budget)

    Le Cuisinier (nr. dwntwn), 1308 W. Burnside St. (224-4260). A/C. Dinner only, Wed.-Sat.; closed Sun., Mon., Tues., and holidays plus two weeks in July. AE, MC, V. Jkt. *Specialties:* mussels normande, confit of duck, leg of lamb w. mustard, sweetbreads w. madeira, filet of beef w. green peppercorn. Menu changes regularly. Limited but respectable wine list. *Note:* The atmosphere and the décor won't lift your spirits, but this little rest. serves the best French food in town. Friendly, competent svce; resv. highly advisable. *French.* **M**

    John's Meat Market (nr. dwntwn), 115 N.W. 22nd Ave. (223-2119). A/C. Lunch Mon.-Fri., dinner nightly; closed holidays. AE, CB, DC, MC, V. Jkt. *Specialties:* steak, stuffed breast of chicken, fish of the day, roast beef, fresh salmon in season. Very good homemade pastry. *Note:* The waiters wear big butchers' aprons, the décor is pleasantly kitsch, and the food, particularly the meat, is faultless. A classic of its kind. *Steak-seafood.* **I**

    Remo's Ristorante Italiano (dwntwn), 1425 N.W. Glisan St. (221-1150). A/C. Dinner only, nightly; closed holidays. AE, MC, V. Jkt. *Specialties:* ravioli al pesto, fettuccine w. salmon, carpaccio, saltimbocca, northern Italian dishes. Good wine list at respectable prices. *Note:* Those who like real Italian food w. not-too-heavy sauces will enjoy this place; likeable atmosphere and décor. Live jazz nightly at the bar. Locally popular; resv. advised. *Italian.* **I**

    Rheinlander (nr. dwntwn), 5035 N.E. Sandy Blvd. (288-5503). A/C. Dinner only, nightly; brunch Sun.; closed Thanksgiving and Dec. 24–25. AE, MC, V. *Specialties:* wienerschnitzel, sauerbraten, rouladen, apfelstrudel. *Note:* Generous portions of authentic German food in an appropriate Bavarian-inn setting. Noisy but cheerful music. Locally popular; very good value. *German.* **I**

    Dan and Louis Oyster Bar (dwntwn), 208 S.W. Ankeny St. (227-5906). A/C. Lunch/dinner daily (till midnight); closed holidays. AE, MC, V. *Specialties:* oysters on the half shell, fried oysters, oyster soup, shellfish, crabs, fisherman's stew, fish of the day. No wine, beer or liquor. *Note:* A true local institution, this venerable seafood rest. has its own oyster beds on the Pacific coast, which tells you something about the quality and freshness of the food here. Since 1865, four generations of fishermen and restaurant-keepers have succeeded to the helm of this establishment, witness the photos, ship models, and family souvenirs that adorn the walls. Often crowded and noisy. Open late evenings. A place you shouldn't miss. *Seafood.* **B–I**

    Uncle Chen (dwntwn), 529 S.W. Third Ave. (248-1199). A/C. Lunch Mon.-Fri., dinner nightly. AE, MC, V. *Specialties:* Szechuan shrimp, General Tso's chicken, typical Hunan and Szechuan dishes. *Note:* The place is modest but the food is serious. Spacious, airy Far Eastern décor. The best Chinese food in the area; locally popular. *Chinese.* **B–I**

    Rose's West (nr. dwntwn), 315 N.W. 23rd Ave. (227-5181). A/C. Breakfast/lunch/dinner daily; closed holidays. DC,

MC, V. *Specialties:* kosher dishes, stuffed cabbage, corned beef, blintzes, over-stuffed sandwiches, Viennese pastry. *Note:* A deli in the grand old New York tradition; the desserts are absolutely superb. Open late; locally popular. Other location: 122nd Ave. N.E. at Glisan St. (254-6547). *American.* **B**

Cafeterias / Fast Food

Original Pancake House (vic.), 8600 S.W. Barbur Blvd. at 24th Ave. (246-9007). Breakfast/lunch only, Wed.-Sun. Has reigned unchallenged over the pancake for more than a quarter of a century—pancakes w. apple, w. orange, w. cointreau, w. cream, w. cherries, and on and on. A local landmark, overrun on wknds. Pleasant colonial-style décor. Well worth the 15-min. drive from dwntwn on I-5S to exit 296B.

BARS & NIGHTCLUBS

Be Bop USA (vic.), 11753 Beaverton Hillsdale Hwy. at Beaverton (644-4433). Rock 'n' roll of the 50s and 60s nightly. Attracts a very young crowd. The biggest weekend party in town. A 20-min. drive from dwntwn on U.S. 26 W and Beaverton-Tigard Hwy. (Ore 217 S).

Goose Hollow Inn (dwntwn), 1927 S.W. Jefferson St. (228-7010). Friendly, congenial pub belonging to Portland's mayor. Locally popular.

Jake's Famous Crawfish (dwntwn), 401 S.W. 12th Ave. (226-1419). Fashionable bar, famous for more than a century. Crowded and noisy. Also an acceptable but overpriced rest. Open nightly.

The Last Laugh (dwntwn), 426 N.W. Sixth Ave. (295-2844). The oldest and best local comedy club; the most famous comics appear here. Also a reputable rest. Open nightly.

Starry Night (dwntwn), 8 N.W. Sixth Ave. (227-0071). Trendy disco; New Wave music.

NEARBY EXCURSIONS

COLUMBIA RIVER GORGE (65 mi., 104 km, east as far as the Hood River via U.S. 30 or I-84): Some of the grandest scenery in the Northwest. The Columbia River, marking the northern border of the state of Oregon, cuts its channel between the steep rock faces of the mountains of the **Cascade Range.** Two fine roads parallel it: I-84, which follows the river at the foot of the gorges, and the scenic U.S. 30, which zigzags along the heights between forest and precipice, passing 11 great waterfalls from **Troutdale** to Bonneville Dam. Unforgettable view from **Crown Point State Park,** rising 1,968 ft. (600 m) above the romantic landscape of fjords delineated by the Columbia River.

About 23 mi. (38 km) from Portland you'll come upon **Multnomah Falls,** second highest (620 ft., 189 m., in two stages) in the U.S., spanning the basalt cliff like the **Latourell Falls** a little farther on, where the river suddenly drops 246 ft. (75 m). And 9 mi. (14 km) east of Multnomah Falls, stop at **Bonneville Dam** to watch the salmon (in springtime) and other kinds of fish (Mar.-Nov.) ascending the Columbia River; spectacular. An excursion well worth taking is the two-hour cruise aboard the paddlewheeler *Columbia Gorge* from **Cascade Locks,** daily mid-June to Sept.; for resv. call 374-8427 or 223-3928.

Don't miss the trip along the Columbia Gorge.

FORT VANCOUVER NATIONAL HISTORIC SITE (10 mi., 16 km, north across the Columbia River in neighboring Vancouver, Washington) (206/696-7655): One of the oldest white settlements in the Northwest. Between 1825 and 1849 this was the center of operations for the legendary Hudson's Bay Company and its fur-trading empire; in 1848 the

U.S. Army built its first military post here. The fort and the stockaded pioneer village have been reconstructed by the National Park Service as a facsimile of the original. A must for history buffs; don't miss it. Open daily.

☀️🔔🔔 **WARM SPRINGS INDIAN RESERVATION** (119 mi., 190 km, SE on U.S. 26): Established by a treaty of 1885, this reserve, inhabited by Paiute and Wasco Indians, is visited every year by thousands of Americans and foreigners, attracted by the hot springs, authentic Indian dances (every Sun. May-Sept.), many open-air activities (horseback riding, rafting, golf, fishing, etc.), very comfortable hotel run by the Inter-tribal Council, and the excellence of its food. Resv. must be made as far ahead as possible. Don't miss the experience.

Where to Stay

🛎 **Kah-Nee-Ta Lodge and Village,** P.O. Box K, Warm Springs, OR 97761 (503/553-1112; toll free 800/831-0100). Besides the hotel's 140 rms, there are a score of rustic cottages and even tepees for lovers of local color. Hotel closed mid-Nov. to mid-Mar. *Hotels and cottages,* **I–M**; *tepees,* **I**

FARTHER AFIELD

☀️🔔🔔 **COLUMBIA RIVER GORGE AND MOUNT HOOD** (190 mi., 360 km, round trip via U.S. 30E, Wash. 14E, I-84W, Ore. 35S, and U.S. 26W): As far as Bonneville Dam, follow the route described above for a visit to the **Columbia Gorge** (see "Nearby Excursions," above). From Bonneville Dam take the Wash. 14 scenic route along the north bank of the Columbia River as far as 🛎 **The Dalles,** the western terminus of the famous Oregon Trail. It was at this once-active little river port that the pioneers from far-off Missouri left their heavy covered wagons for boats, in which they traveled to the mouth of the Columbia River on the last stage of their long odyssey. See mementoes of the period at the **Fort Dalles Museum,** 15th and Garrison Sts. (296-4547), open daily May-Sept., Wed.-Sun. the rest of the year; and at the **Wasco County Courthouse,** 406 W. 2nd St. (296-4798), open Tues.-Sat., Apr.-Oct.

After a look at the dam and enormous lock on the Columbia River at the **Dalles Dam and Reservoir,** 3 mi. (4.8 km) east on I-84, open daily in summer, Mon.-Fri. the rest of the year, return to the Hood River on the Interstate which follows it. The very scenic Ore. 35S will then take you through the wooded mountains of the **Cascade Range** to the winter-sports resort of 🔔🔔 **Mount Hood Meadows,** halfway up the 11,235-ft. (3,424-m) **Mount Hood,** highest peak in Oregon. Wonderful view of the surrounding crests; however, novices are not advised to try climbing Mount Hood.

Return to Portland on U.S. 26. Don't miss this trip; it's a nature lover's delight.

Where to Stay En Route

☀️🛎🛎 **Columbia Gorge,** 4000 W. Cliff Dr., Hood River, OR 97031 (503/386-5566; toll free 800/345-1921). 46 rms. Handsome 1920s hotel overlooking the gorges. Excellent rest. **E–VE**

☀️🛎🛎 **Timberline Lodge,** 6 mi. (10 km) NE on U.S. 26 in the Timberline Ski Area, OR 97028 (503/272-3311). 59 rms. Picturesque resort hotel at the foot of Mount Hood. **I–M**

☀️🔔🔔 **MOUNT ST. HELENS NATIONAL VOLCANIC MONUMENT** (210 mi., 336 km, round trip via I-5N, Wash. 504E, and the reverse on the way back): This national monument, with an area of about 110,000 acres (44,517 ha.), was created as recently as 1982; it encomcompasses Mount St. Helens itself and the whole area devastated by the volcano's brutally sudden eruption on May 18, 1980, after a century of deceptive slumber. The gigantic explosion threw ashes and burning gas 12 mi. (19 km) up into the atmosphere, and caused the death of 60 people. Five subsequent eruptions reduced the surrounding countryside to ashes and created some startling lunar landscapes. The risk of yet further eruptions has led the park rangers to close the slopes of Mount St. Helens for a radius of 20 mi. (32 km) around the crater. Having lost 1,300 ft. (396 m) of its height in the course of the first eruption Mount St. Helens now reaches an elevation of only 8,377 ft. (2,554 m).

Two scenic roads are still open year round; you can take Wash. 503 to **Yale Lake,** south of the volcano, or Wash. 504 to the visitor center on **Silver Lake,** west of Mount St. Helens. The **visitor center** (206/276-6644), open daily, has much movie and still-photo documentation of the 1980 eruption, as well as a giant model of the volcano. The forest roads to the east of Mount St. Helens (FR25, FR81, FR83, and FR90 in particular), from which you can get the most spectacular views, are generally impassable in bad weather, and closed by snow Oct.-May. For highway information in the volcano area, call 206/696-7500. In summer, 100 climbers a day are allowed to climb as far as the crater under the supervision of guides from the U.S. Forest Service.

It's well worth going out of your way to visit Mount St. Helens and the surrounding countryside.

☼🏖🎒 PACIFIC COAST, SALEM, AND OREGON CITY

(380 mi., 608 km, round trip via U.S. 30W, U.S. 101S, U.S. 20E, and I-5N): Wonderful seascapes and picturesque fishing villages along the Pacific coast between **Astoria** (particularly fine view from the **Astoria Column** at the mouth of the Columbia River) and **Newport,** 135 mi. (216 km) to the south. For a detailed description of this part of the itinerary, see Chapter 46 on the Pacific Coast.

You return to Portland via U.S. 20E and I-5N, stopping at 🏖 **Salem,** capital of the state of Oregon. Visit the **State Capitol,** a handsome marble building in Greek Revival style, at Court and Summer Sts. (378-4423), open daily; also **Mission Mill Village,** 1313 Mill St. SE (585-7012), open Tues.-Sat., an interesting group of carefully restored old houses.

Your last stop will be at 🏖 **Oregon City,** at the foot of the falls on the Willamette River; the **McLoughlin House National Historic Site** at 713 Center St. (656-5146), open Tues.-Sun., is a perfect example of an 1845 colonial residence. This splendidly restored museum-home was built by the former administrator of the Hudson's Bay Company and of the British territories in the Northwest from 1824 to 1846.

If only for the beauty of the scenery, you should take this trip.

Where to Stay En Route

☼🛏🛏🛏 **Salishan Lodge,** on U.S. 101, Gleneden Beach, OR 97388 (503/764-2371). 151 rms. One of the best hotels in the U.S. Contemporary urbanity on Siletz Bay. **E–VE**

🛏🛏🛏 **Embarcadero Resort,** 1000 S.E. Bay Blvd., Newport, OR 97365 (503/265-8521). 110 rms. Luxurious hotel-marina on the Yaquina River. **M–E**

🛏🛏 **Tolovana Inn,** 3400 S. Hemlock St., Tolovana Park, OR 97145 (503/436-2211). 180 rms. Comfortable vacation motel w. views of the ocean and Haystack Rock. **I–M**

CHAPTER 45

SEATTLE

□ □ □

Hidden away at the head of the fjord called **Puget Sound,** almost surrounded by water, crowned from afar by the snowy pyramid of **Mount Rainier,** 14,140 ft (4,392 m) high, and the crests of the **Cascade Mountains,** the "San Francisco of the North" rejoices in some of the country's most magnificent scenery. Like its California equivalent, Seattle is fortunate in having a setting and a climate that are an inseparable part of its identity.

Named after the Indian chief Noah Seathl, who in 1851 gave a friendly reception to the first white settlers, five families from the Midwest, Seattle was originally no more than a village of trappers and loggers. Its prosperity came first with the Klondike gold rush of 1897, and subsequently with the two natural resources that it has been so generously endowed with in both quantity and quality: lumber and fish. The millions of ties that went into the construction of the first western railroads came mostly from around Seattle and from the state of Washington. Though the famous 605-ft (184-m) **Space Needle,** left over from the 1962 "Century 21 Exposition," and its attendant downtown high-rises have supplanted what was once a forest of Douglas pines, lumber still accounts for a good deal of the local wealth, as do the sea (one out of every six inhabitants owns a boat) and its products. The leading fishing port in the U.S., Seattle is also (and today more importantly) the capital of the aerospace industry. Almost one out of every two airliners now in service in the Western world first took off from **King County International Airport,** headquarters of the mighty Boeing Corporation.

Today a busy harbor, looking out toward Alaska and Asia, the largest city in the state of Washington has grown again from its ashes after a disastrous fire in 1889 spared only the picturesque **Pioneer Square** enclave, once the heart of the ill-famed Skid Row district. Since every cloud has a silver lining, the soggy climate of the "Emerald City," as Seattle is sometimes called, has made it one of the greenest places in the U.S. Moreover, within easy reach the tourist will find the magnificent forests of **Olympic National Park,** while the superb snowfields of **Snoqualmie National Forest** await the skiing enthusiast. If you enjoy the pleasures of the table, you'll find in the city's restaurants the whole gamut of local seafood which is the gastronomic glory of the Pacific Northwest: oysters from Olympia and Quilcene, Chinook salmon from the Copper River, Columbia River sturgeon, squid from Puget Sound, and Dungeness crabs, to name only the most enticing. As to the people of Seattle, they are among the most friendly and hospitable in the U.S..

Author Mary McCarthy, the late choreographer Robert Joffrey, and the jazz musician and arranger Quincy Jones were all born in Seattle.

BASIC FACTS: State of Washington. Area Code: 206. Time Zone: Pacific Time. ZIP Code: 98101. Founded: 1851. Approximate population: city, 496,000; metropolitan area, 2,300,000. 18th-largest metropolitan area in the U.S.

CLIMATE: Slickers and umbrellas are appropriate in Seattle at all times of year.

With an annual average of 160 days of rainfall, the better part of it between October and April, it's one of the dampest cities in the country. Warmed on one side by the Japan Current in the Pacific, and protected on the other by the Cascade range, Seattle enjoys a temperate climate even in winter (Jan. average, 41°F, 5°C), while in summer the mercury rarely rises above 78°F (25°C); the average for July is 66°F (19°C).

DISTANCES: Portland, 175 mi. (280 km); Salt Lake City, 834 mi. (1,335 km); San Francisco, 810 mi. (1,295 km); Vancouver, 144 mi. (230 km); Yellowstone, 762 mi. (1,219 km).

ARRIVAL & TRANSIT INFORMATION

AIRPORT: Sea-Tac International Airport (SEA), 14 mi. (23 km) south. For information, call 433-5217.

U.S. AIRLINES: Alaska (433-3100), America West (763-0737), American (241-0920), Continental (624-1740), Delta (433-4711), Eastern (622-1881), Hawaiian (toll free 800/367-5320), Northwest (433-3500), Pan Am (toll free 800/221-1111), San Juan Airlines (toll free 800/438-3880), TWA (447-9400), and United (447-3700).

FOREIGN CARRIERS: Air Canada (622-5509), British Airways (toll free 800/247-9297), Japan Airlines (toll free 800/525-3663), and SÁS (toll free 800/221-2350).

CITY LINK: The **cab** fare from the airport to downtown is about $22–$24; time, 25 min. Bus: **Gray Line Airport Express** (626-6088); leaves approx. every 20 min., serving principal downtown hotels; fare, $6; time, about 25 min.

Excellent **public transportation** by bus, trolley car, and streetcar (free in downtown). Spectacular **monorail** link between Seattle Center and Westlake Mall at Fourth Ave. and Pine St., leaving every 15 min. from 10 a.m. until midnight; fare, 50¢; time, 95 seconds. Don't miss it. For information on public transportation, call Metro Transit System (447-4800).

Cabs are expensive and their drivers not always honest.

You won't need to rent a car unless you're planning excursions (recommended) around Puget Sound or into the surrounding mountains.

CAR RENTALS (at Sea-Tac International Airport unless otherwise noted): Avis (433-5231); Budget (433-5243); Dollar (433-5825); Hertz (433-5264); National (433-5501); Thrifty, 18836 Pacific Hwy. South (246-7565). For downtown locations, consult the local telephone directory.

LIMOUSINE SERVICES: Carey Limousine (toll free 800/336-4646) and Star Limo Service (824-1124).

TAXIS: May be hailed on the street, taken from the waiting lines outside major hotels, or summoned by phone. Recommended companies are Farwest Cabs (292-0569), and Yellow Cab (622-6500).

TRAIN: AMTRAK, King St. Station, Third Ave. and Jackson St. (464-1930).

BUS: Greyhound, Eighth Ave. and Stewart St. (624-3456).

INFORMATION & TOURS

TOURIST INFORMATION: The **Seattle Convention and Visitors Bureau,** 666 Stewart St., WA 98101 (206/447-4240).

GUIDED TOURS: ☼ **Bill Speidel Underground Tours,** 610 First Ave. (682-1511): Conducted tours of the original houses and shops on Pioneer Square, spared by the great fire of 1889 and now 10 ft (3 m) below the surface. Unusual and entertaining. Reservations a must; tours daily.

Gray Line Tours (bus or boat), 720 S. Forest Ave. (624-5813): Conducted tours of the city and surroundings, serving principal hotels.

Seattle Harbor Tours (boat), Pier 56, Seneca St. (623-1445): Boat trips in the harbor and on Elliott Bay; daily May-Oct.

Washington State Ferries (boat), Pier 52, Marion St. (464-6400): Many ferry routes across Puget Sound; splendid scenery at a very low price. Operates year round.

SIGHTS, ATTRACTIONS, & ACTIVITIES

ADVENTURES: **Orion River Expeditions,** 1516 11th Ave. NW (322-9130): Air-rafting down the rivers of Washington State, of the Cascade Range, or of British Columbia; trips last one to five days. Apr.-Sept.

ARCHITECTURAL HIGHLIGHTS: ☼🔔 **Boeing Field–King County International Airport,** 5 mi. (8 km) SE on Fourth Ave. (344-7380): The testing ground for Boeing Corp.; from an observation deck, you can watch the evolutions of 727s, 737s, 747s, 757s, and 767s as they come off the production line. Superb Museum of Flight (see "Museums of Science and History," below). For aviation buffs. Open daily.

☼🔔 **Evergreen Point Floating Bridge,** on Wash. 520E between Seattle and the suburb of Bellevue: The longest (7,514-ft, 2,291-m) floating bridge in the world, with 33 pontoons. Very fine view of Lake Washington; should positively be seen.

🔔 **The Kingdome,** 201 S. King St. (340-2100): Impressive 60,000-seat covered stadium in the heart of downtown. The Seattle Mariners and Seattle Seahawks play their home games here; also rock concerts and trade shows. Adjoining is the **Royal Brougham Sports Museum.** Conducted tours Mon.-Sat., mid-Apr. through Nov.; Mon.-Fri. the rest of the year. Worth seeing.

☼🔔🔔 **Lake Washington Canal,** linking Puget Sound to Lake Union: After those of the Panama Canal, the largest locks in the Western Hemisphere. An impressive sight. An unobstructed view of the seagoing traffic moving through the **Hiram M. Chittenden Locks** may be had from Seaview Ave. NW or 54th St. NW. Must certainly be seen.

☼🔔 **Pier 59,** Alaskan Way at the foot of Pike St.: The jewel of Seattle's waterfront rejuvenation program, with two of the city's most popular tourist attractions: the **Omnidome Theater** (622-1868), open daily, with its giant circular screen for 70-mm movies; and the remarkable **Seattle Aquarium** (see "Museums of Science and History," below). Don't miss it.

☼🔔🔔 **Seattle Center,** Fifth Ave. and Harrison St. (684-7200): A 73-acre (30-ha.) tourist and arts complex on the site of the 1962 World's Fair. Comprises several museums, an opera house, theater, convention hall, covered stadium, dozens of shops and restaurants, and the Space Needle, a

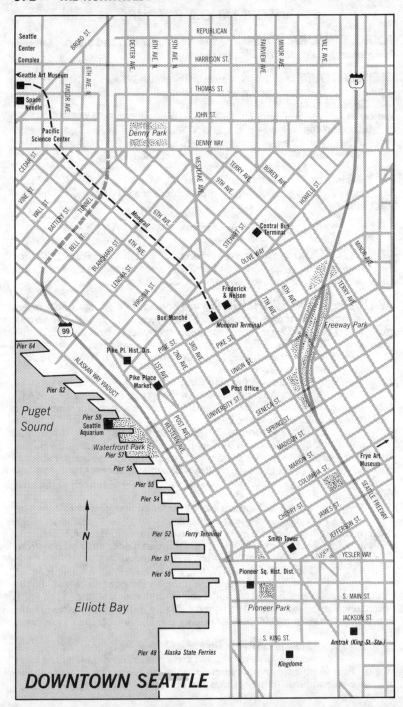

DOWNTOWN SEATTLE

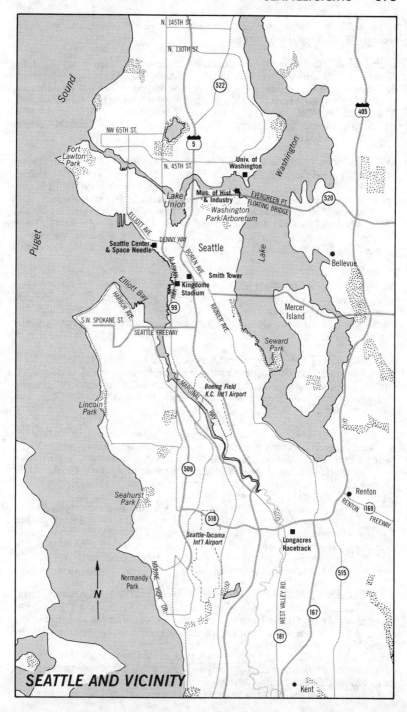

SEATTLE AND VICINITY

spectacular 605-ft (184-m) tower (see "Panoramas," below). A monorail takes you from Westlake Mall, at Fourth Ave. and Pine St., to the Seattle Center in 95 seconds. Open daily; don't miss it.

DEEP-SEA FISHING: If you dream of catching salmon (chum, Coho, or blackmouth), Seattle is where your dream can come true. Many charter boats go daily into Puget Sound from Piers 54 and 56. Some recommended operators are **Emerald City Charters** (624-3931), **Ledger Marine Charters** (283-6160), and **Major Charters** (783-8873).

Also recommended, at Edmonds, just north of Seattle, is **Captain Coley's Charters** (778-4110).

INDUSTRIAL TOURS: ✳ **Boeing 747 Plant,** on Wash. 526 in Everett, 29 mi. (47 km) north on I–5 to exit 189 (342-2121): The assembly plant for the jumbo jets and the 767s; largest covered space in the world. Bus tours (90 min.) Mon.-Fri. year round. Impressive. Reservations required; shouldn't be missed.

Château Sainte Michelle, 14111 N.E. 145th St. in Woodinville, 15 mi. (24 km) NE via I–90 and Wash. 405 (488-1133): Fine 87-acre (35-ha.) estate of vineyards with a pretty château modeled on those in the bordeaux country of France. Tour of the cellars and tasting daily in summer, Mon.-Fri. the rest of the year.

MARKETS: ✳ ⚱ **Pike Place Market,** First Ave. and Pike St. (625-4764): Since 1907 this colorful covered market has been displaying its stalls of fish, fruit, or vegetables side by side with jewelers' booths, fabric shops, junk dealers, little restaurants, etc. Picturesque, noisy, and enjoyable. Well worth seeing; open daily in summer, Mon.-Sat. the rest of the year.

MUSEUMS OF ART: ⚱ **Frye Art Museum,** 704 Terry Ave. (622-9250): Very rich private collection of European paintings, emphasizing the Munich and Vienna Schools, as well as 19th- and 20th-century American works; also interesting temporary exhibitions. A new wing houses a collection of Alaskan art. Should be seen; open daily.

⚱ **Modern Art Pavilion,** Second Ave. North and Thomas St. (447-4670): Annex of the Seattle Art Museum, in the heart of the Seattle Center, devoted to contemporary art. Remarkable works by modern painters of the Pacific School, particularly Mark Tobey, owing much to Chinese philosophy and Zen Buddhism. Also major paintings by Morris Graves, Andy Warhol, Kenneth Callaham, and John Koenig. Shouldn't be missed; open Tues.-Sun.

✳ ⚱ **Seattle Art Museum,** 14th Ave. and E. Prospect St., Volunteer Park (625-8900): The beautiful Fuller collection of Far Eastern (Chinese jade, Haniwa pottery figures) and Inuit art, the White collection of African art, and the Kress collection of works from the Italian Renaissance and the golden age of Dutch painting; also interesting temporary shows, particularly of Indian art from the Pacific Northwest. Don't miss it; open Tues.-Sun.

MUSEUMS OF SCIENCE AND HISTORY: ✳ ⚱ **Burke Museum,** University of Washington campus, N.E. 45th St. at 17th Ave. NE (543-5590): Fine museum devoted to the natural history and ethnology of the Pacific Rim; one of the finest U.S. collections of Indian art (particularly some superb masks) from the Pacific Northwest. Must positively be seen; open Tues.-Sun.

⚱ **Klondike Gold Rush National Historical Park,** 117 S. Main St. (442-7220): Recapitulates the epic of the gold rush to Alaska in 1897–1898; many photographs from the period, as well as original tools and possessions of the Klondike miners. Picturesque and instructive; open daily.

☀☄ **Museum of Flight,** 9404 E. Marginal Way South, King County International Airport (764-5700): Long tucked away into the historic "Red Barn," a turn-of-the-century structure in which the first Boeing aircraft were assembled in 1916, this very fine aeronautical museum has since 1987 had a new and worthier setting, adjoining Boeing Corp.'s test field. The $15-million glass-and-steel building houses some 30 aircraft from the heroic age, beginning with the 1916 B&W Boeing and ending with the B-47 bomber. Also a gallery devoted to space exploration: "Twenty-Five Years of Manned Space Flight." An absolute must for aviation buffs. Open daily; 10 min. from downtown.

☄ **Museum of History and Industry,** 2700 24th Ave. East (324-1125): Remarkable panorama of the history of Boeing Corp., and of the city since its foundation in 1851. Objects salvaged from the great fire of 1889, mementoes of the gold rush, maritime exhibition, etc. Must positively be seen. Open daily.

☄ **Nordic Heritage Museum,** 3014 N.W. 67th St. (789-5707): Devoted to the enormous human and cultural contribution of the Scandinavian peoples to the Pacific Northwest, from the 18th century to the present day. Also temporary exhibitions of modern Scandinavian art and folk art. Interesting. Open Tues.-Sun.

☀☄☄ **Pacific Science Center,** 200 Second Ave., Seattle Center (443-2001): Ultramodern museum, nicknamed the "Cathedral of Science." Spectacular design by Minoru Yamasaki (creator of New York's World Trade Center), with decorative arches, pools, and fountains. From volcanology to astronomy and the exploration of space; particularly interesting are an enormous fiberglass model of the moon, a NASA space module, a scale model of Puget Sound complete with miniature waves and tides, and a reconstruction of a Pacific Northwest Indian longhouse. Fascinating; open daily.

☀☄☄ **Seattle Aquarium,** Pier 59, at the foot of Union St. (625-4357): One of the finest aquariums on the West Coast. Through the underwater viewing dome you can watch while, all around you, the sharks, octopuses, fish, and all kinds of sea creatures strut their stuff in the 400,000-gallon (1.5-million-liter) pool. Truly spectacular; you shouldn't miss it. Open daily.

☄ **Wing Luke Memorial Museum,** 407 Seventh Ave. South (623-5124): Illustrates Chinese immigration into the northwestern U.S. from the 1860s to the present day. Galleries devoted to Far Eastern art and folklore. Exhibitions of photography and Chinese calligraphy. A must for history buffs; open Tues.-Sun.

PANORAMAS: ☀☄☄ **Ballard Bridge,** reached via 15th Ave. NW: Spectacular view of Lake Union and the Fishermen's Terminal looking from south to north; turn around and look south and you'll see the city with Mount Rainier in the distance. Don't miss it.

☀☄ **Columbia Center Building,** Columbia St. and Fifth Ave. (386-5151): The tallest high-rise in Seattle: 954 ft (290 m) and 76 stories. The Observation Platform on the 73rd floor offers a breathtaking view of the downtown buildings, Puget Sound, and Mount Rainier. Open Mon.-Fri., 9:30 a.m. to 6 p.m.; don't miss it.

☀☄☄ **Space Needle,** Seattle Center, Fifth Ave. and Harrison St. (443-2100): Giant tower on three legs, 605 ft (184 m) high, with glass-walled elevators, revolving restaurant, and observation platform 520 ft (160 m) up. The most beautiful view of Seattle, with an unmatched panorama of the bay, the city, and the mountains. Since it was opened in 1962 it has become Seattle's emblem; don't fail to visit it. Open daily till midnight (till 1:30 a.m. in summer).

PARKS AND GARDENS: � **Arboretum,** Lake Washington Blvd. between E. Madison and Montlake (543-8800): More than 5,000 species of trees and plants from around the world, with a particularly fine display of azaleas and rhododendrons. Lovely Japanese garden, gift of Seattle's twin Japanese city, Kobe. Fine view of Lake Washington. A must; open daily.

☼⚐ **Carkeek** (N.W. 110th St.) and **Golden Garden** (Seaview Ave. NW) **Parks:** Two big parks on the shore of Puget Sound; splendid view of the fjord and the distant mountains. Great for picnics; swimming, too, for the foolhardy (water temperature in summer, 54°F, 12°C).

☼⚐ **Discovery Park,** 3801 W. Government Way (625-4636): On a headland overlooking the entrance to the Washington Ship Canal, this large (more than 500 acres, 200 ha.) public park, with its undulating meadows and woodlands, gives you a superb view over Puget Sound from Magnolia Bluff. Two-mi. (3.2-km) beach, but no swimming. Picnic areas, hiking trails. The **Daybreak Star Indian Cultural Center,** with its exhibitions of Indian arts and crafts, is open Mon.-Fri.; the park itself is open daily from dawn to 11 p.m. Don't miss it.

☼⚐ **Freeway Park,** in the heart of downtown Seattle: Represents a successful attempt by the city fathers to "cover the ditch" created by sunken motorways in the center city. Part of it sits atop I–5 and part above an underground municipal parking garage. It boasts an engaging man-made stream and cascade (with a window behind it through which you can watch the traffic passing below); trails for urban hill-climbers; and pleasingly varied plantings. An elegant, urbane oasis above the traffic.

☼⚐ **Gas Works Park,** N. Northlake Way and Meridian Ave. (625-4671): Pretty 20-acre (8-ha.) park around an old gas works, deftly converted into a modern sculpture; fine view of the city, Union Lake, and the passing ships. Don't miss it; open daily.

☼⚐ **Seward Park,** Lake Washington Blvd. and S. Juneau St.: Popular park and beach, with swimming from June to early Sept., on Lake Washington, with the snowy peak of Mount Rainier as a backdrop. Wonderful view. Open daily.

☼⚐ **Volunteer Park,** 15th Ave. and E. Prospect St. (625-4043): At the top of Capitol Hill, this beautiful public park around the Seattle Art Museum offers a clear view of the Olympic Mountains, the Space Needle, and Puget Sound. Observation platform on a Gothic Revival water tower, 520 ft (159 m) high (no elevator). Worth seeing.

☼⚐ **Waterfront Park,** Alaskan Way: Picturesque walk along the dockside. At Pier 59 there's the last word in great aquariums (see the Seattle Aquarium, above); there are gardens at the water's edge from Pier 71 to Pier 89. Wonderful view of Puget Sound and its shipping. Don't miss it.

⚐ **Woodland Park,** 50th St. and Phinney Ave. North (789-7919): Huge park on Green Lake, whose western section is a zoo of very modern design with more than 1,000 animals. Splendid rose garden. Worth a visit; open daily.

PERFORMING ARTS: For daily listings of all shows and cultural events, consult the entertainment pages of the daily papers *Post Intelligencer* (morning) and *Seattle Times* (evening).

Bagley Wright Theater, 225 W. Mercer St., Seattle Center (443-2222): Interesting post-modern design crossed with art nouveau. Classic and contemporary theater. Home of the famous Seattle Repertory Theater (Oct.-Apr.)

Bathhouse Theatre, 7312 W. Green Lake Dr. North (524-9109): Experimental theater.

Coliseum, Seattle Center (684-7200): Rock concerts, big-name shows.

A Contemporary Theatre/ACT, 100 W. Roy St. (285-5110): Modern theater, comedy, drama. One of the major resident theaters in the country.

Empty Space Theater, 95 S. Jackson St. (467-6000): Experimental theater.

5th Avenue Theater, 1308 Fifth Ave. (625-1900): Broadway shows, pop concerts.

Opera House, Seattle Center (443-4711): Concerts, ballet. Home of the Seattle Opera Association (Sept.-May; director, Speight Jenkins), the Pacific Northwest Ballet, and the Seattle Symphony (Sept.-Apr.; principal conductor, Gerard Schwarz).

Paramount Theater, 907 Pine St. (682-1414): Elegantly restored old theater; big-name shows.

Pioneer Square Theater, 512 Second Ave. (622-2016): Modern and off-Broadway theater.

Seattle Center Playhouse, 225 W. Mercer St., Seattle Center (624-2992): Modern and experimental theater; home of the Intiman Theatre Co.

SHOPPING: Food Circus Court, Center House, 305 Harrison St., Seattle Center (684-7200): Cooking and food products from around the world (26 shops), set in an indoor garden with fountains. Perfect for a meal on the run.

Pier 70, 2815 Alaskan Way (448-0708): Souvenir and clothing shops, exotic boutiques, and restaurants in a huge warehouse building by the old harbor. Amusing and picturesque. Open daily.

Uwajimaya, Sixth Ave. South and King St. (624-6248): The largest Asian supermarket in the U.S.; foods and gifts. Open Mon.-Sat.

Ye Olde Curiosity Shop, Pier 51, 601 Alaskan Way, Waterfront (682-5844): Wonderfully kitschy bazaar, almost a century old—museum and souvenir shop at the same time. Many Far Eastern goods. Not to be missed; open daily.

SPECIAL EVENTS: For the exact schedule of events below, consult the **Seattle Visitors and Convention Bureau** (see "Tourist Information," above).

International Film Festival (late Apr. to mid-May): A flourishing tradition since 1974.

Asian Week (early May): Colorful parades; shows. The big day for Seattle's Oriental communities.

Pacific Northwest Arts and Crafts Fair (end of July): Very popular arts-and-crafts show, held at Bellevue, 4 mi. (6.5 km) east on I-90.

Wagner Festival (end of July): Complete "Ring" cycle, alternately in German and English.

Seattle Seafair (late July to early Aug.): Processions, regattas, marathon, ship review.

SPORTS: Seattle has four professional teams:

Baseball (Apr.-Oct.): Mariners, Kingdome (628-3300).
Basketball (Oct.-Apr.): Supersonics, Coliseum (281-5850).
Football (Aug.-Dec.): Seahawks, Kingdome (827-9766).
Ice Hockey (Oct.-Apr.): Breakers, Seattle Center Arena (684-7200).

Horse Racing

Longacres Racetrack, Jackson Ave. SW, Renton (251-8720), 11 mi. (17 km) SE on I-5 and I-405: Racing Fri.-Mon., Apr. to mid-Oct.

STROLLS: ※ ⚓ **Fishermen's Terminal,** W. Emerson St.: The largest fishing harbor in the U.S., and winter quarters of the Alaska fishing fleet. Hundreds of boats of all sizes are moored along the Washington Ship Canal. Many seafood restaurants. Fine view from Ballard Bridge. Not to be missed.

International District, between Fifth and Eighth Aves. South, S. Yesler Way, and S. Dearborn St.: Seattle's Chinatown and Japantown. Many Far Eastern shops and restaurants, Japanese theater, Chinese opera house, Buddhist temple. At the intersection of King and Maynard Sts. is a fine gateway presented by the city of Taipeh. Lively and picturesque; should definitely be seen.

Pioneer Square District, between First Ave., James St., and Yesler Way: This is where Seattle was founded in 1851. Yesler Way, called "Skid Row" in the days of the 19th-century gold rush, was the "hottest" street in this pleasure district. The street was named "Skid Row" because in the earliest days of Seattle logs were "skidded" (dragged by teams of horses) down here from the surrounding hills for the construction of the first houses. These once built, the street was almost abandoned and became the preferred resort of drunks and bums. Today it's lined with shops, art galleries, and congenial restaurants. On Pioneer Square itself there's a 59-ft (18-m) totem pole carved by the Tlingit Indians. Very lively, especially after dark; not to be missed.

Waterfront Drive, Alaskan Way along Elliott Bay: Souvenir shops, Indian, Inuit, and Far Eastern craft shops, bars, and seafood restaurants are arrayed in dozens along the piers. The elevated highway (Alaskan Way Viaduct) offers a fine view of harbor and bay. Not to be missed.

WINTER SPORTS RESORTS: ☼ ᎈᎈ **Alpental,** 54 mi. (86 km) SE on I-90 and Alpental Rd. (236-1600): Eight lifts. Open mid-Nov. to Apr.

Crystal Mountain, 80 mi. (128 km) SE via I-5, Wash. 169, Wash. 410, and Crystal Mountain Rd. (663-2265): Nine lifts; lovely resort on the slopes of Mount Rainier. Open Nov.-Apr.

Ski Acres, 58 mi. (92 km) SE on I-90 (236-1600): 13 lifts. Open mid-Nov. to Apr.

Snoqualmie Summit, 56 mi. (89 km) SE on I-90 (236-1600): 12 lifts. Open mid-Nov. to Apr.

ACCOMMODATIONS

See the listing of toll-free numbers in the Appendix.

Room Rates in Seattle	
B (Budget)	up to $30
I (Inexpensive)	$30–$60
M (Moderate)	$60–$90
E (Expensive)	$90–$140
VE (Very Expensive)	$140 and up

Personal Favorites (in order of preference)

The Westin (dwntwn), 1900 Fifth Ave. at Westlake, WA 98101 (206/728-1000; toll free, see Westin). 875 rms, A/C, color TV, in-rm movies. AE, CB, DC, MC, V. Valet garage $10, pool, health club, sauna, two rests. (including the Palm Court), coffeeshop, three bars, 24-hr rm svce, disco, hrdrsr, boutiques, drugstore, free crib. *Note:* Flagship of the admirable Westin hotel chain. Two circular towers, 40 and 45 stories high, in the dwntwn business district. The rms, huge and comfortable, w. mini-bars, all have a spectacular panoramic view of city, mountains, or Puget Sound. Elegantly redecorated interior; efficient svce; good luxury rest. (Palm Court). Big business and group clientele. Seattle's most glittering hotel. Interesting wknd packages. **E–VE**

※☀️🛎️🛎️🛎️ **The Sorrento** (dwntwn), 900 Madison St., WA 98101 (206/622-6400; toll free, see Preferred). 76 rms, A/C, cable color TV. AE, MC, V. Valet parking $7, rest. (Hunt Club), bar, 24-hr rm svce, free crib, concierge. *Note:* Luxurious small palace hotel in the European style, three-quarters of a century old and now restored to its pristine glory. Period furniture; spacious, comfortable rms w. mini-bars; personalized svce. The Hunt Club is a highly regarded rest. The VIP's favorite; a good place to stay. **E–VE**

🛎️🛎️🛎️ **Holiday Inn Crowne Plaza** (formerly the Park Hilton; dwntwn), Sixth Ave. and Seneca St., WA 98101 (206/464-1980; toll free, see Holiday Inns). 415 rms, A/C, color TV, in-rm movies. AE, CB, DC, MC, V. Valet parking $8, pool, health club, sauna, two rests. (including Juniper's), bar, rm svce, nightclub, free crib, concierge. *Note:* The luxury version of the Holiday Inn style, in a 34-story glass-and-concrete tower in the heart of the business district. Very modern interior and facilities; spacious rms w. view, some w. refrigerators. Four-story, tree-planted lobby; VIP suites from the 32nd to 34th floors. Efficient svce. Group and convention clientele. **E–VE**

※☀️🛎️🛎️ **Edgewater Inn** (nr. dwntwn), 2411 Alaskan Way, Pier 67, WA 98121 (206/728-7000; toll free 800/624-0670). 230 rms, A/C, color TV. AE, CB, DC, MC, V. Free valet parking, rest. (Bayside), bar, rm svce, nightclub, hrdrsr, drugstore, free crib. *Note:* Modern, comfortable hotel right on the water. If your room overlooks the bay, you can rent a rod at the desk, fish from your balcony, and take your catch down to the rest. to be cooked (but if you want such a rm, you must reserve it well ahead!). Good value; 5 min. from dwntwn. **M**

🛎️🛎️ **Mayflower Park Hotel** (dwntwn), 405 Olive Way, WA 98101 (206/623-8700; toll free 800/426-5100). 190 rms, A/C, color TV, in-rm movies. AE, CB, DC, MC, V. Valet parking $3, rest., bar, rm svce, free crib. *Note:* Elderly hotel, completely renovated, in the heart of town a stone's throw from the waterfront. Comfortable and well run; spacious rms w. slightly faded charm; friendly svce. Good value; clientele of regulars. **I–M**

🛎️ **Day Inn Towne Center Inn** (dwntwn), 2205 Seventh Ave., WA 98121 (206/448-3434; toll free Days Inns). 92 rms, A/C, cable color TV. AE, CB, DC, MC, V. Free parking, rest., bar, rm svce, free crib. *Note:* Excellent value right in the business district. Rms adequately large and comfortable; reception and svce with a smile. Group and business clientele. 5 min. from the Seattle Center. **I**

Other Accommodations (from top bracket to budget)

🛎️🛎️🛎️ **Four Seasons Olympic** (dwntwn), 411 University St., WA 98101 (206/621-1700; toll free, see Four Seasons). 451 rms, A/C, in-rm movies. AE, CB, DC, MC, V. Valet garage $10, pool, health club, sauna, two rests. (including the Georgian Room), coffeeshop, bars, 24-hr rm svce, disco, hrdrsr, drugstore, boutiques, free crib, concierge. *Note:* For decades regarded as the great lady of the Seattle hotel scene, the Olympic has recaptured its former grandeur after a complete remodeling in 1982. The Italian Renaissance–style structure, in the heart of Seattle, is a designated historic monument. Very spacious, comfortable rms w. mini-bars; urbanely elegant interior. Well-regarded rest.; exemplary svce. Big business and VIP clientele. A very fine place to stay. **VE**

※※ Ⅼ Ⅼ Ⅼ **Alexis Hotel** (dwntwn), 1007 First Ave., WA 98104 (206/ 624-4844; toll free 800/426-7033). 51 rms, A/C, color TV, in-rm movies. AE, CB, DC, MC, V. Valet parking $8, two tennis courts, rest. (Café Alexis), bar, 24-hr rm svce, free breakfast, free crib, concierge. *Note:* All the charm and elegance of a magnificently restored luxurious private home from around 1900. Elegant, tastefully decorated interior; spacious rms w. period furniture and mini-bars, some w. balconies and fireplaces. Personalized svce of a high order; excellent rest. Very conveniently located an easy walk from the business district and the Pike Place Market. The favorite of those in-the-know. **E–VE**

Ⅼ Ⅼ Ⅼ **Sheraton Hotel and Towers** (dwntwn), 1400 6th St., WA 98101 (206/621-9000; toll free, see Sheraton). 840 rms, A/C, color TV, in-rm movies. AE, CB, DC, MC, V. Valet parking $9, pool, health club, sauna, rest. (Fuller's), coffeeshop, bars, 24-hr rm svce, nightclub, hrdrsr, drugstore, free crib, concierge. *Note:* Big, modern 35-story tower, right in the business district, whose ineffably insipid exterior is belied by a carefully thought-out, imaginative scheme of interior decoration involving some 2,000 art objects, paintings, and sculptures by local artists. Spacious, ultra-comfortable rms, most looking out on Puget Sound or the mountains. Three VIP floors. Fuller's is the city's best rest. Flawless reception and svce. Group and upscale business clientele. **E–VE**

Ⅼ Ⅼ **Meany Tower Hotel** (formerly the University Hotel; nr. dwntwn), 45th St. and N.E. Brooklyn Ave., WA 98105 (206/ 634-2000; toll free 800/634-2010). 155 rms, A/C; color TV, in-rm movies. AE, CB, DC, MC, V. Free parking, rest., coffeeshop, bar, rm svce. *Note:* Modern 16-story tower nr. the university, 10 min. from dwntwn. Excellent reception; spacious, comfortable rms, most w. panoramic view of Lake Washington and the mountains. Good value. Group clientele. **M**

Ⅼ Ⅼ **Best Western Continental Plaza** (nr. dwntwn), 2500 Aurora Ave. North, WA 98109 (206/284-1900; toll free, see Best Western). 98 rms, A/C, cable color TV. AE, CB, DC, MC, V. Free parking, pool, coffeeshop (breakfast and lunch only), rm svce, crib $6. *Note:* Modern, very comfortable motel 15 min. from dwntwn. The rms, most w. balconies, look out on Lake Union and the mountains. Good value; appeals to motorists, since it's 5 min. from the entrance to I-5. **I–M, but lower rates out of season**

Ⅼ **Imperial Inn** (dwntwn), 325 Aurora Ave. North, WA 98109 (206/441-0400; toll free, see Imperial Inns). 59 rms, A/C, cable color TV. AE, CB, DC, MC, V. Free parking, pool, adjoining rest. *Note:* Typical but very acceptable small motel, next to all the attractions of the Seattle Center. Inviting, well-designed rms, some w. kitchenettes. Friendly svce; good overall value. **I**

Ⅼ **Vance Hotel** (dwntwn), 620 Stewart St., WA 98101 (206/ 441-4200; toll free 800/426-0670). 164 rms (116 w. bath), no A/C; color TV. AE, CB, DC, MC, V. Free garage, coffeeshop, bar, valet svce, free crib. *Note:* Aging hotel, rather outmoded as to comfort, in the very center of Seattle; principal attractions are the excellent location and the low rates. Friendly reception and svce. **I**

Airport Accommodations

Ⅼ Ⅼ Ⅼ **Red Lion Inn Sea-Tac** (vic.), 18740 Pacific Hwy. South, WA 98188 (206/246-8600; toll free, see Red Lion Inns). 850 rms, A/C, cable color TV. AE, CB, DC, MC, V. Free parking, pool, health club, two rests. (including Maxi's), coffeeshop, bars, rm svce, disco, hrdrsr, free crib, concierge. *Note:* Huge, ultramodern luxury motel in a 28-acre (11-ha.) garden, capped by a 14-story tower w. glass-walled elevators. Spacious rms w. balconies and superb views of Lake Washington and the mountains. Comprehensive facilities. Efficient reception and svce; group and business clientele. Opposite the airport (free limo.), and 20 min. from dwntwn. **E**

♀ **Motel 6** (vic.), 18900 47th Ave. South, WA 98188 (206/241-
🔑 1648). 147 rms, A/C, color TV, in-rm movies. DC, MC, V.
Free parking, pool. *Note:* Unequalled value 3 min. from the airport; ideal if
you're driving. 20 min. from dwntwn. **B**

YMCA / Youth Hostels
AYH International Hostel (dwntwn), 84 Union St., WA 98122 (206/622-
5443). 125 beds. Typical youth hostel.
YMCA (dwntwn), 909 Fourth Ave., WA 98104 (206/382-5000). 212 rms.
Men, women, families. Health club, pool.

RESTAURANTS

Seattle Restaurant Prices	
(per person, excluding drinks and service charges)	
B (Budget)	up to $15
I (Inexpensive)	$15–$25
M (Moderate)	$25–$40
E (Expensive)	$40–$60
VE (Very Expensive)	$60 and up

Personal Favorites (in order of preference)
🍷🍷 **Fuller's** (dwntwn), in the Sheraton Hotel and Towers (see "Ac-
🍷 commodations," above) (447-5544). A/C. Lunch Mon.-Fri.,
dinner Mon.-Sat.; closed Sun. AE, CB, DC, MC, V. Jkt (J&T at dinner). *Specialties:* timbale of mousse of scallops w. Dungeness crabmeat; cream of corn w. garlic and jalapeño sauce; raw oysters w. raspberry vinegar and cracked-pepper sauce; roast sweetbreads w. shrimp; broiled salmon w. truffles, leeks, and cream of port wine; swordfish w. orange butter and onion conserve. Menu changes daily. Superb list of French and American wines, emphasizing the finest vintages of the Northwest. *Note:* By far the most elegant rest., serving the most sophisticated food, in Seattle. The light, imaginative recipes of the young chef, Caprial Pence, feature local seafood. The décor is embellished by many works of northwestern artists such as Morris Graves and Mark Tobey, and by a remarkable collection of glass from the local Pilchuck School; it's a happy coincidence that the rest. bears the name of the late founder of the Seattle Art Museum. Svce a touch pretentious. Resv. strongly advised; big business clientele. *American.* **M–E**

🍷🍷 **Rosellini's Other Place** (dwntwn), 96 Union St. (623-7340).
🍷 A/C. Lunch Mon.-Fri., dinner Mon.-Sat.; closed Sun. and holidays. AE, CB, DC, MC, V. Jkt. *Specialties:* salade impromptu, marinated scallops w. ginger and chives, poached sable fish w. white wine and cream, salmon w. julienne of vegetables and mustard butter, seafood and fish of the day, game and venison (in season). Fine wine list. *Note:* The elegant, polished cuisine of Rosellini's Other Place makes it one of the best rests. in the northwestern U.S. The trout come from its own fishpond, the wild boar from a California ranch, and the game from its own hunting preserve. Unusually good local seafood. The

rest.'s recent move has been accomplished without the loss of any of its tradition-al merits—quite the contrary. Now a stone's throw from the Pike Place Market, it offers you a lovely view out over the water in a splendid art deco setting. Very good svce; a fine place. *Continental.* **I–M**

Green Lake Grill (nr. dwntwn), 7850 Green Lake Dr. North (522-3490). A/C. Lunch Mon.-Fri., dinner nightly; closed holidays. AE, CB, DC, MC, V. *Specialties:* oyster and salmon caviar pancakes, Alaska king salmon broiled w. thyme and horseradish butter, baked rabbit w. sweet peppers, rockers iko (spiced seafood stew), tuna w. mussels and chanterelle mushrooms, duck ravioli w. sake and ginger. Very good homemade pies. *Note:* Since he opened his first rest. in 1979, Karl Beckley has been recognized as one of the best younger chefs in the area, and this new rest. confirms his reputation. Light, imaginative cuisine in an elegant setting north of Green Lake; courteous, diligent svce. Locally popular; resv. advised. 25 min. from dwntwn. *American.* **I–M**

Jake O'Shaughnessey's (nr. dwntwn), 100 Mercer St. (285-1897). A/C. Dinner only, nightly; closed holidays. AE, DC, MC, V. *Specialties:* Puget Sound sea stew, roast saloon beef in salt crust, barbe-cued salmon, blackberry ice cream. *Note:* Despite its Irish name this local land-mark, decorated in the manner of a 19th-century saloon, serves 100% American food such as the barbecued salmon, which attracts devotees throughout Seattle. Well-stocked bar with more than 20 brands of scotch. Unfortunately no resv. *American.* **I**

Emmett Watson's Oyster Bar (dwntwn), 1916 Pike Pl. (448-7721). Lunch only, Mon.-Sat. (from 11 a.m. to 5 p.m.); closed Sun. and holidays. No credit cards. *Specialties:* oysters (Quilcenes, Canterburies, Olympias, Middlebrooks, etc.) on the half shell, chowder, clams, ceviche. More than 50 brands of beer on draft or in bottle. *Note:* The best-known eating place in Pike Place Market, offering one of the widest selections of oysters on the West Coast, all of exemplary freshness and quality. No interior decoration to speak of: just a dozen bar stools and a few outside tables in fine weather. Quick, efficient svce. Local color guaranteed. *Seafood.* **B**

Bangkok Café (dwntwn), 219 Broadway Ave. East (328-1660). A/C. Lunch/dinner daily. MC, V. *Specialties:* thom yum goong (sweet-and-sour shrimp soup w. mushrooms and lemon grass); cur-ried beef; shrimp sautéed with garlic, onions, and ginger; Thai barbecued chick-en. *Note:* In this city of multitudinous exotic rests., this is one of the few to maintain the authenticity of its food, rather than pandering to Western tastes. Plain décor; exceptionally friendly and attentive svce. Locally popular. *Thai.* **I**

Other Restaurants (from top bracket to budget)

Canlis (nr. dwntwn), 2576 Aurora Ave. North (283-3313). A/C. Dinner only, Mon.-Sat.; closed Sun. and holidays. AE, CB, DC, MC, V. Jkt. *Specialties:* pan-fried oysters, shrimp Capri, lamb chops, steak, poached salmon w. sauce hollandaise, mahi-mahi (Hawaiian-style dol-phin), salade Canlis. *Note:* Flagship of a chain famous throughout the West Coast and Hawaii, this rest. has been serving excellent broiled meats and uncommonly fresh seafood for more than 30 years, w. a slight aura of the exotic thrown in. Plushy atmosphere; excellent svce; very fine view over Lake Union and the city. Locally popular; resv. recommended. *Steak-seafood.* **M**

Rosellini's Four 10 (dwntwn), Fourth Ave. and Wall St. (728-0410). A/C. Lunch Mon.-Fri., dinner Mon.-Sat.; closed Sun., Jan. 1, and Dec. 25. AE, CB, DC, MC, V. Jkt. *Specialties:* rack of lamb provençal, steak au poivre, fresh pasta, salmon stuffed w. shrimp, scaloppine alla marsala, sweetbreads Régence, excellent homemade pastry, peerless wine list. *Note:* Long a Seattle favorite, the rest. draws its inspiration from the Italian origins of the Rosellini family. Its pastas are superb, and the more elaborate dishes no less so. Modern, elegant décor; VIP and upscale business clientele. For so successful a rest., resv. are imperative. Exemplary svce. *Continental-Italian.* **I–M**

☼☋🍸 **Le Gourmand** (dwntwn), 425 N. Market St. (784-3463). A/C. Dinner only, Wed.-Sat.; closed Sun., Mon., and Tues. MC, V. *Specialties:* parsleyed ham, roast kid w. green onions and rosemary, scallops w. riesling and fennel, filet of salmon braised w. sorrel, roast duck w. morels, lamb chops w. mustard, civet of rabbit w. pinot noir. Remarkable desserts. Menu changes every two weeks. *Note:* Although this modest little rest.—half Parisian bistro, half country inn—can accommodate only 30 diners, Le Gourmand has been acknowledged for more than a decade as one of the best places to eat in Seattle. Bruce Naftaly and his wife, Robin Sanders (a remarkable pastrycook), have created a harmonious blend of French and American nouvelle cuisine. Peaceful, intimate atmosphere; very friendly svce; excellent value. Considering how successful—and how small—the place is, resv. are an absolute must. *French-American.* **I (prix fixe)**

☋🍸 **Le Provençal** (vic.), 212 Central Way, in Kirkland, 30 min. from dwntwn via the Evergreen Point Floating Bridge (827-3300). A/C. Lunch Tues.-Fri., dinner nightly; closed holidays. AE, CB, DC, MC, V. *Specialties:* frogs' legs provençale, salmon in pastry shell, cassolette of seafood, roast rack of lamb w. garlic and herbs, fish of the day, dessert cart. Menu changes regularly. Good wine list. *Note:* Charming little country inn, typically French. The very Mediterranean cuisine of owner-chef Philippe Gayte justifies the rest.'s name. Cheerful, friendly svce. Business clientele; resv. advised. An excellent place to eat. *French.* **I (prix fixe)**

☋🍸 **Mikado** (dwntwn), 514 S. Jackson St. (622-5206). A/C. Dinner only, Mon.-Sat.; closed Sun. AE, DC, MC, V. *Specialties:* sushi bar, crabmeat batayaki, tempura, teriyaki, sukiyaki. *Note:* The best Japanese rest. in Seattle (which has a significant Japanese community), a stone's throw from the Kingdome. You can choose between a Western setting and the traditional tatami mats. All the fish dishes are admirable. Swift, efficient kimono-clad svce. *Japanese.* **I**

☼☋🍸 **Ray's Boat House** (nr. dwntwn), 6049 Seaview NW (789-3770). A/C. Lunch Mon.-Fri., dinner nightly; closed Jan. 1, Thanksgiving, and Dec. 24–25. AE, CB, DC, MC, V. *Specialties:* chowder, broiled salmon w. sorrel, crab, oysters, scallops, smoked black cod, calamari in black-bean sauce. Good list of northwestern wines. *Note:* Burned to the ground in 1987, the rest. has risen from its ashes like a phoenix. As with other Seattle seafood rests., fresh salmon is a house specialty at Ray's. Pretty, countrified décor w. lots of paneling and greenery; splendid view of Shilshole Bay and the mountains. Engagingly romantic atmosphere in the evenings. Popular, so resv. advised. 20 min. from dwntwn. *Seafood.* **I**

☋🍸 **Settebello** (dwntwn), 1525 E. Olive Way at Denny Way (323-7772). A/C. Lunch Mon.-Fri., dinner Mon.-Sat.; closed Sun. and holidays. AE, CB, DC, MC, V. *Specialties:* panzotti alla genovese w. walnut sauce, ravioli, osso buco alla milanese, veal cutlet w. rosemary, poached salmon w. tomatoes and basil, tiramisù, sherbet. Very good homemade desserts. Menu changes regularly. *Note:* With its rustic red-tiled floor and its happy, rather noisy atmosphere, the setting is authentic Italian. So is the food. Svce w. a smile. Very popular locally; excellent value; resv. advised. *Italian.* **I**

🍸 **Four Seas** (dwntwn), 714 S. King St. (682-4900). A/C. Lunch Mon.-Sat., dinner nightly (until midnight); closed Jan.

1, Thanksgiving, and Dec. 25. AE, MC, V. *Specialties:* sweet-and-sour pork, Cantonese beef, moo goo gai pan, garlic spareribs. *Note:* The best rest. in Chinatown, and one of the most elegant. Modern Far Eastern décor; rather sophisticated Cantonese food; inefficient svce. Locally popular. *Chinese.* **B–I**

☀☺ **Ivar's Acres of Clams** (dwntwn), Pier 54, at the foot of Madison St. (624-6852). A/C. Lunch/dinner daily; closed Thanksgiving and Dec. 25. AE, MC, V. *Specialties:* fish soup, clam chowder, shellfish, smoked black cod, curried poached halibut, broiled or barbecued fish. *Note:* The most popular of Seattle's innumerable seafood rests., directly on the waterfront near the ferry terminal. Oyster bar open till 2 a.m.; open-air terrace in summer. Generally packed at lunch. Resv. only for groups of six or more. Fine view of Elliott Bay. A local institution since 1938. *Seafood.* **B–I**

Cafeterias / Fast Food

Rosellini's Gourmet Kitchen (dwntwn), Fourth Ave. and Vine St. (448-0136). Lunch/dinner Mon.-Sat. (until 6 p.m.). AE, CB, DC, MC, V. *Specialties:* sandwiches, salads, chili, fresh pasta, homemade pastry. *Note:* This cafeteria observes the same high standards of quality as the Rosellini family's other establishments (see Rosellini's Other Place and Rosellini's Four 10, above). All the materials are choice, and the prices are affordable. Crowded at lunch.

BARS & NIGHTCLUBS

Astor Park (dwntwn), 415 Leonora St. (625-1578). Fashionable disco; New Wave music.

Celebrity Bar & Grill (dwntwn), 315 Second Ave. South (467-1111). This congenial, lively singles bar on Pioneer Square is a favorite with local yuppies. Open nightly.

Comedy Underground (dwntwn), 222 S. Main St. (628-0303). Typical comedy club, presenting the biggest names in the genre.

F. X. McRory's (nr. dwntwn), Occidental Ave. and King St. (623-4800). Oyster bar, very popular with the locals. Huge selection of beer and bourbon. On the noisy side, but entertaining; also an acceptable rest. Nightly until 2 a.m.

Jake O'Shaughnessey's (nr. dwntwn), 100 Mercer St. (285-1897). Lively, noisy Irish pub (see "Restaurants," above). Open nightly till 2 a.m.

Jazz Alley (dwntwn), Sixth Ave. at Lenora St. (441-9729). The best jazz club in town; intimate and engaging.

Sunday's (dwntwn), 620 First Ave. North (284-0456). Another trendy disco. Open nightly.

NEARBY EXCURSIONS

☀☒☒ **MOUNT RAINIER NATIONAL PARK** (95 mi, 153 km, SE via I-5, Wash. 7, and Wash. 706): Mountain scenery in all its grandeur; many glaciers and fields of eternal snow. Wash. 706, open year round, takes you as far as **Paradise Visitor Center,** 5,398 ft (1,646 m) up. If you intend to climb the rest of the way to the 14,410-ft (4,392-m) summit of this great volcano, now 2,000 years dormant, you'll need wiry legs and some mountaineering experience even in the company of your officially licensed guides.

The most popular of the 300 mi. (483 km) of hiking trails in the park is the **Wonderland Trail,** which winds around the slopes of the mountain, crossing in succession deep forests, wildflower-covered alpine meadows, and glaciers. The 140 mi. (224 km) of surfaced road that encircles the highest peak in the Cascades will afford you fabulous views of Mount Rainier's three crests and some of its 26 glaciers; Wash. 410 and Wash. 123 are particularly rewarding.

Don't miss this trip. For information, contact the Superintendent, Mount

Rainier National Park, Tahoma Woods, Star Route, Ashford, WA 98304 (206/ 569-2211).

Where to Stay

☀️ 🔑🔑 **Paradise Inn,** on Wash. 706 (20 mi., 32 km, east of the Nisqually entrance to the park), Ashford, WA 98304 (206/ 569-2275). 127 rms (95 w. baths). *Note:* Very pretty rustic chalet built in the 1920s in an outstandingly beautiful location. **I–M**

☀️ 👓👓 ## MOUNT ST. HELENS NATIONAL VOLCANIC MONUMENT (153 mi., 245 km, south via I-5S and Wash. 504E): One of the most recently active of American volcanoes, recording a major eruption on May 18, 1980. Breathtaking lunar landscapes. Highways are closed for a 20-mi. (32-km) radius around the crater, but many hiking trails open to the public. For more details, see Chapter 44 on Portland.

☀️ 👓👓 ## OLYMPIC NATIONAL PARK (reached by ferry to Winslow, then 89 mi., 142 km, NW via Wash. 305, Wash. 3, Wash. 104, and U.S. 101): More than 1,430 sq. mi. (3,700 km²) of unspoiled wilderness, with astonishing contrasts between the glaciers of **Mount Olympus** (7,965 ft, 2,428 m), the luxuriant forests of the slopes facing the ocean, and the little desert islands along the Pacific. Rains of tropical violence fall daily from Oct. to Apr. on the west face of the park (average annual rainfall, 140 in., 356 cm), so that the thickly wooded slopes of the region are referred to as "rain forests." Abundant wildlife: black bear, eagles, elk, deer, mountain lion, seal, and sea elephant. More than 600 mi. (966 km) of hiking trails crisscross the park, and around it runs a magnificent 330-mi. (531-km) circular highway, the **Olympic Peninsula Scenic Drive** (U.S. 101). **Visitor Center** at 600 E. Park Ave., Port Angeles (206/ 452-4501, ext. 230). Park open year round; don't miss it. You can combine it with a trip to Port Townsend (see below).

☀️ 👓👓 ## PORT TOWNSEND (reached by ferry to Winslow, then 49 mi., 78 km, NW via Wash. 305, Wash. 3, Wash. 104, and Wash 20): Charming little port town on Puget Sound, with fine San Francisco–style pastel-washed Victorian houses and splendid seascapes, and two delightful 19th-century inns. Port Townsend is well worth visiting; you can do so along with Olympic National Park (see above).

Where to Stay

☀️ 🔑🔑 **Manresa Castle,** 7th and Sheridan Sts., Port Townsend, WA 98368 (206/385-5750). 42 Victorian-style rms, most overlooking the bay. AE, MC, V. **I–M**

☀️ 🔑🔑 **James House,** 1238 Washington St., Port Townsend, WA 98368 (206/385-1238). 12 comfortable rms w. period furniture and pretty views. MC, V. **I–M**

🔔 ## SNOQUALMIE NATIONAL FOREST (about 50 mi., 80 km, east on I-90): 1,220,000 acres (490,000 ha.) of deep forests, lakes, mountains, waterfalls, superb scenery, and well-equipped winter sports resorts, all less than an hour's drive from Seattle. Many excursions. Don't miss this trip.

Where to Eat

🍷🍷 **Salish Lodge,** on Wash. 202 at North Bend (206/888-4230). Breakfast/lunch/dinner daily. AE, CB, DC, MC, V. *Note:* Very popular locally. *American.* **I**

TILLICUM VILLAGE (on Blake Island, reached by boat from Pier 56; 206/ 329-5700): Although many tourists come here, I was not impressed with this re-creation of life in a 19th-century Indian village, the price for charcoal-broiled salmon ($25), or the folk-dance exhibition.

FARTHER AFIELD

🔭 NORTH CASCADES AND GLACIER NATIONAL PARKS

(1,548 mi., 2,476 km, round trip via I-5N, Wash. 20E, Wash. 155S, Wash. 174E, U.S. 2E, Wash. 25N, Wash. 20E, U.S. 2E, U.S. 89N, Going-to-the-Sun Rd. West, U.S. 2W, U.S. 93S, and I-90W): An ideal one-week trip for lovers of the wide-open spaces, taking in two of the Northwest's loveliest national parks, North Cascades National Park and Glacier National Park, on the Canadian frontier.

☼ 🔭 North Cascades National Park

You come first to North Cascades National Park, 132 mi. (211 km) from Seattle, its 504,000 acres (204,000 ha.) of magnificent mountain scenery—glaciers (318 of them), innumerable lakes, and majestic crests covered with bristling forests—sitting astride the Canadian border. Many hiking trails crisscross this expanse of unspoiled wilderness north of the Cascades. It took 15 million years of glacial erosion to carve the granite into narrow valleys and abrupt crests like **Goode Mountain** (9,220 ft, 2,810 m) and **Mount Shuskan** (9,127 ft, 2,782 m). Watered by the moist breezes from the Pacific, the western slope of the park is luxuriantly wooded and abounds in wild animals (grizzly, black bear, elk, wolves, eagles), whereas its eastern counterscarp is characterized by sparser growths of conifers and brush. Camping, fishing, rock climbing, hiking in summer; cross-country skiing in winter. Well worth going out of your way for.

Information Centers are open in summer at Marblemount and Colonial Creek (206/856-8700).

☼ 🏛 Grand Coulee Dam and Roosevelt Lake

Continue on scenic Wash. 20, one of the most spectacular highways in the state of Washington, to **Grand Coulee Dam.** At 5,223 ft (1,592 m) wide and 550 ft (168 m) high, this impressive piece of engineering and the generating station that it houses make up one of the largest reinforced-concrete structures in the world (total weight used, 20 million tons). Open daily; don't miss it; for information, call 509/633-1570.

Penned back by the dam is the 151-mi. (243-km) **Roosevelt Lake,** a popular vacation and water-sports area. Following the shore of Roosevelt Lake and continuing to the east, you pick up the scenic Wash. 20 again at Kettle Falls. From here, crossing the northern part of Idaho, you come upon the fish-filled **Lake Pend Oreille** and the **Kaniksu National Forest,** before reaching the incomparably lovely wilderness of Glacier National Park.

☼ 🏛 Glacier National Park

This and Yellowstone are America's two most beautiful national parks. Lying in the northern part of Montana, 611 mi. (978 km) northeast of Seattle on the Canadian border (it is the U.S. section of the **Waterton-Glacier International Peace Park,** of which the adjoining Canadian section is the Waterton Lakes National Park in Alberta, Canada), this huge expanse of mountainous territory covers 1,583 sq. mi. (4,100 km²) and is bisected from north to south by the Continental Divide. There is a particularly striking contrast between its two faces: the western face is humid, with pines, aspens, and red cedars flourishing below the meadows on the precipitous crests; while the eastern face is drier, windy, and often rendered dangerous by the Chinook. With its 60 glaciers (some of them accessible), its dozens of azure lakes, its waterfalls, and its forests, the park is definitely alpine in character. It shelters a wealth of wildlife: grizzly, black bear, elk, bighorn sheep, and mountain goat, to name only a few.

The **Going-to-the-Sun Road,** 50 mi. (80 km) of unbelievable hairpin bends, crosses the park from side to side through **Logan Pass** (closed by snowfalls from mid-Oct. to mid-June), 6,664 ft (2,031 m) above sea level, affording you some unforgettable views of the scenery.

It's worth coming to the Northwest just to see this park. There are many campsites and motels inside the park, often full in July and Aug. (more than two million people come here every year). For information, contact the Superintendent, Glacier National Park, West Glacier, MT 59936 (406/888-5441).

Leaving the park via U.S. 2W and U.S. 93S, you follow the shore of the enormous **Flathead Lake** for some 20 mi. (32 km) to I-90W, on which you return to Seattle, 472 mi. (755 km) west.

⚓ Spokane

On the way you should stop at Spokane, Washington's second-largest city. The very fine **falls** on the Spokane River are illuminated at night. See also the magnificent Gothic **Cathedral of St. John the Evangelist,** 1125 S. Grand Blvd. (509/838-4277), open daily, and **Riverfront Park,** site of the 1974 World's Fair, for the first international exhibition for the protection of the environment.

Then it's back to Seattle on I-90W. If you're a nature lover, the glorious scenery you'll encounter on this trip will thrill you.

Where to Stay En Route

COEUR D'ALENE, IDAHO. 🔑🔑🔑 **Coeur d'Alene Resort,** south of I-90 Bus., Coeur d'Alene, ID 83814 (208/765-4000). 340 rms. AE, MC, V. *Note:* Large, modern 18-story hotel on Coeur d'Alene Lake. Spectacular. **M–E**

GLACIER NATIONAL PARK. ☀ 🔑🔑 **Glacier Park Lodge,** on Mont. 49 (near the intersection with U.S. 2), East Glacier Park, MT 59434 (406/226-5551). 155 rms. MC, V. *Note:* Large, picturesque hotel w. splendid views, open mid-June to mid-Sept. **I–M**

🔆🔑🔑 **Lake McDonald Lodge,** Going-to-the-Sun Rd., West Glacier, MT 59936 (406/226-5551). 102 rms. MC, V. *Note:* Rustic hotel and bungalows on Lake McDonald; lovely views. Open June to mid-Sept. **I–M**

🔆🔑🔑 **Many Glacier,** U.S. 89, East Glacier Park, MT 59434 (406/ 226-5551). 210 rms. MC, V. *Note:* Superbly located on Swiftcurrent Lake; open June to mid-Sept. **I–M**

🔑🔑 **Izaak Walton Inn,** U.S. 2, Essex, MT 59916 (406/888-5700). 30 rms. MC, V. *Note:* Older, historic hotel south of the park; open year round. **I**

🔑🔑 **St. Mary Lodge,** junction of U.S. 89 and Going-to-the Sun Rd., St. Mary, MT 59434 (406/732-4431). 105 rms. AE, MC, V. *Note:* Very inviting motel on the river. Open mid-May to Oct. **I**

GRAND COULEE DAM, WASHINGTON. 🔑 **Coulee House,** Roosevelt Way at Birch St., Coulee Dam, WA 99116 (509/633-1101). 61 rms. AE, DC, MC, V. *Note:* Comfortable little motel w. a view of the dam. **I**

SPOKANE, WASHINGTON. 🔑🔑🔑 **Cavanaugh's Inn at the Park,** 303 W. North River Dr., Spokane, WA 99201 (509/326-8000). 266 rms. AE, CB, DC, MC, V. *Note:* Ultra-comfortable motel across from Riverfront Park. **M–E**

ԱԱԱ **Westcoast Ridpath Hotel,** 515 W. Sprague at First Ave., Spokane, WA 99210 (509/838-2711). 350 rms. *Note:* Inviting hotel in the heart of dwntwn. **I—M**

⚓ THE PACIFIC COAST, FROM NEAH BAY TO HOQUIAM-ABERDEEN (408 mi., 653 km, round trip by

ferry to Winslow, then Wash. 305N, Wash. 3N, Wash. 104N, U.S. 101N, Wash. 112W, Wash. 112E, U.S. 101S, U.S. 12E, Wash. 8E, U.S. 101S, and I-5N): Magnificent coastal route requiring three to four days, and taking in **Port Townsend** (see "Nearby Excursions," above), the ❋ **Makah Indian Reservation, Olympic National Park** (see "Nearby Excursions," above), and the twin towns of **Hoquiam-Aberdeen,** with numerous stretches of scenic highway along the **Straits of San Juan de Fuca** and the Pacific coast (for details, see Chapter 46 on the Pacific Coast).

On the way back, stop at ❋ ⚓ **Olympia,** the capital of Washington State, an old, delightful, flower-planted city at the head of Puget Sound. While there, be sure to see the imposing Doric **Legislative Building** on Capitol Way (586-8687), open Mon.-Fri., with its 287-ft- (88-m-) high dome; also the **State Capitol Museum,** 211 W. 21st Ave. (753-2580), open Tues.-Sun., with interesting works of art and historical material displayed in a gracious Spanish-style building dating from 1920.

Drive back to Seattle on I-5N by way of **Tacoma,** birthplace of Bing Crosby. If you love the sea, this is the drive for you.

For recommended accommodations in Quinault and Hoquiam-Aberdeen, see Chapter 46 on the Pacific Coast.

⚓ VICTORIA AND VANCOUVER, BRITISH COLUMBIA (by hydrofoil or ferry in summer to Victoria; 144 mi., 230

km, north on I-5 to Vancouver): Two captivating Canadian cities which attract many tourists. There's a complete contrast between the English Tudor of Victoria and the 20th-century modernism of Vancouver. The Seattle-Victoria ferry is operated by BC Steamship Co., Pier 69, 2700 Alaskan Way, Seattle (441-5560); the crossing takes 4½ hours, and there are two daily from May to the beginning of Oct. The hydrofoil, operated by Clipper Navigation, Pier 69, 2701 Alaskan Way, Seattle (448-5000), takes only two hours, and there are daily trips year round.

For tourist information, contact the **Vancouver Tourism Information Center,** 562 Burrard St., Vancouver, B.C. V6C 2J6 (604/683-2000); or **Victoria Tourism,** 812 Wharf St., Victoria, B.C. V8W 1T3 (604/382-2127). Both cities amply justify the side trip.

Note: U.S. citizens need no passports to cross into Canada, but are advised to be in possession of proof of citizenship (birth certificate, voter's registration, or the like). Non-U.S. nationals should carry their passports, with a valid U.S. visa, to be sure of being readmitted to the U.S.

CHAPTER 46

THE PACIFIC COAST🔥🔥

□ □ □

From the Olympic Mountains to San Francisco

Favored by a spring-like climate for eight months of the year, the Pacific coast extends for hundreds of miles, its long, sandy beaches often almost deserted—perhaps because the icy currents sweeping down from the Arctic make bathing hazardous as well as uncomfortable. Nature is usually benign here —with some catastrophic exceptions, such as the earthquake that all but razed San Francisco to the ground in 1906, or the eruption of **Mount St. Helens** in 1980, after 123 years of slumber, which killed 35 people and did tens of millions of dollars of damage.

While the winters in northern California are relatively dry, the Oregon coast, and the Washington coast even more, can expect regular heavy showers from November to March; the Olympic Mountains, in the extreme NW, hold the U.S. record for rainfall with an average 142 in. (3,556 mm) annually. As a result, the vegetation is often lush; not for nothing is Washington called "The Evergreen State."

For the 1,060 miles (1,700 km) between the Canadian border and San Francisco, the Pacific coast alternates rocky shores, immense forests of giant conifers, swift-running rivers down which you can raft, and long stretches of white-sand beach punctuated by dozens of picturesque little fishing ports. Between the ocean and the coastal mountains of the **Coast Ranges** and the **Cascade Range** lie several national parks, among the most beautiful in the West and well worth seeing. Outstanding among them are the extraordinary **Olympic National Park** with its impenetrable rain forests; **Redwood National Park** with its thousand-year-old sequoias; **Crater Lake Park,** where one of the world's loveliest lakes (also, at 1,932 ft, 589 m, the deepest in the U.S.) lies in the crater of an extinct volcano; and **Oregon Caves National Monument** with its superb caverns of marble.

In short, a bounteous landscape, still largely unspoiled, which continues southward for several hundred miles until it meets the "civilized," built-up coast of southern California.

BASIC FACTS: States of Washington, Oregon, and California. Area Codes: 206 (Washington), 503 (Oregon), 707 (California). Distance from Cape Flattery (Washington) to San Francisco: about 1,060 mi. (1,700 km).

CLIMATE: Two parallel mountain ranges running a little inland, the Coast Ranges and the Cascade Range, shelter the Pacific coast against the chill winds from the northeast, so that its climate from the Canadian border to San Francisco is uniformly temperate. In winter the thermometer seldom goes below 42° – 46° F (6° – 8° C), while in summer temperatures hover around 68° F (20° C), ideal for a visit. Spring is measurably warmer and dryer than fall; the (very wet) rainy season lasts from Oct. to Mar.

ARRIVAL & TRANSIT INFORMATION

AIRPORTS: The **Eureka-Arcata-Eureka Airport** (ACV), 16 mi. (25 km) north.

Portland International Airport (PDX): See Chapter 44 on Portland.

San Francisco International Airport (SFO): See Chapter 51 on San Francisco.

Sea-Tac International Airport (SEA): See Chapter 45 on Seattle.

AIRLINES: At the **Eureka-Arcata** airport: American (toll free 800/433-7300) and United (toll free 800/241-6522).

At the Portland, Seattle, and San Francisco airports: see Chapters 44, 45, and 51 respectively.

BUS OR CAR RENTAL? The Greyhound Bus Co. has excellent service along the whole Pacific coast. However, the distances are so great, and the attractions so many, that it makes a lot of sense to rent a car or a mobile home with unlimited mileage. Rates are usually lowest in California.

CAR RENTAL: See Chapters 44 on Portland, 45 on Seattle, and 51 on San Francisco.

TRAIN: For the AMTRAK stations in Portland, Seattle, and San Francisco, see Chapters 44, 45, and 51 respectively.

BUS: Greyhound has terminals along the Pacific coast at 956 S.W. 10th St., Newport, Ore. (503/265-2253), and 1603 4th St., Eureka, Calif. (707/442-0370).

For terminals in Portland, Seattle, and San Francisco, see Chapters 44, 45, and 51 respectively.

INFORMATION, TOURS, ADVENTURES, & SPECIAL EVENTS

TOURIST INFORMATION: Information on the Pacific coast is available from both state government and local sources.

State Government Sources

California Office of Tourism, 1121 L St., Sacramento, CA 95814 (916/322-2881).

Oregon Economic Development Dept. – Tourism Division, 595 Cottage St. NE, Salem, OR 97310 (503/378-3451).

Washington Travel Development Division, 101 General Administration Bldg., Olympia, WA 98504 (206/753-5600).

Local Sources

Astoria Chamber of Commerce, Port of Astoria Bldg. (P.O. Box 176), Astoria, OR 97103 (503/325-6311).

Coos Bay Chamber of Commerce, 50 E. Central Ave., Coos Bay, OR 97420 (503/269-0215).

Eureka Chamber of Commerce, 2112 Broadway, Eureka, CA 95501 (707/442-3738).

Newport Chamber of Commerce, 555 S.W. Coast Hwy., Newport, OR 97365 (503/265-8801).

For **Portland, Seattle,** and **San Francisco,** see Chapters 44, 45, and 51 respectively.

GUIDED TOURS: For **Portland, Seattle,** and **San Francisco,** see Chapters 44, 45, and 51 respectively.

For **other localities,** consult the local *Yellow Pages* under "Sightseeing."

ADVENTURES: Six- to eight-hour trips down the Rogue River by raft or motorboat:

From Gold Beach, Ore.

Court's White Water Trips (503/247-6504), Apr.-Nov.; **Jerry's Rogue Jet Boat** (503/247-7601), mid-May to Oct.; and **Mail Boat Whitewater Trips** (503/247-7033), mid-May to Oct.

From Grants Pass, Ore.

Hellgate Excursions, 971 S. 6th St. (503/479-7204), mid-May through Sept.

SPECIAL EVENTS: For exact dates of the events listed below, check with the chambers of commerce listed under "Tourist Information" (above) as well as with those below.

Crescent City Chamber of Commerce, Cultural Center, 1001 Front St. (P.O. Box 246), Crescent City, CA 95531 (707/464-3174).

Depoe Bay Chamber of Commerce, P.O. Box 21, Depoe Bay, OR 97341 (503/765-2889).

Port Orford Chamber of Commerce, Battle Rock Park, U.S. 101S (P.O. Box 637), Port Orford, OR 97465 (503/332-8055).

Astoria, Ore.

Scandinavian Midsummer Festival (mid-June): Parades, folk dancing, craft shows.

Crescent City, Cal.

World Championship Crab Races (end of Feb.).
July 4th Celebration (July 4): Parades, marathon, fireworks.

Depoe Bay, Ore.

Fleet of Flowers Ceremony (Memorial Day): Commemoration of victims of the sea, with religious service and chaplets of flowers thrown into the water.

Eureka, Cal.

Rhododendron Festival (late Apr. to early May): Parades, races, art shows, etc.

Newport, Ore.

Loyalty Days and Sea Fair Festival (late Apr. to early May): Regattas, boat review, art shows, etc.

Port Orford, Ore.

Port Orford Jubilee Celebration (July 4): Commemoration of the Battle of Battle Rock against the Indians; giant barbecue, parade, fireworks.

A NORTH TO SOUTH ITINERARY

The section of this guide devoted to the Pacific coast has been organized as an itinerary, starting at Neah Bay and ending in San Francisco, a distance of about 1,060 mi. (1,700 km). You may choose not to drive the whole distance; the key cities of Seattle, Portland, and San Francisco, as well as many points in between, are linked by air, bus, and train. Car rentals are not hard to find; bear in mind, however, that rates are often markedly lower in California than in Washington and Oregon, and that there may well be a significant charge if you rent a car in one state and drop it off in another. In any case, it shouldn't be difficult to select from the following travel plan the parts that appeal to you most!

From	To	Distance
Neah Bay	Quinault	113 mi. (182 km)
Quinault	Hoquiam-Aberdeen	40 mi. (64 km)
Hoquiam-Aberdeen	Westport	20 mi. (32 km)
Westport	Long Beach	75 mi. (120 km)
Long Beach	Astoria	23 mi. (36 km)
Astoria	Fort Clatsop Nat'l Memorial	6 mi. (10 km)
Fort Clatsop	Seaside	10 mi. (18 km)
Seaside	Cannon Beach	8 mi. (13 km)
Cannon Beach	Tillamook	39 mi. (62 km)
Tillamook	Pacific City	27 mi. (43 km)
Pacific City	Lincoln City	15 mi. (24 km)
Lincoln City	Depoe Bay	12 mi. (19 km)
Depoe Bay	Devil's Punchbowl State Park	5 mi. (9 km)
Devil's Punchbowl	Newport	8 mi. (12 km)
Newport	Yachats	24 mi. (39 km)
Yachats	Sea Lion Caves	15 mi. (24 km)
Sea Lion Caves	Florence	12 mi. (19 km)
Florence	Reedsport	32 mi. (51 km)
Reedsport	Coos Bay	27 mi. (44 km)
Coos Bay	Bandon	24 mi. (38 km)
Bandon	Port Orford	27 mi. (43 km)
Port Orford	Gold Beach	53 mi. (84 km)
Gold Beach	Crescent City	59 mi. (95 km)
Crescent City	McKinleyville	70 mi. (112 km)

McKinleyville	Eureka	10 mi. (16 km)
Eureka	Avenue of the Giants	41 mi. (65 km)
Avenue of the Giants	Fort Bragg	86 mi. (138 km)
Fort Bragg	Noyo	2 mi. (4 km)
Noyo	Mendocino	5 mi. (8 km)
Mendocino	Point Arena	35 mi. (56 km)
Point Arena	Fort Ross	48 mi. (76 km)
Fort Ross	Bodega Bay	22 mi. (36 km)
Bodega Bay	Point Reyes Nat'l Seashore	32 mi. (50 km)
Point Reyes	San Francisco	35 mi. (56 km)

Room Rates Along the Pacific Coast

(see the listing of toll-free numbers in the Appendix)

B (Budget)	up to $30
I (Inexpensive)	$30–$60
M (Moderate)	$60–$90
E (Expensive)	$90–$140
VE (Very Expensive)	$140 and up

Pacific Coast Restaurant Prices

(per person, excluding drinks and service charges)

B (Budget)	up to $15
I (Inexpensive)	$15–$25
M (Moderate)	$25–$40
E (Expensive)	$40–$60
VE (Very Expensive)	$60 and up

NEAH BAY: At the western tip of the **Olympic Peninsula** the little ports of **Neah Bay** and **Sekiu,** about 12 mi. (19 km) apart, are very popular sportfishing resorts (boat rentals). At Neah Bay is the interesting archeological museum of the **Makah Indian Reservation,** on B/A Hwy. 1 (206/645-2711), open daily in summer, Wed.-Sun. the rest of the year; it houses more than 55,000 works of art or handcrafts, some of them over 500 years old.

QUINAULT: Starting point for a visit to **Olympic National Park,** a superb and inviolate nature reserve covering 1,420 sq.

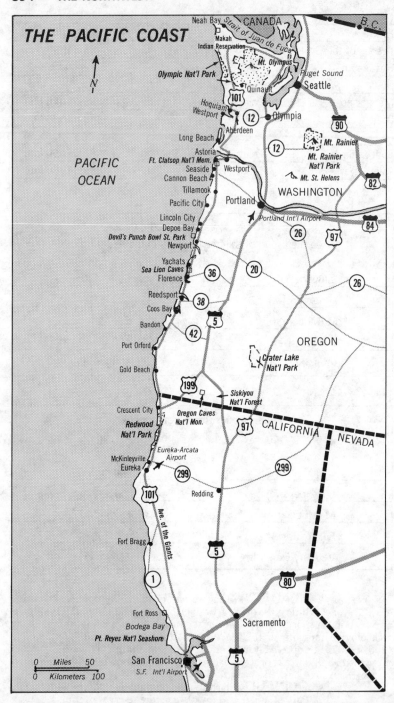

THE PACIFIC COAST

CANADA

B.C.

Neah Bay

Strait of Juan de Fuca

Makah
Indian Reservation

Olympic Nat'l Park

Mt. Olympus

Puget Sound

Quinault

Seattle

Hoquiam
Westport

101

12

Olympia

90

Aberdeen

Long Beach

Astoria

Ft. Clatsop Nat'l Mem.

Seaside

Cannon Beach

Tillamook

Pacific City

Lincoln City

Depoe Bay

Devil's Punch Bowl St. Park

Newport

Yachats

Sea Lion Caves

Florence

Reedsport

Coos Bay

Bandon

Port Orford

Gold Beach

Westport

Portland

Portland Int'l Airport

26

97

84

36

20

38

5

42

WASHINGTON

12

Mt. Rainier

Mt. Rainier
Nat'l Park

Mt. St. Helens

82

OREGON

26

*Crater Lake
Nat'l Park*

PACIFIC
OCEAN

Crescent City

*Redwood
Nat'l Park*

McKinleyville

Eureka

199

*Siskiyou
Nat'l Forest*

*Oregon Caves
Nat'l Mon.*

97

CALIFORNIA

NEVADA

*Eureka-Arcata
Airport*

299

101

Redding

Ave. of the Giants

Fort Bragg

1

Fort Ross

Bodega Bay

Pt. Reyes Nat'l Seashore

San Francisco

S.F. Int'l Airport

299

5

80

Sacramento

5

N

0 Miles 50

0 Kilometers 100

mi. (4,794 sq. km), whose treasures include the glaciers of **Mount Olympus,** rain forests, desert isles along the Pacific shore, and a unique population of wildlife. Beautifully situated on the shores of Lake Quinault, with views of wonderful scenery. Be sure to see the rain forest and the Enchanted Valley. Open year round; don't miss it. For details, see Chapter 45 on Seattle.

Where to Stay

Lake Quinault Lodge, South Shore Rd., Quinault, WA 98575 (206/288-2571; toll free 800/562-6672). 54 rms. AE, MC, V. Free parking, pool, sauna, boating, beach, rest., bar. *Note:* Comfortable little country inn on Lake Quinault. Rms w. balconies, some w. fireplaces. Friendly reception; very acceptable rest. For nature lovers. **I–M**

Where to Eat

Lake Quinault Lodge, South Shore Rd. (206/288-2571). Breakfast/lunch/dinner daily. AE, DC, MC, V. *Specialties:* fresh salmon, fish of the day, shellfish, steak, roast beef. *Note:* Pretty rustic décor w. clear view of Lake Quinault and the mountains. Admirable hotel food; cheerful svce. Resv. advised; a good place to eat. *Steak-seafood.* **B–I**

HOQUIAM-ABERDEEN: Picturesque harbor town on Grays Harbor Gulf, comprising the twin cities of **Hoquiam,** the commercial and fishing port, and **Aberdeen,** with its woodworking plants and fish canneries. Worth a look.

Where to Stay

Nordic Inn, 1700 S. Boone St., Aberdeen, WA 98520 (206/ 533-0100). 66 rms, cable color TV. AE, CB, DC, MC, V. Free parking, rest., bar, nightclub, free crib. *Note:* Typical but inviting motel; spacious rms w. refrigerators; acceptable rest. Good value. **I**

Red Lion, 521 W. Wishkah St., Aberdeen, WA 98520 (206/ 532-5210; toll free, see Red Lion Inns). 67 rms, color TV, in-rm movies. AE, CB, DC, MC, V. Free parking, crib $5. *Note:* Modern motel not far from dwntwn Aberdeen. Nearby rest. Spacious, serviceable rms; free morning coffee. **I, but lower rates Oct.-May**

Westwood Lodge, 910 Simpson Ave., Hoquiam, WA 98550 (206/532-8161). 65 rms, color TV, in-rm movies. AE, MC, V. Free parking, nearby coffeeshop, crib $5. *Note:* Conventional, unpretentious motel; comfortable rms, some w. kitchenettes. Free a.m. coffee; good value. **I**

Where to Eat

Bridge's, 112 North G St. (206/532-6563). A/C. Lunch/ dinner daily; closed holidays. AE, DC, MC, V. *Specialties:* seafood, fish, red meat, oysters. *Note:* Praiseworthy seafood rest. nr. the harbor; everything is absolutely fresh. Attractive modern décor; good svce; no-smoking area. *Steak-seafood.* **B–I**

WESTPORT: This little port, with its fleet of 150 charter boats, is a favorite summer resort for sportfishing (salmon, bass, halibut, etc.). Its **Westport Aquarium,** 321 Harbor St. (206/268-0471), open daily Apr.-Dec., is justly renowned. The nearby **Twin Harbors State Park** has beautiful beaches, but swimming is hazardous.

Where to Stay

🛏🛏 **Château Westport** (formerly the Canterbury), on Wash. 105, Westport, WA 98595 (206/268-9101). 110 rms, cable color TV. AE, CB, DC, MC, V. Free parking, pool, crib $3. *Note:* Inviting motel on the beach. Spacious rms w. balconies and refrigerators, some w. kitchenettes. Pleasant reception and svce; free a.m. coffee; nearby rest. **I, but lower rates Oct.-Apr.**

Where to Eat

🌣🍸🍸 **Sourdough Lil's,** 202 Dock St. (206/268-9700). Lunch/dinner daily; closed Oct. 15 to Jan. MC, V. *Specialties:* fish of the day, shellfish, roast beef, steak. *Note:* Like a 1900s saloon, w. ragtime piano and banjo, and songs w. the diners joining in the chorus. Good fish and meat. Entertaining atmosphere. *Steak-seafood.* **B–I**

🌣🍶 **LONG BEACH:** Sweeping 28 mi. (45 km) in a single stretch, this is one of the world's longest sand beaches. **Wash. 103,** the coast road from Long Beach to **Oysterville,** is a scenic highway; it will take you to **Fort Canby** (206/642-3078), open daily, mid-May to Oct. On Wash. 101 you'll find **Fort Columbia** (206/777-8221), open daily in summer, Wed.-Sun. the rest of the year. From either one of these meticulously restored military posts dating from pioneer days, there's a wonderful view of the mouth of the Columbia River; you shouldn't miss it.

Where to Stay

🛏🛏 **Chautauqua Lodge,** 304 14th St. NW, Long Beach, WA 98631 (206/642-4401). 120 rms, cable color TV. AE, MC, V. Free parking, pool, sauna, adjoining rest., bar, disco, free crib. *Note:* Large, modern motel w. direct beach access; huge, well-designed rms w. balconies and refrigerators, some w. kitchenettes. Good svce; a fine place to stay. **I–M, but lower rates out of season**

🛏 **O'Connor's Shaman,** 115 3rd St. South, Long Beach, WA 98631 (206/642-3714). 40 rms, cable color TV. AE, MC, V. Free parking, pool, adjoining coffeeshop, free crib. *Note:* Typical motel nr. the beach; huge inviting rms, some w. kitchenette and fireplace. **I, but lower rates Oct.-May**

IN NEARBY CHINOOK. **Youth Hostel,** Fort Columbia State Park, Chinook, WA 98614 (206/777-8755). 23 beds. Open year round.

Where to Eat

🍸 **Surfside,** in the Surfside Inn, 31512 J Pl. (206/665-5211). Lunch/dinner daily; closed Dec. 25. MC, V. *Specialties:* seafood, steak, Japanese dishes. *Note:* This rest., specializing in dependably fresh seafood, also offers a pretty ocean view. Dancing Fri. and Sat. evenings. *American-Japanese.* **B–I**

🌣🍶 **ASTORIA:** Dating from 1811, this is one of the oldest American Fur Co. Today it's a charming little fishing port with a strong flavor of the 19th century. If you climb the 128 steps of the **Astoria Column** you'll be rewarded with a wonderful view. There's also the interesting **Columbia River Maritime Museum** at 17th St. and Marine Dr. (503/325-2323), open daily. You should certainly see Astoria.

Where to Stay

♟♟ **Red Lion Inn,** 400 Industry St., Astoria, OR 97103 (503/325-7373; toll free, see Red Lion Inns). 124 rms, color TV, in-rm movies. AE, CB, DC, MC, V. Free parking, rest., coffeeshop, bar, disco, crib $5. *Note:* Wonderfully located facing the harbor and the Columbia River. Spacious, comfortable rms w. balconies and fine view; acceptable rest.; airport limo. A fine place to stay. **I–M, but lower rates out of season**

♟ **Rivershore,** 59 W. Marine Dr., Astoria, OR 97103 (503/325-2921). 43 rms, color TV, in-rm movies. AE, CB, DC, MC, V. Free parking. *Note:* Modest small motel on the Columbia River; adjoining coffeeshop. Spacious, serviceable rms, some w. refrigerators. **I, but lower rates out of season**

Where to Eat

♟♟ **Pier 11 Feed Store,** 77 11th St. (503/325-6101). A/C. Lunch/dinner daily; closed Thanksgiving and Dec. 25. MC, V. *Specialties:* fish of the day, shellfish, red meats; interesting wine list. *Note:* As its name tells you, the rest. occupies a 19th-century grain and feed warehouse on the docks, w. a good view of the Columbia River. Faultless food and svce. *Steak-seafood.* **B–I**

※☀☆☆ **FORT CLATSOP NATIONAL MEMORIAL:** A major landmark in the Winning of the West, marking the limit of the territory explored by the famous expedition of Lewis and Clark. Leaving St. Louis, Mo., in May 1804 on the orders of Pres. Thomas Jefferson, the two officers and their 27 companions crossed the northwestern U.S. in search of the quickest way to the Pacific Ocean. They reached the mouth of the Columbia River in Nov. 1805 and returned to a hero's welcome in St. Louis in Sept. 1806. It was thanks to Lewis and Clark that Americans began to recognize the enormous dimensions of their nation, or rather of the continent with which it was co-extensive. Fort Clatsop, completely reconstructed using original documents, now houses an interesting museum on the odyssey of Lewis and Clark; you'll find it on U.S. 101A (503/861-2471), open daily. Don't miss it.

☆ **SEASIDE:** A well-known oceanside resort for more than a century, with a fine 2-mi. (3-km) beach. At 200 N. Promenade St. there's an interesting aquarium (503/738-6211), open daily Mar.-Nov., Wed.-Sun. the rest of the year.

Where to Stay

♟ **Best Western Seashore Resort,** 60 N. Promenade St., Seaside, OR 97138 (503/738-6368; toll free, see Best Western). 43 rms, cable color TV. AE, CB, DC, MC, V. Free parking, pool, sauna, adjoining coffeeshop. *Note:* Modern motel on the ocean; comfortable rms (the best looking out on the beach); family packages. **I–M**

♟ **City Center,** 250 First Ave. at Columbia St., Seaside, OR 97138 (503/738-6377). 34 rms, color TV, in-rm movies.

MC, V. Free parking, pool, sauna, crib $5. *Note:* Small, well-run conventional motel; nearby coffeeshop, free a.m. coffee; some rms w. kitchenettes. **I, but lower rates Oct.-May**

Where to Eat

The Crab Broiler, intersection of U.S. 26 and U.S. 101 (503/738-5313). A/C. Lunch/dinner daily; closed Thanksgiving, Dec. 24–25, and early Jan. AE, MC, V. *Specialties:* fish of the day, seafood, lobster. *Note:* Agreeable rustic atmosphere (four fireplaces, garden view) and excellent seafood impeccably broiled or otherwise prepared. Very good svce; resv. advised. *Seafood.* **B–I**

CANNON BEACH: Another very popular resort, with a beach 6.8 mi. (11 km) long; its principal feature is a huge solitary rock, 235 ft (72 m) high just offshore from the beach, known as **Haystack Rock.** Flourishing artists' community. From here you have your choice of two interesting excursions: to the 3,820-ft (1,000-m) **Saddle Mountain,** for its views of the coast and the ocean; or to **Ecola Park** on the shoreline, with its seabirds and seals; you should certainly see it.

Where to Stay

IN NEARBY TOLOVANA PARK. The **Tolovana Inn,** 3400 S. Hemlock St., Tolovana Park, OR 97145 (503/436-2211). 180 rms, cable color TV. AE, MC, V. Free parking, pool, sauna, rest., bar, disco, free crib. *Note:* Large vacation motel w. direct access to beach. Spacious, comfortable rms w. private patios or balconies and refrigerators, some w. kitchenettes. Ask for a rm looking out on the ocean and Haystack Rock. Interesting family discounts. **I–M**

TILLAMOOK: Nicknamed "Little Holland" because of its dikes and dairy farms. **Loop Rd.** is a very beautiful scenic highway 19 mi. (31 km) long around **Cape Meares** and the Pacific shore. Don't miss it.

Where to Stay

Best Western Mar-Clair, 11 Main Ave., Tillamook, OR 97141 (503/842-7571; toll free, see Best Western). 47 rms, cable color TV. AE, CB, DC, MC, V. Free parking, pool, sauna, coffeeshop, free crib. *Note:* Modern motel in the center of town; comfortable rms, some w. kitchenettes. Solarium. **I, but lower rates out of season**

Where to Eat

Victory House, 1st and Pacific Sts. (503/842-4111). Lunch/dinner daily; closed Thanksgiving and Dec. 25. AE, CB, DC, MC, V. *Specialties:* sandwiches, steak, fish of the day. *Note:* Engaging Victorian décor; food acceptable but no more; friendly svce. In the center of town. *Steakseafood.* **B–I**

PACIFIC CITY: Famous for its fishermen and their wooden dories which can ride the long Pacific swells (for a small fee you can come along). On your way, stop to look at the ocean from **Cape Lookout,** 18 mi. (30 km) north.

🔔 **LINCOLN CITY:** A popular town for summer homes, with five communities grouped around a beach 3.7 mi. (6 km) long. Many art galleries and crafts shops.

Where to Stay

☀🔔🛏🛏 **Inn at Spanish Head,** 4009 S. U.S. 101, Lincoln City, OR 97367 (503/996-2161). 146 rms, cable color TV. AE, CB, DC, MC, V. Free valet parking, pool, sauna, rest., bar, nightclub, free crib. *Note:* Elegant hostelry of Spanish design on the water. Vast, comfortable rms, most w. private balconies or patios and ocean view, all w. kitchenettes. Adjoining beach. Good svce; a fine place to stay. **M−E, but lower rates out of season**

🛏🛏 **Shilo Inn,** 1501 N.W. 40th St., Lincoln City, OR 97367 (503/994-3655; toll free 800/222-2244). 186 rms, color TV, in-rm movies. AE, CB, DC, MC, V. Free parking, pool, sauna, rest., bar, disco, free crib. *Note:* Three-story motel (no elevator) overlooking the ocean; spacious, comfortable rms w. fireplaces, the best w. a fine view. Free airport limo. Very commendable rest. Good value. **I−M**

🔔🛏 **Nidden Hof,** 136 N.E. U.S. 101, Lincoln City, OR 97367 (503/994-8155). 29 rms, cable color TV. AE, DC, MC, V. Free parking, nearby coffeeshop, crib $5. *Note:* Engaging little motel across from D River Park. Inviting rms w. balconies. Beach nearby. **I, but lower rates Nov.- May**

IN NEARBY GLENEDEN BEACH. The ☀🛏🛏🛏🛏 **Salishan Lodge,** U.S. 101, Gleneden Beach, OR 97388 (503/764-2371; toll free, see Preferred). 151 rms, cable color TV. AE, MC, V. Free covered parking, pool, tennis court, golf course, sauna, health club, rest. (Dining Room), coffeeshop, bar, rm svce, disco, hrdrsr, art gallery, boutiques, crib $6, concierge. *Note:* One of the best hotels in the country; up-to-date elegance in the middle of 617 acres (250 ha.) of woods and gardens. Wonderful setting between the forest and Siletz Bay. Inviting, comfortable two-story buildings overlooking the golf course; spacious rms w. fireplaces, private balconies and patios, the best w. ocean view. Rest. of a high order; excellent svce. A memorable place to stay. **E−VE, but lower rates Nov.-Apr.**

Where to Eat

🍸 **Shilo Inn** (formerly Henry Thiele's), in the Shilo Inn (see "Where to Stay," above) (503/994-5255). Breakfast/lunch/dinner daily. AE, CB, DC, MC, V. *Specialties:* potato pancakes, roast beef, fish of the day. *Note:* Laudable German-inspired dishes, but also good seafood. Lovely ocean view; dancing nightly. Resv. advised. *German-seafood.* **B−I**

IN NEARBY GLENEDEN BEACH. 🍸🍸🍸🍸 **The Dining Room,** in the Salishan Lodge (see "Where to Stay," above) (503/764-2371). A/C. Dinner only, nightly (two seatings, at 6 and 10 p.m.). AE, CB, DC, MC, V. Jkt. *Specialties:* Dungeness crab, Chinook salmon, filet of sole, chateaubriand, Oregon lamb chops. Very good wine list, with more than 1,000 labels. *Note:* One of the best rests. on the Pacific coast. Three-level dining rm, recently renovated, elegantly paneled and w. a pretty view over the bay. Carefully worked-out cuisine, based on remarkably fine local produce—seafood, lamb, game, wild mushrooms, etc. Exemplary svce. Resv. a must, especially on wknds. *Continental-seafood.* **M−E**

🔔 **DEPOE BAY:** Tiny, picturesque fishing port; you must stop to look at the **Spouting Horns,** rock formations that spout like geysers under the violent assault of the waves. Don't miss them.

Where to Stay

Surfrider, U.S. 101, Depoe Bay, OR 97341 (503/764-2311). 40 rms, color TV, in-rm movies. AE, MC, V. Free parking, pool, sauna, rest., bar, disco, crib $2. *Note:* Small, likeable, serviceable motel at the water's edge; comfortable rms w. balconies overlooking the Pacific. Excellent reception. **I–M, but lower rates Oct.-May**

Holiday Surf Lodge, U.S. 101, Depoe Bay, OR 97341 (503/765-2133). 84 rms, cable color TV. AE, MC, V. Free parking, pool, health club, nearby rest., free crib. *Note:* Typical motel w. direct beach access. Functional rms, some w. private patios and kitchenettes, most w. ocean view. Free morning coffee. **I–M**

DEVIL'S PUNCH BOWL STATE PARK: A strange rock, hollowed out like a swimming pool, which fills at each high tide. Beach; aquatic garden. From **Cape Foulweather,** so named by the British navigator Capt. James Cook in 1778, you'll have a fine view of the ocean. Should definitely be seen.

NEWPORT: One of the busiest fishing ports on the Pacific coast, with fine Victorian houses and colorful docks. **Hatfield Marine Science Center,** Marine Science Dr. (503/867-3011), open daily, is an excellent museum of oceanography affiliated with Oregon State University. There's also a renowned saltwater aquarium, **Underseas Gardens,** at 267 S.W. Bay Blvd. (503/265-2206), open daily; shouldn't be missed.

Where to Stay

Embarcadero Resort, 1000 S.E. Bay Blvd., Newport, OR 97365 (503/265-8521; toll free 800/547-4779). 110 rms, no A/C, cable color TV. AE, CB, DC, MC, V. Free parking, pool, sauna, marina, boating, rest. (Embarcadero), bar, rm svce, disco, crib $5. *Note:* Luxurious vacation hotel on the Yaquina River, w. marina and boat dock. Elegant, comfortable rms, all w. private balconies or patios, some w. kitchenettes. Flawless reception and svce; excellent rest.; beautiful views. One of the best places to stay on the West Coast. **M–E, but lower rates Nov.-Apr.**

Newport Hotel (formerly the Hilton Inn), 3019 N. Coast Hwy., Newport, OR 97365 (503/265-9411). 150 rms, color TV, in-rm movies. AE, CB, DC, MC, V. Free parking, pool, rest., bar, rm svce, disco, free crib. *Note:* Modern six-story motel w. balconies and direct beach access. Spacious, comfortable rms; efficient svce; interesting family discounts. Wonderful ocean view. **I–M**

Jolly Knight, 606 S.W. Coast Hwy., Newport, OR 97365 (503/265-7723). 43 rms, color TV, in-rm movies. AE, MC, V. Free parking, adjoining 24-hr rest., free crib. *Note:* Small, unpretentious oceanfront motel; spacious, serviceable rms, the best with a fine view. **I, but lower rates Oct.-May**

Youth Hostel, 212 N.W. Brook St., Newport, OR 97365 (503/265-9816). 24 beds. Open year round.

Where to Eat

Embarcadero, in the Embarcadero Resort (see "Where to Stay," above) (503/265-8521). A/C. Lunch/dinner daily, brunch Sun. AE, CB, DC, MC, V. Jkt. *Specialties:* fish of the day, shellfish, steak.

Note: All-purpose seafaring décor but pretty view of the harbor. First-class food; absolutely fresh seafood. *Steak-seafood.* **B–I**

YACHATS: Fashionable seaside resort with a beautiful fine-sand beach and a very craggy shoreline. The coastal highway here is beautiful beyond description.

Where to Stay
Adobe Hotel, U.S. 101 (P.O. Box 219), Yachats, OR 97498 (503/547-3141). 58 rms, cable color TV. AE, CB, DC, MC, V. Free parking, pool, sauna, rest., bar, crib $4. *Note:* Appealing little motel right on the ocean; huge, inviting rms w. fireplaces and refrigerators, most w. balconies, the best overlooking the Pacific. Cheerful reception and svce; free morning coffee. An excellent place to stay. **I–M, but lower rates out of season**

Where to Eat
River View Inn, U.S. 101 (503/547-4132). Lunch/dinner Tues.-Sun.; closed Mon. and Dec. 24. AE, MC, V. *Specialties:* fish, steak. *Note:* Small, modest, unpretentious rest., serving food that's commendable but no more. *Steak-seafood.* **B–I**

SEA LION CAVES: On U.S. 101 (503/547-3111). A basalt grotto 1,500 ft (450 m) long, 208 ft (63 m) below the surface, inhabited by a seal colony. Open daily; touristy, but spectacular nonetheless.

FLORENCE: A charming little town with a wealth of flowers on the Siuslaw River, very near a chain of lakes and the **Siuslaw National Forest.** It marks the northern boundary of the **Oregon Dunes National Recreation Area,** a huge sandspit 50 mi. (80 km) long, whose dunes rise as high as 524 ft (160 m). Dunebuggy rides available (503/271-3611). Shouldn't be missed.

Where to Stay
Le Château, 1084 Coast Hwy., Florence, OR 97439 (503/ 997-3481). 48 rms, color TV, in-rm movies. AE, MC, V. Free parking, pool, sauna, nearby coffeeshop, crib $4. *Note:* Typical vacation motel w. direct beach access. Spacious rms; functionally comfortable; cheerful reception; free morning coffee. **I, but lower rates Oct.-Apr.**

Where to Eat
Windward Inn, 3757 U.S. 101 (503/997-8243). A/C. Breakfast/lunch/dinner Tues.-Sun.; closed Mon., Thanksgiving, and Dec. 24–25. AE, CB, DC, MC, V. *Specialties:* fish of the day, very fine red meats, fresh fruit and vegetables. *Note:* The two major achievements of this excellent rest., much appreciated by those in-the-know, are the low prices it charges for materials of the highest quality, and its well-stocked wine list. *Steak-seafood.* **B–I**

REEDSPORT: Both saltwater and freshwater fishing enthusiasts can enjoy themselves here at the head of **Winchester Bay.** The headquarters of the **Oregon Dunes National Recreation Area** (see above) is here, at 855 Highway Ave. (503/271-3611).

▲ **COOS BAY:** The world's biggest lumber port; also a busy fishing port. At **North Bend,** on the same bay, there's an interesting museum devoted to the settlement of Oregon, the **Coos County Historical Museum,** Simpson Park on U.S. 101 (503/756-6320), open Tues.-Sun., June-Sept.; Tues.-Sat. rest of year.

☀ ▲▲ Crater Lake National Park

Some 182 mi. (292 km) SE of Coos Bay via Ore. 42 and Ore. 38 is one of the loveliest mountain lakes in the U.S., or indeed in the world, in the caldera of the extinct volcano **Mount Mazama.** A violent eruption some 6,600 years ago created this steep-sided, circular basin, 7 mi. (11 km) across and, at 1,932 ft (589 m), the deepest lake in the country. The reflection of the surrounding peaks and craters in its clear dark-blue waters delineates a surprisingly beautiful volcanic landscape. **Rim Drive,** a 33-mi. (53-km) scenic highway, follows the shoreline; there are many **hiking trails,** including a steep path leading up to Watchman's Peak (8,022 ft, 2,457 m) with its unparalleled view. There are **observation platforms,** which can be reached by car, at the top of Cloudcap (8,060 ft, 2,457 m) and Pinnacles (5,585 ft, 1,672 m), strange needles of tufa and pumice carved out by erosion. Many wild animals live around Crater Lake: black bear, elk, red fox, coyote, wildcat, and others; fish, on the other hand, are few and fishing is strictly regulated. Boat rides may be taken on the lake, but be careful if you go swimming: the water is ice-cold even in summer.

Given the status of a national park in 1902, Crater Lake is open year round (except for the northern entrance, which is closed mid-Oct. to mid-June because of snowslides). At any time of year take warm clothing—it snows 10 months out of the 12. Campsites and a rustic motel are inside the park.

For **information,** contact the Superintendent, Crater Lake National Park, P.O. Box 7, Crater Lake, OR 97604 (503/594-2211). A trip not to be missed.

Where to Stay

♌♌ **Thunderbird Motor Inn,** 1313 N. Bayshore Dr., Coos Bay, OR 97420 (503/267-4141; toll free, see Red Lion Inns). 168 rms (half w. A/C), cable color TV. AE, CB, DC, MC, V. Free parking, pool, rest., bar, rm svce, disco, crib $5. *Note:* In a lovely situation w. a view of the bay. Vast, inviting rms; up-to-date, comfortable facilities, good svce; free airport limo. **I–M**

Youth Hostel, 438 Elrod, Coos Bay, OR 97420 (503/267-6114). 20 beds. Open late May to Sept.

▲ **BANDON:** Little harbor, very popular with tourists, at the mouth of the Coquille River. Lovely beaches famed for the agates and other semiprecious stones you can pick up here.

Where to Stay

♌ **Bandon Beach Motel,** 110 W. 11th St., Bandon, OR 97411 (503/347-2103). 28 rms, color TV, in-rm movies. AE, MC, V. Free parking, adjoining coffeeshop, crib $4. *Note:* Tiny motel on a cliff overlooking the beach; decent standard of comfort; some rms w. balconies and kitchenettes. **I, but lower rates Oct.-May**

Youth Hostel, 375 2nd St., Bandon, OR 97411 (503/347-9533). 35 beds. Open year round.

Where to Eat

☙ **Bandon Boatworks,** 275 Lincoln Ave. SW (503/347-2111). Lunch/dinner Tues.-Sun.; closed Mon. and holidays. MC, V. *Specialties:* fish of the day, steak, milk-fed veal, Mexican dishes. *Note:* Excellent fish, as well as some good Mexican dishes on wknds. Nice view of the jetty and lighthouse. Congenial atmosphere; good svce. *American-Mexican.* **B–I**

☀☙ **PORT ORFORD:** Some of the loveliest seascapes on the Oregon coast. In 1851 the little port was the scene of a bloody battle between Indians and white settlers. At ☙ **Cape Blanco,** 7½ mi. (12 km) NW on U.S. 101, there's a strange black-sand beach which you have to see.

Where to Stay

☙ **Sea Crest,** U.S. 101, Port Orford, OR 97465 (503/332-3040). 18 rms, cable color TV. MC, V. Free parking, nearby coffeeshop, crib $3. *Note:* Mini-motel w. ocean and mountain views. Rms no better than serviceable, but inviting garden and cheerful reception. **I, but lower rates out of season**

☙ **GOLD BEACH:** Owes its name to the gold nuggets that used to be found at the mouth of the **Rogue River** until, in 1861, a lamentable flood swept them all out to sea. Fine excursions into the nearby **Siskiyou National Forest;** also rafting down the Rogue River (see "Adventures," above). Worth the side trip.

Where to Stay

☀☙☙ **Tu Tu Tun Lodge,** 96550 N. Bank Rogue, Gold Beach, OR 97444 (503/247-6664). 18 rms. MC, V. Free parking, pool, fishing, putting green, rest., bar, crib $6. *Note:* Charming country cottage on the Rogue River; boat trips available. Spacious, inviting rms w. balconies; well-stocked library for inveterate idlers. An agreeable, relaxing stopover. Free airport limo.; closed Nov.-Apr. **E**

☙ **Ireland's Rustic Lodges,** 1120 S. Ellensburg, Gold Beach, OR 97444 (503/247-7718). 29 units, cable color TV. No credit cards. Free parking, private beach, nearby coffeeshop, crib $5. *Note:* Pretty little bungalows in a garden overlooking the ocean; the best have ocean views. Spacious rms w. balconies, some w. kitchenettes and fireplaces. Good value on balance. **I–M, but lower rates Oct.-May**

☙ **CRESCENT CITY:** The first important town across the northern border of California, deriving its name from its crescent-shaped coastline. Interesting saltwater aquarium, **Undersea World,** 304 U.S. 101S (707/464-3522), open daily. From here you can easily venture into Redwood National Park with its amazing sequoia forests. Don't miss it.

☀ ☙ Redwood National Park

Just 4 mi. (6 km) east of Crescent City, this forest of giant sequoias (redwoods), 46 mi. (75 km) long by 6 mi. (10 km) wide, stands on the shore. Some redwoods, more than ten centuries old, have grown to 295 ft (90 m); the present record is held by the prosaically nicknamed **Tall Tree,** 368 ft (112 m) high, with a diameter of 14 ft (4.20 m). This is the largest-known living creature in the world. Abundant wildlife: elk, deer, mountain lion, bald eagle, brown pelican, and peregrine falcons. The park is traversed by a splendid scenic highway, U.S. 101. Many hiking trails, campsites, and picnic areas.

There are three other redwood forests nearby: **Jedediah Smith State Park, Del Norte Coast State Park,** and **Prairie Creek State Park;** along with Redwood National Park they make up the **Redwood Empire,** a vast tract of woodlands extending from the northern border of California to the outskirts of San Francisco.

For **information,** contact the Superintendent, Redwood National Park, 1111 2nd St., Crescent City, CA 95531 (707/464-6101). Don't miss it.

☀ ☖ Oregon Caves National Monument

These marble caverns, 85 mi. (136 km) NE of Crescent City via U.S. 199 and Ore. 46, comprising a number of evocatively named chambers—Paradise Lost, Ghost Chamber, Joaquin Miller's Chapel—were discovered in 1874 by a hunter in pursuit of a bear; they are among the most unusual and beautiful in the U.S. Their air temperature is a constant 42°F (6°C). Tours (exhausting) daily year round. For **information,** contact Oregon Caves National Monument, Cave Junction, OR 97523 (503/592-3400).

Around the caves is ☖ **Siskiyou National Forest,** whose cedars—200- to 300-year-old pine trees growing as tall as 130 ft (40 m)—conifers, orchids, and rare plants make it a botanist's paradise.

Where to Stay

Royal Inn, 102 L St. at Front St., Crescent City, CA 95531 (707/464-4113). 30 rms, cable color TV. AE, MC, V. Free covered parking, nearby rest., free crib. *Note:* A fine ocean view is the main attraction of this typical small motel. Spacious rms w. balconies; free morning coffee. **I, but lower rates out of season**

IN NEARBY SMITH RIVER. The ☖☖ **Best Western Ship Ashore,** U.S. 101, Smith River, CA 95567 (707/487-3141; toll free, see Best Western). 35 rms, cable color TV. AE, CB, DC, MC, V. Free parking, coffeeshop, bar, disco, grocery store, crib $6. *Note:* Small, modern motel overlooking the ocean; comfortable rms w. balconies and Pacific or river views. Boat rentals for sportfishing. Free morning coffee. Parking for motor homes. **I–M, but lower rates out of season**

IN NEARBY KLAMATH. The **Youth Hostel,** 14480 U.S. 101, Klamath, CA 95548 (707/482-8265). 29 beds. Open Nov.-Apr.

Where to Eat

Harbor View Grotto, Citizen's Dock (707/464-3815). A/C. Lunch/dinner daily; closed Thanksgiving and Dec. 25. No credit cards. *Specialties:* clam chowder, seafood, ribs of beef, steak. *Note:* Classic fish rest. on the docks; absolutely fresh seafood nicely prepared. From the upstairs rm you have a harbor view. *Steak-seafood.* **B–I**

McKINLEYVILLE: Look over the world's largest totem pole, 162 ft (50 m) high and weighing 26 tons. It was carved from the trunk of a single tree, more than 500 years old.

EUREKA: This very busy port town has a sheltered harbor at the head of **Humboldt Bay,** but is often foggy even in summer.

Many beautiful frame houses (wood is the principal local resource). See the splendid 1885 ⌂ **Carson Mansion** at 143 M St., a perfect specimen of Victorian architecture, unfortunately not open to visitors.

A dozen miles to the south, the little town of ⌂ **Ferndale** is a living museum of the Victorian style.

Where to Stay

☼ ♘ � **Eureka Inn,** 7th and F Sts., Eureka, CA 99501 (707/442-6441; toll free 800/862-4906 in California). 110 rms, cable color TV. AE, CB, DC, MC, V. Free parking, pool, sauna, rest., coffeeshop, rm svce, nightclub, free crib, concierge. *Note:* Elegant, comfortable Tudor-style inn dating from 1922; huge, inviting rms w. private patios or balconies. Exemplary svce; very commendable rest.; free airport limo. An excellent place to stay. **M–E**

♘ **Royal Pacific,** 1304 4th St., Eureka, CA 99501 (707/443-3193; toll free 800/235-3232). 50 rms, color TV, in-rm movies. AE, CB, DC, MC, V. Free parking, pool, sauna, adjoining coffeeshop, bar, crib $5. *Note:* Well-kept conventional motel; inviting rms w. balconies; free morning coffee. **I–M**

IN NEARBY ARCATA. ♘ **Motel 6,** 4755 Valley West Blvd., Arcata, CA 95521 (707/822-7061). 81 rms, A/C, color TV, free in-rm movies. DC, MC, V. Free parking. Pool. No bar or rest. Free crib. *Note:* Unbeatable value 10 min. from dwntwn Eureka. Serviceable comfort; friendly reception. Ideal for the budget traveler. **B**
Youth Hostel, 1390 Eye St., Arcata, CA 95521 (707/822-9995). 20 beds. Open from late May to Sept.

IN NEARBY FERNDALE. The ☼ ♘♘ **Gingerbread Mansion,** 400 Berding St., Ferndale, CA 95536 (707/786-4000). 8 rms. MC, V. Free parking, rest., free breakfast. *Note:* Delightful turn-of-the-century Victorian house in a very pretty English-style garden in the heart of Ferndale's historic district. Elegant rms w. period furniture, some without baths. Impeccable reception and svce. Resv. essential, well ahead. **I–M**

Where to Eat

☼ ♟♟ **Lazio's Seafood,** 4 C St. on Humboldt Bay (707/442-2337). Breakfast/lunch/dinner daily; closed holidays. AE, CB, DC, MC, V. *Specialties:* crab, fresh seafood, sourdough bread. *Note:* Opened in 1946 in an old fish cannery, this rest. is the proud possession of the Lazio family, fishermen from father to son for more than a century. The seafood is superb, as you'd expect. Pretty maritime décor; attentive svce. *Seafood.* **B–I**

♟ **Samoa Cookhouse,** Samoa Blvd. (707/442-1659). Breakfast/lunch/dinner daily; closed Thanksgiving and Dec. 25. AE, CB, DC, MC, V. *Specialties:* barbecued meats, western-style food. *Note:* This locally popular place is more like a museum than a rest., w. its many mementoes of pioneer days. Tasty country cooking; excellent value. Don't miss it. *American.* **B**

☼ ♟♟ **AVENUE OF THE GIANTS:** An extraordinary slash through the middle of the sequoias of **Humboldt National Forest,** the Avenue of the Giants runs parallel to U.S. 101 for 33 mi. (52 km), beginning south of Pepperwood, like a sort of giant green tunnel; it's a sight you should try to see.

Where to Stay

IN GARBERVILLE. The ☀ ℓ ℓ **Benbow Inn,** 445 Lake Benbow Dr., Garberville, CA 95440 (707/923-2124). 55 rms, cable color TV. AE, MC, V. Free parking, private beach, golf course, boating, rest., bar, nightclub. *Note:* An old English manor house on the shore of a wooded lake, for a perfect picture-postcard vacation. Charming décor and reception. Avoid the upper floors—no elevators. Closed early Dec., and from Jan. 2 to mid-Apr. **M**

IN PIERCY. The ℓ **Hartsook Inn,** 900 U.S. 101, Piercy, CA 95467 (707/247-3305). 62 rms, color TV (in lounge). AE, MC, V. Free parking, private beach, rest., crib $3. *Note:* Spacious, comfortable rms in little bungalows along the Eel River in a 30-acre (12-ha.) park. Very acceptable rest; friendly reception and svce. Closed Oct.-Apr. **I–M**

Where to Eat

IN GARBERVILLE. The ♈ **Benbow Inn,** in the Benbow Inn (see "Where to Stay," above) (707/923-2124). Breakfast/lunch/dinner daily; closed Jan. to mid-Mar. AE, MC, V. *Specialties:* fresh salmon in season, veal Italian style, fish of the day, sweetbreads Marnie, rack of lamb. *Note:* Praiseworthy hotel rest. in a pretty waterside park w. open-air dining in summer. Faultless food; agreeable background music. *Continental-seafood.* **B–I**

☀🔔 **FORT BRAGG:** This charming little harbor town, originally founded in 1857 and standing in the center of a superb stretch of rocky coast, was rebuilt after the 1906 earthquake that also destroyed San Francisco. The scenery is lovely. Take a ride on the **California Western Railroad,** a Far West–style line which follows the Noyo River through some magnificent redwood (sequoia) forests as far as Willits; it leaves from Laurel St. (707/964-6371). The round trip takes seven hours, and operates daily year round.

Where to Stay

🔔 **Harbor Lite Lodge,** 120 N. Harbor Dr., Fort Bragg, CA 95437 (707/964-0221). 70 rms, color TV, in-rm movies. AE, CB, DC, MC, V. Free parking, beach, sauna, nearby coffeeshop, crib $5. *Note:* Vacation motel a stone's throw from the beach. Inviting rms w. balconies, the best overlooking Noyo harbor. Direct beach access; good value. **I–M, but lower rates out of season**

Where to Eat

♈ **The Restaurant,** 418 N. Main St. (707/964-9800). Lunch/ dinner Thur.-Tues.; closed Wed., three weeks in Mar., Thanksgiving, and Dec. 25. MC, V. *Specialties:* fresh salmon in season, pork schnitzel, trout stuffed w. crabmeat, saltimbocca of chicken. *Note:* This little rest. in the heart of dwntwn serves some rather unusual fare at a very reasonable price. Resv. advised. *Continental.* **B–I**

🔔 **NOYO:** Picturesque little fishing village at the mouth of the Noyo River. The **Mendocino Coast Botanical Gardens,** on Calif. 1 (707/964-4352), open daily, is a magnificent 17-acre (6.8-ha.) flower garden overlooking the ocean; you shouldn't miss it.

☀ 🔔 **MENDOCINO:** Very pretty little harbor town perched on a rock, which has retained a carefully cultivated 19th-century flavor with its Victorian houses, artists' colony, art galleries, antique dealers, and tourist restaurants. Worth seeing.

Another 3.7 mi. (6 km) south, 🏕 **Van Damme State Park** on Calif. 1 is a very unusual pigmy forest. The poverty of the soil has stunted the trees so that some of them, as much as 20 years old, are only 3 ft (1 m) tall and 2 in. (6 cm) through the trunk; definitely well worth seeing.

Where to Stay

☀ 🍷 🍷 **Mendocino Hotel,** 45080 Main St., Mendocino, CA 95460 (707/937-0511; toll free 800/421-6662). 51 rms, A/C, cable color TV (in most). AE, MC, V. Free parking, rest., bar, rm svce, free breakfast. *Note:* Picturesque hotel from the 1870s, wonderfully well restored. The rms, some without bath, are inviting and tastefully decorated; a certain number have balconies and fireplaces. Laudable rest. Lovely views of the harbor and ocean; attentive reception and svce; free airport limo. A fine place to stay, but you must reserve well ahead of time. **E–VE, but lower rates out of season**

IN NEARBY LITTLERIVER. The ☀ 🍷🍷 **Heritage House,** 5200 Calif. 1, Littleriver, CA 95456 (707/937-5885). 69 rms. No credit cards. Free parking, rest., bar. *Note:* Delightfully romantic little cottages on a cliff overlooking the ocean. The main building dates from 1877. Elegant old furniture; spacious, attractive rms w. private balconies or patios, the best overlooking the Pacific. Renowned rest. In spite of the high rates, this is a very good place to stay; you have to reserve well in advance. Closed Dec.-Jan. **E–VE**

Where to Eat

☀ 🍷 **Café Beaujolais,** 961 E. Ukiah St. (707/937-5614). Breakfast/lunch daily, dinner Thurs.–Sun.; closed Thanksgiving, Dec. 25, and Jan.-Feb. No credit cards. *Specialties:* white-bean and tomato soup, polenta, fresh salmon (in season), waffles, coffee cake. *Note:* Delightful bistro; décor a faithful Victorian re-creation w. an outdoor patio for fine days. Traditional but pleasing food. Resv. advisable. *Continental-seafood.* **B–I**

☀ 🍷 **Mendocino Hotel** (see "Where to Stay," above) (707/937-0511). Breakfast/lunch/dinner daily. MC, V. *Specialties:* fish of the day, steak, homemade cakes. *Note:* The dining rm of that magnificent designated landmark, the 1878 Mendocino Hotel. Charming and picturesque; the setting deserves better in the way of food. Resv. advised. *Steak-seafood.* **B–I**

IN NEARBY LITTLERIVER. The ☀ 🍷🍷 **Ledford House,** Calif. 1 (707/937-0282). Dinner only, nightly; brunch Sun.; closed Thanksgiving, early Dec., and Dec. 25. No credit cards. Jkt. *Specialties:* shrimp cannelloni, fish of the day, baked lamb. *Note:* Beautiful, inviting century-old house looking out on the ocean; inspired cuisine and some fine California wines. Attentive svce; resv. a must. *Continental-seafood.* **I–E**

IN NEARBY ALBION. The ☀ 🍷🍷 **Albion River Inn,** 3790 Calif. 1 (707/937-4044). Dinner only, nightly. MC, V. Jkt. *Specialties:* pasta primavera, linguine w. clams, bouillabaisse, fish of the day. *Note:* Delightful little inn perched on a cliff over-looking Albion Cove. Simple but careful cuisine; many works by local artists adorn the walls. Romantic atmosphere; resv. advised. A fine place. *Continental-seafood.* I

POINT ARENA: Beautiful ocean view from Point Arena, with its famous lighthouse; **Manchester Beach** is nearby.

Where to Stay

IN NEARBY GUALALA. The ☼ ⌘ ♨ **St. Orres,** Calif. 1, Gualala, CA 95445 (707/884-3303). 17 rms, cottages. MC, V. Free parking, sauna, rest., bar, free breakfast. *Note:* Charming tiny inn, w. architecture reminiscent of a Russian dacha and its onion-domed towers, facing the ocean; inviting rms w. balconies (some without bath), or little individual redwood cottages. Unusual interiors w. lovely old paneling. Top-quality rest.; direct beach access. One of the best places to stay on the coast. **M (rooms), M–E (cottages)**

Where to Eat

IN NEARBY GUALALA. The ☼ ♈♈ **St. Orres,** in the St. Orres Hotel (see "Where to Stay," above) (707/884-3335). Dinner only, nightly, brunch Sun.; closed Jan. No credit cards. Jkt. *Specialties:* rack of lamb dijonnaise, roast quail, New York steak, fish of the day. *Note:* Pretty stained-glass window and old paneling; very successful French-inspired cuisine. Charming, romantic atmosphere; resv. a must. *Continental.* **M (prix fixe)**

FORT ROSS: The main Russian outpost in America, this trading post was founded in 1812 by the Russian-American Co. as a base for seal hunting. It was sold in 1841 to the Swiss John Sutter, founder of Sacramento and an important figure in the early development of California. There remain only the fine Russian Orthodox chapel, dating from about 1820, and a few other buildings from the fort. It's on Calif. 1 (707/865-2391), open daily, and you should certainly see it.

BODEGA BAY: Attractive little harbor at the head of a very deep bay. Bodega Bay was the setting for Alfred Hitchcock's movie *The Birds.*

Where to Stay

Best Western Bodega Bay Lodge, Calif. 1, Bodega Bay, CA 94923 (707/874-3525; toll free, see Best Western). 78 rms, cable color TV. AE, CB, DC, MC, V. Free parking, pool, sauna. *Note:* Functional motel overlooking Bodega Bay and Doran Park beach. Spacious rms w. balconies, some w. fireplaces and refrigerators. Nearby rest.; adjoining golf course; free morning coffee. Rates on the high side for an ordinary motel. **M–E**

POINT REYES NATIONAL SEASHORE (35 mi., 56 km, NW of San Francisco): 74,000-acre (29,960-ha.) wildlife reserve on the Pacific; see Chapter 51 on San Francisco.

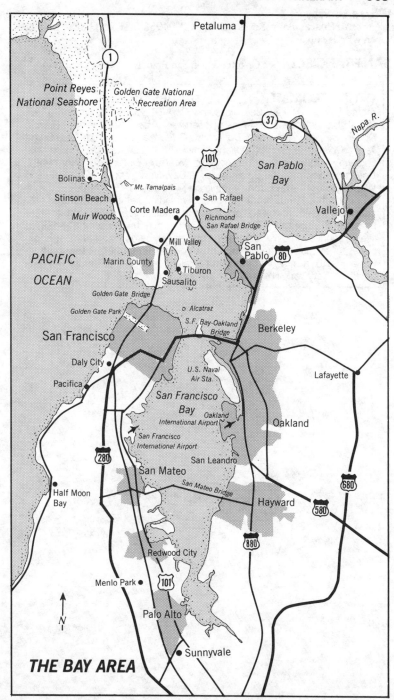

THE BAY AREA

Where to Stay

Youth Hostel, Point Reyes Station, CA 94956 (415/663-8811). 44 beds. Open wknds only.

SAN FRANCISCO: See Chapter 51 on San Francisco.

OTHER FROMMER TRAVEL GUIDES: *Dollarwise USA* complements 13 other Dollarwise Guides and 3 $-A-Day Guides dealing with individual U.S. states and areas: *Dollarwise Alaska, Dollarwise Florida, Dollarwise New York State, Dollarwise California & Las Vegas, Dollarwise Texas, Dollarwise Cruises, Dollarwise Mid-Atlantic States, Dollarwise New England, Dollarwise South-Atlantic States, Dollarwise Northwest, Dollarwise Southwest, Hawaii on $50 a Day, New York on $50 a Day,* and *Washington, D.C., & Historic Virginia on $40 a Day.*

In contrast to the book you are now reading, which highlights 57 U.S. cities and scenic areas, each of the above guides treats one particular state or area in the fullest detail setting forth scores of hotel, restaurant, and sightseeing suggestions. Frommer travel guides can be obtained at most bookstores, or by mailing the appropriate amount (turn to the last few pages in this guide) to Frommer Books, Prentice Hall Trade Division, One Gulf + Western Plaza, New York, NY 10023.

PART SEVEN

THE WEST

CHAPTER 47

LAS VEGAS

□ □ □

"The Gambling Capital of the World" bears no relation to any ordinary city. It is a huge, enthralling slot machine that functions around the clock. This brilliant, showy outburst of neon and glass plumb in the middle of the Mojave Desert is well worth going out of your way to see. Arriving by air at night is a whole show in itself.

Las Vegas (a name which in Spanish means "valley of fertile farmland") was founded in the mid-19th century by Mormons on the colonial trail from Santa Fe to California. Thereafter it went into a long decline until the construction of the Union Pacific's first line of track in 1905. The adoption of new gambling laws by the State of Nevada in 1931 made the fortune of Las Vegas, which the writer Tom Wolfe has called "the most American of American cities." The population has grown from barely 8,000 in 1940 to 620,000 today. This figure does not include the 15 or 16 million tourists who come, year after year, to try their luck at the casino tables or the famous slot machines. Las Vegas has some 33,000 slot machines, about one for every six inhabitants, and 1,300 blackjack tables. In this city everything revolves around gambling, an industry with annual revenues of almost $3 billion, and there are slot machines even in the rest rooms. Nevada's largest city cannot show a single monument or museum worthy of its standing; its only gesture in the direction of culture is the big floor show, presenting the brightest stars in the firmament of entertainment, from Jerry Lewis or Frank Sinatra to Liza Minnelli, and from Sammy Davis, Jr., to Donna Summer or Julio Iglesias.

The glittering palaces along the "Strip," Las Vegas's main drag, offer their rooms at bargain-basement prices. Food at the city's 725 restaurants, cafeterias, and snackbars costs half what it would anywhere else in the country. But don't mistake this for philanthropy or hospitality. It reflects, rather, a (justified) expectation that the visitor or conventioneer, bitten by the gambling fever, will rush to unload his precious dollars on the green baize of the tables or in the slots of the "one-armed bandits" before the plane or the bus comes to take him away again.

If gambling, show business, and conventions are Las Vegas's principal industries, the dozens of "wedding chapels," open until midnight on weekdays and around the clock on weekends, represent the brighter side of the local economy. Las Vegas has more churches, chapels, and other places of worship per thousand inhabitants than any other city in the country. Every year, under the accommodating laws of Nevada, more than 60,000 "marriages on the wing" are performed in Las Vegas by an army of ministers familiarly known as "Marryin' Sams"—between games of poker, blackjack, or baccarat.

Thanks to its low car-rental rates Las Vegas is also a good base for excursions nearby (**Lake Mead, Valley of Fire, Hoover Dam, Red Rock Canyon, Mount Charleston**) or farther afield (the **Grand Canyon** of the Colorado, **Death Valley,** the **Utah national parks**).

BASIC FACTS: State of Nevada. Area Code: 702. Time Zone: Pacific Time (3 hrs behind New York City). ZIP Code: 89114. Founded: 1855. Approximate population: city, 200,000; metropolitan area, 620,000.

CLIMATE: Dry heat and a cloudless sky are the rule here. Summer is a scorcher (as high as 104°F, 40°C, or even higher, in July-Aug.). Spring and fall are more temperate (68°–77°F, 20°–25°C, on the average), but as always, in the desert the nights can be chilly. In winter, although the sun still shines (as it is guaranteed to do for 320 days a year), temperatures vary around a mean of 50°F (10°C).

DISTANCES: Denver, 780 mi. (1,248 km); Los Angeles, 282 mi. (451 km); Phoenix, 285 mi. (456 km); Salt Lake City, 439 mi. (702 km); San Francisco, 568 mi. (908 km).

ARRIVAL & TRANSIT INFORMATION

AIRPORT: McCarran International Airport (LAS), 10 mi. (6 km) south, handles more charter traffic than any other airport in the world. Spectacular futurist décor. Information: 798-5410.

AIRLINES: Air Nevada (736-8900), America West (736-1737), American (385-3781), Continental (383-8291), Delta (731-3111), Northwest (385-2400), Scenic Air Lines (739-1900), Southwest (382-1221), TWA (385-1000), United (395-3222).

CITY LINK: Your cab fare to the Strip will run about $10 (to dwntwn, $15); time, about 15–20 min. Bus: Gray Line Airport Express (toll free 800/634-6570) leaves every 10 min. for the Strip, every 45 min. for dwntwn. Serves principal hotels; fare, $4; time, about 25–35 min.

Cabs are expensive; public transportation (bus, Las Vegas Transit System) is low priced and relatively efficient (but should be avoided at night); for information, call 384-3540. Bus no. 6 runs the whole length of the Strip. Walking can be exhausting, particularly in summer; the city's avenues are unending, straight as a die, and without the least patch of shade or the smallest tree; remember that summer temperatures are in the range of 95°–104°F (35°–40°C). Air-conditioned cars can be rented anywhere at attractive prices.

CAR RENTAL (at McCarran International Airport unless otherwise noted): Abbey, 3751 Las Vegas Blvd. (736-4988), a local company with attractive rates; Avis (739-5595); Budget (735-9311); Dollar (739-8400); Hertz (736-4900); National (739-5391); Thrifty (736-4706). (All except Abbey and Avis offer free pickup/delivery at place of residence.) For dwntwn locations, consult the local telephone directory.

LIMOUSINE SERVICES: Bell Limousine (736-4428), Dav El Limos (toll free 800/922-0343).

TAXIS: Cabs may be hailed on the street or taken from the lines outside the big hotels, but it's more convenient to use the phone. Recommended companies: Checker (873-2227), Desert Cab (736-1702), Whittlesea Blue Cab (384-6111), Yellow Cab (873-2227).

TRAIN: AMTRAK Station, Union Plaza, 1 Main St. (toll free 800/872-7245).

BUS: Greyhound, 200 S. Main St. (384-9561).

INFORMATION & TOURS

TOURIST INFORMATION: The **Las Vegas Chamber of Commerce,** 2301 E. Sahara Ave., NV 89105 (702/457-4664).

Las Vegas Convention and Visitors Authority, Convention Center, 3150 Paradise Rd., NV 89109 (702/733-2323).

For a **recorded message** listing current events and shows, call 457-4664.

GUIDED TOURS: American Sightseeing (384-1230) and **Gray Line Tours** (384-1234): Guided (bus) tours of the city, serving the principal hotels.

Lake Mead Yacht Tour (boat), Nev. 41, **Boulder Harbor** (736-6180): 1½ hour excursions on Lake Mead as far as Hoover Dam; daily, year round.

SIGHTS, ATTRACTIONS, & ACTIVITIES

ADVENTURES: Black Canyon, Inc. (boat), P.O. Box 96, Boulder City, NV 89005 (293-3776): Rafting down the Colorado River from Boulder City; summer only.

Scenic Airlines (air), 241 E. Reno Ave. (739-1900): Air trips over the Grand Canyon. Also **Air Nevada,** 6005 S. Las Vegas Blvd. (736-8900): One-day excursion, including lunch, $180; daily, year round.

ARCHITECTURAL HIGHLIGHTS: ※ ⚖ **Circus Circus,** 2880 Las Vegas Blvd. (734-0410): Looking like the Big Top of some gigantic circus, this is the most originally designed hotel-casino in Vegas. While the gamblers are trying their luck at the casino tables, trapeze artists, tightrope walkers, and acrobats are strutting their stuff overhead. Worth seeing.

⚖ **Convention Center,** 3150 Paradise Rd. (733-2323): One million square feet (300,000 square meters) of covered exhibition space make this modern steel-and-concrete structure the country's largest one-level convention hall. It has room for more than 7,000 participants at meetings or banquets. Las Vegas has developed the convention business (the city averages one a day) into a source of revenue second only to gambling. Should be seen.

CHURCHES/SYNAGOGUES: The **Wedding Chapels:** With some 30 of these institutions at last count, Las Vegas can style itself the country's wedding capital as well as its gaming capital. There is only one requirement under Nevada law: that both prospective spouses be over 18 (or over 16 with parental consent). No blood test is asked for; no time-consuming banns need be read. All you need is a $25 license—obtainable at Clark County Court House, 3rd and Carson Sts. (385-3156), open daily—and the wedding chapel will do the rest! They are open from 8 a.m. to midnight Mon.-Fri. and around the clock on weekends. The cost of solemnizing a marriage, including the minister's fee and the hired witnesses, generally runs $60–$100.

HISTORIC BUILDINGS: ⚖ **Old Las Vegas Fort,** 908 Las Vegas Blvd. North (382-7198): Built in 1855 by a group of 30 Mormon pioneers from Utah, this fort, originally designed to protect the settlers from attack by Indians, is the oldest building in the entire state. Open Sat.-Mon. For lovers of the Old West.

MUSEUM OF ART: ⚖ **Art Museum,** 3333 W. Washington Ave. (647-4300): Works by local and other American artists; interesting temporary exhibitions. Open Tues.-Sun.

MUSEUMS OF SCIENCE AND HISTORY: ⚱ Imperial Palace Auto Collection, 3535 Las Vegas Blvd. (731-3311): This collection of more than 200 valuable antique cars is to be found on the fifth floor of the Imperial Palace Hotel parking garage. It includes the King of Siam's 1928 Delage, Howard Hughes's 1954 Chrysler, an armored Mercedes which once belonged to Hitler, and other cars formerly the property of Al Capone, Eleanor Roosevelt, etc. A must for antique-car enthusiasts. Open daily.

⚱ **Las Vegas Museum of Natural History,** 3700 Las Vegas Blvd. South (798-7757): This spectacular brand-new natural-history museum displays one of the country's largest collections of prehistoric animals, with life-size animated models of dinosaurs, triceratops, etc. Don't miss it. Open daily.

☼ ⚱ **Liberace Museum,** 1775 E. Tropicana Ave. (798-5595): An entire museum devoted to the self-glorification of the late pianist and showman Liberace: from his collection of antique cars and pianos to his glittering million-dollar wardrobe. The triumph of unrestrained Hollywood kitsch. Well worth seeing. Open daily.

⚱ **U.N.L.V. Museum of Natural History,** 4505 Maryland Pkwy. (739-3381): Fauna and flora of the Mojave Desert; interesting collection of Native American objects. Worth a visit. Open Mon.-Sat.

NIGHT TIME ENTERTAINMENT: ☼ 🎰 Casino Center, around Fremont and Main Sts.: The heart of the city's gaming kingdom; the country's (and perhaps the world's) largest concentration of casinos and gambling houses. Particularly spectacular after dark, when Fremont St., better-known to locals as "Glitter Gulch," is illuminated to daytime levels by an extravagance of lights and multi-colored neon signs. The sight shouldn't be missed.

☼ 🎰 **"The Strip,"** Las Vegas Blvd. between Tropicana Rd. and Sahara Ave.: The name is a pun, with references both to striptease and to neon strip-lighting; it describes the city's 3-mi. (5-km) multicolored light show offered by its principal hotels, casinos, and nightclubs. The sight of "the Broadway of Las Vegas" after dark is fascinating indeed, and worth the trip all by itself.

PANORAMAS: ⚱ Sky Room, 100 E. Fremont St. (387-6468): A bar-restaurant-dance hall on the 23rd floor of the Mint Hotel, in the heart of dwntwn. Offers the most spectacular after-dark view of the city (admission charge). Glass-walled elevator. Worth seeing; open daily.

PERFORMING ARTS: For current listings of shows and cultural events, consult the entertainment pages of the daily papers, *Las Vegas Review-Journal* (morning and evening) and *Las Vegas Sun* (morning), as well as the monthly *Nevada*.

Artemus W. Ham Concert Hall, U. of Nevada campus, 4505 Maryland Pkwy. (739-3801): Opera, ballet, jazz, and concerts; home of the Nevada Dance Theater.

Judy Bayley Theater, U. of Nevada campus, 4505 Maryland Pkwy. (739-3641): In the little plaza adjoining the theater, be sure to take a look at Claes Oldenburg's colossal (39-ft, 13-m) sculpture *Flashlight*. Modern and classical theater; big-star shows.

Theater Under the Skies, Spring Mountain Ranch (see "Nearby Excursions," below) (875-4141): Open-air shows; modern and experimental theater. June-July.

Thomas and Mack Center, U. of Nevada campus, 4505 Maryland Pkwy. (739-3900): Pop and rock concerts.

SPECIAL EVENTS: For exact dates, consult the **Las Vegas Convention and Visitors Authority** (see "Tourist Information," above).

Helldorado Festival (May): Rodeos, street parades, beauty contest.

Jaycee State Fair (late July to early August): Carnival, big-star shows, livestock shows.

National Finals Rodeo (Dec.): The "Super Bowl" of professional rodeos.

SPORTS: Baseball (Apr.-Aug.): Stars, Cashman Field (386-7200).

THEME PARKS: ⚲ **Bonnie Springs Ranch,** 20 mi. (32 km) west on W. Charleston Blvd. (875-4191): Pioneer village of 1843, with nicely restored saloons and stores. Far Western railroad. Shows. Comic gun battles between sheriff and outlaws. Western buffs will enjoy it. Open daily.

⚲ **Wet 'n Wild,** 2600 Las Vegas Blvd. South (737-7873): Huge aquatic amusement park; the artificial surf has 4-ft (1.2-m) waves. The giant slide is 75 ft (23 m) high; also waterfalls, shooting the rapids, etc. Locally popular. Open daily Apr. to mid.-Sept.

WINTER SPORTS RESORTS: ⚲ **Mount Charleston Park** and **Lee Canyon,** 34 mi. (55 km) NW on U.S. 95 and Nev. 157: Beautiful pine forest rising to 11,918 ft (3,623 m) on Mount Charleston, and winter-sports resort at Lee Canyon, both very popular at all times of year. For a report on snow conditions during the skiing season, call 385-0181. Three ski lifts.

The ❋ ⚲ **Mount Charleston Inn,** 2 Kyle Canyon Rd., Mount Charleston, NV 89124 (872-5500), is a likeable chalet with a rest. serving very acceptable meat and game dishes. Open daily; 63 rms. I

ACCOMMODATIONS
See the listing of toll-free numbers in the Appendix.

Room Rates in Las Vegas	
B (Budget)	up to $30
I (Inexpensive)	$30–$60
M (Moderate)	$60–$90
E (Expensive)	$90–$140
VE (Very Expensive)	$140 and up

A Note on Accommodations: Over and above the gamblers and the entertainment fans (some of the top shows in the country are given in Las Vegas), there is a year-round crush of groups and conventions filling the 58,000 available hotel rooms, so reservations are essential. If you call toll free 800/634-6681 (or locally 735-8166) you'll be told what rooms are available at any given moment, and you can make your reservation on the spot. Note that at certain times of the year some hotels require a minimum stay of three nights.

Personal Favorites (in order of preference)
❋ ⚲⚲⚲⚲ **Caesars Palace** (nr. dwntwn), 3570 Las Vegas Blvd. South, NV 89109 (702/731-7110; toll free 800/634-6001 for rm

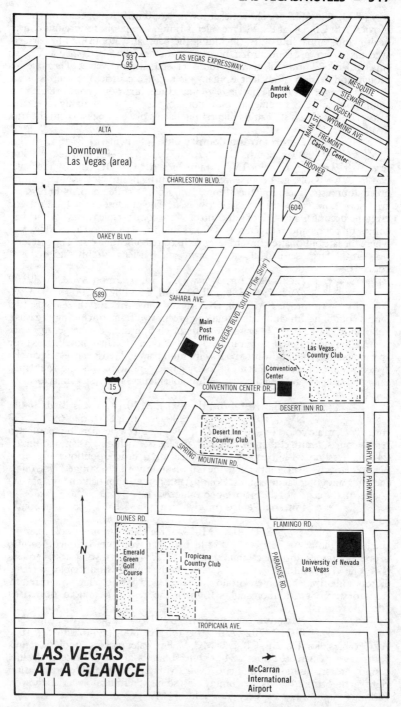

*LAS VEGAS
AT A GLANCE*

resv., 800/634-6581 for show ticket resv.). 1,650 rms, A/C, color TV, in-rm movies. AE, CB, DC, MC, V. Free valet parking, two pools, four tennis courts, health club, sauna, four rests. (including the Bacchanal Room), 24-hr bars, rm svce, disco, shows, casino, hrdrsr, boutiques, cinema, crib $10. *Note:* Las Vegas's super-palace: 22 floors of marble, stucco, crystal, and red velvet. The style—a Hollywood version of ancient Roman—is rather eccentric; the waitresses are dressed straight out of the movie *Ben Hur.* Huge, luxurious, comfortable rms; sumptuous suites. Svce diligent to the point of excess. Several highly acceptable rests. The Las Vegas style at its highest pitch; this place alone is worth the trip. **E–VE**

≗≗≗ **Desert Inn and Country Club** (nr. dwntwn), 3145 Las Vegas Blvd. South, NV 89109 (702/733-4444; toll free, see Preferred). 819 rms, A/C, color TV, in-rm movies. AE, CB, DC, MC, V. Free valet parking, two pools, golf course, ten tennis courts, health club, sauna, putting green, four rests. (including the Monte Carlo Room), coffeeshop, 24-hr bars, rm svce, shows, hrdrsr, boutiques, free crib. *Note:* The quietest of the local palaces; even the décor has a degree of self-control. Very comfortable rms w. private balconies or patios and refrigerators. Remarkable rm svce. Good rests. This was where the late billionaire Howard Hughes liked to come for a rest. The best location on the Strip, set in 160 acres of lawns and gardens. Highly regarded golf course. **E–VE**

≗≗≗ **Alexis Park** (nr. dwntwn), 375 E. Harmon Ave., NV 89109 (702/796-3300; toll free 800/223-0888). 500 suites, A/C, color TV, in-rm movies. AE, CB, DC, MC, V. Free parking, three pools, two tennis courts, health club, sauna, putting green, two rests. (including Pegasus), coffeeshop, 24-hr bars, 24-hr rm svce, night club, hrdrsr, concierge, free crib. *Note:* The newest, finest flower in the local bouquet of deluxe hotels. Has only spacious suites, splendidly fitted out, with mini-bars and refrigerators. Exemplary reception and svce. Ten acres of lovely gardens w. waterfalls and fountains, only a few steps away from the Strip. Admirable luxury hotel rest. Caters to VIPs. **E–VE**

≗≗ **Frontier Hotel** (nr. dwntwn), 3120 Las Vegas Blvd. South, NV 89109 (702/794-8200; toll free 800/634-6996). 593 rms, A/C, cable color TV. AE, CB, DC, MC, V. Free valet parking, pool, two tennis courts, health club, putting green, two rests. (including Diamond Jim's), 24-hr coffeeshop, 24-hr bars, rm svce, shows, casino, hrdrsr, boutiques, free crib. *Note:* Relatively small compared to the Hilton-style giants, but nonetheless offers the full gamut of local diversions. Comfortable rms w. mini-bars and private balconies. In the center of the Strip. Good value. **M–E**

≗≗ **Imperial Palace** (nr. dwntwn), 3535 Las Vegas Blvd. South, NV 89109 (702/731-3311; toll free 800/634-6441). 2,100 rms, A/C, color TV. AE, CB, DC, MC, V. Free valet parking, pool, six rests. (including the Ming Terrace), six 24-hr bars, rm svce, entertainment, casino, hrdrsr, boutiques, antique-car museum, crib $8. *Note:* This vast 19-story barracks is decorated in would-be Far Eastern style, but the rms are comfortable, w. refrigerators and private balconies. Group clientele. Good overall value, w. rate reductions for stays of two or more nights. Right on the Strip. **I–M (single rooms); M (double rooms)**

≗≗ **Hacienda** (nr. dwntwn), 3950 Las Vegas Blvd. South, NV 89119 (702/738-8911; toll free 800/634-6713). 814 rms, A/C, cable color TV. AE, CB, DC, MC, V. Free valet parking, pool, six tennis courts, rest. (Charcoal Room), 24-hr coffeeshop, 24-hr bar, rm svce, night life, casino, hrdrsr, boutiques, free crib. *Note:* Modern, comfortable hotel-casino right on the Strip; spacious, welcoming rms, some w. refrigerators. Friendly svce. Parking for motor homes. Very good value. **I–M**

Motel 6 (nr. dwntwn), 195 E. Tropicana Blvd., NV 89109 (702/736-4904). 580 rms, A/C, color TV, free in-rm movies. DC, MC, V. Free parking, pool, nearby rest., free crib. *Note:* Vegas's best bargain, offering functional but inviting rms at unbeatable prices. A few steps away from the Strip and the airport. Free breakfast. **B**

Western (nr. dwntwn), 899 E. Fremont St., NV 89101 (702/384-4620; toll free 800/634-6703). 115 rms, A/C, color TV. AE, CB, DC, MC, V. Free parking, coffeeshop, 24-hr bar, casino, free breakfast, crib $3. *Note:* Modest, functional motel 5 min. from dwntwn. Very good value for those on a limited budget. **B**

Other Accommodations (from top bracket to budget)

Bally's–Las Vegas (formerly the MGM Grand; nr. dwntwn), 3645 Las Vegas Blvd. South, NV 89109 (702/739-4111; toll free 800/634-3434). 2,830 rms, A/C, color TV. AE, CB, DC, MC, V. Free valet parking, pool, ten tennis courts, health club, sauna, six rests. (including Gigi), 24-hr coffeeshop, six 24-hr bars, rm svce, nightlife, shows, casino, cinema, hrdrsr, boutiques, free crib. *Note:* Gigantic hotel-casino comprising two modern 26-story towers. Completely renovated since a fire which caused 84 deaths in 1980, and now the masterpiece of Las Vegas kitsch. Spacious, comfortable rms, good sports facilities, good svce, but so-so rests. Intrusive group and convention clientele. Puts on some of the best shows in Vegas. Right on the Strip. **M–E**

Hilton Las Vegas (nr. dwntwn), 3000 Paradise Rd., NV 89109 (702/732-5111; toll free, see Hilton). 3,174 rms, A/C, cable color TV. AE, CB, DC, MC, V. Free valet parking, pool, health club, sauna, six tennis courts, putting green, 11 rests. (including Le Montrachet), coffeeshop, four 24-hr bars, rm svce, disco, shows, hrdrsr, boutiques, free crib. *Note:* With 30 floors of glass and concrete, this is not only the largest hotel in Vegas but the largest resort hotel in the world. It's taken by assault year round by the throngs of package tourists and conventioneers. Spacious rms w. balconies; lively ambience. In spite of the hotel's size the svce is good. Inside, a "children's hotel" offers childcare for parents trying their luck at the tables. Renovated after a fire in 1981. Very near the Strip and the Convention Center. **M–E**

Sands (nr. dwntwn), 3555 Las Vegas Blvd. South, NV 89109 (702/733-5000; toll free 800/634-6901). 720 rms, A/C, color TV, in-rm movies. AE, CB, DC, MC, V. Free valet parking, two pools, six tennis courts, health club, putting green, two rests. (including the Regency Room), 24-hr coffeeshop, 24-hr bars, rm svce, shows, casino, hrdrsr, boutiques. *Note:* With its 18-story round white tower and semicircular balconies the Sands looks like a huge lighthouse set down in the middle of the Strip. Spacious, well-laid-out rms w. private balconies or patios, the nicest overlooking the garden. First-class reception and svce; well-regarded luxury-hotel rest. One of the best hotels in Vegas. **M–E**

Tropicana Ramada Resort (nr. dwntwn), 3801 Las Vegas Blvd. South, NV 89109 (702/739-2222; toll free, see Ramada). 1,900 rms, A/C, color TV. AE, CB, DC, MC, V. Free valet parking, pool, health club, sauna, golf course, four tennis courts, four rests. (including Rhapsody), two 24-hr coffeeshops, 24-hr bars, rm svce, disco, shows, casino, hrdrsr, boutiques, crib $10. *Note:* One of Vegas's crowning glories since 1957. Opulent, flamboyant décor. Sophisticated sports facilities including air-conditioned indoor tennis courts. Home of the "Folies Bergères" show. Huge, comfortable rms w. private balconies; beautiful garden w. waterfalls and lagoons. VIP floors. On the Strip, very nr. the airport. **M–E**

Holiday Inn–Hotel Casino (nr. dwntwn), 3475 Las Vegas Blvd. South, NV 89109 (702/369-5000; toll free, see Holiday

Inns). 1,000 rms, A/C, color TV, in-rm movies. AE, CB, DC, MC, V. Free valet parking, pool, health club, sauna, rest. (Claudine's), two 24-hr coffeeshops, 24-hr bars, 24-hr rm svce, entertainment, casino, hrdrsr, boutiques, free crib. *Note:* The world's largest Holiday Inn, in size and in number of rooms. Built to resemble a giant Mississippi paddle-wheeler and topped by an ultramodern tower, it is unusual enough to surprise even those well acquainted with the Las Vegas style of architectural extravagance. Comfort and facilities are above the Holiday Inn standard, but the svce doesn't measure up. Group and convention clientele. In the heart of the Strip. **M–E**

☼ ♀♀♀♀ **Golden Nugget** (dwntwn), 129 E. Fremont St., NV 89125 ௹௹௹௹ (702/385-7111; toll free 800/634-3454). 1,903 rms, color TV, in-rm movies. AE, CB, DC, MC, V. Free parking, pool, health club, sauna, three rests. (including Elaine's), 24-hr coffeeshop, 24-hr bars, rm svce, entertainment, casino, hrdrsr, free crib. *Note:* An unlikely marriage between a marble-fronted Victorian house abundantly paneled in mahogany, and an ultramodern tower (Town House Tower) with sumptuous duplex suites. The opulent interior in the style of the Roaring '20s is sufficient justification for a visit. Huge, ultra-comfortable rms, excellent svce. Boasts Vegas's most expensive ($1,500-a-night) suite. Recently rejuvenated at a cost of $75 million. Along with Caesars Palace, this is the most spectacular hotel in Las Vegas, and a very good value. Right in the middle of Casino Center with its bustling nightlife. **M**

♀♀♀ **Sahara** (nr. dwntwn), 2535 Las Vegas Blvd. South, NV ௹௹௹ 89109 (702/737-2111; toll free 800/634-6666). 932 rms, A/C, color TV. AE, CB, DC, MC, V. Free valet parking, two pools, health club, sauna, putting green, three rests. (including House of Lords), coffeeshop, 24-hr bars, rm svce, disco, shows, casino, hrdrsr, boutiques, crib $8. *Note:* Built in 1952 at the north end of the Strip, this is another Las Vegas classic, to which several newer structures have been added including a 24-story tower. It's still Las Vegas style, but with a touch of class as well. Large rms w. balconies and refrigerators. Excellent svce., but resv. not always honored. House of Lords is a good rest. **M**

♀♀ **Mint Motel and Casino** (dwntwn.), 100 E. Fremont St., NV ௹௹ 89101 (702/387-6468; toll free 800/622-6468). 289 rms, A/C, color TV, in-rm movies. AE, CB, DC, MC, V. Free parking (valet parking $3), pool (in summer), rest. (Sky Room, on the 23rd floor), two coffeeshops, 24-hr bars, 24-hr rm svce, disco, casino, crib $7. *Note:* Comfortable balconied rms and good svce in the heart of dwntwn Vegas. Fine after-dark view from Top of the Mint, but the food is uninteresting. Elegant décor and a friendly atmosphere; a favorite with those in-the-know. Very good value. **I–M**

♀♀ **Union Plaza Hotel** (dwntwn), 1 Main St., NV 89125 (702/ ௹௹ 386-2110; toll free 800/634-6575). 1,020 rms, A/C, color TV, in-rm movies. AE, CB, DC, MC, V. Valet parking $3, pool, tennis court, health club, rest. (Center Stage), coffeeshop, 24-hr bar, rm svce, shows, casino, boutiques, crib $8. *Note:* Modern comfort and facilities housed in two 25-story towers in the heart of dwntwn Vegas, adjoining the Greyhound bus terminal and the AMTRAK train station. Inviting rms w. balconies and refrigerators. From the rest. there's a spectacular view of the dwntwn casino-hotels. Good overall value. **I–M**

♀ **La Quinta** (nr. dwntwn), 3782 Las Vegas Blvd. South, NV ௹ 89109 (702/739-7457; toll free, see La Quinta). 114 rms, A/C, color TV, in-rm movies. AE, CB, DC, MC, V. Free parking, pool, coffeeshop, free airport limo, free crib. *Note:* Modern, comfortable motel right on the Strip, pleasantly decorated in the style of a Spanish hacienda. Commodious, well-laid-out rms. Good value. **I–M**

☼♀♀ **Circus Circus Hotel** (nr. dwntwn), 2880 Las Vegas Blvd. ௹௹ South, NV 89109 (702/734-0410; toll free 800/634-3450).

2,793 rms, A/C, color TV. AE, CB, DC, MC, V. Free valet parking, three pools, two rests., two 24-hr coffeeshops, 24-hr bars, casino, circus, hrdrsr, boutiques, crib $4. *Note:* Right on the Strip, w. a newly constructed 29-story tower adjoining the original building. The interior is the most enterprising in all of Las Vegas, with trapeze artists and tightrope walkers cavorting above the heads of the casino gamblers beneath a pink-and-white make-believe circus marquee. The favorite hotel of parents with children. Huge, inviting rms; acceptable buffet meals at modest prices. Very good value. Worthwhile discounts at weekends. Enormous parking lot for RVs. **B–I**

Vegas World (nr. dwntwn), 2000 Las Vegas Blvd. South, NV 89104 (702/382-2000; toll free 800/634-6277). 600 rms, A/C, cable color TV. AE, CB, DC, MC, V. Free valet parking, pool, rest., coffeeshop, two 24-hr bars, casino, entertainment. *Note:* Huge 23-floor motel right on the Strip, decorated in the style of *2001: A Space Odyssey*. Functional and comfortable; good value. **I**

Bali Hai (nr. dwntwn), 336 Desert Inn Rd., NV 89109 (702/734-2141; toll free 800/624-7215). 171 rms, A/C, color TV. AE, CB, DC, MC, V. Free parking, two pools, two tennis courts, coffeeshop, crib $5. *Note:* Elderly but very well-maintained motel very near the Strip, w. huge, inviting refrigerator-equipped rms (some w. kitchenettes). Friendly reception and svce. Very good value. **B–I**

Mini Price Inn (nr. dwntwn), 4155 Koval Lane, NV 89109 (702/731-2111; toll free 800/634-6541). 360 rms, A/C, color TV. AE, CB, DC, MC, V. Free parking, two pools, 24-hr rest., 24-hr bar, casino. *Note:* Modest but very acceptable motel right near the Strip and the huge Bally's–Las Vegas. Functional comfort at rock-bottom prices, as the name implies. Worthwhile weekend discounts. Wonderful for slender budgets. **B**

YMCA / Youth Hostel

AYH Hostel (nr. dwntwn), 1208 Las Vegas Blvd. South (702/382-8119). Youth hostel.

RESTAURANTS

Las Vegas Restaurant Prices	
(per person, excluding drinks and service charges)	
B (Budget)	up to $15
I (Inexpensive)	$15–$25
M (Moderate)	$25–$40
E (Expensive)	$40–$60
VE (Very Expensive)	$60 and up

Personal Favorites (in order of preference)

Delmonico's (nr. dwntwn), in the Riviera Hotel, 2901 Las Vegas Blvd. South (735-5110, ext. 363). A/C. Dinner only, nightly; closed Christmas week. AE, CB, DC, MC, V. Jkt. *Specialties:* mussels dijonnaise, snails in pastry crust, coquilles St. Jacques sautéed w. oregano, bouillabaisse, lamb sausage Calabrian style. Fine wine list. *Note:* Very elaborate classic haute cuisine of French origin. Elegant wood-and-leather interior in tawny hues. Svce exemplary in all particulars. One of the few Las Vegas rests. that has retained both quality and seriousness. Resv. a must. *French-continental.* **M–E**

    Le Montrachet (nr. dwntwn), in the Hilton Las Vegas Hotel (see "Accommodations," above) (732-5111). A/C. Dinner only, nightly. AE, CB, DC, MC, V. Jkt. *Specialties:* warm foie gras w. apples, avocado soup w. red peppers, lobster w. basil butter, Dover sole meunière, medaillon of veal w. lime. Big wine list w. 400 varieties. *Note:* This newcomer on the local gastronomic scene has been quickly recognized as one of the best rests. in Las Vegas, thanks to its talented young chef Christopher Mihy. The interior—marble hall, leather chairs, and damask-clad walls—is a little overdone. Very good svce; resv. strongly advised. *French.* **M–E**

    Bacchanal Room (nr. dwntwn), in Caesars Palace (see "Accommodations," above) (734-7110). A/C. Dinner only, Thurs.-Mon.; closed Tues., Wed. AE, CB, DC, MC, V. Jkt. *Specialties:* The prix-fixe menus (seven courses from hors d'oeuvres to dessert, accompanied by three different wines) change regularly. French-inspired continental food. *Note:* Local taste apparently requires that every waitress wear a peplum while the waiters are tricked out as Roman centurions—but the food generally meets high standards. Prices match the opulent "Pompeian" scheme of decoration. Resv. required. Two seatings nightly. *Continental.* **E (prix fixe)**

    Port Tack (nr. dwntwn), 3190 W. Sahara Ave. (873-3345). A/C. Open daily around the clock; closed holidays. AE, CB, DC, MC, V. *Specialties:* lamb chops, catch of the day, salmon steak, roast beef, Maine lobster, Alaska king crab. *Note:* Along with its sister establishment (**Starboard Tack,** 2601 Atlantic Ave.; 457-8794), this is one of the rests. most favored by the locals. Charming rustic-seafaring décor; likeable relaxed atmosphere and some of the best seafood in town. *Steak-seafood.* **I–M**

    André's (nr. dwntwn), 401 S. 6th St. (385-5016). A/C. Dinner only, nightly; closed holidays and three weeks in Aug. AE, DC, MC, V. Jkt. *Specialties:* endive salad w. smoked breast of chicken, poached salmon w. celery, sole Véronique, chicken in cream and mushrooms. Dessert cart. More than 300 varieties on the wine list. *Note:* Charming French-style inn away from the noisy crowds of dwntwn Las Vegas. Chef André Rochat produces attractive meals, impeccably prepared and served, in generous portions and at relatively low prices. An excellent place, locally popular; resv. required. *French.* **I–M**

    Vineyard (nr. dwntwn), 3630 Maryland Pkwy. (731-1606). A/C. Lunch/dinner daily; closed holidays. AE, MC, V. Jkt. *Specialties:* fresh homemade pasta (fettuccine Alfredo, lasagna, cannelloni), pizza, chicken cacciatore, veal parmigiana, scampi sauté. *Note:* Straightforward Italian-inspired food in a Neapolitan-operetta setting (with appropriate background music). Friendly, smiling svce. Attracts crowds from the community. No. resv. *Italian.* **I**

    Garcia's (nr. dwntwn), 1030 E. Flamingo Rd. (731-0628). A/C. Lunch/dinner daily; closed Thanksgiving, Christmas. *Specialties:* chimichangas, fajitas, tacos, enchiladas, fried ice cream. *Note:* Authentic Mexican food and excellent margaritas in a brightly colored hacienda setting. In the hottest days, the profusion of plants creates the pleasant illusion that you're in a green, growing garden. Attentive svce. Locally popular. *Mexican.* **B**

    Chin's (nr. dwntwn), 3200 Las Vegas Blvd. South (733-8899). A/C. Lunch/dinner daily. AE, MC, V. *Specialties:* shark's-fin soup, spring rolls, chicken w. strawberries, beef à la Chin's, crystal shrimp, crispy pudding. *Note:* In the unanimous view of the purists this is the best little Far Eastern rest. on the Strip. Authentic (if slightly Americanized) Chinese food; for instance, the chicken w. strawberries is a local variant on the classic Chinese lemon chicken. The result is almost always delicious, and the décor is elegant; accordingly the place has been very successful, and resv. are strongly advised. Valet parking. *Chinese.* **I**

Other Restaurants (from top bracket to budget)

🍷🍷🍷 **Monte Carlo Room** (nr. dwntwn), in the Desert Inn (see "Accommodations," above) (733-4444). A/C. Dinner only, nightly. AE, CB, DC, MC, V. Jkt. *Specialties:* scampi sautéed w. garlic, steak marchand de vin, veal Dornandig, quails Véronique, noisette of lamb bourgeois, hobo steak, flambé desserts. *Note:* Elegant and (for a Vegas rest.) relatively restrained décor. The quality of the food is on a par with the hotel's reputation. Polished svce. Resv. advised. *Continental.* **M–E**

🍷🍷🍷 **Ah-So Japanese Steak Garden** (nr. dwntwn), in Caesar's Palace (see "Accommodations," above) (731-7110). A/C. Dinner only, nightly. AE, CB, DC, MC, V. Jkt. *Specialties:* teppanyaki (broiled steak, lobster, and vegetables), sushi. *Note:* The chefs wield their knives w. devilish dexterity under the eyes of the diners, in a charming plastic reproduction of a Japanese tea house, complete w. gardens, streams, and miniature bridges. Friendly, efficient svce. Resv. advised. *Japanese.* **M (prix fixe)**

☀️🍷🍷🍷 **Lilly Langtry's** (dwntwn), in the Golden Nugget (see "Accommodations," above) (385-7111). A/C. Dinner only, nightly. AE, CB, DC, MC, V. Jkt. *Specialties:* pressed duck w. almonds, lemon chicken, chow si fun, moo goo gai pan, ginger beef. *Note:* The best Cantonese, or indeed Chinese, rest. in Las Vegas. Delicate cuisine, artistically presented and served. The Victorian rococo interior is a delight to the eye. Excellent svce; resv. a must. *Chinese.* **E**

🍷🍷🍷 **Tillerman** (nr. dwntwn), 2245 E. Flamingo Rd. (731-4036). A/C. Dinner only, nightly; closed holidays. AE, CB, DC, MC, V. Jkt. *Specialties:* broiled steak, catch of the day. *Note:* In this light-filled space w. its green plants, its giant ficus trees, and its enormous skylights, you have the agreeable feeling that you're dining under the stars. First-quality meat and fish impeccably prepared. Excellent svce; one of Vegas's most highly recommended rests. *Steak-seafood.* **I–M**

🍷🍷 **Golden Steer Steak House** (nr. dwntwn), 308 W. Sahara Ave. (384-4470). A/C. Dinner only, open nightly till midnight; closed Thanksgiving, December 25. AE, CB, DC, MC, V. *Specialties:* giant (1½-lb.) steaks, steak au poivre, rack of lamb, fresh pasta (first-rate ravioli and linguine with clams), game, roast suckling pig. Good wine list. *Note:* Remarkable steakhouse, but often crowded and noisy; a local favorite for almost 25 years. Western-1890s décor; exemplary svce; resv. advised. Valet parking. *Steak-American.* **I–M**

🍷🍷 **Pamplemousse** (nr. dwntwn), 400 E. Sahara Ave. (733-2066). A/C. Dinner only, nightly. AE, CB, DC, MC, V. *Specialties:* onion soup w. grated cheese, burgundy snails, fresh seafood, roast duckling à l'orange, soufflés, tarte tatin (apple tart). Good list of California wines. *Note:* Charming little French rest. w. a romantic country-inn décor; small garden inviting on fine days. Chef Georges La Forge offers classic but polished cuisine; attentive svce. Fine place, locally very popular, so resv. advisable. *French.* **I–M**

🍷🍷 **Alpine Village Inn** (nr. dwntwn), 3003 Paradise Rd. (734-6888). A/C. Lunch Mon.-Fri., dinner nightly; closed Thanksgiving, Christmas Day. AE, CB, DC, MC, V. *Specialties:* sauerbraten, wienerschnitzel, frikadellen, fondue bourguignonne, apfel strudel. German beers. *Note:* Decorated as a Swiss-Bavarian chalet, somewhat incongruous where the mercury goes up to 95°F (35°C) in the shade! Plentiful, decent food; efficient svce (in

Tyrolean costume). There's a noisy piano bar/tavern in the cellar. A Las Vegas landmark since 1950, opposite the Las Vegas Hilton. Valet parking. *German-continental*. **I**

     🍷 **Battista's Hole in the Wall** (nr. dwntwn), 4041 Audrie St.
     🍸 (732-1424). A/C. Dinner only, nightly; closed Thanksgiving and the last two weeks in Dec. AE, CB, DC, MC, V. Jkt. *Specialties:* fresh home-made pasta (spaghetti cacciatore, lasagne, etc.), scampi, eggplant parmigiana. *Note:* The most Italian of Vegas's Italian rests.; the décor and the agreeable at-mosphere suggest an old trattoria, and the resemblance is enhanced when the owner, Battista Locatelli, belts out a few operatic arias. Unlimited free house wine. Locally popular; resv. advised. *Italian*. **I**

     🍷 **Golden Wok** (nr. dwntwn), 504 S. Decatur Blvd. (878-1596).
     🍸 A/C. Lunch/dinner daily. AE, MC, V. *Specialties:* hot-and-sour soup, shrimp princess, chicken kung pao, moo shu pork. *Note:* A good Chi-nese rest. offering Cantonese and Szechuan dishes, well liked by the Chinese community (always a good sign) in Las Vegas. Modern décor w. a profusion of plants. Efficient svce. Other location: 4760 S. Eastern Ave. (456-1868). *Chinese*. **B–I**

     🍷 **El Burrito Café** (nr. dwntwn), 1919 E. Fremont St. (387-
     🍸 9246). A/C. Lunch/dinner daily. No credit cards. *Specialties:* burritos, chicharrones, tacos. *Note:* Very acceptable small Mexican rest. offering guaranteed local color; tiny and often overcrowded. Resv. advised. *Mexican*. **B**

     🍷 **Golden Nugget Buffet** (dwntwn), in the Golden Nugget (see
     🍸 "Accommodations," above) (385-7111). A/C. Lunch/dinner daily. *Specialties:* barbecued spareribs, roast beef, Chinese dishes, hamhock w. sauerkraut, salads, good desserts (including bread pudding). Un-beatable value (especially if you're starving) in the heart of dwntwn; excellent food, and fill your plate as often as you choose. Locally popular. *American-continental*. **B (prix fixe)**

Cafeterias / Specialty Spots

     Herbie K. (nr. dwntwn), Fashion Show Mall, 3200 Las Vegas Blvd. South (369-5837). The best deli in town, and a favorite with Jerry Lewis. Giant sand-wiches, homemade soups, corned beef, pastrami, brisket. Open daily.

OTHER FROMMER TRAVEL GUIDES: *Dollarwise USA* comple-ments 13 other Dollarwise Guides and 3 $-A-Day Guides dealing with indi-vidual U.S. states and areas: *Dollarwise Alaska, Dollarwise Florida, Dollarwise New York State, Dollarwise California & Las Vegas, Dollarwise Texas, Dollarwise Cruises, Dollarwise Mid-Atlantic States, Dollarwise New England, Dollarwise South-Atlantic States, Dollarwise Northwest, Dollarwise Southwest, Hawaii on $50 a Day, New York on $50 a Day,* and *Washington, D.C., & Historic Virginia on $40 a Day.*

BARS & NIGHTCLUBS

HOTEL SHOWS: No city in the world boasts more bars, casinos, discos, shows, or strip joints to the square mile than Las Vegas. All the major hotels offer, besides several bars and discos apiece, very high-quality shows, of which the most popular are those at **Bally's–Las Vegas, Caesars Palace,** the **Desert Inn,** the **Dunes Hotel,** the **Hilton Las Vegas** (Moulin Rouge Revue), **Sahara, Sands, Stardust** (Lido de Paris Revue), and **Tropicana** (Folies Bergère Revue).

OTHER CHOICES: Botany's (nr. dwntwn), 1700 E. Flamingo Rd. (737-6662). Trendy disco; also a good Créole rest. Open daily around the clock.

Silver Dollar Saloon (nr. dwntwn), 2501 E. Charleston Blvd. (382-6921). Live country music; certified cowboy setting. Open nightly.

State Street (nr. dwntwn), 2570 State St. (733-0225). Bar-rest. favored by show-business stars (Frank Sinatra, Eddie Murphy, Don Rickles, and Engelbert Humperdinck in particular). Very acceptable Italian food; excellent live jazz. The owner is the actor Gianni Russo, who played Carlo in *The Godfather*. Open nightly till 5 a.m.

For lovers of the female form divine and of (relatively) daring floor shows: **Cabaret** (nr. dwntwn), 4416 Paradise Rd. (733-8666).

Crazy Horse Saloon (nr. dwntwn), 4034 Paradise Rd. (732-1116).

Palomino Club (nr. dwntwn), 1848 Las Vegas Blvd. North (642-2984).

NEARBY EXCURSIONS

LAKE MEAD AND HOOVER DAM (27 mi., 43 km, SE on U.S. 93): This beautiful man-made lake, one of the largest in the world, is 116 mi. (180 km) long; it was formed by the construction of the Hoover Dam, which holds back the waters of the Colorado River after it passes through the Grand Canyon. The azure waters are as deep as 590 ft (180 m). Fishing, waterskiing, and sailing are on offer along the 550 mi. (880 km) of shoreline, and each year more than seven million visitors come here. The 726-ft (221-m) dam and the impressive generating plant date from 1935, and are ranked among the country's greatest architectural achievements. Visitor Center open daily (702/293-8367); don't miss it.

OVERTON (65 mi., 104 km, NE on I-15 and Nev. 169): Just 5 mi. (8 km) south of this former 19th-century Mormon colony lies a huge Indian settlement, along the banks of the Muddy River, which 1,200 years ago was peopled by the ancestors of the Hopi. Interesting museum at the dig **(Lost City Museum),** with a rich archeological collection (397-2193). Open daily.

You can advantageously combine this excursion with a visit to the **Valley of Fire** (see below); it's worth the side trip.

RED ROCK CANYON (15 mi., 24 km, west along Charleston Blvd.): Wonderful rocky gorges of white and reddish sandstone, with spectacular views. Lovely 13-mi. (21-km) panoramic drive. Visitor Center (363-1921). Well worth the side trip.

SPRING MOUNTAIN RANCH (18 mi., 29 km, west along W. Charleston Blvd.) (875-4141): This fine 528-acre ranch, very near Red Rock Canyon, dates back to the 1870s, and has been the property of the German steel tycoon Alfred Krupp and then of Howard Hughes. It now belongs to the State of Nevada. Open daily, and interesting.

VALLEY OF FIRE STATE PARK (58 mi., 93 km, NE on I-15): Very beautiful rock-strewn desert of reddish hue (whence the name), overlooking Lake Mead, formed 150 million years ago. A spectacular sight at sundown, and offers some astonishing landscape panoramas at any time. Many petroglyphs (Indian rock drawings). Camping permitted. Visitor Center open daily year round. A must-see.

GHOST TOWNS: **Calico,** 143 mi. (230 km) SW on I-15: The most picturesque and best preserved of California's ghost towns. There were rich silver mines here in the 1880s, and the place had as many as 3,000 inhabitants; today there are a dozen. After the restoration undertaken in

1950, Main Street looks as though it has been taken bodily from a John Ford western. It's on the main highway to Los Angeles; don't miss it. For information, call 619/254-2122.

    Goodsprings, 38 mi. (60 km) SW by I-15 and Nev. 161: At its height around a century ago this little gold-rush town boasted as many as 2,000 inhabitants. The **Pioneer Saloon** is a magnificent period piece. Worth the detour.

NATIONAL PARKS NEARBY

DEATH VALLEY (142 mi., 228 km, NW on U.S. 95, Nev. 373 and Cal. 190): America's most beautiful desert; see Chapter 48 on Death Valley.

GRAND CANYON OF THE COLORADO (291 mi., 465 km, SE on U.S. 93, I-40, and Ariz. 64): One of the seven natural wonders of the world. See Chapter 41 on the Grand Canyon.

ZION NATIONAL PARK (162 mi., 260 km, NE on I-15 and Utah 9) and **Bryce Canyon** (243 mi., 389 km, east on I-15 and Utah 20, U.S. 89, and Utah 12): Two of the country's best-known national parks. See Chapter 32 on Utah's national parks.

CHAPTER 48

DEATH VALLEY NATIONAL MONUMENT🌡️🌡️🌡️

□ □ □

Long the unchallenged domain of the Panamint Indians, an offshoot of the Shoshone, Death Valley is one of the two or three most enthralling natural wonders in the United States. If you are fortunate enough to set eyes on it for the first time from atop the rocky platform symbolically named **Dante's View,** you may well feel that you are present at the Creation. At the foot of the dizzying sheer drop of 5,120 ft (1,600 m) there sprawls in blinding clarity the vast expanse of the salt flats and the lowest point on the continent, 282 ft (86 m) below sea level. On the other side of **Devil's Golf Course** and its weird salt formations, the eternal snows of distant Mt. Whitney rise in striking contrast with the dun-colored rocks and sun-blasted dunes. This two-billion-year-old valley, once the bed, not of a river, but of an Ice Age sea, is home to a surprisingly diverse animal life. Among its denizens are no less than 36 species of mammals, including coyote, porcupine, and kangaroo rat; dozens of insect and reptile species, including the formidable rattlesnake; and birds, notably crows and vultures. Certain kinds of small fish such as the pupfish can be found nowhere on earth except in the scanty waters of this splendid but terrifying blast furnace: **Salt Creek,** notably, or the palm groves of **Furnace Creek** in the center of the valley. The region was named when a group of California-bound pioneers died of thirst and fatigue while attempting to cross the valley on Christmas Day 1849. The area experienced short-lived activity in the 1880s when the borax mines were discovered, and borax, with its many industrial uses, became known as "the white gold of the desert."

Two excellent paved highways span the valley north to south and east to west, and this living desert museum is today one of the most popular tourist spots in California. The extraordinary landscapes, veiled during the heat of the day by a soft-hued, ever-changing haze, draw thousands of visitors to the three lone motels in Death Valley each winter and spring (only two of them stay open in summer). It goes without saying that reservations are highly recommended, except in summer, when Death Valley is virtually abandoned by tourists because of the scorching heat.

HINTS TO MOTORISTS: When visiting Death Valley by car, drive at a moderate speed, especially during the summer, to avoid overheating the engine. Before you set out, make sure that you have a full tank of gas, check your oil, and deflate the tires by a couple of pounds below normal pressure. If you break down between Death Valley Junction and Furnace Creek, or between Stove Pipe Wells and Scotty's Castle, there won't be a living soul within 30 miles! When driving on unpaved roads, *always* have with you a few gallons of reserve water; in summer, an untrained person will die of dehydration in three hours under the Death Valley sun. In any case, don't make the trip except in an air-conditioned car.

BASIC FACTS: State of California (extending into Nevada). Area Code: 619. Time Zone: Pacific Time (three hours behind New York). Zip Code: 92328. A National Monument since 1933. Area: 3,123 sq. mi. (one-fifth of it below sea level). Approximate dimensions: 140 mi. (225 km) long, 4–16 mi. (6–26 km) wide. Recommended time for visiting: Oct. to late Apr.

CLIMATE: As you might expect from its name, Death Valley is one of the most inhospitable areas on the planet. In summer, temperatures frequently reach 113°F (45°C) in the shade (the record, set in July 1913, is 134°F, 56.7°C). From late Oct. to Apr., on the other hand, the mercury rarely goes above 86°F (30°C) in the daytime, with very cool nights, especially during the winter months (record low: 15°F, –9°C). Rainfall is practically nonexistent—less than two inches (5 cm) per year.

DISTANCES: Las Vegas, 142 mi. (228 km); Los Angeles, 305 mi. (490 km); Reno, 285 mi. (456 km); San Francisco, 531 mi. (851 km).

ARRIVAL & TRANSIT INFORMATION

NEAREST AIRPORTS: The **Death Valley Municipal Airport** (DTH): 1 mi. (2 km) west.
    Las Vegas McCarran International Airport (LAS): 142 mi. (228 km) SE.
    Los Angeles International Airport (LAX): 305 mi. (531 km) SW.

AIRLINES: Air Nevada (800/634-6377) offers charter flights from Las Vegas to Death Valley Municipal Airport. For other airlines, see the Las Vegas and Los Angeles chapters.

CAR RENTAL: See the Las Vegas and Los Angeles chapters.

TRAIN: For the closest AMTRAK station, see the Las Vegas chapter.

BUS: For the closest bus stations, see the Las Vegas chapter.
    Greyhound does not serve Death Valley, but the Las Vegas–Tonopah–Reno Stage Line company (LTR), 200 S. Main St., Las Vegas (384-1230), makes daily runs between Beatty (North entrance of Death Valley) and Las Vegas. Given the long distances involved, however, renting a car with unlimited mileage (preferably in California where the rates are lowest) is the best plan.

INFORMATION

TOURIST INFORMATION: Superintendent, Death Valley National Monument, Death Valley, CA 92328 (619/786-2331).
    Visitor Center at Furnace Creek, open daily; also a desert museum.

SIGHTS, ATTRACTIONS, & ACTIVITIES

ARCHITECTURAL HIGHLIGHTS: ☀ ♟♟ **Scotty's Castle,** 52 mi. (84 km) NW of Furnace Creek on Cal. 190 and Grapevine Rd.). The valley's only monu-

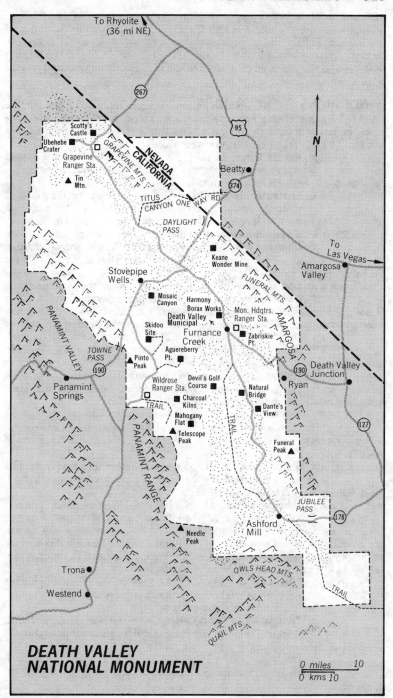

DEATH VALLEY
NATIONAL MONUMENT

ment worthy of the title, a mirage in the middle of the desert. Wealthy Chicago businessman Albert Johnson and his friend, Walter Scotty, a professional cowboy from the Buffalo Bill troupe, built this sumptuously decorated and improbable castle in Hollywood Hispano-Moorish style between 1922 and 1931. Don't miss it—you may never see anything else like it! Guided tours promptly on the hour. Open daily.

PANORAMAS & EXCURSIONS (all distances measured from Furnace Creek):

Aguereberry Point, 48 mi. (77 km) west. A wonderful view of the valley, especially in the afternoon, from an altitude of 6,275 ft (1,961 m). The last 5 mi. (8 km) of the ascent are unpaved. Worth the trip.

Artists Drive, 11 mi. (18 km) south. Narrow, one-way road amid splendid gorges and multicolored landscapes. A treat for color photographers. An absolute must-see.

Badwater, 16 mi. (26 km) south. This spring is the source of undrinkable water, which never dries up even in the middle of summer. Next to the lowest point on the American continent (282 ft, 86 m, below sea level), it's also the hottest place in the valley. Not to be missed.

Charcoal Kiln, 61 mi. (98 km) SW: Beehive-shaped charcoal kilns from pioneer days. Picturesque. The last two miles of the road are unpaved. See it.

Dante's View, 23 mi. (38 km) SE. One of the most breathtaking landscapes in creation, this panoramic platform 5,475 ft (1,669 m) high offers an unforgettable view of the valley. The road up is very steep and quite hard on the transmission. Worth the trip all by itself.

Devil's Golf Course, 8 mi. (12 km) south. A vast salt flat studded with 20-inch- (50-cm-) high salt rocks that really lives up to its name. See it.

Golden Canyon, 4 mi. (6 km) south. This 0.6-mi. (1-km) footpath cuts through splendid rock formations of gold, bright red, ochre, and bronze. A photographer's dream.

The Racetrack, 83 mi. (134 km) NW. This long clay valley, the scene of strange geological displacements, is one of the valley's biggest mysteries. Unpaved road for the last 27 mi. (44 km). For lovers of legends.

Sand Dunes, 21 mi. (35 km) NW. Enormous sand dunes perpetually reshaped by the wind. A miniature Sahara in the middle of California. An absolute must-see.

Telescope Peak, 65 mi. (104 km) SW. The highest point in the valley, at 11,049 ft (3,368 m). From **Mahogany Flat** (the last 2 mi., 4 km, unpaved), a 6.8-mi. (11-km) steep and arduous footpath leads to the summit, where you may enjoy an exceptional view of Death Valley and the neighboring mountains. Do not undertake this trip in summer. In any case, consult the ranger station in neighboring **Wildrose.**

Titus Canyon, 33 mi. (54 km) north. The 26 mi. (42 km) of the one-way track through this steep gorge are accessible only to four-wheel-drive vehicles. Superb landscapes.

Twenty-Mule-Team Canyon, 6 mi. (10 km) SE. A tortuous, unpaved, one-way route zigzags through this splendid rocky setting. Not to be missed.

Ubehebe Crater, 55 mi. (88 km) NW. The only volcanic crater in the area is 2,560 ft (800 m) across and 390 ft (122 m) deep. Worth a look.

※🔭🔭 **Zabriskie Point,** 6 mi. (10 km) SE. Strange, rocky "dunes" in tawny shades offering a superb view of the valley, Telescope Peak, and the Panamint Mountains, especially at sunrise and sunset. The setting for the Antonioni film of the same name. Not to be missed.

ENTERTAINMENT: ※🔭🔭 **Amargosa Opera House,** intersection of Cal. 127 and 190, Death Valley Junction (31 mi., 50 km, SE of Furnace Creek on Cal. 190) (619/852-4316). The smallest opera house in the world. Martha Becket plays and dances solo to Offenbach's *La Vie Parisienne, Swan Lake,* and other classics. Surprising show and décor. Open Mon., Fri., and Sat. evenings Oct.-May. Not to be missed.

GHOST TOWNS (all distances measured from Furnace Creek). 🏛 **Harmony Borax Works,** 1 mi. (2 km) north. Remains of an old borax mine. From here borax was transported to the Mojave railway, 162 mi. (260 km) farther south, on heavy carts which, even in the hottest weather, were drawn by the unbelievably enduring "twenty-mule teams."

🏛 **Panamint City,** 77 mi. (124 km) SW. Remains of a 19th-century mining town. On the way, visit another ghost town, **Ballarat.** Difficult access road.

※🏛 **Rhyolite,** 36 mi. (59 km) NE. Vestiges of one of the most famous 1904 Gold Rush towns, which had as many as 10,000 inhabitants around 1910. See the unusual house made of 50,000 bottles.

🏛 **Skidoo,** 46 mi. (74 km) west. Former miners' camp that has been periodically revitalized over the course of a century. The last stretch of the access road is difficult. Had as many as 500 inhabitants in its day, circa 1906.

NATIONAL PARKS NEARBY: ※🏛 Sequoia National Park, 362 mi. (580 km) west on Cal. 190, 178, 65, and 198. This kingdom of the forest giants is barely 87 mi. (140 km) away as the crow flies, but almost 375 mi. (600 km) by road, a spectacular route through Panamint Valley and Sequoia National Forest. Not to be missed. For the park itself, see chapter on Sequoia.

SUGGESTED TOURING ITINERARIES IN THE VALLEY

※🏛 **NORTH CIRCUIT** (150 mi., 241 km, r.t. from Furnace Creek): Visit **Rhyolite** (see "Ghost Towns," above), **Titus Canyon** (four-wheel-drive vehicles only), **Scotty's Castle** (see "Architectural Highlights," above), and **Ubehebe Crater** (see "Panoramas & Excursions," above). Optional excursion to **Racetrack** for four-wheel-drive vehicles only.

※🔭🔭 **WEST CIRCUIT** (126 mi., 202 km, r.t. from Furnace Creek): Visit **Sand Dunes, Aguereberry Point, Charcoal Kilns,** and optional excursions to **Telescope Peak** (for all of which, see "Panoramas & Excursions," above).

※🔭🔭 **SOUTH CIRCUIT** (88 mi., 142 km, r.t. from Furnace Creek): Visit **Zabriskie Point, Twenty-Mule Team Canyon, Dante's View, Golden Canyon, Artists Drive, Devil's Golf Course,** and **Badwater** (for all of which, see "Panoramas & Excursions," above). The most spectacular circuit through the valley.

ACCOMMODATIONS & RESTAURANTS

See the listing of toll-free numbers in the Appendix.

Room Rates in Death Valley	
B (Budget)	up to $30
I (Inexpensive)	$30–$60
M (Moderate)	$60–$90
E (Expensive)	$90–$140
VE (Very Expensive)	$140 and up

Personal Favorites (in order of preference)

🗝 **Furnace Creek Inn,** Cal. 190, Furnace Creek, CA 92328 (619/786-2361). 69 rms, A/C, color TV (in the lobby). AE, CB, DC, MC, V. Free parking, pool, tennis, sauna, horseback riding, rest., coffeeshop, bar, rm svce, disco, library, service station. *Note:* Very busy luxury motel built in 1927 in a vaguely Spanish, massive, and ungraceful idiom. Vast rms that are functional at the expense of elegance; the best open onto a lovely tropical garden w. palm trees. Antiquated plumbing and other facilities, unprofessional personnel. The pretentious rest. (jacket required, servers in long dresses) offers mediocre food. An ideal point of departure for a number of valley excursions (Dante's View, Badwater, and Zabriskie Point are less than 30 min. away by car). Motel is open mid-Oct. to mid-May only. Free airport shuttle. **VE**

🗝 **Stove Pipe Wells,** Cal. 190, Stove Pipe Wells Village, CA 92328 (619/786-2387). 75 rms, A/C. MC, V. Free parking, pool, golf, tennis, horseback riding, coffeeshop, bar, grocery store, service station, crib, $5. *Note:* This small motel offering functional comfort appears to rise out of the desert like a mirage amid a dramatic dune landscape. Mediocre cafeteria but a pleasant bar. Svce less than friendly. Motel open year round. **I–M (lower off-season rates)**

🗝 **Furnace Creek Ranch,** Cal. 190, Furnace Creek, CA 92328 (619/786-2345; toll free 800/528-6367). 224 rms/bungalows, A/C, color TV (in most rooms). AE, CB, DC, MC, V. Free parking, pool, golf, tennis, horseback riding, coffeeshop, rest. (winter), bar, movie theater (in season), grocery stores, service station. *Note:* Classic motel built in a sort of oasis shaded by palm, date, and other trees. Inviting rms (some w. balconies) and bungalows plus an adequate cafeteria. Ideal place from which to explore the whole valley. Adjacent motor-home parking. Motel open year round. Organizes guided tours of Death Valley. **I–M (lower off-season rates)**

☼🍷 **Scotty's Castle,** Grapevine Rd., Grapevine Canyon, CA 92328. Cafeteria open 9 a.m. to 6 p.m. year round. Service station. Across from the astonishing Scotty's Castle. A green oasis in the heart of the desert.

CHAPTER 49

RENO ⚱

□ □ □

And Lake Tahoe

"**T**he biggest little city in the world," coyly announces an enormous arch spanning over the main street of this former gold prospectors' town, 120 years old. Long known as the world capital of divorce, Reno today has also become the capital of love at first sight, to judge from the innumerable "Wedding Chapels" where, for the modest sum of $60 to $80—credit cards accepted—those aged 18 and over who wish to be married can be lawfully wedded instantly, day or night, seven days a week. This is possible because Nevada law is particularly liberal in matters of marriage and divorce. In the case of divorce, the law requires the petitioner to be a resident of Nevada for six weeks before the granting of the decree; marriage, however, requires but one formality: the purchase of a $25 license from the Marriage Bureau at the Washoe County Courthouse, S. Virginia and Court Sts., Reno, NV 89520 (702/785-4172); open daily from 8 a.m. to midnight. The ceremony at the Wedding Chapel, which lasts no more than ten minutes, requires two witnesses (provided by the chapel if necessary). Flowers (plastic), rice, and the obligatory "Wedding March" cost extra. More than 30,000 such instant weddings are performed annually in Reno. It was in Reno that the author of this guide experienced "the happiest day of his life" (according to his wife, Nicole, anyway).

Though honeymooners constitute a significant part of the local hotel trade (the number of honeymoon suites in the great hotels and even in motels is beyond number), the bulk of business is provided by lovers of roulette, baccarat, and slot machines. Though less flashy and ostentatious, Reno is a sort of replica of Las Vegas, about 400 mi. (700 km) away across the desert. As at Las Vegas, slot machines greet the visitor right at the airport, overflow from the casinos onto the sidewalks of **Virginia St.**—the local Broadway or Wilshire Blvd.—and clatter away day and night in the gaming room of the largest casino-hotel in the world, **Bally's Reno.**

You should not, however, allow the lure of gambling to distract you altogether from the splendid scenery in the nearby **Sierra Nevada,** beginning with **Lake Tahoe** and **Pyramid Lake,** two of the most beautiful mountain lakes in the U.S. Not far from Lake Tahoe, the ghost town of **Virginia City,** one of the great gold-rush towns of the 19th century, preserves its old houses and saloons almost intact, like something right out of a western.

BASIC FACTS: State of Nevada. Area Code: 702 (or 916 in South Lake Tahoe, Tahoe Vista, and Kings Beach, California). Time Zone: Pacific Time. ZIP Code: 89501. Founded: 1868. Approximate population: city, 102,000; metropolitan area, 240,000.

CLIMATE: Reno, in the heart of the desert, enjoys a dry climate, sunny and invigorating. Summers are dazzlingly bright, but only moderately hot (July average, 68°F, 20°C). Spring and fall are usually chilly; at night the temperature falls rapidly. Due to the altitude (4,498 ft, 1,370 m), winter offers a standing invitation to skiers in the area's resorts (Jan. average, 34°F, 1°C).

DISTANCES: Las Vegas, 447 mi. (715 km); Los Angeles, 470 mi. (752 km); Portland, 574 mi. (918 km); Salt Lake City, 523 mi. (837 km); San Francisco, 229 mi. (366 km).

RENO

ARRIVAL & TRANSIT INFORMATION

AIRPORT: Reno-Cannon International Airport (RNO), 4 mi. (6 km) SE. For further information call 328-6499.

AIRLINES: America West (348-2777), American (329-9217), Continental (322-9075), Delta (323-1661), Northwest (toll free 800/225-2525), and United (329-1020).

CITY LINK: The cab fare from the airport to downtown is about $6; time, about 10 min.

Bus: **Airport Limousine** (702/323-3727), serves major downtown hotels; fare, $3; time, about 15 min.

LTR Stage Lines (702/323-3088), serves the Lake Tahoe area.

Except for nearby excursions (recommended), the small size of the town makes renting a car unnecessary. Public transportation (bus) is not very efficient.

CAR RENTAL (all at the airport unless otherwise indicated): Avis (785-2727); Budget (785-2545); Dollar (348-2800); Hertz (785-2511); National (785-2756); and Thrifty, 2697 Mill St. (329-0096). For downtown locations, consult the local telephone directory.

LIMOUSINE SERVICES: Bell Limousine (786-3700), Dav-El Limousine (toll free 800/922-0343), and Executive Limousine (826-7776).

TAXIS: Taxis are relatively affordable, but few in number. They can be called by telephone or taken from the waiting lines outside the major hotels. Recommended companies: **Reno-Sparks Cab** (331-4141), **Whittlesea Checker Taxi** (323-3111), and **Yellow Cab** (331-7171).

TRAIN: AMTRAK Station, Commercial Row and Lake St. (329-8638; toll free 800/872-7245).

BUS: Greyhound, 155 Stevenson St. (322-2970).

INFORMATION & TOURS

TOURIST INFORMATION: The **Greater Reno Chamber of Commerce,** 133 N. Sierra St., NV 89505 (702/329-3558).

Reno-Sparks Convention and Visitors Authority, 4590 S. Virginia St. (P.O. Box 837), NV 89504 (702/827-7366; toll free 800/367-7366).

Reno-Tahoe Visitors Center, 135 N. Sierra St., NV 89505 (702/348-7788).

GUIDED TOURS: Gray Line Tours (bus), 1675 Mill St. (329-1147): Guided tours of the city and surrounding area.

Horizon Helicopters (helicopter), 485 S. Rock Blvd. (786-6060): Helicopter tours over Lake Tahoe, Virginia City, etc. Spectacular. Reservations essential.

Reno-Tahoe Tour Co. (bus), 1325 Airmotive Way (322-6343): Guided tour of Lake Tahoe, Virginia City, Carson City, etc.

Zephyr Balloons (balloon), 120 Mary St. (329-1700): Balloon tours over the Reno and Lake Tahoe region. Truly spectacular.

SIGHTS, ATTRACTIONS, & ACTIVITIES

ADVENTURES: Ram River Expeditions (boat), 4050 Falling Water Dr. (746-1400): Air-rafting down the Truckee River (May-Sept.).

ARCHITECTURAL HIGHLIGHTS: ☀ 🔭 **Bally's Grand–Reno,** 2500 E. 2nd St. (789-2000): The largest casino-hotel in the world, with 2,000 slot machines, 102 blackjack tables, dozens of poker, baccarat, and roulette tables, and 50 bowling lanes. A veritable city within the city. A must-see.

🔔 **Pioneer Theater Auditorium,** S. Virginia and State Sts. (786-5105): A 1,400-seat concert hall; an unusual piece of modern architecture, crowned with a geodesic dome. Home of the Nevada Opera, the Nevada Festival Ballet, and the Reno Philharmonic. Worth looking over.

MUSEUMS OF ART: 🔔 **Sierra Nevada Museum of Art,** 549 Court St. (329-3333): Located in the neo-Georgian Hawkins House, a designated historic monument, this museum displays an interesting collection of works by contemporary artists of the American West, including paintings, sculpture, prints, decorative arts, and Native American art. Also temporary exhibitions. Worth a visit. Open Tues.-Sun.; closed Mon.

MUSEUMS OF SCIENCE AND HISTORY: 🔔 **Fleischmann Planetarium,** 1650 N. Virginia St. (784-4811): Very modern in conception, this planetarium is located on the University of Nevada–Reno campus. Laser shows, museum of astronomy, telescopes available for stargazing. A treat for lovers of astronomy. Open daily.

Harold's Club Gun Collection and Museum, 250 N. Virginia St. (329-0881): Very fine collection of old firearms, from 16th-century Chinese cannon to the Remingtons, Colts, and Winchesters of the Old West. More than 500 different items, some of them very interesting. On the second floor of Harold's Club, one of the oldest casinos in Nevada (1935). Interesting. Open daily.

☀🔭 **Harrah's Automobile Museum,** E. 2nd St. at Glendale Ave., Sparks (355-3500): Billing itself as "one of the great national treasures of America," this automobile museum has as fine a collection as any in the U.S. More than 1,200 old vehicles, many of them extremely rare or one of a kind, splendidly restored. Free hourly shuttle from Harrah's Hotel in downtown Reno. Not to be missed. Open daily.

🔔 **Liberty Belle's Slot Machine Collection,** 4250 S. Virginia St. (826-2607): An amusing collection of old player pianos and slot machines (the oldest dating from 1898), maintained by the Liberty Belle Saloon. Worth a look. Open daily.

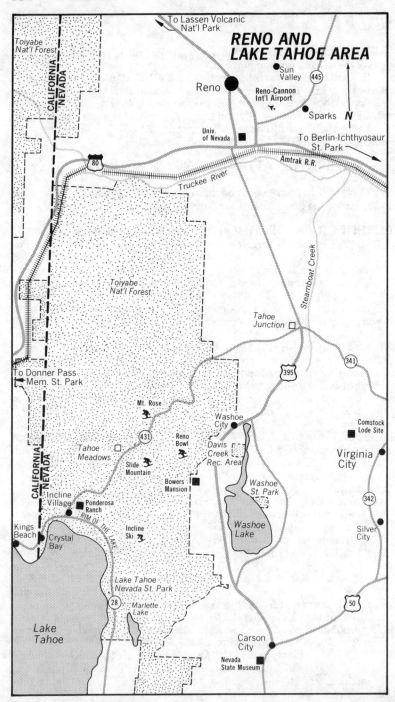

🔔 **MacKay Mining Museum,** 9th and N. Virginia Sts. (784-6988): Extensive geological collection (minerals, precious stones, fossils, etc.). Displays on the history of the gold rush. A facility of the MacKay School of Mines, one of the oldest (1874) and most highly regarded mining schools in the U.S. Interesting. Open Mon.-Fri.

🔔 **Nevada Historical Society Museum,** 1650 N. Virginia St. (789-0190): Displays on the prehistory and modern history of Nevada. Beautiful collection of Native American artifacts. Mementoes of the Winning of the West. Worth a visit; open Wed.-Sun.

NIGHTLIFE: As in Las Vegas, the most important aspect of nightlife in Reno, Sparks, and South Lake Tahoe is to be found in the gaming rooms of the casinos. Most of the big hotels—**Bally's, Harrah's, Caesar's,** the **Hilton, John Ascuaga's Nugget**—also offer frequent floor shows, big-name performers, discos, bars, etc. (see "Accommodations," below).

PERFORMING ARTS: For daily listings of all shows and cultural events, consult the entertainment pages of the daily morning paper *Reno Gazette Journal* and the monthly *Nevada* magazine.

Church Fine Arts Theater, on the University of Nevada–Reno campus, 9th and N. Virginia Sts. (784-6505): Classical and contemporary plays, and musicals. Home of the Nevada Repertory Theater.

Little Theater, 690 N. Sierra St. (329-0661): Modern theater. Drama and comedy (Sept.-June). Also offers children's theater.

Pioneer Theater Auditorium, S. Virginia and State Sts. (786-5105): Classical music concerts, opera, ballet, recitals. Home of the Nevada Festival Ballet (Sept.-Jan.), the Nevada Opera (Oct.-Apr.), and the Reno Philharmonic (Oct.-Apr.), under Ron Daniels, principal conductor.

Reno-Sparks Convention Center, 4590 S. Virginia St. (827-7600): Pop concerts. Hosts an International Jazz Festival annually in Mar.

Trinity Episcopal Church, Rainbow Island Ave. (702/329-4279): Concerts by the Reno Chamber Orchestra (Oct.-Apr.)

Wingfield Riverside Park, S. Arlington Ave. at Island St. (702/851-0759): Free outdoor concerts in this park on the banks of the Truckee River. Mon.-Fri. at noon, June-Aug.

SPECIAL EVENTS: For the exact schedule of events below, consult the **Reno-Sparks Convention and Visitors Authority** (see "Tourist Information," above), the **Carson City Chamber of Commerce,** 1191 S. Carson St., Carson City, NV 89701 (702/882-1565), or the **Lake Tahoe Visitors Authority,** 3050 U.S. 50, South Lake Tahoe, CA 95706 (916/544-5050).

Silver State Square Dance Festival (Reno; May): One of the most important square-dance festivals in the U.S. More than 7,000 dancers come from all over the U.S. and Canada to take part. A great spectacle, and a tradition for over 40 years.

Reno Rodeo (Reno; five days in mid-June): A rodeo festival famous throughout the West. Those not wearing western dress are fined. Exciting atmosphere.

Shakespeare Festival (Lake Tahoe; Aug.): *The* place to be for theater lovers in summer. Shakespearean plays performed outdoors in the lovely natural setting of Sand Harbor State Park.

Great Reno Balloon Race (Reno; Sept.): A hot-air-balloon race, usually with more than 100 entrants. In Rancho San Rafael Park.

☀ **National Championship Air Races** (Reno; four days in mid-Sept.): Prop-plane races, the most famous such competition in the world. Also an aerobatics display. Truly spectacular. Stead Air Field.

Nevada Day Celebration (Carson City; four days in late Oct.): Parades, a "powwow," grand costume ball. Commemorates Nevada's joining the Union in 1864.

SPORTS: Reno has one minor-league professional team:

Baseball (Apr.-Sept.): Padres, Moana Stadium (702/825-0678).

THEME PARKS: ☼ ♨ **Ponderosa Ranch,** at Incline Village, 35 mi. (56 km) SW via U.S. 395, Nev. 431, and Nev. 28 (831-0691): This legendary ranch above Lake Tahoe was owned by the Cartwright family in the television series "Bonanza." Reconstructed western frontier town with a general store, a saloon, a firehouse, and a little church. Tours on horseback or by stagecoach. Entertaining. Open daily.

WINTER SPORTS RESORTS: ♨ **Alpine Meadows,** 48 mi. (76 km) SW via I-80 and Calif. 89 (916/583-4232): 13 lifts; open mid-Nov. to June.

♨ **Donner Ski Ranch,** 43 mi. (68 km) SW on I-80 (916/426-3635): Four lifts; open Dec.-Apr.

♨♨ **Heavenly Valley,** 59 mi. (94 km) south via U.S. 395 and U.S. 50 (702/541-1330): 19 lifts; open mid-Nov. to mid-May.

♨ **Mt. Rose Ski Resort,** 24 mi. (38 km) SW via U.S. 395 and Nev. 431 (702/849-0704): Five lifts; open mid-Nov. to Apr.

♨♨ **Northstar,** 39 mi. (62 km) SW via I-80 and Calif. 267 (916/562-1010): Nine lifts; open Nov.-Apr.

☼ ♨♨♨ **Squaw Valley,** 44 mi. (70 km) SW via I-80 and Calif. 89 (916/583-6985): A famous resort, scene of the Winter Olympics in 1960. 27 lifts; open mid-Nov. to Apr.

ACCOMMODATIONS

See the listing of toll-free numbers in the Appendix.

Room Rates in Reno	
B (Budget)	up to $30
I (Inexpensive)	$30–$60
M (Moderate)	$60–$90
E (Expensive)	$90–$140
VE (Very Expensive)	$140 and up

Personal Favorites (in order of preference)

☼ ♔♔♔♔ **Bally's Reno** (nr dwntwn), 2500 E. 2nd St., NV 89595 (702/789-2000; toll free 800/648-5080). 2,000 rms, A/C, color TV. AE, CB, DC, MC, V. Free valet parking, pool, two health clubs, sauna, eight tennis courts, bowling (50 lanes), seven rests. (including the Café Gigi), 24-hr bars, rm svce, floor shows, casino, hrdrsr, boutiques, two movie theaters, crib $8, free airport shuttle. *Note:* The wildest of the great American casino-hotels. On the ground floor, 163,000 sq. ft. (1.5 ha.) in area, this 26-story giant houses the world's largest casino, with 2,000 slot machines and more than 120 roulette, blackjack, and baccarat tables. The hotel's theater boasts the world's largest stage. The interior decoration is in a nouveau-riche Hollywood style, but the rms (w. refrigerators) are vast and comfortable. Very extensive sports facilities. Efficient svce, despite the hotel's size; decent rests. Usually overcrowded and noisy. Worth a trip all by itself. Very good value. Attractive wknd packages. Parking for campers. **M**

    Harrah's Reno (dwntwn), 219 N. Center St., NV 89504 (702/786-3232; toll free 800/648-3773). 565 rms, A/C, color TV, in-rm movies. AE, CB, DC, MC, V. Free valet parking, pool, health club, sauna, three rests. (including the Steak House), 24-hr coffeeshop, bars, rm svce, floor shows, casino, hrdrsr, boutiques, free crib, free airport shuttle. *Note:* A casino-hotel in the great Las Vegas tradition, luxurious and flashy, in a noisy area of dwntwn Reno. The best floor shows in Reno. Modern and comfortable rms (the best are in the new tower). Caters to groups. Good rest. (Steak House). **M–E, but lower rates out of season**

    Eldorado Hotel (dwntwn), 4th and Virginia Sts., NV 89505 (702/786-5700; toll free 800/648-5966). 411 rms, A/C, cable color TV. AE, CB, DC, MC, V. Free valet parking, pool, three rests. (including the Vintage Steak House), 24-hr coffeeshop, bars, rm svce, floor shows, casino, free crib. *Note:* Big casino-hotel in the middle of dwntwn Reno. Spacious, comfortable rms w. refrigerators. Good svce. Rather noisy neighborhood. Caters to groups and conventions. Acceptable rests. Good value. **I–M**

    John Ascuaga's Nugget Hotel (nr dwntwn), 1100 Nugget Ave., Sparks, NV 89431 (702/356-3300; toll free 800/648-1177). 610 rms, A/C, cable color TV. AE, CB, DC, MC, V. Free valet parking, pool, three rests. (including Trader Dick's), 24-hr coffeeshop, 24-hr bars, rm svce, floor shows, disco, casino, hrdrsr, free crib. *Note:* Ultramodern 28-story casino-hotel. Comfortable, spacious rms w. balconies. Efficient reception and svce. Obtrusive group clientele. Good value. 15 min. from dwntwn. **I–M**

    Fitzgerald's (dwntwn), 255 N. Virginia St., NV 89501 (702/785-3300; toll free 800/648-5022). 345 rms, A/C, cable color TV. AE, CB, DC, MC, V. Free valet parking, two 24-hr rests., 24-hr bars, rm svce, floor shows, casino, free crib. *Note:* Pleasant modern hotel in the heart of Reno. Comfortable, well-furnished rms. Friendly svce. Good value. **I–M**

    Motel 6 East (nr dwntwn), 866 N. Wells Ave., NV 89512 (702/786-9852). 142 rms, A/C, color TV, free in-rm movies. DC, MC, V. Free parking, pool. *Note:* One of the best hotel values in Reno. Comfortable modern rms. Eight min. from dwntwn. **B**

Other Accommodations (from top bracket to budget)

    Hilton Reno (formerly the Sahara; dwntwn), 225 N. Sierra St., NV 89501 (702/322-1111; toll free, see Hilton). 599 rms, A/C, color TV. AE, CB, DC, MC, V. Free valet garage, rest., 24-hr coffeeshop, 24-hr bars, rm svce, casino, floor shows, hrdrsr, free crib. *Note:* Big Las Vegas–style casino-hotel. Pleasant, spacious rms (ask for one w. a view of the Sierra). Vast gaming rooms at street level. Rather noisy area. Acceptable rest. (Top of the Hilton). Good svce. Caters to groups and package tours. In the heart of dwntwn Reno. **I–M**

    Peppermill (nr dwntwn), 2707 S. Virginia St., NV 89502 (702/826-2121; toll free 800/648-6992). 542 rms, A/C, color TV. AE, CB, DC, MC, V. Free valet parking, pool, health club, two rests. (including Le Moulin), coffeeshop, 24-hr bars, rm svce, casino, nightclub, hrdrsr, free crib. *Note:* A 15-story casino-hotel recently modernized and enlarged. Comfortable rms (especially the new wing). Efficient svce. Caters to groups and conventions. Good value. Situated 5 min. from the airport (free shuttle) and 8 min. from dwntwn (free shuttle). **I–M**

    Nugget Motor Lodge (nr dwntwn), 1225 B St., Sparks, NV 89431 (702/356-3300; toll free 800/648-1177). 159 rms, A/C, color TV. AE, CB, DC, MC, V. Free parking, pool, adjoining rest., 24-hr rm svce, free crib. *Note:* Very inviting motel 15 min. from dwntwn. Huge, comfortable rms w. balconies or private patios. Very good value. Casinos nearby. **I–M**

    Circus Circus (dwntwn), 500 N. Sierra St., NV 89503 (702/329-0711; toll free 800/648-5010). 1,625 rms, A/C, color TV. AE, CB, DC, MC, V. Free valet parking, rest., 24-hr coffeeshop, bars, casino, crib $4. *Note:* Clever décor, like a gigantic, multicolored circus tent. Circus shows and gambling all over the place; worth a look. Serviceably comfortable; attractive rates. A good choice in the center of Reno, much frequented by families. **B–I, but lower rates out of season**

    Motel 6 West (nr dwntwn), 1400 Stardust St., NV 89503 (702/747-7390). 122 rms, A/C, color TV, free in-rm movies. DC, MC, V. Free parking, pool. *Note:* One of the best values in Reno. Comfortable, modern rms. 5 min. from dwntwn. **B**

RESTAURANTS

Reno Restaurant Prices	
(per person, excluding drinks and service charges)	
B (Budget)	up to $15
I (Inexpensive)	$15–$25
M (Moderate)	$25–$40
E (Expensive)	$40–$60
VE (Very Expensive)	$60 and up

Personal Favorites (in order of preference)

    La Table Française (nr dwntwn), 3065 W. 4th St. (323-3200). A/C. Dinner only, Tues.-Sat.; closed Sun., Mon., and holidays. AE, CB, DC, MC, V. Jkt. *Specialties:* snails w. Roquefort, confit of duck, quail w. fresh fruit, scallops w. leeks and ginger, spiced duck w. honey, game (in season), hazelnut chocolate mousse cake. Menu changes regularly. Good wine list. *Note:* The retirement in 1984 of Yves Pimparel, head chef and source of inspiration for this excellent French rest., made many fear the worst. But his daughter, Muriel, who has succeeded him, has a master's touch, and this remains the best rest. in Reno. The cooking is a perfect blend of French and Californian nouvelle cuisine. Charmingly got up as both inn and windmill. Well-trained staff; romantic atmosphere. Resv. essential. 8 min. from dwntwn. *French-Continental.* **I–M**

    Steak House (dwntwn), in Harrah's Reno (see "Accommodations," above) (786-3232). A/C. Lunch Mon.-Fri., dinner nightly (until midnight), Sun. brunch. AE, CB, DC, MC, V. Jkt. *Specialties:* frogs' legs provençal, steak Diane, scallops Ste-Michelle, médaillons of beef w. shallot-truffle sauce, noisette of lamb w. avocado. Very good desserts. *Note:* Despite its name, the specialty of this rest. is not its good, big steaks—which are, nonetheless, excellent—but subtler dishes such as sautéed mahi-mahi (Hawaiian dolphin) and excellent curries. Elegant décor; good svce. On the ground floor of Harrah's. *Continental.* **I–M**

    Leonardo's (nr dwntwn), 2450 S. Virginia St. (827-6200). A/C. Dinner only, nightly; closed Thanksgiving and Dec. 25. AE, CB, DC, MC, V. Jkt. *Specialties:* fettuccine Alfredo, lasagne, eggplant parmigiana, scampi alla ventuno, spaghetti alla Pavarotti (w. garlic, green peppers, and chicken livers), saltimbocca, crêpes Da Vinci (filled w. strawberries). Very nice wine list (the best in Reno). *Note:* The favorite rest. of the show-biz crowd, as witness the numerous signed photos of stars on the walls. Excellent Italian cuisine, impeccably prepared and served. Popular locally; resv. strongly advised. *Italian.* **I–M**

    Ichiban (dwntwn), 635 N. Sierra St. (323-5550). A/C. Lunch Mon.-Thurs., dinner nightly; closed holidays. AE, CB, DC, MC, V. *Specialties:* sushi, tempura, teppanyaki, chicken teriyaki. *Note:* The best Japanese food in Reno. Rather banal Far Eastern décor. Attentive svce. Popular locally; resv. advised. *Japanese.* **I**

    Mollie's Garden (dwntwn), in Fitzgerald's (see "Accommodations," above) (785-3300). A/C. Breakfast/lunch/dinner (around the clock). AE, CB, DC, MC, V. *Specialties:* stews, daily specials, steak, salads. *Note:* Honest country cooking; relaxed atmosphere; very good value. *American.* **B**

Other Restaurants (from top bracket to budget)

    Top of the Hilton (dwntwn), in the Hilton Reno (see "Accommodations," above) (322-1111). A/C. Dinner nightly, Sun. brunch. AE, CB, DC, MC, V. Jkt. *Specialties:* Burgundy snails, veal Oscar, scampi provençale, duckling Madagascar, bouillabaisse, steak Diane. *Note:* From the 21st floor of the Hilton Reno, this deluxe rest. offers a spectacular view of the city and surrounding mountains. Flawless traditional hotel cuisine; elegant décor and svce; very high prices by local standards. Resv. advised. *Continental.* **M**

    Café Gigi (nr dwntwn), in Bally's Reno (see "Accommodations," above) (789-2266). A/C. Dinner only, nightly. AE, CB, DC, MC, V. Jkt. *Specialties:* tournedos, steak Diane, pepper steak, lamb chops Vert Pré, roast saddle of veal, crêpes Suzette. *Note:* Despite the décor—Hollywood version of the Palace of Versailles—the food is good, though the svce is needlessly fussy and prices rather high by local standards. On the ground floor of Bally's Reno. Resv. recommended. *French-continental.* **M**

    China Seas (nr dwntwn), in Bally's Reno (see "Accommodations," above) (789-2268). A/C. Dinner only, Mon.-Sat.; closed Sun. AE, CB, DC, MC, V. Jkt. *Specialties:* duck w. almonds, Cantonese lobster, Mongolian beef, chicken w. cashew nuts, Mandarin shrimp. *Note:* One of the few acceptable Far Eastern rests. in Reno, serving pleasing, if Americanized, Chinese food. Banal modern décor; offhand svce. On the ground floor of Bally's Reno. Resv. essential. *Chinese.* **I–M**

    Presidential Car (dwntwn), 250 N. Virginia St. (329-0881). A/C. Dinner only, nightly. AE, CB, DC, MC, V. *Specialties:* roast beef, catch of the day, cheesecake. *Note:* Clever 19th-century railroad setting; good though unimaginative food; efficient svce. *Steak-seafood.* **I**

    Louis Basque Corner (dwntwn), 301 E. 4th St. (323-7203). A/C. Lunch Mon.-Fri., dinner nightly. AE, CB, MC, V. *Specialties:* tripe, chicken basquaise, paella, coq au vin, braised calves' sweetbreads, mutton stew, leg of lamb. *Note:* This rest., w. its family atmosphere and walls decorated w. earthenware and pictures from the Pyrenees, features Basque cooking, both French and Spanish (there are many shepherds of Basque origin in Nevada). Robust, delicious food that treats your wallet gently, served in the generous portions you'd expect. Congenial atmosphere; a great place to eat. Very popular locally. *French-Spanish.* **B–I**

 ☕ **El Borracho** (nr dwntwn), 1601 Virginia St. (322-0313). ☒ A/C. Lunch/dinner daily (until 2 a.m.); closed Thanksgiving and Dec. 25. AE, CB, DC, MC, V. *Specialties:* chiles rellenos, tacos, enchilada verde, fajitas, flauta encantada. *Note:* A little Mexican place, popular locally. Authentic, unpretentious food. Good value. Pretty hacienda décor. *Mexican.* **B**

LAKE TAHOE

ACCOMMODATIONS

See the list of toll-free numbers in the Appendix.

Room Rates in Lake Tahoe	
B (Budget)	up to $30
I (Inexpensive)	$30–$60
M (Moderate)	$60–$90
E (Expensive)	$90–$140
VE (Very Expensive)	$140 and up

Personal Favorites (in order of preference)

 ♗♗♗♗ **Harrah's Lake Tahoe,** U.S. 50 and Stateline Ave., Stateline, NV 89449 (702/588-6611; toll free 800/648-3773). 540 rms, A/C, color TV, in-rm movies. AE, CB, DC, MC, V. Free valet parking, pool, health club, sauna, five rests. (including The Summit), 24-hr coffeeshop, 24-hr bars, rm svce, floor shows, casino, disco, hrdrsr, boutiques, free crib, concierge, free airport shuttle. *Note:* Prestigious casino-hotel with a 393-ft- (120-m-) long gaming room. Its floor shows and amenities rival the best in Las Vegas. Spacious rms, modern and elegant (the best have a view of Lake Tahoe), w. mini-bars; outstanding svce; good rests. Excellent location between the lake and the mountain. A very fine hotel, and you pay accordingly. **E–VE, but lower rates out of season**

 ♗♗ **Tahoe Marina Inn,** Lake Tahoe Blvd., South Lake Tahoe, CA 95705 (916/541-2180). 77 rms (45 w. kitchenettes), color TV, in-rm movies. AE, CB, DC, MC, V. Free parking, pool, sauna, private beach, coffeeshop nearby, free airport shuttle. *Note:* Very comfortable motel right on the lake. Many rms w. private balconies or patios. One of the best values in the whole region. Splendid view. **M–E**

Sierra House Inn, 968 Park Ave., South Lake Tahoe, CA 95729 (916/541-4800). 59 rms, cable color TV. AE, CB, DC, MC, V. Free parking, pool, sauna, coffeeshop nearby, free crib, free airport shuttle. *Note:* Pleasant little motel a stone's throw from Lake Tahoe. Spacious rms w. private balconies or patios. Very good value. Friendly reception and svce. **I–M, but lower rates out of season**

Cedar Glen Lodge, 6589 N. Lake Blvd., Tahoe Vista, CA 95732 (916/546-4281; toll free 800/341-8000). 31 rms, cable color TV. AE, CB, DC, MC, V. Free parking, pool, sauna, private beach, coffeeshop nearby, free crib. *Note:* Charming little motel beside Lake Tahoe, surrounded by pretty gardens. Cozy rms w. private patios (half w. kitchenettes). Calm, countrified atmosphere. Friendly svce. Very good value overall. **I–M, but lower rates out of season**

Other Accommodations (from top bracket to budget)

Hyatt Lake Tahoe, Lakeshore Blvd., Incline Village, NV 89450 (702/831-1111; toll free, see Hyatt). 460 rms, A/C, color TV, in-rm movies. AE, CB, DC, MC, V. Free valet parking, pool, health club, two tennis courts, golf, private beach, bicycles, two rests. (including Hugo's Rôtisserie), 24-hr coffeeshop, 24-hr bar, rm svce, casino, hrdrsr, boutiques, free crib, concierge. *Note:* Luxurious casino-hotel in a lovely wooded setting on the shores of Lake Tahoe. Spacious, ultra-comfortable rms w. fireplaces and balconies, the best overlooking the lake. Efficient svce; very acceptable rest. Ideal for a long vacation stay. Two VIP floors. **M–E, but lower rates out of season**

High Sierra, U.S. 50, Stateline, NV 89449 (702/588-6211; toll free 800/648-3395). 536 rms, A/C, color TV, in-rm movies. AE, CB, DC, MC, V. Free valet parking, pool, sauna, two rests. (including Stetson's), 24-hr coffeeshop, 24-hr bars, rm svce, casino, hrdrsr, boutiques. *Note:* Classic Las Vegas–style casino-hotel, with 1,200 slot machines, dozens of gaming tables, big-name entertainment. Western décor. Pleasant, large rms (some w. balconies and lake views). Good svce. Attractive vacation packages; good value. Caters to groups. **M–E, but lower rates out of season**

Tahoe Beach and Ski Club, 3601 Lake Tahoe Blvd., South Lake Tahoe, CA 95705 (916/541-6220; toll free 800/822-5962). 150 rms, no A/C, cable color TV. AE, CB, DC, MC, V. Free parking, pool, sauna, skiing, waterskiing, private beach, marina nearby, rest., bar, free airport shuttle. *Note:* Very comfortable motel beside Lake Tahoe. Spacious, pleasant rms (some w. balconies). Impeccable svce. Very good location between the lake and the ski slopes. Good value. **M–E, but lower rates out of season**

Royal Valhalla, 4104 Lakeshore Blvd., South Lake Tahoe, CA 95729 (916/544-2233). 80 rms, no A/C, cable color TV. AE, CB, DC, MC, V. Free parking, pool, private beach, valet svce. *Note:* Comfortable little motel w. direct access to the beach. Nice, big rms w. lake or mountain views (most w. private patios or balconies; one-third w. kitchenettes). Good svce. Free morning coffee. Just minutes from the casinos of Stateline. Good overall value. **I–M, but lower rates out of season**

Motel 6, 2375 Lake Tahoe Blvd., South Lake Tahoe, CA 95731 (916/542-1400). 140 rms. A/C, color TV, free in-rm movies. DC, MC, V. Free parking, pool. *Note:* Unbeatable value two steps from the lake. Modern and comfortable. Midway between the ski slopes and the casinos. **B**

RESTAURANTS

Lake Tahoe Restaurant Prices	
(per person, excluding drinks and service charges)	
B (Budget)	up to $15
I (Inexpensive)	$15–$25
M (Moderate)	$25–$40
E (Expensive)	$40–$60
VE (Very Expensive)	$60 and up

Personal Favorites (in order of preference)

♟♟♟ **Le Petit Pier,** 7250 N. Lake Tahoe Blvd., Tahoe Vista (916/546-4464). A/C. Dinner only, Wed.-Mon.; closed Tues. AE, CB, DC, MC, V. Jkt. *Specialties:* country pâté, braised pheasant forestière, tournedos w. marrow in marchand de vin sauce, quail w. green peppercorns. Good wine list. *Note:* Some of the best fare in Lake Tahoe, w. a lovely view of the mountains thrown in. Fine French dining, elaborate and elegant. Preppie atmosphere. Excellent svce. Resv. advised. *French.* **I–M**

♟♟♟ **La Cheminée,** 8504 N. Lake Tahoe Blvd., Kings Beach (916/546-4322). A/C. Dinner only, Thurs.-Mon.; closed Tues., Wed., and the first two weeks in May and Nov. AE, MC, V. Jkt. *Specialties:* terrine of smoked salmon, braised pheasant w. poached quenelles, roast duck w. green peppercorns. The menu changes regularly. Very good desserts. Fine selection of French and California wines. *Note:* The daily menu, written by hand in French, reflects the seasonal availability of ingredients as well as bearing testimony to the imagination and talent of the team in the kitchen. Elegant décor and atmosphere. Resv. indispensable, since the rest. is such a hit. A fine place to eat, but very pricey. *French.* **M**

♟♟ **Swiss Chalet,** Lake Tahoe Blvd. at Sierra Blvd., South Lake Tahoe (916/544-3304). A/C. Dinner only, Tues.-Sun.; closed Mon., Easter, Thanksgiving, and Dec. 25. AE, MC, V. *Specialties:* schnitzel St. Moritz, sauerbraten, steak, veal Cordon Bleu, daily catch. *Note:* Décor and atmosphere of an alpine chalet. French- and German-inspired cooking. Warm and cozy. A landmark since 1957. Resv. recommended. *Continental.* **I–M**

Other Restaurants (from top bracket to budget)

☼ ♟♟♟ **The Summit,** in Harrah's Lake Tahoe (see "Accommodations," above) (702/588-6611). A/C. Dinner only, nightly. AE, CB, DC, MC, V. Jkt. *Specialties:* lobster bisque, red snapper Rockefeller, rack of lamb Pontchartrain, saddle of veal Black Forest, tournedos Alaska, pheasant w. sauerkraut in champagne sauce, bananas Foster, soufflé Grand Marnier. Good wine list. *Note:* Superb view of lake and mountains from the 18th floor of Harrah's. The décor is exceedingly elegant. Rather pompous luxury-hotel cuisine, but impeccably prepared and served. Stylish and classy. Very high prices by local standards. Resv. strongly advised. *Continental.* **M–E**

♟♟ **Chart House,** Kingsbury Grade (1.5 mi, 2.5 km, off U.S. 50), Stateline (702/588-6276). A/C. Dinner only, nightly; closed Dec. 26. AE, MC, V. *Specialties:* filet of beef teriyaki, roast beef, catch of the day. *Note:* Congenial little rest. w. a fine panoramic view of Lake Tahoe from the heights of Stateline. Good food w. no fuss. Friendly svce. A good spot, away from the hustle and bustle of the big casino-hotels along the lake. *American.* **I–M**

🍷🍷 **La Playa,** 7046 N. Lake Blvd., Tahoe Vista (916/546-5903). No A/C. Dinner nightly, brunch Sun. AE, DC, MC, V. Jkt. *Specialties:* roast quail, rack of lamb, tournedos, swordfish steak, catch of the day. Skimpy wine list. *Note:* Charming inn on the shores of Lake Tahoe. Conventional cooking, but very well done. Open-air patio for fine-weather dining, w. views of the lake and the mountains. Friendly reception and svce. A fine place to eat. Resv. recommended. *Continental.* **I–M**

🍷 **Sierra Room,** in Harrah's Lake Tahoe (see "Accommodations," above) (702/588-6611). A/C. Breakfast/lunch/ dinner (around the clock). AE, CB, DC, MC, V. *Note:* Americanized Chinese food, 24 hrs a day. A few dishes are very acceptable. Often packed. All-purpose modern décor. *Chinese.* **B–I**

NEARBY EXCURSIONS

☼🔔 **BERLIN-ICHTHYOSAUR STATE PARK** (175 mi., 280 km, SE via I-80, U.S. 50, Nev. 361, and Nev. 844): Unknown to most tourists, this park, lying east of Gabbs in Union Canyon, is nonetheless fascinating for two reasons. First, it includes the ghost town of **Berlin,** a former miners' community which had several hundred inhabitants at the turn of the century, but has been completely abandoned for more than 75 years. The second and more important of the park's attractions is its large number of fossilized ichthyosaur remains. These enormous prehistoric reptiles, up to 65 ft (20 m) long, with characteristics of both fish and lizard, made their appearance on the planet some 185 million years ago and became extinct 115 million years later. A total of 34 fossilized ichthyosaurs has been discovered so far in the Shoshone Mountains, all uncovered by water erosion during the last glacial period. Guided tours of the park and Berlin are offered Sat. and Sun. at 11 a.m., May-Sept. The park is open daily mid-June to Labor Day, Fri.-Mon. the rest of the year, but is always closed during bad weather. Well worth a visit.

🔔 **CARSON CITY** (30 mi., 48 km, south on U.S. 395): Founded in 1858, Carson City—named after the famous scout Kit Carson, who undertook the first explorations of Nevada, in 1843–1845—is one of the smallest state capitals in the U.S. Nonetheless, the city has a beautiful group of Victorian mansions. The **State Capitol** on N. Carson St., opened in 1871, with its typical silver dome symbolic of Nevada's principal mineral resource, is worth a look. The **Nevada State Museum** deserves a visit, with interesting displays of relics from the days of the pioneers and prospectors; you'll find it on N. Carson and Robinson Sts. (885-4810), open daily.

☼🔔 **DONNER PASS MEMORIAL STATE PARK** (43 mi., 68 km, SW on I-80): This mountain pass was the scene of a famous episode in the history of the westward expansion. In October 1846, 89 pioneers attempting to cross the Sierra Nevada found their way blocked by the snows of an unusually early winter. With no food left, and unable to go on through the blizzards, 42 of them died from hunger and exhaustion. The other 47 survived only by resorting to cannibalism. A museum on the old U.S. 40 (916/587-3841), open daily, traces the story of the Donner party. Well worth going out of your way for.

FORT CHURCHILL HISTORIC STATE MONUMENT
(85 mi., 136 km, SE via Nev. 341, U.S. 395, U.S. 50, and Nev.
28): Remains of a small fort used by the U.S. Army in the 1860s in the war
against the Paiute tribe. The fort also served as a staging post for the riders of the
Pony Express. Visitor center open daily (702/577-2345).

On the way, visit **Virginia City** (see below). Worth a side trip.

LAKE TAHOE (34mi., 54 km, SW via U.S. 395 and Nev.
431, or U.S. 395 and U.S. 50): Lying in the heart of the Sierra
Nevada at an altitude of 6,230 ft (1,899 m), this superb mountain lake, its azure
depths reaching down to 1,600 ft (490 m), is among the country's greatest tourist attractions. Surrounded by granite peaks and coniferous forests, this immense
stretch of water (200 sq. mi., 520 km²) is bordered by a very beautiful scenic road
about 60 mi. (100 km) long. At the southwestern end of the lake, be sure to see
the enchanting **Emerald Bay** and **Eagle Falls,** which plunges 1,508 ft (460 m)
down the mountainside. There are many hotels and restaurants in South Lake
Tahoe, Incline Village, Crystal Bay, Stateline, and other towns on the lake (see
Lake Tahoe "Accommodations" and "Restaurants," above). Ideal for lovers of
water sports, the lake has no fewer than 12 public beaches. Paddlewheel boat trips
aboard M.S. *Dixie* depart from the Zephyr Cove Marina, 4 mi. (6.5 km) north of
Stateline on U.S. 50 (702/588-3508), open daily May-Oct. Lake Tahoe alone is
worth the trip to Reno.

LASSEN VOLCANIC NATIONAL PARK (150 mi., 240
km, NW via U.S. 395, Calif. 36, and Calif. 89): The southernmost outpost of a long chain of volcanic mountains in the Cascade Range, which
stretches from Mount Baker, Mount Rainier, and Mount St. Helens (Washington) in the north, by way of Mount Hood and Crater Lake (Oregon) in the middle, to Mount Shasta (California) in the south, Lassen Peak is one of the only two
active volcanos in the continental U.S. (the other being Mount St. Helens).

Lassen Peak, named after the Danish explorer Peter Lassen, has not erupted
since 1921, but it could happen at any time. The landscape is strange and awe-
inspiring, with desolate fields of lava, black ash, plumes of smoke and sulfurous
vapors, little lakes teeming with fish, thick forests, and muddy hot springs. The
10,457-ft (3,187-m) summit of Lassen Peak, with a superb panoramic view of the
area, can be reached by a two- to three-hour walk up a marked trail. There is also a
fine scenic drive 30 mi. (48 km) long between the park's southern entrance and
Manzanita Lake (Lassen Park Rd.).

The park is open year round, but heavy snowslides prevent access to Lassen
Park Rd. and certain areas of the park from late Oct. through early June. Seven
fully equipped campgrounds. Well worth a detour. For **information,** contact the
Superintendent, Lassen Volcanic National Park, Mineral, CA 96063 (916/595-
4444). **Visitor center** open in summer on Manzanita Lake.

Where to Stay
Childs Meadow Resort, on Calif. 89 (9 mi, 14 km, S. from the SW entrance
to the park), Box 3000, Mill Creek, CA 96061 (916/595-4411). 47 rustic but
comfortable motel rms. I

PYRAMID LAKE (36 mi., 58 km, NE via I-80 and Nev.
447; return by Nev. 445): Last vestige of the prehistoric inland
sea known as Lake Lahontan, Pyramid Lake, 30 mi. (48 km) long by 9 mi. (14
km) wide, is strangely, captivatingly beautiful, surrounded by bald and barren
mountains whose tawny red hues are reflected in its crystalline blue waters. Gen.
John C. Frémont, the first white man to explore the region, in 1844 christened it

Pyramid Lake on account of the conical shape of several islands of porous volcanic rock that rise from its center. The largest of these, Anahoe Island, serves as a sanctuary for a colony of 10,000 white pelicans. Pyramid Lake is also famous for its rainbow and cutthroat trout, which weigh up to 50 lbs. (23 kg), as well as for the curious qui-ui fish, a prehistoric survival. Fishing permits are issued at the offices of the Native American reservation at Sutcliffe, Pyramid Lake Indian Tribal Enterprises, Star Rte. (702/673-6335). The northern part of the lake, with its strange lunar landscapes, is sacred ground to the Paiute people, and off-limits to tourists. Not to be missed.

VIRGINIA CITY (25 mi., 40 km, SE on U.S. 395 and Nev. 341): This, the most famous mining town of the Old West, is not, properly speaking, a ghost town—about 700 people still live here today. Founded in 1859 on the site of the richest vein of gold and silver in Nevada, the legendary Comstock Lode—which alone produced more than $1 billion worth of precious metals—Virginia City in its heyday during the 1870s boasted up to 30,000 inhabitants. As evidence of its unabashed wealth at the time, the town could show off four banks, six churches, a luxurious opera house in which the great Caruso once sang, six theaters, and the only elevator between Chicago and San Francisco, not to mention 110 saloons, by official count.

Clinging to the slopes of Mount Davidson, Virginia City has been in large part restored as it was in its golden age in the 19th century, its principal street (C St.) lined with covered galleries and wooden sidewalks, many small museums (**The Way It Was Museum, The Wild West Museum, Nevada State Fire Museum,** etc.), the offices of the *Territorial Enterprise,* where Mark Twain worked as a reporter, and many saloons with picturesque names (the Bucket of Blood Saloon, the Delta Saloon with its famed Suicide Table, etc.). Also not to be missed are **Piper's Opera House,** B and Union Sts. (702/847-0433), open daily mid-May through Sept. (by appointment the rest of the year), and **The Castle,** a luxurious Norman-style manor built in 1868 by the superintendent of the Empire Mine, at 70 B St. (702/847-0275), open daily.

An entertaining little steam train, the **Virginia and Truckee Railroad** (702/847-0380), operating daily May-Oct., links Virginia City with Gold Hill. Truly spectacular **camel races** take place on Labor Day weekend. Visitor center, open daily, C St. between Taylor and Union Sts. (702/847-0311).

A visit to Virginia City is truly not to be missed.

Where to Stay En Route

In Virginia City, **The Gold Hill Hotel,** on Nev. 341, P.O. Box 304, Virginia City, NV 89440 (702/847-0111). 14 rms. Nevada's oldest hotel (1859). Rooms furnished w. period antiques (some w. fireplaces). Charming and colorful. **I–M**

YOSEMITE NATIONAL PARK (177 mi., 283 km, south on U.S. 395 and Calif. 120): Breathtaking waterfalls and superb granite peaks. One of the two or three most beautiful national parks in the U.S. A must-see. Note that Calif. 120 is closed in winter, necessitating a detour on Calif. 108. For more information, see Chapter 53 on Yosemite National Park.

FARTHER AFIELD

LAKE TAHOE AND VIRGINIA CITY (145 mi., 232 km, round trip via U.S. 395S, Nev. 431S, Calif. 28S, Calif. 89S, U.S. 50E, Nev. 341N, and U.S. 395N): Your first stop will be at **Mount Rose Ski Resort,** a very popular winter sports resort in a lovely natural setting. Make a detour to see ☀ 📭 **Ponderosa Ranch** at Incline Village, which served as the setting for the television series "Bonanza" (see "Theme Parks," above).

Then take the successive scenic highways along ☀ 📭 **Lake Tahoe,** with its splendid scenery (Calif. 28, Calif. 89, and U.S. 50; see "Nearby Excursions," above). Along the way, don't miss **Squaw Valley,** the famous resort where the 1960 Winter Olympics were held. At the southern end of the lake, stop off at beautiful ☀ 📭 **Emerald Bay State Park,** where the water is as clear as crystal. At **Stateline,** on the California-Nevada border, there are many luxury hotels and casinos.

Now on to 🏛 **Carson City,** the state capital and a city of Victorian charm (see "Nearby Excursions," above).

Your last stop on this two- or three-day journey should be at ☀ 📭 **Virginia City,** the most famous gold rush town in the West, which looks like something out of a John Ford or Sam Peckinpah movie. Then back to Reno on U.S. 395N.

A very full itinerary, worth the trip to Reno for its own sake.

CHAPTER 50

THE CALIFORNIA COAST♨

□ □ □

San Francisco to San Diego

From lovely San Diego on the Mexican border to the extraordinary panorama of **San Francisco,** 560 mi. (900 km) to the north, the California coast offers the visitor some of the country's most spectacular landscapes. It is an unexpected patchwork of fertile valleys, great cities, and unspoiled forests of pine or sequoia, of rocky headlands and wonderful beaches (though the currents sweeping in from the north can often chill the water). The California coast, however, is more than a colorful tract of American geography; it embodies a typically Californian way of life compounded of sun, relaxation, and communion with nature.

From the steep cliffs of **Big Sur,** a favorite meeting place for America's literary bohemia, to the fine sand beaches of **Santa Barbara** or **Huntington Beach,** the surfer's paradise, this great "Pacific Riviera" is a standing invitation to travelers, and to lovers of beauty. Thus the motorist who takes the celebrated coastal Hwy. 1 (Cal. 1), the "Cabrillo Highway," will encounter the fabled castle of the billionaire William Randolph Hearst at **San Simeon;** the rosary of Franciscan missions that runs the length of the coast from **San Juan Bautista** to **San Juan Capistrano;** the period charm of the old Spanish colonial settlements like **Monterey,** so beloved by John Steinbeck; the trendy elegance of **Carmel;** the flashier luxury of **La Jolla,** with its Riviera-like beauty; or the mighty silhouette of **Morro Rock,** the Gibraltar of the West Coast, whose massive 563-ft (172-m) bulk looms over the Pacific. And let's not overlook the untold wealth of the late J. Paul Getty's Roman villa at **Malibu,** or the incredible **"Seventeen-Mile Drive"** (27-km) between Carmel and Monterey, past centuries-old cypresses, and tidal rocks covered with sea anemones and peopled with sea lions and elephant seals, where every winter and spring you may watch the passing migration of the gray whales. The California coast, goal of any east-west trip across the U.S., will never cease to enchant the visitor.

For detailed information on the larger cities along the California coast, see the chapters on **Los Angeles, San Diego,** and **San Francisco.**

Note: The name "California," used by the first Spanish conquistadors, comes from a tale of medieval chivalry, and denotes a legendary isle lying to the east of Paradise, inhabited by dusky Amazons and by gryphons, with eagles' heads and lions' bodies.

BASIC FACTS: State of California. Area Codes: 619 (San Diego); 714 (San Bernardino); 213 (Los Angeles); 805 (Santa Barbara); 408 (Monterey); 415 (San Francisco). Time Zone: Pacific Time. Founded: 1769 (San Diego); 1770 (Monterey); 1776 (San Francisco). Approximate distance from San Francisco to San Diego: 604 mi. (974 km).

CLIMATE: The California coast is no less fortunate in its climate than in its scenery. In winter (though this is no name by which to call such a season), the mercury never dips below 46°F–50°F (8°C–10°C), though there can be heavy rains at times in the northern and central parts of the state. Summer is very hot but dry; spring and autumn are wonderful to behold, and filled with unbelievably vibrant light, especially in the south. Aside from a few short weeks of bad weather in winter, this is a year-round paradise.

ARRIVAL & TRANSIT INFORMATION

AIRPORTS: There are five major airports on the California coast:
   Los Angeles International Airport (LAX) (see the Los Angeles chapter).
   Monterey Peninsula Airport (MRY), 4 mi. (6.5 km) SE.
   San Diego Lindbergh International Airport (SAN) (see the San Diego chapter).
   San Francisco International Airport (SFO) (see the San Francisco chapter).
   Santa Barbara Municipal Airport (SBA), 10 mi. (16 km) west.

AIRLINES: See the Los Angeles, San Diego, and San Francisco chapters for listings of domestic and international airlines.

CAR RENTAL: See the Los Angeles, San Diego, and San Francisco chapters.

BUS OR CAR RENTAL?: Greyhound buses provide frequent, convenient service for the entire coastal region of California. On the other hand, car-rental rates in the state are very low—and the possibilities for interesting side trips are almost unlimited—so it's a very good idea to rent a car, or mobile home, with unlimited mileage.

TRAIN: The Amtrak stations are: in Salinas (Monterey), 40 Railroad Ave. (toll free 800/872-7245); in San Luis Obispo, Santa Rosa and Railroad Ave. (805/541-5028); in Santa Barbara, 209 State St. (805/687-6848); see the Los Angeles, San Diego, and San Francisco chapters for offices in these cities.

BUS: In addition to the Greyhound offices in San Francisco, Los Angeles, and San Diego (see these chapters for details), there are California coastal offices at 351 del Monte Ave., Monterey (408/372-1419); 150 South St., San Luis Obispo (805/543-2123); 34 W. Carrillo St., Santa Barbara (805/966-5786).

INFORMATION & TOURS

TOURIST INFORMATION: For general information on the region, write or call the **California Office of Tourism,** 1121 L St., Sacramento, CA 95814 (916/322-2881). For more specific information, contact the following:
   Los Angeles Visitors & Convention Bureau (see the chapter on Los Angeles).
   Monterey Chamber of Commerce, 380 Alvarado St., CA 93940 (408/649-1770).
   San Francisco Visitors Bureau (see the chapter on San Francisco).
   San Luis Obispo Chamber of Commerce, 1039 Chorro St., CA 93401 (805/543-1323).
   Santa Barbara Chamber of Commerce, 1330 State St., CA 93102 (805/965-3021).

GUIDED TOURS: See the chapters on San Francisco, Los Angeles, and San Diego; for other cities, look under "Sightseeing" in the local *Yellow Pages*.

SPECIAL EVENTS: For exact dates on the events listed below, consult the local chambers of commerce listed under "Tourist Information" (above), as well as the **Carmel Business Association,** Vandervort Court, on San Carlos, CA 93921 (408/624-2522), the **Oxnard Convention & Visitors Bureau,** 325 Esplanade Dr., CA 93030 (805/485-8833), the **San Clemente Chamber of Commerce,** 1100 N. El Camino Real, CA 92672 (714/492-1131), the **Santa Cruz Convention and Visitors Bureau,** Church and Center Sts., CA 95061 (408/423-6927), the **Solvang Chamber of Commerce,** 1623 Mission Dr., CA 93463 (805/688-3317), and the **Ventura Visitor and Convention Bureau,** 785 S. Seaward Ave., CA 93001 (805/648-2075).

Carmel
Carmel Bach Festival (last two weeks in July, beginning of Aug.): Concerts, poetry recitations, theater.

Monterey
Monterey Jazz Festival (end of Sept.): Attracts the biggest names in jazz today.

Oxnard
Channel Islands Harbor Parade (early Dec.): Spectacular naval parade with decorated and illuminated boats.

Pebble Beach
Classic Cars Elegance Contest (end of Aug.): Almost 200 classic cars, from the Bugatti Royale to the Cord L-29. One of the world's largest rallies of luxury cars.

San Clemente
La Cristianita Pageant (end of July): Commemorates the first baptisms by the Spanish missionaries.

San Luis Obispo
Mozart Festival (early Aug.): Concerts, choirs, recitals.

Santa Barbara
Old Spanish Days Festival (early Aug.): Parades, historic pageants.

Santa Cruz
Cabrillo Music Festival (end of July to early Aug.): Classical and contemporary music; one of California's most celebrated festivals.

Solvang
Danish Days Festival (3rd wknd in Sept.): Costume festival celebrating the Danish national holiday.
Theaterfest (July to the end of Sept.): Open-air theatricals.

Ventura
County Fair (Oct.): Parades, carnival, rodeo, cattle show. Lively and very colorful.

Distances from San Francisco

To:	Mi.	Km	To:	Mi.	Km
Santa Cruz	81	131	Oxnard	421	679
San Juan Bautista	115	185	Malibu	455	734
Castroville	132	213	Pacific Palisades	463	747
Monterey	143	231	Santa Monica	472	761
17-Mile Drive	145	234	Los Angeles	490	790
Carmel	157	253	Huntington Beach	520	839
Big Sur	184	297	Newport Beach	526	848
San Simeon	248	400	Laguna Beach	535	863
Morro Rock	276	445	San Juan Capistrano	547	882
San Luis Obispo	290	468	San Clemente	554	894
Lompoc	327	527	Oceanside-Carlsbad	580	935
Solvang	339	547	La Jolla	589	950
Santa Barbara	386	623	San Diego	604	974
Ventura	413	666			

Room Rates Along the California Coast
See the listing of toll-free numbers in the Appendix.

B (Budget)	up to $30
I (Inexpensive)	$30–$60
M (Moderate)	$60–$90
E (Expensive)	$90–$140
VE (Very Expensive)	$140 and up

California Coast Restaurant Prices
(per person, excluding drinks and service)

B (Budget)	up to $15
I (Inexpensive)	$15–$25
M (Moderate)	$25–$40
E (Expensive)	$40–$60
VE (Very Expensive)	$60 and up

A NORTH-TO-SOUTH ITINERARY

SAN FRANCISCO and environs (0 mi.): See the chapter on this city.

SANTA CRUZ (81 mi., 131 km): Busy fishing port with a long pier and 28 mi. (45 km) of public beaches much frequented by swimmers. Last refuge of the hippies. Reproduction, one-half original size, of the Santa Cruz Mission, destroyed by an earthquake in the 19th century and now undergoing restoration. At **Año Nuevo State Reserve** (21 mi., 34 km, north on Cal. 1), the unusual spectacle of hundreds of sea lions, elephant seals, and other marine animals lazily sunning themselves on the rocks. At **Felton** (7 mi., 11 km, north on Cal. 9) is the Roaring Camp and Big Trees Railroad (408/335-4484), where a picturesque little train from the early West will take you through the sequoia forests (daily May-Sept.). Worth the side trip.

Where to Stay

Dream Inn, 175 W. Cliff Dr., CA 95060 (408/426-4330). 164 rms, A/C, cable color TV. AE, CB, DC, MC, V. Free parking, pool, rest., bar, rm svce, disco, free crib. *Note:* Modern ten-floor motel, comfortable and attractive; the best rooms (w. balconies) overlook the beach. Good svce. Direct access to beach. **E-VE**

Where to Eat

Crow's Nest, 2218 E. Cliff Dr. (408/476-4560). Lunch/dinner (till 2 a.m.) daily; closed Thanksgiving, Dec. 24 and 25. AE, MC, V. Specialties: fresh salmon in season, fish of the day, steak. *Note:* Likeable fish rest. standing on the jetty of the yacht basin; beautifully fresh fish prepared without any imagination. Svce with a smile. Terrace for fine days, with view of the harbor. No resv. *Steak-Seafood.* **B-I**

IN NEARBY CAPITOLA. Shadowbrook, 1750 Wharf Rd. (408/475-1511). Lunch/dinner daily, May-Sept.; dinner only, daily the rest of the year. Specialties: fresh salmon in season, abalone, excellent meat. *Note:* One of the coast's most popular rests., reached by a little funicular from the highway, below which it stands on the edge of a pretty inlet, surrounded by greenery. Good svce; resv. advised; dancing nightly in summer. *Steak-Seafood.* **I**

SAN JUAN BAUTISTA (115 mi., 185 km): The **Mission of San Juan Bautista,** 2nd & Mariposa Sts. (408/623-4528), open daily. California's largest Franciscan mission (1797), and one of the best preserved. Fine **plaza** with many buildings from the 1850s, including the splendid Plaza Hotel at 2nd St. (408/623-4881), open daily. Shouldn't be missed.

Where to Eat

Cademartori's, 1st & San José Sts. (408/623-4511). Lunch/dinner Tues.-Sun.; closed Mon., July 4, and three weeks in Dec. AE, DC, MC, V. Specialties: veal parmigiana, saltimbocca, abalone, homemade pasta. *Note:* This Italian-American rest. occupies a former outbuilding of the San Juan Bautista Mission, standing in a beautiful garden. It offers honorable, meticulous cuisine and a wonderful view over the San Joaquin Valley. Open-air patio in summer; a good place. *Italian-American.* **B-I**

CASTROVILLE (132 mi., 213 km): In this town, modestly styling itself the "artichoke capital of the world," you may try this delicious vegetable prepared in every conceivable way—fried, boiled, as a cream soup, sautéed, or even in a cake—at the Giant Artichoke Restaurant. Entertaining festival every Sept., with election of an "artichoke queen."

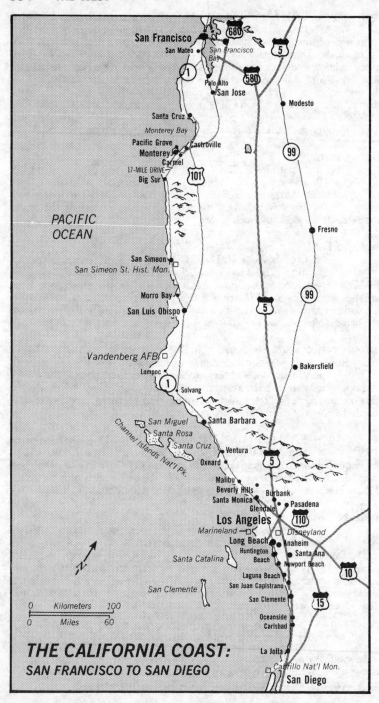

THE CALIFORNIA COAST:
SAN FRANCISCO TO SAN DIEGO

Where to Stay

IN NEARBY SALINAS. ⓣ **Motel 6,** 1010 Fairview Ave., CA 93901 (408/758-2122). 78 rms, color TV, free in-rm movies. DC, MC, V. Free parking, pool, free crib. *Note:* A small, reasonably priced motel offering serviceable comfort on a shoestring. An unbeatable value. **B**

☼ 👓 **MONTEREY** (143 mi., 231 km): Lively and colorful, Monterey is the most Spanish of Californian towns, still evidencing many traces of its colonial days: the **Presidio** (1846), seat of the Spanish government, on Pacific St. (408/647-5414), open Mon.-Fri.; the old **Custom House** (1827), 1 Custom House Plaza; the **Royal Presidio Chapel,** at 550 Church St., founded by Spanish settlers in 1770; **California's First Theater,** the oldest theater in the state, at Pacific & Scott Sts. (408/375-4916), where performances have been given without interruption since 1847; the **Colton Hall Museum,** formerly the City Hall, at 522 Pacific St., whose cellar was used as a prison during the Mexican War. There are some charming old houses, one of which, at 530 Houston St., belonged to Robert Louis Stevenson, the author of *Treasure Island*.

You should also see the harbor district and **Cannery Row,** made famous by John Steinbeck; at 886 Cannery Row (408/375-3333) is the splendid, ultramodern **Monterey Bay Aquarium,** open daily, with more than 5,000 specimens including many sharks and giant octopi; it was used as a setting for the movie *Star Trek IV*.

Where to Stay

☼ 🐚🐚🐚🐚 **Monterey Plaza,** 400 Cannery Row, CA 93940 (408/646-1700; toll free 800/631-1339). 290 rms, A/C, cable color TV. AE, CB, DC, MC, V. Valet gar. $6, private beach, rest. (Delfino), coffeeshop, bar, rm svce, boutiques, concierge. *Note:* The most recent of Monterey's palaces; three elegant four-story Spanish colonial buildings on Cannery Row halfway between Fisherman's Wharf and the Aquarium. The interior decoration, featuring Oriental rugs, teak panels, a profusion of marble, objets d'art, and period furniture, comes together in a magnificent triumph of luxury and sophistication. Huge, comfortable rooms, most w. ocean view; impeccable svce. Admirable Italian rest. A physical-fitness center, w. its own hot springs, is being built next to the hotel. One of the best places on the Pacific Coast. **E–VE** ꮮꮮꮮ **Hyatt Regency,** 1 Old Golf Course, CA 93940 (408/372-1234; toll free, see Hyatt). 579 rms, color TV, in-rm movies. AE, CB, DC, MC, V. Free parking, two pools, six tennis courts, golf course, health club, two rests. (including the Peninsula), rm svce, bars, disco, beauty parlor, concierge, free crib. *Note:* One of the best hotels along the California coast; modern and elegant, with almost 15 acres of gardens facing the Del Monte golf course. Excellent svce; favored by groups and wealthy sports-lovers. Recently modernized and enlarged. Two VIP floors. **E–VE**

ꮮ **Cypress Tree Inn,** 2227 Fremont Rd., CA 93940 (408/372-7586). 55 rms, cable color TV. AE, MC, V. Free parking, rest., crib $4. *Note:* Typical small motel, modest but well run. Enormous rms w. balconies and mini-refrigerators (some w. kitchenettes). Free morning coffee. Located five min. from dwntwn and from Monterey State Beach. **I–M; out-of-season discounts**

ꮮ **Motel 6,** 2124 Fremont St., CA 93940 (408/646-8585). 51 rms, color TV, free in-rm movies. DC, MC, V. Free parking, pool, free crib. *Note:* Small budget hotel nr. dwntwn, adequately comfortable. Unbeatable value. **B**

Where to Eat

🌣 ♟♟♟ **The Old House in Old Monterey** (formerly Gallatin's), 500 Hartnell St. (408/373-3737). A/C. Dinner only, daily. AE, MC, V. Jkt. Specialties: confit of duck, shrimp à la dijonnaise, mushrooms à la George. Menu changes regularly; very good wine list. *Note:* This distinguished French rest., in a splendid 19th-century dwelling house, was recently acquired by Léonce Picot, owner of several celebrated rests. in Florida (including Casa Vecchia and Down Under). Sumptuous setting w. antique furniture, rich rugs, and dazzling flower arrangements. Classic French cuisine impeccably prepared and served; stylishly elegant. Resv. recommended. *French.* **I–M**

♟♟ **Sardine Factory,** 701 Wave St. (408/373-3775). A/C. Dinner only, daily; closed for one week at Christmas. AE, CB, DC, MC, V. J&T. Specialties: fish of the day, shellfish, broiled shrimp w. shallots, veal cardinal. Fine list of reasonably priced wines. *Note:* This famous rest., though its former glory has perhaps faded a trifle, still overlooks the beautiful bay. Exemplary meat and fish prepared in a rather outdated fashion. Engagingly got up as a tropical greenhouse. Svce so-so. Comfortable, welcoming bar. Resv. advisable. Valet parking. *Continental-Seafood.* **I–M**

♟ **The Fishery,** 21 Soledad Dr. (408/373-6200). A/C. Lunch Tues.-Fri.; dinner Tues.-Sat; closed Sun., Mon., all Dec. & Jan. MC, V. Specialties: fishburgers, broiled filet of Coho salmon, catfish Louisiana style, Thai-style seafood platter, squid. *Note:* The community's favorite fish rest., serving the freshest possible food prepared w. some exotic touches (Malaysian and Thai recipes in particular) and at very acceptable prices. Rather elaborate Oriental decor. Fast, deft svce. In view of its popularity, resv. advised. *Seafood.* **B–I**

🌣 🔭🔭 **"SEVENTEEN-MILE DRIVE"** (between **Monterey** and **Carmel,** 145 mi., 234 km): One of the country's most scenic roads, it circles the Monterey Peninsula along the shore. **Cypress Point** features a superb cypress grove at the edge of the ocean. At **Seal Rock** there are large numbers of marine animals as well as dream houses and the world-famous **Pebble Beach golf course.** If you saw nothing else in California, this would still make the trip worthwhile, as attested by the 1½ million visitors who come here every year.

🌣 🔭🔭 **CARMEL** (157 mi., 253 km): This charming little artists' community, spruce and covered in flowers, has become a fashionable tourist attraction and a Shangri-La for lucky retirees. In 1986 Carmel elected a very dark-horse candidate as its mayor—the actor Clint Eastwood. Along Ocean Ave. and the nearby streets are many open-air restaurants, art galleries, and boutiques. See the beautiful **San Carlos Borromeo Mission** (1770), and the tomb of Fray Junipero Serra, founder of the California missions, at 3080 Rio Rd. (408/624-3600), open daily. The **Biblical Garden** at Lincoln St. and Seventh Ave. has a complete collection of the trees, plants, and flowers mentioned in the Bible or originating in the Holy Land.

Point Lobos State Reserve (3 mi., 5 km, south along Cal. 1), with its rocks thronged with sea lions and sea-birds, and its centuries-old cypress trees, is a must for nature-lovers. There is a popular Bach Festival at the end of July. Make a point of coming here, but try to avoid the crowds on summer weekends.

Where to Stay

Quail Lodge, 8205 Valley Green Dr., CA 93923 (408/624-1581; toll free, see Preferred). 96 rms (cottages), A/C, cable color TV. AE, CB, DC, MC, V. Free parking, two pools, tennis court, putting green, sauna, bicycles, rest. (Covey), two bars, rm svce, disco, hrdrsr, library, concierge. *Note:* Delightful country inn set in beautiful gardens w. duck ponds, adjoining the Carmel Valley golf course. Luxuriously decorated rms w. fireplaces, mini-bars, patios, and private balconies. Polished, attentive svce; elegantly romantic atmosphere. Interesting golf and tennis packages. **VE**

La Playa, Camino Real at 8th St., CA 93921 (408/624-6476; toll free 800/582-8900). 75 rms, A/C, cable color TV. AE, MC, V. Free parking, pool, rest., bar, rm svce, free crib. *Note:* Attractive Spanish colonial hotel dating from the early 20th century, w. an entirely renovated interior. Enormous, comfortable rms with mini-refrigerators and private patios, the best offering a view of the ocean and the Point Lobos wildlife reserve. Inviting gardens; efficient svce. **E–VE**

Pine Inn, Ocean Ave. at Monte Verde St., CA 93921 (408/624-3851). 49 rms, cable color TV. AE, MC, V. Free parking, rest., bar, rm svce, crib $5. *Note:* Charming older hotel almost on the beach; comfortable rms w. brass beds and fine views, each decorated in a different style. Fine Victorian décor with stained glass and old floor lamps. Svce and reception both leave something to be desired. **M–E**

Jade Tree Inn, Junipero & Sixth Aves., CA 93921 (408/624-1831). 55 rms, cable color TV. AE, MC, V. Free parking, pool, nearby coffeeshop, crib $5. *Note:* Inviting small motel near the San Carlos Borromeo Mission; large, comfortable rms w. fireplaces and shaded patios, some w. ocean view. You are made welcome with a smile here. **I–M**

IN NEARBY PEBBLE BEACH. The Lodge, 17-Mile Dr. (3 mi., 5 km, north of Carmel), CA 93953 (408/624-3811). 163 rms, A/C, cable color TV. AE, CB, DC, MC, V. Free valet parking, private beach, pool, 12 tennis courts, three golf courses, sauna, riding, sailing, three rests., coffeeshop, bar, 24-hr rm svce, disco, hrdrsr, boutiques, concierge, free crib. *Note:* Pure luxury on the ocean. Exceptional comfort and svce; tasteful décor with period furniture and many artworks. Spacious rms w. fireplaces and mini-bars, and balconies or patios w. a view of the ocean (in the better ones) or the golf course. Excellent rest. (Club XIX). Remarkable sports facilities. Airport limo. Interesting golf and wknd packages. Resv. should be made well in advance. One of the 12 best hotels in the country. **VE**

Where to Eat

Crème Carmel, San Carlos St. & Seventh Ave. (408/624-0444). A/C. Dinner only, daily; closed Jan. 1, Dec. 25. MC, V. Specialties: rack of lamb, bass stuffed with crabmeat, red snapper Hawaiian, filet of beef au cabernet, roast duck, soufflés. The menu changes regularly. *Note:* Small (35-seat) rest. w. a warm, vital ambience. Modern Californian cuisine, elegant and imaginative, but feebly supported by the wine list. Svce is the best; an excellent place to eat. Resv. a must. *American-Continental.* **I**

Rio Grill, Cal. 1 at Rio Rd. (408/625-5436). Lunch/dinner daily. MC, V. "Firecracker," catfish Créole, broiled rabbit, quesadillas, excellent homemade desserts. Menu changes daily. *Note:* Under the same management as the Fog City Diner in San Francisco and Mustards Grill in Napa Valley, this fashionable rest. offers inventive and elegant California cuisine. Décor recalls the Indian pueblos of New Mexico: adobe walls, heavy exposed beams, and cactus. Svce on the relaxed side, but a very congenial atmosphere. A discovery. *American.* **I**

Rocky Point, Cal. 1 at Rocky Point, 12 mi. (19 km) south of Carmel (408/624-2933). Lunch/dinner daily; closed Thanksgiving, Dec. 25. AE, MC, V. Specialties: meat from the broiler, swordfish, barbecued chicken. *Note:* Perched on a cliff, this popular rest. looks right out over the ocean and its wildlife (the rocks below are floodlit at night). Satisfying steaks and irreproachably fresh fish of the day. Resv. advised. *Steak-Seafood.* **I**

Shabu Shabu, Carmel Plaza, Mission St. between Ocean Ave. & 7th (408/625-2828). Lunch Mon.-Sat., dinner nightly. MC, V. Specialties: tempura, teriyaki, shabu shabu (steak, tofu and vegetables). Note: Tasteful, traditional Japanese country-style restaurant w. three selections cooked at your table. Named for its specialty. *Japanese.* **B–I**

Scandia, Ocean Ave. at Lincoln St. (408/624-5659). A/C. AE, MC, V. Breakfast/lunch/dinner daily. Specialties: frikadeller, leg of lamb, veal Oscar, fish of the day. *Note:* A corner of Scandinavia beneath the California sun. Tasty, attractively priced food served w. a smile, against a backdrop of melodious classical music. Locally popular. *Scandinavian-American.* **B–I**

IN NEARBY PEBBLE BEACH. ▼▼▼ **Club XIX,** at the Lodge (see "Where to Stay," above) (408/625-1880). A/C. Lunch/dinner daily. AE, CB, DC, MC, V. Jkt. Specialties: abalone, filet of beef en croûte, fresh salmon in season, veal chasseur, rack of lamb bouquetière, soufflé Grand Marnier. Good wine list. *Note:* Elegant, sumptuous rest. appropriate to a palatial hotel. Classic but delicate French cooking. Magnificent view of Pebble Beach golf club and the ocean. Exemplary svce. Dining by candlelight. One of the best on the coast. Resv. advised. *French.* **I–M**

BIG SUR (184 mi., 297 km): In the 1950s this was the haunt of America's literary bohemians. Its splendid rocky cliffs and its pine and redwood forest have served as backdrop for innumerable movies, TV series, and novels. Henry Miller, who passed his last years here, devoted one of his most famous passages to the place. Very beautiful beach, deserted more often than not. Well worth visiting.

Where to Stay

Ventana Inn, Cal. 1 at Ventana Village, CA 93920 (408/667-2331; toll free 800/628-6500). 40 rms, A/C, color TV, in-rm movies. AE, DC, MC, V. Free parking, pool, sauna, solarium, rest., bar. *Note:* One of the most widely known hotels on the California coast, w. a spectacular ocean view. Very comfortable rms w. fireplaces, balconies, and mini-bars, but even so, rates are excessive for the quality of the svce and facilities. Free breakfast. **VE**

Big Sur Lodge, Cal. 1, CA 93920 (408/667-2171). 61 cottages; no TV, no telephones in rms. MC, V. Free parking, pool, sauna, coffeeshop, market. *Note:* Comfortable bungalows (some w. fireplaces and kitchenettes) in the midst of a grove of redwoods, which is part of Pfeiffer–Big Sur State Park. Very rustic atmosphere; ideal for family parties. **M**

Where to Eat

Ventana, at the Ventana Inn (see "Where to Stay," above) (408/667-2331). Lunch/dinner daily. AE, DC, MC, V. Specialties: veal with tomato and artichoke hearts, fish and meat from the broiler, rack of lamb, very good homemade desserts. Fine list of California wines. *Note:* Beautiful greenhouse of a dining rm looking out over the ocean (*ventana* is the Spanish word for window); cedar paneling, warm colors. Overhanging the water is a terrace where you can enjoy your meal in the open air. Modern California-style cuisine; friendly, relaxed svce. One of the best-known establishments on the coast. Resv. required for dinner. *American.* **I–M**

Nepenthe, Cal. 1, 3 mi. (5 km) south of the entrance to the state park (408/667-2345). Lunch/dinner daily. AE, MC, V. Specialties: ambrosia burger, steak broiled over wood fire, broiled fish, roast chicken. *Note:* From its clifftop, this well-known country inn gives you a splendid view of the sea. Limited menu of food straightforwardly prepared, at reasonable prices. The atmosphere is enjoyable, if slightly touristy. Good svce. *American.* **B–I**

HEARST-SAN SIMEON STATE HISTORICAL MONUMENT

(248 mi., 400 km): The imposing Spanish-Moorish castle that crowns the hill of **Cuesta Encantada** was designed and built by the newspaper magnate William Randolph Hearst, and is without a doubt America's most extravagant and insanely baroque edifice. Hearst's larger-than-life-size eccentricities were the inspiration of Orson Welles' masterpiece, *Citizen Kane.* From 1919 until Hearst's death in 1951, armies of workers labored on the enormous mansion standing in its splendid Italianate gardens—but it is still unfinished in spite of the $30 million (in comparatively uninflated money!) spent on it. The interior, a mixture of Etruscan, Roman, Greek, Gothic, and Renaissance styles, holds hundreds of works of art which Hearst's unbridled passion for collecting, and his wealth, led him to acquire in Europe for immense sums. Don't miss the enormous banquet hall, Neptune's swimming pool, the great salon with its priceless tapestries, and the owner's lavish private quarters. Several guided tours daily, of which tour no. 1, leaving hourly on the half hour, is the most interesting. For information on timetables and prices, call 805/927-2000; for resv. (advisable), call 619/452-1950 (or toll free 800/446-7275 in California).

Where to Stay

San Simeon Pines Resort, 7200 Moonstone Beach Dr., San Simeon, CA 93452 (805/927-4648), 1½ mi. (2.5 km) south of the Hearst Castle. 60 rms, color TV, in-rm movies. AE, MC, V. Free parking, pool, golf, beach, nearby coffeeshop, crib $5. *Note:* Comfortable little motel on the beach; some rms w. terraces and extensive view. Ideal for visiting the castle. Free morning coffee. Agreeable svce and reception. Good value. **I–M**

Best Western Cavalier Inn, 9415 Hearst Dr., San Simeon, CA 93452 (805/927-4688; toll free, see Best Western), 3 mi. (5 km) south of the Hearst Castle. 90 rms, color TV, in-rm movies. AE, CB, DC, MC, V. Free parking, two pools, coffeeshop, rm svce, boutiques, free crib. *Note:* Modern, functional beachfront motel; comfortable rms with private balconies and mini-refrigerators (most w. fireplaces), the best w. ocean view. Good svce; good value. **I–M**

Where to Eat

IN NEARBY CAMBRIA. **Brambles Dinner House,** 4005 Burton Dr., Cambria

(805/927-4716), 9 mi. (15 km) south of Hearst Castle. Dinner only, daily; closed Dec. 25. AE, CB, DC, MC, V. Specialties: fresh salmon in season, steak broiled over wood, roast beef with Yorkshire pudding. *Note:* Fine Victorian house, tastefully decorated. First-rate broiled meat and fish. Thoughtful svce, romantic atmosphere. Resv. advisable in summer. *Steak-Seafood.* **I–M**

♇ **Grey Fox Inn,** 4095 Burton Dr. at Center St. (805/927-3305). Breakfast/lunch/dinner daily; brunch Sun.; closed Dec. 25. AE, MC, V. Specialties: chicken Kiev, roast beef, fish of the day, fresh vegetables. *Note:* Charming little rest. (seats barely 40) with slightly nostalgic decor. Open-air dining in good weather. Meticulous cuisine and svce; very good value. *American-Continental.* **B–I**

🔻 **MORRO ROCK** (276 mi., 445 km): Called the "Gibraltar of the Pacific," this 563-ft (172-m) monolith of volcanic rock dominates the approach to the pretty fishing port of **Morro Bay.** Beautiful nearby beaches include **Cayucos Beach, Atascadero Beach,** and **Morro Strand Beach.** Very near here, in the marshes at the mouth of **Los Oros Creek,** the largest wetlands on the California coast, live no fewer than 250 varieties of birds.

Where to Stay

☀️♟♟♟ **Inn at Morro Bay** (formerly the Best Western Golden Tee), 19 Country Club Dr., CA 93442 (805/772-5651; toll free 800/321-9566). 97 rms, color TV, in-rm movies. AE, CB, DC, MC, V. Free parking, pool, fishing, rest. (Bay Room), bar, rm svce, disco, crib $5. *Note:* Pleasant motel almost in the ocean, exactly halfway between San Francisco and Los Angeles. Private marina; golf course adjoining. Comfortable rms w. balconies; view over the bay and Morro Rock. Amiable, competent svce; very acceptable rest. All in all, good value; recommended. **M–E**

♟♟ **Bay View,** 225 Harbor St., CA 93442 (805/772-2771; toll free 800/742-8439). 22 rms, color TV, in-rm movies. AE, CB, DC, MC, V. Free parking, whirlpool bath, nearby coffeeshop, crib $4. *Note:* Small, rustic motel near the water. Large, comfortable rms w. fireplaces and mini-refrigerators, the best w. ocean view. Free morning coffee. Price a little steep for what's on offer. **I–M, but lower rates off-season**

♟ **Motel 6,** 298 Atascadero Rd., CA 93442 (805/772-5641). 72 rms, color TV, free in-rm movies. DC, MC, V. Free parking, pool, free crib. *Note:* Small budget hotel, adequately comfortable. Unbeatable value. **B**

Where to Eat

🍸🍸 **Dutch's Fine Dining,** 2738 N. Main St. (805/772-8645). Lunch Mon.-Fri.; dinner daily; brunch Sun. AE, CB, DC, MC, V. Specialties: sole à la cardinal, broiled lobster, crab Quo Vadis. *Note:* An outstanding place for seafood-lovers: absolutely fresh produce prepared with real talent. The old stone house is massive but comfortable and inviting. Open-air terrace in summer. *Seafood-Continental.* **B–I**

☀️🔻 **SAN LUIS OBISPO** (290 mi., 468 km): Founded in 1772 by the Spanish Franciscan Fray Junipero Serra, this commercial town, overlooked by four cone-shaped volcanic peaks, is the site of the magnificent **San Luis Obispo de Tolosa Mission,** now a parish church and museum, at Monterey and Broad Sts. (805/543-6850), open daily. Very near the mission is the interesting **San Luis Obispo County Historical Museum,** 696 Monterey St. (805/543-0638), open Wed.-Sun., devoted to the history of the Spanish colonial era. Some 19th-century commercial buildings should not be overlooked: Sinsheimer Bros. at 849 Monterey St. and Ah Louis Store at 800 Palm St. A must-see.

Where to Stay

☀🛏🛏 **Madonna Inn,** 100 Madonna Rd., CA 93401 (805/543-3000). 109 rms, cable color TV. No credit cards. Free parking, rest., bar, rm svce, disco, free crib. *Note:* The craziest hotel in the entire West—a rococo four-story building with no elevators, where every room is decorated in a different style or period, from tropical jungle to fake Louis XVI—not to mention the room w. artificial moonlight or the celestial suite full of cherubs. A triumph of Hollywood kitsch and bad taste. Some of the rooms (the Cloud Nine Suite, w. angels, or the Elegance Room, in lavender, blue, and pink) are booked three to six months ahead. Well worth a visit. Rest. (Gold Rush Room) acceptable but no more. Svce doesn't measure up. **M–E**

🛏 **Motel 6,** 1433 Calle Joaquin, CA 93401 (805/549-9595). 87 rms, color TV, free in-rm movies. DC, MC, V. Free parking, pool, free crib. *Note:* Small budget hotel, adequately comfortable. Unbeatable value. **B**

IN NEARBY AVILA BEACH. The 🛏🛏🛏 **San Luis Bay Inn,** Avila Rd., CA 93424 (805/595-2333; toll free 800/592-5928). 75 rms, A/C, cable color TV. AE, MC, V. Free parking, pool, tennis court, golf, rest. (Cove), bar, rm svce, disco, free airport limo, crib $10. *Note:* Beautiful resort hotel a few feet from the beach. The best rms (w. balconies) look out over Avila Beach and the charming little port of San Luis. Excellent svce; one of the best hotels on the Pacific coast. Resv., several weeks ahead, are a must. Lovely gardens. Deep-sea fishing. **E**

IN NEARBY LOS OLIVOS. The ☀🛏🛏 **Los Olivos Grand Hotel,** 2860 Grand Ave., CA 93441 (805/688-7788; toll free 800/626-7249). 21 suites, A/C, cable color TV. AE, MC, V. Free parking, pool, rest., bar, rm svce. *Note:* In the heart of the Santa Ynez Valley, this delightful turn-of-the-century inn boasts some 20 luxurious suites, each decorated in the style of a famous European impressionist painter. Magnificent gardens; svce and reception very polished; rest. offers truly remarkable French cooking. A peaceful, sophisticated retreat a little more than two hrs by road from Los Angeles. Children under 16 not admitted. **VE**

Where to Eat

☀🍷 **Gold Rush Room,** at the Madonna Inn (see "Where to Stay," above) (805/543-3000). A/C. Dinner only, daily. No credit cards. Specialties: abalone, filet mignon, seafood. *Note:* Decorated, as is the rest of the hotel, in dubious taste; the restrooms in the basement alone are worth the visit all by themselves. Cuisine and svce are unwarrantably pretentious. Dancing. May interest novelty-hunters. *Seafood-American.* **I**

🏛 **LOMPOC** (327 mi., 527 km): Near **Vandenberg Air Force Base** and its missile launchers, this little town of 20,000 people accounts for more than half of all the flower seeds sold throughout the world. North 3 mi. (5 km) along Cal. 246 is **La Purisima Concepcion Mission,** founded in 1787 and rebuilt in 1812, at Purisima Rd. & Mission Gate Rd. (805/733-3713), open daily. It is one of the finest, and best restored, in California, with beautiful gardens. A must-see.

☀🏛 **SOLVANG** (339 mi., 547 km): A little corner of Scandinavia in the heart of California. Founded by Danish settlers in 1911, this unexpected glimpse of old Europe, with its windmills, bakeries, and dove-cotes, attracts many tourists. You'll like the stores and restaurants. The attractive **Santa Ines Mission,** at 1760 Mission Dr. (805/688-4815), is open daily. A must-see.

Where to Stay

☀☆♟♟♟ **Alisal Guest Ranch,** 1054 Alisal Rd., CA 93463 (805/688-6411), 3 mi. (5 km) south of Solvang. 66 rms & three bunga-lows, cable color TV in main lounge. MC, V. Free parking, pool, tennis court, golf, riding, boats, rest., bars, rm svce, disco. *Note:* A real stock ranch carrying more than 2,000 head of cattle on almost 9,900 acres of rolling land with a large private lake. For lovers of the Far Western way of life there are horseback riding and open-air barbecues. Very comfortable; relaxed svce and reception. Excellent value. **VE (Modified American Plan)**

♟ **Best Western King Frederik,** 1617 Copenhagen Dr., CA 93463 (805/688-5515; toll free, see Best Western). 46 rms, A/C, cable color TV. AE, CB, DC, MC, V. Free parking, pool, nearby coffeeshop, free breakfast, crib $4. *Note:* Charming little Scandinavian-style motel; comfortable rms w. balconies; in the heart of town. Good value. **I–M**

Where to Eat

☀☆♟♟ **Danish Inn,** 1547 Mission Dr. (805/688-4813). A/C. Breakfast/lunch/dinner daily. AE, MC, V. Specialties: smör-gåsbord, beef Lindström, veal Oscar, fresh salmon, rack of lamb, Danish pastries. *Note:* This spruce, comfortable rest. with its Scandinavian contemporary décor (try to sit in the Windmill Room) is deservedly a favorite with visitors to Solvang. *Scandinavian-Continental.* **B–I**

☀☆♟♟ **SANTA BARBARA** (386 mi., 623 km): Enchanting seaside resort at the foot of the Santa Ynez Mountains which has be-come a favorite home for movie stars and the California rich. Many Spanish-style adobe houses. The **Santa Barbara Mission** (1786), E. Los Olivos & Upper La-guna Sts. (805/682-4713), with its twin pink-and-white towers, is one of the state's most popular tourist attractions. Nicknamed "the queen of the missions" because of its architectural splendor, it has a wonderful view over the town and the ocean. Open daily.

Other remarkable specimens of the colonial style include the Spanish-Moorish palace of the **County Courthouse,** 1100 Anacapa St., and the **Presidio** (1782), 123 E. Cañon Perdido (805/966-9719), one of the four fortresses built by the Spanish in California. And don't overlook the very beautiful **Museum of Art** at 1130 State St. (805/963-4364), open Tues.-Sun., renowned for its collec-tion of Greek and Roman art; or the picturesque **De La Guerra Plaza** and **El Paseo,** a group of courtyards, plazas, and alleys dating from 1827 and now boasting art galleries, boutiques, and sidewalk cafés.

See also the unusual giant fig tree, over 110 years old, whose trunk—151 ft (46 m) high—can shade 10,000 people from the sun (**Moreton Bay Fig Tree,** Chapala & Montecito Sts.). Not to be missed.

Where to Stay

♟♟♟♟ **Four Seasons Biltmore,** 1260 Channel Dr., CA 93108 (805/969-2261; toll free, see Four Seasons). 229 rms & 11 cottages (2–8 persons each), color TV, in-rm movies. AE, CB, DC, MC, V. Free valet parking, two pools, sauna, tennis court, putting green, beach, rest., coffeeshop, bar, rm svce, disco, drugstore, concierge. *Note:* One of the oldest palace hotels on the California coast, housed in a beautiful Spanish-Moorish building at the edge of the ocean surrounded by 19 acres of superb tropical gardens. Luxurious rms

w. private balconies and unobstructed view of either the Santa Ynez Mountains or the Pacific. Efficient svce. Has ranked as one of the country's finest hotels since it opened in 1927. **VE**

☀☙♟♟♟ **El Encanto Hotel & Garden Villas,** 1900 Lasuen Rd., CA 93103 (805/687-5000). 100 cottages, color TV, in-rm movies. AE, MC, V. Free valet parking, pool, tennis court, rest. (Dining Room), bar, rm svce, disco, concierge, free airport limo, free crib. *Note:* Captivating adobe cottages nestling in a glorious exotic garden, thick w. eucalyptus trees, which looks clear over the Pacific and the Santa Barbara heights. Luxurious, comfortable suites w. private balconies or patios. Exemplary svce (the beds are turned down every day). Rest. highly recommended. This place has the style and atmosphere of a European resort hotel. **E–VE**

♟♟ **Miramar Hotel-Resort,** 1555 S. Jameson Lane, CA 93108 (805/969-2203; toll free 800/322-6983). 200 rms, color TV. AE, CB, DC, MC, V. Free parking, two pools, four tennis courts, saunas, health club, private beach, rest., coffeeshop, rm svce, hrdrsr, crib $8. *Note:* With its unusual blue roof, this old (and somewhat dated) palace right on the ocean is the connoisseurs' favorite. Commodious, comfortable rms or individual cottages w. kitchenettes. Caters to groups and conventions. Direct beach access. Svce inconsistent. The ideal place for railroad buffs (there's a miniature train running across the garden!). On balance, good value. **M–E**

♟ **Motel 6 Beach,** 443 Corona del Mar, CA 93103 (805/564-1392). 52 rms, color TV, free in-rm movies. DC, MC, V. Free parking, free crib. *Note:* Small, reasonably priced motel, near the beach as its name suggests, and a few steps from the zoo. Unsurpassable value. **B**

♟ **Motel 6 State Street,** 3505 State St., CA 93105 (805/687-5400). 60 rms, color TV, free in-rm movies. DC, MC, V. Free parking, pool, free crib. *Note:* Another small, reasonably priced motel eight min. from dwntwn. Serviceable comfort on a shoestring; another unbeatable value. **B**

IN NEARBY MONTECITO. The ☀ ♟♟♟ **San Ysidro Ranch,** 900 San Ysidro Lane, Montecito, CA 93108 (805/969-5046). 38 cottages, cable color TV in lounge. AE, MC, V. Free parking, pool, tennis court, riding, rest., two bars, rm svce, disco, crib $15. *Note:* The small hotel of your dreams, in a 494-acre garden surrounded by mountains. For nearly a century the little white cottages have been home to some of the greatest names in art and politics, including Sir Winston Churchill, Somerset Maugham, and Sir Laurence Olivier. President and Mrs. Kennedy spent their honeymoon here. Huge, sumptuous rms, some w. fireplaces. Exemplary svce. Very good rest. (Plow and Angel). Resv. essential—and well in advance. Very highly recommended; the only California hotel that belongs to the prestigious French Relais et Châteaux association. **E–VE**

IN NEARBY REFUGIO PASS. The ☀ ♟ ♟ **Circle Bar B Guest Ranch,** 1800 Refugio Rd. (1¼ mi. south of Refugio Pass), Goleta, CA 93017 (805/968-1113). 12 rms. AE, MC, V. Free parking, pool, riding, rest., bar, shows (June-Oct.). *Note:* This rustic ranch on 988 unspoiled acres some 20 mi. (32 km) north of Santa Barbara is a big attraction: its next-door neighbor is Rancho del Cielo, the country home of Pres. Ronald Reagan. Simple but comfortable rms, agreeable atmosphere. Heavily attended theatrical shows in summer. Resv. advised a number of weeks ahead. Well worth a stay. Very fine view of the ocean and the Channel Islands. **M–E (Modified American Plan)**

Where to Eat

♟♟♟♟ **Michael's Waterside Inn,** 50 Los Patos Way (805/969-0307). A/C. Lunch daily (except Tues. & Sat.); dinner Wed.-

Mon.; closed Tues. AE, MC, V. Jkt. Specialties: soufflé suissesse, salmon w. lime butter, pigeon w. shallot sauce, tournedos w. red wine and mushrooms. Remarkable desserts, particularly the roulé marquis. *Note:* Elegant Victorian house which has quickly earned itself a reputation for some of the finest food on the coast. The talented chef, Michael Hutchings, a graduate of London's famous La Gavroche, presides over a light, elegant cuisine, much sought after by celebrities and movie stars. A fine establishment w. attentive svce; resv. a must. *French-Continental.* **M–E**

☖☖☖ **El Encanto Dining Room,** at El Encanto Hotel & Garden Villas (see "Where to Stay," above) (805/687-5000). Dinner only, daily. AE, MC, V. Jkt. Specialties: vol-au-vent of snails w. peppers, médaillon of veal Baumanière, pheasant w. almonds and amaretto, marzipan tart. Fine wine list. *Note:* Imposing, palatial, 1930s-style dining rm, whose enormous bay window gives a clear view of the city and its lights. Open-air terrace in summer. Urbane, up-to-date French-inspired cuisine; svce exemplary in all respects; romantic atmosphere. Resv. a must. Highly recommended. *French-Continental.* **I–M**

☖ **Pescados,** 422 N. Milpas St. (805/965-3805). Lunch/dinner daily. MC, V. Specialties: burritos and seafood fajitas, broiled fish of the day, tacos, frijoles negros. *Note:* Outstandingly fresh fish and shellfish, imaginatively prepared Mexican fashion. Charming rustic-modern décor. A successful rest., popular in the community, where on some days you may have a long wait for a table. Friendly, efficient svce; one of the best little rests. on the coast. *Seafood-Mexican.* **B–I**

☖ **La Super-Rica,** 622 N. Milpas St. (805/963-4940). Lunch/dinner daily. No credit cards. Specialties: tacos, frijoles and chorizos, broiled chicken. *Note:* The tireless Mama Gonzalez, bustling behind her stoves, keeps a sharp eye on the preparation of her sauces, marinated meats, and spiced frijoles to ensure that they will be to the taste of her regular customers. Absolutely authentic cooking; the décor is insignificant—but so are the prices. Inviting covered patio for lunch or dinner al fresco. Has a large local following. *Mexican.* **B**

IN NEARBY MONTECITO. The ☖ **Cafe del Sol,** 516 San Ysidro Rd. at Cal. 192 (805/969-0448). A/C. Lunch/dinner daily; closed Dec. 25. AE, MC, V. Specialties: classic Mexican dishes as well as good fish, lobster, frogs' legs, and steaks. *Note:* Pleasant hacienda décor, further brightened w. growing plants; gracious, congenial svce. A good spot. *American-Mexican.* **B–I**

IN NEARBY OJAI. The ❀ ☖☖☖ **Ranch House,** 102 Besant Rd. (805/646-2360). A/C. Lunch/dinner Wed.-Sun.; closed Mon.-Tues. and hols. AE, MC, V. Specialties: crab voisin, beef Bali Hai, chicken au champagne, pork au Cointreau, fish of the day, excellent desserts. Choice wine list. *Note:* One of the most innovative rests. in California; chef Alan Hooker's cuisine is refined and inventive. Herbs and vegetables fresh from the garden; excellent home-baked bread and pastry. Likeable waitresses will tell you about the specials for the day, and you'll enjoy the garden. Background music is classical and agreeable. Two sittings a night, at 6 and 8:30 p.m. *American-Continental.* **I–M**

⛪ **VENTURA** (413 mi., 666 km): The **San Buenaventura Mission,** 211 E. Main St. (805/643-4318), was the last (1782) to be founded by the great Franciscan missionary, Fray Junipero Serra. It still has its original wooden bells. Open daily. Interesting **County Museum** at 100 E. Main St. (805/653-0323), open Tues.-Sun., and fascinating **archeological excavations** in progress at 113 E. Main St. Worth the detour.

An Offshore Side Trip

☀️🔭 **Channel Islands National Park** (about 10 mi., 16 km, off-shore): Group of five small uninhabited islands stretching for some 150 mi. (242 km) parallel to the coast. The five islands—**Anacapa, San Miguel, Santa Barbara, Santa Cruz,** and **Santa Rosa**—are now marine-life sanctuaries; their flora and fauna are different from those of the mainland, and include 830 species not found anywhere else in California. But it is the animal and marine life that constitutes their principal attraction: sea anemones, sea urchins, abalone, crayfish, dolphins, sponges, foxes, seabirds, and half a dozen varieties of sea lions, for a start.

Camping is allowed, by previous arrangement, on Anacapa and Santa Barbara. For park information, contact the Superintendent, Channel Islands National Park, 1901 Spinnaker Dr., Ventura, CA 93001 (805/644-8262).

The islands can be reached only by boat from Oxnard or Ventura on the mainland. The recommended carrier is **Island Packers Company,** 1603 Anchors Way Dr., Ventura (805/642-1393). You shouldn't miss this trip.

Where to Stay

🍷🍷 **Pierpoint Inn,** 550 San Jon Rd., CA 93001 (805/643-6144).
🛏️🛏️ 80 rms, color TV. AE, CB, DC, MC, V. Free parking, pool, tennis court, rest., bar, rm svce, disco, free crib. *Note:* Small, charming English-style inn; rms (w. balconies or terraces) are pleasing and almost all offer a fine view of Pierpoint Bay. Good rest.; interesting wknd packages. Good value. **I—M**
🍷 **Motel 6,** 2145 E. Harbor Blvd., CA 93003 (805/643-5100).
🛏️ 200 rms, color TV, free in-rm movies. DC, MC, V. Free parking, pool, free crib. *Note:* Small, reasonably priced motel; serviceable comfort. Unsurpassable value. **B**

Where to Eat

🍷 **Sportsman,** 53 S. California St. (805/643-2851). A/C. 🍸 Lunch/dinner daily; closed hols. MC, V. Specialties: broiled meat and fish, roast beef sandwiches. *Note:* The simple, unpretentious cuisine rates a big hand. Lovers of hunting and fishing will enjoy the décor. Popular in the community. *Steak-Seafood.* **B—I**

🔔 **OXNARD** (421 mi., 679 km): Like Ventura, a departure point for trips to the **Channel Islands,** 10 mi. (16 km) offshore, where tens of thousands of birds, sea lions, and other marine animals can be seen in their natural environment. Worth the side trip. (See "An Offshore Side Trip" under Ventura, above.)

Where to Stay

🍷🍷🍷 **Casa Sirena Marina,** 3605 Peninsula Rd., CA 93030 (805/985-6311; toll free 800/228-6026). 274 rms, color TV. AE, CB, DC, MC, V. Free parking, two pools, three tennis courts, putting green, saunas, bicycles, marina, rest. (Lobster Trap), two bars, rm svce, free airport limo, free crib. *Note:* Vast, well-equipped resort hotel. Rms w. balconies and harbor view. Ideal for visits to the Channel Islands. A little boisterous and overcrowded. Good rest.; worthwhile discount packages. **I—M**

Where to Eat

🍷🍷 **Lobster Trap,** at Casa Sirena Marina (see "Where to Stay," above) (805/985-6361). A/C. Breakfast/lunch/dinner daily; brunch Sun. AE, CB, DC, MC, V. Specialties: abalone, fish of the day, shellfish, red meats. *Note:* Good hotel cuisine, well prepared w. few surprises. Fine view over the yacht basin and beyond. Slowish svce. Agreeable oyster bar. *Steak-Seafood.* **B–I**

☀☖☖☖ **MALIBU** (455 mi., 734 km): Immense fine-sand beach. Home of such movie celebrities as Sylvester Stallone, Robert Redford and Steven Spielberg. Don't miss the **J. Paul Getty Museum,** one of the two or three wealthiest in the world. There is an exact replica of the 1st-century A.D. "Villa of the Papyrus" from Herculaneum near Naples. (See "Museums" in the Los Angeles chapter.)

☖ **PACIFIC PALISADES** (463 mi., 747 km): Resort town and, like Malibu, home to many movie and television stars. **Will Rogers State Park,** on Sunset Blvd. between Amalfi Dr. and Brooktree Rd., former ranch home of the famous movie cowboy and humorist, is worth a visit (see the Los Angeles chapter).

Where to Eat
Gladstones 4 Fish (see the Los Angeles chapter).

☖ **SANTA MONICA** (472 mi., 761 km): Enormous, busy beach. Picturesque pier with amusements.

Where to Eat
Michael's (see the Los Angeles chapter).

☖☖☖ **LOS ANGELES** (490 mi., 790 km): See the Los Angeles chapter for information on the city and its surroundings.

☖ **HUNTINGTON BEACH** (520 mi., 839 km): Another vast beach popular with surfers and skindivers (beware sharks!).

☀☖ **NEWPORT BEACH** (526 mi., 848 km): One of California's smartest and most fashionable beaches, with its splendid homes and luxury boutiques and restaurants—but also a very busy fishing port **(Newport Pier)** for more than a century. The beauty of its coastal scenery has earned it the nickname "the American Riviera." The **Harbor Art Museum** at 850 San Clemente Dr. (714/759-1122), open Tues.-Sun., makes this a mecca for lovers of the avant-garde and of American experimental art. Well worth the detour.

☖ **LAGUNA BEACH** (535 mi., 863 km): Very beautiful, fashionable beach lying at the foot of steep hills. Many boutiques and open-air restaurants. Nearby is the **Lion Country Safari** theme park, with African wildlife in a natural habitat (see the Los Angeles chapter).

Where to Stay
☖☖ **Casa Laguna Inn,** 2510 S. Coast Hwy., CA 92651 (714/494-2996). 20 rms, A/C, cable color TV. AE, DC, MC, V. Free parking, pool. No bar or rest. *Note:* Enticing little Spanish colonial–style inn w. panoramic view of the Pacific. As far as you can get from production-line tourism. Elegantly decorated rms, each in a different style. Private, luxuriant patios and gardens. Polished svce and welcome. Interesting vacation packages. **E–VE**
☀☖☖ **Ben Brown's Aliso Creek Inn,** 31106 Coast Hwy., South Laguna, CA 92677 (714/499-2271). 61 rms w. kitchenettes,

cable color TV. AE, MC, V. Covered parking, pool, golf, sauna, rest., bar, rm svce, disco, crib $3. *Note:* Likeable little hotel hidden in a peaceful inlet beside the ocean. Huge, comfortable rms w. balconies. Very acceptable rest. Hard-working, congenial svce. A nice place, one hr by car from Los Angeles. **E**

⚱⚱ **Hotel Laguna,** 425 S. Coast Hwy., CA 92651 (714/494-
⚱⚱ 1151). 70 rms, color TV. AE, CB, DC, MC, V. Free parking, private beach, rest. (Claes), bar, rm svce, disco. *Note:* For more than 50 years the Hotel Laguna has been the delight of summer vacationers, captivated by the convenience of its private beach in the center of town. The best rms look over the ocean. Good svce and adequate rest. **M, but off-season reductions**

IN NEARBY LAGUNA NIGUEL. The ⚱⚱⚱⚱ **Ritz Carlton,** 33533 Ritz Carlton Dr., CA 92677 (714/240-2000; toll free 800/241-3333). 393 rms, A/C, color TV, in-rm movies. AE, CB, DC, MC, V. Free valet parking, two pools, four tennis courts, golf, health club, two rests. (including the Dining Room), coffeeshop, bars, 24-hr rm svce, disco, hrdrsr, boutiques, concierge, free crib. *Note:* On its clifftop overlooking the Pacific, this four-story palace opened in 1984 is one of the latest blossoms of American luxury hotelkeeping. Mediterranean-style architecture surrounded by magnificent gardens w. fountains and covered patios. Splendid view of the ocean and Catalina Island. No visiting VIP can afford to miss it, which is why resv. must be made many days, or weeks, ahead. Sumptuous rms w. private balconies, mini-bars, and period furniture. Many antiques and works of art are displayed in the public rooms and foyer of this palace. Ultra-polished svce and reception. The Dining Room is one of the best rests. on the West Coast. VIP floor. Free bus to the beach at the foot of the cliff. Has style and quality both. **VE**

IN NEARBY EL TORO. Coto de Caza, 22000 Plano Trabuco Rd., Trabuco Canyon, CA 92679; take the El Toro Rd. E exit off I-5 (714/858-1500). 100 rms, cable color TV. AE, MC, V. Free parking, 2 pools, 10 tennis courts, bowling, riding, shooting, hunting, sauna, hlth club, bicycles, rest. (Silverado Dining Room), bar, cinema, disco; crib $10. *Note:* Enormous game reserve—as its name suggests—with more than 4940 acres (2,000 ha) at the foot of the Santa Ana Mountains, and just 20 min. from the ocean. Paradise for hunters (pheasant, quail, woodpigeon) and sports enthusiasts (the hotel has a computer-equipped medical center that offers personalized diet and exercise programs). Friendly svce, pleasant rms. Attractive half-board packages. **E**

Where to Eat

⚱⚱ **Las Brisas,** 361 Cliff Dr. (714/497-5434). A/C. Breakfast/
lunch/dinner daily; brunch Sat., Sun.; closed Thanksgiving, Dec. 24. AE, CB, DC, MC, V. Specialties: fish Mexican style, sopa de frijol, carne asada, enchiladas, and squid. *Note:* Inviting terrace overlooking the ocean, or a comfortable dining room w. indoor waterfall. Good Mexican cuisine tailored to North American tastebuds. Has had a large following in the community for many years. Resv. a must. Valet parking. *Mexican-Seafood.* **I**

⚱ **Beach House,** 619 Sleepy Hollow Lane (714/494-9707).
Breakfast/lunch/dinner daily; closed Thanksgiving, Dec. 25. AE, MC, V. Specialties: Maine lobster, fish kebab, abalone amandine, good desserts. *Note:* Likeable fish rest. w. ocean view. Open-air terrace in good weather. A relaxed place. *Seafood.* **B–I**

IN NEARBY LAGUNA NIGUEL. ⚱⚱⚱⚱ **The Dining Room,** at the Ritz Carlton Laguna Niguel (see "Where to Stay," above) (714/240-5008). A/C. Dinner only, daily. AE, CB, DC, MC, V. J&T. Specialties: ragoût of snails w. chanterelles, sweetbreads in flaky pastry w. morels, rabbit sauté w. mustard, paupiettes of sole w. sauce caviar, medallions of veal w. cream of truffles, broiled filet of beef w. shallots, roast duckling w. cherries and port wine, vacherin w. white chocolate, fresh fruit sherbet. Very fine wine list. *Note:* While it lacks the unobstructed view of the Pacific and Catalina Island enjoyed by most of the rms in the Ritz Carlton, this palatial rest., w. its old master paintings and crystal chandeliers, is redolent of luxury and good taste. Quite remarkable classic French cuisine (but prices to match). Svce polished to a high gloss. Distinguished background music. Resv., several days ahead, a must unless you're staying at the hotel. Some of the finest food in southern California. *French-Continental.* **M–E**

SAN JUAN CAPISTRANO (547 mi., 882 km): Perched between mountain and sea, the **San Juan Capistrano Mission** is the most famous, and probably the most beautiful, in California; take I-5, leave it at the Ortega Hwy. exit; open daily (714/493-1424). Founded in 1776 by Fray Junipero Serra, this lovely mission, laid out in the shape of a Latin cross, was almost entirely destroyed by an earthquake in 1812. There survive the Serra Chapel, the ruins of the cloister, and a little museum surrounded by superb tropical gardens where, every year, the swallows come to nest on the first day of spring.

Don't overlook the **Regional Library & Cultural Center,** at 31495 El Camino Real (714/493-1752), open Mon.-Sat., whose elegant post-modern architecture bears the name, and the stamp, of Michael Graves.

Where to Stay

Best Western Capistrano Inn, 27174 Ortega Hwy., CA 92675 (714/493-5661; toll free, see Best Western). 108 rms, A/C, color TV, in-rm movies. AE, CB, DC, MC, V. Free parking, pool, 24-hr rest. adjoining, bar, rm svce, crib $4. *Note:* Comfortable motel very near the famous San Juan Capistrano Mission. Agreeable rms, some w. balconies; a perfect stopover for visiting the mission. Free morning coffee. **I–M**

IN NEARBY CAPISTRANO BEACH. The **Best Western Marina Inn,** 24800 Dana Point Harbor Dr., Dana Point, CA 92629 (714/496-1203; toll free, see Best Western). 135 rms (one-third w. kitchenettes), A/C, color TV, in-rm movies. AE, CB, DC, MC, V. Free parking, pool, sauna, rest. adjoining, free crib. *Note:* Modern, functional motel overlooking the pleasure-boat harbor of Dana Point, where boats may be hired. Commodious rms w. balconies, the best overlooking the Pacific. Free morning coffee. **M**

Where to Eat

El Adobe, 31891 Camino Capistrano (714/493-1163). A/C. Lunch/dinner daily; closed Labor Day, Dec. 25. AE, MC, V. Specialties: all kinds of red meat. *Note:* Old (1766) courthouse, a designated historical monument, converted into a handsome rest. Menu limited, but first-class meats. Enjoyable atmosphere, w. a roof which opens in summer. Resv. advised. *Steak-American.* **B–I**

SAN CLEMENTE (554 mi., 894 km): Beach resort made fashionable by former Pres. Richard Nixon, who made his summer home there (Casa Pacifica) during his term of office.

Where to Eat

Sandtrap, 2391 S. El Camino Real (714/492-4653). A/C. Lunch/dinner daily; closed Labor Day, Dec. 25. MC, V. Specialties: roast beef, steak broiled over a wood fire, fish of the day. *Note:* Inviting small rest. nr. the San Clemente beach. Much-frequented piano bar. *Steak-Seafood.* **B–I**

🔭🔭 **OCEANSIDE-CARLSBAD** (580 mi., 935 km): Miles of beach, almost deserted except for surfers and surf fishers. Four mi. east along Cal. 76 stands the imposing **San Luis Rey de Francia Mission** (619/757-3651), one of the few in California that was *not* founded by the tireless Fray Junipero Serra, but rather by one of his assistants, Father Lasuén. Dedicated to the canonized King Louis IX of France, it once housed 3,000 Indians, and still displays many mementoes of Spanish colonial days in its remarkable museum. It continues to serve its original purpose as a parish church and school for the surrounding Indian reservations. Open daily.

A further 48 mi. (77 km) east along Cal. 76 is the famous 🔭🔭 **Mount Palomar Observatory** with its 200-inch (5.1-m) reflector telescope, one of the world's largest. The dome may be visited daily; for information, call 619/742-3476. Well worth going out of your way for (see the San Diego chapter).

Where to Stay

♟♟♟ **La Costa Hotel & Spa,** Costa del Mar Rd., Carlsbad, CA 92008 (619/438-9111; toll free 800/854-6564). 485 rms or individual cottages, A/C, cable color TV. AE, CB, DC, MC, V. Free parking, three pools, 25 tennis courts, two golf courses, sauna, hot spring, riding, five rests. and bars, coffeeshop, rm svce, hrdrsr, boutiques, free crib. *Note:* Resting on almost 5,000 wooded acres nr. the ocean, this is one of the finest vacation complexes on the West Coast. Comfortable, luxuriously equipped rms or suites. Impeccable svce; excellent facilities. A paradise for sports-lovers or those taking a cure, but priced accordingly (some suites run $900 a day). Wknd and American Plan packages are interesting. For those who love going on a diet. **VE**

♟ **Best Western Beach View,** 3180 Carlsbad Blvd., Carlsbad, CA 92008 (619/729-1151; toll free, see Best Western). 41 rms, A/C, cable color TV. AE, CB, DC, MC, V. Free parking, pool, sauna, beach, nearby coffeeshop, crib $6. *Note:* Friendly small motel facing the beach; comfortable rms w. mini-refrigerators, some also w. balconies or fireplaces, the best overlooking the ocean. Reception with a smile. **M**

♟ **Motel 6,** 1403 Mission Ave., Oceanside, CA 92054 (619/721-6662). 79 rms, color TV, free in-rm movies. DC, MC, V. Free parking, free crib. *Note:* Small, reasonably priced motel; serviceable comfort. Unsurpassable value. **B**

IN NEARBY RANCHO SANTA FE. The ☀♟♟ **Inn at Rancho Santa Fe,** Linea del Cielo, CA 92067 (619/756-1131). 79 rms, A/C, color TV. AE, CB, DC, MC, V. Free parking, pool, tennis court, golf, riding, rest., bar, rm svce, crib $10. *Note:* Deluxe motel and pleasing bungalows set in 19 acres of beautiful gardens; ideal for lovers of sports and fresh air. Very satisfactory rest. Spacious rms w. private patios, some w. kitchenettes. Good svce, good value. **M–E**

Where to Eat

IN NEARBY RANCHO SANTA FE. 🍴🍴 **Mille Fleurs,** 6009 Paseo Delicias (619/756-3085). A/C. Lunch/dinner daily; closed Dec. 25. AE, MC, V. Jkt. Specialties: soup à la moutarde, fresh foie gras and smoked salmon maison, sweetbreads au madère, veal cutlet w. wild mushrooms, original desserts. Somewhat skimpy wine list. *Note:* Everything here bears the delectable imprint of romance, from the Spanish décor with its patios and enormous open fireplaces to the open-air terrace for lunch and the profusion of green houseplants. The young German chef, Martin Woesle, was trained at the famous L'Aubergine in Munich; he offers a vibrant contemporary cuisine. The exceptional fresh fruits and vegetables come from the well-known Chino ranch nearby. Congenial ambience and background music. Resv. a must. *French-Continental.* **I–M**

IN NEARBY DEL MAR. 🍴 **When in Rome,** 828 U.S. 101N (619/944-1771). Dinner only, Tues.-Sun.; closed Mon., hols. AE, MC, V. Specialties: fresh homemade pasta, filet of beef w. peppers, scaloppine w. lemon, broiled fish, chicken cacciatore. *Note:* One of southern California's best Italian rests., serving light, delicate food. The colonnaded rm is full of light; the svce comes with a smile; this is a first-rate place. *Italian.* **I**

☀️🍴 **LA JOLLA.** (589 mi., 950 km): California's most sought-after summer resort, a sort of West Coast equivalent of Europe's Amalfi or Juan-les-Pins. Beautiful beaches hidden by little inlets, luxurious oceanfront homes, open-air stores and restaurants. Important museums, particularly the **Museum of Contemporary Art.** (See "Nearby Excursions" in the San Diego chapter.)

Where to Eat

See the San Diego chapter for the following restaurant recommendations: **Gustaf Anders, Su Casa, Mandarin House, Alfonso's Hideaway,** and **El Chalan.**

🍴 **SAN DIEGO.** (604 mi., 974 km): See the San Diego chapter for information on the city and its surroundings.

CHAPTER 51

SAN FRANCISCO 🔥🔥🔥

□ □ □

And the California Wine Country

They say that "If you live in San Francisco, you never have to take a vacation." Where else would you find a more beautiful sight than its bay? Or a more enjoyable climate than the 59°F (15°C) average, winter and summer alike, which makes San Francisco the world's first naturally air-conditioned city? Tourists—3½ million of them every year—and longtime residents alike share a love at first sight for this charming, colorful city.

Luxurious mansions jostling little pastel-colored cottages on steep hillsides; the old **cable cars** struggling up, or hurtling down, the precipitous streets; the cutting edge of the **Transamerica Pyramid** towering above the exotic pagodas of Chinatown, the largest Far Eastern community outside Asia; the huge, flamboyant silhouette of the **Golden Gate Bridge** framed against the Pacific; the splendid backdrop of San Francisco Bay, with the dark island of Alcatraz anchored amid its icy blue waves, especially at sunset—all these are the details of an amazing urban composition.

But the splendor of the scenery is not, by itself, enough to explain why everybody is captivated by "the Pearl of the West Coast"; after all, a recent Gallup Poll established that San Francisco tops the list of cities "where every American dreams of going to live." Although today's San Francisco, standing at the crossroads of East and West, is one of the world's great financial clearinghouses, the city came on the scene comparatively late. The first men to explore the Pacific coast, the Portuguese Juan Rodríguez Cabrillo and the English Sir Francis Drake, both missed the narrow passage into the bay. It was not until 1776 that the great Franciscan missionary to California, Fr. Junipero Serra, built the **Mission Dolores,** dedicated to St. Francis of Assisi, a little south of the site of the present imposing City Hall. At the same time, there arose on what is now **Portsmouth Square,** at the edge of Chinatown, a little hamlet which the Spaniards called Yerba Buena ("Good Herbs"). Some 70 years later, on July 19, 1846, when Capt. John B. Montgomery of the U.S.S. *Portsmouth* took possession of the town in the name of the people of the United States, it was still no more than a little settlement of trappers and whalers.

The discovery in 1848 of the first veins of gold in California's rocks touched off the famous "gold rush" in the following year, and the population of the town exploded in the space of two years from 900 inhabitants to 50,000. Since then nothing—not even the terrible earthquake of 1906, which registered 8.2 on the Richter Scale, or the conflagration that followed it—has impaired the magnetic attraction of "Baghdad on the Bay" for generations of immigrants. Chinese, Mexicans, Japanese, Italians, White Russians, French Basques, Filipinos, Germans, and Irish have all been drawn hither, and have all contributed to the city's cosmopolitan character. Even now, 43% of its inhabitants are first- or second-generation Americans, and newspapers are published here in 13 languages besides English. The beneficent effects of the melting pot have made of this poly-glot place the most amusing, the most tolerant, and the most sophisticated city in the U.S. In spite of the pervasive fear of AIDS, San Francisco has more gay people (80,000) of both sexes in relation to its population (barely 750,000 inhabitants) than any other American city; there are even gay deputy mayors on the city coun-cil of America's "spiritual capital" of homosexuality. This same respect for mi-nority rights, reinforced by a tradition of nonconformity, has brought to birth in San Francisco a number of contemporary ideologies: the beatniks in the '50s, stu-dent protest at **Berkeley** and the hippies in the '60s, the psychedelic movement at the beginning of the '70s, and so on. The flip side of the coin is a disquieting multiplication of sects, "religions," and small extremist groups like the Black Panthers, the Symbionese Liberation Army, or the fundamentalist sect whose members committed mass suicide at Jonestown.

Another cloud on the horizon is the proximity of the **San Andreas Fault,** which runs 560 mi. (900 km) along the California coast, and keeps San Francisco permanently at risk of another earthquake like that of 1906; there is even a tele-phone number (329-4025) which San Franciscans can call for current informa-tion on shocks registered by local seismographs.

Continuing a century-old tradition, three renowned universities, the Ro-man Catholic **University of San Francisco,** founded in 1855, with 7,000 stu-dents; the **University of California at Berkeley,** founded in 1868, with 32,000 students; and **Stanford University** at **Palo Alto,** founded in 1891, with 13,000 students, make San Francisco one of the most important centers of higher educa-tion and research in the country.

No trip to California can be called complete without an attentive visit to this joyful, flamboyant city which has inspired so many poets, movie directors, novel-ists, and songwriters. From the gaudy frontages of **Chinatown** to the sublime panorama of the bay seen from the Golden Gate, by way of the roller-coaster con-tours of **Telegraph Hill,** the arrogant high-rises of the **Financial District,** where such great corporations as Chevron, Bank of America, Bechtel, Wells Fargo, and Levi Strauss make their headquarters, or the sea scent of **Fisherman's Wharf,** San Francisco is unique. Its immediate, and more distant, surroundings are in them-selves worth the visit, beginning with the charming little ports of **Sausalito** and **Tiburon** across the bay, and moving on to the renowned vineyards of the **Napa Valley,** the magnificent **Seventeen Mile Drive** between Monterey and Carmel —one of the most spectacular highways in the U.S.—and the legendary **Silicon Valley,** headquarters of electronics research and development for the entire country, with one of the heaviest concentrations of high-tech industries in the world. As for longer trips, the motorist's hardest problem is to choose among **Sequoia** and **Yosemite National Parks** (see Chapters 52 and 53), the mountain grandeur of **Lake Tahoe** (see Chapter 49 on Reno), or Calif. 1, the wonderful coast road from San Francisco to Los Angeles, better known as the **Cabrillo Hwy.** (see Chapter 50 on the California Coast).

Food is not the least of San Francisco's attractions. Along with New York and New Orleans, the Golden Gate City is one of the three gastronomic capitals of the U.S. Its Chinese and Japanese restaurants are among the best in the world, and its French and Italian restaurants are every bit as good. Not to mention its renowned restaurants serving seafood and a whole gamut of exotic cuisines: Ko-rean, Filipino, Mexican, Indian, Javanese, Armenian, Caribbean, Vietnamese, and many more. In spite of their boast that their city has more restaurants per capita (more than 4,300) than any other in the country, the favorite sport of San Franciscans seems to be discovering new ones. Note also that, although the city can claim more international-class hotels for its size than any other in the U.S., they're very often completely booked; reservations should be made far in ad-vance.

There is no end to the list of the Golden Gate City's famous children. They include the writers Jack London and Irving Stone, the poet Robert Frost, the movie director Mervin LeRoy, the newspaper magnate William Randolph Hearst, the dancer Isadora Duncan, the banker and statesman Robert S. McNamara, the actor Clint Eastwood, the musician Carlos Santana, and the singer Johnny Mathis.

Warning: Never use the abbreviation "Frisco" for "San Francisco"; the inhabitants consider it insulting.

BASIC FACTS: State of California. Area Code: 415. Time Zone: Pacific Time. ZIP Code: 94101. Founded: 1776. Approximate population: city, 745,000; metropolitan area, 5,820,000. Fourth-largest metropolitan area in the U.S.

CLIMATE: "Disconcerting" is the mildest word that can be applied to San Francisco's climate; Mark Twain wrote, "The coldest winter I ever spent was a summer in San Francisco." There are so many micro-climates that meteorologists run out of technical terms for them. In broad terms, late spring, summer, and a good part of the fall are sunny but cool; temperatures average 61° F (16° C) from June to Oct. Winter is gloomier, though the mercury rarely drops below 58° F (10° C) in Dec.-Jan. Showers are frequent from Nov. to March, as is morning fog over the bay in summer and fall.

DISTANCES: Denver, 1,234 mi. (1,975 km); Las Vegas, 568 mi. (908 km); Los Angeles, 381 mi. (608 km); Portland, 634 mi. (1,015 km); Reno, 229 mi. (366 km); Salt Lake City, 750 mi. (1,200 km).

ARRIVAL & TRANSIT INFORMATION

AIRPORTS: The Oakland International Airport (OAK), 18 mi. (28 km) SE (577-4000).

San Francisco International Airport (SFO), 16 mi. (26 km) south (761-0800), one of the most up-to-date in the country, ranking fifth in volume of traffic among U.S. airports.

DOMESTIC AIRLINES: Alaska (931-8888), American (398-4434), America West (839-1292), Braniff (toll free 800/272-6433), Continental (397-8818), Delta (552-5700), Eastern (474-5858), Hawaiian (toll free 800/367-5320), Northwest (392-2163), Pan Am (toll free 800/221-1111), San Francisco Helicopter (toll free 800/435-9736), Southwest (885-1221), TWA (864-5731), United (397-2100), and USAir (toll free 800/428-4322).

FOREIGN CARRIERS: Air Canada (toll free 800/422-6232), British Airways (toll free 800/247-9297), Canadian Airlines International (toll free 800/426-7000), and Lufthansa (toll free 800/645-3880).

CITY LINK: The **cab** fare from San Francisco airport to downtown is about $26–$28; time, about 30 min. Cab fare from Oakland airport to downtown, about $30; time, about 35 min. Bus: **Airporter** (495-8404), leaving the San Francisco airport every 15 min.; serves principal hotels downtown, in the financial district, and around Fisherman's Wharf, and the Airlines Terminal at Taylor and Ellis Sts.; fare, $6; time, about 40 min. **Bay Area Airporter** (632-5506) also links Oakland airport and the Airlines Terminal; fare, $7; time, 50 min. Van: **Bay Area SuperShuttle** (558-8500) serves all the downtown hotels; fare, $8. Helicopter: **San Francisco Helicopter** (toll free 800/435-9736) connects the two airports with downtown San Francisco; fare, $45–$60; time, 12–18 min., both according to destination. Municipal bus (Samtrans): Lines 7b and 7f connect downtown San Francisco and the two airports; fare, $1.25; time, about 50 min.

The public transportation system, both surface by bus and streetcar, the SAMTRANS (761-7000) and the MUNI (673-6864), and by express subway, BART (788-2278), is excellent throughout the Bay Area. Cabs are numerous but very expensive.

Given the attractive rates offered in California and the large number of enticing excursions around San Francisco, it's highly advisable to rent a car with unlimited mileage. *Warning:* When parking on a hill in San Francisco, it's mandatory to turn your front wheels inward toward the curb to prevent the vehicle from slipping.

CAR RENTALS (at the San Francisco International Airport unless otherwise indicated): Avis (877-6780); Budget (877-4477); Dollar (952-6200); Hertz (877-1600); National (877-4745); Pacific Car Rental (local agency with attractive rates), 1849 Bayshore Blvd., in Burlingame (692-2611); Thrifty, Union Square (673-6675). For downtown locations, consult the local telephone directory.

LIMOUSINE SERVICES: Carey Limousine (468-7550), Dav El Limousine (toll free 800/922-0343), and Four Star Limousine (386-9220).

TAXIS: Cabs may be hailed on the street, taken from the waiting lines outside major hotels, or better still, summoned by phone. Fares are very high. De Soto Cab (673-0333), Luxor Cab (282-4141), Veteran's Cab (552-1300), and Yellow Cab (626-2345).

TRAIN: AMTRAK, Transbay Terminal, 425 Mission St. (982-8512); avoid this neighborhood after dark. There is a regular shuttle-bus link with the station at Oakland, terminus for the major routes to the east and along the Pacific coast.

BUS: Greyhound, 50 7th St. (558-6789).

INFORMATION & TOURS

TOURIST INFORMATION: The **San Francisco Convention and Visitors Bureau,** 900 Market St., CA 94101 (415/391-2000).

Visitor Information Center, Hallidie Plaza, Powell and Market Sts. (415/974-6900).

International Visitors Center, 312 Sutter St., Suite 402 (415/986-1388); reception facilities for foreign visitors.

San Francisco Chamber of Commerce, 465 California St., CA 94104 (415/392-4511).

For a **telephone recording** with an up-to-date listing of cultural events and shows, call 415/391-2001.

GUIDED TOURS: Alcatraz Tours (boat), Pier 41, The Embarcadero (546-2805): Conducted tours of the penitentiary; it's advisable to make reservations, one or more days in advance in summer, through Ticketron (392-7469). Not to be missed.

Bay cruises (boat), Blue & Gold Fleet, Pier 39, The Embarcadero (781-7877), and Red & White Fleet, Pier 43½, The Embarcadero (546-2896): Boat trips on the bay; wonderful views. Daily, year round; not to be missed.

Commodore Helicopters (helicopter), Pier 43, The Embarcadero (981-4832): Helicopter trips over the bay; unforgettable. Daily.

Express Tours (bus), serving the principal hotels (621-7738): One-day excursions to Yosemite National Park, Lake Tahoe, Hearst Castle, etc.

Gray Line Tours (bus), 425 Mission St. (2nd floor) (558-9400): Many tours in the city and surroundings.

Lorrie's Tours (minibus), 770 Post St. (626-2113): Visiting and tasting in the wine cellars of Napa Valley: one-day trip.

Wine Adventures, Inc. (bus), P.O. Box 3273, Yountville, CA 94599 (707/944-8468): One- or several-day visits to Wine Country cellars.

SIGHTS, ATTRACTIONS, & ACTIVITIES

ARCHITECTURAL HIGHLIGHTS: ❀ ♨ **Alcatraz Island,** a rocky island in the bay, reached by boat from Pier 41: Nicknamed "The Rock," this former fort, converted in 1934 to a high-security prison, numbered among its famous inmates Al Capone, Alvin Karpis, Robert Stroud (alias "The Birdman of Alcatraz"), "Doc" Barker, and "Machine Gun" Kelly. Owes its name to the innumerable pelicans (*alcatraces* in Spanish) that used to roost there. Reputed to be "the prison from which no one escapes," the penitentiary was closed in 1963 by order of then–Attorney General Robert Kennedy because of its excessive operating costs; it has been converted into a museum visited by 800,000 people a year. It was occupied by a group of Native Americans from 1969 to 1971, by way of a symbolic protest. The visit is worthwhile, because the experience is unique and the island affords you an otherwise-unobtainable view of the bay, but it's a tiring excursion. Open daily (see "Guided Tours," above).

❀♨ **Bank of America,** 555 California St. (433-7500): For many years the largest commercial bank in the world, the Bank of America was founded by Peter Giannini, the son of poor Italian immigrants. It has more than $80 billion in deposits. Claims to have invented the country's first bank credit card, BankAmericard, now known as VISA. Its head office is housed in this imposing marble-clad 52-story high-rise (see "Panoramas," below).

♨ **Castro Theater,** Castro and 18th Sts. (621-6120): Extravagant 1930s-style movie house in the heart of the gay district. Worth seeing.

♨ **City Hall,** Civic Center Plaza (554-4000): Imposing 1915 building in the French classical revival idiom, capped by a dome higher than the Capitol's in Washington. Should be seen.

♨ **Cow Palace,** Geneva Ave. and Rio Verde, 7 mi. (11 km) south on U.S. 101 (469-6000): Exhibition park and 14,000-seat concert hall in art deco style. Worth a look.

❀♨ **Embarcadero Center,** Clay and Sacramento Sts. between Drumm and Battery Sts.: The new business district, with a group of high-rises by the well-known architect John Portman. Pedestrian walkways at several levels, fountains, modern sculpture, open-air concerts on fine days. You have to see it.

♨ **Ferry Building,** Embarcadero and Market Sts. (332-6600): Once the terminal for the ferries that crisscrossed the bay in all directions before the construction of the Golden Gate and Bay Bridges. Its 236-ft (72-m) tower, erected in 1903, is a copy of the Moorish La Giralda tower in Seville. Today it houses the Port Authority; ferries leave for Sausalito from the southern end of the building. Should be seen.

❀♨♨♨ **Golden Gate Bridge,** linking San Francisco to Sausalito to the north of the bay: Designed by Joseph Strauss, the world's most famous (and most beautiful) bridge was built between 1933 and 1937 at a cost of $35 million. Its construction was a technological masterpiece, involving 200,000 tons of steel, 523,000 cu. yds. (400,000 cu. m) of cement, and 80 mi.

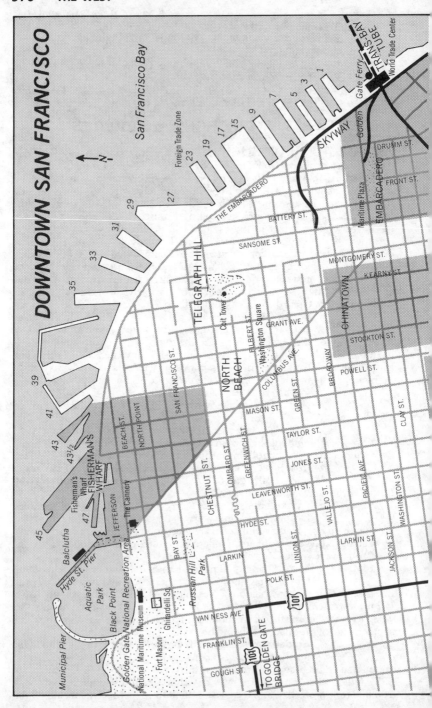

DOWNTOWN SAN FRANCISCO

San Francisco Bay

N→

Foreign Trade Zone

TRANS-BAY TUBE

Golden Gate Ferry

World Trade Center

SKYWAY

Maritime Plaza

DRUMM ST.

EMBARCADERO

FRONT ST.

THE EMBARCADERO

BATTERY ST.

SANSOME ST.

MONTGOMERY ST.

KEARNY ST.

CHINATOWN

STOCKTON ST.

TELEGRAPH HILL

Coit Tower

FILBERT ST.

GRANT AVE.

Washington Square

NORTH BEACH

COLUMBUS AVE.

BROADWAY

POWELL ST.

GREEN ST.

MASON ST.

GREENWICH ST.

TAYLOR ST.

CLAY ST.

JONES ST.

PACIFIC AVE.

WASHINGTON ST.

CHESTNUT ST.

LOMBARD ST.

LEAVENWORTH ST.

VALLEJO ST.

JACKSON ST.

SAN FRANCISCO ST.

HYDE ST.

UNION ST.

LARKIN ST.

BEACH ST.

NORTH POINT

Fisherman's Wharf

FISHERMAN'S WHARF

The Cannery

JEFFERSON

BAY ST.

Russian Hill Park

LARKIN

POLK ST.

101

Balclutha

Hyde St. Pier

Golden Gate National Recreation Area

National Maritime Museum

Fort Mason

Ghirardelli Sq.

VAN NESS AVE.

Aquatic Park

Black Point

FRANKLIN ST.

101

TO GOLDEN GATE BRIDGE

Municipal Pier

GOUGH ST.

(128 km) of high-tension steel cable. It's also the world's most "deadly" bridge; 11 people were killed during construction, and another 700 have committed suicide from it since it was opened on May 28, 1937. The shining Golden Gate Bridge towers 220 ft (67 m) above the waters of the bay, and is used every day by almost 100,000 vehicles. Maintenance for the two 746-ft (227-m) towers and the 8,856-ft (2.7-km) span is provided by a team of 25 painters, who use two tons of red lead every week. Unforgettable view of San Francisco and the bay (overlook parking at the north end of the bridge). There's a toll, for southbound vehicles only. Worth the trip to San Francisco all by itself.

Levi Strauss Factory, 250 Valencia St. (544-6000): This is where, around the middle of the 19th century, Levi Strauss created history's first pair of blue jeans—and it's still operating. Adopted first by the miners of the gold rush, then by cowboys, blue jeans still serve as an emblem of American life. Tours Wed. Resv. requested.

Louise M. Davies Symphony Hall, Van Ness Ave. and Grove St. (431-5400): Home of the San Francisco Symphony Orchestra. Opened in 1980, this ultramodern 3,000-seat concert hall by Skidmore, Owings and Merrill has extremely sophisticated acoustics. Worth seeing.

Transamerica Pyramid, 600 Montgomery St. (983-4000): Designed by architect William Pereira, this 48-floor pyramid capped by a knife-edged stainless-steel and aluminum point cost $34 million to build, and is considered by many to be the most spectacular and original high-rise in the U.S. Since the 853-ft (260-m) building was completed in 1972, it has become one of the emblems of San Francisco. A sight not to be missed.

War Memorial Opera House, Van Ness Ave. and Grove St. (864-3330): Home of the San Francisco Opera since its inauguration (1932). In 1945 the United Nations came into existence in this auditorium, and in 1951 it witnessed the signing of the American-Japanese peace treaty. Worth seeing.

BEACHES: **Baker Beach,** Lincoln Blvd., Presidio: Wonderful for sunbathing, but no swimming allowed.

Ocean Beach, Great Highway: 4 mi. (6 km) of beaches and dunes, much frequented by hang-glider enthusiasts. Swimming here is unsafe.

Phelan Beach, Sea Cliff and 29th Aves.: Small fine-sand beach near Lincoln Park; swimming permitted in summer.

Stinson Beach, 16 mi. (25 km) NW on Calif. 1: Pretty beach at the foot of a mountain; swimming permitted in summer.

CABLE CARS: San Francisco's open-air cable cars—drawn by cables as the name implies—the city's most famous tourist attraction since 1873, were suspended from service from Sept. 1982 to the spring of 1984 for an overhaul of their traction system. Since this involuntary interruption, the city's engaging streetcars, with standing passengers clustering on the steps like bunches of grapes, are once again scaling the steep streets of Nob Hill and Russian Hill, whose gradient in places reaches 21%. Of the 19th century's eight lines and 112 mi. (180 km) of area reached, only three lines remain today, covering 11 mi. (17 km): No. 59 (Powell-Mason), No. 60 (Hyde-Powell), and No. 61 (California–Van Ness). There is a flat $2 fare; the most scenic line is No. 60, from Hyde St. to Powell St.

CHURCHES/SYNAGOGUES: **St. Mary's Cathedral,** Geary and Gough Sts. (567-2020): San Francisco's new (1970) cathedral, a spectacular modern building designed by the Italian architect Pier Luigi Nervi on the site of the old basilica, which burned down in 1962. It comprises four soaring vaults of concrete clad in white Italian travertine, which meet at a height of 196 ft (60 m) in the shape of a cross. Don't miss the futuristic sculpture above the altar. Open daily.

HISTORIC BUILDINGS: ☀ ⚖ **Haas-Lilienthal House,** 2007 Franklin St. (441-3004): Dating from 1886, this magnificent example of Queen Anne–style Victorian is one of the few private houses that survived the 1906 earthquake. Very fine furniture of the period. Open Wed. and Sun. afternoons; should be seen.

⚡⚖⚖ **Mission Dolores** (sometimes called **Mission San Francisco de Asis**), 16th and Dolores Sts. (621-8203): Sixth of the 21 missions built in California by the Franciscan Fr. Junipero Serra, this is the historic birthplace of San Francisco (1776). A fine Spanish Colonial building of whitewashed adobe brick that survived three major earthquakes. In the little cemetery adjoining are the graves of the first settlers and of the Indians who built the mission. Beside it, and in startling contrast to the primitive humility of the mission itself, is the huge Basilica of Mission Dolores, a pompous piece of Spanish-Mexican baroque. Open daily; don't miss it.

⚡⚖ **Whittier Mansion,** 2090 Jackson St. (567-1848): Built in 1896 by a wealthy businessman named William Whittier, this imposing Romanesque mansion with its red sandstone facing and stout anchoring towers is also a survivor of the 1906 earthquake. It's now the home of the California Historical Society. Sumptuous rococo interior; be sure to see the Turkish Smoking Room. Don't miss it.; open Wed., Sat., and Sun. afternoons.

MUSEUMS OF ART: ☀ ⚖⚖ **Asian Art Museum,** Golden Gate Park (668-8921): The collection of Avery Brundage, once president of the International Olympics Committee, includes more than 10,000 works of art from Japan, China, Korea, etc., some more than 3,000 years old; their value, particularly that of the T'ang ceramics and the Khmer sculptures, is impossible to estimate. Because of the size and importance of the collection, it is exhibited in rotation. One of the most beautiful Far Eastern museums in the world, housed in the right wing of the M. H. De Young Museum (see below). An absolute must; open Tues.-Sun.

⚡⚖⚖ **California Palace of the Legion of Honor,** Lincoln Park (221-4811): The only museum in the U.S. entirely devoted to the art of France. Master paintings from the 16th to the 20th century: Fragonard, Georges de la Tour, Corot, Monet, Cézanne, etc. Fine Gobelin tapestries and an exceptional graphic-arts collection with more than 100,000 drawings, engravings, and illustrated books. Sculptures by Rodin. The Beaux Arts building, dating from 1924, is an exact replica of the Palace of the Legion of Honor in Paris. Fine surrounding park and splendid view of the Golden Gate; not to be missed. Open Wed.-Sun.

⚖ **Mexican Museum,** Fort Mason Center, Bldg. D, Laguna St. and Marina Blvd. South (441-0404): Temporary exhibitions and permanent collection of Mexican art from the pre-Columbian and colonial periods to the present day. Also works by modern Mexican-American artists. Worth the side trip. Open Wed.-Sun.

⚡⚖⚖ **M. H. De Young Museum,** Golden Gate Park (221-4811): One of the best art collections in the U.S., with superb representation in Asian art (see Asian Art Museum, above), but no less so in African, Egyptian, European, Polynesian, and other sectors—all housed in an 1894 building which was once part of the California Midwinter International Exposition. Among the best-known works on display are a *Madonna and Child* by Tintoretto, El Greco's *St. John the Baptist,* Frans Hals's *Cavalier in White,* and

Bellini's *Portrait of the Doge Leonardo Loredano*. Note also the very fine John D. Rockefeller collection of American art, with such major works as Charles Willson Peale's *Self-Portrait* and Charles Demuth's *Blue Plums*. Not to be missed; open Wed.-Sun.

    Museum of Modern Art, Van Ness Ave. and McAllister St. (863-8800): The best of contemporary art; hundreds of remarkable paintings and sculptures from Matisse and Mark Rothko to Jackson Pollock and Clyfford Still. Occupies the third and fourth floors of the Veterans Bldg. Definitely worth a visit; open Tues.-Sun.

MUSEUMS OF SCIENCE AND HISTORY: *Balclutha,* Pier 43, The Embarcadero (929-0202): A maritime museum, in an authentic British Cape Horner, built in 1886, which rounded the Horn 17 times. Worth a visit; open daily.

    Cable Car Barn Museum, Washington and Mason Sts. (474-1887): Picturesque museum of San Francisco's own streetcars, including the first to be put into service in 1873. Movies, old photos, etc. See the strange traction system of the famous cable cars; not to be missed. Open daily.

    California Academy of Sciences, Golden Gate Park (750-7145): Comprehensive museum of natural history, including the **Morrison Planetarium** and the renowned **Steinhart Aquarium,** with more than 14,000 sea creatures. Fine collection of fossils and of North American birds. The new **Earth and Space Hall** features a very realistic reproduction of an earthquake. Well worth visiting; open daily.

    Chinese Historical Society of America, 17 Adler Pl. (391-1188): Illustrates the important part played by Chinese immigrants in the founding of San Francisco and the settlement of the American West. Unusual mementoes; fine collection of photographs. A must for history buffs; open Tues.-Sat.

    Exploratorium, 3601 Lyon St. (563-3200): This remarkably well-conceived and instructive museum of science and technology was opened in 1969, in a sort of imitation Greco-Roman temple originally built as the Palace of Fine Arts for the 1915 Panama-Pacific International Exposition. It offers more than 600 participatory exhibits in the fields of science, art, and human perception. Fascinating; you mustn't miss it. Open Wed.-Sun.

    Maritime Museum, Polk and Beach Sts. (556-8177): Interesting maritime museum in an Edwardian casino. Ship models and objects illustrating the history of navigation on the Pacific coast. The "floating" section of the museum is moored at the adjoining Hyde St. Pier: it comprises half a dozen carefully restored old ships, including the three-master *C. A. Thayer* (1895), the paddlewheel ferryboat *Eureka* (1890), the schooner *Alma* (1891), and the tug *Hercules* (1907). Worth visiting. Open daily.

    Old U.S. Mint, 5th and Mission Sts. (974-0788): Along with those in Denver and Philadelphia, one of the country's three mints. A fine 19th-century classical revival building. Note the impressive heap of gold ingots in the circular vault. Numismatic museum. Open Mon.-Fri.

    U.S.S. *Pampanito,* Pier 45, The Embarcadero and Taylor St. (929-0202): World War II submarine which took part in the Pacific campaigns. Visiting the interior of the vessel requires a certain aptitude for gymnastics! Open daily.

    Wells Fargo Bank History Museum, 420 Montgomery St. (396-2619): "History Room" with a Far Western stagecoach (Wells Fargo began life as a stagecoach company). Mementoes of the 1848 gold rush and the 1906 earthquake. Picturesque. Open Mon.-Fri.

NIGHTTIME ENTERTAINMENT: Ever since the 19th century, when the legendary Barbary Coast was an irresistible attraction to sailors, adventurers, settlers, and gold prospectors, San Francisco has believed in thinking big about its nightlife. Witness today the porno dives and risqué nightclubs of Broadway and Columbus Ave., the domain of the topless, of dancing nude couples, and of mud-wrestling women. The biggest concentration of nightlife is in the **North Beach** neighborhood, particularly around Washington Square, but jazz joints, bars, nightclubs, comedy clubs, and discos flourish all over town. As a general rule, nightclubs are not permitted to serve alcoholic beverages after 2 a.m. (see "Bars and Nightclubs," below).

OUTDOOR ART AND PLAZAS: ⚓ **Embarcadero Center,** Clay and Sacramento Sts. between Drumm and Battery Sts.: The sidewalk galleries and plazas of this ultramodern complex are embellished with monumental sculptures by Willi Gutmann, Louise Nevelson, and Nicholas Schöffer, as well as with many paintings and tapestries. At the eastern end of the center is an astonishing futuristic fountain by Armand Vaillancourt; should not be missed.

   ⚓ **St. Mary's Square,** California and Quincy Sts.: Resplendent stainless-steel statue by Benjamino Buffano of Sun Yat-sen, founder and first president of the Republic of China, who lived in San Francisco for a while. Should be seen.

PANORAMAS: ⚓ **Bank of America,** 555 California St. (433-7500): In the heart of the financial district, the West Coast's answer to Wall Street. Bar-restaurant (so-so), the Carnelian Room, on the 52nd floor (admission charge); one of the finest views of the city. Open daily.

   ☼⚓⚓ **Coit Tower,** Telegraph Hill Blvd.: This 210-ft (64-m) tower, erected in 1933 on the top of Telegraph Hill as a memorial to the city's volunteer firemen, offers as beautiful a panorama of the bay as you're likely to find, especially at dawn or sunset. Don't miss it. Open daily (elevator).

   ☼⚓⚓⚓ **Golden Gate Bridge,** north of Presidio Park: Wonderful panorama of the city and bay, looking south; overlook parking at the northern end of the bridge. Worth the trip all by itself (see "Architectural Highlights," above).

   ⚓⚓ **San Francisco–Oakland Bay Bridge,** between San Francisco and Oakland: Opened six months before the Golden Gate, on Nov. 12, 1936, this enormous two-deck bridge has a particularly spectacular view of the city and bay, looking west; a sight not to be missed.

   Sausalito and **Tiburon:** See "Nearby Excursions," below.

   ⚓⚓ **Twin Peaks,** Twin Peaks Blvd.: Nicknamed "los pechos de la Chola" (the Indian woman's breasts) by the first Spanish settlers, these twin peaks, 910 ft (277 m) high, are famous for their clear view of San Francisco and the bay, especially along Market St. Not to be missed, particularly at twilight.

PARKS AND GARDENS: ⚓ **Angel Island,** in the bay, reached by boat from Pier 43½: Small garden-island reserved for pedestrians, cyclists, and picnickers, with dozens of free-roaming stags and does. Frequent boat service daily in summer; weekends only the rest of the year. Fine view of the town.

   ☼⚓⚓ **Golden Gate Park,** bounded by Lincoln Way, Great Hwy., and Fulton and Stanyan Sts. (558-4268): Lying on the ocean to the west, this magnificent 1,017-acre (412-ha) park, one of the most beautiful in the U.S., was reclaimed beginning in 1868 from a tract of bare sand dunes. Contains more than 6,000 different species of trees and plants, including acacia, spruce, and eucalyptus. Several museums (see above). Splendid Japanese garden and tropical hot houses. An absolute must.

Golden Gate Promenade, Marine Dr. between Fort Point and Fort Mason: Landscaped park along the shore of the bay; from Fort Point you have a clear view of the bridge and the city skyline.

Harding Park, Lake Merced and Sloat Blvds.: Huge ocean-front park taking in Lake Merced (canoeing, fishing), a modern zoo, and a public golf course. Very popular with San Franciscans in summer.

Lincoln Park, 34th Ave. and Clement St.: On the ocean at the NW extremity of the city; very fine view of the Golden Gate Bridge, the city, and the Pacific.

The Presidio, Richardson Ave. and Lombard St. (561-3870): The headquarters of the U.S. Sixth Army is on the site occupied by the original Spanish garrison fort in 1776, and lies in 1,450 acres (588 ha.) of park and shady garden. Enter from Lombard and Lyon Sts. to the east, or 25th Ave. and El Camino del Mar to the west; there's a lovely scenic drive between these two points. Don't miss it.

Seal Rocks, Point Lobos Ave.: Reefs thronged with elephant seals, sea lions, marine birds, and other ocean life. Fine ocean view; don't miss it.

Sigmund Stern Memorial Grove, along Sloat Blvd. nr. 19th Ave. (398-6551): Natural amphitheater sheltered by eucalyptus, red woods and fir trees. On summer Sunday afternoons hosts free outdoor concerts, Broadway musicals, operas, and ballets. This 63-acre grove is also the perfect place for barbecues and picnics.

PERFORMING ARTS:
For daily listings of all shows and cultural events, consult the entertainment pages of the daily papers *San Francisco Chronicle* (morning) and *San Francisco Examiner* (evening), especially their joint Sunday edition.

Note that **STBS,** a kiosk on Stockton St. at Union Square (433-7827), provides half-price, cash-only, in-person sales of unsold tickets for day-of-performance events.

Civic Auditorium, Civic Center (431-5400): Recitals; concerts by the San Francisco Pops Orchestra.

Club Fugazzi, 678 Green St. (421-4222): An old North Beach standby; cabaret-style shows.

Curran Theater, 445 Geary St. (673-4400): Musicals, Broadway hits.

Geary Theater, 415 Geary St. (673-6440): Home of the American Conservatory Theater; classical and contemporary theater (Oct.-June).

Golden Gate Theatre, Taylor, Golden Gate, and Market Sts. (775-8800): Contemporary theater, Broadway hits.

Herbst Theatre, Civic Center (431-4500): Ballet, opera, concerts, children's shows.

Louise M. Davies Symphony Hall, Civic Center (431-4500): Home of the San Francisco Symphony, under principal conductor Herbert Blomstedt (Sept.-May); recitals, concerts.

Mason Street Theater, 340 Mason St. at Geary (981-0371): Off-Broadway theater, comedy.

Masonic Auditorium, 1111 California St. (776-4917): Classical concerts, recitals, ballet.

Orpheum Theatre, 1192 Market St. (474-3800): Drama, comedy, touring companies. Home of the Civic Light Opera (May-Dec.).

Palace of Fine Arts Theatre, 3601 Lyon St. (921-9968): Opera, concerts. The International Film Festival is held here annually.

Sigmund Stern Memorial Grove, Sloat Blvd. and 19th Ave. (398-6551): A 25,000-seat open-air auditorium; symphony concerts, opera, jazz, ballet. Free shows every Sun. at 2 p.m. from June to mid-Aug., a tradition more than 50 years old.

Theatre on the Square, 450 Post St. (433-9500): Contemporary theater, drama, comedy.

War Memorial Opera House, Civic Center (864-3330): Home of the San Francisco Ballet, oldest company in the U.S. (Jan.-May), and of the San Francisco Opera Company (Sept.-Dec.).

SHOPPING: The Cannery, 2801 Leavenworth St. at Jefferson (771-3112): A 19th-century fruit-processing factory, now a deluxe shopping center, with 50 boutiques, stores, and restaurants, a stone's throw from Fisherman's Wharf. Open daily.

Cost Plus Imports, 2552 Taylor St. (928-6200): Gadgets and objects from around the world at rock-bottom prices, a stone's throw from Fisherman's Wharf. Open daily.

Cow Hollow, Union St. between Van Ness Ave. and Steiner St.: The district for antique dealers and smart stores, with many bars and restaurants. Used as a setting for the movie *The Conversation*. Picturesque old houses.

Crocker Galleria, 50 Post St. (392-5522): Opened in 1982, this innovative shopping arcade is arranged on three levels under a spectacular glass canopy 70 ft (21 m) high and 275 ft (83 m) long; it resembles the well-known Galleria Vittorio Emmanuele in Milan. More than 50 shops, stores, and restaurants.

Ghirardelli Square, 900 North Point St. (775-5500): Incorporated into a former chocolate factory near Fisherman's Wharf, this picturesque shopping complex, embellished with patios and fountains, is a textbook example of urban renewal. A round 100 shops and restaurants. Very popular with tourists. Open daily.

Pier 39, The Embarcadero (981-7437): Yet another example of the city's talent for converting old industrial buildings (in this instance, a commercial dock not far from Fisherman's Wharf) into lively modern shopping centers. More than 140 different shops and restaurants. Open-air shows. Open daily.

SPECIAL EVENTS: For the exact schedule of events below, consult the **San Francisco Convention and Visitors Bureau** (see "Tourist Information," above).

Chinese New Year (late Jan. to Feb.): Colorful dragon procession and fireworks through Chinatown's streets.

International Film Festival (late Mar. to Apr.): The oldest film festival in the U.S., and one of the most distinguished, held at the Palace of Fine Arts.

Cherry Blossom Festival (Apr.): Festival of the Japanese community, timed to coincide with the flowering of the cherry trees in Japantown. Flower show, Japanese art festival.

Gay Freedom Day (Apr.): Tumultuous parade of the San Francisco gay community; colorful.

Midsummer Music Festival (June-Aug.): Open-air classical music festival in the Sigmund Stern Memorial Grove.

San Francisco Marathon (mid-July): Third in importance (after Boston and New York) in the U.S.; attracts more than 10,000 participants.

Columbus Day Parade (Oct.): Parades, drum majorettes, and oom-pah-pah oom-pah-pah; the Italian community festival at North Beach and Fisherman's Wharf.

Grand National Livestock (late Oct. to early Nov.): Horse show, cattle fair, rodeos. Cowboy atmosphere. At the Cow Palace.

SPORTS: San Francisco has four professional teams:

Baseball (Apr.-Oct.): Athletics, Oakland Coliseum (638-0500); Giants, Candlestick Park (467-8000).

Basketball (Oct.-Mar.): Golden State Warriors, Oakland Coliseum (638-6000).

Football (Aug.-Dec.): 49ers, Candlestick Park (468-2249).

Horse Racing

Bay Meadows Racecourse, Bayshore Frwy. (U.S. 101) and Hillsdale Blvd., San Mateo, 20 mi. (35 km) south (574-7223): Thoroughbred racing, Wed.-Sun., early Sept. through Jan.

Golden Gate Fields, 1100 Eastshore Hwy., Albany, across the San Francisco–Oakland Bay Bridge (526-3020): Thoroughbred racing Feb.-June and harness racing mid-June to mid-Aug., Tues.-Sat.

Deep-Sea Fishing

Sport-fishing enthusiasts will find a charter fleet based year round at Fisherman's Wharf, with boats going out every day at dawn, particularly during salmon season (mid-Feb. to mid-Nov.). Average cost is $40 per person. Some recommended operators include **Captain Ron's Pacific Charters** (285-2000), **Ketchikan Sport Fishing Boat** (981-6269), **Lucky Lady Fishing** (826-6815), and **Wacky Jacky Sportfishing** (586-9800).

STROLLS: ⚱ **Castro Street,** around Market St.: The heart of San Francisco's most important gay neighborhood. Bars, restaurants, movie houses, and stores all—or almost all—bear the impress of one of the largest and most organized homosexual communities in the U.S., 80,000 strong.

Chinatown, bounded by Broadway, Bush, Kearny, and Stockton Sts.: With 80,000 inhabitants, the largest Chinese city outside Asia. Pagoda roofs, tea houses, dragon-shaped lamps, and gaudy shopfronts make this the most picturesque neighborhood in the city; its restaurants are among the best in the country, and foodstalls are justly renowned. You should see the Chinatown Gateway Arch at Grant Ave. and Bush St., the monumental entry to Chinatown; Old St. Mary's Church, the former cathedral built in 1854, at Grant Ave. and California St.; the Buddha Universal Church on Washington St. across from Portsmouth Square, the largest Buddhist temple in the U.S.; and the surprising statue of Sun Yat-sen, founder and first president of the Republic of China, on St. Mary's Square. Tours organized by the Chinese Cultural Center, 750 Kearny St. (986-1822). Don't miss it.

Filbert Street, between Hyde and Leavenworth Sts.: The steepest street in San Francisco, at an angle of 31.5°. Spectacular; has to be seen.

Fisherman's Wharf, Jefferson St. between Hyde and Powell Sts.: Once the city's fishing port, with more than 400 boats; today excessively commercialized. Cafés, bars, restaurants (mostly mediocre) in a fairground atmosphere. The most popular tourist attraction in the U.S. after Walt Disney World, drawing 13 million visitors a year. Nevertheless, worth a glance.

49 Mile Drive: A 49-mi. (78-km) circular drive, marked by signs showing a blue-and-white seagull. The trip can be made by car inside a day, and will take you to most of the city's tourist attractions: Chinatown, Nob Hill, Fisherman's Wharf, Golden Gate Park, Mission Dolores, the Civic Center, Golden Gate Bridge, Telegraph Hill, etc. A free map of the route may be obtained from the Visitor Information Center, Hallidie Plaza (lower level), Powell and Market Sts. You should plan to make the trip.

☼⚲ **Japantown,** Geary and Post between Fillmore and Laguna Sts.: San Francisco's Japanese quarter, designed by Minoru Yamasaki, architect of the World Trade Center in New York. Many stores, tea houses, and Japanese restaurants; kabuki theater; Cultural Center with interesting temporary exhibitions. Note the handsome Peace Plaza with its monumental gate, Japanese gardens, and Peace Pagoda. Martial-arts demonstrations; Japanese music and dance. Worth a look.

☼⚲ **Lombard Street,** between Hyde and Leavenworth Sts.: The twistiest (and most flower-planted) street in San Francisco, with ten hairpin bends in less than 500 ft (150 m). One of the chase sequences in the movie *Bullitt* was shot here; a sight not to be missed.

⚲ **Nob Hill,** around California and Taylor Sts.: "Millionaires' Hill," rising to a height of 376 ft (115 m). Once home to California gold-mining and railroad tycoons ("Nob" is a contraction of "Nabob"); now a neighborhood of luxury hotels and smart apartment buildings. Note the Gothic Revival Grace Cathedral at Sacramento and Taylor Sts., and the Masonic Temple at California and Taylor Sts. Elegant.

☼⚲ **North Beach,** around Washington Square: The city's Little Italy and Greenwich Village, both. In spite of its name, it has no beach; it's more like a neighborhood in Genoa or Bologna. A multitude of food shops, *trattorie,* cafés, strip joints, nightclubs (this is where the "topless" phenomenon first saw the light, to say nothing of beatniks and hippies). A colorful neighborhood, where at least a third of San Francisco's 150,000 Italians make their homes. You should visit the **City Lights bookstore** at 261 Columbus Ave. (362-8193), a shrine of modern American poetry made famous by Lawrence Ferlinghetti; also the nearby bar, **Vesuvio's Cafe,** 255 Columbus Ave. (362-3370). An absolute must.

⚲ **Russian Hill,** around Green and Leavenworth Sts.: In the 19th century this was the artists' and writers' quarter; now it's one of the city's smartest residential neighborhoods. Dozens of interesting homes and buildings along Green St.; worth seeing.

⚲ **SoMa** (South of Market Street), bounded by Mission, First, Townsend, and Division St.: San Francisco's version of New York's SoHo. Once the rough, threatening preserve of butcher supply houses, winos, struggling artists, and gay men dressed in black-leather motorcycle outfits, SoMa has suddenly become fashionable. Now the streets are lined w. hit restaurants, art galleries, night clubs, and trendy fashion outlets. Worth a glance.

☼⚲⚲ **Telegraph Hill,** around Lombard and Kearny Sts.: The steepest of San Francisco's hills, rising up to the Coit Tower and its famous view. A tangle of steep lanes, flights of steps, tiny gardens, and enchanting old frame houses on Montgomery St., Filbert Steps St., Greenwich Steps, Calhoun Terrace, Alta St., and so on. A demanding walk, but you mustn't miss it.

☼⚲ **Union Square,** Post and Geary Sts.: The heart of the city's shopping district, with shops, department stores, hotels, restaurants, and fashionable bars. Very lively. On the east side of the square, with its gardens and fountain by Ruth Azawa, is the elegant little Maiden Lane, lined with luxury shops. In the 19th century it was the most ill-famed street on the famous Barbary Coast, the old red-light district destroyed by the 1906 earthquake. Should be seen.

THEME PARKS: ☼⚲ **Marine World Africa USA,** Marine World Pkwy., in Vallejo, 30 mi. (48 km) NE on I-80 (707/643-6722): Huge theme park and zoo with over 1,000 animals, from killer whale and dolphin to elephant and tiger. Also such water sports as boating and waterskiing; animal acts. Open daily year round; 40 min. from downtown. Ferry service from Fisherman's Wharf (50 min.) by Red and White Shuttle Line (546-2896). Worth the side trip.

    ⚓ **Marriott's Great America,** in Santa Clara, 45 mi. (72 km) SE on U.S. 101 (408/988-1800): A 100-acre (40-ha.) amusement park with more than 100 attractions including a giant roller coaster. Variety shows. Reconstructions of pioneer villages. Open daily in summer, weekends only in spring and fall; closed in winter.

ZOOS: ☼ ⚓ **San Francisco Zoo,** Sloat Blvd. at the Pacific Ocean (661-2023): Zoo of very modern design on the ocean. More than 1,000 animals from around the world, including such rarities as a white tiger, dwarf hippopotamus, okapis, and koalas. Fine collection of apes and exotic monkeys. Mini-train for visitors. You should see it, if only for the beauty of the setting. Open daily.

ACCOMMODATIONS
See the listing of toll-free numbers in the Appendix.

Room Rates in San Francisco	
B (Budget)	up to $30
I (Inexpensive)	$30–$60
M (Moderate)	$60–$90
E (Expensive)	$90–$140
VE (Very Expensive)	$140 and up

Personal Favorites (in order of preference)

    🛎🛎🛎🛎 **The Stanford Court** (dwntwn), 905 California St., CA 94108 (415/989-3500; toll free, see Preferred). 402 rms, A/C, cable color TV. AE, CB, DC, MC, V. Valet garage $14, two rests. (including Fournou's Ovens), bars, rm svce, hrdrsr, boutiques, free crib, concierge. *Note:* The European-style grand hotel at its best. From the Tiffany-style stained-glass dome in the lobby to the four-poster beds in the rms or the miniature TV sets in the marble bathrooms, you'll find a happy combination of luxury and elegance in an atmosphere reminiscent of a private club. Svce is exemplary, and the rest. one of the most popular in San Francisco. In the heart of the fashionable Nob Hill district. This is one of the 12 best hotels in the U.S. Big business clientele; no groups, no conventions. A San Francisco landmark since 1912. **VE**

    ☼🛎🛎🛎🛎 **Mandarin Oriental** (dwntwn), 222 Sansome St., CA 94104 (415/885-0999; toll free 800/663-0787). 160 rms, A/C, cable color TV. AE, CB, DC, MC, V. Parking $15, health club, rest. (Silks), bar, 24-hr rm svce, nightclub, boutiques, free crib, concierge. *Note:* A grand hotel in the sky, on the top 11 floors of twin 48-story towers, linked by "skybridges" with an unparalleled view of the city and the bay. On each floor there are no more than seven very spacious rms or suites w. private balconies, mini-bars, and wonderful views. Ultra-luxurious pastel-toned décor and furnishings. Exemplary svce; fine quality rest.; well-equipped business center. Belongs to Hong Kong's Mandarin chain of luxury hotels. **VE**

    🛎🛎🛎 **Portman** (dwntwn), 500 Post St., CA 94102 (415/771-8600; toll free 800/553-6465). 331 rms, A/C, color TV, in-rm movies. AE, CB, DC, MC, V. Valet garage $16, rest. (Portman Grill), bar,

24-hr rm svce, nightclub, free crib, concierge. *Note:* The first hotel in the U.S. to bear the name of the famous architect John Portman, who himself conceived and carried through this luxury hotel for the business traveler, opened in 1988. Spectacular 17-story lobby w. fountain and modern sculptures. Spacious, elegant rms; outstanding rm svce. The airport limo (there's a charge) is a Rolls-Royce. Well-equipped business center; VIP and upscale business clientele. **VE**

Sherman House (nr. dwntwn), 2160 Green St., CA 94123 (415/563-3600; toll free 800/345-3457). 158 rms, A/C, cable color TV. AE, MC, V. Garage $10, rest., 24-hr rm svce. *Note:* Enchanting four-story Victorian house (no elevator), regarded as the "in" place to stay in San Francisco. Perfection in every detail, from the luxurious Second Empire décor of its rms (w. fireplaces and four-poster beds) to the inspired cuisine of Swiss chef Paul Grutter and the faultless svce; you'll have a memorable stay here. Frequented by show-biz personalities (Bill Cosby and Johnny Carson among them) who appreciate its intimacy and elegance. You'll have to reserve a long time in advance. **VE**

Mansion Hotel (nr. dwntwn), 2220 Sacramento St., CA 94115 (415/929-9444). 19 rms, no A/C. AE, DC, MC, V. Limited parking, rest. (reserved for hotel guests), rm svce, free breakfast, concierge. *Note:* Elegant Queen Anne–style home in the heart of Pacific Heights, a designated historic landmark, w. a score of comfortable period-furnished rms. Interesting, unusual ambience and décor; note the sculptures by Benjamino Buffano. Highly recommended rest. Winning reception and svce; concerts every evening; nice little private garden—in a word, everything you could want if you hate mass tourism. **E–VE**

Beresford (dwntwn), 635 Sutter St., CA 94102 (415/673-9900; toll free 800/227-4048). 114 rms, A/C, color TV. AE, CB, DC, MC, V. Garage $11, coffeeshop (breakfast and lunch only), bar. *Note:* Charming old British hotel atmosphere, a stone's throw from Union Square. Rms a little small but comfortable; private garden; courteous, efficient svce. Very good value; clientele of regulars. **I–M**

Cartwright (dwntwn), 524 Sutter St., CA 94102 (415/421-2865; toll free 800/227-3844). 119 rms, A/C (in a third of the rms), color TV. AE, DC, MC, V. Parking $6, coffeeshop (breakfast and lunch only), rm svce (breakfast only), free crib. *Note:* Small hotel nr. Union Square, aging but remarkably well run. Rms relatively small but comfortable and prettily decorated, w. views over the city. Rather noisy neighborhood. Good value; clientele of regulars. **M**

Oxford Hotel (dwntwn), Mason and Market Sts., CA 94102 (415/775-4600; toll free 800/553-1900). 114 rms, no A/C, color TV (in most rms). AE, CB, DC, MC, V. Parking $5, rest., bar, valet svce, free breakfast. *Note:* Small, modest centrally located family hotel; pleasing, serviceable rms; very good reception. Acceptable German-style bierkeller. An excellent place to stay, at very reasonable prices. **I–M**

Other Accommodations (from top bracket to budget)

Four Seasons Clift (dwntwn), 495 Geary St., CA 94102 (415/775-4700; toll free, see Four Seasons). 329 rms, A/C, color TV, in-rm movies. AE, CB, DC, MC, V. Valet parking $15, two rests. (including the French Room), two bars, 24-hr rm svce, free crib, concierge. *Note:* Distinguished old grand hotel, elegantly and tastefully decorated; spacious rms w. mini-bars. The personalized svce is quite remarkable. Renowned rest. and wine cellar; superb bar (Redwood Room). Upscale business clientele. One of the best places to stay in San Francisco since 1915. Interesting wknd discounts. **VE**

🏨🏨🏨🏨 **The Mark Hopkins** (dwntwn), 1 Nob Hill, CA 94108 (415/ 392-3434; toll free, see Inter-Continental). 392 rms, A/C, color TV. AE, CB, DC, MC, V. Valet garage $15, two rests. (including Nob Hill), coffeeshop, two bars (including the famous Top of the Mark, with 360° panoramic views of the city), 24-hr rm svce, nightclub, hrdrsr, boutiques, free crib, concierge. *Note:* All the great have patronized this local institution, from Frank Sinatra to the late Emperor of Ethiopia, Haile Selassie. From "Millionaires' Hill"—Nob Hill—this elegant caravanserai overlooks Chinatown and the financial district; the rms on the upper floors (w. balconies) have a superb view of the bay. Polished, efficient svce; one of the best-known bars in San Francisco. Has recently opened its doors to groups. Interesting wknd packages. **VE**

☀🏨🏨🏨 **Campton Place** (formerly the Drake Wiltshire Hotel; dwntwn), 340 Stockton St., CA 94108 (415/781-5555; toll free 800/647-4007). 126 rms, A/C, color TV, in-rm movies. AE, DC, MC, V. Valet parking $20, rest. (Campton Place), bar, rm svce, free crib, concierge. *Note:* Small luxury hotel just off Union Square, entirely renovated at a cost of $18 million. All the comfort, elegance, and refinement of a European grand hotel. Soundproofed rms w. period furniture and marble bathrooms. Polished, attentive svce; butlers available as needed! Rest. of a very high order; roof garden. The favorite of those in-the-know. **VE**

🏨🏨🏨 **The Donatello** (formerly the Pacific Plaza; dwntwn), 501 Post St., CA 94102 (415/441-7100; toll free 800/227-3184). 95 rms, A/C, color TV. AE, CB, DC, MC, V. Valet garage $16, health club, rest. (Donatello), bar, rm svce, free crib, concierge. *Note:* One of the new stars of the local luxury-hotel scene, just off Union Square. Elegant Italian Renaissance décor; spacious, elegant rms w. balconies, mini-bars, and a profusion of houseplants. Personalized svce; serene, intimate ambience. Very good Italian rest. Clientele of VIPs and wealthy Europeans. Member of the prestigious Relais et Châteaux hotel chain. **VE**

☀🏨🏨🏨 **Fairmont Hotel and Tower** (dwntwn), 950 Mason St., CA 94106 (415/772-5000; toll free, see Fairmont). 595 rms, A/C, color TV, in-rm movies. AE, CB, DC, MC, V. Valet garage $16, health club, five rests. (including Mason's), bars, 24-hr rm svce, disco, hrdrsr, boutiques, concierge, crib $30. *Note:* A venerable, reputable grand hotel now topped by a rather brutally modern tower. The older (and better) part of the hotel, destroyed in the 1906 earthquake, was rebuilt in the following year. Still has style in spite of the throng of conventioneers, but sometimes crowded and noisy. Flawless comfort and svce. Wonderful view of the whole city from the Crown Room rest. at the top (reached by an outside, glass-walled elevator). Roof garden. Boasts the most expensive suite in the U.S., at $5,000 a night plus tax. VIP and upscale business clientele. Was the model for the TV series "Hotel." **VE**

🏨🏨🏨 **Hyatt Regency San Francisco** (dwntwn), 5 Embarcadero Center, CA 94111 (415/788-1234; toll free, see Hyatt). 803 rms, A/C, color TV, in-rm movies. AE, CB, DC, MC, V. Valet garage $18, four rests. (including the Equinox), revolving bar at the top, 24-hr rm svce, disco, hrdrsr, boutiques, free crib, concierge. *Note:* Building of interesting futuristic structure, inspired by the Aztec pyramids, in the Embarcadero Center, within easy reach of the business district; dramatic 17-story lobby w. indoor gardens, fountains, and sculpture. Modern, comfortable rms, but mediocre svce. Group and business clientele; very lively. Two VIP floors. Wknd discounts. **VE**

🏨🏨🏨 **Ramada Renaissance** (dwntwn), 55 Cyril Magnin St., CA 94102 (415/392-8000; toll free, see Ramada Inns). 1,115 rms, A/C, color TV, in-rm movies. AE, CB, DC, MC, V. Valet garage $14, health club, sauna, two rests., two bars, 24-hr rm svce, disco, hrdrsr, drugstore, free crib, concierge. *Note:* A 32-story glass-and-steel building of daring design, halfway between Union Square and the Moscone Convention Center, and on the edge of the entertainment district. Spacious, ultra-comfortable rms, some w. good views. A wealth of works of art and period furniture. No-smoking rms; VIP floor. Personalized svce; very popular w. business travelers. Interesting wknd discount. **E–VE**

Sheraton Palace (dwntwn), 2 New Montgomery St., CA 94105 (415/392-8600; toll free, see Sheraton). 588 rms, A/C, color TV, in-rm movies. AE, CB, DC, MC, V. Valet garage $15, two rests. (including the Garden Court), coffeeshop, three bars, 24-hr rm svce, nightclub, free crib. *Note:* Charming century-old Victorian hotel, tastefully renovated, very nr. the Moscone Convention Center and the financial district. Once patronized by presidents and celebrities such as Enrico Caruso and Sarah Bernhardt. Beautiful period decoration, particularly the sumptuous Garden Court Rest. w. its enormous stained-glass dome and crystal chandeliers. Remarkably spacious, comfortable rms; very good svce. Business clientele; good overall value. **E–VE**

Miyako (nr. dwntwn), 1625 Post St., CA 94115 (415/922-3200; toll free 800/533-4567). 208 rms, A/C, color TV, in-rm movies. AE, CB, DC, MC, V. Garage $10, rest. (Bamboo Grove), bar, rm svce, boutiques, free crib. *Note:* Modern, comfortable tower right in the Japan Center, 15 min. from dwntwn. Choice of Western or Japanese-style rms. Efficient bilingual svce; acceptable rest. but no more. Clientele of Japanese tourists and American business travelers. Exotic. **E–VE**

Queen Anne (nr. dwntwn), 1590 Sutter St., CA 94109 (415/441-2828). 49 rms, no A/C, color TV. AE, CB, DC, MC, V. Free parking, no bar or rest., valet svce, free breakfast, free crib, concierge. *Note:* Beautiful century-old Victorian building, a designated historic landmark, now elegantly restored. Each rm or suite (some w. fireplaces) is decorated in a different style. Much period furniture; fine carved staircase. Romantic atmosphere; attentive reception and svce. Excellent place to stay, 10 min. from dwntwn. **E–VE**

Holiday Inn Financial District (dwntwn), 750 Kearny St., CA 94108 (415/433-6600; toll free, see Holiday Inns). 566 rms, A/C, color TV, in-rm movies. AE, CB, DC, MC, V. Free garage, rooftop pool, rest., bar, rm svce, nightclub, boutiques. *Note:* Enormous 27-floor tourist barracks nr. Chinatown; all rms have balconies, many overlook the bay. The essence of Holiday Inns. Group and business clientele; rates are too high for what it is. **E**

Bedford (dwntwn), 761 Post St., CA 94109 (415/673-6040; toll free 800/227-5642). 143 rms, no A/C, color TV, in-rm movies. AE, CB, DC, MC, V. Valet parking $11, rest., bar, valet svce, free crib. *Note:* Venerable but very well-maintained hotel three blocks from Union Square. Rms are spacious enough and comfortable; all have refrigerators. Friendly reception and svce. Business and group clientele. **M–E**

Canterbury–Whitehall Inn (dwntwn.), 750 Sutter St., CA 94109 (415/474-6464; toll free 800/227-4788). 250 rms, A/C, color TV, free in-rm movies. AE, DC, MC, V. Garage $8, rest., bar, rm svce, florist. *Note:* Charming older hotel in the heart of dwntwn. Much antique furniture. Intimate atmosphere, comfortable rms. The rest., Lehr's Greenhouse, is indeed a sort of tropical greenhouse, and worth seeing. Friendly, cheerful svce; rather noisy. **M–E**

Chancellor (dwntwn), 433 Powell St., CA 94102 (415/362-2004; toll free 800/428-4748). 140 rms, no A/C, color TV. AE, CB, DC, MC, V. Garage $14, rest. (By the Square), bar, valet svce, free crib.

Note: Modernized old hotel centrally located in the heart of San Francisco. Original Edwardian décor w. marble lobby, orchids, and potted palms. Comfort and svce above average; acceptable rest. Good value. **M**

Seal Rock Inn (nr. dwntwn), 545 Point Lobos Ave., CA 94121 (415/752-8000). 27 rms, no A/C, color TV. AE, CB, DC, MC, V. Free covered parking, pool, rest. (breakfast and lunch only), valet svce. *Note:* Charming little rococo hotel right on the ocean. Fine view of the Pacific and the reefs populated with sea creatures. Spacious, inviting rms w. fireplaces, some w. kitchenettes and refrigerators. Private garden and patio. An excellent place to stay if you like to be away from it all; 25 min. from dwntwn. **M, but lower rates from mid-Sept. to mid-May**

El Cortez (dwntwn), 500 Geary St., CA 94102 (415/775-5000). 170 rms, no A/C, color TV. AE, CB, DC, MC, V. Garage $10, rest., bar, valet svce. *Note:* The spirit of the 1930s, a stone's throw from Union Square. The décor is wilting a little, but the rms are spacious and well equipped, most with kitchenettes. La Mère Duquesne is a laudable rest. Good value. **I–M**

Airport Accommodations

Amfac Hotel (formerly the Airport Marina; vic.), 1380 Bayshore Hwy., Burlingame, CA 94010 (415/347-5444; toll free, see Amfac). 329 rms, A/C, color TV, in-rm movies. AE, CB, DC, MC, V. Free parking, pool, rest., coffeeshop, bars, hrdrsr, boutiques, free crib. *Note:* Large, modern, functional ten-story hotel. Efficient svce; comfortable, well-soundproofed rms, some w. refrigerators, many overlooking the bay. 5 min. from the airport; free 24-hr limo. Ideal for a stopover between flights. 25 min. from dwntwn. **E**

Accommodations in the Vicinity

Claremont Resort Hotel (vic.), Domingo and Ashby Aves., Oakland, CA 94623 (415/843-3000; toll free, see Preferred). 239 rms, A/C, color TV. AE, CB, DC, MC, V. Valet parking $10, pool, health club, ten tennis courts, sauna, rest. (Pavilion Room), coffeeshop, bar, rm svce, disco, hrdrsr, florist, crib $10. *Note:* Splendid castle built in the '20s on 20 acres (8 ha.) of park and garden. Elegant Victorian décor w. period furniture, Oriental rugs, and a fine collection of artwork. The guestbook bears the signatures of innumerable celebrities, from former President Harry S Truman to actor Clint Eastwood. Spacious, inviting rms, the best overlooking San Francisco Bay; excellent rest.; unusually polished svce. A tranquil green oasis 35 min. from dwntwn San Francisco. **E–VE**

Alta Mira Hotel (vic.), 125 Bulkley Ave., Sausalito, CA 94965 (415/332-1350). 36 rms and 14 cottages, no A/C. AE, CB, DC, MC, V. Free valet parking, rest., bar, valet svce. *Note:* Enchanting little hotel on the heights of Sausalito, looking out over the bay and the splendid panorama of San Francisco. Elegantly decorated rms, some w. views of the city and the Golden Gate. Individual cottages w. fireplaces. Attentive, personalized svce; acceptable rest. An elegant, comfortable haven of peace 25 min. from dwntwn across the Golden Gate Bridge. Resv. advised, well ahead of time. **M–E**

Casa Madrona (vic.), 801 Bridgeway, Sausalito, CA 94965 (415/332-0502). 29 rms and 5 cottages, no A/C. AE, MC, V. Free parking, rest., bar, rm svce. free breakfast. *Note:* Italianate mansion dating from 1885. Period furniture in the rms, some of which have refrigerators, fireplaces, and balconies; those in the new wing are particularly comfortable. Courteous reception and svce; romantic atmosphere; pretty, country-style décor.

Very praiseworthy rest. serving French-Californian food. You should reserve far in advance. **M–E (hotel), VE (cottages)**

YMCA / Youth Hostels

Golden Gate Hostel (vic.), 941 Fort Barry Rd., Sausalito, CA 94965 (415/ 331-2777). 60 beds; resv. a must in summer. Rustic youth hostel set among trees and gardens. 30 min. from dwntwn, across the Golden Gate Bridge.

San Francisco International Hostel (nr. dwntwn), Bldg. 240, Fort Mason, San Francisco, CA 94123 (415/771-7277). 165 beds. Youth hostel offering limited comfort. Resv. advised. 20 min. from dwntwn.

YMCA (dwntwn), 166 Embarcadero, San Francisco, CA 94111 (415/392-2191). 250 rms. Men and women. Very centrally located. Pool, rest.

YMCA (nr. dwntwn), 220 Golden Gate Ave., San Francisco, CA 94102 (415/885-0460). 100 rms. Men and women. Health club, pool. 5 min. from dwntwn.

RESTAURANTS

San Francisco Restaurant Prices	
(per person, excluding drinks and service charges)	
B (Budget)	up to $15
I (Inexpensive)	$15–$25
M (Moderate)	$25–$40
E (Expensive)	$40–$60
VE (Very Expensive)	$60 and up

Personal Favorites (in order of preference)

♟♟♟♟♟ **Campton Place Restaurant** (dwntwn), in the Campton Place (see "Accommodations," above) (781-5155). A/C. Breakfast/lunch/dinner daily, brunch Sun. AE, CB, DC, MC, V. J&T. *Specialties:* poached eggs on scones w. ham and orange hollandaise, stuffed lobster w. garlic sauce, lamb chops w. wild-onion cakes, sautéed veal steak w. white truffles, poached sea bass w. seafood, broiled quail w. fried sweet potatoes, rock lobster w. blue-corn cakes. Very good list of California wines; menu changes regularly. *Note:* Bradley Ogden, one of the most talented exponents of American nouvelle cuisine, makes it a point of honor to use only the finest regional ingredients, drawn from the four corners of the U.S. The result is an imaginative, sophisticated bill of fare deserving all manner of high praise. Plush, intimate decorative scheme in tones of taupe and salmon-pink w. some exotic Oriental touches. Flawless svce; so successful that you must reserve several days ahead. One of the 12 best rests. in the U.S. Valet parking. *American.* **E–VE**

♟♟♟♟ **Chez Panisse** (vic.), 1517 Shattuck Ave., Berkeley (585-5525). A/C. Lunch/dinner Mon.-Sat. (café), dinner Tues.-Sat. (rest.); closed Sun. AE, DC, MC, V. *Specialties:* broiled salmon w. sage vinaigrette, pigeon w. basil, stuffed pheasant broiled on a spit, very good cheese and homemade desserts. Menu changes regularly. Skimpy wine list. *Note:* It was in this discreet café-rest. near the famous Berkeley campus that, in 1972, Alice Waters launched her culinary revolution, taking French nouvelle cuisine recipes and adapting them to American palates and ingredients. The dishes offered range from simple country fare (leg of lamb w. white beans) to more sophisticated confections such as the gratin of zucchini and scallops w. saffron. California art nouveau décor; relaxed svce. Well worth the 30-min. drive from San Francisco, but resv. must be made several days in advance for the rest. on the ground floor. The upstairs café, serving less elaborate food, accepts no resv., so you can look forward to a wait. One of the 12 best rests. in the U.S. *French-American*. **I−M (café), E (restaurant)**

♟♟♟ **The Mandarin** (nr. dwntwn), Ghirardelli Square, 900 North Point St. (673-8812). A/C. Lunch/dinner daily; closed Thanksgiving and Dec. 25. AE, CB, DC, MC, V. Jkt. *Specialties:* shark's-fin soup, ginger crab, beggar's chicken, diced squab, Mongolian hot-pot, duck smoked over tea leaves. *Note:* The delightful décor of this rest. (in Ghirardelli Square, a charmingly remodeled old chocolate factory) blends a Chinese and contemporary European aesthetic w. exposed beams and carved paneling. Fine view of the bay (ask for a table nr. the window). Delicate, innovative cuisine; some dishes such as Peking duck and beggar's chicken must be ordered 24 hrs in advance. Confused, perfunctory svce. Resv. advised. *Chinese*. **I−M**

♟♟ **Taxi** (dwntwn), 374 11th St. (558-8294). A/C. Lunch Mon.-Sat., dinner nightly. AE, CB, DC, MC, V. *Specialties:* beer and cheese soups, swordfish steak w. three-pepper cream, filet of smoked pork w. black-eyed peas, broiled chicken w. chili butter, lamb chops w. gingered garlic. Excellent desserts, but wine list on the short side. Menu changes regularly. *Note:* In the heart of SoMa (South *Of MA*rket St.), the new fashionable neighborhood very near the Civic Center, this converted warehouse serves light, imaginative, authentically Californian cuisine. Excellent svce; unusually subdued décor. Patronized by artists and trendy intellectuals. Locally popular; resv. strongly advised. *American*. **I**

☼♟♟ **Tadich Grill** (dwntwn), 240 California St. (391-2373). A/C. Lunch/dinner Mon.-Fri. (until 9 p.m.); closed Sat., Sun., and holidays. No credit cards. Jkt. *Specialties:* tortellini Alfredo, sole Rex, fresh salmon, cioppino (California seafood stew), broiled sea bass, shrimp Diablo, steak, lamb chops, catch of the day. Excellent cheesecake. *Note:* The oldest rest. in San Francisco, dating from the gold-rush year 1849, can still delight lovers of steak and seafood after all the intervening generations. Choice ingredients prepared in exemplary fashion; the old-pub décor is original. Ultra-professional svce. Packed at lunch, mostly w. bankers and businesspeople; no resv., but you can have an agreeable wait at the bar nr. the entrance. *Steak-seafood*. **I−M**

♟♟ **Fog City Diner** (dwntwn), 1300 Battery St. (982-2000). A/C. Lunch/dinner daily. MC, V. Jkt. *Specialties:* fried filet of catfish, Tex-Mex, and Cajun hors d'oeuvres, chili hot dogs, homemade sausage w. polenta, broiled steak w. tomato aïoli, crab cakes, papaya-and-avocado salad, catch of the day, crème brûlée cake. Remarkable list of California wines. *Note:* The quintessence of California cuisine: fresh, light, and tasty. Noisy, relaxed atmosphere in an amusing chrome-and-neon setting. The fashionable place at the foot of Telegraph Hill; trendy patrons; resv. advised. Same management as Mustards Grill in the Napa Valley (see "The California Wine Country," below). *American*. **I**

♟ **Cadillac Bar** (dwntwn), 1 Holland Court (543-8226). A/C. Lunch Mon.-Fri., dinner Mon.-Sat.; closed Sun. AE, CB, DC, MC, V. *Specialties:* tacos, carnitas, broiled fish Veracruzana, crabmeat enchiladas, Botana platter (half chicken, steak, carnitas, queso flameado). Excellent house margaritas. *Note:* In a huge converted warehouse w. immensely high ceilings, very nr. the Moscone Convention Center, Cadillac attracts a host of devotees of real Mexican food. The chefs perform before your eyes, behind great walls of glass. Congenial but noisy atmosphere, w. the inevitable mariachi band. Prompt, cheerful svce. Locally popular, especially at lunch. *Mexican.* **I**

🍸 **Yuet Lee Seafood** (dwntwn), 1300 Stockton St. (982-6020). A/C. Lunch/dinner Wed.-Mon.; closed Tues. No credit cards. *Specialties:* clams in black-bean sauce, fried calamari and oysters, steamed rockfish, lobster sautéed w. garlic, fried shrimps w. chili, catch of the day broiled, fried, or poached. *Note:* Hong Kong–style seafood rest., very popular w. those in-the-know. The Formica décor, appropriate to the combined retail-fish-store-and-rest. operation, is no asset, but the seafood is absolutely fresh and cooked to perfection. No wine or beer (you may bring your own). Prices are stiff for a Chinese rest. *Chinese-seafood.* **I–M**

Other Restaurants (from top bracket to budget)

🍸🍸🍸 **Masa's** (dwntwn), in the Vintage Court Hotel, 648 Bush St. (989-7154). A/C. Dinner only, Tues.-Sat.; closed Sun. and Mon. AE, MC, V. Jkt. *Specialties:* filet of lamb w. green peppercorn and Zinfandel sauce, stuffed quail w. wild rice and mousse of red peppers, linguine w. truffles, mussel soup w. saffron, boudin of lobster, pheasant w. morel mushrooms. Very good desserts, particularly the frozen praline soufflé. Remarkable wine list. *Note:* The most innovative rest. serving French nouvelle cuisine in San Francisco. After the founder, Masataka Kobayashi, died lamented by all in 1985, he was succeeded by the talented Bill Galloway, then more recently by the young Julian Serrano, whose cuisine is both delicate and inspired; the appearance of his dishes is in itself a feast for the eye. Modern paneled décor w. superb flower arrangements, but a tiny space w. only 14 tables. Flawless svce. Resv. indispensable, several days or weeks ahead. A very good place indeed, but the prices are stiff. Valet parking. ($5) *French.* **E–VE**

🍸🍸 **Fleur de Lys** (nr. dwntwn), 777 Sutter St. (673-7779). A/C. Dinner only, Mon.-Sat. (two seatings, at 6:30 and 9 p.m.); closed Sun. and holidays. AE, CB, DC, MC, V. J&T. *Specialties:* foie gras w. braised endives in ginger sauce, consommé of snails, médaillon of veal w. red-pepper mousse, marinated squab in juniper-berry sauce, lamb cutlets and vegetable mousse in thyme sauce, scallops and salmon in orange butter, lobster w. olives and sautéed fennel, filet of venison w. pepper-and-cinnamon sauce, tropical sherbets. Large wine list. *Note:* High-flown décor in a sort of campy *Thousand and One Nights* style, but the cuisine of Hubert Keller, a disciple of the famous French chef Roger Vergé, is a miracle of lightness and delicacy. Reception and svce flawless in all respects. The favorite rest. of San Francisco society. Resv. a must; a very fine place to eat. Valet parking ($4). *French.* **E–VE**

🍸🍸 **Donatello** (dwntwn), in the Donatello (see "Accommodations," above) (441-7182). A/C. Breakfast/lunch/dinner daily. AE, CB, DC, MC, V. J&T. *Specialties:* fresh homemade pasta, lobster and scallop ravioli, wild-mushroom risotto, médaillon of lamb w. herbs and juniper berries, stuffed quail w. sausage, bacon and broiled polenta, filet of pork w. apples and grappa, roast veal w. bacon and vodka; excellent desserts. Very fine list of Italian wines. *Note:* The best, and most expensive, of San Francisco's innumerable Italian rests., on the ground floor of the luxurious Donatello Hotel. Northern Italian food which avoids the beaten path. Decorated in a classic, tasteful combination of tapestries, Italian marble, and pastel colors. Attentive, polished svce. Upscale business clientele. Resv. necessary; valet parking. *Italian.* **M–E**

🍸🍸 **Ernie's** (dwntwn), 847 Montgomery St. (397-5969). A/C. Dinner only, nightly; closed holidays and the first two weeks in Jan. AE, CB, DC, MC, V. J&T. *Specialties:* cream of clams, smoked salmon w. fennel, poached oysters w. leeks, gingered duck, caviar of eggplant and chervil in sauce vierge, seafood stew w. capers, saddle of lamb en rognonnade, chicken w. cream of pears and endives, orange soufflé. Very fine wine list. *Note:* A haunt of celebrities, local or passing through, this San Francisco landmark has recently updated its menu w. some very nouvelle cuisine dishes. Edwardian kitsch interior complete w. brocade, red velvet, and crystal chandeliers. Exemplary svce; resv. essential; valet parking ($4). *Continental.* **M–E**

Stars (nr. dwntwn), 150 Redwood Alley (861-7827). A/C. Lunch Mon.-Fri., dinner nightly, brunch Sun. AE, DC, MC, V. Jkt. *Specialties:* chilled avocado soup w. chili, marinated salmon, oysters w. spiced lamb sausage, tuna steak w. ginger and coriander vinaigrette, braised lamb shank w. curried mayonnaise, James Beard's apple pie. Enormous list of California wines in all price ranges. *Note:* Jeremiah Tower, who forsook architecture for the stove, is one of the gurus of contemporary American cuisine; he works wonders w. light sauces, unexpected taste combinations, and a mesquite grill. Engaging old-fashioned brasserie setting, with retro posters for decoration. Relaxed but efficient svce. Heavily patronized by lawyers and politicians (the Civic Center is within easy reach); resv. strongly advised. *American.* **M–E**

Doros (dwntwn), 714 Montgomery St. (397-6822). A/C. Lunch Mon.-Fri., dinner Mon.-Sat.; closed Sun., holidays, and the first two weeks in July. AE, CB, DC, MC, V. J&T. *Specialties:* fresh homemade pasta, saltimbocca alla romana, veal piccata w. capers, rack of lamb, sautéed veal w. mushroom and eggplant, cold poached salmon. Has one of the largest wine lists in the U.S. *Note:* Another long-standing favorite w. San Francisco's business community. Kitschy décor; European cuisine w. a strong Italian flavor, nicely prepared and served. Peaceful, discreet atmosphere; well-heeled clientele. Resv. a must. Valet parking ($4). *Continental.* **M–E**

Modesto Lanzone (dwntwn), 601 Van Ness Ave. (928-0400). A/C. Lunch Mon.-Fri., dinner Mon.-Sat.; closed Sun., holidays, and two weeks in Sept. AE, CB, DC, MC, V. Jkt. *Specialties:* fresh homemade pasta, gnocchi, roasted rabbit w. endive, stuffed breast of veal, lamb medallions, chicken cacciatore. Good wine list. *Note:* It's generally agreed that San Francisco, w. its very important Italian community, counts a dozen or so of excellent Italian rests. Among the best is Modesto Lanzone. The house-made pastas would be enough to rate it an honorable mention. Elegant, comfortable atmosphere; generally packed; resv. advised. *Italian.* **M**

Empress of China (dwntwn), China Trade Center, 838 Grant Ave. (434-1345). A/C. Lunch/dinner daily. AE, CB, DC, MC, V. Jkt (J&T at dinner). *Specialties:* duck smoked over tea leaves, lobster Cantonese, quail Imperial, steamed pork, Mongolian lamb, diced squab w. chestnuts. *Note:* Overlooking all of Chinatown with the bay as a backdrop, the Empress of China is San Francisco's most refined and elegant rest. The huge dining room, w. its panoramic view, is a veritable museum crammed w. paintings, precious porcelains, and Chinese antiques. The food is a blend of Cantonese, Peking, and Szechuan traditions, w. a touch of individual genius. Svce efficient but curt. Resv. advised. *Chinese.* **I–M**

Jack's (dwntwn), 615 Sacramento St. (986-9854). A/C. Lunch Mon.-Fri., dinner nightly; closed holidays. No credit cards. J&T. *Specialties:* oysters, cracked crab w. mayonnaise, filet of sole Marguéry, sautéed sweetbreads, rack of lamb w. potatoes boulangère, English-style lamb chops, banana fritters w. brandy. Fine wine list. *Note:* In business since 1864 and rebuilt after the 1906 earthquake, this local landmark much patronized by the business community is of particular interest for its excellent fish and seafood. Very good svce for steady customers (not so for newcomers); clientele of regulars. Resv. advised. *Continental-seafood.* **I–M**

☖☖ **Gaylord India** (nr. dwntwn), Ghirardelli Square, 900 North Point St. (771-8822). A/C. Lunch/dinner daily, brunch Sun.; closed Thanksgiving and Dec. 25. AE, CB, DC, MC, V. Jkt. *Specialties:* chicken tikka masala, chicken tandoori, lamb w. cream and walnuts, curries. *Note:* All the subtle flavors of true Indian cuisine; luxurious décor and splendid views of the bay from every table. Attentive svce; agreeable background music. Resv. advised. *Indian.* **I–M**

☖☖ **Greens** (nr. dwntwn), Bldg. A, Fort Mason (771-6222). A/C. Lunch/dinner Tues.-Sat.; brunch Sun.; closed Mon. MC, V. *Specialties:* fresh pasta w. vegetables, homemade soups, mixed salads, pizza provençale, vegetable soufflés, quiches, vegetable hotpot, good homemade desserts. List of French and California wines at reasonable prices. *Note:* Purists look on this as the crowning glory of California vegetarian cuisine; the excellent chef, Deborah Madison, devises light, sophisticated, innovative dishes. The floor-to-ceiling windows give you a superb view of the bay and the Golden Gate Bridge. Very popular w. the business community at lunch; 10-min. drive from dwntwn. Resv. a must. *American.* **I–M**

☖☖ **Le Central** (dwntwn), 453 Bush St. (391-2233). A/C. Lunch Mon.-Fri., dinner Mon.-Sat.; closed Sun. and holidays. AE, DC, MC, V. *Specialties:* celery rémoulade, leeks vinaigrette, saucisson chaud, cassoulet, choucroute garnie, salmon w. butter nantais. Good homemade desserts; interesting wine list. *Note:* You'll find this congenial, authentically French brasserie a stone's throw from Chinatown. The list of daily specials is, very properly, hung on the wall. Flavorful, filling *cuisine bourgeoise;* not-very-efficient svce; Parisian-bistro atmosphere. Draws a crowd of reporters and politicians; resv. advised, particularly at lunch. *French.* **I–M**

☼☖☖ **Sam's Grill** (dwntwn), 374 Bush St. (421-0594). Lunch/dinner Mon.-Fri. (until 8:30 p.m.); closed Sat., Sun., and holidays. MC, V. *Specialties:* clams Elizabeth, deviled crab, broiled sole petrale, catch of the day, shellfish. *Note:* Comfortable and congenial rather than elegant, this old fish rest., always overrun at lunchtime, is a contemporary (1867) of its deadly rival, Tadich Grill. Both serve absolutely choice seafood at reasonable prices. Crowded and noisy at noon; no resv., unfortunately. *Seafood.* **I–M**

☖☖ **Scott's Seafood** (nr. dwntwn), 2400 Lombard St. (563-8988). Lunch/dinner daily; closed Thanksgiving, Dec. 25–26. AE, CB, DC, MC, V. *Specialties:* fisherman's stew, sole petrale, fried calamari, sautéed seafood, catch of the day, shellfish. Good desserts. *Note:* In a small, two-story rowhouse typical of San Francisco, this rest. has achieved great local popularity by serving simple food without fuss, and the freshest fish you could ask for. Cheerful svce; often crowded. No dinner resv. are taken, so wait can be very long. Another location: 3 Embarcadero Center (981-0622); both are excellent places to eat. *Seafood.* **I–M**

☼☖☖ **Yamato** (dwntwn), 717 California St. (397-3456). A/C. Lunch Tues.-Fri., dinner Tues.-Sun.; closed Mon. and holidays. AE, CB, DC, MC, V. Jkt. *Specialties:* teriyaki, sukiyaki, tempura, sesame chicken, shabu shabu, sushi. *Note:* With its miniature waterfalls, gardens, and indoor pools, the oldest Japanese rest. on the West Coast is a masterpiece of architectural elegance. The same elegance is evident in its cuisine. Discreet, efficient svce (in kimono). You can choose between Western-style dining and a tatami room. Locally popular; resv. highly advisable. *Japanese.* **I–M**

☖ **Little Joe's** (dwntwn), 523 Broadway (433-4343). A/C. Lunch/dinner Mon.-Sat.; closed Sun. and holidays. No credit cards. *Specialties:* minestrone, spaghetti al pesto, calamari in red wine sauce, roast chicken w. rosemary, beef tongue w. green sauce, saltimbocca, cacciucco alla livornese (fish soup). *Note:* A landmark of the Italian district of North Beach, in a huge, virtually undecorated old warehouse. Tasty, reasonably priced Italian food prepared by an army of cooks who bustle around their stoves under the admiring eyes of the patrons. Congenial atmosphere. Unfortunately no resv., and a wait is very likely. Very good value. *Italian.* **I**

☀�‍♀ **MacArthur Park** (dwntwn), 607 Front St. (398-5700). Breakfast/lunch Mon.-Fri., dinner nightly; closed holidays. AE, MC, V. *Specialties:* eggs Benedict, ratatouille, smoked pork ribs, barbecued steak, seafood platter, catch of the day broiled on a wood fire, Judy's mud pie. Good list of California wines. *Note:* In a prettily converted old warehouse w. an indoor garden and aviary, MacArthur Park serves fashionable but unpretentious and tasty bistro food. A likeable place w. amicable service. Resv. advised. Valet parking at dinner; the bar is popular at the day's end. *American-Continental.* **I**

☀ **Pacific Heights** (nr. dwntwn), 2001 Fillmore St. (567-3337). A/C. Lunch Mon.-Fri., dinner nightly, brunch Sun. AE, MC, V. *Specialties:* oysters on the half shell, shellfish, mesquite-grilled catch of the day. Good list of California wines at reasonable prices. *Note:* San Francisco's best oyster bar; on any given day it serves at least ten different varieties of the succulent bivalve from both Pacific and Atlantic. The other seafood offered is also impeccably fresh. Charming Victorian décor. A very fine place; excellent value. Resv. advised; valet parking at dinner. *Seafood.* **I**

☀ **Schroeder's** (dwntwn), 240 Front St. (421-4778). A/C. Lunch/dinner Mon.-Fri. (till 9 p.m.); closed Sat., Sun., and holidays. AE, MC, V. *Specialties:* sauerbraten, wienerschnitzel, potato pancakes, Schweitzer bratwurst, apple strudel. *Note:* Since 1893 this splendid bierkeller has been the delight of all who love German food. Bavarian interior; generous helpings; efficient but rather chilly svce; very good value. A very fine specimen of the family rest. Resv. encouraged. *German.* **I**

☀☍ **Buena Vista Café** (dwntwn), 2765 Hyde St. (474-5044). A/C. Breakfast/lunch/dinner daily (bar open till 2 a.m.). No credit cards. *Specialties:* eggs Benedict, enchiladas, steaks, daily specials. *Note:* One of the most famous cafés in San Francisco, w. a fine view of the bay and Alcatraz Island. Best known for its gin fizzes and other cocktails, but the food is also laudable. Very popular with tourists. Claims to have launched the fashion for Irish coffee in the U.S. No resv. *American.* **B–I**

☍ **Yank Sing** (dwntwn), 427 Battery St. (362-1560). A/C. Lunch daily (from 10 a.m. to 3 p.m.). AE, MC, V. *Specialties:* Cantonese dim sum (barbecued pork, shrimp, vegetables, etc.). *Note:* The décor is nothing to speak of, and the svce is somewhat nonchalant, but Yank Sing serves the best dim sum (a kind of hot and cold mixed hors d'oeuvres) in Chinatown, wheeled by your table, one dish after another, on trays. Delicious and relatively cheap. Another location: 53 Stevenson St. (495-4510). *Chinese.* **B–I**

☀☍ **Obrero Hotel** (dwntwn), 1208 Stockton St. (989-3960). No A/C. Dinner only, nightly. No credit cards. *Specialties:* homemade soup, cassoulet, pasta w. clams, oxtail ragoût, roast lamb, roast beef, sole Rex. Wine or beer. *Note:* The last of San Francisco's legendary Basque hotels, serving traditional boardinghouse meals at long, family-style tables. Hearty dinner in a friendly atmosphere. Only one sitting, at 6:30 p.m. every evening. Guaranteed local color. Resv. advised. Unbeatable value. *French.* **B**

Cafeterias / Fast Food

Mama's (dwntwn), 398 Geary St. (788-1004). Breakfast/lunch/dinner daily (till 1 a.m.). AE, DC, MC, V. *Specialties:* roast chicken, sandwiches, daily specials, good homemade desserts. Beer and wine. *Note:* Excellent cafeteria food; inviting atmosphere. Locally popular.

Salmagundi (dwntwn), 442 Geary St. (441-0894). Open daily (till midnight). No credit cards. *Specialties:* homemade soup, quiche, salad, homemade desserts. Beer and wine. *Note:* Praiseworthy, well-prepared food; very popular at lunchtime. Other locations: 2 Embarcadero Center (982-5603), open till 9 p.m.; 1236 Market St. (431-7337), open till 9 p.m.

WHERE TO EAT WHAT

American: Campton Place (ΥΥΥΥ), Chez Panisse (ΥΥΥΥ), Stars (ΥΥ), Fog City Diner (ΥΥ), Green's (ΥΥ), Taxi (ΥΥ), Buena Vista Café (Υ), MacArthur Park (Υ).

Chinese: Empress of China (ΥΥΥ), The Mandarin (ΥΥΥ), Yank Sing (Υ), Yuet Lee Seafood (Υ).

Continental (European): Ernie's (ΥΥΥ), Jack's (ΥΥΥ), Doros (ΥΥ), MacArthur Park (Υ).

Cafeterias/Fast Food: Mama's, Salmagundi.

French: Chez Panisse (ΥΥΥΥ), Masa's (ΥΥΥΥ), Fleur de Lys (ΥΥΥ), Le Central (ΥΥ), Obrero Hotel (Υ).

German: Schroeder's (Υ).

Indian: Gaylord India (ΥΥ).

Italian: Donatello (ΥΥΥ), Modesto Lanzone (ΥΥ), Little Joe's (Υ).

Japanese: Yamato (ΥΥ).

Mexican: Cadillac Bar (Υ).

Seafood: Jack's (ΥΥΥ), Tadich Grill (ΥΥ), Sam's Grill (ΥΥ), Scott's Seafood (ΥΥ), Pacific Heights (Υ), Yuet Lee Seafood (Υ).

Vegetarian: Green's (ΥΥ).

Late-Night Service (closing time in parentheses): Buena Vista Cafe´ (2 a.m.), Mama's (1 a.m.), Salmagundi (midnight).

BARS & NIGHTCLUBS

☼ **Caffè Trieste** (dwntwn), 609 Vallejo St. (392-6739). The city's best-known literary café; since it opened in 1956, this longtime haunt of the Beat poets has played host to every prominent literary figure in town. Francis Ford Coppola wrote the script of *The Godfather* here. Italian-bohemian atmosphere. Open daily.

Carnelian Room (dwntwn), 52nd floor, Bank of America Bldg., 555 California St. (433-7500). Fine view of San Francisco Bay. The rest. (mediocre), is open to the public only for dinner. Agreeable bar. Open nightly.

☼ **Eli's Mile High Club** (vic.), 3629 Martin Luther King Way, Oakland (655-6661). The best blues joint on the West Coast; worth the trip across the bay. The patrons are a very Berkeley crowd.

Finocchio's (dwntwn), 506 Broadway (982-9388). The best-known night-spot featuring female impersonators in the U.S. Open Tues.-Sun.

Great American Music Hall (dwntwn), 859 O'Farrell St. (885-0750). Live big-name rock and jazz concerts. Open nightly.

Hard Rock Café (dwntwn), 1699 Van Ness Ave. (885-1699). Facsimile of the famous London nightclub of the same name. Hard rock; youthful patrons. Good hamburgers; locally very popular. Open nightly.

Harry's Bar and Grill (dwntwn), 500 Van Ness Ave. (864-2779). Inviting bar across from City Hall, a hangout for local politicians. Relaxed, congenial atmosphere. Also an Italian rest. serving good risotto, broiled dishes. Open nightly.

Kimball's (dwntwn), 300 Grove St. at Franklin St. (861-5585). Highly regarded jazz club featuring the biggest names in the business (Wed.-Sat.). Also a very acceptable rest., open nightly.

Milestones (nr. dwntwn), 376 5th St. (777-9997). One of the newest, and best, of San Francisco's jazz clubs; locally popular. Open nightly.

Oasis (nr. dwntwn), 11th and Folsom Sts. (621-8119). Fashionable disco in what used to be a public swimming pool; outlandish hi-tech décor. Youthful, trendy clientele. Open nightly.

Park Exchange (dwntwn), 600 Montgomery St. (983-4800). Disco in a tropical glass house at the base of the Transamerica Pyramid. Well-brought-up yuppie clientele.

Perry's (dwntwn), 1944 Union St. (922-9022). Singles bar in the New York tradition; youthful, relaxed atmosphere. Also an unassuming rest. Recommended as a premier pickup spot; open nightly till midnight.

Pier 23 Café (dwntwn), Pier 23, The Embarcadero (362-5125). Good, live Dixieland and a very fine view of harbor and bay. A likeable place; also a very commendable rest. Wed.-Sun.

Punch Line (dwntwn), 444 Battery St. (397-4337). The best and best known of the city's comedy clubs; showcases beginners as well as established stars. Very popular locally. Open Tues.-Sun.

Specs (dwntwn), 12 Adler St. (421-4112). Congenial pub frequented by artists, writers, etc., from the bohemian North Beach neighborhood. Literary atmosphere. Open nightly.

The Stone (dwntwn), 412 Broadway (391-8282). The fashionable rock joint. Youthful, trendy clientele. Open nightly.

Top of the Mark (dwntwn), in the Mark Hopkins Hotel (see "Accommodations," above) (392-3434). Elegant panoramic bar in a superb art deco setting. Dancing; fine view of the bay. Open nightly till 1:30 a.m.

Venetian Room (dwntwn), in the Fairmont Hotel and Tower (see "Accommodations," above) (772-5226). Star-studded shows, from Tony Bennett to Tina Turner. Luxurious baroque setting. Open Tues.-Sun.

Washington Square Bar and Grill (dwntwn), 1707 Powell St. (982-8123). Lively bar-saloon; also an acceptable Italian rest., but the food is only an excuse to talk, celebrate, and rub elbows w. those in the know. Agreeable jazz piano. Open nightly.

Wolfgang's (dwntwn), 901 Columbus Ave. (474-2995). Live rock, reggae, and jazz; youthful, very with-it atmosphere. The trendy place. Open nightly.

NEARBY EXCURSIONS

BERKELEY (12 mi., 20 km, east via the San Francisco–Oakland Bay Bridge and I-80): A cosmopolitan place filled with museums, libraries, theaters, bookstores, and other cultural sites, this city of 120,000 on the east side of San Francisco Bay became a symbol for a generation. The Free Speech Movement—the first campus revolt of the 1960s—began here, capturing the attention of the nation. The University of California's largest campus (32,000 students), Berkeley is one of the oldest (1868) and most famous schools in the country. Among its 1,600 faculty members are no fewer than 12 Nobel Prize winners and 76 members of the prestigious National Academy of Sciences. From its 307-ft (93-m) campanile, a copy of that on the Piazza San Marco in Venice, you'll have a wonderful view (there's an elevator). The **Visitor Center** in the Student Union Building, Bancroft Way and Telegraph Ave. (642-5215), organizes guided tours of the campus Mon.-Fri. You should also see the university's very beautiful **Art Museum** at 2626 Bancroft Way (642-1207), open Wed.-Sun. Don't miss Berkeley.

MUIR WOODS NATIONAL FOREST (16 mi., 25 km, north via the Golden Gate Bridge, U.S. 101, and Calif. 1):

Splendid redwood forest, with some trees, more than 2,000 years old, growing 230 ft (70 m) or more. From the top of nearby Mount Tamalpais (2,604 ft/794m) there's a magnificent view over San Francisco Bay and the Pacific. You should make this trip. No camping or picnicking permitted. For more information contact the Site Manager, Mill Valley, CA 94941 (415/388-2595).

OAKLAND (10 mi., 16 km, east across the San Francisco–Oakland Bay Bridge): This busy port and industrial city, founded in 1850, has a large black community (the Black Panthers originated here), and one of the most beautiful, and original, museums to be found on the West Coast. The **Oakland Museum**, at 1000 Oak St. (273-3514), open Wed.-Sun., is the work of architect Kevin Roche; its tiered design, with terraced gardens, is quite outstanding. It houses rich material on California art and history, as well as paintings by Hans Hofmann and a splendid film library. Worth a visit.

Note also the picturesque **Jack London Square** around the Inner Harbor, with restaurants, bars, and shops got up in the turn-of-the-century spirit of Jack London's life and writings. The novelist lived in the vicinity, and wrote a number of his books at Heinold's First and Last Chance Saloon, 56 Jack London Square. Don't fail to make this trip.

POINT REYES NATIONAL SEASHORE (35 mi., 56 km, north via the Golden Gate Bridge, U.S. 101, and Calif. 1): A 70,000-acre (28,000-ha.) wildlife reserve on a peninsula jutting out into the Pacific, harboring more than 300 species of birds and mammals. The landscape is beautifully flower-bedecked from Feb. to July. Beaches; camping; swimming permitted in summer. For lovers of authentic nature. **Visitor center** at Drakes Beach (663-1092); open Sat., Sun., and holidays.

SAN RAFAEL (19 mi., 30 km, north via the Golden Gate Bridge and U.S. 101): The **Mission San Rafael Arcángel,** 20th and next-to-last of those founded by the Franciscans in California, was built in 1817 and rebuilt in 1949 on the original site at 1104 Fifth Ave. at A St. (456-3016), open daily. Worth the detour.

See also the very fine **Marin County Civic Center,** one of the last major works of the great Frank Lloyd Wright, who died in 1959 before it was completed; it's 2 mi. (3.2 km) north on San Pedro Rd. (499-7407). Conducted tours by appointment, Mon.-Fri.

SAUSALITO (8 mi., 12 km, north via the Golden Gate Bridge and U.S. 101): The California equivalent of a fashionable European resort like Juan-les-Pins or Portofino, equally attractive to millionaires, artists, and hippies. This gracious pleasure harbor lies across the Golden Gate Bridge from San Francisco, with a wonderful view of the bay. Many shops and art galleries; congenial bars and restaurants. You should see the **San Francisco Bay and Delta Model,** 2100 Bridgeway (332-3870), open Tues.-Sat., an enormous (2-acre, 0.8-ha.) hydraulic model which faithfully reproduces the tidal action and marine currents of San Francisco Bay. Sausalito definitely deserves a visit.

SILICON VALLEY: See "South of the Bay and Silicon Valley," under "Farther Afield," below.

TIBURON (18 mi., 28 km, north via the Golden Gate Bridge, U.S. 101, and Calif. 131): Another charming little pleasure harbor near Sausalito, north of the bay. Wonderful view of San Francisco. Many bars, fashionable shops, and fish and seafood restaurants with fine views of the bay. A place that contrives to be both elegant and relaxing; you should see it.

THE CALIFORNIA WINE COUNTRY

California, which produces more than 70% of all U.S. wines, boasts more than 250 wineries grouped in three main regions. The Central Valley around Fresno produces mass-market table wines. Santa Clara and Monterey, south of San Francisco Bay, produce light, likeable wines, particularly whites. Finally, the Napa Valley and Sonoma Valley areas, north of San Francisco Bay, indisputably produce the state's finest wines, beginning with the renowned Cabernet Sauvignon.

VISITING THE WINERIES: Napa Valley and Sonoma Valley, about 50 mi. (80 km) NE of San Francisco, are known as "Wine Country." You can arrange for visits and tastings at many of its wineries; for information, contact the **Napa Valley Chamber of Commerce,** P.O. Box 636, Napa, CA 94559 (707/226-7455), and the **Sonoma Valley Visitors Bureau,** 453 E. 1st St., Sonoma, CA 95476 (707/996-1090). Among the most interesting wineries are:

Calistoga

Calistoga is 29 mi. (46 km) NW of Napa on Calif. 29.

Sterling Vineyards, a lovely estate with the look of an Italian monastery, at 1111 Dunaweal Lane (707/942-5151), is open for (tiring) visits daily.

On the way, see 🏛 **Old Faithful Geyser,** 1299 Tubbs Lane (707/942-6463), which erupts 65 ft (20 m) into the air at intervals of about 40 min.

Napa

Napa, 44 mi. (70 km) north of San Francisco via I-80 and Calif. 29, is one of the centers of wine making in California.

Clos du Val, 5330 Silverado Trail (707/252-6711), is open daily.

Oakville

Oakville is 13 mi. (20 km) NW of Napa on Calif. 29.

Mondavi, 7801 St. Helena Hwy. (707/963-9611), is in a graceful building modeled on a Franciscan mission; open daily.

Rutherford

Rutherford is 15 mi. (26 km) NW of Napa on Calif. 29.

Beaulieu Vineyard, 1960 St. Helena Hwy. (707/963-2411), has cellars dating from the turn of the century; open daily.

Inglenook Vineyards, on Calif. 29 (707/967-3300), is in a fine 1883 Gothic Revival cellar house and has an interesting museum of viticulture; open daily.

St. Helena

St. Helena is 19 mi. (30 km) NW of Napa on Calif. 29.

Beringer Vineyard, 2000 Main St. (707/963-7115), has huge underground cellars dating from 1876; open daily.

At **Christian Brothers,** 100 South St. (707/963-4480), the 1889 cellar house is one of the largest in the world, belonging, as its name indicates, to a religious order; visits by appointment.

Heitz Wine Cellars, 436 St. Helena Hwy. (707/963-3542); open daily.

Charles Krug, 2800 Main St. (707/963-2761), open daily. The handsome décor dates from 1861.

Louis Martini Winery, 254 St. Helena Hwy. (707/963-2736); open daily.

Finally, **Spring Mountain Winery** is headquartered in the manor house from the TV series "Falcon Crest," 2805 Spring Mountain Rd. (707/963-5233); open daily.

Sonoma

Sonoma, 16 mi. (25 km) west of Napa on Calif. 12, along with Napa is the center of the California wine industry. These vineyards, of which Europe is now envious, were started in the 1820s by Spanish Franciscan missionaries, and have been tended since then by German, French, Hungarian, and Italian growers. The vintage is harvested from Sept. to early Nov. Some of the more interesting wineries are:

Buena Vista Winery, 18000 Old Winery Rd. (707/938-1266), open daily, is the oldest wine-making estate in California, founded in 1857 by the Hungarian Agoston Haraszthy. Classical concerts in summer.

Sebastiani Vineyards, 389 4th St. East (707/938-5532), has an interesting museum of viticulture and collection of antique carved vats; open daily.

On the way, take a look at ⚓ **Jack London State Historic Park,** on Calif. 12 at **Glen Ellen,** where the famous author of *Call of the Wild* killed himself in 1916; he's buried here. Beautiful scenery; museum open daily. Also, be sure to see the ⚓ **Mission San Francisco Solano** with its pretty plaza, 21st and last of the missions founded in California by the Spanish Franciscans, in 1823. It's on E. Spain St. and 1st St. East (707/938-1519); open daily.

Yountville

Yountville is 10 mi. (16 km) NW of Napa on Calif. 29.

Domaine Chandon, California Dr. (707/944-2280), is the U.S. property of the great French champagne house of Moët et Chandon. Cellars open to visitors daily May-Oct., Wed.-Sun. the rest of the year. You'll learn about all the different stages in the manufacture of champagne.

BALLOON EXCURSIONS:
For an unforgettable overview of the Napa Valley take a hot-air-balloon ride. Offered by **Balloon Aviation of Napa Valley,** 2299 3rd St., Napa (707/252-7067), and **Once in a Lifetime Balloon Co.,** P.O. Box 795, Calistoga (707/942-6541). Cost is $150 per person including brunch.

FOOD AND LODGING IN WINE COUNTRY:
As you might imagine, where there is wine, there are restaurants—and places to bed down for the night as well.

Rutherford

⚘♨♨♨♨ **Auberge du Soleil,** 180 Rutherford Hill Rd., Rutherford, CA 94573 (707/963-1211). 48 rms. The most chic and best-known place to stay in the Wine Country. A very luxurious European-style inn with a remarkable rest. (see below). Member of the prestigious Relais et Châteaux hotel chain. **VE**

⚘♈♈♈♈ **Auberge du Soleil** (see above). Lunch/dinner daily. Quite remarkable French-Californian nouvelle cuisine and a superb setting, with a view clear across the Napa Valley. A wonderful place to eat, but the prices are very high (specially the wine list). **E**

Santa Rosa

♨♨ **El Rancho Tropicana,** 2200 Santa Rosa Ave., Santa Rosa, CA 95401 (707/542-3655). 300 rms. Hollywood-style grand hotel; amusing décor. **I–M**

Sonoma

☼♈♊♊ **Sonoma Hotel,** 110 W. Spain St., Sonoma, CA 95476 (707/
996-2996). 17 rms. Lovely old (1872) hotel, tastefully renovated. **I–M**

♈ **Au Relais,** 691 Broadway (707/996-1031). Lunch/dinner
daily. French *cuisine bourgeoise.* A likeable place, and very good
value. **I**

St. Helena

☼♊♊♊ **Wine Country Inn,** 1152 Lodi Lane, St. Helena, CA 94574
(707/963-7077). 25 rms. Charming old country inn. **E–VE**

♈ **Tra Vigne,** 1050 Charter Oak Ave. (707/963-4444). Lunch/
dinner daily. Refined Italian-Californian cuisine in a stunning
setting. **I–M**

Yountville

☼♈♊ **Burgundy House,** 6711 Washington St., Yountville, CA
94599 (707/944-2855). Tiny inn with only 6 rms; elegantly
countrified. **M–E**

♈ **The Diner,** 6476 Washington Ave. (707/944-2626).
Breakfast/lunch/dinner Tues.-Sun.; closed Mon. Mexican-
American food. **B**

☼♈♈♈ **Domaine Chandon,** California Dr. (707/944-2892).
Lunch/dinner Wed.-Sun.; closed Mon. and Tues. Remarkable
French food. **M–E**

♈ **Mustards Grill,** 7399 St. Helena Hwy. (707/944-2424).
Lunch/dinner daily. Excellent entrées grilled over a wood fire;
locally popular. **I–M**

FARTHER AFIELD

☼♒ **CALIF. 1, THE COASTAL HIGHWAY** (398 mi., 639 km,
round trip via I-280S, Calif. 17S, and Calif. 1S and 1N): One of
the most beautiful drives in the U.S. For a good way it follows the old Camino
Real, the 200-year-old highway of the Spanish Franciscan missions. You'll see
Monterey, 17-Mile Drive, Carmel, Big Sur, and the **Hearst Castle** (see Chapter
50 on the California Coast); then back to San Francisco by the coastal road. Can
readily be combined with a visit to areas south of the bay and Silicon Valley (see
below). You shouldn't miss this two-to three-day trip.

☼♒ **LASSEN NATIONAL PARK** (246 mi., 394 km, NE via I-5,
Calif. 36, and Calif. 89): One of the only two active volcanoes
on the U.S. mainland (the other is Mount St. Helens). Rugged scenery. For details, see Chapter 49 on Reno.

☼♒ **REDWOOD EMPIRE** (345 mi., 552 km, round trip via
U.S. 101N, Calif. 20W, and Calif. 1S): Magnificent redwood
forests inland, and wonderful seascapes along the Pacific coast; can easily be
combined with a visit to the vineyards of the **Wine Country** (see above).
You'll pass through **Clear Lake,** a huge mountain lake with fishing and sailing;
the picturesque fishing ports of **Fort Bragg** and **Mendocino; Noyo,** with its
superb 17-acre (6.8-ha.) botanic garden overlooking the Pacific; and **Fort Ross,**
a Russian trading post founded in 1812. It still has many of its original buildings, including its Russian Orthodox chapel; for details, see Chapter 50 on
the California Coast. Your last stop might be **Point Reyes Nation Sea-**

shore (see "Nearby Excursions," above). A two- to three-day trip you shouldn't miss.

Where to Stay En Route

☼ 🛏🛏 **Heritage House,** 5200 Calif. 1, Littleriver, CA 95456 (707/ 937-5885), south of Fort Bragg. 69 rms. Delightful little cottages on the ocean. Good rest. Closed Dec.-Feb. **E−VE**

☼ 🛏🛏 **St. Orres,** on Calif. 1, Gualala, CA 95445 (707/884-3303), between Mendocino and Fort Ross. Charming tiny (17 rms) inn; excellent rest. **M**

☼ 🔭🔭 **SACRAMENTO AND LAKE TAHOE** (448 mi., 716 km, round trip via I-80E, Calif. 89S, U.S. 50W, and I-80W): Lake Tahoe is one of the loveliest mountain lakes in the U.S. (see Chapter 49 on Reno), in an area which offers all kinds of recreational sports in summer, and many ski resorts in winter.

On the way you pass through 🔭🔭 **Sacramento,** capital of the state of California, with a history as interesting as any city in the West. Now nicknamed the "Camellia Capital of the World," it first rose to prominence as a center of the 1848–1849 gold rush. You should certainly see the 🔭 **State Capitol,** more than a century old and now sumptuously restored, on 10th St. at Capitol Mall (916/324-0333), open daily. Take in **Sutter's Fort State Historic Park,** a fort built in 1839 by the Swiss John Sutter, founder of Sacramento, at 2701 L St. (916/445-4209), open daily. Finally, visit the **Old Sacramento Historic District,** a picturesque old neighborhood along the Sacramento River, restored to the way it looked in the period 1850–1880. Some buildings you shouldn't overlook: the **Old Eagle Theater,** oldest in California (1849), at Front and J Sts., open Tues.-Sun.; the **California State Railroad Museum,** as fine as any in the country, 111 I St., open daily; and the **Hastings Building,** once the western terminus of the legendary Pony Express, whose hundred dauntless horsemen (one of them the great Buffalo Bill) used to cover in ten days, at full gallop, the 1,965 mi. (3,145 km) between St. Joseph, Missouri (see Chapter 28 on Kansas City), and Sacramento. It was only the coming of the telegraph, in the 1860s, that put an end to their feats. The Hastings Building also at one time housed the California Supreme Court. It's at 2nd and J Sts.; open daily.

Near Sacramento are many ※ **mining towns** from the gold-rush days; among the most picturesque are **Coloma** (where gold was first discovered in 1848), **Placerville, Fair Play, Rough and Ready, Grass Valley,** and **Nevada City.**

This spectacular trip will take you three to four days; it shouldn't be missed.

Where to Stay in Sacramento

🛏🛏🛏 **Clarion,** 700 16th St., Sacramento, CA 95814 (916/444-8000). 239 rms. Elegantly renovated old hotel standing in a lovely garden across from the Governor's Mansion. Commendable rest. **M−E**

🛏🛏 **Woodlake Inn,** 500 Leisure Lane, Sacramento, CA 95815 (916/922-6251). 314 rms. Luxurious convention hotel located on a private lake. **M**

🛏 **Motel 6,** 1415 30th St., Sacramento, CA 95816 (916/457-0777). 94 rms. Motel, no-frills but acceptable, near Sutter's Fort and the State Capitol. **B**

Where to Eat in Sacramento

🍸🍸 **Biba,** 2801 Capitol Ave. (916/455-2422). Lunch/dinner daily. All the mainstays of Italian cuisine, impeccably prepared and served. *Italian.* **I−M**

☼ ☖ **Firehouse,** 1112 2nd St. (916/442-4772). Lunch Mon.-Fri., dinner Mon.-Sat.; closed Sun. A handsome antique setting in an 1853 firehouse. *Continental-American.* **I–M**

☼ ☖ **SEQUOIA NATIONAL PARK** (270 mi., 432 km, SE via I-580, I-5, and Calif. 198): The kingdom of the forest giants. See Chapter 52 on Sequoia National Park.

☼ ☖☖ **SOUTH OF THE BAY AND SILICON VALLEY** (155 mi., 248 km, round trip via U.S. 101S and I-280N): Start with a visit to ☼ ☖ **Stanford University,** Camino Real (Calif. 82) at **Palo Alto,** a sort of brain factory with no fewer than ten Nobel laureates on the faculty. With 13,000 students, it's one of the most highly regarded of U.S. universities, particularly in the fields of technology, medicine, and high-tech electronics. Elegant red-tiled Romanesque buildings; you get a good view of the campus from the 285-ft (87-m) Hoover Tower. Campus open daily; for information on times, check with the Information Center at the end of Palm Dr. (415/723-2560). Don't miss it.

Stop off at ☼ **Marriott's Great America,** the huge theme park at **Santa Clara** (see "Theme Parks," above).

Though ☼ **Silicon Valley** (named after the silicon chips on which electronic circuits are based) may not be found on most maps, for two decades a surprising number of very bright people have been working here. For a radius of 30 mi. (50 km) around **Sunnyvale, Los Altos, Mountain View,** and **Santa Clara,** yesterday's almond and orange groves have given way to research centers and the futurist factories where tomorrow's (or the day after tomorrow's) computers are designed. Some 3,000 corporations in all, from giants like National Semiconductor and Intel to workshops employing half a dozen people, make Silicon Valley the world capital of electronics. As a living illustration of "neocapitalism," not only are the technicians and researchers employed in Silicon Valley among the best-paid employees in the U.S., but also many participate in the management, and in the profits, of their firms.

Drive 3 mi. (5 km) south of Santa Clara, to ☼ **San Jose,** the former state capital, to see the ☖ **Egyptian Museum** and its important collection of antiquities at 1342 Naglee Ave. (408/287-2807), open daily; ☖ **Alum Rock Park,** 16240 Alum Rock Ave. (408/259-5477), and the curious rock formations that have earned it the name of "Little Yosemite"; the ☖ **Lick Observatory,** with its 36-in. (91-cm) telescope, 25 mi (40 km) SE on Mount Hamilton (408/274-5061), with visits by appointment daily, for astronomy buffs; the **Mirassou** wine cellars, 3000 Aborn Rd. (408/274-4000), open daily; and above all the unbelievable ☼ ☖☖ **Winchester Mystery House,** 525 S. Winchester Blvd. (408/247-2101), open daily, with its 160 bedrooms, 13 baths, 2,000 doors, 10,000 windows, 47 fireplaces, secret corridors, blank walls, trap doors, and false staircases. This was the last home of Sarah Winchester, widow of the famous gunmaker, and during the last 38 years of her life (1884–1922) she never stopped adding to the house—a clairvoyant had told her that she would not die as long as she went on building! It cost her $6 million—a much huger sum then than now.

Your last stop will be in **Saratoga,** where you should visit the elegant ☖ **Villa Montalvo,** with its art galleries and beautiful gardens, at 15400 Villa Montalvo Rd. (408/741-3421); gardens open daily, galleries open Thur.-Sun. Also the **Paul Masson** winery, 13150 Saratoga Ave. (408/675-2481), open daily; there are classical and jazz concerts June-Sept.

This trip can be made inside a day, but it's best combined with the itinerary along Calif. 1, the Coastal Highway (see above).

Where to Eat in Silicon Valley

Lion and Compass, 1023 N. Fair Oaks Ave., Sunnyvale (408/ 745-1260). Lunch Mon.-Fri., dinner Mon.-Sat.; closed Sun. AE, CB, DC, MC, V. The valley's best-known rest. *Continental.* **I–M**

MacArthur Park, 27 University Ave., Palo Alto (415/321-9990). Lunch Sun.-Fri., dinner nightly. Noisy but congenial rest. in a converted railroad station. *American.* **I**

YOSEMITE NATIONAL PARK (210 mi., 336 km, east via I-580, I-205, and Calif. 120): Nature in the raw; don't miss it. See Chapter 53 on Yosemite.

CHAPTER 52

SEQUOIA NATIONAL PARK

□ □ □

And Kings Canyon

Domain of the giant trees, Sequoia National Park is, after Yellowstone, the oldest national park in the U.S. Set up in 1890 to safeguard the redwood (sequoia) forests on the slopes of the **Sierra Nevada,** the park's magnificent scenery embraces granite mountain-crests, canyons, mountain lakes and dense forests. Around Sequoia and the adjoining **Kings Canyon National Park,** inaugurated in 1940, lie giant mountain peaks including **Mount Whitney,** highest in the "lower 48" (14,495 ft., 4,418 m), **Split Mountain** (14,054 ft., 4,285 m), and **Mount Goethe** (13,274 ft., 4,047 m). But though the natural setting is incomparable, the main interest of the two parks is their forests of giant conifers.

The redwood, or sequoia, owes its name to the famous Indian leader Sequoyah, inventor of the alphabet in which the Cherokee language is written. The tree has been known to grow as high as 295 ft. (90 m), with a circumference at the base of 98 ft. (30 m) or more. Its bark, 2 ft. (60 cm) thick, is resistant to both fire and insects. The largest redwood now standing in the Park, the **General Sherman Tree,** stands more than 275 ft. (84 m) tall, and its estimated age of 2,500 years makes it the oldest living creature on earth.

In spite of the huge area they cover, Sequoia and Kings Canyon National Parks have only 75 mi. (120 km) of surfaced roads between them; points off these highways can be reached only on horseback or on foot. There are, however, 900 mi. (1,450 km) of walking trails. Sequoia National Park, while it remains open year round, can be negotiated only with chains or snowtires from Oct. through May; Kings Canyon is closed all winter.

The three motels in the two parks have a limited capacity of 300 rooms; reservations should therefore be made far in advance.

BASIC FACTS: State of California. Area Code: 209. Time Zone: Pacific Time. ZIP Code: 93262. Approximate Area: 1,300 sq. mi. (3,370 km²). Founded: 1890 (Sequoia); 1940 (Kings Canyon).

CLIMATE: Icy and snowy in winter (the snowfall can reach 13 ft., 4 m, and the thermometer sometimes drops to −4° F, −20° C), the climate of Sequoia National Park is brisk and invigorating at all times of the year. Even in midsummer, bring warm clothes for the evenings.

DISTANCES: Las Vegas, 506 mi. (810 km); Los Angeles, 220 mi. (354 km); Sacramento, 257 mi. (411 km); San Francisco, 270 mi. (432 km).

ARRIVAL & TRANSIT INFORMATION

AIRPORTS NEARBY: The **Fresno Municipal Airport** (FAT), 70 mi. (112 km) W.

Visalia Municipal Airport (VIS), 45 mi. (72 km) NE.

AIRLINES (at the Fresno Municipal Airport unless otherwise noted): American Eagle (toll free 800/433-7300), American Eagle (at the Visalia Airport: toll free 800/433-7300), Continental (456-1166), Delta (toll free 800/221-1212), and United (252-5711).

BUS OR CAR RENTAL?: Given the distances and the attractive rates offered in California, the sensible solution is to rent a car with unlimited mileage.

CAR RENTALS (all at the Fresno Municipal Airport): Avis (251-5001), Budget (251-5515), Hertz (251-5055), and National (251-5577).

TRAIN: The nearest AMTRAK station is at Tulare and Q Sts., Fresno (toll free 800/872-7245).

BUS: There is no regular bus service to Sequoia or Kings Canyon National Park.

The nearest regular-service bus stations, both Greyhound, are at 1033 Broadway, Fresno (268-9461), and 24 S. Court St., Visalia (734-3507).

INFORMATION & SIGHTSEEING

INFORMATION: Contact the **Superintendent**, Sequoia and Kings Canyon National Parks, Ash Mountain, Three Rivers, CA 93271 (209/565-3341).

Visitors centers are located at Lodgepole, Giant Forest, and Grant Grove.

SCENERY AND SIGHTS: ☼ ஃ **Cedar Grove,** reached on Calif. 180: The village at the dead end of Kings Canyon River South Fork. The surrounding peaks look down on the riverbed from a height of more than a mile (1,600 m). Road closed in winter only. A wonderful sight.

ஃ **Crystal Cave,** 6 mi. (9 km) east of Giant Forest Village: Splendid limestone cavern with astonishing mineral growths; the temperature inside holds steady near 50°F (10°C). Vehicle road, then foot trail; mid June-mid Sept., daily. Must be seen.

☼ஃ **Giant Forest,** around Giant Forest Village on Calif. 198: Here you'll find the biggest redwoods in the Park, including the **General Sherman Tree,** 275 ft. (84 m) high and 103 ft. (32 m) around the base, with an estimated weight of 2,000 tons. There's enough wood in the tree to build 40 five-room cabins. At about 2,500 years, this is the world's oldest living creature. Don't miss it.

☼ஃ **Grant Grove,** intersection of Calif. 180 and Calif. 198: Stand of giant redwood including the second-tallest in the park, the **General Grant Tree,** 267 ft. (81 m) high and 107 ft. (33 m) around. Not to be missed.

ஃ **High Sierra Trail:** 40-mi. (64-km) hiking trail linking Giant Forest Village to the western tip of the park and the John Muir Trail. Splendid scenery. For walkers in good physical shape.

☼ஃ **John Muir Trail:** A hiking trail about 80 mi. (128 km) long, running north-south along the eastern edge of the park. Won-

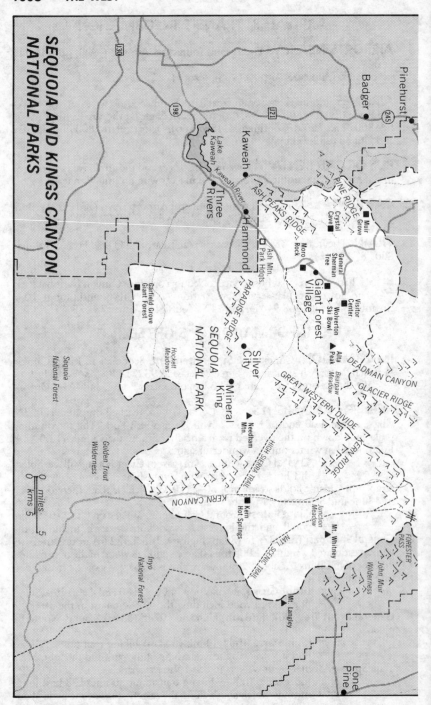

SEQUOIA AND KINGS CANYON
NATIONAL PARKS

Pinehurst
Badger
245
J21
J30
198
Kaweah
Lake Kaweah
Kaweah River
Three Rivers
Hammond
ASH PEAKS RIDGE
Park Hdqts.
Ash Mtn.
PINE RIDGE
Crystal Cave
Muir Grove
General Sherman Tree
Moro Rock
Giant Forest Village
Wolverton Ski Bowl
Visitor Center
Alta Peak
Bearpaw Meadow
DEADMAN CANYON
GLACIER RIDGE
PARADISE RIDGE
Garfield Grove Giant Forest
Hockett Meadows
SEQUOIA NATIONAL PARK
Silver City
Mineral King
Needham Mtn.
GREAT WESTERN DIVIDE
KERN RIDGE
HIGH SIERRA TRAIL
KERN CANYON
Kern Hot Springs
Junction Meadow
NAT'L SCENIC TRAIL
Mt. Whitney
FORESTER PASS
Sequoia National Forest
Golden Trout Wilderness
Inyo National Forest
John Muir Wilderness
Mt. Langley
Lone Pine

0 miles 5
0 kms 5

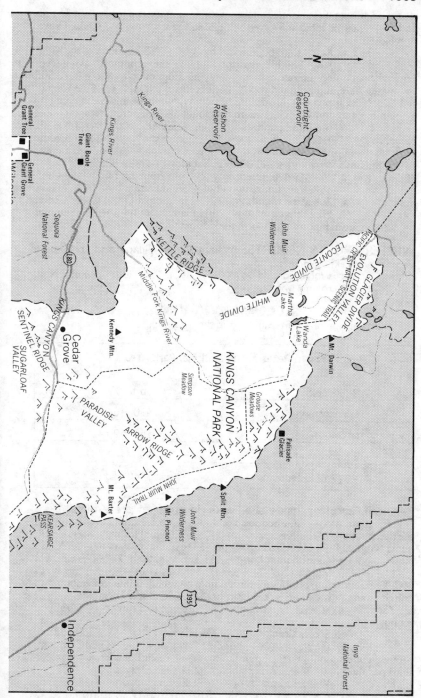

derful landscapes. For seasoned walkers with some mountain experience. Horses and mules may be hired at Wolverton Stables, Grant Grove, and Cedar Grove. Spectacular.

☀️🔍 **Kings Canyon,** reached by Calif. 180: The gorges of the Kings River South Fork display some of the most breathtaking scenery in the park: steep granite cliffs and dizzying drops of up to 8,216 ft. (2,505 m), frozen lakes, and giant redwoods. Their beauty is reminiscent of the Yosemite Valley (see Chapter 53). Road closed in winter. Not to be missed.

☀️🏛️ **Moro Rock,** 4 mi. (6 km) south of Giant Forest Village: One of the most impressive granite monoliths in the Sierra Nevada range, rising 2,080 ft. (1,300 m) above the banks of the Kaweah River Middle Fork. There's a path to the top, from which you'll have a fine all-around view of the mountains and the surrounding forest. Shouldn't be missed.

🏛️ **Muir Grove,** reached by footpath from Lost Grove on Calif. 198: Very fine redwood stand. A must-see.

🏛️ **Zumwalt Meadow,** reached by footpath from Cedar Grove: Huge alpine meadow, particularly beautiful when the summer wildflowers are in bloom. Well worth the side trip.

WINTER SPORTS RESORTS: 🔔 Giant Forest Village and Lodgepole:
Cross-country skiing; no lifts.

🔔 **Wolverton Ski Bowl** (565-3381): Three lifts: open mid-Nov. to mid-Apr.

ACCOMMODATIONS

See the listing of toll-free numbers in the Appendix.

Room Rates in the National Park Area	
B (Budget)	up to $30
I (Inexpensive)	$30–$60
M (Moderate)	$60–$90
E (Expensive)	$90–$140
VE (Very Expensive)	$140 and up

Personal Favorites Inside the Parks (in order of preference)

For reservations inside Sequoia and Kings Canyon National Parks, contact the **Reservations Manager,** Sequoia and Kings Canyon Hospitality Service, Sequoia National Park, CA 93262 (209/561-3314).

🛎️ **Giant Forest Lodge,** on Calif. 198, Giant Forest Village, CA 93262 (209/565-3314). 246 rms (half w. baths), no A/C. MC, V. Free parking, bicycles for rent, skiing, horseback riding, coffeeshop, bar, crib $4. *Note:* Rustic motel in the heart of the redwood forest; cottages w. basic comforts. So-so cafeteria. Some bungalows have open-air barbecues. Open year round. **I–M**

🛎️ **Stony Creek Lodge,** Generals Hwy., Sequoia National Park, CA 93262 (209/561-3314). 11 rms. no A/C. MC, V. Free parking, coffeeshop (open till 8 p.m.). *Note:* Small, rustic but relatively comfortable hotel deep in the forest. Acceptable cafeteria. Open May–Sept. only. **M**

🛎️ **Wilsonia Lodge,** on Calif. 180, Kings Canyon National Park, CA 93633 (209/335-2310). 51 rms (9 w. bath), no A/C.

MC, V. Free parking, coffeeshop (open till 8 p.m.), bar, grocery store, shower room. *Note:* Cottages and bungalows w. basic comforts; most have canvas roofs and no electricity. For lovers of the great outdoors. Open May-Oct. only. **I**

Personal Favorites Outside the Parks (in order of preference)

Best Western Holiday Lodge, on Calif. 198, Three Rivers, CA 93271 (209/561-4119; toll free, see Best Western). 47 rms, A/C, cable color TV. AE, CB, DC, MC, V. Free parking, pool, free coffee in rms, fishing; rest. half mi. away, crib $4. *Note:* Smart little motel looking out on the Kaweah River. Spacious rms w. balconies, some w. fireplaces and refrigerators. Inviting tree-shaded pool. Serviceable facilities; good value. 10 min. by car from the western entrance to the park. **I–M**

The River Inn, 45176 Sierra Dr. (Calif. 198), Three Rivers, CA 93271 (209/561-4367). 12 rms, A/C, cable color TV. MC, V. Free parking, adjoining cafeteria and grocery store. *Note:* Tiny motel overlooking the Kaweah River in a pretty, natural setting. Comfortable rms w. balconies and refrigerators. 15-min. drive from the western entrance to the park. **I**

Lazy J Ranch, 39625 Sierra Dr., Three Rivers, CA 93271 (209/561-4449). 18 rms, A/C, color TV, in-rm movies. AE, MC, V. Free parking, pool, free coffee in rms, adjoining cafeteria. *Note:* Small rustic cottages, some w. kitchenettes and refrigerators, on the Kaweah River. Only moderately comfortable, but well situated. 15-min. drive from the western entrance to the park. **I–M**

NEARBY EXCURSIONS

HANFORD (63 mi., 100 km, SW on Calif. 198): Founded in 1882 to house the immigrant Chinese working on the Southern Pacific Railroad, this was one of the country's largest Chinatowns in the 19th century. From its pioneer past there remain today only a few buildings around China Alley, scrupulously restored, including a Taoist temple and one of the most remarkable restaurants in the U.S.

Where to Eat

Imperial Dynasty, 2 China Alley, 7th and Green Sts. (209/582-0196). Dinner only, Tues.-Sun.; closed Mon. Run by the Wing family since 1883, this rest., whose food is a strange but wholly successful blend of French and Chinese traditions, is well worth going out of your way for. **I–M**

GHOST TOWNS: Mineral King and **Silver City,** on Mineral King Rd., reached by driving 3 mi. (4 km) north of Three Rivers on Calif. 198: The remains of two towns from gold-rush days; a stretch of the road is unsurfaced. Closed in winter.

FARTHER AFIELD

DEATH VALLEY NATIONAL PARK (362 mi., 580 km, east via Calif. 198, Calif. 65, Calif. 178, and Calif. 190): The distance is barely 87 mi. (140 km) as the crow flies, but almost 375 mi. (600 km) along the often spectacular roads through Sequoia National Forest and the Panamint Valley. Loveliest of American deserts; don't miss it. (See also Chapter 48 on Death Valley.)

YOSEMITE NATIONAL PARK (178 mi., 284 km, NW via Calif. 198, Calif. 180, and Calif. 41): One of the country's most beautiful national parks (see Chapter 53).

YOSEMITE NATIONAL PARK🌵🌵🌵

□ □ □

The surpassing beauty of Yosemite National Park should be seen for the first time in May or June, when the waterfalls, swollen by snowmelt, plunge dizzily out of the sky for hundreds of feet to the rocks below. Some, like **Yosemite Falls,** the world's second largest after Angel Falls in Venezuela, are as much as 2,425 ft. (739 m) from lip to basin—13 times as high as Niagara! In summer and fall the falls dry up, but you can still contemplate the grandeur of the million-year-old glacial **Yosemite Valley,** walled in by steep granite cliffs 5,000 ft (1,500 m) high. On the uplands, stands of giant redwoods and plateaus covered in flowery meadows contribute to a landscape whose unspoiled splendor may remind you of Yellowstone.

This huge wildlife reserve deep in the **Sierra Nevada** (naturalists have counted no fewer than 220 species of birds and 75 of mammals—including deer, wild goat, black bear, and coyote) draws more than three million visitors each summer. Because it's within relatively easy reach of San Francisco or Los Angeles, it has become one of California's most popular tourist attractions; in July and August the cars move nose-to-tail along its two main access roads. Yet until as late as 1851, when the Yosemite Gap was first discovered by the white soldiers of the Mariposa Battalion, this had been for 4½ millennia the secret kingdom of the Miwok Indians and their forebears. They called it Ahwahnee, "the deep grassy valley."

When you set eyes on the Yosemite Valley and the peaks of the **High Sierras** from the lookout at **Glacier Point,** or when you see **El Capitan,** a monolith 2½ times as high as the Rock of Gibraltar, whose lowering granitic mass forms a kind of natural fortress in a bend of the valley, you'll feel that scenery of this magnificence is enough to make the trip worthwhile in spite of the crowds of summer holidaymakers and weekenders.

Yosemite National Park (the name is a corruption of *U-zu-mate,* the Indian word for grizzly bear) is open year round.

BASIC FACTS: State of California. Area Code: 209. Time Zone: Pacific Time. Zip Code: 95389. Founded: 1890. Area: 1,190 sq. mi. (3,082 km²).

CLIMATE: As in most of the western national parks, spring and fall, both sunny but cool, are the best times for seeing Yosemite. Runoff from the snowmelt swells the waterfalls to their heaviest rate of flow in spring. Fall paints the forests in a splendor of glowing bronze. Summer is dry and reasonably warm, averaging 71°F (22°C), but if you come in summer you'll find too many other people who've had the same idea. In winter the snow can lie more than 13 ft. (4 m) deep, and daytime temperatures average 34°F (1°C). Cross-country skiers take note: information on snow conditions can be obtained by calling 209/372-1338.

DISTANCES: Las Vegas, 465 mi. (745 km); Los Angeles, 315 mi. (504 km); Reno, 177 mi. (283 km); San Francisco, 210 mi. (336 km).

ARRIVAL & TRANSIT INFORMATION

NEAREST AIRPORTS: The largest nearby is Fresno Municipal Airport (FAT), 97 mi. (156 km) SW. Other local airports include Merced Municipal Airport (MCE), 82 mi. (131 km) west; and Modesto Municipal Airport (MOD), 103 mi. (165 km) west.

AIRLINES (all at the Fresno airport): American (toll free 800/433-7300), Continental (456-1166), Delta (toll free 800/221-1212), and United (252-5711).

BUS OR CAR RENTAL?: Given the distances to be covered, and the attractive rates offered in California, the best solution is to rent a car with unlimited mileage.

CAR RENTAL (at the Fresno airport unless otherwise indicated): Avis (251-5001); Budget (251-5515); Hertz (251-5055); Hertz, Merced Municipal Airport (384-1627); and National (251-5577).

TRAIN: Nearest AMTRAK station is at 24th and K Sts., Merced (toll free 800/872-7245).

BUS: There is no regular bus service to Yosemite National Park. There are daily shuttle buses between Merced and Yosemite; for information and timetable, call YTS Bus Lines (722-0366); resv. are a must.

   The nearest Greyhound bus stations are at 1033 Broadway in Fresno (268-9461) and at 725 W. Main St. in Merced (722-2121).

INFORMATION & TOURS

TOURIST INFORMATION: Superintendent, **Yosemite National Park,** P.O. Box 577, CA 95389 (209/372-0200).

   There are **visitors centers** at Tuolumne Meadows (summer only) and Yosemite Village (year round).

   For information on one- to seven-day trips on foot or on horseback, and for reservations, call 209/252-4848. For information on activities in the park, call 209/372-4845. For weather and highway conditions, call 209/372-4605.

GUIDED TOURS: Golden Eagle Tours (airplane), Fresno Municipal Airport (255-8900): Flights over Yosemite National Park and the peaks of the High Sierras. Spectacular.

   Shuttle Bus: There is free shuttle-bus service in the valley, leaving from the visitors center at Yosemite Village (summer only).

   Yosemite Mountain–Sugar Pine Railroad (steam train), on Calif. 41 in Fish Camp, 4 mi. (6 km) south of the southern entrance to the park (209/683-7273): Beautiful ride across the Sierras on a little narrow-gauge railroad; amusing. Open daily mid-Apr. to mid-Oct.; closed the rest of the year (see The Narrow Gauge Inn under "Accommodations," below).

   Yosemite Transportation System (bus): Trips around the park, starting from The Ahwahnee in Yosemite Village (252-4848).

SIGHTS & ATTRACTIONS

SCENERY AND SIGHTS: ☀ ♨ **Waterfalls:** Most of these are in Yosemite Valley; they reach their most impressive proportions in the spring, dry up in the summer heat from mid-July to Aug., and revive with the first storms of autumn. The most spectacular are **Yosemite Falls,** with a total height of 2,425 ft (739 m) in three stages; **Bridal Veil Fall,** 620 ft (189 m); and **Nevada Fall,** 594 ft (181 m). One of the great beauties of nature which you should not miss.

☀ **Giant Sequoias Stands:** The finest is **Mariposa Grove,** near the southern entrance. It includes the 2,700-year-old Sequoia **Grizzly Giant,** 209 ft (64 m) high and 34 ft (11 m) in diameter. Worth the side trip.

☀ ♨ **Glacier Point,** 5 mi. (8 km) SE of Yosemite Village by (difficult) footpath, or 36 mi. (57 km) by road: Splendid panoramic view of the valley 3,254 ft (992 m) below, the waterfalls, and the peaks of the Sierra Nevada: **North Dome, Basket Dome, Mount Watkins, Half Dome,** and others. Hiking trail or vehicle road (open in summer only). The finest view in the park; shouldn't be missed.

☀ ♨ **Tuolumne Meadows,** 55 mi. (89 km) NE of Yosemite Village: Wonderful unspoiled grassland in a lovely mountain setting; a paradise for campers and hikers. Abundant wildlife including black bear and deer. Access road closed in winter. Well-known rock-climbing school (372-1244), open Oct.-May. Must definitely be seen.

☀ ♨ **Yosemite Valley,** west of Yosemite Village: Enclosed valley such as you might find in the Alps, about 8 mi. (13 km) long, coming to a dead end. Walled in by vertical granite cliffs 3,300 ft (1,000 m) high, over which, when the snow melts, tumble dizzying waterfalls. Most impressive is **El Capitan,** a 3,591-ft (1,095-m) monolith, the dream (or nightmare) of every rock climber. It's worth coming to the park just to see this spectacular valley; now that you're here, don't miss it.

WINTER SPORTS RESORTS: ♨ **Badger Pass Ski Area,** 21 mi. (33 km) south of Yosemite Village via Calif. 41 and Glacier Point Rd. (372-1330): Five lifts; cross-country skiing. Open late Nov. to mid-Apr.

♨ **Yosemite Valley:** Cross-country skiing only; late Nov. to mid-Apr. For a **recording** giving snow conditions, call 372-1338.

OTHER FROMMER TRAVEL GUIDES: *Dollarwise USA* complements 13 other Dollarwise Guides and 3 $-A-Day Guides dealing with individual U.S. states and areas: *Dollarwise Alaska, Dollarwise Florida, Dollarwise New York State, Dollarwise California & Las Vegas, Dollarwise Texas, Dollarwise Cruises, Dollarwise Mid-Atlantic States, Dollarwise New England, Dollarwise South-Atlantic States, Dollarwise Northwest, Dollarwise Southwest, Hawaii on $50 a Day, New York on $50 a Day,* and *Washington, D.C., & Historic Virginia on $40 a Day.*

In contrast to the book you are now reading, which highlights 57 U.S. cities and scenic areas, each of the above guides treats one particular state or area in the fullest detail, setting forth scores of hotel, restaurant, and sightseeing suggestions. Frommer travel guides can be obtained at most bookstores, or by mailing the appropriate amount (turn to the last few pages in this guide) to Frommer Books, Prentice Hall Trade Division, One Gulf + Western Plaza, New York, NY 10023.

ACCOMMODATIONS

See the listing of toll-free numbers in the Appendix.

Room Rates in the Yosemite National Park Area	
B (Budget)	up to $30
I (Inexpensive)	$30–$60
M (Moderate)	$60–$90
E (Expensive)	$90–$140
VE (Very Expensive)	$140 and up

Personal Favorites Inside the Park (in order of preference)

To make reservations at the four following hotels, contact the **Yosemite Park and Curry Co.,** Yosemite National Park, CA 95389 (209/252-4848).

Unless the contrary is specifically indicated, none of the following hotels is air-conditioned.

☀☟♨♨ **The Ahwahnee,** on Calif. 140 in Yosemite Village, Yosemite National Park, CA 95389 (209/252-4848). 121 rms, some w. A/C, some w. color TV. AE, CB, DC, MC, V. Free parking, pool, two tennis courts, horseback riding, bicycling, rest. (resv. required), bar, rm svce, nightclub, crib $5. *Note:* Luxurious 1920s hotel built like a fortress, w. stone walls and exposed beams. Huge, comfortable rms, some w. fireplaces and balconies; also 24 rms in adjoining cottages. The interior is rustic but elegant. Rest. so-so (jkt required at dinner) w. wonderful views of the surrounding peaks. Offhand svce. Noisy and crowded in summer. Open year round. Among the celebrities who have stayed here over the years: Herbert Hoover, John F. Kennedy, Walt Disney, Queen Elizabeth II and the Duke of Edinburgh, Sir Winston Churchill, and Gertrude Stein. Resv. a must, a very long way ahead, especially in summer. **VE**

☀☟♨♨ **Wawona Hotel,** on Calif. 41, Yosemite National Park, CA 95389 (209/252-4848). 105 rms (a third w. baths), color TV in bar. AE, CB, DC, MC, V. Free parking, pool, golf course, tennis court, horseback riding, rest. (resv. indispensable), bar. *Note:* Charming old hotel in the Victorian style dating from 1856 in a beautiful country setting. Deer roam freely across the lawn. The rms provide only rather primitive comforts; cheerful reception and svce; good rest. Stagecoach rides in the countryside around. The favorite hotel of those in-the-know. Open Apr.-Nov.; a 40-min. drive from Yosemite Village. **I–M**

♨ **Yosemite Lodge,** at the intersection of Calif. 140 and Calif. 41, Yosemite National Park, CA 95389 (209/252-4848). 484 rms (75% w. baths), 179 bungalows (half w. baths). AE, CB, DC, MC, V. Free parking, pool, horseback riding, bicycling, rest., coffeeshop, bar, crib $5. *Note:* Relatively modern motel surrounded by very rustic bungalows; comforts are rudimentary but there's a fine view out over the valley. Overrun in summer. Nonexistent svce. Open year round. **M (in lodge); I (in bungalows)**

♨ **Curry Village Motel,** at the intersection of Calif. 140 and Calif. 41, Yosemite National Park, CA 95389 (209/252-4848). 190 rms and bungalows (only half w. baths), and 420 tents. AE, DC, MC, V. Free parking, pool, skating, bicycling, horseback riding, coffeeshop, bar, camping facilities, crib $5. *Note:* Motel and bungalows are functionally comfort-

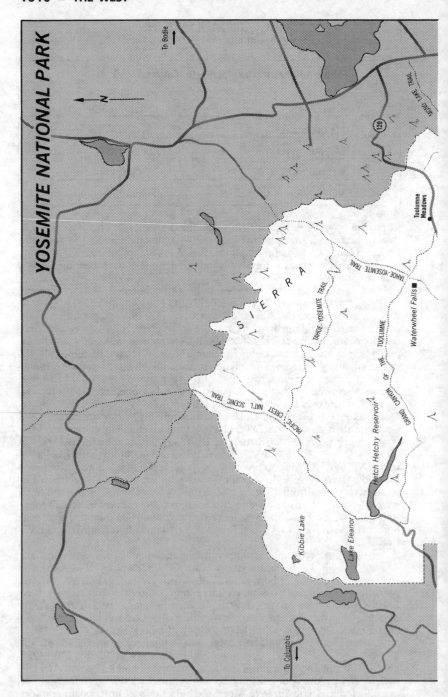

YOSEMITE NATIONAL PARK

To Bodie

N

120

Tuolumne Meadows

MONO LAKE TRAIL

S I E R R A

TAHOE-YOSEMITE TRAIL

TAHOE-YOSEMITE TRAIL

Waterwheel Falls

GRAND CANYON OF THE TUOLUMNE

PACIFIC CREST NAT'L SCENIC TRAIL

Hetch Hetchy Reservoir

Lake Eleanor

Kibbie Lake

To Columbia

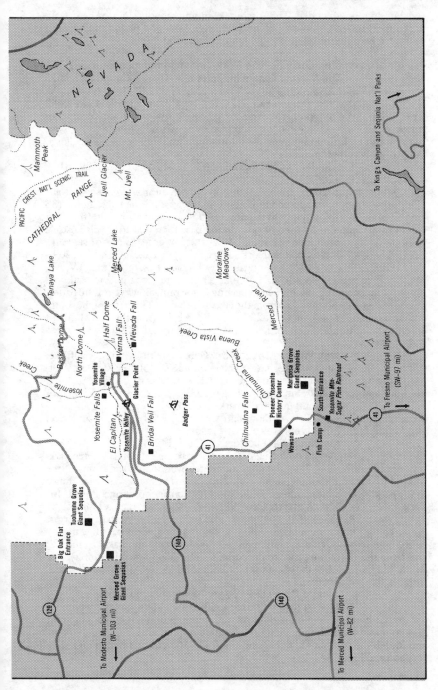

able but no more than that. The Yosemite climbing school is located here. Rafting trips organized in summer. Nonexistent svce. For open-air enthusiasts; open Mar.-Oct. **I–M (in motel or bungalows); B (in tents)**

Personal Favorites Outside the Park (in order of preference)

☀☇♨♨ **The Narrow Gauge Inn,** on Calif. 41, Fish Camp, CA 93623 (209/683-7720). 27 rms, color TV. AE, CB, DC, MC, V. Free parking, pool, rest., bar, rm svce, crib $6. *Note:* Charming little alpine chalet 4 mi. (6 km) from the southern entrance to the park; rms w. private balconies or patios and fine mountain view. Very acceptable rest.; friendly reception and svce. Excursions in a little steam train; for information, call 209/683-7273. Closed Jan. to mid-Mar. **I–M**

♨♨ **Boulder Lodge,** on Calif. 158, June Lake, CA 93529 (619/648-7533). 60 rms, cable color TV. AE, MC, V. Free parking, pool, sauna, tennis court, fishing, skiing in winter, nearby coffeeshop. *Note:* Comfortable motel, with less comfortable bungalows, on June Lake, 22 mi. (35 km) SE of the eastern entrance to the park via U.S. 395 and Calif. 120 (the latter closed in winter). Friendly reception. A good base for a visit to Devils Postpile National Monument. Open year round. **I–M, but lower rates out of season**

☀☇♨♨ **Pines Chalets,** North Shore Rd., Bass Lake, CA 93604 (209/642-3121). 84 bungalows w. kitchenettes, cable color TV. AE, MC, V. Free parking, beach, health club, tennis court, boating, waterskiing, nearby coffeeshop, bar, disco. *Note:* Engaging frame bungalows w. private patios, some w. fireplaces, an easy walk from the lake. It's 18 mi. (28 km) from the southern entrance to the park via Calif. 222 and Calif. 41, far from the hurly-burly of Yosemite's vacationers; ideal for families. Open year round. **E, but lower rates out of season**

♨ **Best Western Yosemite Gateway Inn,** 40530 Calif. 41, Oakhurst, CA 93644 (209/683-2378; toll free, see Best Western). 52 rms, A/C, color TV, in-rm movies. AE, CB, DC, MC, V. Free parking, pool, adjoining rest. *Note:* Small, appealing motel deep in the woods, 15 mi. (24 km) from the southern entrance to the park on Calif. 41. Very comfortable rms, some w. kitchenettes, most w. mountain views. Cheerful reception and svce; good value. **I–M, but lower rates out of season**

♨ **Yosemite View Lodge,** on Calif. 140, El Portal, CA 95318 (209/379-2681). 65 rms, cable color TV. MC, V. Free parking, nearby coffeeshop. *Note:* Small rustic motel overlooking the rapids of the Merced River (ask for a rm w. river view), 2 mi. (3 km) from the western entrance to the park. Acceptable comforts; some rms w. balconies and refrigerators. **I–M**

♨ **Best Western Lake View,** 30 Main St., Lee Vinning, CA 93541 (619/647-6543; toll free, see Best Western). 45 rms, A/C, color TV, in-rm movies. AE, CB, DC, MC, V. Free parking, nearby coffeeshop, crib $5. *Note:* Typical small motel very near Mono Lake, 14 mi. (22 km) from the eastern entrance to the park on Calif. 120 (closed in winter), and 21 mi. (33 km) south of the ghost town of Bodie on U.S. 395. Functionally comfortable; free coffee in rms. **I**

♨ **Ducey's Bass Lake Lodge,** North Shore Rd., Bass Lake, CA 93604 (209/642-3131). 40 rms and bungalows (two-thirds without baths). MC, V. Free parking, private beach, boating, rest., bar, disco (in season). *Note:* Modest, unpretentious motel 18 mi. (28 km) from the southern entrance to the park via Calif. 222 and Calif. 41. Attractively situated on a lake; very acceptable rest. **M**

RESTAURANTS

Yosemite National Park Area Restaurant Prices (per person, excluding drinks and service charges)	
B (Budget)	up to $15
I (Inexpensive)	$15–$25
M (Moderate)	$25–$40
E (Expensive)	$40–$60
VE (Very Expensive)	$60 and up

Personal Favorites (in order of preference)

☼ ♈♈♈ **Erna's Elderberry House,** Victoria Lane at Calif. 41, Oakhurst (683-6800). A/C. Lunch Wed.-Fri., dinner Wed.-Mon., brunch Sun.; closed Tues. MC. Jkt. *Specialties:* Brie-and-artichoke quiche, curried lamb w. celeriac, broiled salmon w. basil butter and tomato purée; remarkable desserts; menu changes regularly. Very good wine list but no hard liquor. *Note:* Some of the best food in California is to be found in this remote little village, nestling in the foothills of the Sierra Nevada some 15 miles from the southern entrance to Yosemite National Park. Chefs Erna Kubin and Fernando Madrigal serve up a wonderful, light, creative cuisine at very attractive prices. Their six-course dinners are a feast for the eye as well as the palate. Elegant Provençal décor; open-air terrace in good weather. Flawless svce. A very fine place—and since a lot of people agree, you should definitely reserve ahead. *French-continental.* **I–M**

♈♈ **The Narrow Gauge Inn,** in the Narrow Gauge Inn (see "Accommodations," above) (683-6446). A/C. Breakfast/lunch/dinner daily (Thurs.-Sat. only from mid-Nov. through Dec.); closed Jan.-Mar. and early Nov. AE, CB, DC, MC, V. *Specialties:* broiled steak and fresh seafood, homemade desserts. *Note:* Chalet-style rest. w. good mountain views. Acceptable but unimaginative food. Rustic décor w. open-air terrace in summer and inviting fireplace in winter. Friendly reception and svce. Good value; resv. advised in summer. *Seafood-American.* **B–I**

♈♈ **Wagon Wheel,** Calif. 140 at 7th St., Mariposa (966-2366). A/C. Dinner only Wed.-Sun.; closed Mon., Tues., and Dec. 25. MC, V. *Specialties:* beef en brochette, steak, catch of the day. *Note:* Engaging little rest. 30 mi. (48 km) from the main entrance to the park. Honest, tasty food; good svce; good value. *Steak-seafood.* **I**

NEARBY EXCURSIONS

☼ ⚱ **BODIE** (96 mi., 153 km, east of Yosemite Village via Calif. 140W, Calif. 120E, U.S. 395N, and Calif. 270E: This old gold prospectors' town had 10,000 inhabitants in 1880 and enjoyed an unhappy celebrity for its violence—seven shoot-outs a week on average. It was destroyed by two great fires, in 1892 and 1932. There remain some interesting survivals, including the church, the school, and the prison; there's also a little museum. Interesting. *Note:* The last 3 mi. (5 km), by unsurfaced road, are impassable in winter.

On the way, visit the large saltwater **Mono Lake** on Calif. 120 (closed in winter), now a refuge for waterfowl; worth seeing.

☼ ⚱ **COLUMBIA** (80 mi., 128 km, NW of Yosemite Village via Calif. 140W, Calif. 120W, and Calif. 49N): One of the best-preserved ghost towns in California. Museums, workshops, and many restored buildings including the picturesque **State Driver's Retreat Saloon,** the **What Cheer Saloon,** and the **City Hotel.** It's certifiably in period, just the way it was in the palmy days of the gold rush.

On the way, take a look at **Sonora,** a place of importance in the Westward Expansion; it's well worth the side trip.

Where to Stay

☼ **City Hotel,** Main St., Columbia, CA 95310 (209/532-1479). 9 rms. AE, MC, V. An Old West period hotel. **M**

NATIONAL PARKS IN THE VICINITY

☼ ⚱ **DEVIL'S POSTPILE NATIONAL MONUMENT** (98 mi., 156 km, SE of Yosemite Village via Calif. 140W, Calif. 120E, U.S. 395S, and Calif. 203W): An unusual sight: hundreds of bluish basalt shafts, 50–60 ft (16–18 m) high and perhaps 100,000 years old, which look like the torn-up pages of a book. All this is set against a luxuriant backdrop of forests, mountain streams, hot springs, and lava flows. Spectacular. Park open mid-June through Oct.; well worth the side trip. *Note:* Calif. 120 is closed in winter.

For **information,** contact the Ranger Station, P.O. Box 501, Mammoth Lakes, CA 93546 (619/934-2289 mid-June through Oct., 209/565-3341 the rest of the year).

☼ ⚱ **SEQUOIA AND KINGS CANYON NATIONAL PARKS** (178 mi., 284 km, SE of Yosemite Village via Calif. 41 and Calif. 180): Forests of giant sequoias and majestic granite crests; not to be missed. See Chapter 52 on Sequoia National Park.

CHAPTER 54

LOS ANGELES

□ □ □

With Hollywood, Disneyland, and Palm Springs

The first great U.S. city designed and built in the Automobile Age, Los Angeles has become a prototype of the modern American metropolis. It consists of a group of distinct urban areas, often a long way apart, which lie like the rim of a wheel around the center city hub, here reduced to its lowest common denominator. The scale of Los Angeles—90 mi. (145 km) long by 50 mi. (80 km) wide— defies belief. Around it lie the suburbs, each of which amounts to a miniature city, from **Glendale, Van Nuys,** and the foothills of the **San Gabriel Mountains** on the north to **Anaheim, Costa Mesa,** and **Long Beach** on the south; from **Ontario** and **Pasadena** on the east to **Santa Monica, Redondo Beach,** and the shores of the Pacific on the west. This vibrant, sprawling city is surpassed only by New York in population, and only by Jacksonville, Florida, in area; at 464 sq. mi. (1,202 km²) it's about half the size of the state of Rhode Island.

A sign of the times: the TV giants, ABC, CBS, and NBC, have ousted the movie studios from Hollywood, the former capital of "the seventh lively art." The run-down slum areas of **Watts** lie a short distance from the daring office skyscrapers of **Bunker Hill** and the twin 52-story towers of **Atlantic Richfield Plaza.** The huge arena of the **Memorial Coliseum,** where the Olympic Games were held in 1932 and 1984, sits cheek-by-jowl with the fairy kingdom of **Disneyland.** The fashionable restaurants of **Sunset Boulevard**—a name dear to all movie addicts—and the plush homes of **Bel Air,** with their azure-blue pools and manicured lawns, coexist with futurist factory buildings or the famous **Stack,** a giant four-level traffic interchange not far from the **Music Center.** Bohemian **Venice,** with its colorful population of roller-skaters, and **South-Central L.A.,** where cocaine wars rage among the teenage gangs, are hardly a half hour's drive from the millionaires' boutiques of **Beverly Hills** or the new business district of **Century City.**

The ever-choked freeways—L.A. is linked by more than 687 mi. (1,100 km) of urban highways—and the oilwells in the heart of the city are parts of its urban landscape, as are the surf on the beaches, the interminable tracts of small suburban houses, the intrusive areas of wasteland, and the purple-colored smog, the city's tribute to the internal-combustion engine. Because of the city's sheer size, its residents ("Angelenos") spend twice as much time every day in their cars as anyone else on the face of the earth. As a result, there are by now innumerable drive-in banks, drive-in restaurants, drive-in movie theaters, and even drive-in churches.

El Pueblo de Nuestra Señora la Reina de Los Angeles de Porciúncula (The Town of Our Lady of Porciúncula, Queen of the Angels)—Los Angeles for short —was founded in 1781 by Don Felipe de Neve, governor of Spanish California;

the site had been explored as early as 1542 by the Portuguese-born navigator, Juan Rodriguez Cabrillo. The California gold rush of 1849 inaugurated a period of rapid growth, further accelerated by the completion of the Southern Pacific's transcontinental railroad in 1876 and the first oil discoveries in 1892. In half a century the city's population grew 2,600%, from 50,000 in 1890 to 320,000 in 1910 and 1,500,000 in 1940. Today this huge urban nebula numbers, with its outlying communities, almost 13 million inhabitants, including at least 2 million "Chicanos" of Mexican origin, and is oriented toward the cutting edge of industry—electronics, aviation, petrochemicals, printing, publishing, tourism, television, movies (more than three-quarters of those made in the U.S.)—but also banking and insurance, to the point where Los Angeles threatens to supersede San Francisco as New York's financial counterpart on the West Coast.

Whether you see it as a dream factory that nurtured the fantasies of generations of Hollywood buffs, or as a nightmare city prefiguring the 21st-century megalopolis, Los Angeles induces in everyone a strange feeling that anything can happen at any moment (a favorite formula of Angeleno Raymond Chandler's fictional detective Philip Marlowe). The city, first of all and most of all, is a patchwork of exotic races and colors: the Far Eastern neighborhoods of **Chinatown, Little Tokyo,** and **Koreatown,** the Mexican stretch along **Olvera Street,** the black slums of **Watts** or the "Latino" ghettos of **East Los Angeles** and **Boyle Heights**—all teeming with tens of thousands of illegal immigrants whose mere presence poses an insoluble problem. The authorities readily admit that if they could, by some extraordinary chance, flush out all these illegals and escort them back to the U.S. border, half the city's restaurants and other businesses would be forced to close their doors for want of unskilled labor.

Angelenos, more relaxed and approachable than the people of the great eastern seaboard cities, emphatically affirm that Los Angeles is principally a state of mind, the so-called mellow way of life, which is special in being "cooler" and more harmonious. True, one humorist has defined the place as "a bunch of suburbs in search of a city," but in spite of its enormous size Los Angeles is truly a whole, and a unique one. **Sepulveda Boulevard,** for example, stretches unbroken for 45 mi. (72 km). In the absence of decent public transportation this city's traffic assumes nightmare proportions every rush hour on the urban highways so misleadingly referred to as "freeways." The interchange between the Harbor and Santa Monica Freeways (I-10 and Cal. 110), in the heart of Los Angeles, holds the world record for traffic density, with peaks of 480,000 vehicles a day. Another, even less enviable record: the country's highest concentration of carbon monoxide pollutants from internal-combustion engines.

After nurturing for many years a cultural inferiority complex toward New York, the U.S. capital of movies, TV, and show business has for more than a decade been living through an intellectual boom—artistic (music, ballet, cinema, architecture, graphic arts), scientific, and cultural. Witness its 35 museums, including the brand-new and spectacular **MOCA** (Museum of Contemporary Art), its hundred or so theaters, 29 symphony and chamber orchestras, 17 theater and opera companies, and 36 ballet companies, some of world class. On the scientific side, thanks to its famous universities and research institutes such as **UCLA, Loyola University, CalTech,** and the **Jet Propulsion Laboratory,** Los Angeles can pride itself on the world's highest concentration of Nobel laureates.

The economic and cultural capital of the West Coast has been called (not without reason) "dynamic," "fascinating," "inhuman"; it may seduce you or shock you, according to your taste. Only one thing is for sure: the visitor who encounters this enormous and sometimes disturbing city for the first time will not soon forget it. In spite of its TV and film portraits, it's relatively safe: FBI statistics rank it 15th among American cities for crime (but first for rape).

Among the city's famous children are President Richard M. Nixon (who was born in the nearby suburb of Yorba Linda), the late Democratic presidential candidate Adlai Stevenson, the sculptor Isamu Noguchi, the late Chief Justice (and former California governor) Earl Warren (who presided over the commission of inquiry on the assassination of President Kennedy), the actresses Marilyn Monroe, Liza Minnelli, Candice Bergen, and Mia Farrow, and the actors Robert Redford, Dustin Hoffman, and Ryan O'Neal.

BASIC FACTS: State of California. Area Codes: 213 (Los Angeles); 818 (San Fernando Valley, Burbank, and Glendale); 714 (Anaheim). Time Zone: Pacific Time (3 hrs behind New York). ZIP Code: 90053. Founded: 1781. Approximate population: city, 3,450,000 (second largest in the U.S.); metropolitan area, 8,260,000 (also second largest), including 150,000 Chinese, 160,000 Japanese, 200,000 Koreans, 950,000 Chicanos of Mexican origin (the official figure, probably understated by 50%), 350,000 Salvadorans, and 60,000 Guatemalans.

CLIMATE: Before the coming of the automobile, Los Angeles had one of the most pleasant climates on the West Coast, dry and sunny, with a mild and rainy winter (lows of 50°F, 10°C), a very tolerable summer averaging 75°F (24°C), in spite of 95°F (35°C) peaks when the hot Santa Ana wind blows out of the desert, and a glorious spring and fall. The smog has ruined everything. Given windless weather and auto pollution, when smog clamps down on the center city and the San Fernando Valley basin, whole districts disappear in the thick, corrosive murk, which sometimes lingers for a full week, especially in summer.

DISTANCES: Denver, 1,059 mi. (1,695 km); Las Vegas, 282 mi. (451 km); Phoenix, 390 mi. (625 km); San Diego, 125 mi. (200 km); San Francisco, 381 mi. (610 km).

ARRIVAL & TRANSIT INFORMATION

Note: Given the sheer size of Los Angeles, the concepts of "downtown" and "suburb" lose all meaning. The places, museums, and monuments referred to below are classified by *districts:* Downtown, Hollywood, Beverly Hills, Santa Monica, etc. Unless otherwise indicated, all phone numbers in this chapter are in area code 213.

AIRPORTS: Los Angeles International Airport (LAX), 17 mi. (27 km) SW. Fourth-largest airport in the world by volume of traffic, handling 41 million passengers a year. Information: 646-5252.

Regional airports include: **Hollywood-Burbank Airport** (BUR), 15 mi. (24 km) NW; **Long Beach Municipal Airport** (LGB), 21 mi. (33 km) SE; **Ontario International Airport** (ONT), 50 mi. (80 km) east; and **Orange County–John Wayne Airport** (SNA), 30 mi. (48 km) SE.

U.S. AIRLINES: Alaska (628-2100), American (935-6045), America West (746-6400), Braniff (toll free 800/272-6433), Continental (772-6000), Delta (386-5510), Eastern (380-2070), Northwest (380-1511), Pan Am (toll free 800/221-1111), Southwest (485-1221), TWA (484-2244), United (772-2121), USAir (toll free 800/428-4322).

FOREIGN CARRIERS: Air Canada (toll free 800/422-6232), Air New Zealand (642-0196), British Airways (toll free 800/247-9297), Canadian (toll free 800/426-7000), Qantas (toll free 800/227-4500), UTA (toll free 800/282-4484).

CITY LINK: The **cab** fare from Los Angeles International to dwntwn is about

$28; to Beverly Hills, $24; to Hollywood, $30; to Santa Monica, about $15. Time, depending on destination and time of day, 35 to 65 min.

Airport bus: Airport Service (778-3141) leaves every 30 min., serving the Greyhound Bus Terminal and the principal hotels dwntwn, in Hollywood, and in Beverly Hills; fare, $7; time, 45 min. to 1 hr 20 min. Super Shuttle (338-1111 or toll free 800/554-6458) provides door-to-door service to any L.A. destination. Fare: $11.

Cabs are expensive, and often impossible to find away from the big hotels. Public transportation is sadly lacking—not even one subway line. For information on the **public bus** service, call RTD (626-4455).

The only solution that makes sense is to rent a car; rates with unlimited mileage in California are among the best in the country.

CAR RENTAL (all at Los Angeles International Airport unless otherwise noted): Avis (646-5600); Budget (645-4500); Dollar (645-9333); Hertz (646-4861); National (670-4950); Rent-A-Wreck, 12333 W. Pico Blvd., Santa Monica (478-0676), offering older cars in good shape at unbeatable rates; Thrifty (645-1880). For dwntwn locations, consult the local telephone directories.

LIMOUSINE SERVICES: American Limousine Service (275-5427), Carey Limousine (275-4153), Royal Coach Livery (toll free 800/423-5288), Scripps Edward Limousine (toll free 800/223-6710), White Tie (553-6060).

TAXIS: Cabs may be hailed on the street, taken from the stands outside the major hotels, or summoned by phone. Drivers do not have a reputation for good service. Recommended companies: Checker (481-1234), Independent (653-5050), Los Angeles Taxi (627-7000), Red Top (988-8515).

TRAIN: AMTRAK, Union Terminal, 800 N. Alameda St., dwntwn (624-0171). An ill-reputed district, dangerous at night.

BUS: Greyhound, 6th and Los Angeles Sts., dwntwn (620-1200).

INFORMATION & TOURS

TOURIST INFORMATION: The **Automobile Club of Southern California,** dwntwn at 2601 S. Figueroa St., CA 90007 (213/741-4070): Practical information for motorists, maps. Fine Colonial building.

Greater Los Angeles Visitors and Convention Bureau, 515 S. Figueroa St., 11th floor, CA 90071 (213/624-7300). Accepts only written requests for information.

Visitors Information Center, in the basement of ARCO Plaza (dwntwn), CA 90071 (213/689-8822): Information on Los Angeles and the metropolitan area; multilingual hostesses. Other location: Hollywood Blvd. at Highland Ave., Hollywood.

GUIDED TOURS: **Burbank Studios Tours,** 4000 Warner Blvd., Burbank (818/985-6000): Tour on foot and by minibus through the movie and TV studios of Warner Bros. and Columbia Pictures. You can watch the shooting of a movie or a TV show being taped. Resv. must be made well ahead. Highly recommended to movie buffs, but exhausting. No movie or still cameras or tape recorders allowed. Price: $20.

Gray Line Tours (bus), 1207 W. 3rd St., dwntwn (213/481-2121): Guided tours of the city; serves principal hotels.

Hollywood Fantasy Tours (bus), 1721 N. Highland Ave., Hollywood

(213/326-8279): Guided tour of the neighborhoods where the movie stars live and other attractions.

Hollywood on Location, 8644 Wilshire Blvd., Beverly Hills (213/659-9165): For movie addicts; maintains an up-to-date schedule of movies currently in production, with practical advice on how to watch.

Mardigras/Buccaneer Cruises (boat), Ports O'Call Village, Harbor Blvd., San Pedro (213/548-1085): One-hour mini-cruises around the Port of Los Angeles and Long Beach. Also dinner cruises. Year round.

Industrial Tours

Lawry's California Center, 570 W. Ave. 26, Los Angeles (225-2491): If you like Lawry's seasonings and food products you won't want to miss the 45-min. conducted tour, which takes in the kitchens where new recipes are tested, and the manufacturing plant (Mon.-Fri.). There are food stores and pleasant restaurants. Open daily year round for lunch, and nightly May-Oct., for dinner. All this stands among very lovely gardens.

SIGHTS, ATTRACTIONS, & ACTIVITIES

ARCHITECTURAL HIGHLIGHTS: 🔔 **Capitol Records,** 1750 Vine St., Hollywood: Amusing structure, shaped like a stack of records, concept of the composer Johnny Mercer and his associate Nat King Cole. No visits, but worth seeing.

🔔 **Civic Center,** between Sunset Blvd., Grand Ave., and 1st St., dwntwn: The administrative center of Los Angeles, comprising **City Hall** (1928), the **Music Center** (see below), and the **Police Building.** Fountains, gardens, interesting modern architecture. Worth seeing.

🔔 **Coca-Cola Bottling Co.,** 1334 S. Central Ave., dwntwn: 1935 bottling plant disguised as an art deco steamboat; a triumph of California kitsch by architect Robert Derrah. No visits but worth a look.

🔔 **Los Angeles Memorial Coliseum,** 3911 S. Figueroa St., dwntwn (747-7111): Built for the 1932 Olympics, this magnificent art deco stadium, with a capacity of 102,000, was completely renovated for the 1984 Olympics. Between times, it houses the home football games of the L.A. Raiders, rodeos, pop concerts, motocross races, etc. Open daily; worth seeing.

🔔 **Los Angeles Times,** 202 W. 1st St., dwntwn (972-5757): Fascinating guided tour of California's largest newspaper, with the fourth-biggest circulation in the country. The sight of the huge news room is worth the trip by itself. Open Mon.-Fri.

☀️🔔 **Music Center,** 135 N. Grand Ave., dwntwn (972-7438): Built in 1964, this is the Los Angeles equivalent of New York's Lincoln Center or Washington's Kennedy Center. Three futurist-looking concert halls—the **Dorothy Chandler Pavilion,** the **Ahmanson Theater,** and the **Mark Taper Forum**—frame a marble plaza with a vast pool and an impressive sculpture by Jacques Lipchitz entitled *Peace on Earth*. Every year the Oscar award ceremony is held here. Open Mon.-Tues. and Thur.-Sat. Must be seen.

🔔 **Pacific Design Center,** 8687 Melrose Ave., West Hollywood (657-0800): Nicknamed "the blue whale," this amazing 1975 tinted-glass building houses showrooms of home furnishings manufacturers. Designed by Cesar Pelli. A sight not to be missed.

🔔 **The "Stack,"** U.S. 110 and U.S. 101, dwntwn: Four-level highway interchange near the Civic Center. Spectacular.

    Tail o' the Pup, 329 N. San Vicente Blvd., West Hollywood (213/652-4517): Bar shaped like a giant hot dog, one of the few surviving relics of California pop architecture. Amusing.

    Union Station, 800 N. Alameda St., dwntwn (624-0171): The city's central station is a magnificent 1939 example of the Hollywood-Spanish style; more than 65 movies have been shot here. Worth seeing, but avoid the neighborhood after dark.

    University of California–Los Angeles (UCLA), 405 Hilgard Ave., Westwood (206-8147): Founded in 1919, the local campus of the University of California moved to its present site in 1929. With 34,000 students it's the state's largest. Among the many points of interest on the huge 410-acre campus are: a very lovely botanic garden with modern sculpture, including works of Matisse and Noguchi; **Schoenberg Hall,** named in memory of the Austrian composer who taught here in the '30s and '40s; and above all the **Wight Art Gallery** (see "Museums of Art," below). Campus open daily.

    Westin Bonaventure Hotel, 404 S. Figueroa St., dwntwn (624-1000): Five huge cylindrical glass towers built in 1976 to the design of architect John Portman. This is Los Angeles' most famous building, and a must for the visitor.

BEACHES: Corona del Mar State Beach, 42 mi. (67 km) SE: One of the most beautiful beaches around Los Angeles, perfect for swimmers.

    Huntington Beach, 36 mi. (58 km) SE: The surfers' paradise; the sport began here in 1907, and the U.S. Championships are held here every year. On the beach is a monument to the Unknown Surfer.

    Laguna Beach, 48 mi. (76 km) SE: The favorite beach for artists and yuppies, reached by a magnificent coastal road from Newport Beach.

    Long Beach, 22 mi. (35 km) S: One of the most popular beaches in the Los Angeles area.

    Malibu, 19 mi. (30 km) West: One of the region's most beautiful, particularly **Malibu Surfrider State Beach,** but with big waves. For experienced surfers.

    Manhattan Beach, 18 mi. (29 km) SW: Agreeable, relatively uncrowded beach, popular with teenagers.

    Santa Monica, 15 mi. (24 km) West: Huge, very popular beach with a picturesque pier and amusement park, somewhat damaged by a tornado.

    Sunset Beach, 33 mi. (54 km) SE: The favorite beach of professional surfers.

    Venice, 16 mi. (26 km) SW: The kingdom of the roller-skaters. "Pop" and amusing by day; riskier after dark. Also popular with bodybuilders (**"Muscle Beach"**).

    Zuma Beach, 25 mi. (40 km) west: The nudists' beach, with great surf.

BROADCASTING AND MOVIE STUDIOS: ABC, 4151 Prospect Ave., Hollywood (557-4396): Tapings of TV shows, open to the public. Tickets must be applied for one or two days in advance. Open daily.

    CBS, 7800 Beverly Blvd., Los Angeles (852-2624): Tapings of TV shows, open to the public. Tickets must be applied for one or two days in advance. Open daily.

    NBC, 3000 W. Alameda Blvd., Burbank (840-3657): The country's largest TV studio. Taping of TV shows, open to the public. Tickets must be applied for one or two days in advance. Also, conducted tour of the studios. Open daily.

Paramount, Bronson and Melrose Aves., Hollywood: The wrought-iron entrance gates were made famous by the movie *Sunset Boulevard*. For movie addicts. No admission to the studio.

☀&& **Universal Studios Tour,** 3900 Lankershim Blvd., Universal City (818/508-9600): A kind of theme park dedicated to the Seventh Art; offers two-hour conducted mini-train tours behind the scenes of Hollywood's largest movie studio. From the *Star Wars* style of attack from outer space through the collapsing railroad bridge, the *Ten Commandments* passage of the Red Sea, the devouring Great White shark from *Jaws,* or the exploits of *King Kong* on the streets of New York to the duel between *Conan the Barbarian* and the giant dragon, nothing, or almost nothing, is spared the sensation-seeking visitor. Kitsch and crowded, but amusing; it draws three million people a year. Open daily except Thanksgiving and Dec. 25. Admission: $17.

CHURCHES/SYNAGOGUES: ☀ && **Crystal Cathedral,** 12141 Lewis St., Garden Grove, 28 mi. (45 km) SE on I-5 (714/971-4013): Philip Johnson's star-shaped, beveled-glass, 3,000-seat church-auditorium, the most modern in the U.S. A spectacular sight, 10 min. by car from Disneyland. Open daily; worth the side trip.

& **Drive-In Church,** 4201 Chapman Ave., Garden Grove: Old drive-in church from the 1950s, a spectacular design by Richard Neutra, one of the progenitors of modern California architecture. Very near the Crystal Cathedral (see above). Worth a look.

& **Wayfarer's Chapel,** 5755 W. Palos Verdes Dr., Rancho Palos Verdes (377-1650): Designed by Lloyd Wright, architect son of the great Frank Lloyd Wright, this splendid 1949 glass-and-sequoia-wood chapel overlooks the Pacific. Open to all denominations. An absolute must-see. Open daily.

HISTORIC BUILDINGS: && **Bradbury Building,** 3rd St. at Broadway, dwntwn (489-1411): One of the country's few office buildings designated as a historic monument (1893). Marble staircases and Victorian wrought-iron balconies. Wonderful interior lobby under an elegant skylight. An absolute must-see. Open Mon.-Sat.

& **Bullocks Wilshire,** 3050 Wilshire Blvd., Los Angeles (382-6161): With its unusual greenish tower and beacon light, this curious 1929 building is one of the most perfect examples of California art deco. Designated a historic monument. Open daily.

& **Casa de Adobe,** 4605 N. Figueroa St., Highland Park (221-2163): An exact replica of an 1850s Mexican hacienda, the building dates from 1918 and is used as an annex to the Southwest Museum (see below). Interesting period decoration and furniture. Worth a visit. Open Tues.-Sun.

El Pueblo de Los Angeles State Historic Park (see "Strolls, Downtown," below).

Gamble House, 4 Westmoreland Pl., Pasadena (tel. 818/793-3334). Probably the finest of the many fine houses built in and around Pasadena by Charles and Henry Greene, in this case for one of the heirs to the Procter and Gamble soap fortune. The Greenes designed everything down to the individual pieces of furniture. The conducted tours are unusually complete and illuminating. A visit to the Gamble House can conveniently be combined with visits to the Huntington Library and the Norton Simon Museum (see below Museums of Art).

☀& **Hollyhock House,** 4800 Hollywood Blvd., Hollywood (662-7272): Built in 1919 as the home of oil heiress Aline Barnsdall, Frank Lloyd Wright's first Los Angeles building was inspired by pre-Columbian themes, and is considered one of his greatest achievements. An absolute must-see. Open Tues.-Thur. and Sat.-Sun.

    🔔 **Lummis Home,** 200 E. Ave. 43, Los Angeles (222-0546): Picturesque turn-of-the-century home of rustic character (rough-hewn stones and exposed beams), once the property of the distinguished historian and archeologist Charles Lummis. Now the headquarters of the Historical Society of Southern California. It can conveniently form part of a combined expedition to the Casa de Adobe (see above) and the Southwest Museum (see "Museums of Science and History," below). Open Wed.-Sun.

    ☀🔔 **Mann's Chinese Theater,** 6925 Hollywood Blvd., Hollywood (464-8111). Opened in 1927 and originally known as Grauman's Chinese Theater, this is probably the world's most famous movie house. Cast in cement on the sidewalk in front of it are the footprints of 160 stars of the silver screen. The architecture is Hollywood Chinese, and the interior is the finest kitsch. Don't miss it.

    🔔 **Mission San Fernando Rey de España,** 15151 San Fernando Mission Blvd., Mission Hills (818/361-0186): Spanish mission founded in 1797 by the indefatigable Fr. Junipero Serra (the 17th of 21 missions built by Spanish religious between 1769 and 1823). Original adobe architecture with walls 4 ft (1.20 m) thick, and a very lovely arcade. Superbly restored, and surrounded by beautiful gardens. Museum. Worth the side trip. Open daily.

    ☀🔔 **Mission San Gabriel Arcangel,** 537 W. Mission Dr., San Gabriel (818/282-5191): The oldest (1771) stone building in California, also the work of Fr. Junipero Serra, and one of the most beautiful of the Spanish missions in the U.S. Renowned for its vineyards; interesting museum. You shouldn't fail to see it.

    🔔 **_Queen Mary,_** Pier J, Long Beach (435-3511): The largest (81,000 tons) and longest ocean liner still afloat. Launched in 1934, this one-time pride of the British merchant marine is now a convention hotel and floating museum. Well worth the visit. Open daily.

    ☀🔔 **Simon Rodia Towers,** 1765 E. 107th St., Watts (569-8181): Eight surrealist metal towers, built single-handed over 33 years with the most incongruous of salvaged material (70,000 shells, bottles, tin cans, tiles, etc.) by an Italian immigrant, Simon Rodia, who died in 1956. An astonishing achievement of naïve art. An absolute must-see.

    🔔 **_Spruce Goose,_** Pier J, Long Beach (435-3511): The world's largest commercial transport plane: wing span, 320 ft (100 m), the length of a football field; take-off weight, 180 tons; intended capacity, 700 passengers. This all-wooden monster, brainchild of billionaire Howard Hughes, made a single hop of one mile (1,600 m) in Los Angeles harbor on Nov. 2, 1947; this was the one and only flight of Hughes's H-2 Hercules, better known ever since by its nickname, "Spruce Goose." It now sits under a 128-ft (40-m) dome next to the _Queen Mary_ (see above). Don't miss it. Open daily.

MARKETS: 🔔 **Farmers Market,** 6333 W. 3rd St., Los Angeles (933-9211): Picturesque covered market with more than 160 food stalls; also vendors of clothing and handcrafts from around the world. An ideal place to eat on the run, but somewhat touristy. Open daily.

    🔔 **Olvera Street,** between Alameda and Main Sts., dwntwn: Lively, colorful Mexican market of **El Pueblo de Los Angeles** (see "strolls: downtown" below). Stalls, handcrafts, restaurants. Very crowded in the evening. Worth a look.

MUSEUMS OF ART: ☀ 👥 **J. Paul Getty Museum,** 17985 Pacific Coast

Hwy., Malibu (458-2003): This is the richest museum in the world, thanks to a bequest from the late oil tycoon J. Paul Getty in 1976; the endowment exceeds $3 billion. Housed in the replica of a Roman villa of the 1st century A.D. (the "Papyrus Villa" at Herculaneum near Naples), the museum displays a fabulous collection of Greek and Roman material, and of European furniture, bronzes, painting, and sculpture from antiquity through the 18th century. Splendid gardens and fountains. Parking space must be reserved ahead. Excellent museum cafeteria. Worth the trip all by itself. Open Tues.-Sun.

Henry Huntington Library, 1151 Oxford Rd., San Marino (818/405-2275): The very rich collection includes almost five million old manuscripts and 500,000 rare books, as well as English 18th- and 19th-century paintings, housed in an elegant Greek Revival building dating from 1911 and recently renovated after a fire. Splendid 200-acre botanic garden. Among the well-known works on exhibit: Gainsborough's *Blue Boy, Pinkie* by Sir Thomas Lawrence, Turner's *The Grand Canal, Venice,* Constable's *View of the Tower,* the Ellesmere Manuscript of Chaucer's *Canterbury Tales,* a 1455 Gutenberg Bible, and a manuscript autobiography of Benjamin Franklin. Don't fail to see it. Open Tues.-Sun.

Los Angeles County Museum of Art (LACMA), 5905 Wilshire Blvd., Los Angeles (857-6111): One of the country's most remarkable museums of art, notwithstanding the controversial modern design by architects William Pereira and Norman Pfeiffer, of which the only successful component is the covered-patio entryway. Splendid collection of impressionists and of contemporary painting and sculpture. Among the well-known exhibits: a supposed portrait of Nicolò Barberini by Lorenzo Lotto, Rembrandt's *Raising of Lazarus,* Georges de la Tour's *The Magdalene with the Candle,* Veronese's *Allegory of Navigation,* Copley's *Portrait of Hugh Montgomerie,* Cézanne's *Still Life with Cherries,* Van Gogh's *St. Paul's Hospital,* Picasso's portrait of Sebastian Juñer Vidal, and the famous *Codex Hammer* of Leonardo da Vinci. In front of the museum is a very fine modern sculpture, *Phoenix,* by Alexander Liberman. Not to be missed. Open Tues.-Sun.

Museum of Contemporary Art (MOCA), 250 S. Grand Ave., dwntwn (621-2766): Five buildings of red sandstone and glass in pure geometric shapes—a cube, a pyramid, the arc of a circle—a masterpiece by the Japanese architect Arata Isozaki, opened in Dec. 1986 at a cost of $23 million. Houses a sumptuous collection of modern painting and sculpture by Mark Rothko, Claes Oldenburg, Franz Kline, Robert Rauschenberg, Roy Lichtenstein, Willem de Kooning, Edward Ruscha, Jackson Pollock, Frank Stella, Ellsworth Kelly, Louise Nevelson, Richard Serra, etc. The temporary exhibitions are often quite enthralling. Don't miss it. Open Tues.-Sun.

Museum of Neon Art (MONA), 704 Traction Ave., dwntwn (617-1580): Here you will learn that even neon can be a means of artistic expression. Surprising and entertaining; worth a visit. Open Tues.-Sat.

Norton Simon Museum, 411 W. Colorado Blvd., Pasadena (818/449-6840): Cultural showcase of the University of California at Los Angeles (UCLA), art in all its forms in a rather disconcerting futurist building. Many modern paintings (Paul Klee, Kandinsky) and sculptures (Rodin's *Burghers of Calais*), but also Far Eastern art (note particularly a group of 10th-century Chola bronzes) and European masters, including Raphael's *Virgin and Child with a Book,* Dierick Bouts' *Resurrection,* Bassano's *The Flight into Egypt, Exotic Landscape* by the douanier Rousseau, Cézanne's *Tulips in a Vase,* Braque's *Still Life with Pipe,* and 88 bronze figurines by Degas. Not to be missed. Open Tues.-Sat.

Pacific Asia Museum, 46 N. Los Robles Ave., Pasadena (818/449-2742): A Chinese-style imperial palace built around a "meditation garden," housing interesting temporary exhibitions of Asian and Pacific art. It is best visited in conjunction with the Huntington Library and Norton Simon Museum (see above). Worth the side trip. Open Wed.-Sun.

☀ 🐚🐚 **Temporary Contemporary Museum,** 152 N. Central Ave., dwntwn (626-6222): This old warehouse in Little Tokyo was used as a temporary shelter for the museum's collection while the new building was under construction; now it serves as an annex, and attracts sizable crowds. Works by Rothko, Rauschenberg, Claes Oldenburg, Roy Lichtenstein, and Jasper Johns, along with many avant-garde American artists. Trendy cultural events in an unexpected setting. Not to be missed. Open Tues.-Sun.

🐚 **Wight Art Gallery,** 405 Hilgard Ave., on the UCLA campus, Westwood (825-1461): An art museum built to house (often very interesting) temporary exhibitions. Also collections of African and Asian art. Adjoining it is a lovely modern-sculpture garden. Deserves a visit. Open Tues.-Sun.

MUSEUMS OF SCIENCE AND HISTORY: 🐚 Cabrillo Marine Museum,
3720 Stephen White Dr., San Pedro (548-7562): Fine oceanographic museum, with no fewer than 34 aquariums containing specimens of more than 100 forms of Pacific marine life. Fascinating. In winter, boat trips are organized for closeup observation of whale migrations. Don't miss visiting here. Open Tues.-Sun.

🐚🐚 **California Museum of Science and Industry,** 700 State Dr., Los Angeles (744-7400): Nicknamed "the museum that loves to be touched," it contains dozens of robots and hands-on displays that involve viewer participation. Brand new IMAX theater with a six-story-high screen. One of the country's best teaching museums; don't miss it. Open daily.

☀ 🐚 **First Interstate Bank Athletic Foundation,** 2141 W. Adams Blvd., Los Angeles, 5 mi. (8 km) SW via the Santa Monica Frwy. (730-9600): A must for all sports fans; the collection contains more than 50,000 items drawn from all kinds of sports, from Jack Dempsey's boxing gloves through the track shoes of sprinter Jesse Owens to the baseball uniforms of Babe Ruth, Lou Gehrig, Stan Musial, and so on. Replicas of medals from the Olympics and other competitions. Also an extensive sports library. Open Tues.-Sun.

☀ 🐚🐚 **George C. Page La Brea Discoveries Museum,** 5801 Wilshire Blvd., Los Angeles (936-2230): More than a million prehistoric fossils (including 9,000 mammals) of creatures engulfed 9,000–40,000 years ago in the nearby "tar pits," dug up and now on exhibit as fragments or reconstructed skeletons, including a ten-ton mammoth and the "La Brea Woman," 9,000 years old. Many stone tools. Dozens of excavations still under way. Fascinating; don't miss it. Open Tues.-Sun.

🐚 **Hollywood Studio Museum,** 2100 N. Highland Ave., Hollywood (874-2276): The old barn where in 1913 Cecil B. deMille shot the industry's first full-length feature, *The Squaw Man,* now a museum with displays and screenings from the heroic days of silent film. Fascinating. Open daily.

🐚 **Hollywood Wax Museum,** 6767 Hollywood Blvd., Hollywood (462-8860): More than 170 movie stars in "flesh and wax" (so to speak), from Marilyn Monroe to Raquel Welch and from Gary Cooper to Paul Newman. The movie industry's answer to Madame Tussaud's. Worth seeing. Open daily.

🐚 **Natural History Museum,** 900 Exposition Blvd., Exposition Park, Los Angeles (744-3414): Interesting museum of natural history and ethnology with important collections of archeology (pre-Columbian art), mineralogy (one of the largest in the world), dioramas of animals in their native habitats, and marine ecology. Worth going out of your way for. Open Tues.-Sun.

      Southwest Museum, 234 Museum Dr., Los Angeles (221-2163): Museum of Native American civilization, designed by the historian Charles F. Lummis around an exceptional collection of Indian art and handcrafts. Will delight devotees of the history of the Old West. Must be seen. Open Tues.-Sun.; closed mid-Aug. to mid-Sept.

      Wells Fargo History Museum, 333 S. Grand Ave., dwntwn (253-3300): It's like being there in the days of the Westward expansion: stagecoaches, a collection of gold nuggets, 19th-century post office, posters, photographs, etc. Amusing. Open Mon.-Fri.

OUTDOOR ART AND PLAZAS: Boyle Heights and East Los Angeles:
These Chicano neighborhoods have some of the finest street murals in the city—on Grand Vista Ave., Alcazar St., Olympic Blvd., Lorena St., Ramona Gardens, Estrada Courts, etc. Dangerous after dark, even in a car.

      The Mall, Main and Los Angeles Sts., nr. City Hall, dwntwn: Gardens, fountains, statuary, and the extraordinary glass **Triforium Tower,** which in the evenings offers a computer-generated symphony of sound and color. Fascinating.

      Venice (see "Strolls, West and North Los Angeles," below): Wonderful pop-art murals in trompe l'oeil on the fronts of several buildings near the Arcades in the center of Venice. Visit not recommended on foot after dark.

PANORAMAS: City Hall, 200 N. Spring St., dwntwn (485-2121): Splen-
did view of the dwntwn high-rises and—on a clear day—of the mountains and the Pacific, from the 22nd floor. Open Mon.-Fri.

      Mullholland Drive, North Beverly Hills: A twisting road which winds across the crest of the Santa Monica Mountains, offering a wonderful view of the city and the ocean in clear weather (best after dark). Very popular with lovers at night.

      Griffith Park (see "Parks and Gardens," below).

PARKS AND GARDENS: Descanso Gardens, 1418 Descanso Dr., La
Cañada (818/790-5571): Some 100,000 camellias bloom here from Nov. to Mar. in the middle of a lovely oak grove. Rosebeds; Japanese garden. Worth the side trip.

      Elysian Park, N. Broadway Ave., Los Angeles: Beautiful 552-acre crescent-shaped landscaped park very near the Dodger stadium. Its hilly terrain offers some fine views of the dwntwn skyline. Should be seen.

      Forest Lawn Memorial Park, 1712 S. Glendale Ave., Glendale (254-3131): This splendid landscaped cemetery is a sort of funerary theme park, unique in the U.S. Many marble and bronze replicas of famous classical sculptures, and a gigantic (192- by 44-ft., 60- by 14-m) *Crucifixion* by Jan Styka, the largest devotional painting in the world. Inspired Evelyn Waugh's novel *The Loved One.* Tombs of Clark Gable and Jean Harlow. An absolute must. Open daily.

      Griffith Park, Los Feliz Blvd. at Vermont Ave., Los Angeles: (665-5188): The country's largest city park (4,107 acres), with a planetarium-observatory from which in fine weather there's a wonderful view of the city, especially at night. Also an ultramodern zoo, transportation museum, lovely rural landscapes, three golf courses, horseback riding, picnic grounds, 50 mi. (80 km) of footpaths. Well worth a visit.

🔔 **Hollywood Bowl,** 2301 N. Highland Ave., Hollywood (850-2000): A 17,000-seat open-air amphitheater with perfect acoustics; every year since 1922 classical jazz and rock concerts as well as variety shows have been given here.

☀️🔔 **Hollywood Memorial Park,** 6000 Santa Monica Blvd., Hollywood (469-1181): The cemetery of the stars: tombs of Rudolph Valentino, Cecil B. deMille, Douglas Fairbanks, Tyrone Power, and dozens of others. Sumptuously kitsch. Open daily. (One great name not to be found here is Marilyn Monroe. Admirers take note: she's buried in a small, charming graveyard such as you might find in a country town, **Westwood Memorial Park,** 1201 Glendon Ave., Los Angeles.)

🔔 **Palisades Park,** Ocean Ave. between Colorado Ave. and San Vicente Blvd., Santa Monica (393-7593): This beautiful park has been called "California's French Riviera." Bordered with palm trees, it snakes along a cliff overlooking, and offering a fine view of, the Pacific, from the Palos Verdes peninsula on the south as far as Malibu to the north. Worth seeing.

🔔 **Will Rogers State Park,** 14253 Sunset Blvd., Pacific Palisades (454-8212): This big public park used to be the ranch of the legendary cowboy-humorist Will Rogers; his personal memorabilia are on display, along with collections of Indian artifacts. Footpaths for strollers, polo matches on Sat. and Sun., picnics, horseback riding.

PERFORMING ARTS:
For current listings of shows and cultural events, consult the entertainment pages of the two daily morning papers, *Los Angeles Times* and *Los Angeles Herald Examiner,* as well as the monthlies *Los Angeles* and *California.* After New York, Los Angeles has more theaters and concert halls (some 200 in all) than any other city in the country.

Ahmanson Theater, 135 N. Grand Ave., in the Music Center, dwntwn (972-7211): Home of the Center Theater Group. Comedy, drama, modern and classical theater; musical comedies and operettas.

Doolittle Theater, 1615 Vine St., Hollywood (462-6666): Musicals, shows, touring companies.

Dorothy Chandler Pavilion, 135 N. Grand Ave., in the Music Center, dwntwn (972-7211): Home of the Los Angeles Philharmonic under principal conductor André Previn (Oct.-May), the Los Angeles Civic Light Opera, Los Angeles Master Chorale, and the Joffrey Ballet.

Embassy Theater, 851 S. Grand Ave., dwntwn (622-3200): Beautiful Beaux Arts building; classical concerts. Home of the Los Angeles Chamber Orchestra.

Greek Theater, 2700 N. Vermont Ave., Griffith Park, Los Angeles (410-1062): Open-air concerts with major pop or rock stars (May-Oct.).

Henry Fonda Theater, 6126 Hollywood Blvd., Hollywood (634-1300): Broadway hits.

Hollywood Bowl, 2301 N. Highland Ave., Hollywood (480-3222): Vast 17,000-seat natural amphitheater. Classical concerts with the Los Angeles Philharmonic; also jazz, rock, and variety shows (June-Sept.).

Los Angeles Theater Center, 514 S. Spring St., dwntwn (627-5599): Ultramodern four-hall complex opened in 1985; home of the Los Angeles Actors' Theater (contemporary and avant-garde theater); also jazz, classical concerts, and ballet. Has a superb skylight and a very fine marble interior.

Mark Taper Forum, 135 N. Grand Ave., in the Music Center, dwntwn (972-7211): Circular theater for chamber-music concerts; the Center Theater Group performs here in its repertory of contemporary plays.

Orange County Performing Arts Center, 600 Town Center Dr., Costa Mesa (714/556-2787): This ultramodern 3,000-seat auditorium was opened in

1986 at a cost of more than $70 million. Now it offers year-round prestige programs: opera, symphony concerts, ballet, etc.

Pantages Theater, 6233 Hollywood Blvd., Hollywood (462-3104): A 1930s art deco movie house, magnificently restored. Musical comedies, Broadway hits, modern plays with famous actors. The Oscar awards were given here from 1949 to 1959.

Pasadena Playhouse, 39 S. El Molino Ave., Pasadena (818/356-7529): Opened in 1925, it is regarded as one of the finest repertory houses for modern and contemporary theater.

Shrine Auditorium, Jefferson Blvd. and Royal St., Los Angeles (749-5123): This enormous (6,300-seat) 1926 hall offers remarkably fine acoustics for its concerts, operas, and ballets.

Shubert Theater, 2020 Ave. of the Stars, ABC Entertainment Center, Century City (557-7777): Musical comedies, star vehicles.

Terrace Theater, 300 E. Ocean Blvd., Long Beach (436-3661): Home of the Long Beach Symphony Orchestra, and the Long Beach Civic Light Opera and Long Beach Ballet companies. Musicals, musical comedies, etc.

Universal Amphitheatre, 3900 Lankershim Blvd., Universal City (818/980-9421): In the Universal Studios complex. Big-name recitals, musicals. Year round.

Westwood Playhouse, 10886 Le Conte Ave., Westwood (208-5454): Near the UCLA campus; contemporary and avant-garde theater.

Wilshire Theater, Wilshire and La Cienega Blvds., West Hollywood (467-1199): Comedy, drama, modern theater.

Wiltern Theater, Wilshire Blvd. and Western Ave., Los Angeles (216-6666): Handsome art deco theater, home of the Los Angeles Opera. Also classical concerts.

SHOPPING: **Atlantic Richfield Plaza,** 505 S. Flower St., dwntwn: The country's largest underground shopping center: dozens of stores, boutiques, art galleries, and restaurants occupying several levels under the giant ARCO/Bank of America Towers. If you suffer from claustrophobia, forget it.

Beverly Center, Beverly and La Cienega Blvds., West Hollywood: Elegant, ultramodern shopping center whose hi-tech architecture seems to be modeled on the Musée Beaubourg in Paris. More than 200 boutiques and stores, 13 restaurants, 15 cinemas and theaters; even a disco. Worth seeing. Open daily.

Edmund's Bookstore, 6658 Hollywood Blvd., Hollywood (463-3273): The best specialist bookstore in the country for the movie industry; a kind of living history of the silver screen. Open Mon.-Sat.

Garment District, Los Angeles St. between 7th St. and Washington Blvd., dwntwn: clothing of all kinds at unbeatable prices for more than half a century, particularly in the **California Mart** or the **Cooper Building.**

Melrose Avenue between La Cienega Blvd. and La Brea Ave., Los Angeles: Trendy fashion boutiques; the California "in" style.

Miracle Mile, Wilshire Blvd. between Highland and Fairfax Aves., Los Angeles: Elegant boutiques and stores carrying the last word from America and Europe.

☀ **Rodeo Drive,** between Santa Monica and Wilshire Blvds., Beverly Hills: The country's, and possibly the world's, smartest street, equivalent to Madison Avenue in New York, Bond Street in London, or the Rue Faubourg St-Honoré in Paris. From Giorgio to Hermès, from Tiffany to Gucci, not to mention the unbelievable Bijan, the most outrageous of luxury boutiques are to be found here. The customers arrive in Rolls-Royces. Unless your wallet is fat, keep it closed—but have a look, anyway.

Seventh Street Market Place, 735 S. Figueroa St., dwntwn: Extraordinary mixture of an underground shopping center, a Japanese garden, and a tropical conservatory, designed by Jon Jerde. Absolutely must be seen. Open daily.

Tower Records, 8801 Sunset Blvd., West Hollywood (657-7300): One of the country's largest record stores. Open daily until midnight.

SPECIAL EVENTS: For exact dates, consult the **Anaheim Visitor and Convention Bureau,** 800 W. Katella Ave., Anaheim, CA 92803 (714/999-8999); the **Long Beach Convention and Visitors Council,** 180 E. Ocean Blvd., Long Beach, CA 90802 (213/436-3645); the **Los Angeles Visitors and Convention Bureau,** 515 S. Figueroa St., Los Angeles, CA 90071 (213/624-7300); or the **Pasadena Chamber of Commerce,** 199 S. Los Robles Ave., Pasadena, CA 91105 (818/795-3355).

Anaheim
Halloween Festival (end of Oct.): Parades; giant masked ball.

Chinatown
Chinese New Year (mid Jan. or early Feb.): Dragon Parade and costumed processions in honor of the Chinese New Year. Picturesque.

Downtown
Cinco de Mayo Procession (May 5): The great annual festival of the Los Angeles Pueblo on Olvera St. in honor of the French defeat at Puebla.

Las Posadas (end of Dec.): Christmas festivities Mexican style at **El Pueblo de Los Angeles;** colorful.

Little Tokyo
Nisei Week (Aug.): Annual Japanese cultural festival, very popular locally.

Long Beach
Long Beach Grand Prix (late Mar. or early Apr.): Formula I Grand Prix along the streets of dwntwn Long Beach; spectacular, drawing more than 200,000 spectators every year.

California Sea Festival (Aug.): Very lively, with boat races, regattas, processions, competitions.

Pasadena
Tournament of Roses (Jan. 1): A great procession of flowers along Orange Grove and Colorado Blvds., with extravagantly decorated floats; a million spectators on the streets and 100 million more watching on television. Timed for a few hours before the Rose Bowl football game.

Pomona
Los Angeles County Fair (end of Sept.): The country's biggest fair-exhibition. 28 mi. (45 km) SE of dwntwn.

SPORTS: Los Angeles is blessed with a multitude of professional teams, as well as three racetracks:

Baseball (Apr.-Sept.): Angels, Anaheim Stadium (714/634-2000); Dodgers, Dodger Stadium (224-1400).

Basketball (Oct. to late Apr.): Clippers, L.A. Sports Arena (748-6131); Lakers, the Forum, Inglewood (673-1300).

Football (Sept.-Dec.): Raiders, L.A. Coliseum (322-5901); Rams, Anaheim Stadium (714/937-6767).

Ice Hockey (Sept. to late Apr.): Kings, the Forum, Inglewood (673-1300).

Horse Racing

Del Mar Thoroughbred Club, Jimmy Durante Dr., Delmar (619/755-1141): Directly on the beach; open late July to mid-Sept.

Hollywood Park, Century Blvd. and Prairie Ave., Inglewood (419-1500). Racing from mid-Apr. to late July and mid-Nov. to the end of Dec.

Santa Anita Park, Huntington Dr. and Baldwin Ave., Arcadia (818/574-7223): Racing from early Oct. to early Nov. and late Dec. to late Apr.

STROLLS: Los Angeles is so big, with so many delightful areas for strolling, that this section is divided into two parts: Downtown, and West and North L.A.

Downtown

Chinatown, around no. 900 N. on Broadway, dwntwn: Stalls, restaurants, pagoda-shaped buildings; a pungent, gimcrack, lively Chinese district.

El Pueblo de Los Angeles, bounded by Macy, Alameda, Spring, and Arcadia Sts., dwntwn (628-1274): The historic heart of Los Angeles since its foundation in 1781. From the Avila Adobe, the city's oldest (1818) house, now a museum of California history, to the Old Plaza Firehouse (1884), and from the Church of Nuestra Señora Reina de los Angeles (1822) to the Merced Theater (1870), El Pueblo can show you a dozen or more 19th-century buildings, carefully restored, along **Olvera Street** and **Old Plaza,** a delightful, shady little square in the purest Spanish-Mexican style, with a wrought-iron bandstand. A living picture of the past, not to be missed. Conducted tours Mon.-Sat.

Financial District, between 3rd, Olive, and Figueroa Sts. and Wilshire Blvd., dwntwn: "The Wall Street of the West Coast." Scarcely 15 years old (until 1957 there was a 13-floor limit on construction because of the earthquake hazard), this new financial district now collects skyscrapers. Among the most striking are the First Interstate Tower, with 62 stories the city's tallest building; the five 35-floor glass cylinders of the Westin Bonaventure Hotel, the 48-story Wells Fargo Building, the Security Pacific Bank (55 stories), and the twin 52-story towers of the ARCO/Bank of America building. A sight not to be missed.

Little Tokyo, 1st St. between Main and San Pedro Sts., dwntwn: Los Angeles, with 160,000 inhabitants who are Japanese or of Japanese descent, is the largest Japanese city outside Asia. Many stores, Buddhist temples, art galleries, restaurants. Exquisite Japanese garden and very active cultural center. Worth seeing.

West and North Los Angeles

Bel Air and Beverly Hills, north of Sunset Blvd.: The two smart neighborhoods of Los Angeles; mansions of millionaires and movie stars hidden behind trees and locked iron gates. Super-deluxe boutiques on Beverly Hills' Rodeo Drive. Even the local post office at 312 S. Beverly Dr. offers valet parking to its customers—which says it all. For a little daydreaming.

Hollywood, around Hollywood Blvd. and Vine St.: Once "the movie Mecca"—but the industry, which was officially born in 1910 when the first studio was built, has now only its former glories to live on. The legendary Hollywood is a community of undistinguished stores, gloomy motels, tattered palm trees, sex shops on Hollywood Blvd., and an intimidating local populace after dark (walking at night is definitely not recommended), but it's still worth a look. Among its attractions are Mann's Chinese Theater (see "Historic Buildings," above), the Hollywood Studio Museum (see "Museums of Science and History," above), and the celebrated Walk of Fame (see below). A laudable attempt to clean up the community, physically and morally, has recently been set in motion.

🔔 **Marina del Rey,** Admiralty Way: Superb marina on the Pacific, where more than 6,000 boats are moored; a favorite place with prosperous bohemia and trendy night-owls. A bogus but picturesque New England fishing village (Fisherman's Village). An absolute must.

🔔 **Pasadena,** via the Pasadena Frwy.: One of the country's scientific strongholds; CalTech (California Institute of Technology), 1201 E. California Blvd., is a veritable hotbed of Nobel laureates in physics and chemistry. It's Visitor Center is at 315 S. Hill Ave. (818/356-6328). The jewel in CalTech's crown is NASA's Jet Propulsion Laboratory, where the *Voyager* space vehicles were assembled, "permitting more astronomical discoveries in two decades than in the preceding two millennia." JPL is open to visitors, by advance resv., twice a month; call 354-8593. See also the entries on the Norton Simon Museum and the Pacific Asia Museum (see "Museums of Art," above).

🔔 **Ports O'Call Village,** Berths 76–79, Harbor Blvd., in San Pedro, 36 mi. (51 km) south along the Harbor Frwy.: Recaptures the atmosphere of a little Spanish-colonial port of the 1850s, with its gas-lit cobbled streets, its dozens of stalls and restaurants. Boat trips around the harbor. Should be seen.

🔔 **Santa Monica Pier,** Ocean Ave., Santa Monica: The granddaddy of California's amusement parks, built on the pier in 1909. The giant carousel figured in the setting of the movie *The Sting*. Well-mannered kitsch.

☀🔔 **Sunset Boulevard,** from Doheny Dr. to Vine St., Beverly Hills / Hollywood: This legendary "main drag of the movies," blazing at night from all its billboards, is the quintessence of Los Angeles' nightlife. Great restaurants, nightclubs, hotels—but also agents, recording and movie studios. The central section of Sunset Blvd., "the Strip," is the stronghold of show business. Not to be missed (at night, for choice).

☀🔔 **Venice,** around Ocean Front Walk and Venice Blvd., Venice: This beach resort was founded in 1904 by Abbot Kinney, an eccentric millionaire who was in love with Venice, and sought to reproduce the city of the doges, canals and all, on the Pacific coast; he even imported genuine gondolas with singing gondoliers. With its eclectic mix of body-builders, roller-skaters, gays, artists, gigantic pop murals ("murales"), and drug dealers, it is today the most bohemian—and the most entertaining—beach in California. Don't miss seeing it.

☀🔔 **"Walk of Fame,"** around Hollywood Blvd. and Vine St., Hollywood: "The promenade of the stars," where nearly 2,000 bronze stars set in the sidewalk evoke the greats of the silver screen; new names are added to the list every month. Worth a snapshot, but don't walk it after dark.

🔔 **Westwood Village,** around Westwood Plaza, Westwood: Los Angeles' "Latin Quarter" or "Greenwich Village"; stroll on the vast UCLA campus (see "Architectural Highlights," above). Dozens of bookstores, record shops, movie houses, restaurants, etc. Very lively, especially after dark.

THEME PARKS: ☀ 🎡 **Disneyland,** 1313 Harbor Blvd., in Anaheim, 24 mi. (38 km) SE on I-5 (714/999-4565): Opened by Walt Disney himself in 1955, this is the archetype of the great American amusement parks. Much smaller than its two Florida siblings, Walt Disney World (opened in 1971) and EPCOT

(1982), Disneyland is still one of the country's most popular tourist attractions, visited so far by more than 250 million people, big and little. From "Sleeping Beauty's Castle" to "Fantasyland" and on to "Pirates of the Caribbean" by way of the Far West train which takes you to "Frontierland," not to mention the mysterious jungle of "Adventureland" or "Carnival in New Orleans," 60 different attractions await the visitor. The latest of these is an outer-space Disneyland, in tune with the times, entitled "Star Tours" and created under the supervision of the famous movie director George Lucas. 45 min. by car from dwntwn. Open daily from late Mar. to mid-Sept. and Wed.-Sun. the rest of the year. Set aside at least one whole day for your visit. Crowded at weekends. Admission: $22. Don't miss this one.

Knott's Berry Farm, 8039 Beach Blvd., in Buena Park, 20 mi. (32 km) SE on I-5 and Cal. 39 (714/220-5200): Ten min. by car from Disneyland you'll find a reconstruction of the Far West: attacks on stagecoaches, ghost town, etc.; also an amusement park with 135 attractions. Big-name shows. This ranks as the country's fourth most popular amusement park, next after the Disney trio. Admission: $16. Open daily. Worth the side trip.

Lion Safari Country, 8800 Irvine Center Dr., in Irvine, 40 mi. (65 km) SE on I-5 (714/837-1200): Hundreds of African animals roaming free on 480 acres of savannah; visitors stay in their cars. Spectacular. Open daily year round.

Six Flags Magic Mountain, 26101 Magic Mountain Pkwy., in Valencia, 32 mi. (52 km) NW on I-5 (805/255-4100): A 260-acre theme park with 100 attractions including the world's largest roller coaster (1.8 mi., 3 km, long with dizzy drops of 92 ft, 30 m); if your heart is weak, don't ride it. Less touristy but no less entertaining than Disneyland. Open daily June-Sept., weekends only the rest of the year.

WINTER SPORTS RESORTS: Angeles National Forest, about 62 mi. (100 km) NE via I-5 and Cal. 2: Mount Waterman, with three ski lifts (818/790-2002); Ski Sunrise, with five lifts (619/249-6150).

Big Bear Lake, 112 mi. (180 km) east via I-10 and Cal. 18: Goldmine, eight lifts (714/585-2519); Snow Summit, 12 lifts (714/866-4621).

Mount Baldy, 51 mi. (82 km) east on I-10 and Cal. 83 (714/981-3344): Four lifts.

ACCOMMODATIONS

See the listing of toll-free numbers in the Appendix.

Room Rates in Los Angeles	
B (Budget)	up to $30
I (Inexpensive)	$30–$60
M (Moderate)	$60–$90
E (Expensive)	$90–$140
VE (Very Expensive)	$140 and up

Note: In a city this big, concepts such as "dwntwn" or "vic." don't apply;

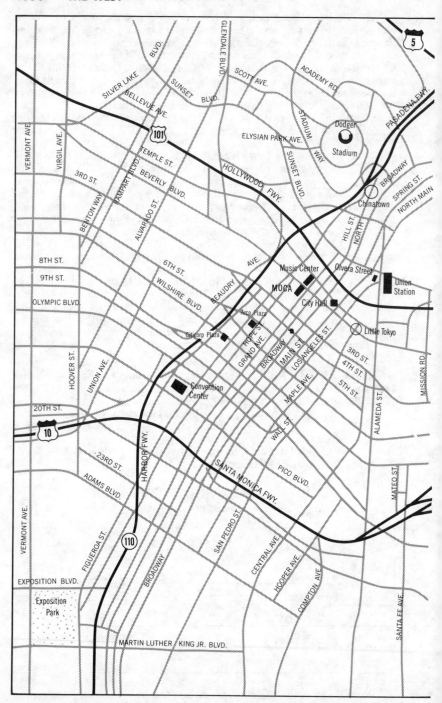

DOWNTOWN LOS ANGELES

Wilshire Blvd., the main east-west artery, is 16 mi. (27 km) long. The hotels (and restaurants) mentioned below are designated by districts (Los Angeles, dwntwn, Beverly Hills, Hollywood, and so on.)

Personal Favorites (in order of preference)

Beverly Hills Hotel, 9641 Sunset Blvd., Beverly Hills, CA 90210 (213/276-2251; toll free 800/792-7637). 325 rms, A/C, color TV, in-rm movies. AE, CB, DC, MC, V. Valet parking $10, pool, two tennis courts, two rests. (including the Coterie), coffeeshop, bar, 24-hr rm svce, hrdrsr, boutiques, crib $25. *Note:* The Beverly Hills Hotel, dating from 1912, is almost as old as the art of the cinema—and a splendid shrine dedicated to it. Producers, newspaper people, past and future stars disport themselves in the 12 acres of gardens, around the pool, or in the Polo Lounge, the bar-rest. of Hollywood biggies. The rms, most w. refrigerators and private balconies or patios, and the bungalows boast Italian-marble bathrooms and a lollipop-pink Beverly Hills–style scheme of decoration. Ask for a bungalow. Excellent rm svce. People go here to see and be seen. One of the 12 best hotels in the country; since its recent purchase by the Sultan of Brunei it has been renovated in the grand manner at a cost of many tens of millions of dollars. **E–VE**

L'Ermitage, 9291 Burton Way, Beverly Hills, CA 90210 (213/278-3344; toll free 800/345-3457). 114 suites, each w. one or two bedrooms. A/C, color TV, in-rm movies. AE, CB, DC, MC, V. Free valet garage, pool, private rest. (Café Russe), bar, roof garden, rm svce, concierge. *Note:* Very luxurious residential hotel in the European manner, in the smartest neighborhood of Beverly Hills. Sumptuously decorated suites w. balconies and mini-bars, some w. kitchenettes. Elegant, intimate setting w. period furniture and numerous works of art by Chagall, Renoir, Van Gogh, and Miró. The svce is of a distinction seldom encountered. The hotel has a presidential super-suite at $1,300 (plus taxes) a night. Setting aside considerations of expense, the best place (along w. the Beverly Hills Hotel) to stay in Los Angeles. **VE**

Hotel Bel Air, 701 Stone Canyon Dr., Westwood Village, CA 90077 (213/472-1211; toll free, see Preferred). 92 rms, A/C, color TV, in-rm movies. AE, CB, DC, MC, V. Free valet garage, pool, rest., bar, 24-hr rm svce, florist, concierge. *Note:* This charming small hotel, in the Spanish mission style, stands among bougainvilleas on a little lake w. swans, breathing a serene intimacy. Elegant rms w. private patios, some w. fireplaces. Honeymooners reserve here months in advance. Fussy rest. (Bel Air Dining Room). Property of the millionaire Hunt family of Texas, and a favorite w. the Establishment. **VE**

Sheraton Grande, 333 S. Figueroa St. (dwntwn), Los Angeles, CA 90071 (213/617-1133; toll free, see Sheraton). 470 rms, A/C, color TV, in-rm movies. AE, CB, DC, MC, V. Valet garage $10, pool, tennis court, three rests. (including Ravel), coffeeshop, two bars, 24-hr rm svce, entertainment, four cinemas, concierge, free crib. *Note:* Brand-new 14-story palace in the heart of dwntwn. Particularly spacious, elegant, comfortable rms, some w. refrigerators. 24-hour valet svce on all floors. Remarkable svce; very complete facilities. The quintessential upper-echelon business hotel. Linked to the dwntwn buildings by a skywalk. **VE**

Disneyland Hotel, 1150 W. Cerritos Ave., Anaheim, CA 92802 (714/778-6600; toll free 800/854-6165). 1,174 rms, A/C, cable color TV. AE, CB, DC, MC, V. Garage $6, three pools, ten tennis courts, private beach, marina, four rests. (including Granville's), coffeeshop, bars, rm svce, disco, boutiques, free crib. *Note:* Both a resort and a convention hotel, this enormous complex is linked directly to Disneyland by monorail. Its three 14-story towers rise around an enormous lagoon/swimming pool. Very comfortable rms w. private balconies or patios and refrigerators. Efficient svce.

Beautiful tropical garden w. waterfalls and little lakes stocked w. goldfish. Somewhat obtrusive package tourists and conventioneers predominate here. 5 min. from the Anaheim Convention Center. **E–VE**

☀☀☂☂ **Roosevelt Hotel,** 7000 Hollywood Blvd., Hollywood, CA 90028 (213/466-7000; toll free 800/858-2244). 400 rms, A/C, color TV. AE, CB, DC, MC, V. Garage $6, pool, rest. (Theodore's), bar, jazz, boutiques, concierge. *Note:* A hallowed spot in the history of the cinema. The first Oscars were awarded here in 1929; it was here also that Clark Gable and Carole Lombard concealed their love affair from the public eye. All the great stars, from Errol Flynn to Douglas Fairbanks and Maureen O'Hara, came here in its heyday. It reopened its doors in 1986 after a $40-million restoration program, and has now recaptured all its former magnificence. The splendid interior is neo-Castilian crossed with art deco. The rooms are comfortable and inviting; the Cinegrill bar is famous. Friendly, smiling svce. The Celebrity Floor is reserved for VIPs. Opposite the renowned Mann's Chinese Theater, in the middle of the "Walk of Fame." **E–VE**

☂☂ **Sportsmen's Lodge,** 12825 Ventura Blvd., Studio City, CA 91604 (818/769-4700; toll free 800/821-8511). 196 rms, A/C, cable color TV. AE, CB, DC, MC, V. Free parking, pool, health club, rest., coffeeshop, bars, rm svce, free crib. *Note:* Luxuriously comfortable motel in a beautiful garden w. swans floating on the lakes. Inviting rms w. private balconies or patios. Attentive svce. Group clientele. Good value. Near Hollywood, Beverly Hills, and Universal Studios; 20 min. from dwntwn. Free limo to Burbank Airport. **M–E**

☂ **Best Western Executive Motor Inn,** 603 S. New Hampshire Ave., Los Angeles, CA 90005 (213/385-4444; toll free, see Best Western). 89 rms, A/C, cable color TV. AE, CB, DC, MC, V. Free parking, health club, sauna, nearby rest. and bar, crib $5. *Note:* Comfortable little Spanish-style motel near the financial district; attentive reception and svce; spacious, well-designed rms w. refrigerators. Good value. 10 min. from dwntwn. **M**

☂ **Hallmark House,** 7023 Sunset Blvd., Hollywood, CA 90028 (213/464-8344). 72 rms, A/C, color TV. AE, CB, DC, MC, V. Free parking, pool. *Note:* Agreeable reception and functional rms, some w. kitchenettes; most have balconies w. a view of the pool and the picnic tables around it. No bar or rest., but good overall value. 5 min. from "the Strip" and the principal attractions of Hollywood. **I**

☂ **Oasis Motel,** 2200 W. Olympic Blvd., Los Angeles, CA 90006 (213/385-4191). 69 rms, A/C, color TV. AE, CB, DC, MC, V. Free parking, pool, adjoining coffeeshop. *Note:* Modest but comfortable small motel 5 min. from the Convention Center and dwntwn Los Angeles. Agreeable reception and svce. Functional rms w. refrigerators; some have kitchenettes. Very good value. **I**

Other Accommodations (from top bracket to budget)

☂☂☂☂ **Beverly Wilshire,** 9500 Wilshire Blvd., Beverly Hills, CA 90212 (213/275-4282; toll free 800/545-4000). 450 rms, A/C, color TV, in-rm movies. AE, CB, DC, MC, V. Valet garage $10, pool, health club, sauna, two rests. (including La Bella Fontana), coffeeshop, three bars, 24-hr rm svce, hrdrsr, florist, free crib. *Note:* Venerable luxury hotel a few steps away from Rodeo Drive and its upscale boutiques. Elegant rms, many w. refrigerators, private patios, or balconies. In the new wing each floor is decorated in the style of a different country. La Bella Fontana is an excellent rest. Exemplary svce, fashionable guest list. A Beverly Hills classic; one of the Hong Kong Regent chain of luxury hotels. **VE**

Westwood Marquis, 930 Hilgard Ave., Westwood Village, CA 90024 (213/208-8765; toll free, see Preferred). 256 suites, A/C, color TV, in-rm movies. AE, CB, DC, MC, V. Valet garage $8, two pools, health club, sauna, rest. (The Dynasty Room), two bars, 24-hr rm svce, hrdrsr, florist, concierge, free crib. *Note:* Modern 17-story luxury hotel originally built as a student residence for nearby UCLA. Has only suites, elegantly decorated and luxuriously equipped. Personalized svce. Clientele drawn from the upper echelons of business and the movies. The neighborhood is lively both day and night. Very good rest. Free limo to Beverly Hills. **VE**

Le Bel Age, 1020 N. San Vicente Blvd., West Hollywood, CA 90069 (213/854-1111; toll free 800/345-3457). 198 suites, A/C, color TV, in-rm movies. AE, CB, DC, MC, V. Free valet parking, pool, health club, two rests. (including Le Bel Age), bar, rm svce, piano bar, hrdrsr, boutiques, concierge. *Note:* First-class hotel very nr. the "Strip"; nothing but spacious, pastel-toned suites w. mini-bars and private balconies. Personalized reception and svce. Elegant European-style décor w. master paintings and antique furniture. A favorite w. those in-the-know. A younger brother of the luxurious L'Ermitage (see above); free Beverly Hills limo. **VE**

Beverly Hilton, 9876 Wilshire Blvd., Beverly Hills, CA 90210 (213/274-7777; toll free, see Hilton). 625 rms, A/C, color TV, in-rm movies. AE, CB, DC, MC, V. Valet garage $8, two pools, health club, four rests. (including L'Escoffier), two coffeeshops, bars, rm svce, disco, hrdrsr, drugstore, boutiques, concierge, free crib. *Note:* The crown jewel of the Hilton chain, remarkably elegant and polished for a hotel of its size. Comfortable rms w. refrigerators and balconies. Efficient, hard-working svce. Very good rests. Favored by the jet set and show business; also by those in-the-know. A little away from downtown Beverly Hills. Very well-equipped business center. Recently completed a $35 million renovation. **E–VE**

Westin Century Plaza, 2025 Ave. of the Stars, Century City, CA 90067 (213/277-2000; toll free, see Westin). 1,072 rms, A/C, color TV, in-rm movies. AE, CB, DC, MC, V. Valet parking $6, two pools, health club, adjoining health club and tennis courts, four rests. (including Yamato), coffeeshop, three bars, 24-hr rm svce, entertainment, hrdrsr, boutiques, concierge, free crib. *Note:* The first modern luxury hotel in the new business district of Century City. Enormous pie-wedge-shaped tourist barracks surmounted by a massive 30-story tower; the interior is, fortunately, more gracious. Vast, comfortable rms w. balconies. Excellent svce. President Reagan occasionally alights in the $3,000-a-night suite here. Caters to package tours and conventions. Inviting garden. **E–VE**

Bel Air Summit, 11461 Sunset Blvd., Bel Air, CA 90049 (213/476-6571). 162 rms, A/C, color TV. AE, CB, DC, MC, V. Free parking, two pools, tennis court, rest. (Caribbean Terrace), bar, rm svce, free breakfast, free crib. *Note:* Small, gracious, comfortable hotel set in a lovely garden and recently renovated. Spacious, elegant rms w. private balconies or patios. Good svce; very commendable rest. Free limo to Beverly Hills business district. **E–VE**

Château Marmont, 8221 Sunset Blvd., Hollywood, CA 90046 (213/656-1010; toll free 800/826-0015). 62 rms and cottages, A/C, color TV. AE, CB, DC, MC, V. Garage $6, pool, rest., bar, rm svce. *Note:* A movie monument, in which innumerable stars (Greta Garbo, Boris Karloff, John Lennon, Robert de Niro, Richard Gere, Sidney Poitier, John Belushi) once lived, or still live, it looks like a fake château rendered in Hollywood kitsch. Spacious rms w. private balconies and refrigerators, or pleasant bungalows around the pool. Small tropical garden. An oasis of rest and peace in the heart of the "Strip." Inconsistent svce. Good value on balance. **E–VE**

New Otani Hotel and Garden, 120 S. Los Angeles St. (dwntwn), Los Angeles, CA 90012 (213/629-1200; toll free 800/421-8795). 448 rms, A/C, color TV, in-rm movies. AE, CB, DC, MC, V. Garage $6, health club, sauna, three rests. (including Commodore Perry's), coffeeshop, two bars, rm svce, hrdrsr, boutiques. *Note:* Japanese style, geared to American taste; modern and well designed. Rms w. tatami mats or Western style, w. refrigerators. Very pretty Japanese garden. Good svce. Business clientele. Very nr. the Little Tokyo business district. Recently renovated at a cost of $2 million. **E–VE**

Hilton Midtown, 400 N. Vermont Ave., Los Angeles, CA 90004 (213/662-4888; toll free, see Hilton). 206 rms, A/C, color TV, in-rm movies. AE, CB, DC, MC, V. Garage $6, pool, health club, sauna, two rests. (including Lotus), 24-hr coffeeshop, bar, rm svce, disco, free crib. *Note:* A brand-new hotel, a very successful essay in Mediterranean architecture. Halfway between Hollywood and the financial district. Spacious, ultra-comfortable rms, some w. refrigerators. Lovely garden w. fountain, waterfall, and little streams. Very efficient svce. Business travelers are well situated here, 10 min. from dwntwn, and there is a fully equipped business center. **E**

The Breakers, 210 E. Ocean Blvd., Long Beach, CA 90802 (213/432-8781; toll free 800/255-5053). 242 rms, A/C, color TV. AE, DC, MC, V. Garage $3, rest., bar, rm svce, disco, crib $10. *Note:* Original art deco building dating from 1926 and elegantly restored in the style of the Roaring '20s. Very comfortable rms, the best w. ocean view; friendly reception and svce. Directly on the beach; ideal for visiting the *Queen Mary* and other neighborhood attractions. **M–E**

Queen Mary Hotel, Pier J at Harbor Scenic Dr., Long Beach, CA 90801 (213/435-3511; toll free 800/421-3732). 390 rms, A/C, color TV, in-rm movies. AE, CB, DC, MC, V. Parking $2, two rests. (including the Promenade Café), bar, rm svce, boutiques. *Note:* The world's largest ocean liner, now a floating hotel, but still with her original art deco scheme of decoration; the svce, however, bears only the remotest resemblance to what it was under the great Cunard Line in the 1930s. Draws many tourists. 45 min. from dwntwn. **M–E**

Sheraton Anaheim, 1015 W. Ball Rd., Anaheim, CA 92802 (714/778-1700; toll free, see Sheraton). 500 rms, A/C, color TV, in-rm movies. AE, CB, DC, MC, V. Free parking, pool, rest., coffeeshop, bar, rm svce, free crib. *Note:* A motel in a Tudor idiom as reviewed and corrected by Hollywood. Comfortable, spacious rms w. mini-bars. Family clientele; ideal for visiting Disneyland (free bus) and Knotts Berry Farm. Good svce. Very good value. **M–E**

Ramada Inn, 12500 E. Firestone Blvd., Norwalk, CA 90650 (213/868-0401; toll free, see Ramada Inns). 268 rms, A/C, cable color TV. AE, CB, DC, MC, V. Free parking, two pools, putting green, 24-hr rest., bar, rm svce, disco, free crib. *Note:* Comfortable motel in a 12-acre garden; spacious, well-designed rms w. private patios. Courteous reception and svce. 10 min. from Disneyland and Knotts Berry Farm. Interesting family packages. Halfway between Disneyland and dwntwn. **M**

Best Western Mikado, 12600 Riverside Dr., North Hollywood, CA 91607 (818/763-9141; toll free, see Best Western). 58 rms, A/C, color TV. AE, CB, DC, MC, V. Free parking, pool, rest., bar, rm svce, free breakfast, crib $10. *Note:* Friendly motel in the hills overlooking Hollywood; vaguely exotic décor. Comfortable rms, friendly reception and svce. Very acceptable Japanese rest. Good value. **M**

Holiday Inn Downtown, 750 Garland Ave. (dwntwn), Los Angeles, CA 90017 (213/628-5242; toll free, see Holiday

Inns). 204 rms, A/C, color TV. AE, CB, DC, MC, V. Free garage, pool, rest. (Pipers), bar, rm svce, free crib. *Note:* Conventional six-story motel very nr. the Convention Center; functionally comfortable. Business clientele. Good value. **I–M**

Hotel Hollywood, 5825 Sunset Blvd., Hollywood, CA 90028 (213/462-5400; toll free 800/445-0021). 90 rms, A/C, cable color TV. AE, CB, DC, MC, V. Garage $5, rest., bar, rm svce, disco, free crib. *Note:* Modern hotel w. a rest. on the top floor offering a fine view of Hollywood and its hills. Spectacular outside elevator. Art deco–style interior. Inviting rms. Free limo to neighboring destinations; ideal for visiting Hollywood and Universal Studios. **I–M**

Best Western Kent Inn, 920 S. Figueroa St. (dwntwn), Los Angeles, CA 90015 (213/626-8701; toll free, see Best Western). 91 rms, A/C, color TV, in-rm movies. AE, CB, DC, MC, V. Free parking, pool, sauna, rest., bar, crib $5. *Note:* A small, functional motel in the heart of dwntwn, nr. the Convention Center. Comfortable rms w. refrigerators. Friendly reception. Business clientele; good value. **I**

Vagabond, 1904 W. Olympic Blvd., Los Angeles, CA 90006 (213/380-9393; toll free, see Vagabond Hotels). 54 rms, A/C, color TV. AE, CB, DC, MC, V. Free parking, pool, adjoining 24-hr coffeeshop, free crib. *Note:* Small, standard, but well-run motel, centrally located 5 min. from the Convention Center. Functional rms; friendly reception. **I**

Westward Ho 7 Seas, 415 W. Katella Ave., Anaheim, CA 92802 (714/778-6900). 175 rms, A/C, color TV. AE, MC, V. Free parking, pool, coffeeship, free breakfast, crib $5. *Note:* Ordinary motel, 3 min. from Disneyland by car. Modest but well run. Free limo to Disneyland. Good value. **I, but out-of-season discounts.**

Motel 6, 1001 San Gabriel Blvd., Rosemead, CA 91770 (818/572-6076). 130 rms, A/C, color TV, free in-rm movies. DC, MC, V. Free parking, pool. cafe adj. open 24 hrs. *Note:* Modern, functional motel at ultra-reasonable prices, 20 min. from dwntwn along Cal. 60 and U.S. 101. Ideal if you're driving; excellent value. **B**

Motel 6, 7450 Katella Ave., Stanton, CA 90680 (714/891-0717). 207 rms, A/C, color TV, free in-rm movies. DC, MC, V. Free parking, pool. *Note:* Typical motel at ultrareasonable prices; ideal as a base for visiting Disneyland and Knott's Berry Farm (10 min. by car). Excellent value. **B**

Airport Accommodations

Amfac Hotel (formerly the Airport Marina), 8601 Lincoln Blvd., Los Angeles, CA 90045 (213/670-8111; toll free, see Amfac Hotels). 750 rms, A/C, color TV, in-rm movies. AE, CB, DC, MC, V. Free parking, pool, golf course, tennis court, health club, two rests., coffeeshop, bars, rm svce, disco, hrdrsr, free airport limo around the clock. *Note:* Ideal for the traveler in transit. Comfortable rms w. private balconies or patios; handsome indoor garden; efficient svce. VIP floor. Very near Marina del Rey and 5 min. from airport. Business and group clientele. **M–E**

Airport Century Inn, 5547 W. Century Blvd., Los Angeles, CA 90045 (213/649-4000; toll free 800/421-3939). 147 rms, A/C, color TV, in-rm movies. AE, CB, DC, MC. V. Free parking, pool, rest., 24-hr coffeeshop, bar, rm svce, free airport limo, crib $4. *Note:* Recently renovated airport motel. Spacious, comfortable rms, the best overlooking the pool. Very efficient svce. A good value, 5 min. from the terminal. **I–M**

YMCA/Youth Hostel

YMCA, 1553 N. Hudson Ave., Hollywood (213/467-4161). 56 rms, pool, health club, coffeeshop. For men and women; also youth hostel.

RESTAURANTS

Los Angeles Restaurant Prices	
(per person, excluding drinks and service charges)	
B (Budget)	up to $15
I (Inexpensive)	$15–$25
M (Moderate)	$25–$40
E (Expensive)	$40–$60
VE (Very Expensive)	$60 and up

Personal Favorites (in order of preference)

Michael's, 1147 3rd St., Santa Monica (451-0843). A/C. Lunch/dinner daily; Sat.-Sun. brunch; closed holidays. AE, CB, DC, MC, V. Jkt. *Specialties:* broiled lobster w. basil and fresh pepper pasta, scallops w. watercress purée, foie gras salad vinaigrette, Oregon salmon w. beurre blanc, pigeon w. leeks and raspberry vinegar, caramelized veal w. lemon. Remarkable desserts (chocolate caramel pie). Fine wine list. *Note:* A shrine of California gastronomy. The cuisine of the young and talented chef, Michael McCarty, though French-inspired, is authentically American, as are the materials he uses. His delicate, imaginative touch is highlighted by his talent for presentation. Elegant neo-modern dining room in the Bauhaus style, w. contemporary works of art worthy of a museum. Charming patio w. umbrella tables for fine days. Friendly, diligent svce. One of the dozen best rests. in the country. Resv. a must. *American.* **E–VE**

L'Ermitage, 730 N. La Cienega Blvd., Los Angeles (652-5840). A/C. Dinner only, Mon.-Sat.; closed Sun., holidays. AE, CB, DC, MC, V. J&T. *Specialties:* mousse of duck liver w. juniper berries, shredded duck w. cabernet, roast pigeon w. cassis, filet de St. Pierre (dory) w. morels, sweetbreads w. wild mushrooms, lobster salad w. zucchini and truffles, sautéed trout w. wood mushrooms, saddle of lamb en croûte, chocolate soufflé. Big wine list. *Note:* Until the death of its chef and owner, Jean Bertranou, this could reasonably have claimed to be the best rest. in the country. Michel Blanchet has succeeded brilliantly in safeguarding his culinary legacy. Food and svce of the highest order, equal to the finest three-star rests. in France. Elegant, recently remodeled décor enhanced by lavish flower arrangements. Pretty covered patio. Valet parking. *French.* **VE**

Saint Estephe, 2640 Sepulveda Blvd., Manhattan Beach (545-1334). A/C. Lunch Tues.-Fri., dinner Tues.-Sat.; closed Sun., Mon., and holidays. AE, CB, DC, MC, V. Jkt. *Specialties:* carne adobada, ravioli w. cream and goat-cheese sauce, blue corn tortillas w. caviar, millefeuille of lobster w. coriander and calabacita, lamb sweetbreads w. chili seeds, salmon and sea bass w. chimayo sauce. Menu changes regularly. Wine list at outrageous prices. *Note:* John Sedlar, in a subtle marriage of French and southwestern U.S. strains, has created an original cuisine which might be dubbed "nouvelle cuisine Santa Fe style." The chili, blue corn, and coriander make up a symphony of unfamiliar flavors which will delight the gourmet. Sober, austere pueblo-style interior with green plants and Peruvian tapestries and wall paintings. One of the great successes of today's Los Angeles cuisine. Resv. advised. 40 min. from dwntwn. *American.* **M**

Scandia, 9040 Sunset Blvd., West Hollywood (278-3555). A/C. Lunch/dinner Tues.-Sat., brunch Sun.; closed Mon., Jan. 1, Dec. 25. AE, CB, DC, MC, V. Jkt. *Specialties:* poached turbot hollandaise, frikadeller, herring filets in sherry, veal Oscar, gravlax w. anise sauce, Viking platter, beef à la Lindstrom, Danish pastries. *Note:* One of Hollywood's most unusual, and most popular, rests. since 1955. Scandinavian décor and food; efficient svce. Resv. suggested but, alas, seldom honored. Open till 1 a.m. The country's finest Scandinavian restaurant. *Scandinavian-continental.* **I–M**

Rebecca's, 2025 Pacific Ave., Venice (306-6266). A/C. Dinner only, nightly. AE, CB, DC, MC, V. *Specialties:* broiled tunafish tostadas w. black beans, ceviche, tamales w. red chili sauce, chiles rellenos w. pork and hazelnut sauce, broiled lobster w. pink-grapefruit salsa, leg of lamb adobado, quesadillas. *Note:* Décor by Frank Gehry, the farthest-out in all Los Angeles, w. crocodiles and other marine monsters in Plexiglas or Formica hanging from the ceiling. But the main reason for a visit to Rebecca's is its remarkable Mexican food, as updated by proprietor Bruce Marder (who also owns the fashionable West Beach Café, see below). Add generously conceived drinks, an interesting wine list at reasonable prices, smiling, helpful svce, and a fashionable clientele which comes more to eat than to see and be seen, and you have the sure-fire formula for Rebecca's overwhelming success. Resv. a must. Valet parking. *Mexican.* **I–M**

Gladstone's 4 Fish, 17300 W. Pacific Coast Hwy., Pacific Palisades (454-3474). A/C. Breakfast/lunch/dinner daily (until midnight). *Specialties:* All kinds of fish and shellfish (the house specialties are broiled over a wood fire), ceviche Peruvian style, chocolate-chip cheesecake. *Note:* An enormous choice of impeccably fresh fish—but make it clear to the server how you want it cooked. Given the quality of the food, the prices are very gratifying. Classical marine décor and ocean view. Good svce. Successful enough that resv. are recommended. Valet parking. Other location: 900 Bayside Dr., Newport Beach (714/645-3474). *Seafood.* **I**

Katsu, 1972 Hillhurst Ave., Los Angeles (665-1891). A/C. Dinner only, nightly. AE, MC, V. *Specialties:* sushi, tempura, kaiseki dinner (Japanese ceremonial banquet). *Note:* A place of pilgrimage for sushi lovers, very near Griffith Park, because of the exceptional freshness of the seafood and the refinement w. which it is prepared and presented. The décor is a rather chilly modern, relieved by a collection of Mineo Mizuno's beautiful ceramics. The sushi is excellent value, but beware of the bill for the kaiseki dinner, which in any case may disappoint you. This is a small rest., so resv. are recommended. *Japanese.* **I**

Pacific Dining Car, 1310 W. 6th St., Los Angeles (438-6000). A/C. Breakfast/lunch/dinner daily (open around the clock). MC, V. Jkt. *Specialties:* excellent steaks broiled to perfection, fish of the day, Caesar salad, cheesecake. *Note:* Since 1921 this authentic railroad diner and its annex have brought joy to Angeleno meat-lovers around the clock. The beef and lamb are of the highest quality, and the wine list includes some remarkable labels at appropriate prices. When you order, make it quite clear how you like your meat cooked. Good svce. Resv. advised. Valet parking at dinner. *Steakhouse.* **M**

Korean Gardens, 950 S. Vermont Ave., Los Angeles (388-3042). A/C. Lunch/dinner daily. AE, MC, V. *Specialties:* juk (rice w. abalone), sinsullo, kunjol pan (vegetable pancake), mandu-kuk (beef bouillon w. dumplings), bul-kogi (marinated beef). *Note:* With some 200,000 Koreans living in Los Angeles, the food here has to be authentic. Many delicate flavors, but spicy-hot dishes as well, thanks to the redoubtable Korean kim chee (highly spiced sauerkraut). Vaguely exotic décor, diligent svce. For lovers of the unusual. *Korean.* **B–I**

R.J.'s. The Rib Joint, 252 N. Beverly Dr., Beverly Hills (274-7427). A/C. Lunch/dinner daily, brunch Sun. AE, CB, DC, MC, V. *Specialties:* barbecued spareribs, short ribs, chili, broiled chicken, fresh fish of the day, chocolate cake. *Note:* A real local institution, w. sawdust on the floor and ceiling fans. Straightforward, tasty food in generous portions, w. more than 55 dishes on the menu. Gigantic salad bar. Very popular locally, so resv. advisable. One of the best buys in Los Angeles. Valet parking. *American.* **B–I**

Other Restaurants (from top bracket to budget)

L'Orangerie, 903 N. La Cienega Blvd., Los Angeles (652-9770). Dinner only, nightly; closed holidays. AE, CB, DC, MC, V. A/C. *Specialties:* fish soup with rouille, médaillons of veal w. three mustards, cassolette of lobster, filet of lamb w. parsley sauce, roast quail w. shallots, broiled sea bass w. Pernod. Unusually good desserts. The wine list is admirable; the prices less so. *Note:* Classical French cooking, contemporary style, in an elegant greenhouse setting composed of high glass bays, mirrors, and green plants. Ultrapolished svce. Favored by local society; a very distinguished environment. Resv. a must. Valet parking. *French.* **E–VE**

Valentino, 3115 Pico Blvd., Santa Monica (829-4313). A/C. Dinner only, Mon.-Sat. (until midnight); closed Sun., holidays. AE, CB, DC, MC, V. Jkt. *Specialties:* gnocchi w. seafood, vegetable risotto, carpaccio of tuna, baby lamb w. broccoli and mousse of lima beans, roulade of swordfish w. shrimp and lime juice, ragoût of kidneys, and venison w. polenta. One of California's finest cellars (50,000 bottles) w. the best wines from California, France, and Italy. *Note:* Unlike the legendary Rudolf Valentino, whose name the rest. has borrowed, the proprietor, Piero Selvaggio, is Sicilian not Apulian. His brilliant, inventive cooking, his luxuriously renovated décor, and his highly polished service combine to make this one of the best rests. on the West Coast. Very fashionable clientele; resv. a necessity. Valet parking. *Italian.* **M–E**

La Toque, 8171 Sunset Blvd., West Hollywood (656-7515). A/C. Lunch Mon.-Fri., dinner Mon.-Sat.; closed Sun., holidays. AE, CB, DC, MC, V. Jkt. *Specialties:* eggs en croûte perfumed w. truffles, fresh tuna tartare, gratin of St. Pierre (dory) w. sea urchins, soufflé of salmon, saddle of lamb w. tarragon. Menu changes regularly. The wine list cannot be described as substantial. *Note:* Ken Frank, one of the most gifted American chefs of his generation, has risen in a comparatively few years to the top of the profession on the wings of his innovative talent, his airy sauces, and the delicacy w. which his dishes are presented. Romantic old-French-inn setting; attentive svce. Resv. necessary. Valet parking. *French.* **M–E**

Chianti, 7383 Melrose Ave., Hollywood (653-8333). A/C. Dinner only, nightly (until midnight); closed holidays. AE, MC, V. Jkt. *Specialties:* fettuccine all'Alfredo, paglia e fieno, saltimbocca alla romana, carpaccio, veal piccata, osso buco, tiramisù. Good list of Italian wines. *Note:* Elegant and sophisticated, this rest. in its venerable art deco setting—a Hollywood classic since 1938—is a must for lovers of northern Italian food, contemporary style. Very good svce; resv. a must. Valet parking. *Italian.* **M–E**

Citrus, 6703 Melrose Ave., Los Angeles (857-0034). A/C. Lunch/dinner Mon.-Sat.; closed Sun. AE, CB, DC, MC, V. Jkt. *Specialties:* cabbage salad w. crabmeat, endive quiche, sautéed salmon w. leek purée, couscous of chicken and spiced lamb sausage, dolphin w. zucchini in sauce verte, oyster flan w. spinach and basil. Remarkable desserts and pastries. *Note:* The truculent but genial Michel Richard, one of the most original young French chefs working in this country, is a virtuoso at combining French and Californian nouvelle cuisine. Immaculate modern décor w. inviting open patio (but uncomfortable chairs). Courteous, efficient svce. Much frequented by movie stars and other celebrities. Resv. essential—this is an "in" place. *French-American.* **M**

The Four Oaks, 2181 N. Beverly Glen Blvd., Bel Air (470-2265). A/C. Lunch/dinner daily. Sun. brunch. AE, MC, V. Jkt. *Specialties:* crayfish salad, sauteed salmon or sea bass, boned rack of lamb, roast squab, sauteed foie gras w onion marmalade and apples, creme brulee. Reasonably priced wine list. *Note:* Cozy country-club ambience complete with bar and fireplace. The delicate and inventive cuisine is nouvelle continental with French overtones. Charming, tree-shaded terrace for alfresco dining. Service is appropriately attentive. *Continental.* **M**

The Palm, 9001 Santa Monica Blvd., West Hollywood (550-8811). A/C. Lunch Mon.-Sat., dinner nightly; closed holidays. AE, CB, DC, MC, V. Jkt. *Specialties:* prime beef, Maine lobster, homemade cheesecake. *Note:* A subsidiary of New York's well-known Palm. Same wonderful steaks, same caricatures on the wall, same enormous helpings (lobsters of 4½ lbs., 2 kg, and up). Noisy, relaxed atmosphere; very good svce (unlike its New York counterpart). *Steak-seafood.* **M**

Patout's, 2260 Westwood Blvd., West Los Angeles (475-7100). A/C. Lunch Mon.-Fri., dinner nightly. AE, DC, MC, V. Jkt. *Specialties:* spaghetti w. shrimp, gumbo, redfish filet and crabmeat in lemon butter, Cajun-style fish, crayfish à l'étouffée (in season), tournedos Patout. *Note:* A sister establishment of the renowned Patout's in New Iberia, Louisiana, this authentic Cajun rest. is a genial goodwill ambassador for bayou country. Fish and shellfish are flown in daily from New Orleans. First-class svce. This place can be highly recommended. Resv. advisable. Valet parking. *Créole.* **M**

The Grill, 9560 Dayton Way, Beverly Hills (276-0615). A/C. Lunch/dinner Mon.-Sat. (until 12:30 a.m.); closed Sun. AE, CB, DC, MC, V. Jkt. *Specialties:* Cobb salad, steak, lamb chops, broiled calves' liver, fish of the day, rice pudding, hot-fudge sundae. *Note:* Tucked away in an alley behind Giorgio's famous boutique on Rodeo Drive, this likeable rest. is a joy to those who like real, unaffected, unpretentious American food—and large helpings of it. For Beverly Hills, the décor is undistinguished. Efficient svce; valet parking. A fine place. *American.* **I–M**

Knoll's Black Forest Inn, 2454 Wilshire Blvd., Santa Monica (395-2212). A/C. Lunch Tues.-Fri., dinner Tues.-Sun.; closed Mon. AE, MC, V. Jkt. *Specialties:* sauerbraten w. potato pancakes, wild boar w. wild rice, roast goose, veal cutlet w. sour cherries, médaillon of venison w. chanterelle mushrooms, Black Forest cake. *Note:* Since 1960 this has been the best place in Los Angeles for lovers of good German food. As well as the classics of German cooking it offers lighter dishes, and some which are unashamedly innovative. Traditional Swiss-Bavarian chalet setting w. a charming garden for open-air meals. Very good svce. *German.* **I–M**

Le Dome, 8720 Sunset Blvd., Los Angeles (659-6919). A/C. Lunch/dinner Mon.-Sat. (until midnight); closed Sun. AE, DC, MC, V. Jkt. *Specialties:* ragoût of veal w. mustard and fresh thyme, cassoulet, calves' liver lyonnaise, rabbit chasseur, calves' tongue gribiche, choucroute garnie, fish of the day. Tempting desserts; good wine list. *Note:* A few really earthy dishes make this luxurious, trendy brasserie one of the most likeable of Los Angeles' fashionable eating-places. Elegant modernist décor. Broad, inviting circular bar. Resv. advised. Valet parking. *French.* **I–M**

The Mandarin, 430 N. Camden Dr., Beverly Hills (272-0267). A/C. Lunch Mon.-Fri., dinner nightly; closed holidays. AE, CB, DC, MC, V. Jkt. *Specialties:* shark's-fin soup, hot-and-sour shrimp, chopped squab in lettuce, Mongolian lamb, Peking duck, beggar-man's chicken, (hot) Szechuan dishes. Fine wine list. *Note:* Same quality and same elaborate décor, w. numerous Far Eastern art objects, as the parent establishment in San Francisco; the food, however, is a little less impressive. Mandarin dinners must be ordered 24 hrs ahead. Impeccable svce. Resv. advisable. Valet parking at dinner. *Chinese.* **I–M**

Primi, 105432 W. Pico Blvd., Los Angeles (475-9235). A/C. Lunch and dinner daily until midnight. AE, DC, MC, V. Jkt. *Specialties:* seafood ravioli, risotto negro (w.squid ink), warm chicken salad w. gorgonzola, a variety of sandwiches, 20 kinds of fresh pâté maison. *Note:* The name Primi refers to the Italian word for hors d' oeuvres, *primi platti,* which is precisely what is offered by this unusual rest. dreamed up by Piero Selvaggio, proprietor of the luxurious Valentino (see above). The "appetizers" here are dishes in their own right, served in small portions. The fixed-price sampling menu (10 small dishes for $25) is a feast for the eye as well as for the palate. Excellent selection of Italian and Californian wines. High-tech décor, with polished steel ceiling, abstract paintings, colored silk hangings, and a black marble bar. Swift, attentive svce. Resv. indispensable, given the rest.'s popularity. *Italian.* **I-M**

West Beach Café, 60 N. Venice Blvd., Venice (823-5396). A/C. Breakfast/lunch Tues.-Sun., dinner nightly until 1:30 a.m. AE, CB, DC, MC, V. Jkt. *Specialties:* water buffalo mozzarella w. pesto, seafood sausage w. herbs, filet mignon tacos, asparagus risotto, roast duck, daily catch, sabayon w. fruit. *Note:* The highly imaginative California-style cuisine and the avant-garde setting with frequently changing modern paintings are the two principal attractions at this stylish rest., while the spectacular bar and fine svce. also contribute to its success. The menu changes regularly, and there is a wide selection of wines by the glass or the bottle. Caters to local artists and trendy Angelenos. Resv. highly recommended. Valet parking. *American.* **I-M**

Antonio's, 7472 Melrose Ave., Los Angeles (655-0480). A/C. Lunch/dinner Tues.-Sun.; closed Mon., July 4, and Labor Day. AE, MC, V. Jkt. *Specialties:* green pepper stuffed w. coriander, chicken pipián, steak w. green sauce, jicama salad, fruit flan. *Note:* Antonio Gutierrez offers delicious and inventive Mexican fare, keeping well off the beaten track of Mexican rest. clichés. Despite a rather loud color scheme, the décor is much less original than the food. Good wine list. Friendly svce. Mariachi bands at dinner. Popular locally. Resv. recommended. Valet parking at dinner. *Mexican.* **I**

Gitanjali, 414 N. La Cienega Blvd., West Hollywood (657-2117). A/C. Dinner only nightly. AE, CB, DC, MC, V. *Specialties:* bhajias, tandoori dishes, chicken tikka, chicken vindaloo, vegetarian dishes. Good wine list. *Note:* One of Los Angeles' oldest and most respected Indian rests. Offers all the subtleties of Punjabi, Kashmiri, Bengali, and Tamil Nadu cooking, spiced with a cunning hand. The décor is a dream of the exotic, with old paintings and copper chandeliers. Good svce, although the waiters are rather absurdly got up as turbaned maharajahs. Resv. advised. *Indian.* **I**

Musso & Frank Grill, 6667 Hollywood Blvd., Hollywood (467-7788). A/C. Lunch/dinner Mon.-Sat.; closed Sun., holidays. AE, CB, DC, MC, V. Jkt. *Specialties:* calves' liver w. onions, bouillabaisse, chicken pot pie, lamb chops, sauerbraten, corned beef and cabbage, creamed spinach, fish of the day. *Note:* Of roughly the same age as the movie industry

(1919), Musso & Frank is a Hollywood monument. The food is uneven, but generally pleasing and substantial; the svce is surly. Comfortable interior with dark-wood paneling and red leather. *Continental-American.* I

♀ **Papadakis Taverna,** 301 W. 6th St., San Pedro (548-1186). ☒ A/C. Dinner only, nightly; closed Mon. MC, V. *Specialties:* moussaka, tiropita, arni psito (roast lamb), shish kebab, baklava. Greek and California wines. *Note:* A more authentic taverna than you might find in Greece, wreathed (as an extra added attraction) in the aromas of the nearby fishing port. A likeable, warm, friendly place, with 100% authentic Greek food and smiling, efficient svce. Locally popular; resv. advised. 10 min. from the port of Long Beach and its tourist attractions. *Greek.* I

♀ **Siamese Princess,** 8048 W. 3rd St., Los Angeles (653-2643). ☒ A/C. Lunch Mon.-Fri., dinner nightly. AE, CB, DC, MC, V. *Specialties:* nam chim salad, mu wan (calamari w. coriander), duck w. ginger, ma haw (spiced pork), chicken wing kai. *Note:* The best of the multitude of Thai rests. that have grown and flourished in California over the past decade. Tasty but delicate food, and (what's uncommon in a Far Eastern rest.) a very good wine list. Slightly kitsch interior with portraits of the Thai royal family on the walls. Very good svce. Resv. advised. *Thai.* I

♀♀ **Yamato,** in the Westin Century Plaza (see "Accommodations," above), Century City (277-1840). A/C. Lunch/dinner daily; closed Labor Day, Thanksgiving, Dec. 25. AE, CB, DC, MC, V. Jkt. *Specialties:* beef sukiyaki, shrimp tempura, teppanyaki, shabu shabu, sushi bar. *Note:* Traditional Japanese décor with meditation garden, but also a conventional Western dining room. The food is perfectly prepared and served. Same management as the well-known rest. of the same name in San Francisco. Locally popular; resv. advised. *Japanese.* I

♀ **Grand Star,** 943 Sun Mun Way, Los Angeles (626-2285). ☒ A/C. Lunch/dinner daily. AE, CB, DC, MC, V. *Specialties:* wonton soup, lobster Cantonese, Mongolian beef, barbecued pork, steamed fish. *Note:* One of Chinatown's best; absolutely authentic food at very moderate prices. Comfortable, intimate atmosphere; a favorite of those in-the-know. *Chinese.* **B–I**

♀ **El Cholo,** 1121 S. Western Ave., Los Angeles (734-2773). ☒ A/C. Lunch/dinner daily; closed Thanksgiving, Dec. 25. AE, MC, V. *Specialties:* enchiladas, tacos, burritos dorados, chiles rellenos, tamales verdes, tostadas. *Note:* Of the innumerable Mexican rests. in Los Angeles, purists think this is the best, with its absolutely authentic food and setting. Comfortable dining rooms and patios. A classic of its kind since 1927; resv. advised. *Mexican.* **B**

☼♀ **Nate 'n Al's,** 414 N. Beverly Dr., Beverly Hills (274-0101). ☒ A/C. Breakfast/lunch/dinner daily (until 8:30 p.m.). CB, DC. *Specialties:* giant sandwiches, herring in sour cream, roast turkey, pastrami, stuffed cabbage, corned beef, homemade cheesecake. *Note:* A Beverly Hills classic since 1945, an authentic New York deli serving generous portions at very modest prices. Unpretentious décor; efficient, smiling svce. Very popular locally, especially at lunchtime. No resv. *American.* **B**

CAFETERIAS/SPECIALTY SPOTS: ☼ **Cassell's,** 3300 W. 6th St., Los Angeles (480-8668). Lunch only, Mon.-Sat. No credit cards. The best hamburgers in all Los Angeles; excellent sandwiches.

Clifton's Cafeteria, 648 S. Broadway, Los Angeles (627-1673). Open daily. No credit cards. Acceptable daily specials, sandwiches. Very good value. Five other locations in the city.

Duke's, 8909 Sunset Blvd., Hollywood (652-9411). Breakfast/lunch daily, dinner Mon.-Fri. No credit cards. Giant sandwiches, 24 kinds of hamburger, very acceptable daily specials. Locally popular.

Original Pantry, 877 S. Figueroa St., Los Angeles (972-9279). Open daily around the clock. No credit cards. Excellent cafeteria food and commendable steaks at very reasonable prices; popular for half a century.

☼ **Pink's,** 711 N. La Brea Blvd., dwntwn (931-4223). Open daily. No credit cards. By general consent the best hot dogs in the city (and a dynamite chili sauce); also good hamburgers. Very popular locally.

WHERE TO EAT IN LOS ANGELES?

American: Michael's (ΨΨΨΨΨ), Saint Estephe (ΨΨΨ), The Grill (ΨΨ), West Beach Café (ΨΨ), Nate 'n Al (Ψ), R.J.'s. The Rib Joint (Ψ)

Chinese: The Mandarin (ΨΨΨ), Grand Star (Ψ)

Continental: Musso & Frank Grill (ΨΨ), The Four Oaks (ΨΨ)

Creole: Patout's (ΨΨ)

Cafeterias/Fast food: Cassell's, Clifton's, Duke's, Original Pantry, Pink's.

French: L'Ermitage (ΨΨΨΨ), L'Orangerie (ΨΨΨΨ), Citrus (ΨΨΨ), La Toque (ΨΨΨ), Le Dome (ΨΨ)

German: Knoll's Black Forest Inn (ΨΨ)

Greek: Papadakis Taverna (Ψ)

Hamburgers: Cassell's

Indian: Gitanjali (ΨΨ)

Italian: Valentino (ΨΨΨΨ), Chianti (ΨΨΨ), Primi (ΨΨ)

Japanese: Katsu (ΨΨ), Yamato (ΨΨ)

Korean: Korean Gardens (Ψ)

Mexican: Antonio's (ΨΨ), Rebecca's (ΨΨ), El Cholo (Ψ)

Scandinavian: Scandia (ΨΨΨ)

Seafood: Gladstone's 4 Fish (ΨΨ)

Steaks, meat: The Palm (ΨΨ), Pacific Dining Car (Ψ)

Thai: Siamese Princess (Ψ)

Late-night service (closing time in parentheses): Chianti (midnight), Gladstone's 4 Fish (midnight), The Grill (12:30 a.m.), Le Dome (midnight), Pacific Dining Car (around the clock), Pink's (3 a.m.), Primi (midnight), Scandia (1 a.m.), Valentino (midnight), West Beach Café (1:30 a.m.)

BARS & NIGHTCLUBS

The insistent rhythm of Los Angeles by night makes it hard to draw up a list of "in" places; discos, bars, and nightclubs grow, wither, and die here with the leaves on the trees. However, here are some more durable names.

Carlos & Charlie's, 8240 Sunset Blvd., Hollywood (656-8830). Very popular singles bar; noisy and absolutely relaxed. Disco-rock music. Respectable Mexican food. Open nightly.

Casey's, 613 S. Grand Ave., dwntwn (629-2353). Favored by yuppies from the dwntwn financial district. Warm paneled interior with sporting posters. Trendy.

Chippendale's, 3739 Overland Ave., West Los Angeles (396-4045). Male striptease. Women's mud-wrestling. Disco nightly.

The Comedy Store, 8433 W. Sunset Blvd., West Hollywood (656-6225). One of the West Coast's best-known and most popular comedy clubs, where the biggest names in the business appear regularly. Trendy people in a trendy place.

☼ **Concerts by the Sea,** 100 Fisherman's Wharf, Redondo Beach (379-4998). One of the city's modern-jazz shrines; Ahmad Jamal and Milt Jackson are here often. Open Thurs.-Sun.

The Ginger Man, 369 N. Bedford Dr., Beverly Hills (273-7585). Likeable bar, with commendable rest., where local celebrities come. Owned by actors Patrick O'Neal and Carroll O'Connor. Open nightly till 2 a.m.

Hard Rock Café, 8614 Beverly Blvd., Los Angeles (276-7605). Facsimile of the well-known London nightclub of the same name; good hamburgers, hard rock, young customers. Open nightly until midnight.

Harry's Bar, 2020 Ave. of the Stars, Century City (277-2333). California branch of the famous bar/rest. in Venice of which Hemingway wrote. Draws mostly TV people (the ABC Entertainment Center is nearby). Also acceptable Italian rest. Open nightly.

☀ **The Improv.,** 8162 Melrose Ave., West Hollywood (651-2583). Granddaddy of the local comedy clubs; shows generally of high quality, sometimes with big-name stars. The rest., despite its name (Hell's Kitchen), is acceptable.

The Palace, 1735 N. Vine St., Hollywood (462-3000). 1930s dance hall, wonderfully restored. Thunderous PA system. Laser machines, TV clips, good live music. Open nightly.

Palomino, 6907 Lankershim Blvd., North Hollywood (818/764-4010). The fashionable country and western place; come in boots and cowboy hat. Open nightly.

☀ **Polo Lounge,** in the Beverly Hills Hotel (see "Accommodations," above), Beverly Hills (276-2251). This bar has been famous for half a century; all the big names of the cinema came here, come here, or will come here to sip their whisky or tomato juice. Ideal for a working breakfast. Open nightly.

Redwoods 2nd Street Saloon, 316 W. 2nd St., dwntwn (617-2867). Most of the customers here work at the *Los Angeles Times*. Setting and atmosphere are comfortable.

Roxy, 9009 Sunset Blvd., West Hollywood (276-2222). The mecca of California rock; music live. Dates vary. Décor in the style of the Roaring '20s.

The Troubadour, 9081 Santa Monica Blvd., West Hollywood (276-1159). Live rock; many pop-rock stars performed here early in their careers, including Joan Baez, Bob Dylan, and Rod Stewart. Open Tues.-Sun.

Variety Arts Center, 940 S. Figueroa St., dwntwn (623-9100). Everyone talks about this big dwntwn nightclub, where you'll find a bar, a musical-comedy theater, a rest., dancing, and a jazz club. Lots of character and style. Open Thurs.-Sat.

Whisky A Go Go, 8901 Sunset Blvd., West Hollywood (652-4202). Big, noisy rock disco. Open nightly.

Yamashiro, 1999 North Sycamore Ave., Hollywood (466-5125). Agreeable bar, poor rest. Splendid nighttime view of the city in clear weather. Open nightly.

NEARBY EXCURSIONS

☀ 🔭 **MISSION SAN JUAN CAPISTRANO** (49 mi., 78 km, along I-5 to the Ortega Hwy. exit) (714/493-1424): Perched between the mountains and the sea, this was the most famous, and probably the loveliest, of California's missions. Founded in 1776 by the Spanish Franciscan Fr. Junipero Serra, it was badly damaged by an earthquake in 1812, but retains part of its cloister, Serra's chapel, ruins of the church with arches and pillars, and the priests' dormitory. In its enchanting gardens thousands of swallows nest from Mar. to Oct.; there's also an interesting little archeological museum. Open daily; don't miss it.

See also the **Regional Library and Cultural Center** at 31495 El Camino

Real (714/493-1752), an elegant post-modern building by Michael Graves. Well worth the side trip. Open daily.

    🔔 **MOUNT WILSON OBSERVATORY** (25 mi., 40 km, NE on Cal. 2) (818/577-1122): This astronomical observatory boasts a 100-inch (2.54-m) telescope; it is reached by a beautiful access road. The observatory itself is closed to visitors, but you can get a magnificent view of the entire Los Angeles region. Worth going out of your way for.

    ☀🔔 **SANTA CATALINA ISLAND (or CATALINA IS-LAND)** (22 mi., 35 km, offshore from Los Angeles): A paradise for bicyclists and big-game fishermen, this 22-mi.- (35-km-) long island, purchased in 1919 by the chewing-gum king William Wrigley, Jr., who had dreams of making it into a second Capri, is now entirely given over to tourism. There's a casino, some decorously rococo hotels, boat trips.

    Two good seafood rests. in the port of **Avalon** are the **Flying Yachtsman,** 403 Crescent Ave. (510-9177), and **Armstrong's,** 306 Crescent Ave. (510-0113), both open for lunch/dinner daily.

    The island can be reached in 20 min. by the **Helitrans** helicopter service, Berth 95, Harbor Blvd., San Pedro (548-1314 for resv., required); or in two hours by boat, **Catalina Island Cruises,** Berths 95 and 96, Harbor Blvd., San Pedro (514-3888).

    Well worth a visit.

    🔔 **WHITTIER** (12 mi., 19 km, SE via Whittier Blvd. and Cal. 72): Visit **Pio Pico State Historic Park,** 6003 Pioneer Blvd. (695-1217). Partially destroyed by flood in 1883, the former residence of Pio Pico, last Mexican governor of California (1852), has been almost entirely restored and offers a fine example of 19th-century colonial architecture. Original furniture and layout. Worth the detour. Open Wed.-Sun.

GHOST TOWNS: Rosamond, 75 mi. (120 km) north on I-5 and Cal. 14: Site of the 19th-century **Tropico Gold Mine** (805/256-2644), which may be visited Thurs.-Sun. The little town from the days of the Westward expansion. has been scrupulously restored.

    Nearby is **Edwards Air Force Base,** where the Space Shuttle lands. Worth the side trip.

NATIONAL PARKS NEARBY: ☀ 🏔 Death Valley, 305 mi. (490 km) NE on I-15, Cal. 127, and Cal. 190: The most beautiful of American deserts, and one of the natural wonders of the world (see Chapter 48 on Death Valley). On the way, stop at 🏔 **Calico,** 10 mi. (16 km) northeast of **Barstow,** a wonderful ghost town from the days of the gold rush (see "Ghost Towns" in Chapter 47 on Las Vegas).

    ☀🔔 **Sequoia National Park,** 220 mi. (354 km) north along I-5 and Cal. 198: The home of the giant trees (see Chapter 52). On the way, see 🔔**Kern County Pioneer Village,** 3801 Chester Ave. (3 mi., 5 km, east of Cal. 99), in Bakersfield (805/861-2132), open daily. This is the largest and best-preserved pioneer village in the entire state; see the Far West in its natural grandeur.

FARTHER AFIELD

    ☀🔔 **JOSHUA TREE NATIONAL MONUMENT** (304 mi., 486 km, round trip via the Pomona Frwy./Cal. 60, I-10, and

Cal. 60E, I-10E., and return): Cactus desert in flower from Mar. to May: a place of wild beauty. The yuccas, or Joshua trees, which have given the park its name, can grow to 64 ft (20 m). From **Salton View** (altitude 4,972 ft, 1,554 m), you can see as far as the Mexican frontier, 93 mi. (150 km) to the south. Splendid rocky landscapes, but watch for the temperature, especially in summer; it can rise high enough to cause engine overheating—and there are only three places in the whole park where you can get water. The **Visitor Center** at Twentynine Palms Oasis (619/367-7511) is open daily.

On the road, go a little out of your way through 🏛 **Riverside,** capital of the "Orange Empire," for a look at two of the most unusual buildings on the West Coast: **Heritage House,** 8193 Magnolia Ave., dating from 1891, an incredible mixture of Spanish, Victorian, and Tudor styles; and the **Mission Inn,** 3649 7th St. at Orange (714/784-0300), a charming Spanish-Moorish hotel, now almost a century old, where many well-known personalities (including Humphrey Bogart and Richard Nixon) have been married in the adjoining wedding chapel. Open daily.

Also visit **Palm Springs** (see below) and **Perris,** the home of hot-air ballooning. Balloon excursions can be arranged, at about $160 an hour for two people, through Dawn Flights (714/244-3511); resv. advisable.

☀🏛🔔🔔 **PALM SPRINGS** (216 mi., 344 km, round trip by I-10E, Cal. 111S, and return): A millionaires' city built in the middle of a desert at the foot of 8,516-ft (2,596-m) **Mount San Jacinto.** Don't miss the trip to the top by cable car on the **Palm Springs Aerial Tramway,** Tramway Rd. (619/325-1391); at 2.5 mi. (4 km) it's the world's longest single-span aerial tramway.

Once no more than a stagecoach stop, Palm Springs has become, in less than a century, one of the snootiest resorts in the country; dozens of celebrities from Bob Hope to Frank Sinatra, from Pres. Ford to Dean Martin, have favored it. Palm Springs and neighboring **Rancho Mirage** boast no fewer than 7,000 pools (one for every five inhabitants), 300 tennis courts, and 40 golf courses. The dry climate and continual (350 days a year) sunshine attract almost two million tourists a year. Hotels offer attractive rates in summer. There's a very fine **Desert Museum,** 101 Museum Dr. (619/325-7186), open Tues.-Sun., Oct.-June.

Where to Stay in the Palm Springs Area

☀🏛🏛🏛🏛 **La Quinta Hotel Golf and Tennis Resort,** 49-499 Eisenhower Dr., La Quinta, CA 92253 (619/564-4111). 270 rms in 63 cottages standing in 26 acres of gardens. One of the finest hotels in the country. Elegant and ultra-chic. Closed June-Sept. **E–VE**

🏛🏛🏛🏛 **Marriott's Rancho Las Palmas,** 41000 Bob Hope Dr., Rancho Mirage, CA 92270 (619/568-2727). 456 rms. Superdeluxe hotel, lovely garden. **VE**

🏛🏛 **Desert Inn,** 155 Belardo Rd., Palm Springs, CA 92262 (619/325-1301). 80 rms. Inviting, comfortable hotel. Bonus is the lovely garden. **M–E**

🏛 **Motel 6,** 595 E. Palm Canyon Dr., Palm Springs, CA 92262 (619/325-6129). 124 rms. Strictly functional motel at unbeatable prices. **B**

Where to Eat in the Palm Springs Area

🍷🍷🍷 **Le Vallauris,** 385 W. Tahquitz-McCallum Way, Palm Springs (619/325-5059). Lunch/dinner daily; closed Aug. AE, CB, DC, MC, V. *French.* **I–M**

Lyons English Grille, 233 E. Palm Canyon Dr., Palm Springs (619/327-1551). Dinner only, nightly. AE, CB, DC, MC, V. *Steak-Continental.* **I**

Medium Rare, 70-064 Cal. 111, Rancho Mirage (619/328-6563). Lunch Mon.-Fri., dinner nightly; closed mid-July to mid-Aug. AE, CB, DC, MC, V. *Continental.* **I**

Billy Reed's, 1800 N. Palm Canyon Dr., Palm Springs (619/325-1946). Three meals daily. MC, V. *American.* **B–I**

☀ COASTAL ROAD CAL. 1 TO SAN FRANCISCO OR SAN DIEGO: One of the country's most spectacular pano-
ramic highways; see chapter on the California Coast.

CHAPTER 55

SAN DIEGO☆☆

□ □ □

Discovered in 1542 by Juan Rodríguez Cabrillo, a Portuguese explorer in the Spanish service, San Diego Bay is one of the most spectacular natural settings on the West Coast. Don Gaspar de Portolá established the first garrison (Presidio) here in 1769 on the site of the present-day **Presidio Park,** thus making San Diego the point of departure for Spanish settlement in California. At the same time, the celebrated Franciscan Fr. Junipero Serra built here the first of the 21 missions that over the next half century he was to string along the Camino Real from the Mexican border to San Francisco, 540 mi. (860 km) to the north. From this storied colonial past California's second-largest city (after Los Angeles) has retained vestiges of Spanish and Mexican as well as American influence.

San Diego is not only an important market for the produce of the fertile lands around it (for example, two-thirds of the avocados consumed in the U.S. are grown here), but a vigorous port and industrial city with its face turned resolutely toward the future, with its centers of electronics, aerospace (General Dynamics), missile technology, medicine (the Salk Institute), and oceanography (Scripps Institution of Oceanography). This southernmost city in California has the 13th-fastest economic growth rate among U.S. metropolitan areas, and its population is keeping pace, rising 44% between 1970 and 1985. Finally, it's the largest naval base in the country after Norfolk, Virginia; the movie *Top Gun* was shot at the **Miramar Naval Air Station** north of San Diego.

For a number of years there has been a huge urban-renewal project in progress in the heart of downtown San Diego, testimony to the city's economic vigor; its symbol is the astonishing **Horton Plaza** commercial complex. At the same time, its gentle climate, its relaxed lifestyle, its exotic overtones (the Mexican city of **Tijuana,** half an hour's drive across the border, attracts 20 million Americans annually), and its setting among green hills rising from the turquoise waters of its bay, combine to make it a vacation and convention city overrun by visitors in summer and winter alike. Tourism ranks third among San Diego's industries, bringing in $2 billion a year. The crime rate, among the lowest in the country, with only nine murders per 100,000 inhabitants, is not the least of its attractions.

Over and above the vestiges of the Spanish Colonial era—including **Old Town** and **San Diego de Alcala,** the oldest Franciscan mission in California (1769)—San Diego offers dozens of miles of superb beaches, a paradise for surfers and scuba-divers; the tropical luxuriance of **Balboa Park** and its world-famous zoo; **Coronado** island and its legendary 19th-century Hotel del Coronado; and the unequalled view of the Pacific from **Point Loma.** The adjoining community of **La Jolla** (a corruption of the Spanish "La Joya," the jewel) is a charming little beach resort which is establishing itself more and more firmly as the chic, trendy place for a vacation home in southern California.

Famous people born in San Diego and La Jolla include the actors Gregory Peck (La Jolla), Robert Duvall, and Cliff Robertson.

BASIC FACTS: State of California. Area Code: 619. Time Zone: Pacific Time. ZIP Code: 92101. Founded: 1769. Approximate population: city, 1,025,000;

metropolitan area, 2,240,000. Seventh-largest city and 19th-largest metropolitan area in the U.S.

CLIMATE: Sheltered at the head of its bay, San Diego lives in a perpetual springtime; the yearly average temperature is 64°F (18°C). Mild in winter though with occasional storms (Jan. avg. 55°F, 13°C), deliciously temperate in spring and fall, quite warm during the summer days (up to 86°F, 30°C) but cool at night the year round, San Diego's climate approaches perfection. You'll need a swimsuit and sunglasses no matter when you come.

DISTANCES: Las Vegas, 331 mi. (550 km); Los Angeles, 125 mi. (200 km); Phoenix, 355 mi. (568 km); San Francisco, 540 mi. (865 km); Tucson, 414 mi. (662 km).

ARRIVAL & TRANSIT INFORMATION

AIRPORT: Lindbergh International Airport (SAN), 3 mi. (5 km) NW (231-7361). Charles Lindbergh's immortal *The Spirit of St. Louis* was built in San Diego, whence the airport's name.

AIRLINES: America West (560-0727), American (232-4051), Braniff (231-0700), Continental (232-9155), Delta (233-8040), Northwest (239-0488), Southwest (232-1221), TWA (295-7009), United (234-7171), and USAir (toll free 800/428-4322).

CITY LINK: The cab fare to city center is about $7-9; time, about 10 min. Bus: **Airporter Express** (231-1123), serving principal downtown hotels; fare, $3. Municipal bus: **San Diego Transit** (#2), stops on Broadway; fare, $1.

The city bus system, the SDTS, is extensive, but slow (information: 233-3004). There is also a modern express trolley system, still at an early stage of development: **San Diego Trolley** (information: 231-8549).

Taxis are reasonably inexpensive, but renting a car with unlimited mileage is advisable, given the large number of attractions outside the city.. California has very favorable car rental rates.

CAR RENTAL (at the airport unless otherwise indicated): Avis (231-7171); Budget (297-3851); Hertz (231-7000); Ladki (local renter with very competitive rates), 929 W. Laurel St. (233-9333); National (231-7100); and Thrifty, 2100 Kettner Blvd. (239-2281).

LIMOUSINE SERVICES: Carey Limousine (225-9551), Coronado Livery Service (435-6310), and VIP Limousine Service (299-7000).

TAXIS: Cabs may be summoned by phone or taken from the waiting lines outside the major hotels. Recommended companies: **Checker Cab** (234-4477), **Coast Taxi** (226-8294), **Orange Cab** (291-3333), and **Yellow Cab** (234-6161).

TRAIN: AMTRAK station, 1050 Kettner Blvd. at C St. (239-9021).

BUS: Greyhound, 120 W. Broadway (239-9171).

INFORMATION & TOURS

TOURIST INFORMATION: The **San Diego Convention and Visitors Bureau,** 1200 Third Ave., Suite 824, CA 92101 (619/232-3101).

Visitor Information Center, 11 Horton Plaza (619/236-1212).

For a **telephone recording** with an up-to-date list of cultural events and shows, call 619/239-9696.

GUIDED TOURS: Gray Line Tours (bus), 1670 Kettner Blvd. (231-9922): Conducted tours of the city and surroundings; serves major hotels.

San Diego Harbor Excursion (boat), Broadway at Harbor Dr. (619/233-6872): Boat trips around the harbor and bay, daily year round.

Tijuana Trolley: Ultramodern public transportation system linking the AMTRAK station at Kettner Blvd. and C St. in downtown San Diego with the Mexican border just this side of Tijuana. Departures every 15 min. from 5 a.m. till 1 a.m. Fare, $2; time, about 40 min. For information, call 619/231-8549.

Whale Watching Trips (boat): The **Natural History Museum,** Park Blvd., Balboa Park (619/232-3821), and the **Scripps Aquarium,** 8602 La Jolla Shores Dr., La Jolla (619/534-4578), organize boat trips to watch whales migrating, from mid-Dec. to mid-Feb. No fewer than 200 of the giant mammals are sighted offshore San Diego every day during this period. Another location: **H. & M. Landing,** 2803 Emerson St. (619/222-1144).

SIGHTS, ATTRACTIONS, & ACTIVITIES

ARCHITECTURAL HIGHLIGHTS: ☼ 🏛 **Horton Plaza,** bounded by First and Fourth Aves., Broadway, and G St.: The farthest-out shopping mall in the U.S. is to be found in the heart of downtown San Diego, featuring the daring post-modern design and pastel mauve, green, orange, and pink décor of architect Jon Jerde. It's an extravagant hodgepodge of façades, colonnades, and porticos which might remind you of a Venetian palace, an art deco theater, or a Spanish mission, but for the unusual modern sculptures. In the midst of all this you'll find mimes, comics, and strolling musicians doing their thing. Construction cost $140 million, and the finished product boasts four department stores, more than 150 retail outlets, restaurants, movie houses, etc. A visit you shouldn't miss. Open daily.

🏛 **University of California at San Diego,** La Jolla Village Dr. and N. Torry Pines Rd., La Jolla (534-4831). Founded in 1912 and now numbering more than 14,000 students, this campus specializes in biological and medical research. Its Cray X-MP 48 computer, one of only six in the world, cost $14 million and is one of the most powerful in existence, operating at a speed of 1.26 billion computations a second. On the lawns of the campus is a fine collection of modern sculpture. Worth seeing.

BEACHES: 🏖 **Borderfield Beach,** 20 mi. (32 km) south via I-5 and Monument Rd.: Right at the Mexican border. Surfing.

🏖 **Coronado Municipal Beach,** 5 mi. (8 km) west on Calif. 75: A family beach.

☼🏛🏖 **La Jolla Cove,** 12 mi. (19 km) NW via I-5 and Ardafer Rd.: The prettiest beach, and the chicest. Wonderful scuba-diving and hang-gliding.

🏖 **Mission Beach,** 8 mi. (12 km) NW on W. Mission Bay Dr.: The favorite of the local younger set.

🏖 **Ocean Beach,** 6 mi. (9 km) west on U.S. 8: Relatively uncrowded.

☼🏛🏖 **Torrey Pines Beach,** 20 mi. (32 km) north via I-5 and County Rd. 21: Huge unspoiled beach in a pine wood. Limited access. Lovely seascapes.

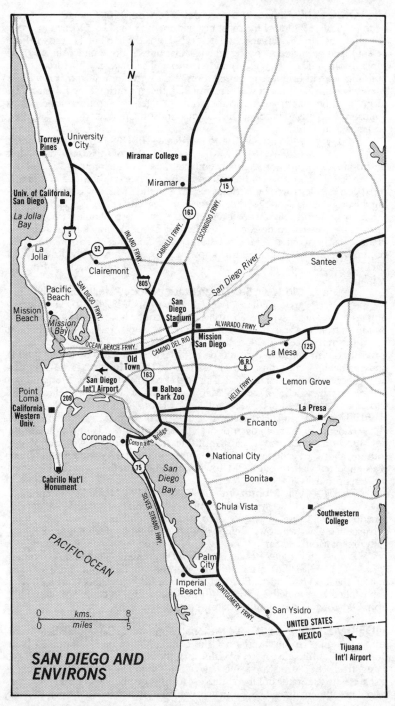

SAN DIEGO AND
ENVIRONS

HISTORIC BUILDINGS: ☼♨ð **Hotel del Coronado,** 1500 Orange Ave., Coronado (435-6611): One of the most historic hotels in the U.S. Opened in 1888, the "Del," as San Diegans affectionately call it, was the first hotel in the world to be equipped with electric power (the installation was done under the personal supervision of Thomas Edison) and elevators. The imposing Victorian frame building, with its bright-red pointed roofs, was a setting for the movie *Some Like It Hot.* Legend has it that it was here, in 1920, that the future King Edward VIII of England first met the woman for whom he later gave up the throne, Wallis Simpson, who was to become Duchess of Windsor. Conducted tours Sat. afternoons; worth seeing.

☼♨ð **Mission San Diego de Alcala,** 10818 San Diego Mission Rd. (283-7319): Known as "The Mother of Missions," this oldest mission in California was originally built on the site of the present-day **Presidio Park** in 1769 by the Spanish Franciscan Fr. Junipero Serra (beatified in 1988 by papal decree). Destroyed by earthquakes in 1803 and 1812, it was rebuilt following the original plans on the banks of the San Diego River in 1813, and is one of the most beautiful religious edifices on the West Coast. Shouldn't be missed; open daily. San Diego de Alcala was the first of the 21 missions built by the Franciscans between the Mexican border and Sonoma, north of San Francisco Bay, along what later became known as El Camino Real (the Royal Way). Each of the 21 missions was built one day's journey on horseback from its neighbors.

☼♨ð **Old Town San Diego State Historic Park,** bounded by Congress, Wallace, Twigg, and Juan Sts. (237-6770): The historic center of San Diego, with its Spanish Colonial adobe houses. Many interesting buildings from the years 1820–1870, lining a huge plaza where cockfights and bullfights were once held. Note the **Casa de Estudillo** (1820), residence of the governor of San Diego when it was part of Mexico. The **Casa de Lopez** (1834) houses a quaint candle museum. The **San Diego Union Building** is the office of a newspaper first published in 1868. The **Seeley Stables** (1869) was long the depot for the stagecoaches of the U.S. Mail. Collection of horse-drawn vehicles. The **Old California Museum,** besides a collection of horse-drawn vehicles, has a model of 19th-century San Diego. At the north corner of the plaza, where the **Casa de Pico,** residence of the first governor of California, once stood, is now the **Bazaar del Mundo,** a replica of a typical Spanish-Mexican marketplace, with craft shops, souvenir shops, art galleries, and restaurants set in courtyards and gardens. There is a signposted walk through Old Town for the benefit of visitors. Shouldn't be missed; open daily.

☼ð **Villa Montezuma,** 1925 K St. (239-2211): Magnificent piece of Victorian architecture contemporary with the Hotel del Coronado (1887). Colorful exterior decoration; very fine rococo interior with superb stained-glass windows. Temporary art exhibitions. Must be seen. Open daily except Mon. and Sat.

ð **Whaley House,** 2482 San Diego Ave. (298-2482): The oldest (1856) brick building in southern California; until 1871 it housed the local law courts. Believed to be haunted by the ghost of a man who was hanged here in 1852. Original furnishings and decoration. An easy walk from Old Town Plaza; should certainly be seen.

MONUMENTS: ☼♨♨ **Cabrillo National Monument,** Catalina Blvd. at Point Loma, 10 mi. (16 km) west on Calif. 209 (293-5450): Dedicated to Juan Rodríguez Cabrillo, discoverer of California, the monument with its lighthouse, dating from 1855, gives you a fine view of San Diego Bay and the Pacific Ocean. It shares with the Statue of Liberty in New York the distinction of being the most-visited monument in the U.S. From here you can watch the offshore migration of the gray whales in mid-Dec. to mid-Feb. Museum. Don't fail to visit. Open daily. The monument closes at sunset.

MUSEUMS OF ART: ❋ ⚏⚏ La Jolla Museum of Contemporary Art, 700

Prospect St., La Jolla (454-3541): If it were only for its site, in a garden overlooking the ocean, this superb museum of modern art would be worth visiting—but there are also works by Roy Lichtenstein, Donald Judd, Ellsworth Kelly, Richard Serra, and many others. Temporary exhibitions of painting, sculpture, photography, design, and architecture. Open Tues.-Sun.; don't miss it.

⚏⚏ **Museum of Art,** Plaza de Panama, Balboa Park (232-7931): A vast panorama of the history of art—European, American, and Far Eastern—in a typical Spanish Colonial building. From Rembrandt and Rubens to Salvador Dalí and the richly wrought frescoes of Mexican artist Diego Rivera. Among the most famous works on display: Zurbarán's *Agnus Dei,* Canaletto's *View of the Mole at Venice,* Frans Hals's *Portrait of Isaac Massa,* and *Still Life* by Juan Sanchez-Cotán. One of the best art museums on the West Coast; don't miss it. Open Tues.-Sun.

⚏ **Museum of Photographic Arts,** Casa de Balboa, Balboa Park (239-5262): Display of photographs old and new by photographers foreign and American; a must for shutterbugs. Open daily.

⚏ **Timken Art Gallery,** Plaza de Panama, Balboa Park (239-5548): In a building which is not among the great successes of modern architecture you'll find a fine collection of Russian icons, 19th-century American painting, and European masters—Brueghel, Rembrandt, Cézanne, and others. Among the best-known paintings here: *Death of the Virgin* by Petrus Christus, *The Parable of the Sower* by Brueghel the Elder, El Greco's *The Penitent St. Peter,* Martin Heade's *Magnolia Grandiflora,* and John Singleton Copley's portrait of *Mrs. Thomas Gage,* a recent acquisition. Open Tues.-Sun.; closed the month of Sept. A must-see.

MUSEUMS OF SCIENCE AND HISTORY: ⚏ Aerospace Museum, Ford

Bldg., Balboa Park (234-8291): History of aviation and space flight from 1880 to the present day. Many models of old aircraft and gliders; also a life-size replica of Lindbergh's legendary *The Spirit of St. Louis,* the original of which was built in San Diego in 1927, and a space capsule. Hall devoted to the heroes and heroines of the story of aeronautics. Well-stocked aviation library. Worth a visit; open daily.

⚏ **Mormon Battalion Memorial,** 2510 Juan St. (298-3317): Military museum dedicated to the memory of 500 soldiers of a Mormon battalion which, during the Mexican War of 1846–1847, made the longest march in the history of the U.S. Army: more than 2,000 miles from Illinois to San Diego. Only 350 of them reached their goal. Also an exhibition on the history of the Mormons. Should be seen; open daily.

⚏ **Museum of Man,** El Prado, Balboa Park (239-2001): Superb natural history museum in an elegant Spanish Colonial building, one of whose notable possessions is the skeleton of Del Mar Man, the oldest humanoid ever found in the U.S. (about 48,000 years old). Giant model of the human body. Fine collection of Hopi and Mayan art. Must definitely be seen. Open daily.

⚏ **Natural History Museum,** Laurel St., Balboa Park (232-3821): Fauna and flora of southern California; the whale skulls are impressive. A seismograph registers all earth tremors, no matter how slight. Should be seen; open daily.

⚏⚏ **Reuben H. Fleet Space Theater,** 1875 El Prado, Balboa Park (238-1168): The largest planetarium in the U.S., with a wholly remarkable audio-visual program. Giant OMNIMAX hemispheric screen for 70-mm projection. Exhibitions on space technology. A must for amateur astronomers; no one should miss it. Open daily.

☼⚲ **Scripps Aquarium-Museum,** 8602 La Jolla Shores Dr., La Jolla (534-2230): On the campus of the University of California at San Diego, this handsome museum of oceanography, one of the best known in the country, displays a comprehensive selection of Californian and Mexican marine life. Beach open to the public, with picnic areas. Don't fail to visit. Open daily.

☼⚲ **Serra Museum,** Presidio Dr., Presidio Park (297-3258): The history of California and its missions, with a valuable antiquarian library, in a charming Spanish Colonial–style building dedicated to the Franciscan missionary Junipero Serra and built on the site of the first Presidio erected by the Spaniards in 1769. Fine view of Mission Bay; shouldn't be missed. Open Tues.-Sun.

⚲ **Star of India,** 1306 N. Harbor Dr., Embarcadero (234-9153): Launched in Britain in 1863 and taken out of service in 1923, this is one of the last great 19th-century sailing ships still afloat. She sailed around the world 21 times. Interesting maritime museum; should be seen. Open daily.

PANORAMAS: ☼ ⚱⚱ **Cabrillo National Monument,** Catalina Blvd. at Point Loma, 10 mi. (16 km) west on Calif. 209 (293-5450): On a promontory overlooking San Diego Bay, the lighthouse and adjoining monument command an unequalled view of the Pacific Ocean to the west, La Jolla to the north, Mexico to the south, and the city to the east. From Dec. to Feb. you can watch from here the migration of the gray whales offshore in the bay. A sight not to be missed. Open daily. The monument closes at sunset.

PARKS AND GARDENS: ☼ ⚱⚱ **Balboa Park,** reached by way of El Prado or Park Blvd. (239-0512): This superb 1,158-acre (468-ha.) tropical park of woods, lawns, and lakes in the heart of San Diego shelters half a dozen museums (see above); a world-famous zoo (see below); the **Spreckels Outdoor Organ,** world's largest open-air organ, with 5,000 pipes; and the **Old Globe Theatre,** a replica of William Shakespeare's theater in London, home to the very popular National Shakespeare Festival (see "Special Events," below); two golf courses; a well-known botanical garden; etc. Shouldn't be missed.

☼⚲ **Mission Bay Park,** West Mission Bay Dr., Sea World Dr., and E. Mission Bay Dr.: 4,600 acres (1,860 ha.) of parkland around the great body of water that is Mission Bay; fishing, waterskiing, surfing, beaches, etc. Beautiful scenery. The famous **Sea World** marine zoo is here. Must definitely be seen; Visitor center at 2688 E. Mission Bay Dr. (276-8200).

⚲ **Presidio Park,** Presidio Dr.: This wooded hill overlooking the **Sierra Museum** (see above) marks the original site of the first Spanish fortifications, built in 1769 (the Presidio). Pretty view of Mission Bay. A must-see.

PERFORMING ARTS: For daily listings of all shows and cultural events, consult the entertainment pages of the daily papers *Evening Tribune* (evening) and *San Diego Union* (morning), as well as the weekly *Del Mar Citizen* and free San Diego *Reader,* and the monthly *San Diego* magazine.

Arts Tix, a kiosk in the Spreckels Theater, 121 Broadway (238-3810), sells tickets for all shows at reduced prices on the day of performance.

Ballet Society of San Diego, 337 W. Washington St. (299-9001): Modern and traditional ballet.

California Theatre, 1122 Fourth Ave. (233-0392): Theater tours, Broadway hits.

Cassius Carter Centre Stage, Balboa Park (239-2255): Drama, musicals, modern theater (Sept.-May); adjoins the Old Globe Theatre.

Civic Theatre, 202 C St. (236-6510): Home of the San Diego Opera, Ian Campbell, director; also of the California Ballet Company.

Gaslamp Quarter Theatre, 547 47th Ave. (234-9583): Contemporary theater.

Golden Hall, 202 C St. (236-6510): Rock concerts, shows by top performers. With the Civic Theatre, part of the huge San Diego Convention and Performing Arts Center.

Lyceum Theatre, 79 Horton Plaza (235-8025): Home of the San Diego Repertory Theatre; drama, comedy.

Marquis Public Theater, 3717 India St. (295-5654): Traditional, contemporary, and experimental theater.

Old Globe Theatre, Balboa Park (239-2255): Replica of Shakespeare's Globe Playhouse in London; destroyed by fire in 1978, it was rebuilt by public subscription. Every summer the National Shakespeare Festival is held here.

Symphony Hall (Fox Theater), 1245 Seventh Ave. (699-4200): Classical concerts and recitals; home of the San Diego Symphony.

Theatre in Old Town, 4040 Twiggs (298-0082): Contemporary theater; musicals.

SHOPPING: Bazaar del Mundo, Juan St., Old Town (296-3161): Picturesque Mexican-style market with restaurants and shops selling clothing, gifts, jewelry, etc. Very aesthetically pleasing. Open daily.

☼ **Horton Plaza,** bounded by First and Fourth Aves., Broadway, and G St. (239-8180): The country's most spectacular shopping center, in the downtown Gaslamp district. Rather disconcerting postmodern architecture, embellished with original sculpture and galleries at several levels. Four department stores, more than 150 stores, restaurants, movie houses. Definitely deserves a visit. Open daily.

La Jolla, around Girard Ave. and Prospect St.: The two shopping streets of this elegant beach resort. Fashionable shops, chic stores, and art galleries. The luxury shopping center at Prospect Point, designed by architect Robert A. M. Stern, is one of the handsomest in the U.S.—with prices to match.

Seaport Village, Pacific Hwy. and W. Harbor Dr. (235-4104): Unusual shopping center on the ocean, which reconstructs the atmosphere of a 19th-century Victorian village in California: 15 restaurants; 70 stores, shops, and art galleries. Wonderful turn-of-the-century-style carousel. Open daily.

Tijuana: See "Nearby Excursions," below.

SPECIAL EVENTS: For the exact schedule of events below, consult the **San Diego Convention and Visitors Bureau** (see "Tourist Information," above).

Fiesta de la Primavera (four days in mid-May): Mariachi concerts, art shows, banjo competition, buffalo barbecue. In Old Town.

Corpus Christi (late May to early June), at the Mission San Antonio de Pala, 50 mi. (80 km) north via I-15 and Calif. 76: Open-air mass, folk dancing. A typical Spanish fiesta celebrated every year since 1816; colorful.

Southern California Exposition (late June to early July): Flower and horse show on the Del Mar Fairgrounds, 9 mi. (14 km) north; very popular locally.

National Shakespeare Festival (mid-June to mid-Sept.): Shakespeare plays in series throughout the summer, at the Old Globe Theatre, Balboa Park. A very well-attended festival.

Festival of Bells (weekend in mid-July): Festival of bells commemorating the foundation of the Mission of San Diego de Alcala on July 17, 1769.

Admission Day (early Sept.): Commemorates California's admission to the Union in 1850. Mariachi concerts, folk dancing, food festival.

Cabrillo Festival (late Sept.): Celebrates the discovery of California. Dancing, folklore displays, parades; very lively.

Mother Goose Parade (Nov.): Amusing parade with costumes based on the Mother Goose tales, at El Cajon, 6 mi. (10 km) NE.

Christmas—Light Boat Parade (third Sun. in Dec.): Procession of illuminated boats in Shelter Yacht Basin, San Diego Harbor.

SPORTS: San Diego has two professional teams:
Baseball (Apr.-Oct.): Padres, Jack Murphy Stadium (283-4494).
Football (Aug.-Dec.): Chargers, Jack Murphy Stadium (280-2111).

Horse Racing

Del Mar Racetrack, County Fairgrounds (755-1141). Thoroughbred racing, Wed.-Mon., late July to mid-Sept.

Deep-Sea Fishing

Every year tens of thousands of rod-and-reel enthusiasts go deep-sea fishing in the waters of southern California, to the Mexican border and beyond: their destined prey include barracuda, sea bass, yellowtail, bonito, and blue marlin. The charter rates for a fully equipped deep-sea-fishing boat are about $400 for a half day of six hours and $500 for a full day of ten hours. Some recommended charterers: **Fisherman's Landing**, 2838 Garrison St. (222-0391); **Lee Palm Sportfishing**, 2801 Emerson St. (224-3857); **Point Loma Sportfishing**, 1403 Scott St. (223-1627); and **Seaforth Boat Rentals**, 1641 Quivira Rd. (223-1681).

STROLLS: ☀☖**Embarcadero,** Harbor Dr. between Market and Grape Sts.: San Diego's fishing and commercial harbor; fine view of bay and shipping. The World War II vessels of the U.S. Navy moored at Broadway Pier may be visited Sat. and Sun. from 1 to 4 p.m.; for information, call 235-3534. Worth a look.

☖ **Gaslamp Quarter,** 5th Ave. between Broadway and Market St.: The 16-block historic district downtown. A lot of work has gone into restoring the old buildings, many of which date to the 1880s. The Gaslamp Quarter Council (410 Island Ave., 233-5227), offers guided tours of the historic buildings and neighborhoods. Worth seeing.

☖ **Harbor and Shelter Islands,** reached via North Harbor Dr. and Rosecrans St.: Two big artificial islands built at the north of the bay on millions of tons of material dredged from the bay itself. A wonderful place for fishing, or loafing, surrounded by marinas, yachts, restaurants, and luxury hotels. Definitely worth seeing.

☀☖☖ **Old Town,** around Wallace, Congress, and Juan Sts.: The historic heart of San Diego, with many shops, restaurants, old houses (see "Historic Buildings," above). Lively and colorful; you shouldn't miss it.

☀☖☖ **Scenic Drive:** A 52-mi. (84-km) loop posted with signs in the form of a blue-and-yellow seagull. In about three hours' driving you'll see most of the tourist attractions described above: the Embarcadero, Shelter Island, Cabrillo National Monument, Old Town, Balboa Park, etc. The drive begins at Broadway Pier. Shouldn't be missed.

THEME PARKS: ☀ ☖☖ **Sea World,** 1720 S. Shores Rd., Mission Bay Park

(226-3901): In a 135-acre (55-ha.) parkland setting, this huge marine-life theme park boasts more than 5,500 sea creatures, including seals, sea elephants, dolphins, and Shamu, the killer whale. Giant 26,400-gallon (100,000-liter) aquarium just for the sharks. Japanese fishing village; Skytower, a 321-ft (98-m) observation tower. A definite must-see; open daily.

    Wild Animal Park, 30 mi. (48 km) NE via I-15 and Calif. 78 (234-6541): A 1,800-acre (730-ha.) reserve with more than 2,200 free-ranging wild animals; lion, zebra, giraffe, rhinoceros, etc. African village. One of the finest safari zoos in the U.S.; you see it by monorail. Not to be missed. Open daily.

ZOOS: ☼ ▲▲ **San Diego Zoo,** Zoo Dr., Balboa Park (234-3153): The handsomest and most inclusive zoo in the U.S., with more than 3,200 wild animals and 3,000 exotic birds drawn from 800 animal species, in 100 acres (40 ha.) of superb undulating tropical gardens with luxuriant vegetation. Among the rarest creatures are Australian koala bears, Komodo dragons (giant lizards from Indonesia), and the only New Zealand kiwis acclimatized to life in the U.S. Your visit can be made by bus, on a moving sidewalk, or by the Skyfari cable car. Not to be missed; open daily.

ACCOMMODATIONS

See the listing of toll-free numbers in the Appendix.

Room Rates in San Diego	
B (Budget)	up to $30
I (Inexpensive)	$30–$60
M (Moderate)	$60–$90
E (Expensive)	$90–$140
VE (Very Expensive)	$140 and up

Personal Favorites (in order of preference)

    Inter-Continental San Diego (dwntwn), 333 W. Harbor Dr., CA 92101 (619/234-1500; toll free, see Inter-Continental). 681 rms, A/C, color TV, in-rm movies. AE, CB, DC, MC, V. Valet parking $8, two pools, four tennis courts, health club, sauna, water sports, private marina w. 450 berths, three rests. (including Las Cascadas), three bars, 24-hr rm svce, nightclub, hrdrsr, boutiques, free crib, concierge. *Note:* San Diego's most spectacular hotel, a splendid modern building w. a mirrored elliptical façade, whose 25 stories overlook Seaport Village and the bay. Ultra-comfortable rms w. private balconies and mini-bars; very complete facilities; very good svce. Lobby richly adorned w. Oriental ceramics and works of art; interior patio embellished w. gardens and waterfalls. Business and group clientele; adjacent 3,000-seat convention hall. **E–VE**

    U.S. Grant (dwntwn), 326 Broadway, CA 92101 (619/233-3121; toll free, see Preferred). 280 rms, A/C, color TV, in-rm movies. AE, CB, DC, MC, V. Valet garage $9, health club, two rests. (including the Grant Grill), bar, 24-hr rm svce, nightclub, concierge. *Note:* Built around 1910 by Ulysses S. Grant, Jr., son of the 18th president of the U.S., this luxurious grand hotel has been sumptuously restored to its original elegance at a cost of $80 million. Works of art, antique furniture, marble floors, and crystal chandeliers adorn the lobby and the public rooms. Rms are huge, and agreeably furnished in Queen Anne style, w. travertine bathrooms. Excellent business rest.; ultra-polished svce; intimacy and distinction. In the heart of dwntwn across from the Horton Plaza Mall. Upscale business clientele. A designated historic monument, reopened in Dec. 1985. Free airport limo. **E–VE**

☀ 🏨🏨🏨 **Humphrey's Half Moon Inn** (nr. dwntwn), 2303 Shelter Island Dr., CA 92106 (619/224-3411; toll free 800/345-9995). 141 rms, A/C, color TV, in-rm movies. AE, CB, DC, MC, V. Free parking, pool, bicycling, putting green, boating, marina, rest. (Humphrey's), bar, rm svce, nightclub, free crib. *Note:* A charming little hotel in a beautiful garden, looking out over glorious San Diego Bay. Pretty South Seas décor; comfortable rms w. balconies (some w. refrigerators); friendly reception and svce. Agreeable rest. w. a view of the harbor; free airport limo. Very good value; an excellent place to stay. **M–E**

🏨🏨🏨 **Town and Country Hotel** (nr. dwntwn), 500 Hotel Circle North, CA 92108 (619/291-7131; toll free 800/854-2608). 960 rms, A/C, color TV, in-rm movies. AE, CB, DC, MC, V. Free parking, four pools, four rests. (including Le Pavillon), coffeeshop, five bars, rm svce, disco, hrdrsr, boutiques, free crib. *Note:* Big convention hotel in 32 acres (12 ha.) of gardens, in Mission Valley, 10 min. from dwntwn and the same from the airport. The largest hotel in San Diego, it's a favorite of groups and conventioneers. Huge rms and very comfortable facilities; efficient svce; good value on the whole. **M–E**

🏨🏨 **Hyatt Islandia** (nr. dwntwn), 1441 Quivira Rd., CA 92109 (619/224-1234; toll free, see Hyatt). 348 rms, A/C, color TV, in-rm movies. AE, CB, DC, MC, V. Free parking, pool, marina, boating, waterskiing, rest. (Islandia Restaurant), coffeeshop, bar, rm svce, disco. *Note:* Modern 17-story tower between the ocean and Mission Bay. Comfortable rms, most w. balconies and refrigerators, overlooking the ocean or the bay. Lovely gardens; impersonal but efficient svce; very convenient location. Group and convention clientele; free airport limo. **E–VE**

🏨🏨 **Holiday Inn Embarcadero** (dwntwn), 1355 N. Harbor Dr., CA 92101 (619/232-3861; toll free, see Holiday Inns). 600 rms, A/C, color TV, in-rm movies. AE, CB, DC, MC, V. Free parking, pool, health club, rest. (Embarcadero Room), coffeeshop, bar, rm svce, disco, boutiques, free crib. *Note:* A typical Holiday Inn, superbly located right on the harbor. The best rms, w. balconies, overlook the bay. Glass-walled outside elevators. Modern, congenial, and noisy; free airport limo. **E**

🏨 **Sands of La Jolla** (vic.), 5417 La Jolla Blvd., La Jolla, CA 92037 (619/459-3336). 38 rms, cable color TV. AE, CB, DC, MC, V. Free parking, pool. *Note:* Small, inviting motel a stone's throw from the beach, 5 min. from La Jolla's shopping district, and 25 min. from dwntwn San Diego. Huge rms, some w. balconies and refrigerators, the best overlooking the ocean. Friendly reception and svce. Good value off-season. **I–M, but lower rates out of season**

🏨 **Friendship Inn Town House Lodge** (dwntwn), 810 Ash St., CA 92101 (619/233-8826; toll free, see Friendship Inns). 55 rms, A/C, color TV. AE, CB, DC, MC, V. Free parking, pool, adjoining 24-hr coffeeshop. *Note:* Modest but very well-run motel very near dwntwn, a stone's throw from Balboa Park and the business district. Serviceably comfortable rms; free coffee in rms; good value. **I**

Other Accommodations (from top bracket to budget)

🏨🏨🏨🏨 **The Westgate** (dwntwn), 1055 Second Ave., CA 92101 (619/238-1818; toll free, see Loews). 223 rms, A/C, cable color TV. AE, CB, DC, MC, V. Valet garage $9, two rests. (including the Fontainebleau Room), bar, rm svce, nightclub, boutiques, free crib, concierge. *Note:* The refined luxury of a great European hotel, w. an authentic Velázquez presiding over the lobby, but lackluster modern architecture. Spacious rms, elegantly decorated in Louis XV or English Regency style, with Italian marble bathrooms. Ultra-polished svce; excellent grand-hotel rest. One of the best hotels on the West Coast, very centrally located; free airport limo. A favorite of those in-the-know. **E–VE**

Hilton Beach and Tennis Resort (nr. dwntwn), 1775 E. Mission Bay Dr., CA 92109 (619/276-4010; toll free, see Hilton). 355 rms, A/C, color TV, in-rm movies. AE, CB, DC, MC, V. Free parking, pool, five tennis courts, health club, private beach, boating, putting green, two rests. (including Tradewinds), two bars, rm svce, disco, free crib. *Note:* Resort hotel of modern design in a 14-acre (6-ha.) tropical garden, right on the water and 10 min. from dwntwn. Comfortable rms w. balconies facing out on Mission Bay. Good sports facilities; efficient svce. Group and convention clientele; free airport limo. **E–VE**

Hotel del Coronado (nr. dwntwn), 1500 Orange Ave., Coronado, CA 92118 (619/435-6611; toll free 800/356-8392). 685 rms (half w. A/C), cable color TV. AE, CB, DC, MC, V. Valet parking $8, two pools, health club, sauna, seven tennis courts, private beach, boating, waterskiing, two rests. (including the Prince of Wales), coffeeshop, bars, 24-hr rm svce, disco, hrdrsr, boutiques, free crib, concierge. *Note:* The empress dowager of local hotels, a 5-min. drive from dwntwn by the San Diego Coronado Bay Bridge; almost every president of the U.S. in the past century, as well as many visiting VIPs, has stayed here. Built in 1888, this was the first hotel in the world to be equipped w. electricity and elevators. Elegant Victorian interior. Direct beach access. Spacious rms w. refrigerators and private patios or balconies, the best w. ocean view. Some shortcomings in comfort and facilities; polished svce; lovely gardens. Part of the movie *Some Like It Hot* was made here. If you cultivate golden moments from the past, this is for you. **E–VE**

Horton Grand Hotel (dwntwn), 311 Island Ave., CA 92101 (619/544-1886; toll free 800/533-4667). 110 rms, A/C. cable color TV. AE, CB, DC, MC, V. Valet parking $2, rest. (Ida Bailey rest.), bar, rm svce, free crib, concierge. *Note:* Charming 19th-century hotel which has retained its Victorian elegance, centrally located in the heart of the Gaslamp district. Superb carved exterior; interior decoration and fittings opulently renovated; impressive grand staircase and picturesque skylight in the lobby. Spacious rms w. fireplaces, some w. balconies. Very agreeable Tea Room. Intimate atmosphere; faultless svce. Upscale business clientele; free airport limo. **E**

La Valencia Hotel (vic.), 1132 Prospect St., La Jolla, CA 92037 (619/454-0771; toll free, see Preferred). 100 rms, A/C, color TV. AE, MC, V. Free valet parking, pool, health club, putting green, three rests. (including the Sky Room), bar, rm svce, nightclub, crib $10. *Note:* A graceful Spanish-Moorish building dating from the 1930s, across from the beach in the midst of the smart stores on Prospect St. and Girard Ave. Spacious, elegant rms w. mini-bars, some w. private balconies or patios, the best w. a fine ocean view. Excellent svce; rest. of quality; inviting gardens. An agreeable air of nostalgia; a very pleasant place to stay. **E**

Best Western Shelter Island Marina Inn (nr. dwntwn), 2051 Shelter Island Dr., CA 92106 (619/222-0561; toll free, see Best Western). 97 rms, A/C, color TV, in-rm movies. AE, CB, DC, MC, V. Free parking, pool, marina, private beach, boating, rest., bar, rm svce, disco, free crib. *Note:* Modern, comfortable motel w. magnificent views of the bay and yacht basin. Spacious rms w. view, some w. patios. Pretty tropical décor. Good reception. Moorings available for boats; free airport limo. Good overall value. **M–E**

𝕃𝕃 **Stardust Hotel and Country Club** (nr. dwntwn), 950 Hotel Circle North, CA 92108 (619/298-0511; toll free 800/223-0888). 216 rms, A/C, color TV, in-rm movies. AE, CB, DC, MC, V. Free parking, pool, eight tennis courts, two golf courses, health club, putting green, 24-hr rest., bars, rm svce, disco, free crib. *Note:* Comfortable, inviting motel 15 min. from dwntwn. Spacious rms, some w. private balconies or patios. Comprehensive sports facilities. Cheerful svce. Group and convention clientele. Good value off-season. **M–E, but lower rates out of season**

𝕃 **7 + 1 Motel** (dwntwn), 1919 Pacific Hwy., CA 92101 (619/232-1077; toll free 800/822-2820). 64 rms, A/C, color TV, in-rm movies. AE, CB, DC, MC, V. Free parking, pool, adjoining coffeeshop. *Note:* Congenial, very well-run motel well located near the Embarcadero. Comfortable rms w. refrigerators, some w. balconies. Friendly reception and svce; free coffee in rms. **I–M, but lower rates out of season**

𝕃 **Padre Trail Inn** (nr. dwntwn), 4200 Taylor St., CA 92110 (619/297-3291). 97 rms, A/C, color TV. AE, CB, DC, MC, V. Free parking, pool, coffeeshop, bar, rm svce. *Note:* Charming little colonial-style motel an easy walk from Old Town. Spacious, inviting rms. Good value. **I**

𝕃 **Motel 6** (nr. dwntwn), 2424 Hotel Circle North, CA 92108 (619/296-1612). 92 rms, A/C, color TV, free in-rm movies. DC, MC, V. Free parking, pool, adjoining rest. *Note:* Unbeatable value a stone's throw from Mission Bay Park and Old Town. Serviceably comfortable. 8 min. from the airport, 10 min. from dwntwn. **B**

Accommodations in the Vicinity

☀𝕃𝕃𝕃 **Rancho Bernardo Inn** (vic.), 17550 Bernardo Oaks Dr., Rancho Bernardo, CA 92128 (619/487-1611; toll free 800/854-1065). 236 rms, A/C, cable color TV. AE, CB, DC, MC, V. Free parking, two pools, two golf courses, 12 tennis courts, putting green, horseback riding, two rests. (including El Bizcocho), bars, rm svce, disco, hrdrsr, drugstore, concierge. *Note:* Luxurious sports-lover's paradise w. two golf courses and 12 tennis courts, near Wild Animal Park and 30 min. from dwntwn. Charming Spanish Mission décor; spacious, elegant rms w. balconies and private patios. Lovely gardens; excellent svce; young, upscale crowd. Well-known tennis school; interesting golf and tennis packages. The ideal vacation hotel. **E–VE**

Airport Accommodations

𝕃𝕃𝕃 **Sheraton Harbor Island** (nr. dwntwn), 1380 Harbor Island Dr., CA 92101 (619/291-2900; toll free, see Sheraton). 710 rms, A/C, color TV, in-rm movies. AE, CB, DC, MC, V. Valet parking $6, two pools, health club, sauna, four tennis courts, marina, boating, two rests. (including Sheppard's), two bars, rm svce, boutiques, free crib, concierge. *Note:* Large, luxurious, modern airport hotel w. very comprehensive facilities. Comfortable rms w. balconies, the best overlooking the bay or the marina. Efficient svce; first-rate rest. VIP suites on the top three floors; beautiful gardens. Business clientele; 2 min. from the airport (free limo). One of the best places to stay in San Diego. **E–VE**

YMCA / Youth Hostels

Point Loma Hostel (nr. dwntwn), 3790 Udall St., CA 92107 (619/223-4778). 60 beds. Youth hostel near Mission Bay Park.

YMCA (dwntwn), 500 W. Broadway, CA 92101 (619/232-1133). 265 rms. Pool, health club, rest. Men and women; also youth-hostel members. Very central.

RESTAURANTS

San Diego Restaurant Prices	
(per person, excluding drinks and service charges)	
B (Budget)	up to $15
I (Inexpensive)	$15–$25
M (Moderate)	$25–$40
E (Expensive)	$40–$60
VE (Very Expensive)	$60 and up

Personal Favorites (in order of preference)

ΨΨΨ **Gustaf Anders** (vic.), 2812 Avenida de la Playa, La Jolla (619/459-4499). A/C. Lunch/dinner daily (until midnight); closed Jan. 1 and Dec. 25. AE, MC, V. Jkt. *Specialties:* fresh pasta w. truffles, salmon marinated w. lemon and dill, filet of beef w. Stilton cheese sauce, ravioli w. foie gras, rabbit liver w. pepper and cognac sauce, young Sonoma lamb w. red pepper, fried trout vinaigrette, bittersweet chocolate mousse. Fine list of California and foreign wines at appropriate prices. Menu changes regularly. *Note:* Brings off the astonishing feat of being at once the most sophisticated and the most relaxing rest. in the area. The light, imaginative cuisine of Gustaf Magnusson and Ulf Anders Strandberg combines Scandinavian influences w. those of California nouvelle cuisine, changing w. the seasons and at the whim of the chefs. Modern, elegant, but rather chilly black-and-white interior; the few works of art on the walls are changed from time to time. Meticulous, discreet svce. Adjoining Caviar Bar for meals on the run. Since 1984 the readers of *San Diego* magazine have rated this the best rest. in town. Resv. strongly advised; 20 min. from dwntwn. *Scandinavian-American.* **E–VE**

☀ΨΨΨ **Anthony's Star of the Sea Room** (dwntwn), 1360 Harbor Dr. (232-7408). A/C. Dinner only, nightly; closed holidays. AE, MC, V. J&T. *Specialties:* clams Genovese, broiled filet of swordfish, sole à l'Admiral, abalone gourmet, salmon in pastry shell, shellfish; strawberries San Diego. Good wine list at high prices. *Note:* One of the best seafood rests. in the country. Enormous choice of absolutely fresh seafood, perfectly cooked. The Ghio family, which directs this luxury establishment, has its own fishing fleet. Fine view of harbor and bay through huge picture windows. Flawless svce; upscale business clientele. *Seafood.* **M–E**

ΨΨΨ **Mille Fleurs** (vic.), Country Square Courtyard, 6009 Paseo Delicias, Rancho Santa Fe (756-3085). A/C. Lunch Mon.-Fri., dinner nightly; closed Dec. 25. AE, MC, V. Jkt. *Specialties:* rack of baby lamb w. garden vegetables, fresh foie gras maison w. sherry vinaigrette, sweetbreads w. madeira, veal cutlet w. morel mushrooms, excellent desserts. Menu changes regularly. *Note:* Chef Martin Woesle did his training at Munich's famous L'Aubergine (a Michelin three-star rest.). Delicate, imaginative French-inspired nouvelle cuisine. Charming, fresh, Mexican-hacienda setting with trompe-l'oeil paintings and a pretty patio. Romantic atmosphere; very good svce. Locally popular so resv. a must. 25 min. from dwntwn. *French.* **M–E**

☀ΨΨ **Dobson's** (dwntwn), 956 Broadway Circle (231-6771). A/C. Lunch Mon.-Fri., dinner Mon.-Sat.; closed Sun. AE, MC, V.

Jkt. *Specialties:* broiled salmon w. three kinds of peppercorns, sautéed scallops provençale, médaillon of veal w. morel mushrooms, sweetbreads w. truffle sauce, chocolate amaretto pecan pie, gâteau St. Honoré. *Note:* Historic old pub, now a hangout for politicians, yuppies, and local businesspeople, particularly at lunch. Nice turn-of-the-century décor agreeably restored. Ask for a table upstairs w. a view of the bar. Usually a lively place; very good food in the heart of dwntwn. Resv. a must. *Continental.* **I–M**

🍸🍸 **Mandarin House** (vic.), 6765 La Jolla Blvd., La Jolla (454-2555). A/C. Lunch Mon.-Fri., dinner nightly. AE, CB, DC, MC, V. *Specialties:* Peking and Szechuan dishes, shrimp velvet, Mongolian beef, Peking duck, chow san shein. *Note:* Locally very popular, Mandarin House is the best Chinese rest. in San Diego, the only great city in California which doesn't feature Chinese food. A particular delight is the chow san shein: beef, shrimp, chicken, and vegetables in a spicy brown sauce. Plush Far Eastern décor; rather brusque svce. Resv. advised. 20 min. from dwntwn. Other location: 2604 5th Ave. (232-1101). *Chinese.* **I**

🍸🍸 **Nino's** (nr. dwntwn), 4501 Mission Bay Dr. (274-3141). A/C. Lunch/dinner Tues.-Sat.; closed Sun. and Mon. AE, CB, DC, MC, V. Jkt. *Specialties:* fresh homemade pasta, sautéed scampi, fried eggplant and zucchini, veal marsala or Florentine, catch of the day. Good desserts. *Note:* Charming Italian rest.; discreet, romantic atmosphere and authentic northern Italian food. Good svce; locally popular—and not large, so resv. essential. 10 min. from dwntwn. *Italian.* **I–M**

🔆🍸 **Casa de Bandini** (nr. dwntwn), 2574 Calhoun St., Old Town (297-8211). A/C. Lunch/dinner daily; closed holidays. AE, DC, MC, V. *Specialties:* crabmeat enchiladas, chimichangas, burritos, fish Veracruz style. Giant margaritas. *Note:* Surrounded by gardens, flowers, and fountains, and adjoining Old Town State Historic Park, this enchanting house built in 1829 by a rich Mexican businessman, Juan Bandini, belongs in a museum of Spanish Colonial architecture. The food draws on traditional Mexican and California recipes; the fish is unusually good. Svce and atmosphere as colorful as the setting; mariachi bands. A must for every visitor. Reserve ahead. *Mexican.* **B–I**

🍸 **Red Sails Inn** (nr. dwntwn), 2614 Shelter Island Dr. (223-3030). A/C. Breakfast/lunch/dinner daily; closed Dec. 25. AE, CB, DC, MC, V. *Specialties:* seafood. *Note:* Very popular with the residents of Shelter Island, Red Sails serves very creditable seafood at very reasonable prices. Fine view of the bay and marina; relaxed atmosphere, raw bar, open-air dining. A landmark for more than half a century. *Steak-seafood.* **B–I**

Other Restaurants (from top bracket to budget)

🍸🍸🍸 **Le Fontainebleau** (dwntwn), in the Westgate (see "Accommodations," above) (238-1818). A/C. Lunch Mon.-Fri., dinner nightly, brunch Sun. AE, CB, DC, MC, V. J&T. *Specialties:* rack of lamb, steak Diane, médaillons of veal Vieux Carré, flaming desserts. Large wine list. *Note:* The lavish Louis XV setting and the tuxedo-clad, white-gloved svce combine to make this the most elegant, and formal, rest. in San Diego. Classic and sophisticated grand-hotel food; background music of distinction. The upscale business favorite, especially at lunch; resv. a must. *French-continental.* **M–E**

🍸🍸🍸 **Sheppard's** (nr. dwntwn), in the Sheraton Harbor Island (see "Accommodations," above) (692-2255). A/C. Dinner only, Tues.-Sat.; closed Sun. and Mon. AE, CB, DC, MC, V. Jkt. *Specialties:* roast filet of lamb w. fennel, fresh salmon w. basil butter, médaillons of veal w. gorgonzola, duckling w. pear brandy, soufflés. Good wine list at decent prices. *Note:* Excellent contemporary California-style food w. a touch of French elegance. Elegant Provençal country-inn décor w. impressionist-style paintings on the walls. Attentive svce. One of San Diego's fashionable rests.; resv. strongly advised. *American.* **M–E**

Papagayo (dwntwn), Seaport Village, 861 W. Harbor Dr. (232-7581). A/C. Lunch Mon.-Sat., dinner nightly. AE, CB, DC, MC, V. Jkt. *Specialties:* shrimp fried w. coconut, brochette of seafood, sea bass Cabo San Lucas style, fish and shellfish marinated in fruit juice and grilled over a mesquite fire. Good wine list. *Note:* This engaging rest. in charming Seaport Village serves what could be described as "Latino seafood." Since it opened it has drawn consistent crowds. Exotic décor and pretty bay view; deft, cheerful svce. A very good place; resv. advised. *Seafood.* **I–M**

La Chaumine (nr. dwntwn), 1466 Garnet Ave., Pacific Beach (272-8540). A/C. Dinner only, Tues.-Sun.; closed Mon. AE, CB, DC, MC, V. Jkt. *Specialties:* frogs' legs provençale, crayfish niçoise, steak bordelaise, rack of lamb liégeoise, excellent desserts; good list of French and California wines. *Note:* Likeable little Parisian bistro w. a charmingly romantic atmosphere. Faultless *cuisine bourgeoise,* remarkable sauces. Svce exemplary in all respects. Locally popular; resv. advised. 15 min. from dwntwn. *French.* **I–M**

The Old Trieste (nr. dwntwn), 2335 W. Morena Blvd. (276-1841). A/C. Lunch Tues.-Fri., dinner Tues.-Sat.; closed Sun., Mon., holidays, the last week in June, and the first week in July. AE, CB, DC, MC, V. Jkt. (at dinner). *Specialties:* fried zucchini, canelloni, scampi, calamari, fresh homemade pasta, veal Florentine, sautéed chicken livers, northern Italian dishes. Very fine wine list. *Note:* The intimate atmosphere of this charming *trattoria* 15 min. from dwntwn sets off to advantage its excellent Italian food. Ultra-professional svce; food-smart clientele. Resv. recommended; parking. *Italian.* **I–M**

Prince of Wales Grill (nr. dwntwn), in the Hotel del Coronado (see "Accommodations," above) (435-6611). A/C. Dinner only, Mon.-Sat.; closed Sun. and holidays. AE, CB, DC, MC, V. Jkt. *Specialties:* rack of lamb crown roast, broiled beef cuts, catch of the day. *Note:* Legend has it that it was in this grand-hotel rest. that the Prince of Wales, the future Edward VIII, first met Mrs. Simpson, the future Duchess of Windsor, for whom he later gave up his throne. The décor is very plush and—as it should be—very British. Excellent broiled foods; flawless svce; resv. a must. *Continental.* **I–M**

Piret's (nr. dwntwn), 902 W. Washington St. (297-2993). A/C. Breakfast/lunch/dinner daily. AE, MC, V. *Specialties:* tarte provençale, fresh homemade pasta, omelette au caviar, broiled chicken w. jalapeño relish, broiled fish, remarkable French pastry. Good selection of French and California wines. *Note:* The flagship of a locally popular chain of French-Californian bistros. The décor is as contemporary and sophisticated as the food. From the croissants to the daily specials, available to stay or to go, everything is delicious and homemade. Svce a touch undependable. No resv.; excellent value. Other locations: 897 First St., Encinitas (942-5152); La Jolla Village Square, La Jolla (455-7955). *French-American.* **I**

Su Casa (vic.), 6738 La Jolla Blvd., La Jolla (454-0369). A/C. Lunch/dinner daily; closed Thanksgiving and Dec. 25. AE, CB, DC, MC, V. Jkt. *Specialties:* crabmeat enchiladas, abalone, Mexican dishes, excellent broiled fish. *Note:* Modeled on an 18th-century hacienda, this picturesque rest. offers some unusual dishes based on old local recipes. Agreeable background music. One of the best Mexican rests. on the California coast. 25 min. from dwntwn. *Mexican.* **I**

Tom Ham's Lighthouse (nr. dwntwn), 2150 Harbor Island Dr. (291-9110). A/C. Lunch Mon.-Fri., dinner nightly, brunch Sun.; closed Dec. 25. AE, CB, DC, MC, V. *Specialties:* scallops, carne asada, broiled sea bass, steak. *Note:* In a genuine 19th-century lighthouse, this popular tourist rest. has a fine view of the bay and the city. Picturesque old interior; very decent if not terribly imaginative food. Good svce; resv. advised. Very good value. *American.* **I**

☼☼♥ **Alfonso's Hideaway** (vic.), 1251 Prospect St., La Jolla (454-2232). A/C. Lunch/dinner daily. AE, MC, V. *Specialties:* carne asada, steak ranchero, burritos, chile colorado, tacos. *Note:* With the Mexican border only 18 mi. (26 km) away, the Mexican food at Alfonso's cannot but be authentic. Some sauces are very spicy, but the steak ranchero is tasty. Charming shady patio. Often crowded and noisy; an excellent, colorful place, 25 min. from dwntwn. *Mexican.* **B–I**

♥ **El Chalan** (vic.), 5621 La Jolla Blvd., La Jolla (459-7707). A/C. Lunch/dinner Wed.-Mon.; closed Tues. AE, MC, V. *Specialties:* ceviche (marinated raw fish), papas relleñas (potatoes stuffed w. meat), pescado Huancaína (fish w. rice), steak Chorrillana (w. garlic and tomatoes). *Note:* As distinct from San Diego's innumerable Mexican rests., El Chalan serves Peruvian food, a touch less highly seasoned but just as tasty. Friendly, congenial atmosphere; resv. advised. 25 min. from dwntwn. *Latin American.* **B–I**

☼☼♥ **Golden Lion Tavern** (dwntwn), 801 Fourth Ave. (233-1131). A/C. Lunch Mon.-Fri., dinner Mon.-Sat.; closed Sun. AE, MC, V. *Specialties:* sandwiches, daily specials, broiled fish; oyster bar. *Note:* Successor to the famous Golden Lion Pub, founded in 1907, this agreeably nostalgic tavern serves commendable food, especially fish. Very popular 49-ft- (15-m-) long bar. Generally crowded. In dwntwn San Diego. *American.* **B–I**

Cafeterias / Fast Food

Hob Nob Hill (dwntwn), 2271 First Ave. (239-8176). Breakfast/lunch/dinner Sun.-Fri.; closed Sat. AE, CB, DC, MC, V. *Specialties:* superb family cooking at very considerate prices: corned beef and cabbage, turkey croquettes, ham and yams, chicken-fried steak, roast pork w. apple sauce, very good homemade desserts. *Note:* A local landmark since 1946. The service is commendable but you may have a long wait; resv. advised.

BARS AND NIGHTCLUBS

Abilene Country Saloon (nr. dwntwn), in the Town and Country Hotel (see "Accommodations," above) (291-7131). Live country music Tues.-Sat.; for would-be cowboys.

Bacchanal (vic.), 8022 Clairemont Mesa Blvd. (560-8022). Rock, disco. Locally popular. Open Wed.-Sat.

Chuck's Steak House (vic.), 1250 Prospect St., La Jolla (454-5325). One of the oldest local jazz clubs; top performers. Wed.-Sun. Good rest.

Catamaran Resort Lounge (nr. dwntwn), 3999 Mission Blvd., Pacific Beach (488-1081). Excellent live jazz, with the best soloists, nightly.

Diego's (nr. dwntwn), 860 Garnet Ave., Pacific Beach (272-1241). Fashionable rock disco with giant video screens; also a commendable Mexican rest. Open nightly.

Halcyon (nr. dwntwn), 4258 W. Point Loma Blvd. (225-9559). Live rock; very popular locally. Open Mon.-Sat.

Marine Room (vic.), 2000 Spindrift Dr., La Jolla (459-7222). This classy oceanfront lounge on the shore has a splendid view of the Pacific. Likeable reception; ditto music. Good rest. adjoining. Open nightly.

Pal Joey's (nr. dwntwn), 5147 Waring Rd., Allied Gardens (286-7873). A rather kitschy big dance hall, 1930s style. Live Dixieland weekends. Near San Diego State University.

Whaling Bar (vic.), in the La Valencia Hotel in La Jolla (see "Accommodations," above) (454-0771). Yuppie bar; well-heeled, trendy patrons. Open nightly.

NEARBY EXCURSIONS

☼🔔 **ANZA BORREGO DESERT STATE PARK** (90 mi., 144 km, NE via I-8, Calif. 79, and Calif. 78): 600,000 acres (240,000 ha.) of largely unexplored desert wilderness adjoining the **Salton Sea,** largest lake in California, 278 ft (85 m) below sea level in the **Colorado Desert** (sailing, water sports, abundant fishing). The contrast between the lake, dotted with holidaymakers, and the nearby desert is particularly striking. Two surfaced roads cross the park from side to side. Among its most remarkable sights are **Font's Point, Borrego Palm Canyon, Split Mountain,** and **Seventeen Palms Oasis.** When the desert plants and shrubs are in flower, from late Jan. to Apr., they are a sight to be seen. *Note:* Temperatures run very high in summer; be sure to carry drinking water. **Visitor center** open daily year round at Borrego Springs (619/767-5311). On the way, visit the mining town of Julian (see below).

☼🔔 **LA JOLLA** (pronounced "La Hoya"; 12 mi., 19 km, NW via I-5, Ardath Rd., and Torrey Pines Rd.): The fashionable place for a summer home, the California equivalent of Palm Beach or Saint Tropez. Lovely beaches, luxurious oceanfront homes, trendy shops, and restaurants. You ought to visit the **Museum of Contemporary Art** with its very fine modern-art collection; and the **Scripps Aquarium-Museum,** one of the most famous museums of oceanography in the world. (See "Museums of Art" and "Museums of Science and History," above). La Jolla shouldn't be missed.

MINING TOWNS: ☼🔔 **Julian,** 64 mi. (102 km) NE via I-8 and Calif. 79: This picturesque prospectors' town, which had several thousand inhabitants in 1885 and barely 1,300 today, still boasts many buildings preserved from its adventurous past, including the very fine **Julian Hotel.** Visit the legendary 🔔 **Eagle Mine,** a gold mine dating from 1870, on C St. (765-9921); open daily.

Where to Stay

☼🔔 **Julian Hotel,** Julian, CA 92036 (619/765-0201). 16 rms. No credit cards. **I–M**

Where to Eat

🍸 **Bailey Barbecue,** 2307 Main St. (765-9957). Open daily. MC, V. **B**

☼🔔🔔 **MOUNT PALOMAR OBSERVATORY** (65 mi., 104 km, NE via I-15 and County Road S.6) (742-3476): One of the most famous astronomical observatories in the world; for two decades its 200-in. (508-cm) telescope, with a 13-ton lens, was the largest in the world (until 1976, when the Russians surpassed it). An impressive sight. Visitors' gallery open daily; well worth the detour. The surrounding mountains are very beautiful.

🔔 **TIJUANA** (18 mi., 28 km, south on I-5): Mexican border town, fake but colorful, full of pleasure spots intended for the tourist. Bullfights every Sunday in summer, dog track, horse races, casino, jai-alai Fri.-Wed. Many tax-free craft shops and bazaars, including **Sara,** 743 Calle Revolución, **Maxim,** 717 Calle Revolución, and **Bazar Las Palomas,** Calle 6 between Revolución and Madero. Open daily.

Note: Foreign drivers must obtain temporary Mexican insurance, for sale at the border. Tourists may be unpleasantly surprised by Tijuana cab fares (see Tijuana Trolley under "Guided Tours," above). No visa is necessary for U.S. citizens visiting Mexico for less than 72 hours, or not traveling more than 75 mi. (120 km) from the border. Tourists of other nationalities should consult the Mexican Consulate in San Diego, 13333 Front St. (231-8414).

Where to Eat

La Escondida de Tijuana, Agua Caliente Blvd. (706/681-4458). Mexican food. Lunch/dinner daily. **B–I**

Reno, Calle 8 and Revolución (706/685-8775). Mexican and American food. Lunch/dinner daily. **I**

PART EIGHT

HAWAII AND ALASKA

CHAPTER 56

HONOLULU AND THE HAWAIIAN ISLANDS

□ □ □

This mecca for honeymooners and middle-class vacationers from the West Coast, the "navel of the Pacific," or as it is also known, the "Aloha State" (*aloha* means "welcome" in Hawaiian), has only three industries: tourism, agriculture —and the armed services! The enormous base at **Pearl Harbor** is both America's shield and her nerve center for Pacific defense. **Waikiki Beach** in Honolulu boasts the world's greatest concentration of hotels, far ahead of Florida, the Balearics, or Hong Kong: 220 hotels to the square mile (80 to the square kilometer), with a total of 32,000 rooms.

Discovered in 1778 by the famous British explorer Capt. James Cook (who was killed the following year by the Hawaiians), the islands have been endowed by nature with some of the planet's lushest landscapes. With its ideal climate and legendary natural beauty, the Aloha State attracts almost five million visitors every year, and some $4 billion of tourist money. Most of these visitors are Americans, but there are a growing number of Japanese, Canadians, and Australians. The usual array of leis and pareos (wrap-around skirts) awaits the battalions of tourists who land every day on charter flights or in tour groups at Honolulu, capital of the island of **Oahu** and principal city of the Hawaiian archipelago.

Besides the swimming and surfing that are almost obligatory on **Waikiki** and **Makaha Beaches,** the visitor will no doubt want to discover all the other local places of pilgrimage: **Pearl Harbor** (where the sunken U.S.S. *Arizona* impressively commemorates Japan's surprise attack on December 7, 1941, and attracts a million visitors a year); **Diamond Head,** a well-mannered volcano overlooking magnificent Honolulu Bay (*honolulu* means "placid bay" in Hawaiian); the splendid **State Capitol,** whose architecture contrives to be at once elegant and daring; **Punchbowl Crater,** a great military cemetery with an unforgettable view of the Waikiki skyscrapers and the ocean beyond; or the famous **Iolani Palace,** the only royal palace ever built on (what later became) American soil.

As with other cities that are financially and otherwise dependent on the tourist industry, Honolulu's Shangri-la image has its flip side: real-estate speculation is out of control, architecture is flashy, atmospheric pollution is bad and getting worse, and local growth industries include prostitution and pickpocketing. If the present rate of construction continues, the island of Oahu just might sink under the weight of concrete.

Alone among the 50 states, Hawaii has a minority (33%) of Caucasian inhabitants. The five main islands of the chain have a population 45% Asian (28% Japanese, 12% Filipino, 5% Chinese), and 20% indigenous (more or less, reflecting many generations of intermarriage), which speaks Hawaiian, a Polynesian-derived language which has only five vowels and seven consonants.

Food is held in high honor in the islands, and some delectable surprises await you, such as pupu (Hawaiian appetizers), opakapaka (steamed fish), lomi-lomi (raw fish marinated with vegetables), laulau (pork and fish wrapped in taro leaves and cooked), mahi-mahi (slices of Pacific dolphin—the fish, not the mammal—fried or broiled), kalua (roast pork), or poi (a gruel made from taro).

The airlines flying between California and Hawaii offer very attractive excursion fares and discount packages for the various islands: **Hawaii,** the largest, with its two active volcanoes (Mauna Loa and Kilauea) and its black sand beaches; **Maui,** with its famous Haleakala nature reserve; **Kauai,** the lush garden island; **Molokai,** famous for its Polynesian temples and for the former leper colony founded by Father Damien.

The Hawaiian Islands were settled comparatively late: it was not until the fifth century of our era that the first inhabitants arrived from the Marquesas, to be followed four or five centuries later by Tahitians. For a long time the archipelago was wholly isolated from the rest of the world, developing a culture which, despite its Polynesian roots, was all its own. The first white missionaries and traders came in the 1820s; not far behind them were the Chinese and Japanese fieldworkers destined for the pineapple and sugarcane plantations (Hawaii is today the largest sugar-growing state in the Union, and the world's largest producer of pineapples). Meanwhile, the indigenous population was decimated by imported diseases to which it had little natural resistance. Those of pure Hawaiian stock now account for only 1.3% of the population of the islands.

BASIC FACTS: Honolulu is the state capital of Hawaii (a word of Polynesian origin meaning "native country"). Area Code: 808. Time Zone: Hawaiian Time (five hours behind New York). ZIP Code: 96815. First European contact: 1778. U.S. possession since: 1898. Became the 50th state of the Union in 1959. Approximate population: city of Honolulu, 410,000; island of Oahu, 760,000; total for the state, 1,060,000.

CLIMATE: The subtropical climate of the Hawaiian Islands can best be described in a single word: delightful. The mean temperature in winter is 68°F (20°C) and in summer 77°F (28°C); from year's end to year's end it doesn't move far from these levels. Even in mid-August the nights are cool and pleasant, thanks to the trade winds. Hours of sunshine at all seasons reach levels unknown in less fortunate regions. Between April and October a south wind known as the "kona" often brings with it brief local downpours.

ARRIVAL & TRANSIT INFORMATION

AIRPORT: Honolulu International Airport (HNL), 5 mi. (8 km) NW. For information call 836-6411.

U.S. AIRLINES: Aloha (836-1111), American (526-0044), Continental (523-0000), Hawaiian (537-5100), Northwest (955-2255), TWA (toll free 800/221-2000), United (547-2211).

FOREIGN CARRIERS: Air New Zealand (toll free 800/521-4059), Canadian (922-0533), Japan Airlines (521-1441), Qantas (toll free 800/227-4500), Singapore Airlines (524-6063), UTA (947-1222).

CITY LINK: Cab fare to Waikiki, about $14–$17 (to dwntwn, $10); time, 20–25 min. Bus: Gray Line Hawaii (834-1033) leaves approx. every 20 min., serving the principal Waikiki hotels; fare, $8; time, approx. 40 min. Cab fares are high, but the public transportation (bus) network is excellent and cheap. The many excursions around Honolulu, and the attractive car-rental rates available in Hawaii, make it advisable to rent a car with unlimited mileage.

CAR RENTAL (all at the Honolulu International Airport): Avis (836-5511); Budget (922-3600); Dollar (926-4242); Hertz (836-2511); National (836-2655); Thrifty (836-2388); Tropical Rent-a-Car (836-1041), a local organization with good rates. For dwntwn locations, consult the phone directory.

LIMOUSINE SERVICES: Carey Limo (836-1422), Dav El Limousines (toll free 800/922-0343), Silver Cloud Limo (524-7999).

TAXIS: In theory cabs can't be hailed on the street, though in practice they often stop. You can phone for a cab from Aloha State Cab (847-3566), Charley's (531-1333), or Sida (836-0011).

BUS: Both in and outside Honolulu the best and cheapest way of getting around is usually the bus service of the Municipal Transit Lines. Information is available in all hotels or from HDT, Mass Transit Division, 725 Kapiolani Blvd. (531-1611).

INFORMATION & TOURS

TOURIST INFORMATION: Statewide, try the **Hawaii Visitors Bureau (HVB),** with headquarters in Honolulu at 2270 Kalakaua Ave., Suite 801, HI 96815 (808/923-1811).

GUIDED TOURS: Ani Ani Glass Bottom Boat, Kewalo Basin (923-2061): On this mini-cruise off Waikiki you may admire the coral gardens and the brightly colored tropical fish through the transparent bottom of your boat.
　　Charley's Sightseeing, 1888 Kalakau Ave. (531-1333): Guided tour of the island by bus or minibus.
　　Gray Line Tours, 435 Kalewa (833-3000): Guided bus tours of city and island; pickup at principal hotels.
　　Pearl Harbor Cruises, Kewalo Basin (536-3641): Three-hour boat tour of Pearl Harbor Bay and the U.S.S. *Arizona* Memorial; two departures daily, at 9:30 a.m. and 1:30 p.m.
　　Royal Helicopters, Waikiki Helipad, 216 Lagoon Dr. (941-4683): Spectacular helicopter trip over the bay and the island; $25–$150, depending on duration.
　　Windjammer Dinner Sail, Pier 7, Honolulu Harbor (521-0036): Entrancing sunset trip and dinner aboard a sailboat.

SIGHTS, ATTRACTIONS, & ACTIVITIES

ARCHITECTURAL HIGHLIGHTS: ☼ 🏛 **State Capitol,** 400 S. Beretania St. (548-2211): This futuristic building, elegantly designed in the form of an open crater (a reference to the volcanic origins of the islands) and surrounded by tall columns symbolizing palm trees, houses the State Legislature. Built in 1969. Open Mon.-Fri. In front of it, note the very fine statue of Queen Liliuokalani, who while a prisoner for nine months in 1894, after the demise of the monarchy, wrote the words of the famous song "Aloha O'e."

BEACHES: ☼ 🏖 **Hanauma Beach,** 10 mi. (16 km) east via Hi. 72: In its conspicuously beautiful setting, this beach is very popular with residents of the area; scuba-diving.

    Kahana Bay, 32 mi. (51 km) north along Hi. 61 and Hi. 83: Deserted and peaceful, far away from the throngs of Waikiki.

    Kailua Beach, 25 mi. (40 km) north along Hi. 61: All kinds of sailing; a quiet family beach.

    Makaha Beach, 38 mi. (60 km) west by H-1 and Hi. 93: The champion surfers' beach; only for the seasoned athlete.

    Sunset Beach, 46 mi. (73 km) NW on H-1, H-2, Hi. 99, and Hi. 83: The most famous surfing beach in all the Hawaiian islands; dangerous in winter.

    Waikiki Beach, Kalakaua Ave.: One of the best-known beaches in the world, with 2½ mi. (4 km) of sand overlooked by a forest of huge hotels. Often crowded. Good for beginning surfers.

    Waimanalo, 19 mi. (30 km) east along Hi. 72: For hang-gliding enthusiasts.

    Waimea Beach Park, 42 mi. (67 km) NW by H-1, H-2, Hi. 99, and Hi. 83: Very popular in summer; only for experienced surfers in winter. In a magnificent setting.

CHURCHES/SYNAGOGUES: ☀ ☖ **Kawaiahao Church,** 957 Punchbowl

St. (538-6267): Nicknamed "The Westminster Abbey of the Pacific," this was the church of the kings of Hawaii from 1842 on. The classic ecclesiastical architecture makes use of an unconventional material: 14,000 blocks of coral cut from the local reefs! The tomb of King Lunalilo is in the garden. Services in Hawaiian and English every Sunday. Open daily; should be seen.

    Royal Mausoleum, 2261 Nuuanu Ave., contains the tombs of the former Hawaiian monarchs of the Kamehameha Dynasty; an unexpected neo-Gothic chapel under the Pacific skies. Open daily.

HISTORIC BUILDINGS: ☖ **Iolani Palace,** King & Richards Sts. (523-0141):

The only royal palace ever built on U.S. territory. It was erected by King David Kalakaua in 1882 and served as a prison for the last monarch, Queen Liliuokalani, in 1894. In the Florentine style; notice the throne room and the grand dining room. A historical curiosity set in beautiful gardens. Very popular public concerts on Fridays. Guided tours Wed.-Sat.; resv. advised.

    Judiciary Building, 417 South St.: Built in 1874, this neoclassical palace, which once housed the Hawaiian parliament, will look familiar to fans of the TV series "Hawaii Five-O," several episodes of which were filmed here. Worth seeing; open Mon.-Fri. Enthroned in front of the building is an imposing copy in gilded bronze of a statue of King Kamehameha I, called "The Napoleon of the Pacific" (the original is on the island of Hawaii). The king wears the *malo,* the great royal cape of feathers, and the traditional Hawaiian headdress. For his feast (Kamehameha Day, June 11), the statue is bedecked with a mass of leis, or necklaces of flowers. Should not be missed.

MARKETS: ☀ ☖ **Tamashiro Market,** 802 N. King St. (841-8047): Colorful

Japanese market very close to the Bishop Museum; piles of fish and shellfish; lots of bustle; nice little Japanese restaurants. Worth a look. Open daily.

MONUMENTS: ☀ ☖☖ **U.S.S. *Arizona* Memorial,** Halawa Gate Boat landing,

Pearl Harbor (422-0561): Impressive memorial erected in the center of Pearl Harbor Bay over the wreck of the battleship *Arizona,* which was sunk with 1,102 of her crew during the Japanese surprise attack on December 7, 1941. The museum, which is open Tues.-Sun., attracts a million visitors a year. U.S. Navy boats leave the Visitor Center for the memorial every 30 min. Can also be reached from Kewalo Basin, near Ala Moana Park (536-3641). Don't miss it.

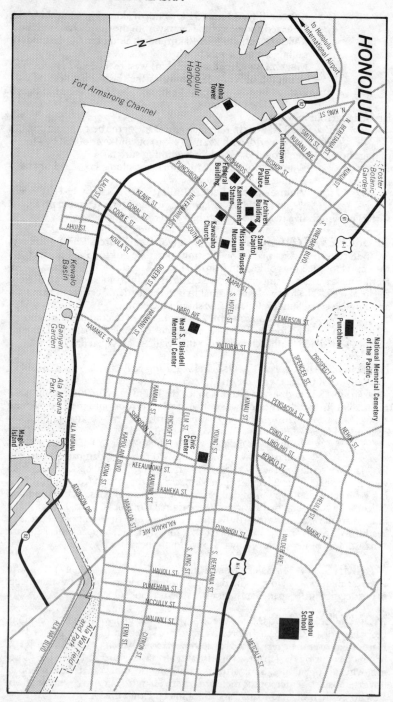

MUSEUMS OF ART: 🌣 ☀ Honolulu Academy of Arts, 900 S. Beretania St.
(538-3693): Graceful modern building with fine collections of Far Eastern (Chinese, Japanese, Korean) as well as European art, including such well-known names as Braque, Van Gogh, Matisse, and Picasso. Among the best-known works on exhibition: Segna di Bonaventura's *Madonna and Child* and John Singleton Copley's portrait of Nathaniel Allen. Must be seen. Open Tues.-Sun.

MUSEUMS OF SCIENCE & HISTORY: ☀ 🏛 Bishop Museum, 1525 Bernice St. (847-1443): This museum, founded in 1898, houses not only the world's richest collection of Polynesian art, but also a center for anthropological research unique in the Pacific Basin. As well as remarkable exhibits of historic objects and handcrafts, it offers regular performances of Hawaiian music and dance. There is also a planetarium. Don't miss this one. Open daily.

🔔 **Falls of Clyde,** Pier 7, Honolulu Harbor (536-6373): Moored at the foot of the Aloha Tower (see "Panoramas," below), this huge sailing ship, built in Scotland in 1878, is one of the last four-masters afloat. For long the principal means of transport among the Hawaiian Islands, she is now a floating museum. Fascinating. Open daily.

🔔 **Fort de Russy Museum,** Kalia Rd. (543-2687): A comprehensive museum of arms, from the primitive weapons used by the natives of Hawaii to those of World War II and Vietnam. For military-history buffs. Open Tues.-Sun.

🔔 **Mission House Museum,** 553 King St. (531-0481): The three missionaries' houses here are the oldest on the islands, dating from 1821, and have their original furnishings and fittings. An interesting glimpse of Hawaiian history. Open daily.

PANORAMAS: 🔔 Aloha Tower, Fort St. Mall (537-9260): Built in 1925, this was long the tallest building on the island. Fine view of the old city and its harbor from the tenth floor (reached by elevator). Once the symbol of the city. Open daily.

☀🔔 **National Memorial Cemetery of the Pacific,** Puowaina Dr. (546-3190): From this enormous military cemetery, lying in the crater of an extinct volcano (also known as Punchbowl Crater) above the city, you'll have a wonderful view of Waikiki and Honolulu harbor. More than 20,000 G.I.s who died in battle are buried here. The view shouldn't be missed. Open daily.

☀🔔🔔 **Round Top Park,** Tantalus & Round Top Drs.: The most spectacular prospect of Honolulu, from a beautiful mountainside tropical park. Don't miss it.

Annabelle's (see "Bars & Nightclubs," below).

PARKS & GARDENS: ☀ 🔔 Diamond Head State Monument, Diamond Rd.: A 400,000-year-old extinct volcano, rearing its 760 ft (232 m) over Waikiki Bay. The interior of the crater may be visited (the path begins at Makalei Place). The volcano owes its name to 19th-century European sailors who mistook shiny volcanic glass for diamonds. A Hawaiian legend has it that the volcano was the dwelling-place of Pele, the goddess of fire. Don't miss it. Open daily.

🔔 **Foster Botanic Garden,** 180 N. Vineyard Blvd. (533-3214): All the flora of the Pacific can be seen at this one spot in the center of Honolulu; spectacular orchid house. Open daily.

🔔 **Kapiolani Park,** Kalakaua & Montserrat Aves.: Hawaii's oldest public park, dating from 1877, boasts a very lovely rose garden, 38-acre zoo, splendid aquarium, public concerts, Hawaiian dances ("Kodak

Hula Show," Tues.-Fri. at 10 a.m.; for information, call 833-1661). For those who like souvenir snapshots of their vacations. Open daily.

    ☀ ♊ **Paradise Park,** 3737 Manoa Rd. (988-2141): Very lovely tropical park with luxuriant orchid garden, bamboo grove, waterfalls, lakes, exotic birds and monkeys, all in their natural state. Don't miss it. 15 min. from dwntwn; open daily.

PERFORMING ARTS: For current listings of shows and cultural events, consult the entertainment pages of the two daily papers, *Honolulu Advertiser* (morning) and *Honolulu Star Bulletin* (evening), as well as the weekly *Sun Press* and the monthly *Honolulu.*

    Blaisdell Center Arena, Ward Ave. & King St. (521-2911): Rock concerts; star-studded shows.

    Blaisdell Concert Hall, Ward Ave. & King St. (537-6191): Home of the Honolulu Symphony Orchestra (principal conductor Donald Johanos), from Oct. to May; also operatic performances Jan.-Feb., recitals, etc.

    John F. Kennedy Theater, University of Hawaii, 1770 East-West Rd. (948-7655): Classical and modern theater, ballet.

    Manoa Valley Theater, 2833 E. Manoa Rd. (988-6131): Home of the Hawaii Performing Arts Company. From Shakespeare to avant-garde theater in a delightfully rustic setting.

    Ruger Theater, Makapuu & Alohea Aves. (734-0274): Home of the Honolulu Community Theater, the islands' best stock company. Drama, comedy, and Broadway hits.

    Waikiki Shell, Kapiolani Park (521-2911): Open-air concerts in summer, including a number by the Honolulu Symphony Orchestra.

SHOPPING: **Ala Moana Center,** Ala Moana Blvd. at Atkinson Dr.: One of the country's largest and newest shopping centers, with more than 200 stores and exotic restaurants. Open daily.

    International Market Place, 2330 Kalakaua Ave.: For quarter of a century this Polynesian version of a Middle Eastern open-air bazaar, with its lantern-decorated giant banyan tree, has been drawing strollers and shoppers in droves. You should certainly take a look. Open daily.

    Royal Hawaiian Shopping Center, 2201 Kalakaua Ave.: Largest in the islands, laid out on three levels along Kalakaua Ave. From luxury fashion boutiques to Hawaiian handcraft stores. Many cafés and restaurants. Street performers (mimes, jugglers, musicians, etc.) and open-air concerts. A must-see. Open daily.

SPECIAL EVENTS: For exact dates, consult the **Hawaii Visitors Bureau (HVB)** (see "Tourist Information," above).

    Chinese New Year (mid-Jan. to Feb.): Parades, costumed processions. Chinatown in Honolulu, and on the other islands.

    Kamehameha Day (June 11): Public holiday in honor of King Kamehameha I (c.1738–1819), the first to establish his rule over the entire island chain. Processions, floats—a very colorful occasion.

    Hula Festival (Aug.): Hawaiian dancing (Honolulu).

    Aloha Week (Sept.-Oct.): Parades, concerts, dances, boat races in Honolulu and the other islands. The archipelago's biggest festival.

    Surfing Championships (Nov.-Dec.): Professional and amateur events. Makaha Beach, and the beaches on the North Shore of Oahu (Sunset and Waimea beaches, for example).

STROLLS: ⌂ **Chinatown,** around King & Smith Sts.: Honolulu's picturesque

Chinese quarter. Buddhist temple, open-air market, and restaurants by day; rather sleazy nightclubs and sex shops after dark.

Waikiki, along Kalakaua Ave.: The heart of the tourist's Honolulu, with dozens of skyscrapers, luxury hotels, restaurants, boutiques, and the world-renowned (and partly man-made) **Waikiki Beach,** nirvana of surfing and other water sports. This stroll you should try not to miss.

ACCOMMODATIONS
See the listing of toll-free numbers in the Appendix.

Room Rates in Hawaii	
B (Budget)	up to $30
I (Inexpensive)	$30–$60
M (Moderate)	$60–$90
E (Expensive)	$90–$140
VE (Very Expensive)	$140 and up

Personal Favorites (in order of preference)

Halekulani Hotel (nr. dwntwn), 2199 Kalia Rd., HI 96815 (808/923-2311; toll free, see Preferred). 456 rms, A/C, color TV, in-rm movies. AE, CB, DC, MC, V. Valet parking $8, pool, private beach, health club, three rests. (including La Mer), two bars and piano bar, 24-hr rm svce, disco, boutique, hrdrsr, concierge. *Note:* Waikiki Beach's super-luxury hotel, set amid five acres of flower gardens. This urbane ultramodern structure occupies the site of a 1920s predecessor, and retains a few vestiges of its distinguished past, notably the bar and two of the three rests. Luxuriously comfortable, spacious rms w. private verandas, mini-bars, and very complete facilities; most have ocean view. The swimming pool, w. its enormous blue mosaic of an orchid, is worth a look all by itself. Svce and reception of the highest order make this a favorite of big business and the jet set. Its name *(halekulani* means in Hawaiian "a house worthy of paradise") is well deserved. **VE**

Kahala Hilton (vic.), 5000 Kahala Ave., HI 96816 (808/734-2211; toll free, see Hilton). 370 rms, A/C, color TV, in-rm movies. AE, CB, DC, MC, V. Free (and valet) parking, sauna, health club, four tennis courts, beach, boats, three rests. (including Maile), bars, 24-hr rm svce, disco, hrdrsr, boutiques. *Note:* A newish 12-story building and a group of charming bungalows, clustered around a tropical lagoon (w. dolphins), far from Waikiki's crowds. Lavish, comfortable rms w. refrigerators and private balconies. Exemplary svce, and one of the city's finest rests. A jewel among local hotels since 1964; its guestbook has been signed by President Reagan and Prince Charles of England, among others. 20 min. from dwntwn. **VE**

Sheraton Waikiki (nr. dwntwn), 2255 Kalakaua Ave., HI 96815 (808/922-4422; toll free, see Sheraton). 1,843 rms, A/C, color TV, in-rm movies. AE, CB, DC, MC, V. Parking $5, two pools, private beach, boats, four rests. (including Kon Tiki), coffeeshop, four bars, rm svce, hrdrsr, boutiques. *Note:* Elegant, modern palace hotel, recently renovated, right on the water in the heart of Waikiki Beach; one of the most highly regarded in Honolulu. Its 30 floors tower above the bay. Large rms w. balconies and ocean or city view. Efficient svce. Luau (including a Polynesian show) Tues. evenings. Group clientele. **E–VE, but lower rates out of season**

☀☿ 🛍🛍 **Colony Surf** (nr. dwntwn), 2895 Kalakaua Ave., HI 96815 (808/923-5751; toll free 800/367-6046). 76 suites and 50 studios, A/C, cable color TV. AE, CB, DC, MC, V. Free valet parking, beach, rest. (Michel's), bar, rm svce, disco. *Note:* Charming small hotel opposite Kapiolani Park in the shadow of Diamond Head, offering remarkably spacious and comfortable studios and mini-suites w. kitchenettes, the best w. a splendid view of the ocean. Highly polished reception and svce. The rest. does not wholly deserve its high reputation. The favorite hotel of those in the know. **E–VE**

🛍🛍 **New Otani** (nr. dwntwn), 2863 Kalakaua Ave., HI 96815 (808/923-1555; toll free 800/421-8795). 138 rms, A/C, color TV. AE, CB, DC, MC, V. Free parking, beach, rest. (Hau Tree Lanai), bar, rm svce, disco. *Note:* Of modest size compared to the giants of Waikiki Beach, this intimate, comfortable hotel across from Kapiolani Park is the favorite of Japanese businessmen. Friendly rms, a little on the skimpy side; excellent svce; very commendable Japanese-American rest. Direct access to the beach. A good place to stay. **M–E**

🛍 **Waikiki Surf** (nr. dwntwn), 2200 Kuhio Ave., HI 96815 (808/923-7671; toll free 800/367-5170). 288 rms, A/C, color TV. AE, CB, DC, MC, V. Free parking, pool, rest., bar, rm svce, free crib. *Note:* Honolulu's big bargain—modern, quiet, and well maintained, five min. from Waikiki Beach. Friendly reception. Some rms w. kitchenettes. One of the best values in the city. Family clientele. **I–M**

🛍 **Outrigger West Hotel** (nr. dwntwn), 2330 Kuhio Ave., HI 96815 (808/922-5022; toll free 800/367-5170). 660 rms, A/C, color TV. AE, CB, DC, MC, V. Parking $4, pool, rest., coffeeshop, bar, rm svce, free crib. *Note:* Another bargain in Waikiki, five min. from the beach. Massive 17-story building, but the balconied rms (some w. kitchenettes) are comfortable enough. Affable reception. Very good value. **M**

Other Accommodations (from top bracket to budget)

🛍🛍🛍 **Hilton Hawaiian Village** (nr. dwntwn), 2005 Kalia Rd., HI 96815 (808/949-4321; toll free, see Hilton). 2,566 rms, A/C, color TV, in-rm movies. AE, CB, DC, MC, V. Gar. $6, three pools, boats, private beach, putting green, gardens, six rests. (including Mahahiki), two coffeeshops, five bars, rm svce (24-hr on VIP floors), disco, more than 100 boutiques (in the Rainbow Bazaar), hrdrsr, private docking, free crib. *Note:* The tallest hotel in the islands, rising 38 floors above Waikiki Beach in the midst of 22 acres of tropical gardens. Wonderful lagoon-style pool surrounded by palm trees. The rms in both towers have a fine ocean view. Commendable standard of comfort; efficient svce. Caters mostly to groups and conventions. Offers sailing trips in a catamaran. Recently underwent a $100-million rejuvenation. **E–VE**

🛍🛍🛍 **Hyatt Regency Waikiki** (nr. dwntwn), 2424 Kalakaua Ave., HI 96815 (808/923-1234; toll free, see Hyatt). 1,234 rms, A/C, color TV, in-rm movies. AE, CB, DC, MC, V. Valet parking $6, pool, private beach, boats, five rests. (including Bagwells 2424), coffeeshop, three bars, rm svce, disco, hrdrsr, 70 boutiques. *Note:* Twin 40-story towers dominating all of Waikiki Bay and constituting a sort of miniature city within the city. The ten-story lobby comes complete w. tropical forest, lagoon, and waterfalls; sumptuous and spectacular. Spacious, elegantly decorated rms, the best overlooking the beach, others the city. Impeccable comfort; exemplary svce. Bagwells 2424 is a very good rest. Interesting vacation and wknd packages. Two floors reserved for VIPs. **E–VE** ꝑꝑꝑ **Ilikai** (nr. dwntwn), 1777 Ala Moana Blvd., HI 96815 (808/ 949-3811; toll free 800/448-8355). 800 rms, A/C, color TV, in-rm movies. AE, CB, DC, MC, V. Gar. $5, two pools, six tennis courts, private beach, two rests. (including Champeaux's, on the 30th floor), bars, rm svce, disco, boutiques, Polynesian show. *Note:* This huge modern tower rising above the Ala Wai yacht basin, a little way from Waikiki Beach, served as a set for episodes of the "Hawaii Five-O" TV series. Very comfortable rms, some w. kitchenettes and most overlooking the ocean. Excellent svce; good rest. Caters mostly to groups. **E–VE**

☀ꝑꝑꝑ **Sheraton Royal Hawaiian Hotel** (nr. dwntwn), 2259 Kalakaua Ave., HI 96815 (808/923-7311; toll free, see Sheraton). 525 rms, A/C, color TV, in-rm movies. AE, CB, DC, MC, V. Parking $5, pool, private beach, two rests. (including the Monarch Room), bars, rm svce, disco, boutiques, Polynesian show. *Note:* "The hotel of kings and presidents," a 1920s palace known as "the pink lady" because of its pastel-colored Spanish-Moorish façade. Loads of rococo charm. Most rms are huge and comfortable but some are a little cramped (avoid those in the new wing). Efficient svce. Luau on Sun. Beautiful tropical gardens. Caters mostly to vacationers. **E–VE**

ꝑꝑ **Holiday Inn Waikiki Beach** (nr. dwntwn), 2570 Kalakaua Ave., HI 96815 (808/922-2511); toll free, see Holiday Inns). 714 rms, A/C, color TV, in-rm movies. AE, CB, DC, MC, V. Parking $3, pool, private beach, rest., coffeeshop, bar, rm svce, disco, crib $10. *Note:* A typical Holiday Inn right on Waikiki Beach, w. a splendid view of the ocean and Diamond Head. Modern and functional; group clientele. Captain's Table is a good rest. Good value out of season. Very close to the zoo and Kapiolani Park. **M–E, but lower rates out of season**

ꝑꝑ **Imperial Hawaii Resort** (nr. dwntwn), 205 Lewers St., HI 96815 (808/923-1827; toll free 800/367-8047, ext. 225). 397 rms, A/C, color TV. AE, CB, DC, MC, V. Free parking, pool, sauna, 24-hr coffeeshop, rest. (Valentino's), disco. *Note:* Classic resort hotel, recently renovated. Rms w. private terraces and ocean view. Modern and comfortable; very good value out of season. A good place to stay. **M–E, but lower rates out of season**

☀ꝑꝑ **Moana Ocean Hotel** (nr. dwntwn), 2365 Kalakaua Ave., HI 96815 (808/922-3111; toll free, see Sheraton). 390 rms, one-third w. A/C, color TV, in-rm movies. AE, CB, DC, MC, V. Gar. $5, private beach, rest. (Banyan Court), bar, rm svce, hrdrsr. *Note:* The oldest (1901) grand hotel on the island; old-fashioned but charming Victorian décor; rooms completely renovated. Direct access to the water. Noisy Polynesian show every night (for the Tihati show you will need resv.). Avoid the rms in the new wing. **M–E, but lower rates out of season**

ꝑꝑ **Outrigger Waikiki** (nr. dwntwn), 2335 Kalakaua Ave., HI 96815 (808/923-0711; toll free 800/367-5170). 523 rms, A/C, color TV, in-rm movies. AE, CB, DC, MC, V. Gar. $5, pool, health club, private beach, three rests., coffeeshop, bar, rm svce, disco, hrdrsr. *Note:* Modern, comfortable hotel, recently renovated, w. direct access to Waikiki Beach, very near the International Market Place. Spacious rms w. refrigerators. Caters to groups and package tours. **M–E**

ꝑꝑ **Inn on the Park** (nr. dwntwn), 1920 Ala Moana Blvd., HI 96815 (808/946-8355; toll free 800/367-5224). 230 rms, A/C, color TV. AE, DC, MC, V. Free parking, pool, rest., two bars, disco, hrdrsr. *Note:* Modern, comfortable hotel. Rms w. terraces and refrigerators, some overlooking the ocean. Very good value. **I–M, but lower rates out of season**

Aloha Surf Hotel (nr. dwntwn), 444 Kanekapolei St., HI 96815 (808/923-0222; toll free 800/367-5205). 204 rms, A/C, color TV. AE, DC, MC, V. Free parking, rest., bar. *Note:* Modest but acceptable hotel, recently modernized and well run, away from the hurly-burly of Waikiki. Good value five min. from the beach. **I–M**

Outrigger Edgewater (nr. dwntwn), 2168 Kalia Rd., HI 96815 (808/922-6424; toll free 800/367-5610). 181 rms, A/C, color TV. AE, CB, DC, MC, V. Free parking, pool, rest., bar, rm svce, disco, hrdrsr, free crib. Serviceable comfort and smiling svce. Very good value, a few steps from the beach. **I–M**

Outrigger Royal Islander (nr. dwntwn), 2164 Kalia Rd., HI 96815 (808/922-1961; toll free 800/367-5170). 104 rms, A/C, color TV. AE, DC, MC, V. Free parking, rest., bar, disco. *Note:* Contemporary comfort; rms w. terraces and a view of Waikiki Beach. Overall good value. **I–M**

Waikiki Marina Hotel (nr. dwntwn), 1956 Ala Moana Blvd., HI 96815 (808/955-0714). 323 rms, A/C, color TV. AE, CB, DC, MC, V. Free parking, pool, nearby rest., bar. *Note:* Modest but acceptable hotel near the Ala Wai Canal. Functional comfort; good value. **I–M**

Airport Accommodations

Best Western Plaza Hotel (formerly the Ramada; vic.), 3253 N. Nimitz Hwy., HI 96819 (808/836-3636; toll free, see Best Western). 268 rms, A/C, color TV, in-rm movies. AE, CB, DC, MC, V. Free parking, pool, rest., bar, rm svce, disco, hrdrsr. *Note:* Modern, friendly eight-story motel 3 min. from the airport and 25 min. from Waikiki. Comfortable rms w. refrigerators; cordial reception and svce. The best place to stay for a stopover between flights, w. free 24-hr airport limousine svce. 5 min. from Aloha Stadium, 10 min. from Pearl Harbor. **I–M, but lower rates out of season**

Accommodations Around the Island of Oahu

Hilton Turtle Bay (formerly the Kuilima Hyatt), Kamehameha Hwy., Kahuku, HI 96731 (808/293-8811; toll free, see Hilton). 487 rms, A/C, color TV, in-rm movies. AE, CB, DC, MC, V. Parking $5, two pools, golf course, ten tennis courts, horseback riding, water sports, private beach, two rests., coffeeshop, two bars, rm svce, disco, hrdrsr. *Note:* Luxury hotel in the middle of a 5-mi. (8-km) beach on the north shore of the island, 1½ hrs by car from Honolulu. Luxury in peace. The huge, comfortable rms overlook the ocean. Excellent svce; very good sports facilities. For lovers of tranquility and of nature. **E–VE**

YMCA/Youth Hostel

Hale Aloha Youth Hostel (nr. dwntwn), 2417 Prince Edward St., HI 96815 (808/946-0951).

RESTAURANTS

Hawaii Restaurant Prices	
(per person, excluding drinks and service charges)	
B (Budget)	up to $15
I (Inexpensive)	$15–$25
M (Moderate)	$25–$40
E (Expensive)	$40–$60
VE (Very Expensive)	$60 and up

Personal Favorites (in order of preference)

☀🍷🍷🍷 **La Mer** (nr. dwntwn), in the Halekulani Hotel (see "Accommodations," above) (923-2311). A/C. Dinner only, nightly. AE, CB, DC, MC, V. Jkt. Specialties: tartare of Hawaiian fish, hot oysters w. leeks, shrimps w. chervil and lemon peel, filet of beef w. sweet peppers, sautéed curried moana, gratin of strawberries; excellent desserts. Menu changes regularly. *Note:* Occupying the original 1920s building of the old Halekulani Hotel, this magnificent rest. looking out to sea is the most elegant, the most polished, and the most costly in Honolulu. Superb, inspired French-Polynesian nouvelle cuisine; first-class svce. The sound of the surf on the nearby beach underlines the elegance of the décor. A first-class establishment in the high style, w. prices to match. Resv. a must. Valet parking. *French-Seafood.* **E–VE**

🍷🍷🍷 **Maile Restaurant** (nr. dwntwn), in the Kahala Hilton (see "Accommodations," above) (734-2211). A/C. Dinner nightly, brunch Sun. AE, CB, DC, MC, V. Jkt. Specialties: snails w. black-bean sauce, potpourri of seafood, roast duckling Waialae, veal w. wild mushrooms, dolphin Caprice. Here nouvelle cuisine scores a triumph under tropic skies, w. superb salads and minimally cooked fish broiled whole. Fine wine list. *Note:* A rather dark, cave-like setting complete w. fountains; smiling, gracious svce in Far Eastern style. One of the best rests. in the islands. Resv. a must. *French-Polynesian.* **M–E**

🍷🍷🍷 **Nick's Fish Market** (nr. dwntwn), in the Waikiki Gateway Hotel 2070 Kalakaua Ave. (955-6333). A/C. Dinner only, nightly (until 2 a.m.). AE, CB, DC, MC, V. Jkt. Specialties: Every imaginable kind of seafood is cooked and served here: Maine lobster, Florida stone crab, and Louisiana soft-shell crab (delivered by air daily) appear cheek by jowl w. Pacific dolphin (mahi-mahi), swordfish, and bass (opaka paka). Excellent bouillabaisse and linguine w. clam sauce. Very good wine list. *Note:* One of the country's outstanding fish rests.; elegant maritime décor; exemplary svce. Resv. a must. Valet parking. *Seafood.* **M**

🍷🍷 **Keo's Thai Cuisine** (nr. dwntwn), 625 Kapahulu Ave. (737-8240). A/C. Lunch Mon.–Sat.; dinner nightly. AE, MC, V. Specialties: spicy chicken soup, minted spring rolls, beef w. coconut milk, garlic shrimp, "Evil Jungle Prince" (chicken w. chili). *Note:* Given the enormous menu w. its more than 200 dishes ranging from the mildest through the moderately spicy to the volcanic, the lover of exotic foods should not fail to visit this friendly, elegant temple of Thai cooking. Charming tropical-garden décor; attentive, efficient svce; an "in" place to eat. Resv. an absolute must. *Thai.* **I**

The Willows (nr. dwntwn), 901 Hausten St. (946-4808). A/C. Lunch/dinner daily; closed hols. AE, CB, DC, MC, V. Specialties: the whole gamut of Polynesian dishes—laulau, limu kohu, lomi-lomi, haupia—as well as scallops Royale and some very good curries. Excellent desserts, such as "Sky High" lemon meringue pie. *Note:* Picture-postcard perfect w. its luxuriant, leafy setting complete w. waterfalls and fishpools; for 40 years it has been a "must" for tourists. Good svce; resv. essential. Valet parking. 10 min. from dwntwn *Polynesian*. **I**

Chez Michel (nr. dwntwn), 444 Hobron Lane (955-7866). A/C. Lunch Mon.-Sat.; dinner daily; closed hols. AE, CB, DC, MC, V. Jkt. Specialties: French cooking w. a dash of the exotic: trout grenoblois, rack of lamb à la jardinière, roast duckling, dolphin provençale, steak tartare, frozen soufflé à l'orange. Fine list of French wines, w. a hundred vineyards represented. *Note:* A local institution. Michel Martin, from Nice, who introduced French cooking to Hawaii in 1946, is still one of its leading exponents in Honolulu. Wood paneling and luxuriant green plants make an attractive setting. Resv. advisable. Very near the yacht basin. Valet parking. *French*. **I–M**

Fisherman's Wharf (nr. dwntwn), 1009 Ala Moana Blvd. (538-3808). A/C. Lunch/dinner daily. AE, CB, DC, MC, V. Specialties: every variety of Pacific seafood, absolutely fresh and at prices easy on your wallet; shrimp Louie salad. *Note:* Honolulu's most popular fish rest.; often crowded and noisy, in spite of which the waitresses contrive to work miracles. Pleasant nautical décor and pretty view of Kewalo yacht basin. No resv. *Seafood*. **I**

King Tsin (nr. dwntwn), 1110 McCully St. (946-3273). A/C. Lunch/dinner daily. AE, CB, DC, MC, V. Specialties: Hunan shrimp, hot-and-sour soup, shrimp in black-bean sauce, Szechuan duck, Mongolian beef, "Beggar's Chicken," Hunan pork w. broccoli. *Note:* The décor of this little rest. is nothing to write home about, but King Tsin's food is 100% authentic, and some of the best Chinese cooking to be found on the island. Some dishes are highly spiced. Repeat customers. A fine place to eat. *Chinese*. **B–I**

Other Restaurants (from top bracket to budget)

Bagwells 2424 (nr. dwntwn), in the Hyatt Regency (see "Accommodations," above) (922-9292). A/C. Dinner only, daily. AE, CB, DC, MC, V. J&T. Specialties: some highly successful variations on the classic themes of European cuisine (trout stuffed w. salmon mousse, braised lobster w. leeks, pheasant w. cabbage, tarragon chicken), as well remarkable seafood and Hawaiian dishes (mahi-mahi, opaka paka). Honolulu's best wine list, w. 300 labels. *Note:* Dignified, elegant luxury hotel dining rm; sumptuously decorated in lively tones of red w. wood paneling and mirrors. Exemplary svce. Resv. advised. Valet parking. *French-Continental*. **M–E**

John Dominis (dwntwn), 43 Ahui St. (523-0955). A/C. Dinner only, daily. AE, CB, DC, MC, V. Jkt. Specialties: every kind of Pacific seafood (grouper, swordfish, tuna, sea bream, crayfish, mackerel, oysters, red snapper) oven-broiled or cooked in its broth, clam chowder, cioppino (a Californian seafood stew). Good wine list. *Note:* One of the best, and handsomest, restaurants in all the islands. Absolutely fresh-caught fish and shellfish. Splendid glass-walled dining rm, from which you can see the sea creatures swimming in their saltwater holding pools carved out of living rock. Splendid view of the harbor, w. Diamond Head in the distance. Cordial, smiling svce, friendly bar; the favorite of the local smart set. Resv. advised. *Seafood-Polynesian*. **M–E**

The Third Floor (nr. dwntwn), in the Hawaiian Regent Hotel, 2252 Kalakaua Ave. (922-6611). A/C. Dinner only, daily. AE,

CB, DC, MC, V. Jkt. Specialties: duck w. peaches, médaillon of veal Black Forest style, lamb cutlets Seville, rack of lamb provençale, seafood casserole w. fennel. Good desserts (ice-cream bonbons); fine wine list. *Note:* Long considered to be Honolulu's finest rest. French-inspired food w. a touch of the exotic. Elegant tropical décor—fountain, pool w. frolicking carp, rattan chairs—and (a little anachronistically) heraldic banners hanging from the ceiling. Svce on the offhand side. Resv. highly advisable. *Continental.* **M–E**

🍷🍷 **Canlis** (nr. dwntwn), 2100 Kalakaua Ave. (923-2324). A/C. Lunch Mon.-Fri.; dinner daily; closed hols. AE, CB, DC, MC, V. J&T. Specialties: steak Pierre, jumbo shrimp, Canlis salad, carefully selected steaks, seafood broiled to order over kiawe wood. Fine wine list at outrageous prices; the finest fish and meat; excellent desserts. *Note:* Elegant, flower-bedecked tropical setting. One of a chain of rests. well known along the West Coast and in Hawaii. Attentive kimono-clad waitresses; resv. advised; valet parking. *Steak-Seafood.* **M–E**

🍷🍷 **Champeaux's** (nr. dwntwn), in the Ilikai Hotel (see "Accommodations," above) (949-3811). A/C. Dinner only, daily; brunch Sun. AE, CB, DC, MC, V. Jkt. Specialties: opakapaka, red snapper Champeaux, island salad. French nouvelle cuisine crossed w. the tropics; salads and desserts not to be missed. *Note:* The quintessential grand-hotel rest. From the 30th floor of the Ilikai, offers a splendid nighttime view of Honolulu. Polished svce; disco too. Resv. advised. *French-Polynesian.* **I–M**

🍷🍷 **Bon Appetit** (nr. dwntwn), 1778 Ala Moana Blvd. (942-3837). A/C. Lunch Mon.–Fri.; dinner, Mon.-Sat.; closed Sun. AE, CB, DC, MC, V. Specialties: mousse of scallops w. caviar, fish soup w. saffron, shrimp ravioli w. cream of morels, duck au poivre vert. Menu changes regularly. *Note:* Guy Banal, formerly the chef at Bagwells 2424 (see above), rules with dexterity and finesse over the stove of this charming French-style bistro located unexpectedly in the middle of the Discovery Bay Shopping Center. Walls decorated w. bamboo; pastel-colored tablecloths. Very friendly reception and svce. If you like authentic French cooking and very low prices, this is one of the best places on the island for you. Resv. advised. *French.* **I–M**

🍷🍷 **Trattoria** (nr. dwntwn), in the Outrigger Edgewater (see "Accommodations," above) (923-8415). A/C. Dinner only, daily. AE, CB, DC, MC, V. Specialties: veal cutlet parmigiana, lobster Fra Diavolo, chicken alla romana, fresh homemade pasta. *Note:* The best Italian rest. in the area. The pastas (canneloni, lasagne) are praiseworthy. Charming Roman-villa décor, but rather noisy. Attentive svce; valet parking. Resv. advised. *Italian.* **I–M**

🍷🍷 **Suntory** (nr. dwntwn), 2233 Kalakaua Ave. (922-5511). A/C. Lunch Mon.-Fri.; dinner daily. AE, MC, V. Specialties: teppanyaki, shabu shabu, sashimi, sushi. In the opinion of connoisseurs, the island's best Japanese rest. Refined, elegant Japanese setting, thoughtful svce. On the 30th floor of the Royal Hawaiian Center. Western-style seating or tatami available. An excellent place. *Japanese.* **I**

🍷 **Wo Fat** (dwntwn), 115 N. Hotel St. (537-6260). A/C. Lunch/dinner daily. AE, CB, DC, MC, V. Specialties: absolutely authentic Cantonese food. *Note:* Honolulu's oldest Chinese rest. (1882), complete w. pagoda roof. A favorite w. the island's Chinese community. Svce a little abrupt. *Chinese.* **B–I**

Cafeteria / Fast Food

Garden Café (dwntwn), Academy of Arts, 900 S. Beretania St. (538-3693). In the museum's modern setting, excellent sandwiches, salads, and lunches. Open Tues.-Sun. No credit cards. Closed June-Sept.

BARS & NIGHTCLUBS

Annabelle's (nr. dwntwn), in the Ilikai Hotel (see "Accommodations," above) (949-3811). Fashionable disco with a fine view over the bay.

Bagwells Lounge (nr. dwntwn), in the Hyatt Regency (see "Accommodations," above) (922-9292). Trendy bar adjoining the restaurant of the same name. Open daily.

Beach Bar (nr. dwntwn), in the Moana Ocean Hotel (see "Accommodations," above) (922-3111). For 80 years this has been Honolulu's most famous bar; the perfect spot for your before-dinner drink. Open daily.

Bobby McGee's Conglomeration (nr. dwntwn), in the Colony Surf (see "Accommodations," above) (922-1282). Favorite yuppie bar/disco. Open daily.

Hilton Dome (nr. dwntwn), in the Hilton Hawaiian Village (see "Accommodations," above) (949-4321). This is where you come to see the well-known Hawaiian singer and showman Don Ho; a real local institution.

Hula's (nr. dwntwn), 2103 Kuhio Ave. (923-0669). Modish disco with a wide-ranging clientele—from punk rockers to gays.

Monarch Room (nr. dwntwn), in the Sheraton Royal Hawaiian Hotel (see "Accommodations," above) (923-7311). Very popular Polynesian show.

Trappers (nr. dwntwn), in the Hyatt Regency (see "Accommodations," above) (922-9292). Piano bar, jazz; intimate and relaxing atmosphere. Open daily.

LUAUS (BUFFET AND POLYNESIAN SHOW)

Polynesian Cultural Center (vic.), one hour from Honolulu by car via Hi. 61 and Hi. 83; transportation (for a fee) available from Waikiki hotels (call 293-3333 for resv.). Open Mon.-Sat. Interesting Polynesian music and dancing. Since the center is run by the Mormons, no alcoholic beverages.

Tihati (nr. dwntwn), in the Moana Ocean Hotel (see "Accommodations," above) (923-2995). The island's best Polynesian show. Open daily.

Also at the **Sheraton Royal Hawaiian Hotel** (Sun.) and the **Sheraton Waikiki** (Tues.) (see "Accommodations," above, for both hotels).

NEARBY EXCURSIONS

☼ **HAIKU GARDENS** (15 mi., 24 km, north on Hi. 61): Tropical jungle with bamboo thickets and giant waterlilies at the foot of the **Koolau Mountains.** An exotic picture-postcard sight. Stop at **Nuuanu Pali Lookout,** offering one of the best views on the island. In 1795 this was the scene of a bloody battle, after which hundreds of the defeated warriors were hurled over the cliff by the soldiers of King Kamehameha.

☼ **POLYNESIAN CULTURAL CENTER** (at Laie, 38 mi., 60 km, north along Hi. 61 and Hi. 83) (293-3333): Seven carefully reconstructed Polynesian villages, representing the whole gamut of Pacific cultures (Hawaii, Tahiti, Samoa, Fiji, Tonga, etc.), standing in 42 acres of beautiful gardens. Excellent displays of folk-dancing (resv. recommended for the evening buffet dinner-shows). Don't miss this one. Not far away is a spectacular Mormon temple (the Mormons manage the Polynesian Cultural Center). Open Mon.-Sat. Bus svce from Honolulu; 1½ hrs.

SEA LIFE PARK (on Makapuu Point at Waimanalo, 16 mi., 26 km, east on Hi. 72) (923-1531): Highly regarded marine zoo opposite the very beautiful Makapuu Beach; offers a complete selection of Pacific marine life from sea anemones to sharks. Whaling museum. 30 min. from dwntwn. Must be seen. Open daily.

☀🔔 **WAIMEA FALLS PARK** (42 mi., 67 km, NW on H-1, H-2, and Hi. 83): 1,680 acres of jungle, tropical gardens, trails, and rock terraces with some very lovely waterfalls in which swimming is permitted. Must be seen. Open daily.

THE OTHER ISLANDS

GETTING THERE: You can get from island to island by recreational tour boats and luxury cruisers (consult your travel agent), or by air. **Aloha Airlines** (808/836-1111), **Hawaiian Airlines** (808/537-5100), and **Mid Pacific Air** (808/836-3313) offer inter-island transportation. Passengers holding full-fare round-trip tickets from the mainland may travel to other islands for an additional charge of about $40–$50 per stopover.

THE ISLAND OF HAWAII: "The Volcano Isle," 40 min. from Honolulu by air (also known as "The Big Island" or "Orchid Island"). At 4,038 sq. mi. (10,460 km²), Hawaii is the largest island in the chain. Its sources of revenue are tropical produce (particularly orchids), cattle rearing, and tourism. The island's largest city (and capital), **Hilo,** acts as food, lodging, and transportation hub (flights to/from the mainland and other islands) for visitors. Hawaii is a micro-cosm of the physical geography of the islands, with its luxuriant vegetation, its white, green, and black sand beaches, and its two active volcanoes: **Kilauea** and the stately **Mauna Loa,** whose 13,000-ft (4,000-m) crest is crowned with snow in winter—an unusual sight in these tropical latitudes. It was from this island that the great Kamehameha, seeking to end the internecine quarrels of the archipela-go, set out to conquer the neighboring islands and unite their people under his rule. Hawaii's southern extremity, **Ka Lae** or **South Cape,** is the southernmost point of U.S. territory.

The Sights

Among the island's most interesting tourist attractions are:

☀🔔 **Akaka Falls,** north of Hilo along the beautiful Hamakua coast road: Lovely park with giant 432-ft (135-m) waterfall.

🔔 **Captain Cook Monument,** at Kealakekua Bay, where the Brit-ish explorer was killed by the Hawaiians in 1779. Splendid ocean view. Daily boat trips from Kailua-Kona.

☀🔔 **Kalapana Beach:** Very popular black sand (powdered lava) beach at the eastern end of the island.

🔔 **Lapakahi State Park:** Site of a 600-year-old fishing village. Don't miss the view.

🔔 **Orchid Farms** around Hilo: Several of these may be visited, particularly **Nani Maui Gardens,** 421 Makalika St. This is the world's largest orchid-exporting center; you should see it. Open daily.

🔔 **Rainbow Falls,** near Hilo: Beautiful waterfalls on the Wailuku River, with guaranteed rainbows on sunny mornings. Splendid trails for walkers.

☀🔔🔔 **Volcanoes National Park,** 29 mi. (47 km) SW of Hilo on Hi. 11: The only U.S. nature reserve with two active volcanoes—Mauna Loa, the more impressive (13,680 ft, 4,275 m), and Kilauea (4,077 ft, 1,274 m). A panoramic ring road, the **Crater Rim Drive,** goes around Kilauea (when it isn't rendered impassable by magma!), and offers a fine view of molten

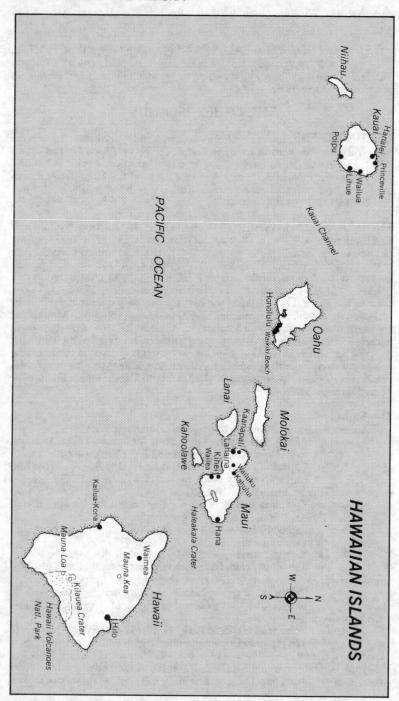

lava flows, forests of giant ferns, and land laid waste by earlier eruptions. If you call 967-7977, a recorded message will advise you of the current level of volcanic activity. You can stay at Volcano House (see below). Interesting museum of volcanology at the park headquarters, open daily. For information: Superintendent, Hawaii Volcanoes National Park, Hawaii, HI 96785 (808/967-7311). Don't fail to visit it.

Where to Stay

Westin Mauna Kea, Kohala Coast, Kamuela, HI 96743 (808/882-7222; toll-free, see Westin). 308 rms, A/C; MAP only. AE. Free valet parking, pool, golf course, 13 tennis courts, sauna, private beach, horseback riding, boats, fishing, four rests. (including the Batik Room), bars, rm svce, disco, hrdrsr, boutiques. *Note:* The islands' luxury hotel par excellence, in an idyllic setting at the foot of an extinct volcano and on its own private beach, on the NW coast of Hawaii. A very successful example of modern architecture; tasteful but sumptuous interior w. many Polynesian art objects. Spacious rms w. mountain or ocean view; also villas for two to four guests. The Batik Room is an excellent rest. Exemplary svce. The golf course is one of the most highly regarded in the country. Everything of the finest and prices to match. One of the 12 best hotels in the U.S. **VE**

Mauna Lani Bay Hotel, Hi. 19, Kohala Coast, Kawaihae, HI 96743 (808/885-6622; toll free 800/367-2323). 351 rms, A/C, cable color TV. AE, CB, DC, MC, V. Free valet parking, pool, golf course, ten tennis courts, sauna, private beach, fishing, boats, horseback riding, four rests. (including the Third Floor), three bars, rm svce, disco, boutiques. *Note:* One of the most luxurious hotels in the Pacific basin; a modern building designed like a ship's prow and standing in its own lovely tropical gardens. Splendid lobby w. indoor pool and palm trees. Elegant, richly furnished rms w. ocean view. Attentive, personalized svce. Caters mostly to groups and conventions. **VE**

Hilton Kona Beach & Tennis Resort, Alii Dr. (P.O. Box 1179), Kailua-Kona, HI 96740 (808/329-3111; toll free, see Hilton). 452 rms, A/C, color TV, in-rm movies. AE, CB, DC, MC, V. Free parking, pool, private beach, golf course, four tennis courts, water sports, horseback riding, four rests. and bars, piano bar, rm svce, disco. *Note:* Futuristic building right on the ocean; beautiful rms w. private patios and spectacular view of the Pacific. Tropical gardens. Comprehensive sports facilities. Good svce. One of the best hotels in the Islands. Group clientele. **E–VE**

Kona Surf Hotel, 78-128 Ehukai St., Keauhou-Kona, HI 96740 (808/322-3411; toll free 800/367-2603). 532 rms, A/C, cable color TV. AE, CB, DC, MC, V. Free parking, two pools, golf course, three tennis courts, sauna, fishing, rest., bars, rm svce, disco, hrdrsr, boutiques. *Note:* Very lovely modern hotel on the ocean. Comfortable rms w. private balconies. Excellent svce. Magnificent tropical gardens. Very good value; the favorite of those in the know. **M–E, but lower rates out of season**

Keauhou Beach, 78-6740 Alii Dr., Keauhou-Kona, HI 96740 (808/322-3441). 317 rms, A/C, color TV. AE, CB, DC, MC, V. Free parking, pool, six tennis courts, sauna, health club, private beach, rest., bar, rm svce, disco. *Note:* Modern, comfortable hotel partly overhanging the water. Huge, well-laid-out rms w. private balconies. Good value, but svce a little undependable. **M–E, but lower rates out of season**

Kona Lagoon Hotel, 78-6780 Alii Dr., Keauhou-Kona, HI 96740 (808/322-2727; toll free 800/367-2603). 454 rms, A/C, color TV. AE, CB, DC, MC, V. Free parking, pool, two tennis courts, rest., bar, rm svce, disco, hrdrsr, boutiques. *Note:* Immaculate luxury hotel on the beach, offering every modern comfort; its ten-acre garden is planted on an old lava bed. Spacious rms, most w. private patio and Pacific view. Group clientele. Svce a little unreliable. **M–E, but lower rates out of season**

☼⏚♨ **Volcano House,** Hi. 11, in Volcanoes National Park, HI 96718 (808/967-7321). 37 rms. AE, CB, DC, MC, V. Free parking, sauna, rest., bar, disco, boutiques. *Note:* One of the loveliest sites in the Islands, in the heart of Volcanoes National Park. Cordial country-inn-style comfort; very acceptable rest. You should reserve as far ahead as possible. Some rms have a fine view of the crater. Open year round. Excellent value. **I–M**

⏚ **Country Club Hotel,** 121 Banyan Dr., Hilo, HI 96720 (808/935-7171). 149 rms, A/C, color TV. AE, CB, DC, MC, V. Free parking, pool, rest., bar, disco. *Note:* Small, modern hotel on the ocean, in tropical gardens surrounded by palm trees. Home-like rms w. private balconies. Svce w. a smile. Interesting vacation packages. Near airport. Good value. **I**

Where to Eat

☼ ♟♟♟ **Batik Room,** in the Westin Mauna Kea (see "Where to Stay," above) (882-7222). A/C. Dinner only, daily. No credit cards. Jkt. Specialties: almond soup, poisson cru à la Tahitienne, coulibiac of dolphin, stuffed squab. A very successful marriage of European and Polynesian cuisines. The menu changes regularly. *Note:* A luxury hotel dining rm at the height of its splendor; exotic setting and stylish svce; the best (and most expensive) food on the island. Resv. a must. *Continental-Polynesian.* **M–E**

♟♟ **S.S. James Makee,** in the Kona Surf Hotel (see "Where to Stay," above) (322-3411). A/C. Dinner only, daily. AE, CB, DC, MC, V. Specialties: European-inspired food w. a touch of the exotic. *Note:* Some interesting dishes, such as médaillon of beef Diablo and shrimp Polynesian, in an attractive nautical setting. Resv. advised. *Continental-Polynesian.* **I–M**

☼ ♟♟ **Parker Ranch Broiler,** Hi. 19 and Hi. 190, Kamuela (885-7366). A/C. Lunch/dinner daily; closed Dec. 25. AE, MC, V. Specialties: grilled red meats and fish. *Note:* The excellent beef is home-reared on the ranch; so are the vegetables, grown without chemical fertilizer. The chef is one of the best on the island; the décor is attractive Victorian. Resv. advised. *Steak-Seafood.* **I**

♟ **K.K.'s Place,** 413 Kilauea Ave., Hilo (935-5216). Lunch/dinner daily. AE, DC, MC, V. Specialties: teppanyaki, tempura. *Note:* Japanese food prepared to the American taste, w. acceptable results, all things considered. *Japanese-American.* **I**

♟ **Spindrifter,** 77-5766 Alii Dr., Kailua-Kona (329-1344). Breakfast/lunch/dinner daily. AE, CB, DC, MC, V. Specialties: fish of the day, scampi, rack of lamb, steak. *Note:* Agreeable open-air restaurant w. ocean view. Decent, unimaginative cooking. *American.* **I**

☼♟ **Volcano House,** in the Volcano House (see "Where to Stay," above) (967-7321). A/C. Lunch/dinner daily. AE, CB, DC, MC, V. Specialties: teriyaki (broiled marinated meat), mahi-mahi (broiled dolphin), steak. *Note:* A superb setting inside Volcanoes National Park itself. Very decent food. Buffet at lunchtime. Friendly svce. Resv. a must. *Japanese-Polynesian.* **I**

MAUI: "The Valley Isle," 25 min. from Honolulu by air. Maui is the second largest of the islands in area: 729 sq. mi. (1,890 km²). It's called the "Valley Isle" because of the long, low-lying fertile isthmus that joins the island's two craggy extremities. On the southeast coast stands the astonishing extinct volcano Haleakala, whose enormous arid crater could hold Manhattan Island. In 1802 King Kamehameha I chose Maui as the site of his capital, Lahaina. Now it's a favorite vacation spot for lovers of big-game fishing and scuba-diving.

The Sights

☀ 🔔 **Haleakala National Park,** 26 mi. (42 km) SE of Kahului on Hi. 37 and Hi. 378: Big nature reserve, over which looms a volcano which has been dormant for 200 years; the huge crater is 6 mi. (10 km) long, 3 mi. (5 km) wide, and about 2,900 ft (900 m) deep. According to Hawaiian legend it was the home of the god Maui, who was able to make the sun stand still in its course. If you want to visit the crater you should be in good shape, and wear stout shoes. Spectacular view of much of the island chain. Visitor Center open daily; for information, call 572-9306.

☀ 🔔 **Iao Valley,** near Wailuku: Wonderful green valley, over which towers a spectacular rock needle 1,170 ft (365 m) high, overgrown with verdure. A must-see.

🔔 **Kaanapali Beach,** near Lahaina: One of the most fashionable beaches in the entire state, on the island's northwest shore.

🔔 **Lahaina:** Picturesque little harbor which was a favorite port of call for whalers in the 19th century. An amusing little train drawn by a steam engine runs a connecting service to Kaanapali. Japanese cultural center. Worth going out of your way for.

Where to Stay

☀ 🛏🛏🛏 **Hyatt Regency Maui,** 200 Nohea Kai Dr., Kaanapali Beach, HI 96761 (808/667-7474; toll free, see Hyatt). 815 rms, A/C, color TV, in-rm movies. AE, CB, DC, MC, V. Free valet parking, two pools, two golf courses, five tennis courts, health club, sauna, boats, four rests. (including the Swan Court), seven bars, rm svce, disco, hrdrsr, boutiques. *Note:* Three ultramodern buildings on the beach w. splendid tropical gardens, indoor waterfalls, and a giant swimming pool. Spacious, comfortable rms. The interior decoration includes many Asian and Polynesian works of art. Excellent svce; comprehensive sports facilities; beautiful setting. Private heliport. Interesting vacation packages. One of Hawaii's best hotels. VIP suites on the top three floors of the main building, including the Islands' most expensive—$1,400 a night. **VE, but lower rates out of season**

🛏🛏🛏 **Inter-Continental Maui Hotel,** 3700 Ala Nui St., Wailea, HI 96753 (808/879-1922; toll free, see Inter-continental). 600 rms, A/C, cable color TV. AE, CB, DC, MC, V. Free valet parking, three pools, two golf courses, 14 tennis courts, private beach, water sports, three rests. (including La Pérouse), four bars, rm svce, disco, hrdrsr, boutiques. *Note:* Luxury hotel on the ocean w. 1,450 acres of tropical gardens and woodlands. Spacious rms w. views of the ocean or Mt. Haleakala. Comfort and facilities above reproach; very good svce; very commendable rests. This is a hotel of quality—one of the finest in the Islands. **E−VE**

🛏🛏 **Kaanapali Beach Hotel,** 2525 Kaanapali Pkwy., Kaanapali, HI 96761 (808/661-0011; toll free 800/227-4700). 431 rms, A/C, color TV, in-rm movies. AE, CB, DC, MC, V. Free parking, pool, tennis court, private beach, boats, rest., coffeeshop, bar, disco. *Note:* Modern deluxe resort hotel, standing almost in the ocean. Relaxed atmosphere; comfortable rms w. private balconies and refrigerators. Agreeable svce; mediocre rest. Good overall value. **E−VE**

🛏 **Maui Lu Resort,** 575 S. Kihei Rd., Kihei, HI 96753 (808/879-5881; toll free 800/227-4700). 170 rms, A/C, cable color TV. AE, CB, DC, MC, V. Free parking, pool, two tennis courts, rest. (Longhouse), bar, disco. *Note:* Hotel decorated in tropical style w. direct beach access. 19 acres of gardens and palm groves. Comfortable rms w. refrigerators, some w. kitchenettes. Inadequate svce, but good overall value. Luaus). **M, but lower rates out of season**

Where to Eat

☀ ♚♚♚ **Gerard's,** in the Plantation Inn, 174 Lahainaluna Rd. Lahaina (661-8939) A/C. Breakfast/lunch/dinner daily. AE, MC, V. *Specialties:* Raw fish à la tahitienne, frog's legs, squid with lime and ginger, bouillabaisse, confit of duck fricassée, partridge à l'étouffée. Desserts are irresistible. The menu changes daily. *Note:* One of the best—if not *the* best—French restaurant in the Islands. The cuisine of master chef Gerard Reversade is a delicate blend of French ideas with Maui-grown ingredients and produce such enchantments as "ahi" (yellow fin tuna) with béarnaise sauce and bean sprouts. Very good wines to complement the food. Brightly-lit decor with period oak and stained glass. Smooth and informal service. Resv. essential.

♚♚♚ **La Pérouse,** in the Inter-Continental Maui Hotel (see "Where to Stay," above) (879-1922). A/C. Dinner only, daily. AE, CB, DC, MC, V. Jkt. Specialties: callaloo crab soup, bouillabaisse, Hawaiian baked fish. Excellent desserts. *Note:* Elegant luxury hotel dining rm in a beautiful Polynesian setting. Attentive svce. One of the best places on the island. Resv. advised. *French-Polynesian.* **M–E**

♚♚ **Chez Paul,** Hwy. 820-C, Olowalu Village. Lahaina (611-3843). A/C Dinner only, Mon.-Sat.; closed Sun. AE, MC, V. Specialties: frogs' legs, roast duck, sauté of veal w. apples and Calvados, mahimahi in beurre blanc, tournedos Madagascar. *Note:* Very good French-inspired food, w. prices to match. Pleasant setting and atmosphere; very popular locally. Resv. advised. *French-Polynesian.* **I–M**

KAUAI: "The Garden Isle," 25 min. from Honolulu by air. **Mt. Waialeale,** a huge (5,080-ft-, 1,570-m-high) extinct volcano, holds the world's wet-weather record, with 350 rainy days and 460 inches (11.45 m) of rainfall yearly! Nicknamed "The Garden Isle" for the luxuriance of its vegetation, Kauai was the first Hawaiian island visited by Captain Cook (1778). It was also the last independent kingdom in the archipelago. Its tortuous contours make for difficult traveling. The capital of the island is **Lihue.**

The Sights

Among the more interesting places to visit are:

☀☖ **Hanalei:** A fashionable spa nestling at the head of a sweeping bay.

☀☖☖ **Na Pali Coast:** This rocky shoreline at the NW end of the island can be reached only by a difficult footpath leading from the termination of Hi. 56. Impressive ridges of rock covered with lush vegetation; this sight alone is worth the trip to Kauai.

☀☖ **Wailua Falls,** north of Lihue: Beautiful falls, and the spectacular **Fern Grotto** carpeted with tropical ferns. Can be reached only by boat from Wailua Marina. Don't miss it.

☀☖☖ **Waimea Canyon State Park,** near Waimea: Magnificent gorges with walls of multicolored rock, reminiscent of Colorado's Grand Canyon. The last section of the road to **Kalalau Lookout** offers some fine views. Don't miss it.

Where to Stay

☀ ♛♛♛ **Sheraton Princeville,** Hi. 56 (P.O. Box 3069), Princeville, HI 96746 (808/826-9644; toll free, see Sheraton). 300 rms, A/C, color TV, in-rm movies. AE, CB, DC, MC, V. Free valet parking, pool, 21 tennis courts, golf course, boats, beach, water sports, horseback riding, three rests. (including Nobles), two bars, rm svce, disco, concierge. *Note:* One of the newer grand luxury hotels in the Islands, built in an original terraced style on a cliff rising from the magnificent Hanalei Bay. Spacious, ultra-comfortable rms w. refrigerators and private patios, the best overlooking the ocean. Very complete sports facilities; can be warmly recommended in spite of its highly expensive rates. **E–VE**

Coco Palms Resort Hotel, Hi. 56 and Hi. 580, Wailua Beach, HI 96766 (808/822-4921; toll free 800/542-2626). 390 rms, A/C, cable color TV. AE, CB, DC, MC, V. Free parking, three pools, nine tennis courts, sauna, private beach, three rests. (including the Coconut Palace), bars, rm svce, disco, hrdrsr, boutiques. *Note:* Very handsome Polynesian-style hotel in a palm grove; a favorite w. honeymooners. The palm grove, 45 acres of splendid tropical gardens, and the lagoons were once part of a royal property. Spacious rms (those in the cottages are preferable). Irreproachable standards of comfort and svce. Coconut Palace rest. highly recommended. Polynesian shows. Good value. For those who love the out-and-out exotic. **M–E**

Stouffer Poipu Beach Hotel, Poipu Rd. (Hi. 520), Poipu, HI 96756 (808/742-1681; toll free, see Stouffer's). 139 rms, A/C, color TV, in-rm movies. AE, CB, DC, MC, V. Free parking, pool, four tennis courts, beach, rest., bar, rm svce. *Note:* Welcoming modern motel on one of the island's most beautiful beaches. Comfortable, spacious rms all w. kitchenettes and refrigerators. Svce w. a smile. A fine place in a very beautiful setting. **M–E**

Kauai Beach Bay Hotel, 484 Kuhio Hwy., Waipouli Beach, HI 96746 (808/822-3441; toll free 800/367-8047). 243 rms, A/C, cable color TV. AE, CB, DC, MC, V. Free parking, pool, tennis court, private beach, rest., bar, disco. *Note:* Functional modern hotel on the site of an old coconut plantation. Large, friendly rms w. private verandas and refrigerators. Good svce. Ideal if you love the beach. **M**

Where to Eat

The Beach House, Lawai Rd., Poipu (742-7575). Lunch/dinner daily; closed Thanksgiving. MC, V. Specialties: every kind of seafood, as well as excellent grilled meats. *Note:* The best rest. on Kauai, according to those who live there, w. absolutely fresh local produce. Beautiful multilevel dining room w. ocean view; don't miss the sunset at dinnertime. *Seafood-Polynesian.* **I–M**

The Coconut Palace, in the Coco Palms Resort Hotel (see "Where to Stay," above) (822-4921). A/C. Dinner only, daily. AE, CB, DC, MC, V. Jkt. Coconut chicken, Cantonese food, creative Polynesian and European dishes. Good wine list. *Note:* One of the best rests. on the island, w. spectacular Polynesian décor. Attentive svce. Resv. advised. *American-Polynesian.* **I–M**

Plantation Gardens, in the Kiahuna Beach Resort, Poipu Rd., Poipu (742-1695). Dinner only, daily. AE, MC, V. Jkt. Specialties: generally successful French-inspired cuisine, w. some exotic touches such as mahi-mahi. *Note:* A lovely old house overlooking tropical gardens. Good svce. Highly regarded locally, so resv. advised. *French-Polynesian.* **I–M**

Barbecue Inn, 2982 Kress St., Lihue (245-2921). A/C. Breakfast/lunch/dinner Mon.-Sat.; closed Sun. AE, MC, V. Specialties: steak teriyaki, shrimp tempura, baked salmon steak, seafood platter, T-bone steak, corned beef and cabbage. *Note:* Decent, flavorful Japanese-American food at delightfully low prices. Décor on the gloomy side, but a likeable place, and very popular locally. Excellent value. *Japanese-American.* **B–I**

MOLOKAI: "The Friendly Isle," 25 min. from Honolulu by air. This rectangular island, 38 mi. (61 km) long by 10 mi. (16 km) wide, was long a religious sanctuary guarded by the Kahuna priesthood from profane intrusion. In the 19th century a Belgian missionary, Joseph de Veuster, known as Father Damien, established a leper colony here. Even today the island is relatively ignored by tourists.

The Sights

☀️🔔 **Halawa Valley,** on the NE of the island: A succession of tidal waves has sharply reduced the once-large population of this fertile valley. Spectacular waterfalls and numerous Polynesian temples *(heiaus)*, once the scene of human sacrifices. Worth the detour.

☀️🔔 **Father Damien's Leprosarium,** at Kalaupapa: Site of the old leprosarium founded in 1873 by the famous Belgian missionary; he himself contracted, and died of, the dread disease, and his tomb is here. Impressive. Over 100 former sufferers of Hansen's disease, as leprosy is now known, remain at Kalaupapa. Open daily (but only to visitors over 16 years old); resv. required at least five days in advance (phone 522-2622).

🔔 **Halawa Beach, One Alii Beach, Moomomi Beach,** and **Kahaiawa Beach** are among the island's many beautiful and deserted beaches.

🔔 **Umilehi Point:** From near here rears the world's highest cliff, towering dizzily 3,216 ft (1,005 m) above the sea.

Where to Stay

☀️🍴🍴 **Kaluakoi Hotel & Golf Club,** Kepuhi Beach, HI 96770 (808/552-2555). 288 rms, A/C, color TV. AE, CB, DC, MC, V. Free parking, pool, golf course, four tennis courts, private beach, two rests., two bars, disco. *Note:* The 32 charmingly pretty Polynesian cottages stand at the water's edge. Tranquil, elegant setting. Spacious, comfortable rms w. refrigerators. Good svce. A great place to stay. **M–E**

🍴 **Wavecrest Resort,** Star Route, Kaunakakai, HI 96748 (808/558-8101). 126 mini-apartments, color TV. MC, V. Free parking, pool, two tennis courts, putting green. *Note:* Modern building, right on the beach, w. mini-apartments for one to six persons, all w. kitchenette and private terrace. Good value for family parties. Minimum stay of three nights. No bar, no rest. **I–M**

🔔 **LANAI:** "The Pineapple Isle," 30 min. from Honolulu by air. This small island, only 17 mi. (27 km) long, is the most authentic—and the least visited—in the Hawaiian chain. It belongs to the food conglomerate, Dole Pineapple Company, and boasts the world's largest pineapple plantation. Tourism is still in its infancy here, so there are superb beaches standing almost empty—particularly 🔔 **Hulo Poe Beach,** ideal for surfers.

THE ISLANDS OF NIHAU AND KAHOOLAWE: These two islands, alone in the chain, have escaped (but for how long?) the tidal wave of tourism. The former is privately owned by the Robinson family; its 250 or so inhabitants speak only Hawaiian. The latter is an arid military reservation, closed to visitors and used as an artillery and bombing range.

CHAPTER 57

ANCHORAGE AND ALASKA♨♨

□ □ □

With its skyscrapers rising against the mountain backdrop, its bustle and its cosmopolitan crowds, Anchorage may at first sight look like the Manhattan of the Far North, but it turns out to have some rustic ways as well. The 20-story hotels and modern office buildings rub shoulders with old frame houses standing in their own little gardens. The brand-new, austerely designed **Convention Center** faces the **Visitors Information Center,** housed in a log cabin which would have been at home in the Gold Rush. It's not uncommon for Alaskans to fly 500 miles (800 km) or more out of the bush to Anchorage to see the latest movie or hear a special concert; parked outside a deluxe French restaurant you may well see a four-wheel-drive wagon which would be more at home on a backcountry trail. This pioneer atmosphere is not the least of Alaska's charms.

The city, founded in 1915 as a work camp on the Alaska Railroad, has grown up slowly around the excellent harbor provided by Cook Inlet (the "anchorage" from which it derives its name). In 1940 the future economic capital of Alaska had barely 3,500 inhabitants; its strategic importance only became apparent during World War II. The first oil discoveries in the Kenai Peninsula in 1957, and those at Prudhoe Bay 11 years later, made the city's fortune. Its population rose from 48,000 in 1970 to the present 230,000—almost half the population of the entire state.

Anchorage nestles at the foot of Cook Inlet, the great arm of the sea discovered two centuries ago by the British explorer James Cook. Today it is the largest city in the state and its economic capital, as well as an important way-station for transpolar air flights, with more than three million passengers passing through its air terminal every year. Even the severe earthquake of 1964, which destroyed part of the city, scarcely checked its growth-oriented civic spirit. Having only just celebrated its 70th birthday, Anchorage is short on historic buildings, but it offers the visitor its incomparable site, two remarkable museums of Indian and Eskimo art, the **Museum of History & Art,** the **Heritage Library & Museum,** and the country's most northerly rose garden. Its location, on the sea and behind the natural barrier of the **Chugach Mountains** to the north and east, gives Anchorage a surprisingly temperate climate. Winter is only a little colder than in Denver or Chicago, and summer is often warmer than in San Francisco.

Anchorage is also an ideal base for exploring the whole of northern Alaska, from **Nome** and **Kotzebue,** in the land of the Midnight Sun and the dogsled, to the **Pribilof Islands** and **Katmai National Park** with their unusual wildlife. Then there are the eternal snows of **Mt. McKinley,** at 20,320 ft (6,193 m) the highest mountain in North America (see below under "Alaska's Highlights").

BASIC FACTS: State of Alaska. Area Code: 907. Time Zone: Alaska Time (4 hours behind New York). ZIP Code: 99502. Founded: 1915. Approximate population: 233,000.

CLIMATE: With its relatively mild winters (averaging 23°F, 3°C. in January), agreeable summers (62°F, 17°C in July), and sunlit autumns (though snow can often fall heavily after mid-October), the climate of Anchorage is far from being the stereotype of Far Northern severity.

The rest of Alaska, on the other hand, does offer wider swings in temperature, differing from one part of the state to another. The south coast is windy and rainy; average temperatures at **Sitka** are 32°F (0°C) in January and 66°F (19°C) in July. The uplands of the interior have a dry, continental climate, with temperatures at **Fairbanks** sometimes rising above 86°F (30°C) in the summer, and falling to −42°F (−40°C) in the winter. The Arctic North, or Far North (a quarter of the state's area lies within the Arctic Circle), is very windy and dry, with truly polar winter readings as low as −79°F (−62°C) and more temperate summers averaging 64°F (18°C); the short summer is followed by a mild fall. At **Barrow,** the northernmost city in the country, the harbor is ice-bound from October to August—but the sun never sets from May 10 to August 2. Equally, it never rises from mid-November to the end of January. Unless you're a winter-sports enthusiast, Alaska is best visited between early June and late September, when average temperatures should run from 35°F (2°C) at the low end to 86°F (30°C) at the highest.

DISTANCES: Denali National Park, 239 mi. (382 km); Fairbanks, 364 mi. (582 km); Haines, 775 mi. (1,240 km); Seward, 127 mi. (203 km); Skagway, 890 mi. (1,424 km); Valdez, 317 mi. (507 km); Whitehorse (Canada), 715 mi. (1,145 km).

ARRIVAL & TRANSIT INFORMATION

AIRPORT: Anchorage International Airport (ANC), 5 mi. (8 km) SW. Information: 266-1437. Other major airports in Alaska are Fairbanks International Airport (FAI), 4 mi. (6.5 km) SE of Fairbanks; and Juneau Municipal Airport (JNU), 8 mi. (13 km) north of Juneau.

DOMESTIC AIRLINES: Alaska (243-3300), American (toll free 800/433-7300), Delta (toll free 800/221-1212), Markair (243-6275), Northwest (243-1123), Reeve Aleutian (243-4700), TWA (toll free 800/221-2000), United (563-2771), Wilburs (243-7878).

FOREIGN CARRIERS: Air France (243-3400), British Airways (toll free 800/247-9297), Japan Airlines (274-3551), KLM (277-1414), Korean Airlines (243-3329), Lufthansa (243-3142), Sabena (243-3324), SAS (243-4106), Swissair (243-7771).

CITY LINK: Cab fare, about $12; time, 15 min. Bus: SERVAIR (243-3310); fare, $6; time, 20 min.; serves principal hotels. The local bus line, the People Mover (264-6543), provides good svce to major dwntwn hotels Mon.-Sat. Given the climate, renting a car for excursions is advisable only Apr.-Sept.

CAR RENTAL (all at Anchorage International Airport): Avis (243-2277), Budget (243-0150), Dollar (243-3312), Hertz (243-3308), National (243-3406). In other cities, check the local phonebook.

LIMOUSINE SERVICES: Dav El Limousines (toll free 800/922-0343).

TAXIS: Few and costly; may not be hailed on the street but must be called by phone: Checker Cab (274-3333), Yellow Cab (272-3401).

TRAIN: Alaska Railroad, 411 W. 1st Ave., Anchorage, AK 99510 (907/265-2623). Serves Anchorage–Fairbanks via Denali National Park and Anchorage–Whittier. Runs year round, with reduced schedules Sept.-May. Resv. a must—at least two weeks ahead.

BUS: White Pass & Yukon Motorcoaches, 743 W. Fifth Ave. (279-0761). Serves Haines and Skagway, and makes connections with the Alaska Marine Hwy. (see "Ferry," below).

FERRY: The **Alaska Marine Highway,** P.O. Box R-JT, Juneau, AK 99811 (907/465-3941), is a kind of seagoing bus, carrying cars and passengers on comfortable, modern ships; it gives the ports of southeastern Alaska on the Inside Passage route (Haines, Juneau, Ketchikan, Petersburg, Sitka, Skagway, Wrangell) a year-round connection to Seattle and to Prince Rupert in Canada. Spectacular landscapes. Another year-round service leaves Whittier, Valdez, and Cordova for Kodiak Island and the Kenai Peninsula. For timetables call: in Anchorage (907/272-7116); Juneau (907/465-3941); Prince Rupert, B.C. (604/627-1744); Seattle (206/623-1970); Skagway (907/983-2941); or toll free 800/642-0066.

INFORMATION & TOURS

TOURIST INFORMATION: Alaska Division of Tourism, Information Office, P.O. Box E-001, Juneau, AK 99811 (907/465-2010), for information on Alaska in general. Anchorage Convention & Visitors Bureau, 201 E. Third Ave., Anchorage, AK 99501 (907/276-4118); also a Visitors Information Center, Log Cabin, 546 Fourth Ave. at F St., Anchorage, AK 99509 (907/274-3531). A recorded message gives information on current cultural and sporting events at 276-3200.

GUIDED TOURS: Alaska Sightseeing Tours (by bus), 349-T Wrangell St., Anchorage, AK 99501 (907/276-1305; toll free 800/637-3334). Guided tours of the principal cities and regions of Alaska, serving Anchorage, Fairbanks, Haines, Juneau, Ketchikan, and Skagway (for local numbers in these cities, consult the telephone book for the appropriate city).

   Era Helicopters, 6160-T S. Airpark Dr., Anchorage, AK 99502 (907/248-4422; toll free 800/843-1947). Helicopter flights over the mountains and glaciers around Anchorage, Fairbanks, Juneau, Prudhoe Bay, or Valdez (for local numbers in these cities, consult the phonebook for the appropriate city).

   Gray Line Tours of Alaska (by bus), P.O. Box 100479-T, Anchorage, AK 99510 (907/276-8866; toll free 800/544-2206). Guided tours of the principal cities and regions of Alaska, serving Anchorage, Fairbanks, Juneau, Ketchikan, Skagway, and Valdez (for local numbers in these cities, consult the phone book for the appropriate city).

SIGHTS, ATTRACTIONS, & ACTIVITIES

ADVENTURE TOURS: Advanced Balloon Adventures, 8701-T Solar Dr., Anchorage, AK 99507 (907/346-3696). Balloon trips over Anchorage and surrounding country; year round.

   Eagle River Float Trip, 200-T N. Franklin St., Juneau, AK 99801 (toll free 800/227-8480). Rafting down the Eagle River in the Chugach Mountains, with transportation from Anchorage; June 1 to Sept. 10.

   Fantasy Airballoon Flights, 12900-T Atherton Rd., Anchorage, AK 99516

(907/345-5521). Balloon trips over Anchorage and surrounding country; year round.

Goose Lake Dog Sled Rides, P.O. Box 757-T, Girdwood, AK 99587 (907/272-3883), 1-hr dogsled rides on trails around Anchorage; Nov. 15 to Apr. 15.

CHURCHES/SYNAGOGUES: ⚱ St. Innocent's Church, 6724 E. 4th St.
(333-9723): Typical Russian Orthodox church; interesting view; can be seen by appointment only.

HISTORIC BUILDINGS: ⚱ Oscar Anderson House, 420 M St. (274-2336).
Built by a Swedish immigrant in 1915, this modest frame house is one of the oldest in the city. Carefully restored, the Anderson House with its great cast-iron stove and its period furniture is a living vestige of the past, with a fine view over Cook Inlet. Open Wed.-Sun., in summer and in Dec.

MUSEUMS: ⚱ Heritage Library & Museum, Northern Lights Blvd. at C St.
(276-1132): Indian and Eskimo handcrafts and mementos of the Gold Rush. Large collection of works on the history of Alaska. Open Mon.-Fri.

⚱ **Museum of History and Art,** 121 W. Seventh Ave. (264-4326): Prehistoric tools, art from the Aleutian, Eskimo, and Athapascan cultures, works of contemporary local artists, works from the 19th century onward inspired by Alaska. Interesting temporary exhibitions. Open Tues.-Sun.

⚱ **Wildlife Museum,** at Fort Richardson, Bldg. 600 (5 mi., 8 km, NE via Glenn Hwy.) (863-8113): Stuffed fish, mammals, and birds, more than 200 specimens covering the whole range of Alaskan wildlife—a must for those interested in zoology. Open Mon.-Fri.

PANORAMAS: ⚱ Earthquake Park, at the western end of Northern Lights
Blvd.: Overlooking Cook Inlet and its seascapes, this beautiful 135-acre (54-ha.) park bears eloquent witness to the violence of the 1964 earthquake. Splendid view of the **Talkeetna Mountains** to the NE and the **Chugach Mountains** to the east.

👓👓 **Resolution Park,** Third Ave. and L St.: This downtown park offers you not only a statue of Captain Cook (who visited these parts in 1778 in his famous ship *Resolution*), but also a very fine view over Cook Inlet and the legendary **Mt. Susitna,** whose shape suggests a sleeping woman. On a fine day you can see as far as **Mt. McKinley,** 140 mi. (225 km) away as the crow flies. A sight not to be missed.

PERFORMING ARTS: For daily listings of all shows and cultural events, con-
sult the entertainment section of the two daily newspapers, the *Anchorage Daily News* (a.m.) and the *Anchorage Times* (p.m.), or call 276-ARTS (276-2787) for a recorded list of current cultural events.

Alaska Repertory Theater, 705 W. Sixth Ave. (276-2327), stages classical, modern, and avant-garde theater. Nov.-Apr.

Egan ConventionCenter, 555 W. Fifth Ave. (278-3831), presents the co-median Larry Beck in his *Alaska Show,* in which the poems of Robert Service are used to evoke the days of the pioneers and the Gold Rush. Daily, June-Sept.

Sydney Laurence Auditorium, Sixth Ave. and F St. (276-8688), is the home of the Anchorage Civic Opera (Sept.-Mar.) and the Anchorage Symphony Orchestra (Nov.-Apr.).

University of Alaska–Anchorage Theater, 3211-T Providence Dr. (786-1800), offers classical and contemporary theater Nov.-Mar.

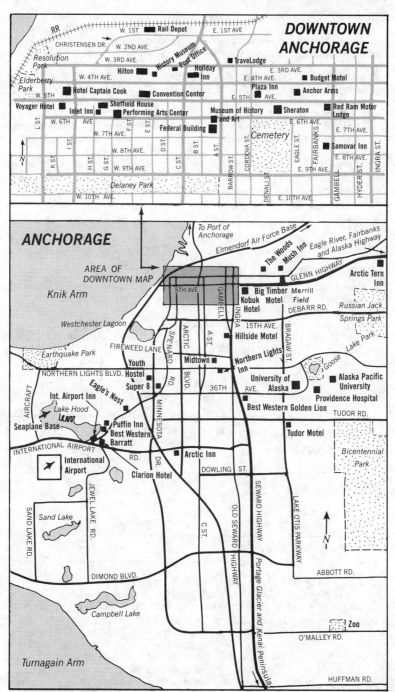

DOWNTOWN ANCHORAGE

RR
W. 1ST — Rail Depot — E. 1ST AVE.
CHRISTENSEN DR.
W. 2ND AVE.
Resolution Park
W. 3RD AVE.
History Museum — Post Office
Elderberry Park
Hilton — Holiday Inn — E. 3RD AVE.
TraveLodge
W. 4TH AVE. — E. 4TH AVE. — Budget Motel
Hotel Captain Cook — Convention Center — Plaza Inn — Anchor Arms
W. 5TH — E. 5TH AVE.
Voyager Hotel — Sheffield House — Museum of History and Art — Sheraton — Red Ram Motor Lodge
Inlet Inn — Performing Arts Center
W. 6TH AVE. — Federal Building — E. 6TH AVE. — E. 7TH AVE.
W. 7TH AVE. — Samovar Inn — E. 8TH AVE.
Cemetery
W. 8TH AVE. — E. 9TH AVE.
W. 9TH AVE.
N
Delaney Park
W. 10TH AVE. — E. 10TH AVE.

K ST., L ST., 1ST., H ST., G ST., F ST., E ST., D ST., C ST., B ST., A ST., BARROW ST., CORDOVA ST., DENALI ST., EAGLE ST., FAIRBANKS, GAMBELL, HYDER ST., INGRA ST.

ANCHORAGE

To Port of Anchorage
Elmendorf Air Force Base
The Woods — Mush Inn
Eagle River, Fairbanks and Alaska Highway
AREA OF DOWNTOWN MAP
5TH AVE. — GAMBELL
GLENN HIGHWAY
Arctic Tern Inn
Knik Arm
Big Timber — Merrill Field
Kobuk Motel Hotel — DEBARR RD.
INGRA
Russian Jack Springs Park
Westchester Lagoon
15TH AVE.
Hillside Motel
BRAGAW ST.
Lake Park
FIREWEED LANE
SPENARD RD. — ARCTIC BLVD. — A ST.
Northern Lights Inn
Goose Lake
Earthquake Park
Youth Hostel
Midtown
University of Alaska
Alaska Pacific University
NORTHERN LIGHTS BLVD.
Super 8
36TH
AVE.
Providence Hospital
Eagle's Nest
MINNESOTA
Best Western Golden Lion
TUDOR RD.
Int. Airport Inn
AIRCRAFT
Lake Hood
Seaplane Base
Puffin Inn
Best Western Barratt
Tudor Motel
INTERNATIONAL AIRPORT
RD. DR.
Arctic Inn
Bicentennial Park
International Airport
DOWLING ST.
Clarion Hotel
JEWEL LAKE RD.
SAND LAKE RD.
Sand Lake
C ST.
OLD SEWARD HIGHWAY
SEWARD HIGHWAY
LAKE OTIS PARKWAY
ABBOTT RD.
DIMOND BLVD.
Portage Glacier and Kenai Peninsula
Campbell Lake
Zoo
O'MALLEY RD.
Turnagain Arm
HUFFMAN RD.

SHOPPING: A few addresses for those interested in authentic Indian and Eskimo artifacts in horn, leather, or wood, jewelry, etc.: **Alaska Heritage Arts,** 211 E. 5th St.; **Alaska Native Arts and Crafts Cooperative,** 425 D St.; **Arctic Cache,** 429 W. 5th St.; **Rusty Harpoon,** 411 W. 4th St.

SPECIAL EVENTS: For a current schedule, inquire at the Anchorage Visitors & Convention Bureau (see "Tourist Information," above).

    Fur Rendez-Vous (Feb.), dogsled races, shows, costume ball, sports events, etc., held at the time of the great annual fur auction.

    Iditarod Trail Sled Dog Race (Mar.), world-famous annual dogsled race from Anchorage to Nome, with more than 50 entries for these two weeks of racing.

    Midnight Sun Baseball, a popular local event held every year at 10 p.m. on June 21.

    Midnight Sun Hot Air Balloon Classic, also on the evening of June 21, attracts dozens of entries.

SPORTS: The **Sled Dog Race Track** on Tudor Rd. pits local against "foreign" champions, Sat. and Sun. only during the winter months. For timetable, call 243-0608.

WINTER SPORTS RESORTS: The popular ⚲ **Alyeska Resort** (40 mi., 64 km, SE via Ak. 1) (783-2222) has four ski lifts and a hotel. Season: Nov.-Apr.; also summer skiing.

ZOOS: The relatively new ⚲ **Alaska Zoo,** 9 mi. (14 km) out via Ak. 1 and O'Malley Rd. (344-3242), offers a full range of native Alaskan animals: polar bears, brown and black bears, foxes, reindeer, moose, etc. Should be seen. Open daily, year round.

ACCOMMODATIONS

See the listing of toll-free numbers in the Appendix.

Room Rates in Anchorage	
B (Budget)	up to $30
I (Inexpensive)	$30–$60
M (Moderate)	$60–$90
E (Expensive)	$90–$140
VE (Very Expensive)	$140 and up

Personal Favorites (from top bracket to budget)

    🛏🛏🛏 **Captain Cook Hotel** (dwntwn), Fifth Ave. & K St., AK 99150 (907/276-6000; toll free 800/323-7500). 600 rms, color TV, in-rm movies. AE, CB, DC, MC, V. Indoor parking $6, pool, three tennis courts, health club, sauna, four rests. (incl. Crow's Nest), 24-hr coffeeshop, four bars, rm svce, disco, boutiques. *Note:* A palace of luxury comprising three modern towers, one of which is crowned by a panoramic rest. (the Crow's Nest) on the 20th floor. Most of the large, comfortable rms offer a fine view of the bay or the mountains. Very good svce; business clientele; in the heart of dwntwn; open year round. **E–VE**

Hilton (dwntwn), Third Ave. & E St., AK 99501 (907/272-7411; toll free 800/445-8667). 591 rms, A/C, color TV, in-rm movies. AE, CB, DC, MC, V. Free gar., pool, sauna, health club, two rests. (incl. Top of the World), bars, rm svce, disco, boutiques. *Note:* Two modern towers with all-around view of Cook Inlet and the mountains from the Top of the World rest. on the top floor. Very comfortable rms; efficient svce; in the heart of dwntwn; open year round. **E−VE**

Sheraton (dwntwn), 401 E. Sixth Ave., AK 99501 (907/276-8700; toll free 800/325-3535). 410 rms, A/C, color TV, in-rm movies. AE, CB, DC, MC, V. Free gar., health club, sauna, rest. (Josephine's), coffeeshop, bars, 24-hr rm svce, disco. *Note:* The most luxurious of Anchorage's large modern hotels. Beautiful foyer with transparent roof and grand staircase in jade; spacious, elegantly decorated rms, excellent svce; the hotel preferred by those in the know. In the heart of dwntwn; open year round. **E−VE**

Holiday Inn (dwntwn), 239 W. Fourth Ave., AK 99501 (907/279-8671; toll free 800/465-4329). 252 rms, A/C, color TV. AE, CB, DC, MC, V. Free parking, pool, sauna, rest. (The Greenery), coffeeshop, bar, rm svce, crib $8. *Note:* Classic, comfortable three-story Holiday Inn with good dwntwn location; caters mostly to groups; open year round. **M−E**

Westmark Hotel (dwntwn), 720 W. Fifth Ave., AK 99501 (907/276-7676; toll free 800/544-0970). 200 rms, color TV, in-rm movies. AE, CB, DC, MC, V. Free parking, health club, rest. (House of Lords), 24-hr coffeeshop, bar, rm svce. *Note:* Modern, comfortable hotel very nr. the Convention Center. Large, comfortable rms w. private balconies, some w. refrigerators. On the top floor the panoramic bar offers an unimpeded view of city, mountains, and ocean. Good svce; business clientele; open year round. **E**

Travelodge Anchorage (dwntwn), 115 E. Third Ave., AK 99501 (907/272-7561; toll free 800/255-3050). 90 rms, A/C, color TV, in-rm movies. AE, CB, DC, MC, V. Free parking, rest. (Coach Room), coffeeshop, bar, rm svce. *Note:* Serviceable, recently renovated hotel w. large, comfortable rms and efficient svce; central dwntwn location. Rates a little high for this kind of hotel. Open year round. **M−E**

Inlet Towers Hotel (nr. dwntwn), 1200 L St., AK 99501 (907/276-0110; toll free 800/544-0786). 136 suites, color TV, in-rm movies. AE, DC, MC, V. Free parking, health club, sauna. *Note:* Ideal for longer stays. Comfortable suites all with fully equipped kitchenettes. Friendly reception and svce; 5 min. by car from dwntwn. Good overall value; open year round. **M**

Northern Lights Inn (nr. dwntwn), 598 W. Northern Lights Blvd., AK 99503 (907/561-5200). 137 rms, color TV. AE, DC, MC, V. Free parking, rest., bar, rm svce, hrdrsr. Free airport limo. *Note:* Comfortable modern hotel halfway between dwntwn and airport. Good svce; caters mostly to business travelers and groups. Good overall value; open year round. **M**

Super 8 Motel (nr. dwntwn), 3501 Minnesota Dr., AK 99503 (907/276-8884; toll free 800/843-1991). 84 rms, color TV, in-rm movies. AE, CB, DC, MC, V. Free parking, adj. rest., free airport limo. *Note:* Modern, functional hotel halfway between dwntwn and the airport. Comfortable rms, free morning coffee; overall good value; open year round. **I**

YMCAs/Youth Hostels

AYH, Minnesota St. & 32nd Ave. (907/276-3635). Youth hostel open year round.

YMCA, 609 F St. (907/279-8522). Men, women, families; open year round.

Airport Accommodations

♟♟ **Best Western–Barratt Inn** (nr. dwntwn), 4616 Spenard Rd., AK 99503 (907/243-3131; toll free 800/528-1234). 217 rms, color TV, in-rm movies. AE, CB, DC, MC, V. Free parking, rest., bar, free 24-hr airport limo svce. *Note:* Welcoming country-style motel near the seaplane base at Spenard Lake, and 3 min. from the international airport. Very comfortable rms, some w. kitchenettes. Acceptable rest., efficient svce, open year round. Ideal for a stopover between flights. **M**

RESTAURANTS

Anchorage Restaurant Prices	
(per person, excluding drinks and service charges)	
B (Budget)	up to $15
I (Inexpensive)	$15–$25
M (Moderate)	$25–$40
E (Expensive)	$40–$60
VE (Very Expensive)	$60 and up

Personal Favorites (From top bracket to budget)

♟♟♟ **Crow's Nest** (dwntwn), in the Captain Cook Hotel (see "Accommodations," above) (276-6000). A/C. Dinner only, Tues.-Sat.; Sun: brunch; closed Mon. AE, CB, DC, MC, V. Jkt. Specialties: salmon stuffed with shrimp, halibut à la Berval, game and venison in season, choice meats, good wine list. *Note:* From the 20th floor of the Captain Cook Hotel, this distinguished rest. offers a fine panorama of the mountains and Cook Inlet. Grand-hotel cuisine supervised by chef Jens Hansen, making full use of local resources in game and seafood. The stylish svce anticipates your needs. Best rest. in all of Alaska; resv. highly advisable. *Continental-seafood.* **M–E**

♟♟ **House of Lords** (dwntwn), in the Westmark Hotel (see "Hotels," above) (907/276-5404). A/C. Lunch Tue.-Fri., dinner Tue.-Sat.; closed Sun. and Mon. AE, MC, V. Jkt. Specialties: filet of halibut Olympia, sole Louis XIV (with shallots and white wine), bouillabaisse, rack of lamb bouquetière, piccata of veal marsala, good wine list. *Note:* Another well-regarded, grand hotel restaurant on the ground floor of the Westmark Hotel. Opulent interior with crystal, pewter, and ancestral portraits. Impeccable cuisine of European inspiration. Very good svce; resv. advisable. *Continental-seafood.* **M**

♟♟ **Marx Bros Café** (dwntwn), 627 W. Third Ave. (907/278-2133). Dinner only, Mon.-Sat.; closed Sun. and holidays. MC, V. Specialties: crab Imperial, fish of the day, venison dishes in season, halibut Macadamia, roast duck with raspberries. *Note:* Located in a picturesque little house built in 1916, this American-style restaurant is very popular locally. Some original dishes; good svce; resv. advised. *American-seafood.* **I–M**

♟♟ **Simon & Seafort's** (dwntwn), 420 L St. (907/274-3502). A/C. Lunch Mon.-Sat., dinner nightly; closed holidays. AE,

MC, V. Specialties: steak, roast beef, fresh homemade pasta, Alaska fish and shell-fish in season, fried zucchini hollandaise, brandy ice cream, very good wine list. *Note:* Pleasantly decorated as a saloon from the days of the Gold Rush. Good, tasty food at very reasonable prices for Alaska. Relaxed setting and fine view of the mountains and Cook Inlet. Try it. *Steak-seafood.* I

🍸 **Clinkerdagger, Bickerstaff & Petts** (nr. dwntwn), 3301 C St. (907/561-5374). A/C. Lunch Mon.-Sat., dinner nightly; closed holidays. AE, MC, V. Specialties: steak, fish of the day, homemade desserts. *Note:* Very popular locally; decorated as an English pub in mock-Tudor. Decent food served in large portions. Resv. advisable. *Steak-seafood.* **B-I**

🍸 **Harry's** (formerly Donovan's; nr. dwntwn), 101 W. Benson Blvd. (907/561-5317). Lunch Mon.-Sat., dinner nightly. MC. Specialties: hamburger, steak, fish of the day, salads. *Note:* This Irish restaurant-pub in the Alaska Pacific Bank Bldg. is best known for its friendly bar and its enormous mixed salads. Acceptable, unpretentious cooking; relaxed atmosphere; good value. *American-steak.* **M-I**

🍸 **Downtown Deli** (dwntwn), 525 W. 4th St. (907/274-0027). Breakfast/lunch/dinner daily. MC. Specialties: homemade soups, sandwiches, corned beef, kosher specialties, fish, daily specials, homemade desserts. *Note:* An Anchorage institution, much patronized by businessmen and local dignitaries. Usually crowded at breakfast and lunch. Friendly, smiling svce. Well-located, very nr. the Captain Cook and Hilton hotels. *American.* **B**

🍸 **Zeppo's Downtown Grill** (dwntwn), 328 G St. (907/272-3663). Lunch/dinner daily (open till 11 p.m. in summer). MC. Specialties: hamburgers, daily specials and fish specials, good wine list. *Note:* Very popular restaurant/wine bar in the center of downtown. No-frills cooking and delightful prices. *American-seafood.* **B**

NEARBY EXCURSIONS

Eklutna (26 mi., 42 km, NE via Ak. 1) is a picturesque Athapascan Indian village whose Russian Orthodox church, St. Nicholas Church (built in 1870), has an interesting collection of icons. The grave-markers in the cemetery are topped, Indian fashion, with a little house for the departed spirit to live in. Here, you can also visit beautiful **Lake Eklutna** and its waterfalls.

Portage Glacier (50 mi., 80 km, SE via Ak. 1) offers an impressive spectacle as it "calves," shedding great pieces of itself which tumble into Portage Lake below. Visitor Center open daily in summer; Definitely worth the trip.

AN ALASKA OVERVIEW

At once the largest and the least populous state in the Union, Alaska runs to extremes in everything: climate, geography, natural resources, and, above all, distances. The south shore of **Misty Fjords National Monument** in the southern part of the state is 1,435 mi. (2,300 km) away from **Barrow,** the northernmost town in the U.S. From the western tip of the great **Aleutian Islands,** pointed toward Siberia like the tusk of an elephant at bay, to the frontier with Canada's Yukon and British Columbia, Alaska (from an Indian word meaning "great land") sprawls across two time zones. Its area of 586,400 sq. mi. (1,520,000 sq. km.) is 2½ times that of Texas, but is home to barely half a million inhabitants, 70,000 of whom are native Indians, Eskimos (Inuit), and Aleuts.

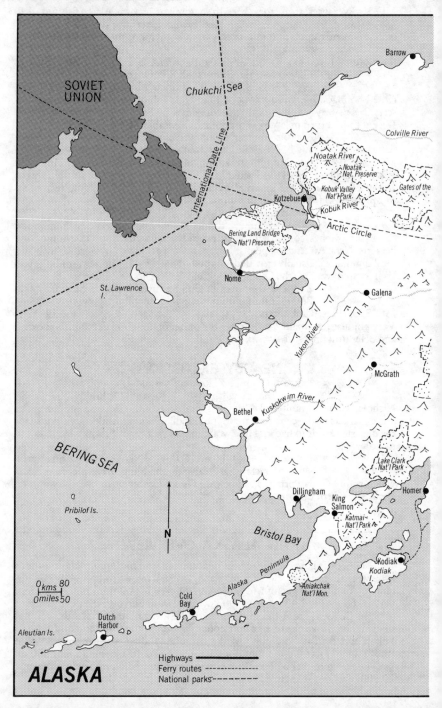

SOVIET UNION

Chukchi Sea

International Date Line

Barrow

Colville River

Noatak River

Noatak Nat'l Preserve

Kobuk Valley Nat'l Park

Gates of the

Kotzebue

Kobuk River

Arctic Circle

Bering Land Bridge Nat'l Preserve

Nome

Galena

St. Lawrence I.

Yukon River

McGrath

Bethel

Kuskokwim River

BERING SEA

Lake Clark Nat'l Park

Dillingham

King Salmon

Homer

Pribilof Is.

Katmai Nat'l Park

N

Bristol Bay

Kodiak

Kodiak I.

Alaska *Peninsula*

Aniakchak Nat'l Mon.

0 kms 80
0 miles 50

Cold Bay

Aleutian Is.

Dutch Harbor

Highways ——————
Ferry routes ------------
National parks ----------

ALASKA

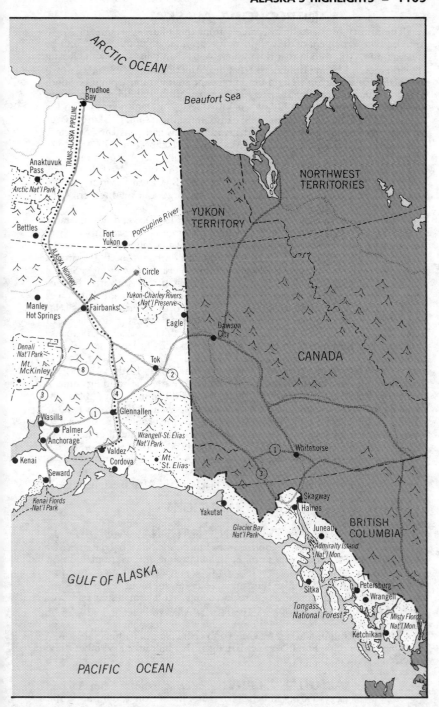

INTRODUCING ALASKA

The history of Alaska is inseparable from that of *Homo sapiens* in North America. The settlement of the continent was begun in 35,000–25,000 B.C. by invaders from Asia who at that time were able to cross what is now the Bering Strait on foot. And it was from Alaska that the "Amerindians" leapfrogged down the Pacific coast, reaching Tierra del Fuego, the southernmost point of South America, a few thousand years later. The history of the state in modern times goes back no further than 1728, when Vitus Bering, a Danish explorer in the service of Tsar Peter the Great of Russia, discovered the 57-mi. (92-km) passage between Siberia and North America that still bears his name. In 1867 Secretary of State William H. Seward purchased Alaska, which had become a Russian colony, for $7.2 million, or around 2¢ per acre—a deal which his political opponents, who knew nothing of the fabulous wealth below Alaska's surface, nicknamed "Seward's Folly," or 'Seward's Icebox." But Seward's vision was corroborated by the gold discoveries of 1896 and the large-scale oil discoveries, the first of which was made in 1957.

Today, Alaska (which became the 49th state in 1959) spends considerably more a year on publicity than the $7.2 million that more than a century ago was the purchase price paid to the Russians for their American colony—because, along with crude oil, fisheries, and forest products, tourism (700,000 visitors a year) is one of the mainstays of the local economy. A visit to the "Frontier State," as it is sometimes called, will give you a deeper insight into Alaska's attraction for lovers of nature, solitude, and wide-open spaces. There are no grander landscapes than the snowy peaks of **Mt. McKinley,** highest in North America, or **Denali National Park;** the mysterious depths of **Tongass National Forest** (twice the size of Ireland) and of **Wrangell–St. Elias National Park;** the blue-shadowed expanse of **Glacier Bay National Park;** the picturesque necklace of islands along the **Inside Passage** with its history-laden little harbors at **Sitka, Petersburg, Ketchikan,** and **Wrangell;** the fissured shores of **Kenai Fjords National Park;** the desolate tundra of **Gates of the Arctic National Park;** the scalding mineral springs of **Circle Hot Springs,** or the "Valley of 10,000 Smokes," in **Katmai National Park.** All of these are unforgettable sights, especially at dawn, or when the summer evenings draw out forever in sunsets of glowing bronze. The state is also heaven on earth for fishermen, hunters (who must have permits), or just plain nature photographers, who won't know where to point their lenses in such a wealth of wildlife: black and brown bear, grizzlies, wolves, mountain goats, Sitka deer, elk, lynx, eagles, caribou, beavers, otters, wolverines, seals, walruses, sea lions—and, unfortunately, mosquitos, the plague of the Alaskan summer.

ALASKA'S HIGHLIGHTS

☖ ADMIRALTY ISLAND NATIONAL MONUMENT

(reachable by seaplane from Juneau and Sitka, or by Alaska Marine Hwy. ferry): Lying at the heart of the Inland Passage, this wild and beautiful island, 100 mi. (160 km) long by 25 mi. (40 km) wide, is inhabited by more brown bears and Sitka deer than humans. Its rain forests, mountain peaks, dozens of lakes and rushing streams, and rocky coasts make it a small-scale replica of Alaska. Admiralty Island is also home to the largest eagle colony in North America.

Shelter: Log cabins and camping sites only. For lovers of nature in the raw.

Information: U.S. Forest Service, 101 Egan Dr., Juneau, AK 99801 (907/586-8751).

🔭 ALEUTIAN ISLANDS (reachable by plane from Anchorage): This island chain stretches more than 1,500 mi. (2,400

km) southwestward from Alaska toward the shores of Asia. Almost uninhabited and rarely visited by tourists in spite of their numerous wildlife reserves, these magnificent windswept islands are a very beautiful destination for the tourist (direct flights between Anchorage and Dutch Harbor/Unalaska). Scene of a 19-day battle in May 1943 between U.S. and Japanese forces, the Aleutians were the only mainland U.S. territory to see combat during World War II. The island of **Attu,** westernmost in the chain, is nearer to Moscow, Beijing, or Tokyo than to Washington, D.C.

Where to Stay

Unisea Inn, Pouch 503-T, Dutch Harbor, AK 99692 (907/581-1325). 46 rms, color TV. MC, V. Rest., bar, boutiques. *Note:* Serviceable, pleasant, welcoming small motel facing the Mall. Open year round. The ideal place to stay for a visit to the Aleutians. **M**

BARROW (reachable by air from Fairbanks or Anchorage): A picturesque Eskimo village whose 2,200 people make their living from fishing and handcrafts, particularly bone carving. Lying 340 mi. (544 km) north of the Arctic Circle, this is the northernmost town in the U.S. At the airport there is a memorial to the cowboy-movie star and humorist Will Rogers and his pilot, Wiley Post, who were killed in an air crash nearby in 1935. The midnight sun shines here for 82 successive days every summer.

Where to Stay

Top of the World, P.O. Box 189-T, AK 99723 (907/852-3900). 40 rms, color TV, cable. AE, MC, V. Adjoining rest. (Pepe's). *Note:* The farthest-north hotel in the Americas. Friendly, refrigerator-equipped rms. Unobstructed view of the Arctic Ocean. Highly recommended Mexican rest.; open year round; entirely redecorated in 1986. About as complete a change of scenery as you can get! **E**

CIRCLE HOT SPRINGS (136 mi., 218 km, NE of Fairbanks along Ak. 2 and 6): Around these hot (139° F, 59° C) springs, discovered in 1897 by a gold prospector, has grown up a spa very popular with Alaskans in winter and with tourists the rest of the year. Thanks to a network of hot-water canals, the market gardeners of the region produce the finest fresh vegetables in Alaska.

COLUMBIA GLACIER: See Valdez.

CORDOVA (reachable by air from Anchorage and Juneau, or by Alaska Marine Hwy. ferry from Whittier and Valdez): This old copper-mining town, which flourished from 1908 to 1938, has taken a renewed lease on life as a busy fishing port. Beautiful site to the east of Prince William Sound. There is an interesting historical museum, the **Cordova Centennial Museum,** Centennial Bldg. (907/424-7443).

DENALI NATIONAL PARK (125 mi., 201 km, south of Fairbanks and 240 mi., 386 km, north of Anchorage on Ak. 3; also reachable by train from Anchorage on the Alaska Railroad, a 7-hr 45-min. trip): This second-largest (9,375 sq. mi., 24,280 sq. km., 2½ times the size of Yellowstone) of our national parks was established in 1917; it is also one of the wildest and most majestic. Almost at the center of the park, and often hidden in summer by clouds, **Mt. McKinley,** the highest peak in North America, stands

20,320 ft tall. An 87-mi. road in the northern part of the park, as well as many trails, allows the visitor to reach the heart of Denali National Park (its name is from an Indian word meaning "the high one"), and to observe its exceptionally rich wildlife—grizzlies, wolves, caribou, elk, and more than 155 species of birds. From both the **Polychrome Overlook** and the **Eielson Visitor Center** (sled-dog demonstrations every day in summer) there are unobstructed views over mountain, forest, and glacier. You'll need warm clothes, a raincoat, and stout shoes.

Information: Superintendent, Denali National Park, P.O. Box 9, Denali Park, AK 99755 (907/638-2238). This park alone is worth the trip to Alaska.

Where to Stay

Denali National Park Hotel, Park Rd., Denali Park, AK 99755 (907/276-7234). 100 rms and 40 sleeping-car compartments. AE, MC, V. Free parking, rest., coffeeshop, bar. *Note:* Adjacent to the Alaska Railroad train station and the Visitor Center, this is the only hotel in the park itself, offering you a choice between friendly rms w. bath or recently modernized sleeping-car compartments without baths. The hotel can arrange excursions in the park, rafting on the river, or flights in light aircraft. Open end of May through Sept. Resv., far in advance, are a must. **M-E**

McKinley Chalets, Park Hwy. (Ak. 3, Mile 238), Denali Park, AK 99755 (907/276-7234). 216 mini-suites. AE, MC, V. *Note:* Rustic but very comfortable chalets, on the bank of the Nenana River, with fine view. Excellent rest. Can arrange park excursions, rafting, or light-aircraft trips. Very near park entrance; caters mostly to groups and conventions. Open mid-May through Sept.; resv. must be made well in advance. **M-E**

FAIRBANKS (365 mi. north of Anchorage by Ak. 3; direct flights from most cities in Alaska; train from Anchorage on the Alaska Railroad, an 11-hr trip): Alaska's second city (pop. 22,600), almost at the geographical center of the state, is first and foremost a supply base for the towns north of the Arctic Circle and for the oilfields of Prudhoe Bay, and thus a busy commercial hub. The most notable of its attractions include:

Alaskaland, Airport Way and Peger Rd. (907/452-4529): This amusement park (open daily) has a replica of a Gold Rush town, open-air museum, restaurant aboard an old paddle-wheel steamer, etc. Entertaining.

Ester (8 mi. SW on Ak. 3) is an authentic turn-of-the-century gold-prospectors' town. The old Cripple Creek District and the Malemute Saloon are worth going out of your way to see.

University Museum, University Campus, College Rd. (907/474-7505), open daily, has an interesting natural-history collection including a 36,000-year-old buffalo, and Indian and Eskimo art and handcrafts. A visit to the ☖ **campus** is recommended.

Four-hr ☖ **cruises** on the Chena and Tanana Rivers aboard picturesque paddle-wheel steamers: *Riverboat Discovery,* Discovery Rd. (907/479-6673), mid-May to mid-Sept. Unusual.

Where to Stay

Captain Bartlett Inn, 1411-T Airport Way, AK 99701 (907/452-1888; toll free 800/544-7528). 200 rms, color TV. AE, DC, MC, V. Free parking, rest. (Sourdough Dining Room), bar, rm svce. Free airport limo. *Note:* Comfortable hotel decorated in a picturesque "Far North" style (the reception area is floored with spruce logs), and boasting "the biggest fireplace in Alaska." Comfortable rms; rest. deserving of respect; winning atmosphere; good svce. Nr. the Alaskaland theme park and the airport (free airport limo); 8 min. from dwntwn. Open year round. **E**

    🛏🛏 **Great Land Hotel** (formerly the Chena View Hotel), 723 First Ave., AK 99701 (907/452-6661). 90 rms, color TV. AE, DC, MC, V. Free parking, rest., bar, rm svce. *Note:* Downtown motel with unimpeded view of the Chena River. Spacious, comfortable rms; friendly welcome and svce; overall good value. Open year round. **M**

    🛏 **Super 8 Motel,** 1909 Airport Way, AK 99701 (907/451-8888; toll free 800/843-1991). 77 rms, color TV, in-rm movies. AE, CB, DC, MC, V. Free parking, adj. rest., free morning coffee, free airport limo. *Note:* Typical motel featuring functional comfort. 8 min. from dwntwn. Open year round. **I–M**

Where to Eat

    ☼🍷🍷 **Sourdough Dining Room** in the Captain Bartlett Inn (see "Where to Stay," above) (452-1888). Lunch/dinner Mon.-Sat. AE, DC, MC, V. Specialties: steak, roast beef, fish of the day, Alaska crab. *Note:* Rustic "Far North" setting with paneling, hunting trophies, and enormous open fireplace. Very acceptable but not particularly imaginative hotel cuisine; attentive svce; relaxed atmosphere. A few steps away from the Alaskaland theme park. *Steak-seafood.* **I–E**

    ☼🍷 **Alaska Salmon Bake,** in the Alaskaland theme park, Airport Way and Peger Rd. (452-7274). Lunch/dinner daily. No credit cards. Fresh salmon, halibut, king crab, barbecued meats. *Note:* A must for every tourist: the Alaska equivalent of a New England clam bake—delicious open-air cooking at a very reasonable price. A colorful, entertaining experience which you shouldn't miss. Free transportation from dwntwn. *Seafood.* **B**

    🍷 **Tiki Cove,** 546 3rd Ave. (452-1484). Lunch/dinner daily. MC, V. Cantonese and Hunan cooking, steak, seafood. *Note:* Worthy (but no more) Chinese food and much-admired Polynesian cocktails in a congenial exotic setting with a fine view of the distant mountains across the Chena River. Locally popular so resv. advisable. *Chinese/American.* **B-I**

    🔔 **FORT YUKON** (reachable by air from Fairbanks): Former Hudson's Bay Co. trading post dating from 1847 and situated astride the Arctic Circle. Attracts many tourists for its authentic Indian handcrafts and its furs. Temperatures as high as 107°F (42°C) in summer and as low as −78°F (−61°C) in winter have been recorded here.

    ☼🔔 **GATES OF THE ARCTIC NATIONAL PARK** (reachable only by charter plane from Fairbanks): Established in 1980, this enormous park lies wholly north of the Arctic Circle. With the adjoining **Kobuk Valley National Park** (weird sand dunes and traces of glacial deposits) and **Noatak National Preserve** (on the trail of caribou, black bears, and wolves), it is one of the last wholly wild reservations in North America. Wonderful mountain and tundra landscapes, with the Noatak River slashing a 62-mi. (100 -km) canyon across this wilderness untouched by human hands. Unfortunately, it's difficult of access for the general run of tourists.

    Information: Superintendent, Gates of the Arctic National Park, 201 First Ave., Fairbanks, AK 99707 (907/456-0281).

    ☼🔔🔔 **GLACIER BAY NATIONAL PARK** (reachable by air or boat from Juneau): One of Alaska's noblest and most impressive natural beauties, this glorious bay, 50 mi. (80 km) long by 2.5–10 mi.

(4–16 km) broad and reminiscent of the Norwegian fjords, is cradled between two mountainous peninsulas whose many glaciers (including the superb **Muir Glacier)** throw off dazzling blue-white reflections. Rearing above the whole is the majestic outline of 15,320-ft (4,663-m) **Mt. Fairweather.** Great chunks of the glaciers are continually falling into the bay with a deafening roar which enhances the fascinating spectacle. Rich wildlife and marine life.

Don't miss the one-to-five-day boat trips across the bay: **Glacier Bay Yacht Tours,** 76 Egan St., Suite 110, Juneau, AK 99801 (toll free 800/426-0600). Enough to make the whole trip worthwhile.

Information: Superintendent, Glacier Bay National Park, Gustavus, AK 99826 (907/697-2230). The park is open from mid-May to the end of Sept.

Where to Stay

Glacier Bay Lodge, Bartlett Cove, Gustavus, AK 99826 (907/697-2225; toll free 800/426-0600). 55 rms. MC, V. Marina, boats, fishing, riding, rest., bar. *Note:* The only hotel in Glacier Bay National Park; the ideal starting-point for trips by boat, by plane, or on foot in Glacier Bay. Elegant rustic architecture in the heart of a forest. Comfortable rms; rest. with a panoramic view. A place that nature lovers won't forget—but you should book far ahead. Open from the end of May through mid-Sept. Campsite adjoining. **E**

Where to Eat

Glacier Bay Lodge Dining Room, in Glacier Bay Lodge (see "Where to Stay," above) (697-2225). Breakfast/lunch/dinner daily; closed end-Sept. through end-May. MC, V. Specialties: salmon, trout, halibut, king crab, shellfish, meats from the broiler. *Note:* Wonderful hotel dining room with a view of Glacier Bay and the mountains which is one of Alaska's finest. Excellent cooking, relying heavily on local seafood. Attentive service; resv. a must. *American-seafood.* **I–M**

HAINES (775 mi, 240 km, SE of Anchorage by the Alaska Hwy. and Haines Hwy.; reachable by air from Juneau, or by the Alaska Marine Hwy. ferry): This little fishing port, tucked between the sea, the Chilkat River, and Mt. Kipinsky at the northern end of the Inside Passage, offers a number of attractions:

The 🔱 **Sheldon Museum,** Main St. at Boat Harbor (907/766-2366), open daily in summer (on Mon. and Wed. the rest of the year), is devoted to the history of the Alaska pioneers and collections of Indian objects.

Fort William H. Seward, Mud Bay Rd. (907/766-2540), open Mon.-Fri., is a turn-of-the-century army post with a replica of a small Indian village (Totem Village). Not to be missed are the demonstrations of Indian dance, on Mon., Wed., and Sat. in summer.

Chilkat Bald Eagle Preserve, adjoining the town, is home from late Oct. to Dec. every year of 4,000 eagles, the world's largest colony of this species.

Where to Stay

Hotel Hälsingland, 13 Ft. Seward Dr., AK 99827 (907/766-2000; toll free 800/542-6363). 60 rms (50 w. bath). AE, CB, DC, MC, V. Free parking, rest. (Commander's Room), bar. *Note:* This picturesque Victorian-style hotel occupies what used to be the officers' quarters of Fort Seward, offering a fine view of the Lynn Canal and the surrounding mountains. Friendly rooms w. functional comfort (most w. private bath). Very creditable rest.; welcome w. a smile. Facing Totem Village and adj. a campsite. Very good value. Open Mar.-Nov. **I-M**

Where to Eat

♈ **Commander's Room** in the Hotel Hälsingland (see "Where to Stay," above) (766-2000). Breakfast/lunch/dinner daily; closed end-Nov. to early Mar. AE, CB, DC, MC, V. *Specialties:* fresh salmon, mackerel, scallops or sauteed prawns, steak. *Note:* Very creditable hotel cuisine served in the former officers' mess of Fort Seward. Fine view of the Lynn Canal and the mountains. Cheerful, friendly service; very good value. *American-seafood.* **B–I**

HOMER (225 mi, 360 km, SW of Anchorage by Ak. 1; reachable by air from Anchorage; Alaska Marine Hwy. ferry connection to Kodiak): A deep-water, ice-free port. Boat trips to the beautiful ⚓ **Kachermark Bay,** rimmed by the Kenai Mountains. A small, well-laid-out natural-history museum is the ⚓ **Pratt Museum,** 3779 Bartlett St. (907/235-8635); open daily May-Sept. (Tues.-Sun. the rest of the year).

JUNEAU (reachable by direct flights from Anchorage or Seattle, or by Alaska Marine Hwy. ferry): Nestling at the feet of the snowcapped **Mt. Juneau** and **Mt. Roberts,** Alaska's picturesque capital is nicknamed "Little San Francisco" because of its narrow streets and the flights of wooden steps hugging the hillsides on which its multicolored houses are built. Besides the ultramodern **State Capitol,** Main and 4th Sts. (admission Mon.-Fri. in summer only), and the elegant **Governor's Mansion,** Calhoun Ave. at 9th St., with its colonial pillars, you should see the unusual Russian-Orthodox ⚓ **St. Nicholas Church,** at 5th and Gold Sts., a wooden octagon dating from 1894 (open daily). The ⚓ **House of Wickersham,** 213 7th St. (907/586-1251), open daily mid-May through Sept., offers you a fine sweeping view, as well as collections of historical memorabilia from the days of the pioneers and the Russian colonists.

The very fine ⚓ **Alaska State Museum,** Whittier St. at Egan Dr. (907/465-2901), open daily, displays an instructive panorama of the history of Alaska's Eskimos and Indians (Aleuts, Athapascans, Tlingits), as well as mastodon tusks more than 50,000 years old, totem poles, etc. Don't miss it.

A short trip (35 mi., 56 km, NW via Glacier Hwy.) to ⚓⚓ **Mendenhall Glacier** should be given high priority. This great river of ice, 12 mi. (19 km) long by 1.5 mi. (2.5 km) wide, is retreating at about 67 ft (21 m) a year; it has taken more than 10,000 years to move 4.3 mi. (7 km) back from the sea, giving birth to a lake at the foot of the dizzying crevasses that fall sheer to the floor of the valley it has carved out. Visitor Center with observatory at the foot of the glacier. Well worth a trip to see.

On ⚓ **Douglas Island,** facing Juneau, is the winter-sports resort of ⚓ **Eagle Crest** (open Dec.-Apr.).

Juneau is also a base for boat trips to the ⚓ **Tracy Arm–Ford's Terror Wilderness,** where the glaciers tumble into fjords 960 ft. (300 m) and more deep.

Where to Stay

♈♈ **Baranof Hotel,** 127 N. Franklin St., AK 99801 (907/586-2660; toll free 800/544-0970). 218 rms, color TV. AE, DC, MC, V. Free parking, rest. (Gold Room), coffeeshop, bar, rm svce. *Note:* The grande dame of local hostelries, right on Franklin St., the historic main street of dwntwn. Opulent decor w. original oil paintings; comfortable rms (some w. kitchenettes); good rest.; attentive svce. Caters mostly to groups; open year round. **M**

♈ **Breakwater Inn,** 1711 Glacier Ave., AK 99802 (907/586-6303). 49 rms, color TV, in-rm movies. AE, CB, DC, MC, V.

Free parking, rest., bar. *Note:* Very comfortable motel with spectacular view of the harbor and the mountains. Pleasant rms w. private balconies (some w. kitchenettes). Smiling svce; good value; open year round. **M**

Northern Light Church, 11th and A Sts. (907/596-9559). Youth hostel, open summer only. **B**

Where to Eat

🍸🍸 **The Diggins,** 340 Whittier Ave., in the Prospector Hotel (586-3737). Breakfast/lunch/dinner daily; also dancing. AE, DC, MC, V. Jkt. *Specialties:* fish of the day and all kinds of seafood; red meats from the broiler. *Note:* Elegant little hotel dining room very close to the harbor. Cuisine mostly seafood, as fresh as you could wish. Very good svce; very popular locally; resv. advised. *American-seafood.* **I–M**

� 🍸🍸 **Silverbow Inn** (in hotel of the same name), 120 2nd St. (586-4146). Lunch/dinner daily; closed holidays. AE, DC, MC, V. Regional French dishes, fish of the day; menu changes regularly. *Note:* Charming old (1914) building, pleasingly restored. Ultraromantic setting (dinner by candlelight) and rather high-flying French-derived cooking. Attentive svce; resv. advisable. *French-American.* **I**

� 🍸 **Second Street Restaurant** (formerly Mike's Place), 1102 2nd St., Douglas (364-3271). Lunch/dinner daily. AE, MC, V. *Specialties:* king crab, fresh salmon, fish of the day, steak. *Note:* Long known as "Mike's Place," this local institution, across the Juneau-Douglas Bridge, prides itself on being one of the oldest restaurants in Alaska. Excellent fish and seafood; spectacular view of Gastineau Channel and the harbor. A very good place; resv. advisable. *American-seafood.* **I**

� **KATMAI NATIONAL PARK** (reachable by air from Anchorage, or from Kodiak as far as King Salmon): A beautiful nature preserve of 4.1 million acres (16,600 sq. km.) in the NE of the Alaska Peninsula. Deep forests shelter brown bears, which are clever salmon-fishers (don't overlook a visit to the 🏛 **McNeil River Sanctuary** at the east end of the park). Many lakes and active volcanoes. The unusually violent eruption of **Mt. Katmai** in 1912 created the lunar landscape of the 🏛 **Valley of Ten Thousand Smokes,** as well as striking cliffs of white ash 90–300 ft (30–100 m) high.

Information: Superintendent, Katmai National Park, P.O. Box 7, King Salmon, AK 99613 (907/246-3305); open early June to Sept.

KENAI (158 mi, 252 km., SW of Anchorage along Ak. 1; or reachable by air from Anchorage): This is the second-oldest city in the state (founded by Russians in 1791) and, thanks to an active offshore drilling program, one of the oil capitals of Alaska. The old **Fort Kenay,** Mission & Overland Aves. (907/283-7294), open daily from June through mid-Sept., was originally built by the U.S. Army in 1869 and rebuilt for the Alaska Centennial in 1967. It faces a fine Russian-Orthodox church of 1896, the 🏛 **Assumption of the Virgin Mary Church,** which is well worth a look.

KENAI FJORDS NATIONAL PARK: See Seward.

KETCHIKAN (reachable by air from Seattle, Juneau, or Sitka; or by Alaska Marine Hwy. ferry): Alaska's southernmost city holds the U.S. record for rainfall—160 in. (4 m) a year! Nicknamed "the world's salmon capital," this important fishing port is also home to the world's largest collection of 🏛🏛 Indian totem poles in **Saxman Totem Park,** 3 mi. (5 km) south on S. Tongass Hwy. (open daily); the **Totem Heritage Center,** 601 Deermount St. (907/225-5900), open daily in summer (Tues.-Fri. the rest of the year); and the **Totem Bight Historical Site,** 10 mi. (16 km) north on N. Tongass Hwy. (open daily). There are more than 60 totem poles in these three locations, and they're worth the trip all by themselves. But while you're here, take a look at the charming little frame houses on Creek St., and visit the interesting **Tongass Historical Museum,** 629 Dock St. (907/225-5600), open daily in summer (Wed.-Sat. the rest of the year), with Indian and Gold Rush exhibits.

Where to Stay

Ingersoll Hotel, 303 Mission St., AK 99901 (907/225-2124; toll free, 800/544-0970). 60 rms, color TV, in-rm. movies; AE, DC, MC, V. Free parking, rest. (Charley's), coffeeshop, bar, rm svce. *Note:* This charming older hotel, at the center of "The Block," the heart of historic Ketchikan, and looming over the harbor, has recently undergone some renovation. Pleasant rooms, locally popular rest, and likeable atmosphere. Open year round. **M**

First United Methodist Church, Grant & Main Sts. (907/225-3780). Youth hostel open from end-May to end-Aug.

Where to Eat

Kay's Kitchen, 2813 Tongass Ave. (225-5860). Lunch only Tues.-Sat.; closed Sun., Mon. MC, V. *Specialties:* soup, crab and shrimp Louie, fish of the day, homemade pie. *Note:* Likeable little restaurant with a view of busy Bar Harbor. Honest, tasty *cuisine bourgeoise;* good-natured welcome and service; excellent value. *American-seafood.* **B-I**

KODIAK (reachable by air from Anchorage or by Alaska Marine Hwy. ferry from Homer and Seward): Capital of Russian America (1784–1799) and now the home port of the state's most important fishing fleet. For an insight into Alaska's Russian heritage, don't fail to visit the **Baranof Museum,** 101 Marine Way (907/486-5920), open daily, Alaska's oldest building (1793), a frame structure which the colony's governor, Alexander Baranof, used for fur storage; or the **Holy Resurrection Church** (1794), again the state's oldest, with its typical bulbous blue domes and some very fine icons and old paintings. The western half of Kodiak Island is a **nature preserve,** rich in wildlife—particularly the giant brown Kodiak bear, which can grow to 1,500 lbs (660 kg); it can be reached by boat or plane from Kodiak.

Information: Kodiak National Wildlife Refuge, 1390 Buskin River Rd., Kodiak, AK 99615 (907/487-2600).

Where to Stay

Shelikof Lodge, 211 Thorsheim Ave., AK 99615 (907/486-4141). 39 rms, color TV; MC, V. Free parking, rest., bar. *Note:* Overlooking the harbor and the city, this modern, comfortable two-story motel is not far from the ferry terminal. Rms recently renovated; acceptable rest.; overall good value. Open year round. **I**

Where to Eat

Captain Keg's, 211 W. Razonof Dr. (486-5469). Lunch/ dinner daily. AE, MC, V. *Specialties:* pizza, sandwiches, fried chicken, steak, hamburger. *Note:* The nautical decor and the showing of silent-film classics have contributed to the success of this pleasant, original eating place. Offers more than 40 brands of domestic and imported beer, as well as a goodly number of Californian and European wines. Agreeable, relaxed atmosphere. *American.* **B–I**

☼ **KOTZEBUE** (reachable only by air, from Anchorage, Fairbanks, and Nome): Just north of the Arctic Circle, this little (pop. 2,000) town is home to one of the oldest Eskimo communities in Alaska, which has lived there at least 300–400 years. It owes its name to the Baltic baron Otto von Kotzebue, who explored these parts around 1840. The ice covering its bay melts in spectacular fashion around the beginning of June. The very modern and interesting ⌂ **Living Museum of the Arctic,** near the airport (907/442-3304), open daily, will show you scenes of everyday Eskimo life (dances, songs, the blanket game, dogsled races, handcraft demonstrations) and well-designed dioramas of the Arctic environment, particularly the region's wildlife. A must.

Where to Stay

☼ ⌂ **Nul-Luk-Vik Hotel,** Box 336-T, AK 99752 (907/442-3331). 85 rms. AE, MC, V. Rest., bar. *Note:* In spite of its tongue-twisting name, this comfortable motel is a favorite with visitors to the Far North; in summer, you can sit at your ease and admire the midnight sun as well as the view of the Arctic Ocean and Kotzebue Sound. Unusual decor; excellent buffet; very good svce. Open year round. **M–E**

MALASPINA GLACIER: See Yakutat.

MENDENHALL GLACIER: See Juneau.

MISTY FJORDS NATIONAL MONUMENT (reachable by boat or seaplane from Ketchikan): Lying between two narrow bays, this lovely natural park, encompassing glaciers, granite cliffs falling sheer into the ocean, and many crystal-clear lakes, marks the southern frontier between Alaska and Canada. Rich wildlife, comprising particularly seals, whales (in the **Behm Canal**), and innumerable waterfowl.

Information: U.S. Forest Service, Federal Bldg., P.O. Box 6137, Ketchikan, AK 99901 (907/225-2148).

MOUNT McKINLEY: See Denali National Park.

☼ **NOME** (reachable only by air, from Anchorage or Fairbanks): Standing on the Bering Sea only an hour's flying time from the Soviet Union, this busy port city reached its apogee in 1898 with the first Gold Rush, which attracted 40,000 prospectors; today it has 2,300 inhabitants. The commercial and economic capital of northwestern Alaska, Nome (a contraction of "No Name") has since 1979 witnessed a sharp upturn in exploration for crude oil, and has also become a tourist center for lovers of fishing, hunting, Eskimo dances, and Indian handcrafts. Nome is also the scene of the celebrated annual ⌂ **Iditarod Trail Race,** the dogsled marathon that is run every March over the 1,049 mi. (1,680 km) of virgin country between Nome and Anchorage.

Where to Stay

☼ ⌂ **Nugget Inn,** Front St. (Box 430-T), AK 99762 (907/443-2323). 47 rms (25% with color TV). AE, MC, V. Rest., bar. *Note:* With its wooden exterior and "Gold Rush" decor, the Nugget Inn might be a set for an adventure movie. Very comfortable rms (the best looking out over the Bering Strait). Likeable bar (Gold Dust Saloon). Svce comes with a smile. Caters mostly to groups and organized tours. Open year round. **M–E**

Community United Methodist Church, W. 2nd & D Sts. (907/433-2865). Youth hostel, open year round.

PETERSBURG (reachable by air from Juneau or Sitka, or by Alaska Marine Hwy. ferry): Nicknamed "Little Norway" because of its many Scandinavian settlers, this charming little fishing port situated at the center of the Inside Passage is a point of departure for boat or seaplane excursions to the spectacular ▲ **Le Conte Glacier,** 25 mi. (40 km) away; for information, contact Viking Travel, Main St., AK 99833 (907/772-3818). The town's ▲ **Clausen Memorial Museum,** 2nd and Fram Sts. (907/772-3598), open daily in summer (on Wed., Thurs., and Sun. the rest of the year), offers a real lure for fishing enthusiasts: the biggest salmon ever caught (126.5 lbs., 57 kg!).

PORTAGE GLACIER: See Anchorage.

PRIBILOF ISLANDS (reachable only by air from Anchorage and Cold Bay): Lost in the Bering Sea, 750 mi. (1,200 km) from Anchorage as the crow flies, this chaplet of green islands shrouded in fog and mist is heaven on earth for naturalists, with more than 200 species of animals and the world's largest seal colony (over a million between May and Sept.); it's the Far North's answer to the Galapagos.

St. Paul, the archipelago's largest island, boasts a picturesque Aleut village with a pretty Russian-Orthodox church. A side trip you shouldn't pass up. Season: early June to late Aug.

Information: Reeve Aleutian Airways, 4700-T International Airport Rd., Anchorage, AK 99502 (907/234-4700).

PRUDHOE BAY (reachable by air from Anchorage and Fairbanks or by car from Fairbanks via Dalton Hwy., 450 mi./720 km): With crude-oil and natural-gas reserves equivalent to 2½ times those of Texas, Alaska's black-gold capital stands amid a flat and desolate landscape on the shores of the Arctic Sea. The terminal of an enormous (800-mi., 1,280-km) pipeline, which since 1977 has linked it to the harbor of Valdez on the Pacific, Prudhoe is a living museum of technology. You will be able to see for yourself the technology involved in tapping a reservoir which lies under the permafrost, with wells that sometimes go to a depth of 1.5 mi. (3,000 m)—and you will see it in a town which in summer is surrounded by herds of wandering caribou and flocks of migrant birds. Don't miss the oilfield installations. Visits from late May to Sept.

Information: Arctic Caribou Lodge (907/659-2371).

Where to Stay

Prudhoe Bay Hotel, Pouch 340004, AK 99734 (907/659-2430). 200 rms. AE, MC, V. Pool, sauna, rest. (no alcoholic beverages since Prudhoe Bay is a "dry" town). *Note:* Large modern hotel adjacent to the airport. Comfortable rms; clientele mostly groups and those with business in the oilfields. Open year round. A boon to the traveler; the nearest town (Barrow) and hotel are 240 mi. away as the crow flies. **M–E**

SEWARD (127 mi., 203 km, south of Anchorage via Ak. 1 and 9; or reachable by air or the Alaska Railroad from Anchorage): Ringed by mountains at the southern tip of the Kenai Peninsula, this little fishing port was badly damaged by the 1964 earthquake. Terminus of the Alaska Railroad, which links it to Fairbanks, the town takes its name from Secretary of State William H. Seward, who negotiated the Alaska Purchase in the 19th century. The tourist office, **Information Cache,** Third Ave. and Jefferson St. (907/224-3094), is housed in the old sleeping car which President Warren G. Harding used on his visit to Alaska in 1923. Be sure, too, to visit 🏛 **St. Peter's Episcopal Church,** Second Ave. and Adams St., for the beautiful painting of the Resurrection, done in 1925 by the Dutch artist Jan van Emple, using Alaskans as models and Resurrection Bay as a background.

Aside from its lovely natural setting, Seward is also the starting-point for excursions, by boat, seaplane, or automobile, to ☀ 🔭 **Kenai Fjords National Park.** Embracing several vast icefields on the eastern slope of the Kenai Mountains (one of which is the **Exit Glacier),** this park, set up in 1980, is a tangled network of fjords and jagged shores, where whales, porpoises, seals, and seabirds hold undisputed sway. Don't pass up this trip.

Information: Superintendent, Kenai Fjords National Park, P.O. Box 1727, Seward, AK 99664 (907/224-3874).

Where to Stay

🏨 **Marina Motel,** Mile 1 Hwy. AK 9, AK 99664 (907/224-5518). 11 rms, color TV, in-rm. movies. AE, CB, DC, MC, V. Free parking. *Note:* Friendly little motel with a splendid view of bay and harbor. Comfortable rms, inviting gardens with picnic area. Free morning coffee; free airport and ferry limo. Open year round. **I—M**

🔭 **SITKA** (reachable by plane from Juneau, Ketchikan, or Seattle; or by Alaska Marine Hwy. ferry): The splendid site was discovered in 1741 by the explorer Vitus Bering, and the town, once nicknamed "the Paris of the Pacific," was picked in 1804 as Alaska's capital by Alexander Baranof, first governor of Russian America; it remained so until 1906, when Juneau was chosen to replace it.

Proud of its history, Sitka offers the visitor many evidences of it Russo-American heritage: 🏛 **St. Michael's Cathedral,** Lincoln St. (907/747-8120), open daily June-Sept. (by appointment the rest of the year), with its valuable icons, is an exact replica of the original Russian Orthodox church of 1844, which was destroyed by fire in 1966. The 🏛 **Russian Bishop's House,** Lincoln St. (907/747-6241), open daily in summer, is Bishop Gregory's log cabin dating from 1842, a designated historic monument.

Among other noteworthy attractions are the 🏛 **Sheldon Jackson State Museum,** Sheldon Jackson College Campus, Lincoln St. (907/747-5228), open daily in summer (daily except Sat. and Mon. the rest of the year), which has memorabilia of the Russian period, as well as Indian and Eskimo masks; and the 🏛 **Sitka National Historic Park,** at the end of Metlakatla St. (907/747-6281), open daily year round, site of the "battle for Alaska" between Russians and Tlingit Indians in 1804, the last stand of the original inhabitants against white domination. Fine collection of 18 Indian totem poles. Every Alaska itinerary should include Sitka.

Where to Stay

☀🏨 **Westmark Shee Atika Lodge,** 330 Seward St., AK 99835 (907/747-6241; toll-free, 800/544-0970). 96 rms, cable color TV. AE, CB, DC, MC, V. Free parking, rest., bar, rm svce. *Note:* Modern hotel opposite the Convention Center, of unusual design which draws heavily on local materials, particularly wood. Comfortable, spacious rms looking out either over the harbor or toward the mountains. Good svce. Open year round. **E**

🏨 **Potlatch House,** 709 Katlian St., AK 99835 (907/747-8611). 30 rms., cable, color TV; AE, DC, MC, V. Free parking, rest., bar. *Note:* Comfortable motel 5 min. by car from dwntwn (free shuttle). Comfortable rms overlooking the harbor or Mt. Edgecumbe. You'll be a welcome, well-looked-after guest. Good value; open year round. **I**

Where to Eat

☆☆ **Channel Club,** Halibut Point Rd., 3-½ mi. (6 km) north of town (747-9916). Dinner only, nightly; closed holidays. AE, DC, MC, V. Jkt. *Specialties:* steak, fresh salmon, king crab, fish of the day. *Note:* Highly regarded locally for its excellent food and its magnificent view of the Western Channel and the impressive Mt. Edgecumbe. Choice seafood and red meats. Resv. highly advisable. *Steak-seafood.* **I–M**

☀ ☖☖ **SKAGWAY** (reachable by air from Haines or Juneau, or by Alaska Marine Hwy. ferry): Formerly the port of entry for the Klondike, Skagway has preserved the appearance and atmosphere of the 1898 Gold Rush better than any other town in Alaska. At that time it boasted 20,000 inhabitants; today, only about 800. ☖ **Broadway,** Skagway's main drag, and the **Trail of '98 Museum,** City Hall, Seventh Ave. & Spring St. (907/983-2420), open daily in summer (by appointment in winter), perfectly reconstruct the age of the 19th-century gold prospectors. Recommended: ☖ *In the Days of '98,* tragicomic melodrama about the Gold Rush, staged in Eagles Hall, 6th St. and Broadway (907/983-2545), presented daily, May to mid-Sept.

On the outskirts, be sure to see the "ghost town" of **Dyea** (11 mi., 18 km NE on the Klondike Hwy.) or **Bennett Lake** (65 mi., 106 km, NE on the Klondike Hwy.), on the edge of which stands the picturesque Canadian village of Carcross. Hardier visitors will brave the rigors of the ☖ **Chilkoot Trail,** a scenic mountain trail once used by the prospectors (three to four days' hike to Lake Bennett).

Skagway is one of the most popular tourist attractions of Alaska; you shouldn't fail to see it.

Where to Stay

☀ ☖ **Golden North Hotel,** 3rd St. and Broadway, AK 99840 (907/ 983-2451). 34 rms. AE, DC, MC, V. Free parking, rest., bar. *Note:* With its singular gilded dome, this agreeable little hotel, a survivor from the Gold Rush, is one of Skagway's most interesting buildings, as well as being the oldest still-functioning hotel in Alaska (since 1897). Comfortable rms with period furnishings, each decorated in a different style. Guaranteed local color. Open year round. **M–E**

☖ **Westmark Inn,** 3rd and Spring Sts., AK 99840 (907/983-2291; toll free 800/544-0970). 200 rms AE, MC, V. Free parking, rest. (Chilkoot Room), coffeeshop, bar. *Note:* Enormous, ungraceful modern motel, whose interior decoration is intended to evoke the great days of the Klondike. Comfortable and functional; favored by rather intrusive tour groups. Free airport and ferry limo. Rates excessive for a motel. Open mid-May to end-Sept. **E**

Where to Eat

☖ **Northern Lights Cafe,** Broadway at 4th (983-2225). Lunch/ dinner daily. MC, V. Fresh salmon, halibut, steak. *Note:* A long-time Skagway classic; decent, unpretentious cooking at very reasonable prices. A boon to the tourist. *American-seafood.* **B–I**

VALDEZ (317 mi., 507 km, NE of Anchorage via Ak. 1 and 4; also reachable by air from Anchorage or Fairbanks, and by Alaska Marine Hwy. ferry from Whittier or Seward): Standing north of the Arctic Circle in a grandly mountainous setting at the foot of Prince William Sound, Valdez, once dubbed "the Switzerland of Alaska," is the terminal of the Prudhoe Bay crude-oil pipeline—and the third-busiest port in the U.S. in terms of tonnage. You can arrange a fascinating visit to the 🏛 **Trans-Alaska Pipeline;** for information, contact the Visitor Center, 245 N. Harbor Dr. (907/835-4630).

Valdez is also the starting point for an expedition to the great 3.7-mi- (6-km-) wide 🔭🔭 **Columbia Glacier** where it falls sheer into the sea. For information, contact Era Helicopters (907/835-2595) or Gray Line Tours (907/835-2357).

Where to Stay

🛏🛏 **Westmark Valdez,** 100 Fidalgo Dr., AK 99686 (907/835-4391; toll free 800/544-0970). 100 rms, cable color TV. AE, MC, V. Free parking, marina, boat, fishing, rest. (Captain's Table), bar, rm svce. *Note:* Comfortable motel on the yacht basin. Spacious, comfortable rms (the best overlooking the harbor). Satisfactory rest. Near Ferry Terminal. Guided tours of Columbia Glacier daily in summer. Open year round. **E**

🛏 **Village Inn,** Meals Ave. and Richardson Hwy. AK 99686 (907/835-4445). 100 rms, color TV. AE, MC, V. Free parking, health club, sauna, rest. (Gay Nineties), bar. *Note:* Modest but well-run motel near the Ferry Terminal offering your choice of functionally comfortable rms (some with private bath) or individual cottages with kitchenettes. Guided tours of Columbia Glacier daily in summer. Open March to end-Sept. **M–E**

🏛 **WRANGELL** (reachable by air from Ketchikan or Juneau, or by Alaska Marine Hwy. ferry): The only city in Alaska to have flown, in succession, the Russian, British, and U.S. flags, Wrangell has also lived through no fewer than three gold rushes, in 1863, 1873, and 1898. Be sure to see the **Bear Tribal House,** Chief Shakes Island (907/874-3505), open varying days and times, for its 🏛 fine carved totem poles, and the 🏛 mysterious Indian rock carvings that may be seen at low tide on the beach near the Ferry Dock.

🔭🔭 **WRANGELL–ST. ELIAS NATIONAL PARK** (reachable by Glenn and Richardson Hwys. to the north of the park, or by boat from Yakutat to the south of the park): With an area of 12,730 sq. mi., (39,270 sq. km.), this is our largest national park—3½ times the size of Yellowstone. The peaks of **Mt. Blackburn** (16,523 ft, 4,995 m,) in the Wrangell Mountains and **Mt. Steller** (10,360 ft, 3,238 m) in the St. Elias Mountains rear above this great stretch of wildland, which, with the adjoining **Kluane National Park,** to the south across the Canadian border, makes up the world's largest assembly of glaciers, other than those of the polar icecaps. Among them is the enormous **Malaspina Glacier,** the biggest icefield in North America.

Information: Superintendent, Wrangell–St. Elias National Park & Preserve, P.O. Box 29-T, Glenallen, AK 99588 (907/822-5235), and at the Ranger Station at Chitina (FR No. 10). For lovers of unspoiled nature-in-the-raw.

🏛 **YAKUTAT** (reachable by air from Anchorage or Juneau): A former Tlingit village, on the sea halfway between Cordova and the Inside Passage, Yakutat is the ideal jumping-off point for a boat or kayak trip along **Russel Fjord** and the **Hubbard Glacier,** or for a flight over the majestic **Malaspina Glacier,** bigger than the State of Rhode Island.

Information: Gulf Air Taxi, Yakutat, AK 99689 (907/784-3240).

SPECIAL EVENTS AROUND ALASKA

For exact dates on the following special events, check with the following sources of travel information:

Cordova Chamber of Commerce, P.O. Box 99-T, Cordova, AK 99574 (907/424-7260).

Fairbanks Convention & Visitors Bureau, 550 First Ave., Fairbanks, AK 99701 (907/456-5774).

Haines Chamber of Commerce, P.O. Box 541-T, Haines, AK 99827 (907/766-2202).

Juneau Convention & Visitors Bureau, 76-T Egan Dr., Suite 140, Juneau, AK 99801 (907/586-1737).

Kodiak Area Chamber of Commerce, P.O. Box 1485-T, Kodiak, AK 99615 (907/486-5557).

Seward Chamber of Commerce, P.O. Box 756-T, Seward, AK 99664 (907/224-3094).

Sitka Convention & Visitors Bureau, 330-T Harbor Dr., Sitka, AK 99835 (907/747-5940).

Skagway Convention & Visitors Bureau, P.O. Box 415-T, Skagway, AK 99840 (907/983-2854).

Valdez Convention & Visitors Bureau, P.O. Box 1603-T, Valdez, AK 99686 (907/835-2984).

Whittier Chamber of Commerce, P.O. Box 608-T, Whittier, AK 99693 (907/472-2337).

CORDOVA: **Ice Worm Festival** (early Feb.): colorful parade through the town's streets led by a 100-ft- (30-m-) long "ice worm" supposed to be emerging from hibernation.

FAIRBANKS: **North American Championship Sled Dog Races** (end of Mar.): hotly contested dog-sled championship.

Yukon 800 River Boat Race (mid-June): outboard-motor boats race 800 mi. (1,280 km) along the Yukon River.

Midnight Sun Baseball: a popular local match played between 10 p.m. and midnight every June 21.

World Eskimo Indian Olympics (end of July): sporting and cultural events bringing together representatives of the main Indian, Eskimo, and Aleut tribes.

HAINES: **Chilkat Dancers** (June-Sept.): twice-a-week displays of Indian dance at Fort William H. Seward.

JUNEAU: **Alaska Folk Festival** (early Apr.): shows, dance, music, arts and crafts exhibits.

Golden North Salmon Derby (Aug.): salmon-fishing championship.

KODIAK: **King Crab Festival** (end of May): annual festival in honor of the region's most famous crustacean.

Cry of the Wild Ram (first two weeks in Aug.): historical evocation of the life of Alexander Baranof, first Russian governor of Alaska; in the Frank Brink Amphitheater, nightly.

Rodeo & State Fair (mid-Aug.): heavily attended fair-exhibition-rodeo.

SEWARD: **Mount Marathon Race** (July 4): with 200 runners from all over the world.

SITKA: **Summer Music Festival** (June): chamber-music recitals.

New Archangel Dancers (June-Sept.): displays of Russian folk dancing; in the Centennial Bldg.

Alaska Day (Oct. 18): annual reenactment of the transfer of authority from Russia to the U.S. on Oct. 18, 1867; on Castle Hill.

SKAGWAY: *In the Days of '98* (mid-May to mid-Sept.): tragi-comic melodrama about the 1898 Gold Rush; staged in Eagles Hall, nightly.

VALDEZ: Winter Carnival (mid-Mar.): dogsled races, dance displays, concerts, festival of food.
Gold Rush Days (early Aug.): can-can dancing, street parades, games, and big free buffet.

WHITTIER: Alaska Crab Festival (mid-Apr.): fishing competition for the largest crab caught.

APPENDIX

□ □ □

STATE TOURIST OFFICES

Alabama: Bureau of Tourism & Travel, 532 S. Perry St., Montgomery, AL 36130 (205/261-4169; toll free 800/252-2262).

Alaska: Division of Tourism, Information Office, P.O. Box E, Juneau, AK 99811 (907/465-2010).

Arizona: Office of Tourism, 1100 W. Washington St., Phoenix, AZ 85007 (602/255-3618).

Arkansas: Department of Parks & Tourism, 1 Capitol Mall, Little Rock, AR 72201 (501/682-7777; toll free 800/643-8383).

California: Office of Tourism, 1121 L. St., Suite 103, Sacramento, CA 95814 (916/322-2881); Chamber of Commerce, Tourism Dept., P.O. Box 1736, Sacramento, CA 95808 (916/444-6670).

Colorado: Tourism Board, 1625 Broadway, Suite 1700, Denver, CO 80202 (303/592-5410; toll free 800/433-2656).

Connecticut: Department of Economic Development, 210 Washington St., Hartford, CT 06106 (203/566-3948).

Delaware: Travel Service, 99 King Hwy. (P.O. Box 1401), Dover, DE 19903 (302/736-4271; toll free 800/441-8846).

District of Columbia: Washington Area Convention & Visitors Association, 1212 New York Ave. NW, Washington, DC 20005 (202/789-7000).

Florida: Division of Tourism, 126 Van Buren St., Tallahassee, FL 32301 (904/487-1462; toll free 800/874-8660).

Georgia: Tourist Division, P.O. Box 1776, Atlanta, GA 30301 (404/656-3590; toll free 800/241-8444).

Hawaii: Visitors Bureau, 2270 Kalakaua Ave., Honolulu, HI 96815 (808/923-1811).

Idaho: Division of Tourism & Industrial Development, Room 108, State Capitol, Boise, ID 83720 (208/334-2470).

Illinois: Office of Tourism, 620 E. Adams St., Springfield, IL 62701 (217/782-7139).

Indiana: Tourism Division, 1 N. Capitol St., Indianapolis, IN 46204 (317/232-8860).

Iowa: Department of Economic Development, Tourism and Film Office, 200 E. Grand Ave., Des Moines, IA 50309 (515/281-3100).

Kansas: Travel & Tourist Division, 400 W. 8th St., 5th floor, Topeka, KS 66603 (913/296-2009).

Kentucky: Department of Tourism, Capitol Plaza Tower, Frankfort, KY 40601 (502/564-4930).

Louisiana: Office of Tourism, P.O. Box 94291, Capitol Station, Baton Rouge, LA 70804 (504/342-8119).

Maine: Publicity Bureau, 97 Winthrop St., Hallowell, ME 04347 (207/289-2423).

Maryland: Division of Tourism Development, 45 Calvert St., Annapolis, MD 21401 (301/974-3517; toll free 800/638-5252).

Massachusetts: Division of Tourism, 100 Cambridge St., Leverett Saltonstall Bldg., 13th Floor, Boston, MA 02202 (617/727-3201).

Michigan: Travel Bureau, Department of Commerce, P.O. Box 30226, Law Bldg., Lansing, MI 48909 (517/373-0670; toll free 800/543-2937).

Minnesota: Tourism Division, 375 Jackson St., St. Paul, MN 55101 (612/296-5029; toll free 800/328-1461).

Mississippi: Department of Tourism & Development, Box 849, Jackson, MS 39205 (601/359-3414).

Missouri: Division of Tourism, 308 E. High St. (P.O. Box 1055), Jefferson City, MO 65102 (314/751-4133).

Montana: Travel Promotion Bureau, 1424 Ninth Ave., Helena, MT 59620 (406/444-2654; toll free 800/548-3390).

Nebraska: Nebraska Travel & Tourism P.O. Box 94666, Lincoln, NB 68509 (402/471-3796).

Nevada: Tourism Travel Division, Capitol Complex, Carson City, NV 89710 (702/885-4322).

New Hampshire: Office of Vacation Travel, 105 Loudon Rd., P.O. Box 856, Concord, NH 03301 (603/271-2343).

New Jersey: Division of Travel & Tourism, P.O. Box 400, Trenton, NJ 08625 (609/292-2470).

New Mexico: Travel Division, 1100 St. Francis Dr., Santa Fe, NM 87503 (505/827-0291; toll free 800/545-2040).

New York: Division of Tourism, State Dept. of Commerce, 1 Commerce Plaza, Albany, NY 12245 (518/474-4116; toll free 800/225-5697).

North Carolina: Travel & Tourism Division, 430 N. Salisbury St., Raleigh, NC 27611 (919/733-4171).

North Dakota: North Dakota Tourism Promotion, Library Memorial Bldg., 600 East Blvd., Bismarck, ND 58505 (701/224-2525).

Ohio: Office of Travel & Tourism, P.O. Box 1001, Columbus, OH 43216 (614/466-8844; toll free 800/282-5393).

Oklahoma: Tourism Promotion Division, 505 Will Rogers Bldg., Oklahoma City, OK 73105 (405/521-2409).

Oregon: Tourism Division, 595 Cottage St. NE, Salem, OR 97310 (503/378-3451; toll free 800/547-7842).

Pennsylvania: Bureau of Travel Development, 416 Forum Bldg., Harrisburg, PA 17120 (717/787-5453; toll free 800/237-4363).

Puerto Rico: Tourism Development Cy., P.O. Box 1546, San Juan, PR 00903 (809/725-2110).

Rhode Island: Tourist Promotion Division, 7 Jackson Walkway, Providence, RI 02903 (401/277-2601).

South Carolina: Division of Tourism, P.O. Box 71, Columbia, SC 29202 (803/734-0127).

South Dakota: Division of Tourism, 711 Wells Ave., Pierre, SD 57501 (605/773-3301; toll free 800/843-1930).

Tennessee: Department of Tourist Development, 601 Broadway (P.O. Box 23170), Nashville, TN 37202 (615/741-2158).

Texas: Travel & Information Division, P.O. Box 5064, Austin, TX 78763 (512/463-8971).

Utah: Travel Council, Council Hall, Capitol Hill, Salt Lake City, UT 84114 (801/538-1030; toll free 800/453-5794).

Vermont: Travel Division, 134 State St., Montpelier, VT 05602 (802/828-3236).

Virginia: State Travel Service, 202 N. 9th St., Richmond, VA 23219 (804/786-4484).

Washington: Travel Development Division, 101 General Administration Bldg., Olympia, WA 98504 (206/753-5600).

West Virginia: Department of Commerce, Division of Tourism, Bldg. 6, Capitol Complex, Charleston, WV 25305 (304/348-2200).

Wisconsin: Division of Tourism, P.O. Box 7606, Madison, WI 53707 (608/266-2161; toll free 800/432-8747).

Wyoming: Travel Commission, I-25 at College Dr., Cheyenne, WY 82002 (307/777-7777).

PRINCIPAL HOTEL/MOTEL CHAINS

For reservations, see "Toll-Free Numbers," below.

Best Western, Best Western Way (P.O. Box 10203), Phoenix, AZ 85604 (602/957-4200).

Four Seasons, 1165 Leslie St., Toronto, ON M3C 2K8, Canada (416/449-1750).

Friendship Inns, 2627 Paterson Plank Rd., North Bergen, NJ 07047 (201/863-3443).

Hilton, 9336 Civic Center Dr., Beverly Hills, CA 90210 (213/278-4321).

Holiday Inns, 3796 Lamar Ave., Memphis, TN 38195 (901/362-4001).

Howard Johnson, Inc., 710 Rte. 46E., Box 2746, Fairfield, NJ, 07007 (201/882-1880).

Hyatt, Madison Plaza, 200 W. Madison St., Chicago, IL 60606 (312/750-1234).

La Quinta Motor Inns, 10010 San Pedro, (P.O. Box 32064), San Antonio, TX 78279 (512/366-6000).

Marriott, 1 Marriott Dr., Washington, DC 20058 (301/380-9000).

Motel 6, 14651 Dallas Pkwy, Dallas, TX 75240 (505/386-6161).

Quality Inns, 10750 Columbia Pike, Silver Spring, MD 20901 (301/593-5600).

Radisson, 12805 Hwy. 55, Minneapolis, MN 55441 (612/540-5526).

Ramada Inns, 3838 E. Van Buren St., Phoenix, AZ 85008 (602/273-4000).

Rodeway Inns, 3838 E. Van Buren St., Phoenix, AZ 85008 (602/273-4550).

Sheraton, 60 State St., Boston, MA 02109 (617/367-3600).

Travelodge, 1973 Friendship Dr., El Cajon, CA 92090 (619/448-1884).

Westin, Westin Bldg., Seattle, WA 98121 (206/443-5000).

TOLL-FREE NUMBERS

Toll-free numbers, recognizable by their "800" area code, are available for your convenience from many airlines, car-rental companies, hotel chains, etc. When you call "1-800" plus a normal seven-digit number, your call is paid for by the subscriber, no matter how far away you may be. Here follows a list of useful toll-free numbers (if you need one not listed here, call 800/555-1212 to reach "information" for all 800 numbers):

AIRLINES: See the individual city chapters for local airline phone numbers.

BUS: Greyhound (800/528-6055); see the individual city chapters for local Greyhound phone numbers.

HOTELS/MOTELS: The following are the national toll-free reservations numbers for the major hotel chains:

Accor (800/221-4542)
Amfac Hotels (800/227-1177)
Best Western (800/528-1234)
Clarion (800/252-7466)
Days Inns (800/325-2525)
Fairmont (800/527-4727)
Four Seasons (800/332-3442)
Friendship Inns (800/453-4511)
Hilton (800/445-8667)
Hyatt (800/228-9000)
Holiday Inns (800/465-4329)
Howard Johnson's (800/654-2000)
Imperial Inns (800/368-4400)
Inter-Continental Hotels (800/332-4246)
La Quinta Motor Inns (800/531-5900)

Loews (800/223-0888)
Marriott (800/228-9290)
Meridien (800/543-4300)
Omni (800/843-6664)
Preferred (800/323-7500)
Quality Inns (800/228-5151)
Radisson (800/333-3333)
Ramada Inns (800/228-2828)
Red Lion Inns (800/547-8010)
Rodeway Inns (800/228-2000)
Sheraton (800/325-3535)
Stouffer (800/468-3571)
Travelodge (800/255-3050)
Treadway Inns (800/752-3297)
Vagabond Hotels (800/522-1555)
Westin (800/228-3000)

CAR-RENTAL AGENCIES:

The following are the national toll-free reservations numbers for the major car-rental chains:

Agency Rent-A-Car (800/321-1972)
Ajax (800/367-2529)
Alamo (800/327-9633)
Americar Rental System (800/336-7400)
Avis (800/331-1212)
Budget (800/527-0700)

Dollar Rent-A-Car (800/421-6868)
General Rent-A-Car (800/327-7607)
Hertz (800/654-3131)
National (800/227-7368)
Rent-A-Wreck (800/535-1391)
Sears Rent-A-Car (800/527-0770)
Thrifty (800/367-2277)

The local numbers for many car-rental agencies will be found in the individual city chapters.

TRAINS:

AMTRAK's 800 numbers vary from state to state; consult local telephone directories. The national toll-free number is 800/872-7245 (USA-RAIL).

Index

Aberdeen (WA), 895
Acadia National Park (ME), 179
Accommodations, 25–7; *see also specific places*
Acoma Pueblo (NM), 778, 795
Active vacations, 7
Adirondack Park (NY), 154–7
Admiralty Island National Monument (AK), 1110
Adventure Island (Tampa, FL), 419–20
Adventure River Water Park (Memphis, TN), 357
Afton Alps Ski Area (MN), 564
Air travel, 19–22
  air courier, flying as, 21
  charters, 21
  discount fares, 20–1
  easy flying hints, 21–2
  foreign visitors, 21
  passes, 21
  regular fare structure, 19–20
  tour packages, 21
Alamo, The (San Antonio, TX), 756
Alamo Village (Brackettville, TX), 766
Alaska, 3, 1099–1124
  Admiralty Island National Monument, 1110
  Aleutian Islands, 1110–11
  Barrow, 1111
  Circle Hot Springs, 1111
  Cordova, 1111
  Denali National Park, 1111–12
  Fairbanks, 1112–13
  Fort Yukon, 1113
  Gates of the Arctic National Park, 1113
  Glacier Bay National Park, 1113–14
  Haines, 1114–15
  Homer, 1115
  Juneau, 1115–16
  Katmai National Park, 1116
  Kenai, 1116
  Ketchikan, 1116–17
  Kodiak, 1117–18
  Kotzebue, 1118
  map, 1108–9
  Misty Fjords National Monument, 1118
  Nome, 1118–19
  overview of, 1107
  Petersburg, 1119
  Pribilof Islands, 1119
  Prudhoe Bay, 1119
  Seward, 1119–20
  Sitka, 1120–1
  Skagway, 1121
  special events, 1122–4
  Valdez, 1121–2
  Wrangell, 1122
  Wrangell–St. Elias National Park, 1122
  Yakutat, 1122
  see also Anchorage

Alaskaland (Fairbanks, AK), 1112
Albany (NY), 154
Albuquerque (NM), 769–81
  accommodations, 773, 775
  arrival and transportation information, 770
  bars and nightclubs, 777
  basic facts, 769
  climate, 769
  distances from, 769–70
  excursions nearby, 777–8
  map, 774
  restaurants, 775–7
  sights, attractions, and activities, 770–2
  tourist information and tours, 770
Alcatraz Island (CA), 975
Aleutian Islands (AK), 1110–11
Alexandria (VA), 284–5
Alpental (WA), 878
Alpine Meadows (CA), 938
Alpine Valley (MI), 479
Alpine Valley (OH), 496
Alpine Valley (WI), 550
Alyeska Resort (AK), 1104
Amargosa Opera House (CA), 931
Ambridge (PA), 236
Amelia Island (FL), 398
American Automobile Association (AAA), 18
American Indian, Museum of the (New York City), 107
American Museum of the Moving Image (New York City), 107
Ameripass, 23, 24
AMTRAK, 22–3
Amusement and theme parks, 6; *see also specific places*
Anaheim (CA), 1034
Anchorage (AK), 1099–1107
  accommodations, 1104–6
  arrival and transportation information, 1100–1
  basic facts, 1099
  climate, 1100
  distances from, 1100
  excursions nearby, 1107
  map, 1103
  restaurants, 1106–7
  sights, attractions, and activities, 1101–4
  tourist information and tours, 1101
Angeles National Forest (CA), 1037
Angel Island (San Francisco, CA), 981
Annapolis (MD), 250, 285–6
Ann Arbor (MI), 487
Año Nuevo State Reserve (CA), 953
Antietam National Battlefield Site and Cemetery (MD), 291
Anza Borrego Desert State Park (CA), 1073
Apache Trail (AZ), 833

1129

NOW, SAVE MONEY ON ALL YOUR TRAVELS!
Join Frommer's™ Dollarwise® Travel Club

Saving money while traveling is never a simple matter, which is why the **Dollarwise Travel Club** was formed 31 years ago. Developed in response to requests from Frommer Travel Guide readers, the Club provides cost-cutting travel strategies, up-to-date travel information, and a sense of community for value-conscious travelers from all over the world.

In keeping with the money-saving concept, the annual membership fee is low — $18 (U.S. residents) or $20 (residents of Canada, Mexico, and other countries)— and is immediately exceeded by the value of your benefits, which include:

1. Any TWO books listed on the following pages.
2. Plus any ONE Frommer City Guide.
3. A subscription to our quarterly newspaper, *The Dollarwise Traveler*.
4. A membership card that entitles you to purchase through the Club all Frommer publications for 33% to 50% off their retail price.

The eight-page *Dollarwise Traveler* tells you about the latest developments in good-value travel worldwide and includes the following columns: **Hospitality Exchange** (for those offering and seeking hospitality in cities all over the world); **Share-a-Trip** (for those looking for travel companions to share costs); and **Readers Ask . . . Readers Reply** (for those with travel questions that other members can answer).

Aside from the Frommer Guides, the Serious Shopper Guides, and the Gault Millau Guides, you can also choose from our Special Editions. These include such titles as **California with Kids** (a compendium of the best of California's accommodations, restaurants, and sightseeing attractions appropriate for those traveling with toddlers through teens); **Candy Apple: New York with Kids** (a spirited guide to the Big Apple by a savvy New York grandmother that's perfect for both visitors and residents); **Caribbean Hideaways** (the 100 most romantic places to stay in the Islands, all rated on ambience, food, sport opportunities, and price); **Honeymoon Destinations** (a guide to planning and choosing just the right destination from hundreds of possibilities in the U.S., Mexico, and the Caribbean); **Marilyn Wood's Wonderful Weekends** (a selection of the best mini-vacations within a 200-mile radius of New York City, including descriptions of country inns and other accommodations, restaurants, picnic spots, sights, and activities); and **Paris Rendez-Vous** (a delightful guide to the best places to meet in Paris whether for power breakfasts or dancing till dawn).

To join this Club, simply send the appropriate membership fee with your name and address to: Frommer's Dollarwise Travel Club, 15 Columbus Circle, New York, NY 10023. Remember to specify which single city guide and which two other guides you wish to receive in your initial package of member's benefits. Or tear out the next page, check off your choices, and send the page to us with your membership fee.

FROMMER BOOKS
PRENTICE HALL TRAVEL
15 COLUMBUS CIRCLE
NEW YORK, NY 10023
212-373-8125

Date_____

Friends:
Please send me the books checked below:

FROMMER™ GUIDES

(Guides to sightseeing and tourist accommodations and facilities from budget to deluxe, with emphasis on the medium-priced.)

☐ Alaska	$14.95	☐ Germany	$14.95
☐ Australia	$14.95	☐ Italy	$14.95
☐ Austria & Hungary	$14.95	☐ Japan & Hong Kong	$14.95
☐ Belgium, Holland & Luxembourg	$14.95	☐ Mid-Atlantic States	$14.95
☐ Bermuda & The Bahamas	$14.95	☐ New England	$14.95
☐ Brazil	$14.95	☐ New York State	$14.95
☐ Canada	$14.95	☐ Northwest	$14.95
☐ Caribbean	$14.95	☐ Portugal, Madeira & the Azores	$14.95
☐ Cruises (incl. Alaska, Carib, Mex, Hawaii, Panama, Canada & US)	$14.95	☐ Skiing Europe	$14.95
		☐ South Pacific	$14.95
☐ California & Las Vegas	$14.95	☐ Southeast Asia	$14.95
☐ Egypt	$14.95	☐ Southern Atlantic States	$14.95
☐ England & Scotland	$14.95	☐ Southwest	$14.95
☐ Florida	$14.95	☐ Switzerland & Liechtenstein	$14.95
☐ France	$14.95	☐ USA	$15.95

FROMMER $-A-DAY® GUIDES

(In-depth guides to sightseeing and low-cost tourist accommodations and facilities.)

☐ Europe on $40 a Day	$15.95	☐ New York on $60 a Day	$13.95
☐ Australia on $30 a Day	$12.95	☐ New Zealand on $45 a Day	$13.95
☐ Eastern Europe on $25 a Day	$13.95	☐ Scandinavia on $60 a Day	$13.95
☐ England on $50 a Day	$13.95	☐ Scotland & Wales on $40 a Day	$13.95
☐ Greece on $35 a Day	$13.95	☐ South America on $35 a Day	$13.95
☐ Hawaii on $60 a Day	$13.95	☐ Spain & Morocco on $40 a Day	$13.95
☐ India on $25 a Day	$12.95	☐ Turkey on $30 a Day	$13.95
☐ Ireland on $35 a Day	$13.95	☐ Washington, D.C. & Historic Va. on	
☐ Israel on $40 a Day	$13.95	$40 a Day	$13.95
☐ Mexico on $35 a Day	$13.95		

FROMMER TOURING GUIDES

(Color illustrated guides that include walking tours, cultural and historic sites, and other vital travel information.)

☐ Australia	$9.95	☐ Paris	$8.95
☐ Egypt	$8.95	☐ Scotland	$9.95
☐ Florence	$8.95	☐ Thailand	$9.95
☐ London	$8.95	☐ Venice	$8.95

TURN PAGE FOR ADDITONAL BOOKS AND ORDER FORM.

0190

FROMMER CITY GUIDES

(Pocket-size guides to sightseeing and tourist accommodations and facilities in all price ranges.)

☐ Amsterdam/Holland	$7.95	☐ Minneapolis/St. Paul	$7.95
☐ Athens	$7.95	☐ Montréal/Québec City	$7.95
☐ Atlantic City/Cape May	$7.95	☐ New Orleans	$7.95
☐ Barcelona*	$7.95	☐ New York	$7.95
☐ Belgium	$7.95	☐ Orlando/Disney World/EPCOT	$7.95
☐ Boston	$7.95	☐ Paris	$7.95
☐ Cancún/Cozumel/Yucatán	$7.95	☐ Philadelphia	$7.95
☐ Chicago	$7.95	☐ Rio	$7.95
☐ Denver/Boulder*	$7.95	☐ Rome	$7.95
☐ Dublin/Ireland	$7.95	☐ San Francisco	$7.95
☐ Hawaii	$7.95	☐ Santa Fe/Taos/Albuquerque	$7.95
☐ Hong Kong*	$7.95	☐ Seattle/Portland*	$7.95
☐ Las Vegas	$7.95	☐ Sydney	$7.95
☐ Lisbon/Madrid/Costa del Sol	$7.95	☐ Tokyo*	$7.95
☐ London	$7.95	☐ Vancouver/Victoria*	$7.95
☐ Los Angeles	$7.95	☐ Washington, D.C.	$7.95
☐ Mexico City/Acapulco	$7.95	*Available June, 1990	

SPECIAL EDITIONS

☐ A Shopper's Guide to the Caribbean	$12.95	☐ Manhattan's Outdoor Sculpture	$15.95
☐ Beat the High Cost of Travel	$6.95	☐ Motorist's Phrase Book (Fr/Ger/Sp)	$4.95
☐ Bed & Breakfast—N. America	$11.95	☐ Paris Rendez-Vous	$10.95
☐ California with Kids	$14.95	☐ Swap and Go (Home Exchanging)	$10.95
☐ Caribbean Hideaways	$14.95	☐ The Candy Apple (NY with Kids)	$12.95
☐ Honeymoon Destinations (US, Mex & Carib)	$12.95	☐ Travel Diary and Record Book	$5.95

☐ Where to Stay USA (Lodging from $3 to $30 a night) $10.95
☐ Marilyn Wood's Wonderful Weekends (Conn, Del, Mass, NH, NJ, NY, Pa, RI, VT) $11.95
☐ The New World of Travel (Annual sourcebook by Arthur Frommer for savvy travelers) $16.95

SERIOUS SHOPPER'S GUIDES

(Illustrated guides listing hundreds of stores, conveniently organized alphabetically by category.)

☐ Italy	$15.95	☐ Los Angeles	$14.95
☐ London	$15.95	☐ Paris	$15.95

GAULT MILLAU

(The only guides that distinguish the truly superlative from the merely overrated.)

☐ The Best of Chicago	$15.95	☐ The Best of Los Angeles	$14.95
☐ The Best of France	$16.95	☐ The Best of New England	$15.95
☐ The Best of Hong Kong	$16.95	☐ The Best of New York	$14.95
☐ The Best of Italy	$16.95	☐ The Best of Paris	$16.95
☐ The Best of London	$16.95	☐ The Best of San Francisco	$14.95

☐ The Best of Washington, D.C. $14.95

ORDER NOW!

In U.S. include $2 shipping UPS for 1st book; $1 ea. add'l book. Outside U.S. $3 and $1, respectively.

Allow four to six weeks for delivery in U.S., longer outside U.S.

Enclosed is my check or money order for $_____

NAME _____

ADDRESS _____

CITY _____ STATE _____ ZIP _____

0190